HELEN PLUM MEMORIAL LIBRARY

P9-BYZ-988

914
ROU
2014

JUN   2014

THE ROUGH GUIDE TO

Europe ON A BUDGET

written and researched by

Eleanor Aldridge, Lauren Atherton, Jonathan Bousfield,
Tim Burford, Kiki Deere, Natasha Foges, Daniel Jacobs, Anna
Kaminski, Ciara Kenny, Norm Longley, John Malathronas,
Neil McQuillian, Jacy Meyer, Roger Norum, Caroline Sieg,
Emma Thomson, Jo-Ann Titmarsh, Andy Turner, Kate Turner,
Steve Vickers, Matt Willis and Martin Zatko

ROUGH GUIDES

roughguides.com

Contents

HELEN PLUM
LIBRARY
LOMBARD, IL

OPPOSITE ALMERÍA, SPAIN PREVIOUS PAGE BURANO, NORTH OF VENICE, ITALY

Introduction to

Europe

Europe presents an irresistible challenge to the budget traveller. A potent mix of culture, landscape and history on the one hand and a cash-gobbling monster on the other, sticking to your daily allowance can prove tricky. But learn to zone out the "Spend! Spend! Spend!" siren song of its myriad restaurants, bars and shops and you'll find that this compact little continent is simply the world's greatest labyrinth. From London's Royal Parks and Amsterdam's canals to İstanbul's Grand Bazaar and the Berlin Wall, just getting tangled up in its sights is a huge draw – you can do the Algarve, the Alps and the Arctic, all in one trip. There's time travel here too: with Stonehenge and Ephesus, cathedrals and castles, châteaux and palaces (not to mention statement-making modern architecture), Europe's man-made structures zoom you through millennia of civilization, a tumultuous history that scars and bejewels the continent by turns.

With its cultural kaleidoscope shifting not just from one country to the next but between towns and villages, relatively short distances can mean profound changes – bang for your backpacking buck, in other words, especially with the average gap year trip getting shorter. And you needn't miss out even in some of the world's most **sophisticated cities**, with many iconic European experiences mercifully light on the pocket: think of *aperitivo* time in Rome, *blini* in Moscow, the freebie wonders at London's British Museum and bargain lunchtime concerts in Paris or Dublin. You will have to spend a few bob, of course. **Accommodation** and travel are bound to devour a fair chunk of your funds; the glass-half-full response is, "What do I spend the rest on?". Start by giving your **taste buds** the ride of their lives, be it in a Lyon *bouchon*, a smoky Turkish *ocakbaşı*, at a market or on the hoof (see Ideas, p.19). Don't be tempted to skip breakfast, either – an oven-fresh croissant or calorie-jammed "full English" is not to be missed, and all the more important in a morning-after-the-night-before context, especially since Europe lives for the wee hours.

ABOVE TAORMINA, SICILY **RIGHT** BRICK LANE, LONDON

Whether it's Berlin and London's hipster dives, flamenco in Seville, Budapest's ruin bars, or the *enotecas* that celebrate Italy's rejuvenated wine industry, there are countless reasons to stay up till sunrise. For fun en masse, check out the continent's **festivals** (see Ideas, p.16) – both traditional and modern – and the outdoor pursuits that animate its wide open spaces (see Ideas, p.21), from horseriding in Bulgaria's Rila Mountains to surfing on Portugal's gnarled Alentejo coast. One advantage of **budget travel** is that it makes splurging all the sweeter – for a little flashpacking guidance, keep an eye out for our Treat Yourself tips throughout the guide.

But for a few exceptions (see p.41), red tape won't be an issue thanks to Europe's unique "open borders" policy – you can travel **hassle-free** between countries that were once fierce enemies. To bolster your funds, consider working (see p.39), which can be a great way to meet people, immerse yourself in a country's day-to-day life and improve your language skills. But a word of caution – while you'll come across sleepy corners where things seem unchanged since some distant "Once upon a time" era, there's an atmosphere of unrest in others. The Eurozone **financial crisis** is rippling across the continent, having already brought down governments from Ireland to Portugal and Slovenia. 2013 saw Spain's unemployment reach record levels, while Athens and İstanbul have experienced violent scenes. When planning your trip and before you set off, keep an eye on the news and scour Twitter, which is also invaluable for up-to-the-minute reviews of new openings and off-the-beaten-track recommendations. The disaffected mood does have one upside: with its citizens so **politically engaged**, this is one of the most interesting times to travel in Europe for decades, and you're bound to have conversations and encounters that define your memories, whichever road you take.

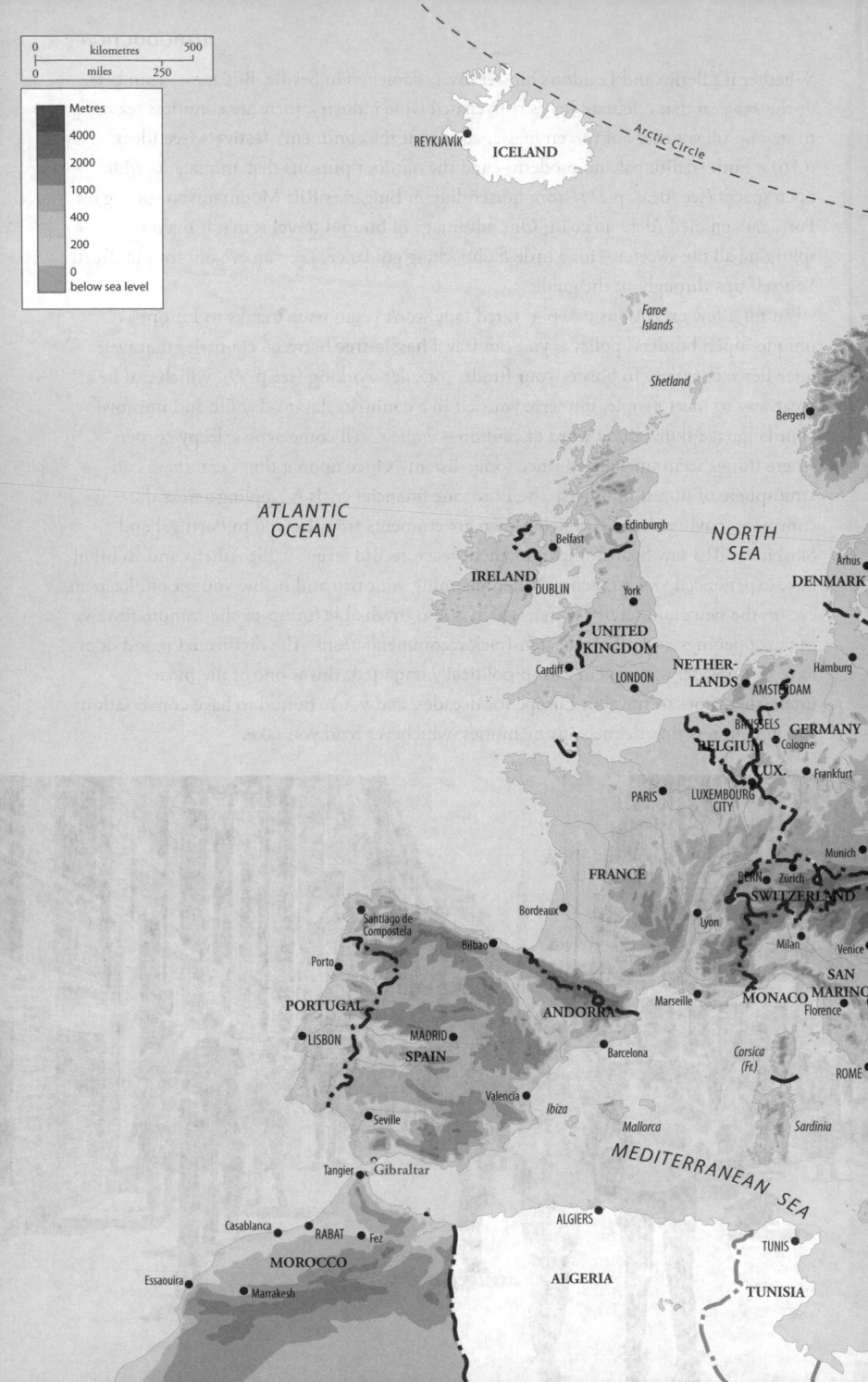

Where to go

Europe has it all: sprawling cities and quaint villages; boulevards, promenades and railways; mountains, beaches and lakes. Some places will be exactly how you imagined: **Venice** is everything it's cracked up to be; springtime in **Paris** has even hardened cynics melting with the romance of it all; and **Oxford**'s colleges really are like Harry Potter film sets. But others will surprise, whether for their under-the-radar nature (see Author picks, p.13) or because they're stuck with an old-established, out-of-date reputation – but then, isn't tweaking your mental map all part of the fun?

Budget travellers are best off combining practicality with stick-a-pin-in-the-map impulsiveness. If you're flying out, look for where the cheap fares will take you and start from there – try our Itineraries section (see pp.22–27) for inspiration. Those getting around by train – still the best option – should note which countries are accessible with an InterRail Global pass and the equivalent Eurail pass (see p.32). Depending on your time and budget, choose one corner of the continent then consider a budget flight for that unmissable experience elsewhere, be it a foodie pilgrimage to **San Sebastián**, a cultural splurge at the **Edinburgh Festival**, or **St Petersburg**'s White Nights.

Great Britain maintains a certain psychological distance from its neighbours, and yet for many it's a European must-do, with iconic sights ranging from Big Ben and the Tower of London to Bath's Royal Crescent. North of the border, the Scottish people's decision in their 2014 independence referendum could bring about Great Britain's biggest constitutional shift since the Act of Union in 1707. **London** has been feeling rather pleased with itself ever since the 2012 Olympics, and their legacy endures in the shape of the Queen Elizabeth Olympic Park. A reuse of the Games site, it's close to the hip, budget-friendly buzz of the city's East End. A quick flight away, **Ireland**'s west coast is an altogether more dramatic slice of the great outdoors, while **Derry-Londonderry**'s artistic vitality saw it crowned UK City of Culture for 2013. With steep fares in Great Britain especially, this is one region to really milk an InterRail card. Those without one should book tickets far in advance, or get ready for some very cosy long-distance bus rides; note that the Eurail Global pass did not include England or Scotland at the time of writing.

The English-Scottish rivalry runs deep but it's not a patch on the Catalan-Spanish equivalent, so be alert to the touted 2014 Catalonia independence referendum – Catalan capital **Barcelona** might just become even more electric than it already is. From there **Madrid** and clubbing hotbed **Ibiza** are within easy reach while, away to the north and east, **France** and **Italy** could exhaust your rail pass in one fell swoop, with some of the world's finest cuisine, architecture, landscape and museums. **Marseille** in the south of France might not be on the traditional must-see lists, but it has renewed vibrancy of late – following a spectacular shake up, the Vieux-Port is studded with gleaming modern architecture quite at odds with the city's gritty reputation. Out west, **Portugal** is relatively easy on the purse strings; its beautiful Douro Rail Route will make a veritable golden ticket of your rail pass, and even the **Algarve** has a thriving hostel scene these days.

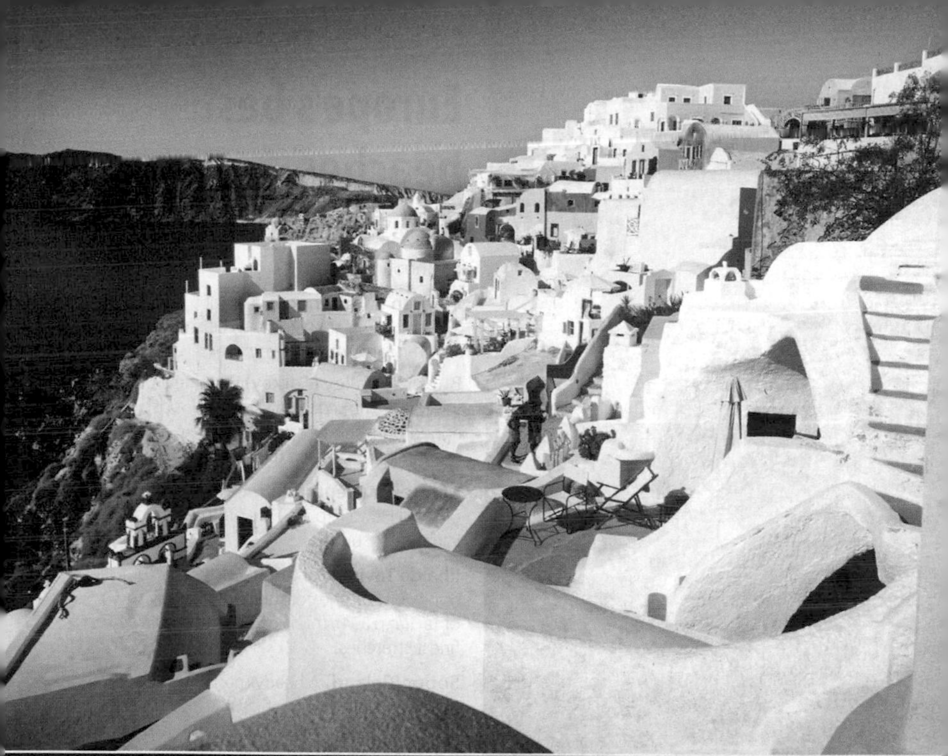

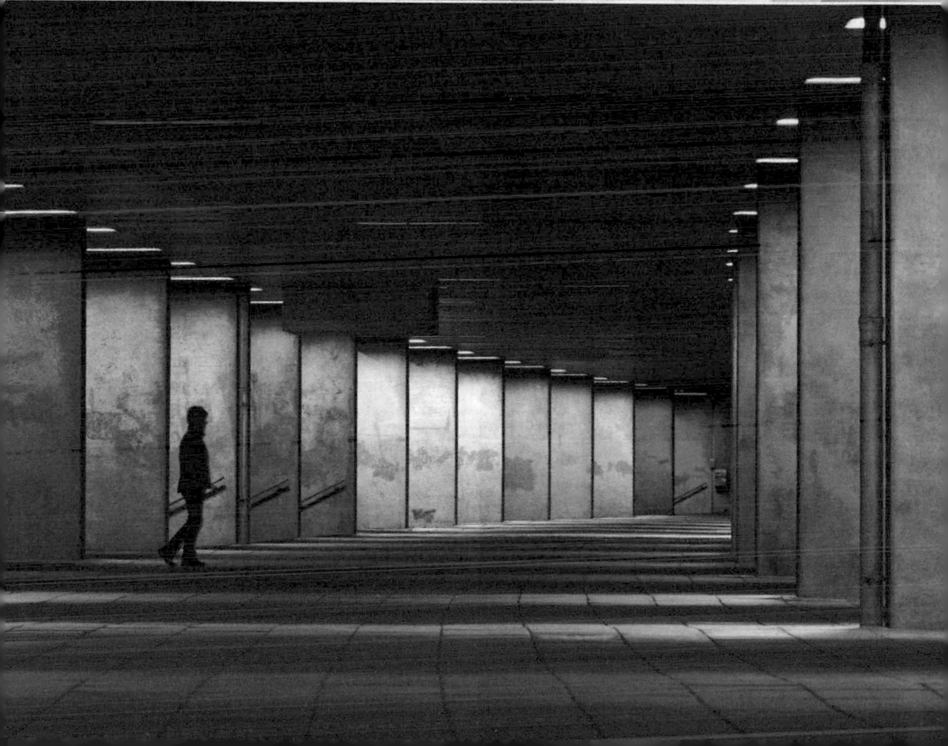

Europe's best beaches

Ses Illetes (Spain) Clubbed out? Formentera's beaches (p.1049) are quieter and wilder than on neighbouring Ibiza.

Mogren (Montenegro) Part of the so-called "Budva Riviera" that stretches either side of Montenegro's party town *par excellence* (p.735).

Butterfly Valley (Turkey) Imagine a Turkish version of *The Beach*, minus the bloodshed, with added butterflies – take a boat here and soak up the trippy hippie vibe (p.1166).

Klitmøller (Denmark) The windswept beaches of "Cold Hawaii" (p.233) are off the wall for all varieties of surfing.

Ilha de Tavira (Portugal) Backed by tufted dunes just off the coast near the pretty town of Tavira (p.894), this is one of the Algarve's finest stretches.

Sopot (Poland) A heady mix of pristine sand and party culture, Sopot (p.846) also boasts Europe's longest wooden pier – ideal for a hangover-busting stroll.

Áyios Prokópios (Greece) Following the herd down to Greece? Hit this lagoon-backed beauty (p.528) armed with a bottle of *kítron*, the local liqueur.

Erraid (Great Britain) Enjoy these perfect slivers of sand – inspiration for Robert Louis Stevenson's *Kidnapped* – on the Isle of Mull (p.493).

Plage de la Rondinara (France) Shaped like a scallop shell, this vies with the turquoise waters of Santa Giulia and Palombaggia for title of "best Corsican beach" (p.349).

Chia (Italy) A sequence of shapely little bays lying just southwest of a quiet Sardinian village (p.679) – nearby lagoons are specked with flamingos, who come here to breed.

Zlatni Rat (Croatia) There's fantastic windsurfing off the island of Brač but the doing-nothing-whatsoever is just as good – try this slender, wishbone-shaped beach (p.172).

Ksamil (Albania) This is still (just about) one of the Mediterranean's unspoiled corners – and with the wonderful ruins of Butrint nearby, the beach at the village of Ksamil (p.60) is an irresistible detour.

FROM TOP SES ILLETES, SPAIN; MOGREN, MONTENEGRO; BUTTERFLY VALLEY, TURKEY

Further south again, voyage to **Morocco** the romantic way – by boat – and splash out on a stay at a traditional riad, where "Europe" can feel very far away indeed

In spite of its famous Europe-Asia split, **Turkey** is supposedly closer to EU accession than Morocco. The Turkish government's violent response to 2013's unrest is likely to have set back that schedule, while nearby **Athens** has experienced similar troubles in recent times. Still, both Athens and **İstanbul** remain excellent budget options. And with these countries' unforgettable ancient sites – not to mention **Greek island** hopping or ballooning above the "fairy chimneys" of Turkey's **Cappadocia** – it's quite possible to feel blissfully removed from current affairs (should you so wish).

The "melting pot" cliché is often applied to İstanbul, but it's a fit for the **Balkans** too. Their rich diversity extends beyond the ethnic and cultural to landscape and urban make-up: the gorgeous coastlines of **Montenegro** and **Albania**; **Croatia**'s islands; **Romania**'s Dracula territory; the monasteries of **Serbia** and bridges of **Bosnia**; the architectural strangeness of Tirana and Skopje, capitals of **Albania** and **Macedonia**. Indeed, with evocative old quarters and (in some cases) relatively recent political turmoil, the Balkans' towns and cities are some of Europe's most fascinating – and affordable.

Into central Europe and the similarities between **Slovenia** and **Slovakia** don't begin and end with phonetics, these near-neighbours rivalling each other for mountain scenery and outdoorsy pursuits. Slovenian capital **Ljubljana** is an elegant charmer, while landlocked Slovakia boasts cutesy **Bratislava** and 2013 European Capital of Culture **Košice**. Industrial **Plzeň** in the **Czech Republic** is set to regenerate around its own Capital of Culture 2015 award, while **Prague** is a treat just the way it is. Given their vast size, you'll be glad that **Poland** and **Ukraine** are enjoying improved infrastructure, a legacy of their stint as co-hosts of the 2012 UEFA European Football Championship – come for big city thrills with the likes of **Warsaw** and **Kyiv**, and a sense of discovery in less-touristed **Wrocław** and **L'viv**.

Once you hit **Germany** and its neighbours, you'll be glad of any money saved further east. That said, as nightlife hubs go, ever-changing **Berlin** is pretty affordable; visit **Munich** for Oktoberfest if you like partying of a more traditional sort. Exploring the compact **Netherlands** by bike is both budget-friendly and oh-so-Dutch, while **Amsterdam** has recently seen a raft of exciting new museum openings. Like the Netherlands, cultural heavyweight **Austria** does a whole lot with its modest size; yet with patches of mountainous terrain, this is one for the skis and snowboard rather than two wheels.

Finally, don't write off **Scandinavia** as unaffordable. Tourist cards, wild camping and university cafeterias – there are ways and means. And even if you can't quite stretch to the latest hot purveyor of "New Danish Cuisine", plenty of **Copenhagen**'s other famous pleasures can be enjoyed on the cheap – bakeries, *bodega* bars and cycling for starters. And the Northern Lights, visible from **Sweden** and **Norway**, might just be the greatest free show on earth. Neighbouring **Finland** serves up everything from the traditional culture of the reindeer-herding Sámi people to 2012 World Design Capital **Helsinki**. From there it's easy to reach the **Baltic** states of Latvia, Estonia and Lithuania. **Tallinn** and **Rīga** are two recent beneficiaries of the European Capital of Culture award, and a little more vibrant for it – or head boldly into **Russia**, where Moscow and St Petersburg have some truly blockbuster sights. From Marrakesh to Moscow – only in Europe.

When to go

Europe is, for the most part, a year-round destination. In terms of budget, it makes sense to travel in the off season (October through to May) – cheaper menus appear on restaurant tables, hotels drop their rates, and haggling over prices becomes a realistic option. This is especially true of tourist hotspots like Paris, Barcelona and Rome, which attract far bigger crowds in July and August.

If you do decide to travel during the peak **summer** season, try heading east – the Balkan coastline, the Slovenian mountains and Baltic cities are all fantastic places for making the most of your money. When tourist traffic dies down as **autumn** approaches, head to the Med. The famous coastlines and islands of southern Europe are quieter at this time of year, and the cities of Spain and Italy begin to look their best. **Wintertime** brings world-class skiing and snowboarding to European mountainsides (though not guaranteed) and countless festive markets pop up in the towns and cities below. There are epic New Year parties everywhere from Moscow to Lisbon and, despite the cold weather elsewhere at this time of year, there's still the possibility of sunshine in Turkey and Morocco. Come **spring** it's worth heading north to the Netherlands, Scandinavia, France and the British Isles, where you'll find beautifully long days and relatively affordable prices before the summer season kicks in around July.

While **weather** extremes are not the issue they are in, say, Asia or Africa, you should still bear them in mind when planning your trip. The Arctic winter in Scandinavia and Russia can bring temperatures as low as -35°C, with the sun barely rising above the horizon for months at a time. Conversely, summer days in central, southern and eastern parts of continental Europe can be sweltering – temperatures of around 40°C are not unheard of.

Author picks

From lungfuls of mountain air to gulps of super-strong beer, via floating taxis and hostels, cycle rides and kayaking, our authors share their top European tips.

Freewheeling Take to two wheels for an exploration of the Loire Valley's Renaissance châteaux, sampling delectable local wines along the way (p.299), or glide around wonderful Copenhagen's famous cycle network (p.213).

Delectable dishes Relish the world's favourite cuisine at an Italian trattoria such as Florence's *Sostanza*, with its tiled walls and communal eating (p.649), and discover that Britain's food ain't all bad at one of its ever-growing network of gastropubs and food markets (p.419).

Watery cities Kayak past medieval spires in Stockholm, Scandinavia's prettiest city, then spend the night aboard a floating hostel (p.1089); cruise along the canals of St Petersburg for a unique perspective on its historic sights (p.930); and absorb Venice's perenially stunning beauty from the seat of an affordable *traghetto* (p.638).

Under-the-radar towns Olomouc, Czech Republic (p.205), is a pint-sized Prague with less people and more charm (and cobblestones), while Berat (p.57) is a gorgeous Albanian town where row after row of Ottoman buildings loom down at you from the sides of a steep valley.

Drinking dens Order a knee-buckling Duvel beer at Brussels' historic *La Fleur en Papier Doré* (p.99) – a time-worn café once the favourite haunt of Surrealist painter Magritte and Tintin creator Hergé – or go oh-so-modern at the *De Prael* brewery (p.787), right in the heart of Amsterdam's Red Light District.

Saddle up Head for Bulgaria's Rila Mountains (p.131) on horseback (or by foot) to enjoy the spectacular scenery spread out beneath Mount Musala (2925m), the Balkan Peninsula's highest peak, or go galloping among the wild ponies on Great Britain's rugged Dartmoor (p.447).

> Our author recommendations don't end here. We've flagged up our favourite places – a perfectly sited hotel, an atmospheric café, a special restaurant – throughout the guide, highlighted with the ★ symbol.

LEFT LOCH LOMOND, SCOTLAND **FROM TOP** VENICE, ITALY; OLOMOUC, CZECH REPUBLIC; STOCKHOLM, SWEDEN

Arts and culture

1 EAST SIDE GALLERY, GERMANY
Page 363
This graffiti-daubed stretch of the Berlin Wall is now under threat.

2 AYA SOFYA, TURKEY
Page 1146
Christianity and Islam meet in one magnificent İstanbul building.

3 BALLET, RUSSIA
Pages 929 & 937
Watch world-class performances at the Bolshoi or Mariinskiy theatres.

4 SISTINE CHAPEL, ITALY
Page 615
Michelangelo's jaw-dropping High Renaissance ceiling still inspires awe.

5 CASA BATLLÓ, SPAIN
Page 1059
Gaudí's masterpieces are inseparable from the Barcelona experience.

6 THE PARTHENON, GREECE
Page 502
The iconic image of Western civilization and template for buildings the world over.

7 STREET MURAL, GREAT BRITAIN
Page 428
Graffiti art animates London's streetscape, particularly the East End.

Festivals

1 ST PATRICK'S DAY, IRELAND
Page 575
Dublin is the epicentre of March 17
shamrock-strewn, Guinness-fuelled fun.

2 BATTLE OF THE ORANGES, ITALY
Page 620
Head to Ivrea for the town's annual
citrus assault – a bruising one-off.

3 ROSKILDE, DENMARK
Page 227
Glastonbury's Scandinavian rival, with
a mass naked run thrown in for good
measure.

4 FESTES DE LA MERCE, SPAIN
Page 1061
Human castles and papier-mâché
"giants" give Barcelona even more
visual pizzazz.

5 FERIA DE ABRIL, SPAIN
Page 1024
Sombreros, flamenco dresses and
dancing – Seville celebrates its
heritage.

6 GLASTONBURY, GREAT BRITAIN
Page 447
You'll probably end up caked in mud,
but this legendary festival is worth it.

7 EXIT FESTIVAL, SERBIA
Page 952
A beautiful fortress setting and
top-name acts – what's not to like?

SİMİTÇİ
09

Eat like a local

1 MARKETS, GREAT BRITAIN
Page 428
Local, seasonal produce and fantastic ethnic diversity – Great Britain is foodie heaven.

2 CURRYWURST, GERMANY
Page 367
After a few steins, nothing else quite hits the spot like this curried street snack.

3 SIMIT, TURKEY
Page 1142
Try one of these fresh bread rings with a little glass of sweet Turkish tea.

4 SMØRREBRØD, DENMARK
Page 211
Open sandwich as art form – dense Danish bread makes these surprisingly filling.

5 PIZZA, ITALY
Page 607
Forget stuffed crust, the Neapolitan pizza is a thing of simple, unadorned beauty.

6 SNAILS, MOROCCO
Page 771
Tease out the flavoursome flesh with a toothpick, then slurp up the broth from your bowl.

7 TAPAS, SPAIN
Page 1000
Small portions, big flavours – Spain's greatest gift to the world's taste buds.

The great outdoors

1 WINTER WONDERLAND
Pages 344 & 824

From Chamonix snowboarding to cross-country skiing in Norway.

2 THE NORTHERN LIGHTS
Pages 827 & 1110

Watch Mother Nature's greatest show in Tromsø or Swedish Lapland.

3 GET YOUR BOOTS ON
Page 349

The GR20 in Corsica is one of countless epic European hikes.

4 GRAB A PADDLE
Pages 892 & 798

Try Portuguese sea-kayaking or simply glide down Utrecht's canals.

5 GIDDY UP
Pages 109, 565 & 573

Belgium's Ardennes region, Hungary's national parks and Ireland's Connemara coast are perfect for a little stirrup time.

6 UNDER CANVAS
Page 37

Camping can help make Europe affordable – and even more beautiful.

7 TWO WHEELS
Pages 219 & 249

From urban trundles around Denmark to thigh-busting marathons deep in the Estonian wilderness.

7

Itineraries

You can't expect to fit everything Europe has to offer into one trip and we don't suggest you try. On the following pages is a selection of itineraries that guide you through the different regions of the continent, taking you from the misty Scottish Highlands to the souks of Morocco. Each of these itineraries could be done in two to three weeks if followed to the letter but don't push it too hard – with so much to see and do you're bound to get waylaid somewhere you love or stray off the suggested route.

BRITAIN AND IRELAND

Home to four proud nations, these two small islands pack in a huge amount – from stately homes and weather-beaten moors to theatre, Premier League football and Europe's best music festivals. Don't forget your brolly, drinking hat and sense of humour.

❶ **London** As the saying goes, when a man is tired of London, he is tired of life. One of the world's greatest cities is also one of the most expensive, but follow our tips to emerge with your wallet intact. **See p.421**

❷ **Oxford** The famous university town offers the chance to punt along the river, admire the college architecture or down a few pints in a student pub. **See p.450**

❸ **Snowdonia** Despite the notoriously unpredictable weather, the Welsh mountains provide excellent hiking and some of Britain's best hostels. **See p.477**

❹ **York** From a Viking museum and medieval streets to the soaring Gothic Minster, if you want to soak up some British history, York is the place to do it. **See p.467**

❺ **Edinburgh** With its stunning cityscape, lively bars and – if you time it right – international festival, the Scottish capital has something for everyone. **See p.479**

❻ **The Highlands** Find your inner Braveheart, knock back some whisky and hike, climb or ski surrounded by Britain's most stunning scenery. **See p.491**

❼ **Belfast** A fascinating if troubled history, friendly locals and access point to one of Europe's natural wonders, the Giant's Causeway. **See p.596**

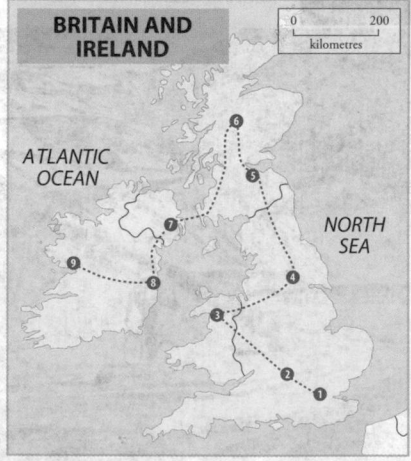

BRITAIN AND IRELAND

0 200 kilometres

ATLANTIC OCEAN

NORTH SEA

ABOVE COSTA DE LA LUZ, SPAIN

❽ Dublin Yep, Guinness really does taste better here, though there's a lot more to see and do in Ireland's sophisticated capital. **See p.575**

❾ Ireland's West Coast From Galway to Cork, this coastline is studded with buzzing towns and beautiful, windswept beaches. **See p.588**

FRANCE AND SWITZERLAND

Still the world's number one tourist destination, France can smugly claim to have it all, from mountains and sun-kissed beaches to unrivalled food and fashion. Pricey it may be, but nearby Switzerland is worth the expense for its attractive, appealingly relaxed cities and the jaw-dropping mountain views.

❶ Paris Laze over a coffee in a Left Bank café, arrange a romantic rendezvous or tick off the many museums in Europe's most elegant capital. **See p.281**

❷ The Loire Valley Some of the most impressive chateaux you'll see in the country grace this bucolic valley, which is also prime vineyard territory. **See p.299**

❸ Bordeaux An elegant, bustling city and world-famous wine-growing region, with some of Europe's finest surf beaches just a short drive away. **See p.308**

❹ The Pyrenees Clear your head after all that wine with the fresh air and fine walks of this mountain range bordering Spain. **See p.316**

❺ The Côte d'Azur Nice, Cannes, Monaco – the names alone ooze glamour, but do you dare dress up and hit one of this chichi region's famed casinos? **See p.322**

❻ Corsica France's adventure playground, Corsica is home to one of Europe's toughest and most rewarding treks, the GR20. **See p.345**

❼ Lyon The country's gastronomic capital – eat at *Le Musée*, a classic *bouchon*, to see how good traditional French cooking can be. **See p.339**

❽ The Alps Try your luck scaling Europe's highest mountains, or spend a season as a ski instructor or chalet monkey. **See p.343 & p.344**

❾ Zürich Laidback Zürich is still one of Europe's clubbing hotspots and has a wonderful riverside setting. **See p.1128**

BENELUX, GERMANY AND AUSTRIA

From fine chocolates and champion beers to fairytale castles, forests and clinking cowbells, this region has something for just about everyone. The cities can pass in a blur of late nights but make time for the scenery too.

❶ Amsterdam Whatever you're looking for – cannabis, clubs, high culture or cuisine – the Netherlands' capital can provide it. **See p.779**

❷ Bruges It may be brazenly touristy but this gem of Flemish architecture is still worth a visit for its atmospheric canals and beautiful buildings. **See p.105**

❸ Cologne Linked to Brussels and beyond by super-fast trains, Cologne makes a perfect first stop in Germany with its spectacular old town and lively festivals. **See p.386**

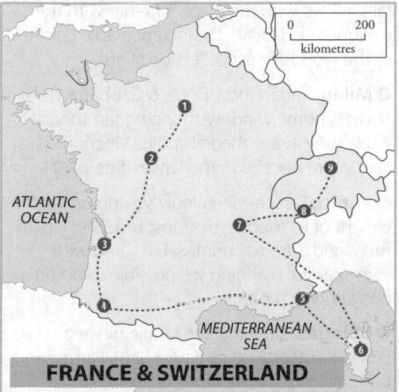

FRANCE & SWITZERLAND

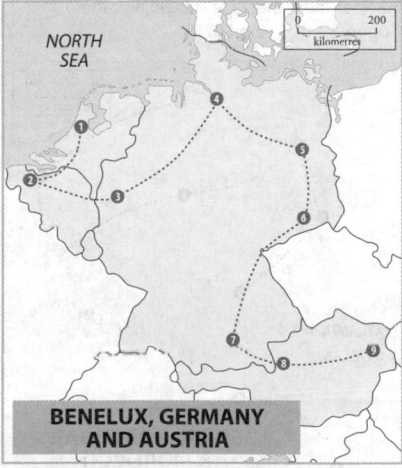

BENELUX, GERMANY AND AUSTRIA

❹ Hamburg Germany's northern gateway boasts a vast port, magnificent red-brick warehouses and a riotous bar and live music scene. **See p.379**

❺ Berlin Some 25 years since the fall of the Wall, Berlin still has a raw, youthful energy that belies its history of division and destruction. **See p.357**

❻ Dresden Bombed to bits in World War II, Dresden is the classic phoenix from the flames story and now one of Europe's favourite backpacker hangouts. **See p.370**

❼ Munich From beer-fuelled thigh-slapping to modern art and mountain scenery, you'll find it all in Bavaria's capital. **See p.405**

❽ Salzburg Hit the Mozart trail, pose Julie Andrews-style in homage to *The Sound of Music* or pull on some skis and head for the mountains. **See p.77**

❾ Vienna Austria's capital is chock-full of palaces, museums and boulevards – with coffee and cake in a grand café never too far away. **See p.65**

SPAIN, PORTUGAL AND MOROCCO

Penélope Cruz, Cristiano Ronaldo, tapas, port and Rioja – it's hard not to warm to the Iberian peninsula. To the south, Morocco is just a short hop across the sea but a different planet in many respects.

❶ Bilbao Capital of the Basque country, Bilbao is Spain's friendliest city and home to one of Europe's most spectacular buildings: the Guggenheim. **See p.1075**

SPAIN, PORTUGAL & MOROCCO

❷ Barcelona Innovative architecture, city beaches, late-night bars and an enchanting old town – you'll find it hard to leave the Catalan capital. **See p.1054**

❸ Ibiza *Amnesia, Pacha, Space* – its nightclubs are famous the world over, but even on Europe's party island there are pockets of idyllic peace and quiet. **See p.1048**

❹ Madrid Take your cue from the locals in the Spanish capital – if you're dining before 10pm, dancing before midnight and asleep before dawn, you haven't experienced a truly Madrileño night out. **See p.1004**

❺ Porto Wander the winding cobbled streets of Portugal's second city – and sample a drop at one (or more) of the countless port lodges. **See p.880**

❻ Lisbon Portugal's immediately likeable capital has a great setting, delicious food and a huge amount of historic interest. **See p.865**

❼ Andalucía Spain in a nutshell – flamenco, fine wines, bullfighting and heat. If you're pushed for time stick to the unmissable cities of Seville and Granada. **See p.1023**

❽ Fez Once across the Straits of Gibraltar, dive head first into Morocco with a stay in this medieval city of labyrinthine alleys, souks and mosques. **See p.756**

❾ Marrakesh Stunning, atmospheric city with the Atlas Mountains as a backdrop and the live circus that is the Jemaa el Fna square at its heart. **See p.767**

ITALY

If there's one country that deserves its own itinerary it's Italy. Almost everyone who visits falls in love with the place, whether with the designer-clad locals, the incomparable cuisine or the world's finest collection of art.

❶ Milan Prada, Gucci, Dolce & Gabbana… Milan is prime window-shopping territory, while the city's cathedral and da Vinci's *The Last Supper* are priceless experiences. **See p.621**

❷ Venice Despite seemingly sinking under the weight of its tourists, the most beautiful city in the world is frankly unmissable – and with some careful planning still possible to do on a budget. **See p.633**

❸ Bologna Capital of the foodie nirvana Emilia-Romagna (think Parma ham, Parmesan, balsamic vinegar), Bologna is a must-do for anyone with a digestive system. **See p.640**

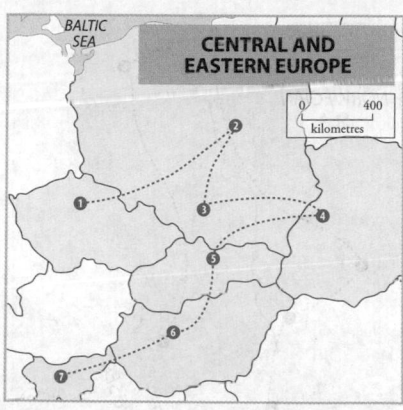

4 Tuscany Birthplace of the Renaissance, Florence rightly pulls in the masses; nearby Siena is just as beautiful, full of fun-loving students and an excellent base to explore the region's hill towns. **See p.644 & p.651**

5 Rome You can hardly "do" Europe and not "do" Rome. Whether you're stuck queuing for St Peter's, the Sistine Chapel or the Colosseum you can at least rest assured that you're about to be wowed. **See p.610**

6 Naples The home of pizza – and the best place to eat it – Naples is also a frenetic, crumblingly attractive city with an intriguing dark side. **See p.659**

7 Pompeii From the ancient graffiti to plaster body casts, seeing a Roman town frozen in time is an experience you won't forget. **See p.664**

8 Matera Try sleeping in a cave in this hand-carved stone city – the perfect introduction to Italy's captivating far south. **See p.667**

9 Sicily Beaches, volcanoes and, in Palermo, one of Italy's most in-your-face cities – Sicilians simply do it better. **See p.669**

CENTRAL AND EASTERN EUROPE

Having long shrugged off the Iron Curtain, the region we used to regard as bleak and distant is now firmly at the beating heart of the continent. With elegant cities and vast tracts of unspoiled countryside, these countries provide a remarkable set of riches.

1 Prague The Czech capital would probably win a pan-European beauty contest for its architecture. As for the beer…well, let's just say you won't be disappointed. **See p.188**

2 Warsaw Beyond the Polish capital's immaculately reconstructed Old Town there are beautiful palaces and parks, not to mention restaurant, club and vodka-soaked bar scenes to explore. **See p.837**

3 Kraków Arty and atmospheric, picture-postcard-pretty Kraków should not be missed, though neither should a sobering trip to nearby Auschwitz. **See p.848**

4 L'viv This Central European gem has good backpacker hostels and a café-jammed, charming Old Town. **See p.1189**

5 Tatra Mountains Stretching between Poland and Slovakia the Tatras are that rare thing – majestic wilderness without hordes of Gore-Tex-clad tourists. **See p.854 & p.970**

6 Budapest Two cities for the price of one: stately, museum-packed Buda and across the not-so-blue Danube, nightlife and restaurant hotspot Pest. **See p.551**

7 Ljubljana Repeat after me: "Lyoo-bly-AH-nah". It may be hard to pronounce but the Slovenian capital is a small, perfectly formed pit stop between central Europe and the Adriatic. **See p.982**

SCANDINAVIA

While it can hit your finances, Scandinavia is worth stretching the budget for. Apart from resembling Europe's answer to Middle Earth it's also full of stylish cities, ingenious design and friendly locals.

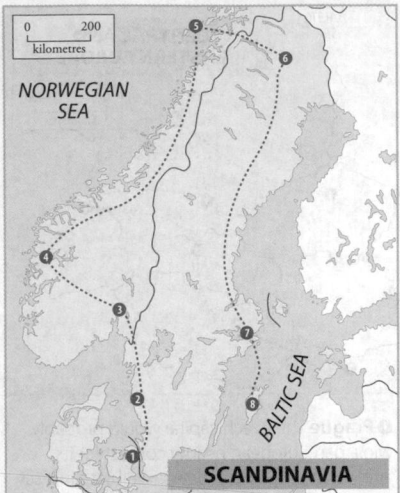

SCANDINAVIA

❶ **Copenhagen** Picturesque and user-friendly, the Danish capital is a lively, welcoming introduction to the region. **See p.213**

❷ **Gothenburg** Sweden's second city boasts elegant architecture, fantastic nightlife and a fully functioning rainforest among its standout attractions. **See p.1098**

❸ **Oslo** Paying €8 for a beer can put people off the Norwegian capital. If you can get over the prices, though, you'll understand why it frequently tops "best places to live" lists. **See p.807**

❹ **The fjords** No trip to Norway would be complete without a visit to the country's western coastline and its magnificent fjords. **See p.816**

❺ **Lofoten Islands** A mild climate, wild scenery and cute, laidback fishing villages pull in the crowds to this remote archipelago in Norway's far north. **See p.824**

❻ **Lapland** Synonymous with Santa, Lapland (whether Swedish or Finnish) fits the winter fantasy perfectly with reindeer, yapping huskies and the staggering Northern Lights. **See p.1110 and p.272**

❼ **Stockholm** Scandinavia's best-looking capital offers up an unspoilt medieval core, über-hip nightlife and, incongruously enough, some fine beaches. **See p.1089**

❽ **Gotland** Sweden's party island buzzes in summer when DJs hit the decks in Visby and the beaches fill with bronzed bodies. **See p.1107**

RUSSIA AND THE BALTIC COAST

Big scary bear it may be, but ever-changing Russia should not be missed, even if it's just to dip into its most "European" city, St Petersburg. Russia's compact Baltic neighbours, meanwhile, provide some of the most beautiful – and most fun – cityscapes in Eastern Europe.

❶ **Moscow** Big, brash, expensive, surreal and exciting, twenty-first-century Moscow is almost a nation in itself and well worth the effort to get to. **See p.922**

❷ **St Petersburg** With jaw-dropping architecture and priceless art collections, Russia's second city is at its best during the midsummer White Nights festival. **See p.930**

❸ **Helsinki** The love child of the Russian and Swedish empires, yet brought up to be proudly Finnish, Helsinki is a fascinatingly schizophrenic capital. **See p.261**

❹ **Tallinn** Having survived its tenure as a cheap stag- and hen-party hub, the beautifully preserved Estonian capital still retains a huge amount of charm. **See p.241**

❺ **Rīga** Larger and more cosmopolitan that its neighbours, Latvia's atmospheric capital is full of architectural treasures and is the gateway to some wonderful coastal scenery. **See p.686**

❻ **Curonian Spit** This narrow strip of lofty sand dunes and dense pine forest is perfect cycling and hiking territory. **See p.713**

❼ **Vilnius** The friendliest and perhaps prettiest of the Baltic capitals, Vilnius's largely undiscovered status means you can enjoy a break from the crowds. **See p.702**

THE BALKANS

A fascinating cultural meeting point, the Balkans today are an exciting, safe and mercifully cheap place to travel. While Croatia

RUSSIA AND THE BALTIC COAST

THE BALKANS

ADRIATIC SEA

0   200
kilometres

❾ Transylvania No, you probably won't see any vampires, but this history-steeped region holds myriad other attractions, from fairytale villages and colourful festivals to tracking wolves in the spectacular Carpathians. **See p.907**

GREECE AND TURKEY

Whether you're interested in classical antiquity and the founding of Western civilization or just sparkling blue seas and sandy beaches, Greece and Turkey are essential destinations.

❶ Kefaloniá Beautiful Kefaloniá is the best place to hop on a moped and find that perfect beach. **See p.539**

❷ Athens Crowded, noisy and polluted the Greek capital may be, but once you've seen the sun set over the Parthenon you'll be hooked. **See p.501**

❸ Íos A favourite among hard-partying backpackers, Íos retains a bohemian, hippie-era charm and is the best stop on the Cyclades island-hopping trail. **See p.529**

❹ Crete Home to the Minotaur and a fair few trashy resorts, Crete also boasts the dramatic Samarian Gorge, Europe's answer to the Grand Canyon. **See p.540**

❺ Ephesus Turkey's best-preserved archeological site is a treasure-trove of ruined temples, mosaics, baths and some spectacular public conveniences. **See p.1162**

❻ Kaş Fill your days mountain biking, paragliding or diving then relive it all in some of the Med's liveliest bars. **See p.1166**

❼ Cappadocia It's a long trip east but Cappadocia's unique volcanic landscape has an irresistible allure – stay in a cave hotel and visit a subterranean city. **See p.1173**

❽ İstanbul Squeeze every kuruş out of your Turkish lira shopping in the bazaars, having a rub down in a hammam and enjoying the surprisingly hectic nightlife. **See p.1145**

and Bulgaria have been on the scene for a while, send a postcard from Bosnia-Herzegovina or Macedonia and you're bound to have someone at home reaching for an atlas.

❶ Dalmatian coast Croatia's dramatic Dalmatian coast and islands are the perfect place to drop out for the summer with unlimited watersports, cheap wine and vitamin D on offer. **See p.167**

❷ Sarajevo War-scarred it may be, but this mini-İstanbul might just be Europe's most welcoming capital – you're unlikely to leave without making a friend or two. **See p.118**

❸ Dubrovnik Rivalling Venice in its day, the "pearl of the Adriatic" has survived centuries of conquest and intrigue, not to mention being on an easyJet flight route. **See p.178**

❹ Budva Montenegro's star resort boasts the requisite pretty old town, but it's the unspoilt beaches and throbbing open-air bars that pull in the party set. **See p.734**

❺ Tirana A charming architectural oddity, Albania's capital is a colourful assault on the eyes – perfect for some urban exploration. **See p.52**

❻ Ohrid Impossibly picturesque, set on the shimmering shores of the eponymous mountain-backed lake, Ohrid is the jewel in Macedonia's crown. **See p.725**

❼ Sofia While no beauty, Bulgaria's laidback capital is an absorbing mix of cultural influences and has some of Eastern Europe's best hostels. **See p.133**

❽ Belgrade Hectic and hedonistic, the Serbian capital is fast attracting the hip crowd thanks to its adrenaline-charged nightlife. **See p.944**

BLACK SEA

0   200
kilometres

AEGEAN SEA

MEDITERRANEAN SEA

GREECE AND TURKEY

RAILWAY ARCHES AND TRAM IN BERLIN

Basics

Getting there

Europe can be easily reached by air from just about anywhere in the world, with flights to all major European cities. It's also possible to arrive by ferry from across the Mediterranean or Black Sea, or on the Trans-Siberian railway from East Asia.

Air fares will always depend on the season; they're usually highest in the summer and over the Christmas period, as well as over public holidays. Note also that flying on weekends or requiring a nonstop journey sometimes adds quite a bit to the round-trip fare. Barring special offers, the cheapest published fares usually require advance purchase of two to three weeks, and impose certain restrictions, such as heavy penalties if you change your schedule. Most cheap fares will only give a partial refund, if any, should you cancel or alter your journey, so check the restrictions carefully before buying. You can often cut costs by going through a youth or student travel specialist (see "Agents"; p.31), which may offer low-cost or special youth or student fares, as well as travel-related services such as travel insurance, rail passes and tours.

If Europe is only one stop on a longer journey, and especially if you are based in Australia or New Zealand, you might consider a Round-the-World (RTW) air ticket. Prices increase with the number of stops – figure on around £750–1200/US$1750–3000/Aus$1750–2500/NZ$2200–4000 for a RTW ticket including one or two European stopovers.

From Britain and Ireland

Heading from Britain to destinations in north-western Europe, it's not just greener to go by train, long-distance bus or ferry – it can be quicker and cheaper too. However, it's normally cheaper to fly than take the train to most parts of southern Europe. From Ireland, you may save a little money travelling by land, sea or even air to London and buying your flight there, but the difference isn't much.

By plane

London is predictably **Britain**'s main hub for air travel, offering the highest frequency of flights and widest choice of destinations from its five airports (Heathrow, Gatwick, Stansted, Luton and City). Manchester also has flights to most parts of Europe, and there are regular services to the Continent from Birmingham, Southampton, Bournemouth, East Midlands, Bristol, Cardiff, Glasgow, Edinburgh, Leeds/Bradford, Liverpool and Newcastle. From the Republic of Ireland, you can fly direct to most major cities in mainland Europe from Dublin, Shannon and Cork. From Belfast, there are direct flights with easyJet to a handful of destinations; otherwise, you'll need to change in London or Manchester.

Budget airlines such as easyJet and Ryanair offer low-cost tickets to airports around Europe (though not always the most convenient airports), and they often have some seriously cheap offers in winter. There are also agents specializing in offers to a specific country or country group on both charters and regular scheduled departures.

EUROPEAN BUDGET AIRLINES

At the time of writing there were 44 budget airlines serving countries in or near Europe. We've listed the more established operators below, but for full details of routes visit Ⓦ flycheapo.com, while Ⓦ skyscanner .net is an invaluable price comparison resource.

Air Berlin Ⓦ airberlin.com
Blue Air Ⓦ www.blueair-web.com
Darwin Ⓦ darwinairline.com
easyJet Ⓦ easyjet.com
Flyhe Ⓦ flybe.com
Fly Niki Ⓦ flyniki.com
Germanwings Ⓦ germanwings.com
Jet2 Ⓦ jet2.com
Norwegian Air Shuttle Ⓦ norwegian.no
Ryanair Ⓦ ryanair.com
Smart Wings Ⓦ smartwings.com
Transavia Ⓦ transavia.com
TUIfly Ⓦ tuifly.com
Vueling Ⓦ vueling.com
Wizz Air Ⓦ wizzair.com

A BETTER KIND OF TRAVEL

At Rough Guides we are passionately committed to travel. We believe it helps us understand the world we live in and the people we share it with – and of course tourism is vital to many developing economies. But the scale of modern tourism has also damaged some places irreparably, and climate change is accelerated by most forms of transport, especially flying. All Rough Guides' flights are carbon-offset, and every year we donate money to a variety of environmental charities.

By train

Direct trains through the **Channel Tunnel** from London to Paris (17 daily, 2hr 30min) and Brussels (10 daily, 2hr 05min) are operated by Eurostar. Tickets for under-26s start at £38 one-way, £66 return. For over-26s, the cheapest and least flexible tickets cost £39 one-way or £69 return. Through-ticket combinations with onward connections from Lille, Brussels and Paris can be booked through International Rail and Rail Europe (see p.32).

Other rail journeys from Britain involve a sea crossing by ferry or, sometimes, catamaran. Tickets can be bought from International Rail, and from most major rail stations or from Dutchflyer (W stenaline.co.uk/ferry/rail-and-sail/holland/) if routed via the Hook of Holland. For some destinations, there are cheaper SuperApex fares requiring advance booking and subject to greater restrictions. Otherwise, international tickets are valid for two months and allow for stopovers on the way, providing you stick to the prescribed route (there may be a choice, with different fares applicable). One-way fares are generally around two-thirds the price of a return fare. If you're under 26 you're entitled to all sorts of special deals, not least cut-price youth fares.

From **Ireland**, direct rail tickets to Europe via Britain generally include both boat connections, and are available from Irish Railways offices in the Republic (☎ 1850 366 222, W irishrail.ie), or Northern Ireland Railways in the North (☎ 028 9066 6630, W translink.co.uk).

For rail passes, contacts and other types of discounted rail travel, see p.32.

By bus

If you're really watching your pennies, a long-distance bus is often the cheapest option, although much less comfortable than the train. The main operator is **Eurolines** (W eurolines.co.uk; W eurolines.ie), which has a network of routes spanning the Continent. Prices can be up to a third less than by train, and there are marginally cheaper fares on most services for those under 26, which undercut youth rail rates for the same journey. There's usually a discount if you buy your ticket in advance, and bigger discounts for journeys booked a week in advance: as an example, current Eurolines fares from London's Victoria Coach Station to Paris or Amsterdam start at £25 for a one-way ticket or £46 for a return booked at least seven days in advance, but special offers are sometimes available. Connecting services from elsewhere in Great Britain add £15 each way to the price of the ticket.

Eurolines also has **Minipass** return tickets from London to two or more European cities, valid for ninety days. Alternatively, you might consider their fifteen- or thirty-day passes, or one of the various passes offered by Busabout for their services around the Continent (see p.33).

By ferry

There are numerous ferry services between Britain and Ireland, and between the British Isles and the European mainland. Ferries from the southeast of Ireland and the south coast of England connect with northern France and Spain; those from Kent in southeast England reach northern France and Belgium; those from Scotland and the east coast and northeast of England cross the North Sea to Belgium, the Netherlands, Germany and Scandinavia.

FERRY OPERATORS

Brittany Ferries UK ☎ 0871 244 0744, W brittany-ferries.co.uk; Ireland ☎ 021 427 7801, W brittanyferries.ie. Cork to Roscoff (April–Nov); Portsmouth to Caen, Cherbourg, Le Havre, St Malo, Bilbao and Santander; Poole to Cherbourg; Plymouth to Roscoff, St Malo and Santander.

Condor Ferries UK ☎ 01202 207216, W www.condorferries.co .uk. Portsmouth to Cherbourg; Portsmouth, Poole and Weymouth to St Malo via Jersey and Guernsey.

DFDS Seaways UK ☎ 0871 522 9955, W dfdsseaways.co.uk. Harwich to Esbjerg (Denmark); Newcastle to Amsterdam; Dover to Calais and Dunkerque; Newhaven to Dieppe; Portsmouth to Le Havre.

Irish Ferries UK ☎ 0871 730 0400, Ireland ☎ 0818 300 400, W irishferries.com. Dublin to Holyhead; Rosslare to Pembroke, Cherbourg (March–Dec) and Roscoff (May–Sept).

My Ferry Link UK ☎ 0844 248 2100, W myferrylink.com. Dover to Calais.

P&O Ferries UK ☎ 0871 664 2121 or ☎ 01304 863000, Ireland ☎ 01 407 3434, W poferries.com. Hull to Zeebrugge and Rotterdam; Dover to Calais; Larne to Cairnryan and Troon (Apr–Oct); Dublin to Liverpool.

Stena Line UK ☎ 0844 470 7070, W stenaline.co.uk; Ireland ☎ 01 204 7777, W stenaline.ie. Harwich to Hook of Holland; Rosslare to Fishguard; Dun Laoghaire and Dublin to Holyhead; Belfast to Cairnryan and Liverpool.

From the US

From the US the best deals are generally from the main hubs such as New York, Washington DC and Chicago to London. Fixed-date advance-purchase tickets for midweek travel to London cost around US$950 in low season (roughly speaking, winter), US$1275 in high season (summer, Christmas and Easter) from New York and Washington DC,

US$1050/1375 from Chicago. A more flexible ticket will set you back around US$2250 out of New York, US$2540 out of Chicago. Fixed-date advance-purchase alternatives include New York to Paris for US$950/1400, US$900/1100 to Frankfurt, US$1000/1150 to Madrid, or US$870/1350 to Athens; flying from Chicago, discounted tickets can be had at US$1150/1400 to Paris, US$1200/1500 to Frankfurt, US$1150/1350 to Madrid, or US$850/1300 to Athens. There are promotional offers from time to time, especially in the off-peak seasons; Virgin Atlantic, for example, sometimes has very cheap New York–London fares in late winter with no advance purchase necessary.

From the west coast the major airlines fly at least three times a week and up to twice daily from Los Angeles, San Francisco and Seattle to the main European cities. Flexible economy-class tickets from LA to London will set you back at least US$2650 in high season. If you can buy your tickets in advance and don't need flexibility, you can get to London for US$1100/1450 (low/high season), to Paris for US$1250/1575, to Frankfurt for US$1300/1675, to Madrid for US$1130/1400, or to Athens for US$1050/1500.

From Canada

Most of the big airlines fly to the major European hubs from Montreal and Toronto at least once daily (three times a week for smaller airlines). From Toronto, London is your cheapest option, with the lowest direct round-trip fare around Can$930/1230. For a flexible economy-class ticket on the same route, you're looking at around Can$2200. Fares from Montreal to Paris start at Can$880/950. Vancouver and Calgary have daily flights to several European cities, with round-trip fares to London from around Can$1200/1475, depending on the season.

From Australia and New Zealand

There are flights from Melbourne, Sydney, Adelaide, Brisbane and Perth to most European capitals, with not a great deal of difference in the fares to the busiest destinations: a return from Sydney to London, Paris, Rome, Madrid, Athens or Frankfurt should be available through travel agents for around Aus$1650 in low season (Australia's summer, Europe's winter) and slightly higher in high season (though you can sometimes get great deals). A one-way ticket costs slightly more than half that,

while a return flight from Auckland to Europe is approximately NZ$2100 in low season and from around NZ$2800 in high season. Asian airlines often work out cheapest, and may throw in a stopover. Some agents may also offer "open jaw" tickets, flying you into one city and out from another, which needn't even be in the same country. For RTW deals and other low-price tickets, the most reliable operator is STA Travel (see below), which also supply packages with companies such as Contiki and Busabout, can issue rail passes, and advise on visa regulations – for a fee they'll even do all the paperwork for you.

From South Africa

Many major airlines fly from Johannesburg and Cape Town to a number of European hubs. Flights from Johannesburg cost about ZAR6700/7000 to Frankfurt in low season/high season, around ZAR7050/7820 to Paris, and slightly more from Cape Town. BA fly direct to London from Johannesburg or Cape Town for around ZAR3000 more. Many of the cheapest deals involve flying via the Middle East with firms such as Turkish or Emirates.

AGENTS

North South Travel UK ☎ 01245 608 291, ⊕ northsouthtravel .co.uk. Friendly, competitive travel agency, offering discounted fares worldwide. Profits are used to support projects in the developing world, especially the promotion of sustainable tourism.

STA Travel UK ☎ 0871 230 0040, ⊕ statravel.co.uk; US ☎ 1 800 781 4040, ⊕ statravel.com; Australia ☎ 134 782, ⊕ statravel.com .au; New Zealand ☎ 0800 474400, ⊕ statravel.co.nz; South Africa ☎ 0861 781 781, ⊕ www.statravel.co.za. Independent and student travel, air tickets, student IDs, travel insurance, car rental and rail passes.

Trailfinders UK ☎ 020 7368 1200, Ireland ☎ 021 464 8800, ⊕ trailfinders.com. One of the best-informed and most efficient agents for independent travellers.

Travel CUTS Canada ☎ 1 800 667 2887, US ☎ 1 800 592 2887, ⊕ travelcuts.com. Canadian youth and student travel firm.

USIT Ireland (Republic) ☎ 01 602 1906, Northern Ireland ☎ 028 9032 4073, Australia ☎ 1800 092 499, ⊕ usit.ie. Ireland's main student and youth travel specialists.

Getting around

It's easy to travel in Europe, and a number of special deals and passes can make it fairly economical too, especially for students and those under 26. Air links are extensive and, thanks to the growing number of budget airlines, flying is often

cheaper than taking the train, but you'll appreciate the diversity of Europe best at ground level, by way of its enormous and generally efficient web of rail, road and ferry connections.

By train

Trains are generally the best way to tour Europe. The rail network in most countries is comprehensive and the region boasts some of the world's most scenic rail journeys. Costs are relatively low, too – apart from Britain, where prices can be absurdly steep – as trains are heavily subsidized, and prices are brought down further by passes and discount cards. We've covered the various passes here, as well as the most important international routes and most useful addresses; frequencies and journey times are given throughout the Guide.

During the summer, especially if you're travelling at night or a long distance, it's best to make **reservations** whenever you can; on some trains (TGV services, for example) it's compulsory. See our "Extra rail charges" box for more on supplements.

For timetables, Ⓦbahn.de is the best online resource, with comprehensive domestic and international rail listings across Europe, while Ⓦseat61.com is another excellent source of information.

Finally, whenever you board an international train in Europe, check the route of the car you are in, since trains frequently split, with different carriages going to different destinations.

Europe-wide rail passes

InterRail

InterRail passes have long been synonymous with young European backpackers travelling across the Continent on the cheap. There are two types of pass available: the **Global Pass** and **One Country Pass**. Both can be bought direct from Ⓦinterrail .com and from main stations and international rail agents in all thirty countries covered by the scheme. To qualify, you need to have been resident in one of the participating countries for six months or more. The only countries in this book not covered by the scheme are Albania, Estonia, Latvia, Lithuania, Morocco and Russia.

InterRail Global Pass The daddy of all rail passes, offering access to almost the entire European rail network. You can choose between five different time periods – continuous blocks of 15 or 22 days or one month – or set amounts of travel – either five days within ten days or ten days within 22 days. Youth (under-26) passes valid for second-class travel start from €184/£156 for five days up to €442/£375 for a month. Note that you cannot use the pass in the country in which you bought it although discounts of up to fifty percent are usually available.

InterRail One Country Pass Same principle as the Global Pass but valid for just one country (or the Benelux zone of Belgium, the Netherlands and Luxembourg). Time periods and prices vary depending on the country. A three-day second-class youth pass will set you back €39/£33 in Bulgaria, €129/£109 in Spain and €147/£125 in France.

Eurail

Non-European residents aren't eligible for InterRail passes. For them the Eurail scheme (Ⓦeurailgroup .org/eurail) offers a range of passes giving unlimited travel in 27 European countries. There are four types of pass – the **Global Pass**, **Select Pass**, **Regional Pass** and **One Country Pass**, all of which should be bought outside Europe. Apart from some One Country passes, all are available at discounted youth (25 or younger) rates for second-class travel and saver rates for adults travelling in groups.

Eurail Global Pass A single pass valid for travel in 24 countries: Austria, Belgium, Bulgaria, Croatia, Czech Republic, Denmark, Finland, France, Germany, Greece, Hungary, Ireland, Italy, Luxembourg, the Netherlands, Norway, Portugal, Romania, Slovakia, Slovenia, Spain, Sweden, Switzerland and Turkey. There are seven different time periods available from ten days' travel within two months, up to three months' continuous travel. Prices start at €435/US$576 for a youth pass valid for fifteen days.

Eurail Select Pass Allows you to select three, four or five bordering countries out of the 24 countries above, plus Montenegro and Serbia, but minus France and Poland. Prices start at €234/US$318 for a three-country youth pass valid for five days' travel within two months.

Eurail Regional Pass Allows travel within two bordering countries. Prices depend on the country combination; for example an Austria–Czech Republic youth pass valid for five days' travel in two

---

EXTRA RAIL CHARGES

Note that even if you've bought an InterRail or Eurail pass, you will still need to pay extra charges or supplements to travel on many high-speed trains (such as Eurostar, TGV and AVE), night trains and those on special scenic routes. Even where there is in theory no supplement, there's often a compulsory reservation fee, which may cost you double if you only find out about it once you're on the train. For details of charges check the InterRail website under "special trains" or "supplements". You can often avoid these charges if you plan your journey within domestic networks.

months will cost you €149/US$202 whereas the same period for Germany–Switzerland costs €242/US$329.

Eurail One Country Pass Offers travel within one of the following eighteen countries (or the Benelux zone of Belgium, the Netherlands and Luxembourg): Austria, Bulgaria, Croatia, Czech Republic, Denmark, Finland, Greece, Hungary, Ireland, Italy, Norway, Poland, Portugal, Romania, Slovakia, Slovenia, Spain and Sweden. Prices vary depending on the size of the country and whether youth passes are available: for example, a youth pass in Denmark valid for three days' travel costs €82/US$111; the same time period costs €177/US$240 in Spain where special youth passes are not available.

Regional rail passes

In addition to the InterRail and Eurail schemes there are a few regional rail passes which can be good value if you're doing a lot of travelling within one area; we've listed some of the main ones below. National rail passes (apart from InterRail and Eurail) are covered in the relevant chapter of the Guide.

Balkan Flexipass Offers unlimited first-class-only travel through Bulgaria, Bosnia-Herzegovina, Greece, Macedonia, Serbia, Montenegro, Romania and Turkey. Prices start at US$243 (youth US$146) for five days' travel in one month.

Brit Rail Pass Ⓦ britrail.com. Allows unlimited travel in Britain and Ireland. Prices start from US$335 (youth US$269) for four days' standard-class travel in one month.

European East Pass Gives five days' travel in a month in Austria, the Czech Republic, Hungary, Poland and Slovakia for US$219, plus up to five additional days at US$31 each.

RAIL CONTACTS
UK

European Rail Ⓣ 020 7619 1083, Ⓦ europeanrail.com. Independent specialists for Continental rail travel

Eurostar Ⓣ 0843 218 6186, outside the UK Ⓣ +44 1233 617 575, Ⓦ eurostar.com. UK to Europe via Channel Tunnel.

International Rail Ⓣ 0871 231 8790, Ⓦ internationalrail.com. Global rail specialist.

InterRail Ⓦ interrail.eu. Main website for buying InterRail passes.

The Man in Seat 61 Ⓦ seat61.com. Comprehensive informational site set up by a rail enthusiast.

Rail Europe Ⓣ 0844 848 4078, Ⓦ raileurope.co.uk. British representative of SNCF French railways, sells rail tickets Europe-wide.

STA Travel Ⓣ 0871 230 0040, Ⓦ statravel.co.uk.

US and Canada

ACP Rail International Ⓣ 1 866 938 7245 or Ⓣ 1 514 733 9865, Ⓦ acprail.com. Eurail agent.

BritRail Travel Ⓣ 1 866 938 7245, Ⓦ britrail.com. British passes.

Eurail Ⓦ eurail.com.

Rail Europe US Ⓣ 1 800 622 8600, Canada Ⓣ 1 800 361 7245, Ⓦ raileurope.com. Official Eurail agent, with wide range of regional and one-country passes.

STA Travel US Ⓣ 1 800 781 4040, Ⓦ statravel.com.

Australia and New Zealand

CIT World Travel Australia Ⓣ 1300 380 992, Ⓦ cittravel.com.au. Eurail and Italian rail passes.

Rail Europe Australia Ⓦ raileurope-world.com.au, New Zealand Ⓦ raileurope.co.nz.

Rail Plus Australia Ⓣ 1300 555 003 or Ⓣ 03 9642 8644, Ⓦ railplus.com.au; NZ Ⓣ 09 377 5415, Ⓦ railplus.co.nz. Eurail and BritRail passes.

STA Travel Australia Ⓣ 134 782, Ⓦ statravel.com.au; New Zealand Ⓣ 0800 474400, Ⓦ statravel.co.nz.

South Africa

Rail Europe Ⓣ 011 628 2319, Ⓦ raileurope.co.za. Official distributor for European rail in South Africa.

STA Travel South Africa Ⓣ 0861 781 781, Ⓦ statravel.co.za.

By bus

Long-distance journeys by bus between major European cities are generally slower and less comfortable than by train and – if you have a rail pass – not necessarily cheaper. If you're only travelling to a few places, however, a bus pass or circular bus ticket can undercut a rail pass, especially for over-26s. There's also the option of a bus tour if you're on a tight schedule or simply want everything planned for you.

Eurolines Ⓦ eurolines-pass.com. Offers the Eurolines pass, valid for travel between 51 cities in twenty countries. It costs £246/€290 (£292/€345 for over-26s) for fifteen days in high season (late June to mid-Sept as well as Christmas/New Year) and £317/€375 (£385/€455) for 30 days. Prices are around a third lower in low season.

Busabout Ⓦ busabout.com. Offers a hop-on, hop-off service throughout Western Europe operating May–Oct. There are three "loops" on offer as well as a Flexitrip Pass where you design your own route. Prices start from £399/€471 for a one-loop pass or £349 /€412 for the Flexitrip Pass.

Contiki Ⓦ contiki.com. Long-established operator offering bus tours throughout Europe for 18- to 35-year-olds from three to 46 days. A twelve-day "European Discovery" tour visiting the Netherlands, Germany, Austria, Italy, Switzerland and France starts at £1168 /€1380 including hotel accommodation and meals.

By ferry

Travelling by ferry is sometimes the most practical way to get around, the obvious routes being from the mainland to the Mediterranean islands, and between the countries bordering the Baltic and Adriatic seas. There are countless routes serving a huge range of destinations, too numerous to outline here; we've given the details of the most useful routes within each chapter.

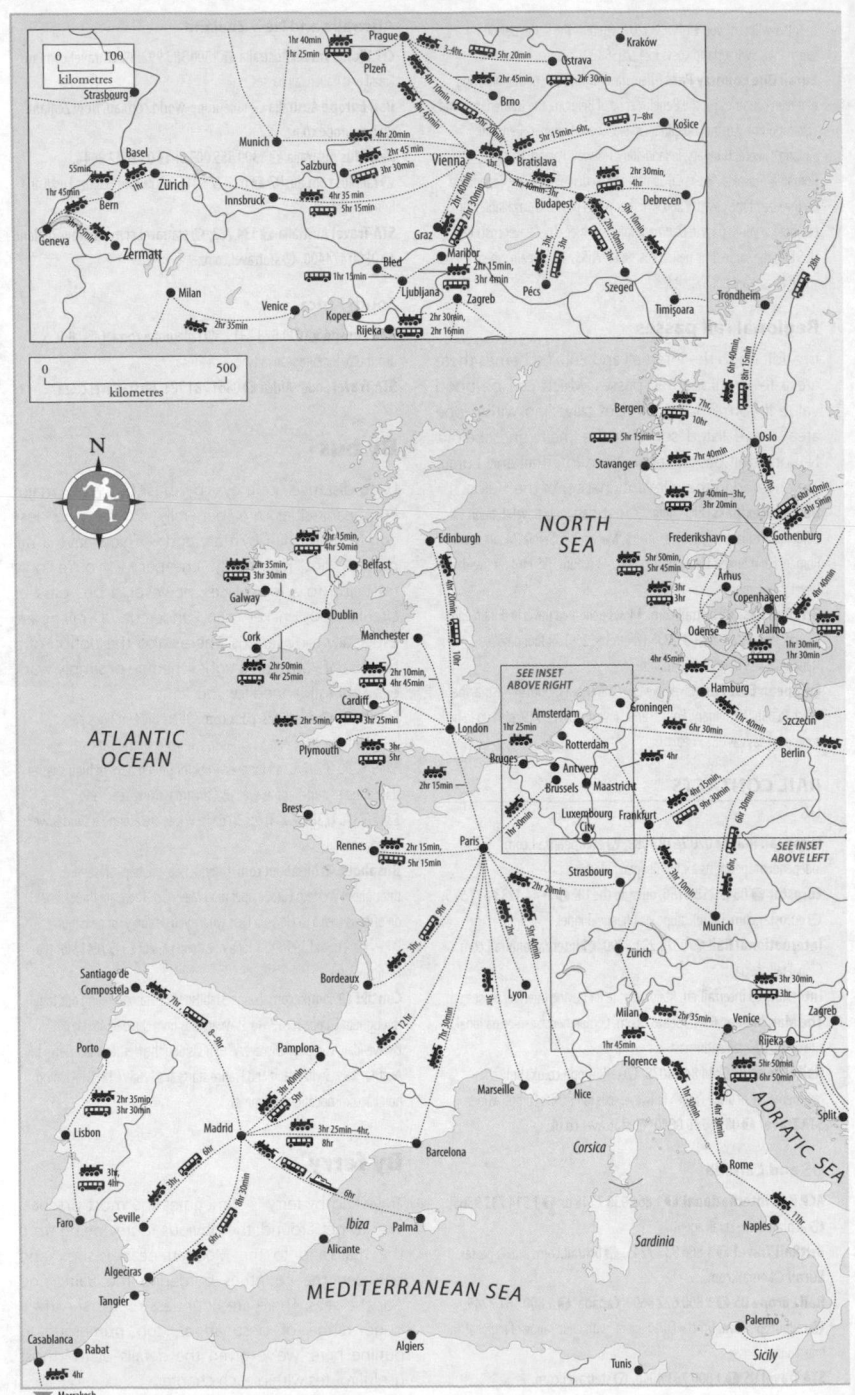

JOURNEY TIMES
BY TRAIN & BUS

By plane

Most European countries now have at least one budget airline selling low-cost flights online, and invariably undercutting train and bus fares on longer international routes. Apart from its environmental impact, travelling by air means you miss the scenery and "feel" for a country that ground-level transport can provide; there's also the inconvenience of getting between airports and the cities they serve, often quite a haul in itself. But, if you're pressed for time, and especially if you want to get from one end of Europe to another, flying is definitely an option. See p.29 for a selective list of budget airlines.

Accommodation

Although accommodation is one of the key costs to consider when planning your trip, it needn't be a stumbling block to a budget-conscious tour of Europe. Indeed, even in Europe's pricier destinations the hostel system means there is always an affordable place to stay. If you're prepared to camp, you can get by on very little while staying at some excellently equipped sites. Come summer, university accommodation can be a cheap option in some countries.

The one rule of thumb is that in the most popular cities and resorts – Venice, Amsterdam, Prague, Paris, Barcelona, the Algarve, and so on – things can get very busy during the peak summer months. Be sure to book in advance regardless of your budget.

Hostels

The cheapest places to stay around Europe are the innumerable hostels that cover the Continent. There are plenty of good-quality independent hostels in most major cities, while many establishments are members of Hostelling International (HI), which incorporates the national youth hostel associations of every country in the world. Most are clean, well-run places, always offering dormitory accommodation, and often a range of private single and double rooms,

or rooms with four to six beds. Many hostels also either have self-catering facilities or provide low-cost meals, and the larger ones have a range of other facilities – a swimming pool and a games room, for example. There is usually no age limit, but where there is limited space priority is sometimes given to those under 26. The best rates are usually available on the hostel website or through booking engines such as Hostelworld (Ⓦ hostelworld.com) or Hostelbookers (Ⓦ hostelbookers.com). Strictly speaking, to use a HI hostel you have to have membership, although if there's room you can stay at most hostels by simply paying a bit extra. If you do plan to stay in hostels, however, it's certainly worth joining, which you can do through your home country's hostelling association. HI hostels can usually be booked through their country's hostelling association website, almost always over the counter at other hostels in the same country, and often through the international HI website Ⓦ hihostels.com.

YOUTH HOSTEL ASSOCIATIONS

USA Ⓣ 1 301 495 1240, Ⓦ hiusa.org.
Canada Ⓣ 613 237 7884, Ⓦ hihostels.ca.
England and Wales Ⓣ 0800 019 1700 or Ⓣ 01629 592 700, Ⓦ yha.org.uk.
Scotland Ⓣ 0845 293 7373, Ⓦ syha.org.uk.
Ireland (Republic) Ⓣ 01 830 4555, Ⓦ anoige.ie.
Northern Ireland Ⓣ 028 9032 4733, Ⓦ hini.org.uk.
Australia Ⓣ 02 9218 9090, Ⓦ yha.com.au.
New Zealand Ⓣ 0800 278 299 or 03 379 9970, Ⓦ yha.co.nz.
South Africa Ⓦ hisouthafrica.com.

Hotels and pensions

With **hotels** you can really spend as much or as little as you like. Most hotels in Europe are graded on some kind of star system. One- and two-star category hotels are plain and simple on the whole, usually family-run, and rooms often lack private facilities; sometimes breakfast won't be included. In three-star hotels rooms will nearly always be en suite and prices will normally include breakfast. In the really top-level places breakfast, oddly enough, isn't always included.

Obviously prices vary greatly, but you're rarely going to be paying less than €26 for a basic double room even in southern Europe, while between the

ACCOMMODATION PRICES

All accommodation prices listed are for high season. The prices we list for hotels, guesthouses, B&Bs, *pensions* and private rooms are for the cheapest double room. For hostels, it is the price of the cheapest dorm bed, and for campsites the cost of a night's stay per person, except where noted.

Netherlands, Scandinavia and the British Isles the average price is around €77. In some countries a pension or **B&B** (also variously known as a guesthouse, *pensão*, *Gasthaus* or numerous other names) is a cheaper alternative, offering just a few rooms of simple accommodation. In some countries these advertise with a sign in the window; in others they can be booked through the tourist office, which may demand a small fee. There are various other kinds of accommodation – apartments, farmhouses, cottages, *gîtes* in France, and more – but most are geared to longer-term stays and we have detailed them only where relevant.

Camping

The **cheapest** form of accommodation is, of course, a campsite. Most sites charge per person, with additional charges per plot and/or per vehicle. Facilities can be excellent, especially in countries such as France where camping is very popular. If you don't have a vehicle you should add in the cost and inconvenience of getting to the site, since most are on the outskirts of towns, sometimes further. Some sites also have cabins, which you can stay in for a little extra, although these are usually fairly basic affairs, only really worth considering in regions like Scandinavia where budget options are thin on the ground. Tourist offices can often recommend well-equipped and conveniently located sites.

As for **camping rough**, it's a fine idea if you can get away with it – though perhaps an entire trip of rough camping is in reality too gruelling to be truly enjoyable. In some countries it's easy – in parts of Scandinavia it's a legal right, and in Greece and other southern European countries you can usually find a bit of beach to pitch down on – but in others it can get you into trouble with the law.

Camping Card International

If you're planning to do a lot of camping, a Camping Card International (**CCI or "carnet"**), which gives discounts on member sites, is a good investment. In

the US and Canada the carnet is available from home motoring organizations, or from Family Campers and RVers (FCRV; ☎ 1 800 245 9755, ⓦ fcrv .org). In the UK and Ireland, the carnet costs £5.50, and is available from the AA in Ireland (☎ 01 617 9999, ⓦ aaireland.ie), or the Caravan Club in the UK (☎ 01342 336633, ⓦ caravanclub.co.uk), or for members only from the Camping and Caravanning Club (☎ 0845 130 7632, ⓦ campingandcaravanning club.co.uk; annual membership £40).

Festivals and annual events

There's always some event or other happening in Europe, and the bigger shindigs can be reason enough for visiting a place. Be warned, though, that if you're intending to visit a place during its annual festival you need to plan well in advance; accommodation can be booked up months beforehand, especially for the most famous events.

Festival calendar

Many of the festivals and annual events you'll come across in Europe have their origin in – and in many cases still represent – religious celebrations, commemorating a local miracle or saint's day. Others are decidedly more secular – from film and music festivals to street carnivals.

JANUARY

Twelfth Night (Jan 6) Rather than Christmas Day, in Spain this is the time for present-giving, while in Orthodox Eastern Europe, Jan 6 is Christmas Day.
La Tamborrada, San Sebastián, Spain (Jan 20) Probably the loudest festival you will encounter as scores of drummers take to the streets of San Sebastián.

FEBRUARY

Berlin Film Festival, Germany (early to mid-Feb) Home of the Golden Bear award, this film bash is geared towards the general public.
Carnival/Mardi Gras (mid-Feb) Celebrated most famously in Venice, but there are smaller events across Europe, notably in Viareggio (Italy), Luzern and Basel (Switzerland), Cologne (Germany), Maastricht (Netherlands) and tiny Binche (Belgium).

MARCH

Las Fallas, Valencia, Spain (March 15–19) The passing of winter is celebrated in explosive fashion with enormous bonfires, burning effigies and plenty of all-night partying.

COUCHSURFING AND AIRBNB

Couchsurfing (ⓦ couchsurfing.com) gives travellers the chance to stay with local people **free of charge**, with hosts verified through references and a vouching system. **Airbnb** (ⓦ airbnb.com) is another good option for budget short-term stays, with (sometimes unusual) lodgings listed by private individuals.

St Patrick's Day (March 17) Celebrated wherever there's an Irish community, in Dublin it's a five-day festival with music, parades and a lot of drinking.

APRIL

Easter Celebrated with most verve and ceremony in Catholic and Orthodox Europe, where Easter Sunday or Monday is usually marked with some sort of procession; note that the Orthodox Church's Easter can fall a week or two either side of the Western festival.

Feria de Abril, Seville, Spain (mid-April) A week of flamenco music and dancing, parades and bullfights, in a frenzied and enthusiastic atmosphere.

King's Day, Amsterdam, Netherlands (April 27) King Willem-Alexander's birthday is the excuse for this anarchic 24-hour drinking and dressing-up binge – remember your orange attire.

MAY

Cannes Film Festival, France (mid/late May) The world's most famous cinema festival is really more of an industry affair than anything else.

PinkPop Festival, Landgraaf, Netherlands (late May/early June) The Netherlands' biggest pop music festival.

JUNE

Festa do São João, Porto, Portugal (June 23–24) Portugal's second city puts on the mother of all street parties, culminating in revellers hitting each other with plastic hammers.

Glastonbury Festival, England (mid/late June) Despite being one of Europe's largest (most expensive) music festivals, Glastonbury is a surprisingly intimate affair thanks to its beautiful setting and hippie vibe.

Roskilde Festival, Denmark (late June/early July) An eclectic range of music (rock, dance, folk) and performance arts, with profits going to worthy causes.

JULY

The Palio, Siena, Italy (July 2 & Aug 16) Italy's most spectacular summer event: a bareback horse race between representatives of the different quarters of the city around the main square.

Montreux Jazz Festival, Switzerland (early July) These days only loosely committed to jazz, this festival takes in everything from folk to breakbeats.

Fiesta de San Fermín, Pamplona, Spain (July 6–14) Anarchic fun, centred on the running of the bulls through the streets of the city, plus music, dancing and of course a lot of drinking.

Exit Festival, Novi Sad, Serbia (early/mid-July) Europe's hippest music festival held in a beautiful fortress and attracting top DJs and artists from around the world.

Avignon Festival, France (early/mid-July) Slanted towards drama but hosts plenty of other events too.

Dubrovnik Summer Festival, Croatia (July & Aug) A host of musical events and theatre performances against the backdrop of the town's beautiful Renaissance centre.

The Proms, London (July–Sept) World-famous concert series that maintains high standards of classical music at egalitarian prices.

Ramadan (June–July in 2014, 2015 & 2016) Commemorating the revelation of the Koran to the Prophet Mohammed, the month of fasting from sunrise until sunset ends with a huge celebration called Eid el-Fitr. Morocco, Turkey, Kosovo, Albania, Bosnia-Herzegovina, plus Muslim areas of Bulgaria and Greece.

AUGUST

Locarno Film Festival, Switzerland (early/mid-Aug) Movies from around the world compete on the banks of Lake Maggiore.

La Tomatina, Buñol, Spain The last Wednesday in August sees the streets of Buñol packed for a one-hour food fight disposing of 130,000 kilos of tomatoes.

Edinburgh Festival, Scotland (last three weeks of Aug) A mass of top-notch and fringe events in every performing medium, from rock to cabaret to modern experimental music, dance and drama.

Notting Hill Carnival, London (last weekend of Aug) Predominantly Black British and Caribbean celebration that's become the world's second-biggest street carnival after Rio.

Venice Film Festival, Italy (late Aug/early Sept) First held in 1932, this is the world's oldest film festival.

SEPTEMBER

Ibiza closing parties, Spain (mostly in Sept) The summer dance music Mecca goes out with a bang in September, with all the main clubs holding closing parties.

Regata Storica, Venice, Italy (early Sept) A trial of skill for the city's gondoliers.

Oktoberfest, Munich, Germany (late Sept/early Oct) A huge beer festival and fair, attracting vast numbers of people to consume gluttonous quantities of beer and food.

Galway International Oyster Festival, Ireland (last weekend in Sept) The arrival of the oyster season is celebrated with a three-day seafood, Guinness and dancing shindig.

OCTOBER

Combat des Reines, Switzerland (early Oct) Quirky cow-fighting contest held to decide the queen of the herd in the Valais region of Switzerland. The main event is the copious drinking and betting on the sidelines (and no, the cows don't get hurt).

NOVEMBER

Bonfire Night, Lewes, England (Nov 5) Huge processions and tremendous fireworks light up this sleepy town every year.

Madonna della Salute Festival, Venice, Italy (Nov 21) Annual candlelit procession across the Grand Canal to the church of Santa Maria della Salute.

DECEMBER

Christmas Festive markets sprout up across the Continent in the run-up to Christmas. One of the best is found in Cologne, Germany.

New Year's Eve Celebrated with fireworks and parties across Europe, it's best experienced in Edinburgh where over a hundred thousand cram the streets for Hogmanay.

Work and study

The best way of getting to know a country properly is to work there and learn the language. Study opportunities are also a good way of absorbing yourself in the local culture, though they invariably need to be fixed up in advance; check newspapers for ads or contact one of the organizations listed opposite.

Working In Europe

There are any number of jobs you can pick up on the road to supplement your spending money. It's normally not hard to find bar or restaurant work, especially in large resort areas during the summer, and your chances will be greater if you speak the local language – although being able to speak English may be your greatest asset in more touristy areas. **Cleaning jobs, nannying** and **au pair** work are also common, if not spectacularly well paid, often just providing room and board plus pocket money. Some of them can be organized on the spot, while others need to be arranged before you leave home.

The other big casual earner is farm work, particularly **grape-picking**, an option from August to October when the vines are being harvested. The best country for this is France, but there's sometimes work in Germany too, and you're unlikely to be asked for documentation. Also in France, along the Côte d'Azur, and in other yacht-havens such as Greece and parts of southern Spain, there is sometimes crewing work available, though you'll obviously need the appropriate experience.

Rather better paid, and equally widespread, if only during the September to June period, is **teaching** English as a foreign language (TEFL), though it's sometimes hard to find English-teaching jobs without a TEFL qualification. You'll normally be paid a liveable local salary, sometimes with somewhere to live thrown in, and you can often supplement your income with more lucrative private lessons. The TEFL teaching season is reversed in Britain and to a lesser extent Ireland, with plenty of work available during the summer in London and on the English south coast (but again, some kind of TEFL qualification is usually required).

A final tip for those hoping to work abroad: buy a book dedicated to the subject. We recommend those published in the UK by Vacation Work; visit ⓦ crimsonpublishing.co.uk for their catalogue. Also try ⓦ studyabroad.com, a useful website with listings and links to study and work programmes worldwide.

Studying in Europe

Studying abroad invariably means learning a language, in an intensive course that lasts between two weeks and three months, and staying with a local family. There are plenty of places you can do this, and you should reckon on paying around £300/US$500 a week, including room and board. If you know a language well, you could also apply to do a short course in another subject at a local university; scan the classified sections of the newspapers back home, and keep an eye out when you're on the spot. The EU runs a programme called Erasmus in which university students from Britain and Ireland can obtain mobility grants to study in one of 32 European countries for between three months and a full academic year if their university participates in the programme. Check with your university's international relations office, or see ⓦ britishcouncil.org/erasmus.

WORK AND STUDY CONTACTS

AFS Intercultural Programs US ☎ 1 800 AFS INFO, Canada ☎ 1 800 361 7248, Australia ☎ 1300131736, NZ ☎ 0800 600 300, SA ☎ 27114310113, ⓦ afs.org. Intercultural exchange organization.
American Institute for Foreign Study US ☎ 1 866 906 2437, UK ☎ 020 7581 7300, Australia ☎ 02 8235 7000, ⓦ aifs.com. Language study and cultural immersion for the summer or school year.
ASSE International UK ☎ 01952 460 733, US ☎ 1 800 677 2773, Canada ☎ 1 800 361 3214, Australia ☎ 03 9775 4711, New Zealand ☎ 0800 488 884, South Africa ☎ 021 790 5637, ⓦ asse .com. International student exchanges and summer language programmes across most of Europe.
British Council UK ☎ 0161 957 7775, ⓦ britishcouncil.org. The Council's Recruitment Group recruits TEFL teachers with degrees and TEFL qualifications for posts, while its Education and Training Group runs teacher exchange programmes and enables those who already work as educators to find out about teacher development programmes abroad.
Council on International Educational Exchange (CIEE) US ☎ 1 207 553 4000, ⓦ ciee.org. Leading NGO offering study programmes and volunteer projects.
Cultural Vistas US ☎ 1 212 497 3500 or ☎ 1 410 997 2200, ⓦ culturalvistas.org. Summer internships in various European countries for students who have completed at least two years of college in science, agriculture, engineering or architecture.
International House UK ☎ 020 7611 2400, ⓦ ihlondon.com. Reputable English-teaching organization that offers TEFL training leading to a Certificate in English Language Teaching to Adults (CELTA), and recruits for teaching positions in Britain and abroad.
World Learning US ☎ 1 800 257 7751 or ☎ 1 802 257 7751, ⓦ worldlearning.org. The Experiment in International Living

(**W** experimentinternational.org) has summer programmes for high-school students, while the School for International Training (**W** sit .edu/studyabroad) offers accredited college semesters abroad, with language and cultural studies, homestay and other academic work.

Travel essentials

Costs

It's hard to generalize about what you're likely to spend travelling around Europe, but it's by and large **not cheap**. Some countries – Norway, Switzerland, the UK – are among the most expensive in the world, while in others (Turkey, for example) you can live quite well on a fairly modest budget. Remember, however, that all of Europe is modern and well touristed which means higher prices than in the developing world. In general, countries in the north and west of Europe are more expensive than those in the south and east, though keep an eye on exchange rates.

Accommodation will be your largest single expense, and can really determine where you decide to travel. **Food and drink** costs also vary wildly, although again in most parts of Europe you can assume that a cheap restaurant meal will cost €10–18 a head, with prices nearer the top end of the scale in Scandinavia, at the bottom end in eastern Europe, and below that in Turkey and Morocco. **Transport** costs are something you can pin down more exactly if you have a rail pass. Nowhere, though, are transport costs a major burden, except perhaps in Britain where public transport is less heavily subsidized than elsewhere.

The bottom line for an average daily budget touring the Continent – camping, self-catering, hitching, etc – might be around €30 a day per person. Adding on a rail pass, staying in hostels and eating out occasionally would bring this up to perhaps €48 a day, while staying in private rooms or hotels and eating out once a day would mean a personal daily budget of at least €94. See the box on opposite for tips on keeping your costs down.

PRICES

At the beginning of each chapter you'll find a guide to "rough costs" including food, accommodation and travel. Prices are quoted in euros for ease of comparison. Within the chapter itself prices are quoted in local currency.

Crime and personal safety

Travelling around Europe should be relatively trouble-free, but, as in any part of the world, there is always the chance of petty theft. Conditions vary greatly depending on the country: in Scandinavia, for example, you're unlikely to encounter much trouble of any kind, whereas in certain areas of metropolises such as London, Paris or Barcelona, the crime rate is significantly higher. Also exercise caution in poorer regions such as Morocco, Turkey and southern Italy.

Safety tips

In order to minimize the risks, you should take some basic precautions. First and perhaps most important, try not to look too much like a tourist. Appearing lost, even if you are, is to be avoided, and it's not a good idea – especially in southern Europe – to walk around flashing an obviously expensive camera or smartphone: the professional bag-snatchers who tour train stations can have your valuables off you in seconds.

If you're waiting for a train, keep your eyes (and hands if necessary) on your bags at all times; if you want to sleep, put everything valuable under whatever you use as a pillow. Exercise caution when choosing a train compartment and avoid any situation that makes you feel uncomfortable. **Padlocking** your bags to the luggage rack if you're on an overnight train increases the likelihood that they'll still be there in the morning. It's also a good idea to wear a **money belt**.

If you're staying in a hostel, take your valuables out with you unless there's a very secure store for them on the premises. It's a good idea to take a photocopy of your passport and send it to your email account, as is leaving a copy of your address book with friends or family.

If the worst happens and you do have something stolen, inform the **police** immediately (we've included details of the main city police stations or tourist police throughout); the priority is to get a statement from them detailing exactly what has been lost, which you'll need for your insurance claim back home.

Customs

Customs and duty-free restrictions vary throughout Europe, but are standard for travellers arriving in the EU at one litre of spirits, four litres of table wine, plus 200 cigarettes (or 250g tobacco, or fifty cigars). There is no duty-free allowance for travel within the EU: in principle you can carry as much in the way of

GETTING BY ON A BUDGET

Buy a rail pass Whether you're planning to take in all of Europe or just a few countries, a rail pass will save you a bundle (see p.32).

Find a roommate Accommodation in hotels, *pensions* and private rooms is cheaper if you share, so buddy up.

Student/youth discounts If you're a student or under 26, make sure you bring your student or youth card (see p.44); always ask about discounts.

Head for the countryside Don't spend more time than you need to in the city – prices will always be highest.

Shun tourist traps Eat and drink with the locals and try regional food as it'll usually be cheaper – and frequently tastier.

Self-cater Markets are full of fresh, seasonal picnic fare which makes self-catering a treat.

Drink at home Have a few drinks before you go out – you can usually pick up booze from local shops at a fraction of the bar price.

Be flexible Transport is often cheaper in off-peak hours.

Sleep on the train Make your longest journeys overnight – you'll forego accommodation costs for the night.

Bargain, bargain, bargain Don't be afraid to haggle (especially in places like Morocco where it's expected), but know when to stop.

duty-paid goods as you want, so long as it is for personal use. Note that Andorra, Gibraltar, the Canary Islands, Ceuta and the Channel Islands are outside the EU for customs purposes. Remember that if you are carrying prescribed drugs of any kind, it might be a good idea to have a copy of the prescription to show to suspicious customs officers. Note also that all EU members restrict the importation from outside Europe of meat, fish, eggs and honey.

Drugs

It's hardly necessary to state that drugs such as amphetamines, cocaine, heroin, LSD and ecstasy are **illegal** all over Europe, and although use of cannabis is widespread in most countries, and legally tolerated in some (famously in the Netherlands, for example), you are never allowed to possess more than a tiny amount for personal use, and unlicensed sale remains illegal. Penalties can be severe (in certain countries, such as Turkey, even possession of cannabis can result in a hefty prison sentence) and your consulate is unlikely to be sympathetic.

Electricity

The supply in Europe is 220v (240v in the British Isles), which means that anything on North American voltage (110v) normally needs a transformer – or at least a plug adapter if the power cord has a built-in transformer. Some countries (notably Spain and Morocco) still have a few

places on 110v or 120v, so check before plugging in or you could fry your electronics. British and Irish sockets take three rectangular pins, elsewhere they take two round pins. A travel plug which adapts to these systems is useful to carry. See ⓦkropla.com for more.

Entry requirements

Citizens of the UK (but not other British passport holders), Ireland, Australia, New Zealand, Canada and the US do not need a **visa** to enter most European countries (current exceptions are listed in the box on below), and can usually stay for between one and three months, depending on nationality. EU countries never require visas from British or Irish citizens. Always check visa requirements before travelling, as they can and do change; this especially applies to Canadian, Australian, New Zealand and South African citizens intending to visit Eastern European countries.

VISA ALERT!

Everyone needs a visa to visit Russia, which must be obtained in advance, and if you're passing through Belarus to get there, you'll need a transit visa for that country as well. Citizens of most countries also need a visa for Turkey, which is available at the border (see p.1140). South Africans need a visa for most European countries, so be sure to check with the appropriate embassy before travelling.

Twenty-six countries (Austria, Belgium, Czech Republic, Denmark, Estonia, Finland, France, Germany, Greece, Hungary, Iceland, Italy, Latvia, Liechtenstein, Lithuania, Luxembourg, Malta, the Netherlands, Norway, Poland, Portugal, Slovakia, Slovenia, Spain, Sweden and Switzerland), known as the Schengen group, now have joint visas which are valid for travel in all of them; in theory, there are no immigration controls between these countries, but there may be spot-checks of ID within their borders.

Gay and lesbian travellers

Gay men and lesbians will find most of Europe a **tolerant** place in which to travel, the west rather more so than the east. Gay sex is no longer a criminal offence in any country covered by this book except Morocco, but some still have measures that discriminate against gay men (a higher age of consent, for example), and Russia has recently introduced a law against "gay propaganda", amid a new wave of homophobia. Lesbianism sometimes escapes such laws on the basis that its existence is not officially recognized, although that is not the case in Russia. For further information, check the International Lesbian and Gay Association's European region website at ⓦ ilga-europe.org.

Health

You don't need to have inoculations for any of the countries covered in this book, although for Morocco and Turkey typhoid jabs are advised, and in southeastern Turkey malaria pills are a good idea for much of the year – check ⓦ cdc.gov/travel for full details. Remember to keep your polio and tetanus boosters up to date.

EU citizens are covered by reciprocal health agreements for free or reduced-cost emergency treatment in many of the countries in this book (main exceptions are Albania, Morocco and Turkey). To claim this, you will often be asked for your proof of residence or **European Health Insurance Card** (EHIC), which you can apply for in Britain at ⓦ ehicdirect.org.uk, and in Ireland at ⓦ ehic.ie. Without an EHIC, you won't be turned away from hospitals but you will almost certainly have to pay for any treatment or medicines. Also, in practice, some doctors and hospitals charge anyway and it's up to you to claim reimbursement when you return home. Make sure you are insured for potential medical expenses, and keep copies of receipts and prescriptions.

Doctors, hospitals and pharmacies

For minor health problems it's easiest to go to a **pharmacy**, found pretty much everywhere. In major cities there should be at least one pharmacy open 24 hours – check any pharmacy window for a rota indicating the branch currently open all night. In cases of serious injury or illness contact your nearest consulate, which will have a list of English-speaking **doctors**, as will the local tourist office. In the accounts of larger cities we've listed the most convenient **hospital** casualty units/ emergency rooms.

Contraceptives

Condoms are available everywhere, and are normally reliable international brands such as Durex, at least in northwestern Europe; the condoms in eastern European countries, Morocco and Turkey are of uncertain quality, however, so it's best to bring your own. **AIDS** is of course as much of a problem in Europe as in the rest of the world, and it hardly needs saying that unprotected casual sex is extremely dangerous; members of both sexes should carry condoms. The **pill** is available everywhere, too, though often only on prescription; again, bring a sufficient supply with you. In case of emergency, the morning-after pill is available from pharmacies without a prescription in Austria, Belgium, Bulgaria, Denmark, Estonia, Finland, France, Greece, Ireland, Lithuania, Morocco, the Netherlands, Norway, Portugal, Sweden, Switzerland, Turkey and the UK.

Drinking water

Tap water in most countries is **drinkable**, and only needs to be avoided in Morocco and parts of Turkey. Unfamiliar food may well give you a small case of the runs, normally over in a day or two.

Insurance

Wherever you're travelling from, it's a very good idea to have some kind of travel insurance. Before paying for a new policy, however, check whether you're already covered: students will often find that their student health coverage extends into the vacations and for one term beyond the date of last enrolment; and some credit cards include travel insurance.

Otherwise you should contact a specialist travel insurance company. A typical policy usually provides cover for the loss of baggage, tickets and – up to a certain limit – cash, as well as cancellation or curtailment of your journey. Most of them

ROUGH GUIDES TRAVEL INSURANCE

Rough Guides has teamed up with WorldNomads.com to offer great travel insurance deals. Policies are available to residents of over 150 countries, with cover for a wide range of adventure sports, 24hr emergency assistance, high levels of medical and evacuation cover and a stream of travel safety information. Roughguides.com users can take advantage of their policies online 24/7, from anywhere in the world – even if you're already travelling. And since plans often change when you're on the road, you can extend your policy and even claim online. Roughguides.com users who buy travel insurance with WorldNomads.com can also leave a positive footprint and donate to a community development project. For more information, go to ⓦroughguides.com/travel-insurance.

exclude so-called dangerous sports unless an extra premium is paid: in Europe this can mean anything from scuba-diving to mountaineering, skiing and even bungee-jumping. With medical coverage, you should ascertain whether benefits will be paid as treatment proceeds or only after you return home, and whether there is a 24-hour medical emergency number. When securing baggage cover, make sure that the per-article limit will cover your most valuable possession.

Internet and email

In many countries **internet cafés** are an increasingly rare sight, as public **wi-fi** – often free – takes over. Most hotels and many cafés offer it on a complimentary basis.

Left luggage (baggage deposit)

Almost every train station of any size has facilities for depositing luggage – either lockers or a desk that's open long hours every day. We've given details in the accounts of the major cities.

Mail

We've listed the central **post offices** in major cities and given an idea of opening hours. Bear in mind, though, that in most countries you can avoid long waits in post offices by buying stamps from newsagents, tobacconists and street kiosks. If you know in advance where you're going to be and when, it is possible to collect letters addressed to you, marked **"poste restante"** and sent to the main post office in any town or city where they will be kept under your name – for at least two weeks and usually for a month. When collecting mail, make sure you take your passport for identification, and be aware that there's a possibility of letters being misfiled by someone unfamiliar with your language; try looking under your first name as well as your surname.

Maps

Though you can often buy maps on the spot, you may want to get them in advance to plan your trip – if you know what you want, the best advice is to contact a firm such as Stanfords in the UK (ⓦstanfords.co.uk) or Rand McNally in the US (ⓦrandmcnally.com); both sell maps online or by mail order. For extensive motoring, it's better to get a large-page road atlas such as Michelin's *Tourist and Motoring Atlas*.

Money

The easiest way to carry your money is in the form of plastic. Hotels, shops and restaurants across the Continent accept major **credit and debit cards**, although cheaper places may not. More importantly, you can use them 24/7 to get cash out of **ATMs** throughout the region, including Morocco and Turkey, as long as they are affiliated to an international network (such as Visa, MasterCard or Cirrus). In some countries **banks** are the only places where you can legally change money, and they often offer the best exchange rates and lowest commission. Local banking hours are given throughout this book. Outside normal hours you can use **bureaux de change**, often located at train stations and airports, though their rates and/or commissions may well be less favourable.

NEWSPAPERS

British and American newspapers and magazines are widely available in Europe, sometimes on the day of publication, more often the day after. They do, however, cost around three times as much as they do at home. Look too for locally produced English-language papers and websites.

Phones

It is nearly always possible, especially in Western Europe, to make international calls from a public call box. Otherwise, you can go to a post office, or a special phone bureau, where you can make a call from a private booth and pay afterwards. Avoid using the phone in your hotel.

To call **any country** in this book from Britain, Ireland, South Africa or New Zealand, dial ☏00, then the country code, then the city/area code (if there is one) without the initial zero – except for the following: Russia and Lithuania (where there is no initial zero); Italy, where the initial zero (or 3 for a cellphone) must be dialled; and Denmark, the Czech Republic, Latvia, Portugal, Spain, Andorra and Gibraltar, where there are no area codes, and the whole number must be dialled. From the US and most of Canada, the international access code is ☏011, from Australia it's ☏0011; otherwise the procedure is the same.

To **call home** from almost all European countries, including Morocco and Turkey, dial ☏00, then the country code, then the city/area code (without the initial zero if there is one), then the local number. The exception is Russia, where you dial ☏8, wait for a continuous dialling tone and then dial ☏10, followed by the country code, area code and number.

For **collect calls**, use the "Home Country Direct" service. In the UK and some other countries, international calling cards available from newsagents enable you to call North America, Australia and New Zealand very cheaply. Most North American, British, Irish and Australasian phone companies either allow you to call home on a credit card, or billed to your home number (contact your company's customer services before you leave to

find out their toll-free access codes from the countries you'll be visiting), or else will issue an international calling card which can be used worldwide, and for which you will be billed at home. If you want a calling card and do not already have one, leave yourself a few weeks to arrange it before leaving.

Mobile/cell phones

North American **cell phones** may not work in Europe – for details contact your provider. Mobiles from the UK, Ireland, Australia and New Zealand and South Africa can be used in most parts of Europe, and a lot of countries – certainly in Western Europe – have nearly universal coverage, but you may have to inform your provider before leaving home to get international access switched on, and you will be charged for receiving calls and even voicemail. Plans were in place at the time of writing to abolish data **roaming charges** when travelling within the EU for residents of the 28 EU member states (plus those of Iceland, Liechtenstein and Norway) from July 2014. The most useful resource for information on phone codes and electrical systems around the world is ⓦkropla.com.

Student and youth discounts

It's worth flashing whichever discount card you've got at every opportunity. If you're a student, an **International Student Identity Card** (ISIC for short) is well worth the investment. It can get you reduced (usually half-price, sometimes free) entry to museums and other sights, as well as qualifying you for other discounts in certain cities. It can also save you money on some transport costs, notably ferries. The card costs £12 in the UK, €15 in Ireland, US$25 in the US, Can$20 in Canada, Aus$25 in Australia, NZ$25 in New Zealand and ZAR100 in South Africa. If you're not a student but under 26, get an International Youth Travel Card, which costs the same and can in some countries give much the same sort of reductions. Both cards are available direct from ⓦisic.org or from youth travel specialists such as STA.

As well as the above options, the **EURO<26** youth card (ⓦeuro26.org) entitles anyone under 26 (or up to 30 in some countries) to a wide range of discounts on transport services, tourist attractions, activities and accommodation for up to a year. It is available online for people living outside Europe and at designated outlets in most of

---

THE EURO (€)

The euro is the currency of 17 EU countries (and a couple of others). Coins come as 1c, 2c, 5c, 10c, 20c, 50c, €1 and €2, with one side of the coin stating the denomination while the other side has a design unique to the issuing country. Euro notes come as €5, €10, €20, €50, €100, €200 and €500. At the time of writing, £1 was worth €1.17, US$1 got you €0.76, Can$1 was €0.72, Aus$1 equalled €0.67, NZ$1 was €0.59 and ZAR1 was €0.08. Check ⓦxe.com for the latest exchange rates.

CLOTHING AND SHOE SIZES

WOMEN'S DRESSES AND SKIRTS

American	4	6	8	10	12	14	16	18
British	8	10	12	14	16	18	20	22
Continental	38	40	42	44	46	48	50	52

WOMEN'S BLOUSES AND SWEATERS

American	6	8	10	12	14	16	18
British	30	32	34	36	38	40	42
Continental	40	42	44	46	48	50	52

WOMEN'S SHOES

American	5	6	7	8	9	10	11
British	3	4	5	6	7	8	9
Continental	36	37	38	39	40	41	42

MEN'S SUITS

American	34	36	38	40	42	44	46	48
British	34	36	38	40	42	44	46	48
Continental	44	46	48	50	52	54	56	58

MEN'S SHIRTS

American	14	15	15.5	16	16.5	17	17.5	18
British	14	15	15.5	16	16.5	17	17.5	18
Continental	36	38	39	41	42	43	44	45

MEN'S SHOES

American	7	7.5	8	8.5	9.5	10	10.5	11	11.5
British	6	7	7.5	8	9	9.5	10	11	12
Continental	39	40	41	42	43	44	44	45	46

Europe (but not France or Germany, nor England or Wales, although it is available in Scotland) for residents – you'll need proof of age and a passport-sized photo. Although the card is valid across the region, prices vary across individual countries (from around €7 to €18), as do the relevant discounts.

Time

This book covers four **time zones** (see map p.46). GMT (Greenwich Mean Time), aka UTC, or Universal Time, is five hours ahead of Eastern Standard Time, eight hours ahead of Pacific Standard Time, eight hours behind Western Australia, ten hours behind eastern Australia, twelve hours behind New Zealand and two hours behind South Africa. Note that all countries in this book (except Morocco) have daylight saving time from March to October, thankfully, they usually all manage to change at the same time. This change, along with daylight saving in North America, Australia and New Zealand, can affect the time difference by an hour either way.

Tourist information

Before you leave, it's worth contacting the **tourist offices** of the countries you're intending to visit for free leaflets, maps and brochures. This is especially true in parts of central and eastern Europe, where up-to-date maps can be harder to find within the country, though note that a few countries do not have any official tourist offices abroad. If there is no office in your home country, apply to the embassy instead.

Once you're in Europe, on-the-spot information is easy enough to find. Most countries have a network of tourist offices that answer queries, dole out a range of (mostly free) maps and brochures, and can often book accommodation, or at least advise you on it. They're better organized in northern Europe – the UK, Scandinavia, the Netherlands, France, Switzerland – with branches in all but the smallest village, and mounds of information; in Greece, Turkey and eastern Europe you'll find fewer tourist offices and they'll be less helpful on the whole, sometimes offering no more than a couple of dog-eared brochures and a photocopied map.

We've given further details, including a broad idea of opening hours, in the introduction for each country.

Travellers with disabilities

Prosperous northern Europe is easier for disabled travellers than the south and east, but the gradual enforcement of EU accessibility regulations is making life easier throughout the European Union at least. Wheelchair access to public buildings nonetheless remains far from common in many countries, as is wheelchair accessibility to public transport. Most buses are still inaccessible to wheel-chair users, but airport facilities are improving, as are those on cross-Channel ferries. As for rail services, these vary greatly: France, for example, provides well for disabled passengers, as do Belgium, Denmark, Switzerland and Austria, but many other countries make little if any provision. For comprehensive info on disabled travel, check out ⓦdisabledtravelers.com.

Women travellers

One of the major irritants for women travelling through Europe is sexual harassment, which in Italy, Greece, Turkey, Spain and Morocco especially can be almost constant for women travelling alone. By far the most common kind of harassment you'll come across simply consists of street whistles and catcalls; occasionally it's more sinister and very occasionally it can be dangerous. Indifference is often the best policy, avoiding eye contact with men and at the same time appearing as confident and purposeful as possible. If this doesn't make you feel any more comfortable, shouting a few choice phrases in the local language is a good idea; don't, however, shout in English, which often seems to encourage them. You may also come across gropers on crowded buses and trains, in which case you should complain as loudly as possible in any language – the ensuing scene should be enough to deter your assailant.

GJIROKASTRA

Albania

HIGHLIGHTS

❶ Tirana Sip espresso in Albania's colourful capital. **See p.52**

❷ Kruja Hilltop scene of national hero Skanderberg's resistance. **See p.56**

❸ Berat Whitewashed Ottoman houses climb the hillsides. **See p.57**

❹ Gjirokastra Charming old town in a superb valley setting. **See p.58**

❺ Ionian Coast Find yourself a deserted beach. **See p.59**

HIGHLIGHTS ARE MARKED ON THE MAP ON P.49

ROUGH COSTS

Daily budget Basic €20, occasional treat €35

Drink Bottle of red wine €4

Food *Qoftë* (minced meat rissoles) €2

Hostel/budget hotel €12/€25

Travel Bus: Tirana–Berat €3.50; train: Tirana–Durrës €0.55

FACT FILE

Population 3.2 million

Language Albanian (*Shqip*)

Currency Lekë (L)

Capital Tirana

International phone code ☎ 355

Time zone GMT +1hr

1

Introduction

Tell your friends or family that you're off to Albania, and you'll likely receive a stock response: "Isn't it dangerous?", "Isn't there a war going on there?", and "Is that even *in* Europe?" are some of the most common. Speak instead to those who have been, and the associations with the country's name become infinitely more positive – you'll hear of rippling mountains, Ottoman architecture, pristine beaches and endlessly hospitable locals. Following decades of isolationist rule, this rugged land still doesn't seem to fit into the grand continental jigsaw, with distinctly exotic notes emanating from its language, customs and cuisine. Pay a visit to this beguiling corner of Europe now, before it garners the popularity it deserves.

Most travellers make a beeline for the capital, **Tirana**, a buzzing city with a mishmash of garishly painted buildings, traditional restaurants and trendy bars. However, those seeking to take Albania's true pulse should head to the mountainous hinterlands, particularly the peaceable hillside towns of **Berat** and **Gjirokastra** – both essentially open-air museums of life in Ottoman times. The muscular, snowcapped peaks of the interior drop down to a series of immaculate beaches, most notably along the **Ionian coastline** in the south of the country, one of the Mediterranean's most remote and least developed stretches.

CHRONOLOGY

168 BC The Romans defeat the Illyrian tribe and establish rule over present-day Albania.
395 AD Division of Roman Empire; Albania falls under the rule of Constantinople.
300s–500s Invasions by Visigoths, Ostrogoths and Huns.
1343 Serbian invasions.
1443–79 Resistance against Ottoman rule, most of it led by national hero Skanderbeg.
1614 Founding of Tirana.
1912 Albania gains independence.
1922 Ahmet Zogu becomes prime minister and president before finally crowning himself King Zog in 1928.
1939 Mussolini annexes Albania; King Zog retreats to the *Ritz* in London.
1946 Proclamation of People's Republic of Albania, led by Enver Hoxha.
1967 "Cultural Revolution" sees agriculture collectivized, religious buildings destroyed and cadres purged.

1979 Mother Teresa, an ethnic Albanian, wins the Nobel Peace Prize.
1990 Thousands scramble into Tirana's Western embassies in an attempt to flee Albania.
1992 The Democratic Party wins elections, ending Communist rule.
1997 Collapse of financial pyramid schemes results in mass bankruptcies.
2000 Artist Edi Rama elected mayor of Tirana.
2009 Albania joins NATO and applies for EU membership.
2013 Edi Rama elected prime minister.

ARRIVAL AND DEPARTURE

It's getting ever easier to **fly** into Albania, with the number of international connections increasing every year. Local low-cost carrier Belle Air (ⓦbelleair.it) flies to Tirana's Mother Teresa airport (ⓦtirana-airport.com) from several Italian cities, as well as London, Athens and Vienna. Direct British Airways flights from London can be quite reasonable, while in warmer months you can fly cheaply to Corfu then get a ferry to Saranda (see p.59). Visas are not required for citizens of most nations; South Africa is a notable exception.

Greece offers by far the simplest international **bus** connections – there are daily services to Tirana from both Athens and Thessaloniki (from €25), and it's also possible to get direct buses to a number of other Albanian cities. From Macedonia there are direct services from Tetovo (west of Skopje) to

Tirana, via Struga and Elbasan. It is still not straightforward to get here from Montenegro – there are no services at all from the capital Podgorica, though there are a couple of daily buses, and some unofficial minivans, linking Shkodra and Ulcinj.

The most interesting form of arrival is by **ferry**. Several operators make overnight sailings to Durrës from Bari in Italy, including Ventouris Ferries (Wventouris.gr; from €56); it's also possible to get to Saranda by ferry from Corfu (Wionian-cruises.com; from €19), with at least two ferries per day making the thirty-minute hop.

GETTING AROUND

Getting from A to B is a little tricky in Albania – you're advised to be flexible, exercise patience, and to treat travel information as a guideline rather than gospel.

Most travel is conducted by **bus**; the vehicles are usually Italian dinosaurs but fares are cheap, and the roads are continually being improved. However, the authorities have steadfastly refused to build any bus stations – fine in smaller towns, but a nightmare in a city as large as Tirana where matters are utterly confusing. Buses are supplemented by minibuses known as **furgons**, which are more numerous but run to no fixed schedule; with no obligation to depart until full, drivers tend to roam around town until they have the required number of passengers, and they make a habit of overcharging foreigners.

Albania also boasts a limited, ageing **train** network. The main line runs from Tirana to Vlora, via Durrës, while there's also a route heading north to Shkodra. InterRail passes are not valid in Albania, and would be pretty pointless in any case.

ACCOMMODATION

Accommodation is surprisingly plentiful for a country with such low tourist numbers, and while state-owned monstrosities were once the norm, a

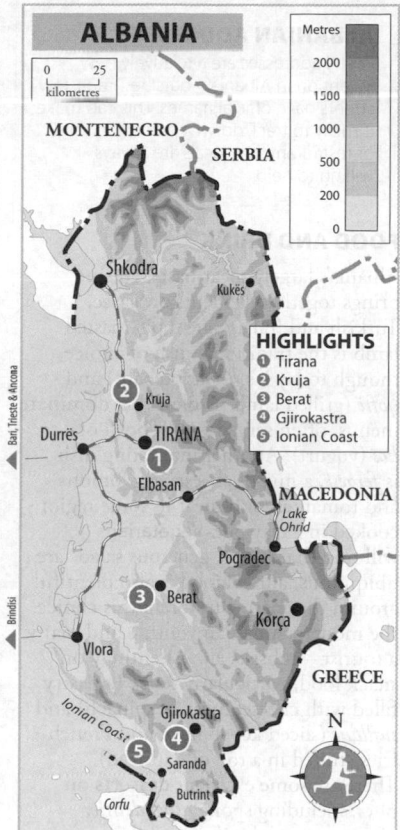

recent building boom has unleashed a whole generation of clean, good-value **hotels**. You should be able to find a double room for under €25 (prices are almost always quoted in euros), and breakfast is usually included. There don't tend to be any set rates for single rooms, but you can expect a small discount from the regular rate. During summer, **private rooms** come into play at beach resorts, and there are now **hostels** in Tirana, Saranda and Berat, charging €10–14 for dorm beds; all have free wi-fi. There are almost no dedicated **campsites**, though the secluded beaches of the Ionian coast are great for those who can manage without facilities. Wild camping is fine in theory, but leaves you at the mercy of the (occasionally corrupt) local police.

1

> **ALBANIAN ADDRESSES**
>
> Postal addresses are a relatively new invention in Albania – outside Tirana, few streets have official names. This can make it tricky to track down a particular hotel or restaurant, but locals are always willing to help.

FOOD AND DRINK

Albania's largely meat-based cuisine brings together elements of Slavic, Turkish and Italian fare. Spit-roasted lamb is the traditional dish of choice, though today it's *qebab* (kebabs) and *qoftë* (grilled lamb rissoles) that dominate menus, often served with a bowl of *kos* (yogurt). Another interesting dish is *fergesë*, a mix of cheese, egg, onions and tomatoes (and meat in some regions) cooked in a clay pot. **Vegetarians** will find that filling, generous salads are ubiquitous, and seafood is also plentiful around the coast. But for all this choice the modern Albanian youth – and many a tourist – subsists almost entirely on snack food, particularly *burek* (a pastry filled with cheese, meat or spinach) and *sufllaqë* (sliced kebab meat and French fries stuffed in a roll of flatbread). There are some excellent **desserts** on offer, including spongy *shendetlije*, cream-saturated *trilece*, and the usual Turkish pastries.

DRINK

As for drinks, **coffee** is king in Albania. Consumed throughout the day, it's traditionally served Turkish-style, with grounds at the bottom (*kafe turke*), though there has recently been a marked shift towards espresso. There are cafés everywhere you look, and it's worth noting that cafés and bars generally melt into the same grey area – what's one by day will usually morph into the other by night.

The alcoholic drink of choice is **rakia** – like coffee, this spirit is something of a way of life in Albania, and usually consumed with meals. The country also produces some **wine**, mostly red, though most locals will admit to a preference for Macedonian fare; Rilindja is a good,

widely sold local label. **Beer** is easy to find, and it's also worth sampling Skënderbeg **cognac**, which is cheap, available in shops everywhere and not too bad at all.

CULTURE AND ETIQUETTE

Albanians tend to go out of their way to welcome foreign guests – partly due to the low number of visitors – and generally do a fine job of eroding popular misconceptions.

Religious practice was largely stamped out following the 1967 Cultural Revolution, meaning that although seventy percent of the population is Muslim, the majority are non-practising; the same can be said of the Christian remainder.

One cultural nicety is that the **body language** used to imply "yes" and "no" is the diametric opposite of what you may be used to – a shake of the head (actually more of a wobble) means "yes", and a nod (actually more of a tilt) means "no". Younger folk and those used to foreigners may well follow international norms, which adds to the confusion.

Tipping at restaurants is generally an exercise in rounding up to the nearest lekë note, but with bigger bills ten percent is the norm. **Smoking** has been officially prohibited in public places since 2007, though the police are too busy smoking to fine anybody, and you'll still see ashtrays on every restaurant table.

SPORTS AND ACTIVITIES

In a mountainous country with a long coastline, the main attractions are pretty obvious – there are some delightful places to **swim** along the Ionian coast, while the most accessible **hiking** is in the national park area of Mount Dajti. More adventurous activities are thin on the ground, with a monopoly of sorts held by Outdoor Albania (☎04 222 7121, ⊛outdooralbania.com), an adventurous young team that can organize treks and **ski-shoeing** trips, or more high-octane fun such as **kayaking** and **paragliding**.

COMMUNICATIONS

Albania's network of **post offices** continues to grow, and most are open Monday to Friday from 9am to 5pm. While their quality of distribution is also improving – from a pretty low base – it's still prudent to hang onto any valuable parcels until you're out of the country. Public **phones** are hard to track down, and almost all use cards; you may be offered these on the street but it's safer – and cheaper – to buy from a post office, many of which will also have public phones of their own. **Wi-fi** is widespread, particularly in cafés, and you'll be able to find a dedicated **internet** café easily enough in urban areas.

EMERGENCIES

Despite its bad rap, the **crime rate** in Albania is actually quite low by European standards, and you're extremely unlikely to find yourself stumbling into one of the famed blood feuds, some of which still bubble away up north. It is, however, worth being aware of a high **road accident** rate made vividly clear by the alarming number of memorial stones by the roadside.

ALBANIAN

Note that the dual nature of Albanian nouns – all have definite and indefinite forms – can cause some confusion with place names. Tirana is alternately referred to as Tiranë, Durrës as Durresi, Berat as Berati, Saranda as Sarandë and Gjirokastra as Gjirokaster.

	ALBANIAN	PRONUNCIATION
Yes	Po	Paw
No	Jo	Yaw
Please	Ju lutem	Yoo lootem
Thank you	Faleminderit	Falemin-derit
Hello/Good day	Tungjatjeta	Toongya-tyeta
Goodbye	Mirupafshim	Meeropafshim
Excuse me	Më falni	Muh falni
Where?	Ku?	Koo?
Good	Mirë	Mir
Bad	Keq	Kek
Near	Afër	Afur
Far	Larg	Larg
Cheap	I lirë	Ee lir
Expensive	I shtrenjtë	Ee shtrenyt
Open	I hapur	Ee hapoor
Closed	Mbyllur	Mbeeloor
Today	Sot	Sawt
Yesterday	Dje	Dye
Tomorrow	Nesër	Nesur
How much is...?	Sa kushton...?	Sa kushton...?
What time is it?	Sa është ora?	Sa ushtu awra?
I don't understand	Unë nuk kuptoj	Oonuh nook koop-toy
Do you speak English?	A flisni anglisht?	Ah fleesnee anglisht?
One	Një	Nyuh
Two	Dy	Deeh
Three	Tre	Treh
Four	Katër	Katur
Five	Pesë	Pes
Six	Gjashtë	Gyasht
Seven	Shtatë	Shtat
Eight	Tetë	Tet
Nine	Nëntë	Nuhnt
Ten	Dhjetë	Dyet

1

EMERGENCY NUMBERS

Police ☎ 129; Ambulance ☎ 127; Fire
☎ 128.

Albania's **hospitals** are in very poor
shape – most locals go abroad for
treatment if they can afford it, and you
should do likewise if possible. There are
very few ambulances, so should you or a
friend come across an accident it's usually
best to hunt down a cab. **Pharmacies**
exist in all urban areas, and are usually
open 9am to 7pm.

INFORMATION

There are a few **tourist information offices**
dotted around, though hours can be
irregular to say the least – they can supply
maps and book accommodation, but
you're better off asking for information at
your hotel or hostel.

MONEY AND BANKS

Albania uses the **lekë** (L), which is also
often used in its singular form, lek. Coins
of 5, 10, 20, 50 and 100 lekë are in
circulation, as are notes of 200, 500,
1000, 2000 and 5000 lekë. Exchange
rates are currently around 140 lekë to
the euro, 165 lekë to the pound, and 110
lekë to the US dollar. Accommodation
prices are quoted in euros at all but the
cheapest places, and some of the more
upmarket restaurants do likewise; in
these you can pay with either currency,
although it often works out more
expensive to pay in lekë. **Banks** are the
best places to exchange money, and are
usually open on weekdays 9am–3pm.

ALBANIA ONLINE

ⓦ**albaniantourism.com** Official site of
the tourist board.
ⓦ**albania-hotel.com** Good for booking
rooms online.
ⓦ**albanianhistory.net** Collection of
historical articles.
ⓦ**tiranatimes.com** Local news site with
up-to-date art and event listings.

ATMs are everywhere in Tirana and easy
to find in any town, while **credit cards** are
increasingly accepted in hotels.

OPENING HOURS AND HOLIDAYS

Few **shops** and restaurants in Albania
have set **working hours**, though you can
expect restaurants to be open from
breakfast to supper, and shops daily from
9am to 5pm. **Museums** are usually closed
on Mondays.

Most shops and all banks and post
offices are closed on **public holidays**:
January 1 and 2, January 6, March 14,
March 22, May 1, October 19,
November 28 and 29, and December
25, as well as at Easter, both Catholic
and Orthodox.

Tirana

Its buildings are painted in lurid
colours, a gigantic, useless pyramid rises
smack in the centre, the main square is
a mess, the roads are potholed, and still
there's no bus station for this city of
almost one million people, and yet
for all these idiosyncrasies **TIRANA** is
undeniably a charmer. The clash of
architectural styles (from Italian to
Communist to postmodern) is most
evident in the central Blloku area,
which was off-limits to all but Party
members during Communist times.
A generation down the line, espresso-
sipping, fun-loving locals and trendy
bar openings are vivid proof that the
city is well on its way to becoming a
"regular" European capital.

Tirana's Ottoman legacy was largely
eroded by former dictator Enver
Hoxha's failed regime, an era still
evidenced by enormous boulevards
and Brutalist architecture. In 2000,
the Edi Rama period began with the
city's charismatic mayor attempting to
paint his city into the modern day;
the resulting streetscape kaleidoscope
performs a continuous palette shift
from lemon to lime, saffron to
cinnamon and burgundy to baby blue.

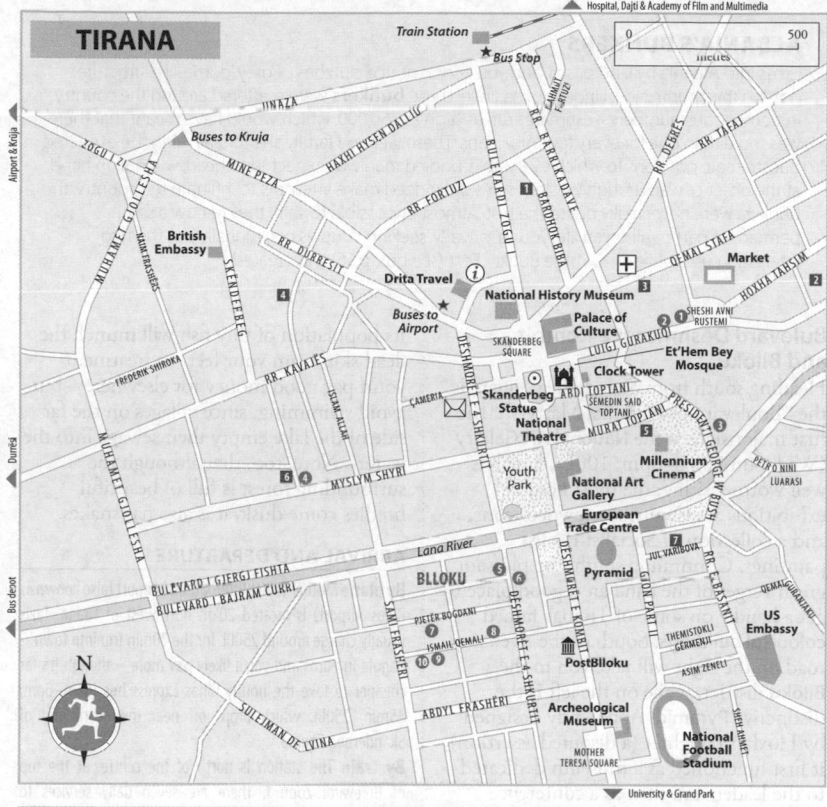

Hospital, Dajti & Academy of Film and Multimedia

TIRANA

Train Station
★ Bus Stop

0 _____ 500
metres

JINAZA

Buses to Kruja

ZOGU I ZI

MINE PEZA

HAXHI HYSEN DALLIU

BULEVARDI ZOGU I

BARDHOK BIBA

RR. FARRIKADATE

RR. DEBRES

RR. TAFAJ

British
Embassy

RR. DURRESIT

RR. FORTUZI

1

QEMAL STAFA

Market

MUHAMET GJOLLESHA

IVAN FRASHERI

SKENDERBEJ

Drita Travel (i)

Buses to
Airport ★

National History Museum

3

HOXHA TAHSIM

2

FREDERIK SHIROKA

RR. KAVAJES

SKANDERBEG
SQUARE

Palace of
Culture

2 **1** SHESHI AVNI
RUSTEMI

LUIGJ GURAKUQI

Et'hem Bey
Mosque

DESHMORET E SHKURTIT

ISLAM ALLA

CAMERIA

Skanderbeg
Statue

⊙ 🏛

Clock Tower

ABDI TOPTANI

SEMEDIN SAID
TOPTANI

PRESIDENT GEORGE W BUSH

3

RR. KAVAJES

National
Theatre

MURAT TOPTANI

PETR O NINI
LUARASI

MUHAMET GJOLLESHA

6 **4** MYSLYM SHYRI

Youth
Park

National Art
Gallery

Millennium
Cinema

European
Trade Centre

Lana River

BULEVARDI I GJERGJ FISHTA

BULEVARDI I BAJRAM CURRI

SAMI FRASHERI

BLLOKU

5

DESHMORET E SHKURTIT

6

Pyramid

7

JUL VARIBOVA

GJON PARI II

RR. E BASANIT

QEMAL GUARNACE

US
Embassy

PJETER BOGDANI

ISMAIL QEMALI

8

DESHMORET E KOMBIT

THEMISTOKLI
GERMENJI

N

SULEJMAN DE LVINA

ABDYL FRASHERI

10 **9**

🏛 PostBlloku

ASIM ZENELI

SHEH AHMET

MOTHER
TERESA SQUARE

Archeological
Museum

National
Football
Stadium

▼ University & Grand Park

ACCOMMODATION			EATING AND DRINKING				
B&B Tirana Smile	**4**	Hostel Albania	**2**	Embelaza Franceze	**5**	Lulishte 1 Maji	**3**	Sky Club	**6**
Capital Tirana	**3**	Kalaja	**5**	Era	**10**	Oda	**2**	Vila 31	**8**
Freddy's Hostel	**1**	Tirana Backpackers	**6**	Patosi	**1**	Radio	**9**		
Green House	**7**			Fish & Squid	**4**	Raum	**7**		

Some locals grumble that their city looks to have fallen victim to a made-for-TV makeover.

WHAT TO SEE AND DO

Tirana is better for strolling than sightseeing, but there's plenty to keep you occupied in the southbound stretch from **Skanderbeg Square** to the **Grand Park**, which narrowly bypasses the trendy **Blloku** district on the way.

Skanderbeg Square

All roads in Tirana lead to **Skanderbeg Square**, centrepoint of the city and, therefore, the nation as a whole. Marked at its southern end by an equestrian statue of national hero Skanderbeg, who led the ultimately unsuccessful resistance to fifteenth-century Ottoman invasions. The imposing **National History Museum** (Tues–Sat 10am–5pm, Sun 10am–2pm; 200L) sits at the north side of the square and is worth a quick visit, particularly for its coverage of Hoxha's concentration camps.

Heading clockwise around the square you'll find the **Palace of Culture**, which houses the National Theatre of Opera and Ballet. Then comes the pretty **Et'hem Bey Mosque**, which was closed off during Communist rule; one sunny day in 1991, thousands flocked here to make use of their new-found religious freedom.

1

ALBANIA'S BUNKERS

Cross into Albania by land or sea, and you'll soon notice clutches of grey, dome-like structures dotting the countryside. Under Hoxha's rule, these **bunkers** were scattered around the country in tremendous numbers – estimates run as high as 750,000, which would have meant that there was more than one for every four Albanians. These were no family shelters, as might be expected, but strategic positions to which every able-bodied man was expected to head, weapon in hand, at the onset of war. Though Western spies did indeed make attempts to infiltrate the country, the bunkers were never really put to the test. Almost impossible to shift, they're now a semi-permanent part of Albanian life; young, privacy-seeking couples occasionally put them to interesting use, while in 2011 the Bunker Fest (see box, p.56) was created.

Bulevard Dëshmorët e Kombit and Blloku

Heading south from Skanderbeg Square is the "Boulevard of National Martyrs". The first major sight is the **National Art Gallery** (Wed–Sun 10am–6pm; 100L), which is well worth visiting; the most notable exhibitions are Onufri's renowned icons, and a collection of Socialist Realist paintings. Continuing south, the pleasant green verges of the **Lana** are a good place to get a handle on some of Tirana's famed **colourful buildings**. South of the river, any road on the right will take you to the **Blloku** district, while on the left is the distinctive **Pyramid**. Apparently designed by Hoxha's daughter (a disputed assertion), it first functioned as a museum dedicated to the leader, and then as a conference centre; it's now dilapidated and defunct, though locals are fond of scaling its walls with a beer in hand. Continuing south, opposite the imposing former Communist Party HQ (now the Prime Minister's residence), the 2013 PostBlloku monument provides an overdue memorial to the years of Cold War paranoia: a restored concrete bunker (see box above) stands alongside a segment of the Berlin Wall and supports from a mine at Albania's notorious Spaç forced labour camp. Walking south again, grandiose buildings line the road until you emerge in Mother Teresa Square, home to a passable **Archeological Museum** (Mon–Fri 10.30am–2.30pm; free).

Grand Park

South of the Archeological Museum, though you'll need to curl west around the hill for access, is the **Grand Park**, whose main feature is an artificial lake to which the Tiranese come for a spot of relaxation.

Its population of tiny fish will munch the dead skin from your feet – a treatment you'd pay good money for elsewhere – but avoid swimming, since villages on the far side of the lake empty their sewage into the waters. Note, too, that although the surrounding forest is full of beautiful fireflies come dusk, it is also has snakes.

ARRIVAL AND DEPARTURE

By plane Mother Teresa International Airport (also known as Rinas Airport) is located 20km northwest of Tirana. Taxis usually charge around 2500L for the 30min trip into town – haggle in euros and you'll likely pay more – though it's far cheaper to take the hourly Rinas Express bus (6am–6pm; 45min; 250L), which drops off near the north end of Skanderbeg Square.

By train The station is north of the centre, at the top of Bulevardi Zogu I. There are seven daily services to Durrës (1hr).

By bus Travelling to or from Tirana by bus is something of a Kafkaesque adventure – the city does not yet have a bus station, so you may be dropped at any one of a dozen places depending upon your point of embarkation, and whether you're travelling by bus or *furgon* – the tourist office can advise . Bus operators serving the route to Durrës and the north tend to use the junction in front of the train station, while those for the south operate from an industrial lot just west of the centre, off Bulevard Gjergj Fishta. With a little more work, the latter may yet become a bus station.

Destinations Athens (3 daily; 12hr); Berat (hourly; 3hr); Durrës (hourly; 40min); Gjirokastra (6 daily; 4hr 30min); Saranda (6 daily; 6hr); Tetovo, for Skopje (2 daily; 9–10hr).

INFORMATION

Tourist office There's an office behind the National History Museum on Ded Gjo Luli (☎04 222 3313), but better advice can be found at one of the hostels. *Tirana Times* (🖥tiranatimes.com) is best for event listings. The irregular *Tirana In Your Pocket* guide (🖥inyourpocket.com) is also a good source of information; you'll find print versions in the hostels and some hotels.

Tours Outdoor Albania (ⓦoutdooralbania.com) and Juicy Tours (ⓦjuicytours.com.au) both organize fascinating out-of-Tirana excursions, including mountain snowshoeing in the winter, kayaking in the summer, and regular cycle trips.

GETTING AROUND

By bus Buses run every 15–30min (6am–10pm) on a few main routes and cost 30L for a one-way ticket.

By taxi Taxis should cost 300–500L for a trip within the city centre (none has a meter), though central Tirana is just about small enough to cover on foot.

ACCOMMODATION

HOSTELS

Freddy's Hostel 75 Bardhok Biba ☎068 203 5261, ⓦfreddyshostel.com. A welcoming family-run place with a variety of cheap, simple rooms to choose from – even in a two-person room you won't be paying much more than dormitory prices. Dorm €12, double €30

★ **Hostel Albania** 56 Beqir Luga ☎067 278 3798, ⓦhostel-albania.com. This hostel is a little tricky to find, but when you're draining a beer in their charming garden you'll be glad you made the effort. Staff are cheery and know the city inside out. Dorm €11

Tirana Backpackers 7 Myslym Shiri ☎068 468 2353, ⓦtiranahostel.com. This centrally located hostel boasts good, dorms and the bar is well stocked with potent home-made *rakia*. They also run some excellent city tours. Dorm €12

HOTELS

★ **B&B Tirana Smile** Bogdanëve ☎04 224 3460, ⓦbbtirana.com. Spotless and charming, this brand-new place has huge, colourful rooms and a very friendly welcome. Breakfast is a mighty feast. Double €45

Capital Tirana Qemal Stafa ☎04 225 8575, ⓦcapitaltiranahotel.com. A friendly place with fresh, modern rooms and a helpfully central location. Double €60

Kalaja 9 Murat Toptani ☎04 225 0000. This is easily the best of the several cheap hotels on this charming, pedestrianized road, its collection of comfy rooms set into a niche in the old castle walls. Double €30

★ TREAT YOURSELF

Green House 6 Iul Varibova ☎04 225 1015, ⓦgreenhouse.al. Artistically designed boutique hotel whose rooms are perhaps the trendiest in the whole country. With doubles from €130, staying here is beyond most backpacker budgets, but do come for the superb on-site restaurant: at 1100L, the veal fillet with truffle sauce is a delectable bargain.

EATING

Embolaza Franceze 1 Dëshmorët e 4 Shkurtit. Come to enjoy cake and coffee served up in a lavish interior. Savoury dishes are available but somewhat overpriced (mains 1000L and up). Daily 8am–11pm.

★ **Era** 33 Ismail Qemali. A hugely popular restaurant with locals and visitors alike – it's attractive yet affordable, service is top-notch, and the menu bursts with delectable local fare. Try the lamb with artichoke and goose fillet with mushroom. Meal with wine under 1000L. Daily 10am–midnight.

Fatosi Luigj Gurakuqi. A cut above most *qofte* snack-shacks – best evidenced by the fact that they're often grilling over a hundred delicious meat rissoles at once. Ten of them, with some bread and fried onion, will set you back just 310L, while the bacon-wrapped shish skewers (100L) are unmissable. Daily 6am–midnight.

Fish & Squid Myslym Shiri. An incredibly cheap seafood option (risotto 280L, stuffed squid 600L) with just one downside: dishes are so small that you'll need a few to fill up, but it's a bargain even so. Daily 10am–10pm.

Lulishte 1 Maji Presidenti George W. Bush. Sprawling family restaurant that serves Italian, Albanian and Mexican meals on the ground floor, and Chinese food upstairs. Mains from 500L. Daily 11am–10pm.

★ **Oda** Luigj Gurakuqi. Small, homely place offering you the chance to eat Ottoman-style meals on Ottoman-style sofas. The stuffed aubergine (700L) is superb, and the offal stew (*tavë dheu*) far better than it sounds; all is best washed down – if you're brave – with a shot of flavoured *rakia*. Daily 11am–11pm.

DRINKING AND NIGHTLIFE

Tirana's nightlife scene moves up a notch with each passing year. Almost everything of note is concentrated in the fashionable Blloku area, where most venues function as cafés by day and as bars come evening.

Radio 29 Ismail Qemali. A trendy bar that's very popular with the city's artier set, making it a good place to meet locals. Open daily though hours vary; usually busy 8pm–midnight.

Raum Pjetër Bogdani. Two upper floors frequented by a young and creative set, who make a sundown shift from coffee to cocktails. Also stages occasional art exhibitions. Daily 10am–late.

Sky Club 5 Dëshmorët e 4 Shkurtit. A top-floor revolving bar with superb city views – this would be incredibly expensive in any other European capital, but here cocktails go for just 400L, and shots of Skenderbeg cognac for 150L. It's also a great place for coffee (150L) in the daytime. Daily 10am–midnight.

Vila 31 31 Ismail Qemali. Hugely popular with preening locals, this trendy café-bar is attached to the former home of one-time dictator, Enver Hoxha – now that's something

1

TIRANA FESTIVALS

Usually held in December, the **Tirana International Film Festival** (⚐ tiranafilmfest.com) has screenings at the Millennium Cinema and National Theatre (⚐ teatrikombetar.gov.al). The **Bunker Fest**, which launched in 2011, is a wild, bunker-based party that usually takes place each May near Durrës – ask at the hostels for details.

---

to ponder over your beer (200L) or cocktail (400L). Daily 7am–2am.

ENTERTAINMENT

Academy of Film and Multimedia 78 Alexsandër Moisiu ☎ 04 236 5188, ⚐ afmm.edu.al. Occasional free screenings of foreign movies (usually Thurs at 7pm).

Millennium Cinema Murat Toptani. Season-old Hollywood films shown in a wonderful old theatre whose outdoor café is a delight on sunny days. Tickets from 300L.

SHOPPING

Tirana has a fascinating daily market (6am–10pm), which sprawls over several blocks north of the Sheshi Avni Rustemi roundabout – Sundays are the best time to go.

Adrion Skanderbeg Square. Has English-language books, newspapers and magazines.

DIRECTORY

Embassies and consulates UK, Skanderberg ☎ 04 223 4973; US, Elbasanit ☎ 04 224 7285.

Exchange Tirana is full of ATMs, and all of the attached banks will be able to exchange cash during business hours.

Hospital Civilian Hospital, Dibrës, northeast of the city centre.

Pharmacies Bulevardi Zogu I (☎ 04 222 2241; Mon–Sat 8am–8pm); Dëshmorët 4 Shkurtit (☎ 04 222 6759).

Post office The office on Çameria is open Mon–Fri 8am–8pm.

Day-trips from Tirana

Local landmarks from which you can peer down on Tirana include the slopes of **Mount Dajti** and the hilltop town of **Kruja**, while also within range is the laidback port of **Durrës**. All can be visited on a day-trip from the capital.

MOUNT DAJTI

The dark, looming shape of **Mount Dajti** is easily visible from Tirana, a temptation that can prove too much for city dwellers, who head to the forested slopes in droves on sunny weekends. The mountain's network of paths feels surprisingly remote even though you're only 25km from the capital. There's no public transport to the mountain, but by taxi it should be no more than 500L to the base of the cable-car system (8am–10pm; 700L return; ⚐ dajtiekspres.com) that whisks passengers to within a slog of the summit. There are a number of restaurants in the area, if you fancy refuelling before heading back to Tirana.

KRUJA

Lofty **KRUJA**, 35km from Tirana, was the focal point of national hero Skanderbeg's resistance to the Ottoman invasions of the fifteenth century, and you'll see his likeness all over town. Most people make a beeline for the **castle**, which houses a number of restaurants and an excellent **History Museum** (Tues–Sun 9am–1pm & 3–6pm; 200L), whose diverting collection of weaponry, icons and the like is augmented by an impressive modern interior. Also within the castle walls is the **Ethnographic Museum** (same times; 300L), housed in a gorgeous building with a serene outdoor courtyard. Souvenir salesmen have taken over the town, and the best place to buy your Albania-flag T-shirt, Skanderbeg statuette or Mother Teresa lighter is the restored **Ottoman bazaar**, just below the castle access road. *Furgons* from Tirana (1hr; 200L) leave regularly from the northwest end of Mine Peza.

DURRËS

Sitting atop a 10km stretch of Adriatic beach, the port city of **DURRËS** (also known as **Durrësi**) is the easiest escape route for sea-seeking Tiranese, and on summer weekends there are few better places to party. There may be far nicer beaches down south, but this one is still pretty fun.

Known as Dyrrhachium, the city was already an important port in Roman times, and was a launchpad for fifth-century Visigoth attacks on Italy, it also served as Albania's capital for a short time after independence. Evidence survives from the city's Roman heyday: a **forum** and **amphitheatre** sit just off opposite ends of the main square, Sheshi i Lirisë, with the latter (daily 8am–8pm; 200L) the largest such construction in the Balkans. In between stands an elegant **mosque**. You can then either follow the old castle wall or cobblestoned Tregëtare downhill to the seafront **promenade**; a ten-minute stroll will bring you to the enjoyable **Archeological Museum** (Tues–Sun 9am–3pm; 200L).

ARRIVAL AND DEPARTURE

By train and bus The train and bus stations sit almost side by side within an easy walk of the main square and the ferry terminal.

By boat The ferry terminal receives regular services from Italy.

ACCOMMODATION AND EATING

Those who don't fancy trawling the beach area (it's packed in summer) will find good eating and sleeping options around the bottom of Tregëtare.

Mediterran Tregëtare ☎ 052 227 074, ✉ mediterran _hotel.dr@hotmail.com. Good value and easy to find, rooms here are spacious and comfortable, and the staff eager to please. Double €25

Arvi Taulantia ☎ 052 230 403, ⊛ hotelarvi.com. Upmarket option with highly presentable rooms – at least by local standards. It's halfway to the museum from the bottom of Tregëtare. Double €60

Southern Albania

With its jumble of rugged mountains fringed by pristine curls of beach, Albania's south is the most appealing part of the country. The interior route boasts the rewarding towns of **Berat** and **Gjirokastra**, each home to whole swathes of Ottoman buildings. Heading on down the Ionian Coast instead, you'll find one of Europe's few unspoilt sections of Mediterranean shore, a near-permanently sunny spot where the

twin blues of sea and sky are ripped asunder by a ribbon of grey mountains – on a clear day you'll be able to see Italy from the 1027m-high **Llogaraja Pass**. Both routes converge at the beach town of **Saranda**, while further south are the fantastic ruins of **Butrint**.

BERAT

There are few better places to be in Albania than standing on the river bridge in the charming, easy-going town of **BERAT**. From this vantage point, you'll be surrounded by huddles of **Ottoman houses**, their dark, rectangular windows staring from whitewashed walls like a thousand eyes. On the south bank is the sleepy **Gorica** district, kept in shadow for much of the day by a muscular backdrop of rock; to the north is the relatively sun-drenched **Mangalemi** district, from which steep, cobblestoned paths lead up to the hill-top **Kalasa**, an old citadel whose wonderful interior is up there with the best old towns in the Balkans.

WHAT TO SEE AND DO

You'll have great views of Berat from the fourteenth-century **Kalasa**, a splendidly restored citadel (daily 9am–9pm; 100L or free out of hours) towering above town, which is accessed via a steep, cobbled road. Unlike other such places in Albania this is still a functioning part of town and home to hundreds, yet almost nothing dilutes its centuries-old vibe; visit at night and you're in for a wonderfully eerie treat. There were once over thirty **churches** here, but just a handful remain; oldest and most beautiful is the thirteenth-century **Church of the Holy Trinity**, sitting on the slope below the inner fortifications. Churches remain locked for most of the year, but you can ask around to find the key-keepers. Also within the grounds is the **Onufri Museum** (Tues–Sun 9am–4pm; 200L), dedicated to the country's foremost icon painter, famed for his use of a particularly vivid red. Heading back down the access road you'll come across the diverting **Ethnographic Museum** (daily: Oct–April 9am–4pm, Sun to 2pm; May–Sept

1

9am–1pm & 4–7pm, Sun 9am–2pm; 200L) and the first of the centre's three main **mosques**.

ARRIVAL AND ACTIVITIES

By bus The central square acts as a bus station of sorts, though it's also possible to pick up or be dropped off at various locations on the main road.
Destinations Gjirokastra (2 daily; 4hr); Saranda (2 daily; 6hr); Tirana (hourly; 3hr).
Tours Rafting excursions (around €50/person) and trips around nearby Mount Tomorri can be organized through Outdoor Albania (⌨ outdooralbania.com). *Berat Backpackers* also lay on occasional tours.

ACCOMMODATION

Berat Backpackers ☎ 069 306 4429, ⌨ berat backpackers.com. Located over the river in Gorica and run by Scott, an affable Geordie, this hostel remains the number one budget choice – the building is a bona fide Ottoman antique, the dorms are cosy, and the garden patio is a delightful place for evening drinks. Dorm €10
Kris Guesthouse ☎ 069 540 0979, ⌨ berat-kris guesthouse.com. Family-run guesthouse located way up in the citadel. The calf muscle-straining climb to the old town and the area's spookily quiet night-time atmosphere mean that it's not for everyone, but it can be an utterly bewitching experience. Dorm €15, double €25
★ **Mangalemi** ☎ 068 232 3238, ⌨ mangalemihotel .com. Near the centre of town, on the road to the citadel, this traditional guesthouse has splendidly decorated rooms that offer excellent value; all are en suite with comfy beds and powerful showers. There's a superb on-site restaurant, and the friendly staff are excellent sources of local information. Double €30

EATING AND DRINKING

Ajka On the Gorica side of the footbridge, this smart place is one of the few local bars which receives female customers. It's also good for coffee; head on up to the roof terrace for the best views. Daily 9am–11pm.
Mangalemi Inside the guesthouse of the same name. Professional service, large portions and reasonable prices – 500L can get you nicely full. The salads are great, or give the stuffed liver a try; head up to the terrace if the weather's nice. Daily 10am–10pm.
Onufri Simple place inside the citadel walls, serving strong coffee and Albanian staples such as *pilaf* and stuffed peppers. Usually open 8am–6pm.
Spëtimi 2 Studenty snack-style joint on the river road, selling good *sufflaqe* (130L) and mouthwatering crêpes (150L). Daily 9am–11pm.
White House ☎ 032 234 570. Riverside restaurant serving the best pizzas in town (from 450L; delivery

service available), as well as seafood dishes and traditional Albanian grub. Daily 9am–10.30pm.

GJIROKASTRA

Sitting proudly above the sparsely inhabited Drinos valley, **GJIROKASTRA** is one of Albania's most attractive towns, and home to some of its friendliest people. Its days as an Ottoman trading hub have bequeathed it a wealth of sparkling **Ottoman houses**, which line a maze of steep, cobbled streets. Gjiro is also etched into the nation's conscience as the birthplace of former dictator **Enver Hoxha**, and more recently the world-renowned author **Ismail Kadare**.

WHAT TO SEE AND DO

The Old Town's centrepiece is its imposing **citadel** (daily 9am–7pm; 200L), which is clearly visible from any point in town. Built in the sixth century and enlarged in 1811 by Ali Pasha Tepelna, it was used as a **prison** by King Zog, the Nazis and Hoxha's cadres; the interior remains suitably spooky. There are also tanks and weaponry to peruse, but most curious is the shell of an **American jet** which was (apparently) forced down in 1957 after being suspected of espionage by the Communist regime. Other than the castle, Gjiro's most appealing sight is its collection of mainly nineteenth-century **Ottoman houses**; there are some prime examples in Partizani, a steep residential area just west of the castle.

ARRIVAL AND DEPARTURE

By bus Buses and *furgons* stop on the highway intersection below the New Town. From here it's a steep, half-hour walk to the Old Town, or a 300L taxi ride.
Destinations Berat (2 daily; 4hr); Saranda (6 daily; 1hr 30min); Tirana (6 daily; 4hr 30min).

ACCOMMODATION

None of these establishments has an address, but they're easy to find. *Gjirokastra* is next to the theatre on the road running under the castle wall, where you'll also find signs to *Kotoni*; *Kalemi* is further up the same road.
Gjirokastra ☎ 084 265 982. Small but modern guesthouse with an excellent location; discounts available outside peak season. Double €25

Kalemi ☎ 084 263 724, ⓦ hotelkalemi.tripod.com. Lofty old building with a variety of pleasant rooms on offer, some with commanding valley views and chunky wooden floors. Double €35

★ **Kotoni** ☎ 084 263 526, ⓦ kotonihouse.com. Cosy Ottoman-era building whose owners may well be the most amiable – and energetic – couple in Gjirokastra. Homely touches include excellent breakfasts and handmade trimmings in the bedrooms. They also organize a variety of interesting tours, including horseriding and picnics on the nearby hills. Double €30

EATING AND DRINKING

Fantazia Uphill from Qafa e Pazarit. Extremely popular café offering splendid valley views, and a variety of teas, coffees (espresso 70L) and alcoholic drinks. Mon–Sat 8am–10pm.

Kujtimi Qafa e Pazarit. Fantastic Albanian meals dished out under the dappled shade of a maple tree. A salad and a small main (the *qoftë* is recommended) will set you back 500L. Daily 9am–9pm.

SARANDA AND AROUND

Staring straight at Corfu, and even within day-trip territory of the Greek island, sunny **SARANDA** is perhaps Albania's most appealing entry point. A recent building boom has eroded some of the town's original genteel atmosphere, but it's still a great place to kick back, stroll along the promenade and watch the sun set over cocktails. There are beaches in town, but better are those near the archeological treasure-trove of **Butrint**, some 25km to the south.

ARRIVAL AND INFORMATION

By bus There's no station, but buses pick up and drop off just north of the centre on Vangjel Pando, with the harbour a 5min walk away downhill.

THE BLUE EYE

On the way between Gjirokastra and Saranda is the wonderful **Blue Eye**, an underwater spring forming a pool of deepest blue. Its setting in a cool, remote grove is quite spectacular – the water is delicious, and you can swim in it until you get the chills (it won't take long, even in summer). Hop on any bus or minivan plying the Saranda–Gjirokastra route, and ask to be let off at the Syri i Kaltër; the pool is 20min from the road on a decent path.

Destinations Athens (2 daily; 10hr); Berat (2 daily; 6hr); Gjirokastra (6 daily; 1hr 20min); Tirana (6 daily; 6hr).

By boat The small terminal on the west side of town has services to Corfu which run at least twice daily year-round, increasing to five per day June–Aug. Tickets (from €19) can be bought from a small office on the access road.

ACCOMMODATION

As elsewhere around the Med, prices are at their highest in July and August. Discounts are negotiable at other times – even the hostels cut their dorm prices by €2 outside the summer months.

HOSTELS

Backpackers SR Mitat Hoxha 10 ☎ 069 434 5426, ⓦ backpackerssr.hostel.com. You're assured a friendly welcome at this small, simple hostel. It's located almost directly opposite the ferry terminal, and its dorms boast sea views; noise from the outside carries in, but guests are usually too busy making their own racket to notice. Dorm €12

★ **Hairy Lemon** Koder 8f ☎ 069 355 9317, ⓦ hairylemonhostel.com. Irish-owned hostel a 10min walk west of the centre, past the ferries. Clean and friendly, with very comfy beds and a great chill-out area for meeting new travel buddies. Dorm €12

HOTELS

Hotel Real Off Abedin Dino ☎ 085 226 361. This is a simple place with spotless but dirt-cheap rooms. It's also a short walk from the seafront, the bus and ferry terminals, and dozens of bars and restaurants. Double €20

Kaonia Jonianet 2 ☎ 085 222 600. The best value of the hotels around the harbour, perhaps because of the unfinished building it's attached to. All rooms have balconies, but not all offer sea views so look before you pay. Double €40

Palma Mitat Hoxha 1 ☎ 085 222 929. Spick-and-span hotel next to the ferry terminal – ask for a balcony room, if you don't mind the noise. Room prices can drop as low as €25 off-season. Double €60

EATING AND DRINKING

The town centre is filled with cheap joints selling *sufflaqe*, *burek* and the like, while there's also the well-stocked Alfa supermarket near the *Backpackers SR* hostel.

Bequa Friendship Park. Off the east side of the park below the bus station, with meat dishes from 250L; real penny-pinchers will appreciate the 60L *pilaf*. Daily 9am–7pm.

Limani Jutting out into the harbour, this sprawling venue is the most popular place in town by some margin, and good for coffee in the morning, pizza for dinner (from 450L), *trilece* for dessert, and ouzo in the evening. Daily 6am–midnight.

1

Paradise Abedin Dino. A winning blend of style, service and good seafood dishes (from 500L) at this waterfront restaurant; it's also a good place for wine. East of town off the Butrint road. Daily 9am–11pm.

NIGHTLIFE

Demi Abedin Dino. Many a backpacker has stumbled back from this bar, a 15min walk east of town along the coastal road, and most notable for its superb views back over Saranda. Daily 10am–2am.

Happy Hour Abedin Dino. Peering out over the prom, this fun bar is worth mentioning for its "Sperm of Barman" shots alone. Open daily from 6pm until last customer leaves.

Viljani Abedin Dino. This prom-side café-bar serves draught beer in ice-cold glasses – enough said. Don't ask for a large one unless you want a full litre of the stuff. Daily 10am–2am.

AROUND SARANDA

The main activity around Saranda is a visit to **Butrint**, which has a fantastic beach nearby at the village of Ksamil.

Butrint

Splendidly sited on an exposed nub of land, the isolated ruins of **BUTRINT**

(daylight hours; 700L) offer a peek into over 2500 years of history, and are a delight to explore on its eucalyptus-lined trails. The area was first developed by the Greeks in the fourth century BC, and the expansive **theatre** and nearby **public baths** were built soon after. Butrint then reached its zenith during Roman times – Julius Caesar stopped by in 44 BC – though most of the statues unearthed from this period are now in the museums of Tirana. You can see most of Butrint's sights on a looped footpath, though do head up to the **Acropolis** for wonderful views.

ARRIVAL AND DEPARTURE

You can pick up *furgons* to Butrint (6 daily; 45min; 100L) at any point on Skënderbeu in Saranda (the road above the prom), but given the paucity of public transport many opt to shell out for a taxi (around €20 including waiting time).

ACCOMMODATION

Livia ☎ 089 212 040, ⓦ www.hotel-livia.com. Way out near the entrance to Butrint, this isolated hotel is fantastic value, with immaculate rooms and an excellent on-site restaurant. Double €35

HALLSTATT

Austria

HIGHLIGHTS

❶ Viennese art Feast your eyes on stunning paintings by Gustav Klimt and Egon Schiele. See p.65

❷ Coffee and cake, Vienna Indulge In mouthwatering treats in one of Vienna's ornate coffeehouses. See p.71

❸ Salzburg A fine Baroque city, home to Mozart and, of course, the sound of music. See p.77

❹ Halstatt Visit this picture-postcard village in the lovely Salzkammergut region. See p.82

❺ Adventure sports, Innsbruck Hiking, mountain-biking and canyoning in the stunning Austrian Alps. See p.86

HIGHLIGHTS ARE MARKED ON THE MAP ON P.63

ROUGH COSTS

Daily budget Basic €60, occasional treat €80

Drink Beer (0.5l €3.70), wine or coffee €3.50

Food Schnitzel €10

Hostel/budget hotel €22/€65

Travel Train: Graz–Vienna €32.50; Vienna–Salzburg €46.80

FACT FILE

Population 8.4 million

Language German

Currency Euro (€)

Capital Vienna

International phone code ☎43

Time zone GMT +1hr

Introduction

Glorious Alpine scenery, monumental Habsburg architecture and the world's favourite musical – Austria's tourist industry certainly plays up to the clichés. However, it's not all bewigged Mozart ensembles and schnitzel; modern Austria boasts some of Europe's most varied museums and contemporary architecture, not to mention attractive and sophisticated cities whose bars, cafés and clubs combine contemporary cool with elegant tradition.

Long the powerhouse of the Habsburg Empire, **Austria** underwent decades of change and uncertainty in the early twentieth century. Shorn of her empire and racked by economic difficulties, the state fell prey to the promises of Nazi Germany. Only with the end of the Cold War did Austria return to the heart of Europe, joining the EU in 1995.

Politics aside, Austria is primarily known for two contrasting attractions – the fading imperial glories of the capital, and the stunning beauty of its Alpine hinterland. **Vienna** is the gateway to much of central Europe and a good place to soak up the culture of *Mitteleuropa*. Less renowned provincial capitals such as **Graz** and **Linz** are surprising pockets of culture, innovation and vitality. **Salzburg**, between **Innsbruck** and Vienna, represents urban Austria at its most picturesque, an intoxicating Baroque city within easy striking distance of the mountains and lakes of the **Salzkammergut**, while the most dramatic of Austria's Alpine scenery is west of here, in and around **Tyrol**, whose capital, **Innsbruck**, provides the best base for exploration.

CHRONOLOGY

1st century BC Romans take over Celtic settlements in present-day Austria.

788 AD Charlemagne conquers Austrian land.

1156 The "Privilegium Minus" gives Austria the status of Duchy.

1278 The Habsburgs seize control of much of modern Austria (except Salzburg), and retain it until World War I.

1683 The Siege of Vienna – the Habsburgs under Leopold I defeat the Ottoman Turks outside Vienna.

1773 Wolfgang Amadeus Mozart becomes Court Musician in Salzburg.

1797 Napoleon defeats Austrian forces, taking Austrian land.

1814 An Austrian coalition force defeats Napoleon. In the Congress of Vienna the Salzburg lands are given to Austria, ending centuries of independence under Prince-Archbishops.

1866 Austrian territory is lost as a result of the Austro-Prussian war.

1899 Sigmund Freud publishes *The Interpretation of Dreams*, introducing the concept of the ego.

1914 The assassination of the Austrian Archduke, Franz Ferdinand, begins the events that lead to World War I.

1920 A new constitution creates the Republic of Austria.

1938 Hitler incorporates Austria into Germany through "Anschluss".

1945 Austria is occupied by Allied forces as World War II ends.

1965 *The Sound of Music* draws attention to Austria on the big screen.

1980s Protests at election of President Kurt Waldheim, due to rumours implicating him in Nazi war crimes.

1995 Austria joins the EU.

1999 The far-right Freedom Party led by Jörg Haider wins 27 percent of the vote in national elections.

2008 The world is enthralled by the case of Josef Fritzl – who imprisoned his daughter in a cellar for 24 years, fathering seven children with her.

ARRIVAL AND DEPARTURE

Austria lies right at the heart of Europe, bordered by seven countries. Excellent transport connections make it an easy stop-off on either a north–south or east–west route through Europe. Vienna has a major international airport, and you can also fly to Salzburg, Innsbruck, Graz and Linz or to the Slovak capital Bratislava, only a 1-hour 15-minute bus journey from Vienna. Vienna is also one of central Europe's major rail-hubs, with **connections** including Budapest, Bratislava and Prague. Trains from Croatia and Slovenia stop in Graz, before

also terminating here. Arriving from northern Italy (Venice, for example), it's likely you'll arrive in Innsbruck, which also has good rail connections with Munich, as does Salzburg.

GETTING AROUND

Austria's **public transport** is fast, efficient and comprehensive. ÖBB (⊚oebb.at; website includes an excellent English-language journey planner) runs a punctual **train** network, which includes most towns of any size. All stations in cities and larger towns have left luggage lockers. An Austria one-country pass with Eurail starts at €79 (3 days validity in 1 month; under-25s), though it's worth checking individual train prices, which can work out cheaper.

Buses (⊚postbus.at) serve remoter villages and Alpine valleys; fares are around €10 per 100km. Daily and weekly regional travelcards (*Netzkarte*), covering both trains and buses, are available in many regions.

Austria is bike-friendly, with **cycle lanes** in all major towns. Many train stations rent **bikes** for around €15 per day.

ACCOMMODATION

Outside popular tourist spots such as Vienna and Salzburg, **accommodation** need not be too expensive. Good-value B&B is usually available in the many small family-run hotels known as *Gasthöfe* and *Gasthäuser*, with prices from €60 per double. In the larger towns and cities a *pension* or *Frühstuckspension* will offer similar prices. Most places also have a stock of **private rooms** or *Privatzimmer*, although in well-travelled rural areas, roadside signs offering *Zimmer Frei* (or vacancies) are common (double room €35–50). Local tourist offices will have lists of these and will often ring around and book something for you.

There are around a hundred **HI hostels** (*Jugendherberge* or *Jugendgästehaus*), run by or affiliated to ÖJHV (⊚oejhv.or.at) or the ÖJHW (⊚oejhw.or.at). Rates are €20–26, normally including breakfast (€1–2 extra for non-members). There are also some excellent **independent hostels** in Salzburg and Vienna, plus affiliated youth hotel chains.

Austria's numerous **campsites** often have laundry facilities, shops and snack bars. Most open May to September, although some open year-round.

AUSTRIA ONLINE

⊚**austria.info** Austrian Tourist Board website.
⊚**tiscover.com** Detailed information on all regions of the country.
⊚**wienerzeitung.at** Website of the official Vienna city authorities' newspaper.

2

FOOD AND DRINK

Austrian food is hearty and traditional; often of good quality, it makes use of local and seasonal ingredients. For ready-made snacks, try a bakery (*Bäckerei*), confectioner's (*Konditorei*) or local market. **Fast food** centres on the *Würstelstand*, which sells hot dogs, *Bratwurst* (grilled sausage), *Käsekrainer* (spicy sausage with cheese), *Bosna* (spicy, thin Balkan sausage) and *Currywurst*. In *Kaffeehäuser* or cafés and bars you can get light meals and **snacks** starting at about €7; look out for the *Tagesmenu*, the lunchtime set menu, which is often excellent value (€8–12 for two courses). Main dishes (*Hauptspeisen*) are dominated by **Schnitzel** (tenderized veal): *Wienerschnitzel* is fried in breadcrumbs, *Pariser* in batter, *Natur* served on its own or with a creamy sauce. Expect to pay €10–15 for a standard main course. There is usually something on offer for vegetarians – more often than not *Käsespätzle*, similar to macaroni cheese. Two seasonal ingredients vegetarians should seek out in spring and early summer are *Bärlauch*, wild garlic, delicious in soups and pasta sauces, and *Spargel*, asparagus, typically the white variety and served with hollandaise.

DRINK

For Austrians, daytime drinking traditionally centres on the **Kaffeehaus**, relaxed places serving alcoholic and soft drinks, snacks and cakes, alongside a wide range of different coffees: a *Schwarzer* is small and black, a *Brauner* comes with a little milk, while a *Melange* is half coffee and half milk; a *Kurzer* is a small espresso; an *Einspänner* a glass of black coffee topped with *Schlag*: whipped cream. A cup of coffee in one of these places is pricey (€3–4), but for this you can linger for hours. Most cafés also offer a tempting array of freshly baked cakes and pastries, as do *Café-Konditorei*

(café-patisseries), where the cakes take centre stage.

Night-time drinking centres on **bars** and **cafés**, although traditional *Bierstuben* and *Weinstuben* are still thick on the ground. Austrian **beers** are of good quality. Most places serve the local brew on tap, either by the *Krügerl* (half-litre, about €3.50), *Seidel* (third-litre, €2–2.50) or *Pfiff* (fifth-litre, €1–1.60). The local **wine**, drunk by the *Viertel* (25cl mug) or the *Achterl* (12.5cl glass), is often excellent. The *Weinkeller* is the place to go for this or, in the wine-producing areas, a *Heuriger* or *Buschenshenk* – a traditional tavern, customarily serving cold food as well.

CULTURE AND ETIQUETTE

Austrian culture and etiquette is much like the rest of Western Europe, with leisurely café culture a central fixture. In restaurants, bars and cafés modest tipping – around ten percent or rounding up to the nearest euro – is expected (pay the waiter or waitress directly).

SPORTS AND ACTIVITIES

With stunning mountain scenery and beautiful lakes, Austria is an ideal destination for all sorts of outdoor sports. **Skiing** and snowboarding are major national pastimes (see box, p.86) and **hiking** and biking trails are clearly marked and graded. Tourist offices will usually have a surfeit of details on local routes and every other possible local activity.

COMMUNICATIONS

Most **post offices** are open Monday to Friday 8am to noon and 2 to 6pm; in larger cities they do without the lunch break and also open Saturday 8 to 10am. **Stamps** can also be bought at tobacconists (*Tabak-Trafik*). You can make

STUDENT DISCOUNTS

It is definitely worth carrying an **ISIC card** (ⓦisic.org) in Austria. Entry to museums and art galleries is costly, particularly in Vienna, and proving your student status will reap substantial savings (often up to fifty percent).

2

LANGUAGE

A high proportion of Austrians speak English, though any attempt at a few phrases of **German** (see box, p.337) will be heartily appreciated. Austrian accents and dialects can be tricky, however – the standard greeting throughout Austria is *Grüss Gott*.

international calls from all public phones, but it's easier to do so from booths at larger post offices. The operator and directory enquiries number is ☎118 11. **Internet access** is widespread (€3–5/hr) and most hostels and hotels have wi-fi.

EMERGENCIES

Austria is law-abiding and reasonably safe. Dial ☎059133 for the nearest police station (*Polizei*). **Pharmacies** (*Apotheke*) follow shopping hours; a rota system covers night-time and weekend opening, with details posted in the window.

INFORMATION

Tourist offices (usually *Information, Tourismusverband, Verkehrsamt* or *Fremdenverkehrsverein*) are plentiful, often hand out free maps and almost always book accommodation.

MONEY AND BANKS

Austria's currency is the **euro** (€). Banking hours tend to be Monday to Friday 8am to 12.30pm and 1.30 to 3pm; Thursday until 5.30pm. Post offices charge slightly less commission on exchange than banks, and, in larger cities, have longer hours.

OPENING HOURS AND PUBLIC HOLIDAYS

Most shops are open all day Monday to Saturday, though in the provinces they can close at lunch and on Saturday

EMERGENCY NUMBERS

Police ☎133; Ambulance ☎144; Fire ☎122.

afternoons. Many **cafés**, **restaurants** and bars also have a weekly *Ruhetag* (closing day). Shops and **banks** close, and most museums have reduced hours, on **public holidays:** January 1, January 6, Easter Monday, May 1, Ascension Day, Whit Monday, Corpus Christi, August 15, October 26, November 1, December 8, December 25 and 26.

Vienna

Most people visit **VIENNA** (Wien) with a vivid image in their minds: a romantic place, full of imperial nostalgia, opera houses and exquisite cakes. Even so, the city can overwhelm with its eclectic feast of architectural styles, from High Baroque through the monumental imperial projects of the late nineteenth century, to the decorative Jugendstil (Art Nouveau) style of the early twentieth, used to great effect on several of the city's splendid U-Bahn stations.

Vienna became an important centre in the tenth century, then in 1278 the city fell to **Rudolf of Habsburg**, but didn't become the imperial residence until 1683. The great aristocratic families flooded in to build palaces in a frenzy of construction that gave Vienna its **Baroque character**. By the end of the Habsburg era the city had become a breeding ground for the ideological passions of the age, and the ghosts of Freud, Klimt and Schiele are now some of the city's biggest tourist draws.

WHAT TO SEE AND DO

Central Vienna is surprisingly compact, with the historical centre, or **Innere Stadt**, just 1km wide. The most important sights are concentrated here and along the Ringstrasse – the series of traffic- and tram-clogged boulevards that form a ring road around the centre. Efficient public transport allows you to cross the city in less than thirty minutes, making even peripheral sights, such as the monumental imperial palace at **Schönbrunn**, easily accessible. However, for all the grand palaces and museums, a trip to Vienna

2

VIENNA

● DRINKING AND NIGHTLIFE

B72	3
Café Leopold	17
Chelsea	6
Espresso	14
Flex	2
Fluc/Fluc Wanne	1
Loos American Bar	10
Passage	16
Rote Bar	12
Wirr	13

● EATING

Aromat	23
Central	5
Dreschler	21
Engländer	7
Europa	20
Kantine	15
Kleines Café	11
Landtmann	4
Prückel	8
Salm Bräu	22
Schnitzelwirt	18
Sperl	19
Trzesniewski	9

Josephinum

Freud Museum

Universität

Rossauer Kaserne

Ringturm

Votivkirche

Schottentor

Börse

Universität

Schottenstift

Museum Judenplatz

Palais Ferstel

Holocaust Memorial

Kirche am Hof

Burgtheater

INNERE STADT

Peterskirche

Rathaus

Herrengasse

Minoriten-kirche

Michaeler-kirche

JOSEFSTADT

Volksgarten

Spanish Riding School

Hofburg

Stallburg

Parliament

Justizpalast

Naturhistorisches Museum

Volkstheater

Volkstheater

Kunsthistorisches Museum

Burggarten

Albertina

SPITTELBERG

Museums Quartier

Staatsoper

Leopold Museum

Museums-quartier

Akademie der bildenden Künste

NEUBAU

Neubaugasse

Secession

Karlsplatz

Theater-an-der-Wein

Majolikahaus

Naschmarkt

Haus des Meeres

Kettenbrückengasse

Schönbrunn

Schönbrunn & Meidling Train Station

---

that's only frantic sightseeing would miss out on European café culture at its very finest: spending a leisurely afternoon nursing a creamy coffee and a piece of cake in one of the grand, shabby-glamorous coffeehouses that the city is famous for.

Stephansdom

The obvious place to begin exploration is **Stephansplatz**, the pedestrianized central square dominated by the hoary Gothic **Stephansdom** (Mon–Sat 6am–10pm, Sun 7am–10pm, except during services; free,

2

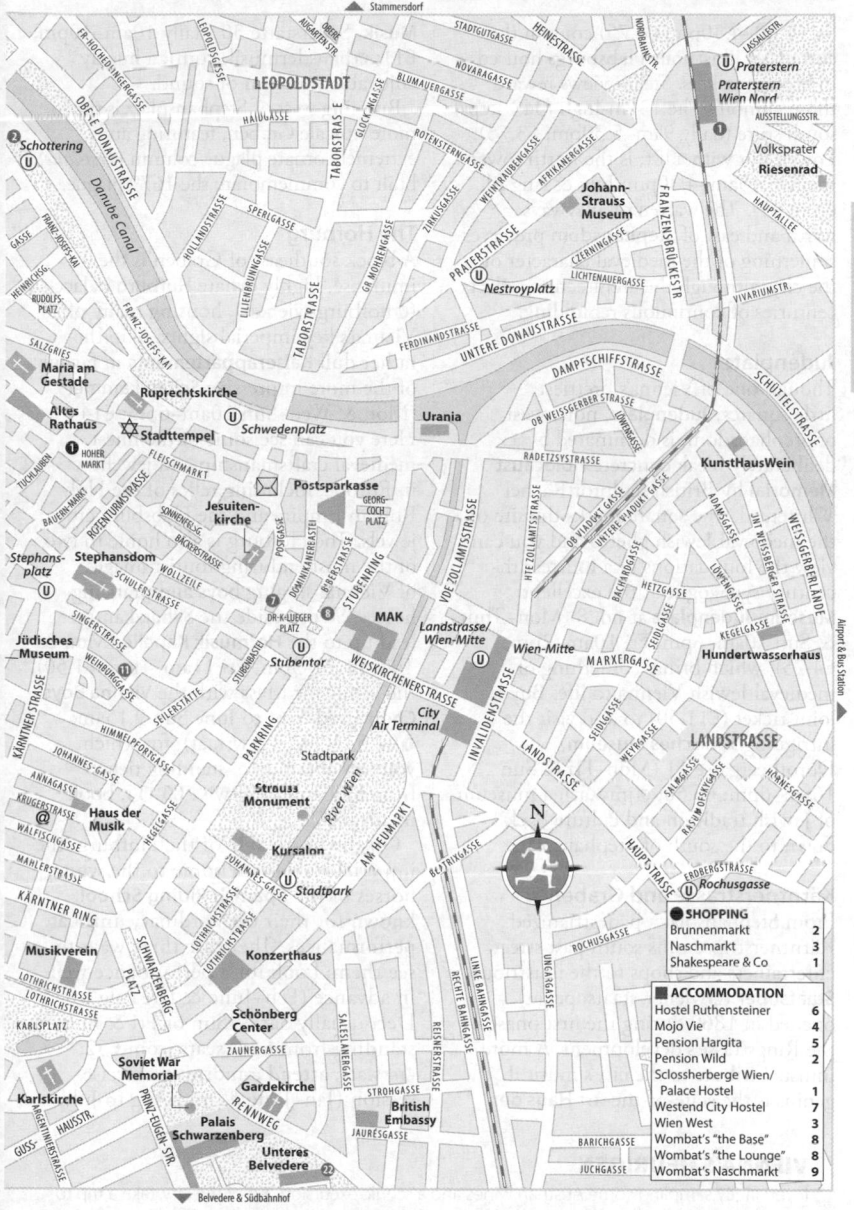

● SHOPPING	
Brunnenmarkt	2
Naschmarkt	3
Shakespeare & Co	1

■ ACCOMMODATION	
Hostel Ruthensteiner	6
Mojo Vie	4
Pension Hargita	5
Pension Wild	2
Sclossherberge Wien/ Palace Hostel	1
Westend City Hostel	7
Wien West	3
Wombat's "the Base"	8
Wombat's "the Lounge"	8
Wombat's Naschmarkt	9

but entry fees to most sections, combined ticket €15.50). It's worth paying to explore the interior more fully, with the highlights of the main section (Mon–Sat 8.30–11.30am & 1–5.30pm, Sun 1–5.30pm; tour with audioguide €5;

English tours April–Oct daily 3.45pm; €5) the Wiener Neustädter Altar, a late Gothic masterpiece, and the tomb of the Holy Roman Emperor Friedrich III. The **catacombs** (tours every 15–30min, Mon–Sat 10–11.30am & 1.30–4.30pm,

2

Sun 1.30–4.30pm; €4.75) contain the entrails of illustrious Habsburgs housed in bronze caskets. Stellar views reward those climbing the 137m-high (343 steps) south spire (daily 9am–5.30pm; €3.75). Lower, but with a lift, is the north tower (daily 8.15am–4.30pm; July & Aug till 6pm; €5). The warren of alleyways north and east of **Stephansdom** preserves something of the medieval character of the city, although the architecture reflects centuries of continuous rebuilding.

Judenplatz

Though one of Vienna's prettiest little squares, **Judenplatz**, northwest of Stephansdom, is dominated by a deliberately bleak concrete **Holocaust Memorial** by British sculptor Rachel Whiteread. The square marks the site of the medieval Jewish ghetto and you can view the foundations of a fourteenth-century synagogue at the excellent **Museum Judenplatz** at no. 8 (Mon–Thurs & Sun 10am–6pm, Fri 10am–2pm; €4.75), which brings something of medieval Jewish Vienna to life. Buy a joint ticket (€11.50) to also visit the intriguing **Jüdisches Museum**, Dorotheergasse 11 (Mon–Fri & Sun 10am–6pm; €6.50; ⓦjmw.at), a museum of Jewish tradition and culture back down to the south of Stephansplatz.

Kärntnerstrasse and Graben

From Stephansplatz, pedestrianized Kärntnerstrasse runs south past street entertainers and shops to the illustrious **Staatsoper** (ⓦwiener-staatsoper.at), opened in 1869 during the first phase of the Ringstrasse's development. A more unusual tribute to the city's musical genius is the state-of-the-art **Haus der Musik**, Seilerstätte 30 (daily 10am–10pm; €11; ⓦhausdermusik.com), a hugely enjoyable museum of sound.

Running west of Stephansplatz is the more upscale Graben, featuring an extremely ornate plague column (*Pestsäule*), built to commemorate the 1679 plague.

The Hofburg

A block southeast of Graben is the immense, highly ornate **Hofburg** palace (ⓦhofburg-wien.at), housing many of Vienna's key imperial sights. Skip the rather dull **Kaiserappartements** in favour of the more impressive **Schatzkammer** (Mon & Wed–Sun 10am–6pm; €14). Here you can see some of the finest medieval craftsmanship and jewellery in Europe, including relics of the Holy Roman Empire and the Habsburg crown jewels. The Hofburg is also home to two of the most enduring tourist images of Vienna: singing boys and prancing horses. Steps beside the Schatzkammer lead up to the **Hofmusik Kapelle** (Mon & Tues 11am–3pm, Fri 11am–1pm; €1.50), the venue for Mass with the **Vienna Boys' Choir** (mid-Sept to June Sun 9.15am; ☎01 533 9927, ⓦwsk.at), for which you can obtain free, standing tickets from 8.30am (otherwise €5–35, book in advance).

On the north side of the Hofburg, the imperial stables are home to the white horses of the **Spanish Riding School**, known for their extraordinary, intricate performances. There are three ways to see them: book for a performance well in advance (Feb–June & late Aug to Dec, usually Sat & Sun or Fri & Sun; standing from €24, seats from €52; ⓦsrs.at); attend a morning exercise session (Jan–June & mid-Aug to July

---

VIENNA'S HEURIGEN

If you fancy sampling some Austrian wines and a scenic excursion out of the city, take a trip to one of the wine-producing villages on Vienna's outskirts. To the north of the Danube, **Stammersdorf** (tram #31 from Schottenring; 40min) is surrounded by vineyards and filled with traditional, family-run *Heurigen* (wine taverns).

Wienhof Wieninger 21 Stammersdorferstr. 78 ⓦheuriger-wieninger.at. A great place to start, with a pleasant garden, buffet and a good selection of own-label whites available by the glass. Mid-April to mid-Dec Thurs & Fri 3pm–midnight, Sat & Sun noon–midnight.

usually Tues–Fri, plus occasional Sat 10am–noon, box office at Josefplatz from 9am; the queue is at its worst early on, but by 11am it's usually easy enough to get in; €12); or join a guided tour of the school and stables (Jan Tues–Sat; Feb, March & Nov Tues–Sun; April–Oct & Dec daily; tours 2pm, 3pm & 4pm; combined tour and training session €27; tickets from visitor centre at Michaelerplatz daily 9am–4pm). Alternatively, if you just want to take a peek at the horses, look into the stables (*Stallburg*) from the glass windows on Reitschulgasse.

Finally, at the Hofburg's easternmost tip, the **Albertina** (daily 10am–6pm, Wed till 9pm; €10.50; w albertina.at), houses one of the world's largest graphic art collections, with works by Raphael, Rembrandt, Dürer and Michelangelo.

The Ring and Rathausplatz

The Ring, the large boulevard that encircles the Innere Stadt, along with its attendant monumental civic buildings, was created to replace the town's fortifications, demolished in 1857; many of these buildings now house museums. On the western section is the showpiece **Rathausplatz**, a square framed by four monumental public buildings: the Rathaus (City Hall), the Burgtheater, Parlament and the Universität – all completed in the 1880s.

The Kunsthistorisches Museum

Of all Vienna's museums, the **Kunsthistorisches Museum** on Burgring still outshines them all (June–Aug daily 10am–6pm, Thurs till 9pm; Sept–May Tues–Sun 10am–6pm, Thurs till 9pm; €14; w khm.at). It's one of the world's greatest collections of Old Masters – comparable with the Hermitage or Louvre. An unrivalled collection of sixteenth-century paintings by Brueghel the Elder, in particular, draws the crowds, while the Peter Paul Rubens collection is also very strong and works by Vermeer and Caravaggio are worth seeking out. A number of Greek and Roman antiquities add breadth and variety. Set aside several hours at least – there is also an excellent

café; a particularly impressive spot for a slice of cake.

The MuseumsQuartier

Just to the southwest of the Ring is Vienna's **MuseumsQuartier** (MQ; w mqw .at), a collection of museums and galleries in the old imperial stables, a mixture of the original buildings with a couple of striking contemporary additions. Stylish outdoor seating, plenty of good cafés and an interesting calendar of events make the area a focus for Vienna's cultural life. The best museum here is the **Leopold Museum** (Mon, Wed & Fri–Sun 10am–6pm, Thurs 10am–9pm; €11.50), with fine work by Klimt and the largest collection in the world of works by Egon Schiele.

The Secession

The eccentric, eye-catching building crowned with a "golden cabbage" by Karlsplatz is the **Secession building** (Tues–Sun 10am–6pm; €8.50), the gallery built as the headquarters of the movement of the same name in 1898, designed by Joseph Maria Olbrech, and decorated by several luminaries of the group, including their first president Gustav Klimt. Their aim was to break with the Viennese establishment and champion new ideas of art and aesthetics, and it still puts on contemporary exhibits. The only permanent artwork is Klimt's *Beethoven Frieze* downstairs.

MAK

On the Ring's eastern section, beyond Stubenring, is the enjoyable **MAK** (Tues 10am–midnight, Wed–Sun 10am–6pm; €10.70, free Sat; w mak.at), an applied arts museum whose eclectic collection spans the Romanesque period to the twentieth century and includes an unrivalled Wiener Werkstätte collection.

The Belvedere

South of the Ringstrasse, the **Belvedere** (daily 10am–6pm; Oberes €10.50, combined ticket €16; w belvedere.at; tram #D from the opera house) is one of Vienna's finest palace complexes. Two magnificent Baroque mansions face each

2

other across a sloping formal garden. The loftier of the two, the **Oberes Belvedere**, has the best concentration of paintings by Klimt in the city, including *The Kiss*, while the Unteres Belvedere and Orangerie show temporary exhibitions.

Schönbrunn

The biggest attraction in the city suburbs is the imperial summer palace of Schönbrunn (ⓦ schoenbrunn.at; ⓤ4 to Schönbrunn), designed by Fischer von Erlach on the model of residences like Versailles. To visit the palace rooms or **Prunkräume** (daily: April–June, Sept & Oct 8.30am–5pm; July & Aug 8.30am–6pm; Nov–March 8.30am–4.30pm) there's a choice of two tours: the "Imperial Tour" (€11.70), which takes in 22 state rooms, and the "Grand Tour" (€14.75 with audioguide, €16.50 with tour guide), which includes all forty rooms. The shorter tour misses out the best rooms – such as the Millions Room, a rosewood-panelled chamber covered from floor to ceiling with wildly irregular Rococo cartouches, each holding a Persian miniature watercolour.
The palace can become unbearably overcrowded at the height of summer, with lengthy queues – it's a good idea to buy tickets in advance online. The splendid Schlosspark (daily dawn–dusk; free) is dotted with attractions, including the Gloriette – a hilltop colonnaded monument, now a café and terrace from which you can enjoy splendid views (daily: April–June & Sept 9am–6pm; July & Aug 9am–7pm; Oct 9am–5pm; €3.50), fountains, a maze and labyrinth (same hours as Gloriette; €4) and Vienna's excellent **Tiergarten** or zoo (daily: Jan, Nov & Dec 9am–4.30pm; Feb 9am–5pm; March & Oct 9am–5.30pm; April–Sept 9am–6.30pm; €14.50; ⓦ zoovienna.at).

ARRIVAL AND DEPARTURE

By plane Vienna Airport (ⓦ viennaairport.com) is around 20km southeast of the city. The cheapest way to reach the centre is to take S-Bahn line ⓢ7 to Wien-Mitte station (every 30min; 24min; €3.80 one-way). The City Airport Train (CAT; every 30min; 16min; €10.50 one-way) to Wien-Mitte is slightly faster. Buses (every 30min; €7.60

one-way) run to ⓤ Schwedenplatz (20min) in the centre and Westbahnhof (45min).
By train Vienna's train stations have been undergoing major redevelopment. Südbahnhof has been incorporated into Wien Hauptbahnhof and will fully exist as the main station by 2015; until then, arrival points are scattered across the city. Trains from the west and Hungary terminate at the Westbahnhof (ⓤ3 five stops from the centre); trains from Bratislava arrive at Südbahnhof (ⓤ Südtiroler Platz and a 5min walk or tram #D); Vienna-Meidling station serves most trains from Graz and the Czech Republic, Poland and Slovenia (ⓤ6 four stops south of Westbahnhof).
Destinations Bratislava (every 30min; 1hr); Budapest (6 daily; 2hr 40min); Graz (hourly; 2hr 30min); Innsbruck (18 daily; 5hr); Linz (every 30min; 1hr 45min); Melk (hourly; 1hr 15min); Prague (5 daily; 4hr 45min); Salzburg (every 30min; 3hr).
By bus Vienna International Bus terminal is at Erdbergstr. (ⓤ Erdberg, southeast of the centre, six stops from Stephansplatz on line ⓤ3).
By boat DDSG (ⓦ www.ddsg-blue-danube.at) boats from further up the Danube, or from Bratislava, dock at Schwedenplatz.
Destinations Bratislava (April–Oct 4 daily; 1hr 15min).

INFORMATION

Tourist information The main tourist office is at Albertinaplatz 1, behind the opera house (daily 9am–6.30pm; ⓣ 01 245 55, ⓦ wien.info).

GETTING AROUND

So many attractions are in or around the Innere Stadt that you can do a great deal on foot.
By public transport The network (ⓦ wienerlinien.at) consists of trams (Strassenbahn or Bim), buses, the U-Bahn (metro) and the S-Bahn (fast commuter trains). U-Bahns run from around 5/6am to 12.30am, with a reduced frequency of roughly every 20min between 1am & 5am (Fri & Sat 24hr); trams run till around midnight. A network of nightbuses centres on Schwedenplatz and Kärtner Ring/Oper.
Tickets Buy your ticket from ticket booths or machines at stations, tobacconists or on board trams and buses (more expensive), then validate it at the start of your journey. One-way tickets are €2 (€2.30 on board buses and trams) and allow unlimited changes in one direction; day passes are better value (24hr/48hr/72hr for €6.70/€11.70/€14.50). The Vienna Card (€19.90) acts as a 72hr travel pass and also gives discounts at attractions. If you have an ISIC card, simply buying a travel pass is a better bet.
By bike Vienna has a very cheap city-wide bike scheme, CityBikes (ⓦ citybikewien.at), with stations all over the city, including behind Stephansdom on Stephansplatz. The

VIENNESE ADDRESSES

Vienna is divided into **numbered districts** (*Bezirke*). District 1 is the Innere Stadt; districts 2–9 are arranged clockwise around it; districts 10–23 are a fair way out. Addresses begin with the number of the district, followed by the street name, then the house number and apartment number.

first hour is free, second is €1, third is €2. Bikes can be rented with a credit card or with a "tourist card" (€2 plus deposit from Royal Tours, Herrengasse 1–3; daily 9–11.30am & 1–6pm).

ACCOMMODATION

For cheaper accommodation booking ahead is essential in summer. Several hostels are near the Westbahnhof, which is an easy few stops into the centre.

HOSTELS

★ **Hostel Ruthensteiner** 15, Robert Hamerlinggasse 24 ☎01 893 42 02, ⓦhostelruthensteiner.com; ⓤWestbahnhof. Excellent, friendly and relaxed hostel an easy walk from the Westbahnhof. There's a spacious leafy courtyard, plus bar, musical instruments, kitchen, barbecue, internet, laundry and free wi-fi. Dorm €17, double €62

★ **Mojo Vie** 7, Kaiserstr. 77/8 ☎0676 55 111 55, ⓦmymojovie.at; ⓤBurggasse-Stadthalle or tram #5 to Burggasse from Westbahnhof. Charming, very stylish alternative to the standard hostel, with a network of local apartments housing dorms (one four-bed, one six-bed) and private rooms. Excellent communal areas and personal, welcoming vibe. Minimum two nights, maximum four people per group. Dorm €20, double €56

Schlossherberge Wien/Palace Hostel 2, Savoyenstrasse 7 ☎01 481 00 30, ⓦhostel.at/hostel -schlossherberge; ⓤOttakring then bus #46b or #146b. Located amid leafy grounds up in the Vienna hills, with a view of the city. All rooms come with showers and access to the massive garden with a volleyball net, and there's free breakfast, lockers and wi-fi. Dorms have a maximum of 4 beds. Dorm €22, double €60

Westend City Hostel 6, Fügergasse 3 ☎01 597 67 29, ⓦwestendhostel.at. A few minutes' walk from the Westbahnhof, this refurbished 211-bed former hotel has friendly staff, en-suite doubles and patio. Dorm €22.50, double €69

Wombat's "the Base" 15, Grangasse 6, and **Wombat's "The Lounge"** Mariahilferstr. 137 ☎01 897 23 36, ⓦwombats.at. A pair of party-orientated *Wombat's* hostels, both near the Westbahnhof. With guest kitchen, laundry and free wi-fi. Dorm €20, double €70

Wombat's Naschmarkt Rechte Wienzeile 35 ☎01 897 23 36, ⓦwombats-hostels.com; ⓤKettenbrückengasse. It's all about location at this newest branch of the *Wombat's* chain, right by the Naschmarkt and within walking distance of the Innere Stadt. It's slick, well equipped, with all dorms en suite, and there's a good bar and communal areas, though inevitably it's a little bland. Dorm €20, double €70

HOTELS AND PENSIONS

Pension Hargita 1/8, Andreagasse 4 ☎01 526 19 28, ⓦhargita.at; ⓤieglergasse. Homely, Hungarian-owned *pension* in a great location just off Mariahilferstr. The interior is decorated with blue country pottery, while the cabin-like common areas are lined with wood. All rooms contain washbasins, though en-suite costs extra. Breakfast €5. Double €54

Pension Wild 8, Lange Gasse 10 ☎01 406 51 74, ⓦpension-wild.com; ⓤVolkstheater. Friendly, laidback *pension*, a short walk from the Ring in a student district behind the university. En-suite costs extra. Especially popular with gay travellers; booking is essential. Double €53

CAMPSITE

Wien Nest 14, Hüttelbergstr. 80 ☎01 914 23 14, ⓦwiencamping.at; bus #148 or #152 from ⓤHütteldorf. In the plush far-western suburbs of Vienna, with two- and four-bed bungalows to rent. Closed Feb. Camping €7.30 per person, plus €7 per tent

EATING

CAFÉS, CHEAP EATS AND SNACKS

Central 1, Herrengasse 14, ⓤHerrengasse. Traditional meeting place of Vienna's intelligentsia, and Trotsky's favourite *Kaffeehaus* – of all Vienna's cafés, perhaps the most ornate. Daily 6/7am–10pm.

Dreschler 6, Linke Wienzeile 22/ Girardgasse 1; ⓤKarlsplatz. Takes the best of the classic Viennese café, and adds a contemporary twist – a stylish remodel and a relaxed vibe during the day through into late evening, when DJs take over. Good snacks, a popular and hearty goulash soup and breakfasts (from €7.50). Only shuts for an hour between 2 and 3am, otherwise open daily 23hr.

★ **Engländer** 1, Postgasse 2; ⓤStubentor. Great *Kaffeehaus* with a long pedigree and food that has a touch of nouvelle cuisine. Snacks €4–12, mains €9–22; two-course lunch menu €10.50, including vegetarian options. Daily 6/7am–1am.

Europa 7, Zollergasse 8; ⓤNeubaugasse. Lively, modern café hosting a young, trendy crowd. Good breakfast menu and weekend breakfast buffet €11.50 (9am–3pm). Different atmosphere in the evening when it morphs into a relaxed bar; frequently hosts DJs on the weekends. Daily 6/7am–5am.

2

Kantine 7, Museumsplatz 1; ⑩ MuseumsQuartier. One of the MuseumsQuartier's cafés, with a varied menu and free wi-fi. The vibe is a tad more upscale than other cafés around town. Daily 6/7am–2am, Sun till midnight.

Kleines Café 1, Franziskanerplatz 3; ⑩ Stephansplatz. Tiny café with outside seating, tucked away in a tranquil cobbled square, serving delicious open sandwiches (from €4.25). Daily 6/7am–9/10pm.

Landtmann 4, Dr Karl Lüger Ring 14; ⑩ Rathaus. One of Freud's haunts, this chandelier-filled perennial favourite feels fit for royals and has always attracted big-name celebrities and politicians, though also welcomes people from all walks of life. Try to score a table next to the huge windows so you can people-watch while devouring a decadent cake. Daily 6/7am–midnight.

Prückel Stubenring 24; ⑩ Stubentor. You could lose hours of your life in a caffeine- and smoke-filled haze here, one of the best and most relaxed of the classic Viennese coffeehouses, with stylish 1950s decor. Live piano music (mainly classical; no cover) Wed–Sat 7pm. Daily 6/7am–midnight.

★ **Sperl** 6, Gumpendorferstr. 11; ⑩ Karlsplatz/Babenbergerstr. With a slightly faded, *fin-de-siècle* interior this is among the finest of the city's coffeehouses, with reasonably priced food (daily special €9–11) and coffee and cake for around €7. Mon–Sat 7am–11pm, Sun 11am–8pm, July & Aug closed Sun.

Trzesniewski Dorotheergasse 1. Just off Graben, this is a great place for a pit stop – grab a couple of small open sandwiches, with pâté toppings such as herring, egg or spicy pepper for €1.50 each, washed down with a *pfiff* (0.2l; €1.20) of beer. Mon–Fri 8.30am–7.30pm, Sat 9am–5pm.

RESTAURANTS

★ **Aromat** Margaretenstr. 52 ☎01 913 24 53; ⑩ Kettenbrückengasse. Just eight tables, and a short, daily changing evening menu (mains €9–12) of imaginative Mediterranean-influenced dishes, plus sweet and savoury crêpes, make this a bit of a treat. Tues–Sun 5–11pm.

Salm Bräu 3, Rennweg 8; tram #71. Not just a bar and not just a restaurant, this brew pub dishes up Viennese staples and huge salads as well as a fine selection of brewed-on-the-premises beers. In summer the long outdoor tables are a fine place to land after touring nearby Belvedere. Daily 11.30am–midnight.

Schnitzelwirt 7, Neubaugasse 52; tram #49. A convivial local favourite set in a wood-panelled space, perfect for getting cosy on cold nights. Great place for *wienerschnitzel* – a bargain at €6.70. Mon–Sat 11am–11pm.

DRINKING AND NIGHTLIFE

If you fancy a bar crawl or live music the string of clubs under the railway arches around ⑩ Thaliastr., Josefstädterstr. and Alserstr. are a good bet.

★ **TREAT YOURSELF**

Loos American Bar 1, Karntnerdurchgang 10; ⑩ Staphansplatz. Designed in the shiny, brash Art Deco style of architect Adolf Loos, and with an old-school feel, this classy joint attracts people of all ages who appreciate an expertly made cocktail. Come early if you want a seat. Daily roughly 6pm till 2am or later.

BARS

Café Leopold 7, Museumsplatz ⑩ cafe-leopold.at; ⑩ MuseumsQuartier. Coolest of the MuseumsQuartier's cafés, in a very stylish glass-walled space attached to the museum. Chic café during the day; DJs and designer gear come out at night. Roughly 6pm till 1am or later.

Espresso 7, Burggasse 57; ⑩ Volkstheater. Chilled bar with street terrace and retro furniture that attracts a multi-aged clientele. Mon–Fri 7.30pm–late, Sat & Sun 10am–late.

Rote Bar 1, Neustiftgasse 1; ⑩ Volkstheater. Set inside the Volkstheater, this sumptuous spot is decked out in red velvet and feels a bit like going back in time. Welcomes all ages but be sure to put on your best threads. Roughly 6pm till at least 1am.

Wirr 7, Burggasse 70 ⑩ www.wirr.at; ⑩ Volkstheater. Day-into-evening café-bar, and "night café" downstairs, with a host of events, including burlesque nights. Popular for weekend brunches and lunches (from €7.50). Daily roughly 6pm till late.

CLUBS AND LIVE MUSIC

B72 8, Hernalser Gürtel Bogen 72–73, under the arches ⑩ b72.at; ⑩ Alserstr. or Josefstadterstr. (between the two). Dark designer club featuring a mixture of DJs and often good live indie bands. Mon–Sat 5pm–4am.

Chelsea 8, Gürtelbögen 29–30, Lerchenfelder Gürtel ⑩ chelsea.co.at; ⑩ Thaliastr. Popular, grungy rock venue with up-and-coming bands. Situated underneath the railway arches on a stretch with several bars. Tues–Sat 6pm–2am.

Flex 1, Am Donaukanal ⑩ flex.at; ⑩ Schottenring. A stalwart in Vienna's club scene, this serious dance-music club by the canal attracts some of the city's best DJs. Thurs–Sat 8pm–4am.

★ **Fluc/Fluc Wanne** 2, Praterstern 5 ⑩ fluc.at; ⑩ Praterstern. Takes shabby-chic to a new level: this upstairs bar (*Fluc*) and underground club (*Fluc Wanne*) inside a former pedestrian tunnel could be mistaken for industrial containers. Come evening they transform into one of the best venues in the city, with interesting electro, house and hip-hop club nights. Both 8pm till 3am or later.

Passage 1, Babenberger Passage, Burgring/Babenbergerstr. ⑩ sunshine.at; ⑪ MuseumsQuartier/Volkstheater. Dressy, futuristic club in a converted pedestrian underpass, attracting a mixed crowd. Roughly 8pm–4am

SHOPPING

Mariahilferstr. is best for high-street clothes shops and the big chains, though Neubaugasse, nearby, is more eclectic. **Brunnenmarkt** Brunnengasse; ⑪ Josefstädter Strasse. Further out, so with a distinctively local feel, Brunnenmarkt sells everything from homewares to Turkish breads and pastries. At Yppenplatz, its northern end, there's a farmers' market on Sat mornings, where you can pick up local produce or stop for brunch at one of the many cafés. Mon–Fri 6am–6.30pm, Sat 6am–2pm.
Naschmarkt ⑪ Karlsplatz. Large famous market with Turkish deli stalls, hip cafés and a plethora of stalls and snack joints, serving everything from falafel to sushi. On Sat mornings a flea market extends south from here near ⑪ Kettenbrückengasse. Mon–Fri 6am–7.30pm, Sat 6am–5pm.
Shakespeare & Co 1, Sterngasse 2 ⑩ shakespeare.co.at; ⑪ Schwedenplatz. Friendly English-language bookshop; also sells translations of Austrian authors. Mon–Fri 10am–6pm, Sat 10am–4pm.

ENTERTAINMENT

The local listings magazine *Falter* (⑩ falter.at) has comprehensive details of the week's cultural programme. The tourist office also publishes the free monthly *Programm*.
Konzerthaus 3, Lothringerstr. 20 ☎ 01 242 002, ⑩ konzerthaus.at. A major classical venue which also hosts occasional performances of jazz and world music.
Musikverein 1, Karlsplatz 6 ☎ 01 505 81 90, ⑩ musikverein-wien.at. Ornate concert hall, bastion of classical music and home to the Vienna Philharmonic.
Staatsoper 1, Opernring 2 ☎ 01 513 15 13, ⑩ wiener -staatsoper.at. One of Europe's most prestigious opera houses. The season runs Sept–June and tickets range from a mere €9 to over €250. They often sell out, but the office also sells hundreds of standing-place tickets (*Stehplätze*) each night 1hr 20min before a performance (from €3/4).

DIRECTORY

Embassies Australia, 4, Mattiellistr. 2–4 ☎ 01 506 740; Canada, 1, Laurenzerberg 2 ☎ 01 531 38 30 00; Ireland, 1, Rotenturmstr. 16–18 ☎ 01 715 42 46; UK, 3, Jauresgasse 12 ☎ 01 71 61 30; US, 9, Boltzmanngasse 16 ☎ 01 31 33 90.
Hospital Allegemeines Krankenhaus, 9, Währinger Gürtel 18–20; ⑪ Michelbeuern-AKH.
Internet Surfland Internet Café, 1, Krugerstr. 10 (daily 10am–11pm; €4.50/30min).
Post office 19; Westbahnhof; Südbahnhof (both 7am–10pm).

Central Austria

West of Vienna, the Danube snakes through the Wachau, one of its most scenic stretches, where castles and vineyards cling to steep slopes above quaint villages. The western end of this 40km stretch is marked by a stunning Baroque monastery in **Melk**. Further west the river steadily loses charm, though it's still a focus for several towns and cities, including **Linz**, whose high-tech Ars Electronica museum is particularly enjoyable. South of the Danube region, the land slowly climbs and rolls into the hills of Styria, with its attractive and bustling capital **Graz**. Northwest of here, the land rises again up to the Salzkammergut, a region of fine Alpine scenery and pretty lakes within easy reach of **Salzburg**. Southwest of the Salzkammergut the peaks really start to soar, and resorts like **Bad Gastein** take full advantage of the landscape and healthy spring waters to offer great skiing and first-rate spa facilities.

2

MELK

For real High Baroque excess, head for the early eighteenth-century **Benedictine monastery** at **MELK** – a pilgrimage centre associated with the Irish missionary St Koloman. The monumental coffee-cake monastery, perched on a bluff over the river, dominates the town. Highlights of the interior (daily: April & Oct 9am–5pm; May–Sept 9am–6pm; tours in English 10.30am & 2.30pm; Nov–March guided, German-language tours only: 11am & 2pm; €8.60, €10.80 with guided tour; ⑩ stiftmelk.at) are the exquisite library, with a cherub-flecked ceiling by Troger, and the rather lavish monastery church, with similarly impressive work by Rottmayr.

ARRIVAL AND INFORMATION

By train The station is at the head of Bahnhofstr., which leads directly into the old quarter.
Tourist information Babenbergerstr. 1 (April & Oct Mon–Fri 9am–noon & 2–5pm, Sat 10am–noon; May & June Mon–Fri 9am–noon & 2–6pm, Sat & Sun 10am–2pm;

July & Aug Mon–Sat 9am–7pm, Sun 10am–noon & 5–7pm; Sept Mon–Fri 9am–noon & 2–5pm, Sat 10am–2pm; ☎ 02 752 52 30 74 10, ⓦ stadt-melk.at). Has a substantial stock of private rooms, though few are central.

ACCOMMODATION

Junges Hotel Melk Abt Karl-Str. 42 ☎ 02 752 526 81, ⓦ melk.noejhw.at. HI hostel a 10min walk from the tourist office. Open March–Oct; reception 4–9pm. Breakfast included. Dorm **€22.80**, double **€48**

LINZ

Away from its industrial suburbs, **LINZ** is a pleasant Baroque city straddling the Danube, and steadily reinventing itself as a city of technology and innovation, most evident in a couple of show-stopping new museums.

WHAT TO SEE AND DO

Linz's two most striking contemporary attractions, Lentos Museum and Ars Electronica Center, face each other on either side of the Danube River. Wander up this way after the sun goes down when both are illuminated – their neon facades glow dramatically opposite each other. To the south of the river is the city's compact Old Town, the hub of which is **Hauptplatz**, with its pastel-coloured facades and central Trinity Column, crowned by a gilded sunburst. Many of the city's liveliest bars are clustered just west of here, around the triangle formed by Hoffgasse, Altstadt and Hahnengasse. Heading south from the Hauptplatz, the busy shopping street Landstrasse leads south towards the train station.

Lentos

A modern addition to the city's cultural scene nestles beside the Danube: the shimmering, hangar-like steel-and-glass **Lentos** (Tues–Sun 10am–6pm, Thurs till 9pm; €7.60; ⓦ lentos.at), which houses contemporary and modern art, including Klimt and Schiele.

Ars Electronica Center

Just across the river is Linz's other major attraction, and worth a trip to the city alone, the unusual, tardis-like temple to science and technology that is **Ars Electronica Center**, Hauptstrasse 2 (Tues, Wed & Fri 9am–5pm, Thurs 9am–9pm, Sat & Sun 10am–6pm; €7.50; ⓦ aec.at). Inside the glowing box of an exterior is an impressive series of interactive high-tech exhibits. One highlight is the "CAVE", a virtual-reality room with 3D projections on the walls and floor. Basement areas explore future developments in biology, materials, the brain and robots – set aside several hours and get stuck into the hands-on experiments.

ARRIVAL AND INFORMATION

By train 2km south of the centre, at the end of Landstr; all trams (lines #1, #2 and #3) from the underground platform at the station (direction "Zentrum") run up Landstr. to Hauptplatz.

Destinations Graz (7 daily; 3hr 30min–3hr 45min); Salzburg (every 30min; 1hr 15min); Vienna (every 30min; 1hr 45min).

Tourist information Alte Rathaus, Hauptplatz 1 (May–Sept Mon–Sat 9am–6.30pm, Sun 10am–7pm; Oct–April Mon–Sat 9am–5pm, Sun 10am–5pm; ☎ 07 32 70 70 20 09, ⓦ linz.at); sells the Linz Card (1 day €16, students €11; 3-day €27, students €21), which includes entry to museums and travel.

GETTING AROUND

By public transport Useful network of trams and buses: "mini" 4-stop ticket €1.20; single journey ("midi", transferable) €2.30; 24hr "maxi" ticket €4.20, under-21s €2.10. The Pöstlingbergbahn from Hauptplatz is a tourist tram (every 30min; 25min one-way; €5.80 return), up to the Pöstlingberg on the north side, a hill with good views over the city and a beer garden.

ACCOMMODATION

Herberge Linz Kapuzinerstr. 14 ☎ 0699 11 80 7003, ⓔ herberge.linz@aon.at. Very central (5min walk west of Hauptplatz, along Promenade off Landstr. then Klammstr.), but bare-bones hostel, with clean basic dorms and kitchens, and some nice outdoor space; check-in 6–8pm only. Dorm **€19**

Jugendherberge Stanglhofweg 3 ☎ 07 32 66 44 34, ⓦ jugendherbergsverband.at; bus #17, #19, #19a, #45a, or #46 to "Leondingerstr". Friendly youth hostel 2km from Hauptbahnhof. All bedrooms are en suite and breakfast is included. Dorm **€19.50**, double **€49**

Wilder Mann Goethestr. 14 ☎ 07 32 65 60 78, ⓦ wildermann.cc; tram one stop from the station to

Goethestr. Simple but friendly and convenient hotel, between the train station and the centre; rooms available with shared facilities or with en-suite showers. Double €45

EATING, DRINKING AND NIGHTLIFE

Alte Welt Hauptplatz 4. Unpretentious bar and wine cellar with tables on a cosy courtyard just off the Hauptplatz and on the main square itself. Hearty, Austrian/Italian-influenced mains €7–16.50. Occasional live music and cabaret. Daily 6pm–2am.

p'aa Altstadt 28. Contemporary vegetarian restaurant, with an imaginative, global menu including curries, Greek, Turkish and Italian-inspired dishes, salads and tasty juices, all using top-quality fresh ingredients. Lunch specials €8.50; evening mains €13.50–17. Mon–Sat 11am–2.30pm & 5.30pm–midnight.

Traxlmayr Promenade 16. Traditional coffeehouse; serves an excellent selection of coffees, and is a good place to treat yourself to a slice of *Linzer Torte*, the town's ubiquitous almond-and-jam cake (€3.60). Mon–Sat 7am–6pm.

GRAZ

Austria's second-largest city, **GRAZ**, owes its importance to the defence of central Europe against the Turks. From the fifteenth century, it was constantly under arms, rendering it more secure than Vienna and leading to a modest seventeenth-century flowering of the arts. Today Graz celebrates its reputation as a city of design, thanks to a clutch of modern architectural adventures and a large student population, and it's a fun place to spend a few days without the tourist traffic of Innsbruck or Salzburg.

WHAT TO SEE AND DO

Graz is compact and easy to explore, with most sights within easy walking distance of its central **Hauptplatz**, with its fantastically decorated Baroque facades.

The Altstadt

From Hauptplatz, it's a few steps to the River Mur and two examples of Graz's architectural renaissance: the **Murinsel** is an ultramodern floating bridge-cum-meeting-place with a café linking the two banks, inspired by an open mussel, while the giant bulbous **Kunsthaus Graz** (Tues–Sun 10am–6pm; €9.50;

🕸 kunsthausgraz.at) is a museum of contemporary art, video installation and photography. Entrance tickets to the Kunsthaus function as a day-pass for several city museums that form part of the Landesmuseum Joanneum (🕸 museum-joanneum.at), a city-wide institution.

Among them (and the best of the bunch) is the **Landeszeughaus** (guided hourly tour Mon & Wed–Sun: April–Oct 10am–6pm; Nov to early Jan & March 10.15am–2.15pm; Sun also 3.15pm), the city armoury on Herrengasse just south of the Hauptplatz, which bristles with sixteenth-century weapons used to keep the Turks at bay.

Schlossberg

To get a view over the city take a trip up the wooded hill that overlooks the town: either walk up the zigzagging stone stairs from Schlossbergplatz or take the lift (daily 8am–12.30am; €0.90 each way) or funicular (April–Sept Mon–Wed & Sun 9am–midnight, Thurs–Sat 9am–2am; Oct–March daily 10am–10pm; €2.30, included in public transport ticket) from Sackstrasse. The **Schloss**, or fortress, was destroyed by Napoleon in 1809; only a few prominent features survive – noticeably the huge sixteenth-century **Uhrturm** (clock tower), and more distant **Glockenturm** (bell tower).

Schloss Eggenberg

Another part of the Landesmuseum Joanneum is the Baroque **Schloss Eggenberg**, 4km west of the city centre (tram #1 from the train station). Designed in imitation of the Escorial for Hans Ulrich von Eggenberg (1568–1634), chief minister to Ferdinand II, the Schloss houses on one floor the Alte Galerie (Tues–Sun: March & Nov 10am–4pm; April–Oct 10am–6pm; €8.70), whose intelligently curated collection includes thirteenth-century devotional works, and a macabre *Triumph of Death* by Jan Brueghel. The palace rooms can only be visited by hourly guided tour (Prunkräume Tues–Sun 10am–4pm, except 1pm; English tours usually available); they were designed as

2

2

■ ACCOMMODATION		●EATING				●DRINKING AND NIGHTLIFE			
Central Campsite	3	Café Promenade	3	La enoteca	5	Flann O'Briens	8	Postgarage	10
Hotel Strasser	1	Glöckl Bräu	6	Mangolds	9	MI	7		
Jufa Graz	2	Hofcafé Edegger Tax	4	Propeller	1	Parkhouse	2		

an allegory of the universe (24 rooms, 365 windows on the outside, four towers and so on); the highlight is the "Room of the Planets", a great hall with an elaborate ceiling and wall paintings depicting the zodiac, and also the three Asian rooms, in particular the one decorated with rare Japanese panels from Osaka.

ARRIVAL AND INFORMATION

By train Graz's train station is on the western edge of town, a 15min walk or short tram ride (#1, #3, #6 or #7) from Hauptplatz.

Destinations Innsbruck (8 daily; 6hr–6hr 15min); Hallstatt via Stainach-Irdning (5 daily; 3hr); Linz (7 daily; 3hr 30min–3hr 45min); Salzburg (7 daily; 4hr); Vienna (hourly; 2hr 30min).

Tourist information Herrengasse 16 (daily: Jan–March & Nov 10am–5pm; April–Sept 10am–6pm; ☎0316 807 50, ⊛graztourismus.at).

GETTING AROUND

By public transport Graz has a good bus and tram network; 24hr ticket €4.40; 1hr ticket €2.10, available from bus drivers, machines on trams, tourist office or transport office on Jakominiplatz south of Hauptplatz.

ACCOMMODATION

Central Campsite Martinhofstr. 3 ☎06 763 78 51 02, ⊛tiscover.at/campingcentral; bus #32 from Jakominiplatz.

Well-equipped campsite south of Graz, with a large swimming pool. Open April–Oct. Camping €9 per person, plus €14 per tent

Hotel Strasser Eggenburger Gürtel 11 ☎03 16 71 39 77, ✆hotelstrasser.at. Located close to the station and a 15min walk from the centre, but don't let the shabby exterior put you off; inside are comfortable, if garish, doubles with TV and massage showers. The 6-person apartments may be an option if you're in a group. Double €64, apartment €180

Jufa Graz Idlhofgasse 74 ☎05 708 32 10, ✆jufa.at; bus #32 from Jakominiplatz. Friendly, modern hostel a 15min walk from both the train station and centre. Has dorms and doubles – including hotel-style rooms with TV and en suite. Good buffet breakfast included and free wi-fi. Dorm €22, double €63

EATING

★ **Café Promenade** Erzherzog-Johann-Allee 1. Attractive, Neoclassical pavilion, with stylish modern decor and a terrace overlooking the Stadtpark. Serves soups (€4–6), salads and mains (€11–15). Daily 7am–11pm.

Glöckl Bräu Glockenspielplatz 2–3. Traditional place, with busy beer terrace serving hearty Austrian dishes like *wienerschnitzel* for under €12. Daily 11am–11pm.

Hofcafé Edegger Tax Hofgasse 8. Sedate, genteel little café, adjoining to a long-established city-centre cake shop. Great for quiet conversations and a relaxing coffee (from €2.20). Mon–Sat 7.30am–7pm.

La enoteca Sackstr. 14 (in courtyard). This wine shop and restaurant, with a small cosy interior and a few courtyard tables, serves a short menu of delicious pasta dishes and antipasti. Evening dishes €6.50–13.50, lunchtime menu of soup, salad and pasta for €6.50 (small portions) or €8 (large). Mon–Sat 10am–7pm.

Mangolds Griesgasse 11. Popular self-service place, with excellent veggie option, with fresh juices and a large salad

---

GRAZ FARMERS' MARKET

The region of Styria (Steiermarkt) is known as a wine-growing and farming region, producing local specialities it is proud of, in particular **Kürbiskernöl** (pumpkin seed oil), which has a delicious, nutty flavour and is used in salad dressings and other dishes on many Graz menus. As a result, Graz's **farmers' market** (Kaiser-Josef-Platz; Mon–Sat 6am–1pm) is particularly good, and an excellent place to buy bottles of Kürbiskernöl, local cheeses, breads, meat and other produce. There are also snack stands, coffee joints and fresh juice bars.

---

bar (pay according to weight: €1.23/100g). Prices twenty percent cheaper after 5pm. Mon–Fri 11am–7pm, Sat 11am–4pm.

Propeller Zinzendorfgasse 17. Convivial student pub with a beer garden and a good menu that ranges from hearty Austrian classics to Asian dishes. The generous portions cost around €8 and there's also an all-you-can-eat student lunch buffet (Mon–Fri 11am–2pm; €7.50). Daily 9am–2am.

DRINKING AND NIGHTLIFE

Flann O'Briens Paradiesgasse. Lively Irish pub, with plenty of outside seating. A haven for English-speaking expats and an easy place to meet people of all nationalities. Guinness €4.60. Daily noon–midnight.

MI Färberplatz 1. Stylish, split-level third-floor café-bar (take the glass lift up), with a designer interior and an attractive roof terrace. Mon–Sat 4pm till at least midnight.

Parkhouse Stadtpark. Buzzing bar in a pavilion, tucked away in the park, with regular DJ nights and a young crowd spilling out onto the grass. Daily 6pm–4am.

Postgarage Dreihackengasse 42 ✆postgarage.at. Puts on an interesting and varied programme of gigs and club nights in the two spaces here – free gigs, gay nights, techno and more. Wed–Sat 7pm–3am.

SALZBURG

For many visitors, **SALZBURG** represents the quintessential Austria, offering ornate architecture, mountain air and the musical heritage of the city's most famous son, Wolfgang Amadeus **Mozart**. The city and surrounding area were for centuries ruled by a series of independent prince-archbishops, and it is the pomp and wealth of their court that is evident everywhere in the fine Baroque Altstadt.

WHAT TO SEE AND DO

Salzburg's compact centre straddles the River Salzach, squeezed between two dramatic mountains – Mönchsberg on the west and Kapuzinerberg on the east. The **west bank** forms a tight-knit network of alleys and squares – Alter Markt, Residenzplatz, Mozartplatz (with obligatory statue of the composer) and Domplatz – overlooked by the medieval **Hohensalzburg fortress** high above.

Residenzplatz

The complex of Baroque buildings at the centre of Salzburg exudes the

2

2

ecclesiastical and temporal power of Salzburg's archbishops, whose erstwhile living quarters – the **Residenz** – dominate the west side of Residenzplatz. You can take a self-guided audio-tour of the lavish **state rooms** (daily 10am–5pm; combined ticket with Residenzgalerie €8.70), and then visit the **Residenzgalerie** (closed Mon), one floor above, whose collection includes a few interesting paintings, most notably the small, almost sketch-like *Old Woman Praying* by Rembrandt.

On the east side of Residenzplatz, accessed from Mozartplatz, is the Neue Residenz, built by Archbishop Wolf Dietrich von Raitenau, and topped by the **Glockenspiel**, a seventeenth-century musical clock which chimes at 7am, 11am and 6pm. It now houses the excellent Salzburg Museum (Tues–Sun 9am–5pm, Thurs till 8pm; July, Aug & Dec also Mon 9am–5pm; €7.60; ⊚salzburgmuseum.at), which, as well as showing some of the archbishop's lavish rooms, explores the history of Salzburg, the rediscovery of Salzburg by Romantic painters and the city's tourist industry.

Domplatz and Franziskanerkirche
The pale marble facade of the **Dom** dominates **Domplatz**, while inside, the impressively cavernous Renaissance structure dazzles with its ceiling frescoes. Across Domplatz, an archway leads through to the Gothic **Franziskanerkirche**, which houses a fine Baroque altar around an earlier *Madonna and Child*. The altar is enclosed by an arc of nine chapels and a frenzy of stucco. Look out for the twelfth-century marble lion that guards the stairway to the pulpit.

Mozarts Geburtshaus and Mozarts Wohnhaus
Getreidegasse, the main street in Salzburg's old town, is lined with opulent boutiques, painted facades and wrought-iron shop signs. At no. 9 is the canary-yellow **Mozarts Geburtshaus** (daily: July & Aug 9am–8pm; Sept–June 9am–5.30pm; €6.70, joint ticket with Wohnhaus €12.50; ⊚mozarteum.at), where the musical prodigy was born (in 1756) and lived until the age of 17.

Between the waves of tour parties it can be an evocative place, housing some fascinating period instruments, including one of his baby-sized violins. Over the Salzach River on Makartplatz is **Mozarts Wohnhaus**, the family home from 1773 till 1787 (same hours; €7.50), containing an engrossing multimedia history of the composer.

Hohensalzburg
Overlooking the city from the rocky mountain, the fortified **Hohensalzburg** (daily: May–Sept 9.30am–7pm; Oct–April 9.30am–5pm; €10.80 including funicular, €8.10 without; ⊚salzburg-burgen.at) is Salzburg's key landmark. You can get up here using the oldest funicular in Austria (daily, every 10min: May, June & Sept 9am–8pm; July & Aug 9am–10pm; Oct–April 9am–5pm; €4 return) from Fesstungsgasse behind the Dom, although the walk up isn't as hard as it looks. Begun around 1070, the fortress gradually became a more salubrious courtly seat. Included in the price is an audioguide tour of the observation tower – with spectacular views – and battlements, separate access to the impressive state rooms and various exhibitions. Entrance to the ramparts is free between early June and late August (7–9.30pm).

Mönchsberg
For some of the best views across to the Hohensalzburg, take the Mönchsberg lift up to the **Mönchsberg** from Anton-Neumayr-Platz (daily 8am–7pm, Wed till 9pm; July & Aug daily till 9pm; €2.50). At the summit, the sleekly concrete-and-glass Museum der Moderne puts on big-name art exhibitions (Tues–Sun 10am–6pm, Wed till 8pm; €8.50). It's a stylish contrast to all the Baroque.

Schloss Mirabell
Across the river from the Altstadt, **Schloss Mirabell** on Mirabellplatz stands on the site of a palace built by Archbishop Wolf Dietrich for his mistress Salome, with whom the energetic prelate was rumoured to have sired a dozen children. The palace's ornate gardens offer a much-photographed view back across the city.

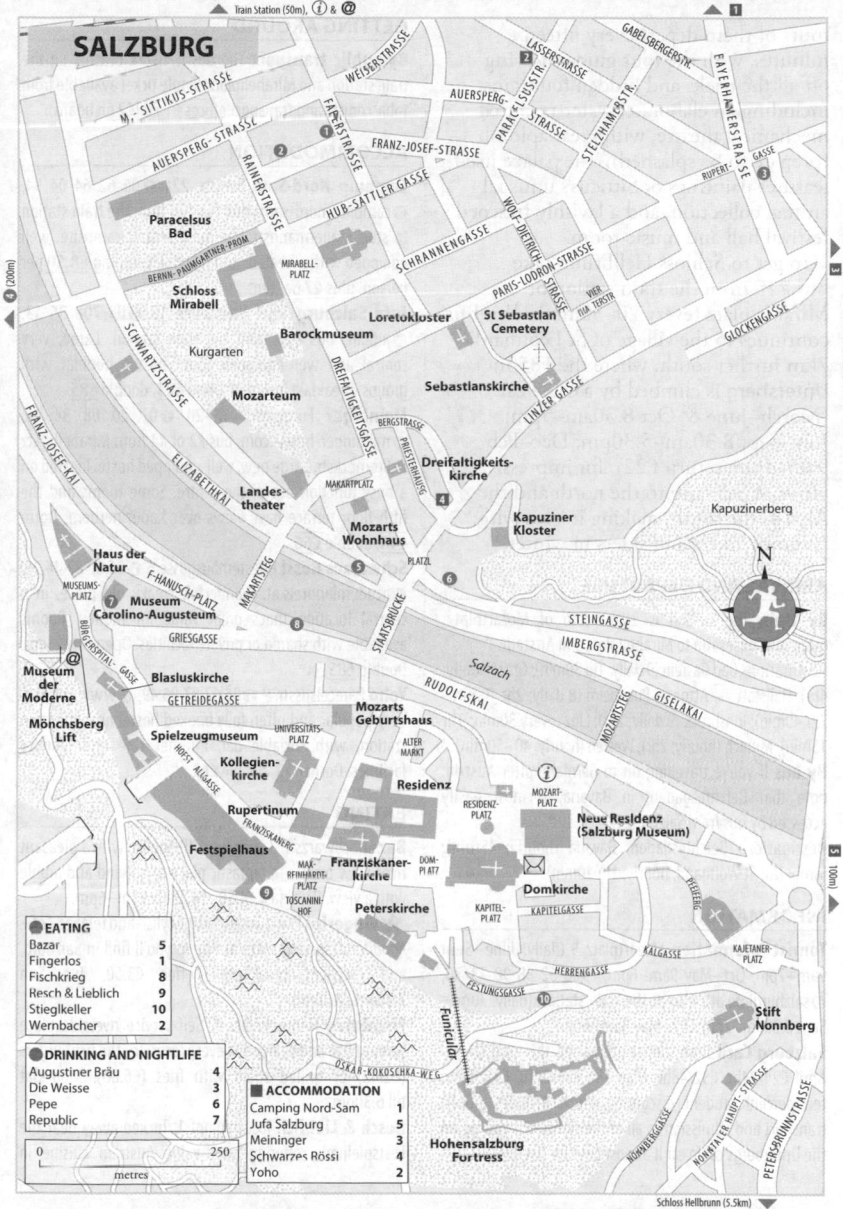

SALZBURG

Train Station (50m), ⓘ & @

2

Paracelsus Bad

Schloss Mirabell

Mirabell-Platz

Barockmuseum

Kurgarten

Loretokloster

St Sebastian Cemetery

Mozarteum

Sebastianskirche

Dreifaltigkeits-kirche

Landes-theater

Makartplatz

Mozarts Wohnhaus

Kapuziner Kloster

Platzl

Kapuzinerberg

N

Haus der Natur

F-Hanusch-Platz

Museums-Platz

Museum Carolino-Augusteum

Griesgasse

Steingasse

Imbergstrasse

Salzach

Museum der Moderne

Blasiuskirche

Getreidegasse

Mönchsberg Lift

Spielzeugmuseum

Universitäts-Platz

Mozarts Geburtshaus

Alter Markt

Rudolfskai

Giselakai

Kollegien-kirche

Rupertinum

Franziskaner-kirche

Residenz

Residenz-Platz

Mozart-Platz

ⓘ

Neue Residenz (Salzburg Museum)

Festspielhaus

Dom-Platz

Domkirche

Peterskirche

Kapitel-Platz

Kapitelgasse

Kalgasse

Kajetaner-Platz

Herrengasse

Festungsgasse

Funicular

Oskar-Kokoschka-Weg

Stift Nonnberg

Hohensalzburg Fortress

EATING
Bazar	5
Fingerlos	1
Fischkrieg	8
Resch & Lieblich	9
Stieglkeller	10
Wernbacher	2

DRINKING AND NIGHTLIFE
Augustiner Bräu	4
Die Weisse	3
Pepe	6
Republic	7

ACCOMMODATION
Camping Nord-Sam	1
Jufa Salzburg	5
Meininger	3
Schwarzes Rössi	4
Yoho	2

0 — 250 metres

Schloss Hellbrunn (5.5km) ▼

Schloss Hellbrunn and the Untersberg

The Italianate palace **Schloss Hellbrunn** (daily: April, Oct & Nov 9am–4.30pm; May, June & Sept 9am–5.30pm; July & Aug 9am–9pm, only Wasserspile after 6pm; €9.80; ⓦhellbrunn.at) on Salzburg's southern fringe – 5km from the city centre – was built in the early seventeenth century by Salzburg's decadent archbishop Marus Sitticus as a place for entertaining. The main attraction is the gardens' impressive array of fountains and watery gimmicks, or *wasserspiele*; guided

2

tours of them depart every fifteen minutes, with the tour guide showing off all the tricks and hidden fountains, including an elaborate, water-powered mechanical theatre, with great aplomb (prepare to be splashed). The palace itself features paintings of Sitticus's unusual animal collection, and a lavishly frescoed festival hall and music room.

To get to Schloss Hellbrunn take bus #25 from the train station or Mirabellplatz (every 20–30min). This bus continues to the village of St Leonhard, 7km further south, where the 1853m **Untersberg** is climbed by a cable car (March–June & Oct 8.30am–5pm; July–Sept 8.30am–5.30pm; Dec–Feb 9am–4pm; return €22), for impressive views of Salzburg to the north and the Alps to the south, making it a hit with summer hikers and skiers in winter.

ARRIVAL AND DEPARTURE

By train The station is 2km north of Mozartplatz; numerous buses run to Mirabellplatz and Altstadt.
Destinations Bad Gastein (9 daily; 1hr 30min); Graz (7 daily; 4hr); Hallstatt via Attnang-Puchheim (8 daily; 2hr 10min–2hr 40min); Innsbruck (9 daily; 2hr); Linz (every 30min; 1hr 15min); Munich (hourly; 2hr); Werfen (hourly; 40–50min).
By bus If you're travelling on to Germany after Austria, note that Berchtesgaden, in Bavaria, is most easily accessed by bus from Salzburg.
Destinations Berchtesgaden, Bavaria (hourly; 45min); Strobl (for St Wolfgang; hourly; 1hr 10min).

INFORMATION

Tourist information Mozartplatz 5 (daily: June–Sept 9am–7pm; Oct–May 9am–6pm; ☏ 06 62 88 98 73 30, ⊚ salzburginfo.at); also at the train station (daily: June–Sept 8.30am–7pm; Oct–May 9am–6pm).
Salzburg Card Both tourist offices sell this card (Nov–April €24/24hr, €32/48hr; May–Oct €26/24hr, €35/48hr; ten percent student discount), which includes public transport and admission to all of the sights – if you go on the Unterbergs cable car it almost pays for itself.

GETTING AROUND

By public transport The bus network centres on the train station and Mirabellplatz. Single ticket available from tobacconists and transport offices €1.70 (€2 on board).

ACCOMMODATION

Camping Nord-Sam Samstr. 22a ☏ 06 62 64 04 94, ⊚ camping-nord-sam.com; bus #23 from the train station to stop Mauermannstr. The most central campsite, well equipped with a heated outdoor pool. Camping €8.50 per person, plus €7 per tent
Jufa Salzburg Josef Preis Allee 18 ☏ 05 708 36 13, ⊚ jufa.at; bus #25 from the train station. Large, very central and well-equipped youth hostel, popular with groups. Breakfast included. Dorm €23, double €85
Meininger Fürbergstr. 18–20 ☏ 07 20 88 34 14, ⊚ meininger-hotels.com; bus #2 or #4 from Mirabellplatz to Sterneckstr. Large new, well-equipped hostel located on a busy junction out of the centre. Some rooms and the fifth-floor terrace have views over Kapuzinerberg. Dorm €16, double €66
Schwarzes Rössl Priesterhausgasse 6 ☏ 06 62 87 44 26, ⊚ academiahotels.at. Wonderful, creaky old place, in a central location that's great value for money. Rooms available with shared or private facilities. Open July–Sept. Double €85
Yoho Paracelsusstr. 9 ☏ 06 62 87 96 49, ⊚ www.yoho.at. Very popular and often fully booked hostel near the train station, with sociable bar, internet café and laundry facilities. Dorm €22, double €67

EATING

Bazar Schwarzstr. 3. Elegant coffeehouse with a pleasant river-view terrace, a fantastic place to unwind and nibble with a view. Breakfast €4.50–14. Daily 7am–6pm.
★ **Fingerlos** Franz-Josef-Str. 9. Stylish and relaxed *Café-Konditorei*, serving cakes as fine as you'll find in Salzburg, and excellent breakfasts. Coffee €3.50. Tues–Sun 7.30am–7.30pm.
Fischkrieg Hanuschplatz 4. Self-service riverside place serving fish and seafood in every form. Try the fishburgers (€2.40) or grilled squid with fries (€6.80). Mon–Sat till 6.30pm.
Resch & Lieblich Toscaninihof 1. Tucked away near the Festspielhaus, offering good-value Austrian cuisine in

THE SOUND OF MUSIC

Salzburg certainly wastes no time cashing in on its connection with the legendary singing Von Trapp family, immortalized in the movie *The Sound of Music*. From its kiosk on Mirabellplatz, Panorama Tours (☏ 06 628 83 21 10, ⊚ panoramatours.com) runs what they dub "**The Original Sound of Music Tour**" (daily 9.30am & 2pm; 4hr; €39) on which you're bussed to the key film locations, such as Hellsbrun Palace and Mondsee Cathedral, played the soundtrack and sent away with a free *edelweiss* souvenir.

dining rooms carved out of the Hohensalzburg cliffs. Daily specials from €8.50. Mon–Sat 11am–11pm.

Stieglkeller Festungsgasse 10. Enormous brewery with a beer terrace overlooking the town. Solid traditional food from €9.20. Daily 11am–11pm, sometimes later at weekends.

Wernbacher Franz-Josef-Str. 5. Classic café with a gorgeous plush 1950s interior. Specials (€10.50–18) change every week, but expect Austrian classics plus American options such as burgers and club sandwiches. Daily 7am–8pm.

DRINKING, NIGHTLIFE AND ENTERTAINMENT

The city hosts dozens of concerts of all musical persuasions year-round; check with Salzburg Ticket Service (Ⓦ salzburgticket.com), in the tourist office on Mozartplatz. The Salzburg Festival (❶ 06 628 04 55 00, Ⓦ salzburgfestival.at), held from late July to late Aug, is one of Europe's premier festivals of classical music, opera and theatre, with many outdoor concerts.

Augustiner Bräu Augustinerstr. 4–6. Fifteen minutes northwest of the centre, this vast beer hall has a raucous open-air terrace. Own-brewed beer is served in huge glasses – €6.30 for 1l. Mon–Fri 3–11pm, Sat & un 2–11pm.

★ **Die Weisse** 10 Rupertgasse. Lively microbrewery, well off the tourist track, with nice little beer garden and great pub food. Goulash and dumplings €11.80. Daily 4–11pm.

Pepe Steingasse 3. Intimate cocktail bar near the river, one of the few places that feels upmarket and can serve a well-prepared drink but is still relaxed. Daily 7pm–3am.

Republic Anton-Neumayr-Platz 2. Stylish restaurant-club, serving food until 11pm (lunch specials €7). The wide-ranging DJ and live music programme (anything from salsa to blues or electro) attracts a young, trendy crowd. Mon–Thurs & Sun 4pm till at least midnight, Fri & Sat till 4am.

DIRECTORY

Consulate UK Alter Markt 4 ❶ 06 646 10 56 17.
Post office Postamt 1010, Residenzplatz 9.

WERFEN

With its impressive fortification and spectacular ice caves, **WERFEN**, 40km south of Salzburg, offers a great day of sightseeing, but arrive early to comfortably see both. The moody castle **Festung Hohenwerfen** (April Tues–Sun 9.30am–4pm; May–Sept daily 9am–5pm; mid-July to mid-Aug daily 9am–6pm; Oct daily 9.30am–4pm; €11.50, €15 with lift), on an outcrop above town, lies a twenty-minute signed walk from Werfen's train station. Though much modified over the years, it has eleventh-century origins, and all the usual components – ornate chapel and torture chamber included – are neatly gathered around a courtyard. There are daily falconry displays (11am & 3pm) too.

Werfen's castle may tower over the town, but up the road at the **Eisriesenwelt ice caves**, it's a mere pimple on the valley floor. The caves are more than two hours' walk from the entrance building, so most visitors take a cable car. Tours (daily, at least hourly: July & Aug 9.30am–4.30pm; May, June, Sept & Oct 9.30am–3.30pm; €20.50 with cable car, €10 without) explore the first kilometre of a 40km network and last around 75 minutes. It's cold enough to require a jumper.

Trains from Salzburg frequently arrive at Werfen's station, from where buses to the caves depart daily at 8.20am, 10.20am, 12.20pm & 2.20pm, with more departures from an official departure point across the river. Bus drivers sell a combined ticket for the ride up, the cable car and the cave (€23.80).

THE SALZKAMMERGUT

The **Salzkammergut**, Austria's lake district, features a spectacular series of lakes and mountains. You can get a feel for the area in a day-trip from Salzburg to St Wolfgang, or on a "Sound of Music tour", but if you want to hike, mountain bike or just chill out, head to a lakeside campsite or B&B for a few days' relaxation – picture-perfect Hallstatt is a good choice.

St Wolfgang

The pretty little village of **ST WOLFGANG**, on the north shore of Wolfgangersee, is undeniably picturesque, though it can get crowded in summer, and provides a good taster of the region, particularly if you take the vintage train to the top of the **Schafberg** peak (May–Oct; €32 return; to avoid queuing, reserve a seat on ❶ 06 13

2

GETTING AROUND THE SALZKAMMERGUT

A single **train** line runs north–south from Attnang-Puchheim via **Bad Ischl** (one of the region's main towns) and **Hallstatt** to Stainach Irdning (hourly; 2hr 9min total journey time), with easy connections **from Salzburg** and Linz at Attnang-Puchheim and **from Graz** at Stainach Irdning. **Buses** run from Salzburg to many villages, with Bad Ischl a useful hub for connections. Hourly buses between Salzburg and Bad Ischl run east along the southern shore of the Wolfgangersee; for St Wolfgang change at **Strobl** for a connecting bus.

82 23 20, 🖰schafbergbahn.at) from a station on the western edge of town.

In town, the **Pfarrkirche**, above the lakeshore, houses a high altar, an extravagantly pinnacled structure 12m in height, completed between 1471 and 1481. It features brightly gilded scenes of the *Coronation of the Virgin* flanked by scenes from the life of St Wolfgang.

ARRIVAL AND INFORMATION

By bus Buses from Strobl (see box above) drop off at both ends of town, before and after the road tunnel that bypasses the centre.

Tourist office The tourist office (Mon–Fri 9am–5pm, Sat 9am–noon; ☎ 06 138 80 03, 🖰wolfgangsee.at) is at the eastern entrance to the road tunnel.

Hallstatt

The jewel of the Salzkammergut is **HALLSTATT**, which clings to the base of precipitous cliffs on the shores of the Hallstättersee, 20km south of Bad Ischl. With towering peaks and a pristine lake, this is a stunning setting in which to hike, swim or rent a boat. Arriving **by train** is an atmospheric and evocative experience; the station is on the opposite side of the lake, and the ferry, which meets all incoming trains, gives truly dramatic views.

WHAT TO SEE AND DO

Hallstatt gave its name to a distinct period of Iron Age culture after Celtic remains were discovered in the salt mines above the town. Many of the finds date back to the ninth century BC, and can be seen in the **Museum Hallstatt** (April & Oct daily 10am–4pm; May–Sept daily 10am–6pm; Nov–March Wed–Sun 11am–3pm; €7.80; 🖰museum-hallstatt.at).

The **Pfarrkirche** has a south portal adorned with sixteenth-century Calvary scenes. In the graveyard outside is a small stone structure known as the **Beinhaus** (daily 10am–5pm), traditionally the repository for the skulls of villagers. The skulls, some quite recent, are inscribed with the names of the deceased and dates of their death, and are often decorated.

The steep Gainswand-Weg starts behind the graveyard, and leads up to the **Salzachtal** (1hr 30min of hard hiking), the highland valley where **salt mines** once ensured the area's prosperity. These can still be viewed, albeit only by guided tour (late April to late Oct daily 9.30am–3/4.30pm; €19). You can also take the **funicular** (late April to late Oct daily 9am–4.30/6pm; €14 return, combined ticket with tour €25) from the suburb of Lahn.

ARRIVAL AND INFORMATION

By train The station is across the lake; ferries (€2.30) are timed to coincide with trains. Return ferry times are posted up at the ferry station and around town; the last train to Hallstatt arrives around 6.30pm.

By bus Buses stop in the suburb of Lahn, a 10min lakeside walk south of the centre.

Tourist information Tourist office at Seestr. 169 (May, June, Sept & Oct Mon–Fri 9am–1pm & 2–5pm; July & Aug Mon–Fri 9am–5pm, Sat & Sun 9am–4pm; Nov–April Mon–Fri 9am–4pm; ☎ 06 134 82 08, 🖰hallstatt.net).

ACCOMMODATION AND EATING

Camping Klausner-Höll Lahnstr. ☎ 06 134 83 22, 🖰camping.hallstatt.net. A short walk from the landing stage at Lahn, on the outskirts of the village. Quiet and well equipped, and also has double rooms. Open mid-April to Oct. Camping **€8.50** per person, plus **€4.70** per tent, double **€47**

Gasthaus zur Mühle Kirchenweg 36 ☎ 06 134 83 18, 🖰hallstatturlaub.at. Small, welcoming bar, restaurant and hostel set back from the landing stage, with a good line in pizzas (from €9). Upstairs are some basic dorm rooms. Dorm **€15**

★ **Gasthof Simony** Markt 105 ☎ 06 134 82 31, 🖰gasthof-simony.at. Located right by the ferry station and the main square, this relaxed, attractive guesthouse has a good range of rooms, with shared or en-suite bathrooms, decorated with traditional wooden furniture and some with balconies overlooking the lake. Good breakfast included. Double €60

BAD GASTEIN

Combining the quiet elegance of an old nineteenth-century spa destination with modern trappings and reasonably modest price tags, the resort of **BAD GASTEIN**, 94km south of Salzburg, is one of Austria's best budget mountain getaways. Note, however, that it's a seasonal destination for winter skiing and high-summer hiking only.

WHAT TO SEE AND DO

The town fills the head of the Gastein valley with most hotels arranged in tiers up either side, and with a waterfall running through the centre. There are some elegant Jugendstil buildings, but the overall impression is of distinctly faded grandeur. The mountains are the chief attraction, served by two gondolas, and are a big draw for winter skiers. The four **ski areas** (w skigastein.com) offer plenty for every standard; day-passes cost €44. In summer, the gondolas serve a web of **hiking trails**, with the 2246m Stubnerkogel mountain trail (late May to mid-Oct 8.30am–4pm; €19.50 return) offering particularly fine views.

Bad Gastein's radon-rich waters have made it a restorative destination since medieval times. To sample them today head to the **Felsentherme**, Bahnhofplatz (daily 9am–9pm; 3hr €20.60; w felsentherme.com), a spa with a collection of pools and saunas, many with splendid views, and a full menu of beauty treatments.

ARRIVAL AND INFORMATION

By train The station is at the top end of the centre, within walking distance of most central accommodation.

Tourist information Kaiser-Franz-Josef-Str. 1, a short walk downhill from the bus and train station (June to mid-July Mon–Fri 8am–6pm, Sat 9am–noon; mid-July to Sept Mon–Fri 8am 6pm, Sat 9am–3pm, Sun 9am–noon; Oct–May Mon–Fri 8am–6pm; t 06 43 23 39 35 60, w gastein .com). Can book private rooms (from €36).

Gastein Card Given out free by hotels and hostels if you stay, and offers discounts on local transport, services and attractions.

ACCOMMODATION AND EATING

Euro Youth Hotel Krone Bahnhofsplatz 8 t 06 43 42 33 00, w euro-youth-hotel.at. Large, sociable hostel close to the station. Offers ski or spa packages. Closes April, May, Oct & Nov. Dorm €17, double €53

Jägerhäusl Kaiser-Franz-Josef-Str. 9 t 06 43 42 02 54. A lively, traditional place to eat, with a big outdoor terrace. Serves pizzas and Austrian classics like *schnitzel* and *käsespätzle* (pasta with cheese; mains €9.50–17). Daily 11am–11pm, sometimes later on busy weekends.

Junge Hotel Bad Gastein Ederplatz 2 t 06 434 20 80, w hostel-badgastein.at. Slick HI hostel, a 10min walk from the train station, away from the centre. Dorm €17, double €50

Western Austria

West towards the mountain province of **Tyrol**, Austria's grandiose Alpine scenery begins to emerge. Most trains from Salzburg travel through a corner of Bavaria in Germany before joining the Inn valley and climbing back into Austria towards **Innsbruck**. A less direct but more scenic route (more likely if you're coming from Graz) cuts by the majestic **Hoher Tauern** – site of Austria's highest peak, the Grossglockner. As Tyrol's main town, Innsbruck offers the most convenient mix of urban sights and Alpine splendour.

INNSBRUCK

Nestled in the Alps and encircled by ski resorts, **INNSBRUCK** is a compact city

OUTDOOR ACTIVITIES IN BAD GASTEIN

Boats can be rented from the boatshed just south of the landing stage (1hr €16). The tourist office can advise on hiking routes and sells local hiking guides. At the southern end of town in the suburb of Lahn is a "Badinsel", an artificial island for sunbathing and swimming (changing facilities nearby).

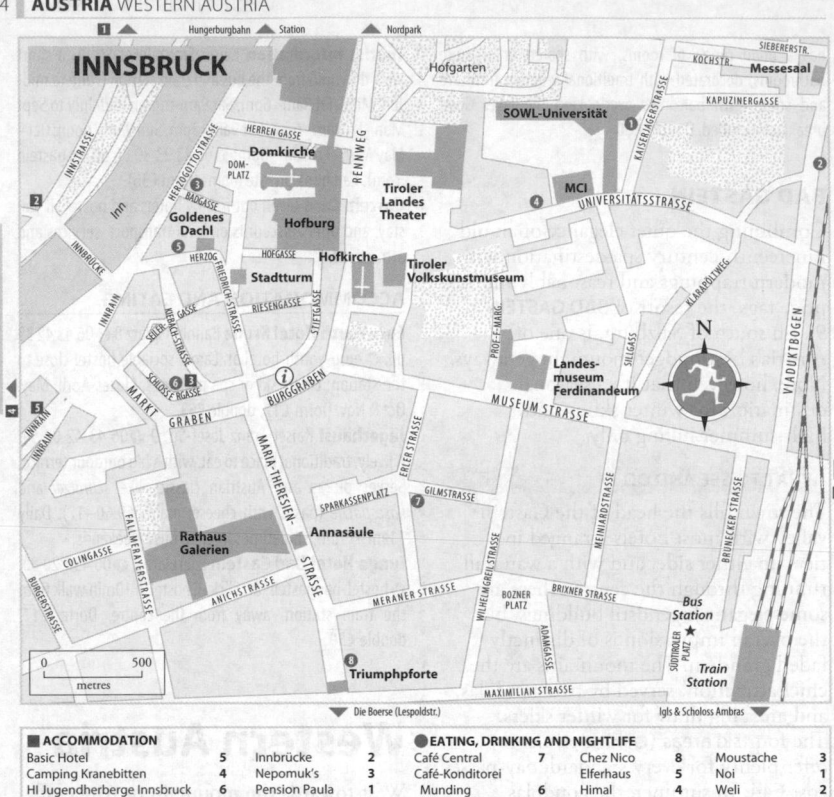

cradled by towering mountains. It has a rich history: Maximilian I based his imperial court here in the 1490s, placing the city at the heart of European politics for a century and a half. This combination of historical pedigree and proximity to the mountains has put Innsbruck firmly on the tourist trail.

WHAT TO SEE AND DO

Most attractions are confined to the central **Altstadt**, bounded by the river and the Graben (Marktgraben and Burggraben), a road that follows the course of the medieval town's moat.

Maria-Theresien-Strasse

Innsbruck's main artery is **Maria-Theresien-Strasse**, famed for the view north towards the great Nordkette, the mountain range that dominates the city. At its southern end the triumphal arch, **Triumphpforte**, was built for the marriage of Maria Theresa's son Leopold in 1756. Halfway along, the **Annasäule**, a column supporting a statue of the Virgin, commemorates the retreat of the Bavarians, who had been menacing Tyrol in 1703. Herzog-Friedrich-Strasse leads on into the centre, opening out into a plaza lined with arcaded medieval buildings. At the plaza's southern end is the **Goldenes Dachl**, or "Golden Roof" (though the tiles are really copper), built in the 1490s to cover an oriel window from which the court of Emperor Maximilian could observe the square below. The **Goldenes Dachl Museum** (May–Sept daily 10am–5pm; Oct & Dec–April Tues–Sun 10am–5pm; €4) is flashy but disappointing, offering a brief glimpse of the balcony.

Domplatz and the Hofburg

Standing on Domplatz, the ostentatious **Domkirche St Jakob** (daily 11am–5pm) is home to a valuable *Madonna and Child* by German master Lucas Cranach the Elder, although it's buried in the fussy Baroque detail of the altar.

The adjacent **Hofburg**, entered around the corner, has late medieval roots but was remodelled in the eighteenth century. Its Rococo state Kaiserapartments are crammed with opulent furniture (daily 9am–5pm, Wed till 7pm; €5.80).

The Hofkirche and Volkskunstmuseum

At the head of Rennweg is the **Hofkirche** (Mon–Sat 9am–5pm, Sun 12.30–5pm; €5.50), which contains the imposing (but empty) **mausoleum of Emperor Maximilian**. This extraordinary project was originally envisaged as a series of 40 larger-than-life statues, 100 statuettes and 32 busts of Roman emperors, but in the end only 32 of the statuettes were completed.

Housed in the same complex, the **Tiroler Volkskunstmuseum** (daily 9am–5pm; combined ticket €11), features a huge collection of folk art and objects including re-creations of traditional wood-panelled Tyrolean interiors.

Landesmuseum Ferdinandeum

A short walk south, the **Landesmuseum Ferdinandeum**, Museumstr. 15 (Tues–Sun 9am–5pm; combined ticket €11) contains one of the best collections of Gothic paintings in Austria; most originate from the churches of the South Tyrol (now in Italy).

Schloss Ambras

Set in attractive grounds 2km southeast of the centre, **Schloss Ambras** (daily 10am–5.30pm, Aug till 6.30pm, closed Nov; €11; tram #6 or #TS bus from the train station) was the home of Archduke Ferdinand of Tyrol. It features the impressive Spanish Hall, built from 1569–71, and exhibitions of armour and curios amassed from around the globe. Don't miss the inner courtyard covered in sixteenth-century frescoes, including depictions of the triumph of Bacchus.

Hungerburg plateau

A good starting point for hikes is the **Nordpark**, on the slopes of the Nordkette range, accessible from the swish Hungerburgbahn cable railway. The Zaha Hadid-designed Congress station (it literally looks like a funky spaceship) is opposite the Hofgarten; take it to Hungerburg, then continue on a two-stage sequence of cable cars to just below the summit (daily 8.30am–5.30pm, Fri also 6–11.30pm; €28 return; ⓦnordkette.com). The rewards are stupendous views of the high Alps and the possibility of all sorts of hikes.

ARRIVAL AND INFORMATION

By train The station is on Südtirolerplatz, east of the old town, an easy walk from the centre.
Destinations Munich (8 daily; 1hr 50min); Salzburg (10 daily; 2hr); Venice (1 daily; 4hr 40min); Vienna (18 daily; 5hr); Zürich (6 daily; 3hr 30min).
By bus The bus station is south of the train station.
Tourist information Tourist office at Burggraben 3 (daily 9am–6pm; ⓣ05 125 98 50, ⓦinnsbruck.info). It sells the Innsbruck Card (24hr/48hr/72hr for €31/€36/€42), which includes public transport, one return trip on all cable-car rides and admission to all the sights.

GETTING AROUND

By public transport Buses and trams; single tickets €2.10, 24hr €4.30. The Sightseer bus stops at main sights (#TS; every 40min; €3.40, included with Innsbruck Card).

ACCOMMODATION

Basic Hotel Innrain 16 ⓣ05 12 58 63 85, ⓦbasic-hotel .at. Despite the name, not the cheapest or most basic option, but a no-frills take on a business hotel; reception open till 10pm (check in with a credit card after then). Free wi-fi. Front-facing rooms are noisy. Double €94
Camping Kranebitten Kranebittner Allee 214 ⓣ05 12 54 67 32, ⓦcampinginnsbruck.com; bus #LK from Boznerplatz, a block west of the station, to Klammstr. Well-equipped campsite 7km west of town. Open May–Oct. Camping €8.90 per person, plus €11 per tent
HI Jugendherberge Innsbruck Reichenauerstr. 147 ⓣ05 12 34 61 79, ⓦyouth-hostel-innsbruck.at; bus #O from Landesmuseum. Large, functional HI hostel on the outskirts of the city. Dorm €22, double €68
Innbrücke Innstr. 1 ⓣ05 12 28 19 34, ⓦgasthof innbruecke.at. Plain but comfortable *Gasthof* on the west bank of the Inn, just over the bridge from the Altstadt. More expensive rooms have en-suite facilities, although most are without. Double €64

2

SKIING AND OTHER ACTIVITIES

Innsbruck is great for outdoor activities; the tourist office has a wide range of brochures. Of Innsbruck's nine **ski areas** the closest to the city is **Nordpark** (see p.85), accessible via the Hungerburgbahn, with its fabulous panoramas, impressive half-pipe and taxing expert-level runs. The other eight ski areas – including the Patscherkofel, Axamer Lizum, Glungezer, Muttereralm, Schlick 2000, Kühtai and Rangger Köpfl. – are all on the opposite, southern, side of the valley and tend to offer much mellower terrain ideal for relaxed, wide-turn skiing. At **Stubai Gletscher** (W stubaier-gletscher.com) glacier skiing is possible during much of the year – Die Böerse at Leopoldstr. 4 (Mon–Fri 9am–6.30pm, Sat & Sun 9am–5pm; T 05 12 58 17 42) arranges skiing day-trips (€79).

In winter, **lift passes** cover all these ski regions individually or in combination for one or more days. The Nordpark, for example, offers day-passes for €32 (less for part of the day). The **Stubaier Gletscher Skipass** covers the whole of the Innsbruck area, includes ski shuttles from the town centre and costs €117 for three days. Passes are available from all lift stations or from the Innsbruck tourist office.

Many **cycling** and mountain-bike routes are accessible from central Innsbruck, though some of the trails are for experts only. For rentals try Die Böerse (see above). Innsbruck's tourist office runs an extensive programme of free guided **walks** – including sunrise and night-time hikes – from June to September.

Nepomuk's Kiebachgasse 16 T 05 12 58 41 18, W nepomuks.at. Slightly ramshackle one-dorm hostel above *Café Munding*, whose owners also run the hostel and serve its good breakfasts. Also has a couple of doubles, though one is windowless and noisy. Dorm €23, double €56

Pension Paula Weiherburggasse 15 T 05 12 29 22 62, W pensionpaula.at; bus #W from the train station. Friendly, good-value *pension* in a chalet on a hillside north of the river – some rooms have balconies and mountain views. Double €58

EATING AND DRINKING

Café Central Gilmstr. 5. Venerable coffeehouse serving up excellent cakes and decent breakfasts (from €6.50). Good spot to linger over a coffee and slice of cake (€2.90–3.60). Daily 7am–6pm.

Café-Konditorei Munding Kiebachgasse 16. Superb cakes and pastries, in a bustling local daytime-only café primed for people-watching. Lots of older ladies but comfortable for people of all ages. Daily 8am–7pm.

Chez Nico Maria Theresienstr 49. While this vegetarian and vegan spot is a tad fancier than most others we list, the two-course lunch special for €13.50 is fab. Portions are substantial and the modern-European creative twist, is superb. Dinner is pricey (€55 for a 5-course menu) so opt for the fantastic-value lunch. Mon & Sat 6.30–10pm, Tues–Fri noon–2pm & 6.30–10pm.

Elferhaus Herzog-Friedrich-Str. 11. Popular old-town beer bar, with a lively atmosphere and big selection of beers. Also serves good basic Austrian food. Daily specials €8.50. Daily 11am–11pm.

Himal Universitätsstr. 13. Stylish Nepalese place serving fresh tasty curries, including an excellent-value lunch deal – two courses for €7.30–7.50, with good veggie options. Mon–Sat 11.30am–2.30pm & 6–10.30pm, Sun 6–10.30pm.

★ **Moustache** Herzog-Otto-Str. 8. A relaxed, studenty bar playing a good soundtrack of mainly British and American alternative tunes. Continue the night at *Aftershave* club below with something on most nights from 10pm. Bar Tues–Sun 11am–2am.

Noi Kaserjägerstr. 1. Excellent, cheap Thai restaurant around the corner from the Hofkirche with tasty lunch menus from €8.30. Daily 5–11pm.

Weli Viaduktbogen 26. Informal, unpretentious café-bar with snacks. Good starting point for exploring the various late-opening bars under the railway arches. Daily 7pm till at least midnight.

DIRECTORY

Consulate UK, Kaiserjägerstr. 1 T 05 12 58 83 20.
Hospital Universitätklinik, Anichstr. 35 (T 05 12 50 40).
Internet Bubble Point, Andreas-Hoferstr. 37 & Brixnerstr. 1 (Mon–Fri 8am–10pm, Sat & Sun 8am–8pm; 15min/€0.70; laundry also available).
Post office Südtiroler Platz 10–12.

BUILDINGS ON MARKT SQUARE, BRUGES

Belgium & Luxembourg

HIGHLIGHTS

❶ **Brussels** See the gold-fringed Grand-Place, Europe's prettiest square. **See p.93**

❷ **Antwerp** Discover the up-and-coming docks of Belgium's hip northern port. **See p.100**

❸ **Ghent** Sip local beers in lively bars and join the Gentse Feesten carnival. **See p.103**

❹ **Bruges** Explore this perfectly preserved medieval town's cobbled streets. **See p.105**

❺ **The Ardennes** Cycle, kayak or hike through gently rolling woods. **See p.108**

❻ **Luxembourg City** Discover the UNESCO-listed old town of this cliff-top capital. **See p.110**

HIGHLIGHTS ARE MARKED ON THE MAP ON P.89

ROUGH COSTS

Daily budget Basic €40, occasional treat €55
Drink Jupiler beer €1.60
Food Mussels with chips €12–20
Hostel/budget hotel €20/€50–70
Travel Train: Brussels–Antwerp €7.10

FACT FILE

Population Belgium: 10.5 million; Lux: 514,862
Language Flemish (Belgium), Letzebuergesch (Lux), French, German
Currency Euro (€)
Capital Brussels; Luxembourg City
International phone code Belgium: ☎32; Lux: ☎352
Time zone GMT +1hr

Introduction

A federal country with three official languages and an ongoing rivalry between its two main groups – Dutch-speaking Flemish and French-speaking Walloons – Belgium's dull reputation is definitely misleading. Lively, cultured cities in the predominantly urban north give way to beautiful forests and rugged hills in the south, while regular, affordable trains and an impressive range of good-value accommodation mean the country is a pleasure to explore. Factor in the Belgians' enthusiasm for beer and fine cuisine, and all the ingredients for a truly memorable trip are in place. With Europe's finest cliff-top city, little Luxembourg certainly does its bit too.

3

Roughly in the middle of Belgium lies the capital, **Brussels**, the heart of the EU and a genuinely vibrant and multicultural city. North of here stretch the flat landscapes of Flemish Belgium, whose main city, **Antwerp**, is a bustling old port with doses of fine art, cutting-edge fashion, and twice as many bars as Amsterdam. Further west, also in the Flemish zone, are the charismatic cities of **Bruges** and **Ghent**, each with a stunning concentration of medieval architecture. To the south of Brussels, Belgium's most scenic region, the Ardennes in Wallonia, has deep, wooded valleys, high elevations and dark caverns, with the town of **Namur** the obvious gateway.

The Ardennes reach across the border into the northern part of the Grand Duchy of Luxembourg, a dramatic landscape of rushing rivers and high hills topped with crumbling castles. The best base for rural expeditions is **Luxembourg City**, an exceptionally picturesque place straddling a steep valley.

CHRONOLOGY

BELGIUM

54 BC Julius Caesar defeats the Belgae tribes.
496 AD The King of the Franks, Clovis, founds a kingdom which includes Belgium.
1400–1500 The Belgian cities of Bruges, Brussels and Antwerp become the European centres of commerce and industry.
1477 Following the marriage of Austrian King Maximilian I and Mary of Burgundy, Belgium becomes part of Austria.
1713 Treaty of Utrecht transfers Belgian territory from French to Austrian rule.

1790 The Belgians form an independent state from Austria, though it does not last long. They are subsequently invaded by Austria, France and the Netherlands in quick succession.
1830 Belgium gains independence from the Netherlands.
1885 King Leopold II establishes a personal colony in the African Congo.
1908 The Belgian government takes over the Congo Free State after reports of Leopold's brutal regime are circulated.
1914–18 Belgium is invaded by Germany and sees heavy fighting before it is liberated.
1940–44 Nazi invasion, and ultimately liberation by Allied forces.
1957 Belgium is a founder member of the European Economic Community (EEC).
1960 Independence granted to the Congo.
1992 Belgium ratifies the Maastricht Treaty on the European Union.
2007 Following the resignation of Prime Minister Guy Verhofstadt, Belgium is without a government.
2011 In December, French-speaking Socialist leader Elio di Rupo is appointed prime minister of a six-party coalition, ending 541 days without a government. This is the longest period a country has ever been without an official government, exceeding Iraq's record of 289 days.
2012 Belgium holds municipal elections. Results show widespread gains for the New Flemish Alliance party seeking autonomy for Dutch-speaking Flanders.
2013 Crown Prince Philippe crowned new Belgian king after the abdication of his father Albert II.

LUXEMBOURG

963 AD Count Siegfried of Ardenne founds the capital of Luxembourg.
1354 Luxembourg's status is raised from fief to duchy by Emperor Charles IV.
1477 The Habsburgs take control of Luxembourg.
1715 Luxembourg is integrated into the Austrian Netherlands.

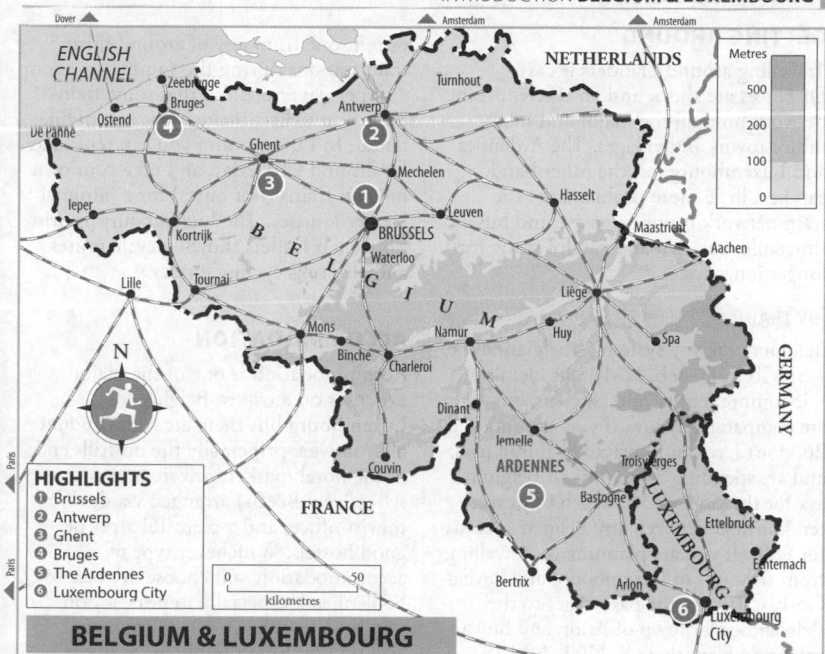

BELGIUM & LUXEMBOURG

1867 Second Treaty of London ensures Luxembourg's independence and neutrality.

1890 Luxembourg announces its own ruling monarchy, relinquishing its ties to the Netherlands.

1914–1918 German occupation.

1920 Joins the League of Nations.

1939–1945 German occupation.

1957 Luxembourg is a founder member of the EEC.

2000 Grand Duke Jean abdicates, handing responsibility over to his son Henri.

2008 Constitutional crisis is provoked by Grand Duke Henri threatening to block a bill legalizing euthanasia. As a result, Parliament approves a reform which restricts the monarch to a purely ceremonial role.

2009 Luxembourg is commended for improving the transparency of its banking systems after being added to a "grey list" of countries with questionable banking arrangements by the G20.

2012 Crown Prince Guillaume weds Belgian Countess Stéphanie de Lannoy at the Notre-Dame Cathedral.

ARRIVAL AND DEPARTURE

BY PLANE

The majority of airborne travel is into Brussels, which has two **airports**: the most conveniently located is Zaventem (also known as Brussels International), while Charleroi (which serves most budget airlines including Flybe and Ryanair) lies about 55km from the centre.

BY TRAIN

There are frequent **rail** connections from London, Paris, Amsterdam and Luxembourg, with almost all international trains arriving at Bruxelles-Midi (Brussel-Zuid), and frequently also stopping in Ghent or Antwerp. Eurostar "Any Belgian Station" tickets are valid to all onward Belgian stations.

BY BUS

Eurolines **buses** from Paris, Amsterdam, London and other destinations stop at Brussels-Nord, as well as Antwerp, Ghent and Bruges.

BY FERRY

Numerous **ferry** services ply between the UK and Belgian ports, including Ramsgate–Ostend (4hr), Rosyth–Zeebrugge (20hr) and Hull–Zeebrugge (15hr).

GETTING AROUND

Travelling around Flanders is easy. Distances are short, and an efficient train network links all the major and many minor towns and villages. The Ardennes and Luxembourg, on the other hand, can be a little more problematic: the train network is not extensive and bus timetables can demand careful study for longer journeys.

BY TRAIN

Belgium's railway system (⟨w⟩belgianrail.be) – SNCB in French, NMBS in Flemish – is comprehensive and efficient, and fares are comparatively low. If you are under 26, don't have an InterRail or Eurail pass, and are spending some time in Belgium, ask for the **Go-Pass 10**, which buys you ten journeys between any Belgian stations for €50. (If you are planning on travelling from Belgium to Luxembourg and have a Go-Pass 10, use the pass to get to the Belgian border town of Arlon and buy an extension from there.) SNCB/NMBS also publishes information on offers and services in their comprehensive timetable book, which has an English-language section and is available at major train stations.

Luxembourg's railways (⟨w⟩cfl.lu) comprise one main north–south route down the middle of the country, with a handful of branch lines fanning out from the capital. There are a number of passes available, giving unlimited train (and bus) travel.

BY BUS

In Belgium **buses** are only really used for travelling short distances, or in parts of the Ardennes where rail lines fizzle out. They're used more in Luxembourg, due to the limited rail network. RGTR (⟨w⟩mobiliteit.lu) has routes across the country. Fares are comparable to those in Belgium.

BY BIKE

The modest distances and flat terrain make **cycling** in Belgium an attractive proposition, though only in the countryside is there a decent network of signposted cycle routes. You can take your own bike on a train for a small fee or rent one from any of around thirty train stations during the summer at about €10 per day; note also that some train excursion tickets include the cost of bike rental. In Luxembourg you can rent bikes for around €10 a day, and take your own bike on trains (not buses) for a minimal fee per journey. The Luxembourg Tourist Office has leaflets showing cycle routes and also sells cycling guides.

ACCOMMODATION

Accommodation is one of the major expenses on a trip to Belgium or Luxembourg but there are some **budget alternatives**, principally the no-frills end of the hotel market, private rooms (effectively B&Bs) arranged via the local tourist office, and a plentiful array of good hostels. Whichever type of accommodation you choose, it's best to book ahead, especially in peak season.

In both countries, prices begin at around €60 for a double room in the cheapest one-star **hotel**; breakfast is normally included. Reservations can be made (for free) through most tourist offices on the day itself; the deposit they require is subtracted from your final hotel bill. **Private rooms** can be booked through local tourist offices too. Expect to pay €40–70 a night for a double, but note that they're often inconveniently situated on the outskirts of cities and towns. An exception is in Bruges, where private rooms – many of them in the centre – can be booked direct.

Belgium has around thirty **HI hostels**, run by two separate organizations: *Vlaamse Jeugdherbergcentrale* in Flanders (⟨T⟩032 32 72 18, ⟨w⟩www.jeugdherbergen.be), and *Jeunesse de Wallonie* in Wallonia (⟨T⟩022 19 56 76, ⟨w⟩lesaubergesdejeunesse.be). Most charge a flat rate per person of €19–25 for a bed in a dormitory or €42–50 for a double room, with breakfast included. Some also offer lunch and dinner for €5–10. Some of the more touristy cities such as Bruges, Antwerp and Brussels also have **privately run hostels**, which normally charge about €20 for a dorm bed. There are ten HI hostels in Luxembourg, all of which are members of the *Centrale des Auberges de Jeunesse Luxembourgeoises* (☏026 27 66 200, ⓦyouthhostels.lu). Dorm bed rates for HI members are around €20, with non-members paying an extra €3. Breakfast is always included; lunch or dinner is €6–8.

In Belgium, there are literally hundreds of **campsites**, anything from a field with a few tent pitches through to extensive complexes. The vast majority are simpler one- and two-star establishments, for which two adults with a tent can expect to pay €10–20 per night; surprisingly, most four-star sites don't cost much more – add about €5. All of Luxembourg's campsites are detailed in the Duchy's free tourist office booklet. Prices vary considerably, but are usually €5–7 per person, plus €5–7 for a pitch. In both countries, campsite phone numbers are listed in free camping booklets, and in Luxembourg the national tourist board (☏042 82 82 10, ⓦvisitluxembourg.com) will make a reservation on your behalf.

FOOD AND DRINK

One of the great pleasures of a trip to **Belgium** is the cuisine, and if you stay away from tourist spots, it's hard to go wrong. Southern Belgian (or Wallonian) cuisine is similar to traditional French, retaining its neighbour's fondness for rich sauces and ingredients. The Ardennes region is renowned for its smoked ham and pâté. **Luxembourg's** food is less varied and more Germanic, but you can still eat out extremely well.

In Flanders the food is more akin to that of the Netherlands, with mussels and French fries the most common dish. Throughout Belgium, pork, beef, game, fish and seafood are staple items, often cooked with butter, cream and herbs, or sometimes in beer; hearty soups are also common. *Hesprolletjes* (chicory and ham

baked in a cheese sauce) and *stoemp* (puréed meat and vegetables) are two traditional dishes worth seeking out. Traditional Flemish dishes such as *waterzooi*, or "watery mess" (fish or chicken stew), and *carbonnade* (beef casserole) are also widely available. There are plenty of good **vegetarian** options too, such as quiche and salad, and you can find vegetarian restaurants in all of the larger cities.

In both countries, **bars** and **cafés** are a good source of inexpensive meals, especially at lunchtime when simple dishes – omelettes, steak, mussels – are offered as a dish of the day (*plat du jour/ dagschotel*) for around €12. **Restaurants** are usually pricier, but the food is generally excellent. **Frituurs** (stands serving chips) are ubiquitous, cheap and usually offer a variety of hot sauces, such as *stoofvlees* (beer-soaked beef).

Belgium is also renowned for its **chocolate**. The big *chocolatiers*, Godiva and Leonidas, have shops in all the main towns and cities, but high-quality chocolate is also available in supermarkets at a much lower price – try the Jacques or Côte d'Or brands.

Beer in Belgium is a real treat. Beyond the common lager brands – Stella Artois, Jupiler and Maes – there are about seven hundred speciality beers, from dark stouts to fruit beers, wheat beers and brown ales. The most famous are the strong ales brewed by the country's six **Trappist monasteries**; Chimay is the most widely available. Luxembourg doesn't really compete, but its three most popular brews – Diekirch, Mousel and Bofferding – complement the food wonderfully.

French **wines** are universally sold, but Luxembourg's wines, especially the *crémant* (sparkling wine), produced along the north bank of the Moselle, are light and refreshing. You'll also find Dutch-style **jenever** (similar to gin) in most bars

3

STUDENT AND YOUTH DISCOUNTS

Most museums and galleries offer substantial discounts to those under 26, even if you don't have an ISIC card. Train travel is also cheaper for travellers aged under 26 if you buy a **Go-Pass 10** (see opposite).

3

LANGUAGE

There are three official languages in **Belgium**: Dutch, French and German. Speaking French in the Flemish north is not appreciated and vice versa. Most Belgians speak English. Natives of **Luxembourg** speak *Letzebuergesch*, a dialect of German, but most people also speak French and German and many speak English too. See p.280, p.357 and p.778 for some basic French, German and Dutch language tips.

EMERGENCY NUMBERS

Belgium Police ☎101; fire and ambulance ☎100.
Luxembourg Police ☎113; fire and ambulance ☎112.

in the north of Belgium, and in Luxembourg home-produced **eau-de-vie**, distilled from various fruits.

CULTURE AND ETIQUETTE

It's nearly impossible to make a faux pas among the Belgians – they're a relaxed bunch who take life at a leisurely pace (so don't be offended if a barman finishes polishing the glasses before serving you). Leave a ten percent tip in restaurants, and greet acquaintances with three kisses, not two.

SPORTS AND ACTIVITIES

The Ardennes is ideal for hiking, kayaking, cycling and horseriding (see p.109 for operators); cross-country skiing is also an option. La Roche-en-Ardenne and Bouillon make excellent bases in Belgium, while in Luxembourg the towns of Vianden and Echternach – each about an hour from Luxembourg City – are popular destinations for hikers and cyclists.

COMMUNICATIONS

Post offices are usually open Monday to Friday 9am–noon and 2–5pm. Some urban post offices also open on Saturday

mornings. Many **public phones** take only phonecards, which are available from newsagents and post offices. **Internet** access is widespread. However, due to more and more hostels, hotels and cafés offering free **wi-fi**, dedicated internet cafés are fast disappearing.

EMERGENCIES

Both countries are safe. However, if you're unlucky enough to have something **stolen**, report it immediately to the nearest police station and get a report number – or better still a copy of the statement itself – for your insurance claim when you get home. With regard to **medical emergencies**, if you're reliant on free treatment within the EU health scheme, try to remember to make this clear to the ambulance staff and any medics you subsequently encounter. Outside working hours, all **pharmacies** should display a list of open alternatives. Weekend rotas are also listed in local newspapers.

INFORMATION

In both Belgium and Luxembourg, there are **tourist offices** even in the smallest of villages. They usually provide free local maps, and the larger towns offer a free accommodation booking service too.

MONEY AND BANKS

Belgium and Luxembourg both use the **euro** (€). **Banks** are the best places to

BELGIUM AND LUXEMBOURG ONLINE

ⓦ**visitflanders.co.uk** Information on Brussels and the Flanders region.
ⓦ**belgiumtheplaceto.be** Information on Brussels and southern Belgium.
ⓦ**visitluxembourg.com** The Luxembourg tourist board's official site.
ⓦ**use-it.be** Excellent online guide for young travellers on Brussels and the Flanders region.

BELGIUM'S PROVINCIAL & LINGUISTIC BORDERS

3

change money and are generally open Monday to Friday 9am–4/4.30pm in both countries, though some have a one-hour lunch break between noon and 2pm, and some close after lunch on Friday. **ATMs** are commonplace.

OPENING HOURS AND HOLIDAYS

In both countries, most shops are closed on Sunday with some only reopening on Monday afternoon, even in major cities. Nonetheless, normal **shopping hours** are Monday to Saturday 9 or 10am to 6 or 7pm, with many urban supermarkets staying open until 8 or 9pm on Fridays and smaller places shutting early on Saturdays. In the big cities, a smattering of convenience stores (*magasins de nuit/ nachtwinkels*) stay open either all night or until around 1 or 2am daily, and some souvenir shops open late and on Sundays too. Most **museums** are closed on Mondays, though look out for occasional late-night openings, especially in Brussels. Restaurants also often close on Mondays. Many **bars** have relaxed closing times,

claiming to stay open until the last customer leaves. Less usefully, many restaurants and bars close for at least a couple of weeks in July or August.

Shops, banks and many museums are closed on the following **public holidays**: New Year's Day, Easter Sunday, Easter Monday, May 1, Ascension Day (forty days after Easter), Whit Sunday, Whit Monday, June 23 (Luxembourg only), July 21 (Belgium only), Assumption (mid-Aug), November 1, November 11 (Belgium only), Christmas Day.

Brussels

Wherever else you go in Belgium, it's hard to avoid **BRUSSELS** (Bruxelles, Brussel), a capital boasting world-class architecture and museums, a well-preserved medieval centre and an energetic nightlife. Since World War II, the city's appointment as headquarters of both NATO and the EU has brought major developments, including a metro,

3

and made Brussels very much an international city. One consequence of its hotchpotch mix of old and new architecture is that it can be a hard place to like at first, especially when compared with its more instantly appealing Flemish neighbours, Ghent and Bruges, but a day or two of wandering around reveals Brussels as much more than the "poor man's Paris".

WHAT TO SEE AND DO

Central Brussels is enclosed within a pentagon of boulevards – the **petit ring** – which follows the course of the medieval city walls. The centre is also divided between the Upper Town and Lower Town, the former being the traditional home of the city's upper classes who kept a beady eye on the workers down below.

The Grand-Place

The obvious point to begin any tour of the **Lower Town** is the **Grand-Place**, the commercial hub of the city since the Middle Ages. With its stupendous spired tower, the **Hôtel de Ville** dominates the square; inside you can view various official rooms (tours in English: Wed 3pm, Sun 10am & 2pm; €3). But the real glory of the Grand-Place lies in its **guildhouses**, mostly built in the early eighteenth century, their slender facades swirling with exuberant carving and sculpture.

The Manneken Pis

Rue de l'Etuve leads south from the Grand-Place down to the **Manneken Pis**, a statue of a little boy pissing that's supposed to embody the city's irreverent spirit, and is today one of Brussels' biggest tourist draws. The original statue was cast in the 1600s, but was stolen several times – the current one is a copy.

Notre Dame de la Chapelle and the Quartier Marolles

Across boulevard de l'Empereur, a busy carriageway that scars this part of the centre, you'll spy the crumbling brickwork of **La Tour Anneessens**, a remnant of the medieval city wall, while

to the south gleams the immaculately restored **Notre Dame de la Chapelle** (June–Sept Mon–Sat 9am–5pm, Sun 11.30am–4.30pm; Oct–May daily 12.30–4.30pm; free), a sprawling Romanesque-Gothic structure founded in 1134 and the city's oldest church. Running south from the church, rue Haute and parallel rue Blaes form the spine of the now gentrified **Quartier Marolles**, traditionally a working-class neighbourhood overlooked by the enormous, scaffold-clad **Palais de Justice**. **Place du Jeu de Balle**, the heart of Marolles, has retained its earthy character and is the site of the city's best **flea market** (daily 7am–2pm; busiest on Sun). Return to the Upper Town using the free glass-walled lift at the junction of rue des Minimes and rue de l'Epee, which drops you off in place Poelaert and offers a panorama of the city.

The Cathédrale

The **Cathédrale** (Mon–Fri 7am–6pm, Sat 8.30am–3.30pm, Sun 2–6pm; €1) lies a couple of minutes' walk to the east of the Grand-Place, at the east end of rue d'Arenberg. It's a splendid Brabantine-Gothic building begun in 1220. Look out also for the gorgeous sixteenth-century **stained-glass windows** in the transepts and above the main doors.

Place Royale

Climb the Mont des Arts – a wide stairway ascending towards **place Royale** – and on the left is the **Old England Building**, one of the finest examples of Art Nouveau in the city. Once a department store, it now holds the **Musée des Instruments de Musique**, at rue Montagne de la Cour 2 (MIM; Tues–Fri 9.30am–5pm, Sat & Sun 10am–5pm; €8, €2 if under 26), which contains an impressive collection of musical instruments and a rooftop café with great views of the city. Back on place Royale, at rue de la Régence 3, the **Musées Royaux des Beaux-Arts** (Tues–Sun 9am–5pm; last ticket 4pm; €8, free first Wed of month) is comprised of two museums: the Musée d'Art Ancien and the new Musée Fin-de-Siècle, which together accommodate a world-class

COMICS IN BRUSSELS

Brussels is a city made for comic book fans. The **Centre Belge de la Bande Dessinée** (Comic Strip Museum; Tues–Sun 10am–6pm; €8, ISIC and IYHF card holders €6; ⓦcbbd.be) at 20 rue des Sables focuses on Belgian comics such as Tintin, Smurfs and so on. For shopping, head to **boulevard Lemonnier** which boasts ten comic book shops, or Multi BD at boulevard Anspach 122. Various walls around the city have been decorated with building-sized scenes from comic strips, and tourist information can supply you with a trail following the major ones.

collection of fine art, including works by Brueghel and Rubens. Major renovations are ongoing. Next door, the **Musée Magritte** (Tues–Sun 10am–5pm, Wed until 8pm; €8, €13 combi ticket with Musées Royaux des Beaux-Arts, free first Wed of month) contains the largest collection of the Surrealist's work in the world. To the northeast of the place Royale, on place des Palais, the haunting remains of the twelfth-century **Palais Coudenberg** (Tues–Fri 10am–5pm, Sat & Sun 10am–6pm; €5), once home to Emperor Charles V, can be found beneath the BELvue museum.

Outside the petit ring

Brussels by no means ends with the petit ring. To the east of the ring road are the glass high-rises of the **EU**, notably the winged **Berlaymont** building beside métro Schuman and, nearby, on rue Wiertz 60, the lavish **European Union Parliament** building, which houses the **Parlamentarium** (Mon 1–6pm, Tues & Wed 9am–8pm, Thurs & Fri 9am–6pm, Sat & Sun 10am–5pm; free), an interactive multimedia visitors' centre explaining the complex workings of parliament.

Just south of the petit ring is the fashionable Ixelles district, filled with excellent examples of Art Nouveau and Art Deco architecture, as well as chic bars and restaurants. Its northern boundary is home to a large African community known as **Matongé**, named after a district of Kinshasa in the Congo. Here you can

explore the shops of **Galerie d'Ixelles** and sample fried plantain from one of the cafés on rue Longue Vie. To the southwest is the Saint-Gilles suburb where, at 25 rue Américaine, the **Musée Victor Horta** (Tues–Sun 2–5.30pm; €8, students €4; ⓦhortamuseum.be) occupies the innovative Art Nouveau architect's former home.

ARRIVAL AND DEPARTURE

By plane The main airport is in Zaventem, 13km northeast of the centre. Trains to the city centre depart from Level -1 (30min; €7.80). No-frills airlines fly into Charleroi, 55km south of Brussels; shuttle buses leave every 30min for Bruxelles-Midi (1hr; €13).

By train Brussels has three main train stations – Bruxelles-Nord, Bruxelles-Central and Bruxelles-Midi, each a few minutes apart. The majority of international trains, including expresses from London, Amsterdam, Paris and Cologne, stop only at Bruxelles-Midi (Brussel-Zuid), roughly 2km southwest of the city centre. Bruxelles-Central is a 5min walk from Grand-Place; Bruxelles-Nord lies in the business area just north of the main ring-road. To transfer from one of the three main stations to another, simply jump on the next available main-line train. Travellers with Eurostar "Any Belgian Station" tickets can do so for free, otherwise you'll have to buy a new ticket.

Destinations Amsterdam (hourly; 2hr 40min); Antwerp (every 30min; 40min); Bruges (every 30min; 1hr); Ghent (every 30min; 40min); London (every 2hr; 2hr); Luxembourg City (hourly; 2hr 50min); Marloie for La Roche-en-Ardennes (hourly; 1hr 50min); Namur (every 30min; 1hr); Ostend (hourly; 1hr 20min); Paris (hourly; 1hr 30min).

By bus Eurolines (ⓦeurolines.co.uk) buses from London-Victoria arrive and depart at the Bruxelles-Nord station complex.

INFORMATION

Tourist office VisitBrussels has offices at rue Royale 2–4 (daily 10am–6pm; ☎02 513 89 40, ⓦvisitbrussels.be) and in the Hôtel de Ville on the Grand-Place (daily

BRUSSELS ONLINE

ⓦ**spottedbylocals.com/brussels** Recommendations for places to eat and visit from local residents.

ⓦ**bestofbrusselsblog.com** City guide blog penned by an American expat working in Brussels.

ⓦ**mysecretbrussels.com** Insider's guide to the city by longtime Brussels resident and journalist Derek Blyth.

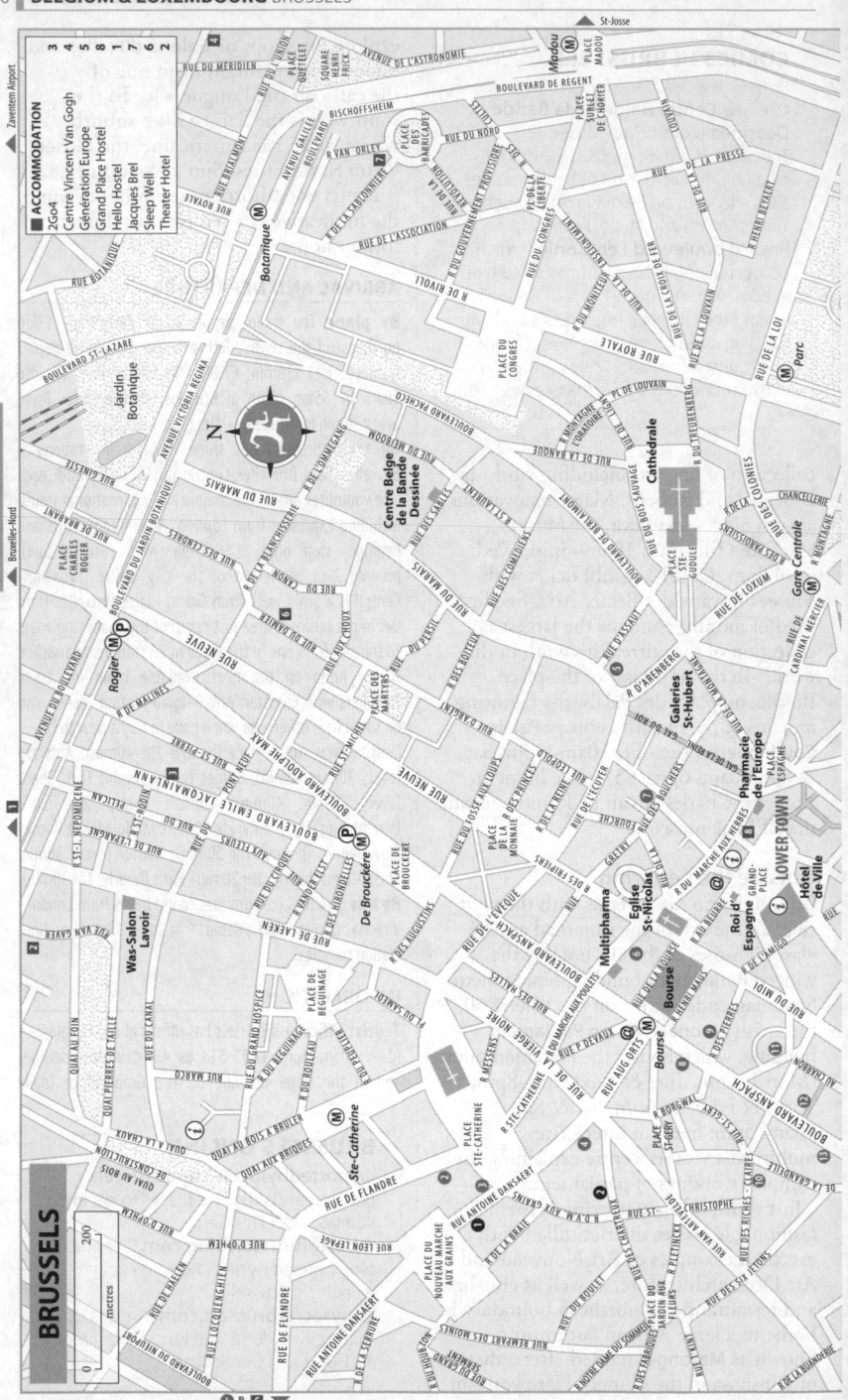

BRUSSELS

ACCOMMODATION
2Go4	3
Centre Vincent Van Gogh	4
Génération Europe	5
Grand Place Hostel	8
Hello Hostel	1
Jacques Brel	7
Sleep Well	6
Theater Hotel	2

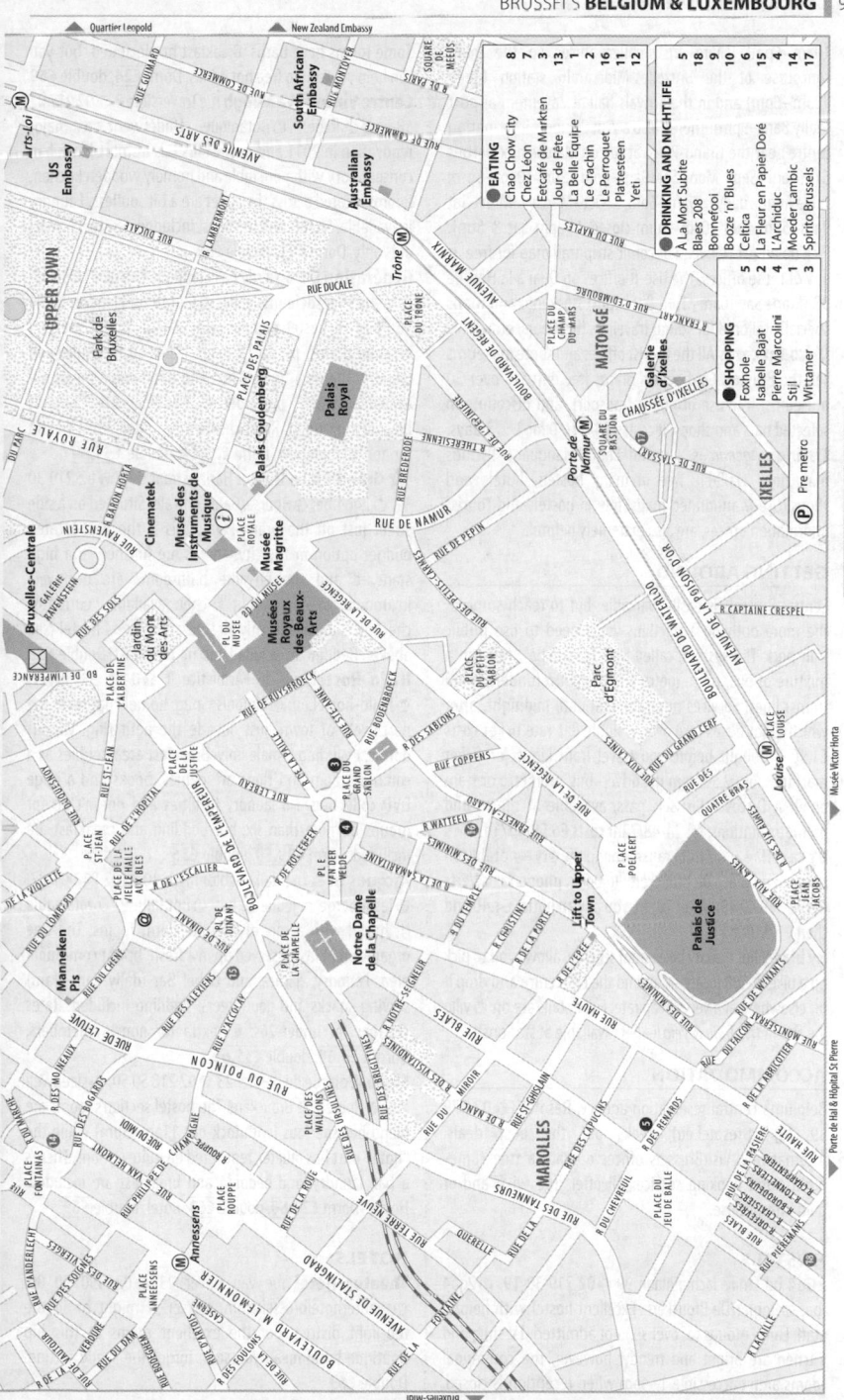

3

● EATING		
Chao Chow City	8	
Chez Léon	7	
Eetcafé de Markten	13	
Jour de Fête	1	
La Belle Equipe	2	
Le Crachin	16	
Le Perroquet	11	
Plattesteen	12	
Yeti		

● DRINKING AND NIGHTLIFE		
À La Mort Subite	5	
Blaes 208	18	
Bonnefooi	9	
Booze 'n' Blues	10	
Celtica	6	
La Fleur en Papier Doré	15	
L'Archiduc	4	
Moeder Lambic	14	
Spirito Brussels	17	

● SHOPPING	
Foxhole	5
Isabelle Bajat	2
Pierre Marcolini	4
Stijl	1
Wittamer	3

IXELLES   Ⓟ Pre metro

3

10am–6pm). There are smaller offices on the main concourse of the Bruxelles-Midi train station (daily 10am–6pm) and in the arrivals hall at Zaventem airport (daily 8am–9pm). There's also a Visit Flanders information centre near the Grand-Place at rue du Marché aux Herbes 61 (April–Sept Mon–Sat 9am–6pm, Sun 10am–5pm; July–Aug daily 9am–6pm; Oct–March Mon–Sat 9am–5pm, Sun 10am–4pm; closed 1–2pm Sat & Sun). Pick up an Art Nouveau or comic strip trail map for free at any of these offices. The Use-It offices on Quai à la Houille 9B (Mon–Sat 10am–1pm & 2–6pm) stock info and maps specially tailored for young travellers (best bars, etc).

Discount cards All the tourist offices and some museums sell the Brussels Card, which grants free entry to over 30 museums, free use of public transport, and discounts in selected bars and shops. It costs €24/34/40 for 1/2/3 days.

Listings *Agenda* is a useful English-language listings magazine, available free in many hostels, hotels and shops. *Use-It* annotated maps, free in hostels and tourist information offices, are also extremely helpful.

GETTING AROUND

Central Brussels is easily walkable, but to reach some of the more outlying attractions you'll need to use public transport. The system, called STIB (ⓦ stib.be), runs on a mixture of bus, tram, métro and prémétro (underground trams) lines. Services run from 6am until midnight, after which night buses take over. A single flat-rate ticket costs €1.90 if bought before you travel from kiosks or ticket machines, or €2.50 from the driver (bus, prémétro or tram only). A Discover Brussels pass, available at métro and prémétro stations, for 24/48/72hr costs €6.50/11/14.

By taxi Hire a taxi from ranks around the city – notably on Bourse and place de Brouckère; to book, phone Taxis Verts (ⓣ 02 349 49 49). After 10pm, you pay an initial €4.40 and then €1.66/km.

By bike Villo! the city bike rental scheme, allows you to pick up a bike at 180 locations around the city centre and drop it off elsewhere at a very cheap rate. Full details are on ⓦ villo .be and in the *Train & Vélo* leaflet (available at stations).

ACCOMMODATION

Belgium's central reservation agency, Resotel (ⓣ 02 779 39 39, ⓦ resotel.eu), seeks out the best deals. Alternatively, VisitBrussels offices operate a free same-night hotel booking service. All offer free wi-fi and/or paid internet use.

HOSTELS

2Go4 bd Emile Jacmainlaan 99 ⓣ 02 219 30 19, ⓦ 2go4 .be; ⓜ Rogier/De Brouckère. Excellent hostel with helpful staff. Large groups (of over six) not admitted. TV snug and kitchen are bright and trendy; however, the communal rooms aren't accessible 1–4pm when reception is closed.

Some rooms have baths. Breakfast not included, but you can help yourself to free hot drinks. Dorm €24, double €69

Centre Vincent Van Gogh rue Traversière 8 ⓣ 02 217 01 58, ⓦ chab.be; ⓜ Botanique. Underwent a major renovation in 2011 and downstairs has a smart black bar, conservatory with pool table and homely wooden kitchen. Rooms located across the street are a bit soulless. Laundry is available. Sheets and breakfast included. 18- to 35-year-olds only. Dorm €21, double €59

Génération Europe rue de l'Eléphant 4 ⓣ 02 410 38 58, ⓦ lesaubergesdejeunesse.be; ⓜ Comte de Flandre. Large 165-bed HI hostel popular with school groups. Several en-suite dorms, plus a TV room, a bar on reception and laundry. There's a tiny kitchen and good-value meals are available when pre-ordered. Bedding and organic breakfast included. Rates cheaper for under-26s. €3 extra for non-HI members. Dorm €23.60, double €55.60

★ **Grand Place Hostel** Haringstraat 6–8 ⓣ 02 219 30 19, ⓦ 2go4.be; ⓜ Bourse/Gare Centrale. Situated on a side street just off the Grand-Place, this is the best-located budget option in the city. Rooms are finished to a high standard and the en-suite bathrooms are positively luxurious. No dorms, but kitchen available. Currently, check-in is inconveniently located at the *2Go4* hostel (see above). Bedding is included, but no breakfast. Double €59

Hello Hostel rue de l'Armistice 1 ⓣ 0471 93 59 27, ⓦ hello-hostel.eu; ⓜ Simonis. Snug, homely option in the northwest of town, just outside the petit ring. Various dorms, including female only. Breakfast area doubles as a common room and there are games, books and a huge DVD collection. No laundry facilities and doesn't accept groups of more than six, but bedding and breakfast are included. Dorm €19.50, double €55

Jacques Brel rue de la Sablonnière 30 ⓣ 02 218 01 87, ⓦ lesaubergesdejeunesse.be; ⓜ Botanique. Comfortable HI hostel with a mix of en-suite dorm rooms. The free organic breakfast is served up in a fresh, bright communal area. Laundry, games, and Babel Bar (daily 7am–1am) serving snacks and good beers. Bedding included. Rates cheaper for under-26s; €3 extra for non-HI members. Dorm €23.60, double €55.60

Sleep Well rue du Damier 23 ⓣ 02 218 50 50, ⓦ sleepwell .be; ⓜ Rogier/De Brouckère. The hostel section's rooms are bland but spacious (with lock-out 11am–3pm) while the "hotel" part has quieter, renovated en-suite options. There's a bar, laundry, and bedding and breakfast are included. Hostel: Dorm €22.50, double €63; hotel: double €69

HOTELS

Theater Hotel rue van Gaver 23 ⓣ 02 350 90 00, ⓦ theaterhotelbrussels.com; ⓜ Yser. It might be in the red-light district, but the excellent rooms at this hip boutique hotel mean you soon forget the seedy setting. Double €63

EATING

Brussels has an international reputation for its food, and even at the dowdiest snack bar you'll find well-prepared *Bruxellois* dishes featuring fusions of Walloon and Flemish cuisine.

CAFÉS

Eetcafé de Markten place du Vieux Marché aux Grains 5; ⓜ Ste-Catherine. Vibrant café offering good-quality hearty salads, sandwiches and soups at very reasonable prices. Mon–Sat 8.30am–midnight, Sun 10am–6pm.

Jour de Fête bd Anspach 181; ⓜ Bourse. Laidback, lunchtime-only café decorated with retro furniture and a menu of just five dishes: one meat, one veg, one fish, one pasta and one seasonal at a bargain €12 each. Tapas buffet too ranging from €6–10. Mon–Fri noon–2.30pm.

Yeti rue de Bon Secours 4–6; ⓜ Bourse. Eco-conscious café which uses only organic, local and/or Fairtrade products. Good breakfasts, sandwiches (€6), teas and popular for Sunday brunch. Tues–Fri 8am–4pm, Sat & Sun 10am–6pm.

RESTAURANTS

Chao Chow City bd Anspach 89; ⓜ Bourse. Chinese food never came so cheap! Offers two dishes for either €3.80 at lunchtime or €5.80 come evening. Options are typed up and posted on a piece of paper in the window. Daily noon–midnight.

Chez Léon rue des Bouchers 18 ⓦ nl.chezleon.be; ⓜ Bruxelles-Central. Touristy, but worth a visit for their reliably tasty mussels, chips and beer "meal deal" (€14.60). Mon–Sat 11.30am–11pm.

La Belle Équipe rue Antoine Dansaert 202 ☎ 02 502 11 02; ⓜ Porte de Flandre. Authentic pizzeria which specializes in gourmet toppings (pizzas around €12). Everyone dines on one long bar top. Delivery service available. Daily 9am–10pm.

★ **Le Crachin** rue de Flandre 12 ⓦ lecrachin.net; ⓜ Ste-Catherine. Breton crêperie serving home-made sweet and savoury buckwheat pancakes and mugs of cider. Mains €12. Mon–Fri noon–2.30pm & 6.30–10.30pm, Sat & Sun noon–10.30pm.

Le Perroquet rue Watteeu 31; ⓜ Louise. Come to this Art Nouveau café for the good-value pittas and salads (€7–14). Mon 6–11.30pm, Tues & Wed noon–midnight, Thurs–Sat noon–1am, Sun noon–11.30pm.

Plattesteen rue du Marché au Charbon 41; Prémétro Bourse. Typical *Bruxellois* dishes are on the menu at this traditional family restaurant, famous for its sunny terrace beneath a cartoon mural. Mains €10. Daily noon–3pm & 6–10pm.

DRINKING AND NIGHTLIFE

Brussels' bars are a joy. St-Géry, just to the west of Bourse, is the place to drink, especially during summer when bars spill out into the square. Rue du Marché au Charbon is the hub of gay nightlife.

BARS

À La Mort Subite rue Montagne aux Herbes Potagères 7 ⓦ alamortsubite.com; ⓜ Gare Centrale. Atmospheric 1920s bar, famous for its Gueuze and Kriek beers. Mon–Sat 11am–1am, Sun noon–midnight.

★ **Bonnefooi** rue des Pierres 8 ⓦ bonnefooi.be; Prémétro Bourse. Live music every night at this hip bar and a great atmosphere in summer when the crowds mingle on the street. Jupiler costs €1 until 10pm daily. Daily 4pm–8am.

Booze 'n' Blues rue des Riches-Claires 20; ⓜ Bourse. Locals swear by this place in spite of the rude owner, returning night after night for the faultless soundtrack of blues and soul music . Daily 7pm–late.

Celtica rue du Marché aux Poulets 55 ⓦ celticpubs.com; Prémétro Bourse. Catch that all-important football match on the big screens here. DJs play every night from 11pm and it has the cheapest happy-hour prices in town – Trappist monastery beers just €2 before midnight. Daily 1pm–late.

La Fleur en Papier Doré rue des Alexiens 55 ⓦ lafleurenpapierdore.be; ⓜ Gare Centrale. Traditional Belgian "brown" bar that was a favourite haunt of Hergé and Magritte. Serves Lambic beer the traditional way, in ceramic mugs. Tues–Sat 11am–midnight, Sun 11am–7pm.

L'Archiduc rue Antoine Dansaert 6 ⓦ archiduc.net; Prémétro Bourse. Legendary Art Deco jazz bar. Things get going around midnight – ring the doorbell to get in. Daily 4pm–5am.

Moeder Lambic place Fontainas 8 ⓦ moederlambic .com; Prémétro Anneessens. Excellent place to try Belgium's many brews, with 46 beers on tap, including Brussels brewed Cantillon – all served to you in snug wooden booths. Daily 11am–1am, until 2am Sat & Sun.

CLUBS

Blaes 208 rue Blaes 208 ⓦ blaes208.be; ⓜ Porte de Hal. A Brussels institution, with big-name DJs usually lined up for its Fuse Sat techno nights. Entry €5 before midnight, €10 after. Usually Wed–Sat, with monthly gay nights.

Spirito Brussels rue de Stassart 18 ⓦ spiritobrussels .com; ⓜ Porte de Namur. A converted Anglican church, this place deserves its reputation as one of the most beautiful clubs in the world. Free entry on Fri, €10 on Sat. Fri & Sat 10.30pm–6am.

SHOPPING

Aside from the Marolles flea market (see p.94), rue Blaes and rue Haute are lined with a mix of affordable and expensive antiques shops. High-street labels can be found on and around rue Neuve.

Foxhole rue des Renards 6. Affordable vintage clothes store. Thurs–Sun 9.30am–6pm.

3

Isabelle Bajart rue des Chartreux 25. Vintage fashion. Mon & Tues noon–7pm, Wed–Sat 11am–7pm.

Pierre Marcolini rue des Minimes 1 (pl du Grand Sablon). Award-winning *chocolatier*. Mon–Wed & Sun 10am–7pm, Thurs & Fri 10am–8pm.

Stijl rue Antoine Dansaert 74. Department store showcasing local and international designers. Mon–Sat 10.30am–6.30pm.

Wittamer pl du Grand Sablon 12. Esteemed *pâtissier* and *chocolatier*. Mon 9am–6pm, Tues–Sat 7am–7pm, Sun 7am–6.30pm.

DIRECTORY

Embassies Australia, av des Arts 56 ☎ 02 286 05 00 ⓜTrone; Canada, av de Tervuren 2 ☎02 741 06 11 ⓜMerode; Ireland, chaussée d'Etterbeek 180 ☎ 02 282 34 00 ⓜSchuman; New Zealand, 7th Floor, av des Nerviens 9–31 ☎02 512 10 40 ⓜSchuman; South Africa, rue Montoyer 17–19 ☎02 285 44 00 ⓜTrone; UK, av d'Auderghem 10 ☎02 287 62 11 ⓜSchuman; USA, bd du Régent 27 ☎02 811 40 00 ⓜArts-Loi/Kunst-Wet.

Hospital Hôpital St Pierre, rue Haute 322 ☎02 535 33 11.

Internet Wi-fi is available at *Aroma Coffee Lounge*, Grand Place 37 (Mon–Sat 8.30am–9pm, Sun 8.30am–10pm), and at *McDonald's* at place de la Bourse 3 (Mon–Wed 8am–midnight, Thurs–Sat 8am–5am, Sun 9.30am–midnight).

Left luggage Self-service lockers at all three main train stations; €3/3.50/4 for a small/medium/large locker for 24hr.

Pharmacies Pharmacie de l'Europe, rue du Marché aux Herbes 109 (Mon–Sat 9am–7pm); Multipharma, rue du Marché aux Poulets 37 (Mon–Fri 9.30am–6.30pm, Sat 10am–6pm).

Post office Bruxelles-Central (Mon & Wed–Fri 8.30am–5pm, Tues 8.30am–6pm).

Northern Belgium

Almost entirely **Flemish-speaking**, the region to the north of Brussels has a distinctive and vibrant cultural identity, its pancake-flat landscapes punctuated by a string of fine historic cities. These begin with **Antwerp**, a large old port that flourished during the sixteenth century and is now Flanders' most forward-thinking city, followed by **Ghent** and **Bruges**, which became prosperous during the Middle Ages on the back of the cloth trade. All three cities have great restaurants and a lively bar scene.

ANTWERP

ANTWERP, Belgium's second city, and the de facto capital of Flemish Belgium, fans out from the east bank of the Scheldt River about 50km north of Brussels. Many people prefer it to the capital; it is an immediately attractive place, famous for Rubens, fashion, diamonds and the best nightlife in Belgium.

WHAT TO SEE AND DO

At the centre of Antwerp is the spacious **Grote Markt**, where the conspicuous **Brabo fountain** features a bronze of Silvius Brabo, the city's first hero, depicted flinging the hand of the giant Antigonus – who terrorized passing ships – into the Scheldt. The north side of Grote Markt is lined with daintily restored sixteenth-century **guildhouses**, while the west is hogged by the handsome **Stadhuis (Town Hall)**.

Onze Lieve Vrouwe Kathedraal

Southeast of Grote Markt, the **Onze Lieve Vrouwe Kathedraal** (Mon–Fri 10am–5pm, Sat 10am–3pm, Sun 1–4pm; €5; ⓦdekathedraal.be) is one of the finest Gothic churches in Europe, dating from the middle of the fifteenth century. Four paintings by Rubens, including his masterpieces *Elevation of the Cross* and *Descent from the Cross*, are displayed here.

Plantin-Moretus Museum

The **Plantin-Moretus Museum** at Vrijdagmarkt 22–23 (Tues–Sun 10am–5pm; €8; ⓦmuseumplantin moretus.be), occupies the grand old mansion of Rubens' father-in-law, the printer Christopher Plantin. It provides a beautiful, richly decorated setting for two

---

FERRIES TO BRITAIN

Belgium's main international ferry port is **Zeebrugge**, just outside Bruges, with ferries from Hull and Rosyth in Great Britain. Ferry companies provide bus connections from the port to the train station. Transeuropa ferries run from Ramsgate to the resort town of **Ostend**, from where trains to Bruges take fifteen minutes.

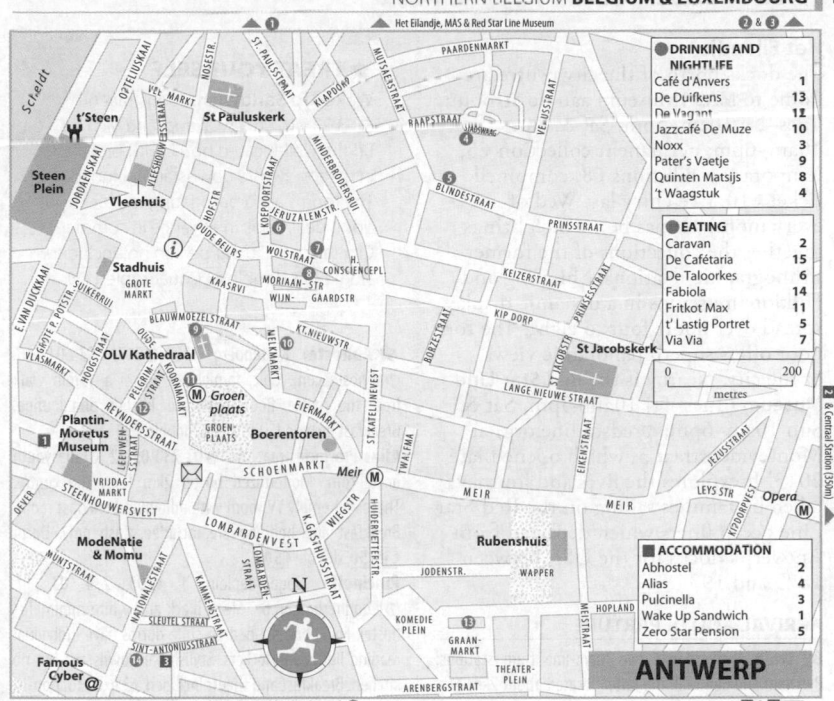

Het Eilandje, MAS & Red Star Line Museum

& Central Station (350m)

DRINKING AND NIGHTLIFE

Café d'Anvers	1
De Duifkens	13
De Vagant	12
Jazzcafé De Muze	10
Noxx	3
Pater's Vaetje	9
Quinten Matsijs	8
't Waagstuk	4

EATING

Caravan	2
De Cafétaria	15
De Taloorkes	6
Fabiola	14
Fritkot Max	11
t' Lastig Portret	5
Via Via	7

ACCOMMODATION

Abhostel	2
Alias	4
Pulcinella	3
Wake Up Sandwich	1
Zero Star Pension	5

ANTWERP

Koninklijk Museum voor Schone Kunsten (closed until 2017) & 15

of the oldest printing presses in the world.

ModeNatie and Museum voor Schone Kunsten

In the heart of the city's fashion quarter along Nationalestraat, the **ModeNatie** (ⓦmodenatie.com) showcases some of the avant-garde fashion for which the city is famous. Part of the building contains **MoMu** (Tues–Sun 10am–6pm; €8; ⓦmomu.be), which has some great fashion displays, from sixteenth-century lace dresses to pieces by Dries van Noten.

About fifteen minutes' walk further south at Leopold de Waelplaats, the **Koninklijk Museum voor Schone Kunsten** (Royal Museum of Fine Arts; ⓦkmska.be) has one of the country's best fine-art collections. Unfortunately, it is closed for renovation until 2017.

North of the Grote Markt

The impressively gabled **Vleeshuis** (Tues–Sun 10am–5pm; €5) is a short walk north of the Grote Markt. Built for the guild of butchers in 1503 and

distinguished by its striped brickwork, it now holds a permanent exhibition covering 600 years of music and dance. Just north of here, along Vleeshouwersstraat, the elegant nave at the sixteenth-century **St Pauluskerk** (April–Oct daily 2–5pm; free) is decorated by a series of paintings depicting the Fifteen Mysteries of the Rosary, including Rubens' exquisite *Scourging at the Pillar* of 1617.

Rubenshuis and St Jacobskerk

Ten minutes' walk east of the Grote Markt is the **Rubenshuis**, at Wapper 9 (Tues–Sun 10am–5pm; €8; ⓦrubenshuis .be); the former home and studio of Rubens, it's now restored as a very popular museum. On his death in 1640, Rubens was buried in the chapel behind the high altar at **St Jacobskerk**, just to the north at Lange Nieuwstraat 73. The church features one of his last works, *Our Lady Surrounded by Saints*, featuring himself as St George, his two wives as Martha and Mary, and his father as St Jerome.

3

Het Eilandje

The docks north of the city centre are home to **MAS** (Museum aan de Stroom; Tues–Fri 10am–5pm, Sat & Sun 10am–6pm; permanent collection €5, temporary exhibitions €8, combined ticket €10, free entry last Wed of every month; ⓦmas.be), which brings together the collections of the former Ethnographic, National Shipping and Folklore museums in a dynamic display spread over floors four to eight. The top floor offers superb panoramic views of the city. Nearby is the **Red Star Line Museum** (Tues–Fri 10am–5pm, Sat & Sun 10am–6pm; ⓦredstarline.org) at Montevideostraat 3, which opened late 2013. It explores the lives and journeys taken by families sailing on the Red Star Line ocean liners which departed from Antwerp's docks for the USA between 1873 and 1934.

ARRIVAL AND DEPARTURE

By train Antwerp has two main-line train stations: Berchem and Centraal. The latter, located about 2km east of the Grote Markt, is the one you want for the city centre.
Destinations Bruges (hourly; 1hr 20min); Brussels (every 30min; 40min); Ghent (every 30min; 50min); Ostend (hourly; 1hr 40min).

INFORMATION

Tourist information Grote Markt 13 (Mon–Sat 9am–5.45pm, Sun 9am–4.45pm; ⓣ03 232 01 03, ⓦvisitantwerpen.be). Centraal Station also has a kiosk.
Discount cards Tourist offices sell the Antwerp City Card: it costs €28, is valid for 48hr, and grants free access to all city museums and churches, as well as 25 percent discount on numerous other attractions and bike rental.

GETTING AROUND

A flat-rate one-way ticket on any part of the city's transport system costs €2; a 24hr pass (*dagpas*) is €6. Tickets are 20 percent cheaper if bought ahead of travel at supermarkets, newsagents or the tourist information office.
By tram/metro Antwerp is easily traversed on foot, but there are very good metro and tram services covering the city. Trams #2 and #15 (direction Linkeroever) run from the tram station beside Centraal Station to the centre; get off at Groenplaats.

ACCOMMODATION

Many mid-priced and budget establishments are around Centraal Station, where you should exercise caution at night.

★ **TREAT YOURSELF**

Wake-Up Sandwich Hoogstraat 68 ⓣ03 225 16 06, ⓦwakeupsandwich.be. Bright, well-located hotel, with breakfast in the lovely café downstairs included. The rooms accommodating four are a good deal. Book in advance in summer. City tax of €2.50 per person not included. Single **€50**, double **€85**, quadruple **€120**.

★ **Abhostel** Kattenberg 110 ⓣ0473 57 01 66, ⓦabhostel.com. Chic, family-run hostel a 15min walk from the centre. Rooftop terrace, kitchen and lounge. Breakfast included. Dorm **€21**, double **€50**
Alias Provinciestraat 256 ⓣ03 230 05 22, ⓦaliasyouth hostel.com. Modernized hostel 2km from the centre. There's a homely TV room with adjoining breakfast room. Breakfast and bedding are included. Cash only. Dorm **€19.50**, double **€50**
Pulcinella Bogaardeplein 1 ⓣ03 234 03 14, ⓦjeugdherbergen.be. Sleek black-and-white minimalist hostel. Four- and six-bed en-suite dorms have individual reading lights and lockers. Stylish bar downstairs but no kitchen. Breakfast and sheets included. €3 extra for non-HI members. Dorm **€23.60**, double **€55.60**
Zero Star Pension Minkelersstraat ⓣ078 05 40 50, ⓦzva.be. If visiting in July and August (closed the rest of the year), this converted gas factory, 3km from the centre, offers the cheapest beds in town and throws in an organic breakfast too. Sheets €4 extra. Dorm **€18**

EATING

Antwerp is full of informal café-restaurants. Several of the best are clustered on Suikerrui and Grote Pieter Potstraat near the Grote Markt, and there's another concentration in the vicinity of Hendrik Conscienceplein. For fast food, try the kebab and falafel places on Oude Koornmarkt, or, of course, any of the *frituurs*.

CAFÉS AND SNACK BARS

★ **Caravan** Damplein 17. Vintage café that puts together picnic hampers and is famous for its weekend *koppijn ontbijt* ("hangover breakfast") served with either a beer or a painkiller. Mains €5–12. Mon, Wed, Thurs 10am–9pm, Fri & Sat 10am–11pm, Sun 10am–7pm.
De Cafétaria Montignystraat 21. Shabby-chic café serving healthy sandwiches (€5), milkshakes, pastries and excellent coffee. Plenty of magazines strewn around to flick through while you eat. Daily 9am–6pm.
Fabiola Sint-Antoniusstraat 4. A rustic café with a fantastic range of croque monsieurs (€4–7). Sweet and

savoury, traditional and gourmet – they're all here. Mon–Wed 10am–5.30pm, Fri & Sat 10am–7.30pm.

Fritkot Max Groenplaats 12. It doesn't look like much but this place might just serve the best chips in town (cornets cost €3) – ideal for a quick refuel between sightseeing. Daily noon–midnight.

Via Via Wolstraat 43 ⓦ viaviacafe.com. Popular travellers' café serving dishes from around the world. Mains €10. Mon–Sat 11.30am–late, Sun 3pm–late.

RESTAURANTS

De Taloorkes Lange Koepoortstraat 61. Five minutes' walk from Grote Markt but a world away from its touristy offerings, this locals' restaurant serves mouth-watering stews and mussels for €15. Daily noon–10pm.

t'Lastig Portret Blindestraat 1. Frequented by university students and teachers, this friendly place is adored for its hearty mains (€11–16) and €9 dish of the day. Mon–Fri 11am–2.30pm & 5–10pm.

DRINKING AND NIGHTLIFE

BARS

De Duifkens Graanmarkt 5. A great place to try local beer Bolleke Koninck. Rumour has it the former owner's ashes are stored in the urn that sits on top of the fireplace! Mon–Fri 11.30am–late, Sat & Sun 10am–late.

De Vagant Reyndersstraat 25. Specialist gin bar serving Belgian and Dutch *jenevers* in comfortable surroundings. Mon–Fri 11am–11pm, Sat & Sun noon–11pm.

Pater's Vaetje Blauwmoezelstraat 1. In the shadow of the cathedral, this old-fashioned pub has a great range of beers and is popular with tourists and locals alike. Fri & Sat 11am–5am, Sun–Thurs 11am–3am.

Quinten Matsijs Moriaanstraat 17. Established in 1545, this is Antwerp's oldest bar. The regal dark-wood interior is ideal for a relaxed quiet drink. Tues–Sat noon–late, Sun noon–8pm.

't Waagstuk Stadswaag 20. Traditional "brown" bar that serves beer the proper way: their Orval is aged for six months and the Hopruiker is on draught, a treat you won't find anywhere else in Belgium. Mon–Thurs 10am–2am, Fri 10am–4am, Sat 2pm–4am, Sun 2pm–10pm.

CLUBS

Café d'Anvers Verversrui 15 ⓦ cafe-d-anvers.com. Club housed in a sixteenth-century church in the red-light district. Mainly house music. Tickets can be bought online and range from €7–15. Thurs 11pm–6am, Fri & Sat 11pm–7.30am.

Jazzcafé De Muze Melkmarkt 15 ⓦ jazzcafedemuze.be. Renowned jazz bar with free live performances Mon–Sat at 10pm and Sun at 3pm. Daily 11am–late.

Noxx Kotterstraat 1 ⓦ noxxantwerp.com. Club in the Het Eilandje district, north of the city centre. Has four rooms,

including the Salle Noire with a 360-degree LED wall. Music varies. Entry on Thurs free, Fri varies, Sat €15. Thurs 10pm–6am, Fri 11pm–6am, Sat 11pm–7am.

SHOPPING

Antwerp offers superb fashion shopping. High-street labels can be found along Meir and Huidevettersstraat, while Kammenstraat is good for vintage clothes shops. The haute-couture boutiques congregate around Nationaalstraat, Kammenstraat and Steenhouwersves. Pricey antiques and cavernous junk shops can be found along Kloosterstraat.

DIRECTORY

Internet Famous Cyber, Nationalestraat 92 (Mon–Thurs & Sun 10am–8pm, Fri 10am–9pm; €1.50/hr).

Left luggage Self-service lockers in the Centraal train station under the stairs, €3/24hr.

Post office Groenplaats 43 (Mon–Wed & Fri 9am–6pm, Thurs 9am–7pm, Sat 9am–3pm).

GHENT

The largest town in Western Europe during the thirteenth and fourteenth centuries, **GHENT** (Gent) was once at the heart of the medieval Flemish cloth trade. It's now the third-largest city in Belgium, and rivals Bruges thanks to its beautiful canals and well-preserved medieval architecture – without the stifling tourism.

WHAT TO SEE AND DO

A captivating university town with a spirited nightlife and its own **castle**, Ghent's main appeal lies in wandering the cobbled streets which line the canalside and sampling the city's bars.

Sint-Baafsplein

Ghent is famous for its three towers in a row. The first of these – and the best place to start exploring – is the mainly Gothic **Sint-Baafskathedraal**, squeezed into the corner of St Baafsplein (April–Oct Mon–Sat 8.30am–6pm, Sun 1–6pm; Nov–March Mon–Sat 8.30am–5pm, Sun 1–5pm). Inside, a small chapel (April–Oct Mon–Sat 9.30am–5pm, Sun 1–5pm; Nov–March Mon–Sat 10.30am–4pm, Sun 1–4pm; €4 includes audioguide; ⓦ sintbaafskathedraal.be). The cathedral holds Ghent's greatest treasure, the

3

3

GHENT

0   100
metres

PATERSHOL

ANSEELE-
PLEIN

Het Gravensteen

VRIJDAGMARKT

BIJ ST
JACOBS

Oude
Vismijn

City Boat
Trips

Stadhuis

EMILE
BRAUNPLEIN

Sint-
Niklaaskerk

Belfort &
Lakenhalle

Sint-
Baafskathedraal

ACCOMMODATION

De Draecke	3
Den Augustijn	1
Hostel 47	2
Hostel Uppelink	4

STAM   St Pieters Station & SMAK

EATING		**DRINKING AND NIGHTLIFE**	
De Lieve	2	Café het Spijker	7
Julie's House	3	Hot Club de Gand	5
Mosquito Coast	8	Pink Flamingos	6
		't Dreupelkot	4
		The White Cat	1

altarpiece of the Adoration of the Mystic Lamb, a wonderful, early fifteenth-century painting by brothers Hubert and Jan van Eyck. It's undergoing a five-year restoration, so a panel may be missing.

On the west side of St Baafsplein lurks the medieval **Lakenhalle** (Cloth Hall), a gloomy hunk of a building. One of its entrances leads to the adjoining **Belfort** (Belfry; daily 10am–6pm; €5; ⓦbelfortgent.be), a much-amended edifice dating from the fourteenth century. A lift climbs up to the roof for excellent views over the city centre. St Niklaaskerk, at the western end of Emile Braunplein, completes the trio.

The Graslei and Patershol

The **Graslei** forms the eastern side of the old city harbour and is home to a splendid series of medieval guildhouses. On warm days it's packed with students sunning themselves, and is the departure point for fifty-minute boat tours (€6.50 in cash)

along the canals. Nearby just to the north are the narrow cobbled lanes and alleys of the **Patershol**, a pocket-sized district that was formerly home to the city's weavers, but is now Ghent's main restaurant quarter. To the west, on Sint-Veerleplein, stands **Het Gravensteen** (Castle of the Counts; April–Sept 10am–6pm, final entry at 5pm; Oct–March 9am–5pm, final entry 4pm; €8 includes movieguide), a spectacular twelfth-century castle, now a chilling torture museum.

SMAK and STAM

Strolling south from the centre along Ghent's main shopping street, Veldstraat, it takes about twenty minutes to reach the old casino, parts of which have been turned into **SMAK** (Citadelpark; Tues–Sun 10am–6pm; €6; ⓦsmak.be), a contemporary art museum well known for its adventurous temporary exhibitions.

Just north, across the canal at Godshuizenlaan 2, is **STAM** (Tues–Sun 10am–6pm; €6; ⓦstamgent.be), detailing the city's history via an array of artefacts, weapons, costumes and coins.

ARRIVAL AND DEPARTURE

By train Of Ghent's two train stations, Gent-Sint-Pieters, about 2km to the south of the city centre, is the handiest for town.

Destinations Antwerp (every 30min; 50min); Bruges (every 20min; 25min); Brussels (every 30min; 40min); Ostend (every 30min; 50min).

INFORMATION

Tourist information Oude Vismijn, Sint-Veerleplein 5 (daily: March 15–Oct 14 9.30am–6.30pm; Oct 15–March 14 9.30am–4.30pm; ☎09 266 56 60, ⓦvisitgent.be).

Discount cards The CityCard Gent grants free entry to all of the city's main museums and monuments, free use of public transport and a complimentary canal cruise. It costs €25 for 48 hours, or €30 for 72 hours, and can be bought from the tourist office, hotels, participating museums and offices of the public transport company De Lijn.

GETTING AROUND

By tram Trams depart from outside the train station. Tram #1 (direction Evergem or Wondelgem) runs up to the Korenmarkt, right in the centre of town, every few minutes. The flat-rate fare for trams is €2/journey; validate the ticket at the machine once you get on.

★ TREAT YOURSELF

Den Augustijn Lange Steenstraat 23 ☎09 334 64 39, ⓦdenaugustijn.be. Single elegant room located in the central and stylish Patershol district. Breakfast isn't included (try the highly recommended Simon Says café just around the corner) but the owners offer free bike rental. Single **€75**, double **€90**.

ACCOMMODATION

The tourist office publishes a comprehensive brochure detailing local accommodation, and operates a free hotel booking service. You can also ask them about camping options out to the west of town.

De Draecke St Widostraat 11 ☎09 233 70 50, ⓦwww .vjh.be/gent. Central option with very friendly staff and no city tax. But there are downsides – the en-suite rooms are unremarkable, communal areas (bar, TV room) are a bit lacklustre and there's no kitchen. Bedding and breakfast included. €3 extra for non-HI members. Dorm **€21.50**, double **€51.40**

Hostel 47 Blekerijstraat 47 ☎0478 71 28 27, ⓦhostel47 .com. Trendy hostel in the north of town. Dorm rooms are finished to a high standard, and ther communal showers and sinks are very swanky. No laundry, and city tax (€2.50) is payable on top, but breakfast and sheets are included. Cash only. Dorm **€26.50**, double **€66**

★ **Hostel Uppelink** Sint-Michielsplein 21 ☎09 279 44 77, ⓦhosteluppelink.com. An excellent new eleven-room hostel overlooking the central Korenlei canal. A few of the dorms – some with exposed-brick walls – sleep just two or four people, and one is for women only. Homely lounge and bar too. Breakfast and sheets, but not city tax (€2.50), are included. Dorm **€22.50**

EATING

Fancier restaurants are concentrated in Patershol, while less expensive options cluster around the Korenmarkt.

De Lieve Sint-Margrietstraat 1. This down-to-earth restaurant is one of the last in town to serve proper Belgian food at honest prices. Try the dish of the day, which usually costs less than €10. Menu is in Dutch only. Mon–Fri 11am–10pm.

Julie's House Kraanlei 13. Visit this wonderful artisanal

bakery for the *gestreken mastellen* – cinnamon cookies that are ironed flat before serving. The €12 breakfast menus are good too. Wed–Sun 9am–6.30pm.

★ **Mosquito Coast** Hoogpoort 28. Travellers' café with bookshelves of guides, two terraces and a menu of filling wraps and international hot dishes for around €16. Also serves Ghent-made aperitif Roomer. Tues–Sat 11am–late, Sun 3pm–late.

DRINKING AND NIGHTLIFE

Ghent boasts an energetic drinking scene thanks to its student population.

BARS

★ **Café het Spijker** Pensmarkt 3. Cosy candelit bar housed in what was a thirteenth-century leprosy shelter. Terrace out the back with lovely views of the canal. Daily 9am–4am.

Pink Flamingos Onderstraat 55. Wacky little place stuffed with kitsch paraphernalia. Attracts a hip crowd, and is a great place for an aperitif or cocktail. DJs play every night from 10pm. Thurs–Sat 2pm–3am.

't Dreupelkot Groentenmarkt 12. The city's last traditional *jenever* bar. It stocks over 215 flavours, all kept at icy temperatures. Mon–Sat 4pm–late.

CLUBS AND LIVE MUSIC

Hot Club de Gand Schuddevisstraatje Groentenmarkt 15b ⓦhotclubdegand.be. Hidden down a narrow alley, this is the best jazz spot in town, with jam sessions on Wed evenings. Daily 3pm–late.

The White Cat Drongenhof 40, Patershol. James Bond-themed basement club in the Patershol district – don't miss the aquarium bar. Live jazz or funk on Fri and Sat. Wed–Sat 9pm–late.

DIRECTORY

Internet Free wi-fi inside the Oude Vismijn (Old Fish Market) and *Café het Spijker* (see above).

Post office Lange Kruisstraat 55 (Mon–Fri 9am–6pm, Sat 9am–3pm).

BRUGES

The reputation of **BRUGES** (Brugge) as one of the most perfectly preserved

GHENT FESTIVAL

For ten days during the second half of July, Ghent transforms into a 24-hour party city as it pulsates with the **Gentse Feesten** (ⓦgentsefeesten.be). Stages are set up in all the main squares and blast out every kind of music. Accommodation can get booked up months before the festival, so be sure to make a reservation, and try to avoid visiting immediately afterwards – everything is shut for the next week or so as the city recovers.

3

3

BRUGES

medieval cities in Europe has made it Belgium's tourist honeypot. Inevitably, the crowds tend to overwhelm the city's charms, but you would be mad to come to Belgium and skip it. Bruges boomed throughout the Middle Ages, its weavers turning English wool into clothing that was exported worldwide. By the end of the fifteenth century, however, Bruges fell into decline and its unique beauty went unnoticed until it was rediscovered some 400 years later, thanks to the popularity of Georges Rodenbach's novel *Bruges-la-Morte*.

WHAT TO SEE AND DO

The older sections of Bruges fan out from two central squares, Markt and Burg.

Markt

Markt, edged on three sides by nineteenth-century gabled buildings, is the larger of the two squares, an impressive open space flanked to the south by the mighty **Belfort** (Belfry; daily 9.30am–5pm; €8), built in the thirteenth century when the town was at its richest. Its tapering staircase leads up to the roof from where there are spectacular views over the city. Also on the square is the new **Historium** (daily 10am–6pm, last tickets 5pm; €11, combi ticket with Groeningemuseum €15; ⍟historium.be), which shows what life was like in Bruges during the fifteenth century through its seven interactive rooms.

The Burg and the Heilig Bloedbasiliek

From the Markt, Breidelstraat leads through to the **Burg**, whose finest building is the **Heilig Bloedbasiliek** (Basilica of the Holy Blood; April–mid-Oct daily 9.30am–noon & 2–5pm; mid-Oct–March Mon, Tues & Thurs–Sun 10am–noon & 2–5pm; €1.50; ⍟holyblood.com). Its Upper Chapel holds a phial of the blood of Christ brought back from Jerusalem by the Crusaders. Stored in a grandiose silver tabernacle, the Holy Blood is still venerated on Ascension Day, when it is carried through the town in a colourful but solemn procession.

The Stadhuis

The **Stadhuis** has a beautiful, turreted sandstone facade, behind which is a magnificent **Gothic Hall** (daily 9.30am–5pm; €4). The price of admission covers entry to the nearby former alderman's mansion. Its Renaissance **'t Brugse Vrije** (daily 9.30am–12.30pm & 1.30–5pm), a ceremonial meeting room, dates from the sixteenth century and features an enormous oak chimneypiece carved in honour of the ruling Habsburgs.

The Groeninge and Gruuthuse museums

The **Groeningemuseum**, at Dijver 12 (Tues–Sun 9.30am–5pm; €8, combi ticket with Historium €15), houses a superb collection of Flemish paintings, including several canvases by Jan van Fyck. Further along the Dijver, at no. 17, the **Gruuthuse Museum** (Tues–Sun 9.30am–5pm; €8) is sited in a rambling fifteenth-century mansion and holds a varied collection of fine art, including intricately carved altarpieces and locally made tapestries.

Onze Lieve Vrouwekerk

The **Onze Lieve Vrouwekerk** (Mon–Sat 9.30am–5pm, Sun 1.30–5pm; €6), on Mariastraat, features a delicate marble statue of *Madonna and Child* by Michelangelo and, in the chancel, the exquisite Renaissance mausoleums of Charles the Bold and his daughter Mary of Burgundy.

Sint-Janshospitaal and Begijnhof

Sint-Janshospitaal (Tues–Sun 9.30am–5pm; €8) has been turned into a lavish museum celebrating the city's history in general and the hospital in particular. In addition, the old chapel displays a small but distinguished collection of paintings by **Hans Memling**.

From Sint-Janshospitaal, it's a quick stroll down to the **Begijnhof** (daily 6.30am–6pm; free), a circle of whitewashed houses around a tidy green that was established in the thirteenth century for pious women who had been widowed by the Crusades. Inside, the **Begijnhuisje** (Mon–Sat 10am–5pm, Sun 2.30–5pm; €2) remains open for visitors. Nearby is the romantic **Minnewater**, often known as the "Lake of Love".

ARRIVAL AND DEPARTURE

By train Bruges's train station is situated 2km southwest of the centre.
Destinations Antwerp (hourly; 1hr 20min); Brussels (every 30min; 1hr); Ghent (every 20min; 25min); Ostend (every 20min; 15min); Zeebrugge (hourly; 15min).

INFORMATION

Tourist information The main office is in the city concert hall at 't Zand 34 (Mon–Sat 10am–5pm, Sun 10am–2pm; ☎05 044 86 86, ⓦvisitbruges.be), with smaller branches on the Markt inside the Historium (daily 10am–5pm) and inside the train station (Mon–Fri 10am–5pm, Sat & Sun 10am–2pm).
Discount card The Brugge City Card (ⓦbruggecitycard .be) grants free access to the main museums and attractions, includes a free canal boat ride and 25 percent discount on bicycle rental and public transport. It costs €38/43 for 48/72hr, and is cheaper for under-26s.

GETTING AROUND

By bus Local buses leave from outside the train station for the main square, the Markt; tickets cost €2 from the driver.

ACCOMMODATION

Bauhaus Langestraat 133–137 ☎05 034 10 93, ⓦst -christophers.co.uk/bruges hostels. Cheerful hostel with its own nightclub. Ask for a bunk in the new section, where "pod" beds have curtains around them for privacy and locker drawers. Guests can claim 10 percent off the bill and free beer at the hostel's excellent bar-restaurant. Free walking tours. Reception located at no. 145. Bedding and breakfast included. Dorm €17, double €50
Lybeer Korte Vuldersstraat 31 ☎05 033 43 55, ⓦhostellybeer.com. Modern hostel a 10min walk from the train station. Rooms are clean, and the common room cosy. Offers free walking tours themed on the film *In Bruges*. Sheets and towels included; breakfast €4 extra. Rates increase by roughly €2 at weekends. Dorm €16, double €50
Passage Dweersstraat 26 ☎05 034 02 32, ⓦpassagebruges.com. This hostel has ten comfortable dormitories; breakfast (€5 extra) is served in the excellent Art Deco restaurant. Next door, the hotel section offers simple but well-maintained doubles, some with shared facilities. Dorm €16, double €52
Snuffel Sleep In Ezelstraat 47–49 ☎05 033 31 33, ⓦsnuffel.be. West of the centre with 4- to 12-bed dorms. Life centres around the laidback, late-opening bar. Free book exchange, kitchen and bike rental (€6/day). Bedding and breakfast included. Dorm €16

EATING

Although many places in Bruges are mediocre and tourist-orientated, it's still possible to find quality, value-for-money food.
De Stoepa Oostmeers 124 ⓦstoepa.be. Mediterranean-style café-bar with a wood-burning stove for the winter months and a quiet, leafy terrace ideal for relaxed summer lunches. Mains €6–8. Tues–Sun 11am–2am.
Friterie 1900 Markt 35. Grab a cornet of traditional

3

3

Belgian *frites* for just €2 at this simple shop-front counter. Mon–Thurs & Sun 10am–midnight, Fri & Sat 10am–1am.

L'Estaminet Park 5. Friendly, candlelit café-bar with a first-rate beer menu and sweet and savoury snacks such as pancakes and toasties for around €8. Tues–Sun 11.30am–late, Thurs 4pm–late.

Medard Sint-Amandsstraat 18. Family-run Italian restaurant famous for its generous portions of spaghetti – just €4 for a huge bowl. Fri–Wed noon–late.

★ **Pas Partout** Jeruzalemstraat 1 ⓦ sobo.be. A cash-and lunchtime-only place, 350m from the centre, that serves the cheapest *steak frites* (€10) in town. Dishes are prepared by once-unemployed individuals who are now learning a new trade. Mon–Sat 11.45am–2pm.

DRINKING AND NIGHTLIFE

Café Vlissinghe Blekersstraat 2 ⓦ cafevlissinghe.be. Open since 1515, this peaceful, tucked-away café is packed with historic relics. Has board games and a large terrace out the back. Wed–Sat 11.30am–late, Sun 11am–7pm.

De Kleine Nachtmuziek Sint-Jakobsstraat 60. Peaceful whisky bar with a jazz and blues soundtrack. Mon, Tues, Thurs–Sun 6pm–late.

Ma Rica Rokk t'Zand 6. Central bar with a tropical holiday-themed interior that attracts a good-looking crowd. Daily: Sept–June 7.30pm–3am; July–Aug 9pm–5am.

't Opkikkertje West-gistelhof 13 ⓦ opkikkertje.be. It's worth seeking out this off-the-beaten-track "brown" bar, just across the river, for the twice-monthly live bands on Sat. Mon, Tues, Thurs, Fri 4.30pm–late, Wed 6pm–late, Sat 5pm–late.

★ **'t Poatersgat** Vlamingstraat 82 ⓦ poatersgat.com. Atmospheric cellar bar with an exemplary beer list. A real locals' hangout. Daily 5pm–late.

SHOPPING

Lace and chocolate are the best gifts to buy in Bruges, and with over 50 chocolate shops, there's no shortage of choice.

't Apostolientje Balstraat 11. Sells a good selection of antique lace. 550m from the centre. Mon–Sat 9.30am–5pm, Sun 9.30am–1pm.

The Chocolate Line Simon Stevinplein 19. Unusual option selling tobacco- and wasabi-flavoured chocolate. Tues–Sat 9.30am–6.30pm, Sun–Mon 10.30am–6.30pm.

DIRECTORY

Internet The city has free wi-fi zones ("ZapFi") in the t'Zand, Markt and Burg squares, but there are no dedicated internet cafés.

Left luggage Located just inside the train station's main entrance, on the left; €3/3.50/4 for small/medium/large self-service locker.

Southern Belgium

South of Brussels lies **Wallonia**, French-speaking Belgium, where a belt of heavy industry interrupts the rolling farmland that precedes the high wooded hills of the **Ardennes**. The latter spreads over three provinces – **Namur** in the west, **Luxembourg** in the south and Liège in the east – and is a great place for hiking and canoeing.

NAMUR

Capital of Namur province, the city of **NAMUR** is a charming place, with an antique centre that boasts a number of first-rate restaurants and bars full of university students. It is also the ideal base from which to explore the Ardennes forest.

WHAT TO SEE AND DO

Straddling the confluence of the rivers Sambre and Meuse, Namur's important strategic location is evidenced by the massive, rambling **citadel** that overlooks the town. One of the largest in Europe, explore it on foot or take the La Citad'n tourist train (daily June to mid-Sept; weekends only mid-Sept to mid-Nov; €2), which departs every twenty minutes from place de l'Ange and rue du Grognon.

At rue de Fer 24 is the **Musée Provincial des Art Anciens** (Provincial Museum of Ancient Arts; Tues–Sun 10am–6pm; €3, audioguide €2), which now houses the Trésor du Prieuré d'Oignies, a spellbinding collection of reliquaries.

In the heart of the old town, at rue Fumal 12, is the **Musée Provincial Félicien Rops** (Tues–Sun 10am–6pm, open Mon July & Aug only; €3, audioguide €2; ⓦ museerops.be). Sexually liberated for his generation, Rops pushed the boundaries in his sketches and paintings – look for his saucy *Les Sataniques* series on the second floor.

A general **market** is held every Saturday on rue de Fer and a flea market every Sunday on quai de la Meuse (both 7am–1pm).

ARRIVAL AND DEPARTURE

By train Namur's train station is 500m north of the centre on place de la Station.

Destinations Brussels (every 30min; 1hr); Luxembourg City (hourly; 1hr 40min); Marloie for La Roche-en-Ardenne (hourly; 35min); Melreux for La Roche-en-Ardenne (hourly; 1hr).

INFORMATION

Tourist information Square Léopold (daily 9.30am–6pm; ☎081 24 64 49, ⓦnamurtourisme.be). There's also a seasonal office (April–Oct daily 9.30am–6pm; ☎081 24 64 48), inside the Halle Al'Chair at rue du Pont 21.

GETTING AROUND

By bike Rent bikes from Maison des Cyclistes inside the train station (€13/day).

By boat From June to Sept Namourette boats taxi passengers across the River Meuse from Grognon to the town of Jambes; €1 one-way. Fifty-minute cruises along the Sambre and Meuse rivers depart from quai des Chasseurs Ardennais (April–June & Sept–Oct 1.30pm, 3pm & 4pm, July–Aug 11am, 1.30pm & 5pm; €6.50).

ACCOMMODATION

Auberge de Jeunesse av Félicien Rops 8 ☎081 22 36 88, ⓦlesaubergedejeunesse.be. This hostel at the southern edge of town offers doubles and three-, four- and five-bed dorms. There's a bar with a terrace overlooking the river, a communal kitchen and another serving breakfast and evening meals (mains €5), TV room, and laundry. It's 3km from the train station: walk along the river or take bus #3 or #4 from the centre (€1.75). Sheets and breakfast included. €3 extra for non-HI members. Dorm €20.60, double €50.20

Gîtes du Vieux Namur rue du Président 32 ☎475 45 76 00, ⓦlesgitesduvieuxnamur.be. Stylish self-catering apartments for stays of two nights or more, located in the centre of old Namur. €85 per night

EATING AND DRINKING

★ **A Table!** rue des Brasseurs 21. Lively café serving organic light bites and veggie options (mains around €13). Tables at the back have views of the Sambre and the citadel. Mon–Wed 11.30am–2.30pm, Thurs–Sat 11.30am–2.30pm & 6.30–9pm.

La Mère Gourmandin rue du Président 13. Serves savoury crêpes from €12 and tumblers of home-made cider. Romantic and candelit at night. Mon–Thurs noon–2pm, Fri & Sat noon–2pm & 6.30–9.30pm.

Piano Bar place Marché-aux-Légumes 10. One of Namur's most popular bars, with live jazz Fri and Sat from 10pm. Mon–Thurs & Sun noon–2am, Fri & Sat noon–4am.

Ursule & Pétula rue de Bruxelles 50. This café specializing in gourmet sandwiches (€4.50) and salads (€6.50) is reassuringly popular with locals. Mon–Fri 10.30am 2pm.

LA ROCHE-EN-ARDENNE

If you've had enough of Belgian cities or flat landscape, head to the **Ardennes** for a change of scene. While its principal town, **La Roche-en-Ardenne**, is packed in the summer (mostly with young families), it remains one of the area's best bases for outdoor activities, and it's easy to escape into the gorgeous surrounding woods. The only downside is that, aside from the town's fairly impressive **castle ruins** (July & Aug daily 10am–6.30pm; April–June, Sept & Oct daily 11am–5pm; Nov–March Mon–Fri 1–4pm; €5), there's not a whole lot to distract you if the weather's bad.

ARRIVAL AND DEPARTURE

By train The nearest stations to La Roche are Marloie and Melreux, both around half an hour away by bus.

By bus Catch bus #3 from Melreux or #15 from Marloie (both: every 2hr; 35min). Passengers are dropped off in the centre of town.

INFORMATION AND TOURS

Tourist information place du Marché 15 (daily 9.30am–5pm, until 6pm July & Aug; ☎084 36 77 36, ⓦla-roche-tourisme.com). Offers internet access.

Ardenne Aventures rue de l'Eglise 35 ☎084 41 19 00, ⓦardenne-aventures.be. Long (€21; 5hr) and short (€16; 1hr 30min) kayak trips year-round, leaving hourly in high season; mountain biking (€25; 4hr); horseriding (€45; 2hr); rafting (Nov–April; €19; 1hr 30min). You can get good rates if you combine two activities on one day.

Brandsport Auberge La Laiterie, Mierchamps 15 ☎084 41 10 84, ⓦwww.brandsport.be. Orienteering (€16.50/half-day); kayaking (€13.50/half-day); caving (€46.50/half-day); archery (€26.50/half-day). Horseriding, abseiling and caving can also be organized.

ACCOMMODATION AND EATING

Camping Le Vieux Moulin Petite Strument 62, about 800m to the south of the town centre along the Val du Bronze ☎084 41 13 80, ⓦstrument.com. Huge campsite with a picturesque setting beside a stream. Open March–Oct 31. €3 per person, plus €9 per tent

La Stradella place du Marché 2. Garish decor, but the wood-fired Italian pizza is worth it. Very central. Daily 11am–3pm & 5–11pm.

Villa Le Monde rue du Nulay 9 ☎0497 21 86 19, ⓦvillalemonde.com. Family-run, travel-themed villa a short walk from the centre of the village, with four en-suite rooms named after songs. Tax €1 per night. Double €73

Luxembourg

Famous as a tax haven, financial centre and headquarters for various European institutions, the **Grand Duchy of Luxembourg**, one of Europe's smallest sovereign states, unsurprisingly gets written off by many travellers. However, this is a mistake: **Luxembourg City** is incredibly charming and well worth visiting for a night or two.

LUXEMBOURG CITY

LUXEMBOURG CITY is one of the most spectacularly situated capitals in Europe. The valleys of the rivers Alzette and Pétrusse, which meet here, cut a green swathe through the city, their deep canyons formerly key to the city's defences.

WHAT TO SEE AND DO

Luxembourg City divides into four distinct sections: the old town (northern side of the Pétrusse valley), which holds most of the city's sights and is the most appealing quarter; the modern city, where the train station is located; the atmospheric valleys of the **Grund** area (east); and the **Kirchberg** section (northeast), home to sleek European Union buildings.

The old town

The UNESCO-listed old town focuses on two squares: the **place d'Armes**, fringed with cafés and restaurants, and the larger **place Guillaume II**, the venue for Luxembourg's main general market (Wed & Sat from 7am). Nearby, on rue du St-Esprit, is the **Musée d'Histoire de la Ville de Luxembourg** (Tues–Sun 10am–6pm, Thurs until 8pm; €5; ⓦmhvl.lu). Levels 0–2 house a permanent exhibition explaining Luxembourg's history, and there's a

glass-walled lift offering dramatic views of the Grund.

A few minutes' walk east of the museum on the montée de Clausen lies the entrance to 17km of underground tunnels known as the **Casemates du Bock** (March–Oct daily 10am–5pm; €3), the earliest of which were excavated in 1644 under Spanish control.

The Grund

The dramatic **chemin de la Corniche** runs along the top of the cliff with great views of the slate-roofed houses of the quaint and leafy **Grund** down below. It leads to the gigantic **Citadelle du St-Esprit**, whose top has been levelled off and partly turned into a verdant park. The Grund is especially worth visiting on Wednesday (when students have a half-day) and Friday nights when its bars kick into action.

Kirchberg

Spread over a large area, the east of the city is largely dominated by European Union buildings; among them, at Park Dräi Eechelen 3, is the **Musée d'Art Moderne Grand-Duc Jean** (Wed–Fri 11am–8pm, Sat–Mon 11am–6pm; €5; ⓦmudam.lu). Down the hill from Mudam, at Park Dräi Eechelen 5, is the new **Musée Dräi Eechelen** (Mon & Thurs–Sun 10am–6pm, Wed 10am–8pm; €5; ⓦm3e.public.lu), a restored fort detailing the Duchy's history.

A good way to see the city is to take the hour-long tours offered by the hop-on, hop-off **sightseeing bus** which leaves from place de la Constitution (April 1–Oct 30 every 20min; €14, valid for 24hr).

ARRIVAL AND DEPARTURE

By train The train station, a 15min walk south of the old town, is the hub of all the city's bus lines. Buses departing from the depot on rue Aldringen will take you back to the train station.
Destinations Brussels (every 30–40min; 2hr 50min); Cologne (hourly; 5hr); Namur (hourly; 1hr 40min); Nancy (every 40min; 1hr 30min); Strasbourg (hourly; 2hr).

INFORMATION

Tourist office place Guillaume II 30 (Mon–Sat 9am–6/7pm, Sun 10am–6pm; ☎022 28 09, ⓦlcto.lu).

Discount card The "muséeskaart" grants access to all city museums, is valid for one or three days and costs €8/12. If travelling outside the capital, the Luxembourg Card grants free entry to 50 museums and tourist attractions in the country and includes free cross-country travel. It is available for 1/2/3 days and costs €11/19/27.

GETTING AROUND

By bike Vél'oh! ⊚veloh.lu. City rental scheme with 72 stations dotted across town. There's a long-term card or a 7-day ticket. Book the latter and you only pay for what you use. Payment with bank card. First 30min free, then €5/24hr.

ACCOMMODATION

There are plenty of cheap hotels around the train station; you'll pay a little more to stay in the more appealing old town – see the tourist information website for listings.
Campsite Kockelscheuer route de Bettembourg 22 ☎ 047 18 15, ⊚ camping-kockelscheuer.jimdo.com; bus #5. A well-equipped campsite 4km/20min bus ride from the city centre, with wi-fi, tennis courts, bowling and golf all available. Open March–Oct 31. **€4** per person, plus **€5** per tent
Luxembourg City-Hostel rue du Fort Olisy 2 ☎ 026 27 66 650, ⊚ youthhostels.lu; bus #9, stop "Umboc". This big, bright HI hostel sits under imposing viaduct arches in the Pfaffenthal district. Offers four- and six-bed dorms (half are en suite) and has a bar-restaurant with terrace, plus a pool table, book exchange and laundry. Shuttle service to/ from station (3km; €3) and airport (6km; €4). €3 extra for non-HI members. Dorm **€23.90**, double **€57.80**

EATING

French cuisine is popular here, but traditional Luxembourgish dishes, such as neck of pork with broad beans (*judd mat gaardebounen*), are found on many menus too.
A La Soupe rue Chimay 9. Trendy soup bar just off place Guillaume II. A bowl plus bread costs €4.50. Mon–Fri 7.30am–7.30pm, Sat 8.30am–7.30pm.
Banana's Bar av Monterey 9. Lively American bar-restaurant whose walls are plastered with old advertising posters. Serves burgers, pastas and salads, all for around

---

★ TREAT YOURSELF

Bodega rue du Curé 5a. Adored by locals, this homely Iberian restaurant has personable service and excellent tapas and steaks. Mains are around €16, but it's worth splashing out. The huge helpings of paella are particularly good, as are the fish and lamb chops. Mon–Sat 11.30am–1am.

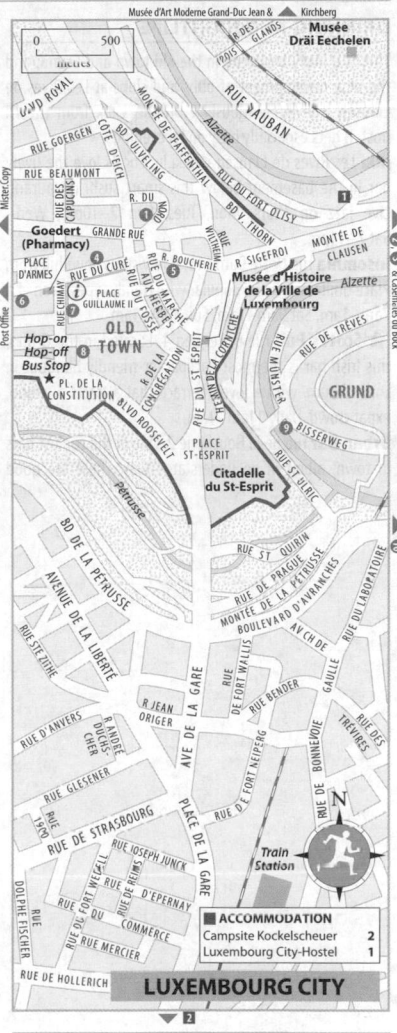

LUXEMBOURG CITY

● EATING		● DRINKING AND NIGHTLIFE	
A La Soupe	7	Ikki	3
Banana's Bar	6	Insomnia	8
Bodega	4	Les Rives de Clausen	2
Chiggeri	1	Scott's Pub	9
D'Artagnan	10	Urban Bar	5

€12. No credit cards. Mon 9am–11pm, Tues–Sat 9am–1am, Sun noon–7pm.
Chiggeri rue du Nord 15. Bohemian bar-restaurant with funky decor. Famous for its *tartiflette* (€20) and 2200-strong wine list that features in the Guinness Book of World Records. Mon–Fri noon–1am, Sat & Sun noon–3am.
D'Artagnan bd du Général Patton 92. Simple restaurant with one winning card: it serves the best horse steak in town (€20.50). Mon noon–2pm, Tues–Fri 7–10pm.

DRINKING AND NIGHTLIFE

There's a lively bar scene in the old town and Grund, and the new development of pubs and clubs at Les Rives de Clausen (rue Emile Mousel 2; 10min walk from the HI hostel) gets especially busy on Fri evenings.

Ikki Les Rives de Clausen ⓦikki.lu. Locals love the lively bar in the basement below this smart sushi restaurant. Live jazz on Thurs. Mon, Tues, Sun 7–10pm, Wed–Sat 7–11pm.

Insomnia rue Notre Dame 15. A few steps downhill from Place Guillaume II and popular with trendy types. Mon–Fri 7am–1am, Sat 9am–1am, Sun 4pm–1am.

★ **Scott's Pub** rue Bisserweg 4. Located in the Grund, this Irish bar is the most backpacker-friendly hangout in Luxembourg, with a lovely terrace that attracts a young, expat crowd. Daily 11am–1am.

Urban Bar rue de la Boucherie 2. One of the coolest bars in town, albeit in an understated way. There are good burgers and a filling dish of the day, and DJs play Wed–Sat. Fri & Sat 11am–2am, Sun–Thurs 11am–1am.

DIRECTORY

Embassies UK, bd Joseph II 5 ☎02 298 64; US, bd Emmanuel Servais 22 ☎04 601 23.

Internet The entire city has a wi-fi network – "Hot City" scratchcards with access codes can be bought from the tourist office (€4.90/2hr; €8.90/48hr). Alternatively, try MisterCopy at bd Prince Henri 9b (Mon–Fri 9am–6pm, Sat 10am–5pm; €6.50/hr).

Luggage storage Located on platform 3CD of the train station (€3/day; daily 6am–9.30pm).

Pharmacies Goedert, place d'Armes 5 (Mon–Sat 8am–6.15pm); um Piquet, rue Aldringen 23 (Mon–Fri 7.30am–6.30pm, Sat 8.30am–1pm).

Post office rue Aldringen 25 (Mon–Fri 7am–7pm, Sat 7am–5pm).

MOSTAR AND NERETVA RIVER

Bosnia-Herzegovina

HIGHLIGHTS

❶ **Sarajevo** One of the friendliest capitals in Europe. **See p.118**

❷ **Jajce** Adorable Bosnian town with a resident waterfall. **See p.122**

❸ **Bihać** Rafting centre focused on the River Una. **See p.123**

❹ **Mostar** Much more than just a bridge. See p.123

❺ **Trebinje** Herzegovina's most appealing town, and another superb bridge. **See p.126**

HIGHLIGHTS ARE MARKED ON THE MAP ON P.115

ROUGH COSTS

Daily budget Basic €25, occasional treat €40

Drink Bosnian coffee €0.50–1

Food *Ćevapčići* (meat rissoles) €2–4

Hostel/budget hotel €12/€25

Travel Bus: Sarajevo–Bihać €25; train: Sarajevo–Mostar €5

FACT FILE

Population 3.9 million

Languages Bosnian, Croatian, Serbian

Currency Convertible Mark (BAM or KM)

Capital Sarajevo

International phone code ☎ 387

Time zone GMT +1hr

Introduction

A land where turquoise rivers run swift and sheep huddle on steep hillsides, Bosnia-Herzegovina is one of Europe's most visually stunning corners. With muezzins calling the faithful to prayer under a backdrop of church bells, it also provides a delightful fusion of East and West in the heart of the Balkans. Appropriately, the country is now marketing itself as the "heart-shaped land", unintentionally revealing more perhaps than just the shape of its borders: this remains a country cleaved into two distinct entities, the result of a bloody war in the mid-1990s. However, while Bosnia-Herzegovina was not too long ago making headlines for all the wrong reasons, it's now busily, and deservedly, re-etching itself on the world travel map as a bona fide backpacker magnet of some repute.

Most travellers spend their time in the country's two major draws: Sarajevo and Mostar. **Sarajevo** has shrugged off its years under siege to become one of Europe's most likeable capitals, while the delightful city of **Mostar** is focused on an Old Bridge that, meticulously rebuilt after destruction during the war, must be the most photographed object in the Balkans. There are also some beguiling smaller towns to choose from, such as Bosnia's **Jajce**, or Herzegovina's **Blagaj**, while outdoor enthusiasts will be in their element in **Bihać**, one of Europe's foremost rafting destinations. **Trebinje** is easily the pick of the towns in the Republika Srpska.

CHRONOLOGY

9 AD Annexed by Rome.
395 Division of Roman Empire; the area that comprises today's Bosnia-Herzegovina stays under the rule of Rome.
553 Emperor Justinian I conquers the area for the Byzantine Empire.
1463 Bosnia falls to the Ottoman Empire.
1482 Herzegovina falls to the Ottoman Empire.
1878 Russian defeat of Turkey sees Bosnia-Herzegovina transferred to Austria-Hungary.
1914 Franz Ferdinand shot in Sarajevo by a Bosnian Serb, eventually leading to World War I.
1918 Bosnia-Herzegovina becomes part of the Kingdom of Serbs, Croats and Slovenes.
1961 Ivo Andrić, born near Travnik, wins the Nobel Prize for Literature.
1984 Sarajevo hosts the Winter Olympics.

1985 Emir Kusturica's film, *When Father Was Away on Business*, set in Bosnia, wins the Palme d'Or at Cannes.
1991 Following fall of Yugoslavia, Croat-Muslim alliance declares independence and makes Sarajevo its capital; Serbs set up their own government just to the east.
1992 Led by Radovan Karadžić, Bosnian Serbs start campaign of "ethnic cleansing".
1993 Fighting breaks out between Croats and Muslims.
1995 NATO shelling ends siege of Sarajevo; peace terms set out by Dayton Agreement.
2001 *No Man's Land* becomes the first Bosnian movie to win an Academy Award.
2008 Radovan Karadžić arrested on charges of war crimes.
2011 Bosnia's Croat, Serb and Muslim political leaders agree to form new central government.
2012 Bosnian Serb military chief Ratko Mladić war crimes trial opens in The Hague.

ARRIVAL AND DEPARTURE

As close to landlocked as it's possible to get, Bosnia-Herzegovina is fairly easy to enter from all sides. There is a daily **train** service from Zagreb in Croatia, which runs through Sarajevo and Mostar en route to Ploče. There are currently no trains from Belgrade or Budapest into Bosnia. **Bus** connections are more numerous and points of origin include Belgrade, Split and Dubrovnik. There are currently no direct **flights** from the UK to Bosnia, but a number of budget carriers fly to Zagreb (see p.159), Zadar (see p.167) and Dubrovnik (see p.178), from where you can get an onward bus.

GETTING AROUND

Bosnia-Herzegovina isn't the easiest country to get around, since much of its transport infrastructure – particularly the rail network – was damaged during the war. Things are improving, however, and decent **bus** services will almost always be able to get you where you want to go; it'll just take a little longer than you might expect – see ⓦbhtourism.ba for schedules. Also note that connections between the Federation and the Republika Srpska aren't regular.

There are also a few **railway** lines across the country, though severe underfunding means that most trains are too slow or irregular to be worth considering; the one exception is the twice-daily route linking Sarajevo and Mostar, which is fabulously scenic.

ACCOMMODATION

There are plenty of **hostels** in both Sarajevo and Mostar (dorm beds costing around €12), as well as **private rooms** in these cities, though they're pretty rare elsewhere. Otherwise, **hotel** accommodation is still pretty cheap in Bosnia-Herzegovina – you should always be able to find a room in the €25–35 range. **Guesthouses** (*pansiona*) are available in some towns, though are nowhere near as numerous as in neighbouring countries. Free **wi-fi** access is now almost standard in all accommodation. There are a few **campsites** dotted around, most with reasonable facilities (ⓦen.camping-info /bosnia-heszegovina). The possible presence of unexploded mines from the war means that wild camping is not a good idea.

A TALE OF TWO ENTITIES

Travellers should be aware that, in many ways, Bosnia-Herzegovina functions as two separate countries. These are not Bosnia and Herzegovina, as one might infer from the name, since these are geographical regions (Bosnia makes up around 80 percent of the country, with Herzegovina a small triangle south of Sarajevo). Rather, the country is split along ethnic lines. To the west, and including Sarajevo, is the **Federation of Bosnia and Herzegovina**, a Muslim-Croat alliance; while to the east and north is the **Republika Srpska**, an ethnic-Serb territory of almost equal size, centred on its capital Banja Luka. To add to the confusion, there are three official languages – all essentially the same – and three presidents. "Most countries just have one idiot in charge", says a local, "but we've got three."

FOOD AND DRINK

Centuries of Ottoman rule have left Turkish fingerprints on the nation's **cuisine**. You'll find *čevapčići* joints everywhere, selling grilled meat rissoles that are usually served up with *somun* (spongy bread) and chopped onion. Similarly hard to avoid are stands selling *burek*, greasy pastries filled with meat, spinach, cheese and sometimes pumpkin or potato; Sarajevo is often rated as the best *burek* city in the Balkans. Soups (*čorba*) and vegetables pop up all over the place on the country's menus, though more often than not the latter are stuffed with mincemeat; **vegetarians** will often have to satisfy themselves with salads, or certain selections from the ubiquitous pizzerias. Sweeties also have a Turkish ring to them, with syrupy *baklava* pastries available everywhere; added to this is an artery-clogging range of creamy **desserts**, most notable of which is *tufahije*, a marinaded apple topped with walnut and cream.

DRINK

The consumption of **coffee** (*kafa*) has been elevated to something approaching an art form (see box opposite). For alcohol, there are a few good domestic **beers** (*pivo*), and Herzegovina produces a lot of **wine** – try Blatina, a local variety of red. There's also *rakia*, a potent spirit as popular by night as coffee is by day. Locals are also fond of telling guests that Bosnian tap water is safe to drink – evidently a major source of pride.

CULTURE AND ETIQUETTE

It's imperative to note that there are three distinct **ethnicities** in Bosnia-Herzegovina – **Bosnian Serb**, mostly Orthodox; **Bosnian Croat**, mostly Catholic; and Muslims known as **Bosniaks**. Of course, all were constituent parts of the bloody war of the mid-1990s; this affected every single person in the country, and reverberations can still be felt today – it's never too far away from people's minds. Some locals are more than willing to talk about their experiences, particularly in Sarajevo, but of course it's best to let them make the first move.

Also worth noting is the **geographical split** evident in the country's name – you'll find yourself using "Bosnian" as an adjective most of the time, and this is accepted, though in Herzegovina it's a *tiny* bit of a faux pas to tell locals how much you're "enjoying Bosnia".

As for the more regular facets of travel etiquette, you should **dress** conservatively around religious buildings, leave small change or a little more as **tips** in a restaurant, and be aware that for all the ethnic rivalry, **smoking** is perhaps the country's dominant religion. Note, too, that most hostels will require you to remove your shoes before entering.

SPORTS AND OUTDOOR ACTIVITIES

Bosnia-Herzegovina is pretty good for outdoor pursuits. Beefy mountains mean that **hiking** is popular, though the continued presence of **landmines** means that you should seek local confirmation that an area is safe before setting off. During winter, a few **ski** slopes around Sarajevo come to life, while there's year-round **rafting** to be had on several of

BOSNIAN COFFEE

Don't dare use the dreaded T-word – although Bosnian coffee is served **Turkish-style**, with hot water poured over unfiltered grounds, locals insist that their variety is unique. It's markedly weaker than Turkish coffee, mainly because of its function as a social lubricant – it's consumed fervidly throughout the day, with different coffee sittings ascribed different terms: *razgalica* in the morning, *razgovoruša* a little later on, and *sikteruša* following a meal. Coffee is **served** on a metal tray from a *džezva*, a cute metal pot, and poured into little tumblers (*fildžan*). Also on the tray will be a *šećerluk*, containing a few cubes of sugar – it's traditional to dip the corner of a sugar cube into your coffee for a flash, nibble it, then let the coffee wash it down. And, most importantly, do as the locals do and take your time.

the country's rushing rivers – the best is the Una, near Bihać.

COMMUNICATIONS

Most **post offices** (*pošta*) are open weekdays from 9am to 5pm, and often on Saturday mornings too. Public **phones** use cards, which can be bought at post offices and kiosks, but it's usually cheaper to make international calls at a post office. **Wi-fi** is common in Sarajevo and Mostar, and where you do find an internet café, expect to pay 1–2KM/hr.

EMERGENCIES

With the war still fresh in many minds, travellers often arrive expecting Bosnia-Herzegovina to be a dangerous place; it will quickly become clear that this is not the case, and that the **crime rate** is very low by European standards. The country's two **police** forces are usually easy to deal with, but keep your passport or a copy handy in case of a spot check. One very important danger to note is the presence of **landmines**. Strewn liberally during the war, the vast majority have now been cleared, and there's no danger in any urban area. In

the countryside, however, it's advisable to stick to clear paths.

Pharmacies usually follow shop hours, though in larger cities you'll find that some stay open until late, and are sometimes open 24 hours.

INFORMATION

Larger cities have **tourist information offices** with plenty of good English materials; some can make accommodation bookings. Free city **maps** are handed out at most hotels and all tourist offices.

MONEY AND BANKS

The currency of Bosnia-Herzegovina is the **convertible mark**, usually abbreviated to KM, though internationally it is BAM. Notes of 5, 10, 20, 50, 100 and 200 KM are in circulation, as are coins of 10, 20 and 50 feninga, and 1, 2 and 5 KM. Exchange **rates** are currently around 1.95KM to the euro, 2.28KM to the pound, and 1.50KM to the US dollar. Accommodation prices are sometimes quoted in euros, as are meals at some upmarket restaurants. In urban areas you won't have to look too far for an **ATM**, and **exchange offices** (*menjačnica*) are plentiful in places used to tourists. **Banks** are usually open weekdays from 9am to 4pm, and often on Saturday mornings too. Credit/debit cards are accepted in most hotels, restaurants and shops.

BOSNIA-HERZEGOVINA ONLINE

Ⓦ **bhtourism.ba** Official tourist board site.
Ⓦ **www.bhmac.org** Contains some useful information about landmine dangers.
Ⓦ **sonar.ba** Excellent site on all things to see and do in Sarajevo.

EMERGENCY NUMBERS

Police ❶ 122; Ambulance ❶ 124; Fire ❶ 123.

4

4

BOSNIAN

The Bosnian language is essentially the same as Serbian, which in turn is essentially the same as Croatian (see p.158), and all three are listed as official languages in Bosnia-Herzegovina. Note that the Republika Srpska uses the **Cyrillic alphabet**, which may cause some problems with street signs, menus and timetables.

OPENING HOURS AND HOLIDAYS

Times are less rigid here than in most countries – **shops** usually open when they want to open, which in most cases is from 10am to 7pm, and in larger cities there's little difference on weekends. All banks and post offices will be closed on **public holidays**: January 1, March 1, May 1 and November 25 – though these dates are far from the end of the story as the Catholic and Orthodox churches celebrate Easter and Christmas at different times, and Muslims celebrate a biannual holiday known as *Bajram*.

Sarajevo

With their imaginations and travel memories fired by spiky minarets, grilled kebabs and the all-pervasive aroma of ground coffee, many travellers see in **SARAJEVO** a Slavic mini-İstanbul. The Ottoman notes in the air are most prominent in Baščaršija, the city's delightful Old Town, which is home to umpteen mosques, bazaars, kebab restaurants and cafés. Further afield, burnt-out buildings evoke the catastrophic war of the mid-1990s, though the fun-loving, easy-going Sarajevans do a great job of painting over the scars of those tumultuous years – it's hard to walk around without being offered coffee, and it's hard to be invited for coffee without making friends.

Sarajevo gained importance during **Roman** times, and after a short slumber was reinvigorated as a trading hub during the **Ottoman** period, but sadly its recent history is far more pertinent. The international spotlight fell on the city as the host of the **1984 Winter Olympics**, but less than a decade later the world's eyes were retrained on it during a **siege** that lasted for almost four years – by some estimates, the longest in military history. Bosnian Serb forces made a near-unbroken ring around the city, shelling major buildings and shooting civilians dead on their way to work, while years of litter lay rotting in the streets. When the ceasefire was announced in 1996, around ten thousand people had been killed; on the ground you may notice some of the many **Sarajevo Roses** – flower-like scars of mortar shell explosions, poignantly filled in with red resin, though now badly fading.

WHAT TO SEE AND DO

The central district of **Baščaršija** is Sarajevo's prettiest and contains most of its sights. Heading west from here, the city's history unravels like a tapestry – Ottoman-era mosques slowly give way to the churches and elaborate buildings of the Austro-Hungarian period, before communist behemoths herald your arrival into "Sniper Alley" and its shells of war.

Baščaršija

The powerful waft of grilled *ćevapi* is a sure sign that you're about to enter **Baščaršija**, whose pedestrianized streets are a delight to wander around, filled to the brim with cafés, snack stands and trinket stalls. It's most logical to approach this district from the east, where you'll find the once-glorious **National Library**. In 1992, a single day's shelling destroyed over three million books, but reconstruction of this pink-and-yellow cream cake of faded beauty is now almost complete. A little way along is the central square, home to **Sebilj**, a small kiosk-like fountain, and **Baščaršija Mosque**. Far more beautiful is the **Gazi Husrev Beg Mosque** just down the way, which is worth a peep inside. Further west, you'll come across the **Bezistan**, an Ottoman-era bazaar now sadly filled with all manner of fake goods unsuited to such an elegant structure.

Baščaršija is also home to the six buildings that make up the **Museum of**

BAŠČARŠIJA

■ ACCOMMODATION

Haris Youth Hostel	1
Hostel City	
Center Sarajevo	4
Hotel Safir	2
Meidan Motel	3
Residence Hostel	5
Traveller's Home	6

● DRINKING & NIGHTLIFE

Baghdad	11
Barhana	4
Cheers!	12
Sarajevo Brewery	14

● EATING

ASDŽ	10
At Mejdan	13
Buregdžinica Bosna	7
Carigrad	6
Ćevabdžinica Petnica	8
Ćevabdžinica Željo	9
Dveri	3
Karuzo	1
Male Daire	5
Maršal Tito	2

Sarajevo – by far the largest is located inside the old Bursa Bezistan bazaar (Mon–Sat 10am–4pm; 2KM), just off the main square, which features a whole host of historical relics, all beautifully presented.

The Latin Bridge and 1878–1918 Museum

Modest in appearance, the **Latin Bridge** has some weighty history behind it – this was the scene of the assassination of Archduke Franz Ferdinand and, by extension, the start of World War I; a plaque on the wall indicates the exact spot where Ferdinand met his fate. Off its northern end, the small, one-room **1878–1918 Museum** (Mon–Fri 10am–6pm, Sat 10am–3pm; 3KM) commemorates the incident, its most significant exhibits being the pistol used by the assassin, Gavrilo Princip, and the subsequent indictment against the perpetrators (there were seven in all). Across the Miljacka River you'll see the fascinating **Papagajka**, a decaying yellow-and-green residential block apparently designed with hovercars in mind – this is how the Jetsons may have lived under Communism.

Ferhadija and around

Along and just off **Ferhadija**, the main pedestrianized thoroughfare, are several points of interest. Dominating the skyline just west of the Bezistan bazaar is the twin-turreted Catholic **cathedral** dating from the 1880s, while, just behind here, along Mula Mustafa Baseskije, stands the **central market place**. It was here, on February 5, 1994, that 68 people were killed following a mortar attack in what became the war's single most infamous incident; a blood red wall is inscribed with the names of all those who died. Adjacent to the cathedral, the superb **Galerija 11/7/95** (daily 10am–7pm; 10KM) is dedicated to the memory of the victims of the 1995 Srebrenica massacre.

"Sniper Alley" museums

Well worth the fifteen-minute walk west of Baščaršija is the **Historical Museum** (Tues–Fri 9am–6pm, Sat & Sun 9am–1pm; 4KM). Don't be put off by the somewhat brutal exterior and shabby entrance, as the permanent exhibition detailing how Sarajevo functioned during the siege is sobering and superbly presented. The exhibits and photos are frequently harrowing, though the most

4

striking aspect is the remarkable resourcefulness Sarajevans displayed, manifest in some ingeniously improvised implements for cooking, lighting, heating and the like. On the other side of the main road stands the **Holiday Inn**, a distinctive yellow building that was the city's only functioning hotel during the siege, and as home to foreign journalists was also one of its safest places.

Of even greater importance during the siege was the tunnel under the airport, part of which is now open as the **Tunnel Museum** which can be visited on daily tours (€12; bookable through hotels or travel agencies). During the siege, Sarajevo's UN-held airport was the only break in the city's surrounding ring of Serb forces – an 800m-long tunnel dug underneath the runways provided, for most locals, the only way into or out of the city. At the museum, you'll be played a home-movie-style DVD that describes the tunnel's creation, and the reasoning behind it, before being led through a small section of the now-collapsed route.

ARRIVAL AND DEPARTURE

By plane Sarajevo's Butmir International Airport is 12km from the city centre, a trip that will cost around 20KM by taxi. Or take tram #3 to the final stop, then hire a cab.

By train The station is located some 1.5km west of Baščaršija. It's a half-hour walk into the centre, a short trip on tram #1, or a 7KM cab ride.

Destinations Mostar (2 daily; 2hr 45min); Zagreb (2 daily; 9hr).

By bus The main bus station is adjacent to the train station. Note that most buses to and from Belgrade (and to other towns in Republika Srpska) use Istočno bus station in the suburb of Dobrinja, in the Serbian part of the city; from here, exit right and walk for some 200m where you catch trolleybus #107 into the centre.

Destinations Belgrade (7 daily; 7hr); Bihać (3 daily; 7hr); Dubrovnik (3 daily; 6hr); Jajce (5 daily; 3hr 30min); Mostar (every 1hr–1hr 30min; 2hr 30min); Novi Sad (4 daily; 8hr); Split (3 daily; 5hr); Travnik (6 daily; 2hr); Zagreb (3 daily; 8hr).

INFORMATION AND TOURS

Tourist information Saraçi 58 (July–Aug daily 10am–10pm; Sept–June Mon–Sat 10am–6pm; ☎ 033 580999, ⓦ sarajevo-tourism.com). You may stumble across a copy of *Sarajevo In Your Pocket*, but failing that, pick up *Sarajevo Navigator*, a useful monthly listings booklet.

Tours Both the *Haris* and *City Center* hostels, as well as numerous agencies, organize tours of surrounding sights, plus "Tunnel Tours" (see above), for about €15.

GETTING AROUND

Public transport An efficient system of buses, trams and trolleybuses operates throughout the city from 5am–1am. Tickets can be bought from a kiosk for 1.60KM, or for 1.80KM from the driver; be sure to validate your ticket on board, as fines are steep and ticket inspectors strict.

Taxis Journey costs start at 2KM, and thereafter it's around 1KM per km; a ride in the centre should cost no more than 5KM.

ACCOMMODATION

The city now has a fair few hostels, though many are unofficial, so best stick to the ones listed here. If you get stuck, dozens of agencies around Baščaršija will be able to set you up with a private room.

HOSTELS

Haris Youth Hostel Vratnik Mejdan 29 ☎ 033 232563, ⓦ hyh.ba. Super-relaxed hostel a 15min walk uphill from the centre. Check in at their office (Mon–Sat 8am–4pm), near the Baščaršija tram stop, and they'll give you a free ride up. Evenings can see anything from barbecues to impromptu guitar sessions. Dorm €15

Hostel City Center Sarajevo Muvekita 2/3 ☎ 033 203213, ⓦ hcc.ba. Extremely clean hostel in a very central location, with four- to ten-bed dorms plus doubles, a cool lounge with PlayStation and musical instruments. Breakfast included. Dorm €14, double €40

Residence Hostel Muvekita 1 ☎ 061 275188, ⓦ residencerooms.com.ba. This large, rambling hostel is more restful than *City Center* across the street, with spacious, high-ceilinged dorms, plus doubles with private bathrooms. Two kitchens for guest use. Breakfast included. Dorm €15, double €40

★ **Traveller's Home** Cumurija 4 ☎ 070 242400, ⓦ myhostel.ba. A warm welcome awaits at this perky hostel near the river, with a good mix of dorms and private rooms, plus kitchen and laundry facilities. Breakfast included. Dorm €15, double €40

HOTELS

Hotel Safir Jagodića 3 ☎ 033 475040, ⓦ hotelsafir.ba. Just north of the Baščaršija tram stop, this quiet, friendly place has eight cool, pastel-coloured rooms, each with a kitchenette, although breakfast is included. Double €72

Mejdan Motel Mustaj-Pašin Mejdan 11 ☎ 033 233563, ⓦ mejdanmotel.com. Nicely tucked into the hillside near the river, this motel feels quite secluded despite its proximity to the centre. Enjoy breakfast on the summery patio. Double €52

EATING

You can't walk more than 10m in Baščaršija without coming across yet another *ćevabdžinica* – note that many do not serve alcohol. *Burek* is similarly easy to hunt down, and many travellers rate it the best in the Balkans.

CAFÉS

At Mejdan Obala Isa Bega Ishakovića. Set in, around and on top of a park-centre pavilion near the Latin Bridge, this is a great place for coffee on a summer's day. Daily 8am–10pm.

Carigrad Sarači 111. Mouthwatering selection of rich cakes, syrupy *baklava* and other sweet sins from just 1.50KM. Note that said desserts actually look bigger on your plate than they do behind the counter. Daily 9am–10pm.

Male Daire Luledina bb. Peace-out café just behind the Baščaršija Mosque, where you can throw down good Bosnian coffee for 1.50KM, and suck on a *nargileh* for just 5KM. Daily 8am–11pm.

Maršal Tito Bihaćka 19. Military-themed café-bar tucked under a wing of the Historical Museum. With socialist realist pictures on the inside and a gunship sitting outside, it's an interesting place to drink and chat. Daily 10am–midnight.

RESTAURANTS

ASDŽ Mali Ćurčiluk 3. Curiously named canteen-style restaurant with rows of simple, tasty local staples to choose from, usually costing around 6KM a plate. Daily 8am–7pm.

Buregdžinica Bosna Bravadžiluk 9. With something as simple as *burek*, there should be very little to choose between purveyors, but the ones on offer here are simply a cut above the rest. Try the pumpkin (*tykva*) variety, with lashings of sour yoghurt (8KM). Daily 7am–10pm.

★ **Ćevabdžinica Petica** Bravadžiluk 21. If you must plump for just one *ćevabdžinica*, make it this one: unlike some places, meats (7KM) are grilled to order, and the service is snappy. Daily 8am–10pm.

Ćevabdžinica Željo Kundurdžiluk 12. Other Baščaršija kebab joints may be a little more polished, but this pair – close by each other – are always packed with locals, who know that they provide the most bang for their buck. 7KM for ten *kebapči* and *somun* (spongy pitta bread). Daily 8am–10pm.

Dveri Prote Bakovića 12. Nicely secreted away, this traditional Bosnian restaurant has a beautifully decorated interior, and the food is heavenly – try the polenta with smoked beef and sour cream (11KM). Daily 9am–11pm.

Karuzo Dženetića Ćikma bb. It's nice to see a chef avoid culinary pigeonholes. Karuzo's Saša brings together meat-free dishes whose variety defies explanation, and sushi (20KM). Somehow, it seems to work. Mon–Fri noon–3pm & 6–11pm, Sat 6–11pm.

DRINKING AND NIGHTLIFE

Sarajevo has a fair few quirky underground bars, which come and go with alarming regularity, so ask around. Locals go out late – most bars only start filling up after midnight, and all these places kick on until 1 or 2am at least.

Baghdad Bazerdžani 6. The white drapes, soft red lighting and mosaic lanterns ensure that, if nothing else, this is probably the best-looking bar in Sarajevo: a relaxing spot for a beer or cocktail, plus DJ sets at weekends.

Barhana Djugalina 8. Set in a tucked-away courtyard, this groovy little bar is the place to come, above all, for a decent rakija. Try to bag one of the candlelit outdoor tables.

Cheers! Muvekita 4. The main reason why those staying at Muvekita's various hostels don't get too much sleep – if you can't beat 'em, join 'em. Raucous fun and regular live music.

Sarajevo Brewery Franjevačka 15. If you like Sarajevsko Pivo, why not head straight for the source? Their city-centre factory has a large, ornate bar out back, where it costs 5KM for a large glass of the good stuff. It's also more or less the only place in which you can try their delicious dark variety.

ENTERTAINMENT

Bosnian Cultural Centre Branilaca Sarajeva 24 ⓦ bkc .ba. Large concert venue.

Chamber Theatre 55 Maršala Tita 56 ⓦ kamernlteatar55 .ba. Homely place used for experimental theatre productions, though rarely in English.

Kinoteka BiH Alipašina 19 ⓦ kinotekabih.ba. Interesting mix of subtitled movies shown weekdays at 7pm.

National Theatre Obala Kilina Bala. The largest theatre in the country, and home to Sarajevo's opera and ballet academies.

4

FESTIVALS IN SARAJEVO

Baščaršija Nights ⓦ bascarsijskenoci.ba. Ballet, theatre, music and art exhibitions throughout July.

Jazz Fest ⓦ jazzfest.ba. Excellent jazz festival, with some stellar names, usually held in November.

MESS ⓦ mess.ba. International, English-centred festival of theatre in October.

Sarajevo Film Festival ⓦ sff.ba. In August, this is now one of the most prestigious film festivals in Europe, and largely focused on the region's own output.

Saravejo Winter ⓦ sarajevskazima.ba. Artistic festival (music, film, visual and performing arts) each February.

Sarajevo War Theatre Gabelina 16. Hosts a fascinating clutch of performances from home and abroad.

SHOPPING

Most useful to travellers is a small area around Mula Mustafa Bašeskije, where you'll find a couple of appealing markets – indoor and outdoor – and a few secondhand clothing stores. One recommended souvenir purchase is a Bosnian coffee set: while whole teams of Baščaršija stands sell cheap ones, Sprečo, at Kovači 15 (Mon–Sat 9am–6pm), offer beautiful hand-made copper-and-tin sets for €30. Also try tracking down Butik Badem on Abadžiluk, which doles out superb Turkish sweets, dried mulberries, and a lot more besides.

DIRECTORY

Embassies and consulates Canada, Grbavička 4 ☎ 033 222033; UK, Tina Ujevića 8 ☎ 033 282200; US, Alipašina 43 ☎ 033 445700.
Hospital Kranjčevićeva 12 ☎ 033 208100.
Internet There's free wi-fi outside the tourist office and increasingly throughout Baščaršija, or try Click Café at Kundurdžiluk 1 (Mon–Fri 9am–9pm; 3KM/hr).
Money Banks and ATMs are everywhere, though there are only a couple of exchange offices in Baščaršija.
Pharmacy Obala Kulina 7 (☎033 272300; daily 8am–8pm) and Zelenih Beretki 28 (☎ 033 626200; Mon–Sat 9am–8pm).
Post office Zmaja od Bosne 88 (Mon–Sat 7am–8pm).

Bosnia

Occupying roughly four-fifths of the country, mountainous Bosnia contains some of the country's most appealing towns, and helpfully all can be visited on a fairly straight route linking Sarajevo and Zagreb. First up, get a sense of medieval history in **Travnik**, Bosnia's former capital, then head to **Jajce**, a tiny town with a waterfall crashing through its centre. Lastly there's laidback **Bihać**, one of Europe's best rafting hotspots.

TRAVNIK

Just a couple of hours out of Sarajevo, **TRAVNIK** is a good day-trip target, though its position on a main transport route detracts slightly from a delightful setting. This was the **Bosnian capital** during the latter part of Ottoman rule, and the residence of high-ranking officials known as viziers – you'll see their tombs (*turbe*) dotted around town. Travnik also gained fame as the birthplace of Ivo Andrić, a Nobel Prize-winning novelist whose *Bosnian Chronicle* was set in his hometown.

The best place to soak up Travnik's history is its majestic fifteenth-century **castle** (10am–6pm; 2KM), built to hold off Ottoman forces but completed a few years too late. It's now great for a clamber around, and provides spectacular views of the surrounding mountains. Just under the castle is **Plavna Voda**, a quiet huddle of streamside **restaurants** where you can eat trout caught further upstream.

JAJCE

Whereas Travnik has grown a little too busy for its size, little **JAJCE** is simply adorable – even its name is cute, a diminutive form of the word "egg", and therefore translating as something like "egglet". The name is said to derive from the shape of an egg jutting up in the Old Town, ringed with walls and topped with an impressive **citadel**. In the Middle Ages, Bosnian kings were crowned just down the hill in the **Church of St Mary** (open to the public); the last coronation, of Stjepan Tomašević, took place here in 1461, but two years later the king had his head lopped off during the Ottoman invasion. Opposite the church are the **catacombs** (no set opening hours; 1KM), essentially an underground church, complete with a narthex, nave, presbytery and baptistry; if you're lucky, you'll find the keyholder in the restaurant opposite. Further downhill, the 21m-high **waterfalls** are a splendid sight, despite the pounding they took during the Bosnian conflict.

ACCOMMODATION AND EATING

Stari Grad Old Town ☎ 030 654006, ⊛ jajcetours.com. One of very few places to stay in Jajce, this lovely hotel, slap-bang in the Old Town, offers tastefully furnished singles, doubles and some suites, all air-conditioned. Breakfast included. Double **€41**
Vodopad Old Town. As with accommodation, there are very few places to eat and drink, but this fun place just

RAFTING IN NORTHWEST BOSNIA

Rafting in the Bihać area is possible year-round – the continuous flow of tourist traffic means that you'll usually be able to join a group (6–10 per boat) in any month, though the main season runs from March to October. Six kilometres from town, **Una Kiro** (☎037 361110, ⓦuna-kiro-rafting.com) is the best established company for foreigners, and has a camping ground next to their base. There are three main routes to choose from; listed per-person prices include equipment and transport, but not meals.

Kostela-Bosanska Krupa An easy 24km, 5hr stretch that's best for novices; €37.

Kostela-Grmuša Short, but packs in some meaty rapids on a 13km, 4hr course; €27.

Štrbački Buk-Lohovo An absolutely terrifying 15km, 4hr route featuring a 25m rapid; €43.

---

inside the gates doles out colossal double-scoop ice creams for just 1.5KM; if the weather's hot don't expect to get through the whole thing before it melts.

BIHAĆ

Herzegovina has no shortage of great **rafting** locales, but Bosnia's **BIHAĆ** beats them all. The crystal-clear **River Una** rushes through town, though it's a little further upstream that you'll find the best rafting; the river is highest in the spring and autumn. Adventure sports aside, Bihać is a pleasant, compact town with a cheerful pedestrianized zone in the centre. Here you'll find the **Church of Zvonik** and **Fathija Mosque**, both visitable, but most interesting is the **Captain's Tower**, once a prison, now a museum (Mon–Fri 9am–4pm, Sat 9am–2pm Sat, closed Sun; 1KM).

ACCOMMODATION

Villa Una ☎037 311393, ⓦvilla-una.com. Great location down by the river, and owned by the same outfit who run local rafting tours, this super value place has a combination of standard and superior rooms, though all are spotlessly clean. Breakfast included. Double €38

Herzegovina

Wedged into the far south of the country, little Herzegovina is less known than its big brother, Bosnia, but this land of muscular peaks and rushing rivers arguably has more to see. Pride of place goes to **Mostar** and its famed Old Bridge, but it's worth venturing outside the city to see little **Blagaj**, or to absorb the religious curiosities of **Međugorje**. Those

on their way to Dubrovnik or Montenegro should also call in at **Trebinje**, by far the most pleasant town in the Republika Srpska.

MOSTAR

On arrival at the train or bus station, you may be forgiven for thinking that the beauty of **MOSTAR** has been somewhat exaggerated. There then begins a slow descent to the Old Town, during which it becomes more and more apparent that it really is a very special place indeed. Attentive ears will pick out rushing streams, salesmen crying their wares, as well as church bells and *muezzins* competing for attention, while steep, cobblestoned streets slowly wind their way down to the fast-flowing, turquoise-blue Neretva River and its Old Bridge, incredibly photogenic even when the Speedo-clad *mostari* – the brave gents who dive from the apex – aren't tumbling into the waters below. The city is becoming ever more popular with tourists, though the dearth of high-end accommodation means that most visit on a day-trip – bad news for anyone on the Old Bridge around lunchtime, though great news for anyone staying the night; the best time to come is first thing in the morning or early evening.

Mostar's history is irrevocably entwined with that of its bridge. Like hundreds of locals, this was to fall victim in 1993 when the Croats and Muslims of the town, previously united against the Serbs, turned on each other: the **conflict** rumbled on for two long years, each side sniping at the other from opposing hills.

4

THE OLD BRIDGE

Transit point, dungeon, tourist attraction, war victim and macho launchpad, Mostar's small, hump-backed **Stari Most** has led an interesting life. With tradesmen terrified by the rickety nature of its wooden predecessor and the fast-flowing Neretva below, it was built in the 1560s at the instigation of Suleyman the Magnificent. Those employed to guard the bridge were called the **mostari**, a term later borrowed when naming the city, and then used to describe the men who dive from the apex, 21m down into the Neretva. After 427 years in service, the bridge was strategically destroyed by Croat forces in November 1993, symbolizing the ethnic division of the city. There then began the arduous process of rebuilding it piece by piece, using new materials but following the same techniques used in its initial construction, before it reopened in 2004. The *mostari* are still there, day after day; they'll try to work the crowd into shelling out an acceptable fee – typically around €25 – before taking the plunge. Join them if you dare, especially in July, when the annual **diving festival** marks the highlight of Mostar's year.

Locals claim that, prior to the war, more than half of the city's marriages were mixed, but the figure has since dwindled to nothing; while relations are now much improved, the truce remains uneasy.

WHAT TO SEE AND DO

The **Old Town**, spanning both sides of the Neretva, contains most things of interest in Mostar, and in its centre is the **Old Bridge**, focal point of the city and the obvious place to kick off your sightseeing. On the eastern bank is the more interesting Muslim part of town, while the west is mainly home to Catholic Croats.

The east bank

Lined with trinket stores, cobblestoned Kujundžiluk climbs uphill, soon leading to the **Koski Mehmed Paša Mosque** (sunrise–sunset). For all its beauty, the panoply of souvenir sellers shows that tourism, rather than religious endeavour, is the current priority; eschew the 8KM it costs to climb the minaret and instead head down to the terrace where you can get superb head-on views of the bridge. Passing another mosque, the road segues quickly into modern Mostar, though pay attention to signs pointing out the **Turkish House** (irregular hours; 2KM) on your left, a fascinating peek into the Ottoman traditions of yesteryear. Above Kujundžiluk you'll see the **Cejvan Cehaj Mosque**, Mostar's oldest, on the way to the **Museum of Herzegovina** (Mon–Fri 9am–2pm, Sat 10am–noon; 2KM).

Between the two lies a Muslim **graveyard**, and it's hard not to be moved when you notice that almost everybody laid to rest here died the same year, 1993.

Old Bridge Museum

Off the eastern end of the bridge is **Helebija**, a tower that now accommodates the enlightening **Old Bridge Museum** (daily except Mon 10am–6pm; 5KM), spread over four levels, and topped with a viewing point. Of most interest is the archeological section, where you can see some of the few remaining chunks of the bridge that weren't swept away, alongside footage of its painstaking rebirth. There's sobering archive footage of the bridge's downfall in the neighbouring **Old Bridge Gallery**, which also stocks a superb range of books on the war and the history of Bosnia in English.

The west bank

Tara, the bridge's western tower, was once a dungeon into which prisoners were thrown to die, either from injury, starvation or – in rainy season – drowning. It's now the base of the diving club, and the **War Photo Exhibition** (daily: June–Sept 9am–9pm; April, May, Oct & Nov 11am–6pm; 6KM), an array of startling shots taken during the troubles by Kiwi photographer Wade Goddard. Just 22 at the time, Goddard spent this period with a family inside the Old Town, wandering the streets to document the hardships. A little zigzagging will bring you to the **Crooked Bridge**

– apparently built as a warm-up for the big boy, and almost as pleasing; although it (just about) remained standing during the war, it did finally collapse in 1999 due to flooding. Further along is the **Tabhana**, a former bathhouse now filled with bars and restaurants. Continue to the end of the street and you'll eventually reach Bulevar, the main road that, during the war, served as the **front line** – still today, the road is lined with a succession of battered buildings.

ARRIVAL AND DEPARTURE

By train The station is in an ugly area to the east of town, a 20min walk from the Old Bridge.
Destinations Sarajevo (2 daily; 2hr 45min).
By bus The station is next to the train station.
Destinations Dubrovnik (5 daily; 4hr); Sarajevo (hourly; 2hr 30min); Trebinje (3 daily; 3hr 30min).

INFORMATION AND TOURS

Tourist office Rade Bitange 5, behind the Tabhana, just west of the Old Bridge (daily: June–Aug 9am–9pm; May & Sept 9am–5pm; ☎ 033 580833, ⓦ turizam.mostar.ba). Limited information available but they can help organize private accommodation.
Tours The high-octane Bata, from *Hostel Majdas* (see below), runs jam-packed full-day tours for €27/ person, including hiking and diving in areas unreachable on public transport – guests usually come back in the late evening covered in sweat and mud, yet happy as Larry.

ACCOMMODATION

The tourist office can help to organize private rooms, which cost €10–25/person depending upon the season, room size and proximity to the Old Bridge.
★ **Hostel Majdas** Pere Lazetića 9 ☎ 061 382940, ⓦ hostelmajdas.com. Friendly, cosy and within easy reach of the stations and the Old Town, this is Mostar's best hostel by a long way. They are four fresh and colourful rooms, a homely lounge and pretty courtyard where guests gather to chat and drink. Moreover, their day-long tours (see above) are astonishingly good. Breakfast included. Dorm €12, double €25
Hostel Nina Celebića 18 ☎ 061 382743. Around 400m from the bridge, on the east bank, this modern, almost apartment-like building has spotless a/c dorms and double rooms. Trout barbecues are often organized in the garden. Station pick-ups and drop-offs on request. Dorm €10, double €30
Kriva Cuprija Crooked Bridge ☎ 036 550953, ⓦ motel -mostar.ba. High-quality rooms beside the rushing waters that surge beneath the Crooked Bridge – make sure that

★ **TREAT YOURSELF**
Muslibegović House Osman Dikića 41 ☎ 036 551379, ⓦ muslibegovichouse.com. A rare and surprisingly affordable chance to stay in a national monument – this home has been in the hands of the noble Muslibegović family for over 300 years. Twelve rooms renovated with tasteful, individual designs, though a strong Ottoman theme prevails throughout; double €90, suites €10 extra.

you're based in this one, and not their sister hotel of the same name, on the other side of the river. Excellent restaurant attached (see below). Double €70
Pansion Oscar Onešćukova 33 ☎ 036 580237. Nicely positioned on the edge of the Old Town (west bank), the a/c rooms at this guesthouse are perfectly adequate for the price; some with bathroom, some without. Breakfast included. Double €30

EATING AND DRINKING

Try to avoid eating noon–2pm, which is when the tour groups are led to their pre-booked seats for pre-cooked meals.
Ali Baba East bank. The word "cavernous" is often misused, but this quirky place – café, bar and club all at once – is housed, literally, in a cave. It's the liveliest place in town of an evening, and summer months see DJs come in to spin some vinyl. The "Ali Baba" sign is on the little-used road entrance (the tunnel leading to it is worth a peek); the one at the lower entrance says "Open Sesame!".
★ **Hindin Han** Jusovina bb. Just off Onešćukova and picturesquely set high above the water with a flower-bedecked terrace, the fine menu here comprises traditional Balkan grilled meats alongside trout, stuffed squid, seafood risotto (14KM) and the like. Daily 11am–11pm.
Kriva Cuprija Crooked Bridge. Excellent value, considering the quality of the food, and an excellent location under the Crooked Bridge. Fresh trout with salad and a berry sauce will cost just 10KM, or try the "Hercegovinan Plate" of rice, lamb and potatoes for only a little more.
Palma Burek Alekse Šantića 13. The best *burek* in town, no question, with meat, cheese or spinach fillings and a dollop of yoghurt (3KM); the café to the rear doles out coffee, big slices of cake and ice cream. Mon–Sat 7am–11pm, Sun 5–11pm.
Štrbački West bank. Okay, so it's a tourist trap, as evidenced by the traditionally uniformed staff. But it's a very nice trap to fall into, since the food's excellent, and fairly priced to boot: try the stuffed peppers for 8KM. In addition, it's one of the few places in the Old Town to serve proper Bosnian coffee.

4

EXCURSIONS FROM MOSTAR

Using Mostar as a base, you have a whole slew of destinations to choose from. Unfortunately, the paucity of public transport means that it's tough to see more than one in a day, and some places aren't accessible at all: often your best option is to visit on a **tour** from Mostar.

Blagaj

Closest to Mostar is the village of **BLAGAJ**, just 12km to the east and accessible by local buses #10, #11 and #12 (7 services a day; 40min; 4KM return). Once you disembark, carry straight ahead through the town to the **Tekija** (daily 10am–6pm). Huddled into a niche in the cliff face, this wonky wooden building was once the residence of dervishes, and the interior – prayer rooms, washroom and kitchen – are all suitably spartan. The *hammam*, meanwhile, remains as it was. Right next to it, a never-ending torrent of water gushes out of the cliff, apparently reaching levels of 43,000 litres per second; some of this is skimmed off to make tea and coffee, which you can order at the adjacent terrace for just 1.5KM, including a chunk of *lokum* (Turkish delight).

Međugorje

Twenty-six kilometres south of Mostar is the curious village of **MEĐUGORIJE**, a mere non-entity until June 1981, when a group of teenagers claimed to have been spoken to by the **Virgin Mary** here. Unlike Lourdes and Fatima, this has not been officially recognized by the Vatican, but that doesn't stop pilgrims arriving in such numbers that there are now thousands of rooms available to accommodate them. The main sights here are the **Church of St James** and the nearby "Weeping Knee" statue, so named as it apparently flouts the laws of thermodynamics by dribbling out a constant flow of fluid. You can reach here on local bus #48 from Mostar, though – get this – they don't run on Sundays.

Počitelj and the Kravice Waterfalls

A few kilometres south of Međugorije is the hillside village of **POČITELJ**, one of the most traditional in Herzegovina. The place is quite stunning, and dotted with remnants from the fifteenth century, most notably a citadel and a terrific mosque. Unfortunately there are no direct buses here, so it's best to join a tour. Groups will likely swing through to see the nearby **Kravice Waterfalls**, which are not accessible on public transport. High, wide and handsome, the pool below is a great place for a dip.

TREBINJE

The Republika Srpska's most appealing town by a country mile, **TREBINJE** is tucked into Herzegovina's southern extremity, and its proximity to Dubrovnik and the Montenegrin border makes it the ideal start or finish line to a race through the country. It's most famed for the sixteenth-century **Arslanagić Bridge** – a longer version of the one in Mostar – which sits a ten-minute walk from the town centre; in what must have been quite a feat, it was moved here, stone by stone, from the village of Arslanagić some 5km away, in 1972.

Back in the centre is the **Old Town**, a pretty warren of streets now largely filled with cafés; better yet for coffee-slurping is elegant **Jovan Dučić Trg**, home to a daily market and almost totally cloaked with maple leaves (*platani*).

There are also a couple of still-functioning **hilltop monasteries**, notably fourteenth-century Tvrdoš 6km west of Trebinje, which are a delight to roam around and well worth the climb.

INFORMATION

Tourist office Jovan Dučić bb (Mon–Fri 8am–6pm, Sat 9am–3pm; ☏ 059 273410, ⊛ trebinjeturizam.br).

ACCOMMODATION, EATING AND DRINKING

Azzovo Stari Grad 14. Cosy, blues- and jazz-orientated bar that's pretty much the most popular meeting place in town. Daily 8am–11pm.
Hotel Platani Cvijetni trg 1 ☏ 059 270420, ⊛ hotel -platani-trebinje.com. Named after the huge plane trees on the square, this imposing stone building is by far the best place to stay in town, and very reasonably priced too. Breakfast included. Double **€50**

RILA MONASTERY

Bulgaria

HIGHLIGHTS

❶ **Aleksandar Nevski Cathedral, Sofia** The capital's most striking building. **See p.135**

❷ **Rila Monastery** Fabulous frescoes deep in the mountains. **See p.139**

❸ **Bansko** Skiing and snowboarding on the cheap, plus cosy traditional pubs. **See p.140**

❹ **Plovdiv's Old Quarter** Ornate Ottoman houses and Roman remains. **See p.142**

❺ **The Black Sea Coast** White sand, watersports and beach bars. **See p.148**

HIGHLIGHTS ARE MARKED ON THE MAP ON P.129

ROUGH COSTS

Daily budget Basic €25, occasional treat €40

Drink Beer (0.5l) €1

Food *Shopska* salad €3

Hostel/budget hotel €10/€25

Travel Train: Sofia–Plovdiv €5; bus: €5

FACT FILE

Population 7.3 million

Language Bulgarian

Currency Lev (Lv)

Capital Sofia

International phone code ☎ 359

Time zone GMT +2hr

5

Introduction

With dramatic mountain ranges, superb beaches, numerous historic towns and a web of working villages with traditions straight out of the nineteenth century, Bulgaria has a wealth of attractions crammed into a relatively compact country. More than anything else, this is a land of adventures: once you step off the beaten track, road signs and bus timetables often disappear (or are only in Cyrillic), and few people speak a foreign language, but almost everyone you meet will be determined to help you on your way.

Bulgaria's image has altered dramatically in recent years, thanks largely to the modernization of the country's tourist infrastructure coupled with soaring foreign interest in inexpensive rural and coastal properties. Independent travel is common: costs are relatively low, and for the committed there is much to take in. Romantic National Revival era architecture, featuring timber frames and floral motifs, is a particular draw, with **Koprivshtitsa**, **Bansko** and **Plovdiv** foremost among examples of the genre. The monasteries are stunning, too – the finest, **Rila**, should be on every itinerary, while for city life aim for **Sofia**, **Plovdiv**, and the cosmopolitan coastal resorts of **Varna** and **Burgas**.

CHRONOLOGY

4000s BC Thracian tribes settle in the area of present-day Bulgaria.
600s BC Greeks settle in the area of present-day Bulgaria.
100s AD Romans invade the Balkan Peninsula.
200 A popular Roman amphitheatre draws people to Serdica (Sofia).
681 The First Bulgarian Kingdom is formed.
864 Bulgaria accepts the Orthodox Church.
1018 The country falls under Byzantine control.
1185 The Byzantines are repelled and the Second Bulgarian Kingdom is proclaimed.
1396 The Ottomans conquer Bulgaria, ushering in almost five hundred years of Turkish rule.
1876 Revolutionaries based at Koprivshtitsa carry out the ill-fated April Rising, which provokes savage Ottoman reprisals.
1877 War of Liberation sees Russia declare war on Turkey to win freedom for Bulgaria.
1886 The Treaty of Bucharest ends the Serbo-Bulgarian war begun the previous year, and Bulgaria gains territory.

1908 Bulgaria declares itself an independent kingdom.
1912 First Balkan War; Bulgaria sustains heavy losses in victory over the Ottomans.
1913 Second Balkan War; previous allies Serbia and Greece defeat Bulgaria.
1914–18 Bulgaria sides with the Central Powers during World War I.
1945 Soviet army invades German-occupied areas of Bulgaria.
1954 Todor Zhivkov becomes head of the Bulgarian Communist Party in power.
1989 Zhivkov ousted among calls for democratization.
1991 New constitution proclaims Bulgaria a Parliamentary Republic.
2001 Former king Simeon II is elected Prime Minister.
2004 Bulgaria joins NATO.
2007 Bulgaria joins the EU.
2009 Zhivkov's former bodyguard, Boiko Borisov, is elected Prime Minister.
2013 Borisov resigns following nationwide protests against poor living standards, rising energy costs, and corruption.

ARRIVAL AND DEPARTURE

The majority of tourists arrive at either of Sofia's two airport terminals, although in summer many fly directly to the coastal cities of Varna and Burgas on charter flights. Frequent **low-cost flights** from London and other European cities to Sofia are provided by easyJet and Wizz Air, which also has summer services to Varna and Burgas. The national carrier Bulgaria Air (⟨⟩air.bg) serves most of Europe but there are no direct flights to or from North America or Australasia.

Bulgaria has land borders with five countries and reliable international **rail** links. Popular routes include from

BULGARIA

HIGHLIGHTS
1. Alexsandar Nevski Cathedral, Sofia
2. Rila Monastery
3. Bansko
4. Plovdiv's Old Quarter
5. The Black Sea Coast

Bucharest to Veliko Tarnovo (5–6hr) or to Sofia (11hr), and from Thessaloniki to Sofia (10hr), while trains from İstanbul traverse the country, stopping at Plovdiv (11hr) and Sofia (14hr) before continuing to Belgrade. Eurolines (ⓦwww.eurolines .bg) runs frequent **bus** services to Sofia from many major European cities and has booking offices in Sofia, Plovdiv, Varna and Burgas.

GETTING AROUND

Public transport in Bulgaria is inexpensive but often slow and not always clean or comfortable. Travelling by **bus** (*avtobus*) is usually the quickest way of getting between major towns and cities. Generally, you can buy tickets (*bileti*) at the bus station (*avtogara*) at least an hour in advance when travelling between towns, but on some routes they're only sold when the bus arrives. On rural routes, tickets are often sold by the driver.

Bulgarian State Railways (BDZh; ⓦbdz .bg) can get you to most towns; trains are punctual and fares low. Express services (*ekspresen*) are restricted to main routes, but on all except the humblest branch lines you'll find so-called Rapid (*burz vlak*) trains. Where possible, use these rather than the snail-like *patnicheski* services. Long-distance or overnight trains have reasonably priced couchettes (*kushet*) and/or sleepers (*spalen vagon*). For these, on all expresses and many rapids, you need **seat reservations** (*zapazeni mesta*) as well as tickets (*bileti*). To ensure a seat in a non-smoking carriage (*myasto za nepushachi*), you will have to specify this when booking. **International tickets** must be bought in advance from the BDZh-Rila office located within stations. Most stations have **left luggage** offices (*garderob*). InterRail and Balkan Flexipass are valid, although it often works out cheaper to buy rail tickets as you go.

5

Cycling in Bulgaria's cities is becoming increasingly popular as cycle lane networks expand, while the country's quiet minor roads linking towns and villages are a delight. Of the few bike rental outfits in Bulgaria, Zig-Zag Holidays in Sofia (⍟zigzagbg.com) is one of the most reliable and also runs organized tours.

ACCOMMODATION

Decent **hostels** charging around 20Lv for a dorm bed and 50–70Lv for double rooms can be found in Sofia, Plovdiv, Veliko Turnovo, Burgas and Varna. Budget **hotels** rent doubles from around 50Lv, a little more in Sofia and Plovdiv, while cosier family-run hotels with similar prices are common on the coast and in touristy towns such as Koprivshtitsa and Bansko.

The best **campsites** (*kamping*; summer only) are dotted along the coast. Campers are charged individually (around 9Lv per person) and two-person chalets (30–40Lv per night) are usually available. Camping rough is technically illegal and punishable with a fine, though authorities usually turn a blind eye. A number of hostels also offer camping space.

FOOD AND DRINK

Sit-down meals are eaten in either a **restorant** (restaurant) or a **mehana** (tavern). There's little difference between the two, save that a *mehana* is likely to offer folksy decor and a wider range of traditional Bulgarian dishes. Wherever you go, you're unlikely to spend more than 25Lv for a main course, salad and drink. The best-known traditional dish is *gyuvech* (which literally means "earthenware dish"), a rich stew comprising peppers, aubergines and beans, to which is added either meat or meat stock. *Kavarma*, a spicy meat stew (either pork or chicken), is prepared in a similar fashion. **Vegetarian meals** (*yastia bez meso*) are hard to obtain, although there is always a plentiful range of salads. *Gyuveche* (a variety of *gyuvech* featuring baked vegetables), *kachkaval pane* (cheese fried in breadcrumbs) and *chuskhi byurek* (baked peppers stuffed with egg and rice) are worth trying.

Foremost among **snacks** are *kebapcheta* (grilled sausages), or variations such as *shishche* (shish kebab) or *kyofteta* (meatballs). Another favourite is the *banitsa*, a flaky-pastry envelope with a filling – usually cheese – sold by bakeries and street vendors in the morning and evening. Elsewhere, *sandvichi* (sandwiches) and *pitsi* (pizzas) dominate the fast-food repertoire. Bulgarians consider their **yogurt** (*kiselo mlyako*) the world's finest, and hardly miss a day without consuming it.

DRINK

The quality of Bulgarian **wines** is constantly improving. Among the best reds are the heavy, mellow Melnik, and rich, dark Mavrud, while Dimyat is a good dry white. If you prefer the sweeter variety, try Karlovski Misket (Muscatel) or Traminer. Cheap native **spirits** are highly potent: *mastika* (like Greek *oúzo*) is drunk diluted with water; *rakiya* – brandy made from either plums (*slivova*) or grapes (*grozdova*) – is generally sipped, accompanied by salad. Bulgarian **beer** is as good as any, but local brands such as Kamenitza, Zagorka and Shumensko must now compete with the likes of Staropramen, Stella Artois and Heineken, which are brewed locally under licence.

Coffee (*kafe*) usually comes *espresso* style. **Tea** (*chai*) is nearly always herbal – ask for *cheren chai* (literally "black tea") if you want the real stuff, normally served with lemon.

CULTURE AND ETIQUETTE

Bulgarians are predominantly Orthodox Christian; Muslims of Turkish descent make up around nine percent of the population. Social etiquette in Bulgaria is still rather formal: shaking someone's hand is the most common form of **greeting** and you should address someone with their title and surname unless you know them well. It is appropriate to wait for the Bulgarian person to decide when

5

BODY LANGUAGE

Bulgarians shake their heads when they mean "yes" and nod when they mean "no" and sometimes reverse these gestures if they know they're speaking to foreigners, thereby complicating the issue further. Emphatic use of the words *da* (yes) and *ne* (no) should help to avoid misunderstandings.

to become less formal with you. When invited to someone's home it is polite to bring a small gift, and something from your own country will be particularly appreciated.

As for **tipping**, leaving a ten percent tip will definitely be well received, although it is not obligatory.

SPORTS AND ACTIVITIES

Bulgaria's mountainous terrain offers plenty of adventurous options. The **ski season** lasts from December to March, and the country has several well-known resorts. Bansko (Wbanskoski.com), in the spectacular Pirin mountain range in the southwest, is the best known, with alpine peaks and challenging runs perfect for experienced skiers and snowboarders. Other large resorts include Pamporovo (Wwinter .pamporovoresort.com) in the Rhodope Mountains, which is the best for beginners, and Borovets (Wborovets-bg .com) in the Rila range; there are also ski facilities on Vitosha Mountain (Wvitoshaski.com), just twenty minutes from the centre of Sofia. For more information see Wbulgariaski.com.

Of all Bulgaria's ranges, the Rila Mountains (Wrilanationalpark.bg) provide some of the country's most attractive **hiking** destinations, including the highest peak – Mount Musala (2925m) – from where a two- to three-day trail leads to Rila Monastery. For the best maps, advice and organized hikes visit Zig-Zag Holidays (Wzigzagbg .com) in Sofia. **Horseriding** is growing in popularity, and a small number of travel agencies can arrange trips of varying length (see box, p.141).

Despite the popularity of team sports such as basketball, handball and volleyball, none generates as much passion as football. Teams in the premier division ("A" Grupa) play on Saturday or Sunday afternoons. **Tickets** are generally cheap (around 5–10Lv) and sold at booths outside the grounds on the day of the match.

COMMUNICATIONS

You'll find that hotels, cafés, bars and restaurants generally offer free wi-fi. **Post offices** (*poshta*) are usually open Monday to Saturday 8.30am to 5.30pm, longer in big towns. **Phonecards** (*fonokarta*) for both Bulfon's orange phones and Betcom's blue phones are available from post offices and many street kiosks and shops. Cheap **SIM cards** from Bulgaria's three main network providers (Mtel, Globul and Vivacom) are widely available. The operator number for domestic calls is ☏121, for international calls ☏123.

EMERGENCIES

Petty theft is a danger on the coast, and the Bulgarian **police** can be slow in filling out insurance reports unless you're insistent. Foreign tourists are no longer a novelty in much of the country, but **women** travelling alone can expect to encounter stares, comments and sometimes harassment, while clubs on the coast are pretty much seen as meat markets. A firm rebuff should be enough to cope with most situations. Note that everyone is required to carry some form of **ID** at all times.

If you need a **doctor** (*doktor*) or dentist (*zabolekar*), go to the nearest hospital (*bolnitsa*), whose staff might speak English or German. Emergency treatment is free of charge, although you must pay for **medicines**. Larger towns will have at least one 24-hour pharmacy.

EMERGENCY NUMBERS

For any emergency dial ☏112

5

INFORMATION

Bulgaria's National Tourist Information Centre, located in Sofia at ploshtad Sveta Nedelya 1 (Mon–Fri 9am–5.30pm; ☎02

933 5826, ⓦbulgariatravel.org), is a smart, modern affair offering free maps and travel advice. Most major towns and cities have local **tourist information**

BULGARIAN

Hotel and travel agency staff in Sofia and the larger towns and coastal resorts generally speak some **English**, but knowledge of foreign languages elsewhere in the country is patchy; younger people are more likely to know a few words of English. Most street signs, menus and so on are written in the **Cyrillic** alphabet, but an increasing number have English transliterations.

	BULGARIAN	**PRONUNCIATION**
Yes	Да	Da
No	Не	Ne
Please	Моля	Molya
Thank you	Благодаря	Blagodarya
Hello/Good day	Добър ден	Dobur den
Goodbye	Довиждане	Dovizhdane
Excuse me	Извинявайте	Izvinyavite
Where?	Къде?	Kude?
Good	Добро	Dobro
Bad	Лошо	Losho
Near	Близо	Blizo
Far	Далече	Daleche
Cheap	Евтино	Eftino
Expensive	Скъпо	Skupo
Open	Отворено	Otvoreno
Closed	Затворено	Zatvoreno
Today	Днес	Dnes
Yesterday	Вчера	Vchera
Tomorrow	Утре	Utre
How much is...?	Колко струва...?	Kolko stroova...?
What time is it?	Колко е часът?	Kolko ai chasut?
I don't understand	Не разбирам	Ne razbiram
Do you speak English?	Говорите ли английски?	Govorite li Angleeski?
Do you have any vegetarian dishes?	Имате ли вегетерианска храна?	Imate li vegitarianska hrana?
Cheers	Наздраве	Nazdrave
The bill, please	Може ли сметката	Mozhe li smetkata
Is this the bus for...?	Това ли е автобусът за...?	Tova li avtobusat za...?
Is this the train to...?	Това ли е влакът за...?	Tova li e vlakut za...?
Have you got a single/double	Имате ли единична двойна стая	Imate li edinichna/dvoyna staya
How much for the night?	Колко струва нощувката?	Kolko struva noshtuvkata?
One	Един/Една	Edin/edna
Two	Две	Dve
Three	Три	Tree
Four	Четири	Chetiri
Five	Пет	Pyet
Six	Шест	Shest
Seven	Седем	Sedem
Eight	Осем	Osem
Nine	Девет	Devet
Ten	Десет	Deset

BULGARIA ONLINE

Ⓦ **bulgariatravel.org** Comprehensive travel information.

Ⓦ **discover-bulgaria.com** Travel information and hotel booking.

Ⓦ **novinite.com** English-language news and features.

Ⓦ **questbg.com** News and features for foreigners living in Bulgaria.

Ⓦ **programata.bg** Up-to-date English-language cultural listings.

centres where staff speak several languages and can provide maps, brochures and leaflets although they aren't usually authorized to make hotel reservations. The best general **maps** of Bulgaria and Sofia are published by Kartografiya and Domino; both are available in Latin alphabet versions and are sold at street stalls, petrol stations and bookshops.

MONEY AND BANKS

Until Bulgaria joins the Eurozone (target date: Jan 1, 2015) the currency remains the **lev** (Lv), which is divided into 100 stotinki (st). There are notes of 2Lv, 5Lv, 10Lv, 20Lv, 50Lv and 100Lv and coins of 1st, 2st, 5st, 10st, 20st and 50st, and 1Lv. Pegged to the euro, the lev is stable, and although hotels and travel agencies frequently quote prices in euros, you will be expected to pay in the local currency. At the time of writing, €1 was equal to 1.95Lv, $1 to 1.50Lv, and £1 to 2.30Lv. Producing a **student ID card** at museums and galleries will often get you a discount of between a third and a half.

Banks are open Monday to Friday 9am to 4pm, and there are ATMs in every town. Private exchange bureaus, offering variable rates, are widespread – but beware of hidden commission charges. Also watch out for black market moneychangers who approach unwary foreigners with offers of better rates; if they sound too good to be true, they are. Many smaller banks and offices won't take travellers' cheques, while credit cards are acceptable at most shops, hotels and restaurants.

OPENING HOURS AND HOLIDAYS

Big-city **shops** and **supermarkets** are generally open Monday to Friday 8.30am to 6pm or later, on Saturday they close at 2pm. The massive malls that have sprung up in recent years are usually open daily from 10am to 10pm. In rural areas and small towns, an unofficial siesta may prevail between noon and 3pm. Many shops, offices, banks and museums are closed on the following **public holidays:** January 1, March 3, Easter Sunday and Monday, May 1, May 24, September 6, September 22, December 25 and December 31. Additional public holidays may occasionally be called by the government.

Sofia

With its drab suburbs and distinct lack of charming old buildings **SOFIA** (София) can seem an uninspiring place to first-time visitors. Yet much has been done in recent years to revitalize the heart of a city with high hopes of becoming European Capital of Culture in 2019. Once you've settled in and begun to explore, you'll find it a surprisingly vibrant city, especially on fine days, when its lush public gardens and pavement cafés buzz with life. Just 8km to the south, meanwhile, looms verdant **Mount Vitosha**, promising fantastic hiking, biking and skiing.

Sofia was founded by a Thracian tribe some three thousand years ago, and various **Roman ruins** attest to its zenith as Serdika, a regional imperial capital in the fourth century AD. The Bulgars didn't arrive on the scene until the ninth century and, with the notable exception of the thirteenth-century Boyana Church, their cultural monuments largely disappeared during Ottoman rule (1396–1878). The architectural legacy of the Ottomans was mostly eradicated following liberation in 1878 and is now visible solely in a couple of stately **mosques**. The finest architecture postdates Bulgaria's liberation: handsome Neoclassical buildings, imposing Soviet-era government offices, vast parks,

5

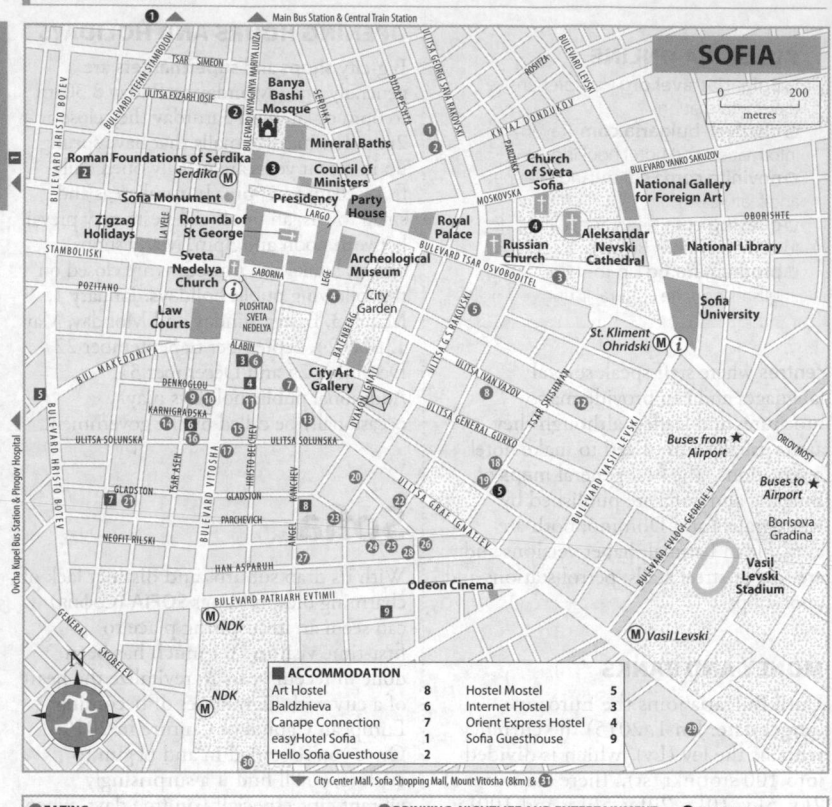

SOFIA

0   200
metres

ACCOMMODATION			
Art Hostel	8	Hostel Mostel	5
Baldzhieva	6	Internet Hostel	3
Canape Connection	7	Orient Express Hostel	4
easyHotel Sofia	1	Sofia Guesthouse	9
Hello Sofia Guesthouse	2		

City Center Mall, Sofia Shopping Mall, Mount Vitosha (8km) & 31

EATING				**DRINKING, NIGHTLIFE AND ENTERTAINMENT**				**SHOPPING**	
Annette	27	Memento Café	10	4 Rooms	13	ID Club	9	Aleksandar	
Art Club Museum Café	4	Pri Yafata	16	Apartment	24	J.J. Murphy's	14	Nevski Market	4
Before & After	15	Slunce Luna	21/26	Bilkovata	18	Jules Verne	5	Elephant Bookstore	5
Divaka	11/23/28	Tea House	1	Blaze	12	Mixtape 5	31	Halite	2
Dream House	6	Ugo	17/20/25	Chervilo	3	My Mojito	8	Tzum	3
Farmer's	7/19			Dada	2	Sofia Live Club	30	Zhenski bazaar	1
				Hambara	22	Swingin' Hall	29		

and the magnificent **Aleksandar Nevski Cathedral**.

WHAT TO SEE AND DO

Most of Sofia's sights are centrally located and within easy walking distance of each other. The pedestrianized Bulevard Vitosha forms the heart of the shopping district and leads north to the Church of Sveta Nedelya, from where bulevard Tsar Osvoboditel passes the major public buildings, culminating with the grand Aleksandar Nevski Church.

Sveta Nedelya Church

At the heart of Sofia is **ploshtad Sveta Nedelya**, a pedestrianized square dominated by the distinctive **Sveta Nedelya Church** (daily 7am–7pm). Dating from 1863, its broad dome dominates the vast interior chamber, and colourful modern frescoes adorn every square centimetre of its walls.

The Largo

Laid out in the 1950s to demonstrate the power of Communist rule, the **Largo** is an elongated plaza flanked on three sides by severe monumental edifices built in Soviet Classicist style. They include the towering monolith of the former **Party House**, originally the home of the Communist hierarchy, and now serving as government offices. The plaza extends westwards to the **Sofia Monument**, the city's symbol which represents the eponymous Goddess of Wisdom. On the northern side of the Largo is the **Council of Ministers**, Bulgaria's cabinet offices.

The Banya Bashi Mosque and the mineral baths

The **Banya Bashi Mosque** was built in 1576 by Mimar Sinan, who also designed the great mosque at Edirne in Turkey. The mosque is not officially open to tourists, but modestly dressed visitors may visit outside of prayer times. Behind stand Sofia's **mineral baths**, housed in a splendid yellow-and-red striped *fin-de-siècle* building. Closed since 1986, it is being restored with a view to reopening as a city history museum in the near future. Locals gather daily to bottle the hot, sulphurous water that gushes from public taps into stone troughs outside, opposite ulitsa Exzarh Iosif.

The Rotunda of St George and the Presidency

Sofia's oldest church, the **Rotunda of St George**, dates back to the fourth century and contains frescoes from the eighth century onwards. It was built upon the Roman foundations of Serdika, which are open to the public and can also be seen in front of the nearby TSUM department store. Surrounding the church is the **Presidency**, guarded by soldiers in colourful nineteenth-century garb (Changing of the Guard hourly).

The Archeological Museum

A fifteenth-century mosque now holds the **Archeological Museum** (daily 10am–6pm; 10Lv; ⊕naim.bg), whose prize exhibit is the magnificent Valchitran Treasure, a Thracian gold cauldron plus cups. Also on show is a collection of Thracian armour, medieval church wall paintings and numerous Roman tombstones.

The City Art Gallery

The **City Art Gallery** (Tues–Sat 10am–7pm, Sun 11am–6pm; free; ⊕sghg.bg) in the City Garden, immediately to the south of ploshtad Aleksandar Batenberg,

stages regular exhibitions of contemporary Bulgarian art. Displays feature the country's best-known artists, including bold expressive pieces by Vladimir Dimitrov (known as "The Master"), and striking abstract works by Georgi Bozhilov-Slona.

The Russian Church and Aleksandar Nevski Cathedral

Built on the site of a mosque in the early twentieth century, the **Russian Church** (daily 8am–7pm) is a stunning golden-domed building with an emerald spire and an exuberant mosaic-tiled exterior, which conceals a dark, candle-scented interior. The nearby **Aleksandar Nevski Cathedral** (daily 7am–7pm, liturgy on Sun at 1pm; free) is one of the finest pieces of architecture in the Balkans. Financed by public subscription and built between 1882 and 1924 to honour the 200,000 Russian casualties of the 1877–78 War of Liberation, it's a magnificent structure, bulging with domes and semi-domes and glittering with gold leaf. Within the gloomy interior, a beardless Christ sits enthroned above the altar, and numerous scenes from his life, painted in a humanistic style, adorn the walls. The crypt, entered from outside (Tues–Sun 10am–6pm; 6Lv), contains a superb collection of icons from all over the country.

The National Gallery for Foreign Art

An imposing nineteenth-century building houses the **National Gallery for Foreign Art** (closed for renovations at the time of writing; ⊕foreignart museum.bg), which devotes a lot of space to Indian woodcarvings and second-division French and Russian artists, though there are a few minor works by the likes of Rodin, Chagall and Kandinsky. Heading west past Aleksandar Nevski Cathedral, you'll pass two recumbent lions flanking the Tomb of the Unknown Soldier, set beside the wall of the plain, brown-brick **Church of Sveta Sofia** which gave the city its name in the fourteenth century.

5

Borisova Gradina

Down bulevard Tsar Osvoboditel, past Sofia University, is **Borisova Gradina**, named after Bulgaria's interwar monarch, Boris III. The park – the largest in Sofia – has a rich variety of flowers and trees, outdoor bars, a couple of football stadiums and two huge Communist monuments.

Mount Vitosha

A wooded granite mass 20km long and 16km wide, **Mount Vitosha**, 8km south of the city, is where Sofians go for picnics and skiing. The ascent of its highest peak, the 2290m **Cherni Vrah**, has become a traditional test of stamina. Getting here on public transport is straightforward, although there are fewer buses on weekdays than at weekends. Take tram #5 from behind the Law Courts to Ovcha Kupel bus station, then change to bus #61, which climbs through the forests towards **Zlatni Mostove**, a beauty spot on the western shoulder of Mount Vitosha beside the so-called **Stone River**. Beneath the large boulders running down the mountainside is a rivulet which once attracted gold-panners. Trails lead up beside the stream towards the mountain's upper reaches: Cherni Vrah is about two to three hours' walk from here. Alternatively, use the Simeonovo cable car (daily in winter, weekends only the rest of the year; 8/10Lv one-way/return) to reach the handful of ski pistes at Aleko (ⓦskivitosha.com) from where it's a two-hour hike up to the Cherni Vrah summit. To reach the Simeonovo lift station take tram #10 from the centre to Hladilnik and change to bus #122.

ARRIVAL AND DEPARTURE

By plane Sofia airport (ⓦsofia-airport.bg) has two terminals: budget carriers arrive at Terminal 1; Bulgaria Air and other major airlines are handled by the newer and smarter Terminal 2. The best way to get into the centre of town from Terminal 1 is to catch *marshrutka* (private minibus) #30, which runs until around 10pm (every 15–30min; 1.50Lv). Bus #84 leaves from Terminal 1 and #284 from Terminal 2; tickets (1Lv) can be bought from the airport newspaper kiosk – you'll need additional tickets

for any oversized bags. Waiting taxis might well try to charge you an exorbitant 40Lv or more, so it's wise to book one at the booth in the arrivals hall (12–15Lv).

By train Trains arrive and depart from Central Station (Tsentralna Gara), a concrete hangar 2km from the centre harbouring a number of exchange bureaus and snack bars, but little else to welcome the visitor. The metro station (5am–midnight) just outside is the quickest and easiest way to reach the centre.

Destinations Bansko (2 daily; 8hr via Septemvri); Belgrade (1 daily; 7hr 30min); Blagoevgrad (7 daily; 3hr); Bucharest (1 daily; 9hr 30min); Burgas (4 daily; 8hr); İstanbul (1 daily; 11hr); Koprivshtitsa (4 daily; 2hr 30min); Plovdiv (13 daily; 2hr 30min); Septemvri (15 daily; 2hr); Thessaloniki (2 daily; 6hr); Varna (6 daily; 7 hr 30min); Veliko Turnovo (10 daily; 4hr via Gorna Oryahovitsa).

By bus Most buses arrive at the terminal, just next to the train station, although some Bansko services and Blagoevgrad buses (for connections to Rila Monastery) use the Ovcha Kupel terminal, 5km southwest of the centre along bul. Tsar Boris III. Buses #11 and #60 head to the centre from here.

Destinations Bansko (6 daily; 3hr); Burgas (hourly; 7hr); Koprivshtitsa (2 daily; 2hr); Plovdiv (hourly; 2hr); Varna (every 30min; 7hr); Veliko Tarnovo (hourly; 4hr).

INFORMATION

Tourist office Both the National Tourist Information Centre at pl. Sveta Nedelya 1 (see p.134) and the Sofia Tourist Information Centre (Mon–Fri 9.30am–6.30pm; ☏02 491 8344, ⓦinfo-sofia.bg), in the underpass at the Kliment Ochridski metro station, provide city maps and local travel advice. An excellent alternative is the friendly travel agency Zig-Zag Holidays (ⓦzigzagbg.com) at bul. Stamboliiski 20 (entrance on ul. Lavele; Mon–Fri 9.30am–6.30pm, daily in summer; ☏02 980 5102), which charges a 5Lv consultation fee, although not for accommodation booking.

GETTING AROUND

Public transport There's a flat fare of 1Lv on all urban routes, whether by bus (*avtobus*), trolleybus (*troleibus*), the two-line metro system, or tram (*tramvai*). Tickets (*bileti*) are sold from street kiosks and can be bought from machines on board trams or from the driver on buses and must be punched once you have entered the vehicle (inspections are frequent and there are 20Lv spot fines for fare dodgers). Kiosks at the main tram stops sell one-day tickets (*karta za edin den;* 4Lv) and a strip (*talon*) of ten tickets (8Lv) – the tickets can only be used by the purchaser and must be used in sequence. Metro tickets can only be bought from metro stations.

Taxis and minibuses The most reliable taxi company is OK Taxis (☏02 973 2121, ⓦoktaxi.net), charging 79st per km until nightfall, 90st afterwards, and 70st initial fare; make sure the driver has his meter running. Additionally, there's a fleet of private minibuses (*marshrutka*), acting like shared taxis and covering around forty different routes across the city for a flat fare of 1.50Lv. Destinations and routes are displayed on the front of the vehicles – in the Cyrillic alphabet – and passengers flag them down like normal taxis, calling out when they want them to stop.

ACCOMMODATION

Sofia has a number of good hostels, and some small, reasonably priced hotels in central locations. All hostels have free wi-fi and breakfast unless otherwise stated.

HOSTELS

Art Hostel ul. Angel Kanchev 21a ☎ 02 987 0545, ⓦ art -hostel.com. Sofia's trendiest hostel, hosting art exhibitions, live music, resident DJs and occasional drama performances. Guests have access to a kitchen and popular tea room-cum-bar with lovely garden, and free computer access. Dorm 20Lv, double 60Lv

Canape Connection ul. Gladston 12a ☎ 02 441 6373, ⓦ canapeconnection.com. Cosy, central hostel with rustic furniture and comfortable, extra-wide beds. Helpful staff are on hand to provide local information, and the breakfast is excellent. Dorm 22Lv, double 70Lv

★ **Hostel Mostel** bul. Makedoniya 2A ☎ 0889 223 296, ⓦ hostelmostel.com. Superb hostel located in a historic building a short walk from the centre. Besides the free all-you-can-eat breakfast, they offer a bowl of pasta and a bottle of beer for every night of your stay. The ground floor has a cavernous, comfortable lounge space with flat-screen TV, DVDs and travel library. Just up the road is the hostel's lively bar. Dorm 20Lv, double 60Lv

Internet Hostel ul. Alabin 50a ☎ 0889 138 298, ⓔ interhostel@yahoo.co.uk. Friendly hostel with kitchen offering spacious but dated doubles, triples and quads, as well as studio apartments. Located on the second floor of a shopping arcade, above the *Dream House* restaurant. Dorm 18Lv, double 50Lv, studio apartment for two 60Lv

Orient Express Hostel ul. Hristo Belchev 8A ☎ 0888 384 828, ⓦ orientexpresshostel.com. Small and homely hostel, with high ceilings, modern fittings combined with antique and salvaged furniture, and TVs in every room. Its fifth-floor position makes for great views from the rooms, but some arduous stair climbing as there's no lift. Friendly and helpful staff. Dorm 22Lv, double 70Lv, apartment 90Lv

Sofia Guesthouse bul. Patriarh Evtimiy 27 ☎ 02 403 0100, ⓦ sofiaguest.com. Large hostel with a very central location and clean, bright rooms, plus a garden and TV lounge. Staff can arrange bike rental, day-trips, and a pick-up/drop-off service from the train and bus stations or airport. Dorm 18Lv, double 56Lv, attic apartment 98Lv

HOTELS

Baldzhieva ul. Tsar Asen 23 ☎ 02 981 1257, ⓦ baldjievahotel.net. Small hotel with a pleasant courtyard garden one block west of bul. Vitosha. The en-suite rooms are clean and simply furnished, and come with phone, fridge, TV and wi-fi. Breakfast not included. Double 58Lv

easyHotel Sofia ul. Aldomirovska 108 ☎ 02 920 1654, ⓦ easyhotel.com. Despite being inconveniently located several blocks west of the centre, this is a great deal for anyone in search of a spotless, cheap en-suite room. Prices vary according to availability. Double 38Lv

★ **Hello Sofia Guesthouse** bul. Stefan Stambolov 12 ☎ 0889 138 298, ⓦ hellosofia.hostel.com. Situated just a short distance from Sofia's thriving Women's Market (Zhenski Bazaar), this delightful guesthouse has been thoughtfully designed and features imaginative styling and home comforts that include widescreen TVs, spacious en-suite bathrooms, and a smart shared kitchen and lounge area. Double 56Lv

EATING

The cheapest places to grab snacks, a beer or a coffee are the many cafés and kiosks on bul. Vitosha and pl. Slaveikov or in the city's public gardens. In recent years soup-focused places such as *Farmer's* (see p.138) have proliferated, serving up generous portions of wholesome, inexpensive fare that's proven immensely popular.

CAFÉS

Art Club Museum Café Corner of ul. Saborna and ul. Lege. Chic café with a pleasant patio, set amid Thracian tombstones next to the Archeological Museum. Live DJs in the basement Thurs, Fri & Sat nights. Serves a variety of light meals, desserts and inventive drinks, such as cappuccino with coconut and banana (5Lv). Open 24hr.

Memento Café bul. Vitosha 32 ⓦ memento.bg. One of the countless cafés that have mushroomed along the city's main commercial strip in recent years, this tiny yet popular spot has a Mediterranean feel and serves top-notch coffee, cakes, and sandwiches. Daily 8am–2am.

★ **Tea House (Chai vuv fabrikata)** ul. Georgi Benkovski 11. Atmospheric traditional teahouse with a formidable array of teas including Kashmiri *chai* and rose, priced from 2.50Lv. Daily 10am–11pm.

RESTAURANTS

Annette ul. Angel Kunchev 27 ⓦ annette.bg. An excellent Moroccan restaurant with tree-shaded outdoor seating and a mouth-watering range of exotic dishes that include chicken baked with pear in wine sauce (13.90Lv). Daily 10am–10pm.

5

Before & After ul. Hristo Belchev 12 ⓦ ba.club-cabaret .net. Elegant and popular restaurant near the *Orient Express Hostel*, with a range of Bulgarian, Turkish and international including some fantastic traditional desserts. Also great for vegetarian options, including grilled vegetables in yoghurt and dill (6Lv). Hosts tango dances on Sun. Daily 10am–midnight.

Divaka ul. Gladston 54, with other branches at ul. Hristo Belchev 16 & ul. 6th Septemvri 41a. Small chain of bright and busy restaurants serving excellent, meat-heavy Bulgarian dishes. Chicken kebab 7.50Lv, vegetarian shish kebab 5.50Lv. Open 24hr.

Dream House ul. Alabin 50a ☎02 980 8163, ⓦ dreamhouse-bg.com. Intimate, friendly and well-established vegetarian restaurant above a shopping arcade. Has a good choice of meals and snacks using seasonal produce, including aubergine couscous (6.80Lv) and Asian bamboo soup (2.90Lv). They also deliver within the city centre area. Daily 11am–10pm.

Farmer's ul. Shishman 24, with another branch at pl. Garibaldi. Smart places serving a great range of soups (2.90Lv) as well as salads, chunky burgers and aubergine sandwiches. Eat-in or takeaway. Daily 9am–10pm.

Pri Yafata ul. Solunska 28 ⓦ pri-yafata.com. Brash but fun take on a traditional *mehana*, complete with live music, costumed staff and a great Bulgarian menu that includes tripe soup (*shkembe churba*; 4.50Lv) and a wide range of grilled meat dishes. Daily 11am–midnight.

★ **Slunce Luna** ul. Gladston 18b & ul. 6th Septemvri 39 ⓦ sunmoon.bg. Popular vegetarian restaurants with rustic furniture and a bakery that supplies both with great wholemeal bread. Daily 9am–11pm.

Ugo bul. Vitosha 45, ul. Neofit Rilski 68 & ul. Han Krum 2 ⓦ ugo.bg. One of the better pizza and pasta restaurant chains in the centre, *Ugo* offers a broad range of dishes 24 hours a day.

DRINKING AND NIGHTLIFE

For evening entertainment, there's an ever-growing number of clubs, most playing a mix of pop, retro, rock or the ubiquitous local "folk pop" (*chalga*). Jazz and Latino music are also popular. Information on the city's small but thriving gay scene can be found at ⓦ gay.bg.

BARS

Apartment ul. Neofit Rilski 68. Stylish and chilled, this eclectic bar-cum-living room occupies a pair of high-ceilinged nineteenth-century flats hung with an intriguing array of artwork. The pricey drinks menu keeps the riffraff at bay. Daily noon–2am.

Bilkovata ul. Tsar Shishman 22. A buzzing, smoky cellar with decent music and a young crowd, *Bilkovata* is something of a local legend: fondly remembered by successive generations of students, arty types and young professionals, it's still going strong. Packed beer garden in summer. Daily 10am–2am.

Dada ul. Benkovski 10 ⓦ dadaculturalbar.eu. *Dada*'s regular cultural evenings – including film screenings and poetry readings – attract a mixed crowd of Bulgarians and expats. Daily noon–2am.

Hambara ul. 6-ti septemvri 22. Hidden behind an unmarked doorway just off the street, this dark, candlelit, stone-floored bar is one of the most atmospheric places in the centre for a long night of drink-fuelled conversation. Live jazz several nights a week. Daily 7pm–2am.

J.J. Murphy's ul. Karnigradska 6 ⓦ jjmurphys.net. Sofia's top Irish bar, offering filling pub grub, big-screen sports and live music at the weekends. Daily noon–1am.

Jules Verne ul. Rakovski 127 (first floor). Simply furnished bar frequented by a vibrant crowd of arty young professionals. Daily 10am–late.

CLUBS

Entrance fees range from nothing to 20Lv depending on the venue; expect to pay more if a major DJ is manning the decks. A valid ID is compulsory.

4 Rooms ul. Angel Kanchev 1. Capacious grungy club with battered furniture and blaring tunes that's a magnet for Sofia's disaffected youth. Daily 5pm–2am.

Blaze ul. Slavyanska 36. Lively bar and club near the university, with a good sound system pumping out mainstream pop for the trendy clientele. Daily 9pm–3am.

Chervilo bul. Tsar Osvoboditel 9 ⓦ chervilo.com. Stylish city centre club offering the latest in house, techno and Latin over two floors. The action spreads out onto the terrace in summer, when it's more like an elite, pay-to-enter pavement café than a club. Café daily 10am–10pm; club Thurs–Sat 10pm–7am.

ID Club ul. Karnigradska 19B ⓦ idclub.bg. A popular gay club with plenty of dancing space that plays retro, *chalga* and pop until the early hours. So-called "face control" (only letting in those who look the part) is strict on busy nights. Daily 9pm–3am.

My Mojito ul. Ivan Vazov 12. This well-established club is one of Sofia's trendiest, with a laidback crowd and DJs playing a mix of mainstream dance and pop. Daily 9pm–5am.

ENTERTAINMENT

LIVE MUSIC

Mixtape 5 NDK underpass beneath Lover's Bridge. Big club with central stage hosting hip local and international bands and DJs. Daily 9pm–late.

Sofia Live Club National Palace of Culture (NDK) ⓦ sofialiveclub.com. Lying deep beneath NDK, a monolithic Communist-era building that dominates central Sofia, this plush club has hosted an impressive number of international world music and jazz groups. Daily 8pm–2am.

Swingin' Hall ul. Dragan Tsankov 8. Cheerful, crowded bar that's been around for years and has live music (usually pop, rock or jazz) on two stages. Tues–Sat 9pm–4am.

CINEMA

Cinema City bul. Stamboliski 101 ☏02 929 2929, ⓦcinemacity.bg. Multi-screen cinema in the Mall of Sofia with lots of snack stands in the vicinity.

Odeon bul. Patriarh Evtimiy 1 ☏02 969 2469. Shows oldies and prize-winning art films past and present. Small bar in the lobby.

SHOPPING

Until recently, the city's pedestrianized central street, bul. Vitosha, was the place where you were most likely to come across familiar high-street shops and brands; some remain but many were replaced by outdoor cafés when the retailers moved into the characterless yet immensely popular malls located south of the centre. Ul. Graf Ignatiev and ul. Tsar Ivan Shishman are now Sofia's busiest central shopping streets, home to numerous bars, cafés and a wide range of small independents selling everything from books to clothes, souvenirs and vegetables.

Aleksandar Nevski Located at the apex of the three central churches on pl. Aleksandar Nevski, this cluster of stalls offers an odd mix of religious paintings, Turkish-influenced silver jewellery, traditional Bulgarian peasant textiles, plus antique and replica Communist items. Be warned that there's Nazi memorabilia on sale too.

Elephant Bookstore ul. Tsar Ivan Shishman 31. A delightfully cosy shop crammed with new and used English books and a mesmerizing array of quirky gifts.

Halite bul. Knyaginy Mariya Luiza, opposite the Banya Bashi Mosque. This elegant building houses Sofia's central food hall with two floors of shops and food stalls.

Tzum Located just outside Serdika metro, this was once the preserve of the party elite and, although it's now been eclipsed by the much larger suburban malls, it remains the centre's premier shopping mall stocked with upmarket and luxury goods.

Zhenski bazaar bul. Stefan Stambolov. One of the city's best outdoor markets, where trinkets, fresh fruit, vegetables and other foodstuffs are on sale.

DIRECTORY

Embassies and consulates Canada, Pozitano 7 ☏02 969 9710; Ireland, Bacho Kiro 26–30 ☏02 985 3425; South Africa, Bacho Kiro 26 (2nd floor) ☏02 939 5015; UK, Moskovska 9 ☏02 933 9222; US, Kozyak 16 ☏02 937 5100.

Hospital Pirogov hospital (bul. General Totleben 21 ☏02 915 4411, ⓦpirogov.bg).

Pharmacy Aronia 2001 at bul. Pencho Slaveikov 6, opposite Pirogov hospital, is open 24hr.

Post office ul. General Gurko 6 (daily 7am–8.30pm).

Southern Bulgaria

The route south from Sofia skirts the Rila and Pirin mountain ranges, swathed in forests and dotted with alpine lakes, and home to Bulgaria's highest peaks. Even those on a tight schedule should find time for a visit to the most revered of Bulgarian monasteries, **Rila**, around 30km east of the main southbound route. **Bansko**, meanwhile, on the eastern side of the Pirin range, boasts a wealth of traditional architecture, as well as being a major ski resort and a good base for hiking. Another much-travelled route heads southeast from Sofia towards İstanbul. The main road and rail lines now linking İstanbul and Sofia essentially follow the course of the Roman Serdica–Constantinople road, running past towns ruled by the Ottomans for so long that foreigners used to call this part of Bulgaria "European Turkey". Of these, the most important is **Plovdiv**, Bulgaria's second city, whose old quarter is a wonderful mixture of National Revival mansions and classical remains. Some 30km south of Plovdiv is **Bachkovo Monastery**, containing Bulgaria's most vivid frescoes.

RILA MONASTERY

As the most celebrated of Bulgaria's religious sites, famed for its fine architecture and mountainous setting – and declared a World Heritage site by UNESCO – the **Rila Monastery** receives a steady stream of visitors, many of them day-trippers from Sofia.

WHAT TO SEE AND DO

Ringed by mighty walls, the **monastery** (daily dawn–dusk; free; ⓦrilamonastery .pmg-blg.com) has the outward

5

appearance of a fortress, but this impression is negated by the beauty of the interior, which even the crowds can't mar. Graceful arches above the flagstoned courtyard support tiers of monastic cells, and stairways ascend to wooden balconies. Bold red stripes and black-and-white check patterns enliven the facade, contrasting with the sombre mountains behind and creating a harmony between the cloisters and the **church**. Richly coloured frescoes shelter beneath the church porch and cover much of its interior. The iconostasis is splendid, almost 10m wide and covered by a mass of intricate carvings and gold leaf. Beside the church is **Hrelyo's Tower**, the sole remaining building from the fourteenth century. Cauldrons, which were once used to prepare food for pilgrims, occupy the soot-encrusted kitchen on the ground floor of the north wing, while on the floors above you can inspect the spartan refectory and panelled guest rooms. Beneath the east wing is the **treasury** (daily 9am–4.30pm; 10Lv), where, among other things, you can view a wooden cross carved with more than 1500 miniature human figures during the 1790s.

ARRIVAL AND DEPARTURE

Joining a day tour from the capital (book through the Sofia Tourist Information Centre; see p.136) is by far the most sensible way of getting here, with the majority costing around 50Lv per person.

ACCOMMODATION

Rila monastery ☎ 07054 2208. It's possible to stay on site in reasonably comfortable rooms. Gates close at 11pm. Double 60Lv
Zodiac 4km beyond the monastery ☎ 0887 362 186, ⓦ camping-zodiac.com. Pleasant campsite occupying an attractive riverside spot, with smart double bungalows and a good restaurant. Camping 10Lv per person, double bungalow 15Lv per person

EATING

For cheap snacks, delicious bread and doughnuts, head for the bakery opposite the East Gate.
Drushliavitsa Built over a stream on the hillside just beyond the East Gate, this traditional-style Bulgarian restaurant offers polite service and shaded outdoor seating. The menu features Bulgarian standards and fresh local trout (7Lv). Daily 10am–10pm.

Rila Situated behind the bakery. Identical in style to the *Drushliavitsa* with a similar menu and prices, but less enthusiastic service. Daily 10am–10pm.

BANSKO

Lying some 40km east of the main Struma Valley route, **BANSKO** (Банско) is the primary centre for walking and skiing on the eastern slopes of the Pirin mountains. Originally an agricultural centre, ski tourism has prompted massive investment in recent years, resulting in the unappealing sight of apartment blocks and hotels squeezed into the backyards of stone-built nineteenth-century farmhouses. Despite this overdevelopment, the central old town, with its numerous traditional pubs hidden away down labyrinthine cobbled streets, is as attractive as ever and the perfect place to wind down after a hard day on the slopes.

Though connected to Sofia and other towns by bus, Bansko can also be reached by a **narrow-gauge railway**, which leaves the main Sofia–Plovdiv line at Septemvri and forges its way across the highlands. It's one of the most scenic trips in the Balkans, but also one of the slowest, taking five hours to cover just over 100km.

WHAT TO SEE AND DO

Bansko centres on the modern pedestrianized ploshtad Nikola Vaptsarov, where the **Nikola Vaptsarov Museum** (daily 9am–noon & 2–5pm; 4Lv) relates to the local-born poet and Socialist martyr. Immediately north of here, ploshtad Vazrazhdane is watched over by the solid stone tower of the **Church of Sveta Troitsa**, whose interior contains exquisite nineteenth-century frescoes and icons. On the opposite side of the square, the **Rilski Convent** houses an icon museum (Mon–Fri 9am–noon & 2–5pm; 4Lv) devoted to the achievements of Bansko's nineteenth-century icon painters.

From the main square, ulitsa Pirin leads north towards the **cable car** (Dec–April daily 8.30am–5pm; 28Lv), where there is a buzzing collection of

HORSERIDING IN THE RILA MOUNTAINS

A unique way to experience the spectacular terrain of the **Rila Mountains** is on horseback. Some of the trails pass through virtually untouched forest areas and alongside staggering glacial lakes; there are also some seriously rocky options for experienced or adventurous riders. The Sofia-based tour operator Horseriding Bulgaria (ul. Orfey 9 ☎02 403 0107, ⓦhorseridingbulgaria.com) offers a number of tours setting out from their Iskar Ranch at the foot of the Rila Mountains, and costing from €600–900 for eight days.

ski-rental shops, bars and restaurants. Ski passes cost 58Lv per day (38Lv for children), and ski and snowboard equipment can be rented for around 30Lv per day. The cable car doesn't operate outside the ski season so the only option for reaching the summit in the summer months is to head west – on foot or by taxi – via a steep 14km uphill climb to the Vihren hut, where cheap dorm **accommodation** (12Lv per person) is available. This is the main trailhead for hikes towards the 2914m summit of **Mount Vihren**, Bulgaria's second-highest peak, or gentler rambles around the meadows and lakes nearby.

ARRIVAL AND DEPARTURE

By train The train station is on the northern edge of town, a 10min walk from pl. Vaptsarov.
Destinations Septemvri (3 daily; 5hr).
By bus The bus station is close to the train station.
Destinations Blagoevgrad (hourly; 1hr); Plovdiv (7 daily; 4hr); Sofia (hourly; 2hr 30min).

INFORMATION

Tourist information The tourist office is on pl. Nikola Vapzarov 1 (Tues–Sat 9am–noon & 1–6pm; ☎0749 88580, ⓦbansko.bg).

ACCOMMODATION

Bisser Family Hotel ul. El Tepe 16 ☎0749 88078, ⓦbisser-bansko.com. Pleasant hotel situated on a quiet street near the centre of town. En-suite rooms, wi-fi and breakfast included. Free daily bus to the lift station. Double 54Lv
Dedo Pene ul. Aleksandar Buynov 1 ☎0749 88348, ⓦdedopene.com. Located just south of pl. Vazrazhdane, there's an array of wonderfully atmospheric rooms in this restored nineteenth-century building. Double 60Lv
Zlatev Guest House ul. Nikola Popfilipov 1 ☎0899 969370. Family-run place in the heart of the old town, offering smart en-suite rooms and a secluded courtyard garden. Double 55Lv

EATING AND DRINKING

★**Dedo Pene** ul. Aleksandar Buynov 1 ⓦdedopene .com. Atmospheric restaurant serving reasonably priced traditional Bulgarian food and Bansko specialities such as *kapama*, a delicious stew of chicken, pork and cabbage. Sit inside among folksy decorations or opt for the vine-shaded courtyard in summer. Daily 11am–1am.
Molerite ul. Glazne 41 ⓦmolerite.com. Two floors of wooden benches and ethnic textiles just north of pl. Nikola Vaptsarov – try the superb local specialities such as roast lamb (17.50Lv) and sword-grilled shish kebabs (15Lv). Turns into a folk-pop disco after about 11pm. Daily 11am–2am.
Oxygen bul. Bulgaria 22. Popular bar in the town centre with a mixed programme of DJ-driven sounds, potent cocktails and good vibes. Daily noon–late.

PLOVDIV

Bulgaria's second-largest city, **PLOVDIV** (Пловдив) has more obvious charms than Sofia, which the locals here tend to look down on. The old town embodies Plovdiv's long history – Thracian fortifications subsumed by Macedonian masonry, overlaid with Roman and Byzantine walls. Great timber-framed mansions, erected during the Bulgarian renaissance, loom over the derelict Ottoman mosques and artisans' dwellings of the lower town. But this isn't just another museum town: the city's arts festivals and trade fairs are the biggest in the country, and its restaurants and bars are equal to those of the capital.

WHAT TO SEE AND DO

Plovdiv centres on the large **ploshtad Tsentralen**, dominated by the monolithic *Hotel Trimontium Princess*.

Ploshtad Dzhumaya

Thronged with promenading Plovdivians and lined with shops, cafés and bars, the pedestrianized ulitsa Knyaz Aleksandar I

5

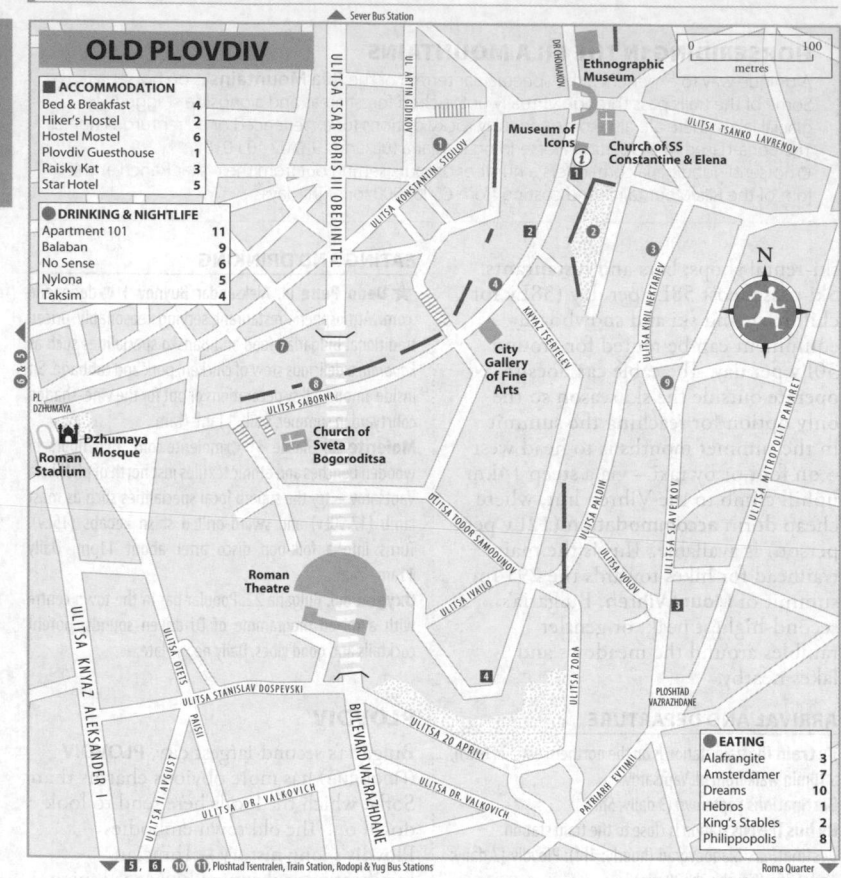

OLD PLOVDIV

■ ACCOMMODATION
Bed & Breakfast	4
Hiker's Hostel	2
Hostel Mostel	6
Plovdiv Guesthouse	1
Raisky Kat	3
Star Hotel	5

● DRINKING & NIGHTLIFE
Apartment 101	11
Balaban	9
No Sense	6
Nylona	5
Taksim	4

● EATING
Alafrangite	3
Amsterdamer	7
Dreams	10
Hebros	1
King's Stables	2
Philippopolis	8

5, **6**, **10**, **11**, Ploshtad Tsentralen, Train Station, Rodopi & Yug Bus Stations
Roma Quarter ▼

leads onto the attractive **ploshtad Dzhumaya** where the substantial ruins of a **Roman stadium** that could hold thirty thousand spectators are on display beneath the square. Among the variously styled buildings here, the renovated **Dzhumaya Mosque**, with its diamond-patterned minaret and lead-sheathed domes, steals the show; it's believed that the mosque dates back to the reign of Sultan Murad II (1359–85).

The Old Quarter
Covering one of Plovdiv's three hills with its cobbled streets and colourful mansions, the **Old Quarter** is a painter's dream and a cartographer's nightmare. As good a route as any is to start from ploshtad Dzhumaya and head east up ulitsa Saborna. Blackened fortress walls dating from Byzantine times

can be seen around Saborna and other streets, sometimes incorporated into the dozens of timber-framed National Revival houses that are Plovdiv's speciality. Outside and within, the walls are frequently decorated with niches, floral motifs or false columns, painted in a style known as *alafranga*. Turn right, up the steps beside the Church of Sveta Bogoroditsa, and continue, along twisting cobbled lanes, to the **Roman Theatre** (daily 9am–6pm; 4Lv), the best preserved in the country, and still an impressive venue for regular concerts and plays (advertised around the town and in the local press).

The City Gallery of Fine Arts and around
The **City Gallery of Fine Arts** (Mon–Fri 9.30am–5.30pm, Sat & Sun

10am–5.30pm; 3Lv, free Thurs; ⑩galleryplovdiv.com) holds an extensive collection of nineteenth- and twentieth-century Bulgarian paintings, including some fine portraits by renowned National Revival realist painter Stanislav Dospevski. A short distance northeast, the **Church of SS Constantine and Elena** contains a fine gilt iconostasis, decorated by the prolific nineteenth-century artist Zahari Zograf, whose work also appears in the adjacent **Museum of Icons** (Mon–Fri 9.30am–5.30pm, Sat & Sun 10am–5.30pm; 3Lv, free Thurs). A little further uphill is the richly decorated Kuyumdzhioglu House, now home to the **Ethnographic Museum** (Tues–Sun 9am–noon & 2–5.30pm; 5Lv, free Thurs). Folk costumes and crafts are on display on the ground floor; upstairs, the elegantly furnished rooms reflect the former owner's taste for Viennese and French Baroque.

ARRIVAL AND DEPARTURE

By train Plovdiv's train station is on bul. Hristo Botev, a 10min bus ride (#20 or #26) south of the centre.
Destinations Burgas (5 daily; 6hr); İstanbul (1 daily; 9hr); Koprivshtitsa (2 daily; 3hr 30min via Karlovo); Sofia (15 daily; 2hr 30min); Varna (8 daily; 8hr 30min).
By bus Two of Plovdiv's three bus stations are near the train station: Rodopi, serving the mountain resorts to the south, is just on the other side of the tracks; Yug, serving Sofia and the rest of the country, is one block east; the third, Sever, is north of the river (bus #3 or #99; 20min) and serves destinations such as Koprivshtitsa and Veliko Tarnovo. Several agencies at Yug station sell tickets for international buses. Hebros Bus (daily 8am–7pm; ☎ 032 626937), a Eurolines agent, can book seats on buses to Greece, Turkey and Western Europe.
Destinations Avtogara Rodopi: Smolyan (hourly; 40min via Bachkovo monastery). Avtogara Sever: Koprivshtitsa (1 daily; 2hr 30min); Veliko Tarnovo (5 daily; 4hr). Avtogara Yug: Burgas (5 daily; 4hr); Sofia (hourly; 2hr); Varna (5 daily; 5hr).

INFORMATION

Tourist information In the old town next to the Museum of Icons at ul. Saborna 22 (Tues–Fri 9am–5.30pm, Sat 10am–2pm; ☎ 032 620433), and in the new town behind the post office at pl. Tsentralen 1 (Mon–Fri 9am–6pm, Sat & Sun 10am–2pm; ☎ 032 656794, ⑩ plovdiv-tour.info). Both offices provide maps and can reserve hotel rooms and arrange excursions.

ACCOMMODATION

Plovdiv's hotel prices are relatively high, but there are several excellent hostels and a few decent-value hotel options.

HOSTELS

★ **Hiker's Hostel** ul. Saborna 53 ☎ 0885 194553, ⑩ hikers-hostel.org. Small but comfortable and friendly hostel in the middle of the old town, with fantastic views and a traditional open fire during winter. Breakfast, wi-fi and computer access are included. Also organizes day-trips in Plovdiv and the surrounding area, and guests can even pitch tents in the back yard. Dorm 14Lv, double 50Lv, camping 10Lv per pitch
Hostel Mostel ul. Petar Parchevich 13 ☎ 0879 100185, ⑩ hostelmostel.com. Charming hostel in the new town, with wi-fi, computer access, breakfast, evening meal and bottle of beer included in the price. Tent space in the yard. Dorm 20Lv, double 52Lv, camping 18Lv per person
Plovdiv Guesthouse ul. Saborna 20 ☎ 032 622432, ⑩ plovdivguest.com. Modern hostel in the old town with six-bed dorms that each have a bathroom. Private en-suite rooms are also available, while breakfast and wi-fi are offered at no extra charge. Dorm 20Lv, double 68Lv
Raisky Kat ul. Slaveikov 6 ☎ 032 268849, ⑩ raiskykat .hostel.com. Dated but welcoming family-run hostel offering doubles and triples with shared bathroom in the old town. Double 46Lv

HOTELS

Bed & Breakfast ul. Knyazh Tseretelev 24 ☎ 0878 434770, ✉ bedbreakfast@abv.bg. Situated high in the old town, this cosy family-run hotel has large, comfortably furnished en-suite rooms. Double 80Lv

---

THE NIGHT TRAIN TO İSTANBUL

There's a nightly **train** to İstanbul, which leaves Plovdiv at 9.15pm and arrives at 8am; tickets cost 51Lv and must be bought in advance from the BDZh-Rila office in Plovdiv's Central Station (Tsentralna Gara; daily 7am–noon & 1–6pm; ☎ 032 643120). Australian, US, UK and most EU citizens require Turkish **visas** (see p.1140) that can only be bought online at ⑩ evisa.gov.tr.

5

★ TREAT YOURSELF

For some of the best wine and food that southern Bulgaria has to offer, head to the restaurant of the *Hebros* hotel at ul. Konstantin Stoilov 51 (☎032 260180, ⒲hebros-hotel.com). The international menu changes from day to day – look out for their delicious home-made meatballs served with tomato and aubergine purée – and there are always vegetarian options and an array of delicious desserts. Main courses are around 25Lv and appetizers, such as stewed snails with wild rice, around 14Lv. Tempting as the food is, it is the wine that really earns *Hebros* its stellar reputation, with recommendations matched to every dish and a tremendous selection from all over Bulgaria and the world; prices range from 15–250Lv a bottle.

Star Hotel ul. Patriarch Evtiimi 13 ☎032 633599, ⒲starhotel.bg. What was once Plovdiv's top Socialist-era hotel is now offering the same faded but comfortable rooms (with a/c and wi-fi) at a fraction of their original price. Central location, but breakfast not included. Double <u>65Lv</u>

EATING

The most atmospheric restaurants are in the old town, many occupying elegant old houses and serving good, traditional Bulgarian food. In the new town, ul. Knyaz Aleksandar I is awash with cheaper fast-food outlets, though better quality can be found away from the main drag.

Alafrangite ul. Kiril Nektariev 17 ⒲alafrangite.eu. Lovely National Revival-style restaurant serving traditional Bulgarian cuisine housed in an old town mansion. Mid-range prices, plus nightly live music in the fig-tree-shaded courtyard. Daily noon–11pm.

Amsterdamer ul. Konstantin Stoilov 10 ⒲plovdiv.amsterdambg.com. Stylish reproduction of a Dutch restaurant serving international and Bulgarian cuisine at mid-range prices. Daily 11am–midnight.

Dreams ul. Knyaz Aleksandar I 42. A popular central spot for coffee, cocktails and cakes. Daily 9am–10pm.

King's Stables ul. Saborna 9a. One of the old town's nicest and most reasonably priced restaurants. Serves large portions of traditional Bulgarian food, including some excellent grilled meat dishes (4–10Lv). The yogurt with home-made blueberry jam is definitely worth trying. There's also a bar that offers equally generous measures of spirits and weekly live music performances. Summer only. Daily 11am–11pm.

Philippopolis ul. Saborna 29, ⒲philippopolis.com. An excellent old town restaurant beneath an art gallery serving well-presented international food in a quiet garden with lovely views. Daily 10am–midnight.

DRINKING AND NIGHTLIFE

The best places to drink are the pavement cafés of ul. Knyaz Aleksandar I. The Kapana area just north of the Dzhumaya mosque is the place to head for late-night tipples and dancing.

Apartment 101 ul. Gladston 8. Just off pl. Tsentralen, this tiny, incredibly popular café-bar is crammed into the first floor of a rickety old building. Daily 8am–midnight, Fri & Sat until 2am.

Balaban ul. Kiril Nektariev 4. Atmospheric old town bar with low ceilings, wood panelling and cheap cocktails. Daily 11am–midnight.

No Sense ul. Evlogi Georgiev 5. Popular place over two floors that's been pumping out retro and rock every night for years. Daily 6pm–4am.

Nylona ul. Benkovski 8. With no sign outside, this dimly lit rock bar in the Kapana area attracts an alternative crowd and hosts irregular live music performances. Daily noon–4am.

Taksim ul. Saborna 47. Cheap, open-air old town hangout with sweeping views of the city. Daily 10am–11pm.

DIRECTORY

Hospital For 24hr emergency treatment try Medicus Alpha at ul. Veliko Tarnovo 21 (☎032 634463, ⒲medicusalpha.com), alongside the park next to pl. Tsentralen.

Internet Most hostels have computer access, and cafés and bars generally offer free wi-fi.

Pharmacy Kamea, ul. Hristo Danov 4, close to pl. Dzhumaya, is open 24hr.

Post office pl. Tsentralen 1 (Mon–Sat 7am–7pm, Sun 7am–11am).

BACHKOVO MONASTERY

Just 30km away and an easy day-trip from the city, the most attractive destination around Plovdiv is **Bachkovo Monastery** (daily 7am–8pm; free). Founded in 1038 by two Georgians in the service of the Byzantine Empire, this is Bulgaria's second-largest monastery. A great iron-studded door admits visitors to the cobbled courtyard, surrounded by wooden galleries and adorned with colourful frescoes. Beneath the vaulted porch of Bachkovo's principal church, **Sveta Bogoroditsa**, are frescoes depicting the horrors in store for sinners; the entrance itself, overseen by the Holy Trinity, is rather more uplifting.

ARRIVAL AND DEPARTURE

Take one of the hourly buses from Rodopi station towards Smolyan; the stop for Bachkovo is 45min from Plovdiv.

ACCOMMODATION AND EATING

It's possible to stay in refurbished rooms in the monastery (☎ 03327 2277; 40Lv/person with hot water and en suite), and there are three restaurants just outside; *Vodopada*, with its mini-waterfall, is the best.

Central Bulgaria

For over a thousand years, Stara Planina – known to foreigners as the **Balkan range** – has been the cradle of the Bulgarian nation. It was here that the Khans established the First Kingdom, and here, too, after a period of Byzantine control, that the Boyars proclaimed the Second Kingdom and created a magnificent capital at **Veliko Tarnovo**. The nearby Sredna Gora (Central Mountains) were inhabited as early as the fifth millennium BC, but for Bulgarians this forested region is best known as the Land of the April Rising, the nineteenth-century rebellion for which the picturesque town of Koprivshtitsa will always be remembered.

Although they lie a little way off the main rail lines from Sofia, neither Veliko Tarnovo nor Koprivshtitsa is difficult to reach. The former lies just south of Gorna Oryahovitsa, a major rail junction midway between Varna and Sofia, from where you can pick up a local bus; the latter is served by the Koprivshtitsa stop, where five daily trains from Sofia are met by local buses to ferry you the 12km to the village itself.

KOPRIVSHTITSA

Seen from a distance, **KOPRIVSHTITSA** (Копривщица) looks almost too lovely to be real, its half-timbered houses lying in a valley amid wooded hills. It would be an oasis of rural calm if not for the tourists drawn by the superb architecture and Bulgarians paying homage to a landmark in their nation's history.

WHAT TO SEE AND DO

All of the town's museums are open 9.30am–5.30pm, with half of them closing on Mondays, and the other half on Tuesdays. You can buy a combined ticket for all six for 5Lv at the tourist office and at any of the museums; otherwise they are priced at 3Lv each. It's also possible to hire an English-speaking guide for a two-hour tour (10Lv).

A street running off to the west of the main square leads to the **Oslekov House** (closed Mon). Its summer guest room is particularly impressive, with a vast wooden ceiling carved with geometric motifs. Cross the Freedom Bridge opposite the information centre to reach **Karavelov House** (closed Tues), the childhood home of Lyuben Karavelov, a fervent advocate of Bulgaria's liberation who spent much of his adult life in exile where he edited revolutionary publications. Near the Surlya Bridge is the birthplace of the poet **Dimcho Debelyanov** (closed Mon), who is buried in the grounds of the hilltop **Church of the Holy Virgin**. A gate at the rear of the churchyard leads to the home of **Todor Kableshkov** (closed Mon), leader of the local rebels. Kableshkov's house now displays weapons used in the Rising and features a wonderful circular vestibule. Continuing south, cross the **Bridge of the First Shot**, which spans the Byala Reka stream, head up ulitsa Nikola Belodezhdov, and you'll come to the **Lyutov House** (closed Tues), once home to a wealthy yogurt merchant and today housing some of Koprivshtitsa's most sumptuous interiors. On the opposite side of the River Topolnitsa, steps lead up to the birthplace of another major figure in the Rising, **Georgi Benkovski** (closed Tues). A tailor by profession, he made the famous silk banner embroidered with the Bulgarian lion and "Liberty or Death!".

5

KOPRIVSHTITSA AND THE APRIL RISING

From the "Bridge of the First Shot" to the "Place of the Scimitar Charge", there's hardly a part of Koprivshtitsa that isn't named after an episode or participant in the **April Rising of 1876**, a meticulously planned grassroots revolution against Ottoman control that failed within days because the organizers had vastly overestimated their support. Neighbouring towns were burned by the *Bashibazouks* – the irregular troops recruited by the Turks to put the rebels in their place – and refugees flooded into Koprivshtitsa, spreading panic. The rebels eventually took to the hills while local traders bribed the *Bashibazouks* to spare the village – and so Koprivshtitsa survived unscathed, to be admired by subsequent generations as a symbol of heroism. Although the home-grown Bulgarian revolution failed, the barbarity of the Turkish reprisals outraged the international community and led to the 1877–78 War of Liberation which won freedom for Bulgaria from over five hundred years of Ottoman rule.

ARRIVAL AND INFORMATION

By train Buses to Koprivshtitsa usually meet trains arriving at the station 12km south of town.

Destinations Burgas (1 daily; 5hr 30min); Plovdiv (6 daily; 5hr); Sofia (5 daily; 2hr); Veliko Tarnovo (3 daily; 7–11hr).

By bus The small bus station is 200m south of the main square.

Destinations Plovdiv (1 daily; 2hr 30min); Sofia (5 daily; 2hr).

Tourist office The tourist office on the main square, pl. 20th April 7 (daily 10am–7pm; ☎07184 2191, ⓦ koprivshtitza.com), sells tickets for Koprivshtitsa's six house museums.

ACCOMMODATION

The tourist office can book private rooms (around 40Lv) in charming village houses. Advance reservations are recommended in summer.

Bolyarka ul. Petar Zhilkov 7 ☎07184 2043. Four-room B&B just uphill from the centre, offering bright, pine-furnished rooms and a lovely garden. Double 40Lv

Panorama ul. Georgi Benkovski 40 ☎07184 2035, ⓦ panoramata.com. A well-run complex south of the centre with smart modern rooms on the ground floor and traditional-style rooms above; most have sweeping views of the town. Double 60Lv

Trayanova Kashta ul. Gerenilo 5 ☎07184 3057. Just up the street from the Oslekov House, with delightful rooms in the National Revival style. Double 40Lv

EATING AND DRINKING

Dyado Liben Inn This fine nineteenth-century mansion opposite the main square serves traditional dishes such as *gyuvech* (meat stew) for around 6–12Lv. Daily 11am–11pm.

Lomeva Kashta A folk-style restaurant just north of the square, serving grills and salads from 6Lv. Daily 10am–midnight.

VELIKO TARNOVO

With its dramatic medieval fortifications and huddles of antique houses teetering over the lovely River Yantra, **VELIKO TARNOVO** (Велико Търново) holds a uniquely important place in the minds of Bulgarians. When the National Assembly met here to draft Bulgaria's first constitution in 1879, it did so in the former capital of the Second Kingdom (1185–1396), whose civilization was snuffed out by the Turks. It was here, too, that the Communists chose to proclaim the People's Republic in 1944.

WHAT TO SEE AND DO

Modern Veliko Tarnovo centres on **ploshtad Mayka Balgariya**: from here bulevard Nezavisimost (which becomes ulitsa. Stefan Stambolov after a few hundred metres) heads northeast into a network of narrow streets that curve above the River Yantra and mark out the old town and its photogenic houses. From ulitsa Stambolov, the narrow cobbled ulitsa Rakovski slopes up into the **Varosh Quarter**, a pretty ensemble of nineteenth-century buildings once home to bustling artisans' workshops and now occupied by clothing and souvenir shops.

Sarafkina House

Clinging to the steep hillside at ulitsa General Gurko 88 is the **Sarafkina House** (Tues–Sat 9am–6pm; 6Lv), whose elegant restored interior is notable for its splendid octagonal vestibule and a panelled rosette ceiling.

Museum of the Bulgarian Renaissance and Constituent Assembly

Designed by the legendary local architect Kolyo Ficheto (1800–81), the blue-and-white building where the first Bulgarian parliament assembled in 1879 is now home to the **Museum of the Bulgarian Renaissance and Constituent Assembly** (Wed–Mon 9am–6pm; 6Lv), where you can see a reconstruction of the original assembly hall, and a collection of icons.

Tsarevets

Ulitsa Ivan Vazov leads directly from the museum to the medieval fortress, **Tsarevets** (daily: April–Oct 8am–7pm; Nov–March 9am–5pm; 6Lv). A successful rebellion against Byzantium was mounted from this citadel in 1185, and Tsarevets remained the centre of Bulgarian power until 1393, when, after a three-month siege, it fell to the Turks. The partially restored fortress is entered via the **Asenova Gate** halfway along the western ramparts. To the right, paths lead round to **Baldwin's Tower**, where Baldwin of Flanders, the so-called Latin Emperor of Byzantium, was incarcerated by Tsar Kaloyan. Visitors can climb up to the parapet of the fully renovated tower for sweeping views of the town.

Don't miss the dramatic twenty-minute Tsarevets Sound and Light show held most evenings during the summer – it's free on public holidays, but on other days you'll have to wait for a large group to fork out for it, otherwise it doesn't go ahead. Call ☎062 636952 for show times.

ARRIVAL AND INFORMATION

By train All trains to Veliko Tarnovo actually stop at Gorna Oryahovitsa station from where bus #10 covers the 13km to the centre (30min). International trains must be booked in advance through the Rila-BDZh office behind the tourist office at ul. Kaloyan 1 (Mon–Fri 8am–noon & 1–4.30pm; ☎062 622042).

Destinations Bucharest (2 daily; 6hr); Burgas (4 daily; 7hr); İstanbul (1 daily; 14hr); Sofia (10 daily; 4hr); Varna (9 daily; 3hr 30min).

By bus Buses to and from Sofia and Varna use the small central bus terminal (*tsentralna avtogara*) just behind the

Tourist Information Centre outside *Hotel Etar*. Buses to Plovdiv, Burgas and Ruse use the western terminal (*avtogara zapad*), 4km southwest of town accessed by bus #10 and trolley buses #1 and #3 from the centre. From Ruse there are two daily buses to Bucharest (1hr 30min). Buses to Athens and İstanbul use the southern bus terminal (*avtogara yug*) which is a 10min walk south of the centre along bul. Hristo Botev.

Destinations Athens (1 daily; 16hr); Burgas (4 daily; 4hr 30min); İstanbul (1 daily; 10hr); Plovdiv (4 daily; 4hr); Ruse (5 daily; 2hr); Sofia (hourly; 4hr); Varna (hourly; 5hr).

Tourist information The tourist office is at bul. Hristo Botev 5 (summer Mon–Fri 9am–6pm, Sat & Sun 9am–5pm; winter Mon–Fri 9am–5pm; ☎062 622148, ⓦvelikoturnovo.info).

ACCOMMODATION

Comfort ul. Paneyot Tipografov 5 ☎062 628728, ⓦhotelcomfortbg.com. A spotless, family-run place, with wi-fi, a/c and splendid views of the Tsarevets fortress. Located just above the Varosh Quarter's bazaar. Double __50Lv__

Hikers Hostel ul. Rezervoarska 91 ☎062 604019 or ☎0889 691661, ⓦhikers-hostel.org. A friendly hostel with quirky wooden furniture tucked away in a narrow street high above the Varosh Quarter, looking out over Tsarevets. There's excellent dorm accommodation, tent space, kitchen and free wi-fi, computer access and pick-up service. Dorm __14Lv__, double __52Lv__, camping __10Lv__ per person

★ **Hostel Mostel** ul. Iordan Indjeto 10 ☎0897 859359, ⓦhostelmostel.com. Located in a beautifully restored nineteenth-century Ottoman building south of the road leading to Tsarevets, with comfortable dorms and private en-suite rooms. Included in the price are a pick-up service, wi-fi, computer access, an all-you-can-eat breakfast, evening meal and a beer for every night of your stay. There's also a barbecue and tent space in the garden. Dorm __20Lv__, double __60Lv__, camping __18Lv__ per person

Nomads Hostel ul. Gurko 27 ☎062 603092 or ☎0886 039705, ⓦnomadshostel.com. A welcoming, cosy and central hostel with helpful staff who can arrange a variety of trips around the region. Wi-fi, computer access and a great organic breakfast are part of the deal. Dorm __18Lv__, double __50Lv__

EATING AND DRINKING

Clun na Architecta ul. Velcho Dzhamdhziyata 14. Tucked away down a quiet alley and partially hewn into a rock face, this pleasant restaurant serves authentic Bulgarian cuisine and has a garden with lovely views. Daily 11am–midnight.

5

Melodie Bar pl. Slaveykov 1. Small, dimly lit jazz bar frequented by locals and expats. Daily 11.30am–2am.

Shastlivetsa ul. Stambolov 79. Perennially popular restaurant with fantastic views that offers local dishes, as well as a large range of pizzas and pastas. Main courses 6–25Lv. Daily 9am–midnight.

Stratilat ul. Rakovski 11. Located at the beginning of the Varosh Quarter, this relaxed café and cake shop occupies a restored old building with plenty of outdoor seating. Daily 10am–10pm.

The Black Sea coast

Bulgaria's **Black Sea** resorts have been popular holiday haunts for more than a century, though it wasn't until the 1960s that the coastline was developed for mass tourism, with Communist party officials from across the former Eastern Bloc descending on the beaches each year for a spot of socialist fun in the sun. Since then, the **resorts** have mushroomed and grown increasingly sophisticated, with the prototype mega-complexes followed by holiday villages. Fine weather is practically guaranteed, and the selling of the coast has been successful in economic terms, but with the exception of ancient **Sozopol** and touristy **Nesebar**, there's little to please the eye. The coast's two main cities – **Varna** and **Burgas** – can both be used as a base for getting to less developed spots, such as the cliffs of **Kamen Bryag** and **Sinemorets**' superb beaches.

VARNA

VARNA (Варна) is a cosmopolitan place, and nice to stroll through: Baroque, nineteenth-century and contemporary architecture are pleasantly blended with shady promenades and a handsome seaside park. As a settlement it dates back almost five millennia, but it wasn't until seafaring Greeks founded a colony here in 585 BC that the town became a port. The modern city is used by both commercial freighters and the navy, as well as being a popular tourist resort in its own right.

WHAT TO SEE AND DO

Social life revolves around **ploshtad Nezavisimost**, where the opera house and theatre provide a backdrop for restaurants and cafés. The square is the starting point of Varna's evening promenade, which flows eastward from here along bulevard Knyaz Boris I and towards bulevard Slivnitsa and the seaside gardens. Beyond the opera house, Varna's main lateral boulevard cuts through ploshtad Mitropolit Simeon to the domed **Cathedral of the Assumption**. Constructed in 1886, it contains a splendid iconostasis and bishop's throne. The **Archeology Museum** on the corner of Mariya Luiza and Slivnitsa (daily 10am–5pm; Ⓦamvarna.com) houses one of Bulgaria's finest collections of antiquities. Most impressive are the skeletons adorned with Thracian gold jewellery that were unearthed in Varna in 1972 and date back almost six thousand years.

South of the centre on ulitsa Han Krum are the extensive remains of the third-century **Roman baths** (Tues–Sun 10am–5pm; 5Lv). It's still possible to discern the various bathing areas and the once huge exercise hall. At the southern edge of the Sea Gardens, the **Navy Museum** (Mon–Sat: summer 10am–6pm; winter 10am–5pm; 5Lv) is worth a trip to see the boat responsible for the Bulgarian Navy's only victory; it sank the Turkish cruiser *Hamidie* off Cape Kaliakra in 1912.

Beaches

Varna's municipal beach offers a perfunctory stretch of sand but little tranquillity as it's dominated by open-air bars and clubs. The beaches at the busy resorts of **Golden Sands** and **Albena** to the north are hardly any quieter, but are certainly wider and much more attractive. Beyond Albena the coastline turns rocky until the villages at **Krapets** and **Durankulak**, just short of the Romanian border, which boast some wonderful undeveloped sandy beaches.

ARRIVAL AND DEPARTURE

By plane Varna's international airport (ⓦ varna-airport
.bg) is about a 15min ride northwest of the city from
opposite the Tourist Information Centre. Take bus #409
(every 15min 6am–11pm; 1–3Lv), or taxis cost 12–15Lv.
By train The train station is a 10min walk south of the
centre along ul. Tsar Simeon.
Destinations Plovdiv (6 daily; 8hr); Sofia (6 daily; 7hr
30min).
By bus The bus terminal is a 10min journey (bus #1,
#22 or #41) northwest of the centre on bul. Vladislav
Varnenchik.
Destinations Albena (6 daily; 30min); Burgas (every
30min; 2hr 30min); Durankulak (1 daily; 2hr 45min);
Golden Sands (every 30min; 20min); Kamen Bryag (4
daily; 2hr 30min); Krapets (1 daily; 2hr 20min); Sofia
(every 30min; 7hr); Sunny Beach (hourly; 2hr 10min);
Veliko Tarnovo (7 daily; 4hr).

INFORMATION

Tourist office pl. Sv. Kiril i Metodi opposite the Cathedral
of the Assumption (summer daily 9am–7pm; winter
Mon–Fri 9am–6pm; ☎052 820690, ⓦ varnainfo.bg). The
staff sell city maps, reserve hotel rooms and organize
excursions.

ACCOMMODATION

Flag Hostel ul. Bratia Shkorpil 13A ☎0897 408115,
ⓦ varnahostel.com. Located a couple of minutes' walk
east of the Cathedral of the Assumption, the hostel
occupies the top floor of a nondescript building and
offers small dorms with wi-fi, a/c and breakfast
included. Dorm 18Lv
Interhotel Cherno More bul. Slivnitsa 33 ☎052
612235, ⓦ chernomorebg.com. Once the city's flagship
Socialist-era hotel, this central, sixteen-floor concrete
monolith now offers its modernized rooms at reasonable
prices. Fabulous views and a top-floor cocktail bar and
restaurant. Double 70Lv
★ **Yo Ho Hostel** ul. Ruse 23 ☎0887 933340,
ⓦ yohohostel.com. Centrally located just off pl.
Nezavisimost, this fun hostel sprawls over several colourful
floors and hosts regular live bands and art exhibitions.
Breakfast, wi-fi, computer access and pick-up service are
all thrown in. Helpful staff can arrange day-trips and bike
rental. Dorm 14Lv, double 40Lv

EATING AND DRINKING

There are plenty of bars to choose from along bul. Knyaz
Boris I, while in summer the beach, reached by steps
from the Sea Gardens, is lined with open-air bars, fish
restaurants and a seemingly unending strip of
nightclubs. Outside high season, though, it's pretty
dismal.

Arkitekt ul. Musala 10. A traditionally furnished wooden
townhouse west of the centre serving authentic Bulgarian
dishes and plenty of grilled meat (from 7Lv), with a
pleasant courtyard garden. Daily 11am–11pm.
Bara bul. Knyazh Boris 24. Quirky first-floor bar with
chessboard ceiling lamps, bathroom mosaics, old furniture
and a great selection of cocktails. Daily noon–2am.
Happy Bar and Grill pl. Nezavisimost. American-style
restaurant with a picture menu offering a mixture of
Bulgarian and international food. The *kashkaval pane*
(battered cheese) is particularly good (4.90Lv). Daily
11am–11pm.
Interhotel Cherno More bul. Slivnitsa 33. Head to the
sixteenth-floor cocktail bar for unrivalled views of the city;
cocktails will set you back 8–12Lv. Daily 11am–1am.
★ **Morske Vulk** ul. Odrin. Just south of pl. Exarch Yosef,
this is one of the friendliest and cheapest restaurants in
town, with a vibrant, alternative crowd and brilliant
Bulgarian dishes, including vegetarian options such as
pizza for around 8Lv. Daily 11am–2am.
Three Lions Pub pl. Slaveikov 1. Thriving English-
themed pub located 100m east of the train station with
regular live rock bands, big-screen TVs and good food.
Daily 11am–1am.

BURGAS

The south coast's prime urban centre
and transport hub, **BURGAS** (Бургас)
provides easy access to the picture-
postcard town of Nesebar to the north
and Sozopol to the south. Bypassed by
most tourists, the pedestrianized city
centre, lined with smart boutiques, bars
and cafés, is pleasant enough, though
Burgas' best features are the well-
manicured **Sea Gardens** overlooking the
beach, and its pier at the eastern end
of town.

ARRIVAL AND INFORMATION

By plane Burgas International Airport (ⓦ bourgas
-airport.com) is 15km north of the centre. Take bus #15
from the central bus station (every 30min from
6am–10pm) or a taxi (15–20Lv).
By train The train station is at the southern edge of town,
near the port.
Destinations Plovdiv (6 daily; 6hr); Sofia (5 daily; 8hr).
By bus The bus station is next to the train station.
Destinations İstanbul (2 daily; 6hr); Nesebar (every
30min; 50min); Plovdiv (4 daily; 4hr); Sinemorets (1 daily;
1hr 30min); Sofia (hourly; 6hr 30min); Sozopol (every
30min; 50min); Varna (hourly; 2hr).
Tourist office Beneath bul. Hristo Botev in the underpass

5

opposite the opera house (Mon–Fri 9.30am–5.30pm; ☎056 841542, ⊛tic.burgas.bg). Provides maps and can make hotel reservations.

ACCOMMODATION

Burgas has a reasonable choice of mid-range hotels but has long suffered from a shortage of budget accommodation.

Burgas Hostel Slavyanska 14 ☎056 825854, ⊛hostelburgas.com. Central hostel with friendly, helpful staff located 10min east of the train station. Offers clean dorms, sea views from its roof terrace, wi-fi, free breakfast, and kitchen and laundry facilities, as well as a free pick-up service from the bus and train stations. Dorm 20Lv, double 50Lv

Fors ul. K. Fotinov 17 ☎056 828852, ⊛hotelfors-bg.com. Smart central hotel with good service, and spotless en-suite rooms with wi-fi and a/c. Double 75Lv

Fotinov ul. K. Fotinov 22 ☎056 993031, ⊛hotelfotinov .com. Pleasant family-run hotel near the *Fors*. Facilities include fitness equipment, wi-fi, sauna and a/c. Double 82Lv

EATING AND DRINKING

Burgas' pedestrianized central boulevards are crammed with bars, cafés and restaurants that spill out onto the streets in summer. There are several pleasant places to eat in the Sea Gardens and plenty more bars along the beach.

Chai vuv Fabrikata Teahouse pl. Troikata 4 ⊛teahouseburgas.bg. Mellow vegetarian restaurant and teahouse facing the central square. Daily 10am–11pm.

Rosé ul. Bogoridi 19 ⊛roserestaurant.bg. Stylish central restaurant serving excellent Mediterranean cuisine at reasonable prices. Daily 10am–midnight.

Zheleznyat Svetilnik ul. K. Fotinov 28. Great traditional-style restaurant with shaded outdoor seating serving typical Bulgarian dishes at mid-range prices with an emphasis on grilled meat. Excellent wine list. Daily 11am–11pm.

NESEBAR

Famed for its delightful medieval churches, nineteenth-century wooden architecture and labyrinthine cobbled streets, **NESEBAR**'s (Несебър) old town, 35km northeast of Burgas, lies on a narrow, man-made isthmus connected by road to the mainland. It was founded by Greek colonists and grew into a thriving port during the Byzantine era; ownership alternated between Bulgaria and Byzantium until the Ottomans captured it in 1453. The town remained an important centre of Greek culture and the seat of a bishop under Turkish rule, which left Nesebar's **Byzantine churches** reasonably intact. Nowadays the town depends on them for its tourist appeal, demonstrated by the often overwhelming stream of summer visitors. Outside the hectic summer season, the place seems eerily deserted, with little open other than a few sleepy cafés.

WHAT TO SEE AND DO

Standing just inside the city gates, the **Archeological Museum** (summer Mon–Fri 9am–8pm, Sat & Sun 9.30am–7pm; winter Mon–Fri 9am–5pm; 5Lv; ⊛ancient-nessebar .com) has an array of Greek tombstones and medieval icons on display. Immediately beyond the museum is **Christ Pantokrator**, the first of Nesebar's churches, currently in use as an upmarket art gallery (summer only Mon–Fri 9am–8pm, Sat & Sun 9.30am–7pm). It features an unusual frieze of swastikas – an ancient symbol of fertility and continual change. Downhill on ulitsa Mitropolitska is the eleventh-century church of **St John the Baptist** (now also an art gallery; same hours), only one of whose frescoes still survives. Overhung by half-timbered houses, ulitsa Aheloi branches off from ulitsa Mitropolitska towards the **Church of Sveti Spas** (summer only Mon–Fri 10am–5pm, Sat & Sun 10am–3pm; 3Lv), outwardly unremarkable but filled with seventeenth-century frescoes.

A few steps to the east lies the ruined **Old Metropolitan Church**, dominating a plaza filled with pavement cafés and street traders. The church itself dates back to the sixth century, and it was here that bishops officiated during the city's heyday. Standing in splendid isolation beside the shore, the ruined **Church of St John Aliturgetos** represents the zenith of Byzantine architecture in Bulgaria. Its exterior employs limestone, red bricks, crosses, mussel shells and ceramic plaques for decoration.

Beaches

Visitors can either head for Nesebar's handful of small beaches or hop on a shuttle bus to the unattractive neighbouring resort of **Sunny Beach** where a great expanse of golden sand studded with thousands of umbrellas stretches for several kilometres along the overdeveloped coastline.

ARRIVAL AND INFORMATION

By bus Buses arrive at either the harbour at the western end of town, or further up Han Krum before turning around to head for the nearby Sunny Beach resort. Bus #1 connects the new and old towns.

Destinations Burgas (every 30min; 50min); Sofia (8 daily; 6hr 30min); Varna (6 daily; 2hr).

Tourist office Located in the centre of the old town at ul. Messemvria 10 (daily 10am–6pm; ☎0554 42611, ⓦ visitnessebar.org).

ACCOMMODATION

You can book private rooms (40–60Lv for a double), many in fine old houses, through Messemvria Tour at ul. Han Krum 16 (daily 8am–6pm) close to the post office in the new town, near the St John the Baptist church.

Lebed ul. Avrora 8a ☎0899 841872. Located on quiet back-streets at the eastern end of the old town, this place offers clean, simple rooms with modern furnishings. Double 50Lv

Tony ul. Kraybrezhna 20 ☎0554 42403. This old town hotel's pleasant, a/c rooms have balconies with sea views and wi-fi. Double 50Lv

EATING AND DRINKING

There are plenty of places to eat, although most restaurants are aimed at the passing tourist crowd, serving predictably mediocre food. Snacks are available from summertime kiosks along the waterfront.

Kapitanska Sreshta ul. Mena 22. Atmospheric fish restaurant housed in a nineteenth-century building with a lovely shaded terrace overlooking the old town's harbour. Daily 10am–midnight.

Neptun ul. Neptun 1. Pleasant outdoor spot on the southeastern tip of the old town with great sea views. Serves a reasonably priced selection of Bulgarian standards. Daily 10am–midnight.

SOZOPOL

SOZOPOL (Созопол) is a busy fishing port and holiday resort, especially popular with Eastern European tourists. Its charm owes much to the **architecture** of the old town, where wooden houses jostle for space on a narrow peninsula, their upper storeys almost meeting across cobbled streets. The oldest settlement in Bulgaria, Sozopol was founded in the seventh century BC by Greek colonists.

WHAT TO SEE AND DO

The **Archeological Museum** (summer daily 9am–7pm; winter Mon–Fri 9am–5.30pm; 4Lv) behind the library holds a worthwhile collection of ancient ceramics, as well as a number of artefacts uncovered in the local area. Further into the town, follow the signs to the **Southern Fortress Wall and Tower Complex** (summer 9am–9pm; open by appointment only in winter; 4Lv; ⓦ sozopol-foundation.com), which gives access to a beautifully restored tower and exhibits dating from the fourth century BC.

Sozopol's two small **beaches** are predictably overcrowded in high season, so it's worth making the short trip north to the emptier beaches around the *Zlatna Ribka* campsite (see p.152).

ARRIVAL AND INFORMATION

By bus Buses from Burgas arrive at pl. Han Krum on the southern edge of the old town. Those from other Bulgarian cities usually arrive and depart from pl. Cherno More in the the new town.

Destinations Burgas (every 30min; 50min); Plovdiv (7 daily; 5hr); Sofia (8 daily; 7hr).

Tourist information In the absence of a municipal tourist office, the best source of information is the Aiatour travel agency located high in the new town at ul. Musala 7 (summer daily 9am–9pm; irregular office hours out of season; ☎0550 23925, ⓦ aiatour.com).

ACCOMMODATION

Accommodation in Sozopol can be even harder to find during summer than in Nesebar, and most places shut down for the rest of the year. The Aiatour travel agency (see above) can arrange private rooms of varying standards (18–30Lv per person).

Art ul. Kiril I Metodii 72 ☎0550 24081, ⓦ arthotel-shh .com. Smart modern hotel and restaurant perched on a rocky cliff at the northern end of the peninsula. Double 70Lv

Rusalka ul. Milet 36 ☎0550 23047. On the south of the peninsula, this is the best-value old town hotel with

5

comfortable a/c rooms overlooking the sea. Breakfast not included. Double 80Lv

Zlatna Ribka 3km north of town on the Burgas bus route ☎0550 22534, ⊛zlatnaribka.bgcamping.com. Popular seaside campsite with great beach: the closer you are to the shore, the pricier the pitch. Camping 30Lv per tent; camper van 35Lv

EATING AND DRINKING

Art ul. Kiril I Metodii 72. Great old town restaurant with outdoor tables on the cliff's edge at the northeastern end of the old town. Serves a mid-priced range of Bulgarian

and international meals. Daily 10am–midnight.

Art Club Mishel ul. Apollonia 39. Central bar and café in a lovely old town building with plenty of comfy outdoor seating. Live jazz most nights. Daily 11am–1am.

Chuchura ul. Ribarska 10. Situated on the western side of the old town, this is a popular traditional-style restaurant with a particularly good selection of fish dishes (20–30Lv). Daily 11am–midnight.

Vyatarna Melnitsa ul. Morski Skali 27. Similar in style and price to the *Chuchura*, the "Windmill" has excellent service and perches on the northern tip of the peninsula. Daily 10am–midnight.

VIS ISLAND

Croatia

HIGHLIGHTS

❶ Amphiteatre, Pula Visit the sixth-largest amphitheatre in the world. **See p.165**

❷ Zadar Visit this buzzing town and discover its unique Sea Organ. **See p.167**

❸ Diocletian's Palace, Split Be amazed by this extraordinary 1700-year-old palace. **See p.169**

❹ Vis Island Relax on the Dalmatian Coast's most laidback island. **See p.175**

❺ Dubrovnik The ancient walled city is hardly undiscovered but can still work its unique magic. See p.178

HIGHLIGHTS ARE MARKED ON THE MAP ON P.155

ROUGH COSTS

Daily budget Basic €50, occasional treat €70

Drink Litre of local wine €6

Food *Čevapčići* (mini kebabs) €5

Private room/hostel €42/€20

Travel Ferry: within Dalmatian islands €5–10; bus: Zagreb–Split €25

FACT FILE

Population 4.4 million

Language Croatian (Hrvatski)

Currency Kuna (kn)

Capital Zagreb

International phone code ☎ 385

Time zone GMT +1hr

6

Introduction

The serpentine coastline and sheer natural beauty of Croatia (Hrvatska) make it an irresistible European destination. Its tourist industry is now fully fledged, but the accompanying development has been fairly unobtrusive and there are still plenty of secluded rocky beaches and pristine old towns to explore. As well as a stunning array of architecture, the country has a rich cultural heritage and a rapidly expanding festival scene. Already a hit destination among those in the know, Croatia's recently acquired EU membership means it's set to grow in popularity.

The capital, **Zagreb**, is a lively central European metropolis, combining elegant nineteenth-century architecture with plenty of cultural diversions and a vibrant bar and club scene. The peninsula of **Istria** contains many of the country's most developed resorts, with old Venetian towns like **Rovinj** rubbing shoulders with the raffish port of **Pula**. Further south lies **Dalmatia**, a dramatic, mountain-fringed stretch of coastline studded with islands. Dalmatia's main towns are Italianate **Zadar** and vibrant **Split**, an ancient Roman settlement and modern port that provides a jumping-off point to offshore destinations like high-society **Hvar**, untamed **Vis** and enchanting **Korčula**.

South of Split lies the medieval walled city of **Dubrovnik**, stuffed full of tourists but still a magical place to be.

CHRONOLOGY

600s Croatian Slavs settle in the region.

925 Tomislav is crowned the first King of Croatia.

1102 Inland Croatia accepts the authority of Hungarian kings.

1400s Coastal Croatia (independent city-state Dubrovnik excepted) falls under Venetian rule.

1526 Habsburg dynasty takes control of inland Croatia after the fall of Hungary to the Ottomans.

1918 After the defeat of the Habsburgs in World War I, Croatia joins the Kingdom of the Serbs, Croats and Slovenes.

1929 The kingdom becomes known as Yugoslavia.

1941 Croatian-Slovene communist Josip Broz Tito leads resistance to the Nazis and local quislings.

1945 Croatia becomes part of the communist Yugoslav federation.

1980 Tito dies without a clear successor, and political paralysis grips the country.

1990 Multi-party elections in Croatia produce a pro-independence majority.

1991 Croatia declares its independence. The Yugoslav army, backed by Serb irregulars, responds with force.

1995 Croatian forces retake areas occupied by Serbs, bringing the war to an end.

1999 Conservative president Franjo Tuđman dies, ushering in a more liberal era in Croatian politics.

2009 Croatia joins the NATO alliance.

2012 Croatian General Ante Gotovina is cleared of all charges on appeal at the International War Crimes Tribunal in the Hague.

2013 Croatia joins the EU on July 1.

ARRIVAL AND DEPARTURE

The principal international **airports** are Dubrovnik, Pula, Rijeka, Split, Zadar and Zagreb. Ryanair runs services to Pula, Rijeka and Zadar and easyJet fly to Zagreb, Split and Dubrovnik. Wizz Air fly to Split, Jet2 fly to Pula, Split and Dubrovnik, and BA fly to Dubrovnik and Zagreb. The national carrier, Croatia Airlines (ⓦcroatiaairlines.com), operates routes throughout Europe.

Ferry routes to Croatia run frequently from Italy: Split and Zadar from Ancona, Split from Pescara, Rovinj from Trieste and Venice, Pula from Venice and Dubrovnik from Bari; see ⓦjadrolinija.hr, ⓦvenezialines.com, ⓦtriestelines.it and ⓦsnav.it.

Croatia is served by many international **buses**, including services from Vienna, Belgrade and Sarajevo, most of them run by Eurolines (ⓦeurolines.com), who are

6

CROATIA

SLOVENIA

LJUBLJANA

ITALY

Trieste

HUNGARY

ZAGREB

Karlovac

Sisak

Osijek

Poreč
Vrsar
Rovinj
Pula ❶

Istria

Rijeka

Krk

Cres
Rab

PLITVICE LAKES
NATIONAL PARK

Gospić

PAKLENICA
NATIONAL
PARK

Petrčane
Zadar ❷

N

**ADRIATIC
SEA**

Knin

BOSNIA -
HERZEGOVINA

SERBIA

Venice
Ancona
Pescara

Šibenik
KRKA
NATIONAL PARK

Dalmatia

SARAJEVO

ITALY

❸ Split

Supetar

Brač

Bol Stari Grad

Vis
Town

Hvar
Town

Jelsa

Komiža *Vis*

Hvar

❹ Vela Luka

Korčula

MONTENEGRO

Korčula
Town

Mljet

❺
Dubrovnik

HIGHLIGHTS
❶ Amphitheatre, Pula
❷ Zadar
❸ Diocletian's Palace, Split
❹ Vis Island
❺ Dubrovnik

0   50
kilometres

Metres

1000
500
200
0

partnered with AutoTrans (⬤autotrans
.hr). Several German cities are connected
with Croatia too; see ⬤touring.de.
For services from Trieste check ⬤auto
stazionetrieste.it.

Croatia is also linked with the rest
of Europe by **rail**; see ⬤bahn.de
for timetables.

GETTING AROUND

Croatia's **train** service is pretty limited;
you're much more likely to use the
excellent **bus** network.

BY BUS

Croatia has an array of local bus
companies. Leading ones include
AutoTrans (⬤autotrans.hr); services are
well integrated and punctual, and bus

stations tend to be well organized. If
you're at a big city bus station, tickets
(*karta*) must be bought from ticket
windows before boarding. Elsewhere, buy
them from the driver. You'll be charged
around 7kn for items of baggage to be
stored in the hold.

BY TRAIN

Croatian Railways (*Hrvatske željeznice*;
⬤hzpp.hr) runs a smooth and efficient
service, but it isn't very extensive. The
most useful route is the Zagreb–Split
line, which is served by high-speed,
tilting trains. Trains (*vlak*, plural *vlakovi*)
are divided into *putnički* (slow ones,
which stop at every station) and IC
(intercity trains that are faster and more
expensive). Timetables (*vozni red*) are
usually displayed on boards in stations

6

– *odlazak* means departure, *dolazak* arrival. **InterRail** passes are valid, and you must pay a small reservation fee for longer journeys.

BY FERRY

Jadrolinija (Ⓦjadrolinija.hr) operates numerous **ferry** services. The Rijeka–Split–Stari Grad (Hvar)–Korčula Town (Korčula)–Sobra (Mljet)–Dubrovnik route runs twice a week in both directions between May and September. The Rijeka to Dubrovnik route (22hr 30min) involves one night on the boat. In addition, ferries and faster catamarans link Split with the islands of Brač, Hvar, Vis and Korčula. **Fares** are reasonable for short trips: Split to Hvar costs 22kn. For longer journeys, prices vary greatly according to the level of comfort. **Book** in advance for longer journeys, wherever possible, and note that ferry timetables change around the end of May and end of September.

ACCOMMODATION

Private rooms (*privatne sobe*) have long been the mainstay of Croatian tourism. Bookings are made through private travel agencies (usually open daily 8am–8/9pm in summer). High-season prices are around €40/310kn for a simple double sharing a toilet and bathroom and €50/375kn upwards for an en-suite double; stays of fewer than three nights are subject to a surcharge. Places fill up quickly in July and August: arrive early or book ahead. Single travellers will find it difficult to get a private room unless they're prepared to pay the price of a double – although outside peak season you can negotiate.

It's very likely you'll be offered a place to stay by elderly ladies waiting outside train, bus and ferry stations, particularly in southern Dalmatia. Don't be afraid to take a room offered in this manner, but be sure to establish the location and agree a price before setting off: expect to pay around twenty percent less than you would with an agency. However you find a room, you can usually examine it

before committing to paying for it. Official establishments with rooms should have a blue plaque saying "*sobe*" or "*apartmani*" outside – if they don't, they're not legal.

Independent **hostels** are cropping up more and more in Croatia – especially in the larger towns. The average price for a dorm bed is 150kn and many also offer private rooms. The Croatian Youth Hostel website (Ⓦhfhs.hr) also has details and prices of HI-affiliated hostels. Campsites usually open just for the summer season; see Ⓦcamping .hr for a list.

FOOD AND DRINK

Croatia has a varied and distinctive range of **cuisine**, largely because it straddles two culinary cultures: the fish- and seafood-dominated cuisine of the Mediterranean and the hearty meat-oriented fare of Central Europe.

For **breakfasts** and **fast food**, look out for bakeries or snack-food outlets selling *burek* (about 15kn), a flaky pastry filled with cheese; or grilled meats such as *čevapčići* (rissoles of minced beef, pork or lamb sold in a bun with relish; 37kn for a dozen from street stalls). Bread (*kruh*) is bought from a *pekarna* (bakery) or a supermarket.

A **restaurant** menu (*jelovnik*) will usually include starters such as *pršut* (home-cured ham) and *paški sir* (piquant hard cheese). Typical mains include some kind of *odrezak* (fillet of meat, often pan-fried), usually either *svinjski* (pork) or *teleški* (veal); and fresh fish, invariably grilled in one piece with head and bones intact. Other coastal staples are breaded or grilled squid (*lignje*), black squid risotto (*crni rižot*), and mixed fish stew (*brudet*). Real delicacies to be tried at least once are *škampi* (unpeeled prawns eaten with your fingers), *oštrige* (oysters), and *jastog* (lobster). No town is without at least one **pizzeria**, serving good stone-baked pizzas (around 40kn). A **konoba** is a no-frills, often family-run restaurant, usually serving local dishes at low prices.

Typical **desserts** include *palačinke* (pancakes) and *sladoled* (ice cream).

DRINK

Croatia is laden with relaxing **cafés** (*kavana*) for daytime drinking. Coffee (*kava*) is usually served black unless specified otherwise – ask for *mlijeko* (milk) or *šlag* (cream). Tea (*čaj*) is less available and drunk without milk.

Croatian **beer** (*pivo*) is of the light lager variety; Velebitsko and Vukovarsko are the best local brands. The local **wine** (*vino*) is consistently good and reasonably cheap: in Dalmatia there are some pleasant, crisp white wines such as Posip and Bogdanjuša, as well as reds derived from the ubiquitous local Plavac grape. Ruling the roost in Istria are Malvazija, a palatable white, and Teran, a light fresh red. Local spirits (*rakija*) include *medica*, a honey-based, slow-burning nectar; *travarica*, a grape brandy infused with herbs; and *Pelinkovac*, a bitter spirit similar to Jägermeister.

CULTURE AND ETIQUETTE

With an almost ninety percent Roman Catholic population, religious holidays in Croatia are celebrated with gusto. A fun-loving people generally, especially among the younger generation, Croatians are welcoming and will happily engage you in conversations about food, wine and politics over a beer or two.

A service charge is not usually added to restaurant bills and it is the norm to leave a **tip** at your discretion (ten percent is quite acceptable).

SPORTS AND OUTDOOR ACTIVITIES

The Dalmatian coast is great for **watersports**, including windsurfing, kite-surfing, wake-boarding and some less hardcore pursuits, such as banana-boating and renting a motorboat. Brač, Hvar and Vis have plenty of well-marked **cycling** and **hiking** trails.

Football remains the nation's favourite diversion. Croatia's national team has

> ### CROATIA ONLINE
> Ⓦ **adriatica.net** Information on the Adriatic resorts and also an accommodation booking service.
> Ⓦ **croatia.hr** Official tourist board site.
> Ⓦ **find-croatia.com** General travel info.
> Ⓦ **istra.hr** Official website for the Istrian peninsula.
> Ⓦ **dalmacija.net** Covers Dalmatia.

consistently proved to be one of the most successful in the whole of Central-Eastern Europe, regularly qualifying for major tournaments – an awesome achievement given Croatia's population of 4.4 million.

COMMUNICATIONS

Post offices (*pošta* or HPT) are discernible by their bright yellow signs and open Monday to Friday 7am to 7pm, Saturday 7am to 2pm. In big towns and resorts, some are open daily and until 10pm. Stamps (*marke*) can also be bought at newsstands, and letterboxes are painted the same yellow as post office signs.

Public **phones** use cards (*telekarta*), which come in denominations of 15kn, 25kn, 50kn and 100kn; buy these from post offices or newspaper kiosks You can also make international calls from the post office. Croatian SIM cards are available for about 100kn. Even small towns have **internet cafés** (expect to pay around 25kn/hr), and many normal cafés offer wi-fi now too.

CRIME AND SAFETY

The crime rate is low by European standards and **police** (*policija*) are generally helpful when dealing with tourists. They often make routine checks on identity cards and other documents, so always carry your passport. In an **emergency**, call ☎112.

HEALTH

EU citizens in possession of a European Health Insurance Card are entitled to free

6

CROATIAN

	CROATIAN	PRONUNCIATION
Yes	Da	Dah
No	Ne	Neh
Please	Molim	Mo-leem
Thank you	Hvala	Hvahlah
Hello/Good day	Bog/Dobar dan	Dobahr dan
Goodbye	Bog/Doviđenja	Doh veedehnyah
Excuse me	Izvinite	Izvineet
Sorry	Oprostite	Auprausteete
Today	Danas	Danass
Good	Dobro	Dobroh
Bad	Loše	Losheh
How much is…?	Koliko stoji…?	Koleekoh sto-yee…?
What time is it?	Koliko je sati?	Koleekoh yeh satee?
I don't understand	Ne razumijem	Neh rahzoomeeyehm
Do you speak English?	Govorite li engleski?	Govoreeteh lee ehngleskee?
Where is…?	Gdje je…?	Gdyeh ye…?
Where are…?	Gdje su…?	Gdyeh soo…?
Entrance	Ulaz	Oolaz
Exit	Izlaz	eezlaz
Tourist office	Turistički Ured	Tooristichkee oored
Toilet	Zahod	Zah-haud
Private rooms	Sobe	Saubey
I'd like to book…	Ja bih revervirala…	Ya bee reserveerahla…
Cheap	Jeftino	Yeftinoh
Expensive	Skupo	Skoopoh
Open	Otvoreno	Otvoreenoh
Closed	Zatvoreno	Zatvoreenoh
One	Jedan	Yehdan
Two	Dva	Dvah
Three	Tri	Tree
Four	Četiri	Cheteeree
Five	Pet	Pet
Six	Šest	Shest
Seven	Sedam	Sedam
Eight	Osam	Osam
Nine	Devet	Devet
Ten	Deset	Deset

emergency care in Croatia but will still pay for certain medicines and treatments – so travel insurance is highly recommended. **Pharmacies** (*ljekarna*) tend to follow normal shopping hours (see opposite) and a rota system covers nights and weekends; details are posted in the window of each pharmacy.

INFORMATION

Most towns of any size have a **tourist office** (*turističke informacije*), which will give out brochures and local maps. Few offices book private rooms, but they will direct you to an agency that does.

MONEY AND BANKS

The local currency is the **kuna** (kn), which is divided into 100 lipa. There are coins of 1, 2, 5, 10, 20 and 50 lipa, and 1kn, 2kn and 5kn; and notes of 5kn, 10kn, 20kn, 50kn, 100kn, 200kn, 500kn and 1000kn. Accommodation and ferry prices are often quoted in euros, but you still pay in kuna. **Banks** (*banka*) are open Monday to Friday 9am to 5pm (sometimes with longer hours in summer), Saturday 8am to 1pm. Money can also be changed in post offices, travel agencies and **exchange bureaux** (*mjenjačnica*). Credit cards are accepted in a large number of hotels and restaurants. At the time of writing £1 = 9kn, €1 = 7.5kn and US$1 = 5.9kn. It's relatively hard to get rid of kuna once you've left Croatia (though exchange offices in neighbouring countries often accept it); spend up or exchange before leaving.

OPENING HOURS AND HOLIDAYS

Most **shops** open Monday to Friday 8am to 8pm, Saturday 8am to 3pm, although many supermarkets, outdoor markets and the like are open daily 7am to 7pm. A handful of newsagents and supermarkets open on Sundays. Many **museums and galleries** are closed on Mondays. Most shops and banks are closed on the following **public holidays**: January 1, January 6, Easter Monday, May 1, Corpus Christi, June 22, June 25, August 5, August 15, October 8, November 1 and December 25 & 26.

Zagreb

Capital of Croatia since 1991, **ZAGREB** has served as the cultural and political focus of the state since the Middle Ages. The city grew out of two medieval communities, Kaptol, to the east, and Gradec, to the west, each sited on a hill and divided by a river long since dried up but nowadays marked by a street known as Tkalčićeva. Zagreb grew rapidly in the nineteenth century, and the majority of its buildings are relatively well-preserved, grand, peach-coloured monuments to the self-esteem of the Austro-Hungarian Empire. Nowadays, with a population reaching almost one million, Zagreb is the style-conscious, boisterous capital of a newly self-confident nation. The city empties in July and August when most locals head for the coast, but there's still enough going on to ensure that a few days here will be well spent.

Central Zagreb falls neatly into three parts. **Donji Grad**, or Lower Town, which extends north from the train station to the main square, Trg bana Jelačića, is the bustling centre of the modern city. Uphill from here, to the northeast and the northwest, are the older quarters of **Kaptol** (the Cathedral Quarter) and **Gradec** (the Upper Town), both peaceful districts of ancient mansions, quiet squares and leafy parks.

Trg bana Jelačića and Ilica

Flanked by cafés, hotels and department stores, **Trg bana Jelačića** is hectic with trams and hurrying pedestrians; the statue in the centre is of the nineteenth-century governor of Croatia, Josip Jelačića.

Running west from the square, below Gradec hill, is **Ilica**, the city's main shopping street. A little way along it and off to the right, you can take a **funicular** (daily every 10min, 6.30am–10pm; 4kn one-way) up to the Kula Lotrščak (see p.161).

Preradovićev Trg and Trg maršala Tita

Head south of Ilica via **Preradovićev Trg**, a small, café-filled square where there's a flower market, and you will reach **Trg maršala Tita**. This grandiose open space is centred on the late nineteenth-century **National Theatre**, in front of which stands *The Well of Life*, a fountain by Croatia's greatest twentieth-century sculptor, Ivan Meštrović.

The Museum of Arts and Crafts and the Ethnographic Museum

The beautiful **Museum of Arts and Crafts**, just west of the National Theatre (Tues–Sat 10am–7pm, Sun till 2pm; 30kn), holds an impressive collection of furniture and textiles dating from the Renaissance to the present day. Nearby on Mažuranićev Trg, the **Ethnographic Museum** (Tues–Sun 10am–6pm; 15kn, free Thurs) displays a collection of costumes from every corner of the country and an array of curios brought back by Croatian explorers from all over the world.

6

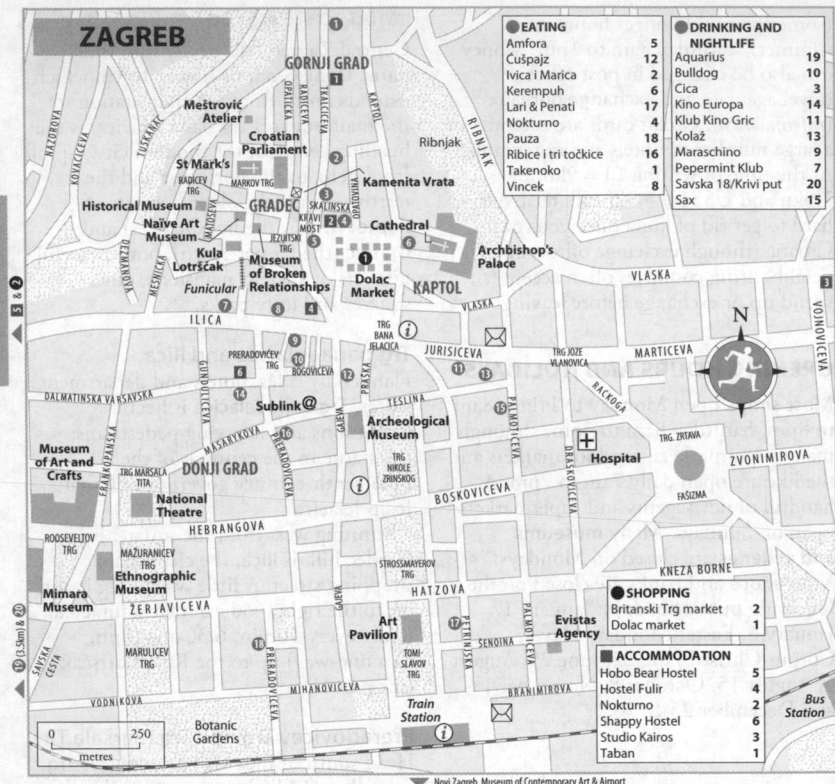

ZAGREB

GORNJI GRAD

Meštrović
Atelier

Croatian
Parliament

St Mark's

Historical Museum

Naïve Art
Museum

Kula
Lotrščak

Museum
of Broken
Relationships

Funicular

GRADEC

Kamenita Vrata

Cathedral

Dolac
Market

KAPTOL

Archbishop's
Palace

Ribnjak

ILICA

Sublink @

Archeological
Museum

Museum
of Art and
Crafts

DONJI GRAD

National
Theatre

Ethnographic
Museum

Mimara
Museum

Art
Pavilion

Evistas
Agency

Train
Station

Botanic
Gardens

Bus
Station

Novi Zagreb, Museum of Contemporary Art & Airport

0   250
metres

●EATING	
Amfora	5
Ćušpajz	12
Ivica i Marica	2
Kerempuh	6
Lari & Penati	17
Nokturno	4
Pauza	18
Ribice i tri točkice	16
Takenoko	1
Vincek	8

●DRINKING AND NIGHTLIFE	
Aquarius	19
Bulldog	10
Cica	3
Kino Europa	14
Klub Kino Gric	11
Kolaž	13
Maraschino	9
Pepermint Klub	7
Savska 18/Krivi put	20
Sax	15

●SHOPPING	
Britanski Trg market	2
Dolac market	1

■ACCOMMODATION	
Hobo Bear Hostel	5
Hostel Fulir	4
Nokturno	2
Shappy Hostel	6
Studio Kairos	3
Taban	1

Mimara Museum

The **Mimara Museum** at Rooseveltov Trg 5 (Tues, Wed, Fri & Sat 10am–5pm, Thurs till 7pm, Sun till 2pm; 40kn) houses one of Zagreb's most prized art collections, a treasure-trove belonging to Zagreb-born Ante Topić Mimara. Highlights include Chinese art from the Shang through to the Song dynasty, as well as a fine collection of European paintings, although some of the attributions (can Zagreb really boast a Rembrandt or a Rubens?) have been questioned by experts.

The Art Pavilion and Archeological Museum

Tomislavov Trg, opposite the train station, is the first in a series of three shaded, green squares that form the backbone of the lower town. Its main attraction is the **Art Pavilion** (Tues–Sat 11am–7pm, Sun 10am–1pm; 20kn), built in 1898 and now hosting art exhibitions in its gilded stucco and mock-marble interior. On the western edge of the most northerly square – tree-lined **Trg Nikole Zrinskog** (or Zrinjevac) – stands the **Archeological Museum** (Tues, Wed, Fri & Sat 10am–6pm, Thurs till 8pm, Sun till 1pm; 20kn), which houses interesting artefacts from prehistoric times to the Middle Ages.

Kaptol and the cathedral

The filigree spires of Zagreb's **cathedral** (daily 7am–7pm) mark the edge of the small district (and street) known as **Kaptol**, ringed by the ivy-cloaked turrets of the eighteenth-century **Archbishop's Palace**. Destroyed by an earthquake in 1880, the cathedral was rebuilt in neo-Gothic style, with a high, bare interior. Behind the altar lies a shrine to Archbishop Stepinac, head of the Croat church in the 1940s, imprisoned by the

HEARTBREAK HOUSE: ZAGREB'S MUSEUM OF BROKEN RELATIONSHIPS

For a voyage into the more tumescent recesses of the human psyche there are few better starting points than Zagreb's **Museum of Broken Relationships** at Ćirilometodska 2 (daily 9am–9pm; 20kn), a travelling art installation that became a permanently grounded museum in 2010. Based on mementoes donated by the public, it's a compelling and unique museum of wistful memory and raw emotion, with exhibits ranging from garden gnomes to prosthetic limbs. Each is accompanied by a text explaining why it was so significant to the donor – some are touching, others quite kinky; and quite a few belong to the obsessive world of a David Lynch movie.

Communists after World War II, and beatified by the pope in 1998.

Gradec and Dolac market

Gradec is the most ancient and atmospheric part of Zagreb, a leafy, tranquil quarter of tiny streets, small squares and Baroque palaces. It begins at the lively **Dolac market** (daily till mid-afternoon), which occupies several tiers immediately behind Trg bana Jelačića; this is the city's main food market, held every morning.

Tkalčićeva

From the far side of Dolac market, **Tkalčićeva** spears north along the path of the dried-up river that used to divide Kaptol and Gradec. Nowadays this is the city's prime people-watching spot – grab a seat at one of the many alfresco bars and cafés for the evening *korzo* (promenade) when well-heeled locals and their pooches strut their stuff.

Entry to Gradec proper from here is by way of **Krvavi Most**, which connects the street with Radićeva. On the far side of Radićeva, the **Kamenita Vrata** is a gloomy tunnel with a small shrine that formed part of Gradec's original fortifications. Close by, the **Kula Lotrščak** (Burglars' Tower; Tues–Sun 11am–7pm; 10kn) marks the top station of the funicular (see p.159) and provides fantastic views over the rest of the city and the plains beyond; a small cannon has been fired from the tower every day at noon since 1877.

The Naïve Art Museum and Church of St Mark

The **Naïve Art Museum**, Cirilmetodska 3 (Tues–Fri 10am–6pm, Sat & Sun 10am–1pm; closed hols; 20kn), provides a captivating introduction to the world of Croatia's self-taught village painters. Just north of here, the focus of **Markov Trg** is the squat **Church of St Mark**, a much-renovated structure, whose striking tiled roof displays the colourful coats of arms of the constituent parts of Croatia.

Museum of Contemporary Art

Arguably Zagreb's most stylish attraction, the **Museum of Contemporary Art** at Avenija Dubrovnik 17 (Tues–Fri & Sun 11am–6pm, Sat 11am–8pm; 30kn; tram #14 to Siget stop) occupies a swish modern building in high-rise suburbs south of the river. The museum showcases both Croatian and international art: works by local iconoclasts Goran Trbuljak, Sanja Iveković and Mladen Stilinović reinforce Croatia's reputation for art that's witty, ironic and understated. The interactively inclined can take a ride on Carsten Holler's toboggan tubes.

ARRIVAL AND DEPARTURE

By plane Zagreb airport is 10km southeast of the city; buses run to the main bus station (every 30min–1hr, 7am–8pm; 30kn).

By train Zagreb's central train station (*glavni kolodor*) is on Tomislavov Trg, on the southern edge of the city centre, a 10min walk from Trg bana Jelačića.
Destinations Belgrade (1 daily; 6hr 40min); Budapest (1 daily; 6hr 30min); Ljubljana (4 daily; 2hr 20min); Munich (2 daily; 8hr 45min); Salzburg (2 daily; 7hr); Sarajevo (1 daily; 9hr); Split (2 daily, one of which overnight; 6hr 20min–8hr 30min); Vienna (1 daily; 6hr 30min).

By bus The main bus station (*autobusni kolodvor*) is a 10min walk east of the train station, at the junction of Branimirova and Držićeva – trams #2 and #6 run between the two, with #6 continuing to the main square.

6

PLITVICE LAKES

Midway between Zagreb and the Dalmatian coast, the **Plitvice Lakes National Park** (daily: April, May, Sept & Oct 8am–6pm; June–Aug 7am–8pm; Nov–March 9am–4pm; April–Oct 110kn, rest of year 80kn; ⊚np-plitvicka-jezera.hr) is the country's biggest single natural attraction. The 8km string of sixteen lakes, hemmed in by densely forested hills, presents some of the most eye-catching scenery in mainland Croatia, with water rushing from lake to lake via a sequence of falls and rapids. Wooden walkways traverse the foaming waters, allowing a close-up view of the scenery. Most backpacker hostels in Zagreb, Zadar and Split offer day-trips to the lakes (expect to pay around 150kn, not including entrance to the park itself). Independent travellers can make it to the lakes by public bus – at least three Zagreb–Zadar and three Zagreb–Split services pass the park entrance.

Destinations Belgrade (daily; 6hr); Dubrovnik (7 daily; 9–11hr); Ljubljana (1 daily; 3hr); Munich (2 daily; 9hr 30min–11hr); Pula (hourly; 4hr–5hr 30min); Rijeka (hourly; 2hr 30min–3hr); Rovinj (7–9 daily; 4hr 30min–6hr); Sarajevo (5 daily; 7–8hr); Split (every 30min; 4hr 45min–8hr 30min); Trieste (1 daily; 4hr); Vienna (2 daily; 6hr); Zadar (hourly; 3–5hr).

INFORMATION

Tourist information Trg bana Jelačića 11 (Mon–Fri 8.30am–8pm, Sat 9am–6pm, Sun 10am–4pm; ☎01 48 14 051, ⊚zagreb-touristinfo.hr). Also at the main railway station (Mon–Fri 9am–9pm, Sat & Sun 10am–5pm); main bus station (Mon–Fri 9am–9pm, Sat & Sun 10am–5pm); and airport (Mon–Fri 9am–9pm, Sat & Sun 10am–5pm).

Discount cards The tourist office sells the Zagreb Card (24hr/60kn, 72hr/90kn), which offers unlimited city transport and good discounts in museums and restaurants – perfect if you plan to do lots.

GETTING AROUND

By tram The easiest way to get about, with sixteen routes. Lines #2 and #6 run between the bus and train stations, #6 taking you into Jelačića, the main crossing point in the city. There's also a four-line network of night services.

By bus The bus network serves the capital's peripheries, setting off from the suburban side of the train station.

Tickets Tram and bus tickets (*karte*), valid for 1hr 30min if travelling in one direction, are sold at kiosks (12kn) or from the driver (15kn); day-tickets (*dnevne karte*) cost 40kn. Validate your ticket by punching it in the machines on board. You can pay for a single journey (12kn) by sending the text message "ZG" to ☎8585.

By taxi There are ranks at the station and the northeast corner of Trg bana Jelačića. The standard rate is 19kn plus 7kn/km, which goes up by twenty percent early in the morning and late at night, on Sun and holidays. Luggage costs 5kn/item. To book, call Cammeo (☎060 7100) or Ekotaxi (☎1414).

ACCOMMODATION

Private rooms Arrange through the Evistas agency at Šenoina 28, midway between the train and bus stations (Mon–Fri 9am–8pm, Sat 9.30am–5pm; ☎01 48 39 554, ⊚evistas@zg.t-com.hr). Rooms from 550kn

★ **Hobo Bear Hostel** Medulićeva 4 ☎01 48 46 636, ⊚hobobearhostel.com; tram #6 from the bus or train station to Frankopanska. Stylish hostel in a great location near Ilica. There's a funky wine-cellar-like common room, free wi-fi and a well-appointed kitchen. Dorm 112kn, double 450kn

Hostel Fulir Radićeva 3a ☎01 48 30 882, ⊚fulir-hostel .com. Tucked in a small courtyard off Tkalčićeva, *Fulir* offers homely dorms with a Rough Guides-esque colour scheme, a kitchen, cosy common room and resident cat. Free wi-fi. Dorm 120kn

Nokturno Skalinska 2a ☎01 48 13 325, ⊚hostel .nokturno.hr. Amazingly central hostel right behind the Dolac. Sunny dorms, free wi-fi and internet, a common room and kitchen all make this a fine choice. Try the restaurant downstairs (see opposite). Dorm 130kn

Shappy Hostel Varšavska 8 ☎01 48 30 483, ⊚hostel -shappy.com. Newish hostel with bright, homely dorms and en-suite doubles. Tucked in beside the Cvijetni

---

★ TREAT YOURSELF

Takenoko Kaptol Centar, Nova ves 17 ☎01 48 60 530, ⊚takenoko.hr. If you like eating quality Asian food in design-conscious interiors then moodily minimalist *Takenoko*, in the Kaptol shopping centre, should do the trick. Most people come here for the excellent sushi, although the menu also sweeps in steaks, teriyaki chicken, a broad range of wok-fried dishes and – fusion fans take note – wasabi-garnished lamb chops and Adriatic fish dressed with Asian spices. Mains around 150kn. Mon–Sat noon–11.30pm, Sun noon–5pm.

shopping centre and with a lively downstairs café, it's an ideal base camp from which to explore the city. Dorm 130kn, double 400kn

Studio Kairos Vlaška 92 ☎01 46 40 680, ⓦstudio -kairos.com; trams #4, #7, #11 and #12 to the Petrova stop. Located a 15min walk east of the main square, this cute and welcoming B&B consists of four small but neat rooms with smart en-suite bathrooms, flat-screen TV, a/c and wi-fi. Most of the rooms are officially twins, but the slide-out, expandable beds will sleep three at a pinch. Double 530kn

Taban Tkalčićeva 82 ☎01 55 33 527, ⓦbuzzbackpackers .com. At the top of the Tkalčićeva café-bar strip and with a well-stocked ground-floor bar of its own, *Taban* offers smartly furnished, well-isolated dorms and neat private doubles with TV. Wi-fi throughout. Dorm 150kn, double 500kn

EATING

Zagreb has plenty of cafés and bars with outdoor seating in the pedestrian area around Gajeva and Bogovićeva, and along trendy Tkalčićeva. For picnic food, head to Dolac market (see p.161).

CAFÉS

Ivica i Marica Tkalčićeva 70. Hansel and Gretel go organic at this gingerbread-house-styled café serving superb wholemeal cakes (16kn/slice). Its restaurant also serves healthy traditional food, including nettle soup and Istrian truffle pasta. Daily noon–11pm.

Vincek Ilica 18. Something of a Zagreb institution, this is the best place in town to stop for ice cream (6kn/scoop), cakes and hot chocolate. Mon–Sat 8.30am–11pm.

RESTAURANTS

Amfora Dolac 2. Next door to the indoor fish market at the Dolac, this cheap-and-cheerful spot serves a fresh fishy menu including fish stew (25kn) and sardines (26kn). Daily 6am–5pm.

Ćušpajz Gajeva 9. The term "soup kitchen" gets a whole new meaning in this intimate little bistro run by Loredana Boban, wife of former football star Zvonimir. Soup of the day 35kn per bowl – crusty bread and salad nibbles included. Daily 11am–6pm.

Kerempuh Kaptol 3, Dolac. Located above the Dolac market (where ingredients are sourced daily), this is a smart, affordable spot to fill up on traditional Croatian favourites. Lunchtime specials 50kn, soup 20kn, veal liver 35kn. Mon–Sat 7am–11pm, Sun 7.30am–4pm.

★ **Lari & Penati** Petrinjska 42a. A small but perfectly formed deli-cum-restaurant with amazingly cheap and classy food, from spare ribs (45kn) to tuna confit and fennel (40kn). All served to a soundtrack of smooth jazz. Mon–Fri 8am–5pm, Sat noon–5pm.

SUMMER IN THE CITY

A lot of Zagreb's clubs and live music venues close down for the summer, when most of the city's hip young things relocate to the Adriatic coast. Keeping life ticking over is the **Strossmartre (Ljeto na Strosu)** season of **open-air concerts and events** in Zagreb's Upper Town, with nightly happenings all summer long. It runs from May to early Sept. Full schedule on ⓦ ljetonastrosu.com.

6

Nokturno Skalinska 4. On a cobbled street off Tkalčićeva, *Nokturno* offers pleasant outdoor seating and tasty pizzas (25–35kn), meat and fish dishes (40–75n), and salads (25kn). Mon–Thurs 8am–midnight, Fri & Sat 8am–1am, Sun 8am–midnight.

Pauza Preradovićeva 34. Adriatic/Far Eastern fusion and lot more besides in one of Zagreb's more adventurous restaurants, offering wok-fried combinations of Adriatic fish and Asian spices, a range of pastas, salads and rice dishes. Mains 70–90kn. Mon–Fri 10am–11pm, Sat noon–5pm.

Ribice i tri točkice Preradovićeva 7/1. A great place to sample Adriatic cuisine without fear of having your wallet emptied afterwards, with traditional Dalmatian dishes (grilled squid, fried anchovies, fillets of hake) served at village-tavern prices (50–60kn for a main). Daily 9am–midnight.

DRINKING AND NIGHTLIFE

Pick up the free monthly *Events and Performances* pamphlet from the tourist office.

BARS

Bulldog Bogovićeva 6. Don't be put off by the name – this is a typically stylish Zagreb bar and pavement café in the town centre, which sometimes features live bands. Daily 9am–1am.

Cica Corner of Tkalčićeva and Skalinska. This café has an eccentric interior filled with washing machines and retro hairdressing chairs, and plenty of outdoor seating. Famous

ZAGREB FESTIVALS

Zagreb offers an impressive array of annual **festivals** and events including INmusic (late June; ⓦinmusicfestival.com), a two-day rock-and-pop festival on the shores of Lake Jarun. The 2013 line-up included Arctic Monkeys, Iggy Pop and Bloc Party. Check with tourist information for details of other events.

6

for its potent fruit- and herb-flavoured brandies (12kn). Daily 8am–midnight.

Kino Europa Varšavska 3. A lovely old interwar cinema that screens art movies, the Europa's café serves as a key meeting point for the city's art-and-culture tribes. There's a good choice of *rakijas* (12kn), and retro discos in the foyer at weekends. Mon–Thurs 8am–11pm, Fri & Sat 8am–2am, Sun noon–10pm.

Klub Kino Gric Jurišićeva 6. Boasts both a private arthouse cinema and a small chilled-out bar with stripy walls. Enjoy a White Russian (30kn) in one of its stylish red director's chairs. Daily 7.30am–11.30pm.

Kolaž Amruševa 11. This semi-submerged straight-gay-whatever bar is only a short stroll from the main square but seems to be in another world. The bare-brick interior and low-key lighting create the ideal ambience for a long night of alcohol-oiled conversation. Daily 9am–midnight.

★ **Maraschino** Margaretska 1. So trendy it hurts, this bar/club features live DJs and a bar made of martini glasses. Try a shot of the eponymous cherry brandy from Zadar (12kn). Mon–Thurs & Sun 7am–1am, Fri & Sat till 4am.

Savska 18/Krivi put Savska 25. Near the Zagreb university students' union, this unassuming hut sucks in a huge cross section of young, boisterous and edgily alternative types, with a smoke-saturated inner sanctum and a vast wooden-bench yard with space for hundreds. Bottled Velebitsko beer (15kn) is the standard order. Daily 8am–1am.

CLUBS

Aquarius Aleja Mira bb ⊛ aquarius.hr; tram #17 from Trg bana Jelačića to Horvati. At the eastern end of Lake Jarun, 6km southwest of the centre, this club specializes in techno and drum'n'bass. International headline acts play here too (tickets from 190kn). Cover charge for club nights 30–40kn. Thurs–Sun 10pm–6am.

Pepermint Klub Ilica 24. Look for the long queue of fashionistas on Ilica to find this fresh and trendy club, which plays a mix of music from funk to soul. Daily 10am–4am.

Sax Palmotićeva 22 ⊛ sax-zg.hr. Fashionable basement club two blocks east of Trg N. Zrinskog, featuring a variety of live music with a jazz bias. Cover charge from 20kn. Tues–Sat 9am–3am.

SHOPPING AND MARKETS

The principal area for shopping is along Ilica, off Trg bana Jelačića, which has several independent stores as well as familiar high-street names, punctuated by handsome coffee shops and a few tempting bakeries.

Britanski Trg market. This bric-a-brac market is a magpie's dream – jewellery, traditional Croatian embroidery, farming implements, binoculars – you name it, it's there. Sun till 2pm.

DIRECTORY

Embassies Australia, Nova Ves 11 ☎ 01 48 91 200; Canada, Prilaz Gjure Deželića 4 ☎ 01 48 81 200; UK, Ivana Lučića 4 ☎ 01 60 09 100; US, Thomasa Jeffersona 2 ☎ 01 66 12 200.

Exchange In the post office on Branimirova or at any bank. Privredna bank at Ilica 5 changes travellers' cheques.

Hospital For emergencies visit Heinzelova 88 ☎ 01 63 02 911.

Internet Wi-fi is widespread. Best of the central internet cafés is *Sublink*, Teslina 12 (Mon–Sat 9am–10pm, Sun 3–10pm, 20kn/hr; ☎ 01 48 19 993, ⊛ sublink.hr).

Left luggage At the train (24hr; 15kn/hr) and bus stations (daily 6am–10pm; 5kn/hr).

Pharmacies 24hr pharmacies at Radiceva 3 and Ilica 301.

Post offices Branimirova 4 (24hr); Jurišićeva 13 (Mon–Fri 7am–9pm, Sat 7am–2pm, Sun 8am–2pm).

Istria

A large peninsula jutting into the northern Adriatic, **Istria** is Croatian tourism at its most developed. Many of the towns here were resorts in the nineteenth century and still attract an annual influx of sun-seekers. Yet the growth of tourism has done little to detract from the essential charm and beauty of the region. Istria's largest centre is the port city of **Pula**, which, with its Roman amphitheatre and other relics of Roman occupation, is a rewarding place to spend a couple of days. On the western side of the peninsula, the town of **Rovinj**, with its cobbled piazzas and shuttered houses, is the very image of Mediterranean chic.

ARRIVAL AND DEPARTURE

By bus and train Travelling on from Istria towards Zagreb or Dalmatia, most routes lead through the port city of Rijeka, from where regular buses run to Zagreb, Pula, Rovinj, Zadar, Split and Dubrovnik. Rijeka's train station is 500m west of the centre at Krešimirova 5. The bus station is on the western fringe of the centre on Trg Žabica.

By ferry Rijeka is also the starting point for the twice-weekly Jadrolinija coastal route to Dubrovnik. The Jadrolinija ferry office (☎ 051 211 444) is at the passenger terminal on the seafront.

PULA

Once the chief port of the Austro-Hungarian Empire, **PULA** is an engaging combination of working port, naval base and vibrant riviera town. The Romans put the city squarely on the map when they arrived in 177 BC, transforming it into an important commercial centre.

The chief reminder of Pula's Roman heritage is its impressive amphitheatre; south of here, the town centre circles a pyramidal hill, scaled by secluded streets, dotted with Roman relics and topped with a star-shaped Venetian fortress.

The amphitheatre

The first-century BC **Roman amphitheatre** (daily 8am–8pm; 40kn) is the sixth largest in the world, and once had space for over 23,000 spectators. The outer shell is fairly complete, as is one of the towers, up which a slightly hair-raising climb gives a good sense of the enormity of the structure and a view of Pula's industrious harbour. The amphitheatre hosts the annual **Pula Film Festival** (wpulafilmfestival.hr) at the end of July, as well as concerts throughout the summer.

The Archeological Museum

A short way south of the amphitheatre is Pula's **Archeological Museum** (Jan–April & Oct–Dec Mon–Fri 9am–2pm; May–Sept Mon–Sat 9am–8pm, Sun 9am–3pm; 20kn), where pillars and toga-clad statues mingle with ceramics, jewellery and trinkets from all over Istria, some of them prehistoric.

The Triumphal Arch and the Temple of Augustus

Central Pula's main street, Giardini, runs south to the first-century BC **Triumphal Arch of the Sergians**, through which the pedestrianized Via Sergia leads to the town's ancient Roman **Forum**, now the square at the centre of Pula's old quarter. On the far side of here, the slim but impressive **Temple of Augustus** was built between 2 BC and 14 AD to celebrate the cult of the emperor; its imposing Corinthian columns, still intact, make it one of the best examples of a Roman temple outside Italy.

Sveta Srca

Several stepped alleyways lead up from Via Sergia towards Pula's fortress-crowned central hill. One of these alleys, De Villeov Uspon, climbs past Sveta Srca ("Sacred Hearts"; Tues–Sun 11am–2pm & 5–9pm; 20kn), a deconsecrated church that now serves as a spectacular exhibition space – there's usually something of artistic or historical interest here over the summer.

By plane Pula's airport is 6km northeast of the city. The bus ride to the centre costs 35kn; taxis are around 100kn.

By train Pula's train station is a 10min walk north of the centre, at the far end of Kolodvorska.

By bus The bus station is 10min northeast of the centre, along Istarska Divizije.

Destinations Dubrovnik (1 daily; 15hr); Rijeka (roughly hourly; 1hr 30min–2hr 30min); Rovinj (roughly hourly; 45min); Split (3 daily; 10hr); Trieste (4 daily; 2hr 45min–3hr 45min); Venice (1 daily; 5hr); Zadar (3 daily; 7hr); Zagreb (hourly; 3hr 30min–5hr).

By ferry Pula's small passenger port is just east of the amphitheatre. Ferries for Venice can be booked through Commodore Travel at Riva 14 (☎052 211 631).

Destinations Venice (May–Oct 2 weekly; 3hr); Zadar (June–Sept 2–5 weekly; 4hr 45min).

Tourist information In the Forum (daily: June–Sept 8am–10pm; Oct–May 9am–5pm; ☎052 212 987, wpulainfo.hr).

Private rooms Book through A Turizam, opposite the cathedral at Kandlerova 24 (Mon–Fri 9am–5pm, Sat 10am–3pm; ☎052 212 212, wa-turizam.hr. Rooms from __100kn__

Hostel Pipištrelo Flaciusova 6 ☎052 393 568. An imaginatively designed hostel decked out in bold greens, yellows and salmon-pinks, with Pop Art adorning the walls of several rooms. There's a small kitchen on the ground floor, a social area next to the reception, and several shelves of books available for exchange. Wi-fi throughout. Dorm __135kn__, double __400kn__

6

PULA: EUROPEAN BASS-CULTURE CAPITAL

For anyone into reggae, dub, jungle, dubstep or any of their bass-heavy offshoots, Pula has emerged as one of the best places in the Mediterranean to spend the summer. Punta Christo, an abandoned seaside fortress just north of town, is the perfect venue for three highly recommended festivals – **Seasplash**, which concentrates on traditional reggae and dub (late July; ⓦseasplash-festival.com); **Outlook**, which focuses on reggae, dubstep and everything beyond (late Aug; ⓦoutlookfestival.com); and the more eclectic **Dimensions**, which ventures towards the outer frontiers of dance culture (early Sept; ⓦdimensionsfestival.com).

Pula Art Hostel Marulićeva 41 ☎098 874 078, ⓦpulaarthostel.com; bus #2a or #3 to Verudela from the bus station. Sociable hostel near central Pula (look out for the distinctive green building) with lots of creative touches, including a mosaic staircase. Free wi-fi and internet. Dorm 130kn

Stoja 3km southeast of town ☎052 387 144, ⓦarenacamps.com; bus #1 from Giardini. Simple campsite on a wooded peninsula with beautiful rocky beaches. Minimum two nights in summer. Camping 64kn per person, plus 84kn per tent.

EATING AND DRINKING

Bistro Dva Ferala Kandlerova 32. *Dva Ferala* attracts a lively local crowd to its street-side seating for cheap Croatian cuisine, including *ćevapčići*, and pork and chips (both 45kn). Mon–Sat 8am–8pm.

Jupiter Castropola 38. Perched on a hill near the fortress, this is a popular pizzeria with pretty Art Deco glass panels and a terrace. Sizeable pizzas from 30kn. Mon–Fri 10am–11pm, Sat noon–11pm, Sun 3–11pm.

Market Narodni Trg. Offers plenty of fresh fruit and veg and has a wealth of local deli products in the cast-iron Art Nouveau pavilion at its centre. Daily 7am–2pm.

Pietas Julia Riva 20. Grab a sofa and an apple martini (36kn) at this fun lounge bar in a pavilion west of the amphitheatre. Free wi-fi. Daily 10am–4am.

Rock Cafe Scalierova 8 ⓦmyspace.com/rockcaffepula. A spacious place with a stage for live music, alcoves decorated with rock-star murals and a lot of fancy wood carving adorning the main bar and the wall panelling. Daily 8am–midnight.

Uljanik Dobrilina 2. Counter-cultural club of many years' standing with a huge beer garden, DJ nights at weekends and live music in the summer. Cover charge varies – often free entry during the summer. Thurs–Sat 9pm–late.

ROVINJ

Once an island, charming **ROVINJ** lies 40km north of Pula. Refreshingly free of traffic, its hotchpotch of cobbled streets, terracotta roofs and shuttered windows teeters over the clear sea, and the harbour is an attractive mix of fishing boats and swanky yachts.

WHAT TO SEE AND DO

From the main square, **Trg maršala Tita**, the Baroque **Vrata svetog Križa** leads up to Grisia Ulica, lined with galleries selling local art. It climbs steeply through the heart of the Old Town to **St Euphemia's Church** (daily: April–June 10am–1pm; July–Sept 10am–6pm), dominating Rovinj from the top of its peninsula. This eighteenth-century Baroque church has the sixth-century sarcophagus of the saint inside, and you can climb its 58m-high tower (same hours; 10kn). Paths on the south side of Rovinj's busy harbour lead south towards **Zlatnirt**, a densely forested cape, crisscrossed by tracks. The best of the **beaches** – all rocky – are here, but you can also try the two islands just offshore: **Sveta Katarina**, the nearer of the two, and **Crveni otok**, just outside Rovinj's bay (linked by boats from the harbour; every hour; 30kn return).

ARRIVAL AND INFORMATION

By bus Rovinj's bus station is a 5min walk southeast of its centre, just off Trg na lokvi, at the junction of Carrera and Carducci.

Destinations Dubrovnik (1 daily; 15hr); Pula (roughly hourly; 45min); Rijeka (5–7 daily; 3hr); Split (1 daily; 11hr); Trieste (2 daily; 2–3hr); Venice (1 daily; 5hr 15min); Zadar (1 daily; 8hr); Zagreb (7–8 daily; 4hr 30min–6hr).

By ferry Rovinj's small passenger port lies just north of the peninsula. Trieste Lines serve Trieste, Venezia Lines serve Venice.

Destinations Trieste (June–Oct 1–2 daily; 1hr 30min–2hr 15min); Venice (summer only, 2 weekly; 3hr 30min).

Tourist information On the waterfront promenade at Obala Pina Budicina 12 (June–Sept daily 8am–10pm; Oct–May Mon–Fri 8am–3pm, Sat 8am–1pm; ☎052 811 566, ⓦtzgrovinj.hr).

ACCOMMODATION

Private rooms Try Natale, opposite the bus station at Via Carducci 4 (Mon–Sat 7.30am–9.30pm, Sun 8am–5pm; ☎052 813 365, ⓦrovinj.com). Rooms from 145kn

Porton Biondi Aleja Porton Biondi 1 ☎052 813 557, ⓦportonbiondi.hr. A pine-shaded campsite with its own beach, 700m north of town. Mid-March to Nov. Camping 45kn per person, plus 25kn per tent

EATING AND DRINKING

Trg Valdibora is home to a small produce market.

Da Sergio Grisia 11. Great pizzas – baby and normal-sized – from 38kn. Much better value than the places on the harbourfront. Daily noon–midnight.

Irish Pub Art Carera 88. Head through the passageway and into the back yard to locate this dark and welcoming drinking den, catering for a mixed bag of locals and tourists. There's a small outdoor terrace, and live music Thurs. Daily 11am–midnight.

Maestral Obala V. Nazora. Located on the seafront towards Zlatni rt, with plenty of pine-shaded outdoor seating, and the fresh seafood (from 40kn) is grilled alfresco. Daily 8am–11pm.

Monte Carlo Svetoga Križa 23. This bar has a gorgeous terrace where you can intersperse drinks with refreshing dips in the sea. Bottled beer 20kn. Daily 8am–1am.

The Dalmatian Coast

Stretching from Zadar in the north to the Montenegrin border in the south, the **Dalmatian Coast** is one of Europe's most dramatic shorelines. All along, well-preserved medieval towns sit beneath a grizzled karst landscape that drops precipitously into some of the cleanest water in the Mediterranean. For centuries, the region was ruled by Venice, spawning architecture that wouldn't look out of place on the other side of the water. The busy northern port city of

Zadar provides a vivacious introduction to the region. Otherwise, the main attractions are in the south: the lively provincial capital **Split**, built around a Roman palace, is served by trains from Zagreb and provides onward bus connections with the walled city of **Dubrovnik**. Ferry and catamaran connections to the best of the islands – Brač, Hvar, Vis and Korčula – are also from Split.

ZADAR

A bustling town of nearly 100,000 people, **ZADAR** is one of the success stories of the Croatian Adriatic, combining ancient and medieval heritage with a vibrant bar scene and the kind of go-ahead architectural projects (such as the *Sea Organ* and the *Greeting to the Sun*) that give the seafront the appearance of an art installation.

WHAT TO SEE AND DO

Zadar displays a pleasant muddle of architectural styles, with Romanesque churches competing for space with modern cafés. The main sights are concentrated in the Old Town, which is hemmed in by the sea; the central Roman Forum is the best place to begin exploring.

The Forum

Zadar's main square – or **Forum** – is dominated by the ninth-century **St Donat's Church** (May–Sept daily 9am–10pm; 10kn), a hulking cylinder of stone with a vast bare interior, built – according to tradition – by St Donat himself, an Irishman who was bishop here for a time. Opposite, the **Archeological Museum** (June–Sept Mon–Sat 9am–9pm; Oct–Nov

6

THE SEA ORGAN AND GREETING TO THE SUN

Zadar's quirkiest feature, the **Sea Organ**, consists of wide marble steps leading into the sea, with a set of tubes and cavities carved underneath, which enable the sea and wind to orchestrate a constant harmony. Emitting a strange sound, a bit like panpipes crossed with whale song, the *Organ* is surprisingly melodic and relaxing. Next to it is another public artwork, **Greeting to the Sun**: a huge disc that accumulates solar power during the day and radiates a multicoloured hypnotic glow by night.

6

Mon–Fri 9am–2pm, Sat 9am–1pm; 15kn), housed in a slick, modern building, has an absorbing collection of Neolithic, Roman and medieval Croatian artefacts.

Behind St Donat's, the twelfth- and thirteenth-century **Cathedral of St Anastasia** has an arcaded west front reminiscent of Tuscan churches. Around the door frame stretches a frieze of twisting acanthus leaves, from which various beasts emerge – look out for the rodent and bird fighting over a bunch of grapes. You can climb the 56m campanile for great views over the city (Mon–Sat 10am–5pm; 10kn).

South of the Forum

Southeast of the Forum lies **Narodni Trg**, an attractive Renaissance square. A little further southeast, on Trg Petra Zoranića, the Baroque St Simeon's Church houses the exuberantly decorated reliquary of St Simeon, commissioned by Queen Elizabeth of Hungary in 1377 and fashioned from 250kg of silver by local artisans.

Overlooking the harbour at Poljana Zemaljskog odbora 1 is the state-of-the-art **Museum of Ancient Glass** (winter Mon–Sat 9am–4pm; summer till 7pm; 30kn), which contains one of the finest collections of ancient Roman glassware outside Italy and affords wonderful views of the harbour, too.

ARRIVAL AND DEPARTURE

By plane Zadar's airport is 12km east of town. Buses (7–14 daily depending on flight schedule 25kn) run into town.

By train and bus The train and bus stations are about 1km east of the town centre, a 20min walk or a hop on bus #5 – tickets cost 10kn from the driver or 16kn (valid for two journeys) from kiosks.

Destinations (train) Split (2 daily; 5hr; change at Knin).

Destinations (bus) Dubrovnik (7 daily; 8hr 30min); Pula (3 daily; 6hr 30min); Rijeka (9 daily; 4hr 30min); Rovinj (1 daily; 8hr); Split (approx every 30min; 3hr–3hr 30min); Zagreb (hourly; 3–5hr).

By ferry Ferries arrive on Liburnska obala, just outside the walls of the Old Town. For Ancona book through Jadrolinija (ⓦ jadrolinija.hr); for Pula through Miatours (see below).

Destinations Ancona (3–6 weekly; 6–9hr); Pula (June–Sept 2–5 weekly; 4hr 45min).

INFORMATION

Tourist information Narodni Trg (June & Sept daily 8am–8pm; July & Aug daily 8am–midnight; Oct–May Mon–Fri 8am–3pm; ☎ 023 316 166, ⓦ tzzadar.hr).

ACCOMMODATION

Private rooms Try Jaderatours, in the Old Town on Elizabete Kotromanić (☎ 023 250 350, ⓦ jaderatours.hr); or Miatours, under the arches near the ferry quays at Vrata sv. Krševana bb (☎ 023 254 300, ⓦ miatours.hr). Rooms from 150kn

Borik Majstora Radovana 7 ☎ 023 332 074, ⓦ camping .hr; bus #5 or #8 from the bus and train stations. Well-equipped campsite near Hostel Zadar. Summer only. Camping 130kn per person and tent

Boutique Hostel Forum Široka 20 ☎ 023 253 031, ⓦ hostelforumzadar.com. Designer hostel decked out by the team responsible for Goli & Bosi in Split (see p.171), offering a mixture of dorm rooms and hotel-standard private doubles (with breakfast included). Free wi-fi and a fully equipped kitchen are yours to use. Dorm 180Kn, double 740Kn

Drunken Monkey Hostel Skenderbega 21 ☎ 099 809 3280. Out in the suburb of Arbanasi but till very handy for bus station and town centre, the Monkey offers clean dorms, a garden with a small pool, cosy communal areas and on-site bar. Free wi-fi and internet access. Dorm 145kn, double 380kn

EATING

For snacks and picnics, the daily market just inside the Old Town walls off Jurja Barakovića is the place to get fruit, vegetables, local cheeses and home-cured hams.

Konoba Na Po Ure Špire Brusine 8. Popular with locals and visitors alike, this homely restaurant is best known for its fish dishes, including heaps of juicy mussels (45kn) and fresh anchovies (25kn). Daily 10am–11pm.

★ **Konoba Skoblar** Trg Petra Zoranića ☎ 023 213 236. Serving up the broad gamut of Dalmatian food at prices that won't lead to tears, Skoblar continues to draw in locals eager for marende (elevenses) or a more expansive mid-afternoon lunch. Daily specials (50kn) are chalked up on a board outside the door. Daily 10am–11pm.

Pet Bunara Trg Pet Bunara. Churning out tasty and trustworthy pizzas (55kn) alongside refined Adriatic-Mediterranean cuisine that makes best use of local ingredients, the "Five Wells" is truly a restaurant for all occasions – and comes well recommended by locals. Daily 8am–1am.

DRINKING AND NIGHTLIFE

Arsenal Trg Tri Bunara ⓦ arsenalzadar.com. Arts centre, lounge bar, restaurant and concert venue, Arsenal is a

6

TISNO FESTIVALS

Tisno, a sprawling seaside village midway between Zadar and Split, shot into the festival limelight in 2012 when it became the new summer home of the Garden organization, the Zadar-based crew responsible for launching the legendary **Garden Festival** in 2007. The festival has grown to become one the Mediterranean's prime summer events and yet has never lost its intimate boutique-festival feel. The Garden Festival site is also used to host several other festivals throughout the summer – July and August is just one huge party if you have the stamina to stick around. Getting there from Zadar or Split is easy – catch an inter-city bus to Šibenik and then change to a local bus to Murter, which calls at Tisno on the way. There's plenty of accommodation too, with apartments and camping on the site itself, or private rooms in Tisno village. **Tickets** for the Tisno festivals hover at around €110, transport and accommodation not included.

Garden Festival Early July; ⍵ thegardenfestival.eu.
Electric Elephant Mid-July; ⍵ electricelephant.co.uk.
Soundwave Festival Late July; ⍵ soundwavecroatia.com.
SuncéBeat Late July to early Aug; ⍵ suncebeat.com.
Stop making Sense Early Aug; ⍵ stopmakingsense.eu.

---

seriously exciting venue. Housed in a restored Venetian warehouse, you can pop in for a reasonably priced breakfast or catch a concert, film or DJ set. Cover charge for some events. Free wi-fi. Mon–Thurs & Sun 8am–midnight, Fri & Sat 8am–2am.

Hitch Kolovare ⍵ hitch-bar.com. With a partially covered terrace jutting out into the Adriatic with views across the straits to the island of Ugljan, this is one of Zadar's best bets for sunset cocktail-sipping and after-sundown clubbing. Daily 7am–5am.

Kult Stomorica 6. One of a number of café-bars tucked down winding Stormica, this fashionable spot has a large wooden terrace area on which to enjoy the pumping music. Daily 7.30am–1am.

★ **The Garden** Bedemi zadarskih pobuna ⍵ watchthegardengrow.eu. This lounge-bar sits high up in the city walls: there are big beds to relax on, cocktail in hand, as well as a dancefloor that regularly boasts big-name DJs (cover charge for popular events). April–Oct daily 11am–2am.

SPLIT

The largest city in the region, and its major transit hub, **SPLIT** is a hectic place, but one of the most enticing spots on the Dalmatian Coast. At its heart lies a crumbling Old Town built within the walls of Diocletian's Palace, and including some of the most outstanding classical remains in Europe.

WHAT TO SEE AND DO

Diocletian's Palace is still the epicentre of the city – lived in almost continuously since Roman times, it has gradually become a warren of houses, tenements and churches. Almost everything worth seeing is concentrated here, behind the waterfront Riva, while to its west is the lush **Marjan peninsula**.

Diocletian's Palace

Built as a retirement home by Dalmatian-born Roman Emperor Diocletian in 305 AD, **Diocletian's Palace** is a jumble of original features and subsequent additions. The best place to start a tour is on its seaward side through the **Bronze Gate**, which once gave direct access to the water. Through the gate, you find yourself in a shady vaulted hall full of souvenir stalls. To your left are the atmospheric **subterranean halls** (daily: May–Sept 8am–8pm; Oct–April 8am–2pm; 10kn) that once sat beneath Diocletian's apartments, and where you can get some idea of the size and layout of his erstwhile home.

Carry on through the vaulted hallways and up the steps to the **Peristyle**, which these days serves as the main town square. At the southern end, more steps lead up to the **vestibule**, an impressive round building that's the only part of the imperial apartments to be left anything like intact, despite losing its dome.

The cathedral

On the eastern side of the Peristyle stands one of two black granite

6

Egyptian sphinxes, dating from around 15 BC, which originally flanked the entrance to Diocletian's mausoleum; the octagonal building, surrounded by an arcade of Corinthian columns, has since been converted into Split's **cathedral** (Mon–Sat 7am–noon & 5–7pm; 15kn; 5kn extra to visit the crypt). The cathedral's striking walnut and oak **doorway** was carved in 1214 and shows scenes from the life of Christ. Inside, the dome is ringed by two series of decorative Corinthian columns and a frieze that contains portraits of Diocletian and his wife. The church's finest feature is a cruelly realistic *Flagellation of Christ* depicted on the Altar of St Anastasius, completed by local artist Juraj Dalmatinac in 1448. To the right of the entrance is the **campanile** (same hours; 10kn), a restored Romanesque structure – from the top, the views across the city are magnificent.

Follow the alleyway directly opposite the cathedral to reach the intriguing **baptistry**, or Temple of Jupiter (same hours as cathedral; 10kn), originally built by a cult in Diocletian's time and later adapted by Christians.

The Golden Gate and Archeological Museum

North of the cathedral, along Diokleci-janova, is the grandest and best preserved of the palace entrances: the **Golden Gate**. Just outside there's a piece by Meštrović, a gigantic statue of the fourth-century Bishop **Grgur Ninski** – rubbing its big toe is said to bring good luck. Fifteen minutes' walk northwest of here, the **Archeological Museum**, at Zrinsko Frankopanska 25 (June–Sept Mon–Sat 9am–2pm & 4–8pm; Oct–May Mon–Fri 9am–2pm & 4–8pm, Sat 9am–2pm; 20kn), contains displays of Illyrian, Greek, medieval and Roman artefacts. Outside, the arcaded courtyard is crammed with gravestones, sarcophagi and decorative sculpture.

The Marjan peninsula

If you want some peace and quiet, and stunning views over the city, head for the woods of the **Marjan peninsula** west of the Old Town. It's accessible via Sperun and then Senjska, which cut up through the slopes of the **Varoš** district. There are tiny rocky **beaches** all round the peninsula.

Meštrović Gallery

The main historical highlight of the Marjan peninsula lies fifteen minutes west of the centre (bus #12 from the seafront). The **Meštrović Gallery**, Ivana Meštrovića 39 (May–Sept Tues–Sun 9am–7pm; Oct–April Tues–Sat 9am–4pm, Sun 10am–3pm; 30kn, includes entrance to Kaštelet), is housed in the ostentatious Neoclassical building that was built – and lived in – by Croatia's most famous twentieth-century artist, the sculptor Ivan Meštrović (1883–1962). This fabulous collection consists largely of boldly fashioned bodies curled into elegant poses. Meštrović's former workshop, **Kaštelet** (same hours), is 200m up the same road, and contains a chapel decorated with his woodcarved reliefs showing scenes from the Stations of the Cross.

ARRIVAL AND DEPARTURE

By plane Split airport is 16km west of town; Croatia Airlines buses connect with scheduled flights and run to the waterfront Riva (30kn); their office at Riva 9 has timetables. Alternatively, the #37 Split–Trogir bus runs from the main road outside the airport to the suburban bus station on Domovinskog rata, just north of the Old Town (every 20min; 20kn). A taxi costs 250kn.

By train and bus Split's main bus and train stations are next to each other on Obala Kneza Domagoja, 5min walk round the harbour from the centre.

Destinations (train) Zadar (change at Knin; 2 daily; 5hr); Zagreb (2 daily, one of which overnight; 6hr 20min–8hr 30min).

Destinations (bus) Belgrade (1 daily, overnight; 11hr 30min); Dubrovnik (make sure you take your passport, as you pass through a short stretch of Bosnia-Herzegovina on the way; 10 daily; 5hr); Pula (3 daily; 13hr); Rijeka (6 daily; 8hr); Sarajevo (4 daily; 6hr 30min–8hr); Trieste (1 daily; 10hr 30min); Zadar (hourly; 3hr–3hr 30min); Zagreb (every 30min; 5hr–8hr 30min).

By boat The ferry terminal and Jadrolinija booking office (ⓦjadrolinija.hr) are both in the harbour, with the latter also selling Krilo Jet and SNAV tickets. Note that services are reduced outside of the summer months.

Destinations Ancona (3 ferries daily; 10hr); Brač (Bol: 1 ferry daily; 55min; Supetar: 1 ferry hourly; 50min); Dubrovnik (2 ferries weekly; 11hr); Hvar (Hvar Town: 1 ferry daily; 1hr; 1 Krilo Jet catamaran daily; 55min; Stari Grad: 7 ferries daily; 2hr); Korčula (Vela Luka: 2 ferries daily; 2hr 45min; 1 catamaran daily; 1hr 45min; Korčula Town: 2 ferries weekly May–Sept; 6hr; 1 Krilo Jet catamaran daily; 2hr 25min); Rijeka (2 ferries weekly; 11hr 30min); Vis (2–3 ferries daily; 2hr 20min; 1 catamaran daily; 1hr 15min).

INFORMATION

Tourist information In the Peristyle of the Palace (June–Sept Mon–Fri 8am–8pm, Sat 8am–7pm, Sun 9am–1pm; Oct–May Mon–Fri 9am–5pm; ☎ 021 345 606, ⓦ visitsplit.com).

Discount card The Splitcard, available from the tourist office (35kn/72hr; free if you're staying 3 days or more), gets you free or discounted entrance to several of the sights, plus reductions on hostels and restaurants.

ACCOMMODATION

Private rooms Book through Turist Biro, Obala narodnog preporoda 12, on the waterfront (☎ 021 347 100, ⓦ turistbiro-split.hr). Rooms from **345kn**

★ **Goli & Bosi** Morpurgova Poljana 2 ☎ 021 510 999, ⓦ gollybossy.com. Sleek hotel decked out in eye-popping black and yellow, with tongue-in-cheek captions along the floors. Also includes the *De Belly Café*, a stylish restaurant and bar in the pretty courtyard outside (mains from 25kn). The smart dorms are the most affordable option and each one is built into its own cubbyhole. Dorm **210kn**, double **650kn**

Hostel Apinelo Petrova 42 ☎ 091 393 1287, ⓔ hostel .apinelo@gmail.com. A restored stone house just outside the Old Town offering neat new dorms and a collection of 2-person apartments, plus a small communal kitchen and free wi-fi. Dorm **120kn**, apartment **500kn**

Silver Central Kralja Tomislava 1 ☎ 021 490 805, ⓦ silvercentralhostel.com. A modern, central hostel with a buzzy common area, bright and breezy dorms and free wi-fi and internet. Dorm **10kn**, doubles at various locations in the centre **525kn**

Split hostel booze & snooze Narodni trg 8 ☎ 021 342 787, ⓦ splithostel.com. In the middle of the old city, this hostel is run by friendly Croatian-Australians who like partying with their guests. Also has a nearby sister hostel – *Split Hostel Fiesta Siesta* – with on-site bar at Kruževićeva 5. Free Internet. Dorm **180kn**, double **530kn**

Villa Varoš Miljenka Smoje 1 ☎ 021 483 469, ⓦ villavaros .hr. Charming and cosy guesthouse in a lovingly restored house in the atmospheric Varoš quarter. Rooms are kitted out with homely, semi-rustic furnishings together with a/c and TV. Double **586kn**

EATING

The daily market at the eastern edge of the Old Town is the place to shop for fruit, veg and local cheeses.

Buffet Fife Trumbićeva obala 11. Near the seafront this is a no-frills local favourite, serving dishes such as stuffed sweet peppers (35kn) and *pašticada* (beef stew with prunes; 45kn) in huge portions. Daily 6am–midnight.

Galija Kamila Tončića 12. Popular pizzeria with a wood-fired oven and pleasant terrace area. Huge salads for around 50kn and obligatory pizzas for 32–57kn. Mon–Sat 8am–11pm, Sun noon–11pm.

★ **Konoba Trattoria Bajamont** Bajamontićeva 3. Grab a seat at an old sewing machine table and watch the chef cook tasty Dalmatian dishes such as asparagus risotto (55kn) and calamari (50kn). Daily 8am–11pm.

Makrovega Leština 2. Hidden away in alleys just west of the Old Town, this chic café is a wonderful source of quality vegetarian food, with tofu and soya put to imaginative uses in a wide-ranging menu. The daily specials (soup, main and salad) are superb value at 60–70kn. Mon–Fri 9am–8pm, Sat 9am–4pm.

DRINKING AND NIGHTLIFE

The beach at Bačvice, a few minutes' walk south past the train station, is a popular party place in summer.

Bifora Bernardinova 5. An indie bar squeezed into one of the Old Town's cutest piazzas, *Bifora* is a fun place to enjoy a cocktail (from 30kn). Mon–Thurs & Sun 7am–1am, Fri & Sat till 2am.

Figa Buvinina 1. This legendary Split bar (formerly known as *Puls*) offers a flashy-looking menu of sandwiches and light bites, a great list of cocktails and shots, and a to-die-for location on one of the Old Town's most atmospheric stepped alleys. Daily 8am–1pm.

Galerija Plavca Marulićeva 3. This bright L-shaped space is not the most atmospheric in town, but it's popular with an arty-if-not-too-earnest local clientele and has a supremely soothing courtyard with outdoor seating. Mon–Thurs & Sun 7am–11pm, Fri & Sat 7am–1am.

Teak Just off Majstora Jurja. A nicely furnished café-bar with a sleek wood interior. Good for a quiet coffee during the day or some funk and something boozy in the evening. Beers from 11kn. Daily 8am–midnight.

DIRECTORY

Exchange At the bus station or any bank.
Hospital Firule, Spinčićeva 1 (☎ 021 556 111).
Internet Caffe Net Com, Grgura Ninskog 9 (daily 10am–10pm).

6

Launderette Modrulj, Šperun (daily: April–Oct 8am–8pm; Nov–March 9am–5pm).
Left luggage At the bus station (daily 7am–9pm; 5kn for first hour, then 1.5kn/hr) and train station (daily 6.30am–10pm; 15kn/hr).
Pharmacy Dobri, Gundulićeva 52 (24hr).
Post office Kralja Tomislava 9 and Obala kneza Domagoja 2 (both Mon–Fri 7.30am–7pm, Sat 7.30am–2.30pm).

BRAČ

BRAČ is a bewitchingly bare, scrub-covered island fringed by fishing ports, coves and beaches. The easiest way to reach Brač is by **ferry** from Split to **Supetar**, an engaging, laidback fishing port on the north side of the island, from where it's an hour's bus journey to **Bol**, a major windsurfing centre on the island's south coast and site of one of the Adriatic's most beautiful beaches, **Zlatni Rat** (Golden Horn).

Supetar

Though the largest town on the island, SUPETAR is a rather sleepy village onto which package tourism has been painlessly grafted. There aren't many sights, save for several attractive shingle **beaches** which stretch west from the harbour, and the **Petrinović Mausoleum**, a neo-Byzantine construction 1km west of town, built by sculptor Toma Rosandić to honour a local-born shipping magnate.

The library, Jobova bb (Mon–Sat 8.30am–1.30pm & 2.30–7.30pm; free), houses the Ivan Rendić Gallery, displaying sculptures by this successful Supetar native who worked around the turn of the twentieth century.

ARRIVAL AND INFORMATION

By ferry There are regular ferries between Supetar and Split (9–14 daily; 50min).
Tourist information Beside the ferry dock at Porat 1 (June–Sept Mon–Sat 8am–11.30am & noon–10pm, Sun 8am–11.30am & noon–3.30pm; Oct–May Mon–Fri 8am–3pm; ☏ 021 630 551, ⊕ supetar.hr).

ACCOMMODATION

Private rooms Available from Atlas (☏ 021 631 105) on the harbourfront at Porat 10, and Start (☏ 021 757 741), opposite the ferry dock. Rooms from <u>**300kn**</u>.

BRAČ ACTIVITIES

Scuba diving Fun Dive Club in the *Supetrus* hotel complex at Put Vela Luke 4 (closed Oct–April; ☏ 098 130 7384, ⊕ fundiveclub.com) rents snorkelling and scuba gear and arranges dives (from 220kn).
Mountain biking ACF at bana J. Jelačiča 14 rents out mountain bikes (80kn/day).

EATING AND DRINKING

There's a supermarket at the harbour.
Benny's Bar Put Vela Luke bb. West of town towards the *Supetrus* hotel complex, *Benny's Bar* has a large outdoor terrace with a pool where you can take in the sea air and enjoy live DJs and cocktails. June–Sept daily 8am–2am.
Bistro Palute Porat 4. The best of the places to eat on the harbourfront: serves good grilled fish from an open wood fire and meat dishes such as mixed skewers with fries (52kn) and goulash (55kn). Daily 8am–midnight.
Konoba Lukin Porat 32. Harbourside seating, a cosy, familial atmosphere and well-prepared local dishes make this the best option for a meal. Cuttlefish salad (60kn) and pizzas (30–40kn). Daily noon–midnight.

Bol

Stranded on the far side of the Vidova Gora Mountains, you cannot help but be overwhelmed by the beauty of **BOL**'s setting, or the charm of its old stone houses. However, the main attraction of the village is its beach, **Zlatni Rat**, which lies to the west of the centre along the wooded shoreline. This pebbly spit juts into the sea like a finger, changing shape from season to season as the wind plays across it. Unsurprisingly, it gets very crowded during summer.

Dramatically perched on a bluff just east of central Bol is the late fifteenth-century **Dominican Monastery** (daily 10am–noon & 5–8pm; 10kn), which boasts an altar painting by Tintoretto.

ARRIVAL AND INFORMATION

By plane Croatia Airlines fly to Bol airport, which is 10km from town, in the summer months.
By bus From Supetar, 14 daily buses make the hour-long trip to Bol's harbour. Some buses take a slower route – check before you leave.
By ferry Ferries dock at the end of the harbour in the middle of town. Note that buses from Jelsa to Hvar Town are not very frequent on Sun.

BOL ACTIVITIES

Hiking The 778m peak of Vidova Gora is within easy reach of Bol: a trail (2hr each way) heads uphill just beyond *Kito Camping* (see below). Check with tourist information for details of the route.

Mountain biking The tourist office has free cycling maps. Next door, *Big Blue Café* rents bicycles (90kn/day).

Watersports Big Blue (April–Nov; ☎021 635 614, ⓦ big-blue-sport.hr), on the path leading to Zlatni Rat, rents windsurfing boards (250kn/day) and sea kayaks (185kn/day).

Destinations Hvar (Jelsa: 1 daily; 20min); Split (1 daily; 55min).

Tourist information In the harbour (June & Sept daily 8.30am–3pm & 5–9pm; July & Aug daily 8.30am–10pm; Oct–May Mon–Fri 8.30am–3pm; ☎021 635 638, ⓦ bol.hr).

ACCOMMODATION

Private rooms Boltours, at Vladimira Nazora 18 (☎021 635 693, ⓦ boltours.com), arrange private rooms and 2-person apartments. Alternatively, try Adria at Bračka Cesta 10 (☎021 635 966, ⓦ adria-bol.hr), a 10min walk west. Rooms from 330kn, apartments from 430kn

Kito Camping Bračke ceste bb ☎021 635 551, ⓦ camping-brac.com. Large, friendly campsite close to the centre of Bol, with kitchens and a nearby supermarket. Camping 69kn per person, plus 25kn per tent

EATING AND DRINKING

Konoba Gušt Frane Radića 14. Inviting place with rustic decor and an extensive menu of traditional Dalmatian dishes features a wide range of fresh fish and a satisfying *pašticada* (70kn). Mid-April to Oct daily noon–1am.

Konoba Mlin Ante Starčevića 11. A lovely restaurant in a pretty old stone mill, with live music and an outdoor wood-fired grill where freshly caught fish are cooked to taste. Mains from 70kn. June–Oct daily 5pm–midnight.

Pizzeria Topolino Frane Radića 1. Located just metres from the sea, *Topolino* offers gorgeous views and a wide range of breakfast dishes, wood-oven-cooked pizzas, fresh salads (from 50kn) and home-made lemonade (18kn). May–Oct daily 8am–11pm.

Varadero Frane Radića. A prime position in the main square with DJs, a twelve-page cocktail menu (from 40kn) and a beach cabin feel – this is the place to be after dark. April–Oct daily 7.30am–2am.

HVAR

One of the most hyped of all the Croatian islands, **HVAR** is undeniably beautiful – a slim, green slice of land punctuated by jagged inlets and cloaked with hills of lavender. Despite Hvar's growing reputation as a high-society party island, tourist development hasn't been too overbearing. The island's Venetian-flavoured centre, **Hvar Town**, offers charm and affordability alongside plentiful opportunities for a cocktail-driven splash-out.

WHAT TO SEE AND DO

Hvar's central main square is flanked by the arcaded bulk of the **Venetian arsenal**, the upper storey of which was added in 1612 to house a **theatre** (summer 9am–1pm & 5–11pm; winter 11am–noon; 20kn), the oldest in Croatia. At the eastern end of the square is the **cathedral** (open mornings before services), a sixteenth-century construction with an eighteenth-century facade – a characteristic mixture of Gothic and Renaissance styles. Inside, the **Bishop's Treasury** (daily: June–Aug 9am–noon & 5–7pm; Sept–May 10am–noon; 20kn) holds a small but fine selection of chalices and reliquaries. The rest of the Old Town stretches back from the piazza in an elegant confusion of twisting lanes and alleys.

Up above, the **fortress** (daily: April & May 9am–4pm; June–Sept 8am–11pm; 25kn) was built by the Venetians in the 1550s and offers gorgeous sweeping views. From here, you can pick out the attractive fifteenth-century **Franciscan Monastery** (May–Oct daily 9am–1pm & 5–7pm; 20kn) to the left of the harbour, and the pleasingly simple monastic church next door.

Beaches and islands

The **beaches** nearest to town are rocky and crowded, so it's best to make your way towards the **Pakleni otoci**. Easily reached by water taxi from the harbour (50–70kn return), the Pakleni are a chain of eleven wooded islands, three of which cater for tourists with simple bars and restaurants: Jerolim, a naturist island, is

6

the nearest; next is Marinkovac; then Sv Klement, the largest of the islands. Bear in mind that camping is forbidden throughout the islands, and that naturism is popular.

ARRIVAL AND DEPARTURE

By boat At least one daily catamaran from Split arrives at Hvar Town itself; seven other ferries head for Stari Grad, 20km east. There's also one daily ferry from Bol on Brač to Jelsa in the centre of the island. Tickets for Krilo Jet catamarans are available from Pelegrini Tours, by the ferry dock at Riva bb (☎021 742 743, ⓦpelegrini-hvar.hr). SNAV (ⓦsnav.it) serve the route from Stari Grad to Peccara, Italy.

Destinations from Hvar Town Korčula Town (1 Krilo Jet catamaran daily; 1hr 15min); Split (daily: 1 ferry; 1hr; 1 Krilo Jet catamaran; 55min); Vela Luka (1 catamaran daily; 45min); Vis (1 ferry weekly; 1hr 30min).

Destinations from Stari Grad Pecara, Italy (July–Sept 1 ferry daily; 4hr 30min).

By bus Buses run from Stari Grad to Hvar Town (6–10 daily; 30min) and from Jelsa to both Hvar Town (3–4 daily; 45min) and Stari Grad (5–11 daily; 15min).

Destinations Jelsa (2–4 daily; 50min); Stari Grad (5 daily; 35min).

INFORMATION

Tourist information Branches at the bus station and on the main square at Trg sv. Stjepana bb (both June & Sept Mon–Sat 8am–1pm & 4–9pm, Sun 10am–noon & 6–8pm; July & Aug daily 8am–2pm & 3–10pm; Oct–May Mon–Sat 8am–1pm; ☎021 741 059, ⓦtzhvar.hr).

ACCOMMODATION

Private rooms Contact Pelegrini Tours (see above). Rooms from 375kn

Camping Mala Milna Milna ☎021 745 013. Terraced site right by the sea, 3km east of Hvar in the village of

HVAR ACTIVITIES

Island tours Secret Hvar (☎021 717 615, ⓦsecrethvar.com) offers 4WD trips on the rough roads of inland Hvar, exploring abandoned villages and lavender plantations. Also kayaking (350kn) and hiking trips (300kn).

Watersports Hvar Adventure at Obala bb, just off the Riva (☎091 228 0088, ⓦhvaradventure.com), run sea kayaking around the Pakleni islands (350Kn), guided hiking (300Kn), sailing (420kn) and rock climbing (400kn).

★ TREAT YOURSELF

Carpe Diem On the main seafront ⓦcarpe-diem-hvar.com. Said to be the best cocktail bar in Croatia, glamorous *Carpe Diem* is the epitome of jet-set. DJs spin crowd-pleasing tunes on the colonnaded terrace overlooking the harbour till the early hours, while skilled bartenders mix a long list of decadent cocktails (from 50kn). There is no cover charge but they do operate a "face control" admissions policy when busy, so it's worth dressing up. Taxi boats outside Carpe Diem transport revellers to its sister venue, *Carpe Diem Beach*, on the island of Marinkovac, which hosts DJ parties every night in peak season (cover charge for major events 100kn; check website for listings). *Carpe Diem* mid-June to late Aug daily 9am–2am; *Carpe Diem Beach* mid-June to late Aug daily 10am–5am.

Milna. With a bit of luck, small-tent travellers might find a pitch right beside the shore. Open May–Sept. Camping 50kn per person, plus 50kn per tent

★ Green Lizard Hostel Lucica ☎021 742 560, ⓦgreenlizard.hr. A funky, family-run hostel uphill from the ferry port, with great sea views, fun cocktail evenings and hammocks to chill out in. Shared kitchen, free internet and wi-fi. Open Easter–Oct. Dorm 150kn, double 350kn

Orange Hostel Lučica 11 (near *Green Lizard*) ☎091 515 7330, ⓦorange.hostel.com. More a peaceful private house than a hostel – there isn't a common room – with a leafy terrace and a mixture of rooms within its tangerine exterior. Double 530kn

EATING

Luna Petra Hektorovića 1. Quality local food imaginatively presented, including excellent grilled fish (120kn) and seafood pastas (70kn) in a modern, white-walled interior with contemporary arty touches. Easter–Dec daily noon–midnight.

Macondo Groda. This place has got style and quality, yet remains informal, and for a slap-up seafood feast there are few better places. The *škampi buzara* (unpeeled prawns in wine sauce; 120kn) is excellent. April–Oct Mon–Sat noon–2pm & 6pm–midnight, Sun 6pm–midnight.

Pizza Kogo Trg sv. St Jepana 34. A popular spot with pew-like seating inside and plenty of tables on the main square too. Reasonably priced mains include salads (45–55kn) and pizzas (45–65kn). Daily: June–Sept 10am–4am; Oct–May 10am–11pm.

DRINKING AND NIGHTLIFE

Hula Hula Majerovica. Hvar's premier après-beach bar, located on the shoreline path just beyond the *Amfora* hotel. Cold beers and cocktails served up on a big seaside terrace scattered with stools and beds, although it's standing-room only on summer nights. May–Sept 9am–midnight.

Kiva Fabrika. Raucously enjoyable black hole of a place in an alleyway just off the portside path. Can be a tight squeeze on summer weekends. Daily 9pm–2am.

Veneranda Club Gornja Cesta bb, west of the harbour. This monastery-turned-club offers international DJs (cover charge 150–200kn), an oxygen bar and wallet-busting cocktails (from 60kn). Regular cover charge 50kn. Summer daily 10pm–5am.

VIS

Wild and hilly, **VIS** is situated further offshore than any of Croatia's inhabited Adriatic islands. Closed to foreigners for military reasons until 1989, the island boasts two good-looking towns, **Vis Town** and **Komiža**, and great beaches and bars. Depending much more heavily on independent travellers and yachters than on the package crowd, it has a laidback atmosphere unique in the Adriatic.

Vis Town

VIS TOWN is a sedate arc of grey-brown houses on a deeply indented bay, above which loom the remains of abandoned agricultural terraces. A five-minute walk east from the harbour is the town's **history museum** (May–Oct Mon–Fri 10am–1pm & 5–9pm, Sat 10am–1pm; 20kn), and not far on from here is the suburb of **Kut**, an atmospheric, largely sixteenth-century tangle of narrow cobbled streets overlooked by summer houses built by the nobles from Hvar. A kilometre further on lies a small British war cemetery, and, just behind it, a pebbly beach. Heading west around the bay soon brings you to a small peninsula where the campanile of the Franciscan monastery of St Hieronymous rises gracefully alongside a huddle of cypresses. The ruins of an ancient Greek cemetery and nearby Roman baths lie just before the monastery.

ARRIVAL, INFORMATION AND TOURS

By boat Ferries and catamarans arrive in the centre of Vis Town's harbour from where buses (5 daily; 15min) depart for Komiža on the western side of the island.
Destinations Hvar (1 ferry weekly; 45min); Split (2–3 ferries daily; 2hr 20min; 1 catamaran daily; 1hr 30min).

Tourist information Just to the right as you leave the ferry dock (May–Sept Mon–Sat 9am–1pm & 6–9pm; Oct–April Mon–Fri 9am–1pm; ☎021 717 017, ⊛tz-vis.hr).

Tours Navigator (☎021 717 786, ⊛navigator.hr), directly in front of the ferry dock, offer island tours, trips to the Blue Cave (see p.176; 230kn) and scooter rental (200kn/hr).

ACCOMMODATION

Private rooms Enquire at Navigator (see above); and Ionios agency, 200m left of the ferry dock at Obala sv. Jurja 37 (☎021 711 532, ⊛ionios@st.t-com.hr), offer a range of rooms and apartments from **200kn**

EATING AND DRINKING

There is a small supermarket near the harbour. Note that eating out on Vis is reasonably expensive and the island is extremely seasonal.

Bejbi Šetalište stare Isse. Pronounced "baby", this is a laidback daytime coffee-drinking spot that bursts into life at night, with a funkily decorated café indoors, and bamboo-shaded bar in the yard. Daily: summer 6am–2am; winter 6am–midnight.

Karijola Šetalište viškog boja 4. Perched on a terrace midway between the town centre and Kut, this is the best place for a quality thin-crust pizza. Settle your stomach with *Karijola*'s range of irresistible *rakijas* – the *rakija od mirte* (grappa flavoured with mistletoe) has proven aphrodisiac qualities. May–Sept 1pm–1am.

Konoba Vatrica Kralija Krešimira. Friendly, family-run restaurant in Kut, specializing in fresh fish cooked over a wood fire. More affordable options are the black squid risotto and macaroni in lobster sauce (both 60kn). May–Sept daily 9am–midnight; Oct–April weekends 5–11pm.

Paradajz Lost Pod Kulom 5. Just off the Riva behind a squat medieval tower, *Paradajz Lost* (a play on words based on the fact that *paradajz* is dialect for "tomato") serves an extensive range of excellent local wines in a courtyard strewn with a jumble of junk-shop furniture. June–Sept daily 8am–2am.

Komiža

KOMIŽA, 10km from Vis Town, is the island's main fishing port – a picturesque town surrounded by lofty mountains. Dominating the southern

6

end of the harbour is the Kaštel, a stubby sixteenth-century fortress, which now holds the charming **Fishing Museum** (June–Sept Mon–Sat 9am–noon & 6–9pm; 15kn). Komiža's nicest beaches are ten minutes south of here, where you'll find a sequence of pebbly coves. Each morning, small boats leave the harbour for the nearby island of Biševo in order to visit the **Blue Cave**, a grotto filled with eerie shimmering light; expect to pay around 140kn for a half-day trip (see p.175).

ARRIVAL, INFORMATION AND TOURS

By bus Buses from Vis Town terminate about 100m behind the harbour.
Tourist information On the Riva just beyond the Kaštel (June–Aug Mon–Fri 8am–1pm & 6.30–8pm, Sat & Sun 6.30–8pm; Sept–May Mon–Sat 8am–1pm; ☎021 713 455, ⊛tz-komiza.hr).
Tours Alternatura, Hrvatskih mučenika 2 (☎021 717 239, ⊛alternatura.hr), organize guided tours of the island's former military facilities, as well as scuba diving, free climbing, sailing in a traditional *falkuša* fishing boat and hang-gliding.

ACCOMMODATION

Private rooms Book through Alternatura (see above), and Srebrna, Ribarska 4 (daily 8am–1pm & 6–10pm; ☎021 713 668, ⊛srebrnatours.hr). Rooms from 250kn

EATING, DRINKING AND NIGHTLIFE

Aquarius Kamenica beach. A popular summertime beach club, with fresh food and cocktails, projections beamed onto the sea, nightly DJs and dancing till dawn. Summer only. 24hr.
Kolđeraj Trg kralja Tomislava 1. This local bakery serves up fresh anchovy pasties (*komiška pogača*; 15kn), as well as other sweet and savoury pastries. Daily 6.30am–2am.
Konoba Bako Gundelićeva 1. Romantic beachside tavern complete with an indoor lobster pond. The fresh fish by the kilo is pricey, but there are also shrimp skewers (60kn) and

frutti di mare (86kn) on offer. Daily: June–Aug 4pm–2am; Sept–May 5–11pm.

KORČULA

Like so many islands along this coast, **KORČULA** was first settled by the Greeks, who gave it the name Korkyra Melaina or "Black Corfu", for its dark and densely wooded appearance. Even now, it's one of the greenest of the Adriatic islands, and one of the most popular. Medieval **Korčula Town** is the island's main settlement.

WHAT TO SEE AND DO

KORČULA TOWN sits on a beetle-shaped hump of land, a beautiful walled city ribbed with narrow alleys. The Venetians first arrived here in the eleventh century, and stayed, on and off, for nearly eight centuries, and their influence is particularly evident in the Old Town.

The Cathedral and Bishop's Treasury

The Old Town huddles around the **Cathedral of St Mark** (Mon–Sat: May & June 9am–2pm; July–Sept 9am–2pm & 5–7pm; Oct–April enquire at the tourist office to visit; 5kn), with a facade decorated with a gorgeous fluted rose window and a bizarre cornice frilled with gargoyles. The interior is one of the loveliest in the region – a curious mixture of styles, ranging from the Gothic forms of the nave to the Renaissance northern aisle, tacked on in the sixteenth century.

The best of the cathedral's treasures have been moved to the **Bishop's Treasury** (same hours as cathedral; 20kn, includes entrance to the cathedral), a couple of doors down. This small collection of fine and sacral art is one

---

MOREŠKA

Performances of Korčula's famous **folk dance**, the **Moreška**, take place outside the main gate to the Old Town every Monday and Thursday evening throughout the summer (tickets available from several agencies including Kaleta, Katun Tours and Atlas, all on Plokata 19, Travnja; 100kn). This archaic, repetitive, sword-based dance is the story of a conflict between the Christians (in red) and the Moors (in black): the heroine, Bula, is kidnapped by the evil foreign king and his army, and her betrothed tries to win her back in a ritualized sword fight which takes place within a shifting circle of dancers.

of the best in the country; look out for the Leonardo da Vinci sketch of a soldier wearing a costume bearing a striking resemblance to that of the Moreška dancers (see box opposite).

The Town Museum and the House of Marco Polo

On the main square, a former Venetian palace holds the **Town Museum** (Mon–Sat: April to mid-June & mid-Sept to Oct 10am–2pm; mid-June to early July 10am–2pm & 6–8pm; early July to mid-Sept 10am–9pm; 15kn), which displays everything from Greek amphorae to nineteenth-century furnishings. It is possible that Marco Polo was born in Korčula, but the seventeenth-century **House of Marco Polo** (daily: June, May & Sept 10am–2pm & 4–8pm; July & Aug 9am–9pm; 15kn) has no link whatsoever with the explorer – there are, however, good views of town from its upper storeys.

Beaches

Your best bet for **beaches** is to head off by water taxi from the old harbour to one of the **Skoji islands** just offshore. The largest and nearest of these is **Badija** (40kn return), where there are some secluded rocky beaches, a couple of snack bars and a naturist section. There's also a sandy **beach** just beyond the village of **Lumbarda**, 8km south of Korčula (hourly buses in summer; 15min).

ARRIVAL AND DEPARTURE

By bus Korčula's bus station is 400m southeast of the Old Town. The bus service from Dubrovnik crosses the narrow stretch of water dividing the island from the mainland, by ferry from Orebić. Korkyra Info (w korkyra .info) also runs a door-to-door minibus service to Dubrovnik (June–Sept daily with frequency depending on demand; 2hr; 148kn).
Destinations Dubrovnik (2 daily; 3hr 30min); Zagreb (1 daily, overnight; 11hr 30min).

By boat Ferry and catamaran services from Dubrovnik, Hvar and Split dock in Korčula Town harbour. In addition, there are also ferry and catamaran services from Hvar and Split to Vela Luka at the western end of the island, from where there's a connecting bus service to Korčula Town (3–6 daily; 1hr 10min). The Jadrolinja ticket office in Korčula Town is at Plokata 19 Travnja. Note that ferry

departures may switch between the west and east harbours in bad weather, so check before you leave. G&V Line catamaran tickets available from Korkyra Info (see above), Krilo Jet catamaran tickets from kiosk at west harbour.
Destinations from Vela Luka Hvar (1 catamaran daily; 45min); Split (2 ferries daily; 2hr 45min; 1 catamaran daily; 2hr).
Destinations from Korčula Town Dubrovnik (May–Sept 2 ferries weekly; 4hr; July & Aug 4 G&V Line catamarans weekly; 2hr 35min); Hvar (1 Krilo Jet catamaran daily; 1hr 15min); Split (May–Sept 2 ferries weekly; 5hr 40min; 1 Krilo Jet catamaran daily; 2hr 25min).

INFORMATION

Tourist information By the western harbour at Obala dr. Franje Tuđmana 4 (June–Sept Mon–Sat 8am–3pm & 5–9pm, Sun 9am–1pm; Oct–May Mon–Sat 8am–2pm; ☎ 020 715 701, w visitkorcula.net).

ACCOMMODATION

Private rooms Kaleta (☎ 020 711 282, w kaleta.hr) and Kantun Tours (also left luggage and bike rental; ☎ 020 715 622, w ikorcula.net), both at Plokata 19 Travnja, offer rooms from 300kn
Apartments Depolo ul. Hrvatske bratske zajednice 62 ☎ 020 721 172 or ☎ 098 357 582, w apartment-korcula .com. Modern apartments on the top two floors of a historic stone house midway between the bus station and the Old Town. They can be rented out as four- to six-person apartments or as smaller two-person units. Two-person apartments 600kn
Campsite Kalac ☎ 020 726 336, w korcula-hotels .com. Korčula's largest campsite, just 3km from town and with 600 pleasant pine-shaded pitches and a small sandy beach. Camping 60kn per person, plus 50kn per tent
Villa Depolo ul. Svetog Nikole bb ☎ 020 711 621, ✉ egon.depolo@du.t-com.hr. Four enormous, tastefully decorated rooms on the seafront, 150m west of the Old Town; several have brilliant sea views. Double 290kn

EATING, DRINKING AND NIGHTLIFE

There's a daily fruit and veg market beside the entrance to the Old Town.
★ **Arsenal Bistro** Vl. Ljiljana Duhović. Just right of the main gate into the Old Town, *Arsenal Bistro* is a real gem, with a changing menu of delicious cooking served in a simple, canteen-like interior; try the mouthwatering home-made macaroni with goulash (50kn). Daily 8am–10pm.
Boogie Jungle Put Lokve w boogie-jungle.com. Located 3km out on the Žrnovo road, on a hill overlooking the town, this alfresco disco grouped around a series of

6

6

curtain-draped pavilions is the place to enjoy wine and cocktails until sunrise. Cover charge 30–70kn. June–Sept daily 10pm–5am.

Dos Locos Šetalište Frana Kršinića. Live DJs and an alfresco bamboo bar draw the crowds to this spot behind the bus station. Cocktails for only 40kn during happy hour (8–10pm). Daily 9am–late.

Massimo Šetalište Petra Kanavelic. This cocktail bar, ensconced in a medieval turret, may be pricey but it's one of the prime spots for admiring a Korčula sunset. You have to go up and down by ladder – worth keeping in mind after a couple of cocktails (from 45kn). Daily 6.30pm–2am.

U Maje i Tonke Trg Korčulanskih klesara i kipara 2 ☎091 799 5549. Traditional staples given the modern bistro treatment, with a superb range of tapas-style nibbles embracing aubergine, goats' cheese and marinated fish. Desserts employ local flavours from carob to basil. A bit too busy in high season – be prepared to take your time. May–Sept daily noon–3pm & 6pm–midnight.

DUBROVNIK

The walled city of **DUBROVNIK**, at Croatia's southern tip, is the country's irresistibly beautiful star attraction. Lapped by the glittering Adriatic Sea, sturdy walls encircle the city's white marble streets, which are lined with imposing Baroque buildings.

First settled by Roman refugees in the early seventh century and given the name Ragusa, the town soon exploited its favourable position on the Adriatic with maritime and commercial genius. By the mid-fourteenth century it had become a successful and self-contained city-state, its merchants trading far and wide. Dubrovnik continued to prosper until 1667, when an earthquake devastated the city. Though the city-state survived, it fell into decline and, in 1808, its political independence was ended by Napoleon.

An eight-month siege by Yugoslav forces in the early 1990s caused much destruction, but the city swiftly recovered.

WHAT TO SEE AND DO

Within its fabulous **city walls**, Dubrovnik is a sea of terracotta roofs punctured now and then by a sculpted dome or tower. The best way to get your bearings is by making a tour of the walls (daily: April–Oct 8am–7.30pm; Nov–March 10am–3pm; 50kn), which are 25m high with all five towers still intact. From here, you get spectacular views of the **Old Town**, bisected by the main street,

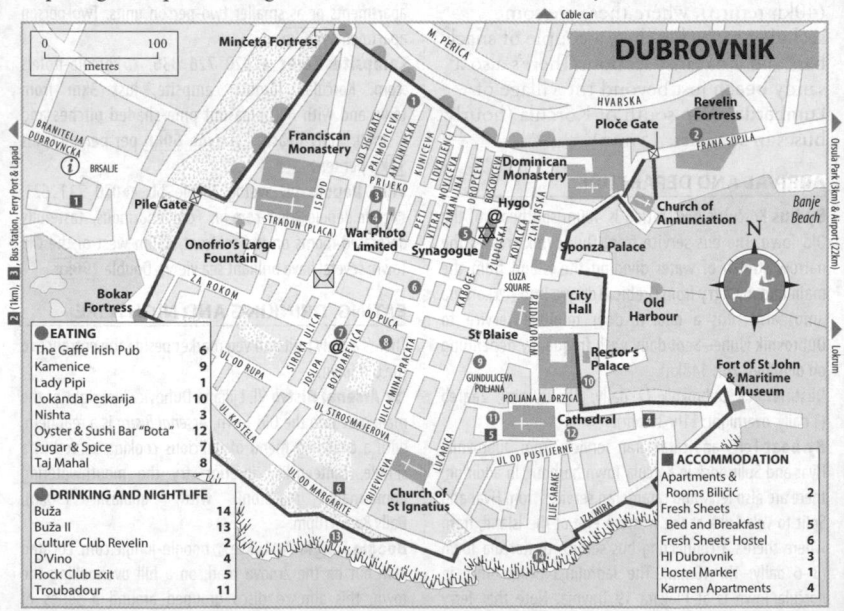

DUBROVNIK

EATING
The Gaffe Irish Pub	6
Kamenice	9
Lady Pipi	1
Lokanda Peskarija	10
Nishta	3
Oyster & Sushi Bar "Bota"	12
Sugar & Spice	7
Taj Mahal	8

DRINKING AND NIGHTLIFE
Buža	14
Buža II	13
Culture Club Revelin	2
D'Vino	4
Rock Club Exit	5
Troubadour	11

ACCOMMODATION
Apartments & Rooms Biličić	2
Fresh Sheets Bed and Breakfast	5
Fresh Sheets Hostel	6
HI Dubrovnik	3
Hostel Marker	1
Karmen Apartments	4

Stradun. The main attractions, all within the walls, can easily be covered in a day and a half.

The Pile Gate

The **Pile Gate**, main entrance to the Old Town, is a fifteenth-century construction complete with a statue of St Blaise, the city's protector, set in a niche above the arch. Just through the gate sits **Onofrio's Large Fountain**, built in 1444, a domed affair at which visitors to this hygiene-conscious city used to have to wash themselves before they were allowed any further.

The Franciscan monastery and Stradun

Opposite Onofrio's Large Fountain, the museum of the peaceful fourteenth-century **Franciscan monastery** complex (daily: summer 9am–6pm; winter 9am–5pm; 30kn) holds some fine Gothic reliquaries and manuscripts tracing the development of musical scoring, together with objects from the apothecary's shop, dating from 1317; there is still a working on-site pharmacy. From here, **Stradun** (also known as Placa), the city's main street, runs dead straight across the Old Town, its limestone surface polished to a shine by thousands of feet. **War Photo Limited**, at Antuninska 6 (May–Oct daily 9am–9pm; 30kn), is a three-storey photo gallery housing changing exhibitions from some of the world's leading photographers – conflict, and its frequently innocent victims, is the main focus.

The far end of Stradun broadens into airy **Luža Square**, the centre of the medieval town and still a hub of activity. On the left, the **Sponza Palace** was once the customs house and mint, with a facade showing off an elegant weld of florid Venetian Gothic and more sedate Renaissance forms. Nowadays it houses free contemporary art exhibitions and a memorial to those who lost their lives during the Dubrovnik siege (daily: May–Oct 9am–10pm; Nov–April 10am–3pm; free).

The Dominican monastery

North behind the Sponza Palace lies the **Dominican monastery**, its arcaded courtyard filled with palms and orange trees. It also houses a small **museum** (daily: summer 9am–6pm; winter 9am–5pm; 20kn), with outstanding examples of local sixteenth-century religious art.

The Church of St Blaise and Rector's Palace

On the south side of Luža Square lies the Baroque-style **Church of St Blaise**. Built in 1714, it serves as a graceful counterpoint to the palace. Outside the church stands the carved figure of an armoured knight – known as **Orlando's Column**, it was once the focal point of the city-state. Adjacent sits the fifteenth-century **Rector's Palace**, the seat of the Ragusan government, in which the incumbent Rector sat out his month's term of office. Today it's given over to the rather uninspiring **City Museum** (daily: April–Oct 9am–6pm; Nov–March 9am–4pm; combined ticket with Maritime Museum and a couple of other sights not covered here – the Ethnographic Museum and Revelin Fortress – 70kn).

The cathedral

The seventeenth-century **cathedral**, south from the Rector's Palace, is a rather plain building, although there's an impressive Titian polyptych of *The Assumption* inside. The **Treasury** (summer daily 8am–5pm; 15kn) boasts a twelfth-century reliquary containing the skull of St Blaise; shaped like a Byzantine crown, it is covered with portraits of saints and frosted with delicate gold and enamel filigree work.

The Fort of St John and Church of St Ignatius

The city's small harbour is dominated by the monolithic hulk of the **Fort of St John**; upstairs it houses a **maritime museum** (Tues–Sun: April–Oct 9am–6pm; Nov–March 9am–4pm; combined ticket with City, Ethnographic Museum and Revelin Fortress 70kn),

6

6

which traces the history of Ragusan sea power through a display of naval artefacts and model boats. Skirting round the city's southern walls you enter one of its oldest quarters, **Pustijerna**, much of which predates the seventeenth-century earthquake. Uphill sits the **Church of St Ignatius**, Dubrovnik's largest, a Jesuit confection modelled on Rome's enormous Gesù church. Steps sweep down from here to **Gundulićeva Poljana**, the square behind the cathedral, which is the site of the city's morning produce market.

The Dubrovnik Cable Car and Mount Srđ

For the best views in town take a ride on the **Dubrovnik Cable Car**, Petra Krešimira (daily: Feb, March & Oct 9am–5pm; April, May & Sept 9am–8pm; June–Aug 9am–midnight; Dec & Jan 9am–4pm; one-way 50kn, return 87kn), whose orange pods soar up to the top of Mount Srđ, offering a fantastic panorama of the city. You can also walk up or down the mountain via the winding footpath known as the Serpentina (90min up; 35min down). Note that the Serpentina is stony and unshaded – strong footwear and water are essential. The fort at Srđ's summit houses the **Museum of the Homeland War** (daily 9am–6pm; 20kn), featuring guns, shell cartridges and a rousing collection of photos.

Beaches

The noisy and crowded main city **beach** is a short walk east of the Old Town; less crowded and somewhat cleaner is the beach on the Lapad peninsula, 5km to the west (bus #6 from the Pile Gate). Or you can catch a boat from the old city jetty (April–Oct daily 8am–6pm; every 30min; 10min; 50kn return) to the wooded island of **Lokrum**. Covered in pine trees, Lokrum is home to an eleventh-century Benedictine monastery-turned-palace and has extensive rocky beaches running along the eastern end of the island – with a naturist section (known as FKK) at the far eastern tip.

ARRIVAL AND DEPARTURE

By plane Atlas buses (30min; 35kn) run to and from the city centre (enquire at the tourist office for times), stopping at the bus terminal in Gruž and outside the cable-car station on Petra Krešimira.

By bus The bus terminal is located in the port suburb of Gruž, 4km west of town. If travelling to Split, take your passport, as you pass through Bosnia enroute.

Destinations Korčula (1–2 daily; 3hr); Montenegro (various towns; 2–4 daily); Pula (1 daily; 15hr); Rijeka (4 daily; 11hr 30min–13hr); Rovinj (1 daily; 16hr); Sarajevo (5 daily; 5–6hr); Split (14–17 daily; 4hr–4hr 30min); Trieste (1 daily; 15hr); Zadar (6–7 daily; 7hr–8hr 30min); Zagreb (8 daily; 11hr).

By boat The ferry terminal is located in the port suburb of Gruž, 4km west of town.

Destinations Bari, Italy (4–6 ferries weekly; 9hr); Korčula (May–Sept 2 ferries weekly; 4hr; July & Aug 4 G&V Line catamarans weekly; 2hr 35min); Rijeka (2 ferries weekly; 22hr 30min); Split (2 ferries weekly; 11hr).

INFORMATION AND TOURS

Tourist information The main branch is on the plaza outside the Pile Gate at Brsalje 5 (daily: July & Aug 8am–10pm; May, June & Sept 9am–9pm; Oct–April 9am–5pm; ☎020 321 561, ⊛tzdubrovnik.hr). There's also one opposite the ferry terminal in Gruž (same hours). The Dubrovnik Card (24hr/72hr/week for 110kn/180kn/220kn; ⊛www.dubrovnikcard.com) offers free entry to eight city attractions and 24hr public transport, and is available from the tourist office.

Tours Adriatic Kayak Tours, Zrinsko Frankopanska 6 (☎020 312 770, ⊛adriatickayaktours.com), organize kayaking tours from 275kn for a half-day to Lokrum island.

GETTING AROUND

By bus City buses #1a or #1b (tickets 12kn from driver or 10kn from kiosk) run from the bus terminal to the main western entrance to the Old Town, the Pile Gate.

★ **TREAT YOURSELF**

Karmen Apartments Bandureva 1 ☎020 323 433, ⊛karmendu.com. Make like a real Ragusan and splash out on a stay at the exquisitely and artfully decorated *Karmen Apartments*. These four homely apartments (sleeping 2–3) are full of personal touches and offer amazing views of the harbour and city walls. Marc, the owner, is a wealth of local information. Apartment **600kn**

DUBROVNIK SUMMER FESTIVALS

The prestigious **Summer Festival** (☎020 326 100, ⓦdubrovnik-festival.hr) from July 10 to August 25 is an enjoyable time to visit, with high-quality classical concerts and contemporary theatre performances in many of the city's courtyards, squares and bastions. Book well in advance or you may end up without a proper seat.

Orsula Park (ⓦparkorsula.du-hr.net), a hillside park 3km out of town on the road to Cavtat, hosts a summer-long season of concerts and DJ events on an outdoor stage; check the website for details.

6

ACCOMMODATION

Private rooms Locals offering private rooms meet bus and ferry arrivals. Alternatively, try Partner Travel/Direct Booker at Pera Čingrije 2 (☎020 638 194, ⓦdirect-booker .com). Central rooms from 450kn, rooms in Gruž and Lapad from 400kn

Apartments & Rooms Biličić Privežna 2 ☎020 417 152 & ☎098 802 111, ⓦdubrovnik-online.com/apartments _bilicic. Well-equipped rooms and four-person apartments a 10min walk uphill from town. There's a gorgeous garden – complete with tortoises – and genial owner Marija offers free picks-ups, internet access and laundry service. Double 450kn, apartment 900kn

★ **Fresh Sheets** Sv Šimuna 15 ☎091 799 2086, ⓦfreshsheetshostel.com. A fun, stylish hostel in a great Old Town location with superb views, free wi-fi and internet, and a communal kitchen. Breakfast included. Dorm 200kn, double 550kn, private rooms (singles and doubles) in neighbourhood from 250kn per person

Fresh Sheets Bed and Breakfast Bunićeva poljana 6 ☎091 896 7509, ⓦfreshsheetsbedandbreakfast.com. A new departure from the *Fresh* team (see above), with a mixture of doubles (some en suite, some shared) and two-person studio apartments in a historic stone building right behind the cathedral. Wi-fi throughout. Double 675kn, studio 1050kn

HI Dubrovnik Vinka Sagrestana 3, follow steps next to *Café Bar Ferrari* on Bana Jelačića ☎020 423 241, ⓦhfhs.hr; connected to Old Town and bus and ferry terminals by buses #1a and #1b, #3, #4, #5, #6 and #7. Well run with clean rooms, a leafy courtyard and free breakfasts. Dorm 160kn

Hostel Marker Svetog Đurđa 6 ☎091 739 7545, ⓦhostelmarkerdubrovnik.hostel.com. A range of comfortable rooms and four-bed apartments spread between five old houses beneath the Lovrjenac Fort. Double 525kn, apartment 1000kn

EATING

There's a morning market (Mon–Sat) at Gundulićeva Poljana in the Old Town, and a supermarket in the same square.

Kamenice Gundulićeva Poljana 8. A simple fish restaurant where waitresses in white clogs serve cheap portions of whitebait (56kn) and locals sometimes break into song over the delicious *kamenice* (oysters; 10kn each). Daily: summer 8am–midnight; winter 8am–9pm.

Lady Pipi Peline bb. Right beneath the city walls, this is one of the best places in the Old Town for local food simply cooked, with an outdoor grill on a vine-covered terrace serving squid, sausages and steaks. Cash only, and no reservations – expect to queue on summer evenings. April–Oct daily 9am–3pm & 6–11pm.

Lokanda Peskarija Na Ponti. Right on the old harbour with a huge terrace and great views, this seafood-only restaurant serves up a small but fantastic menu including mussels (60kn) and a fish platter (180kn for two people). Daily 8am–1am.

★ **Nishta** Prijeko bb. A meal at this stylish vegetarian café makes a welcome change from Croatia's meat and fish staples. A healthy portion of vegetable curry will set you back 85kn and there is a fresh salad bar too (30–59kn). March–Dec Mon–Sat noon–11pm.

Oyster & Sushi Bar "Bota" Od Pustijerne bb ☎020 324 034. Worth splashing out on, *"Bota"* offers fresh-as-you-like sushi and sashimi for 7kn/piece, and tempura oysters (12kn/piece) straight from the restaurant's renowned oyster farm in Mali Ston. April–Oct daily 10am–1am.

Taj Mahal Nikole Gučetića 2. Don't be fooled by the name – *Taj Mahal*, tucked away off the Stradun, offers traditional Bosnian dishes such as stuffed aubergines (40kn), veal in pastry (80kn) and *baklava* (25kn) in an exotic interior. Daily 10am–11pm.

The Gaffe Irish Pub Miha Pracata 4. Ignore the sports pub exterior – *The Gaffe* offers excellent hearty home cooking at reasonable prices. Low-season lunch specials such as beef stew and dumplings are only 30kn. Food served at lunchtime only. Daily 9am–1am.

DRINKING AND NIGHTLIFE

★ **Buža** Accessed from Ilije Sarake. Reached via a hole in the city walls, this is a stunning spot for a dip in the sea and a drink, with a cluster of tables perched on rocky terraces. Its more expensive (34kn/beer) sister bar, *Buža II*, is at Crijeviceva 9. Both daily 10am–late, depending on the weather.

6

Culture Club Revelin Sv. Dominika 3 ⓦ clubrevelin .com. The stocky Revelin Fort makes an amazing venue for club nights and gigs, attracting international DJs such as Darren Emerson – check their website and posters for listings and cover charge. Wed–Sat 10pm–late.

D'Vino Palmotićeva 4a. There are quite a few wine bars lurking in the Old Town's alleys but *D'Vino* is one of the oldest and best. The alley invariably fills with enthusiastic imbibers on warm summer evenings. Daily noon–2am.

Rock Club Exit Boškovićeva 2. A year-round favourite with locals, although it loses out in the summer months due to its first-floor location. Setting the tone are album covers and rock-star photos on the walls, and more or less permanently hard-riffing background music. Daily 6pm–2am.

Troubadour Bunićeva Poljana 2. A buzzing bar run by three musical brothers, with a great view of the cathedral. Live music – usually jazz – every night. Beer 35kn. Daily 9am–2am.

DIRECTORY

Consulates UK, Vukovarska 22/1 ☎ 020 324 597.
Hospital Roka Mišetića 2 ☎ 020 431 777.
Internet Hugo Internet, Prijeko 13 (7kn/15min, 10kn/30min).
Left luggage Bus station (daily 4.30am–10.30pm; first hour 5kn, thereafter 1.5kn/hr).
Pharmacy Kod Zvonika, Stradun (Mon–Sat 7am–8pm).
Post office Široka (Mon–Fri 7.30am–9pm, Sat 10am–5pm).

TÝN CHURCH AT DUSK, PRAGUE

Czech Republic

HIGHLIGHTS

❶ Prague Row through the golden city at dusk. See p.188

❷ Sedlec ossuary See human bones in the subterranean ossuary at Sedlec. **See p.197**

❸ Český Krumlov Forget the Renaissance ever ended at this fairytale town. **See p.199**

❹ Plzeň Visit the home of Pilsner Urquell, the original lager. See p.200

❺ Karlovy Vary Indulge in some spa treatments at this lovely town in the mountains. **See p.201**

❻ Olomouc Discover the capital of an ancient empire. See p.205

HIGHLIGHTS ARE MARKED ON THE MAP ON P.185

ROUGH COSTS

Daily budget Basic €40, occasional treat €50

Drink Pilsner Urquell €1.50

Food Pork and dumplings €4

Hostel/budget hotel €14/€40

Travel Train: Prague–Karlovy Vary €12; bus: €6

FACT FILE

Population 10.5 million

Language Czech

Currency Czech koruna (Kč)

Capital Prague

International phone code ☎420

Time zone GMT +1hr

Introduction

"Prague never lets you go", said Franz Kafka, "this dear little mother has claws". Prague gets her golden claws into tourists too, and few ever make it outside the capital. But those who tear themselves away won't be sorry; the colonnade- and park-filled spa towns, Bohemia's Renaissance breweries and hilltop ruins, and the tumbling vineyards and underground bars of Moravia are worth exploring.

Sitting in the centre of Europe, with Germany to the west, Poland to the north, Slovakia to the east and Austria in the south, the Czech Republic is firmly entrenched in Central Europe. Although the country is small, the variety in landscape and architecture is enormous, encompassing the forests and rolling countryside of **Bohemia**, peaceful spa towns like Karlovy Vary, **Moravia**'s spectacular karst region and historic towns like **Olomouc** and Český Krumlov.

CHRONOLOGY

Fourth century BC The Celtic "Boii" tribe inhabit the area now known as Bohemia.

500s AD Slavic tribes arrive.

830 AD The Great Moravian Empire is established on the Morava River.

907 Hungarians conquer the Great Moravian Empire.

1355 Charles IV, "the father of the Czech nation", is crowned Holy Roman Emperor.

1415 Protestant reformer Jan Hus is burned at the stake, sparking decades of religious conflict.

1458 George of Poděbrady is crowned.

1526 King Ferdinand I, a Habsburg, takes the Czech throne, and begins a project of re-Catholicization.

1620 The Protestant nobility is defeated by Catholic forces at the Battle of White Mountain.

1800s Rapid growth in nationalism and industrialization.

1918 The independent republic of Czechoslovakia is founded at the end of World War I.

1938 German troops annex Sudetenland in western Czechoslovakia.

1945 German occupation ends as the Allies move in.

1948 The Communist Party seizes control of Czechoslovakia.

1968 The "Prague Spring" sees a brief period of political liberalization, the USSR responds by invading.

1989 The Velvet Revolution. Czechoslovakia becomes a democracy.

1993 The Czech Republic and Slovakia peacefully separate into two states.

2004 The Czech Republic joins the EU.

2007 The Czech Republic joins the EU's Schengen Treaty free movement zone.

2013 First direct presidential election is held, and Miloš Zeman becomes the new president.

ARRIVAL AND DEPARTURE

There are direct flights from more than a dozen UK airports, and from New York JFK, to Václav Havel Airport Prague (☎ 220 113 314, ⊛ prg.aero/cs), 10km northwest of the city. Several international routes (including one from London Stansted by Ryanair, and from London Luton via Wizz Air) serve Brno (⊛ brno -airport.cz). There are a couple of flights a week between Karlovy Vary (⊛ airport-k -vary.cz) and Russia. Prague is served by direct **train** services from numerous major European cities, including Bratislava, Berlin, Vienna and Budapest.

Eurolines (⊛ eurolines.com) runs good international **bus** services to the Czech Republic, as does Orange Ways (⊛ orange ways.com). Student Agency (⊛ student agencybus.com) has international routes but also runs between Prague and other Czech cities.

GETTING AROUND

Czech public transport is affordable and reliable. For train and bus times go to ⊛ idos.cz.

BY TRAIN

The Czech Republic has one of the most comprehensive **rail** networks in Europe. Czech Railways (České dráhy (ČD);

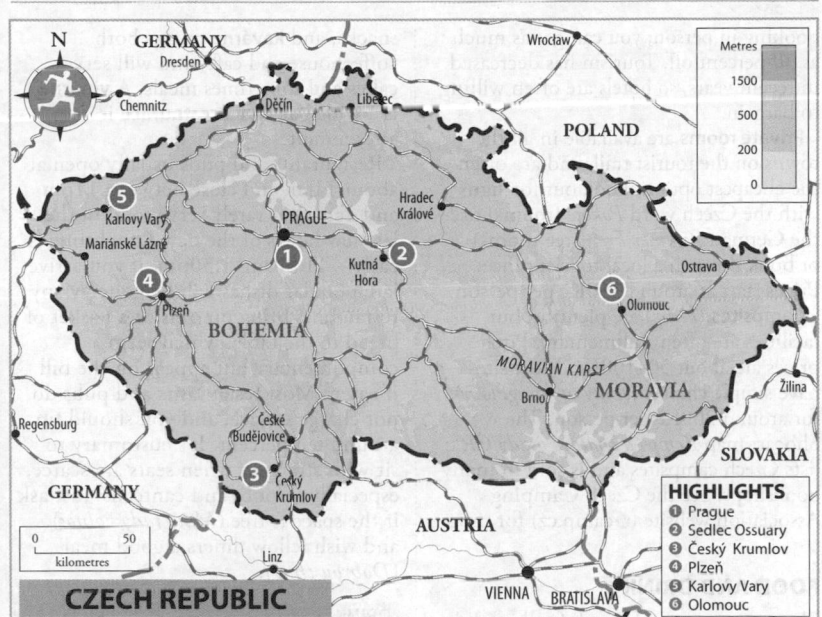

N

GERMANY
Dresden

Chemnitz Děčín Liberec

POLAND

Wrocław

Metres
1500
500
200
0

⑤ Karlovy Vary

Mariánské Lázně

PRAGUE **①**

Hradec
Králové

④

Plzeň

Kutná
Hora **②**

BOHEMIA

Ostrava

⑥ Olomouc

MORAVIAN KARST

MORAVIA

Žilina

Brno

Regensburg

České
Budějovice

SLOVAKIA

GERMANY

③ Český
Krumlov

AUSTRIA

HIGHLIGHTS
❶ Prague
❷ Sedlec Ossuary
❸ Český Krumlov
❹ Plzeň
❺ Karlovy Vary
❻ Olomouc

0   50
kilometres

Linz

CZECH REPUBLIC

VIENNA BRATISLAVA

7

Ⓦcd.cz) runs two types of train: *rychlík* (R) or *spěšný* (Sp) trains are faster, only stopping at major towns, while *osobní* trains stop at every small station, averaging 30km per hour. Fast trains are further divided into SuperCity (SC), which require reservations, EuroCity (EC) or InterCity (IC), which charge a supplement, and Expres (Ex), which don't. **Tickets** (*jízdenky*) for domestic journeys can be bought at the station (*nádraží*) before or on the day of departure. ČD runs reasonably priced **sleepers** to a number of neighbouring countries, which you should book in advance. **InterRail** and Eurail passes are valid in the Czech Republic.

BY BUS

Regional **buses** are mostly run by the state bus company, Česká státní automobilová doprava (ČSAD), or ICOM, plus a number of smaller private operators. **Bus stations** are often alongside train stations; some have ticket offices but you can usually buy tickets from the driver. For long-distance journeys it's a good idea to book your ticket at least a day in advance or if you want to guarantee yourself a seat.

The Student Agency (Ⓞ841 101 101, Ⓦstudentagency.cz, Ⓦstudent agencybus .com) runs an excellent, reasonably priced bus service, with direct routes between popular destinations. Tourbus also has good domestic bus connections (Ⓦtourbus.cz).

BY BICYCLE

Cycling is popular in the Czech Republic, and the varied countryside provides good terrain whatever your level. Regional cycling maps (Ⓦshocart.cz) are sold in bookshops. There's bike rental in all major cities and some smaller towns. See Ⓦcyklistevitani.cz for more information.

ACCOMMODATION

Accommodation will be the largest chunk of your daily expenditure. The Czech Youth Hostel Association is affiliated with Hostelling International (Ⓞ224 914 062, Ⓦczechhostels.com) and offers accommodation across the country. Smaller hostels and B&Bs are often understaffed; confirm your arrival time beforehand or you risk being locked out. Check if there's an online discount before

7

booking in person; you can get as much as 30 percent off. Tourism has decreased in recent years, so hotels are often willing to bargain.

Private rooms are available in all the towns on the tourist trail, and are often the cheapest option. Look out for signs with the Czech word *Pokoje* (rooms) or the German *Zimmer Frei* (free rooms) or book through a local tourist office. Prices start at around 350Kč per person.

Campsites (*kemp*) are plentiful but facilities are often rudimentary. Pitch prices are about 50–100Kč. Most sites have simple **chalets** (*chaty* or *bungalovy*) for around 200Kč per person. The Shocart map *Kempy a chatové osady ČR* lists Czech campsites and is sold in many bookshops. See the Czech Camping Association website (ⓦcamp.cz) for more.

FOOD AND DRINK

The great mystery of Czech food is where the summer menu went. Pork, game, dumplings and cabbage are perfect in the icy Eastern winters but depressing on a hot day. Czech staples like roast duck (*pečená kachna*), beef in cream sauce (*svíčková na smetaně*) or baked pork (*vepřové výpečky*) are omnipresent, and can be delicious or boring, depending on the chef. Desserts include strudel (*závin*), fruit dumplings (*ovocné knedlíky*) and crêpes (*palačinky*).

Prague and bigger towns offer a big choice of non-Czech restaurants, and even small towns have a pizzeria and a Chinese restaurant. **Vegetarian** food is easier to come by in cities, but in rural areas the choice is usually between fried cheese (*smažený sýr*) and fried cauliflower (*smažený květák*).

A **samoobsluha** or **bufet** is a self-service canteen selling cheap meals, sandwiches and snacks. A **bageterie** is a sandwich shop, and a **pekařství** is a bakery, which often sells open sandwiches as well as bread, rolls, buns and cakes – not to be confused with a **cukrárna**, or cake shop. A **pivnice** is a pub without food, a **hospoda** or **hostinec** is a pub that serves meals. A **čajovna** is a teahouse, which might serve snacks, and **kavárna** means both coffeehouse and café, and will serve cakes and sometimes meals. A **vinárna** is a wine bar and a **restaurace** is a restaurant.

Restaurants and pubs usually open at about 11am and close between 11pm and 2am, but rarely serve food in the last few hours of the day. Lunchtime is early – 11.30am–1.30pm; if you arrive late popular dishes will be gone. Many restaurants bring pretzels or a basket of bread to the table, which seem complimentary but appear on the bill if eaten. Most restaurants and pubs do not charge service, and you should **tip** around ten percent. It's customary to sit with strangers when seats are scarce, especially in pubs and canteens: just ask if the space is free (*Máte tady volno?*), and wish fellow diners a good meal (*Dobrou chuť*).

DRINK

The Czechs drink more **beer** (*pivo*) per capita than anyone else in the world – hardly surprising given the high quality and low price of Czech beer. The most famous brands are Pilsner Urquell, from Plzeň, and Budvar, from České Budějovice. Even small canteens and cafés have beer on tap. Southern Moravia is a wine-growing region, and produces some good whites. Other specialities include *slivovice*, devilishly strong plum brandy, and Becherovka, herb liquor.

CULTURE AND ETIQUETTE

It can be easy to mistake the Czechs' shyness for surliness, and people who actually speak pretty good English will often tell you that they don't speak it at all – it's often from lack of confidence rather than unfriendliness, and if you can get past some initial resistance, people are usually helpful and kind. Obviously, it helps if you learn some basic words – *Dobrý den* (hello), *Na shledanou* (goodbye), *Prosím* (please) and *Děkuji vam* (thank you) will take you far.

Ten percent is usual for **tips**, depending on the establishment: give fifteen percent for more upmarket places.

SPORTS AND ACTIVITIES

Football is the country's second national sport. In Prague, you can see two of the tops teams, Sparta (w sparta.cz) and Slavia (w slavia.cz). Matches are usually on Saturdays from August to November and March to May.

The main national craze is **ice hockey**: you can watch matches in bars in most towns in the Czech Republic, or arrange to see games in stadiums during the season (book tickets through w sazkaticket.cz).

There are plenty of **outdoor activities** such as cycling, hiking and rock climbing to be enjoyed in Bohemia, as well as **caving** in the Moravian karst.

COMMUNICATIONS

Most **post offices** (*pošta*) are open Monday to Friday 9am to 5pm, Saturday 9am to noon. Signs over the counters show where to queue: *známky* (stamps), *dopisy* (letters) or *balíky* (parcels). Stamps are also sold at newsagents and kiosks.

CZECH

7

	CZECH	PRONUNCIATION
Yes	*Ano*	Ah-no
No	*Ne*	Neh
Please/You're welcome	*Prosím*	Pro-seem
Thank you	*Děkuji*	Dye-koo-yi
Good day/Hello	*Dobrý den*	Dob-ree den
Goodbye	*Na hledanou*	Nash-leh-dan-oh
Excuse me	*Promiňte*	Prom-in-teh
Sorry	*Pardon*	Pardon
Where?	*Kde?*	Kde?
Good	*Dobrý*	Dobree
Bad	*Špatný*	Shpatnee
Near	*Blízko*	Bleez-ko
Far	*Daleko*	Dah-lek-o
Cheap	*Levný*	Levnee
Expensive	*Drahý*	Dranee
Open	*Otevřeno*	Ot-evsh-en-o
Closed	*Zavřeno*	Zavsh-en-o
Today	*Dnes*	Dnes
Yesterday	*Včera*	Vch-er-a
Tomorrow	*Zítra*	Zeet-ra
How much is it?	*Kolik to stojí?*	Kol-ik toh sto-yee?
What time is it?	*Kolik je hodin?*	Kol-ik ye hod-in?
I don't understand	*Nerozumím*	Ne-rozoo-meem
Do you speak English?	*Mluvíte Anglicky?*	Mluv-ee-te ang-lit-skee?
I don't know Czech	*Nerozumím Český*	Ne-rozoo-meem Chess-kee
Toilet	*Toaleta*	Toh-aleta
Square	*Náměstí*	Nam–yest-yee
Station	*Nádraží*	Nah-dra-shee
Platform	*Nástupiště*	Nah-stoopish-tyeh
One	*Jeden*	Yed-en
Two	*Dva*	Dva
Three	*Tři*	Trshi
Four	*Čtyři*	Shtiri
Five	*Pět*	Pyet
Six	*Šest*	Shest
Seven	*Sedm*	Sed-um
Eight	*Osm*	Oss-um
Nine	*Devět*	Dev-yet
Ten	*Deset*	Dess-et

7

EMERGENCY NUMBERS

Police ☎158; Fire ☎150; Ambulance ☎155; General emergency number, EU-wide ☎112.

Some **public phones** only take phone cards (*telefonní karty*), available from post offices, kiosks and some shops. You'll find **internet cafés** in bigger towns; they usually charge 60–100Kč per hour.

EMERGENCIES

Like any major city Prague has a **pickpocket** problem. Danger-spots are Old Town Square, Charles Bridge, Wenceslas Square, the #22 tram and in the metro. The area around hlavní nádraží (main station) and the park at Karlovo náměstí (Charles Square) are used by drug addicts and prostitutes at night. By law you should carry your **passport** with you.

Pharmacies (*lékárna*) are easy to find but not always English-speaking. If you need a repeat prescription take the empty bottle or remaining pills.

INFORMATION

Most towns have a **tourist office** (*informační centrum*) with English-speaking staff. You can find **maps** (*mapa*) in tourist offices, bookshops and petrol stations.

CZECH REPUBLIC ONLINE

Ⓦ **czech.cz** Basic information on the Czech Republic.
Ⓦ **expats.cz** Website for Prague's expat community with useful practical information and events listings.
Ⓦ **praguepost.com** Online and print English-language news.
Ⓦ **radio.cz/english** News and cultural events.
Ⓦ **ticketpro.cz**, Ⓦ **ticketstream.cz**, Ⓦ **ticketsbti.cz** Three good sites for finding out what's on in Prague and booking tickets online. Ticketstream and Ticketpro also have events outside of Prague.
Ⓦ **slovnik.cz** Online dictionary.

STUDENT DISCOUNTS

Student discounts can be up to half-price. Bring an ISIC card, as many places won't recognize university cards.

MONEY AND BANKS

The local **currency** is the Czech crown, or koruna česká (Kč), though some tourist-oriented services list prices in euros. At the time of writing £1 = 29Kč, €1 = 25Kč and $1 = 19Kč. **Banks** are usually open Monday to Friday 9am to 5pm and there are plenty of ATMs.

OPENING HOURS AND HOLIDAYS

Most shops are open Monday to Friday 9am to 5 or 6pm. Smaller shops close for lunch between noon and 2pm and some stay open late on Thursdays. In larger towns some shops stay open all day at weekends, and the corner shops (*večerka*) stay open daily till 10 or 11pm. Museums, galleries and churches are generally open daily; synagogues are closed on Saturdays and Jewish holidays. Many attractions are closed on Mondays.

Public holidays include January 1, Easter Monday, May 1, May 8, July 5 and 6, September 28, October 28, November 17, December 24–26.

Prague

Historical, whimsical, hedonistic and cynical, **PRAGUE** bewilders its visitors – and charms them. Since the Iron Curtain fell in 1989, tourism and investment have poured in, turning the previously ramshackle Communist capital into a buzzing Western metropolis.

Prince Bořivoj, an early Christian, founded the first Czech dynasty in 870, and his grandson, Prince Václav (the Good King Wenceslas of the song), became the Czech patron saint before being offed by his younger brother Boleslav I. Prague experienced a golden age under the urbane emperor, **Charles IV**, a polylingual patron of the arts whose court was the heart of fourteenth-century Europe. Charles founded the university as well as an entire new quarter, Nové Město, and built the Charles Bridge and St Vitus'. A long period of Austro-Hungarian rule gave Prague its Teutonic facades and high-minded coffeehouses, while the National Revival reasserted the Slavic identity of the city and the onion dome rose again. The short-lived First Republic, modelled on American democracy, crashed when Nazi troops marched into Czechoslovakia, and President Beneš's decision to accept German "protection" was a dark moment in the nation's history, but saved the city from decimation. In 1948 Communism arrived in a wave of stained concrete, bringing a few architectural pearls along with the swine. The period since 1989 has seen rapid construction, but with a few exceptions, such as Jean Nouvel's Golden Angel in Smíchov, Karlín's Danube building and the playful Dancing House, it's been conservative and timid. Not so the restaurants, hotels, bars and clubs, which have re-awoken Prague's slumbering decadence.

WHAT TO SEE AND DO

Flowing from the east towards Germany, the Vltava divides Prague in the centre. Hradčany and Malá Strana, once home to the Austro-Hungarian elite, sit primly on the left bank, faced by the noisier commercial quarters, Staré Město, Josefov and Nové Město.

Hradčany, which houses the castle and St Vitus' Cathedral, tumbles into **Malá Strana** (Little Quarter), a maze of cobbles, carved doorhandles and stickleback roofs. The Czech senate's Baroque gardens, which back onto Malostranská metro, are open daily from noon till 4pm.

Over the river is **Staré Město** (Old Town), a delicate web of alleys and passages running towards Staroměstské náměstí, the old market square. Within Staré Město is the old Jewish quarter, **Josefov**, which now encloses a luxury shopping district.

Nové Město (New Town), the most central part of the modern city, spans the largest area of old Prague, with blocks stretching south and east of the old town in long strides.

Prague Castle

Once the heart of the Holy Roman Empire, **Prague Castle** (sights daily 9am–4/5pm; grounds daily 5/6am–11pm/midnight; ⊕hrad.cz) is home to the Czech president and crown jewels. Wandering is free, but to enter the buildings you need to buy a **ticket** (250–350Kč, valid for two days), which come in long-visit or short-visit options and are available at the Castle Information Centre, opposite the cathedral entrance.

St Vitus' Cathedral

Medieval **St Vitus' Cathedral**, which broods over the Prague skyline, is scarcely visible close up; the Third Courtyard surrounds it too tightly. The **Chapel of sv Václav**, by the south door, was built in the fourteenth century to commemorate the Czech prince Saint Wenceslas (Václav), murdered by his brother Boleslav I. A door in the south wall leads to the coronation chamber, which houses the **crown jewels**.

Old Royal Palace

The **Old Royal Palace** (Starý královský palác), across the courtyard from the south door of the cathedral, was home to Bohemian royalty from the eleventh to the seventeenth centuries. The massive **Vladislav Hall** (Vladislavský sál), where the early Bohemian kings were elected, is still used for the most important state events.

Basilica of St George

The **Basilica of St George** (Bazilika sv Jiří), with its beautiful Romanesque interior, was originally built in 1173. Concerts are often held here. The nearby Convent of Saint George houses a collection of sixteenth- to eighteenth-century Czech art.

Golden Lane

Golden Lane (Zlatá ulička), round the corner from the basilica, is a street of

7

7

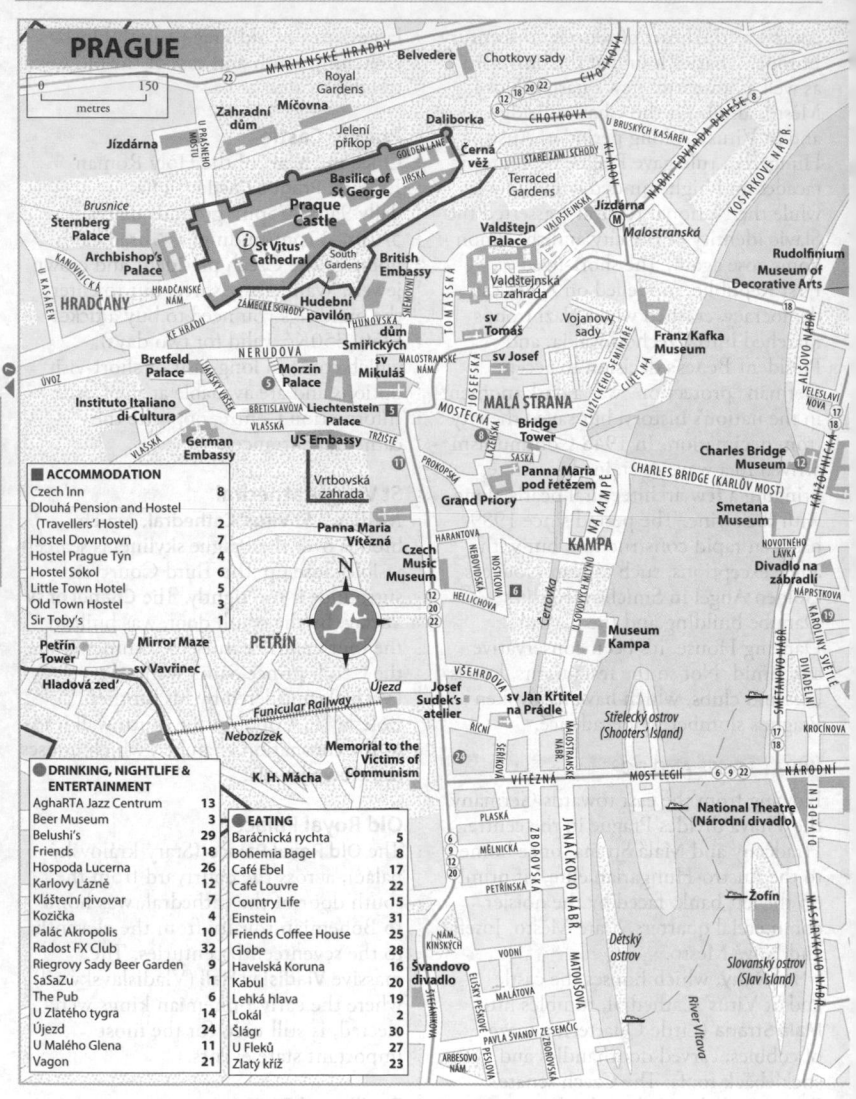

toy-sized tradesmens' cottages, as bright and compact as a watercolour box. Franz Kafka briefly lived at no. 22, his sister's house, during World War I.

The Royal Gardens

North of the castle walls, cross the **Powder Bridge** (Prašný most) to reach the **Royal Gardens** (Královská zahrada; April–Oct daily 10am–6pm; free), and enjoy the view over Little Quarter surrounded by fountains, sloping lawns and almond trees.

Hradčanské náměstí

Aristocratic palaces lie across Hradčanské náměstí like a pod of beached whales. A passage down the side of the Archbishop's Palace leads to **Šternberg Palace** (Tues–Sun 10am– 6pm; 150Kč), home to a European **art collection** that contains pieces by

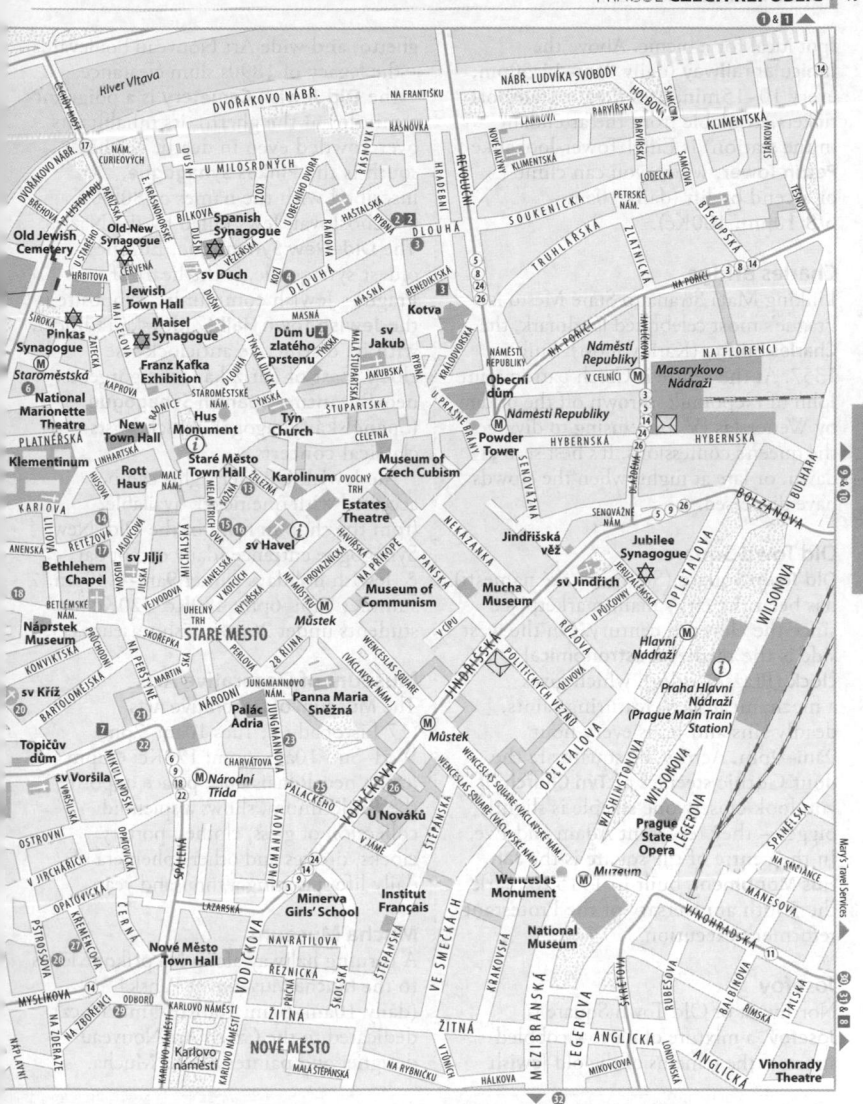

Rubens, Cranch and El Greco. At Jiřská 3 is **Lobkowicz Palace** (daily 10am–6pm; 275Kč; ⓦlobkowicz.cz), full of aristocratic bric-a-brac. A passage at Pohořelec 8 leads to **Strahov Monastery** (Strahovský klášter) with its exquisite Baroque library (daily 9am–noon & 1–5pm; 80Kč; ⓦstrahovskyklaster.cz), which displays peculiar and sublime artefacts from illuminated manuscripts to dried whale penises.

Sv Mikuláš

Malostranské náměstí, the main square in Malá Strana, forms a ring around the flamboyant church **St Nicholas** (daily 9am–4/5pm; 70Kč), a triumph of Baroque whimsy with one of the most overlooked interiors in the city.

Petřín

Head south down Karmelitská and you will see **Petřín hill** rising above, a bucolic

7

spot ideal for a picnic. Above the **funicular railway** (daily 9am–11.30pm; every 10–15min; uses Prague transport tickets, available from the attendant in the station) is Eiffel Tower-lookalike **Petřín Tower**, which you can climb or ascend by lift (daily 10am–6/8/10pm; 100Kč).

Charles Bridge

Linking Malá Strana to Staré Město is Prague's most celebrated landmark, the **Charles Bridge** (Karlův most), built in 1357. At the centre is Czech patron saint John of Nepomuk, thrown off the bridge by Wenceslas IV for refusing to divulge the queen's confessions. It's best seen at dawn, or late at night, when the crowds have dispersed.

Old Town Square

Old Town Square (Staroměstské náměstí) has been the city's main marketplace since the eleventh century. On the west side is the medieval **astronomical clock** (Pražský orloj), which gives a mechanical show featuring saints, deadly sins and Jesus every hour 9am–9pm. Across the square are the dour Gothic steeples of **Týn Church**; if you look closely one steeple is slightly bigger – they represent Adam and Eve. In the centre of the square is the **Jan Hus Monument**, built in 1915 to mark the 500th anniversary of the Protestant reformer's execution.

Josefov

Northwest of Old Town Square is **Josefov**, a mixture of narrow cobbled streets – the remains of the old Jewish ghetto, and wide Art Nouveau boulevards – the legacy of 1890s slum clearance.

The **Old Jewish Cemetery** is a poignant reminder of the ghetto, its inhabitants overcrowded even in death. To the south is the **Pinkas Synagogue**, inscribed with the names of 80,000 Czechoslovak Jews killed by the Nazis. The **Old–New Synagogue**, Europe's oldest synagogue, is the heart of Prague's Jewish community. Opposite is the **Jewish Town Hall** (Židovská radnice), with its distinctive anticlockwise clock. East of Pařížská is the gorgeous neo-Byzantine **Spanish Synagogue** (Španělská synagoga), which hosts classical concerts.

The Jewish Quarter sights can be accessed with one ticket, available from the shop in front of the Old–New Synagogue entrance (daily except Sat & Jewish holidays winter 9am–4.30pm, summer 9am–6pm; 480Kč, 320Kč for students under 26; ⊛jewishmuseum.cz).

Museum of Decorative Arts

The **Museum of Decorative Arts** (17 Listopadu 2; Tues 10am–7pm, Wed–Sun 10am–6pm; 120Kč; ⊛upm .cz), a neo-Renaissance palace opposite the Rudolfinum, shows a splendid collection of glass, clothes, pottery, clocks, dresses and other ephemera of daily life spanning a thousand years.

Mucha Museum

A turning halfway along Na příkopě leads to the **Mucha Museum** at Panská 7 (daily 10am–6pm; 180Kč; ⊛mucha.cz), dedicated to the Czech Art Nouveau designer and painter Alfons Mucha.

FRANZ KAFKA

Franz Kafka was born in 1883 to middle-class Czech Jewish parents who ran a haberdashery in Old Town. His ambivalent relationship with Prague is reflected in his trademark tone of anxious claustrophobia – "A cage went in search of a bird", he once jotted in a notebook. You can see the building where he slaved away as a clerk at **na poříčí 7**, and his homes on **Golden Lane** (no. 22) and **Old Town Square** (Oppelt building). Kafka went to fortnightly meetings at **Café Louvre** (see p.195) and also frequented **Café Savoy** in Malá Strana, where he first met the actor Isaac Lowy, who re-awakened his interest in Jewish culture. At the **Kafka Museum** at Cihelna 2b (daily 10am–6pm; 180Kč; ⊛kafkamuseum.cz) you can see first editions and manuscripts, personal letters, diaries and drawings – a peephole into one of the most intriguing minds of the twentieth century.

Municipal House

Squatting ponderously on one edge of náměstí Republiky is the **Municipal House** (Obecní dům), a delightful example of Czech Art Nouveau containing a concert hall, restaurant, café and frescoes by Mucha. You can get in by taking the overpriced guided **tour** (two or three daily; 290Kč), or drink tea in the gilded café and enjoy a decent Czech meal in the basement for rather less.

Museum of Communism

Situated, with delicious irony, above *McDonald's*, the **Museum of Communism** on Na Příkopě 10 (daily 9am–9pm; 190Kč; ⓦmuzeumkomunismu.cz) draws a detailed picture of life behind the Iron Curtain in all its grim monotony, from propaganda and labour camps to shopping and TV.

Wenceslas Square

The greasy axle of modern Prague is **Wenceslas Square** (Václavské náměstí), a mass of shabby gift shops and strip clubs. It was here that protesters gathered to topple Communism in the Velvet Revolution. At the top end is a statue of St Wenceslas on his horse. Below is a small **memorial** to 21-year-old student **Jan Palach**, who burnt himself to death in protest against the Russian invasion of '68, becoming a symbol of Czech resistance.

The Museum of Modern Art

Take tram #12 from outside ⓜMalostranska to the **Museum of Modern Art** (Veletržní palác; Tues–Sun 10am–6pm; 180Kč), a stately piece of 1920s functionalism housing works by Klimt, Picasso and the French Impressionists.

DOX Centre for Contemporary Art

DOX (Sat–Mon 10am–6pm, Wed–Fri 11am–7pm, closed Tues; 180Kč, students 90Kč; ⓦdox.cz) showcases modern painting, sculpture, architecture, design and photography. One of the most intriguing venues in town, it's hosted the likes of Andy Warhol and Damien Hirst, as well as Czechs such as sculptor David Černý and émigré architect Jan Kaplický.

ARRIVAL AND DEPARTURE

By plane Prague's airport (*letiště*), Václav Havel Airport Prague (ⓦprg.aero), is 10km from the city centre. The best way of getting into town is to catch a bus and then a metro. Bus #119 (4am–midnight; every 7–15min; 20min) goes to ⓜDejvická on line A, and bus #179 to ⓜNové Butovice on line B. "Fixed-price" taxis are expensive, at about 700Kč to the centre.

By train If you're coming by train you'll arrive at one of Prague's four stations: Praha hlavní nádraží (Prague Main Station), where most international trains arrive/depart; Praha Holešovice station; Praha Masarykovo; or Praha Smíchov. All four are adjacent to metro stations.

Destinations Berlin (every 2hr; 4hr 45min); Bratislava (4 daily; 4hr); České Budějovice (up to 10 daily; 2hr 40min–3hr); Dresden (5 daily; 2hr 15min); Karlovy Vary (3 daily; 3hr 20min); Olomouc (1–2 hourly; 2hr 15min–3hr 30min); Plzeň (hourly; 1hr 40min); Vienna (3 daily; 4hr 45min).

By bus The main bus station is Praha-Florenc on the eastern edge of Staré Město, and right next to ⓜFlorenc (line B). At night it's a shady place, so don't loiter. Most buses depart from Praha-Florenc. For Student Agency buses, book ahead (see p.185) at their main office in the Florenc bus station.

Destinations Berlin (3 daily; 4hr 45min–5hr 15min); Bratislava (up to 8 daily; 4hr 30min); Brno (every 30min–1hr; 2hr 20min–3hr); České Budějovice (up to 10 daily; 2hr 30min–3hr 25min); Český Krumlov (up to 6 daily; 3hr, typically leaves from Na Knížecí bus station near metro Anděl); Karlovy Vary (hourly; 2hr 10min–2hr 40min); Kutná Hora (hourly on weekdays; 1hr 15min); Plzeň (hourly; 1hr); Vienna (6 daily; 4–5hr).

INFORMATION

Tourist information The Prague Information Service (Pražská informační služba – PIS) is free and can provide maps and brochures, and help with accommodation and tickets. There are several branches around town (Mon–Fri 9am–6/7pm, Sat 9am–3/5pm; April–Oct also Sun 9am–5pm; ⓦpraguewelcome.com), including inside Hlavní nádraží (Main Station), at the Charles Bridge in the Lesser Town Bridge Tower, Staroměstské náměstí 5 (Old Town Square), and Rytířská 31 near ⓜMuztek.

GETTING AROUND

By metro The metro (daily 5am–midnight) is fast, reliable and – with only three lines – easy to navigate.

By tram Running every 3–20min, Prague's trams cross the city's hills and cobbles with great dexterity. Tram #22, which runs through Vinohrady and Hradčany, is an option if you want to sightsee. Night trams (numbers #51–#59; midnight–4.30am; every 30min) all pass through Lazarská in Nové Město.

7

RIVER CRUISE

Prague is most beautiful from the water. Boat trips down the Vltava last between an hour and a day; there are lunch and dinner cruises and jazz and club boats with live music. Buy tickets on the riverbank at Čechův Bridge or Embankment nábřeži, or pre-book with Prague Boats (☎ 224 810 030, ⓦ prague-boats.cz; prices start at 240Kč), or Jazzboat (☎ 731 183 180, ⓦ jazzboat.cz; 590Kč with option for dinner).

By taxi Prague cabbies are notoriously wily, so it is best to call a taxi – AAA has English-speaking operators (☎ 14 0 14), as does Profi Taxi (☎ 14 0 15). If you have to hail a cab, look for the Fair Place taxi sign, get a quote beforehand, and ask for a receipt (*účtenka*).

Travel passes If you're planning to use public transport regularly you can buy a travel pass (110Kč/24hr, 310Kč/72hr); remember to validate it once. Another option is Praguecard (ⓦ praguecard.biz), which costs €55 (1408Kč), students €42 (1075Kč), and gives you three days of transport and entry to 50 attractions. To receive the card with transport it must be booked online.

Tickets Buy tickets at tobacconists, kiosks or the ticket machines inside metro stations and by some tram stops, and validate them by stamping them in the yellow machines on board trams or at the metro entrance. There are two main tickets: the 32Kč ticket is valid for 90min; the 24Kč is valid for 30min. Plain-clothes inspectors check tickets and there is a fine of 800Kč on the spot if you don't have a valid ticket.

Bike rental Praha Bike (Dlouhá 24; daily 9am–8pm; ⓦ prahabike.cz) rents bikes and organizes tours around Prague for 490Kč for a tour (2hr 30min) or 500Kč for an 8hr rental. City Bike (Královdvorská 5; daily 9am–7pm, ⓦ citybike-prague.com) offers bike rental with an optional MP3 audio tour (550Kč for 8hr).

ACCOMMODATION

Prague has hundreds of hotels and hostels, and prices are similar to any other European capital. The central hotels are located in Staré Město, Nové Město and Malá strana, or you can go further out to pay less. Vinohrady is picturesque, with great wine bars and restaurants, Žižkov is down at heel but lively at night, Vyšehrad is pretty and sedate. There are plenty of travel agencies, but it's cheaper to book direct. You can find apartments and rooms on ⓦ prague-city-apartments.cz, ⓦ praguecentralapartments.com and ⓦ pragueclassicrental.cz. The Charles University offers student rooms over the summer; contact the booking office at Voršilská 1, Nové Město (Mon–Fri only; ☎ 224 930 010; beds July to mid-Sept; from 350Kč).

★ **Czech Inn** Francouzská 76, Vinohrady ☎ 267 267 600, ⓦ czech-inn.com. With its oak floors, brushed aluminium and discarded backpacks Czech Inn seems like the product of a tryst between a youth hostel and a luxury hotel. It's on the edge of the town centre in the great Vinohrady neighbourhood and has a café-bar with live music, great staff and a 24-hour reception. Room options include dorms, private (both en-suite and shared bath) and apartments. Go by metro to Náměstí Míru, then tram #4 or #22 to Krymská. Dorm 350Kč, double 1565Kč

Dlouhá Pension and Hostel (Travellers' Hostel) Dlouhá 33, Staré Město ☎ 224 826 662, ⓦ travellers.cz; Ⓜ Náměstí Republiky. Large party hostel a 5min walk from Old Town Square and next door to Roxy music club. There's a kitchen and a 24hr reception. Breakfast included. Dorm 350Kč, double 800Kč

Hostel Downtown Národní 19, Nové Město 224 240 570, ⓦ hosteldowntown.cz. Clean, garishly decorated HI-affiliated hostel. Room options include dorms as well as private rooms with either shared or private baths. Dorm 550Kč, double 2080Kč

Hostel Prague Týn Týnská 19, Staré Město ☎ 224 808 301, ⓦ hostelpraguetyn.com; Ⓜ Náměstí Republiky. Newly done up hostel offering a free breakfast. Located just 200m to Old Town Square. A bit small, but clean and colourful. Prices quoted in euros but they accept koruna as well. Dorm 355Kč/€13.90

Hostel Sokol Nosticova 2, Malá strana ☎ 257 007 397, ⓦ hostelsokol.cz. Immaculate, spartan dorms full of brass and white linen overlooking the river, originally built for Communist athletes. Dorm 350Kč

Little Town Hotel Malostranské náměstí 11/260, Malá strana ☎ 242 406 964, ⓦ littletownhotel.cz; Ⓜ Malostranská. In the shadow of St Nicholas Cathedral, this hostel-hotel mix is fresh, if a little barren. Choose from dorms or private en suite or private shared bath rooms. Dorm 500Kč, double 1000Kč

Old Town Hostel Benediktská 2, Staré Město ☎ 224 829 058, ⓦ oldpraguehostel.com. Bright, compact hostel on a quiet central street. Breakfast included. Doubles have shared bathrooms. Dorm €14.90 (381Kč), double €48 (1229Kč)

Sir Toby's Dělnická 24 ☎ 246 032 610, ⓦ sirtobys.com; Ⓜ Nádraží Holešovice or tram stop Dělnická. Upmarket suburban hostel with a garden, cellar bar, lounge, large kitchen and dorms that look like pricey hotel rooms stretched. Dorm 390Kč, double 1700Kč

EATING

There was a time when Prague food was limited to meat and dumplings, but now you can find anything from French and Korean to Mexican and Chinese. Restaurants are affordable, especially at lunchtime (11.30am–1.30pm) when pubs and bistros run cheap daily offers. Prices soar in the tourist district but quality lags behind. Prague has a thriving café culture, and watching the comings and goings from an old-fashioned coffeehouse, with a slice of strudel or honey cake and a book, is one of the city's great pleasures.

CAFÉS

Bohemia Bagel Masná 2, Staré Město ⓦ bohemiabagel .cz. Start out the day with a hearty breakfast (served all day), or refuel with a sandwich or burger. Decent vegetarian options. Daily 8am–9pm.

Café Ebel Řetězová 9, Staré Město ⓦ ebelcoffee.cz. Excellent place to escape the crowded streets and indulge in a good cup of coffee, breakfast or light snack. Mon–Fri 8am–8pm, Sat & Sun 8.30am–8pm.

★ **Café Louvre** Národní 22, Nové Město ⓦ cafelouvre .cz. Lovely Art Nouveau coffeehouse as rich and delectable as the classic sacher torte. There's a billiard hall, good-value lunch menu and a shady terrace. Mon–Fri 8am–11.30pm, Sat & Sun 9am–11.30pm.

Friends Coffee House Palackého 7, Nové Město ⓦ milujikavu.cz. Try their freshly roasted coffee and home-made sandwiches or sip on a glass of wine. Hosts music performances, readings and photograph exhibitions. Mon–Fri 9am–9pm, Sat & Sun noon–8pm.

Globe Pštrossova 12, Nové Město ⓦ globebookstore.cz. Modern café-bookshop popular with Prague's American crowd. Weekend brunches and weekday happy hours. Mon–Thurs 9.30am–midnight, Fri–Sun 9.30am–1am.

Šlágr Francouzská 72, Vinohrady ⓦ kavarnaslagr.cz. A popular, dimly lit, jazz-infused lovesong to the lost coffeehouses of '20s Prague. Delicious home-made cakes. Daily 10am–10pm.

Zlatý kříž Jungmannovo nám. 19, Nové Město ⓦ lahudkyzlatykriz-praha.cz. A meaty slice of real Czech culture, this popular stand-up lunch-bar serves Prague's best *chlebíčky* (ornate open sandwiches) for only 16Kč, plus cold cuts, rolls and beer on tap. Mon–Fri 7am–7pm, Sat 9am–3pm.

RESTAURANTS

Baráčnická rychta Tržiště 23, Malá strana ⓦ baracnickarychta.cz. Popular local stashed in a back alley in the tourist district. Good food, outdoor seating in the quiet courtyard and Svijany, a superb beer, on tap. Mains 150–295Kč. Mon–Sat 11am–11pm, Sun 11am–9pm.

Country Life Melantrichova 15, Staré Město ⓦ countrylife.cz. Around the corner from Old Town Square, this vegetarian lunch spot gets packed. Cafeteria style, food is priced by weight (a plateful should be 100–120Kč). Hot and cold offerings, plus free water. Mon–Thurs 10.30am–7.30pm, Fri 10.30am–5pm, Sun noon–6pm.

Einstein Rumunská 25, Vinohrady ⓦ pizza-einstein.cz. Good and extensive Italian menu – the pizza is probably

the best of the lot. Great garden and ISIC discount. Mains 79–166Kč. Daily 11am–11pm.

Havelská Koruna Havelská 21, Staré Město ⓦ havelska -koruna.cz. Not for the health-conscious, with all of the Bohemia grandma's favourite dishes inelegantly plopped on a plate. Located a 2min walk from Old Town Square. Mains 89–150Kč. Daily 10am–8pm.

Kabul Karolíny Světlé 14, Staré Město ⓦ kabulrestaurant .cz. Super Afghani restaurant a 5min from Old Town Square with a nice lunch menu and lovely back garden. Mains 90–280Kč. Daily noon–11pm.

Lehká hlava Boršov 2, Staré Město ⓦ lehkahlava.cz. Cure for Czech pub fatigue – bright, chic, non-smoking and vegetarian. Daily lunch menu for 108Kč. Mains 150–195Kč. Mon–Fri 11.30am–11.30pm, Sat & Sun noon–11.30pm.

Lokál Dlouhá 33, Staré Město ⓦ ambi.cz. A restaurant chain trying to re-create the charm of a little Czech pub on a cleaned up scale. It's very popular and the best bet for some authentically tasty Czech food. Mains 134–142Kč. Mon–Fri 11am–1am, Sat noon–1am, Sun noon–10pm.

U Fleků Křemencova 11, Nové Město ⓦ ufleku.cz. The look is there, and the beer is worth the trip, but the place can be a bit touristy. Food is pure Czech. Mains 189–329Kč. Daily 10am–11pm.

DRINKING AND NIGHTLIFE

Pubs close between 11pm and 2am so for late-night drinking head to the city centre's bars and clubs. All-night bars with gambling (*herna*) are dotted around Prague, but are grubby and unsafe. Pub crawls are a good way to cover a lot of ground: one popular company is Prague Pub Crawl (ⓦ pubcrawl.cz; 490Kč), or for something perhaps more sedate, join the Sandemans beer tour (ⓦ newpraguetours .com; 350Kč), which meets daily at 6pm on Old Town Square.

BARS AND PUBS

Beer Museum Dlouhá 46, Staré Město ⓦ praguebeermuseum.com. No glass cases or fossils in sight in this relaxed central pub – just a line of taps as long as a Louvre corridor. Daily noon–3am.

Belushi's Odborů 4, Nové Město ⓦ belushis.com. Trendy, dimly lit bar and music club in the ground floor of Mosaic House hostel, which moonlights as a sports bar (mostly hockey and football) and serves decent meals. The stream of hostel guests creates a gregarious atmosphere. Daily 7am–1am.

Hospoda Lucerna Vodičkova 36, Nové Město ⓦ hospodalucerna.cz. Long, loud bar popular with everyone. Decent meals and a bit of history – the pub dates back to 1908. Mon–Thurs 11am–2am, Fri 11am–3am, Sat noon–3am, Sun noon–1am.

Klášterní pivovar Strahovské nádvoří 301, Hradčany ⓦ klasterni-pivovar.cz. Reward yourself for the steep walk

7

up Petřin with a delicious beer – dark and light – brewed by the monks at Strahov Monastery. Daily 10am–10pm.

Kozička Kozí 1, Staré Město ⓦ kozicka.cz. Popular place to start and round off an evening; the underground place stays open later than most and also serves proper meals. Mon–Thurs noon–4am, Fri 5pm–4am, Sat 6pm–4am, Sun 7pm–3am.

★ **Riegrovy Sady Beer Garden** Riegrovy sady, Vinohrady. Pints are sold out of one hut, sausages out of another. There's a big screen for sport, table-football and table-hockey. Alternatively, you can buy your beer in a plastic cup and drink it in the park, with cherry blossom rustling above. Daily noon–2am (dependent on weather).

The Pub Veleslavínova 3, Staré Město ⓦ thepub.cz. Self-service pub with a tap on every table. The amount of beer (Pilsner Urquell) you've consumed is projected on a big screen to encourage inter-table rivalry. Mon–Thurs 11am–1am, Fri 11am–3am, Sat noon–3am, Sun noon–11pm.

U Zlatého tygra Husova 17, Staré Město ⓦ uzlatehotygra .cz. If you like authenticity, this tobacco-smoked local full of noisy old men is the place for you. Pilsner on tap. Just 5min from Old Town Square. Daily 3–11pm.

CLUBS

Friends Náprstkova 1, Staré Město ⓦ friendsclub.cz. Low-key gay bar that transforms into a raucous club on Fri and Sat nights. Daily 6pm–3am, Fri & Sat till 5am.

Karlovy Lázně Novotného lávka 1, Staré Město ⓦ karlovylazne.cz. Hyper-kitsch super-club next to the Charles Bridge; techno on the top floor, progressively more retro as you descend towards the internet café in the lobby. Daily 9pm–5am.

Palác Akropolis Kubelíkova 27, Žižkov. Art Deco mammoth Akropolis is a maze of live music, theatre, dancing and eating, offering rock, house, pop, hip-hop, reggae and the rest. Mon–Thurs 11am–12.30am, Fri–Sun 11am–1.30am.

Radost FX Club Bělehradská 120, Vinohrady ⓦ palacakropolis.cz. Popular central club decorated like a faux-oriental brothel and famous for its nightly parties. Visit during the day for a decent vegetarian meal. Daily 10pm–5am.

SaSaZu Bubenské nábřeží 306, Holešovice ⓦ sasazu.com. Shiny goliath of Prague nightlife modelled on the slick clubs of New York's meatpacking district, with an oriental fusion restaurant. Fri & Sat 10pm–5am.

Újezd Újezd 18, Malá strana ⓦ klubujezd.cz. Three-floor club popular with the young, hedonist set. Mix of live music and DJs; the bottom floor is a pub and the corridors serve as an art gallery. Daily 2pm–4am.

ENTERTAINMENT

You can find entertainment listings on the sometimes difficult to navigate Prague Events Calendar (ⓦ pragueeventscalendar.cz), expat websites Expats.cz (ⓦ expats.cz) and Prague.tv (ⓦ prague.tv), or in the Day&Night section of the rather overpriced English-language paper *The Prague Post* (sold in the kiosks on Wenceslas Square).

LIVE MUSIC

AghaRTA Jazz Centrum Železná 16, Staré Město ⓦ agharta.cz. Prague's best jazz club, with a good mix of top international names and local acts. Daily from 9pm.

U Malého Glena Karmelitská 23, Malá Strana ⓦ malyglen.cz. Tiny, popular jazz venue in a Little Quarter cellar with a restaurant upstairs. Daily from 9.30pm.

Vagon Národní třída 25, Nové Město ⓦ vagon.cz. Smoky music club playing a mix of rock and reggae, bursting at the seams with long-haired students and ageing rockers. Daily from 9pm.

CLASSICAL MUSIC, OPERA AND BALLET

Small classical concerts are held in churches in the tourist district every night – you'll be pelted with fliers as you walk through town, or you can find listings online (see p.193).

Národní Divadlo (National Theatre) Národní 2, Nové Město ⓦ narodni-divadlo.cz. Grand monument to nineteenth-century nationalism, built with a brick from every village in the country. Ballet and opera performed by national and touring companies. You can also get information on ballet and opera being shown at both the State Opera (Wilsonova 4, Nové Město) and Stavovské divadlo (Ovocný trh 1, Staré Město).

Obecní dům Nám. Republiky 5, Staré Město ⓦ obecnidum.cz. Grand Art Nouveau building hosting a range of classical concerts and festivals.

Rudolfínum Alšovo nábřeží 12, Staré Město ⓦ ceskafilharmonie.cz. This neo-Renaissance concert hall next to the river houses the Czech Philharmonic Orchestra, creators of a thousand film soundtracks.

THEATRE

Lanterna Magika Národní 4 ⓦ narodni-divadlo.cz. A blend of circus, puppetry and dance. Czech theatre minus the language barrier.

National Marionette Theatre Žatecká 1 ⓦ mozart.cz. Giant marionettes miming to a CD of Mozart's *Don Giovanni*. Silly but good fun.

Švandovo divadlo Štefánikova 57 ⓦ svandovodivadlo .cz. Czech theatre with English subtitles. Sit in the balcony for best view.

CINEMA

Kino Lucerna Štěpánská 61, Nové Město ⓦ lucerna.cz /kino.php/pronajmy.php. Nestling inside a shopping arcade off Wenceslas Square, Lucerna is a flamboyant, pint-sized Art Nouveau cinema. Czech, international, old, new films and a quiet vintage bar.

Kino Světozor Vodičkova 41, Nové Město ⓦ kinosvetozor .cz. New releases, classics, art-house and documentaries.

ACTIVITIES

Boating Žofín or Střelecký island. Pedalo and rowing boat rental from little firms on the river islands opposite the National Theatre. April–Oct; passport kept as deposit, approx 100Kč/hr.

HC Slavia 02 Arena, Libeň, ⓦ hc-slavia.cz. Nothing beats an ice hockey match, beer in one hand and sausage in the other, surrounded by a thousand bellowing Czechs.

Podoli Swimming Complex Podolska 74, ⓦ pspodoli .cz. Olympic-sized indoor and outdoor pools, waterslides, saunas and lawn for sunbathing. Take tram #3 or #17 to Kublov.

SHOPPING

Bontonland Václavské náměstí 1. Music and film emporium buried bunker-like under Wenceslas Square.

Palladium Náměstí Republiky 1. Central mall with major European brands, supermarkets and a food court.

Pařížská This street named "Paris" resembles the broad leafy boulevards of France's capital, and houses Cartier, Hermes, Louis Vuitton et al. There's more shopping on nearby Celetná and Karlova.

Shakespeare and Sons U lužického semináře 10. Little Quarter English-language bookshop.

DIRECTORY

Embassies and consulates Australia (honorary), Klimentská 10, Nové Město ☎ 221 729 260; Canada, Muchova 6, Hradčany ☎ 272 101 800; New Zealand, Václavské náměstí 11, Nové Město ☎ 234 784 777; Ireland, Tržiště 13, Malá Strana ☎ 257 530 061; UK, Thunovská 14, Malá Strana ☎ 257 402 111; US, Tržiště 15, Malá Strana ☎ 257 022 000.

Hospital Na Františku Hospital, Na Františku 8, Staré Město ☎ 222 801 211 (24hr number, English spoken).

Internet Most hostels and hotels offer wi-fi free (or for a small fee). Elsewhere in the city, try Click Internet Cafe, Malé Náměstí 13, which has internet terminals, direct connections and wi-fi. It also offers international calling and Skype booths (daily 10am–11pm; internet 2Kč/min). Globe (see p.195) has internet terminals (Mon–Thurs 9.30am–midnight, Fri–Sun 9.30am–1am; 2Kč/min).

Left luggage There are lockers or left-luggage offices at all train stations.

Pharmacies Palackého 5, Nové Město (24hr; ☎ 224 946 982); Belgická 37, Vinohrady (24hr; ☎ 222 513 396).

Post office Jindřišská 14, Nové Město (daily 2am–midnight, but service is slow outside office hours).

Bohemia

Prague is circled by the region of **Bohemia**, which covers the western two-thirds of the Czech Republic. To the west of Prague is **Karlovy Vary**, a picturesque spa town in the woody Sudeten hills, while southeast of there is **Plzeň**, brimming with industrial vigour and Pilsner Urquell beer. Travelling east towards Slovakia you'll reach **Kutná Hora**, with its sinister bone church. South of Prague, close to the Austrian border, is another beer-brewing giant, **České Budějovice**, home of Budweiser, and **Český Krumlov**, with its rose-coloured churches and frescoed palaces.

KUTNÁ HORA

A short bus ride from Prague, **KUTNÁ HORA** has a handful of tourist attractions and a sleepy, provincial atmosphere. Beneath the town are kilometres of exhausted silver and gold mines. From 1308, Bohemia's royal mint at Kutná Hora converted its silver into coins that were used all over Central Europe, but when the mines ran dry the town dwindled.

WHAT TO SEE AND DO

Kutná Hora's old town is so small it can be explored in a couple of hours. Most of the main attractions sit between main square Palackého náměstí and the Cathedral of sv Barbora ten minutes to the southeast.

Sedlec ossuary

The town's most popular attraction is the ghoulish **ossuary** (*kostnice*), which houses 40,000 human skeletons (daily: April–Sept 8am–6pm; Oct & March 9am–5pm; Nov–Feb 9am–4pm; 90Kč, students 60Kč; ⓦ ossuary.eu) arranged in intricate patterns by local oddball František Rint, a carpenter, in 1870. Take bus #1 or #4 from Kutná Hora to Sedlec.

Cathedral of sv Barbora

The **Cathedral of sv Barbora** (Tues–Sun: Oct–April 10am–4pm; May–Sept 9am–5.30pm; 60Kč, students 40Kč), a

7

Gothic masterpiece dedicated to the patron saint of miners, is approached by a street lined by Baroque saints and angels. To the right is the former Jesuit College, now the Kutná Hora Arts Centre.

Italian Court

From Palackého náměstí head down 28 října to the **Italian Court**, where coins were once minted. Exhibits re-create working conditions, and there's an exhaustive collection of Kutná Hora coins. Entrance is by guided tour only (daily: April–Sept 9am–6pm; March & Oct 10am–5pm; Nov–Feb 10am–4pm; 100Kč).

Mining Museum

In a medieval fort at the junction of Barborská and Ruthardská is the **Mining Museum** (Tues–Sun: April & Oct 9am–5pm; May, June & Sept 9am–6pm; July & Aug 10am–6pm; ⓦcms-kh.cz, 160Kč), where tourists can stroll the ancient mines in white coats and goggles.

ARRIVAL AND INFORMATION

By train Trains leave from Prague Main Station. Kutná Hora's station is out of town, near Sedlec (useful for visiting the ossuary). Take #1 or #4 bus into the town centre.
Destinations Prague (7 daily; 1hr).
By bus Buses leave from Prague's Florenc station.
Destinations Prague (2 daily; 1hr 30min).
Tourist office Palackého náměstí 377 (April–Sept daily 9am–6pm; Oct–March Mon–Fri 9am–5pm, Sat & Sun 10am–4pm; ☏327 512 378, ⓦkutnahora.cz). Can book private rooms and has internet access.

EATING AND DRINKING

Barborská Barborská 35. Miniature cocktail bar with a friendly vibe. Mon–Thurs 4pm–1am, Fri & Sat 4pm–3am.
Dačický Rakova 8. Meaty Czech comfort food and local dark beer in arched, dimly lit beerhall. Mains 119–499Kč. Daily 11am–11pm.
Kavárna na Kozím Plácku Dačického náměstí 10 ⓦkoziplacek.cz. Comfy interior filled with serious coffee lovers. Daily 10am–10pm.

ČESKÉ BUDĚJOVICE

ČESKÉ BUDĚJOVICE is a sweet kernel of medieval town inside a tough shell of industrial sprawl. It was built in 1265,

and its history has been connected with beer since the beginning, when citizens brewed lager for the Holy Roman Emperor. In the seventeenth century war and fire devastated the town, but it was lavishly rebuilt by the Habsburgs. Today its elegant arcades and winding backstreets are the perfect place to enjoy a Budvar beer – which is, after all, the reason most people come here.

WHAT TO SEE AND DO

The compact medieval town centre forms a grid around magnificent **Přemysla Otakara II Square**, one of Europe's largest marketplaces. Just off the square is Black Tower (Černá věž; July & Aug daily 10am–6pm; Sept–June Tues–Sat 10am–6pm; 30Kč, students 20Kč), which you can climb for good views.

Budvar brewery

The **Budvar brewery** is 2.5km up the road to Prague, on Karolíny Světlé (bus #2). You'll need to book ahead for a one-hour English tour (March–Dec daily 9am–5pm; Jan & Feb Tues–Sat 9am–5pm; 100Kč; ☏387 705 347, ⓦvisitbudvar.cz).

ARRIVAL AND DEPARTURE

By train The town's train station is a 10min walk from the old town: head west along Lannova třída. There are several daily direct trains from Prague; it's possible to visit as a day-trip, but if you want to visit the brewery consider staying overnight. There's left luggage storage.
Destinations Brno (4 daily; 4hr 27min); Český Krumlov (6 daily; 50min); Plzeň (every 2hr; 1hr 57min).
By bus The bus station is by the train station. It has left luggage facilities. Like trains, there are several direct buses from Prague.
Destinations Brno (3 daily; 4hr 15min); Český Krumlov (approx every 30min; 35–45min).

INFORMATION

Tourist office Náměstí Přemysla Otakara II. 1 (June–Sept Mon–Fri 8.30am–6pm, Sat 8.30am–5pm, Sun 10am–4pm; Oct–May Mon–Fri 9am–4pm, Sat 9am–1pm; ☏386 801 413, ⓦc-budejovice.cz).

ACCOMMODATION

Penzion Centrum Biskupská 3 ☏387 311 801, ⓦpenzioncentrum.cz. Renovated central townhouse with bright, comfortably furnished rooms with en suite facilities. The price includes breakfast. Double 1500Kč

U solné brány Radniční 11 ☎386 354 121, ⓦhotelusolnebrany.cz. Tucked into the old town walls, this small hotel has pleasant, relaxed service and tasteful, plain rooms with satellite TV. Breakfast included. Double 1990Kč

Ubytovna u nádraží Dvořákova 14 ☎972 544 648, ⓦubytovna.vors.cz. České Budějovice isn't the cheapest city to stay in, so this is a decent choice for affordable accommodation, located in a dour housing block a 10min walk from the centre. The rooms are private but have shared facilities. Double 760Kč

EATING AND DRINKING

Café au Chat Noir Náměstí Přemysla Otakara II. 21. Relaxed, Parisian-style café on the main square. Mon–Fri 9am–10pm, Sat 10am–10pm, Sun 2–10pm.

Hladový vokno Hroznová 34 ⓦhladovyvokno.cz. When your budget's tight and your belt's loose head to *Hladový vokno* (Hungry Window) for a hefty kebab or burger (34–75Kč). Mon–Thurs 10.30am–11pm, Fri 10.30am–12.30am, Sat 5pm–12.30am.

Indická Resaurace Chelčického 10 ⓦindickarestaurace .cz. Climb a poky private staircase to find this well-loved Indian restaurant, known for warm service and lovingly cooked food. Lunch specials 75–125Kč, mains 110–270Kč. Mon–Sat 11am–11pm.

Masné Krámy Krajinská 13 ⓦmasne-kramy.cz. Locals call it "the beer church" – an arched lofty Renaissance meat-market devoted to local beer. Don't miss the excellent unfiltered yeast beer (*kroužkovaný ležák*). Mains 128–349Kč. Mon–Sat 10.30am–11pm, Sun 10.30am–9pm.

Pavlač Hroznova 9. Popular place just off the main square with a wide-ranging menu including vegetarian options. Mains 115–255Kč. Daily 10am–11pm.

Singer Pub Česká 55. Noisy, affable local frequented by Erasmus students. Mon–Thurs 11am–midnight, Fri 11am–3am, Sat 6pm–3am, Sun 6pm–midnight.

ČESKÝ KRUMLOV

Tiny, red-roofed **ČESKÝ KRUMLOV** nestles between two bends in the Vltava River like a patch of wild strawberries. More often than not, tour buses unload crowds of visitors at the city gates at noon and pick them up in the afternoon, creating a five-hour stampede through the narrow streets. The only solution is to stay overnight; there's too much to see in a day anyway. The town's been a UNESCO World Heritage Site since 1992.

WHAT TO SEE AND DO

The twisting River Vltava divides the town into two: circular Staré Město on the right bank and the Latran quarter on the left.

Krumlov Chateau

Krumlov Chateau (April, May, Sept & Oct 9am–5pm; June–Aug 9am–6pm, closed Mon year round) rises above the Latrán quarter. You can stroll through the castle's grounds and main courtyards day or night, but to go inside you'll have to pay for one of the three guided tours (130–300Kč). Climb the tower for beautiful views and explore the chateau's geometrical gardens and two theatres, the exquisite Rococo Chateau Theatre, and the cunning Communist Revolving Theatre, which spins on a mechanical axis.

The Eggenberg Brewery

A world away from the gleaming, modern breweries at Plzeň and České Budějovice is the **Eggenberg**, which opened in 1630. Tours cost from 100Kč (daily at 11am; ☎380 711 225, ⓦeggenberg.cz). The restaurant serves good traditional food.

Egon Schiele Art Centrum

Just off the main square, on Široká, is the wonderful **Egon Schiele Art Centrum** (daily 10am–6pm; 120Kč; ☎380 704 011; ⓦschieleartcentrum.cz), devoted to the eponymous Austrian painter, who moved here in 1911 and caused outrage by painting nude teenagers and putting his feet on café tables. There are also temporary exhibitions of contemporary art and design.

ARRIVAL AND DEPARTURE

By train The train station is 1km south of the centre. If you come by train you will have to change at České Budějovice. Destinations České Budějovice (6 daily; 50min); Plzeň (every 2hr, change at České Budějovice; 2hr 57min); Prague (5 daily, change at České Budějovice; 3hr 40min).

By bus The bus station is a 5min walk northeast of the inner town.

Destinations České Budějovice (2 hourly; 50min); Linz (2 daily; change in České Budějovice; 2hr 35min); Prague (7 daily; Student Agency bus; 2hr 55min); or 3hr 30min (local bus, involves 1 change).

7

INFORMATION AND TOURS

Tourist office Náměstí Svornosti 2 (April, May, Sept & Oct Mon–Fri 9am–6pm, Sat & Sun 9am–6pm, closed noon–1pm; June–Aug Mon–Fri 9am–7pm, Sat & Sun 9am–7pm, closed 1–2pm; Nov–March Mon–Fri 9am–5pm, Sat & Sun 9am–5pm, closed noon–1pm; ☏ 380 704 622, ⓦ ckrumlov.info). Internet access (5Kč/5min).

Tours and rental Expedicion (Soukenická 33 ⓦ expedicion.cz) offer fishing, horseriding, bike riding, climbing, skijoring, canoeing and expeditions involving combinations of the above. Rafting/kayaking from 500Kč/person, fishing 790Kč/5hr, horseriding 300Kč/hr. Vltava Sport Service (Hradební 60 ⓦ ckvltava.cz) rents bikes, scooters, canoes and rafts. Bikes 320Kč/day, boat rental from 400Kč/4hr trip.

ACCOMMODATION

Hostel 99 Věžní 99 ☏ 775 276 253, ⓦ hostel99.cz. A kitchen, table tennis, movies, informative staff, a bar and (overpriced) restaurant. Come summer the dorms resemble high-school pyjama parties. The rafting pub crawl is famous. Dorm **300Kč**, double **800Kč**

Hostel Merlin Kájovská 59 ☏ 606 256 145, ⓦ hostelmerlin.com. Clean, cheap rooms overlooking the river with shared bathrooms and a kitchen. Dorm or double **250Kč** per person

★ **Krumlov House Hostel** Rooseveltova 68 ☏ 380 711 935, ⓦ krumlovhostel.com. A renovated Renaissance bakery as warm and cheering as fresh bread. There are private rooms and dorms, a common room, large kitchen and movies. Dorm **300Kč**, double **500Kč**

U Čerta a Káči Dlouhá 100 ☏ 777 615 903, ⓦ certakaca.cz. This central *pension* looks like a dolls' house, with low wooden beams, heart-print curtains and a minute kitchen. Double **950Kč**

Vodácký kemp Nové Spolí ☏ 777 640 946, ⓦ kempkrumlov.cz. Basic campsite in a picturesque spot by the river, 2km from the town, reachable by the #3 bus from the train or bus station. May–Sept. **55Kč** per person, plus **30Kč** per tent

EATING AND DRINKING

Antre Horní 2 ⓦ klubantre.cz. Dapper '30s café and music club in the municipal theatre. Breakfast, snacks and cakes, cocktails, wine, beer and live jazz. Daily 10am–midnight.

Cikánská Jizba Dlouh. 31. *Cikánská Jizba* (Gypsy Bar) is a standard Czech pub every night except Fridays, when talented local Roma musicians play. Daily noon–midnight.

Egon Schiele Café Široká 71 ⓦ egonschielecafe.com. A snug sitting room of a gallery café which locals say serves the best coffee in Krumlov. There's chess, board games,

> ### ČESKÝ KRUMLOV FESTIVALS
> **Five Petalled Rose Festival** Every June at the solstice. Medieval fair with jousting, fencing and theatre in the park.
> **International Music Festival** Every July–Aug. Large multi-genre music festival which usually attracts a few big names.

books and wi-fi. The cheesecake (*tvarohový dort*) is a sad dieter's happy dream. Daily 10am–7pm.

Na Louži Kájovská 66. The best Czech cooking in town. Come at lunchtime, as the chef only cooks once a day and popular dishes run out. Don't miss the fruit dumplings (*ovocné knedlíky*), pastry-and-fruit parcels slippery with melted butter and sprinkled with hard sweet cheese and brown sugar. Mains 85–185Kč. Daily 10am–11pm.

Pizzeria Nonna Gina Klášterní 52. Authentic, Italian family-owned restaurant; even the olive oil comes from the family's vineyard in Italy. Mains 90–160Kč. Daily 11am–11pm.

U dwau Maryí Parkán 104. Ye olde Bohemian food as it never was, but who's complaining? Gruel, rabbit, mead and millet on a riverside terrace. Mains 130–185Kč. Daily 11am–11pm.

PLZEŇ

Tough, industrial **PLZEŇ** (Pilsen) was built on beer and bombs. Founded in 1292, the city swelled in the nineteenth century when the Industrial Revolution brought an ironworks and an armaments factory, and diversified to cars and trams under Communism. Most tourists come to pay their respects to Plzeň's beloved son, Pilsner Urquell. The town's diverse architecture and unpretentious vigour are strong secondary attractions. The city was also named European Capital of Culture 2015, so some general sprucing up as well as an increase in public events can be expected.

WHAT TO SEE AND DO

The main square, náměstí Republiky, is dominated by the Gothic **Cathedral of sv Bartoloměj**, with the tallest spire in the country (103m). Opposite is the Italianate town hall, built in the Renaissance but sgraffitoed last century. Nearby **Velká synagogue** (April–Oct Sun–Fri, except Jewish holidays 10am–6pm; 60Kč adults, 40Kč students), the third largest in the world, was once the heart of the town's large Jewish community, decimated by the Holocaust, and now houses exhibitions.

Pilsner Urquell and Brewery Museums

The star attraction in Plzeň is 12° Plzeňský Prazdroj, better known as **Pilsner Urquell** (Original Pilsner; English guided tours daily 12.45pm, 2.15pm or 4.15pm; 190Kč). **Pivovarské Brewery Museum**, in the original brewery, provides some history and a film on brewing (daily: April–Nov 10am–6pm; Dec & Feb–March 10am–5pm; museum only 90Kč, combined ticket 250Kč; ☎377 062 888, ⓦprazdrojvisit.cz/en).

Plzeň's Historical Underground

While you are at the Brewery Museum don't miss **Plzeň's Historical Underground** (Plzeňské historické podzemí; daily: April–Nov 10am–6pm; Dec–March 10am–5pm; English tour daily at 1pm; 100Kč, students 70Kč; ☎377 235 574, ⓦplzenskepodzemi.cz), 500m of tunnels under the town. The tunnels were once part of an underground network of passages that rivalled the streets above.

ARRIVAL AND INFORMATION

By bus You can get to Plzeň from Prague in around 1hr by bus from Zličín with Student Agency. The bus terminal is on the west side of town, a 10min walk from the centre.
Destinations Karlovy Vary (6 daily; 1hr 30min–1hr 50min); Prague (hourly; 1hr–1hr 30min).
By train The main train station (Hlavní nádraží) is just east of the city centre, a 10min walk away.
Destinations České Budějovice (every 2hr; 1hr 56min); Prague (hourly; 1hr 30min).
Tourist office Náměstí Republiky 41 (daily: April–Sept 9am–7pm; Oct–March 9am–6pm; ☎378 035 330, ⓦpilsen.eu).

ACCOMMODATION

Euro Hostel Na Roudné 13 ☎377 259 926, ⓦeurohostel .cz. No-frills dorms and doubles a 10min walk from the centre. Opt out of breakfast, which is overpriced. Dorm from 390Kč, double from 900Kč
Pension City Sady 5 května 52 ☎377 326 069, ⓦpensioncityplzen.cz. Slightly tired rooms in a convenient location by the river. Breakfast included. Double 1450Kč

Pension Stará Plzeň Na Roudné 12 ☎377 259 901, ⓦpension-sp.cz. Rustic house and stables converted into a handsome old-fashioned pension. Double 800Kč
Pension V Solní Solní 8 ☎377 236 652, ⓦvolny.cz /pensolni. Cosy three-room *pension* off the main square. Book in advance. Double 1020Kč

EATING AND DRINKING

Anděl Bistro Bezručova 7 ⓦandelcafe.cz. Central restaurant with extraordinarily fresh and healthy lunch specials. 75–120Kč. Mon–Fri 9am–4.30pm.
CrossCafe Anglické nábřeží 1 ⓦcrosscafe.cz. Fantastic views at this American-style coffee shop at the top of Plzeň's only skyscraper. Mon–Fri 7.30am–9pm, Sat & Sun 11am–9pm.
Francis Náměstí Republiky 3. 50s rock-playing student bar-café with a wood-burning stove for winter, a courtyard for summer, sausages for the hungry and books for the antisocial. Mon–Fri 3–10pm.
Měšťanská Beseda Kavárna Kopeckého sady 13. Opulent Art Nouveau interior, beer on tap, old men grimacing over chessboards and delectable honey chocolates (*medový koule*) make this the place for a rainy afternoon. Mon–Fri 9am–11pm, Sat 11am–11pm, Sun 11am–9pm.
Na Parkánu Veleslavínova 4 ⓦnaparkanu.com. It's the Brewery Museum pub, but lusty portions, unfiltered beer and decent prices make it popular with locals. Cheap lunch menu 11am–2pm. Mains 75–250Kč. Mon–Wed 11am–11pm, Thurs 11am–midnight, Fri–Sat 11am–1am, Sun 11am–10pm.

KARLOVY VARY

You would be forgiven for thinking you took a wrong turn and left the Czech Republic when you got into the heart of **Karlovy Vary**. The freshly painted spa town, awash with fur caps and poodles in Dior handbags, feels decidedly un-Czech, largely due to its popularity with Russia's wealthy set and partly because tourists outnumber locals. Peter the Great, Goethe and Beethoven all visited the town, and the old-style pleasures of spa life – hiking in the forest, bathing in hot spring water, and eating sweet nut wafers (*oplatky*) to chase away the taste of the water – are still the best.

The town is orientated to Russian tourists, so finding English-speakers is harder than elsewhere (bring your phrasebook). Euros are readily accepted.

7

WHAT TO SEE AND DO

Walking into town with the Communist eyesore *Thermal Hotel* on your right, you'll pass a series of slender white colonnades built over the springs, which can be sampled for free. The grandest is **Mill Colonnade** (Mlýnská kolonáda), containing five springs. Further up Lázeňská street are **Market Colonnade** (Tržní kolonáda), a delicate wooden construct, and the Communist-era **Hot Spring Colonnade** (Vřídelní kolonáda), a spring so hot and powerful that spa guests breathe the vapours instead of drinking the water.

Hiking

The cool pine forests surrounding Karlovy Vary are perfect for **hiking**, and there are dozens of well-marked trails. One popular route goes from *Grand Hotel Pupp* to a viewing tower and hilltop restaurant *Diana*, 1.5km away. If you don't want to walk you can ride the **funicular** (daily: Feb–March & Nov–Dec 9am–5pm; April, May & Oct 9am–6pm; June–Sept 9am–7pm; 70Kč return).

Moser glassworks and museum

Luxury glass manufacturer **Moser** lies in the town's suburbs. You can tour the glassworks and glass museum (Kpt Jaroše 46; tours every 30min; daily 9am–2.30pm; 180Kč, students 100Kč; ☎353 416 132, ⊛moser-glass.com). Take bus #22 or #1 from Tržnice to the Moser stop.

Spa treatments

Sampling the waters is free, but you'll need to buy a drinking cup from a kiosk, or bring a plastic bottle. To avoid the bitter taste, wallow in the waters instead; the cheapest option is the *Thermal Hotel*'s springwater hilltop pool (daily 10am–8pm, last entrance 7pm;

180Kč for 180min, 140Kč with ISIC). Follow the signs for "Bazén" (pool). If you'd prefer to be coated in mud or steamed in brine try the modern spa centre at *Carlsburg Plaza* hotel (Mariánskolázeňská 23; daily 8am–8pm; ⊛carlsbad-plaza.com).

ARRIVAL AND INFORMATION

By train Trains from Prague arrive at Horní station, to the north of town. Trains from Mariánské Lázně arrive at Dolní station, close to the main bus station and town centre.

Destinations Plzeň (3 daily; 3hr, with a change at Mariánské Lázně; 1 daily; 3hr 14 min, direct); Prague (5 daily; 3hr 20min).

By bus Buses run to the spa from both train stations. If you're bussing from Prague, alight one stop early at Tržnice, right in the centre. The Student Agency bus from Prague Florenc is your best option (9 daily; ☎800 100 300, ⊛studentagencybus.com).

Destinations Plzeň (hourly; 1hr 30min–1hr 50min); Prague (hourly; 2hr 15min).

Tourist office T.G. Masaryka 53 (Mon–Fri 8am–6pm, Sat & Sun 10am–1pm & 1.30–5pm; ☎355 321 171, ⊛karlovyvary.cz). There's also tourist information at the Hot Spring Colonade (see above).

ACCOMMODATION

Avoid the hotels that cluster around the spas: they're designed and priced for Russian oligarchs. Guesthouses and B&Bs are located around the bus and train stations. Private rooms are good value and can be booked through the tourist office. Karlovy Vary is generally not budget orientated – be prepared to stay outside the city for something affordable.

Březový Háj Campsite ☎353 222 665, ⊛brezovy-haj .cz. Located on a riverbank, *Březový*, 3km from the centre, has tennis courts, a pool and bungalows. Catch the Březova bus from Tržiště bus station. April–Sept. Bed in bungalow 200Kč

Chebský Dvůr/Egerlander Hof Tržiště 39 ☎353 229 332, ⊛egerlanderhof.eu. Clean, basic rooms above a pub in the heart of the spa district. Double 1100Kč

Kavalerie T.G. Masaryka 43 ☎353 229 613, ⊛kavalerie .cz. On the main street connecting the bus station and the centre, *Kavalerie* is a B&B over a café with homely rooms.

INTERNATIONAL FILM FESTIVAL

The **Karlovy Vary Film Festival** (⊛kviff.com) comes to town every July, bringing a smattering of A-listers and a carnival atmosphere. Anyone can buy tickets (65Kč) or day passes (200Kč/day) to the films, which range from Hollywood blockbusters to low-budget European indies. The town gets crowded so book accommodation and travel in advance.

There are two tiers: economy and standard (the difference is mostly in size), plus apartments. Price refers to two people with breakfast included. Economy 1170Kč, standard 1320Kč

Maltézský Kříž Stará Louka 50 ☎ 353 169 011, ⓦ maltezskykriz.cz. If you have a little more to spend, this central boutique hotel offers better quality at a lower price than any other central hotel. It's becoming popular so book in advance. Includes breakfast. Double 2800Kč

EATING AND DRINKING

To avoid the overpriced restaurants and pubs, picnicking is the cheapest eating option; there are supermarkets and bakeries on T.G. Masaryka.

Foopaa Jaltská 7 ⓦ foopaa.cz. The biggest cocktail menu In town at this central bar, which moonlights as a club on Fri and Sat nights. Closed Sun.

Kavárna Čas T.G. Masaryka 3. Quiet little cinema coffee shop filled with the scent of popcorn and sweets, free of tour groups and serving excellent Italian espresso. Daily 10am–8pm.

KusKus Bělehradská 8 ⓦ kus-kus.cz. Charming café serving organic, vegetarian and vegan sandwiches, salads, cakes and snacks, eat-in or takeaway. Mon–Fri 7.30am–3pm.

Rad's Baguettes Zeyerova 2 ⓦ radsbaguettes.cz. The only inexpensive sandwich shop in the centre, with sandwiches, panini and baguettes. Up to 42Kč. Mon–Fri 7am–6pm, Sat 8am–noon.

Tandoor I.P. Pavlova 25 ⓦ tandoor-kv.cz. It's hard to find, stashed down a private driveway, but the pleasant food, friendly service and decent prices are worth the effort. Mon–Sat noon–9pm, Sun noon–6pm.

U Švejka Stará Louka 10. The least overpriced of the central restaurants. High prices are balanced by large portions. Daily 11am–11pm.

Moravia

Eastern **Moravia** (Morava) moves at a slower pace than Bohemia, but is warmer and more relaxed. It shares borders with Poland to the north, and Slovakia and Austria to the south. In the southeast of Moravia is bustling, industrial **Brno**, with red-brick houses and wide boulevards, and travelling north you'll reach **Olomouc**, an ancient city bursting with youthful energy.

BRNO

BRNO evolved into today's handsome, red-brick city during the nineteenth century, when it was a major textile producer and known as "rakouský Manchestr" (Austrian Manchester). The capital of Moravia, Brno's vital energy has produced eleven universities, a powerful economy and a number of famous Czechs, including inventor of genetics Gregor Mendel, composer Leoš Janáček and novelist Milan Kundera.

WHAT TO SEE AND DO

Triangular **Svobody Square** (náměstí Svobody) sits funnel-like on the high street, Masarykova. To the right is Zelný trh, the old medieval Cabbage Market, still bustling with vegetable traders hawking onions and daffodils. **Špilberk Castle**, which houses historical exhibitions, dominates the skyline to the west, in a standoff with the hilltop **Cathedral of St Peter and St Paul** to the south.

Capuchin crypt
Below the Cabbage Market is the Capuchin monastery, with its popular **crypt** (May–Sept Mon–Sat 9am–noon & 1–4.30pm, Sun 1–4.30pm; Feb–April & Oct–Nov closed Mon; mid-Dec to mid-Feb Sat 9am–noon & 1–4.30pm), which houses a charming collection of mummified monks.

7

BURČÁK

September ushers in **vinobraní**, boisterous festivals marking the wine harvest. Revellers dance, drink and feast in an event that dates back to the Middle Ages, and the star of the show is **burčák**, wine fresh from the press. Sweet and bubbly, it's only part fermented so it tastes as innocent as peach juice, but it's up to 8 percent alcohol. It's only available from the end of August to the end of November at festivals, wine bars and markets. There are festivals all over the country, though the best are in wine country, Moravia. For more information, check ⓦ wineofczechrepublic.cz.

7

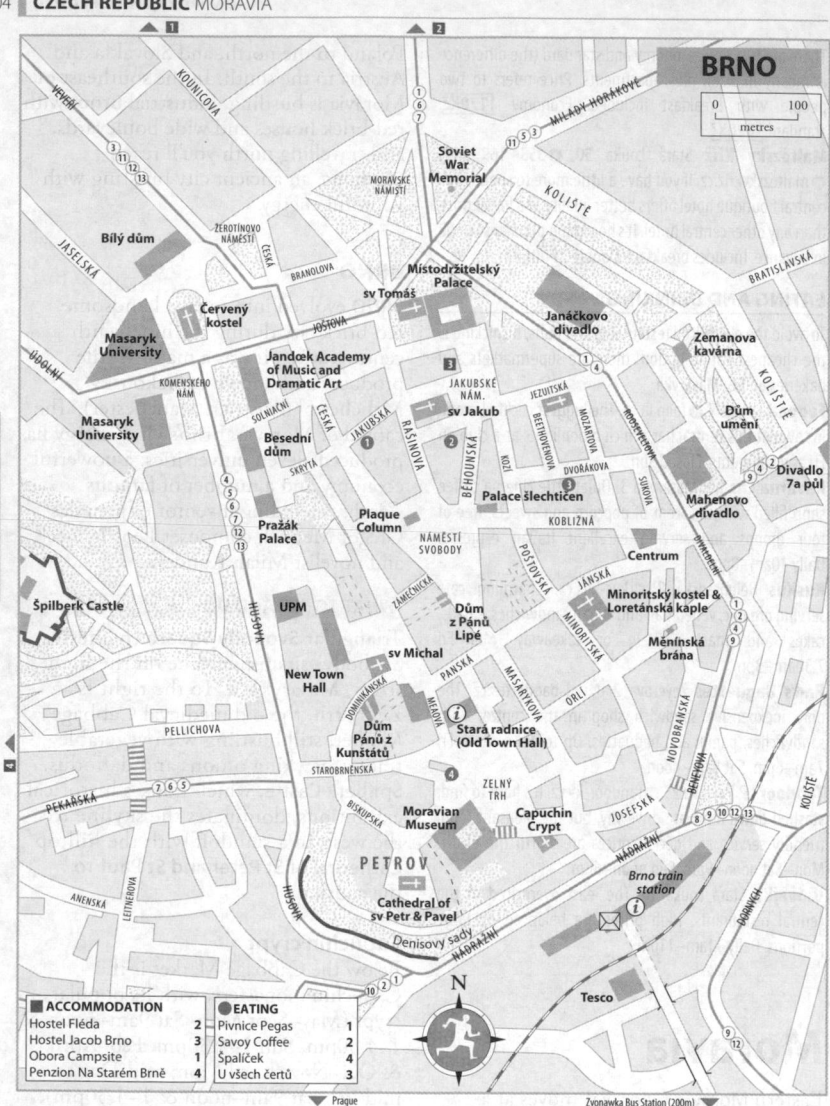

BRNO

0 — 100 metres

Soviet War Memorial

Bílý dům

Červený kostel

sv Tomáš

Místodržitelský Palace

Janáčkovo divadlo

Zemanova kavárna

Masaryk University

Jandœk Academy of Music and Dramatic Art

Masaryk University

Besední dům

sv Jakub

JAKUBSKÉ NÁM.

Dům umění

Divadlo 7a půl

Špilberk Castle

Pražák Palace

Plaque Column

NÁMĚSTÍ SVOBODY

Palace šlechtičen

Mahenovo divadlo

Centrum

Minoritský kostel & Loretánská kaple

UPM

Dům z Pánů Lipé

Měnínská brána

sv Michal

New Town Hall

Dům Pánů z Kunštátů

Stará radnice (Old Town Hall)

ZELNÝ TRH

Moravian Museum

Capuchin Crypt

PETROV

Brno train station

Cathedral of sv Petr & Pavel

Denisovy sady

Tesco

N

ACCOMMODATION

Hostel Fléda	2
Hostel Jacob Brno	3
Obora Campsite	1
Penzion Na Starém Brně	4

EATING

Pivnice Pegas	1
Savoy Coffee	2
Špaliček	4
U všech čertů	3

Prague

Zvonawka Bus Station (200m)

The Old Town Hall

On Stará Radnice is the **Old Town Hall**, packed with strange artefacts clothed in fantastical legends. The tower (April–Sept daily 9.30am–5.30pm; 20Kč) offers panoramic views of Brno.

Brno Underground

It's possible to explore the renovated cellars beneath the Cabbage Market, including a labyrinth with an ossuary

filled with 50,000 skeletons (Tues–Sun 9am–6pm; 160Kč).

ARRIVAL AND INFORMATION

By plane Brno's Tuřany airport (brno-airport.cz) is 8km from the centre. From the airport, take bus #76 to the main bus station. Both Ryanair and Wizz Air fly to Brno.

By train Brno's main train station is on the edge of the city centre; it has lockers and a 24hr left-luggage office.

Destinations Bratislava (direct trains every 2hr; 1hr 30min); České Budějovice (every 2hr; 4hr 30min); Olomouc (hourly; 1hr 33min–2hr 15min).
By bus The bus station sits beside the train station.
Destinations Olomouc (2–3 hourly; 1hr–1hr 50min); Prague (3 hourly; 2hr 40min).
Tourist office Old Town Hall at Radnická 8 (Mon–Fri 8am–6pm, Sat 9am–5pm, Sun 9am–3pm; ☎542 427 150, ⓦticbrno.cz).

ACCOMMODATION

Brno hosts trade fairs from August to October, February and April, as well as a Moto GP in August, so book in advance during those months, and expect higher prices.
Hostel Fléda Štefánikova 24 ☎731 651 005, ⓦhostelfleda.com. Graffiti-daubed 48-bed hostel above Brno's coolest nightclub, *Club Fléda*, which feels like a high school after a student revolution. Catch tram #1 or #6 to Hrnčířská. Doubles have shared baths. Dorm <u>300Kč</u>, double <u>800Kč</u>
Hostel Jacob Brno Jakubské náměstí 7 ☎542 210 466, ⓦhosteljacob.cz. Clean and bright hostel with private rooms. The 37-bed *Jacob* is centrally located and has a well-equipped kitchen. Breakfast included. Dorm <u>500Kč</u>, double <u>1340Kč</u>
Obora Campsite Rakovecká 72 ☎546 223 334, ⓦautocampobora.cz. Lake-side campsite 15min from the train station (tram #1 to the zoo, then bus #103). May–Sept. Bungalow <u>230Kč</u> per person, camping <u>80Kč</u> per person plus pitch
Penzion Na Starém Brně Mendlovo náměstí 1a ☎543 247 872, ⓦpension-brno.com. Genteel B&B in a former monastery. Go through Vankovka shopping centre from the train and bus stations and take tram #1 to Mendlovo náměstí. Double <u>1200Kč</u>

EATING AND DRINKING

As Brno gets classier, so do its restaurants and prices. It's still a university town though, so join the queues at one of the food stands on either Kobližná or Benešova for a cheap and filling *gyro* or pizza.
Pivnice Pegas Jakubská 4. Gregarious microbrewery rambling through numerous oak-panelled rooms. Dumplings with everything, wheat beer and a table shortage. Mains 90–365Kč. Mon–Sat 9am–midnight, Sun 11am–11pm.
Savoy Coffee Jakubské náměstí 1 ⓦsavoy-brno.cz. Regal coffeehouse returned to its functionalist glory after decades as a Communist button shop. Mon–Fri 9am–midnight, Sat & Sun 11am–midnight.
Špalíček Zelný trh 12. Meat-and-potatoes Moravian cuisine, Starobrno beer, outdoor seating above the vegetable market and a 149Kč 3-course lunch menu. Mains 89–300Kč. Daily 11am–11pm.

U všech čertů Dvořákova 6/8 ⓦucertu.cz. Popular pub with a good beer list and tasty food to go with it. Lunch specials 98Kč, mains 138–210Kč. Daily 11am–11pm.

OLOMOUC

"They say we are going to Olomutz," wrote Tolstoy, "and Olomutz is a very decent town." It's strange that few people have discovered how right he was. In the Middle Ages **Oloumouc** was the capital of the Great Moravian Empire, and its wealth crystallized into magnificent palaces and churches before trickling away to Brno carrying a wave of industrial sprawl. The unspoilt city centre is home to 25,000 students, who ensure a rich supply of lively bars, cafés and clubs.

7

WHAT TO SEE AND DO

The old town clusters around two adjacent squares, **Horní** (upper) and **Dolní** (lower). The town hall on Horní has an astronomical clock, an object of exuberant Communist kitsch covered with gesticulating blonde peasants. Nearby is the polygonal Holy Trinity Column, protected by UNESCO, the largest plague column in the country.

Cathedral of sv Václav and the Archdiocesan Museum

Dwarfing tiny Václavské Square is the **Cathedral of sv Václav**, originally a Romanesque basilica, which contains a **crypt** (May–Oct Mon–Wed 10am–5pm, Thurs 9am–4pm, Fri & Sat 9am–5pm, Sun 11am–5pm) packed with reliquaries. Next door is the **Archdiocesan Museum** (Tues–Sun 10am–6pm; 50Kč), showcasing more than a thousand years of local history and a mind-blowing collection of church bling. The highlight is a gold-plated carriage covered with romping cherubs.

Olomouc Museum of Art

With interesting permanent exhibitions and great temporary ones, the **Olomouc Museum of Art** on Denisova (Tues–Sun 10am–6pm; 50Kč; ⓦolmuart.cz) puts on an enjoyable stroll through twentieth-century Czech art.

7

FESTIVAL FRENZY

With its long-held reputation as a centre of culture and the arts, Olomouc is a natural home for festivals. April brings **Academia Film** (Ⓦafo.cz), screening international science documentaries, and flower festival **Flora Olomouc** (Ⓦflora-ol.cz). In May is the **Dvořák Festival** (Ⓦmfo.cz); actually a celebration of all the major Czech composers. The **Olomouc City Festival** (Ⓦolomouc.eu) is held at the beginning of June, and the end of the month sees **Beerfest** (Ⓦbeerfest.cz), an enjoyable combination of beer, rock music and gastronomy. The **Summer of Culture in Olomouc** (Ⓦolomouc.eu) runs through July and August offering theatre, music and exhibitions throughout the city. In September, there's the **Organ Music Festival** and **Fall Festival of Sacred Music**.

ARRIVAL AND INFORMATION

By train The train station is 1.5km east of the centre; catch tram #2, #4 or #6 to get into town.
Destinations Brno (5 daily; 1hr 30min–2hr 20min); Prague (hourly; approx 2hr 10min).
By bus The bus station is 3km east of the city centre; catch tram #4.
Destinations Brno (hourly; approx 1hr 30min).
Tourist office Town Hall, Horní náměsti (daily 9am–7pm; ☎585 513 385, Ⓦtourism.olomouc.eu).

ACCOMMODATION

Arigone Univerzitní 20 ☎585 232 351, Ⓦarigone.cz. Excellent boutique hotel in a delightful old house in the heart of the historical centre. Double 2290Kč
Pension Moravia Dvořákova 37 ☎603 784 188, Ⓦpension-moravia.com. Large suburban house converted into a welcoming B&B, 10min from the centre. Double 900Kč
Pension U Jakuba 8. května 9 ☎585 209 995, Ⓦpensionujakuba.cz. Affordable central hotel so hygienic it must be wrapped in plastic. Double 1190Kč, 4-bed apartment 2460Kč
★ **Poets' Corner Hostel** Sokolská 1 ☎777 570 730, Ⓦhostelolomouc.com. Friendly, laidback central hostel in two brightly painted '30s flats, run by lifelong travellers. 8-bed dorms, double and triple rooms, kitchen and self-catering facilities, bikes for rent, laundry services, common room and informative staff. Dorm 300Kč, double 900Kč, triple 1200Kč

EATING AND DRINKING

CAFÉS AND RESTAURANTS

Café 87 Denisova 47. Fresh sandwiches, good coffee, ideal street-gazing and famous chocolate pie. Mon–Fri 7.30am–9pm, Sat & Sun 8am–9pm.
Café Dolce Vita Tř. 1. máje 38. Smart non-smoking café with well-priced food, delicious coffee and

friendly service. Mon–Fri 8am–8pm, Sat 9am–8pm, Sun 2–8pm.
Green Bar Ztracená 3 Ⓦgreenbar.cz. Self-serve vegetarian restaurant with fresh hot and cold dishes, salads and desserts. Pay by weight, 21Kč per 100g. Mon–Fri 10am–5pm.
Nepálská restaurace Mlýnská 4 Ⓦnepalska.cz. Nepalese restaurant with an excellent 110Kč lunch special and mains ranging 110–180Kč. Shares its space with a decent Irish pub. Mon–Thurs 11am–1am, Fri–Sat 11am–2am, Sun 11am–8pm.
★ **Moritz** Nešverova 2 Ⓦhostinec-moritz.cz. The finest microbrewery in Olomouc, serving light, delicate lager and hearty Moravian cuisine. There's a beer garden in the summer with live music. Try the open sandwiches with bitter *tvarůžky* cheese marinated in beer, or the roast duck with cabbage and dumplings. Mains 125–299Kč. Sun–Thurs 11am–11pm, Fri & Sat 11am–midnight.

BARS AND CLUBS

15Minut Komenského 31. A few steps away from university dorms and filled with wildly enthusiastic students every weekend. Their riotous two-day Erasmus Party in September is infamous. Daily 6pm–4am.
Koktejly & sny Uhelná 8 Ⓦkoktejlyasny.cz. "Cocktail and Dreams" is a throwback to the '50s, and if you can overlook the kitsch, you'll appreciate their excellent cocktails. Mon–Wed 8am–midnight, Thurs–Fri 8am–1am, Sat 10.30am–1am, Sun 10.30am–9pm.
The Black Stuff Irish Pub 1. máje 19 Ⓦblackstuff.cz. Toy-town railway tunnel meets hobbit drinking hole, popular with students. Seven beers on tap. Mon–Thurs 4pm–2am, Fri 4pm–3am, Sat 5pm–3am, Sun 5–11pm.
Vertigo Klub Univerzitní 6 Ⓦklubvertigo.cz. Named after Hitchcock's dreamy noir masterpiece, this atmospheric underground student bar is filled with loquacious philosophy students and a smell that isn't quite tobacco. Daily 6pm–2am.

Denmark

HIGHLIGHTS

❶ Copenhagen by bike Explore one of the world's best cycle networks. **See p.213**

❷ Kødbyen Dance all night in the capital's hipster hotbed. **See p.222**

❸ Hans Christian Andersens Hus The legendary author's fairytale museum. **See p.227**

❹ Århus Get in touch with your inner cool in this jazz Mecca. **See p.230**

❺ Smørrebrød Aalborg's sleek harbour-front *Utzon Restaurant* is famous for its take on this Danish classic. **See p.235**

❻ Skagen Breathtaking, heather-topped, sand-dune beaches. **See p.235**

HIGHLIGHTS ARE MARKED ON THE MAP ON P.209

ROUGH COSTS

Daily budget Basic €50, occasional treat €80

Drink Carlsberg (pint) €5

Food *Pølser* (Danish hot dog) €3.50

Hostel/budget hotel €23.50/€65

Travel Train: Copenhagen–Århus, €50; bus: €40

FACT FILE

Population 5.6 million

Language Danish

Currency Danish krone (kr)

Capital Copenhagen

International phone code ☎45

Time zone GMT +1hr

Introduction

Denmark has achieved nothing short of the unthinkable over the past decade: from a little-known, little-understood country wedged between mainland Europe and the rest of Scandinavia to an international cultural powerhouse with Michelin-starred restaurants, multiple hit TV shows and fashion stars. But this international renown doesn't make the country any less thrilling to navigate on the ground and on a budget. Food-wise, you'd be hard pressed to find better butter, bacon and beer anywhere around, with some mean cheeses and pastries to boot. But don't expect this health-conscious people to sit around feasting all day: a bunch will have jogged past your table before you can say smørrebrød, and cycling is ubiquitous. With agriculture its primary industry, technological innovation and a focus on green energy is a big part of the economy of daily life. Culturally, too, it hits all the right marks. Expect impeccable design and great musical offerings (especially jazz) at every turn. What's more, an ultra-efficient transport infrastructure makes Denmark one of Europe's most enjoyable countries to explore.

8

The nation has preserved a distinct national identity, exemplified by the universally cherished royal family and the reluctance to fully integrate with the EU (the Danish rejection of the euro was more about sovereignty than economics). There's also a sense of a small country that has long punched above its weight: it once controlled much of northern Europe and still maintains close ties with Greenland, its former colony.

Geographically, three main landmasses make up the country – the islands of Zealand and Funen and the peninsula of Jutland, which extends northwards from Germany. Most visitors make for **Zealand** (Sjælland), and, more specifically, **Copenhagen**, an exciting focal point with a beautiful old centre, a good array of museums and a boisterous nightlife. **Funen** (Fyn) has only one real urban draw, **Odense**, once home to Hans Christian Andersen; otherwise, it's renowned for cute villages and sandy beaches. **Jutland** (Jylland) has, as well as scenery alternating between lonely beaches, gentle hills and heathland, two of the liveliest Danish cities in **Århus** and **Aalborg**.

CHRONOLOGY

400 BC "Tollund Man" lives; his preserved body is discovered in a bog in 1950, and provides evidence of habitation during the Iron Age.

500 AD First mention of the "Dani" tribe is made by foreign sources.

695 First Christian mission to Denmark.

825 First Danish coinage introduced.

1397 The Union of Kalmar unites Denmark, Sweden and Norway under a single Danish monarch.

1536 Reformation leads to the establishment of the Danish Lutheran Church.

1629 Sweden heavily defeats Charles IV's Denmark in the Thirty Years' War, resulting in Danish territorial losses.

1814 Denmark cedes Norway to Sweden.

1836 Hans Christian Andersen writes "The Little Mermaid".

1849 Constitutional monarchy established.

1864 Defeat by Prussia results in the loss of much territory.

1914 Neutrality is adopted during World War I.

1918 The vote is granted to all Danes.

1934 Children's playtime is transformed by the invention of Lego by Ole Kirk Christiansen.

1940 Nazi invasion meets minimal resistance.

1945 Denmark is liberated by Allied forces.

1979 Greenland is given greater autonomy by the Danish.

1989 First European country to legalize same-sex marriages.

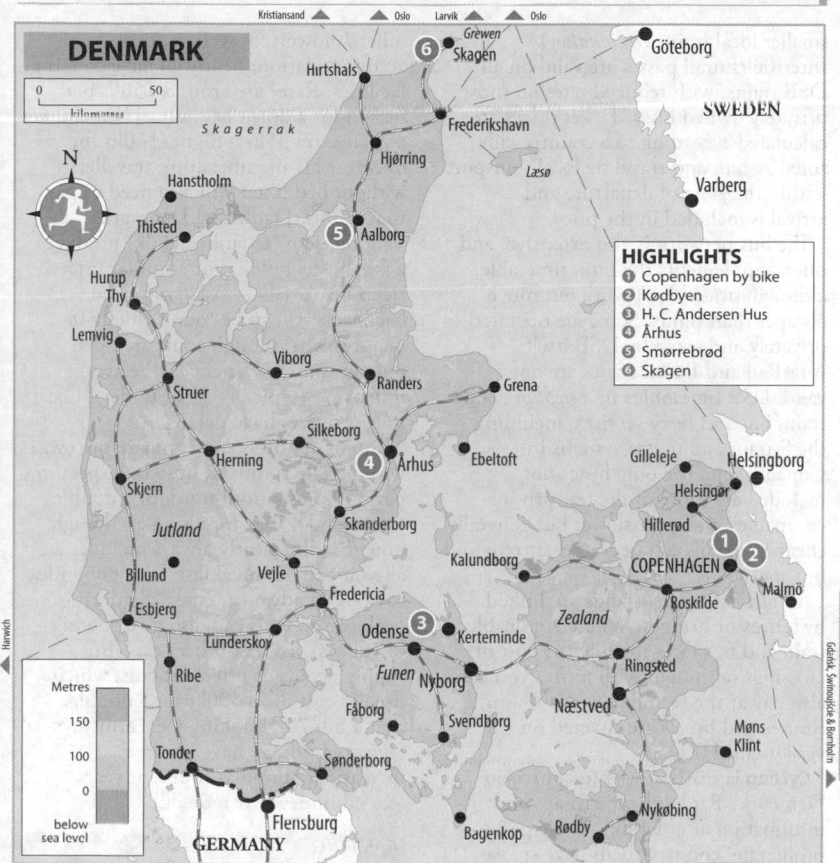

DENMARK

HIGHLIGHTS
1. Copenhagen by bike
2. Kødbyen
3. H. C. Andersen Hus
4. Århus
5. Smørrebrød
6. Skagen

1991 Danish police fire on protestors demonstrating against the country's acceptance of the Maastricht Treaty.
1992 Denmark wins European Football Championships.
2004 Crown Prince Frederick marries Tasmanian Mary Donaldson in a lavish ceremony.
2006 Cartoon depictions of the Prophet Mohammed in Danish newspapers spark mass protests in the Muslim world.
2009 UN climate change summit takes place in Denmark; the hoped-for global treaty does not materialize.
2011 Denmark criticized for reimposing border controls to stop flow of illegal immigration.

ARRIVAL AND DEPARTURE

Visitors usually arrive in Copenhagen, either flying in to gleaming **Kastrup Airport** or pulling in to the city's **Central Station**, connected with the European rail network via Germany and, across the spectacular Øresund bridge, to Sweden. Most international buses also arrive at Central Station. In addition, the **regional airports** at Aalborg, Århus and Billund handle a growing number of budget flights, mostly operated by Ryanair. There are regular **ferry services** to and from the UK (via Esbjerg), to Sweden/Norway (via Frederikshavn or Hirtshals) and to the Faroe Islands/Iceland (via Hirtshals).

GETTING AROUND

Denmark has a swift, easy-to-use public transport system. Danish State Railways (Danske Statsbaner or DSB; ⓦdsb.dk) runs an exhaustive and reliable **rail** network supplemented by a few privately owned rail lines. Services range from the large inter-city expresses (*lyntog*) to smaller local trains (*regionaltog*). InterRail/Eurail passes are valid on all DSB trains, with reduced rates on most privately owned lines. Ticket prices are calculated according to a countrywide zonal system and travel by local transport within the zone of departure and arrival is included in the price.

The **bus** network is also extensive, and often supplements the train timetable, although prices don't work out much cheaper than trains. Some are operated privately and some by DSB itself; InterRail and Eurail passes are not valid. DSB **timetables** or *køreplan* detail train, bus and ferry services, including the S-train and metro systems in Copenhagen. The only buses not included are those of the few private companies: these are slower but generally cheaper; details can be found at train and bus stations.

All of Denmark's islands are linked by **ferries** or bridges. Where applicable, train and bus fares include the cost of crossings (although with ferries you can also pay at the terminal and walk on). Routes and prices are covered on the very useful HI map.

Cycling is the best way to appreciate Denmark's flat landscape (maps and information at ⓦdcf.dk). Cycle paths proliferate, country roads have sparse traffic and all large towns have cycle tracks. Bikes can be rented at hostels, tourist offices and some train stations, as well as from bike rental shops (80–100kr/day, 350–400kr/week; 200–500kr deposit). All trains and most long-distance buses accept bikes, but you'll have to pay according to the zonal system used to calculate passenger tickets (12–60kr); 48kr to take your bike from Copenhagen to Århus by train, or 80kr by bus. Reservations (30kr extra) are recommended (and obligatory on many trains May–Aug).

ACCOMMODATION

Accommodation is a major expense, although there is a wide network of good-quality **hostels**. Most have a choice of private rooms, often with en-suite toilets/showers, as well as dorm accommodation; nearly all have cooking facilities. Rates are around 150kr per person for a dorm bed; non-HI members pay an extra 35kr a night (160kr for one-year HI membership); travellers without bed linen will also need to pay to rent this. Danhostel Danmarks Vandrerhjem (ⓦdanhostel.dk) produces a free hostel guide. For a similar price, **sleep-ins** (smaller hostels aimed at backpackers) can be found chiefly in major towns, though some are open only in summer. There can be an age restriction (typically 35 or under). Local tourist offices have details.

Rooms at **hotels** can compare pricewise with private rooms in hostels. Expect to pay 550kr as a minimum for a double room (and 450kr for a single), though note that this nearly always includes an all-you-can-eat breakfast. It's a good idea to book in advance, especially during peak season (this can also give you big discounts). Tourist offices can also supply details of **private rooms**, which usually cost 300–400kr for a double, plus a 50–70k booking fee. **Farmstays** (*Bondegårdsferie*) have become increasingly popular in recent years (see ⓦbondegaardsferie.dk).

CAMPING

If you plan to **camp**, you'll need an international camping carnet, or a Camping Key Scandinavia (110kr), which is available at official campsites. A Transit Card (35kr) can be used for a single overnight stay. Most campsites are open from April to September, while a few stay open all year. There's a rigid **grading system**: one-star sites have toilets and showers; two-stars also have basic cooking facilities and a food shop within 2km; three-stars include a laundry and a TV room; four-stars also have a shop, while five-stars include a cafeteria. Prices are 75–100kr per person. Many campsites also have **cabins** to rent, usually with cooking facilities, for 2500kr–6000kr per week for a six-berth place, although they are often fully booked in summer months in advance (though occasionally you'll be able to rent a cabin for just a few days for around 300kr per night). Tourist offices offer a free leaflet listing all sites. **Camping rough** without permission is illegal, and an on-the-spot fine may be imposed. Good English-language information is available at ⊛dk-camp.dk.

FOOD AND DRINK

Traditional **Danish food** is often characterized by rather stodgy meat or fish and veg combos, although the quality of ingredients is invariably excellent, especially these days with many chefs espousing the farm-to-plate or organic cooking ethos. Specialities worth seeking out include *stegt flæsk med persille sovs* (thinly sliced fried pork with boiled potatoes and parsley sauce) and the classic *røget sild* (smoked herring). **Breakfast** (*morgenmad*) is a treat, with almost all hotels and hostels offering a spread of cereals, freshly made bread, cheese, ham, fruit juice, milk, coffee and tea, for around 60kr (if not included in room prices). **Brunch**, served in most cafés from 11am until mid-afternoon, is a popular, filling option for late starters and costs 80–100kr. The traditional **lunch** (*frokost*) is *smørrebrød* – slices of rye bread heaped with meat, fish or cheese, and assorted trimmings – sold for 40–80kr a piece and very filling. An excellent-value set lunch can usually be found at restaurants and *bodegas* (bars selling no-frills food). *Tilbud* is the "special", *dagens ret* the "dish of the day"; expect to pay around 80kr for one of these, or 120–180kr for a three-course set lunch. The latest craze is smushi, the Danish take on sushi (about 50kr per piece).

For daytime **snacks**, there are hot-dog stands (*pølsevogn*) on all main streets and at train stations, serving hot dogs (*pølser*), toasted ham-and-cheese sandwiches (*parisertoast*) and chips (*pommes frites*) for around 25kr. Bakeries and cafés sell Danish pastries (*wienerbrød*), tastier and much less sweet than the imitations sold abroad, and *rundstykker* (literally "round pieces"), a type of crispy bread roll. Restaurants are pretty expensive for dinner (reckon on 130–200kr), but you can usually find a Middle Eastern or Thai place offering **buffets** for around 80–100kr. Kebab shops are also very common and often serve pizza slices from around 30kr. If you plan on **self-catering**, head for the good-value Netto or Fakta supermarkets.

DRINK

The most sociable places to **drink** are pubs (variously known as a *værtshus*, *bar* or *bodega*) and cafés, where the emphasis is on **beer**. The cheapest is bottled lager – the so-called gold beer (Guldøl or Elefantøl; 25–35kr/bottle) is the strongest. Draught lager (Fadøl) is more expensive and a touch weaker, but tastes fresher. The most common brands are Carlsberg and Tuborg, although microbreweries are now common with many pubs making their own beer on the premises. Most international **wines** (from 40kr) and **spirits** (20–40kr) are widely available. There are many varieties of **schnapps**, including the potent Aalborg-made Aquavit.

CULTURE AND ETIQUETTE

Denmark is a liberal and tolerant country. The defining aspect of culture here, in fact, is *hygge*: spending quality time with friends or loved ones over good food and a drink. Remember that the Danish language doesn't have a specific word for "please", so don't be upset if Danes leave it out when talking to you in English (which most Danes speak amazingly well). When wandering about, be sure you don't stray into the cycle lanes alongside most roads, and be aware that

8

DENMARK ONLINE

⊛ **visitdenmark.com** The excellent website of the Danish Tourist Board.
⊛ **cphpost.dk** News and reviews from the *Copenhagen Post*, the capital's English-language weekly.
⊛ **aok.dk** Listings for most of Zealand; some pages in English.
⊛ **rejseplanen.dk** Public transport journey planner (with English-language option).

locals will almost always wait for the green "walk" light at pedestrian crossings – even when there isn't a car in sight.

Tipping is not expected, as service charges are included in hotel, restaurant and bar bills; however, if you think you've had particularly good service it's not unheard of to leave a few kroner. **Smoking** is banned in most restaurants, cafés and bars.

SPORTS AND OUTDOOR ACTIVITIES

Football (soccer) is by far the most popular **sport** in Denmark. The biggest teams are FC Copenhagen and Brøndby (both from the capital) who play in the twelve-team Superliga (⒲dbu.dk). As for **outdoor activities**, there's a series of cycle routes and hiking paths (⒲dvl.dk). Watersports are also popular. Over 200 beaches having Blue Flag status and the extensive fjords of Zealand and Jutland provide further variety for the recreationally minded; ask at tourist offices where the best swimming is. Klitmøller on Jutland is the surfing capital.

COMMUNICATIONS

Post offices are open Monday to Friday from 9.30/10am to 5/6pm and Saturday from 9.30/10am to noon/2pm, with reduced hours in smaller communities. You can buy stamps from most newsagents. If you're in Denmark long-term, consider buying a **Danish SIM** for your mobile – prepaid cards from operators such as Telmore and CBB are available from petrol stations and post offices from 99kr. **Internet access** is free at libraries and some tourist offices, most towns have internet cafés, and omnipresent coffee chain *Baresso* offer free wi-fi.

EMERGENCY NUMBERS

All emergencies ☏112.

EMERGENCIES

Danish **police** are generally courteous and most speak English. For **prescriptions**, doctors' consultations and dental work – but not hospital visits – you have to pay on the spot.

INFORMATION

Most places have a **tourist office** that can help with accommodation. They're open daily in the most popular spots, but have reduced hours from October to March. All airports and many train stations also offer a hotel booking service.

MONEY AND BANKS

Currency is the **krone** (plural kroner), made up of 100 øre. It comes in notes of 50kr, 100kr, 200kr, 500kr and 1000kr, and coins of 50øre, 1kr, 2kr, 5kr, 10kr and 20kr. **Banking hours** are Monday to Friday from 9.30/10am to 4pm, Thursday until 5.30/6pm. Banks are plentiful and are the easiest place to **exchange cash** and travellers' cheques, although they usually charge around 30kr per transaction. Forex bureaux tend to charge 20kr to exchange cash and 10kr for travellers' cheques, but are scarce. Most airports and ferry terminals have late-opening exchange facilities, and ATMs are widespread. At the time of writing, €1 = 7.5kr, US$1 = 5.7kr and £1 = 8.7kr.

OPENING HOURS AND HOLIDAYS

Standard **shop hours** are Monday to Thursday from 9/10am to 5.30/6pm, Friday from 9/10am to 7/8pm, Saturday

STUDENT AND YOUTH DISCOUNTS

Your **ISIC card** will get you thirty to fifty percent off most museum and gallery admission prices, although free entry is often available on Wednesdays and Sundays. If you're staying long-term a **DSB Wildcard** (185kr) offers fifty percent off train fares for a year (⒲dsb.dk).

DANISH

	DANISH	PRONUNCIATION
Yes	*Ja*	Ya
No	*Nej*	Nye
Please	*Vær så venlig*	Verso venly
Thank you	*Tak*	Tagg
Hello/Good day	*Goddag*	Go-day
Goodbye	*Farvel*	Fah-vell
Excuse me	*Undskyld*	Unsgul
Good	*God*	Got
Bad	*Dårlig*	Dohll
Near	*Nær*	Neh-a
Far	*Fjern*	Fee-ann
Cheap	*Billig*	Billie
Expensive	*Dyr*	Duy-a
Open	*Åben*	Oh-ben
Closed	*Lukket*	Lohgget
Ticket	*billet*	bill-le
Today	*Idag*	Ee-day
Yesterday	*Igår*	Ee-goh
Tomorrow	*Imorgen*	Ee-mon
How much is...?	*Hvad koster...?*	Val kosta...?
I'd like...	*Jeg vil gerne ha...*	yai vay gerna ha...
What time is it?	*Hvad er klokken?*	Val eayr cloggen?
Where is...?	*Hvor er...?*	Voa eayr...?
A table for...	*et bord till...*	et boa te...
I don't understand	*Jeg forstår ikke*	Yai fusto igge
Do you speak English?	*Taler de engelsk?*	Tayla dee engellsgg?
One	*En*	Ehn
Two	*To*	Toh
Three	*Tre*	Tray
Four	*Fire*	Fee-a
Five	*Fem*	Fem
Six	*Sex*	Sex
Seven	*Syv*	Syu
Eight	*Otte*	Oddeh
Nine	*Ni*	Nee
Ten	*Ti*	Tee

8

from 9am to 1/2pm (though in larger cities, several will stay open until 5pm on Saturday). Many larger shops and department stores are also open on Sundays for limited hours. All shops and banks are closed, and public transport and many museums run to Sunday schedules on **public holidays**: January 1; Maundy Thursday to Easter Monday; Prayer Day (4th Fri after Easter); Ascension (fortieth day after Easter); Whit Sunday and Monday; Constitution Day (June 5); December 24 (pm only); December 25 and 26. On **International Workers' Day**, May 1, many offices and shops close at noon.

Copenhagen

Split by lakes and surrounded by sea, an energetic and hip waterside vibe permeates **COPENHAGEN** (København), one of Europe's most user-friendly (and trendy) capitals. It's a welcoming, compact city with a centre largely given over to pedestrians (and cyclists) with an emphasis on café culture and top-notch museums by day, and a cracking live music, bar and club scene by night. Festivals like **Distortion** (June) and the **Jazz Festival** (July) show the city off at its coolest and most inventive.

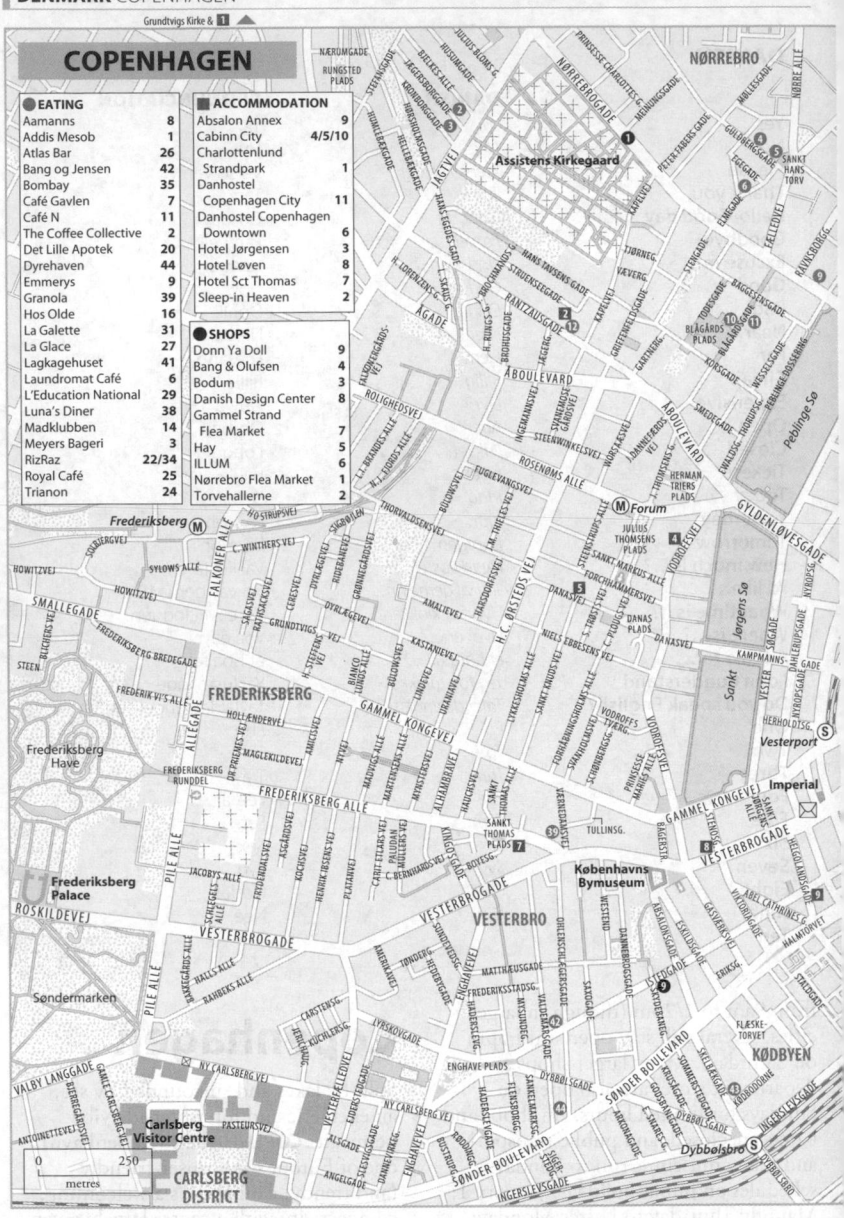

COPENHAGEN

● EATING

Aamanns	8
Addis Mesob	1
Atlas Bar	26
Bang og Jensen	42
Bombay	35
Café Gavlen	7
Café N	11
The Coffee Collective	2
Det Lille Apotek	20
Dyrehaven	44
Emmerys	9
Granola	39
Hos Olde	16
La Galette	31
La Glace	27
Lagkagehuset	41
Laundromat Café	6
L'Education National	29
Luna's Diner	38
Madklubben	14
Meyers Bageri	3
RizRaz	22/34
Royal Café	25
Trianon	24

■ ACCOMMODATION

Absalon Annex	9
Cabinn City	4/5/10
Charlottenlund Strandpark	1
Danhostel Copenhagen City	11
Danhostel Copenhagen Downtown	6
Hotel Jørgensen	3
Hotel Løven	8
Hotel Sct Thomas	7
Sleep-in Heaven	2

● SHOPS

Donn Ya Doll	9
Bang & Olufsen	4
Bodum	3
Danish Design Center	8
Gammel Strand Flea Market	7
Hay	5
ILLUM	6
Nørrebro Flea Market	1
Torvehallerne	2

Until the twelfth century, when **Bishop Absalon** built a castle on Christiansborg's present site, there was little more than a tiny fishing settlement to be found here. Trade and prosperity flourished with the introduction of the Sound Toll on vessels in the Øresund, and the city became the Baltic's principal harbour, earning the name **København** ("merchants' harbour"). By 1443, it had become the Danish capital. A century later, Christian IV created Rosenborg

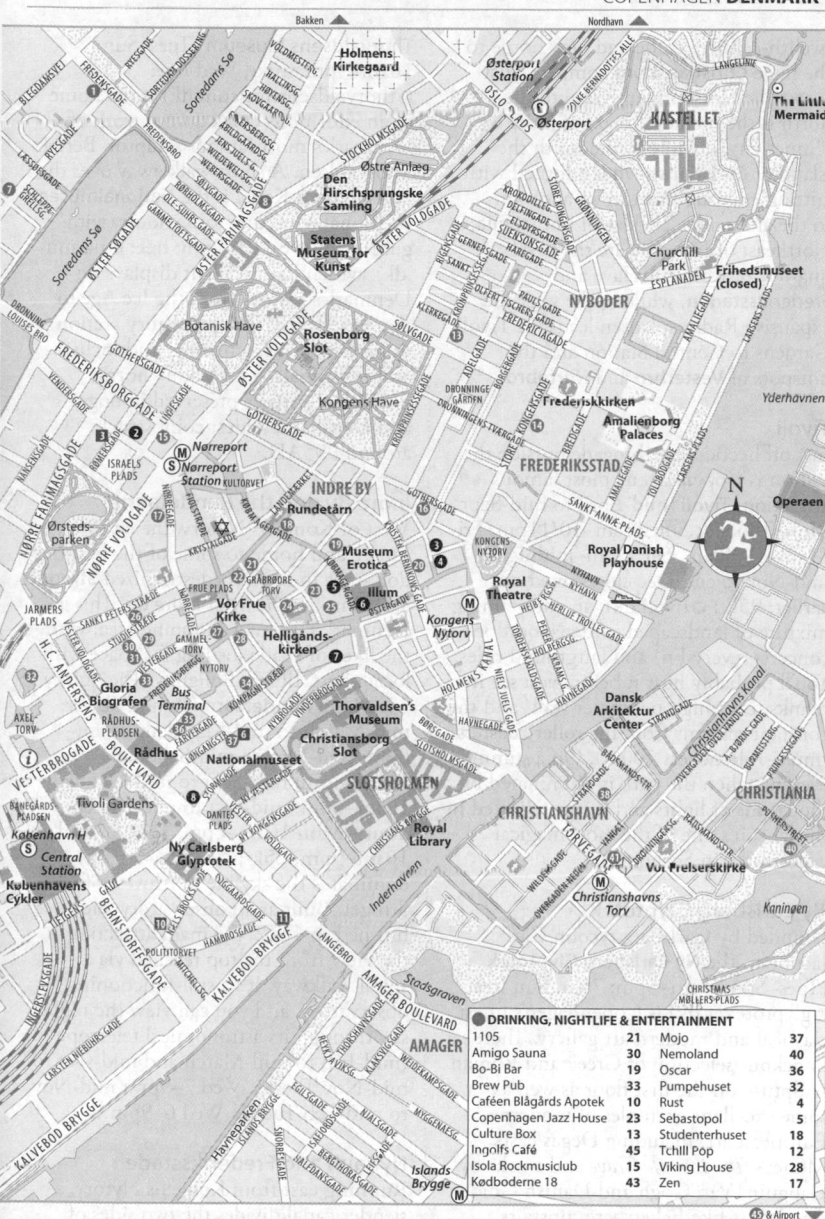

DRINKING, NIGHTLIFE & ENTERTAINMENT			
1105	**21**	Mojo	**37**
Amigo Sauna	**30**	Nemoland	**40**
Bo-Bi Bar	**19**	Oscar	**36**
Brew Pub	**33**	Pumpehuset	**32**
Caféen Blågårds Apotek	**10**	Rust	**4**
Copenhagen Jazz House	**23**	Sebastopol	**5**
Culture Box	**13**	Studenterhuset	**18**
Ingolfs Café	**45**	Tchlll Pop	**12**
Isola Rockmusiclub	**15**	Viking House	**28**
Kødboderne 18	**43**	Zen	**17**

Castle, Rundetårn and the districts of Nyboder and Christianshavn, and in 1669 Frederik III graced the city with its first royal palace, Amalienborg. Since then, various kings and merchants have built up the city to be the amalgam of architectural styles and landscapes that you see today.

WHAT TO SEE AND DO

The historic core of the city is **Slotsholmen**, originally the site of the twelfth-century castle and now home to the huge **Christiansborg** complex. Just across the Slotsholmen Kanal to the north is the medieval maze of **Indre By** ("inner city"), while to the south the island of **Christianshavn** is adorned with cutting-edge architecture in addition to the alternative enclave of **Christiania**. Northeast of Indre By are the royal quarters of Kongens Have and **Frederiksstaden**, while to the west the expansive Rådhuspladsen leads via Tivoli Gardens to Central Station and the hotspots of **Vesterbro** and **Nørrebro**.

Tivoli

Just off hectic Vesterbrogade outside the station is Copenhagen's most famous attraction, **Tivoli** (mid-April to mid-Sept Mon–Thurs & Sun 11am–10/11pm, Fri 11am–12.30am, Sat 11am–midnight; mid-Nov to end Dec closes one hour earlier; 95kr; ⓦtivoli.dk), an entertaining mixture of landscaped gardens, outdoor concerts (every Fri) and fairground rides. You'll probably hear it before you see it, thanks to its high perimeter walls and the constant screams from the roller coasters (multi-ride tickets 200kr). On a summer evening when the park is illuminated by thousands of lights and lamps reflected in the lake, it's one of the most magical experiences in Scandinavia.

Ny Carlsberg Glyptotek

Founded by Carlsberg tycoon Carl Jacobsen, the **Ny Carlsberg Glyptotek** (Tues–Sun 11am–5pm; 75kr, Sun free; ⓦglyptoteket.dk) is Copenhagen's finest classical and modern art gallery. There's a knockout selection of Greek and Roman sculpture on the first floor as well as some excellent examples of modern European art, including Degas casts, Monet's *The Lemon Grove* and works by Gauguin, Van Gogh and Danish Golden Age artists like Eckersberg, upstairs. Wind up your visit with a slice of delicious cake in the café beside the delightfully domed winter garden.

Thorvaldsens and the National museums

On the north side of Slotsholmen, the **Thorvaldsens Museum** (Tues–Sun 10am–5pm; 40kr, Wed free; ⓦthorvaldsensmuseum.dk) is the home of an enormous collection of work of Denmark's most famous sculptor, Bertel Thorvaldsen. A short walk away over the Slotsholmen Kanal is the **Nationalmuseet** (National Museum; same hours, with guided tours Sun at 2pm; free; ⓦnatmus .dk), which has excellent displays on Denmark's history from the Ice Age to the present day. The prehistory section in particular is fascinating, and includes amber animals, gold Viking horns, numerous corpses preserved in bogs and Denmark's oldest coin, struck around 995AD.

Indre By and the Rundetaarn

West of Kongens Nytorv, the city's largest square and home to some of the best hot dog stalls in town, pedestrianized **Strøget** leads into the heart of **Indre By**. This is Denmark's premier shopping area, with the likes of Prada jostling for space with local giant, Illums Bolighus. The quirky 35m-high **Rundetaarn** (Round Tower; mid-March to mid-May daily 10am– 6pm; mid-May to mid-Sept daily 10am–8pm; mid-Sept to mid-Oct daily 10am–6pm; mid-Oct to mid-March Thurs–Mon 10am–6pm, Tues & Wed 10am–9pm; 25kr; ⓦrundetaarn.dk) dominates the skyline northwest of Strøget. Built as an observatory and finished in 1642, the main attraction is the view from the top reached via a spiral walkway. It's a still-functioning observatory, and you can view the night sky through its astronomical telescope (mid-Feb to mid-March and mid-Oct to mid-Nov Tues & Wed 7–9pm; mid-Nov to mid-Feb Tues & Wed 6–9pm).

Nyhavn and Frederiksstaden

Running east from Kongens Nytorv, a slender canal divides the two sides of **Nyhavn** ("new harbour"), picturesquely lined with colourful eighteenth-century houses – now bars and cafés – and thronged with tourists year-round. Just north of Nyhavn, the royal district of **Frederiksstaden** centres on cobbled Amalienborg Slotsplads, home to the four

COPENHAGEN ON A BUDGET

Europe's fifth most expensive city, Copenhagen can be a tricky place to get by on a budget, but with a bit of planning you can make the most of your wallet. Museums with **free admission** include the Nationalmuseet (National Museum), the Frihedsmuseet (Museum of the Danish Resistance) and the Statens Museum for Kunst (National Gallery), (see opposite & below), while many others offer free entry one day per week. Another great free activity in summer is swimming in Copenhagen harbour's outdoor pool on Islands Brygge, southwest across the canal from Indre By. You should also consider buying a CPHCARD (see p.219). As for getting around, you can walk to most places, use the free city bikes or take the harbour bus-boats. The city has plenty of free music on offer, including concerts at Tivoli almost weekly during summer. As for accommodation, having your own bed linen and HI card can save you upwards of 100kr nightly.

Amalienborg royal palaces. Two remain as royal residences, and there's a changing of the guard at noon if the monarch is home. In the opposite direction is the great marble dome of **Frederikskirken**, also known as Marmorkirken or marble church (Mon–Thurs 10am–5pm, Fri–Sun noon–5pm; admission to dome 1pm & 3pm Sat & Sun, plus Mon–Fri June–Aug; free), modelled on St Peter's in Rome. Further along Bredgade and down Esplanaden, a German armoured car commandeered by the Danes to bring news of the Nazi surrender marks the entrance to the **Frihedsmuseet** (Museum of the Danish Resistance Movement; Tues–Sun 10am–3pm, May–Sept until 4pm; free; ⊕frihedsmuseet.dk).

Kongens Have and Rosenborg Slot

West of Frederikskirken, **Kongens Have** is the city's oldest public park and a popular spot for picnics. Within the park is the fairytale **Rosenborg Slot** (daily: May, Sept & Oct 10am–4pm, June–Aug 10am–5pm, Jan–April & Nov to mid-Dec 11am–2pm; 80kr; ⊕dkks.dk), the castle that served as the principal residence of Christian IV. The highlight is the downstairs treasury, where a gilded throne and the **crown jewels** and rich accessories worn by Christian IV are on display.

The Botanisk Have and art galleries

The **Botanisk Have** (Botanical Garden; May–Sept daily 8.30am–6pm, Oct–April Tues–Sun 8.30am–4pm; free; ⊕botanik .snm.ku.dk), on the west side of Kongens Have, is dotted with greenhouses and rare plants. The neighbouring **Statens Museum for Kunst** (National Gallery; Tues–Sun 10am–5pm, Wed till 8pm; free, entry fee for some special exhibitions; ⊕smk.dk) has bright and spacious galleries holding a vast collection of art, from minor Picassos to major works by Matisse and Titian. Across the park on Stockholmsgade, **Den Hirschsprungske Samling** (The Hirschsprung Collection; daily except Tues 11am–4pm; 75kr, free on Wed; ⊕hirschsprung.dk) holds a collection of twentieth-century Danish art, including work by the Skagen artists (see box, p.235), renowned for their use of light.

Little Mermaid

Just north of the **Kastellet**, a star-shaped fortress with five bastions on a corner overlooking the harbour, sits the diminutive (and in all honesty, anticlimactic) **Little Mermaid**, a magnet for tourists since her unveiling in 1913. A bronze statue of the Hans Christian Andersen character, it was sculpted by Edvard Eriksen and paid for by the founder of the Carlsberg brewery. Over the years she's been the victim of several attacks, having her head and arms chopped off and even being blown up by a bomb in 2003 – and also spent much of 2010 at Shanghai's Expo – but she remains the most enduring symbol of the city.

Christianshavn

From Christiansborg, a bridge crosses to **Christianshavn**, built by Christian IV in the early sixteenth century and nicknamed "Little Amsterdam" thanks to

8

its small canals, cute bridges and Dutch-style houses. Reaching skywards on the far side of Torvegade is one of the city's most recognizable features, the copper and golden spire of **Vor Frelsers Kirke** (daily 11am–3.30pm; tower Mon–Sat 10am–7.30pm, Sun 10.30am–7.30pm; free, tower 35kr; ⓦvorfrelserskirke.dk). Also worth a look is the canalside **Dansk Arkitektur Center** (daily 10am–5pm, Wed till 9pm; 40kr, students 25kr or free for architecture students; ⓦdac.dk), at Strandgade 27B, with regular exhibitions on design and architecture plus an excellent café and bookshop.

Christiania

Christiania is a former barracks area colonized by hippies after declaring itself a "free city" in 1971. It has evolved into a self-governing entity based on collective ownership, with quirky buildings housing alternative small businesses such as a bicycle workshop and women's smithy, as well as art galleries, cafés, restaurants, Copenhagen's best falafel stand, music venues and Pusherstreet, once an open hash market. There are guided tours of the area (late June to Aug daily 3pm; rest of the year Sat & Sun only; 40kr; ☎32 95 65 07, ⓦrundvisergruppen.dk), starting at the main gate by Prinsessegade, but it's just as fun to wander around on your own. No photos are allowed, unless by special permission. The neighbourhood has been racked by controversy since the off, sitting as it does on prime real estate while its population remain exempt from the taxes most Danes pay. Although the area's future is threatened by moves from the Danish conservative government, as its residents may tell you, the places earns its keep: it's one of Copenhagen's most visited attractions, and justifiably so.

Vesterbro

Directly behind the train station begins **Vesterbro**, home to Copenhagen's red-light district and one of the most cosmopolitan areas in the city. It has a great selection of shops, bars and restaurants as well as the **Københavns Bymuseum** at Vesterbrogade 59 (City

Museum; daily 10am–5pm, Wed till 9pm; 40kr, free on Fri), which covers the city's history, with an elaborate banquet hall upstairs used for classical concerts. While the area is perfectly safe to walk around, male travellers may want to give Istedgade (one of the main thoroughfares) a wide berth at night to avoid being propositioned.

Carlsberg Visitors Centre

"Probably the best beer in the world" claims the advert. Well, you can decide for yourself at the **Carlsberg Visitors Centre** (Tues–Sun 10am–5pm; 70kr; ⓦvisitcarlsberg.dk) along Gamle Carlsberg Vej (buses #18 and #26). As well as learning how to create the perfect pint at the Jacobsen Brewhouse, you also get to sample two beers from a choice of Carlsberg, Tuborg and Jacobsen brews.

Nørrebro

Nørrebro, an edgy area northwest across the canal from Indre By (accessible from the centre via buses #3A, #4A or #5A or a 25min walk), is crammed with some of Copenhagen's best cafés, bars and clubs, centred on Sankt Hans Torv. Caution is advised, particularly at night: but it's home to most of Denmark's most happening hangouts and the resplendent **Assistens Kirkegård**, a tranquil cemetery which locals use as a park in summer, and that has Hans Christian Andersen among its permanent residents.

ARRIVAL AND DEPARTURE

By plane Kastrup airport is 11km southeast of the centre, and is served by a main-line train to Central Station (5am–midnight every 10min; midnight–5am hourly; 12min; 36kr).

By train Trains pull into Central Station (Københavns Hovedbanegård or Københavns H on tickets) near Vesterbrogade.

Destinations Aalborg (every 30min; 4hr 20min–5hr); Århus (every 30min; 2hr 50min–3hr 40min); Hamburg (hourly; 4hr 30min–5hr 45min); Helsingør (every 20min; 50min); Malmö (several hourly; 35min); Odense (3 hourly; 1hr 15min–1hr 30min); Roskilde (every 20min; 30min).

By bus Long-distance buses from elsewhere in Denmark stop at or near the Central Station.

Destinations Aalborg (3–5 daily; 4hr 45min); Århus (6–7 daily; 3hr); Malmö (hourly; 55min).

By boat Ferries dock an S-train ride away north of the centre at Nordhavn (two stops from Nørreport station).

INFORMATION

Tourist information Vesterbrogade 4a, across from Central Station ☎70 22 24 42, ⓦvisitcopenhagen.com (May, June & Sept Mon–Sat 9am–6pm, Sun 9am–4pm; July & Aug daily 9am–7pm; Oct–April Mon–Fri 9am–4pm, Sat 9am–2pm). Accommodation (including private rooms) can be booked for free via their website. Note that pickpockets operate in the tourist office and thefts are common: be vigilant with your possessions (the same applies in the train station).

Discount cards If you're sightseeing on a tight schedule, the CPHCARD (ⓦcopenhagencard.com; 299/529kr for 24/72hr) is valid for the entire public transport network (including all Zealand) and gives entry to most attractions in the area. It's available at tourist offices, hotels, travel agents and the train station.

GETTING AROUND

By Metro, S-tog and bus An integrated network of buses, electric S-trains (S-tog) and an expanding metro covers the city (5am–1am); night buses (*natbus*) take over after 1am, along with metro services on Thurs, Fri and Sat nights, though the latter are less frequent. Night fares are double daytime fares, and if you're taking your bike, you'll need to buy a special ticket. Free route maps are available from stations.

Tickets The cheapest ticket is the *billet* (24kr for two zones), valid for an hour's unlimited travel. You can also buy a *Klippekort* containing ten *billets* (150kr for two zones). Other options include the CPHCARD (see above) and the city card (for the four main city transport zones; 75/190kr for 24/72hr). Seven-day flexicards (different zone combinations available) are good money-saving devices for those on a slightly longer stay. Single *billets* can be bought onboard buses; all other tickets can and should be bought at train stations/newsagents. Make sure you validate your ticket before boarding at the yellow ticket-punching machines on the platform. Plain-clothes ticket inspectors operate on almost all train routes: there are instant 600kr fines for travelling without a ticket; don't even bother trying to play ignorant – your defence won't be bought, as all transport signs are printed bilingually in Danish and English.

By bike The city's brand new-Gobike scheme (April–Nov; ⓦgobike.com) allows you to borrow any of 1260 hi-tech bikes from racks across the city. Integrated with onboard GPS and a tablet computer, the bikes feature navigation with route planning and map display, as well as real-time information on available bikes and docking stations all over the city. Payment is made by credit card, with charges varying based on the amount of time the bicycle is rented for (at press time the pricing details were still unavailable). Lower-tech cycle rental is available from CPH Bike Rental, Turesensgade 10 (daily 10am–6pm; from 50kr/6hr; profits go to helping cycling in Africa; ⓦcph-bike-rental.dk), and Københavns Cykelbørs, Gothersgade 157 (Mon–Fri 9am–5.30pm, Sat 10am–1.30pm, plus June–Aug Sun 10am–1.30pm; from 75kr/day; ⓦcykelborsen.dk); the latter also rents out hi-tech bicycles with GPS computers that have built-in guides of the city.

ACCOMMODATION

Copenhagen has a very good selection of hostels, mainly concentrated in the city centre and Nørrebro. Booking ahead is recommended on weekends and during summer months; otherwise turn up as early as possible during the day to ensure a bed. Hotel prices can verge on the astronomical, but there are often online deals available and a few cheaper options in the centre. Private rooms (around 400kr) booked through the tourist office are usually an S-train ride away from the centre. Breakfast is not included, unless otherwise stated.

HOSTELS

Danhostel Copenhagen City H.C. Andersens Boulevard 50 ☎33 11 85 85, ⓦdanhostelcopenhagencity.dk. Priding itself as Europe's largest "designer" youth hostel, this thousand-bed monster is friendly, efficient and centrally located in a multistorey building overlooking the harbour. There's a guest kitchen, a convivial café-bar and free wi-fi. Bikes for 100kr/day. All rooms en suite. Dorm __155kr__, double __425kr__

COPENHAGEN TOURS

When the weather's good, it's well worth forking out on a **city tour** to familiarize yourself with Copenhagen. There are hop-on/hop-off open-top **bus tours** around the key city sights (195kr; ⓦsightseeing.dk) and also Netto Boats (March–Oct 9.40am–8pm; 40kr; ⓦnetto-baadene.dk) operating hour-long canal and harbour **boat tours** past the old stock exchange (not open to the public), the island of Holmen and the Little Mermaid, leaving regularly from Nyhavn. For bike enthusiasts (see above), the best option is Bike Mike (daily 10.30am, plus April–Oct Wed & Sat 2.30pm; 290kr for 3hr including bike rental; ☎26 39 56 88, ⓦbikecopenhagen -withmike.dk), with themed **cycle tours** departing from Sankt Peders Stræde 47 in the Latin Quarter.

8

8

Danhostel Copenhagen Downtown Vandkunsten 5 ☎70 23 21 10, ⓦcopenhagendowntown.com. Affable hostel with mostly small four-person dorms and thirty private rooms, along with a cool café-bar, free wif-fi, pool table, chill-out cushions and a bang-in-the-centre location. Dorm 100kr, double 350kr

Hotel Jørgensen Rømersgade 11 ☎33 13 81 86, ⓦhoteljoergensen.dk. Hostel offering six- to ten-bed dorms and basic rooms (with cable TV; 10 have their own bathroom), with a buffet breakfast included. Common room with TV, pool and table football. A stone's throw from Nørreport station on Israels Plads. Dorm 160kr, double 650kr

Sleep-in Heaven Struenseegade 7, Nørrebro ☎35 35 46 48, ⓦsleepinheaven.com. Welcoming, irreverent hostel in a quiet spot next to Assistens Kirkegård. Six- or twelve-bed mixed dorms, plus double rooms (shared bathroom). Age limit 35; breakfast 40kr. Open 24hr; pool table; bar; free internet. Bus #12/#69, nightbus #92N from the centre (10min). Dorm 144kr, double 620kr

HOTELS

Absalon Annex Helgolandsgade 15 ☎33 24 22 11, ⓦabsalon-hotel.dk. Basic, slightly worn rooms with TV and shared bathroom in a one-star annexe of this three-star hotel. Price includes a good breakfast buffet. Single 450kr, double 650kr

Cabinn City Mitchellsgade 14 ☎33 46 16 16, ⓦcabinn .com. Clean cabin-style rooms close to Tivoli and the station. All are en suite and have TV; breakfast is 70kr extra. Two other branches in Frederiksberg. Single 495kr, double 625kr

Hotel Løven Vesterbrogade 30 ☎33 79 67 20, ⓦloevenhotel.dk. A real bargain for such a central location, in a historic nineteenth-century building (ring the bell marked "1st floor Løven" for admittance), with 46 airy and spacious rooms spread over five floors; most have a fridge, and some have a/c and bathroom. No breakfast but has kitchen for self-catering. Occasional deals for longer stays. Reservations essential in summer. Double 590kr

Hotel Sct Thomas Frederiksberg Allé 7 ☎33 21 64 64, ⓦhotelsctthomas.dk. This gem of a three-star spot offers boutique-ish rooms close to hip Værnedamsvej and a short walk from glorious Frederiksberg Gardens. It's a bit of a trek from the city centre, but the friendly owners and very reasonable rates more than compensate. Double 695kr

CAMPSITES

Charlottenlund Strandpark Strandvejen 144, Charlottenlund ☎39 62 36 88, ⓦcampingcopenhagen .dk. Beautifully situated 6km from Copenhagen at Charlottenlund Beach and with good, clean facilities. Very busy in summer. S-train line A, B or C to Svanemøllen then

★ **TREAT YOURSELF**

Truth be told, Copenhagen's main pedestrian street, Strøget, can seem bleak compared to the rest of the city, but it's worth exploring for the tucked-away gem that is the **Royal Smushi Café** (Amager Torv 6; Mon–Fri 10am–7pm, Sat 10am–6pm, Sun 11am–5pm; ⓦroyalsmushicafe.dk). In a peaceful courtyard off the main drag, this state-of-the-art café is the place to come for *smushi*: a mix of Danish *smørrebrød* and Japanese fusion cuisine. You'll need 135kr to sample three *smushi* (the herring is best); other lunch items are 85–145kr.

bus #14. Closed mid-Oct to early March. 100kr per person, plus 35kr per tent

EATING

Mixing Michelin stars with budget bars, Copenhagen delights with its tremendously varied eating scene – which has helped to plant it on the map as Scandinavia's most sophisticated city. Head out of the centre as locals do towards Nørrebro and Vesterbro for the best deals. For self-caterers, bakeries are a good option, while for takeaway *smørrebrød* try the outlets at Centrum Smørrebrød, Vesterbrogade 6C; or Klemmen at Central Station. There are Netto supermarkets at Nørre Voldgade 94, Nørrebrogade 43 and Landemærket 11. If you fancy really getting to know the locals while filling up on home-made Danish food, you could always book a Dine With the Danes evening, a long-running initiative which gets travellers into contact with locals who cook, serve and share a meal with you (ⓦdinewiththedanes.dk; from 400kr).

CAFÉS

Bang og Jensen Istedgade 130 ⓦbangogjensen.dk. With high stucco ceilings, a mahogany counter left over from its former incarnation as a pharmacy, and plenty of swagger, this hip Vesterbro café-bar will never go out of fashion. Their casual bistro fare includes nachos with jerk chicken (80kr) and croque chèvre sandwiches (73kr). Big with local musicians, artists and social entrepreneurs. Tends to pack out before concerts in nearby Vega. Mon–Fri 7.30am–2am, Sat 10am–2am, Sun 10am–midnight.

Café Gavlen Ryesgade 1 ⓦcafegavlen.dk. With breakfasts (from 40kr), delicious cakes (40kr) baked daily on the premises and good *smørrebrød* (44kr), this café is chic enough to grace Montparnasse: at night, speciality beers and cocktails replace the delicious coffee as the drink of choice. Mon–Thurs 9am–midnight, Fri & Sat 9am–2am, Sun 9am–11pm.

Dyrehaven Sønder Blvd 72 ⓦdyrehavenkbh.dk. Cool café-bar-restaurant popular with in-the-know locals and expats. It serves real down-home Danish dishes such as *kartoffelmed* (black bread with potatoes; 55kr) and grilled mackerel with lemon and dill (144kr). Mon–Fri 9am–2am, Sat 10am–2am, Sun 10am–midnight.

Granola Vernedamsvej 5. Feel-good retro coffee bar serving delicious ice cream on one of the city's trendiest streets. Breakfasts from 35–140kr. Daily 7am–midnight.

La Galette Larsbjørnsstræde 9 ⓦlagalette.dk. Authentic Breton pancakes made with organic buckwheat and an array of fillings – from ham and eggs to smoked salmon and caviar. Pancakes 30–120kr. Mon–Sat noon–4pm & 5.30–10pm, Sun 4–10pm.

Laundromat Café Elmegade 15 ⓦthelaundromatcafe .com. You can tell a good-value, popular café by the crowds, right? They certainly flock to this place, where breakfast goodies start at 45kr and big brunches at 88kr. Great cakes and coffees. Other branches in Frederiksberg (Gammel Kongevej 96) and Østerbro (Århusgade 38). Mon–Fri 8am–midnight, Sat & Sun 10am–midnight.

Luna's Diner Sankte Anne Gade 5 ⓦlunasdiner.dk. Bright little café in Christianshavn with street-front seating, the best milkshakes in town (56kr), burgers (128kr) and a popular weekend veggie brunch until 3pm (189kr, but you'll never eat it all). Mon–Thurs 9.30am–midnight, Fri & Sat 9.30am–1am, Sun 9.30am–11pm.

★ **The Coffee Collective** Jaegersborggade 10 ⓦcoffeecollective.dk. The best café in town, bar none. The joint is run by a former world champion barista. Ethically sourced coffee (espresso 20kr; long white 30kr), ultra-knowledgeable staff and coffee roasted right in front of you during the day. Mon–Fri 7.30am–7pm, Sat 9am–6pm, Sun 10am–6pm.

RESTAURANTS

Aamanns Øster Farimagsgade 10 ⓦaamanns.dk. Good place for cheap *smørrebrød* and other Danish dishes (from 50kr). Eat in or take away. Take away Mon–Fri 10.30am–8pm, Sat 11am–4.30pm, Sun noon–4.30pm; restaurant Wed–Sat noon–4pm & 6–11pm, Sun noon–4pm.

Atlas Bar Larsbjørnsstræde 18 ⓦatlasbar.dk. Busy basement bar-restaurant with an imaginative range of world food from ostrich and Japanese beef to Mexican vegetarian burritos. Mains from 100kr. Mon–Sat noon–10pm.

Bombay Lavendelstræde 13 ⓦeatatbombay.dk. The city's best Indian, with curries to eat in or take away for 115kr. Tues–Sun 4–11pm.

Café N Blågårdsgade 17 ⓦcafe-n-2200.dk. Bargain veggie burgers (49kr) and a "special" dish-of-the-week (from 89kr) make this fabulous veggie/vegan café-restaurant a handy pit stop for budget-conscious travellers. Home-made bread, great coffee and pavement seating. Mon–Fri 8am–9pm, Sat & Sun 9am–9pm.

Det Lille Apotek Store Kannikestæde 15 ⓦdetlilleapotek.dk. "The little pharmacy" proclaims itself as the oldest restaurant in Copenhagen. Though their food is admittedly average (and the meat-heavy mains are pricey), the whole place has a great olde-worlde atmosphere and they do some decent-value lunches (from 98kr). Daily 11.30am–midnight.

Hos Olde Store Regnegade 26 ⓦhos-olde.dk. Initimate bar with an antiquarian decor, offering plenty of *smørrebrød* (69kr), such as sausage with onion and aspic

8

COPENHAGEN'S BEST BAKERIES

The Danes take their bakeries seriously and you'll see them all around Copenhagen. The range of loaves and pastries on offer is almost intimidating, but staff will happily advise. As well as *rundstykker* and flaky pastries, most bakeries offer affordable sandwiches. The following five are among the city's best:

Emmerys Frederiksholms Kanal 1, Nørrebrogade 8, and Østerbrogade 51, among others ⓦemmerys.dk. Trendy bakery chain with organic bread and filling sandwiches (from 49kr). Mon–Fri 7am–6pm, Sat & Sun 7am–4/5pm.

Lagkagehuset Torvegade 45 ⓦlagkagehuset.dk. Opposite the Christianshavn metro station, this justifiably popular bakery offers a bewildering range of breads baked in stone ovens, as well as great pastries (from 15kr) and fruit-covered cakes. Mon–Thurs 6am–7pm, Fri 6am–7.30pm, Sat & Sun 6am–7pm.

La Glace Skoubougade 3 ⓦlaglace.dk. Set just east of

Gammel Torv, Copenhagen's oldest confectioner (dating to 1870) is an essential stop for cakes and freshly made hot chocolate. Mon–Fri 8.30am–6pm, Sat 9am–6pm, Sun 10am–6pm.

Meyers Bageri Jaegersborggade 9 ⓦclausmeyer.dk. The focus is on bread here: it comes out of the oven the moment before the store opens, and the variety of loaves is incredible. Also at Store Kongensgade 46. Mon–Fri 7am–6pm, Sat & Sun 7am–4pm.

Trianon Hyskenstræde 8, east of Nytorv ⓦtrianon.dk. Purveyors to the queen – so the standard of breads and pastries here is top-notch. Mon–Fri 7.30am–5.30pm, Sat 8.30am–5pm.

8

and various herring dishes. Has live jazz on Wed evenings. Daily noon–9.30pm.

★ **L'Education National** Larsbjornstrade 12 ⓦ leducation.dk. Cute brasserie with friendly staff: the tasty French food is cheap (lunch mains from 75kr) but the service and intimate atmosphere (candles and checked tablecloths) make the experience memorable. Mon–Sat 11.30am–10pm.

Madklubben Store Kongensgade 66 ⓦ madklubben .info. Down-at-heel affordable chain restaurant that does simple Danish dishes (250kr for four courses). Efficient staff. Branches at Tivoli (Vesterbrogade 31630) and in Vesterbro (Vesterbrogade 62). Mon–Sat 5.30pm–midnight.

RizRaz Kompagnistræde 20 ⓦ rizraz.dk. Stylish, time-tested Mediterranean chain with an excellent vegetarian buffet (lasagne/pizza/salad) for 79kr (99kr after 4pm) and great large weekend brunches (95kr; 10am–4pm). Another branch at Store Kannikestræde 19. Mains around 139kr. Mon–Fri 11.30am–midnight, Sat 10am–midnight, Sun 10am–midnight.

DRINKING AND NIGHTLIFE

These days, Nørrebro vies for *the* place to be with hip Kødbyen, the city's still-functioning meatpacking district just southeast of Tivoli, where arty bars and clubs have taken over old warehouses. Bars across the city are generally open until midnight or 1am Mon–Wed & Sun, and until at least 2am Thurs–Sat.

BARS

1105 Kristen Bernikows Gade 4 ⓦ 1105.dk. It ain't cheap, but then the bartender here is inventor of the "Copenhagen", the city's signature cocktail. Phenomenal drinks and plenty of beautiful people. Wed, Thurs & Sat 8pm–2am, Fri 4pm–2am.

Bo-Bi Bar Klareboderne 4 ☏ 33 12 55 43. Simple, red hole-in-the-wall home to Copenhagen's oldest bar counter (from 1917), great cheap bottles of Danish and Czech beers, and a refreshingly diverse clientele of students, artists and writers. Daily noon–2am.

Blågård's Apotek Blågårds Plads 20 ⓦ kroteket.dk. Unpretentious bar with a mixed crowd: students like the cheap beer, and an older crowd come for regular live blues/ jazz. Two dozen of the beers on offer are home brews, which change regularly. Give the Vesterweisse, the summer wheat ale, a try. Daily noon–2am.

Brew Pub Vestergarde 29 ⓦ brewpub.dk. Popular micobrewery bang in the centre of town, with a range of ales (40/58kr for small/large) and a great beer garden. Mon–Thurs noon–midnight, Fri & Sat noon–2am.

Ingolfs Café Ingolfs Alle 3 ⓦ ingolfskaffebar.dk. South of the centre in Amager via bus #5a, this is a mellow, Bohemian café-bar serving daytime organic brunches and often erupting into a live music venue at sundown. Come

here for recuperation the morning after, then get the party started all over again. Mon & Tues 10am–10pm, Wed–Sat 10am–midnight, Sun 10am–9pm.

Nemoland Fabriksområde 52, Christiania ⓦ nemoland .dk. Run by Christiania residents, this is one of the city's most popular open-air bars, with picnic tables and decent café food. In winter, the crowd moves indoors to the pool tables and backgammon boards. Mon–Thurs 10am–1am, Fri–Sat 10am–3am, Sun 10am–1am.

Oscar Rådhuspladsen 77 ⓦ oscarbarcafe.dk. Bright and lively café-bar in a perfect location off Rådhuspladsen; popular with a gay clientele. DJs spin till late at weekends. Happy hour (5–9pm) has 33kr Carlsbergs, and there are good sandwiches and burgers (from 79kr) too. Sun–Thurs 11am–11pm, Fri & Sat 11am–2am.

Sebastopol Sankt Hans Torv 2 ⓦ sebastopol.dk. Trendy café-bar with a retro feel on the Sankt Hans Torv square. Small/large beer 34/50kr. Good brunches too (from 80kr). Mon–Thurs 8am–midnight, Fri 8am–1am, Sat 9am–1am, Sun 9am–10pm.

Studenterhuset Købmagergade 52 ⓦ studenterhuset .com. Friendly student hangout by the Rundetaarn, with table football and pinball machines. Live music Thurs–Sat and an international party every Wed for Erasmus students. Cakes from 15kr; large beer 25kr (a student card gets you a third off all prices). Happy hour (Daily 7–10pm, plus Fri noon–10pm) gets you two draught beers for 35kr. Mon–Sat 11am–midnight (sometimes later).

★ **Tchili Pop** Rantzausgade 28 ⓦ tjili.dk. *Tchili Pop's* oh-so-cool clientele keep coming back here for the laidback vibe and great live music sessions from up-and-coming Danish bands. It's one of Nørrebro's best bars. Mon & Tues 10am–midnight, Wed 10am–1am, Thurs 10am–2am, Fri & Sat 10am–3am, Sun 10am–midnight.

Viking House Vimmelskaftet 49 ⓦ thevikinghouse.dk. Touristy but boisterous joint pumping out rock/heavy metal classics and with live music at weekends. In something of a drinkers' wasteland, and always lively, especially on Wed, when beers are 25kr. Sun–Thurs noon–5am, Fri & Sat 10am–8am.

CLUBS

Culture Box Kronprinsessegade 54A ⓦ culture-box.dk. Stylish basement club and easily the best electronica venue in town. Cover charge 50–120kr. Fri & Sat 9pm–late.

Isola Rockmusiclub Linnésgade 16A ⓦ isolabar.dk. Intimate club/bar playing mostly soul, rock and R&B. Free entry. Thurs–Sat 8pm–5am.

Kødboderne 18 Kødboderne 18 ⓦ kb18.net. Club/live music venue in the heart of Kødbyen hosting everything from electronica to blues/rock, and a renowned Sat club night. Definitely an *it* place to go out in Copenhagen. Cover charge 60kr. Thurs 9pm–3am, Fri & Sat 9pm–7/8am.

Rust Guldbergsgade 8 ⓦ rust.dk. Popular club and

concert venue playing indie, rock and hip-hop. Cover charge 40–80kr. Wed–Sat 9pm–5am.

Zen Nørregade 41 ☎ 33 11 00 46, ⓦ zen.dk. Exclusive, chic and not always easy to get into, this trendy spot offers phat beats, plenty of pretension and young people grinding on the dancefloor. Caveat emptor. Thurs–Sat 11pm–4am.

SHOPPING

CLOTHES

Istedgade and the parallel Vesterbrogade have the best selection of boutiques including vintage and little-known designer wear.

Donn Ya Doll Istedgade 55 ⓦ donnyadoll.dk. Has a great range of gadgets and Scandinavian designer labels. Mon–Fri 11am–6pm, Sat 10am–4pm.

DANISH DESIGN

Bang & Olufsen Østergade 18 ⓦ bang-olufsen.dk. This flagship store sells audiophile stereo gear, top-end TVs and mobile-related sound products. Mon–Thurs 10am–6pm, Fri 10am–7pm, Sat 10am–4pm.

Bodum Østergade 10 ⓦ bodum.com/dk. Offer a range of imaginative kitchenware including their classic cafetiére. Mon–Thurs 10am–6pm, Fri 10am–7pm, Sat 10am–4pm.

Danish Design Center HC Andersens Boulevard 27 ⓦ ddc.dk. Have a peek inside the gift shop here which sells loads of cool and wacky designer gadgets. Mon–Fri 8am–6pm, Sat & Sun 10am–6pm.

Hay Pilestræde 29 ⓦ hay.dk. Sells colourful, funky and affordable household accessories and *objets d'art*. Mon–Fri 10am–6pm, Sat 11am–4pm.

ILLUM Østergade 52 ⓦ illum.dk. Hard to miss, halfway down Strøget, this is Copenhagen's premier department store; worth visiting just to marvel at the interior. Mon–Sat 10am–8pm, Sun 11am–6pm.

MARKETS

Gammel Strand flea market Gammel Strand 26. The most central market, celebrated but pricey, focusing on antiques. Fri & Sat 8am–5pm.

Nørrebro Flea Market Just outside Assistens Cemetery along Nørrebrogade. Head out here for cheaper deals on everything from porcelain to clothes. May to mid-Oct Sat 7am–2pm.

Torvehallerne Israels Plads ⓦ torvehallernekbh.dk. Copenhagen's new food market, near Norreport station, is

an evocative covered market with stalls selling fairly upscale foodstuffs. Mon–Thurs 10am–7pm, Fri 10am–8pm, Sat 10am–6pm, Sun 11am–5pm.

ENTERTAINMENT

CINEMA

Grand Mikkel BryggersGade 8 ☎ 33 15 16 11, ⓦ grandteatret.dk. Stylish arthouse cinema with a great café and lively events programme (films around 80kr).

Imperial Ved Vesterport 4 ☎ 70 13 12 11, ⓦ imperialbio .dk. Copenhagen's largest cinema, with only one theatre. which can fit over 1100 people. Seats from 75–105kr.

LIVE MUSIC

As well as the options below, check out the programmes at *Vega* at Enghavevej 40 in Vesterbro and *Rust* (see opposite).

Copenhagen Jazz House Niels Hemmingsensgade 10 ⓦ jazzhouse.dk. The city's premier jazz venue. Daily 7pm–late.

Mojo Løngangsstræde 21C ⓦ mojo.dk. Atmospheric, divey blues venue with live acts every night. Entrance free or 70–120kr. Daily 8pm–5am; happy hour 8–10pm.

Pumpehuset Studiestræde 52 ⓦ pumpehuset.dk. Two concert venues in one, set into a former salt warehouse, with a total capacity of 1000. Hosts Danish bands and also attracts international names such as Kaiser Chiefs and Röyksopp. Entrance 50–250kr.

OPERA AND THEATRE

If you're under 25 (or if you're buying after 4pm on performance day) then you may be able to get tickets at half price for the venues below; ask at the Royal Theatre box office for details.

Operaen Christianshavns Torv ⓦ operaen.dk. The city's spectacular opera house is as much an architectural as a musical attraction. Cheap tickets on the day of the performance can cost as little as 100kr. Guided tours July to late Aug (advance booking essential, 100kr).

Royal Theatre Kongens Nytorv ⓦ kgl-teater.dk. Denmark's oldest and grandest theatre hosts ballet, opera, drama and concerts.

Skuespilhuset Sankt Annæ Plads 36 ⓦ kgl-teater.dk. Strikingly modern waterside building with three stages, one of which can be opened for alfresco performances. All plays are in Danish; the café has a great harbourside view. Guided tours early July to early Aug (100kr; daily 4pm).

8

GAY COPENHAGEN

The Danish capital has a small but lively **gay scene** and hosts regular festivals and events including an annual Gay Pride march and one of the world's oldest LGBT film festivals, MIX, held each October (ⓦ mixcopenhagen.dk). There are several gay **clubs** and numerous **bars** across the city; the big **sauna** is Amigo Sauna (Studiestrade 21a; ⓦ amigo-sauna.dk). Check out ⓦ visitcopenhagen.com/gay and ⓦ copenhagen-gay-life.dk for more information.

Embassies Australia, Dampfærgevej 26 ☎ 70 26 36 76; Canada, Kristen Bernikowsgade 1 ☎ 33 48 32 00; Ireland, Østbanegade 21 ☎ 35 47 32 00; UK, Kastelsvej 36–40 ☎ 35 44 52 00; US, Dag Hammarskjölds Allé 24 ☎ 33 41 71 00.

Exchange Den Danske Bank at the airport (daily 6am–8.30pm); Forex and X-Change at Central Station (daily 7/8am–9pm).

Hospital Rigshospitalet, Blegdamsvej 9 ☎ 35 45 35 45.

Internet The Royal Library's Black Diamond site at Søren Kierkegaards Plads 1 in Slotsholmen has free internet/wi-fi in a hugely impressive harbourside complex.

Left luggage Lockers at Central Station by the entrance on Reventlowsgade, from 30kr for 24hr.

Pharmacies Steno Apotek, Vesterbrogade 6C; Sønderbro Apotek, Amagerbrogade 158. Both 24hr.

Police In Central Station and at Halmtorvet 20, off Lille Istedgade.

Post office Købmagergade 33 and at Central Station.

DAY-TRIPS FROM COPENHAGEN

When the weather's good, you can top up your tan at the **Amager Strandpark beach**, just 5km from the centre (bus #12 or take the metro to Øresund, Amager Strand or Femøren then a 5min walk). If Tivoli hasn't exhausted your appetite, then make for the world's oldest amusement park at **Bakken** (ⓦbakken.dk; April–Aug daily noon/2pm–10pm/11pm/midnight; multi-ride ticket 219kr/249kr), close to the Klampenborg stop at the end of lines C and F+ on the S-train about 10km north of downtown. Besides slightly sinister clowns and vintage roller coasters it offers pleasant woods and nearby beaches to wander around.

There are two more excellent attractions on Zealand's northeastern coast. In the affluent town of **HILLERØD** at the end of S-train line C is the spectacular multi-turreted **Frederiksborg Slot** (daily: April–Oct 10am–5pm; Nov–March 11am–3pm; 75kr; ⓦfrederiksborgslot .dk), a seventeenth-century castle built by Christian IV surrounded by an ornamental lake and housing Denmark's national portrait gallery. Further north in **HUMLEBÆK**, and a short walk from its train station, is **Louisiana**, an outstanding modern art gallery, at Gammel Strandvej 13 (Tues–Fri 11am–10pm, Sat & Sun

11am–6pm; 110kr; ⓦlouisiana.dk). The gallery's setting is worth the journey alone – a harmonious blend of art, architecture and the natural landscape.

The rest of Zealand

As home to Copenhagen, **Zealand** is Denmark's most visited region, and, with a swift metropolitan transport network covering almost half of the island, you can always make it back to the capital in time for an evening drink. North of Copenhagen, **Helsingør** (Elsinore) is the departure point for ferries to Sweden and the site of legendary Kronborg Castle. To the west, and on the main train route to Funen, is **Roskilde**, with an extravagant cathedral that served as the resting place for Danish monarchs, and a superb location on the Roskilde fjord, from where five Viking boats were salvaged and are now displayed in a gorgeous, specially built museum.

HELSINGØR

Despite its status as a busy ferry port, **HELSINGØR** is a laconic, likeable town with some major historical attractions. Its position on the narrow strip of water linking the North Sea and the Baltic brought the town prosperity when, in 1429, the Sound Toll was imposed on passing vessels. Today it remains an important waterway, with ferries to and from Helsingborg in Sweden accounting for most of Helsingør's through-traffic and innumerable cheap booze shops.

WHAT TO SEE AND DO

The town's single great tourist draw is **Kronborg Castle** (daily: June–Aug 10am–5.30pm; Sept–May 11am–4pm; Nov–March closed Mon; 75kr; ⓦkronborg.dk), principally because of its literary associations as Elsinore Castle, the setting for Shakespeare's *Hamlet*. There's no evidence Shakespeare ever visited Helsingør, and the tenth-century character Amleth on whom his hero was based long predates the castle. Nevertheless, the cottage industry of Hamlet souvenirs thrives here like it's nobody's business. The present castle dates from the sixteenth century when it jutted into the sound as a formidable warning to passing ships not to consider dodging the toll, and it remains a grand affair, enhanced immeasurably by its setting; the interior, particularly the royal chapel, is spectacularly ornate. Beneath the castle are the casemates, gloomy cavernous rooms that served as soldiers' quarters during times of war.

The big new attraction just south is the revamped former shipyard area where the recently opened **Maritime Museum of Denmark** (Ny Kronborgvej 1; June–Aug daily 10am–5.30pm; April–Oct daily 11am–4pm; Nov–March Tues–Sun 11am–4pm; 100–120kr; ⓦmfs.dk) is now one of the country's premiere places to learn about Denmark's seafaring past and present. Set underground in the old dry docks next to the Castle, the structure was built to a cost of 130 million kroner and opened in mid-2013. The building comprises a continuous ramp that loops around the dock walls, allowing for unobstructed views from the Castle. Inside, the technologically advanced, well-curated collections are dedicated to the country's maritime history, with informative exhibits that span Viking, medieval and modern seafaring, exploration and merchant shipping. In addition to videos and interactive exhibits on ships and life at sea, there are other unique finds, including a colossal Maersk freight container. Exhibits include relics from Denmark's conquests in Greenland, India, the West Indies and West Africa, as well as the world's oldest surviving ship's biscuit (1852). The area is also the site of the **Culture Yard** (Mon–Fri 10am–9pm, Sat & Sun 10am–4pm; free; ⓦkulturvaerftet.dk), a theatre, concert venue, library and café-restaurant housed in an innovatively designed glass-steel structure created from old wharf buildings. Its attached **Værftsmuseum** (Mon 2–6pm, Tues–Sat 10am–2pm, Sun 2–6pm; free) gives an insight into local maritime heritage.

The medieval quarter

Helsingør's well-preserved **medieval quarter** is dominated by **Stengade**, the main shopping street, linked by a number of narrow alleyways to Axeltorv, the town's small market square and a nice place to enjoy a beer. Near the corner of Stengade and Skt. Annagade is Helsingør's cathedral, **Skt. Olai Kirke** (Mon–Sat: May–Aug 10am–4pm; Sept–April 10am–2pm; free; ⓦhelsingoerdomkirke.dk), while beyond is **Skt. Mariæ Kirke** (mid-May to mid-Sept Tues–Sun 10am–3pm, mid-Sept to mid-May Tues–Sun 10am–2pm, free; guided tours at 2pm Mon–Fri; 20kr), whose Karmeliterklostret, built circa 1400, is now the best-preserved medieval monastery in Scandinavia (guided tours only; arrange via the church office). Its former hospital now contains the **Town Museum** (Tues–Sun noon–4pm, Sat till 2pm; 20kr), which displays an unnerving selection of surgical tools used in early brain operations.

The northern coast of Zealand is scattered with quaint little fishing villages: consider a trip to **Gilleleje**, where you can buy fresh fish directly from the fishermen (connected by train to Helsingør).

ARRIVAL AND INFORMATION

By train The train station is on Jernbanevej, a 2min walk south of the centre.

Destinations Copenhagen (every 20min; 45min); Gilleleje (every 30min; 40min); Hillerød (hourly; 30min).

Tourist office Havnepladsen 3, just opposite the train station (Jan–June & Sept–Dec Mon–Fri 10am–4pm; July Mon–Fri 10am–5pm, Sat & Sun 10am–2pm; Aug same hours, closed Sun; ☏49 21 13 33, ⓦvisitnorthsealand.com).

> ### FERRIES TO SWEDEN
>
> The main ferry operator between Helsingør and **Helsingborg** in Sweden is Scandlines (ⓦscandlines.dk), making the twenty-minute crossing every fifteen to thirty minutes (55kr return). All services leave from the main terminal by the train station. Eurail is valid on Scandlines while InterRail and the Copenhagen Card give a 25 percent discount.

8

ACCOMMODATION

Danhostel Helsingør Nordre Strandvej 24 ☎ 49 28 49 49, ⓦ helsingohostel.dk. Beautifully located hostel in a restored villa right on the beach (suitable for swimming) 2km north of town; bus #340 from the station (8min; get off at Højstrup Trinbraet stop). Rents bikes for 75kr/day. The cheapest rooms share baths off the corridor. Dorm 185kr, double 450kr

Helsingor Camping Strandalleen 2 ☎ 49 28 49 50 ⓦ helsingorcamping.dk. Near *Danhostel* on the same bus route, this magnificent site has great coastal views across to Kronborg Slot. 70kr per person, plus 50kr per tent; cabins from 250kr

EATING AND DRINKING

Café Brostraede Brostraede 1. Unpretentious café with limited seating but the best sandwiches around (44kr) and organic beers; down a tiny alley linking the port with the old town. Mon–Fri 10.30am–5.30pm, Sat 10.30am–3pm.

Ole Jensen Stenegade 19. Don't consider stocking up on picnic items anywhere else. The cheese selection at this supermarket/deli, particularly, will wow you. Mon–Thurs 9.30am–5.30pm, Fri 9.30am–6pm, Sat 9am–3pm.

ROSKILDE

Once the capital of Denmark, **ROSKILDE** is worth a visit even if you can't make it to its famous annual rock festival (see opposite). Its **Viking Ship Museum** is a world-class attraction, while the cathedral and old centre are lovely to wander around. One of Denmark's most colourful markets takes place on Wednesday and Saturday on the square outside the cathedral.

WHAT TO SEE AND DO

The fabulous **Roskilde Domkirke** (April–Sept Mon–Sat 9am–5pm, Sun 12.30–5pm; Oct–March Tues–Sat 10am–4pm, Sun 12.30–4pm; 60kr; ⓦ visit.roskildedomkirke.dk) was founded by Bishop Absalon in 1170 and largely completed by the fourteenth century. It's stuffed full of dead Danish monarchs including twenty kings and seventeen queens. The most impressive chapel is that of Christian IV, full of bronze statues, frescoes and vast paintings of scenes from his reign. The current queen, the charismatic Margrethe II, has also expressed a desire to be buried here.

Next door is Roskilde Palace, housing the diverting **Museum of Contemporary Art** (Tues–Fri 11am–5pm, Sat & Sun noon–4pm when there are exhibitions on; 40kr, Wed free; ⓦ samtidskunst.dk).

Viking Ship Museum

Fifteen minutes' walk north of the centre on the banks of the fjord is the modern **Viking Ship Museum** (late June to Aug daily 10am–5pm; Sept to mid-June daily 10am–4pm; 115kr May–Sept, otherwise 80kr; ⓦ vikingshipmuseum.dk).
Inside, five superb specimens of Viking shipbuilding are displayed: a deep-sea trader, a merchant ship, a warship, a fishing vessel and a longship preserved incredibly from 1042, each retrieved from the fjord where they were sunk to block invading forces. Two life-size models of ships are next door, which you can board after trying on traditional Viking clothes. Outside, you can watch boat-building and sail-making using only tools and materials available during the Viking era; when the weather allows, you can also experience a replica ship's seaworthiness on the fjord – you'll be handed an oar when you board and be expected to pull your weight as a crew member (50min; 80kr on top of the museum ticket; minimum twelve people). It's a humbling experience when you consider that similar ships made it all the way to Greenland.

ARRIVAL AND INFORMATION

By train The train station is at the southern edge of town. Destinations Copenhagen (every 20min; 30min); Odense (every 30min; 1hr 10min).

By bus The bus station is within the same complex as the train station. Destinations Copenhagen (several hourly; 40min).

Tourist office On the main square, Stændertorvet 1 (Mon–Fri 10am–5pm, Sat 10am–1pm; ☎ 46 31 65 65, ⓦ visitroskilde.com).

Cycle rental Jupiter Cykler Roskilde at Gullandsstræde 3 offer cycle rental (75kr per day; 500kr deposit). Mon–Thurs 9am–5.30pm, Fri 9am–6pm, Sat 9am–2pm.

ACCOMMODATION

Roskilde Camping Baunehøjvej 7 ☎ 46 75 79 96, ⓦ roskildecamping.dk. 4km north of town via Frederiksborgvej on bus route 603, the campsite here has a

ROSKILDE FESTIVAL

Book well in advance if you wish to stay during the **Roskilde Festival** (ⓦ roskilde-festival.dk), one of the largest open-air music festivals in Europe, attracting almost 100,000 people annually. Tickets go on sale in December and tend to sell out quickly. The festival usually takes place in early July, and there's a special free campsite beside the festival site, to which shuttle buses run from the train station every few minutes.

gorgeous grassy, woodsy setting on the edge of the fjord. It's quite windy round here. Pitch 80kr, cabin 400kr

Roskilde Vandrerhjem Vindeboder 7 ☎ 46 35 21 84, ⓦ danhostel.dk/roskilde. Beautifully situated modern hostel of 40 rooms in the harbour area near the Viking Museum. Dorm 200kr, double 450kr

EATING AND DRINKING

Café Druedahls Skomagergade 40 ⓦ cafedruedahls .dk. Popular café just south of the cathedral, with a range of beers and sandwiches. Offers a good-value brunch for 119kr, weekend buffet 119kr. Mon–Sat 11am–8.30pm.

Gimle Helligkorvej 2 ⓦ gimle.dk. Set just 10min east of the tourist office, this café/live music venue serves burgers (99kr) and sandwiches (459kr); also turns into a club Fri & Sat nights. Tues & Wed noon–midnight, Thurs noon–2am, Fri & Sat noon–5am, Sun 10am–5pm.

Konditor Bager Algade 6 ⓦ konditor-bager.dk. Under new management, this is Roskilde's best bakery; breads and cakes 8–15kr. Mon–Fri 6.30am–5pm, Sat 7am–3pm.

Funen

Funen is the smaller of the two main Danish islands. Its pastoral outlook and laidback fishing villages along the coast draw many visitors, but the main attraction is **Odense**, Denmark's third city and the birthplace of writer Hans Christian Andersen and composer Carl Nielsen.

ODENSE

Named after Odin, chief of the pagan gods, **ODENSE** (pronounced Own-suh) is well over a thousand years old. An attractive little place, with a lush location on the River Odense Å, it has an engaging cultural scene and a surprisingly energetic nightlife with a focus on live music: it's one of Denmark's most enchanting places to spend a few days.

WHAT TO SEE AND DO

Odense's inner core is a network of cobbled streets flanked by photogenic medieval houses.

H.C. Andersens Hus and H.C. Andersens Barndomshjem

The city's (perhaps the country's) best attraction is the **H.C. Andersens Hus** at Bangs Boder 29 (June–Aug daily 9am–6pm; Sept–May Tues–Sun 10am–4pm; 85kr; ⓦ museum.odense.dk), where the writer was born in 1805. The museum includes a library of Andersen's works and audio recordings of some of his best-known fairytales read by the likes of Sir Laurence Olivier. There's also intriguing paraphernalia including school reports, manuscripts, paper cuttings and drawings from his travels. The most striking feature, aside from the diminutive house itself, is the series of murals by Niels Larsen Stevns (1930) depicting different stages of Andersen's life. Check out the telling quotes on Andersen's unconventional looks and talent: "He is the most hideous man you could find but has a poetic childish mind", commented one contemporary.

Down the road, at Munkemøllestræde 3–5, is the tiny **H. C. Andersens Barndomshjem** (Childhood Home; daily 10am–4pm; 30kr; ⓦ museum.odense.dk) where the writer lived between the ages of two and fourteen.

The city centre

On Skt. Knuds Plads just southwest of the Rådhus (town hall) is the crypt of Gothic **Odense Cathedral** (April–Oct daily 10am–5pm; Nov–March 10am–4pm; free; ⓦ odense-domkirke.dk). Also known as Skt. Knuds Kirke, this travertine church holds the remains of King Knud II and his brother Benedikt, both murdered in 1086 at the altar of

8

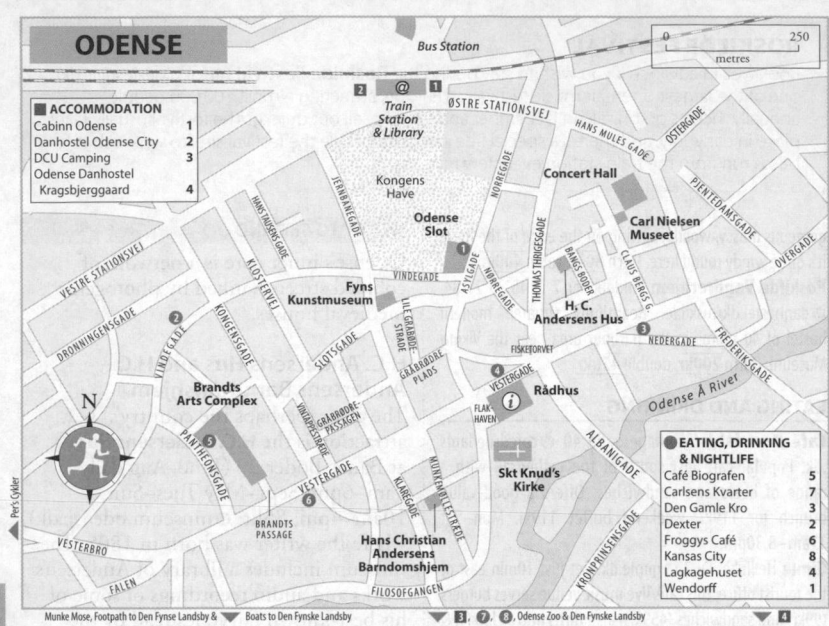

nearby Skt. Albani Kirke. Don't miss the splendiferous gold-leaf-coated altarpiece inside by Lübeck master Claus Berg.

At Jernbanegade 13, the **Fyns Kunstmuseum** (Funen Art Gallery; Tues–Sun 10am–4pm; 60kr; ⊚museum .odense.dk) focuses on late nineteenth-century Danish art including stirring works by Vilhelm Hammershøi and Skagen artist P.S. Krøyer.

Over at the Odense Concert Hall the city's other famous son, Carl Nielsen (one of Europe's leading nineteenth-century composers), also has a riveting museum devoted to his life, **Carl Nielsen Museet** (Jan–April Thurs & Fri 3–7pm, Sat & Sun 11am–3pm; May–Aug Wed–Sun 11am–3pm; Sept–Dec Thurs & Fri 3–7pm, Sat & Sun 11am–3pm; free; ⊚museum.odense.dk).

Just off Vestergade, west of the centre is the **Brandts Arts Complex**. Once a large textile mill, the area has been beautifully converted and now features an art school, cinema, music library and three museums (Tues, Wed & Fri–Sun 10am–5pm, Thurs noon–9pm; 80kr combined ticket; ⊚brandts.dk). In the large hall that once housed the huge machinery is the

Kunsthallen, which displays works by the cream of new talent in art and design, and the **Museet for Fotokunst**, featuring changing photography exhibitions. On the third floor the **Danmarks Mediemuseum** chronicles the development of printing, bookbinding and illustrating from the Middle Ages to the present day.

Den Fynske Landsby and Odense Zoo

South of the centre at Sejerskovvej 20 is **Den Fynske Landsby** (Funen Village; April–June & mid-Aug to late Oct Tues–Sun 10am–5pm; July to mid-Aug daily 10am–6pm; 60/85kr; ⊚museum .odense.dk), a living, breathing nineteenth-century village made up of buildings brought here from all over Funen, including a windmill and a school. In summer, free shows are staged at the open-air theatre. Buses #110 and #111 run to the village from the bus station.

It's infinitely better, however, to walk to the museum by following the river south about 4km via the ornamental park of Munke Mose. Boats also run there hourly (75kr return) via **Odense Zoo** (daily

10am–4/5pm winter, 10am–6/7pm summer; 150kr; ⦿odensezoo.dk), which has Northern Europe's largest exclusively African safari park.

ARRIVAL AND INFORMATION

By train Odense train station is part of a large shopping mall 5min walk north of the centre.

Destinations Århus (every 30min; 1hr 40min); Copenhagen (3 hourly; 1hr 15min–1hr 30min); Esbjerg (hourly; 1hr 20min–2hr).

By bus Long distance buses terminate at the train station.

Destinations Århus (2 daily; 1hr 50min); Copenhagen (hourly; 2hr).

Tourist office At Vestergade 2 near the Rådhus (Sept–June Mon–Fri 9.30am–4.30pm, Sat 10am–1pm; July & Aug 9.30am–6pm, Sat 10am–3pm, Sun 11am–2pm; ☎63 75 75 20, ⦿visitodense.com).

Bike rental CSV Cykeludlejning, at Nedergade 36; rents bikes (100kr/day, plus 500kr deposit).

Internet Free access in the library at the train station.

Left luggage At the train station behind the ticket office; 50kr for 24hr (daily 5am–1.15am).

ACCOMMODATION

HOSTELS

Danhostel Odense City Østre Stationsvej 31 ☎66 11 04 25, ⦿cityhostel.dk. Conveniently located in a former hotel next to the train station, this five-star hostel has clean rooms, 24hr automated check-in and a good café with buffet breakfast for 69kr. Dorm 250kr, double 570kr

Odense Danhostel Kragsbjerggaard Kragsbjergvej 121 ☎66 13 04 25, ⦿odense-danhostel.dk. Sister hostel to the city branch, this one is set in a manor house surrounded by woodland 2km south of the centre (bus #61 & #63 from the station). Breakfast 65kr. Rents on a per-room basis (2- to 8-person rooms available, so works out cheap if you're in a big group). Double 495kr, dorm 200kr

HOTEL

Cabinn Odense Østre Stationsvej 7–9 ☎63 14 57 00, ⦿cabinn.com. Budget chain hotel close to the train station. All rooms are short on space but are en suite and have TV. Free internet access; buffet breakfast 70kr. Double 625kr

CAMPSITE

DCU Camping Odensevej 102 ☎66 11 47 02, ⦿camping -odense.dk. Located near Den Fynske Landsby on the outskirts of Odense, this campsite has mini-golf and a heated pool. Take bus #22 from the train station towards Højby. 78kr per person, plus 25kr per tent; cabins from 550kr

EATING

Café Biografen Brandts Passage 39–41 ⦿cafebio.dk. Trendy bar attached to an artsy cinema, adorned with classic film posters. The bar gets going with thirtysomethings later on. Club sandwich 79kr; coffee 22kr. Brunch buffet (Fri–Sat till 2pm) 109kr. Mon–Thurs 10.30am–11pm, Fri 10.30am–midnight, Sat 10am–midnight, Sun 10am–10.30pm.

Den Gamle Kro Overgade 23 ⦿dengamlekro.eu. Set within a seventeenth-century courtyard, this traditional restaurant offers perhaps the best gastronomic experience in Denmark. There's a basement wine cellar and a host of delicious smørrebrød (mostly 71–93kr); mains like the trout fillet start at 208kr. Mon–Sat 11am–10pm, Sun 11am–9pm.

Froggys Café Vestergade 68 ⦿froggyscafe.dk. Bang-in-the-centre café-bar serving delicious salads (92kr) and the legendary Froggy's burger (119kr). Brunches from 75kr. DJs at weekends. Mon–Wed 9am–midnight, Thurs 9am–2am, Fri & Sat 9.30am–5am, Sun 9.30am–midnight.

Lagkagehuset Vestergade 1 ⦿lagkagehuset.dk. The Danish chain has finally made it to Odense, wowing locals with their renowned scrumptious cakes. Mon–Fri 6.30am–7pm, Sat & Sun 6.30am–6pm.

Wendorff Asylgade 16 ⦿wendorff.dk. Wonderful bakery with two counters teeming with bread and cakes (9–15kr). Mon–Fri 7am–6pm, Sat & Sun 7am–4pm.

DRINKING AND NIGHTLIFE

★ **Carlsens Kvarter** Hunderupvej 19 ⦿carlsens.dk. Cosy bar in the style of a country pub, with a relaxed atmosphere and Odense's best selection of beers (around 27kr for bottles), including all the Belgian Trappist ales. Mon–Sat noon–1am, Sun 1–7pm.

Dexter Vindegade 65 ⦿dexter.dk. Jazz, blues and folk venue with live music 2–3 times a week (entry 80–180kr, depending on the group playing) and a free jam night on Mon evenings. Good range of international beers too.

Kansas City Munkebjergvej 140 ⦿kansascity.dk. This old clothes factory is now an experimental music venue epitomizing everything that's great about the local music scene: watch this space for tomorrow's big Danish names in the music biz. It's 2km south of the centre via bus #29 or #63. Fri & Sat 7pm–late.

Jutland

Long ago, the Jutes, the people of **Jutland**, were a separate tribe from the more warlike Danes who occupied the eastern islands. By the Viking era, however, the battling Danes had spread west, absorbing the Jutes, and real power gradually shifted towards Zealand, where it has largely stayed ever since. Nevertheless, **Århus**, Denmark's second city halfway up the eastern coast, and **Aalborg**, capital of northern Jutland, are vibrant, cosmopolitan urban centres that draw those who dare to venture on from the other, more frequently visited centres. Further inland, the landscape is dramatic – stark heather-clad moors, fjords and dense forests, while north of Aalborg the landscape becomes increasingly wind-battered and stark until it reaches **Skagen**, on the peninsula's tip.

ARRIVAL AND INFORMATION

By train You can reach the Jutland ferry terminals by train from other parts of the country. The train station in Esbjerg is at the end of Skolegade, with trains to and from Copenhagen (3hr 10min). All buses and most trains in Frederikshavn terminate at the central train station, a short walk from the town centre; some trains continue to the ferry terminal itself.

By boat Jutland has two main international ferry ports. Esbjerg has overnight ferries to and from Harwich, in the UK; bus #5 connects the passenger harbour with the centre (a 15min walk). Frederikshavn, in the far north of the region (2hr 45min by train from Århus), has express ferries to Sweden and Norway. Its ferry terminal is near Havnepladsen, not far from the centre.

Destinations Harwich (UK), Götaborg (Sweden), Oslo (Norway).

Tourist offices The tourist office in Esbjerg is at 33 Skolegade (Sept–June Mon–Wed & Fri 10am–4pm, Thurs 10am–6pm; ☎75 12 55 99, ⓦvisitesbjerg.dk). In Frederikshavn, the tourist office is close to the ferry terminal at Skandiatorv 1 (Jan to late June & early Aug to Dec Mon–Fri 9am–4pm, Sat 10am–1pm, late June to early Aug Mon–Sat 9am–6pm, Sun 9am–2pm; ☎98 42 32 66, ⓦvisitfrederikshavn.dk).

ÅRHUS

Denmark's second-largest city, **ÅRHUS**, is an instantly likeable assortment of intimate cobbled streets, sleek modern architecture, brightly painted houses and student hangouts. It's small enough to get to grips with in a few hours, but lively enough to make you linger for days – an excellent music scene (especially for jazzophiles), interesting art, pavement cafés and energetic nightlife all earn it the unofficial title of Denmark's capital of culture.

WHAT TO SEE AND DO

Århus's main street, the pedestrianized Ryesgade/Søndergade, leads down from the train station, across the river and into the main town square, Bispetorvet. Running parallel one block west of Rysegade is Park Alle with the functionalist 1941 **Rådhus** (city hall), designed by Arne Jacobsen and Eric Moller (guided tours including the bell tower can be arranged through the tourist office; see p.232). The square itself is dominated by the fifteenth-century **Domkirke** (May–Sept Mon & Wed–Sat 9.30am–4pm, Tues 10.30am–4pm; Oct–April Mon & Wed–Sat 10am–3pm, Tues 10.30am–3pm; ⓦaarhus-domkirke .dk), a massive Gothic church with exquisite frescoes as well as a miniature Danish warship hanging from the ceiling. The area to the north, known as the Latin Quarter, is crammed with browsable shops, galleries and modern cafés.

ARoS

AROS (Tues & Fri–Sun 10am–5pm, Wed & Thurs till 10pm; 100kr; ⓦaros.dk) is one of Europe's most beautiful contemporary buildings and a fantastic modern art museum. It contains seven floors of works from the late eighteenth century to the present day, accessed from a centrepiece spiral walkway reminiscent of New York's Guggenheim. The Skagen artists head the fine collection of home-grown art: the likes of Warhol are also represented along with the eerie 5m-high *Boy*, by Australian sculptor Ron Mueck. Its standout permanent exhibit is artist Olafur Eliasson's fantastical addition to the roof, known as *Your Rainbow Panorama*. Suspended between city and sky, and loosely inspired by Dante's *Divine Comedy*, this 150m circular pathway spans the colour spectrum and gives panoramic views out to the city.

Den Gamle By

A short walk northwest of the centre is one of the city's best-known attractions, **Den Gamle By**, on Viborgvej (The Old

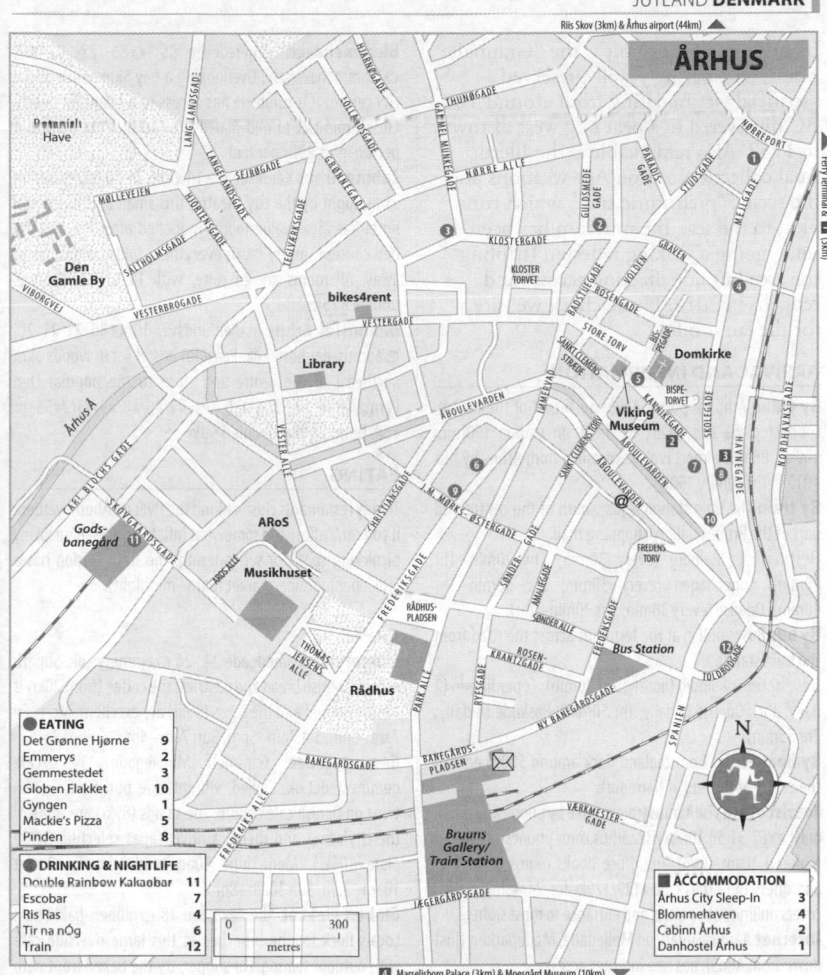

Riis Skov (3km) & Århus airport (44km) ▲

ÅRHUS

Ferry Terminal & ⚓ (3km)

EATING

Det Grønne Hjørne	9
Emmerys	2
Gemmestedet	3
Globen Flakket	10
Gyngen	1
Mackie's Pizza	5
Pinden	8

DRINKING & NIGHTLIFE

Double Rainbow Kakaobar	11
Escobar	7
Ris Ras	4
Tir na nOg	6
Train	12

ACCOMMODATION

Århus City Sleep-In	3
Blommehaven	4
Cabinn Århus	2
Danhostel Århus	1

0   300
metres

▣ Marselisborg Palace (3km) & Moesgård Museum (10km) ▼

Town; daily: Jan 11am–3pm; early Feb to late March 10am–4pm; late March to June 10am–5pm; July to mid-Aug 10am–6pm; mid-Aug to Dec 10am–5pm; 60–135kr; ⓦdengamleby.dk), an open-air museum of traditional Danish life, with 75 half-timbered townhouses and actors in contemporary dress. Many buildings date from the 1800s, but a new town expansion just finishing up at press time features shops and homes from the 1920s and 1970s. You can enter places such as a pastry shop, a haberdashery and a gynaecologist clinic, and there are also pony rides, a bookshop and a working central telephone switchboard. Close by

are the pleasant **botanical gardens** (Mon–Sat 1–3pm, Sun 11am–3pm; free).

Marselisborg Palace and Moesgård Museum

Marselisborg Skov, 2km south of the centre, is the city's largest park, and home to the summer residence of the Danish royals: its landscaped grounds can be visited when the monarch isn't staying (usually at all times outside Easter, Christmas and late June to early Aug).

Ten kilometres south of Århus, the **Moesgård Museum** (ⓦmoesmus.dk), reached direct by bus #6, details Danish civilizations from the Stone Age onwards.

8

Its most notable exhibit is the "Grauballe Man", an amazingly well-preserved sacrificial victim dating from around 100 BC discovered in a peat bog west of town in 1952. Also remarkable is the Illerup Ådal collection of Iron Age weapons and the scenic "prehistoric trail" which runs 3km to the sea. The museum has been undergoing a striking redesign (tripling the area but not affecting access) and reopens in 2014. Please check website for the latest info.

ARRIVAL AND INFORMATION

By plane Århus airport is 44km northeast of the centre, connected via bus #925x to the train station (50min; 100kr). Billund airport is also accessible from Århus by bus #913X (1hr 30min; 190kr).

By train The train station is just south of the centre and part of the Bruuns Gallery shopping mall.

Destinations Aalborg (every 30min; 1hr 20min–1hr 40min); Copenhagen (every 30min; 2hr 50min–3hr 40min); Odense (every 30min; 1hr 30min–2hr).

By bus Buses pull in at the terminus across the road from the train station.

Destinations Aalborg (hourly; 2hr 30min); Copenhagen (2 daily; 3hr); Odense (2 daily, 1hr 50min); Roskilde (4 daily; 2hr 55min).

By boat Ferries from Zealand dock around 500m east of the centre at the end of Nørreport.

Tourist office VisitAarhus (contactable by phone and email only; ☎ 87 31 50 10, ⓦ visitaarhus.com; phones answered Mon–Fri 10am–3pm). The office books rooms (70kr fee) and offers the Århus Card (129/179kr for 24/48hr), which covers unlimited bus travel and entrance to most sights.

Internet Aarhus Library on Møllegade, Mølleparken (just down from ARoS), has free internet access.

GETTING AROUND

By bus A basic ticket costs 20kr from machines in the back of the bus and is valid for any number of journeys for 2hr from the time stamped on it.

By bike From April to Oct you can borrow one of the 450 free city bikes (ⓦ aarhusbycykel.dk) dotted around the city centre (20kr coin deposit). Outside this period, bikes4rent at Skanderborgvej 107 (ⓦ bikes4rent.dk) rents out bikes from 75kr/day, with a 300kr deposit.

ACCOMMODATION

Århus City Sleep-In Havnegade 20 ☎ 86 19 20 55, ⓦ citysleep-in.dk. The most central hostel, with facilities including a guest kitchen, pool and TV rooms and a courtyard for summer barbecues. Organic breakfast is 70kr; also has free internet access. Dorm 180kr, double 500kr

Blommehaven Ørneredevej 35 ☎ 86 27 02 07, ⓦ blommehaven.dk. Overlooking a bay 5km south of the city centre, this campsite has access to a beautiful beach. Closed mid-Oct to mid-March (bus #6 or #19). 78kr per person, plus 20kr per tent

Cabinn Århus Kannikegade 14 ☎ 86 75 70 00, ⓦ cabinn .com. Right by the city theatre, this small and functional hotel has great-value rooms modelled after the Murphy bed concept: pretty much everything folds up and packs away. All rooms are en suite, with TV and telephone. Double 625kr

Danhostel Århus Marienlundsvej 10 ☎ 86 21 21 20, ⓦ aarhus-danhostel.dk. Peaceful hostel set in woods 3km northeast of the centre and close to the popular Den Permanente beach via buses #1/#6/#8/#9/#16/#56 or #58. Dorm 250kr, double 550kr

EATING

Trendy restaurants cluster along the river on Åboulevarden: if you can't afford the somewhat inflated prices, it's a lovely picnicking spot. For self-catering, the train station has a late-opening supermarket (8am–midnight).

CAFÉS

Emmerys Guldsmedgade 24–26 ⓦ emmerys.dk. Superb organic Danish bread and pastries; the coffee (from 20kr) is freshly ground and the cakes (35kr) are excellent. Mon–Fri 7am–6pm, Sat 7am–5pm, Sun 7am–4pm.

Gemmestedet Gammel Munkegade 1 ⓦ cafe gemmestedet.dk. Chilled, vibrant café putting a Turkish twist on Danish café culture. The salads (89kr) are some of the city's best and there's a novel tapas selection (large plate 105kr). Mon–Thurs 10am–midnight, Fri & Sat 10am–2am, Sun 10am–8pm.

Globen Flakket Åboulevarden 18 ⓦ globen-flakket.dk. Locals flock for the brunches at this large riverside café with outdoor seating. For supper, try the baked trout with ratatouille and grilled lemon, and side it with one of their microbrewery beers. The weekend brunch buffets are a big hit (98kr). Mon–Thurs 8.30am–midnight, Fri 8.30am–2am, Sat 9am–2am, Sun 9am–10pm.

RESTAURANTS

Det Grønne Hjørne Frederiksgade 60 ⓦ dgh-aarhus.dk. Great choice for a big feed on the cheap with an all-you-can-eat buffet (noon–4pm, 69kr; 4.30–10pm, 99kr). Mon–Sat noon–11pm.

Gyngen Mejlgade 53 ⓦ gyngen.dk. Impressive veggie burgers (120kr) and a mean chilli con carne with crème fraîche (78kr). Live music Tues–Sat (entrance 100–150kr). Tues 11am–4pm & 7pm–2am, Wed–Fri 11am–2am, Sat 6pm–2am.

★ **Mackie's Pizza** Sankt Clemens Torv 9 ⓦ mackiespizza.dk. Zany pizza joint with diner-style interior full of sports and music memorabilia. Delectable pizzas (from 65kr), with the rule that you have to eat them cutlery-free. Mon–Sat noon–11pm, Sun noon 10pm.

Pinden Skolegade 29 ⓦpinden.dk. The best place in town for traditional Danish food including a knockout *stegt flæsk med persille sovs* (pork in a creamy parsley sauce) for 105kr. All-you-can-eat Sat lunch buffet 139kr, 12.30–3.30pm (except June to early Sept). Mon–Wed noon–11pm, Thurs–Sat noon–1am.

DRINKING AND NIGHTLIFE

Double Rainbow Kakaobar Skovgaardsgade 3. Small underground cultural space and café that organizes music, cultural events and buzzy, off-the-wall parties. Their coffee and hot chocolate are fantastic. Daily 11am–8pm (often later).

Escobar Skolegade 32. Popular student hangout with cheap beer (draught 40kr), loud music (frequently metal) and friendly bar staff. Sun–Thurs 7pm–3am, Fri 2pm–5am, Sat 7pm–5am.

Ris Ras Mejlgade 24 ⓦcaferisras.dk. Chilled student hangout with a vast range of beers. No food served, but you're welcome to bring your own. Mon–Thurs noon–2am, Fri–Sat noon–3am, Sun 2–7pm.

Tir na nÓg Frederiksgade 40 ⓦtirnanog.dk. Large, lively Irish bar with big-screen football and live folk/rock music Thurs, Fri & Sat from 11pm. Pint of Carlsberg 30kr noon–7pm. Open till 3am.

Train Toldbodgade 6 ⓦtrain.dk. Århus's most popular nightclub is also a concert venue that pulls in some big-name DJs and international acts. Entry fees for club nights 20–100kr, or up to 225kr for concerts (tickets are 25kr more expensive at door).

NORTHWEST OF ÅRHUS

Mainland Denmark's loveliest scenery lies northwest of Århus, with the big draw being the country's first national park, **Thy** (ⓦnationalparker.naturstyrelsen.dk), created in 2008. It's a lonely tract of wild beach and inland heath containing the Danish surfing Mecca of **Klitmøller**, and backing onto vast fjords such as **Limfjorden**, producing some of the world's finest oysters.

ARRIVAL AND INFORMATION

By train Trains run from Århus to Struer (hourly; 2hr 10min) and then on into the park.

Tourist information There's an information centre at Stenbjerg Landing (May–Oct 11am–3pm) on bus route #320 from Harup Thy train station.

AALBORG

North Jutland's main city, **AALBORG** has undergone a renaissance in recent years. Long renowned for its raucous nightlife and nearby Viking burial ground, the city of 130,000 has now redeveloped its waterfront with hugely impressive results to showcase its industrial heritage, while not detracting from its substantial medieval core. It's also the main transport terminus for the region, and makes an exciting stopover on the way north to Skagen.

WHAT TO SEE AND DO

Huge investment on the stretch of Aalborg facing Limfjorden has transformed the once industrial **waterfront** district into a centre for design and entertainment, while there's plenty of historical charm in the sights and cobbled streets of the **old town**.

Kunsten Museum of Modern Art and Aalborg Tower

Those after a culture fix should head to the **Kunsten Museum of Modern Art** (Tues–Sun 10am–5pm; 75kr, free in Dec; ⓦkunsten.dk), a stunning modern art gallery close to a sculpture park (take bus #15 or walk ten minutes west of the train station). Just west of here, up a staircase through woods, is the **Aalborg Tower** (late March to Oct 10/11am–5pm; 40kr), with spectacular city views and a bistro restaurant.

The old town

Aalborg's well-preserved **old town** centres on the Gothic cathedral, the **Budolfi Kirke** (June–Aug Mon–Fri 9am–4pm, Sat 9am–noon; Sept–May Mon–Fri 9am–3pm, Sat 9am–noon; ⓦaalborgdomkirke.dk). On the other side of Østerågade, the sixteenth-century **Aalborghus Castle** is notable for its dungeon (May–Oct Mon–Fri 8am–3pm; free) and underground passages (till 9pm).

Leading down to the waterfront is bar-lined **Jomfru Ane Gade**, Aalborg's booziest street.

Waterfront

The waterfront is still in the development phase, with a cruise-ship terminal,

8

landscaped park and more restaurants/bars on the cards, but for now the showpiece attraction is **Nordkraft** (Kjellerups torv 5; ⓦnordkraft.dk), housed in a former power station five minutes' walk east of the centre, near the big new shopping centre Friis, and containing a cinema, theatre/concert venue, several restaurants and the relocated tourist office. Just north, towards the water, stands the **House of Music** (ⓦmusikkenshus.dk), a new cultural and performance space, and home to the Royal Academy of Music from spring 2014. A short walk west is the **Utzon Center** (Tues–Sun 10am–5pm; 60kr; ⓦutzoncenter.dk), designed by the man who gave the world the Sydney Opera House, Jørn Utzon. Utzon was born in Aalborg and left the city this fitting architectural masterpiece, inspired by the old shipyards hereabouts, shortly before his death. It's a showcase for contemporary design and has a wonderful café. A ten-minute walk further west is the distinctive **V&S Distillery** at Olesens Gade 1, home of the potent Scandinavian spirit Aquavit, though unfortunately they only offer tours for large groups.

Lindholm Høje

A few kilometres north of Aalborg via bus #2 (15min), atmospheric **Lindholm Høje** (Lindholm Hills; free) is Scandinavia's largest Viking burial site with more than seven hundred graves. It's best to visit early or late in the day as the slanting sunlight glints off the burial stones, many of which are set in the outline of a Viking ship. It's worth stopping by the site's impressive **museum** (April–Oct daily 10am–5pm; Nov–March Tues–Sun 10am–4pm; 60kr).

ARRIVAL AND INFORMATION

By plane Aalborg airport (served by budget airline Norwegian from London Gatwick three times a week) is 7km northwest of the centre and connected by bus #2 (20min; 20kr).

By train The train station is on J.F. Kennedys Plads, 10min walk southwest of the centre. Left-luggage lockers are available (20kr for 24hr).

Destinations Århus (every 30min; 1hr 20min–1hr 40min); Copenhagen (every 30min; 4hr 20min–5hr); Frederikshavn (hourly; 1hr 10min).

By bus The bus terminal is on J.F. Kennedys Plads, just next to the train station.

Destinations Århus (via Hobro; 1–2 daily; 4hr); Copenhagen (3 daily; 5hr 30min); Odense (via Hobro; 4 weekly; 4hr).

Tourist office In the Nordkraft building, Kjellerups torv 5 (Mon–Fri 10am–5.30pm, Sat 10am–2pm; ☎99 31 75 00, ⓦvisitaalborg.com). Helpful service and touch-screen information; they sell the Aalborg Card here (225kr for 48hr), which gives you free public transport, free admission to most attractions and discounts in cafés/shops.

Internet There's free access in the city library at Rendsburggade 2.

ACCOMMODATION

Cabinn Aalborg Fjordgade 20 ☎96 20 30 00, ⓦcabinn .com. Modern hotel with small, clean, en-suite rooms next to the Riis shopping centre. Free wi-fi. Breakfast 70kr. Double **675kr**

Danhostel Aalborg ☎98 11 60 44, ⓦdanhostelaalborg .dk. Large, well-equipped hostel 3km west of the town on the Limfjord bank beside the marina – take bus #13 to the Egholm ferry junction and continue on foot for 5min following the signs. Dorm **375kr**, double **600kr**, cabin **460kr**

Strandparken Skydebanevej 20 ☎98 12 76 29, ⓦstrandparken.dk. Pleasant campsite 2km west of the centre with access to an open-air swimming pool and beach. Closed mid-Sept to late March. **80kr** per person, plus **30kr** per tent

EATING AND DRINKING

Jomfru Ane Gade is packed with late-opening bars, clubs and restaurants offering bargain food/drink deals.

Flammen Østerågade 27 ⓦrestaurant-flammen.dk. Great new buffet restaurant with a dozen odd meats and salads; which has taken the city by storm. It's a chain, but doesn't feel like one. Sun–Wed 5.30–9.30pm, Thurs–Sat 5–11pm.

Irish House Østerågade 25 ⓦtheirishhouse.dk. Popular pub serving traditional Irish food (until 9pm) and ales, with regular drinks deals. Live music Thurs–Sat, jam sessions on Mon and sport on TV most evenings. Mon–Wed 1pm–1am, Thurs 1pm–2am, Fri & Sat noon–4am, Sun 2pm–midnight.

Penny Lane Boulevarden 1 ⓦpennylanecafe.dk. Buzzing café serving filling sandwiches (85kr), lunches (from 95kr) and brunches from 105kr. Mon–Thurs 8am–6pm, Fri 8am–7pm, Sat 8am–4pm.

★ **Søgaards Bryghus** CW Obels Plads 1A ⓦsoegaardsbryghus.dk. One of Denmark's best brewpubs with any of some 85 brews concocted here. The food is first-rate too (they do a serious steak). Sunday all-you-can-eat brunch buffet 170kr, dinner mains 188–258kr. Mon–Thurs 11am–11pm, Fri & Sat 11am–late, Sun 10.30am–9pm.

Studenterhuset Gammeltorv 11, opposite Budolfi Domkirke ⓦstudenterhuset.dk. Student-run music venue/café: the place to catch local Danish bands. International student night on Wed. Also has a book exchange library and free internet. Coffee 14kr; large beer 29kr. Mon, Tues & Thurs 11.30am–midnight, Wed 11.30am–1am, Fri 11.30am–2am, Sat 3pm–2am.

Utzon Restaurant Slotspladsen 4 ⓦutzoncafeog restaurant.dk. Opened in May 2013, this swish spot inside the Utzon centre has excellent vistas of the fjord (and seating in both an atrium and terrace). Does good, affordable takes on *smørrebrød*. Tues–Sun 10am–5pm.

SKAGEN

About 100km north of Aalborg, **SKAGEN** lies at the very top of Denmark amid breathtaking heather-topped sand dunes. A popular resort, it attracts thousands of visitors annually thanks to its artistic links to the past and spectacular seafood restaurants.

WHAT TO SEE AND DO

Much of Skagen's appeal lies in aimlessly wandering its marina or cycling out to its fabulous beaches. There is one star sight, however – the **Skagen Museum** (signposted from train station; May–Aug daily 10am–5pm, Wed till 9pm; Sept–April Tues–Sun same hours; 90kr; ⓦskagensmuseum.dk), displaying much of the work of the influential Skagen artists (see box below). Nearby, at Markvej 2–4, is the home of one of the group's leading lights and his wife, herself a skilful painter: the **Michael and Anna Anchers Hus** (April & Oct Tues–Sun 11am–3pm; May–Sept daily 1–5pm; Nov Sat 11am–3pm; 80kr; ⓦanchershus .dk). Around 1.5km southwest of the hostel is the **Buried Church**, which was

engulfed by sand drift in 1795 and subsequently abandoned. Today the white spire is all that remains amid the dunes. **Old Skagen**, 4km west of the centre, is where Denmark's jet set have their villas: head to the **Solnedgangspladsen** here to watch the spectacular sunsets.

Grenen

Denmark's northernmost tip is at **Grenen**, 3km from Skagen along Strandvej and the beach, where two seas – the Kattegat and Skagerrak – meet, often with a powerful clashing of waves. You can get here by tractor-drawn bus (April to mid-Oct; 25kr return) – although it's an enjoyable walk through beautiful seaside scenery. At the tip you'll find some fascinating World War II heritage, an ambient restaurant and kilometres of blissful quiescence.

ARRIVAL AND INFORMATION

By train The Skagen train station is on Sct. Laurentii Vej, the town's main thoroughfare. It's served by privately operated trains from Frederikshavn (50 percent discount with Eurail/InterRail) roughly once an hour.
Destinations Frederikshavn (hourly; 35min).

Tourist office Vestre Strandvej 10, close to the marina (Jan to mid-late June & mid-Aug to late Dec Mon–Fri 9.30am–4pm & Sat 10am–1/2pm; late June to mid-Aug Mon–Sat 9am–4pm & Sun 10am–2pm; ☏98 44 13 77, ⓦskagen-tourist.dk). Can arrange private rooms (around 350kr for 75kr fee).

Bike rental Skagen Cykeludlegning by the train station (90kr/day, plus 200kr deposit).

ACCOMMODATION

Danhostel Skagen Rolighedsvej 2 ☏98 44 22 00, ⓦdanhostelskagen.dk. A little way out of the centre, but the rooms are clean and good value. Breakfast 50kr. The nearest train station is actually Frederikshavnsvej. Reservations essential in summer. Closed Dec to mid-Feb. Dorm <u>160kr</u>, double <u>560kr</u>

8

THE SKAGEN ARTISTS

Skagen has long been popular with artists thanks to the warm, golden sunlight that illuminates its coastal scenery. During the 1870s, a group of painters inspired by naturalism settled here and began to paint the local fishermen working on the beaches, as well as each other. The **Skagen artists**, among them Michael and Anna Ancher and P.S. Krøyer, stayed until the turn of the century and achieved international recognition for their work, now on display at the Skagen Museum.

Grenen Camping Fyrvej ☏ 98 44 25 46, ⓦ grenen camping.dk. By the beach 1.5km along the road to Grenen. Closed mid-Sept to late March. <u>76–89kr</u> per person, plus <u>165–230kr</u> per tent

EATING, DRINKING AND NIGHTLIFE

Skagen has fantastic "fresh-off-the-boat" seafood: treat yourself to a blowout meal at one of the marina restaurants, such as *Pakhuset* at Rødspættevej 6.

★ **Brøndums Hotel** Anchersvej 3 ⓦ broendums-hotel .dk. Near the Skagen Museum and historically more important, as it was here that the Skagen Artists met, ate, stayed and socialized. You can do the same in the wonderfully atmospheric hotel restaurant; *smørrebrød* is a somewhat affordable 80–130kr. Daily noon–10pm.
Buddy Holly Havnevej 16 ⓦ buddy-skagen.dk. Skagen's liveliest club, with plenty of drinks deals. Courtyard in back. Daily 10pm–5am.
Jacobs Café & Bar Havnevej 4 ⓦ jakobscafe.dk. Lively café-bar with outside seating and free wi-fi. Sandwiches 90–125kr. Sun–Thurs 9am–9.30pm, Fri & Sat 9am–10pm.

8 THE FAROE ISLANDS

Accessible only via plane or ferry, the remote and otherworldly Faroe Islands comprise an archipelago of eighteen wild, green and steeply pitching isles buffeted by North Atlantic winds, making for days of unforgettable adventure and some fascinating insight into Denmark's former colonial territories (though islanders prefer the term "autonomous region"). The islands are characterized by Denmark's most dramatic scenery and an abundance of sheep – which, incidentally, outnumber humans and have fuelled the trade in Faroese woollen products since being worn by the cast in the iconic Danish TV-series *The Killing*. Krone is the currency, and Danish and English are understood.

WHAT TO SEE AND DO

The world's smallest capital city, **Torshavn**, a tranquil port of colourful turf-roofed houses, is the obvious starting point for island explorations. The historic **Tingenes** area by the harbour is where most of the interest lies in town, along with the islands' now-famous woollen handicrafts showcased at Gudrun & Gudrun (Dalagøta 12; Mon–Fri 10am–5.30pm,

Sat 10am–2pm; ⓦ gudrungudrun.com). Northwest, on the island of Eysturoy, and connected by bus #400 from Torshavn, is **Leirvik**, a fishing village well known for its engaging **Boat Museum** (harbourfront; May–Sept Mon–Sat 10am–5pm; contact Torshavn tourist office before visiting). Further northwest from Torshavn is **Viðoy**, a wild island boasting some of Europe's highest sea cliffs and a haven for birdlife. To reach the cliffs at **Cape Enniberg**, head to the village of Viðareiði (bus #400 from Torshavn to Klaksvik then bus #500; eight daily; 140kr) from where it's a tough, mountainous walk. The remotest of the Faroe Islands is spectacular **Mykines**, to the extreme west of the archipelago. Truly lost in time, it has some of the Faroes' best hiking. Get to Mykines via helicopter from Vágar Airport (ⓦ atlantic.fo; 145kr) or boat from nearby Sørvágur (summer only; 60kr; ⓦ ssl.fo).

ARRIVAL AND INFORMATION

By plane Vagar Airport, 30km west of Torshavn, is connected to the capital by bus (ten daily; 55min; 90kr). Atlantic Airways (ⓦ atlantic.fo) is the sole carrier operating flights to the Faroe Islands.
Destinations Copenhagen (2 daily; 1hr 20min).
By boat Ferries dock in the centre of Torshavn; passages are operated by Smyril Lines (ⓦ smyrilline.com).
Destinations Hirtshals (1–2 weekly; 38hr).
Tourist office í Gongini 9. Can advise on accommodation, activities and transport on all the islands (☏ 298 20 61 00 or 298 30 24 25, ⓦ visitfaroeislands.com). Pick up the excellent English-language leaflet "Walking The Faroe Islands". Due to extreme conditions, a guide for any hike on the Faroes is strongly recommended.

ACCOMMODATION, EATING AND DRINKING

Áarstova Gongin 1 ⓦ aarstova.fo. Brilliant, snug restaurant in one of Torshavn's oldest houses, specializing in Faroese cuisine. Get your salted fish and wind-dried lamb here. Mains from 265kr. Daily 5.30pm–midnight.
Café Natur Aarvegur 7. The liveliest joint in town. Renovated harbourside café-bar sporting the Faroes' best beer selection, with live music at weekends. Daily 11am–11.30pm.
Kerjalon Hostel Oyggjarvegur 45 ☏ 298 31 75 00, ⓦ hotelforoyar.com. The best budget accommodation in Torshavn, located next to the *Hotel Føroyar*. Dorm <u>175kr</u>

OLD TOWN, TALLINN

Estonia

HIGHLIGHTS

❶ Tallinn's Old Town Wander this beautifully preserved corner of the city. **See p.242**

❷ Lahemaa National Park Pristine wilderness on Estonia's north coast. **See p.249**

❸ Saaremaa A perfect island getaway with a beautiful castle and relaxing spa hotels. See p.250

❹ Pärnu Beach Enjoy a bracing dip in the Baltic or a mud bath in a local spa. **See p.251**

❺ Tartu Party the night away with the student population of Tartu. **See p.252**

HIGHLIGHTS ARE MARKED ON THE MAP ON P.239

ROUGH COSTS

Daily budget Basic €50, occasional treat €70

Drink Le Coq beer €2.50

Food Blood sausage and sauerkraut €5

Hostel/budget hotel €22/€45

Travel Bus: Tallinn–Saaremaa €15; Tartu–Tallinn €11

FACT FILE

Population 1.3 million

Language Estonian

Currency Euro (€)

Capital Tallinn

International phone code ☎ 372

Time zone GMT +2hr

9

Introduction

Visitors to Estonia encounter a mix of urbanity and wilderness, of the medieval and the contemporary, with crumbling castles and colourful design permeating urban landscapes. An efficient transport system makes it easy to get around, and the tech-savvy, dynamic residents welcome visitors with open arms. Friction between older generations of Russians and Estonians is a throwback to the Soviet era, while younger people mix freely, and those who get past the Estonians' natural reserve find them to be gregarious, uninhibited hosts.

Estonia's capital, **Tallinn**, has a magnificent medieval centre and lively nightlife, rivalled only by that of **Tartu**, an exuberant university town. **Pärnu**, a popular seaside resort, boasts fantastic sandy beaches. For inexpensive spa treatments, a fine castle and unspoilt countryside head for the island of **Saaremaa**, while **Lahemaa National Park**, outside Tallinn, offers a taste of pristine wilderness.

CHRONOLOGY

100s AD Tacitus refers to the Aestii people – the forebears of the Estonians.

1154 Estonia depicted on a map of the world for the first time.

1219 Danish conquer North Estonia, ushering in over a century of Danish rule.

1227 German crusaders invade the rest of Estonia.

1346 Danish territories in Estonia sold to the German Livonian Order.

1525 First book printed in the Estonian language.

1561 Livonian Order surrender their Estonian territory to Sweden.

1625 Sweden takes control over all Estonia.

1632 Estonia's first university opens in Tartu.

1721 Russia defeats Sweden in the Northern War and takes over Estonia.

1816 Serfdom is abolished in Estonia.

Late 1800s The spread of the Estonian language in schools is instrumental in increasing Estonian nationalism.

1918 Estonia states its claim to independence but is invaded by the Red Army, starting the Estonian War of Independence.

1920 The Russians are defeated, giving Estonia full independence.

1934 Authoritarian rule is established by Prime Minister Konstantin Pats.

1940 Soviets invade Estonia, ushering in Communist rule.

1944 After four years of Nazi German occupation, the Soviet occupation returns.

1988 The "Singing Revolution" begins with huge crowds gathering to sing patriotic songs.

1991 The fall of the Soviet Union leads to Estonian independence.

2004 Estonia joins NATO and the EU.

2007 Estonia is the first country to introduce internet voting for national elections.

2009 Estonia rides the global economic crisis better than her Baltic neighbours.

2011 The euro becomes Estonia's official currency.

ARRIVAL AND DEPARTURE

The compact and ultramodern **Tallinn Airport** (⊕tallinn-airport.ee) is served by several European capitals, including London, Dublin, Frankfurt, Barcelona and Stockholm. Ryanair, easyJet, airBaltic and national carrier Estonian Air (⊕estonian-air.ee) are among the main airlines. International **bus lines**, such as Ecolines (⊕ecolines.net) and Lux Express (⊕luxexpress.eu), connect Tallinn via Tartu or Pärnu to Russia (Moscow, St Petersburg), Latvia (Rīga), Lithuania (Vilnius, Kaunas) and Germany (Berlin), among others. The only international **rail services** from Estonia are the daily train from Tallinn to St Petersburg and the overnight train to Moscow – book seats in advance. Tallinn can also be reached by **ferry** from Helsinki, Finland, and from Stockholm, Sweden.

HIGHLIGHTS
1. Tallinn's Old Town
2. Lahemaa National Park
3. Saaremaa
4. Pärnu Beach
5. Tartu

GETTING AROUND

Bus tickets can be bought either from the bus station ticket office or directly from the driver. Online schedules are available at ⓦtpilet.ee; buy tickets in advance if you're travelling in the height of summer or at weekends.

The **rail network** is limited, but trains are as fast as buses and slightly cheaper. Check ⓦedel.ee for times and prices; purchase your ticket from the conductor.

The bigger cities have efficient **public transport** systems, and are well geared towards being explored by **bike**, as are the islands such as Saaremaa. Due to the scarcity of public transport on the islands, many locals hitchhike; the usual precautions apply.

ACCOMMODATION

Though cheaper than in Western Europe, accommodation in Estonia will still take a large chunk out of most budgets. Tallinn has a vibrant **youth hostel** scene, though outside of the capital, some **hostels** are just student dorms converted for the summer. Beds cost €16–22 per

person. Youth hostels aside, booking a **private room** is often the cheapest option (€23–27/person). This can be arranged through tourist offices or private agencies. There are also plain guesthouse or *pension* rooms for €25–35 per person including breakfast, though the cheapest of these are not always centrally located.

FOOD AND DRINK

Mainstays of **Estonian cuisine** include soup (*supp*), dark bread (*leib*) and herring (*heeringas*), culinary legacies of the country's largely peasant past. Typical national dishes are *verevorst* (blood sausage) and *karbonaad* (pork chop), both traditionally served with *mulgikapsad* (sauerkraut). Various kinds of smoked fish, particularly eel (*angerjas*), perch (*ahven*) and pike (*haug*), are popular too, as are **Russian dishes** such as *pelmeenid* (ravioli with meat or mushrooms). Both Tallinn and Tartu also boast an impressive choice of ethnic **restaurants**. Outside these two cities, **vegetarians** will find their choice to be more limited.

When eating out, it's cheaper to head for bars and cafés, many of which serve **snacks** like pancakes (*pannkoogid*) and salads (*salatid*). A modest meal in a café costs €6–8, while in a typical restaurant two courses and a drink comes to around €25. **Self-catering** poses no major problems, as supermarkets and fresh produce markets are plentiful.

ESTONIA ONLINE

ⓦ**visitestonia.com** Extensive tourist board site covering all things Estonian.
ⓦ**baltictimes.com** English-language weekly newspaper.
ⓦ**inyourpocket.com** Excellent guide covering Tallinn, Tartu and Pärnu.

9

ESTONIAN

	ESTONIAN	PRONUNCIATION
Yes	*Jah*	Yah
No	*Ei*	Ey
Please	*Palun*	Palun
Thank you	*Aitäh/tänan*	Ayteh, tanan
Hello/Good day	*Tere*	Tere
Goodbye	*Head aega*	Heyad ayga
Excuse me	*Vabandage*	Vabandage
Where?	*Kus?*	Kus?
Student ticket	*Õpilase pilet*	Ypilahse pilet
Toilet	*Tualett*	Tualet
I'd like	*Ma sooviksin*	Mah sawviksin
I don't eat meat	*Ma ei söö*	Mah ay serr
The bill, please	*Palun arve*	Pahlun ahrrve
Good/Bad	*Hea/Halb*	Heya/Holb
Near/Far	*Lähedal/Kaugel*	Lahedal/Cowgal
Cheap/Expensive	*Odav/Kallis*	Odav/Kallis
Open/Closed	*Avatud/Suletud*	Avatud/Suletud
Today	*Täna*	Tana
Yesterday	*Eile*	Eyle
Tomorrow	*Homme*	Homme
How much is…?	*Kui palju maksab…?*	Kuy palyo maksab…?
What time is it?	*Mis kell praegu on?*	Mis kell prego on?
I don't understand	*Ma ei saa aru*	May saaru
Do you speak English?	*Kas te räägite inglise keelt?*	Kas te raagite inglise kelt?
One	*Üks*	Uks
Two	*Kaks*	Koks
Three	*Kolm*	Kolm
Four	*Neli*	Neli
Five	*Viis*	Vees
Six	*Kuus*	Koos
Seven	*Seitse*	Seytse
Eight	*Kaheksa*	Koheksa
Nine	*Üheksa*	Ooheksa
Ten	*Kümme*	Koome

Restaurant opening hours tend to be between noon and midnight; cafés are open from 9am to 10pm or later.

DRINK

Estonians are enthusiastic drinkers, with **beer** (*õlu*) being the most popular tipple. The principal local brands are Saku and A. Le Coq, both of which are lager-style brews, although both companies also produce stronger, dark beers – the most potent being found on the islands (*Saaremaa õlu* is the best known). In bars a lot of people favour **vodka** (*viin*) with mixers while local alcoholic specialities include **hõõgvein** (mulled wine) and **Vana Tallinn**, a pungent dark liqueur which some suicidal souls mix with

vodka. **Pubs and bars** – most of which imitate global models – are taking over, especially in Tallinn. If you're not boozing, head for a *kohvik* (café); **coffee** (*kohvi*) is usually of the filter variety, and **tea** (*teed*) is served without milk (*piima*) or sugar (*suhkur*) – ask for both if necessary. Bars are usually open from noon until 2 or 4am on weekends.

CULTURE AND ETIQUETTE

Estonians tend to be reserved when you first meet them, though if you are lucky enough to be invited to a local home, you will see their warm and generous side. Unused to loud displays of emotion, they are scandalized by the loutish behaviour of foreign stag parties, although they do enjoy sociable drinking. A ten percent **tip** is sufficient in restaurants to reward good service; otherwise just round up the bill.

SPORTS AND OUTDOOR ACTIVITIES

Football and **basketball** are the national sports; for the former, go to the A. Le Coq Arena (Asula 4c; ☎627 9940), whereas Tallinn's Saku Suurhall (Paldiski mnt 104b; ☎665 9534) is the best place to see a basketball game. In the summertime, Estonia becomes a haven for **watersports**: windsurfing, kayaking, canoeing or simply hitting the beach. **Hiking**, **biking** and **horseriding** are popular both on the Estonian mainland and on the islands off its coast, such as Saaremaa and Hiiumaa. Almost twenty percent of Estonia is protected land, divided between four **national parks** and numerous **nature reserves**, which are home to many species of wild animals and birds. National parks are best visited between May and September; RMK (ⓦrmk.ee) manages the protected areas and campsites.

COMMUNICATIONS

Post offices (*postkontor*) are open Monday to Friday 8am to 6pm and Saturday 9am to 3pm. Most **public phones** take phonecards (available at kiosks and post offices) for local and long-distance calls. Alternatively, you can either purchase a local starter kit (which includes a SIM card and free talk time) for your mobile phone, or use a mobile phone from another European country, since it is relatively inexpensive; consult your service provider about roaming charges. **Internet cafés** have become scarce due to the proliferation of free wi-fi hotspots; free wi-fi is offered by most cafés and restaurants, and by all accommodation options in this chapter.

EMERGENCIES

Theft and street crime are at relatively low levels. The **police** (*politsei*) are mostly

---

EMERGENCY NUMBERS

Police ☎110; Fire & ambulance ☎112.

---

young and some speak English. **Emergency health care** is free and, in Tallinn at least, emergency operators speak English.

INFORMATION

Tourist offices (ⓦvisitestonia.com) can be useful for booking B&Bs and hotel rooms, as well as good-quality free **maps**; most bookshops also have good map sections. The *In Your Pocket* guides (ⓦinyourpocket.com) are excellent listings guides, available from tourist offices and kiosks for €2.50 or can be downloaded free from their website.

MONEY AND BANKS

Currency is the euro (€), which is divided into 100 cents. Notes come as 5, 10, 20, 50, 100, 200 and 500 euros, and **coins** as 1, 2, 5, 10, 20 and 50 cents, and 1 and 2 euros. Bank (*pank*) opening hours are Monday to Friday 9am to 4pm, with most also open on Saturday from 9am to 2pm. **ATMs** are widely available. **Credit cards** can be used in most hotels, restaurants and stores, but outside urban areas cash is preferred.

OPENING HOURS AND HOLIDAYS

Most **shops** open Monday to Friday 10am to 6pm and Saturday 10am to 3pm, but many larger ones stay open later and are also open on Sundays. **Public holidays**, when most shops and all banks are closed, are: January 1, February 24, Good Friday, Easter Monday, May 1, June 23 and 24, August 20, December 25 and 26.

Tallinn

TALLINN, Estonia's compact, buzzing capital, with its enchanting heart surrounded by medieval walls, has been

9

shaped by nearly a millennium of outside influence. While the fairy-tale Old Town has become the ideal weekend getaway for city-break tourists, the Estonian capital's growing importance as a regional centre for business, arts and technology has provided it with a go-ahead contemporary feel coupled with bags of hedonistic energy.

WHAT TO SEE AND DO

The heart of Tallinn is the **Old Town**, still largely enclosed by the city's medieval walls. At its centre is the **Raekoja plats**, the historic marketplace, above which looms **Toompea**, the hilltop stronghold of the German knights who controlled the city during the Middle Ages. East of the city centre there are several places worth a visit, such as **Kadriorg Park**, a peaceful wooded area with a cluster of historic buildings, the forested island of **Aegna** and the **Lauluväljak** amphitheatre.

Raekoja plats

Raekoja plats, the cobbled market square at the heart of the Old Town, is as old as the city itself. On its southern side stands the fifteenth-century **Town Hall** (Raekoda), boasting elegant Gothic arches at ground level, and a delicate steeple at its northern end. Near the summit of the steeple, **Vana Toomas**, a sixteenth-century weather vane depicting a medieval town guard, is Tallinn's city emblem. The well-labelled and informative **museum** inside the cellar hall (May–Sept Mon–Sat 10am–4pm; rest of the year closed weekends; €4) depicts Tallinn town life through the ages, and there is a good view from the belfry. For an even better view of the town square,

climb the spiral staircase of the **Town Hall Tower** (Raekoja Torn; May–Sept daily 11am–6pm; €3).

Church of the Holy Ghost and St Nicholas's Church

The fourteenth-century **Church of the Holy Ghost** (Pühä Vaimu kirik; Mon–Sat: May–Sept 9am–5pm; rest of the year 10am–3pm; €1) on Pühavaimu is the city's oldest church, a small Gothic building with stuccoed limestone walls, stepped gables, carved wooden interior, a tall, verdigris-coated spire and an ornate clock from 1680 – the oldest in Tallinn.

Contrasting sharply is the late Gothic **St Nicholas's Church** (Niguliste kirik; Mon–Wed & Sun 10am–5pm; museum €3.50), southwest of Raekoja plats. Dating back to the 1820s and rebuilt after being mostly destroyed in a 1944 Soviet air raid, it now serves as a museum of church art, including medieval burial stones and the haunting *Danse Macabre* ("Dance With Death") by Bernt Notke. It also hosts free organ recitals (Sat & Sun 4pm).

Toompea and the Aleksander Nevsky Cathedral

Toompea is the hill where the Danes built their fortress after conquering what is now Tallinn in 1219. According to legend, it is also the grave of **Kalev**, the mythical ancestor of the Estonians. Approach through the sturdy gate tower – built by the Teutonic Knights to contain the Old Town's inhabitants in times of unrest – at the foot of Pikk jalg. This is the cobbled continuation of Pikk, the Old Town's main street, that climbs up to Lossi plats, dominated by the impressively cake-like **Aleksander Nevsky Cathedral** (daily 8am–7pm). Bristling with domes, this structure was built at the end of the nineteenth century for the city's Orthodox population – an enduring reminder of the two centuries Tallinn spent under tsarist rule.

At the head of Lossi plats, the pink **Toompea Castle** stands on the original Danish fortification site. Today's castle is the descendant of a stone fortress built by

---

THE TALLINN CARD

To do a lot of sightseeing in a short space of time, it can be really worth your while to pick up a **Tallinn Card** (Ⓦtallinncard.ee; €24/32/40 for 24/48/72hr), which gives you unlimited free rides on public transport as well as free entry to a plethora of attractions and discounts in shops and restaurants. Check website for details.

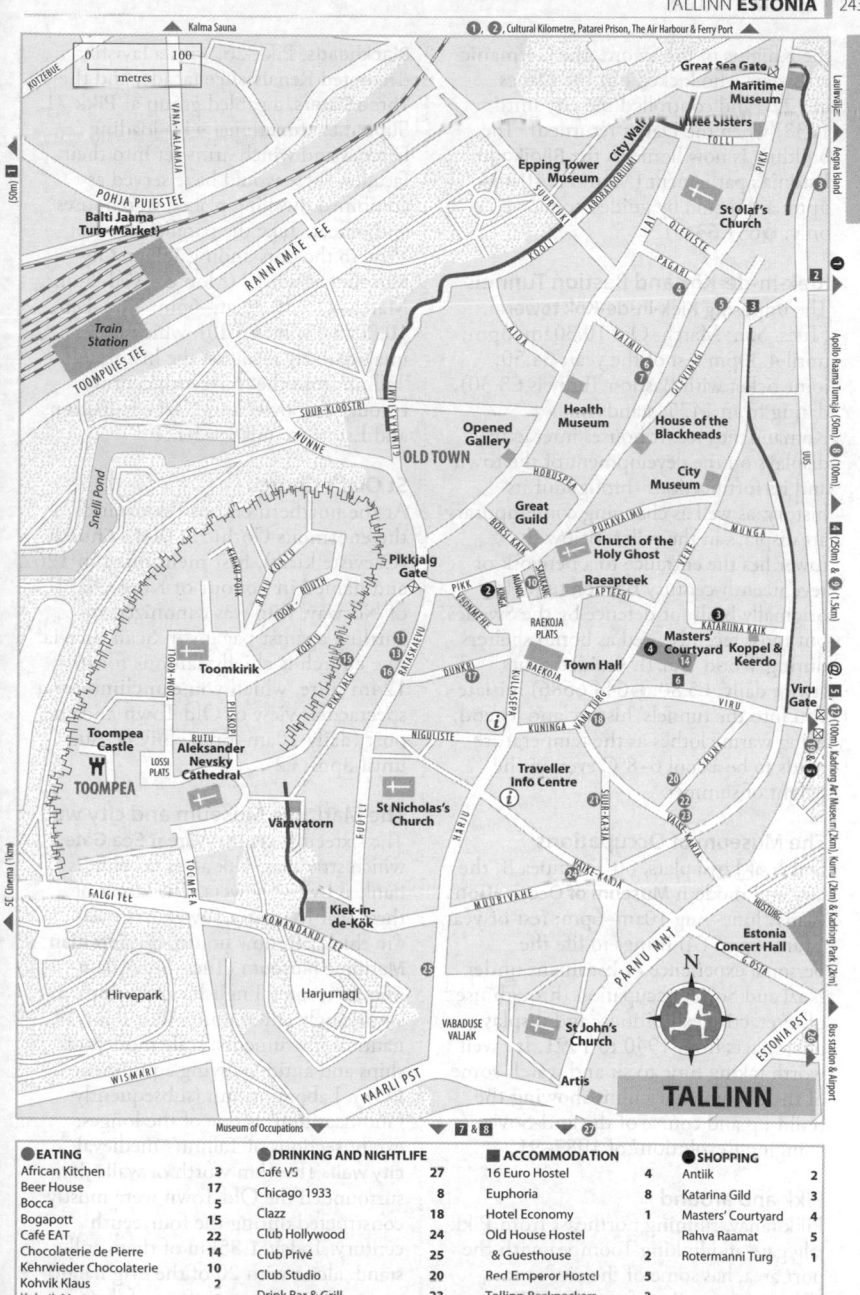

Great Sea Gate
Maritime Museum
Three Sisters
City Wall
Epping Tower Museum
St Olaf's Church
Balti Jaama Turg (Market)
POHJA PUIESTEE
Train Station
TOOMPUIES TEE
RANNAMÄE TEE
SUUR-KLOOSTRI
NUNNE
Opened Gallery
OLD TOWN
Health Museum
House of the Blackheads
City Museum
Great Guild
Church of the Holy Ghost
Pikkjalg Gate
Raeapteek
Toomkirik
RAEKOJA PLATS
Masters' Courtyard
Koppel & Keerdo
Town Hall
Viru Gate
Toompea Castle
LOSSI PLATS
TOOMPEA
Aleksander Nevsky Cathedral
Väravatorn
St Nicholas's Church
Traveller Info Centre
Kiek-in-de-Kök
Hirvepark
Harjumägi
Estonia Concert Hall
VABADUSE VALJAK
St John's Church
Artis
TALLINN
N
Snelli Pond

Museum of Occupations   7 & 8   27

● EATING		● DRINKING AND NIGHTLIFE		■ ACCOMMODATION		● SHOPPING	
African Kitchen	3	Café VS	27	16 Euro Hostel	4	Antiik	2
Beer House	17	Chicago 1933	8	Euphoria	8	Katarina Gild	3
Bocca	5	Clazz	18	Hotel Economy	1	Masters' Courtyard	4
Bogapott	15	Club Hollywood	24	Old House Hostel		Rahva Raamat	5
Café EAT	22	Club Privé	25	& Guesthouse	2	Rotermanni Turg	1
Chocolaterie de Pierre	14	Club Studio	20	Red Emperor Hostel	3		
Kehrwieder Chocolaterie	10	Drink Bar & Grill	23	Tallinn Backpackers	3		
Kohvik Klaus	2	Hell Hunt	4	Tallinn			
Kohvik Moon	1	Kodu Baar	6	Boutique Hostel	6		
Lido	26	Rock Café	9	The Monk's Bunk	7		
More	19	St Patrick's	21				
Õ	12	Von Krahli Bar	13				
Texas Honky Tonk & Cantina	7						
Vanaema Juures	16						
Von Krahli Aed	11						

9

the Knights of the Sword, the Germanic crusaders who kicked out the Danes in 1227 and controlled the city until 1238 (when the Danes returned). The building is now home to the **Riigikogu**, Estonia's parliament (Mon–Fri 10am–4pm; admission by guided tour only; ☎631 6345).

Kiek-in-de-Kök and Bastion Tunnels

The imposing **Kiek-in-de-Kök tower** (Tues–Sun: March–Oct 10.30am–6pm; until 4.30pm rest of the year; €4.50; joint ticket with Bastion Tunnels €8.30), dating from 1475, stands on Komandandi tee. It houses interactive displays on the development of the town and its fortifications throughout its history, as well as changing contemporary art displays in the cellar. Below the tower lies the entrance to a network of seventeenth-century **bastion tunnels**, originally built for defence by the Swedes but most recently used as bomb shelters during World War II. Guided tours (twice daily; €5.80; ☎644 6686) initiate you into the tunnels' history and legend; bring warm clothes as the temperature tends to be a cool 6–8°C even in the height of summer.

The Museum of Occupations

South of Lossi plats, on Toompea 8, the airy and modern **Museum of Occupations** (daily: June–Aug 10am–6pm; rest of year 11am–6pm; €4) brings to life the personal experience of Estonians under Nazi and Soviet occupation through use of interactive exhibitions, and displays of artefacts from 1940 to 1991. It's well worth taking time to sit and watch some of the documentary films showing the build-up and course of the anti-Soviet "Singing Revolution" of 1987–91.

Pikk and around

Pikk tänav, running northeast from Pikk jalg gate and linking Toompea with the port area, has some of the city's most elaborate examples of **merchants' houses** from the Hanseatic period, including the **Great Guild** at Pikk 17, headquarters of the German merchants who controlled the city's wealth; the **House of the Blackheads**, Pikk 26, with a lavishly decorated Renaissance facade; and the **Three Sisters**, a gabled group at Pikk 71. Supremely functional with loading hatches and winch-arms set into their facades, these would have served as combined dwelling places, warehouses and offices. Take the parallel street of Vene to the outstanding **Tallinn City Museum** at no. 17 (Mon & Wed–Sun: March–Oct 10.30am–6pm; Nov–Feb 10.30am–5pm; €3.20), which imaginatively recounts the history of Tallinn from the thirteenth century through to Soviet and Nazi occupations and Estonian independence.

St Olaf's Church

At the northern end of Pikk stands the enormous Gothic **St Olaf's Church** (Oleviste kirik), first mentioned in 1267 and named in honour of King Olaf II of Norway, who was canonized for battling against pagans in Scandinavia. The church is chiefly famous for its 124m spire, which you can climb for a spectacular view of Old Town and the port (daily 10am–6pm, July & Aug until 8pm; €2).

The Maritime Museum and city wall

The sixteenth-century **Great Sea Gate**, which straddles Pikk at its far end, is flanked by two towers. The larger of these, Fat Margaret Tower, has walls 4m thick and now houses the **Estonian Maritime Museum** (Tues–Sun 10am–6pm; €4; some English captioning), a surprisingly entertaining four floors of nautical instruments, scale models of ships and antique diving equipment. Down Laboratoriumi (subsequently Gümnaasiumi) is one of the longest extant sections of Tallinn's medieval **city wall**. The 4km worth of walls that surrounded the Old Town were mostly constructed during the fourteenth century. Today, 1.85km of them still stand, along with 20 of the original 46 towers. You can enter three of the oldest towers, Nunne, Kuldjala and Sauna, from Gümnaasiumi 3 (Mon–Wed & Fri noon–6pm, Sat & Sun 11am–4pm; €1.50).

The Cultural Kilometre and Patarei Prison

Just north of the Old Town, the Cultural Kilometre (Kultuurikilomeeter) is a footpath that runs through an intriguing stretch of post-Soviet, post-industrial Tallinn. It begins beside the Kultuurikattel ("The Culture Boiler"), a former power station now being converted into an arts venue. The power station's iconic chimney is where Russian film director Andrei Tarkovsky shot key seasons of existential classic, *Stalker*. From here the path heads west past a small fishing harbour, and the Estonian Design House at Kalasadama 8, where young designers display and sell their wares. The path continues past the atmospheric old houses of the Kalamaja district before arriving at Patarei Prison Museum (May–Sept daily noon–7pm; €2; ℗patarei.org), a nineteenth-century fortress that was turned into a jail in 1920. Abandoned in 2004, it remains in pretty much the same state it was left in, providing an eerie, unsettling and unforgettable experience for visitors.

The Air Harbour

The Cultural Kilometre terminates outside Estonia's most astounding museum attraction, the Air Harbour (May–Sept daily 10am–7pm; Oct–April Tues–Sun 11am–7pm; €8; ℗lennusadam .eu), a huge hangar built by the Russians in World War I to house a fleet of sea planes. A masterpiece of modern construction, this cavernous concrete space was reopened in 2012 as an extension of the Maritime Museum (see opposite). A system of raised walkways takes you past the exhibits – including fishing boats, mines, a replica World War I biplane and naval guns. The *pièce de résistance* is the Lembit submarine, built for the Estonian navy in Barrow-in-Furness in the 1930s. Outside, ice-breaker *Suur Tõll* and several other ships are moored.

Kadriorg Park

Kadriorg Park, a heavily wooded area 2km east of the Old Town along Narva maantee, was laid out according to the instructions of Russian tsar Peter the Great. The main entrance to the park is at the junction of Weizenbergi tänav and J. Poska (tram #1 or #3 from Viru väljak). Weizenbergi cuts through the park, running straight past **Kadriorg Palace**, a Baroque residence designed by the Italian architect Niccolò Michetti, which Peter had built for his wife Catherine. The palace houses the **Kadriorg Art Museum** (May–Sept Tues & Thurs–Sun 10am–5pm, Wed 10am–8pm; Oct–April closed Tues; €4.80), with a fine collection of Dutch and Russian paintings.

KUMU

Marking the eastern end of Kadriorg Park is the immense, futuristic-looking **KUMU** (May–Sept Tues & Thurs–Sun 11am–6pm, Wed 11am–8pm; Oct–April closed Tues; €5.50; ℗ekm.ee), a must-see for anyone interested in Estonian art in the twentieth century. It's certainly a wide-ranging collection: surrealism, pop art and abstraction flourished during the Soviet period, despite official hostility to such modernist excesses.

Aegna Island

An hour's ride on the boat (May–Sept Mon & Wed–Fri 3 daily, Sat & Sun 4 daily; double-check timetable with tourist office) from **Pirita harbour** (bus #1, #34 or #38 from the underground stop at the

---

ESTONIA'S SONG FESTIVAL

The **Lauluväljak** at Narva maantee 95 (℗lauluvaljak.ee), just to the northeast of Kadriorg Park, is a vast amphitheatre which is the venue for Estonia's **Song Festivals**. These gatherings, featuring a choir 25,000-strong, are held every five years, and have been an important form of national expression since the first all-Estonia Song Festival held in Tartu in 1869. The grounds were filled to their 45,000-person capacity during summer 1988 when people assembled here spontaneously to sing patriotic songs in protest against Soviet rule, in what became known as the "**Singing Revolution**". The next Song Festival is in July 2014.

9

Viru Centre; €7.50 return), tiny peaceful **Aegna** is an excellent day-trip destination. Its forest-covered interior and clean beaches attract locals who camp here in the summer.

ARRIVAL AND DEPARTURE

By plane The Lennart Meri Tallinn Airport (*lennu jaam*) is 3km southeast of the city centre and linked to the Viru shopping mall by bus #2 (every 20min, 6am–midnight; €1.60), a 5min walk from the Old Town's Viru Gate.

By train Tallinn's train station (*balti jaam*) is at Toompuiestee 35, just northwest of the Old Town, a 10min walk to the Town Square. There are ATMs by the front doors.

Destinations Moscow (1 daily at 5.50pm; 15hr); Pärnu (2 daily; 2hr 40min); St Petersburg (1 daily at 7.40am; 6hr 40min); Tartu (8 daily; 2hr 30min).

By bus The city's bus terminal (*autobussi jaam*) is at Lastekodu 46, 2km southeast of the centre; there is an ATM and luggage storage. Trams #2 and #4 run from nearby Tartu mnt. to Viru väljak at the eastern entrance to the Old Town; alternatively, take any bus heading west along Juhkentali.

Destinations Kuressaare (up to 16 daily; 4hr 30min); Pärnu (every 30min, 6.20am–9pm; 2hr); Riga (11 daily; 4hr 30min); St Petersburg (6–8 daily; 7–9hr); Tartu (every 30min, 5.45am–11pm; 2hr 30min); Vilnius (2 daily; 9–10hr).

By boat Arriving by sea, the passenger port (*reisisadam*) is just northeast of the centre at Sadama 25. For updated schedules see ⓦ portoftallinn.com.

Destinations Helsinki (10–15 daily; 1hr 30min–3hr 30min); Stockholm (1 daily at 6pm; 16hr).

INFORMATION

Tourist information Tourist office at ullasseppa 4 (May–Sept Mon–Fri 9am–7pm, Sat & Sun 10am–5pm; Oct–April Mon–Fri 9am–5pm, Sat 10am–3pm; ☎645 7777, ⓦ tourism.tallinn.ee). You can also buy the Tallinn Card here (see box, p.242).

GETTING AROUND

By public transport Tallinn has an extensive tram, bus and trolleybus network. Locals travel for free; non-Tallinners must buy tickets (*talongid*) from the driver (€1.60); or buy an e-ticket from a post office or news kiosk (€2 deposit necessary), topping it up according to what you think you will need – single journeys cost €1.10 (24/72hr €3/€5).

ACCOMMODATION

Demand for budget accommodation still outstrips supply in summer, so book in advance. You can find central and excellent-value private rooms at Mere 4 with Bed & Breakfast Rasastra (Mon–Sat 9.30am–6pm, Sun 9.30am–5pm; ☎661 6291, ⓦ bedbreakfast.ee), an agency offering accommodation in family homes throughout the Baltics, as well as private apartments for longer stays.

16 Euro Hostel Roseni 9 ☎501 3046, ⓦ 16eur.ee. Just outside the Old Town walls, this tastefully decorated cheapie haven offers free use of sauna and swimming pool (9–11am) to complement your stay in one of its en-suite rooms or dorms. Dorm €13, double €32

Euphoria Roosikrantsi 4 ☎5837 3602, ⓦ euphoria.ee. A four-storey hostel with a great communal atmosphere, impromptu jam sessions, clean dorms and a couple of rooms, all with shared facilities. You can smoke a hookah and even paint your own mural in the large common room. Dorm €13, double €38

Hotel Economy Kopli 2c ☎667 8300, ⓦ economyhotel .ee. Refurbished 1920s hotel offering modern and comfortable rooms overlooking the train station area on the outskirts of the Old Town. Breakfast is included, as is wi-fi in the lobby. Double €65

Old House Hostel & Guesthouse Uus 26 ☎641 1281, ⓦ oldhouse.ee. Renovated, quiet Old Town house with attractive dorms and a handful of cosy twin rooms with shared bath, guest lounge and kitchen. Wi-fi available. Dorm €15, double €29

Red Emperor Hostel Aia 10 ☎608 7387, ⓦ redemperorhostel.com. Ideally located on the eastern

---

TALLINN TOURS

Tallinn can be explored in many different ways. Here are some of the more innovative tours:

City Bike Tours Uus 33 ☎511 1819, ⓦ citybike.ee. Tours of the Old Town and beyond run by young, energetic guides, as well as a "Legends and Secret Tunnels" afternoon walking tour. Groups can try the weird and wonderful "Conference Bike". Guided and self-guided tours of Lahemaa National Park available.

EstAdventures ☎5308 8373, ⓦ estadventures.ee. Small-group tours of Tallinn ("Legends of Tallinn"

comes particularly recommended), as well as day-trips to Lahemaa National Park.

Tallinn Traveller Info Info Tent opposite the tourist office June–Aug (daily 10am–10pm); otherwise call ☎5837 4800 (ⓦ traveller.ee). The excellent and inexpensive "Chill-out Tour", "Beautiful Bike Tour" or the "Funky Bike Tour" present Tallinn and its environs in a novel way, led by young, knowledgeable, multilingual student guides.

fringes of the Old Town, *Red Emperor* offers a choice of brightly decorated rooms ranging from quads to 10-bed dorms. Additional facilities include free wi-fi, kitchen and a next-door bar with pool tables. Dorm €10

Tallinn Backpackers Olevimägi 11 ☎644 0298, ⊚tallinnbackpackers.com. This party spot encourages bonding between fellow international travellers, be it through video screenings, communal dinners or drink-your-own-height-in-beer-cans on "Wizard Wednesdays". Don't count on getting much sleep! Dorm €16

Tallinn Boutique Hostel Viru 5 ☎644 6050, ⊚tallinnboutiquehostel.com. The calmer sister hostel to *Tallinn Backpackers* with quiet singles, doubles and triples, as well as access to all *Tallinn Backpackers'* facilities and an invitation to join their raucous parties, but with the option of actually sleeping afterwards. Double €32

★ **The Monk's Bunk** Tatari 1 ☎636 3924, ⊚themonks bunk.com. Relatively new hostel that's sociable without being a stag party magnet, and with staff who go out of their way to keep guests entertained with a variety of day-trips, tours and pub crawls. Spacious dorms have comfortable beds and there is an on-site bar and cinema room. Dorm €10

EATING

Self-caterers can try the Rimi supermarket at Aia 7 or else buy some cheap fresh produce at the Balti Jaama Turg (train station market) behind the train station.

CAFÉS, CHEAP EATS AND SNACKS

Bogapott Pikk jalg 9. This tiny family-run Tallinn institution, surrounded by part of the medieval wall, serves delicious sandwiches, coffee and pastries while you look around the art shop and ceramics studio. Coffee €1.60. Mon–Sat 10am–6pm, Sun 10am–5pm.

Café EAT Sauna 2. Popular with students, this basement establishment offers different kinds of *pelmeenid* (dumplings) and doughnuts, sold by weight (€0.65/100g). Cheap and very filling. Pint of cider €2.50. Mon–Sat 11am–9pm.

Chocolaterie de Pierre Vene 6. Quaint café with vintage furnishings and a cobbled-alley terrace. Pierre's handmade chocolates are the stars of the show, although all manner of other sweets are on offer too. Carrot cake €3.50. Daily 9am–11pm.

Kehrwieder Chocolaterie Saiakang 1. Dark, warren-like cellar café filled with quirky old furniture, famous for its great handmade chocolates and gourmet coffees, though the latter don't come cheap. Coffee €2.40. Mon–Thurs & Sun 8am–11pm, Fri & Sat 8am–1am.

Kohvik Klaus Kalasadama 8. In the same building as the Estonian Design House and perfectly situated for an assault on the Cultural Kilometre (see p.245), *Klaus* is a chic and cheery place in which to indulge in salads, pastas and

main meals, as well as kick-start espressos and a full range of alcohol. Mon 9am–10pm, Tues–Fri 9am–11pm, Sat 10am–11pm, Sun 10am–10pm.

Lido Solaris shopping centre, Estonia pst 9. It's a fast-food chain, captain, but not as we know it: traditional dishes from Estonia and all over the Baltic, some of which (potato pancakes, grilled meats) are cooked in front of you as you pass along the endless canteen counter. Scale models of Estonian buildings fill the dining space, staff in national costume man the tills. Fill your plate for under €4. Daily 9am–9pm.

More Viru Keskus shopping centre. Located on the top floor of the Rahvu Raamat bookshop in the Viru Centre, *More* represents the aristocratic end of the order-at-the-counter market, with Tallinn's beautiful things queuing up to grab an equally beautiful range of soups, pastries and cakes. The coffees and leaf teas are also top notch. Quiche €4.10. Daily 9am–9pm.

RESTAURANTS

African Kitchen Uus 34. Wide selection of peanut, coconut and rice dishes, some spicy and many vegetarian, prepared by a Nigerian chef and served in a jungle-themed lounge. Tasty smoothies (€3.70) and mains (€6.50–14). Daily noon–midnight.

Beer House Dunkri 5. Vast, popular beer cellar which brews its own ales and serves up generous portions of imaginative meat dishes, such as elk and wild boar, as well as good, solid sausage-and-mash combos. Mains €8–12. Live music nightly. Daily 11am–midnight.

★ **Bocca** Olevimägi 9. A chic cocktail spot in the evenings, this slick Italian restaurant with superbly executed dishes won't blow a hole in your budget if you stick to the soups and pastas. Try the linguine with grilled prawns and scallops (€12). Mon–Thurs noon–11pm, Sat noon–midnight, Sun 1–10pm.

Kohvik Moon Vorgu 3. Just outside the Old Town near the start of the Cultural Kilometre, *Moon* ("Poppy") serves up Baltic-Mediterranean cuisine in contemporary

---

★ **TREAT YOURSELF**

Ö Mere pst. 6e ☎661 6150. The decor – sedate charcoal and cream – is simplicity itself, so your attention is directed at the exquisitely presented, modern Estonian dishes made from locally sourced, seasonal ingredients. Try the eel poached in apple wine (€13), the venison steak in wild mushroom sauce (€19), and finish off with chocolate fondue with home-made blueberry ice cream (€8). Mon–Thurs noon–11pm, Fri & Sat noon–midnight, Sun 1–10pm.

9

surroundings. Borshch €3, duck breast €10. Dishes of the day are a steal at €5. Mon–Sat noon–11pm, Sun 1–9pm.

Texas Honky Tonk & Cantina Pikk 43. This kitschy, lively Texan saloon attracts a quota of homesick Americans and anyone else hungry for ribs, burritos, tacos and burgers. A good place to sink a beer on the courtyard terrace. Mains €8–10. Mon–Thurs & Sun noon–midnight, Fri & Sat noon–1am.

Vanaema Juures Rataskaevu 10/12. A Tallinn favourite for many years, "Grandma's Place" serves no-nonsense Estonian home food in a cosy cellar setting. Try Grandma's elk roast, the meatballs or the lamb in blue cheese sauce. Mains €6–10. Mon–Sat noon–10pm, Sun noon–6pm.

Von Krahli Aed Rataskaevu 8. The self-styled "Embassy of Pure Food" delivers delicious and imaginative fusion dishes, including many vegetarian options, such as pasta with tofu (€4) and pumpkin risotto (€6.50). Mon–Sat noon–midnight, Sun noon–6pm.

DRINKING, NIGHTLIFE AND ENTERTAINMENT

Most of Tallinn's popular clubs cater for a mainstream crowd. More underground, cutting-edge dance music events change location frequently and are advertised by flyers, or try asking around in the city's hipper bars; expect to pay €4–10 admission.

BARS

Café VS Pärnu mnt. 28. By day, this is a cool café with purple/silver industrial decor and, randomly enough, great Indian food; start out with a masala omelette for €4.80. By night, it morphs into a chilled-out DJ venue, though if you order the chicken biriyani to go with your late-night beats, be sure to bring a friend – portions are generous (€7). Mon–Thurs & Sun noon–midnight, Fri & Sat noon–2am.

Drink Bar & Grill Väike-Karja 8. The patrons at this lively bar are a mixed bunch: locals, backpackers and expats – but all are united in their love of unusual beers, organic ciders and the bar's own house brew. Daily noon–midnight.

Hell Hunt Pikk 39. Lively pub packed with expats and locals most nights. It's spacious, friendly and serves its own excellent light and dark Hunt beer. Daily noon–2am.

★ **Kodu Baar** Vaimu 1. This artsy-student-local bar hidden round a corner from the well-trodden thoroughfares of touristy Tallinn offers a nice mixture of grungy minimalism and domestic comfort, with distressed walls and dim lighting in one room; sofas, standard lamps and bookshelves in another. There's a good range of beer in bottles and Czech Kozel on draught. Occasional gigs and DJ evenings add to the fun. Daily 4pm–4am.

St Patrick's Suur-Karja 8. The pick of Tallinn's Irish pubs, set in a beautifully restored medieval house and popular with expats, tourists and locals alike. Your fourth Saku Originaal beer comes free. Mon–Thurs & Sun 11am–2am, Fri & Sat 11am–4am.

Von Krahli Bar Rataskaevu 10/12. "Krahl" to regulars, this large hip hangout is always packed with a mix of local students and bohemian types. Frequent live music – from alternative to reggae to hip-hop. Good, cheap food: huge daily specials €4. Mon–Thurs & Sun noon–1am, Fri & Sat noon–3am.

CLUBS

Club Hollywood Vana-Posti 8 ⊛ clubhollywood.ee. Large Old Town dance club playing techno, R'n'B and hip-hop. Very popular with a younger crowd as well as tourists. Cover €3–8; free entry for women on Wed. Wed–Sat 11pm–5am.

Club Privé Harju 6 ⊛ clubprive.ee. Style-conscious temple to cutting-edge dance culture, often attracting big-name DJs; check the schedule. Over 20s only. Entry €7–14. Thurs 11pm–5am, Fri & Sat midnight–6am.

Club Studio Sauna 1 ⊛ clubstudio.ee. A regular menu of house and cutting-edge dance music styles, plus frequent appearances from big-name visiting DJs, make *Studio* the place to be for the knowledgeable, party-hungry clubber. Entry €7–10. Wed–Sat 11pm–5am.

SAUNAS

The first thing to do when you go to an Estonian **sauna** is get completely naked, though in mixed saunas wrapping a towel around you is at your own discretion. Once you get used to the heat, scoop some water onto the hot stones; it evaporates instantaneously, raising the temperature. Once everyone is sweating profusely, some might gently swat themselves or their friends with birch branches; this increases circulation and rids the body of toxins. Don't overdo it – ten minutes should be long enough, but get out immediately if you start to feel dizzy. Locals normally follow up with a plunge into a cold lake, although a cold shower will suffice. A good place to start is **Kalma** at Vana-Kalamaja 9a (Mon–Fri 11am–10pm, Sat & Sun 10am–11pm; men €8–9, women €6.50–8; ☎ 627 1811, ⊛ kalmasaun.ee) – Tallinn's oldest public bath (built in 1928), containing private saunas for rent as well as men's and women's general baths (complete with swimming pool).

LIVE MUSIC

Chicago 1933 Aia 3 ⓦchicago.ee. The name says it all: this swinging joint successfully re-creates the ambience of the 1930s in the Windy City, its patrons sliding into dark wood booths to enjoy some excellent live blues. Entry €14. Mon–Thurs & Sun noon–midnight, Fri & Sat noon–3am.

Clazz Vana Turg 2 ⓦclazz.ee. One of the most popular venues in the Old Town for nightly live music – from blues to jazz to Latin. Shorter hours in winter. Fri & Sat 11am–4am, rest of week until 2am.

Rock Café Tartu mnt 80d, 3rd floor ⓦrockcafe.ee. Two-storey rock club in a warehouse near the bus station, with a superb sound system and excellent live acts – largely rock, but also occasional blues. Check the schedule before heading out. Entry €4–15. Open gig nights only (usually Fri & Sat) 10pm–3am.

CINEMAS

5D Cinema Endla 45 (Kristiine Centre) ⓦ5dcinema.ee. This state-of-the-art cinema drags you right into the movie with its combination of moving seats, 3-D imagery, scents and even water misting. Intense. Entry €5–6.50.

Artis Estonia pst. 9 ⓦkino.ee. Shows a full range of independent films. Entry €4.20–6.

SHOPPING

Antiik Kinga 5. Come here for all your collectable Soviet kitsch, including a number of Lenin busts. Mon–Sat 10am–6pm, Sun 10am–3pm.

Katarina Gild Katarina käik. Alleyway just off Vene crammed with high-quality, highly original craft shops selling ceramics, stained glass, linen and more. Mon–Sat 11am–6pm.

Masters' Courtyard Vene 6. Courtyard housing some of Tallinn's most original art and craft shops, and galleries, where you can find special ceramics, glassware, woodworks and candles for a very reasonable price. Mon–Fri 10am–6pm, Sat & Sun 10am–4pm.

Rahva Raamat Vire Centre, Viru väljak. Large bookshop with numerous English-language books and travel guides. Daily 9am–9pm.

Rotermanni Turg Roseni. Local foodstuffs (Tues–Sat), including a lot of organic produce and delicious snacks. Crafts and collectables on Sun. Tues–Sun 10am–6pm.

DIRECTORY

Embassies Canada, Toomkooli 13, 2nd floor ☎627 3311; Ireland, Vene 2, 2nd floor ☎681 1888; UK, Wismari 6 ☎667 4700; US, Kentmanni 20 ☎668 8100.

Exchange Outside banking hours, try Tavia at Aia 5, though their overnight rates are not as favourable as their day rates.

Hospital Tallinn Central Hospital, Ravi 18 ☎620 7040. English-speaking doctors available. Or call the Tallinn First Aid hotline on ☎697 1145 for advice in English.

Left luggage At the bus station (Mon–Sat 6.30am–10pm, Sun 7.45am–8pm; €4/24hr).

Pharmacies Aia Apteek, Aia 7 (9am–9.30pm); Tõnismäe Apteek, Tõnismägi 5 (24hr).

Police Pärnu mnt. 11 ☎612 4200.

Post office Narva mnt. 1, opposite the *Viru Hotel* (Mon–Fri 7.30am–8pm; Sat 8am–6pm).

The rest of Estonia

There are several attractions outside Tallinn that are well worth visiting, such as the vast, beautiful expanse of **Lahemaa National Park** and the pretty island of **Saaremaa**, home to the Bishop's Castle. The seaside resort of **Pärnu** is a slightly livelier affair, but outshone in vibrancy by the buzzy university town of **Tartu**.

LAHEMAA NATIONAL PARK

The largest of Estonia's national parks, 725-square-kilometre **Lahemaa** lies an hour's drive or bus ride from Tallinn. It stretches along the north coast, comprising lush forests, pristine lakes, and ruggedly beautiful coves and wetlands. The land is dotted with erratic boulders (giant rocks left over from the last Ice Age) and tiny villages throughout, while the forest is home to brown bears, wild boar, moose and lynx. The park is best explored by bicycle, as the villages are all connected by good paved roads. Parts of the park are doable as a day-trip, but you may well be charmed into staying longer.

EXPLORING THE PARK

If you go with Tallinn's City Bike Tours (see box, p.246), this is the day route that offers an excellent introduction to the park: start in the village of **Palmse**, where you can take in the grand German manor (10am–7pm May–Sept; shorter hours rest of year; €4); and cycle 8.5km northeast to **Sagadi Manor**, a well-preserved eighteenth-century aristocratic home (May–Sept daily 10am–6pm by prior appointment only), before heading north for 3km to **Oandu** – the start of

9

several nature trails. Just before the fishing village of **Altja**, 2km to the north, you'll find the 1km **Beaver Trail**, where you can see dams built by beavers and stop for lunch at *Altja Korts* – an attractive tavern serving tasty fresh dishes, such as grilled salmon with grated potato pancakes (mains €8). From Altja you can cycle around the coast of the **Vergi peninsula**, taking in the picturesque villages (17km) surrounded by pine forest, before ending up on the wide, clean, windswept beach in **Võsu**. A seaside trail heads north from Võsu for 6km before arriving at the attractive village of **Käsmu**, which has a superb nautically themed **museum** (9am–6pm; donations) started by a local collector many years ago; look out for the giant sea mines in the front yard.

If you have any energy left, you can then tackle the rugged cycle trails along the western half of the Käsmu peninsula before getting picked up. Travelling independently, you can take the bus to Käsmu (see below), do the trail in reverse and then cycle up from Palmse to Võsu (6km) for an overnight stay before catching a bus back to Tallinn the following day.

ARRIVAL AND INFORMATION

By bus There are buses from Tallinn to Võsu (3 daily; 1hr 25min), Käsmu and Altja (1–2 daily each; 1hr 10min–1hr 45min). For Palmse you can take a Rakvere- or Narva-bound bus from Tallinn to Viitna (hourly; 1hr) and hike or hitchhike the remaining 7.2km, or else catch a bus from Võsu (1 daily).

Lahemaa National Park Visitor Centre Located in tiny Palmse (daily: May–Aug 9am–7pm; Sept 9am–5pm; ☎ 329 5555, ⓦ lahemaa.ee). The helpful staff at the visitor centre can advise on accommodation, biking and hiking trails, and nature tours, and provide a detailed map of the area.

GETTING AROUND

By bike Cycling is the best way to get around (locals do hitchhike, but the usual precautions apply). You can rent a bicycle at the *Palmse Hotel* (€4/hr or €15/day) and Sagadi Manor (see p.249), though bikes are sturdier and better maintained at Tallinn's City Bike Tours (see box, p.246), which also arranges transfers and day-trips to Lahemaa.

ACCOMMODATION

There are guesthouses and places to eat in Palmse, Sagadi, Altja, Võsu and Käsmu, as well as campsites,

huts and forest houses throughout, maintained by RMK (ⓦ rmk.ee).

Metsa Puhkemaja Võsu ☎ 323 8431, ⓦ mpm.pri.ee. Simply furnished doubles and triples with shared facilities, kitchen facilities and a sauna. Free wi-fi throughout. Double **€30**

Toomarahva Turismitalu Altja ☎ 505 0850, ⓦ toomarahva.ee. A lovely traditional farmstead complete with thatched roof, log-panelled rooms, and a sauna hut at the bottom of a blissful garden. Hay bales **€5**, double **€40**

SAAREMAA

The island of **SAAREMAA**, off the west coast of Estonia, is claimed by many to be one of the most authentically Estonian parts of the country. Buses from Tallinn, Tartu and Pärnu come here via a ferry running from the mainland village of Virtsu to Muhu Island, which is linked to Saaremaa by a causeway. The principal attraction is Kuressaare's thirteenth-century castle, one of the finest in the Baltic region, but the rest of the island also deserves exploration; **cycling** is the best way to get around.

Kuressaare

In **Kuressaare**'s Kesk väljak (main square) you'll find the yellow-painted **Town Hall**, dating from 1670, its door guarded by stone lions. From the square, Lossi runs south to the magnificent **Bishop's Castle** (Piiskopilinnus), set in the middle of an attractive park and surrounded by a deep moat. The formidable structure dates largely from the fourteenth century and is protected by huge seventeenth-century ramparts. The labyrinthine keep houses the **Saaremaa Regional Museum** (May–Aug daily 10am–7pm; Sept–April Wed–Sun 11am–6pm; €5; students €2.50), a riveting collection of displays charting the culture, nature and history of the island (including an excellent section on Soviet occupation) You can also climb the watchtowers, one of which houses stunning contemporary art and photography exhibitions.

Around the island

Cycling is a wonderful way of seeing Saaremaa, with its alternating landscapes of pine forest, tiny villages and vast fields.

Highlights include the 37km route north from Kuressaare to **ANGLA**, its five much-photographed wooden windmills by the roadside. Halfway along, **KAALI** village, home to a giant meteorite crater thought to be at least 4000 years old, makes a worthy detour.

Ten kilometres southwest of Kuressaare, you can stop at **JARVE**, the local beach hangout, or do the 47km down to the tip of the Torgu peninsula, which ends in an amazing view from the jagged cliffs.

ARRIVAL AND INFORMATION

By bus From the bus station on Pihtla in Kuressaare, turn left onto Tallinna to reach the main square.
Destinations Leisi (5–6 daily; 55min); Pärnu (4 daily; 3hr); Tallinn (up to 18 daily; 4hr 30min); Tartu (2 direct daily; 6hr).
Tourist information The tourist office is in the Town Hall at Tallinna 2 (June–Aug Mon–Fri 9am–6pm, Sat & Sun 10am–4pm; Sept–May Mon–Fri 9am–5pm; ☎ 453 3120, Ⓦ kuressaare.ee & Ⓦ saaremaa.ee).

GETTING AROUND

By bike Bike rental from Bivarix Rattapood, Tallinna 26 (Mon–Fri 10am–6pm, Sat 10am–2pm; €8/4hr, €15/day).

ACCOMMODATION

Kraavi Holiday Cottage 500m southeast of the castle at Kraavi 1, Kuressaare ☎ 5335 8784, Ⓦ kraavi.ee. Family-run guesthouse offering cosy, spacious doubles and triples with a hearty breakfast included and free wi-fi. Use of sauna and bikes is extra. Little English spoken but the hostess is very welcoming. Double **€34**
Ovelia Majutus Suve 8, Kuressaare ☎ 455 5732, Ⓦ ovelia .ee. Friendly and clean guesthouse with basic rooms, some with TVs. Some are also en suite, and have a shared kitchen. A 10min walk from the bus station. Double **€40**
Piibelehe Holiday Home Piibelehe 4, Kuressaare ☎ 453 6206, Ⓦ piibelehe.ee. On the outskirts of town, this place has a number of airy guest rooms, some en suite and with use of a kitchen; camping also available. Discounts for multi-day stays. Camping **€2** per person, plus **€6** per tent, double **€38**

EATING AND DRINKING

Classic Café Lossi 9, Kuressaare. A great little spot to sample some of the best coffee and food in town while sitting in a cosy nook, surrounded by black-and-white photos of Kuressaare. Coffee €1.50. Daily 8.30am–8pm.
Kodulinna Lokaal Tallinna mnt. 12, Kuressaare. Popular café on the main square dishing up inexpensive soups and light meals. Try the Saaremaa-style potato pancake (€2.60). Mon–Thurs & Sun noon–2am, Fri & Sat till 5am.

Veski Pärnu 19, Kuressaare. Popular pub in an old windmill serving imaginative dishes. Try the wild boar with ginger and honey on barley mash (€11) or the miller's wife's cottage cheese dessert (€4). Mon–Thurs noon–9pm, Fri & Sat till 10pm.

PÄRNU

PÄRNU, Estonia's main seaside resort, comes into its own in summer, when it fills up with locals and tourists, and hosts daily cultural and musical events.

WHAT TO SEE AND DO

Rüütli, cutting east–west through the centre, is the Old Town's main pedestrianized thoroughfare, lined with shops and a mix of seventeenth- to twentieth-century buildings, while parallel Kuninga boasts the largest concentration of restaurants. The entertaining **Pärnu Museum** is at Rüütli 53 (Mon–Sat 11am–7pm; €4/students €3), tracing local history from 9000 BC up until World War II; ask for the information sheet in English. The oldest building in town is the **Red Tower** (Punane Torn; Tues–Sun 10am–5pm; free), a fifteenth-century remnant of the medieval city walls at Hommiku 11, a block north from Rüütli.

Follow Nikolai south from the centre and you'll reach the **Kunsti Museum** (daily 9am–9pm; €2; Ⓦ chaplin.ee), set in the former Communist Party HQ at Esplanaadi 10. It holds excellent temporary exhibitions of contemporary art. South of here Nikolai joins Supeluse, which leads to the beach, passing beneath the trees of the shady Rannapark. Just beyond the sand dunes lies Pärnu's main attraction: the wide, clean sandy **beach**,

---

★ TREAT YOURSELF

Spa Hotel Rüütli, Kuressaare Pargi 12 ☎ 452 2133, Ⓦ saaremaaspahotels.eu. Non-guests are welcome to sample a variety of inexpensive "medical" and "wellness" spa treatments at this hotel, including "Charcot's Shower" – strip naked and be pummelled with strong jets of water (€10). Treatments take place 8am–3pm; book in advance.

9

lined with see-saws, changing booths and volleyball nets.

ARRIVAL AND INFORMATION

By train The train station is about 5km east of the centre at Riia mnt. 116.

Destinations Tallinn (2 daily; 2hr 30min).

By bus The bus station is on Pikk in the Old Town (information & ticket office round the corner at Ringi 3; daily 6.30am–7.30pm). Luggage storage by platform 8 (Mon–Fri 8am–7.30pm, Sat & Sun 9am–5pm; €3/day).

Destinations Kuressaare (4–5 daily; 3hr); Rīga (3 daily; 2hr 30min); Tallinn (at least 1 hourly, 4.40am–8.30pm; 2–3hr); Tartu (up to 16 daily; 2hr 30min).

Tourist information The tourist office at Uus 4 (mid-May to mid-Sept daily 9am–6pm, mid-Sept to mid-May Mon–Fri 9am–5pm, Sat 10am–2pm; ☎447 3000, ⓦ visitparnu.com) stocks extensive information on Pärnu and surrounding area.

ACCOMMODATION

Hommiku Hostel & Guesthouse Hommiku 17 ☎445 1122, ⓦ hommikuhostel.ee. Both hostel and guesthouse-style accommodation are on offer at this attractive central budget option: all doubles and triples are en suite and have their own kitchenettes; singles share a bathroom. Wi-fi and cable TV throughout. Dorm **€20**, double **€58**

Hostel Lõuna Lõuna 2 ☎443 0943, ⓦ hostellouna.eu. Centrally located, with spartan, spacious dorms and basic rooms with shared facilities, popular with local students. Functional, wi-fi-equipped en suites on the ground floor. Dorm **€15**, double **€45**

Terve Hostel Ringi 50 ☎529 8168, ⓦ terve.ee. Cosy family-run guesthouse just south of the town centre, offering airy, clean rooms with shared facilities, plus use of jacuzzi, guest kitchen and wood-fired sauna. Double **€50**

EATING AND DRINKING

Club Str& Tammsaare pst. 35. A seafront hotel club with quirky decor attracting a mixed crowd of locals and tourists, and some decent DJs. Entry €7. Age 21-plus. Fri & Sat 11pm–4am.

★ Postipoiss Vee 12. Wooden tavern, invoking nostalgia for tsarist Russia with its decor, and specializing in delicious Russian cuisine. You can't go wrong with home-made *pelmeni* (meat dumplings) in chanterelle sauce. Get in early to beat the groups. Mains €4–6. Mon–Thurs & Sun daily noon–11pm, Fri & Sat till 2am.

Rüütlihoov Rüütli 29. This lively pub has friendly service and live music on weekends. The outdoor terrace is a good spot for a cold beer (€2.50). Mon–Thurs & Sun noon–10pm, Fri & Sat till midnight.

Si-Si Restaurant and Lounge Supeluse 21. Located inside a mansion with an attractive garden, this excellent Italian restaurant serves authentic dishes such as aubergine baked with mozzarella and tagliatelle with shrimp and courgettes, to a contented beach crowd. Mains €6–17. Daily noon–11pm.

Sõõrikubaar Pühavaimu 15. An essential stop for caffeine addicts, this popular little café also does tasty pastries and *sõõrikud* (Estonian doughnuts). Mon–Fri 8am–7pm, Sat & Sun 9am–5pm.

Steffani Nikolai 24. Extremely popular restaurant with a wide choice of tasty pizza and pasta dishes (huge calzone €7). Runs a popular second branch between Ranna pst. and the beach in the summer, serving similar fare. Mon–Thurs & Sun 11am–11.30pm, Fri & Sat till 1.30am.

KINHU

A short boat ride from Pärnu lies an island stuck in a delightful time warp. The four hundred or so inhabitants of **Kinhu** sustain a traditional way of life that you won't find on the Estonian mainland. You'll find young women wearing traditional striped woollen skirts, just like their great-grandmothers, and see little old ladies riding old-fashioned Soviet motorcycles with sidecars (there are no cars on the island).

ARRIVAL AND DEPARTURE

By boat To get here, take a ferry from the ferry quay at Kalda 2 in Pärnu (1–2 Wed–Sun; 2hr 30min).

ACCOMMODATION

Rock City Guesthouse Sääre village ☎5626 2181, ⓦ rockcity.ee. One of the few places to stay, this is a simply furnished building set among trees near the shore. Open June–Aug only. Double **€45**

TARTU

Just over two hours southeast of Tallinn, **TARTU** is in many ways the undiscovered gem of the Baltic States, a small-scale university town that is full of youthful energy but happily free from the city-break tourism that tends to swamp the Estonian capital. With plenty of diversions, and events all year round, it's worth a stay of a couple of days.

WHAT TO SEE AND DO

The city's centre is its cobbled Raekoja plats, fronted by the Neoclassical Town Hall, a pink-and-white edifice with the

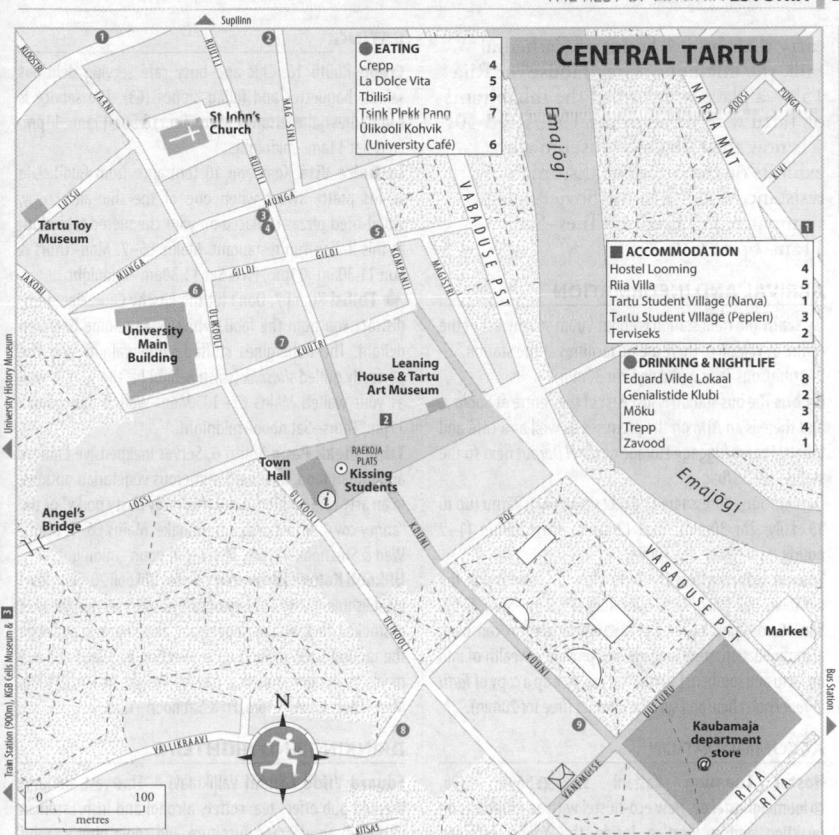

CENTRAL TARTU

EATING

Crepp	4
La Dolce Vita	5
Tbilisi	9
Tsink Plekk Pang	7
Ülikooli Kohvik (University Café)	6

ACCOMMODATION

Hostel Looming	4
Riia Villa	5
Tartu Student Village (Narva)	1
Tartu Student Village (Pepleri)	3
Terviseks	2

DRINKING & NIGHTLIFE

Eduard Vilde Lokaal	8
Genialistide Klubi	2
Möku	3
Trepp	4
Zavood	5

"Kissing Students" statue in the fountain in front of it. The northeast corner features the **Leaning House** (a wonky-looking structure that is still essentially sound), home of the **Tartu Art Museum** (Wed–Sun noon–6pm; €2.25), with edgy temporary exhibitions downstairs and works by Estonian masters upstairs. The Neoclassical theme continues in the cool white facade of the main **Tartu University** building at Ülikooli 18, just north of the square. Upstairs you can look at the Student Lock-up, where students were incarcerated in the nineteenth century for such offences as the late return of library books and duelling (weekdays 11am–5pm; €1; joint ticket with the Art Museum on the ground floor €2). About 100m beyond the university is the red-brick Gothic **St John's Church** (Tues–Sat 10am–6pm; church free; tower €1.60), founded in 1330, and most

famous for over one thousand pint-sized terracotta sculptures set in niches around the main entrance, although only about two hundred still survive.

Cathedral Hill and around

Behind the Town Hall, Lossi climbs Cathedral Hill, a pleasant park with the remains of the red-brick **Cathedral** at the top, housing the University History Museum (June–Aug daily 10am–5pm; May & Sept Wed–Sun 11am–5pm; Oct & Nov Sat & Sun 11am–5pm; €1.60). Inside are some weird and wonderful scientific instruments, and a viewing terrace on one of the former cathedral towers. Nearby is the **Sacrifice Stone**, left over from Estonia's pagan past; students now burn their lecture notes on it after the exams. Behind the stone you'll find **Kissing Hill**, where newlywed grooms

9

carry their brides. South of Cathedral Hill, the infamous "Grey House" at Riia 15b – a place which filled the inhabitants of Tartu with dread in the 1940s and 50s – is now the **KGB Cells Museum** with exhibits on deportations, Estonian resistance and life in the Soviet gulags, summarized in English (Tues–Sat 11am–6pm; €2).

ARRIVAL AND INFORMATION

By train The train station is about 900m southwest of the centre at Vaksali 6. There are no facilities at the station.
Destinations Tallinn (8 daily; 2hr 30min).

By bus The bus station is just east of the centre at Soola 2, and there is an ATM on the premises as well as a café and toilets. There's luggage storage at *Hotel Dorpat* next to the station (€1.50/bag).
Destinations Kuressaare (3 direct daily; 6hr); Pärnu (up to 15 daily; 2hr 30min); Rīga (2 daily; 5hr); Tallinn (1–2 hourly, 3am–9pm; 2hr 30min).

Tourist information The Tartu Visitors' Centre inside the old Town Hall (Mon 9am–6pm, Tues–Fri 9am–5pm, Sat & Sun 10am–2pm; ☎744 2111, ⓦvisittartu.com) can book accommodation, store luggage and provide a wealth of info on Tartu and southern Estonia. You can pick up a copy of *Tartu in Your Pocket* here and surf the internet (free for 20min).

ACCOMMODATION

Hostel Looming Kastani 38 ☎5699 4398, ⓦloominghostel.ee. New eco-hostel with an emphasis on recycling and a location inside the Young Estonian Creativity Centre, with bright decor, friendly young staff, comfy, brand-new beds and a spacious guest lounge. Dorm €15, double €33

Riia Villa Riia 117a ☎738 1300, ⓦriiavilla.ee; bus #1, #8, #18 or #22 up Riia to Soinaste bus stop. West of Old Town, this tranquil guesthouse is well worth seeking out. Each of the six en-suite rooms has its own theme; choose "Glamorous Simplicity" or "Kleopatra's Room". Wi-fi available. Double €38

Tartu Student Village Narva mnt. 27 & Pepleri 14 ☎742 7608, ⓦtartuhostel.eu. Cheap and fairly central accommodation in summer at two locations. The Narva branch offers spartan en-suite rooms with kitchenettes and internet connection, while the Pepleri branch has more of the same plus self-contained 2-person apartments with TV, internet and sauna access (€6/hr), ideal for a longer stay. Book in advance. Double €40, apartment €50

★ **Terviseks** Raekoja Plats 10 ☎565 5382, ⓦterviseksbbb.com. Backpacker-favourite-turned-B&B run by friendly, energetic young staff, with spacious, brightly decorated doubles and dorms, modern lounge and gleaming kitchen. Special touches include reading lights by each bed and a guitar for guest use. Dorm €15, double €30

EATING

Crepp Rüütli 16. Chic and busy café serving delicious salads, baguettes and filling crêpes (€3). The service is sometimes quite leisurely. Mon–Thurs & Sun 11am–11pm, Fri & Sat 11am–midnight.

La Dolce Vita Kompanii 10 (entrance from Gildi). Life seems pretty sweet when one of the thin-and-crispy, wood-fired pizzas is placed on your chequered tablecloth at this Italian-run restaurant. Mains €6–7. Mon–Thurs & Sun 11.30am–11pm, Fri & Sat 11.30am–midnight.

★ **Tbilisi** Küüni 7. Don't let the kitschy Caucasian decor distract you from the food, which is a genuine Georgian delight. The aubergines stuffed with walnuts and the perfectly grilled *shashlik* (shish kebab) hit the spot as well as your wallet. Mains €7–10. Mon–Wed & Sun noon– 11pm, Thurs–Sat noon–midnight.

Tsink Plekk Pang Küütri 6. Serves inexpensive Chinese and Indian food, including numerous vegetarian options, in an arty café ambience. Try the "rusty busty porky" or the "angry cow", or just grab a milkshake. Mains €6–8. Mon– Wed & Sun noon–11pm, Thurs–Sat noon–midnight.

Ülikooli Kohvik (University Café) Ulikooli 20. Split-level establishment with an elegant café upstairs serving the likes of smoked duck with roast beetroot, and a bargain buffet on the ground floor, dishing up a selection of salads and hot meals to hungry students; pay by weight at €0.70/100g. Mon–Thurs noon–11pm, Fri & Sat noon–1am.

DRINKING AND NIGHTLIFE

Eduard Vilde Lokaal Vallikraavi 4. This vast, literary-themed pub offers tea, coffee, alcohol and Irish/Estonian pub grub amid grand furniture and sepia photographs, while the lively summer terrace is perfect for beer and snacks. Mon–Thurs noon–midnight, Fri & Sat noon–2am, Sun noon–11pm.

★ **Genialistide Klubi** Magasini 5 ⓦgenklubi.ee. Tartu's self-styled "subcultural centre", this eclectic boho venue is a café (with a varied and tasty food menu) by day and an indie bar-club by night, attracting a mixed, arty crowd. Music and events vary, as do opening times; check the website for details. Mon–Sat noon–3am.

Möku Rüütli 18. Convivial basement bar not much bigger than a cupboard, attracting a crush of people that usually spreads out to cover the adjoining pavement. Good choice of draught beers. Daily 6pm–3am.

Trepp Rüütli 16. Upstairs from *Crepp* (see above), this typically Tartu-esque slice of student bohemia features bare wooden floors, matt black furnishings, and a dangerously long and tempting menu of shots and spirits. Mon–Thurs 7pm–2am, Fri & Sat 7pm–3am.

Zavood Lai 30. Legendary student hangout with post-industrial decor, table football, eccentric indie sounds and a menu of cheap and tasty food chalked up on the blackboard. Mon–Thurs & Sun 7pm–4am, Fri & Sat 7pm–5am.

SAUNA, KUOPIO

Finland

HIGHLIGHTS

❶ **Design District, Helsinki** Sample the shops, cafés and nightlife of this vibrant and trendy area of the capital. **See p.266**

❷ **Lenin Museum, Tampere** Fascinating museum delving into the relationship between Lenin and Finland. **See p.269**

❸ **Olavinlinna Castle, Savonlinna** One of the best-preserved medieval castles in northern Europe. **See p.270**

❹ **Saunas** Don't be shy – strip off and join the locals. **See p.271**

❺ **Sámi Culture, Inari** One of Europe's last frontiers, where nomadic reindeer herders live in harmony with snowmobiles. **See p.274**

HIGHLIGHTS ARE MARKED ON THE MAP ON P.257

ROUGH COSTS

Daily budget Basic €40, occasional treat €65

Drink Salmiakki €4–6 shot

Food Reindeer stew with potatoes €10

Hostel/budget hotel €22/€45

Travel Train: Helsinki–Rovaniemi €87; bus: Helsinki–Tampere €27

FACT FILE

Population 5.4 million

Language Finnish and Swedish

Currency Euro (€)

Capital Helsinki

International phone code ☎ 358

Time zone GMT +2hr

10

Introduction

Drawing strong cultural influences both from its easterly neighbour, Russia, and from the West, Finland remains one of Europe's most enigmatic countries. It's a land best known for its laconic, pithy people with a penchant for kicking back in a sauna au naturel, and for its quirky and bizarre annual festivals – its strangeness is a good part of the country's charm. And while it's far from a budgeteer's paradise, there are definitely ways to save – that is, if you know where to drink.

The Finnish landscape is mostly flat and punctuated by huge forests and lakes, but has wide regional variations. The south contains the least dramatic scenery, but the capital, **Helsinki**, more than compensates, with its brilliant *fin-de-siècle* architecture and superb collections of late modern and contemporary artworks, as does the former capital of **Turku**, with some great museums and nightlife. Stretching from the Russian border in the east to the industrial city of **Tampere**, the vast waters of the **Lake Region** provide a natural means of transport for the timber industry – indeed, water here is a more common sight than land, with many towns lying on narrow ridges between lakes. North of here, the gradually rising fells and forests of **Lapland** are Finland's most alluring terrain and are home to the Sámi, semi-nomadic reindeer herders. For a few months on either side of midsummer, the midnight sun is visible from much of the region; in the dead of winter much of the north of the country in shrouded in polar darkness.

CHRONOLOGY

1800 BC Tribes from Russia settle in Lapland.
98 AD Roman historian Tacitus writes first recorded reference of the "Fenni".
1150s Sweden invades southwestern Finland.
1293 Sweden defeats Finland again, establishing dividing lines between the Catholic West and Orthodox East.
1642 First complete Finnish translation of the Bible produced.
1721 In the Treaty of Uusikaupunki, Sweden cedes Finnish land to Russia.
1809 Russians take Finland after military victory over Sweden.
1812 Helsinki is declared capital of Finland.

1858 Confusion caused as Russia forces Finns to drive on the right-hand side of the road.
1860 Finland acquires its own currency, the markka.
1906 Finland gains its own national parliament. Finnish women are the first in the world to receive full political rights.
1917 Finland declares independence from Russia.
1939–40 Soviet troops invade Finland but meet fierce resistance during the "Winter War".
1941 Under the Moscow Peace Treaty, the southeast territory of Karelia is ceded to the Russians.
1952 Helsinki holds the Olympic Games.
1987 Finnish company Nokia begins to make hand-held mobile phones.
1995 Finland joins the EU.
2000 Tarja Halonen becomes the first female president.
2002 Finland adopts the euro.
2006 National celebrations as Finnish death metal group Lordi win Eurovision song contest.
2008 Ex-president Martti Ahtisaari awarded the Nobel Peace Prize.
2009 Finnish government sells its share in Santa Park, signalling that the global economic crisis has reached the North Pole.
2011 The conservative National Coalition wins Finland's parliamentary elections, with the populist, anti-immigration and anti-EU True Finns party coming in third, causing alarm around Europe.
2013 World Orienteering Championships held in northern city of Vuokatti.

ARRIVAL AND DEPARTURE

There are over twenty airports dotted around the country (information at ⓦfinavia.fi/en), but you're most likely to arrive at Helsinki Vantaa, Tampere Pirkkala or Lappeenranta Airport, which are the main hubs for **international flights**. British Airways (ⓦba.com), Finnair (ⓦfinnair .com) and Norwegian (ⓦnorwegian.no) fly

FINLAND

HIGHLIGHTS
1. Design District, Helsinki
2. Lenin Museum, Tampere
3. Olavinlinna Castle, Savonlinna
4. Saunas
5. Sámi Culture, Inari

into Helsinki and Ryanair into Tampere from the UK, but the biggest low-cost airline in Finland is Blue1 (ⓦblue1.com), which offers routes to and from most major European cities. **Ferries** arrive from Tallinn in Estonia or Stockholm at Helsinki and Turku; contact either Silja Line (ⓦtallinksilja.com) or Viking Line (ⓦvikingline.fi) for tickets and timetables. Another popular route into the country is overland by **train** from St Petersburg to Helsinki, which thanks to a high-speed rail link takes less than three hours.

GETTING AROUND

For the most part trains and buses integrate well, and you'll only need to plan with care when travelling through the more remote areas of the far north and east.

BY TRAIN

Trains are operated by Finnish State Railways (VR; ⓦvr.fi). Comfortable Express and InterCity trains, plus faster, tilting Pendolino trains, serve the principal cities several times a day. If you're travelling by night train, it's better to go for the more expensive sleeper cars if you want to get any rest, as no provision is made for sleeping in the ordinary seated carriages. Elsewhere, especially on east–west hauls through sparsely populated regions, trains are often tiny or replaced by buses on which rail passes are still valid. InterRail (and Eurail) passes are valid on all trains. The best timetable is the *Rail Pocket Guide*, published by VR and available from all train stations and tourist offices.

10

Buses – privately run, but with a common ticket system – cover the whole country, but are most useful in the north. Tickets can be purchased at bus stations and most travel agents; only ordinary one-way tickets can be bought on board. The timetable (*Pikavuoroaikataulut*), available at all main bus stations, lists all bus routes, or check ⓦmatkahuolto.fi. The private company Express Bus (ⓦexpressbus.fi) sells some particularly cheap fares – often as low as €2 – though you must book at least five days in advance for the most rock-bottom fares.

Domestic flights can be comparatively cheap as well as time-saving, especially if you're planning to visit Lapland and the far north. Finnair (ⓦfinnair.com) and Blue1 (ⓦblue1.com), a subsidiary of SAS, operate the most flights, though Norwegian (ⓦnorwegian.com) also runs a few domestic routes. The cheaper tickets are generally only available if booked well in advance.

Cycling can be an enjoyable way to see the country at close quarters, particularly because the only appreciable hills are in the farthest stretches of the north. You can take your bike along with you on an InterCity train for a €10 fee (reservations rarely necessary), and most youth hostels, campsites and some hotels and tourist offices offer bike rental from around €10 per day, or €45 per week; there may also be a deposit of around €30.

ACCOMMODATION

There's a good network of 65 official **HI hostels** (ⓦhostellit.fi) as well as a few independents. Most charge €5–6 for breakfast and bed linen is often extra (€4–7), so if you're on a tight budget it's worth bringing your own sheets. Dorms are almost always single-sex. The free *Finland: Budget Accommodation* booklet, available from any tourist office, contains a comprehensive list of hostels and campsites.

Hotels are expensive. Special offers in summer mean that you'll be able to sleep well on a budget in high season, but may have difficulty finding anything affordable out of season – the reverse of the norm. In many towns you'll also find **tourist hotels** (*matkustajakoti*) offering fewer frills for €35–50 per person, and **summer hotels** (*kesähotelli*; June–Aug only), which offer decent accommodation in student blocks for €25–45 per person.

Official **campsites** (*leirintäalue*) are plentiful. The cost to camp is roughly €12–15 per pitch, plus €4–5 per person, depending on the site's star rating. Most open from May or June until August or September, although some stay open longer and a few all year round. Many three-star sites also have cottages, often with TV, sauna and kitchen. To camp in Finland, you'll need a Camping Key Scandinavia, available at every site (and online: ⓦcamping.fi) for €16 and valid for a year. Camping rough is illegal without the landowner's permission – though in practice, provided you're out of sight of local communities, there shouldn't be any problems.

FOOD AND DRINK

Finnish food is a mix of Western and Eastern influences, with Scandinavian-style fish specialities and exotic meats such as reindeer and elk alongside dishes that bear a Russian stamp – pastries, and casseroles strong on cabbage and pork. Also keep an eye out for *karjalan piirakka* – oval-shaped pastries containing rice and mashed potato, served hot with a mixture of finely chopped hard-boiled egg and butter. *Kalakukko* is another inexpensive delicacy, if an acquired one: a chunk of bread with pork and whitefish baked inside it; it's legendary around Kuopio but available almost everywhere. Slightly cheaper but just as filling, *lihapiirakka* are envelopes of sweet pastry filled with rice and meat – ask for them with mustard (*sinappi*) and/or ketchup (*ketsuppi*).

Breakfasts (*aamiainen*) in hotels usually consist of a buffet of herring, eggs, cereals, cheese, salami and bread, while you can lunch on the economical **snacks** sold in market halls (*kauppahalli*) or adjoining cafés. Most train stations and some bus stations and supermarkets also have cafeterias offering a selection of snacks, greasy nibbles and light meals, and street stands (*grillis*) turn out burgers and hot dogs for around €3. Otherwise, campus **mensas** are the cheapest places to get a hot dish (around €4); theoretically, you have to be a student, but you're only asked for ID on occasion. In regular restaurants or *ravintola*, **lunch** (*lounas*) deals are good value, with many places offering a lunchtime buffet table (*voileipäpöytä* or *seisovapöytä*) stacked with a choice of traditional goodies for a set price of around €10. Pizzerias are another good bet, serving lunch specials for €7–9. For **evening meals**, a cheap pizzeria will serve up standard plates of meat and two veg, while in Helsinki and the big towns there's usually a good range of options, including Chinese, Thai and possibly Indian.

DRINK

Most restaurants are fully licensed, and many are frequented more for drinking than eating. **Bars** are usually open till midnight or 1am (and clubs until 2am or 3am) and service stops half an hour before closing. You have to be eighteen to buy beer and wine, twenty to buy spirits, and some places have an age limit of twenty-four. The main – and cheapest – outlets for takeaway alcohol are the ubiquitous government run **ALKO** shops (Mon–Thurs 9am–8pm, Fri 9am–8pm, Sat 9am–6pm).

Beer (*olut*) falls into three categories: "light beer" (I-Olut), like a soft drink; "medium strength beer" (*keskiolut*; III-Olut), perceptibly alcoholic, sold in supermarkets and cafés; and "strong beer" (A-Olut or IV-Olut), on a par with the stronger European beers, and only available at licensed restaurants, clubs and ALKO shops. Strong beers, such as Lapin Kulta and Koff, cost about €1.30 per 300ml bottle at a shop or kiosk. Imported beers go for €2.20–3 per can. Finlandia **vodka** is €20 for a 700ml bottle; Koskenkorva, a rougher vodka, is €15. You'll also find Finns knocking back **salmiakki**, a premixed vodka/liquorice cocktail which looks, smells and tastes like cough medicine, and *fisu*, another inexplicably popular drink that blends Fisherman's Friend lozenges with Koskenkorva.

CULTURE AND ETIQUETTE

To an outsider, the percipient and proud Finns can seem almost alarmingly pithy, withdrawn and at times downright odd: little value is put on exuberance, and you can have an entire conversation with a Finn without their making any discernible facial expression.

Underneath this reserve, of course, Finnish people are as full of enthusiasm and affection as any other nation. This is a people whose aversion to small talk and affinity for the awkward moment is rivalled only by their remarkable ability to drink several times their body weight in grain alcohol in an evening's sitting. Their underlying bonhomie does come out when there's drink around, but alcohol abuse really has long been a noticeable problem here, and it's wise to avoid trying to keep up with the Finnish capacity for drinking.

Tipping is rare in Finland, and **buying rounds** is absolutely unheard of. Service is usually included in restaurant bills, although it's common to round the bill up to the nearest convenient figure when

10

FINLAND ONLINE

ⓦ **visitfinland.com** The official Finnish Tourist Board site.
ⓦ **finland.fi** A well-run, informative government site on Finnish culture and society.
ⓦ **sauna.fi** Everything you ever wanted to know about saunas but were afraid to ask, from the Finnish Sauna Society.
ⓦ **festivals.fi** A comprehensive listing of festivals throughout Finland.

10

FINNISH

Stress on all Finnish words always falls on the first syllable.

	FINNISH	PRONUNCIATION
Yes	*Kyllä*	Koo-leh
No	*Ei*	Ay
Thank you	*Kiitos*	Keetos
Hello/Good day	*Hyvää päivää*	Hoo-veh pai-veh
Goodbye	*Näkemiin*	Nek-er-meen
Excuse me	*Anteeksi*	Anteksi
Where?	*Missä?*	Miss-eh?
Good	*Hyvä*	Hoo-veh
Bad	*Paha*	Paha
Near	*Lähellä*	Le-hell-eh
Far	*Kaukana*	Kau-kanna
Cheap	*Halpa*	Halpa
Expensive	*Kallis*	Kallis
Open	*Avoinna*	Avoyn-na
Closed	*Suljettu*	Sul-yet-oo
Today	*Tänään*	Ten-ern
Yesterday	*Eilen*	Aylen
Tomorrow	*Huomenna*	Hoo-oh-menna
How much is…?	*Kuinka paljon maksaa…?*	Koo-inka pal-yon maksaa…?
What time is it?	*Paljonko kello on?*	Palyonko kello on?
I don't understand	*En ymmärrä*	Enn oomerreh
Do you speak English?	*Puhutteko englantia?*	Poohut-tuko englantia?
One	*Yksi*	Uksi
Two	*Kaksi*	Kaksi
Three	*Kolme*	Col-meh
Four	*Neljä*	Nel-yeh
Five	*Viisi*	Veesi
Six	*Kuusi*	Coosi
Seven	*Seitsemän*	Sayt-se-men
Eight	*Kahdeksan*	Cah-deksan
Nine	*Yhdeksän*	Oo-deksan
Ten	*Kymmenen*	Kummenen

paying in cash (the same applies for taxi fares).

SPORTS AND OUTDOOR ACTIVITIES

The winter landscape lends itself to **cross-country skiing**, the season lasting from December until January in the south and April in northern and central Finland. There are ski slopes, too – see ⓦ ski.fi for more information – and several operators offering off-piste skiing. Watery pursuits like **kayaking** (or kitesurfing on the frozen lakes in the winter) are a worthwhile option in the lake regions, especially around Lake Inari. Popular national **sports** include the distinctively Finnish *pesäpallo*, similar to baseball, and ice hockey.

COMMUNICATIONS

Communications are dependable and quick. Free **internet access** is readily available, either at the tourist office or local library (booking sometimes required), and major towns and cities often have free, comprehensive wi-fi. **Post offices** are generally open 9am to 6pm Monday to Friday, with later hours in Helsinki. Public **phones** have been swiftly phased out in favour of mobile service; if you plan to make a lot of calls in Finland, invest in a Finnish SIM card for use in your phone. €20 will get you a Finnish number with about sixty minutes of domestic calling time or several hundred domestic text messages. Directory enquiries are ☎118 (domestic) and ☎020208 (international).

EMERGENCIES

You hopefully won't have cause to come into contact with the Finnish **police**, though if you do they are likely to speak English. As for **health problems**, if you're insured you'll save time by seeing a doctor at a private health centre (*lääkäriasema*) rather than waiting at a national health centre (*terveyskeskus*), though you're going to pay for the privilege. Medicines must be paid for at a **pharmacy** (*apteekki*), generally open daily 9am to 6pm; outside these times, a phone number for emergency help is displayed on every pharmacy's front door.

INFORMATION

Most towns have a **tourist office**, some of which will book accommodation for you, though in winter, their hours are much reduced and some don't open at all. You can pick up the decent map of Finland free from tourist offices.

MONEY AND BANKS

Finland's currency is the **euro** (€). Banks are generally open Monday to Friday 9am to 4pm. Some **banks** have exchange desks at transport terminals, and **ATMs** are widely available. You can also change money at hotels, but the rates are generally poor. **Credit cards** are widely accepted right across the country.

OPENING HOURS AND HOLIDAYS

Most **shops** generally open Monday to Friday 9am to 6pm, Saturday 9am to 4pm. Along with banks, they close on **public holidays**, when most public

---

EMERGENCY NUMBERS

☎112 for all emergency services.

---

transport and museums run to a Sunday schedule. These are: January 1, January 6 (Epiphany), Good Friday and Easter Monday, May 1, Ascension (mid-May), Whitsun (late May), Midsummer (late June), All Saints' Day (early Nov), December 6 and 24 to 26.

10

Helsinki

Instantly loveable, **HELSINKI** is remarkably different from the other Scandinavian capitals, and closer both in mood and appearance to the major cities of Eastern Europe. For a century an outpost of the Russian Empire, Helsinki's very shape and form derives from its more powerful neighbour. Yet during the twentieth century it became a showcase for independent Finland, much of its impressive architecture reflecting the dawning of Finnish nationalism and the rise of the republic. Today, visitors will find a youthful buzz on the streets, where the boulevards, outdoor cafés and trendy restaurants are crowded with Finns taking full advantage of the short summer. At night the pace picks up in Helsinki's solid selection of lounges, cafés, bars and clubs.

WHAT TO SEE AND DO

Following a devastating fire in 1808, and the city's designation as Finland's capital in 1812, Helsinki was totally rebuilt in a style befitting its new status: a grid of wide streets and Neoclassical brick buildings modelled on the then Russian capital, St Petersburg.

Esplanadi and Senate Square

Esplanadi, a wide, tree-lined boulevard across a mishmash of tramlines from the harbour, is Helsinki at its most charming. At its eastern end, the **City Museum** at Sofiankatu 4 (Mon–Wed & Fri 9am–5pm, Thurs 9am–7pm, Sat & Sun 11am–5pm; free; ⊛hel.fi) offers a record of 450 years of Helsinki life in an impressive permanent exhibition called "Helsinki Horizons".

To the north is Senate Square (Senaattintori), dominated by the

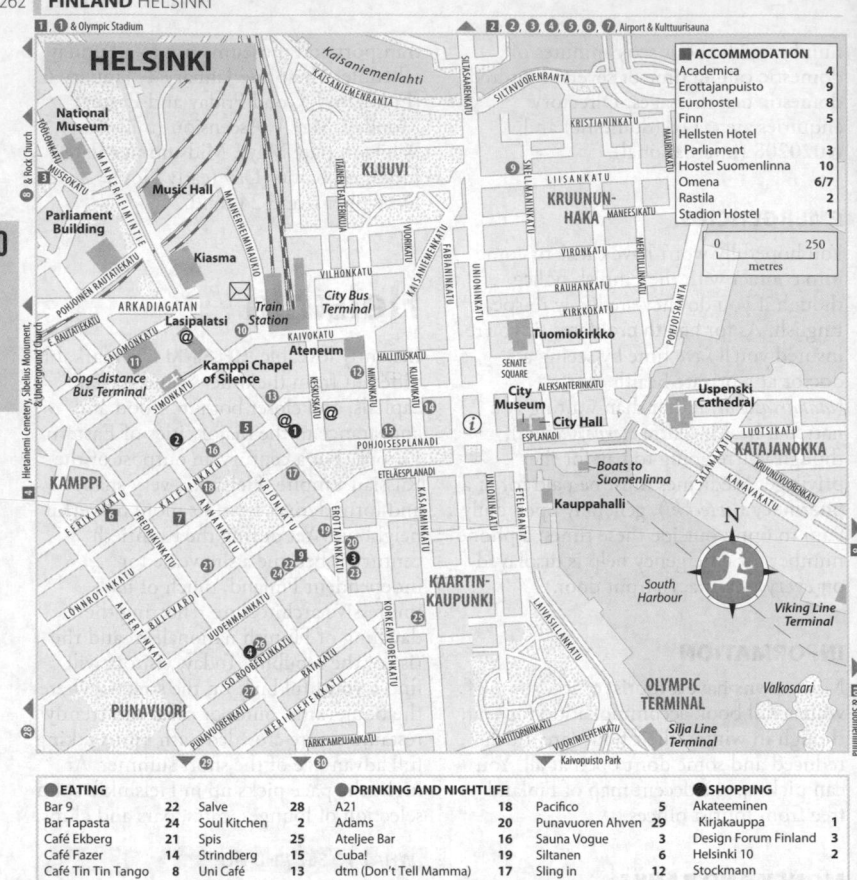

HELSINKI

National Museum

Music Hall

Parliament Building

Kiasma

Long-distance Bus Terminal

Lasipalatsi

Kamppi Chapel of Silence

Ateneum

Train Station

City Bus Terminal

KAMPPI

PUNAVUORI

KLUUVI

KRUUNUN-HAKA

SENATE SQUARE

City Museum

City Hall

Tuomiokirkko

Uspenski Cathedral

KATAJANOKKA

Boats to Suomenlinna

Kauppahalli

KAARTIN-KAUPUNKI

South Harbour

Viking Line Terminal

OLYMPIC TERMINAL

Valkosaari

Silja Line Terminal

Kaivopuisto Park

N

0   250
metres

■ ACCOMMODATION	
Academica	4
Erottajanpuisto	9
Eurohostel	8
Finn	5
Hellsten Hotel Parliament	3
Hostel Suomenlinna	10
Omena	6/7
Rastila	2
Stadion Hostel	1

● EATING				● DRINKING AND NIGHTLIFE				● SHOPPING	
Bar 9	22	Salve	28	A21	18	Pacifico	5	Akateeminen	
Bar Tapasta	24	Soul Kitchen	2	Adams	20	Punavuoren Ahven	29	Kirjakauppa	1
Café Ekberg	21	Spis	25	Ateljee Bar	16	Sauna Vogue	3	Design Forum Finland	3
Café Fazer	14	Strindberg	15	Cuba!	19	Siltanen	6	Helsinki 10	2
Café Tin Tin Tango	8	Uni Café	13	dtm (Don't Tell Mamma)	17	Sling in	12	Stockmann	
Lupolo	27	Villipuutarha	4	Karaoke Bar Restroom	30	The Tiger	11	Department Store	1
Pelmenit	7	Vltava	10	Korjaamo	1	We Got Beef	26	Stupido	4
Pompei	9			Liberty or Death	23	Zetor	13		

exquisite form of the **Tuomiokirkko** (Cathedral; June–Aug daily 9am–midnight; Sept–May Mon–Sat 9am–6pm, Sun noon–6pm; ⓦhelsinginseurakunnat.fi). After the elegance of the exterior, the spartan Lutheran interior comes as a disappointment; more impressive is the gloomily atmospheric **crypt** (June–Aug daily 9am–midnight; Sept–May Mon–Sat 9am–6pm, Sun noon–6pm entrance on Kirkkokatu), now often used for exhibitions.

Uspenski Cathedral

The square towards the eastern end of Aleksanterinkatu is overlooked by the onion domes of the Russian Orthodox **Uspenski Cathedral** (May–Sept Mon–Fri 9.30am–4pm, Sat 9.30am–2pm, Sun noon–3pm, Oct–April closed Mon; tram #3). Inside, there's a glitzy display of icons. Beyond is **Katajanokka**, a wedge of land extending between the harbours; with its beautiful Art Nouveau architecture it's one of the city's most atmospheric places to walk around.

Kiasma and Lasipalatsi

Kiasma is Helsinki's museum of contemporary art (Tues 10am–5pm, Wed–Fri 10am–8.30pm, Sat 10am–6pm, Sun 10am–5pm; €10; ⓦkiasma .fi), its gleaming steel-clad exterior and hi-tech interior making it well worth a visit. Temporary exhibitions feature everything from paintings to video installations. Opposite is the **Lasipalatsi**, a multimedia complex situated in a renovated 1930s classic Functionalist building, now home to a number of cool shops and cafés.

Kamppi Chapel of Silence

This tranquil, award-winning space (Mon–Fri 7am–8pm, Sat & Sun 10am–6pm; ⓦevl.fi) on busy Narinkka Square (locally referred to as Kamppi Square) is a non-ecumenical structure designed to instil a sense of calm in anyone needing respite from the hustle and bustle of downtown.

Parliament and National Museum

North along Mannerheimintie past the train station and the Kiasma museum is the multi-columned and rather solemn 1931-era **Parliament Building** (guided tours only; free). There's more information on the parliament from the attached visitor centre at Arkadiankatu 3 (Mon–Fri 10am–4pm). North of here is the **National Museum** (Tues–Sun 11am–6pm; €8; ⓦnba.fi), its design drawing on the country's medieval churches and granite castles. The exhibits, from prehistory to the present, are exhaustive; concentrate on a few specific sections, such as the fascinating medieval church art and the ethnographic displays.

Olympic Stadium

Nearly 4km north of the train station along Mannerheimintie, the **Olympic Stadium** is clearly visible; originally intended for the 1940 Olympics, it hosted the second postwar games in 1952, though it is now used primarily for large concerts. Its **tower** (Mon–Fri 9am–9pm, Sat & Sun 9am–6pm; €5; ⓦstadion.fi) gives an unsurpassed view over the city and the southern coast.

Rock Church

About 1.5km west of the train station, at Lutherinkatu 3, is the late 1960s **Rock Church** (Temppeliaukio kirkko; Mon–Sat 10am–5pm, Sun 11.45am–5pm; June–Aug open 45 minutes later; closed during services; tram #3B), blasted from a single lump of granite. It's a thrill to be inside, beneath its domed copper roof.

Kulttuurisauna

This contemporary sauna (ⓦkulttuurisauna.fi) is the first new public sauna to be built in Helsinki in decades. Set on the Hakaniemenranta waterfront northeast of the Tuomiokirkko, the large room is one of the most energy-efficient saunas in the world, featuring a wood-heated furnace, solar panels and eco-friendly passive heat storage systems. Afterwards, visitors can cool off by taking a dip in the sea.

Suomenlinna

Built on five interconnected islands by the Swedes in 1748 to protect Helsinki from seaborne attack, the fortress of **Suomenlinna**, fifteen minutes away by boat, is the biggest sea fortress in the world. Reachable by ferry (hourly; €5 return) from the harbour, it's also a great place to walk around on a summer afternoon, with superb views back across the water towards the capital: you can either visit independently or take one of the hour-long summer **guided walking tours**, beginning close to the ferry stage and conducted in English (June–Aug daily 11am, 12.30pm & 2.30pm; Sept–May Sat & Sun 1.30pm; €9/4, according to high/low season). Suomenlinna has a few museums, none particularly riveting, but the best of the lot is **Suomenlinna Museum** (daily: May–Sept 10am–6pm; Oct–April 10.30am–4.30pm; €6.50), which contains a permanent exhibition on the island.

ARRIVAL AND DEPARTURE

By plane Vantaa airport (ⓦhelsinki-vantaa.fi) is 20km to the north, connected by Finnair buses to the central train station (every 20min; €6.30).

Destinations Ivalo (for Inari; 1–2 daily; 1hr 30min–2hr 30min); Oulu (13–15 daily; 1hr); Rovaniemi (5 daily; 1hr 15min).

By train The train station is in the heart of the city on Kaivokatu.

Destinations Oulu (11 daily; 6hr 10min–9hr); Rovaniemi (4 daily; 10hr 20min–12hr 55min); St Petersburg (2 daily; 3hr 30min); Tampere (hourly; 2hr); Turku (hourly; 2hr).

10

10

By bus The long-distance bus station is under the Kamppi shopping centre on Simonkatu.
Destinations Porvoo (15 daily; 1hr); Turku (hourly; 2hr 30min–2hr 50min).
By ferry Terminals are less than 1km from the centre; take tram #3T or #3B.
Destinations Stockholm (3 daily; 16hr); Tallinn (hourly; 1hr 30min–4hr).

INFORMATION

Tourist office The excellent City Tourist Office at Pohjoisesplanadi 19 (mid-May to mid-Sept Mon–Fri 9am–8pm, Sat & Sun 9am–6pm; mid-Sept to mid-May Mon–Fri 9am–6pm, Sat & Sun 10am–4pm; ☎09 3101 3300, ⓦvisithelsinki.fi) hands out the useful, free listings magazines *Helsinki This Week* and *City*.
Discount card If you're staying a while, consider purchasing a Helsinki Card (€38/48/58 for 24/48/72hr), giving unlimited travel on public transport and free entry to more than fifty museums.

GETTING AROUND

The city's transport system (trams, buses and a limited metro) is very efficient.
Tickets One-way tickets can be bought on board (€2.80) or from the bus station, tourist office or kiosks around the centre (€2.20), while a tourist ticket (€8/16/24/32 for one/three/five/seven days) permits unlimited use of the whole network for the period covered. Tram #3T/#3B follows a useful figure-of-eight route around the centre.
Spårakoff Pub Tram One unique way to get around town is on the Spårakoff Pub Tram (mid-May to late-Aug; €8; ⓦwww.sinebrychoff.fi), a bright red streetcar that prowls about city streets with thirty passengers and unlimited reserves of Koff beer. With regular departures, it's a great way to see the city (sober or otherwise), since the route takes in most major downtown sights, including Linnanmäki, Töölö Bay and the Olympic Stadium. There is a toilet on board.

ACCOMMODATION

Hostel beds are in short supply, especially during summer, so booking ahead is sensible, either direct or through the Hotel Booking Centre at the train station for a fee of €5 in person or for free by phone, email or online (Mon–Fri 9am–4.30/6pm, Sat 10am–4/5pm, June–Aug also open Sun 10am–4/5pm; ☎09 2288 1400, ⓦhelsinkiexpert.com).

HOSTELS

Academica Hietaniemenkatu 14 ☎09 1311 4334, ⓦhostelacademica.fi. On the fringes of the city centre with single-sex dorms and double rooms. Breakfast and bed linen included in the price. June–Aug only. Tram #3T (stop "Kauppakorkeakoulu"). Dorm €27.50, double €65

★ **Erottajanpuisto** Uudenmaankatu 9 ☎09 642 169, ⓦerottajanpuisto.com. Sociable, hip and atmospheric hostel (think shabby couches) in a grand old building on Helsinki's best street for bar-hopping. Dorm €28, double €68

Eurohostel Linnankatu 9 ☎09 622 0470, ⓦeurohostel.fi. The biggest hostel in Finland, close to the ferry terminals and with a free sauna. Dorm €27.10, double €54.20

Hostel Suomenlinna ☎09 684 7471, ⓦhostelhelsinki.fi. Easily the most idyllic place to stay, and located on the fortress island of Suomenlinna (see p.263). Dorm €25, double €64

Stadion Hostel Olympic Stadium ☎09 477 8480, ⓦstadionhostel.fi. Some 2km out of the centre and often crowded, but cheap and open all year. Tram #3T, #4, #7 or #10 to the stadium, then follow the signs. Dorm €23, double €54

HOTELS

Finn Kalevankatu 3b ☎09 684 4360, ⓦhotellifinn.fi. Peaceful and recently redone modern rooms on the top floor of an office block, virtually in the city centre. Double €79

Hellsten Hotel Parliament Museokatu 18 ☎09 251 1050, ⓦhellstenhotels.fi. Sleek, large and well-appointed apartment-style rooms that are perfect for groups of friends. Operates another similar hotel in Katajanokka. Double €75

Omena Eerikinkatu 24 & Lönnrotinkatu 13 ⓦomenahotels.com. Helsinki's best deals can often be found at either of these two centrally located, self-service, internet-reserved hotels. Rooms are very sleek. Double €45

CAMPSITE

Rastila Karavaanikatu 4 ☎09 107 8517, ⓦrastilacamping.fi. Great camping spot with cabins and dorms in an attached hostel. It's 13km east of the city centre, near the end of the metro line (Vuosaari) and served by night buses #90N till 1.30am during the week and 4.15am Fri & Sat. Camping €5 per person plus €14 per pitch, dorm €21, double €62, cabin €79

EATING

Many places offer good-value lunchtime deals, and there are plenty of affordable ethnic restaurants and fast-food *grillis* for the evenings. At the end of Eteläesplanadi the *kauppahalli* (Mon–Fri 8am–7pm, Sat 8am–4pm) is good for snacks and sandwiches. Another great bargain are the numerous university student cafeterias around the city.

CAFÉS

Café Ekberg Bulevardi 9 ⓦ cafeekberg.fi. Nineteenth-century fixtures and a *fin-de-siècle* atmosphere, with starched waitresses bringing expensive sandwiches and pastries to marble tables. Lunch €9.30. Mon–Fri 7.30am–7pm, Sat 8.30am–5pm, Sun 9am–5pm.

Café Fazer Kluuvikatu 3 ⓦ fazer.fi. Owned by Finland's biggest chocolate company, with celebrated cakes and pastries. Lunch €9.70. Mon–Fri 7.30am–10pm, Sat 9am–10pm, Sun 10am–6pm.

★ **Café Tin Tin Tango** Töölöntorinkatu 7 ⓦ tintintango .info. Somewhat quirky café-bar with a laundry machine and sauna (book a day in advance) en route to the Olympic Stadium. Slough off the travel dirt and have a beer at the same time. Full breakfasts around €10. Mon–Thurs 7.30am–midnight, Fri 7am–2am, Sat 9am–2am, Sun 10am–midnight.

Strindberg Pohjoisesplanadi 33 ⓦ strindberg.fi. A classic Finnish café: the upstairs restaurant serves contemporary Scandinavian cuisine, while the street-level café is one of the places in town to see and be seen. Mains around €20. Mon 9am–11pm, Tues–Sat noon–midnight, Sun 10am–10pm.

Uni Café Mannerheimintie 3 ⓦ hyyravintolat.fi. Cheap, filling dishes at this university cafeteria right in the city centre, with meals from €6. Mon–Fri 11am–7pm, Sat 11am–6pm.

Villipuutarha Kaarlenkatu 13 ⓦ villipuutarha.fi. Superb, dainty little spot great for cakes in Kallio. Mon, Tues & Fri 11am–7pm, Sat 10am–6pm.

RESTAURANTS

Bar 9 Uudenmaakatu 9 ⓦ bar9.net. Though known as a great, unpretentious neighbourhood bar, they also serve excellent food all day. Massive grilled ham and cheese sandwiches, spicy pastas and salads from €8. Mon–Fri 11am–2am, Sat & Sun noon–2am.

Bar Tapasta Uudenmaankatu 13 ⓦ marcante.fi. Bustling evening tapas joint, with Spanish beers and wine to accompany the fairly authentic food. Tapas from €4. Tues–Thurs 5pm–late, Fri & Sat 4pm–late.

Lupolo Punavuorenkatu 3 ⓦ lupolo.fi. Casual, very unpretentious (if slightly cramped) spot with super-friendly staff and great, innovative dishes that profile fresh local cuisine. Tues–Sat 5pm–late.

Pelmenit Kustaankatu 7. This affordable hole-in-the-wall East European restaurant does amazing home-style comfort food such as blini, borsch and *pelmeni* (dumplings) for under €10. Mon–Thurs 11am–5pm, Fri–Sun 10am–10pm.

Pompei Snellmaninkatu 16 ⓦ ravintolapompei.com. Excellent, down-at-heel neighbourhood Italian restaurant run by a friendly Neopolitan. Good salads and pastas, and especially great pizzas from €10. Grappa and limoncello to boot. Mon–Fri 11am–9pm, Sat noon–9pm.

Salve Hietalahdenranta 11 ⓦ ravintolasalve.fi. Unselfconsciously old-school sailors' restaurant at the end of Bulevardi that's been serving up the same heavy Finnish fare for over a century. Well worth a visit. Lunch from €8. Mon–Fri 10am–midnight, Sun 10am–11pm.

Soul Kitchen Fleminginkatu 26–28 ⓦ soulkitchen.fi. American-style restaurant serving southern specialities such as macaroni cheese and succulent BBQ ribs. Aretha and Ray play the tubes. Daily 3pm–midnight.

Spis Kasarmikatu 26 ⓦ spis.fi. New new-Nordic, 18-seat vegetarian restaurant that's big on the ideals of locavorism, stocking everything – from music to utensils to food – from the Nordic countries. Get there early or make a reservation. Tues–Sat 5pm–midnight.

Vltava Elielinaukio 2 ⓦ vltava.fi. Pronounced "Valltava", this Czech restaurant just next to the train station serves massive grilled sausage and steak dishes sided with a great collection of pilsners. Sun & Mon 10am–midnight, Tues–Thurs 10am–3pm, Fri & Sat 10am–4am.

DRINKING AND NIGHTLIFE

Drinking in Helsinki is about as autonomic an activity as breathing for city residents. Wednesday is a popular night for going out, while on Friday and Saturday it's best to arrive as early as possible to get a seat. Several venues put on a steady diet of live music and there are occasional free gigs on summer Sundays in Kaivopuisto Park, south of the centre. There's also a wide range of clubs and discos, which charge a small admission fee (€5–10). For details of what's on, read the back page of the culture section of *Helsingin Sanomat*, or the free fortnightly English-language paper *City*, found in record shops, bookshops, department stores and tourist offices.

BARS

A21 Annankatu 21 ⓦ a21.fi. This award-winning bar offers excellent if slightly pricey cocktails, designer seating and cliques of there-to-be-seen clientele. Wed & Thurs 6pm–1am, Fri & Sat 6pm–3am.

Ateljee Bar *Hotel Torni*, Yrjönkatu 26. The best views of Helsinki from this stylish (but expensive) rooftop bar. Mon–Thurs 2pm–2am, Fri & Sat noon–2am, Sun 2pm–1am (outside of summer, closes one hour earlier).

Cuba! Erottajankatu 4 ⓦ cubacafe.fi. Popular bar with a decent-sized dancefloor that puts on electronica, rock, pop and house music in addition to some steamy salsa nights. Tues 5pm–midnight, Wed & Thurs 5pm–2am, Fri & Sat 5pm–4am.

Karaoke Bar Restroom Tehtaankatu 23A ⓦ karaokebar .net. One-time public lavatory rebuilt as a karaoke bar, with large gold-framed paintings on the walls. Popular with local F1 champion Kimi Räikkönen and stag dos, so consider yourself forewarned. Mon–Fri 3pm–2am, Sat & Sun 2pm–2am.

10

Liberty or Death Erottajankatu 5 Ⓦlibertyordeath.fi. Small exposed-brick cocktail bar that feels something like a Nordic speakeasy, with candles, jazz and regular changing menus of drinks bearing names such as Jabberwocky and Mutineer. As hip as you'll find in Helsinki. Mon–Thurs 4pm–2am, Fri & Sat 4pm–2am.

Pacifico Helsingkatu 15 Ⓦpacifico.fi. Cavernous tavern that was once a former movie theatre. Great Sunday brunches too. Wed–Fri 8pm–2am, Sat 11am–2am, Sun 11am–4pm.

Punavuoren Ahven Punavuorenkatu 12 Ⓦkalaravintolat.fi. One of Helsinki's best *olutravintoloja* ("beer restaurants"), this tranquil dive is very local, with Finns of all ages sporting berets, moustaches and pipes, and scores of international beers in bottles and on draught. Late June to mid-Aug Mon–Thurs 4pm–2am, Fri 4pm–3am, Sat 3pm–3am, Sun 3pm–midnight; mid-Aug to late June Mon–Thurs 2pm–2am, Fri 2pm–3am, Sat noon–3am, Sun noon–midnight.

Siltanen Hämeentie 13B Ⓦsiltanen.org. This great little red-brick spot is a Kallio favourite for local artists and musicians. They often play Finnish music from the 60s. Great spot for its hulking large breakfasts and brunches (€16) too. Mon–Thurs & Sun 11am–2am, Fri & Sat 11am–3am.

Sling in Mikonkatu 8 Ⓦslingin.fi. Best – and best-priced – cocktails in Helsinki, with knowledgeable bartenders who do the classics and their own inventive concoctions. Awkwardly located on the second floor of a shopping mall across from the train station – though perhaps this is a reason to go. Enter on Kaivokatu. Mon–Thurs 5pm–2am, Fri 3pm–3am, Sat & Sun 5pm–3am.

We Got Beef Iso Roobertinkatu 21. For over a decade now, Helsinki's hippest-of-the-hipster bars has been the place to come hear DJs spin reggae, ska and funk, with a small dancefloor out the back. Wed–Sat 6pm–4am.

Zetor Kaivopiha, Mannerheimintie 3 Ⓦzetor.net. This classic Finnish bar-restaurant is filled with old rusty tractors and serves drinks and eats all day and night until 3.30am. A great place to try *sahti* – Finnish home-brewed ale. Sun & Mon noon–midnight, Tues noon–3am, Wed–Sat noon–4am.

CLUBS

Adams Erottajankatu 15–17 Ⓦravintolaadams.fi. Helsinki's hippest new dance club, while fairly small, fancies itself rather VIP. Also has a great restaurant open Tues–Sat 5–11pm. Fri–Sun 10pm–4am.

Korjaamo Töölönkatu 51B Ⓦkorjaamo.fi. This well-managed cultural centre puts on a series of superb indie rock, electronica and avant-garde concerts throughout the year, and also has a great bar. Opening hours depend on gigs and events.

The Tiger 1A Urho Kekkosenkatu Ⓦthetiger.fi. This extremely popular sprawling nightclub consists of several levels, multiple black-marble dancefloors, large terrace lounges and VIP rooms. Fri–Sun 10pm–4am.

GAY HELSINKI

The gay scene in Helsinki has shrunk somewhat in recent years, but it's still lively. For the latest details, pick up a copy of the widely available monthly *Z* magazine – in Finnish only but with a useful listings section – or drop into the state-supported gay organization SETA, Pasilanraitio 5 (Ⓣ044 511 2134, Ⓦseta.fi).

dtm (Don't Tell Mamma) Mannerheimintie 6 B Ⓦdtm.fi. The capital's legendary gay nightclub has moved house, but still has all the charm: drag shows, gay karaoke and regular house music parties. Mon–Sat 9pm–4am.

Sauna Vogue Sturenkatu 27A Ⓦsaunavogue.net. Finland's only gay sauna, with a bar, steamroom, terrace and masseur. €18 entry. Mon & Tues 3–10pm, Wed–Sun 3–11pm.

SHOPPING

Look out for Design District stickers, marking the city's most interesting boutiques and designer shops.

Akateeminen Kirjakauppa Ⓦakateeminen.com. Next door to Stockmann Department Store (see below) is the city's best bookshop, with thousands of titles in English. Mon–Fri 9am–9pm, Sat 9am–6pm, Sun noon–6pm.

Design Forum Finland Erottajankatu 7 Ⓦdesignforum.fi. Comprehensive shop, café and studio space devoted to Finnish design: clothes, homeware, ceramics and jewellery. Mon–Fri 11am–7pm, Sat 11am–6pm.

Helsinki 10 Eerikinkatu 3 Ⓦhelsinki10.fi. Some great clothing brands from Finland and further afield at this lovingly stocked boutique. Mon–Fri 11am–7pm, Sat 10am–6pm.

Stockmann Department Store Corner of Aleksanterinkatu and Mannerheimintie Ⓦstockmann.com. Sprawling Constructivist edifice selling everything from bubble gum to Persian rugs. Mon–Fri 9am–9pm, Sat 9am–6pm, Sun noon–6pm.

Stupido Iso Roobertinkatu 23 Ⓦstupido.fi. Independent record shop with a dedicated Finnish section featuring a lot of heavy metal and Europop. A good place to pick up flyers and listings too. Mon–Fri 11am–7pm, Sat 11am–5pm.

DIRECTORY

Embassies Australia (honorary consulate), Museokatu 25b Ⓣ09 4777 6640; Canada, Pohjoisesplanadi 25b Ⓣ09 228 530; Ireland, Erottajankatu 7A Ⓣ09 646 006; South Africa, Rahapajankatu 1A Ⓣ09 6860 3100; UK, Itäinen Puistotie 17 Ⓣ09 2286 5100; US, Itäinen Puistotie 14a Ⓣ09 616 250.

Exchange Apart from the banks, try Change Group at the airport (6am–8/9pm) or Forex at the train station (Mon–Fri 8am–10pm, Sat & Sun 9am–7pm).

Hospital Marian Hospital, Lapinlahdenkatu 16 ☎09 310 6611.

Internet Cafe Aalto, Akateeminen Kirjakauppa, Keskuskatu 1; mhar in the Lasipalatsi, Mannerheimintie 22–24; Robert's Coffee, Aleksanterinkatu 52.

Left luggage Lockers (€3 and up) in the long-distance bus station (Mon–Thurs & Sat 9am–6pm, Fri 8am–6pm), and in the train station (daily 6.30am–10pm).

Pharmacy Yliopiston Apteekki (☎0300 20 200, toll call), Mannerheimintie 96, is open 24hr; its branch at Mannerheimintie 5 is open daily 7am–midnight.

Post office Elielinaukio 2F (mid-Aug to late-May Mon–Thurs 8am–10pm, Fri 8am–10pm, Sat & Sun noon–6pm; late May to mid-Aug Mon–Thurs 9am–8pm, Fri 9am–6pm, Sat & Sun noon–6pm).

PORVOO

About 50km east of Helsinki, **PORVOO** is one of the oldest towns on the south coast and one of Finland's most charming. Its narrow cobbled streets, lined by small colourful wooden buildings, give a sense of Finnish life before the capital's bold squares and Neoclassical geometry. Close to the station, the **Johan Ludwig Runeberg House**, Aleksanterinkatu 3 (May–Aug Mon–Sat 10am–4pm, Sun 11am–4pm; Sept–April Wed–Sun noon–4pm; €6), is where the famed Finnish poet lived from 1852; one of his poems provided the lyrics for the Finnish national anthem.

The old town is built around the hill on the other side of Mannerheimkatu, crowned by the fifteenth-century **Tuomiokirkko**, where Alexander I proclaimed Finland a Russian Grand Duchy and convened the first Finnish Diet. The cathedral survived a serious arson attack in 2006 and reopened two years later. The town's past can be explored in the **Porvoo Museum** (May–Aug Mon–Sat 10am–4pm, Sun 11am–4pm; Sept–April Wed–Sun noon–4pm; €6) at the foot of the hill in the main square.

ARRIVAL AND INFORMATION

By bus Buses run daily from Helsinki to Porvoo (€11.80 one-way; 1hr).

Tourist office Rihkamakatu 4 (Mon–Fri 9am–7pm, Sat & Sun 10am–5pm; ☎040 489 9801, ⓦporvoo.fi).

ACCOMMODATION

Porvoo Hostel Linnankoskenkatu 1–3 ☎019 523 0012, ⓦwww.porvoohostel.fi. Cosy 29-bed hostel, with 10 rooms. There's an indoor pool and sports facilities nearby. Dorm €22, double €26

Sun Camping Porvoo Kokonniemi Uddaksentie 17 ☎019 581 967, ⓦsuncamping.fi. Campsite 1.5km from the town centre. June–Aug only. €5.50 per person, plus €15 per tent

EATING

Hanna Maria Välikatu 6 ⓦhanna-maria.fi. The cheapest place to eat in the Old Town, with lunches that range €7–9. Mon–Sat 8am–5pm, Sun 10am–5pm.

10

The southwest

The region immediately west of Helsinki comprises swathes of interminable forests interrupted only by modest-sized patches of water and wooden villa towns. The far southwestern corner is rather more interesting, with islands and inlets around a jagged shoreline, a spectacular archipelago stretching halfway to Sweden and some distinctive Finnish–Swedish coastal communities.

TURKU

Co-host of the European Capital of Culture during 2011 (along with Tallinn), **TURKU** was once the national capital, but lost its status in 1812 and most of its buildings in a ferocious fire in 1827. These days it's a small and sociable city, bristling with history, culture and a sparkling nightlife, thanks to the students from its two universities.

WHAT TO SEE AND DO

To get to grips with Turku and its pivotal place in Finnish history, cut through the centre to the Aura River which splits the city. This tree-framed space was, before the great fire of 1827, the bustling heart of the community.

Tuomiokirkko

Overlooking the river, the **Tuomiokirkko** (daily 9am–7/8pm except during services) was erected in the thirteenth

10

century and is still the centre of the Finnish Lutheran Church. Despite repeated fires, a number of features survive, and there's a small museum in the south gallery.

Turku Art Museum

The **Turku Art Museum** (Tues–Fri 11am–7pm, Sat & Sun 11am–5pm; €8) is housed in a lovely building constructed in 1904. It contains one of the better collections of Finnish art, with works by all the great names of the country's nineteenth-century Golden Age plus a commendable stock of modern pieces.

Aboa Vetus and Ars Nova

Turku's newest and most splendid museum is the combined **Aboa Vetus and Ars Nova** (daily 11am–7pm, Sept–March closed Mon; €8; guided tours July–Aug daily 11.30am), along the riverbank. Digging the foundations of the modern art gallery revealed a warren of medieval lanes, now on show. The gallery comprises 350 striking works plus temporary exhibits, and there's a great café too.

Turku Castle

Crossing back over Aurajoki and down Linnankatu and then heading towards the mouth of the river will bring you to **Turku Castle** (Tues–Sun 10am–6pm; €8). If you don't fancy the walk, hop on bus #1 from the market square. The featureless exterior conceals a maze of cobbled courtyards, corridors and staircases, with a bewildering array of finds and displays – a 37-room historical museum. The castle probably went up around 1280; its gradual expansion accounts for the patchwork architecture.

ARRIVAL AND INFORMATION

By train The train station is just north of the city centre. It takes roughly 15 minutes to walk into town, or you could take local bus #1.

Destinations Helsinki (hourly; 2hr); Tampere (9 daily; 1hr 40min).

By bus The bus station is next to the train station.

Destinations Helsinki (hourly; 2hr 15min–3hr 50min); Tampere (every 30min; 2–3hr).

By ferry From the Stockholm ferry, take the train to the terminal, 2km west, or catch bus #1 to Linnankatu.

Destinations Stockholm (4 daily; 10–11hr).

Tourist office Aurakatu 4 (April–Sept Mon–Fri 8.30am–6pm, Sat & Sun 9am–4pm; Oct–March Mon–Fri 8.30am–6pm, Sat & Sun 10am–3pm; ☎02 262 7444, ⓦ visitturku.fi).

ACCOMMODATION

Campsite Ruissalo ☎02 262 5100. On the island of Ruissalo, which has two sandy beaches and overlooks Turku harbour. June–Aug; bus #8. **€5** per person, plus **€16** per tent

Hostel Turku Linnankatu 39 ☎02 262 7680, ⓦ hostelturku.fi. One of the cleanest, most efficient and best-run hostels in Finland, situated right by the river. Pine floors, comfy sofas as well as three large kitchens, laundry, personal lockers, an internet café and inexpensive bicycle rental service. Take bus #1 or #30. Dorm **€23**

Linnasmaki Lustokatu 7 ☎02 4123 500, ⓦ linnasmaki .fi. Basic 56-room year-round hostel in the Christian Institute, 4km from town (bus #14 or #15). Dorm **€30**

Omena Hotelli Humalistonkatu 7 ⓦ omenahotels.com. Alvar Aalto fans might fancy a stay in this building designed by Finland's most famous architect. The hotel is modern and self-service, with an automated reception area. Double **€45**

★ **River Hostel Turku** Linnankatu 72 ☎040 689 2541, ⓦ msborea.fi. Permanently docked on the river, the S/S *Borea* is the most exciting place to stay in Turku on a budget. The appeal lies not in the tidy, en-suite cabin rooms, but in the quirky experience of staying on an ex-cruise ship. Double **€78**

Tuure Bed and Breakfast Tuureporinkatu 17 C ☎02 233 0230, ⓦ tuure.fi. Clean, pleasant little guesthouse with friendly proprietors in the centre of town, where 15 rooms are located in something of a drab office building. Double **€58**

EATING AND DRINKING

Fresh produce is sold in the *kauppatori* (market square), near the tourist office, every day; in summer it's full of open-air cafés; nearby, the effervescent market hall or *kauppahalli* (Mon–Fri 8am–5pm, Sat 8am–2pm) offers a slightly more upmarket choice of delis and other places to eat. A drink at one of the many floating bar-restaurants moored along Itäinen Rantakatu is a popular summer tradition.

CAFÉS AND RESTAURANTS

Assarin Ullakko Rehtorinpellonkatu 4a. This rock-bottom-priced student cafeteria ("The Assistant's Attic") offers a lively atmosphere great for meeting local students. Lunch costs €5.45 (50 percent discount for students). Mon–Thurs 10.30am–3.30pm, Fri 10.30am–3pm, Sat 11.30am–4pm.

Blanko Aurakatu 1 ⓦblanko.net. Ever-popular bar-restaurant just opposite the tourist office. Good lunches and drum 'n' bass and house DJs till 3am at weekends. Lunches from €7.90, dinners double that. Mon & Tues 11am–11pm, Wed & Thurs 11am–midnight, Fri & Sat 11am–3pm, Sun noon–6pm.

Tintå Läntinen Rantakatu 9 ⓦtinta.fi. Wines and pizzas, with solid lunches around €15. Mon 11am–midnight, Tues–Thurs 11am–1am, Fri 11am–midnight, Sat noon–2am, Sun noon–midnight.

Viikinkiravintola Harald Aurakatu 3 ⓦravintolaharald.fi. With whittled furnishings, earthenware plates and heads of game mounted on the walls, this Viking-style restaurant also does great, hearty meals. Lunches from €8 served until 3pm. Mon–Thurs 11am–10pm, Fri 11am–11pm, Sat noon–11pm, Sun 1–10pm.

BARS AND CLUBS

B4R Kristiinankatu 4 ⓦbar4.fi. This spot offers a solid collection of various beers and drinks. Mon–Thurs 4pm–2am, Fri–Sun 4pm–3am.

Dynamo Linnankatu 7 ⓦdynamoklubi.com. A rocking bar set across two floors, with red velour chairs and olive leather couches. Only really gets going around 1am, when the dancefloor becomes packed and sweaty. Tues–Sat 9pm–4am.

Klubi Humalistonkatu 8 ⓦklubi.net. Cavernous, student venue featuring live bands and DJ nights – for listings, check the posters liberally applied to lampposts all over town. Wed 10pm–4am, Thurs–Sat 9pm–4am.

Monk Humalistonkatu 3 ⓦmonk.fi. Cool spot with lots of live jazz. Mon 9pm–1am, Fri–Sat 9pm–4am.

The Lake Region

About a third of Finland is covered by the **Lake Region**, a massive area of bays, inlets and islands interspersed with dense pine forests. Despite holding much of Finland's industry, it's a tranquil, verdant area, and even **Tampere**, a major industrial city, enjoys a peaceful lakeside setting. The eastern part of the region is the most atmospheric: slender ridges furred with conifers link the few sizeable landmasses. The regional centre, **Savonlinna**, stretches gorgeously across several islands and boasts a fine medieval castle, inside which a superb opera festival is held every summer, while bustling **Kuopio** offers a good taste of the region.

TAMPERE

Scandinavia's largest inland city, **TAMPERE** is a leafy place of cobbled avenues, sculpture-filled parks and two sizeable, placid lakes. It was long a manufacturing centre, but thanks to an impressive arts patronage, it has become one of Finland's most enjoyable cities, with free outdoor concerts, a healthy nightlife and one of the best modern art collections in the country.

WHAT TO SEE AND DO

The main streets run off either side of Hämeenkatu. To the left, up slender Hämeenpuisto, the **Lenin Museum** at no. 28 (Mon–Fri 9am–6pm, Sat & Sun 11am–4pm; €5) commemorates the revolutionary's ties with Finland and his life in general; the absorbing exhibition has a devoted, trainspotter feel. Moomin fans shouldn't miss the adorable **Moomin Museum** (Tues–Fri 9am–5pm, Sat & Sun 10am–6pm; €6), a respectful and exhaustive overview of Tove Jansson's creations; it is temporarily being housed in a section of the otherwise uninspiring **Art Museum of Tampere** (Tues–Sun 10am–6pm; €6) at Puutarhakatu 34. If you're looking for more representative Finnish art you might be better off visiting the **Hiekka Art Gallery**, a few minutes' walk away at Pirkankatu 6 (Tues–Thurs 3–6pm, Sun noon–3pm; €7). Better still is the tremendous **Sara Hildén Art Museum** (daily 10/11am–6/7pm, closed Mon Oct–April; €10, includes admission to Särkänniemi amusement park and Näsinneula observation tower), built on the shores of Näsijärvi, a quirky collection of Finnish and foreign modern works; take bus #16 (or #4 in summer) from the centre.

ARRIVAL AND INFORMATION

By plane Bus #61 operates between the airport and the city centre, taking 40min. Tampere-Pirkkala Airport is located 13km southwest of the city; the bus (ⓦairpro.fi) costs €6.

By train The train station is at Rautatienkatu 25, at the end of Hämeenkatu.

Destinations Helsinki (hourly; 2hr); Kuopio (daily; 3hr 15min–4hr 10min); Oulu (14 daily; 4hr 35min–8hr

10min); Savonlinna (5 daily; 5hr 30min–6hr 30min); Turku (8–11 daily; 1hr 40min).

By bus The long-distance bus station is in the town centre, off Hämeenkatu.

Tourist office In the train station (Sept–May Mon–Fri 9–5pm; June–Aug Mon–Fri 9am–6pm, Sat & Sun 10am–3pm; ☎ 03 5656 6800, ⓦ gotampere.fi).

10 ACCOMMODATION

Dream Hostel Åkerlundinkatu 2 ☎ 045 236 0517, ⓦ dreamhostel.fi. This cosy spot features modern furnishings and pretty much every amenity you could imagine, including a sauna and gym. Dorm €22

Härmälä Campsite ☎ 020 719 9777. 4km south of the city centre in gorgeous wooded environs with cabins; bus #1. Early May to late Sept. €5 per person, plus €15 per pitch, cabin €46

Omena Hotelli Hämeenkatu 7 & Hämeenkatu 28 ⓦ omenahotels.com. These two excellent, self-service hotels have no reception and you must book online, but they offer some of the best deals in town. Double €45

EATING

Gopal Ilmarinkatu 16 ⓦ gopal.fi. Wonderful, friendly vegetarian Indian lunch spot just off the central *tori* where you pay what your food weighs (€1.85 per 100g). Mon–Fri 11am–5pm, Sat noon–4pm.

Kahvila Runo Ojakatu 3 ⓦ kahvilaruno.fi. With some great Finnish rustic furniture, this bookish, high-ceilinged space has plenty of charm and is the best place for a coffee and cake in town. Mon–Fri 9am–8pm, Sun 10am–8pm.

Salud Tuomiokirkonkatu 19 ⓦ salud.fi. A lively Spanish restaurant serving mixed tapas plates and an amply sized weekday lunch buffet, both for around €10. Mon–Fri 11am–late, Sat noon–late, Sun 1pm–late.

Tivoli Smørrebrød & Øl Itäinenkatu 9–13. Good selection of Nordic sandwiches and beers in this resto-pub set in the Finlayson factory area. Mon & Tues 11am–9pm, Wed & Thurs 11am–10pm, Fri 11am–11pm, Sat noon–11pm, Sun noon–9pm.

DRINKING

Klubi Tullikamarinaukio 2 ⓦ klubi.net. Busy nightclub and concert venue in an old customs house behind the train station. Also serves affordable lunches. Wed 10pm–4am, Thurs–Sat 9pm–4am.

Telakka Tullikamarin aukio 3 ⓦ telakka.eu. Though this resto-pub does have good meals (from €13.50), it is better known as the most popular watering hole among local university students. Set a few minutes' walk north of the train station. Mon & Tues 11am–midnight, Wed & Thurs 11am–2am, Fri 11am–3am, Sat noon–3am, Sun noon–midnight.

Vanha Monttu Hämeenkatu 17 ⓦ vanhamonttu.net. Cellar bar filled with ex-punk and hard-rocker kids and lots of naff memorabilia on the walls. The lively drunken karaoke nights are a particularly good spot to see the Finnish national character up close. Sun–Wed 11am–2am, Thurs–Sat 11am–3am.

SAVONLINNA AND AROUND

SAVONLINNA is one of the most relaxed towns in Finland, renowned for its **opera festival** (☎ 015 476 750, ⓦ operafestival.fi) in July. It's packed throughout summer, so book well ahead if you're visiting at this time. Out of peak season, its streets and beaches are uncluttered, and the town's easy-going mood and lovely setting – amid a confluence of forests and lakes – make it a pleasant place to linger.

WHAT TO SEE AND DO

The best locations for soaking up the atmosphere are the **harbour** and **market square** at the end of Olavinkatu, where you can cast an eye over the grand *Seurahuone* hotel, with its Art Nouveau fripperies. At the square, try the Savonlinna speciality known as "*lörtsy*", a delicious meat-and-rice-filled pastry packed with condiments. Follow the harbour around picturesque Linnankatu, or around the sandy edge of Pihlajavesi, which brings you to atmospheric and surprisingly well-preserved **Olavinlinna Castle** (hourly guided tours Jan–May Mon–Fri 10am–4pm, Sat & Sun 11am–4pm; June to mid-Aug daily 10am–6pm; mid-Aug to mid-Dec Mon–Fri 10am–4pm, Sat & Sun 11am–4pm; €8), perched on a small island. Founded in 1475, the castle witnessed a series of bloody conflicts until the Russians claimed possession of it in 1743 and relegated it to the status of town jail.

Nearby is the **Savonlinna Provincial Museum** in Riihisaari (Tues–Sun 11am–5pm, plus Mon same times June–Aug; €5), which occupies an old granary and displays an intriguing account of the evolution of local life, with rock paintings and ancient amber carved with human figures.

ARRIVAL AND INFORMATION

By train There are two train stations: be sure to get off at Savonlinna-Kauppatori, just across the main bridge from the tourist office.
Destinations Parikkala (for Helsinki; 6 daily; 50min); Punkaharju (6 daily; 30min); Tampere (5 daily; 5hr 30min–6hr 30min). Both destinations are reached from either train station in Savonlinna.
By bus The bus station is off the main island, but within easy walking distance of the town centre.
Destinations Kuopio (3–5 daily; 2hr 45min–4hr 35min).
Tourist office Puistokatu 1 (July to early Aug Mon–Sat 10am–6pm, Sun 10am–2pm; rest of year Mon–Fri 9am–5pm; ☎ 0600 30 007, ⓦ savonlinna.travel).

ACCOMMODATION

Perhehotelli Hospitz Linnankatu 20 ☎ 015 515 661, ⓦ www.hospitz.com. Attractive, central hotel. Prices go up by some 50 percent during the opera festival. Double **€98**
Savonlinna SKO Hostel Opistokatu 1 ☎ 015 72 910, ⓦ www.sko.fi. Likeable summer (June–Aug) hostel in the town's Christian Institute. 6km from the city centre. Double **€90**
S/S Heinävesi Savonlinna harbour ☎ 0500 653 774, ⓦ www.savonlinnanlaivat.fi. In the summer, this steamship offers 34 beds in spartan, comfy on-board cabins. Double **€70**
Vuohimäki Camping Vuohimäentie 60 ☎ 015 537 353, ⓦ suncamping.fi. The nearest campsite, though still a good 7km from the centre. Early June to late Aug; bus #4. **€5** per person plus **€15** per pitch (€14 in total for only one person).

EATING AND DRINKING

Good, cheap food is available at the pizza joints along Olavinkatu and Tulliportinkatu.
Majakka Satamakatu 11. Tasty Finnish nosh, with some good deals at lunchtime (from €7.40). Mon–Sat 11am–1am, Sun noon–midnight.
Paviljonki Rajalahdenkatu 4. The restaurant of a local cookery school, serving a small selection of Finnish and continental mains, such as spareribs with BBQ-sauce and sugared apple (from €16.90). Daily 11am–4pm.

KUOPIO

The pleasant lakeside town of **KUOPIO** is best known for its enormous smoke sauna, the biggest in the world, and makes for a worthwhile pit stop on your way north to Lapland. One of the best times to visit is during the annual **Kuopio Dance Festival** (ⓦ www.kuopiodance festival.fi) in mid-June.

WHAT TO SEE AND DO

Built on a grid system, the centre is easy to navigate. Just south of the train station is the main square, the *kauppatori*.

Museums

From the main square Kauppakatu leads east to the **Kuopio Museum** (Tues–Sat 10am–5pm; €7) at no. 23 with two floors of natural and cultural history. Further up the road, at no. 35, the **Kuopio Art Museum** (Tues–Sat 10am–5pm; €5) is housed in a converted bank. The thoughtfully curated temporary exhibitions focus mainly on modern Finnish art. Around the corner on Kuninkaankatu, the **Victor Barsokevitsch Photographic Centre** (June–Aug Mon–Fri 10am–6pm, Sat & Sun 11am–4pm; Sept–May Tues–Fri 11am–5pm, till 7pm on Wed, Sat & Sun 11am–3pm; summer €5, winter €4) is a real find – one of the best photography galleries in the country, with changing exhibitions.

Woodsmoke sauna

Kuopio's **woodsmoke sauna** (Tues year-round, plus Thurs June–Aug; €12; ⓦ rauhalahti.fi), set at the *Jätkänkämppä Lumberjack Lodge*, is the main draw in town, and about as quintessentially Finnish an experience as you'll find: there are traditional Finnish evenings each night the sauna is open, which often include a Lumberjack Show and great dinner buffet from mid-May to mid-August (€21). The lodge is located 4km south of the centre in the *Rauhalahti* spa hotel complex.

ARRIVAL AND INFORMATION

By train Kuopio's train station is located just north of the *kauppatori*.
Destinations Helsinki (12 daily; 4hr 45min–5hr 10min); Oulu (4 daily; 4hr–4hr 30min); Rovaniemi (5 daily; 6hr 30min–14hr 30min); Savonlinna (9 daily; 2hr 45min–4hr); Tampere (daily; 3hr 15min–4hr 10min).
By bus The bus station sits opposite the train station.
Destinations Savonlinna (3–5 daily; 2hr 45min–4hr 35min).
Tourist office Within the City Hall at Haapaniemenkatu 17 (June–Aug Mon–Fri 9.30am–5pm (plus July Sat 9.30am–3pm); rest of year Mon–Fri 9.30am–4pm; ☎ 017 182 584, ⓦ visitlakeland.fi).

10

ACCOMMODATION

Hostelli Hermanni Hermanninaukio 3e ☎040 910 9083, ⓦhostellihermanni.fi. Comfortable if basic hostel 1.5km out of town. Dorm €30, double €50

Matkalukeskus Rauhalahti Katiskaniementie 8, 5km from the city centre ☎017 473 000, ⓦrauhalahti.fi. Attractive lakeside campsite with cottages, a hostel and space for tents (late May to late Aug). Camping €5 per person plus €13 per tent, cottage €32, double €92. The nearby spa hotel (☎03 060 830), part of the same establishment but with a different reception, offers rooms too. Double €80

Youth Hostel Virkkula Asemakatu 3 ☎044 449 6822, ⓦkuopionsteiner.fi. Summer hostel in a colourful converted school just by the train station. Early June to mid-Aug. Dorm €25

EATING AND DRINKING

★ **Café Kaneli** Kauppakatu 22 ⓦkahvilakaneli.net. Charming little café cluttered with knick-knacks and pictures, serving great coffee and cake. Mon, Tues, Thurs, Fri 9.30am–6pm, Wed 9.30am–7.30pm, Sat 11am–4pm, Sun 11am–3pm.

Sampo Kauppakatu 13. Proudly traditional fish restaurant that has been serving Finnish dishes loved by locals since 1931. Mains around €14. Mon–Thurs 11am–10pm, Fri & Sat 11am–midnight, Sun noon–10pm.

Wanha Satama At the harbour ⓦwanhasatama.net /aukioloajat. Set in a former customs house, this modern Finnish restaurant is popular on sunny summer evenings, offering up inexpensive sandwiches and salads and more expensive local dishes. Open daily, though exact hours are complicated (check the website).

The north

The northern regions make up a vast portion of Finland: a full one third of the country lies north of the Arctic Circle. It's sparsely populated, with small communities often separated by long distances and little of anything in between besides tundra-like plains or dense forests. The coast of Ostrobothnia is affluent due to the adjacent flat and fertile farmland; busy and expanding **Oulu** is the region's major city, though it maintains a pleasing small-town atmosphere. Further north is the wild territory of **Lapland**, its wide-open spaces home to several thousand Sámi, who have lived more or less in harmony with this

harsh environment for millennia. Up here are two good bases: the buzzing town of **Rovaniemi** and, further north, the quiet village of **Inari**, Lapland's de facto capital and a great jumping-off point for trips to more remote bits of the region; there is an extensive bus service and regular flights from Helsinki. Make sure you try Lappish **cuisine**, too – fresh cloudberries, smoked reindeer and wild salmon are highlights.

OULU

OULU, with its renowned university, is a leading light in Finland's burgeoning computing industry and a great place to pause on your way up north, with a good collection of restaurants and cafés and a pulsing nightlife, especially in the warmer months. On Kirkkokatu, the copper-domed and stuccoed **Tuomiokirkko** (June–Aug daily 11am–8/9pm; Sept–May Mon–Fri noon–1pm) seems anachronistic amid the bulky blocks of modern Oulu. Across the small canal just to the north, the **Northern Ostrobothnia Museum** (Tues–Sun 10am–5pm; €4) has a large regional collection with a good Sámi section.

ARRIVAL AND INFORMATION

By train The train station is located a few blocks east of the *kauppatori* and *kauppahalli*.
Destinations Helsinki (11 daily; 6hr 10min–9hr); Rovaniemi (7 daily; 2hr 15min–2hr 45min); Tampere (14 daily; 4hr 35min–8hr 10min).

By bus The bus station is located just next to the train station.
Destinations Helsinki (6 daily; 9hr 45min–13hr 30min); Rovaniemi (7 daily; 3hr 10min–5hr 35min).

Tourist office Torikatu 10 (Mon–Thurs 9am–5pm, Fri 9am–4pm; mid-June to Aug until 5pm, plus Sat 10am–4pm; ☎08 5584 1330, ⓦoulutourism.fi).

ACCOMMODATION

Nallikari Holiday Village ☎044 703 1353, ⓦcampingfinland.fi. Campsite with cabins on Hietasaari Island, 4km from town; take bus #17 from Isokatu in the town centre. Cabins €40, camping €4 per person plus €13 per tent

Välkkylätalo Ylioppilaantie 2 ☎010 272 2987, ⓦosao .fi. Fairly central summer hostel with bland but acceptable rooms. Double €45

EATING, DRINKING AND NIGHTLIFE

45 Special Saarisonkatu 12 ⓦ 45special.com. Legendary rock club with three floors and frequent live bands; the Sunday jams are a good bet. Most concerts are free, those that cost are rarely more than €5.

Finlandia Hallituskatu 31. No-nonsense pizzeria that is one of the cheapest places for a dinner in town. Daily until late.

Never Grow Old Hallituskatu 13–17 ⓦ ngo.fi. With swinging wicker bungalow chairs, a painted Caribbean beachscape and reggae music all night long, this quirky bar is perfect for late-night dancing most nights of the week. Mon–Thurs 10.30am–1pm, Fri 10.30am–5am, Sat 11am–5am, Sun noon–midnight.

Valve Café Hallituskatu 7 ⓦ kulttuurivalve.fi. Oulu's youth and cultural centre has a relaxed courtyard café that's super in the afternoons. Films are screened every evening in the same building. Mon–Fri 9am–2.30pm.

Vox Pakkahuoneenkatu 8 ⓦ viinibaarivox.fi. This wine bar has become popular with the town's yuppie hipster set. Mon–Thurs 11am–midnight, Fri 11am–2am, Sat 4pm–2am, Sun 4pm–midnight.

ROVANIEMI

Easily reached by train, **ROVANIEMI** is touted as the capital of Lapland, and while its fairly bland shopping streets can't compare to the surrounding rural hinterland, the town's Arctic sensibility makes it worth spending a day here while gearing up for an exploration of the Northern Finnish hinterlands. The best way to prepare yourself for what lies further north is to visit the 172m-long glass tunnel at Arktikum at Pohjoisranta 4 (June–Aug daily 9am–6pm; mid-Jan to May and Sept to Nov Tues–Sun 10am–6pm; Dec to mid-Jan daily 10am–6pm; €12; ⓦ arktikum.fi). Subterranean galleries house Sámi crafts, costumes and displays on all things circumpolar. The **midnight sun** is visible from Rovaniemi for several weeks each side of midsummer. The best vantage points are either the striking bridge over the Ounaskoski or atop the forested and mosquito-infested hill, Ounasvaara, across the bridge.

Two of the biggest attractions are outside town. **The Arctic Circle**, 8km north, is connected by the hourly bus #8 from the railway station (€6.80 return). A few paces north of the circle is the **Santa**

Claus Village (early Jan to May 10am–5pm; June–Aug 9am–6pm, Sept–Nov 10am–5pm; Dec to early Jan 9am–7pm; free), a large log cabin where you can meet Father Christmas (and purchase his various paraphernalia) all year round.

ARRIVAL AND INFORMATION

By plane The airport is located 10km north of town, and connected by bus (€7).
Destinations Helsinki (5 daily; 1hr 15min).
By train The train station is just outside the town centre, at Ratukatu 3.
Destinations Helsinki (4 daily; 10hr 20min–12hr 55min); Oulu (7 daily; 2hr 15min–2hr 45min).
By bus The bus station is just west of the centre, off Postikatu, a few minutes' walk east from the train station.
Destinations Inari (4 daily; 4hr 40min–7hr 50min); Nordkapp, Norway (June to late Aug 1 daily; 10hr 35min).
Tourist office Maakuntakatu 29-31 (mid-June to mid-Aug Mon–Fri 9am–6pm, Sat & Sun 9am–3pm; rest of the year Mon–Fri 9am–5pm; ☎016 346 270, ⓦ visitrovaniemi.fi).

ACCOMMODATION

Guesthouse Borealis Asemieskatu 1 ☎016 342 0130, ⓦ guesthouseborealis.com. Wonderful family-run spot with colourful rooms and great service. Double **€64**

Hostel Rudolf Koskikatu 41, book via ☎016 321 321, ⓦ rudolf.fi. Modern hostel with colourful rooms a 10min walk from the centre. There are no staff on site; check-in and reservations are handled by the *Hotel Santa Claus*, Korkalonkatu 29. April–Nov. Dorm **€40**, double **€61**

Ounaskoksi Camping ☎016 345 304. Campsite on the far bank of Ounaskoski, facing town – a 20min walk from the station. Mid-May to late Sept. **€7.50** per person plus **€14** per tent

EATING AND DRINKING

Café and Bar 21 Rovakatu 21 ⓦ cafebar21.fi. Somewhat low-key spot big with younger folk, serving salads, waffles, smoothies and coffee. Mon & Tues 11am–9pm, Wed & Thurs 11am–midnight, Fri 11am–2am, Sat noon–2am, Sun noon–9pm.

★ **Kauppayhtiö** Valtakatu 24. Unexpectedly fantastic café-bar with a mishmash of retro furniture. DJs at the weekend and a gallery at the back. Mon, Tues & Thurs 11am–8pm, Wed 11am–10pm, Fri & Sat 11am–3am.

Kotilelpomo Antinkaapo Rovakatu 13 ⓦ antinkaapo.com. The best café in town serves a wide range of cakes and pastries. Mon–Fri 7.30am–5pm, Sat 10am–2pm.

Monte Rosa Pekankatu 9 ⓦ monterosa.fi. Rovaniemi's best Italian restaurant, with excellent pan pizzas and pasta dishes, from €9.20. Mon–Fri 5–11pm, Sat 3–11pm, Sun 5–10pm.

Zoomit Korkalonkatu 29. Modern, if somewhat gaudy, bar that's been around for a few years now but is still popular with local university students. Mon, Tues, Thurs 11am–noon, Wed 11am–1pm, Fri & Sat 11am–2am, Sun noon–11pm.

INARI

10

A half-day bus ride north of Rovaniemi, **INARI** lies along the fringes of Inarijärvi, one of Finland's largest lakes, and makes an attractive base from which to further explore this part of Lapland. In the town itself, the excellent **SIIDA** (Sámi Museum; Tues–Sun: June to mid-Sept 9am–8pm; mid-Sept to May 10am–5pm; €10; ⓦ siida.fi) has an outstanding outdoor section giving you an idea of how the Sámi survived in Arctic conditions in their tepees, or *kota*, while the indoor section has a well-laid-out exhibition on all aspects of life in the Arctic. Towards the northern end of the village, summer **boat tours** (€20) depart from under the bridge to the ancient Sámi holy site on the island of **Ukonkivi**. If walking's your thing then check out the pretty **Pielpajärvi Wilderness Church**, a well-signposted 7km (2hr) hike from the village.

ARRIVAL AND INFORMATION

By plane Ivalo airport in Törmänen is roughly 50km southeast of Inari. Other than car rental, the only remotely affordable way to reach Inari from here is by taking a taxi to Ivalo centre (€15), then a bus to Inari (€8.20).
Destinations Helsinki (from Ivalo; 1–2 daily; 1hr 30min–2hr 30min).

By bus Buses stop outside the tourist office, in the centre of town, before continuing to Karasjok in Norway and – from June to late Aug only – Nordkapp, about the most northerly point in mainland Europe.
Destination Ivalo (3–5 daily; 35min); Rovaniemi (3–4 daily; 5hr 5min–6hr 20min).
Tourist office The helpful tourist office (mid-Sept to May Tues–Sun 10am–5pm; June to mid-Sept daily 9am–8pm; ☏ 040 168 9668, ⓦ saariselka.fi) is in the SIIDA museum complex. Staff here can advise on guided snow-scooter trips in winter and fishing trips in summer – as well as trips across the Russian border to Murmansk.

ACCOMMODATION

Finding accommodation should not be too problematic, though Inari does get very busy during the summer.
Lomakylä Inari Inarintie 26 ☏ 016 671 108, ⓦ saariselka.fi. A brief walk from town, these lakeside log cabins are open year-round and most have private bath. Cabin €23, camping €10
Uruniemi Campsite 2km south of the village ☏ 016 671 331, ⓦ uruniemi.com. In a lovely location right by the lake, with cabins and rooms arranged around manicured grounds. Oct–May advanced booking obligatory. Camping €5 per person, plus €5 per tent, cottage from €27
★ **Villa Lanca** Opposite the tourist office ☏ 040 748 0984, ⓦ villalanca.com. Cheery guesthouse with gorgeous rooms. Double €79

EATING

Aanaar Saarikoskentie 2. The restaurant inside the *Inarin Kultahovi* hotel dishes up the best meals in town, including reindeer carpaccio and skewered tiger prawns, with mains €12–25. Daily 11am–10.30pm.
Sarrit Inarintie 46. Inside the SIIDA museum, this restaurant prepares excellent Arctic dishes, including a succulent baked salmon fillet with hollandaise sauce. Hours same as SIIDA museum (above).

THE SEINE, VIEWED FROM NOTRE-DAME, PARIS

France

HIGHLIGHTS

❶ **Paris** Explore some of Europe's best museums, restaurants and nightlife. **See p.281**

❷ **Reims** Treat yourself to champagne tasting and a cellar tour. **See p.296**

❸ **Strasbourg** A city of striking architecture and hearty Alsatian food. **See p.305**

❹ **Perpignan** Savour a sangria in the picturesque village of Collieure. **See p.321**

❺ **Marseille** Cycle along the dazzling Corniche for free. **See p.329**

❻ **Corsica** Marvel at the fiery red Calanques on Ile de la Beautè. **See p.345**

HIGHLIGHTS ARE MARKED ON THE MAP ON P.277

ROUGH COSTS

Daily budget Basic €50, occasional treat €75

Drink Glass of wine €3, beer €3

Food Baguette/sandwich €3–5

Hostel/budget hotel €16–35/€40–60

Travel Train: Paris–Nice €60

FACT FILE

Population 66 million

Language French

Currency Euro (€)

Capital Paris

International phone code ☎ 33

Time zone GMT +1hr

Introduction

France is one of Europe's most stylish and dynamic countries. The largest country in Western Europe, it offers a variety of cultural and geographical experiences unmatched across the continent. Yet, despite its size, it's surprisingly easy to explore, with a fantastic high-speed train network which means that within hours of indulging in the café culture of the capital, you could be swimming in the clear waters of the Côte d'Azur.

11

Paris continues to captivate visitors with its world-class museums, distinctive neighbourhoods and exuberant nightlife. To the west, **Normandy** boasts some of the country's greatest Romanesque architecture, while the lush countryside and rocky coastline of neighbouring **Brittany** provide great surroundings for getting away from it all. To the east, you'll find the rolling vineyards and elegant towns of Champagne and **Burgundy**, while south lie the châteaux of the **Loire Valley** and the gorgeous hills and valleys of the **Dordogne** beyond. The Atlantic coast has a misty charm, including low-key **La Rochelle** and the surfing capital of **Biarritz**. Though most people push on south to the country's most obvious attractions, there's a lot to be said for exploring the Germanic towns of **Alsace** in the east and the high and rugged heartland of the **Massif Central**.

France's gastronomic capital, **Lyon**, acts as a gateway to the heady southern region of **Provence**, characterized by beautiful countryside, charming towns and sublime food. The **Côte d'Azur** retains something of its old glamour, while **Marseille** is more worthy of exploration than its reputation would have you believe. The very south of the country, marked by the canyons of the **Pyrenees**, hides the dream-like fortress of Carcassonne, and provides some of the country's best walking territory, alongside the **Alps**. The student cities of **Montpellier** and **Toulouse** should be stops on any budget traveller's itinerary, boasting cheap restaurants, excellent nightlife and a relaxed ambience.

CHRONOLOGY

51 BC Julius Caesar conquers Gaul.

486 AD Clovis I, leader of the Franks, establishes his rule over Gaul.

800 Charlemagne rules as King of the Franks.

1066 William, the Duke of Normandy, invades England and is crowned King of England.

1337 The Hundred Years' War with England begins.

1431 After leading the French army to victory, Joan of Arc is burnt at the stake for heresy, at the age of 19.

1589 Henry IV is the first of the Bourbon dynasty to become King of France. Enforces Catholicism on the country.

1789 The French Revolution ends the rule of the monarchy and establishes the First Republic.

1804 Napoleon I declares himself Emperor of the French Empire.

1815 Napoleon I is defeated at the battle of Waterloo; the monarchy is restored.

1871 Defeat in the Franco-Prussian War leads to the creation of the Third Republic.

1872 Monet ushers in the Impressionist Movement.

1889 Eiffel Tower is built, making it the tallest building in the world.

1905 Church and State are legally separated.

1914–18 World War I – over 1.5 million Frenchmen killed.

1939–44 Nazi Germany occupies France, leading to four years of fascist rule under the Vichy regime. France is liberated by Allied forces in August 1944.

2002 The euro replaces the franc.

2005 Civil unrest and riots across the country after the death of two teenagers who were running from police in one of Paris' impoverished housing estates.

2007 Nicolas Sarkozy is elected President, narrowly beating Ségolène Royal, France's first female presidential candidate.

2011 Full-face veils are banned from public places.

2012 Socialist François Hollande is elected President.

2013 France's first gay marriage takes place in Montpellier.

HIGHLIGHTS
1. Paris
2. Reims
3. Strasbourg
4. Perpignan
5. Marseille
6. Corsica

FRANCE

11

ARRIVAL AND DEPARTURE

The main hub for arrivals by **plane** is Paris Charles de Gaulle, which is served by both major and budget airlines. In addition, there are around forty other airports, including Lyon, Nice, La Rochelle and Marseille. France has excellent **train** connections to the rest of Europe. The main access point is Paris: Gare du Nord links to Belgium, Germany and the UK; Gare de Lyon to Italy; and Gare d'Austerlitz to Spain. There are also excellent connections from the south of France to Italy and Spain.

The Eurolines **coach service** (@eurolines.com) connects most European countries to France; the main arrival point in Paris is the *gare routière* in the suburb of Bagnolet.

GETTING AROUND

France has one of the most extensive **rail** networks in Western Europe, run by the government-owned SNCF (@sncf.com). Bus services tend to be uncoordinated and are best used only as a last resort.

Train fares are reasonably high, but you can make savings by booking well in advance; Paris to Lyon, for example, can cost €27, but will be double that if booked on the day of travel.

InterRail and Eurail passes are valid on normal trains at all times. The high-speed TGVs (*Trains à Grande Vitesse*) require reservations (€9), and there is a supplement to travel on certain other trains (from €1). Tickets (not passes) must be stamped in the orange machines in front of the platform on penalty of a steep fine. All but the smallest stations have an information desk but only a handful have left-luggage facilities. The word *autocar* on a timetable indicates that it's an **SNCF bus service**, on which rail tickets and passes are valid.

Bikes that can be dismantled go free on all trains – if you can't collapse your bike then it can still travel free as long as the train doesn't require reservations and there's room. If you're catching a train that requires a reservation, your bike will also need a booking, and you'll have to pay a flat fee of €10. Bike rental shops (charging around €15 per day) are plentiful and many towns also have bike-sharing schemes.

ACCOMMODATION

Outside the summer season and school holidays, it's generally possible to turn up in any town and find accommodation. However, many hostels get booked up with school groups, so where possible it's worth reserving in advance.

All **hotels** are officially graded and are required to post their tariffs inside the entrance. Most **hostels** in France are operated by FUAJ, the French youth hostel association (part of the worldwide Hostelling International; ⓦhihostels .com). Many of the hostels are situated some distance from the centre of town, and the quality varies widely – from old-fashioned institutional accommodation to bright, modern, well-situated buildings. Many FUAJ hostels close in the middle of the day so you are unable even to leave your bags, and all require that you vacate the rooms by around 10am, even if you're not checking out. Almost all hostels provide bed linen, and most offer a free breakfast. **Gîtes d'étape** provide bunk beds and simple kitchen facilities in rural areas for climbers, hikers, cyclists, etc – they are listed, along with mountain refuges, on ⓦgites -refuges.com. Local **campsites** provide a good budget alternative as they are generally clean, well equipped and often enjoy prime locations. Ask tourist offices for lists of sites or consult ⓦcampingfrance.com.

FOOD AND DRINK

Eating out in France isn't particularly cheap, but the quality of the food is often excellent and, even in the big cities, it's usually easy to find somewhere you can enjoy a *plat* and a glass of wine for under €15.

Generally the best place to eat **breakfast** (*petit déjeuner*) is in a bar or café. Most serve *tartines* (baguette with butter and/ or jam) and croissants until around 11am. Coffee is invariably served black and strong – *un café* is an espresso, while *un café crème* is made with hot milk. Tea (*thé*) and hot chocolate (*chocolat chaud*) are also available – though the former is served without milk unless you request it on the side.

Cafés are often the best option for a light **lunch**, usually serving omelettes, sandwiches (generally half-baguettes filled with cheese or meat) and *croque-monsieur* (toasted ham and cheese sandwich; €5–8), as well as more substantial meals. Crêperies are ubiquitous throughout France and are usually very reasonably priced (from €5). Most cafés and restaurants have a midday *formule* (a set menu starting at around €12) of two or three courses, which will often allow you to enjoy high-quality restaurant food that you wouldn't otherwise be able to afford. Most restaurants serve food from noon to 2pm and 7 to 11pm.

Vegetarian restaurants are becoming more common, especially in large cities, and if you make it clear that you're *un végétarien(ne)*, something can normally be arranged in all but the most basic of places.

DRINK

Drinking is an important part of French life, with the local bar playing a central

FRANCE ONLINE
ⓦ**tourisme.fr** French Tourist Board.
ⓦ**franceguide.com** Links to many tourist offices.
ⓦ**discoverfrance.net** Useful tourist information, with links to other sites.
ⓦ**viafrance.com** Information on festivals, expos, events and concerts.

STUDENT AND YOUTH DISCOUNTS

Most museums and attractions offer a student or under-26 discount, which can be anything up to a third off. To make the most of these, buy an **ISIC** (International Student) or **IYTC** (International Youth) card. For more information see ⓦisiccard.com. It's also worth noting that many museums have free entry on the first Sunday of every month.

---

social role. **Wine** (*vin*) is the national drink, and drunk at just about every meal or social occasion. Even the most basic of cafés usually offer a wide range of French wines by the glass, and ordering a *pichet* or a carafe (usually ranging from a quarter bottle to a half bottle) is often great value.

Beer can be very expensive, especially if ordered by the pint. Beer on tap (*à la pression*) is the best value – ask for *une pression* or *un demi* (0.33 litre). Spirits such as **cognac** and **armagnac**, and of course the notorious **absinthe**, are widely drunk but not cheap. A pleasant, inexpensive pre-dinner drink is *un kir*, a mix of white wine and crème de cassis, and if you're in the south of France it's definitely worth sampling the local **pastis**, drunk over ice and diluted with water – very refreshing on a hot day.

CULTURE AND ETIQUETTE

Making an effort to speak French, however dreadful your accent, is always highly appreciated; a few basic words will get you a lot further than any amount of grimacing and pointing.

It's customary to **tip** porters, tour guides, taxi drivers and hairdressers, around ten percent. Restaurant prices almost always include a service charge, so only leave an additional cash tip if you feel you've received service out of the ordinary.

SPORTS AND OUTDOOR ACTIVITIES

The main sport in France is undoubtedly **football**. The French football league (ⓦlfp.fr) is divided into Ligue 1 (the highest), Ligue 2 and National. Match tickets are available from specific club websites, or in the town they are playing – ask at the local tourist office.

Rugby is another major pursuit,

especially in the southwest, and the country often puts up a good showing in the Six Nations tournament. Further details of rugby fixtures can be found at ⓦfrancerugby.fr. The annual Tour de France, an epic 3000km **cycle race** across the country every July (ⓦletour.fr), is one of the country's most popular sporting events. The best **skiing** is in the Alps, and it's usually possible to ski from November to April. Prices can be high, however, so it's worth checking package prices in resort towns such as Chamonix (see p.344). France is also traced with lots of long-distance footpaths, known as *sentiers de grande randonnée* or GRs, and facilities for **hikers** are generally very good, including mountain refuges and excellent information centres in major hiking regions. The most popular areas for hiking are the Pyrenees and the Alps, though the Massif Central has some impressive, off-the-beaten-track routes.

COMMUNICATIONS

Post offices (*la poste*) are widespread and generally open from 8.30am to 6.30pm Monday to Friday, and 8.30am to noon on Saturday. **Stamps** (*timbres*) are also sold in *tabacs* (newsagents). For all calls within France you must dial the entire ten-digit number, including area code. The number for directory enquiries is ⓘ12. Almost all hotels and hostels, as well as an increasing number of campsites, offer wi-fi.

EMERGENCIES

There are two main types of **police**, the Police Nationale and the Gendarmerie

---

EMERGENCY NUMBERS

Police ⓘ17; Ambulance ⓘ15; Fire ⓘ18; or ⓘ112 for all three.

11

FRENCH

	FRENCH	PRONUNCIATION
Yes	*Oui*	Whee
No	*Non*	No(n)
Please	*S'il vous plait*	See voo play
Thank you	*Merci*	Mersee
Hello/Good day	*Bonjour*	Bo(n)joor
Goodbye	*Au revoir/à bientôt*	Orvoir/abyantoe
Excuse me	*Pardon*	pardo(n)
Today	*Aujourd'hui*	Ojoordwee
Yesterday	*Hier*	Eeyair
Tomorrow	*Demain*	Duhma(n)
What time is it?	*Quelle heure est-il?*	Kel ur et eel?
I don't understand	*Je ne comprends pas*	Je nuh compron pah
How much?	*Combien?*	Combyen?
Do you speak English?	*Parlez-vous anglais?*	Parlay voo onglay?
Where's the…?	*Où est…?*	Oo ay…?
Entrance	*Entrée*	Ontray
Exit	*Sortie*	Sortee
Tourist office	*Office de tourism*	Ofees der toureesmer
Toilet	*Toilettes*	Twalet
Hotel	*Hôtel*	Otel
Youth hostel	*Auberge de jeunesse*	Obairjh der jherness
Church	*Église*	Ay-gleez
Museum	*Musée*	Mewzay
What time does the… leave?	*À quelle heure part…?*	A kel et par…?
Boat	*Le bateau*	Ler bato
Bus	*Le bus*	Ler bews
Plane	*L'avion*	Lavyon
Train	*Le train*	Ler trun
Ticket	*Billet*	Beelay
Do you have a… room?	*Avez-vous une chambre…?*	Avay voo ewn shombrer…?
Double	*Avec un grand lit*	Avek un grand lee
Single	*À un lit*	A un lee
Cheap	*Bon marché*	Bo(n) marchay
Expensive	*Cher*	Share
Open	*Ouvert*	Oovair
Closed	*Fermé*	Fermay
One	*Un*	Uh(n)
Two	*Deux*	Duh
Three	*Trois*	Trwah
Four	*Quatre*	Kattre
Five	*Cinq*	Sank
Six	*Six*	Seess
Seven	*Sept*	Set
Eight	*Huit*	Wheat
Nine	*Neuf*	Nurf
Ten	*Dix*	Deess

11

Nationale, and you can report a theft, or any other incident, to either.

To find a **doctor**, ask for an address at any *pharmacie* (chemist) or tourist information office. Consultation fees for a visit will be around €25 and you'll be given a *Feuille de Soins* (Statement of Treatment) for any insurance claims. EU citizens are, with an EHIC, exempt from charges (see p.42).

INFORMATION

Most towns and villages have an *Office de Tourisme*, giving out local information and free maps. The larger ones can book accommodation anywhere in France, and most can find you a local room for the night, albeit with an added service charge.

MONEY AND BANKS

The currency of France is the **euro** (€). Standard **banking hours** are Monday to Friday 9am to noon and 2 to 4.30pm; in cities, some also open on Saturday morning. **ATMs** are found all over France and most accept foreign cards. Credit cards are generally accepted by most shops, restaurants and hotels.

OPENING HOURS AND HOLIDAYS

Basic **working hours** are 9am to noon/1pm and 2/3 to 6.30pm. The traditional closing **days** for shops (and some restaurants) are Sunday and Monday. **Museums** are usually closed on Mondays, with reduced opening hours outside of summer. All shops, museums and offices are closed on the following **national holidays**: January 1, Easter Sunday and Monday, Ascension Day, Whit Monday, May 1, May 8, July 14, August 15, November 1, November 11, December 25.

Paris

All the clichés about **PARIS** are true – stylish, romantic, glamorous and utterly compelling – yet it retains surprises that continue to delight even the most seasoned visitors. The landscape of the city changes as you cross from *quartier* to *quartier*, and each area has a distinct style and atmosphere – from historic **St-Germain** and the genteel Luxembourg Gardens to the vibrant Marais, abuzz with bars and cafés, and the steep cobbled streets of **Montmartre**. Paris is small for a capital city, and the best way to explore it is on foot – or do as the locals do and rent a bike (see p.289). Of course, it goes without saying that the café, bar and restaurant scene here is among the best in Europe, even for travellers on a budget.

WHAT TO SEE AND DO

Paris is split into two halves by the Seine. On the north of the river, the **Right Bank** (*Rive droite*) is home to the *grands boulevards* and its most monumental buildings, many dating from the civic planner Baron Haussmann's nineteenth-century redevelopment. Most of the major museums are here, as well as the city's widest range of shops around rue de Rivoli and Les Halles.

The **Left Bank** (*Rive gauche*) has a noticeably different feel. A legendary bohemian hangout since the nineteenth century, some of the city's most evocative streets can be found here. These days much of the area has given in to commerce, though it's not hard to discover some of its old spirit if you wander off the main roads around boulevard St-Germain and St-Michel.

Parts of Paris, of course, don't sit so easily within such definitions. **Montmartre**, rising up to the north and dominated by the great white dome of Sacré Coeur, has managed to retain a village-like feel despite its tourist popularity, and the islands of the Seine (de la Cité and St-Louis), though touristy themselves, retain a charming, old-fashioned atmosphere within their side streets. In recent years, Paris's once run-down **eastern districts** have also been revitalized and are now home to some of the city's best nightlife.

11

PARISIAN ARRONDISSEMENTS

Paris is divided into twenty postal districts, known as *arrondissements*, which are used to denote addresses. The first, or *premier* (abbreviated as 1er), is centred on the Louvre and the Tuileries, with the rest (abbreviated as 2e, 3e, 4e etc) spiralling outwards in a clockwise direction.

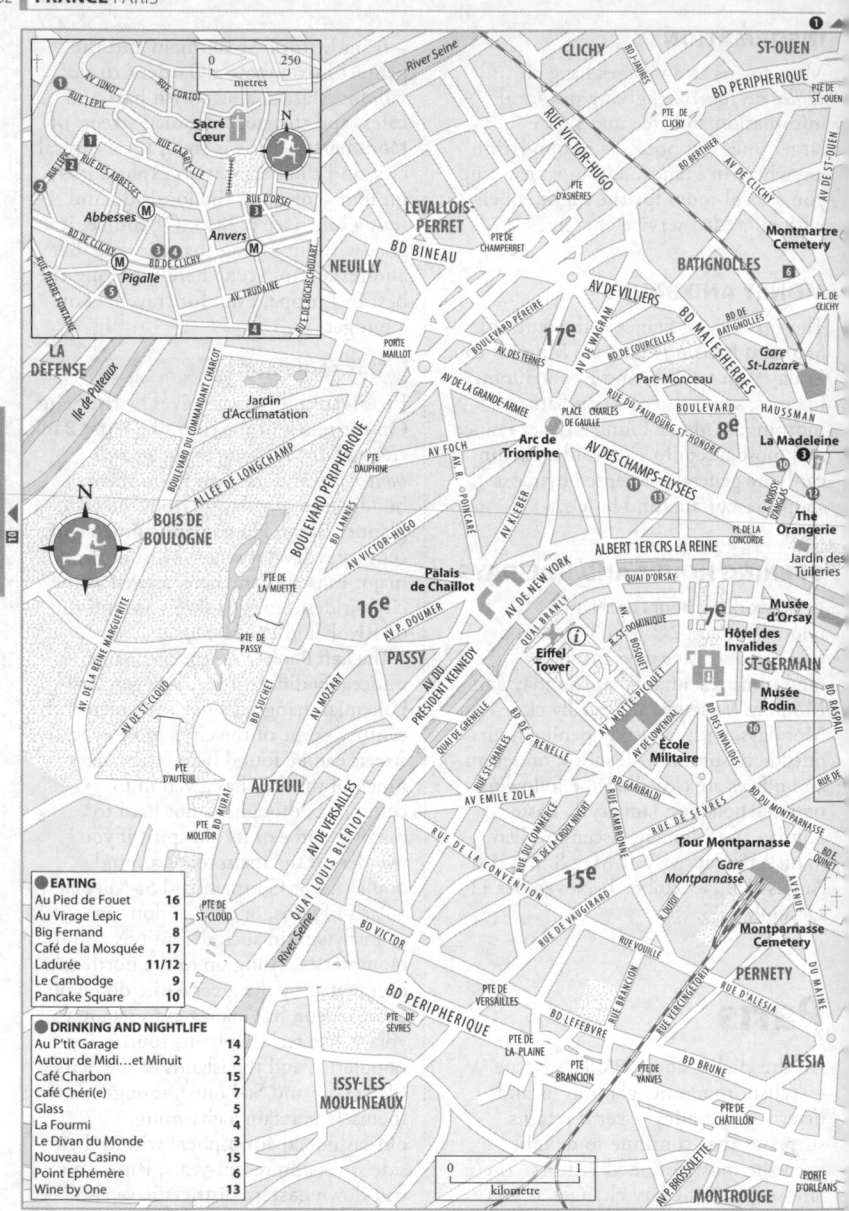

EATING

Au Pied de Fouet	16
Au Virage Lepic	1
Big Fernand	8
Café de la Mosquée	17
Ladurée	11/12
Le Cambodge	9
Pancake Square	10

DRINKING AND NIGHTLIFE

Au P'tit Garage	14
Autour de Midi…et Minuit	2
Café Charbon	15
Café Chéri(e)	7
Glass	5
La Fourmi	4
Le Divan du Monde	3
Nouveau Casino	15
Point Éphémère	6
Wine by One	13

The Arc de Triomphe, Champs-Élysées and around

The **Arc de Triomphe** (daily: April–Sept 10am–11pm; Oct–March 10am–10.30pm; €9.50; Ⓜ Charles-de -Gaulle-Etoile), at the head of the Champs-Élysées, is an imposing Parisian landmark, matched only by the Eiffel Tower, and offers panoramic views from the top. The celebrated **avenue des Champs-Élysées** is now, unfortunately, home to little more than a constant stream of tourists and too many chain shops. It leads to the vast, usually

■ ACCOMMODATION	
Camping Bois de Boulogne	10
Bonsejour Montmartre	1
Eldorado	6
Le Village	3
Mama Shelter	11
Oops!	13
Peace & Love	7
Plug-Inn	2
St Christopher's Inn	5/8
The Loft	9
Woodstock Hostel	4
Young and Happy	12

● SHOPPING	
Hédiard	3
Galeries Lafayette	2
Marché aux Puces de St-Ouen	1

11

traffic-clogged **place de la Concorde**, whose centrepiece, a gold-tipped obelisk from the temple of Luxor, was presented to the city by the viceroy of Egypt in 1829. Beyond lies the formal **Jardin des Tuileries** (daily: April–Aug 7am–9pm; Sept–March 7.30am–7.30pm;

ⓂConcorde), the perfect place for a stroll with its grand vistas and symmetrical flowerbeds. Towards the river, the **Orangerie** (Mon & Wed–Sun 9am–6pm; €7.50; Ⓦwww.musee-orangerie.fr; ⓂConcorde) displays Monet's largest water-lily paintings in a specially designed room, as well as works by Cézanne, Matisse, Utrillo and Modigliani.

The Louvre

On the east side of the Jardin des Tuileries is arguably the world's most famous museum, the **Louvre** (Mon, Thurs, Sat & Sun 9am–6pm; Wed & Fri 9am–9.45pm; €11; Ⓦlouvre.fr; ⓂPalais Royal-Musée du Louvre/Louvre-Rivoli). The building was first opened to the public in 1793 and within a decade Napoleon had made it the largest art collection on earth with the takings from his empire, which explains the remarkably eclectic collection.

The main entrance is via I.M. Pei's iconic glass pyramid, but you can sometimes avoid the (lengthy) queues by entering through the Louvre Rivoli métro station or through the Louvre Carousel shopping arcade. Most people head straight for Da Vinci's *Mona Lisa*, but it's definitely worth exploring some of the other sections such as **Sculpture**, which covers the entire development of the art in France from Romanesque to Rodin.

The Pompidou Centre

From the Louvre, it's a short walk to the **Pompidou Centre** on place Georges-Pompidou (Mon & Wed–Sun 11am–10pm; free; Ⓦcentrepompidou.fr; ⓂRambuteau), famous for its striking design masterminded by Renzo Piano and Richard Rogers, who had the innovative idea of turning its insides out to allow for maximum space inside. The main reason to visit is the hugely popular **Musée National d'Art Moderne** (Mon & Wed–Sun 11am–9pm; €11–13), one of the world's great collections of modern art, spanning the period from 1905 to the present day, and taking in Cubism, Surrealism and much more along the way.

The Marais

Just east of the Pompidou Centre lies the **Marais**, one of Paris's more striking *quartiers*. This chic district is defined by its designer boutiques and trendy café-bars; it's also one of the city's main gay hotspots. The **Musée d'Art et d'Histoire du Judaïsme**, 71 rue du Temple (Mon–Fri 11am–6pm, Sun 10am–6pm; €6.80; Ⓦmahj.org; ⓂRambuteau), pays homage to the area's Jewish roots, with a major display of Jewish artefacts and historical documents as well as paintings by Chagall and Soutine. A short walk east brings you to the seventeenth-century Hôtel Juigné Salé, which holds the **Musée Picasso**, 5 rue de Thorigny (Ⓦmusee-picasso.fr; closed at the time of writing for a major renovation; ⓂSt-Sébastien Froissart), housing a substantial collection of the artist's personal property.

Bastille

Southeast of the Marais is the traffic-choked **place de la Bastille**, the site of the Bastille prison that was famously stormed in 1789, starting the French Revolution. Now the place is marked by the Colonne de Juillet, topped by a green bronze figure of Liberty, and by the strikingly modern Opéra Bastille.

Île St-Louis and Île de la Cité

A short walk southwest from place de la Bastille and across the pont de Sully brings you to the peaceful **Île St-Louis**, its main road, rue St-Louis en l'Île, lined with shops and restaurants.

Pont St-Louis bridges the short distance to **Île de la Cité**, where the city first started in the third century BC, when a tribe of Gauls known as the Parisii settled here. The most obvious attraction is the astounding Gothic **Cathédrale de Notre-Dame** (Mon–Fri 8am–6.45pm, Sat & Sun 8am–7.15pm; free; Ⓦnotredamedeparis.fr; ⓂCité), which dates from the mid-fourteenth century and was extensively renovated in the nineteenth. It's worth climbing the towers (daily: April–Sept 10am–6.30pm; Oct–March 10am–5.30pm; July & Aug Fri & Sat until 11pm; €8.50) for an up-close view of the gargoyles and tower architecture.

At the western end of the island lies **Sainte-Chapelle**, 4 bd du Palais (daily: March–Oct 9.30am–6pm; Nov–Feb 9am–5pm; €8.50; ⓂCité). One of the finest achievements of French Gothic style, it is lent fragility by its height and huge expanses of glorious stained glass.

The Eiffel Tower

Gustave Eiffel's iconic tower is, rightly or wrongly, the defining image of Paris for most tourists. Hugely controversial on its 1889 debut, it has come to be recognized as one of the city's leading sights. If you wish to pay it a visit (daily: mid-June to Sept 1 9am–midnight; Sept 2 to mid-June 9am–11pm; €8.50 to second floor, €14.50 to top; ⓦ tour-eiffel.fr; ⓜ Bir Hakeim/RER Champ de Mars-Tour Eiffel), be prepared for frustratingly long queues. It's at its most impressive at night, when fully illuminated – especially from the opposite side of the river.

Les Invalides and the Musée Rodin

A short walk from the Eiffel Tower is the Hôtel des Invalides, easily spotted by its gold dome. Built as a home for invalid soldiers on the orders of Louis XIV, it now houses the giant **Musée de l'Armée**, 129 rue de Grenelle (daily: April–Oct 10am–6pm; Nov–March 10am–5pm; €9.50; ⓦ musee-armee.fr; ⓜ Varenne). Military buffs will be fascinated by the vast collection of armour, uniforms, weapons and Napoleonic relics, and the wing devoted to World War II.

Immediately east, on 77 rue de Varenne, the **Musée Rodin** (Tues–Sun 10am–5.45pm; €9; ⓦ musee-rodin.fr; ⓜ Varenne) contains many of Rodin's greatest and most famous works, including *The Thinker* and *The Kiss*. The collection is housed in an elegant eighteenth-century mansion, the Hôtel Biron, surrounded by a serene sculpture garden.

Musée d'Orsay

In a beautifully converted train station by the river, the celebrated **Musée d'Orsay**, 62 rue de Lille (Tues–Sun 9.30am–6pm; Thurs until 9.45pm; €9; ⓦ musee-orsay.fr; RER Musée d'Orsay/ⓜ Solférino), is much more compact and manageable than the Louvre. Covering the periods between the 1840s and 1914, the collection features legendary artists such as Renoir, Van Gogh and Monet, and famous works including Manet's *Le Déjeuner Sur L'Herbe* and Courbet's striking *The Origin Of The World*. The queues are always long, but booking

tickets the day before at the advance ticket office on site will allow you priority entrance.

The Latin Quarter

The neighbourhood around the boulevards St-Michel and St-Germain has been known as the **Quartier Latin** since medieval times, when it was the home of the Latin-speaking universities. It is still a student-dominated area – its pivotal point being **place St-Michel** – now sadly dominated by tacky tourist traps. There are, however, some excellent bars and restaurants nearby.

Immediately south of here stand the prestigious Sorbonne and Collège de France universities, the jewels in the crown of French education and renowned worldwide. Nearby, the elegant surroundings of the **Jardin du Luxembourg** (daily dawn to dusk; RER Luxembourg) are perfect for a leisurely picnic.

St-Germain

The northern half of the *6ᵉ arrondissement* is an upmarket and expensive part of the city, but fun to wander through. The area is steeped in history: Picasso painted *Guernica* in rue des Grands-Augustins; in rue Visconti, Delacroix painted and Balzac's printing business went bust; and in the parallel rue des Beaux-Arts, Oscar Wilde died quipping "Either the wallpaper goes or I do." **Boulevard St-Germain** is home to the famous *Flore* and *Deux Magots* cafés, both with rich political and literary histories; however, the astronomical prices mean that gawping rather than sipping is the best option.

Montparnasse

Southeast of the Luxembourg gardens is Montparnasse, which has somewhat lost its lustre since the erection of the hideous 59-storey skyscraper, **Tour Montparnasse**. This has rightly become one of the city's most hated landmarks since its construction in 1973, a sole redeeming feature being the view it offers if you take the lift to the 56th floor (daily: April–Sept 9.30am–11.30pm; Oct–March 9.30am–10.30pm; €13.50;

11

11

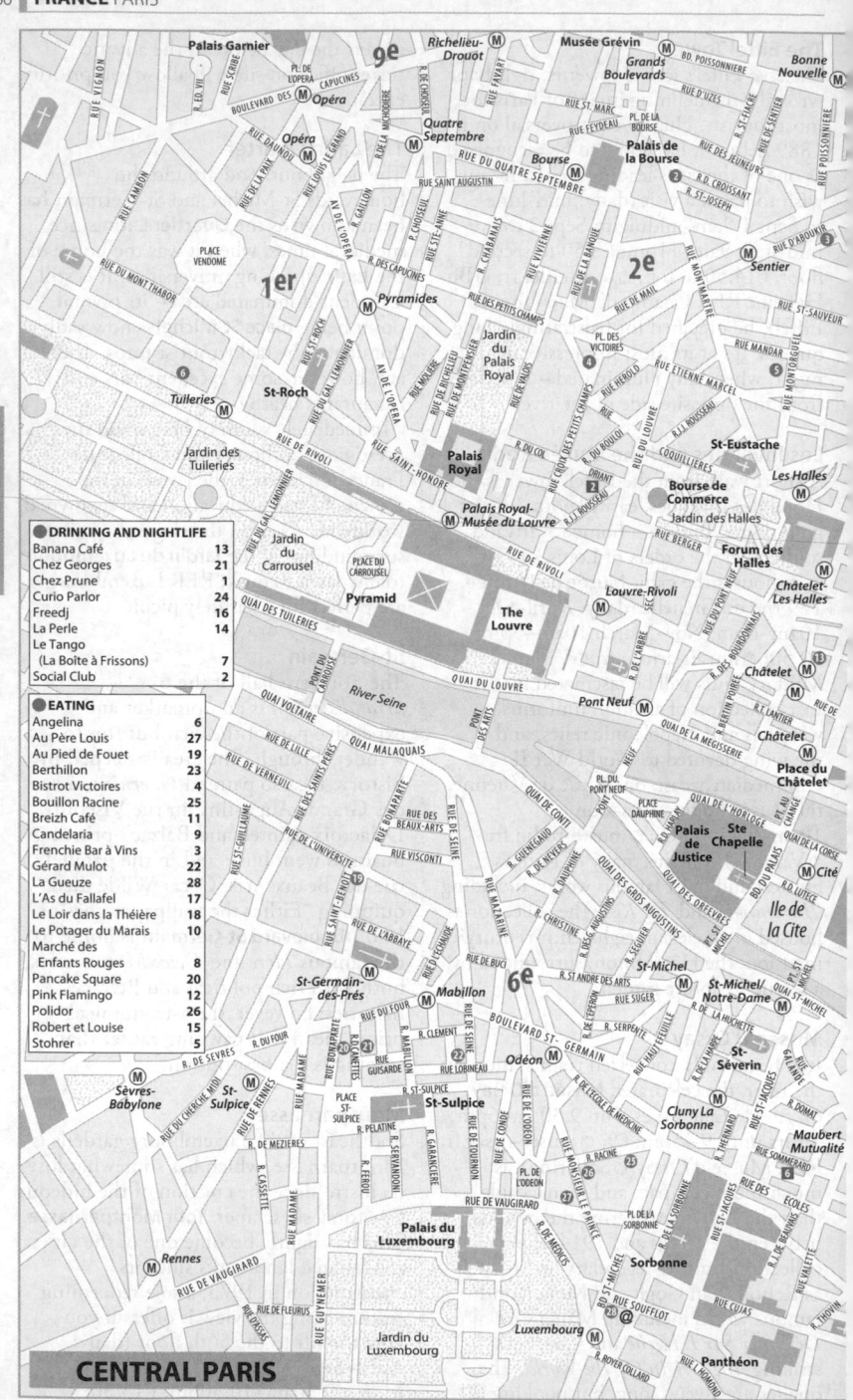

DRINKING AND NIGHTLIFE

Banana Café	13
Chez Georges	21
Chez Prune	1
Curio Parlor	24
Freedj	16
La Perle	14
Le Tango	
(La Boîte à Frissons)	7
Social Club	2

EATING

Angelina	6
Au Père Louis	27
Au Pied de Fouet	19
Berthillon	23
Bistrot Victoires	4
Bouillon Racine	25
Breizh Café	11
Candelaria	9
Frenchie Bar à Vins	3
Gérard Mulot	22
La Gueuze	28
L'As du Fallafel	17
Le Loir dans la Théière	18
Le Potager du Marais	10
Marché des	
Enfants Rouges	8
Pancake Square	20
Pink Flamingo	12
Polidor	26
Robert et Louise	15
Stohrer	5

CENTRAL PARIS

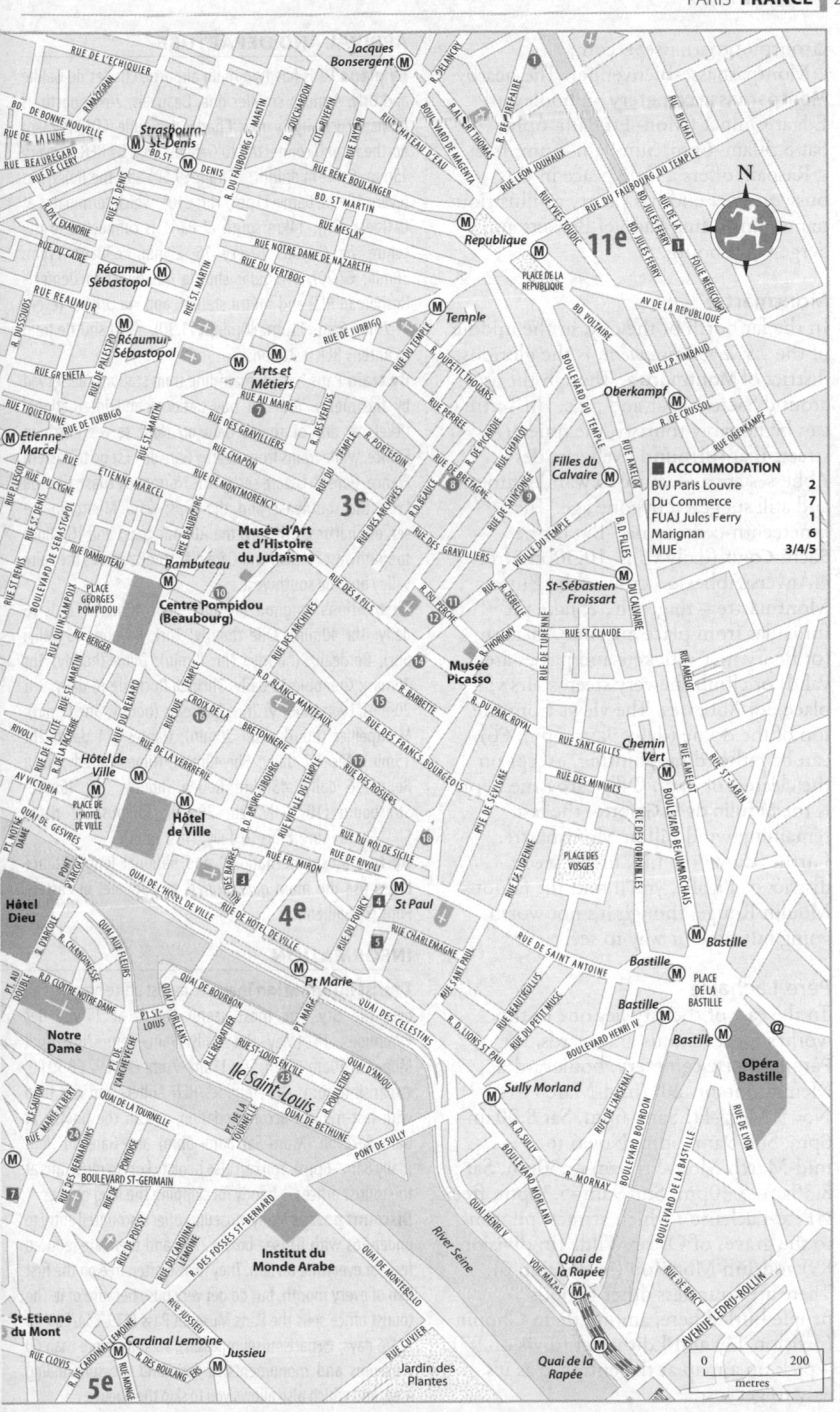

ACCOMMODATION	
BVJ Paris Louvre	2
Du Commerce	7
FUAJ Jules Ferry	1
Marignan	6
MIJE	3/4/5

11

ⓦ tourmontparnasse56.com;
ⓜ Montparnasse-Bienvenüe). The nearby
Montparnasse cemetery on boulevard
Edgar Quinet (Mon–Fri 8am–6pm,
Sat 8.30am–6pm, Sun 9am–6pm; free;
ⓜ Raspail) offers a little peace in this
busy *quartier* and has plenty of illustrious
names, including Samuel Beckett and
Serge Gainsbourg.

Montmartre

In the far north of the city, in the middle
of the *18e arrondissement*, is the glorious
district of **Montmartre**. Though the area
around Sacré-Cœur and place du Tertre
can be horribly touristy, the quieter
streets that surround lively rue des
Abbesses are a pleasure to wander around,
and still suggest a bygone age. The
nineteenth-century neo-Byzantine
Sacré-Cœur (daily 6am–10.30pm; free;
ⓜ Anvers/Abbesses) crowns the Butte
Montmartre – to get there, take the
funicular from place Suzanne Valadon
(ordinary métro tickets and passes are
valid) or climb the very steep stairs via
place des Abbesses. The views from the
top of the dome (daily 9am–6pm; €6)
can be rather disappointing, except on
the clearest of days. Off nearby rue Lepic
is the **Moulin de la Galette**, the last
remaining windmill in Montmartre.
Further down the hill, in the seedy
district of Pigalle, you'll find the famous
Moulin Rouge, though it's not worth
going out of your way to see.

Père-Lachaise

To the east of the city lies one of the
world's most famous graveyards, the
Père-Lachaise cemetery, boulevard de
Ménilmontant, 20e (mid-March to
Nov 5 Mon–Fri 8am–6pm, Sat 8.30am–
6pm, Sun 9am–6pm; Nov 6 to
mid-March Mon–Fri 8am–5.30pm, Sat
8.30am–5.30pm, Sun 9am–5.30pm; free;
ⓜ Père-Lachaise), which attracts pilgrims
to the graves of Oscar Wilde (in division
89) and Jim Morrison (in division 6).
There are countless other famous
people buried here, among them Chopin
(division 11) and Edith Piaf (division 97)
– pick up a map at the entrance as it's
easy to get lost.

ARRIVAL AND DEPARTURE

By plane Paris has two main airports: Charles de Gaulle
and Orly. A much smaller one, Beauvais, 76km north, is
primarily used by Ryanair. Charles de Gaulle (CDG) is 23km
northeast and connected to Gare du Nord by RER B (every
15min, 5am–midnight; 25min; €9.50) and the Roissybus
(every 15min, 6am–11pm; 1hr; €10), which terminates at
ⓜ Opéra. Orly, 14km south of Paris, is connected to the
centre via Orlybus (every 15–20min, 5.30am–11pm;
30min; €7.20), a regular shuttle bus direct to Denfert-
Rochereau RER and métro station, and via Orlyval (every
4–7min, 6am–11pm; 30min; €11.30), a fast shuttle train
to Antony RER B station.
By train Paris has six main-line train stations, all served
by the métro. You can buy national and international
tickets at any of them. Gare du Nord serves northern
France, while trains from nearby Gare de l'Est go to eastern
France. Gare St-Lazare serves the Normandy coast; Gare de
Lyon the southeast and the Alps; Gare Montparnasse
serves Chartres, Brittany, the Atlantic coast and TGV lines
to southwest France; and Gare d'Austerlitz serves the Loire
valley and the southwest.
Destinations Avignon (12 daily; 2hr 40min); Calais (6
daily; 1hr 40min); Lille (hourly; 1hr); Bayonne (5 daily;
5hr); Bordeaux (hourly; 3hr 20min); Dijon (hourly; 1hr
30min); Grenoble (5 daily; 3hr); La Rochelle (6 daily; 3hr
20min); Lyon (hourly; 2hr); Marseille (hourly; 3hr 15min);
Montpellier (hourly; 3hr 20min); Nantes (11 daily; 2hr
15min); Nice (7 daily; 5hr 40min); Nîmes (hourly; 3hr);
Reims (6 daily; 45min); Rouen (hourly; 1hr 15min);
Strasbourg (10 daily; 2hr 20min); Toulouse (7 daily;
5hr–6hr 30min); Tours (6 daily; 1hr 15min).
By bus Most international and national long-distance
buses use the main *gare routière* at Bagnolet in eastern
Paris (ⓜ Gallieni).

INFORMATION

Tourist information There are tourist office branches all
over the city. The most useful one is at 25 rue des
Pyramides 1er (May–Oct daily 9am–7pm; Nov–April
Mon–Sat 10am–7pm, Sun 11am–7pm; ☏ 08 92 68 30 00,
ⓦ parisinfo.com; ⓜ Pyramides/RER Auber) and can help
with last-minute accommodation, as can the booths at
Gare de Lyon (Mon–Sat 8am–6pm) and Gare du Nord
(daily 8am–6pm). You can also book tickets to museums at
the tourist offices – handy for skipping the long queues.
Discount passes Many museums offer discounted entry to
under-26s with ID (see box, p.279), and there are reduced
fees for everyone on Sun. They're also often free on the first
Sun of every month, but do get very busy because of it. The
tourist office sells the Paris Museum Pass (€39/€54/€69 for
2/4/6 days; ⓦ parismuseumpass.fr), valid for more than 60
museums and monuments in Paris and the surrounding
area, and which also allows you to skip the queues.

GETTING AROUND

Tickets Single tickets (€1.70) are valid on buses, the métro and, within the city limits (zones 1–2), the RER rail lines. If you're going to be using a fair bit of public transport, it makes more sense to buy a *carnet* of ten tickets (€13.30).

By métro The métro (Mon–Thurs & Sun 5.30am–12.30am, Fri & Sat 5.30am–2am) is an easy way of travelling around the city. The various lines are colour-coded and numbered, and the name of the train's final destination is visible.

By train Longer journeys across the city, or out to the suburbs, are best made on the underground RER express rail network.

By bus The bus network runs Mon–Sat 5.45am–8.30pm or 12.30am depending on the route, with a greatly reduced service on Sun. Night buses (ⓦnoctilien.fr) run 1am–5.30am (every 30min–1hr) on over 40 routes.

By bike There are over 1500 locations in the city from where you can rent a bike as part of the city's Velib scheme (€1.70/day, €8/week; first 30min free, €1/30min thereafter; ⓦvelib.paris.fr). You'll need a credit card for a deposit in case the bike is damaged. When you've finished with them, bikes can be deposited at any of the Velib stands in the city.

By taxi Taxis are plentiful after dark and can be hailed on the street. Rates start at €2.50, with a minimum charge of €6.20.

ACCOMMODATION

Accommodation is a lot more expensive in Paris than elsewhere in the country, and it's best to book in advance. The city has a good selection of independent youth hostels, some of which are more like boutique hotels than the usual standard of French hostel. All properties listed below have wi-fi and most hostels provide a rudimentary breakfast.

HOSTELS

BVJ Paris Louvre 20 rue Jean-Jacques Rousseau ☏ 01 53 00 90 90, ⓦbvjhotel.com; ⓜLouvre Rivoli; map pp.286–287. The most central hostel in Paris, close to the Louvre and Les Halles, is rather institutional but excellently located. Dorm €30, double €70

FUAJ Jules Ferry 8 bd Jules-Ferry, 11ᵉ ☏ 01 43 57 55 60; map pp.286–287. With a great position in the lively area by the Canal St Martin, this is a popular hostel despite being a little careworn. Dorms are on the small side. Dorm €26.50

Le Village 20 rue d'Orsel, 18ᵉ ☏ 01 42 64 22 02; map pp.282–283. A friendly, independent hostel with good facilities, smarter than average dorms and an on-site bar. It might be located in the least picturesque area of Montmartre, but has a lovely terrace with views of the Sacré-Coeur. Dorm €28, double €85

MIJE ☏ 01 42 74 23 45, ⓦmije.com; ⓜSt-Paul or Pont-Marie; map pp.286–287. A group of three hostels – *Le Fauconnier* (11 rue du Fauconnier), *Le Fourcy* (6 rue de Fourcy) and *Maubuisson* (12 rue des Barres) – situated just a few hundred metres apart in a set of magnificent mansions. Rooms are simple, but all guests can eat at *Le Fourcy's* decent restaurant. There's a 1am curfew and additional obligatory purchase of MIJE membership (€2.50; valid for a year). Dorm €32, double €80

Oops! 50 ave des Gobelins, 13ᵉ ☏ 01 47 07 47 00, ⓦoops-paris.com; ⓜPlace d'Italie; map pp.282–283. The city's first and much imitated, "design hostel", situated south of the Latin Quarter near Place d'Italie. All rooms are en suite and kept very clean, though doubles can be seriously overpriced in high season. Dorm €34, double €100

Peace & Love 245 rue La Fayette, 19ᵉ ☏ 01 46 07 65 11, ⓦparis-hostels.com; ⓜJaurès or Stalingrad; map pp.282–283. Right opposite the Canal St Martin, this small, welcoming hostel is a good choice if sleep isn't high on your priorities, with a cheap, popular bar that's open till 2am. Prices vary considerably with demand. Dorm €28, double €60

Plug-Inn 7 rue Aristide Bruant, 18ᵉ ☏ 01 42 58 42 58, ⓦplug-inn.fr; ⓜAbbesses; map pp.282–283. Small and swish hostel with designer decor and a great location on the slopes of Montmartre. The only downside is that some rooms are a little cramped. Dorm €28, double €95

★ **St Christopher's Inn** 5 rue de Dunkerque, 10ᵉ ☏ 01 40 34 34 40, ⓦstchristophers.co.uk; ⓜGare du Nord; map pp.282–283. This whopper of a hostel (it has over six hundred beds) opened in 2013 and it's a very slick operation: dorm beds all have lockable storage cages and USB points in the headboard, plus there are two on-site restaurants and a bar. Other perks include phones for free international calls, a female only floor and a slew of nightly activities. There's a particular focus on private rooms here (4-bed apartments from €150), whereas their purpose-built "canal" branch (159 rue de Crimée, 19ᵉ) has a higher proportion of dorm beds. Dorm €35, double €80

The Loft 70 rue Julien Lacroix, 20ᵉ ☏ 01 42 02 42 02, ⓦtheloft-paris.com; ⓜBelleville; map pp.282–283. This boldly decorated hostel in up-and-coming Belleville is smart and stylish, but the paper-thin walls and pop-rock endlessly pumped into the corridors mean it doesn't quite live up to its boutique hotel aspirations. Dorm €38, double €90

Woodstock Hostel 48 rue Rodier, 9ᵉ ☏ 01 48 78 87 76, ⓦwoodstock.fr; ⓜAnvers; map pp.282–283. This friendly, no-frills hostel has a great location just a few streets away from Montmartre. Private rooms aren't en suite, but they're some of the cheapest in Paris. Additional charge of €3 for Fri and Sat night stays. Dorm €25, twin €54

Young and Happy 80 rue Mouffetard, 5ᵉ ☏ 01 47 07 47 07, ⓦyoungandhappy.fr; ⓜMonge/Censier-Daubenton; map pp.282–283. In the heart of a student enclave in the Latin Quarter, this establishment has a youthful atmosphere that more than lives up to its name. Dorm €23, twin €65

11

★ TREAT YOURSELF

Mama Shelter 109 rue de Bagnolet 20ᵉ ☎01 43 48 48 48, ⓦmamashelter.com; map pp.282–283. Doodle-covered blackboard ceilings and a graffiti theme distinguish this cool, Philippe Starck-designed hotel. If the iMac, mini-bar and free movies in your room aren't enough of a distraction, facilities include a restaurant, pizzeria, bar and rooftop terrace. Book early for their ludicrously cheap starting rate. Double €89

HOTELS

Bonsejour Montmartre 11 rue Burq, 18ᵉ ☎01 42 54 22 53, ⓦhotel-bonsejour-montmartre.fr; ⓂAbbesses; map pp.282–283. In a great position just off lively rue des Abbesses, this charming family-run hotel offers great-value doubles and singles. The rooms are peaceful but not polished (en-suite bathrooms will be installed from 2014 onwards), and the best have small balconies. Book direct for the best rates. Double €70

Du Commerce 14 rue de la Montagne-Ste-Geneviève, 5ᵉ ☎01 43 54 89 69, ⓦcommerce-paris-hotel.com; ⓂMaubert-Mutualité; map pp.286–287. Bright and welcoming budget hotel on a quiet street in the heart of the Latin Quarter. The rooms are decorated in a cheery mix of oranges, pinks and greens, and there's a small dining area with a microwave on the ground floor. Double €68

Eldorado 18 rue des Dames, 17ᵉ ☎01 45 22 35 21, ⓦeldoradohotel.fr; ⓂPlace de Clichy; map pp.282–283. Eclectic budget hotel near busy Place de Clichy and a 5min walk from Montmartre, with a bohemian atmosphere, quirkily decorated rooms and a good attached bar. Book well in advance. Double €80

Marignan 13 rue du Sommerard, 5ᵉ ☎01 43 54 63 81, ⓦhotel-marignan.com; ⓂMaubert-Mutualité; map pp.286–287. Excellent backpacker-oriented hotel, with laundry facilities, a kitchen and a good choice of triples and singles. The ebullient proprietor is a mine of information on Paris. Breakfast included. Double €78

CAMPSITE

Camping Bois de Boulogne Allée du Bord de l'Eau ☎01 45 24 30 00, ⓦcampingparis.fr; shuttle bus to and from ⓂPorte Maillot; map pp.282–283. The city's major campsite is situated in the beautiful Bois de Boulogne and offers a range of facilities including showers, a canteen and bike rental. Camping €20 per person and tent

EATING

Eating out in Paris need not be an extravagant affair, and even at dinner, it's possible to have a meal for around €15. Make a reservation Thurs–Sat evening if you can.

CAFÉS, CHEAP EATS AND SNACKS

Angelina 226 rue de Rivoli, 1ᵉ ⓂTuileries; map pp.286–287. Drinking a cup of the decadent *chocolat chaud à l'ancienne* (€7.90) at this historic tearoom is a Paris institution. Mon–Fri 7.30am–7pm, Sat & Sun 8.30am–7pm.

Berthillon 31 rue St-Louis-en-l'Île, 4ᵉ ⓂPont Marie; map pp.286–287. Expect long queues for some of the best ice creams and sorbets in the city; the divine flavours include salted caramel and earl grey. Single scoop €2.50. Wed–Sun 10am–8pm.

Bouillon Racine 3 rue Racine 6ᵉ ⓂCluny-La Sorbonne; map pp.286–287. One of a few surviving *bouillons* (soup kitchens) that opened in the early 1900s, featuring gloriously extravagant Art Nouveau decor. Head to the bar-cum-tearoom on the ground floor where they now serve Belgian beers (*demi pressions* from €4.30) and waffles. Daily noon–11pm.

TOP THREE PARISIAN PATISSERIES

You can't walk far in Paris without stumbling over a **patisserie**, many of which have been serving cakes for hundreds of years. Here are three of the best that are worth braving the queues for:

Gérard Mulot 76 rue de Seine, 6ᵉ ⓂOdéon; map pp.286–287. This justifiably famous patisserie is usually crammed with locals. The many delights include lemon meringue tart (€5) and red fruit *millefeuille* (€4.20). Mon, Tues and Thurs–Sun 7am–8pm.

Ladurée 75 av des Champs-Élysées 8ᵉ ⓂGeorge V; map pp.282–283. Famous for its delectable *macarons* (€1.85/piece), which come in flavours such as salted caramel and orange blossom. Indulge in one of their

many treats over a cup of their delicate tea in this ornate tearoom, or head to the more intimate branch at 16 rue Royale. Tearoom Mon–Thurs 7.30am–11.30pm, Fri 7.30am–12.30am, Sat 8.30am–12.30am, Sun 8.30am–11.30pm.

Stohrer 51 rue Montorgueil, 2ᵉ ⓂÉtienne-Marcel; map pp.286–287. The city's oldest patisserie serves arguably its most divine selection of cakes – try a rum baba (variations from €4), which was actually invented here. Daily 7.30am–8.30pm.

11

Café de la Mosquée 39 rue Geoffroy-St-Hilaire, 5ᵉ; ⓜ Place Monge; map pp.282–283. Attached to La Grande Mosquée, this Moorish café is an oasis of calm. Mint tea (€2.50) and baklava (€2.50 per piece) are on offer in the intricately tiled salon de thé, or you can smoke shisha in the courtyard. Daily 9am–11pm.

★ **L'As du Fallafel** 34 rue des Rosiers, 4ᵉ; ⓜ Saint-Paul; map pp.286–287. Everyone has a favourite falafel joint on this street, but the queues attest to *L'As du Fallafel's* popularity. Their signature combination – pitta bread stuffed full of falafel, cabbage, aubergine, hummus and yogurt – costs €5.50 to take away. Mon–Thurs & Sun noon–midnight.

Le Loir dans la Théière 3 rue des Rosiers, 4ᵉ; ⓜ St-Paul; map pp.286–287. The Sun brunch is especially popular at this laidback, cosy café, as are their excellent cakes (€4–6.50). Get there early to bag a comfy leather armchair. Daily 10am–7pm.

★ **Marché des Enfants Rouges** 39 Rue de Bretagne, 3ᵉ; ⓜ Filles du Calvaire; map pp.286–287. Not a café, but the oldest market in Paris. Take your pick from the freshly cooked food available at the stalls (including French, Moroccan and Italian) then grab a spot at the shared picnic tables. Tues, Wed & Thurs 8.30am–1pm & 4–7.30pm, Fri & Sat 8.30am–1pm & 4–8pm, Sun 8.30am–2pm.

RESTAURANTS

Au Père Louis 38 rue Monsieur le Prince, 6ᵉ ☎ 01 43 26 54 14; ⓜ Odéon; map pp.286–287. This cosy, labyrinthine restaurant is a great choice for a long, relaxed meal. The menu is packed with classic dishes including onion soup (€9) and *tarte tatin* (€7.50). Daily noon–3pm & 7pm–midnight.

★ **Au Pied de Fouet** 45 Rue de Babylone, 7ᵉ ☎ 01 47 05 12 27; ⓜ Saint-François-Xavier; map pp.282–283. Tiny and charmingly old-fashioned restaurant with red-check tablecloths, picture-cluttered walls and wonky floors. Try the *pâté de campagne* (€3.50) and *bavette* (€10) with wine from €2.90 a glass. There's another branch at 3 Rue Saint-Benoît, 6ᵉ. Mon–Sat noon–4.30pm & 7.30–11pm.

Au Virage Lepic 61 rue Lepic, 18ᵉ ☎ 01 42 52 46 79; ⓜ Abbesses; map pp.282–283. Simple, good-quality food (*plats* from €15), focusing on meat and game, served in a friendly, traditional bistro. Mon, Wed & Thurs–Sun 7–11pm.

Big Fernand 55 rue du Faubourg Poissonnière, 9ᵉ; ⓜ Poissonnière or Cadet; map pp.282–283. Run by a young and jolly team, this is *the* place to satisfy a burger craving in Paris. Try one of their creations like *Le Bartholomé* (beef patty with raclette and caramelized onions; €12) or build your own. Mon–Sat noon–2.30pm & 7.30–10.30pm.

Bistrot Victoires 6 rue de la Vrillière, 2ᵉ ☎ 01 42 61 43 78; ⓜ Bourse; map pp.286–287. A convivial local bistro, tucked away near the Palais Royale. The fantastic old bar and big mirrors lend it a timeless appeal, and the food is

surprisingly cheap for this part of the city (*poulet roti* €10). Daily noon–3pm & 7–11pm.

Broizh Café 109 rue Vieille du Temple, 3ᵉ ☎ 01 42 72 13 77; ⓜ Saint-Sébastien-Froissart; map pp.286–287. Authentic Breton *galettes* and crêpes (from €4) served in a refreshingly modern interior. The *galette complète* (ham, cheese and egg) is particularly good, as is the salted caramel crêpe. Wed–Sat 11.30am–11pm. Sun 11.30am–10pm.

★ **Candelaria** 52 rue de Saintonge, 3ᵉ; ⓜ Saint-François-Xavier; map pp.286–287. The queue usually snakes out the door for the excellent Mexican food here. There's no menu, but tortilla chips and home-made guacamole (€5) are a must, as are their potent margaritas (€5). There are just six stools and scruffy sharing tables for diners (no reservations), with a crowded, dark cocktail bar behind. Restaurant Mon–Wed & Sun 12.30–11pm, Thurs–Sat 12.30pm–midnight, bar daily 6pm–2am.

La Gueuze 19 rue Soufflot, 5ᵉ; ⓜ Cluny-La Sorbonne; map pp.286–287. There are Belgian beers aplenty (*demi pressions* from €5) in this Flemish-themed restaurant near the Jardin du Luxembourg, with *moules mariniéres* (€10) the most popular accompaniment to a brew. Daily noon–2am.

Le Cambodge 10 avenue Richerand, 10ᵉ; ⓜ Goncourt; map pp.282–283. A laidback Cambodian restaurant with a unique ordering system where you write (or draw) your choice on a notepad. Try the *bo bun*, a fragrant noodle dish with beansprouts, carrots and peanuts (from €10). Mon–Sat noon–2.30pm & 7–11pm.

Le Potager du Marais 22 rue Rambuteau, 3ᵉ ☎ 01 57 40 98 57; ⓜ Rambuteau; map pp.286–287. Smart vegetarian restaurant serving interesting organic dishes like quinoa burgers with vegan cheese (€18) and spinach and walnut lasagne (€17). Wed–Sun noon–4pm & 7pm–midnight.

Pancake Square 4 rue de Surène, 8ᵉ ☎ 01 42 65 20 27; ⓜ Madeleine; map pp.282–283. A nautical-themed crêperie with a great range of *galettes* such as the *savoyarde* (raclette, potatoes, bacon and cream; €10) and *pichets* of Breton cider (€8). There's another branch at 10 rue des Canettes, 6ᵉ. Mon–Sat noon–2.30pm and 7–10pm.

Pink Flamingo 105 rue Vieille du Temple 3ᵉ ☎ 01 42 71 28 20; ⓜ Saint-Sébastien-Froissart; map pp.286–287. The inventively named pizzas (from €13) at the Marais branch of this eclectic pizzeria include the Gandhi (sag paneer, baba ganoush and mozzarella) and the Bjork (smoked salmon, lumpfish caviar and crème fraîche). Tues–Fri noon–3pm & 7–11.30pm, Sat & Sun noon–4pm & 7–11.30pm.

Polidor 41 rue Monsieur-le-Prince, 6ᵉ ☎ 01 43 26 95 34; ⓜ Odéon; map pp.286–287. Historic bistro that was a favourite of James Joyce and Hemmingway; service can be short-tempered but the food is good and reasonably priced. Try the *boeuf bourguignon* (€12). Daily noon–2.30pm & 7pm–midnight.

Robert et Louise 64 rue Vieille du Temple, 3ᵉ ☎ 01 42 78 55 89; ⓜ Rambuteau or Saint Paul; map, pp.286–287. The

11

11

★ TREAT YOURSELF

Frenchie Bar à Vins 6 rue du Nil, 2ᵉ ❶01 40 39 96 19; Ⓜ Sentier; map pp.286–287. Across the road from their very chic (and very popular) restaurant, this modern, bare-brick wine bar offers a more accessible taste of Gregory Marchand's cooking. He's worked in London (under Jamie Oliver) and New York, the influences of which can be seen in both his food and cosmopolitan clientele. All dishes are designed to share; expect savoury options like papardelle with rabbit ragu (€14) followed by a divine chocolate pot with olive oil and sea salt (€9). Wines (from €6 a glass) are exceptionally well chosen. Mon–Fri 7–11pm.

unassuming facade of this Marais institution doesn't betray anything of the restaurant's rustic, down-to-earth interior. The ground-floor dining room is permeated by the heady smell of the wood fire, over which the signature dish, *côte de boeuf pour deux* (€42), is beautifully cooked. The weekday lunch menu (€12) is excellent value. Tues 7–11pm, Wed–Sun noon–2.30pm & 7–11pm.

DRINKING AND NIGHTLIFE

Drinks are charged according to where you sit, with supplements for drinking on the terrace. The old working-class districts east of the Canal St Martin continue to hold some of the city's liveliest nightlife, while the Marais is the place to head for chic café-bars and trendy gay spots. The university quarter near St-Germain-des-Prés is also worth exploring. Most places are open all day until around 2am, and many offer an early-evening "happy hour". For listings, pick up the weekly guide *Pariscope*, which has a small section in English.

BARS

Au P'tit Garage 63 rue Jean-Pierre Timbaud, 11ᵉ Ⓜ Parmentier; map pp.282–283. A young and rowdy crowd pack out this scruffy bar; expect to see plenty of double denim and check shirts. Cheap and sugary caipirinhas (€6.50) fuel the rock'n'roll atmosphere. Daily 5pm–2am.

Café Charbon 109 rue Oberkampf, 11ᵉ; Ⓜ Parmentier or rue Saint-Maur; map pp.282–283. Long a stalwart of the rue Oberkampf scene, the popularity of *Café Charbon* hasn't waned. The classic brasserie decor – oxblood booths, chandeliers and high ceilings – dates from the early twentieth century, while the attached club, *Nouveau Casino* (see opposite), opened in 2001. Wine starts at €4, with cocktails from €8. Mon, Tues & Sun 9am–2am, Wed–Sat 9am–4am.

★**Café Chéri(e)** 44 boulevard de la Villette, 19ᵉ; Ⓜ Belleville; map pp.282–283. This friendly neighbourhood bar is a great place to get a feel for Belleville's laidback "bobo" (bourgeois bohemian) vibe. Old school desks have been resurrected to provide the seats on the street, while the interior hosts exhibitions and DJs (Thurs–Sat). Happy-hour deals include overflowing glasses of wine for €3.50. Daily 11am–2am.

Chez Georges 11 rue des Canettes, 6ᵉ; Ⓜ Mabillon or Saint-Sulpice; map pp.286–287. Fantastic, old-fashioned cellar wine bar (wine by the glass from €3.50), popular with students and older locals alike. Tues–Sat noon–2am.

Chez Prune 36 rue Beaurepaire, 10ᵉ Ⓜ Jacques Bonsergent; map pp.286–287. As you might guess from the shabby-chic decor, mosaic floors and yellow walls, this relaxed café-bar is the quintessential canal-side hipster hangout. Wine from €3.50 a glass. Mon–Sat 8am–2am, Sun 10am–2am.

Glass 7 Rue Frochot, 9ᵉ; Ⓜ Pigalle; map pp.282–283. Located in the seedy but slowly gentrifying area south of Pigalle (dubbed "SoPi"), *Glass* is a little slice of Americana in Paris. Ignore the menacing bouncer; there's a great atmosphere inside this small, packed bar. Try one of their whisky-based cocktails (€10) or craft beers (from €4). Tues, Wed & Sun 8pm–3am, Fri & Sat 8pm–5am.

La Fourmi 74 rue des Martyrs, 18ᵉ; Ⓜ Pigalle; map pp.282–283. Refreshingly casual Montmartre café-bar with comfy red velvet benches, high ceilings and an enormous chandelier made from old wine bottles. Affordable beers (from €4) and cocktails keep things lively well into the night. Mon–Thurs 8am–2am, Fri & Sat 8am–4am, Sun 10am–2am.

La Perle 78 rue Vieille du Temple, 3ᵉ; Ⓜ Rambuteau or Saint-Sébastien-Froissart; map pp.286–287. This gay-friendly Marais bar might appear unremarkable, but it becomes enormously popular on weekend evenings. Prices aren't bad for this part of town either, with 50cl beers from €6.70 and wine from €3.50 a glass. Daily 8am–2am.

Wine by One 27 rue de Marignan, 8ᵉ; Ⓜ Franklin D. Roosevelt; map pp.282–283. An unpretentious concept wine bar with over 100 wines to sample from snazzy self-service machines. Load a €2 card with as much money as

★ TREAT YOURSELF

Curio Parlor 16 rue des Bernardins, 5ᵉ Ⓜ Maubert-Mutualité; map pp.286–287. Look for a small placard by the door to find this intimate speakeasy, decked out with flocked wallpaper, stags' heads and taxidermy parrots. Their unusual concoctions include the *gusanos* (tequila, agave honey, mint and ginger ale; €12) or try a nip of their speciality, Japanese whisky. Tues–Thurs 7pm–2am, Fri & Sat 7pm–4am.

you wish, then choose a wine to taste; prices start at €0.90 for a small sip. Tues–Fri noon–11pm, Sat 3–10pm.

CLUBS AND LIVE MUSIC

Autour de Midi...et Minuit 11 rue Lepic, 18ᵉ ⓦ autourdemidi.fr; ⓜ Blanche; map pp.282–283. A cosy subterranean jazz club with free jam sessions on Tues and Wed. Tues–Sat, hours vary.

Le Divan du Monde 75 rue des Martyrs, 18ᵉ ⓦ divandumonde.com; ⓜ Pigalle; map pp.282–283. Small venue with an eclectic selection of live music and occasional big-name rock acts. See website for gig times.

Nouveau Casino 109 rue Oberkampf, 11ᵉ ⓦ nouveau casino.net; ⓜ Parmentier or rue Saint-Maur; map pp.282–283. Electro- and indie-dominated club and venue housed in an old leather tannery behind *Café Charbon* (see opposite). The line-up includes a mix of DJ sets and indie acts like Haim. Entry prices up to €15. Tues–Sun, hours vary.

Point Ephémère 200 quai de Valmy 10ᵉ ⓦ pointephemere.org; ⓜ Jaurès; map pp.282–283. Grungy, concrete-floored bar, restaurant, club and gallery, which spills out onto the bank of the canal. Expect a mix of exhibitions, DJs, live acts and secret gigs for the likes of Foals. *Demi pressions* are a steal from €2.50. Mon–Sat noon–2am, Sun noon–9pm.

Social Club 142 rue Montmartre, 2ᵉ ⓦ parissocialclub .com; ⓜ Bourse; map pp.286–287. Head to this central club to see big name techno and electro DJs. Recent line-ups have included SBTRKT and Simian Mobile Disco. Wed 11.30pm–3am, Thurs–Sat 11pm–6am.

GAY AND LESBIAN PARIS

Paris has a well established gay scene concentrated mainly in the Halles, Marais and Bastille areas. For information, check out *Têtu* (ⓦ tetu.com), France's biggest gay monthly magazine, or visit the main information centre, Centre Gai et Lesbien de Paris, 63 rue Beaubourg, 3ᵉ (ⓣ 01 43 57 21 47, ⓦ centrelgbtparis.org; ⓜ Ledru-Rollin/Bastille).

Banana Café 13 rue de la Ferronnerie, 1ᵉʳ ⓦ bananacafeparis.com; ⓜ Châtelet; map pp.286–287. Seriously hedonistic club-bar, packing in the punters with up-tempo clubby tunes and go-go boy shows. Cocktails are just €4 during the 6–11pm happy hour. Daily 6pm–5am.

Freedj 35 rue Ste-Croix-de-la-Bretonnerie, 4ᵉ; ⓜ Hôtel-de-Ville; map pp.286–287. A stylish club in the heart of the Marais, attracting a young, trendy crowd. Daily 6pm–4am.

Le Tango (La Boîte à Frissons) 13 rue au Maire, 3ᵉ ⓦ boite-a-frissons.fr; ⓜ Arts-et-Métiers; map pp.286–287. This old dancehall welcomes a mixed gay, lesbian and straight crowd for ballroom dancing before the music gives way to disco around 1am. There's usually a €9 entrance fee. Fri & Sat 10.30pm–5am, Sun 6–11pm.

ENTERTAINMENT

CINEMA

Tickets cost around €10 and discounts are offered across the city on Wed. Films are identified as either *v.o.*, which means they're shown in their original language, or *v.f.*, which means they're dubbed into French.

Cinémathèque Française 51 rue de Bercy, 12ᵉ ⓦ cinematheque.fr; ⓜ Bercy. Housed in a striking Frank Gehry-designed building, Cinémathèque Française screens a range of films from avant-garde pieces to homages to Hollywood stars.

Le Champo 51 rue des Ecoles, 5ᵉ ⓦ lechampo.com; ⓜ Cluny-La Sorbonne. This Latin Quarter cinema has been screening films since 1938. They now show an interesting selection of art-house classics and run *les nuits du Champo*: a night of three films followed by breakfast for €15.

THEATRE, OPERA AND CLASSICAL MUSIC

Along with concert venues, theatres offer standby tickets at a reduced rate. These are generally only released around 20min before the performance, and many offer discounted tickets to students.

Cité de la Musique 221 av Jean-Jaurès, 19ᵉ ⓦ cite -musique.fr; ⓜ Porte-de-Pantin; map pp.282–283. Modern venue in Parc de la Villette with an eclectic music programme that covers Baroque, contemporary works and world music. Tickets around €20.

Comédie-Française ⓦ comedie-francaise.fr. For classical theatre by the likes of Molière or Racine, head to a production by this venerable company, staged in several theatres across Paris. Tickets from €10.

Palais Garnier Place de l'Opéra, 9ᵉ ⓦ opera-de-paris.fr; ⓜ Opéra; map pp.286–287. The city's original opera house stages both operas and ballets within its lavish interior. Tickets from €5.

SHOPPING

Galeries Lafayette 40 bd Haussmann, 9ᵉ ⓦ galerieslafayette.com; ⓜ Chaussée d'Antin-La Fayette; map pp.282–283. This massive department store sells everything from lingerie and designer fashion to books and DVDs. Worth a visit just to gawp at the astonishing architecture. Mon–Wed, Sat & Sun 9.30am–8pm, Thurs 9.30am–9pm.

Hédiard 21 place de la Madeleine, 8ᵉ ⓦ hediard.fr; ⓜ Madeleine; map pp.282–283. Gastronomes will be in seventh heaven in this shop, where the finest foods have been sold since 1854. Mon–Sat 9am–8pm.

Marché aux Puces de St-Ouen Rue des Rosiers, 18ᵉ ⓦ les-puces.com; ⓜ Porte de Clignancourt; map pp.282–283. Bargain hunters congregate on this massive flea market (Europe's largest), with over 2500 stalls – be prepared to haggle. Mon, Sat & Sun 9am–6pm.

11

DIRECTORY

Embassies and consulates Australia, 4 rue Jean Rey, 15ᵉ ☎ 01 40 59 33 00; Canada, 35 av Montaigne, 8ᵉ ☎ 01 44 43 29 00; Ireland, 4 rue Rude, 16ᵉ ☎ 01 44 17 67 00; New Zealand, 7 rue Léonard de Vinci, 16ᵉ ☎ 01 45 01 43 43; UK, 35 rue du Faubourg-St-Honoré, 8ᵉ ☎ 01 44 51 31 00; US, 2 av Gabriel, 8ᵉ ☎ 01 43 12 22 22.

Exchange A good *bureau de change* is the Comptoir des Tuileries, at 53 rue Vivienne, 2ᵉ (Mon–Fri 9.30am–7pm, Sat 1–5.30pm; ☎ 01 42 60 17 16).

Hospital Contact SOS-Médecins (☎ 01 47 07 77 77) for 24hr medical help, or dial ☎ 15 for emergencies.

Left luggage Lockers (€5.50–9.50) are available at all train stations.

Pharmacy Dérhy (☎ 01 45 62 02 41), 84 av des Champs-Élysées' is open 24hr.

Post office 52 rue du Louvre, 1ᵉʳ (Mon–Sat 7.30am–6am, Sun 10am–midnight).

DAY-TRIPS FROM PARIS

Within easy day-trip distance from Paris are two of the country's most popular sights – stately **Versailles** and Monet's beautiful garden at **Giverny**.

Versailles

The **Palace of Versailles** (Tues–Sun: April–Oct 9am–6.30pm; Nov–March 9am–5.30pm; €18 palace and gardens, €15 palace only; ⓦ en.chateauversailles.fr) is the epitome of decadence and luxury, with its staggeringly lavish architectural splendour that is a homage to its founder, the "Sun King" Louis XIV. The **ornamental gardens** (daily: April–Oct 8am–8.30pm; Nov–March 8am–6pm) are particularly splendid and ostentatious, complete with canals, boating lakes and fountains. The easiest way to get to Versailles is on the half-hourly RER line C to Versailles-Rive Gauche (40min; €6.70 return).

Giverny

Less than an hour northwest of Paris, **GIVERNY** is famous for **Monet's house and gardens**, complete with water-lily pond (April–Oct daily 9.30am–6pm; €9.50; ⓦ fondation-monet.com). Monet lived here from 1883 until his death in 1926 and the gardens that he laid out were considered by many – including Monet himself – to be his "greatest masterpiece"; the best months to visit are May and June, when the rhododendrons flower around the lily pond and the wisteria hangs over the Japanese bridge, but it's overwhelmingly beautiful at any time of year. To get here, take a train to nearby **Vernon** from Paris-St-Lazare (around 5 daily; 45min; €27.80 return), then either rent a bike from the café opposite the station (€14 for the day) or take the shuttle bus (€8 return; see website for times).

Northern France

Northern France includes some of the most industrial and densely populated parts of the country. However, there are some curiosities hidden away in the far northeastern corner. **Lille** with its *vieux ville* is lovely to amble around, while **Boulogne** is the most interesting port town. Further south, the *maisons* and vineyards of **Champagne** are the main draw, for which the best base is **Reims**, with its fine cathedral.

BOULOGNE

BOULOGNE is a pleasant Channel port with a long, sandy stretch of beach. Its **ville basse** (Lower Town), where the main port is located, is somewhat run-down, but within the medieval ramparts of the **ville haute** (Upper Town) rising above, there's a twelfth-century castle, a cathedral and a range of cafés and restaurants.

ARRIVAL AND INFORMATION

By train The train station is a 15min walk from the centre of the *ville basse*.

Destinations Calais (hourly; 35min); Paris (7 daily; 2–3hr); Lille (4 daily; 1hr).

Tourist information The main tourist office is in Nausicaá aquarium, boulevard St-Beauve (Mon–Sat 10.30am–12.30pm & 2–5.30pm, with longer hours in summer; ☎ 03 21 10 88 10, ⓦ tourisme-boulognesurmer.com).

ACCOMMODATION AND EATING

Citron Basilic 69 Grande Rue ☎ 03 21 92 65 61. Small, modern restaurant offering two-course *formules* for €13.90: dishes might include rabbit terrine or chicken and courgette risotto. Tues–Thurs noon–2.30pm, Fri & Sat noon–2.30pm & 7–10pm.

11

FUAJ Bologne-sur-Mer 56 place Rouget de Lisle ☎ 03 21 99 15 30, ⓦ fuaj.org. The cheapest beds in town are at this friendly hostel opposite the station. It has a small bar with a pool table and *babyfoot*. Dorm **€21.50**

Opal Inn 170 bvd Sainte Beuve ☎ 03 21 32 15 15, ⓦ hotel-opalinn.com. Behind a rather drab frontage lies this smart, modern three-star, nicely decorated in hues of lilac. Facilities include a 24hr bar, super-cheap room service and sea views. Double **€69**

CALAIS

CALAIS is one of the main ports for ferries to and from the UK. Unless you have an early-morning departure there's little reason to make a special stop here.

ARRIVAL AND DEPARTURE

By train Calais Ville is in the town centre; Calais Frethun is on the outskirts.

Destinations Lille (hourly; 30min–1hr 30min); Paris (4 daily; 1hr 45min).

By ferry For last-minute ferry bookings contact P&O Ferries (☎ 0825 120 156).

ACCOMMODATION AND EATING

Centre Européen de Séjour Avenue du Maréchal de Lattre de Tassigny ☎ 03 21 34 70 20; bus #3 from Calais Ville station. Decent hostel with small dorms and an on-site restaurant. Dorm **€21.50**

Histoire Ancienne 20 rue Royale ☎ 03 21 34 11 20. Family-run restaurant with a good-value *menu gourmand* (three courses €18.90) featuring dishes like salmon in a béarnaise sauce. Mon noon–2.30pm, Tues–Sat noon–2.30pm and 6–11pm.

Hotel Particulier Richelieu 17 rue Richelieu ☎ 03 21 34 61 60, ⓦ hotel-richelieu-calais.co.uk. Delightful small hotel with individually decorated rooms (some with claw-foot tubs); don't be put off by the unpromising modern exterior. Double **€55**

LILLE

LILLE is a lively, modern city which is well worth visiting for a day or two. The winding, cobbled streets of the old town are lined with traditional patisseries, brasseries and a range of upmarket shops. The **Grand-Place**, also known as place du Général de Gaulle, is a busy square dominated by the old exchange building (**Vieille Bourse**), which now houses an afternoon book market (Tues–Sun 1–7pm). South of the old quarter lies the

modern place Rihour, beyond which is the **Palais des Beaux-Arts**, place de la République (Mon 2–6pm, Wed–Sun 10am–6pm; €6.50; ☎ 03 20 06 78 00, ⓦ pba-lille.fr), a notable fine arts museum with an excellent collection of Renaissance art and varying exhibitions.

ARRIVAL AND INFORMATION

By train Gare Lille-Flandres is on place de la Gare; Gare Lille-Europe is a 2min walk further east and has faster services.

Destinations from Gare Lille-Europe Brussels (hourly; 35–50min); Calais (hourly; 30min); London (hourly; 1hr 30min); Lyon (7 daily; 3hr); Paris (every 30min; 1hr).

Tourist information The tourist office is in Palais Rihour (Mon–Sat 9am–6pm, Sun 10am–noon & 2–5pm; ⓦ lilletourism.com).

ACCOMMODATION

Faidherbe 42 place de la Gare ☎ 03 20 06 27 93, ⓦ hotel-faidherbe-lille.fr. Just opposite the station, this simple hotel is clean and welcoming. The cheapest rooms (with bathrooms down the hall) are great value. Double **€44**

FUAJ Lille 12 rue Malpart ☎ 03 20 57 08 94, ⓦ fuaj.org. Basic FUAJ hostel, centrally located near the Hôtel de Ville. Breakfast is included and there are simple cooking facilities. Note that reception is closed 11am–3pm. Dorm **€21.50**

Hotel Kanaï 10 rue de Bethune ☎ 03 20 57 14 78, ⓦ hotelkanai.com. This stylish boutique hotel has a great location on a pedestrianized road in the heart of the city. As Lille is geared to business travellers, you can grab a real bargain at weekends. Double **€70**

EATING AND DRINKING

Estaminet Chez la Vielle 60 rue de Gand ☎ 03 28 36 40 06. One of a few remaining *estaminets* (traditional Flemish bistros) in Lille, where hops dangle from the beams lining the ceiling. Start with a traditional blackcurrant and juniper liqueur (€4) before tucking into filling dishes like black pudding and apple tart (€12.30). Tues–Sat noon–2pm & 7–11pm.

L'Illustration 18 rue Royale. The pick of the bars on this lively stretch, thanks to the friendly bartenders and retro-pop soundtrack. They serve a good range of beers (from €4.50 for 50cl) and wine (from €3 a glass). Mon–Sat 12.30pm–3am, Sun 12.30pm–2am.

MEERT 27 rue Esquermoise. A grand *patisserie* and *confiserie* selling all manner of pastries and chocolates, which you can eat in their *salon de thé* or take away. The éclairs (€2.50) are divine. Tues–Thurs 10.30am–7.30pm, Fri 9.30am–7.30pm, Sat 9am–7.30pm, Sun 9am–6pm.

11

REIMS

REIMS is located at the heart of the Champagne region, so if you fancy a tipple or two it's worth stopping by. The town is also home to the spectacular Gothic **Cathédrale Notre Dame** (daily 7.30am–7.30pm), one of the most beautiful in France. The interior is renowned for the stained-glass designs by Marc Chagall in the east chapel and glorifications of the champagne-making process in the south transept.

If you're in town for the **champagne**, head to the tourist office for details of which *maisons* are currently offering tours; all have English-speaking guides. Cellar tours involve a small fee which includes a tasting at the end. The atmospheric *caves* of **Taittinger**, 9 place St-Niçaise (March–Nov Mon–Sat 9.30am–5.30pm; Dec–March Mon–Fri 9.30am–5.30pm; €16; ⓦ taittinger.fr) are the only cellars you can visit without an appointment. Other good houses to visit are **Mumm**, 34 rue du Champ-de-Mars (€13; ⓦ mumm .com), and the prestigious **Veuve Clicquot**, 1 place des Droits-de-l'Homme (€25; ☎03 26 89 53 90, ⓦ veuve-clicquot.fr).

ARRIVAL AND INFORMATION

By train The train station is a short walk north of the centre.
Destinations Paris (5 daily; 50min).
Tourist information Reims Tourisme (ⓦ reims-tourism .com) has two offices: outside the station on Parvis de la Gare (Mon–Thurs & Sat 8.30–11am & noon–6pm, Fri 8.30–11am & noon–7pm, Sun 11am–5pm) and opposite the cathedral at 2 rue Guillaume de Machault (April–Oct Mon–Sat 9am–7pm, Sun 10am–6pm; Nov–March Mon–Sat 9am–6pm, Sun 10am–4pm).

ACCOMMODATION

CIS de Champagne Parc Léo Lagrange ☎03 26 40 52 60, ⓦ cis-reims.com; tram A or B to "Comédie". The only dorm accommodation in Reims is predominantly group-oriented and a 15min walk from the train station. Dorm **€21.50**
Hotel Monopole 28 place Drouet d'Erlon ☎03 26 47 10 33. Like all of Reims's budget hotels, the *Monopole* is a little careworn, though it's cheap, friendly and well located on bustling place Drouet d'Erlon. Double **€45**

EATING AND DRINKING

Bisrot du Forum 6 place du Forum ☎03 26 47 56 58.

Tartares are the speciality at this casual bistro, from the classic *boeuf* (€15) to a tomato, feta and cucumber vegetarian option (€13). Daily 8am–12.30am.
Waïda 3–5 place Drouet d'Erlon ☎03 26 47 44 49. An old-fashioned bakery offering a mix of savoury and sweet pastries to eat in or take away; it's a good spot for a simple breakfast of baguette with butter and jam (€2.30). Tues–Fri 7.30am–7.30pm, Sat 7.30am–8pm, Sun 8am–1.30pm & 3.30–7.30pm.

Normandy and Brittany

To the French, the essence of **Normandy** is in its food and drink: this is the land of butter and cream, cheese and seafood, cider and calvados. Many of the towns also have great historic importance: **Rouen** is where Joan of Arc was burned at the stake; **Bayeux** is rightly celebrated for its eponymous tapestry; the 80km stretch of northern coastline was the site of the **D-Day landings**; and the granite spectacle of **Mont St-Michel** dates back to the thirteenth century. The striking coastline, sandy beaches and lush countryside of **Brittany** seem to belong to a very different part of France; it seems almost unbelievable that these verdant pastures are within easy reach of Paris. People here are both fiercely proud and defiantly isolationist.

ROUEN

ROUEN is a city of impressive churches, half-timbered houses and small cobbled streets. The town's focal point is place du Vieux-Marché, where Joan of Arc was burned at the stake in 1431. The old market square leads onto rue du Gros-Horloge, which has a colourful one-handed clock arching over the street. Walking along here brings you to the impressive **Cathédrale de Notre-Dame** (Mon 2–6pm, Tues–Sat 9am–7pm, Sun 8am–6pm), a Gothic masterpiece built in the twelfth and thirteenth centuries. The cathedral is best known as the subject of a series of paintings by Monet which explore the interaction between light and shadow on its facade.

★ TREAT YOURSELF

Gill Côté Bistro 14 place du Vieux Marché, Rouen ☎ 02 35 89 88 72. While the local two Michelin star restaurant, *Gill*, might be out of reach, its smart bistro offshoot is great value. Expect beautifully executed classics like gazpacho with goats' cheese mousse (€7.50) followed by lamb shank with honey and fennel (€15.90). Daily noon–2.30pm & 5.30–10.30pm.

ARRIVAL AND INFORMATION

By train The station is a 10min walk from the centre.
Destinations Caen (6 daily; 1hr 45min); Paris (hourly; 1hr 10min).

Tourist information The tourist office is opposite the cathedral at 25 place de la Cathédrale (May–Sept Mon–Sat 9am–7pm, Sun 9.30am–12.30pm & 2–6pm; Oct–April Mon–Sat 9.30am–12.30pm & 1.30–6pm; ⓦ rouentourisme.com).

ACCOMMODATION

FUAJ Rouen 3 rue du Tour, route de Darnétal ☎ 02 35 08 18 50, ⓦ fuaj.org; bus #2 or #3 to "Auberge de Jeunesse". Housed in a former dyeworks, this modern hostel has good communal areas. Dorm **€22.50**
★ **Le Sisley** 51 rue Jean Lecanuet ☎ 02 35 71 10 07, ⓦ hotelsisley.fr. Take your pick from Monet, Manet, Degas or Renoir – each room here is decorated in the style of one of the great Impressionist painters. Some of the colours are pretty loud, but it has bags of personality. Double **€56**

EATING AND DRINKING

Brasserie Paul 1 place de la Cathédrale ☎ 02 35 71 86 07. An archetypal French brasserie, where you can have a good meal of *escargots* (€8.90), chicken in cider sauce (€10.90) and local cheeses. Daily 10am–11pm.
Crêperie la Regalière 12 rue Massacre ☎ 02 35 15 33 33. Located just off the Rue du Gros Horloge, this is a great place to sample traditional Norman *galettes* (from €7) and ciders (€2.90). Tues–Sat noon–11pm.
La Boîte à Bières 35 rue Cauchoise. Studenty bar with a great atmosphere and occasional live music. There are ten beers on tap and a huge range by the bottle. Tues–Sat 5pm–2am.

BAYEUX

BAYEUX's world-famous **tapestry** depicting the 1066 invasion of England by William the Conqueror is one of the highlights of a visit to Normandy. The 70m strip of linen, embroidered over nine centuries ago, is housed in the **Centre Guillaume le Conquérant**, rue de Nesmond (daily: April–Oct 9am–5.45pm, Nov–March 9.30–11.45am & 2–5.15pm; €9). The **cathedral**, place de la Liberté (daily: Jan–March 9am–5pm; April–June & Oct–Dec 9am–6pm; July–Sept 9am–7pm), is a spectacular thirteenth-century edifice, with some parts dating back to the eleventh century.

ARRIVAL AND INFORMATION

By train Bayeux's train station is on the southern side of town, just off boulevard Sadi Carnot.
Destinations Caen (hourly; 20min); Paris (3 daily; 2hr 15min).

Tourist information The tourist office is at Pont St-Jean (daily 10am–12.30pm & 2–5.30pm, with later opening in July and Aug; ☎ 02 31 51 28 28, ⓦ bayeux-bessin -tourisme.com).

ACCOMMODATION AND EATING

De la Gare 26 place de la Gare ☎ 02 31 92 10 70, ⓦ hotel -delagare-bayeux.fr. Home to Normandy Tours (see box, p.298), this conveniently situated hotel has fourteen rooms and a simple brasserie. Double **€34**
Fringale 43 rue St-Jean ☎ 02 31 21 34 40. The best of the restaurants on this pedestrianized street, serving traditional *menus* from €17; try the French onion soup. Mon & Wed–Sun noon–2pm & 6.30–10pm.
Mogador 20 rue A. Chartier ☎ 02 31 92 24 58, ⓦ hotel -mogador-bayeux.fr. A small hotel in the centre of town offering homely doubles as well as quads and triples. Double **€53**

ST-MALO

ST-MALO is a beautiful Breton coastal town with cobbled streets surrounded by medieval ramparts. You can easily spend a lazy day or so ambling through the lanes and strolling along the beaches. The **town museum**, in the castle to the right as you enter the main city gate, Porte St-Vincent (daily: April–Sept 10am–12.30pm & 2–6pm; Oct–March 10am–noon & 2–6pm; €6), covers the city's eventful history, which has encompassed colonialism, slave-trading and privateers. The **Cathédrale St-Vincent** (daily 9.45am–6pm) on place Jean de Châtillon was severely damaged during World War II, as was most of the old town, but has since been restored.

11

D-DAY BEACHES

On June 6, 1944, 135,000 Allied troops stormed the beaches of Normandy in **Operation Overlord**. After heavy fighting, which saw thousands of casualties on both sides, the Allied forces took command of all the beaches, which was a major turning point of World War II. The 80km stretch of coastline north of Bayeux that saw the D-Day landings includes: **Omaha**, now home to the Musée Mémorial d'Omaha Beach (daily: mid-Feb to mid-March 10am–12.30pm & 2.30–6pm; mid-March to mid-Feb 9.30am–6.30pm; €6; ⓦ musee-memorial-omaha.com), where exhibits include uniforms and a tank; and **Arromanches**, 10km northwest of Bayeux, which was the main unloading point for cargo (some four million tonnes of it). The interesting museum at Arromanches, **Musée du Débarquement**, place du 6 Juin (daily: Feb–April & Nov 10am–12.30pm & 1.30–5pm; May–Aug 9am–7pm, Sept 9am–6pm; €7.50; ⓦ musee -arromanches.fr), has further information on France's liberation.

One of the best ways to see the beaches is on a tour: contact Normandy Sightseeing Tours (from €45; ☎ 02 31 51 70 52, ⓦ d-daybeaches.com), or Normandy Tours (€50; ☎ 02 31 92 10 70, ⓦ normandy-landing-tours.com)

There are also plenty of windsurfing, sailing and wakeboarding opportunities at **Surf School St-Malo**, just off chaussée du Sillon along the bay at 2 avenue de la Hoguette (☎ 02 99 40 07 47, ⓦ surfschool.org).

ARRIVAL AND INFORMATION

By train The station is a 20min walk east from the walled town.
Destinations Dol de Bretagne (hourly; 15min); Paris (2 daily; 3hr 20min); Rennes (hourly; 1hr).
Tourist information The tourist office is on Esplanade St-Vincent (Mon–Sat 9am–1pm & 2–6pm, with longer hours in summer; ⓦ saint-malo-tourisme.com).

ACCOMMODATION

Centre Patrick Varangot 37 avenue du Révérend Père Umbricht ☎ 02 99 40 29 80, ⓦ centrevarangot.com; bus #3 to "Auberge de Jeunesse". Spotlessly clean hostel located 1.5km from the train station and 150m from the beach. Book well in advance. Dorm **€21**
Cité d'Alet Allée Gaston ☎ 02 99 81 60 91, ⓦ ville-saint -malo.fr. Perfectly positioned campsite on a peninsula by the beach. Amenities include a café, shop and showers. Camping **€14.40** per person and tent
Port Malo Hotel 15 rue Ste-Barbe ☎ 02 99 20 52 99, ⓦ hotel-port-malo.com. Inside the walls, this quaint hotel has surprisingly modern rooms, plus there's a bar right downstairs. Double **€62**

EATING AND DRINKING

Coquille d'Oeuf 20 rue de la Corne de Cerfs ☎ 02 99 40 92 62. Service can be a little slow at this cosy restaurant, but their unusual dishes (such as scallops in a Thai-style sauce; €15) are worth the wait. Daily 7–10pm.
La Brigantine 13 rue de Dinan ☎ 02 99 56 82 82. You won't find an English menu at this contemporary crêperie,

but there is one British concession: the "queen mum", a marmalade and chocolate crêpe flambéed in whisky (€6.90). Daily noon–10pm, closed Tues & Wed in winter.
La Java 3 rue Ste-Barbe. Fantastically cluttered and quirky cider bar with swings rather than stools at the bar and a toilet hidden in an old confessional. This is a great place to sample a *kir Breton* (cassis and cider; €3.80). Daily 9am–9pm, sometimes later.

MONT ST-MICHEL

Although part of Normandy, the island of **MONT ST-MICHEL** is easily reached from Brittany and can be visited on a day-trip from St-Malo. It's the site of the striking Gothic **Abbaye du Mont-Saint-Michel** (daily: May–Aug 9am–7pm; Sept–April 9.30am–6pm; €9), known as La Merveille, which is visible from all around the bay. The granite structure was sculpted to match the contours of the hill, and the overall impression is stunning. At the time of writing there was a controversial plan in progress to replace the mainland causeway with a bridge (due to be completed by 2015), returning Mont St-Michel to a true island once more.

ARRIVAL AND INFORMATION

By coach The easiest way of getting here is to take a Keolis coach (ⓦ destination-montsaintmichel.com) from Dol de Bretagne (€6.50 one-way) or Rennes (€12.40 one-way). You can reach Dol by train from St-Malo (hourly; 15min) and regular trains run from Paris to Rennes (hourly; 2hr 10min).
By train Very infrequent trains (2–4 daily; 20min) run from Dol de Bretagne to Mont St-Michel's nearest station, Pontorson, where shuttle buses connect to the island (10 daily; 15min).

Tourist information The helpful Tourist Information Centre is on the mainland (daily 10am–6pm, with longer opening in summer; ☎02 14 13 20 15, ⓦ bienvenueaumontsaintmichel.com)

The Loire Valley

With countless **châteaux** overlooking the stunning river and panoramic views over some of France's best vineyards, the Loire Valley is deservedly one of the country's most celebrated regions. Alongside the magnificent châteaux there are numerous lovely towns, including laidback **Saumur**, historic **Orléans** and the fairytale towns of **Amboise** and **Chinon**. The cathedral city of **Tours** is the best base for exploring the castles, while the modern metropolis of **Nantes** holds some unusual attractions.

NANTES

Part of Brittany until the 1960s, **NANTES** has transformed itself in the last decade. The star attraction is the **Machines de l'Île** (varied opening hours, see website; €8 for elephant ride or a spin on the carousel; ⓦ lesmachines-nantes.fr), home to a disarmingly realistic mechanical **elephant** which takes regular walks along the riverside, and an intricate, multi-level merry-go-round.

Back in the centre of town, the **Château des Ducs** (courtyard, ramparts and garden daily: July & Aug 9am–8pm; Sept–June 10am–7pm; free), built by two of the last rulers of independent Brittany, François II and his daughter Duchess Anne, is now home to the high-tech **Musée d'Histoire de Nantes** (July & Aug daily 10am–7pm; Sept–June Tues–Sun 10am–6pm; €5). In 1800 the castle's arsenal exploded, shattering the stained glass of the **Cathédrale de St-Pierre et St-Paul** (April–Oct 8am–7pm; Nov–March 8am–6pm), 200m away, just one of many disasters that have befallen the church.

ARRIVAL AND INFORMATION

By train The train station, on rue de Richebourg, is a 10min walk from the centre or a short tram ride to "Commerce".

Destinations Le Mans (for connections to Tours; hourly; 1hr 30min); Paris (hourly; 2hr 30min).
Tourist information The tourist office is at 9 rue des Etats opposite the Château des Ducs (June–Sept daily 9am–7pm; Nov–May Wed–Sun 2–6pm; ☎02 72 64 04 79, ⓦ nantes-tourisme.com).

ACCOMMODATION

FUAJ La Manu 2 place de la Manu ☎02 40 29 29 20, ⓦ fuaj.org; tram #1 to "Manufacture". Nantes' basic HI hostel is housed in an old tobacco factory a little east of the centre. Dorm **€20.70**
Saint Daniel 4 rue du Bouffay ☎02 40 47 41 25, ⓦ hotel -saintdaniel.com. You couldn't ask for a more central location, although the surrounding streets can be a little noisy at night. Rooms are plain but clean, and the staff are welcoming. Double **€45**

EATING AND DRINKING

Café Cult 2 rue des Carmes ☎02 40 47 18 49. Splashes of magenta and orange paint liven up this historic building. Grab one of the coveted tables outside on place du Change for classic bistro dishes (€21 for two courses) and wonderfully cheap wine (from €2.70 a glass). Mon 7.30–10pm, Tues & Wed noon–2.30pm & 7.30–10pm, Thurs & Fri noon–2.30pm & 8–11pm, Sat 8–11pm.
La Ribouldingue 33 rue de Verdun. Table football, pinball and DJ sets are among the draws at this industrial-themed bar. Drinks are cheap, too, with cocktails from €6, shooters from €3 and half-litre beers for just €4. Mon 4pm–2am, Tues–Sat 11am–2am, Sun 2–8pm.
Le Bistroquet 87 rue du Maréchal Joffre ☎02 40 74 09 44. The food at this retro bistro-cum-diner – such as duck and foie gras filo parcels – is inventive but unpretentious. The lunch menu (€12) is particularly good value. Mon noon–2pm, Tues–Sat noon–2pm & 7–11pm.

TOURS AND AROUND

The elegant and compact regional capital **TOURS** makes a good base. The city has two main areas, situated on either side of the central rue Nationale. To the east loom the extravagant towers and stained-glass windows of the **Cathédrale St-Gatien** (daily 9am–7pm), with some handsome old streets behind. Adjacent, the **Musée des Beaux-Arts** (Mon & Wed–Sun 9am–12.45pm & 2–6pm; €5), on place François Sicard, has some beautiful paintings in its collection, notably Mantegna's *Resurrection*. The **old town** crowds around medieval place Plumereau, on the west side of the city,

11

11

its half-timbered houses now packed with innumerable bars and restaurants.

ARRIVAL AND INFORMATION

By train The station is located to the south of the city on rue Édouard Vaillant.

Destinations Amboise (hourly; 20min); Chenonceaux (7–10 daily; 25min); Chinon (5–10 daily; 45min); Orléans (6–8 daily; 1hr 15min); Paris (4–6 daily; 1hr 20min); Saumur (6–8 daily; 45min).

Tourist information The tourist office at 78–82 rue Bernard-Palissy, in front of the train station (April–Sept Mon–Fri 8.30am–7pm, Sat & Sun 10am–12.30pm & 2.30–5pm; Oct–March Mon–Sat 9am–12.30pm & 1.30–6pm, Sun 10am–1pm; ☎02 47 70 37 37, ⓦtours -tourisme.fr), can arrange tours of the châteaux if you're short on time.

ACCOMMODATION

Val de Loire 33 bd Heurteloup ☎02 47 05 37 86, ⓦhotel-chambre.hotelvaldeloire.fr. The best option near the station, this hotel has fourteen spacious rooms which are nicely decorated and double-glazed. Double **€55**

★ **Vendome** 24 rue Roger Salengro ☎02 47 64 33 54, ⓦhotelvendome-tours.com. Although it's a 15min walk from place Plumereau, this charming hotel (renovated in 2013) has individually decorated rooms, the best of which overlook a courtyard filled with lilacs and wisteria in spring. The owners are particularly helpful and serve excellent breakfasts (€6) in the chintzy dining room. Double **€44**

EATING AND DRINKING

Comme Autre Fouée 11 rue de la Monnaie ☎02 47 05 94 78. An old-fashioned restaurant specializing in the miniature sweet and savoury dough-based snacks, *fouée*, with local fillings such as *andouillette* and mustard (*menus* from €18). Tues & Wed 7–10.30pm, Thurs–Sat noon–2.30pm & 7–10.30pm.

Le Marché Gourmand 27 rue du Grand-Marché ☎02 47 64 50 38. Resolutely modern bistro serving artfully presented dishes; mains (from €16) might include pork fillet in creamy *romarin* sauce. Daily noon–2pm & 7.30–10.30pm.

Les Trois Orfèvres 6 rue des Orfèvres ⓦ3orfevres.com. This bar-club is a popular choice for tourists and students

alike, with a rock-heavy soundtrack, dedicated *soirées étudiante* and bottled beers from €5. Wed–Sat 11pm–6am.

Villandry

One of the Loire's most popular châteaux, **Villandry** (daily 9am–5pm, with later opening in summer; €9.50, €6.50 gardens only; ⓦchateauvillandry.fr) lies around 20km west of Tours. It boasts extraordinary ornamental Renaissance gardens that have marvellous views over the River Cher. The château itself dates from 1536 and has an interesting collection of Spanish paintings dating back to the seventeenth century.

ARRIVAL AND DEPARTURE

By bike There's no public transport, but Villandry is easy to reach by bike from Tours: cycle direct (20km) or take your bike on the train (3 daily; 12min) to Savonnières, 5km away.

By bus Shuttle buses operate July & Aug between Tours and the château (2–3 daily; 35min; timetables at ⓦtourainefilvert.com).

Chenonceau

Perhaps the finest Loire château is **Chenonceau** (daily 9am–5pm, with some later opening in summer; €11; ⓦchenonceau.com), straddling the river 30km east of Tours. As with Villandry, the stunning formal gardens and beautiful river views are the highlight. The château's charming interior is preserved in pristine condition and houses an excellent collection of paintings and tapestries.

ARRIVAL AND DEPARTURE

By train Regular trains run from Tours to the adjacent village of Chenonceaux (10 daily; 25min) – note the additional "x" that differentiates it from the château.

CHINON

The ancient town of **Chinon** is an attractive and tranquil place to stop, with

---

CYCLING THE LOIRE VALLEY

The **Loire à Vélo** scheme provides over 300km of safe cycling routes, with cycle paths meandering along the river all the way from Orléans to Angers (ⓦloire-a-velo.fr has all the details). You can rent bikes in Tours from **Detours de Loire**, 35 rue Charles Gille (☎02 47 61 22 23, ⓦlocationdevelos.com), who allow you to drop the bike off at another town in their network for a small fee, depending on how far you've travelled.

opportunities for kayaking on the River Vienne. The ruined **fortress** overlooking the town (daily 9.30am–5pm, till 7pm July & Aug; €7.50; ⊛forteressechinon.fr) offers glorious views and is a fascinating relic of France's historic past: parts of it date from the twelfth and thirteenth centuries. Today it's been sensitively renovated, with interactive guidebooks and video projections that bring the ruins to life.

ARRIVAL, INFORMATION AND TOURS

By train The station, a 15min walk east of town, has good connections to Tours (8 daily; 50min).

Tourist information The tourist office is on place Hofheim (May–Sept daily 10am–7pm; Oct–April Mon–Sat 10am–12.30pm & 2.30–6pm; ☎02 47 93 17 85, ⊛chinon-valdeloire.com).

Kayak tours CLAN (daily April to mid-Oct; ☎06 23 82 96 33, ⊛loisirs-nature.fr), on quai Danton next to the campsite, offer combined kayak and bike excursions and also rent sit-on kayaks (€7/hr).

ACCOMMODATION AND EATING

Agnès Sorel 4 quai Pasteur ☎02 47 93 04 37, ⊛hotel -agnes-sorel.com. Delightful, family-run hotel well worth the schlep to the other side of town. The best of the modern, crisply decorated rooms have river views. Double €55

Camping Île-Auger quai Danton ☎02 47 93 08 35, ⊛camping-chinon.com. A 5min walk from the town, this campsite enjoys a lovely location by the river. Open April–Oct. Camping €4.90 per person and tent

L'Ardoise 42 Rue Rabelais ☎02 47 58 44 78. A smart but relaxed restaurant with a suntrap terrace hidden upstairs. The lunch menu offers exceptional value: three courses for €15 or the plat du jour (such as a cod and courgette "crumble") for €8. Mon noon–2pm, Wed–Sun noon–2pm & 7–10.30pm.

SAUMUR AND AROUND

SAUMUR is a peaceful, pretty riverside town, famous for its sparking wine and as a centre of spirit distillation. The **Distillerie Combier**, 48 rue Beaurepaire, offers bilingual tours and tastings (3 guided tours daily: Jan–March Wed–Sat; April, May and Oct Tues–Sun; June–Sept daily; €4); it is most well known for triple sec, but also produces a fiery absinthe. Above town, the **château** (Tues–Sun 10am–1pm &

2–5.30pm, with longer hours in summer; €9; ⊛chateau-saumur.com) boasts great views but only one wing is open to the public.

ARRIVAL AND INFORMATION

By train The station is on the north bank of the river; head over two bridges to the town.

Destinations Nantes (6 daily; 1hr–1hr 30min); Tours (8 daily; 50min).

Tourist information The tourist office is on quai Carnot (Oct to mid-May Mon–Fri 9.15am–12.30pm & 2–6pm; mid-May to Sept Mon–Fri 9.15am–7pm; erratic Sun opening throughout the year; ☎02 41 40 20 60, ⊛ot-saumur.fr).

ACCOMMODATION

Flower Camping Rue de Verden, l'Île d'Offard ☎02 41 40 30 00, ⊛saumur-camping.com. This combined campsite and centre de séjour has a swimming pool, small bar and restaurant. As a family-oriented place, the hostel's 2- to 8-bed dorms work like hotel rooms; no-one shares with strangers. Camping €13.50 per pitch, dorm first person €26.50, with fee of €12.50 for each additional guest

Le Londres 48 rue d'Orléans ☎02 41 51 23 98, ⊛www .lelondres.com. Light, bright and immaculately decorated hotel, with splashes of colour breaking up the smart white theme. Double €60

EATING AND DRINKING

L'Alchimiste 6 rue de Lorraine ☎02 41 67 65 18. The simple, modern décor lets the food shine here. Their €17 two-course menu includes delicious seasonal dishes like langoustine risotto and rhubarb tart. Tues–Sat noon–1.30pm & 7.30–10pm.

Abbaye de Fontevraud

The immense **Abbaye de Fontevraud** (Tues–Sun 10am–5pm, with later opening in summer; €9.50; ⊛abbayedefontevraud.com), 15km southeast of Saumur, was founded in 1099 as both a nunnery and a monastery with an abbess in charge. Its chief significance is as the burial ground of the Plantagenet kings and queens, notably Henry II, Eleanor of Aquitaine and Richard the Lionheart; some of the tombs are extraordinarily elaborate.

ARRIVAL AND DEPARTURE

By bus The only way to get here by public transport is on the irregular bus #1 from Saumur (4 daily; 25min).

11

AMBOISE

Situated on the banks of the Loire, **AMBOISE** is a beautiful if heavily visited town. The main sight is the **Château Royal d'Amboise** (daily 9.30am–12.30pm & 2–5pm, with longer hours in summer; €10.50; ⓦchateau-amboise.com), holding a majestic spot overlooking the river. It was built in the eleventh century and saw further additions by successive royals. Leonardo da Vinci's final residence, **Clos–Lucé**, is also located here (daily 10am–6pm; €13.50; ⓦvinci -closluce.com), housing a collection of some of his inventions with models dotted around the surrounding gardens.

ARRIVAL AND INFORMATION

By train The station is a 15min walk north of town on the opposite bank of the river.
Destinations Orléans (10 daily; 1hr); Tours (hourly; 20min).
Tourist information The tourist office is by the river on quai du Général de Gaulle (Mon–Sat 10am–6pm, Sun 10am–12.30pm; ☎02 47 57 09 28, ⓦamboise-valdeloire .co.uk).

ACCOMMODATION

Café des Arts 32 rue Victor Hugo ☎02 47 57 25 04, ⓦwww.cafedesarts.net. This pleasant café has a collection of 2- to 8-bed rooms hidden upstairs, all kitted out with sturdy pine bunks. It's not a hostel, so you don't share, but the prices are just as reasonable. Double €42
Camping de L'Île d'Or 100 rue de l'Île d'Or ☎02 47 57 23 37, ⓦcamping-amboise.com. A peaceful campsite located at the eastern end of Île d'Or. Camping €2.80 per person, plus €3.70 per tent
Le Blason 11 place Richelieu ☎02 47 23 22 41, ⓦleblason.fr. Built as a school in 1490, this charming hotel has exposed beams in all of the rooms. It's slightly old-fashioned, but full of character. Double €53

EATING AND DRINKING

Anne de Bretagne 1 place du Chateau ☎02 47 57 05 46. This simple crêperie is a good choice for an affordable meal. Try a glass of the local sparkling wine (€3.60) before a filling *galette paysanne* (bacon, egg, cheese and potato; €7.30). Daily noon–10pm.
Le Shaker 3 quai Francois Tissard, l'Île d'Or. With views across the water to the château, this riverside cocktail bar and *glacier* serves gigantic, fruity creations from €9 and non-alcoholic shakes for €5. Tues–Sun 6pm–3am.

ORLÉANS

Due south of Paris, **ORLÉANS** became legendary when Joan of Arc delivered the city from the English in 1429. Stained-glass windows in the nave of the enormous, Gothic **Cathédrale Sainte-Croix** (daily 9.15am–6pm) tell the story of her life, from her childhood through to her heroic military career and her eventual martyrdom. Immediately opposite, the **Musée des Beaux-Arts** (Tues–Sun 10am–6pm; €4) has an excellent collection of French paintings.

ARRIVAL AND INFORMATION

By train The station is a 15min walk north of the centre.
Destinations Amboise (10 daily; 1hr); Paris (hourly; 1hr); Tours (8 daily; 1hr 15min).
Tourist information The tourist office is at 2 place de l'Etape (Mon 2–5pm, Tues–Sat 10am–1pm & 2–5pm, with longer hours in summer; ☎02 38 24 05 05, ⓦtourisme-orleans.com).

ACCOMMODATION

Auberge de Jeunesse 7 av de Beaumarchais, 10km south of the city ☎02 38 53 60 06, ⓦaubergedejeunesseorleans .fr; tram A to "Université l'Indien". Pleasant modern hostel with helpful staff, although it's a bit of a trek from the centre of town. Dorm €16
St Martin 52 bvd Alexandre Martin ☎02 38 55 02 28, ⓦhotel-st-martin.fr. Budget hotels are thin on the ground in Orléans, so try this three-star – part of the dependable *Logis* group – with enormous double beds and bold graphic furnishings. Double €69

EATING AND DRINKING

Au Bon Marché 12 place du Châtelet ☎02 38 53 04 35. This congenial restaurant serves faultless bistro classics made from fresh, local ingredients. You can't go wrong with the excellent *bavette* (€13.50) and a glass of Loire red (€4). Daily noon–2pm & 7–10pm.
Le Garage 195 rue de Bourgogne. Rock'n'roll memorabilia fills all the available space in this bar, with everything from

> ★ **TREAT YOURSELF**
>
> **De L'Abeille** 64 rue Alsace-Lorraine ☎02 38 53 54 87, ⓦhoteldelabeille.com. A luxurious, family-run boutique hotel, decorated with beautiful wallpaper and antique furniture. In summer you can enjoy views over to the cathedral from their roof terrace. Three- and four-bed rooms available. Double €89

records to birdcages dangling from the ceiling. Potent mojitos and 50cl *pressions* for €5 make it a popular choice. Mon 11.30am–2.30pm & 5pm–1am, Tues–Sat 11.30am–2.30pm & 5.30pm–2am.

Burgundy

Burgundy has some charming towns and villages, as well as some of the country's finest food and drink. **Dijon**, the capital, is an affluent town with great shops and lovely architecture. Heading south, the small town of **Beaune** is a good place to sample the best of the region's famous wine, and to try local specialities such as *escargots à la bourguignonne* and *bœuf bourguignon*.

DIJON

Most famous for its mustard, **DIJON** is an elegant, historic town, based around a range of classical squares and narrow, winding streets. The Palais des Ducs, in the heart of the city, is notable both for the fifteenth-century **Tour Philippe le Bon** (tours departing from the tourist office roughly hourly: April–Sept Tues–Sun; Oct–March Tues, Sat & Sun; €3) and the fourteenth-century **Tour de Bar**, which houses the magnificent **Musée des Beaux-Arts** (Mon & Wed–Sun: May–Oct 9.30am–6pm; Nov–April 10am–5pm; free), with its collection of paintings ranging from Titian and Rubens to Monet and Manet. Just to the north lies the stunning thirteenth-century Gothic **church of Notre-Dame** (Mon–Sat 10am–4.30pm), the exterior north wall of which holds a well-worn sculpted owl (*chouette*), which people touch for luck.

ARRIVAL AND INFORMATION

By train Dijon's train station is a 15min walk west from the centre.
Destinations Beaune (every 30min; 20min); Lyon (hourly; 1hr 40min–2hr); Paris (hourly; 1hr 35min).
Tourist information The tourist office is at 11 rue des Forges (April–Sept Mon–Sat 9.30am–6.30pm, Sun 10am–6pm; Oct–March Mon–Sat 9.30am–1pm & 2–6pm, Sun 10am–4pm; 08 92 70 05 58, visitdijon.com); there's another branch in the station with the same hours.

ACCOMMODATION

CRIS Dijon 1 av Champollion 03 80 72 95 20, cri-dijon.com; bus #3 to "CRI-Dallas". The local hostel is comfortable, cheap and has good self-catering facilities. The only drawback is that it's 2.5km from the centre. Dorm **€20.90**
Le Jacquemart 32 rue Verrerie 03 80 60 09 60, hotel-lejacquemart.fr. A traditional hotel with warmly furnished rooms, the best with faux-marble bathrooms. The cheaper rooms aren't en suite. Double **€38**
Le Sauvage 64 rue Monge 03 80 41 31 21, hotellesauvage.com. Beautifully restored fifteenth-century hotel in a central location with a good restaurant. Double **€52**

EATING AND DRINKING

Chez Copains 10 Rue Quentin 03 80 40 20 10. The friendly, young proprietors and ingredients sourced in the adjacent market make this restaurant a hit. Try a Burgundian classic like *œufs en meurette* (poached eggs in red wine; £7). Tues–Thurs noon–2pm & 7–10.30pm, Fri & Sat noon–2.30pm and 7–11pm.
Chez Nous Impasse Quentin. In an alleyway just off rue Quentin, this bar is something of a local institution, with 50cl *pressions* from €4 and wine from €2. Mon 4pm–midnight, Tues 10am–1am, Wed & Thurs 11am–1am, Fri & Sat 10am–2am.
L'Assommoir Tome II 41 rue Monge. Vintage cartoons paper the walls of this hip little bar. The cocktails are particularly good – try the *negroni* (€7.50) – and there are regular DJ sets and live music. Mon–Sat 5pm–2am, Sun 4–10pm.

11

BURGUNDY VINEYARDS

The Burgundy vineyards are justly famous for their complex wines, made predominantly from Pinot Noir and Chardonnay grapes. The best way to explore them is on the **Route des Grand Crus** (route-des-grands-crus-de-bourgogne.com), which takes in such places as **Vougeot** and **Puligny Montrachet**, famous for their high-calibre reds and whites respectively. The wine is cheaper if bought from source – expect to pay around €10 for a good bottle and €20 and upwards for an excellent one. If you fancy learning more about the wines, the **École des Vins de Bourgogne** in Beaune, 6 rue du 16e Chasseurs (03 80 26 35 10, ecoledesvins-bourgogne.com), offers crash courses in wine appreciation, some in English.

11

BEAUNE

At the heart of the Côte d'Or region, **BEAUNE** is home to some of Burgundy's most prestigious wine cellars, many of which can be visited on guided tours (ask at the tourist office).

Its other major attraction is the fifteenth-century hospital, the **Hôtel-Dieu** (daily 9am–6.30pm; €7, including audioguide), now a museum with re-creations of the original wards and an exhibition of paintings and tapestries. On nearby rue d'Enfer is the old-fashioned **Musée du Vin** (Wed–Sun: April–Sept 10am–8pm; Oct–March 11am–5pm; €5.60), which explains the history of the region's wine industry. The **Marché aux Vins** (daily: April–Sept 9.30am–5.30pm; Oct–March 9.30–11.30am & 2–5.30pm; €10 for 8 wines) is a rather more taster-friendly experience, offering a self-guided tour of their modern cellars with some delectable wines to taste along the way.

ARRIVAL AND INFORMATION

By train Beaune station is a 10min walk east of the centre.
Destinations Dijon (every 30min; 20min).
Tourist information The tourist office is at 6 bd Perpreuil (Mon–Sat 9am–noon & 1–6pm, Sun 10am–12.30pm & 1.30–5pm, with longer hours in summer; ☏ 03 80 26 21 30, ⓦ ot-beaune.fr).

ACCOMMODATION AND EATING

Bistrot Bourguignon 8 rue Monge ☏ 03 80 22 23 24. Beaune's first wine bar has a good-value lunch menu featuring classics like *confit canard* (€13), with wine from €3 a glass. Daily 11am–2pm & 6–11pm.
Foch 24 bd Maréchal Foch ☏ 03 80 24 05 65, ⓦ hotelbeaune-lefoch.fr. Eleven pleasant rooms above a little café, run by a helpful family. Double €45
Les Cent Vignes 10 rue Auguste Dubois ☏ 03 80 22 03 91, ⓔ campinglescentvignes@mairie-beaune.fr. Located just 1km out of Beaune, this good-value campsite has showers and a shop. Camping €4.30 per person, plus €5.60 per tent

Alsace and Lorraine

Dominated by the remarkable city of **Strasbourg**, Alsace often bears more similarity to Germany or Switzerland than to the rest of the country. The *mélange* of cultures is at its most vivid in the string of little wine towns that punctuate the **Route des Vins** along the eastern margin of the wet and woody Vosges mountains. The province of **Lorraine** is home to elegant eighteenth-century **Nancy**. Food and drink is excellent in the region: from local brew Kronenbourg to delicious white Rieslings and Gewürztraminers, the alcohol is excellent, and the *winstubs* (or wine rooms) that dominate towns offer inexpensive, unpretentious food based around pork, veal and beef, often in stews or casseroles.

NANCY

NANCY, capital of Lorraine, is a refined and beautiful town of opulent squares and splendid boulevards. At the centre is **place Stanislas**, a supremely graceful square dominated by the **Hôtel de Ville**. The roofline of this UNESCO World Heritage Site is topped by florid urns and lozenge-shaped lanterns dangling from the beaks of gilded cockerels. On the west side of the square, the **Musée des Beaux-Arts** (Mon & Wed–Sun 10am–6pm; €6; ⓦ mban.nancy.fr) boasts work by Caravaggio, Delacroix, Matisse and Picasso as well as contemporary installations. A little to the north the **Musée Lorrain**, 64 Grande-Rue (Tues–Sun 10am–12.30pm & 2–6pm; €5.50), devoted to Lorraine's history, is housed in the splendid Palais Ducal.

ARRIVAL AND INFORMATION

By train Nancy's station is a 10min walk from place Stanislas.
Destinations Lyon (3 daily; 4hr); Paris (6 daily; 1hr 30min); Strasbourg (7 daily; 1hr 30min).
Tourist information The tourist office is at 1 place Stanislas (April–Oct Mon–Sat 9am–7pm, Sun 10am–5pm; Nov–March Mon–Sat 9am–6pm, Sun 10am–1pm; ☏ 03 83 35 22 41, ⓦ nancy-tourisme.fr).

ACCOMMODATION

Château de Rémicourt 149 rue de Vandoeuvre ☏ 03 83 27 73 67, ⓦ fuaj.org; bus #134 or #135 from outside the station to "Lycée Stanislas". The local hostel is a 20min bus ride from town, but it's spacious and friendly. Dorm €14.70

Le Flore 8 rue Raymond Poincaré ⊙ 03 83 37 63 28, ⓦle
-flore-nancy.fr. Simply decorated hotel convenient for the
station, with fluffy towels and cosy flower-print duvets.
Double €48

EATING AND DRINKING

Bouche à L'Oreille 17 rue Stanislas ⊙ 03 83 37 22 87. This
bric-a-brac cluttered restaurant is the place to indulge a
cheese craving; they have a huge range of *tartiflettes* (from
€11.50) and fondues (from €15.95). Mon noon–1.30pm,
Tues–Fri noon–1.30pm & 7–10pm, Sat 7–10.30pm.
Le Potager 25 rue des Maréchaux. Modern café serving
over twenty plate-sized "bruschettas" from €8 – try the
classic tomato, olive oil and basil or the more filling potato,
ham and raclette option. Tues–Sat noon–2pm & 7–10pm.

STRASBOURG

STRASBOURG is a major city with the feel
of a charming provincial town. It has one
of the loveliest cathedrals in France, an
ancient but active university and is the
current seat of the Council of Europe
and the European Court of Human
Rights, as well as part-time base of the
European Parliament.

WHAT TO SEE AND DO

The **Grand Île** section of the city is the
most striking, centred on two main
squares, the busy **place Kléber** and, to the
south, **place Gutenberg**, named after the
fifteenth-century pioneer of printing type.

Cathédrale de Notre-Dame

The major landmark is the **Cathédrale de
Notre-Dame** (daily 7–11.20am &
12.35–7pm; free), which beautifully
combines ostentatious grandeur with
chocolate-box fragility. Climb to the
top platform for stunning views to the
Black Forest (€5), and don't miss the
tremendously complicated **astrological
clock** (noon–12.30pm; €2), built in
1842. Visitors arrive in droves to witness
its crowning performance – striking the
hour of noon with unerring accuracy
at 12.30pm.

Musée de l'Oeuvre Notre-Dame

The **Musée de l'Oeuvre Notre-Dame**, 3
place du Château (Tues–Fri noon–6pm,
Sat & Sun 10am–6pm; €6), houses the
original sculptures from the cathedral

exterior, as well as some of Europe's
finest collected stained glass. A particular
highlight is *Les Amants Trépassés* in
room 23, which shows two lovers
being punished, and makes the average
Hollywood horror film look mild
in comparison.

Petite France

Divided into three small islands by
picturesque canals, the beautiful **Petite
France** is made up of winding streets
bordered by sixteenth- and seventeenth-
century houses. The name Petite France
was given to the area by the Alsatians
in the seventeenth century, having been
a quarantine area for patients of a
devastating sixteenth-century venereal
disease attributed to the French.

Musée d'Art Moderne et Contemporain

The **Musée d'Art Moderne et
Contemporain**, 1 place Hans Jean Arp
(Tues–Sun 10am–6pm; €7), stands on
the west bank of the river and houses an
impressive collection featuring Monet,
Kandinsky, Klee and Picasso.

ARRIVAL AND INFORMATION

By train The station is a 15min walk west from place
Kléber.
Destinations Nancy (7 daily, 1hr 15min); Paris (hourly;
2hr 20min).
Tourist information The main tourist office is at 17
place de la Cathédrale (daily 9am–7pm; ⊙ 03 88 52 28 28,
ⓦ otstrasbourg.fr).

ACCOMMODATION

Hotels get booked up early when the parliament is in
session (one week a month); check ⓦeuroparl.europa.eu.
Camping de la Montagne Verte 2 rue Robert Forrer
⊙ 03 88 30 25 46, ⓦaquadis-loisirs.com; tram B or C to
"Montagne Verte". Located just 3km away from the centre,
this leafy campsite has an on-site shop and bike rental.
Camping €9.80 per person and tent
Ciarus 7 rue de Finkmatt ⊙ 03 88 15 27 88, ⓦciarus.com.
Pleasant and central hostel, set around a pretty internal
courtyard and with a very cheap on-site restaurant.
Dorm €27
Le Colmar 1 rue du Maire Kuss ⊙ 03 88 32 16 89, ⓦhotel
-lecolmar.com. One of the best budget options just a short
walk from the train station, this cheery hotel has a few
en-suite rooms and a good buffet breakfast. Double €42

11

STRASBOURG

0   100
metres

■ ACCOMMODATION
Camping de la
  Montagne Verte   2
Ciarus   1
Le Colmar   3

● EATING AND DRINKING
Chez Yvonne   1
Jeanette et les Cycleaux   4
L'Académie de la Bière   2
L'Epicerie   3

EATING AND DRINKING

Chez Yvonne 10 rue du Sanglier ☎ 03 88 32 84 15. If it's old-world Alsatian atmosphere you're looking for, you can't do better than this old-fashioned *winstub*, with its lacy lamps, wood-panelling and hearty, traditional dishes like coq au Riesling (€15.90). Daily noon–2.30pm & 6pm–midnight.

Jeanette et les Cycleaux 30 rue des Tonneliers. Trendy, chilled-out bar serving wine (from €3.50), milkshakes and light snacks. Daily 11am–1am.

L'Académie de la Bière 17 rue Adolphe-Seyboth. Head here for an enormous range of French and German beers: there are 15 on tap with half-litres from €5.50. Daily 11am–4am.

L'Epicerie 6 rue Vieux Seigle. A lovely café with vintage decor, situated in a reconstructed grocer's. Try one of their delicious *tartines* (open sandwiches) from €5.50. Daily 11.30am–1.30am.

The southwest

The southwest of France has a varied landscape, stretching from the vast horizons of Poitou-Charente to the ordered rows of Bordeaux's vineyards and the lush, heady green of the Dordogne. The Atlantic coast, lacking the busy glitz of the Côte d'Azur, has a slow, understated charm, best seen in **La Rochelle**. Further south, **Bordeaux**, justifiably famous for its wines, is a cosmopolitan and lively city that's worth a few days' exploration – from here, it's easy to strike east to **Périgueux**, a good base for exploring the nearby prehistoric caves, or south to the Basque coast, home to **Biarritz**, the country's surf capital, and **Bayonne**, with its fine old timber-framed buildings and excellent chocolatiers.

The Pyrenees, marking the very south of France, are home to some of the country's best walking and one of its most vibrant cities, the rose-brick university town of **Toulouse**, whose youthful energy is matched only by **Montpellier**. Medieval **Carcassonne**, between the two, is undoubtedly the biggest tourist trap of the region, but it's hard not to be wowed when you first see its fairytale spires rising above the surrounding buildings.

LA ROCHELLE

The lively port town of **LA ROCHELLE** has an exceptionally beautiful seventeenth- and eighteenth-century centre and is a very pleasant place to linger for a few days. Granted a charter by Eleanor of Aquitaine in 1199, it rapidly became a port of major importance, trading in salt and wine. Following a makeover in the 1990s, which established a university, pedestrianized the centre and moved out the fishing operation, La Rochelle has become the largest Atlantic yachting port in Europe, without the exclusivity of some of its Mediterranean counterparts.

WHAT TO SEE AND DO

The heavy Gothic gateway of the Porte de la Grosse Horloge straddles the entrance to the old town, dominating the pleasure-boat-filled inner harbour, which is guarded by two of La Rochelle's three sturdy towers, **Tour de la Chaîne** and **Tour St Nicholas** (daily: April–Sept 10am–6.30pm; Oct–March 10am–1pm & 2.15–5.30pm; €8.50 for all three towers). Behind the Grosse Horloge, the main shopping street, rue du Palais, is lined with eighteenth-century houses and arcaded shop fronts. The **Musée du Nouveau Monde**, 10 rue Fleuriau (Oct–June Mon & Wed–Fri 9.30am–12.30pm & 1.30–5pm, Sat & Sun 2–6pm; July–Sept Mon & Wed–Fri 10am–1pm & 1.45–6pm, Sat & Sun 2–6pm; €4.50), commemorates the town's dubious fortunes from slavery, sugar, spices and coffee. For beaches – and bicycle paths – you're best off crossing over to the **Île de Ré**, a narrow, sand-rimmed island immediately west of La Rochelle (take one of the Rébus buses from place de Verdun). Out of season it has a slow, misty charm, centred on the cultivation of oysters and mussels; in summer it's packed to the gills.

ARRIVAL AND DEPARTURE

By plane La Rochelle airport is located 2.5km northwest of the city. For the centre, take the #7 bus (every 30min, 6.52am–7.53pm; 15min) and get off at stop "Place de Verdun". On Sun take bus #47 to "Place de Verdun" (9 daily, 8.30am–7.05pm; 15min). Tickets cost €1.30 and can be bought on board (@ yelo.agglo-larochelle.fr).

By train From the train station, it's a 7min walk down av du Général de Gaulle to the town centre.
Destinations Bordeaux (6 daily; 2hr 20min); Cognac (6 daily; 1hr 20min–2hr); Nantes (4 daily; 1hr 50min); Poitiers (12 daily; 1hr 45min).

INFORMATION

Tourist information 2 quai Georges Simenon, Le Gabut (April & May Mon–Sat 9am–6pm, Sun 10.30am–5.30pm; June & Sept Mon–Sat 9am–7pm, Sun 10.30am–5.30pm; July & Aug Mon–Sat 9am–8pm, Sun 10am–6pm; Oct–March Mon–Sat 9am–6pm, Sun 10am–1pm; ☎ 05 46 41 14 68, @ larochelle-tourisme.fr).
Internet Le Continuum, 9 ter rue Amelot, near the market (Mon–Sat 10.30am–7.30pm; €2/hr).

GETTING AROUND

By bike There are 47 stations across the city where you can make use of the free bike service (credit card authorization required; first 30min free; €1/30min thereafter). Alternatively, there is daily bike rental available through the tourist office (free first 2hr; €1.10/hr thereafter), who also offer free city bicycle maps (@ yelo.agglo-larochelle.fr).

ACCOMMODATION

FUAJ La Rochelle Av des Minimes ☎ 05 46 44 43 11, @ fuaj.org. Modern hostel, well positioned by Port des Minimes, a 30min walk from the station. Recently refurnished, the bright, nicely decorated rooms are all en suite; dinner is available (from €6) and outdoor activities are often organized. From the station, follow signs to Porte des Minimes. Reception 8am–10pm. Dorm €17.50, double €45
Hotel de l'Océan 36 cours des Dames ☎ 05 46 41 31 97, @ hotel-ocean-larochelle.com. This small, friendly hotel is decked out in blues and yellows. Rooms are en suite, and those at the front have excellent views of the port. Double €65
Hotel les Rosiers 56 boulevard André Sautel ☎ 05 46 67 42 27, @ hotel-lesrosiers.com. Located a short walk from the old town, what this basic hotel lacks in style it compensates for in price. More expensive en suites also available. Double €40
Le Soleil Av Crépeau ☎ 05 46 44 42 53. This municipal campsite has ping-pong, pétanque and hot showers, and allows barbecues. Fabulously located right by the sea, and just 800m from the town centre. Open mid-June to mid-Sept. Camping €9.70 per person and tent

EATING, DRINKING AND NIGHTLIFE

Corrigans 20 rue des Cloutiers @ corrigans.fr. A low-key but convivial little place down a quiet street near the market. Serves reasonably priced beer, with Irish music sessions every Sun. Tues–Sat 6pm–2am, Sun 7pm–1am.

11

11

Isêo Gourmet 2 rue des Cloutiers, Place du Marché. A modern version of the traditional *traiteur* offering *nem* (fried Vietnamese rolls, from €3.20 for two) and sushi (from €4.20 for eight). Daily 11am–3pm & 5–9pm, Sat 11am–3pm & 5–10pm, Sun 11am–2pm & 5–9pm.

La Guignette 8 rue Saint Nicolas ☎05 46 41 05 75. Formerly a sailor's haunt, this is a wine bar beloved of students, who come at *l'heure de l'apéro* for a glass of its eponymous aperitif – white wine flavoured with fruit. Mon–Sat 10am–noon & 4–8pm.

L'Amaranthe 14 rue Bletterie ☎05 17 83 07 21. Sitting only fifteen, it's all rather cosy but the changing menu offers fresh, inventive dishes and the €12 lunch menu is excellent value. Mon, Tues & Thurs–Sat noon–2pm & 7.30–11pm, Wed & Sun noon–2pm.

Le Piano Pub 12 cour du Temple ☎05 46 41 09 52. One of a number of venues on this pleasant courtyard, this is popular with a student-age crowd and hosts the occasional rock gig. Daily 7pm–2am.

COGNAC

COGNAC is shrouded in the heady scent of its famous brandy. Of the various cognac *chais* (distilleries) huddled around the end of the Grande-Rue, **Baron Otard** is one of the best choices for a guided tour (April–Oct daily 11am–5pm; Nov & Dec Mon–Fri except bank holidays 11am–5pm; €9; ⓦbaronotard.com), which recounts a history of the site, the principles of making cognac and, most importantly, a tasting.

ARRIVAL AND INFORMATION

By train Gare SNCF, Bvd de Paris.
Destinations Bordeaux (frequent; 1hr 50min–2hr 50min).
By bus The *gare routière* is located at Au Pied du Pont du Guit.
Destinations Angouleme (9 daily, 6.20am–6.15pm; 50min).
Tourist information 16 rue du 14 Juillet (May, June & Sept Mon–Sat 9.30am–5.30pm; July & Aug Mon–Sat 9am–7pm, Sun 10am–4pm; Oct–April Mon–Sat 10am–5pm; ☎05 45 82 10 71, ⓦtourism-cognac.com).
Internet Je Console, 24 allée de la Corderie (Mon 2–7pm, Tues–Sat 9.30am–7pm; €3.50/hr).

ACCOMMODATION AND EATING

Le Cellieur place 4-6 rue du 14 Juillet ☎05 45 82 25 46. A friendly local's haunt renowned for its traditional home-cooked food. Good-value *plats* (€8.50) and *formule* (€13.50) with a menu that changes daily. Mon–Fri noon–2pm & 7–10pm, Sat 7–10pm.

L'Oliveraie 6 place de la Gare ☎05 45 82 04 15, ⓦoliveraie-cognac.com. If you get carried away with the brandy and need to stay the night, this place has simple rooms and a swimming pool. Double **€70**

BORDEAUX

Though crammed with grand old buildings, **BORDEAUX** still has a surprisingly youthful feel. Café culture is in full swing here – indeed, one of the most pleasurable things about a visit to the city is sitting out on a sun-drenched terrace enjoying a glass or two of the region's fabulous wines. If you have time, and want to find out more about the justifiably world-famous wines of the region, it's definitely worth doing a wine tour (see box, p.310).

(see box, p.310).

WHAT TO SEE AND DO

The centre of Bordeaux bends around the east bank of the **Garonne** River in a crescent moon shape – and is colloquially known as *Porte de la Lune*.

Le Triangle d'Or and Quinconces

The "golden triangle", full of chic Parisian boutiques, runs between **place Gambetta**, with its eighteenth-century Porte Dijeaux, place de la Comédie with the classical 1780 **Grand Théâtre**, and place Tourny at the peak. In a breathtaking nineteenth-century colonial warehouse to the north of the vast Esplanade des Quinconces is the unmissable **CAPC musée**, 7 rue Ferrère (Tues–Sun 11am–6pm, Wed till 8pm; permanent collection free, temporary exhibitions €5). This is the finest contemporary art exhibition space in France, displaying pioneering national and international works with admirable use of space and lighting. The permanent collection includes Richard Long and Gilbert & George, but the temporary installations are often the most exciting.

Sainte-Catherine, Saint Pierre and Place de la Victoire

The central pedestrian artery, **rue Ste-Catherine**, leads down from place de la Comédie to the city's best historical museum, the **Musée d'Aquitaine**, 20 cours

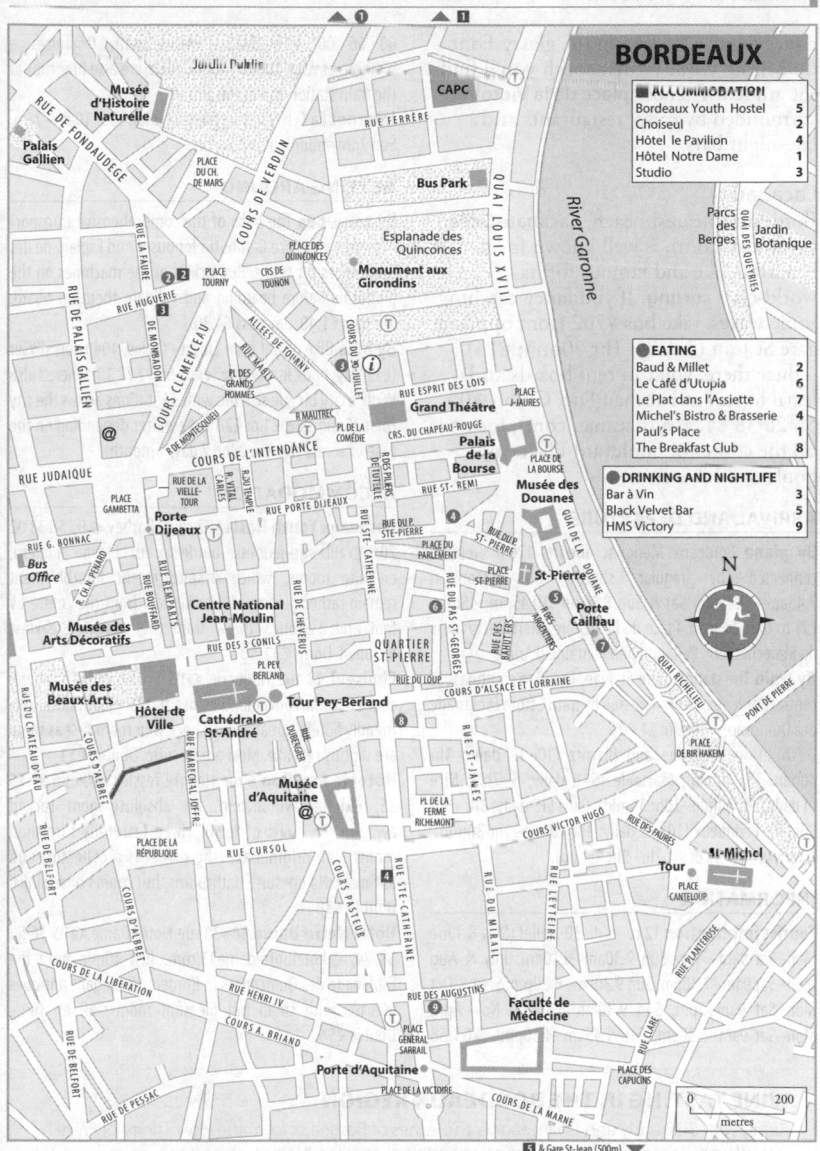

BORDEAUX

■ ACCOMMODATION

Bordeaux Youth Hostel	5
Choiseul	2
Hôtel le Pavilion	4
Hôtel Notre Dame	1
Studio	3

● EATING

Baud & Millet	2
Le Café d'Utopia	6
Le Plat dans l'Assiette	7
Michel's Bistro & Brasserie	4
Paul's Place	1
The Breakfast Club	8

● DRINKING AND NIGHTLIFE

Bar à Vin	3
Black Velvet Bar	5
HMS Victory	9

Pasteur (Tues–Sun 11am–6pm; free or €5 for temporary exhibitions), which illustrates the history of the region from prehistoric times through to the 1800s. A few streets north stands the **Cathédrale St-André** (Mon 3–7.30pm, Tues–Sat 10am–1pm & 3–7.30pm, Sun 9.30am–1pm & 3–7.30pm), with its exquisite stained-glass windows and slender twin spires. Around the corner at 20 cours d'Albret, the **Musée des Beaux-Arts** (Mon & Wed–Sun 11am–6pm; free or €5 for temporary exhibitions) displays works by Rubens, Matisse and Renoir, as well as Lacour's evocative 1804 Bordeaux dockside scene, *Quai des Chartrons*. To the east of the centre lies the striking **place de la Bourse**, best viewed from the river's edge, reflecting in the glassy Font du Miroir, while farther south you'll find the student-friendly **place de la Victoire**, surrounded by cafés, restaurants and late-night bars.

Lacanau

Bordeaux's nearest beach, **Lacanau-Océan** (Ⓦ lacanau.com), is well known for its beautiful lake and famous for its world-class **surfing**. If you fancy catching some waves, take bus #702 from opposite gare St Jean (3 daily; 1hr 50min; €14) – once there, you can rent boards and learn to surf at Lacanau Surf Club (Ⓣ 05 56 26 38 84, Ⓦ surflacanau.com), located on the corner of boulevard Plage and boulevard Liberty.

ARRIVAL AND DEPARTURE

By plane Bordeaux Mérignac airport, 12km west, is connected by regular shuttle bus (Mon–Fri 7.45am–10.45pm, Sat & Sun 8.30am–10.45pm; 45min; €7) to Gare St Jean, Place de la Victoire, Mériadeck/Cours du Maréchal Juin, Pellegrin and Fontaine d'Arlac.

By train The station, Gare St-Jean, lies 2km southeast of central Bordeaux, easily accessed by tram C from Esplanade des Quinconces (10min; €1.40).

Destinations Bayonne and Biarritz (10–12 daily; 1hr 40min–2hr 10min); Marseille (5–6 daily; 6–7hr); Nice (4 daily; 8hr 30min–10hr 10min); Paris (19 daily; 3hr–3hr 30min); Périgueux (10–12 daily; 1hr 10min–1hr 30min); Toulouse (10–17 daily; 2hr–2hr 45min).

INFORMATION

Tourist information 12 cours du 30-Juillet (May & June Mon–Sat 9am–7pm, Sun 9.30am–6.30pm; July & Aug Mon–Sat 9am–7.30pm, Sun 9.30am–6.30pm; Sept & Oct Mon–Sat 9am–7pm, Sun 9.30am–6.30pm; Nov–April Mon–Sat 9am–6.30pm, Sun 9.45am–4.30pm; Ⓣ 05 56

00 66 00, Ⓦ bordeaux-tourisme.com). Organizes a plethora of wine and city tours. There are also branches at the train station and at the airport.

Internet La Cyb, 23 cours pasteur (Mon–Sat 10am–2am, Sun 2pm–midnight; €2.50/hr).

GETTING AROUND

By tram/bus The hubs of the comprehensive transport networks are place Gambetta for buses and Esplanade des Quinconces for trams. Buy tickets at the machines on the platforms before boarding and validate them on board; 1hr pass €1.40, day pass €4.30.

By bike Bike rental from Liberty Cycles, 104 cours d'Yser (€12/day; book in advance; Ⓣ 05 56 92 77 18). There's also VCub, a city bicycle scheme with 31 stations across the city (first 30min free, €1 or €2/hr thereafter depending on the type of access chosen: 24hr, 7 day, 1 month).

ACCOMMODATION

Bordeaux Youth Hostel 22 cours Barbey Ⓣ 05 56 33 00 70, Ⓦ auberge-jeunesse-bordeaux.eu. Clean, modern, en-suite rooms, which despite recent refurbishment remain rather gloomy. A 15min walk from the centre by foot and a stone's throw from the station. Breakfast included. Dorm **€22.50**

Choiseul 13 rue Huguerie Ⓣ 05 56 52 71 24, Ⓦ hotel choiseul.com. Conveniently close to place Gambatta, this friendly hotel is great value. Check your room first as some are slightly cell-like. Most are en suite. Double **€51**

Hôtel le Pavillon 6 rue Honoré Tessier Ⓣ 05 56 91 75 35, Ⓦ hotelpavillon.com. An absolute gem tucked away in the heart of town. Three tastefully furnished rooms with original art (the owner is a collector) and antiques. No en-suite bathrooms, but rooms have sinks. Double **€30**

Hôtel Notre Dame 36–38 rue Notre Dame Ⓣ 05 56 52 88 24, Ⓦ hotelnotredame33.com. Just 10min from the Esplanade des Quinconces in Bordeaux's elegant antiques quarter, with small but pleasant rooms, all en suite. Double **€56**

WINE TASTING IN THE BORDEAUX REGION

Along with Burgundy and Champagne, the wines of Bordeaux form the Holy Trinity of French **viticulture**. Bordeaux is mostly a red-wine region, growing high-class (and more expensive) **Cabernet Sauvignon** on the Left Bank (the countryside to the west of the Garonne River and Gironde estuary), while smaller growers make predominantly Merlot and Cabernet-Franc-based wines on the Right Bank. There are also some very good white wines, mainly from the Pessac and Graves regions to the south and southeast – largely based on **Sauvignon Blanc** and **Semillon**, that come in both dry and sweet forms. The easiest way to taste the wines is in the village of **St Emilion**, to the east of Bordeaux, where there are many wine shops that hold wine tastings. L'Envers du Décor, 11 rue du Clocher (Ⓣ 05 57 74 48 31), is a good choice and has reasonable prices. The Bordeaux tourist office (see above) has information on château visits and wine tastings, and organizes a good variety of half and full-day wine tours of the area.

La Villa Zénith 16 av Adjudant Guittard, Lacanau ☎ 06 84 60 88 08, ⱳ lacanau-zenith.com. Located 200m from the beach, with comfy dorms, garden, cooking facilities and equipment lockers. Dorm €25

Studio 26 rue Huguerie ☎ 05 56 48 00 14, ⱳ hotel -studio-bordeaux.fr. Book well in advance for this backpackers' favourite. Its central location, clean en-suite rooms and helpful owner ensure its continuing popularity. Double €32

EATING

Baud & Millet 19 rue Huguerie. Enjoy a leisurely glass of wine (from €4), and cheese and charcuterie (€12.50) at this fantastic wine shop where the friendly Monsieur Baud speaks excellent English. Mon–Sat 10am–11pm.

Le Café d'Utopia 5 place Camille Jullian. A lively, casual place in a beautiful old building that houses the Utopia arthouse cinema. Try one of their huge hot sandwiches (from €6.90) or delicious gourmet salads (from €12.90). May–Sept Mon–Fri noon–10.30pm, Sat & Sun noon–12.30am; Oct–April Mon–Fri noon–3pm & 7–10.30pm, Sat & Sun noon–10.30pm.

Le Plat dans l'Assiette 8 rue Ausone ☎ 05 56 01 05 01. One whole menu on a plate – that's the hook here – but it's no haute cuisine gimmick; the cheapest of the *assiettes* – the *éphémère* at €16.50 – still crams in goat's cheese, *magret séché* and Serrano ham in among the relatively healthy stuff. Tues–Sat noon–2.30pm & 7.30–10.30pm.

Michel's Bistro & Brasserie 15 rue du Pas-Saint Georges. The bargain €1 coffee aside, Michel's great value lunch menu (€11.90), local wine (€2.90) and sunny corner terrace justifies a stop at this charming bistro. Mon–Sat 8/9am–2am, Sun 11am–11pm.

Paul's Place 76 Rue Notre Dame. Paul graciously welcomes you into his place, a delightful treasure-trove of old books, paintings, and curios, while his son Jack prepares the good-value menu (€12.50). Host to regular film nights, poetry readings and gigs. Tues & Wed noon– 2pm, Thurs–Sat noon–11pm, Sun 4–7pm.

The Breakfast Club 27 Ayres Street. This slice of chintzy (northern) England, run by the charming English/French duo Laure and Merve, serves vein-busting fry-ups (€10) and a proper brew (Yorkshire tea, naturally). Mon–Sat 10am–6pm, Sun 11am–5pm.

DRINKING AND NIGHTLIFE

Bar à Vin 3 cours du 30 Juillet. As promoters for Bordeaux wine growers and home to a wine-tasting school, the bar here is a good place to sample the region's excellent wines (from €2.50), best enjoyed with one of the wonderful cheese plates (€7). Mon–Sat 11am–10pm.

Black Velvet Bar 9 rue du Chai des Farines ☎ 09 51 34 28 73. The atmospheric arches host regular concerts and open mic nights every Sun – doubly intoxicating when

combined with the happy hour (5–8pm). Mon–Sat 5pm–2am, Sun 5pm–midnight.

HMS Victory 3 Place Général Sarrail ☎ 05 56 92 70 47. Expect a packed dancefloor and merrymaking spilling onto the terrace at this lively student pub where you're welcome to bring your own food. Live music and happy hours Thurs–Sat. Daily 2pm–2am.

PÉRIGUEUX

The bustling market town of **PÉRIGUEUX**, with its beautiful Renaissance and medieval centre, makes a fine base for visiting the **Dordogne**'s prehistoric caves.

WHAT TO SEE AND DO

The centre of town focuses on **place Bugeaud**, west of which is the striking **Cathédrale St-Front** (daily 8.30/9am–7/8pm) – its square, pineapple-capped belfry surging above the roofs of the surrounding medieval houses. During a nineteenth-century restoration, the architect Paul Abadie added five Byzantine domes to the roof, which served as a prototype for his more famous Sacré Coeur in Paris (see p.288). Heading north along rue St-Front, you'll reach the **Musée d'Art et d'Archéologie du Périgord**, at 22 cours Tourny (Mon & Wed–Fri 10.30am–5.30pm, Sat & Sun 1–6pm; €4.50), which boasts some beautiful Gallo-Roman mosaics found locally.

ARRIVAL AND INFORMATION

By train The station is a 10min walk to the west of place Bugeaud.

Destinations Bordeaux (13 daily; 1hr 10min–1hr 30min); Les Eyzies (2–6 daily; 35min); Paris (12 daily; via Libourne or Limoges; 4–5hr).

Tourist information The tourist office, at 6 place Francheville (daily 9/10am–12.30pm & 2–6/7pm; ☎ 05 53 53 10 63, ⱳ tourisme-perigueux.fr), has a factsheet detailing how to get to the caves and back in a day (see p.312).

Internet Ouratech, 1 place du Général Leclerc (Mon–Sat 10am–7pm, €3/hr).

ACCOMMODATION

Camping Barnabé 80 rue des Bains ☎ 05 53 53 41 45, ⱳ www.barnabe-perigord.com. This peaceful campsite enjoys an excellent position on the banks of the River Isle. Plots are shady, and there's a bar, ping-pong and mini-golf

11

on site. To get there cross pont des Barris and follow the south riverbank for 20min. Camping €4.80 per person, plus €4 per tent

★ **Des Barris** 2 rue Pierre Magne ☎05 53 53 04 05, ⊚hoteldesbarris.com. A lovely little eighteenth-century hotel with twelve simple but attractive wood-furnished rooms. All are en suite and the best have views across the river to the cathedral. Double €55

Le Midi 18 rue Denis-Papin ☎05 53 53 41 06, ⊚hotel -du-midi.fr. Excellently located opposite the station, this family-run bar-hotel offers the cheapest rooms in town. Double €48

EATING AND DRINKING

Cocotte et Cie 17 rue Voltaire ☎05 53 53 16 49. A popular choice, with a lovely terrace ideal for enjoying such reasonably priced food as *confit de canard* (€9) or the lunch menu (€13.50). Mon–Sat noon–3pm & 6–11pm.

L'Eden 3 rue Aubergerie ☎05 53 06 31 08. An intimate restaurant serving up old-style Périgord cooking with great care and skill, using local ingredients. The *menus* are recommended – €13.50 at lunchtime and €28.50 in the evening. Tues noon–1.30pm, Wed–Sat noon–1.30pm & 7.30–9.30pm.

Les Toqués 38 rue Pierre Semard. An Irish pub/gig venue with over 160 bottled beers and 7 on tap. The place accelerates from quiet evening drinks to no-holds-barred rowdiness at the drop of a hat. Tues & Wed 10am–10pm, Thurs–Sat 10am–midnight.

VÉZÈRE VALLEY CAVES

This lavish cliff-cut region, riddled with **caves** and subterranean streams, is half an hour or so by train from Périgueux. Cro-Magnon skeletons were unearthed here in 1868, and since then an incredible wealth of archeological evidence about the life of late Stone Age people has been found. The paintings that adorn the caves are remarkable not only for their age, but also for their exquisite colouring and the skill with which they were drawn.

WHAT TO SEE AND DO

The centre of the region is **LES EYZIES**, a rambling, somewhat unattractive village dominated by tourism. Worth a glance before or after visiting the caves is the **Musée National de la Préhistoire** (June & Sept daily except Tues 9.30am–6pm; July & Aug daily 9.30am–6.30pm; Oct–May daily except Tues 9am–12.30pm & 2–5.30pm; €5).

Font de Gaume caves

Just outside Les Eyzies, off the road to Sarlat, the **Grotte de Font-de-Gaume** (Mon–Fri & Sun: mid-May to mid-Sept 9.30am–5.30pm; mid-Sept to mid-May 9.30am–12.30pm & 2–5.30pm; €7.50; ☎05 53 06 86 00) contains dozens of polychrome paintings, the colour remarkably preserved by a protective layer of calcite. The tours last 45 minutes but only 180 people are admitted each day with a maximum of twelve people per group, so to be sure of a place you should reserve in advance by phone or arrive before 9.30am.

The Cap Blanc frieze

The **Abri du Cap Blanc** (daily: mid-May to mid-Sept 10am–6pm; €7.50; ☎05 53 06 86 00) is a steep 7km bike ride from Les Eyzies. This is not a cave but a rock shelter, containing a 15,000-year-old frieze of horses and bison, the only exhibited prehistoric sculpture in the world. To visit the cave during low season contact the reception centre at the Font-de-Gaume cave in Les Eyzies (see above).

Grotte des Combarelles

Three kilometres from Les Eyzies is the **Grotte des Combarelles** (Mon–Fri & Sun: mid-May to mid-Sept 9.30am–5.30pm; mid-Sept to mid-May 9.30am–12.30pm & 2–5.30pm; €7), whose engravings of humans, reindeer and mammoths from the Magdalanian period (about 20,000 years ago) are the oldest in the region.

Lascaux

Up the valley of the Vézère River to the northeast, Montignac is more attractive than Les Eyzies. Its prime interest is the cave paintings at nearby **Lascaux** – or, rather, the tantalizing replica at Lascaux II (obligatory 40min guided tour April–June & Sept daily 9.15am–6pm; July & Aug daily 9am–7pm; Oct–March Tues–Sun 10am–12.30pm & 2–5.30pm; €9; tickets must be bought in advance from the tourist office, see opposite); the original has been closed since 1963 due to deterioration caused by the breath and body heat of visitors.

Produced 17,000 years ago, the paintings are considered the finest prehistoric works in existence.

INFORMATION

Les Eyzies The tourist office at 19 rue de la Préhistoire (June–Sept Mon–Sat 9am–7pm, Sun 9/10am–noon & 2–5/6/7pm; Oct–May Mon–Sat 9am–noon & 2–6pm, also Sun April & May 10am–noon & 2–7pm; ☎ 05 53 06 97 05, ☯ leseyzies.com) has information on private rooms in the area, offers internet access and also rents out bikes (€14/day).

Montignac The tourist office (July & Aug daily 9am–7pm; Sept–June Mon/Tues–Fri/Sat 9.30/10/10.30am–12.30pm & 2–5/6pm; ☎ 05 53 51 82 60, ☯ tourisme-vezere.com) is located at place Bertrand-de-Born.

ACCOMMODATION

Hôtel de la Grotte 63 rue du 4 Septembre, Montignac ☎ 05 53 51 80 48, ☯ hoteldelagrotte.fr. Montignac is short on moderately priced accommodation but this is the best option in town, with a nice restaurant as well (*menus* from €12.50). Double €61

Le Moulin du Bleufond, Montignac ☎ 05 53 51 83 95, ☯ bleufond.com. Montignac also has a campsite on the riverbank. Closed mid-Oct to March. Camping €7 per person, plus €8.50 per tent

BIARRITZ

A former Viking whaling settlement, **BIARRITZ** became famous in the nineteenth century when Empress Eugénie came here with the last French Emperor, Napoleon III. He built her a seaside palace in 1855 and an impressive list of kings, queens and tsars followed, bringing *belle époque* and Art Deco grandeur to the resort. Today Biarritz is the undisputed surf capital of Europe, hosting the prestigious weeklong Surf Festival in July, which includes a longboard competition and nightly parties on the Côte des Basques beach. Despite its surf cachet, the town feels as though its glory days are well past, and it's actually a rather traditional (and tacky) seaside resort that can't compete with the Côte d'Azur.

WHAT TO SEE AND DO

The town's beaches are the main attraction. The best surfing is on the long competition beach, **plage de la Côte des Basques**, to the south – those less interested in surfing should try the intimate **Port-Vieux** beach for a calmer swim. A free beach shuttle, the Océane bus (Ligne 10), connects all the major beaches from Anglet to Ilbarritz in high season, departing from Biarritz Gare or outside the municipal casino on 1 Boulevard du Général de Gaulle (June & Sept daily, every 20min, 7.20am–11am & every 15min, 11am–8pm; ☯ anglet-tourisme.com).

The **Musée de la Mer** (April, May, June, Sept & Oct daily 9.30am–8pm; July & Aug daily 9.30am–midnight; Nov–March Tues–Sun 9.30am–7pm; €13.50; ☯ museedelamer.com), opposite Rocher de la Vierge, has an interesting aquarium taken from the Bay of Biscay, and a rooftop seal pool. **Asiatica**, at 1 rue Guy Petit (Mon–Fri 2–6.30pm; July & Aug Mon–Fri 10.30am–6.30pm, Sat & Sun 2–7pm; €10), uphill and left off avenue Foch, houses one of Europe's most important collections of oriental art.

ARRIVAL AND DEPARTURE

By plane Aérodrome Biarritz-Bayonne-Anglet is connected to the town centre by Chronoplus bus line #14 (€1). Line #C (direction Bidart Izarbel) connects to Biarritz Gare.

By train The station lies 3km from the centre in La Négresse. Bus #A1 and #10 run between the station and the town centre. Bus #C serves Bayonne.

Destinations Bayonne (14 daily; 15–30min); Paris (5 daily, connect in Bayonne; 5hr–6hr 15min).

11

PELOTE BASQUE

The fastest ball game in the world, **pelote** (or *pilota* in Basque) consists, in essence, of propelling a ball (*pelote*) against a wall (*fronton*) so that your opponent cannot return it, sometimes at speeds of over 300km per hour. There are over twenty versions, with different courts, rackets and balls.

The biggest tournaments in Biarritz – the Open in July and the Gant d'Or in August, played in the parc Mazon on avenue Joffre and the Plaza Berri on avenue Foch – are great spectacles.

By bus The main bus hub is by the *Hotel de Ville* on Square d'Ixelle. Line #A1 and #A2 connect to Bayonne centre (every 10–20min; 40min).

Destinations Bilbao (2 daily; 2hr 55min); San Sebastian (2 daily at 12.15pm & 6.45pm; 1hr 45min).

INFORMATION

Tourist information Tourist office at square d'Ixelles (Jan–March Mon–Fri 9am–6pm, Sat 10am–noon & 2–5pm, Sun 10am–1pm; April to mid-June Mon–Fri 9am–6pm, Sat & Sun 10am–5pm; mid-June to late June & Sept Mon–Fri 9am–7pm, Sat & Sun 10am–6pm; July & Aug daily 9am–7pm; ☎ 05 59 22 37 00, ⊛ tourisme.biarritz.fr).

GETTING AROUND

By bus Local operator Chronoplus have an information kiosk (☎ 05 59 24 26 53, ⊛ chronoplus.eu) near the main bus hub. Two free shuttle services operate from Square d'Ixelle (Mon–Sat 7.30am–7.30pm) – one for the town centre (every 10min) and another for the suburb of Saint-Charles (every 20min).

By scooter Rent a Bike, 24 rue Peyroloubilh (☎ 05 59 24 94 47), rents scooters and beach buggies; ID and credit card required (€12/day).

ACCOMMODATION

Atalaye 6 rue des Goélands ☎ 05 59 24 06 76. The faded seaside glamour still charms, with some rooms offering views of the ocean. Double **€50**

Biarritz Camping 28 rue Harcet ☎ 05 59 23 00 12, ⊛ biarritz-camping.fr. A spacious and well-equipped campsite, just a short walk from the beach and 2km from the centre of town. Open late March to early Oct. Camping **€28** for two people plus tent

FUAJ Biarritz 8 rue Chiquito de Cambo ☎ 05 59 41 76 00, ⊛ fuaj.org; bus #2, #9, or route B bus on Sun to "Bois de Boulogne". Just 1.5km from the beach and close to the station and the lake, this fantastic hostel has two- to four-bed dorms, rents out bicycles and has some good deals on surf lessons. Dorm **€19.50**

Hotel de la Plage 3 Esplanade du Port Vieux ☎ 05 59 23 95 19, ⊛ hoteldelaplage-biarritz.com. Bright, nicely furnished rooms (some overlooking the beach) lend this hotel an airy feel. And at just 50m from the sea, the location is superb. Double **€60**

La Marine 1 rue des Goélands ☎ 05 59 24 34 09, ⊛ hotel-lamarine-biarritz.com. A fresh-feeling place, painted crisp blue and white. The only downside to its central location is the noise from revellers outside. Double **€45**

EATING AND DRINKING

Bar Jean 5 rue des Halles ☎ 05 59 24 80 38. Don't miss this local tapas favourite, which serves plates of the excellent local ham (€12.50) and sangria (€3.50). Very

popular so worth booking ahead. Mon & Thurs–Sun 9am–3pm & 6.30pm–2am.

Bleue de toi 30 rue Mazagran. They've done a lot with this crêperie's small size – stylishly decorated, there's a tiny mezzanine space and tables outside. The midday menu features a glass of cider, a *galette* (try the *forestière*) and a sweet crêpe for dessert. April–Sept daily 11am–11pm.

Casa Juan Pedro Quai du Petit Port. Occupies a uniquely picturesque spot but doesn't make you pay for the privilege. Try the grilled sardines (€8.50). April–Sept daily noon–11pm.

Crampotte 30 Port des Pêcheurs ☎ 05 35 46 91 22. An ideal place for an aperitif in the early evening, overlooking the pretty Petit Port. Try the plates of basque ham and cheese (to share €8.90) with a glass of basque *cidre* (€2.70). Daily 9am–2.30pm & 6–11pm.

Les Halles place Sobradiel. This recently restored *halles* is a fantastic spot to savour fresh, inexpensive seafood and local delicacies. Try fresh oysters and a glass of wine at *L'Ecaillerie*, a simple seafood stand that supplies most restaurants in town, yet whose €5-or-less dishes don't reflect restaurant prices. Daily 7am–1.30pm.

Sideria Hernani 29 av du Maréchal Joffre. Heavy wooden tables, barrels and local warmth accompany excellent Basque cuisine and cider. The *côte de boeuf* (€38 for two people) is huge but well worth it. Daily 8pm–midnight.

BAYONNE

Capital of the French Basque country and home of the bayonet, **BAYONNE** lies 6km inland at the junction of the Nive and Adour rivers. Having escaped the worst effects of mass tourism, it remains a cheerful and pretty town, with the shutters on the older half-timbered houses painted in the distinctive Basque tones of green and rust-red.

WHAT TO SEE AND DO

The town's two medieval quarters line the banks of the Nive, whose quays are home to many bars and restaurants. Grand Bayonne on the west bank is the administrative and commercial centre, while Petit Bayonne, to the east, has a more bohemian feel and is full of places to eat and drink.

Petit Bayonne

On **quai des Corsaires**, along the Nive's east bank, stands the **Musée Basque** (April–June & Sept Tues–Sun

10am–6.30pm; July & Aug daily 10am–6.30pm, Thurs till 8.30pm, Oct–March Tues–Sun 10.30am–6pm; €6.50), which provides a comprehensive overview of modern Basque culture.

Grand Bayonne

The **Cathédrale Ste-Marie** (Mon–Sat 10–11.45am & 3–5.45pm, Sun 3.30–6pm), across the Nive, looks best from a distance, its twin spires rising with airy grace above the houses; the **cloister** (daily 9am–12.30pm & 2–5/6pm; free) rewards a visit with a good view of the stained glass and buttresses. Chocolate-making techniques were brought here by Jewish chocolatiers fleeing the Spanish Inquisition. It was here that a devilish brew, hot chocolate, was introduced to the country, much to the distaste of the Catholic Church due to its aphrodisiac qualities – the best place in town to try it is *Cazenave* (see below).

ARRIVAL AND DEPARTURE

By train Bayonne's train station is in the St-Esprit quarter on the opposite bank of the Adour from the centre, a 10min walk over the Pont St-Esprit. Buses from Biarritz also arrive here.

Destinations Bordeaux (6–12 daily; 1hr 40min–2hr 10min); Hendaye (for the Spanish border; 14 daily; 35min); Lourdes (5–8 daily; 1hr 45min–2hr); Paris (14–16 daily, some indirect; 4hr 45min–6hr); St Sébastien (from Hendaye; every 30min; 45min); Toulouse (7–12 daily; 3hr 10min–4hr 40min).

INFORMATION

Tourist information Take rue Bernède from the Hôtel de Ville, to place des Basques, where the tourist office (July & Aug Mon–Sat 9am–7pm, Sun 10am–1pm; Sept–June Mon–Fri 9am–6.30pm, Sat 10am–6pm; ☎08 20 42 64 64, ⚇bayonne-tourisme.com) has an excellent scheme that lends bikes for free.

Internet CyberNetCafé, 9 place de la République (Mon–Sat 8am–8pm, Sun 10am–8pm; €3/hr).

GETTING AROUND

By bus There are free shuttle buses operating within the centre (Mon–Sat 7.30am–7.30pm), one of which departs from the train station at Place Perreire.

ACCOMMODATION

Hôtel des Arceaux 26 rue Port-Neuf ☎05 59 59 15 53. Many rooms don't have exterior windows, which can prove

stuffy on hot days, but the hotel nevertheless has a pleasantly quirky character. Double **€66**

Hôtel le Port Neuf 44 rue Port-Neut ☎05 59 25 65 03. Excellently located within the picturesque old town and a 10min walk from the station. The rooms are stylishly furnished with en-suite bathrooms. Double **€60**

Monbar 24 rue Pannecau, Petit Bayonne ☎05 59 59 26 80. Though slightly shabby and old-fashioned, this quiet family-run hotel has clean, bright en-suite rooms and a friendly owner. Double **€32**

Monte Carlo 1 rue Sainte Ursule ☎05 59 55 02 68. Basic and charmless rooms, albeit with a winning location opposite the station. The restaurant and bar below may prove noisy at night. Double **€30**

EATING AND DRINKING

★ **Auberge du Petit Bayonne** 23 rue des Cordeliers ☎05 59 59 83 44. The welcome is warm and the food hearty at this husband-and-wife-run place. Menus are €10.50–19. The lamb sweetbread with cèpes is excellent, but you must try the roasted suckling lamb (*agneau de lait*) when it's available. Mon & Thurs–Sat noon–2.30pm & 7.30–10pm, Tues & Sun noon–2.30pm.

Bistrot Ste-Cluque 9 rue Hugues, St-Esprit ☎05 59 55 82 43. Make sure you try the local cured ham (€7.50), flavoured with salt from nearby mines, at this jolly bistro by the station; three-course dinner menu €18. Daily noon–2pm & 7–10.30pm.

Cazenave 19 Arceaux du Pont-Neuf. The pick of the chocolatiers; try the famous *chocolat mousseux* – delicious, hand-whipped hot chocolate served with chantilly cream (€5.20) – with a serving of their hot, buttered toast (€3). Tues–Sat 9.15am–noon & 2–7pm.

En Equilibre 19 rue des Cordeliers ☎05 59 59 46 98. A hearty traditional menu best savoured at lunchtime (€13; evening menu €19); the camembert entrée and main of duck breast with sour cherry compote is delicious. Mon 7.30–10.30pm, Tues–Sat noon–2.30pm & 7.30–10.30pm.

Trinquet Saint-André Bar-Brasserie 3 rue du Jeu de Paume. An airy canopied terrace adjoins this cool little bar. The lunch *formule* is excellent value (€8–15) and it's a lovely spot to relax to the sound of *trinquet* (an indoor ball game similar to squash) played in the seventeenth-century hall next door. Mon–Wed & Fri 9am–3pm & 5pm–midnight, Thurs and Sat 9am–midnight.

LOURDES AND AROUND

In 1858 Bernadette Soubirous, the 14-year-old daughter of a poor local miller in **LOURDES**, had eighteen visions of the Virgin Mary in a spot called the Grotte de Massabielle. Miraculous cures at the grotto

11

HIKING IN THE PYRENEES

From either Gavarnie or Barèges, a few hours on the Pyrenees-spanning **hiking trail**, GR10, or the harder HRP (Haute Randonnée Pyrénéenne), brings you to staffed alpine refuges (rough camping is not generally allowed in the park). In summer, serious and properly equipped hikers may wish to continue on the trails, which are well served with refuges, though the weather and terrain make them highly dangerous in winter. The Lourdes and Bayonne tourist offices have information, or check ⓦ lespyrenees.net.

---

soon followed and Lourdes grew exponentially; it now sees six million Catholic pilgrims a year and whole streets are devoted to the sale of religious kitsch. At the **grotto** itself – a moisture-blackened overhang by the riverside with a statue of the Virgin inside – long queues of the faithful process through. Above looms the first, neo-Gothic church built here, in 1871, and nearby the massive subterranean **basilica** has a capacity of twenty thousand.

ARRIVAL AND INFORMATION

By train Lourdes train station is on the northeastern edge of town.
Destinations Biarritz (frequent; 2hr 20min–4hr 10min); Toulouse (frequent; 2–3hr).
By bus The *gare routière* is located in the central place Capdevieille. There are two public transport networks, Ma Ligne and TER Midi-Pyrenees.
Destinations from Ma Ligne Barèges (1 daily at 5pm; 1hr 17min); Gavarnie (June–Sept 1 daily at 9.04am; 1hr 40min).
Destinations from TER Midi-Pyrenees Barèges (7 daily; 1hr 5min).
Tourist information For the tourist office on place Peyramale (Mon–Sat 9am–noon & 2–5.30/6/6.30/7pm; Easter–Oct also Sun 10am–12.30/6pm; ☏ 05 62 42 77 40, ⓦ lourdes-infotourisme.com), turn right outside the train station, then left down Chaussée Maransin.

ACCOMMODATION

Hotel Croix des Nordistes 29 bd de la Grotte ☏ 05 62 94 28 57, ⓦ hotelcroixdesnordistes-lourdes.com. There's an abundance of inexpensive hotels in Lourdes, including this simple place. Double €42
Plein Soleil 11 av du Monge ☏ 05 62 94 40 93, ⓦ camping -pleinsoleil.com. A well-equipped campsite with swimming pool, on-site bar and spotless facilities within close proximity of Lourdes. Camping €22.50 for two people and tent

Gavarnie and Barèges

From Lourdes train station, several SNCF buses run daily to **Gavarnie** and **Barèges**, two resorts near the heart of the Parc National des Pyrénées Occidentales.

Gavarnie is smaller and pricier than Barèges, but has an incomparable natural amphitheatre towering above, forming the border with Spain. For more on hiking in the park, see box above.

ACCOMMODATION

Camping La Bergerie Chemin du Cirque, Gavarnie ☏ 05 62 92 48 41, ⓦ camping-gavarnie-labergerie.com. A lovely campsite with good facilities and on-site bar. The pitches are discreetly located in terraces to preserve the beauty of the surrounding landscape. Camping €3.80 per person and tent
Gîte L'Oasis 2 Pass Toys, Barèges ☏ 05 62 92 69 47, ⓦ gite-oasis.com. A comfortable family-run gîte. Rooms are en suite, cosily furnished, and some have mountain views with balconies. Breakfast included with doubles; dorms are half-board. Dorm €36, double €24
La Ribère Route de Labatsus, Barèges ☏ 05 62 92 69 01, ⓦ laribere.com. One of the highest campsites in the French Pyrenees, offering stunning mountain views. Over 50 terrace-based pitches, with good, clean facilities. Camping €14 for two people and tent

TOULOUSE

TOULOUSE is one of the most vibrant provincial cities in France, thanks to its sizeable student population – second only to that of Paris. The city has long been a centre for aviation – St-Exupéry and Mermoz flew out from here on their pioneering flights over Africa in the 1920s – and has more recently been developed as the country's centre of high-tech industry.

WHAT TO SEE AND DO

The centre of Toulouse is a rough hexagon clamped around a bend in the wide, brown Garonne River.

Place du Capitole and the old city

The **place du Capitole** is the site of Toulouse's town hall and a prime meeting place, with numerous cafés and a weekday market. South of the square,

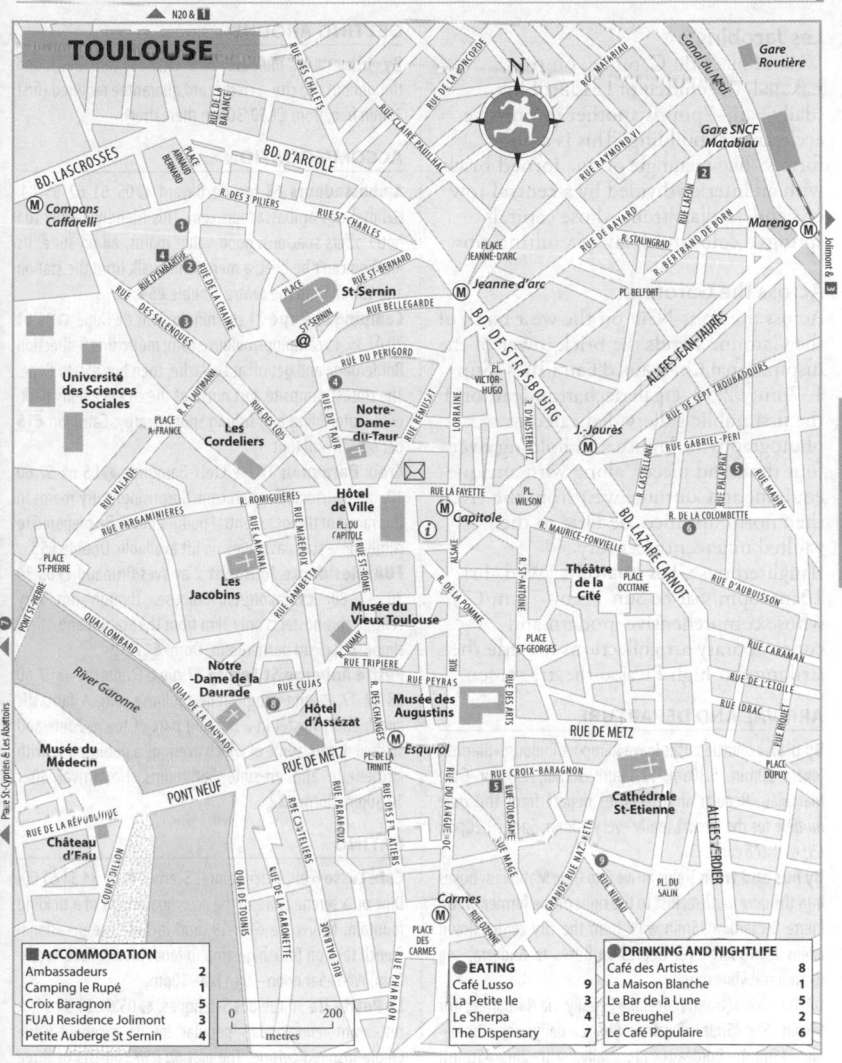

and east of rue Alsace-Lorraine, lies the **old town**. The predominant building material is the flat Toulousain brick, whose cheerful rosy colour gives the city its nickname of *ville rose*. Best known of these buildings is the Hôtel d'Assézat, west towards the river end of rue de Metz, which houses the marvellous private art collection of the **Fondation Bemberg** (daily 10am–12.30pm & 1.30–6pm, Thurs till 9pm; €8), including excellent works by Bonnard.

St-Sernin

Rue du Taur leads northwards from place du Capitole to place St-Sernin and the largest Romanesque church in France, **Basilique de St-Sernin** (June–Sept Mon–Sat 8.30am–7pm, Sun 8.30am–7.30pm; Oct–May Mon–Sat 8.30am–6pm, Sun 8.30am–7.30pm). Dating back to 1080, it was built to accommodate passing hordes of Santiago pilgrims and is one of the loveliest examples of its kind.

Les Jacobins

West of place du Capitole, on rue Lakanal, the church of **Les Jacobins** (daily 9am–7pm) is another impressive ecclesiastical building. This is a huge fortress-like rectangle of unadorned brick, with an interior divided by a central row of slender pillars from whose capitals springs a colourful splay of vaulting ribs.

Across the Garonne

Across the Pont-Neuf on the west bank of the Garonne stands the brick tower of the inspirational **Chateaux d'Eau** (Tues–Sun 1–7pm; €2.50; ⓦgaleriechateaudeau.org) the first public gallery in France dedicated to photography in France and holding over four thousand pieces, along with antique equipment. Continue west from the river, then north up Allées de Fitte to the vaulted nineteenth-century slaughterhouse, **Les Abattoirs** (Wed–Fri 10am–6pm, Sat & Sun 11am–7pm; €7), whose comprehensive modern and contemporary art collections include the striking 8m-high Picasso theatre screen.

ARRIVAL AND DEPARTURE

By plane Shuttle buses leave Aéroport Toulouse-Blagnac (every 20min, 5.30am–12.15am; 30min; €5) for Gare Matabiau. Regular shuttle buses depart from the *gare routière* for the airport (daily every 20min, 5am–9.20pm; €5; ⓦtisseo.com).

By bus and train Trains arrive into Gare Matabiau, buses into the *gare routière*, just to the right of the former on Bd Pierre Semard, a 15min walk from the city centre down allées Jean-Jaurès. For details on buses to Andorra, see ⓦandorrabybus.com.

Destinations (train) Barcelona (3 daily, via Narbonne; 4hr 50min–5hr 45min); Bayonne (18–22 daily; 2hr 30min–3hr 45min); Bordeaux (16 daily; 2hr–2hr 45min); Carcassonne (18 daily; 45min–1hr 15min); Lourdes (9–14 daily; 2hr); Lyon (10–14 daily; 4–6hr); Marseille (9–12 daily; 3hr 50min–5hr 50min); Paris (8–12 daily; 5–7hr). Destinations (bus) Andorra (2 daily; 3hr 30min).

INFORMATION

Tourist information Tourist office at place Charles de Gaulle by Capitole *métro* station (June–Sept Mon–Sat 9am–7pm, Sun 10.30am–5.15pm; Oct–May Mon–Fri 9am–6pm, Sat 9am–12.30pm & 2–6pm, Sun 10am–12.30pm & 2–5pm; ☎05 40 13 15 31, ⓦtoulouse-visit.com).

Internet Nethouse, 1 rue de Trois Renards (Mon–Sat 9am–9pm; €3/hr).

GETTING AROUND

By bike Vélô Toulouse bike stands can be found throughout the city – credit card guarantee required (first 30min free, from €1.50/30min thereafter).

ACCOMMODATION

Ambassadeurs 68 rue de Bayard ☎05 61 62 65 84, ⓦhotel-des-ambassadeurs.com. This friendly, family-run hotel offers spacious, good-value rooms, all en suite. Its location can't be beat, a mere 5min walk from the station and 15min from the centre. Double €54

Camping le Rupé 21 chemin du Pont de Rupé ☎05 61 70 07 35, ⓦcamping-toulouse.com; métro line B direction Borderouge and get off at La Vache, then bus #59 to Rupé. The closest campsite, just north of the city in a leafy park, with waterskiing and fishing spots nearby. Camping €15 per person and tent

Croix Baragnon 17 rue Croix-Baragnon ☎05 61 52 60 10, ⓦhotelcroixbaragnon.com. Surprisingly airy rooms in this rarest of things, a central budget hotel. Be prepared to climb some stairs as there's no lift available. Double €55

FUAJ Residence Jolimont 2 av Yves Brunaud ☎05 34 30 42 80, ⓦfuaj.org/en/Toulouse. Though not very central, this hostel is only 1km from the station and offers simple but clean dorm rooms. Dorm €17.50

Petite Auberge St Sernin 17 rue d'Embarthe ☎07 60 88 17 17, ⓦgite-compostelle-toulouse.com. A fantastic and friendly hostel in a buzzing part of town. Four- and six-bed dorms, some of which overlook a public park, with kitchenette and en-suite bathrooms. No arrival after 10.30pm. Dorm €22

EATING

Café Lusso 6 bis, place Saintes Scarbes ☎05 34 31 61 09. Dine on a serene *place* to the accompaniment of a tinkling fountain. Mains are €14–19, and include the occasional French take on British gastropub food. Mon & Tues noon–2pm, Wed–Sat noon–2pm & 8–10pm.

La Petite Ile 30 rue des Salenques, ☎05 61 21 54 31. A restaurant *reunaionnais* popular for its excellent-value Creole-inspired cuisine. The *plat du jour* consists of three changing dishes – a *rougail* (typical Creole dish using spices and tomatoes), a curry and a masala – and, at €6.90, is a bargain given the huge portions. Takeaway Thurs only 6–7pm. Mon–Wed & Fri noon–3.30pm, Thurs noon–3.30pm & 7–10.30pm.

Le Sherpa 46 rue du Taur. The extensive menu of this busy crêperie and tea place is not only cheap (from €3) but encompasses every possible combination of filling. Daily 11am–midnight.

DRINKING AND NIGHTLIFE

Café des Artistes 13 place Daurade. A table on the sun-drenched terrace overlooking the Garonne is a deservedly popular spot. Come evening, it's perfect with a beer (€3) from their wide ranging selection. Mon–Wed 11am–1am, Thurs–Sat 11am–2am, Sun noon–10pm.

La Maison Blanche 10 rue Arnaud Bernard ⓦ café -maison-blanche.fr. Sizzling, and not just because of the crowds that flock to this happening little venue, an Association Bar (you must register to gain free admittance) committed to staging fantastic live music. By day the café serves coffee (€1) and tapas (€2), come night the wine flows (€1.50) and the party truly begins. Mon–Fri 1pm–midnight, Sat 4pm–1am.

Le Bar de la Lune 22 rue Palaprat. Relax with one of 120 types of beer (bottles such as Duvel from €5, a *demi* of well-kept beer €2) in this friendly little bar where the volume allows for conversation. Mon–Fri 7pm–2am, Sat 8pm–3am, Sun 6pm–2am.

Le Breughel 30 rue de la Chaine. A 35-year-old bar with over 30 different, mainly Belgian, beers (from €4) and an infectiously lively atmosphere. Crowds regularly spill onto the neighbouring Place des Tiercerettes as impromptu live music fills the air. Daily 5pm–2am, Sat till 3am.

Le Café Populaire 9 rue de la Colombette. This long-standing drinking den serves arguably the cheapest pints in the city (€2.50), which goes some way to explaining its buzzy atmosphere. Happy hour 7.30–8.30pm. Mon–Fri 9am–2am, Sat till 3am; closed Aug.

The Dispensary 1 rue Marthe Varsi. With its rock & roll aesthetic, impressive cocktail menu and delicious burgers (€12), this is an excellent option. Tues & Wed 5pm–2am, Thurs & Fri noon–2am, Sat noon–3am, Sun noon–midnight.

CARCASSONNE

The fairytale aspect of **CARCASSONNE**'s old town (la Cité) was the inspiration for the castle in Walt Disney's *Sleeping Beauty*. Viollet-le-Duc rescued it from ruin in 1844, and his rather romantic restoration has been furiously debated ever since. Unsurprisingly, it's become a real tourist trap, its narrow lanes lined with innumerable souvenir shops and regularly crammed with hordes of day-trippers.

WHAT TO SEE AND DO

The **Cité** is a 25-minute walk from the station (20min from the new town) – well worth it to get a full view of the fortress from below. There's no charge for admission to the main part of the Cité, or the grassy *lices* (moat) between the walls. However, to see the inner fortress of the **Château Comtal** (daily guided tours every 30min, 10am–5/6.30pm; €8.50), with its small museum of medieval sculpture, and to walk along the walls, you have to join one of the 45-minute tours from the ticket office. In addition to wandering the town's narrow streets (though they can be a bit of a squeeze in summer), don't miss the beautiful, thirteenth-century church of **St-Nazaire** (daily 9am–noon & 2–7pm) at the end of rue St-Louis.

ARRIVAL AND INFORMATION

By train The station is on the northern edge of the new town, at the end of av du Maréchal Joffre, from where it's a 35min walk to the Cité (very steep for the last 5min) or catch #4 from the bus stop on bd Omer Sarraut (Mon–Sat hourly, 7am–7pm; €1.20).

Destinations Barcelona (6 daily, via Narbonne; 4hr–5hr 10min); Montpellier (14 daily; 1hr 15min–1hr 45min); Nice (6 daily, via Marseille; 4–5hr); Paris (11–16 daily; 3–6hr); Perpignan (13 daily; 1hr 30min–2hr 15min); Toulouse (18–22 daily; 45min–1hr 15min).

Tourist information There are three tourist office branches, the main one at 28 rue de Verdun; another at av du Maréchal Joffre near the station and the third at the Porte Narbonnaise in the Cité (April–June & Sept–Oct Mon–Sat

11

CYCLING THE CANAL DU MIDI

The 240km-long **Canal du Midi**, which begins in Toulouse and ends at Sète, opening onto the Mediterranean, is a UNESCO World Heritage Site and renowned for its beauty. The towpath that runs along the canal beneath the dappled light of the plane trees is a picturesque cycle route, and you can explore this stretch of the canal by cycling between Carcassonne and Trèbes or Castelnaudary. Bikes can be rented from Génération VTT, Canal du Midi port opposite the station in Carcassonne (April–Oct daily 9.30am–1.30pm & 2.30–6.30pm; from €10/2hr; ☏ 06 09 59 30 85, ⓦ generation-vtt.com).

For a more leisurely ride, take a boat trip along the canal and enjoy the wonderful views of the medieval castle and the vineyards of the Carbadès with Carcassonne Croisières (April–Oct daily; €8.50–11; ☏ 04 68 71 61 26, ⓦ carcassonne-croisiere.com). Enquire at the Carcassonne tourist office (see above) for details of more excursions.

9am–6pm, Sun 9am–1pm; July & Aug daily 9am–7pm; Nov–March Mon–Sat 9am–12.30pm & 1.30–5.30pm; ☎ 04 68 10 24 30, ⓦ carcassonne-tourisme.com).

ACCOMMODATION

Campéole la Cité Route St-Hilaire ☎ 04 68 10 01 00, ⓦ campingcitecarcassonne.com. A lovely riverside location (less than 10min from the Cité) and good sporting facilities. Accommodation in fixed tents or on-site mobile homes (min two nights July & Aug). Camping **€26.70** per one/two people and tent, fixed tent **€55**

★ **FUAJ Carcassone** Rue du Vicomte Trencavel ☎ 04 68 25 23 16, ⓦ fuaj.org. A fantastic hostel in an unsurpassable position in the heart of la Cité. Dorms are comfortable, facilities are modern and clean, and breakfast is substantial. There's also table tennis, themed nights in the bar, bike rental and organized trips to the surrounding countryside. Dorm **€22.80**

Hotel du Pont Vieux 32 rue Trivalle ☎ 04 68 25 24 99, ⓦ hoteldupontvieux.com. Some rooms have tired decor but the building is atmospheric nevertheless, with a lovely garden behind ivy-covered walls, and the more expensive rooms offering views of the Cité. There's a roof terrace, too, with spectacular views. Double **€59**

Notre Dame de l'Abbaye 103 rue Trivalle ☎ 04 68 25 16 65, ⓦ abbaye-carcassonne.com. A tranquil option, this former abbey has spick-and-span dorms and a beautiful garden. Camping is possible within the grounds. Breakfast included except for campers. Dorm **€20**, double **€49**, camping **€12** per person and tent

EATING AND DRINKING

La Tête de l'Art 37 bis rue Trivalle. A wonderfully atmospheric café/bar just outside the battlements, filled with pieces of art belonging to the charismatic owner/artist Jean-Marc Tilcké, who runs the art gallery opposite. Daily 10am–10.30pm.

L'Auberge des Lices 3 rue Raymond-Roger Trencavel. Set nicely apart from the main tourist traffic in the Cité. The cheapest menu (€19) features cassoulet. Mon, Tues & Thurs–Sun noon–2pm & 7.30–10pm; open Wed eve July & Aug.

Le Ponte Vecchio 22 rue Trivalle ☎ 04 68 71 33 17.

Combining the romance of Italy with the fine dining of France, this intimate restaurant oozes plenty of charm. The generous €20 menu offers cassoulet and an unmissable dessert list. Mon, Sat & Sun 7–10.30pm, Tues–Fri noon–2pm & 7–10.30pm.

Le Trivalou 69 rue Trivalle ☎ 04 68 71 23 11. Options may be limited but the cooking is excellent: the €21 *menu* of asparagus terrine entrée, sautéed lamb morsels and delicious lavender crème brûlée is well worth the indulgence. Wed–Sun noon–10.30pm.

MONTPELLIER

MONTPELLIER is a vibrant city, renowned for its ancient university, once attended by such luminaries as Petrarch and Rabelais. Most of the central area is pedestrianized, which lends itself to unhurried exploration and many enjoyable evenings at terrace cafés.

WHAT TO SEE AND DO

At the city's hub is place de la Comédie, a grand oval square paved with cream-coloured marble and surrounded by cafés. The Opéra, an ornate nineteenth-century theatre, presides over one end, while the other end leads onto the pleasant Champs de Mars park. Nearby, at 39 bd Bonne Nouvelle, the much-vaunted **Musée Fabre** (Tues–Sun 10am–6pm; €6) has a wide art collection stretching from the Renaissance to the modern day, housed in a number of exceptionally beautiful buildings. The tangled, hilly lanes of Montpellier's old quarter lie behind the museum, and are full of seventeenth- and eighteenth-century mansions and small museums. The **Jardin des Plantes** (Tues–Sun noon–6/8pm; free), just north of the old town, with its alleys of exotic trees, is France's oldest

---

MONTPELLIER MARKETS

"Allez-allez-allez!" is the call of Montpellier's stallholders in the many **markets** around town. Here are three of the best.

Les Halles Jacques-Coeur Opposite the tram on boulevard Antigone. Stalls sell fresh local produce and home-cooked food. Mon–Sat 8am–9pm, Sun 8am–3.30pm.

Marché Paysan Across the *place* from Les Halles Jacques-Coeur. A farmers' market specializing in local produce, seafood and local crafts. Sun 8am–1pm.

Plan-Cabanes Faubourg du Courreau and Gambetta. The most fun of all the city's markets – here you can eat Arab and African cuisine for next to nothing. Daily 7.30am–1.30pm.

botanical garden, founded in 1593. Opposite the gardens lies the **university quarter**, with its beautiful old buildings and lively café life.

ARRIVAL AND DEPARTURE

By plane The airport is 8km to the west of Montpellier, by the beaches, connected to the city by *navettes* (€1.50 single or €2.40, including one bus or tram connection in town). Airport shuttle #120 runs to Place de l'Europe Tramway station, line 1, rue Poséidon (Mon–Sat 8.45am–11pm & Sun 10.45am–11pm; 15min); going the other way it runs daily 5.30am–8pm (15min).
By bus and train The train station, Gare St Roch, is 5min away from the *gare routière*, on the southern edge of town, a short walk down rue de Maguelone from the centre.
Destinations (train) Avignon (12 daily; 1hr); Barcelona (4 daily, 2 via Port-Bou; 4hr 20min–7hr); Carcassonne (9 daily; 1hr 25min–1hr 45min); Marseille (10 daily; 1hr 30min–2hr 20min); Nîmes (frequent; 30min); Paris (12 daily; 3hr 30min); Perpignan (16 daily; 1hr 30min–2hr).

INFORMATION

Tourist information Near place de la Comédie (July–Sept Mon–Fri 9am–7.30pm, Sat & Sun 9.30am–6pm; Oct–June Mon–Sat 10am–6pm, Sun 10am–5pm; ☎04 67 60 60 60, ⊛ot-montpellier.fr).
Internet Cyberstade, 6 rue Jules-Ferry.

ACCOMMODATION

FUAJ Montpellier Rue des Écoles-Laïques ☎04 67 60 32 22, ⊛fuaj.org; tram stop "Louis Blanc". While the central location lends a real party atmosphere (noise can be a problem), the interior of this handsome building is tired and awaiting refurbishment. Closed noon–3pm. Dorm **€21.20**
Le Mistral 25 rue Boussairolles ☎04 67 58 45 25, ⊛hotel-le-mistral.com. Simple, pleasant rooms; the location on a quiet street within a 5min walk of Place de la Comédie makes this is a solid option. Double **€64**
Les Étuves 24 rue des Étuves ☎04 67 60 78 19, ⊛hoteldesetuves.fr. A small family-run hotel, full of *belle époque* touches. The spotless, white rooms have en-suite showers or baths. Double **€37**
Nova 8 rue Richelieu ☎04 67 60 79 85, ⊛hotelnova.fr. Ideally situated within close proximity to the station and old town, this hotel offers clean, spacious rooms at a bargain price, but it's the friendly welcome that's hard to beat. Double **€48**

EATING AND DRINKING

Barberousse 6 rue Boussairolles. Wooden from top to toe, with barrels for tables, this place feels a little like a ship's hold. Given that it's a *rhumerie* with nearly 80

different kinds available, you might find the floor starts listing too. Happy hour 6–8pm. Mon–Sat 6pm–1am.
La FaBRik 12 rue Boussairolles. Live music (think rock, blues, jazz and Irish), Belgian beers, whiskies from around the world and the occasional indoor boules tournament at this hipster hotspot. Tues–Sat 8pm–1am.
La Tomate 6 rue Four des Flammes ☎04 67 60 49 38. Truly a city institution, not least because of the prices – a midday menu is just €9.10, while the €12.95 evening menu offers fish soup and cassoulet among its options. Tues–Sat noon–2pm & 7.30–10.30pm.
Le Bookshop Café 8 rue du Bras de Fer. A peaceful spot located down a picturesque passageway in the old quarter. Choose a special tea blend (€2.20) and a book from their well-stocked shelves of English titles. Mon–Fri 1–7pm, Sat 10am–7pm.
Pizzeria Don Peppino 13 rue Sainte Croix ☎04 67 52 89 75. Dine on the picturesque terrace beside the cathedral or within the cave-like interior at this atmospheric pizzeria in the heart of the old town (from €7.50 large/€5.50 small). Tues–Sat noon–10.30pm.

PERPIGNAN

This far south, climate and geography alone ensure a palpable Spanish influence, but **PERPIGNAN** is actually Spanish in origin and home to the descendants of refugees from the Spanish Civil War. It's a cheerful city, with Roussillon's red-and-yellow-striped flag atop many a building, and makes an ideal stop-off en route to Spain or Andorra.

WHAT TO SEE AND DO

The centre of Perpignan is marked by the palm trees and smart cafés of **place Arago**. From here rue d'Alsace-Lorraine and rue de la Loge lead past the massive iron gates of the classical **Hôtel de Ville** to the tiny **place de la Loge**, the focus of the old heart of the city. Just north up rue Louis-Blanc is one of the city's few remaining fortifications, the crenellated fourteenth-century gate of **Le Castillet**, now home to the **Musée de l'Histoire de la Catalogne Nord**, a fascinating museum of Roussillon's Catalan folk culture (Tues–Sun 10.30am–6pm; €4).

ARRIVAL AND INFORMATION

By train The station is a 15min walk from the city centre.
Destinations Barcelona (5 daily; 2hr 50min–5hr); Carcassonne (via Narbonne; 13–16 daily; 1hr 30min–2hr);

11

Montpellier (16–20 daily; 1hr 30min–2hr); Paris (10–16 daily; 5hr–9hr 20min); Toulouse (16 daily; 1hr 30min–2hr).

By bus The bus station is by Pont Arago, on av du Général Leclerc.

Tourist information In the Palais des Congrès at the end of bd Wilson (Mon–Sat 9am–6/7pm, Sun 10am–1/4pm; ☎ 04 68 66 30 30, ⓦ perpignantourisme.com).

Internet GamesNet at 45 bis av du Général Leclerc (Mon–Fri 8.15am–1am, Sat 1pm–1am, Sun 1–8pm; €2/hr).

ACCOMMODATION

Camping Catalan Route de Bompas ☎ 04 68 63 16 92, ⓦ camping-catalan.com. A lively campsite 5km from the centre, with a swimming pool and frequent pétanque competitions. Ask for shade as not all pitches have it. Camping **€16.28** per person and tent

FUAJ Perpignan Parc de la Pépinière ☎ 04 68 34 63 32, ⓦ fuaj.org/perpignan. Backing onto a busy road isn't ideal but noise is limited and location is convenient for the station (5min). Dorms are basic, but staff are friendly and helpful, and the breakfast is excellent. Closed 10am–5pm. Dorm **€18.17**, double **€19.37**

Hotel de la Loge 1 rue des Fabriques d'en Nabot ☎ 04 68 34 41 02, ⓦ hoteldelaloge.fr. A beautiful hotel dating from 1650. Rooms have original beams, traditional Catalan furniture and some look out onto the lovely inner courtyard – all in all, a bargain. Double **€55**

Hotel du Berry 6 av du Général de Gaulle ☎ 04 68 34 59 02, ⓦ hotelduberry.com. Close to the station, the rooms (all en suite) really are basic but a night's sleep doesn't come much cheaper. Double **€40**

EATING AND DRINKING

Crêperie Bretonne 8 rue du Maréchal Foch. You may find yourself eating on the back of an old Renault Prairie at this charming crêperie, replete as it is with a dazzling array of vintage paraphernalia. Crêpes €3.20–8.90. Mon–Sat noon–2pm & 7–11pm.

El Serrano 16 rue de la Cloche d'Or. Tiny deli-café on a side street near Musée Rigaud offering excellent plates (€4–7.50) of *manchego*, *jambonserrano* and *pata negra salamanca*, alongside *pichets* of wine (€4) or sangria (€5). Tues–Sat 8am–7pm.

La Cafétière 17 rue de l'Ange. Located in a quiet courtyard, this distinguished café is a specialist in the brewing of aromatic teas and coffees. Select one of their slow-roasted coffee beans from the bean-filled drawers, perfectly accompanied by a home-made pastry (€5). Tues–Sat 9am–7pm.

VIP 4 rue Grande des Fabriques ☎ 04 68 51 02 30. Not easy to find, though its quality means that locals will be able to direct you. Crisp white tablecloths and a strong meat presence on the menu. You won't go wrong with the *plat du jour* (€10). Mon–Fri noon–2pm & 7.30–10pm, Sat & Sun noon–2pm & 7.30–11pm.

Provence and the Côte d'Azur

Provence is held by many to be the most irresistible region in France, with attractions that range from the high mountains of the southern Alps to the wild plains of the **Camargue**. Though technically part of the neighbouring region of Languedoc, the old Roman town of **Nîmes** is a good place to start exploring, as is nearby **Arles**, most famous for Van Gogh's paintings and a great place to indulge in the area's café culture. **Avignon**, home of a wonderful summer festival, is so crammed full of history that it can sometimes feel like a living museum, while just to the north, in **Orange**, lies Europe's best-preserved Roman theatre. Most of the region's towns are full of cobbled streets lined with brightly coloured, shuttered buildings, which are a delight to explore, and none more so than **Aix-en-Provence**.

By contrast, **Marseille**, France's second city, still hasn't shaken off its gritty image. Yet it rewards a little exploration and is home to some of the area's finest food. It also makes a good base for exploring the stunning **Calanques**. The Côte d'Azur certainly lives up to its name – taking a train along the coast reveals sparkling turquoise sea, packed in many places with the glitzy yachts of the rich and famous. **Nice** has all the trappings of a jet-set

---

THE CÔTE VERMEILLE

The **Vermilion Coast** (ⓦ collioure.com) is named for its richly coloured rocks, which attracted artists such as Picasso, Dalí and Matisse. The latter's 1905–06 paintings of Collioure saw the birth of Fauvism, the forerunner to Cubism. Aside from these colourful rocks, the coast is also home to some lovely beaches and charming fishing towns. Over ten trains a day run between Perpignan and Collioure (25min).

> **PONT DU GARD**
>
> This stunning vestige of a 50km aqueduct built in the first century AD to carry spring water from Uzès to Nîmes is a poignant memorial to the hubris of Roman civilization. It sits peacefully in the valley of the Gardon River, and is a great place to cool off on hot summer days. Tours are run from the informative museum on the left side of the valley; to get there, take a bus from Nîmes to Uzès, where six *navettes* run to the Pont each day; bring a swimsuit, walking shoes and a picnic (@ot-pontdugard.com).

lifestyle, yet it feels a little more down-to-earth than nearby **Cannes**, and makes a great base for exploring small villages in the hills and other seaside towns.

NÎMES

NÎMES is intrinsically linked to two things: ancient Rome – whose influence is manifest in some of the most extensive **Roman remains** in Europe – and denim, a word corrupted from *de Nîmes*. First manufactured as *serge* in the city's textile mills, denim was exported to America to clothes workers, where a certain Mr Levi Strauss made it world-famous. These days, the town has a relaxed charm, and, with an excellent hostel as well, makes for a good place to relax for a few days.

WHAT TO SEE AND DO

The old centre of Nîmes spreads northwards from place des Arènes, site of the magnificent first-century Les Arènes (daily 9/9.30am–5/6/7pm; €7.80), one of the best-preserved Roman arenas in the world. Turned into a fortress by the Visigoths while the Roman Empire crumbled, the arena went on to become a huge medieval slum before it was fully restored. Now, with a retractable roof, it hosts opera, an international summer jazz festival and bullfights during the high-spirited Ferías on Pentecost and the third weekend of September. Another Roman survivor can be found northeast along boulevard Victor Hugo – **La Maison Carrée** (daily: April–Sept 10am–6.30/7pm; Oct–March 10am–4.30/6pm; €4.80), a compact temple built in 5 AD and celebrated for its harmony of proportion – the entrance price includes a 3-D film about Roman Nîmes.

ARRIVAL AND DEPARTURE

By plane The airport is 8km to the south, accessible by *navettes* leaving from av Feuchères, in front of the bus and train stations.

By bus and train Nîmes' adjacent bus and train stations are at the end of av Feuchères, a short walk southeast from the amphitheatre. Regional buses leave from bays situated at the rear.

Destinations Arles (6 daily; 25min); Avignon (16 daily; 30min); Clermont-Ferrand (3 daily; 5hr); Lyon (9 daily; 1hr 20min); Marseille (14 daily; 50min–1hr 20min); Montpellier (frequent; 30min); Nice (6 daily, via Marseille; 4–5hr); Paris (11 daily; 3hr); Perpignan (13 daily; 2hr 10min–2hr 40min).

INFORMATION

Tourist information Tourist office on 6 rue Auguste, by the Maison Carrée (Mon–Sat 8.30/9am–6.30/7/8pm, Sun 10am–5/6pm; @04 66 58 38 00, @ot-nimes.fr); buy the monument and museum pass (€11) here, which gives access to the town's attractions for three days.

Internet Nîmes Internet Centre, 4 rue des Greffes (Mon–Fri 10am–10pm, Sun 3–10pm; €3/hr).

ACCOMMODATION

Acanthe du Temple 1 rue Charles Babut @04 66 67 54 61, @hotel-temple.com. The rooms are basic but it's the service provided by owner Eric (who speaks English) that makes this place the pleasure that it is. Double €62

Cesar 17 av Feuchéres @04 66 29 29 90, @hotel-nimes .net. A fine choice, 2min from the station, and with some rooms overlooking the elegant Av Feuchéres. Check your room first as some look onto a fire escape. Double €55

★ **FUAJ Nîmes** 257 chemin de l'Auberge de Jeunesse, Cigale @04 66 68 03 20, @fuaj.org; bus #i (Alès or Villeverte direction) from the station to Stade. In a beautiful hillside arboretum, 2km west of Nîmes, this friendly, well-equipped hostel offers modern two-, four- or six-bed dorms and camping within their picturesque grounds. Dorm €15.55, double €36, camping €7.05 per person and tent

EATING AND DRINKING

★ **À la Tchatche** 4 rue Saint-Antoine. A wonderful *bistrot à vins* with a young, convivial owner fiercely proud of

11

11

the local provenance of all his produce, not least his mother's cured duck (€6.50). The *champignons à la brandade* (€4.50) are superb, as is the *pélardon* cheese with herbed honey (€6). Wed–Sat 10am–3pm & 6pm–1am.

Halles Auberge Central Halles. A popular counter bar in the bustling halles. Watch as the chefs prepare bold regional dishes such as *coeur de canard au balsamique* (€7.50). Tues–Fri 10.30am–2pm, Sat & Sun 10.30am–2.30pm.

Le Ciel de Nimes Third Floor, Carré d'Art ☎ 04 66 36 71 70. This rooftop bar/restaurant offers fantastic new perspectives of La Maison Carée from above. As dusk falls enjoy a cocktail (€6.90) and the spectacular views from the terrace. Tues–Sun 10am–6pm, Fri & Sat 7.30pm–1am.

Le Petit Mas Corner of rue Fresque and rue de la Madeleine ☎ 04 66 36 84 25. Generous salads are the thing at this buzzing little spot. The €13.50 midday *formule* of tapas and a *plat du jour* or salad is excellent value. Mon–Sat 11am–3pm & 6.30pm–1am.

Maison Villaret 13 rue de la Madelaine. Since its foundation in 1775, this beautiful family bakery has become renowned for its trademark *croquant Villaret*, a small, almond-flavoured biscuit, now a city speciality. Mon–Sat 7am–7.30pm & Sun 8am–7pm.

Wine Bar "Le Cheval Blanc" 1 place des Arènes. With a terrace overlooking the arena this Parisian-brasserie-style place is perfect for a tipple. The €12.50 lunch menu is excellent value. Mon–Sat noon–2pm & 7–11pm/midnight.

ARLES

ARLES is a lovely, relaxed little Provençal town, steeped in Roman history. In 1888, Vincent Van Gogh was drawn in by the picturesque town, where he painted *Starry Night* and *Night Café*, but also got into a drunken argument with Gauguin and cut off the lower part of his left ear. Today Arles, as home to the École Nationale de Photographie and host to the summer photographic **festival**, Les Rencontres (July to mid-Sept; ⓦ rencontres-arles.com), is the centre of French photography.

WHAT TO SEE AND DO

The focal point for tourists in Arles is the striking **amphitheatre** (Arènes), at the end of rue Voltaire (daily: May–Sept 9am–7pm; Oct, March & April 9am–6pm; Nov–Feb 10am–5pm; €6), built at the end of the first century. The surrounding Rond-Point des Arènes is

crammed full of touristy shops, cafés and restaurants, and can get very crowded on summer days. No original Van Gogh paintings remain in Arles, but the Fondation Van Gogh – which moved in 2010 from the Palais de Luppé to a temporary space at 17 rue des Suisses before moving again in spring 2012 to a new permanent home at the Hôtel Léautaud de Donines (5 place Honoré Clair) – exhibits works based on his masterpieces by well-known contemporary artists such as Hockney and Bacon. On place de la République you'll find the **Cathédrale St-Trophime**, whose doorway is one of the most famous examples of twelfth-century Provençal carving, depicting a Last Judgement trumpeted by rather enthusiastic angels.

Cirque Romain

The best insight into Roman Arles is at the **Musée de l'Arles Antique** (Mon & Wed–Sun 10am–6pm; €6), west of the town centre, by the river. The fabulous mosaics, sarcophagi and sculpture illuminate Arles' early history.

Place Constantin

Housed in a splendid medieval building once used by the Knights of the Order of Malta, the **Musée Réattu** (10 rue du Grand Prieuré; Tues–Sun 11am–7pm; €8; ⓦ museereattu.arles.fr) hosts a fine collection of modern art, including sketches and sculptures by Picasso. Opposite are the remains of the fourth-century **Roman baths** (daily: March & April 9am–noon & 2–6pm; May–Sept 9am–noon & 2–7pm; Oct 9am–noon & 2–6pm; Nov–Feb 1–5pm; €3).

ARRIVAL AND INFORMATION

By train The train station is 5min walk from the amphitheatre on av Paulin.

Destinations Avignon (11–16 daily; 20min–1hr); Lyon (7–9 daily; 2hr 20min–2hr 55min); Marseille (15–20 daily; 45min–1hr); Montpellier (15–20 daily; 55min); Nîmes (8–11 daily; 25min).

Tourist information The main tourist office is located opposite rue Jean Jaurès on bd des Lices (Jan–March, May & Dec Mon–Sat 9am–4.45pm, Sun 10am–1pm; Oct Mon–Sat 9am–6.45pm; April–Sept Mon–Sat 9am–5.45pm, Sun 10am–1pm; ☎ 04 90 18 41 20,

THE CARRIÈRES DE LUMIÈRES

Just outside of Les Baux-de-Provence, a fortified village 15km northeast of Arles, lie some bauxite quarries that have been turned into a unique audiovisual experience called the **Carrières de Lumières** (daily: April–Sept 10am–6pm; Oct–March 10am–5pm; €8.50; ☎04 90 54 47 37, ⓦ carrieres-lumieres.com). Vast images are projected onto the floors, ceilings and walls of this cavernous quarry to the accompaniment of music, giving a unique resonance within the space. Wandering through these vast spaces and enveloped within a spectacular shifting projection of colours and shapes is a mind-blowing experience. Ligne 59 bus (6 daily, 7.45am–6.15pm; 35min; €2.20) departs from Arles' train station to Les Baux-de-Provence village from where it is a short walk to the quarries.

ⓦ arlestourisme.com), and provides a hotel booking service. There's also a handy tourist office in the train station (April–Sept daily 10am–1pm & 3–7pm).
Internet Cyber City, 31 rue Voltaire (Mon–Sat 7am–10pm, Sun 9am–1pm; €3/hr).

ACCOMMODATION

De la Muette 15 rue des Suisses ☎04 90 96 15 39, ⓦ hotel-muette.com. A bargain slap-bang in the centre of the old town, and recently refurbished as well – all cool greys and browns with bare stone walls. Double €65
Du Musée 11 rue du Grand Prieuré ☎04 90 93 88 88, ⓦ hoteldumusee.com. A stylish hotel in a seventeenth-century building with some rooms (some more spacious than others) looking onto a delightful inner courtyard. Double €65
FUAJ Arles 20 av du Maréchal-Foch ☎04 90 96 18 25, ⓦ fuaj.org. The somewhat old-fashioned dorms are clean and airy, and there's a bar on site. Often gets overrun with noisy school kids, but the location is good – just 5min from town and a 15min walk from the station. Closed 10am–5pm. Dorm €19.10
Le Régence 5 rue Marius Jouveau ☎04 90 96 39 85, ⓦ hotel-regence.com. In the heart of the old district and within a 5min walk of the station. Rooms are clean and bright with some overlooking the tranquil Rhône River. Bike rental is available. Double €55

EATING AND DRINKING

Café la Nuit 11 Place du Forum. The café immortalised in Van Gogh's *Café Terrace at Night*, this remains *the* spot to

enjoy this pretty Roman *place*. Fine for a drink but avoid the poor, overpriced food. Daily 8am–11pm.
Cuisine de Comptoir 10 rue Liberté. A simple, stylish place serving up excellent *tartines* on fine *poilâne* bread (€10–15). It's no sandwich bar, though – served with soup (often gazpacho) and salad, they're worth savouring with a glass of wine. Mon–Sat 9.30am–2.30am & 7pm–midnight.
La Fee Gourmande 39 rue Dulau ☎04 90 18 26 57. A friendly, unpretentious establishment with menus and *plats* from €13. Excellent home cooking is offered, with melt-in-your-mouth slow-cooked lamb the house speciality. Wed–Sun noon–1.30pm & 7.30–9.30pm.
Le 16 16 rue du Dr-Fanton ☎04 90 93 77 36. A traditional little bistro serving a good-value lunch *formule* at €14.50 and dinner *formule* at €19. Mon–Fri noon–1.45pm & 7–9.30pm, Sat noon–1.45pm.

THE CAMARGUE

The flat, marshy delta immediately south of Arles – **the Camargue** – is a beautiful area, used as a breeding ground for the bulls that participate in local *corridas* (bullfights), and the white horses ridden by their herdsmen. The wildlife of the area also includes flamingos, marsh birds

★ TREAT YOURSELF

Le Calendal Hotel 5 rue Porte de Laure ☎04 90 96 11 89, ⓦ lecalendal.com. Mere steps from Arles' amphitheatre, this sunny hotel is a great choice if you feel like splashing out. Rooms are bright and decorated in traditional Provençal colours without being twee; all are en suite, with air conditioning and satellite television. The real selling point is the gorgeous garden at the back. Prices occasionally include use of the Roman baths-inspired spa – check ahead. Double €129

VAN GOGH'S ARLES

The tourist office (see opposite) issues a good booklet of themed **walking tours** in Arles (€1). The best of these is the Van Gogh trail which, by following various markers on the pavements, takes you to the sites of his most famous paintings – it's fascinating to see how the town has changed since he was here.

11

and sea birds, and a rich flora of reeds, wild flowers and juniper trees. The only town is **SAINTES-MARIES-DE-LA-MER**, best known for the annual Gypsy Festival held each May. It's a pleasant if touristy place, with some fine sandy beaches. If you're interested in birdwatching or touring the lagoons, your first port of call should be the tourist office (see below).

ARRIVAL AND INFORMATION

By bus Buses arrive and depart from bd Georges Clemenceau in Saintes-Maries-de-la-Mer. Destinations Arles (5–7 daily; 1hr).

Tourist information The tourist office at 5 av Van Gogh, Saintes-Maries-de-la-Mer (daily: July & Aug 9am–8pm; Sept–June 9am–5/7pm; ☎04 90 97 82 55, ⓦ saintesmaries.com), can tell you where to rent bicycles, horses or 4WDs, if you prefer to explore the delta alone.

AVIGNON

AVIGNON, great city of the popes and for centuries one of the major artistic centres of France, is today one of the country's biggest tourist attractions and is always crowded in summer. It's worth putting up with the inevitable queues and camera-wielding hordes to enjoy the unique stock of monuments, churches and museums of this immaculately preserved medieval town. During the **Avignon festival** in July (see box, p.328), it's the only place to be – around 200,000 spectators come here for the show, though, so doing any normal sightseeing becomes virtually impossible.

WHAT TO SEE AND DO

Central Avignon is enclosed by thick medieval walls, built by one of the nine popes who based themselves here in the fourteenth century, away from the anarchic feuding and rival popes of Rome. Place de l'Horloge is lined with cafés and market stalls on summer evenings, beyond which towers the enormous **Palais des Papes** (daily: March–June 9/9.30am–6.30/7pm; July & Aug 9am–8/8.30pm; Sept–Nov 9am–7pm; Nov–Feb 9.30am–5.45pm; €10.50, joint ticket with Pont St-Bénézet €15). Save your money, though: the

denuded interior gives little indication of the richness of the papal court, although the building is impressive for sheer size alone. The nearby **Musée du Petit Palais** (Mon & Wed–Sun 10am–1pm & 2–6pm; €6) houses a collection of religious art from the thirteenth to sixteenth centuries. Jutting out halfway across the river is the famous **Pont St-Bénézet** (also known as Pont d'Avignon; same hours as Palais des Papes; €3.50). The struggle to keep the bridge in good repair against the ravages of the Rhône was finally abandoned in 1660, three and a half centuries after it was built, and today just four of the original 22 arches survive.

On the south side of the city, the wonderful private collection of Jacques Doucet is on display at the **Musée Anglandon-Dubrujeaud**, 5 rue Laboureur (April–Nov Tues–Sun 1–6pm; Nov–March Wed–Sun 1–6pm; €6). The former home of museum founders Jean-Angladon Dubrujeaud and his wife Paulette Martin Avignon, it now houses some important pieces by Degas, Cézanne, Picasso, Modigliani and the only painting by Van Gogh displayed in Provence.

ARRIVAL AND DEPARTURE

By train Avignon's main train station is opposite the porte de la République on bd St-Roch, just 5min from the central place de l'Horloge. A regular shuttle bus (2–4 hourly; 13min; €1.20; ⓦ tcrf.com) runs to the separate TGV station, 3km to the southeast, from just inside porte de la République.

Destinations from Gare SNCF Arles (frequent; 20–40min); Lyon (10 daily; 2hr 20min); Nîmes (15 daily; 20–40min); Toulouse (11 daily, 8 via Nîmes or Montpellier; 3hr 10min–4hr 30min).

Destinations from Gare TGV Lyon (2 hourly; 1hr 5min–1hr 30min); Nice (12 daily; 3hr–4hr 10min); Paris (15 daily; 2hr 40min–3hr 30min).

INFORMATION

Tourist information The tourist office at 1 cours Jean-Jaurès (April–Oct Mon–Sat 9am–6pm, Sun 10am–5pm; Nov–March Mon–Fri 9am–6pm, Sat 9am–5pm, Sun 10am–noon; ☎04 32 74 32 74, ⓦ avignon-tourisme.com) has an accommodation booking service and offers English-language tours.

Internet Cybert Média at 22 rue Portail Matheron

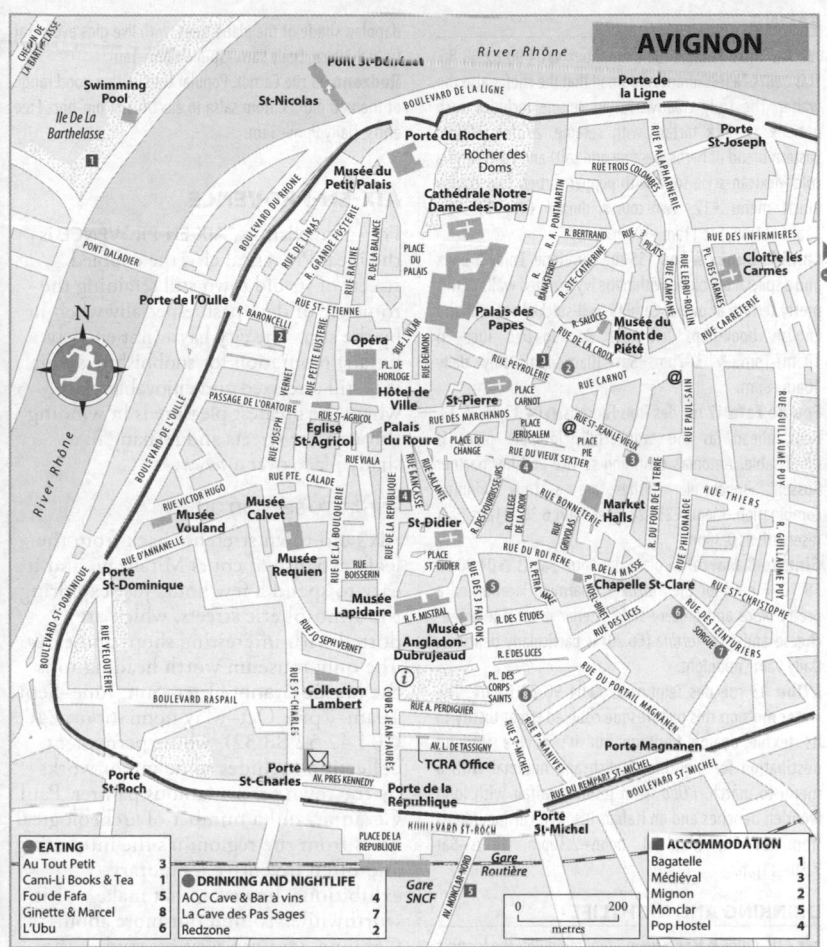

AVIGNON

● EATING	
Au Tout Petit	3
Cami-Li Books & Tea	1
Fou de Fafa	5
Ginette & Marcel	8
L'Ubu	6

● DRINKING AND NIGHTLIFE	
AOC Cave & Bar à vins	4
La Cave des Pas Sages	7
Redzone	2

■ ACCOMMODATION	
Bagatelle	1
Médiéval	3
Mignon	2
Monclar	5
Pop Hostel	4

(daily: Jan–July & Sept–Dec 9.30am–11pm; Aug 10am–9pm; €3/hr).

ACCOMMODATION

Bagatelle 25 allée Antoine-Pinay ☎ 04 90 86 30 39, ⓦ campingbagatelle.com. A 20min walk from the station, this is the nearest campsite to town, with an adjoining hostel offering small, clean dorms and some private rooms. The on-site bar and restaurant have the feel of an old-fashioned holiday camp. Camping €18.51 per person and tent, dorm €19.90, double €37

Médiéval 15 rue Petite-Saunerie ☎ 04 90 86 11 06, ⓦ hotelmedieval.com. A former aristocratic townhouse with a grand staircase. Though the decor is a little tired, it's kept very clean and the studios are good value for longer stays. Double €73

Mignon 12 rue Joseph Vernet ☎ 04 90 82 17 30, ⓦ hotel-mignon.com. Rooms decked out in Provençal colours, all with satellite TV, a/c and wi-fi. Breakfast is included and can be enjoyed in your room for no extra charge. Double €62

Monclar 13–15 av Monclar ☎ 04 90 86 20 14, ⓦ hotel-monclar.com. An attractive eighteenth-century house with a pleasant garden, situated outside the town walls, close to the train station. Rooms are clean and bright and there's free internet access. Double €62

Pop Hostel 17 rue de la République ☎ 04 32 40 50 60, ⓦ pophostel.fr. Behind the nineteenth-century façade of this high-quality hostel lie stylish, inviting rooms and a smart bar/lounge. Dorms are 4-, 6- or 8-bed with shared bathrooms, and there are also doubles and private dorms for 3 or 5 people. Dorm €14, private dorm €20, double €25

11

EATING

★ **Au Tout Petit** 4 rue d'Amphoux ☎ 04 90 82 38 86. This gem of a restaurant is so small that the chef is also the waiter. The truly creative fusion cuisine includes such options as duck tartare with sesame, za'atar (Middle Eastern blend of herbs, sesame and salt) and curry, and a cold Mexican-style soup with pepper sorbet. Two-course lunch menu €12, two-course dinner €16. Tues–Fri 11am–11pm, Sat 11am–10pm.

Cami-Li Books & Tea 155 rue Carreterie. Enjoy a book and a special tea blend within the ivy-covered walls of this pretty terrace at owner Camili's well-stocked secondhand English bookshop. Jan–June & Aug–Dec Tues–Fri 10am–1pm & 3–7pm, Sat 10am–4pm; July daily 10am–8pm.

Fou de Fafa 17 rue des Trois Faucons ☎ 04 32 76 35 13. Book ahead, as this wonderfully intimate place is unmissable. Antonia's charming service and her partner Russell's spectacular dishes are a truly winning combination. Menu €23–28. Tues–Sun 6.30–11pm (last reservations 9.30pm).

Ginette & Marcel 25 place des Corps Saints ☎ 04 90 85 58 70. Famed for their tartines, charming location on a pretty place and grocery-style interior decor. The three-cheese-and-pear tartine (€6.20) is particularly delicious. Daily 9am–midnight.

L'Ubu 13 rue des Teinturiers ☎ 04 90 80 01 01. The water mills on this picturesque cobbled street testify to its textile dyeing heritage but it's now a thriving destination for nightlife. Stylish and minimal with a menu to match, L'Ubu is an intimate affair with long wooden benches and an Italian-inspired cuisine. Mains from €12.50. Mon–Fri noon–2.30pm, Thurs–Sat 7.30–11pm.

DRINKING AND NIGHTLIFE

★ **AOC Cave & Bar à vins** 5 rue Trémoulet. The friendly staff will guide you through the selection of over 150 wines, much of which is the local Côtes du Rhône (from €2.50 a glass). Tues–Fri noon–2pm & 6pm–1am, Sat 6pm–1am.

La Cave des Pas Sages 41 rue des Teinturiers. A happening little bar where you can hang out beneath the dappled shade of the plane trees, with live gigs every Sat from 8.30pm. Daily 9am–3pm & 6pm–1am.

Redzone 25 rue Carnot. Popular club, with a good range of themed nights, from salsa to electro and hip-hop. Free entry. Daily 9pm–3am.

AIX-EN-PROVENCE

For many visitors, **AIX-EN-PROVENCE** is the ideal Provençal city, the cobbled streets of its old town still retaining the romance of days past, especially when lit by the sun. The city has a (not entirely unfair) reputation for snobbishness, but it is still a relaxed and enjoyable place, where the greatest pleasure is in winding through the streets and relaxing in a shady place over a *pastis*.

WHAT TO SEE AND DO

Aix's old town stretches back from the leafy expanse of cours Mirabeau, and it's easy to spend a few hours just exploring the atmospheric streets, which are dotted with interesting shops and cafés. The only museum worth heading to is the **Musée Granet** (Tues–Sun: June–Sept 10am–7pm; Oct–May noon–6pm; €4; ☎04 42 52 88 32), whose permanent collection includes some minor works by the town's most famous painter, Paul Cézanne, and a number of archeological finds from the region; it's the interesting and often inventive temporary exhibitions, however, that make a visit worthwhile. To find out more about Cézanne, you can visit his studio, the **Atelier Cézanne** (daily: April–June & Sept 10am–noon & 2–6pm; July & Aug 10am–6pm; Oct–March 10am–noon & 2–6pm; €5.50; ☎04 42 21 06 53, ⓦatelier-cezanne.com), a ten-minute walk from the north end of the Vieille

---

AVIGNON FESTIVAL

During Avignon's three-week July **festival** (☎04 90 27 66 50, ⓦfestival-avignon.com), over one hundred venues show multiple plays every day, alongside opera, classical music and film. The most popular aspect of the festival is probably the **street performers** – musicians, magicians, dancers, jugglers, clowns, artists and mime acts – who bring great colour and noise to the city. Make sure you book your hotel early.

   The biggest fringe festival in the world, **Le Festival Off**, runs simultaneously, comprising hundreds of independent companies and representing the very best of cutting-edge fringe theatre and performance (ⓦavignonleoff.com).

PASS CÉZANNE

A **Pass Cézanne** (€15; available April–Oct) is worth considering if you're visiting all of the sites related to the painter.

Ville; it looks exactly the same as it did at the time of his death. There are also weather-dependent tours available (bookable in advance at tourist office) to the Carrières de Bibemus, a wild, colourful landscape where the painter spent a great deal of time between 1895 and 1904.

ARRIVAL AND DEPARTURE

By train The SNCF station is located on rue Gustave-Desplaces, just 5min southwest of the old town. It's more likely that you'll arrive at the TGV station, 8km southwest of Aix and linked by regular *navette* (every 30min; 15min; €3.80) to the *gare routière* on av de l'Europe.
Destinations from Gare SNCF Marseille (every 20min; 30–45min).
Destinations from Gare TGV Avignon (22 daily; 20min); Lyon (20 daily; 1hr 30min); Marseille (frequent; 15min); Paris (12 daily; 3hr).

INFORMATION

Tourist information The tourist office at 300 av Giuseppe Verdi, just west of Place du General du Gaulle (June–Sept Mon–Sat 8.30am–8pm, Sun 10am–1pm & 2–6pm; Oct–May Mon–Sat 8.30am–7pm, Sun 10am–1pm & 2–6pm; 04 42 16 11 61, aixenprovencetourism.com). Offers a hotel booking service and arranges tours to Cézanne's home (€5.50).
Pass Aix Pays d'Aix Offering excellent value, this €2 pass provides discounted admission to the principal museums, plus half-price guided tours and reduced rates at wineries.
Internet Netgames, rue de l'Aumone Vielle (Mon–Sat 11am–midnight, Sun 2–10pm; €2/hr).

AIX STREET MARKETS

You cannot visit Aix and miss the colourful, vibrant **street markets** with which the town is synonymous. Held all year round, three times a week on Tuesdays, Thursdays and Saturdays, the flower market opposite the town hall, the antiques market on Place de Verdun and the farmers' market on Place Richelme are particularly unmissable.

ACCOMMODATION

Auberge de Jeunesse 3 av Marcel Pagnol 04 42 20 15 99, auberge-jeunesse-aix.fr; bus #4 from the *gare routière* to Vasarely. Situated 2km out of the city, offering modern dorms, a bar with cheap beers and inclusive breakfast. No communal kitchen facilities. Closed 2–4.30pm. Dorm €21.10, double €23
Hôtel Paul 10 av Pasteur 04 42 23 23 89, aix-en-provence.com/hotelpaul. A good budget option a 10min walk from the centre, with basic clean rooms, albeit rather tired. No credit cards accepted and expensive wi-fi and parking charges. Double €55
Le Manoir 8 rue d'Entrecasteaux 04 42 26 27 20, hotelmanoir.com. Centrally located but feels tucked away with an olde-worlde grandness that is very appealing. Bright, spacious rooms furnished in the Provençal style. Breakfast is served in the fourteenth-century cloister. Double €77

EATING AND DRINKING

Bar Brigand Place Richelme (Place des Sangliers). A satisfyingly grungy little pub so beloved of the town's hipsters they spill out onto the street, especially during happy hour (daily 6.30–8.30pm; pint €3.50). Mon–Sat 11.30am–2am, Sun 6pm–2am.
La Calèche 10 rue de la Masse. The menu is wide-ranging but really it's all about the excellent pizza here, with bases singed just-so in the wood-fired oven (€10–13). Daily noon–3pm & 7pm–midnight.
Le Bouddoir Place des Tanneurs. A lovely place for a coffee on this little terrace beside a tinkling fountain. Come evening it livens up and makes a perfect spot to enjoy one of their cocktails (€6.90). Mon–Sat 9am–2am, Sun 4–11pm.

MARSEILLE

France's second most populous city, **MARSEILLE** has been a major centre of international maritime trade ever since it was founded by Greek colonists 2600 years ago. Like the capital, the city has suffered plagues, religious bigotry, republican and royalist terror, had its own Commune and Bastille-storming, and it was the presence of so many revolutionaries from this city marching to Paris in 1792 that gave the name Marseillaise to the national anthem. A working city with little of the glamour of its ritzy Riviera neighbours, it is nevertheless a vibrant, exciting place, with a cosmopolitan population including many Italians and North Africans.

11

The old harbour, or **Vieux Port**, is the hub of the town and a good place to indulge in the sedentary pleasure of observing the city's street life over a *pastis*. Two fortresses guard the entrance to the harbour and the town extends outwards alongside the harbour from its three quais.

Musée des Civilisations d'Europe et de la Méditerranée (MuCEM)

One of two fortresses guarding the harbour entrance, medieval Fort St-Jean, has been converted (with the addition of a modernist annexe) by Algerian-born architect Rudy Ricciotti into the **Musée des Civilisations d'Europe et de la Méditerranée** or **MuCEM** for short (Mon & Wed–Sun: May–Oct 11am–7pm, Fri till 10pm; Nov–April 11am–6pm, Fri till 10pm; €5, €8 incl temp exhibition; ⓦmucem.org). With an enormous collection totalling a million works, and encompassing a broad range of disciplines including archeology, art history, sociology, religion and more, the museum transcends national boundaries to trace the important phases of Mediterranean civilization and culture through a series of permanent and temporary exhibitions.

There is a 115m-long bridge joining the fort to the new annexe, and a second bridge connecting the port and the church of St Laurent in the Panier district, linking the oldest parts of the city with the newly rejuvenated docklands.

LE CORBUSIER

If you're interested in architecture, it's definitely worth taking the short bus journey out to Le Corbusier's **La Cité Radieuse**. Completed in 1952, this seventeen-storey block of flats is surprisingly striking even today, and you can take the lift up to the rooftop to enjoy fantastic views of the city and the surrounding area. You can even enjoy a drink while you're here (see p.333). Take bus #21 from Centre Bourse to the Le Corbusier stop.

Villa Méditerranée

Next to the MuCEM the spectacular **Villa Méditerranée** (Tues–Thurs noon–7pm, Fri noon–10pm, Sat & Sun 10am–7pm; ⓦvilla-mediterranee.org), designed by the Italian architect Stegano Boeri, is a new venue for exhibitions and events dedicated to the opening of dialogue between Mediterranean nations. There is an exciting programme of screenings, concerts, exhibitions and conferences; see website for details.

Euroméditerranée

The focus of the city's long-term regeneration plans is concentrated around the formerly industrial dockland area north of the Vieux Port, rechristened Euroméditerranée. These ambitious redevelopment plans are currently transforming the hitherto neglected area surrounding the **Cathédrale de la Major** (Tues–Sat 10am–7pm), an imposing nineteenth-century structure overlooking the modern docks. The vast J1 Hangar, converted from a former ferry terminal, is currently used as a commercial space with bars, restaurants and a gallery, but its future is far from certain. South from the cathedral on avenue de la Tourette sits a low modernist structure built in 1948, formerly a sanitary station used to screen newly arrived immigrants, and now the home of the **Musée Regards de Provence** (Mon–Thurs, Sat & Sun 10am–6pm, Fri 10am–9pm; €6). The museum houses the Fondation Regards de Provence's 850-strong collection of art from, and about, Provence, as well as frequent temporary exhibitions and a permanent exhibition telling the compelling story of the building and its role in the lives of immigrants entering the city.

Le Panier

On the northern side of the harbour is the original site and former old town of Marseille, known as **Le Panier**. During the occupation, large sections were dynamited by the Nazis to prevent resistance members hiding in the small,

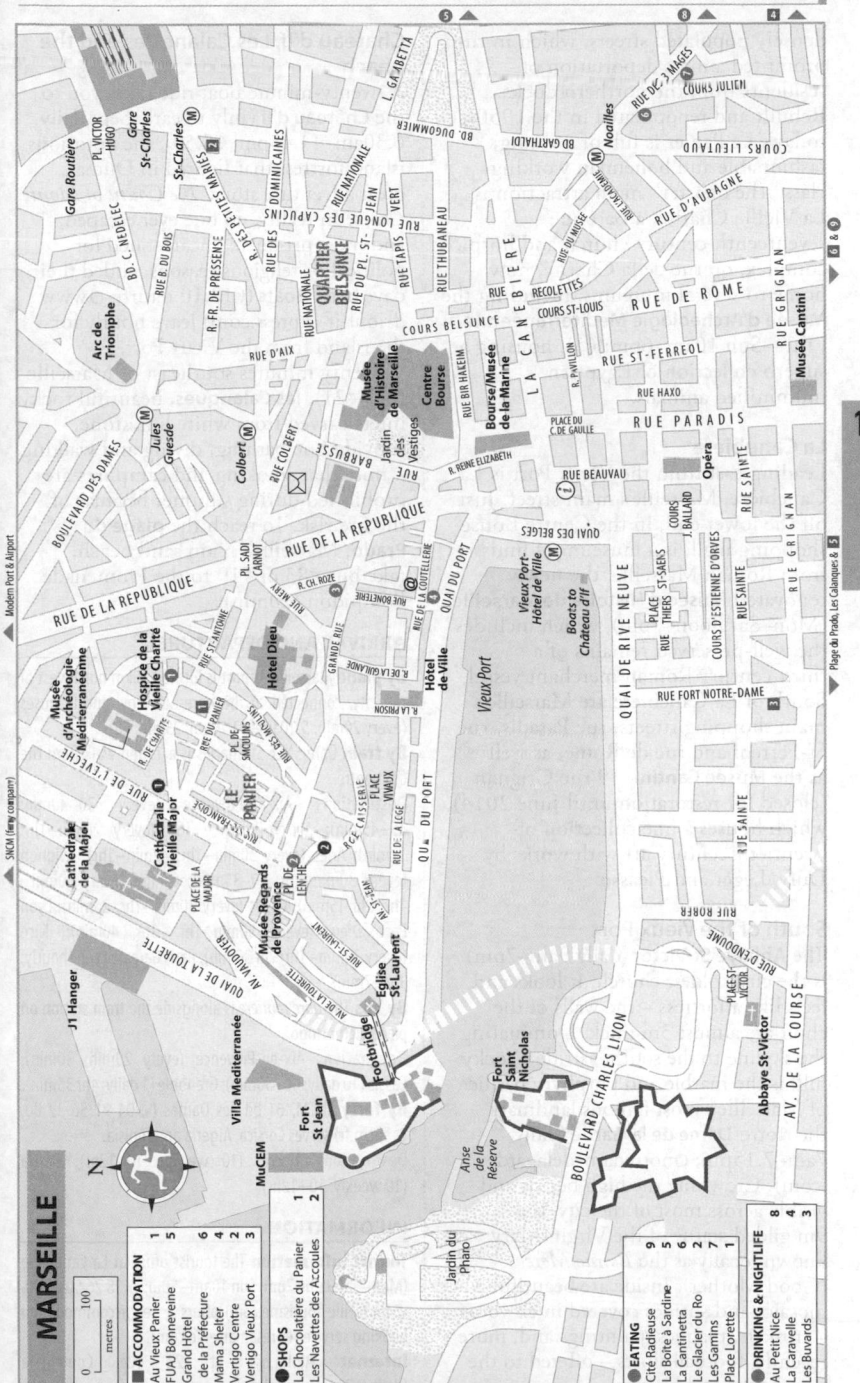

MARSEILLE

0   100
metres

■ ACCOMMODATION
Au Vieux Panier   1
FUAJ Bonneveine   5
Grand Hôtel
de la Préfecture   6
Mama Shelter   4
Vertigo Centre   2
Vertigo Vieux Port   3

● SHOPS
La Chocolatière du Panier   1
Les Navettes des Accoules   2

● EATING
Cité Radieuse   9
La Boîte à Sardine   5
La Cantinetta   6
Le Glacier du Ro   7
Les Gamins   2
Place Lorette   1

● DRINKING & NIGHTLIFE
Au Petit Nice   8
La Caravelle   4
Les Buvards   3

11

11

densely populated streets, which in turn prompted a mass deportation of residents from the northern docks. Rebuilt and repopulated in the 1950s, today's Le Panier is full of a young, fashionable and bohemian working class. The quarter's main attraction is La Vieille Charité, a Baroque seventeenth-century church and hospice complex, on rue de la Charité, now home to several museums, including the **Musée d'Archéologie Méditerranéenne** (Tues–Sun 10am–6pm; €5), housing a superb collection of Egyptian mummified animals.

La Canebière

Leading east from the Vieux Port is La Canebière, Marseille's main street. Just off the lower end, in the Centre Bouse shopping mall, is a museum of finds from Roman Marseille, the newly renovated **Musée d'Histoire de Marseille** (Mon–Sat noon–7pm), which includes the well-preserved remains of a third-century Roman merchant vessel. South of La Canebière are Marseille's main shopping streets, rue Paradis, rue St-Ferréol and rue de Rome, as well as the **Musée Cantini**, 19 rue Grignan (closed for restoration until June 2014), which houses a fine collection of twentieth-century art with works by Dufy, Léger and Picasso.

South of the Vieux Port

The **Abbaye St-Victor** (daily 9am–7pm) is the city's oldest church. It looks and feels like a fortress – the walls of the choir are almost 3m thick. Dominating the skyline to the south, astride a rocky hill, is the marble and porphyry basilica of Marseille's most famous landmark, the **Notre-Dame de la Garde** (daily 7am–7.15pm; ⍟notredamedelagarde .com). Crowning the high belfry, and visible across most of the city, is a 9m gilded statue of the Virgin Mary, known locally as the *Bonne Mère* (Good Mother). Inside are beautiful mosaics and shrines covered in ex-votos – trinkets, plaques, paintings and, more recently, football shirts – offered to the Saints for good luck.

Chateau d'If, Les Calanques and the beach

A twenty-minute boat ride takes you to the **Château d'If** (July to early Sept daily 6.30am–11.45pm; €5.50), the notorious island fortress that figured in Dumas' great adventure story, *The Count of Monte Cristo*. In reality, no one ever escaped, and most prisoners, incarcerated for political or religious reasons, ended their days here. **Boats** (€10.10 return; ⍟www .frioul-if-express.com) leave hourly for the island from the Vieux Port.

Twenty minutes southeast of Marseille (bus #21), **les Calanques**, beautiful rocky inlets carved from white limestone, provide fine bathing, diving and walking – note that smoking and campfires are prohibited during summer because of the fire risk. To reach the **plage du Prado**, Marseille's main sand beach, take bus #83 or #19 to the Promenade Pompidou (20min).

ARRIVAL AND DEPARTURE

By plane Marseille Airport is located 20km northwest of the city, connected to the gare SNCF by shuttle buses (every 20min, 5.10am–12.10am; 25min; €8).

By train Gare SNCF St-Charles is a 15min walk from the city centre.

Destinations Aix-en-Provence (every 30–40min; 35–45min); Aix-en-Provence TGV (every 20min–1hr; 12min); Arles (every 30min–1hr; 42min–1hr); Avignon (every 30min–1hr; 30–35min); Cannes (every 30min–1hr; 2hr 15min); Cassis (every 30min–1hr; 25min); Lyon Part Dieu (every 30min–1hr; 1hr 40min); Nice (every 30min–1hr; 2hr 30min); Paris Gare de Lyon (hourly; 3hr 17min).

By bus The *gare routière* is alongside the train station at place Victor Hugo.

Destinations Aix-en-Provence (every 20min; 30min); Cassis (10 daily; 40–50min); Grenoble (1 daily; 4hr 35min).

By ferry SNCM, 61 bd des Dames (☎04 91 56 32 00, ⍟sncm.fr) serves Corsica, Algeria and Tunisia.

Destinations Ajaccio (10 weekly; 10–12hr); Bastia (10 weekly; 10–12hr).

INFORMATION

Tourist information The tourist office at La Canebière (Mon–Sat 9am–7pm, Sun 10am–5pm; ☎08 26 50 05 00, ⍟marseille-tourisme.com) offers a free accommodation booking service (⍟resamarseille.com).

Internet Alpha.net at 22 rue Coutellerie (daily 7.30am–midnight).

GETTING AROUND

By public transport Marseille has an efficient public transport network (⦿rtm.fr). The metro runs Mon–Fri 5am–10.30pm, Sat & Sun till after midnight; trams run 5am to after midnight. *Solos* (single tickets; €1.50) can be used on journeys combining all three modes of transport if used within an hour; *cartes journées* (day passes; €5) can be bought from métro stations and on buses.

By bike Blue bicycles belonging to Le Vélo scheme (⦿levelo-mpm.fr) can be rented from 130 self-service rental points throughout the city using a bank card (€1 for 7-day membership; usage first 30min free, €1 for each additional 30min).

By ferry RTM runs a ferry between the Vieux Port and Pointe Rouge in the south of the city for easier access to the beaches and Les Calanques (daily every hour: March to mid-May 7am–7pm; mid-May to mid Sept 7am–10pm; €2.50).

ACCOMMODATION

FUAJ Bonneveine Impasse Dr Bonfils, off av Joseph Vidal ⦿04 91 17 63 30, ⦿fuaj.org; bus #44 to the Bonnefon stop. At 5km from the city, yet in a fantastic location near Les Calanques and just 200m from the beach, this is a brilliant hostel, with friendly staff and clean dorms (2–6 beds). Tours, sea kayaking and horseriding can be arranged, and there's a bar on site. Dorm €22

Grand Hôtel de la Préfecture 9 bv Louis Salvator ⦿04 91 33 99 81, ⦿hoteldelaprefecture.fr. A once-grand place with a rich history now providing bargain rooms just minutes from the Vieux Port. Double €44

Mama Shelter 63 rue de la Louhière ⦿04 84 35 20 00, ⦿mamashelter.com. Combining both luxury and practicality, a night at *Mama*'s includes a Mac TV, free

---

★ TREAT YOURSELF

Au Vieux Panier 13 rue du Panier ⦿06 32 19 90 05, ⦿auvieuxpanier.com. In the heart of the trendy Le Panier district and 500m from the Vieux Port, the rooms of this seventeenth-century, former Corsican grocery store have been transformed into ephemeral works of art. Each year a different artist is commissioned to design a room within the house, creating unique spaces each with a distinctive atmosphere, equipped with en-suite bathrooms and design touches. There is a lounge area and exhibition space, communal kitchen and a beautiful roof terrace offering spectacular views of the ocean and the landmarks of Marseilles. A truly spellbinding experience. Double €90

---

movies and a kitchenette. The lively terrace bar is so happening there's no need to leave – unless you wish to visit the private beach. Double €49

Vertigo Centre 42 rue Petits Mariés ⦿04 91 91 07 11, ⦿hotelvertigo.fr. Mere steps from the train station, this excellent hostel has bright, spacious dorms, all en suite, as well as a number of private rooms – the "deluxe" have private balconies. Staff are friendly and helpful, and there's a good kitchen, garden and a cheap bar. Dorm €25, double €65

Vertigo Vieux Port 38 rue Fort Notre Dame ⦿04 91 54 42 95, ⦿hotelvertigo.fr. A marvellous hostel spread across two former warehouses, each with quality modern art (all local commissions) on display. The communal spaces are very well conceived, the dorms are airy and breakfast is included. Dorm €25, double €65

EATING

Cité Radieuse 280 bd Michelet. Head to the third floor of Le Corbusier's magnificent apartment building (see box, p.330) and have a drink on the terrace of the retro-futuristic café. Tues–Sat noon–10pm.

La Boîte à Sardine 2 bd de la Liberation ⦿04 91 50 95 95, ⦿laboiteasardine.com. There's thankfully no tinned fish on the menu – rather, it depends on that morning's catch but usually includes 5–6 different fresh fish (€12–18), oysters and shellfish. Reservation essential. Tues–Sat 11am–3pm.

Le Glacier du Roi 4 place de Lenche. An artisan glacier with over 24 seasonal-based flavours. The *navettissimo* flavour is delicious – a blend of biscuit crumbs and orange flower water inspired by the traditional *navette* biscuits of Marseille. Two scoops €3.50. Tues–Sun 8.30am–7.30pm.

Les Gamins 11 cours Julien ⦿04 91 42 49 03. With its retro interior and stylish clientele it might appear all surface here, but the home-cooked ingredients suggest otherwise. The menu features ten different burgers, ranging from veggie to deluxe foie gras (€11–15). Tues–Sat noon–10.30pm.

Place Lorette 3 place de Lorette. Within stone-vaulted rooms, this Moroccan tea salon is elegantly furnished with traditional Moroccan textiles and furniture. Savour a pot of mint tea (€5) and pastry (€2) on the pretty terrace. Tues–Sun 11am–8pm.

★ TREAT YOURSELF

La Cantinetta 24 cours Julien ⦿04 91 48 10 48. Savour classic Italian dishes (€9–19) in the sun-dappled garden or the convivial dining room of this gregarious restaurant that's evocative of a huge Italian family reunion. Reservation essential. Tues–Sat noon–2pm & 8–10.45pm.

11

11

DRINKING AND NIGHTLIFE

Au Petit Nice 28 place Jean Jaurès. An institution among the locals for its cheap beer (€2) and constantly bustling terrace. It remains the spot to soak up the ambience of the Cours Julien district. Daily 10am–2am.

La Caravelle *Hotel Belle-Vue*, 34 Quai du Port. The balcony of this intimate tapas bar overlooking the Vieux Port is a majestic spot come evening. Aperitifs and free tapas are served 6–9pm with live jazz every Wed & Fri evening. Daily 7pm–1am.

Les Buvards 34 grand rue. This inviting wine bar is essential for sampling delicious organic wines (€3–4 per glass). Charismatic owner Frédéric Coachon will delight in sharing his knowledge and expertise. Mon–Sat 10am–1am.

SHOPPING

La Chocolatière du Panier 47 rue du Petit Puit. A beautiful old shop spanning three generations. With over 300 varieties on offer these seasonal creations are artisanal, inventive and delicious. Mon–Sat 10am–1pm & 2.30–6.30pm.

Les Navettes des Accoules 68 rue Caisserie. Renowned for their croquants, macaroons, canistrelli and of course the orange-flavoured *navette* biscuits which any self-respecting gourmet must sample. Mon–Sat 9am–7pm.

CANNES

Fishing village turned millionaires' playground, **CANNES** is best known for the International Film Festival, held in May, during which time it is overrun by the denizens of Movieland, their hangers-on and a small army of paparazzi. The seafront promenade, **La Croisette**, and the Vieux Port form the focus of Cannes' eye-candy life, while the old town, **Le Suquet**, on the steep hill overlooking the bay from the west, with its quaint winding streets and eleventh-century castle, is a pleasant place to wander.

ARRIVAL AND INFORMATION

By train The station is on rue Jean-Jaurès, a short walk north of the centre.

Destinations Marseille (frequent; 2hr); Monaco (frequent; 1hr–1hr 10min); Nice (frequent; 25–35min).

Tourist information The main tourist office is in the Palais des Festivals on the waterfront (daily 9/10am–7/8pm; ☎04 92 99 84 00, ⓦcannes.travel). There is also a booth at the station (Mon–Sat 9am–1pm & 2–6pm).

Internet Instant Photo, 11 rue Marechal Joffre (Mon–Sat 9.30am–1pm & 2.30–7pm; €3/hr).

ACCOMMODATION

Albe 31 rue du Bivouac Napoléon ☎04 97 06 21 21, ⓦalbe-hotel.fr. A good-value two-star with bright and clean, a/c rooms, just one street from the Palais and the beach. Double €69

Cybelle 14 rue du 24 août ☎04 93 38 31 33, ⓦhotelcybelle.fr. Excellent value considering the location and the price-hiking reputation of this town. The decor is by no means chic but rooms feel clean and crisp. Double €58

Parc Bellevue 67 av Maurice Chevalier ☎04 93 47 28 97, ⓦparcbellevue.com; bus #2 from the train station. The nearest campsite is in the suburb of La Bocca, 3km to the west of Cannes; most plots are shaded and there is a 40m pool. Camping €4 per person, plus €13.50 per tent

PLM 3 rue Hoche ☎04 93 38 31 19, ⓦhotel-cannes-plm .com. A comfortable little hotel close to the station and a short walk from the beachfront. Rooms are decorated in soothing, neutral colours and there's free wi-fi. Double €54

EATING AND DRINKING

Chez Vincent & Nicolas 90 rue Meynadier ☎04 93 68 35 39. An original choice, with flamboyant staff, inventive food and a lovely setting. Try the scallops wrapped in bacon; meat or fish mains start at around €16. Daily 6.30–11.30pm.

La Crêperie 66 rue Meynadier. Cheerful little crêperie with a good-value *menu* served all day: a savoury and a sweet crêpe, plus a glass of cider or wine for €11. Tues–Sat 10am–10pm.

Le Bistrot Gourmand 10 rue Docteur Pierre Gazagnaire. A couple of minutes northwest of the marina, this place offers film-star food on a budget – truffle-infused dishes are one of their hallmarks. *Formules* €15–29. Tues–Sat noon–2pm & 7–9.30pm, Sun noon–2pm.

Lemonot 12 rue Hélène Vagliano. A few minutes southeast of the train station, with fabulously fresh ingredients and excellent Lebanese *meze*. *Formules* €10–19. Tues–Sat 9am–8pm.

Morrison's Irish Pub 10 rue Teisseire. As is frequently the case in France, the most popular bar in town is Irish, and this down-to-earth place makes a pleasant change from Cannes' A-list ambience. Happy hour daily 5–8pm. Mon–Fri 5pm–2am, Sat & Sun 1pm–2am.

ANTIBES

The charming medieval town of **ANTIBES** has stupendous sea views shared by the Alps soaring majestically in the distance.

Only 11km east of Cannes and easily visited as a day trip, it has largely escaped the glitzy exclusivity and overdevelopment blighting so many neighbouring resorts, although the sea is still awash with millionaires' yachts.

WHAT TO SEE AND DO

The town's bustling streets are animated by many bars and restaurants, and there's a fine market selling fresh produce and local crafts (food June–Aug daily 6am–1pm; Sept–May Tues–Sun 6am–1pm; crafts mid-June to Sept Tues–Sun 3pm–midnight; Oct to mid-June Fri–Sun 3pm–midnight). Antibes also has an excellent **Picasso** collection on Place Mariejol where you can see some of his lesser-known works in beautiful surroundings (mid-June to mid-July Tues–Sun 10am–6pm; mid-July to Aug Tues, Thurs, Sat & Sun 10am–6pm, Wed & Fri 10am–8pm; mid-Sept to mid-June Tues–Sun 10am–noon & 2–6pm; €6; ☎04 92 90 54 20, ⬛antibes-juanlespins.com).

Antibes boasts some of the Riviera's most irresistible beaches – the long, sandy **Plage de la Salis** and the smaller **Plage de la Garoupe** are both free and unspoilt by big hotels.

ARRIVAL AND DEPARTURE

By train There are connections with Cannes (frequent; 7–10min) and Nice (frequent; 20–25min).
By bus There are connections with Cannes (every 20min; 30–35min) and Nice (every 20min; 45min–1hr10min).

NICE AND AROUND

NICE, capital of the French Riviera and France's fifth-largest city, grew into a major tourist resort in the nineteenth century, when large numbers of foreign visitors – many of them British – were drawn here by the mild Mediterranean climate. The most obvious legacy of these early holidaymakers is the famous **promenade des Anglais** stretching along the pebble beach, which was laid out by nineteenth-century English residents to facilitate their afternoon stroll by the sea. These days, Nice is a busy, bustling city, but it's still a lovely place, with a beautiful location and attractive historical centre.

WHAT TO SEE AND DO

The old town, a rambling collection of narrow alleys lined with tall, rust-and-ochre houses, centres on place Rossetti and the Baroque **Cathédrale Ste-Réparate**. It's worth making nearby Le Château one of your first stops to take in the view, which stretches across the town and west over the bay. It's a steep walk up, or there's a lift, tucked just under the stairs (free) on the western side. A short walk north through the old town takes you to the promenade des Arts, where the **Musée d'Art Moderne et d'Art Contemporain** (Tues–Sat 10am–6pm; free) has a collection of Pop Art and neo-Realist work, including pieces by Andy Warhol and Roy Lichtenstein.

Cimiez

Up above the city centre is Cimiez, a posh suburb that was the social centre of the town's elite some seventeen centuries ago, when the city was capital of the Roman province of Alpes-Maritimae. To get here, take bus #15 from in front of the train station. The **Musée d'Archéologie**, 160 av des Arènes (Mon & Wed–Sun 10am–6pm; free) houses excavations of the Roman baths, along with accompanying archeological finds. Overlooking the museum is the wonderful **Musée Matisse** (Mon & Wed–Sun 10am–6pm; free): Nice was the artist's home for much of his life and the collection covers every period. Nearby, the beautiful **Musée Chagall**, 16 av du Docteur Ménard (Mon & Wed–Sun 10am–5/6pm; €7.50–9.50), exhibits dazzlingly colourful biblical paintings, stained glass and book illustrations.

Day-trips from Nice

Nice is an excellent base from which to explore the surrounding beaches and picturesque resorts of the Riveria. The medieval **ÈZE VILLAGE** is a labyrinthine maze of vaulted passages and stairways, its streets winding around a cone of rock below the corniche. Towering 470m above sea level, it offers spectacular panoramic views of the coast. Take bus #112 or #82 to Èze Vllage from tram stop Garibaldi (hourly; 30min)

11

11

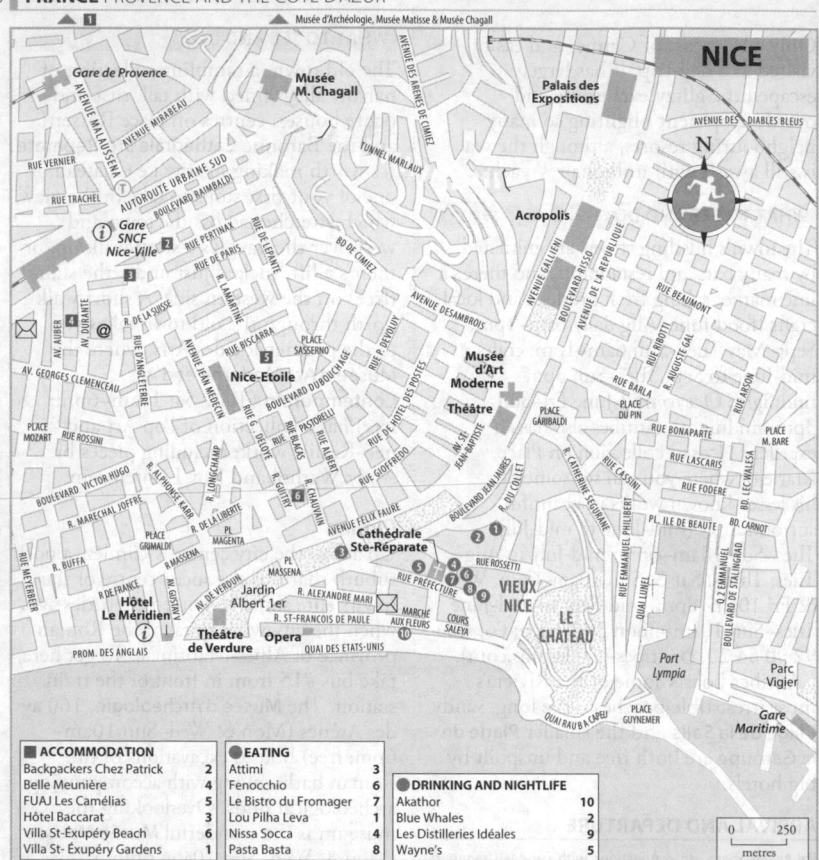

■ ACCOMMODATION	
Backpackers Chez Patrick	2
Belle Meunière	4
FUAJ Les Camélias	5
Hôtel Baccarat	3
Villa St-Éxupéry Beach	6
Villa St-Éxupéry Gardens	1

● EATING	
Attimi	3
Fenocchio	6
Le Bistro du Fromager	7
Lou Pilha Leva	1
Nissa Socca	4
Pasta Basta	8

● DRINKING AND NIGHTLIFE	
Akathor	10
Blue Whales	2
Les Distilleries Idéales	9
Wayne's	5

ARRIVAL AND DEPARTURE

By plane Nice airport is 6km southwest of the city, connected to the main train station, Nice-Ville, by two fast buses: #98 (every 20min, 5.52am–11.37pm) or #99 (every 30min, 8am–9pm); the single fare of €4 allows unlimited travel on the Lignes d'Azur network for one day. The slower regular bus #23 (every 30min, daily 6am–8.50pm; €1) also serves the main train station.

By train The main train station, Nice-Ville, is a 10min walk northwest from the centre, on av Thiers. The nearby Gare de Provence serves small stations between Nice and Digne-les-Bains.

Destinations from Nice-Ville Antibes (every 10–30min; 18–29min); Avignon TGV (10 daily; 2hr 50min–3hr 35min); Cannes (every 10–30min; 27–42min); Genoa (7 daily via Ventimiglia; 3hr–4hr 30min); Marseille (17 daily; 2hr 30min–2hr 45min); Milan (7 daily via Ventimiglia; 4hr 50min–6hr 10min); Monaco (frequent; 15min); Paris (14 daily; 5hr 45min–6hr 25min).

By bus There is no actual *gare routière*. Instead buses

depart from the main thoroughfares in central Nice – Av St Jean Baptiste, Promenade des Anglais, and place Massèna. Check ◍ lignesdazur.com for details.

Destinations Antibes (every 10–20min; 50min); Cannes (every 10–30min; 1hr 30min); Èze-sur-Mer (up to 5 hourly; 32min); Èze Village (6 daily; 30min); Monaco (up to 5 daily; 43min).

By ferry SNCM (🕿 04 93 13 66 59, ◍ sncm.fr) and Corsica Ferries (🕿 08 25 09 50 95, ◍ corsica-ferries.fr) operate services to Corsica from the Gare Maritime. SNCM's services run during July & Aug only but Corsica Ferries run all year round.

Destinations (SNCM) Ajaccio (2 weekly; 7hr); Bastia (5 weekly; 6hr); Calvi (6 weekly; 6hr); Ile Rousse (9 weekly; 5hr).

Destinations (Corsica Ferries) Ajaccio (5 weekly; 6hr 30min); Bastia (9 weekly; 5hr 15min); Calvi (6 weekly; 5hr 45min); Ile Rousse (9 weekly; 3hr 55min).

INFORMATION

Tourist information The main tourist office branch is at

5 promenade des Anglais (Mon–Sat 8/9am–6/8pm; mid-June to mid-Sept also Sun 9am–7pm; ☎ 08 92 70 74 07, ⓦ nicetourisme.com), with outlets at the airport and next to the station.

Internet Nice Nett, 19 rue Paganini (daily 9am–11pm; €3/hr).

GETTING AROUND

By bus and tram Buses and trams in Nice and surrounding towns are run by Lignes d'Azur (ⓦ lignesdazur .com). Single tickets for both buses and trams cost €1, and day pass tickets (€4) are also available.

By bike Nice's on-street bicycle rental scheme, Vélo Bleu (ⓦ velobleu.org), has 120 rental stations scattered throughout the city. You have to sign up online or at the bike station (€1/day, €5/week, ☎ 04 30 00 30 01), after which the first 30min is free; thereafter it costs €1 for the subsequent 30min and then €2/hr. Payment by credit card only.

ACCOMMODATION

Backpackers Chez Patrick First floor, 32 rue Pertinax ☎ 04 93 80 30 72, ⓦ backpackerschezpatrick.com. A friendly hostel with dorms of 3–6 beds close to the station, with no curfew. Lacks a kitchen or communal space. Check-in from 2.30pm. Dorm €28

Belle Meunière 21 av Durante ☎ 04 93 88 66 15. In a beautiful old building close to the station and a short walk from town, this friendly hotel offers simple but pleasant rooms and dorms. Breakfast included, and there's free parking. Dorm €20, double €58

FUAJ Les Camélias 3 rue Spitalieri ☎ 04 93 62 15 54, ⓦ fuaj.org. In an excellent, central location, not far from the old town, this is a great, friendly hostel with clean, modern dorms and a good bar on site. Dorm €26.90

Hôtel Baccarat 39 rue d'Angleterre ☎ 04 93 16 14 25. This large hostel has mixed dorms (4–12 beds), kitchen and a communal space. They have a flexible, helpful attitude, too, in spite of the 3–6am curfew. Private doubles are also good value. Dorm €22, double €40

Villa St-Éxupéry Beach 6 rue Sacha Guitry ☎ 04 93 16

---

13 45, ⓦ villahostels.com. Another excellent hostel from the people behind *Villa St-Éxupéry Gardens*. The atmosphere feels slightly chaotic but its location can't be beat. Dorm €30

★ **Villa St-Éxupéry Gardens** 22 av Gravier ☎ 04 93 84 42 83, ⓦ villahostels.com; tram from the station towards Las Planas and get off at "Comte de Falicon". Housed in a beautiful monastery above town, this is deservedly popular. Most dorms are en suite and some have terraces with stunning city views. The bar, housed in the old chapel, serves beer and wine for €1 and is packed every night. Dorm €30

EATING

Attimi 10 place Masséna ☎ 04 93 62 00 22. This bright terrace restaurant specializes in regional Italian dishes using organic, seasonal produce. Their specialities include colourful salads (from €7.50) and enormous pizza (from €10.50). Daily noon–midnight.

Fenocchio 2 place Rossetti. The master ice-cream maker of Nice, with a huge variety of flavours, such as vanilla, rose and black pepper. One scoop €2. Daily 10am–midnight.

Lou Pilha Leva 10 rue Collet. A self-proclaimed institution, this is nevertheless one of the best places in town to try *socca* chickpea flatbreads (€2.80) – classic Nice fast food – and *petits farcis* stuffed vegetables (€5.70). Daily 11am–8/9pm (later in summer).

Nissa Socca 7 rue Sainte Reparate ☎ 04 93 80 18 35. In a touristy location but serving good Niçois specialities. Try the generous *daube de boeuf* with gnocchi (€12). *Menu* €18. Mon, Tues & Thurs–Sun noon–2.30pm & 7–10.30pm.

Pasta Basta 18 rue de la Prefecture ☎ 04 93 80 03 57. No-frills pasta place with fresh and dried pasta varieties, and a choice of sauces. Pasta from €4.80, sauce from €3.50, and rough wine by the *pichet* from €4. Daily noon–10.30pm.

DRINKING AND NIGHTLIFE

Akathor 32 cours Saleya. The fifty different European beers on offer attract both locals and tourists in their droves. Regular live music; pint €4–6. Daily 5.30pm–2am.

Blue Whales 1 rue Mascoïnat. A relaxed place, with a long happy "hour" (6.30pm–midnight), and live music throughout the week, as well as DJs. Daily 6.30pm–4.30am.

Les Distilleries Idéales 40 rue de la Préfecture. This pleasant terrace bar in the heart of the old town has ten different draught beers (from €4.30), snacks (from €4.20) and a happy hour (6–9pm). Daily 9am–midnight.

Wayne's 15 rue de la Préfecture. Live music and DJ sets every night at this boisterous Irish bar, which heaves with backpackers and Anglophone expats. Happy hour 5–8pm. Daily 10.30am–2am.

11

★ **TREAT YOURSELF**

Le Bistro du Fromager 29 rue Benoît Bunico ☎ 04 93 13 07 83. The cheesiest restaurant in Nice, their every offering is built around France's fantastic *fromage*, coupled with wine from the cellar. The cooking is excellent, the produce local and the atmosphere buzzy, though the price is around €25 per person. Booking recommended. Mon–Sat 7.30–10pm.

11

MONACO

The tiny independent principality of **MONACO** rears up over the rocky Riviera coast like a Mediterranean Hong Kong. The 3km-long state consists of the old town of Monaco-Ville; Fontvieille; La Condamine by the harbour; Larvotto, with its artificial beaches of imported sand; and, in the middle, **MONTE CARLO**. There are relatively few conventional sights – indeed, Monaco seems composed of little other than roads, fast cars and apartment blocks – but one worth heading to is the superb (though expensive) **Musée Océanographique** on avenue St-Martin (daily 9.30/10am–6/7/7.30pm; €14), which displays a living coral reef, transplanted from the Red Sea into a 40,000-litre tank. If you want to try your luck at the famous **casino** (over-18s only; daily 2pm–very late), you'll have to dress smartly – no shorts or T-shirts – and show your passport.

ARRIVAL AND INFORMATION

By train Monaco train station is underground, reached from av Prince-Pierre. Bus #4 (direction Larvotto) takes you from the train station to the Casino-Tourism stop, near the tourist office.
Destinations Nice (up to 4 hourly; 20min); Cap d'Ail (frequent; 3min).
By bus Buses following the lower corniche or autoroute stop at place d'Armes by the *gare* SNCF and in Monte Carlo.
Tourist information Tourist office at bd des Moulins (Mon–Sat 9am–7pm, Sun 10am–noon; ☎07 92 16 61 16, ⓦ visitmonaco.com).

ACCOMMODATION

Hôtel de France 6 rue de la Turbie ☎07 93 30 24 64, ⓦ monte-carlo.mc/france. Comfortable and clean, this is as cheap as they come for a hotel room in the centre, though planned improvement works may push prices up. Double **€116**
RIJ Villa Thalassa ☎04 93 78 18 58, ⓦ clajsud.fr. This clean and welcoming hostel is just 2km away from Monte Carlo along the coast near a good beach at Cap d'Ail. You can walk here in 30min from the city, or get the train to Cap d'Ail. Dorm **€18.50**

EATING AND DRINKING

Avenue 31 31 av Princesse Grace ☎07 97 70 31 31. Stylish, modern brasserie opposite the beach with an eclectic *carte*. Lunchtime *formules* from around €17. Daily noon–2.30pm & 8–10.45pm, Fri & Sat till 11.45pm.
Stars 'n' Bars 6 quai Antoine 1er. This feisty, well-known bar on the quai serves up good-value food (for Monaco). Pizzas from €9; happy hour 5.30–7.30pm. Daily 11am–midnight.
Virage 1 quai Albert 1er. For an affordable glimpse of this town's bling soul you could try the weekly €20 lunchtime menu (main course, dessert, drink) at this fancy ice-white bar-restaurant with excellent harbour views. Mon–Sat noon–11.30pm, Sun 11.30am–5pm.

The southeast

The southeast of France encompasses a geographically varied area, from the thick forests of the Massif Central to the dramatic peaks of the Alps. The Massif Central, not the most accessible part of the country, is worth going out of your way for, especially to see the dramatic landscape that surrounds **Le Puy-en-Velay**, which makes an excellent base for exploration. Most travel in the region will require passing through **Lyon**, a beautiful city that's worth lingering over, especially to sample some of its exquisite restaurants. From here, a few hours on a train will take you to **Grenoble**, hemmed in by snowcapped mountains, and to **Chamonix**, which really comes alive during the ski season, and is a great place for extreme sports throughout the year.

LE PUY-EN-VELAY

LE PUY sprawls across a broad basin in the mountains, a muddle of red roofs and poles of volcanic rock; both landscape and architecture are completely theatrical. The town is a good base for explorations of the Massif Central – the tourist office (see opposite) is well stocked with information to help you plan your visit.

The **cathedral**, at the top of Mont Corneille, with its small, almost Byzantine cupolas and Romanesque facade, dominates the old town. The nearby **church of St-Michel** (daily: May–Sept 9am–6.30/7pm; Oct–Nov 9.30am–noon & 2–5.30pm; Dec–March 2–5pm; €3.50), at the top of Rocher d'Aiguilhe, is an eleventh-century construction that appears to have grown out of the rock.

ARRIVAL AND INFORMATION

By train The train station is on place du Maréchal Leclerc, a 15min walk from the tourist office.
Destinations Lyon (10 daily; 2hr 20min); Paris (8 daily via St Etienne and/or Lyon; 4hr 25min–5hr 30min).
Tourist information Tourist office on place du Clauzel (daily: July & Aug 8.30am–7pm; Sept–June 8.30am–noon & 1.30–6.15pm, closed Sun Oct–Easter; ⓣ 04 71 09 38 41, ⓦ ot-lepuyenvelay.fr).

ACCOMMODATION

Bouthézard ⓣ 04 71 09 55 09; bus #6 from chemin de Roderie. The municipal campsite is a 30min walk north from the station. Open mid-March to mid-Oct. Camping **€2.90** per person, plus **€2.75** per tent
FUAJ Centre Pierre Cardinal 9 rue Jules Vallès ⓣ 04 71 05 52 40, ⓦ fuaj.org. Even cheaper than *Le Régional* are this hostel's old but clean dorms. There are basic breakfasts (€3) and cooking facilities, and reservations are compulsory for weekend stays. Check-in Mon–Sat 2–11.30pm only, Sun 6–9pm. Dorm **€11.50**
Le Régional 36 bd du Maréchal Fayolle ⓣ 04 71 09 37 74, ⓦ hotelleregional.fr. A basic hotel attached to a friendly bar, offering cheap and comfortable doubles with shared bathroom. Double **€26**

EATING

Âme des Poètes 16 rue Séguret. In a lovely spot by the cathedral serving inexpensive regional food such as green lentil lasagne with salad (€14). Daily 11am–11pm.
Marco Polo 46 rue Raphaël. The freshly cooked pasta is the thing at this Italian restaurant with a beautiful vaulted cellar just moments from the cathedral. Tues–Sat 11.30am–3pm & 7–11pm.

LYON

It's hardly surprising that **LYON** is France's gastronomic capital, with more restaurants per square metre than anywhere else on earth. Lyon also has a vibrant nightlife and cultural scene, the highlight of which is the summer-long festival Les Nuits de Fourvière, celebrating theatre, music and dance.

WHAT TO SEE AND DO

The city is split into three by its two rivers – the Saône and the Rhône. The elegant city centre, **Le Presqu'Île**, is made up of grand boulevards and public squares, while across the Saône lies the beautifully preserved and atmospheric old Renaissance quarter of Vieux Lyon.

Le Presqu'Île

North from Gare de Perrache, the pedestrian rue Victor-Hugo opens out onto the vast place Bellecour, which dwarfs even its statue of Louis XIV on horseback. On rue de la Charité, the **Musée des Tissus et des Arts Decoratifs** (Tues–Sun 10am–5.30pm; €10) has an interesting collection of fabrics, clothes and tapestries dating from ancient Egypt to the present, alongside a collection of period furnishings. Northwest of place Bellecour, on the east bank of the Saône, the quai St-Antoine is lined every morning with a colourful food market; a book market takes place just upriver on Sundays.

North and inland from the river, Place des Terreaux is home to the **Musée des Beaux-Arts** (daily except Tues 10/10.30am–6pm; €7 for permanent collections, €9 for temporary exhibitions, €12 for both). This absorbing collection includes ancient Egyptian, Greek and Roman artefacts as well as works by Rubens, Renoir and Picasso.

La Croix-Rousse

North of place des Terreaux, the old silk weavers' district of **La Croix-Rousse** has an authentic, creative feel to it. It is still a working-class area, but today only twenty or so people work on the computerized looms that are kept in business by the restoration and maintenance of tapestries within France's palaces and châteaux. The famous *traboules*, or covered alleyways, that run between streets were originally used to transport silk safely through town, later serving as wartime escape routes and hideouts for la Résistance. Look out for the small signs dotted about on walls in this area – follow the arrows to do a self-guided walking tour.

Vieux Lyon

The streets on the left bank of the Saône form an attractive muddle of cobbled lanes and Renaissance facades. The **Musée des Marionnettes du Monde & Musée**

11

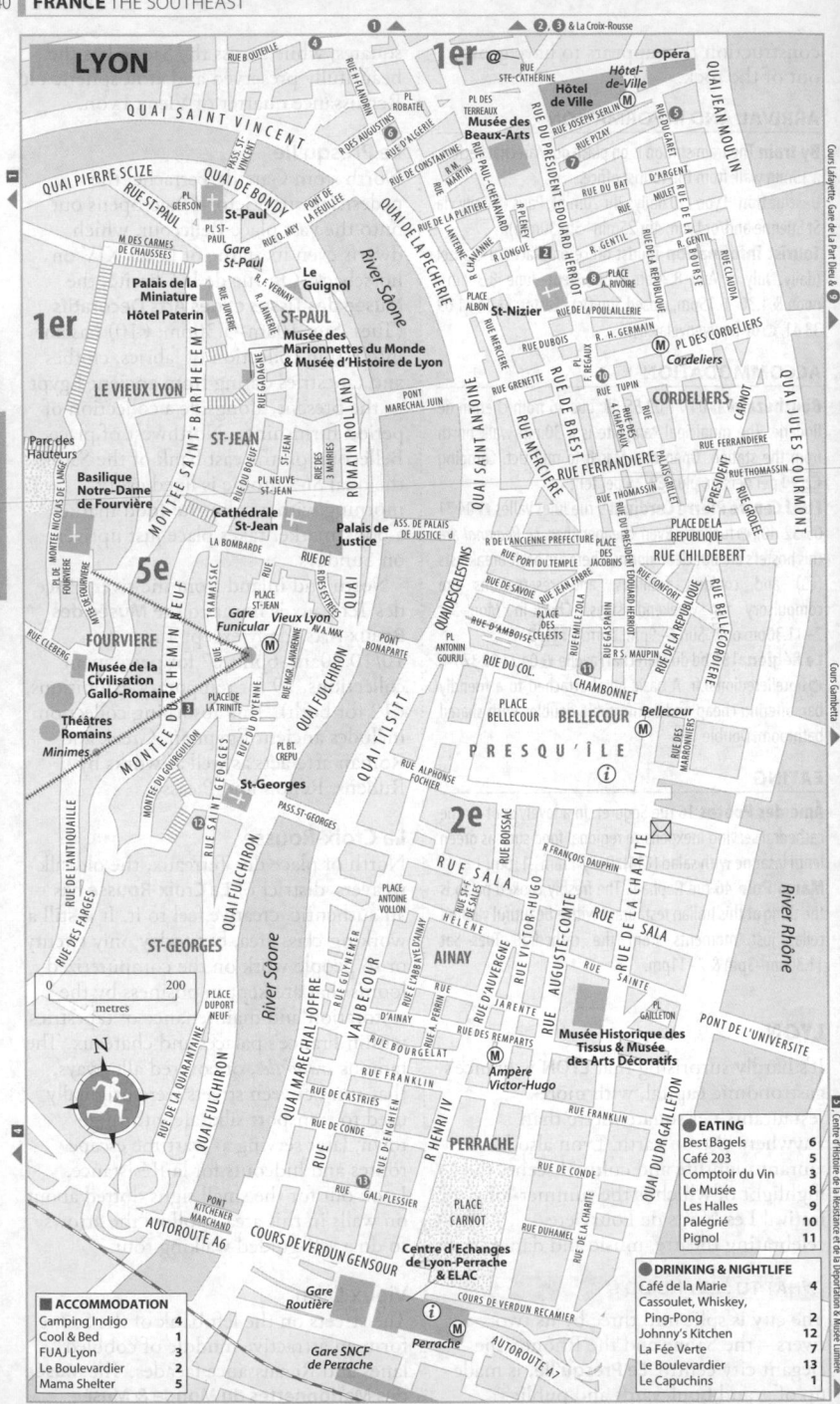

LYON

ACCOMMODATION

Camping Indigo	4
Cool & Bed	1
FUAJ Lyon	3
Le Boulevardier	2
Mama Shelter	5

EATING

Best Bagels	6
Café 203	5
Comptoir du Vin	3
Le Musée	8
Les Halles	9
Palégrié	10
Pignol	11

DRINKING & NIGHTLIFE

Café de la Marie	4
Cassoulet, Whiskey, Ping-Pong	2
Johnny's Kitchen	12
La Fée Verte	7
Le Boulevardier	13
Le Capuchins	1

Cours Lafayette, Gare de la Part Dieu & →

Cours Gambetta →

Centre d'histoire de la Résistance et de la Déportation et Musée Lumière →

d'Histoire de Lyon, in the **Musée Gadagne** (Wed–Sun 11am–6.30pm; €6), place du Petit Collège, is well worth an hour or two of your time, containing not just Lyon's famous puppets but also a collection of puppets from around the world. At the southern end of the rue St-Jean lies the **Cathédrale St-Jean**; though damaged during World War II, its thirteenth-century stained glass is in perfect condition.

Lyon Romain

Just beyond the cathedral, on avenue Adolphe-Max, is a funicular station, from which you can ascend (€2.40/return) to the two **Roman theatres** on rue de l'Antiquaille (daily 7am–7/9pm; free), and the excellent **Musée de la Civilisation Gallo-Romaine**, 17 rue Cléberg (Tues–Sun 10am–6pm; €4), containing mosaics and other artefacts from Roman Lyon. Crowning the hill, the **Basilique de Notre-Dame** (daily 9am–7pm) is a gaudy showcase of multicoloured marble and mosaic, and there are fantastic views over the city from the gardens at the back of the church.

Elsewhere in the city

Reminders of the war are never far away in France, and the **Centre d'Histoire de la Résistance et de la Déportation**, 14 av Berthelot (Wed–Sun 10am–6pm; €4), tells of the courage and ingenuity of the French Resistance. It also serves as a poignant memorial to the city's deported Jews. To the southeast of town, the **Musée Lumière**, 25 rue du Premier-Film (Tues–Sun 10am–6.30pm; €6), houses the Lumière brothers' cinematograph, which in 1895 projected the world's first film.

ARRIVAL AND DEPARTURE

By plane Tram–train *le Rhône Express* runs from Part-Dieu main-line station to Lyon-St-Exupéry airport (every 15min, 6am–9pm; every 30min, 5am–6am & 9pm–midnight; €15).

By train The main TGV train station, Gare de la Part-Dieu, is on bd Marius-Vivier-Merle, in the heart of the commercial district on the east bank of the Rhône, and connected to the centre by métro. Other trains arrive at the Gare de Perrache, by the southern edge of the centre on the Presqu'île.

Destinations Arles (7 daily; 2hr 40min); Avignon TGV (16 daily; 1hr 10min); Dijon (17 daily; 1hr 40min–2hr 45min); Geneva (13–15 daily; 1hr 45min–2hr 50min); Grenoble (frequent; 1hr–2hr 10min); Marseille (frequent; 1hr 45min–3hr 45min); Paris (every 30min; 1hr 50min–2hr 10min); Turin (via Chambery; 4 daily; 4–5hr).

INFORMATION

Tourist information Tourist office at place Bellecour (daily 9am–6pm; ☎04 72 77 69 69, ⓦen.lyon-france.com).

Internet Raconte-moi La Terre, 14 rue du Plat (Mon noon–7.30pm, Tues–Sat 10am–7.30pm; €2/hr); an internet café/bookshop specializing in travel literature.

GETTING AROUND

By public transport Tickets for all city transport cost a flat €1.60, or buy the tourist office's *liberté* ticket for a day's unlimited travel on trams, buses and métro (€5).

By bike Vélo'v is a citywide cycling scheme where you take and leave a bike from one of about a hundred sites around town (€1.50/day ticket; first 30min free; ⓦvelov.grandlyon.com; credit card authorization required).

ACCOMMODATION

Camping Indigo Porte de Lyon ☎04 78 35 64 55, ⓦcamping-lyon.com; bus #89 from the bus station in Gare de Vaise, north of the city. The closest campsite to town, with a bar, restaurant, internet and a summer swimming pool. Camping **€20.25** per person and tent

Cool & Bed 32 Quai Arloing ☎04 26 18 05 28, ⓦcoolandbed.com. Located in a quiet courtyard next to the Saône River and a 20min walk from the old town (10min walk from metro stop Valmy), this is an excellent new hostel with stylish facilities and friendly staff. Dorm **€20**

★ **FUAJ Lyon** 41–45 montée du Chemin Neuf ☎04 78 15 05 50. An excellent hostel, well worth the hike up from the métro station (Vieux Lyon; alternatively, take funicular to Minimes and walk down) for the fantastic views of the city from its terrace. Dorms are comfortable and clean, staff friendly and helpful, and there's a good bar. Dorm **€21**

> If you're staying in Lyon for up to 3 days then consider investing in the **Lyon City Card** (1/2/3 days for €21/€31€41), an easy, good-value way of enjoying the city. It offers unlimited access to all public transport and free entrance to over 20 museums and temporary exhibitions. For an additional €3, you get unlimited access to the Vélo'v city bikes.

11

★ Le Boulevardier 5 rue de la Fromagerie ☎ 04 78 28 48 22, ⊛leboulevardier.fr. On a peaceful street but centrally located, this recently restored hotel offers en-suite rooms furnished with vintage touches. Worth staying for the attached bar alone (see below). Double €49

Mama Shelter 13 rue Domer ☎04 78 02 58 00, ⊛mamashelter.com. Another ultra-cool offering from the *Mama* family. Minimal, contemporary, with quality touches and a luxuriously comfortable bed. Location is excellent (only three metro stops from the Gare de la Part-Dieu). Double €49

EATING

Best Bagels 1 place Tobie Robatel. With four different addresses throughout the city this bagel-bar is no longer a secret but its success is all in the name. Bagel, drink and accompaniment €6.95. Mon & Tues 11.30am–10pm, Wed–Sat 11.30am–11pm, Sun 11am–2.30pm.

Café 203 9 rue du Garet. This delightful café attracts a young crowd and has an excellent €13.30 *formule – plat au choix* (such as *terrine de poisson* or an oriental-inspired prawn pasta) plus a delicious dessert. Daily 7am–2am.

Comptoir du Vin 2 rue de Belfort ☎04 78 39 89 95. A fantastic local *bouchon* in the heart of the trendy Croix-Rousse district. Dishes are generous and delicious – the *andouillete* with mustard sauce (€10) is excellent. *Menu* €10–16. Mon–Fri noon–2pm & 7–11pm.

★ Les Halles 102 cours Lafayette. Lyon's covered market has enough gorgeous produce to keep a gourmand happy for weeks – a great stop on sunny days when you can pick up everything you need for a picnic. Tues–Sat 7am–noon & 3–7pm, Sun 7am–noon.

Palégrié 8 rue Palais Grillett ☎04 78 92 94 84. Innovative, exquisitely executed flavours complemented and enhanced by simple ingredients. At €22.50, the lunch

---

★ TREAT YOURSELF

Le Musée 2 rue Forces ☎04 78 37 71 54. How the owner maintains this level of personal service is a marvel; he explains the menu in person and, after dining, takes guests out to the back of the restaurant to see the *traboule* (ancient passageways used by the city's silk manufacturers). The food is simple *bouchon* cooking (a heavily meat-orientated style particular to Lyon) at its best: *quenelle* (poached fish or meat-with breadcrumbs), pig's cheek *à la lyonnaise*, *escargots* with *pistou* (Provençal cold sauce, similar to pesto). *Menu* €20–22. Tues–Sat noon–2pm & 7.30–9.15pm.

---

menu is excellent value considering the quality. Booking essential. Mon–Fri noon–2.30pm & 7–11pm.

Pignol 8 place Bellecour. Justifiably famous Lyonnaise patisserie, serving a mouthwatering array of sweet treats to eat in or take away, and a number of savoury lunch dishes such as *croque monsieur* (€6.80). Daily 8am–7.30pm.

DRINKING AND NIGHTLIFE

Café de la Mairie 4 place Sathonay. One of a number of low-key places on this pleasant *place* and a lovely spot for an early-evening sundowner. Mon–Sat 7am–1am.

Cassoulet, Whiskey, Ping-pong 4 rue de Belfort. Apart from offering what it says on the sign – the owner's three favourite things – this little bar has good jazz, cheap beer and wine, and a great atmosphere. Cassoulet €10, whiskey from €2. Tues–Sat 6pm–1am.

Johnny's Kitchen 48 rue St Georges. This Irish bar is where it's at, with a lively atmosphere, jovial bar staff and a great location in the old town. And sure, you're in gastronomic Lyon, but don't be embarrassed to order one of the burgers (€10 with fries and salad). Pints €4.50. Mon–Fri noon–1am, Sat & Sun noon–3am.

La Fée Verte 4 rue Pizay. A small dedicated *absinthe* bar where DJs play accessible hip-hop and electro. *Absinthe* €2.70. Mon 9pm–3am, Tues & Wed 9pm–1am, Thurs & Fri 9pm–4am, Sat 6pm–4am.

Le Boulevardier 5 rue de la Fromagerie. A great little bar with a charming, relaxed feel that matches the jazz played here (both live and recorded). A good place to start or finish your night off (wine €2.50, *demi* €2.70). Mon–Sat 7/8am–8pm, Sun 9am–3pm; till 3am Fri & Sat if there's a gig.

Le Capuchins 14 rue des Capuchins. This is popular with music types and the poster-strewn walls reveal a lively scene in Lyon. There's gigs downstairs on Sat and live DJ sets every Fri (*demi* €2.70). Daily 4pm–1am.

GRENOBLE

The economic and intellectual capital of the French Alps, **GRENOBLE** is a thriving city, beautifully situated on the Drac and Isère rivers and surrounded by mountains. The old centre, south of the Isère, focuses on place Grenette and place Notre-Dame, both popular with local students, who lounge around in the many outdoor cafés. The central **Musée de Grenoble**, 5 place Lavalette (Mon & Wed–Sun 10am–6.30pm; €8, free first Sun each month), is considered, by dint of its twentieth-century masterpieces, to be one of the best in Europe and includes works by Matisse, Chagall and Gauguin.

HIKING IN THE ALPS

There are six **national and regional parks** in the Alps – Vanoise, Écrins, Bauges, Chartreuse, Queyras (the least busy) and Vercors (the gentlest) – each of which covers ideal walking country, as does the **Route des Grandes Alpes**, which crosses all the major massifs from Lake Geneva to Menton and should only be attempted by seasoned hikers. All walking routes are clearly marked and equipped with refuge huts, known as **gîtes d'étape** (🅦gites-refuges .com). The Maisons de la Montagne in Grenoble (see below) and Chamonix (see p.344) provide detailed information on GR paths (an abbreviation of Grande Randonnée meaning "long ramble"), and local tourist offices often have maps of walks in their areas. Bear in mind that anywhere above 2000m will only be free of snow from early July until mid-September.

Grenoble's highlight, however, especially in good weather, is the trip by **téléphérique** (May–Sept daily; Oct–April Tues–Sun; first ascent between 9.15am and 11am, last descent between 6.30pm and 12.15am according to the season; €4.95/7.15 one-way/return) from the riverside quai Stéphane Jay up to Fort de la Bastille on the steep slopes above the north bank of the Isère. It's a hair-raising ride to an otherwise uninteresting fort, but the views over the mountains and down onto the town are stunning, and the walk down is lovely and tranquil.

ARRIVAL AND INFORMATION

By bus and train The train and bus stations are on the northwestern edge of the city, at the end of av Félix Viallet, a 10min walk to the centre.
Destinations (train) Chamonix (5–9 daily with connections; 4hr 15min); Lyon (frequent; 1hr 15min–1hr 45min); Paris (8 daily direct; 3hr); Turin (2–3 daily, via Chambéry; 3hr 30min–3hr 50min).
Tourist information Tourist office at 4 rue de la République, near place Grenette (Mon–Sat 9am–6.30pm, May–Sept Sun 9am–2pm; Oct–April Sun 10am–1pm; 🅣04 76 42 41 41, 🅦grenoble-tourisme.com).
Internet Cyber Phone 38, 2 bis rue Tres Cloître (Mon–Sat 9am–8pm; €2/hr).
Hiking information Maison de la Montagne, 3 rue Raoul Blanchard (Mon–Fri 9.30am–12.30pm & 1–6pm, Sat 10am–1pm & 2–5pm; 🅦grenoble-montagne.com).

GETTING AROUND

By bus and tram There are three main tram lines and buses that operate within the city (🅦tag.fr). A single ticket (€1.50; day pass €4.40) is valid for one hour on the TAG network, including changing vehicles.
By bike Bike rental at Métro Vélo, Place de la Garem, lower level of the station (Mon–Fri 7am–8pm, Sat & Sun 9am–noon & 2–7pm; 🅦metrovelo.fr; €3/24hr).

ACCOMMODATION

Alizé 1 place de la Gare 🅣04 76 43 12 91, 🅦hotelalize .com. Just across the road from the station, Grenoble's cheapest hotel offers a friendly welcome and basic but surprisingly spacious and airy rooms. Double €42
★ **FUAJ Grenoble** 10 av du Grésivaudan 🅣04 76 09 33 52; bus #1 to la Quinzaine (the best option) or tram A to la Rampe. This smart, modern, eco-friendly hostel has ultra-clean dorms and a good atmosphere. There's excellent information about hiking in the area and skiing in winter; unfortunately it's 5km from the centre of town. Dorm €21
Hôtel de l'Europe 22 place Grenette 🅣04 76 46 16 94, 🅦hoteleurope.fr. Faded grandeur in a seventeenth-century building with a central location overlooking the square. Rooms are generally small, and the cheapest have shared bathrooms. Double €50
Hôtel Victoria 17 rue Thiers 🅣04 76 46 06 36, 🅦hotelvictorlagrenoble.com. A charming hotel in a quiet street close to town. Some rooms are spacious with traditional decor but some look onto grey rooftops; most are en suite. Double €64
Les Trois Pucelles 🅣04 76 96 45 73, 🅦www.camping -trois-pucelles.com; tram C in the direction of Le Prisme and get off at Mas des Îles. Located 4km from Grenoble, in Seyssins, this campsite has 65 pitches, two swimming pools and a restaurant in an arboretum by the Drac River (400m south of Mas des Îles). Open all year. Camping €10 per person and tent.

EATING AND DRINKING

Café des Arts 36 rue St-Laurent 🅦lecafedesarts38.fr. This intimate venue with stone walls and low lighting is suitably atmospheric for its programme of live jazz. Check website for details. Daily 8pm–midnight.
Chez Mémé Paulette 2 rue St Hughes 🅣04 76 51 38 85. A cheerful little place crammed with wooden tables and rustic warmth, and specializing in regional dishes such as *tartines* (€5.55) and *cocottes* (baked eggs; €5.95). Booking recommended Fri & Sat evening. Daily noon–11.30pm.
Ciao a Te 2 rue de la Paix 🅣04 76 42 54 41. The interior of this family-run *ristorante* may be a little dated but it's all

11

11

★ TREAT YOURSELF

One of the most exhilarating experiences you can have in the Alps is not on the ground, but in the air. A number of companies operate **tandem paragliding flights**, which allow you to take in the fantastic scenery from a different perspective. Fly Chamonix (📞610 28 20 77, 🌐fly-chamonix.com) offers tandem flights from €100 – for more information, or to book a flight, head to Chamonix Freeride Centre, 280 rue Paccard, Chamonix (daily 9am–noon & 3–7pm).

about the classic Italian cuisine. From *panzarotti* (a filled savoury pastry, like calzoni) to pasta to octopus salad, it's consistently excellent, though not cheap. Booking recommended. Tues–Sat noon–1.30pm & 7–9pm.

K Fée des Jeux 1 quai Stéphane Jay. A unique place specializing in board games, Sun brunch and, strangely, mead. The food is good value too, particularly the €7.50 salads. Kitchen Wed–Sat noon–2pm, Sun 10.30am–noon; bar Wed–Fri 6pm–1am, Sat 2pm–1am, Sun 2–6pm.

L'As de Pique 14 rue Lieutenant 📞04 76 87 32 91. Enjoy a glass of wine (€2) in this pleasantly atmospheric and retro bar. The adjoining restaurant serves the regional speciality *Ravioles de Royans* (dishes €14–22) daily: bar 6–11pm; restaurant 7.30–10.45pm.

Mark XIII 8 rue Lakanal. A two-floor bar and venue that draws in an exciting depth and variety of underground electronic DJ talent (progressive house, drum'n'bass, techno, ambient). Tues–Sat 6pm–1am.

CHAMONIX AND MONT BLANC

At 4810m, **Mont Blanc** is both Western Europe's highest mountain and the Alps' biggest draw. Nestled at its base, the town of **CHAMONIX** is lively year-round; in summer it's popular for rock climbing and hiking, while in winter its draw is the area's vast skiing possibilities. The pricey **téléphérique** (daily every 15min, 7.10/8.10am–4.30/5pm; early July to mid-Aug 6.30am–5/5.30pm; mid-Sept to early Nov 8.30am–3.30/4pm; €50 return; 📞04 50 53 22 75) soars to the Aiguille du Midi (3842m), a terrifying granite pinnacle on which the cable-car station and a restaurant are precariously balanced. Here, the view of Mont Blanc, coupled with the altitude, will literally leave you breathless. Book the

téléphérique ahead to avoid the queues and get there early, before the clouds and the crowds close up.

ARRIVAL AND DEPARTURE

By train Chamonix train station is 3min walk from the centre, down av Michel Croz. Behind it, at Montvers station, a mountain train serves the glaciers.
Destinations Grenoble (2 daily, via St Gervais; 6hr 10min); Lyon (8 daily, via St Gervais; 4–5hr).

By bus Buses leave from in front of the train station.
Destinations Courmayeur, Italy (2–6 daily; 45min); Geneva (2–5 daily; 2hr).

INFORMATION

Tourist information The tourist office at 85 place du Triangle-de-l'Amitié (mid-April to late June Mon–Sat 9am–12.30pm & 2–6pm; July to mid-Sept daily 9am–7pm, until 9pm Sat; mid-Sept to Christmas holidays 9am–12.30pm & 2–6pm, closed Sun in Oct & Nov; Christmas holidays to mid-April daily 8.30am–7pm; 📞04 50 53 00 24, 🌐chamonix.com) is able to book accommodation, provide good information on local activities and advise on weather and snow conditions.

Hiking information The Maison de la Montagne on place de L'Église is the place for organizing climbing, trekking, mountain biking and parapenting. On the top floor, the l'Office de Haute Montagne (daily 9am–noon & 3–6pm; 📞04 50 53 22 08, 🌐ohm-chamonix.com) offer general advice on mountain conditions and activities. They also have good information about the Gîtes de Montagne that are situated along the major hiking trails.

ACCOMMODATION

Camping Les Marmottes 140 chemin des Doux 📞04 50 53 61 24, 🌐camping-lesmarmottes.com. Situated off the main road south of Chamonix, this campsite is linked to the town via a free bus service. Facilities include a games room, use of barbecues and a laundry, and it enjoys great views of Mont Blanc. Camping **€6.20** per person, plus **€5.40** per tent

FUAJ Chamonix-Mont Blanc 127 Montée J. Balmat, les Pélerins d'en Haut 📞04 50 53 14 52, 🌐fuaj.org; bus #3 from the town centre or the train to Les Pélerins. Situated in a traditional chalet 2km out of the centre, this hostel has good dorms and a friendly atmosphere, but no on-site kitchen. Closed noon–5pm & 7.30–8.30pm. Dorm **€23.50**

★ **Gite Vagabond** 365 av Ravanel-le-Rouge 📞04 50 53 15 43, 🌐gitevagabond.com. This lively and friendly hostel is a good choice year-round and invaluably cheap for the ski season (book ahead). Dorm **€21**

Hôtel de l'Arve 60 impasse des Anémones 📞04 50 53 02 31, 🌐hotelarve-chamonix.com. Open year-round with an excellent, central location, this chalet-style accommodation is a relative snip. Double €70

EATING AND DRINKING

Chambre 9 272 av Michel Croz. A renowned, loud and lively bar on the ground floor of the *Gustavia* hotel, full of young, dancing tourists. Daily noon–2am.

La Calèche 18 rue Paccard ☎04 50 55 94 68. The decor, chock-a-block with traditional paraphernalia from ice picks to stuffed animals, provides a truly atmospheric backdrop for the rich regional cuisine, though it's slightly overpriced (*menu* from €24). Daily noon–2.30pm & 7–11pm.

MBC 350 Route du Bouchet. This microbrewery is perfect for those who find *bière blonde* doesn't quite hit the spot in the mountain air. Burger lovers will be satisfied, too. Food served 4–11pm. Spring & autumn 4pm–1am; summer & winter daily 4pm–2am.

Moö Bar Cuisine 239 Avenue Michel-Croz. A laid-back Swedish-run bar-restaurant serving good-value dishes such as the *plat du jour* (€10.90) or pulled-pork burger €12.90 – all dishes served with salad. The bar has regular live bands. Daily 9am–late.

Poco Loco 47 rue Paccard. It doesn't look like much but this sliver of a snack bar does what it does – toasted sandwiches and other *sur le pouce* (on the go) goodies – very well and very generously. Daily 11am–2am.

Corsica

Known to the French as the "île de beauté", Corsica has an amazing diversity of natural landscape. Being one-third national park, its magnificent rocky coastline is interspersed with outstanding beaches, while the interior mountains soar as high as 2706m. Two French *départements* divide Corsica, each with its own capital: Napoleon's birthplace, **Ajaccio** on the southwest coast; and **Bastia**, which faces Italy in the north. The old capital of **Corte** dominates the interior, backed by a formidable wall of mountains. Of the coastal resorts, **Calvi** draws tourists with its massive citadel and long sandy beach; while **Bonifacio**'s Genoan houses perch atop limestone cliffs, overseeing the clearest water in the Mediterranean, on the island's southernmost point. Still more dramatic landscapes lie around the **Golfe de Porto** in the far northwest, where the famous red cliffs of the **Calanches de Piana** rise over 400m.

ARRIVAL AND DEPARTURE

By plane Air France (✪airfrance.fr) and its partner company Air Corsica (CCM; ✪aircorsica.com) have regular flights to Corsica's four airports at Ajaccio, Bastia, Calvi and Figari (near Bonifacio). It's often possible to get discounts if you are under 25. Bastia's airport, Poretta, is 20km south of town. Shuttle buses (35–40min; €9) meet all flights and stop outside the train station in the centre of town.

By ferry The three principal ferry companies serving the island are Corsica Ferries (✪corsica-ferries.com), Moby (✪moby.it) and SNCM (✪sncm.fr). Prices are between €30 and €80, with the cheapest from the Italian ports. Routes are scaled back in winter (Oct–March) to several journeys a week; check websites for details. Bastia's port is in the north of town, a 5min walk from the centre.

Destinations from Nice Ajaccio (6 weekly; 6hr 15min–7hr); Bastia (8 weekly; 5hr 20min–7hr 30min); Calvi (1 daily; 5hr 45min).

Destinations from Marseille Ajaccio (10 weekly; 11–12hr); Bastia (14 weekly; 11–13hr).

Destinations from Livorno, Italy Bastia (22 weekly; 4hr).

Destinations from Genoa, Italy Bastia (1 daily; 4hr 45min).

Destinations from Savona, Italy Bastia (14 weekly; 6hr).

Destinations from Santa-Teresa-di-Gallura, Sardinia Bonifacio (2–8 daily; 1hr).

Destinations from Porto Torres, Sardinia Ajaccio (1 weekly; 4hr 30min).

GETTING AROUND

Corsica is somewhat difficult to navigate if relying on public transport, with services slow and infrequent. The unofficial websites ✪corsicabus.org and ✪train-corse .com are helpful for train and bus timetables. Bastia is the island's main transport hub – while there's little of particular interest here, there's a good chance that you'll pass through the town at least once during your visit.

By train Corsica's narrow-gauge railway crosses the mountains to connect the island's main towns along the most scenic of lines. Lines run from Calvi to Ponte Leccia in the interior and from Ajaccio to Bastia. InterRail and other cards reduce the fare to half for all services, or you could buy a *Carte Zoom*, which gives one week's unlimited train travel for €49. The cards are available from any station. For up-to-the-minute timetable information call the stations at Calvi (☎04 95 65 00 61), Bastia (☎04 95 32 80 61) or Ajaccio (☎04 95 23 11 03). Bastia's station is located west of place St-Nicolas.

Destinations from Bastia Ajaccio (2–4 daily; 3hr 30min); Calvi (change at Ponte Leccia; 1–2 daily; 3hr); Corte (2–4 daily; 1hr 45min).

11

11

By bus Buses are infrequent between the larger towns and rarely reach the interior villages; main routes include Bastia–Porto Vecchio, Ajaccio–Bastia and Calvi–Bastia. Services are scaled back drastically Nov–May. Buses arrive in, and depart from, Bastia via either Rond Point de la Prefacture, near the train station, or rue du Nouveau Port.
Destinations from train station Calvi (2 daily at 10.30am & 5pm; 2hr–2hr 30min).
Destinations from rue du Nouveau Port Ajaccio (Mon–Sat 2 daily at 7.15am & 3pm; 3hr); Corte (Mon–Sat 2 daily at 7.15am & 3pm; 1hr 15min); Porto Vecchio (June–Sept 2 daily at 8.30am & 4pm; 3hr).

By scooter With little public transport and many secluded beaches to visit, the roads that undulate and meander around Corsica mean it's a great place to rent a scooter. Try Scootloc at Place du Marché in Ajaccio (€39–45/day; ☎ 06 26 17 31 07), Scoot Rent at 3 quai Banda del Ferro in Bonifacio (€45/day; ☎ 06 25 44 22 82) or Garage d'Angeli at 4 rue Villa St-Antoine in Calvi (€35–50/day; ☎ 04 95 65 02 13).

By car This is by far the most convenient way to get around Corsica. Hertz (w hertz.fr), Europcar (w europcar .com) and Avis (w avis.fr) all have offices in the big towns and airports, with prices starting from €70/day.

AJACCIO

Set in a magnificent bay, **AJACCIO** has all the ingredients of a Riviera-style town with its palm trees, spacious squares, glamorous marina and street cafés.
Napoleon was born here in 1769, but did little for the place except to make it the island's capital for the brief period of his empire. It is, however, a lovely place to spend time, particularly around the harbour and narrow streets inland from the fifteenth-century **Genoese** citadel. The **Musée Fesch**, rue Cardinal-Fesch (May–Sept Mon, Wed & Sat 10.30am–6pm; Thurs, Fri & Sun noon–6pm; July & Aug open until 8.30pm Fri; Oct–April Mon, Wed & Sat 10am–5pm, Thurs, Fri & Sun noon–5pm; €8), is home to the country's most important collection of Renaissance paintings outside Paris, including works by Botticelli, Titian and Poussin. The best beach to head to is **plage Trottel**, ten minutes southwest from the centre along the promenade.

ARRIVAL AND DEPARTURE

By plane The airport, Napoleon Bonaparte, is 8km southeast and connected to the town by *navette* (shuttle bus; €5; w corsicabus.org); taxis cost around €25.

By train The train station is a 10min walk north along the seafront.
Destinations Bastia (2–4 daily; 3hr 30min); Calvi (change at Ponte Leccia; 1–2 daily; 4hr 30min); Corte (2–4 daily; 2hr).
By bus and ferry The ferry port and bus station occupy the same building off quai L'Herminier.
Destinations (bus) Bastia (2 daily; 3hr); Bonifacio (1–2 daily; 3hr 15min); Corte (2 daily; 1hr 45min).

INFORMATION

Tourist information 3 bd du Roi Jérôme (April–June, Sept & Oct Mon–Sat 8am–7pm, Sun 9am–1pm; July & Aug Mon–Sat 8am–8pm, Sun 9am–1pm & 4–7pm; Nov–March Mon–Fri 8am–12.30pm & 2–6pm, Sat 8.30am–12.30pm & 2–5pm; ☎ 04 95 51 53 03, w ajaccio -tourisme.com).
Internet Cyber Espace, 1 rue Dr Versini (daily 11am–9pm; €2/hr).

ACCOMMODATION

Budget accommodation in Ajaccio is hard to find and hotels get booked up quite quickly. The tourist office can provide a list of those available as well as private apartments to rent.
Camping de Barbicaja Route des îles Sanguinaires ☎ 04 95 52 01 17; bus #5 from place Général-du-Gaulle. The most convenient campsite is 3km out of town, near the beach, a short bus ride away. Closed Oct–April. Camping **€8.60** per person and tent
Marengo 2 rue Marengo ☎ 04 95 21 43 66, w hotel -marengo.com. A sweet little hotel with spacious, clean rooms. The cheapest have shared toilets, while some lead onto a floral courtyard. Double **€75.80**
Pension de Familie Tina Morelli 1 rue Major Lambrochini ☎ 04 95 21 16 97. The tired grandeur of this old guesthouse belongs to another era. Tina Morelli, the proprietress, provides wonderful home cooking (see opposite) and comfortable, traditionally furnished rooms. Breakfast included. Double **€80**

EATING AND DRINKING

Da Mamma 3 Passage Guingette ☎ 04 95 21 39 44. The set €17 *menu* (entrée, *plat* and dessert) doesn't compromise on quality in this traditional restaurant, pleasantly situated in the shade of a magnificent rubber tree (mains €12–25, *menu* €12–21). Tues–Sat 11am–2pm & 7.30–10.30pm, Sun 7.30–10.30pm.
Le Grand Café Napoleon 10 Cours Napoleon ☎ 04 95 21 42 54. One of the oldest, grandest establishments in Ajaccio where you can eat in style – though not necessarily pay the price. The weekday three-course *menu du marché* is excellent value at €16 for refined French cuisine in an opulent setting. Daily noon–2pm & 7.30–10pm.

Marché Campinchi Place César Campinchi. This market is a great place to stock up on fresh fruit and veg, plus cheese and Corsica's famed charcuterie at its cheapest. Tues–Sun 8am–noon.

Pension de Familie Tina Morelli 1 rue Major Lambrochini ☎ 04 95 21 16 97. The restaurant of the Morelli family *pension* has been serving delicious home-cooked French cuisine since the 1960s. The three-course set menu is simplicity at its best with a *pichet* of wine for €15/person. Mon–Sat 7–9.30pm.

Vino de Diablo Port de l'Amirauté. A party place with live music and a lovely expansive terrace on the port. Three tapas and a drink for €13; good lunch *menu* at around the same price. Mon 11am–11pm, Tues & Wed 11am–midnight, Thurs–Sat 11am–2am.

LE GOLFE DE PORTO

Corsica's most startling landscapes surround the **Golfe de Porto**, on the west coast. A deep blue bay enfolded by outlandish red cliffs, among them the famous **Calanches de Piana** rock formations, the gulf is framed by snow-topped mountains and a vast pine forest. The entire area holds endless possibilities for outdoor enthusiasts, with a superb network of marked trails (free maps available from the Ajaccio tourist office) and **canyoning** routes, perfect bays for **kayaking** and some of the finest **diving** sites in the Mediterranean.

Porto

Less adventurous visitors can explore the coast on one of the excursion boats from the village of **PORTO**, the gulf's main tourist hub.

ARRIVAL AND INFORMATION

By bus Buses arrive and depart from opposite the pharmacy. The local bus operator is Autocars SAIB (ⓦ autocarslledebeaute.com).

Destinations Ajaccio (Oct–April 1–2 daily; 2hr); Calvi (mid-May to Sept 1 daily; 2hr 30min); Corte (July–Oct 1 daily; 2hr 45min).

Tourist information Quartier la Marine (May to mid-June & mid- to late Sept Mon–Fri 9am–6pm, Sat 9am–4pm, Sun 9am–1pm; mid-June to mid-Sept Mon–Sat 9am–7pm, Sun 9am–1pm; Oct–April Mon–Fri 9am–5pm, Sat 9am–1pm; ☎ 04 95 26 10 55, ⓦ porto-tourisme.com).

ACCOMMODATION AND EATING

The village has a huge range of accommodation. For an inexpensive meal, try one of the pizzerias lining the roadside above the marina.

Camping Oliviers Along from the supermarket on the main road east from the village ☎ 04 95 26 14 49, ⓦ camping-oliviers-porto.com. Lovely campsite, with pitches under the shade of olive trees. Amenities include a bar, swimming pool, gym, hot tub, a hammam and massages. Also 2-person wooden chalets with terrace and private. Camping €9.80 per person, plus €3.50 per tent, chalet €111

Le Romulus Cours Napoléon. A good-value Italian, offering pizza, pasta dishes and lasagne. The terrace is a particularly lovely spot come evening. Mon–Sat noon–2pm & 7–10.30pm.

Le Vaïta Route de la Marine ☎ 04 95 26 13 33, ⓦ le-vaita .com. The best option of the cheaper hotels, with an adjoining restaurant, and located a 15min walk from the centre. Pretty basic but comfortable rooms with en suite. Double €79

CALVI

Seen from the water, the great citadel of **CALVI** resembles a floating island, defined by a hazy backdrop of snow-capped mountains. The island's third port, it draws thousands of tourists for its 6km of sandy beach. The **ville haute**, a labyrinth of cobbled lanes and stairways encased by a citadel, rises from **place Christophe Colomb**, which links it to the town and marina of the *ville basse*. The square's name derives from the local belief that the discoverer of the New World was born here, in a now ruined house on the edge of the citadel. To reach the public **beach**, keep walking south, past the boats in the marina, and – unless you want to pay for a lounger and waited service – past the private beach bars.

ARRIVAL AND DEPARTURE

By plane Calvi's Ste-Catherine airport is 7km southeast of town, connected only by taxis (€17–19).

By train The train station, on av de la République, is just off the marina to the south of the town centre. All services go via Ponte Leccia.

Destinations Ajaccio (1–2 daily; 4hr 45min); Bastia (1–2 daily; 3hr 15min); Corte (1–2 daily; 3hr).

By bus Buses to and from Bastia and Calenzana stop in place Porteuse d'Eau, next to the station. Porto buses stop outside the Super U supermarket 200m south of the train station.

11

Destinations Bastia (Mon–Sat 2 daily at 7.15am & 2pm; 2hr–2hr 15min); Porto (May to late Sept daily at 3.30pm, except Sun May, June & mid- to late Sept; 2hr 30min).
By ferry The ferry port is on the opposite side of the marina, below the citadel.

INFORMATION

Tourist information Tourist office at Port de Plaisance (April–Oct daily 9am–noon & 3–6.30pm; Nov–March Mon–Sat 9am–noon & 2–6pm; ☎04 95 65 16 67, ⓦbalagne-corsica.com).

ACCOMMODATION

Du Centre 14 rue Alsace-Lorraine ☎04 95 65 02 01. The most convenient budget accommodation, hidden away in the *ville basse*, with modest and well-kept rooms. Double €59

La Pinède ☎04 95 65 17 80, ⓦcamping-calvi.com; infrequent beach train (*ferrovière*; around 5 daily) serves Île Rousse – get off at the "Tennis" stop. Campsite sheltered in the pine forest behind the public beach, with a bar and a good shop. If you're walking it's 2km along av de la République. Open mid-March to mid-Nov. Camping €9.50 per person, plus €3.50 per tent

U Carabellu Route de Pietra-Maggiore ☎04 95 65 14 16, ⓦclajsud.fr. Book ahead for this hostel, with tidy spacious dorms and a great out-of-town location overlooking the bay. From the station, turn left down av de la République, then right at the Total garage after 500m and keep walking for 3.5km. Also offers full- and half-board options. Dorm €18.50

EATING AND DRINKING

Bar de la Tour Quai Landry. A lovely spot overlooking the water, and a great place for an early-evening beer. Daily noon–1am.

Best Of 1 rue Clemenceau, Port de Plaisance Area. The wood-fired bread topped with local specialities, panini and sandwiches made here are perfect for a snack on the move. Daily 11.30am–10pm.

La Tire Bouchon 15 rue Clemenceau ☎04 95 38 21 87. Serving traditional Corsican cuisine such as veal stew or tagliatelle with *brocciu* (fresh ewe's or goat's cheese). Mains €12–20, *menu* €19. April–Oct daily noon–2pm & 7–11pm.

Pizzeria Cappuccino Quai Landry ☎04 95 65 11 19. This restaurant has a great atmosphere and serves up good-value *calzones* (from €11.50) and pasta. Daily noon–3pm & 6–11pm.

CORTE

Perching on the rocky crags of the island's spine, **CORTE**, the island's only interior town, is regarded as the spiritual capital of Corsica, as this is where **Pasquale Paoli** had his seat of government during the brief period of independence in the eighteenth century. Paoli founded a university here and its student population adds some much-needed life. For outdoor enthusiasts, this is also an ideal base for **trekking** into the island's steep valleys, with two superb gorges stretching west into the heart of the mountains.

WHAT TO SEE AND DO

The main street, **cours Paoli**, runs the length of town, culminating in **place Paoli**, a pleasant market square lined with cafés. A cobbled ramp leads up to the **ville haute**, where you can still see the bullet marks made by Genoese soldiers during the War of Independence in tiny **place Gaffori**. Continuing north you'll soon come to the gates of the **citadelle**, whose well-preserved ramparts enclose the **Museu di a Corsica** (April to mid-June Tues–Sun 10am–6pm; mid-June to mid-Sept daily 10am–8pm; mid-Sept to Oct daily 10am–6pm; Nov–Dec & mid-Jan to March Mon–Sat 10am–5pm; €5.30). The best views of the citadel, the town and its valley are from the **Belvédère**, a man-made lookout post on the southern end of the ramparts.

ARRIVAL AND INFORMATION

By train Corte's train station is 1km south east of town at the foot of the hill near the university.
Destinations Ajaccio (2–4 daily; 2hr); Bastia (2–4 daily; 1hr 30min); Calvi (1–2 daily via Ponte Leccia; 2hr 30min).
By bus Some buses stop at the south end of cours Paoli, others go to the station.
Destinations Ajaccio (Mon–Sat 2 daily at 9am & 4.15pm; 1hr 45min); Bastia (Mon–Sat 3 daily at 7.45am, 9.30am & 4.40pm; 1hr 15min).
Tourist information In the *citadelle* (summer Mon 10am–1pm & 3–6pm, Tues–Sat 9am–6pm; winter Mon–Fri 9am–noon & 2–5pm; ☎04 95 46 26 70, ⓦwww.corte-tourisme.com).

ACCOMMODATION

Ferme Équestre l'Albadu Ancienne route d'Ajaccio ☎04 95 46 24 55. The nicest of the local campsites, located

THE GR20

The **GR20 hiking trail** stretches across Corsica's dramatic granite spine from Calenzana in the north to Conza in the south. Covering a breathtaking landscape, the route takes you through some lush countryside and over the snowcapped peaks of the heart of the island. It is manageable for anyone in reasonable shape with basic trekking common sense, but proper hiking equipment is essential, as are nerves of steel for the ropes and vertical staircases built into the mountainside. Covering a distance of 180km, it takes around two weeks to complete, walking 2–6hr per day; red and white waymarks show the route, which is well serviced with bunked **mountain refuges**. Although the refuges cook and sell food, several days' supplies and a good stock of water are recommended. Do not attempt the route outside of the summer months; even then there is some residual snow in parts.

Buses go from Calvi to Calenzana (July & Aug 2 daily; Sept–June 4 weekly Mon, Tues, Thurs & Fri; 30min; €8), where the walk begins. Accommodation details and more information about the route itself can be found at Ⓦcorsica.forhikers.com/gr20. Detailed maps can be obtained from the Calvi tourist office.

11

15min walk from town – follow the main road south down the hill from place Paoli and take the second right after the second bridge. Camping €5 per person, plus €2.50 per tent

HR Allée du 9 Septembre ☎04 95 45 11 11, Ⓦhotel-hr .com. Cheap and cheerful rooms in an old converted police station southwest of the station and just 10min from the centre. Double €45

Le Torrent Santo Pietro di Venaco ☎04 95 47 00 18. In a village just outside Corte, this hotel in a nineteenth-century building on a hillside has seen better days but is certainly atmospheric. Double €73

EATING AND DRINKING

A Merenda 3 cours Paoli ☎04 95 46 30 99. A friendly bistro with a pretty terrace, serving good-value *plats* (try the breaded veal cutlet in cream), burgers or quick snacks such as panini, crêpes and pasta dishes. Daily 11.30am–midnight.

Café du Cours 22 rue Paoli. Student nights and well-priced drinks at this busy bar which also has internet access, some live Corsican bands and daytime left-luggage facilities; *demi* €3. Daily noon–1am.

U Museu 1 rampe Ribanelle ☎04 95 61 08 36, Ⓦrestaurant-umuseu.com. Huddled beneath the citadel walls, this place serves a superb goat's cheese salad and tasty wild-boar stew; three-course menu €15. Daily noon–2.15pm & 7–10.15pm.

BONIFACIO

The port of **BONIFACIO** has a superb, isolated position on a narrow peninsula of dazzling white limestone at Corsica's southernmost point, only an hour away by boat from Sardinia. For hundreds of years the town held the most powerful fortress in the Mediterranean and was a virtually independent republic. Nowadays, people are met with sights of precariously balanced houses edging their way into the sea. Bonifacio has become a chic holiday spot, sailing centre and deluxe day-trip.

WHAT TO SEE AND DO

The **ville haute** is connected to the marina by a steep flight of steps at the west end of the quay, at the top of which you can enjoy glorious views across the straits to Sardinia. Within the massive fortifications of the citadel is an alluring maze of cobbled streets which bring you back down to the marina, where a **boat excursion** (around €17.50; try Rocca Croisières, Ⓦrocca-croisieres.com) round the base of the cliffs gives a fantastic view of the town and the **sea caves**. Some outstanding beaches lie near Bonifacio, most notably the shell-shaped **plage de la Rondinara**, 10km north; further north still, off the main Porto Vecchio road, the **plages de Santa Giulia** and **Palombaggia** wouldn't look out of place in the Maldives. Buses (July & Aug 4 daily at 7.20am, 8.30am, 12.45pm & 5pm; Sept–June Mon–Sat 3 daily at 7.20am, 8.30am & 12.50pm; 30min) make the journey from Bonifacio to Porto Vecchio, passing the turn-off for la Rondinara. From Porto Vecchio a beach bus runs in July and August to Palombaggia (3 daily at 9.45am, 1.45pm, 4.20pm; 45min) and another to Santa Giulia (Mon–Sat 4

11

daily at 9.50am, 12.10pm, 3.05pm & 6.30pm; 20min).

ARRIVAL AND DEPARTURE

By plane Figari Sud-Corse Airport is located 20km from Bonifacio. There are regular *navettes* to and from the airport (every 30min; €10; ⓦ corsicabus.org).

By bus Buses stop in the car park at the base of the harbour.

Destinations Ajaccio (Mon–Sat 1–2 daily; 3hr 30min); Porto Vecchio, for connections to Bastia (July & Aug 4 daily at 7.20am, 8.30am, 12.45pm & 5pm; Sept–June Mon–Sat 3 daily at 7.20am, 8.30am & 12.50pm; 30min).

By ferry Boats from Santa-Teresa-di-Gallura on Sardinia dock at the far end of the quay at the bottom of the hill.

Destinations Santa-Teresa-di-Gallura (2–8 daily; 1hr).

INFORMATION

Tourist information The tourist office is based in the *ville haute*, at the bottom of rue Fred Scamaroni (mid-April to Oct daily 9am–7pm; July & Aug daily 9am–8pm; Oct to mid-April Mon–Fri 10am–5pm; ⓣ 04 95 73 11 88, ⓦ bonifacio.fr).

Internet Scara Lunga, quai Jérôme Comparetti.

ACCOMMODATION

Hôtel des Étrangers av Sylvère Bohn ⓣ 04 95 73 01 09. An absolute bargain just north of the harbour, offering spick-and-span rooms with tiled floor, plus more expensive rooms with a/c. Double **€44**

L'Araguina 33 av de Bonifaccio ⓣ 04 95 73 02 96, ⓦ camping-araguina-bonifacio.com. The only campsite close to the town has lumpy and sandy pitches but loans out tents and sleeping bags for those unprepared. It's north from the marina, 1km out of town with an unfortunate roadside location. Camping **€7.10** per person, plus **€3.20** per tent

Royal 8 rue Fred Scamaroni ⓣ 04 95 73 00 51, ⓦ hotel-leroyal.com. A good option in the centre of town, only minutes away from the tourist office. Don't let the slightly faded blue carpet and curtain-less showers put you off – the beds are comfy and it offers a decent night's sleep. Double **€60**

EATING AND DRINKING

B'52 Quai Camparetti. A laidback and tasteful late-night bar with tapas bites to accompany the house cocktails. Tues–Sat 7pm–1am.

Cantina Doria Rue Doria ⓣ 04 95 73 40 59. A charming little place with odds and ends strung from the rafters, and serving traditional, hearty, Corsican specialities – try the fish soup or charcuterie. Three-course menu for €16.50. Mon–Sat noon–2pm & 7–10.30pm.

Kissing Pigs 15 quai Banda del Ferro ⓣ 04 95 73 56 09. In spite of the prevailing pig theme (excellent *charcuterie*), the *aubergine à la bonifacienne* is one of the highlights and the €19 *châtaignes* ("chestnuts") *menu* is a steal. Worth reserving a table on the terrace for a dreamy view of the port. Daily 11.30am–3.30pm & 7–11pm.

Germany

HIGHLIGHTS

❶ **Berlin** Dramatic history and gritty modernity combine in this most untamed of European capitals. **See p.357**

❷ **Dresden** Glorious Baroque architecture by day; decadent bar-crawling by night. **See p.370**

❸ **Dom, Cologne** Cologne's cathedral is Gothic grandeur on a massive scale. **See p.386**

❹ **Heidelberg** Great romantic setting, buzzing student life and the best castle ruins in Germany. **See p.398**

❺ **Oktoberfest, Munich** The world's most famous beer festival. **See p.409**

HIGHLIGHTS ARE MARKED ON THE MAP ON P.353

ROUGH COSTS

Daily budget Basic €55, occasional treat €70

Drink Beer (half-litre) €2.70

Food Schnitzel €8

Hostel/budget hotel €25/€35

Travel Train: Munich–Berlin €79–139

FACT FILE

Population 81.8 million

Language German

Currency Euro (€)

Capital Berlin

International phone code ☎49

Time zone GMT +1hr

Introduction

Berlin and Munich deservedly draw the crowds, but the rest of Germany is often underrated as a destination, despite its picture-postcard medieval villages, dynamic modern cities and swathes of idyllic countryside. But those who do explore more widely will find a rich regional diversity, which harks back to a time when the country was made up of a patchwork of independent states, and a robust respect for the past. There are plenty of unique customs, festivals, castles, historic town centres, food, beers and wines to discover. Juxtaposed with all this tradition is – in Germany's cities at least – an embracing of modernity, something that's rarely found in Europe. Here inventiveness is celebrated in dynamic modern architecture, slick engineering, cutting-edge contemporary art museums and luxurious spas.

12

No German city celebrates innovation and creativity quite like **Berlin**, which bursts with youth, art and energy. Counter-culture also thrives in the other great eastern German city of **Dresden**, which is also known for its Baroque finery. This, too, is a key draw in the many palaces of **Potsdam**, while small but cultured **Weimar** is another significant town that rewards travel in this region.

In northern Germany the large, bustling harbour city of **Hamburg** with its rambunctious nightlife is a key draw. Further south, straddling the banks of the River Rhine, **Cologne** is another dynamic city, famed for a skyline dominated by a spectacular cathedral begun in 1248, and its huge and decidedly impious Carnival celebrations.

Munich is the key city in southern Germany, with its fine museums and bustling beer halls, but in general the region is best appreciated in smaller towns which preserve the country's pastoral and romantic side. Among them are the beautiful university town of **Heidelberg; Trier** with its many Roman remains; the spa town of **Baden-Baden**; and the attractive and youthful town of **Freiburg**. Many of Germany's scenic highlights can be found in the south too, including the **Bavarian Alps** along the Austrian border; the **Bodensee** (Lake Constance) near the Swiss border; the **Black Forest** and the **Rhine Valley**, whose majestic sweep has spawned a rich legacy of legends and folklore.

CHRONOLOGY

57 BC Julius Caesar invades and conquers "Germania Inferior".

800 AD Charlemagne, the Frankish ruler over territory including Germany, is crowned Holy Roman Emperor.

1438 Habsburg dynasty rules over Germany with election of Albert I.

1517 Martin Luther writes his *95 Theses* against corruption in the Catholic Church, a protest that culminates in the Protestant Reformation.

1648 End of the Thirty Years' War between European Catholic and Protestant powers leads to the division of Germany into princely states.

1806 Napoleon dissolves the Holy Roman Empire.

1871 Unification of Germany under Chancellor Otto von Bismarck, after German success in the Franco-Prussian War.

1880s Bismarck establishes German colonies in Africa.

1918 Germany is defeated in World War I; the Treaty of Versailles enforces heavy reparation payments upon Germany.

1919 The Weimar Republic is established.

1923 Hyperinflation causes economic meltdown.

1933 Hitler becomes Chancellor of Germany.

1939 World War II begins as Germany invades Poland.

1939–45 Millions die in Nazi concentration camps during the Holocaust.

1945 Germany is defeated, the Allies occupy the country.

1949 Germany is divided between Communist East and Democratic West.

1961 The Berlin Wall is constructed.

1989 Following mass protests, the Berlin Wall is torn down.

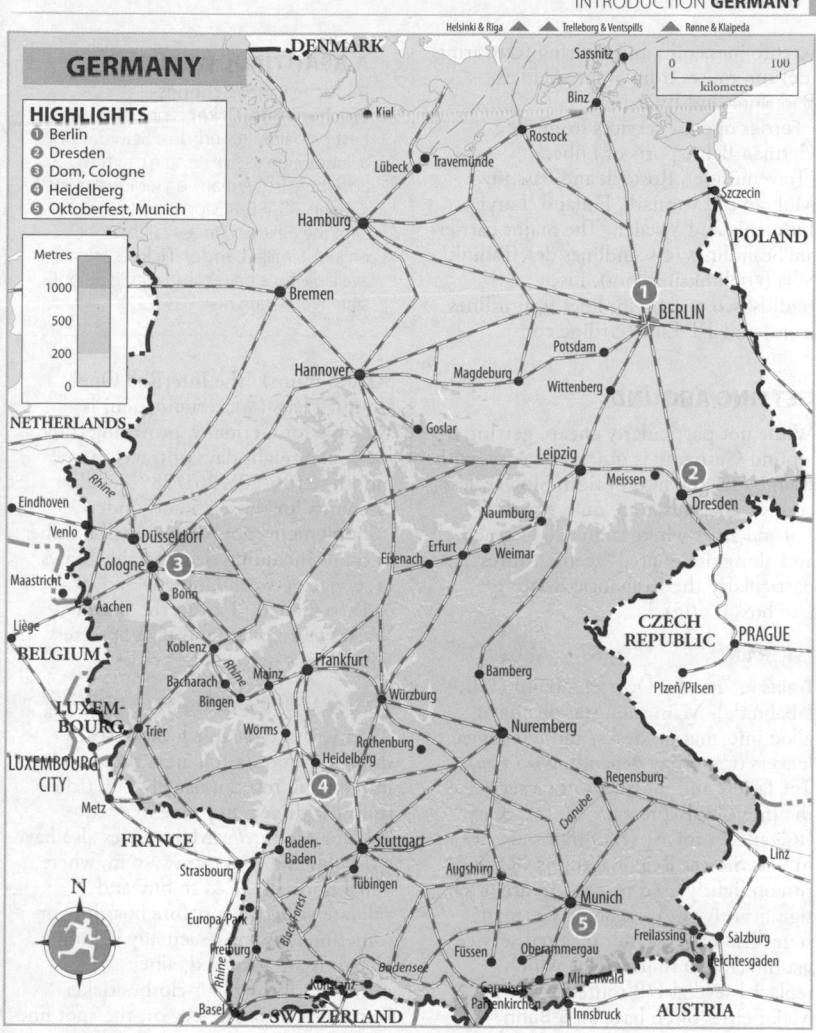

Helsinki & Rīga ▲▲   Trelleborg & Ventspills   ▲ Rønne & Klaipeda

GERMANY

HIGHLIGHTS
1 Berlin
2 Dresden
3 Dom, Cologne
4 Heidelberg
5 Oktoberfest, Munich

Metres
1000
500
200
0

1990 The two Germanys are reunited.

2002 Germany reluctantly abandons the Deutschmark and joins the euro.

2005 Angela Merkel becomes first female – and first eastern German – Chancellor.

2009–2013 Euro crisis; Germany emerges as the dominant power in the euro bloc and starts moves towards a banking union.

ARRIVAL AND DEPARTURE

Flying is the cheapest and most convenient way to get to Germany from outside Europe and even from many other European countries thanks to the proliferation of discount airlines. The largest airport is Frankfurt Airport (FRA), and there are over forty others to choose from.

Germany is well connected by train and bus with destinations throughout continental Europe. Check Deutsche Bahn's website (wbahn.de) for international routes; several private bus companies, such as BerlinLinienBus (wberlinlinienbus.de), Gulliver's (wgulliver.de), MeinFernbus (wmeinfernbus.de), Eurolines (w eurolines.com) and Touring (w touring .de) run routes from as far afield as Barcelona and Bucharest.

Ferries operate services from the German Baltic ports of Lübeck (Travemünde), Rostock and Sassnitz-Mukran to Denmark, Finland, Latvia, Lithuania and Sweden. The major carriers are Scandlines (w scandlines.de), Tallink/ Silja (w tallinksilja.com), Lisco (w dfdslisco.com), Finnlines (w finnlines .com) and TT-Line (w ttline.com).

GETTING AROUND

While not particularly cheap, getting around Germany is quick and easy, with **train** by far the best option. Slower, less comfortable **buses** are only worth it in rural areas where trains don't reach and along designated "scenic routes", particularly the Romantic Road (see box, p.405).

BY TRAIN

Trains are run by Deutsche Bahn (DB; w bahn.de). Main train stations have good information desks, and left-luggage lockers (€3–6/day depending on size). The fastest and most luxurious service is the InterCityExpress (ICE). InterCity (IC) and EuroCity (EC) trains are next in line. Slower Regional trains (RE/RB) run on lightly used routes and are often significantly cheaper. Some German states also offer a faster regional service via InterRegio trains (IRE) which replaced several DB routes in 2001. Major cities often have an **S-Bahn** commuter rail network.

With **standard tickets**, valid for two days, you can make as many stops along the way as you'd like. So if you're heading to Berlin from Cologne, you can take a day in Hannover on your way for no extra charge. A return ticket costs the same as two one-way tickets. Tickets are a lot cheaper if booked for set journeys in advance (up to three days before) – with 25 and 50 percent discounts often available – and there are numerous discount passes for groups and individuals (see box above). InterRail and Eurail are both valid (including on

A BEAUTIFUL WEEKEND

Deutsche Bahn's **Schönes-Wochenende-Ticket** is one of the best bargains around: on a Saturday or a Sunday, up to five people can travel anywhere in Germany on regional trains (S-Bahn, RB, IRE, RE) for a day (midnight–3am the next day) for €42 (if bought online). Similar **Länder-Tickets** are available for a day's travel within a single state (9am–3am next day; €22).

S-Bahn trains). The InterRail One Country Pass (w interrailnet.eu) is available for Germany, providing three, four, six or eight days of travel in one month (€186/205/261/289 – with discounts for those 25 and under).

Supplements apply on a small number of trains including sleepers; the Thalys (a service between Cologne and Brussels or Paris Gare du Nord); the Berlin–Warszawa Express; and ICE Sprinters – fast trains between key cities.

BY LOCAL BUS AND TRAM

All cities have reliable local **buses**, though in more rural areas they can be infrequent. You can usually buy tickets from the driver; stops are marked "H" for *Haltestelle*. Major cities also have a **U-Bahn** and/or a tram system, where you'll normally need to buy and validate your ticket before boarding or, sometimes, as you're actually boarding. U-Bahns are patrolled, albeit infrequently, by plain-clothes ticket inspectors who will levy on-the-spot fines on passengers without valid tickets.

BY BICYCLE

Cyclists are well catered for: many smaller roads have cycle paths, and bike-only lanes are ubiquitous in cities, where it's often a great way to get around. There are also some excellent long-distance cycle routes. Many train stations have bicycle rental outlets (around €15/day). Deutsche Bahn offers its own service, Call A Bike (w callabike.de), where you call ☎07000 522 5522, give your credit card number and obtain a code to open a bike lock. When you return the bike, your credit card is charged according to how long you've used it (€0.08/min up to a maximum of €15/day). Bikes need their own ticket (*Fahrradkarte*) on a train: €5/day on regional trains and €9/day on IC/EC trains. Bikes are not allowed on ICE services.

ACCOMMODATION

It's often best to reserve **accommodation** in advance, especially in the cities, where trade fairs and seasonal tourism can create high demand. Nearly all tourist offices will reserve accommodation for a fee.

You're never far away from a large, functional **HI hostel** (*Jugendherberge*) run by DJH (@jugendherberge.de) – but they are often block-booked by school groups, so reserve in advance, and they aren't particularly cheap (around €22, including breakfast and sheets). There are usually no curfews or lockouts, but reception hours may be limited. **Independent hostels** are a much better choice in cities – friendly, relaxed and often an excellent source of local advice; however, many have started to book their beds budget-airline-style: the bigger the demand and the closer to the arrival day you book, the more you pay. Expect to pay €15–30; breakfast and sheets are not always included. The Backpacker Network Germany (@backpackernetwork.de) lists many options.

Hotels are graded, clean and comfortable. In rural areas, prices start at about €30 for a double room; in cities, at about €50. *Pensions* and **B&Bs** are plentiful; local tourist offices will have a list (or look for signs saying *Fremdenzimmer* or *Zimmer frei*).

Even the most basic **campsites** have toilets, washing facilities and a shop. For a complete list of campsites see @bvcd.de.

FOOD AND DRINK

German **food** is both good value and high quality, and though traditionally solid and meat-heavy, there's often a wide range of international choices in cities at least: Italian restaurants are the most reliable, but Greek, Turkish and Chinese places are also common. Some hotels and guesthouses include **breakfast** in the price of the room – typically including cold meats and cheeses, bread and jams. Traditionally **lunch** tends to be treated as the main meal, with good-value daily menus on offer. Pubs and inns – a **Gaststätte**, **Gasthaus** or **Gasthof** – are usually cosy and serve hearty home cooking, particularly pork and sausages along with distinct regional variations.

The distinction between café, restaurant and bar is often blurred, with many offering good simple breakfasts, salads and some mains. *Gaststätten*– along with the brewery-affiliated *Brauhäuser* – also offer their own beer alongside filling soups, salads and snack dishes. The easiest option for snacks, however, is to head for the ubiquitous **Imbiss** street stalls and shops, which range from traditional *Wurst* sellers to popular *döner kebap* places.

Traditional German cuisine generally offers little for **vegetarians**, but nowadays you should be able to find vegetarian food in all but the most diehard of country inns.

DRINK

For **beer** drinkers, Germany is paradise. Munich's beer gardens and beer halls are the most famous drinking dens in the country, offering a wide variety of premier products, from dark lagers through tart *Weizens* to powerful *Bocks*. Cologne holds the world record for the number of city breweries, which all produce the beer called *Kölsch*, but wherever you go you can be fairly sure of getting a locally brewed variety. There are also many high-quality German **wines**, especially those made from the Riesling grape. Finally, **Apfelwein** is a sour variant of cider beloved in and around Frankfurt.

CULTURE AND ETIQUETTE

Most Germans are friendly, hospitable and helpful, and if you stand at a corner long enough with map in hand, someone's bound to volunteer help. **Jaywalking** is illegal in Germany; only cross on the green man, as you could be fined if caught

12

12

GERMANY ONLINE
Ⓦ **bahn.de** German railways.
Ⓦ **germany.travel** Official tourist board site.
Ⓦ **stadtplandienst.de** City maps.
Ⓦ **webmuseen.de** Information on the country's museums (also available as an app).

– but are most likely to get off with highly disapproving looks from passers-by even in the largest of cities.

The German approach to paying at a café is a little different. If you're in a group, you'll be asked if you want to pay individually (*getrennt*) or all together (*zusammen*). To **tip in a café**, round your bill up to the next €0.50 or €1 and give the total directly to the waiter; at restaurants you'll be expected to leave around ten percent of the bill.

SPORTS AND OUTDOOR ACTIVITIES

Bundesliga football (Ⓦbundesliga.de/en) is the major spectator sport in Germany, with world-class clubs playing in top-notch stadiums. Tickets can be purchased from the clubs' websites; important matches sell out well in advance.

Germany's great outdoors has a lot to offer, particularly to **hikers** and **cyclists**. The most popular regions for hiking are in the Black Forest and the Bavarian Alps, but there are well-maintained, colour-coded hiking routes all over Germany. The country is crisscrossed with long-distance cycling routes. The cycling page on Germany's tourism website (Ⓦgermany-tourism.de/cycling) is excellent for planning.

COMMUNICATIONS

Post offices are open Monday to Friday 8am to 6pm and Saturday 8am to 1pm. Call shops are the cheapest way to **phone** abroad, though you can also do this from any payphone except those marked "National"; phonecards are widely available. The operator is on ☏03.

Internet access is widespread; expect to pay €1–2 per hour. As Germans have not taken to wi-fi in a big way, don't expect many cafés or bars to offer free access; often you have to pay in hotels or, indeed, hostels.

EMERGENCIES

The **police** (*Polizei*) treat foreigners with courtesy. Reporting thefts at local police stations is straightforward, but there'll be a great deal of bureaucracy to wade through. Doctors generally speak English. **Pharmacies** (*Apotheken*) can deal with many minor complaints; all display a rota of local pharmacies open 24 hours.

INFORMATION

You'll find a good **tourist office** in every town, with a large amount of literature and maps; town and regional tourist websites are usually excellent. City tourist offices often offer discount cards, which typically cover public transport and free or discounted entry to major sights. These can be worthwhile, but check first what discounts are offered – sometimes they're no better than the student price. All museums and attractions offer huge reductions for students and young people.

MONEY AND BANKS

German currency is the **euro** (€). **Exchange facilities** are available in most banks, post offices and commercial exchange shops called *Wechselstuben*. The Reisebank has branches in the train stations of most main cities (generally open daily, often till 10/11pm). Basic **banking hours** are Monday to Friday 8.30am to noon and 1.30 to 3.30/4pm, Thursdays till 5/6pm. **Credit cards** are generally accepted – but certainly not universally – with budget restaurants, cafés and many shops requesting cash. **ATMs** are widespread.

EMERGENCY NUMBERS
Police ☏110; Fire & Ambulance ☏112.

GERMAN

Pronunciation Consonants: "w" is pronounced like the English "v" and the "v" like "f"; "sch" is pronounced "sh"; "z" is "ts". The German letter "ß" is a double s. Vowels: a is like in "car", e is "eh", "ie" and "i" are "ee", "ei" is "eye", "eu" is "oy"; u is "oo", o is "awe", ä is like in "ma'am", ü is like the French "plus" and ö like the French "oeuf".

	GERMAN	**PRONUNCIATION**
Yes	*Ja*	Yah
No	*Nein*	Nine
Please	*Bitte*	Bitteh
Thank you	*Danke*	Duhnkeh
Hello/Good day	*Guten Tag*	Gooten tahg
Goodbye	*Tschüss, ciao,* or *auf Wiedersehen*	Chuss, chow, or owf veederzain
Excuse me	*Entschuldigen Sie, bitte*	Enshooldigen zee bitteh
Today	*Heute*	Hoyteh
Yesterday	*Gestern*	Gestern
Tomorrow	*Morgen*	Morgen
I don't understand	*Ich verstehe nicht*	Ich vershtayeh nicht
How much is…?	*Wieviel kostet…?*	Vee feel costet…?
Do you speak English?	*Sprechen Sie Englisch?*	Shprechen zee aing lish?
I'd like a beer	*Ich hätte gern ein Bier*	Ich hetteh gairn ein beer
Entrance /exit	*der Eingang/der Ausgang*	dare eingahng/dare owsgahng
Toilet	*das WC/die Toilette*	dahs vay-tsay/dee toyletteh
HI hostel	*die Jugendherberge*	dee yougendhairbairgeh
Main train station	*der Hauptbahnhof*	howptbahnhof
Bus	*der Bus*	dare boos
Plane	*das Flugzeug*	das floog-tsoyg
Train	*der Zug*	dare tsoog
Cheap/expensive	*Billig/teuer*	Billig/toy-er
Open/closed	*Offen/auf geschlossen/zu*	Uhffen/owf gehshlossen/tsoo
One	*Eins*	Einz
Two	*Zwei*	Tsveye
Three	*Drei*	Dry
Four	*Vier*	Fear
Five	*Fünf*	Foonf
Six	*Sechs*	Zex
Seven	*Sieben*	Zeeben
Eight	*Acht*	Ahkt
Nine	*Neun*	Noyn
Ten	*Zehn*	Tsehn

12

OPENING HOURS AND HOLIDAYS

Shops open at 8am and close around 6 to 8pm weekdays and 2 to 4pm on Saturdays; they are generally closed all day Sunday, though regulations vary by state. Exceptions are pharmacies, petrol stations and shops in and around train stations, which stay open late and at weekends. **Museums** and **historic monuments** are, with few exceptions (mainly in Bavaria), closed on Monday. **Public holidays** are: January 1, January 6 (regional), Good Friday, Easter Monday, May 1, Ascension Day, Whit Monday, Corpus Christi (regional), August 15 (regional), October 3, November 1 (regional) and December 25 and 26.

Berlin

Energetic and irreverent, **BERLIN** is a welcoming, exciting city where the speed of change over the past few decades has been astounding. With a long history of decadence and cultural dynamism, the revived national capital has become a

12

magnet for artists and musicians. Culturally, it has some of the most important archeological collections in Europe, as well as an impressive range of galleries and museums, and an exuberant, cutting-edge nightlife.

The city resonates with modern European history, having played a dominant role in Imperial Germany, both during the Weimar Republic after 1914 and in the Nazis' Third Reich. After 1945 the city was partitioned by the victorious Allies and, as a result, was the frontline of the Cold War. In 1961, its division into two hostile sectors was given a very visible expression by the construction of the notorious Berlin Wall. After the Wall fell in 1989, Berlin became the national capital once again in 1990. These days, parliament (**Bundestag**) sits in the renovated Reichstag building, and the city's excellent museum collections have been reassembled. The physical revival of

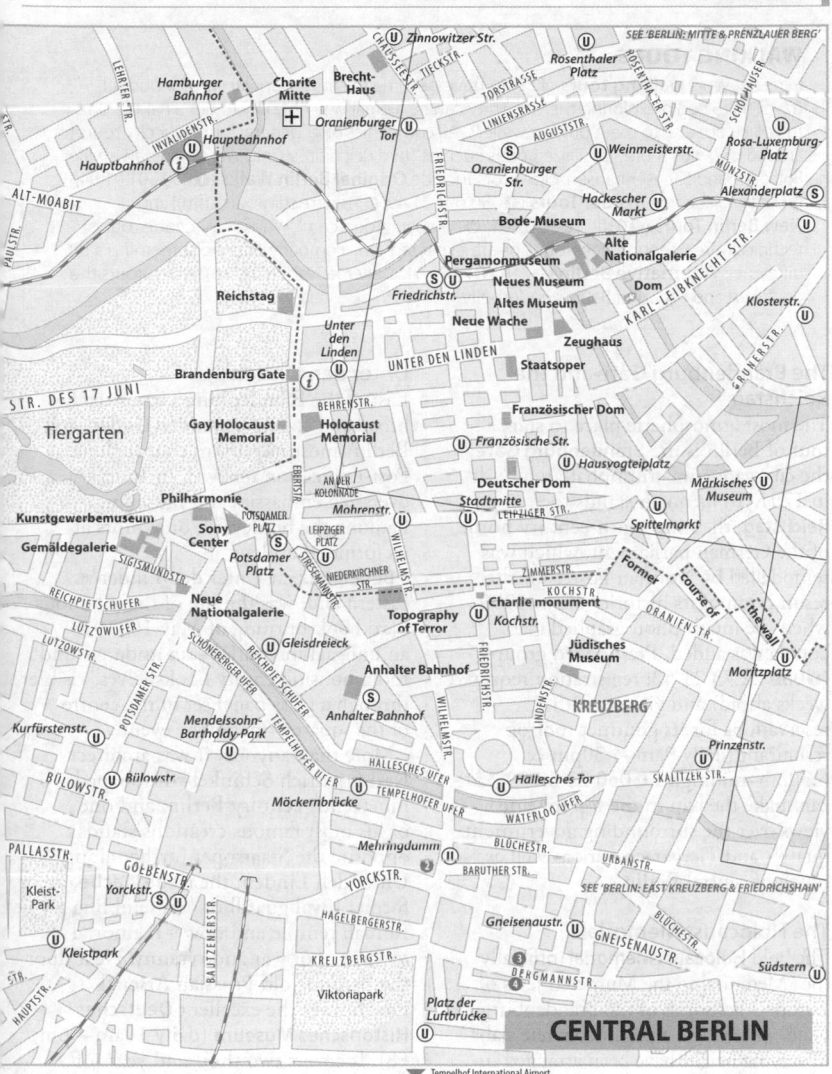

CENTRAL BERLIN

12

Berlin has put it at the forefront of contemporary architecture, and there is a plethora of dramatic new buildings around the city.

WHAT TO SEE AND DO

Most of Berlin's main sights are in the central **Mitte** district, which extends from the leafy boulevard of Unter den Linden to the bustling area of restaurants, shops and bars around Hackescher Markt a short walk

northeast. To the south lies Potsdamer Platz and the museums of the Kulturforum. This overlooks the Tiergarten park while further west lies the adjacent area City West, a neighbourhood known for its shopping, particularly along the Ku'damm. The residential city districts beyond Mitte – particularly **Kreuzberg**, **Prenzlauer Berg**, **Friedrichshain** and **Neukölln** – have many of the city's liveliest hangouts.

12

WALKING TOURS

In recent years **walking tours** of Berlin have become the most popular way for budget travellers to begin exploring the city. They can be a great way not only to get a handle on the place but also to meet other travellers. All companies offer general four-hour city tours for around €12, plus more specialized ones such as Third Reich sites; Cold War Berlin; Jewish life; Potsdam; and Sachsenhausen. Operators include **Original Berlin Walks** (☏030 301 91 94, ⊚berlinwalks.com); **Insider Tours** (☏030 692 31 49, ⊚insiderberlintours.com); and **New Berlin Tours** (☏030 510 50 03 01, ⊚newberlintours.com), whose city-centre tour is technically free, though generous tips are expected. One company offering something a bit different is **Alternative Berlin** (☏0162 819 82 64, ⊚alternativeberlin.com), which tours the graffiti art and squats of Berlin's underbelly.

The Brandenburg Gate and the Reichstag

The most atmospheric place to start a tour of Berlin is the **Brandenburg Gate**, the city-gate-cum-triumphal-arch built in 1791. To its north stands the **Reichstag**, the nineteenth-century home of the German parliament, which was remodelled by Norman Foster for the resumption of its historic role in 1999, when the much-photographed glass cupola was added. Pre-booked groups (☏030 22 73 21 52; registration required weeks ahead) and visitors with reservations for its gourmet rooftop restaurant (daily 9am–4.30pm & 6.30pm–midnight; ☏030 22 62 99 33) can make the trip to the top for fine views over the surrounding government quarter and Tiergarten park as well as much of central Berlin.

The Holocaust Memorials

The bold **Holocaust Memorial** (officially the "Memorial to the Murdered Jews of Europe") lies south of the Brandenburg Gate, where 2711 upright concrete slabs of varying height have been arranged in a dizzying grid. The exhibition in its underground information centre (*Ort der Information*; Tues–Sun: April–Sept 10am–8pm; Oct–March 10am–7pm; free) is carefully presented and moving. Over the road, on the fringes of the Tiergarten park, another concrete oblong forms the **Gay Holocaust Memorial**, which remembers those convicted of homosexual acts under the regime. The whole construction leans to one side, so is defiantly not straight, and has a small window behind which a film of two men kissing permanently plays.

Unter den Linden

East of the Brandenburg Gate stretches broad and stately **Unter den Linden**, once Berlin's most important thoroughfare. Post-unification renewal, including oversized embassies and museums flanking the boulevard, only hints at its former grandeur.

Bebelplatz, at Unter den Linden's eastern end, was the site of the infamous Nazi book-burning of May 10, 1933; an unusual memorial – an underground room housing empty bookshelves, visible through a glass panel set in the centre of the square – marks the event.

More than anyone, it was architect Karl Friedrich Schinkel who shaped nineteenth-century Berlin, and one of his most famous creations stands opposite the Staatsoper further along Unter den Linden: the **Neue Wache**, a former royal guardhouse resembling a Roman temple and now a memorial to victims of war and tyranny. Next door the Baroque old Prussian Arsenal now houses the excellent **Deutsches Historisches Museum** (daily 10am–6pm; €8). It covers two thousand years of German history in imaginative displays that often focus on social history, making good use of the vast selection of artefacts in the collection: from a seventeenth-century Turkish tent taken during the siege of Vienna to parallel displays of life in 1950s East and West Berlin.

The Gendarmenmarkt

Following Charlottenstrasse south from Unter den Linden, you come to the elegant **Gendarmenmarkt**, where the **Französischer Dom** and lookalike

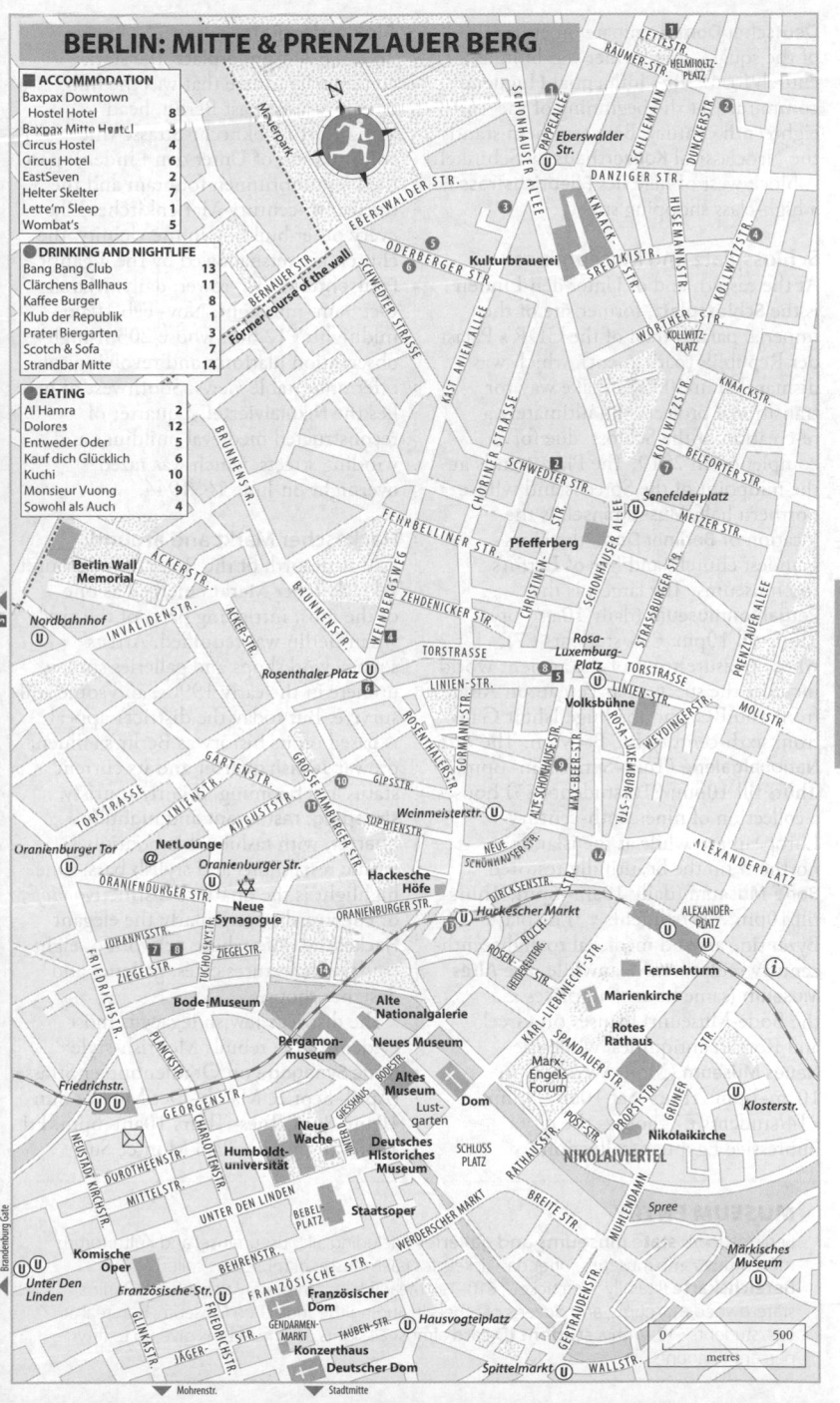

BERLIN: MITTE & PRENZLAUER BERG

■ ACCOMMODATION

Baxpax Downtown Hostel Hotel	8
Baxpax Mitte Hostel	3
Circus Hostel	4
Circus Hotel	6
EastSeven	2
Helter Skelter	7
Lette'm Sleep	1
Wombat's	5

● DRINKING AND NIGHTLIFE

Bang Bang Club	13
Clärchens Ballhaus	11
Kaffee Burger	8
Klub der Republik	1
Prater Biergarten	3
Scotch & Sofa	7
Strandbar Mitte	14

● EATING

Al Hamra	2
Dolores	12
Entweder Oder	5
Kauf dich Glücklich	6
Kuchi	10
Monsieur Vuong	9
Sowohl als Auch	4

12

12

Deutscher Dom dominate on either side of the square. The former was built as a church for Berlin's influential Huguenot community at the beginning of the eighteenth century. Between them stands the Neoclassical **Konzerthaus** by Schinkel. A block west of here lies **Friedrichstrasse**, a high-class shopping street.

Schlossplatz and Museuminsel

At the eastern end of Unter den Linden is the **Schlossplatz**, former site of the imperial palace, then of the GDR's Palast der Republik (parliament), which was dismantled in 2008 to make way for transitional projects and ultimately a re-creation of the Schloss, due for completion in 2019. The Platz stands at the midpoint of the Spree island whose northern half, **Museuminsel**, is the location of **Berliner Dom**, the city's grandest church, and five of Berlin's top museums. The largest is the **Pergamonmuseum** (daily 10am–6pm, Thurs till 10pm; €14/students €7), whose treasure-trove of the ancient world includes the spectacular Pergamon Altar, from 160 BC, and the huge Ishtar Gate from sixth-century BC Babylon. The **Alte Nationalgalerie** (Tues–Sun 10am–6pm, Thurs till 10pm; €10/students €5) houses a collection of nineteenth-century European art, while at the island's northern tip the beautifully restored **Bode-Museum** (daily 10am–6pm, Thurs till 10pm; €10/students €5) displays Byzantine art and medieval to eighteenth-century sculpture. Meanwhile, the **Altes Museum** (same hours and prices as the Bode-Museum) focuses on Greek and Roman antiquities, while the **Neues Museum** (Mon–Wed & Sun 10am–6pm; Thurs–Sat 10am–8pm; €14/students €7) houses the city's impressive Egyptian collection.

Alexanderplatz

To reach **Alexanderplatz**, the stark commercial square that was the hub of communist East Berlin, head along Karl-Liebknecht-Strasse (the continuation of Unter den Linden), past the Neptunbrunnen fountain and the thirteenth-century Marienkirche. Like every other building in the vicinity, the church is overshadowed by the gigantic **Fernsehturm** (TV tower; daily: March–Oct 9am–midnight; Nov–Feb 10am–midnight; €12.50), whose 203m-high observation platform and revolving café offer unbeatable views. Southwest of here lies the **Nikolaiviertel**, a quarter of reconstructed medieval buildings and winding streets, which was razed overnight on June 16, 1944.

Hackescher Markt and around

The area north of the River Spree around ⑤Hackescher Markt emerged as one of the most intriguing parts of the city when Berlin was reunified. Artists' squats, workshops and galleries sprang up here in the early 1990s, and some still survive. But today the district's appeal is based on its history as Berlin's affluent prewar **Jewish quarter** and its current status as a booming, if fairly touristy, **shopping**, **restaurant** and **nightlife quarter**, with fashionable boutiques, ethnic restaurants and stylish bars. One highlight is the quarter's distinctive *Höfe*, or courtyards; particularly the elegant **Hackesche Höfe** whose network of eight courtyards features cafés, galleries and designer shops.

The district's Jewish legacy is most evident in the rebuilt Moorish-style **Neue Synagoge** on Oranienburger Strasse (April–Sept & March–Oct Mon & Sun 10am–8pm, Tues–Thurs 10am–6pm, Fri 10am–5pm; Nov–Feb Mon & Sun

---

MUSEUM ENTRY

Berlin's superb **state museums and galleries** (including all Museuminsel and Kulturforum museums; ⓦsmb.museum) offer day-tickets for each cluster of museums called a **Bereichskarte** (literally "area ticket"; €10–19). Meanwhile, a three-day ticket for all Berlin's state-owned museums, and dozens of others including the Jüdischen Museum, is a steal at €24/students €12. With a **student ID card** almost all sights and museums give up to fifty percent discounts.

10am–6pm, Tues–Thurs 10am–6pm,
Fri 10am–2pm; €4/students €3). Little
remains of the building beyond the
facade, but there are exhibitions on
the history of the synagogue and on
Jewish culture.

Potsdamer Platz

The heart of prewar Berlin lay to the
south of the Brandenburg Gate, around
Potsdamer Platz, which for decades lay
dormant and bisected by the Berlin Wall.
Post-reunification, huge commercial
development has produced a business
district that gathers around the impressive
Sony Center, with its cinema, shops and
attractive atrium.

The Kulturforum

Just west of Potsdamer Platz lies the
Kulturforum, a gathering of museums
centred on the unmissable
Gemäldegalerie (Tues–Sun 10am–6pm,
Thurs till 10pm; €10/students €5; ⑨ &
⑩ Potsdamer Platz), with its world-class
collection of Old Masters. The
interconnected building to the north
houses the **Kunstgewerbemuseum**
(Tues–Fri 10am–6pm, Sat & Sun
11am–6pm; same ticket), a sparkling
collection of European arts and crafts.
A couple of minutes' walk to the south,
the **Neue Nationalgalerie** (Tues–Sun
10am–6pm, Thurs 10am–10pm, Sat &
Sun 11am–6pm; €10/students €5) hosts
temporary modern art exhibitions and
has a good permanent collection of
twentieth-century German paintings,
including Berlin portraits and cityscapes
by George Grosz and Otto Dix.

The course of the Wall

It's now more than twenty years since the
Berlin Wall came down, and recently an
increased effort has been made to
remember the impact of the Wall and
those who died trying to cross it. Much
of the course is marked by a row of two
cobblestones, with info boards at key
points. There are also several stretches
preserved as memorials. Immediately
east of Potsdamer Platz, a sizeable,
crumbling section of Wall runs along
Niederkirchnerstrasse, beside the

captivating **Topography of Terror** (daily
10am–8pm; free), a museum on the
former site of the Gestapo and SS
headquarters which documents their
chilling histories.

To the east, Niederkirchnerstrasse
meets Friedrichstrasse at the site of the
Wall's most infamous crossing:
Checkpoint Charlie. Here, along with
a reconstruction of the checkpoint,
is a fascinating open-air display on the
Wall's history.

At Bernauer Strasse, just north of
Mitte, there's a short stretch of wall that
has been preserved as the **Berlin Wall
Memorial**. This is the only section where
the two parallel walls plus "death strip"
between remain, viewable from a
lookout at the small documentation
centre over the road. Extending from
the no-man's land for several blocks is a
stretch of memorials with plaques,
images and buttons to press that tell
you stories of life in a city with the wall
and stories of escape attempts (Tues–
Sun: April–Oct 9.30am–7pm; Nov–
March 9.30am–6pm; free;
⑨ Nordbahnhof/⑩ Bernauer Str.).

Stretching along the River Spree, near
Friedrichshain, a roughly 1km-long
section of the Wall known as the
East Side Gallery (⑨ Ostbahnhof) is
covered with paintings by international
artists, originally done in the months
after the fall of the Iron Curtain, but
touched up since. Sadly, bits and pieces
of this stretch of the wall were removed
in 2013 to make way for commercial
building sites and luxury apartments.
Whether the remaining sections will be
protected from such treatment in future
remains to be seen.

Jüdisches Museum

Daniel Libeskind's striking zinc-skinned
Jüdisches Museum, Lindenstr. 9–14 in
west Kreuzberg (Jewish Museum; Mon
10am–10pm, Tues–Sun 10am–8pm;
€7/students €3.50; ⑩ Hallesches Tor/
Kochstr.), is part museum, part
memorial. Its lower ground level is
Libeskind's reflection on three strands
of the Jewish experience in Berlin – exile,
Holocaust and continuity – and is a

12

12

BERLIN: EAST KREUZBERG & FRIEDRICHSHAIN

▼ **5** (500m) & Berlin Brandenburg Airport (17km)

■ ACCOMMODATION		● EATING		● DRINKING AND NIGHTLIFE			
Baxpax Kreuzberg Hostel	3	Burgeramt		Ankerklause	14	Privatclub	8
Hüttenpalast	5	Frühstücksklub	3	Astro	1	Rosi's	6
Jetpak Alternative	4	Burgermeister	7	Berghain	2	SO 36	13
Odyssee Globetrotter Hostel	1	Il Casolare	15	Cassiopeia	5	Watergate	9
Ostel	2	Knofi	12	Hops & Barley	4		
		Kvartira Nr. 62	10	Madame Claude	11		

disorientating but compelling experience. You are then directed to the upper two floors, a more conventional exhibition which documents the culture, notable achievements and history of Berlin's Jewish community.

Ku'damm and around
The focus of the city's western side, a short walk south of Bahnhof Zoo station, is the start of the Kurfürstendamm, or **Ku'damm**, a 3.5km strip of ritzy shops, cinemas, bars and cafés. Western Berlin's most famous landmark here is the **Kaiser-Wilhelm-Gedächtniskirche**, mostly destroyed by British bombing in 1943, the broken spire left as a reminder of the horrors of war, with a modern church built alongside. The spire's exterior is currently covered by a clever exterior made to look like a modern high-rise building as renovation works (expected to continue into 2014) attempt to halt the decay.

Tiergarten
Berlin Zoo, beside Zoologischer Garten station, forms the beginning of the giant **Tiergarten**, a restful expanse of woodland and a good place to wander along the banks of the Landwehrkanal. Strasse des 17 Juni heads all the way through the Tiergarten to the Brandenburg Gate, with the **Siegessäule**, the iconic victory monument, at the central point.

Schloss Charlottenburg

The sumptuous **Schloss Charlottenburg** is on Spandauer Damm 10–22 (Old Palace; Tues–Sun: April–Oct 10am–6pm; Nov–March 10am–5pm, €15/students €11; 10min walk from ⑤ Westend or bus #M45 from Zoo). Commissioned by the future Queen Sophie Charlotte in 1695, it was added to throughout the eighteenth and early nineteenth centuries. Admission to the Old Palace includes a tour of the main state apartments and self-guided visits to the private chambers, while the New Wing includes an array of paintings by Watteau and other eighteenth-century French artists.

The Olympiastadion

Located at the far west of the city is the site of the 1936 Olympics, and of the 2006 Football World Cup final, the **Olympiastadion**, one of the very few impressive Nazi-era buildings to have survived. If you can't make it to a Hertha BSC (ⓦ herthabsc.de) match, you can visit at other times (daily 9am–4/7/8pm; €5/students €4; various tours available €9–12; ⓦ olympiastadion-berlin.de; ⓞ or ⑤ Olympiastadion).

ARRIVAL AND DEPARTURE

By plane Berlin's two international airports (ⓦ berlin-airport.de) both lie within easy reach of the city centre via public transport. The closer of the two is Tegel airport (TXL), from which a frequent #TXL express bus runs to the Hauptbahnhof and Alexanderplatz, while #X9 express or local #109 buses run to Bahnhof Zoo (all covered by a public transport zone AB ticket; €2.30). Schönefeld (SXF) is southeast of the centre and reachable via S-Bahn line S9 to Alexanderplatz, the Hauptbahnhof and Bahnhof Zoo (every 30min; 30min); bus #X7 runs to nearby ⓤ Rudow. A public transport zone ABC ticket (€3) covers journeys from Schönefeld into the centre. Berlin Brandenburg International (BBI) – which will incorporate Schönefeld – will open eventually; at the time of writing the due date was set for sometime in 2014, but don't hold your breath; the project has been delayed countless times and will likely be delayed again. When it does open, Tegel will shut its doors.

By train The huge Hauptbahnhof northeast of the Brandenburg Gate is well connected to the rest of the city by S- and U-Bahn.

Destinations Cologne (hourly; 5hr 20min); Dresden (every 2hr; 2hr); Frankfurt (hourly; 4hr); Hamburg (hourly; 1hr 40min); Hannover (hourly; 2hr); Leipzig (hourly; 1hr 15min); Munich (hourly; 6hr); Paris (4 daily, including overnight; 8–10hr); Prague (every 2hr; 4hr 40min); Warsaw (5 daily; 5hr 25min); Weimar (every 2hr; 2hr 20min).

By bus Most international buses stop at the bus station (ZOB), Masurenallee 4-6, which is linked to the Ku'damm area by many buses, including the #M49 service, and U-Bahn line #2 from Kaiserdamm station.

Destinations Cologne (hourly; 6hr); Frankfurt (hourly; 4hr 30min); Hamburg (hourly; 1hr 50min); Hannover (hourly; 2hr 30min); Leipzig (hourly; 1hr 20min); Munich (hourly; 6hr).

INFORMATION

Tourist information Main tourist office at the Hauptbahnhof (daily 8am–10pm; ☎ 030 25 00 25, ⓦ visitberlin.de), with branches at Brandenburg Gate (daily 10am–7pm); Kurfürstendamm 21 (Mon–Sat 10am–8pm, Sun 9.30am–6pm); and in the ALEXA shopping centre, Alexanderplatz (Mon–Sat 10am–8pm).

Discount passes The WelcomeCard (Berlin AB: 48hr/72hr/5-day for €18.50/€24.50/€31.50; Berlin and Potsdam ABC: 48hr/72hr/5-day for €20.50/€26.50/€36.50; ⓦ berlin-welcomecard.de) provides free travel and up to fifty percent off at many of the major tourist sights, though not those on the Museuminsel, and many of the discounts are the same as student prices.

GETTING AROUND

BVG (ⓦ bvg.de) operate an efficient, integrated system of U- and S-Bahn train lines, buses and trams, though cycling in Berlin is also very easy.

By U- and S-Bahn Trains run daily 4.30am–12.30am (Fri & Sat all night).

By bus and tram The city bus network – and the tram system in eastern Berlin – covers the gaps left by the U-Bahn; several useful tram routes centre on Hackescher Markt, including the #M1 to Prenzlauer Berg. Night buses and trams operate, with buses (around every 30min) generally following U-Bahn line routes; free maps are available at most stations.

Tickets Available from machines at U-Bahn stations, on trams or from bus drivers: zone AB single ticket €2.40; zone ABC single €3.10; short-trip ticket (Kurzstreckentarif) for 3/6 train or bus/tram stops €1.40; zone AB day ticket €6.50; for 2/3/5 days the WelcomeCard (see above) is good value. Validate single tickets in the yellow or red machines on platforms before travelling.

By bike Many hostels rent out bikes for around €12–15 per day, as do Fat Tire beneath the TV tower at Alexanderplatz (daily 9.30am–6pm, till 8pm April–Sept;

12

12

☎030 240 479 91, ⓦfattirebiketours.com/berlin). They also offer bike tours (€24/adults, €22/students for 4hr 30min).

ACCOMMODATION

Berlin has plenty of great hostels, primarily in Mitte, Prenzlauer Berg, Kreuzberg and Friedrichshain; several new options are more like budget hotels and are often the best choice for private rooms. Try to book at least a couple of weeks in advance in high season. A few of the larger hostels vary their prices considerably depending on demand. All hostels listed have wi-fi.

HOSTELS

Baxpax Downtown Hostel Hotel Ziegelstr. 28 ☎030 27 87 48 80, ⓦbaxpax.de; Ⓢ & ⓤFriedrichstr; map p.361. This hostel is a little more hotel-like than its sister branches. Most rooms en suite; sheets cost €2.50. Dorm €24, double €100

Baxpax Kreuzberg Hostel Skalitzer Str. 104 ☎030 69 51 83 22, ⓦbaxpax.de; ⓤGörlitzer Bahnhof; map p.364. One of a trio of backpacker outfits with clean, bright rooms, and offering cooking facilities and bike rental. Dorm €16, double €105

Baxpax Mitte Hostel Chausseestr. 102 ☎030 28 39 09 65, ⓦbaxpax.de; ⓤZinnowitzer Str.; map p.361. Same vibe as *Baxpax* hostels listed elsewhere but in a fantastic location amid oodles of bars and restaurants. Dorm €20, double €89

Circus Hostel Weinbergsweg 1a, Mitte ☎030 20 00 39 39, ⓦcircus-berlin.de; ⓤRosenthaler Platz; map p.361. Clean, welcoming fun and deservedly popular base in a great location between Mitte and Prenzlauer Berg, with helpful staff and its own bar. Dorm €20, double €58

★ **EastSeven** Schwedter Str. 7, Prenzlauer Berg ☎030 93 62 22 40, ⓦeastseven.de; ⓤSenefelderplatz; map p.361. Cosy, small, independent hostel with kitchen and pretty garden, including a barbecue. Some nice touches, such as communal meals on Mon, discounts in local shops and good tips on nearby clubs. Dorm €20, double €57

Helter Skelter Kalkscheunenstr. 4–5, Mitte ☎030 28 04 49 97, ⓦhelterskelterhostel.com; ⓈFriedrichstr; map p.361. Lively and central old-school backpackers' place with kitchen and sheets included – and breakfast too if you stay three nights. Dorm €17, double €65

★ **Jetpak Alternative** Görlitzerstr. 38 ☎030 62 90 86 41, ⓦjetpak.de; ⓤSchlesisches Tor; map p.364. Attractive high-end hostel in a gritty neighbourhood close to all the action in Kreuzberg and Friedrichshain. Perks include free internet, a buffet breakfast and under-floor heating, along with bicycle rental, laundry facilities and cheap beer. Dorm €28

Lette'm Sleep Lettestr. 7, Prenzlauer Berg ☎030 44 73 36 23, ⓦbackpackers.de; ⓤEberswalder Str.; map p.361. Chilled-out hostel with free internet, a kitchen and a good

location, on a particularly attractive square in Prenzlauer Berg. Dorm €17, double €72

Odyssee Globetrotter Hostel Grünberger Str. 23, Friedrichshain ☎030 29 00 00 81, ⓦglobetrotterhostel .de; ⓤFrankfurter Tor; map p.364. Young, well-organized hostel with quirky, individually designed rooms and a guest kitchen, ideally situated for the Friedrichshain nightlife scene – though a touch far from the sights. Dorm €14, double €48

Ostel Wriezener Karree 5 ☎030 25 76 86 60, ⓦostel.eu; ⓈOstbahnhof; map p.364. Novelty *Ostalgie*-themed hostel and hotel, all authentically decked out GDR-style, though with some very modern facilities such as free wi-fi. Breakfast €8. Dorm €23, double €73

Wombat's Alte Schönhauser Str. 2 ☎030 84 71 08 20, ⓦwombats-hostels.com/berlin; ⓤRosa-Luxemburg-Platz; map p.361. Bright, friendly and well-equipped new hostel in a great location near some good bars. All dorms are en suite, the spacious, 2-person apartments with kitchens are particularly stylish and the roof bar has superb views over the city. Breakfast €4. Dorm €26, double €72, apartment €84

HOTELS

Circus Hotel Rosenthalerstr. 1 ☎030 20 00 39 39, ⓦcircus-berlin.de; ⓤRosenthaler Platz; map p.361. Fantastic and stylish budget hotel run by the *Circus Hostel* over the road. Helpful staff provide tons of local advice and some nice extras like free loans of laptops to take advantage of the hotel's free wi-fi. Good breakfasts (€9) are also offered and all rooms are en suite, though those overlooking the street are a little noisy. Double €95

Hüttenpalast Hobrechtstr. 65/66 ☎030 37 30 58 06, ⓦhuettenpalast.de; ⓤHermannplatz; map p.364. Funky and quirky place with its own garden and café on the border of trendy Kreuzberg and Neukölln, offering standard hotel rooms, wooden cabanas or vintage caravans. Breakfast €6.50 (cabanas and caravans include morning coffee and croissant). Free wi-fi. Double €85, caravan/cabin €65

EATING

Many cafés, bars and restaurants serve food, with plenty offering a good weekend brunch. The bustling Kreuzberg/ Neukölln Turkish market (Tues & Fri noon–6pm), on the Maybach Ufer (ⓤSchönleinstr. or Kottbusser Tor), is great for cheap breads, vegetables, meat and Turkish sweets.

CAFÉS, CHEAP EATS AND SNACKS

Al Hamra Raumerstr. 16, Prenzlauer Berg ⓤEberswalder Str. or ⓈPrenzlauer Allee; map p.361. Relaxed, extremely popular Arabian-style café-bar. Good food and cheap drinks every day – Sun brunch until 5pm is especially tasty (€10). Daily 11am–11pm.

Burgeramt Frühstücksklub Krossener Str. 22, on Boxhagener Platz; ⊕ Frankfurter Tor or ⑤ Warschauer Str.; map p.364. *Imbiss* place with a slightly eccentric line in burger toppings – pineapple, teriyaki and gouda appear together – but there are plenty of classic and veggie versions, making it a perfect bar-hopping pit stop in Friedrichshain. Burgers €3–6. Daily 11am–midnight.

Burgermeister Oberbaumstr. 8; ⊕ Schlesisches Tor; map p.364. Cult burger joint in converted old Prussian public toilets by the elevated underground station at Schlesisches Tor, serving fresh and delicious burgers (€2–4) that could hold their own in far classier surroundings. Has a couple of places to sit, but mostly it's standing room only and often packed. Mon–Thurs 11am–2am, Fri & Sat 11am–4am, Sun 3pm–2am.

Curry 36 Mehringdamm 36, west Kreuzberg; ⊕ Mehringdamm; map pp.358–359. One of the best places to try Berlin *Currywurst* (€1.80) – a traditional fast-food combo of grilled sausage, hot tomato sauce and curry powder. Daily 10am–4am.

Dolores Rosa-Luxemburg-Str. 7, Mitte; ⑤ & ⊕ Alexanderplatz; map p.361. Mouthwatering California-style Mexican fast food, complete with San Francisco decor and a predictable concentration of expats. Burritos from €4. Daily 11am–11pm.

Entweder Oder Oderberger Str. 15, Prenzlauer Berg; ⊕ Eberwelder Str.; map p.361. Friendly, typically Prenzlauer Berg café-bar, with a tasty menu of German dishes that's perfect for a hangover-beating breakfast: a big platter for two costs €14.50. Daily 11am–11pm.

Kauf dich Glücklich Oderberger Str. 44, Prenzlauer Berg; ⊕ Eberwelder Str.; map p.361. Super cute, café-bar-waffle shop and ice-cream parlour combination, all done out in Fifties retro furniture (that's for sale). Daily 8am–6pm.

Knofi Bergmannstr. 11 & 98, west Kreuzberg; ⊕ Mehringdamm; map pp.358–359. The *Gözsies* – filled Turkish crêpes – are cheap (€5), huge and delicious at this lively local Mediterranean café (no. 11) and deli (no. 98); there's the same menu of soups, salads and some hot dishes at both, and a smaller choice at their other branch (Oranienstr. 179; ⊕ Kottbusser Tor; map p.364), where you can get a plate of salads and pâtés for €8. All branches daily 8am–9pm.

Kvartira Nr. 62 Lübbener Stra. 18; ⊕ Schlesisches Tor; map p.364. Atmospheric Russian café in 1920s-era dark red and gold decor serving Russian classics such as *borscht* (€4), delicious *pelimi* (dumplings; €5) and tea flavoured with jam – as well as some great chocolate cake. Daily 8am–9pm.

Sowohl als Auch Kollwitzstr. 88, Prenzlauer Berg; ⊕ Eberswalder or Senefelderplatz; map p.361. Excellent cake selection, with an extensive coffee and tea menu to boot; also popular for breakfast. Daily 8am–10pm.

RESTAURANTS

Il Casolare Grimmstr. 30, Kreuzberg ☎ 030 69 50 66 10; ⊕ Schönleinstr.; map p.364. Always packed Italian restaurant in a lovely, leafy canal-side spot that's famous for its great wafer-thin pizzas (from €8) and brusque service. Daily 11am–11pm.

Kuchi Gipsstr. 3, Mitte; ⊕ Weinmeister Str.; map p.361. Deliciously fresh, imaginative sushi, all prepared in front of you, is the speciality at this stylish Mitte restaurant. Well worth the slightly higher prices: sushi selection from around €10, stir-fried noodles with tofu €11. Daily 11.30am–11pm.

Monsieur Vuong Alte Schönhauser Str. 46, Mitte; ⊕ Weinmeisterstr.; map p.361. Small, hip and popular Vietnamese place with a high-quality, low-price menu that changes daily. Meals €9. Daily 11am–midnight.

DRINKING AND NIGHTLIFE

Berlin's nightlife ranks among the best in the world and is centred on several different neighbourhoods. As Hackescher Markt and Oranienburger Str. become more upmarket and touristy, the best bars tend to be in the inner-city residential areas: in Prenzlauer Berg, try the area around Kastanienallee for places with a relaxed, neighbourhood feel; in Friedrichshain, the Simon-Dach-Str. is a premier twenty-something late-night hangout; while many of the city's best clubs and prime alternative hangouts are in the vicinity or in the adjoining ramshackle district of Kreuzberg and Neukölln.

BARS

Ankerklause Kottbusser Damm 43, Neukölln; ⊕ Schönleinstr.; map p.364. This everything-goes bar with a nautical theme is open all day until late, with a deck overlooking the canal, a cosy interior with comfy booths, a jukebox and a laidback vibe. They also dish up basic food like nachos and sandwiches (€4–12) until about 9pm. Daily 11am till at least 2am.

GAY BERLIN

Berlin's diverse **gay scene** is spread across the city, but there's a discernible gay village just south of ⊕ Nollendorfplatz in Schöneberg. Here you'll find bars like *Heile Welt* (see p.368), where you can pick up gay listings magazine *Siegessäule* (ⓦsiegessaeule.de), also available in many local cafés and shops. Look out for Club nights by GMF (ⓦgmf-berlin.de) at various venues, including Sundays at **Weekend** and visit **Berghain** (see p.368), a mixed venue with a strong gay presence. The Christopher Street Day Gay Pride festival takes place every year in June (ⓦcsd -berlin.de).

12

Astro Simon-Dach-Str. 40, Friedrichshain; ⓤ Frankfurter Tor; map p.364. Kitschy, always-packed pre-club bar with different DJs nightly and plenty of trendoids flaunting their purple hair and tattooed arms. Daily 6pm–2am.

Heile Welt Motzstr. 5; ⓤ Eberswalder Str.; map pp.358–359. One of Berlin's youngest and trendiest gay bars with great cocktails and a convivial atmosphere. Daily 6pm–late.

Hops & Barley Wühlischstr. 22–23; ⓤ & ⓢ Warschauer Str.; map p.364. One of Berlin's better spots to drink beer brewed on the premises, offering seasonal beers and signature brews like the malty dunkles (dark), a refreshing pilsner and tart cider. Daily 11am–11pm.

Klub der Republik Pappelallee 81, Prenzlauer Berg; ⓤ Eberswalder Str.; map p.361. With fire-escape steps up to the entrance, cheap drinks and frequent live DJs, this fabulous chilled-out lounge-bar gets the shabby-retro look just right. Thurs–Sun 7pm till at least 3am.

Madame Claude Lübenner Str. 19, Kreuzberg; ⓤ Frankfurter Tor & ⓢ Warschauer Str.; map p.364. Quirky, grungy subterranean space with furniture stuck to the ceiling (is that an upside-down chair?), making you think you've leapt into a rabbit hole. Gets packed later on and features DJs spinning a mix of techno, house, funk, rock and a mish-mash of whatever they're in the mood for. Tues–Sat 7pm till at least 3am.

Prater Biergarten Kastanienallee 7–9; ⓤ Eberswalder Str.; map p.361. Large and relaxed Prenzlauer Berg beer garden. The attached Gaststätte serves German classics year-round. Daily (weather permitting) noon till at least 11pm, later in summer.

Scotch & Sofa Kollwitzstr. 18, Prenzlauer Berg; ⓤ Senefelderplatz; map p.361. Trendy, relaxed pre-club bar with free internet and a loyal crowd. Daily 4am till at least 2am.

Strandbar Mitte Monbijoustr. 3, Mitte; ⓢ Hackescher Markt; map p.361. Popular, seasonal city beach bar with sand and deckchairs overlooking the River Spree. Great spot to lounge in the afternoon with a beer, attracting a mixed, 20–40-something crowd. April–Oct daily 9am–late.

CLUBS

Don't bother turning up before 1am at Berlin's clubs. To find out what's on, pick up one of the listings magazines,

Zitty (ⓦ zitty.de), Tip (ⓦ tip-berlin.de) or the English-language Exberliner (ⓦ exberliner.com).

Bang Bang Club Choriner Str. 34. Mitte ⓦ bangbang-club.de; ⓢ Hackescher Markt; map p.361. Studenty indie club, which is one of the locations of the excellent Karrera Klub (ⓦ karreraklub.de), and puts on good gigs. Thurs–Sun 9pm till well into the following day.

Berghain Am Wriezener Bahnhof, Friedrichshain ⓦ berghain.de; ⓢ Ostbahnhof; map p.364. Legendary techno club in a huge former power station, attracting a mixed gay-straight crowd; entrance policy is strict and generally turns away anyone who looks like a foreign backpacker. Upstairs Panorama Bar Fri & Sat, Berghain usually Sat only, till well into Sun; see website for exact times.

★ **Cassiopeia** Revaler Str. 99 ⓦ cassiopeia-berlin.de; ⓢ & ⓤ Warschauer Str.; map p.364. Shambolic former squat with a mad combination of skate-park, climbing wall, cinema, beer garden and four dancefloors. Always worth a look. Wed–Sun 8pm till well into the following day.

Clärchens Ballhaus Auguststr. 24 ⓦ ballhaus.de; ⓢ Hackescher Markt; map p.361. Dancehall that harks back to 1913, hosting a range of dance nights with instruction – check website for times and styles. Also dishes up great pizzas. Daily 4pm till at least midnight.

Kaffee Burger Torstr. 60, Mitte ⓦ kaffeeburger.de; ⓤ Rosenthaler Platz/Rosa-Luxemburg-Platz; map p.361. Small, former GDR bar decorated in deep flushed red, with an eclectic range of live music, spoken word events and club nights, including the infamously funky Russian disco twice monthly. Daily 6pm till at least midnight.

Privatclub Pücklerstr. 34 (under the Markthalle café), Kreuzberg ⓦ privatclub-berlin.de; ⓤ Görlitzer Bhf; map p.364. Intimate basement club with an eclectic range of club nights (soul, Balkan-electronica and indie) and the occasional live gig. Fri & Sat 9pm till at least 2am.

★ **Rosi's** Revalerstr. 29, Friedrichshain ⓦ rosis-berlin.de; ⓢ Warschauer Str.; map p.364. Quirky and hugely fun with Berlin's hallmark unfinished and improvised feel. There's a sense of crashing a house party here, with a small kitchen and living room to hang out in between bouts on dancefloors where indie or techno pounds. Outdoor table tennis too. Daily 9pm till at least 2am.

SO 36 Oranienstr. 190, Kreuzberg ⓦ so36.de; ⓤ Görlitzer Bhf; map p.364. Cult punk club with a large gay and lesbian following. Sun's Café Fatal – ballroom dance class at 7pm, dancing from 8pm – is a fantastically friendly gay and mixed free-for-all. Also frequent live music. See website for exact times.

Watergate Falckensteinstr. 49 ⓦ water-gate.de; ⓤ Schlesisches Tor.; map p.364. Futuristic club with impressive light installations and a glorious riverside location; music is varied but mostly electronic. Wed–Sun 8pm till well into the following day.

BERLIN BY PUB CRAWL

If you fancy exploring Berlin's legendary nightlife in the company of other young travellers, consider joining a **pub crawl tour**. For around €13 you'll be taken to half a dozen watering holes and a club (cover included). All companies offering walking tours (see box, p.360) also organize pub crawls.

ENTERTAINMENT

If you're hunting for cut-rate last-minute tickets to just about any kind of show or event, try Hekticket (☎ 030 230 99 30, ⓦ hekticket.de), which sells half-price tickets from 2pm and has two locations: Hardenberg Str. 29a, Charlottenburg, opposite the main entrance to Ⓤ & Ⓢ Zoologischer Garten, and Karl-Liebknecht-Str. 12, Mitte, north of the TV tower, Ⓤ & Ⓢ Alexanderplatz.

CineStar Potsdamerstr. 4 ⓦ cinestar.de; Ⓤ & Ⓢ Potsdamer Platz; map pp.358–359. Cinema in the Sony Center on Potsdamer Platz that screens films in English; €8/€6.50 students.

Philharmonie Herbert-von Karajan-Str. 1 ☎ 030 25 48 80, ⓦ berliner-philharmoniker.de; Ⓤ & Ⓢ Potsdamer Platz; map pp.358–359. Custom-built home of the world's most celebrated orchestra, the Berlin Philharmonic.

Staatsoper Unter den Linden 7 ☎ 030 20 35 40, ⓦ staatsoper-berlin.org; Ⓢ & Ⓤ Friedrichstr; map p.361. Excellent operatic productions in one of central Berlin's most beautiful buildings.

DIRECTORY

Banks and exchange ATMs and exchange at the airports, and major stations including Reisebank, at the Hauptbahnhof (daily 8am–10pm).

Embassies and consulates Australia, Wallstr. 76–79 ☎ 030 880 08 82 31; Canada, Leipziger Platz 17 ☎ 030 20 31 20; Ireland, Jägerstr. 51 ☎ 030 22 07 20, ⓦ embassyofireland .de; New Zealand, Friedrichstr. 60 ☎ 030 20 62 10, ⓦ nzembassy.com; South Africa, Tiergartenstr. 18 ☎ 030 22 07 30, ⓦ suedafrika.org; UK, Wilhelmstr. 70–71 ☎ 030 20 45 70, ⓦ gov.uk/government/world/germany.de; US, Clayallee 170 ☎ 030 830 50, ⓦ germany.usembassy.gov.

Hospital There's an emergency room at Campus Charité Mitte, entrance Luisenstr, 65/66, Mitte (☎ 030 450 50).

Internet NetLounge, Auguststr. 89 (Mon–Fri 10am–6pm, Sat 10am–4pm; €2.50/30min).

BARGAINS AND BOUTIQUES

Boutiques and local designers are in good supply in Berlin, though bargains are rare. The area just northeast from Ⓢ Hackescher Markt is the best place for a cluster of boutiques. Head to Prenzlauer Berg (from Kastanienallee to Helmholzplatz) for high-quality, high-priced **local designers**, and to the Boxhagener Platz area of Friedrichshain for the latest hipster apparel. Flea markets (*Flohmärkte*) abound in Berlin; head to the Mauerpark in Prenzlauer Berg (Sun 8am–6pm; tram #M10 to Bernauer Str./ Wolliner Str.) for the best bargains.

Pharmacy Apotheke Haupbahnhof, at the Hauptbahnhof (24hr).

Post office The post office (Postämt) with the longest hours is at Bahnhof Friedrichstr., at Georgenstr. 12 (Mon–Fri 6am–10pm, Sat & Sun 8am–10pm).

DAY-TRIPS FROM BERLIN

Easy and engaging day-trips using the S-Bahn include the town of **Potsdam**, just southwest of Berlin, famous for the lavish summer palaces and gardens of the Prussian royalty at Sanssouci. Just beyond Berlin's northern edge lies the sombre site of the former **Sachsenhausen** concentration camp.

Potsdam: Park Sanssouci

Stretching west from **POTSDAM**'s town centre is Park Sanssouci (park entry free, but €2 donation requested for which you get a useful map; day ticket for all sights €19/students €14), a dazzling collection of eighteenth- and nineteenth-century Baroque and Rococo palaces and ornamental gardens that were once the fabled retreat of the Prussian kings. Dotted with follies, fountains and themed gardens, it's a place you could easily lose a day exploring. **Schloss Sanssouci** (Tues–Sun: April–Oct 10am–6pm; €14/students €10; Nov– March 10am–5pm; €10/students €7), the star attraction, was a pleasure palace completed in 1747, where Frederick the Great could escape the stresses of Berlin and his wife. Head here first, as tickets are timed and sell out fast. East of the palace is the **Bildergalerie** (May–Oct Tues–Sun 10am–6pm; €3.50/students €3), a restrained Baroque creation with paintings by Rubens, Van Dyck and Caravaggio. On the opposite side of the Schloss, the **Neue Kammern** (April Mon & Wed–Sun 10am–6pm; May–Oct Tues–Sun 10am–6pm; Nov–March Mon & Wed–Sun 10am–5pm; €4/students €3) was originally used as an orangery and later converted into a guest palace in similar lavish Rococo style.

West of here, the **Orangery** (April Sat & Sun 10am–6pm; May–Oct Tues–Sun 10am–6pm; €4/students €3, tower €2), a later, Neoclassical palace built by

12

Frederick William IV in 1826, features the astonishing Raphael Hall, covered with quality copies of many of Raphael's most famous works. At the west end of the 1.5km-long stylized gardens stands the massive Rococo **Neues Palais** (Mon & Wed–Sun: April–Oct 10am–6pm; Nov–March 10am–5pm; €6.50/ students €5.50), which has an exquisitely opulent interior.

ARRIVAL AND INFORMATION

By train and bus Take ⓢ #7 (every 10min; 35min; zone C) or a regional train to Potsdam. From Potsdam train station, take bus #695 (every 20min) or #X5 to Schloss Sanssouci (2km); #695 also stops at the Neues Palais, the Orangery and the Dachhaus.

Tourist information Potsdam tourist office is in the train station (April–Oct Mon–Sat 9.30am–8pm, Sun 10am–4pm; Nov–March Mon–Fri 9.30am–6pm, Sun 10am–4pm). Sanssouci's main information office is by the windmill (Historische Mühle; daily: March–Oct 8.30am–5pm; Nov–Feb 9am–4pm) near the Schloss Sanssouci entrance.

Gedenkstätte Sachsenhausen

Over 200,000 people were imprisoned at **Sachsenhausen concentration camp** between 1936 and 1945, of which many tens of thousands died at the hands of the Nazis. Some original buildings have been turned into a memorial with exhibitions (daily: mid-March to mid-Oct 8.30am–6pm; mid-Oct to mid-March 8.30am–4.30pm; free audio tour €3; leaflet €0.50; ⓦstiftung-bg.de/gums/en /index.htm).

ARRIVAL AND DEPARTURE

By train and bus Take ⓢ #1 to Oranienburg (every 10min; 50min; zone C), and then bus #804 or #821, or walk for 20min, following the signs to Sachsenhausen.

Eastern Germany

Berlin stands apart from the rest of the East, but its dynamism finds an echo in the two other main cities in the region: particularly **Dresden**, the beautiful Saxon capital so ruthlessly destroyed in 1945, now rebuilt and thriving, and **Leipzig**, which provided the vanguard of the 1989

revolution. Both combine some interesting sights and excellent museums and galleries, with a fun, irreverent bar and club scene. Equally enticing are some of the smaller places, notably the beautiful, diminutive **Weimar**, the fountainhead of much of European art and culture, while small-town **Meissen** retains the appearance and atmosphere of prewar Germany.

DRESDEN

Once generally regarded as Germany's most beautiful city, **DRESDEN** survived World War II largely unscathed until the night of February 13, 1945. Then, in a matter of hours, it was reduced to ruins in saturation bombing, with around 18,000 to 25,000 people killed. Post-reunification, the city has slotted easily into the economic framework of the reunited Germany, and most of the historic buildings have been brilliantly restored in an ambitious and hugely successful project. Its physical revival is reflected in its resurgent nightlife, with the thriving Neustadt-centred scene a hedonistic surprise.

WHAT TO SEE AND DO

The city's main sights are in the picturesque **Altstadt**, which stretches along the southern bank of the River Elbe. The grand Baroque set pieces are centred on **Theaterplatz** – with the Zwinger, Residenzschloss and Semperoper (the grand opera house) – and **Neumarkt** further east. Between the two is Augustusstrasse, along which runs a porcelain-tiled mural, while the formal **Brühlsche Terrasse** is an elegant promenade along the river. The southern part of the Altstadt is more prosaic, though the large 1960s Prager Strasse, which runs down to the Hauptbahnhof, is useful for high-street shopping. North of the river, the **Neustadt** is the best place to eat, drink and sleep.

The Frauenkirche

Dominating Dresden Altstadt's skyline is the elegant, soaring dome of the Baroque **Frauenkirche** (Mon–Fri 10am–noon &

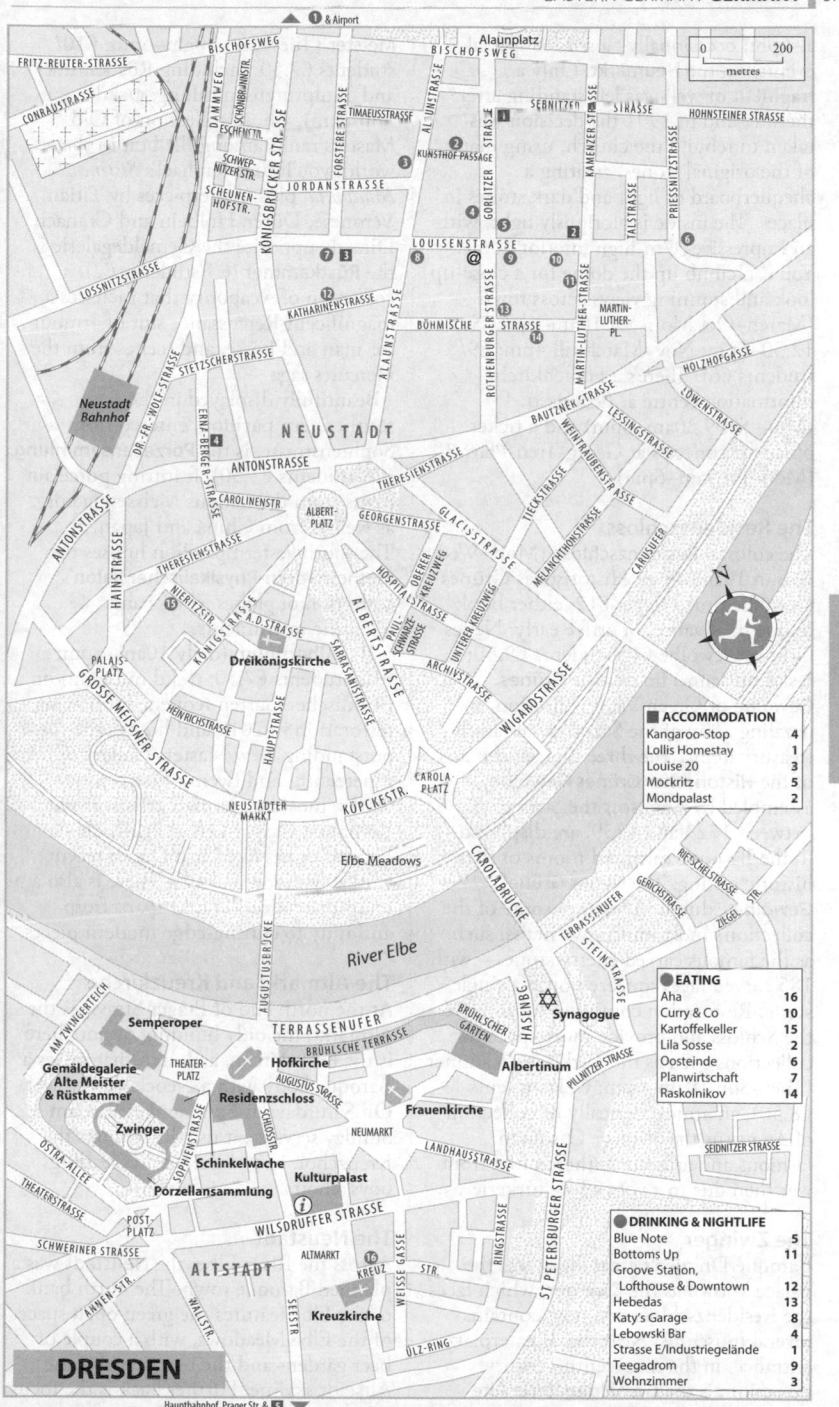

1 & Airport

0 — 200
metres

ALAUNPLATZ

12

N

ACCOMMODATION
Kangaroo-Stop	4
Lollis Homestay	1
Louise 20	3
Mockritz	5
Mondpalast	2

EATING
Aha	16
Curry & Co	10
Kartoffelkeller	15
Lila Sosse	2
Oosteinde	6
Planwirtschaft	7
Raskolnikov	14

DRINKING & NIGHTLIFE
Blue Note	5
Bottoms Up	11
Groove Station, Lofthouse & Downtown	12
Hebedas	13
Katy's Garage	8
Lebowski Bar	4
Strasse E/Industriegelände	1
Teegadrom	9
Wohnzimmer	3

DRESDEN

Hauptbahnhof, Prager Str. & **5**

12

1–6pm; occasionally closed for special events) on the **Neumarkt**. Only a fragment of wall was left standing after the war, and in 1991 the decision was taken to rebuild the church, using many of the original stones, creating a chequerboard of light and dark stones in places. The inside is gloriously light, with an impressive 37m-high interior dome. You can climb up the dome for a close-up look and stunning views across town (March–Oct Mon–Sat 10am–6pm, Sun 12.30–6pm; Nov–March till 4pm; €9/students €6). There's a Frauenkirche information centre at Galeriestr. 1 (Mon–Sat 9.30am–6pm) and a ticket office for concerts at Georg-Treu-Platz 3 (Mon–Fri 9am–6pm).

The Residenzschloss

The colossal **Residenzschloss** (Mon–Wed & Sun 10am–6pm; Historisches Grünes Gewölbe timed ticket €12, either book online in advance, or arrive early; Neues Grünes Gewölbe €12/students €9.50; ⊛skd.museum) houses the **Grünes Gewölbe** or Green Vault collection, a dazzling array of the Saxon royal family's treasury items. The three thousand items of the **Historisches Grünes Gewölbe**, assembled by Augustus the Strong between 1723 and 1730, are displayed in the Baroque mirrored rooms of their historic setting. The **Neues Grünes Gewölbe** exhibition features some of the collection's most impressive items, such as the famous carved cherry stones – with 185 carved faces squeezed onto a single stone. Restoration continues to improve the Schloss and provide more space for collections such as the Türkische Kammer (Tues–Sun 10am–6pm; €11/students €8.50), an atmospherically lit collection of Augustus the Strong's Ottoman fashions and armour, gathered first from war then due to a vogue for "turkerie".

The Zwinger

Baroque Dresden's great glory was the palace known as the **Zwinger**, which faces the Residenzschloss and now contains several museums. Near the Theaterplatz entrance, in the nineteenth-century extension, is the **Gemäldegalerie Alte Meister** (Tues–Sun 10am–6pm; €10/students €7.50, including Rüstkammer and Skulpturensammlung; ⊛skd .museum), whose collection of Old Masters ranks among the best in the world: you'll find Raphael's *Sistine Madonna*, plus masterpieces by Titian, Veronese, Dürer, Holbein and Cranach. Directly opposite the Gemäldegalerie is the **Rüstkammer** (€3/students €2), a collection of weaponry that includes a magnificent Renaissance suit of armour for man and horse, and scenes from the Hercules saga.

Beautifully displayed in the southeastern pavilion, entered from Sophienstrasse, is the **Porzellansammlung** (€6/students €3.50), featuring porcelain items from the famous Meissen factory, as well as from China and Japan. The southwestern pavilion houses the **Mathematisch-Physikalischer Salon**'s collection of globes, clocks and scientific instruments.

The **Albertinum** (daily 10am–6pm; €10/students €7.50; ⊛skd.museum) on Brühlischer Garten reopened following restoration in 2010 and houses the outstanding New Masters Gallery of nineteenth- and twenty-first-century works, most by German artists: from Romantic Caspar David Friedrich via Expressionists like Otto Dix to recent works by modern artists. There is also a sculpture collection that spans from antiquity to cutting-edge modern pieces.

The Altmarkt and Kreuzkirche

At the north end of Prager Strasse is the **Altmarkt**; the only building of note here is the **Kreuzkirche**, a church that mixes a Baroque body with a Neoclassical tower. On Saturdays at 6pm, and at 9.30am Sunday services, it usually features the Kreuzchor, one of the world's leading boys' choirs.

The Neustadt

Across the River Elbe, the **Neustadt** was a planned Baroque town. The north bank of the Elbe features the green open space of the Elbe Meadows, with a couple of beer gardens and the best views of the Altstadt skyline. Further back is the focus of the city's gentrification, with a burgeoning art scene; wander through the bohemian **Kunsthof passage** with its courtyards, houses and arty shops.

ARRIVAL AND DEPARTURE

By plane Dresden Airport (🖥 dresden-airport.de) is connected to the Hauptbahnhof and the Neustadt Bahnhof by 🚊 2 (every 30min; 13–23min; €2.20).

By train Dresden has two main train stations – the Hauptbahnhof, south of the Altstadt, and Neustadt Bahnhof, at the northwestern corner of the Neustadt. Destinations Berlin (every 2hr; 2hr 15min); Frankfurt (hourly; 4hr 45min); Leipzig (every 30min; 1hr 15min–1hr 40min); Meissen (every 30min; 40min); Prague (every 2hr; 2hr 10min); Weimar (hourly; 2hr 10min); Wrocław (3 daily; 3hr 30min).

INFORMATION

Tourist information Tourist office in the Kulturpalast on Altmarkt (Mon–Fri 10am–7pm, Sat 10am–6pm, Sun 10am–3pm; 🕿 0351 501 601 60, 🖥 dresden-tourist.de).

Discount passes The good-value Dresden-City-Card (€26/48hr) covers public transport, entrance to all Dresden state museums, except the Historisches Grünes Gewölbe, and sundry discounts. The Dresden Regio-Card (€78/5-day) extends to regional transport.

GETTING AROUND

By public transport The network of trams, buses and S-Bahn is frequent and reliable, though the main sights are easily walkable. Trams #8 (to Theaterplatz) and #7 (to Synagoge by Brühlischer Garten) are useful for getting between the Neustadt and Altstadt. One-way €2.20; day ticket €5.50.

ACCOMMODATION

Kangaroo-Stop Erna-Berger-Str. 8–10, Neustadt 🕿 035 13 14 34 55, 🖥 kangaroo-stop.de. Cheap, spacious hostel with a kitchen on a quiet street 3min from the Neustadt Bahnhof, 10min from the bar district. Dorms in one building and apartments (holding from upwards of 2 people) and private rooms in another. Dorm €25, double €44, apartment €78

★ **Lollis Homestay** Görlitzer Str. 34, Neustadt 🕿 035 18 10 84 58, 🖥 lollishome.de. This wonderfully cosy hostel is in the centre of the lively Neustadt, with friendly staff, quirky rooms, a kitchen (plus free communal dinners weekly) and bikes for rent – though the central location means it can be loud at night. Tram to Alaunplatz or 20min from Neustadt Bahnhof. Sheets €2 extra. Both dorms and rooms €2 extra at weekends. Dorm €13, double €46

Louise 20 Louisenstr. 20, Neustadt 🕿 035 18 89 48 94, 🖥 louise20.de. Bright, quiet, though slightly bland, hotel-quality hostel in a courtyard in the bar district. Dorm €17, double €40

Mockritz Boderitzer Str. 30 🕿 035 14 71 52 50, 🖥 camping-dresden.de; bus #76 from the Hauptbahnhof. Basic campsite with some nice shady spots. Open year-round. Reception 8–11am & 4–9pm. Camping €6.50 per person, plus €4.50 per tent

Mondpalast Louisenstr. 77, Neustadt 🕿 035 15 63 40 50, 🖥 mondpalast.de; tram to Louisenstr., Pulsnitzerstr. or a 20min walk from the Neustadt Bahnhof. Another great backpackers' place with a kitchen and en-suite doubles on one of the Neustadt's main thoroughfares. Bike rentals €8/day. Sheets €2. Dorm €18, double €44

EATING

Aha Kreuzstr. 7, Altstadt. Slightly hippy-ish fair-trade café and shop, with a good-value menu of soups and healthy mains like potato and leek soup, and caesar salad. Daily 10am–7pm.

Curry & Co Louisenstr. 62, Neustadt. This ultra-hip, minimalist *Currywurst* joint is a basic stand that serves up cheap, quick and satisfying meals on the go. *Currywurst* and fries €5. Daily 10am–11pm.

Kartoffelkeller Nieritzstr. 11, Neustadt. Potato served in myriad ways, in a beautiful cellar space, at good rates. Roast potatoes with herring fillets €10. Mon–Sat noon–10pm.

Lila Sosse Kunsthof passage, Alaunstr. 70, Neustadt. A cool bistro in a pretty courtyard that prepares modern German dishes from €13. A great spot for relaxing and unwinding. Daily 10am–11pm.

Oosteinde Preissnitzstr. 18, Neustadt. Delicious, good-value food served under a low vaulted roof or outside in a peaceful beer garden. Burgers from €7, mains from €8. Daily 11am–11pm.

Planwirtschaft Louisenstr. 20, Neustadt. Popular café-bar-restaurant and *Biergarten* with great breakfast buffet (Mon–Fri €10, Sat & Sun €12). Convivial tables set under trees offer the chance to chat with new friends. Daily noon–11pm.

Raskolnikov Böhmische Str. 34, Neustadt. A large, rambling, bohemian Russian bar-café and restaurant. Great food and atmospheric beer garden that gets very crowded on weekends. Daily 11am–11pm.

DRINKING AND NIGHTLIFE

With over 130 bars and clubs clustered around a handful of narrow streets, the Neustadt provides something for everyone. For nightlife listings, pick up a copy of *Sax* or *Dresdner* (German only) from kiosks or backpacker hostels.

BARS

Blue Note Görlitzer Str. 2b, Neustadt 🖥 bluenote -dresden.de. Dark and boozy jazz bar, packed to the gills

12

every night for its live music. If you want to snag a seat get there early, as in when it opens. Daily 7pm till at least midnight.

Bottoms Up Martin-Luther-Str. 31, Neustadt. Down a quiet backstreet away from the main action, this easy-going café-bar and beer garden is an unpretentious favourite with good weekend breakfasts. Mon–Fri 7pm till at least midnight, Sat & Sun 9am–midnight.

Hebedas Rothenburger Str. 30, Neustadt. Grungy atmospheric bar that epitomizes the Neustadt alternative scene. The crowd is composed of mostly 20-somethings. Daily 7pm till at least midnight.

Lebowski Bar Gorlitzerstr. 53, Neustadt. Kick back with a cocktail (a white Russian, of course, just like the Dude) while the Big Lebowski plays in the background. Daily 6pm till at least 1am.

Teegadrom Louisenstr. 48, Neustadt. An alternative to the Neustadt hipster scene: calm and candlelit, with board games and a mixed crowd of 20- and 30-somethings. Daily 4pm till at least midnight.

Wohnzimmer Alaunstr. 27/Jordanstr. 19, Neustadt. Two levels of living-room-themed bar, with comfy couches and a good selection of cocktails including mojitos and martinis. Daily 8pm till at least 1am.

CLUBS

Groove Station, Lofthouse & Downtown Katherinenstr. 11–13, Neustadt ⓦ groovestation.de, ⓦ lofthouse-dresden.de & ⓦ downtown-dresden.de. Set around a courtyard, this rough-and-ready rock, hip-hop and dance bar/live music complex has been a Neustadt cornerstone for years. Thurs–Sat 8pm till at least 2am.

Katy's Garage Alaunstr. 48, Neustadt ⓦ katysgarage.de. Neustadt institution – and one of the few clubs to open daily – with a chilled beer garden at the front, and club behind (from 8pm); Mon is student night. Daily 5pm till at least 1am.

Strasse E/Industriegelände Werner-Hartmann-Str. 2 ⓦ strasse-e.de; tram #7 or #8 to Industriegelände, along Hermann-Mende-Str. then right onto Werner-Hartman-Str. Industrial area turned club/venue mini-city north of the Neustadt, where there's always something on. Daily 7pm till at least 2am.

DAY-TRIPS FROM DRESDEN

Around Dresden there is stunning scenery in **Saxon Switzerland** and the quaint unspoilt town of **Meissen**, making the city a good base for exploring the region. Both are within Dresden's regional transport network, and the three-day Dresden Regio-Card is good value for week-long stays (see p.373).

Sächsische Schweiz (Saxon Switzerland)

The **Sächsische Schweiz** (Saxon Switzerland) region southeast of Dresden is a natural wonderland of majestic sandstone mountains, offering ample opportunities for hiking, cycling and climbing. One classic route is the 115km Malerweg (Painter Route), overnighting in the tourist-friendly villages along the way. There are countless day hikes as well, such as Königstein to Rathen via Lilienstein (7km), through woods and open vistas.

ARRIVAL AND INFORMATION

By S-Bahn and bus It's easy to visit this region from Dresden; just take ⓢ#1 (every 30min; three-zone ticket €5.90) to Kurort Rathen, Königstein or Bad Schandau and follow trailheads from there; local buses also connect these towns.

Tourist information The tourist office in Dresden (see opposite) sells maps and gives information on the Sächsische Schweiz, or check out ⓦ saechsische-schweiz.de.

Meissen

The cobbled square and photogenic rooftop vistas are reason enough to visit the porcelain-producing town of **MEISSEN**, which, unlike its neighbour Dresden, survived World War II almost unscathed.

Walking towards the centre from the **train station** (a 20min walk over the railroad bridge or the Altstadtbrücke; both are signposted), on the opposite side of the River Elbe, you see Meissen's commandingly sited castle almost immediately, rising just back from the Elbe's edge. The **Albrechtsburg** (daily: March–Oct 10am–6pm; Nov–Feb 10am–5pm; €10/students €6) is a late fifteenth-century combination of military fortress and residential palace, which housed a porcelain factory in the eighteenth and nineteenth centuries. Much of its current interior is nineteenth century, with murals celebrating Saxon history. Cocooned within the castle precinct is the Gothic **Dom** (daily: April–Oct 9am–6pm; Nov–March 10am–4pm; €3.50/students €2.50); inside, look out for the brass tomb-plates of the Saxon dukes.

The **Staatliche Porzellan-Manufaktur Meissen** is at Talstr. 9 (daily: May–Oct 9am–6pm; Nov–April 9am–5pm; €10/students €6), about 1.5km south of the central Markt. This is the most famous factory to manufacture Dresden china, whose invention came about when Augustus the Strong imprisoned the alchemist Johann Friedrich Böttger, ordering him to produce gold. Instead, he accidentally invented the first true European porcelain. You can view many of the factory's finest creations in the attached **museum** (same hours) and shop.

ARRIVAL AND INFORMATION

By S-Bahn S-Bahn line 1 from Dresden to Meissen station (35–40min).

Tourist information Meissen's tourist office is located on Markt 3 (April–Oct Mon–Fri 10am–6pm, Sat & Sun 10am–3pm; Nov–March Mon–Fri 10am–5pm, Sat 10am–3pm, Jan closed weekends; ☎03521 419 40, ⊛ touristinfo-meissen.de).

LEIPZIG

LEIPZIG has always been among the most dynamic of German cities. With its influential and respected university, and a tradition of trade fairs dating back to the Middle Ages, there was never the degree of isolation from outside influences experienced by so many cities behind the Iron Curtain. Leipzigers have embraced the challenges of reunification, and the city's imposing monuments, narrow cobbled backstreets and wide-ranging nightlife make for an inviting visit.

WHAT TO SEE AND DO

Most points of interest lie within the old centre, a compact mix of traditional and often strikingly modern, with several *Passagen*, or covered shopping arcades, often with stylish Art Nouveau touches running between the main streets.

Nikolaikirche and Markt

Following Nikolaistrasse due south from the train station brings you to the **Nikolaikirche**, a rallying point during the collapse of the GDR, when its weekly peace prayers, which had been going on

for several years, escalated into large protests. Although a sombre medieval structure outside, inside the church is a real eye-grabber thanks to rich decoration, works of art and pink columns with palm-tree-style capitals. A couple of blocks west is the Markt, whose eastern side is entirely occupied by the **Altes Rathaus**, built in the grandest German Renaissance style with elaborate gables and an asymmetrical tower. To the rear of the Altes Rathaus is the Baroque **Alte Handelsbörse**, formerly the trade exchange headquarters. South of the Markt is **Mäddler Passage**, an elegant arcade famous for the restaurant *Auerbach's Keller*, which features in Goethe's *Faust*.

Museum der bildenden Künste

Immense and striking, the modern perspex-skinned cube of the **Museum der bildenden Künste**, at Katharinenstr. 10 (Tues & Thurs–Sun 10am–6pm, Wed noon–8pm; €6/students €4), houses a distinguished collection, from Old Masters through to twentieth-century artists, and is particularly strong on Leipzig-born Max Beckmann. Traditional galleries are interspersed with airy, two-storey spaces that feature contemporary pieces, many by local artists. The result is imaginative and playful, and showcases some of the work of a thriving local art scene. To explore it further, check out the excellent **Galerie für Zeitgenössische Kunst**, Karl-Tauchnitz-Str. 11, just outside the Ring southwest of the centre (Gallery for Contemporary Art; Tues–Fri 2–7pm, Sat & Sun noon–6pm; €5/students €3); it has a second gallery in the **Spinnerei** galleries complex in an old cotton mill west of the centre (❸ Plagwitz; ⊛ spinnerei.de).

The Thomaskirche and Bach-Museum

Just southwest of the Markt, on Thomaskirchof, stands the **Thomaskirche**, where Johann Sebastian Bach served as cantor for the last 27 years of his life. Predominantly Gothic, the church has been altered through the centuries. The most remarkable feature is its musical

12

12

tradition: the Thomanerchor choir, which
Bach once directed, can usually be heard
on Fridays (6pm), Saturdays (3pm) and
during the Sunday service (9am). Directly
across from the church is the **Bach-
Museum** (Tues–Sun 10am–6pm; €8/
students €6), which showcases Bach
relics such as his manuscripts and
evokes his period and music through
modern displays.

Runde Ecke and Zeitgeschichtliches Forum

In the autumn of 1989 Leipzig was at
the forefront of protests against the
GDR, and one focus for this was the
Runde Ecke, at Dittrichring 24, the city's
headquarters for the Stasi, East
Germany's secret police (daily 10am–
6pm; free; helpful English audioguide
€3). Much of it has been preserved as it
was, complete with a Stasi official's office,
making it a fascinating trawl through the
methods and machinery of the Stasi.

Less atmospheric but slicker is the
Zeitgeschichtliches Forum (Tues–Fri
9am–6pm, Sat & Sun 10am–6pm; free;
ask for English notes), just south of
the Markt at Grimmaische Str. 6, a
multimedia museum on the history of
the GDR.

The Grassi museums

Just east of the centre is the **Grassi museum**
complex, which houses a trio of museums
at Johannisplatz 5–11 (Tues–Sun
10am–6pm; combined ticket €14/students
€10; tram #4, #7, #12 or #15 to
Johannisplatz), with the **Museum für
Angewandte Kunst** (Applied Arts; €6/
students €4) the star, a huge and well-
displayed collection of decorative arts. The
other two are the **Museum für Völkerkunde**
(Ethnology; €7/students €3.50) and the
Museum für Musikinstrumente (Musical
Instruments; €6/students €3.50).

ARRIVAL AND INFORMATION

By plane Leipzig-Halle Airport (W leipzig-halle-airport
.de) is connected with the main train station by the Airport
Express train (every 30min; 15min).
By train Leipzig's enormous Hauptbahnhof is at the
northeastern corner of the Ring, which encircles the old
part of the city.

Destinations Berlin (hourly; 1hr 20min); Dresden (every
30min; 1hr 15min–1hr 40min); Frankfurt (hourly; 3hr
30min); Meissen (hourly; 1hr 20min); Weimar (hourly; 1hr).
Tourist information Tourist office beside the Museum
der bildenden Künste at Katharinenstr. 8 (Mon–Fri
9.30am/10am–6pm, Sat 9.30am–4pm, Sun 9.30am–
3pm; ✆ 0341 71 04 260, W leipzig.de); staff can book
private rooms (free service). Their Leipzig Card (1/3-day for
€9.50/€20), which covers public transport and various
discounts, is unlikely to work out as good value –
particularly if you get student discounts, which are often
the same.

GETTING AROUND

By tram and bus A network of trams and buses centring
on the Hauptbahnhof covers places outside the city centre;
trams #9 and #11 are useful for Karl-Liebknecht-Str. Up to
four stops (Kurzstrecke) €1.60, one-way ticket €2.10, day
ticket €5.20.

ACCOMMODATION

Auensee Gustav-Esche-Str. 5 ✆ 034 14 65 16 00,
W camping-auensee.de; tram #10 or #11 (direction Wahren/
Schkeuditz) to Annaberger Str., then bus #80 to Auensee.
This campsite is open year-round, with bungalow doubles
also available. Reception daily: April–Oct 8am–1pm &
2–9.30pm; Nov–March 8am–1pm & 2–5.30pm. Camping
__€7__ per person, plus __€4__ per tent, bungalow __€30__
Central Globetrotter Kurt-Schumacher-Str. 41 ✆ 034
11 49 89 60, W globetrotter-leipzig.de. Popular backpacker
spot 3min walk north of the station. Sheets €3, sleeping
bags not allowed. Dorms €2 extra at weekends. Dorm __€15__,
double __€38__
Rizz City Karl-Liebknecht-Str. 40 ✆ 034 12 11 33 05; tram
#10 or #11 to Südplatz. Excellent *pension* between the hip
Südvorstadt neighbourhood and the centre, though front
rooms can suffer traffic noise. Quads available, breakfast
not included. Double __€75__
Sleepy Lion Jacobstr. 1 ✆ 034 19 93 94 80, W hostel
-leipzig.de. This is a spacious, well-run hostel west of the
centre, 15min walk from the station. Sheets €2.50,
sleeping bags not allowed. Dorms €2 extra at weekends.
Dorm __€14__, double __€45__

EATING, DRINKING AND NIGHTLIFE

Gottschedstr., just west of the Thomaskirche, is lined with
attractive cafés and bars, while Karl-Liebknecht-Str., a
couple of tram stops south of the centre (#10 or #11), is
lively and studenty.
Ilses Erika Bernhard-Göring-Str. 152, Südvorstadt
W ilseserika.de; tram to Connewitz Kreuz. Indie bar, club
and music venue Thurs–Sat; beer garden all summer long.
Attracts a nice mix of ages and people from students to
families with kids in the beer garden. Daily 11am–11pm.

Kickers in Karl-Liebknecht-Str. 82; tram #10 or #11 to Südplatz. Small, relaxed bar with free table football, loud music and a very studenty feel to it. Daily from around 6pm to midnight, weekends till 3am.

Luise Busestr. 4, corner of Gottschedstr. Chic café-bar with an attractive, vaguely Pop Art decor, serving excellent breakfasts (from €5) and pasta dishes. Daily 6pm–midnight.

Moritzbastei Universitätsstr. 9 ⓦ moritzbastei.de. A cavernous student cellar bar and club in the centre, with lots of events, including live music. There are also beer gardens and a cheap student canteen. Daily 4pm–1am.

naTo Karl-Liebknecht-Str. 46, Südvorstadt ⓦ nato-leipzig .de; tram #10 or #11 to Südplatz. Popular bar, live music venue and cinema showing a mix of German faves and international stuff, sometimes with subtitles but often dubbed. Daily 5 or 6pm till at least midnight.

Zur Pleissenburg Ratsfreischulstr. 2, just south of Thomaskirche off Burgstr. Great value pub-restaurant in the centre serving hearty German food. Daily specials from €6. Daily 5/6pm till around 11pm.

WEIMAR

Despite its modest size, **WEIMAR** has played an unmatched role in the development of German culture: Goethe, Schiller and Nietzsche all made it their home, as did the architects and designers of the Bauhaus school. The town was also chosen as the drafting place for the constitution of the democratic republic established after World War I, a regime whose failure ended with the Nazi accession. Add to this the town's cobbled streets and laidback, quietly highbrow atmosphere, and Weimar makes an attractive stop for a day or two.

WHAT TO SEE AND DO

Weimar's main sights are concentrated in the city's walkable centre, south of the main train station and on the west side of the River Ilm. The meadow-like **Park an der Ilm** stretches 2km southwards from the **Schloss** on both sides of the river. The former concentration camp at **Buchenwald** is a bus ride to the northwest.

The Schloss and Markt

Weimar's former seat of power was the **Schloss**, set by the River Ilm at the eastern edge of the town centre, a Neoclassical complex of a size more appropriate for ruling a mighty empire. It's now a museum (Tues–Sun: April–Oct 10am–5.30pm; Nov–March 10am–4pm; €4/students €3), with a collection of Old Masters on the ground floor, including pieces by both Cranachs and Dürer, while the first-floor rooms are grand Neoclassical chambers, with lavish memorial rooms to great poets – most notably Goethe and Schiller. South of nearby Herderplatz is the spacious **Markt**, lined with a disparate jumble of buildings, the most eye-catching of which is the green and white gabled Stadthaus on the eastern side, opposite the neo-Gothic Rathaus.

The Goethewohnhaus und Nationalmuseum

On Frauenplan, south of the Markt, is the **Goethewohnhaus und Nationalmuseum** (Tues–Sun: April–Sept 9am–6pm, Sat till 7pm; Oct 9am–6pm; Nov–March 9am–4pm; combined €10.50/students €8.50; Nationalmuseum only €4/students €3.50). Goethe lived here for some fifty years until his death in 1832, and the house is atmospherically preserved as it was in his lifetime, complete with his extensive collections and the chair in which he died.

Theaterplatz and around

Weimar's most photographed symbol is the large double statue of Goethe and Schiller. It stands in the centre of Theaterplatz, a spacious square west of the Markt. The **Nationaltheater** on the west side of the square was founded and directed by Goethe, though the present building is a modern copy. Directly opposite is the small but interesting **Bauhaus museum**, with a collection of artefacts from the school (daily 10am–6pm; €5/students €4).

Schillerstrasse snakes away from the southeast corner of Theaterplatz, with **Schillerhaus** at no. 12 (Tues–Sun: April–Sept 9am–6pm, Sat till 7pm; Oct 9am–6pm; Nov–March 9am–4pm; €6/students €5), the home of the poet and dramatist for the last three years of his life.

12

Konzentrationslager Buchenwald

The **Konzentrationslager Buchenwald** (Tues–Sun: April–Oct 10am–6pm; Nov–March 10am–4pm; free; ⓦbuchenwald.de) is situated north of Weimar on the Ettersberg heights, and can be reached by bus #6 (hourly from Goetheplatz and the train station). Over 240,000 prisoners were incarcerated in this concentration camp, with 65,000 dying here. Very few original buildings remain, but an audioguide (€4) and the historical exhibition paint a vivid picture of life and death in the camp.

ARRIVAL AND INFORMATION

By train Weimar's train station, on the Leipzig line, is a 20min walk north of the main sights.

Destinations Dresden (hourly; 2hr 10min); Eisenach (every 30min; 45min–1hr 10min); Frankfurt (hourly; 2hr 30min); Leipzig (hourly; 1hr).

Tourist information Tourist office at Markt 10 (April–Oct Mon–Sat 9.30am–7pm, Sun 9.30am–3pm; Nov–March Mon–Fri 9.30am–6pm, Sat & Sun 9.30am–2pm; ☎03643 545 407, ⓦweimar.de).

ACCOMMODATION

DJH Germania Carl-August-Allee 13 ☎036 43 85 04 90, ⓦdjh-thueringen.de. Neat and tidy HI hostel between the station and the centre. Spaces are nothing special but always spotlessly clean. Dorm €29

★ **Labyrinth Hostel** Goetheplatz 6 ☎036 43 81 18 22, ⓦweimar-hostel.com. Fantastic, central and friendly hostel, each of whose attractive spotless rooms were individually designed by different local artists. There's a good kitchen, a relaxed communal area and a courtyard. Dorm €14, double €48

Savina Meyerstr. 60 ☎036 438 66 90, ⓦpension-savina .de. Convenient *pension* where the cosy, spotless and simply furnished rooms come with en-suite bathrooms and kitchenettes. A fine choice. Double €63

EATING, DRINKING AND NIGHTLIFE

ACC Burgplatz 1. A relaxed bar and restaurant with quiet candlelit tables lining a cobbled side street, free internet and an upstairs gallery. Mains from €8. Daily 11am–11pm/midnight.

Estragon Herderplatz 3. Small café that's part of an organic supermarket, with a daily-changing menu of tasty, filling soups (€3–5) and a salad bar (pay by weight). Mon–Fri 10am–7pm, Sat 10am–4pm.

Giancarlo's Schillerstr. 11. Gloriously old-fashioned Italian ice-cream parlour, with over sixty home-made flavours – try the bitter chocolate – or there are extravagant sundaes

and waffles. The €2 breakfast (9–11am) of coffee and a croissant, doughnut or roll is unbeatable value. Daily 9am–10pm, sometimes later in summer.

Kasseturm Goetheplatz 10. Student club in an atmospheric brick tower, which has some good live music nights, always sweaty and occasionally rowdy. Mon–Sat 8pm till at least 1am.

EISENACH: THE WARTBURG

A small town on the edge of the Thuringian Forest, **EISENACH** is home to the best-loved medieval castle in Germany, the **Wartburg.** The castle complex (guided tour only daily, every 15min: April–Oct 8.30am–5pm; Nov–March 9am–3.30pm; €10/students €5.50; English translation available), first mentioned in 1080, includes one of the best-preserved Romanesque palaces this side of the Alps, as well as newer additions, including the Festsaal, a nineteenth-century interpretation of medieval grandeur so splendid that Ludwig II of Bavaria had it copied for his fairytale palace, Neuschwanstein. The tour takes you through its ornately decorated rooms. Also on view is a small exhibition of paintings – including some elegant portraits by Cranach – and the **Lutherstube**, the room in which Martin Luther translated the New Testament into the German vernacular while in hiding in 1521–22.

ARRIVAL AND INFORMATION

By train Eisenach is 45min–1hr 10min from Weimar by train (every 30min), and can be done as a day-trip. The Wartburg is a good hour's walk from the train station (you can get a map from DB information at the train station or tourist office). From the station head southwest along Wartburgallee; after 20–30min, at Reuter Villa, there's a signposted footpath up to the Wartburg – it's a pretty steep 30min climb from here. Bus #10 runs hourly (April–Oct) from the train station to the Eselstation (donkey station), from where it's a 15min steep climb to the castle.

Tourist information Tourist office at Markt 9 (Mon–Fri 10am–5pm, Sat & Sun 10am–4pm; ☎036 917 92 30, ⓦeisenach.de).

ACCOMMODATION AND EATING

There's a traditional restaurant at the Wartburg, cheap and tasty Thuringian *Rostbratwurst* stalls near the donkey station and a dozen or so cafés and restaurants around the Markt in the town centre.

DJH Artur Becker Mariental 24 ☎036 91 74 32 59, ⊕djh-thueringen.de; bus #3 or #10. Clean and friendly hostel, a 30min walk from the station; it's on the Wartburg side of town (at the bottom of the hill; about 30min walk from the top). Dorm €24

Northern Germany

Hamburg, Germany's second city, is infamous for the sleaze and hectic nightlife of the Reeperbahn strip – but it is far more than this, with a sophisticated cultural scene, handsome warehouse quarter and big-city allure. Another maritime city, **Lübeck**, has a strong pull, with a similar appeal to the mercantile towns of the Low Countries. To the south lies **Hannover**, worth a visit for its museums and gardens. The province's smaller towns present a fascinating contrast – the former silver-mining town of **Goslar**, in particular, is unusually beautiful.

HAMBURG

Stylish media centre and second-largest port in Europe, **HAMBURG** is undeniably cool – more laidback than Berlin or Frankfurt, more sophisticated than Munich, and with nightlife to rival the lot. Its skyline is dominated by the pale green of its copper spires and domes, but a few houses and churches are all that's left from older times. Though much of the subsequent rebuilding isn't especially beautiful, the result is an intriguing mix of old and new, coupled with an appealing sense of open space – two-thirds of Hamburg is occupied by parks, lakes or canals.

WHAT TO SEE AND DO

Much of the fun of Hamburg is in exploring different quarters, each with a distinct feel and purpose. The centre, defined by the Binnenalster and Aussenalster lakes to its northeast, and the docks and port to the south, is focused on the oversized **Rathaus**. The streets that span north, particularly **Jungfernstieg** and around, are classy and commercial. But the focus of Hamburg is the **docks** and **warehouses** along the Elbe River. North from the port are the best neighbourhoods after dark: **St Pauli** and its infamous Reeperbahn, the studenty **Schanzenviertel** further north, and chic **Altona** off to the west.

The Rathaus

The commercial and shopping district centres on **Binnenalster** lake and the neo-Renaissance **Rathaus** (guided tours several times daily in English: Mon–Thurs 10am–3pm, Fri 10am–1pm, Sat 10am–5pm, Sun 10am–4pm; €3.50), a magnificently pompous demonstration of the city's power and wealth in the nineteenth century.

Nikolaikirche and St Michaelis

Hamburg's skyline is punctuated by a series of church spires – it's worth climbing one to appreciate the surrounding watery expanses. The most dramatic ascent is the glass lift up through the skeletal spire of **Nikolaikirche** on Willy-Brandt-Strasse, which is pretty much all that remains of the church, the rest having been destroyed in 1943. A small, poignant exhibition is displayed in the crypt (daily: May–Sept 10am–8pm; Oct–April 10am–5pm; €4.50 for spire and exhibition). Hamburg's city church is the elegant Baroque **St Michaelis**, on Englische Planke. Its interior is whiter than ever following restoration, and you can go up the tower (daily: May–Oct 9am–7.30pm; Nov–April 10am–5pm; €4.50/students €4) for a panorama over the docks.

The waterfront

From the red-brick **Speicherstadt** immediately south of the Markt, via eye-catching new developments of the **HafenCity** area to the impressive utilitarian **port** to the west, Hamburg's waterfront is its most distinctive area. With its tall, ornate warehouses, the nineteenth-century Speicherstadt quarter is the most attractive part to wander and crisscross the bridges at will – Hamburg

12

Superbude St. Georg & 5

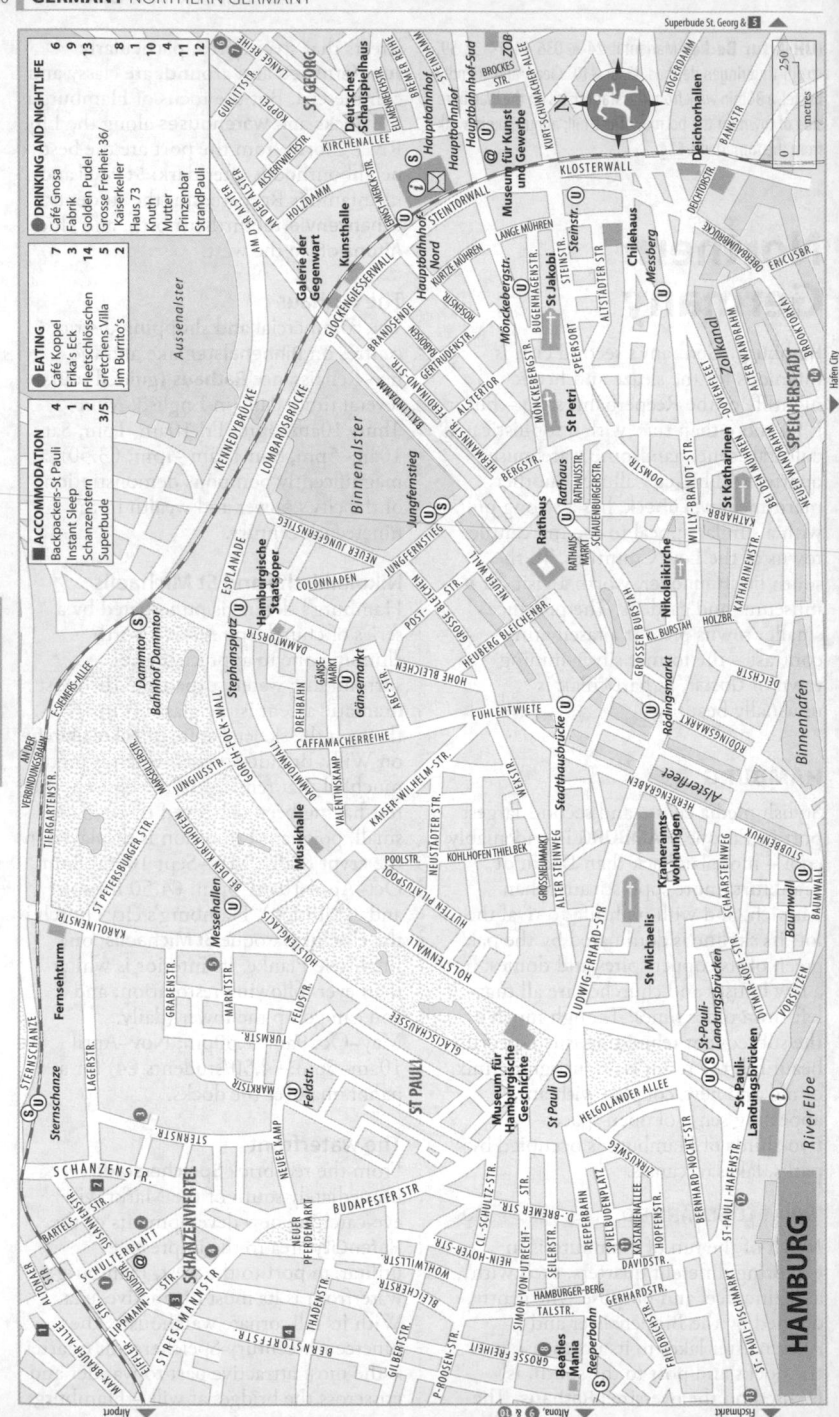

ACCOMMODATION

Backpackers-St Pauli	4
Instant Sleep	1
Schanzenstern	2
Superbude	3/5

EATING

Café Koppel	7
Erika's Eck	1
Fleetschlösschen	14
Gretchens Villa	5
Jim Burrito's	2

DRINKING AND NIGHTLIFE

Café Gnosa	6
Fabrik	9
Golden Pudel	13
Grosse Freiheit 36/ Kaiserkeller	8
Haus 73	1
Knuth	10
Mutter	4
Prinzenbar	11
StrandPauli	12

HAMBURG

has more of them than Venice or Amsterdam. Its modern counterpart behind is HafenCity, a 25-year docklands development project with futuristic architecture, such as the Elbephilharmonie concert hall.

Further west, the harbour area is dominated by the solid wharf building of St Pauli Landungsbrücken, while west again along Hafenstrasse is the location for the legendary **Fischmarkt**. Come early on Sunday and you'll find yourself in an amazing trading – and drinking, as it's a post-club institution – frenzy; everything is in full swing by 6am then all over by 10am. Around the harbour you can pick up many one-hour **boat tours** (prices start at €14), giving an intriguing look at the port and its industrial containers.

St Pauli and the Schanzenviertel

The former dockers' quarter, **St Pauli**, is now the red-light district and nightlife centre. Its main artery is the **Reeperbahn** – ugly and unassuming by day, blazing with neon at night. Running off here is Grosse Freiheit, the street that famously hosted The Beatles' first gigs – the junction of the two is now Beatles-Platz, with a sculpture of the Fab Four and a nearby museum, Beatles Mania (daily 11am–6pm; €13/students €10), with memorabilia.

The neighbourhood north of here, centred on Schulterblatt, is the **Schanzenviertel** (or Schanze), home to a riotously good fun, scruffy and studenty bar scene and cool urban ateliers.

The Kunsthalle

Just northeast of the Hauptbahnhof, on Glockengiesserwall, is the **Kunsthalle**, Hamburg's unmissable art collection (Tues–Sun 10am–6pm, Thurs till 9pm; €12/students €6). The main building features an outstanding collection, ranging from Old Masters to the twentieth century, and includes works by Rembrandt and Munch. An attached glass cube, reached via an underground passageway, houses the **Galerie der Gegenwart** (Contemporary Art; same ticket), with late twentieth-century works plus big temporary exhibitions and installations.

ARRIVAL AND DEPARTURE

By plane Hamburg Airport, roughly 11km north of the city, is connected with the main train station via S-Bahn line S1 (every 10min; 25min; €2.90). Lübeck Airport is connected to Hamburg bus station by a shuttle bus (timed to flights; 1hr 15min; €10).

By train The Hauptbahnhof is at the eastern end of the city centre.

Destinations Århus (2 daily; 5hr); Berlin (hourly; 1hr 40min); Copenhagen (4 daily; 5hr); Frankfurt (hourly; 4hr); Hannover (every 30min; 1hr 35min); Lübeck (every 30min; 40min); Munich (hourly; 6hr–6hr 30min).

INFORMATION

Tourist information Tourist office in the Hauptbahnhof (Mon–Sat 9am–7pm, Sun 10am–6pm; ☎ 040 30 05 13 00, ⓦ hamburg-tourismus.de). Also at the airport (daily 5.30am–11pm) and St Pauli–Landungsbrücken 4/5 (Mon–Wed 9.30am–6pm, Thurs–Sat 9.30am–7pm, Sun 9am–6pm).

Discount pass The Hamburg Card (€10.50/22.50/37 for 1/3/5 days) gives reduced admission to some of the city's museums as well as free use of public transport.

GETTING AROUND

By public transport Hamburg is big, so its extensive public transport network, made up of U-Bahn, S-Bahn and buses, can come in handy. A short trip costs €1.80, a one-way trip €2.90, a day ticket €5.70 (after 9am, €7 before); a day ticket for up to five people is €10.90, and a three-day ticket €19.

By bike Bike rental from Fahrradladen St Georg, Schmilinskystr. 16, 10min from Hauptbahnhof (Mon–Fri 10am–7pm, Sat 10am–1pm; €6/12 for half day/day) and Fahrradstation, Schlüterstr. 11 (ⓢ Dammtor; Mon–Fri 9am–6pm; €6/12 for half day/day).

ACCOMMODATION

Backpackers-St Pauli Bernstorffstr. 98 ☎ 040 23 51 70 43, ⓦ backpackers-stpauli.de; ⓤ Feldstr. Small backpacker hostel run by St Pauli locals, well located for both St Pauli and the Schanze, with a good communal area and bar next door. Sheets €2 (own sleeping bags not permitted). Dorm €22, double €70

Instant Sleep Max-Brauer-Allee 277 ☎ 040 43 18 23 10, ⓦ instantsleep.de; ⓢ & ⓤ Sternschanze. Located in the lively Schanze area, this laidback, basic hostel has the cheapest beds in town as well as a kitchen and internet access, though it's on a noisy corner above a bar. Dorm €23, double €55

Schanzenstern Bartelsstr. 12 ☎ 040 439 84 41, ⓦ schanzenstern.de; ⓢ & ⓤ Sternschanze. Eco-hostel in the Schanze area, with an attached organic restaurant. Sheets included. Dorm €22, double €57

12

Superbude Juliusstr 1–7 ☎040 807 91 58 20, Ⓦsuperbude.de; Ⓤ & Ⓢ Sternschanze. Trendy and hip hotel-hostel hybrid. No dorms per se but they will book multiple same-sex singles into larger rooms on request, the communal areas are stylish and it's smack in the middle of St Pauli. Free wi-fi. Double €104

EATING

Café Koppel In Koppel 66 arts centre, Lange Reihe 75, northeast of the train station in St Georg district; Ⓤ & Ⓢ Hauptbahnhof. Relaxed but classy vegetarian café-restaurant that's part of an arts centre, with a small menu of home-made daily specials (around €8), delicious cakes and a pretty summer garden. Daily 8am–10pm.

Erika's Eck Sternstr. 98; Ⓤ & Ⓢ Sternschanze. This is a firm student favourite, serving huge portions of traditional German dishes almost round the clock, making it popular post-clubbing. Mon–Fri 5pm till 2pm the next day, Sat & Sun 5pm–9am.

Fleetschlösschen Brooktorkai 17; Ⓤ Messberg. Atmospheric little café in a small building in the Speicherstadt – worth stopping in at to browse through its collection of books on Hamburg and the harbour. Good coffee and a short menu of fairly standard pasta dishes. Daily 8am–9pm.

Gretchens Villa Marktstr. 142; Ⓤ Messehallen. Cute, bright little café with a short daytime menu and heavenly cakes – a good spot for people-watching on this street of stylish shops. Tues–Fri 10am–7pm, Sat & Sun 11am–7pm.

Jim Burrito's Schulterblatt 12, Schanzenviertel; Ⓤ & Ⓢ Sternschanze. Laidback Schanze take on Mexican: tasty, cheap and filling, if not particularly spicy (a range of chilli sauces is to hand), and with a nicely shabby charm to the place. Burritos €5–9. Daily 11am–11pm.

DRINKING AND NIGHTLIFE

Hamburg's nightlife is outstanding: the Schanzenviertel for studenty bar-crawling; St Pauli for clubs and live music venues; while Altona attracts an older, more relaxed crowd. For information on the gay scene check *Hinnerk* (German only) magazine, available from the tourist office, cafés and bars.

BARS

Café Gnosa Lange Reihe 93; Ⓢ St Pauli. Well-known gay bar-café northeast of the train station that also attracts a mixed non-gay crowd. Packed at weekends. Marvellous cakes for €3, and good breakfasts. Daily 8am–8pm.

Knuth Grosse Rainstr. 21; Ⓢ Altona. Relaxed but stylish neighbourhood café-bar with comfy chairs and a convivial atmosphere where you can lounge and read or just grab a bite. Daily 8am till at least 10pm.

Mutter Stresemannstr. 11; Ⓤ & Ⓢ Sternschanze. Small, atmospheric retro-styled bar that's often the last to shut. Attracts a mix of ages and manages to be hip without any attitude. Daily 5pm–late.

StrandPauli Hafenstr. 89; Ⓤ & Ⓢ Landungsbrücken. Cool urban beach-bar on the old wharf, with cocktails, Caribbean vibes and an unrivalled view of the port. Roughly June–Sept daily noon–midnight.

CLUBS AND LIVE MUSIC

Fabrik Barnerstr. 36 Ⓦfabrik.de; Ⓢ Altona. Major live music and club venue in Altona, with a huge range of music and occasional mixed gay nights. Daily 8pm till at least 3am.

Golden Pudel Am St Pauli Fischmarkt 27 Ⓦpudel.com; Ⓢ Reeperbahn or Ⓤ & Ⓢ Landungsbrücken. Often packed and raucous club in what looks like a squat on the harbour. Hosts some great local DJs playing electro, dub and hip-hop. Daily 7pm till at least 4am.

Grosse Freiheit 36/Kaiserkeller Grosse Freiheit 36 Ⓦgrossefreiheit36.de; Ⓤ St Pauli or Ⓢ Reeperbahn. A tourist attraction in itself, *Grosse Freiheit 36* books major acts most weekends, with an emphasis on goth and rock. The massive *Kaiserkeller* below plays mostly alternative music, and is famous for hosting The Beatles in the early 1960s. Mon & Wed–Sat 7pm till at least 3am.

Haus 73 Schulterblatt 73 Ⓦdreiundsiebzig.de; Ⓤ & Ⓢ Sternschanze. Something is always on in this ramshackle building, somewhere between a community centre and a club, from dance classes to film and reggae club nights. Mon–Sat 7pm till at least midnight, usually later at weekends.

⭐ **Prinzenbar** Kastanienallee 20 Ⓦprinzenbar.net; Ⓤ St Pauli or Ⓢ Reeperbahn. This wonderfully atmospheric venue, all crumbling Baroque cherubs, chandeliers and dark corners, hosts small club nights and live gigs; mainly indie. Tues–Sat 7pm till at least midnight.

DIRECTORY

Bank and exchange Reisebank, at the train station.

Consulates New Zealand, Domstr. 19 ☎040 442 55 50; UK, Neuer Jungfernstieg 20 ☎040 448 032 36; US, Alsterufer 28 ☎040 411 711 00.

Internet In the basement of the Saturn department store, southern building of the main train station (Hauptbahnhof-Süd; 30min/€1.50). Also Teletime on Schultterblatt (30min/€1).

Pharmacy At the Hauptbahnhof (daily 7am–11pm).

Post office At the Hauptbahnhof (Mon–Fri 8am–6pm, Sat 8am–12.30pm).

LÜBECK

Just an hour from Hamburg, **LÜBECK** makes a great day-trip. Set on an egg-shaped island surrounded by the water defences of the River Trave and the city moat, the pretty Altstadt is a compact place to wander, with many small lanes and courtyards to explore.

WHAT TO SEE AND DO

The city's emblem – and your first view of the Altstadt as you approach from the station – is the twin-towered, leaning **Holstentor** (daily: Jan–March 11am–5pm; April–Dec 10am–6pm; €6/students €3.50), with a small city museum inside. Straight ahead, over the bridge and up Holstenstrasse, the first church on the right is the Gothic **Petrikirche**; an elevator goes to the top of its spire (daily 9am–9pm, from 10am Oct–March; €4/students €3) for great views over the town. Back across Holstenstrasse is the Markt and the elaborate **Rathaus**. Just behind, you'll find **Konditorei-café Niederegger**, a renowned shop crammed with marzipan products and a free museum dedicated to the sugary substance.

Behind the north wing of the town hall stands the **Marienkirche**, Germany's oldest brick-built Gothic church. The interior makes a light and lofty backdrop for treasures like a 1518 high altar. The church's huge bells remain embedded in the floor where they fell when the church was bombed in 1942.

Katharinenkirche, on the corner of Königstrasse and Glockengiesserstrasse, has three sculptures on its facade by Ernst Barlach; only three of the nine commissioned in the early 1930s had been completed when his work was banned by the Nazis. To the north at Königstrasse 9–11 are the **Behnhaus** and the **Drägerhaus**, two patricians' houses now converted into a museum (Tues–Sun: Jan–March 11am–5pm; April–Dec 10am–5pm; €6/students €3.50) housing modern and nineteenth-century paintings. More art – excellent medieval plus modern exhibitions – can be found in the **St Annen Museum** (April–Dec Tues–Sat 10am–5pm, Jan–March from 11am; €6/students €3) in a former convent, which also has good displays on merchant life in Lübeck.

ARRIVAL AND DEPARTURE

By plane Bus #6 goes from Lübeck airport to the train station (every 20min; 25min; €2.70).

By train The train station is 5min west of the Altstadt: walk down Konrad-Adenauer-Str. to the Holstentor.

Destinations Copenhagen (4 daily; 4hr 20min); Hamburg (every 30min; 40min).

By ferry Lübeck's port, Travemünde, is 20min by train from Lübeck. Lisco Baltic Service (☎045 02 88 66 90, ⊛dfdslisco.com) travel to Rīga; Finnlines (☎045 028 05 43, ⊛ferrycenter.fi) to Helsinki and Malmö; and TT-Line (☎045 028 01 81, ⊛ttline.com) to Trelleborg.

Destinations Helsinki (9 weekly; 28hr); Malmö (3 daily; 8–9hr); Rīga (2 weekly; 35hr); Trelleborg (4 daily; 7hr).

INFORMATION

Tourist information Tourist office at Holstentorplatz 1 (June–Sept Mon–Fri 9.30am–7pm, Sat 10am–4pm, Sun 10am–2pm; Oct–May Mon–Fri 9.30am–6pm, Sat 10am–3pm; Dec also Sun 10am–2pm; ☎018 058 89 97 00, ⊛luebeck.de). It has a café, arranges walking tours and has information on boat tours.

Discount passes The Happy Day Card (€12/14/17 for 24/48/72hr) covers public transport and up to a fifty percent discount at museums. Combined museum tickets are also available: two museums in three days (€10/students €6), three in three days (€14/students €8), all museums in one week (€19/students €10).

EATING

Hüxstr, which runs east from the Markt, has several good cafés and bars.

Cole Street Beckergrube 18, west of the Markt, off Breite Str. Named after a south London street where the owner once lived, this shabby-chic café and bar is good for a light bistro lunch or a drink.

HANNOVER

HANNOVER is a major transport hub and trade-fair city and, unfortunately, it looks the part; in other words it looks fairly dull. The city's showpiece – refreshingly – is not a great cathedral, palace or town hall, but a series of **gardens** and first-class **museums**. Hannover's location at the intersection of major cross-country rail lines and its lack of budget accommodation make it a perfect candidate for a pit stop on your way to somewhere else.

WHAT TO SEE AND DO

Hannover's commercial centre is a short walk southwest of the train station. The best **museums** are further south, on the other side of Friedrichswall, while the splendid **royal gardens** are northwest of the centre. The centre is pretty bland, but

12

there are some attractive corners and interesting neighbourhoods if you explore a bit further out.

The Altes Rathaus and Marktkirche

A short distance southwest of the train station, a few streets of rebuilt half-timbered buildings convey some impression of the medieval town. The elaborate brickwork of the high-gabled fifteenth-century **Altes Rathaus** is impressive, despite the modern interior. Alongside is the fourteenth-century red-brick Gothic **Marktkirche**, with some miraculously preserved stained glass.

Niedersächsisches Landesmuseum and Sprengel Museum

Southeast of the Marktkirche, across Friedrichswall on Willy-Brandt-Allee, is the **Niedersächsisches Landesmuseum** (Tues–Sun 10am–5pm, Thurs till 6.30pm; €5/students €3.50, free Fri 2–4pm; ⓦAegidientorplatz), housing a fine collection of paintings from the Middle Ages to the early twentieth century, plus archeology and ethnology collections. A bit further down the road lies the **Sprengel Museum** (Tues–Thurs & Sun 10am–7pm, Fri & Sat 10am–9pm; €7.50/students €4, higher during special exhibitions; ⓦsprengel-museum.de), with a first-rate collection of twentieth- and twenty-first-century painting and sculpture.

The Neues Rathaus

West of the Landesmuseum on Friderichswall is the vast, green-domed **Neues Rathaus**, built at the start of the twentieth century. In the foyer are four models of Hannover in 1689, 1939, 1945 and today, illuminating the extent of wartime loss, something that is all too clear as you look over the city from the top of the town hall's **dome** (Mon–Fri 9am–6pm, Sat & Sun 10am–6pm; €3/students €2), reached via a curved lift.

The gardens

The royal gardens of **Herrenhausen**, featuring Europe's biggest fountain, stretch out northwest of the centre. Proceeding north from town along Nienburger Strasse, the **Georgengarten**, an English-style landscaped garden, is to the left, a foil to the city's pride and joy, the magnificent formal **Grosser Garten** beyond (daily 9am till dusk; €5; trams #4 and #5 to Herrenhäuser Gärten, main entrance just by the stop on Herrenhäuser Str.). If possible, time your visit to coincide with the fountain displays (late March to late Oct daily 11am–noon & 2/3–5pm). Directly opposite, on Herrenhäuser Strasse, is the entrance to **Berggarten**, the botanic garden (same hours and ticket).

ARRIVAL AND DEPARTURE

By plane Hannover Airport and the train station are connected with S-Bahn line #5 (every 30min; 20min; €3.30).

By train The train station is in the centre of town, just northeast of main shopping district Kröpcke.

Destinations Amsterdam (every 2hr; 4hr 20min); Berlin (hourly; 1hr 40min); Cologne (hourly; 2hr 40min); Frankfurt (hourly; 2hr 20min); Goslar (hourly; 1hr); Hamburg (every 30min; 1hr 35min); Munich (hourly; 4hr 20min–4hr 40min).

INFORMATION

Tourist information Tourist office across from the train station, Ernst-August-Platz 8 (Mon–Fri 9am–6pm, Sat 9am–2pm; May–Sept also Sun 9am–2pm; ☎0511 123 451 11, ⓦhannover-tourism.de).

GETTING AROUND

By public transport The best of Hannover is outside the centre, so its excellent transport network of tram/U-Bahn, S-Bahn and buses – centred on the Hauptbahnhof, Kröpcke and Aegidientorplatz – is useful. The tram/U-Bahn network has some overground tram lines (such as #17 and #10) and some hybrid tram/U-Bahn lines where central stops are underground, with lines emerging above ground to become street-level trams further out (such as #4 and #5). One-way tickets €2.40, day tickets €4.40.

Discount pass The Hannover Card (individual €11.20/16, up to 5 people €19.80/31 for 1/3 days) covers public transport and provides discounts to the main museums and sights.

ACCOMMODATION

There are very few budget options in Hannover, and prices double or more during trade fairs.

Flora Heinrichstr. 36 ☎051 138 39 10, ⓦhotel-flora -hannover.de. Spotless hotel with slightly old-fashioned furniture, located behind the train station. The welcome is always very warm and the front-desk staff overly helpful. Breakfast included. Double **€65**

Hostel Hannover Lenaustr. 12 ☎051 11 31 99 19, ⓦhostelhannover.de; trams #10 & #17 to Goetheplatz. Basic but friendly, this slightly old-fashioned hostel has decent communal areas but packed dorms. Though it's located outside the centre, it's good for the Linden-Limmer nightlife. Check-in 8–11am & 5–8pm. Sheets €4. Prices €5 extra at weekends and trade fairs. Dorm **€18**

EATING AND DRINKING

In the centre, slightly twee, touristy Kramerstr. and Knochenhauerstr. near the Markt are your best options. More fun for nightlife is the sprawling Linden-Limmer district west of the centre, particularly around Goetheplatz or midway along Kötnerholzweg. Lister Meile, behind the station, is also a good bet.

Café Glocksee Glockseestr. 35 ⓦcafe-glocksee.de; tram #10 to Goetheplatz. Great, scruffy little club and venue; head along Lenaustr. and it's the graffitied building at the end (entrance round the back). Mon–Sat 8am–midnight.

Café Safran Königsworther Str. 39, corner of Braunstr; tram #10 to Glocksee. This laidback café-bar has some sort of cheap deal every day, such as beer and a pizza for €7. Daily 11am–10pm.

Markthalle Karmaschstr. 49, near the Markt. The indoor market is packed full of dozens of food stalls – German, Italian, Spanish, Turkish and Japanese, and even a cocktail bar – selling good-value meals. It's also a very popular after-work spot for a quick drink. Mon–Wed 7am–8pm, Thurs & Fri 7am–10pm, Sat 7am–4pm.

Spandau Projekt Engelbosteler Damm 30; ⓤChristuskirche. Cool, retro-styled café-bar on a street of restaurants north of the centre. There are Italian dishes and Thai veggie curries at fair prices plus organic breakfast buffets at weekends. Daily 8am–9pm.

BREMEN

Famous for a fairytale of four animal musicians, **BREMEN** is an attractive small city located about an hour from Hannover and Hamburg. Maritime trade via the Weser River led to it becoming a wealthy medieval merchant city with a liberal mindset, something for which Bremen remains famous today. Their legacy is such attractive architecture as one of the finest town squares in North Germany, listed as a UNESCO World Heritage Site, and a small but enjoyable nightlife district.

WHAT TO SEE AND DO

The town's geographic and cultural heart is the **Markt**, with a **Rathaus** fronted by a fabulous Renaissance facade of ornate allegorical carving. Rooms within (Mon–Sat hourly 11am–6pm except 2pm, Sun 11am; €5.50) live up to the looks, especially the Güldenkammer with gilded Jugendstil leather wall-hangings. Outside, a statue of Roland, a chivalric knight and protector of civic rights, brandishes a sword at the **Dom** opposite, to champion the citizens' independence from the archbishops; a church lackey burned down its wooden predecessor. Running south off the Markt, **Böttcherstrasse** was remodelled in the 1920s from a decaying alley into a "Kunst Schau" (Art Show) by a team of avant-garde artists, notably sculptor Bernhard Hoetger. Here, the **Paula-Modersohn-Becker Museum** (Tues–Sun 11am–6pm; €6/students €3) contains artworks by an artist from a local art colony at Worpswede, while revamped Gothic merchant's house **Roselius-Haus** (same ticket) displays late medieval art and furniture.

South of the Dom is the **Schnoorviertel**, the traditional quarter of fishermen, sailors and craftsmen on the Weser's banks at the edge of the old town. Today the cottages contain upmarket boutiques, galleries and restaurants – touristy, certainly, but cute nonetheless. East of the Schnoor, the **Kunsthalle** (Tues 10am–9pm, Wed–Sun 10am–5pm; €7) has an excellent gallery of German and international art, including works by Rubens and Delacroix, alongside works by Worpswede artists.

ARRIVAL AND INFORMATION

By train Head straight out of the train station; it's a 10min walk into the centre.
Destinations Hamburg (every 30min; 1hr); Hannover (hourly; 1hr 20min).
Tourist information Tourist office just off Markt on the corner of Obernstr. and Liebfrauenkirchhof (Mon–Fri 10am–6.30pm, Sat & Sun 10am–4pm; ☎0421 308 00 10, ⓦbremen-tourism.de). Smaller office in the train station (Mon–Fri 9am–7pm, Sat & Sun 9.30am–6pm).

12

ACCOMMODATION, EATING AND DRINKING

In the centre, Schlacte is a line of bars on the riverbank, while the main bar and nightlife district is the Ostertorviertel east of the old town.

Piano Fehrfeld 64. Lazy-paced café-bar at the heart of the Ostertorviertel whose menu of pizzas, pastas and steaks, most priced under €15, is popular with everyone from families to friends. Daily 9am–1am.

Ratskeller Am Markt 21. Touristy and not cheap at around €16 a main, but the cellar restaurant beneath the Rathaus is one of the most famous in Germany for historic atmosphere as much as traditional cooking. Daily 11am–11pm.

Townhouse Am Dobben 62 ☎ 042 17 80 15, ⊛ townside .de; tram #6 from the train station. Friendly modern hostel in Bremen's nightlife district, with eco ethics such as Fairtrade products as well as a kitchen and women's dorm. Dorm €16, double €55

Central Germany

12

Central Germany is the country's most populous region and home to its industrial heartland – the Ruhrgebiet. **Cologne** stands out here, with its reminders of long centuries as a free state, cheek-by-jowl bars and a populace that's legendary for its friendliness. Neighbouring **Bonn**, Beethoven's birthplace, makes for a good day-trip, while nearby **Aachen** is of interest as the first capital of the Holy Roman Empire. To the south, the Rhineland-Palatinate (*Pfalz*) is famed for the romantic vineyard-lined stretch of the Rhine from Cologne to Mainz, which passes through a gorge of impressive rock outcrops, studded with the sort of castles that have given rise to many a fairytale. Nowadays pleasure cruisers – and a railway line – make the attractive journey through the gorge, and beyond to the state capital of **Mainz**, where the printing press was invented, as celebrated in the excellent Gutenberg Museum. The Mosel, which joins the Rhine near the city of Koblenz, has a similar parade of vineyards and ruined castles leading south to the ancient town of **Trier**, with its extraordinarily well-preserved Roman remains – possibly the best outside Italy. To the northeast, in the state of Hesse,

dynamic **Frankfurt** dominates, with its financial sector providing the region's economic powerbase.

COLOGNE (KÖLN)

COLOGNE (Köln) has a population of one million, and its huge Gothic Dom is Germany's most visited monument. Despite its long history, much of the city is modern – the legacy of World War II – but though it's not the most beautiful city in Germany, it's certainly one of the liveliest and friendliest. Try to catch the annual pre-Lent **Carnival** – when huge parties fill the streets – or the summer Christopher Street Day (Gay Pride) celebrations, which can attract up to a million visitors. Cologne has a long and glorious history – as a Roman colony (Colonia), a pilgrimage centre, trading city, marketer of eau de Cologne and recently as Germany's media capital.

WHAT TO SEE AND DO

Cologne's major sights are all within walking distance of the train station, in a dense centre on the west bank of the Rhine.

The Dom

Begun in 1248, and only finished in 1880, Cologne's gigantic **Dom** (daily: May–Oct 6am–9pm; Nov–April 6am–7.30pm) is one of the largest Gothic buildings ever built and its archbishop was one of the seven Electors of the Holy Roman Empire. Its treasures are many and it's worth paying €1 for the explanatory English booklet inside. Climb the 509 steps to the top of the south tower (daily: March, April & Oct 9am–5pm; May–Sept 9am–6pm; Nov–Feb 9am–4pm; €3 or combination ticket with Domschatzkammer €6) for a breathtaking panorama over the city and the Rhine. The **Domschatzkammer** (daily 10am–6pm; €5) in the vaults on the north side of the building contains a stunning array of treasury items.

Museum Ludwig and the Römisch-Germanisches Museum

In a modern building next to the Dom,

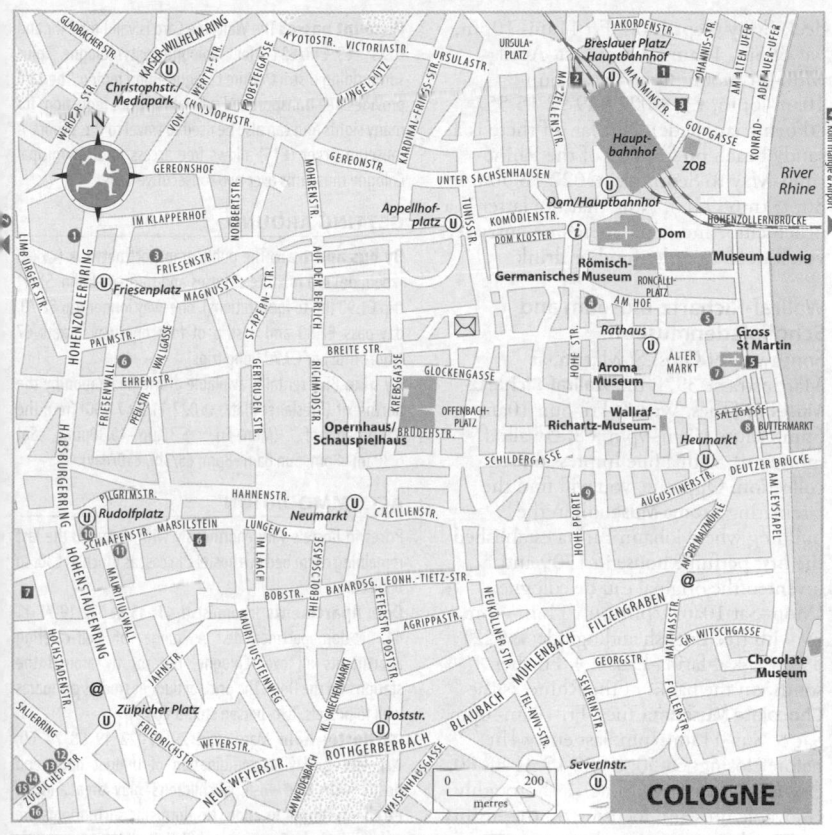

■ ACCOMMODATION		● EATING		Pizzeria Bella Italia 1	6	Greencomm at Nachtflug	1
Dom Apartments	3	Della Rosa	14			MTC	12
Höstel Köln	6	Culux	10			Stiefel	13
Köln-Deutz City Hostel	4	Früh am Dom	4	● DRINKING & NIGHTLIFE		Underground	2
Meininger	7	Gaffel Haus	7	Biermuseum	8	Venue	9
Müller	1	Habibi	15	Ex-Corner	11		
Stapelhäuschen	5	Päffgen	3	Filmdose	16		
Station Backpacker's	2	Peters Brauhaus	5				

the spacious **Museum Ludwig** (Tues–Sun 10am–6pm, first Thurs in month 10am–10pm; €10, first Thurs in month €5; ☎022 122 12 61 65, ⓦmuseenkoeln .de) is one of Germany's premier collections of modern art, particularly strong on American Pop Art and German Expressionism. The neighbouring **Römisch-Germanisches Museum** (Tues–Sun 10am–5pm, first Thurs in month 10am–10pm; €8; ⓦmuseenkoeln .de/roemisch-germanisches-museum) was built directly over its star exhibit, the Dionysus Mosaic, which can be viewed *in situ*. The finest work of its kind in

northern Europe, it was created for a patrician villa in about 200 AD.

Gross St Martin and the Rhine

For nearly six hundred years, the tower of **Gross St Martin**, one of Cologne's twelve Romanesque churches, was the dominant feature of the city's skyline. Just behind it is the best spot to enjoy the Rhine, a grassy promenade stretching between the Hohenzollern and Deutzer bridges. For the best view of the Altstadt, cross the river by the footway along the first bridge to reach the **Köln Triangle** skyscraper at Ottoplatz 1, which has an observation deck (May–Sept Mon–Fri 11am–10pm, Sat & Sun 10am–10pm; Oct–April Mon–Fri noon–6pm, Sat & Sun 10am–6pm; €3; ☎022 349 92 15 55, ⓦkoelntriangle.de). Not far off there is a sandy beach on km 689 of the Rhine (mid-May to Sept; free; ☎022 16 50 04 30, ⓦkm689.de). Note that the latter is a beach club, and while there's no entry fee you'll need to order food or drink.

Wallraf-Richartz-Museum and Schokoladenmuseum

Southwest of Gross St Martin, at Martinstrasse 39, is the **Wallraf-Richartz-Museum** (Tues, Wed & Fri–Sun 10am–6pm, Thurs 10am–9pm; €8; ⓦwallraf .museum), with a fine Impressionist collection. Opposite, you will find the fascinating **Aroma Museum**, in the building where Johann Farina established the first perfume house in 1709 and invented the original eau de cologne (Mon–Sat 10am–7pm, Sun 11am–4pm; €9 with free English audioguide; ☎0221 399 8994, ⓦfarina-haus.de). Further south, on the banks of the Rhine, is the **Chocolate Museum** (Tues–Fri 10am–6pm, Sat & Sun 11am–7pm, last entry 1hr before closing; €8.50; ☎022 19 31 88 80, ⓦschokoladenmuseum.de), a thoroughly enjoyable museum focusing on the history and production of chocolate.

ARRIVAL AND DEPARTURE

By plane Cologne/Bonn Airport is connected to the train station with line ⓢ13 (every 20min; 15min; €2.70). Destinations London (easyJet; 1hr 15min).

By train The Hauptbahnhof is immediately north of the Dom in the centre of the city.

Destinations Aachen (every 30min; 36–52min); Amsterdam (every 2hr; 2hr 40min); Berlin (hourly; 4hr 28min); Bonn (frequent; 20–30min); Brussels (7 daily; 1hr 50min); Frankfurt (10–11 daily; 1hr 10min); Heidelberg (every 30min–1hr 30min; 2hr 40min); Mainz (1–2 hourly; 1hr 45min); Munich (hourly; 4hr 32min–5hr 53min); Paris Gare du Nord (4 daily; 3hr 17min); Stuttgart (1–2 hourly; 2hr 13min).

By bus The bus station (ZOB) is directly behind the train station on Johannisstr.

INFORMATION

Tourist information Main office opposite the Dom (Mon–Sat 9am–8pm, Sun 10am–5pm; ☎022 122 13 04 00, ⓦcologne-tourism.de). Staff can book hotel rooms.

Discount passes The Welcome Card is valid for 24hr and costs €9/€13/€24 for Cologne city/Cologne plus surrounding district/entire Cologne-Bonn region. The card provides free transport and substantial price reductions for many sights and can also be used to travel to the airport. A museum ticket (€15) allows free access to all municipal Cologne museums over two consecutive days.

GETTING AROUND

By bus and tram The public transport network (ⓦkvb -koeln.de) is a mixture of buses and trams/U-Bahn. Short trip €1.90 (up to four stations), one-way longer trip €2.70, day-pass €7.80 and a strip of four one-way tickets €7 (short trips) or €9.70 (long trips).

By bike Bike rental is available at the Radstation by the north exit (Breslauer Platz, ☎022 11 39 71 90) from the Hauptbahnhof (Mon–Fri 5.30am–10.30pm, Sat 6.30am–8pm, Sun 8am–8pm; €5/3hr, €10/day).

ACCOMMODATION

Prices in hostels vary enormously with demand; the last remaining dorm bed in a hostel can cost as much as €30, so book early.

Dom Apartments Johannisstr 43–45 ☎022 19 77 11 44, ⓦdomapartment.de. A range of self-catering apartments all over Cologne, but mostly around the station and the Dom. The price of budget studios compares well to hostels. Two-person studio €69

★ **Hostel Köln** Marsilstein 29 ☎022 19 98 77 60, ⓦhostel.ag. Stylish combination of budget hotel and hostel with free wi-fi, a children's play area and an excellent, central location. No dorms as such; rooms are only sold whole. Breakfast included. Double €49

Köln-Deutz City Hostel Siegesstr. 5 ☎022 181 47 11, ⓦkoeln-deutz.jugendherberge.de. Large and functional DJH hostel close to Deutz station, directly across the Rhine from the Altstadt. Standard facilities include a disco room. Normally booked by large groups. Good weekend deals online. Dorm €28.50, double €65

Meininger Engelbertstr. 33–35 ☎022 199 76 09 65, ⓦmeininger-hotels.com. This branch of the hostel chain has a great location and a wide range of services: free wi-fi, kitchen, bar, laundry facilities (€5) and bike rental €12. Dorm €17, double €57

Müller Brandenburgerstr. 20 ☎022 19 12 83 50, ⓦhotel -mueller-koeln.de. Homely, simple three-star hotel, one of a cluster of budget hotels behind the station. Breakfast €7. Free wi-fi. Double €69

Stapelhäuschen Fischmarkt 1–3 ☎022 12 72 77 77, ⓦkleines-stapelhaeuschen.de. Charming Altstadt hotel-restaurant rebuilt to resemble its seventeenth-century appearance, and located by Gross St Martin. Rooms overlooking the river are the nicest. Double €63.80

Station Backpacker's Marzellenstr. 44–56 ☎022 19 12

53 01, ⓦ hostel-cologne.de. Large, privately run hostel just north of the station, with 24hr reception, kitchen and free internet. Breakfast €5. Weekend supplement €6. Dorm **€17**, double **€48**

EATING

The Altmarkt area is the main focus of nightlife for visitors, though locals tend to prefer the western part of the city along the Ring, while students gather around Zülpicher Platz.

Bella Rosa Heinsberger Str. 11a. One of a handful of good-value Italian restaurants in the student area. Big portions and a young, friendly crowd. Pizza and pasta €4–7. Mon–Thurs & Sun 8am–1am, Fri & Sat 8am–3am.

Culux Rudolfplatz 7. A fast-food restaurant with a difference: choose one of 25 kinds of sausage, plus a drink, sauce and side for €7.30. Veggie wraps €3.40, salads from €7.90. Mon & Tues noon–11pm, Wed & Thurs noon–midnight, Fri & Sat noon–1am, Sun 1–11pm.

Früh am Dom Am Hof 12–18. Located opposite the Dom, this huge, heavily touristed *Brauhaus* serves excellent food. Main courses from around €10, snacks €5. Daily 8am–midnight.

Gaffel Haus Alter Markt 20–22. Typical, old-style restaurant, serving huge portions and house beer; much cosier than most. Light Cologne specialities from around €4; hamburger €6.50. Daily 11am–1am.

★ **Habibi** Zülpicher Str. 28. Serving arguably the best falafel in Germany, this Lebanese restaurant in the student neighbourhood stays open for late-night munchies. Takeaway falafel in pita €1.90. Mon–Thurs & Sun 11am–1am, Fri & Sat 11am–3am.

Päffgen Friesenstr. 64–66. Less touristy than the places near the Dom, with a younger clientele and *Kölsch* brewed on the premises. Mains from €10. Mon–Thurs & Sun 10am–midnight, Fri & Sat 10am–12.30am.

★ **Peters Brauhaus** Mühlengasse 1 ☎ 022 12 57 39 50. Reservations only to eat in this popular beer tavern, but it's worth visiting if only to admire the grand Art Deco room. The pork knuckle (*Schweinehaxe*) is a 1kg monster dish (€15). Daily 11am–12.30am.

Pizzeria Bella Italia 1 Friesenwall 52. Super-cheap Italian with pasta dishes and pizzas from €4; needless to say, its benches are packed shoulder-to-shoulder. Mon–Thurs 11.30am–10pm, Fri & Sat 11.30am–1am, Sun 2–10pm.

DRINKING AND NIGHTLIFE

Cologne's unique beer, *Kölsch*, is a light, aromatically bitter brew served in small, thin glasses.

Biermuseum Buttermarkt 39. Loud, busy Altstadt bar tucked away near the river, serving 18 beers on tap and countless more in bottles, all costing less than €3. Daily 2pm–3am.

Filmdose Zülpicher Str. 39 ⓦ filmdose-koeln.de. Quiet wine bar that's packed with students; it has a cabaret stage used for live theatre during term time. Hamburger €3, chips €1.50. Mon–Fri 9am–1am, Fri & Sat 9am–3am.

Greencomm at Nachtflug Hohenzollernring 89 ⓦ greencomm.de. Monthly after-hours club playing prog trance and house in one of the chic venues on the Ring. Free before 8am, €13 after. 1st Sun of the month 6am–late.

MTC Zülpicher Str. 10 ⓦ mtcclub.de. Studenty venue featuring live rock and metal bands. Go early to avoid the long queues. Live shows from 8pm. Fri & Sat punk parties 11pm–late.

Stiefel Zülpicher Str.18. Dilapidated and relaxed punk-rock bar in a student quarter that's packed with cheap restaurants and lively bars. A great place to down a beer or shoot pool. Mon–Thurs 6pm–2am, Fri & Sat 6pm–5am, Sun 7pm–1am.

Underground Vogelsanger Str. 200 ⓦ underground -cologne.de; ⓣ Venloer Str. Great for live gigs, especially rock and punk, the *Underground* has a beer garden and a big indie/alternative following. May–Sept daily 5pm–late; Oct–April Wed–Sat 6.30pm–late.

GAY NIGHTLIFE

The gay scene in Cologne is second only to Berlin's. See ⓦ heart-of-cologne.de.

Ex-Corner Schaafenstr. 57–59 ⓦ i-like-x.de. This corner bar is one of a triangular cluster of gay bars just south of Rudolfplatz and is busy every night of the week. Daily 7pm–5am.

Venue Hohe Str. 14 ⓦ venue-cologne.de. The biggest, loudest, brashest gay club in Cologne, with different music nights attracting a variety of clubbers every weekend; free wi-fi. Cover €8, Fri & Sat 11pm–late.

DIRECTORY

Internet Gigabyte, Hohenzollernring 7–11 (24hr; €0.50–1.50/hr; ☎ 022 165 02 64 42, ⓦ giga-byte.info). Giant internet café with 130 terminals.

12

COLOGNE'S CARNIVAL

Though Cologne's **carnival** actually begins as early as November 11, the real business starts with Weiberfastnacht on the Thursday prior to Lent. The city goes wild for the next five days until Ash Wednesday; prepare yourself for drunken dancing in the streets and wild costumes. The best of the numerous parades are the alternative **Geisterzug Saturday night**, complete with fire-juggling and drumming, and the spectacular **Rose Monday Parade**, which features music, floats and political caricatures.

Hospital Out of hours medical service (☎ 01805 04 41 00; calls 14 cents/min).

Left luggage At the train station (€3/2hr, €6/24hr).

Pharmacy At the north exit from the train station (Mon–Fri 6am–10pm, Sat 8am–10pm, Sun 10am–6pm); there's also a digital notice board giving details of out-of-hours service.

Post office Breite Str. 6–26 (Mon–Fri 9am–7pm, Sat 9am–2pm).

BONN

A great day-trip from Cologne, lovely, riverside **BONN** was West Germany's unlikely capital from 1949 until unification in 1990. But even with its role diminished, Bonn is still worth a visit to see the birthplace of Ludwig van Beethoven, a string of top-rated museums and an attractive Old Town.

WHAT TO SEE AND DO

The small pedestrianized **Old Town** (Altstadt) centres on two spacious squares. The square to the south is named after the **Münster**, whose central octagonal tower and spire are the city's most prominent landmarks. The **Market square** (Marktplatz) is dominated by the pink Rococo **Rathaus** and hosts a market every day except Sunday.

The Beethoven-Haus and the Schloss

A couple of minutes' walk north of Marktplatz, at Bonngasse 20, is the **Beethoven-Haus** (April–Oct Mon–Sat 10am–6pm, Sun 11am–6pm; Nov–March Mon–Sat 10am–5pm, Sun 11am–5pm; €5; ☎ 228 98 17 50, ⓦ beethoven-haus-bonn.de), where the composer was born in an attic room in 1770. Beethoven left Bonn for good aged 22, but the city nevertheless has the best collection of memorabilia of its favourite son. To the east is the Baroque **Schloss**, once the seat of the Archbishop-Electors of Cologne and now part of the university.

The Museumsmeile

The **Museumsmeile** (ⓤ Heussallee/ Museumsmeile) is home to the **Kunstmuseum** at Friedrich-Ebert-Allee 2 (Tues & Thurs–Sun 11am–6pm, Wed 11am–9pm; €7; ⓦ kunstmuseum-bonn .de), with its fine Expressionist collection.

Next door is the **Kunst- und Ausstellungshalle** (Tues & Wed 10am–9pm, Thurs–Sun 10am–7pm; prices depend on exhibition, around €10; ☎ 022 89 17 12 00, ⓦ bundeskunsthalle .de), an arts centre hosting major temporary exhibitions. The Kunstmuseum's other neighbour is the **Haus der Geschichte** at Willy-Brandt-Allee 14 (Tues–Fri 9am–7pm, Sat & Sun 10am–6pm; free; ⓦ hdg.de), a fascinating museum exploring German history from the end of World War II to the present.

ARRIVAL AND INFORMATION

By train and bus Bonn's train station lies in the middle of the city; just to the east is the bus station, whose local services, along with the trams, form part of a system integrated with Cologne's (see p.388).

Tourist information Windeckstr. 1, am Münsterplatz (Mon–Fri 10am–6pm, Sat 10am–4pm, Sun 10am–2pm; ☎ 022 877 50 00, ⓦ bonn-region.de).

Discount pass The Bonn Regio WelcomeCard (valid 24hr; €9/€12//€24 for city of Bonn/greater Bonn/Cologne-Bonn region) is a great deal, providing free travel and free admission to almost all museums and sights.

EATING AND DRINKING

Cassius Garten Maximilianstr. 28d, across from the station. Offers daily-changing hot vegetarian and vegan specials, buffet-style meals (pay by weight €1.70/100g), and great soups from €2.50. Mon–Sat 8am–8pm.

Pawlow Heerstr. 64. Fashionable café-bar in the bohemian Nordstadt district, with benches outside, great coffees and small measures of wine for tight budgets from €2. On weekends after 10pm it becomes a club. Mon–Thurs 11am–1am, Fri & Sat 11am–late, Sun 10am–1am.

Zebulon Stockenstr. 19. This Altstadt bar is a big favourite with students, especially English-speaking ones studying abroad. Mon–Fri 4pm–1am, Sat noon–1am, Sun 5–11pm.

AACHEN

AACHEN has a laidback atmosphere that reflects its large student population, making it a good day-trip from Cologne or a stopover between countries. Bordering Belgium and the Netherlands, it was the hub of Charlemagne's Europe-wide eighth-century empire. The choice was partly strategic but also because of the presence of hot springs. Relaxing in these waters was one of the emperor's favourite pastimes, and they remain a major draw at the luxurious **Carolus Thermen**, a spa northeast of the centre (daily 9am–11pm, last entry 9.30pm; with sauna Mon–Fri €30/day; Sat & Sun €32/day; without sauna Mon–Fri €15/day; Sat & Sun €16/day; ⓦcarolus-thermen.de).

WHAT TO SEE AND DO

The surviving architectural legacy of Charlemagne is small, but its crowning jewel, the former **Palace chapel**, has pride of place at the heart of the **Dom** (daily: Jan–March 7am–6pm; April–Dec 7am–7pm; ⓦaachendom.de), a UNESCO World Heritage Site. At the rear end of the chapel, the gilded shrine of Charlemagne, finished in 1215 after fifty years' work, contains the emperor's remains, while the gallery has the imperial throne, viewable only on a tour (English tour daily at 2pm; €4; tickets from Dominformation opposite Schatzkammer). Next to the Dom is the dazzling treasury or **Schatzkammer** (Jan–March Mon 10am–1pm, Tues–Sun 10am–5pm; April–Dec Mon 10am–1pm, Tues–Sun 10am–6pm; €5; entrance on Johannes-Paul-II-Strasse). Its highlights are the tenth-century Lothar Cross and a Roman sarcophagus once used as Charlemagne's coffin. The emperor's palace once extended as far as the expansive **Markt**. Here two of the palace towers remain, incorporated into the fourteenth-century **Rathaus**, whose facade is lined with the figures of fifty Holy Roman Emperors, 31 of whom were crowned in Aachen. The glory of the interior (daily 10am–6pm; €5) is the well-restored Kaisersaal, repository of the reproduction crown jewels.

ARRIVAL AND INFORMATION

By plane The Aachen/Maastricht airport is 41km from Aachen. There's a regular Airport Express bus from Aachen central station to the airport (1–2 hourly; 45min; €10); timetable at ⓦ paxmax.de.
Destinations London Stansted (Ryanair; 1hr).
By train The centre is 10min walk from the train station – down Bahnhofstrasse, then left into Theaterstrasse.
Destinations Brussels (hourly; 1hr 15min); Cologne (every 20min; 35–55mins); Liège (1–2 hourly; 25–50mins); Paris Gare du Nord (4 daily; 2hr 36min).

Tourist information In the Elisenbrunnen on Friedrich-Wilhelm-Platz (Jan–March Mon–Fri 9am–6pm, Sat 9am–2pm; April–Dec Mon–Fri 9am–6pm, Sat 9am–3pm, Sun 10am–2pm; ☏0241 180 29 60, ⓦ aachen.de).

EATING AND DRINKING

The student quarter centres on Pontstrasse – which leads northeast out of the Markt – and is lined with bars, cheap cafés and restaurants.
Kittel Pontstr. 39. Relaxed bohemian café with daily student breakfast specials and great inexpensive food, with pasta from €5. DJs on the decks from 8pm Sat. Daily 10am–1am.
Leo van den Daele Büchel 18. Historic wood-clad café with great cakes and particularly good *Printen*, a spiced gingerbread that's the main local speciality. Breakfasts from €6. Mon–Fri 9am–6.30pm, Sat 9am–6pm, Sun 10am–6pm.
Sowiso/Ocean Pontstr. 164–166. One of a cluster of lively sports and cocktail bars, with student-friendly prices, plentiful outdoor seating and a cheerful atmosphere. Guinness on tap, Jägermeister €1.50. Daily 10am–late.

MAINZ

At the confluence of the Rhine and Main rivers, **MAINZ** is an agreeable mixture of old and new, with an attractively restored centre and a jovial populace who are responsible for Germany's second-biggest carnival bash after Cologne. Its long-standing ecclesiastical power aside – the archbishop of Mainz was the head of German bishops – the city is also famous for Johannes Gutenberg, who invented printing here around 1450.

WHAT TO SEE AND DO

Rearing high above central Mainz, the **Dom** (March–Oct Mon–Fri 9am–6.30pm, Sat 9am–4pm, Sun 1–2.30pm & 3.30–6.30pm; Nov–Feb Mon–Fri 9am–5pm, Sat 9am–4pm, Sun 1–2.30pm & 3.30–5pm) is unusual for sharing its outer walls with rows of eighteenth-century houses. Inside, the choirs at both ends indicate it as an imperial cathedral, with one for the emperor and the other for the clergy; seven coronations have taken place here. The bustling **market square** outside (markets Tues, Fri & Sat 7am–2pm) adjoins Liebfrauenplatz and the

12

fascinating **Gutenberg Museum** (Tues–Sat 9am–5pm, Sun 11am–3pm; €5; ⓦgutenberg-museum.de). The latter pays tribute to one of the greatest inventions of all time, which enabled the mass-scale production of books; don't miss the original Gutenberg Bibles on the third floor. Its extension next door is the **Druckladen** (Printing shop; Mon–Fri 9am–5pm, Sat 10am–3pm; free; ☏061 31 12 26 86, ⓦgutenberg-druckladen .de), where visitors are shown how to hand-set type, and can buy posters and souvenirs.

ARRIVAL AND DEPARTURE

By plane Mainz Is served via Frankfurt airport; take ⓢ8 to Mainz Hauptbahnhof (2 hourly; 25min).
By train The station is a 15min walk northwest of the city centre; head down Bahnhofstr. or take a tram or bus to Höffchen (single ticket €2.60).
Destinations Cologne (1–3 hourly; 1hr 22min–1hr 55min); Frankfurt (frequent; 40min); Heidelberg (8 daily; 55min); Stuttgart (1–2 hourly; 1hr 30min).
By boat KD Lines sail along the Rhine between Mainz and the city of Koblenz via Bacharach (late April to early Oct 1–2 daily; 5hr 30min/2hr 30min to Bacharach; ☏0221 208 83 18; ⓦk-d.com).

INFORMATION

Tourist information Brückenturm am Rathaus (Mon–Fri 9am–6pm, Sat 10am–4pm, Sun 11am–3pm; ☏06131 28 62 10, ⓦinfo-mainz.de). Tricky to find, with an isolated position: it's elevated above the street beside a pedestrian bridge.
Discount pass The MainzPlus card, sold at the tourist office and in the Local Transport Office in front of the central station at Bahnhofplatz 6a, costs €9.95 and allows you free access to all museums and free transport in the Mainz/Wiesbaden conurbation for 48hr.

GETTING AROUND

By bike Bike rental from Mainzer Rad Verleih Bingerstr 19 (on the viaduct south of the station; deposit €50 with ID, then from €8.90/day; ☏06131 33 61 225, ⓦcjd-mainz.de).

ACCOMMODATION

DJH Otto-Brunfels-Schneise 4 ☏061 318 53 32, ⓦdiejugendherbergen.de; buses #62 & #63 from the Hauptbahnhof to stop "Am Viktorstift/*Jugendherberge*". Modern HI hostel, with single, twin and four-bed rooms, in the wooded heights of Weisenau and with a great view over the Rhine. Breakfast €5.50. Dorm **€21.50**, double **€54**

Stadt Coblenz Rheinstr. 49 ☏061 316 29 04 44, ⓦstadtcoblenz.de. Conveniently located near the Dom, this is the only cheap option in the centre, although some rooms suffer from street noise (and from the Cuban bar below). Breakfast €6, free wi-fi, but odd reception hours; call first. Double **€55**

EATING, DRINKING AND NIGHTLIFE

Mainz boasts more vineyards on its outskirts than any other German city; its many lovely wine bars are the best places to sample their produce.
Altdeutsche Weinstube Liebfrauenplatz 7. The oldest wine bar in town (established 1462) offering daily dishes for €11. Local wine €3. Mon–Fri 4pm–midnight, Sat & Sun 11.30am–midnight.
★ **Codex** Liebfrauenplatz 5. Popular café with daily specials and standard German dishes for €7–8. Good beer (€3.50), friendly service and free wi-fi. Mon–Thurs 9am–1am, Fri & Sat 9am–2am, Sun 10am–1am.
Heiligeist Mailandsgasse 11. Attractive and inexpensive bistro in the Gothic vaults of a fifteenth-century hospital; mains (average €10) feature *Cronstarte*, a kind of local pizza-cum-pancake. Mon–Fri 4pm–1am, Sat & Sun 9am–2am.

THE RHINE GORGE

North of Mainz, the Rhine snakes west to **BINGEN**, where the spectacular 80km-long **Rhine Gorge** begins. Its most famous sight is the **Lorelei**, a rocky projection between Oberwesel and St Goar, where legend has it that a blonde maiden would lure passing mariners to their doom with her song. The region is best visited by boat or by bike, spending a night in Bacharach, but if you're pressed for time, the train will do.

ARRIVAL AND DEPARTURE

By train The railway between Mainz and Koblenz runs along the riverbank, offering wonderful gorge views from the windows; sit on the right.
By boat Some river cruises depart from Mainz, but Schifffahrt Rhein begin at Bingen (ⓦschifffahrt-rhein.de). The full one-way boat fare from Bingen to Koblenz is €34.10.

Bacharach

Pretty, half-timbered **BACHARACH**, 15km from Bingen, huddles behind a fourteenth-century wall, which you can walk along for a brilliant view. The town is chock-full of alleyways and quirky buildings, such as the celebrated **Altes Haus** at Oberstrasse 61, so wonky it seems to lean in all directions at once. Many of them house *Weinstuben* (wine bars), where you should try local favourite *Hahnenhof* Riesling.

ACCOMMODATION

Im Malerwinkel Blücherstrasse 41–45 ☎ 067 43 12 39, ⓦ im-malerwinkel.de. The best budget hotel is this lovely half-timbered place built into the old town wall; the path into town next to the brook nearby is a delight. Free wi-fi. Double €68

Jugendherberge Bacharach ☎ 067 43 12 66, ⓦ djh .de. The twelfth-century castle of Burg Stahleck above town houses what is probably Germany's most atmospheric hostel. It's a steep uphill climb to get there, but the views of the Rhine Valley are worth it; book well in advance as prices rise with demand. Dorm €20.50, double €52

TRIER

Birthplace of Karl Marx, and the oldest city in Germany, **TRIER** was once the capital of the Western Roman Empire. Nowadays, it's merely a regional centre for the upper Mosel valley, giving it a relaxed air. Despite a turbulent history, the city's past is well preserved, particularly in the most impressive group of Roman remains north of the Alps.

WHAT TO SEE AND DO

The centre corresponds roughly to the Roman city and can easily be covered on foot. From the train station, it's a few minutes' walk down Theodor-Heuss-Allee to the **Porta Nigra**, Roman Trier's northern gateway (daily: March & Oct 9am–5pm; April–Sept 9am–6pm; Nov–Feb 9am–4pm; €3). From here,

Simeonstrasse runs down to the **Hauptmarkt**, a busy pedestrian area, where market stalls sell groceries and flowers. At the southern end of the Hauptmarkt, a half-hidden Baroque portal leads to the exquisite Gothic church **St Gangolf**, built by the burghers of Trier to aggravate the archbishops, whose political power they resented.

The Dom and Konstantinbasilika

Up Sternstrasse from the Hauptmarkt, the magnificent Romanesque **Dom** (daily: April–Oct 6.30am–6pm; Nov–March 6.30am–5.30pm; ⓦ dominformation.de) lies on the site of the one built in the fourth century by Emperor Constantine. The present church dates from 1030, and the original facade has not changed significantly since then. From here, take Liebfrauenstrasse and turn left on An der Meerkatz, to the **Konstantinbasilika** (April–Oct daily 10am–6pm; Nov–March Tues–Sat 11am–noon & 2–4pm, Sun noon–1pm). Built as Emperor Constantine's throne hall, its dimensions are awe-inspiring: 36m high and 71m long, it is completely self-supporting. It became a church for the local Protestant community in the nineteenth century.

The Rheinisches Landesmuseum and the Kaiserthermen

Just beyond some formal gardens southwest of the Konstantinbasilika, the **Rheinisches Landesmuseum** (Tues–Sun 10am–5pm; €6; ⓦ landesmuseum-trier .de) is easily the best of Trier's museums, with a permanent display that conveys the sophistication and complexity of Roman civilization; the prize exhibits are

12

BOAT TRIPS ON THE MOSEL

The stretch of the Mosel connecting Trier with the city of Koblenz cuts a sinuous and attractive gorge that gives Germany some of its steepest vineyards and best full-bodied wines. **Boats** offer an ideal way to explore the valley: Personen-Schiffahrt Gebrüder Kolb (ⓦ moselfahrplan .de) offer regular sailings from Trier to Bernkastel-Kues, while the separately run ship, *Princesse Marie-Astrid* (ⓦ visitmoselle.lu/en/boat-princesse-marie-astrid), sails along the Luxembourg border on the upper Moselle; Mosel-Schiffs-Touristik (ⓦ moselpersonenschifffahrt.de) concentrate on the middle leg around Traben-Trarbach and Bernkastel-Kues; while Köln-Düsseldorfer (ⓦ k-d.com) cover the northern stretch between Cochem and Koblenz. Pick up the latest timetables at the tourist information office in Trier.

the richly sculpted tombstones from Neumagen and the collection of Roman mosaics, the largest north of the Alps. A few minutes' walk further south, the **Imperial Baths** (daily: March & Oct 9am–5pm; April–Sept 9am–6pm; Nov–Feb 9am–4pm; €3) was one of the largest bath complexes in the Roman world. The extensive underground heating system has survived, and you can walk through its passages.

The Karl-Marx-Haus

Southwest of the Hauptmarkt, the **Karl-Marx-Haus**, Brückenstrasse 10 (April–Oct daily 10am–6pm; Nov– March Mon 2–5pm, Tues–Sun 11am– 5pm; €4 includes free audio guide; ⊛fes .de/Karl-Marx-Haus), is where Karl Marx was born. It now houses a modern three-storey museum on his life and work, as well the influence of his ideas in history up to the present.

ARRIVAL AND INFORMATION

By train The train station is slightly east of the centre. Walk 500m straight up the Christophstrasse, to reach the Porta Nigra and get your bearings.

Destinations Cologne (hourly; 2hr 45min–3hr 30min); Luxembourg (1–2 hourly; 47min).

Tourist office At the Porta Nigra (Jan & Feb Mon–Sat 10am–5pm, Sun 10am–1pm; March & April Mon–Sat 9am–6pm, Sun 10am–3pm; May–Oct Mon–Sat 9am–6pm, Sun 10am–5pm; Nov & Dec Mon–Sat 9am–6pm, Sun 10am–3pm; ☎0651 97 80 80, ⊛trier -info.de).

Discount cards The Antiquity Card (€9) includes free admission to the Landesmuseum and two Roman structures plus reductions for other sights. The Trier-Card (€9.90/3 days) also covers transport, but only provides discounts to the museums.

GETTING AROUND

By bike Bike rental in the bicycle underground garage next to the Porta Nigra (mid-April to Oct Mon–Sat 9am–6pm, Sun 10am–5pm; €10/day). Also inside the train station by platform 11 (mid-April to Sept daily 9am–6pm; Oct to mid-April Mon–Fri 10am–6pm, Sat 10am–2pm; €10/day).

ACCOMMODATION

Camping Treviris Luxemburgerstr. 81 ☎065 18 20 09 11, ⊛camping-treviris.de. Campsite on the western bank of the Mosel, over the Konrad-Adenauer bridge, with a

beer garden and barbecue. Open April–Oct. Camping **€5.80** per person, plus **€5.50** per tent

DJH An der Jugendherberge 4 ☎065 114 66 20, ⊛djh.de; buses #5, #7, #8 and #12. Spotless modern HI hostel, with games rooms and sports facilities. Some single-bed rooms. Dorm **€21.50**, double **€54**

Hille's Gartenfeldstr. 7 ☎065 17 10 27 85, ⊛hilles -hostel-trier.de. Homely, clean and sociable independent hostel 10min walk south of the station. Breakfast €6, sheets €3. Dorm **€14**, double **€50**

EATING, DRINKING AND NIGHTLIFE

Alt Zalawen Zurlaubener Ufer 79. This traditional tavern, complete with outdoor seating overlooking the Mosel, makes an excellent place to try out the local cider, Viez. Meat platter €6. April–Oct daily 3–11pm; Nov–March Mon–Sat 3–11pm.

Astarix Karl-Marx-Str. 11. This relaxed student bar is your best bet for good and inexpensive food, and there's often live music at night. Difficult to find, with the entrance down a side alley. Pizzas €3.50–5. Mon–Thurs 11.30am–11pm, Fri & Sat 11.30am–11.30pm, Sun 1–11.30pm.

Irish Club Trier Jakobstr. 10 ⊛irishpub-trier.de. Central, reliably popular and fun bar offering quiz nights, karaoke, live bands and DJs at weekends. Pint of Guinness €5.50. Mon–Thurs & Sun noon–1am, Fri & Sat noon–2am.

FRANKFURT (AM MAIN)

Straddling the River Main just before it meets the Rhine, **FRANKFURT** is known as Germany's financial capital and the home of the European Central Bank. But it also has some of Germany's best museums and some excellent (if expensive) nightlife. Over half of the city, including almost all of the centre, was destroyed during World War II and the rebuilders often opted for innovation over restoration, resulting in an architecturally mixed skyline – part quaint, Germanic red sandstone, part skyscraper, giving rise to the name *Mainhattan*.

WHAT TO SEE AND DO

Frankfurt's centre is defined by its old city walls, now a semicircular stretch of public gardens. Presided over by the gabled **Römer** or town hall, the broad, irregular piazza of **Römerberg** is the historical and geographical heart of the Altstadt, where Charlemagne built his fort to protect the original *frankonovurd* (Ford of the Franks). The whole quarter was flattened

■ ACCOMMODATION		● EATING		● DRINKING & NIGHTLIFE		
Fair Hotel	1	Bayram	8	Adolf Wagner	12	Main Café	9
Five Elements	2	Café Karin	6	CK Studio	1	Zum Eichkatzerl	10
Frankfurt Hostel	4	Die Kuh die Lacht	2/7	Club Voltaire	3		
Little Paris	5	Metzgerei Ebert	4	Cooky's	5		
United Hostel	3			Fichtekränzi	11		

by bombing in 1944, but the most
significant landmarks were rebuilt or
restored afterwards and there are now
moves to rebuild more of the original
houses. Each December, Römerberg is
the focus for Frankfurt's delightful
Christmas Market.

Kaiserdom

The Altstadt's most significant survivor
is the thirteenth-century church of
St Bartholomäus, known as the
Kaiserdom (daily 8am–8pm; free), where
for two centuries Holy Roman Emperors
were crowned. To the right of the choir is
the restored **Wahlkapelle** (electoral

chapel), where the seven Electors would
choose the Holy Roman Emperor. You
can climb up the tower for a great view
of the city (April–Oct Tues–Fri 10am–
5pm, Sat & Sun 11am–5pm; €4). If
taking the lift is more your thing, you can
try the 200m ride up to the 55th floor of
the **Main Tower** at Neue Mainzer Strasse
52–58 (April–Oct Mon–Thurs & Sun
10am–11pm, Fri & Sat 10am–11pm;
Nov–March Mon–Thurs & Sun
10am–7pm, Fri & Sat 10am–9pm; €5).

Goethehaus

Although completely destroyed in a 1944
bombing raid, the mansion at Grosser

Hirschgraben 23–25 (Mon–Sat 10am–6pm, Sun 10am–5.30pm; €7), where Johann Wolfgang Goethe was born in 1749 and lived on and off until his move to Weimar in 1775, has been painstakingly reconstructed. Paintings and furniture had thankfully been evacuated prior to the bombing, and were so effectively reassembled during the restoration of 1947–51, that the resulting house feels "lived in". The adjoining museum gives you an excellent overall description of Germany's literary giant. A must.

Museum für Moderne Kunst

Dividing Braubachstrasse from Berliner Strasse at the eastern end of the Altstadt is the **Museum für Moderne Kunst** (MMK, Domstrasse; Tues & Thurs–Sun 10am–6pm, Wed 10am–8pm; €10, ⓦmmk-frankfurt.de), a three-storey affair featuring major modern artists such as Lichtenstein and Beuys, alongside innovative temporary exhibitions.

Sachsenhausen and Museumsufer

For a laidback evening out, head for **Sachsenhausen**, the city-within-a-city on the south bank of the Main. The network of streets around Affentorplatz is home to the apple-wine (*Ebbelwei*) houses, while the Schaumainkai – also known as **Museumsufer** – is lined with excellent museums. Pick of the bunch is the **Städel**, located at no. 63 (Tues, Fri, Sat & Sun 10am–6pm, Wed & Thurs 10am–9pm; €12; ⓦstaedelmuseum.de), which was extended in a major building project in 2009–11. All the big names in German art are represented, including Dürer, Holbein and Cranach – as well as other European masters from Rembrandt to Picasso. The **Deutsches Filmmuseum** at no. 41 (Tues & Thurs–Sun 10am–6pm, Wed 10am–8pm; €5; ⓦdeutsches filmmuseum.de) has its own cinema and is popular for foreign films and arthouse screenings. Another engaging choice is the lively **Museum für Kommunikation** at no. 53 (Tues–Fri 9am–6pm, Sat & Sun 11am–7pm; €3; ⓦmfk-frankfurt.de), installed in a bright, glassy modern building, whose exhibits include a Salvador Dalí lobster telephone.

ARRIVAL AND DEPARTURE

By plane Frankfurt Airport (ⓦfrankfurt-airport.com) is Germany's busiest. It has its own train station, with regular rail links to many German cities and Frankfurt's Hauptbahnhof (Ⓢ8 and Ⓢ9; 11min; €4.25). The deceptively named Frankfurt Hahn Airport (ⓦhahn -airport.de) actually lies midway between Trier and Koblenz. It is connected to Frankfurt by bus that stops just south of the station (15 daily; 1hr 45min; €14; timetable at ⓦbohr-omnibusse.de).

By train From the Hauptbahnhof it's a 15min walk to the centre; take Ⓤ4 or Ⓤ5, or tram #11 or #12. There is a left-luggage facility here.

Destinations Berlin (hourly; 4hr 10min); Cologne (1–3 hourly; 1hr–1hr 20min); Hamburg (hourly; 3hr 55min); Hannover (1–2 hourly; 2hr 19min–3hr); Heidelberg (hourly; 52min); Mainz (frequent; 30min); Munich (hourly; 3hr 15min); Nuremberg (1–2 hourly; 2hr 5min).

By bus The bus station is just south of the Hauptbahnhof. Destinations Cologne (5 daily; 3hr); Munich (5 daily; 6hr); Stuttgart (5 daily; 6hr).

INFORMATION

Tourist information In the train station (Mon–Fri 8am–9pm, Sat & Sun 9am–6pm; ☎069 21 23 88 00, ⓦfrankfurt-tourismus.de), and also at Römerberg 27 (Mon–Fri 9.30am–5.30pm, Sat & Sun 10am–4pm). They can book accommodation.

Discount passes The Frankfurt Card (€9.20/13.90 for 1/2 days) can be bought from tourist offices and allows travel throughout the city, plus fifty percent off entry charges to most museums. The Museumsufer Ticket (€18) provides free entrance to 34 museums over two consecutive days.

GETTING AROUND

By public transport Frankfurt has an integrated public transport system (ⓦrmv.de) made up of S-Bahn, U-Bahn and trams. Short trip €1.60 (allowed destinations shown on every stop), longer trip €2.60, day ticket €6.40 (€8.30 includes airport).

ACCOMMODATION

Accommodation is pricey, thanks to the business clientele; rates can triple during or just before trade fairs. The flipside is that they tumble at weekends (when you are strongly advised to come).

Fair Hotel Mainzer Landstr. 120 ☎069 74 26 28, ⓦfairhotelfrankfurt.de. Pleasant budget hotel just north of the train station, away from the sleazier streets. Rooms without WC 20 percent cheaper. Good weekend rates. Double **€60**

Five Elements Moselstr. 40 ☎069 24 00 58 85, ⓦ5elementshostel.de. Lively new hostel a short walk from the main station, with 24hr reception, all-you-can-eat breakfast until midday, laundry and free wi-fi (in your room). The bar area is a great place to socialize and there's live music every Sat. Dorm €18, double €36

Frankfurt Hostel Kaiserstr. 74 ☏069 247 51 30, ⓦfrankfurt-hostel.com. Very close to the station with bar till 5am and 24hr reception. Sheets and breakfast included, locker rental €2. Free wi-fi at reception. Dorm €19, double €49

★ **Little Paris** Karlruherstr. 8 ☏069 273 99 63, ⓦlittle -paris-hotel.de. Delightful little hotel in a side street south of the station, where each room is designed around a French movie star. Breakfast and wi-fi included. An excellent choice. Double €55

United Hostel Kaiserstr. 52 ☏069 256 67 80 00, ⓦunited-hostel-frankfurt.com. A lot of money has been spent on this bright and hip 2012 hostel: it has double-glazed windows, hotel-quality bathrooms, huge kitchen and a cinema-size TV screen. Breakfast €4.50, Free wi-fi. Dorm €17

EATING AND DRINKING

Bayram Münchnerstr. 29. Turkish restaurant and kebab house going since 1991, popular and highly recommended by the locals. All food is fresh and cooked on a wooden grill. Massive portions for €8.50. Daily 8am–midnight.

Café Karin Grosser Hirschgraben 28. Frankfurt institution that's friendly, unpretentious and well worth a visit. Breakfast till 6pm (from €3.20) and bistro-bar in the evenings; pasta €9.80. Mon–Sat 9am–midnight, Sun 10am–7pm.

★ **Die Kuh die Lacht** Schillerstr. 28 & Friedensstr. 2. Excellent burgers – including meat-free falafel and nut options – with side dishes ranging from fries to salad or veggie tempura. Classic burger €6.50 plus free wi-fi. Both branches Mon–Sat 11am–11pm, Sun 11am–10pm.

Metzgerei Ebert Grosse Eschenheimer Str. 5. A family butchery which also sells cooked food in Frankfurt's pedestrian area. A plateful of Frankfurters and potato salad costs €5.40. Try the famous *Zeppelinwurst*, produced with a patented recipe since 1909. Mon–Fri 8.30am–7pm, Sat 9am–6pm.

NIGHTLIFE

Apfelwein (acidic cider) is Frankfurt's speciality, and Sachsenhausen's taverns are the most atmospheric places to try it.

Adolf Wagner Schweizer Str. 71. One of the most popular of the *Apfelwein* taverns, with a lively clientele of all ages and a cosy terrace. Meals from €9, *Apfelwein* €1.80. Daily 11am–midnight.

CK Studio Alte Gasse 5, ⓦck-studio.eu. The top gay club in Frankfurt in the middle of the gay area, albeit with rather expensive drinks. Entrance €10. Fri 10pm–late, Sat 11pm–late.

Club Voltaire Kleine Hochstr. 5. Politically committed, alternative bar and club with various events from art exhibitions to live music (entry €5–10). Beer €2.50. Mon Sat 6pm–1am, Sun 6pm–midnight.

Cooky's Am Salzhaus 4 ⓦcookys.de. Stylish hip-hop, house and soul club north of Berliner Strasse, hosting popular DJ nights plus occasional live acts. Beer €3.50, entry €5–10. Tues–Sun 10pm–late.

Fichtekränzi Wallstr. 5. Lovely *Apfelwein* tavern with a tree-shaded courtyard, wood-panelled interior and a more extensive menu than many. "Frankfurt butcher's platter" €7.30. Daily 5–11.30pm.

Main Café Schaumainkai 50. Situated on the river quay, this is the perfect place to sit on the grass, drink beer and chill, while watching the skyscrapers of "Mainhattan" opposite. Mon–Sat 10am–late, Sun 11am–4.30pm.

Zum Eichkatzerl Dreieichstr. 29, Sachsenhausen. An excellent, traditional *Apfelwein* tavern with a large courtyard and some veggie options; main courses from €7. Mon–Fri 5pm–1am, Sat & Sun 4pm–1am.

DIRECTORY

Consulates Australia, Main Tower, 28th floor Neue Mainzer Str. 52–58 ☏069 90 55 80; UK, Barclays Capital, Bockenheimlandstr. 38–40 ☏069 71 67 53 45; US, Giessenerstr. 30 ☏069 753 50.

Hospital Bürgerhospital, Nibelungenallee 37–41 ☏069 15 00 00.

Internet Internet Callshop, Kaiserstr. 70 (daily 9am–11pm; €2/hr); Internet Phoneshop, Kaiserstr. 81 (Mon–Sat 9am–11pm, Sun 10am–11pm; €2/hr).

Pharmacy At the train station, lower concourse (Mon–Fri 6.30am–9pm, Sat 8am–9pm, Sun 9am–8pm).

Post office Branches at the train station (Mon–Fri 7am–7pm, Sat 9am–4pm) and Goetheplatz 6 (Mon–Fri 9.30am–7pm, Sat 9am–2pm).

Baden-Württemberg

The southwestern state of **Baden-Württemberg** is Germany's most prosperous. The motorcar was invented here in the late nineteenth century, and the region has stayed at the forefront of technology ever since, with **Stuttgart** still the home of Daimler (Mercedes) and Porsche. Baden-Württemberg is also home to the famous university city of **Heidelberg**. Baden-Württemberg's scenery is wonderful: its western and southern boundaries are defined by the Rhine and its bulge into Germany's largest lake, the **Bodensee** (Lake Constance). Within the curve of the river lies the **Black Forest**, source of another of the continent's principal waterways, the Danube.

HEIDELBERG

Quintessentially German and home to Germany's oldest university, **HEIDELBERG** lies majestically on the banks of the swift-flowing Neckar, 85km south of Frankfurt. For two centuries, it has seduced travellers, most notably Mark Twain, like no other German city and it still draws them to its bosom. The centrepiece is the **Schloss**, a compendium of magnificent buildings, made more atmospheric by their ruined condition; this is one castle where you

won't end up traipsing through over-decorated bedchambers. The rest of the city has some good museums, but the main appeal lies in its picturesque cobbled streets, crammed with traditional restaurants and student pubs. In spring and early summer the streets hum with activity and late-night parties – by July and August, most students have left, to be replaced by swarms of visitors.

WHAT TO SEE AND DO

The dominating **Heidelberg Schloss** (daily 8am–6pm; €6 with a Bergbahn ticket, guided tours €4, audioguide €4; ⓦschloss-heidelberg.de) can be reached from the Kornmarkt by the *Bergbahn* funicular (every 10min; €6 return along with castle entry), which continues to the **Königstuhl** viewpoint (€12 return); you can also walk up in ten minutes via the

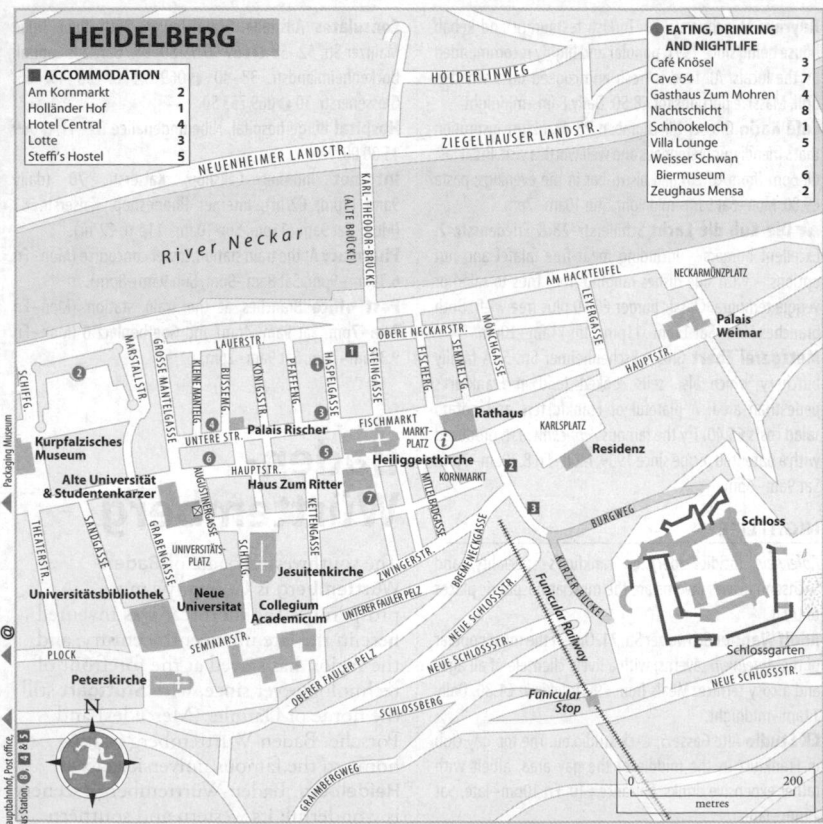

12

HEIDELBERG

■ ACCOMMODATION

Am Kornmarkt	2
Holländer Hof	1
Hotel Central	4
Lotte	3
Steffi's Hostel	5

● EATING, DRINKING AND NIGHTLIFE

Café Knösel	3
Cave 54	7
Gasthaus Zum Mohren	4
Nachtschicht	8
Schnookeloch	1
Villa Lounge	5
Weisser Schwan Biermuseum	6
Zeughaus Mensa	2

HÖLDERLINWEG

ZIEGELHAUSER LANDSTR.

NEUENHEIMER LANDSTR.

River Neckar

KARL-THEODOR-BRÜCKE (ALTE BRÜCKE)

AM HACKTEUFEL

NECKARMÜNZPLATZ

Palais Weimar

LAUERSTR.

OBERE NECKARSTR.

HAUPTSTR.

MARSTALLSTR.

GROSSE MANTELGASSE

KLEINE MANTELG.

BUSSEMG.

KÖNIGSSTR.

PFAFFENG.

HASPELGASSE

STEINGASSE

FISCHERG.

SEMMELSG.

MÜNCHGASSE

LEYERGASSE

Kurpfälzisches Museum

UNTERE STR.

Palais Rischer

FISCHMARKT

MARKT-PLATZ (i)

Rathaus

KARLSPLATZ

Residenz

Alte Universität & Studentenkarzer

HAUPTSTR.

AUGUSTINERGASSE

Haus Zum Ritter

Heiliggeistkirche

KORNMARKT

MITTELBADGASSE

KETTENGASSE

BURGWEG

Schloss

THEATERSTR.

SANDGASSE

GRABENGASSE

SCHULG.

UNIVERSITÄTS-PLATZ

Jesuitenkirche

ZWINGERSTR.

BREMENECKGASSE

KURZER BUCKEL

Funicular Railway

Universitätsbibliothek

Neue Universität

Collegium Academicum

UNTERER FAULER PELZ

NEUE SCHLOSSSTR.

Schlossgarten

PLÖCK

SEMINARSTR.

OBERER FAULER PELZ

NEUE SCHLOSSSTR.

NEUE SCHLOSSSTR.

Peterskirche

SCHLOSSBERG

Funicular Stop

N

GRAIMBERGWEG

Packaging Museum

Hauptbahnhof, Post office.

Bus Station, ① ④ & ⑤

0   200

metres

steep Burgweg. At the southeastern corner is the most romantic of the ruins, the **Gesprengter Turm**; a collapsed section lies intact in the moat, leaving a clear view into the interior. The **Schloss** is in fact a group of Renaissance palaces that now also contains the diverting Pharmacy Museum with exhibits in English (same hours as the Schloss; €6), and the **Grosses Fass**, an eighteenth-century wine barrel capable of holding 220,000 litres.

The Altstadt

The **Altstadt**'s finest surviving buildings are grouped around the sandstone **Heiliggeistkirche** on Marktplatz. Note the tiny shopping booths between its buttresses, a feature ever since the church was built. The striking Baroque **Alte Brücke** is reached from the Marktplatz down Steingasse; dating from the 1780s, it was painstakingly rebuilt after being blown up during World War II. The **Palais Rischer** on Untere Strasse (now a private dwelling) was the most famous venue for the university's *Mensur*, or fencing match; wounds were frequent and prized as badges of courage – for optimum prestige, salt was rubbed into them, leaving scars that remained for life. Universitätsplatz, the heart of the Old Town, is flanked by the eighteenth-century **Alte Universität** (April–Oct Tues–Sun 10am–6pm; Nov–March Tues–Sat 10am–4pm; €3) with its impressive conference room **Alte Aula** (1886) and the **Neue Universität**, erected with US funds in 1931. The oddest of Heidelberg's traditions was that its students didn't come under civil jurisdiction: offenders were dealt with by the university authorities, and could serve their punishment at leisure. The **Studentenkarzer** (Students' Prison) around the corner at Augustinergasse 2 (same hours and ticket as Alte Universität) was used from 1778 to 1914; its spartan cells are covered with some fantastic graffiti.

Finally, if you are into quirky museums, check out the wonderful **Packaging Museum** at Hauptstrasse 22 (Wed–Fri 1–6pm, Sat & Sun 11am–6pm; €3.50; ⓦverpackungsmuseum.info), displaying consumer products like 1890s carbolic toilet paper, 1900 Knorr cubes and 1907 Persil washing powder.

ARRIVAL AND DEPARTURE

By plane The Baden-Airpark (ⓦbadenairpark.de) is connected to Heidelberg train station by bus (4 daily; 1hr 45min; €20).
Destinations London (Ryanair).

By train and bus Heidelberg's train and bus stations are next to each other in an anonymous quarter 20min walk west of the Altstadt. Buses #32 and #33 run into the old centre.
Destinations Frankfurt (1–2 hourly; 54min); Mainz (1–2 hourly; 51min); Munich (every 2hr; 3hr); Stuttgart (1–2 hourly; 45min).

INFORMATION

Tourist information In the Rathaus on Marktplatz (Mon–Fri 8am–5pm, Sat 10am–5pm; ☏ 062 215 84 02 24, ⓦheidelberg-marketing.de) and on the square outside the station (April–Oct Mon–Sat 9am–7pm, Sun 10am–6pm; Nov–March Mon–Sat 9am–6pm).

Discount pass The Heidelberg card (1/2/4 day for €12.50/€14.50/€16.50) provides free transport in the city, free entry to the Schloss and reductions in museums, attractions and restaurants.

Internet Try the difficult to find, but fast and cheap, Matrix Internet Café, Plöck 93 (Mon–Fri 9.30am–7pm, Sat 10am–4pm; €1/hr; ☏ 062 218 93 60 41, ⓦcopy-matrix.de).

GETTING AROUND

By bus and tram Heidelberg is small, but the bus and tram system is useful for journeys from the train or bus stations. A bus between the station and the old town is €1.10 one-way; longer trip €2.20; day ticket €6.

By bike Bike rental at An der Alten Brücke Neckarstaden 52, by the Old Bridge (Tues–Fri 10am–1pm & 2–6pm, Sat 10am–6pm; Sun appointment only 2–6pm; €5/hr or €15/day; ☏ 062 216 54 44 60; ⓦfahrradverleih-heidelberg.de).

ACCOMMODATION

Hotels are often booked solid and are expensive; book months in advance for July & Aug.

Am Kornmarkt Kornmarkt 7 ☏ 062 212 43 25, ⓦhotelamkornmarkt.de; bus #33, get off at Bergbahn. Excellent-value hotel in a 600-year-old building underneath the castle. Large rooms each with a different colour scheme but not all en suite. Continental buffet breakfast €9. Free wi-fi at reception. Double **€70**

Hotel Central Kaiserstr. 75 ☏ 062 212 06 41, ⓦhotel-central-heidelberg.de. Sparkling and airy, if rather bland, modern hotel near the train station. One of the best-value places in town that's likely to have a bed with breakfast. Wi-fi €6/3hr. Double **€75**

12

12

★ **TREAT YOURSELF**

Holländer Hof Neckarstaden 66
☎062 216 05 00, ⊛hollaender-hof.de.
Possibly the most comfortable hotel
in this most romantic of towns, with
dreamily furnished rooms facing the
Old Bridge full of German *Gemütlichkeit*.
Breakfast and half a bottle of sparkling
wine included. Double **€120**

★ **Lotte** Burgweg 3 ☎062 217 35 07 25, ⊛lotte
-heidelberg.de; bus #33, get off at Bergbahn. The cheapest
option inside the Old Town, this is an old-fashioned yet
modern hostel with two well-equipped kitchens, washing
facilities and free wi-fi. Dorm **€23**, double **€64**

Steffi's Hostel Alte Eppelheimer Str. 50 ☎062 217 78 27
72, ⊛hostelheidelberg.de. Independent hostel in a former
brick factory with a clanky, noisy lift a short walk from the
train station. Perks include big kitchen, free wi-fi and bike
rental (€20 deposit). Breakfast €3. Dorm **€18**, double **€56**

EATING, DRINKING AND NIGHTLIFE

Because of its large student community Heidelberg
punches well above its weight in nightlife. The focus is
Untere Strasse and the Rathausplatz, but there are many
clubs dotted around the new city as well.

Café Knösel Haspelgasse 20. Chic café with enormous
cakes at this popular corner spot; coffee €3.90, simple daily
mains around €9. Mon–Fri noon–3pm & 6–10pm, Sat &
Sun noon–10pm.

Cave 54 Krämmergasse 2 ⊛cave54.de. The oldest
student jazz club in Germany, this is a famous venue: Ella
Fitzgerald and Louis Armstrong, among others, have
graced it with their presence. Their 9pm Sun jam is
legendary. €5 cover. Daily 8pm–late.

Gasthaus Zum Mohren Untere Str. 5. One of several hip,
young drinking spots along this alley, with various nightly

THE HEIDELBERG KISS

The **Knösel Chocolaterie** at Haspelgasse
16 (not to be confused with the *Knösel
Café* nearby; Tues–Sat 11am–6pm) is
home to the famous *Heidelberger
Studentenkuss*, a dark chocolate filled
with praline and nougat on a waffle
base (€2.25). The sweet has remained
unchanged since 1863 when the male
students were not allowed to talk to
chaperoned girls and their only means of
showing their affection (and passing on a
secret message) was by impishly offering
this small confectionery.

events. On Thurs ladies drink champagne free all night.
Fri–Thurs 4pm–3am, Fri & Sat 1pm–3am.

Nachtschicht Bergheimer Str. 147 ⊛nachtschicht.com.
Popular club in a former factory with hip-hop, disco and
house nights. Just north of the train station. Cover €6.
Thurs 10pm–3am, Fri 8pm–3am, Sat 11pm–4am.

★ **Schnookeloch** Haspelgasse 8. The oldest tavern in
town and still cosy. Drink beer from a boot (€7) and eat
unfinishable schnitzels for €12. Daily 11am–1am.

★ **Villa Lounge** Hauptstr. 187. Popular to the point of
bursting with under 25s who flock there for the various
cheap drink specials. If you're lucky you'll be in town when
they offer cocktails for €4, or announce their all-night
Happy Hour. Mon–Wed & Sun 9am–1am, Thurs–
Sat 9am–3am.

Weisser Schwan Biermuseum Hauptstr. 143. Spacious
establishment offering 28 types of beer and much loved by
the locals for its good-value lunch menu. Try its *Fleischkäse*
for €6.90. Daily 11am–11.45pm.

Zeughaus Mensa Im Marstallhof. Inside the old barracks
is a student refectory open to everyone. Fill up from a basic
warm buffet and pay by weight. Around €6 for a plateful.
Daily 11am–10pm.

FREIBURG (IM BREISGAU)

FREIBURG basks in the laidback
atmosphere you'd expect from Germany's
sunniest city. It's been a university town
since 1457 and its youthful presence
is maintained all year round with a
varied programme of festivals. It's a
thoroughly enjoyable place to visit, and
makes the perfect urban base for
exploring the surrounding **Black Forest**.
Home of the cuckoo clock and source of
the Danube, the Black Forest, stretching
170km north to south, and up to 60km
east to west, is Germany's largest and
most beautiful forest. Its name reflects
the mountainous landscape darkened
by endless pine trees and, as late as the
1920s, much of this area was eerie
wilderness, a refuge for boars and bandits.
Nowadays, many of its villages are geared
toward tourism, brimming with souvenir
shops, while old forest trails provide easy
and enjoyable hiking.

WHAT TO SEE AND DO

The city's most impressive sight is the
dark-red sandstone **Münster** (daily
8am–8pm), with its intricate openwork
spire. Begun in about 1200, the church

has a masterly Gothic nave, with flying buttresses, gargoyles and statues – the stained-glass windows are all original, having survived World War II. From the tower (April–Oct Mon–Sat 9.30am–5pm, Sun 1–5pm; Nov–March Tues–Sat 9.30am–5pm, Sun 1–5pm; €1.50) there's a fine panorama of the city and the surrounding forested hills. Walking south from here on Kaiser-Josef-Strasse, Freiburg's central axis, you come to the **Martinstor**, one of two surviving towers of the medieval fortifications. Just southeast of here is the main channel of the *Bächle* (medieval rain canals supplying water in case of fire); follow it along Gerberau, to the **Schwaben Tor**, the other thirteenth-century tower. Nearby, at Oberlinden 12, you can find Germany's oldest surviving inn, **Zum Roten Bären** (established 1120).

Schauinsland

The hills of the Black Forest almost rise out of Freiburg's Altstadt, giving the town a hugely convenient outdoorsy playground for hikers and mountain bikers, and the tourist information office has an abundance of good maps, as well as suggestions for numerous trailheads accessible by public transport. The largest of these forested peaks, **Schauinsland**, lies 7km south of the city and is easily ascended, thanks to the Schauinslandbahn cable car (daily: Jan–June & Oct–Dec 9am–5pm; July–Sept 9am–6pm; one-way €8.50, return €12; ☎0761 4511 777, ⓦschauinslandbahn.de; tram #2 to Günterstal terminus then bus #21). From its summit a five-minute walk leads to a lookout tower and the top of several well-marked trails. These offer first-class hiking and mountain biking – partly because almost the entire 14km journey back to Freiburg is downhill – with great views along the way.

ARRIVAL AND DEPARTURE

By plane Basel airport – now renamed EuroAirport Basel-Mulhouse-Freiburg – is 70km south of Freiburg but serves the town with an hourly bus to the train station (€25 single, €40 return; 50min; ⓦfreiburger -reisedienst.de).

By train The train station is on Bismarckallee about a 10min walk west of the city centre. A 24hr ticket for all city buses and trams costs €5.50.
Destinations Basel (2 hourly; 40min–1hr); Frankfurt (hourly; 2hr 10min); Stuttgart (hourly; 2hr); Zürich (hourly; 2hr 11min).
By bus The bus station is on Bismarckallee just below the train station.
Destinations Munich (3–4 daily; 3hr 45min).

INFORMATION AND TOURS

Tourist information Rathausplatz 2–4 (June–Sept Mon–Fri 8am–8pm, Sat 9.30am–5pm, Sun 11am–noon; Oct–May Mon–Fri 8am–6pm, Sat 9.30am–2.30pm, Sun 10am–noon; ☎076 13 88 18 80, ⓦfreiburg.de). For €3, they'll also find you a room.
Tours Tours in English (1hr 30min) are offered by Freiburger Leben (May–Oct Wed–Fri 10am & 2pm, Sat 10.30am, noon & 3.30pm; €9; ☎076 11 37 69 18; ✉info @freiburgerleben.com).

ACCOMMODATION

★ **Black Forest Hostel** Kartäuserstr. 33 ☎076 18 81 78 70, ⓦblackforest-hostel.de; tram #1 from the station to Schwabentorbrücke. Buzzing backpackers' hostel in an old factory, and by far the best place to stay in town. Well-equipped kitchen, wi-fi, and bikes for €5/day. Sheets €3. Dorm **€14**, double **€50**
Camping Hirzberg Kartäuserstr. 99 ☎076 13 50 54, ⓦfreiburg-camping.de; tram #1 to Musikhochschule, then turn left through the subway, cross the river and follow the signs. The most accessible (on foot) of Freiburg's three campsites. Open all year Camping **€7.80** per person, plus **€5** per tent
Helene Staufenerstr. 46 ☎076 14 52 10 29, ⓦhotel -helene-freiburg.de. Just over 1km south of the train station, just beyond the Dreisam River, this is the best-value central hotel in Freiburg. Breakfast buffet included. Double **€66**
KL Freiburg Kartäuserstr. 41 ☎076 12 11 16 30, ⓦkl -freiburg.de. Very modern and clean hotel-cum-hostel, not far from the centre, with a cafeteria offering three meals. Though it's almost always full, it's worth trying, especially if you are a student, as you get a fifteen percent discount. Breakfast included. Double **€69**

EATING, DRINKING AND NIGHTLIFE

Freiburg has better nightlife than larger towns; pick up a free *Fipps* magazine to see what's on.
Jazzhaus Schnewlinstr. 1 ☎076 13 49 73, ⓦjazzhaus.de. Club in an old wine cellar attracting a range of ages and hosting all manner of musical events, from world music concerts to blues, jazz, rock and hip-hop. Club night cover €7. Fri & Sat club nights 11pm–4am, gigs 8–11pm.

12

EUROPA PARK

Germany's largest **theme park** (daily: April–Oct 9am—6pm; Nov & Dec 11am–7pm; €39; ☎078 22 77 66 88; ⓦeuropapark.de) lies on the French border near Freiburg and it's great fun. Fairytale figures like Rapunzel and Hansel & Gretel battle it out with eleven roller coasters for your attention during the day, while variety shows, cinemas, pop concerts and restaurants in individual country-themed quarters entertain you at night. To reach it, take the local train from Freiburg to Ringsheim (hourly; 30min) and the #7231 shuttle bus from the station (2 hourly; 10min; €2.10). You can stay overnight at the Europa-park campsite (**€10.50** per person and tent).

Karma Bertoldstr. 51–53 ⓦkarma-freiburg.de. The *Karma* complex has everything you need: a café-bar, a good Indian restaurant with weekday lunch specials (around €6) and a club in the cellar (cover €6). Café-bar Mon–Thurs 9.30am–2am, Fri & Sat 9.30am–3am, Sun 9am–1am; restaurant Mon–Thurs & Sun 11am–11pm, Fri & Sat 11am–1am; club Fri & Sat 11pm–6am.

Markthalle Martinsgässle 235 & Grünewalderstr. 4 (two entrances). Food court that bustles with locals visiting different kiosks for quality regional Swabian and international dishes. Mon–Thurs 8am–8pm, Fri & Sat 8am–midnight.

★ **Martin's Bräu** Fressgässle 1. Typical *bierstube* brewing its own beer and offering cheap local specialities for €7–8 and standard dishes like spaghetti bolognese (€7.30). Mon–Thurs & Sun 11am–midnight, Fri & Sat 11am–2am.

Schlappen Löwenstr. 2 ⓦschlappen.com. Cool café-bar attracting mainly a student clientele that starts as a restaurant and a pub, and ends as a club with music late at night. Try the *Maultaschen* for €6.70, washed down with one of the many beers on sale (€3). Mon–Wed 11am–1am, Thurs 11am–2am, Fri & Sat 11am–3am, Sun 3pm–1am.

STUTTGART

In the centre of Baden-Württemberg, 85km southeast of Heidelberg, **STUTTGART** is home to the German success stories of Bosch, Porsche and Mercedes. Founded in 950 as a stud farm (*Stuotgarten*) by Duke Liudolf of Swabia, it became a town only in the fourteenth century. Though not the most beautiful of cities, it has some unique museums and sparkling nightlife.

WHAT TO SEE AND DO

From the train station, Königstrasse passes the brutalist modern Dom and enters Schlossplatz, on the south of which is the **Altes Schloss**, built to defend Duke Liudolf's stud farm and now home to the **Württemberg State Museum** (Tues–Sun 10am–6pm; €5.50; ⓦlandesmuseum-stuttgart.de). This large and richly varied museum explores the history of the region from the Stone Age to the present through archeological exhibitions as well as arts and crafts. Northeast of Schlossplatz at Konrad-Adenauer-Strasse 30–32 is the **State Gallery**, one of Germany's most visited art museums (Tues & Thurs 10am–8pm, Wed & Fri–Sun 10am–6pm; €5.50; Wed & Sat free; ⓦstaatsgalerie.de). There's an Old Masters section as well as a New Gallery focusing on various schools within twentieth-century art movements.

The Mercedes and Porsche museums

As much as they are collections of vintage cars, the Mercedes and Porsche museums are also temples to fine engineering, human ingenuity and thousands of hours of careful hard work. So slick are the museums – their modern architecture airy and futuristic, the displays self-confident, seamless and high-tech – that they can't fail to inspire. The **Mercedes-Benz-Museum** (Tues–Sun 9am–6pm; €8/students €4; Ⓢ1 to Neckarpark/Mercedes Benz; ⓦmercedes-benz-classic.com) is strong on the early parts of motoring history, since its founders invented both the motorbike and motorcar. A special extra is the race simulator (€4), which allows you to feel like Stirling Moss or Lewis Hamilton for five minutes. The **Porsche Museum** (Tues–Sun 9am–6pm; €8/students €4; Ⓢ6 to NeuwirtshausPorscheplatz; ⓦporsche.com) is no less flashy – and it allows you to pose inside a Carrera GTS. Dozens of priceless, highly polished examples of engineering at its finest are

THE PIG MUSEUM

The absolute must-see in Stuttgart is the **Schweinemuseum** (daily 11am–7.30pm; €4.90; ⓦ schweinemuseum.de; ⓤ Schlachthof), a private museum displaying all things cultural, educational and kitsch about our porky friends – from Disney cartoons and a teratogenic two-headed stuffed piglet to a roomful of piggy banks – over two floors and 40,000 exhibits. An adjacent inn allows you to fill your belly accordingly.

explained by an intelligent audioguide and touch-screen monitors. The success of the brand is underlined by a display of some of Porsche's 28,000 trophies.

ARRIVAL AND DEPARTURE

By plane Stuttgart Airport is linked to the train station by ⓢ2 and ⓢ3 (frequent; 30min). GermanWings and BA serve London while Lufthansa serve Birmingham and Manchester.

By train Stuttgart's train station is located in the centre of town.

Destinations Berlin (4–5 daily; 5hr–5hr 45min); Cologne (8 daily; 2hr 14min); Frankfurt (hourly; 1hr 17min); Hamburg (6–7 daily; 5hr 30min); Konstanz (10 daily; 2hr 20min); Munich (1–2 hourly; 2hr 15min); Zürich (every 2hr; 3hr).

By bus There's no bus station in the centre because of redevelopment. Some buses use the station at Hafenbahnstr. 15 in Obertürkheim, while others use Burgunderstr. 39 in Zuffenhausen. Both are 15–20min by S-Bahn from the central train station.

INFORMATION

Tourist information Opposite the train station at Königstr. 1a (Mon–Fri 9am–8pm, Sat 9am–6pm, Sun 1–6pm; tours & tickets ☎ 071 12 22 81 11, hotel bookings ☎ 071 12 22 81 00; ⓦ stuttgart-tourist.de). There's another branch at the airport, in Terminal 3 (Mon–Fri 8am–7pm, Sat 9am–1pm & 1.45–4.30pm, Sun 10am–1pm & 1.45–5.30pm).

Discount passes The StuttCard (€9.70/3 day) covers free admission to various attractions and numerous reductions; the Combination StuttCard (€18/3 day) also includes use of local public transport.

GETTING AROUND

By public transport A day ticket for the extensive integrated public transport network costs €6.10, a one-way ticket €2.

ACCOMMODATION

Alex 30 Alexanderstr. 30 ☎ 071 18 38 89 50, ⓦ alex30 -hostel.de; ⓤ Olgaeck. Established independent hostel near the Bohnenviertel. Has a bar, café, kitchen and terrace. Wi-fi is subject to a one-off charge of €1. Breakfast buffet €8. Dorm **€24**, double **€58**

DJH Haussmannstr. 27 ☎ 071 16 64 74 70, ⓦ jugendherberge-stuttgart.de; ⓤ 15 to Eugensplatz. Large, well-organized but still run-of-the-mill DJH hostel. Dorm **€25.60**, double **€60.20**

Inter Hostel Paulinenstr. 16 ☎ 071 166 48 27 97, ⓦ inter-hostel.com; ⓤ Österreichischer Platz. Modern, friendly, funky hostel right in the centre, with spartan but large rooms, three kitchens over six floors and price reductions for long stays. Big buffet breakfast for €7. Free wi-fi. Dorm **€23**, double **€60**

Schwabennest Hospitalstr. 9 ☎ 071 129 68 10, ⓦ schwabennest.wix.com/schwabennest1. Spotless guesthouse above a Swabian restaurant, and one of the few central bargains. Some rooms are en suite. Breakfast €7.50. Double **€55**

EATING, DRINKING AND NIGHTLIFE

Stuttgart is surrounded by vineyards, and its numerous *Weinstuben* are excellent places to try good-quality local wines at low cost. It is also one of the best cities for nightlife in Germany with the focus below Schlossplatz and west of Rotebühlplatz.

Die Kiste Hauptstätterstr. 35 ⓦ kiste-stuttgart.de. Live venue with Guinness on tap offering interesting jazz sessions as well as performances by local indie rock bands. Entrance €5. Mon–Thurs 6pm–1am, Fri & Sat 6pm–2am.

★ **Lehmann** Seidenstr. 20 ⓦ lehmannclub.de. One of techno's cathedrals with a reputation inside Germany second only to legends like Berlin's *Berghain*. Cover €10–12. Fri & Sat 11pm–late.

★ **Mata Hari** Geißstr. 3. Standing room only in this bar/café, very popular with the under 25s, and always packed to the rafters. Champagne €4, beer €3, daily dish €7. Mon–Thurs & Sun 2pm–2am, Fri & Sat 2pm–3am.

Palast der Republik Friedrichstr. 27. Offbeat cult place: a former public loo that's now a beer kiosk. On sunny days drinkers line the pavement outside and (amazingly for

---

★ **TREAT YOURSELF**

Sautter Johannesstr. 28 ☎ 071 16 14 30, ⓦ hotel-sautter.de; ⓤ Schloss/ Johannesstrasse. Good, central, quiet business hotel with special deals on weekends and a restaurant attached offering local specialities. Breakfast and wi-fi included. Double **€82**

12

Germany) DJs play loud music on the pavement at night. Beer €3.30. Mon–Wed 11am–2am, Thurs–Sat 11am–3am, Sun 3pm–midnight.

Schönbuch Bräuhaus Bolzstr. 10. Independent brewery and associated beer hall and garden in the middle of the pedestrian district with filling lunch dishes for €7. Try a half-litre of its Ur-Edel lager for €3.50 and swoon. Mon–Wed & Sun 11am–midnight, Thurs–Sat 11am–1am.

Udo's Snack Calverstrasse 23. Hole-in-the-wall snack bar offering quality burgers for €4 and loud techno for free: an irresistible combination that's been going strong for over 30 years. Mon–Wed 11am–10pm, Thurs 11am–11pm, Fri & Sat 11am–1am.

KONSTANZ AND THE BODENSEE

In the far south, hard on the Swiss border, **KONSTANZ** lies at the tip of a tongue of land sticking out into the huge **Bodensee** (Lake Constance). The town itself is split by the lake, giving Konstanz the air of a sea town. Its convivial atmosphere is best experienced in the summer, when street cafés tempt prolonged stays and the water is a bustle of sails.

WHAT TO SEE AND DO

Konstanz's most prominent building is the **Münster** church, dating from the Romanesque period and located in the heart of the Altstadt (Mon–Sat 10am–5.30pm, Sun 12.30–6pm; free). The regional highlights are two small Bodensee islands. The nearby **Mainau** island (daily dawn to dusk; €17.50; ⓦmainau.de) has a royal park featuring magnificent floral displays, formal gardens, greenhouses, forests, a butterfly house and a handful of well-placed restaurants. The tranquil island of **Reichenau**, 8km west of Konstanz, has a Romanesque Benedictine Abbey which is a UNESCO World Heritage Site.

ARRIVAL AND INFORMATION

By train The train station is at the southern edge of the city on the border with Switzerland. For Reichenau take the regional "Seehas" train to Reichenau station (frequent; 9min), then change to bus #7372 to "Mittelzell" (frequent; 15min).

Destinations Munich (2 hourly; 4hr 15min–5hr); Zürich (hourly; 1hr 20min).

Tourist information Beside the train station at Bahnhofplatz 43 (April–Oct Mon–Fri 9am–6.30pm, Sat 9am–4pm, Sun 10am–1pm; Nov–March Mon–Fri 9.30am–6pm; ⓣ075 31 13 30 30, ⓦkonstanz-tourismus .de); staff can book private rooms.

GETTING AROUND

By bike Bike rental from Kultur-Rädle, Bahnhofplatz 29 (Easter–Oct Mon–Fri 9am–12.30pm & 2.30–6pm, Sat 10am–4pm, Sun 10am–12.30pm; Nov–Easter Mon–Fri 9am–12.30pm & 2.30–6pm, Sat 10am–4pm; €12/day; ⓣ07531 273 10; ⓦkultur-raedle.de).

By boat You can get information on cruises and ferries from the Bodensee-Schiffsbetriebe (BSB) at Hafenstr. 6 (ⓣ075 313 64 00, ⓦbsb-online.com). Their ferries run regularly around the lake and they also offer scenic trips to Switzerland.

ACCOMMODATION

Campingplatz Bruderhofer Fohrenbühlweg 45 ⓣ075 313 13 88, ⓦcampingplatz-konstanz.de; bus #1 to Tannenhof then a 10min walk. One of two pleasant neighbouring campsites on the lakeshore 4km northeast of the centre and around 1km from the car-ferry dock. Camping €4.50 per person, plus €6.80 per tent

DJH Konstanz Zur Allmannshöhe 16 ⓣ075 313 22 60, ⓦjugendherberge-konstanz.de; bus #4 to Jugendherberge. Excellent hostel uniquely located in an old water tower, 5km out of town. Those over 26 pay €4.50 extra. Dorm €23.60

Bavaria

Bavaria (Bayern), Germany's largest federal state, fills the southeast of the country, providing its entire border with Austria. It's the home of almost all German clichés: beer-swilling men in *Lederhosen*, piles of *Sauerkraut* and sausages galore. But that's only a small part of the picture, and one that's almost entirely restricted to the Bavarian Alps that lie south of the magnificent state capital, **Munich**. Eastern Bavaria – whose capital is **Regensburg** – is dominated by rolling forests where life revolves around logging and minor industries like glass production. To the north, **Nuremberg** is the hub of Protestant **Franconia** (Franken), a region known for its vineyards and natural parks as well as

THE ROMANTIC ROAD

The charming, picturesque **Romantic Road** (Ⓦ romantischestrasse.de) is perhaps Germany's most famous and best-loved tourist route, running from the vineyards of Würzburg in northern Bavaria over 385km of pastoral scenery and quaint medieval villages to the fairytale castle of Füssen in the south. From April to October, Touring (Ⓣ 069 719 12 62 68, Ⓦ touring-travel.eu) runs one bus daily in each direction between Frankfurt and Füssen via Munich, up and down the Road, with short stops in many of the towns (12hr 20min).

beautifully preserved and atmospheric medieval towns – notably **Rothenburg ob der Tauber**, which is but a highlight among the glut of attractive places that dot Bavaria's **Romantic Road**.

MUNICH

Founded in 1158, **MUNICH** (München) has been the capital of Bavaria since 1504, and as far as the locals are concerned it's the centre of the universe. Impossibly energetic, it bursts with a good-humoured self-importance that is difficult to dislike. After Berlin, Munich is Germany's most popular city – and with its compact, attractive old centre it's far easier to digest. It has a great setting, with the mountains and Alpine lakes just an hour's drive away. The best time to come is from June to early October, when the beer gardens, cafés and bars are in full swing – not least for the world-famous **Oktoberfest** beer festival.

WHAT TO SEE AND DO

Just ten minutes' walk east of the train station, the twin onion-domed towers of the red-brick Gothic Frauenkirche (Dom; Mon–Wed, Sat & Sun 7am–7pm, Thurs 7am–8.30pm, Fri 7am–6pm) form the focus of the city's skyline. The pedestrian shopping street, **Kaufingerstrasse**, just below, heads east to the centre and the main square, the Marienplatz.

Marienplatz

The **Marienplatz** is the bustling heart of Munich, thronged with crowds being entertained by street musicians and artists. At 11am and noon (also 5pm March–Oct), the square fills with tourists as the glockenspiel in the **Neues Rathaus** (Marienplatz 8; Tower May–Oct daily 10am–7pm; Nov–April Mon–Fri 10am–5pm; €2.50) jingles into action. To the right is the plain Gothic **Altes Rathaus**, whose tower now houses a vast toy collection in the **Spielzeugmuseum** (daily 10am–5.30pm; €4).

Alter Peter and the Viktualienmarkt

On the south side of Marienplatz, the **Peterskirche** tower (summer Mon–Fri 9am–7pm, Sat & Sun 10am–7pm; winter Mon–Fri 9am–6pm, Sat & Sun 10am–6pm; €1.50) offers the best views of the Altstadt. Directly below, you'll find the **Viktualienmarkt**, an open-air food market selling everything from *Weisswurst* and beer to fruit and veg. West of here, at Sendlinger Str. 62, stands the pint-sized **Asamkirche** (Mon–Fri 7.30am–6pm; Sat 8am–7pm, Sun 8am–3pm; free), one of the most splendid Rococo churches in Bavaria.

The Hofbräuhaus and the Residenz

Northeast of Marienplatz is the **Hofbräuhaus**, Munich's largest and most famous drinking hall (see p.408). North of here, on Residenzstrasse, is the entrance to the palace of the Wittelsbachs, the immense **Residenz** (daily: April to mid-Oct 9am–6pm; mid-Oct to March 10am–5pm; €7; Ⓦ residenz-muenchen.de). One of Europe's finest Renaissance buildings, it was so badly damaged in the last war that it had to be almost totally rebuilt. The splendid 66m-long Antiquarium, the oldest part of the palace, is the highlight of the visit. A separate ticket is necessary to see the fabulous treasures of the **Schatzkammer** (same hours as the Residenzmuseum; €7/€11 combined ticket with Residenz); the star piece is the dazzling stone-encrusted statuette of St George, made around 1590. Across Odeonsplatz from the Residenz is one of

12

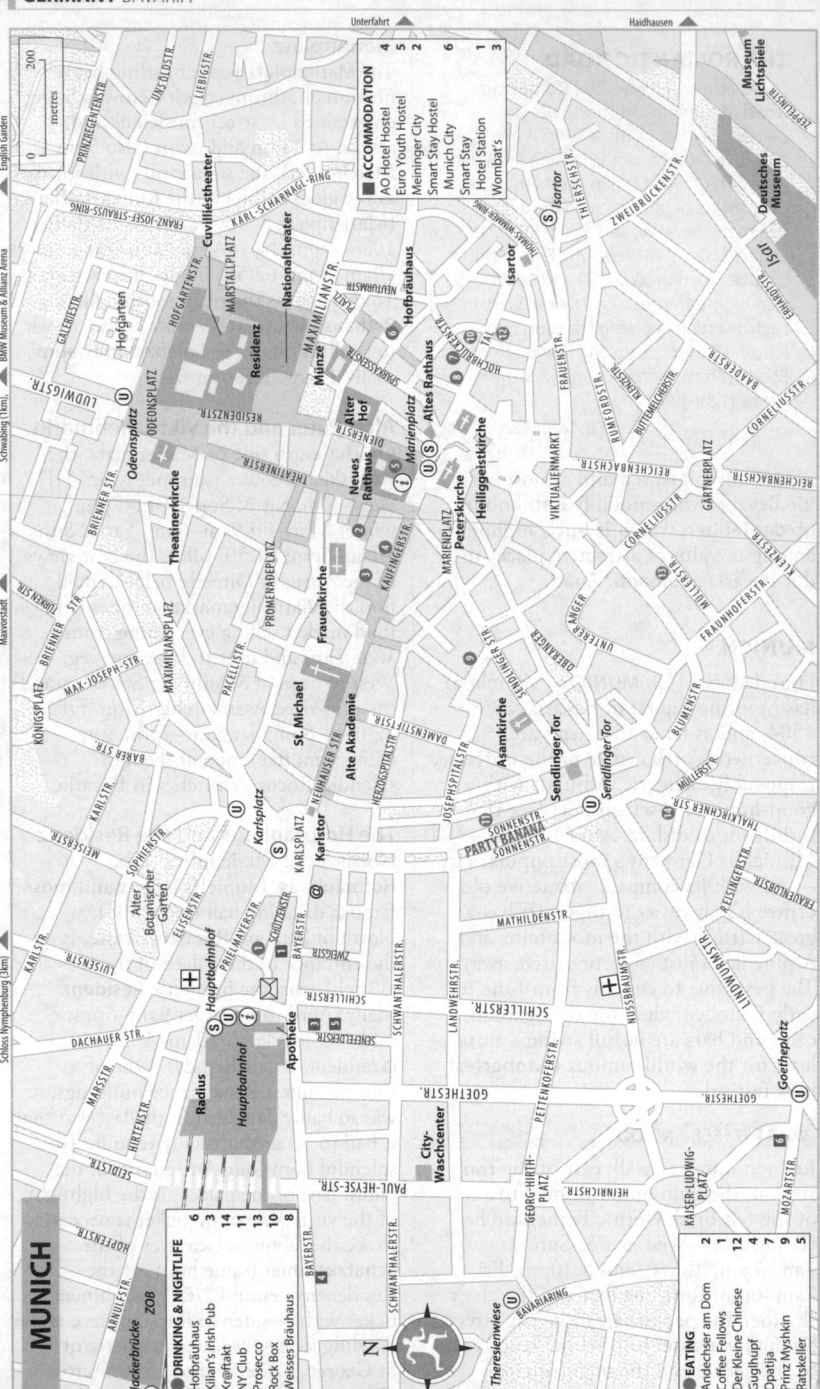

MUNICH

12

ACCOMMODATION
AO Hotel Hostel	4
Euro Youth Hostel	5
Meininger City	2
Smart Stay Hostel	6
Munich City	1
Smart Stay Hotel Station	3
Wombat's	

● DRINKING & NIGHTLIFE
Hofbräuhaus	6
Kilian's Irish Pub	3
Kraftakt	14
NY Club	11
Prosecco	13
Rock Box	10
Weisses Bräuhaus	8

● EATING
Andechser am Dom	2
Coffee Fellows	1
Der Kleine Chinese	12
Guglhupf	4
Opatija	7
Prinz Myshkin	9
Ratskeller	5

the city's most regal churches, the **Theatinerkirche**, whose golden-yellow towers and green copper dome add a splash of colour to the roofscape.

The Deutsches Museum

Munich's most impressive museum – the **Deutsches Museum** at Museumsinsel 1 (daily 9am–5pm; €8.50; ⓦdeutsches -museum.de) – occupies a midstream island in the Isar, southeast of the centre. Covering every conceivable aspect of scientific and technical endeavour, from historical scientific instruments to the latest medical research, this is the most compendious collection of its type in Germany.

The English Garden

Munich's open central park is a delight to walk around in, especially in the summer. Check out the **Munich surfers** at the bottom of the garden on Prinzregentenstrasse, walk up for a Hofbräu beer and a sausage in the **Chinesischen Turm** (daily 10am–11pm), lie naked if you dare in the nudist section in the middle of the garden (west of the stream) or rent a pedalo on the large lake at the top.

North Munich

There are two main attractions a short trip north of the centre: right by U-Bahn Olympiapark you can find **BMW World** (daily 7.30am–midnight; free), in reality a big showroom for the car giant's latest models but impressive nevertheless, and the **BMW museum** (Tues–Sun 10am–6pm; €9) opposite, with vintage cars and motorcycles on display as well as electric cars and hydrogen engine models. Further north is the futuristic **Allianz Arena**, home of **Bayern Munich** and the site of its very interesting museum (daily except match days 10am–6pm; €12, audioguide €3, combi ticket with Arena tour €19) where the club's silverware (and goldenware) is on display along with photos, mementoes, videos and biographies of their greats, with Beckenbauer's presence towering throughout.

West Munich

Schloss Nymphenburg (daily: April to mid-Oct 9am–6pm; mid-Oct to March 10am–4pm; €6/€11.50 combined ticket for all Nymphenburg attractions, €5/€8.50 in winter; ⓦschloss -nymphenburg.de), the summer residence of the Wittelsbachs, is reached by tram #17 from the train station. Its kernel is a small Italianate palace begun in 1664 for the Electress Adelaide, who dedicated it to the goddess Flora and her nymphs – hence the name.

ARRIVAL AND DEPARTURE

By plane Munich's airport, Franz Josef Strauss Flughafen (ⓦmunich-airport.de), is connected to the Hauptbahnhof by Ⓢ1 and Ⓢ8 (frequent; buy a Munich day card).

By train The Hauptbahnhof is at the western end of the city centre.

Destinations Berlin (1–2 hourly; 6hr–6hr 25min); Cologne (1–2 hourly; 4hr 37min); Hamburg (1 hourly; 6hr); Heidelberg (4 daily; 3hr); Innsbruck (every 2hr; 1hr 52min); Nuremberg (2 hourly; 1hr 15min); Regensburg (hourly; 1hr 27min); Salzburg (1–2 hourly; 1hr 30min–2hr); Stuttgart (1–2 hourly; 2hr 17min); Vienna (5 daily; 4hr 17min).

By bus The bus station (ZOB) is on Arnulfstrasse, behind the train station.

Destinations Freiburg (4 daily; 4hr 45min).

INFORMATION AND TOURS

Tourist information There are tourist offices at Bahnhofplatz 2 (Mon–Sat 9am–8pm, Sun 10am–6pm; ⓦmuenchen.de) and in the Neues Rathaus on Marienplatz (Mon–Fri 10am–8pm, Sat 10am–4pm, Sun 10am–2pm), either of which can book you rooms (from around €50). There is also a telephone accommodation line ☏089 23 39 65 00.

Tours Mike's Tours Bräuhausstr. 10 (10am–8pm; ☏089 25 54 39 87, ⓦmikesbiketours.com) does popular, fun and tongue-in-cheek-y English-only bike tours around Munich and beyond as well as bike rentals. Cheap "backpacker rate" for students or residents of hostels. A 4hr tour of Munich costs €25 (students €15), simple bike rental €12–€15/day. Also does a Neuschwanstein tour by coach for €49 (students €39).

GETTING AROUND

By public transport Short trips (*Kurzstrecke*: up to two S- or U-Bahn stops, or up to four bus or tram stops) on Munich's public transport system (ⓦmvv-muenchen.de) cost €1.30. Longer one-zone trips cost €2.60. One-day and

12

12

three-day passes, valid for all public transport, are a good investment at €5.80/€14.30 with reductions for two. Also available are strip cards (€12.50 for 10); stamp two strips for every zone crossed – the zones are shown on maps at stations and tram and bus stops. For short trips, only one strip needs to be stamped.

ACCOMMODATION

The cheap hotel area is south of the station below the length of Bayerstrasse. Cheap – or any – accommodation can be hard to find during the Oktoberfest, when prices rocket.

AO Hotel Hostel Bayerstr. 75 ☎089 45 23 57, ⓦaohostels.com. Modern hotel-cum-hostel with clean, warm rooms on the large side. Room prices follow the airline model; the earlier you book, the less the cost. Wi-fi free at reception but €5/day in your room. Breakfast €6, sheets €3. Dorm €15, double €60

★ **Euro Youth Hotel** Senefelderstr. 5 ☎089 59 90 88 11, ⓦeuro-youth-hotel.de. Good atmosphere and location in an 1880s building that survived the war, with late-closing bar (3am; beer 0.5l €2.90) and friendly staff. Free sheets. Breakfast €4.50 extra for dorm beds. Various tours stop at the hostel for pick-ups. Dorm €17.50, double €60

Meininger City Landsbergerstr. 20 ☎089 55 05 30. Functional, well-managed hostel about 15min from the station. Every room/dorm has shower and WC, while the singles and doubles have a TV and phone. Beer garden good in the summer. Buffet breakfast included. Dorm €16.50, double €62

Smart Stay Hostel Munich City Mozartstr. 4 ☎089 558 79 70, ⓦsmart-stay.de; U-Bahn to Goetheplatz. Welcoming hostel within spitting distance of the Oktoberfest grounds, a 15min walk south from the train station. Breakfast buffet and sheets included. Dorm €14.90, double €89

Smart Stay Hotel Station Schützenstr. 7 ☎089 552 52 10, ⓦsmart-stay.de. Good location between the station and the centre, but overlooking a pedestrianized street. What this clean, basic hotel lacks in charm it makes up for in convenience. Buffet breakfast €6.50. Dorm €20, double €79

Wombat's Senefelderstr. 1 ☎089 59 98 91 80, ⓦwombats -hostels.com. Modern, lively and central with a great bar, winter garden and friendly staff. Breakfast €3.80. Wi-fi on ground floor only. Dorm €26, double €80

EATING

A good place to fuel up is the bustling Viktualienmarkt, which has an array of outdoor or stand-up eating options.

★ **Andechser am Dom** Weinstr. 7a, behind the Dom. Traditional place serving solid Bavarian food and beer from the Andechs monastic brewery. Mains €12; half-litre of its Helles Bier €3.60. Daily 10am–1am.

Coffee Fellows Schützenstr. 14 ⓦcoffee-fellows.de. A café chain with excellent coffee and cakes, as well as free wi-fi for 30/60min depending on how much you spend, otherwise €5/hr. Mon–Thurs 7am–10.30pm, Fri 7am–11.30pm, Sat 8am–11.30am, Sun 8am–9.30pm.

Der Kleine Chinese Im Tal 28. Cheap, filling Chinese dishes served all day in this tiny restaurant and takeaway near Marienplatz. Mains €5.50–7.50. Daily 11am–10pm.

★ **Guglhupf** Kaufingerstr. 5. Hidden within the shopping arcades of Kaufingstrasse is this great café, your best option for a sit-down meal in the centre. Great selection of salads for €7; schnitzel and chips €10 as well as Apfelstrudel with ice cream for €6. Mon–Sat 8am–8pm, Sun 10am–7pm.

Opatija Hochbrückenstr. 3. Excellent, cosy Croatian restaurant that looks unaffordably grand until you look at the prices. Simple mains from €6. Daily noon–10pm.

Prinz Myshkin Hackenstr. 2 ☎089 26 55 96. Best vegetarian in the city, with international dishes served beneath a high vaulted ceiling. Lunch special €7.50. Daily 11am–12.30am.

DRINKING AND NIGHTLIFE

The main focus for clubbers is the "Party Banana" semicircle on the inner ring road between Maximilianplatz and Sendlinger Tor. For listings check out the English-language website *MunichFound* (ⓦmunichfound.de) or the free magazine *In München* (in German).

Hofbräuhaus Platzl 9. The most famous and touristy of the beer halls, but beer and food prices are reasonable. *Mass* (1l beer) €7.30. Daily 9am–11.30pm.

Kilian's Irish Pub am Dom Frauenplatz 11. One of the most popular meeting places for expats and their local friends, this pub offers Murphy's on tap, massive hamburgers (€8–9), fish and chips (€10.90) as well as live music every night at 8pm. Mon–Thurs 4pm–1am, Fri & Sat 11am–2am, Sun noon–1am.

★ **Rock Box** Im Tal 15, entrance on Hochbrückenstr ⓦrockboxbar.de. Lounge-club in a tiny but

---

★ **TREAT YOURSELF**

Ratskeller Marienplatz 8 ☎089 219 98 90. The labyrinthine cellar of the Neues Rathaus is always full – nowadays mostly with tourists. The food is hearty and good, everything from *Weisswurst* with bread (€5) to elegant seasonal dishes including game. Two-course lunch menu with drink €13. Daily 10am–midnight.

OKTOBERFEST

The huge **Oktoberfest** (ⓦoktoberfest.de) held on the Theresienwiese fairground for sixteen days following the penultimate Saturday in September, is an orgy of beer drinking spiced up by hairy fairground rides. The event began with a fair held to celebrate a Bavarian royal wedding in October 1810; it proved so popular that it's been repeated ever since.

tried-and-tested venue full of young locals, all of whom are eager to practise their English on you. Cocktails €8. DJs on Fri & Sat. Mon–Wed 3pm–1am, Thurs–Sat 3pm–4am, Sun 7pm–2am.

Weisses Bräuhaus Im Tal 7. Famous for its *weissbier* (€3.60) and a little cosier than the *Hofbräuhaus*. It offers *Blitzessen* (something along the lines of "snack blitzkrieg") till 5pm: one dish for €5.90. Daily 8am–12.30am.

GAY AND LESBIAN NIGHTLIFE
Munich has a lively and visible gay scene mostly south of the Sendlinger Tor.

Kr@ftakt Thalkirchnerstr. 4, ⓦkraftakt.com. Café bar, attracting a young crowd with a sun terrace and a comfortable large lounge. Beer €3.10. Mon–Thurs & Sun 10am–1am, Fri & Sat 10am–3am.

NY Club Sonnenstr. 25 ⓦnyclub.de. Munich's top gay club, with lush decor and a great sound system; international DJs play on Sat. Fri 10pm–late, Sat 11pm–late.

Prosecco Theklastr. 1 ⓦprosecco-munich.de. Tiny bar that blends Alpine kitsch with every other variety of decorative excess. The music is a mix of German *Schlager* tunes (schmaltzy German pop) and Eurodisco hits. Thurs–Sat 9pm–late.

DIRECTORY

Consulates Canada, Tal 29 ☎089 219 95 70; Ireland, Denninger Str. 15 ☎089 20 80 59 90; South Africa, Sendlinger-Tor-Platz 5 ☎089 231 16 30; UK, Möhlstr. 5 ☎089 21 10 90; US, Königinstr. 5 ☎089 288 80.

Hospital 24hr A&E at Rotkreuz Krankenhaus Nymphenburger Str. 163 (☎089 13 03 25 43).

Internet Call Center Bayerstr. 1 (Mon–Sat 10am–8pm; €1.5/hr).

Left luggage At the train station (€1–3/day depending on size).

Pharmacy Munich airport (daily 6.30am–9pm). For 24hr pharmacies call ☎089 59 44 75.

Post office Bahnhofplatz 1 (Mon–Fri 8am–8pm, Sat 9am–4pm).

KZ-GEDENKSTÄTTE DACHAU

On the northern edge of Munich, the town of **Dachau** was the site of Germany's first **concentration camp** (daily 9am–5pm; free; English audioguide €3.50; maps free). Many original buildings still stand, including the crematorium and gas chamber; a replica hut gives an idea of the conditions prisoners endured. In the former maintenance building there's a sobering exhibition in English detailing the history of the camp, including graphic colour film shot at liberation. There's also a 22-minute documentary film in English shown five times daily (10am–3pm). Dachau's S-Bahn station is on line ⓢ2 from the central station (20min); from the S-Bahn take bus #726 to the KZ-Gedenkstätte stop (Mon–Fri & peak time Sat every 20min, Sun every 40min).

THE BAVARIAN ALPS

12

It's amid picture-book mountain scenery that you'll find the classic Bavarian folklore and customs, and the **Bavarian Alps** encompass some of the most famous places in the province, such as the fantasy castle of **Neuschwanstein** and Hitler's **Eagle's Nest** near Berchtesgaden. Visit these hotspots outside the July and August peak season and you'll find the crowds less oppressive. Note that the popular resort of Berchtesgaden is more easily accessible from Salzburg (see p.77).

Neuschwanstein and Schloss Hohenschwangau

Lying between the Forggensee reservoir and the Ammer mountains, **FÜSSEN** and the adjacent town of **SCHWANGAU** are the bases for visiting Bavaria's two most popular castles. **Schloss Hohenschwangau** (obligatory guided tours daily: April–Sept 9am–6pm; Oct–March 10am–4pm; €10.50/€23 combined ticket with Neuschwanstein, ⓦhohenschwangau.de), originally built in the twelfth century but heavily restored in the nineteenth, was where "Mad" King Ludwig II spent his youth. Ludwig's stamp is firmly imprinted on **Schloss Neuschwanstein** (guided tours daily: April–Sept 8am–5pm; Oct–March 9am–3pm; €12/€23 combined ticket with Schloss Hohenschwangau; tickets for both castles can only be bought at the ticket centre at Alpseestrasse 24, Hohenschwangau village; ⓦneuschwanstein.de), the storybook castle which he had built on a crag overlooking Hohenschwangau. The inspiration for Disneyland's castle, it's an architectural hotchpotch with a stunning Byzantine throne hall. Still incomplete at Ludwig's death, it's a monument to a sad and lonely character.

ARRIVAL, INFORMATION AND TOURS

By train Take the train to Füssen (every 2hr from Munich; 2hr) and then bus #73 or #78 to Hohenschwangau.

Tourist information Füssen's tourist office, Kaiser-Maximilian-Platz 1 (Mon–Fri 9am–5pm, Sat 10am–4pm; ☏083 629 38 50, ⓦfuessen.de), can book accommodation.

Tours Füssen is also the end of the Romantic Road from Würzburg via Augsburg (see box, p.405), served by special tour buses in season. You can visit both of the area's castles in a day; get a Bayern Ticket from Munich Central station for €22, which allows unlimited transport in Bavaria until 3am next day including city transport in Munich.

ACCOMMODATION

HI hostel Mariahilferstr. 5 ☏083 62 77 54, ⓦfuessen .jugendherberge.de. The nearest hostel is in Füssen, a 10min walk from the train station. The many mountain-bike trails nearby render this hostel particularly attractive to cyclists. Dorm **€19.70**, double **€49**

Berchtesgaden

Almost entirely surrounded by mountains at Bavaria's southeastern extremity the area around **BERCHTESGADEN** has a

---

HITLER'S HIDEOUT

Berchtesgaden is indelibly associated with **Adolf Hitler**, who rented a house in the nearby village of Obersalzberg, which he later enlarged into the **Berghof**, a stately retreat where he could meet foreign dignitaries. High above the village, Hitler's *Kehlsteinhaus*, or "**Eagle's Nest**", survives as a restaurant, and can be reached by bus and lift from Obersalzberg (mid-May to late-Oct daily 8.30am–4pm; €16.10 bus and lift return ticket; ⓦkehlsteinhaus.de).

---

magical atmosphere, especially in the mornings, when mists rise from the lakes and swirl around lush valleys and rocky mountainsides.

Unsurprisingly, Berchtesgaden has some great **mountain walks** to take you away from the summer crowds (the tourist office has maps), though the star attraction is the stunning emerald **Königssee**, Germany's highest lake, which bends around the foot of the towering **Watzmann** (2713m), 5km south of town – regular buses run out here – and there are year-round **cruises** (April–Oct daily 9am–4.15pm; €16.30 return). The town is also home to an unexpected diversion, the **Salzbergwerk**, a historic salt mine that's been refurbished with an hour-long amusement-park-like ride/tour through its underground caverns (tours daily: May–Oct every 10min, 9am–5pm; Nov–April every 25min, 11am–3pm; €15.50; ☏865 26 00 20, ⓦsalzzeitreise. de).

ARRIVAL AND INFORMATION

By bus and/or train Direct bus from Salzburg (hourly; 45min). If coming from Munich you must change at Freilassing (1 hourly; 2hr 55min), so it's actually quicker and no more costly to take a direct Munich–Salzburg train (1–2 hourly; 1hr 30min), and then change to the aforementioned bus.

Tourist information The tourist office is opposite the train station (June to mid-Oct Mon–Fri 8.30am–6pm, Sat 9am–5pm, Sun 9am–3pm; mid-Oct to May Mon–Fri 8.30am–5pm, Sat 9am–noon; ☏086 52 96 70, ⓦberchtesgadener-land.info).

ACCOMMODATION

DJH Berchtesgaden Struderberg 6 ☏086 529 43 70, ⓦberchtesgaden.jugendherberge.de. Berchtesgaden's youth hostel is in the Strub district west of the town centre and has views of the Watzmann massif. Breakfast included. Dorm **€20.80**, double **€49.80**

Haus Achental Ramsauer Strasse 4 ☏086 52 45 49, ⓦgaestehaus-achental.de. A friendly alternative to the youth hostel, located close to the station, this is a large, typically Bavarian family hotel complete with hanging geraniums on balconies. Breakfast included. Double **€68**

REGENSBURG

The undisturbed medieval ensemble of central **REGENSBURG**, stunningly located on the banks of the Danube midway between Nuremberg and Munich, can easily be visited as a day-trip, but it makes a tempting overnight stop too. Getting lost in the web of cobbled medieval lanes, nursing a drink in one of the sunny squares or cycling along the Danube are the main draws here. It's also a university city, with a lively nightlife scene for its size.

WHAT TO SEE AND DO

A good place to start is the twelfth-century **Steinerne Brücke**, the only secured crossing along the entire length of the Danube at the time it was built. At the southern end of the bridge, it's worth climbing the **Brückturm** (April–Oct Tues–Sun 10am–5pm; €2.50), the last survivor of the bridge's watchtowers, for excellent views of the old town and river. Just south, the Gothic **Dom** (daily: April–Oct 6.30am–6pm; Nov–March 6.30am–5pm), begun in 1273, has some beautiful fourteenth-century stained-glass windows. Regensburg's medieval **Rathaus** contains the magnificent fourteenth-century Gothic Reichssaal, which was, from 1663 to 1806, the fixed venue for the imperial Diet or Reichstag of the Holy Roman Empire. It can now be visited as part of the **Reichstagsmuseum** (guided tours in English daily: April–Oct 3pm; Nov, Dec & March 2pm; €8). There's also a prison and torture chamber in the basement. In the southern part of the Altstadt is **Schloss Thurn und Taxis** (guided tours in English July to mid-Sept daily 1.30pm; €12.50; ⓦthurnundtaxis .de), one of the largest inhabited palaces in Europe, occupying the converted monastic buildings of the abbey of St Emmeram.

ARRIVAL AND INFORMATION

By train Maximilianstr. leads straight from the train station north to the centre.
Destinations Munich (hourly; 1hr 33min); Nuremberg (hourly; 1hr); Vienna (every 2hr; 4hr).
Tourist information Tourist office at Rathausplatz 4 (April–Oct Mon–Fri 9am–6pm, Sat 9am–4pm, Sun 9.30am–4pm; Nov–March Mon–Fri 9am–6pm, Sat 9am–4pm, Sun 9.30am–2.30pm; ☎0941 507 44 10, ⓦregensburg.de).

GETTING AROUND

By bike Bike rental from Bikehaus, Bahnhofstr. 18 (☎094 15 99 88 08; €13/24hr), on the left as you leave the Hauptbahnhof on the northern (Altstadt) side.

ACCOMMODATION

Brook Lane Hostel Obere Bachgasse 21 ☎094 16 90 09 66, ⓦhostel-regensburg.de. Independently run hostel in the Altstadt, with accommodation in snug dorms or spartan singles and doubles. Open 24hr. Dorm €16, double €52
DJH Regensburg Wöhrdstr. 60 ☎094 14 66 28 30, ⓦregensburg.jugendherberge.de. Youth hostel on an island in the Danube, within easy walking distance of the Altstadt. Breakfast included. Dorm €24

EATING AND DRINKING

★ **Dicker Mann** Krebsgasse 6 ☎094 15 73 70. Vine-covered and candlelit café-restaurant on a tiny side street off Haidplatz serving delicious, good-value meals. Breakfast from €4.50, dinner specials from around €8. Daily 9am–1am.
Fürstliches Brauhaus Waffnergasse 6–8. The Thurn und Taxis' *Brauhaus*, with a copper microbrewery behind the bar, a shady beer garden and own-brew Helles, Marstall Dunkell and Braumeister Weisse beers. Light meals from €7, main courses around €9. Mon–Fri 11am–midnight, Sat & Sun 10am–midnight.
Wurstkuchl Historische Wurstküche Thundorfer Str. 3. Next to the Steinerne Brücke and looking like somewhere a hobbit might grill sausages, this institution originally functioned as the stonemasons' and dock workers' kitchen and has a menu dominated by the delicious Regensburg sausages (plate of 6 €9). Daily 8am–7pm.

NUREMBERG

In many minds, the medieval town of **NUREMBERG** (Nürnberg) conjures up images of the Nazi rallies, the 1935 "Nuremberg Laws" which deprived Jews of their citizenship and forbade them relations with Gentiles, and then the war-crime trials. Yet all this infamy is a world away from the friendly, bustling city of today. Nuremberg's relaxed air makes a day spent exploring its half-timbered houses, fine museums and beer halls hard to beat.

WHAT TO SEE AND DO

Meticulous postwar rebuilding means you'd never guess that World War II bombs reduced ninety percent of Nuremberg's centre to rubble. The

12

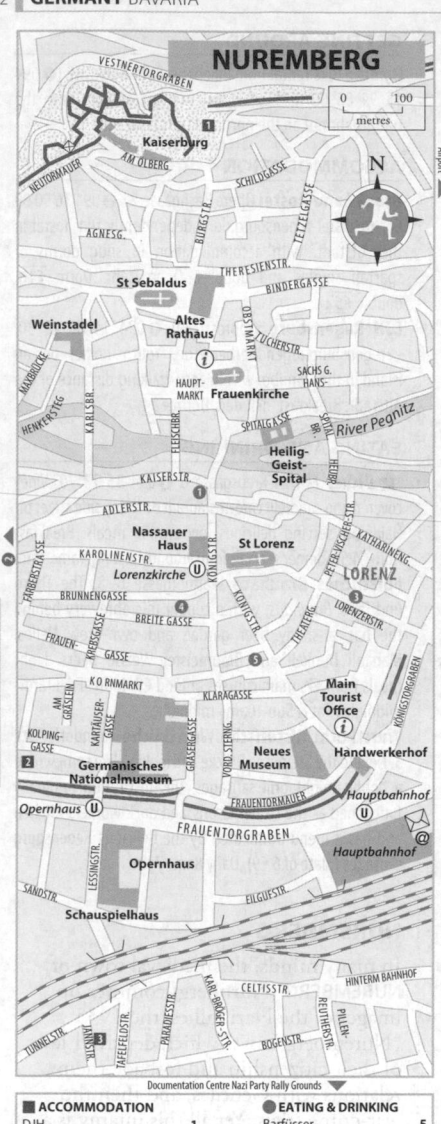

Oct–March 10am–4pm; €8; €6.50 for Palas, museum and tower; €3.50 for tower and well only), which forms the northwest corner of the Medieval fortifications, was where Holy Roman Emperors held their "Reichstag" or imperial diet in the Middle Ages. Guided tours visit the Palas (or castle keep) and the Tiefer Brunnen – the castle's 47m-deep well. Tickets are also valid for the castle museum and the **Sinwellturm tower**, which can be climbed for great views.

The Germanisches Nationalmuseum

The sprawling **Germanisches Nationalmuseum**, Kartäusergasse 1 (Tues & Thurs–Sun 10am–6pm, Wed 10am–9pm; €7; ⓦgnm.de), presents the country's cultural history through its large, important collection of artefacts and art from German central Europe, from the Bronze Age to the present. Look out for the first globe, made by Martin Behaim in 1492 – just before Columbus "discovered" America.

The Fascination and Terror exhibition

The Nazi Party rallies were held on the Zeppelin and March fields in the suburb of Luitpoldhain. Here, the gargantuan but never-completed Congress Hall houses the **Documentation Centre Nazi Party Rally Grounds** (Mon–Fri 9am–6pm, Sat & Sun 10am–6pm; €5; ⓦmuseen .nuernberg.de; tram #9 to Doku-Zentrum), an unmissable multimedia exhibition documenting the history of the rally grounds and the ruthless misuse of power under National Socialism.

ARRIVAL AND DEPARTURE

By plane The U2 underground service connects Nürnberg airport with the train station (every 10–12min; 13min).
By train The Hauptbahnhof is just outside the southern edge of the city walls; follow Königstr. into the centre.
Destinations Augsburg (every 30min–1hr 30min; 1hr 10min); Berlin (every 30min–1hr 30min; 5hr 10min);

reconstructed medieval core is compact, surrounded by ancient city walls and neatly bisected by the River Pegnitz.

The Kaiserburg

The **Kaiserburg** (imperial castle; guided tours daily: April–Sept 9am–6pm;

Frankfurt (every 30min–1hr; 2hr 10min); Leipzig (every 2hr; 3hr 45min); Munich (every 30min; 1hr 10min–1hr 25min); Regensburg (hourly; 55min); Vienna (every 3hr; 4hr 56min); Würzburg (2–4hr; 1hr).

INFORMATION

Tourist information Tourist office at the entrance to the Altstadt opposite the Hauptbahnhof (Mon–Sat 9am–6pm, Sun 10am–4pm; ☎091 12 33 60, ⚐tourismus-nuernberg.de). Smaller office at Hauptmarkt 18, in the Altstadt (Mon–Sat 9am–5pm; May–Oct also Sun 10am–4pm; Dec Mon–Sat 9am–6pm, Sun 10am–6pm; ☎091 12 33 60).

Discount pass The Nürnberg Card (€23/2 days) covers public transport plus entrance to museums.

GETTING AROUND

By public transport There are U-Bahn, tram, and bus systems; a one-way trip costs €2.20, a day ticket (or a ticket for Sat & Sun) €4.30.

By bike Nuremberg also has a Parisian-style public bike rental network, NorisBike (€1/30min, €8/24hr; ⚐norisbike .de), with 66 rental points across the city. You can register as a user and pay by credit card at the rental station.

ACCOMMODATION

DJH Burg 2 ☎091 12 30 93 60, ⚐nuernberg .jugendherberge.de; ⚐#2 to Rathenauplatz, then bus #36 to Burgstr. The HI hostel has a wonderful location in the fifteenth-century imperial stables next to the Kaiserburg, overlooking the Altstadt, a 25min walk from the Hauptbahnhof. Dorm €25.10

Lette'm Sleep Frauentormauer 42 ☎091 19 92 81 28, ⚐backpackers.de. This friendly and popular hostel offers free wi-fi, a kitchen and secure storage. Bed linen costs €3. Dorm €18, double €55

Pension Vater Jahn-Parma Jahnstr. 13 ☎091 144 45 07, ⚐hotel-vaterjahn-parma.de. Immaculate and friendly guesthouse just south of the Opernhaus on the other side of the railway tracks, close to the Hauptbahnhof and Altstadt. Double €52

EATING AND DRINKING

There are plenty of snack stops in the pedestrian shopping zone and at the Hauptbahnhof; bars and cafés are scattered throughout the Altstadt.

Barfüsser Hallplatz 2. This popular beer hall in cavernous cellars brews its own beer and serves good food. Daily specials from €10; six *Bratwurst* €8.50. Daily 11am–11pm.

Bratwurst Herzle Brunnengasse 11. A bit less obviously tourist-oriented than some options, *Herzle* is a great place for sampling Nuremberg's mini-sausages. Six *Bratwürste* €6.60. Mon–Sat 11am–11pm.

Mach 1 Kaiserstr. 1–9 ⚐mach1-club.de. Stylish club with a main floor pumping house and electro sounds, a futuristic tunnel and a more intimate lounge area. Thurs Sat 11am–11pm.

Souptopia Lorenzerstr. 27. If you're sick of sausage, head for this little wonder, where seven types of soup are on offer daily, including at least one vegan option. Large bowl of soup from €6.20. Mon–Fri 11am–7pm, Sat 11am–5pm.

★ **Treibhaus** Karl-Grillenberger-Str. 28. Refreshingly out of the way yet still in the Altstadt, (close to ⚐Weisser Turm) this hip café-bar offers everything you need from morning to night, with breakfasts from €2.50, salads from €6 and cocktails from €4.50. Mon–Wed 8am–1am, Thurs & Fri 8am–2am, Sat 9am–2am, Sun 9.30am–1am.

ROTHENBURG OB DER TAUBER

The **Romantic Road** (see box, p.405) winds its way along the length of western Bavaria, running through the most visited – and most beautiful – medieval town in Germany: **ROTHENBURG OB DER TAUBER**. This fairytale location is besieged with tour groups during the day, so spend the night – or at least an evening – to appreciate it in relative peace.

WHAT TO SEE AND DO

The views of the surrounding countryside from the fourteenth-century town walls are magnificent, but Rothenburg's true charms lie among its medieval houses and cobbled streets.

Marktplatz and St Jakobs-Kirche

The focus of the Altstadt is the sloping **Marktplatz**, dominated by the arcaded front of the Renaissance Rathaus; the narrow, 60m tower of the Altes Rathaus (April–Oct daily 9.30am–12.30pm & 1–5pm; Nov & Jan–March Sat & Sun noon–3pm; Dec Mon–Thurs & Sun 10.30am–2pm & 2.30–6pm, Fri & Sat 10.30am–2pm & 2.30–8pm; €2) provides the best views. The other main attractions on the Marktplatz are the mechanical figures on the facade of the **Ratsherrntrinkstube**. Eight times a day these figures re-enact an episode in which former mayor Nusch allegedly saved Protestant Rothenburg from the wrath of Catholic General Tilly during the Thirty Years' War, by downing three

12

litres of wine in one go. Northwest of the Marktplatz is the impressive Gothic **St Jakobs-Kirche** (daily: April–Oct 9am–5pm; Nov & Jan–March 10am–noon & 2–4pm; Dec 10am–4.45pm; €2). Don't miss the exquisite Heilig-Blut-Altar, a masterpiece of woodcarving by Tilman Riemenschneider, tucked away on an upper level.

The Mittelalterliches Kriminalmuseum

Of the local museums, the most interesting is the **Mittelalterliches Kriminalmuseum** at Burggasse 3–5 (daily: Jan, Feb & Nov 2–4pm; March & Dec 1–4pm; April 11am–5pm; May–Oct 10am–6pm; €4.50; ⊙www .kriminalmuseum.rothenburg.de.), which contains collections of medieval torture instruments and related objects, such as the beer barrels that drunks were forced to walk around in.

ARRIVAL AND INFORMATION

By train A 10min walk east of the centre. From the station head left on Bahnhofstr., then right on Ansbacherstr., which takes you straight through Röder city gate.
Destinations Würzburg (hourly; 1hr 10min).

Tourist information Tourist office in the Ratsherrntrinkstube on Marktplatz (April–Oct & Dec Mon–Fri 9am–6pm, Sat & Sun 10am–4pm; Nov & Jan–March Mon–Fri 9am–5pm, Sat 10am–1pm; ☎09861 404 800, ⊙rothenburg.de).

ACCOMMODATION AND EATING

DJH Mühlacker 1 ☎098 619 41 60, ⊙rothenburg .jugendherberge.de. Housed in two beautifully restored buildings and a modern annexe off the bottom of Spitalgasse. Dorm €23

Gästehaus Raidel Wenggasse 3 ☎098 61 31 15, ⊙gaestehaus-raidel.de. Located in a wonderfully creaky 600-year-old building, this guesthouse oozes character, with lots of antiques and a feeling of yesteryear. Double €72

Roter Hahn Obere Schmiedgasse 21 ☎098 61 97 40. Franconian regional specialities in the historic setting of a fourteenth-century inn, with main courses from €11. Daily 11am–11pm.

BRITISH MUSEUM, LONDON

Great Britain

HIGHLIGHTS

❶ **The British Museum** Arguably the world's finest museum. **See p.424**

❷ **Bath** Regency and Roman splendour in England's most beautiful city. **See p.443**

❸ **York** Medieval city bursting with bars and bistros. **See p.467**

❹ **Hiking Wales** Dream-like hikes from the Brecon Beacons to Snowdonia. **See p.475 & p.477**

❺ **Edinburgh Festival** The world's biggest arts festival. **See p.479**

❻ **Over the sea to Skye** Craggy peaks and Celtic mysteries. **See p.494**

HIGHLIGHTS ARE MARKED ON THE MAP ON P.417

ROUGH COSTS

Daily budget Basic €50, occasional treat €75

Drink Lager €4

Food Fish and chips €8

Hostel/budget hotel €23/€70–93

Travel Train: London–Brighton €18–30; bus: London–Manchester €6–33

FACT FILE

Population 63 million (includes Northern Ireland)

Language English

Currency Pound Sterling (£)

Capital London

International phone code ☏44

Time zone GMT

13

Introduction

A famous British newspaper headline in the 1950s declared: "Fog in Channel, Continent Cut Off". Britain's outlook on the world has always been unique, born of its status as an island nation on the western edge of Europe. And yet within this compact territory there's not just one country but three – England, Wales and Scotland – and a multitude of cultural identities: God forbid you should call a Scot or a Welshman English.

London, the capital, is the one place that features on everyone's itinerary. **Brighton** and **Canterbury** offer contrasting diversions – the former a lively seaside resort, the latter one of Britain's finest medieval cities. The southwest of England holds the rugged moorlands of **Devon**, the rocky coastline of **Cornwall**, and the historic spa city of **Bath**, while the chief attractions of central England are the university cities of **Oxford** and **Cambridge**, and Shakespeare's hometown **Stratford-upon-Avon**. Further north, the former industrial cities of **Manchester**, **Liverpool** and **Newcastle** are lively, rejuvenated places, and **York** has splendid historical treasures, but the landscape, especially the uplands of the Lake District, is the biggest magnet. For true wilderness, head to the **Welsh mountains** or **Scottish Highlands**. The finest of Scotland's lochs, glens and peaks, and the magnificent scenery of the West Coast islands, can be reached easily from **Glasgow** and **Edinburgh** – the latter perhaps Britain's most attractive urban landscape.

CHRONOLOGY

54 BC The Romans attack Britannia but are forced back until a successful invasion in 43 AD.
1066 AD Duke William II of Normandy defeats the last Anglo-Saxon ruler, King Harold II, at the Battle of Hastings.
1215 The Magna Carta forms the basis upon which English law is built.
1301 Edward I conquers Wales, giving his heir the title Prince of Wales.
1534 Henry VIII breaks with the Catholic Church. The Head of State becomes Head of the Church of England.
1603 King James VI of Scotland also becomes James I of England in the Union of the Crowns.

1653–58 A brief period of republicanism under Oliver Cromwell, following the English Civil War.
1707 The Act of Union unites the parliaments of Scotland and England, with the addition of Ireland in 1800.
1800s The Industrial Revolution helps Britain to expand her empire and become a dominant world force.
1914–18 Britain fights in World War I.
1928 Women attain full suffrage after a hard-fought campaign.
1939–45 Britain fights in World War II. London and other major centres are heavily bombed during the Blitz.
1947 Indian independence from British rule heralds the gradual demise of the British Empire.
1960s The Beatles sing their way through the swinging sixties.
1979 Margaret Thatcher becomes Britain's first female Prime Minister.
1998 Devolution in Scotland and Wales.
2005 On July 7 London is rocked by terrorist bombings, leaving 52 dead.
2012 London hosts the Olympics.

ARRIVAL AND DEPARTURE

If you're travelling from outside mainland Europe or Ireland, clearly the

"**Great Britain**", or just "Britain", is a geographical term encompassing England, Scotland and Wales, including their islands. However, it can also be used politically, in the context of central government, "British" nationals, or for national teams at sporting events such as the Olympics, in which case it includes Northern Ireland. "**United Kingdom**" is a political term, referring to the sovereign state of England, Scotland, Wales and Northern Ireland. In this guide Northern Ireland is covered with the rest of the island in the Ireland chapter.

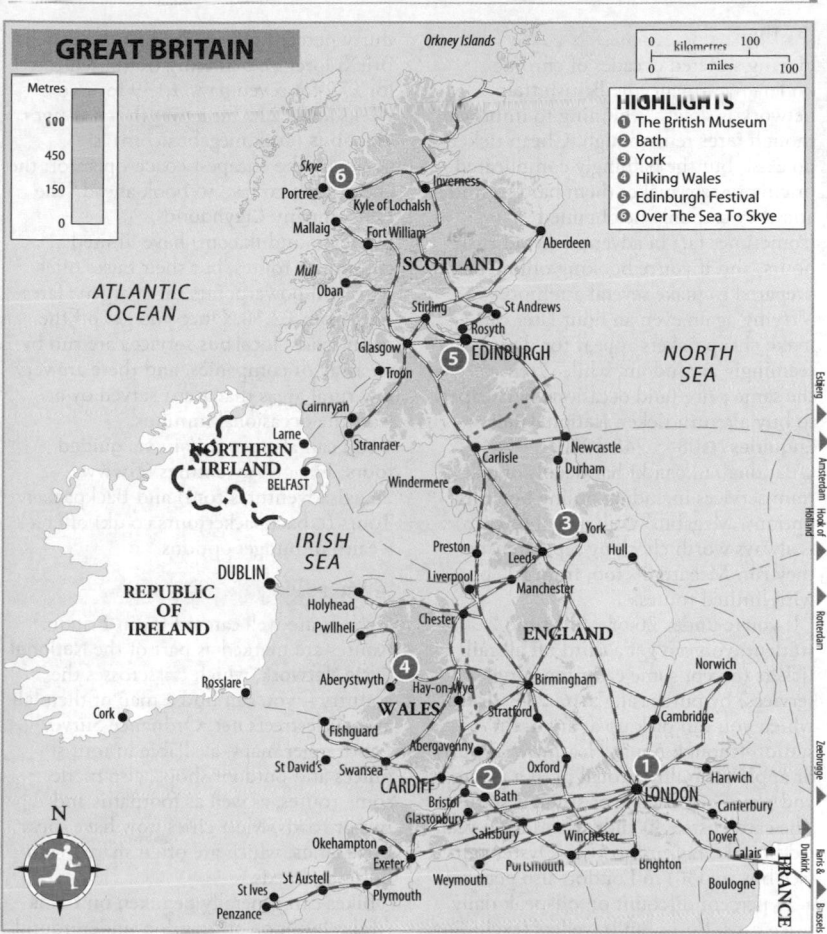

GREAT BRITAIN

Metres
600
450
150
0

kilometres 100
miles 100

HIGHLIGHTS
❶ The British Museum
❷ Bath
❸ York
❹ Hiking Wales
❺ Edinburgh Festival
❻ Over The Sea To Skye

Orkney Islands

Skye ❻
Portree
Mallaig
Inverness
Kyle of Lochalsh
Fort William
Aberdeen

SCOTLAND

Mull
Oban
Stirling
St Andrews
Glasgow
Rosyth
Troon
❺ EDINBURGH

ATLANTIC
OCEAN

NORTH
SEA

Cairnryan
Larne
Stranraer
Carlisle
Newcastle
Durham

**NORTHERN
IRELAND**
BELFAST
Windermere

IRISH
SEA

Preston
❸ York
Hull

DUBLIN
Liverpool
Leeds
Manchester

**REPUBLIC
OF
IRELAND**
Holyhead
Pwllheli
Chester
ENGLAND

Rosslare
Aberystwyth
Hay-on-Wye ❹
Birmingham
Norwich

Cork
WALES
Stratford
Cambridge

Fishguard
Abergavenny
St David's
Swansea
CARDIFF
Oxford
Harwich
❷
Bristol
Bath
LONDON ❶
Canterbury

Okehampton
Glastonbury
Salisbury
Winchester
Dover
Calais

Exeter
Weymouth
Portsmouth
Brighton
Boulogne

St Ives
St Austell
Plymouth
Penzance

N

Esbjerg ▶
Amsterdam, Hook of Holland ▶
Rotterdam ▶
Zeebrugge ▶
Paris & Brussels ▶
Dunkirk
FRANCE

Roscoff & Santander ▼
Bilbao, Cherbourg, Le Havre Caen, St-Malo ▼ & Santander ▼
Dieppe ▼

only direct route to Britain is by **plane**. Long-haul flights land at a range of destinations throughout the UK, including Manchester, Edinburgh and Glasgow, though most air passengers still find themselves passing through London's main airports – Gatwick, Heathrow, Stansted and Luton – the latter two the principal hubs of no-frills carriers like Ryanair and easyJet, which also operate out of smaller regional airports around the country and provide many internal flights.

Greener alternatives for getting to Britain from mainland Europe include the **Eurostar** (ⓦeurostar.com) high-speed train from Paris or Brussels

to St Pancras International in London, Eurolines **bus** (ⓦeurolines .co.uk), or **ferry**: boats from Ireland, France, Belgium, the Netherlands, Denmark and Spain dock at ports across the UK.

GETTING AROUND

Most places are accessible by train and/or coach (as long-distance buses are known), though costs are among the highest in Europe. **Traveline** (ⓣ0871 200 2233, ⓦtraveline.org.uk) is a national service that can advise on trains, coaches, ferries and, most usefully, local buses.

13

BY TRAIN

Having suffered decades of chronic under-investment, the British **train** network is slowly beginning to improve, though **fares** remain high. Cheap tickets do exist, but the bafflingly complicated pricing system makes them hard to find, and they can only be obtained (sometimes far) in advance. Avoid rush hours, and if you're booking online be prepared to make several attempts – trying again even an hour later can make cheap tickets appear (or disappear) seemingly at random, while often it's the same price (and occasionally cheaper) to buy a return ticket. **National Rail Enquiries** (☎0845 748 4950, ⊚nationalrail.co.uk) has details of all train services including online booking options. Megabus (⊚uk.megabus.com) is always worth checking separately as they run Megatrains too, from £1, but with limited routes.

If you're under 26 or a full-time student, you can get a third off all rail tickets (except some early-morning services) by purchasing a **16–25 Railcard**, which you can pick up at any train station (though not at Heathrow airport) or apply for online. You'll need a photo and proof of your age or student status. The card costs £30 and is valid for a year. Adding the railcard to your Oyster card (see box, p.430) in London also gets you a 34 percent discount on off-peak daily price caps. European travellers (excluding British residents) are also eligible for an **InterRail Great Britain Pass** (⊚interrailnet .com; see p.32). Prices start from £126/£186 for three days' train travel in one month for under/over-25s.

BY BUS

Long-distance buses are referred to as **coaches** in Britain. Services between cities are frequent and inexpensive especially compared to trains; however, long journeys take considerably longer. **National Express** (☎08717 818178, ⊚nationalexpress.com) serve the most routes, and prices sometimes start from just £1. If you're a student or under 26 you can buy a National Express Coachcard (£10), which gives up to thirty percent off standard fares, or their BritXplorer Pass offering unlimited travel for £79 for seven days, £139 for two weeks and £219 for a month for all ages. **Megabus** (⊚uk.megabus.com) is generally the cheapest coach operator; the cheap seats go fast, so book ahead. The US company **Greyhound** (⊚greyhounduk.com) have limited commuter routes, but their buses offer wi-fi and powerpoints for chargers; fares start from £2.50. Once you get off the main roads, **local bus services** are run by an array of companies, and there are very few rural areas that aren't served by at least the occasional minibus.

You can also see Britain via **guided tours**; Haggis Adventures (⊚www .haggisadventures.com) and Backpacker Tours (⊚backpackertours.co.uk) offer a wealth of budget options.

BY BIKE

Cyclists are well catered for in Britain. Routes are marked as part of the **National Cycle Network**, which crisscrosses the country – you can find a map of them all at ⊚cyclestreets.net. Ordnance Survey Landranger maps, available in tourist offices and outdoor shops, also mark some routes, as well as footpaths and minor roads. Most cities now have some **cycle lanes**, which are often shared with buses and taxis.

Bikes can generally be taken on **trains** (though not on all London underground trains; see ⊚tfl.gov.uk for details of when and where you can take a bike). Some train companies may charge you and/or require you to book in advance. National Express **coaches** only take bikes if they can fold and are bagged. Folded bikes are accepted on London buses.

ACCOMMODATION

Accommodation in Britain is expensive and it's a good idea to reserve in advance. Many tourist offices will book rooms for you, although expect to pay a small fee for this, as well as putting down a deposit.

Britain has an extensive network of **HI hostels** operated by the Youth Hostel Association (⊚yha.org.uk for England

and Wales; ⓦsyha.org.uk for Scotland). A bed for the night with YHA can cost as little as £10, but in cities except to pay up to £25. YHA membership (£13.95/year) will save you £3 per night. Most places of interest will also have at least one **independent hostel**, which will generally be of a comparable standard and price but often more centrally located.

In tourist cities it's hard to find a double room in a **hotel** for less than £65 a night, though there are a few cheaper chain hotels: Premier Inn (ⓦpremierinn.com) sometimes offer identikit rooms from £29 while Travelodge (ⓦtravelodge.co.uk) can be as low as £21 per room when there are deals on. EasyHotel (ⓦeasyhotel.com) have small rooms decked out in their signature orange; London rooms start at £29, Edinburgh rooms from £25. A nicer option for budget accommodation, and often cheaper outside London (particularly if you're on your own), are **guesthouses** and **B&Bs** – usually a comfortable room in a family home, plus a substantial breakfast – starting at around £30 a head. Tourist offices often have a list of nearby accredited B&Bs.

There are more than 750 official **campsites** in Britain, charging from around £5 per person. Camping wild in England and Wales requires the landowner's permission, while in Scotland it is mostly legal as long as you're unobtrusive and leave the site as you found it.

FOOD AND DRINK

Long lampooned as a culinary wasteland, Britain has seen a transformation in both the quality and variety of its restaurants over the past two decades. **Modern British cuisine** – in effect anything inventive – has been at the core of this change, though wherever you go you'll find places serving Indian, Italian and Chinese food, and often plenty of other international cuisines. If you're on a tight budget, the temptation is still to head for the nearest fast-food joint, but with a little effort, alternatives can easily be found, with even higher-end establishments often offering reasonably priced lunchtime or early-evening deals.

Wherever you stay you'll almost certainly be offered an "**English breakfast**" – basically eggs, bacon, sausage, and any combination of fried or grilled sides such as tomatoes, mushrooms, black pudding, bread and baked beans; you'll also be given the option of cereal, toast and fruit. Every major town will have upmarket restaurants and so-called **gastropubs** serving daintily presented cuisine, but traditional British cooking – the mainstay of pub food – is hearty and filling. Typical dishes include the quintessential fish and chips, steak and kidney pie, shepherd's pie (minced lamb topped with mashed potato), and – mainly on Sundays – roast dinners, served with roast potatoes, veg and (particularly with beef) Yorkshire pudding, made from savoury batter. Britain is one of Europe's better countries for **vegetarians**, and wherever you eat there'll always be at least one veggie choice.

DRINK

Drinking traditionally takes place in the **pub**, where beer – sold by the pint or half-pint – generates most of the business, although wine, bottled beer and spirits are also popular. Despite the popularity of cold, fizzy lager, traditional British beer, known as real ale or bitter, is undergoing something of a renaissance; richer and often darker than lager, and served at cellar temperature rather than chilled, it comes in thousands of varieties. In England pubs are generally open Monday to Saturday from 11am to 11pm, and on Sunday from noon to 10.30pm (though changes to licensing laws mean many places now open longer than that at weekends); hours are often longer in Scotland, while Sunday closing is common in Wales.

In Scotland, the national drink is of course **whisky**. The best – and most expensive – are single malts, best drunk neat or with a splash of water to release the flavour.

CULTURE AND ETIQUETTE

Famed for their stiff upper lip and polite reticence, the British do tend to be more reserved than their continental

13

counterparts. Possibly the most cosmopolitan place in Europe – in the larger cities anyway – Britain has developed a reputation for liberal tolerance and benefits from a diverse range of faiths, creeds and colours.

Tipping is expected (if not mandatory) in restaurants; around ten percent of the total is the norm. Technically this is optional, though you will be frowned at if you ask for it to be removed. It's also customary to tip taxi drivers a similar amount, though it is not necessary to tip bar staff at bars and pubs.

SPORTS AND OUTDOOR ACTIVITIES

Football (soccer) is a British obsession. "The beautiful game" was codified here in 1863, and seeing a match is a must for any sports fan, though for top games it can be extremely difficult and costly to acquire tickets. To guarantee seeing a Premier League match choose a lesser-known club: in London, Fulham (Ⓦfulhamfc.com). **Rugby** and **cricket**, though popular, do not generally inspire the same fervent tribalism as football, and consequently can offer a more relaxed spectator experience. You can turn up and buy tickets on the day for domestic matches at Lord's cricket ground in London (Ⓦlords.org) during the season (April–Sept). Tennis fans make a beeline for the world-famous championships at **Wimbledon** (Ⓦwimbledon.com). It's not a cheap day out, but ground tickets cost just £8–20, a few pounds less after 5pm.

Britain's diverse geography and geology, with access to large bodies of fresh and salt water, mean that venues for **outdoor pursuits** are easily accessible. **Walking** is one of the finest ways to see the country, and an excellent infrastructure of long-distance footpaths crisscrosses Britain (Ⓦwalkingbritain.co.uk). The uplands of Wales (Ⓦvisitwales.co.uk /active), Scotland (Ⓦactive.visitscotland .com) and the English Lake District (Ⓦgolakes.co.uk) are particularly good for hiking, climbing and watersports, while Devon and Cornwall (Ⓦvisitsouthwest. co.uk) have the best **surfing** in the UK.

BRITAIN ONLINE
Ⓦ**visitbritain.com** Official tourist board site with links to regional sites.
Ⓦ**transportdirect.info** Information on nationwide transport.
Ⓦ**streetmap.co.uk** Detailed UK street maps.

COMMUNICATIONS

Wi-fi is widespread, and access is offered at most accommodation, including hostels. **Internet cafés** can be found in larger towns; prices vary and are sometimes extortionate; £3–5 per hour is not uncommon. **Post offices** open Monday to Friday 9am to 5.30pm, and some open on Saturday 9am to noon. **Public phones** (operated mainly by BT) are disappearing fast; phonecards to make calls to mobiles or internationally can be bought from postoffices and newsagents – most also accept credit cards. For the **operator**, call ☎100 (domestic) or 155 (international).

EMERGENCIES

Police are approachable and helpful. Tourists aren't a particular target for criminals except in the crowds of the big cities, where you should be on your guard against **pickpockets**. Britain's bigger conurbations all contain areas where you may feel uneasy after dark, but these are usually away from tourist sights.

For health complaints that require immediate attention, go to the **emergency** department of the local hospital (known as A&E). These are run by the **National Health Service** (NHS; Ⓦnhs.uk to find your nearest) and will be free at the time of treatment, though depending on your country (some have mutual agreements with Britain) you may get billed later. For minor injuries you can also use NHS **walk-in clinics**. **Pharmacies** dispense only a limited range of drugs without a doctor's prescription. Most are open standard shop hours, though in large towns there may be ones that stay open late or even 24hr; local newspapers carry lists of late-opening pharmacies.

13

EMERGENCY NUMBERS
Police, fire and ambulance ☎ 999 or 112.

INFORMATION

Tourist offices exist in virtually every British town, offering information and a basic range of maps. **National parks** (ⓦ www.nationalparks.gov.uk) also have their own information centres, which are better for guidance on outdoor pursuits. The most comprehensive series of **maps** is produced by the **Ordnance Survey** (ⓦ ordnancesurvey.co.uk) – essential if you're planning serious hiking.

MONEY AND BANKS

The **pound sterling** (£), divided into 100 pence, remains the national currency. There are coins of 1p, 2p, 5p, 10p, 20p, 50p, £1 and £2; and notes of £5, £10, £20 and £50; notes issued by Scottish banks are legal tender but sometimes not accepted south of the border. At the time of writing, £1 was worth €1.18 and $1.52. Normal **banking hours** are Monday to Friday 9.30am to 5pm, though branches are increasingly open on Saturday mornings. **ATMs** accept a wide range of debit and credit cards, but note that freestanding ATMs usually charge around £2 to take money out on top of your bank charges, so try and go to one attached to a bank. Shops, hotels, restaurants and most other places readily accept **credit cards** for payment.

OPENING HOURS AND HOLIDAYS

General **shop hours** are Monday to Saturday 9am to 5.30/6pm, although many places in big towns are also open Sunday (usually 11am–5pm in England and Wales, longer in Scotland) and until 7/8pm – or later – at least once a week. **Public holidays** are: January 1, January 2 (Scotland only), Good Friday, Easter Monday (not Scotland), first Monday and last Monday in May, last Monday in August, St Andrew's Day (Nov 30, or nearest Mon if weekend; Scotland only),

Christmas Day and Boxing Day (Dec 25 & 26) – though in practice it's only on January 1, January 2 (Scotland only) and Christmas Day that everything shuts down; on other holidays, many shops in larger towns and cities – as well as nearly all sights – remain open.

London

With a population of around 8 million, **LONDON** sprawls over an area of more than 600 square miles either side of the River Thames. The city exudes an undeniable buzz of success; it is where the country's news, art and money are made, and the pace of life is fast (just watch commuters bolting down the escalators). However, high-octane excitement comes at a price, with accommodation and transport costs among the most expensive in the world. The high living costs are nevertheless put up with by most Londoners precisely because there is just so much to see and do here, much of it free.

Skip exorbitantly priced palaces in favour of London's (mostly free) world-class museums and galleries and be sure to visit at least a couple of the outdoor spaces; London is one of the world's greenest cities, with many parks, cemeteries and canals to explore. London's famous department stores and offbeat weekend **markets** offer limitless **shopping**, while its cultural scene caters for all tastes and budgets, churning out everything from epic theatre productions to experimental live music. While **food** can be expensive, London's multicultural society means that there is a stunning variety of cuisine, often very affordable.

WHAT TO SEE AND DO

The majority of sights are north of the **River Thames**, and a good place to start is the political and regal centre; the area around Whitehall, with **Trafalgar Square** at one end, **Parliament Square** at the other and **Buckingham Palace** off to the side.

13

, Hampstead & Luton Airport (60km)   Highgate, Markets & (200m)

LONDON

■ ACCOMMODATION			
Aviva Studio Apartments	10	Palmers Lodge Swiss Cottage	1
Clink 78	4	Pride of Paddington	8
Generator	5	Ridgemount Hotel	6
Great Eastern	7	Russell's	2
Lee Valley Camping		St Christopher's Inn	9
and Caravan Park	3	Travel Joy	11

Camden Road Station

Camden Market

Primrose Hill

St John's Wood

PRINCE ALBERT ROAD

Mornington Crescent

St Pancras International Station

Camden Town

London Zoo

Regent's Canal

PARK ROAD

WELLINGTON ROAD

ELGIN AVENUE

MAIDA VALE

ST JOHN'S WOOD ROAD

EVERSHOLT STREET

PANCRAS ROAD

Euston Station

Euston

University College Hospital

EUSTON ROAD

Warren Street

Euston Square

Regent's Park

Great Portland Street

Goodge Street

BLOOMSBURY

Warwick Avenue

LITTLE VENICE

WESTWAY

EDGWARE ROAD

Marylebone

Baker Street

MARYLEBONE ROAD

Regent's Park

TOTTENHAM COURT ROAD

GOWER ST.

Marylebone Station

Edgware Road

GLOUCESTER PLACE

BAKER STREET

Mortimer Street

SEE WEST END MAP FOR DETAIL

Tottenham Court Road

Paddington Station

St Mary's Hospital

Paddington

PRAED STREET

WIGMORE STREET

SEYMOUR ST.

OXFORD CIRCUS

Oxford Circus

OXFORD STREET

WARDOUR ST.

SHAFTESBURY AVENUE

SOHO

BAYSWATER

GLOUCESTER TERRACE

SUSSEX GARDENS

CRAVEN ST.

Marble Arch

Selfridge's ❶

Bond Street

BROOK STREET

REGENT ST.

Leicester Square

LEICESTER SQUARE

Marble Arch

BAYSWATER ROAD

Speaker's Corner

BERKELEY STREET

PICCADILLY CIRCUS

Piccadilly Circus

TRAFALGAR SQUARE

Lancaster Gate

PARK LANE

SOUTH AUDLEY ST.

CURZON ST.

Green Park

Kensington Gardens

Hyde Park

The Serpentine

Serpentine Gallery

Wellington Arch

PICCADILLY

Green Park

THE MALL

St James's Park

Green Park

CONSTITUTION HILL

KENSINGTON ROAD

Royal Albert Hall

Knightsbridge

Hyde Park Corner

Buckingham Palace

BIRDCAGE WALK

PARLIAMENT SQUARE

Victoria and Albert Museum

Harrods ❷

Queen's Gallery

St James's Park

Science Museum

PONT STREET

BROMPTON ROAD

SLOANE STREET

BELGRAVE SQUARE

EATON SQUARE

GROSVENOR PL.

VICTORIA STREET

GREAT PETER ST.

Victoria

HORSEFERRY ROAD

PAGE ST.

Natural History Museum

CROMWELL ROAD

South Kensington

EBURY STREET

BUCKINGHAM PALACE ROAD

Victoria Coach Station

Victoria Station

VAUXHALL BRIDGE ROAD

REGENCY ST.

Tate Britain

Royal Court

SLOANE SQUARE

Sloane Square

OLD BROMPTON ROAD

FULHAM ROAD

KING'S ROAD

PIMLICO RD

BELGRAVE ROAD

WARWICK WAY

Pimlico

CHELSEA

Curzon Chelsea

ST GEORGE'S DR

CAMBRIDGE ST.

0	metres	100
0	yards	100

● EATING			
A.Gold	19	Monmouth	
Ciao Bella	17	Coffee Company	27
E. Pellicci	13	Paul Rothe & Son	24
F. Cooke	5	Simpson's Tavern	26
Mandalay	16	Sông Què	7
		Tayyabs	23

Heathrow Airport (24km)

Notting Hill & Portobello Road Market

& Kensington

& Earls Court

Fulham

Gatwick Airport (48km)   (800m)

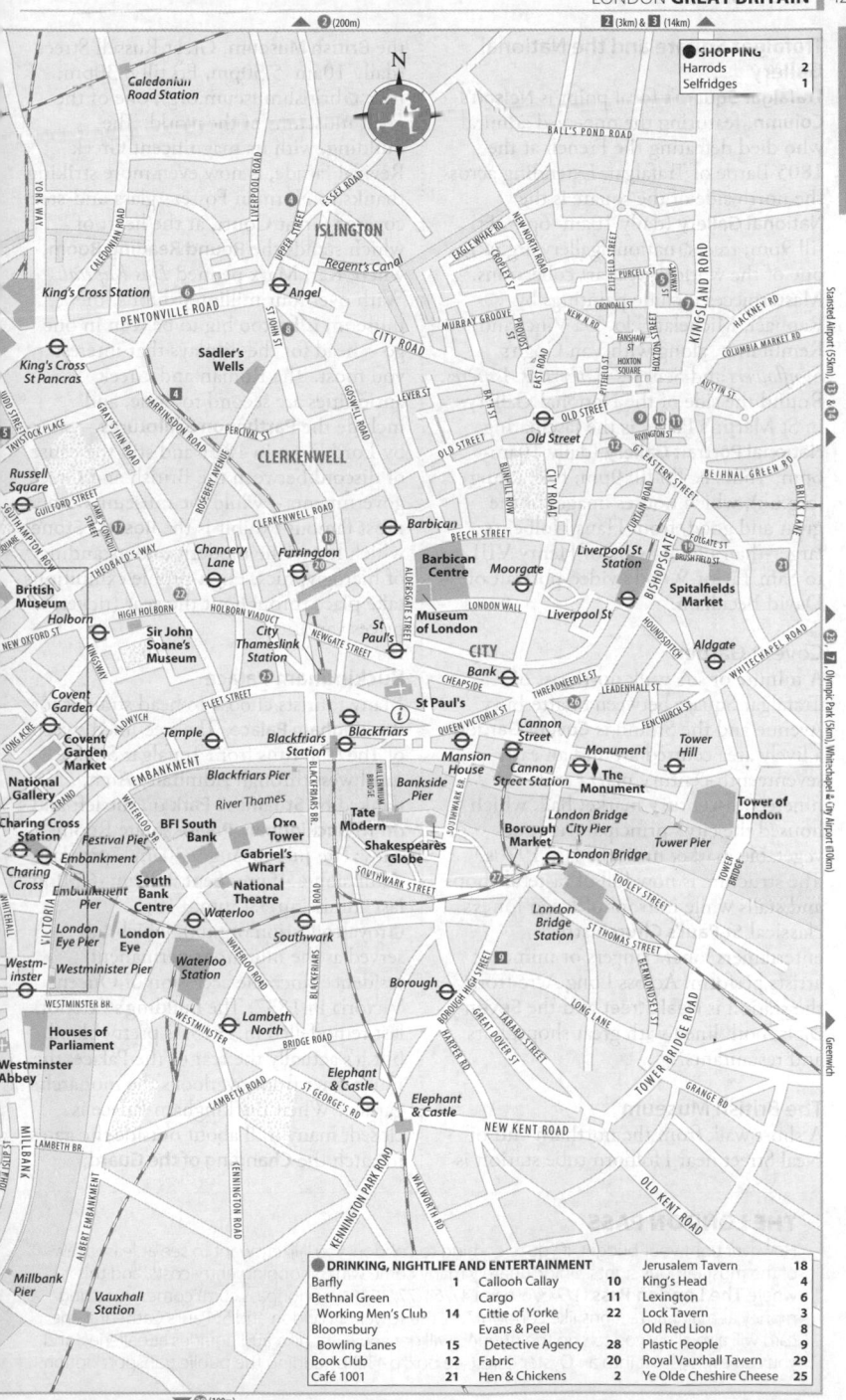

▲ ② (200m)

2 (3km) & **3** (14km) ▲

Stansted Airport (55km), **13** & 84
28, 7, Olympic Park (5km), Whitechapel & City Airport (10km)
Greenwich

● **SHOPPING**
Harrods	2
Selfridges	1

● **DRINKING, NIGHTLIFE AND ENTERTAINMENT**

Barfly	1	Callooh Callay	10	Jerusalem Tavern	18
Bethnal Green		Cargo	11	King's Head	4
Working Men's Club	14	Cittie of Yorke	22	Lexington	6
Bloomsbury		Evans & Peel		Lock Tavern	3
Bowling Lanes	15	Detective Agency	28	Old Red Lion	8
Book Club	12	Fabric	20	Plastic People	9
Café 1001	21	Hen & Chickens	2	Royal Vauxhall Tavern	29
				Ye Olde Cheshire Cheese	25

▼ ㉙ (100m)

13

Trafalgar Square and the National Gallery

Trafalgar Square's focal point is **Nelson's Column**, featuring the one-eyed admiral who died defeating the French at the 1805 Battle of Trafalgar. Extending across the north side of the square is the **National Gallery** (daily 10am–6pm, Fri till 9pm; free; ⓦnationalgallery.org.uk), one of the world's great art collections. Masterpieces include paintings by Raphael, Michelangelo, Da Vinci and Rembrandt, along with Van Gogh's *Sunflowers* and Seurat's *Bathers at Asnières*. Round the side of the National Gallery, in St Martin's Place, is the fascinating **National Portrait Gallery** (daily 10am–6pm, Thurs & Fri till 9pm; free; ⓦnpg.org.uk), which houses images of the great and good, from Hans Holbein's larger-than-life drawing of Henry VIII to Sam Taylor-Wood's video portrait of David Beckham.

Covent Garden

A minute or so's walk northeast of Trafalgar Square between Shaftesbury Avenue and the Strand is **Covent Garden**, a lively area centred around an early seventeenth-century piazza and nineteenth-century market hall, which housed the city's principal fruit and vegetable market until the late 1970s. The structure is now full of tasteful shops and stalls while in front of Inigo Jones's classical **St Paul's Church** street entertainers, opera singers or mime artists perform. Across Long Acre from the station is **Neal Street** and the **Seven Dials**, both lined with great shops, bars and restaurants.

The British Museum

A short walk from the northern end of Neal Street near Holborn tube station is the **British Museum**, Great Russell Street (daily 10am–5.30pm, Fri till 8.30pm; free; ⓦbritishmuseum.org), one of the great museums of the world. The building, with its magnificent Greek Revival facade, is now even more striking thanks to Norman Foster's glass-and-steel covered Great Court, at the heart of which stands the **Round Reading Room**, where Karl Marx penned *Das Kapital*. With over four million exhibits, the museum is far too big to be seen in one go – head for the displays that interest you most. The Roman and Greek antiquities are second to none, and include the **Parthenon Sculptures** – taken by Lord Elgin in 1801 and still the cause of discord between the British and Greek governments – while the museum's other most famous exhibit is the **Rosetta Stone**, which led to the modern understanding of hieroglyphics. High-profile exhibitions take place throughout the year (ticket prices vary).

Buckingham Palace

Many tourists choose to head straight for **Buckingham Palace**. The tree-lined sweep of **The Mall** runs from Trafalgar Square southwest through Admiralty Arch, flanked by **St James's Park** on the left and on to **Buckingham Palace** (State Rooms daily: late July to Aug 9.30am–7pm, last admission 4.45pm; Sept 9.30am–6.30pm, last admission 3.45pm; £19; ⓦroyalcollection.org.uk), which has served as the monarch's permanent residence since the accession of Queen Victoria in 1837. The building's exterior, last remodelled in 1913, is pretty bland, but it's actually the rear of the Palace: the much finer front overlooks the monarch's garden. When Buckingham Palace is closed, many mill about outside the gates to catch the **Changing of the Guard**;

THE LONDON PASS

However tight your budget, if you're coming to London, you'll likely want to see at least a few of the most famous sights. Unfortunately many come with whopping entry costs, and this is where **The London Pass** (1/2/3/6-day £47/64/77/102; ⓦlondonpass.com) comes in. Saving money at major attractions like London Zoo, the Tower of London and St Paul's Cathedral, the card will also allow you to skip the queues, will get you extras like audioguides at galleries, and you can even turn it into an Oyster card (see box, p.430) by adding the public transport option.

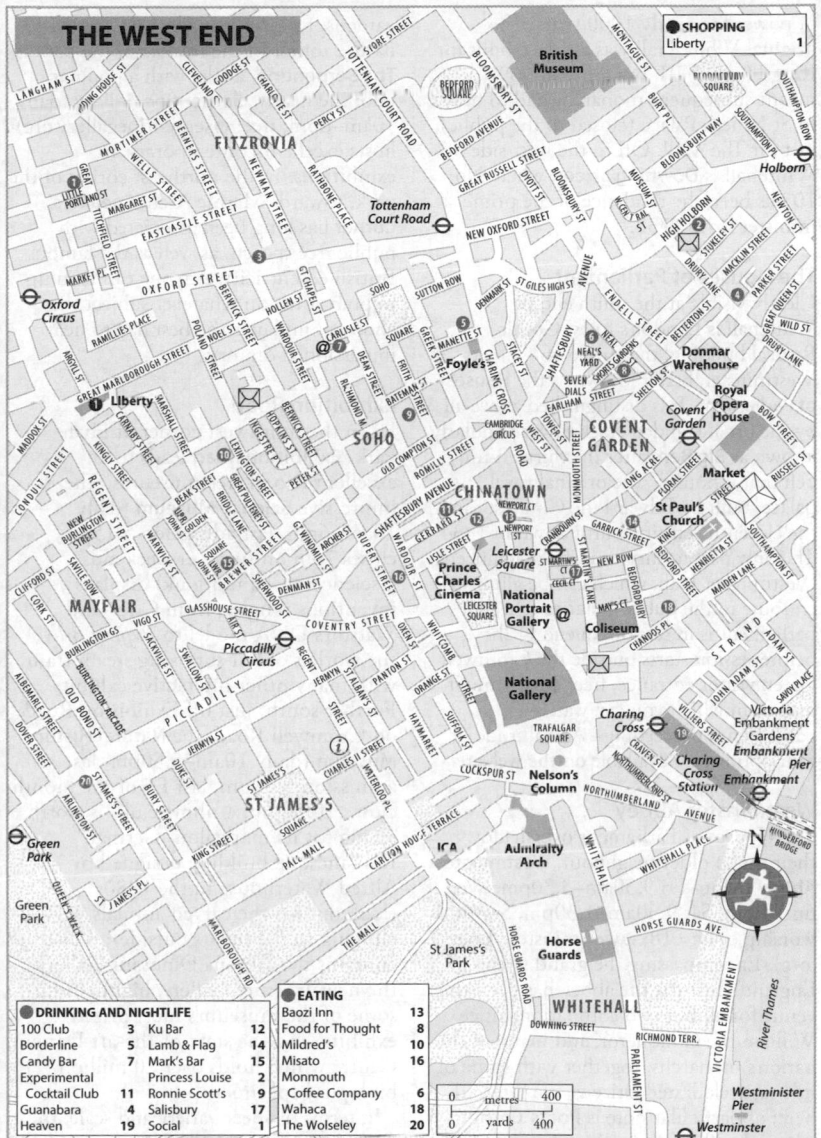

THE WEST END

● SHOPPING	
Liberty	1

● DRINKING AND NIGHTLIFE			
100 Club	3	Ku Bar	12
Borderline	5	Lamb & Flag	14
Candy Bar	7	Mark's Bar	15
Experimental		Princess Louise	2
Cocktail Club	11	Ronnie Scott's	9
Guanabara	4	Salisbury	17
Heaven	19	Social	1

● EATING	
Baozi Inn	13
Food for Thought	8
Mildred's	10
Misato	16
Monmouth	
Coffee Company	6
Wahaca	18
The Wolseley	20

however, you're better off heading for **Horse Guards** over the other side of the park, where there's a more elaborate equestrian ceremony (Mon–Sat 11am, Sun 10am) and where the Olympic beach volleyball tournament took place in 2012. From Buckingham Palace you can retrace your steps to go down Whitehall towards

Westminster, or head west through Green Park to Hyde Park Corner.

Whitehall and Westminster

Whitehall, flanked by government buildings, leads off south from Trafalgar Square towards the area known as **Westminster**, the country's political seat

13

of power for nearly 1000 years. The original White Hall was a palace built for King Henry VIII, but a fire in 1698 meant subsequent monarchs had to move to St James's Palace (closed to the public), just off The Mall. Off to the west side of Whitehall is **Downing Street**, where No. 10 has been the residence of the prime minister since 1732.

The Houses of Parliament

Clearly visible at the south end of Whitehall is London's finest Gothic Revival building, the Palace of Westminster, better known as the **Houses of Parliament**. It is distinguished above all by the ornate, gilded clock tower popularly known as **Big Ben**, after the thirteen-ton bell that it houses. The original royal palace, built by Edward the Confessor in the eleventh century, burnt down in 1834. The only part to survive is the magnificent Westminster Hall, which can be glimpsed en route to the **public galleries** (check parliament is in session; queue 1–2hr before session starts outside the Cromwell Green visitor entrance; free; ⓦparliament .uk) from which you can watch parliament's proceedings. A multitude of tour options are available on the website.

Westminster Abbey

The Houses of Parliament overshadow their much older neighbour, **Westminster Abbey** (Mon–Fri 9.30am–3.30pm, Wed until 6pm, Sat 9.30am–1.30pm, Sun for worship only; £18; ⓦwestminster-abbey .org). Encompassing the grand sweep of England's history, the abbey has been the venue for all but two coronations since William the Conqueror, and many of the nation's monarchs, together with some of its most celebrated citizens, are interred here; of particular note is **Poets' Corner**, where the likes of Chaucer, Tennyson and Charles Dickens are buried. More recently, the abbey was the venue chosen for the 2011 wedding of Prince William and Kate Middleton, now the Duke and Duchess of Cambridge.

Hyde Park

Central London's largest green space, **Hyde Park** is made up of manicured gardens, forest-like glades and shaded nature zones. In the middle of the park is **The Serpentine**, a lake with a popular lido; the nearby **Serpentine Gallery** (daily 10am–6pm; free; ⓦserpentinegallery.org) hosts excellent contemporary art exhibitions. In the northeast corner of the park, towards Marble Arch, **Speakers' Corner** has long been associated with public free speech, as well as the famous British eccentricity. Anyone can turn up to pour forth on whatever subject they choose; Sunday is the best day to hear impassioned oratory.

Exhibition Road

From the southwest corner of Hyde Park, **Exhibition Road** leads to an excellent trio of free museums. The impressive **Science Museum** (daily 10am–6pm, last admission 5.15pm, closes 7pm on summer weekends; ⓦsciencemuseum.org.uk) displays inventions ranging from Crick and Watson's DNA model to *Puffing Billy*, the world's oldest surviving steam train, with many other interactive exhibits. Further south, just off Exhibition Road on Cromwell Road, the **Natural History Museum** (daily 10am–5.50pm, last admission 5.30pm, last Fri of the month closes 10.30pm; ⓦnhm.ac.uk) is worth seeing for its marvellous German Romanesque building designed by Alfred Waterhouse in the 1880s (look out for the carved animals clinging to the pillars outside); it also contains the famous Dinosaur Gallery, the new Treasure Gallery, highlighting some of the museum's most prized exhibits, and the state-of-the-art Darwin Centre which holds over 20 million biological specimens.

In terms of sheer variety and scale, the nearby **Victoria and Albert Museum** (daily 10am–5.45pm, closes 10pm Fri; ⓦvam .ac.uk) is the greatest museum of applied arts in the world. In addition to its displays on fashion through the ages, the most celebrated of the exhibits are the *Raphael Cartoons*, fashion from the eighteenth century through to modern *haute couture*, and the enormous Ardabil carpet, the oldest in the world.

South Kensington tube is the closest to all three museums and has an underground walkway connecting them.

Tate Britain

A short walk from Parliament Square west along Millbank, **Tate Britain** (daily 10am–6pm; free; ⑩tate.org.uk) displays British art from 1500 onwards, including a whole wing devoted to Turner. The permanent galleries usually include a selection of works by the likes of Hogarth, Constable and Bacon, and the gallery hosts the controversial Turner Prize for contemporary British artists each year, along with other temporary exhibitions (entry charges apply). The **Tate to Tate Boat** carries passengers from Millbank to Tate Modern on Bankside (see below; every 40min during Tate opening hours; £5.50 one-way or £3.70 with a Travelcard).

South Bank

The **South Bank** forms the stretch by the Thames roughly from Westminster Bridge to London Bridge (a 50min walk). The riverside footpath buzzes with life, as people stroll and jog past street entertainers and art installations, or sit out at the many restaurants. The focal point is the **London Eye** (daily 10am–8.30/9.30pm; £19.20; ten percent discount if bought online; ⑩londoneye .com), a 135m-tall observation wheel that revolves above the river. Head north from here past the brutalist **South Bank Centre** (see p.435) – which encompasses the Royal Festival Hall and the Hayward Gallery – the adjacent **National Theatre** and **British Film Institute**. You'll pass craft shops and restaurants in Gabriel's Wharf and the OXO Tower before reaching Bankside (see below).

Bankside and Tate Modern

Contemporary **Bankside** is dominated by **Tate Modern** (daily 10am–6pm, Fri & Sat till 10pm; free; ⑩tate.org.uk), built in a minimalist postwar power station. There are pricey temporary exhibitions (around £10; book ahead for major exhibitions), but as the permanent collection includes works by just about every famous modern artist including Monet, Bonnard, Matisse, Picasso, Dalí, Mondrian, Warhol and Rothko, you should get your fill of modern art for free.

Directly outside Tate Modern is Norman Foster's **Millennium Bridge**, which, with its spectacular views, will take you across the river to the City of London and St Paul's Cathedral.

Globe Theatre to London Bridge

Dwarfed by Tate Modern is **Shakespeare's Globe** (⑩shakespearesglobe.com), a reconstruction of the polygonal playhouse where most of the Bard's later works were first performed. If you're happy to stand in the pit, you can catch a show from as little as £5. A short stroll further east winds away from the river under Victorian railway arches to **London Bridge** and the popular **Borough Market** (see box, p.428), a fantastic place to refuel.

The City of London

Follow the commuters as they trudge over London Bridge to the **City of London**. Despite the newer development of Canary Wharf stealing many companies further east, the area remains London's financial hub. Out of office hours, the City can feel hauntingly empty, but its charm lies in magnificent buildings interspersed with tiny chapels on narrow, winding streets.

St Paul's Cathedral

On the western edge of the City is one of London's most famous landmarks, **St Paul's Cathedral** (Mon–Sat 8.30am–4pm; £15; ⑩stpauls.co.uk). The most distinctive feature of architect Christopher Wren's Baroque edifice is the vast dome, one of the largest in the world. Highlights include the **Whispering Gallery**, up in the dome, so-called because words whispered to the wall on one side are clearly audible on the other; the broad exterior Stone Gallery; and the uppermost Golden Gallery, which offers panoramas over London. The **crypt** is the resting place of Wren, Turner, Reynolds and other artists, but the most imposing sarcophagi are those occupied by the Duke of Wellington and Lord Nelson.

13

Museum of London

Just north of St Paul's, situated in the 1970s-designed **Barbican Centre**, is the **Museum of London** (daily 10am–6pm; free; ⓦmuseumoflondon.org.uk). It tells the story of the city from prehistoric times to the present day, with particularly interesting displays on Roman London and the Great Fire, plus the Lord Mayor's state coach dating to 1757. The Barbican Centre itself (ⓦbarbican.org.uk) is one of London's cultural hotspots, housing cinemas, theatres and galleries.

Tower of London

Despite all the hype, and the entrance fee, the **Tower of London** (daily: March–Oct 9/10am–5.30pm; Nov–Feb 9/10am–4.30pm; £20.90 or £18 if booked online; ⓦhrp.org.uk), on the river a mile southeast of St Paul's by Tower Bridge, remains one of London's most remarkable buildings. Begun by William the Conqueror, and pretty much completed by the end of the thirteenth century, the Tower is the most perfectly preserved (albeit heavily restored) medieval fortress in the country. The central **White Tower** holds part of the Royal Armouries collection, and, on the second floor, the Norman Chapel of St John, London's oldest church. Close by is Tower Green,

where two of Henry VIII's wives were beheaded. The Waterloo Barracks house the **Crown Jewels**, among which are the three largest cut diamonds in the world.

The East End

A short walk from the Tower brings you to Aldgate and the start of the **East End**. The area has always drawn large immigrant populations due to its proximity to the river – it has been in turn Huguenot, Jewish and, most recently, Bangladeshi and Pakistani. Walk down Whitechapel Road from Aldgate and you'll pass one of Britain's largest mosques, as well as the excellent **Whitechapel Gallery** (Tues–Sun 11am–6pm, Thurs until 9pm; free; ⓦwhitechapelgallery.org), which shows off a cutting-edge mix of contemporary art. **Brick Lane** meanders off to the left (take Osborn St), lined with curry houses, trendy street markets, retro shops and boutiques.

At the other end of Brick Lane are the funky, creative areas of **Shoreditch**, **Hoxton** and **Old Street**. The area is a fun place to go out in the evening, and is full of boutique restaurants, galleries, cafés and design stores. A two- to three-mile walk further east down Whitechapel Road brings you to what was once a desolate industrial area, transformed into

MARKETS

At the weekend, visit one of London's high-quality markets: some are well established, some trendy pop-ups, but wherever you go, you're sure to find tasty food and a lively, relaxed atmosphere. Unless specified, markets tend to run 10am–5pm.

Borough ⓣ London Bridge; map pp.422–423. Where serious foodies stock up on hard-to-source ingredients. Not cheap, but there are free tasters and cheaper gourmet snacks. Mon–Wed 10am–3pm, Thurs 11am–5pm, Fri noon–6pm, Sat 8am–5pm.

Brick Lane and Spitalfields ⓣ Liverpool St; map pp.422–423. Technically two separate markets, but punters wander between the two on Sun, when Brick Lane is thick with food stalls. Spitalfields draws an eclectic mix of artists, jewellers and designers in a restored covered market. Brick Lane Sun 9am–5pm; Spitalfields Mon–Fri 10am–5pm, Sun 9am–5pm.

Camden ⓣ Camden Town; map pp.422–423. A punk hangout in the 1970s, with plenty of Dr. Martens and

studded jackets still on offer today, mixed with every other sub-culture going. Daily 10am–6pm.

Columbia Road Shoreditch High Street Overground; map pp.422–423. An easy walk from Brick Lane, this lovely plant and flower market is also full of boutique stores and hip coffee shops. Sun 8am–3pm.

Greenwich Cutty Sark DLR; map pp.422–423. Covered market with quirky handmade gifts and crafts (Tues, Wed & Fri–Sun) as well as vintage clothes stores and antiques (Tues, Thurs & Fri). Tues–Sun 10am–5.30pm.

Portobello Road ⓣ Notting Hill; map pp.422–423. The most iconic London market thanks to the film Notting Hill, with stalls peddling antiques, rare books and vintage finds (Sat only), as well as fashion and crafts. Mon–Wed 9am–6pm, Thurs 9am–1pm, Fri & Sat 9am–7pm.

13

the Olympic Park for the 2012 Games. The site reopened as the **Queen Elizabeth Olympic Park** in July 2013 (Ⓦnoordinary park.co.uk), with major sporting and events venues surrounded by parkland, plus Anish Kapoor's 115m-high *Orbit*, Britain's largest piece of public art, whose sky-high platforms offer fantastic views across London.

Regent's Park and Camden

As with almost all of London's royal parks, Londoners have Henry VIII to thank for **Regent's Park**, which he confiscated from the Church for yet more hunting grounds. Flanked by some of the city's most elegant residential buildings, the park is home to **London Zoo** (daily 10am–4/6pm; £21.50; Ⓦzsl.org), one of the world's oldest and most varied collections of animals. Take the tube to Baker Street, Regent's Park or Great Portland Street to enter the park at its southernmost edge and walk north to the zoo, or get the tube to **Camden Town** with its famous **market** (see box opposite) and music scene, and walk west down **Regent's Canal**, which runs through the middle of the zoo.

Hampstead Heath and Highgate Cemetery

Camden gives way to the affluent suburb of Hampstead and to wild **Hampstead Heath**, which offers the perfect antidote to London's highly manicured parks. East of Hampstead is **Highgate Cemetery**, ranged on both sides of Swains Lane (Ⓞ Highgate/Archway). Karl Marx lies in the East Cemetery (Mon–Fri 10am–5pm, Sat & Sun 11am–5pm; £4; Ⓦhighgate -cemetery.org); more atmospheric is the overgrown West Cemetery (guided tours only: March–Nov Mon–Fri 2pm, Sat & Sun hourly 11am–4pm; Dec–Feb Sat & Sun hourly 11am–3pm; £12, includes entry to East Cemetery), with its spooky Egyptian Avenue and terraced catacombs.

Greenwich

One of London's most beguiling spots, and offering respite from the frenetic centre, **Greenwich** is worth the short trip. Transport links are good: there are regular riverboats (see p.431), trains from London Bridge, or the DLR scoots from Bank via the redeveloped Docklands south to the **Cutty Sark** (daily 10am–5pm, last admission 4pm; entry by timed ticket only, best to pre-book online; £12; Ⓦrmg.co.uk). This famous tea clipper has recently been dazzlingly restored after a devastating fire, and now you can walk beneath the 143-year-old hull, as well as stroll the decks and explore the hold. Hugging the riverfront to the east is Wren's beautifully symmetrical Baroque ensemble of the **Old Royal Naval College** (daily 10am–5pm; free; Ⓦornc.org). Across the road, the **National Maritime Museum** (daily 10am–5pm, closes 8pm Thurs; free; Ⓦnmm.ac.uk) has model ships, charts and globes, and hosts sea-themed exhibitions. From here Greenwich Park stretches up the hill, crowned by the Wren-inspired **Royal Observatory** (daily 9am–5pm; free), where you can straddle the Greenwich Mean Time meridian.

ARRIVAL AND DEPARTURE

BY PLANE

Flying into London, you'll arrive at one of the capital's five international airports: Heathrow (Ⓦheathrowairport.com), Gatwick (Ⓦgatwickairport.com), Stansted (Ⓦstansted airport.com), Luton (Ⓦwww.london-luton.co.uk) or City (Ⓦlondoncityairport.com). EasyBus (Ⓦeasybus.co.uk) has buses from Gatwick, Stansted and Luton to central London from £2, while National Express operate from all airports. From Heathrow, Gatwick and Stansted, there are express trains every 15min that will get you there faster than other modes of transport, but at around £20 for a single ticket, it's not cheap; fares are often discounted online.

Heathrow 15 miles west. Served by Piccadilly Line on the Tube (every few min, 6am–11.50pm; 1hr; £5.50 cash or £5/3 Oyster peak/off-peak). In addition to the express train services (see above), Heathrow Connect trains offer a slower stopping service to Paddington Station (every 30min; 25min; £9.50). National Express coaches go to Victoria Coach Station (every 10–15min; 50min; £6). After midnight, night bus #N9 runs to Trafalgar Square (every 20min; 1hr 10min; £2.40 cash/1.40 Oyster).

Gatwick 30 miles south. Connected by several train companies: Southern trains run on the same route as the Gatwick Express, but are cheaper (every 15min; 35min; £14.40), and First Capital Connect trains run to London Bridge, Blackfriars and St Pancras International (every 15min; 30–40min; around £10).

13

Stansted 34 miles northeast. Regular National Express services run to Victoria Coach Station via Baker Street and Marble Arch (every 15min; 1hr 45min; £10), or Liverpool Street (every 15min; 1hr–1hr 15min; £8); Terravision buses also go to Victoria and Liverpool Street (every 20–40min; 40–55mins; £6–9).

Luton 37 miles north. Served by shuttle buses to Luton Airport Parkway station, from which there are services to St Pancras (every 5–20min; 25–45min; £13.50) and other stations with First Capital Connect (see Gatwick). Green Line bus #757 also runs from the airport terminal into central London (every 20min–1hr; 1hr 30min; £17 or £25 return within 3 months).

London City 10 miles east. Served by the Docklands Light Railway (DLR), with regular services to Bank (every 8–15mins; 22min; £4.50 cash or £3.20/2.70 Oyster peak/off-peak).

BY TRAIN

Eurostar services from Paris or Brussels terminate at St Pancras International. Trains from the English Channel ports arrive at Victoria, Waterloo or Charing Cross stations, while those from elsewhere in Britain come into one of London's numerous main-line termini (namely Waterloo and Paddington from the southwest, Euston or King's Cross from the north, and Liverpool Street from the east), all of which have Tube stations.

Destinations Bath (every 30min; 1hr 30min); Brighton (every 15min; 1hr 5min); Bristol (every 15min; 1hr 20min–1hr 45min); Brussels (7 daily; 2hr–2hr 15min); Cambridge (every 15min; 45min); Cardiff (every 15min; 2hr 10min); Dover (every 30min; 1hr 10min–2hr); Durham (every 30min; 2hr 45min–3hr); Edinburgh (every 30min; 4hr 20min–5hr 40min); Glasgow (hourly; 4hr 30min–5hr 40min); Lille (8 daily; 1hr 20min–1hr 40min); Liverpool (every 20min; 2hr 10min–2hr 30min); Manchester (every 20min; 2hr 10min); Newcastle (every 30min; 2hr 50min–3hr 15min); Oxford (every 10–20min; 1hr–1hr 50min); Paris (hourly; 2hr 20min–2hr 45min); Penzance (13 daily;

5hr 10min–8hr 10min); Stratford-upon-Avon (hourly; 2–3hr); York (every 30min; 1hr 50min–2hr 20min).

BY BUS

Long-distance buses from around Britain and continental Europe arrive at Victoria Coach Station, a 500-yard walk south of Victoria train station.

Destinations Amsterdam (4 daily; 11–12hr); Bath (every 1hr 30min; 2hr 50min–3hr 20min); Berlin (4 weekly; 20hr); Brighton (hourly; 2hr–3hr 15min); Bristol (hourly; 2hr 45min); Cambridge (every 1hr–1hr 30min; 2hr 10min–2hr 30min); Cardiff (hourly; 3hr 10min–3hr 25min); Dover (hourly; 2hr 30min–3hr); Dublin (1 daily; 12hr 30min); Durham (4 daily; 6–7hr); Edinburgh (2 daily; 9hr–9hr 45min); Glasgow (5 daily; 8hr 15min–9hr 45min); Inverness (1 daily; 12hr 35min); Liverpool (every 2hr; 4hr 40min–5hr 45min); Manchester (hourly; 4hr 35min–5hr 20min); Newcastle (5 daily; 6hr 25min–7hr 25min); Oxford (every 20–30min; 1hr 50min–2hr); Paris (4 daily; 8hr 30min); Penzance (5 daily; 8hr 20min–9hr 55min); Stratford-upon-Avon (3 daily; 3hr 15min–3hr 25min); York (4 daily; 4hr 50min–5hr 25min).

INFORMATION

Tourist information London's flagship tourist office is the City of London Information Office (Mon–Sat 9.30am–5.30pm, Sun 10am–4pm; ☏ 020 7332 1456, ⓦ visitlondon.com), opposite St Paul's Cathedral. There are other branches all over the city – the website details them on a map.

GETTING AROUND

Transport for London (TfL) oversees the city's public transport, and their website (ⓦ tfl.gov.uk) is a vital tool for all Londoners and visitors to help navigate this enormous city by tube, bus, boat or bike. It can even help you plan walking routes or look up reliable taxi companies. TfL's six tourist information centres are in the following major stations: Piccadilly Circus tube station, Heathrow Terminals

---

OYSTER CARDS

The cheapest way to pay for all public transport in London is to use an **Oyster** touch card (ⓦ tfl.gov.uk; £5 refundable deposit), valid on the underground, buses, trams, the DLR, the London Overground rail network and most National Rail services in London, and will give you money off some riverboats. You can store cash on the card ("pay as you go") as well as weekly travel cards; simply "top up" at stations or Oyster Ticket Stops, including newsagents and other shops (look for the Oyster logo outside). When using an Oyster, one-way bus fares are almost halved (£2.40 to £1.40) and tube fares in Zone 1 are reduced from £4.50 if paying cash to £2.10. If you pay as you go, you'll be charged no more than the maximum daily cap (currently £8.40 peak or £7 off-peak for Zones 1 and 2). Consider buying a week's **Travelcard** (from £30.40) if you're staying for several days and plan on making lots of journeys. You can buy pre-loaded cards before you come to the UK (ⓦ visitorshop.tfl.gov.uk). Even without Oyster, a one-day (£8.80/7.30 peak/off-peak) paper Travelcard will still save you pounds.

13

1, 2 and 3, Euston, Liverpool Street, Victoria and King's Cross (all open daily; see website for hours). There's also a 24hr phone line for information on all services, including up-to-date closures or diversions (☎ 0043 222 1234).

BY UNDERGROUND

The quickest way to get around is via the London Underground network, known as "the tube" (daily 5.30/7.30am–12.30am approx; check "first and last" tube on TfL website). It can be staggeringly expensive without an Oyster card (see box opposite). Tickets must be bought in advance from the machines or booths in station entrance halls and need to be kept until the end of your journey so that you can leave the station. If you use Oyster, be sure to always touch the card reader on the way in and out of each station. If you cannot produce a valid ticket or Oyster card on demand, you'll be charged an on-the-spot penalty fine of £80. Bear in mind that during rush hour the tube is heaving with commuters and best avoided, especially if you are laden with baggage. Within central London always check whether walking will be quicker – Covent Garden and Leicester Square stations are just a 4min walk apart.

BY BUS

A great way to see the city, especially from the top of London's famous red double-deckers. Many run 24hr, though be aware that night buses prefixed with the letter "N" may not run the same route as their day counterpart. If you don't have an Oyster card, you will need to buy a single ticket (£2.40) from the machine at the bus stop before boarding (in central London), or, outside of the centre, simply pay the driver (use small change). If you have a contactless debit/credit card, you can use it to cover the "pay as you go" fare of £1.40. Hail buses by sticking your arm out. Most buses are modern, but classic London Routemaster buses, complete with conductor, still run on two routes: Charing Cross station to the Tower of London (#15) and Kensington High St to Aldwych (#9).

BY BOAT

Riverboat services on the Thames are a pleasant and quick way to get between east and west. Having an Oyster or a paper Travelcard will get you a third off riverboat tickets (otherwise £3.30 single), while if you've got a pay-as-you-go Oyster you'll get ten percent off single fares. Westminster Pier, Embankment Pier and Waterloo Pier are the main central embarkation points and there are regular sailings to Bankside, London Bridge, Tower Bridge and Greenwich. Timings and services alter frequently so pick up the *Thames River Services* booklet from a TfL travel information office, or see ⓦ tfl.gov.uk/river.

BY TAXI

If you're in a group, London's metered black cabs (just wave to hail one when their orange "taxi" light is illuminated)

can be a viable way of travelling. Cost depends on time of day, distance travelled and travel time and there's a minimum £2.40 fare. A two-mile journey (10–20min) should cost around £11 (6am–8pm). To book in advance, call ☎ 020 7272 0272. Minicabs look just like regular cars and are considerably cheaper than black cabs (a black cab to Heathrow will cost up to £85, while a minicab will charge £40–60), but need to be booked by phone in advance. To get numbers for local registered minicab companies, download the Cabwise app, text CAB to ☎ 60835, or call the travel information number above.

BY TRAIN AND TRAM

There is a variety of different train lines in London. The Overground and the Docklands Light Railway (DLR) are operated by TfL and form part of the Tube map – most interchanges are as simple as on the tube. National Rail services from London out to Greater London suburbs and commuter towns are run by outside agents, but you can use Oyster cards for most journeys in and around the city (details on TfL website). Oyster can also be used on the trams in south London.

BY BIKE

The public bike rental scheme is available to all (ⓦ www .tfl.org.uk; credit or debit card needed to hire at docking stations found all over central London). "Boris Bikes", named after the mayor who installed them, cost £2 to rent for the day or £10 for a week, then you pay an hourly incremental charge after that; as the first half an hour is free, so long as you keep docking the bikes and picking up new ones, it can be a great and cheap way to see London. Alternatively, you can find standard rental shops through the London Cycling Campaign (ⓦ lcc.org.uk). Pick out cycle-friendly routes using the free guides available from transport information offices, or check the TfL website.

ACCOMMODATION

Where to stay can be a difficult question in a city London's size. West London offers easy access to the museums and central London, though it tends to be the most expensive part of town for eating and nightlife. Northeast London is currently London's hippest area, with a vibrant atmosphere and the best nightlife in town. Leafy northwest London provides unrivalled access to London's best green spaces, while anywhere near the South Bank will be central enough to walk into the West End while offering the chance to explore off-the-beaten track neighbourhoods south of the river. The Visit London hotel booking service (☎ 0845 644 3010, ⓦ visitlondon.com) will get you the best available prices with no additional charge. Student rooms are also available July–Sept; try Imperial College (☎ 020 7594 9507, ⓦ imperial.ac.uk/summeraccommodation) or LSE

13

(☎020 7955 7676, ⓦlsevacations.co.uk). For classy, modern budget B&Bs, try the Bed and Breakfast Club (ⓦthebedandbreakfastclub.co.uk).

HOSTELS

The YHA (see p.418) has eight HI-affiliated London hostels, all in unbeatable locations (Oxford Street, Holland Park, St Pancras, St Paul's, Central near Regent's Park), Earls Court and Thameside), and most offer cheap twins and doubles as well as dorms. Prices shown are examples of the cheapest weeknight dorm in high season; in low season beds start from around £15. A continental breakfast is included at the hostels below unless specified.

Clink78 78 King's Cross Rd ☎020 3475 3000, ⓦclinkhostels.com; ⓤKing's Cross; map pp.422–423. Quirky hostel housed in a Victorian courthouse with dorms of various sizes (some of which are girls-only) painted in cheerful colours. Chill-out space is in the actual courtrooms, while the cheapest of the private rooms are the cramped former police cells. Dorm £19, double £66

Generator 37 Tavistock Place ☎020 7388 7666, ⓦgeneratorhostels.com; ⓤRussell Square; map pp.422–423. Huge, raucous party hostel with clubby, neon-lit social spaces and a youthful clientele. Dorm £27.50, double £66

★ **Great Eastern** 1 Glenaffric Ave ☎020 7531 6514, ⓦbestplaceinns.com; Island Gardens DLR station; map pp.422–423. Tucked out of the way in Docklands by the Thames, this hostel, one of a growing chain, is a 10min walk from Greenwich via a foot tunnel, and 5min on the DLR to Canary Wharf tube. It's situated above a remodelled pub, with sparkling facilities and great lounge area. Dorm £20

★ **Palmers Lodge Swiss Cottage** 40 College Crescent ☎020 7483 8470, ⓦpalmerslodges.co.uk; ⓤSwiss Cottage; map pp.422–423. One of a chain of boutique hostels, this is a superb option with disabled access in a converted Victorian mansion, retaining much of its period character. Dorm £17, double £84

Pride of Paddington 1–3 Craven Rd ☎020 7402 2156, ⓦtheprideofpaddington.co.uk; ⓤPaddington; map pp.422–423. Opposite Paddington station and great for Hyde Park and central London, this renovated hostel above a pub is basic but spotless. Cooked breakfast included. Dorm £27

St Christopher's Inn 121 Borough High St ☎020 7939 9710, ⓦst-christophers.co.uk; ⓤLondon Bridge; map pp.422–423. Cheerful party hostel in a series of buildings near London Bridge. *The Village* has a nightclub and comedy bar; *The Inn* is above a pub and a little more tranquil, while *The Oasis* is exclusively for women. Dorm £16, double £45

Travel Joy 111 Grosvenor Rd ☎020 7834 9689, ⓦtraveljoyhostels.com; ⓤPimlico or bus #24 from central London; map pp.422–423. Right on the river in tranquil Pimlico, this friendly hostel is set above the *King William IV* pub, with a terrace hosting barbecues on sunny days and live music events on Sat. Dorm £22, double £100

HOTELS, B&BS AND SELF-CATERING

Most budget hotels and B&Bs in central London are grotty or old-fashioned; with a short commute from the centre, you get much better value for money. See p.419 for budget chain hotels.

★ **Aviva Studio Apartments** 42 Glenthorne Rd ☎07976 020304, ⓦavivastudio-apartments.co.uk; ⓤHammersmith; map pp.422–423. On a residential street in West London but with plenty of local restaurants and just 5min from the tube, these well-equipped apartments are clean and comfortable, and the owners are friendly and knowledgeable about the local area. Double £55

Ridgemount Hotel 65–67 Gower St ☎020 7636 1141, ⓦridgemounthotel.co.uk; ⓤEuston Square; map pp.422–423. What you sacrifice in style and room size, you make up for in location in Bloomsbury and, as a bonus, you get a spotless and friendly hotel to boot. Double £76

★ **Russell's** 123 Chatsworth Rd, Hackney ☎0797 666 9906, ⓦrussellsofclapton.com; Homerton Overground or #38 bus from central London; map pp.422–423. The out-of-the-way location (15min walk from the Overground station) in a formerly insalubrious part of Hackney means you get a boutique B&B offering vintage-style luxury for tiny prices, not to mention a great breakfast. A good location for exploring trendy Shoreditch and Dalston. Double £85

CAMPSITE

Lee Valley Camping and Caravan Park Meridian Way, Enfield ☎020 8803 6900, ⓦvisitleevalley.org.uk; train from Liverpool St to Edmonton Green then #W8 bus; map pp.422–423. For a completely different London experience, try a four-person wood cabin or two-person cocoon in a leisure complex including golf course and cinema in North London. You can pitch your own tent, too. Camping £9.50 per person and tent, cocoon £35, cabin £50

EATING

Few cities can match London for the sheer diversity of eating experiences on offer. You'll find restaurants from every country on earth, with pubs just as likely to offer Thai green curry as steak and ale pie. With so much choice, it's not hard to eat well on a budget.

CAFÉS, CHEAP EATS AND SNACKS

★ **A. Gold** 42 Brushfield St; ⓤLiverpool Street; map pp.422–423. Right by Spitalfields Market (see box, p.428),

LONDON STREET FOOD

London's latest trend is for **gourmet street food**, and food vans are popping up all over the capital selling everything from pulled-pork sandwiches to custard tarts. Locations change frequently, but the following (along with Portobello Market; see box, p.428) are good bets for a gourmet lunch on a budget.

Broadway Market From London Fields Park to the Regent's Canal; London Fields rail or Haggerston Overground. There's been a produce market on this site in Hackney since the 1890s; these days over a hundred stalls sell everything from gourmet sausage rolls to cupcakes. Sat 9am–5pm.

Real Food Market Behind the Royal Festival Hall on the South Bank ⏰Waterloo. Delicious organic food

served direct from producers – a great place for a snacky lunch on the South Bank. Fri noon–8pm, Sat 11am–8pm, Sun noon–6pm.

Whitecross Street Market Whitecross Street ⏰Barbican. Latin American street food is a speciality at this bustling food market in the heart of the City. Thurs & Fri 11am–5pm.

---

this superb traditional food shop sells old-fashioned sweets, teas and chutneys, but the main draw is the tasty, made-to-order sandwiches, crammed with gourmet ingredients such as roast beef, Yorkshire pudding and horseradish sauce (£4–5; Mon–Fri only). Mon–Fri 10am–4pm, Sat & Sun 11am–5pm.

★ **E. Pellicci** 332 Bethnal Green Rd; ⏰Bethnal Green; map pp.422–423. Run by the Pellicci family since the 1900s and a favourite haunt of gangster brothers the Krays, this is the most elegant and cosy greasy spoon in town. Mon–Sat 7am–4pm.

F. Cooke 150 Hoxton St; ⏰Old Street; map pp.422–423. Get the very traditional London pie, mash & liquor (parsley gravy) with the house chilli vinegar for under £4.30, or if you dare, a jellied eel in this spit 'n' sawdust family-run place. Mon–Thurs 10am–7pm, Fri & Sat 9.30am–8pm.

Food For Thought 31 Neal St; ⏰Covent Garden; map p.425. Subterranean vegetarian café serving wholesome salads, soups and mains for around £6. Mon–Sat noon–8.30pm, Sun noon–5.30pm.

Monmouth Coffee Company 27 Monmouth St, Seven Dials; ⏰Holborn; map p.425; also at Borough Market (see box, p.428); ⏰London Bridge; map pp.422–423. *Monmouth* have built a name for themselves for making the best coffee in London – look out for other cafés selling

their blends. Mon–Sat 8am–6.30pm; Borough branch Mon–Sat 7.30am–6pm.

Paul Rothe & Son 35 Marylebone Lane ☎020 7935 6783; ⏰Bond Street; map p.425. Established in 1900 and still run by the Rothes. Marvel at the variety of jams in the window, and also at the low prices of their British breakfast and lunches. Sandwiches from £3.20, jacket potatoes from £4.50. Mon–Fri 8am–6pm, Sat 11am–5pm.

RESTAURANTS

Baozi Inn 26 Newport Court ☎020 7287 6877; ⏰Leicester Square; map p.425. So authentic you may not recognize anything on the menu, but this place serving Beijing and Chengdu street food is a treat for the taste buds. Mains £7.50. Mon–Thurs & Sun noon–10.30pm, Fri & Sat noon–midnight.

★ **Ciao Bella** 86–90 Lamb's Conduit St ☎020 7242 4119; ⏰Russell Square/Holborn; map pp.422–423. Jolly, extremely popular old-style Italian, serving huge plates of pasta or pizza from £7. Mon–Sat noon–11.30pm, Sun noon–10.30pm.

Mandalay 444 Edgware Rd ☎020 7258 3696; ⏰Edgware Road; map pp.422–423. A real gem, serving pure, freshly cooked, unreconstructed Burmese cuisine. Lunch deal £4.50 (Mon–Fri). Mon–Sat noon–2.30pm & 6–10.30pm.

Mildred's 45 Lexington St ☎020 7494 1634; ⏰Oxford Circus or Piccadilly Circus; map p.425. Intimate veggie restaurant and bar with an imaginative menu featuring burgers, curries and stir-fries. Mains around £9. Mon–Sat noon–11pm.

Misato 11 Wardour St; ⏰Piccadilly Circus; map p.425. Japanese café known for its converse qualities of enormous portions for minuscule prices: you can get a big meal for around £7. Daily noon–11pm.

Simpson's Tavern Ball Court, 38½ Cornhill ☎020 7626 9985; ⏰Bank; map pp.422–423. This historic chophouse, tucked away down a Dickensian alley in the City, dates back to 1757 and the interior and menu seem to have

---

★ TREAT YOURSELF

The Wolseley 160 Piccadilly; ⏰Piccadilly Circus; map p.425. Traditional British afternoon tea doesn't come much more special than this: exquisite cream teas from £9.75 in the beautiful Art Deco surroundings of the opulent Wolseley. Don't worry about dressing up; the experience is surprisingly relaxed. Afternoon tea served Mon–Fri 3–6.30pm, Sat 3.30–5.30pm, Sun 3.30–6.30pm.

13

changed little since. Settle into one of the wood-panelled booths and feast on door-stop sandwiches (from £3) or hearty mains such as pork, leek and cider pie (£8.50). Mon–Fri 8am–4pm.

Sông Quê 134 Kingsland Rd ☎020 7613 3222; Hoxton Overground; map pp.422–423. On a strip of road packed with Vietnamese restaurants, the basic decor here belies the excellent food and efficient service. Mains around £7. Mon–Fri noon–3pm & 5.30–11pm, Sat noon–3pm, Sun noon–10.30pm.

Tayyabs 83–89 Fieldgate St ☎020 7247 6400; ⓤAldgate East; map pp.422–423. Close to, but not on, Brick Lane (home to pushy curry touts), this Pakistani restaurant is popular for its grills, naan and bring-your-own-alcohol policy. Come early or be prepared to queue. Mains from £6. Daily noon–11.30pm.

Wahaca 66 Chandos Place; ⓤCharing Cross or Covent Garden; map p.425. Now one of a small London chain (other central branches in Soho and the South Bank), this vast basement restaurant serving Mexican street food is always packed. It's noisy and fun, and the tapas-size servings of tacos, tostadas and quesadillas are delicious. The sharing platter (£19.95) is good value. Mon–Sat noon–11pm, Sun noon–10.30pm.

DRINKING AND NIGHTLIFE

From Victorian pubs serving ale to old gents, to hip bars and clubs frequented by an eternally young, edgy clientele, London has it all. To the east, a thriving bar and club scene around Shoreditch, Hoxton and Old Street is still going strong, though the coolest of the cool are increasingly shifting their parties elsewhere.

BARS AND PUBS

Book Club 100 Leonard St ⓦwearetbc.com; ⓤLiverpool Street/Old Street; map pp.422–423. With a bar serving food, along with cheaper and better cocktails than other bars in the area, this hip Shoreditch hangout also boasts a ping-pong room, exhibitions, film screenings and live music. Mon–Wed 8am–midnight, Thurs & Fri 8am–2am, Sat 10am–2am, Sun 10am–midnight.

Café 1001 91 Brick Lane ⓤAldgate East/Liverpool St; map pp.422–423. Sprawling, grungy bar above a heaving café. Squishy sofas, and free live music and cinema draw a laidback hipster crowd. Daily 6am–midnight.

★ **TREAT YOURSELF**

If you fancy a change from pints of lager, head for one of the city's stylish **cocktail bars** for a barrel-aged daiquiri or smoky negroni. The drinks are pricey (£8–13), but they pack a punch, and the bars are open till the early hours. For speakeasy-style cool, try *Evans & Peel Detective Agency*, 310c Earls Court Rd (ⓤEarls Court; map pp.422–423), while *Callooh Callay*, 65 Rivington St (ⓤOld Street; map pp.422–423), boasts creative cocktails and a party vibe. The *Experimental Cocktail Club* at 13A Gerrard St (ⓤLeicester Square; map p.425), accessed via an unmarked doorway in Chinatown, has an appealingly clandestine feel, while *Mark's Bar*, 66 Brewer St, Soho (ⓤPiccadilly Circus; map p.425), has a great cocktail list and lavish decor.

★ **Jerusalem Tavern** 55 Britton St ⓤFarringdon; map pp.422–423. Cool Clerkenwell's the setting for this packed pub, serving some of the best ales in London from barrels in the wall. Mon–Fri 11am–11pm.

Lamb & Flag 33 Rose St ⓤCovent Garden or Leicester Square; map p.425. A respite from hectic Covent Garden, this compact, atmospheric pub was once known as the *Bucket of Blood* – after the prize fights held here. Mon–Sat 11am–11pm, Sun noon–10.30pm.

Lexington 96 Pentonville Rd ⓤAngel; map pp.422–423. This luxuriously decorated bourbon joint puts on events like a pop pub quiz, as well as cheap live music and club nights upstairs. Mon–Wed & Sun noon–2am, Thurs noon–3am, Fri & Sat noon–4am.

Lock Tavern 35 Chalk Farm Rd ⓤChalk Farm; map pp.422–423. This laidback Camden pub is ever-popular, thanks to its free live music, tasty food and buzzing atmosphere. The garden out back is in high demand on summer weekends. Mon–Thurs noon–midnight, Fri & Sat noon–1am, Sun noon–11pm.

Salisbury 90 St Martin's Lane ⓤLeicester Square; map p.425. Beautiful old gin palace packed with original features, dark wood, mirrors and glassware in the heart of

---

DRINKING ON A BUDGET

For a break from London's sky-high drink prices check out the sensitively restored Victorian pubs owned by the **Sam Smith's** brewery. Prices are kept low as everything, including spirits and soft drinks, comes from the same brewery; a pint of lager starts at just £2.50. The *Cittie of York*, 22 High Holborn (ⓤChancery Lane; map pp.422–423), or *Ye Olde Cheshire Cheese* at 145 Fleet St (ⓤBlackfriars; map pp.422–423), and *The Princess Louise* at 208 High Holborn (ⓤHolborn; map p.425) all have historical interiors, but there are plenty of others.

Theatreland. Mon–Thurs 11am–11.30pm, Fri & Sat 11am–midnight, Sun noon–10.30pm.

Social 5 Little Portland St ⓣ Oxford Circus; map p.425. Cosy retro bar with booths upstairs and a buzzing club below with DJs playing everything from rock to hip-hop for a truly hedonistic crowd. Mon–Wed noon–midnight, Thurs–Sat noon–1am.

CLUBS

Bethnal Green Working Men's Club 42 Pollard Row ⓦ workersplaytime.net; ⓣ Bethnal Green; map pp.422–423. This East End club puts on an eclectic array of events, from cabaret and performance art to themed club nights. Entry from £5. Opening times vary; see website.

Bloomsbury Bowling Lanes Basement of *Tavistock Hotel*, Bedford Way ⓦ bloomsburybowling.com; ⓣ Russell Square; map pp.422–423. Get your glad rags on for subterranean karaoke, bowling, cocktails and dancing, with different nights spinning funk, rockabilly and disco. Mon–Thurs noon–midnight, Fri & Sat noon–2am, Sun noon–11pm.

Cargo 83 Rivington St ⓦ cargo-london.com; ⓣ Old Street; map pp.422–423. Live music bar/club with globally influenced music, trendy crowds and a laidback vibe. Mon–Thurs 6pm–1am, Fri & Sat 6pm–3am, Sun 6pm–midnight.

Fabric 77a Charterhouse St ⓦ fabriclondon.com; ⓣ Farringdon; map pp.422–423. Probably London's most famous club, and one that keeps drawing the crowds despite the hefty entry fee (around £17). Get there early or buy your ticket online to avoid queues. Fri is usually drum 'n' bass and dubstep; Sat & Sun are house, electronica and techno. Fri 10pm–6am, Sat 11pm–8am, Sun 11pm–5am.

Guanabara Parker St ⓦ guanabara.co.uk; ⓣ Holborn; map p.425. Nightly samba, bossa-nova and Latin beats keep the punters on the dancefloor at this fun Brazilian club. Free Mon & Tues; Wed & Thurs £5 after 9pm, Fri £10 after 9pm, Sat £10 after 8pm, Sun £5 after 8pm. Mon–Sat 5pm–2.30am, Sun 5pm–midnight.

Plastic People 147 Curtain Rd ⓦ plasticpeople.co.uk; ⓣ Old Street/Liverpool Street; map pp.422–423. This tiny basement club makes an intimate venue for house, hip-hop, funk and jazz and is many people's first choice for a fun night out in the East End. Entrance £7–10. Thurs around 10pm–2am, Fri & Sat 10pm–4am.

LIVE MUSIC VENUES

100 Club 100 Oxford St ⓦ the100club.co.uk; ⓣ Tottenham Court Rd; map p.425. Historically important venue – the Sex Pistols played here – in a very central location hosting quality new talent. Daily roughly 7.30pm–2am.

Barfly 49 Chalk Farm Rd ⓦ mamacolive.com; ⓣ Camden Town/Chalk Farm; map pp.422–423. Where a large array of punk, rock and indie bands make their debut, with club

nights too. Mon & Thurs 3pm–2am, Tues & Wed 3pm–1am, Fri & Sat 3pm–3am, Sun 3pm–midnight.

Borderline Orange Yard, Manette St ⓦ mamacolive.com; ⓣ Tottenham Court Road; map p.425. Count on this intimate venue for live rock and Americana. Good place to catch new bands. Also weekly rock, pop and indie nights. Mon–Wed 11pm–3am, Thurs–Sat 11pm–4am.

Ronnie Scott's 47 Frith St ⓦ ronniescotts.co.uk; ⓣ Tottenham Court Rd; map p.425. London's most famous jazz club; big-name acts play in the dimly lit, red-velvet downstairs club. Less pricey and great fun is Wed's late-night jam session (from 9.30pm; £5, or £8 after 11pm) in the upstairs bar. Mon–Sat 6pm–3am, Sun 6.30pm–midnight.

South Bank Centre Belvedere Rd, by Waterloo Bridge ⓦ southbankcentre.co.uk; ⓣ Waterloo; map pp.422–423. Vast arts complex, showcasing high-quality music of all genres; it includes the Royal Festival Hall and the Purcell Room, both top classical music venues.

GAY AND LESBIAN NIGHTLIFE

Candy Bar 4 Carlisle St ⓦ candybarsoho.com; ⓣ Tottenham Court Road; map p.425. Lesbian bar/club offering a retro-style cocktail bar-cum-pool room upstairs, and a noisy, beery ground-level cruising area. Different events every night, from live acts to film screenings. Free entry; £5 after 9pm Fri & Sat. Mon & Wed–Sat 4pm–3am, Tues 4–11pm, Sun 4pm–12.30am.

Heaven Under The Arches, Villiers St ⓦ heavennightclub-london.com; ⓣ Charing Cross/Embankment; map p.425. Britain's most popular gay club, this legendary, 2000-capacity club continues to reign supreme. Free entry vouchers on website. Regular club nights Mon & Thurs–Sat; for other events see website.

Ku Bar 30 Lisle St ⓦ ku bar.co.uk; ⓣ Leicester Square/Tottenham Court Rd; map p.425; smaller branch at 25 Frith St. Ever-popular bar over three floors with a huge variety of inventive club nights. Tues is lesbian night. Free entry; £5 after 11pm Fri & Sat. Mon–Sat noon–3am, Sun noon–midnight.

Royal Vauxhall Tavern 372 Kennington Lane ⓦ rvt.org.uk; ⓣ Vauxhall; map pp.422–423. From cabaret to comedy and from bingo to disco, the *RVT* has it all. An international gay institution. Entry around £7. Check website for event times.

ENTERTAINMENT

CINEMAS

BFI Under Waterloo Bridge, South Bank ⓦ bfi.org.uk; ⓣ Waterloo; map pp.422–423. Serious arts cinema showing up to ten different films each day and screening the London Film Festival (Oct) and London Lesbian and Gay Film Festival (late March).

Coronet 103 Notting Hill Gate ⓦ coronet.org; ⓣ Notting

13

CULTURE ON THE CHEAP

Many **theatres** offer student discounts, and have standing, restricted view, or standby tickets available last minute. Try ⓦlastminute.com, who have cheaper tickets for most of the big shows, or there's the TKTS booth in Leicester Square selling half-price tickets (Mon–Sat 9am–7pm, Sun 10.30am–4.30pm) for that day's performances, with tickets also available up to a week in advance. For classical music, between July and September, you can't beat the **Proms** (ⓦbbc.co.uk/proms), the annual classical music festival held at the Royal Albert Hall. Simply queue up a few hours before the performance to get £5 standing tickets.

Hill Gate; map pp.422–423. Dating back to 1898 and with tiered, red-velvet seating, the Coronet has a decrepit but elegant air. Its prices are cheaper than West End cinemas, and tickets cost just £3.50 on Tues (and on Mon for students).

Prince Charles 2–7 Leicester Place ⓦprincecharlescinema .com; ⓣLeicester Square; map p.425. The bargain basement of London's cinemas, with a programme of newish movies, singalong events and cult favourites.

THEATRES

Though dominated by big musicals, there's no shortage of other world-class performances. Another option is theatre pubs, where experimental performances are shown in intimate pub settings before moving on to bigger things. Check out the *Old Red Lion*, 418 St John's St (ⓣAngel; map pp.422–423), the *King's Head*, 115 Upper St (ⓣAngel or Highbury & Islington; map pp.422–423), or the *Hen & Chickens*, 109 St Paul's Rd (ⓣ Highbury & Islington; map pp.422–423).

Coliseum St Martin's Lane ⓦeno.org; ⓣLeicester Square; map p.425. Home to the English National Opera, and more radical and democratic than the Royal Opera House, with opera (in English) and ballet.

Donmar Warehouse 41 Earlham St ⓦdonmar warehouse.com; ⓣCovent Garden; map p.425. Formerly the spiritual home of director Sam Mendes, and the best bet for a central off-West End show. Front-row tickets £10 on Mon when bought two weeks in advance (see website).

Institute of Contemporary Arts (ICA) Nash House, The Mall ⓦica.org.uk; ⓣCharing Cross; map p.425. Set within historic Nash House, the enduringly cutting-edge ICA has several galleries, a theatre and two cinemas, and puts on a varied programme of talks and events.

National Theatre by Waterloo Bridge, South Bank ⓦnationaltheatre.org.uk; ⓣWaterloo; map pp.422–423. The NT has three separate theatres and consistently good productions. With tickets often going on sale at £10, it's no wonder that some performances sell out months in advance. If you haven't booked, ask about discounted day seats or £5 standing tickets.

Royal Court 50–51 Sloane Square ⓦroyalcourttheatre .com; ⓣSloane Square; map pp.422–423. With an emphasis on new work by cutting-edge young writers, this intimate space is a great place to catch emerging talent. All seats £10 on Mon.

Sadler's Wells Rosebery Ave ⓦsadlerswells.com; ⓣAngel; map pp.422–423. London's biggest dance venue puts on a truly varied mix of contemporary dance – from tap to hip-hop – as well as more traditional forms such as ballet and flamenco.

SHOPPING

London's up there with Paris and New York for the sheer variety of its shopping, and there are many stores and boutiques you simply won't find anywhere else. If you're on a budget, window-shopping is still a great way of spending time; better still, visit one of the capital's many markets (see box, p.428). Westfield, the mammoth mall with outlets in west London (ⓣShepherd's Bush) and east London (ⓣStratford and Stratford Overground), has all the big names, both high-end and high-street. For shopping by street, see box opposite.

Harrods Brompton Road ⓣKnightsbridge; map pp.422–423. London's grandest department store and a major tourist attraction; check out the incredible food hall with its Arts and Crafts tiling. Daily 10am–8pm, Sun noon–6pm.

Liberty Great Marlborough Street ⓣOxford Circus; map p.425. Famous for its iconic prints, with jewellery, scarves, bags and designer clothes in opulent surroundings. Mon–Sat 10am–8pm, Sun noon–6pm.

Selfridges Oxford Street ⓣMarble Arch/Bond Street; map pp.422–423. A better bet than Harrods for clothes, Selfridge's is famous for its creative window displays, selling pretty much everything from sushi to stationery. Just off Regent Street is the elegant mock-Tudor branch. Mon–Sat 9.30am–9pm, Sun noon–6pm.

DIRECTORY

Banks and exchange Shopping areas such as Oxford St and Covent Garden are littered with private exchange offices, but their rates are usually worse than the banks. Any post office (see p.420) will exchange money commission-free and any large bank will offer competitive rates.

Embassies Australia, Corner of Aldwych with the Strand ☎020 7379 4334 (ⓣHolborn/Temple); Canada, 1 Grosvenor Square ☎020 7258 6600 (ⓣBond Street), in the next few years due to relocate to Canada House, Trafalgar

13

QUINTESSENTIAL LONDON SHOPPING STREETS

Charing Cross Road A great place to pick up reading material. Rummage in one of the many secondhand bookshops, or browse new titles in Foyles.

Covent Garden Plenty of high-street stores, plus independent fashion outlets around the Neal St area, Floral St, Seven Dials and Long Acre.

Knightsbridge to Sloane Square Every high-end designer has their flagship store near here.

Oxford Street London's most famous and frequented shopping strip, home to gargantuan branches of high-street shops including Topshop, Primark and Nike Town.

Soho and Carnaby Street Seedy Soho is crammed with quirky fashion shops, independent record stores and erotica. At its western boundary, Carnaby Street (⊗carnaby.co.uk) trades heavily on its association with the swinging Sixties, but is still a good bet for cool trainers and young fashion.

Square (opposite National Gallery); Ireland, 17 Grosvenor Place ☎020 7235 2171 (⊕Hyde Park Corner); New Zealand, 80 Haymarket ☎020 7930 8422 (⊕Piccadilly Circus); South Africa, South Africa House, Trafalgar Square ☎020 7451 7299 (⊕Charing Cross); United States, 24 Grosvenor Square (☎020 7499 9000); ⊕Bond Street.

Hospitals St Mary's Hospital, Praed St (☎020 3312 6666; ⊕Paddington); University College Hospital, 235 Euston Rd (☎0845 1555 000); ⊕Euston Square or Warren Street).

Internet There's a 24hr internet café at 11 Charing Cross Rd (£1/hr).

Left luggage At all airport terminals and major train stations.

Pharmacy Boots at Piccadilly Circus is open until midnight (6pm on Sun), or Zafash at 233 Old Brompton Rd is 24hr (⊕Earls Court).

Post office 24 William IV St (Mon & Wed–Fri 8.30am–6.30pm, Tues 9.15am–6.30pm, Sat 9am–5.30pm; ⊕Leicester Square/Charing Cross).

Southeast England

Nestling in self-satisfied prosperity, **southeast England** is the richest part of Britain. Swift, frequent rail and coach services make it ideal for **day-trips** from London. The medieval ecclesiastical power base of **Canterbury** is full of history, while on the coast the upbeat, hedonistic resort of **Brighton** is London's summer playground by the sea.

DOVER

DOVER is the main port of entry along this stretch of coast, and the country's busiest. **Ferries** sail to Calais and Dunkirk from the Eastern Docks.

ARRIVAL AND INFORMATION

By train The main train station is Dover Priory, a 10min walk west of the centre and served by shuttle buses from the Eastern Docks.

Destinations Canterbury (2 hourly; 16–27min) and London (2 hourly; 1–2hr).

By bus Coaches to London pick up from both the docks and the town-centre bus station on Pencester Road.

Destinations London (hourly; 2hr 30min–3hr 20min).

Tourist information The tourist office is in Dover Museum, Market Square (daily 9.30/10am–3/5pm; Oct–March closed Sun; ☎01304 201066, ⊗whitecliffscountry.org.uk).

CANTERBURY

CANTERBURY, still home to England's pre-eminent Archbishop, was one of medieval Europe's hottest pilgrimage destinations, as Chaucer's *Canterbury Tales* attest. Pilgrims flocked to the shrine of Archbishop Thomas à Becket, who was brutally murdered in the cathedral nave in 1170, victim of an unseemly spat between Church and State. Enclosed on three sides by medieval walls, quaint Canterbury now hosts a sizeable student population and great food and shopping options, but the main draw for visitors is still the towering edifice of the cathedral.

WHAT TO SEE AND DO

Built in stages from 1070 onwards, **Canterbury Cathedral** (Mon–Sat 9am–5.30pm, crypt opens 10am, Sun 12.30–2.30pm; ⊗canterbury-cathedral .org; £9.50) derives its distinctive

13

presence from the perpendicular thrust of its late Gothic towers, dominated by the central, sixteenth-century Bell Harry tower. In the northwest transept, a modern sculpture, portraying ragged swords, is suspended over the place where Becket met his violent end. You'll also want to see the Romanesque arches of the crypt, one of the few remaining visible relics of the Norman cathedral with religious murals dating back to the eleventh century.

East of the cathedral, across the ring road, are the evocative ruins of **St Augustine's Abbey** (April–Sept daily 10am–6pm; Oct Wed–Sun 10am–5pm; Nov–March Sat & Sun 10am–4pm; £5), on the site of a church founded by St Augustine, who began the conversion of the English in 597.

The best exposition of local history is provided by the **Beaney House of Art & Knowledge**, 18 High St (Mon–Wed, Fri & Sat 9am–5pm, Thurs 9am–7pm, Sun 10am–5pm; free; ⓦcanterbury.co.uk), which also has an array of exhibition galleries on subjects as diverse as ancient Greek art and Dutch stained glass, plus paintings from the seventeenth century onwards.

ARRIVAL AND DEPARTURE

By train Canterbury has two train stations: Canterbury East for most services from London Victoria and Dover Priory, and Canterbury West for services from London Charing Cross via Waterloo East and London Bridge, as well as high-speed trains from St Pancras – the stations are 10min south and northwest of the centre respectively.

Destinations Brighton (change at Ashford International; hourly; 2hr 15min); Dover (every 30min; 30min); London St Pancras (hourly; 1hr); London Victoria (every 30min; 1hr 35min); London Charing Cross via Waterloo East and London Bridge (every 30min; 1hr 40min).

By bus The bus station is at St George's Lane, below the High St.

Destinations Dover (hourly; 40min); London (hourly; 2hr).

INFORMATION

Tourist information The tourist office is located in the Beaney (see above; same hours; ☎01227 378100).

Internet *La Trappiste*, a café and restaurant at 1 Sun St (daily 8am–11pm), offers free internet to customers.

ACCOMMODATION

★ **Arthouse B&B** 24 London Rd ☎01227 453032, ⓦarthousebandb.com. A 10min walk from the centre, this unique arty, 2-room B&B in an old fire station makes up with character what it lacks in quantity. Double **£60**

Kipps Canterbury 40 Nunnery Fields ☎01227 786121, ⓦkipps-hostel.com. Homely independent hostel near Canterbury East station and an easy walk to the centre. There's a communal kitchen, free wi-fi and a garden with pool table. Dorm **£19.50**, double **£66**

EATING AND DRINKING

Canterbury can be an expensive town for food if you're trying to avoid the chain restaurants, with some surprisingly upmarket places, but there are some excellent budget finds tucked away.

Boho Café 27 High St. Stylishly furnished with retro collectables, and with a cute garden out back, *Boho* is good for delicious breakfasts, generous sandwiches (around £5), fish dishes and home-made burgers. Mon 9am–5pm, Tues–Sat 9am–9pm, Sun 10am–5pm.

The Dolphin 17 St Radigund's St. Chilled-out, slightly shabby pub with a roaring fire in winter and a sun-trap garden in summer, plus a good range of local ales and simple pub food. Mon–Sat noon–11.30pm/12.30am, Sun noon–10.30pm.

★ **The Farmhouse** 11 Dover St ☎01227 456118, ⓦthefarmhousecanterbury.co.uk. Trendy but relaxed bar-restaurant with 1950s furniture and a retro jukebox serving pricey Modern British cuisine all day, as well as a slap-up breakfast (£5 for the works; daily except Mon). Live music and DJs at weekends (small entry fee). It also puts on club nights and live music, focusing on indie and folk. Tues–Thurs 9am–11pm, Fri & Sat 9am–2am, Sun 11am–5pm.

★ **Goods Shed** Canterbury West station. Top-notch local picnic ingredients and cheap lunch specials in this atmospheric café and farmers' market. Head for *Patrick's Kitchen* – a gourmet takeaway stall – for delicious sausage rolls (70p). Tues–Sat 9am–7pm, Sun till 4pm.

BRIGHTON

BRIGHTON has been a magnet for day-tripping Londoners since the Prince Regent (later George IV) started holidaying here in the 1770s with his mistress, launching a trend for the "dirty weekend". One of Britain's most entertaining seaside resorts, the city has emerged from seediness to embrace a new, fashionable hedonism, becoming one of the country's gay centres. This

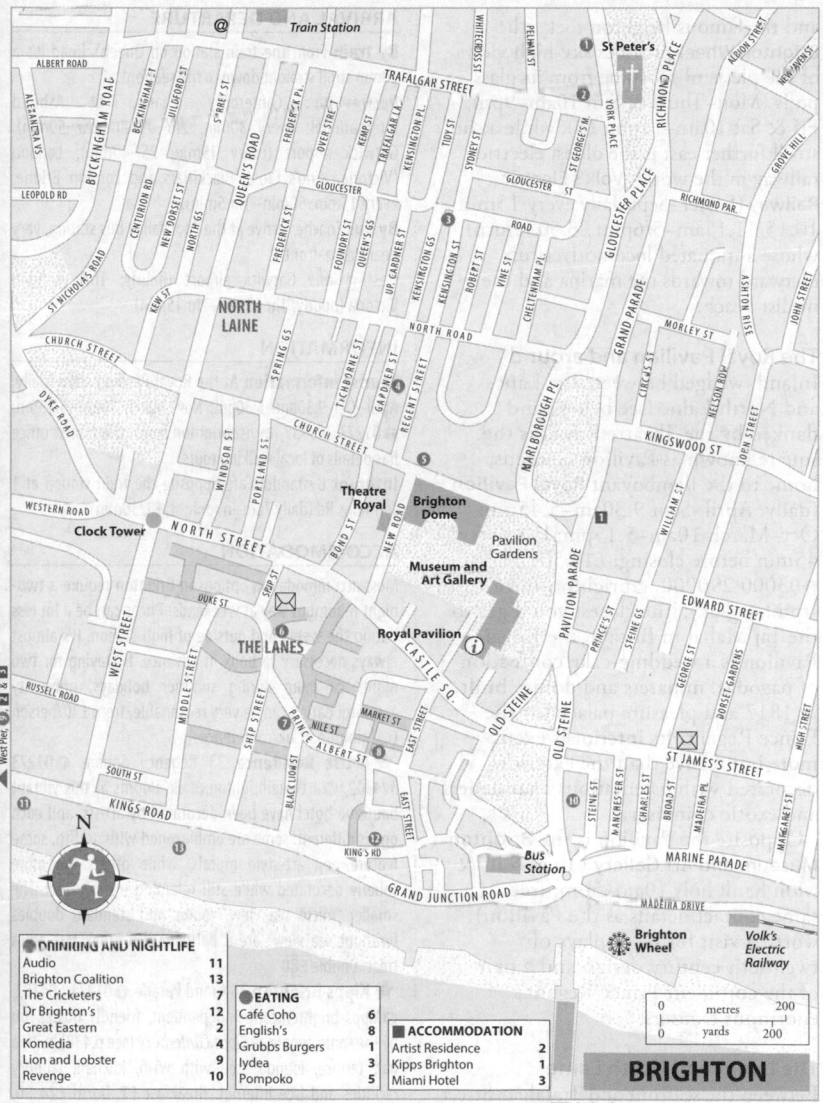

BRIGHTON

▼ Brighton Pier

factor – along with a large student presence – has endowed Brighton with a buzzing nightlife scene, and there's a colourful music and arts festival (⊚brightonfestival.org), which runs for three weeks in May.

WHAT TO SEE AND DO

Most people head straight for the beach, a four-mile-long stretch of pebbles bordered by a balustraded promenade. Brighton's cultural attractions and the shops and cafés of The Lanes are a short stroll from here.

The seafront

The wonderfully tacky half-mile-long **Brighton Pier** is an obligatory call; it's a huge amusement arcade, peppered with booths selling fish and chips, candyfloss

13

and the famous Brighton rock. The **Brighton Wheel** provides sky-high views of the pier and coastline from its glass pods (Mon–Thurs & Sun 10am–9pm, Fri & Sat 10am–11pm; £8), while a short stroll further east is the oldest electric railway in the world, **Volk's Electric Railway** (Easter–Sept daily every 15min, 10.15/11.15am–5/6pm; £3.50 return), whose antiquated locomotives run eastward towards the marina and the nudist beach.

The Royal Pavilion and around

Inland, wedged between The Lanes and North Laine (see below) and flanked by the Theatre Royal, is the square known as Pavilion Gardens, home to the flamboyant **Royal Pavilion** (daily: April–Sept 9.30am–5.45pm; Oct–March 10am–5.15pm; last entry 45min before closing; £10.50; ☎03000 290900, ⓦbrighton-hove -rpml.org.uk). The closest you'll get to the Taj Mahal in Britain, the Royal Pavilion is a wedding-cake confection of pagodas, minarets and domes built in 1817 as a pleasure palace for the Prince Regent. Its interior is even more impressive than the exterior, decorated with ostentatious chandeliers and exotic chinoiserie.

Opposite the Pavilion is the **Brighton Museum and Art Gallery** (Tues–Sun & Mon bank hols 10am–5pm; free; same contact details as the Pavilion), worth a visit for its displays of twentieth-century design and a pair of the corpulent Prince Regent's enormous trousers.

The Lanes and North Laine

Between the seafront and Trafalgar Street lie Brighton's "lanes", offering some of the UK's best shopping. The narrow alleys of **The Lanes** preserve the layout of the fishing port that Brighton once was, while to the north the arty, bohemian quarter of **North Laine** is not in fact one road but many thin streets. Both are packed with stalls, independent secondhand clothes-, record- and bookshops, quirky boutiques and cosy coffeehouses.

ARRIVAL AND DEPARTURE

By train From the train station on Queen's Road it's a 10min stroll straight down to the seafront.

Destinations Canterbury (change at Ashford International; every 30min; 2hr 25min–2hr 50min); Gatwick airport (every 15min; 25–40min); London (Victoria, King's Cross, Blackfriars and London Bridge; every 15min; 50min–1hr 5min).

By bus Coaches arrive at the Pool Valley bus station, very near the seafront.

Destinations Gatwick airport (hourly; 1hr); London Victoria (hourly; 1hr 50min–2hr 15min).

INFORMATION

Tourist information At the Royal Pavilion shop (daily: April–Oct 9.30am–5.30pm; Nov–March 10am–5.15pm; ☎01273 290337, ⓦvisitbrighton.com), the tourist office has details of local walking tours.

Internet Bystander Café opposite the train station at 1 Terminus Rd (daily 7am–midnight; £1/30min).

ACCOMMODATION

Most accommodation options in Brighton require a two-night minimum stay at weekends. Prices can be a lot less during the week, and outside of high season. It's almost always necessary to book in advance. If staying for two nights or more during summer holidays, university accommodation can be very reasonable, from £30/person (ⓦbrighton.ac.uk/conferences).

★ **Artist Residence** 33 Regency Square ☎01273 324302, ⓦarthotelbrighton.co.uk. Rooms at this vibrant boutique hotel have been decorated by artists, and each one is different: some are emblazoned with graffiti, some feature pop art-style murals, while others are more soberly decorated while still retaining an arty feel. The smaller "micro sea view" rooms and standard doubles (without sea view) are a bargain, and breakfasts are a treat. Double £80

★ **Kipps Brighton** 76 Grand Parade ☎01273 604182, ⓦkipps-brighton.com. Independent, friendly hostel run by the same people as Kipps Canterbury (see p.438), with a bar, terrace, lounge area with wi-fi, kitchen, laundry facilities and free internet. Breakfast £1. Dorm £24.50, double £80

Miami Hotel 22 Bedford Square ☎01273 778701, ⓦthemiamihotel.co.uk. Despite the unpromising name, this is a handsome grade II-listed regency townhouse just a short stroll from the beach and town centre. The rooms are spotless (some with sea views and balconies), and attached kitchenettes allow you to self-cater too. Double £45

EATING

Café Coho 53 Ship St. This bijou café with a handful of outdoor tables is a great spot for people-watching in The

★ TREAT YOURSELF

English's 29–31 East St ☎01273 327980. Superior seafood in appealingly old-school surroundings. The two-course set menu is great value at £14.95, with dishes such as mussels steamed in cider followed by haddock in a pesto crust: worth missing breakfast and lunch for. Daily noon–10pm.

Lanes. It does posh overstuffed sandwiches (bacon, brie and cranberry £4.25), as well as delicious cakes and coffee. Mon–Fri 8am–6pm, Sat & Sun 9am–6pm.

Grubbs Burgers 13 York Place & 89 St James' St. This Brighton micro-chain is legendary for its succulent burgers, with around 15 inventive combos, including, surprisingly, many vegetarian options. Burger and fries/wedges £5. Daily noon–midnight/1am.

★ Iydea 17 Kensington Gardens. Veggie café with an emphasis on quick eats and friendly service; expect delicious globally influenced mains (£4.70–7.70 including two sides), tempting breakfasts, as well as cakes, salads, smoothies and organic beer and wine. Daily 9/9.30am–5.30pm.

Pompoko 110 Church St. Extremely popular no-frills Japanese with speedy service and tasty rice dishes such as sweet and sour prawns (£4.60), with everything on the menu under £5. Daily 11.30am–11pm.

DRINKING AND NIGHTLIFE

Packed with bars, pubs and clubs, Brighton's frenetic nightlife can compete with that of many larger cities. For full listings, pick up a copy of *The Brighton Magazine* or check out ⓦ brighton.co.uk. Brighton has a lively gay scene; check out the free listings magazine *3Sixty*.

PUBS

★ The Cricketers 15 Black Lion St. This historic pub – Brighton's oldest – was immortalized by Graham Greene in the classic *Brighton Rock*, and its cosy, rich-red interior with plenty of hidden nooks has changed little since. A good selection of ales, and the food's good too (sandwiches with fries £7.25). Mon–Fri 11am–midnight, Sat & Sun 11am–2am.

Dr Brighton's 16 Kings Rd. Friendly gay pub on the seafront, popular with all ages. On Mon, Tues, Thurs & Sun the happy hour lasts all day. Mon–Thurs 1pm–midnight, Fri & Sat 1pm–2am, Sun 1–11pm.

Great Eastern 103 Trafalgar St. A tiny, 150-year-old traditional pub, serving over 60 American whiskies. Live music on Thurs and DJs every other Fri/Sat, as well as traditional roast lunches on Sun. Mon–Thurs & Sun noon–midnight, Fri & Sat noon–1am.

★ Lion and Lobster 24 Silwood St. A classic pub serving excellent food in rambling dining quarters (book at weekends), and a two-storey outdoor terrace. Burger and fries £9. Mon–Thurs 11am–1am, Fri & Sat 11am–2am, Sun noon–midnight.

CLUBS AND LIVE MUSIC VENUES

Audio 10 Marine Parade ⓦ audiobrighton.com. "A clubber's club", it proclaims on its website, and one of Brighton's best; draws some big-name acts and DJs from all genres. Bar Mon–Fri 4pm–2/3am, Sat & Sun 2pm–2/3am; club Tues–Thurs 11pm–3am, Fri & Sat 11am–4am.

Brighton Coalition 171–181 Kings Rd Arches ⓦ drinkinbrighton.co.uk/coalition. Right on the seafront, this club puts on a range of events, from club nights to karaoke. Thurs hosts *Secret Discotheque*, dedicated to pop, with cheap drinks and popular with students. Daily 10pm–late.

Komedia 44 Gardner St ⓦ komedia.co.uk. Cool venue offering everything from cabaret and comedy to rock gigs, club nights and spoken word. Live music nights vary 7.30–11pm; club nights Fri & Sat 11pm–3am; comedy Thurs, Fri & Sun 8–10.30pm, Sat 7–9.30pm & 11pm–1.30am.

Revenge 32 Old Steine ⓦ revenge.co.uk. Brighton's biggest gay club is a three-floor affair, including a roof terrace, with a cheesy soundtrack. Bar Mon–Wed & Sun noon–1am, Thurs 9pm–1am, Fri & Sat noon–6am; club Tues–Sat 10.30pm–5am.

The West Country

England's **West Country** is not a precise geographical term, but as a broad generalization, the cosmopolitan feel of the southeast begins to fade into a slower, rural pace of life from **Salisbury** onwards, becoming more pronounced the further west you travel. In Neolithic times a rich and powerful culture evolved here, shown by monuments such as **Stonehenge** and **Avebury**. Urban attractions include vibrant **Bristol** and the elegant Regency spa town of **Bath**, while those in search of rural peace and quiet should head for the compelling bleakness and ancient woods of **Dartmoor**. The southwestern extremities of Britain include some of the country's most beautiful stretches of coastline: with rugged, rocky shores and

13

excellent white sandy beaches, **Cornwall** is one of Britain's busiest corners over the summer.

SALISBURY

Modern **SALISBURY** was founded after clergy living in the fort at **Old Sarum**, two miles north of the city, moved down the valley and created a walled sanctuary and the magnificent cathedral at the site where five rivers meet. Unlike most British towns, the centre follows a grid pattern, so it is easy to find your way from the train station off Fisherton Street east over the River Avon to the bus station and Market Square (market on Tues & Sat), or to the Cathedral south down the High Street through North Gate.

WHAT TO SEE AND DO

The city's dominant feature is the elegant spire of its **cathedral** (Mon–Sat 9am–5pm, Sun noon–4pm; £6.50 includes 45min tour or £10 for 1hr 30min tour including spire; ⊕salisburycathedral.org.uk), the tallest in the country, rising over 400ft. The cathedral was almost entirely completed in the thirteenth century. Don't miss the world's oldest working clock, dating to 1386, which resides in the north aisle. A lofty octagonal **chapterhouse**, approached via the cloisters (Mon–Sat 9.30/10am–4.30pm, Sun 12.45–3.45pm; free), holds one of the four extant copies of the 1215 **Magna Carta**, England's most famous constitutional document, as well as one of the finest medieval friezes in Europe depicting famous Old Testament stories.

Most of Salisbury's remaining sights are grouped in a sequence of graceful historic houses around **Cathedral Close**. The **Salisbury and South Wiltshire Museum** on West Walk (Mon–Sat 10am–5pm; June–Sept also Sun noon–5pm; £6; ⊕salisburymuseum.org .uk) is a good place to bone up on the Neolithic history of the region before heading out to Stonehenge.

ARRIVAL AND DEPARTURE

By train The station is on the northwest edge of town, a 10min walk to the cathedral or a 30min stroll through town to *Salisbury YHA*.

Destinations Bath (every 30–40min; 55min–1hr 5min); Bristol (every 30–40min; 1hr 10min–1hr 50min); Exeter (for Dartmoor; hourly; 1hr 55min–2hr 10min); London (every 30min; 1hr 30min).
By bus Buses terminate behind Endless St, a short walk northeast of the cathedral.
Destinations Bath (1 daily; 1hr 20min); Bristol (1 daily; 2hr 10min); London (3 daily; 3hr 10min–3hr 30min).

INFORMATION

Tourist information Tourist office on Fish Row, just off Market Square (Mon–Fri 9am–5pm, Sat 10am–3/4pm, Sun 10am–2pm; ☎01722 342860, ⊕visitwiltshire.co.uk).

ACCOMMODATION

Alderbury Caravan & Camping Park Southampton Rd, Whaddon ☎01722 710125, ⊕alderburycaravanpark .co.uk; bus #X7. Three miles south of Salisbury, this pleasant and friendly campsite is easily reached from the city centre (15min). Camping **£6.50** per person and tent
Salisbury YHA Milford Hill House, Milford Hill ☎0845 371 9537, ⊕yha.org.uk. Excellent hostel in a historic house, just 10min walk east of the city centre in a secluded setting. Dorm **£22.50**, double **£57**

EATING AND DRINKING

★ **Gallery Café at Fisherton Mill** 108 Fisherton St. Fantastic café-cum-art-and-craft gallery where you'll likely get a great stone-baked bread sandwich (£5.60) as watch sculptors or milliners at their craft. Tues–Fri 10am–5pm, Sat 9.30am–5pm.
★ **Haunch of Venison** 1 Minster St. Tiny, atmospheric old pub supposedly home to the ghost of the "Demented Whist Player", whose amputated mummified hand resides in a nook in a side room as a warning to card game cheats everywhere. Also boasts an outstanding whisky selection. Mon–Sat 11am–11pm, Sun noon–11pm.

STONEHENGE AND AVEBURY

In deepest darkest Wiltshire, between Salisbury and Bath, the countryside was once home to a thriving Neolithic civilization, the greatest legacy of which is **Stonehenge** (daily: mid-March to April, May & Sept to mid-Oct 9.30am–6pm; June–Aug 9am–7pm; mid-Oct to mid-March 9.30am–4pm; last admission 30min before closing; £8). Built in several distinct stages and adapted to the needs of successive cultures, the first stones were raised about 3500 BC and during the next six hundred years, the incomplete blue-stone circle was transformed into the familiar formation observed today. The way in which the sun's rays penetrate the enclosure at dawn on midsummer's day has led to speculation about Stonehenge's role as either an astronomical observatory or a place of sun worship. During normal visiting hours the stones are cordoned off – you see them from about 100m away.

The only way to enter the circle itself is to **pre-book** for entry outside standard visiting hours (£16.30; ☏0870 333 0605, ⓦenglish-heritage.org.uk), or to go on the evening of the summer solstice, when tens of thousands of revellers party at the stones until sunrise (see the website for details). A new visitor centre, due to open 1.5 miles away at Airman's Corner in January 2014, will have displays on the history of the site as well as reconstructed Neolithic huts.

Salisbury also serves as a base for visiting the Neolithic site around thirty miles north at **AVEBURY**. The **stone circles** were probably erected some 4000 years ago, and the main circle – with a diameter of some 1300ft – easily beats Stonehenge in terms of scale. For more on the monoliths, and for a guided tour (1–2 daily; £3) that will make the site come to life, enquire at the two small National Trust **museums** in the village (daily 10/10.30am– 4/6pm; £4.40 for both, £1 off if arriving by public transport).

ARRIVAL AND DEPARTURE

By bus You can get to Stonehenge from Salisbury on the #X5 bus (every 30min–1hr; £6.40 return) to Amesbury, then a two-mile walk. More conveniently, take a hop-on tour bus (every 30min–1hr, 9.30am–5pm; £12). For Avebury, catch the #2 to Devizes from Salisbury bus station, then change for the #49 to Avebury (every 1–2hr; 1hr 30min–2hr). From Bath, try Mad Max tours who'll take you to both sites (daily; £32.50 for a full day; ☏07990 505970, ⓦmadmaxtours.co.uk).

BATH

BATH is surely the prettiest small city in Britain. It became important under the Romans who worshipped at the hot springs, creating the eponymous **baths**, one of Britain's top sights. Revived and reconstructed in the eighteenth century as a retreat for the wealthy and fashionable, the city has a harmonious and elegant look, constructed from the local honey-coloured sandstone and still retaining the genteel air of refinement Jane Austen satirized in her novels *Persuasion* and *Northanger Abbey*. However, the large student population makes this a vibrant place to be and there are numerous festivals throughout the year, such as the eclectic two-week International Music Festival in May and, naturally, the Jane Austen Festival in September, when a regency dress parade takes place. See ⓦvisitbath.co.uk for all festivals.

WHAT TO SEE AND DO

Bounded on three sides by the River Avon, Bath's core is relatively compact. From Bath Spa train station, head north along Manvers Street which becomes Pierrepoint Street in the direction of Pulteney Bridge and turn off left up York Street to reach the Abbey, Roman Baths and tourist office. Carry on winding northwest from the Abbey until you reach Queen Square and walk through Royal Victoria Park to reach the most famous streets in Bath, the Royal Crescent and Royal Circle.

The Roman Baths and Bath Abbey

The Romans considered natural hot springs a gift from the gods, and Bath's, being the only ones in Britain, received very special treatment when they conquered in 43 AD. Hidden underground for years, the springs were rediscovered by the Victorians and made into the wonderfully interactive **Roman Baths museum** (daily: March–June, Sept & Oct 9am–6pm; July & Aug 9am–10pm; Nov–Feb 9.30am–5.30pm; last entry 1hr before closing; £12.75, July & Aug £13.25, combined ticket with Fashion Museum £16.25; ⓦromanbaths .co.uk). Highlights include the almost perfectly preserved bronze head of Minerva, Roman goddess of the sacred spring, a large portion of the decorative front of the Temple that would have stood as part of the bath complex, as well

13

★ **TREAT YOURSELF**

Follow in the footsteps of the Romans and pamper yourself in stylish, contemporary surroundings at **Thermae Bath Spa** (daily 9am–9.30pm; ⍵ thermaebathspa .com), Britain's only natural hot spa. A two-hour session, with access to the spectacular open-air rooftop pool, costs £26.

as the extensive warren of spa rooms. The **Pump Room**, built in the eighteenth century, is now a restaurant and tearoom; the Roman Baths entrance ticket entitles you to a free glass of the tepid ferrous spa water inside.

The Royal Crescent and Assembly Rooms

The best of Bath's eighteenth-century architecture is on the high ground to the north of the town centre, where the well-proportioned Georgian urban planning is showcased by the elegant **Circus** and adjacent **Royal Crescent**. The first house to be built here, no. 1 (Mon noon–5pm, Tues–Sun 10.30am–5pm; £8.50; ⍵ no1royalcrescent.org.uk), has been sumptuously restored to its former glory; you can wander the elegant Georgian rooms above stairs, as well as the original servants' quarters.

Just east of the Circus, the elegant **Assembly Rooms** (daily 10.30am–5/6pm; £2, or included with entry to the Fashion Museum) were the hub of fashionable Georgian society. The building also houses the fascinating **Fashion Museum** (daily: Jan, Feb, Nov & Dec 10.30am–4pm; March–Oct 10.30am–5pm; £7.75 or joint ticket with Roman Baths £16.25; ⍵ museumofcostume.co.uk).

The Holburne Museum

A ten-minute walk from the centre along Great Pulteney St, the **Holburne Museum** (Mon–Sat 10am–5pm, Sun 11am–5pm; free; ⍵ holburne.org) is an excellent fine-arts collection housed in a stately villa with a bold glass extension. On display are paintings by Gainsborough, who was born in Bath, and his contemporaries Stubbs and Zoffany, as well as some fine Dutch paintings and exquisite small-scale sculptures, ceramics and porcelain.

ARRIVAL AND DEPARTURE

By train Bath Spa train station is on Dorchester St at the end of Manvers St, 5min south of the Abbey.

Destinations Bristol (every 20min; 15–45min); London (every 30min; 1hr 30min); Oxford (change at Didcot Parkway; every 30min–1hr; 1hr 10min–1hr 30min); Salisbury (every 30min–1hr; 55min–1hr 5min).

By bus The bus station is along from the train station on Dorchester St.

Destinations Bristol (every 20min; 1hr); Bristol Airport (hourly; 1hr 15min); Glastonbury (1 direct daily from Bath Spa; 1hr); London (hourly; 2hr 45min–3hr 55min).

INFORMATION

Tourist information The tourist office is just off the Abbey churchyard (Mon–Sat 9.30am–5.30pm, Sun 10am–4pm; ☎ 0906 711 2000, ⍵ visitbath.co.uk). Daily walking tours set off from the Pump Room (10.30am & 2pm; Sat 10.30am only; free, 2hr).

Internet @Internet, 13 Manvers St (9am–9pm; £1/20min).

ACCOMMODATION

Bath YHA Bathwick Hill ☎ 0845 371 9303, ⍵ yha.org.uk; bus #18 or #U18. Stunning HI hillside villa a good mile uphill east of town with restaurant and bar. Dorm __£19.50__, double __£44__

Bath YMCA Broad St Place ☎ 01255 325900, ⍵ www .bathymca.co.uk. Large, no-frills hostel in a pretty enclave in the centre of town. Wi-fi and basic breakfast included. Dorm __£21__, double __£60__

University of Bath Claverton Down ☎ 01225 386079, ⍵ bath.ac.uk/accommodation. Simply furnished, great-value en-suite rooms at the university, east of the centre, with hotel-style extras such as free toiletries, tea and coffee; most rooms are available July–Sept but some can be booked all year. Double __£60__

White Hart Inn Widcombe Hill ☎ 01225 313985, ⍵ whitehartbath.co.uk. Well worth the 10min walk from the station, and although it is a bit further out from the centre, this old inn with a restaurant and bar downstairs, plus a little sun-trap garden, offers simple but excellent-value accommodation. Dorm __£15__, double __£40__

EATING, DRINKING AND NIGHTLIFE

★ **The Bell Inn** 103 Walcot St ⍵ thebellinnbath.co.uk. Everything you could want from a neighbourhood pub: a range of beers, a mixed and lively crowd, a garden, live music most days and vinyl DJs at weekends, plus good roasts at weekends and barbecues in summer. Mon–Sat 11.30am–11pm, Sun noon–10.30pm.

Made by Ben 100 Walcot St. Delicious gourmet sandwiches, pies, quiches and cakes. There's a handful of tables out back, or you can take away (quiche with salad £6). Mon–Fri 10am–5pm, Sat 9am–5pm, Sun 11am–4pm.

Moles 14 George St ⓦmoles.co.uk. This popular live-music venue attracts a good mix of bands, and the club nights (Tues–Sat) are a good bet for a fun night out. Tues–Sat 10pm–3/4am.

The Raven 6–7 Queen St ⓦtheravenofbath.co.uk. Not content with its reputation for micro-brewed ales, relaxed atmosphere and evening entertainments like storytelling, this pub also serves up fantastic pies with mash and gravy (£8.80). Mon–Thurs & Sun 11.30am–11pm, Fri & Sat 11.30am–midnight.

★ **Wild Cafe** 10a Queen St. A trendy local favourite for brunch (served all day) with great organic and fairtrade food, low prices and the boast that it is powered by renewable energy. English breakfast £6.95. Mon–Fri 8am–5pm, Sat 9am–6pm, Sun 10am–5pm.

Yak Yeti Yak 12 Pierrepont St ☎01225 443473. Not the cheapest, but you may not get another Nepalese meal this good in Britain; the 3-course set meal is a good deal (£10.50 noon–2pm & before 6.30pm). Booking essential at weekends. Mon–Thurs & Sun noon–2pm & 6–10.30pm, Fri & Sat noon–2pm & 5–10.30pm.

BRISTOL

Situated on a succession of chunky hills twelve miles west of Bath and just inland from the mouth of the River Avon, **BRISTOL** grew rich on transatlantic trade – the slave trade, in particular – in the early part of the nineteenth century. It remains a wealthy, commercial centre, and is home to a population of around 450,000, a major university, a thriving music scene that produced some of the most significant artists of the Nineties (Portishead, Tricky, Massive Attack), and Banksy – guerrilla artist and *agent provocateur* whose subversive stencils adorn neglected city walls throughout the world. More ethnically diverse than other cities in the Southwest, Bristol manages to combine clued-up arty urban culture with enticing green spaces and striking industrial architecture. In August, the city hosts Europe's largest hot-air balloon fiesta – a spectacular sight.

WHAT TO SEE AND DO

The city centre is an elongated traffic interchange, known as the **Centre Promenade**. Walking from the station, detour via the church of **St Mary Redcliffe** (Mon–Sat 8.30am–5pm, Sun 8am–8pm; donation expected), a glorious Gothic confection begun in the thirteenth century, before continuing across the river, through elegant Queen's Square. The southern end of the centre gives way to the city's **Floating Harbour**, an area of waterways that formed the hub of the old port. It is now the location of numerous bars and restaurants as well as **M Shed** (Tues–Sun 10am–5/6pm; free), a museum dedicated to the city's history, with engaging, interactive exhibits, and two of Bristol's contemporary arts venues: the **Arnolfini** (ⓦarnolfini.org.uk; free), a cool, white gallery and performing arts space, and the **Watershed** (ⓦwatershed .co.uk), a cinema complex with an excellent café. Just north of here, **College Green** is overlooked by the city's Gothic Revival **cathedral** and the curvaceous red-brick Council House. A short walk west along the southern side of the harbour, or a brief ride on the ferry (£1.50; 10min), brings you to Isambard Kingdom Brunel's majestic **SS Great Britain** (daily 10am–4.30/5.30pm; £12.95; ⓦssgreatbritain.org), the world's first propeller-driven iron ship, which first launched from here in 1843.

Stokes Croft

The main road leading north from the centre, **Stokes Croft**, has become the city's cultural pulse as artists and creative types have turned what was until recently a grotty road littered with derelict buildings into a buzzing and fashionable part of the city with an array of vintage shops, cool cafés and street art.

Clifton

Reached by bus #8 from the Centre Promenade, genteel **Clifton Village** is a great place to wander, with airy terraces, enticing pubs and upmarket antiques shops. Overhanging the limestone abyss of the Avon Gorge is the **Clifton Suspension Bridge**, another creation of the indefatigable engineer Brunel. From the Clifton side of the Suspension Bridge, **the Downs**, the city's largest green space,

13

stretches north for a couple of miles. On the way back down to the centre, don't miss the **City Museum and Art Gallery** (daily 10am–5/6pm; free; ⊛bristol.gov .uk/museums), home to Banksy's controversial *Paint Pot Angel* sculpture.

ARRIVAL AND DEPARTURE

By plane Bristol airport is eight miles south of town. Regular buses run to the stations and the city centre (30min), as well as to Bath (1hr 15min).

By train The main station, Bristol Temple Meads, is a 5min bus ride southeast of the centre (bus #8 or #9), or a 15min walk.

Destinations Bath (every 10–30min; 11–14min); Cardiff (every 20min; 40min–1hr); Exeter for Dartmoor (every 30min; 1hr–1hr 50min); Penzance (5 daily; 4hr 15min); Oxford via Reading or Didcot Parkway (every 30min; 1hr–1hr 30min); Salisbury (every 30min–1hr; 1hr 10min); York (hourly; 4hr).

By bus Close to the Broadmead shopping centre on Marlborough St.

Destinations Bath (every 20min; 1hr); Cardiff (every 1–2hr; 1hr 10min); Glastonbury (some via Wells; every 30min; 1hr 20min); Oxford (1 daily; 2hr 50min); Penzance (6 daily; 5hr 50min–8hr); Salisbury (1 daily; 2hr 10min).

INFORMATION

Tourist information Tourist office at E Shed, Canons Rd, just off Centre Promenade on the water (Mon–Fri & Sun 11am–4pm, Sat 10am–4pm; ☎0906 7112191, ⊛visitbristol.co.uk). Website has a useful "Free days out" section including downloadable audio walking tours; the tourist office sells tickets for tours of the city's street art (2hr; £7.50 per person).

Internet *Bristol YHA* (see below) has a pleasant café with internet access (£3/hr).

ACCOMMODATION

Bristol Backpackers 17 St Stephen's St ☎0117 9257900, ⊛bristolbackpackers.co.uk (bookings by phone only). Loud, convivial place in the heart of the centre, with friendly staff, a late bar and internet access. Dorms are clean and spacious. Dorm £16, double £38

Bristol YHA 14 Narrow Quay ☎0845 3719726, ⊛yha .org.uk. This splendidly situated hostel is set in an old wharfside building – a former grain house – next to the Arnolfini. The rooms are clean and tidy and the staff are keen to help. Internet costs extra. Dorm £20, double £48

Clifton House 4 Tyndall's Park Rd ☎0117 9735407, ⊛cliftonhousebristol.com. Boutique B&B in a Victorian villa in Clifton, behind the museum, offering en-suite triple and quad rooms with a luxurious feel. Full English breakfast included. Double £75

EATING

Boston Tea Party 75 Park St, 156 Cheltenham Rd, 97 Whiteladies Rd & 1 Princess Victoria St, Clifton. Chain of cafés dotted around the Southwest, each with its own personality and an emphasis on locally sourced produce. Cooked breakfast £6.50. Mon–Sat 7/7.30am–7/8pm, Sun 8/9am–7pm.

★ **Canteen** 80 Stokes Croft. In a refurbished 1960s office block, this cooperative-run bar with restaurant serves subsidized delicacies such as mussels in white wine for just £7. Plus live alternative music for all tastes in the evening. Music starts around 9.30pm or from 4pm Sun. Mon–Thurs & Sun 10am–midnight, Fri & Sat 10am–1am.

Mud Dock 40 The Grove. Bike shed café-restaurant on the quayside, with dishes such as spinach and feta omelette on the £5 weekday lunch menu and great views from their balcony over the water. Mon 10am–5pm, Tues–Fri & Sun 10am–10pm, Sat 9am–10pm.

No. 1 Harbourside 1 Canon's Rd. The sister venue to *Canteen*, next to the tourist office, serves similarly fantastic and cheap food (mains from £6), with live music Wed & Thurs from 9.30pm, Fri & Sat from 11pm, and a craft market Sat & Sun 11am–4pm. Mon–Thurs & Sun 10am–midnight, Fri & Sat 10am–2am.

St Nicolas' Market Corn St. For a budget meal on the go, try this great market, with a huge array of local and ethnic food stalls. Mon–Sat 9.30am–5pm.

★ **Thali Cafe** 12 York Rd, Montpelier, 1 Regents St, Clifton, & 1 William St, across the river from Temple Meads. Colourful mini-chain of Bristol Indian restaurants serving up a fantastic range of street food and thalis on the cheap (£8.50). Clifton daily noon–10/10.30pm; Montpelier Mon–Fri 6–11pm, Sat & Sun 10am–11pm; William St daily 6–11pm.

DRINKING, NIGHTLIFE AND ENTERTAINMENT

For nightlife and music listings check out the magazine *Venue* (⊛venue.co.uk), available at any newsagent.

Apple Welsh Back, at the end of King St. A fantastic array of West Country ciders, cider cocktails and snacks such as sausage rolls (£2.95), all served on a floating canal boat on the harbour. Mon–Sat noon–midnight, Sun noon–10.30pm.

Coronation Tap 8 Sion Place. A Clifton institution overlooking the Suspension Bridge, this pub is famous for its Exhibition Cider, a lethal brew restricted to half-pint measures. Mon–Fri 5.30–11pm, Sat & Sun 7–11pm.

Lakota 6 Upper York St, Stokes Croft ⊛lakota.co.uk. Bristol's biggest and most famous club, three-storey *Lakota* is popular with hardcore ravers for its dedication to underground dance music; nights vary from drum 'n' bass to dubstep to house. The monthly, trance-oriented *Tribe of Frog* night is legendary. Hours vary; check website.

13

GLASTONBURY FESTIVAL

The world-famous **Glastonbury Festival** (ⓦglastonburyfestivals.co.uk), held annually over the last weekend in June, is one of the West Country's biggest draws. When first hosted in 1970, this small-scale event cost £1, but nowadays it draws 175,000-plus people to its binge of music and hedonism – the tickets (£205 plus booking fees) sell out in hours. The cost may be exorbitant, but there's still nothing else quite like it.

Old Vic King St ⓣ0117 9877877, ⓦbristololdvic.org.uk. Britain's longest continuously running theatre has recently undergone a state-of-the-art refurbishment and now offers several diverse performance spaces.

★ **Start The Bus** 7–9 Baldwin St ⓦstartthebus.tv. A buzzing live music bar with local art on the walls, delicious diner-style food (2 for 1 burgers on Tues) and a happy crowd. Mon–Wed & Sun noon–1am, Thurs noon–2am, Fri & Sat noon–3am.

★ **Thekla** The Grove, East Mud Dock ⓦtheklabristol .co.uk. Legendary riverboat venue staging eclectic events, gigs and Bristol's best club nights. Gig times vary, club nights Thurs–Sat 9.30/10pm–3/4am.

DARTMOOR

DARTMOOR, an expanse of uplands some 75 miles southwest of Bristol, is one of England's most beautiful wilderness areas. It's home to an indigenous breed of **wild pony** and dotted with **tors**, natural outcrops of granite. The area is renowned for outdoor pursuits, from cycling and horseriding to canoeing and climbing. Don't go unprepared, especially if you plan to camp, as the moor has an unforgiving weather system and explorers regularly get lost in its thick fogs. The northern part of the moor is more easily accessible from Exeter while the southern moor is best approached from Plymouth.

Okehampton

The wildest parts of the moor, around its highest points of **High Willhays** and **Yes Tor** (which at over 2000ft are classified them as southern England's only mountains), are a few miles south of the market town of **OKEHAMPTON**, served by regular buses from Plymouth and Exeter. Some of the starkly beautiful terrain around here is used by the Ministry of Defence as a firing range. The excellent, if petite, **Museum of Dartmoor Life** is at 3 West St (Easter–Dec Mon–Fri

10.15am–4.15pm, Sat 10.15am–1pm; £2.50; ⓣ01837 52295, ⓦmuseumofdartmoorlife.org.uk).

ARRIVAL AND INFORMATION

By train and bus There are train stations at Exeter, Newton Abbot, Totnes, Ivybridge and Plymouth; buses run from these towns onto the moor. The Haytor Hoppa bus runs on Sat (May–Oct 4 daily) from Newton Abbot or Bovey Tracey (both serviced by frequent buses from Exeter) up to the northeast corner of the moor.

Tourist information Tourist office located off Fore Street, Okehampton (summer Mon–Sat 10am–5pm; winter Mon, Fri & Sat 10am–4.30pm; ⓣ01837 53020, ⓦokehamptondevon.co.uk).

Visitor centres There are three visitor centres (all April–Sept daily 10am–5pm, reduced hours Thurs–Sun in winter) in the park: Haytor information centre (ⓣ01364 661520); Postbridge information centre (ⓣ01822 880272); and the main High Moorland Visitor Centre in Princetown (ⓣ01822 890414).

Websites Check out ⓦwww.dartmoor-npa.gov.uk (with free downloadable walks) to help plan your trip; MOD website ⓦwww.access.mod.uk gives details of times when it's safe to walk the moor.

ACCOMMODATION

★ **Sparrowhawk Backpackers** 45 Ford St, Moretonhampstead ⓣ01647 440318, ⓦsparrowhawk backpackers.co.uk. A converted barn with a dorm in the old hayloft, plus comfortable if basic private rooms. There's a relaxing communal area including a large kitchen and a sunny courtyard. Dorm __£17__, double __£38__

CAMPING ON DARTMOOR

Camping wild on certain common land in Dartmoor is permitted for one or two nights, though you shouldn't pitch on farmland, within 100m of a road, house or on an archeological site; check out ⓦwww.dartmoor-npa.gov.uk/visiting /active-dartmoor/camping for a helpful map. Always obtain consent from the landowner if pitching on private land and follow the backpacking code of conduct.

13

YHA Dartmoor Bellever ☎ 0845 371 9622, ⓦ yha.org.uk. This remote and cosy *YHA* hostel, a mile south of Postbridge, makes a great base for local circular walks. There are basic bunks in the dorms upstairs and a social area with books and games downstairs. Small discount for arrival on foot/bike. Dorm **£18**

YHA Okehampton Klondyke Rd ☎ 01837 53916, ⓦ yha .org.uk. There's a *YHA* hostel and activity centre in a converted goods shed at Okehampton station. On-site restaurant. Dorm **£24**, camping **£10.50** per person and tent

PENZANCE AND AROUND

The busy market and port town of **PENZANCE** forms the natural gateway to the westernmost extremity of Cornwall, the Penwith Peninsula, and has the best transport links – all the major sights in the region can be reached on day-trips from here.

WHAT TO SEE AND DO

Although Penzance itself makes a pleasant base, the real attractions are a bus ride away along the coast.

St Michael's Mount

The view east across the bay is dominated by **St Michael's Mount** (ⓦ stmichaels mount.co.uk), site of a fortified medieval monastery perched on an offshore pinnacle of rock. At low tide, the Mount is joined by a cobbled causeway to the mainland village of Marazion (regular buses from Penzance); at high tide, a boat can ferry you over (£2 each way). You can amble partway along the Mount's shoreline, but most of the rock lies within the grounds of the **castle**, now a stately home (April–Oct Mon–Fri & Sun 10.30am–5pm; £7.60).

The Minack Theatre

Clinging to a craggy cove near Porthcurno beach, seven miles west of Penzance, the **Minack Theatre** (daily: April–Sept 9.30am–5.30pm plus evening performances; Oct–March 10am–4pm; site closed when performances are in progress, see website; £4 entrance to site during day, performance prices vary; ⓦ minack.com) is a splendid sight, a craggy amphitheatre using the sea as a backdrop and with seats carved into the rocks. From Penzance, buses #501 and #1A drop you in Porthcurno, from where it is a 400m steep climb to the theatre, or the #504 will take you all the way.

ARRIVAL AND DEPARTURE

By train The train station is at the northeastern end of town, a step away from Market Jew St.
Destinations Bristol (5 daily; 4hr 10min); London (7 daily; 5hr 40min–6hr 5min); Par (for Newquay; every 30min–1hr; 1hr–1hr 10min); St Ives (change at St Erth; every 45min–1hr; 20–50min).
By bus The bus station is next to the train station at the northeastern end of town.
Destinations Bristol (4 daily; 6hr 10min–7hr 55min); Land's End (every 30min; 55min); London (4 daily; 8hr 35min–10hr); Newquay (3 daily; 1hr 35min–2hr 5min); St Ives (hourly; 50min).

INFORMATION

Tourist information There's a National Trust visitor centre just outside the train and bus stations (Mon, Tues, Wed, Fri & Sat 10am–4pm; ☎ 01736 335530, ⓦ purelypenzance.co.uk).
Internet Penzance Computers, 36b Market Jew St (Mon–Sat 9am–6pm, Sun 10am–4pm; £3.75/hr).

GETTING AROUND

By bus The open-top Cornwall Explorer (#300) is a hop-on-hop-off service stopping at Land's End, St Ives,

---

THE EDEN PROJECT

One of Cornwall's major draws, occupying a 160-ft-deep disused clay pit, the **Eden Project** (daily: April–Oct 9am–6pm; Nov–March 10am–4pm; school holidays 10am–6pm; last entry 1hr 30min before closing; £23.50; ticket valid for one year, discounts if arriving by public transport or booking online; ⓦ edenproject.com) showcases the diversity of the planet's plant life in a stunningly landscaped site. The centrepiece is two vast geodesic "biomes", or conservatories, one holding plants more usually found in Mediterranean zones, and the larger housing the **world's largest indoor rainforest**; a new canopy walkway allows you to take in the view from the treetops. For an additional £10 you can glide above the biomes on England's longest zip wire. The Eden Project lies four miles northeast of St Austell in Bodelva (bus #101 from St Austell train station or #527 from Newquay). Arrive early and allow at least half a day for a full exploration.

Marazion/St Michael's Mount and Penzance (3 daily; £7.20/day; ⓦfirstgroup.com).

Travel card "Ride Cornwall" day ticket (£10; available from train station ticket offices or on buses) gives you unlimited access to buses and trains in the county, and to Plymouth in Devon.

ACCOMMODATION

Penzance Backpackers Alexandra Rd (no number; about halfway up) ☎01736 363836, ⓦpzbackpack.com. Good independent hostel on a quiet tree-lined road 15min walk from the station. With kitchen, cosy lounge and wi-fi. Dorm **£16**, double **£36**

Penzance YHA Castle Horneck, Alverton ☎0845 371 9653, ⓦyha.org.uk. Beautifully converted and refurbished Georgian manor house about a mile from the centre, off the Land's End road. Dorm **£21**, double **£46**

★ **Whitesands Hotel** Sennen, near Whitesand Bay and Land's End ☎01736 871776, ⓦwhitesandshotel.co.uk. In between Penzance and St Ives, this quirky hotel offers themed rooms and a cheaper surf lodge with dorms and its own kitchen, as well as tipis and yurts. On-site bar, restaurant and barbecue. Buses from Land's End and St Ives stop outside. Dorm **£25**, double **£50**, camping **£15** per person and tent, yurt **£14** per person (minimum 2)

EATING AND DRINKING

Archie Browns Bread St. Welcoming veggie café and health-food shop using locally sourced ingredients. Specialities include mango and sweet potato curry, black bean stew and homity pie. Breakfasts from £2.60. Mon–Sat 9am–5pm.

★ **Mackerel Sky** 45 New St ☎01736 448982. Excellent café-restaurant serving great seafood (try the crab rarebit; £7.95), as well as non-fishy options such as burgers, roasts and sandwiches. Tues, Wed & Sun 10am–5pm, Thurs–Sat 10am–late.

The Turk's Head Chapel St ☎01736 363093. Ancient inn with a piratical heritage that includes a smugglers' tunnel. Touristy, but fun, and with good food. Mon–Sat 11.30am–11pm, Sun noon–10.30pm.

ST IVES

Across the peninsula from Penzance, the fishing village of **ST IVES** is the quintessential Cornish resort, featuring a muddle of narrow streets lined with whitewashed cottages, sandy beaches and squawking seagulls. The village's erstwhile tranquillity attracted several major artists throughout the twentieth century, including Ben Nicholson and Barbara Hepworth, and every other shop in town is a gallery making the most of its arty heritage. There is even a diminutive outpost of the **Tate gallery** empire here overlooking Porthmeor Beach (rotating exhibitions; March to late July, Sept & Oct daily 10am–5.20pm; late July & Aug daily 10am–6.20pm; Nov–Feb Tues–Sun 10am–4.20pm; £7.70 or £11 combined with Barbara Hepworth Museum; ⓦtate .org.uk/stives). The charming **Barbara Hepworth Museum and Garden** on Barnoon Hill (same hours as Tate St Ives; £6.60) preserves the studio of the modernist sculptor.

Of the town's three beaches, the largest, north-facing **Porthmeor**, occasionally has good surf; rent a board (£10/2hr) or take a lesson at the St Ives Surf School (£30/2hr; ☎01736 793938, ⓦstivessurfschool.co.uk). Alternatively, ramble along the coastal path south towards **Zennor** for beautiful views of craggy coves and wild flowers.

ARRIVAL AND INFORMATION

By train The train station is at Porthminster Beach. Destinations London (via St Erth; 7 daily; 5hr 35min–6hr 20min); Penzance (hourly; 30–50min).

By bus The bus station is at The Malakoff, next to the train station. Destinations Penzance (every 30min–1hr; 45min).

Tourist information The St Ives Visitor and Information Centre (May Mon–Fri 10am–3pm, Sat 11am–3pm; June Mon–Fri 10am–4pm, Sat 11am–4pm, Sun 11am–3pm; July–Sept Mon–Fri 10am–5pm, Sat & Sun 11am–4pm; Oct–April Mon–Fri 10am–3pm; ☎0905 2522250; ⓦstivestic.co.uk) is in the Guildhall. Walking tours (Wed 11am all year, plus March–Oct Mon & Thurs 11am; £5) leave from here.

Internet There's internet access at the tourist office (£1/15min).

ACCOMMODATION AND EATING

Blas Burgerworks The Warren ☎01736 797272. Tuck into the best burgers in the Southwest, with a great choice for vegetarians, too: specialities include halloumi stack with caper aioli and black bean burger with guacamole. Daily noon–10pm.

St Ives Backpackers The Gallery, Town Centre ☎01736 799444, ⓦbackpackers.co.uk/st-ives. The rambling *St Ives Backpackers* hostel occupies an enormous old Wesleyan chapel on The Stennack. It's built around a central courtyard where barbecues are organized in summer. Dorm **£17.95**, double **£40**

13

NEWQUAY

Buffeted by Atlantic currents, Cornwall's north coast is the area of the West Country most favoured by the **surfing** set. King of the surf resorts is tacky **NEWQUAY**, whose seven miles of golden sands, including Fistral Beach, host surfing championships. Equipment can be rented on most beaches or from one of the surf shops around town.

ARRIVAL AND INFORMATION

By plane Newquay's airport is three miles north of town; bus #556 runs to the centre (hourly; 20min).

By train The train station (change in Par or Plymouth) is just east of the centre.
Destinations London (5 daily; 5hr–5hr 15min); Penzance (6 daily; 2hr 5min–2hr 30min).

By bus The bus station is on Manor Rd.
Destinations Eden Project (hourly; 1hr 5min); St Ives (every 30min; 1hr 5min).

Tourist information Tourist office at Marcus Hill (Mon–Fri 9.15am–5.30pm, Sat & Sun 10am–4pm, reduced hours in winter; ☎01637 854020, ⓦvisitnewquay.org). Has a left luggage facility and books surfing lessons.

ACCOMMODATION

Matt's Surf Lodge 110 Mount Wise ☎01637 874651, ⓦmatts-surf-lodge.co.uk. No-frills rooms come with great views at Newquay's original surf lodge. Breakfast and linen are included, and free tea and coffee, a DVD lounge and cheap bar are further pluses. Dorm £15, double £40

Newquay International Backpackers 69 Tower Rd ☎01637 879366, ⓦbackpackers.co.uk/newquay. Among numerous campsites and hostels is this hospitable if rather cramped place, with a sunny courtyard, kitchen and lounge. Dorm £18, double £38

Central England

Encompassing both the old industrial towns and cities of the Midlands and some postcard-pretty countryside, alongside some of England's major cultural landmarks, **CENTRAL ENGLAND** defies easy categorization. With close on a million residents, Birmingham is the Midlands' largest city, but despite boasting one of the best concert halls in the country, is still unlikely to feature on a whistle-stop national tour. More appealing for a quick fix of history and culture are

Stratford-upon-Avon, birthplace of William Shakespeare, and the rival university cities of **Oxford** and **Cambridge**.

OXFORD

Thoughts of **OXFORD** inevitably conjure up the university, revered as one of the world's great academic institutions. The city's skyline is dominated by its "dreaming spires", while its streets form a dense maze of historic honey-stone buildings, containing the university's 38 colleges. Although in term time you're never far from the university or its thousands of students, Oxford is a sizeable city, and the combination of workaday vitality with sleepy academic tradition is a distinct part of its appeal. Note that access to colleges may be restricted during examinations – especially in May and June – as well as conferences and functions.

WHAT TO SEE AND DO

Start by ascending the spire of the University Church, **St Mary the Virgin**, on the High Street (Mon–Sat 9.30am–4.30/5.30pm, Sun 11.45am–4.30pm; £3) to orientate yourself with fantastic panoramic views.

Christ Church College and the cathedral

One of the wealthiest and most ostentatious of Oxford's colleges, Christ Church (Mon–Sat 9/10am–4.30pm, Sun 2–4.30pm; £8) was founded by Cardinal Wolsey in 1524; these days, a great number of its visitors come to see its grand **dining hall** (often closed 11.40am–2.30pm), which featured in the *Harry Potter* films. The college chapel is in fact the city of Oxford's **cathedral**. Christ Church's **Picture Gallery**, through the Canterbury Gate off Oriel Square (Jan–May & Oct–Dec Mon & Wed–Sat 10.30am–1pm & 2–4.30pm, Sun 2–5pm; June Mon & Wed–Sat 10.30am–5pm, Sun 2–5pm; July–Sept Mon–Sat 10.30am–5pm, Sun 2–5pm; £3 or £1.50 if paying to enter the college), is also worth a peek for its prestigious Old Master paintings and drawings.

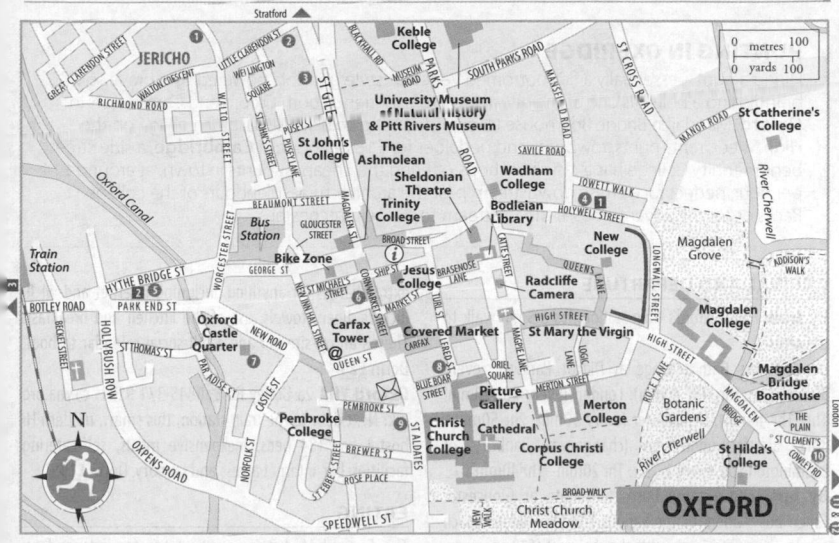

■ ACCOMMODATION		● EATING				● DRINKING & NIGHTLIFE			
Hollywell Bed & Breakfast	1	Atomic Burger	11	G&D's	2/9/12	The Bear	8	The Eagle & Child	3
Oxford Backpackers	2	Big Bang	7	Kazbar	10	The Bridge	5	Raoul's	1
Oxford YHA	3	Edamamé	4			The Cellar	6		

Christ Church Meadow, Merton and Magdalen

South of Christ Church, **Christ Church Meadow** offers scenic views and gentle walks – either east along Broad Walk to the River Cherwell or south along New Walk to the Thames (referred to hereabouts as the Isis). From the Broad Walk, paths lead to **Merton** (Mon–Fri 2–5pm, Sat & Sun 10am–5pm; £2), among the oldest and prettiest of Oxford's colleges. Nearby Rose Lane emerges at the eastern end of the High Street opposite **Magdalen College** (pronounced "maudlin"; daily 1–6/7pm; £5), which boasts its own deer park and a prestigious college choir.

The Bodleian Library and around

Just north of the High Street span the buildings that make up the **Bodleian Library** (term time: Mon–Fri 9am–10pm, Sat 9am–4pm, Sun 11am–5pm; holiday time: Mon–Fri 9am–7pm, Sat 10am–4pm; reading rooms by guided tour only, 6 tours daily; quadrangles and exhibition room free, tours from £7; ⑩www .bodleian.ox.ac.uk/bodley), the second-largest collection of books in the country.

The most dramatic library building (although inside it is just a reading room) is the Italianate **Radcliffe Camera** (tours Wed, Sat & Sun; booking essential; £13; ⑦01865 287400).

University museums

A couple of minutes' walk north along Parks Road and through the Natural History Museum lies the **Pitt Rivers Museum** (Mon noon–4.30pm, Tues–Sun 10am–4.30pm; free; ⑩www.prm.ox.ac .uk). Its fascinating anthropological collection includes totem poles, swords and opium pipes. Five minutes west of the **Sheldonian** (Mon–Sat 10am–12.30pm & 2–3.30/4.30pm; £2.50), Oxford's historic theatre – used for music recitals and lectures, as well as graduation ceremonies – is the mammoth Neoclassical edifice containing the **Ashmolean Museum** (Tues–Sun 10am–6pm; last Fri of the month also open 7–10.30pm; free; ⑩ashmolean.org). Collections include an array of Islamic, Indian and Oriental antiquities, the world's largest hoard of Raphael drawings and a Stradivari "Messiah" violin dating to 1716.

13

PUNTING IN OXBRIDGE

Hiring a punt – essentially a flat-bottomed Venetian-style gondola powered by a brave soul brandishing a pole – is one of the finest ways to experience both Oxford and Cambridge. In **Oxford**, Magdalen Bridge Boathouse (Ⓦoxfordpunting.co.uk), just past the college on the High Street, rents punts, rowboats and pedaloes for £18 per hour. In **Cambridge**, a side street behind Trinity College has a range of shops offering the cheapest punts in town, at around £14 per hour, perfect for a cruise downstream past the architectural splendours of the college Backs or, for the adventurous, a trip upstream to rural Grantchester.

ARRIVAL AND DEPARTURE

By train From Oxford's train station, it's a 5min walk to the centre.

Destinations Bath (change at Didcot Parkway; every 30min–1hr; 1hr–1hr 40min); London (every 20–30min; 1hr–1hr 40min); Manchester (every 30min; 2hr 50min–3hr); Stratford-upon-Avon (change at Banbury or Leamington Spa; every 1–2hr; 1hr 20min–1hr 40min).

By bus Long-distance buses terminate at Gloucester Green bus station. Of the various London–Oxford coach services, the #X90 is currently the cheapest (£13 one-way; Ⓦoxfordbus.co.uk).

Destinations Cambridge (every 30min; 3hr–3hr 20min); Gatwick Airport (hourly; 2hr–2hr 30min); Heathrow Airport (every 30min; 1hr 20min); London (every 10–15min; 1hr 40min); Stratford-upon-Avon (1 daily; 1hr 5min).

INFORMATION AND TOURS

Tourist information Tourist office at 15 Broad St (Mon–Sat 9.30am–5pm, Sun 10am–3.30pm; ☎01865 252200, Ⓦvisitoxfordandoxfordshire.com). You can book walking tours here (£8), or buy the visitors' guide (£1), which details a self-guided walk.

Internet C-Work, North Bailey House, New Inn Hall St (Mon–Sat 9am–9pm, Sun 9am–7pm; £1/30min).

GETTING AROUND

By bike For bike rental, head to Bike Zone at 28–32 St Michael's St, off Cornmarket St (☎01865 728877, Ⓦbike -zone.co.uk; £18/day); advance booking necessary.

ACCOMMODATION

Oxford has a good choice of hostels, and, out of term time, some colleges also make student rooms available to tourists (Ⓦoxfordrooms.co.uk). Wherever you stay, it's advisable to book in advance.

Holywell Bed & Breakfast 14 Holywell St ☎01865 721880, Ⓦholywellbedandbreakfast.com. Set in a Grade II-listed house, this three-room B&B has bags of charm. Rooms are spacious and cosily furnished and the breakfasts are tasty; blueberry pancakes are a speciality. Double **£85**

★ **Oxford Backpackers** 9a Hythe Bridge St ☎01865 721761, Ⓦhostels.co.uk. Very backpacker friendly; no

extra charges for anything, including internet and wi-fi, lockers, linen, towels, use of the kitchen and breakfast. There's an on-site bar and a full social calendar to boot. Dorm **£21**

Oxford YHA 2a Botley Rd ☎0845 371 9131, Ⓦyha.org .uk. Next door to the train station, this smart, modern HI hostel has 184 beds, inexpensive meals, self-catering facilities, bar, internet access and laundry. Dorm **£19**

EATING

The Covered Market is your best bet for independent, daytime cafés, while the Jericho district (north of the centre) or the Cowley Rd out east are great for independent cafés and restaurants.

★ **Atomic Burger** 96 Cowley Rd. With comic books for wallpaper and breakfasts named after John Hughes characters, this place is an ode to Americana. As for burgers, there's a choice from the Big Kahuna (with pineapple, Swiss cheese and teriyaki sauce; £8.75) to the plain Forrest Gump (£6.75). All available in beef, chicken or veggie. Mon–Fri 10am–2.30pm & 5–11pm; Sat & Sun 10am–11pm.

Big Bang 42 Oxford Castle Quarter. The mix-and-match menu of British gourmet sausages and quality mash is the big draw here, but they also do great breakfasts (till 3pm; £6.95 for the works). There's a barbecue terrace and weekly live jazz too. The £5 midweek lunch menu for students is a bargain. Mon–Sat 10am–11pm, Sun 10am–10pm.

Edamamé 15 Holywell St ☎01865 246916. Terrific Japanese food at fair prices – it's no wonder the queue for this tiny restaurant snakes down the street. Wed 11.30am–2.30pm, Thurs 5–8.30pm, Fri & Sat 11.30am–2.30pm & 5–8.30pm, Sun noon–3.30pm.

★ **G&D's** *George & Davis* 55 Little Clarendon St, Jericho; *George & Danver* 94 St Aldates; *George & Delila* 104 Cowley Rd. Fantastic Oxford mini-chain of ice-cream cafés – they make their own. Also great for bagels and coffee. All branches daily 8am–midnight.

Kazbar 25–27 Cowley Rd. Authentic Spanish food served in a Moroccan ambience is a winning combination. The mouthwatering array of tapas (normally £3.50–5) is half-price 5–6pm Mon–Fri & Sun. Mon–Thurs 5pm–midnight, Fri 5pm–12.30am, Sat noon–12.30am, Sun noon–11pm.

13

DRINKING AND NIGHTLIFE

For listings of gigs and other events, consult *Daily Info*, a poster put up in colleges and all around town on Tues and Fri (ⓦ dailyinfo.co.uk).

The Bear 6 Alfred St. Oldest pub in Oxford with very low ceilings, real ales and snippets from interesting neckties – proffered by their owners in exchange for a pint. Mon–Thurs 11am–11pm, Fri & Sat 11pm–midnight, Sun 11.30am–10.30pm.

The Bridge 6 Hythe Bridge St ⓦ bridgeoxford.co.uk. Mainstream club plying drunken punters (mostly students) with commercial dance, r'n'b and pop. Mon–Sat 9pm–2am.

The Cellar Frewin Court, off Cornmarket St ☎ 01865 244761, ⓦ cellaroxford.co.uk. Probably the closest you get to a serious club in Oxford. Nightly music, often live acts, attracts a more discerning breed of music lover. Tickets around £6. Daily 7.30pm–2/3am.

The Eagle & Child 49 St Giles. This pub was once the haunt of J.R.R. Tolkien, C.S. Lewis and other literary types, and still attracts an engaging mix of professionals and academics. Food is available too. Mon–Thurs 11am–11pm, Fri & Sat 11am–midnight, Sun noon–10.30pm.

★ **Raoul's** 32 Walton St ⓦ raoulsbar.com. A great cocktail bar with posh cocktails made with home-made and locally sourced ingredients (try the Jamboree: cucumber vodka and strawberry preserve, lemon, nettle cordial, marmalade bitters and cassis; £6.50). Mon, Tues & Sun 4pm–midnight, Wed–Sat 4pm–1am.

STRATFORD-UPON-AVON

The pretty town of **STRATFORD-UPON-AVON** is synonymous with its famous citizen, William Shakespeare, who was born here in 1564. The town revels in its links to the bard and successfully plays up the "merrie olde England" image. Most people come to see the five attractively restored Shakespeare-related properties, but you could save your money and simply soak up the atmosphere by meandering along the river, lined with Tudor buildings.

Top of everyone's Bardic itinerary is **Shakespeare's Birthplace** (daily: April–June, Sept & Oct 9am–5pm; July & Aug 9am–6pm; Nov–March 10am–4pm; £14.95 including Nash's House/New Place & Hall's Croft, or pass to all five houses £22.50; ⓦ shakespeare.org.uk) on Henley Street. Pass through the tacky visitor centre to the heavily restored building where the great man was born to gain some understanding of his beginnings.

A short walk away on Chapel Street are **Nash's House/New Place** (daily: April–Oct 10am–5pm; Nov–March 11am–4pm; for ticket see above). The former was once the property of Thomas Nash, first husband of Shakespeare's granddaughter, Elizabeth Hall, and is kitted out with period furnishings and temporary exhibitions. Next door is New Place, the site of Shakespeare's last home, where he died in 1616. The house is long gone, but recent excavations on the site unearthed some interesting finds, now on public display here. A five-minute walk away, Old Town Street is home to the medieval **Hall's Croft** (same hours and ticket as Nash's House/New Place), former home of Shakespeare's eldest daughter, Susanna, and her husband, John Hall.

About half a mile west of the town centre in Shottery is the thatched, wood-beamed **Anne Hathaway's Cottage** (same hours as Shakespeare's Birthplace, but closes 5pm July & Aug; £9, or pass to all five houses £22.50), surrounded by beautiful gardens said to be where Shakespeare courted Anne. Two and a half miles from here (clearly signposted) is Shakespeare's mother's family home, now called **Mary Arden's Farm** (mid-March to early Nov daily 10am–5pm; £9.95, or pass to all five houses

---

THE ROYAL SHAKESPEARE COMPANY

Don't go to Stratford without seeing a play at the Royal Shakespeare Theatre (box office Mon–Sat 10am–6pm; ☎ 0844 800 1110, ⓦ www.rsc.org.uk), home to the fantastically talented **Royal Shakespeare Company**. The Company works on a repertory system, which means you could see three or four different plays in a visit of a few days (though not all by the Bard himself). Tickets start at £5 for standing room, rising to £60 for the best seats in the house. Note that the most popular shows get booked up months in advance.

13

£22.50): a classily re-created Tudor working farm complete with rare-breed animals, as well as weavers, falconers and farmers in period costume.

Back in town, a short walk from Hall's Croft towards the river, is the handsome **Holy Trinity Church** (March & Oct Mon–Sat 9am–5pm, Sun 12.30–5pm; April–Sept Mon–Sat 8.30am–6pm, Sun 12.30–5pm; Nov–Feb Mon–Sat 9am–4pm, Sun 12.30–5pm). William and Anne Shakespeare are buried here in the chancel (£2, or free with ticket to one of Shakespeare's houses).

ARRIVAL AND INFORMATION

By train Stratford's train station is on the northwestern edge of town, a 10min walk from the centre.
Destinations London Marylebone (5 daily; 2hr–2hr 50min); Oxford (change at Banbury or Leamington Spa; 6 daily; 1hr 20min–1hr 40min).
By bus Long-distance buses pull into the Riverside Station on the east side of the town centre, off Bridgeway.
Destinations London (3 daily; 3hr 15min–3hr 25min); Oxford (1 daily; 1hr).
Tourist information Tourist office at Bridgefoot, opposite Bancroft Gardens (March–Oct daily 9am–5.30pm; Nov–Feb Mon–Sat 9am–5.30pm, Sun 10am–4pm; ☎01789 264 293, ⓦdiscover-stratford .com); can book accommodation and sell tickets for local attractions and transport, and there's internet access and a café. Open-top bus tours of the town depart from here (ⓦwww.citysightseeing-stratford.com).

ACCOMMODATION

★ **Hamlet House** 52 Grove Rd ☎07968 702434, ⓦhamlethouse.com. Friendly B&B a 5min walk from the centre, with quirky themed rooms and a resident parrot named Dolly. Free internet, bikes and jumbo breakfasts, with specialities such as omelette cooked with herbs from the garden. Double <u>£55</u>
Stratford YHA Hemmingford House, Alveston ☎0845 371 9661, ⓦyha.org.uk; buses #X15, #18A and #X18 from Bridge St or bus station. Rambling Georgian mansion with its own café-bar on the edge of the pretty village of Alveston, two miles east of town. Dorm <u>£16.50</u>, double <u>£36</u>

EATING AND DRINKING

Hole in the Wall Guild St. Pizza kitchen and bar with a roof terrace and live music weekly. Good-value food (Moroccan spiced chicken pizza £8.95) and pop art Shakespeares on the walls. Mon–Wed & Sun noon–11pm, Thurs noon–midnight, Fri & Sat noon–1am.

Old Thatch Tavern Market Place. The only thatched building in the centre of Stratford, and one of the few historic inns that hasn't lost its character, this cosy pub has good British food and ales. Mon–Sat 11.30am–11pm, Sun noon–6pm.
Real Tea Café 40a Wood St. The perfect antidote to the multitude of twee tearooms, this funky café has 35 types of tea, each brewed to perfection. Mon–Sat 9am–5pm, Sun 10am–5pm.

CAMBRIDGE

Tradition has it that the University of **CAMBRIDGE** was founded by refugees from Oxford, who fled that town after one of their number was lynched by hostile townsfolk in the 1220s; there's been rivalry between the two institutions ever since, though nowadays it's manifested in the annual boat race. What distinguishes Cambridge from its counterpart is "**the Backs**", the green swathe of land straddling the River Cam, which overlooks the backs of the old colleges and provides the town's most enduring image of grand academic architecture. As in Oxford, access to the colleges may be restricted during examinations, conferences and functions. For four days in late July, the town hosts the popular **Cambridge Folk Festival** (ⓦcambridgefolkfestival.co.uk).

WHAT TO SEE AND DO

Cambridge city centre is bound to the west by the Cam and is dominated by historic university buildings. A logical place to start a tour is King's Parade, originally the medieval High Street.

King's College

Flanking King's Parade, **King's College** has a much-celebrated, extraordinarily beautiful **chapel** (term time Mon–Sat 9.30/9.45am–3.15/3.30pm, Sun 1.15–2.30pm; rest of year daily 9.30/9.45am–4.30pm; £7.50; ⓦwww .kings.cam.ac.uk) and is home to an equally vaunted choir (term time Evensong Mon–Sat 5.30pm, Sun 10.30am & 3.30pm). At the northern end of King's Parade, the **Senate House** is the scene of graduation ceremonies.

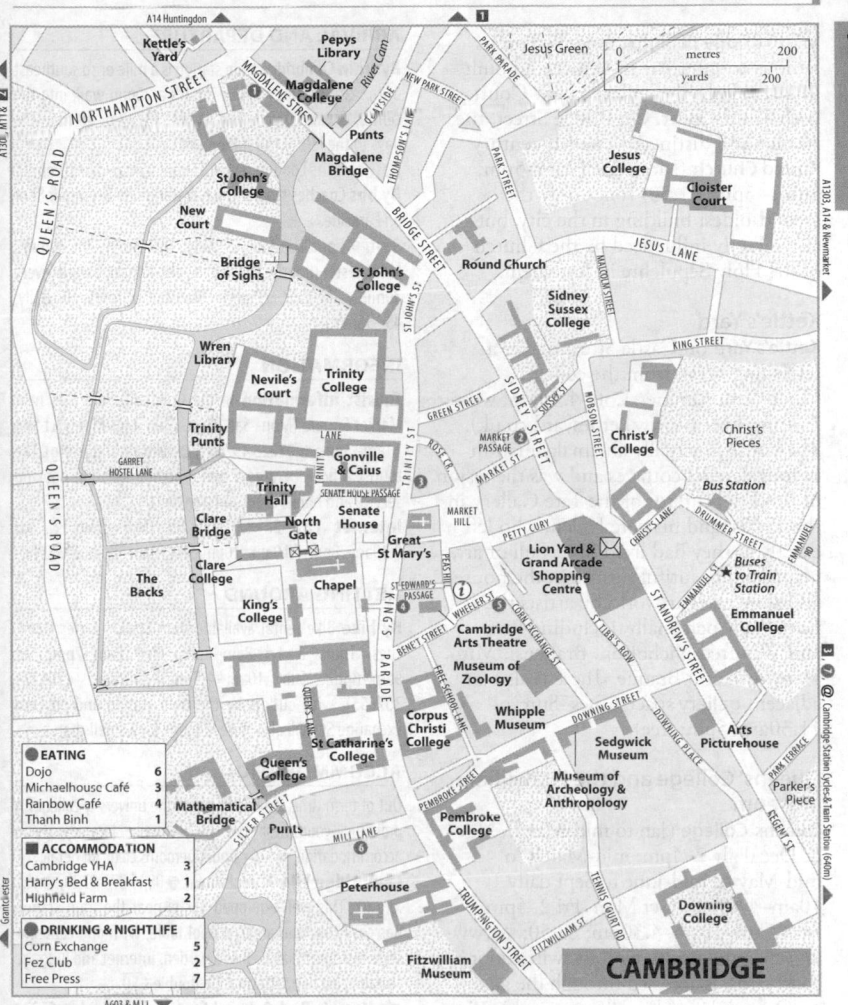

A14 Huntingdon

Kettle's Yard

Pepys Library

Jesus Green

metres 200
yards 200

NORTHAMPTON STREET

Magdalene Street

Magdalene College

Punts

Magdalene Bridge

Jesus College

Cloister Court

St John's College

New Court

Bridge of Sighs

St John's College

Round Church

JESUS LANE

Sidney Sussex College

KING STREET

Wren Library

Nevile's Court

Trinity College

LANE

Trinity Punts

Gonville & Caius

MARKET PASSAGE

Christ's College

Christ's Pieces

Bus Station

Trinity Hall

North Gate

Senate House

MARKET ST

DRUMMER STREET

Clare Bridge

Great St Mary's

PETTY CURY

Lion Yard & Grand Arcade Shopping Centre

Buses to Train Station

Clare College

Chapel

Emmanuel College

The Backs

King's College

Cambridge Arts Theatre

KING'S PARADE

Museum of Zoology

Whipple Museum

Arts Picturehouse

Parker's Piece

St Catharine's College

Corpus Christi College

Sedgwick Museum

Museum of Archeology & Anthropology

Queen's College

Mathematical Bridge

Punts

Pembroke College

Downing College

Peterhouse

Fitzwilliam Museum

CAMBRIDGE

● EATING
Dojo 6
Michaelhouse Café 3
Rainbow Café 4
Thanh Binh 1

■ ACCOMMODATION
Cambridge YHA 3
Harry's Bed & Breakfast 1
Highfield Farm 2

● DRINKING & NIGHTLIFE
Corn Exchange 5
Fez Club 2
Free Press 7

Trinity College

Just north of King's, **Trinity College**
(ⓦwww.trin.cam.ac.uk) is the largest of
the Cambridge colleges. Beyond the
Great Gate lies the vast asymmetrical
expanse of Great Court, which displays a
fine range of Tudor buildings, the oldest
of which is the fifteenth-century clock
tower – the annual race against its
midnight chimes is now common
currency thanks to the film *Chariots of
Fire*. The west end of Nevile's Court is
enclosed by the beautiful **Wren Library**
(term time Mon–Fri noon–2pm, Sat
10.30am–12.30pm; rest of year Mon–Fri

only; free). Back outside Trinity, it's a
short hop to the River Cam, where you
can go **punting** – the quintessential
Cambridge pursuit (see box, p.452).

St John's College and the Round Church

Founded by Henry VII's mother, Lady
Margaret Beaufort, **St John's College**
(daily 10am–5pm, closes 3.30pm Jan,
Feb, Nov & Dec; £5; ⓦwww.joh.cam
.ac.uk) is worth a quick peek for its chapel
ceiling depicting saints and scholars
standing shoulder to shoulder, as well as
its mishmash of architectural styles. The

13

lovely **Bridge of Sighs**, modelled on its famous counterpart in Venice and built in 1813, links the college's New Court with Third Court. On Bridge Street, the strange and distinctive twelfth-century **Round Church** (Mon–Sat 10am–5pm, Sun 1–5pm; £1.50) is not only the second-oldest building in the city, but also directly influenced by the Church of the Holy Sepulchre in Jerusalem.

Kettle's Yard

Kettle's Yard on Castle Street makes a refreshing break from the colleges (Tues–Sun: summer 1.30–4.30pm; winter 2–4pm; free; ⊕www.kettlesyard.co.uk). The house is actually an amalgamation of four derelict cottages and was the vision of Jim Ede, curator of the Tate Gallery in the 1920s, and his wife Helen, who left it exactly as they had lived in it. Full of art, plants and beautiful furniture, the house also showcases artworks by artists the Edes knew personally, including Ben and Winifred Nicholson, Brancusi, Miró, Hepworth and Braque. There is also an adjacent **gallery** space (Tues–Sun 11.30am–5pm; free).

Queens' College and the Fitzwilliam Museum

Queens' College (Jan to mid-March, Nov & Dec daily 2–4pm; mid-March to mid-May & mid-June to Sept daily 10am–4.30pm; Oct Mon–Fri 2–4pm, Sat & Sun 10am–4.30pm; £2.50; ⊕www.queens.cam.ac.uk), with its twin Tudor courtyards, is accessed through the gate on Queen's Lane. Equally eye-catching is the wooden Mathematical Bridge over the Cam, a copy of the mid-eighteenth-century original which, it was claimed, would stay in place even if the nuts and bolts were removed. From Queens', it's a short stroll in the opposite direction from the colleges down Trumpington Street to the excellent **Fitzwilliam Museum** (Tues–Sat 10am–5pm, Sun noon–5pm; free; ⊕www.fitzmuseum.cam.ac.uk). The ground floor contains classical antiquities, including a large Egyptian collection, while the first floor displays applied arts and European painting, including masterpieces by Rubens, Hogarth, Renoir and Picasso.

ARRIVAL AND DEPARTURE

By train Cambridge train station is a mile or so southeast of the city centre, off Hills Rd. It's a 20min walk into the centre, or take shuttle bus #1, #2, #3, #7 or #8 from the bays to the left of the station exit.

Destinations London (every 15min; 45min–1hr 30min).

By bus Coaches stop at the bus station on Drummer St or on Parkside.

Destinations London (13 daily; 1hr 45min–2hr 30min); Manchester (hourly; 3hr 35min–4hr 40min); Oxford (every 30min; 3hr–3hr 20min); Stansted Airport (9 daily; 45–55min).

INFORMATION

Tourist information In the Guildhall, Peas Hill, near Market Square (Mon–Sat 10am–5pm, plus May–Oct Sun 11am–3pm; ☎01223 457581, ⊕visitcambridge.org). The tourist office operates a useful accommodation booking service and books tours and transport.

Internet CB1 at 32 Mill Rd (Mon–Thurs & Sat 9.30am–8pm, Fri 9am–10pm, Sun 10am–8pm; £1.80/hr).

GETTING AROUND

By bike Bike rental available from Station Cycles (Mon, Tues, Thurs & Fri 8am–6pm, Wed 8am–7pm, Sat 9am–6pm, Sun 10am–4/5pm; £10/day; ☎01223 307655), with outlets by the train station and on Corn Exchange St. Will also store luggage for a small charge.

ACCOMMODATION

Out of term time, staying in one of the university colleges is probably your best bet for centrally located, cheap accommodation; see ⊕cambridgerooms.co.uk for details.

Cambridge YHA 97 Tenison Rd ☎0845 371 9728, ⊕yha.org.uk. This well-equipped hostel near the train station has cosy common areas, a pool table, wi-fi and canteen-style restaurant, as well as a garden. Internet and luggage storage cost extra. Dorm £22, double £50

★ **Harry's Bed & Breakfast** 39 Milton Rd ☎01223 503866, ⊕welcometoharrys.co.uk. This welcoming B&B with four cosy en-suite rooms is an easy 10min walk from the centre. The Full English is top-notch. Double £75

Highfield Farm Long Rd, Comberton ☎01223 262308, ⊕highfieldfarmtouringpark.co.uk; bus #18 or #18A. Rural family-run campsite, five miles west of the city (25min by bus). Open April–Oct. Cash only. Camping £13.50 per person and tent

EATING

Dojo 1 Miller's Yard. Extremely popular pan-Oriental noodle bar with outdoor seating serving up high-quality Asian dishes (pad thai £8.20). Mon–Thurs noon–2.30pm & 5.30–11pm, Fri noon–4pm & 5.30–11pm, Sat & Sun noon–11pm.

13

Michaelhouse Café St Michael's Church, Trinity St. Appealing café in a church nave with an emphasis on local produce. Mains from £7.25; "hungry student" deal (Mon–Fri 2.30–3.30pm) offers the usual lunch mains for £3.95. Mon–Sat 8am–5pm.

★ **Rainbow Café** 9A King's Parade. This award-winning veggie and gluten-free café is hugely popular, with a global menu of hearty, freshly made dishes, from enchiladas (£8.95) to Latvian potato bake (£9.95). Tues–Sat 10am–10pm, Sun 10am–4pm.

Thanh Binh 17 Magdalene St. Good Vietnamese cuisine including excellent *pho* (£9.50) and unusual durian fruit ice cream. Lunch menu £9.95 for two courses. Mon–Sat noon–2pm & 6–10pm.

DRINKING AND NIGHTLIFE

To find out about current club nights, theatre productions and comedy nights, browse the flyers hanging from the railings down King's Parade.

Corn Exchange Corn Exchange St ☎01223 357851, ⓦ www.cornex.co.uk. Largest music venue in the city with all the big names in music, dance and comedy passing through on tour. Booking essential.

★ **Fez Club** 15 Market Passage ⓦ cambridgefez.com. A much-loved Cambridge institution, the *Fez*'s eclectic music policy keeps it ahead of the competition. Mon's *Jam Hot* is student night. Fills up quickly so it's best to join the queue by 11pm. Entry £3–6. Daily 10pm–3am.

★ **Free Press** 7 Prospect Row. In the backstreets behind Emmanuel College this tiny local has real ales, a beer garden, great food and is well off the tourist trail. Mon–Thurs noon–2pm & 6–11pm, Fri & Sat noon–11pm, Sun noon–2.30pm & 7–10.30pm.

Northern England

The great outdoors grabs the headlines in lake-laden, mountain ravine-scored **Northern England**. The best-known area is the **Lake District**, encompassing picturesque stone-built villages, sixteen huge lakes and England's highest mountains. Less explored but equally beautiful is **Northumberland** in the northeast and the southern **Peak District**. Northern England is also home to some of the country's major cities, including **Manchester** and **Liverpool** in the west and **Newcastle** in the northeast – they each combine the ostentatious civic architecture of nineteenth-century capitalism with vigorous twenty-first-century renewal. The ecclesiastical hotbeds of **Durham** and **York** are unmissable, their famous cathedrals providing a focus for fascinating, medieval-themed meanderings.

MANCHESTER

Sprawling northern metropolis **MANCHESTER** has one of the country's most vibrant social and cultural scenes, enlivened by the student population of its two major universities, its stylish Gay Village, the glitzy Curry Mile and its buzzing, bohemian Northern Quarter. In many ways it is the flagship for multifaceted Britishness: it shot to prominence courtesy of its Industrial Revolution riches, later becoming a powerhouse of music and football.

WHAT TO SEE AND DO

From the main Piccadilly train station, it's a few minutes' walk northwest to **Piccadilly Gardens**, an obvious starting point for an exploration of the city.

Manchester Art Gallery

The **Manchester Art Gallery** (daily 10am–5pm, till 9pm Thurs; free; ⓦ manchestergalleries.org) has a fine collection of Pre-Raphaelite paintings, Impressionist pictures of Manchester by Adolphe Valette and an excellent interactive gallery. It is located a quarter of a mile from the gardens, on Mosley Street. Just to the west, the **Town Hall** (Mon–Fri 9am–5pm, free; guided tours Tues and occasional Sun 11am; £5) is the country's pinnacle of Victorian civic aspiration: check out the Ford Madox Brown murals inside.

Royal Exchange Theatre and National Football Museum

St Ann's Square is home to the wonderful **Royal Exchange Theatre** (ⓦ royalexchange.co.uk). If you don't have time to see a show, pop in and have a look at the building – formerly the Cotton Exchange – whose florid, pink marble columns and lofty cupolas

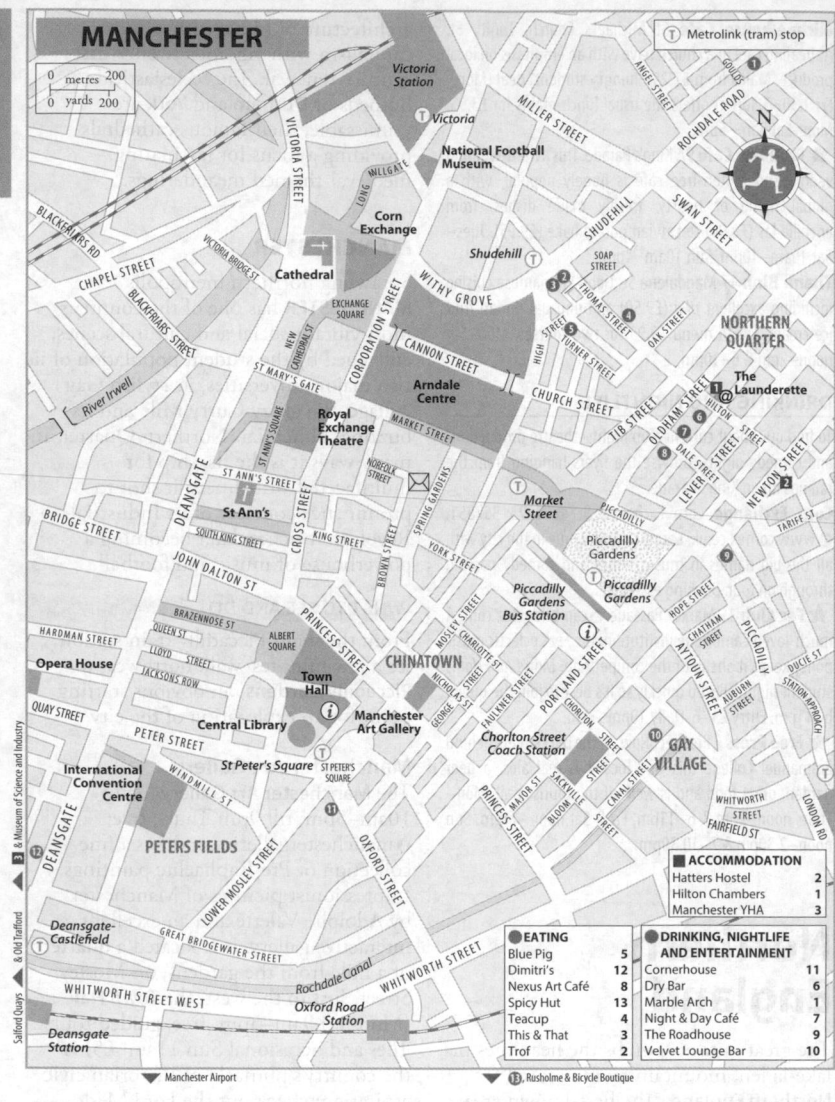

surround the spherical performance space, an egg-like module squatting in the centre. A short walk north in Cathedral Gardens you'll find the **National Football Museum** (☏0161 870 9275, ⓦnationalfootballmuseum.com), a spectacular, wedge-shaped glass building housing artefacts that tell the story of football, from its earliest beginnings around the world to the birth of the women's game.

Museum of Science and Industry
South down Deansgate and right onto Liverpool Road, the superbly informative **Museum of Science and Industry** (daily 10am–5pm; free; ⓦmosi.org.uk) celebrates the triumphs of industrialization. Exhibits include working steam engines, textile machinery, a hands-on science centre and atmospheric re-creations of period rooms. There's also a chance to walk through a

13

rebuilt Victorian sewer, complete with nasty whiffs and pongs.

Salford Quays and Old Trafford

Metrolink trams from Piccadilly and Deansgate-Castlefield run to Harbour City, jump-off point for the revamped **Salford Quays**, scene of a massive urban renewal scheme in the old dock area. Centrepiece is the spectacular waterfront arts hub, **The Lowry** (daily 9.30/10am–8pm; free; ⊕ thelowry.com), housing theatres and galleries, where room is always made for the work of the artist L.S. Lowry, best known for his "matchstick men" scenes. You can also get here by walking down the docks from the Salford Quays tram stop. A footbridge runs across the docks to the **Imperial War Museum North** (daily 10am–5pm; free; ⊕ north .iwm.org.uk), a striking aluminium-clad building imaginatively exploring the effects of war since 1900. Looming nearby is **Old Trafford**, home of Manchester United Football Club, whose museum, a must-see for any football fan, is situated in the Sir Alex Ferguson Stand (northern side of stadium; daily 9.30am–5pm; museum & tour £16, museum only £11; advance booking essential for tours ☎ 0161 868 8000, ⊕ manutd.com; Metrolink towards Altrincham to Old Trafford, or towards Eccles to Exchange Quay).

ARRIVAL AND DEPARTURE

By plane The airport is ten miles south, with a fast, frequent train service to Manchester Piccadilly (every 5–10min; 15–20min; £4.70).
By train Most trains arrive at Piccadilly station, on the city's east side.
Destinations Chester (every 30min; 1hr–1hr 30min); Edinburgh (every 2hr; 3hr 20min); Glasgow (4 daily; 3hr 10min); London (3 hourly; 2hr 10min); Liverpool (frequent; 45min–1hr 10min); Newcastle (hourly; 2hr 40min); York (3 hourly; 1hr 25min).
By bus Long-distance coaches stop at Chorlton St coach station, just west of Piccadilly station.
Destinations Chester (3 daily; 1hr 15min–1hr 40min); Glasgow (4 daily; 4–5hr); Liverpool (at least hourly; 55min); York (via Leeds; 18 daily; 2hr 20min–2hr 40min).

INFORMATION

Tourist information Manchester Visitor Centre is in Piccadilly Plaza, on Portland St (Mon–Sat

9.30am–5.30pm, Sun 10.30am–4.30pm; ☎ 0871 222 8223, ⊕ visitmanchester.com).
Internet The Launderette, 19 Hilton St, doubles as a cybercafé (Mon–Fri 7.30am–7pm, Sat 8am–5pm, Sun 10am–2pm; 50p/15min).

GETTING AROUND

By bike Bike rental from Bicycle Boutique, Hillcourt St (Mon–Fri 8.30am–6.30pm, Sat & Sun 10am–4pm; £15/day, £12/day Sat & Sun; ☎ 0161 273 7801).

ACCOMMODATION

Hatters Hostel 50 Newton St ☎ 0161 236 9500, ⊕ hattersgroup.com. Old and a little rough around the edges, this hostel is a good option if you want to party and just need somewhere cheap to lay your head. Dorm **£14.50**, double **£42**
Hilton Chambers 15 Hilton St ☎ 0161 236 4414, ⊕ hattersgroup.com. This clean Northern Quarter hostel has a roof terrace, complimentary all-day breakfast and is a little fresher-feeling (and more expensive) than its sister property on Newton St. Prices go up at weekends. Dorm **£15**, double **£55**
★ **Manchester YHA** Potato Wharf, Castlefield ☎ 0871 371 9647, ⊕ yha.org.uk. Close to the Museum of Science and Industry, this swanky HI hostel (all dorm rooms have en-suite bathrooms) has a great canalside location. Dorm **£23**, double **£49**

EATING

For cheap eats, head a few blocks east of the Town Hall to Chinatown, or Wilmslow Rd in Rusholme (bus #18 from the city centre; 25min), otherwise known as "Curry Mile", featuring some of Britain's best budget Asian cooking.
Blue Pig 69 High St. Parisian-style bar-restaurant whose deli menu includes tasty local cheeses and hearty sharing boards (£13.95; fish, meat and veggie versions available). Daily 10am–midnight/1am.
Dimitri's 1 Campfield Arcade, Deansgate. Serving a medley of Greek, Italian and Spanish cuisine, *Dimitri's* feels consistently lively, with good-value lunchtime offers like five small dishes for £10 Mon–Thurs & Sun. Mon–Thurs & Sun 11am–midnight, Fri & Sat 11am–2am.
Nexus Art Café 2 Dale St. Not-for-profit café opened by a group of Methodists. Serves tasty sandwiches and jacket potatoes (from £3), and acts as a hub for local artists. Mon–Sat 11am–7pm, Sun noon–6pm.
Spicy Hut 35 Wilmslow Rd. Garishly decorated, long-standing and unpretentious curry house on the Curry Mile. They do a mean madras (£8.40). Mon–Sat 5pm–midnight/1am/2am, Sun 2pm–midnight.
Teacup 55 Thomas St. Feel-good food like eggs Benedict (£8) draws a mostly young crowd to this relaxed café, whose menu of loose-leaf teas includes a

13

MANCHESTER MUSIC

In 1978, local TV personality Tony Wilson founded **Factory Records** and gave voice to a musical movement that came to define both Manchester and Britain's post-punk musical soundscape. Bands like Joy Division and New Order emerged and embraced the new electronic music that was played at Factory's club, **The Hacienda**, the prototype for the industrial warehouse spaces ubiquitous in club design today. *The Hacienda* closed in 1997 but its legacy lives on, with places like the *Night & Day Café* (26 Oldham St; ⓦ nightnday.org) and the *Roadhouse* (8 Newton St; ⓦ theroadhouselive.co.uk) providing stages for up-and-coming talent.

hangover-busting herbal brew. Mon–Thurs & Sun 10am–6pm, Fri & Sat 10am–8pm.

This & That 3 Soap St. Hard to spot but worth seeking out, this canteen-style curry place is frequently full up. The house special – three curries poured over rice – costs just £4.90. Mon–Thurs 11.30am–4.30pm, Fri & Sat 11.30am–8pm, Sun 11.30am–4pm.

Trof 8 Thomas St ☏ 0131 833 3197. Coffee, sandwiches, burgers, beer: whatever your craving, *Trof* can oblige. Expect eclectic cocktails and events like Sun's roast dinner-and-vinyl session. Mains from £7.50. Mon–Thurs 10am–midnight/1am, Fri & Sat 9/10am–3am, Sun 9am–midnight.

DRINKING, NIGHTLIFE AND ENTERTAINMENT

Manchester has no shortage of places to drink. The two best-known areas are the Northern Quarter, around Oldham St, and the Gay Village, around Canal St. For details of nightlife, consult Fri's *Manchester Evening News*.

Cornerhouse 70 Oxford St. With celebrity patrons Danny Boyle and Helen Mirren, this chic venue's status as café, bar, gallery and leading independent cinema seems assured. Mon–Thurs 9.30am–11pm, Fri & Sat 9.30am–midnight, Sun 11am–10.30pm.

Dry Bar 28–30 Oldham St. A "Madchester" institution and a catalyst for much of what goes on in the Northern Quarter. A downstairs music venue hosts DJs and live bands. Mon–Thurs 11am–midnight, Fri & Sat 11am–4am, Sun 11am–midnight.

★ **Marble Arch** 73 Rochdale Rd. Out-of-the-way, lavish-looking brew pub with vaulted ceilings and sloping floors, concocting its own ales. Food (mains around £14) is relatively expensive. Mon–Thurs & Sun noon–11pm, Fri & Sat noon–midnight.

Velvet Lounge Bar 2 Canal St. Elegant, opulent Gay Village cocktail bar, decorated with plush velvet curtains and zebra-striped chairs. Mon–Wed 4pm–12.30am, Thurs 4pm–1am, Fri & Sat 4pm–2am, Sun 2pm–12.30am.

PEAK DISTRICT

The wild, cavern-riddled **PEAK DISTRICT** lies between Manchester and Sheffield, and is Britain's oldest and most easily

accessed national park. The main centres are **Buxton**, just outside the park boundaries, **Castleton** to the northeast and **Bakewell** in the southeast.

WHAT TO SEE AND DO

The sedate Victorian spa town of **Buxton** should be your first stop if coming by train from Manchester. The town is centred around nineteenth-century pleasure gardens complete with a pavilion theatre and the legendary **St Ann's Well**, where the famous mineral water is sourced. There are spectacular caverns just outside town at **Poole's Cavern** (daily: March–Oct 9.30am–5pm; Nov–Feb Sat & Sun 10am–4pm; ⓦ poolescavern.co.uk; £8.80), but you're better off heading to **Castleton**, a beautiful stone village 10 miles northwest with its three showcaves and dozens more challenging subterranean passageways to explore (details at the visitor centre, see opposite). A five-mile hike or one stop on the Hope Valley line further brings you to **Edale**, where the area's best hike to **Kinder Scout** (8 miles) begins. From **Bakewell**, famed for its jam-filled pudding, it's a ten-minute ride with bus #215 or #218 to **Chatsworth House** (get off at Baslow; house open 11am–5.30pm, last admission 4.30pm; garden 11am–6pm, last admission 5pm; £19; ☏ 01246 565300, ⓦ chatsworth.org), one of Britain's grandest country houses set in a 35,000-acre estate with a garden featuring the stately home's iconic cascades, as well as woods, valleys, fountains and tumbling rivers.

ARRIVAL AND INFORMATION

By train Trains from Manchester Piccadilly run to Buxton (hourly; 1hr) and Hope (every 1–2hr; 50min), two miles east of Castleton.

13

By bus Several direct buses per day run from Manchester to Bakewell (2hr) and Buxton (1hr 20min). TransPeak buses run hourly between Bakewell and Buxton (30min); other routes include the #173 (Castleton–Bakewell) and the #68 (Buxton–Castleton).

Tourist information The main offices are at Pavilion Gardens in Buxton (daily: 9am–5pm; ☎ 01298 25106) and Castleton's National Park Centre, Buxton Rd (daily: Jan–March 10.30am–4.30pm/5pm; April–Dec 10/10.30am–5/5.30pm; ☎ 01629 816572, ⊛ www.peakdistrict.gov.uk).

ACCOMMODATION AND EATING

Castleton YHA Castleton ☎ 08453 719628, ⊛ yha.org.uk. YHA hostel in a fabulous Gothic mansion just outside Castleton: extensive grounds have their own livestock, and there's also a planetarium and a Celtic roundhouse for campfires. Dorm **£23**

Ye Olde Cheshire Cheese Inn How Lane, Castleton. Pretty old coaching inn selling sandwiches (£5.25 with Cheshire cheese and apple chutney), plus home-made pies. Food daily noon–8.30/9pm.

Youlgreave YHA Fountain Square, Youlgreave ☎ 0845 3719151, ⊛ yha.org.uk; bus #170/#171. A 42-bed hostel in a converted Victorian shop, 3 miles outside Bakewell. Dorm **£18.40**

LIVERPOOL

Thanks to an astounding twenty-first-century revival, **LIVERPOOL** leads the way as the region's most liveable, loveable big city: a major turnaround from its infamous post-war poverty. The rediscovered sense of cultural pride is almost as palpable as in the days when it was Britain's main transatlantic port and the empire's second city. The Albert Dock has been the focus of regeneration, where converted warehouses and glitzy, glassy architecture showcase Liverpool's cultural spoils. Acerbic wit and loyalty to one of the city's two football teams are the linchpins of Liverpool's identity, along with an underlying pride in the local musical heritage; fair enough from the city that produced The Beatles.

WHAT TO SEE AND DO

From Lime Street train station it's a short walk to William Brown Street and the impressive **Walker Art Gallery** (daily 10am–5pm; free; ⊛ liverpoolmuseums .org.uk/walker), which takes you on a jaunt through British art history: Hogarth, Gainsborough, Hockney and local boy Stubbs are all well represented: be sure to see Ben Johnson's vivid 2008 Liverpool cityscape.

The Waterfront

It's a twenty-minute walk west from the Walker Art Gallery to the **Pier Head** and Liverpool's waterfront, where it's worth taking a "Ferry 'cross the Mersey" (as sung by Gerry and the Pacemakers) to Birkenhead for the views back towards the city; ferries serve commuters during rush hours (£2.60/£4 return during morning/afternoon), but in between there are hourly cruises with commentary (£8). Just behind the ferry terminal, but best seen from the river itself, stands the grandiose **Royal Liver Building**, with its enormous clock faces and local mascots – a Liver bird perched on each tower.

A short stroll south is the **Albert Dock** where you'll find the **Tate Liverpool** (daily 10am–5.50pm; free; ⊛ tate.org.uk /liverpool), northern home of the national collection of modern art.

THE FAB FOUR

Liverpool's most famous sons, The Beatles, account for a large number of the city's tourist attractions, with plenty of pubs and shops providing a high dose of Fab Four nostalgia. Spread over two venues on Albert Dock and Pier Head is **The Beatles Story** (daily: April–Oct 9am–7pm; Nov–March 10am–6pm; last admission 5pm; £12.95; ⊛ beatlesstory.com), a multimedia attempt to capture the essence of the band's rise. Buses depart twice daily from Albert Dock's tourist information centre for a two-hour **Magical Mystery Tour** (book on ☎ 0151 236 9091 or at tourist offices; £15.95) of sites associated with the band, such as Penny Lane and Strawberry Fields. Real fans will also want to visit **20 Forthlin Rd**, once home of the McCartney family, and the **Mendips**, the house where John Lennon lived between 1945 and 1963 (both are accessible on a pre-booked minibus tour Feb–Nov Wed–Sun; £20; ☎ 0151 427 7231, ⊛ nationaltrust.org.uk). Finish your Fab tour with a night at **The Cavern Club** (see p.463).

13

Occupying the other side of the dock is the **Merseyside Maritime Museum** (daily 10am–5pm; free; @liverpoolmuseums .org.uk/maritime), now incorporating the **International Slavery Museum**.

The cathedrals

To the east of the city, at either end of Hope Street, stand two very different but equally powerful twentieth-century cathedrals. The Roman Catholic **Metropolitan Cathedral** (daily 7.30am–5/6pm; donation requested), a ten-minute walk up Mount Pleasant, is a vast inverted funnel of a building, while the pale red Anglican **Liverpool Cathedral** (daily 8am–6pm; free) is the largest in the country: a muscular, neo-Gothic creation, designed by Sir Giles Gilbert Scott in 1903 but not completed until 1978. Climb the colossal tower (£5) to get fabulous 360-degree city views. On clear days it's possible to see Blackpool Tower, 28 miles to the north.

ARRIVAL AND DEPARTURE

By plane Liverpool John Lennon airport is nine miles southeast of the city, with Arriva's #500 buses (every 30min) heading to the Liverpool One bus station in the city centre.

By train Regional destinations like York, Crewe and Manchester arrive and depart from Liverpool Lime Street station, on the eastern edge of the city centre, as do services to and from London Euston.

Destinations Cardiff (via Crewe/Chester/Birmingham; 3–4 hourly; 4hr); Liverpool (frequent; 45min–1hr 10min); York (hourly; 2hr 15min).

By bus Regional coaches stop on Norton St, northeast of Liverpool Lime Street.

Destinations Cardiff (1–2 daily; 6hr 20min); Chester (4 daily; 50min); Manchester (every 30min; 1hr); Newcastle (4 daily; 5–6hr); Oxford (2 daily; 5hr–5hr 40min).

By boat P&O ferries from Dublin dock at Liverpool Freeport, 5 miles north of the centre. Stena Line ferries for Belfast dock at the Seacombe 12 Quays Ferry Terminal, across the river from Albert Dock.

Destinations Belfast (1–2 daily; 8hr); Dublin (3 daily; 8hr).

INFORMATION

Tourist information Albert Dock (daily: April–Sept 10am–5.30pm; Oct–March 10am–5pm; @0151 233 2008, @visitliverpool.com). There are also branches at St Georges Place (daily 10am–5pm) and Liverpool John Lennon airport (daily 8am–6pm).

Internet Liverpool Central Library, William Brown St (free; @0151 233 5835).

ACCOMMODATION

Embassie Hostel 1 Falkner Square @0151 707 1089, @embassie.com. This nineteenth-century house and former Venezuelan consulate exudes character, with a games room, two kitchens and a garden. Breakfast included. £5 extra Fri & Sat. Dorm **£16**

International Inn 4 South Hunter St, off Hardman St @0151 709 8135, @internationalinn.co.uk. Converted Victorian warehouse with en-suite, four- to ten-person dorms and helpful staff. Adjacent café has internet access; also cheap doubles and apartments. Dorm **£17**, double **£38**, apartment **£65**

Liverpool YHA 25 Tabley Street, off Wapping @0845 371 9527, @yha.org.uk. Reliable HI hostel to the south and east of Albert Dock, with smart three- to six-bed rooms, all with private bathrooms. Dorm **£20**, double **£50**

The Old Dairy 39a Kempton Rd @theolddairyliverpool .co.uk; bus #14/#79c/#79d from Queen Square. Popular guesthouse a couple of miles from the centre, with clean doubles (most en-suite). Double **£45**

EATING

Apart from the places below, Liverpool's Chinatown, around Berry and Nelson Streets, is a good spot to look for cheap food.

Cuthbert's Bakehouse 103 Mount Pleasant. Relaxed coffee shop with a cosy living-room feel (think net curtains and mismatched chairs), plus a little garden. The sugary-sweet peanut butter slices cost £1.80. Mon–Fri 9am–5.30pm, Sat 10am–5pm.

Egg 16–18 Newington. Gem of a veggie/vegan café doing mammoth quiches, salads and vegan-friendly cakes. Bring your own wine. It's on the second floor. Mains from £4.75. Mon–Fri 9am–10.30pm, Sat & Sun 10am–10.30pm.

Kimo's 38–44 Mount Pleasant. Moroccan-style café-restaurant serving healthy salads (from £4), plus burgers, pizzas and Moroccan dishes. Mains from £6.50. Daily 10am–11pm.

Lucha Libre 96 Wood St, adjacent to FACT. Mexican place serving street food (think fish tacos, quesadillas and burritos) in a lively restaurant setting. Wash down the spiciness with an ice-cold tamarind soda (£2.75). Daily noon–10/11pm.

DRINKING AND NIGHTLIFE

Serious clubbers and live-music fans gravitate towards the streets around Wolstenholme Sq, while the Cavern Quarter around Mathew St is home to myriad cheesy late-night bars, often Beatles-themed. The evening paper, the *Liverpool Echo*, has what's-on listings.

Alma Da Cuba St Peters' Church, Seel Street. Catholic church spectacularly converted into a softly lit restaurant, which turns into a pumping party venue later on in the night. Mon–Wed & Sun 11am–12am, Thurs–Sat 11am–2am.

The Baltic Fleet 33a Wapping. Supposedly haunted, this brew pub is a crumbling relic surrounded by newly built hotel blocks. Daily noon–late.

★ **Berry and Rye** 48 Berry Street. Hidden behind an all-black shop front (no sign) is this speakeasy-style cocktail bar specializing in, as the name suggests, whiskey and gin. Knowledgeable staff and candlelit snugs make it a good pre-club bar. Tues–Sat 5pm–2am, Sun 7pm–1am.

The Cavern Club 8–10 Mathew St ⓦcavernclub.org. Rebuilt version of The Beatles' original venue, hosting live bands every day (nightly admission charge of up to £4 Thurs–Sun). Daily 10am–midnight/2am.

Leaf on Bold St 65–67 Bold St. An unusual combination of teashop, bar and venue for self-expression, with regular yoga classes, clothing fairs and Scrabble sessions. Mon–Thurs 9am–midnight, Fri 9am–2am, Sat 10am–2am, Sun 10am–midnight.

Nation Wolstenholme Square ⓦcream.co.uk and ⓦchibuku.com. Nightclub hosting Liverpool's most infamous nights – *Cream* and *Chibuku*. See website for specific times.

The Philharmonic 36 Hope St. Fabulous, ornate pub with mosaic floors, gilded wrought-iron gates and marble decor in the gents. Skip the food in favour of the guest ales. Daily 11am–midnight.

ENTERTAINMENT

FACT 88 Wood St ⓦfact.co.uk. The Foundation for Art and Creative Technology shelters two galleries showing film/video/new media projects, an arthouse cinema and café-bar. Mon–Sat 10am–9pm, Sun 11am–9pm.

Liverpool Academy 11–13 Hotham St ⓦo2academyliverpool.co.uk. The best medium-sized live music venue in town, with good club nights.

Playhouse Williamson Square ⓦeverymanplayhouse.com. Respected theatre staging everything from black comedies to children's plays. Box office Mon–Sat 10am–6pm.

CHESTER

Genteel **CHESTER** boasts Britain's most intact city walls and unique medieval Rows (covered walkways high above street level lined with shops and cafés). Timber-framed houses sit sedately beside the River Dee, which in Roman times made it a port and one of the most important strongholds in the empire. These days, Chester makes a good base for visiting Liverpool or North Wales.

Walking the 2.5 miles round the Roman **city walls** is the best introduction to the city. Outside the walls to the east on Vicar's Lane is Britain's largest **Roman Amphitheatre** (daily; free) hinting at Chester's former importance within the empire. For more on the Romans, visit the red-brick **Grosvenor Museum** (Mon–Sat 10.30am–5pm, Sun 1–4pm; free) on Grosvenor Street or sign up for a guided city tour with a Roman centurion at the **Roman Tours Shop** next door (tours daily noon & 3pm). The northeastern section of the walls skirts the 1000-year-old **Cathedral** (Mon–Sat 9am–5pm, Sun 11am–4pm; donation requested), a grand monastic complex with wonderfully preserved cloisters. Another fun way to explore is via a river or canal boat: **Roman High Tea Cruises** (daily 4pm; £12) run by **Mill Hotel & Spa** (ⓞ01244 350 035, ⓦmillhotel.com) throw in cakes and sandwiches with their canal cruise, leaving from outside the hotel on Milton Street.

ARRIVAL AND INFORMATION

By train Trains arrive and depart from the station on the eastern edge of the city, a 10min walk from the centre.
Destinations Conwy (hourly; 1hr); Liverpool (every 15min; 45min); London (hourly; 2hr); Manchester (2–3 hourly; 1hr 15min).
By bus Coaches stop just north of Princess St, in the city centre.
Destinations Liverpool (4 daily; 1hr); Manchester (4 daily; 1hr 30min).
Tourist information The main tourist office is inside the town hall on Northgate St (daily 9am–5.30pm; ⓞ08456 477 868). Sells maps (£1.50) for self-guided tours of the city.

ACCOMMODATION AND EATING

Blue Moon Cafe 23 The Groves. Down on the riverfront, this 1950s/60s-themed café serves great, filling breakfasts (£4.95) as well as hot mains like fish and chips. Daily 10am–4.30pm.
The Brewery Tap 52–54 Lower Bridge St. Seventeenth-century hall with great cask ales and meals – like grilled ox heart – for £8.95. Mon–Thurs noon–11pm, Fri & Sat noon–midnight, Sun noon–10.30pm.
Chester Backpackers 67 Broughton St ⓦchesterbackpackers.co.uk. The best budget option in town: a quirky former pub that also offers long-term rates. Dorm £15.95, double £40

13

THE LAKE DISTRICT

The site of England's highest peaks and its biggest concentration of lakes, the glacier-carved **Lake District National Park** is the nation's most popular walking area. Weather here in Cumbria changes quickly, but the sudden shifts of light on the bracken-bedaubed moorland, and on the slate of the local buildings, are part of the area's appeal. The region is informally divided into the South Lakes, including **Windermere** and **Ambleside**, and the North Lakes, which include **Keswick**.

ARRIVAL AND DEPARTURE

By train Departing from London, use the main-line service from Euston to Glasgow, disembarking at Lancaster or Oxenholme. Within the Lake District only Windermere and Kendal are accessible by train, on a branch line from Oxenholme.
Destinations from Windermere Lancaster (5 daily; 40min); Oxenholme (hourly; 20min).
Destinations from Kendal Lancaster (5 daily; 25min); Oxenholme (hourly; 5min).
By bus National Express coaches run daily from London Victoria and Manchester to the Lake District.
Destinations from Windermere London (1 daily; 8hr 10min); Manchester (via Preston; 1 daily; 5hr 20min).
Destinations from Kendal London (1 daily; 7hr 45min); Manchester (via Preston; 1 daily; 5hr).

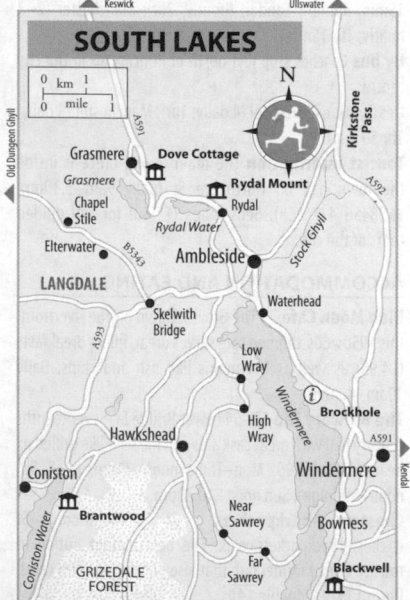

SOUTH LAKES

Keswick — Ullswater

0 km 1
0 mile 1

N

Old Dungeon Ghyll

Grasmere ● Dove Cottage
Grasmere 🏛
Chapel
Stile ●   Rydal Mount 🏛
Elterwater ●   ● Rydal
Rydal Water
Ambleside ●
LANGDALE
Skelwith
Bridge ●   Waterhead
Low
Wray ●
Hawkshead ●   High   ℹ Brockhole
Wray   A591
Coniston ●   Windermere
🏛
● Brantwood   Near
Sawrey ●   ● Bowness
GRIZEDALE   Far   Blackwell
FOREST   Sawrey   🏛
Lakeside

Kirkstone Pass
A591
A592
Stock Ghyll
Windermere
Kendal
Coniston Water

GETTING AROUND

By bus Stagecoach buses go everywhere in the region, and offer Explorer Tickets, valid across all of Cumbria and Lancashire (1/3 days for £10.30/£22). Tourist offices provide a complete list of services, but the main routes are #555 from Lancaster to Kendal, Windermere, Ambleside, Grasmere and Keswick, and the summer-only open-top #599, from Bowness to Ambleside via Windermere and Brockhole.

Windermere and Bowness

Windermere is the largest of the lakes, with its main town of **WINDERMERE** set a mile or so back from the water. Other than the short climb up to the viewpoint of **Orrest Head** (30min), it offers little to do, but it is the region's main service centre.

There are also buses (#555 from outside the train station) to the **Lake District National Park Visitor Centre** at Brockhole, which has an excellent information centre as well as exhibitions on the Lake District past, present and future (daily: mid-March to Oct 10am–5pm; Nov to mid-March 10am–4pm; free; ☎015394 46601). Boats (£7.40) to the Visitor Centre run from Ambleside (see opposite).

For trips onto Lake Windermere itself, catch bus #508/#599/#800 from outside Windermere train station to the more photogenic, but often more crowded, lakeshore town of **BOWNESS**. Lake **ferries** (☎015394 43360, ⓦwindermere-lakecruises.co.uk) run to Lakeside at the southern tip (£10 return) or to Waterhead (for Ambleside) at the northern end (£10 return); a 24-hour Freedom of the Lake ticket costs £18.

INFORMATION

Tourist information The Windermere tourist office is located outside the train station (daily 9/9.30am–4.30/5pm; ☎01539 446499).

GETTING AROUND

By bike Bikes can be rented from Country Lanes at Windermere train station (£20/day; ☎01539 444544, ⓦcountrylaneslakedistrict.co.uk).

ACCOMMODATION

Brendan Chase 1 College Rd, Windermere ☎015394 45638, ⓦbrendanchase.co.uk. Backpacker-friendly B&B with flowery en-suite rooms, free wi-fi and a living room decorated by the team on TV's The Hotel Inspector. Double __£60__

> ## ACCOMMODATION IN THE LAKES
> There are 25 YHA **youth hostels** in the region, including one in each of the areas listed here, with the exception of Bowness: see ⓦ yha.org.uk for details – but be aware that hostels can get both busy and expensive in summer. **Campsites** also proliferate, some in exceptional locations. For more information visit the official site of the Cumbria Tourist Board, ⓦ golakes.co.uk.

Lake District Backpackers' Lodge High St, Windermere ☎ 015394 46374, ⓦ lakedistrictbackpackers .co.uk. This little hostel just downhill from the station has cosy yet simple dorms. Booking ahead is recommended; cash only if paying on arrival. Breakfast included. Dorm £15, double £35

EATING AND DRINKING

The Elleray Victoria Street, Windermere ☎ 015394 88464, ⓦ elleraywindermere.co.uk. Handily located a short walk from the train station, this place does good-value pub food (lunch £5 daily noon–3pm). Mon–Thurs & Sun noon–11pm, Fri & Sat noon–midnight.

The Hole in't Wall Low Side, behind the church in Bowness ☎ 015394 43488. Don't miss the chance to enjoy a pint of cask ale (£3.25) at the oldest hostelry in Bowness, once supposedly frequented by Dickens. Mon–Sat 11am–11.30pm, Sun 11am–10.30pm.

Lazy Daisy's Crescent Road, Windermere ☎ 015394 43877, ⓦ lazydaisyslakelandkitchen.co.uk. Welcoming coffee shop with sandwiches and snacks (from £5.75) on offer throughout the day and a more sophisticated evening menu that includes fish dishes and salads. Daily 9am–9pm.

McClure's College Road, Windermere ☎ 015394 42636, ⓦ wmcclure.co.uk. Warehouse-like cash and carry tucked away off the main street. A cheap place to stock up on snacks when planning a long hike. Mon–Fri 8am–5pm, Sat 8am–12.30pm, Sun 9.30am–11.30am.

Ambleside

Pretty but touristy, **Ambleside** is good for stocking up on outdoor gear, and makes a reasonable base between the north and south lakes. The **Ambleside Armitt Museum** (Mon–Sat 10am–5pm; £3.50; ⓦ armitt.com) exhibits items of local geological, archeological and literary interest.

INFORMATION

Tourist information Limited info is available at The Hub of Ambleside (look for the post office sign) by the Market Cross (daily 9am–5/5.30pm; ☎ 01539 432582).

ACCOMMODATION

Ambleside Backpackers Old Lake Rd ☎ 015394 32340, ⓦ englishlakesbackpackers.co.uk. Independent

family-run hostel located in a quiet part of town, with immaculate dorms. Breakfast included. Dorm £19

Ambleside Youth Hostel Waterhead ☎ 0845 3719620. Recently refurbished YHA hostel in a prime lakeside location. There are superb views across the water and excellent facilities, including a licensed restaurant. Dorm £21

EATING AND DRINKING

Bizzy Lizzy's Lake Rd. Home-made soups (£3.60) and local ice cream (from £1.60) are sold at this teashop overlooking Loughrigg. Daily 10.30am–4/5pm.

Zeffirelli's Compston Road. A cinema with its own daytime café and a pizza restaurant (margherita £8.45). Daily 10am–10pm.

Elterwater and Langdale

The #516 Stagecoach bus from Ambleside runs four miles west to the charming hamlet of **ELTERWATER**. The valley here offers dramatic scenery and plenty of good walking, including up to Stickle Tarn and the peaks of **Langdale** (including England's highest point, Scafell Pike). The *Sticklebarn Tavern*, two miles beyond Elterwater on the same bus route, is a good place to start from, though you should make sure you have good shoes, waterproofs and a map. If you need some relaxation after a long day's walking, the *Langdale Hotel* down the road from *Baysbrown Campsite* lets non-residents use its pool, spa and sauna (£9.75 for a day pass).

ACCOMMODATION AND EATING

★ **Baysbrown Campsite** A few minutes' walk west from the centre of Chapel Stile ☎ 01539 437150. Canny campers shun the expensive hotels in favour of this spectacular site, which has views down the valley. Camping £5 per person and tent

Brambles Café In the centre of Chapel Stile. Attractive little café serving coffee, light meals and toasted teacakes (£1.70) to a friendly mix of tourists and locals. Daily 9am–5pm.

Keswick and Derwent Water

Principal hiking and tourist centre for the northern lakes, **KESWICK** (pronounced

13

LAKE DISTRICT LUMINARIES

The lakeland landscape has been an inspiration to some of England's most revered literary figures. **William Wordsworth** lived at both Rydal Mount (March–Oct daily 9.30am–5pm; Nov–Feb Wed–Sun 11am–4pm; £6.75, gardens only £4.50), three miles northwest of Ambleside on the #555 bus, and the more interesting Dove Cottage, Grasmere (daily 9.30am–4.30/5.30pm; closed Jan; £7.50), which still holds many of Wordsworth's possessions. Both he and his sister Dorothy lie in simple graves in the village churchyard of St Oswald's.

   Beatrix Potter, author, illustrator and botanist, lived at Hill Top (Mon–Thurs, Sat & Sun: mid-Feb to mid-March 10.30am–3.30pm; mid-March to mid-May 10.30am–4.30pm; mid-May to Aug 10.30am–5.30pm; Sept & Oct 10.30am–4.30pm; £8.50; ticket numbers limited; ⓦnationaltrust.org.uk), a lovely seventeenth-century house in the hamlet of Near Sawrey. You can take a ferry from Bowness (see p.464) and cover the steep two miles to the house on foot or by minibus. Get there early to beat the crowds.

   From the village of Coniston, reached by bus #505 from Windermere or Ambleside, you can take the wooden *Coniston Launch* (£10.50 return; ☏01768 775753, ⓦconistonlaunch.co.uk) to the elegant lakeside villa, Brantwood (daily 10.30am–4/5pm; £7.20, gardens only £4.95), once home of artist and critic **John Ruskin**. The house is full of Ruskin's own drawings and sketches, as well as items relating to the Pre-Raphaelite painters he inspired.

"kez-ick") lies on the shores of **Derwent Water**. The **Keswick Launch** (mid-March to Nov & school hols daily; Dec to mid-March Sat & Sun; £9.50 return trip; ☏01768 772263, ⓦkeswick-launch.co.uk) runs right around the lake, and you can get off at Hawes End for the climb up **Cat Bells** (1481ft), best of the lakeside vantage points. From Keswick you can hike up to Latrigg (1203ft; 3hr) for breathtaking views or the more challenging **Skiddaw** (3050ft; 5hr), among the more straightforward of the area's many true mountain hikes. Walks round the lake via **Borrowdale**, perhaps the most beautiful valley in England, take three to five hours, depending on whether you stick to the lakeside or climb above it. A mile and a half's stroll eastwards is **Castlerigg Stone Circle** (free), a Neolithic monument commanding a spectacular view.

ARRIVAL AND INFORMATION

By bus The terminal is behind Booths Foodstore, off Keswick's Main St.

Destinations Ambleside (up to 20 daily; 45min); Grasmere (up to 20 daily; 30min); Kendal (up to 20 daily; 1hr 30min); Windermere (up to 20 daily; 1hr 10min).

Tourist information Moot Hall, Market Square (daily 9.30am–4.30/5.30pm; ☏01768 772645).

GETTING AROUND

By bike Bike rental available from Keswick Mountain Bikes, Southey Hill (daily 9am–5.30pm; ☏01768 775202, ⓦkeswickmountainbikes.co.uk; £20/day).

ACCOMMODATION

Denton House Penrith Rd ☏01768 775351, ⓦdentonhouse-keswick.co.uk. Sprawling, laidback hostel that focuses on the Lake District's outdoor attractions, and can organize activities in the area. Dorm **£18**

Keswick Camping Crow Park Rd ☏01768 772392, ⓦcampingandcaravanningclub.co.uk. Very convenient location west of town, 5min from the bus station and right on the shores of Derwent Water. Booking advised. Camping **£9.65** per person, plus **£7.20** per tent

YHA Keswick Station Rd ☏08453 719746, ⓦyha.org.uk. Well-maintained YHA hostel in a serene riverside spot with impressive mountain scenery. The restaurant here is licensed and does cheap evening meals. Dorm **£20.50**

EATING, DRINKING AND ENTERTAINMENT

Dog and Gun Lake Rd. Keswick's best pub, with local beers on tap and a kitchen turning out pub food, including a celebrated goulash (£6.95/9.95, depending on size). Daily noon–11pm.

The George 3 St John's St. Old coaching inn with Jennings ales on tap, serving a much-in-demand Cow Pie (£11.95 for a half portion). Daily 11am–11pm/midnight.

Lakeland Pedlar Henderson's Yard, off Main St. Keswick's most agreeable café: vegetarian-friendly, with excellent home-made cakes and scones, as well as soups and sandwiches. Try the "boneshaker" salad with organic bread (£5). Daily 9am–4/5pm.

Theatre by the Lake Lake Rd ☏01768 774411 ⓦtheatrebythelake.co.uk. Located right on the edge of town, close to Derwent Water, this theatre has two stages hosting drama, dance, music and the odd bit of stand-up.

YORK

Affluent **YORK** is a layer cake of history: the Romans used the city as their capital in northern Britain, as did Edwin of Northumbria, whose conversion to Christianity in 627 granted it huge spiritual importance. Then the Vikings swept through in 866, and ruled until 954, when Eric Bloodaxe lost Jorvik – as it was then known – to King Edred, who brought it into his unified England. Today its sinuous century-old cobbled streets are filled with cafés and craft shops, surrounded by picturesque medieval ramparts and centred on the spectacular Gothic Minster.

WHAT TO SEE AND DO

Start your sightseeing with a stroll along the **city walls** (daily till dusk), a three-mile circuit that takes in the various medieval "bars", or gates, with fine views of the Minster. Guided walks (daily 10.15am, plus 2.15pm April–Sept & 6.45pm July & Aug; free; 2hr) depart from outside the art gallery in Exhibition Square; just turn up.

York Minster

Ever since Edwin built a wooden chapel on the site, **York Minster** (Mon–Sat 9am–5pm, Sun noon–5pm; £10 for Minster only) has been the centre of religious authority for the north of England. Most of what's visible now was built in stages between the 1220s and the 1470s, and today it ranks as the country's largest Gothic building. Inside, the scenes of the East Window, completed in 1405, and the abstract thirteenth-century Five Sisters window, represent Britain's finest collection of stained glass. If you want to climb the central tower, which gives views over the medieval pattern of narrow streets to the south known as **The Shambles**, you'll need to buy a combined ticket costing £15.

Yorkshire Museum

Southwest of the Minster, just outside the city walls, Museum Gardens leads to the ruins of the Benedictine abbey of St Mary and the **Yorkshire Museum** (daily 10am–5pm; £7.50, or £10 including the Castle Museum; ⓦyorkshiremuseum.org.uk), which contains much of the abbey's medieval sculpture, and a selection of Roman, Saxon and Viking finds.

Jorvik, Dig and Castle Museum

From the Minster, shopping streets spread south and east, focusing eventually on Coppergate, former site of the city's Viking settlement. The blockbuster experience that is **Jorvik Viking Centre** (daily: April–Oct 10am–5pm; Nov–March 10am–4pm; Oct half-term until 6pm; ⓦjorvik-viking-centre.co.uk; £9.75) provides a taste of the period through a re-creation of Viking streets, complete with appropriate sounds and smells. It gets very busy at peak period, and you may want to book your tickets online to save hassle. Just north of here, within St Saviour's Church, is **Dig** (daily 10am–5pm; £5.50 or £13.25 including Jorvik; ⓦdigyork.com), a hands-on museum where visitors carry out their own archeological excavation, discovering artefacts and learning about the science and processes of archeology.

Further south, the superb **Castle Museum** (daily 9.30am–5pm; £8.50) has full-scale re-creations of life in bygone times, with evocative street scenes of the Victorian and Edwardian periods.

ARRIVAL AND DEPARTURE

By train York's train station lies outside the city walls on Station Rd.

Destinations Edinburgh (every 30min; 2hr 25min–2hr 40min); London (every 30min; 2hr–2hr 20min); Manchester (every 15–30min; 1hr 30min); Newcastle (every 30min; 1hr).

By bus Long-distance coaches drop off/pick up outside the train station, as well as on Rougier St, 200m northeast, just before Lendal Bridge.

Destinations Edinburgh (1 daily; 6hr 15min); Glasgow (1 daily; 7hr 30min); London (4 daily; 5hr 30min); Manchester (hourly via Leeds; 2hr 35min); Newcastle (2 daily; 2hr 20min).

INFORMATION

Tourist information 1 Museum St (Mon–Sat 9am–5/5.30pm, Sun 10am–4pm; ☎01904 550099, ⓦvisityork.org).

Discount card York Pass (£34 for one day), which includes access to nearly all the sights.

Internet Computer terminals are available in cocktail bar,

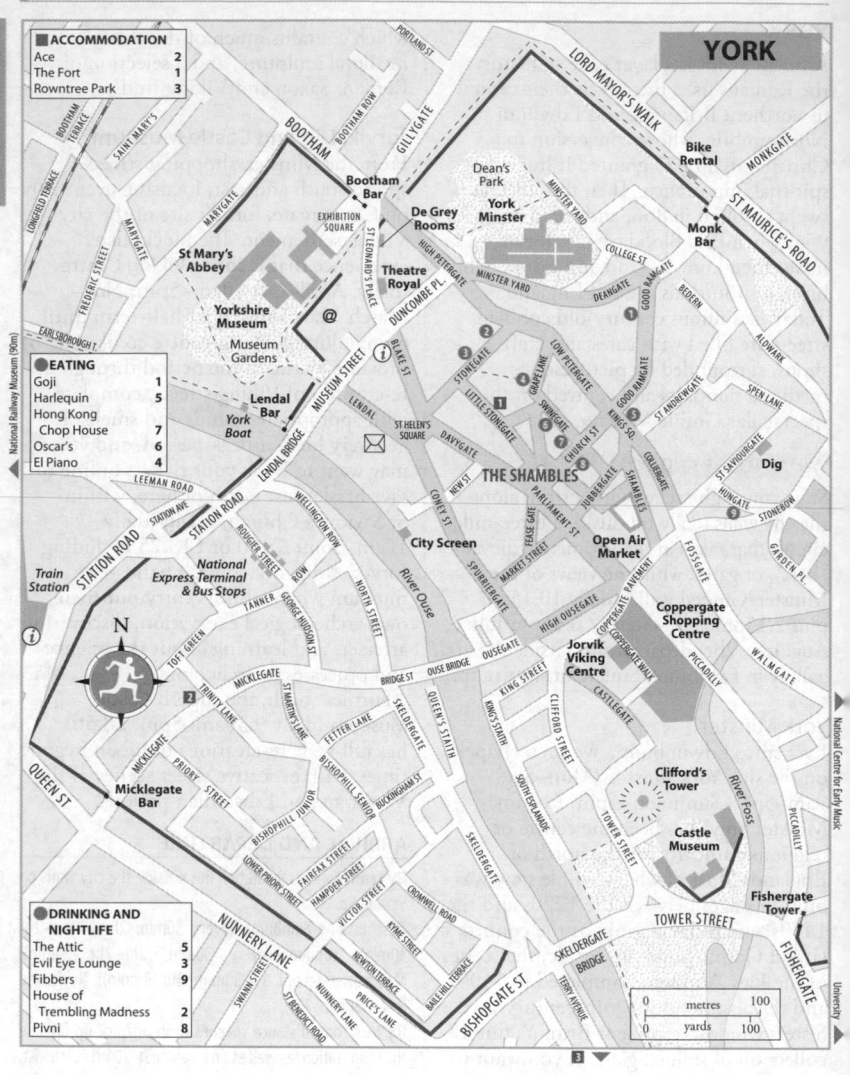

York

ACCOMMODATION
Ace	2
The Fort	1
Rowntree Park	3

EATING
Goji	1
Harlequin	5
Hong Kong Chop House	7
Oscar's	6
El Piano	4

DRINKING AND NIGHTLIFE
The Attic	5
Evil Eye Lounge	3
Fibbers	9
House of Trembling Madness	2
Pivni	8

Evil Eye Lounge, 42 Stonegate (Mon–Sat 10am–midnight/1am, Sun 11am–midnight; £1/30min, 3.3p/min thereafter).

ACCOMMODATION

Outside of term time, the University of York (☎01904 328431, ⓦyork.ac.uk) rents out good-value double rooms at its campus on a night-by-night basis.

Ace 88–90 Micklegate ☎01904 627720, ⓦacehotelyork .co.uk. Wonderful boutique hostel in a Grade 1-listed Georgian terrace house. Expect stone-flagged floors, wood-panelled rooms, a basement games room, a secluded courtyard and a sauna. Several of the private rooms available are more luxurious than most B&Bs. Dorm **£16**, double **£80**

The Fort 1 Little Stonegate ☎01904 639573, ⓦthefortyork.co.uk. York does upper-end budget well these days: bang in the centre, spacious rooms with flat-screen TVs and local artwork. Rooms are en suite; there's a bar-café downstairs. Dorm **£18**, double **£58**

Rowntree Park Terry Ave ☎01904 658997, ⓦcaravan club.co.uk. Conveniently placed campsite on the banks of the River Ouse, just south of town, within easy walking distance. Camping **£7.90** per person, plus **£10.20** per tent

EATING

El Piano 15–17 Grape Lane. Bright, family-run vegan restaurant serving plenty of nut-free and raw dishes (mains £9.95), with flavours from South America, Spain and East Africa. Mon–Sat 11am–11pm, Sun noon–9pm.

Goji 36 Goodramgate. Vegetarian café/deli with its own gallery. Great sandwiches and salads, cheese selections, vegan wines and a convivial courtyard. Meals £7. On Fri/Sat eve it also does inventive evening meals, including a garlicky mushroom burger (£9.25). Mon–Thurs 9.30am–4.30pm, Fri 9.30am–4.30pm & 6.30–11pm, Sat 9.30am–5pm & 6.30–11pm, Sun 11am–4.30pm.

★ **Harlequin** 2 King's Sq. Tourists usually flock to Bettys on St Helen's Sq, ignoring this (much cheaper) first-floor tearoom, which serves excellent lunches and ethically sourced coffee (espresso £1.75). Mon–Sat 10am–4pm, Sun 11am–3pm.

Hong Kong Chop House 33 Swinegate. Lantern-lit Chinese restaurant specializing in Hakka cuisine. As the owners are proudly superstitious, every dish on the menu is priced with a lucky number eight as the last digit. At £8.88, the stir-fried duck is the luckiest dish going. Daily noon–2pm & 4.30–11pm.

Oscar's 27 Swinegate. Lively wine bar and restaurant, with lasagnes, curries and the like for £7.95. Also has a two-for-one cocktail deal from 10pm nightly. Mon–Sat 11.30am–midnight/1am, Sun 11.30am–midnight.

DRINKING AND NIGHTLIFE

The Attic 2 King's Sq, on the second floor, above *Harlequin*. A youthful, art-filled coffee shop run by the same team as *Harlequin*, with occasional cabaret nights and bottled craft beer. Thurs noon–6pm, Fri & Sat noon–8pm.

Evil Eye Lounge 42 Stonegate. Inviting bar with comfy sofas, an encyclopaedic range of spirits, quaffable cocktails and great Southeast Asian food. Shots around £3. Mon–Sat 10am–midnight/1am, Sun 11am–midnight.

Fibbers Stonebow House, Stonebow ⓦ fibbers.co.uk. Long-established, this is still York's best live music venue, with guitar bands playing most nights of the week. Most gigs start at 7.30pm, though see website for exact times.

House of Trembling Madness 48 Stonegate. Sequestered away above a bottle shop and serving a great range of Belgian beers in a shadowy, candlelit hall. Try the £1.50 "Viking willies" (salamis) kept behind the bar. Daily 10/11am–midnight.

Plvni 6 Patrick Pool. A proper beer drinkers' pub in a timber-framed building dating back to 1190. While some of the bottled beers go for up to £20, the ales on tap are much cheaper. Mon–Sat 11.30am–11.30pm/11.45pm, Sun noon–11.30pm.

ENTERTAINMENT

City Screen 13–17 Coney St ⓦ picturehouses.co.uk. Arthouse cinema with a riverside café bar and live music. Also screens Hollywood films. See website for individual show times.

National Centre for Early Music St Margaret's Church, Walmgate ⓦ ncem.co.uk. Hosts a prestigious early music festival in July, plus world, jazz and folk gigs throughout the year. See website for specific show times.

DURHAM

A "perfect little city" according to travel writer Bill Bryson, **DURHAM** is known for its spectacular cathedral and castle perched high on a bluff enclosed by a loop of the River Wear (pronounced "weer"). Once one of northern England's power bases, today it's a quiet provincial city with a strong student presence. Visit as a day-trip from Newcastle or stay over to soak up the medieval vibe.

WHAT TO SEE AND DO

Durham hit the limelight after the remains of St Cuthbert, the patron saint of Northumbria, were moved here in the ninth century because of Viking raids. His shrine at the eastern end of the beautiful eleventh-century **cathedral** (Mon–Sat 9.30am–6pm, Sun 12.30–5.30pm; till 8pm daily mid-July to early Sept; ⓦ durhamcathedral.co.uk; donation requested) soon became a pilgrimage site. The cathedral is England's finest example of Norman architecture, and also contains the tomb of the Venerable Bede, the country's first historian. The **tower** gives breathtaking views (Mon–Sat 10am–3/4pm; £5). On the opposite side of Palace Green is the **castle** (regular guided tours; £5; ☎ 0191 3342 932), a much refurbished Norman edifice that's now a university hall of residence. A half-hour stroll follows a pathway on the wooded riverbank below the cathedral and castle, all the way around the peninsula.

South of the centre on Elvet Hill the engrossing **Oriental Museum** (Mon–Fri 10am–5pm, Sat & Sun noon–5pm; £1.50), run by Durham University, is the country's only museum dedicated exclusively to oriental art. It hit headlines when, in 2012, bungling burglars broke

13

in to steal £2m of Chinese artefacts, only to forget where they had stashed them. The thieves were arrested, and the artefacts were later recovered on wasteland south of the city.

ARRIVAL AND INFORMATION

By train Durham train station is a 10min walk from the centre, via either of the two main river bridges.
Destinations London (hourly; 3hr); Newcastle (every 20min; 20min); York (4 hourly; 45min).
By bus The bus station is just south of the train station on North Rd.
Destinations London (3 daily; 7hr); Newcastle (every 30min; 50min).
Tourist information A phone line (☎ 03000 262626) has replaced Durham's tourist office. However, the World Heritage Site Visitor Centre, near the castle at 7 Owengate, can help with most enquiries (daily 9.30am–4.30/5/6pm).

ACCOMMODATION

Durham University has rooms available – including within the castle – at Easter and from July to Sept (☎ 0800 289 970, ⓦ dur.ac.uk/conferences).
Castle View Crossgate ☎ 0191 386 8852, ⓦ castle-view .co.uk. The best-value guesthouse with homely rooms, internet access and great views of Durham. Double **£80**
YHA Durham City St Chad's College, near the cathedral ☎ 0191 334 3358, ⓦ yha.org.uk. Open only during the summer holidays and at Easter, this well-located college block has great-value rooms, some of which are en suite. Double **£25**

EATING, DRINKING AND ENTERTAINMENT

Compared with Newcastle down the road, Durham's no clubbers' paradise, but there are plenty of lively bars as well as some nice old-fashioned pubs.
★ **Flat White** 21a Elvet Bridge. Home-made cakes are served on floral plates at this café/wine bar just off Saddler St, whose stone walls and wooden beams are decorated with colourful sprigs of dried flowers. Cheap breakfasts (from £3.25) and excellent coffee. Mon–Sat 9.30am–5.30pm, Sun 10am–4pm.
Gala Theatre & Cinema Millennium Place ⓦ galadurham.co.uk. Durham's large theatre and cinema complex hosts drama, concerts, comedy shows and film nights. Daily 10am–late.
Vennel's Café Saddler's Yard, off Saddler St. Café serving everything from cakes to pies and quiches (£4.85) in a lovely little hidden courtyard. Mon–Sat 9.30am–5pm, Sun 10.30am–5pm.
The Victoria Inn 86 Hallgarth St. Splendidly British, this pub retains its original interior, with three separate rooms

warmed by smouldering coal fireplaces. Make time for a pint of bitter (£3.20). Daily 11.45am–3pm & 6–11pm.

NEWCASTLE-UPON-TYNE

NEWCASTLE-UPON-TYNE has shaken off its image as being all bare-chested football fans and raucous nightlife. While still possessing both in abundance, this formerly industrial city is now as trendy as it is tough, and more about culture than clubbing. It's streets ahead of its rivals in the northeast, and has a slew of fine galleries and arts venues, as well as a handsome Neoclassical downtown area fanning out from the lofty Grecian column of **Grey's Monument**, the city's central landmark. Facing Newcastle across the Tyne is rejuvenated Gateshead, a former industrial area and now the hub of the city's art scene.

WHAT TO SEE AND DO

Arriving by train from the south, your first view is of the **River Tyne**, flanked by redeveloped quaysides and crossed by a series of bridges linking Newcastle to the **Gateshead** side of the river. Most famous is the single steel-arched **Tyne Bridge**, built in 1928 and complemented by the hi-tech "winking" **Millennium Bridge**, a wonderful sweeping arc of sparkling steel channelling pedestrians cross-river. North of the centre is student- and bar-filled Jesmond, while east is the trendy, regenerated area of Ouseburn.

Laing Gallery, Baltic and The Sage

The northeast's main art collection is housed in the **Laing Gallery** on New Bridge Street (Tues–Sat 10am–5pm, Sun 2–5pm; free; ⓦ twmuseums.org.uk/laing), but is overshadowed by the excellent **Baltic** (Baltic Centre for Contemporary Art; daily 10/10.30am–6pm; free; ⓦ balticmill.com) next to the Millennium Bridge in Gateshead. One of the biggest contemporary galleries outside London, this converted former flour mill accommodates exhibition spaces, artists' studios, a café-bar and two restaurants. On a similarly ambitious scale, the Baltic has been joined by the **Sage Gateshead** (daily roughly 9am–11pm; free;

ⓦ thesagegateshead.org), a billowing steel, aluminium and glass structure by Norman Foster. The programme of concerts (classical and contemporary) and activities here has transformed this side of the river.

ARRIVAL AND DEPARTURE

By plane The airport is five miles north, served by the local Metro system (DaySaver ticket for unlimited rides in all three zones £4.40).

By train Newcastle's Central Station is a 2min walk from the centre.

Destinations Durham (around 3 hourly; 10–15min); Edinburgh (every 30min; 1hr 30min); Glasgow (every 30min, most via Edinburgh; 2hr 30min–3hr); London (every 30min; 3hr–3hr 15min); York (up to 5 hourly; 1hr–1hr 15min); Manchester (via York; every 15min; 2hr 35min–3hr 20min).

By bus The coach station, on St James's Boulevard, is a few mins' walk west of the station.

Destinations Durham (every 30min; 50min); Edinburgh (3–4 daily; 2hr 40min–3hr 10min); Glasgow (2 daily; 3hr 30min–4hr 30min); Liverpool (6 daily; 5hr 25min–6hr 50min); London (8 daily; 6hr–7hr 45min); Manchester (9 daily; 5hr 30min); York (2 daily; 2hr 30min).

By ferry The ferry port (for crossings from Amsterdam) is in North Shields, seven miles east, with connecting buses running to the centre.

Destinations Amsterdam (1 daily; 15hr 30min).

INFORMATION

Tourist information The main tourist office is at Central Arcade (Mon–Sat 9.30am–5.30pm, Sun 10am–4pm; ☎ 0191 277 8000). The City Library can also provide tourist information.

Internet Newcastle City Library, 33 New Bridge St West (Mon–Thurs 8.30am–8pm, Fri 8.30am–5.30pm, Sat 9.30am–5.30pm, Sun 11am–5pm; ☎ 0191 277 4100; free for members – join at front desk).

ACCOMMODATION

The University of Northumbria (☎ 0191 227 4209, ⓦ northumbria.ac.uk) and Newcastle University (☎ 0191 222 6318, ⓦ ncl.ac.uk) offer good-value, summertime B&B (mostly single rooms) in their halls of residence.

Albatross Backpackers Inn 51 Grainger St ☎ 0191 233 1330, ⓦ albatrossnewcastle.co.uk. The most convenient place to stay in Newcastle, this large, friendly hostel is both cheap and central. Dorm £16.50, double £45

Euro Hostel 17 Carliol Square ☎ 0845 490 0371, ⓦ euro -hostels.co.uk/newcastle. Clean, smart rooms at this 256-bed converted warehouse hostel on top of one of the city's best bars. All rooms are en suite. Dorm £16.50, double £45

EATING

Many restaurants are grouped around Bigg Market, a block west of Grey St.

Nudo 54–56 Low Friar St. Plush, popular noodle house with sushi from £2.50 and noodle dishes for £6.50–8. Authentic dishes include grilled eel, Japanese style. Daily noon–10pm.

Kafeneon 8 Bigg Market. Central, Greek bar/restaurant with a bargain happy-hour menu (5–8pm) that gets you two courses for £8.90. Mon–Sat 11am–10pm.

Pink Lane Coffee Pink Lane. Well-run speciality coffee shop just up from the station with staff that really know their beans. Sandwiches too (£3–3.50). Mon–Fri 7.30am–6pm, Sat 9am–5pm, Sun 10am–4pm.

Scrumpy Willow and the Singing Kettle 89 Clayton St. Cool café in a converted house doing a roaring trade in veggie fare, like the famous dhal, plus great coffee and scrummy cakes (£2.50). Mon–Sat 10am–7/8pm.

DRINKING AND NIGHTLIFE

Free monthly entertainment listings magazine, *The Crack*, available in pubs and record shops, is the best way to find out what's on.

The Cluny Lime St, Ouseburn. Live music venue hosting rising stars from around the globe. Glorious burgers (£6.95) and a good international beer selection. Mon–Sat 8–11pm/midnight, Sun 8–10.30pm.

Digital Times Square ⓦ yourfutureisdigital.com. Proud owner of the best sound system in the city. Plenty of world-class DJs have headlined here, with last Fri of the month hosting *Turbulence*: Northern England's best drum 'n' bass night. The music policy otherwise runs the full gamut from eighties cheese through to rave, with an indie night on Thurs. See website for opening and closing times.

The Forth Pink St ⓦ theforthnewcastle.co.uk. Great pre-club spot with an innovative food menu (mains from £8.25), good music, an open fire and a roof terrace. Mon–

★ TREAT YOURSELF

Blackfriars Friars Street ☎ 0191 261 5945. Claiming to be Britain's oldest continually used dining room and located in a thirteenth-century monastery, with several cosy eating areas, one with a monastic-style banqueting table. Overlooking a lush central courtyard, it serves well-priced mains like pan haggerty (a northeastern speciality of potatoes, onions and cheese) for around £12. Go there for lunch or an early evening meal on a weekday to get the best deals. Worth the splurge. Mon–Sat noon–2.30pm & 5.30pm–late, Sun noon–4pm.

13

Wed noon–11pm, Thurs & Fri noon–midnight, Sat 11am–midnight, Sun noon–11pm.
Powerhouse 7–19 Westmoreland Rd. The northeast's biggest gay club, playing something for everyone until 4am over three floors. Often cheap drinks before midnight. Mon & Thurs–Sun 11/11.30pm–4am.

HADRIAN'S WALL

Hadrian's Wall, once separating Roman England from barbarian Scotland, can be a wonderfully atmospheric place, especially on a rainy day, when it's not difficult to imagine Roman soldiers gloomily contemplating their bleak northern posting from atop the wall. Nowadays the **Hadrian's Wall Path**, an 84-mile way-marked trail (5–7 days) runs coast to coast across Northumberland and Cumbria. It starts at **Segedunum**, Wallsend, four miles east of Newcastle, the last outpost of Hadrian's great border defence. You can visit the excavations (daily: April–Oct 10am–5pm; Nov–March 10am–3pm; £5.25; ⓦWallsend). Otherwise, the best jumping-off point and base for longer exploration is the abbey town of **HEXHAM**, 45 minutes west of Newcastle by train or bus. Some of the finest preserved sections of wall include **Housesteads** (daily 10am–4/6pm; £6.20), the most complete Roman fort in Britain, set in spectacular countryside, and the partly re-created fort and lively museum at **Vindolanda** (daily 10am–5/6pm; £6.50). The circular route starting and finishing at the HI hostel, *Once Brewed* (see below), provides a decent walk, covering around 7.5 miles and taking in both Housesteads and Vindolanda, as well as some dramatic scenery. For a break from the Romans, visit **All Out Adventures** (ⓦalloutadventures.co.uk) at **Slaley Hall** near Hexham, where you can try your hand at a host of outdoor activities from archery to a Segway safari (£20–60).

ARRIVAL AND INFORMATION

By bus The Hadrian's Wall #AD122 bus (up to 5 daily Easter–Oct, though not all services cover the whole route; 1-day ticket £9, 3-day £18, 7-day £36) runs between Hexham and Carlisle via all the main sites. The first service of the day runs all the way from Newcastle Central Station, so it's possible to hop on there, too. The year-round #685 bus runs from Carlisle to Housesteads via Haltwhistle (on the Newcastle–Carlisle train line).

Tourist information Hexham has a tourist office in the main car park (April–Oct Mon–Sat 9.30am–5pm, Sun 11am–4pm; Nov–March Mon–Sat 10am–4.30pm; ☎01434 652220) and there's also a National Park Centre at the HI hostel, *Once Brewed* (see below; April–Oct daily 9.30am–5pm; Nov–March Sat & Sun 10am–3pm; ☎01434 344396, ⓦvisitnortheastengland.com).

ACCOMMODATION AND EATING

Hadrians Wall Camping Melkridge, Haltwhistle ☎01434 320495, ⓦhadrianswallcampsite.co.uk. Small, level site near the Wall with a centrally heated bunk barn. Camping **£10** per person and small tent, bunk barn **£15**
Once Brewed ☎0845 371 9753, ⓦyha.org.uk. HI hostel in a modern, purpose-built block 15 miles west of Hexham and within easy walking distance of the wall. Dorm **£18.50**, double **£40**
Twice Brewed Inn ☎01434 344534, ⓦtwicebrewedinn .co.uk. Friendly pub on the same site as *Once Brewed* with simple rooms, food (served till 8.30pm) and local beers. Double **£59**

LINDISFARNE (HOLY ISLAND)

Accessed by a sandy causeway at low tide only, magical emerald-green **LINDISFARNE** (ⓦwww.lindisfarne.org .uk), topped by its distinctive, stumpy castle, has been one of Britain's most important pilgrimage destinations since 635 AD, when St Aidan's monastic order settled here. From the **Lindisfarne Centre** (see below), it's a short walk to the ruined eleventh-century **Lindisfarne Priory** (April–Oct daily 10am–4/6pm; Nov–March Sat & Sun 10am–4pm, £5.20), burial place of St Cuthbert, on the site of St Aidan's original monastery. The island is also Britain's best puffin-spotting site.

ARRIVAL AND INFORMATION

By bus Arriva bus #X15 runs from Newcastle Haymarket to Beal (6 daily Mon–Sat; 2hr 20min). From here you can take bus #477 (7 daily; 15min) to Holy Island. Connections are dependent on tide times, so check before travelling (☎01670 533998, ⓦlindisfarne.org.uk).
Tourist information Available at the Lindisfarne Centre, Marygate (daily 10am–5pm; exhibition £3).

Wales

Picturesque **WALES** has long appealed to English holidaymakers, drawn by unspoilt countryside, in which the population of sheep vastly outnumbers that of humans. The relationship between Wales and England, however, has never been entirely easy. Fed up with demarcation disputes, the eighth-century Mercian king Offa constructed a dyke to separate the two countries: the 177-mile **Offa's Dyke Path** still (roughly) marks the border to this day, though Wales passed under English rule in the late thirteenth century. The arrival, in 1999, of the National Assembly for Wales, the first all-Wales tier of government for nearly six hundred years, may well indicate that power is shifting back, although so far it's a slow trickle. Regardless, Wales retains a strong national identity, most clearly manifested in the Welsh language (see box below).

Much of the country, particularly the **Brecon Beacons** in the south and **Snowdonia** in the north, is relentlessly mountainous and offers wonderful walking terrain, while **Pembrokeshire** to the west boasts lonely coastline. The biggest towns, including the capital **Cardiff** in the south, **Aberystwyth** in the west, and **Caernarfon** in the north, all cling to the coastal lowlands, but even then the mountains are only a short bus-ride away. **Holyhead**, on the island of **Anglesey**, is the main British port for ferry sailings to Dublin.

CARDIFF

Though once shackled to the fortunes of the coal-mining industry, Wales' capital city, **CARDIFF** (Caerdydd), has been revitalized over the past decade, not least due to the arrival of the Welsh Assembly. The city's narrow Victorian arcades are interspersed with new shopping centres and wide pedestrian precincts.

WHAT TO SEE AND DO

Cardiff's city centre extends north of Cardiff Central train station. To the west of the centre, overlooking the River Taff, is the gleaming **Millennium Stadium** (wmillenniumstadium.com); Cardiff's main historical landmark, the castle, is a short stroll northeast of here.

Cardiff Castle and the National Museum

Cardiff Castle (daily 9am–5/6pm; £11; wcardiffcastle.com) is the historical heart of the city. Standing on a Roman site developed by the Normans, the castle was embellished by the English architect William Burges in the 1860s, and each room is now a wonderful example of Victorian "medieval" decoration: the Banqueting Hall and Fairytale Nursery steal the show. Five minutes' walk northeast, the **National Museum Cardiff** in Cathays Park (Tues–Sun 10am–5pm, free; wwww.museumwales.ac.uk) houses a fine collection of Impressionist paintings, together with natural history and archeological exhibits.

WELSH CULTURE AND LANGUAGE

Indigenous **Welsh culture** survives largely through language and song. Music, poetry and dance are celebrated at Eisteddfod festivals throughout the country; most famous is the annual Royal National Eisteddfod (weisteddfod.org.uk) in different locations across the country in early August.

The **Welsh language** has undergone a revival and you'll see it on road signs all over the country, although you're most likely to hear it spoken in the north, west and mid-Wales, where for many, it's their first language. Some Welsh place names have never been anglicized, but where alternative names do exist, we've given them in the text.

SOME BASICS

Hello	*Helo*	Hello
Goodbye	*Hwyl*	Huh-will
Please	*Os gwelwch chi'n da*	Oss gway-look un tha
Thank you	*Diolch*	Dee-ol'ch

13

Cardiff Bay

A half-hour walk south of the centre is the **Cardiff Bay** area, also reached by bus #7 from Cardiff Central, or a train from Queen Street. Once known as Tiger Bay, the long-derelict area has seen massive redevelopment since the Welsh Assembly opened. The **Wales Millennium Centre** dominates, with its huge theatre (see opposite). Nearby is the Cardiff Bay **Visitor Centre** (see below), known as "The Tube" for its unique, award-winning design. There are also waterfront walks, glittering millennium architecture and an old Norwegian seamen's chapel, converted into a cosy café.

Around Cardiff

St Fagans: National History Museum

(daily 10am–5pm; free; ⓦ museumwales .ac.uk) is four miles west of the centre on bus #32A/#320/#322. Set in 100 acres of parklands, this open-air museum is home to reconstructed rural and industrial heritage buildings that tell the story of Wales.

ARRIVAL AND DEPARTURE

By plane Cardiff Airport is around 35min west of the centre; bus #X91 (roughly every 2hr) runs to Cardiff Central train station.

By bus Long-distance coaches and buses from the airport arrive at the bus terminal, right beside Cardiff Central train station, south of the city centre off Penarth Rd. Destinations Abergavenny (hourly; 1hr 30min–2hr 20min); Aberystwyth (3 daily; 3hr 50min); Brecon (8 daily; 1hr 25min); Bristol (hourly; 1hr 15min); London (hourly; 3hr 20min–3hr 50min).

By train Long-distance services (including all those listed) arrive and depart from Cardiff Central. Some local trains also depart here, while others use Queen St station, east of the centre. Destinations Abergavenny (every 30min; 40min); Birmingham (hourly; 2hr); Bristol (Temple Meads; every 30min; 50min); Conwy (3 daily; 4hr 20min); London (every 30min; 2hr 10min); Manchester (hourly; 3hr 25min); Pembroke (2 daily; 3hr).

INFORMATION

Tourist information The Old Library on The Hayes (Mon–Sat 9.30am–5.30pm, Sun 10am–4pm; ☎ 029 2087 3573, ⓦ visitcardiff.com), and Cardiff Bay Visitor Centre (daily 10am–6pm, occasionally until 7.30pm when events take place; ☎ 029 2087 7927). The former is home to The Cardiff

Story (Mon–Sat 10am–5pm, Sun 11am–4pm; free), an interactive museum that uses videos, sound effects and smells to show how the city went from "coal to cool".

Internet Cardiff Central Library, The Hayes (☎ 029 2038 2116, ⓦ cardiff.gov.uk; free). More than 90 computers available for public use, though you'll need to join the library, so bring one piece of ID.

ACCOMMODATION

Big Sleep Hotel Bute Terrace, near Cardiff International Arena ☎ 029 2063 6363, ⓦ thebigsleephotel.com. Trendy, central budget hotel with modern interiors and clean rooms with wi-fi access and flat-screen TVs. Double **£29**

NosDa Studio Hostel 53–59 Despenser St ☎ 029 2037 8866, ⓦ nosda.co.uk. Just across the river from the centre, opposite the Millennium Stadium, this place offers good facilities at knockdown prices. Dorms are bright and modern and there's a bar, terrace, internet access, chill-out area and 24hr reception. Breakfast included. Dorm **£16**, double **£23**

★ **River House Backpackers** 59 Fitzhamon Embankment, along the riverbank ☎ 029 2039 9810. Spotlessly clean, this riverside hostel feels more like a private home than a budget crash pad. There are two private rooms plus a mix of 4- and 6-bed dorms, which share a well-equipped kitchen, dining area, living room and decked outside seating area. Free breakfast, wi-fi, coffee and tea, plus occasional free food and drink. Dorm **£18**, double **£42**

EATING, DRINKING AND NIGHTLIFE

Clwb Ifor Bach (The Welsh Club) 11 Womanby St ⓦ clwb.net. Little club playing an eclectic range of music from house and techno to punk and indie. Regular live bands. Entry usually £3–10. Tues–Sat 10pm–2/3am.

La Crêperie de Sophie 16 High St Arcade. Breakfast, lunch and afternoon tea are served at this well-priced crêpe place, which has a takeaway counter at street level and a busy little dining area downstairs. Sweet and savoury crêpes from £2.99. Mon–Fri 11am–5pm, Sat 10am–5pm, Sun 11am–4pm.

Madame Fromage 18 Castle Arcade. Cheese experts, serving up delicious soups (£4.50 with bread), cold platters and larger bites in a pretty Victorian arcade opposite the castle. Mon–Fri 10am–5.30pm, Sat 9.30am–6pm & occasional Sun 11am–4pm.

Milgi Lounge 213 City Rd. Colourful veggie restaurant serving cocktails (from £5.95) in the student district, a mile and a half north of the centre. Mon–Thurs & Sun 11am–midnight, Fri & Sat 11am–12.30am.

Zerodegrees 27 Westgate St. Sleek, glass-fronted bar-restaurant and microbrewery close to the Millennium Stadium. Stone-fired pizzas from £7.95. Mon–Sat noon–midnight, Sun noon–11pm.

ENTERTAINMENT

Wales Millennium Centre ☎029 2063 6464, ⊚wmc.org.uk. Cardiff Bay's arts hub has a wide-ranging, year-round programme that includes opera, ballet, contemporary dance, music and comedy.

CHEPSTOW AND TINTERN ABBEY

South Wales' main historical treasure is accessible from the sleepy market town of **CHEPSTOW** (Cas-Gwent), bunched around Britain's first stone **castle** (March–Oct daily 9am–5/6pm; Nov–Feb Mon–Sat 10am–4pm, Sun 11am–4pm; £4.50; ⊚cadw.wales.gov.uk), built by the Normans in 1067. Nothing in town, however, can match the six-mile stroll north along the Wye to the romantic ruins of **Tintern Abbey**, built in 1131 and now in a state of majestic disrepair (same hours as castle; £4.50).

ARRIVAL AND DEPARTURE

By bus If you don't fancy walking, catch bus #69 (every 2hr), which runs from Chepstow to Tintern and on to Monmouth, eight miles north.
Tourist information For information on Chepstow and the Offa's Dyke Path contact the tourist office on Bridge Street (daily: April–Oct 9.30am–5.30pm; Nov–March 10am–3.30pm; ☎01291 623772, ⊚chepstow.co.uk).

ACCOMMODATION

St Briavels Castle HI hostel ☎01594 530 272, ⊚hihostels.com, bus #69. The cheapest place to stay is some way out of town: this spooky HI hostel occupies a moated Norman castle seven miles northeast of Chepstow. Dorm £17.50

THE BRECON BEACONS

The **Brecon Beacons National Park** (⊚breconbeacons.org) is a vast area of rocky uplands that makes perfect walking country, though tough: the SAS use the terrain for training. The Beacons themselves, a pair of 2900ft-high hills accessed from Brecon town, share the limelight with the **Black Mountains** in the park's eastern portion, which rise north of pretty Crickhowell. In 2013, the national park was named as one of the world's first "dark sky reserves" in an attempt to stop light pollution ruining views of the starry night skies.

Crickhowell and around

Friendly **CRICKHOWELL** (Crughywel) lies five miles west of Abergavenny and makes a picturesque base. A great six-mile hike into the **Black Mountains** from here takes you through remote countryside to tiny **Partrishow Church**; inside, you'll find a rare carved fifteenth-century rood screen complete with a dragon, and an ancient mural of the grim reaper. For more dramatic scenery, the six-and-a-half-mile round trip to Table Mountain (1481ft) or the still-longer hike up to **Sugar Loaf** (1955ft), offer great views of the Black Mountains.

Brecon

The largest of the central Brecon Beacons rise just south of **BRECON** (Aberhonddu), a lively little town eight miles west of Crickhowell known for its mid-August international jazz festival (⊚brecon jazz.com). Accommodation is scarce during the festival and prices high, so book ahead.

Hay-on-Wye

To the north of the Black Mountains, on the border with England, charming **Hay-on-Wye** is famous as the secondhand book capital of the world and is home to Britain's leading literary festival (annually in late May; ⊚hayfestival.com).

ARRIVAL AND INFORMATION

By bus Stagecoach's (⊚stagecoachbus.com) #T4 bus service runs from Cardiff to Brecon (every 2hr; 1hr 30min), where you can transfer to their #X43 service to Crickhowell (hourly; 25–45min) and Abergavenny (hourly; 40min–1hr). Buses from Hereford in England (accessible by rail) travel to Hay-on-Wye (#39) and Brecon.

TOURIST INFORMATION

Crickhowell The tourist office (Mon–Sat 10am–5pm,

THE BEACON WAY

The 100-mile **Beacon Way** traverses the entire Brecon Beacons National Park from Abergavenny to Llangadog (allow 8 days). Check what weather to expect before setting out as conditions change rapidly on the hills. Regular trains run from Cardiff to Abergavenny.

13

Sun 10am–1.30pm; ☎01873 811970) is on Beaufort Street; the bus from Brecon stops nearby on the square.
Brecon For details of the numerous hiking routes call in at the tourist office in Brecon's Cattle Market car park (Mon–Sat 9.30am–4.45pm, Sun 10am–4pm; ☎01874 622485).

ACCOMMODATION AND EATING

CRICKHOWELL

Riverside Campsite ☎01873 810397. The best-value accommodation in town, located by the impressive seventeenth-century river bridge. March–Oct only. Vehicles incur an extra £2 charge. Camping £2 per person, plus £6 per tent

BRECON

YHA Brecon Two miles east of Brecon at Groesfford ☎0845 371 9506, ⓦyha.org.uk. A mile off the Abergavenny bus route, this Victorian house has reasonable dorms and private rooms sleeping two, some with en-suite facilities. Dorm £18.50, double £38

HAY-ON-WYE

The Bridge 4 Bridge St ☎01497 822952, ⓦthebridgehay .co.uk. Pick of the crop is a small, family-run B&B serving excellent cooked breakfasts, though these are not included in the room price. Double £56
Kilvert's Inn The Bullring. Has superior pub food, good cask ales and pricy rooms named after literary greats from Roald Dahl to Shakespeare. Double £80

PEMBROKESHIRE AND ST DAVID'S

The sleepy town of **Pembroke** (Penfro), accessible by train from Cardiff, is a handy jumping-off point from which to explore the southern part of the **Pembrokeshire Coast National Park** (ⓦpcnpa.org.uk), which covers 240 square miles of wooded estuaries, rocky cliffs and isolated beaches. Walkers can hail buses that run along the coast.

St David's

Around thirty miles north of Pembroke, the city of **ST DAVID'S** (Tyddewi), Britain's smallest, is one of the most enchanting spots in Britain (ⓦstdavids.co.uk). Its beautiful **cathedral** (daily 9am–5.30pm; £3 donation requested), delicately tinted purple, green and yellow by a combination of lichens and geology, hosts a prestigious classical music festival in late May or early June. Nearby the remains of the magnificent fourteenth-century **Bishop's Palace** (March–Oct daily 9.30am–5/6pm; Nov–Feb Mon–Sat 10am–4pm, Sun 11am–4pm; £3.20) add to the wonderful setting.

ARRIVAL AND INFORMATION

By bus Travel first to Haverfordwest, served by frequent trains from Cardiff (every 1–2 hr; 2hr 30min) and National Express buses from Pembroke (2 daily; 35min). From here take hourly bus #411 sixteen miles west to St David's.
Tourist information There's a national park visitor centre in town at the Oriel y Parc Landscape Gallery (daily: March–Oct 9.30am–5.30pm; Nov–Feb 10am–4.30pm; ☎01437 720392, ⓦpembrokeshirecoast.org.uk).

ACCOMMODATION

YHA St David's Llaethdy, close to Whitesands Beach ☎0845 371 9141, ⓦyha.org.uk. Converted farmhouse that appeals to surfers and climbers, who get a kick out of exploring the surrounding coastline. Dorm £21, double £52

ABERYSTWYTH

ABERYSTWYTH, a lively, thoroughly Welsh seaside resort of neat Victorian terraces, has a thriving student culture. The flavour of the town is best appreciated from the seafront, where one of Edward I's castles bestrides a windy headland to the south. There's also a Victorian **camera obscura** (£1), which can be reached via the clanking **cliff railway** (daily April–Oct 10am–5pm; otherwise limited timetable in operation; £4 return). For a more extended rail trip, you could take the popular **Vale of**

FERRIES TO IRELAND

Two ferries to Rosslare in Ireland (4hr; ⓦirishferries.com) leave from **Pembroke Dock**, two miles north of Pembroke, every day. About 17 miles further north, at the end of the main train line from Cardiff and London, is **Fishguard** (Abergwaun), another embarkation point for Rosslare, with Stena Line ferries departing twice daily (3hr 30min; ⓦstenaline.co.uk). **Holyhead** (Caergybi), on Anglesey, is the busiest Welsh ferry port, with several ferries and catamarans operated by Stena Line and Irish Ferries leaving for Dublin each day (2hr 20min–3hr 15min).

13

CLIMBING SNOWDON

The longest but easiest ascent of the mountain is the **Llanberis Path**, a signposted five-mile hike (3hr), manageable by anyone reasonably fit. Alternatively, take the steam-hauled **Snowdon Mountain Railway** (mid-March to early Nov daily; £35 return; a cheaper diesel service costs £27; ⊚ www.snowdonrailway.co.uk), which operates from Llanberis (see below) to the summit, weather permitting. Whenever you come, make sure you're equipped with suitable shoes, warm clothing, and food and drink to see you through any unexpected hitches.

Rheidol narrow-gauge steam train to **Devil's Bridge**, a canyon where three bridges span a dramatic waterfall (late March to Oct; £16 return).

ARRIVAL AND INFORMATION

By train The train station is 10min south of the seafront, reached by walking up Terrace Rd.

Tourist information The tourist office is also on Terrace Rd, near the junction with Bath St (Mon–Sat 10am–5pm, plus same hours on Sun July & Aug; ☎ 01970 612125).

ACCOMMODATION AND EATING

Maes y Mor 25 Bath St ☎ 01970 639270, ⊚ maesymor .co.uk. While the town seafront is lined with genteel guesthouses, this smart place, located a block back, is the best deal around, with a self-catering kitchen available. Double **£45**

The Treehouse 14 Baker St ⊚ treehousewales.co.uk. Welcoming, vegetarian-friendly café-deli above an organic food shop that sells fresh fruit and veg. Mains from £5.95. Mon–Fri 10am–5pm, Sat 9am–5pm.

SNOWDONIA NATIONAL PARK

Jagged peaks, towering waterfalls and glacial lakes – it's not surprising that walkers congregate in large numbers in **Snowdonia National Park** (⊚ visitsnowdonia.info), with a steady stream of tourist traffic even in the bleakest months. The park covers an enormous area stretching from Aberdyfi in the south to Conwy on the north coast; its highlight, though, is the glory of North Wales – **Mount Snowdon**, at 3560ft the highest mountain in England and Wales, and the blue-grey, slate towns and villages that surround the peak.

GETTING AROUND

By bus and train There are two main access routes. From Porthmadog, a few miles north of Harlech (both on the local rail network), buses skirt the base of Snowdon north to Caernarfon and Llanberis; main-line trains from Crewe

and Chester hug the north coast through Bangor to Holyhead, passing through Llandudno Junction and Conwy (the latter is a request stop).

Llanberis

LLANBERIS is a lacklustre lakeside village in the shadow of **Snowdon** and a convenient base for exploring the area. The slate quarries that seared Llanberis's surroundings now lie idle, but the **Welsh Slate Museum** (Easter–Oct daily 10am–5pm; Nov–Easter Mon–Fri & Sun 10am–4pm; free; ⊚ museumwales.ac.uk) remains as a memorial.

ARRIVAL AND INFORMATION

By bus Regular buses run the seven miles southeast from Caernarfon (see p.478), stopping on the high street. Sherpa Bus services encircle Snowdon itself; a £6.80 "Red Rover" ticket lets you ride all day.

Tourist information The tourist office is a few minutes' walk away from the high street on the A4086, inside the Electric Mountain building (Mon, Tues & Fri–Sun 10am–4pm; ☎ 01286 870765, ✉ llanberis.tic@gwynedd.gov.uk).

ACCOMMODATION

There's a good choice of accommodation for walkers. The Sherpa Bus provides access to several well-equipped HI hostels (⊚ yha.org.uk), each at the base of a footpath up the mountain.

Bryn Gwynant YHA Nant Gwynant, 10 miles south of Llanberis along the A498 ☎ 0845 371 9108, ⊚ yha.org.uk /hostel/bryn-gwynant. YHA hostel in a converted Victorian mansion, with views across Llyn Gwynant lake to Snowdon itself. Dorm **£17.50**, double **£52**

Llanberis YHA Llwyn Celyn, Llanberis ☎ 0845 371 9645 ⊚ yha.org.uk/hostel/llanberis. Close to local amenities and the start of the Llanberis Path (the fastest route up Snowdon). Rain-soaked walkers can make use of the laundry facilities and drying room. Dorm **£15**, double **£50**

Pen-y-Pass YHA Five miles south of Llanberis along the A4086 ☎ 0845 371 9534, ⊚ yha.org.uk/hostel/pen-y -pass. Secluded hostel along the Pen-y-Pass mountain pass, with dorms and private rooms, some of which are en suite. Dorm **£15**, double **£45**

13

EATING

Pete's Eats 40 High St. Stodgy snacks are served at this brightly painted corner café, with baguettes from £3.60 and a good selection of cakes. Daily 8am–8/9pm.

CAERNARFON

CAERNARFON is a handy springboard for trips into Snowdonia. **Caernarfon Castle** (daily: March–Oct 9.30am–5/6pm; Nov–Feb Mon–Sat 10am–4pm, Sun 11am–4pm, £5.25), built in 1283, is arguably one of the most splendid castles in Britain, with atmospheric towers and rambling stone passageways. It's here that heirs to the throne, the princes of Wales, are ceremonially invested.

ARRIVAL AND INFORMATION

By bus Buses stop at the station on Penllyn, just across Castle Square from the tourist office.
Tourist information Castle St (April–Oct daily 9.30am–4.30pm; Nov–March Mon–Sat 10am–3.30pm; ☎ 01286 672232, ☜ visitsnowdonia.info).

GETTING AROUND

By bike Bike rental available from Beics Menai, 1 Slate Quay, southeast of the castle (☎ 01286 676804, ☜ beicsmenai.co.uk; £22/8hr).

ACCOMMODATION AND EATING

Black Boy Inn Northgate St ☎ 01286 673604, ☜ black-boy-inn.com. Smart (but pricey) en-suite rooms. Also serves great pub food (mains from £7.45) and Welsh cream teas. Double £63
Totters 2 High St ☎ 01286 672963, ☜ totters.co.uk. A sparkling-clean independent backpacker hostel that provides excellent budget accommodation. Dorm £17, double £40

NORTH WALES COAST

From Caernarfon, buses run northwest via Bangor to the pretty little island of **Anglesey** (Ynys Môn), connected to North Wales by the Menai Bridge, built by Thomas Telford in 1826. Beside the bridge is the big draw of **Beaumaris Castle** (March–Oct daily 9.30am–5/6pm; Nov–Feb Mon–Sat 10am–4pm, Sun 11am–4pm; £3.80), reached by bus #53, #57 or #58 from Bangor. The giant castle was built in 1295 by Edward I to guard the straits and has a fairytale moat enclosing its

twelve sturdy towers. Eighteen miles east of Bangor, at the medieval walled coastal town of Conwy, is another of King Edward's masterpieces, **Conwy Castle** (same hours as Beaumaris; £5.75).

ACCOMMODATION

YHA Conwy Larkhill, Sychnant Pass Rd ☎ 0845 371 9732, ☜ yha.org.uk. Just west of the centre, Conwy's modern HI hostel has views across to the castle. Dorm £18, double £35

Scotland

With its kilted bagpipers, brooding castles on craggy highland hilltops, mystery-steeped lochs and whisky, **SCOTLAND** has a unique character, which is apparent as soon as you cross the border from England. This is partly due to the Scots, unlike the Welsh, successfully repulsing the expansionist designs of England down the centuries. Although the "old enemies" formed a union in 1707, Scotland retained many of its own institutions, notably distinctive legal and educational systems. However, Scottish **political nationalism** has been on the rise since 1997's referendum, when the Scottish people voted in favour of devolution. The Scottish Parliament held its first meeting in 1999, and the 2011 elections saw the Scottish National Party (SNP) gain a historic majority: a first for a Scottish political party in the modern era and a telling step towards increased independence. Buoyed by its continued success, the SNP-led government announced its intention to hold a **referendum** on complete independence in late 2014 – a move that could have profound effects on the way the country is run.

Most of Scotland's population clusters around the two principal cities: stately **Edinburgh**, the national capital, with its magnificent architecture and imperious natural setting, and revitalized **Glasgow**, a former Industrial Revolution powerhouse now renowned for its culture, nightlife and cuisine. Outside this Central Belt, Scotland is overwhelmingly rural, and just beyond Glasgow the wild, mountainous,

13

loch-strewn bulk of the **Highlands** rears up and doesn't stop until it hits the north coast. Off the west coast lie the majority of Scotland's beach-fringed islands, surviving largely on fishing and agriculture. All this makes for terrific outdoor fun, with many of the most scenic spots – such as the famous **Loch Lomond** and **Loch Ness** – easily accessible.

EDINBURGH

EDINBURGH, so said former resident Robert Louis Stevenson, "is what Paris ought to be". For many centuries Scotland's capital rivalled Europe's greatest cities in terms of learning, cultural clout and setting. It straddles two extinct volcanoes, Castle Rock – topped with an imposing castle – and Arthur's Seat, which shelters the official residence of the Royal Family in Scotland. In between is a beautiful city, made up of steeply twisting alleyways (wynds) and stone-built houses. The population usually hovers around the half-million mark, but swells massively in high season, peaking in August during the **Edinburgh Festival**.

WHAT TO SEE AND DO

The centre has two distinct parts. The castle rock is the core of the medieval city – the **Old Town** – where nobles and servants lived side by side for centuries within tight defensive walls: Edinburgh earned its nickname "Auld Reekie" from the smog and smell generated by the cramped inhabitants. To the north, the

New Town, designed by eminent architects of the day, was begun in the late 1700s: still largely intact, it's an outstanding example of Georgian town planning.

The Old Town and castle

The cobbled **Royal Mile** – composed of Castlehill, Lawnmarket, High Street and Canongate – is the central thoroughfare of the **Old Town**, running down to the Palace of Holyroodhouse from the **castle** (daily 9.30am–5/6pm; £16; ⓦedinburghcastle.gov.uk), a formidable edifice perched on sheer volcanic rock. Within its precincts are St Margaret's Chapel, dating from 1110 and containing the ancient Honours of Scotland (also known as the Scottish Crown Jewels) and the even older Stone of Destiny, coronation stone of the kings of Scotland. There's a large military museum here, too, and the castle esplanade provides a dramatic setting for the Military Tattoo, an unashamed display of martial pomp staged during the Festival. Year-round, at 1pm (Mon–Sat), a cannon shot is fired from the battlements.

National Museum of Scotland

Further down at the eastern end of Lawnmarket, George IV Bridge leads south from the Royal Mile to Chambers Street; here the recently revamped **National Museum of Scotland** (daily 10am–5pm; free; ⓦnms.ac.uk) is home to many of the nation's historical treasures, ranging from Celtic pieces to twentieth-century icons.

THE EDINBURGH FESTIVAL

By far the biggest arts event in Europe, August's **Edinburgh Festival** is really a multitude of festivals, mostly theatre-based, attracting artists, performers, comedians and tourists in their thousands. **The Edinburgh Festival Fringe** (ⓦedfringe.com), begun as a sideline to the International Theatre Festival to showcase alternative performances, is now the largest draw, mainly for its up-and-coming and big-name comedians. But with a ticket even on the Fringe often hitting £10 or more, and accommodation prices soaring, the only way to experience the Festival cheaply is often to work at it. Anything and everything becomes a venue, and every venue needs box office, front of house, technical and bar staff. You won't make much money, but you'll often end up with accommodation and free passes for your venue's shows, and sometimes others. The main Fringe venues to approach are the Assembly Rooms (ⓦassemblyfestival.com), Gilded Balloon (ⓦgildedballoon.co.uk), Underbelly (ⓦunderbelly.co.uk) and Pleasance (ⓦpleasance.co.uk/edinburgh). The Book Festival (ⓦedbookfest.co.uk) is also a good bet.

13

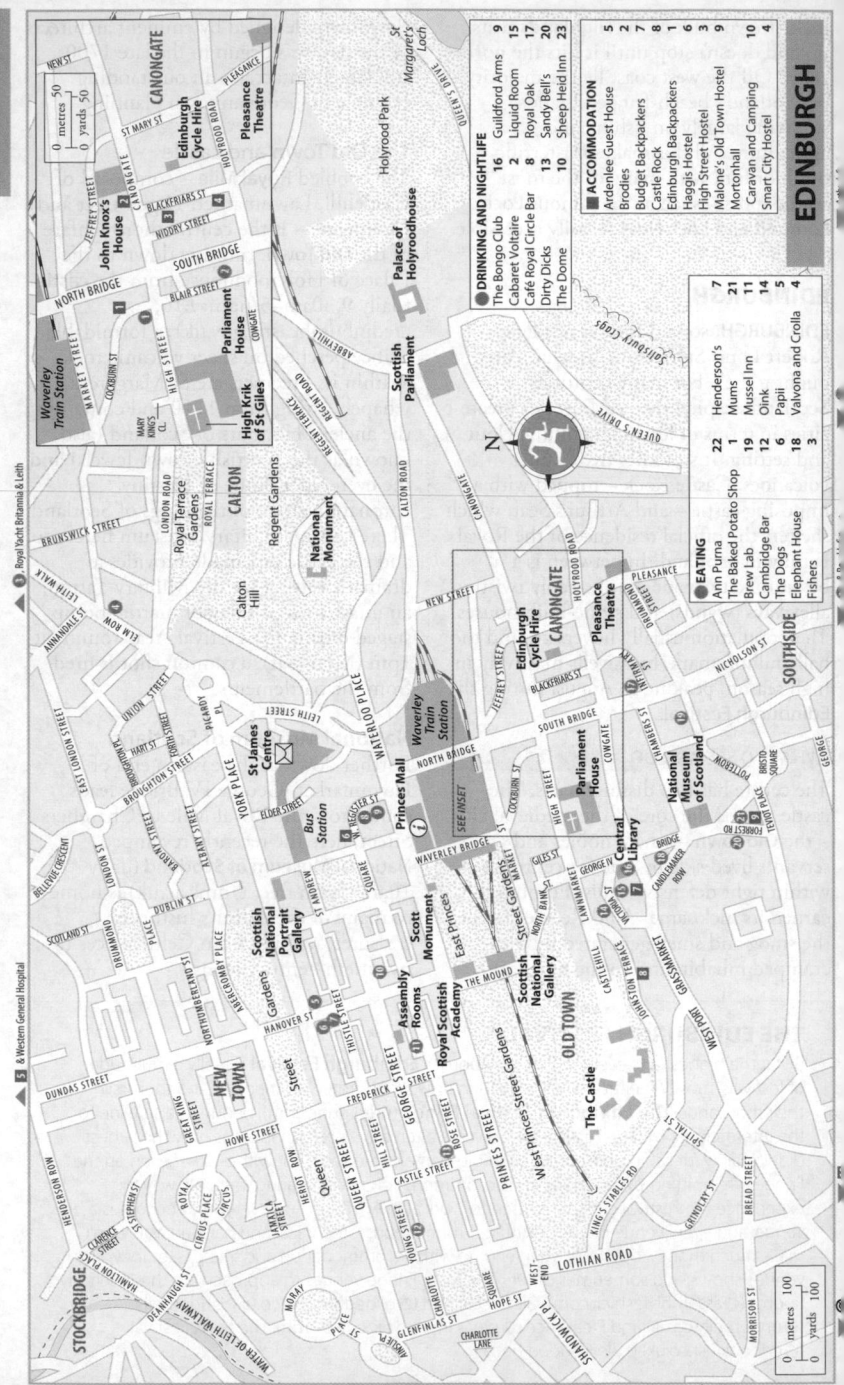

EDINBURGH

● **DRINKING AND NIGHTLIFE**

The Bongo Club	16	Guildford Arms	9
Cabaret Voltaire	2	Liquid Room	15
Café Royal Circle Bar	8	Royal Oak	17
Dirty Dicks	13	Sandy Bell's	20
The Dome	10	Sheep Heid Inn	23

■ **ACCOMMODATION**

Ardenlee Guest House	5	
Brodies	2	
Budget Backpackers	7	
Castle Rock	8	
Edinburgh Backpackers	1	
Haggis Hostel	6	
High Street Hostel	3	
Malone's Old Town Hostel	9	
Mortonhall Caravan and Camping	10	
Smart City Hostel	4	

■ **EATING**

Ann Purna	22	Henderson's	7
The Baked Potato Shop	1	Mums	21
Brew Lab	19	Mussel Inn	11
Cambridge Bar	12	Oink	14
The Dogs	6	Papii	5
Elephant House	18	Valvona and Crolla	4
Fishers	3		

13

High Kirk of St Giles and Parliament House

Back on the Royal Mile, High Street starts at Parliament Square, dominated by the **High Kirk of St Giles** (May–Sept Mon–Fri 9am–7pm, Sat 9am–5pm, Sun 1–5pm; Oct–April Mon–Sat 9am–5pm, Sun 1–5pm; £3 donation) with its crown-shaped spire and Thistle Chapel sporting some impressive mock-Gothic woodcarving. On the south side of Parliament Square are the Neoclassical law courts, incorporating the seventeenth-century **Parliament House**, under whose spectacular hammerbeam roof the Scottish parliament met until the 1707 Union.

John Knox's House and Scottish Parliament

The final section of the Royal Mile, Canongate, starts just beyond **John Knox's House** (Mon–Sat 10am–6pm, plus July & Aug Sun noon–6pm; £4.25; ⊚ scottishstorytellingcentre.co.uk), atmospheric home of the city's fierce Calvinist cleric, now joined to the Scottish Storytelling Centre. The road leads to the new **Scottish Parliament** (Mon–Sat 9/10am–5/6pm except during February recess; free), a costly, controversial but undoubtedly striking piece of contemporary architecture.

The Palace of Holyroodhouse and Arthur's Seat

The Royal Family's official Scottish residence is the imposing **Palace of Holyroodhouse** (daily: April–Oct 9.30am–6pm; Nov–March 9.30am–4.30pm; £11), which has been entwined with its fair share of historical figures including Oliver Cromwell and Mary

Queen of Scots. The public are admitted to the sumptuous state rooms unless the royals are in residence, The **Queen's Gallery** (same hours; £6.25) displays works of art from the royal collection. The palace looks out over Holyrood Park, from where fine walks lead along the **Salisbury Crags** and up **Arthur's Seat** beyond; a fairly stiff climb is rewarded by magnificent views over the city and the Firth of Forth.

The New Town

The wide grassy valley of Princes Street Gardens marks a clear divide between the Old and New Towns. Along the north side runs **Princes Street**, the main shopping area. Splitting the gardens halfway along is the **Scottish National Gallery** (daily 10am–5pm, Thurs till 7pm; free; ⊚ nationalgalleries.org), an Athenian-style sandstone building. One of the best small collections of pre-twentieth-century art in Europe, it displays works by major European artists including Botticelli, Titian, Rembrandt, Gauguin and Van Gogh. Look out for Sir Henry Raeburn's charming *Skating Minister* – a postcard favourite. The gallery is linked, via a Neoclassical underground chamber, to the **Royal Scottish Academy** (Mon–Sat 10am–5pm, Sun noon–5pm; free), an exhibition space originally designed in 1826.

The Scott Monument and Calton Hill

Northeast of the National Gallery you can climb the peculiar Gothic spire of the **Scott Monument** (daily: April–Sept 10am–6/7pm; Oct–March 9/10am–4/6pm; £4), a tribute to Scottish author Sir Walter Scott. Further on down Princes Street **Calton Hill** rises up above

---

HAUNTED EDINBURGH

From serial-killing corpse-dealers Burke and Hare to the malevolent Mackenzie Poltergeist, the winding streets and underground vaults of the Old Town shelter a multitude of spooks, and several entertaining **ghost tours** operate around the High Street. Some favour a historical approach while others lean firmly toward the high theatrical, using "jumper-ooters" – usually costumed students – to scare unsuspecting tour-goers. **The Real Mary King's Close** (☏ 0845 070 6244, ⊚ realmarykingsclose.com; £12.95), off the Royal Mile, is a tour (every 15min: April–July, Sept & Oct daily 10am–9pm; Aug daily 9am–9pm; Nov–March Mon–Thurs & Sun 10am–5pm, Fri & Sat 10am–9pm; 1hr) of an intact old close built over after the plague, offering a fine balance between the informative and the chilling.

13

the New Town and is worth climbing, both for the citywide views and for the surreal collection of Neoclassical follies, including the unfinished **National Monument**, perched on the very top.

Scottish National Portrait Gallery

North of Princes Street is the broad avenue of Queen Street, at whose eastern end stands the **Scottish National Portrait Gallery** (daily 10am–5pm, Thurs till 7pm; free). The remarkable red-sandstone building is modelled on the Doge's Palace in Venice; inside, the collection of portraits offers an engaging procession through Scottish history from Robert Burns to Sean Connery.

Scottish Modern Art Galleries

In the northwest corner of the New Town lies **Stockbridge**, a smart residential suburb with vintage shops, cool cafés and a bohemian vibe. From here Belford Road leads up to the **Scottish National Gallery of Modern Art** (daily 10am–5pm; free), whose two buildings (named Modern One and Modern Two) offer an accessible introduction to all the notable movements of twentieth-century art, with a sculpted garden area designed by Charles Jencks.

Leith

Once rough-round-the-edges Leith, Edinburgh's historic port two miles northwest of the city centre, has been revitalized in recent years and now has a cool collection of lively waterside bars and restaurants. It's home to the Royal Yacht

Britannia (daily: April–June & Oct 9.30am–4pm; July–Sept 9.30am–4.30pm; Nov–March 10am–3.30pm; £12; ⓦroyalyachtbritannia.co.uk), the Queen's former luxury yacht, now berthed at Ocean Terminal. The vessel has hosted some of the world's most important figures in its 44 years of service and kick-started Leith's regeneration when it came to rest in the port here.

ARRIVAL AND DEPARTURE

By plane Edinburgh airport is eight miles west of the centre; there are bus connections around the clock to the city, and the new tram service is set to be in operation from summer 2014, connecting the airport with the city centre.
By train Edinburgh's Waverley Station is bang in the centre, just south of Princes St.
Destinations Aberdeen (hourly; 2hr 30min); Durham (every 30min; 1hr 45min); Glasgow (every 15min; 50min); Inverness (10 daily; 3hr 30min); Leuchars (for St Andrews; every 30min; 1hr 10min); London (1–2 hourly; 4–8hr); Newcastle (3 hourly; 1hr 30min); Stirling (every 30min; 50min); York (3 hourly; 2hr 30min).
By bus Edinburgh Bus Station is on Elder Street, just south of York Place, and is served by a mixture of long-distance and local buses.
Destinations Aberdeen (hourly; 3hr); Glasgow (every 15min; 1hr 15min); Inverness (every 1–2hr; 3hr 35min–4hr 35min); London (4 daily; 8hr 45min–10hr); Manchester (3 daily; 5hr 40min–6hr 25min); Newcastle (5 daily; 2hr 40min–3hr 20min); St Andrews (hourly; 1hr 45min–2hr); Stirling (at least hourly; 1hr 10min–2hr 10min).

INFORMATION

Tourist information 3 Princes St, above the station on the top level of Princes Mall (July & Aug Mon–Sat 9am–8pm, Sun 10am–8pm; Sept–June Mon–Sat

---

EDINBURGH OUTDOORS

Many of Scotland's outdoor features can be enjoyed – albeit on a more limited scale than in the Highlands – within striking distance of the capital. The **Pentland Hills** are ideal for moderate but scenic walking (take Lothian bus #4, #10, #11, #15, #16 or #27, or Stagecoach #101, #102). At **Glentress** (First bus #62), an area of forest near Peebles, about an hour south of Edinburgh, you can rent mountain bikes to enjoy the purpose-built tracks and runs (ⓦglentressbikehire.co.uk; £26 per day). Edinburgh also has some pleasant **beaches**: it's worth making the hour or so trip out along the east coast to find the best ones. First buses #124, #X24 and #X25 stop at Longniddry and beautiful Gullane, each with shallow, sandy bays and surprisingly warm water. Also consider the jaunt to **Rosslyn Chapel** (April–Sept Mon–Sat 9.30am–6pm, Sun noon–4.45pm; Oct–March Mon–Sat 9.30am–5pm, Sun noon–4.45pm; £9; ⓦrosslynchapel.com), seven miles south of Edinburgh on Lothian bus #15, a fifteenth-century mystery-steeped chapel in a wooded glen. With Dan Brown famously giving it a starring role in his bestselling novel *The Da Vinci Code*, it's now firmly on the tourist trail.

9am–5/7pm, Sun 10am–5/7pm; ☎0131 473 3868, ⓦvisitscotland.com). There's also one at the airport.

Discount card An Edinburgh Pass includes a free airport transfer and access to more than 30 of the city's attractions (1-day pass/2-day/3-day £30/40/50). The pass can be obtained from the main tourist office.

GETTING AROUND

By bus Lothian buses (ⓦlothianbuses.com) run from Princes St to Leith (bus #10/#12/#16/#22 via Leith Walk). There's a good city-wide bus service, although the extensive roadworks in preparation for the trams mean they're often diverted; day-passes are available on board (both Lothian and First have day passes for £3.50, but be aware that the two firms don't accept each other's passes – and neither company gives change).

By bike Edinburgh Cycle Hire, 29 Blackfriars St (☎0131 556 5560, ⓦcyclescotland.co.uk). This place rents bikes (from £15/70/day/week) and can offer cycling tours of Scotland. Edinburgh itself is hard work, but there's pleasant cycling along the canal as far as Glasgow.

ACCOMMODATION

If you want to stay during the Festival (early Aug to early Sept), you'll need to book months in advance and, in many cases, be prepared to pay more than the high season prices listed here. Minto St, which starts about a mile and a half south of the train station, and Pilrig St, just west of Leith Walk, hold myriad B&Bs.

HOSTELS

Brodies 93 High St ☎0131 556 2223, ⓦbrodieshostels .co.uk. Its location on the Royal Mile is hard to argue with, but there's a severe lack of space for socializing. Dorm £13, double £65

Budget Backpackers 37–39 Cowgate ☎0131 226 6351, ⓦbudgetbackpackers.com. Fun, youthful hostel, in a handy location just off Grassmarket, with a technicolor bar area and relaxed chill-out room, plus a decent range of dorms. Recommended. Dorm £12.50, double £48

★ **Castle Rock** 15 Johnston Terrace ☎0131 225 9666, ⓦscotlandstophostels.com. Friendly 200-bed hostel tucked below the castle ramparts. It comes with a comfortable lounge, period features and, apparently, its own ghost. Dorm £14.50, double £45

Edinburgh Backpackers 65 Cockburn St ☎0131 220 2200, ⓦhoppo.com. Big hostel with a great central location in a side street off the Royal Mile. Rooms are of a good standard and clean. They also have self-catering apartment-style doubles. Dorm £13, double £55

Haggis Hostel 5/3 West Register St ☎0131 557 0036, ⓦhaggishostels.co.uk. Small, clean, fresh-feeling dorms high up in a building near Princes St. TV room, laundry facilities, clean showers and breakfast provided. Not to be

confused with Princes St East Backpackers, one floor up. Dorm £20

High Street Hostel 8 Blackfriars St ☎0131 557 3984, ⓦscotlandstophostels.com. Large hostel in a sixteenth-century building just off the Royal Mile, with basic rooms, a mural-filled lounge area and a huge kitchen. A little grubby, but with friendly staff and a good location. Dorm £26.50, double £72

Malone's Old Town Hostel 14 Forrest Rd ☎0131 226 5954, ⓦmalonesedinburgh.com. Dorms at this hostel above an Irish bar are a little stark, but they're clean and share bright, spotless bathrooms. Good location near Grassmarket. Dorm £17

Smart City Hostel 50 Blackfriars St ☎0131 524 1989, ⓦsmartcityhostels.com. This modern hostel has spotless, hotel-standard en-suite rooms and dorms, with a stylish bar, terrace and restaurant. Dorm £24, double £89

GUESTHOUSE

Ardenlee Guest House 9 Eyre Place ☎0131 556 2838, ⓦwww.ardenlee.co.uk. Welcoming guesthouse near the Royal Botanic Garden with comfortable rooms. Double £80

CAMPSITE

Mortonhall Caravan and Camping 38 Mortonhall Gate, Frogston Rd East ☎0131 664 1533, ⓦmortonhall .co.uk; bus #11 from Princes St. Friendly site set in landscaped grounds four miles south of the city centre. Camping £12 per person and tent.

EATING

Edinburgh has one of Britain's best eating scenes, and a thriving café culture

CAFÉS, CHEAP EATS AND SNACKS

The Baked Potato Shop 56 Cockburn St. Long the best place in town for tatties (potatoes): try the vegetarian haggis filling. Small potatoes £3.99. Daily 9am–9pm, with longer hours in summer.

Brew Lab 6–8 South College St. Artisan coffee bar favoured by design-conscious students, who come for the locally made cakes and pastries (from £1.80), exposed brick interiors and free wi-fi. Daily 8/9am–6pm.

Elephant House 21 George IV Bridge. Popular café with a cavernous back room, famous as the birthplace of Harry Potter. Simple dishes like chilli con carne cost £4.75. Daily 8/9am–10/11pm.

Oink 34 Victoria St. Busy little takeaway shop specializing in hog roast rolls (look for the pig in the window). Choose your bread, stuffing and sauce, then tuck in (from £3.60). Daily 11am–5pm, but may close earlier if pork runs out.

Papii 101 Hanover St. Smart, pastel-coloured interiors make this bright café a popular place to stop for a fruit smoothie (£3.10), or coffee made from locally roasted

13

beans. Mon–Fri 7.30am–4pm, Sat 9am–5pm, Sun 10am–4pm.

Valvona and Crolla 19 Elm Row. Stylish deli (Scotland's oldest) doing picnic treats with a Mediterranean slant (great Italian wines and cheeses). Mon–Thurs 8.30am–6pm, Fri & Sat 8am–6.30pm, Sun 10.30am–4pm.

RESTAURANTS

Ann Purna 45 St Patrick Square. Swankily decorated vegetarian Indian restaurant: quite possibly Scotland's best. Mains £12–14. Daily noon–11pm.

Cambridge Bar 20 Young St. A wide range of home-made burgers, with a mass of different toppings to choose from, starting at £6.45. Daily noon–11pm/midnight/1am.

The Dogs 110 Hanover St. There are two menus at this no-nonsense Scottish restaurant: a good-value lunch menu (until 4pm the haggis, bacon and black pudding hash costs £6.35) and a pricier evening one. Daily noon–10pm.

Fishers 1 The Shore, Leith. Among several seafood restaurants on this upmarket stretch beside Leith docks, *Fishers* keeps its prices reasonable and its atmosphere congenial, with high-quality fish sourced from around Scotland's coast. Mains £12–19. Daily noon–10.30pm.

Henderson's 94 Hanover St. Family-run veggie and vegan place combining a bistro, gallery and basement restaurant with a deli selling good organic bread. Mains in the bistro from around £6. Mon–Sat 8am–10pm, plus Sun 11am–4pm in Aug and Dec.

★ **Mums** 4a Forrest Rd. Gravy-drizzled comfort food in a laidback diner. *Mums* serves up more than a dozen types of mashed potato with its gluten-free sausages (from £6.95), and has a good selection of bottled Scottish ales and ciders to wash the food down with. Daily 9/10am–10pm.

Mussel Inn 61–65 Rose St. Shellfish restaurant with a sister branch in Glasgow; you can feast here on a kilo of mussels for around £10. Mon–Thurs noon–3pm & 5.30–10pm, Fri–Sun noon/12.30–10pm.

DRINKING AND NIGHTLIFE

Hardcore clubbers head over to Glasgow, but Edinburgh still has a lively nightlife. Pick up a copy of *The List* or *The Skinny* to find out what's going on. If you're just out for a drink, try the New Town's traditional pubs, or the bar-restaurants along the waterfront in Leith. The top of Leith Walk is the place for gay nightlife.

PUBS AND BARS

★ **Café Royal Circle Bar** 19 West Register St. Make a point of visiting this Grade A listed pub, arguably Edinburgh's most beautiful watering hole. There's a pricier restaurant below serving seafood (mains from £10.50). Mon–Sat 11am–11pm/midnight/1am, Sun 12.30–11pm.

Dirty Dicks 159 Rose St. Interiors cluttered with old curios, cask-conditioned ales, an animated atmosphere

and legendary steak-and-ale pies (£8.95). Daily 11am/noon–1am.

The Dome 14 George St. Opulent bar/restaurant/garden-café with a vast, magnificent domed drinking area in Edinburgh's eighteenth-century Physician's Hall. The house wine is £5.50 a glass. Mon–Sat noon–midnight/1/2am, Sun 10am–midnight.

Guildford Arms 1–5 West Register St. Beautiful New Town Victorian pub, bedecked with chandeliers and serving real ales. Draught beers from £3.20. Mon–Sat 11am–midnight, Sun noon–11.30pm.

Sheep Heid Inn 43–45 The Causeway, Duddingston. Edinburgh's oldest pub with great ales, tasty food and the world's oldest-known skittle alley. It's a tad out of town, a 20min walk around the southern edge of Holyrood Park, but the extensive wine list (£4–6 per glass) makes it worth the effort. Mon–Thurs 11am–11pm, Fri & Sat 11am–midnight, Sun 12.30–11pm.

CLUBS AND LIVE MUSIC

The Bongo Club 66 Cowgate ⓦ thebongoclub.co.uk. Now in a new location beneath Central Library, this legendary Edinburgh club hosts reggae, funk, soul, drum 'n' bass and electro. Don't miss the monthly Fri-night funk institution that is *Four Corners*. Club nights 11pm–3am (see website for days).

Cabaret Voltaire 36–38 Blair St ⓦ thecabaretvoltaire .com. Eclectic beats and the occasional live band. The house cocktails – including an Edinburgh iced tea – start at £6. Most nights 11pm–3am (see website for days).

Liquid Room 9c Victoria St ⓦ liquidroom.com. Hosts house nights and cheap, midweek indie parties. It's also a popular live venue; Kasabian, Feeder and the Dead Kennedys have all graced the stage. Most nights keep going until 3am (see website for details of specific nights).

Royal Oak 1 Infirmary St ⓦ royal-oak-folk.com. The venue for Scottish folk music, where you'll hear plenty of talented people any night of the week, and it's definitely not all old fogies. Music: Mon–Thurs 9pm–1am, Fri 9pm–1.30am, Sat 6pm–1.30am, Sun 4pm–midnight.

Sandy Bell's 25 Forrest Rd. Music fans and whisky drinkers prop up the long, mirror-backed bar at this corner pub, which has live folk music nightly from 9.30pm. The malt of the month costs £2.70. Daily noon–1am.

DIRECTORY

Banks and exchange Several big bank branches on and around St Andrew's Square, Hanover St and along George St. Alternatively, the tourist office at Princes Mall has an exchange booth.

Embassies and consulates Australia (Honorary Consulate) 5 Mitchell St ☎ 0131 538 0582; Canada: Mr John Rafferty ☎ 07702 359 916; US, 3 Regent Terrace ☎ 0131 556 8315.

SCOTLAND'S MUSIC FESTIVALS

The summer festival season is a great time to visit Scotland. For mainstream acts, check out **T in the Park**, near Kinross (July; @tinthepark.com), and **Rock Ness**, on the edge of Loch Ness (June; @rockness.co.uk). For something more alternative, try **Loopallu**, in the Highlands at Ullapool (September; @loopallu.co.uk), or the **Wickerman Festival** (July; @thewickerman festival.co.uk), near Dundrennan in Dumfries and Galloway, which culminates in the burning of a huge wicker effigy.

Hospitals Royal Infirmary, Old Dalkieth Rd ☎0131 536 1000; Western General Hospital, Crewe Rd South ☎0131 537 1000 for minor injuries.

Internet Here Internet Café, 23 Leven St (Mon–Fri 10am–8pm, Sat & Sun 10/11am–6pm; £1.95/hr).

Left luggage At Waverley Station (£7 per item/day).

Pharmacy Boots, 101–103 Princes St (Mon–Sat 8am–7/8pm, Sun 10am–6pm).

Post office St James' Shopping Centre, near the eastern end of Princes St (Mon–Sat 9/9.30am–5.30pm).

GLASGOW

Having shrugged off its post-industrial malaise, rejuvenated **Glasgow**, Scotland's largest city, has undergone a revamp these last two decades and now basks in the light of its outstanding achievement: epitomized in its successful application to host the 2014 Commonwealth Games. The River Clyde on which it sits now bustles again with prosperity; the city's also home to one of the world's best art schools and a fantastic live music scene. The city is rightly favoured by many for its down-to-earth ambience, die-hard "Glesga" party spirit and innovative architecture ranging from lavish eighteenth-century mansions through to cutting-edge twenty-first-century design.

WHAT TO SEE AND DO

Glasgow's centre lies on the north bank of the River Clyde, around the grandiose **George Square**, a little way east of Central Station. Here, in the West End and on the South Side, lies the legacy of grand civic buildings that led the Victorians to label Glasgow the "second city of the Empire".

The Gallery of Modern Art

Just south of George Square, down Queen Street, is the **Gallery of Modern Art** (daily 10/11am–5pm, till 8pm Thurs; free; @glasgowlife.org.uk), a lavish

eighteenth-century construction housing an exciting collection of contemporary Scots art, notably by Toby Paterson and John Byrne.

The National Piping Centre

Just across from Glasgow's Theatre Royal at 30–34 McPhater Street, the **National Piping Centre** (Mon–Fri 9am–5pm, Sat 9am–1pm; £4.50; @thepipingcentre.co.uk) tells the story of the Scottish bagpipe, from its role in clan conflicts to the seemingly impossible task of putting pipe music to paper. Attached is the independently run hotel, *The Pipers' Tryst* (see p.488).

Cathedral and Necropolis

Northeast of George Square is the **cathedral** on Castle Street (Mon–Sat 9.30am–4.30/5.30pm, Sun 1–4/5pm). Originally built in 1136, it's the only Scottish mainland cathedral to have escaped the country's sixteenth-century religious reformers. The adjacent **Necropolis**, a hilltop cemetery for the magnates who made Glasgow rich, has great views across the city.

Kelvingrove Art Gallery and the West End

The boundaries of the leafy **West End** are marked by the magnificent, Baroque crenellations of **Kelvingrove Art Gallery** (daily 10/11am–5pm; free; @glasgowlife .org.uk), which houses pieces by Rembrandt, Degas, Millet, Van Gogh and Monet, as well as an impressive body of Scottish painting. Don't miss Dalí's *Christ of St John of the Cross* – an arresting vision of the Crucifixion.

River Clyde

The **Riverside Museum** along Glasgow's redeveloped waterfront at 100 Pointhouse Place (daily 10/11am–5pm; free;

GLASGOW

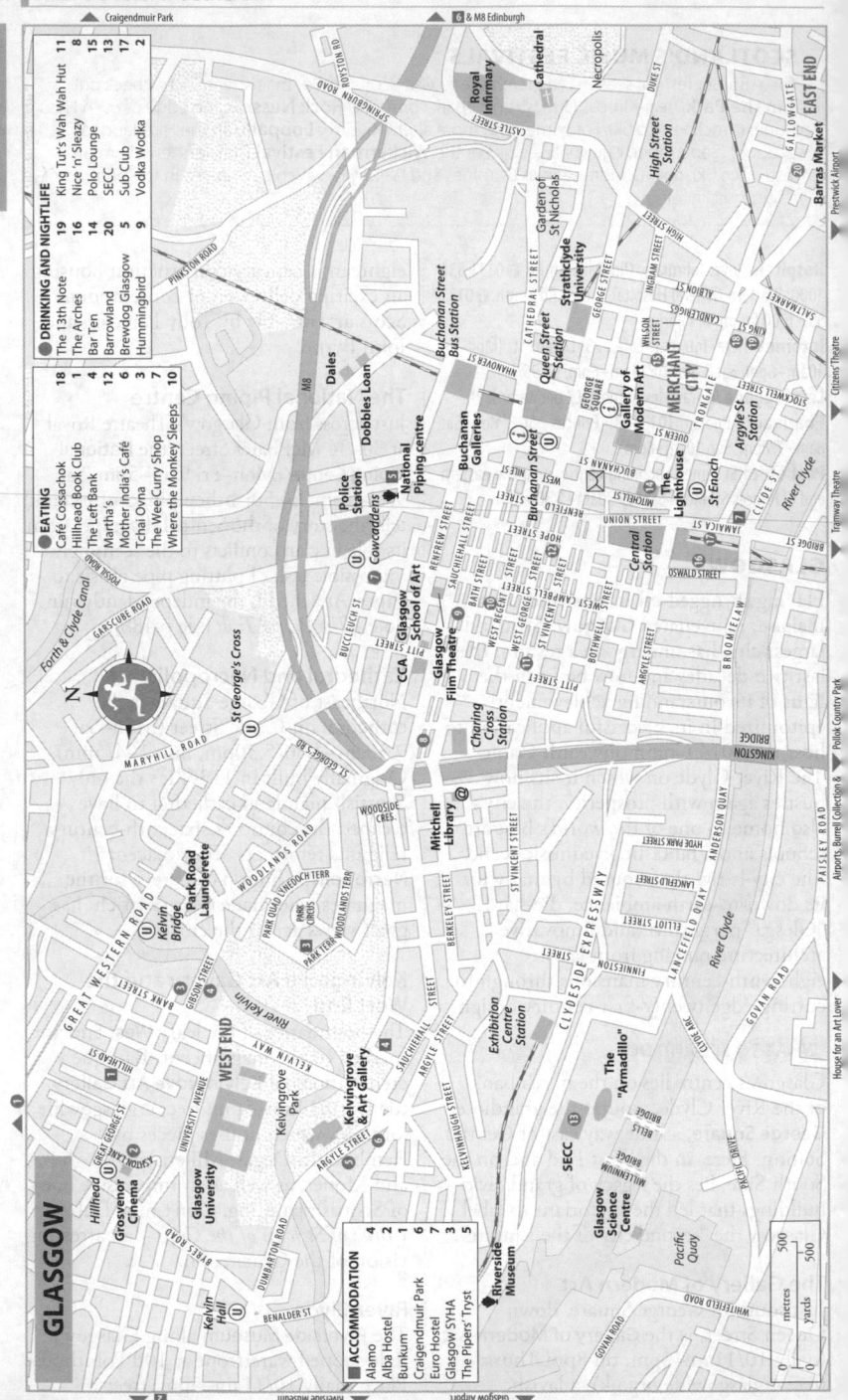

ACCOMMODATION

Alamo	4
Alba Hostel	2
Bunkum	1
Craigendmuir Park	6
Euro Hostel	7
Glasgow SYHA	3
The Pipers' Tyst	5

EATING

Café Cossachok	18
Hillhead Book Club	1
The Left Bank	4
Martha's	12
Mother India's Café	6
Tchai Ovna	3
The Wee Curry Shop	7
Where the Monkey Sleeps	10

DRINKING AND NIGHTLIFE

The 13th Note	19	King Tut's Wah Wah Hut	11
The Arches	16	Nice 'n' Sleazy	8
Bar Ten	14	Polo Lounge	15
Barrowland	20	SECC	13
Brewdog Glasgow	5	Sub Club	17
Hummingbird	9	Vodka Wodka	2

CHARLES RENNIE MACKINTOSH

There aren't many architects who have made a bigger impression on a city than **Charles Rennie Mackintosh** (1868–1928). Little-appreciated in his lifetime, his fascinating, pioneering building designs around the city are among the best examples of early modernist architecture, and are now finally getting the recognition they deserve. See his work for yourself at his first commission, the **Lighthouse** (Mitchell Lane; Mon–Sat 10.30am–5pm, Sun noon–5pm; free; ⓦthelighthouse.co.uk), **Glasgow School of Art** (167 Renfrew St; 3–10 tours daily, depending on season; £9.75; ☎0141 353 4500, ⓦwww.gsa.ac.uk), **House for an Art Lover** (Bellahouston Park; daily 10am–1pm/4.30pm, call ahead on ☎0141 353 4770 to check exact times; £4.50; ⓦwww.houseforanartlover.co.uk) and the **Willow Tearooms** (217 Sauchiehall St; Mon–Sat 9am–5pm, Sun 11am–5pm) where you can appreciate the architecture over tea and cakes.

ⓦglasgowlife.org.uk) showcases the city's shipbuilding heritage. The area is also home to the wonderful **Glasgow Science Centre**, 50 Pacific Quay (daily 10am–5pm, closed Mon & Tues in winter; £9.95). In summer you can also take a cruise from the quay outside here on the world's last ocean-going paddle steamer (☎0845 130 4647, ⓦwaverleyexcursions.co.uk) to Dunoon (£27), Greenock (£15) and Rothesay (£29), as well as other destinations around the Clyde Estuary.

The Burrell Collection

About four miles south of the centre, in **Pollok Country Park** (bus #3/#45/#48/#57 from Union Street, or train to Pollokshaws West), is the astonishing **Burrell Collection**, housed in a custom-built gallery (daily 10/11am–5pm; free; ⓦglasgowlife.org.uk). Works by Memling, Cézanne, Degas, Bellini and Géricault feature among the paintings, while in adjoining galleries pieces from ancient Rome, Greece, China and medieval Europe are exhibited.

ARRIVAL AND DEPARTURE

By plane Glasgow Airport lies eight miles west of the city, with regular buses shuttling to Buchanan St bus station; Glasgow Prestwick airport, thirty miles south, is connected to the city centre by trains (3 hourly) and buses.

By train Glasgow has two main train stations, around 10min walk apart: Central serves all points south and west, as well as Edinburgh; Queen St serves Edinburgh and the north.

Destinations from Queen Street Balloch (every 30min; 45min); Edinburgh (every 15min; 50min); Inverness (some change at Perth; every 2hr; 3hr 25min); Mallaig (for Skye; 2–3 daily; 5hr 15min); Oban (for Mull; 2 daily; 3hr);

Newcastle (most change in Edinburgh; every 30min–1hr; 2hr 30min–3hr); Stirling (every 30min; 25–40min).

Destinations from Glasgow Central Edinburgh (up to 4 hourly; 1hr–1hr 30min); Liverpool (via Wigan/Preston; every 30min; 3hr 30min); London (hourly; 4hr 30min–5hr 30min); Manchester (3 direct, around 23 daily via Preston/Carlisle; 3hr 15min–3hr 45min).

By bus Buchanan St bus station sits at the northern end of Buchanan St.

Destinations Edinburgh (every 15min; 1hr 10min); Inverness (every 1hr 30min; 3hr 30min–4hr 30min); Liverpool (1 daily; 6hr 30min); London (6 daily; 8hr–9hr 45min); Manchester (7 daily; 4hr 45min–5hr 30min); Newcastle (4 daily; 4hr–4hr 30min); Oban (for Mull; 3 daily; 3hr); St Andrews (hourly; 2hr 30min); Skye (3 daily; Kyle of Lochalsh 5–6hr, Portree 6–7hr, Uig 7–8hr); Stirling (up to 3 per hour; 45min–1hr 45min).

INFORMATION

Tourist information The tourist office is at 170 Buchanan St, just west of Glasgow Queen St (Mon–Sat 9am–6pm, Sun noon–4pm; ☎0141 204 4400, ⓦseeglasgow.com); there's a smaller office at the airport.

GETTING AROUND

Glasgow's central grid pattern makes navigation by foot relatively simple. The Strathclyde Travel Centre, at Buchanan St bus station (Mon–Sat 6.30am–10.30pm, Sun 7am–10.30pm), has information on all public transport, as well as discount passes.

By subway The subway is cheap and easy, operating on a circular chain of fifteen stations with a flat fare of £1.40 (Discovery Ticket £3.80 for a day's unlimited travel).

By bike Dales at 150 Dobbies Loan has mountain bikes to rent (Mon–Fri 9am–6pm, Thurs 9am–7pm, Sat 9am–6pm, Sun 11am–4pm; £20/day; ☎0141 332 2705).

ACCOMMODATION

Alamo 46 Gray St ☎0141 339 2395, ⓦalamoguesthouse .com. Quiet and attractive Victorian tenement near Kelvingrove Park, with 12 immaculate rooms and a

13

resident cat. The more affordable rooms are downstairs. Call for the best rates. Double **£68**

Alba Hostel 6 Fifth Av ☎0141 334 2952, ⓦalbahostelglasgow.co.uk. This good-value West End hostel is a little out of town but has its own car park, making it a good bet for drivers. Cheap rates for long-term stays. Dorm **£15**, double **£40**

Bunkum 26 Hillhead St ☎0141 581 4481, ⓦbunkumglasgow.co.uk. Welcoming, family-run hostel in a great position close to the university in a stately Victorian terrace. Dorm **£14**, double **£36**

Craigendmuir Park Clayhouse Rd, Stepps ☎0141 779 4159, ⓦcraigendmuir.co.uk. Large, well-equipped campsite four miles northeast of the centre; take a train to Stepps, from where it's a 15min walk. Camping **£14.25** per person and tent

Euro Hostel 318 Clyde St ☎08455 399 956, ⓦeuro -hostels.co.uk/glasgow. There's usually still room at this huge, soulless hostel when the rest of Glasgow is booked up. The bar at street level sells cheap cocktails Mon–Thurs & Sun. Dorm **£12**, double **£28**

Glasgow SYHA 8 Park Terrace ☎0141 332 3004, ⓦglasgowhostel.co.uk. Refurbished hostel in a listed building beside Kelvingrove Park, a handy location for going out in the West End. All rooms are en suite and of a high standard. Dorm **£20.50**, double **£57**

The Pipers' Tryst 30–34 McPhater St, at the National Piping Centre ☎ 0141 353 5551. Reliable, great-value mid-range hotel with tartan-wrapped beds and its own bar selling a good selection of single malts. Double **£65**

EATING

Café Cossachok 10 King St. Russian restaurant, gallery and live venue that envelops diners in soft red light and haunting violin music. The menu (mains from £9.50) includes Slavic staples like *borshch*. Tues–Sat 11am–11pm, Sun 4–11pm.

★ **Hillhead Book Club** 17 Vinicombe St. Attractive bar-restaurant in an old cinema, with a high, sculpted ceiling lit up by huge lanterns. There are two menus (one for veggies), and the well-presented mains all cost less than £10. Also a ping-pong table for pre-club fun. Mon–Fri 11am–10pm, Sat & Sun 10am–10pm.

The Left Bank 33–35 Gibson St. Airy restaurant with a monumental all-day brunch at weekends and innovative lunches with an Indian/Middle Eastern slant from £5.25. Mon–Fri 9am–midnight, Sat & Sun 10am–midnight/1am.

Martha's 142a St. Vincent St. With a mission to bring fast, healthy food to the people of Glasgow, this slick café turns out subtly spiced veggie and meat dishes, serving them either as a main course with rice, or as a takeaway wrap (from £3.95). Mon–Fri 7.30am–4pm, Sat 11am–4pm.

Mother India's Café 1355 Argyle St. Value for money and an innovative, tapas-style approach to curry make this

bustling place near Kelvingrove Museum a winner. Dishes from £3.75. Daily noon–11pm/midnight.

Tchai Ovna 42 Otago Lane. Enchanting "magic teashop", tucked down a lane in the West End. Sample exotic teas in an atmosphere that's part opium den, part hippy commune. Excellent vegetarian food for under £5. Daily 11am–11pm.

The Wee Curry Shop 7 Buccleuch St. Tiny establishment offering excellent-value Indian food for around £6–8. Mon–Sat noon–2.30pm & 5.30–10/10.30pm, Sun 5.30–10.30pm.

Where the Monkey Sleeps 182 West Regent St. Breath of fresh air in the city centre: a basement coffee shop attracting a student crowd with good tunes and cheap bagels (from £3.20). Mon–Fri 7am–4pm.

DRINKING AND NIGHTLIFE

Pubs and clubs cluster around the city centre, the suave Merchant City to the east of Queen St, and the West End around Ashton Lane, a cobbled street strung with fairy lights and lined with bars and restaurants.

PUBS AND BARS

Bar Ten 10 Mitchell Lane. A great pre-club bar with DJs. Its industrial interior is the work of Ben Kelly, designer of Manchester's fabled, but now demolished, *Hacienda*. Food also available, with mains around £7–8. Daily 11am–midnight.

Brewdog Glasgow 1397 Argyle St. The place to come for top-quality craft beers by the Scottish brewery Brewdog. There's usually at least half a dozen IPAs on tap, plus occasional guest ciders. Feeling brave? Try the 9.2% Hardcore IPA (£3.50 for half a pint). Mon–Sat noon–midnight, Sun 12.30pm–midnight.

★ **Hummingbird** 186 Bath St. One of several cheap bars along Bath St, *Hummingbird* is cool and dingy, with candles hanging from the ceiling in birdcages. Does a good line in gourmet burgers (from £7.50) and has cocktails named after subjects like travel, politics and food. Mon–Thurs noon–1am, Fri & Sat noon–3am.

Vodka Wodka 31–35 Ashton Lane. Always busy, with a popular garden area round the back, this student-friendly bar stocks vodkas from countries as diverse as Poland, Sweden, England and New Zealand. The cocktail of the day costs £5. Daily noon–midnight.

CLUBS AND LIVE MUSIC

The 13th Note 50–60 King St ⓦ13thnote.co.uk. A Glasgow institution hosting up-and-coming bands from metal to indie via acoustic rock. Also serves great veggie food. Daily noon–midnight.

The Arches 30 Midland St/253 Argyle St (two entrances) ⓦwww.thearches.co.uk. Cavernous club and live venue under Central Station that pulls off gigs, theatre shows and lysergic club nights with equal aplomb. The bigger nights can go on till 4/5am. See website for specific event times.

Barrowland 244 Gallowgate ⓦglasgow-barrowland .com. Glasgow's most famous live venue, with a medium-size capacity for soon-to-be-big bands and more established acts. Gig nights 7–11pm.

King Tut's Wah Wah Hut 272a St Vincent St ⓦkingtuts .co.uk. Famous as the place where Oasis were discovered, and still hosting excellent gigs. Mon–Sat noon–1am, Sun 5pm–1am.

Nice 'n' Sleazy 421 Sauchiehall St ⓦnicensleazy.com. Late-night bar, with the best jukebox in town and great gigs in its sweaty basement. Daily noon/1pm–3am.

Polo Lounge 84 Wilson St. Popular gay club that mixes refined drinking upstairs with a packed, cruisey dancefloor in the basement. Tues, Thurs & Sun 11pm–3am, Wed & Fri 10pm–3am, Sat 9pm–3am.

SECC Exhibition Way ⓦsecc.co.uk. The Scottish Exhibition and Conference Centre, including the famous "Armadillo" building, hosts the big-name touring bands and comedy acts. Hours vary depending on show (see website).

Sub Club 22 Jamaica St ⓦsubclub.co.uk. Underground club and purveyor of the finest techno and electro, regularly hosting DJs from Glasgow, London and beyond. Fri & Sat 11pm–3am, plus some midweek parties (see website).

ENTERTAINMENT

Centre for Contemporary Arts (CCA) 350 Sauchiehall St ⓦcca-glasgow.com. Cultural centre that has a reputation for a programme of controversial performances and exhibitions.

Citizens' Theatre 119 Gorbals St ⓦcitz.co.uk. South Side theatre famous for sourcing top Scottish talent. Also hosts hands-on workshops, including afternoon play-reading sessions.

Glasgow Film Theatre 12 Rose St ⓦgft.org.uk. This wonderful cinema shows art films and old favourites, as well as documentaries by British filmmakers.

The Grosvenor Ashton Lane ⓦgrosvenorcafe.co.uk. Independent cinema/café that also hosts live music and screenings in Kelvingrove Park. Cinema 10am/noon–10pm daily.

DIRECTORY

Hospital Royal Infirmary, 84 Castle St (☎0141 211 4000).
Internet Mitchell Library, North St: wi-fi access and 100 PCs for public use (Mon–Sat 9am–5/8pm; free for members).
Pharmacy Boots, Buchanan Galleries (Mon–Sat 8.45am–6.15pm with late opening Thurs, plus Sun 10am–6pm).
Police Pitt St (☎0141 532 2000).
Post office 59 Glassford St (Mon–Sat 8.30am–5.30pm).

STIRLING

13

STIRLING's strategic position between the Lowlands and Highlands at the easiest crossing of the River Forth has shaped its major role in Scottish history. Its steep cobbled streets and stupendous castle atop a crag have also earned the city somewhat flattering comparisons to a mini-Edinburgh.

WHAT TO SEE AND DO

Imperiously set on a rocky volcanic outcrop, the atmospheric **castle** (daily 9.30am–5/6pm; £13) combined regal and military functions. Highlights within the complex are the **Royal Palace**, dating from the late Renaissance, and the earlier **Great Hall**, with its restored hammerbeam roof. The oldest part of Stirling huddles around the streets leading up to the castle. Look out for the Gothic, timber-roofed **Church of the Holy Rude** (daily 10am–5pm), where the infant James VI – later James I of England – was crowned King of Scotland in 1567. From here, Broad Street slopes down to the lower town, passing the **Tolbooth**, the city's arts and cultural centre. Stirling is famous as the scene of Sir William Wallace's victory over the English in 1297, a crucial episode in the Wars of Independence. The Scottish hero was commemorated in the Victorian era with the **Wallace Monument** (daily: April–June, Sept & Oct 10am–5pm; July & Aug 10am–6pm; Nov–March 10.30am–4pm; £8.25), a bizarre Tolkienesque tower providing stupendous views – finer even than those from the castle.

ARRIVAL AND INFORMATION

By train The train station is just east of the centre in the lower part of town.
Destinations Aberdeen (hourly; 2hr 10min); Edinburgh (every 30min; 1hr); Glasgow (3 hourly; 30–40min); Inverness (6 daily; 2hr 45min).
By bus Long-distance buses depart from beside the train station.
Destinations Edinburgh (up to 3 hourly; 2hr 10min); Glasgow (1–2 hourly; 40min); St Andrews (every 2hr; 1hr 50min).
Tourist information Old Town Jail, St John St (daily 10am–5pm; ☎01786 475 019, ⓦvisitscotland.com). There's also a desk at 1–5 Port St (Mon–Fri 10am–5pm).

13

ACCOMMODATION

Willy Wallace Hostel 77 Murray Place ☎01786 446773, ⓦwillywallacehostel.com. Lively and welcoming backpacker hostel with a comfy common room where you can watch TV or play video games. Dorm £17, double £40

Witches Craig Campsite Blairlogie ☎01786 474947, ⓦwitchescraig.co.uk; bus #62. Picturesque site three miles east of town. Closed Nov–March. Camping £9.75 per person and tent

EATING AND DRINKING

La Ciociara 41 Friars St. Good-value Italian in the heart of Stirling. The buffet lunch on Thurs and Fri costs £5.95. Daily 11am/noon–10/11pm.

The Portcullis Castle Wynd. Right by the castle, this eighteenth-century hotel has one of the city's best bars, complete with beer garden and fire. It also serves reasonable pub food (mains from £9.50) too. Daily 11.30am–midnight.

ST ANDREWS

The country's oldest university town and a major golfing hotspot, plush **ST ANDREWS** lies on a gorgeous stretch of the Fife coast 56 miles northeast of Edinburgh. With Prince William as a former alumnus and its seven swanky golf courses being both the oldest and most revered in the world, it's unsurprising the town has a self-important air. Having attracted a well-to-do crowd for several centuries, it's on the pricey side, too.

WHAT TO SEE AND DO

Located on the northwestern fringes of town, the **Old Course** is St Andrews' most famous golf course and – according to Jack Nicklaus – the world's best. At the course's southern end, towards the waterfront, is the **British Golf Museum** (daily: March–Oct 9.30/10am–5pm; Nov–March 10am–4pm; £6.50); if you want to step onto the famous fairways, head to the **Himalayas** putting green, located right by the first hole and only £2 per round. A wonderful crescent of sandy beach sweeps north from the Old Course; immediately south of it runs North Street, one of St Andrews' two main arteries, largely taken up with grand university buildings.

The castle and cathedral

The ruined **castle** (daily 9.30am–4.30/5.30pm; £5.50, combined ticket with cathedral £7.20) sits on North Street, while a short distance further along the coast is the equally ruined Gothic **cathedral** (same hours; £4.50 or £7.20 with combined ticket), the mother church of medieval Scotland and the largest and grandest ever built in the country.

ARRIVAL AND INFORMATION

By train There are no direct trains, though frequent buses connect with the train station five miles away in Leuchars.

By bus The bus station is west of town on City Rd.

Destinations Edinburgh (hourly; 1hr 50min); Glasgow (hourly; 2hr 30min).

Tourist information 70 Market St (Mon–Sat 9.15/9.30am–5/7pm, plus Sun April to mid-Oct 10/11am–4/5pm; ☎01334 472021, ⓦvisitstandrews.com).

ACCOMMODATION AND EATING

If you want to stay in summer or during one of the big golf tournaments, when accommodation is in short supply, it's worth booking ahead.

Cairnsmill Caravan Park ☎01334 473604, ⓦcairnsmill.co.uk. A large, family campsite a mile from town with its own swimming pool and games room. Camping £10 per person and tent

Ogstons 147 North St. This fantastic building contains a great restaurant (most mains £9–14), bar and a cosy basement music lounge. Mon–Thurs 11am–9.30pm, Fri & Sat 11am–10pm, Sun 11am–9.30pm.

St Andrews Tourist Hostel St Mary's Place ☎01334 479911, ⓦstandrewshostel.com. Nicely decorated hostel with clean, basic dorm rooms, a well-equipped kitchen and comfy lounge. A 10min walk from the castle. Dorm £14

LOCH LOMOND AND THE TROSSACHS

Lying at the heart of the **Trossachs National Park**, **Loch Lomond** – the largest stretch of fresh water in Britain – is the epitome of Scottish scenic splendour, thanks in large part to the ballad that fondly recalls its "bonnie, bonnie banks". From the main hub at **BALLOCH**, at the loch's southwestern tip, you can take a cruise around the 33 islands nearby (☎01389 752376, ⓦsweeneyscruises.com; £9/hr). The **western shore** is easily accessible by bus from Balloch, with the A82 zipping along its banks. The **eastern shore**, however, is much more peaceful, as large sections of it are only accessible via the footpath which forms part of the West Highland Way. The easiest hike to the graceful peak of **Ben Lomond** (3192ft) is from **Rowardennan** (3hr), accessible in summer by ferry from Inverbeg on the western shore or alternatively by catching the McGills bus #309 from Balloch to Balmaha (roughly hourly; 30min) and hiking the remaining seven miles.

ARRIVAL AND INFORMATION

By train The easiest way to get to the loch is to take one of the frequent trains from Glasgow Queen St Station to Balloch.
Destinations Glasgow (every 30min; 45min).
Tourist information The tourist office is opposite Balloch's train station in the Old Station Building (daily: summer 9.30am–6pm; winter 10am–5pm; ☎01389 753533, ⓦvisitscotland.com). The office has details of the wide choice of campsites and B&Bs in all the villages.

ACCOMMODATION

Rowardennan Hostel North of Balloch on the eastern side of the loch ☎01360 870259, ⓦsyha.org.uk. Remote hostel with tantalizing views across the loch – see above for details on how to get here. Dorm <u>£18</u>, double <u>£42</u>

THE HIGHLANDS

The beguiling **Highlands** are a stunning mix of bare hills, green glens and silvery lochs, which extend up to the country's northern coast. The distances involved, along with scarce public transport, mean that you'll need several days to explore any one part properly. **FORT WILLIAM** is the Highlands' key outdoor base, served by train from Glasgow and bus from Inverness. On the outskirts of town is the **Nevis Range**, with skiing in winter and mountain biking in summer, and, sixteen miles south, **Glen Coe**, where soaring scenery and poignant history combine like nowhere else in the country. If you want to climb **Ben Nevis** (Britain's highest peak), the easiest route (7hr return) begins just outside town, but make sure you wear suitable clothing, as capricious weather conditions and poor visibility can

HIGHLAND TOURS
A couple of rival companies offer lively minibus tours designed specifically for backpackers: **Haggis** (☎08452 578345, ⓦhaggisadventures.com) and **Macbackpackers** (☎0131 558 9900, ⓦmacbackpackers.com) depart from Edinburgh on trips lasting between one and ten days, covering the likes of Loch Ness, Skye and the Highlands. Three-day tours to Skye cost around £110.

combine to make the ill-prepared hiker extremely vulnerable. Fort William also marks one end of the West Highland Way, which runs all the way to Glasgow. **AVIEMORE**, at the foot of the looming **Cairngorm** range, now a national park, is also a good base for challenging hiking, ancient pine forests and winter sports. With **outdoor activities** the big draw across the region, most tourist information centres and hostels carry information on local hiking routes and adventure sports.

ARRIVAL AND DEPARTURE

By train Some scenic spots are served by ScotRail's train network (ⓦscotrail.co.uk), which has good-value travel passes available.

ACCOMMODATION AND EATING

FORT WILLIAM

Glen Nevis Hostel ☎01397 702336, ⓦsyha.org. It's better to stay in Glen Nevis than Fort William itself: try this SYHA hostel at the foot of Ben Nevis, a 2.5-mile walk or £7 taxi ride out of town (try Alistair's Taxis on ☎01397 252525). Dorm <u>£22</u>

AVIEMORE

Cairngorm Hotel Opposite the train station on Grampian Rd. Serving reasonably priced pub-style food (mains £9–11), much of it sourced from Scotland. Food daily noon–9.30pm.
Glenmore Lodge ☎01479 861256, ⓦglenmorelodge .org.uk. As well as running excellent, though expensive, outdoor courses, this famous lodge also offers en-suite rooms on a B&B basis. Double <u>£74</u>
SYHA hostel Grampian Road ☎01479 810345, ⓦsyha .org. Just south of the train station, this SYHA is well equipped for hikers. Dorms are simple, but there's a handy drying room and a sociable dining space. Dorm <u>£17</u>, double <u>£45</u>

13

INVERNESS

Lying 160 miles north of Edinburgh, **INVERNESS** is the capital of the Highlands: a grey but affable town with a vibrant dining scene and a wonderful setting at the mouth of the River Ness. The chief historical attraction nearby is the ever-popular **Culloden Visitor Centre** (daily: April–Oct 9am–5.30/6pm; Nov–March 10am–4pm; £10.50), six miles east on bus line #2B from the city centre. In 1746, Culloden Moor was the scene of the last pitched battle on British soil, when Bonnie Prince Charlie's Jacobite army was crushed in just forty minutes, ending Stuart ambitions of regaining the monarchy forever. Infinitely more dramatic is **Cawdor Castle** (May–Oct daily 10am–5.30pm; £9.75), twelve miles northeast, a fairytale fourteenth-century castle and legendary home of Shakespeare's Macbeth. There's no direct bus from Inverness, so you'll need to take the #10 bus to Nairn and transfer there to #252, walking the last ten minutes or so to the castle.

ARRIVAL AND DEPARTURE

By plane Inverness airport is seven miles northeast of the town, from where there's a regular bus into the city (roughly every 30min; 25min).

By train The train station is just northeast of the centre on Station Sq.

Destinations Aviemore (every 1–2hr; 35–45min); Edinburgh (8 daily; 3hr 15min–4hr 45min); Glasgow (4 direct daily, or change at Perth; 3hr 20min); Kyle of Lochalsh (for Skye; Mon–Sat 4 daily; Sun 1 daily; 2hr 30min); Stirling (some change at Perth; 11 daily; 2hr 30min–3hr).

By bus The bus station is just northwest of the train station.

Destinations Edinburgh (8 daily; 3hr 20min–4hr 40min); Fort William (via Loch Ness, every 2hr; 1hr 50min); Glasgow (5 daily; 3hr 30min–4hr 30min); Stirling (2 daily; 3hr 20min).

INFORMATION

Tourist information Castle Wynd (April–Oct Mon–Sat 9am–5/6pm, Sun 9.30/10am–4/5pm; Nov–March Mon–Sat limited hours; ☎01463 234353, ⓦinverness-scotland .com). Will find rooms for a small fee and does bike rental.

ACCOMMODATION AND EATING

Bazpackers 4 Culduthel Rd ☎01463 717663, ⓦbazpackershostel.co.uk. The smallest hostel in town, and the best, with an open fire, friendly staff and views over the River Ness. Dorm **£17**, double **£44**

Hootananny 67 Church St. Lively pub that has live gigs and good Scottish food like haggis in puff pastry for £3.45. Mon–Thurs noon–1am, Fri & Sat noon–3am, Sun 6.30pm–midnight.

Inverness Student Hotel 8 Culduthel Rd ☎01463 236556, ⓦinvernessstudenthotel.com. This welcoming hostel has great views, a quiet location by the castle and a good range of dorms. Dorm **£18**

Inverness YHA Victoria Rd ☎01463 231771, ⓦsyha.org .uk. Large, modern HI hostel with excellent facilities, though it's not the most central option. Dorm **£25**

La Tortilla Asesina 99 Castle St. Snug Spanish restaurant with tapas from £3.75. The menu also includes plenty of veggie options, like meat-free paellas and goat's cheese omelettes. July & Aug daily noon–11.30pm; Sept–June Mon–Thurs & Sun noon–10.30pm, Fri & Sat noon–11.30pm.

LOCH NESS

Loch Ness forms part of the thickly forested natural fault line of the Great Glen, which slices across the southern edge of the Highlands between Inverness and Fort William. Most visitors are eager to catch a glimpse of the elusive **Loch Ness Monster**: to find out the whole story, take a bus to **DRUMNADROCHIT**, fourteen miles southwest of Inverness, where the **Loch Ness Exhibition Centre** (daily: Easter–Oct 9/9.30am–5/6pm; Nov–Easter 10am–3.30pm; £6.95; ⓦlochness.com) attempts to breathe life into the old

---

MIDGE ALERT

During the summer months, particularly in wetter areas, the Highlands and Islands are blighted by **midges** – tiny biting insects that appear in swarms. If you're camping or hiking, make sure you have insect repellent – locals swear by Avon's Skin So Soft moisturizer – or a midge hood, a net fitting over a wide-brimmed hat which, while making no concessions to fashion, should protect the face. Even a light breeze will blow the midges away, though, so try and pick somewhere that isn't completely still to camp.

13

THE LOCH NESS MONSTER

Tales of **Nessie** date back at least as far as the seventh century, when the monster came off second best in an altercation with St Columba. However, the possibility that a mysterious prehistoric creature might be living in the loch only attracted worldwide attention in the 1930s, when sightings were reported during the construction of the road along its western shore. Numerous appearances have been reported since, but even the most high-tech surveys of the loch have failed to come up with conclusive evidence.

myth. A couple of miles south, the ruined **Castle Urquhart** (daily: April–Sept 9.30am–6pm; Oct until 5pm; Nov–March until 4.30pm; £7.90) is one of Scotland's most beautifully sited fortresses.

THE ISLE OF MULL AND AROUND

The **Isle of Mull** is the most accessible of the Hebridean islands off Scotland's west coast: just 45 minutes by ferry from **Oban**, which is linked by train to Glasgow. Its three hundred miles of rugged coastline are the main draw, peppered with castles, beautiful beaches, idyllic chocolate-box villages like Tobermory, and Iona, the birthplace of Christianity in Britain.

Craignure and Tobermory

CRAIGNURE is the ferry terminal for boats from Oban. Just outside is dramatic thirteenth-century **Duart Castle** (April Mon–Thurs & Sun 11am–4pm; May to mid-Oct daily 10.30am–5pm; £5.75), two miles' walk along the bay: you can peek in the dungeons and ascend to the rooftops. Mull's "capital" **TOBERMORY**, 22 miles northwest of Craignure, is easily the most attractive fishing port in the west of Scotland, with brightly coloured houses and boats sheltering in a bay backed by a steep bluff.

Fionnphort and Staffa

Some 35 miles west of Craignure, tiny **Fionnphort** is nevertheless one of Mull's

metropolises. A few miles south at Knockvologan is the gorgeous sandy beach of **Erraid**, inspiration for Robert Louis Stevenson's thriller *Kidnapped*. The Iolaire (☎01681 700358; ⓦstaffatrips.co.uk; £30; also stops on Iona) runs from Fionnphort to **Staffa**, a moody, uninhabited basaltic island marking the northern end of the Giant's Causeway (see p.600) with the cathedral-like **Fingal's Cave**, whose haunting noises inspired Mendelssohn's *Hebrides Overture*.

Isle of Iona

Serene little **Iona** has been a place of pilgrimage for several centuries: it was here that St Columba fled from Ireland in 563 AD and established a monastery subsequently responsible for the conversion of more or less all of pagan Scotland. The present **abbey** (daily 9.30am–4.30/5.30pm; £5.50) dates from 1200, while Iona's oldest building, **St Oran's Chapel**, lies just south. It stands at the centre of the burial ground, Reilig Odhrain, which is said to contain the graves of sixty kings.

ARRIVAL AND INFORMATION

By ferry Regular ferries (up to 7 daily; 45min) run from Oban, priced at £5.40 one-way. Iona is served by Calmac ferries (at least 6 daily; 10min) from Fionnphort

Tourist information The island's main tourist office is at The Pier, Craignure (April to mid-Oct Mon–Fri 8.30am–5.15/7pm, Sat 9am–5.15/6.30pm, Sun 10/10.30am–5.15/7pm; mid-Oct to March Mon–Sat 9am–5pm, Sun 10.30am–noon & 3.30–5pm; ☎01680 812377, ⓦvisitscottishheartlands.com).

Explore Mull Visitor Centre On the edge of Main Street's car park, Tobermory (daily 9am–5pm; ☎01688 302875, ⓦexploremull.com). Can arrange trips and accommodation.

ACCOMMODATION

Iona Hostel A mile from the ferry, Iona ☎01681 700781, ⓦionahostel.co.uk. Camping is not permitted on the island, but this excellent hostel has comfortable beds and superb views. Dorm **£19.50**

Tobermory Youth Hostel Main Street, Tobermory, Mull ☎01688 302481. Dorms here are a little stark, but the setting – among multicoloured harbour-front houses – is undeniably pretty. Open March–Oct only. Dorm **£17.75**

13

ISLAND-HOPPING

The sea off Scotland's west coast is dotted with islands, from tiny rocks to substantial landmasses. The main ferry company, **Caledonian MacBrayne** (CalMac; ⓦcalmac.co.uk), connects most of them, and offers a range of island-hopping trips. **Arran**, **Islay** and the **Small Isles** (Rum, Muck and Eigg) are all worth visiting, too.

THE ISLE OF SKYE

The deeply indented coastline, azure water and spectacular summits of the **Isle of Skye** make it one of the most captivating spots in Britain. The island's stunning topography once shielded Bonnie Prince Charlie from capture by government forces; now the high, jagged peaks of the **Cuillin** ridge are Britain's best (and most demanding) walking and climbing terrain. Equally dramatic are the rock formations of the **Trotternish peninsula** in the north.

Elgol and the Cuillins

The best approach to the **Cuillins** is by #55 bus from Broadford on the dramatic road to **ELGOL**, from where there are boat trips on the *Bella Jane* (late March to Oct daily; one-way £14, return £24; ☎0800 731 3089, ⓦbellajane.co.uk) to stunning Loch Coruisk, where there's a seal colony. With adequate planning, you can hike from the loch up into the Cuillins or back to Elgol. Serious hikers also head for **GLENBRITTLE**, west of the Cuillins, where there's an HI hostel (see below).

Portree, Old Man of Storr and Uig

Skye's capital is **PORTREE**, an attractive fishing port in the north of the island, with several **hostels** (see below). Some nine miles from Portree on the **Trotternish peninsula** are Skye's geological highlights: a 165ft sea stack called the **Old Man of Storr** and, soaring above Staffin Bay ten miles north, the **Quiraing** – a spectacular forest of rock formations. The tranquil village of **UIG**, on the west coast, has ferries to the islands of the Outer

Hebrides, as well as an HI hostel (see below).

ARRIVAL AND INFORMATION

By train Skye is connected to the mainland via a bridge to Kyle of Lochalsh, from where several trains daily serve Inverness (2hr 35min). Trains also run from Mallaig to Glasgow (3 daily; 5hr 20min).

By ferry Ferries run between Armadale in southeastern Skye and Mallaig on the mainland (April–Oct 6–8 daily; 30min).

By bus Regular buses link Skye with Glasgow (3 daily; 7hr).

Tourist information Portree has the island's main tourist office just off Bridge Rd (Mon–Sat 9am–5/6pm, plus April–Oct Sun 10am–4pm; ☎01478 614906).

ACCOMMODATION

GLEN BRITTLE

Glenbrittle Hostel Glen Brittle ☎01478 640278, ⓦsyha.org.uk. No-frills youth hostel with a self-catering kitchen and a small shop selling snacks and supplies. Closed Oct–Feb. Dorm £18

PORTREE

Portree Independent Hostel ☎01478 613737, ⓦhostelskye.co.uk. Cheery, paint-daubed hostel in the middle of Skye's attractive capital. Cosy living room and free tea and coffee. Dorm £17

UIG

Uig Hostel Just off the A87 ☎01470 542746, ⓦsyha.org.uk. Great base for walking in an old maternity hospital on Skye's western edge. Good-sized rooms and spacious "waiting areas". Closed Oct–March. Dorm £17.50

Uig Bay Campsite ☎01470 542714, ⓦuig-camping-skye.co.uk. This very friendly campsite with views over the land and sea also rents out bikes (£12/day). Open year-round. Camping £6 per person and tent

EATING

BROADFORD

Harbour Restaurant Main St. Popular place serving an unlikely mix of Scottish and Spanish flavours, including traditional desserts (from £4). Daily 10am–10pm; closed Tues in winter.

PORTREE

Café Arriba Quay Brae. Chilled café on the road up from the harbour, with inventive pasta dishes, stews and burgers for around £6–7. Daily 7am–6pm.

FRESCO AT THE PALACE OF KNOSSOS, CRETE

Greece

HIGHLIGHTS

❶ **Athens** Roam the Acropolis and hit the capital's clubs. **See p.501**

❷ **Olympia** Discover where the Games were born. **See p.515**

❸ **Meteora** Awe-inspiring Byzantine monasteries in a magical setting. **See p.518**

❹ **Thessaloníki** A multicultural hub, springboard to Northern Greece and Vergína. **See p.520**

❺ **Santoríni** Take in the sunset from Ía on this spectacular island. **See p.530**

❻ **Knossos** Visit the legendary home of the Minotaur. **See p.540**

HIGHLIGHTS ARE MARKED ON THE MAP ON P.497

ROUGH COSTS

Daily budget Basic €30, occasional treat €40

Drink Ouzo €3

Food *Souvláki* (shish kebab) €3

Hostel/budget hotel €15/€40

Travel Bus: Athens–Delphi €15; ferry: Athens–Crete €36

FACT FILE

Population 11.2 million

Language Greek

Currency Euro (€)

Capital Athens

International phone code ☏ 30

Time zone GMT +2hr

Introduction

With 227 inhabited islands and a landscape that ranges from Mediterranean to Balkan, Greece has enough appeal to fill months of travel. The beaches are distributed along a convoluted coastline, with cosmopolitan resorts lying surprisingly close to remote islands where boats may call only once or twice a week. The initial glimpse of sapphire water or the discovery of millennia-old ruins bordered by ancient olive groves is intoxicating, and it's the mingling of history and hedonism that ensures Greece's enduring appeal. Island-hopping is still popular, but if you're on a tight budget, consider exploring the mainland or the Peloponnese by bus, or save on multiple ferry trips by focusing on a few highlights.

The country is the sum of an extraordinary diversity of influences. Romans, Arabs, Frankish Crusaders, Venetians, Slavs, Albanians, Turks, Italians, as well as the thousand-year Byzantine Empire, have all been and gone since the time of Alexander the Great. Each has left its mark: the **Byzantines** through countless churches and monasteries; the **Venetians** in impregnable fortifications such as Monemvasiá in the Peloponnese; the **Franks** with crag-top castles, again in the Peloponnese but also in the Dodecanese and east Aegean. Most obvious, perhaps, is the heritage of four hundred years of **Ottoman Turkish** rule, which exercised an inestimable influence on music, cuisine, language and way of life.

Even before the fall of Byzantium in the fifteenth century, Greek peasants, fishermen and shepherds had created one of the most vigorous and truly **popular cultures** in Europe, which found expression in song and dance, costumes, embroidery, furniture and the distinctive whitewashed houses. Though having suffered a decline under Western influence, Hellenic culture – architectural and musical heritage in particular – is undergoing a renaissance.

CHRONOLOGY

c. 800 BC Homer writes *The Iliad* and *The Odyssey*.
776 BC First Olympic Games are held in Olympia.
438 BC The building of the Parthenon is completed.
399 BC The trial and execution of Socrates, the founding father of philosophy, takes place.
387 BC Plato establishes the Athens Academy.
323 BC Alexander the Great dies heralding the beginning of the Hellenistic period.
146 BC Greece becomes a province of the Roman Empire.
330 AD The Roman capital moves to Constantinople and the Byzantine Empire is established. Christianity becomes dominant religion.
1453 Ottoman Turks invade Constantinople. End of the Byzantine Empire.
1821 Greek National Revolution against Ottoman rule.
1832 The Treaty of London recognizes Greek Independence. Greece becomes a monarchy under King Otto I.
1833 Athens becomes the capital of modern Greece.
1864 King Otto ousted, King George I introduces parliamentary democracy.
1896 The first modern Olympic Games are held in Athens.
1912–13 During the Balkan wars Greece doubles its size, gaining Thessaloníki and parts of Macedonia and Thrace.
1940–41 Greece is invaded and occupied by German, Italian and Bulgarian armies. Liberation comes in October 1944 with the help of heavy resistance fighting.
1945–49 Greek Civil War between Communists and pro-Western forces.
1952 A new constitution is passed which retains the monarchy as head of state.
1967 Military coup led by Colonel George Papadopoulos.
1974 Turkish invasion of Cyprus. The colonels' junta collapses. New constitution established and the monarchy abolished with a referendum.
1981 Greece joins the EU.
2002 Greece adopts the euro.
2010 The economic crisis forces the Greek government to seek help from the European Union and the IMF. A heavy recession follows, which continues for years.

14

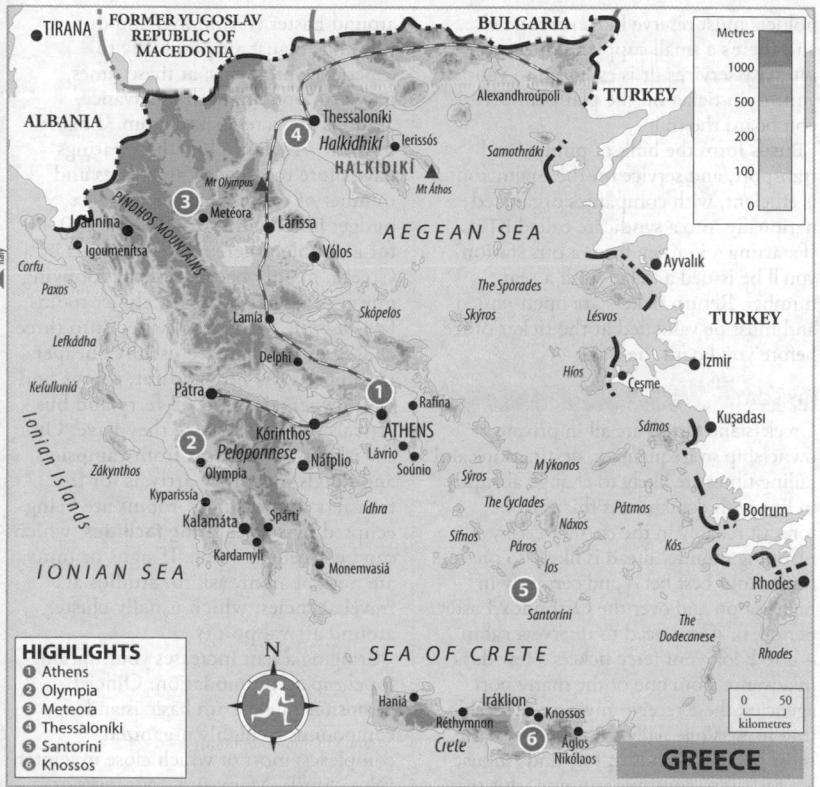

HIGHLIGHTS
1 Athens
2 Olympia
3 Meteora
4 Thessaloníki
5 Santoríni
6 Knossos

N

GREECE

ARRIVAL AND DEPARTURE

There are international **airports** on the mainland at Athens and Thessaloníki, both well connected with their respective cities. Other destinations served by budget flights include Crete, Corfu and Rhodes, as well as numerous other mainland and island destinations.

By **boat**, there are regular ferries from Ancona, Bari, Brindisi, Trieste and Venice in Italy, arriving at Corfu, Kefalloniá, Igoumenítsa and Pátra. Eurail and InterRail pass holders travel free with Superfast Ferries (W superfast.com) from Ancona and Bari to Igoumenítsa, Greece's third passenger port after Pireás and Pátra. From here, there are four daily onward bus services to Athens and two to Thessaloníki (for Bulgaria, Romania or Turkey), though you should get any necessary visas in Athens. You can also travel by boat from Turkey to the

Dodecanese and the northern Aegean islands (Rhodes, Kós, Sámos, Híos and Lésvos), and from Albania to Corfu.

By bus, **land** crossings into Greece are possible from Albania, Macedonia, Bulgaria, Romania and Turkey, all arriving in Thessaloníki, from where onward travel to the rest of the country is easy and straightforward. Note that since January 2011 there are no more international trains into Northern Greece.

GETTING AROUND

BY TRAIN AND BUS

The limited **rail** network has become even more so with the financial crisis, and only the lines Athens–Salonika and Athens–Kiáto, as well as local tourist lines (or Odontotós, see box, p.511), are reliable. **Eurail** and **InterRail** are valid, though pass

14

holders must reserve like everyone else, and there's a small supplement on the intercity services. It is essential to validate your train ticket on the platform before you board the train.

Buses form the bulk of public land transport, and service on the major routes is efficient, with companies organized nationally into a syndicate called **KTEL**. If starting a journey from a bus station, you'll be issued a ticket with a seat number. Return tickets are open-ended and must be validated at the ticket office before you board the bus.

BY BOAT

Greek **island ferries** are all in private ownership so frequencies, destinations and sailing times are likely to change abruptly in line with demand. As this can't be forecast reliably in the current crisis, planning months ahead is likely to prove futile. Your best bet – and certainly in high season and over the Orthodox Easter period, or if you need to reserve a cabin – is to book your ferry tickets a few days in advance from one of the many port agencies; these receive any new timetable info first. While daily boats between the most popular islands in July and August are certain to continue running, this may not be the case outside of these months. The cheapest ticket is "deck class". Leave plenty of time for your journey as ferries are often late, or take longer to reach their destinations than scheduled.

Hydrofoils and high-speed catamarans are roughly twice as fast and twice as expensive as ordinary ferries. In season, *kaïkia* (caïques) sail to more obscure islets. For more information on ferry and hydrofoil schedules, see ⓦgtp.gr.

BY BIKE AND SCOOTER

Once on the islands, almost everybody rents a **scooter** or a bicycle. Scooters cost from €12 a day, bikes a bit less. To rent a scooter you must produce a motorcycle licence from your country of origin.

ACCOMMODATION

Most of the year you can turn up pretty much anywhere and find a **room**. Only around Easter (Orthodox) and during July and August are you likely to experience problems; at these times, it's worth booking well in advance.

Hotels are categorized from "Luxury" down to "E-class", but these ratings have more to do with amenities and number of rooms than pricing – a budget hotel will typically cost €30–60 for a double. There are few **hostels** in Greece, mainly because of the lobbying power of owners of privately let rooms (*dhomátia*). These are divided into three classes (A–C), and are usually cheaper than hotels. As often as not, rooms find you: owners descend on ferry and bus arrivals to fill any space they have. On the islands, minibuses from campsites and hotels meet new arrivals for free transfers. Increasingly, rooms are being eclipsed by **self-catering facilities**, which can be excellent value. If signs or touts are not apparent, ask for studios at travel agencies, which usually cluster around arrival points.

Bringing a tent increases your options for cheap accommodation. Official **campsites** range from basic island compounds to highly organized complexes, most of which close in winter (Nov–April). Many sites rent tents or have more permanent accommodation in the form of cabins and bungalows. Rough camping is forbidden.

FOOD AND DRINK

Eating out in Greece is popular and reasonably priced: €10–15 per person for a meal with beer or cheap wine. Typical **taverna** dishes to try include *moussaka* (aubergine and meat pie), *yígandes* (giant haricot beans in tomato sauce), *tzatzíki* (yogurt, garlic and cucumber dip),

---

BUDGET EATING

Head to a supermarket and stock up on Greek yogurt and honey for breakfast and buy *tyrópites* and *spanakópites* (cheese and spinach pies respectively) from a bakery for lunch. **Snacks** are one of the pleasures of Greek eating. Good budget food chains include *Woodys* and *Everest*.

melitzanosaláta (aubergine dip), *khtapódhi* (octopus) and *kalamarákia* (fried baby squid). Quintessentially Greek establishments *ouzerí* and *mezedhópolia* serve filling *mezédhes* (the Greek version of tapas) with drinks, adding up to a substantial meal. Note that people eat late: 1.30–3pm for lunch & 9–11.30pm for dinner, although most places serve food all day.

As for **drinks**, the traditional coffee shop or **kafenío** is the central pivot of rural life; like tavernas, these range from the sophisticated to the old-fashioned. Their main business is sweet Greek coffee, but they also serve spirits such as aniseed-flavoured *ouzo* and brandy, as well as beer and soft drinks. Islanders take pre-dinner *ouzo* an hour or two before sunset: you'll be served a glass of water alongside, to be tipped into your *ouzo* until it turns milky white. **Bars** are ubiquitous in the largest towns and resorts. Drinks, at €5.50–8, are invariably more expensive than at a *kafenío*.

CULTURE AND ETIQUETTE

It is important to be respectful when visiting one of Greece's many **churches** or **monasteries**, and appropriate clothing should be worn – covered arms and legs for both sexes. The more popular sites often provide such clothing, should you be without it. Photography is also banned in sacred places. Another important part of Greek life is the afternoon **siesta**, when peace and quiet are valued. In restaurants, **tipping** is normally expected and usually customers leave a little more for service. **Topless bathing** is the norm on virtually all Greek beaches, but, especially in smaller places or town beaches, check first before stripping off. Full nudity is tolerated only at designated or isolated beaches.

SPORTS AND OUTDOOR ACTIVITIES

The larger islands and resorts on the mainland have countless opportunities for **watersports** – including waterskiing, windsurfing, diving and snorkelling.

GREECE ONLINE

Ⓦ **visitgreece.gr** Greek National Tourist Organization site.
Ⓦ **trainose.gr** Greek trains.
Ⓦ **odysseus.culture.gr** Greek Ministry of Culture site; the most up-to-date source for museum and archeological sites' opening times.

14

There are usually information kiosks at the main beaches. The country's mountainous landscape provides plenty of **walking** and **climbing** options. The most rewarding areas are in northern Greece, concentrating around Mount Olympus to the east and the Epirus region to the northwest. Always wear sturdy walking boots for long treks, and carry plenty of water. If you want to do some serious hiking, it's worth buying a specialist map.

COMMUNICATIONS

Post offices operate Monday to Friday 7.30am to 2pm. **Stamps** can also be bought at designated postal agencies inside newsstands or stationers. **Public phones** are mainly card-operated; buy phonecards from newsagents and kiosks. It's possible to make collect (reverse-charge) or charge-card calls from these phones (Ⓣ 139 for international operator), but you need €2.50 credit on a Greek phonecard to begin. If you're in the country for more than a week or so it's worth buying a **pay-as-you-go SIM card** available from mobile-phone shops; you can get your phone unlocked there, too. **Internet cafés** have become almost completely obsolete; Greeks have embraced wi-fi so completely that almost every café, bar and restaurant has a strong signal.

PERÍPTERA PAVEMENT KIOSKS

You can't walk far in Greece without coming across a *períptero* pavement kiosk. Selling everything from bus tickets to condoms, razors and stationery, they're often the first port of call for directions, too. Many are open 24 hours.

14

EMERGENCY NUMBERS
Police ☎ 100; Ambulance ☎ 166; Fire
☎ 199; Tourist police ☎ 171.

EMERGENCIES

The most common causes of a run-in
with the **police** are drunken loutishness
and camping outside an authorized site.

For minor medical complaints go to the
local **pharmacy**, usually open Monday
to Friday 8am to 2pm. Details of places
open out-of-hours are posted in all
pharmacy windows. For serious medical
attention you'll find English-speaking
doctors in all bigger towns and resorts;
consult the tourist police for names.
Emergency treatment is free in state

GREEK

	GREEK	PRONUNCIATION
Yes	Ναί	Né
No	Όχι	Óhi
Please	Παρακαλώ	Parakaló
Thank you	Ευχαριστώ	Efharistó
Hello/Good day	Γειά σας/Χαίρετε	Yá sas/Hérete
Goodbye	Αντίο	Adío
Excuse me	Συγνώμη	Signómi
Sorry	Λυπάμαι	Lipáme
When?	Πότε?	Póte?
Where?	Πού?	Poú?
Good	Καλό	Kaló
Bad	Κακό	Kakó
Near	Κοντά	Kondá
Far	Μακριά	Makriá
Cheap	Φτηνό	Ftinó
Expensive	Ακριβό	Akrivó
Open	Ανοιχτό	Anikhtó
Closed	Κλειστό	Klistó
Today	Σήμερα	Símera
Yesterday	Χθές	Khthés
Tomorrow	Αύριο	Ávrio
How much is...?	Πόσο κάνει...?	Póso káni...?
What time is it?	Τί ώρα είναι?	Tí óra íne?
I don't understand	Δέν καταλαβαίνω	Thén katalavéno
Do you speak English?	Ξαίρετε Αγγλικά?	Ksérete angliká?
Do you have a room?	Έχετε ένα ελεύθερο δωμάτιο?	Éhete éna eléfthero domátio?
Where does this bus go to?	Πού πηγαίνει αυτό τό λεωφορείο?	Poú piyéni aftó tó leoforío?
What time does it leave?	Τί ώρα φεύγει?	Tí óra févyi?
A ticket to...	Ένα εισιτήριο γιά...	Éna isitírio yiá...
I'm going to...	Πάω στό...	Páo stó...
Can I have the bill please?	Τό λογαριασμό παρακαλώ?	Tó loghariazmó, parakaló?
One	Ένα /Μία	Éna/mía (for 1am/pm)
Two	Δύο	Dhýo
Three	Τρία/Τρείς	tría/trís(for 3am/pm)
Four	Τέσσερα/Τέσσερεις	Téssera/tésseris (for 4am/pm)
Five	Πέντε	Pénde
Six	Έξι	Éxi
Seven	Εφτά	Eftá
Eight	Οκτώ	Októ
Nine	Εννέα	Enéa
Ten	Δέκα	Théka

14

FAR FROM AN OPEN AND SHUT CASE

The only evidence of the crisis ravaging Greece at the moment which tourists are likely to notice is the **erratic opening times** of state museums, tourist offices or archeological sites. This is easy to explain: depending on money allotted, museums employ extra staff for the summer season with its longer operating hours. But even when they know they have the money, new anti-corruption laws mean that they have to go through a lengthy public tender process even when employing guards for a few months in the summer. As a result, you may find that even in June, summer hours have not yet started, or that winter hours (normally Tues–Fri 8am–3pm) apply throughout the year. For this reason, we highly recommend that you do your sightseeing in the mornings.

---

hospitals, though you'll only get the most basic level of nursing care.

INFORMATION

National Tourist Organization (EOT) offices have been scaled down considerably during the economic crisis. You can only find them in the largest of towns and resorts; in other places, try the municipal tourist offices, which are mostly open only in the summer, or private local agencies near the ports or bus stations.

MONEY AND BANKS

Greece's currency is the **euro** (€). **Banks** are normally open Monday to Thursday 8am to 2.30pm, Friday 8am to 1.30pm. They charge a flat fee (€2–3) to change money, the National Bank usually being the cheapest; travel agencies and designated exchange booths give a poorer rate, but often levy a sliding commission, which makes them better than banks for changing small amounts. **ATMs** accept foreign cards and **credit cards** are generally accepted in most hotels, restaurants and shops, though in isolated areas cash will prove useful.

STUDENTS AND YOUTH DISCOUNTS

Many state-owned **museums and sites** are free for students from EU countries (a valid student card is required, but not necessarily an ISIC). Non-EU students generally pay half-price.

OPENING HOURS AND HOLIDAYS

Shops generally open from 8.30/9am to 2.00/2.30pm Monday to Saturday with afternoon shopping 5.30/6pm to 8.00/8.30pm on Tuesday, Thursday and Friday. Tourist areas have shops and offices that often stay open right through the day. On Sunday shops are generally closed. In rural areas **public transport** reduces dramatically or ceases completely, so be careful not to get stranded. Opening hours for **museums** and **ancient sites** change with exasperating frequency, though all state museums are closed on Monday. Smaller sites may close for a siesta (even when they're not supposed to), as do monasteries. The country's ongoing financial crisis has also affected opening hours – see box above. There's a vast range of **national holidays** and **festivals**. The most important, when almost everything will be closed, are: January 1 and 6, first Monday of Orthodox Lent (March 3, 2014, February 23, 2015), March 25, May 1, Orthodox Easter Sunday and Monday (20/21 April, 2014, 12/13 April, 2015), Whit Monday (June 9, 2014, June 1, 2015), August 15, October 28, December 25 and 26.

Athens

Exasperating and exhilarating, **ATHENS** has been inhabited continuously for over seven thousand years. Vastly improved by a vigorous scrub for the 2004 Olympics, it now has an efficient, user-friendly metro and its mix of contemporary culture, nightlife and

14

heritage rivals that of almost any European city. Part of Athens' charm is the mix of retro and contemporary: cutting-edge clothes shops and designer bars stand by the remnants of the Ottoman bazaar, while modernist 1960s apartment blocks stand shoulder-to-shoulder with Neoclassical mansions.

Athens' Acropolis, protected by a ring of mountains and commanding views of all seagoing approaches, was a natural choice for prehistoric settlement. Its development as a city-state reached its zenith in the fifth century BC with a flourish of art, architecture, literature and philosophy that has pervaded Western culture ever since. The **ancient sites** are the most obvious of Athens' attractions, but the pleasant cafés, markets and landscaped stair-streets, the startling views from the hills of **Lykavitós** and **Filopáppou**, and, around the foot of the Acropolis, the scattered monuments of the Byzantine and nineteenth-century town, all have their appeal.

WHAT TO SEE AND DO

Pláka is the best place to begin exploring the city. One of the few parts of Athens with unified architecture, its narrow streets and stepped lanes are flanked by nineteenth-century Neoclassical houses. The interlocking streets provide countless opportunities for watching the world – or at least, the tourists – go by. While the Acropolis complex is an essential sight, it can be rewarding to stumble across smaller and more modest relics, such as the fourth-century BC Monument of Lysikrátis, or the first-century Tower of the Winds. Or take a walk through the pleasant National Gardens, away from the chaos of Athens' traffic-choked streets. Save some energy for the balmy evenings, however – with fantastic restaurants and funky bars, Athens knows how to juxtapose the ancient with the modern.

The Acropolis

A rugged limestone outcrop, watered by springs and rising abruptly from the plain of Attica, the **Acropolis** (daily: summer 8am–7pm; winter 8am–sunset; €12, non-EU students €6, EU students free; ticket valid for four days and allows free access to all other ancient sites nearby, which all have same hours) was one of the earliest settlements in Greece, supporting a Neolithic community around 5000 BC. During the ninth century BC, it became the heart of the first Greek city-state, and in the fifth century BC, Pericles had the complex reconstructed under the direction of architect and sculptor Pheidias, producing most of the monuments visible today, including the Parthenon. Having survived more or less intact for over two millennia, the Acropolis was blown up by a shell in 1687 during the Ottoman-Venetian war. In 1811 Lord Elgin controversially sawed off parts of the frieze (the "Elgin Marbles"), which he later sold to the British Government. While the original religious significance of the Acropolis is now nonexistent, it is still imbued with a sense of majesty. The vistas alone are worth the climb, as the Acropolis's height affords a rare bird's-eye view over the capital. Go early or late to beat the crowds and savour a moment alone with this icon of Western civilization.

The Parthenon

With the construction of the **Parthenon**, fifth-century BC Athens reached an artistic and cultural peak. No other monument in the ancient Greek world had achieved such fame, and it stood proud as a symbol of the greatness and the power of Athens. The first and largest building constructed by Pericles' men, the temple is stunning, achieving an unequalled harmony in temple architecture. Built on the site of earlier temples, it was intended as a new sanctuary for Athena and a house for her cult image, a colossal statue decked in ivory and gold plate that was designed by Pheidias and considered one of the Seven Wonders of the Ancient World; unfortunately the sculpture was lost after the fifth century AD.

The Erechtheion

To the north of the Parthenon stands the **Erechtheion**, the last of the great works of Pericles. The building is intentionally unlike anything else found among the remnants of ancient sites. The most bizarre and memorable feature is the Porch of the Caryatids, as the columns are replaced by six maidens from the town of Caryae (Caryatids) holding the entablature gracefully on their heads. The significance of this design continues to puzzle both historians and visitors.

The Acropolis Museum

The **Acropolis Museum** (April–Oct Tues–Thurs, Sat & Sun 8am–8pm, Fri 8am–10pm; Nov–March Tues–Thurs 9am–5pm, Fri 9am–10pm, Sat & Sun 9am–8pm; €5; ⓦ theacropolismuseum .gr), opened in 2009, sits in a striking, purpose-built building at the foot of the rock, and stands above a set of excavations visible through the see-through floor. It contains nearly all the portable objects removed from the Acropolis since 1834. Prize exhibits include the *Moschophoros*, a painted marble statue of a young man carrying a sacrificial calf; the graceful sculpture of Athena Nike adjusting her sandal, known as *Nike Sandalízoussa*; and four Caryatids from the Erechtheion. Athens now has a suitable facility for the storage and display of the Elgin Marbles – but whether the British Museum will return them remains to be seen.

Herodes Atticus Theatre and Theatre of Dionysus

Dominating the southern slope of the Acropolis hill is the second-century Roman **Herodes Atticus Theatre**, restored for performances of music and classical drama during the summer festival (the only time it's open). The main interest hereabouts lies in earlier Greek sites to the east, pre-eminent among them the **Theatre of Dionysus**. Masterpieces of Aeschylus, Sophocles, Euripides and Aristophanes were first performed here, at one of the most evocative locations in the city. The ruins are impressive; the theatre, rebuilt in the fourth century BC, could hold some seventeen thousand spectators.

The Ancient Agora

Northwest of the Acropolis, the **Ancient Agora** was the nexus of ancient Athenian city life, where acts of administration, commerce and public assembly competed for space. The site is a confused jumble of ruins, dating from various stages between the sixth century BC and the fifth century AD. For some idea of what you are surveying, head for the **museum** in the rebuilt Stoa of Attalos. At the far corner of the precinct sits the nearly intact but distinctly clunky Doric Temple of Hephaistos, otherwise known as the **Thissíon** from the exploits of Theseus depicted on its friezes.

The Roman Forum

The **Roman Forum**, or Roman agora, was built as an extension of the Hellenistic Agora by Julius Caesar and Augustus. The best-preserved and most intriguing of the ruins, though, is the graceful, octagonal structure known as the **Tower of the Winds**. It was designed in 50 BC by the Macedonian astronomer Andronicus, and served as a compass, sundial, weather vane and water clock powered by a stream from one of the Acropolis springs. Each face of the tower is adorned with a relief of a figure floating through the air, personifying the eight winds.

Sýndagma Square and the National Gardens

All roads lead to Platía Syndágmatos – **Sýndagma Square** – with its pivotal metro station. It is geared to tourism, with a main post office, banks, luxury hotels and travel agents grouped around it. Behind the Neoclassical parliament buildings off the square, the **National Gardens** provide the most refreshing spot in the city, a shady oasis of trees, shrubs and creepers. South of the gardens stands **Hadrian's Arch**, erected by the Roman emperor to mark the edge of the classical city and the beginning of his own. Directly behind are sixteen surviving columns of the 104 that originally comprised the **Temple of Olympian Zeus** – the largest temple in Greece, dedicated by Hadrian in 132 AD.

14

14

ATHENS

▲ Ambelókipi

Ambelókipi, Kifissiá, Marathon, Airport, 3 & 6 ▲

■ **ACCOMMODATION**
Athens Backpackers	10
Athens Studios	11
Athens Style	4
Camping Athens	1
Camping Bacchus	3
Dióskouros	5
Guest House	7
John's Place	12
Marble House	6
Orion	8
Phaedra	6
Student and	
Travellers' Inn	
Youth Hostel	9
Pagration	

● **DRINKING AND NIGHTLIFE**
Baba Au Rum	12
Bios	8
Booze	11
Brettos	18
Closer	2
Gagarin 205	1
Hoxton	15
Mamácas	16
Mike's Irish Bar	6
Nixon	7
Six D.O.G.S.	13

● **EATING**
Amvrosia	19
Barba Yannis	3
Dhióskouri	17
Doris	9
Rozalia	4
Taverna tou Psyrri	10
Thanásis	16
To Athinaïkón	5

● **SHOPPING**
Eleftheroudhakis	1
Monastiráki	
flea market	2

KYPSÉLI

Pedhíon Áreos

Lykavitós Theatre

LYKAVITÓS

Funicular

Áyios Yeóryios

Evangelismos Hospital

EXÁRHIA

Lófos Stréfi

National Archeological Museum

Polytekhnío

National Library

Omonía

National Theatre

Metaxourvío

Larissis Train Station

Peloponnissou Train Station

▼ Liossíon 260 Bus Station, 1 & 3

14

LOCAL BUSES
▽ A Dháfni, Eefsína
▽ B Soúnio
▽ C #051 terminal

National Gallery
Evangelismós
Museum of Cycladic & Ancient Greek Art
British Council
Benáki Museum
Presidential Palace
Panathenaic Stadium
Ardhittós
PANGRATI
METS
First Cemetery

National Gardens
Parliament
Záppio
Temple of Olympian Zeus
Hadrian's Arch
MAKRIYIANNI

National Bank
City of Athens Mus.
Cathedral
Cine París
PLAKA
Monument of Lysikrátis
Theatre of Dionysus
Acropolis
Acrópoli
Acropolis Museum
MITSAÍON

Flower Market
Roman Forum
Tower of the Winds
Stoa
Ancient Agora
ACROPOLIS
Erechtheion
Parthenon
Asklepíon
Herodes Atticus Theatre
Areopagus
Ayi Apóstoli
Trissaíon
Thissío
Monastiráki

Central Market
Commercial Bank
EOLOU
ATHINAS
PSYRRÍ

Keramikós
Hill of the Nymphs
Hill of the Pnyx
Ay. Dhimítrios
Prison of Socrates
Monument of Philopáppou
FILOPAPPOU HILL
Dora Stratou Theatre
KOUKAKI
ANO PETRALONA

metres
0   250

14

Town museums

At the northeastern corner of the National Gardens is the fascinating and much-overlooked **Benáki Museum**, Koumbári 1 (Wed & Fri 9am–5pm, Thurs & Sat 9am–midnight, Sun 9am–3pm; €7, students €5; Thurs free; benaki.gr), with a well-organized collection that features Mycenaean jewellery, Greek costumes, memorabilia of the Greek War of Independence and historical documents, engravings and paintings.

Taking the second left off Vassilísis Sofías after the Benáki Museum will bring you to the **Museum of Cycladic and Ancient Greek Art**, Neofýtou Dhouká 4 (Mon & Wed–Sat 10am–5pm, Thurs 10am–8pm, Sun 11am–5pm; €7, Mon €3.50, 19–26 years €3.50, free under 19; Ⓦcycladic.gr), impressive for both its subject and the quality of its displays.

To the northwest, beyond Omónia, the fabulous **National Archeological Museum**, Patissíon 44 (summer Mon 1–8pm, Tues–Sat 8am–8pm, Sun 8am–3pm; winter daily 8am–3pm; €7, students €3; check Ⓦodysseus.culture.gr for free days), contains gold from the grave circle at Mycenae, including the so-called Mask of Agamemnon, along with an impressive classical art collection and findings from the island of Thíra, dating from around 1450 BC, contemporary with the Minoan civilization on Crete.

ARRIVAL AND INFORMATION

BY PLANE

The Suburban Rail line whisks you from Eleftheríos Venizélos airport, 33km southeast of Athens, to Laríssis train station (hourly, 5.10am–11.30pm; €8), involving a change at Nerantziótissa, where you can also transfer to metro Line #1. Although this is the quickest mode of transport, the airport is also directly connected to metro Line #3 (every 30min, 6.30am–11.30pm; €8). Bus #X93 serves the Kifissoú bus station at 100 Kifissoú St (every 30min; 1hr 10min). The #X95 bus from outside Arrivals goes direct to Sýndagma Square (every 10min; 1hr 15min). The #X96 runs to Pireás port (every 30min; 1hr 40min) and the #X97 to Dafni Metro station (every 30–40min; 1hr 10min). All tickets cost €5 one-way and service is 24/7. A fixed-fare taxi to the centre will cost you €35 or, from midnight to 5am, €50.

BY TRAIN

Thessaloníki trains arrive at the Laríssis train station to the northwest of the city centre, with its own metro station on Line #2. For some destinations in the Peloponnese you may need to take the Suburban Rail to Kórinthos and change there.

Destinations Kórinthos (7/8 daily; 1hr 20min); Thessaloníki (8 daily; 4–7hr).

BY BUS

Buses from northern Greece and the Peloponnese arrive at Kifissoú bus station, 10min from the centre by bus #051 (5am–midnight). Buses from central Greece arrive closer to the centre at Liossíon bus station, 260 Liossíon St, north of the train station. From here bus #024 goes to Sýndagma Square (5am–midnight). Most international buses drop off at the train station or Kifissoú; a few will drop you right in the city centre upon request. Attica buses to Lávrio, Rafína and Soúnio leave from the KTEL/Mavromatéon terminal at the southwest corner of the Pédhion Áreos park.

Destinations from Kifissoú Corfu (3 daily; 11hr); Igoumenítsa (4 daily; 7hr); Ioánnina (8 daily; 8hr); Kalamáta (9 daily; 2hr 30min–3hr 30min); Kefalloniá (6 daily; 8hr); Kórinthos (every 30min; 1hr 20min); Mycenae-Fíkhti (hourly; 2hr 30min); Náfplio (hourly; 2hr 30min); Pátra (every 30min; 2hr 30min–3hr); Pýrgos (10 daily; 5hr); Spárti (12 daily; 4hr); Thessaloníki (12 daily; 6hr 30min).

Destinations from Liossíon Delphi (6 daily; 3hr); Kými, for Skýros ferries (5 daily; 3hr 30min); Tríkala (8 daily; 4hr 30min); Tripoli (12–15 daily; 2hr 15min); Vólos (12 daily; 5hr).

Destinations from KTEL/Mavromatéon Rafína (every 30min; 1hr 30min); Sounio (hourly; 2hr); Lávrio (1–2 hourly; 1hr 30min).

BY BOAT

The port of Pireás (the last stop on metro Line #1; the station is a few steps from the quay), effectively an extension of Athens, is the main terminus for international and inter-island ferries. Blue-and-white buses shuttle passengers around the port for free. The other ports on the east coast of the Attic peninsula, Rafína and Lávrio, are alternative departure points for many of the Cycladic and northeastern Aegean islands. Frequent buses connect them with Platia Eghýptou in central Athens. Note that the schedules detailed here are subject to change (see p.498).

Destinations from Pireás Hánia (1–3 daily; 9hr); Íos (1–2 daily; 3hr 30min–10hr); Iráklion (1–3 daily; 12hr); Kós (1–2 daily; 7–12hr); Lésvos (1–3 daily; 9–11hr); Mýkonos (2–4 daily; 3hr 30min–5hr 30min); Náxos (3–4 daily; 5–8hr); Páros (3–4 daily; 3–7hr); Pátmos (1–3 weekly;

7–12hr); Rhodes (1–3 weekly; 11–23hr); Santoríni (1–5 daily; 4–10hr); Sífnos (1–2 daily; 3–5hr); Sýros (3–4 daily; 3–5hr).

INFORMATION

Tourist information The GNTO Information Desk is at Dhionysíou Areopayítou 18-20 (Mon–Fri 9am–7pm, Sat, Sun & holidays 10am–4pm; ☎210 331 0392, ✉info @gnto.gr; Ⓜ Akropolis).

GETTING AROUND

All public transport operates daily 5am–midnight. At the weekend (Fri & Sat), the metro and tram operates until 2.30am.

Tickets Single-journey tickets are valid on all forms of transport for 90min (€1.40). Travelcards are also available (€4/€14 for 24hr/7-day). If you travel without a valid ticket you are liable for a fine up to sixty times the value of your ticket.

By bus and trolley Athens' bus and trolley network is extensive but very crowded at peak times. Tickets for buses (€1.20) must be bought in advance from kiosks and validated once on board.

By tram A useful tram line runs from Sýndagma through Athens to the seaside resorts of Glyfádha and Voúla.

By metro Line #1 runs from Pireás to Kifissiá, with central stops at Thissío, Monastiráki and Omónia; Line #2 runs from Anthoúpolis to Áyios Dhimítrios via Sýndagma and a station at the foot of the Acropolis; Line #3 heads east from Monastiráki to Dhoukíssis Plakendías (with special metro cars continuing direct to the airport). They generally operate 5am–12.30am (until 2.30am Fri & Sat). Tickets (€1.20; Ⓦ stasy.gr) are available at all stations from automatic coin-op dispensers or staffed windows. They must be validated before boarding.

By taxi Taxis can be fairly expensive. Drivers will often pick up several passengers along the way, each paying the full fare for their journey – so if you're picked up by an already occupied taxi, memorize the meter reading; you'll pay from then on, including a €1.50 minimum charge.

ACCOMMODATION

The city can be deserted in Aug when a lot of establishments close for vacations and the nightlife moves to the islands and to the seaside.

HOSTELS

★ **Athens Backpackers** Makri 12, Makriyiánni ☎210 9224 044, Ⓦ backpackers.gr. Relaxed hostel in a prime location with clean, simple dorms, internet access, rooftop bar with Acropolis views and a buzzing atmosphere. The €6 walking tour makes it a great place to meet fellow travellers. Very popular, so best to book ahead. Dorm **€22.50**

Athens Style Aghias Theklas 10, Monastiráki ☎210 3225 010, Ⓦ athenstyle.com. Pleasant hostel with roof terrace, wi-fi, free breakfast and a great location a few minutes' walk from Monastiráki metro. Private rooms and studio apartments (4 beds) available. Rooms are more expensive at weekends. Dorm **€22**, double **€75**, apartment **€96**

Dióskouros Guest House Pittakoú 6 ☎210 3248 165, Ⓦ hoteldioskouros.com. Very basic and cheap hostel in the Pláka area, good at organizing further trips to the islands. Also has female-only dorms. Prices include continental breakfast. No private bathrooms. Dorm **€20**, double **€50**

Student and Travellers' Inn Kydhathinéon 16, Pláka ☎210 3244 808, Ⓦ studenttravellersinn.com. Popular, clean and well-run official HI hotel-cum-hostel in a prime location close to nightlife. Cheerful rooms, as well as luggage storage, free wi-fi access and a garden bar with big screen. Dorm **€21**, double **€35**

Youth Hostel Pagration Dhamáreos 75, Pangráti ☎210 7519 530, Ⓦ athensyhostel.com; trolley #2 or #11. In a congenial (if remote) neighbourhood with cooking and laundry facilities. No curfew; own keys. Beds 10–20 percent cheaper off season. Dorm **€10**

HOTELS AND APARTMENTS

★ **Athens Studios** Veikou 3a, Makriyiánni ☎210 9235 811, Ⓦ athensstudios.gr. Well-priced serviced studios (holding 1–2) run by the team at *Athens Backpackers*. Simple, spacious and clean with kitchen, TV, laundry and wi-fi. Extra sleepers can be accommodated on fold-out beds. There's also a six-bed apartment. Luggage storage €7/day. Breakfast included. Studio **€60**, apartment **€155**

John's Place Patróöu 5, Pláka ☎210 3229 719. Dark, basic rooms with shared bath, albeit neat and well kept by the friendly owner. Centrally located in a peaceful backstreet off Mitropóleos, with a cheap restaurant on the ground floor. Double **€50**

CRIME

Though safer than many European cities, Athens has seen a **crime rise** in the last few years as the result of tensions between new immigrant communities and the police, an increase in drug use and unemployment, and the city's history of anti-establishment feeling. Though not quite no-go areas as such, it's nevertheless best to avoid walking in parks after dark (especially Pedhíon Áreos), in unlit areas around Omónia Square and in the backstreets behind the Athens Polytechnic. Petty theft is also on the up, especially in the centre and around Ⓜ Victoria.

14

Marble House Cul-de-sac off Anastasíou Zínni 35, Koukáki ☎210 9228 294, ⓦmarblehouse.gr. Peaceful, welcoming *pension* south of the Acropolis. Most rooms en suite and with balcony; all rooms have fans and fridge. Free wi-fi. Open March–Dec. Double €40

Orion Emmanouíl. Benáki 10, Exárhia ☎210 330 2388, ⓦorion-dryades.com. Quiet, well-run budget hotel across from the Lófos Stréfi park – a steep final walk to get there, yet close to many attractions. Rooftop kitchen and common area with an amazing view. Double €35

Phaedra Adhriánou & Herefóndos 16, Pláka ☎210 3238 461, ⓦhotelphaedra.com. Cheerful and clean rooms with a/c, just over half of which are en suite. Excellent location on a pedestrianized street overlooking a Byzantine church and the Acropolis. Double €60

CAMPSITES

These campsites are not easily served via public transport.
Camping Athens Leofóros Athinón 198–200 ☎210 5814 114, ⓦwww.campingathens.com.gr. Located 7km west of Athens, this is the closest campsite to the city. Decent facilities, minimarket and snack bar. Camping €8.50 per person, plus €5 per tent

Camping Bacchus 4km from Lávrio signposted on the road to Soúnio ☎22920 39571. Very convenient for the Lávrio ferries and it's by the seaside, too. Free wi-fi. Camping €7.50 per person, plus €7 per tent

EATING

Despite the touts and tourist hype, Pláka provides a pleasant setting for an evening meal, though for good-value, good-quality cuisine, outlying neighbourhoods such as Psyrrí, Sýndagma, Gázi and Exárhia are better bets. If you want to leave other tourists behind, take metro Line #1 and try the cafés and restaurants around Metro Maroússi, Neo Irákleio and Kifissiá up north.

Amvrosia Dhrákou 3–5. Located right by Syngroú-Fix metro station, this is the best grill on this pedestrian street and always packed. Good takeaway *ghýros* (Greek kebabs), or enjoy a whole roast chicken at outdoor tables. Kebabs €6–9. Daily noon–12.30am.

Barba Yannis Emmanouíl Benáki 94, Exárhia. Vast menu of inexpensive oven-cooked food, served both indoors – in a charmingly old-fashioned interior – and out. Mains €5–8. Mon–Fri 8am–1am, Sat 9am–6pm.

Dhióskouri Dhioskoúron 13, Pláka. Popular, atmospheric café with an unbeatable view of the Agora, where cold drinks and coffees take precedence over slightly pricey snacks. *Mezédhes* €5–9. Daily noon–late.

Doris Praxitélous 30. Daytime-only restaurant with a loyal local clientele. Ignore the dodgy decor and tuck into hearty stews and cheap pasta. Greek doughnuts (*loukoumádhes*) are a speciality. Mains from €6. Free wi-fi. Daily noon–6.30pm.

Rozalia Valtetsíou 58, Exárhia. A great all-round *mezédhes*-and-grills taverna with an extensive menu. There's also a garden, open in summer. *Mezédhes* €5. Daily noon–2am.

Taverna tou Psyrri Aischýlou 12, Psyrrí. Straightforward taverna, the best in a cluster, that excels in grilled/fried seafood, vegetable starters and wine from basement barrels. Arrive early (remember Greeks eat late) or wait for a table (no reservations). Mains €8–9. Daily 11.30am–12.30am.

Thanásis Mitropóleos 69, Monastiráki. Reckoned to serve the best *souvláki* (€2) and Middle Eastern kebabs in this district. Always packed with locals at lunchtime, but worth the wait. Take away or eat in. Kebab platter €8.90. Daily 9am–2am.

To Athinaïkón Themistokléous 2, corner with Panepistimíou. In business since 1932, this is a sophisticated *ouzerí* with marble tables and old posters, popular with local workers at lunch; strong on fresh seafood. Great prices, too (€7–8). Mon–Sat 11.30am–12.30am.

DRINKING, NIGHTLIFE AND ENTERTAINMENT

Clubs and bars do not start filling up until after midnight and stay open until dawn. If you have no idea where to go, just get off at Metro Kerameikós around midnight and walk around.

BARS

★ **Baba Au Rum** Kleitíou 6, Sýndagma. This trendy bar has colourful decor and offers a great selection of enormous cocktails (€9); 150 types of rum on offer. Mon–Thurs 7pm–late, Fri–Sun noon–late.

Booze Kolokotróni 57–59. Dark, cavernous space with a cool daytime crowd draped at long tables supping draught beer (€3) and playing board games. Stick around at night for DJs, exhibitions and the latest from the Athens avant-garde. Daily 11am–late.

Brettos Kydathinéon 41, Pláka. With colourful bottles and wooden barrels lining the walls, this is a sophisticated spot which oozes reminders of its hundred-year-plus history. *Ouzo* €3.50; cocktails €8. Daily 10am–2am.

Closer Ippokrátous 150, Exárhia. The entrance looks like a normal house door, but walk up the stairs where the DJs play some of the latest and most innovative rock/indie music. It gets busier after 1am. Mid-Sept to mid-June daily 10pm–6am.

Hoxton Voutádon 42, Gazi. Hip, industrial-style bar-club playing rock, electro and pop to Gazi scenesters; always popular, always cool, mutating over the years to keep abreast of every fashion. Daily 9pm–3am.

Mike's Irish Bar Sinópis 6, Pyrgos Athinón, Ambelókipi. A lively watering hole which has something to suit

THE ATHENS FESTIVAL

The **Athens Festival** (📞 210 327 2000, 🌐 greekfestival.gr), from June to late August, encompasses classical Greek theatre, contemporary dance, classical music, big-name jazz, traditional Greek music plus rock concerts. Most performances take place at the Herodes Atticus Theatre – an atmospheric venue on a warm summer's evening. There are also bus excursions to the great ancient theatre at Epidaurus (see p.512). The main festival box office is at Panepistimíou 39; tickets from €15.

everyone, including karaoke, live music and big screens for sport. Guinness drinkers are especially well catered for. Daily 8pm–4am.

Nixon Agisiláou 61b, Gazi. One of Athens' trendiest and busiest bars, where you can meet young locals sipping cocktails at €8 a go. Tourist-free – so far. Mid-Sept to mid-May daily 8pm–late.

CLUBS AND LIVE MUSIC

Bios Peireós 84 🌐 bios.gr. Around the corner from *Nixon* (see see above), *Bios* comprises a small, cosy bar upstairs, and a raw, minimalist club downstairs with an adjoining terrace. From the Stereo MCs to Performance Art – you'll find it here. Fri & Sat 10pm–late.

Dora Stratou Theatre Filopáppou Hill 🌐 grdance.org. Dancers, singers and folk musicians unite to give spectators an insight into local Greek traditions. Tickets from €15. Late May to mid-Sept Wed–Fri 9.30pm, Sat & Sun 8.15pm.

Gagarin 205 Liossíon 205 🌐 gagarin205.gr. Located near Attikí metro station, this is the place to watch the best international up-and-coming bands and more established acts. Check the website for details. Prices vary. Gigs start around 9.30pm.

Mamácas Persefónis 41, Gazi 🌐 mamacasbar.gr. Blinding white inside, this is a high-class restaurant by day and Athens' prime dance club by night, with well-known international DJs every week; check website for details. Cover charges €10–15. Wed–Sat midnight–late.

⭐ **Six D.O.G.S.** Avramiotou 6-8, Monastiraki 🌐 sixdogs .gr. A garden bar with an indoor live venue that has taken Athens by storm; there's hardly a local under 30 who hasn't passed through its doors. Its eclectic choice of international bands and a large, shady garden have played as important a role in its popularity as its reasonable prices (beer €5; cocktails €7). Concert prices vary. Bar daily 10am–4am, concerts 10pm–late.

SHOPPING

For high-street shopping, head to the boutique stores around Kolonáki square. Souvenir shops abound in Pláka, where leather goods and jewellery are excellent value.

Eleftheroudhákis Nikis 20, on Sýndagma Square. The largest stock of foreign-language books in town, plus walking maps. Mon, Wed & Sat 9am–5pm, Tues, Thurs & Fri 9am–9pm.

Monastiráki flea market An interesting selection of weird and wonderful goods for sale. Sun is the best time for a visit, when the market expands into the surrounding streets. The nearby Central Market sells local foods. Daily; hours vary according to stall.

DIRECTORY

Embassies and consulates Australia, Kifissías & Alexándhras Level 6 Thon Bldg 📞 210 870 4000; Canada, Ioánni Yennadhíou 4 📞 210 727 3400; Ireland, Vassiléos Konstandínou 7 📞 210 723 2771/2; New Zealand, Kifissiás 76 📞 210 692 4136; UK, Ploutárhou 1, Kolonáki 📞 210 727 2600; US, Vassilísis Sofías 91 📞 210 721 2951/9.

Hospitals Evangelismós (📞 213 20 41 000) is the most central, but KAT (📞 213 20 86 000), way out in Maroússi, is the designated Greater Athens emergency hospital. Both have their own metro stops.

Internet Though there are no internet cafés as such, there's free wi-fi access around Sýndagma Square, 🌐 Thissíon and at Platía Kotziá. Across the city as a whole, it's hard to find a café not offering its own wi fi.

Left luggage Many hotels store luggage for free. Or try Pacific Travel Services, Níkis 26, Sýndagma (Mon–Sat 9am–8pm, Sun 9am–2pm; price according to size, see website: 📞 210 3241 007, 🌐 pacifictravel.gr /baggage.html).

Post office Main branch by Sýndagma Square has the longest hours (Mon–Fri 7.30am–8pm, Sat 7.30am–2pm, Sun 9am–1pm). Another branch at corner of Aiólou and Stadhíou (Mon–Fri 7.30am–8pm).

STARLIT CINEMAS

Outdoor cinema is a charming Greek tradition and there are hundreds of alfresco screens throughout the country. A balmy evening watching a classic in a bougainvillea-draped courtyard with a few beers is hard to beat. Try the centrally located Cine Paris at Kydhathinaíon 22 in Athens ((🌐 cineparis.gr) or the Cinema Kamari just outside Kamari on Santoríni (🌐 cinekamari.gr; see p.530). Both open mid-May to mid-Sept.

14

CAPE SOÚNIO AND TEMPLE OF POSEIDON

The 70km of shoreline south of Athens has good but highly developed beaches. At weekends the sands fill fast, as do innumerable bars, restaurants and clubs. But for most visitors, this coast's attraction is at the end of the road. **Cape Soúnio** is among the most imposing spots in Greece, and on it stands the fifth-century BC **Temple of Poseidon** (daily 10am–sunset; €4, students €2), built in the time of Pericles as part of a sanctuary to the sea god. In summer you've faint hope of solitude unless you arrive before the tours do, but the temple is as evocative a ruin as Greece can offer. Doric in style, it preserves sixteen of its thirty-four columns, and the view is stunning. Below the promontory lie several coves, the most sheltered of which is a five-minute walk east from the car park and site entrance.

The main Soúnio **beach** is more crowded, but has a group of tavernas at the far end, which – considering the location – are reasonably priced. Buses to Soúnio leave every hour from Athens' KTEL/Mavromatéon terminal. They alternate between coastal and inland services, the latter slightly longer and more expensive. Take the coastal route, which takes around two hours.

The Peloponnese

The appeal of the **Peloponnese** is hard to overstate. The **beaches** of this southern peninsula are among the finest and least developed in the country, while its ancient sites include the Homeric palace of Agamemnon at **Mycenae**, the Greek theatre at **Epidaurus** and the sanctuary of **Olympia**, host to the Olympic Games for a millennium. Medieval remains run from the fabulous castle at **Acrocorinth** and the strange tower-houses and frescoed churches of the **Máni**, to the extraordinary Byzantine towns of **Mystra** and **Monemvasiá**. The Peloponnese also boasts Greece's most spectacular train

route, an hour-long journey on the **rack-and-pinion rail line** from Dhiakoftó to Kalávryta (see box opposite).

ARRIVAL AND DEPARTURE

By bus and train The usual approach from Athens is on the frequent buses and trains that run via modern Kórinthos (Corinth).

By boat From Italy and the Adriatic, Pátra (see p.516) is the main port of the Peloponnese, although some ferries from the Ionian Islands arrive at Kyllíni.

KÓRINTHOS

Whoever possessed **Kórinthos** – the ancient city that displaced Athens as capital of the Greek province in Roman times – controlled both the trade between northern Greece and the Peloponnese, and the short cut between the Ionian and Aegean seas. It's unsurprising, therefore, that the city's history is a catalogue of invasions and power struggles, until it was razed by the Romans in 146 BC. The site lay in ruins for a century before being rebuilt, on a majestic scale, by Julius Caesar in 44 BC. St Paul stayed for 18 months and preached there in 51/52 AD.

WHAT TO SEE AND DO

Nowadays, the remains of the city occupy a rambling site below the acropolis hill of Acrocorinth, itself littered with medieval ruins. To explore both you need a full day, or better still, to stay close by. The modern village of ARHÉA KÓRINTHOS spreads around the main archeological zone, where you'll find plenty of places to eat and sleep, including a scattering of **rooms** to rent in the backstreets.

Arhéa Kórinthos

The main excavated site (Tues–Sun 8am–3pm; €6) is dominated by the remains of the Roman city. You enter from the south side, which leads straight into the **Roman agora**. The real focus, however, is a survival from the classical Greek era: the fifth-century BC **Temple of Apollo**, whose seven austere Doric columns stand slightly above the level of the forum.

DHIAKOFTÓ TO KALÁVRYTA RAILWAY

A contender for one of Europe's quirkiest railway journeys, the **rack-and-pinion rail line** (Odontotós; ⓦodontotos.com) from Dhiakoftó to Kalávryta is a must for any visitor to the region (2–3 daily; €19 return). Trains grind their way up vertiginous slopes, rattle through tunnels and clank over crazily narrow bridges on their way through the dramatic Vouraikós Gorge.

Acrocorinth

Towering 575m above the lower town, **Acrocorinth** (Tues–Sun 8am–3pm; €2) is an amazing mass of rock still largely encircled by 2km of wall. During the Middle Ages this ancient acropolis of Kórinthos became one of Greece's most powerful fortresses. It's a 4km climb (about 1hr), but well worth it. Amid the sixty-acre site, you wander through a jumble of semi-ruined chapels, mosques, houses and battlements, erected in turn by Greeks, Romans, Byzantines, Franks, Venetians and Ottomans.

ARRIVAL AND DEPARTURE

By train Kórinthos is connected to Athens via the suburban rail line to Eleftherios Venizélos airport. The train station is 3km from town with special shuttles running between the two.
Destinations Athens (6 daily; 1hr 30min).
By bus The KTEL bus station is at Dimokratías 4, some 200m east of the centre.
Destinations Ancient Kórinthos (hourly; 20min); Árgos (hourly; 1hr); Dhiakoftó (4 daily; 45min–1hr 30min); Kalamáta (7 daily; 3hr 15min–4hr); Mycenae-Fíkhti (hourly; 30min); Pátra (6 daily; 1hr 50min–2hr 30min); Náfplio (7 daily; 1hr 20min); Spárti (8 daily; 4hr).

ACCOMMODATION

Hotel Korinthos Damaskenou 26 ☎27410 26710, ⓦkorinthoshotel.gr. One block from the port and three blocks from the bus station, this small but friendly hotel is very popular with local students. Free wi-fi. Book online for price reductions. Breakfast €5. Double **€50**
Marinos Rooms Arhéa Kórinthos, Sysyphus St ☎27410 31994, ⓦmarinos-rooms.com. Very popular, family-run hotel right by Ancient Kórinthos with comfortable rooms. Book in advance. Decent restaurant downstairs. Breakfast included. Double **€50**

MYKÍNES (MYCENAE)

Southwest of Kórinthos, the ancient site of **MYCENAE** is tucked into a fold of the hills just 2km northeast of the modern village of **Mykínes**. Agamemnon's citadel, "well-built Mycenae, rich in gold", as Homer wrote, was uncovered in 1874–76 by the German archeologist Heinrich Schliemann, who was convinced that Homer's epics had a factual basis. Brilliantly crafted gold and sophisticated architecture bore out the accuracy of Homer's words. The buildings unearthed by Schliemann show signs of having been occupied from around 1950 BC until 1100 BC, when the town, though still prosperous, was abandoned. No coherent explanation has been found for this event, but war between rival kingdoms was probably a major factor.

WHAT TO SEE AND DO

You enter the **Citadel of Mycenae** (daily: summer 8am–6pm; winter 8am–3pm; €8, students €4) through the mighty **Lion Gate**. Inside the walls to the right is **Grave Circle A**, the cemetery which Schliemann believed contained the bodies of Agamemnon and his followers, murdered on their triumphant return from Troy. In fact the burials date from about three centuries before the Trojan war, but they were certainly royal, and the finds are among the richest yet unearthed. Schliemann took the extensive **South House**, beyond the grave circle, to be the Palace of Agamemnon. But a much grander building was later discovered on the summit of the acropolis. Rebuilt in the thirteenth century BC, it is, like all Mycenaean palaces, centred on a **Great Court**. The small rooms to the north are believed to have been royal apartments, and in one of them the remains of a red stuccoed bath have led to its fanciful identification as the place of Agamemnon's murder.

14

Outside the walls of the citadel lay the main part of the town, and extensive remains of **merchants' houses** have been uncovered near to the road. A few minutes' walk down the road is the astonishing **Treasury of Atreus**, a royal burial vault entered through a majestic 15m corridor.

ARRIVAL AND DEPARTURE

By bus There are three daily morning buses from Náfplio (see below) stopping at the gate, with three more returning in the afternoon.

ACCOMMODATION

The modern village of Mykínes has one main street, where all accommodation and places to eat are located.

Camping Atreus ☎ 27510 76221. This shady campsite comes equipped with clean facilities, a swimming pool and a good family restaurant on site. Open May–Sept. Camping **€6** per person, plus **€3.80** per tent

Oraia Eleni (Belle Hélène) ☎ 27510 76225. Once the home of archeologist Heinrich Schliemann, this hotel looks a bit run-down, but it's full of history. What's more, its rooms are spacious and the shared bathrooms spotless. Breakfast included. Double **€40**

NÁFPLIO

NÁFPLIO, 44km south of Kórinthos, a lively, beautifully sited town with a faded elegance, inherited from when it was briefly modern Greece's first capital, makes an attractive base for exploring the area or for resting up by the sea.

WHAT TO SEE AND DO

The main fort, **Palamídhi** (daily: summer 8am–7pm; winter 8am–4.30pm; €4), is most directly approached by 999 stone-hewn steps up from Polyzoïdhou Street. Within its walls are three self-contained castles, all built by the Venetians in the 1710s. To the west, the **Acronafplía** fortress (free to enter) occupies the ancient acropolis, whose walls were adapted by successive medieval occupants. The third fort, the photogenic **Boúrtzi** (free to enter), occupies the islet offshore from the harbour and allowed the Venetians to close the shallow shipping channel with a chain. In the town itself, **Platía Syndágmatos**, the main square, is

a great place to relax over a coffee. There's also a thriving nightlife, with a string of bars along the waterfront at Bouboulínas.

ARRIVAL AND DEPARTURE

By bus Buses arrive on Syngroú, just south of the interlocking squares Platía Trión Navárhon and Platía Kapodhístria.

Destinations Árgos (every 30min; 30min); Athens (hourly; 3hr); Epidaurus (4 daily; 45min); Mycenae (3–4 daily; 1hr); Trípoli (2–4 daily; 1hr).

ACCOMMODATION AND EATING

Dimitris Bekas Rooms Efthimiopoúlou 26 ☎ 27520 24594. Don't be disheartened by the stone steps leading up to this welcoming *pension* – the views from the roof terrace are stunning. It is located close to the centre of the old town. Double **€25**

Old Mansion Siokóu 7. Bustling taverna serving up Greek favourites to the accompaniment of live traditional music at weekends. Mains €8–15. Daily noon–midnight.

EPIDAURUS

From the sixth century BC to Roman times, **EPIDAURUS**, 30km east of Náfplio, was a major spa and religious centre; its **Sanctuary of Asclepius** was the most famous of all shrines dedicated to the god of healing. The magnificently preserved 14,000-seat theatre (daily: summer 8am–8pm; winter 8am–5pm; €6) is the venue for evening **classical-theatre performances** during the Athens and Epidaurus Festival (June–Aug; ⓦ greekfestival.gr).

ACCOMMODATION AND EATING

Camping Nicholas I & II Paleá Epídavros ☎ 27530 41297/41445, ⓦ nicolasgikas.gr. Two campsites, 2.5km apart, which have wonderful pitches among orange and mulberry groves, right on the beach. An on-site taverna, *Mouria*, serves *Nicholas I* and has played host to many a celebrity appearing at the Epidaurus Festival – from Pavarotti to Dame Helen Mirren. Open May–Sept. Book ahead. Camping **€6.50** per person, plus **€5.50** per tent

SPÁRTI (ANCIENT SPARTA)

Today, **SPÁRTI**, 112km southwest of Náfplio, is just a large provincial town. As the ancient Spartans left no tangible cultural legacy like the Athenians, don't expect any ruins of note. Because of its good road connections, however, and decent hotels and restaurants, it is best suited for an overnight stay and a day-trip to **Mystra** (see below).

ARRIVAL AND DEPARTURE

By bus The KTEL bus station is at the far eastern end of Lykoúrgou, a 10min walk from the centre.
Destinations Areópoli (2 daily; 2hr); Athens (10 daily; 4hr); Kalamáta (2 daily; 2hr 30min); Kórinthos (8 daily; 2hr); Monemvasiá (3 daily; 2hr 30min); Mystra (hourly; 30min); Yíthio (5 daily; 1hr).

ACCOMMODATION

Apollon Thermopýlon 84 ☎ 27310 22491. This friendly hotel, which has clearly seen better days, has plenty of clean and comfortable en-suite rooms. Basic breakfast included; free wi-fi (stronger at reception). Double €40
Hotel Cecil Paleológou 125 ☎ 27310 24980. A warm welcome awaits at this centrally located small hotel, with clean en-suite rooms equipped with a/c, free wi-fi and TV. No breakfast. Double €55

EATING

Diethnés Paleológou 105. The garden here is an oasis of calm, and especially atmospheric in the evenings. Hearty Greek favourites are dished up to the sound of birdsong. Meals around €12–15. Daily noon–midnight.
Zeus Paleológou 72. Modern Greek cuisine in minimalist surroundings and a wide selection of local wines. A bit pricey but worth it; specialities include roast goat and artichoke bake (€10–12). Daily noon–midnight.

MYSTRA (MYSTRÁS)

A glorious, airy place, hugging a steep flank of the Taïyetos mountains, **MYSTRA** is an astonishingly complete Byzantine city that once sheltered a population of some twenty thousand. The castle on its summit was built in 1249 by Guillaume II de Villehardouin, fourth Frankish Prince of the Morea (as the Peloponnese was then known), and together with the fortresses of Monemvasiá and the Máni it guarded his territory. In 1262 the Byzantines drove out the Franks and established the Despotate of Mystra.

To explore the site of the **Byzantine city** (daily 8am–3pm; €5), take the bus from Spárti which stops at the village of Néos

Mystrás and then continues up the hill. Make for the top entrance, then explore a leisurely downhill route. Following this course, the first identifiable building you come to is the fourteenth-century church of **Ayía Sofía**. The **Kástro**, reached by a path that climbs directly from the upper gate, maintains the Frankish design of its thirteenth-century construction, though modified by successive occupants. Heading down from Ayía Sofía, there are two possible routes. The right fork winds past the ruins of a Byzantine mansion, while the left fork passes the massively fortified **Náfplio Gate** and the vast, multistorey complex of the **Despots' Palace**. At the **Monemvasiá Gate**, linking the upper and lower towns, turn right for the **Pandánassa convent**, which is perhaps the finest that survives in the town. Further down on this side of the lower town make sure you see the diminutive **Perívleptos monastery**, whose single-domed church, partly carved out of the rock, contains Mystra's most complete cycle of frescoes. The **Mitrópolis**, or cathedral, immediately beyond the gateway, ranks as the oldest of Mystra's churches, built from 1270 onward.

ACCOMMODATION

Castle View Néos Mystrás ☎ 27310 83303, ⊛ castleview .gr. Shady and quiet, this campsite is 500m from the village. A small pool and a good traditional taverna are just two of its attractions. Open April–Oct. Camping €6 per person, plus €4 per tent
Paleologio Mystras 2.5km from Spárti, 4km from Néos Mystrás ☎ 27310 22724; buses to Néos Mystrás stop at the entrance (tell the driver in advance). Well-run campsite with good facilities (wi-fi, laundry, minimarket). Open all year. Camping €6.50 per person, plus €3.50 per tent

MONEMVASIÁ

Set impregnably on a great eruption of rock connected to the mainland by a causeway, the Byzantine seaport of **MONEMVASIÁ** is a place of grand, haunted atmosphere. At the start of the thirteenth century it was the Byzantines' sole possession in the Morea, eventually being taken by the Franks in 1249 after three years of siege. Regained by the Byzantines as part of the ransom for the

14

14

captured Guillaume de Villehardouin, it served as the chief commercial port of the Despotate of the Morea. At its peak in the Byzantine era, Monemvasiá had a population of almost sixty thousand.

WHAT TO SEE AND DO

A causeway connects the mainland village of **Yéfira** to Monemvasiá. The twenty-minute walk provides some wonderful views, but there is also a free shuttle bus. The **Lower Town** once sheltered forty churches and over 800 homes, though today a single main street harbours most of the restored houses, plus cafés, tavernas and a scattering of shops. The foremost monument is the **Mitrópolis**, the cathedral built by Emperor Andronikos II Komnenos in 1293, and the largest medieval church in southern Greece. Across the square, the tenth-century domed church of **Áyios Pétros** was transformed by the Ottomans into a mosque and is now a small **museum** of local finds (Tues–Sun: summer 9am–4pm; winter 8am–3pm; €2). Towards the sea is a third church, the **Khrysafítissa**, with its bell hanging from an old acacia tree in the courtyard. The climb to the **Upper Town** is highly worthwhile, not least for the solitude. Its fortifications, like those of the lower town, are substantially intact; within, the site is a ruin, though infinitely larger than you could imagine from below.

ARRIVAL AND INFORMATION

By bus Intercity buses arrive in the village of Yéfira on the mainland. A free daily shuttle leaves for Monemvasiá every 10–15min. For all onward destinations change in Spárti.
Destinations Spárti (4 daily; 1hr 30min).
Tourist information Malvasia Travel (by the bus stop) has taken over by default all tourist information services. It also sells bus tickets.

ACCOMMODATION

There is cheap accommodation in Yéfira, but if Monemvasiá has cast its enchanting spell over you, then splash out to stay on the rock itself.
Dina's House Kastro, Monemvasiá ☎ 27320 61311, ⓦ gr.monemvasia-online.com/dina. Self-contained apartments with all mod cons inside a part of the old castle. Top marks for atmosphere. Haggle and you could get rooms cheaper than the quoted price. Double **€55**

★ **Malvasia** Kastro, Monemvasiá ☎ 27320 61160, ⓦ malvasiahotel-traditional.gr. A peaceful hotel full of charm, retaining many traditional features. The views from the more expensive rooms are breathtaking; they could really make your holiday. Breakfast, a/c, satellite TV, all included. Double **€60**

EATING

Matoula Kastro, Monemvasiá. This long-running family restaurant has plenty of fresh fish on offer, and a shady terrace on which to enjoy the food and the views. Mains €10. Daily noon–11pm.
To Kanoni Kastro, Monemvasiá. A small and friendly place inside the castle with split-level seating, offering a variety of vistas from its balcony. Mains €7–10. April–Oct daily noon–midnight.

YÍTHIO

YÍTHIO, Sparta's ancient port, is the gateway to the dramatic Máni peninsula and one of the south's most attractive seaside towns. Its low-key harbour, with occasional ferries, has a graceful nineteenth-century waterside, while out to sea, tethered by a long narrow causeway, is the islet of **Marathoníssi** (ancient Kranae), where Paris and Helen of Troy spent their first night after her abduction from Sparta.

ARRIVAL AND DEPARTURE

By bus Buses from Athens and Spárti drop you close to the centre of town, at the bus station located on Vassiléos Pávlou.
Destinations Areópolis (4 daily; 30min); Athens (4–6 daily; 5hr); Kalamáta (2 daily; 2hr); Kórinthos (6 daily; 2hr 45min); Spárti (6 daily; 50min); Trípoli (3 daily; 2hr 30min).

ACCOMMODATION

★ **Meltemi** On the Yíthio–Areópoli road ☎ 27330 23260, ⓦ campingmeltemi.gr. Excellent campsite served by four buses from Yíthio (ask the driver to stop at the site), where facilities include pool with a bar, restaurant and free wi-fi. Also 2-person bungalows. Disabled access. Open April–Oct. Camping **€6** per person, plus **€5** per tent, bungalow **€30**
Rooms Matina Vassiléos Pávlou 19 ☎ 27330 22518. Little English is spoken but the owner is very welcoming. Rooms are spacious and airy, and there's a small terrace too. No breakfast. Double **€50**
Saga Pension Tzanetáki ☎ 27330 23220, ⓦ sagapension .gr. Looks like a Greek apartment block, but it contains

spacious and comfortable rooms, most with balconies towards the sea. There's also a popular restaurant downstairs. Breakfast €5. Double **€50**

EATING

Barba Sideris Ermoú & Xantháki. A taverna right by the sea, specializing in skewered and grilled meat dishes. Feast for €15–20. Daily noon–midnight.

To Korali Plateía Yíthiou. This is the place to do as the locals do – order some *ouzo* and watch the world go by from the corner of the square. Mains €10–15. Daily noon–midnight.

THE MÁNI PENINSULA

The southernmost peninsula of Greece, the **Máni peninsula**, stretches from Yíthio in the east and Kalamáta in the west down to Cape Ténaro, mythical entrance to the underworld. It's a wild and arid landscape with an idiosyncratic culture and history: nowhere else in Greece seems so close to its medieval past. There are numerous opportunities for outdoor activities too.

Areópolis

The quickest way into the Máni is to take a bus from Yíthio to **AREÓPOLIS**, gateway to the so-called Inner Máni. For onward travel to the Outer Máni, a change at Oítylo is involved. Should you get stuck overnight, there are a few decent hotels.

ARRIVAL AND DEPARTURE

By bus The bus station is in the main square, Platía Athánatos.

Destinations Oítylo (3 daily; 20min); Yíthio (4 daily; 30min).

ACCOMMODATION

Hotel Kouris Main Square 27330 51340. Not the best-looking hotel facade in Greece but all rooms are en suite and have balconies, plus it's the cheapest option in town. Breakfast included. Double **€50**

Tsimova 17 March Square 27330 51301. A renovated tower-house in the old lower town, full of character and charm. Ask to see the owner's ancient rifle collection. Breakfast included. Double **€50**

Kardhamýli and Outer Máni

Various attractions lie to the north of Areópolis, along the 80km road to Kalamáta, which has views as dramatic

and beautiful as any in Greece. There are numerous cobbled paths for hiking and a series of **small beaches**, beginning at **NÉO OÍTILO** with its fine sandy beach, and extending more or less through to Kardhamýli. The fishing village of **ÁYIOS NIKÓLAOS** has the best fish tavernas and rooms. **STOÚPA**, with possibly the best beach, is now geared towards British tourism, with several small hotels, two **campsites**, supermarkets and tavernas.

KARDHAMÝLI, 8km north of Stoúpa, remains a beautiful place despite its commercialization and busy road, with a long pebbly beach and the restored tower-house quarter of **ANO KARDHAMÝLI**. Tourism has picked up recently, mainly due to the film *Before Midnight* (2013), starring Ethan Hawke and Julie Delpy, which was filmed here.

ARRIVAL AND INFORMATION

By bus Buses stop in Kardhamýli next to the main square.
Destinations Kalamáta (1–4 daily; 45min).

Tourist information There's no tourist office as such, but Wunder Travel (27210 73141, wundertravel.gr) has bus timetables and provides information on the region.

ACCOMMODATION

Iphigenia Rooms Kardhamýli 27210 73648. A wonderful base for exploring the area, with apartments featuring small kitchenettes and bougainvillea-draped balconies. Some have great views over the Messenian Gulf. Only 100m from the seafront. No breakfast. Double **€50**

Lela's Kardhamýli 27210 73541, or mobile 6977 716 017 in winter. Tucked away (look for signs from the main road), these rooms occupy a prime position beside the sea. There's also a good taverna (see below). No breakfast. Double **€50**

EATING AND DRINKING

★ **Lela's** Kardhamýli. With an ever-changing menu, *Lela's* is ideal for a delicious, home-cooked meal. She used to be the cook for English author Patrick Leigh Fermor while he lived in Kalamitsi, one village down. Go early to grab a table with the best views. Mains €8. Daily noon–11pm.

OLYMPIA

The historic resonance of **OLYMPIA**, which for over a millennium hosted the

14

Panhellenic Games, is rivalled only by Delphi or Mycenae. Its site, too, ranks with this company, for although the ruins are confusing, the setting is as perfect as could be imagined: a luxuriant valley of wild olive and plane trees beside the twin rivers of Alfiós and Kladheós, overlooked by the pine-covered Mount Kronion.

WHAT TO SEE AND DO

The entrance to the **ancient site** (summer Mon–Fri 8am–8pm, Sat & Sun 8am–3pm; winter daily 8am–3pm; €6, or €9 with museum; ☏ 26240 22517) leads along the west side of the sacred precinct wall, past a group of public and official buildings. Here the fifth-century BC sculptor Pheidias was responsible for creating the great gold-and-ivory cult statue in the focus of the precinct, the great Doric **Temple of Zeus**. The smaller **Temple of Hera**, behind, was the first built here; prior to its completion in the seventh century BC, the sanctuary had only open-air altars. Rebuilt in the Doric style in the sixth century BC, it's the most complete structure on the site. However, it's the 177m track of the **Stadium** itself that makes sense of Olympia: the start and finish lines are still there, as are the judges' thrones in the middle and seating banked to each side, which once accommodated up to thirty thousand spectators. Finally, in the **archeological museum** (summer Mon 10am–5pm, Tues–Fri 8am–8pm, Sat & Sun 8am–3pm; winter Mon 10am–5pm, Tues–Sun 8am–3pm; €6, or €9 with site), the centrepiece is the statuary from the Temple of Zeus, displayed in the vast main hall. Most famous of the individual sculptures is the **Hermes of Praxiteles**, dating from the fourth century BC; one of the best preserved of all classical sculptures, it retains traces of its original paint.

ARRIVAL AND DEPARTURE

By bus Most people arrive at Olympia via Pýrgos, which has frequent buses to the site. The bus stop is at the end of Praxitéles Kondhýli.
Destinations Pýrgos (hourly; 45min); Trípoli (2 daily; 3hr 30min).

ACCOMMODATION

Camping Diana ☏ 26240 22314/22425, ⓦ camping diana.gr. The closest campsite, 1km from the site, has many good facilities (pool, internet, café bar, currency exchange), but there's not much to do except visit Olympia. Open all year. Camping **€7** per person, plus **€5** per tent

Youth Hostel Praxitéles Kondhýli 18, Olympia ☏ 26240 22580. This "old school" hostel is in the centre of the village but that is its only selling point. There's a curfew of 11pm, and common areas including toilets are, let's say, not exactly kept spic-and-span. Sheets €2. Dorm **€10**

EATING

Yéfsis Mélathron Yeoryíou Doúma 3, Olympia. Family taverna with a welcoming atmosphere, offering many vegetarian dishes such as *ladhera*, as well as large *souvláki* portions (€6) and traditional veal and chicken stews at good prices. Daily noon–midnight.

PÁTRA

The city of **PÁTRA** is the third largest in the country, and connects the mainland to Italy and the Ionian Islands. Unlike many other destinations in the Peloponnese, Pátra is a thriving working city and has a life of its own which extends far beyond tourism, despite the number of travellers passing through. There are enough sites and museums to fill a day's sightseeing, though most people choose to pass through rather quickly. The city is best enjoyed in the evening, when thousands of party-going university students transform the streets. At the heart of the drinking scene is Aghíou Nikoláou, a pedestrian street crammed with bars. The Patras Carnival (ⓦ carnivalpatras.gr) is the best-known in Greece.

ARRIVAL AND DEPARTURE

By train The train station is by the port on Óthonos Amalías, but there are only a few commuter lines; Intercity trains no longer run.
By bus Buses arrive at the KTEL Achaïa bus station at Zaïmi 2, corner of Othonos Amalias.
Destinations Athens (every 30min; 2hr 30min–3hr); Ioánnina (2 daily; 5hr); Kalamáta (2 daily; 4hr); Pýrgos (9–12 daily; 2hr).
By ferry Ferries from all departure points arrive at the port close to the bus and train stations.

Destinations Ancona (2–3 daily; 20–21hr); Bari (1–2 daily; 16hr); Brindisi (3–7 weekly; 13–16hr); Corfu (1 daily; 6 7hr); Igoumenítsa (1 daily; 0 10hr); Itháki (2 daily; 6hr); Kefalloniá (2 daily; 2hr 30min–5hr); Venice (4–6 weekly; 30–32hr).

INFORMATION

Tourist information Agorá Argýri, Aghíou Andréou 12 (daily 7.30am–10pm; 2610 461740/1). One of the best, most helpful and well-manned tourist offices in Greece.
Tourist Police Goúnari 52, by the Italian ferry terminal (2610 455 833).

ACCOMMODATION

Pension Nicos Patréos 3 2610 623 757. Rooms (most en suite) are a little small, but this hotel is convenient for the port, train and bus stations, and there's a rooftop bar for coffee and beers. Double €35
Youth Hostel Iróön Polytekhníou 62 2610 427 278, patrasrooms.gr. Located 800m north of the bus terminal on the coastal road, this stone villa has the cheapest beds in town. The owner also rents apartments behind the bus station. Dorm €12, double €40

The centre and north

Central and northern Greece has a multi-faceted character, encompassing both ancient and modern, from the mythical home of the gods on **Mount Olympus** to the urban splendour of **Thessaloníki**, and a plethora of landscapes. The highlights lie at the fringes: site of the ancient oracle **Delphi**, and further northwest at the otherworldly rock-monasteries of **Metéora**. Access to these monasteries is through **Kalambáka**, beyond which the **Katára pass** over the Píndhos mountains provides a stunning backdrop. En route lies **Métsovo**, perhaps the easiest location for a taste of mountain life, though blatantly commercialized. Nearby **Ioánnina**, once the stronghold of the notorious Ali Pasha, still retains a lot of character. To the south, closer to Athens, is the monastery of **Ósios Loukás**, one of Greece's finest Byzantine buildings and worth a detour en route to Delphi.

DELPHI

With its position on a high terrace overlooking a great gorge, in turn dwarfed by the ominous crags of Parnassós, it's easy to see why the ancients believed the extraordinary site of **DELPHI**, 150km northwest of Athens, to be the centre of the Earth. But what confirmed this status was the discovery of a chasm that exuded strange vapours and reduced all comers to frenzied, incoherent and obviously prophetic mutterings. For over a thousand years a steady stream of pilgrims toiled their way up the dangerous mountain paths to seek divine direction, until the oracle eventually expired with the demise of paganism in the fourth century AD. Today it makes for a pleasant day-trip from the capital.

14

WHAT TO SEE AND DO

You enter the **Sacred Precinct of Apollo** (daily: summer 7.30am–8pm; winter 8am–3pm; €6, or €9 with museum) by way of a small agora, enclosed by ruins of Roman porticoes and shops selling votive offerings. The paved **Sacred Way** begins after a few stairs, zigzagging uphill between the foundations of memorials and treasuries to the **Temple of Apollo**. The theatre and stadium used for the main events of the Pythian games are on terraces above the temple. The **theatre**, built in the fourth century BC, was closely connected with Dionysus, god of drama and wine. A steep path leads up through pine groves to the stadium, which was banked with stone seats in Roman times.

The **museum** (summer daily 9am–4pm; winter Tues–Sun 8am–3pm; €6, or €9 with site) contains a collection of ancient sculpture matched only by finds on the Acropolis in Athens; the most famous exhibit is *The Charioteer*, one of the few surviving bronzes of the fifth century BC. Following the road east of the sanctuary towards Aráhova, you reach a sharp bend. To the left, the celebrated **Castalian spring** still flows from a cleft in the cliffs, where visitors to Delphi were obliged to purify themselves. Across and below the road

14

from the spring is the **Marmaria** or Sanctuary of Athena Pronoia (same hours as main site; free), the "Guardian of the Temple". The precinct's most conspicuous building is the **Tholos**, a fourth-century BC rotunda whose purpose remains a mystery. Above the Marmaria, a **gymnasium** also dates from the fourth century BC, though it was later enlarged by the Romans.

ARRIVAL AND DEPARTURE

By bus The small bus station is on Pávlou & Fridheríkis, at the opposite end of the modern town of Delphi to the archeological site.

Destinations Athens (4 daily; 3hr); Pátra (1–2 daily; 3hr); Thessaloníki (1 daily; 5hr).

ACCOMMODATION

Apollon Camping 1.5km west towards Ámfissa ☎ 22650 82750, ⊛ apolloncamping.gr. A good camping option and the closest to Delphi. Swimming pool, minimarket and good views towards the Corinthian Gulf are on offer. Open all year. Camping **€7.50** per person, plus **€3.50** per tent

Athina Pávlou & Fredheríkis 55, Delphi ☎ 22650 82239. Most rooms at this guesthouse face the valley for spectacular views, and all have a/c and access to wi-fi. Breakfast included. Open April–Oct. Double **€35**

Sibylla Pávlou & Fredheríkis 9, Delphi ☎ 22650 82335, ⊛ sibylla-hotel.gr. Located close to the archeological site, rooms are spotless and comfortable, and staff are helpful. There's also a basic self-service breakfast available for €1.50. Double **€30**

EATING

Taverna Vakhos Apóllonos 31 ⊛ vakhos.com. This taverna combines a wonderful setting and mouthwatering food. The menu includes plenty of home-made fare, including wine and baklava. Good choice of vegan and vegetarian options. Mains €6–8. Daily noon–11pm.

KALAMBÁKA AND METÉORA

Few places are more exciting to arrive at than **KALAMBÁKA** and the neighbouring village of **Kastráki**, about twenty minutes' walk away. Your eye is immediately drawn to the weird grey cylinders of rock overhead – these are the outlying monoliths of the extraordinary valley of **Metéora**. The earliest religious communities in the valley emerged during the late tenth century, when

hermits made their homes in the caves that score many of the rocks. In 1336 they were joined by two monks from Mount Áthos, one of whom established the first monastery here.

WHAT TO SEE AND DO

Today, put firmly on the map by films such as the James Bond classic *For Your Eyes Only*, the four most visited monasteries are essentially museums. Only two others, Ayías Triádhos and Ayíou Stefánou, continue to function with a primarily religious purpose. Each monastery levies an **admission charge** of €2 and operates a strict **dress code**: skirts for women (supplied at the monasteries), long trousers for men and covered arms for both sexes.

Beyond the monastery of **Ayíou Stefánou**, firmly planted on a massive pedestal, stretches a chaos of spikes, cones and stubbier, rounded cliffs. Visiting the monasteries demands a full day, which means staying two nights nearby. Opening times are highly volatile because of particular saints' days, masses, fast days etc, so call from your hotel before you leave.

Ayíou Nikoláou Anápavsa and Varlaám

From Kastráki, the fourteenth-century **Ayíou Nikoláou Anápavsa** (Mon–Thurs, Sat & Sun 9am–1.30pm; €2; ☎ 2432 022375) is reached first. Some 250m past the car park and stairs to Ayíou Nikoláou, a clear path leads up a ravine between assorted monoliths; soon, at a fork, you've the option of bearing left (for Megálou Meteórou; see below) or right to **Varlaám** (summer Mon–Thurs, Sat & Sun 9am–4pm; winter Mon–Wed, Sat & Sun 9am–3pm; €2; ☎ 2432 022277), which is one of the oldest and most beautiful monasteries in the valley.

Megálou Meteórou and Roussánou

From the fork below Varlaám the path also takes you northwest to **Megálou Meteórou** (summer Mon & Wed–Sun 9am–5pm; winter Mon & Thurs–Sun 9am–4pm; €2; ☎ 2432 022278), the grandest of the monasteries and also the highest. Next you follow trails until you reach the signed access path for the tiny, compact convent of **Noussánou** (summer Mon, Tues & Thurs–Sun 9am–6pm; winter Mon, Tues & Thurs–Sun 9am–2pm; €2; ☎2432 022649).

Ayías Triádhos and Ayíou Stefánou

It's less than a half-hour from Roussánou to the vividly frescoed **Ayías Triádhos** (summer Mon, Wed & Fri–Sun 9am–6pm; winter Mon, Tues & Fri–Sun 9am–2pm; €2; ☎2432 022220), approached up 130 steps carved through a tunnel in the rock. **Ayíou Stefánou** (Tues–Sun: summer 9am–1.30pm & 3.30–5.30pm; winter 9am–1pm & 3–5pm; €2; ☎2432 022279), the last of the monasteries, lies a further fifteen minutes' walk east of Ayías Triádhos; bombed in World War II, it's the one to omit if you've run out of time.

ARRIVAL AND DEPARTURE

By train Kalambáka train station is located 100m south of the bus station.
Destinations Athens (4 daily; 5hr); Thessaloníki (2 daily; 3hr).
By bus Buses arrive at the bus station in Kalambáka on Ikonómou. Most long-distance buses from Thessaloníki or the south involve a change at Tríkala.
Destinations Ioánnina (2–3 daily; 3hr); Métsovo (3 daily; 1hr 30min); Tríkala (hourly, 30min).

ACCOMMODATION

Hotel Metéora Ploutárhou 13 ☎24320 22367, ⌨hotel-meteora.gr. The pick of the Kalambáka hotels. Great value for the high standard, the en-suite rooms come with wi-fi, a/c and delicious breakfasts. Double €40
★ **Hotel Tsikeli** Kastráki ☎24320 22438, ⌨tsikelihotel.gr. A wonderful, relaxing guesthouse, with simple rooms, free wi-fi and stunning views. Breakfast is served in the lush garden. Haggle for a lower price off-season. Double €45
Plakias Kastráki ☎24320 22504, ⌨meteora-plakias.gr. A homely feel accompanies these clean and crisp en-suite rooms, not far from the main square, although the ground-floor rooms sacrifice their views of Metéora. Breakfast included. Double €35
Vrachos At the entrance to Kastráki ☎24320 22293, ⌨campingkastraki.gr. A well-equipped campsite with a large swimming pool (with view of the rocks) and caravans to rent. Also offers rock-climbing lessons. Camping €8 per person and tent

EATING

Bakaliarákia Below the square and behind the church in Kastráki, a traditional taverna, with cheap fried cod and house wine. Mains €5–7. Daily noon–11pm.
Parádhissos Kastráki. This taverna offers a spacious terrace with beautiful views and a variety of barbecued specialities. Mains €5–8. Daily noon–11pm.

IOÁNNINA

The fortifications of **IOÁNNINA**'s old town, former capital of the Albanian Muslim chieftain Ali Pasha, are punctuated by towers and minarets. From this base Ali, "the Lion of Ioánnina", prised from the Ottoman Empire a fiefdom encompassing much of western Greece. Disappointingly, most of the city is modern and undistinguished; however, the fortifications of Ali's citadel, the **Kástro**, survive more or less intact. Apart from this, the most enjoyable quarter is the old **bazaar** area, outside the citadel's main gate.

On the far side of the lake from Ioánnina, the island of **Nissí** is served by water-buses (every 30min; €2) from the quay northwest of the Froúrio. Its village, founded during the sixteenth century, is flanked by several beautiful, diminutive monasteries, with the best thirteenth-century frescoes in **Filanthropinón**.

ARRIVAL AND INFORMATION

By bus The local and Intercity KTEL station is at Yeoryíou Papandhreou.
Destinations Athens (7 daily; 7hr 30min); Igoumenítsa (5–7 daily; 2hr 30min); Pátra (2 daily; 3hr 30min); Thessaloníki (5–6 daily; 3hr).
Tourist information Dhodhónis 39 (Mon–Fri 7am–3pm; ☎26510 41868, ✉eotioan@otenet.gr). This tourist office can provide information on the whole Epirus region.

ACCOMMODATION

Filyra Andhroníkou Paleológou 18 ☎26510 83560 71460, ⌨hotelfilyra.gr. Not quite a hotel, but five bright, modern two-person studios with small kitchenettes, ideal for self catering, located in the historic Kástro; the owner also has several properties nearby. Studio €65
Limnopoula Kanari 10 ☎26510 25265; #7 bus. This pleasant and highly atmospheric lakeshore campsite is 2km out of town on the Pérama/airport road. Open April–Oct. Camping €9 per person, plus €2 per tent

14

EATING

Fysa Roufa Georgiou Avéroff 55. This popular family restaurant serves oven-baked dishes (on the large side) and specializes in tripe soup. Mains €5–8. 24hr.

★ **To Souvlaki tou Vounou** Amfithea ⓦ soublakibounou.gr. A 10min drive from the centre by car or taxi, this grill taverna is in a fantastic location by the lake and is a top recommendation by the locals. Athens prices but it's worth it. Free wi-fi. Mains €10–12. Daily noon–2am.

THESSALONÍKI

Second city of Greece, **THESSALONÍKI** feels more Central European and modern than Athens. During the Byzantine era, it was the second city after Constantinople, enjoying a cultural "Golden Age" until the Ottoman conquest in 1430. As recently as the 1920s, the city's population was as mixed as any in the Balkans: besides the Greeks there were Turks, who had been in occupation for close on five centuries, Slavs, Albanians, and the largest European **Jewish** community in the Mediterranean – 80,000 at its peak. Finally, with a student population of 120,000, the city's **nightlife** is buzzing, with many bars and clubs concentrated either in the regenerated warehouse area of **Ladhádhika** by the port or further up in **Valaoritou Street**.

WHAT TO SEE AND DO

Today, Thessaloníki boasts many excellent sights – including a superb archeological museum and some lovely frescoed Byzantine churches – but the most obvious pleasures of Greece's second city are in its street-life: its myriad bars, first-rate restaurants and pumping clubs.

The Archeological Museum

The renovated **Archeological Museum** (summer Mon 1–8pm, Tues–Sun 8am–8pm; winter daily 8.30am–3pm; €6, €8 combined with the Byzantine museum) is on Andronikou 6, a few paces from the White Tower. The museum's highlights are the "Macedonian gold" rooms on the ground floor, containing precious finds from various tombs in the area. There are startling

amounts of gold and silver – masks, crowns, necklaces, earrings, bracelets – all of extraordinary craftsmanship.

The Museum of Byzantine Culture and White Tower

The well-curated **Museum of Byzantine Culture** at 2 Stratou Ave (same hours as–and just east of the Archeological Museum; €4), is also worth a look for its finely preserved tombs, splendid mosaics, icons and jewellery. Close by, on the waterfront, Thessaloníki's enduring landmark, the **White Tower** (Tues–Sun 8.30am–3pm; €3), the last surviving bastion of the city's medieval walls, tells the story of the city through a high-tech multimedia exhibit. Go to the top for an unforgettable view of the city.

Churches

Among the city's many **churches**, the unmissable ones are Áyios Geórgios or "Rotónda", in the east of the city, originally a Roman rotunda built in 306 AD, decorated with golden mosaics; Áyios Dhimítrios (built originally in 413 AD, though the current building dates from 1948) with several seventh-century mosaics and the relics of the saint; the eighth-century Ayía Sofía, a few blocks west of "Rotónda", with superb mosaics of the Ascension and the Virgin Enthroned; and nearby Panayía Ahiropíitos (fifth century AD), the largest Palaeochristian church in the Balkans.

The photography museum

If, after all the icons and alabaster, you feel like something a little more contemporary, the excellent portside **Museum of Photography** (Tues–Fri 11am–7pm, Sat & Sun 11am–9pm; €2) is worth a few hours' exploration. In 2014 it will be hosting the international Photo Biennale, with talks and presentations in various languages.

ARRIVAL AND INFORMATION

By plane From the airport, 16km out at Mikrá, buses #78 (every 15–20min, 5.30am–11pm) and #78N (every 30min, 11pm–5.30am) run to the train station and KTEL bus terminal (€0.90). Taxi €20.

14

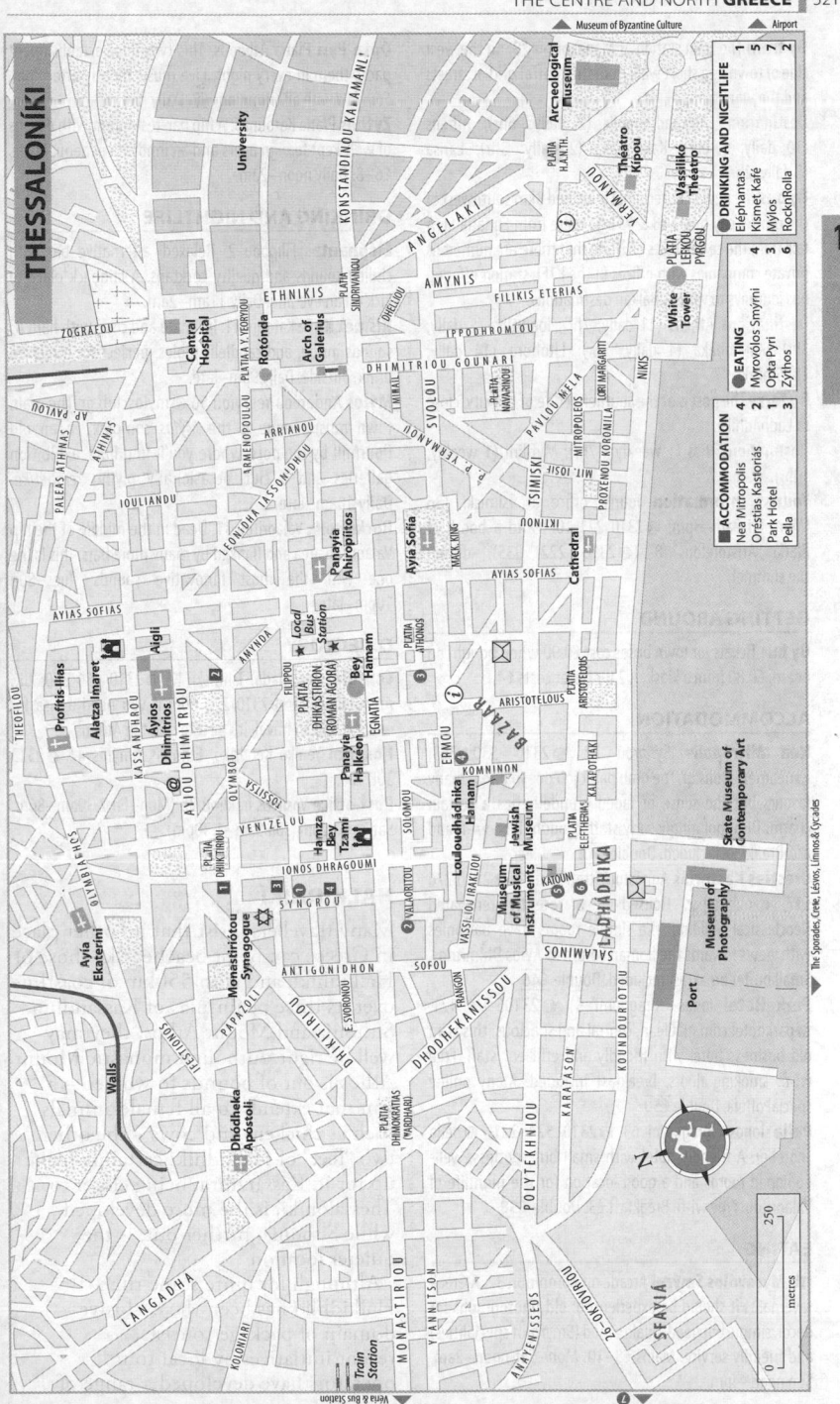

THESSALONÍKI

Museum of Byzantine Culture ▲   Airport ▲

DRINKING AND NIGHTLIFE
Eléphantas	1
Kismet Kafé	5
Mylos	7
RocknRolla	2

EATING
Myrovólos Smýrni	4
Opta Pyrí	2
Zýthos	1

ACCOMMODATION
Nea Mitropolis	4
Oréstias Kastorías	2
Park Hotel	1
Pella	3

The Sporades, Crete, Lésvos, Limnos & Cyclades ▶

◀ Véria & Bus Station   🄸 ▼

14

By train The train station at Monastiriou 28, on the west side of town, is a short walk from the central grid of streets and the waterfront.

Destinations Alexandroupolis (2 daily; 6hr); Athens (10 daily; 5–6hr); Kalambáka (2 daily; 3hr); Larisa (8 daily; 2hr).

By bus The new KTEL terminal is located 3km southwest of the centre; city buses #8 & #31 go there from Egnatía St. A taxi from the centre costs €6. Note that there are numerous private companies with offices in the KTEL station offering bus journeys to various Balkan destinations.

Destinations Athens (11 daily; 7hr); Ioánnina (5 daily; 3hr); Kalambáka (4 daily; 3hr); Litóhoro (14 daily; 1hr 5min).

By ferry The port is at the southern edge of the city, close to Ladhádhika.

Destinations Híos (1 weekly; 17hr); Mytilini (1 weekly; 14hr).

Tourist information Tourist office at Tsimiskí 136 (Mon–Fri 8am–3pm; ☎ 2310 221 100) and a booth at Platía Aristotelous 8 (☎ 2310 222 935), during the summer.

GETTING AROUND

By bus Tickets for town buses cost €0.90 when bought on board, €0.80 from a kiosk. A 24hr ticket costs €4.

ACCOMMODATION

Nea Mitrópolis Syngroú 22 ☎ 2310 530 363, ⓦ neametropolis.gr. The drab paint job doesn't do it many favours but the sense of faded grandeur has a certain charm. Disappointingly surly staff, though. Free wi-fi and a/c. Breakfast included. Double €42

Oréstias Kastoriás Agnóstou Stratiótou 14 ☎ 2310 276 517, ⓦ okhotel.gr. Housed in a recently renovated Neoclassical building, the simple rooms have balconies with views towards the Roman Forum or Áyios Dhimítrios. Small buffet breakfast included. Double €46

Park Hotel Íonos Dhragoúmi 81 ☎ 23105 24 121, ⓦ parkhotel.com.gr. Clean, central and spacious, this is an old business hotel with friendly and efficient staff. Free wi-fi, smoking floors, breakfast included. Many online special offers. Double €50

Pella Íonos Dhragoúmi 63 ☎ 2310 524 221, ⓦ pella -hotel.gr. A friendly hotel with small but spotless, well-equipped rooms and a good location for the nightlife of Valaoritou. Free wi-fi. Breakfast €3. Double €50

EATING

★ **Myrovólos Smýrni** Arcade off Komninón 32. A Greek taverna as it should be experienced: old photographs for decor, simple but good-quality food (Smyrniot specialities) and friendly service. Mains €8–10. Mon–Sat noon–2am, Sun noon–4pm.

Opta Pyri Platía Áthonos. This two-floor establishment packs them in every night. Live music nightly after 8pm. *Souvláki* with all trimmings €7. Daily noon–2am.

Zýthos Platía Katoúni 5. A hip bar-restaurant with dozens of well-kept foreign beers and an innovative menu. Mains €6–8. Daily noon–2am.

DRINKING AND NIGHTLIFE

Eléphantas Filíppou 2. Relaxed, alternative bar with chilled sounds and quality cocktails. A laidback place to kick off an evening. Daily 11am–2am.

Kismet Kafé Katoúni 11. Intimate and cosy, with hard DJ sounds inside, and candlelit tables, perfect for a relaxed drink, outside. Daily 9pm–late.

Mýlos Andhréou Yeoryíou 56 ⓦ mylosclub.gr. The main town music venue is the *Mýlos* complex, in an old flourmill by the port, where you'll find bars, exhibition galleries and a club occasionally plying *rembétika*. Daily 10am–late.

RocknRolla Valaoritou 31. Dead in the middle of the hip Valaoritou area and flanked by many more bars, this is the one with the most innovative sounds. Tues–Sun 10pm–late.

DIRECTORY

Consulates Canada, Tsimiskí 17 ☎ 2310 256 350; UK, Aristotélous 21 ☎ 2310 278 006; if you need a visa for onward Balkan travel, it's best to get it in Athens.

Hospital Yenikó Kendrikó, Ethnikís Amýnis 41 ☎ 2313 308 100.

Post office Vasiléos Irakliou 38 (Mon–Fri 7.30am–8pm, Sat 7am–2pm, Sun 9am–1.30pm).

HALKIDHIKÍ

Many travellers insist that no other place in Greece can boast beaches like those of Halkidhikí, and with 550km of coastline over its three peninsulas of Kassándhra, Sithonía and Mount Athos, they may well be right. Although monastic Mount Athos is out of bounds to women – a ban that extends to all female animals such as chickens and cows – the other two "feet" of Halkidhikí certainly make up for it. Kassándhra, being closer to Thessaloníki, is the more developed, while Sithonía, further out, is the quieter location.

Although for quite some time Halkidhikí has been the exclusive domain of package tourists, recent initiatives by local tour operators have developed a range of backpacker-oriented activities including mountain biking, watersports, hiking and horseriding (@gohalkidiki.com)

Several archeological sites aside – including Stáyira, the birthplace of Aristotle – the most interesting cultural event in Halkidhikí is the Sáni Festival in the town of Sáni (July & Aug; @sanifestival.gr), which brings together world-class rock and jazz acts, as well as Greek superstars.

ARRIVAL AND DEPARTURE

By bus Regular buses and mini-buses to Halkidhikí leave from Thessaloníki airport.

ACCOMMODATION

Camping Blue Dream Sáni ☏ 23750 41449, @campingbluedream.gr. High-quality campsite dead on the beach with restaurant and lively beach bar; conveniently situated for the Sáni Festival. Open May–Sept. Camping **€7.20** per person, plus **€6.30** per tent

Camping Valti Sykiá ☏ 23750 41449, @camping -valti.com. Shaded leafy family campsite on a superb beach on the eastern side of Sithonía; beach bar also offers meals. Open May–Oct. Camping **€5** per person, plus **€4** per tent

VERGÍNA (ANCIENT AEGAE)

In 1977, archeologists discovered the burial sanctuary of the ancient Macedonian dynasty, including Alexander the Great's father and son, at the village of **VERGÍNA**. The four **Royal Tombs** (summer Mon 10am–6pm, Tues–Sun 8am–8pm; winter Tues–Sun 8am–3pm; €8) constitute the focus of an unmissable underground museum. It features delicate gold and silver funerary

artefacts, the facades of the tombs, the kings' armours, frescoes (uniquely, with perspective) and the ashes of the deceased royals in ornate ossuaries.

ARRIVAL AND DEPARTURE

By bus It's easy to make this a day-trip from Thessaloníki: hourly buses run to Véria (1hr; €9 return), from where eleven onward buses per day cover the final 20min to modern Vergína village (€3.20 return, taxi €15 one-way).

MOUNT OLYMPUS AND LITÓHORO

Highest, most magical and most dramatic of all Greek mountains, **Mount Olympus** – the mythical seat of the gods – rears straight up nearly 3000m from the shores of the Thermaïkós Gulf. Dense forests cover its lower slopes and its wild flowers are gorgeous. If you're well equipped, no special expertise is necessary to reach the top between mid-June and October, though it's a long hard pull, and its weather is notoriously fickle. The usual approach to Mount Olympus is via **LITÓHORO** on the eastern slopes, a pleasant village in a magnificent mountain setting. You can buy a proper **map** of the range in Athens, Thessaloníki or Litóhoro.

ARRIVAL AND DEPARTURE

By bus Litóhoro's KTEL terminal is just south of the main square.

Destinations Thessaloníki (hourly; 1hr 15 min).

ACCOMMODATION

Hotel Enipéas Litóhoro ☏ 23520 84328, @www.hotel -enipeas.gr. This hotel, with a central location and balconied rooms with views over a gorge, is the best-value

---

CLIMBING MOUNT OLYMPUS

Four to five hours' walking along the well-marked, scenic E4 long-distance path up the Mavrólongos canyon brings you to **Priónia**, from where there's a sharper three-hour trail-climb to the *Spilios Agapitos* refuge (see p.524). It's best to stay overnight here, as you need to make an early start for the three-hour ascent to **Mýtikas**, the highest peak (2917m) – the summit frequently clouds over towards midday. The path continues behind the refuge, reaching a signposted fork above the tree line in about an hour; straight on, then right, takes you to Mýtikas via the ridge known as Kakí Skála, while the other fork, an abrupt right, continues for an hour to the *Yiosos Apostolidhis* hut (see p.524). From the hut there's an enjoyable loop down to the **Gortsiá** trailhead and from there back down into the Mavrólongos canyon, via the medieval monastery of Ayíou Dhionysíou. If you are short of time, you can hike the short 30-minute trail along Enipéas Gorge to the village's water reservoir.

14

★ **TREAT YOURSELF**

Gastrodrómio en Olympo Ayíou Nikoláou 36, Litóhoro ☎ 23520 21300, ⓦ gastrodromio.gr. Who would have thought that Litóhoro would sport one of the most acclaimed restaurants in Greece? If you make it there, splash out on casseroles with locally sourced meats and mountain herbs, fresh fish and a platter with thirty different types of Greek cheeses. Three-course menu from €10. Booking recommended July & Aug. Daily noon–late.

accommodation in the village. Free wi-fi. Breakfast included. Double €50

Seaside Hostel Gritsa, 5km from Litóhoro ☎ 23520 61406, ⓦ summitzero.gr. You can combine a stay by the sea and a climb up Mount Olympus by staying at this seaside hostel. Prices are a bit steep, but the whole place is highly congenial plus they organize hikes and mountain-bike rides on Mount Olympus. Dorm €15

Spilios Agapitos ☎ 23520 81800; **Yiosos Apostolidhis** (no phone). A couple of basic refuges on the slopes of Mount Olympus. *Spilios Agapitos* open mid-May to mid-Oct; *Yiosos Apostolidhis* open mid-June to mid-Sept. Both dorm €10 per person; *Spilios Agapitos* also camping €4.20 per person and tent

The Cyclades

The **Cyclades** (pronounced with a hard C throughout) is the most satisfying Greek archipelago for island-hopping, with its vibrant capital on **Sýros**. The majority of the islands are arid and rocky, with brilliant-white, cuboid architecture, making them enormously popular with tourists. **Íos**, the original hippie island, is still a backpacker's paradise, while **Mýkonos** – with its teeming old town, nudist beaches and highly sophisticated clubs and bars (many of them gay) – is by far the most visited (and most expensive) of the group. Arriving by ferry at the partially submerged volcanic caldera of **Santoríni**, meanwhile, is one of the world's great travel adventures. **Páros**, **Náxos** and **Sífnos** are nearly as popular, while the one major ancient site worth making time for is **Délos**, the commercial and religious centre of the classical Greek world. Note that accommodation prices quoted below can be thirty to forty percent cheaper outside July and August.

ARRIVAL AND DEPARTURE

By boat Almost all of the Cyclades are served by boats from Pireás, but there are also ferries from Rafína, one hour by bus north of Athens.

SÝROS

Sýros is the most populous island in the archipelago, and **ERMOÚPOLIS** is its capital and port (and capital of the Cyclades as a whole). It's a lively spot, bustling with a commercial life that extends far beyond tourism. Crowned by two imposing churches, the Catholic Capuchin **Monastery of St Jean** in the medieval quarter of Ano Sýros, and the Orthodox **Anástasis**, the city is one of the most religiously and culturally diverse places in the whole of Greece.

ARRIVAL AND INFORMATION

By ferry The ferry port is in the centre of Ermoúpolis. Destinations Íos (5–6 weekly; 4–7hr); Mýkonos (3–5 daily; 50min); Náxos (1–2 daily; 1hr 30min–2hr); Pireás (3–5 daily; 2hr 30min–4hr); Santoríni (1–2 daily; 3–6hr); Sífnos (2–3 weekly; 2hr 30min).

Tourist information Teamwork, Akti Papagou 18 (☎ 22810 83400, ⓦ teamwork.gr), is the best place to go to ask for directions, accommodation and tours.

ACCOMMODATION

Kastro Rooms Kalomenopoúlou 12 ☎ 22810 88064/82394. Spacious rooms in a beautiful old mansion house near the main square, with access to a communal kitchen. No breakfast. Double €40

Palladion Proïou 3 ☎ 22810 86400, ⓦ palladion-hotel.com. Quiet, clean, recently renovated and with rooms overlooking a garden – this place is excellent value. Breakfast included. Double €55

EATING

Stin Ithaki tou Aí Klonos & Stefanou. Tucked down a side street, this welcoming taverna has all the Greek classics and vibrant bougainvillea overhead. Mains €10. Daily noon–midnight.

Yiannena Platía Kanári. Popular, friendly spot, seemingly unchanged since the 1950s, serving great seafood and other Greek standards. Mains €7. Daily 11am–1am.

SÍFNOS

Although **Sífnos** – notable for its classic Cycladic architecture and pottery – often gets crowded, its modest size makes exploring the picturesque island a pleasure, whether by the excellent in-season bus service or on foot over a network of old stone pathways.

KAMÁRES, the port, is tucked in at the base of high, bare cliffs in the west. A steep twenty-minute bus ride takes you up to **APOLLONÍA**, a rambling collage of flagstones, belfries and flowered courtyards. The island bank, post office and tourist police are all located here. As an alternative base, head for **KÁSTRO**, a short bus ride below Apollonía on the east coast; built on a rocky outcrop with an almost sheer drop to the sea on three sides, this medieval capital of the island retains much of its character. The island's finest beach is, however, **VATHÝ**, a fishing village regularly connected by bus to and from Apollonía.

ARRIVAL AND INFORMATION

By boat The ferries dock at the port of Kamáres. Destinations Íos (1–3 weekly; 3hr); Mýkonos (1 weekly; 5hr); Pireás (2–4 daily; 3–5hr); Santoríni (2 weekly; 4hr 30min); Sýros (2–3 weekly; 2hr 30min–5hr).
Tourist information There is an information booth opposite the dock (summer only Mon–Fri 8am–3pm).

ACCOMMODATION

The Aegean Thesaurus agency (☎22840 33527) in Kamáres should be able to help with rooms.
★ **Hotel Stavros** Kamáres ☎22840 33383, ⓦsifnostravel.com. These crisp en-suite rooms, some with kitchenettes, have balconies with beach views. There's also a decent book exchange in the reception. No breakfast. Double €50
Makis Camping Kamáres ☎22840 32366, ⓦmakiscamping.gr. A campsite with excellent facilities – including a laundry open to non-guests – as well as studios (holding 1–2 people). Open May–Sept. Camping €8 per person, plus €4 per tent, studio €50

MÝKONOS

Mýkonos has become the most popular and expensive of the Cyclades, visited by several million tourists a year. If you don't mind the crowds, the upmarket capital, **MÝKONOS TOWN** (also known as

DAY-TRIP TO DÉLOS

Boats from the west end of Mýkonos harbour leave for ancient **Delos** (€38 return), the sacred isle, where Leto gave birth to Artemis and Apollo. It's worth a half-day trip for the magnificent views across to the nearby Cyclades from Mount Kýnthos (a 15min walk to the top), and for the archeological site (Tues–Sun 8.30am–3pm; €5) with remains of ancient temples, mosaics and its monumental lion avenue.

14

HÓRA), is still the most beautiful and vibrant of all island capitals. Dazzlingly white, it's the archetypal Greek island town with sugar-cube buildings stacked around a cluster of seafront fishermen's dwellings.

The closest **beach** is **Áyios Stéfanos**, 4km north and connected by a very regular bus service, though **Platýs Yialós**, 4km south, is marginally less crowded. A bus service from Mýkonos town and a *kaïki* service from **Órnos**, 2km south, connect almost all the beaches east of Platýs Yialós: gorgeous, pale-sand **Parága** beach, popular with campers; **Paradise**, well sheltered by its headland dominated by the eponymous campsite and club; and **Super Paradise**, partly nudist and gay. Probably the island's best beach is **Eliá** – mainly gay – on the south-central coast: a broad, sandy stretch with a verdant backdrop. Less busy, but harder to get to, are **Kaló Livádi**, **Kalafátis** and **Liá** further east, as well as the northern, more windswept beaches of **Fteliá** and **Áyios Sóstis**.

ARRIVAL AND DEPARTURE

By plane The airport is about 3km out of town, a short taxi ride away (€8–10). Buses to the north terminal are infrequent (€1).
By ferry Boats dock at the "new" port (a short walk north of town) where the bus station is also situated. *Kaïkia* to Délos (see box above) leave from the west end of Mýkonos harbour.
Destinations Íos (3–4 weekly; 2hr–5hr 30min); Náxos (2–4 daily; 45min–3hr); Páros (2–3 daily; 50min); Pireás (3–4 daily; 3hr 30min–5hr 30min); Santoríni (2–4 daily; 2hr 15min–7hr); Sífnos (occasional; 3hr 30min); Sýros (1–3 daily; 45min–1hr 15min).

14

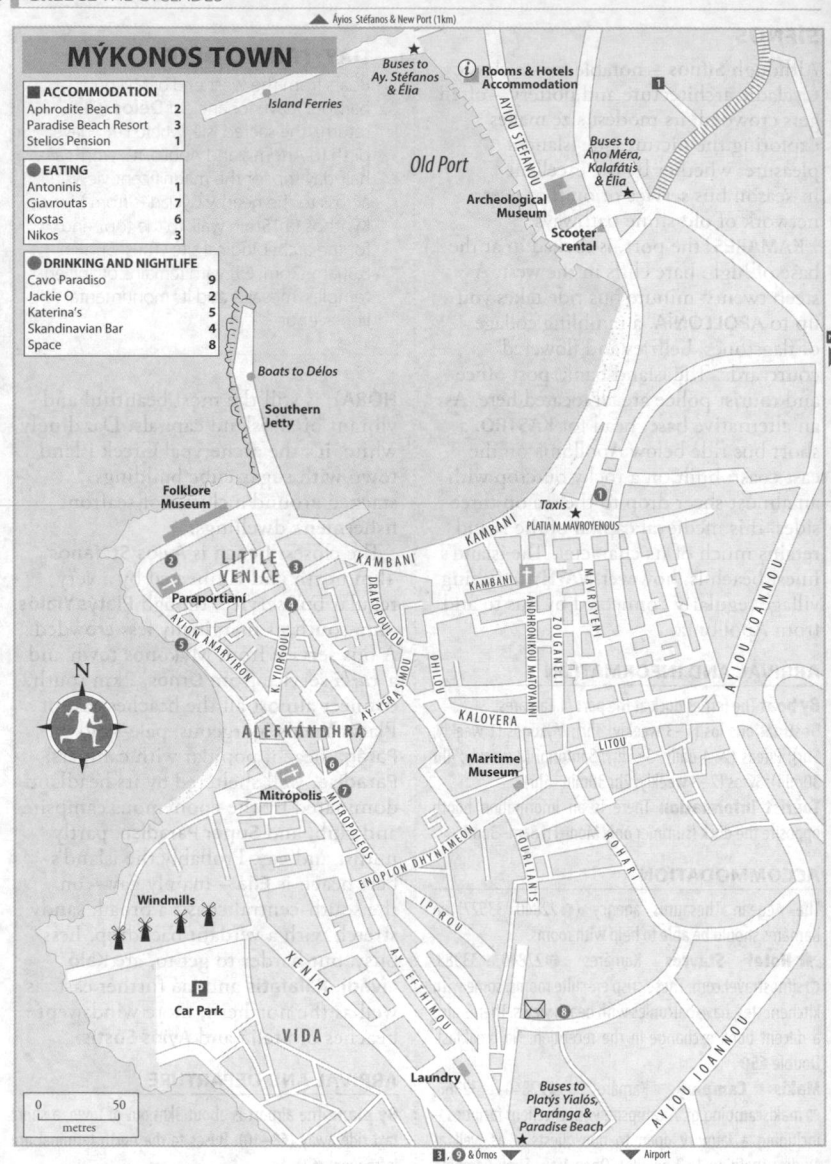

Áyios Stéfanos & New Port (1km)

MÝKONOS TOWN

■ ACCOMMODATION
Aphrodite Beach	2
Paradise Beach Resort	3
Stelios Pension	1

● EATING
Antoninis	1
Giavroutas	7
Kostas	6
Nikos	3

● DRINKING AND NIGHTLIFE
Cavo Paradiso	9
Jackie O	2
Katerina's	5
Skandinavian Bar	4
Space	8

Buses to
Ay. Stéfanos
& Élia

Rooms & Hotels
Accommodation

Island Ferries

Old Port

AYIOU STEFANOU

Buses to
Áno Méra,
Kalafátis
& Élia

Archeological
Museum

Scooter
rental

Southern
Jetty

Boats to Délos

Folklore
Museum

Taxis
PLATIA M.MAVROYENOUS

LITTLE
VENICE

KAMBANI

Paraportianí

KAMBANI

AYION ANARYIRON

DRAKOPOULOU

IONIAS

K. YIORGOULI

DHILOU

AY. YERA

KAMBANI

ANDRONIKOU MATOYANNI

ZOUGANELI

MAVROYENI

AYIOU IOANNOU

ALEFKÁNDHRA

KALOYERA

LITOU

Maritime
Museum

Mitrópolis

MITROPOLEOS

ENOPLON DHYNAMEON

IPIROU

TOURLIANIS

ROHARI

N

Windmills

Car Park

VIDA

XENIAS

AY. EFTHIMIOU

Laundry

Buses to
Platýs Yialós,
Paránga &
Paradise Beach

AYIOU IOANNOU

0   50
metres

&, & Órnos   Airport

INFORMATION

Tourist information Rooms and Hotels Accommodation, basically two offices in the old port (April–Oct daily 9.30am–5pm), can help you with accommodation, maps and activities; one office deals with hotels (☎22890 24540), the other with rented rooms (☎22890 24860).

Tourist police Office located opposite the airport (☎22890 22482).

GETTING AROUND

By bus Buses for Kalafátis and all beaches east of town leave from the terminus next to the island ferries. A second bus terminus, for beaches to the south, is located at the other end of town.

ACCOMMODATION

Aphrodite Beach ☎22890 71367, ⓦaphrodite -mykonos.gr. A four-star hotel at Kalafátis, 18km from town, with a selection of hostel-style bunk-bed accommodation (note that you can't just rent a bed; you need to take a whole dorm). Reserve before you go, as there are often block-bookings by tour groups. Open April–Oct. Dorm €140

Paradise Beach Resort ☎ 22890 22129, ⓦ paradise -greece.com. An industrial-size (and feel) campsite on the eponymous beach also offering cabins and bungalows. Don't go there If you want a quiet holiday. Open April–Oct; prices tumble outside July & Aug. Camping €10 per person, plus €5 per tent, cabin €50, bungalow €90

Stelios Pension ☎ 22890 24641 or 22890 26779. A whitewashed Mykoniot-style building, with comfortable rooms, located off steps leading up from behind the OTE telecommunications office. Open April–Oct. Double €90

EATING

Antoninis Platía Mantó. A reliable choice on the main square, serving Greek family cooking since 1955. Go to the kitchen to choose your dish. Mains €12. Daily noon–late.

Giavroutas Mitropóleos 11. Sometimes it feels like this place is open 24/7, a basic taverna that has been serving clubbers with munchies for decades. Mains €8. Open April–Oct. Daily noon–7am.

Kostas Mitropóleos 5. Small, excellent restaurant buried deep in the town's labyrinthine centre, and serving everything from seafood to grills. Mains €12. Daily 6pm–2am.

Nikos Aghias Monís Square. A popular option, strong on fresh fish but also serving traditional Greek cuisine. Get there before 10pm to find a table (no reservations). Mains €15. Daily noon–2am.

DRINKING AND NIGHTLIFE

★ **Cavo Paradiso** Paradise Beach ⓦ cavoparadiso.gr. Close to the *Paradise Beach Resort*, this packed after-hours club features regularly in the top-ten lists of clubs worldwide. Open 2–3 times a week (1am–9am); check the website.

Jackie O Below Paraportianí church ⓦ jackieomykonos .com. The busiest of three gay clubs in a row below the church of Paraportianí. Top floor (if you can reach it through the crowd) is a bit quieter. Daily 10pm–6am.

Katerina's Little Venice. Low-key decor combined with sea views from the terrace makes this a relaxing place for a drink. Cocktails €10. Daily noon–late.

Skandinavian Bar K. Yeorgouli. A good choice for the backpacker set, this buzzing, inexpensive multi-bar complex is housed around a small square. Plenty of room for dancing, too. May–Sept daily 8pm–late.

Space Lákka Square. The largest dance club in town, home to a host of resident and guest DJs. May, June & Sept Fri & Sat; July & Aug daily midnight–8am.

PÁROS

With its old villages, monasteries, fishing harbour and labyrinthine capital, **Páros** has everything one expects from a Greek island, including a vibrant nightlife, four blue flag beaches and boat connections to virtually the entire Aegean.

PARIKIÁ, the main town, has ranks of white houses punctuated by the occasional Venetian-style building and church domes. Just outside the centre, the town also has one of the most interesting churches in the Aegean – the fourth-century **Ekatondapylianí** (daily 7am–9pm; free). The place culminates in a seaward Venetian **kastro**, whose surviving east wall incorporates a fifth-century BC round tower. The second-largest village of Páros, **NÁOUSSA**, a twenty-minute bus ride from Parikiá, retains much of its original character as a fishing village with winding, narrow alleys and simple Cycladic houses.

ARRIVAL AND INFORMATION

By ferry All ferries dock at Parikiá, the main town.
Destinations Íos (2–3 weekly; 2–3hr); Mýkonos (1–2 daily; 45min–1hr); Náxos (2–3 daily; 35min); Pireás (3–5 daily; 3–4hr); Santoríni (1–3 daily; 3hr); Sífnos (2 weekly; 2hr 45min); Sýros (6–8 weekly; 2hr 40min).
Tourist information Located in the windmill in the centre of the roundabout opposite the quay (summer only, during ferry arrivals).

GETTING AROUND

By bus The bus stop is centrally located in Parikiá next to the quay. There are buses to Náoussa every 30min in July & Aug, less frequently at other times.

ACCOMMODATION

★ **Captain Manólis** Market St, Parikiá ☎ 22840 21244, ⓦ paroswelcome.com. Central but unbelievably quiet and freshly renovated; all rooms have garden views and free wi-fi. Breakfast €5. Double €55

Dina Market St, Parikiá ☎ 22840 21325, ⓦ hoteldina .com. Small family *pension*, showcasing the Cycladic colours of white and blue; it's obsessively clean and right in the middle of the action. Double €65

★ **Kriós Beach Camping** 2km from Parikiá ☎ 22840 21705, ⓦ krios-camping.gr. Excellent facilities in a shady site. Occasional parties that include plate smashing. Free wi-fi and pool. Open May–Sept. Camping €8 per person, plus €4 per tent

Young Inn Náoussa ☎ 6976 415 232, ⓦ young-inn.com.

14

14

Comfortable en-suite bedrooms, some with kitchenettes. A sociable place, as there are all kinds of organized activities. Breakfast costs extra. Free transfers to the port. Open April–Oct. Dorm €8, double €30

EATING, DRINKING AND NIGHTLIFE

Dubliner/Paros Rock By the bridge, Parikiá. Young, lively and OTT, this complex of bars and clubs is where you will probably end up dancing after a night drinking in town. Cocktails €7–8. Entrance with first drink €5. June–Sept daily 11pm–6am.

Happy Green Cows Just behind the National Bank in Parikiá, this place serves excellent, inventive vegetarian food in kitsch, colourful surroundings. Carnivore concessions include fish and chicken. Mains €12. April–Oct daily 7pm–2am.

Tráta Parikiá. Down a side street off the road heading east out of town, this popular taverna specializes in seafood. Mains €8. April–Oct daily noon–midnight.

NÁXOS

Náxos is the largest and most fertile of the Cyclades, with high mountains, intriguing central valleys, a spectacular north coast, sandy beaches in the southwest, and Venetian towers and fortified mansions scattered throughout.

WHAT TO SEE AND DO

A long causeway protecting the harbour connects **NÁXOS TOWN** with the islet of Palátia, where the huge stone portal of an unfinished sixth-century BC **Temple of Apollo** still stands. Most of the town's life goes on down by the port or in the streets just behind it; the quaint Old Market Street has narrow stone paths leading to small shops and a handful of restaurants and cafés. From here, stepped lanes lead up past crumbling balconies and through low arches of the **Bourgo** to the fortified medieval **kastro**, near the **Archeological Museum** (Tues–Sun 8.30am–3pm; €3), with its important Early Cycladic collection. The town has a laidback feel, with unashamedly long happy hours which last for most of the day. There's a thriving nightlife, with plenty of bars scattered along the waterfront.

Beaches

The island's best **beaches** are regularly served by buses in season. Within Náxos Town itself is **Áyios Yeóryios**, a long sandy bay, part of the hotel and restaurant quarter. A short bus ride south, however, you'll find the more inviting **Áyios Prokópios** and **Ayía Ánna** beaches, with plenty of rooms to let and many good tavernas. Beyond the headland stretches **Pláka** beach, a 5km-long vegetation-fringed expanse of white sand, which comfortably holds the summer crowds of nudists and campers from the two campsites nearby.

ARRIVAL AND INFORMATION

By plane The airport is a 10min taxi ride south of Náxos Town (€10).

By ferry Boats dock at the quay at the northern end of Náxos Town.

Destinations Íos (4–5 weekly; 1hr 30min); Mýkonos (1–3 daily; 3hr); Páros (2–3 daily; 45min); Pireás (2–3 daily; 4hr–5hr 30min); Santoríni (1–2 daily; 1hr 15min–3hr 30min); Sífnos (1 weekly; 3hr 30min); Sýros (4–5 weekly; 2hr 30min).

Tourist information You can obtain information at Zas Travel (☎ 22850 23330) or Auto Tour car rental (☎ 22850 25480) opposite the quay, where you can pick up leaflets or leave your luggage (both daily 9.30am–9.30pm).

GETTING AROUND

By bus The bus stop in Náxos Town is opposite the quay.

ACCOMMODATION

Camping Marágas ☎ 22850 24552, ⓦ maragascamping. gr. A shaded campsite yet right on Maragas beach and the closest to town. Also offers double rooms. Discounts for students. Open April–Oct. Camping €9 per person and tent, double €40

★ **Camping Pláka** Ayía Anna ☎ 22850 42700/42031, ⓦ plakacamping.gr. Flanked by the imaginatively named *Pláka I* and *Pláka II* hotels, this large modern site with its own sandy beach (50m away), surf school and restaurant feels more like a resort than a campground. Camping €9 per person and tent

Despina's Rooms Náxos Town ☎ 22850 22356. Hidden (but well signposted) beneath the castle in the Bourgo. Rooms are small but clean and airy, with shared bathroom and balconies with sea views. Double €35

EATING AND DRINKING

Elia Old Market St, Náxos Town. Housed in a beautiful stone building, this smart café-bar has live music and an enticing atmosphere. Also serves breakfast and lunch. Cocktails €8. Daily 9am–3pm & 7pm–late.

Manólis Garden Old Market St, Bourgo. A peaceful spot

for an evening meal, with traditional Greek dishes. Mains €8–10. May–Oct daily 6pm–1am.

Molos Ayios Prokópios. Commanding the best part of the beach and serving traditional Greek fare, this is the pick of the seaside tavernas. Mains €8. May–Oct daily 9am–1am.

Íos

Once a hippie hangout, Íos remains popular with a younger crowd seeking fun and sun, and as party capital of the Aegean, the island provides this in abundance. However, although no other island attracts more under-25s, Íos has miraculously maintained much of its traditional Cycladic charm, with picture-perfect whitewashed houses and churches. Lively nights lead to lazy days, perfect for exploring the island beaches.

WHAT TO SEE AND DO

Don't expect a quiet stay in the town of HÓRA, as every evening the streets throb to music with the larger **clubs** clustered near the bus stop. To get the most out of the nightlife, start around 11pm with the bars and clubs around the central square, which tend to close at 3am. Around this time the larger clubs on the main street begin to liven up, and the party continues (even if you don't) until 9am.

Mylopótas and Manganári

The most popular stop on the island's bus routes is **MYLOPÓTAS**, site of a magnificent beach where there's a mini-resort (run by Far Out Camping; see below) offering plenty of activities including quad biking, watersports and diving, as well as parties. It gets very crowded, so for a bit more space, head away from the Mylopótas bus stop, where there are dunes behind the beach. From Yialós, boats depart daily at around 10am to **MANGANÁRI** on the south coast, where there's a superb blue flag beach.

ARRIVAL AND DEPARTURE

By ferry Boats dock at the quay in Yialós. Regular buses connect the port to Hóra and Mylopótas (every 15min, 8am–12.30am), but many hotels and hostels offer free transfers.

Destinations Mýkonos (1–2 daily; 1hr 40min); Náxos (4–5 weekly; 45min–3hr); Páros (2–4 weekly; 5hr); Pireás (1–2 daily; 3hr 20min); Santoríni (2–3 daily; 35min–1hr 30min); Sífnos (2–3 weekly; 3–5hr); Sýros (3–5 weekly; 5hr 30min).

ACCOMMODATION

Far Out Camping Mylopótas ☎ 22850 91468, ⊛ faroutclub.com. By far the most popular campsite, thanks to its facilities and fun factor. Two-person bungalows also available. Open April–Sept. Camping €8 per person and tent (free Sept with own tent), bungalow €36

★ **Francesco's** Hóra Old Town ☎ 22860 91223, ⊛ francescos.net. A favourite option with the backpacker set, who come for the only dorm beds in town as well as private rooms. Lively bar and terrace with sea views, late breakfast till 2pm and a pool with a view. Much cheaper in June and Sept. Dorm €20, double €70

Lófos Hóra ☎ 22860 91481. Right up from the archeological site, this shaded, family-owned complex with basic but well-furnished rooms is very convenient for access both to the bus stop and the Hóra nightlife opposite. Open May–Oct. Double €40

EATING

Ali Baba's Hóra. Thai chefs dish up generous portions of authentic Thai food, served with the famous fishbowl cocktails. Stir-fries €10. May–Oct 6pm–midnight.

Lord Byron Hóra. An intimate restaurant with funky decor, serving generous meze plates to share (€12). A restaurant for those with an appetite. May–Oct daily 6pm–1am.

★ **Mario's** Top of the stairs from Mylopótas beach. Perched at a curve on the road to Hóra with spectacular views and enormous pizzas (€9). April–Oct daily noon–midnight.

DRINKING AND NIGHTLIFE

Red Bull Bar Main square. Small bar specializing in dance music – and the well-known energy drink, mixed with large doses of spirits. Cocktails €7. May–Oct daily 10pm–3am.

Scorpion Main street. Huge nightclub, packed to the rafters, and with a dancefloor that throbs well beyond dawn. Entry €10 including a free drink. July & Aug daily 1am–late.

Slammer Bar Main square. Legendary bar, although beware of saying the word "slammer" too loudly. Plays popular music ranging from the Eighties to current tunes. Entry €5 including a free drink. May–Oct daily 10pm–3am.

Sweet Irish Dreams Main street, in front of the church. Satisfy your cravings for a pint of the black gold here and dance till dawn on the tables. Entry €7 including a free drink. June–Sept 6pm–late.

14

14

SANTORÍNI (THÍRA)

Santoríni is the epitome of relaxation, with its sun-drenched beaches and ambling, whitewashed stone paths. The island (a partially submerged volcanic caldera poking above the ocean's surface in five places) is a welcome destination to those who have spent too many nights partying on Íos. As the ferry manoeuvres into the great bay, gaunt, sheer cliffs loom hundreds of metres above. Nothing grows to soften the view, and the only colours are the reddish-brown, black and grey pumice strata layering the cliff face of **Thíra**, the ancient name of Santoríni. Despite a past every bit as turbulent as the geological conditions that formed it, the island is now best known for its spectacular views, dark-sand beaches and light, dry white wines.

WHAT TO SEE AND DO

Regular buses meeting the ferries at **Órmos Athiniós** make their way to the island's capital **FIRÁ**, half-rebuilt after a devastating earthquake in 1956 and lurching dementedly at the cliff's edge. Besieged by day-trippers from cruise-ships, it's somewhat tacky and commercialized, though watching the sunset from a cliff-hugging terrace of any of the overpriced restaurants you'll understand why it's so popular. There's no shortage of **rooms** in the area, though most are expensive. The town boasts a couple of **museums**: the **Archeological Museum** (Tues–Sun summer 9am–4pm; winter 8am–3pm; €3) near the cable car and the astonishing **Museum of Prehistoric Thíra** (Mon & Wed–Sun: summer 9am–4pm; winter 8am–3pm; €3), between the cathedral and the bus station, where you will find a range of stunning artefacts documenting an advanced civilization that perished forty centuries ago.

Around the island

Near the northwestern tip of the island is one of the most dramatic towns of the Cyclades, **ÍA**, a curious mix of pristine white reconstruction and tumbledown ruins clinging to the cliff face. With a post office, travel agencies and an

> ### BOAT TRIPS TO THE VOLCANO
> Take a **boat trip** (€10–30) from Firá or Ía to explore the magma-encrusted islets of the caldera and to swim in the sulphurous hot springs. You can book trips of varying lengths from your accommodation or a travel agent.

excellent **youth hostel** (see opposite), it makes a good base from which to explore the island. Santoríni's **beaches** are bizarre: long black stretches of volcanic sand that get blisteringly hot in the afternoon sun. There's little to choose between **KAMÁRI** and **PERÍSSA**, the two main resorts: both have long beaches and a mass of restaurants, rooms and apartments, although Períssa gets more backpackers.

At the southwestern tip of the island, evidence of a Minoan colony was unearthed at **Akrotíri** (summer Tues–Sun 8.30am–3pm; €5; bus from Firá or Períssa), a town buried under banks of volcanic ash. Nearby is the spectacular, red-sand **Kókkini Ámmos** beach.

ARRIVAL AND DEPARTURE

By plane The airport is on the east side of the island. While buses run to Firá and Monólithos beach (€1.60), they are infrequent and there are fewer than forty taxis on the island (fare to Firá €15). Try to negotiate a free transfer with your hotel.

By ferry Most boats arrive at the somewhat functional port of Órmos Athiniós from where buses depart for the island's capital.

Destinations Íos (1–3 daily; 30min–1hr); Iráklion (1–3 daily; 1hr 30min–5hr); Mýkonos (1–3 daily; 2hr 30min); Náxos (2–4 daily; 1hr 20min); Páros (2–3 daily; 3hr 30min–6hr); Pireás (3–5 daily; 4–9hr); Sífnos (1–2 weekly; 4–5hr); Sýros (5–6 weekly; 5–8hr).

GETTING AROUND

By bus In contrast to the airport, bus services are plentiful enough between Firá and other destinations around the island, but timetables vary widely from month to month.

ACCOMMODATION

Kykladonisia Firá ☎22860 22458, ⓦsantorinihostel .com. Sleek, upmarket hostel with a swimming pool, single-sex dorms and free wi-fi. Try to get one of the rooms with a sunset view. Prices skyrocket in Aug. Dorm €25, double €67

★ San Giorgio Firá ☎ 22860 23516, ⊛ sangiorgiovilla
.gr. Tucked away to the left of the car park next to the main
square, this hotel has clean, excellent-value rooms with
a/c, some with balconies. No breakfast. Open April–Nov.
Double €60

Santorini Camping Firá ☎ 22860 22944, ⊛ santorini
camping.gr. A shady campsite with a pool, restaurant and
internet access, 350m from Firá centre. Prices range widely
according to season. Camping €10 per person and tent,
dorm €15

Youth Hostel Ía ☎ 22860 71465 ⊛ santorinihostel.gr. An
excellent hostel with a terrace and shady courtyard, a bar
and clean dorms, albeit with a short season – late May to
Sept. Dorm €18

The Dodecanese

The **Dodecanese** islands lie so close to the
Turkish coast that some are almost within
hailing distance of the shore. They were
only included in the modern Greek state
in 1948 after centuries of occupation
by Crusaders, Ottomans and Italians.
Medieval **Rhodes** is the most famous, but
almost every one has its classical remains,
its Crusader castles, its traditional
villages and grandiose, Italian-built Art
Deco public buildings. The main islands
of Rhodes, **Kós** and **Pátmos** are well
connected with each other, and none is
hard to reach.

ARRIVAL AND DEPARTURE

By ferry Rhodes is the principal transport hub, with ferry
services to Turkey, as well as connections with Crete, the
northeastern Aegean islands, selected Cyclades and the
mainland.

RHODES

It's no surprise that **Rhodes** is among
the most visited of Greek islands. Not
only is its east coast lined with sandy
beaches, but the core of the capital is
a beautiful and remarkably preserved
medieval city.

WHAT TO SEE AND DO

RHODES TOWN divides into two unequal
parts: the compact old walled city and the
new town sprawling around it in three
directions. There's plenty to explore in

the rest of the island too, not least
charming **Haráki** and lively **Líndhos**.

Rhodes Town

First thing to meet the eye, and
dominating the northeast sector of the
city's fortifications, is the **Palace of the
Grand Masters** (June–Aug Mon
9am–4pm, Tues–Sun 8am–7.30pm;
Sept–May Tues–Sun 8am–3pm; €6). Two
excellent **museums** occupy the ground
floor: one devoted to medieval Rhodes,
the other to ancient Rhodes. The heavily
restored **Street of the Knights** (Odhós
Ippotón) leads due east from the front of
the palace. The "Inns" lining it housed the
Knights of St John for two centuries, and
at the bottom of the slope the Knights'
Hospital now houses the **Archeological
Museum** (same hours; €6), where the star
exhibits are the two famous statues of
Bathing Aphrodite and the *Marine Venus*,
the last of which inspired a book by
Lawrence Durrell. Heading south, it's
hard to miss the most conspicuous
Ottoman monument in Rhodes, the
candy-striped **Süleymaniye Mosque**, now
only open for major events and weddings.
The only Muslim sight you can visit is
the **Hafiz Ahmed Aga Library**, which was
built in 1793 and still contains 1256
manuscripts out of the original 1995
(Mon–Sat 9.30am–3pm; €1).

ARRIVAL AND INFORMATION

By plane Rhodes' Diagoras airport lies 15km east of
Rhodes Town. Buses leave frequently for the centre
(€2.30). A taxi to town costs €20–24. Rhodes is also
connected directly with many European capitals via
charter flights.
Destinations Athens (4–5 daily; 1hr); Iráklion (1 daily;
55min); Thessaloníki (1 daily; 1hr 15min).
By ferry Ferries dock at the port of Akandia east of the Old
Town; cruise ships anchor at Kolóna; pleasure boats and
local traffic still use Mandhráki. There's a ticket office at
Kolóna (7.30am–9pm).
Destinations Iráklion (1–2 weekly; 10–14hr); Kós (2–4
daily; 2hr 30min–3hr); Marmaris (1–2 daily; 1–2hr);
Pátmos (2 daily; 5hr); Pireás (9–12 weekly; 10–20hr);
Santoríni (4–5 weekly; 6–7hr); Sýros (3–4 weekly; 9hr).
By bus Buses for the rest of the island leave from two
departure points on Averoff St.
Destinations Faliraki (2 hourly; 35min); Líndhos
(13 daily; 1hr).

14

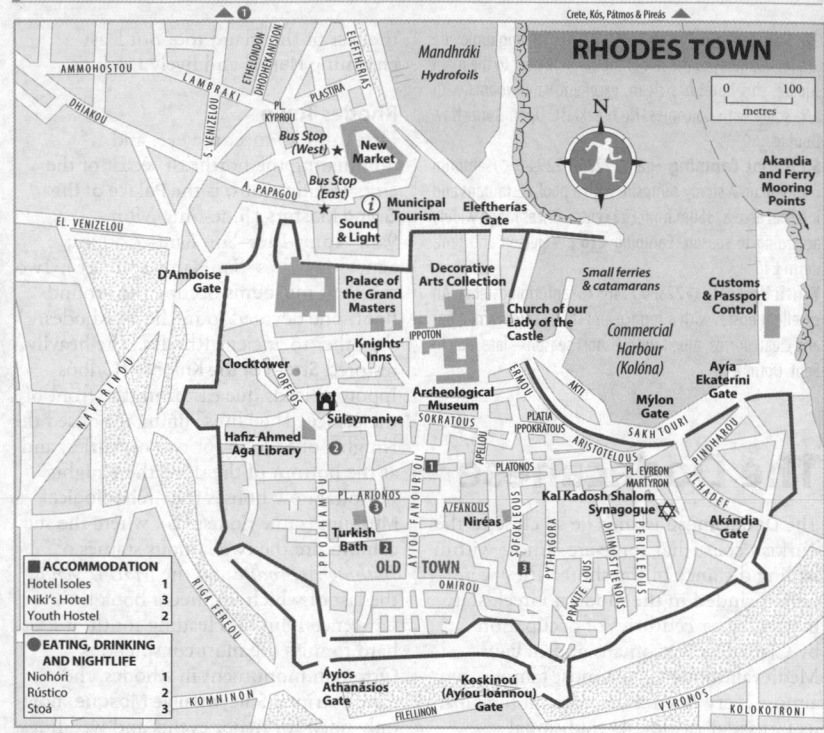

RHODES TOWN

ACCOMMODATION
Hotel Isoles	1
Niki's Hotel	3
Youth Hostel	2

EATING, DRINKING AND NIGHTLIFE
Niohóri	1
Rústico	2
Stoá	3

Tourist information The municipal tourist office is at Platia Rimini (Mon–Fri 7am–3pm; ☎22410 3545; ⊛rhodes.gr). They can provide you with maps and bus timetables.

ACCOMMODATION

Hotel Isoles Evdhóxou 75, Old Town ☎22410 20682, ⊛hotelisoles.com. Simple, clean hotel in a converted Ottoman house with a beautiful roof terrace and charming Italian owners. Free wi-fi. Breakfast included. Double **€60**

★ **Niki's Hotel** Sofokléous 39, Old Town ☎22410 25115, ⊛nikishotel.gr. Wonderful views over the old town from the roof garden, and breakfast (€5) served outside on a lovely patio. Very quiet, despite being close to all-night bars. Free wi-fi. Double **€50**

Youth Hostel Ergíou 12, Old Town ☎22410 30491, ✉hostel-gr19@gmail.com. A friendly hostel with four-bed dorms and double rooms. The dorms are basic, but the studios are carefully restored with original features retained. Free wi-fi. Dorm **€10**, double **€30**

EATING, DRINKING AND NIGHTLIFE

Niohóri Ioánni Kazoúli 29, New Town. This family restaurant is worth the 10min walk out of the old town, as it serves Greek cuisine at very reasonable prices (mains

€5–7). They also own the butcher's opposite, where all meat is sourced. Daily 1–11pm.

Rústico Ippodhámou 3-5, Old Town. Busy taverna under a shady vine with a wide range of choices: from seafood and traditional Greek dishes to Italian pasta. Two-course menus plus aperitif for €10–12. Daily 10am–midnight.

★ **Stoá** Menekléous 32, Old Town. Opposite the old Turkish Baths, this is one of the few busy bars in the Old Town not catering solely to tourists. Come to one of its many Greek live music nights and make friends with every young person on the island. Cocktails €6. Daily 10am–late.

Faliráki and Haráki

Heading down the east coast from Rhodes Town, you reach the island's mega-resort of **Faliráki**. A few years back, the name was synonymous with 18–30s drink-and-disgrace antics, but the authorities have clamped down and the place is much friendlier and amenable as a result, while the nearby Water-Park also attracts many families. That's not to say that its notorious nightlife has abated: its two main streets are called Bar Street and Club Street, after all.

The giant promontory of **Tsambíka**, 26km further south, is the first place to seriously consider stopping – there's an excellent beach just south of the headland. The best overnight base on this stretch of coast is probably **HARÁKI**, a tiny port with rooms and tavernas overlooked by a ruined castle.

Líndhos and around

LÍNDHOS, Rhodes' number two tourist attraction, lies 12km south of Haráki, its charm undiminished by commercialism and crowds. On the steep hill above the town, the Doric **Temple of Athena** and Hellenistic stoa (porch-like building used for meetings and commerce), as well as the Knights' castle, stand inside the town's famed Akropolis (Tues–Sun: June–Aug 8am–7.40pm; Sept–May 8am–2.40pm; €6). Líndhos's two beaches on either side of the Akropolis are crowded in the summer; you'll find better ones heading south past Lárdhos, the start of 15km of intermittent coarse-sand beach up to and beyond the growing resort of **Yennádhi**. Inland near here, the late Byzantine frescoes in the village church of **Asklipió** are among the best on Rhodes.

KÓS

Kós is the largest and most popular island in the Dodecanese after Rhodes, and there are superficial similarities between the two. Like its rival, the harbour here is also guarded by a castle of the Knights of St John, the streets are lined with ambitious Italian public buildings, and minarets and palm trees punctuate extensive Greek and Roman remains.

Mostly modern **KÓS TOWN**, levelled by a 1933 earthquake, fans out from the harbour. Apart from the castle, the town's main attraction is its wealth of Hellenistic and Roman remains. It's also one of the few spots in Greece where cycling is positively encouraged, and cycle lanes traverse the whole of Kós Town.

The Archeological Museum and castle

The **Archeological Museum** at Platía Eleftherías is currently being extended with a tentative opening date of 2015. Next to it, scaffolding from the **Castle** (Tues–Sun 8am–2.30pm; €3) props up the branches of the so-called Hippocrates plane tree, which does have a fair claim to being one of the oldest trees in Europe.

The Asklepion and Platáni

Hippocrates is honoured by the **Asklepion** (summer Tues–Fri 8am–8pm, Sat–Mon 8am–3pm; winter Tues–Fri 8am–3pm; €4), a temple to Asklepios and renowned centre of Hippocratic teaching, 45 minutes on foot (or a short bus ride) from town. The road to the Asklepion passes through the village of **PLATÁNI**, where Turkish owners run a couple of well-regarded tavernas.

Beaches

To get to the **beaches** you'll need to use buses or rent scooters or bikes. Around 12km west of Kós Town, **Tingáki** is easily accessible but busy. **Mastihári**, 30km from Kós Town, has a decent beach and private rooms for rent. Continuing west, buses run as far as **Kéfalos**, which covers a bluff looking back along the length of Kós. Well before Kéfalos are **Áyios Stéfanos**, where the exquisite remains of a mosaic-floored fifth-century basilica overlook tiny Kastrí islet, and **Kamári**, the package resort just below Kéfalos. Beaches begin at Kamári and extend east past Áyios Stéfanos for 7km, almost without interruption; **Paradise** has the most facilities, but **Magic** (officially Polémi) and **Langádhes** are calmer and more scenic.

By plane The airport lies 24km southwest of Kós Town. Bus #2 serves the town centre (every 10–20min, 8am–3.15pm; €3.20). A taxi costs €38. There are also many charter flights to Western Europe.
Destinations Athens (1 daily; 1hr); Iráklion (1 daily; 1hr).
By ferry Boats arrive at the harbour, to the north of the centre in Kós Town.
Destinations Bodrum (1–2 daily; 30–45min); Pátmos

14

14

(1–3 daily; 2hr 30min); Pireás (1 daily; 15hr); Rhodes (1–4 daily; 3hr).

By bus Island buses arrive 400m inland from the port, with a ticket and information booth at 7 Kleopátras street. For times and destinations see ⓦ ktel-kos.gr

Tourist information Artemisías 2 (Mon–Fri: May–Oct 8.30am–3pm; Nov–April 8.30am–2.30pm; ☏ 22420 29910, ⓔ eotkos@otenet.gr). There's also a kiosk at the port (summer Mon–Sat 8am–11pm; ☏ 22420 24460).

ACCOMMODATION

Hotel Afendoúlis Evripílou 1, Kós Town ☏ 22420 25321, ⓦ afendoulishotel.com. Homely en-suite rooms with balconies are set around a mezzanine floor, and there's a warm family welcome. Double €50

Hotel Sonia Irodhótou 9, Kós Town ☏ 22420 28798, ⓦ hotelsonia.gr. A freshly renovated place set around a shady garden with a veranda, whose informative owners welcome late arrivals. TV, a/c, free wi-fi; breakfast €5. Double €40

EATING

Ambavris 1.5km inland in the eponymous hamlet on the road to Platáni. This taverna may be some distance out of town, but it has an excellent selection of *mezédhes* (€25 for two) and is popular with the locals. May–Oct daily 6–11pm.

Koako Vasiléos Yeoryíou 6, Kós Town. Located in a residential area by the marina, this restaurant has a varied Greek menu, including fish dishes and good cheap house wine. Mains €6–8. Daily noon–midnight.

PÁTMOS

St John the Apostle reputedly wrote the Book of Revelation in a cave on **Pátmos**, and the monastery that commemorates him, founded here in 1088, dominates the island both physically and politically. Although the monks no longer run Pátmos as they did for more than six centuries, their influence has stopped most of the island going the way of Mammon like Rhodes or Kós.

WHAT TO SEE AND DO

SKÁLA, the port and main town, is the only busy part of the island, crowded with day-trippers from Kós and Rhodes. **HÓRA** is a beautiful little town whose antiquated alleys conceal over forty churches and monasteries, plus dozens of shipowners' mansions dating from the seventeenth and eighteenth centuries.

Monastery of St John

The **Monastery of St John** (Mon, Wed, Fri & Sat 8am–1.30pm, Tues, Thurs & Sun 8am–1.30pm & 4–6pm; monastery & treasury €4) shelters behind massive defences in the hilltop capital of Hóra. Buses go up (€1), but the thirty-minute walk along a beautiful old cobbled path is much more worthwhile.

Monastery of the Apocalypse

Just over halfway up the hill to Hóra is the **Monastery of the Apocalypse** (same hours; €2), built around the cave where St John heard the voice of God issuing from a cleft in the rock. This is merely a foretaste, however, of the main monastery, whose fortifications guard a dazzling array of religious treasures dating back to medieval times.

Beaches

The bay north of the main harbour in Skála shelters **Méloï beach**, with a well-run campsite. For swimming, the second beach north, **Agriolivádhi**, is usually less crowded. From Hóra a good road runs above the package resort of Gríkou to the isthmus of **Stavrós**, from where a thirty-minute trail leads to the excellent beach, with one seasonal taverna (summer *kaïki* from Skála). There are more good beaches in the north of the island, particularly **Livádhi Yeránou**, shaded by tamarisk groves and with a decent taverna, and **Lámbi**, with volcanic pebbles and another quality taverna.

ARRIVAL AND INFORMATION

By ferry Boats arrive at the harbour, in the middle of Skála.

Destinations Kós (1–3 daily; 2hr 30min); Pireás (4–5 weekly; 6–10hr); Rhodes (2–4 daily; 5–9hr); Syros (1–2 weekly; 4hr).

By bus The bus stop is next to the harbour; most journeys take about 10min.

Destinations Hóra (7–11 daily); Gríkou (8 daily); Kámbos (4 daily).

Tourist information The tourist office is located close to the police station opposite the harbour (summer Mon–Sat 9am–2.30pm & 6.30–9pm, Sun 10.30am–2.30pm; ☎ 22470 31666) and can assist with accommodation.

ACCOMMODATION

Siroco Cochlakas, Skála ☎ 22470 33262, ⓦ siroco.patmos .eu. Situated 5min from the port, these fully equipped self-contained, two-person apartments with kitchenette have large private balconies and beautiful sunset views. Apartment **€70**

Stefanos Camping Melóï ☎ 22470 32415 or 31821. Well-equipped family campsite, with many – albeit small-scale – facilities and a taverna nearby. Open May–Sept. Camping **€8** per person, plus **€2** per tent

EATING

Art Café Skála, behind the post office. Excellent bar-café with flickering candles, views to the harbour and the monastery, draught beer and a breezy roof garden. Great place to relax. Daily 7pm–late.

Hiliomodhi Skála. As the nautical decor suggests, this is the place for fish and seafood dishes and it won't leave you disappointed. Grilled octopus (**€8**) a speciality. Daily 5pm–1am.

Northeastern Aegean

The seven scattered islands of the northeastern Aegean form a rather arbitrary archipelago. Local tour operators do a thriving business shuttling passengers for absurdly high tariffs between the easternmost islands and the Turkish coast. Sámos is overrun with package tours but tranquil **Lésvos** (or **Mytilíni**) has a more low-key appeal.

LÉSVOS (MYTILÍNI)

Lésvos, birthplace of Sappho, the ancient world's foremost female poet, may not at first seem particularly beautiful, but the craggy volcanic landscape of pine and olive groves grows on you. Despite the inroads of tourism, this is still essentially a working island, with few large hotels outside the capital, Mytilíni, and the resorts of Skála Eressoú and Mólyvos.

Few people stay in the town of **MYTILÍNI** but do pause long enough to peek at the new **Archeological Museum**, 8 Noemvriou St (Tues–Sun 8am–3pm; €3), with its superb Roman mosaics. Sleepy **MÓLYVOS**, also known as Míthymna, on the northwestern coast, is easily the most attractive spot on Lésvos, and the place you should visit first on the island. Tiers of sturdy, red-tiled houses mount the slopes between the picturesque harbour and the Genoese castle. Wandering through the cobbled streets is a pleasure, since the town's hillside location provides plenty of stunning vistas across the sweeping bay. The main lower road, past the tourist office, heads towards the picturesque harbour, where there are some good-quality seafood tavernas. Lésvos's best beach is at **SKÁLA ERESSOÚ** in the far southwest, and attracts gay women the world over. Cheap rooms generally outnumber hotels except during the International Women's Festival in September (ⓦ womensfestival.eu) when you are advised to book well in advance. **PLOMÁRI** in the southeast, claiming to be the *ouzo* capital of Greece, is another good base, though it lacks beaches within walking distance.

ARRIVAL AND INFORMATION

By plane The airport is 8km southeast of the capital Mytilíni. Bus into town every 30min (10min; €2)
Destinations Athens (4–5 daily; 1hr); Iráklion (2–3 weekly; 1hr 15min); Rhodes (1 daily; 45min); Thessaloníki (1 daily; 50min).

By ferry Boats arrive at the quay in Mytilíni. On arrival, turn left to reach the town centre.
Destinations Ayvalik/Dikili, Turkey (daily; 1hr 30min); Pireás (1–2 daily; 8–10hr); Thessaloníki (1–2 weekly; 15hr).

By bus The bus station in Mytilíni is located at the southwestern end of the waterfront, near Platía Konstandinopóleos.

Tourist information Aristárhou 6, Mytilíni, near the quay (Mon–Fri 8am–3pm; ☎ 22510 42511/42512, ⓔ pyt_mitilinis@gnto.gr).

ACCOMMODATION

Hotel Sappho 12 Theofrastou St, Skála Eressoú ☎ 22530 53233. A hotel that attracts mostly gay women although it doesn't have a single-sex policy as such. Good café-bar,

14

free wi-fi, a/c, pet-friendly. Breakfast €7. Open April–Nov. Double **€40**

Mólivos Camping Mólyvos ☎ 22530 71169, ⓦ campinglesvos.gr. A shady campsite with minimarket, snack bar and tent rental, 800m from town. Open May–Oct. Camping **€5** per person, plus **€2** per tent

Nassos Guest House Mólyvos, up from the tourist office ☎ 69420 46279, ⓦ nassosguesthouse.com. A charming, converted Turkish house built around 1900. There are fine views of the town from the rooms and the terrace. No breakfast. Double **€30**

EATING

The Captain's Table Mólyvos. Set among the fishing boats in the picturesque harbour, with good fish as well as traditional dishes. Fish €7–8. Daily 5.30pm–midnight.

To Hani Mólyvos. Near the market, this restaurant-grill was established in 1959 and has been serving delicious meals ever since, complemented by a wonderful terrace with views over the town towards the sea. Mains €6–8. Daily 8am–midnight.

The Sporades

The **Sporades**, scattered across the northwestern Aegean, are an easy group to island-hop. The three northern islands – package-tourist haven Skiáthos, Alónissos and **Skópelos**, the pick of the trio – have good beaches, transparent waters and thick pine forests. **Skýros**, the fourth of the Sporades, is isolated from the others and less scenic, but with perhaps the most character; for a relatively uncommercialized island within a day's travel of Athens it's unbeatable.

SKÓPELOS

More rugged yet better cultivated than neighbouring Skiáthos, **Skópelos** is also very much more attractive. **SKÓPELOS TOWN** slopes down one corner of a huge, almost circular bay. There are dozens of rooms to let – take up one of the offers when you land or visit the Roomowners Association (see below) for vacancies. Within the town, spread below the oddly whitewashed ruins of a Venetian *kastro*, are an enormous number of churches – 123 reputedly, though some are small enough to be mistaken for houses.

Beaches

Buses run along the island's one asphalt road to Loutráki about seven times daily, stopping at the turn-offs to all the main beaches and villages. **Stáfylos** beach, 4km out of town, is the closest, but it's small, rocky and increasingly crowded; the overflow, much of it nudist, flees to **Valanió**, just east. Much more promising, if you're after relative isolation, is sandy **Limnonári**, a fifteen-minute walk or short *kaïki* ride from **AGNÓNDAS** (which has tavernas and rooms). The large resort of **Pánormos** has become overdeveloped, but slightly further on, **Miliá** offers a tremendous 1500m sweep of tiny pebbles beneath a bank of pines.

ARRIVAL AND DEPARTURE

By ferry Boats arrive at the quay in the middle of Skópelos Town. The island also has another small port at Loutráki.
Destinations Áyios Konstandínos (4 daily; 1hr 20min); Skiáthos (6 daily; 45min–1hr); Vólos (4–6 daily; 1hr 30min–3hr).

By bus The bus stop is next to the quay, near the taxi rank. In addition to destinations listed (all with journey times of less than 30min), buses also stop at Pánormos and Stáfylos.
Destinations Agnóndas (6–8 daily); Miliá (3–5 daily); Loutráki (4–6 daily).

ACCOMMODATION

The Roomowners Association, opposite the quay (daily 9.30am–2pm; ☎ 24240 24576), has lists of the island's accommodation.

Archontiko Skópelos Town ☎ 24240 22049. This welcoming guesthouse has traditional decor and a homely atmosphere, situated on a quiet, cobbled street just off the harbour. No a/c, wi-fi or breakfast, but very atmospheric. Double **€35**

Hotel Regina Skópelos Town ☎ 24240 22138. Close to the waterfront, these spacious en-suite rooms have large double beds and balconies. Breakfast included. Double **€55**

EATING

Alexander Skópelos Town. A delightful garden restaurant, serving traditional Greek food alongside more unusual local specials, such as pork with plums. Mains €7–12. Daily 7pm–late.

O Molos Old Harbour, Skópelos Town. A reliable taverna on the waterfront, serving typical Greek cuisine. Mains €7–8. Daily noon–midnight.

SKÝROS

Skýros remained until the 1980s a very traditional and idiosyncratic island. Some older men still wear the vaguely Cretan costume of cap, vest, baggy trousers, leggings and clogs, while the women favour yellow scarves and long embroidered skirts. Skýros also has a particularly lively *Apokriátika* or pre-Lenten **carnival**, featuring the "Goat Dance", performed by masked revellers in the village streets.

WHAT TO SEE AND DO

A **bus** connects Liniariá – a functional little port with a few tourist facilities – to **SKÝROS TOWN**, spread below a high rock rising precipitously from the coast. Traces of classical walls can still be made out among the ruins of the Venetian *kastro*; within the walls is the crumbling, tenth-century monastery of **Áyios Yeóryios**. Despite the town's peaceful afternoons, the narrow streets come alive in the evening, as the sun sets behind the hills, bathing the white buildings in a soft light. There are several hotels and plenty of **rooms** to let in private houses; you'll be met with offers as you descend from the bus. The campsite is down the hill at the fishing village of **MAGAZIÁ**, with rooms and tavernas fronting the island's best beach.

ARRIVAL AND DEPARTURE

By plane There is a small domestic airport on the northern tip of the island, 10km from the town. There are no buses; a taxi to town costs about €15.
Destinations Athens (3 weekly; 40min); Thessaloníki (3 weekly; 40min).
By ferry Boats arrive at the functional port of Linariá. Buses meet the boats and connect the port to Skýros Town.
Destinations Kými (2–4 daily; 1hr 40min).

ACCOMMODATION

Hotel Elena Skýros Town ✆ 22220 91738. Centrally located, with tiled floors, white walls and wooden furniture. Rooms are clean and comfortable. A/c and free wi-fi available, but no breakfast. Double **€35**

EATING

Adráchti Skýros Town. Tasty local dishes are served on a rooftop terrace with a panoramic view over the town. Mains around €8. Daily noon–midnight.

Nostos Café Skýros Town. On the central square above the bank, this is the perfect place for a pre-dinner drink as you watch the sunset from the terrace. Daily 6pm late.
O Pappous k'Ego Skýros Town. This popular spot opens for dinner only and serves Skyriot specialities such as goat in lemon sauce. Tables spill out onto the cobbled pavement. Mains €5–9. Daily 6pm–late.

Ionian islands

The six **Ionian islands** are geographically and culturally a mixture of Greece and Italy. Floating on the haze of the Adriatic, their green silhouettes come as a surprise to those more used to the stark outlines of the Aegean. The islands were the Homeric realm of Odysseus, and here alone of all modern Greek territory the Ottomans never held sway. After the fall of Byzantium, possession passed to the Venetians, and the islands became a keystone in that city-state's maritime empire from 1386 until its collapse in 1797 when they passed to the French, the British and finally the Greeks in 1864. Tourism has hit **Corfu** in a big way but none of the other islands has endured anything like the same scale of development. For a less sullied experience, head for **Kefalloniá**.

CORFU (KÉRKYRA)

A visit to **Corfu** is an intense experience, if sometimes a beleaguered one, for it has more package hotels and holiday villas than any other Greek island. The commercialism is apparent the moment you step ashore at the ferry dock, or cover the 2km from the airport. That said, **CORFU TOWN**, the capital, has a buzzy appeal: cafés on the Esplanade and in the arcaded Listón have a civilized air, and become lively bars when the sun sets. The rest of the island is dotted with some lovely beaches and appealing villages.

WHAT TO SEE AND DO

Corfu Town and around

In Corfu Town, the Palace of Sts Michael and George at the north end of

14

the Spianádha is worth visiting for its private **Asiatic Museum** (Tues–Sun: summer 8am–8pm; winter 8.30am–3pm; €3), **Modern Art Gallery** (Tues–Sun 9am–4pm; €4) and **Byzantine Museum** (Tues–Sun 9am–3pm; €2); sadly the **Archeological Museum** is currently closed until at least 2015. A combined ticket for all museums plus the **Old Fort** (daily: summer 8am–sunset; winter 8.30am–3pm; €4) costs €8. The island's patron saint, Spyrídhon, is entombed in a silver-covered coffin in his own church on Vouthrótou, and four times a year, to the accompaniment of much celebration and feasting, the relics are paraded through the streets. Some 5km south of town lies the picturesque convent of **Vlahérna**, which is joined to the plush mainland suburb of Kanóni by a short causeway; the tiny islet of **Pondikoníssi** in the bay is visited by frequent *kaïkia* (€3 return).

Vátos and Pélekas

Much of the island's coastline has been remorselessly developed; the tiny village of **VÁTOS**, just inland from west-coast Érmones, is the one place within easy reach of Kérkyra Town that has an easy, relaxed feel to it and reasonable rooms and tavernas. It's the best option for independent travellers, and there's a free bus service to the beach of Glyfádha. Thanks to the village's hilltop location, there are some fine views over the surrounding countryside towards the coast. Nearby **PÉLEKAS** is rather busy and also inland but it's a good alternative base.

Áyios Górdhis and around

Further south, **ÁYIOS GÓRDHIS** beach is more remote but that hasn't spared it from the crowds who come to admire the cliff-girt setting. **Áyios Yeóryios**, on the southwest coast, consists of a developed area just before its beautiful beach, which extends north alongside the peaceful Korissíon lagoon. **Kávos**, near the cape itself, rates, with its many clubs and discos, as the nightlife capital of the island; for daytime solitude and swimming, you can walk to beaches beyond the nearby hamlets of Spartérá and Dhragotiná.

ARRIVAL AND DEPARTURE

By plane The airport is 2km south of Corfu Town. Local buses #2 and #3 leave from 500m north of the terminal gates. A taxi costs €12. There are charter flights from all over Europe.

Destinations Athens (2–3 daily; 1hr).

By ferry Boats arrive at the new port, 1km west of Corfu Town.

Destinations Saranda, Albania (1 daily; 1hr); Brindisi (3–5 weekly; 4–9hr); Igoumenítsa (8–10 daily; 1hr 15min); (Venice 1–2 weekly; 24hr).

By bus The long-distance bus terminal is on Avramíou in Corfu Town.

Destinations Athens (1–3 daily; 10hr); Thessaloníki (1 daily; 7hr).

GETTING AROUND

By bus The local bus stop is at Platía Saróko in Corfu Town, where there's also a kiosk with timetable information.

ACCOMMODATION

Hotels are expensive in Corfu Town. Use the online website ⓦ holidaysincorfu.gr to book a room or a studio directly.

CORFU TOWN

Atlantis Ksenophóntos Stratigoú 48 Corfu ☏ 26610 35560, ⓦ atlantis-hotel-corfu.com. Conveniently located near the New Port. Rather colourless and functional, but offering large rooms with a/c and a good breakfast included. Double €75

★ **Dionysus Camping Village** Dhassiá, 8km north of Corfu Town ☏ 26610 91417, ⓦ dionysuscamping.gr; bus #7 (tell the bus driver to stop). Campsite with excellent facilities, pitches under olive trees and sporting activities on offer. Open April–Oct. Camping €6.50 per person, plus €4.50 per tent

AROUND THE ISLAND

Corfu Traveler's Inn Áyios Górdhis ☏ 26610 53935, ⓦ corfubackpackers.com. Beachside accommodation with plenty of activities on offer. Prices include free pickup, breakfast and dinner. Dorm €25

Pension Martini Pélekas ☏ 26610 94326, ⓦ pensionmartini.com. Friendly owners offer simple rooms which have balconies with great views; there's a lush garden too. Double €30

The Pink Palace Áyios Górdhis ☏ 26610 53103/4, ⓦ thepinkpalace.com. Raucous but fun youth-orientated holiday complex (though no upper age limit), with jacuzzis, club, sports facilities, hairdressers, money exchange and more. Prices include free pickups as well as breakfast and dinner. Dorm €21, double €50

EATING AND DRINKING

CORFU TOWN

Aleko's Beach On the jetty below the Palace of Sts Michael and George, serving typical Greek cuisine and seafood. Go later in the evening to soak up the atmosphere. Mains €7–9. May–Sept daily 11am–midnight.

Mikro Café Theotóki & Kotárdou 42. A delightful café-bar with an inviting garden, perfect for a morning coffee or an evening drink. Beers €3, cocktails €6.50. Daily 10am–midnight.

To Paradosiakon Solomoú 20. This colourful restaurant with pavement seating serves traditional dishes such as beef onion stew and chicken or veal in tomato sauce. Mains €7–9. April–Oct daily 10am–midnight.

PÉLEKAS

Jimmy's Opposite a tiny, yellow church near the crossroads of the roads to the beach and Kaiser's Throne lookout point. This friendly taverna serves excellent food all day, including vegetarian dishes and local specials. Mains €7–9. Daily noon–late.

Zanzibar Below the central square on the road to Corfu Town. Very popular bar with an extensive cocktail menu and DJs in the evenings. Beers €5, cocktails €7. Easter–Oct 7pm–late.

KEFALLONIÁ

Kefalloniá is the largest, and, at first glance, least glamorous, of the Ionian islands; the 1953 earthquake that rocked the archipelago was especially devastating here, with almost every town and village levelled and rebuilt. Since the 2001 film adaptation of Louis de Bernières' novel, *Captain Corelli's Mandolin*, the island has attracted increasing numbers of tourists.

WHAT TO SEE AND DO

There's plenty of interest: beaches to compare with the best on Corfu, good local wine and the partly forested mass of Mount Énos (1628m). The island's size, skeletal bus service and shortage of summer accommodation make renting a motorbike or car a must for extensive exploration.

Argostóli

ARGOSTÓLI, with daily ferries to Kyllíni on the mainland, is the bustling, concrete island capital. The town's **Archeological Museum** (Tues–Sun

8.30am–3pm; €3) is second only to Corfu's in the Ionian archipelago.

North of the island

Heading north, you come to the beach of **Mýrtos**, considered the best on the island, although lacking in facilities; the closest places to **stay** are nearby Dhiváráta and almost bus-less **Ássos**, a beautiful fishing port perched on a narrow isthmus linking it to a castellated headland. At the end of the line, pretty **Fiskárdho**, with its eighteenth-century houses, is the most expensive place on the island; the main reason to come would be for the daily **ferry** to Lefkádha island, and crossings to Itháki.

The east coast

Busy **SÁMI**, set against a natural backdrop of verdant, undulating hills, nestles itself into a sweeping bay. The town is the second port on the island, with boats to Itháki and Pátra. However, **AYÍA EFIMÍA**, 10km north, makes a far more attractive base. Between the two towns, 3km from Sámi, the **Melissáni cave** (summer daily 8.30am–6.30pm; winter Sat & Sun 10am–4pm; €6), a partly submerged, Capri-type "blue grotto", is well worth a stop. Southeast from Sámi are the resorts of **PÓROS**, with regular ferries to Kyllíni.

ARRIVAL AND INFORMATION

By plane Kefalloniá International airport lies 9km south of Argostóli with many flights to European destinations. There are no public buses, and taxis to town cost €12.

By ferry Ferries from Kyllíni dock at Póros and Argostóli. Ferries from Pátra dock at Sámi while departures for Zákynthos leave from Pessádha.

Destinations from Argostóli Kyllíni (1 daily; 2hr 15min).
Destinations from Póros Kyllíni (3–5 daily; 1hr 15min).
Destinations from Sami Pátra (1–2 daily; 3hr 30min).
Destinations from Pessádha Zákynthos (2 daily; 1hr 30min).

By bus The bus station in Argostóli is just past the causeway, on I. Metaxa.

Destinations Athens (3 daily; 7hr); Ayía Efimía (4 daily; 40min); Fiskárdho (2 daily; 1hr 30min); Póros (2 daily; 30min); Sámi (4 daily; 40min).

Tourist information Customs Office Pier (Mon–Fri 7am–2.30pm; ☎ 26710 22248).

ACCOMMODATION

★ **Hotel Melissani** Dihalion 23, Sámi ☎ 26740 22464,

14

14

GREECE IN THE MOVIES

It's no surprise that Greece's photogenic sea, sands and dazzling light have provided the set for numerous films. Worth seeking out before your trip are **Shirley Valentine** (1989), the story of a downtrodden housewife's discovery of Mýkonos (see p.525) and alfresco love; the romantic musical comedy **Mamma Mia** (2008), filmed on Skópelos (see p.536); the tender **Before Midnight** (2013), shot around Kardhamýli (see p.515); and the Bond film **For Your Eyes Only** (1981), set amid the spectacular cliff-top monasteries of the Metéora (see p.518).

ⓦ melissanihotel.gr. An interestingly if idiosyncratically decorated hotel. The thirteen en-suite rooms have balconies or verandas with sea views. Huge reductions (forty percent) outside July & Aug. Breakfast €7. Open May–Oct. Double €65

Karavomilos Beach 1km outside Sámi ☎ 26740 22480, ⓦ camping-karavomilos.gr. A shady campsite near the beach, 1km from town. Open May–Sept. Camping €8.50 per person, plus €6 per tent

Olga A Tritsi 82, Argostóli ☎ 26710 24981, ⓦ olgahotel.gr. Beautiful, centrally located Neoclassical hotel with large rooms (fridge and a/c) by the quayside. Good online bargains. Breakfast €5. Double €55

EATING AND DRINKING

Captain's Table I. Metaxa & 21 Maïou, Argostóli. A waterfront restaurant with a nautical theme serving everything from home-made pizza to fresh fish. Always busy, with mains priced €8–10. Daily noon–midnight.

Mermaid Restaurant Sámi. In a wonderful location on the seafront, this friendly restaurant uses local produce to create hearty dishes. Mains €7–9. May–Oct daily noon–midnight.

Tzívras Vandhóroui 1, Argostóli. Small traditional restaurant near the market with all Greek fare cooked to a high standard. Good vegetarian selection. Daytime only. Daily 11am–5pm.

Crete

CRETE is distinguished as the home of the **Minoan** civilization, Europe's earliest, which made the island the centre of a maritime trading empire as early as 2000 BC and produced artworks unsurpassed in the ancient world. The capital, **Iráklion**, is not the prettiest town on the island, although visits to its superb Archeological Museum and the Minoan palace at nearby **Knossos** are all but compulsory. There are other great Minoan sites at **Mália** on the north coast and at **Phaestos** in the south. Near the

latter are the remains of the Roman capital at **Gortys**.

Historical heritage apart, the main attractions are that inland this is still a place where traditional rural life continues, and that the island is big enough to ensure that, with a little effort, you can still get away from it all. There's also a surprisingly sophisticated club scene in the north-coast cities, and plenty of manic, beer-soaked tourist fun in some resorts in between.

IRÁKLION

The best way to approach bustling **IRÁKLION** is by sea; that way you see the city as it should be seen, with Mount Ioúktas rising behind and the Psilorítis range to the west. As you get closer, it's the fifteenth-century city walls that first stand out, still dominating and fully encircling the oldest part of town, and finally you sail in past the great Venetian fort defending the harbour entrance. The excellent **Archeological Museum**, at Xanthoudhidhou 1 (summer Mon 1–8pm, Tues–Sat 8am–8pm, Sun 8am–3pm; winter Mon 11am–5pm, Tues–Sun 8am–3pm; €4; €10 incl. Knossos), hosts a collection that includes almost every important prehistoric and Minoan find on Crete.

ARRIVAL AND DEPARTURE

By plane Nikos Kazantzakis airport is 4km east of the city, from where buses run to the centre (every 10min; €1.10). A taxi costs €14.

Destinations Athens (4–6 daily; 50min); Thessaloníki (1 daily; 1hr 15 min).

By bus For all points along the north-coast highway and Knossos use bus station A close to the ferry dock; services on inland routes to the south and west (for Phaestos, for example) leave from a terminal outside the city walls at Haniá Gate (station B).

Destinations from bus station A Hersónissos (every 15–30min; 40min); Knossos (every 10min; 20min); Mália (every 15 30min; 1hr); Réthymnon (hourly; 1hr 30min); Sitía (4 daily; 3hr 15min).

Destinations from bus station B Phaestos (8 daily; 1hr).

By ferry Boats dock at the quay at the eastern end of town. As you arrive, turn right to reach the centre.

Destinations Mýkonos (1–2 daily; 5hr); Páros & Cyclades (1–2 daily; 4hr); Santoríni, Milos and Pireás (5–7 daily; Pireás 6–10hr); Rhodes (2 weekly; 12–13hr).

INFORMATION

Tourist information Xanthoudhidhou 1, next to museum (daily: summer 9am–5pm; winter 9am–2.30pm; ☎ 2810 246298/99). There is also an information office at the airport.

ACCOMMODATION

★ **Kronos** Sof. Venizelou 2 and M. Agarathou ☎ 2810 282 240, ⊛ kronoshotel.gr. Maybe the best budget hotel, with a great view to the sea. Its common areas are leather-clad while the spacious rooms have a/c and wi-fi; the buffet breakfast (included) is quite good, too. Double €57

Lena Lahaná 10 ☎ 2810 223280, ⊛ lena-hotel.gr. Two-star hotel, in a residential street 500m from the harbour. Quiet, functional and cheerful with a/c or fans in every room plus free wi-fi. Breakfast included. Double €55

Rea Kalimeráki 1 ☎ 2810 223 638, ⊛ hotelrea.gr. A clean and comfortable *pension* in a quiet and convenient central location, with super-friendly staff. Breakfast €3. Open March–Nov. Double €35

EATING

Ippókambos Sofoklí Venizélou 3. The locals' choice for *mezédhes* and the freshest seafood. Authentic and delicious. Mains €6–9. Mon–Sat noon–midnight.

Pagopoiíon Platía Ayíou Títou. This is a chic and sleek bar-restaurant occupying a prime spot in the city; a super-cool setting in an old ice house is the place to experience a night out in Iráklion. Entry €5. Daily 11pm–late.

Perí Oréxeos Koráï 10. A good choice for innovative Cretan cuisine (such as a feta burger). There's a pleasant

terrace too, for lazy breakfasts and snacks. Mains from €8. Daily noon–1am.

KNOSSOS AND PHAESTOS

The largest of the Minoan palaces, **KNOSSOS** (daily: April–Sept 8am–8pm; winter 8.30am–3pm; €6) reached its cultural peak over 3500 years ago. Evidence of a luxurious lifestyle is plainest in the **Queen's Suite**, off the grand **Hall of the Colonnades** at the bottom of the stunningly impressive **Grand Staircase**. The site was excavated by Sir Arthur Evans from 1900 onwards. At the same time, the Italian Federico Halbherr was excavating the Minoan Palace at **PHAESTOS**, 35km west of Gortys (see below). Unlike the reconstruction work at Knossos, however, Phaestos remains totally pristine, which, to many, adds to its value and magnificence (summer Mon–Sat 8am–8pm, Sun 8am–3pm; winter daily 8am–3pm; €4).

GORTYS

About 1km west of the village of Áyii Dhéka, where the bus drops you off, **GORTYS** (summer daily 8am–8pm; winter Tues–Sun 8am–3pm; €3) is the ruined capital of the Roman province of Cyrenaica, which included not only Crete but also much of North Africa. If you walk here from Áyii Dhéka you'll get an idea of the huge scale of the place at its height in the third century AD. At the main entrance to the fenced site, north of the road, is the ruined but still impressive basilica of **Áyios Títos**, the island's first Christian church and burial place of the saint (Titus) who converted Crete and was also its first bishop. Beyond this is

14

THESEUS AND THE MINOTAUR

Legend has it that King Minos built the labyrinth at Knossos to contain the **minotaur**. This terrifying creature with a man's body and a bull's head fed on fresh maidens and young men – until Theseus, prince of Athens, arrived to slay the monster, and, with Minos's daughter Ariadne's help, successfully escaped the maze. Too bad our hero subsequently ditched Ariadne on Náxos; yet she fared well marrying the god Dionysus. On the way back, Theseus forgot to change the ship's sails from black to white – a signal to his father, Aegeus, that he'd survived and slayed the Minotaur – and caused his father's suicide from grief. Aegeus jumped from Cape Soúnio (p.510) into the sea that was subsequently named after him.

14

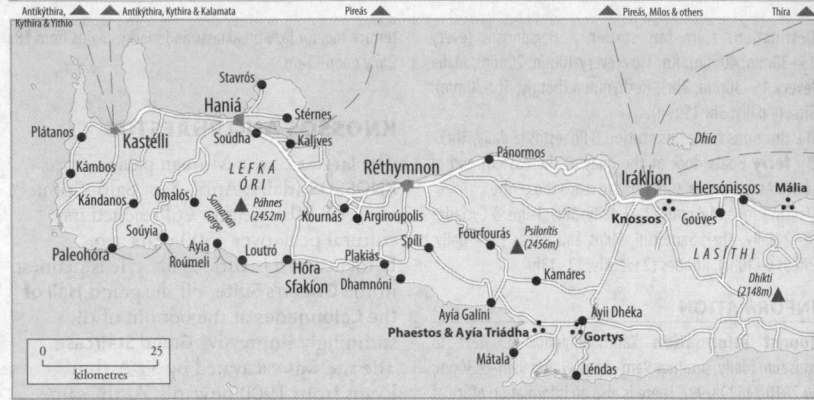

the **Odeion**, which houses the most important discovery on the site, the **Law Code** – ancient laws inscribed on stones measuring about 10m by 3m.

HERSÓNISSOS AND MÁLIA

The coast east of Iráklion was the first to be developed, and is still the domain of the package tourist. There are some good beaches, but all of them fully occupied. The heart of the development lies around **HERSÓNISSOS** and **MÁLIA**, which these days form virtually a single resort. If it's the party-holiday spirit you're after, this is the place to come. Hersónissos is perhaps slightly classier, but Mália was a bigger place to start with, which means there's a real town on the south side of the main road, with more chance of reasonably priced food and accommodation. Wherever you go, you'll have no problem finding bars, clubs and English (or Irish or even Dutch) pubs.

SITÍA

Sleepy **SITÍA**, the port and main town of the relatively unexploited eastern edge of Crete, may be about to wake up. For the moment, though, it still offers a plethora of waterside restaurants, a long sandy beach and a lazy lifestyle little affected by the thousands of visitors in peak season. There are several cheap **rooms** around Kondhiláki, a few streets back from the harbour. At the eastern end of the island, **VÁÏ BEACH** is the most famous on Crete,

thanks to its ancient grove of palm trees. In season, though, its undoubted charms, now fenced off, are diluted by crowds of day-trippers. Other beaches at nearby **Ítanos** or **Palékastro** – Crete's main windsurfing centre – are less exotic but emptier. Or head further south – at **Káto Zákros** the pebbly beach is right by another important Minoan palace.

ARRIVAL AND INFORMATION

By bus The bus station is on the southern edge of town, a short walk from the town's centre.
Destinations Áyios Nikólaos (6–7 daily; 1hr 30min); Iráklion (4–6 daily; 3hr 15min); Vaï (3 daily; 1hr).
By ferry The harbour is located 500m north of town.
Destinations Iráklion, Santoríni and on to Pireás (2 weekly; 15–16hr); Kásos, Karpathos, Halki and Rhodes (2 weekly; Rhodes 9hr).
Tourist information Tourist office on the seafront (Mon–Fri 8am–3pm).

ACCOMMODATION AND EATING

Arhontikó Kondhiláki 16. This welcoming, family-run old Neoclassical guesthouse has clean and simple rooms, and a leafy garden at the front. Fab owners. No breakfast. Double **€30**
Stéki Papandhréou 10. Preferred and much recommended by locals, this is one of the oldest restaurants in Sitía, offering locally sourced meats, freshly caught fish, but also many vegetarian options using local greens. Mains €7–8. Daily noon–midnight.

RÉTHYMNON

West of Iráklion, the old town of **RÉTHYMNON** is a labyrinthine tangle of Venetian and Turkish houses set around

CRETE

Pláka

Áyios
Nikólaos

Váï

Sitía

Zákros

Káto
Zákros

Myrtos   Ierápetra

Kásos, Kárpathos, Rhodes & Hálki

an enclosed sixteenth-century harbour
and wide sandy beach. Medieval minarets
lend an exotic air to the skyline, while
dominating everything from the west is
the superbly preserved outline of the
Venetian fortress (summer 8am–7pm;
winter 10am–5.30pm; €4). Much of the
pleasure is in wandering the streets of the
old town once the sun has set; there's an
unbroken line of tavernas, cafés and
cocktail bars right around the waterside
and into the area around the old port.
Better-value places are found around the
seventeenth-century Venetian **Rimóndi
Fountain**, an easily located landmark.
The heart of Réthymnon's sparkling
nightlife centres on the old port from
around midnight.

ARRIVAL AND INFORMATION

By bus The bus station is to the west of the city; head
around the inland side of the fortress to reach the centre.
Destinations Haniá (hourly; 1hr); Iráklion (hourly; 1hr
30min).
Tourist information Mégaro Delfíni at
Sofoklí Venizelou (Mon–Fri 8am–3pm; ☎ 28310 29148,
✉ gry_rethymnon@gnto.gr).

ACCOMMODATION

Barbara Dokimáki Rooms Dhambérgi 14 ☎ 28310
22607. Pleasant en suite rooms with kitchenettes, set
around a small courtyard or terrace area. Double **€45**
Camping Elizabeth Missiria, 4km east of Réthymnon
☎ 28310 28694, ✇ camping-elizabeth.net. This campsite
is in the hotel strip along the beach, served by frequent
buses. Also rents bungalows (€38). Open May–Oct.
Camping **€7.50** per person, plus **€5.40** per tent
Olga's Pension Soulíou 57 ☎ 28310 53206. These small
but attractive rooms are individually decorated and have
free wi-fi and a/c. The flower-filled roof garden is a gem.
Breakfast included. Double **€50**
Youth Hostel Tombázi 41 ☎ 28310 22848, ✇ yhrethymno
.com. This friendly and relaxed hostel has clean facilities,
cheap breakfasts and free wi-fi access. Dorm **€10**

EATING, DRINKING AND NIGHTLIFE

Metropolis Neárchou 15 ✇ metropolis-crete.com.
A funky bar with DJs from a local, eponymous radio
station, and a scattering of themed events, karaoke and
live music. March–Nov 10pm–late.
Opera Club Salamínos 12. The town's biggest nightclub,
with occasional live gigs from bands and Greek acts
(normally starting at 8.30pm, prices vary). June–Sept
daily 10pm–late.
Rock Club Cafe Ioulías Petichaki 6. With three bars and a
long dancefloor, this is a long-standing favourite near the
harbour playing mainstream sounds. Drinks €7. June–
Sept daily midnight–6am.
Stella's Kitchen Soulíou 55, at *Olga's Pension* (see above).
Popular with the locals, this café is good for breakfasts and
great-value daily specials, a couple of which are always
vegetarian. Mains €5–6. Daily 8am–9pm.
★ **To Pigádhi** Xanthoúdhidhou 31. This unpretentious
restaurant is great value and recommended by all locals.
There's an atmospheric garden and excellent food with
attentive service. Mains €7–12. May–Oct noon–midnight.

PLAKIÁS

Réthymnon lies at one of the narrower
parts of Crete, so it's relatively quick to

14

HIKING THE SAMARIAN GORGE

The **Samarian Gorge** – one of Europe's longest – is an easy day-trip from Haniá (May–Oct
only), as there are regular buses. If you do it, though, be warned that you will not be alone:
dozens of coachloads set off before dawn from all over Crete for the dramatic climb into the
White Mountains and the long (at least 4hr) walk down. At the bottom of the gorge is the
village of Ayía Roúmeli from where boats will take you east to Hóra Sfakíon and your bus
home, or west towards the pleasant resorts of Soúyia and Paleohóra. The mountains offer
endless other **hiking challenges**: Soúyia and Paleohóra are both good starting points, as
is Loutró, a tiny place halfway to Hóra Sfakíon, accessible only by boat.

14

cut across from here to the south coast. The obvious place to head is **PLAKIÁS**, a growing resort that's managed to retain a small-town atmosphere. There are numerous **rooms**, though it becomes very busy in August.

ACCOMMODATION

Appolonia Camping ☎ 28320 31318 or 31507, ⓦ apollonia-camping.gr. Charming family campsite with snack bar, basketball court, pool and a children's pool only 50m from the beach. Open April–Oct. Camping €7 per person, plus €4 per tent

Youth Hostel ☎ 28320 32118, ⓦ yhplakias.com. Proud to be the most southerly hostel in Europe, it is set in an olive grove and, with its relaxed atmosphere, it feels like a taverna. Book well ahead. Open Easter–Oct. Dorm €10

HANIÁ

HANIÁ is the spiritual capital of Crete; for many, it is also the island's most attractive city – especially in spring, when the snowcapped peaks of the Lefká Óri (White Mountains) seem to hover above the roofs.

WHAT TO SEE AND DO

The **port area** is the oldest and the most interesting part of town. The little hill that rises behind the landmark domes of the quayside Mosque of the Janissaries is called **Kastélli**, site of the earliest Minoan habitation and core of the Venetian and Turkish towns. Beneath the hill, on the inner harbour, the arches of sixteenth-century Venetian arsenals survive alongside remains of the outer walls. Behind the harbour lie the less picturesque but livelier sections of the old city. Around the cathedral on Halídhon are some of the more animated shopping areas, particularly leather-dominated **Odhós Skrydhlóf**.

Beaches

Haniá's **beaches** all lie to the west: the packed city beach is a ten-minute walk beyond the Maritime Museum, but for good sand you're better off taking the bus from the east side of Platía 1866 along the coast road to Kalamáki. In between you'll find emptier stretches if you're prepared to walk some of the way.

ARRIVAL AND INFORMATION

By plane The airport is located in Acrotiri, 15km from town. Buses run to town (every 2hr, 6.15am–9.50pm; €2.30). Taxis cost €30.
Destinations Athens (3–4 daily; 50min).
By bus The bus station is on Odhós Kydhonías, within easy walking distance of the centre.
Destinations Iráklion (hourly; 3hr); Omalós (for the Samarian Gorge; 4 daily when the gorge is open; 1hr); Réthymnon (hourly; 1hr).
By ferry Ferries dock about 10km away at the port of Soúdha: there are frequent city buses that will drop you by the market on the fringes of the old town. There are also ferries from nearby Kastélli to Yíthio (2 weekly; 7–8hrs).
Destinations Pireás (1 daily; 10hr).
Tourist information Mégaro Pántheon at Kriari 40 (Mon–Fri 8am–3pm; ☎ 28210 92943, ✉ gry_chania@gnto.gr).

ACCOMMODATION

Camping Chania 5km west of town ☎ 28210 31138, ⓦ camping-chania.gr. Small site, but it has a pool, a restaurant and is close to no less than four beaches. Get there by city bus (any west-heading destination) from Platía 1866. Open March–Oct. Camping €5 per person, plus €4 per tent

Earini Rooms Halídhon 27 ☎ 28210 57666, ⓦ earini.gr. A hospitable welcome and decent rooms can be found at this well-situated guesthouse opposite the archeological museum. Special discounts for students. Double €45

Mme Bassia Betólo 45–51 ☎ 28215 02750, ⓦ mme bassia.gr. A charming *pension* with a homely atmosphere in the harbour backstreets. The traditionally decorated rooms are a good size, and there's a tiny roof garden too. Breakfast €5.50. Double €30

Pension Nora Theotokopoúlou 60 ☎ 28210 72265, ⓦ pension-nora.com. Charming a/c, en-suite rooms in an old wooden Turkish house, with access to a shared kitchen. Prices vary and so does the room size and facilities. No breakfast. Double €35

EATING AND DRINKING

Ellotia Pórtou 6. It's a tad difficult to find this cosy garden taverna, but it's worth it, as it serves delicious traditional fare in a leafy setting. Grills €7–9. Daily noon–midnight.
Fáka Arholéontos 15. Not facing the port and thus considerably cheaper, this is nevertheless one of the best budget restaurants in Haniá, whose quality hasn't diminished through the years. Cretan lyra-based folk music at the weekends. Daily noon–midnight.
★ **Tamam** Zambelíou 49. A converted Turkish bathhouse with an adventurous local menu. Especially popular with vegetarians and wine-lovers. Mains €8–10. Daily noon–1am.

SZECHENYI BATHS, BUDAPEST

Hungary

HIGHLIGHTS

❶ **Castle hill, Budapest** The heart of historic Buda. **See p.551**

❷ **Thermal Baths, Budapest** Wallow in the city's historic baths. **See p.554**

❸ **Siófok** A must if you're a party animal. See **p.559**

❹ **Badacsony** Enjoy wines and walks in this gorgeous region. **See p.561**

❺ **Pécs** Explore this compact town's UNESCO treasures. **See p.562**

❻ **Valley of the Beautiful Woman, Eger** Taste local wines in the valley's cellars. See **p.564**

HIGHLIGHTS ARE MARKED ON THE MAP ON P.547

ROUGH COSTS

Daily budget Basic €60, occasional treat €70

Drink Beer (large) €1–1.50

Food Goulash €2–3

Hostel/pension €15–40

Travel Train: Budapest–Eger €8.50

FACT FILE

Population 10 million

Language Hungarian

Currency Forint (Ft)

Capital Budapest

International phone code ☏36

Time zone GMT +1hr

Introduction

Bordered by countries as diverse as Austria, Serbia and Ukraine, Hungary is a crossroads at the centre of the continent – what was once known as Mitteleuropa – and it fuses old Europe and new in its mix of Habsburg grandeur and Communist-era grittiness. There is a Central European solidity to its food, buildings and culture, but the more exotic, and undeniably romantic, founding myth of the nomadic, warrior Magyars from the Central Asian steppe is also key to Hungarians' fiery national pride.

15

Budapest, the capital, is a city of imposing scale and wide Danube vistas, split by the river into historic Buda and buzzy Pest, and offering both the old (imperial-era boulevards, Art Nouveau coffeehouses, bubbling Turkish baths) and the new (quirky warehouse bars and summer riverboat clubs). A few hours' travel beyond Budapest is enough to access Hungary's other key charms, from Serb-influenced **Szentendre**, a short way north along the Danube bend, to the lush wine-growing **Badacsony** region on the shores of **Lake Balaton** to the southwest. Balaton, the "nation's playground", also plays host to crowded summer party resorts such as **Siófok**, or gentler **Keszthely**. Hungary's three most culture-rich towns beyond Budapest are scattered across the country but not to be missed: **Sopron**, close by the border with Austria; **Pécs**, on the far southern tip, ringed by alpine hills; and **Eger**, just northeast of Budapest, a mellow, historic city famous for its Bull's Blood wine. Across southeast Hungary stretches the enormous Great Plain, covering half the country and home to some beautiful national parks and the cities of **Szeged**, **Kecskemét** and **Debrecen**.

CHRONOLOGY

9 BC Area around the Danube is conquered by the Romans.
434–453 AD Attila the Hun's feared empire is centred in modern-day Hungary.
568 The Avars, nomads from Inner/Central Asia, arrive.
Around 896 The Magyars in Hungary begin the *honfoglalás* or land-taking (conquest of the region).
1000 Kingdom of Hungary established by King Stephen.
1242 The Mongols attack Hungary.

1526 The Hungarian army is defeated by the Ottomans in the Battle of Mohács and the country is split into three regions, under different forms of government.
1552 The Hungarians hold back the Turks at the Eger fortress – a major date in national consciousness.
1699 The Turks are defeated and expelled from Hungary by the Austrian Habsburgs.
1867 In order to quell separatist calls, Austria accepts greater Hungarian autonomy – in what is known as the Compromise – and the dual monarchy of Austria-Hungary is formed.
1896 Huge celebrations across Hungary for the millennial anniversary – 1000 years since the arrival of the Magyars.
1918 After World War I, Austria-Hungary is split into two countries.
1920 Treaty of Trianon in which Hungary loses two-thirds of its prewar territory.
1919–41 The right-wing dictatorship of Admiral Horthy.
1938 Hungarian journalist László Bíró invents the ballpoint pen.
1944 Germany occupies Hungary and installs the Arrow Cross party (Hungarian fascists) in government.
1944–45 Hungary's large prewar Jewish community is decimated as Jews are deported and ghettoized under Nazi occupation.
1945 Soviets invade Hungary.
1947 Soviets consolidate their postwar power in Hungary.
1956 National uprising against Soviet occupation is brutally repressed.
1989–91 Collapse of Communism in the Soviet Union and the eastern bloc.
1990 Hungary's first free elections held.
2004 Hungary joins the EU.
2010 Pécs becomes European City of Culture.

ARRIVAL AND DEPARTURE

Flights to Budapest arrive at Ferenc Liszt (formerly Ferihegy) airport, 20km from the centre; bus and metro connect into

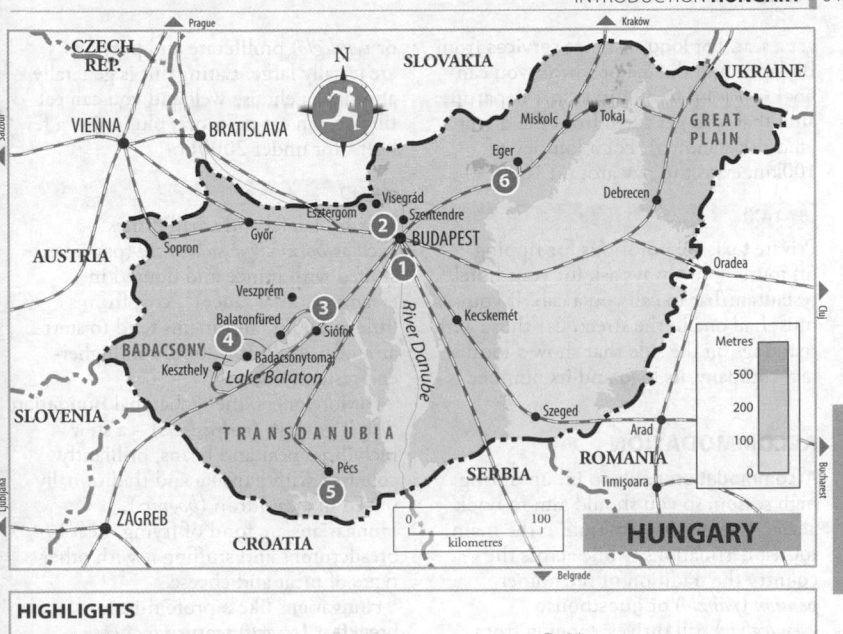

HIGHLIGHTS

❶ Castle hill, Budapest
❷ Thermal Baths, Budapest
❸ Siófok
❹ Badacsony
❺ Pécs
❻ Valley of the Beautiful Woman, Eger

Budapest, but most convenient is the airport bus that will take you straight to your accommodation. Wizzair also flies directly from London to Debrecen.

Most international **trains** arrive at Keleti station in Budapest, although Nyugati and Déli also handle some international arrivals. Global or One Country InterRail passes are valid on all trains. International **buses** are generally operated by Eurolines, or Volánbusz, its Hungarian associate. The international terminal is at Népliget (blue metro) in Budapest. Mahart operates **hydrofoils** from Vienna which dock at the International Landing Stage on Belgrád rakpart in Budapest.

GETTING AROUND

Public transport in Hungary is cheap, clean and fairly reliable. The only problem can be getting information, as English is by no means uniformly spoken. If you are in Hungary for long or if you travel there frequently, you may want to consider buying a **Hungary Card** (ⓦhungarycard.hu), which offers savings in transport, accommodation and museums all over the country, and is valid for one year.

BY TRAIN

Intercity **trains** (marked "IC" on the timetable) are the fastest way of getting to the major towns. Seat reservations, a separate numbered piece of card available at any MÁV office (ⓦmav-start.hu), are compulsory for services marked ❻ on timetables, and cost around 480Ft extra. You can buy **tickets** (*jegy*) for domestic services at the station (*pályaudvar* or *vasútállomás*) on the day of departure, but it's best to buy tickets for international trains (*nemzetközi gyorsvonat*) at least 36 hours in advance. When buying your ticket, specify whether you want a one-way ticket (*egy útra*), or a return (*retur* or *oda-vissza*).

BY BUS

Volánbusz (ⓦvolanbusz.hu) runs the bulk of Hungary's **buses**, which are often the quickest way to travel between the smaller towns. Arrive early to confirm times and get a seat. For **long-distance services** from Budapest and the major towns, you can book a seat up to 30min before departure; after that, you get them from the driver (and risk standing). For a journey of 100km, expect to pay around 1600Ft.

BY TAXI

Private **taxis** are notorious for ripping off tourists, so always ask for your hotel/restaurant/bar to call you a cab. If you must hail one in the street, use those with markings on the side that show a local taxi company, its logo and its number.

ACCOMMODATION

Accommodation tends to fill up during high season, so you should aim to book ahead. **Hostels** are common in the main tourist destinations, while across the country the tradition of the homely *pension* (*panzió*) or **guesthouse** (*vendégház*) still thrives, ranging from rooms in private homes to more professional outfits. Here, expect to pay from 8000Ft for a double. If you're really strapped for cash, try for **university dorms** – rooms are rented out in July and August, and often available at weekends year-round; local tourist offices can assist with bookings. **Private rooms** (*vendégszoba*) and apartments are also affordable and can be arranged through Ibusz, the nationwide agency (🔴ibusz .hu), or local tourist offices. Doubles range from 4000Ft in provincial towns to around 6000Ft in Budapest. Outside Budapest and Lake Balaton (where prices in the summer can double), a three-star **hotel** (*szálló* or *szálloda*) will charge from around 12,000Ft for a double; solo travellers may have to pay this too, since singles are not always on offer.

Campsites range from deluxe to third class. In high season, expect to pay around 2000Ft for two people with a tent, and up to twice as much around Lake Balaton.

FOOD AND DRINK

You are unlikely to go hungry in Hungary. Cafés and restaurants (*étterem* or *vendéglő*) proliferate and portions are usually large. Eating out is generally affordable: choose well and you can eat till you can eat no more, plus enjoy a few beers, for under 2000Ft.

FOOD

Kebabs, falafel and small dishes – such as *hortobágyi palacsinta* (pancakes stuffed with mince and doused in creamy paprika sauce) – cost from as little as 600Ft, and mains tend to start around 1200Ft (or 2000Ft in higher-end restaurants).

For foreigners, the archetypal **Hungarian dish** is goulash (*gulyásleves*) – a stew including meat and beans, brilliantly coloured with paprika and traditionally served in a cauldron (*bogrács*). Hungarians are fond of frying meat in breadcrumbs and stuffing it with other types of meat and cheese.

Hungarians like a protein-heavy **breakfast** (*reggeli*) featuring cheese, eggs and salami, plus bread and jam. **Coffeehouses** (*kávéház*) are increasingly trendy and you'll find many serving breakfast and coffee with milk (*tejeskávé*) or whipped cream (*tejszínhabbal*). For most Hungarians coffee means one thing: espresso (*eszpresszó*).

Traditionally, **lunch** is the main meal of the day, and lunch set menus (*napi menü*) can be a highly affordable way of eating out. You won't want for **snacks**, particularly sweet ones: the old-fashioned *cukrászda* or patisserie with tempting displays of elaborate cakes is a staple of every town centre. Marzipan is a national favourite, as is ice cream (*fagylalt*). **Pancakes** (*palacsinta*, from around 350Ft) are very popular, as are strudels (*rétes*; about 600Ft).

DRINK

Hungary's mild climate and diversity of soils are ideal for **wine** (*bor*), which is cheap whether you drink it by the bottle (*üveg*) or the glass (*pohár*). Hungary's best-known wine-producing region is the Tokaj-Hegyalja, known predominantly for dessert wine. *Bikavér*, produced around Eger and meaning "Bull's Blood", is a robust red. Good whites can be found around the Badacsony in the Balaton region and near Sopron.

Wine bars (*borozó*) are common, but the best way to taste is at source at the wine cellars (*borpince*) around Pécs and Eger. Harder drinkers favour **brandy** (*pálinka*), with popular flavours being distilled from apricots (*barack*), plums (*szilva*) or pears (*körte*). Local **beers** (*sör*) to try are Soproni Ászok and Pécsi Szalon.

CULTURE AND ETIQUETTE

Hungarians are generally very ready to help if you need directions or assistance. The biggest barrier can be language – in Budapest you can survive on English but elsewhere you will likely need to muster a little German, as well as the polite basics in Hungarian. Never say "thank you" when paying; this is understood in Hungary as "keep the change". If you want to leave a tip, ten percent will do, and, in restaurants, is expected.

Hungary's dominant **religion** is Catholicism but there are many Protestant churches. Respectful clothing is expected in places of worship. **Women travellers** should not expect any particular hassle in Hungary.

SPORTS AND OUTDOOR ACTIVITIES

Hungary is a predominantly rural country, one-fifth covered in forests. The Great Plain, especially the area around Kecskemét and the Kiskunság National Park, offers some of the best **horse riding** in Europe as well as fantastic horse shows during the summer. It's cheapest to select an independent horseriding operator .

Cycling is very well provided for: Tourinform (see box below)can provide cycling maps with recommended routes, and bikes can be rented in most towns at reasonable prices. Particularly scenic cycling routes can be found around Lake Balaton. There are limited **hiking** opportunities in Hungary; however, walks in the Badacsony region offer stunning views over Lake Balaton.

HUNGARY ONLINE

ⓦ **tourinform.hu** National tourist office.
ⓦ **ibusz.hu** Handy portal for viewing and booking cheap private rooms all across Hungary.
ⓦ **budapestinfo.hu** Comprehensive site with up-to-the-minute listings.
ⓦ **bkv.hu** Timetables and info for all public transport in Budapest.
ⓦ **elvira.hu** Train timetables for Hungary.
ⓦ **volan.eu** Bus timetables for the whole country.
ⓦ **jegymester.hu** Buy tickets for events and exhibitions online.

15

COMMUNICATIONS

Post offices (*posta*) are usually open Monday to Friday 9am to 5pm, but you can find some in the big shopping centres that are open during the weekend as well. There are few **public phones** left: they use cards that can be bought from post offices and newsstands. To make national calls, dial ☏06, wait for the buzzing tone, then dial the area code and number. To make an international call, dial ☏00, wait for the buzzing tone, then dial the country code and number. **Internet cafés** are on the wane (cost is usually 200–400Ft/hr), because all hotels, hostels (certainly those covered), as well as many cafés and bars, offer free wi fi.

EMERGENCIES

Tourists are treated with respect by the **police** (*rendőrség*) unless they're suspected of smuggling drugs or driving under the influence of alcohol. Most police have some German, but rarely any other foreign language. Always carry a photocopy of your passport. **Pharmacies** are identifiable by their green cross signs. Opening hours are generally Monday to Friday 9am to 6pm, Saturday 9am to noon; signs in the window give the location of all-night pharmacies (*ügyeletes gyógyszertár*). Those in the big shopping centres are open every day. Tourist offices can direct you to local medical centres or doctors' surgeries (*orvosi rendelő*); these will probably be in private (*magán*) practice, so be sure to carry health

15

insurance. EU citizens have reciprocal arrangements for emergency treatment, but only at state hospitals.

MONEY AND BANKS

Currency is the **forint** (Ft or HUF), which comes in notes of 500Ft, 1000Ft, 2000Ft, 5000Ft, 10,000Ft and 20,000Ft, and in coins of 5Ft, 10Ft, 20Ft, 50Ft, 100Ft and 200Ft. At the time of writing, €1=265Ft, US$1=185Ft, and £1=300Ft. Standard **banking hours** are Monday to Friday 8am to 5pm, Saturday 8am to noon. You can find some open on Sundays in the big shopping centres.

HUNGARIAN

	HUNGARIAN	PRONUNCIATION
Yes	*Igen*	I-gen
No	*Nem*	Nem
Please	*Kérem*	Kay-rem
Thank you	*Köszönöm*	Kur-sur-nurm
Hello/Good day	*Jó napot*	Yo nopot
Goodbye	*Viszontlátásra*	Vee-sont-lar-tarsh-rar
Excuse me	*Bocsánat*	Botch-ah-not
Good	*Jó*	Yo
Bad	*Rossz*	Ross
Today	*Ma*	Ma
Yesterday	*Tegnap*	Teg-nop
Tomorrow	*Holnap*	Hall-nop
How much is…?	*Mennyibe kerül ?*	Men-yi-beh keh-rool…?
What time is it?	*Hány óra van?*	Hine-ora von?
I don't understand	*Nem értem*	Nem air-tem
Do you speak English?	*Beszél Angolul?*	Beh-sail ong-olool?
Where is/are?	*Hol van/vannak?*	Hawl-von/von-nok?
Entrance	*bejárat*	beyah-rot
Exit	*kijárat*	kiyah-rot
Women's toilet	*női*	nuy
Men's toilet	*férfi mosdó*	fayr-fi maws-daw
Toilet	*WC*	vait-say
Hotel	*szálloda*	sahlaw-da
Railway station	*vasútállomás*	voh-sootal-law-mass
Bus/train stop	*megálló*	meh-gall-oh
Plane	*repülőgép*	repoo-lur-gepp
Near	*közel*	kur-zel
Far	*távol*	tav-oll
Single room	*egyágyas szoba*	eggy-ah-yas saw-ba
Double room	*kétágyas szoba*	kay-ta-yas soba
Cheap	*Olcsó*	Ol-cho
Expensive	*Drága*	Drah-ga
Open	*Nyitva*	Nyeet-va
Closed	*Zárva*	Zah-rva
One	*Egy*	Eggy.
Two	*Kettö*	Ket-tur
Three	*Három*	Hah-rom
Four	*Négy*	Naidge
Five	*Öt*	Urt
Six	*Hat*	Hot
Seven	*Hét*	Hait
Eight	*Nyolc*	Nyolts
Nine	*Kilenc*	Kee-lents
Ten	*Tíz*	Teez

EMERGENCY NUMBERS

Police ☎ 107 (24hr hotline ☎ 01 438 8080); Ambulance ☎ 104; Fire ☎ 105.

ATMs are widespread, and you can use a **credit/debit card** to pay in many hotels, restaurants and shops.

OPENING HOURS AND HOLIDAYS

Shops are generally open Monday to Friday 10am to 6pm, Saturday 10am to 1pm, and closed on Sundays and public holidays including January 1, March 15, Easter Monday, May 1, Whit Monday, August 20, October 23, November 1, December 25 and 26. Shopping centres operate later hours and are generally open every day, and Tesco – which in Hungary is a fully fledged department store – is often open 24/7.

Budapest and around

Over two million people – one-fifth of Hungary's population – live in **BUDAPEST**, and it is the political, cultural and commercial heart of the country. After the 1867 Compromise, which gave the Hungarian monarchy equal status with Austria under the final half-century of the Habsburg Empire and ushered in a high age of Hungarian nationalism, the city was rapidly developed to become a standing celebration of Hungarian culture and power. The sheer scale of its vast iconic buildings, from the castle to the Parliament to the Gellert Baths, testifies to Hungary's central role in European history.

Pest is located on the eastern bank of the Danube and **Buda** on the hilly west bank. Since the unification of these two distinct cities in 1873, the **Danube** (Duna) is less a dividing line, more the heart of the capital itself, providing its most splendid vistas, from both banks. Each of Budapest's 23 districts (*kerületek*) is designated on maps

and at the beginning of addresses by a Roman numeral; "V" is Belváros (inner city), on the Pest side; "I" is the Castle district in Buda.

Castle Hill (Várhegy) is the crowning feature of the **Buda** side; a plateau 1.6km long, it rises steeply from the Danube bank, bearing the imposing Buda Palace, a web of cobbled streets and the Mátyás Church, symbolic of Hungarian nationalism. **Pest** is thick with hip cafés and bars, as well as being home to the historic Belváros (central old town) and the intimate Jewish district.

Buda: Castle Hill

Castle Hill stands on the western bank of the **Chain Bridge** (Széchenyi lánchíd), opened in 1849, and – amazingly – the first permanent bridge between Buda and Pest. From Clark Ádám tér on the Buda side, you can reach Castle Hill on the dinky nineteenth-century funicular or **Sikló** (daily 7.30am–10pm; 1000Ft) or take bus #16/16A from Széll Kálmán tér metro station direction Disz tér.

Mátyás Church and Fishermen's Bastion

On **Szentháromság tér**, the busy square at the heart of Buda, stands the bright-roofed **Mátyás Church** (Mon–Sat 9am–5pm, Sun 1–5pm; 1000Ft). Inside, the church is fabulously exuberant, with the original thirteenth-century structure used as the base for a late nineteenth-century redesign in a Romantic Nationalist style. The splendid gold leaf and nationalist motifs clearly reclaimed the church as Hungarian – it had been a mosque for a time under Ottoman rule. A statue of **King Stephen** (Szent Istvan) on horseback stands outside – he is revered as the founder of the Hungarian state and the one responsible for converting Hungarians to Christianity.

Behind the church is the neo-Romanesque **Fishermen's Bastion** or Halászbástya, constructed in 1902 on the spot supposedly defended in the past by the guild of fishermen against would-be invaders. Today it's an excellent place for

15

15

looking out across the river to the splendid Parliament building rising up on the east bank.

Buda Palace

Topping the crest of Castle Hill, close by the point where the funicular railway emerges, stands **Buda Palace**. The fortifications and interiors have been endlessly remodelled, with the palace's destruction in World War II only the latest in a long line of onslaughts since the thirteenth century. The **National Gallery** (Tues–Sun 10am–6pm, last ticket 5.15pm; 1200Ft; ☎01 201 908, ⓦwww.mng.hu), which occupies the central wings B, C and D of the palace compound, contains Hungarian art from the Middle Ages onwards, including heavily symbolic nineteenth-century representations of idealized national myths.

On the other side, facing the Palace's Lion Courtyard, the **Budapest History Museum** in Wing E (Tues–Sun: March–Oct 10am–6pm; Nov–Feb 10am–4pm; 1500Ft; ☎01 487 8800, ⓦbtm.hu) gives some further historical context with a gathering of artefacts from Budapest's dark ages and medieval past, but is rather old-fashioned, and arguably underwhelming for the price.

Gellért Hill

Close by the Szabadság híd (Freedom bridge) on the Buda side is **Gellért Hill** (Gellérthegy), home to the best known of the city's baths, Gellért Baths (see box, p.554) and topped by the **Liberation Monument**, constructed in 1947 to commemorate Hungary's liberation from Nazi rule. Depicting a woman holding aloft the palm of victory, it is one of the few Soviet monuments to survive the fall of the Iron Curtain *in situ* (most have been destroyed or moved out of town to the Statue Park). Below, the **Citadella**, a mock-medieval fortress built by the Habsburgs to cow the population after the 1848–49 revolution, hugs the west bank of the Danube.

Statue Park

The **Statue Park** (Szoborpark; daily 10am–sunset; 1500Ft; ☎01 424 7500,

ⓦmementopark.hu), on the Buda side of the river 15km south of town, houses statues of Marx, Engels, Lenin and friends, as well as heroic scenes from Communist legend, and is a lively glimpse into the Communist past of eastern Europe for the uninitiated. Bus #150 departs from Kosztolányi tér every 20/30 min; get off at the Szoborpark stop. The easiest option, but far from cheap, is to take the private tour bus from Deák tér (daily 11am & 3pm; 4900Ft return, includes entrance fee).

Pest: around Vörösmarty tér

Central **Vörösmarty tér** is flooded with crowded café terraces; it's worth stopping to savour the sweet delights on offer at the **Gerbeaud** patisserie (see box, p.557), a favourite *belle époque* high-society haunt. By *Gerbeaud*'s terrace is the entrance to the Underground Railway (Földatti Vasút), the first metro line on the continent, and the second in the world after London's, when it opened in 1896. It is now a UNESCO World Heritage Site.

Váci utca, a mix of chic shops and tourist tat stalls, runs south from **Vörösmarty tér**. Past the Pesti Theatre, where the twelve-year-old Franz (Ferenc) Liszt made his concert debut, Váci utca continues south to the **Central Market Hall** (Mon 6am–5pm, Tues–Fri 6am–6pm, Sat 6am–3pm), a grand high-roofed hall whose stalls are laden with paprika, *pálinka*, local wines and enough sausages and hams to satisfy the most voracious meat-eater.

National Museum

At Muzeumkörút 14–16 (the road named after it) and easily accessed by ⓜKálvin tér, is the grandiose Neoclassical **National Museum** (Tues–Sun 10am–6pm; 1100Ft; ☎01 338 2122, ⓦhnm.hu), which gives a comprehensive overview of Hungarian history from the Magyar tribes' arrival to the collapse of Communism.

The Great Synagogue and Jewish quarter

On the corner of Wesselényi and Dohány utca stands the **Great Synagogue** or Dohány Street synagogue (March

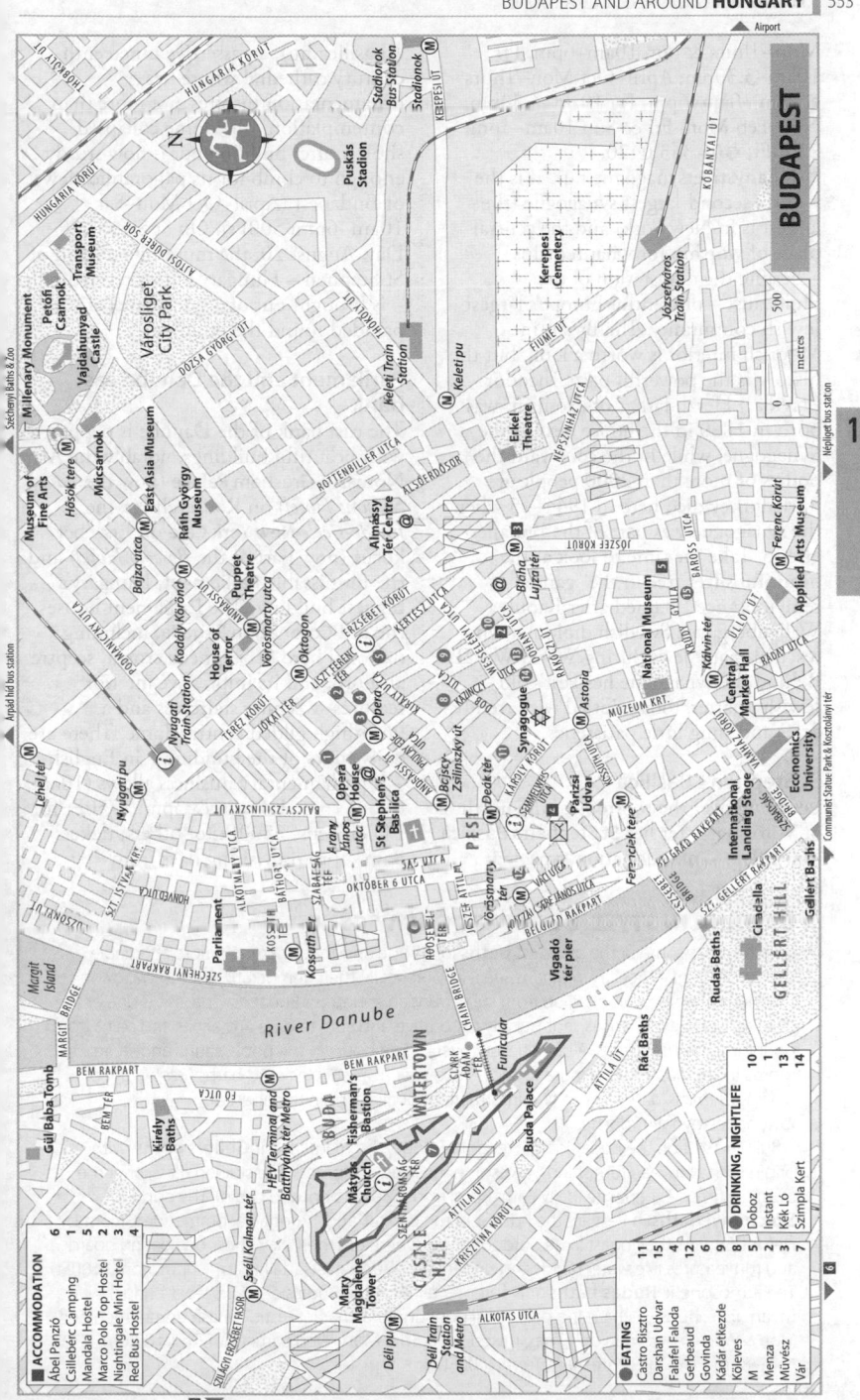

BUDAPEST

ACCOMMODATION
Abel Panzió	6
Csillebérc Camping	1
Mandala Hostel	5
Marco Polo Top Hostel	2
Nightingale Mini Hotel	3
Red Bus Hostel	4

EATING
Castro Bisztro	11
Darshan Udvar	15
Falafel Faloda	4
Gerbeaud	12
Govinda	6
Kádár étkezde	9
Köleves	8
M	5
Menza	2
Művész	3
Vár	7

DRINKING, NIGHTLIFE
Doboz	10
Instant	1
Kék Ló	13
Szimpla Kert	14

15

6

15

Mon–Thurs & Sun 10am–6pm, Fri 10am–3.30pm; April–Oct Mon–Thurs & Sun 10am–6pm, Fri 10am–4.30pm; Nov–Feb Mon–Fri & Sun 10am–4pm; 2250Ft; ☎01 343 0420, ⓦdohanystreetsynagogue.hu). It is the world's second-largest synagogue (the largest is in New York) and the central place of worship for what remains – despite the devastation of the Holocaust – of Central Europe's largest Jewish community. The Byzantine-Moorish interior is worth a look, but the history is the powerful part: Theodor (Tividar) Herzl, father of Zionism, was born in 1860 in the house next to the Synagogue, while in the courtyard the bodies of more than 2000 people are buried; they died here in 1944–45 when the synagogue was part of the Budapest ghetto. Take the time to look at the beautiful silver tree in the "garden of remembrance", named after Raoul Wallenberg, the Swedish diplomat who rescued many Jews during World War II. Behind the synagogue lies Pest's old Jewish quarter, today dotted with trendy cafés and snug little patisseries.

St Stephen's Basilica

Looming over the rooftops to the north of Vörösmarty tér lies **St Stephen's Basilica** (daily 9am–7pm; donation expected; ⓦbasilica.hu), an assertive nineteenth-century cathedral whose heavy ornamentation inspires awe more than contemplation. The dome collapsed shortly after building but is now sturdy enough to climb for its panoramic views of Budapest (April–Oct Mon–Sat 10am–6pm; 500Ft). On St Stephen's Day, August 20, the mummified hand of St Stephen – Hungary's most revered relic – is brought out of a side-chapel and paraded round the building.

Parliament and the Danube east bank

The east bank of the Danube is peppered with beautiful buildings, notably the Art Nouveau **Gresham Palace** (now the *Four Seasons Hotel*) on Roosevelt tér, the *fin-de-siècle* **New York Cafe** on Erszébet körút (now part of the *Boscolo Hotel*) and the unmissable **Parliament**, Hungary's biggest building. The Parliament houses the old **Coronation Regalia**, including national hero St Stephen's crown, sceptre and orb, and its impressive interior features sweeping staircases and a 96m-high gilded central dome. There are daily **tours** of the building – in English – if parliamentary business allows (10am, noon, 1pm, 1.45pm & 3pm; 1750Ft for EU citizens, 3500Ft for others; tickets 8am–4pm on visiting days from

---

BATHING IN STYLE: BUDAPEST'S SPA SCENE

Budapest has some of the grandest **baths** in Europe and they are much more affordable than you might expect: Hungarians see it as practically their democratic right to wallow in the thermal waters bubbling up from subterranean springs. A Budapest spa visit is one of the city's must-do experiences, fantastically restorative and sure to ease any aches and pains from pounding the city streets. A basic ticket covers three hours in the pools, sauna and steam rooms (*gözfürdő*). You pay more to access extra services such as mud baths (*iszapfürdő*) or massages (*masszázs*). You can find information for all baths in Budapest at ⓦbudapestgyogyfurdoi.hu.

Built in 1913 on the Buda side of Freedom Bridge, the magnificent **Gellért baths**, with original Art Nouveau furnishings, awesome mosaics, sculptures and stained glass, offer the most exclusive experience (daily 6am–8pm; from 5300Ft pool and cabin). The popular **Széchenyi Baths** in Pest are the hottest in the capital, and strongly recommended. Right by Heroes' Square, they boast large outdoor pools where old men play chess on floating boards, and fun features like water rapids and underwater bubble jets (daily 6am–10pm; from 4600Ft). The atmospheric **Rudas baths** at Döbrentei tér 9 on the Buda side of Erszébet bridge, meanwhile, house a charming octagonal pool under a characteristic Turkish dome (men only Mon & Wed–Fri, women only Tues, mixed Sat & Sun; Mon–Wed 6am–6pm, Thurs & Sun 6am–8pm, Fri & Sat 10pm–4am; from 3000Ft).

Parliament's Gate X or in advance from ⓦjegymester.hu/parlament).

Andrássy út

To the east of St Stephen's Basilica, **Andrássy út** runs dead straight for 2.5km, a wide avenue lined with grand if sometimes tumbledown buildings. Look out for the magnificent Opera House at no. 22. At no. 60, out east towards Hosök tere, is the **House of Terror** (Tues–Sun 10am–6pm; 2000Ft; ☎01 374 2600, ⓦterrorhaza.hu). Once the headquarters of the fascist Arrow Cross and later of the Communist secret police (the ÁVO), the House of Terror is now a hard-hitting museum to the "dual terror" of Fascism and Communism. Original footage, photographs and interviews with survivors are powerfully used to tell the story of the twin tyrannies that Hungary suffered in the twentieth century. Not to be missed.

Hosök tere – Heroes' Square

The bombastic **Hosök tere** (Heroes' Square) was created to mark the 1000th anniversary of the Magyar conquest in 1896, and its triumphant conquerors and rearing horses recall a time when Hungarian nationalism was at full throttle. Its centrepiece is the **Millenary Monument**, portraying the Magyar leader Prince Árpád, and the surrounding semicircle of greats of Hungarian history includes King Stephen and Lajos Kossuth. The latter headed Hungary's short-lived independent government after the 1848 revolution. Also on **Heroes' Square** is the **Museum of Fine Arts** at Szent György tér 2 (Tues–Sun 10am–6pm, last entry 5pm; 1800Ft; ☎01 469 7289, ⓦszepmuveszeti.hu), with a good collection of paintings by big names including Brueghel, Rembrandt and El Greco.

Behind the museum lies **Budapest Zoo** at Állatkerti körút 12 (daily 9am–sunset; 2500Ft; ☎01 273 4900, ⓦzoobudapest .com), which may not top the city's attractions for grown-ups but does feature some striking architecture; let's hope its animal inhabitants appreciate it. Opposite the zoo are the yellow neo-Baroque **Széchenyi baths** (see box opposite).

The Városliget and Vajdahunyad Castle

The **Városliget** (City Park), which starts just behind the Hosök tere, holds the **Vajdahunyad Castle**, a somewhat kitsch imitation Transylvanian castle which incorporates no fewer than 21 architectural styles from across Hungary's regions and was built in 1896 as a celebration of Hungarian art and design. In the courtyard is a statue of the monk Anonymus – a celebrated twelfth-century chronicler of Hungarian history. An artificial lake at the foot of the castle is filled with water for rowing and pedaloes in summer, and ice-skating in winter.

15

ARRIVAL AND DEPARTURE

BY PLANE

From Ferenc Liszt (formerly Ferihegy) airport, 16km from the centre of Budapest, an airport shuttle minibus (☎01 296 8555, ⓦairportshuttle.hu) will deliver you to any address you ask for (3200Ft one-way, 5550Ft return to the city centre; tickets from their office in the terminal building). The journey is cheaper but by no means quick or convenient by public transport: take airport bus #200E (every 15min, 5.05am–11.45pm) to Kobánya-Kispest metro station, and from there it's ten metro stops to the centre (Deák tér station). You need two tickets for each leg of the journey (350Ft each if you buy them from the newsagents at the airport terminal). Use only the official Fő taxis at the airport; they have fixed prices depending on which sector of the city you are travelling to (5900–6500Ft to the centre).

BY TRAIN

There are three main train stations, all of which are directly connected by metro with Deák tér metro station. Keleti (Eastern; ☎01 313 6835) handles most international trains; Nyugati (Western; ☎01 349 0115) receives domestic trains mostly from the Danube Bend; and Déli (Southern; ☎01 355 8657) has domestic services from Lake Balaton. For general train information see ⓦelvira .hu; you can book tickets in advance from abroad on ☎01 371 9449.

Destinations from Keleti Bratislava (8 daily; 2hr); Bucharest (1 daily; 14hr 30min); Eger (8 daily; 2hr); Kraków (1 daily; 10hr 30min); Pécs (hourly; 3hr); Prague (9 daily; 7hr); Sopron (10 daily; 2hr 30min–3hr 20min); Vienna (9 daily; 3hr); Zagreb (1 daily; 6hr 20min).

Destinations from Nyugati Kecskemét (hourly; 1hr 20min); Szeged (hourly; 2hr 20min).

Destinations from Déli Keszthely (7 daily; 3hr 11min); Siófok (12 daily; 1hr 30min–2hr 20min).

15

BY BUS

The central bus station is at Népliget (blue metro) while Stadionok bus station (red metro) serves areas east of the Danube.

Destinations from Népliget Badacsony (2 daily; 3hr); Bratislava (2 daily; 2hr 50min); Eger (1–2 hourly; 1hr 50min–2hr 10min); Kecskemét (hourly; 1hr 15min–1hr 45min); Keszthely (6 daily; 2hr 30min); Kraków (2 weekly; 7hr); Pécs (8 daily; 3hr); Prague (1 daily; 7hr 15min); Sopron (8 daily; 3hr); Szeged (6 daily; 3hr); Vienna (5 daily; 2hr 55min).

BY BOAT

Regular passenger cruises on the Danube are operated by Mahart (May–Sept; ☎01 484 4013, ⊛mahart.info), leaving from Vigadó tér pier. International hydrofoils dock at Belgrád rakpart.

Destinations from Vigadó tér pier Szentendre Belgrád rakpart (April Sat & Sun 10am; May–Sept daily 10am; 1hr 30min); Vienna (Mon & Wed 9am; 6hr 30min).

INFORMATION AND TOURS

Tourist information There are several Tourinform offices in Budapest. The main one is at Süto utca 2, just around the corner from Deák tér metro (daily 8am–8pm; ☎01 438 8080). Other branches are at Liszt Ferenc tér 11 (April–Oct daily noon–8pm; Nov–March Mon–Fri 10am–6pm; ☎01 322 4098) and Ferihegy Airport Terminal 2A/2B (daily 9am–10pm).

Discount passes A Budapest Card (4500/7500/8900Ft for 24/48/72hr; ⊛budapest-card.com), available at the airport and town tourist offices, hotels and major metro stations, gives unlimited travel on public transport, free or discounted admissions to museums and attractions, and discounts on the airport minibus. Prices and offers change every April, so check before buying. All museums offer reduced entry to students.

Tours Budapest Tours offer various free excursions (☎20 534 5819, ⊛freebudapesttours.hu), the most popular of which is the Orientation Tour (10.30am from Deák tér; 2hr 30min). Budapest Underguide (☎30 908 1597, ⊛underguide.com) offer many specialized tours in English, of which their "Tipsy" tour (a pub crawl at €95 for four including a few drinks) is particularly recommended.

GETTING AROUND

Tickets A basic 350Ft ticket is valid for a journey along a single metro line and also for a single journey on buses, trolleybuses, trams and the HÉV suburban train as far as the city limits. You can buy tickets from metro stations and punch in the machines at the station entrance before the journey starts, or on board buses, trolleybuses and trams. There are 24/72hr (1650/4150Ft) and seven-day (4960Ft) travel cards which are valid on all metro lines and bus lines within the city of Budapest.

By metro The metro (daily 4.30am–11.15pm) has three lines (yellow, red and blue) intersecting at Deák tér; services run every 2–15min. You must use a new ticket for each connection if you are changing metro lines, or else buy a transfer ticket for 530Ft which allows one change. If you don't have the correct ticket you can be fined up to 12,000Ft.

By bus and tram Buses (*busz*) generally run every 10–15min. Express buses, with the red suffix "E", go nonstop between termini. Trams (*villamos*) and trolleybuses (*trolibusz*) run regularly throughout the day. Most nightbuses have three-digit numbers which begin with a 9 (apart from the #6), and run every 30–60min between around midnight and dawn along routes with a night service.

By taxi Avoid hailing a taxi on the street; you are liable to get ripped off; ask your hotel or restaurant to call a cab. If you must use one, try Főtaxi (☎01 222 2222, ⊛fotaxi.hu), or the English-speaking Citytaxi (☎01 211 1111, ⊛citytaxi.hu). Other good, trustworthy firms are Taxi Plus (☎01 888 8888, ⊛taxiplus.hu), Taxi4 (☎01 444 4444, ⊛taxi4.hu) and Taxi2000 (☎01 200 0000, ⊛taxi2000 .hu). Charges are 300Ft (flag drop) plus around 240Ft/km.

ACCOMMODATION

If you want to be close to Budapest's nightlife, cafés and central sights, the best places to stay are districts V, VI and VII in Pest; the level of competition among hostels keeps prices down.

Ábel Panzió XI, Ábel Jenő utca 9 ☎01 209 2537, ⊛abelpanzio.hu. Fantastic 1913 Art Nouveau villa, in a green residential street away from Budapest's hectic rhythm. Buffet breakfast included. Double **€60**

Csillebérc Camping XII, Konkoly Thege Miklos utca 21 ☎01 395 6537, ⊛csilleberciszabadido.hu; bus #90 from Széll Kálmán tér to the Csillebérc stop. Large, well-equipped site in the Buda hills offering a range of bungalows. Although geared mostly to Hungarian students, it's the only camping option within close distance of Budapest. Open all year. Camping **800Ft** per person, plus **1400Ft** per tent

★ **Mandala Hostel** VIII, Krúdy Gyula 12 ☎01 789 9515, ✉mandalahostel@gmail.com. Beautifully decorated boutique hostel in a listed 1909 Art Nouveau building. Large six- to eight-bed dorms in open-plan/loft style, rather than the usual bunkbeds. Dorm **€8**, double **€15**

Marco Polo Top Hostel VII, Neár utca 6 ☎01 413 2555, ⊛marcopolohostel.com. Very well-organized hostel with double rooms and twelve-bed dorms that are separated by curtains so they don't feel cramped (though they get hot in the summer). The bar downstairs is the starting point of pub crawls. Wi-fi on first floor only. Dorm **€14.50**, double **€50**

★ **Nightingale Mini Hotel** VIII, József Körút 2 ☎70 947 9676, ✉nightingale.minihotel.budapest@gmail.com. Very fresh, chic decor in this friendly hostel-without-dorms dead on Blaha Lujza tér, offering doubles and triples only. All rooms but one have their own bathroom. Smoking rooms available. Double €30

Red Bus Hostel V, Semmelweis utca 14 ☎ 01 266 0136, ⓦ redbusbudapest.hu. Located 2min from Deák tér, a small, friendly, quiet, strictly non-smoking hostel with reasonably modern decor. Book online for cheap prices. Dorm €11, double €35

EATING

There are some great eating-out options in Budapest, and it's also easy to refuel cheaply and on-the-go at the growing numbers of outlets serving falafel, kebabs and hummus-based snacks.

CAFÉS, CHEAP EATS AND SNACKS

Falafel Faloda VI, Paulay Ede utca 1. Perennially popular falafel vendor. You are given a pitta and you stuff in the falafel and salad yourself. Prices from 860Ft. Mon–Fri 10am–8pm, Sat 10am–6pm.

Govinda V, Vigyázó Ferenc utca 4. Vegetarian Indian dishes at low prices. Its "Ayurvedic menu" including main, salad and (non-alcoholic) drink costs 1450Ft. Mon–Fri 11am–9pm, Sat noon–9pm.

Müvész VI, Andrássy út 29. Classic old coffeehouse, across from the Opera House, decorated in the old style with chandeliers and dark furnishings. Try a slice of Dobos cake for 850Ft. Mon–Sat 9am–10pm, Sun 10am–10pm.

★ **Vár** I, Dísz tér 8. The only budget option on the Buda hill, this is a great self-service café with filling dishes for under 1000Ft. Even if you're not hungry, have a seat to sip the best cappuccino in Budapest. June–Aug daily 8am–10pm; Sept–May daily 8am–8pm.

RESTAURANTS

Castro Bisztro V, Madách Imre tér 3. Shabby-chic bistro close to Deák tér, with laidback feel and eclectic decor including chintzy floral tablecloths. Goulash 950Ft. Mon–Wed 11am–midnight, Fri 11am–1am, Sat noon–1am, Sun 2pm–midnight.

Darshan Udvar VIII, Krúdy Gyula utca 7. Part of a cluster of bar-restaurants in a cul-de-sac off a charming pedestrianized street. Offers pizzas alongside other Italian – and Hungarian – specialities with mains around 1350Ft. Daily 11am–midnight.

Kádár étkezde VII, Klauzál tér 9. Highly affordable, heart-warming home cooking in the old Jewish quarter – a truly authentic experience, with a daily menu in Hungarian only. Salt beef a speciality (1400Ft). Tues–Sat 11.30am–3.30pm.

Kőleves VII Kazinczy utca 41. Fun, upbeat restaurant with a beer garden, using fresh, high-quality ingredients in inventive Hungarian fusion dishes – soups are cooked traditionally with a hot stone.

★ **TREAT YOURSELF**

Gerbeaud V. Vörösmarty tér 7–8 ⓦ gerbeaud.hu. A Budapest institution, and the archetype and pinnacle of the much-loved Hungarian patisserie, specializing in cream-laden confections. A cheesecake will set you back 2450Ft while a cappuccino costs 990Ft. Daily 9am–9pm.

Two-course lunch menu 1000Ft. Mon–Fri 11.30am–1am, Sat & Sun noon–1am.

M VII Kertesz utca 48 (off Liszt Ferenc tér) ☎ 01 322 3108. Cosy little restaurant that feels at once low-key and very special (great for a romantic meal), with quirky interior design and delicious Hungarian-inspired food; watch out: the desserts are particularly generous. Mains from 1200Ft. Reservation recommended. Mon–Fri 6pm–midnight, Sat & Sun noon–midnight.

★ **Menza** VI, Liszt Ferenc tér 2. Stylish, if self-consciously so. Enjoy Hungarian dishes alfresco on the see-and-be-seen Liszt Ferenc tér, where you can easily pick up its wi-fi signal, strong enough for an army base. The ever-changing lunch menu for 990Ft is a steal. Daily 10am–1am.

DRINKING, NIGHTLIFE AND ENTERTAINMENT

District VII with its atmospheric "ruin pubs", namely bars inside "run down" buildings, is where you should be headed. The fortnightly *Budapest Funzine* (ⓦ www .funzine.hu) is a free publication in English for nightlife and events updates, available from hotels, cafés and tourist information points. Tickets for most music events can be bought through Ticket Express (VI, Andrássy út 18; ☎ 30 303 0999, ⓦ eventim.hu). Also check out ⓦ festivalcity.hu for information on Budapest's numerous festivals.

★ **Doboz** VII, Klauzál utca 10. The latest "in" ruin venue in Budapest set around an inner courtyard where a King Kong made out of planks is climbing a plane tree; anyone over 25 might feel out of place. Draught beer 360Ft. Fri & Sat cover 1000Ft. Mon & Tues 5pm–3am, Wed & Thurs 5pm–5am, Fri & Sat 5pm–6am.

Instant VI, Nagymező utca 38. Labyrinthine venue set around an open courtyard with an offbeat energy and surreal, arty decor. It doesn't fill up until 1am. Mon–Thurs & Sun 4pm–6am, Fri & Sat 4pm–11am.

★ **Kék Ló** VII, Kazinczy utca 11. If you feel overwhelmed by *Szimpla Kert*, pop in to the quieter, more fashionable *Kék Ló* opposite. Apart from its microbrewery beer selection (280Ft), it also sells designer clothes. Mon–Thurs noon–midnight, Fri noon–2am, Sat 4pm–2am, Sun 4pm–midnight.

15

Szimpla Kert VII, Kazinczy utca 14 ⓦszimpla.hu. The original "ruin pub" occupies a chaotic warehouse space with seven bars and a smokers' yard, but is far too often full with stag parties and hostel pub crawls. Daily noon–4am.

DIRECTORY

Embassies and consulates Australia, XII, Királyhágó tér 8–9 ❶01 457 9777, ⓦhungary.embassy.gov.au; Canada, XII, Ganz utca 12–14 ❶01 392 3360; Ireland, V, Szabadság tér 7 ❶01 301 4960; New Zealand Consulate, VII, Nagymező utca 47 ❶01 302 2484; UK, V, Harmincad utca 6 ❶01 266 2888; US, V, Szabadság tér 12 ❶01 475 4400, ⓦhungary.usembassy.gov.

Hospitals Medical help 24hr at V, Semmelweis utca 14/b (entrance on Gerlóczy utca), near Astoria, ❶01 311 6816; and at weekends at II, Ganz utca 13–15 ❶01 202 1370.

Internet Electric Café, VII, Dohány utca 37 (daily 9am–midnight; ⓦelectriccafe.hu); Fougou, VII, Wesselenyi utca 57 (daily 7am–2am; ⓦfougou.uw.hu); Yellow Zebra Bikes VI, Lázár utca 16 (daily: April–Oct 9.30am–7pm; Nov–March 10am–6.30pm; ⓦyellowzebrabikes.com). All 200Ft/hr.

Pharmacies The pharmacy at Teréz körút 41, near Oktogon, is open 24hr; pharmacies inside shopping centres also tend to be open longer hours.

Police The tourist police office is located inside the main Tourinform office, V, Sütő utca 2. The police phone hotline is ❶01 438 8080 (24hr).

Post office V, Petőfi utca 13 (Mon–Fri 10am–7pm); the branch on VI, Teréz körút 51, also opens Sat (8am–1pm).

SZENTENDRE

SZENTENDRE on the west bank of the **Danube Bend** is a popular day-trip from Budapest, a picturesque if rather touristy "town of artists" with narrow cobbled streets and quaint houses.

WHAT TO SEE AND DO

Szentendre was originally populated by Serbs seeking refuge from the Ottomans in the late seventeenth century and the Serbian cultural imprint remains, particularly in the rococo **Blagovestenska Church** (April–Oct Tues–Sun 10am–5pm; May & Nov Fri–Sun 10am–5pm; Jan & Feb open for worship only; 300Ft; ❶26 312 399), on the north side of the main square, **Fő tér**. Just around the corner at Vastagh György utca 1 is the **Margit Kovács Museum** (daily 10am–6pm; 1000Ft; ❶26 310 244), displaying the lifetime work of Hungary's greatest

ceramicist and sculptor, born in 1902.

There's a charming view over Szentendre's steeply banked rooftops and gardens from the hilltop **Templom tér**, above Fő tér, where the **Serbian Orthodox Cathedral** is visible inside its walled garden; tourists are generally not admitted, but you can see the cathedral iconostasis and treasury in the adjacent museum (Jan & Feb Sat & Sun 10am–4pm; March–Dec Tues–Sun 10am–6pm; 600Ft; ❶26 312 399). Try and spend some time here, as there are at least half a dozen more art collections, exhibitions or galleries worth more than a look. Don't miss the **Marzipan Museum** with its sculpted pastries at Dumtsa Jenő utca 12 (April–Oct 9am–7pm; Nov–March daily 9am–6pm; 500Ft; ❶26 310 545). There are spring-welcoming folk dances on March and April weekends, music festivals over the summer and a rich programme leading to New Year's Eve. Ask Tourinform for details.

ARRIVAL AND INFORMATION

By train HÉV trains depart from Batthyány tér in Budapest. Szentendre's train station is located a 5min walk south of town. If you have a Budapest travel card, and you're travelling by train, you only have to pay a small surcharge of around 600Ft return at the ticket office Destinations Budapest (2–7 hourly; 40min).

By boat Boats depart from Budapest's Vigadó tér pier (1 daily; 1hr 30min). Szentendre's docking station is 100m north of the town centre.

Tourist information Tourinform, Dumtsa Jenő utca 22 (June–Aug Mon–Fri 10am–6pm, Sat & Sun 10am–4pm; Sept–May Mon–Fri 9am–4.30pm, Sat & Sun 10am–2pm; ❶26 317 965, ⓦiranyszentendre.hu).

ACCOMMODATION

Centrum Panzió Bogdanyi utca 15 ❶26 302 500, ⓦhotelcentrum.hu. Homely, moderately plush rooms with modern bathrooms, just opposite the riverbank. Breakfast 1000Ft. Double **€50**

Ilona Panzió Rákóczi F utca 11 ❶26 313 599. Simple rooms in a pleasant location in the heart of the old quarter. Breakfast included. Double **8000Ft**

Pap-Sziget Pap Island, 1.5km north of town ❶26 310 697, ⓦcamping-budapest.com; Pap Sziget bus from Ujpest metro station north of Budapest. Well-organized campsite with two-person caravans, bungalows and motel rooms to rent. Very convenient for the Hungaroring Formula 1 car races. Open May–Sept only. Camping

4000Ft for two people and tent, double 6400ft, caravan 4,960Ft, bungalow 4800Ft

EATING AND DRINKING

Aranysárkány Alkotmány utca 1a. Cosy, popular and traditionally filling Magyar cuisine in Hungary's first ever private restaurant, established in 1977. Try goulash soup served in bread casing for 1100Ft. Daily noon–midnight.

Görög Kancsó Duna Korzó 9. A Greek restaurant with a summer-holiday feel and sophisticated decor; offers glass-enclosed seating along the main Danube bank. Great moussaka for 1990Ft. Free wi-fi. June–Aug daily 9.30am–midnight; Sept–May Mon–Thurs 9.30am–10pm, Fri–Sun 9.30am–11pm.

Palapa Batthyani utca 2 just off Dumtsa Jenő utca ☎ 26 302 418. Brightly decorated, fun Mexican outfit with lively garden and tequila cocktails. Mains from 1700Ft. Daily noon–10pm.

Western Hungary

The major tourist attraction to the west of the capital is **Lake Balaton**, dubbed the "Hungarian sea", and all that remains of the Pannonian Sea which once covered this part of Europe. Its built-up southern shore features loud resorts such as **Siófok**, which brands itself as the "Capital of Summer", while gentler **Keszthely** perches on the western tip. Worth a visit if you fancy a spot of swimming during the day while boozing and dancing at night, Siófok is Hungary's answer to the notorious nightlife of resorts such as Kavos, Malia and Magaluf – without the Mediterranean coyness. By contrast, the four villages that cluster around **Badacsony**, a hulk of volcanic rock on the northern shore of the lake, are very charming indeed and the perfect starting point for walks and wine-tasting tours in the Balaton region. Being flat, the lakeshore lends itself to cycling and there are plenty of places where you can rent a bike for around €4–5/day.

The wider region of **Transdanubia** – of which Lake Balaton and Badacsony are part – is the most ethnically diverse in the country. Its valleys and hills, forests and mud flats have been settled by Magyars, Serbs, Slovaks and Germans, and occupied by Romans, Ottomans and Habsburgs. Its towns have been through multiple evolutions and it shows: the delightful **Sopron** has a gorgeous medieval centre, Roman ruins and Baroque finery to its name, while **Pécs** boasts the country's best-preserved Ottoman mosque as well as some fascinating early Christian excavated finds.

SIÓFOK

The biggest, trashiest resort on Balaton, **SIÓFOK** throbs with summer crowds intent on sunbathing, boozing and clubbing. The two main resort areas are Aranypart (Gold Shore) to the east of the centre and Ezüstpart (Silver Shore) to the west. Though the central stretch of sand consists of a paying **beach** (daily mid-May to mid-Sept 7am–9pm; 1000Ft), there are free beaches 1km either side. You can rent windsurfing equipment and wakeboards from 1500Ft per hour at most beaches.

ARRIVAL AND INFORMATION

By train The train station is on Fő utca at the centre of town.

Destinations Budapest (6–7 daily; 1hr 30 min); Keszthely (6–7 daily; 1hr 30min).

By bus The bus station is at Fő utca 71–81 (☎ 84 310 220). Local bus #1 goes along the west shore and #2 goes along the east shore, which includes the two main campsites.

Destinations Budapest (4 daily; 1hr 30min–2hr 30min); Keszthely (2 daily; 1hr 30min); Pécs (8 daily; 2hr 30min–3hr).

Tourist information The Tourinform office is inside the Víztorony (Water Tower), the town's landmark on the main square (June–Aug Mon–Sat 8am–8pm, Sun 9am–1pm; Sept–May Mon–Fri 8am–4.30pm, Sat 9am–1pm, ☎ 84 310 117, ⊕ siofokportal.com).

ACCOMMODATION

Hostels are geared towards Hungarian students, so you'd be better off on a campsite. Tourinform can book you private rooms, of which there are plenty during the summer.

Aranypart Camping Szent László utca 185 ☎ 84 353 899, ⊕ balatontourist.hu; bus #2, Szabadifürdő stop. Located 3km east of the centre, this is a large, well-equipped campsite that also has 4-person bungalows to rent. Mid-April to mid-Sept. Camping 1250Ft per person, plus 750Ft per tent, bungalow 21,000Ft

15

15

Ifjúság Camping Siófok-Sóstó, Pusztatorony tér ☎84 352 851, ⓦbalatontourist.hu; bus #2, final stop. This smaller, quiet campsite lies 9km east of the centre, not on Balaton itself, but on the shore of a fishing lake. Also has 2-person bungalows. Open mid-April to mid-Sept. Camping <u>1050Ft</u> per person, plus <u>650Ft</u> per tent, bungalow <u>4200Ft</u>

EATING

★ **Amigo** Fő utca 99. Good value pizzeria offering much more than pizzas, with a roast pork platter, for example, at 1300ft. Well worth walking the 200m east from the bus station. Mon–Thurs & Sun 11am–midnight, Fri & Sat 11am–1am.

Café Roxy Szabadság tér 1. Very pleasant and central wood-panelled café-restaurant; great for a relaxed glass of wine, mid-morning coffee or oven-baked pizza (from 1400Ft). Daily: June–Aug 8am–1am; Sept–May 8am–11pm.

DRINKING AND NIGHTLIFE

Siófok's nightlife is very much geared towards bringing together the sexes, to put it mildly.

Flört Sió utca 4 ⓦflort.hu. High-energy techno club with special nights such as *XXLparty* and – no prizes for guessing the theme – *Sex in the Club*. Still, Tiësto, Sasha, Paul van Dyk and many more top DJs have appeared here. Aug daily 10pm–7am, otherwise occasional nights throughout the year.

Palace Dance Club Siófok-Ezüstpart, Vécsey Károly utca 20 ⓦpalace.hu. Siófok's most notorious club, open since 1990 andstill going strong. Two floors of house, dance and techno, while the second floor is a lap dance bar. Special party buses will whisk you there for free if you call ☎30 200 8888. June–Aug on party nights (no fixed days) 10pm–late.

KESZTHELY

KESZTHELY is a gentler counterpart to brash Siófok, with a pleasant waterfront encompassing two bays (one for swimming, the other for ferries) with stretches of grass and small paying beaches (Városi Strand 1000Ft; Helikon Strand and Libás Strand 600Ft) that give peaceful views over the seemingly never-ending lake.

WHAT TO SEE AND DO

Walking up from the train station along Martírok útja, you'll pass the **Balaton Museum** on your left at Muzeum utca 2 (May–Oct Tues–Sun 10am–6pm; Nov–April Tues–Sat 9am–5pm; 700Ft;

☎83 312 351, ⓦbalatonimuzeum.hu), hosting exhibits on the region's history and wildlife. Kossuth utca, swarming with cafés and shops, leads up towards the beige, Baroque **Festetics Palace**, which also houses hunting, coach and model railway museums (June–Sept daily 9am–6pm; Oct–May Tues–Sun 10am–5pm; 2000Ft just for the palace, 3300Ft for all museums except the wine museum; ☎83 314 194, ⓦhelikonkastely.hu). The third largest palace in Hungary, it was built in 1745 by Count György Festetics, who attracted the leading lights of the eighteenth-century literary and high society scenes. Highlights include the mirrored ballroom, but, given the entry fee, those on a budget may prefer to admire the exterior and pretty surrounding gardens. The palace stages regular summer concerts and in its cellars you can find the **Wines of Balaton museum** exhibiting 1500 wines (Tues–Sun 10am–5pm; 600Ft just for the visit; 1500Ft includes three tastings; 2500Ft includes five tastings).

ARRIVAL AND INFORMATION

By train The train station is located a 15min walk south of the centre at the junction of Kazinczy utca and Mártirok utca.

Destinations Budapest (7 daily; 3hr); Siófok (7 daily; 1hr 30min).

By bus The bus station is next to the train station, at Kazinczky utca.

Destinations Badacsony (7 daily; 30 min); Budapest (6 daily; 2hr 30min); Pécs (4 daily; 3hr); Siófok (2 daily; 1hr 30min); Sopron (2 daily; 3hr).

By ferry The quay is a 10min walk south of the centre, along Erzsébet királyné útca.

Destinations Keszthely (mid-July to Aug 1 daily; 2hr).

Tourist information Tourinform, Kossuth Lajos utca 30 (mid-June to Aug Mon–Fri 9am–7pm, Sat & Sun 10am–4pm; Sept Mon–Fri 9am–6pm, Sat 9am–4pm; Oct to mid-June Mon–Fri 9am–5pm, Sat 9am–1pm; ☎83 314 144, ⓦwest-balaton.hu).

ACCOMMODATION

Ambient Hostel Sopron utca 10 ☎30 460 3536, ⓦkeszthely-apartman.fw.hu. Clean and bright dorms, en-suite doubles and small apartments for two or more are offered in this handily located hostel next to the Festetics Palace. Dorm <u>2290Ft</u>, double <u>6200Ft</u>, apartment <u>7990Ft</u>

Castrum Camping Móra Ferenc utca 48 ☎ 83 312 120, ⓦ castrum.eu. Over 150 pitches in this large campsite 300m from the lakefront, while hedges and trees provide plenty of shade. Open mid-April to Sept. Camping **1300Ft** per person, plus **1600Ft** per tent

Kristály Hotel Lovassy utca 20 ☎ 83 319 999, ⓦ kristalyhotel.hu. Conveniently placed for the station, the lake and the town centre, this is a comfortable three-star hotel open year-round with large, airy rooms and a small spa with massage services (from €18). Double **€70**

EATING AND DRINKING

Gizella Hélikon utca 4. Family tavern, just south of the main square with wood-and-lace decor. Office workers come here for their lunch, which consists of a simple but price-busting three-course menu at 1000Ft. Also 50cm pizzas from 1100Ft. Daily 11am–9pm (menu till 3pm).

John's Pub Kossuth Lajos utca 46 ⓦ johnspubkeszthely .hu. Saloon-style bar with a long but affordable cocktail list and music late into the night. Daily lunch menu for 1000Ft. Club nights at weekends. Mon–Thurs noon–midnight, Fri & Sat noon–4am.

Margaréta Bercsényi Miklós utca 60. Charming service and an excellent, varied Hungarian menu. Dish of the day costs 950Ft. Daily 11am–10pm.

BADACSONY

The **BADACSONY** – a hefty hunk of volcanic rock, forming a plateau visible from many kilometres around – is the iconic centre-point of the beautiful wine-growing region that is named after it. Four villages nestle at its feet, and it makes for a lovely base for walks, wine tasting and swimming in Lake Balaton. In particular, **Badacsonytomaj** has a small-scale sweetness and its charms are only enhanced by sampling a glass of local wine – never hard to come by, given the abundance of boutique wine cellars and roadside bars (*borozó*). You can rent bikes at various points along Park utca, the main road by the lake. The area is surrounded by clean, paying beaches (Strandfürdő 700Ft).

WHAT TO SEE AND DO

The Baroque **Róza Szegedy House** (March–June & Sept–Oct Tues–Sun 10am–6pm; July & Aug daily 10am–7pm; Nov–Feb Fri–Sun 11am–4pm; 500Ft) is on Kisfaludy utca, the only road going uphill from Római utca. The

walk is a steep but picturesque 2.5km through the Badacsony vineyards. A little further up stands **Rose Rock** (Rózsa kő), where local legend has it that if a man and woman sit together with their backs facing Lake Balaton and think about each other, they will marry within a year. The Rose Rock is a good starting point for an invigorating hike to the Kisfaludy lookout tower (437m) and, twenty minutes further north, the Stone Gate (Kőkapu), formed by two great basalt towers. Both points offer splendid views of the lake and the patchwork of Badacsony's vineyards.

ARRIVAL AND INFORMATION

By train The train station is opposite the ferry pier on Park utca.
Destinations Budapest (3 daily; 3hr 30min).
By bus There is no bus station as such. The bus stop is on Park utca by the ferry pier.
Destinations Keszthely (7 daily; 30min).
By ferry The ferry docking is in the middle of town. It operates mid-July to Aug only.
Destinations Keszthely (1 daily 2hr).
Tourist information Park utca 14 (Jan–April & Sept–Dec Mon–Fri 9am–3pm; May & June daily 9am–5pm; July & Aug daily 9am–9pm; ☎ 87 531 013, ⓦ badacsony.com). They can book accommodation and hiking tours in English.

ACCOMMODATION

★ **Borbaratok** Római utca 88, Badacsonytomaj ☎ 87 471 000, ⓦ borbaratok.hu. Outstanding *panzió*, with large, beautifully comfortable rooms. Excellent restaurant with superb Hungarian dishes (open mid-March to Dec 11.30am–9pm). Breakfast included. Double **13,780Ft**

Tomaj Camping Balaton utca 13, Badacsonytomaj ☎ 87 471 321, ⓦ tomajcamping.hu. Pretty campsite by the lakeside, also known as the "Riviera", around a 10min walk east of the train station. Also rents wooden bungalows with kitchenette. Open April–Sept. Camping **950Ft** per person, plus **1700Ft** per tent; bungalow **8000Ft**

EATING AND DRINKING

Bacchus Kossuth Lajos utca 1 ⓦ bacchusinfo.hu. With gorgeous views over the lake, *Bacchus* is a perfect spot for sampling local wines and Hungarian countryside dishes. Mains from 1000Ft. May–Oct daily 10am–10pm.

SOPRON

SOPRON, a captivating town close to the Austrian border, retains its original

15

15

medieval layout with no fewer than 240 listed buildings. From its fourth-century Roman-era town walls to its Baroque central square, it is steeped in history.

WHAT TO SEE AND DO

The horseshoe-shaped **Belváros** (inner town) is north of Széchenyi tér and the main train station. At its southern end, beautiful **Orsolya tér** (Bear Square) features Renaissance edifices and the white and cream Gothic church. Heading north towards the main square, **Új utca** (New Street – actually one of the town's oldest thoroughfares) is a gentle curve of perfectly preserved homes painted in red, yellow and pink. At no. 22 stands a **medieval synagogue** (April–Oct Tues–Sun 10am–6pm; 800Ft; ☎99 311 327) that flourished when the street was Zsidó utca (Jewish Street).

Fő tér

Fő tér features an exquisite assembly of Gothic and Baroque architecture. Its centrepiece is the **Goat Church** at Templom utca 1 (April–Oct Tues–Sun 10am–noon & 1–5pm; Nov–March 10am–noon & 1–3pm; 300Ft), so called because, legend has it, its construction in the thirteenth century was financed by a goatherd whose flock unearthed a cache of loot. The attached **Chapter house** (same hours; combined ticket 700Ft; ☎99 523 768), which served as a prayer house and burial chapel, is thought to be one of Hungary's best examples of Gothic religious architecture. The Renaissance **Storno House**, at Fő tér 8, has a pretty good exhibition of the colourful history of Sopron county (April–Oct Tues–Sun 10am–6pm; Nov Tues–Sun 10am–2pm; Dec–March Tues–Sun 10am–4pm; 1000Ft; ☎99 311 327).

Firewatch Tower

North of Storno House rises Sopron's symbol, the **Firewatch Tower** (April, Sept & Oct Tues–Sun 10am–6pm; May–Aug Tues–Sun 10am–8pm; Nov Tues–Sun 10am–2pm; Dec–March Tues–Sun 10am–4pm; 1200Ft), founded upon the stones of a fortress originally laid out by the Romans. From the top there's a

stunning bird's-eye view of the town. The **Gate of Loyalty** at the base of the tower commemorates the townsfolk's decision to remain part of Hungary when offered the choice of annexation to Austria in 1921.

ARRIVAL AND INFORMATION

By train The station is on Mátyás Király utca, 500m south of Széchenyi tér and the old town.
Destinations Budapest (10 daily; 2hr 40min–3hr 30min); Vienna (1–2 hourly; 1hr 10min).
By bus The station is northwest of the old town, a 5min walk along Lackner Kristóf utca from Ógabona tér.
Destinations Keszthely (2 daily; 3hr); Pécs (1 daily; 6hr).
Tourist information Tourinform is inside the Liszt Cultural Centre at Liszt Ferenc utca 1 (Mon–Fri 9am–5pm, Sat 9am–noon; ☎99 517 560, ⓦ sopron.hu).

ACCOMMODATION AND EATING

Cézár Cellar Hátsókapu utca 2. A shabby exterior hides a cosy candlelit medieval cellar serving local beers, wines and meat and cheese boards from 480Ft. Mon–Sat 4pm–midnight, Sun 4–11pm.
Jégverem Panzió Jégverem utca 1 ☎99 510 113, ⓦ jegverem.hu. Pleasant if twee little rooms in a 250-year-old inn. It also has a restaurant where a basic two-course menu is available for 750Ft on weekdays. Double **8900Ft**
Park Hostel Ady Endre utca 31 ☎20 558 4410, ⓦ parkhostel.hu; bus #1 or #10. Large, fresh and friendly yellow-and-pine hostel opposite the Elizabeth Gardens (Erzsébet Kert), which is also walkable from the centre (15min). Dorm **2800Ft**

PÉCS

PÉCS is everyone's second-favourite town after Budapest, with a strong religious and scholarly heritage (Hungary's first university was founded here in 1367) and remarkable history, today captured by its landmark mosque, synagogue and cathedral plus a clutch of fascinating Roman-era finds. The surrounding Mecsek hills help create a warm microclimate in the Pécs basin.

WHAT TO SEE AND DO

Pécs is a small and navigable town, its cultural attractions concentrated in the **Belváros** (Old Town), radiating outwards from Széchenyi tér. Start with the synagogue by Kossuth tér, then head through charming Jokai tér towards the leafy western side, where you'll find the magnificent Peter and Paul cathedral.

Synagogue and Mosque of Gázi Kászim Pasha

Heading up Bajcsy-Zsilinszky utca from the bus terminal you'll pass the imposing **synagogue**, which dominates Kossuth tér (May–Sept Mon–Fri & Sun 10am–5pm; 300Ft; ☎72 315 881). The beautiful nineteenth-century interior is hauntingly impressive. Over 4000 Pécs Jews perished in the Holocaust and only a tenth of that number live in Pécs today. During the Ottoman occupation (1543–1686), Pécs' chief church, in a commanding position on Széchenyi tér 2, was converted into the **Mosque of Gázi Kászim Pasha** (mid-April to mid-Oct Mon–Sat 9am–5pm, Sun noon–4.30pm; mid-Oct to mid-April Mon–Sat 10am–2pm, Sun noon–4pm; 400Ft; ☎72 321 976, ⓦdzsami.hu), which now stands as the last remaining of 17 mosques the Ottomans built in Pécs. The building has again been converted to serve as a church – and a cross is placed atop the crescent on its roof – but the underlying design is unmistakably Islamic.

Archeological World Heritage Sites and cathedral

From the centre of town, follow either Káptalan or Janus Pannonius utca towards the pristine Art Nouveau **Peter and Paul Basilica** (April–Oct Mon–Sat 9am–5pm, Sun 1–5pm; Nov–March Mon–Sat 10am–4pm, Sun 1–4pm; 1200Ft includes Treasury, Lapidarium and Crypt; ☎72 513 057, ⓦpecs .egyhazmegye.hu). Topped with all twelve Apostles, it is built on an epic scale. Nearby at Szent Istvan tér 17 (in the gardens just below the steps to the cathedral) is the **Cella Septichora visitor centre**, giving access to a wealth of Roman early Christian archeological remains (April–Oct daily 10am–6pm; Nov–March Tues–Thurs 10am–4pm, Fri–Sun 10am–5pm; 1700Ft; ☎72 510 628, ⓦpecsorokseg.hu). Pécs fell under Roman rule as the empire expanded into the Balkans in the second century, and

became Christian with the conversion of the Emperor Constantine in 313 AD. The excavated rooms include the Peter and Paul burial chamber and a Christian cemetery site. Visitors can get a 360-degree view through glass panels placed above, below and on the side of the chambers.

15

ARRIVAL AND INFORMATION

By train The train station is a 20min walk south of the centre on Indóház tér. Sadly, there are no more international trains south from Pécs.
Destinations Budapest (9 daily; 3hr).

By bus The bus station is northeast of the train station by the Arkád shopping centre.
Destinations Budapest (8 daily; 3hr); Siófok (1–2 daily; 3hr 30min 4hr); Sopron (1 daily; 6hr); Szeged (11 daily; 3hr 30min–4hr).

Tourist information Tourinform is at Széchenyi tér 7 (April–Oct Mon–Fri 9am–5pm, Sat 9am–1pm; Nov–March Mon–Fri 9am–5pm, Sat 9am–1pm; ☎72 213 315, ⓦiranypecs.hu). They rent bikes (2500Ft/day) and can book accommodation and English-language tours.

ACCOMMODATION

Arkadia Hunyádi utca 1 ☎72 512 550, ⓦhotel arkadiapecs.hu. Central but quiet three-star hotel with sophisticated grey-black decor over two buildings: choose between modern cool and older trad. Free parking and breakfast included. Double €60

Fönix Hotel Hunyádi utca 2 ☎72 311 680, ⓦfonixhotel .com. Just north of Széchenyi tér, the simple en suite rooms in this hotel offer good value. Breakfast included. Double 8800Ft

★ **Hungária Apartmanház** Hungária utca 17 ☎72 251 184, ⓦapartmanhotelpecs.hu. Superb self-catering modern studio apartments with cable TV, wooden floors, kitchenette and wi-fi. Washing facilities on site (€2). Free parking, no breakfast. Apartment €35

NAP Hostel Kiraly utca 23–25 ☎72 950 684, ⓦnaphostel.com. Centrally located hostel with bright but crammed dorms and graffiti-style decor. Entrance through *Nappali Bar* below. Dorm €10, double €44

EATING

If you are stuck, head for the Arkád shopping centre (daily 8am–8pm) where there are many fast-food outlets offering Asian, Italian, Turkish, American and Hungarian food.

Az Elefánthoz Jokai tér 6. Excellent Italian serving delicious thin-crust pizzas on Pécs' best square for people-spotting. Beers 420Ft, pizzas from 1500Ft. Mon–Thurs & Sun 11.30am–11pm, Fri & Sat 11.30am–midnight.

★ **Flekken 1** Hungária utca 16. Popular budget tavern just off the centre with wide selection of dishes from pizzas (980Ft) to goulash (690Ft) and huge salads (Caesar 940Ft). Daily 11am–11pm.

Flekken 2 Opposite *Flekken 1* at Hungária utca 13. As cheap and popular as *Flekken 1*, but only does lunches. Two-course menu 850Ft. Daily 11am–3pm.

DRINKING AND NIGHTLIFE

Etkező Király utca 2. All-night café-bar and restaurant by the National Theatre with club nights on the first floor on Sat. Beer 340Ft, mains from 1200Ft. Daily 8am–2am.

Ti-Ti-Tá Líceum utca 4. The main club/bar and live music venue in Pécs, offering a variety of events. Whether you like reggae, rock or techno, you'll find it here late into the night. Entrance fee varies depending on act. Beer 600Ft. Fri & Sat 10pm–4am.

Eastern Hungary

The gorgeous town of **Eger**, set among the rolling Bükk hills, is an absolute must on any trip to Hungary long enough to allow you to foray beyond Budapest. Just a twenty-minute walk southwest of the centre of town lies the "Valley of the Beautiful Woman" (*Szepasszony-vólgy*), crammed with boutique wine cellars clustered close together – an integral part of a trip to Eger.

EGER

Atmospheric **EGER** boasts a fabled fortress which famously repulsed Ottoman attack in 1552, expansive cobbled streets and a feeling of bonhomie which must have something to do with its famous Bull's Blood cuvée wine (*Egri Bikavér*); a white wine version (*Egri Csillagok*) was launched with much expectation in 2012 and is equally delicious.

WHAT TO SEE AND DO

Eger's historic centre stretches either side of the main square, **Dobó István tér**, extending to the compact, cobbled streets around the castle, northeast of the centre.

Cathedral
The splendid Neoclassical **cathedral** or basilica on Pyrker tér (☎36 470 970, ⊛eger-bazilika.plebania.hu; Mon–Sat 8.30am–6pm, Sun 1–6pm; 300Ft) is the country's second-largest church after Estergom. Painted a Habsburg royal yellow, it is five minutes' walk southwest from the main square, approached by a grand set of steps. Inside, it is cheerfully decorated with toffee-coloured columns and pastel frescoes. The **Lyceum** opposite the cathedral is worth visiting for its library (Feb, March & mid-Oct to mid-Dec Sat & Sun 9.30am–1.30pm; April to mid-Oct Tues–Sun 9.30am–3.30pm; 800Ft; ☎36 325 211). The **observatory**, located at the top of the tower in the east wing of the Lyceum (same hours; 1000Ft), houses a nineteenth-century camera obscura.

Archbishop's Palace
On pleasant, pedestrianized Széchenyi Istvan utca 3 stands the **Archbishop's Palace**, currently under restoration and due to open in late 2014. It is a u-shaped Baroque building whose right wing houses the treasury and a history of the bishopric of Eger. Walk down Sandor utca, cross the bridge and head to the left to see Eger's minaret extending skyward, an iconic memento of Eger's years under Ottoman occupation (April–Sept 10am–6pm; Oct to early Nov 10am–5pm; 250Ft).

Castle
Uphill from Dobó István tér is the castle (daily March & Oct 8am–6pm; April & Sept 8am–7pm; May–Aug 8am–8pm; Nov–Feb 8am–5pm; 400Ft; ☎36 312 744, ⊛egrivar.hu). It is certainly worth paying to enter the castle grounds – you get a powerful sense from the inside of the sheer scale of the fortress, which is very well preserved. You can easily imagine the soldiers and local women (who volunteered to join in) in 1552 seeing off a Turkish force six times their number. The museum and the casements inside are visited separately (April Tues–Sun 9am–5pm; May–Oct Tues–Sun 10am–5pm; Nov–March Sat & Sun 10am–4pm; 1400Ft).

ARRIVAL AND INFORMATION

By train The station is on Állomás tér. The centre is a 10min walk to the right of Deák Ferenc utca, just up from the station.

Destinations Budapest (9 daily; 2hr).

By bus The bus station is at Barcóczy utca 2 behind the Basilica (☎ 36 517 777).

Destinations Budapest (1–2 hourly; 1hr 50min–2hr 10min); Debrecen (8 daily; 2hr 45min).

Tourist information The Tourinform office is at Bajcsy-Zsilinszky utca 9 (mid-March to mid-June & Sept–Nov Mon–Fri 9am–5pm, Sat 9am–1pm; mid-June to Aug Mon–Fri 9am–6pm, Sat & Sun 9am–1pm; Dec to mid-March Mon–Fri 9am–5pm; ☎ 36 517 715, ⓦ eger.hu).

GETTING AROUND

By bike You can rent bikes from Eger Bike at Bajcsy-Zsilinszky utca 17–19 (☎ 30 233 5814, ⓦ egerbike.hu) for 3000Ft/day.

ACCOMMODATION

As in most of Hungary, colleges convert their dorms to hostels in July and Aug. Try Wigner Jenő at Racóczi St 2 (☎ 36 537 000, ✉ kiss.ferenc@wigner.sulinet.hu) or St Hedvig at Dobó tér 6 (☎ 36 320 788, ✉ kissne@szenthedvig.hu).

Aphrodite Apartments Dobó utca 22 ☎ 36 415 535, ⓦ aphroditeapartmentsandcafe.com. Great-value large self-catering apartments in the middle of the historic centre, holding up to 4 people. Price includes wi-fi, parking and a room service breakfast. Reception at *Görög Café* next door. Apartment **14,500Ft**

Tourist Motel Mekcsey utca 2–4 ☎ 36 411 101. Cheap, basic motel just along from the castle; most rooms are without their own WC. Breakfast 700Ft. Double **5600Ft**

Tulipán Szépasszonyvölgy 71 ☎ 36 311 542, ⓦ tulipancamping.com. Modern, leafy but basic campsite in the Szépasszony Valley – but, with 80-odd wine cellars within walking distance, who cares? Open mid-March to mid-Oct. Camping **800Ft** per person, plus **900Ft** per tent

EATING AND DRINKING

Biboros Bajcsy-Zsilinszky utca 6. The main watering hole of the Eger youth, this popular bar with a great inner courtyard stays busy until the early hours. Beer 270Ft. Mon–Fri 11am–3am, Sat 1pm–3am, Sun 3pm–midnight.

Palacsintavár Dobó utca 9. A true Eger institution, with a terrific range of filling sweet and savoury pancakes (around 1200Ft) and a diverting interior filled with displays of retro cigarette packets, matches and the odd goldfish. Tues–Thurs noon–midnight, Fri & Sat noon–11pm, Sun noon–8pm.

Várkert Étterem Dózsa György tér 8. Traditional Hungarian food (mains 1400Ft) in the pedestrianized area below the castle walls. Daily 11.30am–10pm.

The Great Plain

Spanning half of Hungary, the **Great Plain** is its key horseriding region – horseriding being a core part of Magyar folklore: this warrior people's stunning success in conquering this part of Europe is often attributed to their skill and agility as archers on horseback. The prime destinations here are **Debrecen**, and the nearby **Hortobagy National Park**. Further south, between the Danube and the Tisza rivers are **Kecskemét** and **Szeged**, both towns with some interesting turn-of-the-twentieth-century architecture and well worth a stop.

KECSKEMÉT

Possible as a day-trip from Budapest, **KECSKEMÉT** is a small town chiefly remarkable for several striking pieces of architecture from Hungary's "Romantic Nationalist" period at the turn of the twentieth century. Its name comes from the Hungarian for goat, *kecske*, as its thirteenth-century bishop apparently used to give the cloven-footed creatures to each new Christian convert.

WHAT TO SEE AND DO

Kecskemét's main attraction is the ornate **Cifra Palace** on Szabadság tér – a large building on a street corner that you might overlook, were it not for the daring Art Nouveau design. Designed by Markus Géza in 1902, it now houses the **Kecskemét Art Gallery** (Tues–Sun 10am–5pm; 550Ft; ☎76 480 776, ✉cifrapalota.kecskemet@gmail .com). Szabadság tér runs into the other main square, Kossuth tér, where the **Town Hall** stands tall, a masterpiece of Romantic Nationalist architecture. You can visit its Ceremonial Hall (Mon–Fri 10am–noon; 710Ft) – ask at Tourinform. Finally, the **Hungarian Photography Museum** at Katona József tér 12 (Wed–Sun 10am–5pm; 500Ft; ☎76 483 221, ⓦfotomuzeum.hu) has excellent exhibitions of photography from the nineteenth century to the present day.

15

ARRIVAL AND INFORMATION

By train It's about a 15min walk down Nagykőrösi utca from the station at Kodaly Zoltan tér 7, towards Szabadság tér.

Destinations Budapest (10–11 daily; 1hr 15min); Szeged (10–12 daily; 1hr).

By bus Located right next to the train station at Noszlopy Gaspár park 1.

Destinations Budapest (hourly; 1hr 15min–1hr 45min); Szeged (9–10 daily; 1hr 40min).

Tourist information Kossuth tér 1, in the corner of the Town Hall (April–Oct Mon–Fri 8am–6pm, Sat 9am–1pm; Nov–March Mon–Fri 8am–4pm; ☏76 481 065, ⊛visitkecskemet.hu). They also offer bike rental (3000Ft/day).

ACCOMMODATION AND EATING

During the summer (July & Aug), hostel accommodation is available in the colleges at Piaristák tér 4 (☏76 486 977) and Nyíri utca 28 (☏76 486 322).

Fábián Panzió Kápolna utca 14 ☏76 477 677, ⊛panziofabian.hu. Very friendly *pension* with smart, spacious rooms around a beautifully tended garden. Note that beds are only 1.95m long. Breakfast 1000Ft. Double 11,000Ft

★ **Lordok Kávezó** Kossuth tér 6–7. Central café with a good self-service section for lunch and dinner (mains 1000Ft). The patisserie offers ginormous gateaux time-stamped for freshness (600Ft). Mon–Fri 7am–10pm, Sun 7am–8pm.

Technika Kavezó Rácoczi utca 2. ⊛technikakavezo.hu. An atmospheric rock club inside the old Kecskemét Synagogue. The mainly student crowd is attracted by the frequent gigs on offer and the cheap beer (400Ft/half litre). Mon noon–11pm, Tues & Wed noon–10pm, Thurs noon–2am, Fri noon–4am, Sat 8pm–4am.

SZEGED

SZEGED, the most sophisticated city in the Great Plain, straddles the River Tisza as it flows south towards Serbia. The present layout of the city, and its beautiful Art Nouveau architecture, date from after the great flood of 1879, when Szeged was rebuilt with strapping new buildings and squares thanks to foreign funding. The student population gives the city a real energy, and it's more than pleasant for a day or two's stopover.

WHAT TO SEE AND DO

Szeged's biggest monument is **Dom tér**, ringed by scholarly cloisters and busts of celebrated Hungarians. It was created in 1920 to complement the enormous double-spired **Votive Church** (daily 9am–7pm; Tower 700Ft; ☏62 420 32, ⊛dom.szeged.hu), which leading townspeople pledged to erect after the great flood. At 12.15pm and 5.45pm, the **Musical Clock** on the south side of the square comes alive, as figurines from inside pop out and trundle around to the chiming of bells.

Móra Ferenc Museum

The **Móra Ferenc Museum** at Roosevelt tér 1–3 (daily 10am–6pm; 900Ft; ☏62 549 040, ⊛www.mfm.u-szeged.hu) contains folk art, fine art and archeological remains offering insight into the Avars, the people who ruled much of the Central-Eastern European Pannonian plain from the sixth to ninth centuries. From the museum, it's a short walk to green, pretty Széchenyi tér, home to the neo-Baroque **town hall** with its decorative tiled roof. Look out for the "Bridge of Sighs", modelled on the Venetian original, which links the hall to a neighbouring house.

Great Synagogue

The **Great Synagogue** at Jósika utca 10 (April–Sept Mon–Fri & Sun 10am–noon & 1–5pm; Oct–March Mon–Fri & Sun 9am–2pm, 400Ft; ☏62 423 849, ⊛zsinagoga.szeged.hu) was built between 1900 and 1903 by architect Lipót Baumhorn. It is one of Hungary's most beautiful buildings, sporting a blue glass dome with stars picked out in gold, and a stunning Art Nouveau interior that is full of life: the frescoes and stained glass replicate exactly the plants and flowers that the then chief rabbi, a keen botanist, estimated would have grown in ancient Jerusalem.

ARRIVAL AND INFORMATION

By train The train station is on Indoház tér, south of the centre, a short tram ride on the #1 or #2 (400Ft).

Destinations Budapest (hourly; 2hr 20min); Kecskemét (hourly; 1hr).

By bus The station is on Mars tér, a 10min walk west from Roosevelt tér down Híd utca.

Destinations Budapest (6 daily; 3hr); Novi Sad (2 daily; 3hr); Pécs (9 daily; 3hr 30min); Subotica (3 daily; 1hr).

Tourist information Tourinform, Dugonics tér 2 (June–Sept Mon–Fri 9am–6pm, Sat 9am–1pm; Oct–May Mon–Fri 9am–5pm; ☎62 488 690, ⓦszeged.hu) Very organized and helpful office; can help with accommodation. Ask for their Art Nouveau walk guide.

ACCOMMODATION

Eötvös Kollegium Tisza Lajos krt 103 ☎62 544 388, ✉szallas@eotvos.u-szeged.hu. During the summer season, Eötvös College rents beds in its dorms right in the centre of town. Email them to book in advance; if they're full they will suggest other colleges. July & Aug only. Dorm 3210Ft

★ **Lila Vendégház** József Attila sgt 9 ☎62 635 166, ⓦlilahaz.hu. Friendly budget hotel with modern, well-furnished rooms, each one with its own small hall – a nice touch. Free parking available, plus cooked breakfast for 1000Ft. Double 9000Ft

Partfürdő Camping Középkikötő sor 1–3 ☎62 430 843, ⓦszegedkemping.hu. Located on the riverbank in Újszeged, a 10min walk from the centre across the Belvárosi bridge, this large campsite has a large swimming pool and private river beach. Open May–Sept. Camping 990Ft per person, plus 390Ft per tent

EATING AND DRINKING

Corso Café Kárász utca 16. Open-fronted café/restaurant in Szeged's pedestrianized heart, attracting a student crowd for its large portions. Mains from 1180Ft. Mon–Sat 9am–1am, Sun 9am–10pm.

Dugonics Teri Kisvendeglő Dugonics tér 2. A patisserie with a good restaurant at the back, where tall indoor yuccas rise above the cherry-wood tables. Three-course menus 800Ft during the week, 1500Ft weekends. Daily 11am–9pm.

★ **Halászcsárda** Roosevelt tér 12–14 ☎62 555 980. A Szeged riverside institution, where a cauldron of brilliant-red fish goulash goes down swimmingly with a glass of local Riesling. Mains from 1800Ft; half-portions available (and, frankly, recommended). Reservation likewise recommended. Daily 11am–11pm.

DEBRECEN

DEBRECEN is where you should go to experience the real Hungary of the *betyar* (cowboys) and the *czardas* (inns). Far from Budapest and its Germanic influences, this is a city where the nineteenth-century patriotism that awoke the Hungarian nation is still running strong, aided and abetted both by a Calvinist stubbornness and by the youthful idealism of its large student population. Although it's Hungary's second city, it is both easy to manage and – with a forest within city limits – as close to nature as a city can be. It is also the gateway to the stunning Hortobagy National Park, a piece of Asian steppe in Central Europe.

WHAT TO SEE AND DO

Debrecen's identity as the centre of Calvinism in Hungary is confirmed by the dominating presence of the **Great Reformed Church** on Kossuth tér (Jan–March Mon–Sat 10am–1pm; April–Nov Mon, Tues & Thurs 10am–4pm, Wed 10am–6pm, Fri 10am–2pm; 400Ft; ☎52 412 695, ⓦnagytemplom.hu). Although the interior is sparse and austere, you can browse the Hungarian Declaration of Independence (in English), which Lajos Kossuth proclaimed here on 13 April 1849, and also see his chair and memorabilia. If you are fit enough, you can climb the Western tower for a bird's-eye view of the city. Behind the church, the **Déri museum** (Tues–Sun 10am–6pm; 800Ft; ☎52 322 207, ⓦwww.derimuzeum.hu) is undergoing renovations until at least 2014, but its pride and joy, **Munkácsy's Jesus Triptych**, should still be on display.

The other focus of the town is conveniently located at the end of the #1 tram line running north from the station via Kossuth tér: the area around the **University** and **The Great Forest** (*Nagyerdő*), which is really a fancy name for the admittedly large city park. There, you can find restaurants and bars dotted around, as well as the much respected **Aquaticum** spa.

ARRIVAL AND INFORMATION

By plane The airport (served by Wizzair) is only about 10min by bus south of the main train station. An airport shuttle runs regularly between the airport and the city, stopping at various points in the centre, all the way to the University (500Ft).
Destinations London Luton (5 weekly; 2hr 35min).
By train The train station is south of town on Petőfi tér and joined to the centre by tram #1.
Destinations Budapest (hourly; 2hr 30min); Hortobagy (10 daily; 45min).

15

By bus The bus station is about a 15min walk west of the centre on Külső-Vásár tér, at the end of Széchenyi utca.
Destinations Eger (8 daily; 2hr 20min); Szeged (3 daily; 5hr).

Tourist information Tourinform is at 20 Piac utca (mid-June to mid-Sept Mon–Fri 9am–5pm, Sat 9am–1pm; mid-Sept to mid-June Mon–Fri 9am–5pm; ☏ 52 412 250). During the summer (mid-June to mid-Sept) there is a manned Kiosk on Kossuth tér (daily 10am–8pm). They offer bicycles for rent (1000Ft/4hr plus 10,000Ft deposit) and sightseeing tours in English (2hr 30min; 2500Ft).

GETTING AROUND

By tram and bus Debrecen's public transport is very easy to negotiate, with a tram line running from the train station north to the University and looping back again, taking in all important sights. A bus ticket costs 300Ft (buy from kiosks). A one-day card valid on trams and buses costs 1200Ft, while a three-day card costs 2400Ft.

ACCOMMODATION

Debrecen University (☏ 52 512 950 & ☏ 52 512 940) offers beds in various student residences around the town during July & Aug.

★ **Régi Posta** Széchenyi utca 6 ☏ 52 325 325, ⓦ regiposta.hu. Great location, great hosts and great inclusive breakfast in the oldest building in Debrecen, where Sweden's Charles XII stayed in 1714 (you can book his room). Free parking and an excellent Hungarian traditional restaurant in the basement. Double **€55**

Szív Panzió Szív utca 11 ⓦ szivpanzio.hu. Spotlessly clean *pension* in a quiet residential street a 10min walk from the station. The red ochre inner courtyard has a covered wooden benchstand, great for sipping a coffee in the summer. Free parking. Breakfast 1000Ft. Double **7800Ft**

EATING, DRINKING AND NIGHTLIFE

Palma Simonyi utca 44. Feels like an English pub, albeit of the gastro persuasion: food is as good as the drinks. Although mains start at 2000Ft, the weekday three-course lunch menu costs only 1100Ft. Daily 10am–midnight.

★ **Roncso** Csapó utca 27 ⓦ roncsbar.hu. When you walk into Debrecen's only "ruin pub" you think you've entered the scene of an Iron Maiden album cover – no wonder, as it belongs to the drummer of local metal band, *Tank Csapda*. Don't worry, they're friendly plus they brew their own beer (360Ft). Mon, Tues & Sun 11am–midnight, Wed & Thurs 11am–2am, Fri & Sat 11am–4am.

GUINNESS STOREHOUSE, DUBLIN

Ireland

HIGHLIGHTS

❶ **Dublin** Visit the home of world-famous Guinness. **See p.575**

❷ **Ring of Kerry** Stunning coastal, mountain and lakeshore scenery on a 179km loop. **See p.589**

❸ **County Clare** Enjoy traditional Irish music in Clare's pubs. **See p.591**

❹ **Slieve League** Witness astounding views from Europe's highest sea cliffs. **See p.595**

❺ **Titanic Quarter, Belfast** Regenerated and fast-developing area, with a showcase museum. See p.598

❻ **Giant's Causeway** Marvel at the astonishing basalt columns. **See p.600**

HIGHLIGHTS ARE MARKED ON THE MAP ON P.571

ROUGH COSTS

Daily budget Basic €50, occasional treat €70

Drink Guinness €4.50/pint

Food Irish stew €10

Hostel/budget hotel €16/€35–45

Travel Train: Dublin–Belfast (2hr 10min) €16; bus: Kilkenny–Dublin (2hr 20min–3hr) €12.50

FACT FILE

Population 6 million

Language English; Gaelic

Currency Euro € (Republic); pound sterling £ (N. Ireland)

Capitals Dublin (Republic); Belfast (N. Ireland)

International phone code ☎ 353 (Republic); ☎ 44 (N. Ireland)

Time zone GMT

Introduction

In both Northern Ireland and the Republic, Ireland's lures are its landscape and people – the rain-hazed loughs and wild coastlines, the talent for conversation and wealth of traditional music. While economic growth has transformed Ireland's cities, the countryside remains relatively unchanged.

Ireland's west draws most visitors; its coastline and islands – especially **Aran** – combine vertiginous cliffs, boulder-strewn wastes and dramatic mountains. The interior is less spectacular, though the southern pastures and low wooded hills are classic landscapes. Northern Ireland's principal highlight is the bizarre basalt formation of the **Giant's Causeway**.

Dublin is an extraordinary mix of youthfulness and tradition, of revitalized Georgian squares and vibrant pubs. **Belfast** has undergone a massive rejuvenation, while the cities of **Cork** and **Galway** sparkle with energy.

No introduction can cope with the complexities of Ireland's **politics**, which still permeate most aspects of daily life in many areas in the North. However, regardless of partisan politics, Irish hospitality is as warm as the brochures say, on both sides of the border.

CHRONOLOGY

c. 3000 BC Neolithic tombs first constructed.

c. 500 BC Celts arrive, heralding the Iron Age.

c.100 BC Romans refer to Ireland as "Hibernia".

432 AD Saint Patrick arrives in Ireland, converting pagans to Christianity.

795 Viking raids on Ireland.

1167 Arrival of Anglo-Norman invaders, ushering in eight hundred years of English rule.

1558–1603 Policy of Plantation of Irish lands under Queen Elizabeth I.

1649–53 Cromwell re-conquers Ireland, after a bloody campaign against Irish Catholics and English Royalists.

1690 Battle of the Boyne marks decisive victory by the Protestant king William of Orange over Catholic James II of England, as he attempted to regain the crown.

1704 Penal Code introduced, barring Catholics from voting, education and the military.

1759 Arthur Guinness begins to brew his famous stout in Dublin.

1798 Rebellion of the United Irishmen led by Wolfe Tone and supported by French troops is suppressed.

1801 Act of Union makes Ireland officially part of Great Britain.

1803 Second United Irishmen Rebellion under Robert Emmet defeated.

1845–49 Potato famine causes widespread starvation and prompts mass migration to the United States.

1879–82 Land War increases support for the Home Rule movement led by Charles Stewart Parnell.

1916 Easter Rising by Irish nationalists is brutally repressed by the British.

1922 Irish War of Independence ends with secession of 26 Irish counties from the UK to form the Irish Free State. Six counties in the North remain part of Great Britain.

1922 James Joyce's *Ulysses* is published.

1949 The Republic of Ireland is declared.

1970s The Provisional IRA steps up violent campaigns in Northern Ireland and the UK.

1972 British troops kill thirteen civilians in Derry, Northern Ireland, in an event known as Bloody Sunday.

1973 Ireland joins the European Community.

1998 Good Friday Agreement signed by the British and Irish governments heralding a new era of peace and cooperation in Northern Ireland.

2002 The euro is introduced in the Republic of Ireland.

2005 The Provisional IRA announces a full ceasefire.

2007 Agreement between rival party leaders, Ian Paisley and Gerry Adams, to share power in an elected assembly for Northern Ireland.

2008 Crisis in the Irish banking system combines with a worldwide recession, bringing an end to economic prosperity.

2010 Police and justice powers for Northern Ireland transferred from London to Belfast; the EU and International Monetary Fund approve an €85billion loan to bail out the Irish economy.

2011 Queen Elizabeth makes historic first State visit to Ireland.

2013 Ireland takes on a six-month presidency of the European Union. The Gathering tourism initiative invites anyone with an interest in Ireland to visit as part of a year-long celebration of Irishness.

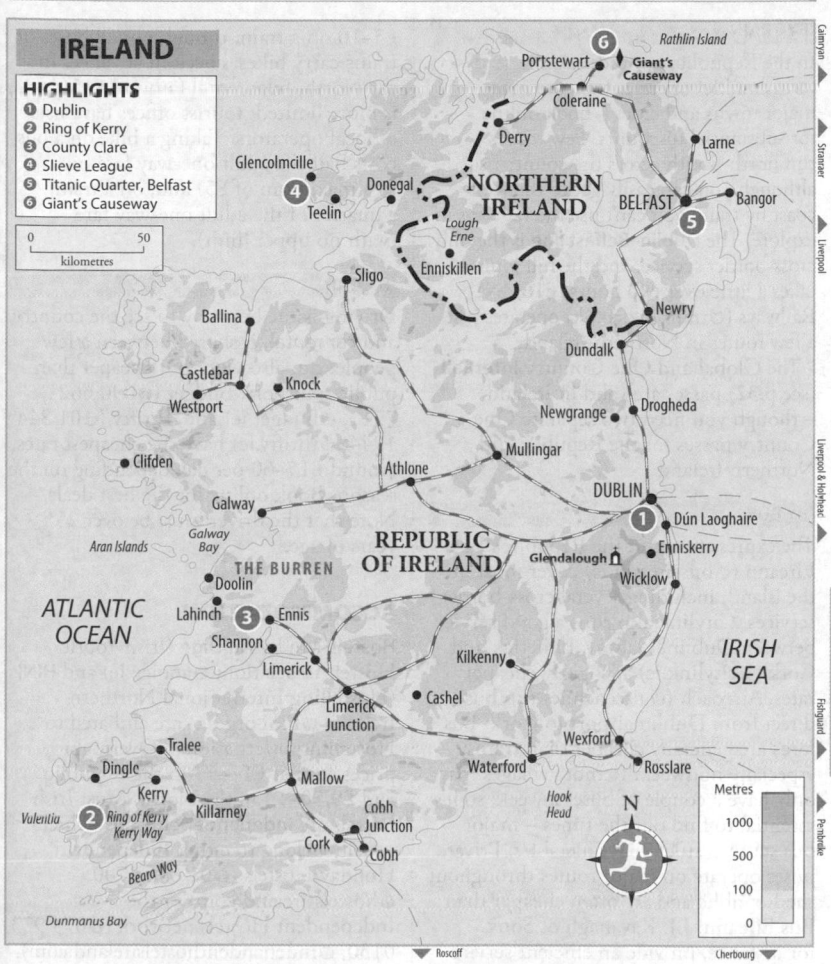

IRELAND

HIGHLIGHTS
1. Dublin
2. Ring of Kerry
3. County Clare
4. Slieve League
5. Titanic Quarter, Belfast
6. Giant's Causeway

0   50
kilometres

Note: There is a possibility the peace walls will come down in Northern Ireland before publication.

ARRIVAL AND DEPARTURE

Ireland has five international **airports**: Dublin, Cork, Shannon and Knock in the Republic, and Belfast International in the North. Regional airports, which also serve Great Britain, are Belfast City, Derry, Donegal, Galway, Kerry and Sligo.

Ferry routes from the UK comprise Cairnryan–Larne, Fishguard–Rosslare, Fleetwood–Larne, Holyhead–Dublin, Holyhead–Dún Laoghaire, Isle of Man–Belfast, Isle of Man–Dublin, Liverpool–Belfast, Liverpool–Dublin, Pembroke–Rosslare, Stranraer–Belfast and Troon–Larne. Travelling by ferry without a vehicle is not expensive (about €60 return), but taking a car is pricey (€200–300 in high season).

GETTING AROUND

You can save money on rail and bus services by booking online and buying multi-journey tickets in advance; the **Freedom of Northern Ireland/Irish Rover** tickets give you unlimited bus/rail travel for three, five, eight or fifteen days. See ⓦtranslink.co.uk or ⓦbuseireann.ie.

BY TRAIN

In the Republic, Iarnród Éireann (wirishrail.ie) operates **trains** to most major towns and cities – book online for substantial discounts. Few routes run north–south across the country, so, although you can easily get to the west coast by train, you can't use the railways to explore. The **Dublin–Belfast line** is the only cross-border service, and the full journey takes a little over two hours (€16). NI Railways (wtranslink.co.uk) operates just a few routes in Northern Ireland.

The Global and One Country **InterRail** (see p.32) passes are valid in Ireland – though you need two separate One Country passes for the Republic and Northern Ireland.

BY BUS

The express **buses** of the Republic's Bus Éireann (wbuseireann.ie) cover most of the island, including several cross-border services. Citylink also runs a good service between Dublin, Galway, Limerick and Cork (wcitylink.ie) at slightly cheaper rates. Aircoach (waircoach.ie) run buses direct from Dublin airport to Cork. Bus **fares** are generally cheaper than trains, especially midweek. Remote villages may only have a couple of buses a week, so it's essential to find out the times – major bus stations stock free timetables. Private buses operate on major routes throughout the Republic and are often cheaper than Bus Éireann: J.J. Kavanagh & Sons, for instance, provide an efficient service from Dublin airport to Shannon airport, Limerick, Galway, Kilkenny and Waterford (☎056 883 1106, wjjkavanagh.ie). In the North, Ulsterbus (wtranslink.co.uk) runs regular and reliable services.

BY BICYCLE

Cycling is an enjoyable and reasonably safe way of seeing Ireland. In the Republic, bikes can be rented in most towns and Raleigh is the main operator (€15/day, €70/week; from €100 deposit, depending on the dealer; ☎01 465 9659, wraleigh.ie); local dealers (including some hostels) are cheaper. It costs an extra €10 to carry a bike on a bus, and

€3–10 on a train, though not all buses or trains carry bikes; check in advance. In the North, bike rental (around £15/day) is more limited; tourist offices have lists of local operators. Taking a bike on a bus costs half the adult one-way fare (up to a maximum of £5) and, on a train, a quarter of the adult one-way fare (with no upper limit).

BY CAR

Driving is the best way to see the country, and **car rental**, if shared between a few people, can also work out cheaper than public transport. Budget (☎090 662 7711, wbudget.ie) and Thrifty (☎01 844 1944, wthrifty.ie) have the cheapest rates, around €15–60 per day depending on the season. Book online for the best deals. Note that the driver must be over 25 years of age.

ACCOMMODATION

Hostels run by **An Óige** (Irish Youth Hostel Association; wanoige.ie) and **HINI** (Hostelling International Northern Ireland; whini.org.uk) are affiliated to Hostelling International. Overnight prices start at €11–17 in the Republic and £9.50–13 in the North. Most Irish hostels are **independent hostels**, which usually belong to either Independent Holiday Hostels (☎01 836 4700, whostels-ireland.com) or the Independent Hostels network (☎074 973 0130, windependenthostelsireland.com). In the Republic, expect to pay €10–18 for a dorm bed, €17–32 (rising to €46 in some Dublin hostels) per person for private rooms where available; in the North, it's £7–12/£14–25.

B&Bs vary enormously, but most are welcoming, warm and clean. Expect to pay from around €30/£25 per person sharing; most **hotels** are a little pricier but you can find bargains online. Booking ahead is always advisable during high season and major festivals.

Camping costs around €8–12 a night in the Republic, £7–10 in the North. In out-of-the-way places it may be possible to camp in the wild, but ask the landowner's permission first: farmers in popular tourist areas may ask for a small fee. Some hostels also let you camp for around €8/£5 per person.

FOOD AND DRINK

Irish **food** is meat-orientated. B&Bs usually provide a "traditional" **Irish breakfast** of sausages, bacon and eggs (although many offer vegetarian alternatives). **Pub lunch** staples are usually meat or fish and two veg, with a few veggie options, while specifically vegetarian places are sparse outside major cities and popular tourist areas. All towns have fast-food outlets, but traditional fish and chips is a better bet, especially on the coast. For the occasional treat, there are some very good seafood restaurants, particularly along the southwest and west coasts. Most towns have daytime cafés serving a selection of affordable hot dishes, salads, soups, sandwiches and cakes.

DRINK

The stereotypical view of the "Irish national pastime" has a certain element of truth; especially in rural areas, the **pub** is the social heart of the community and the focus for the proverbial **craic** (pronounced "crack"), a particular blend of Irish fun involving good company, witty conversation and laughter, frequently against a backdrop of music. The classic Irish drink is **Guinness**, which is made in Dublin, while the Cork stouts, Beamish and Murphy's, have their devotees. For English-style keg **bitter**, try Smithwicks. Irish **whiskeys** are world-famous – try Paddy's, Jameson's or Bushmills.

CULTURE AND ETIQUETTE

With the huge influx of visitors to Ireland in recent years, the country has acquired an increasingly **cosmopolitan** feel, particularly in the big cities, but the sense of national identity and heritage remains strong. Traditional music sessions are still the primary form of evening entertainment in pubs, especially in rural areas.

Despite the decreasing influence of Catholicism in Ireland, family values still reign. It's hard to miss the hospitality and friendliness that most clearly define the Irish.

Smoking is banned in all indoor public places. In restaurants and cafés, a ten percent **tip** is generally expected.

SPORTS AND OUTDOOR ACTIVITIES

Walking and **cycling** in Ireland are great ways of enjoying the country's beautiful landscapes (see ⓦirishtrails.ie for suggested routes). There are great opportunities for **horseriding** (see ⓦdiscoverireland.ie); a lovely ride is along the white sands of Connemara. **Watersports** are popular: Ireland is increasingly praised for its surfing spots, such as Portrush in the north, Bundoran in Donegal, and Lahinch in Clare (see ⓦisasurf.ie).

The two great Gaelic sports, **hurling** (the oldest field game in Europe, and similar to hockey) and **Gaelic football** (a mixture of soccer and rugby, but predating both these games), are very popular spectator sports. Croke Park Stadium in Dublin is home to the big fixtures (see ⓦgaa.ie and ⓦcrokepark.ie for information and tickets).

Horse racing (ⓦgoracing.ie) looms large on the sporting agenda: you'll never be far from a race in Ireland, whether it's a big racecourse like Galway or a soggy village affair in the middle of nowhere.

COMMUNICATIONS

Main **post offices** are open Monday to Friday 9am to 5.30pm, Saturday 9am to 1pm. Stamps and phonecards are also often available in newsagents. **Public phones** are becoming increasingly rare, but internet shops with phones for national and international calls can be found in most towns. **International calls** are cheaper at weekends or after 6pm (Mon–Fri). To call the Republic from Northern Ireland dial ☎00353 followed by the area code (without the initial 0) and the local number (note cross-border calls are charged at the international rate). Call centres offer cheaper international

16

IRELAND ONLINE

ⓦdiscoverireland.ie Fáilte Ireland website with comprehensive tourist information.

ⓦdiscovernorthernireland.com Northern Ireland Tourist Board.

ⓦheritageireland.com Information on Ireland's main heritage sites.

ⓦntni.org.uk Details of the National Trust's properties in Northern Ireland.

ⓦvisitdublin.ie Accommodation, eating and drinking listings for the capital.

rates than public telephones. To call the North from the Republic use the code ☎048, followed by the eight-digit local number. **Internet access** is widely available and costs about €3/£2.50 per hour; it's generally cheaper in big towns and cities.

EMERGENCIES

16

The Republic's police are known as the **Gardaí** (pronounced "gar-dee"), while the **PSNI** (Police Service of Northern Ireland) operates in the North. **Hospitals** and medical facilities are high quality; you'll rarely be far from a hospital, and both Northern Ireland and the Republic are within the European Health Insurance Card scheme. Most **pharmacies** open standard shop hours, though in large towns some may stay open until 10pm; they dispense only a limited range of drugs without a doctor's prescription.

INFORMATION

Tourist offices are abundant in Ireland, in the smaller as well as larger towns on the tourist trail. **Fáilte Ireland** provides tourist information in the Republic; the **Northern Ireland Tourist Board** in the North. They provide free maps of the city/town and immediate vicinity, and sell a selection of more extensive and specialized maps.

EMERGENCY NUMBERS

In the Republic ☎112 or 999; in Northern Ireland ☎999.

MONEY AND BANKS

Currency in the Republic is the **euro** (€), in Northern Ireland the **pound sterling** (£). Standard **bank hours** are Monday to Friday 9.30am to 4.30pm (Republic and Northern Ireland). There are **ATMs** throughout Ireland – though not in all villages – and most accept a variety of cards. The exchange rate at the time of writing was €1.15/£1.

OPENING HOURS AND HOLIDAYS

Business hours are roughly Monday to Saturday 9am to 6pm, with some late evenings (usually Thurs) and Sunday opening. **Museums** and attractions are usually open regular shop hours, though outside the cities, many only open during the summer. Some museums are closed on Mondays. **Cafés** usually open daily from 8am–6pm, and most **restaurants** from noon–10pm. **Pubs** operate strict trading hours, and those without a late-night licence must close at 11.30pm Sunday to Thursday and 12.30am on Friday & Saturday. **Nightclubs** close at 2.30am.

Public holidays in the Republic are: Jan 1, St Patrick's Day (March 17), Easter Monday, May Day (first Mon in May), June Bank Holiday (first Mon in June), August Bank Holiday (first Mon in Aug), October Bank Holiday (Halloween, last Mon in Oct), December 25 and 26. Note that some places may also close on Good Friday. In the North: January 1, St Patrick's Day (March 17), Good Friday, Easter Monday, May Day (first Mon in May), Spring Bank Holiday (last Mon in May), July 12, August Bank Holiday (last Mon in Aug), December 25 and 26.

STUDENT DISCOUNTS

A **student card** usually gives reduced entrance charges of up to fifty percent, and if you're visiting sites run by the Heritage Service in the Republic (ⓦheritageireland.ie) it's worth buying a **Heritage Card** (€21, students €8), which provides a year's unlimited admission.

THE IRISH LANGUAGE

Though **Irish** is the first language of the Republic, you'll rarely hear it spoken outside the areas officially designated as *Gaeltacht* ("Irish-speaking"), namely West Cork, West Kerry, Connemara, some of Mayo and Donegal, and a tiny part of Meath. However, two important words you may encounter sometimes appear on the doors of pub toilets: *Fir* (for men) and *Mná* (for women). You'll also find the word *Fáilte* (welcome) popping up frequently as you enter towns and tourist spots. A few other words to get your tongue round:

Sláinte	cheers, good health
Gardaí	police
An lár	city centre
Dia dhuit	hello
Slán	goodbye

More information on the Gaeltacht areas is available at ⓦgaelsaoire.ie.

Dublin and around

Set on the banks of the River Liffey, **DUBLIN** is a splendidly monumental city with a cosmopolitan feel and an internationally renowned nightlife. It was the centre of Ireland's booming economy during the "Celtic Tiger" years up to 2007, which brought rejuvenation and renewed energy, and which still remains despite high unemployment.

Dublin began as the Viking trading post **Dubh Linn** (Dark Pool), which soon amalgamated with the Celtic settlement of **Baile Átha Cliath** (Town of the Hurdle Ford) – still the Irish name for the city. The city's fabric is essentially **Georgian**, hailing from when the Anglo-Irish gentry invested their income in new townhouses. After the 1801 Act of Union, Dublin entered a long economic decline, but remained the focus of much of the agitation that eventually led to independence.

The city is an excellent base for excursions to the picturesque mountains, lakes, forested estates and rural villages of **County Wicklow**, or to the five-thousand-year-old passage tombs at **Newgrange** in the Boyne Valley, County Meath.

WHAT TO SEE AND DO

Dublin's fashionable **Southside** is home to the city's trendy bars, restaurants and shops – especially in the cobbled alleys of **Temple Bar** leading down to the **River Liffey** – and most of its historic monuments, centred on **Trinity College**, **Grafton Street** and **St Stephen's Green**. But the **Northside**, with its long-standing working-class neighbourhoods and inner-city communities, is the real heart of the city. Across the bridges from Temple Bar are the shopping districts around **O'Connell Street**, where you'll find a flavour of the old Dublin. Here, you'll also come across a fair amount of graceful – if slightly shabby – residential streets and squares, with plenty of interest in the museums and cultural hotspots around the elegant **Parnell Square**.

The Vikings sited their assembly and burial ground near what is now **College Green**, a three sided square where Trinity College is the most famous landmark.

Trinity College

Founded in 1592, Trinity College played a major role in the development of a Protestant Anglo-Irish tradition: right up to 1966, Catholics had to obtain a special dispensation to study here, though now they make up the majority of the students. The stern grey and mellow red-brick buildings are ranged around cobbled quadrangles in a larger version of the quads at Oxford and Cambridge. **The Old Library** (May–Sept Mon–Sat 9.30am–5pm, Sun 9.30am–4.30pm; Oct–April noon–4.30pm; €9, students €8; ⓦbookofkells.ie) owns numerous Irish manuscripts; pride of place goes to the illustrated ninth-century **Book of Kells**, which contains the four Gospels written in Latin on vellum, the script

16

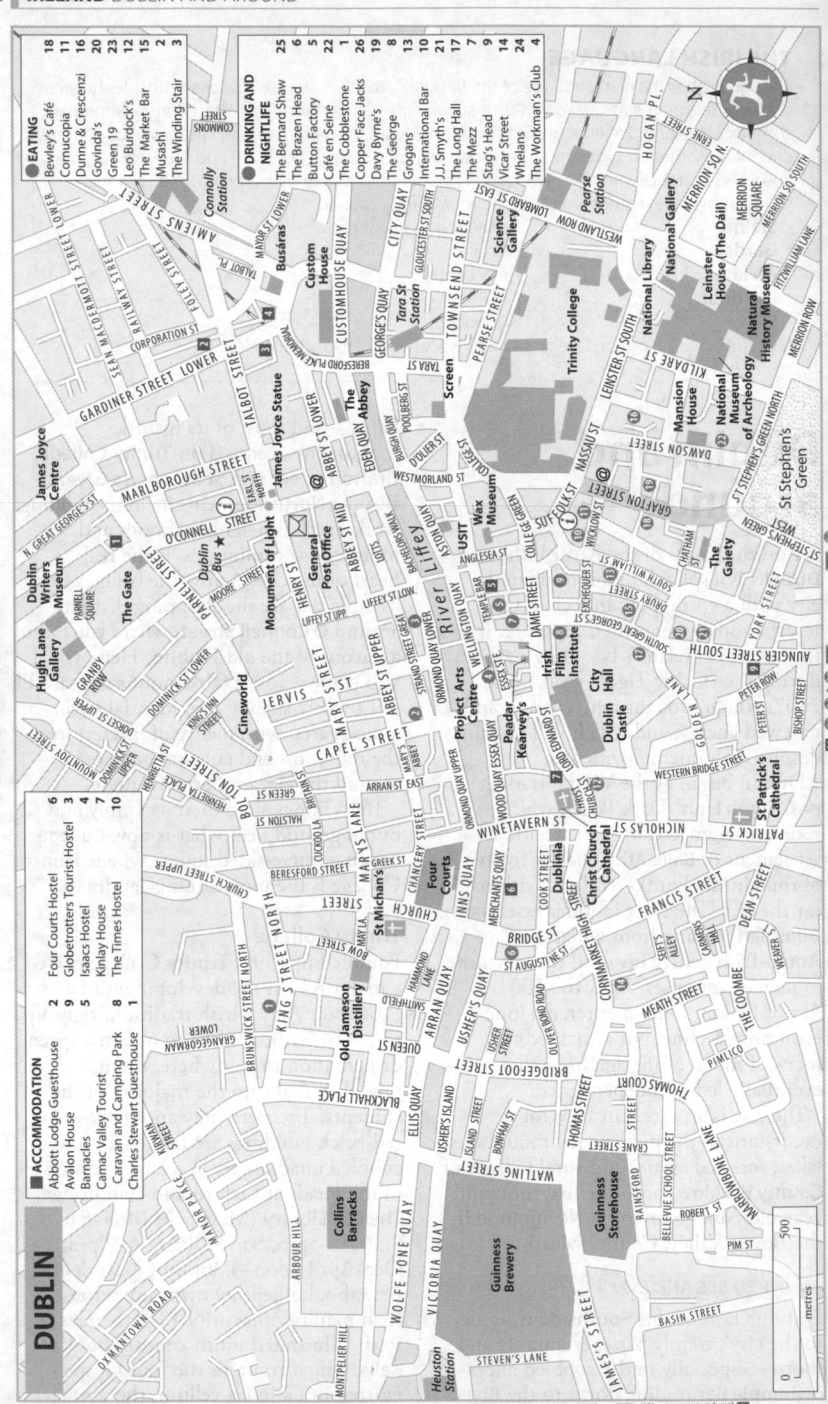

DUBLIN

■ ACCOMMODATION
Abbott Lodge Guesthouse	2
Avalon House	9
Barnacles	5
Camac Valley Tourist	
Caravan and Camping Park	8
Charles Stewart Guesthouse	1
Four Courts Hostel	6
Globetrotters Tourist Hostel	3
Isaacs Hostel	4
Kinlay House	7
The Times Hostel	10

● EATING
Bewley's Café	18
Cornucopia	11
Dunne & Crescenzi	16
Govinda's	20
Green 19	23
Leo Burdock's	12
The Market Bar	15
Musashi	2
The Winding Stair	3

● DRINKING AND NIGHTLIFE
The Bernard Shaw	25
The Brazen Head	6
Button Factory	5
Café en Seine	22
The Cobblestone	1
Copper Face Jacks	26
Davy Byrne's	19
The George	8
Grogans	13
International Bar	10
J.J. Smyth's	21
The Long Hall	17
The Mezz	7
Stag's Head	9
Vicar Street	14
Whelans	24
The Workman's Club	4

16

adorned with patterns and fantastic animals intertwined with the text's capital letters. The first of the great Irish illuminated manuscripts, the **Book of Durrow**, which dates from between 650 and 680, is also on display.

Grafton Street and around

Just south of College Green, the streets around pedestrianized **Grafton Street** frame Dublin's quality shopping area – featuring boutiques, department stores and designer outlets, as well as some secondhand, more alternative, shops. At the southern end of Grafton Street lies **St Stephen's Green**, whose pleasant gardens and ponds are a nice picnic spot on a sunny day. Running parallel to Grafton Street, Kildare Street harbours the imposing **Leinster House**, built in 1745 as the Duke of Leinster's townhouse, and now the seat of the Irish parliament, the **Dáil** (pronounced "doyle").

National Museum of Archaeology and the Natural History Museum

Alongside the Dáil is the **National Museum of Archaeology** (Tues–Sat 10am–5pm, Sun 2–5pm; free; ⍵museum.ie), the repository of the treasures of ancient Ireland. Much of its prehistoric gold was found in peat bogs, along with the Lurgan Longboat and the collection of "Bog Bodies", preserved victims of Iron Age human sacrifice. The Treasury and the Viking exhibitions display such masterpieces as the Ardagh Chalice and Tara Brooch – perhaps the greatest piece of Irish metalwork – and St Patrick's Bell.

The **Natural History Museum** (Tues–Sat 10am–5pm, Sun 2–5pm; free) has more than 10,000 animals from Ireland and overseas on display, some dating from the eighteenth century when the museum was first opened.

Merrion Square and the National Gallery

The back of Leinster House overlooks **Merrion Square**, the finest Georgian plaza in Dublin. No. 1 was once the home of Oscar Wilde, and a flamboyant statue on the green opposite shows the writer

draped insouciantly over a rock; on Sundays the square's railings are adorned with artwork for sale. On the west side of the square, the **National Gallery** (Mon–Sat 9.30am–5.30pm, Thurs until 8.30pm, Sun noon–5.30pm; free) features a collection of works by European Old Masters and French Impressionists, but the real draw is the trove of Irish paintings, best of which is the permanent exhibition devoted to Ireland's best-known painter, Jack B. Yeats.

Temple Bar and the Wax Museum

Dame Street, leading west from College Green, marks the southern edge of the **Temple Bar** quarter, where you'll find a hub of lively restaurants, pubs, boutiques and arts centres. At night the area plays host to tourists out looking for a good time, as well as to stag and hen parties – so expect a particularly raucous kind of fun.

The **National Wax Museum** (daily 10am–7pm; €12; ⍵waxmuseumplus.ie) houses an entertaining who's who of Ireland's most famous celebrities, politicians and historical figures, with interactive exhibits.

Dublin Castle

Tucked away behind City Hall, **Dublin Castle** (Mon–Sat 10am–4.45pm, Sun noon–4.45pm; €4.50; ⍵www.dublin castle.ie) was founded by the Normans, and symbolized British power over Ireland for seven hundred years. Though parts date back to 1207, it was largely rebuilt in the eighteenth century following fire damage. Tours of the State Apartments reveal much about the extravagant tastes and foibles of the viceroys, and the real highlight is the excavations in the Undercroft, where elements of Norman and Viking Dublin are still visible. The Clock Tower building now houses the **Chester Beatty Library** (Mon–Fri 10am–5pm, Sat 11am–5pm, Sun 1–5pm; Oct–April closed Mon; free; ⍵cbl.ie), a sumptuous and massive collection of books, objects and paintings amassed by the twentieth-century American collector Sir Arthur Chester Beatty on his travels around Europe and Asia.

16

16

Christ Church Cathedral

Over the brow of Dublin Hill, **Christ Church Cathedral** (June–Sept Mon–Sat 9am–7pm, Sun 12.30–2.30pm & 4.30–6pm; Oct–May Mon–Sat 9am–5pm, Sun 12.30–2.30pm; €6; ⓦchristchurchdublin.ie) was built between 1172 and 1240 and heavily restored in the 1870s. The crypt museum now houses a small selection of the cathedral's treasures, the least serious of which include a mummified cat and rat, found trapped in an organ pipe in the 1860s.

St Patrick's Cathedral

Five minutes' walk south from Christ Church is Dublin's other great Norman edifice, **St Patrick's Cathedral** (Mon–Sat 9am–5pm, Sun 9–10.30am & 12.30–2.30pm; €5.50; ⓦstpatrickscathedral.ie), founded in 1191, and replete with relics of Jonathan Swift, author of *Gulliver's Travels*, its dean from 1713 to 1747.

Guinness Brewery

West of Christ Church, the **Guinness Brewery** covers a large area on either side of James's Street. Guinness is the world's largest single beer-exporting company, dispatching some 300 million pints a year. Set in the centre of the brewery, the **Guinness Storehouse** (daily 9.30am–5pm; July & Aug until 7pm; €16.50 including pint of Guinness, ten percent discount if you book online; ⓦguinness-storehouse .com) serves as a kind of theme park for Guinness-lovers – and even if you're not a fan, you can't fail to be entertained by the interactive displays and activities, which include learning how to pour the perfect pint and watching some of those great Guinness TV ads again. Visits to the Storehouse end with reputedly the best pint of Guinness in Dublin, in the panoramic *Gravity Bar* at the top of the building, with amazing views over the city.

Irish Museum of Modern Art

Regular buses (#26, #51, #79 and #90) run along The Quays to Heuston Station from where it's a five-minute walk to the **Royal Hospital Kilmainham**, Ireland's first Neoclassical building, dating from 1680, which now houses the **Irish Museum of Modern Art** (Tues–Sat 10am–5.30pm, Wed opens 10.30am, Sun noon–5.30pm; free; ⓦimma.ie). Its permanent collection of Irish and international art includes works by Gilbert and George, Damien Hirst, Sean Scully, Francesco Clemente and Peter Doig.

General Post Office and the Monument of Light

Halfway up O'Connell Street looms the **General Post Office** (Mon–Sat 8.30am–6pm; free), the insurgents' headquarters in the 1916 Easter Rising; only the frontage survived the fighting, and you can still see where bullets were embedded in the pillars. The building is still a functioning post office, and home to an interesting **museum** (Mon–Sat 10am–5pm; €2; ⓦanpost.ie/historyandheritage) documenting the history of the postal service in Irish society. Across the road on the corner of Essex Street North is a **statue of James Joyce**. At the same junction, where the city's most famous landmark, Nelson's Pillar, once stood (it was blown up by the IRA on the fiftieth anniversary of the Easter Rising in 1966), stands a huge, illuminated stainless-steel spire – the **Monument of Light** – representing the city's hopes for the new millennium.

Parnell Square

At the northern end of O'Connell Street lies Parnell Square, one of the first of Dublin's Georgian squares. Its plain red-brick houses are broken by the grey-stone **Hugh Lane Gallery** (Tues–Thurs 10am–6pm, Fri & Sat 10am–5pm, Sun 11am–5pm; free; ⓦhughlane.ie), once the Earl of Charlemont's townhouse and the focus of fashionable Dublin. The gallery exhibits work by Irish and international masters, and features a reconstruction of Francis Bacon's working studio. Almost next door, the **Dublin Writers Museum** (Mon–Sat 10am–5pm, Sun 11am–5pm; €7.50; ⓦwritersmuseum.com) whisks you through Irish literary history from early Christian writings up to Samuel Beckett. Two blocks east of Parnell Square, at 35 North Great George's St, the **James Joyce Centre** (Tues–Sat 10am–5pm, Sun noon–5pm; €5; ⓦjamesjoyce.ie) runs intriguing walking tours of the novelist's haunts (€10, combined tickets with the Dublin Writers Museum are available, ☎01 878 8547).

Old Jameson Distillery

Fifteen minutes west of O'Connell Street, on Bow Street, is the **Old Jameson Distillery** (Mon–Sat 9am–6pm, Sun 10am–6pm; €14; ⓦjamesonwhiskey.com). Tours cover the history and method of distilling what the Irish called *uisce beatha* (anglicized to whiskey and meaning "water of life") – which differs from Scotch whisky by being three times distilled and lacking a peaty undertone – and end with a tasting session. The Distillery also has two **bars**, which pride themselves on their Jameson cocktails, and a **restaurant** (9am–4.45pm; light lunch €7).

Phoenix Park

Phoenix Park is one of the world's largest urban parks, a great escape from the hustle and bustle of the centre (bus #10 from O'Connell Street or #25 from Wellington Quay); originally priory land, it's now home to the Presidential Lodge, **Áras an Uachtaráin** (free tours every Sat 10.30am–4.30pm; ⓦpresident.ie), and **Dublin Zoo** (daily: Feb 9.30am–5pm; March–Sept 9.30am–6pm; Oct 9.30am–5.30pm; Nov–Jan 9.30am–4pm; €16; ⓦdublinzoo.ie).

ARRIVAL AND DEPARTURE

By plane The airport (ⓦdublinairport.com) is 10km north of the city; Airlink buses #747 and #748 run to Busáras bus station (every 10–20min; 30min; €6 one-way, €10 return), or there are regular Dublin Bus services #16A, #41, #41B & #41C (every 10–20min; €1.85). Aircoach (ⓦaircoach.ie) run services to the city centre and South Dublin (€6–14 one-way/€10–21 return depending on distance travelled), and a cheap, comfortable coach all the way to Cork (€15/22) and Belfast (€16/23). A taxi to Dublin centre should cost €25.

By train Trains terminate at either Connolly Station on the Northside, or Heuston Station on the Southside.

Destinations (Connolly) Belfast (8 daily Mon–Sat, 5 Sun; 2hr 10min); Drogheda (33 daily; 30min–1hr); Rosslare (3–6 daily; 3hr); Sligo (6–11 daily; 3hr 10min–3hr 30min).

Destinations (Heuston) Cork (12–15 daily; 2hr 50min); Ennis (4 daily, via Limerick; 2hr 55min–3hr 40min); Galway (9–11 daily; 2hr 20min–2hr 50min); Kilkenny

(6 daily Mon–Sat, 4 on Sun; 1hr 40min–1hr 50min); Killarney (7 daily; 3hr 30min–3hr 50min); Westport (3 daily; 3hr 20min–3hr 40min).

By bus Bus Éireann coaches arrive at Busáras bus station, off Beresford Place, just behind The Custom House; private buses use a variety of central locations.

Destinations Belfast (20 daily; 2hr 55min); Cashel (6 daily; 2hr 50min); Cork (6 daily; 4hr 25min); Derry (11 daily; 4hr); Donegal town (11 daily; 3hr 45min–4hr 10min); Doolin (2 daily; 6hr 15min); Drogheda (35 daily; 1hr 20min); Ennis (13 daily; 4hr 20min–6hr 50min); Enniskillen (11 daily; 2hr 20min–3hr); Galway (15 daily; 3hr 30min); Kilkenny (7 daily; 2hr 10min–2hr 30min); Killarney (5 daily; 6hr 10min); Newgrange (3 daily; 1hr 40min–1hr 55min); Portrush (1–2 daily; 5hr 40min); Rosslare Harbour (18 daily; 3hr 20min); Sligo (7 daily; 4hr); Westport (4 daily; 5hr–5hr 40min).

By boat Ferries dock at either Dún Laoghaire, 10km south of the city centre, from where DART railway connects to the city (every 20min; €2.80; 20min), or at the closer Dublin Port, where the #53B bus (€2.40; 35min) meets arriving ferries; through-coaches from Britain usually drop you at Busáras.

INFORMATION AND TOURS

Tourist office Suffolk St, off College Green (Mon–Sat 9am–5.30pm, Sun 10.30am–3pm; ⓦvisitdublin.com), with branches at 14 Upper O'Connell St, the Dún Laoghaire ferry terminal and the airport.

Travel agency USIT on Aston Quay, by O'Connell Bridge (Mon–Fri 10am–6.30pm, Thurs until 7pm, Sat 9.30am–5pm; ☎01 602 1904, ⓦusit.ie).

Bus tours City Sightseeing (ⓦcitysightseeingdublin .com) and Dublin Bus Tours (ⓦdublinsightseeing.ie) run similar hop-on, hop-off tours to all the major sights in the city (€18); both collect from the front of Trinity College.

Walking tours Tour Gratis (ⓦneweuropetours.eu) operate free walking tours, picking up from all of the listed hostels (see p.580) every morning. The fantastic 1916 Rebellion walking tours (March–Oct Mon–Sat 11.30am, Sun 1pm; meet at the *International Bar*, 23 Wicklow St; €12; ⓦ1916rising.com) visit sights of interest relating to the 1916 Rising.

Organized pub crawls Dublin Literary Pub Crawl (April–Oct daily 7.30pm; Nov–March Thurs–Sun 7.30pm; meet at *The Duke Pub*, 9 Duke St; €12; ⓦdublinpubcrawl.com); and the more raucous Backpacker Pubcrawl (May–Sept daily 8pm; Oct–March Thurs–Sat 8pm; meet at *Peadar Kearney's Bar* on Dame St; €12; ⓦbackpackerpubcrawl.com).

GETTING AROUND

Pre-paid Leap Cards, available online (ⓦleapcard.ie; refundable deposit of €5) or from newsagents, are valid on Dublin Bus, LUAS trams, DART and commuter rail services, and work out cheaper than paying cash fares.

16

By bus Dublin has an extensive route network and all buses are exact fare only. Fares range from €0.65 for short city-centre journeys to €2.80, and a one-day bus pass is €6.90. Free bus timetables are available from Dublin Bus, 59 Upper O'Connell St. Nitelink night buses cost €5.70.

By tram The LUAS tram service operates along two routes: from Connolly Station to Tallaght via Abbey St to Heuston Station, and from St Stephen's Green to Sandyford. Tickets cost €1.60–2.70 one-way, €3.10–5.10 return.

By train The DART railway links Howth and Malahide to the north of the city with Bray and Greystones to the south via Pearse, Tara St and Connolly stations in the city centre (maximum fare €4). A trip on the DART is an activity in itself, affording stunning views of the Dublin suburbs and coastline. Get off at Howth, Malahide, Sandymount, Dún Laoghaire, Killiney, Bray or Greystones for pleasant seaside walks.

Bike rental Cycle Ways, 185 Parnell St ☎ 01 873 4748.

ACCOMMODATION

Although Dublin has lots of accommodation, anywhere central will probably be full at weekends, around St Patrick's Day (March 17), at Easter and in high summer, so it's wise to book ahead (preferably online). The cheaper places are generally north of the river, especially around the bus and train stations northeast of the centre. All hostels listed provide free breakfast.

HOSTELS

Avalon House 55 Aungier St ☎ 01 475 0001, ⓦ avalon -house.ie. Bustling and friendly hostel with slightly cramped dorms but plenty of twin or four-bedded rooms. Performers get a free night's accommodation for an evening recital in the café. Dorm €12, double €50

Barnacles 19 Temple Lane ☎ 01 671 6277, ⓦ barnacles .ie. Hugely popular hostel on a cobbled street in the heart of Temple Bar. Dorm €17.50, double/twin €68

★ **Four Courts Hostel** 15–17 Merchants Quay ☎ 01 672 5839, ⓦ fourcourtshostel.com. In a very central location, this hostel is housed in Georgian buildings overlooking the River Liffey. Excellent facilities and helpful staff. Dorm €15, double/twin €48

Globetrotters Tourist Hostel 46 Gardiner St Lower ☎ 01 873 5893, ⓦ globetrottersdublin.com. Upmarket hostel where security-locked dorms and individual bed lights make for a peaceful night's sleep. There's a pretty Japanese garden, and all prices include a full Irish breakfast. Dorm €12, double €69

Isaacs Hostel 2–5 Frenchman's Lane ☎ 01 855 6215, ⓦ isaacs.ie. Housed in an eighteenth-century wine warehouse with its own restaurant and a free sauna in the basement. Close to the bus station. Dorm €15

Kinlay House 2–12 Lord Edward St ⓦ kinlaydublin.ie. Large, friendly and popular hostel right beside Christ Church Cathedral. Dorm €12.50, double/twin €60

★ **The Times Hostel** 8 Camden Place ☎ 01 475 8588, ⓦ timeshostels.com. Small and convivial hostel close to some of the city's best pubs and restaurants, with free pancake breakfasts and organized tours, pub crawls and game nights. Dorm €14, double €60

GUESTHOUSES

Abbott Lodge Guesthouse 87–88 Gardiner St Lower ☎ 01 836 5438, ⓦ abbott-lodge.com. Georgian townhouse with large, high-ceilinged rooms and floral bedspreads. Welcoming and family run with plenty of kitsch decor involving fake flowers and ornaments. Single €65, double €80

Charles Stewart Guesthouse 5/6 Parnell Square ☎ 01 878 0350, ⓦ charlesstewart.ie. Very reasonably priced accommodation in elegant Georgian surroundings, opposite the Gate Theatre. Double/twin €62

CAMPSITE

Camac Valley Tourist Caravan and Camping Park Naas Rd, Clondalkin ☎ 01 464 0644, ⓦ camacvalley.com. The most convenient campsite, with excellent facilities, located on the N7, a 35min drive from the centre. Bus #69 from the centre (Aston Quay, near O'Connell Bridge) stops right outside the campsite. The last bus is at 11.15pm, so if you're any later, a taxi (around €25) is your only option. €10 per person

EATING

★ **Bewley's Café** 78 Grafton St. An old Dublin institution, and a favourite haunt of Ireland's literary luminaries, including Joyce, Kavanagh, Beckett and O'Casey. Lounge over a coffee and croissant for breakfast or enjoy good pasta (€10), pizza (€12) or salad (€8) for lunch or dinner. You can also catch a lunchtime play or music recital in the theatre upstairs. Daily 8am–10pm.

Cornucopia 21 Wicklow St. One of the city's few vegetarian cafés and very popular for its generous portions of home-made soups, salads, curries and gratins. Mains €8–12. Mon–Sat 8.30am–9pm, Sun noon–8.30pm.

Dunne & Crescenzi 14–16 South Frederick St. Authentic Italian restaurant serving delicious bruschetta (€5.50), antipasti, panini and simple pasta dishes (from €12), washed down with the cheapest (yet very palatable) house wine in Dublin. Daily 8am–late.

Govinda's 4 Aungier St. Huge helpings of dhal and rice and tasty vegetarian curries (€7), plus daily veggie specials, served by very friendly staff. Mon–Sat noon–9pm.

Green 19 19 Camden St. Simple yet top-quality dishes like slow-braised pork belly with a chorizo cassoulet or corned beef with mash and parsley sauce, all priced at €10. Excellent cocktails and a funky vibe complete the picture. Mon–Sat 10am–11pm, Sun noon–10pm.

★ TREAT YOURSELF

For high-end organic Irish food, it is hard to beat **The Winding Stair** (40 Ormond Quay; ☎ 01 872 7320, ⓦ winding-stair.com). Dishes are thoughtfully prepared using ingredients from small, carefully selected producers. The menu changes daily, but expect dishes like steamed cockles and mussels with Clogherhead crab and Irish rib-eye steak with roasted garlic truffle butter. The dining room is bright and airy, with gorgeous views over the River Liffey. Mains €22. Daily noon–10.30pm.

Leo Burdock's 2 Werburgh St. Dublin's best fish and chips – takeaway only. Fresh cod is €5.95. There's another branch on Liffey St Lower. Daily noon–midnight.

★ **The Market Bar** 14 Fade St. Dublin's first gastro-bar serving tapas with an Irish twist in a converted abattoir. Tapas €4–12. Daily noon–midnight.

Musashi 15 Capel St. Chow down on some of the city's finest (and cheapest) sushi, accompanied by a jazz soundtrack. BYOB. Daily noon–10pm.

DRINKING AND NIGHTLIFE

Most of Dublin's eight hundred pubs serve food as well, and can be the best place to sample traditional Irish cuisine. The music scene – much of which is pub-based – is changeable, so it's always best to check the listings magazines like *Hot Press* (€3.50). See ⓦ dublineventguide.com for listings of free events, or *In Dublin* (ⓦ indublin.ie) and *Totally Dublin* (ⓦ totallydublin.ie). Camden Street is the best place to find live rock; hit Temple Bar for clubs playing pop and dance music, as well as touristy traditional sessions.

BARS

★ **The Bernard Shaw** 11–12 South Richmond St ⓦ bodytonicmusic.com. The walls of this "bar, café and creative space" are covered in graffiti outside and the works of local artists inside. There's a colourful beer garden, nightly DJs playing everything from reggae to house, a pool table and a Big Blue Bus serving excellent pizzas (€8). Mon–Fri 8am–midnight/1am, Sat & Sun 4pm–midnight/1am.

Café en Seine 39–40 Dawson St ⓦ cafeenseine.ie. Join Dublin's well-heeled professionals for a cocktail or two in an Art Nouveau-style café-bar with three floors and five bars. Daily noon–late.

Davy Byrne's 21 Duke St ⓦ davybyrnes.com. An object of pilgrimage for *Ulysses* fans, since Leopold Bloom stopped here for a snack. Attracts a sophisticated crowd and also serves good food (traditional Irish stew €12). Mon–Wed

11am–11.30pm, Thurs & Fri 11am 12.30am, Sat 10.30am–12.30am, Sun 12.30–11pm.

Grogans 15 South William St ⓦ groganspub.ie. Popular spot among Dublin's bohemian set, with paintings by local artists adorning the walls. On sunny evenings the crowd spills onto the pedestrian street outside. Mon–Thurs 10.30am–11.30pm, Fri & Sat 10.30am–12.30am, Sun 12.30–11pm.

The Long Hall 51 South Great George's St. Victorian pub encrusted with mirrors and antique clocks. Mon–Wed 4–11.30pm, Thurs 1–11.30pm, Fri & Sat 1pm–12.30am, Sun 1–11pm.

Stag's Head 1 Dame Court, Dame St, almost opposite the Central Bank. Wonderfully intimate pub, full of mahogany, stained glass and mirrors. Very popular with local Dubliners, and does good pub lunches. Mon–Sat 10.30am–1am, Sun 10.30am–midnight.

CLUBS

Button Factory Curved St ⓦ buttonfactory.ie. Housed in the refurbished Temple Bar Music Centre, this is the place to find top Irish and international DJs in the Thurs–Sat club. Opening hours are erratic but club nights are 11pm–2.30am.

Copper Face Jacks 29–30 Harcourt St ⓦ copperfacejacks.ie. The most popular of several similar venues along Harcourt St, and notorious for its pop tunes and groups of single lads and lasses looking for a good time. Daily 9pm–2.30am.

The George South Great George's St ⓦ thegeorge.ie. Dublin's oldest and most popular gay bar and club. Mon 2–11.30pm, Tues–Fri 2pm–2.30am, Sat 12.30pm–2.30am, Sun 12.30pm–1.30am.

The Workman's Club 10 Wellington Quay ⓦ theworkmansclub.com. A maze of interconnecting rooms in a red-brick building fronting the River Liffey houses dancefloors, venues for live music and poetry readings, themed bars and a rooftop terrace. Daily 5pm–3am.

LIVE MUSIC

★ **The Brazen Head** 20 Lower Bridge St ⓦ brazenhead.com. The oldest pub in Dublin, with traditional music nightly from 9.30pm. Daily until late.

The Cobblestone 77 King St North ⓦ cobblestonepub.ie. Atmospheric pub on the edge of the Smithfield Plaza, famous for its nightly traditional sessions. Daily until late.

International Bar 23 Wicklow St ⓦ international-bar.com. Large saloon with rock bands, jazz and a comedy club upstairs or in the cellar. Daily until late.

J.J. Smyth's 12 Aungier St ⓦ jjsmyths.com. One of the few places to catch local jazz and blues talent. Opening hours depend on gigs and events.

The Mezz 23–24 Eustace St ⓦ mezz.ie. Café-bar with live rock, jazz, blues funk, soul and reggae every night. Bar food served 2.30–9.30pm. Mains from €7. Opening hours depend on gigs and events.

Vicar Street 58–59 Thomas St ⓦ vicarstreet.com. One of the city's finest music venues, offering a varied programme of major music and comedy acts. Opening hours depend on the events programme.

Whelans 25 Wexford St ⓦ whelanslive.com. Notorious music pub and club attracting a host of up-and-coming international stars as well as local talent. Daily until late.

ENTERTAINMENT

THEATRES

Dublin's theatres are among the finest in Europe, offering a good mix of classical and more avant-garde performances. Tickets start at around €20, with concessions offered on Mon–Thurs nights and for matinees. Check the *Event Guide* (ⓦ eventguide.ie) for performances.

The Abbey Lower Abbey St ⓦ abbeytheatre.ie. Ireland's most historic theatre, founded in 1899 by W.B. Yeats to promote Irish culture and drama.

The Gaiety South King St ⓦ gaietytheatre.ie. Dublin's oldest and most ornate theatre, showing pantomimes and popular plays.

The Gate 1 Cavendish Row ⓦ gate-theatre.ie. Showcases contemporary Irish drama, alongside European classics.

CINEMAS

Cineworld Parnell St ☎ 1520 880 444, ⓦ cineworld.ie. Seventeen-screen multiplex.

Irish Film Institute 6 Eustace St, Temple Bar ☎ 01 679 5744, ⓦ irishfilm.ie. Shows classics and new independent films, and has a good bar and restaurant.

Screen D'Olier St ☎ 0818 300 301, ⓦ screencinema.ie. Arthouse and independent films.

SHOPPING

Charity and secondhand Camden Street has some good charity shops, while Harlequin, Castle Market, and Wild Child on Drury Street sell vintage gear.

High street and department stores Try Grafton Street and Henry Street for high-street shops, including Topshop (top of Grafton St) and Penny's (37 O'Connell St), which sells ridiculously cheap clothes, shoes and accessories. Dundrum (Mon–Fri 9am–9pm, Sat 9am–7pm & Sun 10am–7pm) is home to the biggest shopping centre in Europe; take LUAS from St Stephen's Green to Balally.

Markets You can pick up some great bargains on retro clothes and accessories and Irish designer goods at Cow's Lane Market in Meeting House Square in Temple Bar (Sat). George's Street Arcade (daily) also has some interesting buys – books, vinyl artwork and clothes.

DIRECTORY

Embassies Australia, Fitzwilton House, Wilton Terrace ☎ 01 664 5300; Canada, 7–8 Wilton Terrace ☎ 01 234

4000; UK, 29 Merrion Rd ☎ 01 205 3700; US, 42 Elgin Rd, Ballsbridge ☎ 01 668 8777.

Exchange General Post Office, O'Connell St; most city centre banks.

Hospitals Southside: St James's, James St ☎ 01 410 3000; Northside: Mater Misericordiae, Eccles St ☎ 01 885 8888.

Internet Central Cybercafé, 6 Grafton St; Global Internet Café, 8 Lower O'Connell St. There are free wi-fi spots around the city centre; look out for the DublinFree mosaics or see ⓦ dublincity.ie for locations.

Left luggage Busáras, Heuston and Connolly stations.

Pharmacy Dame Street Pharmacy, 16 Dame St; O'Connell's, 55 O'Connell St.

Post office GPO O'Connell St (Mon–Sat 8.30am–6pm); St Andrew's St (Mon–Fri 9am–6pm, Sat 9am–1pm).

COUNTY WICKLOW

Referred to as the "Garden of Ireland", the picturesque mountains, lakes, forested estates and rural villages of **County Wicklow** provide a stunning backdrop for a bracing country walk or scenic drive. Given its proximity to the capital, the region is easily visited on a day-trip from Dublin, but there are plenty of B&Bs and hostels in the area.

The wonderfully unspoilt 127km mountain trail, the **Wicklow Way**, bisects the Wicklow Mountains, looping through glacial valleys, farmland and forests. The trail passes through the villages of **Roundwood, Rathdrum** and **Enniskerry**, from where the eighteenth-century **Powerscourt Estate** gardens and waterfall (house and gardens daily 9.30am–5.30pm; €8.50, waterfall only €5.50; ⓦ powerscourt.ie) are easily accessible.

Some 30km south of Enniskerry, the beautifully tranquil monastic site of **Glendalough** ("valley of the two lakes") forms one of the most dramatic landscapes in the country. The monastery was founded in the sixth century by St Kevin, and the 30m-high tapering round tower on the bank of the Lower Lake has epitomized mystical Ireland in tourist brochures for decades.

ARRIVAL AND DEPARTURE

By bus You can get to the three villages of Roundwood, Rathdrum and Enniskerry (all on the Wicklow Way) on bus #44 from O'Connell Street in Dublin city centre (hourly; €2.80). For Glendalough, take the St Kevin's bus (4 daily;

€13 one-way/€20 return; ⓦ glendaloughbus.com) from outside the Mansion House on Dawson Street.

INFORMATION AND TOURS

Tourist office The Glendalough visitor centre is at Lower Lake (daily 9.30am–6pm, closes 5pm March–Oct; €3), and the Wicklow Mountains National Park Information Centre (Upper Lake; May–Sept daily 10am–5.30pm; Oct–Feb Sat & Sun 10am–dusk; ⓦ wicklowmountainsnationalpark.ie) can provide information on walking routes.

Tours The visitor centre at Lower Lake runs tours (daily 2pm) of Glendalough monastic site. Several companies run day-tours to Glendalough from Dublin (including Over the Top Tours, ⓦ overthetoptours.com, and Wild Wicklow Tours, ⓦ wildwicklow.ie; both €25–28).

ACCOMMODATION

Glendalough Hostel On the R757 near the Upper Lake ☏ 0404 45342, ⓦ anoige.ie. Ideally located in an old lodge near the monastic settlement. Dorm **€16**, twin **€50**

NEWGRANGE

One of the foremost visitor attractions in the country, **Brú na Bóinne** ("the palace of the Boyne") encompasses the 5000-year-old passage graves of **Newgrange**, Knowth and Dowth. Three rotund mounds of earth rise above these Neolithic graves – now excavated and reconstructed – south of the River Boyne in County Meath.

The **exhibition** (€3, €6 with entrance to Newgrange and €11 for all three passage graves) in the visitor centre (see below) includes information on the sites, how they were built and the artwork of enigmatic spirals carved into the stone walls. There is also a full-scale replica of the chamber at Newgrange as well as a model of one of the smaller tombs at Knowth.

The **guided tour** of Newgrange is led by the visitor centre (see below), and includes a simulation of the rising sun during the winter solstice, during which the rays of light enter through a strategically positioned slit above the entrance, casting first light on the burial chamber before spreading along the 19m length of the passage.

ARRIVAL AND INFORMATION

By bus To get to the visitor centre, take the Bus Éireann service #100 from the Busáras bus depot in Dublin city centre (see opposite) to Drogheda, from where shuttle bus #163 connects to the visitor centre.

Tourist information Access to the monuments is by guided tour from the visitor centre only (daily: May–Sept 9am–6.30pm; Oct–April 9.30am–5pm; ⓦ newgrange .com), located on the south side of the River Boyne, 5km east of the village of Slane.

The southeast

The southeast is Ireland's sunniest and driest corner. The region's medieval and Anglo-Norman history is richly concentrated in **Kilkenny**, a bustling, quaint inland town, while to the west, at the heart of County Tipperary, is the **Rock of Cashel**, a spectacular natural formation topped with Christian buildings from virtually every period. In the southwest, **Cork** is both relaxed and spirited, the perfect place to ease you into the exhilarations of the west coast.

16

KILKENNY

KILKENNY is Ireland's finest medieval city, its castle set above the broad sweep of the River Nore and its narrow streets laced with carefully maintained buildings. In 1641, the city became the virtual capital of Ireland, with the founding of a parliament known as the Confederation of Kilkenny. The power of this short-lived attempt to unite resistance to English persecution of Catholics had greatly diminished by the time Cromwell's wreckers arrived in 1650. Kilkenny never recovered its prosperity, but enough remains to indicate its former importance.

WHAT TO SEE AND DO

Left at the top of Rose Inn Street is the broad **Parade**, which leads up to the castle. To the right, the High Street passes the eighteenth-century **Tholsel**, once the city's financial centre and now the town hall.

Rothe House

Beyond the Tholsel is **Parliament Street**, the main thoroughfare, where the **Rothe**

House (April–Oct Mon–Sat 10.30am–
5pm, Sun 3–5pm; Nov–March Mon–Sat
10.30am–4.30pm; €5; ⓦrothehouse
.com) provides a unique example of an
Irish Tudor merchant's home, comprising
three separate houses linked by
cobbled courtyards.

St Canice's Cathedral

The thirteenth-century **St Canice's
Cathedral** (June–Aug Mon–Sat
9am–6pm, Sun 2–6pm; Sept–March
Mon–Sat 10am–1pm & 2–4/5pm, Sun
2–4/5pm; €4; ⓦstcanicescathedral.com)
has a fine array of sixteenth-century
monuments, many in black Kilkenny
limestone. The **round tower** next to the
cathedral (June–Aug Mon–Sat
9am–6pm, Sun 2–6pm; Sept–March
Mon–Sat 10am–1pm & 2–4/5pm, Sun
2–4/5pm; €3; combined ticket with
cathedral €6) is the only remnant of a
monastic settlement reputedly founded
by St Canice in the sixth century; there
are superb views from the top.

Castle

It's the imposing twelfth-century **Castle**,
though, which defines Kilkenny
(tours daily: 9/9.30am–4.30/5.30pm;
€6; ⓦkilkennycastle.ie). Its library,
drawing room, bedrooms and Long
Gallery of family portraits are open
for viewing, as is the **Butler Gallery**
(daily 10am–1pm & 2–4.30/5.30pm;
free; ⓦbutlergallery.com), housing
exhibitions of modern art.

ARRIVAL AND DEPARTURE

By train The train station is just north of the centre, off
John Street.
Destinations Dublin (7 daily; 1hr 40min–2hr).
By bus The bus station is next to the train station, off John
Street. Some services stop on Patrick Street.
Destinations Cork (3 daily; 2hr 50min); Dublin (6 daily;
2hr 15min–2hr 45min).

INFORMATION

Tourist office Rose Inn St, in the sixteenth-century Shee
Alms House (May–Sept Mon–Sat 9.30am–5.30pm; Oct–
April Tues–Sat 9.30am–1pm & 2–5pm; ☎ 056 775 1500;
ⓦkilkennytourism.ie).
Listings The weekly *Kilkenny People* (€1.80) has listings
information. See also ⓦkilkenny.ie.

Festivals The town is renowned for The Cat Laughs
comedy festival in June (ⓦthecatlaughs.com) and its Arts
Festival in August (ⓦkilkennyarts.ie).

ACCOMMODATION

★ **Kilkenny Tourist Hostel** 35 Parliament St ☎ 056
776 3541, ⓦkilkennyhostel.ie. An excellent budget option
in a rambling Georgian building. Dorm €15, double €36
MacGabhainn's Backpackers Hostel 24 Vicar St ☎ 056
777 0970, ⓦmacgabhainns-backpackers.hostel.com.
Small and friendly hostel in the centre of town, with a
barbecue area for sunny days. Dorm €15
Tree Grove camping Danville House, New Ross Rd
☎ 056 777 0302, ⓦtreegrovecamping.com. Campsite
1.5km south of the city on the R700, open March–Nov 15.
Bike rental available. €8 per person

EATING

Billy Byrne's 39 John St ☎ 056 772 1783. Fine pub
lunches for €9. Food served 10am–6pm.
★ **Café Sol** William St ☎ 056 776 4987. Award-winning
café-restaurant which is pricey in the evenings, but good
for salads and light mains (from €8) at lunch. Mon & Tues
11.30am–5pm, Wed–Sun 11.30am–9.30pm.
Gourmet Store 56 High St. Hummus, panini, bagels and
wraps made to order at this little deli. From €3.
Mon–Sat 8am–6pm.
Kyteler's Inn St Kieran St ⓦkytelersinn.com. Decent pub
grub (from €10) in medieval surroundings, accompanied
by regular traditional music sessions. Food served noon–
9pm. Daily until late.

DRINKING AND NIGHTLIFE

Parliament Street and Ormonde Street are best for live
traditional and rock music; John Street has a more
commercial feel with clubs and pop music.
Edward Langton's 69 John St. Swanky hotel with four
bars and a popular club open Tues, Thurs & Sat
10pm–2.30am. There's a swing club on Thurs–Sat in the
67 Bar and regular comedy nights, live music and theatre
in the Set Theatre. Also serves good pub grub (mains €12)
from noon to 10pm daily.
The Pumphouse 26–28 Parliament St. Popular with
young and old, locals and travellers alike. Music most
nights, and there's also a pool table. Sun–Thurs
2–11.30pm, Fri & Sat 2pm–12.30am.
★ **Ryans** 62 Friary St ⓦryanskilkenny.com. Intimate,
candlelit bar with traditional music on Thurs and jazz, blues,
rock and open-mic sessions other nights. Daily until late.
Tynan's 2 Horseleap Slip, St John's Bridge. Riverside bar
with cosy Victorian interior and beer garden; there are still
relics from its days as a pharmacy and grocery store. Late
bar Mon, Wed & Thurs; live music Mon–Thurs from 9pm.
Daily until late.

THE ROCK OF CASHEL

The extraordinary **ROCK OF CASHEL** (daily: March–May 9am–5.30pm; June–Sept 9am–7pm; Oct 9am–5.30pm; Nov–Feb 9am–4.30pm; €6) appears as a mirage of crenellations rising bolt upright from the vast encircling plain and is where St Patrick reputedly used a shamrock to explain the doctrine of the Trinity. **Cormac's Chapel**, built in the 1130s, is the earliest and most beautiful of Ireland's Romanesque churches, and the limestone **Cathedral**, begun in the thirteenth century, is a fine example of Anglo-Norman architecture, with its Gothic arches and lancet windows. The tapering **round tower** is the earliest building on the Rock, dating from the early twelfth century. The **Cashel Heritage Centre** (daily 9.30am–5.30pm; closed Sat & Sun Nov–Feb; free; ⓦcashel.ie) on Main Street has a small exhibition that covers the history of the town.

ARRIVAL AND DEPARTURE

By bus Cashel is most often visited as a day-trip from Cork or Kilkenny; buses from Cork drop off outside *The Bakehouse* bakery, those from Kilkenny and Dublin on the other side of the street.

ACCOMMODATION

★ **Cashel Lodge** Dundrum Rd ⓣ062 61003, ⓦcashel -lodge.com. A beautifully renovated coach house blessed with spectacular views and located close to the Rock. Dorm €20, double €65, camping €10

EATING AND DRINKING

The Bakehouse 7 Main St. Cosy café offering fresh baked scones, pastries, soups and sandwiches (€5–7). Daily 8am–5.30pm.
Mikey Ryan's Bar 76 Main St. Atmospheric traditional pub with occasional live music. Fresh soup and sandwiches served Mon–Sat noon–3pm.

CORK

Everywhere in **CORK** there's evidence of its history as a great mercantile centre, with grey-stone quaysides, old warehouses, and elegant, quirky bridges spanning the River Lee to each side of the city's island core – but the lively atmosphere and large student population, combined with a vibrant social and cultural scene, are equally powerful draws. Massive stone walls built by invading Normans in the twelfth century were destroyed by William III's forces during the **Siege of Cork** in 1690, after which waterborne trade brought increasing prosperity, as witnessed by the city's fine eighteenth-century bow-fronted houses and ostentatious nineteenth-century churches.

WHAT TO SEE AND DO

The graceful arc of **St Patrick's Street** – which with **Grand Parade** forms the commercial heart of the centre – is crammed with major chain stores. Just off here on Princes Street, the **English Market** (Mon–Sat 9am–5.30pm) offers the chance to sample local delicacies like *drisheen* (a peppered sausage made from a sheep's stomach lining and blood). On the far side of St Patrick's Street, chic Paul Street is a gateway to the bijou environs of French Church Street and Carey's Lane. The west of the city is predominantly residential, though Fitzgerald Park is home to the **Cork Public Museum** (Mon–Fri 11am–1pm & 2.15–5pm, Sat 11am–1pm & 2.15–4pm, plus April–Sept Sun 3–5pm), which focuses on Republican history.

Shandon area

North of the River Lee is the historic **Shandon area**, a reminder of Cork's eighteenth-century status as the most important port in Europe for dairy products. The striking **Cork Butter Exchange** survives, stout nineteenth-century Neoclassical buildings given over to craft workshops. At one corner of the old butter market on O'Connell Square is the **Cork Butter Museum** (March–June & Sept–Oct 10am–5pm; July & Aug 10am–6pm; Nov–Feb Sat & Sun 10am–3.30pm; €4; ⓦcorkbutter .museum), which exhibits, among other items, a keg of thousand-year-old butter. Behind the square is the pleasant Georgian church of **St Anne's Shandon** (March–Oct Mon–Sat 10am–4pm, Sun 11.30am–3.30pm; June–Sept Mon–Sat 10am–5pm, Sun 11.30am–4.30pm; Nov–Feb Mon–Sat 11am–3pm, closed

16

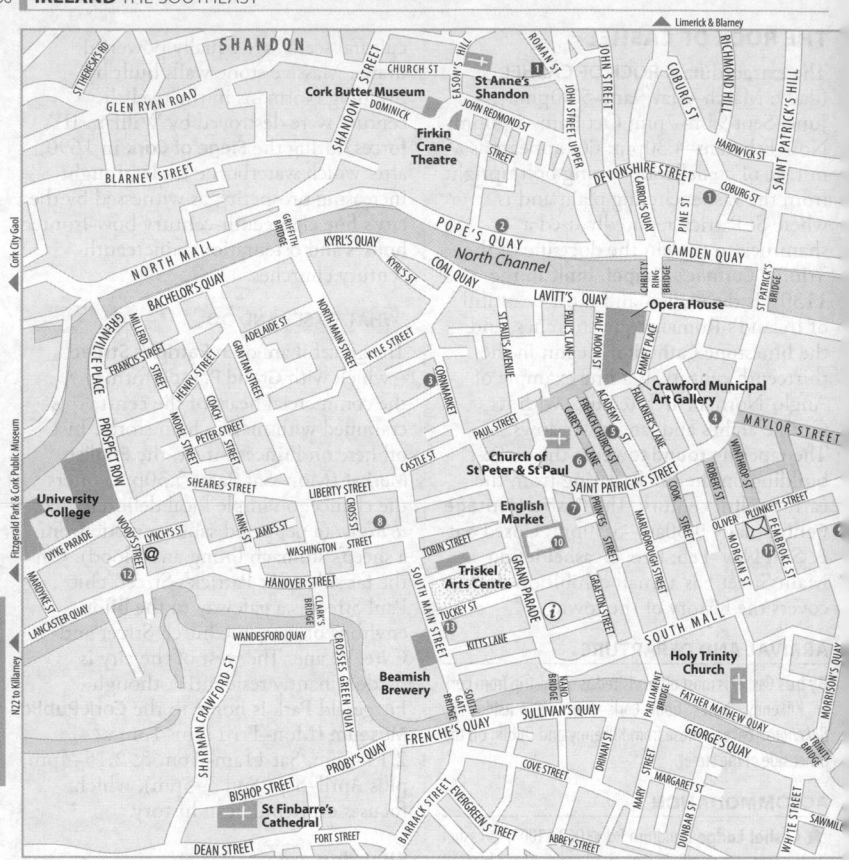

Sun; €6), easily recognizable from all over the city by its weather vane – a 3.5m salmon. The church tower gives excellent views over the city and an opportunity to ring the famous bells. Around 2km west along North Mall, in the Sunday's Well area of the city, is the nineteenth-century **Cork City Gaol** (daily: March–Oct 9.30am–5pm; Nov–Feb 10am–4pm; €8; ⓦ corkcitygaol.com), with wax figures and an excellent audioguide focusing on social history.

ARRIVAL AND DEPARTURE

By train The train station is 1km east of the city centre on Lower Glanmire Road.

Destinations Dublin (15 daily Mon–Sat, 12 Sun; 2hr 35min–3hr 35min); Killarney (8 daily; 1hr 30min–2hr).

By bus The bus station is on Parnell Place by Merchant's Quay.

Destinations Cashel (6 daily; 1hr 35min–1hr 50min); Dublin (6 daily; 4hr 25min); Galway (13 daily; 4hr 20min); Kilkenny (3 daily; 3hr 10min–4hr 15min); Killarney (11 daily; 2hr).

By ferry Boats from Roscoff arrive at Ringaskiddy, 13km from town. A shuttle bus runs to the centre.

INFORMATION

Tourist office Grand Parade (Mon–Sat 9.30am–5pm, July & Aug also Sun 10am–5pm; ☎ 021 425 5100, ⓦ discoverireland.ie/southwest).

Internet Internet Exchange, Wood St; €3/hr.

Festivals Cork's international jazz festival takes place in late October (ⓦ corkjazzfestival.com) and there's a film festival in November (ⓦ corkfilmfest.org).

ACCOMMODATION

Aaran House Tourist Hostel Lower Glanmire Rd ☎ 021 455 1566, ⓔ tracy_flynn3@hotmail.com. Friendly and very convenient for train and bus stations. Dorm €14, twin/double €38

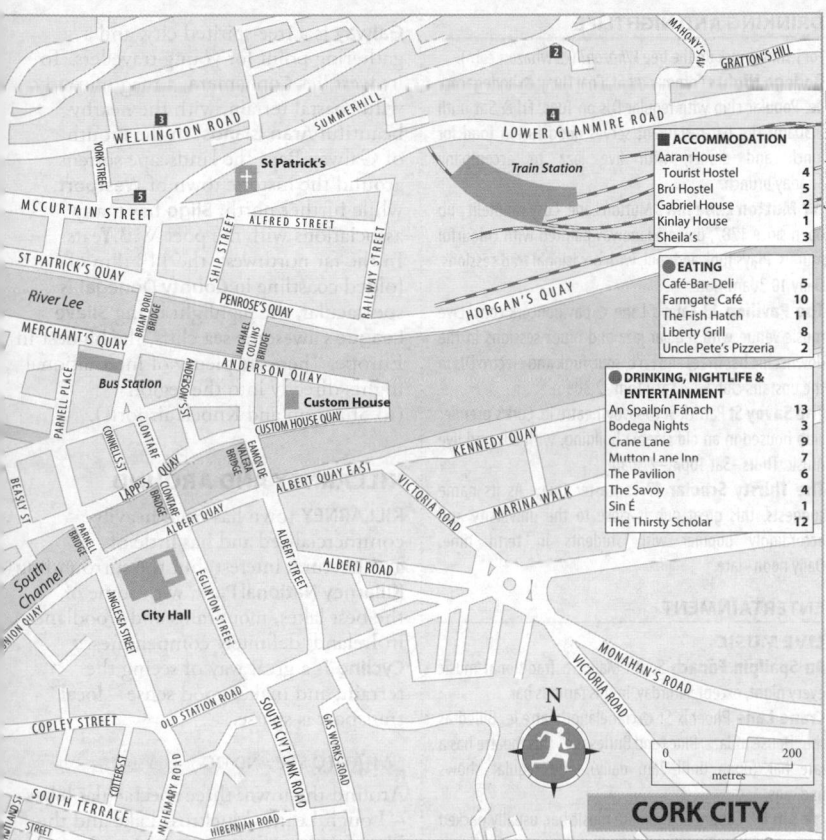

ACCOMMODATION
Aaran House	
Tourist Hostel	4
Brú Hostel	5
Gabriel House	2
Kinlay House	1
Sheila's	3

EATING
Café-Bar-Deli	5
Farmgate Café	10
The Fish Hatch	11
Liberty Grill	8
Uncle Pete's Pizzeria	2

DRINKING, NIGHTLIFE & ENTERTAINMENT
An Spailpín Fánach	13
Bodega Nights	3
Crane Lane	9
Mutton Lane Inn	7
The Pavilion	6
The Savoy	4
Sin É	1
The Thirsty Scholar	12

CORK CITY

16

Brú Hostel 57 McCurtain St ☎021 455 9667, ⓦbruhostel .com. Enjoy modern facilities at the affordable hostel with a bar attached, where guests can claim a free pint. Live music every night. Dorm €17, double €48

Gabriel House Summerhill North ☎021 450 0333, ⓦgabrielhousebb.com. This old Christian Brothers building has been beautifully renovated and now offers quality accommodation with sweeping views of the city. Single €50, double €80

Kinlay House Bob & Joan's Walk, off Upper John St, Shandon ☎021 450 8966, ⓦkinlayhousecork.ie. With great facilities (self-catering, kitchen, laundry, service, health club), this large but friendly hostel is in a lovely part of town near St Anne's Shandon. Dorm €15, double €50

★ **Sheila's** 4 Belgrave Place, Wellington Rd ☎021 450 5562, ⓦsheilashostel.ie. Set back from the hustle and bustle of town, *Sheila's* is comfortable, clean and well run, with extras such as a small cinema room and a sauna (€2). Dorm €16, double/twin €38

EATING

Café-Bar-Deli 18 Academy St. This ever-popular restaurant serves delicious pasta dishes (from €9) and pizza (from €7). Mon–Sat 12.30–9/10pm, Sun 2–8pm.

★ **Farmgate Café** English Market ⓦfarmgate.ie. Enjoy wholesome, fresh food sourced from the surrounding market in a bustling atmosphere. Mains €9–14, gourmet sandwiches €7. Mon–Sat 8.30am–5pm.

The Fish Hatch *Imperial Hotel*, Pembroke St. Cook-to-order takeaway offering premium fresh fish, hand-cut chips and mushy peas with a hint of mint. Posh fish and chips at their best. Cod meal €8.50. Daily noon–late.

Liberty Grill 32 Washington St ⓦlibertygrill.ie. Brunch (served till 5pm Mon–Sat) and burgers – try the lamb and feta one – are this restaurant's specialities. Mains from €10. Mon–Sat 8am–9pm.

★ **Uncle Pete's Pizzeria** 31 Pope's Quay ⓦunclepetes .ie. Grab a €2 slice of thin-crust pizza from this quality Italian takeaway. Toppings encompass anything from king prawns to black pudding. Daily noon–late.

DRINKING AND NIGHTLIFE

For listings, pick up the free *Whazon?* (ⓦ whazon.com).

Bodega Nights Cornmarket St, Coal Quay ⓦ bodegacork.ie. Popular club with regular DJs on Tues, Fri & Sat until 2.30am. The bar-restaurant serves good fusion food for lunch and dinner, with live jazz to accompany Sunday brunch.

★ **Mutton Lane Inn** 3 Mutton Lane. Cosy candlelit pub open since 1787, down a laneway painted with colourful murals. Plays funk and soul, with occasional trad sessions. Daily 10.30am–late.

The Pavilion 13 Carey's Lane ⓦ pavilioncork.com. Live music venue with regular jazz and blues sessions in the downstairs bar (free) and r'n'b, soul, funk and electro DJs in the upstairs club Fri & Sat 11pm–2.30am.

The Savoy St Patrick St ⓦ savoytheatre.ie. Cork's premier club housed in an old cinema building, with DJs and live music. Thurs–Sat 10pm–2.30am.

The Thirsty Scholar 17 Lancaster Quay. As its name suggests, this great pub is close to the university and accordingly popular with students in term time. Daily noon–late.

ENTERTAINMENT

LIVE MUSIC

An Spailpín Fánach South Main St. Traditional music every night, except Saturday, in this famous bar.

Crane Lane Phoenix St ⓦ cranelanetheatre.ie. Billed as the "House of Jazz, Blues and Burlesque", this theatre has a late bar (open until 2am daily), and regular shows and gigs.

★ **Sin É** 8 Coburg St. Intimate music bar, usually packed for its traditional sessions and other live music on Tues–Thurs from 9.30pm and Fri and Sun at 6.30pm.

THEATRE AND CINEMA

Triskel Arts Centre Tobin St ☎ 021 427 2022, ⓦ triskelart.com. A lively spot housed in the eighteenth century Christchurch, with cinema, exhibitions, readings and concerts.

The west coast

If you've come to Ireland for mountainous scenery, sea and remoteness, you'll hit the jackpot in County Kerry. By far the most visited areas are the town of **Killarney** and a scenic route around the perimeter of the Iveragh Peninsula known as the **Ring of Kerry**. In the heart of the Burren, **Doolin** in County Clare is a marvellous spot for **traditional music**.

Galway is a free-spirited city, and a gathering point for young travellers. To its west lies **Connemara**, a magnificently wild coastal terrain, with the nearby beautiful **Aran Islands**, in the mouth of Galway Bay. The landscape softens around the historic town of **Westport**, while further north, **Sligo** has many associations with the poet W.B.Yeats. In the far northwest, the 1134km of folded coastline in **County Donegal** is spectacular, the highlight being **Slieve League**'s awesome sea cliffs, the highest in Europe. There are plenty of international flights directly into the region (to Shannon and Knock airports).

KILLARNEY AND AROUND

KILLARNEY town has been heavily commercialized and has little of architectural interest, but the surrounding **Killarney National Park**, with some of the best lakes, mountains and woodland in Ireland, definitely compensates. **Cycling** is a great way of seeing the terrain, and makes good sense – local transport is sparse.

WHAT TO SEE AND DO

Around the town, three spectacular **lakes** – Lough Leane, Muckross Lake and the Upper Lake – form an appetizer for MacGillycuddy's Reeks, the highest mountains in Ireland.

Knockreer Estate

The entrance gates to the **Knockreer Estate**, part of the Killarney National Park, are just over the road from Killarney's cathedral. Tall wooded hills, the highest being **Carrantuohill** (1041m), form the backdrop to **Lough Leane**, and the main path through the estate leads to the restored fifteenth-century tower of **Ross Castle** (March–Oct 9.30am–5.45pm; €6, gardens free), the last place in the area to succumb to Cromwell's forces in 1652.

Muckross Estate

Two kilometres south of Killarney is the **Muckross Estate**, where you should aim first for **Muckross Abbey**. Founded by the

Franciscans in the mid-fifteenth century, it was suppressed by Henry VIII, and later, finally, by Cromwell. Back at the main road, signposts point to **Muckross House** (daily: July & Aug 9am–7pm; Sept–June 9am–5.30pm; €7.50 or €12.50 joint ticket with farm; ⓦ muckross -house.ie), a nineteenth-century neo-Elizabethan mansion with wonderful gardens and a traditional working farm. The estate gives access to well-trodden paths along the shores of Muckross Lake where you can see one of Killarney's celebrated beauty spots, the **Meeting of the Waters**. Close by is the massive shoulder of Torc Mountain, shrugging off **Torc Waterfall**. The Upper Lake is beautiful, too, with the main road running along one side up to **Ladies' View**, from where the view is truly spectacular.

Gap of Dunloe and the Black Valley

West of Killarney lies the **Gap of Dunloe**, a natural defile formed by glacial overflow that cuts the mountains in two. *Kate Kearney's Cottage*, a pub located 10km from Killarney at the foot of the track leading up to the Gap, is the last fuelling stop before *Lord Brandon's Cottage*, a summer tearoom (June–Aug 10am–5pm), 11km away on the other side of the valley. The track winds its way up the desolate valley between high rock cliffs and waterfalls, past a chain of icy loughs and tarns to the top, to what feels like one of the most remote places in the world: the **Black Valley**, named after its entire population perished during the famine (1845–49). There's a wonderfully isolated An Óige hostel here (see below).

The quickest way to Killarney from here is to carry on down to *Lord Brandon's Cottage* and take the boat back across the Upper Lake.

ARRIVAL AND DEPARTURE

By train The train station is on Park Road, a short walk east of the centre.
Destinations Cork (8 daily; 1hr 20min–1hr 40min); Dublin (7 daily; 3hr 15min–3hr 30min).
By bus The bus station is next to the train station on Park Road.
Destinations Cork (13 daily; 1hr 35min–1hr 50min); Dingle (2–5 daily; 2hr–2hr 40min); Dublin (10 daily; 6hr 10min–7hr 30min); Waterville (1 daily; 1hr 55min).

INFORMATION

Tourist office Beech Road off New Street (daily 9am–6/8pm; ☏ 064 31633, ⓦ discoverireland.ie /southwest).
Internet Leaders, 9 Beech Rd; Web-Talk, 53 High St.
Listings *The Kerryman* (€2) ⓦ kerryman.ie.

ACCOMMODATION

Black Valley Hostel Beaufort ☏ 064 34712, ⓦ anoige .ie. Ideally located for nature lovers, with the Kerry Way, Killarney National Park, the MacGillycuddy Reeks and Carrantuohill mountain close by. Sits 22km from Killarney; follow signs for Black Valley off the Killarney to Kenmare Rd. Dorm €14, twin €38
★ **Dunloe View Hostel** 8km west of Killarney town on the Ring of Kerry (N72) road ☏ 064 664 4187, ⓦ dunloeviewhostel.ie. Pleasant hostel on a working farm, overlooking the MacGillycuddy Reeks. Dorm €17, double €45
Flesk Caravan and Camping Muckross Rd ☏ 064 663 1704, ⓦ killarneyfleskcamping.com. 1.5km south of the centre on the N71 Kenmare road. €25 per pitch plus two adults
Neptune's Town Hostel Bishop's Lane, off New St ☏ 064 663 5255, ⓦ neptuneshostel.com. Large, welcoming hostel with colourful rooms. Dorm €14, double €40
The Súgan Hostel Lewis Rd ☏ 064 663 3104, ⓦ killarneysuganhostel.com. Cosy, family-run hostel with colourful decor. There's also bike rental, cheaper if you're a guest. Dorm €12, double €40

EATING AND DRINKING

The Country Kitchen 17 New St. Cheap, hearty food, including full Irish breakfast (€9). Mon–Sat 9.30am–6pm.
★ **Courtney's** 24 Plunkett St ⓦ courtneysbar.com. Huge and informal bar, popular with young people for its midweek traditional sessions, live bands on Fri and DJ sets on Sat. Daily until late.
McSorley's 10 College St ⓦ mcsorleyskillarney.com. Traditional music in the main bar every night until around 10pm in summer, followed by a live band. The upstairs club is the biggest in Killarney. Daily until 2am.
O'Connor's Bar 7 High St. Old and intimate little pub with local Irish musicians on Thurs and Fri. You can book Gap of Dunloe tours here (see above). Daily until late.

THE RING OF KERRY

Most tourists view the spectacular scenery of the 179km **Ring of Kerry**, west of

16

Killarney, without ever leaving their tour coach or car – so anyone straying from the road, or waiting until the afternoon, will experience the slow twilights of the Atlantic seaboard in perfect seclusion.

GETTING AROUND

By bus Buses from Killarney circle the Ring in summer (May–Sept 2 daily; from €20 return). The public bus departs from the bus station and private tour operators (book through the tourist office in Killarney) from their respective offices in town. For the rest of the year, buses travel only the largely deserted mountain roads, as far as Cahersiveen.

By bicycle Cycling the Ring (216km) takes at least three days. Most of the route is off the main road, but it is well signposted and passes through the main towns and villages. Several places in Killarney offer bike rental for around €15 per day, including O'Sullivan's Cycles (ⓦ killarneyrentabike.com) on Lower New Street, beside the entrance to Killarney National Park.

16 DINGLE

The fishing village of **DINGLE** is the best base for exploring the peninsula. Formerly Kerry's leading port in medieval times, then later a centre for smuggling, the town's main attractions nowadays are aquatic: the star of the show is undoubtedly **Fungi** the dolphin, who's been visiting the town's harbour since 1983 (boats offer trips out to see him from around €16).

ACCOMMODATION

Hideout Hostel Dykegate St ☎066 915 0559, ⓦ thehideouthostel.com. The best budget option in town, combining a communal hostel feel with the comfort of a small hotel. Dorm €16, double €40

Rainbow Hostel 1km west of the centre in Miltown ☎066 915 1044, ⓦ rainbowhosteldingle.com. Laidback family-run hostel on the edge of town. Dorm €16, double €40, camping €9

EATING AND DRINKING

Goat Street Café Upper Main St. Colourful and friendly café offering soups, salads, curries and home-baked desserts made using local organic produce. Mon–Sat 10am–4pm, plus Thurs–Sat 6–8.30pm.

John Benny's Strand St ⓦ johnbennyspub.com. Popular pub renowned for its excellent fresh oysters, seared king scallops and seafood pies. There's live music Mon–Sat. Daily until late.

O'Flaherty's Bar Bridge St ⓦ oflahertysbardingle.com. The proprietor Fergus leads local and visiting musicians in nightly trad sessions in a space packed with memorabilia documenting the history of Dingle. Mon–Thurs 11am–11.30pm, Fri & Sat 11am–12.30am, Sun noon–11pm.

SLIGO

SLIGO is, after Derry, the biggest town in the northwest of Ireland. The legacy of **W.B. Yeats** – perhaps Ireland's best-loved poet – is still strongly felt here: the **Yeats Memorial Building** on Hyde Bridge (Mon–Fri 10am–5pm; free; ⓦ yeats-sligo .com) features a photographic exhibition and film on his life, while the poet's Nobel Prize for Literature and other memorabilia are on show in the **Sligo County Museum** in the library on Stephen Street (Tues–Sat 10am–noon & 2–4.30pm; free). **The Model Arts Centre** on The Mall (Tues–Sat 10am–5.30pm, Sun noon–5pm; free; ⓦ themodel.ie) has works by the poet's brother, **Jack B. Yeats**, along with a broad collection of modern Irish art.

ACCOMMODATION

Gyreum Riverstown, 20km south of Sligo town ☎071 916 5994, ⓦ gyreum.com. A unique eco-lodge in a giant green mound rising out of the Sligo hills, modelled as a "modern-day cairn" with spectacular views spanning five counties. Dorm €15

Railway Hostel 1 Union Place ☎071 914 4530, ⓦ therailway.ie. Small and homely hostel with comfortable communal areas and a lovely kitchen. Dorm €16, double €40

Tree Tops B&B Cleveragh Rd, 1km southeast along Pearse Rd ☎071 916 0160, ⓦ streetsligo.com. Bright and comfortable rooms with sparklingly white bedspreads, great breakfasts and friendly hosts. Single €40, double €72

EATING AND DRINKING

Café Society 3 Teeling St ⓦ cafe-society.tripod.com. An eclectic menu of burgers, curries (from €6) and sandwiches served until 9pm. Mon–Fri 8.30am–8.30pm, Sat 10am–7pm.

Hargadon's 4–5 O'Connell St ⓦ hargadons.com. Award-winning but reasonably priced pub grub, including an excellent seafood chowder, home-made pâté and fresh seafood. The three-course menu of the day is a steal at €9.95. There's also a wine shop attached. Mon–Sat noon–3.30pm & 4–9pm.

Shoot the Crows Gratton St. One of the best places in Sligo for live traditional music. There are also regular sessions in *Farley's* and *Furey's*, both on Bridge Street. Opening hours depend on gigs.

DINGLE PENINSULA

The **Dingle Peninsula** is a place of intense, shifting beauty: spectacular mountains, long sandy beaches and splinter-slatted rocks. The highlight is the stunning promontory of **Slea Head**, which has fabulous views over to the **Blasket Islands**.

The Irish-speaking area west of Dingle is rich in relics of the ancient Gaelic and early Christian cultures. The spectacular fort of **Dún Beag** (daily Feb–Nov 10am–5pm; €3; w dunbegfort.com) is about 6km west of Ventry village, and has four earthen rings as defences and an underground escape route by the main entrance. West of the fort, the hillside above the road is studded with stone beehive huts, cave dwellings, forts, churches, standing stones and crosses – over five hundred in all. The beehive huts were built and used for storage up until the late nineteenth century, but standing among ancient buildings – such as the **Fahan group** – you're looking over a landscape that's remained essentially unchanged for centuries.

GETTING AROUND

Public transport in the west of the peninsula amounts to a very irregular bus from Dingle to Dunquin, making cycling the best way to explore.

COUNTY CLARE

Some 40km northwest of Ennis in **County Clare** is the tiny seaside village of **DOOLIN**, famed for a steady, year-round supply of **traditional music**.

The village is the perfect base from which to explore the mystically barren expanse of **The Burren**, a vast landscape of cracked limestone terraces stretching to the wild Atlantic Ocean. The area is dotted with well-preserved megalithic remains such as the **Poulnabrone Dolmen** (on the R480, 20min drive from Doolin), an imposing tomb constructed from three massive limestone slabs dating from 2500 BC. The

Cliffs of Moher, 4km south of Doolin, are the area's most famous tourist attraction, with their great bands of shale and sandstone rising 200m above the waves.

A **ferry** (April–Sept) runs from Doolin pier to the **Aran Islands** (see p.593). **LAHINCH**, a small village 20km south of Doolin, attracts hordes of surfers (see below) for its famous beach break.

INFORMATION

Tourist office The visitors' centre is beside the car park in Doolin (daily: March & Oct 9am–6pm; April 9am–6.30pm; May & Sept 9am–7pm; June 9am–7.30pm; July & Aug 9am–9pm; Nov–Feb 9am–5pm; €6; w cliffsofmoher.ie) and can organize tours to O'Brien's Tower, built in 1835 as a viewing point for visitors.

Surfing You can rent boards from Lahinch Surf Shop (☏ 065 708 1543, w lahinchsurfshop.com) or organize lessons at the Lahinch Surf School (☏ 087 960 9667, w lahinchsurfschool.com).

ACCOMMODATION

★ **Aille River Hostel** ☏ 065 707 4260, w ailleriverhosteldoolin.ie. Renovated three-hundred-year-old cottage with camping facilities (enquire for prices), beautifully located overlooking the Aille River in the centre of Doolin village. Dorm €16, double €45

★ **Doolin Hostel** Sea Rd ☏ 087 282 0587, w doolinhostel.ie. Doolin's oldest hostel has been completely renovated and feels more like a modern hotel, with a coffee shop on site serving fresh cakes and scones. Dorm €15, double €46

Lahinch Hostel Church St, Lahinch ☏ 065 708 1040, w lahinchhostel.ie. Basic dormitory accommodation popular with surfers. Dorm €15

Rainbow Hostel ☏ 065 707 4415, w rainbowhostel.net. A welcoming, family-run place offering bike rental (€8–12/day) and free guided walks of the area around Doolin. Dorm €16, double €40

EATING AND DRINKING

Doolin Café w thedoolincafe.com. The self-proclaimed philosophy here is "why buy it when you can make it", with all dishes on the seasonal menu made using local artisan produce. The veggie breakfast with home-made baked beans and grilled halloumi is a real treat. Daily 8.30am–4pm, plus Thurs–Mon 6.30–9.30pm.

O'Connor's w gusoconnorsdoolin.com. One of three pubs in Doolin famous for their nightly traditional music sessions, offering giant portions of steaming mussels (€12) and other fresh seafood dishes. If you can't find a seat here, try *McGann's* or *McDermott's* close by. Mon–Thurs 10am–11.30pm, Fri & Sat 10am–12.30am, Sun 10am–11pm.

16

GALWAY

County **GALWAY** is home to the country's largest Irish-speaking Gaeltacht region, and as a lively university city, its reputation as party capital of Ireland is well justified. University College Galway guarantees a high number of young people in term time, but the energy is most evident during Galway's **festivals**, especially the lively **Arts Festival** in the last two weeks of July (ⓦgalway artsfestival.com), and the **Galway Races** in the last week of July (ⓦgalwayraces.com).

WHAT TO SEE AND DO

Granted city status in 1484, **Galway** developed in the Middle Ages into a flourishing centre of trade with the Continent, a period of prosperity that is evident in its impressive architecture.

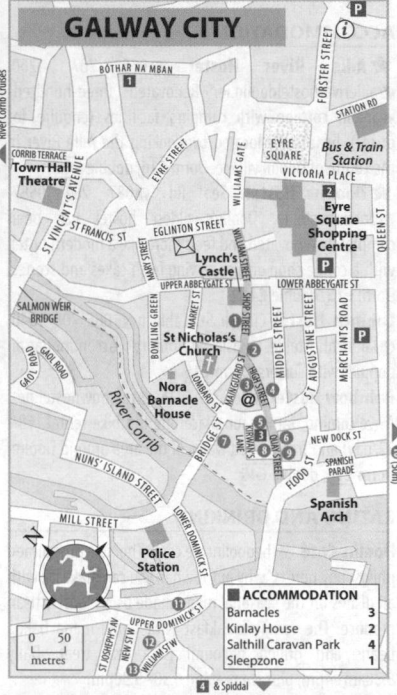

Merchant townhouses line pedestrianized Shop Street, where buskers perform at all hours of the day and night outside some of the city's liveliest bars and cafés. **Lynch's Castle** on Shop Street, which now houses the Allied Irish Bank, dates from the fifteenth century and is a fine example of a medieval townhouse, with its stone facade decorated with carved panels, gargoyles and a lion devouring its prey.

Down by the River Corrib stands the **Spanish Arch**, a sixteenth-century structure that was used to protect galleons unloading wine and rum. Across the river lies the **Claddagh** district, the old fishing village that once stood outside the city walls and gave the world the Claddagh ring as a symbol of love and fidelity. Past the Claddagh the river widens out into **Galway Bay**; for a pleasant sea walk follow the road until it reaches **Salthill**, the city's seaside resort. There are several beaches along the promenade, though for the best head 5km from Salthill to **Silverstrand** on the Barna road.

ARRIVAL AND DEPARTURE

By train The train station is off Eyre Square, on the northeast edge of the city centre.
Destinations Dublin (9–11 daily; 2hr 30min–3hr).
By bus The bus station is located on Forster Street, beside the train station.
Destinations Cork (12 daily; 4hr 25min); Doolin (4 daily; 1hr 40min–2hr 50min); Dublin (15 daily; 3hr 30min–3hr 45min); Killarney (7 daily; 4hr 40min); Westport (6 daily; 1hr 35min–3hr 45min).

INFORMATION

Tourist office Forster St (daily 9am–5.45pm; ☎091 537 700, ⓦirelandwest.ie).
Internet Hotlines, 4 High St.

ACCOMMODATION

Barnacles 10 Quay St ☎091 568 644, ⓦbarnacles.ie. Buzzing hostel conveniently located for pubs and cafés on Quay St; the larger dorms are a little crowded, but smaller ones are bright and comfortable. Dorm €15, double €47
Kinlay House Merchant's Rd ☎091 565 244, ⓦkinlaygalway.ie. Enormous, impersonal hostel just off Eyre Square. Day-trips to the Aran Islands, the Cliffs of Moher and Connemara depart right outside the door. Dorm €18, double €55

GALWAY CITY

■ ACCOMMODATION
Barnacles	3
Kinlay House	2
Salthill Caravan Park	4
Sleepzone	1

● EATING
Da Tang Noodle House	4
Eight Bar and Restaurant	10
Fat Freddy's	9
La Salsa	3
McCambridges	1
McDonagh's	8

● DRINKING AND NIGHTLIFE
Blue Note	12
Crane Bar	13
The Living Room	7
The Quays	6
Róisín Dubh	11
Taaffe's	2
Tigh Neachtain	5

Salthill Caravan Park Ballyloughlane, Renmore ☎ 091 523 972, ⌨ salthillcaravanpark.com. Family-run park located right on the beach, less than 2km from the centre April–Sept. €10 per person

★ **Sleepzone** Bóthar na mBan, Wood Quay ☎ 091 566 999, ⌨ sleepzone.ie. Ultramodern hostel with a mini-hotel feel, bright en-suite rooms and a huge communal kitchen. Dorm €15, double €60

EATING

★ **Da Tang Noodle House** 2 Middle St ⌨ datangnoodlehouse.com. Excellent noodle soups (€10), dim sum and salads in pretty surroundings. Lunch €6–9, dinner €12–14. Daily noon–10pm.

★ **Eight Bar and Restaurant** 8 Dock Rd ☎ 091 565111, ⌨ eight.ie. With a focus on locally sourced seasonal ingredients and a menu that changes daily, this place caters for serious foodies, with fresh seafood, quality cuts of meat, hearty stews and innovative salads. Mains €15. Daily noon–3pm & 6–10pm.

Fat Freddy's The Halls, Quay St ⌨ galwayrestaurants.net. Good pizzas, salads and antipasti at this fun, colourful bistro. Mains €10–15. Daily noon–10pm.

La Salsa 6 Mainguard St. Mexican takeaway offering giant burritos, nachos and burgers. €4–7. Daily noon–midnight.

McCambridges 38–39 Shop St ⌨ mccambridges.com. The queues run out the door every lunchtime at this gourmet deli renowned for its sandwiches, wraps and rolls (€3–5). Mon–Sat 8am–7pm, Sun noon–6pm.

McDonagh's 22 Quay St ⌨ mcdonaghs.net. A must for the freshest seafood at any time of day. The takeaway next door has a few informal tables and is much cheaper than the restaurant. Mains €8–34. Mon–Sat 5–10pm; takeaway daily noon–midnight.

DRINKING AND NIGHTLIFE

The Quay St area leading down to the river is known as the "Left Bank" due to the proliferation of popular pubs, restaurants and cafés. See the weekly *Galway Advertiser* (free; ⌨ advertiser.ie/galway) or *Galway City Tribune* (€1.60) for listings.

Blue Note 3 West William St. Atmospheric pub with intimate booths and snugs, a heated smoking garden, and DJs most nights.

★ **Crane Bar** 2 Sea Rd ⌨ thecranebar.com. Holds revered traditional music sessions nightly from 9pm.

The Living Room 5 Bridge St. Popular late-night bar on three levels with retro decor. DJ Thurs–Sun.

The Quays Quay St. One of the city's best-loved pubs, whose atmospheric interior was taken from a medieval French church. Daily until late.

Róisín Dubh Dominick St ⌨ roisindubh.net. Popular music bar and venue which plays host to top-class Irish

and international acts. Opening hours depend on gigs and events.

Taaffe's 19 Shop St. One of the best places to hear traditional music, where there are nightly sessions until late.

Tigh Neachtain 17 Cross St ⌨ tighneachtain.com. Old-fashioned pub that attracts an eccentric, arty crowd. Great live music, too. Daily until late.

THE ARAN ISLANDS

The **Aran Islands** – **Inishmore, Inishmaan** and **Inisheer**, 50km out across the mouth of Galway Bay – are spectacular settings for a wealth of early remains and some of the finest archeological sites in Europe. The isolation of the Irish-speaking islands prolonged the continuation of a unique, ancient culture into the early twentieth century.

Inishmore

Inishmore is a great tilted plateau of limestone with a scattering of villages along the sheltered northerly coast. The land slants up to the southern edge, where dramatic cliffs rip along the entire shoreline. As far as the eye can see is a tremendous patterning of stone, the bare pavements of grey rock split into bold diagonal grooves and latticed by dry-stone walls.

16

WHAT TO SEE AND DO

Most of Inishmore's sights are to the northwest of **KILRONAN**, the island's principal town, where minibuses and ponies and traps offering island tours (see p.594) wait by the pier. Past the *American*

GETTING TO THE ISLANDS

Daily ferries to Inishmore run year-round (less frequent to the other islands), departing from Galway city, Rossaveal (30km west by bus) and Doolin in County Clare. A return trip costs around €25. Book tickets in Galway city through Aran Island Ferries, 4 Forster St (☎ 091 568 903, ⌨ aranislandferries.com); or O'Brien Shipping (☎ 065 707 4455, ⌨ doolinferries .com) – both companies have desks in the Galway tourist office. You can also fly with Aer Árann Islands (☎ 091 593 034, ⌨ aerarannislands.ie) for €45 return.

Bar and up the hill to the west of Kilronan is a small settlement called Mainistir, from where it's a short signposted walk to the twelfth-century **Teampall Chiaráin** (Church of St Kieran). five kilometres west along the main road from here is Kilmurvey, a small cluster of houses with a sandy beach which is a fifteen-minute walk from the most spectacular of Aran's prehistoric sites, **Dún Aonghasa**, accessed via its **visitor centre** (April–Oct 9.45am–6pm; Nov–March 9.30am–4pm; closed Mon & Tues in Jan & Feb; €3). The spectacular fort, which is 2500 years old, is perched on the edge of a sheer cliff, beaten relentlessly by the Atlantic Ocean below. The **Seven Churches**, just east of the village of Eoghanacht, is a monastic site dating from the ninth century, believed to be one of the most significant medieval pilgrimage destinations in the west of Ireland.

ARRIVAL AND DEPARTURE

By ferry Boats from Galway city, Rossaveal and Doolin (see box, p.593) dock at Kilronan.

INFORMATION AND TOURS

Tourist office Just west of where the ferry docks at Kilronan (daily: March–Oct 10am–5pm; Nov–Feb 11am–5pm; ☎ 099 61263).

Tours Seasonal minibuses (€10) run tours up through the island's villages. Pony-and-trap tours depart from the pier (€40 for a group of up to 4 people).

Bike rental Mullin's and BNN's near the pier (€10/day).

ACCOMMODATION

Accommodation can be booked through the Kilronan tourist office, or when you buy your ferry ticket in Galway.

Kilronan Hostel Kilronan ☎ 099 61255, ⓦ kilronanhostel.com. Cheery hostel with great facilities. Very convenient for the ferry. Dorm €17, double €45

Mainistir House Hostel Mainistir ☎ 099 61318, ⓦ aranislandshostel.com. A 20min walk west from the pier, this peaceful hostel offers a renowned "all you can eat" buffet every night for €15. Dorm €16, double €50

EATING AND DRINKING

Seafood is the island's great speciality, with most of the popular restaurants located in Kilronan.

The Old Courthouse (The Ould Pier). Simple and cheap place serving fresh fish and chips and seafood chowder, with a few outdoor tables. Closed Nov–Feb. Daytime only.

★ **Joe Watty's Bar** A great pub with traditional music most nights; serves good soups and stews, from €6. Food served daily noon–9pm.

Inishmaan

Compared to Inishmore, **Inishmaan** is lush, with stone walls forming a maze that chequers off tiny fields of grass and clover. The island's main sight is **Dún Chonchubhair**: built sometime between the first and seventh centuries, its massive oval wall is almost intact and commands great views. Ask at the *Teach Ósta* pub for information (☎ 099 73003) – it's a warm and friendly place that also serves snacks in summer.

ACCOMMODATION

An Dún ☎ 099 73047, ⓦ inismeainaccommodation.ie. Comfortable B&B right on the sea, also near Dún Chonchubhair. March–Nov only. Double €76

Ard Álainn ☎ 099 73027, ⓦ galway.net/pages/ard -alainn. Perched on a hill near Dún Chonchubhair offering lovely views over the island and neighbouring Inishmore. April–Sept only. Double €55

Inisheer

Inisheer, less than 3km across, is the smallest of the Aran Islands, and tourism plays a key role here. A great plug of rock dominates the island, its rough, pale-grey stone dripping with greenery, topped by the fifteenth-century **O'Brien's Castle**, standing inside an ancient ring fort. Set around it are low fields, a small community of pubs and houses, and windswept sand dunes.

INFORMATION

Tourist office The Inisheer Island Cooperative hut by the pier (Mon–Sat 10.30am–3.30pm, summer only; ☎ 099 75008, ⓦ inisoirr-island.com) will give you a map and a list of B&Bs.

ACCOMMODATION

Brú Radharc na Mara ☎ 099 75024 ⓦ bruhostelaran .com. Comfortable and clean family-run hostel, offering tours of the island on request. March–Oct only. Dorm €15, double €40

Campsite This campsite has toilets and washing facilities, and is near the pier. May–Sept only. Free

Radharc an Chláir Castle Village ☎ 099 75019. Bright yellow bungalow by the castle offering views across the sea to the Cliffs of Moher. Double €70

EATING AND DRINKING

Óstán Inis Oírr ⓦostaninismeain.com. Tasty meals are available daily at the island's only hotel,
Tigh Ned's The place to head for music, coffee and snacks.

DONEGAL TOWN

DONEGAL TOWN is focused around its old marketplace – The Diamond – and makes a fine base for exploring the stunning coastal countryside and inland hills and loughs. Just about the only sight in the town itself is the well-preserved shell of **O'Donnell's Castle** on Tírchonaill Street by The Diamond (April–Oct daily 10am–6pm; Nov–March daily 9.30am–4.30pm; €4), a fine example of Jacobean architecture. On the left bank of the River Eske stand the few ruined remains of **Donegal Friary**, while on the opposite bank a woodland path known as Bank Walk offers wonderful views of **Donegal Bay** and the **Blue Stack Mountains**.

ARRIVAL AND DEPARTURE

By bus The stop for Bus Éireann departures and arrivals is outside the *Abbey Hotel*.
Destinations Derry (3–7 daily; 1hr 30min); Dublin (9–11 daily; 3hr 30min–5hr 55min); Glencolmcille (2 daily; 1hr 25min); Sligo (8 daily; 1hr).

INFORMATION

Tourist office The Quay (June–Aug Mon–Sat 9am–5.30pm, Sun 11am–3pm; Sept–May Mon–Sat 9am–5pm; ☎074 972 1148, ⓦdiscoverireland.ie /northwest).

ACCOMMODATION

There are dozens of B&Bs in Donegal – you can book at the tourist office.
Atlantic Guesthouse Main St ☎074972 1187, ⓦatlanticguesthouse.ie. Family-run establishment in the centre of town with bright and cheery rooms. Double **€52**
★ **Donegal Town Independent Hostel** ☎074972 2805, ⓦdonegaltownhostel.com. Just past the roundabout on the Killybegs Rd, a 5min walk from town, this peaceful and very friendly hostel also has camping. Dorm **€17**, double **€42**, camping **€9** per person

EATING AND DRINKING

The Blueberry Tea Room Castle St. Good-quality, reasonably priced food served in a very cosy atmosphere. It has an internet café upstairs. Mains up to €12. Mon–Sat 9am–7pm.

The Reel Inn Bridge St. A lively bar packed with local old-timers, even at midday. Traditional music every night.
Simple Simon The Diamond. Deli in an organic food store offering healthy takeaway lunches (€2–5). Mon–Sat 10am–6pm.

SLIEVE LEAGUE

To the west of Donegal town lies one of the most stupendous landscapes in Ireland. There are two routes up to the ridge of **Slieve League**: a back way following the signpost to Baile Mór just before Teelin, and the road route from Teelin to Bunglass, a sheer 300m above the sea. The former path has you looking up continually at the ridge known as One Man's Pass, on which walkers seem the size of pins, while the front approach swings you up to one of the most thrilling cliff scenes in the world, the **Amharc Mór**. On a good day you can see a third of Ireland from the summit.

GLENCOLMCILLE

Since the seventh century, following Columba's stay in the valley, **GLENCOLMCILLE** has been a place of pilgrimage: every June 9 at midnight the locals commence a three-hour barefoot itinerary of the cross-inscribed slabs that stud the valley basin, finishing up with Mass at 3am in the small church. If you want to attempt *Turas Cholmcille* ("Columba's Journey") yourself, get a map of the route from the Glencolmcille Hill Walkers Centre, which also has lovely modern budget accommodation (see below), or the **Folk Village Museum** (Easter–Sept Mon–Sat 10am–6pm, Sun noon–6pm; €4.50; ⓦglenfolkvillage .com), a cluster of replica, period-furnished thatched cottages.

ACCOMMODATION

Dooey Hostel ☎074 973 0130. A path to the left of the Folk Village Museum leads to this very basic but wonderfully positioned hostel run by a chatty local lady called Mary and her son Leo. Dorm **€15**, double **€30**
Ionad Siul Guesthouse ☎074 973 0302, ⓦionadsuil .ie. Very modern and comfortable rooms at the Glencolmcille Hill Walkers Centre, with use of a cosy communal area and self-catering facilities. Double **€50**

16

EATING AND DRINKING

An Cistin Part of the Foras Cultúir Uladh Irish language and culture complex, and the best place for food and drink.

Biddy's Bar Main St. Small bar located in the centre of town. In the summer there's live music most nights, from traditional and folk to blues.

Roarty's Main St. Good for a drink and lively traditional music sessions most nights.

Northern Ireland

In 1998, after thirty years of the Troubles in Northern Ireland, its people overwhelmingly voted in support of a political settlement and, it was hoped, an end to political and sectarian violence between Catholic republicans and Protestant unionists. For a time the political process gradually inched forwards, hampered by deep mistrust and suspicion on both sides. In recent years, however, considerable headway has been made in the peace process, with the resumption of devolved government in Northern Ireland, and a greater sense of hope evident on both sides of the community. **Belfast** and **Derry** are lively and attractive cities which have benefited from considerable investment and regeneration in recent years, and the northern coastline – especially the bizarre geometry of the **Giant's Causeway** – is as spectacular as anything in Ireland.

BELFAST

A quarter of Northern Ireland's population lives in the capital, **BELFAST**.

While the legacy of **the Troubles** is clearly visible in areas like West Belfast – where peace walls currently divide Catholic and Protestant communities and political murals adorn street corners – security measures have been considerably eased, though there are certain flashpoints such as the Short Strand and the Ardoyne, which remain inadvisable to visit.

The city is going from strength to strength, with a flourishing arts scene and many new restaurants and clubs. Despite its turbulent history, the city is imbued with a new zest for life, and a palpable cross-community desire for a peaceful future.

WHAT TO SEE AND DO

City Hall is the central landmark of Belfast, and divides the city conveniently into north and south. The area to the north of it, known as the **Cathedral Quarter**, contains most of Belfast's official buildings, as well as the main shopping areas, cosy pubs and cool warehouse restaurants. The southern section of the city, the so-called **Queen's Quarter**, hosts many of the city's museums and student bars, while the **Titanic Quarter** across the river is the city's most recently developed area.

Donegall Square and around

Belfast City Hall, presiding over central Donegall Square, is an austere Presbyterian building (tours Mon–Fri 11am, 2pm & 3pm, Sat 2pm & 3pm; free). At the northwest corner of the square stands the **Linen Hall Library** (Mon–Fri 9.30am–5.30pm, Sat

---

POLITICAL MURALS

The Republican and Loyalist **murals** on the Falls and Shankill roads in West Belfast are a must-see. There are over two thousand examples of this political artwork in Northern Ireland altogether, mostly painted during the height of the Troubles to represent the political and religious loyalties of the respective communities. More recently, community-led, apolitical murals are becoming increasingly common. The open-topped Belfast City Sightseeing buses include the murals in their tour of Belfast, departing every 30–45min from Castle Place (£12.50, student £10.50). Taxi Trax (Castle Junction on King St, near City Hall; £25/car; ☎028 9031 5777, ⓦ taxitrax.com) offer bespoke taxi tours including West Belfast, but the most interesting way of viewing the murals is to take a walking tour with political ex-prisoners, who present both Republican and Loyalist viewpoints (tours Mon–Sat 11am & Sun 2pm; 2hr; £8; assemble at the bottom of Divis Towers, Falls Rd; ☎028 9020 0770, ⓦ coiste.ie).

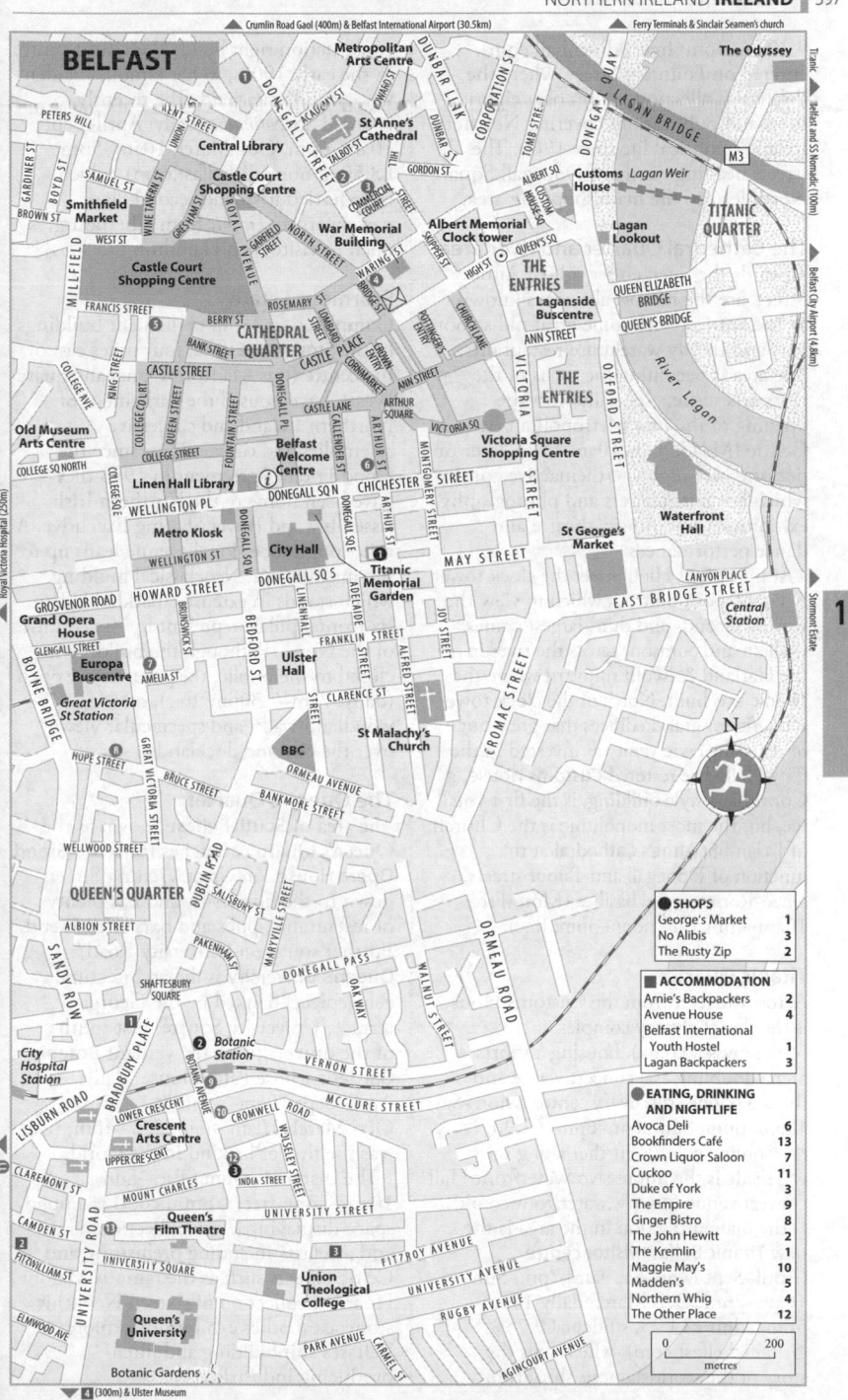

BELFAST

Crumlin Road Gaol (400m) & Belfast International Airport (30.5km)

Ferry Terminals & Sinclair Seamen's church

The Odyssey

Metropolitan Arts Centre

St Anne's Cathedral

Central Library

Castle Court Shopping Centre

Smithfield Market

Castle Court Shopping Centre

War Memorial Building

Albert Memorial Clock tower

Customs House — Lagan Weir

Lagan Lookout

TITANIC QUARTER

Titanic
Belfast and SS Nomadic (100m)
Belfast City Airport (4.8km)
Stormont Estate

CATHEDRAL QUARTER

THE ENTRIES

Laganside Buscentre

Queen Elizabeth Bridge

Queen's Bridge

River Lagan

Old Museum Arts Centre

Belfast Welcome Centre

Victoria Square Shopping Centre

THE ENTRIES

Linen Hall Library

Metro Kiosk

City Hall

St George's Market

Waterfront Hall

Grand Opera House

Europa Buscentre

Great Victoria St Station

Titanic Memorial Garden

Ulster Hall

Central Station

BBC

St Malachy's Church

QUEEN'S QUARTER

Botanic Station

City Hospital Station

Crescent Arts Centre

Queen's Film Theatre

Union Theological College

Queen's University

Botanic Gardens

Royal Victoria Hospital (250m)

Ulster Museum (300m)

16

N

0 — 200 metres

● SHOPS
George's Market	1
No Alibis	3
The Rusty Zip	2

■ ACCOMMODATION
Arnie's Backpackers	2
Avenue House	4
Belfast International Youth Hostel	1
Lagan Backpackers	3

● EATING, DRINKING AND NIGHTLIFE
Avoca Deli	6
Bookfinders Café	13
Crown Liquor Saloon	7
Cuckoo	11
Duke of York	3
The Empire	9
Ginger Bistro	8
The John Hewitt	2
The Kremlin	1
Maggie May's	10
Madden's	5
Northern Whig	4
The Other Place	12

9.30am–4pm; free; ⓦlinenhall.com), entered on Fountain Street, where the Political Collection houses over eighty thousand publications covering Northern Ireland's political life since 1966. The streets heading north off Donegall Square North lead to the main shopping area.

The Cathedral Quarter and river area

Towards the river, either side of Ann Street, are the narrow alleyways known as **The Entries**, with some great old saloon bars and trendy warehouse restaurants. The area is becoming the focus of the city's arts scene, especially with the opening of the new Metropolitan Arts Centre (MAC; daily 10am–7pm, later on performance nights; ⓦthemaclive.com) which hosts regular art and photography exhibitions, and music, theatre and dance performances.

At the end of High Street the clock tower is a good position from which to view the world's second- and third-largest cranes, Goliath and Samson, across the river in the Harland & Wolff shipyard where the **Titanic** was built. North of the clock tower is a series of grand edifices that grew out of the same civic vanity as invested in the City Hall. The restored **Customs House**, a Corinthian-style building, is the first you'll see, but the most monolithic is the Church of Ireland **St Anne's Cathedral** at the junction of Donegall and Talbot streets, a neo-Romanesque basilica (Mon–Fri 10am–4pm, Sun noon–3pm; free).

Titanic Quarter

Across the river from the Customs House is the sleek **Odyssey** complex (ⓦtheodyssey.co.uk), housing a sports arena doubling as a concert venue and the **W5 science discovery centre** (Mon–Sat 10am–6pm, Sun noon–6pm; £7.90; ⓦw5online.co.uk). Further along the waterside is the impressive Waterfront Hall concert venue (ⓦwww.waterfront.co.uk).

The main attraction in the area is the new **Titanic Belfast visitor centre** (April–Sept Mon–Sat 9am–7pm, Sun 10am–7pm; Oct–March daily 10am–5pm; adult £14.75, student £9.75; ⓦtitanicbelfast.com), which tells the story of the world-famous ship from construction right beside the visitor centre in the early 1900s, to her famous maiden voyage and tragic end. The recently restored SS *Nomadic* (daily: April–Sept 10am–6pm, Oct–March 10am–5pm; £8.50; ⓦnomadicbelfast.com), which once ferried first- and second-class passengers to *Titanic* from Cherbourg, is open to visitors on Hamilton Dock.

Stormont Estate

Completed in 1938, parliament buildings in the **Stormont Estate**, four miles east of the centre (bus #4a from Donegall Square West), have housed the parliament of Northern Ireland and successive assemblies and conventions; since the Good Friday Agreement in 1998 they have been home to the Northern Irish Assembly and Power Sharing Executive. A mile-long processional avenue leads up to the magnificent, Neoclassical building, which stands in extensive parkland. The six frontal pillars represent the six counties of the North. Although the building is closed to the public, the grounds are open (daily: 7am–7.30pm; free), offering woodland walks and spectacular views over the city and docklands.

The Queen's Quarter

The area of **South Belfast** known as the Queen's Quarter stretches from the **Grand Opera House**, on Great Victoria Street, down to the university, and has plenty of restaurants, pubs and bars at each end. Further south on University Road, **Queen's University** is the architectural centrepiece, flanked by the Georgian terrace, University Square. Just south of the university are the verdant **Botanic Gardens** whose Palm House (daily: April–Sept 10am–noon & 1–5pm; Oct–March 10am–noon & 1–4pm; free) was the first of its kind in the world.

The **Ulster Museum** (Tues–Sun 10am–5pm; free; ⓦnmni.com) is a huge space displaying a rich collection of art and artefacts including prehistoric and Celtic objects such as the famous Malone Hoard, a collection of sixteen Neolithic stone axes; other exhibitions explore Belfast's shipbuilding and linen-producing industries.

ARRIVAL AND DEPARTURE

By plane Belfast International Airport is 30km west of town (buses every 10–30min to Europa bus station; £7 one-way, £10 return; ☎ 028 9448 4848, ⓦ belfastairport .com); George Best Belfast City Airport is 4.8km northeast (bus #600 every 20min to city centre 5.30am–10pm; £2.50 return; ☎ 028 9093 9093, ⓦ belfastcityairport.com).

By train Most trains call at the central Great Victoria Street Station, though those from Dublin and Larne terminate at Central Station on East Bridge Street. Destinations Coleraine (9–10 daily; 1hr 20min–1hr 45min); Derry (5–9 daily; 2hr 30min); Dublin (8 daily; 2hr 10min); Larne Harbour (9–25 daily; 1hr 10min).

By bus Buses from Derry, the Republic, the airports and ferry terminals arrive at Europa Buscentre beside Great Victoria Street train station; buses from the north coast use Laganside Bus Centre in Queen's Square. A regular Centrelink bus connects all bus and train stations. Destinations Derry (11–32 daily; 1hr 50min); Dublin (20 daily; 3hr); Enniskillen (5–16 daily; 2hr–2hr 20min).

By boat Ferries from Stranraer dock at Corry Rd (taxi £9), and those from Liverpool further north on West Bank Rd (taxi £8), while ferries from Cairnryan dock 30km north at Larne (bus or train to centre).

INFORMATION

Tourist office The Belfast Welcome Centre, 10–12 Donegall Square North (Mon–Sat 9am–5.30/7pm, Sun 11am–4pm; ☎ 028 9024 6609, ⓦ visit-belfast.com).

GETTING AROUND

Information on all buses and trains is available at ☎ 028 9066 6630 or ⓦ translink.co.uk.

By bus The city is served by Metro bus service. Day tickets for the whole network cost £3.70 Mon–Sat. One-way tickets cost £1.20–1.80. The metro kiosk in Donegall Square West provides free bus maps. Ulsterbus serves outlying areas.

Discount passes The one-, two- or three-day Belfast Visitor Pass (£6.50/£10.50/£14) offers unlimited travel and discounts for visitor attractions around the city.

Bike rental Lifecycles, Unit 35, Smithfield Market (£10/ day, £16 for 2hr guided tour).

ACCOMMODATION

★ **Arnie's Backpackers** 63 Fitzwilliam St ☎ 028 9024 2867, ⓦ arniesbackpackers.co.uk. Cheerful and relaxed independent hostel with a homely atmosphere and colourful garden, near the university. Dorm **£12**, twin **£44**

Avenue House 23 Eglantine Ave ☎ 028 9066 5904, ⓦ avenueguesthouse.com. A homely guesthouse in a red-brick Victorian townhouse, with a warm welcome, pretty garden and great breakfasts. Double **£70**, triple **£80**

Belfast International Youth Hostel 22–32 Donegall Rd ☎ 028 9031 5435. Large, well-equipped but characterless modern HINI hostel, just west of Shaftesbury Square. Dorm **£11**, double **£42**

Lagan Backpackers 121 Fitzroy Ave ☎ 028 9514 0049, ⓦ laganbackpackers.com. Friendly, clean and comfortable place in an old red-brick house, with free English breakfast included and regular barbecue nights in summer. Dorm **£10**, double **£35**

EATING

Many of the best places to eat and the liveliest pubs are located in the Cathedral Quarter, with plenty of budget options and student bars around Great Victoria Street and in the university area.

Avoca Deli Arthur St ⓦ avoca.ie. Gourmet deli counter in the centre of town offering quality soups, salads and mains to eat in or take away. £4–9. Mon–Sat 9.30am–6pm, Sun 12.30–6pm.

Bookfinders Café 47 University Rd. Bohemian café at the back of a charmingly messy bookshop. Poetry nights on Fridays from 8pm. Lunch from £3. Mon–Sat 10am–5.30pm.

★ **Ginger Bistro** 7–8 Hope St ⓦ gingerbistro.com. Fresh seasonal ingredients are sourced locally from farmers and fishermen, and whipped into tasty and imaginative dishes with an international twist. Mains £13–20. Tues–Sat noon–3pm & 5–9.30pm.

Maggie May's 45 Botanic Ave ⓦ maggiemaysbelfast .co.uk. Huge, economically priced portions in this cosy café with lots of veggie choices, open for lunch and dinner. Sandwiches from £3, mains £5. Daily 8.30am–10.30pm.

The Other Place 78 Botanic Ave ⓦ theotherplace.co.uk. Fine breakfasts, and plenty of pizzas, pastas and baked potatos (£5–10). Daily 8am–10pm.

DRINKING AND NIGHTLIFE

Belfast's best entertainment is pub music, though there's also a vibrant club scene and plenty of DJ bars. For listings check *The Big List* (free; ⓦ thebiglist.co.uk), available in pubs, record shops and hostels, and the Belfast Telegraph (70p; ⓦ belfasttelegraph.co.uk).

PUBS

★ **Crown Liquor Saloon** 46 Great Victoria St ⓦ crownbar.com. The city's most famous pub, decked out like a spa bath, with a good range of Ulster food, such as champ and colcannon (both potato dishes) and Strangford oysters in season. Mon–Wed 11.30am–11pm, Thurs–Sat 11.30am–midnight, Sun 12.30–1pm.

Cuckoo 149 Lisburn Rd. Quirky bar popular with students, with a graffitied floor, cuckoo clocks on the walls, and jam jars of cocktails (£4.95). Daily until 1am.

Duke of York 7–11 Commercial Court ⓦ dukeofyorkbelfast.com. Traditional bar on one of Belfast's oldest, cobbled streets, with regular live trad

16

sessions, an upstairs disco and a courtyard area which gets packed on sunny days. Daily until late.

The Empire 42 Botanic Ave ⓦthebelfastempire.com. Music hall and cellar bar in a converted church, with nightly live music or comedy. Opening hours depend on gigs and events.

The John Hewitt 53 Donegall St ⓦthejohnhewitt .com. Owned by Belfast Unemployed Resource Centre, this popular bar has some of Belfast's best traditional music sessions on Tues, Wed and Sat evenings, blues on Thurs and jazz on Fri.

Madden's 52–74 Berry St. Unpretentious and atmospheric pub, with regular traditional music sessions (Fri & Sat).

CLUBS

The Kremlin 90 Donegall St ⓦkremlin-belfast.com. Northern Ireland's biggest gay venue, with a host of events throughout the week.

Northern Whig 2–10 Bridge St ⓦthenorthernwhig .com. Massive upmarket bar in the premises of the old newspaper, featuring pre-club DJs most nights.

SHOPPING

The main shopping area is the long stretch of Donegall Place and Royal Avenue, where you'll find big fashion and retail names. The big shopping centres are Victoria Square on Victoria Street and Castle Court on Royal Avenue. Away from main thoroughfare Royal Avenue are more alternative and more locally inspired outlets. Unsurprisingly, things get more alternative in the university area.

George's Market May St, east of City Hall. Specializes in food on Friday and artisan produce at the weekends. Fri 6am–2pm, Sat 9am–3pm, Sun 10am–4pm.

No Alibis 83 Botanic Ave ⓦnoalibis.com. A great independent bookshop specializing in crime. It often holds music events and readings. Opening hours depend on events.

The Rusty Zip 28 Botanic Ave ⓦtherustyzip.com. Full of vintage gems, from lace 1930s blouses to 1980s sequined jumpsuits. Mon–Wed, Fri & Sat 10am–6pm, Thurs 10am–8pm, Sun 2–5pm.

DIRECTORY

Exchange The Belfast Welcome Centre (see p.599), and all major bank branches.

Hospitals Belfast City Hospital, Lisburn Rd (☎028 9032 9241); Royal Victoria, Grosvenor Rd (☎028 9024 0503).

Internet Belfast Welcome Centre, 47 Donegall Place.

Left luggage Belfast Welcome Centre, 47 Donegall Place.

Police North Queen St ☎028 9065 0222.

Post office Castle Place.

THE GIANT'S CAUSEWAY

Since 1693, when the Royal Society publicized it as one of the great wonders of the natural world, the **Giant's Causeway** has been a major tourist attraction. Lying 65 miles northwest of Belfast, it consists of an estimated 37,000 polygonal basalt columns; it's the result of a massive subterranean explosion some sixty million years ago which spewed out a huge mass of molten basalt onto the surface which, as it cooled, solidified into massive polygonal crystals. Taking the 1km path down the cliffs from the visitor centre (daily: Feb, March & Oct 9am–6pm; April–June & Sept 9am–7pm; July & Aug 9am–9pm; Nov–Jan 9am–5pm; £8.50; ⓦgiantscauseway ireland.com), or the shuttle bus (every 15min; £2 return), brings you to the most spectacular of the blocks where many people linger, but if you push on, you'll be rewarded with relative solitude and views of some of the more impressive formations high in the cliffs. One of these, **Chimney Point**, has an appearance so bizarre that the ships of the Spanish Armada opened fire on it, believing that they were attacking Dunluce Castle, a few kilometres further west. An alternative 3.2km circuit follows the spectacular cliff-top path from the visitor centre, with views across to Scotland, to a flight of 162 steps leading down the cliff to a set of basalt columns known as the **Organ Pipes**.

THE MOURNE MOUNTAINS

If you're based in Belfast but fancy a day-trip out of the metropolis, the beautiful **Mourne Mountains** provide the perfect escape. The mountain range comprises twelve peaks, of which Slieve Donard, at 850m, is the highest in Northern Ireland. From Belfast, buses #20, #720 and #237 run from the Europa Buscentre to Newcastle (up to 15 daily; 1hr); from Newcastle, the Mourne Rambler service (June–Aug) tracks a loop through the area (£5.50 day-ticket; ⓦmourne-mountains.com).

GETTING TO THE GIANT'S CAUSEWAY

By train Trains from Belfast go to Coleraine, where there's a regular connection to Portrush; from either, you can catch the "open-top" bus (July & Aug 4 daily; £4.30) to the Causeway, or from Portrush there's bus #172, both running via Bushmills. A restored narrow-gauge railway runs between Bushmills and the Causeway (July & Aug 7 daily, plus some days in other months; 20min; one-way £5.25, return £6.75; ☎028 2073 2844).

By bus A direct coach (Goldline Express #221) runs from the Belfast Europa Buscentre to the Causeway in July & August (4 daily; 1hr 35min; one-way £11.50, return £17.50). The Antrim Coaster coach (Goldline Express #252) runs from Larne direct to the Causeway (2 daily; April–Sept only; 2hr 30min; one-way £10, return £17.50) and on to Coleraine via Bushmills, Portrush and Portstewart, Antrim Glens and stunning seascapes en route.

Carrick-a-Rede

Don't miss the **Carrick-a-Rede Rope Bridge**, which sits 13km east of the Causeway (daily: March–Oct 10am–6/7pm, June–Aug 10am–7pm, weather permitting; £5.60; ⓦnationaltrust.org.uk). For the past two hundred years, fishermen had reputedly erected a bridge from the mainland cliffs to Carrick-a-Rede island over a vast chasm, so they could check their salmon nets. Now, the National Trust is in charge. Venturing across the swaying rope bridge high above the water is an exhilarating experience, but not for the faint-hearted.

ARRIVAL AND DEPARTURE

By bus Ulsterbus #252 runs between Bushmills and the rope bridge via the Causeway in summer months.

PORTSTEWART

PORTSTEWART is a pleasant coastal resort ten miles west of the Giant's Causeway, with a long sandy beach and good surf. Barmouth Wildlife Reserve behind the strand has bird hides offering opportunities to view waterfowl, waders and nesting birds.

INFORMATION

Ocean Warriors 80 The Promenade ☎028 7083 6500, ⓦoceanwarriors.co.uk. Surf shop offering boards and wetsuits for sale or rent.

ACCOMMODATION

Rick's Causeway Coast Hostel 4 Victoria Terrace ☎028 7083 3789, ⓦrickscausewaycoast.hostel.com. The bus stop for the Giant's Causeway is 100m from the hostel. Dorm £12, double £36

EATING AND DRINKING

Harbour Café 18 The Promenade. Huge, hearty portions of lasagne, roast dinners and fish and chips (from £7.50) served up by friendly staff daily. There's an ice-cream parlour too for a sweet treat. Open daily.

Shenanigans 78 The Promenade ⓦshenanigans portstewart.com. The steaks, fresh fish and vegetables used for the seasonal menu in this gastropub are all sourced in Northern Ireland. The meal deal for two including wine is just £20. They serve a great strawberry daiquiri (£5.90) in the bar, and there's a popular student nightclub *Havana* upstairs (Thurs–Sat open until 1am).

DERRY-LONDONDERRY

DERRY-LONDONDERRY (traditionally referred to as "Derry" by Nationalists, "Londonderry" by Unionists – and now often pinned together as "Derry-Londonderry") lies at the foot of Lough Foyle, less than three miles from the border with the Republic. The city presents a beguiling picture, its two hillsides terraced with pastel-shaded houses punctuated by stone spires, and, being seventy percent Catholic, has a very different atmosphere from Belfast. Despite the Catholic dominance, from Partition in 1921 until the late 1980s, the Protestant minority maintained control of all important local institutions. The situation came to a head after the Protestant Apprentice Boys' March in August 1969, when the police attempted to storm the Catholic estates of the Bogside. In the ensuing tension, British troops were widely deployed for the first time in Northern Ireland. On January 31, 1972, the crisis deepened when British paratroopers opened fire on civilians, killing thirteen unarmed demonstrators in what became known as **Bloody Sunday**.

16

Derry-Londonderry is now greatly changed: tensions eased considerably here long before Belfast, although defiant murals remain and marching is still a contentious issue. The city centre has undergone much regeneration, and Derry-Londonderry's justifiable reputation for innovation in the arts resulted in it becoming the UK City of Culture in 2013 (ⓦcityofculture2013.com).

WHAT TO SEE AND DO

You can walk the entire mile-long circuit of Derry-Londonderry's seventeenth-century **city walls** – some of the best-preserved defences in Europe. Reinforced by bulwarks, bastions and an earth rampart with parapet, the walls encircle the original medieval street pattern with four gateways – Shipquay, Butcher, Bishop and Ferryquay.

The **Bogside murals** are in the streets that were once the undisputed preserve of the IRA, and **Free Derry Corner** marks the site of the original barricades erected against the British army at the height of the Troubles. Nearby are the Bloody Sunday and Hunger Strikers' memorials. Further along the city wall is the **Royal Bastion**, former site of the Rev. George Walker statue which was blown up in 1973. It is in Walker's and their predecessors' memory that the Protestant Apprentice Boys march around the walls every August 12. The new **Peace Bridge** crosses the River Foyle to the redeveloped Ebrington Square, a former World War I military base that has been transformed into an outdoor event space.

ARRIVAL AND DEPARTURE

By plane City of Derry airport (☎028 7181 0784, ⓦcityofderryairport.com) is 7 miles northeast, connected to the centre by the Airporter bus (£5).

By train Trains from Belfast arrive on the east bank of the Foyle with a free connecting bus to the bus station.

Destinations Belfast (4–9 daily; 2hr 30min); Coleraine (5–9 daily; 1hr).

By bus The station is on Foyle Street, beside Guildhall Square.

Destinations Donegal (3–7 daily; 1hr 25min–1hr 45min); Dublin (11 daily; 4hr); Enniskillen (5–15 daily; 2hr–4hr 20min); Sligo (3–5 daily; 2hr 30min).

INFORMATION

Tourist office 44 Foyle St (July–Sept Mon–Fri 9am–7pm, Sat 9am–6pm, Sun 10am–5pm; Oct–June Mon–Fri 9am–5pm, Sat 10am–5pm, Sun 10am–4pm; ☎028 7126 7284, ⓦderryvisitor.com).

Tours City Tours offer walking tours of the walls (11 Carlisle Rd; daily 10am, noon & 2pm; £4; ☎0771 293 7997, ⓦderrycitytours.com) and taxi tours (£25/hr for 4 people), which explore fifteen hundred years of history and provide an introduction to the Bogside murals.

Internet Webcrawler Cyber Café, 52 Strand Rd.

ACCOMMODATION

Derry City Independent Hostel 44 Great James St ☎028 7128 0524, ⓦderry-hostel.co.uk. A friendly, bohemian hostel with furniture from around the world. Hosts regular barbecues in the summer. Dorm **£14**

★ **Dolce Vita** 46 Great James St ☎028 7137 7989. Run by the people at *Derry City* hostel (see above), the adjacent building has private double and twin rooms in a similar style. Double **£36**

★ **The Saddler's House** 36 Great James St ☎028 7126 9691, ⓦthesaddlershouse.com. Beautifully decorated Georgian townhouse run by knowledgeable hosts and serving excellent breakfasts. This, together with its sister B&B *The Merchant House*, is a real treat. They also have self-catering cottages and 2-bed apartments available to rent. Late-night revellers not welcome. Double **£60**

EATING

Badgers Bar & Restaurant 16–18 Orchard St. Located in the heart of the city, close to the walls, this hugely popular bar serves good pub grub using locally sourced ingredients. Daily noon–10pm.

★ **Café del Mondo** Shipquay St ⓦcafedelmondo.org. Not-for-profit café and restaurant located in the Craft Village modelled on a nineteenth-century square, serving excellent-value stews, soups and salads from around the world. Hosts poetry readings and live music in the evenings. Mains £3.50–8. Café daily 8.30am–6pm; restaurant daily 6pm–midnight.

DRINKING AND NIGHTLIFE

Bound for Boston 27–31 Waterloo St. This live music venue has a great beer-garden and seven pool tables. Daily until late.

Peadar O'Donnell's/The Gweedore Bar 59–63 Waterloo St ⓦpeadars.com. Traditional and contemporary music every night until late.

Sandino's Café Bar Water St ⓦsandinos.com. Intimate candlelit café-bar with a Che Guevara theme downstairs, and a live music venue upstairs, which opens late. Traditional music on Sun from 5pm.

DUOMO, FLORENCE

Italy

HIGHLIGHTS

❶ Turin Enjoy modern art and Slow Food in this bustling city. **See p.620**

❷ Venice Visit St Mark's Square after midnight when it's almost tourist-free. **See p.633**

❸ Florence Marvel at Renaissance masterpieces. See p.644

❹ Pompeii and Herculaneum Explore the evocative remains of two cities buried by ash. See p.664

❺ Matera A cavernous city with dwellings entirely hewn out of rock. **See p.667**

❻ Taormina Breathtaking views of Mount Etna at this former bohemian retreat. **See p.673**

HIGHLIGHTS ARE MARKED ON THE MAP ON P.605

ROUGH COSTS

Daily budget Basic €35, occasional treat €50

Drink Wine €2.50/glass

Food Local pasta dish €5–8; pizza slice €2

Hostel/budget hotel €15–30/€45–60

Travel Train: Rome–Naples; bus: €15

FACT FILE

Population 60 million

Language Italian

Currency Euro (€)

Capital Rome

International phone code ☎39

Time zone GMT +1hr

17

Introduction

Of all the countries in Europe, Italy is perhaps the hardest to classify. A modern industrialized nation and a harbinger of global style, its designers lead the way with each season's fashions. But it is also a Mediterranean country, with all that that implies. If there is a single national characteristic, it is to embrace life to the full, manifest in its numerous local festivals and in the importance placed on good food. There is also, of course, the country's enormous cultural legacy: Tuscany alone has more classified historical monuments than any country in the world, and every region holds its own treasures.

Italy wasn't unified until 1861, a fact that's borne out by the regional nature of the place today. The well-to-do cities of **Turin** and **Milan** epitomize the wealthy, industrial north; to their south is **Genoa**, a bustling port with a long seafaring tradition. By far the biggest draw in the north is **Venice**, a unique and beautiful city – though you won't be alone in appreciating it. The centre of the country, specifically **Tuscany**, boasts classic, rolling countryside and the art-packed towns of Florence, Pisa and Siena, while neighbouring **Umbria** has a quieter appeal. **Rome**, the capital, harbours a dazzling array of ancient and Renaissance gems. South of here in Campania, **Naples**, a vibrant, unforgettable city, is the spiritual heart of the economically undeveloped Italian south, while close by are fine ancient sites and the spectacular **Amalfi Coast**. The region of Basilicata is home to spellbinding **Matera**, a unique troglodyte settlement where cave dwellings are carved into rock. Puglia, the "heel" of Italy, has underrated pleasures – most notably **Lecce**, a Baroque gem of a city. **Sicily** is a law unto itself, with attractions ranging from Hellenic remains to the drama of Mount Etna, and the beguiling city of Palermo. **Sardinia**, too, feels far removed from the mainland, especially in its relatively undiscovered interior.

CHRONOLOGY

753 BC Rome founded by Romulus and Remus.
509 BC The city becomes a Republic.
49 BC Julius Caesar wages war against the Senate and extends the Roman Empire across Europe.
80 AD Building of the Colosseum.

476 Last Roman Emperor Romulus Augustus overthrown by barbarians.
756 Papal States created after Frankish forces defeat the Lombards.
1173 Building of the Tower of Pisa begins.
1512 Michelangelo completes his frescoes in the Sistine Chapel, as the Italian Renaissance flourishes.
1804 Napoleon declares himself emperor of Italy.
1814 Following Napoleon's defeat, Italy is divided into various states.
1861 Unification of Italian states into a Kingdom by Giuseppe Garibaldi.
1898 First Italian football league established.
1915 Italy joins World War I on the side of the Allies.
1922 Fascist Benito Mussolini becomes prime minister.
1929 The Lateran Treaty declares Vatican City an independent state. It is the smallest state in the world.
1940 Italy enters World War II on the side of the Nazis.
1943 Allies capture Sicily and imprison Mussolini. Italy declares war on Germany.
1945 Mussolini is captured and executed by Italian Communists.
1946 Republic replaces the monarchy.
1957 The Treaty of Rome establishes the European Economic Community.
2007 Silvio Berlusconi wins a third term as prime minister, amid persistent allegations of corruption.
2009 Earthquake in L'Aquila, around 100km east of Rome, kills over 260 people and leaves thousands homeless.
2011 Silvio Berlusconi steps down as prime minister and is succeeded by Mario Monti.
2013 Pope Benedict XVI unexpectedly resigns and is replaced by Francis I.

ARRIVAL

BY PLANE

The majority of tourists arrive at the

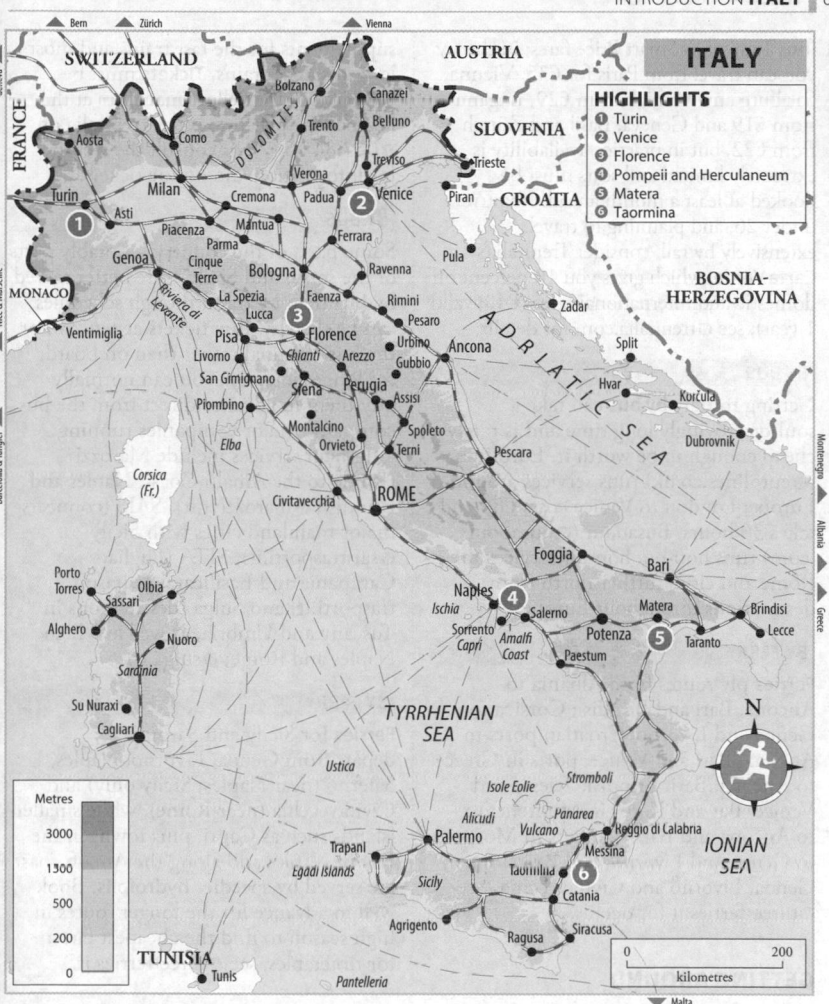

ITALY

HIGHLIGHTS
1. Turin
2. Venice
3. Florence
4. Pompeii and Herculaneum
5. Matera
6. Taormina

airports of Rome or Milan, although low-cost European airlines Ryanair and easyJet also offer services to Bari, Bologna, Brindisi, Genoa, Naples, Palermo, Parma, Perugia, Pisa, Rimini, Turin and Venice, plus destinations in Sardinia and Sicily. Budget Italian airline blu-express (ⓦblu-express.com) flies from France, Spain, Greece, Russia and Turkey to Rome, as well as between many Italian cities; Meridiana (ⓦmeridiana.it) has routes between many European and Italian cities. From North America, national carrier Alitalia (ⓦalitalia.com) runs direct flights to Milan, Rome and Venice, with numerous connecting flights to other cities, although you may find cheaper deals with US airlines such as Delta and American Airlines. Meridiana operates direct flights from New York to Cagliari, Catania, Olbia, Naples and Palermo. The cheapest option, though, can be to fly to London and get a budget flight onward from there.

BY TRAIN

Train travel from the UK often works out more expensive than flying, but there is a vast choice of routes, mostly arriving in Milan. From elsewhere in Europe, look

17

into Trenitalia's Smart Price fares; in theory you can travel from Paris for €35, Vienna, Salzburg and Munich from €29, Lugano from €19 and Geneva, Basil and Zürich from €22, but in practice availability is extremely limited and seats must be booked at least a month ahead. If you're under 26, and planning to travel extensively by rail, consider Trenitalia's **Carta Verde**, which gives you 10 percent off domestic and international fares (€40; valid 1 year); see ⓦtrenitalia.com for details.

BY BUS

Getting to Italy **by bus** can take a soul-destroyingly long time and is rarely cheap enough to be worth it. Eurolines (ⓦeurolines.co.uk) runs services around Europe; London to Venice costs €88 and takes 30 hours. Busabout (ⓦbusabout .com) runs hop-on, hop-off services to Rome and cities further north from destinations throughout Europe.

BY FERRY

Ferries ply routes from Albania to Ancona, Bari and Brindisi; Corsica to Genoa and Livorno; Croatian ports to Ancona, Bari and Venice; ports in Greece to Ancona, Bari, Brindisi, Trieste and Venice; Bar and Kotor in Montenegro to Ancona and Bari; Tangiers in Morocco to Genoa and Livorno; and Barcelona to Genoa, Livorno and Civitavecchia. See ⓦdirectferries.it for details.

GETTING AROUND

BY TRAIN

The rail network is extensive, less so in the south, though delays are common. **Trains** are operated by Italian State Railways (Ferrovie dello Stato or FS; ⓦtrenitalia .com). For most journeys you'll have a choice between Eurostar – expensive but fast – the slower, mid-priced Intercity and the cheap, snail-paced Diretto, Interregionale and Regionale. Seat reservations are obligatory on Eurostar and Intercity lines, and should be made a week in advance on busy routes. **InterRail** and **Eurail** passes are valid on the whole FS network, though you'll pay

supplements for the fast trains and most long-distance trains. **Tickets** must be validated in the yellow machines at the head of the platform. Call Trenitalia on ☎06 6847 5475 or consult the website for information and online tickets.

BY BUS

Some parts of the country – notably parts of the south and Sicily – are better served by **bus** than by train, though schedules can be sketchy. Buy tickets at *tabacchi* or the bus terminal rather than on board; for longer journeys you can normally buy them in advance direct from the bus company. Major companies running long-haul services include Marozzi (Rome to the Amalfi Coast, Naples and Brindisi; ⓦmarozzivt.it), SAIS (connects major mainland cities with Sicily; ⓦsaistrasporti.it), SITA (Puglia, Campania and Basilicata; ⓦsitasud trasporti.it) and Sulga (destinations in Tuscany and Umbria, as well as Milan, Naples and Rome; ⓦsulga.it).

BY FERRY

Ferries for Sicily and Sardinia depart from Genoa, Livorno, Naples, Salerno (near Naples; Sicily only) and Civitavecchia (near Rome), while smaller islands such as Capri, plus towns in the Bay of Naples and along the Amalfi coast, are served by speedier **hydrofoils**. Book well in advance for the longer routes in high season to find the cheapest fares; for timetables, see ⓦdirectferries.it.

ACCOMMODATION

Book **hotels** in advance in the major cities and resorts, especially in summer. Rates vary greatly, but on average you can expect to pay €60 for a double without private bathroom (*senza bagno*) in a one-star hotel, and at least €80 for a double in a three-star. Very busy places might ask you to book a minimum of three nights.

B&Bs and **agriturismi** (farmstays) can make a good-value alternative. They are often in spectacular locations and provide excellent Italian home cooking, though you may need a car to get to them: ask for a list from the local tourist office.

There are **hostels** in every major Italian city, charging €15–30 per person for a dorm bed, though for two people travelling together, this isn't much cheaper than a budget hotel room. You can see the full list of Italy's HI hostels on ⓦaighostels.it. Alternatively, **student accommodation** is a popular budget option in university towns (July and August only), or ask the tourist board about local **case per ferie**, usually religious houses with rooms or beds to let. They can be better value than hostels but often have curfews. Short-term flat rentals often work out much cheaper than staying in hotels, in particular in larger cities like Rome and Florence. ⓦcross-pollinate.com lists rooms and apartments for rent in a number of Italian cities.

There are plenty of **campsites**, and in most cases you pay for location rather than facilities, which can vary enormously. Daily prices are around €7 per person, plus €10 for a two-person tent. See ⓦcamping.it for information.

FOOD AND DRINK

There are few places in the world where you can eat and drink as well as in Italy. If you eat only pizza and panini, you'll be missing out on the distinctive **regional cuisines**; don't be afraid to ask what the *piatti tipici* (local dishes) are. Most Italians start their day in a bar, with a cappuccino and a *cornetto* (croissant), a **breakfast** that should cost around €2 if you stand at the counter – or at least double that if you take a seat. At **lunchtime**, bars sell *tramezzini*, sandwiches on white bread, and panini. Another stopgap are *arancini*, fried meat- or cheese-filled rice balls, particularly prevalent in the south. Italian **ice cream** (*gelato*) is justifiably famous and usually costs €1.50–2.50 a cup or cone. **Markets** sell fresh, tasty produce for next to nothing, and work out much cheaper than supermarket shopping.

The ultimate budget option for sit-down food is **pizza**. Although trattorias or restaurants often offer a fixed-price *menù turistico*, it's generally better to steer clear if you want an

APERITIVO TIME

When you're strapped for cash but want to have a good time, it's worth remembering that between about 6 and 9pm, most bars either bring you **snacks** or have an *aperitif* buffet if you buy a drink. These snacks are often substantial enough to fill you up, so you'll be able to save on buying dinner.

authentic experience. A **trattoria** is traditionally cheaper than a restaurant, offering *cucina casalinga* (home-style cooking). But in either, pasta dishes go for around €5–9; main fish or meat courses for €7–15. Order vegetables (*contorni*) separately. Afterwards there's fruit (*frutta*), desserts (*dolci*) and liquors such as *grappa* and *limoncello*.

DRINK

Bars are less social centres than functional places for a quick coffee or beer. You pay first at the cash desk (*la cassa*), present your receipt (*scontrino*) and give your order. Coffee comes small and black (*caffè*), with a dash of milk (*macchiato*), iced (*shakerato*) in summer, or there's the ever-popular *cappuccino*. Tea (*tè*) comes with lemon (*con limone*) unless you ask for milk (*con latte*); it's mainly served cold as ice-tea (*tè freddo*). A *spremuta* is a fresh orange juice; crushed-ice fruit *granite* are refreshing in summer.

Wine is invariably drunk with meals, and is very cheap. Go for the local stuff: ask for *un mezzo* (a half-litre) or *un quarto* (a quarter) *della casa* (house). Bottles are pricier but still good value; expect to pay at least €12 in a restaurant. The cheapest and most common brands of **beer** (*birra*) are the Italian Peroni and Moretti. Draught beer (*alla spina*) is served in measures of a pint (*una media*) and half-pint (*piccola*). A generous shot of spirits, limoncello, or grappa – made from grape pips and stalks – costs from €2. Amaro is a bitter after-dinner liqueur. Drinking in bars (*locali*) can be pricey – around €5 for a beer and €5–9 for a cocktail – while drinking in clubs can be ruinous, although the entrance fee of €10–15 usually includes one drink.

STUDENT AND YOUTH DISCOUNTS
Entrance to many of Italy's state-owned museums and archeological sites is free or reduced for
EU citizens aged under 25. Students are often eligible for discounts too; carry a valid ISIC card
or equivalent. For one week each year, usually in April, publicly owned museums and sites
open their doors for free for the Settimana della Cultura (Cultural Heritage Week).

Most places will be happy to serve
you **tap water** (*acqua dal rubinetto*). For
bottled water, ask for *acqua naturale*
(still) or *acqua frizzante* (sparkling).

CULTURE AND ETIQUETTE

Italy remains strongly **family-oriented**,
with an emphasis on the traditions and
rituals of the Catholic Church, and it's not
unusual to find people living with their
parents until their early thirties. While the
north is cosmopolitan, the south can be
rather provincial; women travelling on
their own may attract unwanted attention
in smaller areas. When entering churches,
ensure that your knees and shoulders are
covered. In towns and villages all over the
country, life stops during the middle of the
day for a long lunch.

Tipping is not a big deal in Italy; in
restaurants – if a service charge is not
included – it's acceptable to reward good
service with a couple of euros. In bars,
some Italians leave a coin on the counter
after finishing their coffee, but it is by no
means expected. Likewise, taxi drivers
will not expect a tip. **Smoking** is outlawed
in all enclosed public places.

SPORTS AND OUTDOOR ACTIVITIES

Spectator sports are popular, particularly
football (*calcio*), though cycling,
motorcycling and motor racing are also
high-profile sports. A football match in
Italy can be an exhilarating experience.
The season runs from the end of August
to May; see ⓦwww.lega-calcio.it for
details of matches; tickets cost from €25.

Campania, Sardinia and Sicily, with
their clear waters, provide excellent
conditions for **scuba diving** and
snorkelling, while Rome, Milan, Turin,
Venice and, at the other end of the
country, Mount Etna in Sicily, are within

easy reach of **ski resorts**. The same
mountainous terrain is perfectly suited to
summertime **hiking**; enquire at local
tourist offices. For mountain biking try
the rolling hills of Umbria and Tuscany,
although serious bikers might consider
the infamous Passo dello Stelvio near the
Swiss border.

COMMUNICATIONS

Post office opening hours are usually
Monday to Friday 8.30am to 6.30pm,
with branches in larger towns also open
Saturdays 8.30am–12.30pm. Stamps
(*francobolli*) can also be bought at *tabacchi*
– ask for *posta prioritaria* if you want
letters to arrive home before you do.
Public **phones** are card-operated; get a
phonecard (*scheda telefonica*) from *tabacchi*
and newsstands for €5/10. For land-line
calls – local and long-distance – dial all
digits, including the area code. Directory
enquiries (⓿1240) are pricey. Most towns
have at least one place with **internet** access;
hourly rates are around €2–4.

EMERGENCIES

Most of the **crime** you're likely to come
across is small-time. You can minimize
the risk of this by being discreet, not
flashing anything of value and keeping
a firm hand on your camera and bag,
particularly on public transport. The
police come in many forms: the *Vigili
Urbani* deal with traffic offences and the
Carabinieri with public order and drug
control; report thefts to the *Polizia di
Stato*. Italy treats soft and hard drugs
offences with equal severity.

Pharmacies (*farmacie*) can give advice
and dispense prescriptions; there's one

EMERGENCY NUMBERS
Police ⓿ 112 for all emergencies.

ITALIAN

	ITALIAN	PRONUNCIATION
Yes/No	Sì/No	See/Noh
Please	Per favore	Pear fah-vure-ay
You're welcome	Prego	Pray-goh
Thank you	Grazie	Grraat-see-ay
Hello/Good day/Hi	Ciao/buongiorno/salve	Chow/boo-on jawr-noh/salvay
Goodbye	Ciao/arrivederci	Chow/arrivi-derchee
Excuse me	Mi scusi	Mee scoo-see
Good	Buono	Bwo-noh
Bad	Cattivo	Cat-ee-voh
Near	Vicino	Vih-chee-noh
Far	Lontano	Lont-ah-noh
Today	Oggi	Ojj-ee
Yesterday	Ieri	Ee-air-ee
Tomorrow	Domani	Doh-mahn-ee
How much is...?	Quanto è...?	Cwan-toe ay...?
What time is it?	Che ore sono?	Keh orr-ay son-noh?
I don't understand	Non capisco	Non kapee-skoe
Do you speak English?	Parla Inglese?	Parr-la inglay-zay?
Ticket	Biglietto	Bil-yettoh
Where is...?	Dov'è...?	Doh-vay...?
Entrance	L'ingresso	Lingress-oh
Exit	L'uscita	Loo-shee-tah
Platform	Il binario	Il bin-ah-ree-oh
Toilet	Il bagno	Il ban-yo
Ferry	Il traghetto	Il trag-ettow
Bus	L'autobus	Lout-o-boos
Plane	L'aereo	Lah-air-ay-oh
Train	Il treno	Il tray-no
I would like a...	Vorrei...	Vorr-ay...
Bed	Letto	Lett-oh
Single/double room	Camera singola/doppia	Cam-errah singolah/doppiah
Cheap	Economico	Eck-oh-no-micoh
Expensive	Caro	Car-oh
Open	Aperto	Apairt-oh
Closed	Chiuso	Queue-zoh
Breakfast	Colazione	Coll-ats-ioh-nay
Hotel	L'hotel	Lott-ell
Hostel	L'ostello	Lost-ellow
One	Uno	Oo-noh
Two	Due	Doo-ay
Three	Tre	Tray
Four	Quattro	Cwattr-oh
Five	Cinque	Chink-way
Six	Sei	Say
Seven	Sette	Set-tay
Eight	Otto	Ot-toe
Nine	Nove	Noh-vay
Ten	Dieci	Dee-ay-chee

open all night in towns and cities (find the address of the nearest on any pharmacy door). For serious ailments, go to the *Pronto Soccorso* (casualty) section of the nearest hospital (*ospedale*).

INFORMATION

Most towns, major train stations and airports have a **tourist office** (*ufficio turistico*), which will give out maps for free. Studio FMB has excellent hiking

ITALY ONLINE

ⓦ **deliciousitaly.com** A guide on food, travel and culture.

ⓦ **italia.it** The official website of Italy's tourist board.

ⓦ **italianreflections.com** Traveller blogs, news and features on the country.

maps covering the north of the country, as does Club Alpino Italiano, available throughout Italy.

MONEY AND BANKS

Italy's currency is the euro (€). You'll get the best rate of exchange at a **bank**; hours are Monday to Friday 8.30am to 1.30pm and 2.30 to 4pm. ATMs (*bancomat*) are widespread. The Italian way of life is cash-based, and many smaller restaurants and B&Bs will not accept credit cards.

OPENING HOURS AND HOLIDAYS

Most shops and businesses open Monday to Saturday 8/9am to 1pm and 4–7/8pm, though in the north, offices work a 9am to 5pm day. Just about everything, with the exception of bars and restaurants, closes on Sunday. Most churches keep shop hours. Museums traditionally open Tuesday to Sunday 9am to 7pm. Most archeological sites open daily from 9am until an hour before sunset.

Many of Italy's inland towns close down almost entirely for the month of August, when Italians head for the coast. Everything closes for national holidays: January 1, January 6, Easter Monday, April 25, May 1, June 2, August 15, November 1, December 8, December 25 and 26.

Rome

Of all Italy's historic cities, **ROME** (Roma) exerts the most fascination. Its sheer weight of history is endlessly compelling. Classical features – the Colosseum, the Roman Forum, the spectacular Palatine Hill – stand alongside ancient basilicas containing relics from the early Christian period, while Baroque fountains and churches define the city centre. But it's not all history and brickwork: Rome has a vibrant, chaotic life of its own, its crowded streets thronged with traffic, locals, tourists and students.

WHAT TO SEE AND DO

Rome's city centre is divided into distinct areas. The **Centro Storico** (historic centre) occupies a hook of land on the east bank of the River Tiber, bordered to the east by Via del Corso and to the north and south by water. The old Campus Martius of Roman times, it became the heart of the Renaissance city and is now an unruly knot of narrow streets holding some of the best of Rome's classical and Baroque heritage, as well as much of its nightlife.

From here, Rome's central core spreads east, across Via del Corso to the major shopping streets around the **Spanish Steps** and the main artery of Via Nazionale, and south to the **Roman Forum**, **Colosseum** and **Palatine Hill**. The west bank of the river is home to the **Vatican** and **St Peter's** and, to the south of these, charming **Trastevere**. East of Termini Station is student-hub San Lorenzo, home to Rome's main university and some of its best nightlife.

The Roman Forum

The best place to start a tour of the city is the **Roman Forum** (daily 8.30am–1hr before sunset; 2-day joint ticket with Colosseum and Palatine Hill, which operate same opening hours, €12), the bustling centre of the ancient city. It's worth getting the audioguide (€5, must be returned by 4.30pm) as there is next to no textual information displayed on site.

Running through the heart of the Forum, the **Via Sacra** was the best-known street of ancient Rome, lined with its most important buildings, such as the Curia – begun in 45 BC, this was the home of the Senate during the Republican period. Next to the Curia is the **Arch of Septimius Severus**, erected in the early third century AD to commemorate the Emperor's tenth anniversary in power. In the centre of the Forum is the **House of the Vestal Virgins**, where the six women charged with keeping the sacred flame of Vesta alight lived. On the far side of the site, the towering **Basilica of Maxentius** is probably the Forum's most impressive relic. From the basilica, the Via Sacra climbs to the **Arch of Titus** on a low arm of the Palatine Hill, its reliefs showing the spoils of Jerusalem being carried off by eager Romans.

Palatine Hill

From the Forum, turn right at the Arch of Titus to reach the **Palatine Hill** (hours and price as per Roman Forum), now a beautiful archeological garden. In the days of the Republic, the Palatine was the most desirable address in Rome. From the **Farnese Gardens**, on the right, a terrace looks back over the Forum, while the terrace at the opposite end looks down on the alleged centre of Rome's ancient beginning – an Iron Age hut, known as the **House of Romulus**, the best-preserved part of a ninth-century BC village.

Close by, steps lead down to the **Cryptoporticus**, a passage built by Nero to link the Palatine with his palace on the far side of the Colosseum. A left turn leads to the **House of Augustus** (Mon, Wed, Sat & Sun 11am–3.30pm), which holds beautiful frescoes dating back to 30 BC and is considered to be among the most magnificent examples of Roman wall paintings anywhere; even the builders' ancient graffiti has been meticulously preserved.

The Capitoline Hill

Formerly the spiritual and political centre of the Roman Empire, the Capitoline Hill lies behind the Neoclassical Vittoriano monument on Piazza Venezia. Atop the Capitoline is **Piazza del Campidoglio**, designed by Michelangelo in the 1530s and flanked by the two wings of one of the city's most important museums of ancient art – and the oldest public gallery in the world, dating back to 1471 – the **Capitoline Museums** (Tues–Sun 9am–8pm; €9.50, student €7.50). The Palazzo Nuovo, the museum's left-hand wing, contains some of the best of the city's Roman and Greek sculpture. Highlights of the Palazzo dei Conservatori opposite include various parts of the colossal statue of the Emperor Constantine which once stood in the Forum, and sixteenth-century frescoes.

Colosseum

Immediately outside the Forum, the fourth-century **Arch of Constantine** marks the end of the Via Sacra. Across from here is Rome's most awe-inspiring ancient monument, the **Colosseum** (hours and price as per Roman Forum; bypass queues by buying tickets at the Palatine Hill; see above). Begun by the Emperor Vespasian in 72 AD, construction was completed by his son Titus about eight years later – an event celebrated with one hundred days of games. The arena was about 500m in circumference and could seat fifty thousand people; the Romans flocked here for gladiatorial contests and cruel spectacles. Mock sea battles were also staged here – the arena could be flooded in minutes. After the games were outlawed in the fifth century, the Colosseum was pillaged for building material, but the magnificent shell remains.

Campo de' Fiori and the Ghetto

From Piazza Venezia, Via del Plebiscito forges west; take a left turn into the maze of cobbled streets that wind down to pretty **Campo de' Fiori**, one-time heart of the medieval city, now home to a colourful produce market (Mon–Sat 6.30am–2pm). Surrounded by bars, it's a great spot to watch the *passeggiata* (early-evening stroll).

A short walk from here, east of Via Arenula, a warren of narrow streets makes up the Ghetto. Having moved here from Trastevere in the thirteenth century, the city's Jews were walled off from the rest of the city in 1556, and subsequently suffered centuries of ill-treatment, culminating in the deportations of World War II, when a quarter of the Ghetto's population died in concentration camps. Today, the area has an intimate, backstreet feel, and is an atmospheric place for a wander and a delicious deep-fried artichoke.

17

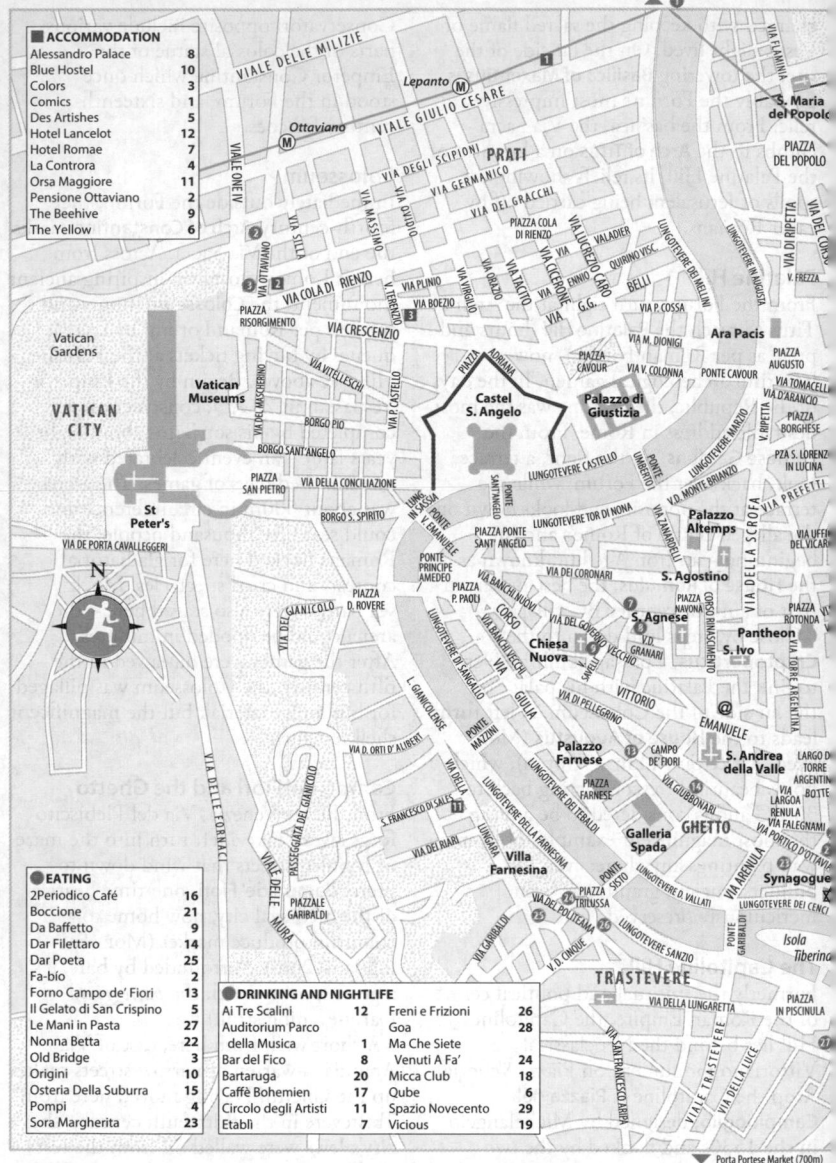

■ ACCOMMODATION	
Alessandro Palace	8
Blue Hostel	10
Colors	3
Comics	1
Des Artishes	5
Hotel Lancelot	12
Hotel Romae	7
La Controra	4
Orsa Maggiore	11
Pensione Ottaviano	2
The Beehive	9
The Yellow	6

● EATING	
2Periodico Café	16
Boccione	21
Da Baffetto	9
Dar Filettaro	14
Dar Poeta	25
Fa-bio	2
Forno Campo de' Fiori	13
Il Gelato di San Crispino	5
Le Mani in Pasta	27
Nonna Betta	22
Old Bridge	3
Origini	10
Osteria Della Suburra	15
Pompi	4
Sora Margherita	23

● DRINKING AND NIGHTLIFE			
Ai Tre Scalini	12	Freni e Frizioni	26
Auditorium Parco della Musica	1	Goa	28
Bar del Fico	8	Ma Che Siete Venuti A Fa'	24
Bartaruga	20	Micca Club	18
Caffè Bohemien	17	Qube	6
Circolo degli Artisti	11	Spazio Novecento	29
Etabli	7	Vicious	19

Porta Portese Market (700m)

Pantheon

One of the Centro Storico's main draws is the **Pantheon** (Mon–Sat 9am–7.30pm, Sun 9am–6pm; free), the most complete ancient Roman structure in the city, finished around 125 AD. Inside, the diameter of the dome and height of the building are precisely equal, and the hole in the dome's centre is a full 9m across; there are no visible arches or vaults to hold the whole thing up – instead, they're sunk into the concrete of the walls of the building. The coffered ceiling was covered in solid bronze until the seventeenth century, and the niches were filled with statues of the gods.

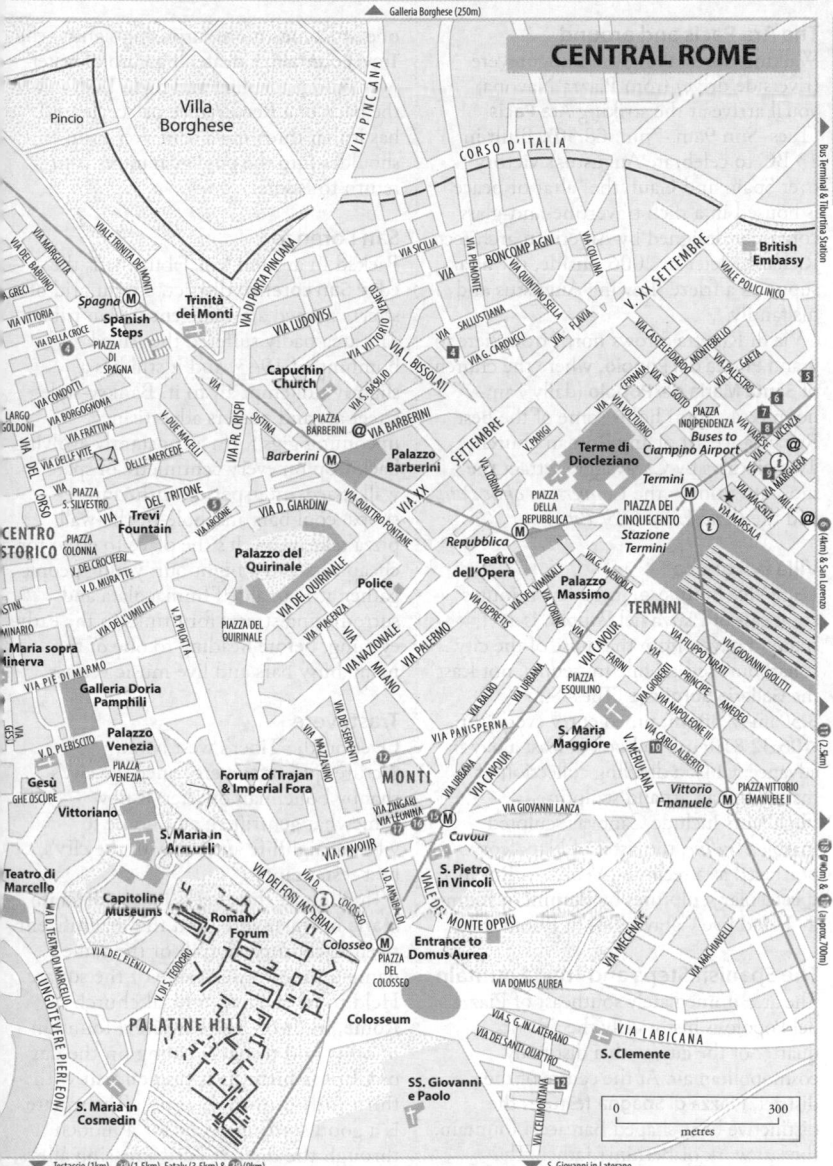

Galleria Borghese (250m)

CENTRAL ROME

Villa Borghese

Pincio

CORSO D'ITALIA

British Embassy

Spagna Ⓜ
Trinità dei Monti

Spanish Steps

Capuchin Church

Barberini Ⓜ
Palazzo Barberini

Terme di Diocleziano

Buses to Ciampino Airport

Termini

PIAZZA DEI CINQUECENTO
Stazione Termini

Trevi Fountain

CENTRO STORICO

Palazzo del Quirinale

Police

Repubblica

Teatro dell'Opera

Palazzo Massimo

TERMINI

S. Maria sopra Minerva

Galleria Doria Pamphili

Palazzo del Quirinale

S. Maria Maggiore

Palazzo Venezia

Gesù

Vittoriano

Forum of Trajan & Imperial Fora

MONTI

Vittorio Emanuele Ⓜ

PIAZZA VITTORIO EMANUELE II

S. Maria in Aracoeli

Cavour

S. Pietro in Vincoli

Teatro di Marcello

Capitoline Museums

Roman Forum

Colosseo Ⓜ

Entrance to Domus Aurea

PALATINE HILL

Colosseum

S. Clemente

VIA LABICANA

SS. Giovanni e Paolo

S. Maria in Cosmedin

0   300
metres

Testaccio (1km), ㉖ (1.5km), Eataly (3.5km) & ㉙ (9km)

S. Giovanni in Laterano

Piazza Navona

A ten-minute stroll west of the Pantheon, **Piazza Navona** is one of the city's most pleasing squares, and follows the lines of the Emperor Domitian's chariot arena. The Borromini-designed church of **Sant'Agnese in Agone** on the west side supposedly stands on the spot where St Agnes, exposed naked to the public in the stadium, miraculously grew hair to cover herself. Opposite, the **Fontana dei Quattro Fiumi** is by Borromini's arch-rival, Bernini; each figure represents one of the four great rivers of the world – the Nile, Danube, Ganges and Plate – though only the horse was actually carved by Bernini.

17

The Ara Pacis and around

Walking north along the Lungotevere (riverside drive) from Piazza Navona, you'll arrive at the striking **Ara Pacis** (Tues–Sun 9am–7pm; €8.50). Built in 13 BC to celebrate Augustus's victory over Spain and Gaul, the "altar of peace" is housed in a slick travertine-and-glass container designed by American architect Richard Meier in 2006. Inside, the altar supports a frieze showing Augustus and his family.

Via di Ripetta arrows north from here to grand **Piazza del Popolo**, where the church of **Santa Maria del Popolo** (daily 7am–noon & 4–7pm) holds some of the best Renaissance art of any Roman church. Two pictures by Caravaggio attract the most attention – the *Conversion of St Paul* and the *Crucifixion of St Peter*.

Villa Borghese

Leafy **Villa Borghese**, just a few minutes' stroll east of Piazza del Popolo, is a tranquil haven from the noise of the city. It harbours several fine museums, not least the **Galleria Borghese** (Tues–Sun 8.30am–7.30pm; timed entry every 2hr; ✆06 32 810; call to book at least a day in advance; €11), a dazzling collection of mainly Italian art and sculpture. Highlights include Canova's sculpted marble *Pauline*, the sister of Napoleon portrayed as a reclining Venus, in Room 1; spectacular sculptures by Bernini in rooms 2–4; and five Caravaggios in Room 8.

The Spanish Steps and Trevi Fountain

The area immediately southeast of Piazza del Popolo is historically the artistic quarter of the city, with a distinctly cosmopolitan air. At the centre of the district, **Piazza di Spagna** features the distinctive boat-shaped Barcaccia fountain, the last work of Bernini's father. The **Spanish Steps** – a venue for international posing – sweep up from the piazza to the sixteenth-century church of **Trinità dei Monti**. From the top of the Spanish Steps, narrow Via Sistina winds down to Piazza Barberini, dominated by Bernini's Fontana del Tritone, its muscular Triton held up by four dolphins. West down Via del Tritone, hidden among a web of narrow streets, is one of Rome's more surprising sights – the **Trevi Fountain**, a deafening gush of water over Baroque statues and rocks built onto the back of a Renaissance palace; legend has it that throwing a coin over your shoulder into the pool guarantees your return to Rome.

San Lorenzo

Packed in around Via Tiburtina is the edgy **San Lorenzo** district, a tight grid of streets named after ancient Italian tribes. The area badly suffered the Allied bombing of 1943, and it still has a slightly unkempt air to it. Banksy-style street art and posters advertising upcoming gigs form a constantly evolving backdrop on every centimetre of spare wall space, interspersed with vintage shops, cool bars and hole-in-the-wall pizza takeaways. It's the place to go to for cheap eats and a night out; young people gather at Piazza dell'Immacolata and surrounding streets for drinks in the early evening, before heading to one of the many busy bars and live music venues.

Trastevere

Over on the Tiber's west bank, picturesque **Trastevere**, once the city's shabby bohemian quarter, is now somewhat gentrified, and home to vibrant nightlife and some of the city's best restaurants.

The hub of the area is **Piazza di Santa Maria in Trastevere**, and the magnificent twelfth-century church of the same name on the western side of the square. Held to be the first official church in Rome, built on a site where a fountain of oil is said to have sprung on the day of Christ's birth, it is resplendent with thirteenth-century mosaics. The square is a good starting point for a mooch through the district's crisscrossing alleys, lined with enticing cafés, bars, markets, boutiques and *gelaterias*.

St Peter's basilica

The **Vatican City**, a tiny territory north of Trastevere, is partly hemmed in by high walls, but opens its doors to the rest of the city in the form of Bernini's **Piazza San Pietro**. **St Peter's Basilica** (daily 7am–6pm;

free) was built to a plan initially conceived at the end of the fifteenth century by Bramante and finished off over a century later by Carlo Maderno, bridging the Renaissance and Baroque eras. The first thing you see, on the right, is Michelangelo's moving *Pietà*, completed when he was just 24. On the right-hand side of the nave, the bronze statue of St Peter was cast in the thirteenth century by Arnolfo di Cambio. Bronze was also used in Bernini's imposing 28m-high *baldacchino*, the centrepiece of the sculptor's embellishment of the interior. To the right of the main doors, you can ascend by stairs or lift to the **roof**, from where there's a steep walk up 320 steps to the **dome** (daily 8am–5pm; €6, €7 with lift), well worth the effort for its glorious views over the city.

The Vatican Museums

A ten-minute walk from the northern side of Piazza San Pietro takes you to the **Vatican Museums** (Mon–Sat 9am–6pm; last admission 4pm; €16, students under 26 €8; last Sun of the month 9am–2pm; last admission 12.30pm; free) – quite simply the largest, richest museum complex in the world, stuffed with treasures from every period of the city's history. The queues to get in can be daunting so it's best to book ahead online (wmv.vatican.va). Highlights include the **Stanze di Raffaello**, a set of rooms decorated for Pope Julius II by Raphael among others, including the *School of Athens* fresco, which depicts his artistic contemporaries as classical figures: Leonardo is Plato and Michelangelo Heraclitus. Further on is the **Galleria Chiaramonte**, a superb collection of Roman statues, and the **Galleria delle Carte Geografiche**, a stunning corridor adorned with incredibly precise, richly pigmented maps of Italy.

The **Sistine Chapel**, of course, is the main draw. Built for Pope Sixtus IV in 1481, it serves as the pope's private chapel and hosts the conclaves of cardinals for the election of each new pope. The paintings down each side wall depict scenes from the lives of Moses and Christ by Perugino, Botticelli and Ghirlandaio,

among others. But it's Michelangelo's ceiling frescoes of the *Creation* that everyone comes to see, executed almost single-handedly over a period of about four years for Pope Julius II. The *Last Judgement*, on the west wall of the chapel, was painted by Michelangelo over twenty years later. The nudity caused controversy from the start, and the pope's zealous successor, Pius IV, insisted that loincloths be added – removed in a recent restoration.

ARRIVAL AND DEPARTURE

By plane Rome has two airports. Leonardo da Vinci, better known as Fiumicino (wadr.it/fiumicino), and Ciampino (wadr.it/ciampino), which is exclusively for low-cost flights. Two train services link Fiumicino to Rome: the Leonardo Express to Termini (every 30min until 11.37pm; 30min; €14), and the FL1 to Trastevere, Ostiense and Tiburtina stations (every 15–30min until 11.27pm; €8). Terravision coach services (every 30min–1hr; 1hr; €4; wterravision.eu) and SIT buses (every 45min; 1hr; €5; wsitbusshuttle.com) travel to Termini station. From Ciampino, Terravision (€4) and SIT buses (€4) make the 40min trip to Termini station.

By train The main train station is Termini, meeting point of the metro lines and city bus routes. Some long-distance services use Stazione Tiburtina. The two stations are connected by metro and bus.

Destinations Bologna (every 15min; 2–4hr); Florence (every 15min; 1hr 20min–3hr 20min); Milan (every 15min; 3hr–6hr 30min); Naples (every 30min; 1hr 10min–2hr 40min); Paris (1 daily; 14hr 50min); Turin (hourly; 4–6hr); Vienna (1 daily; 13hr 20min); Zürich (via Milan; 5 daily; 6hr 50min–7hr 30min).

By bus Domestic bus services use the bus terminal outside Stazione Tiburtina (wTiburtina).

Destinations Agrigento (1 daily; 12hr); Amalfi (1 daily; 4hr); Bologna (2 weekly; 4hr 30min); Florence (1–2 daily; 3hr 20min); Lecce (4 daily; 8hr 30min); Naples (1 daily; 2hr); Palermo (1 daily; 11hr); Perugia (5 daily; 2hr 20min); Sorrento (2 daily; 4hr).

INFORMATION AND TOURS

Tourist office The department of tourism Roma Capitale (wturismoroma.it) has a tourist information booth at Termini Station at platform 24 (daily 8am–7.30pm), and green tourist information kiosks (PIT) near every major sight (daily 9.30am–7pm), as well as at both of the city's airports at arrivals (Fiumicino daily 8am–7.30pm; Ciampino daily 9am–6.30pm). w060608.it is a council-run tourist website; you can also call ☎06 0608 for information in English (daily 9am–9pm).

17

ROME ONLINE

ⓦ **buzzinrome.com** Eating and drinking listings, as well as tips on shopping.
ⓦ **wantedinrome.com** Up-to-date information on what's happening in Rome, from concerts to exhibitions.
ⓦ **romeing.it**. Insider guide to Rome's events, cultural scene and lifestyle.
ⓦ **heartrome.com** Blog on food and travel in the capital.

Discount passes The Roma Pass (€30 for three days; ⓦ romapass.it) gives you free access to all public transport within the city, as well as free entry to the first two sites you visit, plus many further discounts. Buy the pass from tourist information kiosks or from participating sites.

Tours Romeing Tours (ⓦ romeingtours.com) run fun walks around the historical centre, while Eating Italy Food Tours (ⓦ eatingitalyfoodtours.com) offer entertaining food and cultural tours.

GETTING AROUND

Tickets Public transport is cheap and reasonably reliable. A day-pass (BIG; €6), one-way ticket (BIT; valid for 100min on all public transport, including one trip on the metro; €1.50), 3-day pass (BTI; €16) or 1-week ticket (CIS; €24) for the metro and bus network can be bought from most newspaper stalls and *tabacchi*, and from ticket machines in metro stations. Stamp tickets to validate them at the entrance gates to metros and on board buses and trams.

By bus The bus network is extensive; useful routes include the #40 from Termini station, which passes through the centre en route to the Vatican, and #116 from the Ⓜ Barberini, which serves both Villa Borghese and the Centro Storico. A network of night buses (*bus notturni*) serves most parts of the city, running until about 5.30am. #N1 follows metro line A; #N2 calls at all stops along metro line B; and #N8 runs from Trastevere to Termini station.

By metro The quickest way to get around, with trains every 3–5min. The city's two metro lines, A and B, meet beneath Termini station and run 5.30am–11.30pm (Fri & Sat till 1.30am).

By taxi Meters start at €3 by day (€4.50 on Sun) and €6.50 after 10pm. Depending on luggage and the time of travel, it should cost around €10 to get from Termini to the centre. You can hail one in the street, or at the ranks at Termini or Argentina (opposite Feltrinelli), or call ☎ 06 3570.

ACCOMMODATION

In high season (April–July, Sept & major religious holidays) Rome is very crowded, so book accommodation as far in advance as possible. Many of the city's hostels and cheaper hotels are located close to Termini station, but it's pretty insalubrious; pay a bit more to stay in the centre if you can.

HOSTELS

Alessandro Palace Via Vicenza 42, Termini ☎ 06 446 1958, ⓦ hostelsalessandro.com. Mock classical paintings decorate the walls of this happening hostel with en-suite a/c dorms, all with lockers and individual plugs. The deck chairs on the rooftop terrace are a great spot to catch some rays. Dorm €26, twin (no double) €110

Comics Viale Giulio Cesare 38, Prati ☎ 06 9437 9873, ⓦ comicsguesthouse.it. Unique quirky hostel with the world's favourite comics characters decorating every nook and cranny; all rooms are immaculate and each has a/c, TV, DVD player and private bath. There's also a chill-out area with beanbags, DVDs and a Playstation. Dorm €30, double €75

La Controra Via Umbria 7, Termini/Centro Storico ☎ 06 9893 7366, ⓦ lacontrora.com. A laidback, quiet hostel where guests socialize at the breakfast table; all dorms have a/c, parquet floors and private bath. Dorm €35, double €110

Orsa Maggiore Via San Francesco di Sales 1a, Trastevere ☎ 06 6840 1725, ⓦ foresteriaorsa.altervista.org. In an exceptional location in Travestere, this municipal-run women's hostel is housed in a former convent. Rooms are ample, bright and functional and the atmosphere calm and laidback. Dorm €26, double with shared bath €72, double with bath €100

Pensione Ottaviano Via Ottaviano 6, Prati ☎ 06 3973 8138, ⓦ pensioneottaviano.com. The dorms are simply furnished and on the cramped side, but *Ottaviano* is a good place to meet other travellers, and there are views of St Peter's from some rooms. They can organize airport transfers from €30. Dorm €25, twin €70

★ **The Beehive** Via Marghera 8, Termini ☎ 06 4470 4553, ⓦ the-beehive.com. This wonderful hostel has spacious rooms with artisan mirrors and designer furnishings, a vegetarian organic café, a massage room and a quiet leafy patio perfect to unwind with a book. Dorm €30, double with shared bathroom €80, double with bathroom €90

★ **The Yellow** Via Palestro 44, Termini ☎ 06 49382 682, ⓦ the-yellow.com. A fun party hostel. The comfortable dorms all have individual hanging bars for clothes as well as personal reading lamps, plugs and lockers. The bustling friendly bar attracts plenty of locals too and the party continues until the wee hours in the soundproof basement. Women-only dorm €17, mixed dorm €25, double €120

HOTELS

★ **Blue Hostel** Via Carlo Alberto 13, Termini ☎ 340 925 8503, ⓦ bluehostel.it. This intimate little hotel with only six doubles has bright and airy rooms with original timber ceilings dating back to 1750; windows give on to a

★ TREAT YOURSELF

Just a stone's throw away from the Colosseum, the family-run **Hotel Lancelot** (Via Capo d'Africa 47 ☎ 06 7045 0615, ⓦ lancelothotel.com; double €196), in a leafy residential neighbourhood has charmingly quaint rooms, some with private balconies; those on the upper floors boast incredible views over the nearby Colosseum. Staff are welcoming and encourage guests to mingle at the convivial breakfast tables. Excellent low-season rates (Jan, Feb & Aug) make the hotel more affordable.

peaceful interior courtyard, which echoes with birdsong and the bells of nearby Santa Maria Maggiore. There's also a private apartment, with kitchen, sleeping 5. Double €120, apartment €170

Colors Via Boezio 31, Prati ☎ 06 687 4030, ⓦ colorshotel .com. Located right by the Vatican, this colourful hotel has spic-and-span rooms with modern amenities. From mid-June to September there are a few dorms available. Dorm €35, double €120

Des Artistes Via Villafranca 20, Termini ☎ 06 4454 365, ⓦ hoteldesartistes.com. The spic-and-span a/c rooms here are spacious and pleasantly decorated with classical prints and wooden furniture; some rooms operate as dorms. There's a large rooftop terrace, perfect to meet other travellers and kick back in the sun in the warmer months. Dorm €32, double €84

Hotel Romae Via Palestro 49, Termini ☎ 06 4463 554, ⓦ hotelromae.com. The functional rooms with sturdy comfy beds all have private bath, a/c, minibar and cable TV; free all-day tea, coffee and fruit. Double €120

EATING

All of Rome's neighbourhoods have at least one food market (generally Mon–Sat 7am–2pm); Campo de' Fiori is the most famous, while Piazza Vittorio Emanuele near Termini sells African fruits and Asian food too. The large food temple Eataly (ⓦ www.roma.eataly.it; Ⓜ Piramide) is home to plenty of superb restaurants, bars and cafés, perfect to sample Italian dishes.

CAFÉS, SNACKS AND ICE CREAM

★ **2Periodico Café** Via Leonina 77, Monti ⓦ 2periodicocafe.it. Arty café in the heart of the Monti district with mismatched furniture, where you can sit back with a good book and a cuppa. Light dishes and mains from €6. It livens up substantially in the evenings when *aperitivo* time kicks in. Daily 9am–1am, Fri & Sat 9am–2am.

Boccione Via del Portico d'Ottavia 1, Ghetto. Historic Jewish bakery with marvellous ricotta and dried fruit-filled cakes. Mon–Thurs 7am–7pm, Fri 7am–3.30pm, Sun 7am–6pm.

Fa-bío Via Germanico 43, Prati. Organic fresh juices made with fruit and/or vegetables for €3.50 and zingy salads with ingredients like tofu, lentils and lovely dressings for €5 are the perfect antidote to too much pizza and sun. Good vegetarian choices. Mon–Fri 9am–6pm, Sat 9am–4pm.

Forno Campo de' Fiori Piazza Campo de' Fiori 22, Centro Storico ⓦ fornocampodefiori.com. This little bakery is the perfect spot to grab some "pizza bianca" (white pizza, focaccia style) or "pizza rossa" (red pizza, with tomatoes) on the go for about €2 a slice. Mon–Sat 7.30am–8pm.

★ **Il Gelato di San Crispino** Via della Panetteria 42, Centro Storico ⓦ ilgelatodisancrispino.it. Close to the Trevi fountain, Rome's best *gelateria* rustles up exceptional ice cream flavours, all made using natural in-season fruits. The signature *crespino al miele* (creamy vanilla with honey) is a must. Mon–Thurs noon–12.30am, Fri & Sat 11am–1.30am, Sun 11–12.30am.

Old Bridge Viale Bastioni di Michelangelo 5, Prati ⓦ gelateriaoldbridge.com. The perfect pit stop for a refreshing ice cream (from €1.50) after a long day of sightseeing at the nearby Vatican Museums. Daily 10am–2am.

Origini Via del Gesù corner Piè di Marmo, Centro Storico. Friendly *gelateria* offering exquisite home-made ice cream (€3), *granite* and yogurt with a choice of toppings (both €4). Staff will happily let you sample the flavours on offer. Daily 10am–11.30pm.

Pompi Via della Croce 82, Centro Storico ⓦ barpompi.it. Savour Rome's best tiramisù (€4) at this long-standing favourite café. The six different flavours include piña colada and banana and chocolate, and come in a little box perfect to take-away and enjoy on nearby Piazza di Spagna. Daily 10am–9.30pm.

RESTAURANTS AND PIZZERIAS

The Centro Storico, Trastevere, Testaccio and Monti are full of small, family-run restaurants.

Da Baffetto Via del Governo Vecchio 114, Centro Storico ⓦ pizzeriabaffetto.it. A real Roman institution that has been going for years – get ready to queue for the exquisite pizzas (from €5) kneaded by the wood-fire oven. Daily 6.30pm–12.30am.

Dar Filettaro Largo dei Librari 88, Centro Storico. A true Rome experience: chaotic and delicious. The order of the day is fried fish (€5), along with whatever salad is in season. Mon–Sat 5–11pm.

Dar Poeta Vicolo del Bologna 45, Trastevere ⓦ darpoeta .com. The pizzas (€5–9) are made using a special dough recipe, with the final result being partially Roman

17

WATER FOUNTAINS

All over Rome, there are small water fountains from which you can drink. The water is ice-cold, clean and free, so bring a water bottle and fill up.

(crunchy) and partially Neapolitan (sloppy). Daily noon–1am.

★ **Le Mani in Pasta** Via dei Genovesi 37, Trastevere ⓦ lemaniinpasta.com. Wonderful home cooking with an emphasis on fish-based dishes and traditional Roman cuisine in the heart of Trastevere – you can peer at the flurry of activity in the kitchen from the welcoming little dining area. *Primi* €9–13. Tues–Sun 12.30–3pm & 7.30–11.30pm.

Nonna Betta Via del Portico d'Ottavia 16, Ghetto ⓦ nonnabetta.it. Authentic Jewish Roman home cooking, with recipes all handed down by grandma Betta. Try the fried artichokes (€5) in season. Good-value set lunches for €15. Small discounts for *Rough Guide* readers and students. Wed–Mon 11.30am–11pm.

Osteria Della Suburra Via Urbana 67, Monti ⓦ osteriadellasuburra.com. Traditional osteria serving *lumache alla romana* (snails €13), *cervelletti d'agnello* (fried lamb brains with courgettes or artichokes; €10) and *coratella d'abbacchio* (mixed offal of lamb with wine and onion; €8). There are also plenty of wonderful home-made pasta dishes (€8–10). Tues–Sun 1–3pm & 7–11pm.

Sora Margherita Piazza delle Cinque Scole 30, Ghetto. This intimate family-run place with a handwritten menu offers all manner of local dishes including handmade pasta (mains €11), served in a tiny dining area where customers inevitably socialize over their dishes. Mon–Fri 12.30–3pm, plus two evening sittings at 8pm & 9.30pm. In winter open Saturdays too.

DRINKING AND NIGHTLIFE

The two main areas to go for a drink are Trastevere and the Centro Storico, particularly around Campo de' Fiori. Bohemian Monti, near the Colosseum, and studenty San Lorenzo are full of bars frequented by locals. For clubs, the door charge can be anything from €5 to €25, and normally includes a complimentary drink.

BARS

★ **Ai Tre Scalini** Via Panisperna 251, Monti. Monti's laidback wine bar with old-school knick-knacks attracts a cool young crowd who are here for the exceptional wine (there are over 250; from €4.50 a glass), which can be enjoyed with top-notch regional dishes (€7.50). Daily 12.30pm–1.30am.

Bar del Fico Piazza del Fico 26, Centro Storico ⓦ bardelfico.com. This trendy spot attracts Rome's cool set, who gather here to mingle over an *aperitivo* (glass of wine €5, cocktails €8) on the leafy cobbled square. Daily 7am–2am.

Bartaruga Piazza Mattei 9, Ghetto ⓦ bartaruga.com. Unique bar decked out like a retro dream with dark undertones, drapes and eclectic period furniture; it featured in Woody Allen's *To Rome With Love*. Cocktails €10. Daily 6pm–1am.

Caffè Bohemien Via degli Zingari 36, Monti ⓦ caffebohemien.it. Intimate boho hangout with mismatched vintage furniture, dim lighting and books lining the walls, perfect for an evening drink (wine €5, cocktails €6). There's an *aperitivo* buffet (7–9pm; €8). Mon, Wed & Thurs 5.30pm–1.30am, Fri & Sat 6pm–2am.

★ **Etabli** Vicolo delle Vacche 9, Centro Storico ⓦ etabli .it. This wonderful wine bar with high ceilings and a cosy fireplace for the winter months hosts live jazz and funky blues bands (Tues & Wed 8.30–11.30pm) and Thursday

FESTIVALS

Festival delle Letterature ⓦ festivaldelleletterature.it. The floodlit Basilica of Maxentius provides a stunning backdrop to readings by international authors. May & June.

Estate Romana & Expo Tevere ⓦ estateromana.comune.roma.it. Events include concerts and cultural happenings – many of them free – in parks and piazzas around town, plus buzzing bars, restaurants and an outdoor cinema set up along the riverbank around Trastevere and the Tiber Island. "Gay Village" (ⓦ gayvillage.it) runs through the summer with music and club nights. June–Sept.

La Festa di Noantri Piazza Santa Maria in Trastevere and around. Trastevere's traditional summer festival in honour of the Virgin, with street stalls selling snacks and trinkets, and a grand finale of fireworks. Last two weeks of July.

RomaEuropa Festival ⓦ romaeuropa.net. A cutting-edge performing arts festival, generally with some big-name acts, in locations around town. Mid-Sept to Nov.

Rome Film Festival ⓦ romacinemafest.it. A host of film stars descend on the city for its annual film festival, and there are English-language screenings all around town. Mid- to end Oct.

jam sessions (8pm–midnight). Wine, tapas (both €5) and cocktails (€8). Daily 6.30pm–1am, Thurs, Fri & Sat until ?am

Freni e Frizioni Via del Politeama 4/6, Trastevere ⓦ freniefrizioni.it. This ex-garage (the name means "Brakes and Clutches"), cluttered with vintage machinery, is a popular early-evening hangout, thanks to its generous *aperitivo* buffet (7–9pm) – just buy a drink (from €6) and dig in. Daily 6.30pm–2am.

Ma Che Siete Venuti A Fa' Via di Benedetta 25, Trastevere ⓦ football-pub.com. Quench your thirst at this tiny drinking hole serving 16 top-notch beers (€4) on tap, to be enjoyed with local and international footie matches on screen. Daily 11am–2am.

CLUBS AND LIVE MUSIC VENUES

For up-to-date info in English, check the Entertainment section of *WHERE Rome* magazine ⓦ wheretraveler.com. Much of the club scene moves down to the beach at Ostia in the summer – look for posters around town.

Auditorium Parco della Musica Viale P. de Coubertin, Flaminio ⓦ auditorium.com. Bus #M from Termini. See big international acts in this magnificent venue, one of the few modern constructions in the city. In the summer gigs are held in the outdoor amphitheatre, which seats 3000.

Circolo degli Artisti Via Casilina Vecchia 42, San Giovanni ⓦ circoloartisti.it. Bus #105 from Termini. Huge bar, disco and garden with live rock, blues and electro; good vintage market some Sundays. Check the website for the latest events.

Goa Via Giuseppe Libetta 13, Ostiense ⓦ goaclub.com. One of Rome's historic clubs, with ethno-industrial decor and big-name DJs spinning techno and house. Thurs–Sat 11pm–4.30am.

Micca Club Via Pietro Micca 7a, Esquilino ⓦ miccaclub .com. This retro club in a brick-vaulted space plays '50s and '60s classics and hosts popular burlesque and cabaret shows. Sun–Thurs 7pm–2am, Fri & Sat 7pm–4am.

Qube Via di Portonaccio 212, Pigneto ⓦ qubedisco.com. Set on three floors, this large popular club hosts university nights on Mondays, gay nights on Fridays and an eclectic mix of DJs on Saturdays, spinning all sorts from '60s to electronica. Check the website for event details. Oct–May Mon, Fri, Sat 10.30pm–3am.

Spazio Novecento Piazza Guglielo Marconi 26 ⓦ spazionovecento.it; ⓜ EUR Palasport. Popular club located in the heart of the Eur district playing house, dance, techno and hosting live events as well as big-name DJs, such as Bob Sinclar. Usually Fri & Sat, but check the website for what's on.

Vicious Via Achille Grandi 7a, Esquilino ⓦ viciousclub .com. Step into this underground joint with dark interiors where a hip crowd soaks in techno, electronica, rock and indie beats. Thurs–Sun 10pm–4am.

ENTERTAINMENT

Cinemas Nuovo Olimpia (Via in Lucina 16g, off Via del Corso) is the main English-language cinema Check ⓦ romereview.com for original-language cinemas and film listings.

Classical music The city's churches host a wide range of concerts, many of them free. The Auditorium Parco della Musica is home to the Accademia di Santa Cecilia, the city's prestigious classical academy.

Opera The opera scene is concentrated on the Teatro dell'Opera, Piazza B. Gigli, in winter (ⓣ 06 481 7003, ⓦ operaroma.it), and moves to the spectacular Terme di Caracalla in summer.

SHOPPING

Shops With the exception of the Galleria Alberto Sordi on Via del Corso, malls and department stores are few and far between. The boutiques around Piazza di Spagna are for big-spenders only, but nearby Via del Corso is lined with shops selling cheap to mid-range clothing, books and CDs. Other mainstream outlets can be found along Via Cola di Rienzo near the Vatican, and Via Nazionale, off Piazza della Repubblica. Via del Governo Vecchio off Piazza Navona has a string of great vintage stores; the alleys off Campo de' Fiori and the streets of San Lorenzo harbour independent jewellery and clothing shops.

Markets Porta Portese flea market is the city's best known (Sun mornings; catch the #H from Termini to Porta Portese), but Via Sannio (Mon–Sat 9am–1.30pm; ⓜ San Giovanni) is also a great place to find vintage bargains.

DIRECTORY

Embassies Australia, Via Antonio Bosio 5 ⓣ 06 852 721; Canada, Via Salaria 243 ⓣ 06 854 441; New Zealand, Via Clitunno 44 ⓣ 06 853 7501; UK, Via XX Settembre 80 ⓣ 06 4220 0001; US, Via V. Veneto 119a ⓣ 06 46 741.

Exchange Offices at Termini station operate out of banking hours.

Hospitals Ambulance ⓣ 118; central hospital: Policlinico Umberto I ⓣ 06 49 971; International Medical Center ⓣ 06 488 2371. The 24/7 multilingual health line ⓣ 06 43 23 62 91 provides assistance with medical-related matters.

Internet Try Lav@sciuga, a laundromat with internet point, at Via Palestro 69 (daily 8am–9pm; €2/hr).

Left luggage At Termini station (daily 6am–11pm; €5 for the first 5hr, then €0.70/hr).

Pharmacy Piram, Via Nazionale 228 (24hr), near Termini. The rota is posted on pharmacy doors.

Police Emergencies ⓣ 112; main police station (*questura*) at Via S. Vitale 15 ⓣ 06 46 861.

Post office Piazza San Silvestro 19 (Mon–Fri 8.30am–7pm, Sat 8.30am–12.30pm).

17

Northwest Italy

The northwest of Italy is many people's first experience of the country, and while it often represents its least stereotypical "Italian" aspect, there are some iconic towns in the area. The vibrant city of **Turin** was the first capital of Italy after the Unification in 1861, and still holds many reminders of its past. **Milan**, the upbeat capital of the heavily industrial region of **Lombardy**, continues to be taken seriously for its business and fashion credentials, while the region of **Liguria** to the south is home to the country's most spectacular stretch of coastline. The chief town of the province is the sprawling port of **Genoa**, while southeast, towards Tuscany, the **Cinque Terre**'s rugged stretch of coastline continues to wow travellers with its cliff-top villages and clear blue waters.

TURIN

Following the 2006 Winter Olympics, **TURIN** (Torino) – a virtual Fiat company town and the home of Vermouth and Lavazza coffee – emerged resplendent with gracious avenues, opulent palaces and splendid galleries. It's a lively, bustling place, with cafés, a fun nightlife and enough contemporary art to rival any European city.

WHAT TO SEE AND DO

The grid plan of the Baroque centre makes finding your way around easy. Via Roma is the central spine, a grand affair lined with designer shops and ritzy cafés and punctuated by the city's most elegant piazzas, notably **Piazza San Carlo**. A five-minute walk northwest brings you to the fifteenth-century Duomo, home of the Turin Shroud, which is kept under wraps and away from the public eye. This piece of cloth, imprinted with the image of a man's body, had long been claimed as the shroud in which Christ was wrapped after his crucifixion, although 1989 carbon-dating tests suggested that it was a medieval fake, made between 1260 and 1390.

BATTLE OF THE ORANGES
In the week leading up to Shrove Tuesday, locals in the town of **Ivrea**, some 55km north of Turin, stage an annual three-day battle armed only with the cheerful-looking but painful-feeling fruit. If you fancy getting juiced – and quite possibly bruised – there are twelve buses daily to Ivrea from Turin.

The **Palazzo Madama**, looming over **Piazza Castello**, is architecturally stunning, and has a collection of Baroque, Gothic, Renaissance and decorative art on show (Tues–Sat 10am–6pm, Sun 10am–7pm, ticket office closes 1hr before; €7.50). East of Via Roma is the **Mole Antonelliana**, which Turin residents proudly call the "Eiffel Tower of Turin", boasting great views over the city from the top of its panoramic lift. The building also contains the excellent **Cinema Museum** (Mon–Fri & Sun 9am–8pm, Sat 9am–11pm; €5 for panoramic lift only, €12 including museum, €9 museum only).

Museums

Turin has a good selection of modern art museums: the **Galleria Civica d'Arte Moderna e Contemporanea (GAM)**, on Via Magenta 31 (Tues–Sun 10am–6pm; €10), holds works dating from the eighteenth century to the present day, by artists such as Giorgio de Chirico and Lucio Fontana. For more contemporary art, it is worth the journey to the **Castello di Rivoli**, 15km outside Turin (Tues–Fri 10am–5pm, Sat & Sun 10am–7pm; €6.50), home to the

SKIING THE VIA LATTEA
The snow-capped peaks surrounding Turin are home to some of the best ski slopes in the region. Known collectively as the **Via Lattea** (ⓦvialattea.it), the eight Italian resorts hosted the 2006 Winter Olympics. Sestriere is the most sophisticated, while Sauze d'Oulx is great for its après-ski scene. All the towns are linked by ski lifts, and a daily ski pass costs an affordable €34. Getting to the slopes involves a train from Turin to Oulx (hourly; 1hr 15min), and then a bus to your chosen destination.

most important collection of postwar art in Italy, with works by Jeff Koons, Carl Andre and Mario Merz. On weekdays, take the metro to Paradiso, then bus #36 to Piazza Martiri Della Libertà, then walk for fifteen minutes.

ARRIVAL AND DEPARTURE

By plane Turin Caselle airport (ⓦaeroportoditorino.it) is 16km north of the city. The best way to reach the centre is by the SADEM bus (Mon–Sat every 15–30min, Sun every 30min; €6.50 (€7 if you buy on board); €5 with Torino+Piemonte Card).

By train The main station is in Porta Nuova, a 15min walk from Piazza Castello.

Destinations Geneva (1 daily; change 3 times; 12hr); Genoa (hourly; 1hr 45min); La Spezia (every 2hr; 3hr 30min); Lyon (2 daily; change at Chambery; 4hr); Milan (frequent; 1hr 50min); Nice (hourly; change at Ventimiglia; 5hr); Paris (2 direct daily; 5hr 45min); Rome (frequent; 4hr 30min); Venice (frequent; 4hr 30min).

INFORMATION

Tourist office Piazza Castello/Via Garibaldi (daily 9am–6pm; ☎011 535 181, ⓦturismotorino.org). There is an office at the Porta Nuova train station (Mon–Sat 9am–6pm, Sun 9am–3pm) and also at the airport.

Discount pass Pick up a Torinot - Piemonte Card (€25/2 days, €29/3 days) for free entrance to over 190 museums and cultural sites, and discounts on theatre and concert tickets.

Internet 1pc4u on Via Verdi 20/g offers cheap access.

Post office Via Alfieri 10.

ACCOMMODATION

Many of Turin's budget hotels are off Via Nizza, just one block over from the train station.

B&B Una stanza in famiglia Via Goito 16 ☎011 536 0398, ⓦunastanzainfamiglia.it. This sunny and spacious family home has some rooms with balconies; it is just a short walk from the station. Double €80

Hotel Due Mondi Via Saluzzo 3 ☎011 650 5084, ⓦhotelduemondi.it. Spacious, comfortable rooms in an old-fashioned boutique-style hotel. Discounts are available. Double €60

Open 011 Corso Venezia 11 ☎011 250 535, ⓦopen011 .it. Welcoming hostel with helpful staff and large, spotless rooms. Take the train to Torino Dora, or get bus #46 (Dora stop), #52 (Viba stop) or #10 from Porta Nuova station. Dorm €18

Paradiso Via Berthollet 3 ☎011 669 8678, ⓦalbergo -paradiso-torino.it. This clean one-star has private bathrooms for every room. The pick of the cheaper hotels in this unappealing district near the train station. Double €45

EATING

Slow Food (ⓦslowfood.com), the non-profit international organization promoting gastronomic traditions and locally sourced produce, was born in Bra, just a few kilometres from Turin. The city is therefore a strong supporter of the movement, with many of its restaurants and food shops serving local dishes, wines and food.

★ **Augusto** Via San Quintino 9/bis ☎011 562 3173, ⓦpizzeriaaugusto.it. Simply the best pizzeria in Turin (large pizzas from €6). Get there early if you want a table outside, or book ahead. Daily except Sat lunch 12.30–2.30pm & 7pm–12.30am.

Mood Libri e Cafè Via Cesare Battisti 3/E ☎011 518 8657, ⓦmoodlibri.it. A popular haunt for students from the nearby university, this bookshop-cum-café serves a hearty Sun brunch for around €10. Daily 9am–9pm.

Tabernalibraria Via Bogino 5 ☎011 812 8028, ⓦtabernalibraria.to.it. Great-value restaurant favoured by students and workers. Vegetarian options and an extensive wine list. A hearty lunch costs €10. Mon–Sat 10am–11pm.

Urbani Via Saluzzo 3. A hit with locals, this is a big, classy place in a shabby part of town. Start talking football with the owner and staff and you will never leave. Pastas from €8 and pizzas from €5. Daily 12.30–2pm & 7.30pm–midnight.

DRINKING AND NIGHTLIFE

The liveliest areas are Il Quadrilatero, a few metres west of Piazza Castello, Via San Quintino, and the Murazzi Piazza Vittorio Veneto area, where people congregate at outside tables.

AEIOU Via Spanzotti 3. Big warehouse-style club for dancing all night; features rock, Cuban, jam sessions, art and theatre projects. Entrance usually free. Tues–Sun 10pm–3am.

Arancia di Mezzanotte One of the best bars on the lively Piazza Emanuele Filiberto. Buzzy place with tables crammed together outside. Tues–Sun 5pm–4am.

★ **Gran Bar** Piazza Gran Madre di Dio 2. Cool wine and coffee bar close to the river and the magnificent Vittorio Veneto Piazza. Espresso is cheap at €1. Daily 7am–2am.

KM5 Bar Via San Domenico 14. Not the most glamorous location but locals flock here for the generous and good-value *aperitivo*. Lots of outdoor seating with DJ every Thurs. Tues–Sun 6.30pm–3am.

MILAN

MILAN (Milano) is the capital of Italy's fashion and design industry, with the reputation as a fast-paced and somewhat unfriendly business city ruled by consumerism and the work ethic. But don't be put off: coupled with the swanky shops and excellent nightlife, Milan

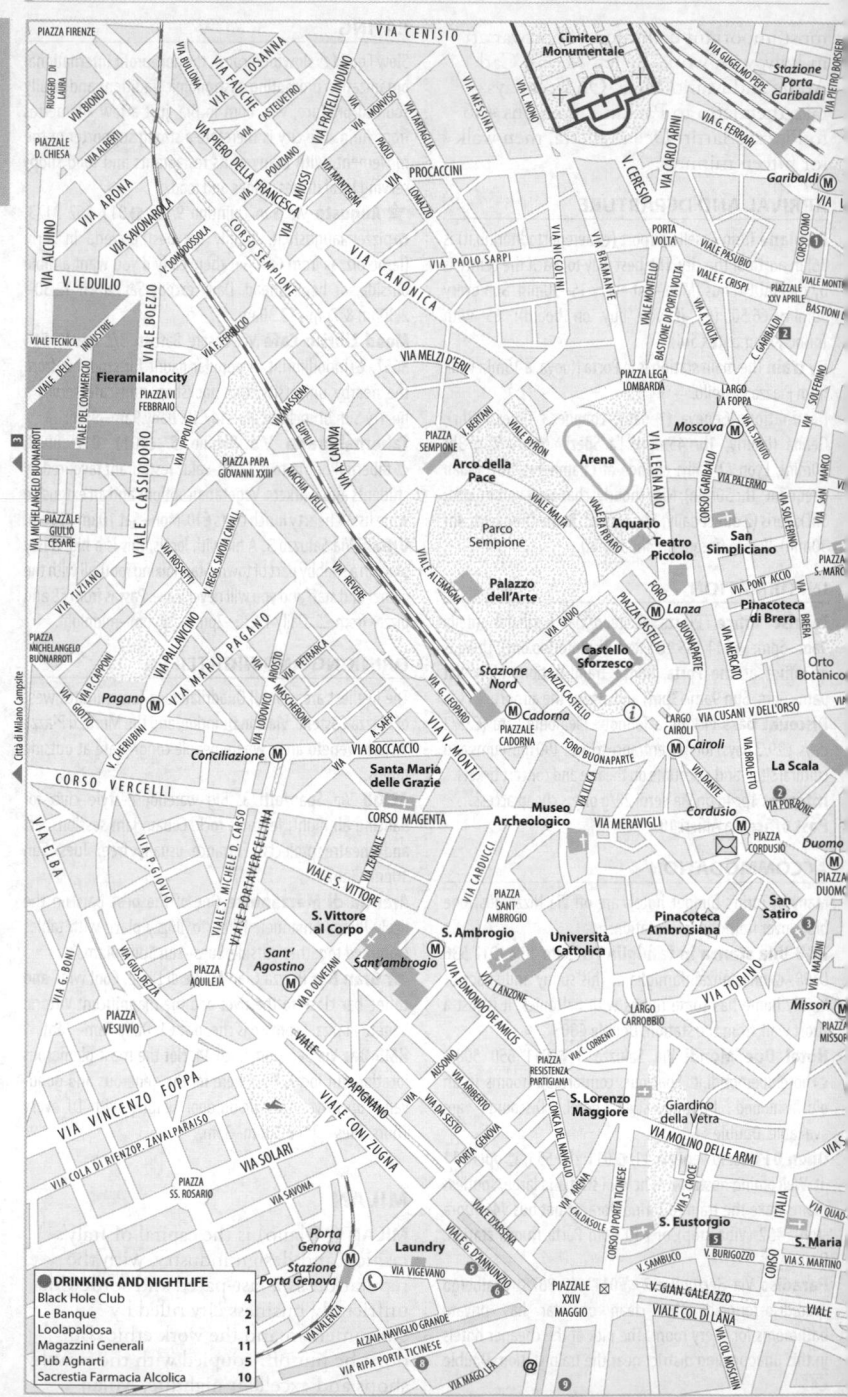

DRINKING AND NIGHTLIFE	
Black Hole Club	4
Le Banque	2
Loolapaloosa	1
Magazzini Generali	11
Pub Agharti	5
Sacrestia Farmacia Alcolica	10

MILAN

ACCOMMODATION
ACISJF	2
Ciao Bella	4
Hotel Due Gardini	1
Ostello Burigoz 11	5
Piero Rotta HI Hostel	3

● **EATING**
La Cozzeria	7
MAG	8
Premiata Pizzeria	6
Princi	3
Slice Café	9

0 ———————— 500
metres

17

boasts a lovely canal area, friendly suburbs and unmissable historical sites – the Gothic cathedral has few peers in Italy, while Leonardo da Vinci's iconic fresco of *The Last Supper* is a must.

WHAT TO SEE AND DO

Piazza del Duomo

A good place to start a tour of Milan is **Piazza del Duomo**, the city's historic centre and home to the world's largest Gothic cathedral (daily 7am–7pm; free; ⓦduomomilano.it), begun in 1386 and not completed until almost five centuries later. The gloomy interior gives access to the cathedral's fourth-century **baptistery** (daily 9.30am–5.30pm; €4) and the **cathedral roof** (Nov–March daily 9am–7pm; April–Oct Mon–Wed 9am–7pm, Thurs–Sun 9am–9pm; €12 by elevator, €7 on foot), where you are surrounded by a forest of lacy Gothic carving and subjected to superb views of the city. On the north side of the piazza, the opulent **Galleria Vittorio Emanuele II** is a cruciform glass-domed gallery designed in 1865 by Giuseppe Mengoni, who was killed when he fell from the roof a few days before the inaugural ceremony. The Galleria leads through to the world-famous eighteenth-century **La Scala** opera house.

Pinacoteca di Brera

At the far end of Via Brera is Milan's most prestigious gallery, the awe-inspiring **Pinacoteca di Brera** (Tues–Sun 8.30am–7.15pm; €6; ⓦwww.brera .beniculturali.it), filled with works looted from the churches and aristocratic collections of French-occupied Italy.

Castello Sforzesco

The **Castello Sforzesco** (castle grounds daily 7am–7pm, closes 6pm in winter; free) rises imperiously from the mayhem of **Foro Buonaparte**, laid out by Napoleon as part of a grand plan for the city. The castle houses the **Museo d'Arte Antica and Pinacoteca** (both Tues–Sun 9am–5.30pm; €3; ⓦmilanocastello.it) – the former contains Michelangelo's *Rondanini Pietà*, the latter paintings by Vincenzo Foppa, the leading Milanese artist before Leonardo da Vinci.

Santa Maria delle Grazie and the Last Supper

South of the Castello, the church of **Santa Maria delle Grazie** is Milan's main attraction. A Gothic pile, partially rebuilt by Bramante (who added the massive dome), it is famous for its fresco of *The Last Supper* by Leonardo da Vinci, which covers one wall of the refectory. Advance booking is essential (viewing Tues–Sun 8.15am–7pm; €10; ⓦmilan -museum.com).

ARRIVAL AND DEPARTURE

By plane Linate (ⓦmilanolinate.eu) is Milan's closest airport, 7km from the city centre and connected by the airport bus to Stazione Centrale (every 30min, 6.05am–11pm; 30min; €5; ⓦatm-mi.it). Ordinary city buses (#73; €1.50) also run every 15min until around midnight from Linate to Piazza San Babila. Malpensa airport (ⓦairportmalpensa.com) is 45km away towards Lago Maggiore and connected by the Malpensa Express train to Cadorna station (every 30min; €11; ⓦmalpensaexpress.it) and by bus with Stazione Centrale (until 11.15pm; 1hr; €10; ⓦmalpensashuttle.it). Bergamo Orio al Serio is 50km away and connected to Stazione Centrale (Orioshuttle every 30min, 4am–11.30pm; 1hr; from €3.50; ⓦorioshuttle.it).

By train Most international trains pull in at the Stazione Centrale, northeast of the centre on Piazza Duca d'Aosta (metro lines MM2 or MM3).

Destinations Bologna (frequent; 1–3hr); Geneva (4 daily; 4hr); Genoa (frequent; 1hr 40min); Lyon (3 daily – 1 direct; change at Chambery or Dijon; 5hr 30min); Paris (4 daily; 7–10hr); Rome (frequent; 3–4hr); Venice (every 30min; 2hr 30min–3hr 30min); Verona (every 30min; 1hr 30min); Vienna (5 daily; 11–14hr; 2 changes); Zagreb (1 daily; 11hr; change at Venice Mestre); Zürich (every 2hr; 3hr 45min).

By bus Buses arrive at and depart from Lampugnano bus station.

Destinations Bologna (3 daily; approx 3hr); Florence (4 daily; 4hr 35min); Naples (1 daily; 11hr); Palermo (2 daily; 20hr); Rome (4 daily; 8hr); Siena (4 daily; 4–5hr); Venice (2 daily; 5hr).

INFORMATION

Tourist office Piazza Castello 1 (Mon–Fri 9am–6pm, Sat 9am–1pm & 2–6pm, Sun & public hols 9am–1pm & 2–5pm; ☎02 7740 4343, ⓦvisitamilano.it). There is also a small kiosk at the Stazione Centrale in front of platforms 13 and 14, but it is often impossibly packed. Both have the ever-helpful free listings guide, *Milanomese*, in Italian and English, and *Hello Milano*.

GETTING AROUND

By bus, metro and tram An efficient network of trams, buses and the metro (stations denoted on map as Ⓜ) runs 6am–12.30am. There are interconnecting stations so you can change from the metro onto the overground and back. For detailed maps and route information head to the ATM office in Duomo metro station (Ⓦ atm.it).

By night bus These take over after the other options close, and run until 1am following the train routes, or until about 3am following alternative routes. Buses #90 & #91 operate 24 hours covering Milan's external ring road.

Tickets Tickets (normally valid 1hr 30min; €1.50) can be used for one journey only on the metro or as many bus and tram journeys as you can make in that time, or a 24hr ticket (€4.50), valid on metro, tram and buses, available from any metro station or *tabacchi*. A 48hr ticket costs €8.25.

Bike sharing This is a great way to see the city. Bikes can be picked up and deposited at various points around the city. You need a credit card to access the service. A daily subscription costs from just €2.50 (Ⓦ bikemi.com).

ACCOMMODATION

There are plenty of one-star hotels, mostly concentrated in the area around Stazione Centrale, and along Viale Vittorio Veneto and Corso Buenos Aires. When there is an "exposition" on (there are about 25 a year, lasting 2–3 days each) prices rocket.

ACISJF Corso Garibaldi 123 ☎02 2900 0164, Ⓦ acisjf -milano.it. Run by nuns and open to women under 25 only, with an 11pm curfew in the week and at midnight at the weekend; it's in a great location on an eclectic bar-lined street. Single €40, twin €60

★ **Ciao Bella** Via Balzaretti 4 ☎02 2395 1135, Ⓦ ciaobellamilan.hostel.com. A welcoming hostel with large en-suite rooms. There is a big colourful sitting room and kitchen as well as a private garden. Take the metro three stops to Piola and walk for 10min. Dorm €20

Hotel Due Gardini Via B Marcello 47 ☎02 295 21093. This friendly spot has a lovely breakfast conservatory and a small garden, and is just a 10min walk from the station. Double €75

Ostello Burigozzo 11 Via Burigozzo 11 ☎02 5831 4675, Ⓦ ostelloburigozzo11.com. Well-equipped hostel superbly located in a vibrant canal area; no curfew. Dorm €19

Piero Rotta HI Hostel Via Salmoiraghi 1 ☎02 3926 7095, Ⓦ hihostels.com. Huge, friendly HI hostel. There is a public swimming pool (June–Sept 10am–7.30pm; €5) around the corner and the pleasant Sitting Bull pub on the nearby roundabout. No curfew. Metro QT8 then a 5min walk down Via Salmoiraghi. Dorm €20.50

EATING

La Cozzeria Via Lodovico Muratori 6. Small and cosy seafood restaurant a short walk from PTA Porta Romano metro. Mussels and chips €15. Tues–Sun 7–10.30pm.

MAG Ripa di Porta Ticinese 43. Trendy coffee and sandwich bar looking out over the canal. On Thurs all cocktails are €5. Tues–Sun 8am–1am

Premiata Pizzeria Alzaia Naviglio Grande 2. Modern pizza restaurant next to the canal; pizzas from €7. The best tables are on its narrow terrace in front of the entrance. Daily 11am–4pm & 6pm–midnight, closed Tues lunch.

★ **Princi** Via Speronari 4. Part of a chain of excellent Milan bakeries serving everything from brioche to pasta from its staggeringly large counter. Mon–Sat 9am–6pm.

Slice Café Via Ascanio Sforza 9. Funky bar with leopard-print sofas on the waterfront; 6–10pm all-you-can-eat buffet with a drink for €8. Daily noon–11pm.

DRINKING AND NIGHTLIFE

Nightlife centres on the streets around the Brera gallery, the club-filled Corso Como, and the Navigli and Ticinese quarters, clustered around Milan's thirteenth-century canals. Drinks go for around €5 a beer and €7 for cocktails.

Black Hole Club Viale Umbria 118 Ⓦ blackholemilano .com. This club is a fair trek from the centre, reached by bus #90, #91, #92 or tram #16. It offers free concert nights and its biggest draw is the massive summer garden. Wed, Fri & Sat 10pm–5am.

Le Banque Via Porrone 6 Ⓦ lebanque.it. Formerly a bank, this grandiose lounge bar-restaurant is close to the cathedral. Dine in a room resembling a king's banqueting hall on huge purple thrones. Excellent large buffet lunch with drinks for €15. Restaurant noon–3.30pm & 8–11pm (closed Sat lunch & Sun); bar Tues–Fri 6pm–1am, until 6am Sat & Sun.

Loolapaloosa Corso Como 15 Ⓦ loolapaloosa.com. Popular pub-style student hangout offering aperitifs (7–10.30pm) and solid tables to dance on to a mixture of pop, old school favourites and Latin. Daily 7pm–5am.

Magazzini Generali Via Pietrasanta 14 Ⓦ magazzinigenerali.it. Enormous warehouse attracting a mixed crowd, playing dance, and occasionally live music by international indie bands. Wed, Fri & Sat from 11.30pm.

★ **Pub Agharti** Via Vigevano 1 Ⓦ aghartipub.com. In summer, drinkers spill out onto the streets from this chilled

---

LA SCALA

The season at **La Scala** (☎02 861 827, Ⓦ teatroallascala.org), one of the world's most prestigious opera houses, runs from December to July. Although seats are expensive and can sell out months in advance, there is often a chance of picking up a seat in the gods (from €25) an hour or so before a performance, by heading to the Theatre ticket office on Via Filodrammatici 2.

17

A DAY-TRIP TO LAKE COMO

Trains leave for Como San Giovanni regularly from Milan's Grand Central station and take 35min, but it is a fair walk to the lake. Cheaper trains from Milan's Cadorna station (every 30min; 1hr 15min; last return train to Milan is around 9pm) head to the more convenient North Lake Como station, which is only a five-minute walk from the lake. You can take a cruise (hop-on, hop-off ticket €8.90; W navigazionelaghi.it) which stops at five points around the lake, and don't miss a wander round the enchanting, relaxed village of **Torno** in the southeast corner of the lake. If you fancy a picnic on Como's beautiful waterfront, drop by the supermarket opposite the North Como train station. Como's tourist offices are on Piazza Matteotit and on Via Maestri Comacini.

popular bar near the canal. Aperitif (6.30–9.30pm) €6. Daily 4pm–3am.

Sacrestia Farmacia Alcolica Via Conchetta 20. Extremely popular place with an underground bar with a lengthy cocktail list and occasional live DJ sets. €6.50 for a cocktail. Daily 6pm–2am.

SHOPPING

The fashion streets of Milan are famous for having some of the most expensive and exclusive shops in the world. For those with cash to flash, wander along Milan's shopping triangle, the famous Quadrilatero della Moda – Via Manzoni, Via Montenapoleone, Via della Spiga and Via Sant Andrea Corso are home to some of the top designer names in the industry. The boutiques in the Navigli area in the southwest of the city have a range of quirkier, affordable clothing (nearest station Ⓜ Porto Genova).

DIRECTORY

Consulates Australia, Via Borgogna 2 ☎ 02 7767 4200; UK, Via San Paolo 7 ☎ 02 723 001; US, Via Principe Amedeo 2/10 ☎ 02 290 351.

Exchange The office in Stazione Centrale is a good bet, or Yex Change on Piazza Duomo.

Hospitals Fatebenefratelli, Corso Porta Nuova 23 ☎ 02 63 631, W www.fbf.milano.it; Ospedale Maggiore Policlinico, Via Francesco Sforza 35 ☎ 02 55 031, W www.policlinico.mi.it.

Internet Grazia, Piazza d'Aosta 14 (Mon–Sat 9am–10pm; €5.60/hr).

Police Piazza San Sepolcro 9 ☎ 02 62 261.

Post office Piazza Cordusio 2 ☎ 02 87 55 77.

GENOA

GENOA (Genova) has retained its reputation as a tough, cosmopolitan port but combines the beauty of Renaissance palaces dotted along the small, winding streets. The birthplace of Christopher Columbus, it was one of the five Italian maritime republics, and reached the height of its power in the fifteenth and sixteenth centuries. After a long period of economic decline, Genoa is successfully cleaning itself up, and the city now offers an interesting mix of ultra-modern architecture and amenities, and old-style streets and restaurants.

WHAT TO SEE AND DO

Genoa spreads outwards from its old town around the port in a confusion of tiny alleyways and old palaces. It is one of the oldest historical centres in Europe, with the buzzing Piazza de Ferrari as the heartbeat of the city.

Palazzo Ducale

From 1384 to 1515, except for brief periods of foreign domination, the doges ruled the city from the ornate, stuccoed **Palazzo Ducale** in Piazza Matteotti (Tues–Sun 10am–1pm & 3–6pm; €5). Decorated with elaborate frescoes, the rooms are a sight to behold. Walk up the tower to the palace's cramped prison cells, which still contain the shackles and scrawled graffiti of prisoners past.

Cattedrale di San Lorenzo

The Gothic **Cattedrale di San Lorenzo** (daily 8am–noon & 3–7pm), complete with Baroque chancel, is home to the Renaissance chapel of St John the Baptist, whose remains once rested in the thirteenth-century sarcophagus. After a particularly bad storm, priests carried his casket through the city to placate the sea, and a commemorative procession takes place each June 24 to honour him. His reliquary is in the **treasury** (tours available Mon–Sat 9am–noon & 3–6pm; €6, including entry to the Diocesan

Museum, same hours), along with a polished quartz plate on which, legend says, Salome received his severed head

The waterfront

After generations of neglect, Genoa's waterfront has recently undergone restoration and is gaining tourist appeal with a huge aquarium and lively markets and cafés near Piazza Caricamento.

Piazza Banchi and around

Behind Piazza Caricamento is a thriving commercial zone centred on **Piazza Banchi**, formerly the heart of the medieval city, off which the long **Via San Luca** leads north to the **Galleria Nazionale di Palazzo Spinola** (Tues–Sat 8.30am–7.30pm, Sun 1.30–7.30pm; €4, €6.50 joint ticket with the Palazzo Reale, €2 18–25 years), displaying work by the Sicilian master Antonello da Messina. North of here is the wonderful **Via Garibaldi**, lined with frescoed and stuccoed Renaissance palaces; a walk down the street at night is a must. Two palaces are now museums housing Genoese paintings: the **Palazzi Bianco and Rosso** (Tues–Fri 9am–7pm, Sat & Sun 10am–7pm; joint ticket €9, ticket also includes Palazzi Tursi), adorned with fantastic chandeliers, mirrors, gilding and frescoed ceilings.

Christopher Columbus House

The childhood home and museum (Sat & Sun 10am–6pm; €5) dedicated to the man who discovered the New World is on Piazza Dante. It is small but gives a fascinating insight into Columbus's life. Highlights include a bell reputedly from his flagship the *Santa Maria*.

ARRIVAL AND DEPARTURE

By plane Genoa's airport (ⓦ www.airport.genova.it) is a 20min bus ride from Stazione Principe and Stazione Brignole, and buses run every 45min; tickets for the Volabus, a coach running to and from the airport, are €6 and are available from stations, tourist offices, *tabacchi* and aboard the bus itself.

By train Most trains stop at Genoa's two stations, Stazione Principe in Piazza Acquaverde and Stazione Brignole in Piazza Verdi. It is an easy walk to the centre from either. There is a metro system that connects the centre with both Brignole and Principe. If you have to travel between the two, take a train, metro or bus #28 or #36.

Destinations Bologna (frequent; 2–3hr); Milan (hourly; 1hr 30min); Naples (direct 2 daily; 8hr); Pisa (frequent; 2hr); Rome (every 2hr; 5–6hr).

By bus Buses arrive at the main bus terminal outside Stazione Principe and Stazione Brignole. From Principe to the centre take the metro or bus #35; from Brignole take the metro or bus #18, #36, #39 or #40.

Destinations Nice (1 daily; 3hr).

By ferry Ferries arrive at Ferry Terminale, a 10min walk downhill from Stazione Principe. Cruise ships arrive at Stazione Marittima.

Destinations Bastia (weekly, daily during summer; 4hr 45min); Olbia (daily in summer; 10hr); Palermo (6 weekly; 20hr); Porto Torres (daily; 11hr).

INFORMATION

Tourist office Piazza De Ferrari, in the Felici Carlo theatre building (daily 9am–1pm & 3–5.30pm; ☎ 010 860 6122, ⓦ genova-turismo.it); a second is on Via Garibaldi (daily 9am–6.30pm; ☎ 010 557 2903). There are also small kiosks at the airport (9am–1pm & 1.30–5.30pm) and on Piazza Caricamento.

Discount passes The tourist office (see above) sells a Genoa pass, which gives you free use of all transport in the city, including lifts and funiculars (€4.50/24hr). The Museum Card gives access to most of the city's museums and free bus travel (€20/2 days). They also sell transport passes for parties of a maximum of four people (€9/24hr).

Internet Non Solo Copie 2, Via Jacopo da Levanto 17 (Mon–Fri 8.30am–6pm, Sat 9am–noon; €3.30/hr).

ACCOMMODATION

The best areas to stay are the roads bordering the old town, and Piazza Colombo and on Via XX Settembre, Genoa's main shopping street near Stazione Brignole.

Astro Via XX Settembre 3/21 ☎ 010 581 533, ⓦ hotelastrogenova.com. Friendly one-star hotel on the seventh floor and very close to Stazione Brignole. The best rooms are the African or flower-themed rooms. Double **€58**

Barone Via XX Settembre 2/23 ☎ 010 587 578, ⓦ hotel baronegenova.it. Small hotel with light rooms and welcoming owners, 200m from Stazione Brignole. Double **€55**

★ **Genova** Passo Costanzi 120 ☎ 010 242 2457, ⓦ ostellogenova.it. Friendly, clean and well-run HI hostel a 30min bus ride from centre with great views over the port. Single-sex dorm beds. Take bus #40 or #640 (evening) from Stazione Brignole. From Stazione Principe take bus #35 to Via Napoli and change to bus #40 or #640, alight at the stop on Via Constanzi, last bus departs Via Napoli around midnight. Dorm **€18**, double **€50**

Villa Doria Via al Campeggio Villa Doria 15/N, Pegli

17 ☎ 010 696 9600, ⓦ camping.it/liguria/villadoria. Leafy campsite 8km from Genoa, with its own café, shop and solarium: take a train to Pegli and then bus #93. **€9** per person, plus **€10** per tent

EATING AND DRINKING

For cheap lunches, snacks and picnic ingredients, try the huge covered Mercato Orientale, halfway down Via XX Settembre in the cloisters of an Augustinian monastery. There are lots of restaurants and bars down Via Ravecca, a few hundred metres southeast of the port. For late-night drinking, head to the bars around Piazza delle Erbe, just south of Palazzo Ducale.

★ **Exultate** Piazza Lavagna 12 ☎ 010 246 8724. Popular pizzeria that brews its own beer. A pizza and a beer will set you back about €10. Lots of tables outside in an intimate piazza. Mon–Fri 11am–2.30pm & 7pm–1am, Sat & Sun 11am–2am.

★ **Gloglo** Piazza Lavagna 19r ☎ 010 254 3361. Aperitifs come with tasty snacks at this relaxed place on a square. Staff are chatty and drinks are generous. Beer €5. Daily noon–midnight.

Il Clan Salita Pallavicini 16 ☎ 010 254 1098, ⓦ ilclan.biz. Trendy bar packed to the rafters with the young and hip. Arrive early to bag one of the loft bed-seats. Cocktail hour starts at 5.30pm. Mon–Sat 5.30pm–1am.

Louisiana Jazz Club Via S. Sebastiano 36r ⓦ louisianajazzclub.com. A drum reveals the entrance to this established and excellent jazz venue. Cocktails and generous snacks are €7. Thurs only 9pm–midnight.

★ **Sa Pesta** Via Giustiniani 16r ☎ 010 246 8336, ⓦ sapesta.it. Extremely popular with locals, this place is well known for its good local cooking. Dishes from €9. Booking a table is essential. Mon–Sat noon–2.30pm, dinner Thurs–Sat pre-booking only.

Trattoria da Maria Via Testadoro 14/b, just off Via XXV Aprile ☎ 010 581 080. No-nonsense, endearingly chaotic place up a grubby side street, which serves up simple Ligurian cooking at rock-bottom prices. Pasta €4.50. Dinner only on Thurs and Fri, lunch Mon–Sat, closed Sun.

THE RIVIERA DI LEVANTE

A superb stretch of lush green hills sheltering beautiful seaside resorts, the **RIVIERA DI LEVANTE** stretches eastwards from Genoa. The ports that once survived on navigation, fishing and coral diving are now well versed in the ways of tourism, and while the resorts are hectic during summer months, the towns are still charming enough to ensure they're worth visiting. The coastline is wild and beautiful in parts and a coastal path

meanders over the cliff-tops to each of the resorts. All the towns can be reached by train and boat.

Santa Margherita Ligure

Pretty **SANTA MARGHERITA LIGURE** is a small, palm-tree-lined resort, with a little pebble beach and concrete jetties to swim from. Quieter than its more famous neighbours, the town has a charming and sleepy fishing village atmosphere.

INFORMATION

Tourist office In the middle of Piazza Vittorio Veneto (Tues–Sat 9.30am–12.30pm & 2.30–5.30pm; ☎ 0185 287 485, ⓦ turismo.provincia.genova.it).

GETTING AROUND

By scooter and bike Scooters and bikes are a fun way of getting around: go to Via XXV Aprile 11 (☎ 0185 284 420, ⓦ gmrent.it).

By boat Boats depart regularly in summer for Rapallo (see below) and the millionaires' playground that is the small village of Portofino (return €9 weekdays, €9.50 Sun & public hols).

ACCOMMODATION

Albergo Annabella Via Costasecca 10 ☎ 0185 286 531. A cheap, comfortable and friendly establishment just off Piazza Mazzini. Double **€65**

Istituto C. Colombo Via Dogali 2a ⓦ istituto-colombo.com. Though fairly basic, the rooms each have a private bathroom. Centrally situated. Dorm **€23**

EATING

Da Pezzi Via Cavour 21 ☎ 0185 285 303. The long-established canteen-like locals' hangout serves pasta, grills and takeaway snacks at affordable prices. Mon–Fri & Sun 11.45am–2pm & 6.15–9.30pm.

Il Faro Via Maraigliano 24a ☎ 0185 286 867. Friendly restaurant with a focus on fish. Lots of tables under the cool portico. Fixed menu €25. Wed–Sun noon–3pm & 8–11pm.

Osteria 7 Via Jacopo Ruffini 36 ☎ 0185 281 703. Great pastas are served on long wooden tables. Seafood, particularly octopus, is a speciality. Expect to pay around €25. Mon, Tues & Thurs–Sun noon–2pm & 7–10pm.

Rapallo

RAPALLO is a lovely Riviera town just a forty-minute train ride from Genoa. Brightly coloured beach huts line parts of the pebbled shore, backed by an intriguing tangle of narrow lanes that are well worth a wander.

INFORMATION

Tourist office Lungo Vittorio Veneto 7 (Tues–Sat 9.30am–1pm & 2–5.30pm, Sat 9.30am–1pm & 3.30–5.30pm; ☎ 0185 230 346, ⓦ turismoinliguria.it).

ACCOMMODATION

Albergo Fernanda 9 Via Milite Ignoto 9 ☎ 0185 502 44, ⓦ hotelfernanda.com. This centrally located townhouse is a 5min walk from the station and is close to a tiny beach. Double **€75**

Rapallo Via San Lazzaro 4 ☎ 0185 262 018, ⓦ campingrapallo.it. This well-equipped campsite is a haven of green and just 2km from the sea. **€7.50** per person, plus **€12.50** per tent

EATING AND DRINKING

★ **Bansin** Via Venezia 105 ☎ 0185 231 119, ⓦ trattoriabansin.it. An authentic trattoria in the heart of the old town with a bargain fixed menu of €7 or €10. Daily noon–2pm & 7.15–10.30pm, closed Sun lunch in summer.

Enoteca Il Castello 10 Lungamare Castello 6 ☎ 0185 52426. This bar has lovely views of the castle and sea as well as an enormous menu of bruschetta (€4). Sat–Tues 11.30am–1am, Wed until 3pm.

CINQUE TERRE

The **CINQUE TERRE** (ⓦ parconazionale5 terre.it) is a series of five beautiful villages – **Monterosso**, **Vernazza**, **Corniglia**, **Manarola** and **Riomaggiore** – perched on tiny cliff-bound inlets lapped by azure-blue sea and linked by a coastal pathway. It's possible to visit all the villages in one day via the pathway, although it can get busy at peak seasons. The liveliest of the villages is probably Monterosso, with its excellent large beach.

ARRIVAL AND INFORMATION

By train Trains from La Spezia in the south and Levanto in the north run three times an hour and stop at each of the villages.

Tourist office Each village has a tourist office at its train station.

GETTING AROUND

Passes The Cinque Terre Card – validity available for 1 weekday (€5) or 2 weekdays (€9) – is sold at the tourist offices (it is slightly more expensive on weekends). The card gives access to the paths and village lifts (where available). Other cards include train and hiking combos (1 day/€10; 2 days/€19).

By boat A boat stops at each of the villages every hour (€15/day; one-stop ticket €8 though prices vary depending on where you start your journey; ⓦ navigazionegolfodeipoeti.it)

ACCOMMODATION

Accommodation tends to be expensive in summer months, at about €120 for a double room, or there are rental apartments that have to be taken for a week at a time. Tiny Manarola is the best of the villages for budget accommodation.

Ostello Cinque Terre Via Riccobaldi 21, Manarola ☎ 0187 920 215, ⓦ hostel5terre.com. Offers gorgeous views, delicious food and chilled-out communal spaces. To get there, head to the top of the town and turn left; it's the green building behind the church. 2-night minimum stay (price is quoted for 2 nights). **€250**

EATING AND DRINKING

A Ca Du Sciensa Piazza Garibaldi 17. A good place for a drink and just a stone's throw from the beach. Also specializes in fish and Ligurian dishes. Sat–Thurs noon–4pm & 6–11pm.

Trattoria Billy Via Aldo Rollando 122 ☎ 0187 920 628, ⓦ trattoriabilly.com. For great views over Manarola and good local food this trattoria is worth the steep uphill walk and the €30–40 bill. Booking is recommended. Daily noon–2.30pm & 6–10.30pm, closed Thurs lunch.

Northeast Italy

Venice, the premier draw in Northeast Italy, is one of Europe's most stunning – and unmissable – cities. The region around it, the **Veneto**, still bears the imprint of Venetian rule and continues to prosper. Gorgeous, vibrant **Verona** plays on its Shakespeare connections and centres on a fairly intact Roman amphitheatre, while nearby **Padua** hums with student activity and has some artistic and architectural masterpieces. South, between Lombardy and Tuscany, **Emilia-Romagna** is the heartland of northern Italy, a patchwork of ducal territories formerly ruled by a handful of families, whose castles and fortresses still stand proudly in well-preserved medieval towns. **Parma** is a wealthy provincial town worth visiting for its easy-going ambience and delicious food as well as masterful paintings by Parmigianino and Correggio. The coast is less interesting but, just south of the Po delta, **Ravenna** boasts probably the finest set of Byzantine mosaics in the world.

17

VERONA

The romantic city of **VERONA**, with its Roman sites and cobbled streets of impressive medieval buildings, stands midway between Milan and Venice. It reached its zenith as an independent city-state in the thirteenth century under the Scaligeri family, who were energetic patrons of the arts; many of Verona's finest buildings date from their rule.

WHAT TO SEE AND DO

The city centre nestles in a deep bend of the River Adige, and the main sight of its southern reaches is the central hub of **Piazza Bra** and its mighty **Roman Arena** (Mon 1.30–7.30pm, Tues–Sun 8.30am–7.30pm; July & Aug closes 3.30pm on performance days; €4.50). Dating from the first century AD, this Roman amphitheatre originally held seating for twenty thousand, and offers a tremendous panorama from the topmost of the 44 marble tiers. It now houses the largest outdoor opera stage in the world (see box below).

Historical centre

To the north of the Roman amphitheatre, Via Mazzini, a narrow traffic-free street lined with expensive clothes shops and pricey *gelaterias*, leads to a number of squares. The biggest and most appealing is Piazza Erbe, a pretty square with a market in the middle and cafés lining either side. From Erbe most of the major sights are within an easy walk. The adjacent Piazza dei Signori is flanked by the medieval **Palazzo degli Scaligeri**. At right angles to this is the fifteenth-century **Loggia del Consiglio**, the former assembly hall of the city council and Verona's outstanding early Renaissance

★ TREAT YOURSELF

Nowadays the Roman Arena is used as an **opera venue** for big summer productions. The sight of the stands lit up by the thousands of candles handed out to the audience is a pretty special one. The ticket office (☎045 800 5151, ☼arena. it) is outside the arena. Prices begin at €23.

building, while, close by, the twelfth-century **Torre dei Lamberti** (June–Sept daily 8.30am–8.30pm, Fri until 11pm; Oct–May daily 8.30am–7.30pm; €4.50 to walk or by lift) gives dizzying views of the city; be prepared to block your ears for the hourly ringing of the tower's bells. **Juliet's house** is situated on the nearby Via Capello 23 (Mon 1.30–7.30pm, Tues–Sun 8.30am–7.30pm; €6) – even if you don't want to pay to go inside the house, you can see the famous balcony, rub the right breast of her statue (supposedly for luck) and read some of the thousands of love messages dotted around the place.

Arche Scaligere and the Duomo

In front of the Romanesque church of **Santa Maria Antica**, the **Arche Scaligere** are the elaborate Gothic funerary monuments of Verona's first family, set in a wrought-iron palisade decorated with ladder motifs, the emblem of the Scaligeri. Nearby, on Via Arche Scaligere 4, is **Romeo's House**, marked by a lopsided sign. Verona's **Duomo**, with its unfinished bell tower (Tues–Sat 10am–6pm, Sun 1.30–5.30pm; €2.50), lies just around the river's bend, a mixture of Romanesque and Gothic styles that houses an *Assumption* by Titian.

Roman theatre

The **Roman theatre** (€4.50), on the north side of the river, is worth climbing up to for its gorgeous views. In July and August, a Shakespeare festival (in Italian, but it's still great to soak up the atmosphere) and a jazz festival make use of this amazing venue (see opposite). If you want even better views of the city head up to Castelo San Pietro for the ultimate views of Verona.

Basilica di San Zeno Maggiore

The **Basilica di San Zeno Maggiore** (Mon–Sat 8.30am–6pm, Sun 12.30–6pm; €2.50) is one of the most significant Romanesque churches in northern Italy. Its rose window, representing the Wheel of Fortune, dates from the twelfth century, as do the magnificent portal and medieval frescoes.

17

ARRIVAL AND DEPARTURE

By train The train station is connected with Piazza Bra by bus #11, #12 or #13. Alternatively, it's a straightforward 15min walk down Corso Porta Nuova.

Destinations Milan (frequent; 1hr 30min–2hr); Padua (frequent; 45min–1hr 30min); Rome (8 direct daily; 3hr); Venice (every 30min; 1–2hr).

INFORMATION

Tourist office Via degli Alpini 9 (Mon–Sat 9am–7pm, Sun 10am–4pm; ⊛ tourism.verona.it).

Discount passes The Verona Card (€15/2 days or €20/5 days) covers most of Verona's museums and churches and can be purchased at the tourist offices, *tabacchis* and most museums.

Exchange Via Cappello 3 (Mon–Sat 9am–8.30pm), or at the station (daily 7.30am–8.30pm).

Festivals If you're interested in the Shakespeare and jazz festivals that take place in the Roman Theatre in the summer, head to the box office on Via Pallone 12 (☎ 045 8011 154 or you can buy at the venue; ticket prices start at €10; ⊛ getticket.it).

Internet The Internet Train on Via San Vitale 5/b (Mon–Fri 7am–9pm, Sat & Sun 2–8pm; €2.50/hr) or Play Caffè on Via Adigetto 47 (daily 10am–12.30am; €2/hr). Verona has free wi-fi, with passes available from the library (Biblioteca Civica) on Via Cappello 43.

ACCOMMODATION

ACISJF-Protezione Della Giovane Via Pigna 7 ☎ 045 596 880, ⊛ protezionedellagiovane.it. For women under 26 only, this simple and clean hostel is right in the old centre. The curfew is 11pm unless you're going to the opera. Take bus #73 or #96/#97 at night from the station to Piazza Erbe, from where it's a 5min walk. Dorm **€22**

★ **B&B Casa Nuvola** Adigetto 21 ☎ 377 441 1906, ⊛ casanuvola.com. This excellent B&B is run by a friendly owner and the rooms are tastefully decorated – some have small balconies. Breakfast is particularly good. Tariffs fluctuate according to what's happening in town, so check before booking. Double **€50**

★ **HI Hostel** Via Fontana del Ferro 15 ☎ 045 590 360, ⊛ hihostels.com. One of Italy's best hostels, housed in a frescoed *palazzo* on the north side of the river, and surrounded by grandiose gardens. Take bus #72, #73 or #90 from the station. Dorm **€20**

EATING AND DRINKING

Retro Gusto Via Berni Francesco 1–3. This restaurant-deli serves wonderful home-made dishes, and has a fantastic wine list. Cheese-tasting platters and other mains from €9. Mon–Sat noon–3.30pm & 7–11pm.

Sottoriva 23 Via Sottoriva 42/a. This bar-restaurant on a lovely quiet street near the river has outdoor seating and

serves cheap pizzas and good salads as well as a large choice of beers. Salads €6.50. Daily 11am–11pm.

Square Via Sottoriva 15. Modern chic bar strong on cocktails. There's a DJ every Thurs evening. Beer and wine €3. Tues–Fri 6.30pm–2am, from 3.30pm on Sat & Sun.

★ **Trattoria Dal Ropetan** Via Fontana del Ferro ☎ 045 803 0040. Small restaurant tucked away among a maze of streets on the north side of the Po. The food is excellent and the friendly owner a law unto himself. Try the *penne del Ropetan* (€7). Booking is recommended. Daily noon–3pm & 7–11pm, closed Tues.

Trattoria l'Altra Colonna Via Tezone 1c ☎ 045 591 455. This place has a real community spirit and is a genuine family affair. No English spoken but this only adds to the charm. They serve an excellent daily pasta for €7. Mon–Sat noon–2.30pm & 7–10.30pm.

PADUA

Hemmed in by industrial sprawl, **PADUA** (Padova) is not the most alluring city in northern Italy. However, it's a particularly ancient place with a relaxed air and a sense of the real Italia. Donatello and Mantegna both worked here, and in the seventeenth century Galileo researched at the university.

WHAT TO SEE AND DO

Cappella degli Scrovegni

Just outside the city centre, through a gap in the Renaissance walls off **Corso Garibaldi**, the stunning Giotto frescoes in the lapis-ceilinged **Cappella degli Scrovegni**, affectionately referred to as the "scrawny chapel" for its diminutive size (slots for a 15 or 20min viewing must be booked, but bookable on the day if there is space; €13; ☎ 049 201 0020, ⊛ cappella degliscrovegni.it), are the main reason for coming to Padua. Commissioned in 1303 by Enrico Scrovegni in atonement for his father's usury, the chapel's walls are covered with breathtakingly detailed and largely well-preserved illustrations of the life of Mary, Jesus and the story of the Passion. It's a bit of a rush to see forty masterpieces in fifteen minutes, but well worth it.

Piazza del Santo

In the southwest of the city, down Via Zabarella from the *cappella*, is the starkly impressive **Piazza del Santo**. The main sight here is Donatello's **Monument to**

17

Gattamelata of 1453, the earliest large bronze sculpture of the Renaissance. On one side of the square, the basilica of San Antonio, or **Il Santo**, was built to house the body of St Anthony (a famous disciple of St Francis of Assisi); the **Cappella del Tesoro** at the far end of the Duomo (daily 7am–12.45pm & 2.30–7.30pm) houses the saint's tongue and chin in a head-shaped reliquary.

The university

From the basilica of San Antonio, Via Umberto leads back towards the university, which was established in 1221, and is older than any other in Italy except Bologna. The main block is the **Palazzo del Bo**, where Galileo taught physics from 1592 to 1610. The major sight is the sixteenth-century **anatomy theatre** (March–Oct tours Mon, Wed & Fri at 3.15pm, 4.15pm & 5.15pm, Tues, Thurs & Sat at 9.15am, 10.15am & 11.15am; Nov–Feb tours Mon, Wed & Fri at 3.15pm & 4.15pm, Tues, Thurs & Sat at 10.15am & 11.15am; €5; ☎049 827 3047, booking possible only for groups of ten or more). The university's botanical garden, the oldest in the world, is a green haven in the city (Via Orto Botanico 15; April–Oct daily 9am–7pm; Nov–March Mon–Sat 9am–3pm; €5; ☎049 827 2119, ⓦwww.ortobotanico.unipd.it).

ARRIVAL AND DEPARTURE

By plane Venice airport is most convenient for Padua there are hourly buses that go to Marco Polo (ⓦveniceairport.it) via central Venice (1hr; €8). Tickets are bought from the kiosk in the bus station, which is next to the railway station.

By train Padua train station is next to the bus station and is at the far end of Corso del Popolo, a 5min walk north of the city walls or a short tram stop away (Padua also has a good tram system).

Destinations Bologna (frequent; 1hr–1hr 30min); Milan (frequent; 2–3hr); Parma (hourly; 2hr 30min; change at Bologna); Venice (every 10min; 45min); Verona (every 20min; 45min–1hr 30min).

INFORMATION

Tourist office Galleria Vicolo Pedrocchi 9, just off Via 8 Febbraio (Mon–Sat 9am–1.30pm & 3–7pm; ☎049 876 7927, ⓦturismopadova.it), plus another at the station (Mon–Sat 9am–7pm, Sun 9am–noon) and a small kiosk in Piazza Del Santo.

Discount passes The tourist office sells the 48hr Padova Card (48hr/€16; 72hr/€21), which gives access to certain museums (including Scrovegni Chapel frescoes), free bus travel and a parking space.

ACCOMMODATION

★ **Albergo Verdi** Via Dondi dall'Orologio 7 ☎049 836 4163, ⓦalbergoverdipadova.it. While it doesn't look much from the outside, *Albergo Verdi* has spacious rooms that are stylish and comfortable. There's a lovely breakfast terrace. Double **€80**

Dante Via San Polo 5 ☎049 876 0408, ⓦhoteldante.eu. This old-fashioned hotel could do with a facelift; however, it is one of the cheaper options and only a stone's throw from the sights. Double **€60**

HI Hostel Via A. Aleardi 30 ☎049 875 2219, ⓦhihostels .com. A large, somewhat soulless hostel, but the cheapest accommodation in town and near all the major sites. 11pm curfew. Bus #12 or #18 from the station (stop at Via Cavalletto). Dorm **€19**

Sporting Center Via Roma 123 ☎049 793 400, ⓦwww .sportingcenter.it. Extremely well-equipped, spacious campsite 15km away in Montegrotto Terme, with a reasonable two-star hotel on site. Also a restaurant, large swimming pool and thermal spa. Served by frequent trains (15min). Double **€63**, camping per person plus tent **€16.50**

EATING AND DRINKING

For eating on the go, there's a daily fruit market on Piazza Erbe, which also has a few cheap restaurants and bars. There is a supermarket, Pam, at Piazzetta-Garzeria della 3 (Mon–Sat 8am–9pm, Sun 8am–2pm). On summer evenings, people sit in the centre of the scruffy Prato della Valle.

Cacao Café Via San Francesco 69. A good place for starting off the day with a brioche and a coffee, or stopping by for an evening drink. Run by the friendly Andrea. Mon 5–10pm, Tues–Fri 9am–10pm, Sat 5–10pm.

Focacceria Padova Garzeria Piazzetta della Garzeria 6. Part of a self-service restaurant chain in northern Italy, this particular restaurant specializes in pizza, focaccia and sandwiches for around €4. Daily 8.30am–10pm.

★ **La Folperia** Piazza della Fruitta. Max and Barbara bring their seafood stall to the square every night. Mouthwatering and generous portions of *gamberi fritta*, calamari and other seafood served on paper plates. Portion around €4. Daily 5–9pm.

★ **Osteria L'Anfora** Via dei Soncin 13 ☎049 656 629. Fantastic *osteria* near Piazza Erbe and one of the few places you want to eat inside rather than outside even on a warm day. Delicious fresh pasta (from €9) is served in a large ramshackle room decorated with the owner's passions in mind. Booking recommended. Mon–Sat 9am–midnight.

VENICE

The first-time visitor to **VENICE** (Venezia) arrives with a heavy load of expectations, most of which won't be disappointed. It is an extraordinarily beautiful city, and the major sights are all they are cracked up to be. The downside is that Venice is very expensive and deluged with tourists. Twenty-seven million come here each year, most seduced by the famous motifs – Carnival (see p.640), glass ornaments and singing gondoliers. To avoid the mêlée, stroll down one of the intriguing and peaceful side streets or take a boat across to the Lido and relax on its lovely beach.

WHAT TO SEE AND DO

Piazza San Marco

Flanked by the Grand Canal, **Piazza San Marco** is probably the busiest square in the whole of Italy, let alone Venice. It's lined with some stunning architecture such as the dominating **Campanile** (Easter–June 9am–7pm; July–Sept 9am–9pm; Oct 9am–7pm; Nov–Easter 9.30am–3.45pm; €8; ⓦwww .basilicasanmarco.com), which began life as a lighthouse in the ninth century, but is in fact a reconstruction: the original tower collapsed on July 14, 1902. It is the tallest structure in the city, and the 98m-high tower provides magnificent views of the neighbouring islands and lagoons, as well as the red-clay rooftops of the city.

Basilica di San Marco

Across Piazza San Marco, the **Basilica di San Marco** (Easter–Oct Mon–Sat 9.45am–5pm, Sun 2–5pm; Nov–Easter Mon–Sat 9.45am–5pm, Sun 2–4pm; free) is the most exotic of Europe's cathedrals, modelled on Constantinople's Church of the Twelve Apostles, finished in

1094 and embellished over the succeeding centuries with trophies brought back from abroad. Inside, a steep staircase leads from the church's main door up to the **Museo di San Marco** and the **Loggia dei Cavalli** (March–Nov 9.45am–5pm; Easter–Oct 9.45am–5pm; €5), where you can enjoy fine views of the city and the Gothic carvings along the apex of the facade. However, it's the **Sanctuary**, off the south transept (Easter–Oct Mon–Sat 9.45am–5pm, Sun 2–5pm; Nov–Easter Mon–Sat 9.45am–4pm, Sun 2–4pm; €2), that holds the most precious of San Marco's treasures, the **Pala d'Oro**, or golden altar panel, commissioned in 976 in Constantinople. This mind-blowingly intricate explosion of gold, enamel, pearls and gemstones is generally considered to be one of the greatest accomplishments of Byzantine craftsmanship. The **Treasury** (Easter–Oct Mon–Sat 9.45am–5pm, Sun 2–5pm; Nov–Easter Mon–Sat 9.45am–4pm, Sun 2–4pm; €3) is a similarly dazzling warehouse of chalices, reliquaries and candelabra, while the tenth-century **Icon of the Madonna of Nicopeia** (in the chapel on the east side of the north transept) is the most revered religious image in Venice. Considered by Venetians to be the protector of the city after being brought here from Constantinople by Doge Enrico Dandolo in 1204, she was carried at the head of the Imperial Army in battles.

Palazzo Ducale

The **Palazzo Ducale** (daily: April–Oct 8.30am–7pm (ticket office closes 1hr earlier); Nov–March 8.30am–5.30pm; €16, €8 with student card; ⓦvisitmuve.it) was principally the residence of the doge. Like San Marco, it has been rebuilt many times since its foundation in the first

---

VENICE ORIENTATION

The 118 islands of central Venice are divided into six districts known as *sestieri*, with that of **San Marco** (enclosed by the lower loop of the Canal Grande) home to most of the essential sights. To the east it's bordered by **Castello**, to the north by **Cannaregio**. On the other side of the Canal Grande is **Dorsoduro**, which stretches from the fashionable quarter at the southern tip of the canal to the docks in the west. **Santa Croce** roughly follows the curve of the Canal Grande from Piazzale Roma to a point just short of the Rialto, where it joins the smartest of the districts on this bank, **San Polo**.

17

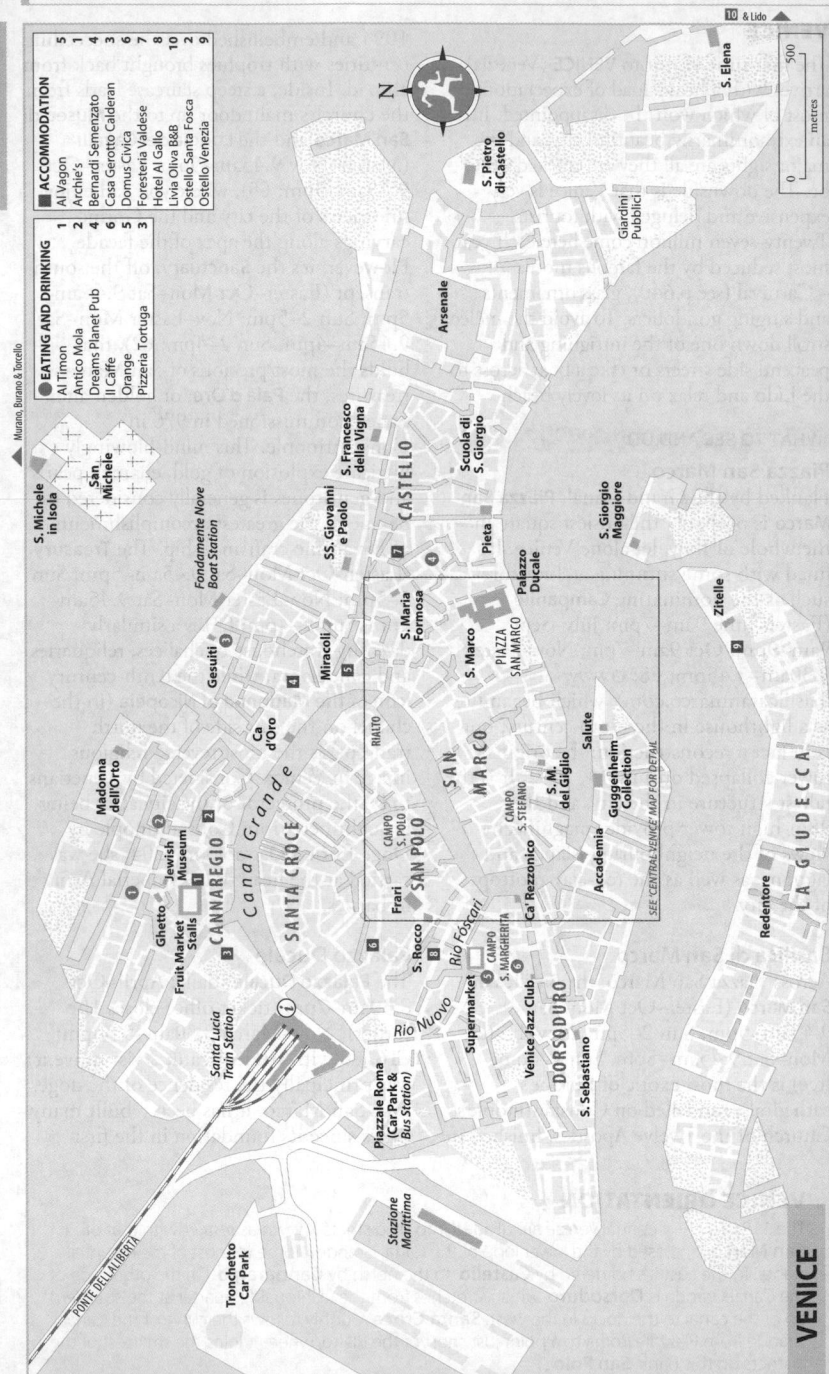

10 & Lido ▲

▲ Murano, Burano & Torcello

VENICE

■ ACCOMMODATION
Al Vagon	5
Archie's	1
Bernardi Semenzato	4
Casa Gerotto Calderan	3
Domus Civica	6
Foresteria Valdese	7
Hotel Al Gallo	8
Livia Oliva B&B	10
Ostello Santa Fosca	2
Ostello Venezia	9

● EATING AND DRINKING
Al Timon	1
Antico Mola	2
Dreams Planet Pub	4
Il Caffe	6
Orange	5
Pizzeria Tortuga	3

N

0 — 500
metres

S. Elena

S. Pietro
di Castello

Giardini
Pubblici

Arsenale

S. Michele
in Isola

San
Michele

S. Francesco
della Vigna

Scuola di
S. Giorgio

CASTELLO

Fondamente Nove
Boat Station

SS. Giovanni
e Paolo

Pieta

S. Giorgio
Maggiore

Gesuiti

Miracoli

S. Maria
Formosa

S. Marco

PIAZZA
SAN MARCO

Palazzo
Ducale

Zitelle

Madonna
dell'Orto

Ca'
d'Oro

RIALTO

SAN
MARCO

S. M.
del Giglio

Salute

Guggenheim
Collection

LA GIUDECCA

Jewish
Museum

Ghetto

Fruit Market
Stalls

CANNAREGIO

Canal Grande

SANTA CROCE

CAMPO
S. POLO

SAN POLO

Frari

S. Rocco

Rio Fóscari

S. Stefano

Ca' Rezzonico

Accademia

SEE CENTRAL VENICE MAP FOR DETAIL

Redentore

Santa Lucia
Train Station

Rio Nuovo

Supermarket

Venice Jazz Club

CAMPO
S. MARGHERITA

DORSODURO

S. Sebastiano

Piazzale Roma
(Car Park &
Bus Station)

Stazione
Marittima

PONTE DELLA LIBERTÀ

Tronchetto
Car Park

years of the ninth century, but the earliest parts of the current structure date from 1340. As well as fabulous paintings and impressive administrative chambers, the Palazzo contains a maze of prison cells, reached by crossing the world-famous **Ponte dei Sospiri** (Bridge of Sighs).

Dorsoduro

In the Dorsoduro area west of San Marco, five minutes' walk from the impressive European art collection in the **Galleria dell'Accademia** (Mon 8.15am–2pm, Tues–Sun 8.15am–7.15pm; €9, €6 for EU 18–25s with ID; ⓦgallerie accademia.org), the unfinished Palazzo Venier dei Leoni is home to the **Guggenheim Collection** (daily except Tues 10am–6pm; €14, €8 students under 26 with ID; ⓦguggenheim-venice.it). Peggy Guggenheim lived here for thirty years until her death in 1979. Her private collection is an eclectic mix of pieces from her favourite Modernist artists, with works by Brancusi, De Chirico, Max Ernst and Malevich.

San Polo

On the northeastern edge of **San Polo** is the former trading district of **Rialto**. It still hosts the lively Rialto market, which is located on the far side of the Rialto bridge and has stalls heaving with fresh fruit and vegetables and a shiny array of fish.

Fifteen minutes' walk west of here is the mountainous brick church **Santa Maria Gloriosa dei Frari** (Mon–Sat 9am–6pm, Sun 1–6pm; €3; ⓦchorusvenezia.org), the main reason people visit San Polo. The collection of artworks here includes a couple of rare paintings by Titian – most notably his radical *Assumption*, painted in 1518. Titian is also buried in the church. At the rear of the Frari is the **Scuola Grande di San Rocco** (daily 9.30am–5.30pm; €10, €8 under-26s, ID needed; ⓦscuolagrandesanrocco.it), home to a cycle of more than fifty major paintings by Tintoretto.

Cannaregio

In the northernmost section of Venice, **Cannaregio**, you can walk from the bustle of the train station to some of the quietest and prettiest parts of the city in a matter of minutes. The district boasts one of the most beautiful *palazzi* in Venice, the **Ca D'Oro**, or Golden House (Mon 8.15am–2pm, Tues–Sat 8.15am–7.15pm, Sun 10am–6pm; €6, €3 EU under-26s with ID; ⓦcadoro.org), whose facade once glowed with gold leaf, and what is arguably the finest Gothic church in Venice, the **Madonna dell'Orto** (Mon–Sat 10am–5pm, Sun noon–5pm; €2.50), which contains Tintoretto's tomb and two of his paintings. Cannaregio also has the dubious distinction of containing the world's first **ghetto**: in 1516, all the city's Jews were ordered to move to the island of the **Ghetto Nuovo**, an enclave that was sealed at night by Christian guards. Even now it looks quite different from the rest of Venice, its many high-rise buildings a result of restrictions on the growth of the area. The **Jewish Museum** (Oct–May 10am–5.30pm; June–Sept 10am–7pm; closed Sat; €4; ⓦmuseoebraico.it) in Campo Ghetto Nuovo organizes interesting tours of the area (daily except Sat Oct–May 10.30am–4.30pm; June–Sept 10am–5.30pm every 30min; €10, €8 including museum admission).

Castello

Campo Santi Giovanni e Paolo is the most impressive open space in Venice after Piazza San Marco, dominated by the huge brick church of **Santi Giovanni e Paolo** (Mon–Sat 9am–6pm, Sun noon–6pm), founded by the Dominicans in 1246 and best known for its funeral monuments to 25 doges. The other essential sight in **Castello** is the **Scuola di San Giorgio degli Schiavoni** (Mon 2.45–6pm, Tues–Sat 9.15am–1pm & 2.45–6pm, Sun 9.15am–1pm; €3), to the east of San Marco, set up by Venice's Slav population in 1451. The building has a superb cycle by Vittore Carpaccio on the ground floor.

Venice's other islands

Immediately south of the Palazzo Ducale, Palladio's church of **San Giorgio Maggiore** (daily: Oct–April 9.30am–12.30pm & 2.30–4.30pm; May–Sept 9.30am–12.30pm & 2.30–6pm; €5) stands on the island of the same name and has two

17

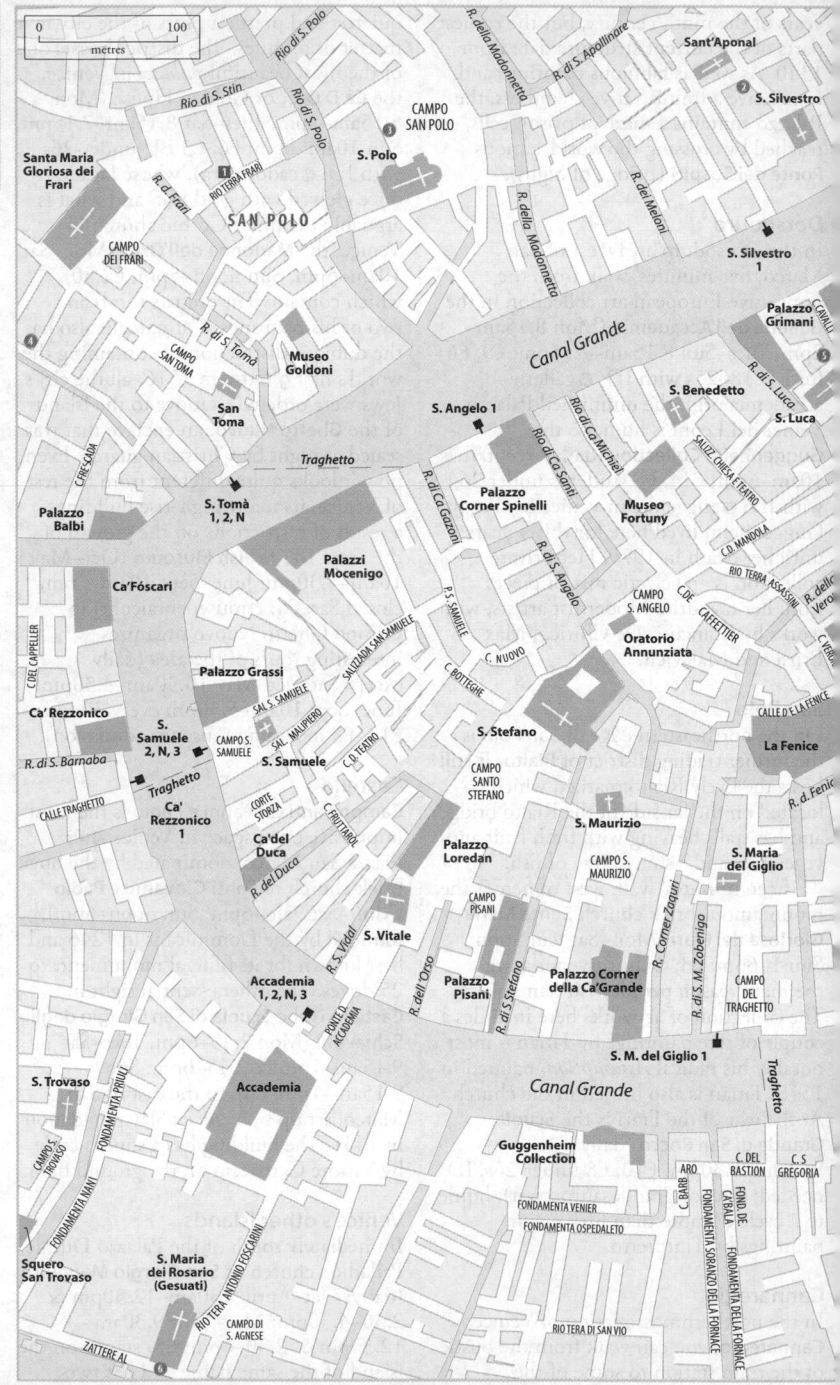

0   100
metres

R. di S. Stin

R. di S. Polo

R. di S. Polo

R. della Madonnetta

R. di S. Apollinare

Sant'Aponal

S. Silvestro

CAMPO SAN POLO

S. Polo

Santa Maria Gloriosa dei Frari

R. d Frari

RIO TERRA FRARI

R. della Madonnetta

R. del Meloni

S. Silvestro 1

SAN POLO

CAMPO DEI FRARI

Palazzo Grimani

Canal Grande

R. di S. Tomà

CAMPO SAN TOMA

Museo Goldoni

S. Benedetto

R. di S. Luca

S. Luca

S. Angelo 1

Rio di Ca' Michiel

SALIZE CHIESA ETEATRO

San Tomà

Traghetto

S. Tomà 1, 2, N

R. di Ca' Gozzon

Palazzo Corner Spinelli

Museo Fortuny

Palazzo Balbi

R. di Ca' Sant

C. D. MANDOLA

RIO TERRA ASSASSIN

R. delle Vero

Ca' Fóscari

Palazzi Mocenigo

R. di S. Angelo

CAMPO S. ANGELO

C. DE. CAFFETTIER

P.S. SAMUELE

C. NUOVO

Oratorio Annunziata

C. VEDA

C. DEL CAPPELLER

Palazzo Grassi

SALIZZADA SAN SAMUELE

C. BOTTEGHE

CALLE D'E LA FENICE

Ca' Rezzonico

SAL. S. SAMUELE

SAL. MALIPIERO

S. Stefano

La Fenice

S. Samuele 2, N, 3

CAMPO S. SAMUELE

S. Samuele

C. D. TEATRO

CAMPO SANTO STEFANO

R. d. Fenic

R. di S. Barnaba

Traghetto

CALLE TRAGHETTO

Ca' Rezzonico 1

CORTE STORZA

C. FRUTTARIÒL

S. Maurizio

CAMPO S. MAURIZIO

S. Maria del Giglio

Ca'del Duca

R. del Duca

Palazzo Loredan

CAMPO PISANI

R. Comer Zaquan

S. Vitale

R. S. Vidal

CAMPO DEL TRAGHETTO

Accademia 1, 2, N, 3

PONTE D. ACCADEMIA

R. dell'Orso

Palazzo Pisani

R. di S. Stefano

Palazzo Corner della Ca'Grande

R. di S. M. Zobenigo

S. Trovaso

Accademia

Canal Grande

S. M. del Giglio 1

Traghetto

Guggenheim Collection

C. BABA

C. DEL BASTION

C. S GREGORIA

CAMPO S. TROVASO

FONDAMENTA PRIULI

FONDAMENTA MANIN

ARO

FONDAMENTA VENIER

FOND. DE. CA' BALA

FONDAMENTA SORANZO DELLA FORNACE

Squero San Trovaso

S. Maria dei Rosario (Gesuati)

RIO TERA ANTONIO FOSCARINI

CAMPO DI S. AGNESE

RIO TERA DI SAN VIO

ZATTERE AI

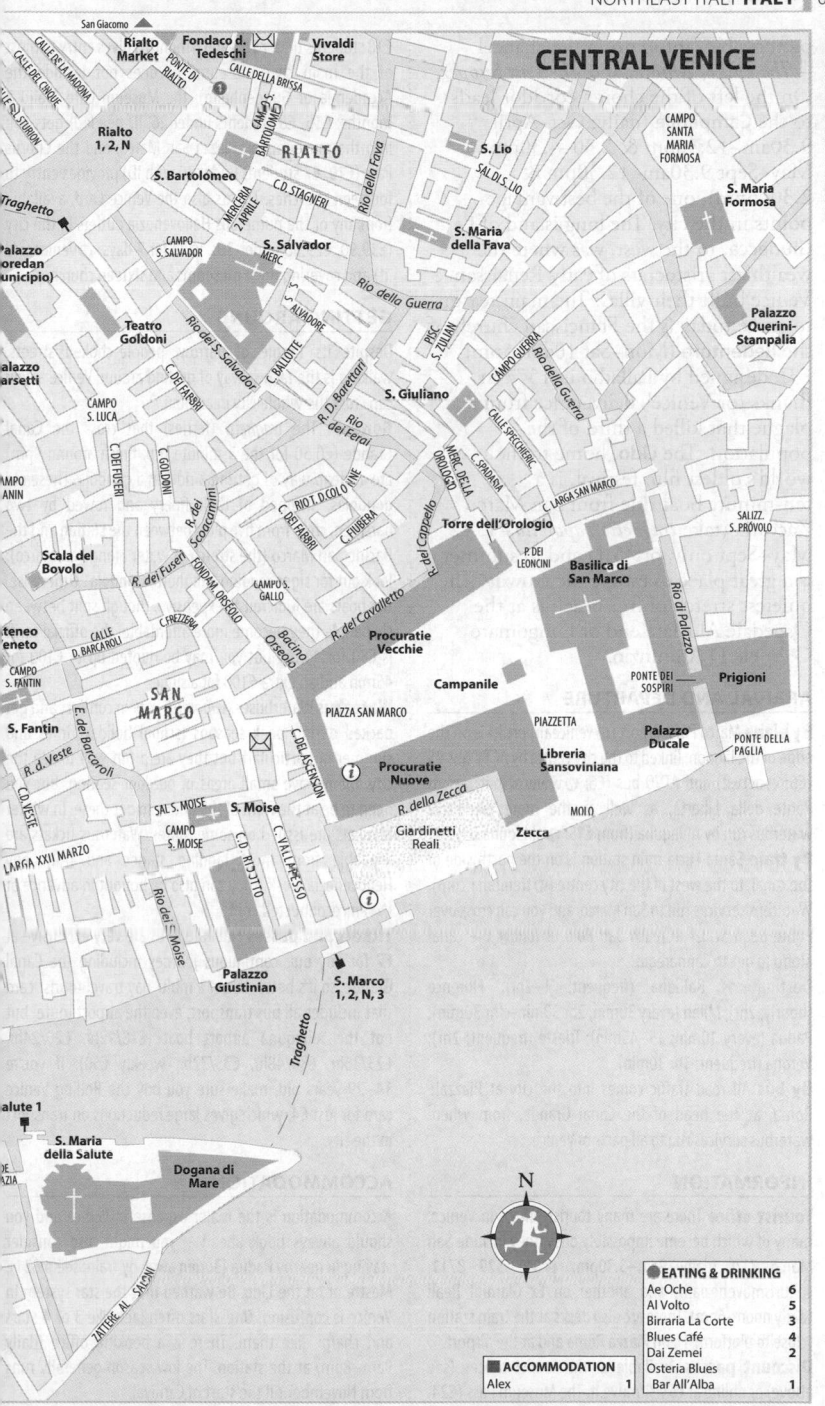

CENTRAL VENICE

San Giacomo
Rialto Market
Fondaco d. Tedeschi
Vivaldi Store
CALLE DEL CINQUE
CALLE (S.) STURION
CALLE DEL CINQUE
CALLE DELLA MADONNA
PONTE DI RIALTO
CALLE DELLA BRISSA
CAMPO S. BARTOLOMIO
Rialto 1, 2, N
RIALTO
S. Lio
SAL DI S. LIO
CAMPO SANTA MARIA FORMOSA
Traghetto
S. Bartolomeo
MERCERIA 2 APRILE
C.D. STAGNERI
Rio della Fava
S. Maria Formosa
Palazzo Loredan (Municipio)
CAMPO S. SALVADOR
S. Salvador
MERC
S. Maria della Fava
S. SALVADORE
C. BALLOTTE
Palazzo Farsetti
Teatro Goldoni
Rio del S. Salvador
Rio della Guerra
Palazzo Querini-Stampalia
CAMPO S. LUCA
C. DEI FARSRI
R. D. Baretteri
PISC. S. ZULIAN
S. Giuliano
CAMPO GUERRA
Rio della Guerra
CAMPO ANIN
C. DEI FUSERI
C. DEI GOLDONI
RIO dei Ferai
CALLE SPECHIERI
MERC. DELLA OROLOGI
C. SPADASA
Scala del Bovolo
R. dei Scoacamini
C. DEI FABBRI
RIO T. D.COLONNE
C. FIUBERA
R. per Cappello
Torre dell'Orologio
C. LARGA SAN MARCO
SALIZZ. S. PRÒVOLO
Ateneo Veneto
R. dei Fuseri
FONDAM. ORSEOLO
C. FREZZERIA
CAMPO S. GALLO
R. del Cavalletto
P. DEI LEONCINI
Basilica di San Marco
CAMPO S. FANTIN
CALLE D. BARCAROLI
Bacino Orseolo
Procuratie Vecchie
Campanile
Rio di Palazzo
S. Fantin
E. del Borcaroli
R. d. Veste
PIAZZA SAN MARCO
PIAZZETTA
PONTE DEI SOSPIRI
Prigioni
C.D.VESTE
SAL S. MOISE
C. VALLARESSO
Procuratie Nuove
Libreria Sansoviniana
Palazzo Ducale
PONTE DELLA PAGLIA
LARGA XXII MARZO
S. Moise
CAMPO S. MOISE
C.D. RIO2TTO
R. della Zecca
MOLO
Zecca
Rio del S. Moise
Giardinetti Reali
Palazzo Giustinian
S. Marco 1, 2, N, 3
Traghetto
Salute 1
S. Maria della Salute
GRAZIA
Dogana di Mare
ZATTERE AL SALONI

N

EATING & DRINKING
Ae Oche	6
Al Volto	5
Birraria La Corte	3
Blues Café	4
Dai Zemei	2
Osteria Blues Bar All'Alba	1

ACCOMMODATION
Alex	1

17

pictures by Tintoretto in the chancel – *The Fall of Manna* and *The Last Supper*. On the left of the choir a corridor leads to the **Campanile** (daily: Oct–April 9.30am–12.30pm & 2.30–4.30pm; May–Sept 9.30am–12.30pm & 2.30–6pm), one of the best vantage points in the city. The long island of **La Giudecca**, to the west, was where the wealthiest aristocrats of early Renaissance Venice built their villas. The main reason to come today is the Franciscan church of the **Redentore** (Mon–Sat 10am–5pm; €3), designed by Palladio in 1577 in thanks for Venice's deliverance from a plague that killed a third of the population. The **Lido**, home to the world's oldest film festival, is a ten-minute boat ride from San Marco Zaccaria (take *traghetto vaporetto* #1, #2 May–Sept only, or #5.1) and in summer is a great place to escape the crowds. The quietest stretch of free beach is at the Ospedale Al Mare end of Lungomare Gabriele D'Annunzio.

ARRIVAL AND DEPARTURE

By plane Marco Polo airport (ⓦveniceairport.it) is on the edge of the lagoon, linked to the city centre by ACTV bus #5 (€6; ⓦactv.it) and ATVO bus (€6; ⓦwww.atvo.it) across Ponte della Libertà, as well as the more expensive waterbus run by Alilaguna (from €15; ⓦalilaguna.it).

By train Santa Lucia train station is on the north side of the canal, to the west of the city centre (ⓦtrenitalia.com). Waterbus services run to San Marco, and you can cross over Ponte degli Scalzi to reach San Polo or follow the canal along to get to Cannaregio.

Destinations Bologna (frequent; 1–2hr); Florence (hourly; 2hr); Milan (every 30min; 2hr 30min–3hr 30min); Padua (every 10min; 15–45min); Trieste (frequent; 2hr); Verona (frequent; 1hr 30min).

By bus All road traffic comes into the city at Piazzale Roma, at the head of the Canal Grande, from where waterbus services run to all parts of Venice.

INFORMATION

Tourist office There are many tourist offices in Venice, many of which become impossibly busy; they include San Marco 71/f (daily 9am–3.30pm; ☎041 529 8711, ⓦturismovenezia.it) and another on Ex Giardini Reali (daily noon–6pm). There are also desks at the train station (close to platform 1), on Piazza Roma and at the airport.

Discount passes Available at the tourist offices (see above) or online at ⓦvisitmuve.it. The Museum Pass (€24,

€18 students under 26, valid 6 months) gives entry to most of the main civic museums (it does not include the Accademia or Guggenheim); the Museum Card (valid 3 months; €16, €8 students under 26, ID needed) gets you into the museums on Piazza San Marco; and the Chorus Pass (€10, €7 students under 30 with ID) provides entry to fourteen churches. There's also the Venice Card, available from any of the numerous Hellovenezia outlets in the city (€39.90, €29.90 under-30s, valid for 7 days; ⓦvenicecard .it) and covering most museums and sixteen churches.

GETTING AROUND

Despite its tangle of narrow–, people-choked streets, walking is the fastest way of getting around Venice – you can cross the whole city in an hour.

Gondola The *traghetti* (ferries) that cross the Canal Grande (€0.50 for the 3-minute trip, finish around 9pm) are a cheap way of getting a ride on a gondola. These old gondolas, stripped of their finery and rowed by two oarsmen, cross from five piers between the station and the Bacino San Marco (the stretch of water along San Marco); look out for signs reading "traghetto Gondola". Otherwise, the boats are ludicrously expensive, though split between six people they become more affordable: the official tariff is €80 for 40min but you may be quoted up to €100 for 45min and an extra €100 for a singer.

Waterbus Waterbuses (*vaporetti*) vary in comfort and get packed during peak seasons (school holiday times and summer in particular) but they are a fun way to see the city. Many have small areas of outdoor seating, but you need to be at the front of the queue to get these. In winter blankets are issued on some routes. Waterbus tickets are available from most landing stages and from any Hellovenezia kiosk. They can also be bought in advance at ⓦveniceconnected.com.

Tickets and passes Flat-rate fares are very expensive at €7 for any one continuous journey including the Canal Grande, so it's better to get a multi-day travel tourist card that includes all bus transport, even the airport route, but not the Alilaguna airport boat (€18/12hr, €20/24hr, €25/36hr, €30/48hr, €35/72hr, weekly €50). If you're 14–29 years old, make sure you buy the Rolling Venice card for just €4, which gives large reductions on transport in the city.

ACCOMMODATION

Accommodation is the major expense in Venice and you should always book ahead – you might also consider staying in nearby Padua (30min away by train; see p.631), Mestre or on the Lido. Be warned that the star system in Venice is confusing. One-stars often look like 3 or 4 stars and charge like them. There is a booking office (daily 9am–8pm) at the station. The low season generally runs from November till the start of Carnival.

Alex Rio Terra Frari San Polo 2606 ☎041 523 1341, ⓦhotelalexinvenice.com; map pp.636–637. Cosy one-star option run by Velice Velia and her son. The best of the bright sunny rooms are the ones with small terraces on the top floor. Double €130

Al Vagon Campiello Riccardo Selvatico, Cannaregio 5619 ☎041 5285 626, ⓦhotelalvagon.com; map p.634. One of the best of the one-star options and close to the Rialto bridge. Rooms are a bit glitzy, but many have fantastic canal views and balconies. Double €100

Archie's Rio Terra Del Cristo 1814b ☎041 720 884, ⓦhostelz.com; map p.634. This place is small, old and a bit shabby, but the owner and his sons are friendly and it is cheap and close to the train station and lots of bars. Dorm €23, double €55

★ **Bernardi Semenzato** Calle dell'Oca, Cannaregio 4366 ☎041 522 7257, ⓦhotelbernardi.com; map p.634. The owners are a delight at this one-star. To capture the best sunsets ask for room 8 in the exquisitely decorated annexe. Some doubles have canal views. Double €80

Casa Gerotto Calderan Campo San Geremia, Cannaregio 283 ☎041 715 562, ⓦcasagerottocalderan.com; map p.634. Large, welcoming place not far from the train station. Some rooms have views over the small square. Dorm €25, double €65

Domus Civica Calle De Le Sechere, San Polo 3082 ☎041 721 103, ⓦdomuscivica.com; map p.634. Very basic hostel in university accommodation just a 10min walk from Santa Lucia train station. Curfew 12.30am. Open mid-June to mid-Sept only. Dorm €39, double €50

Foresteria Valdese Santa Maria Formosa, Castello 5170 ☎041 528 6797, ⓦforesteriavenezia.it; map p.634. Pleasant hostel in an eighteenth-century palace. Head from Campo Santa Maria Formosa along Calle Lunga, and it's at the foot of the bridge at the far end. Dorm €35

Hotel Al Gallo Calle del Forno, S. Croce 88 ☎041 523 6761, ⓦalgallo.com; map p.634. Very close to the bus station, this hostel cum hotel offers free tea and coffee in the common room. Double €89

★ **Livia Oliva B&B** Via Aldo Mauzio 5, Lido ☎041 526 2981; map p.634. An unbeatable choice on the Lido, close to the ferry station and near a lovely sandy beach. The rooms are spotless and there's a lovely terrace overlooking the quiet canal-lined street. Double €58

Ostello Santa Fosca S. Maria dei Servi, Cannaregio 2372 ☎041 715 775, ⓦsantafosca.com; map p.634. This student hall of residence in a former convent is basic but does have a kitchen and cheap internet and plenty of outdoor sitting areas. Dorm €30

Ostello Venezia Fondamenta delle Zitelle, Giudecca 86 ☎041 523 8211, ⓦhostelvenice.org; map p.634. The official HI hostel, in a superb location with views of San Marco from the island of Giudecca. Curfew 11pm. Waterbus #2 from the station. Large place, but get there early morning or book. Dorm €24

EATING

Venice is full of great restaurants but it can be a minefield to find cheap places. Many appear to offer good value, but be careful to check about cover charges (€1.50/person) and service (12–15 percent) before you take the plunge. Pizzerias and self-service places are the best bet, and avoid the tourist hotspots like Piazza San Marco where prices rocket. There is a supermarket on Salizada 5817 selling cheap sandwiches and pastries.

★ **Ae Oche** Zattere Venezia 1414, ☎041 520 6601, ⓦaeoche.com; map pp.636–637. This pizzeria chain has three restaurants in great locations in Venice – this one is on the water's edge. You can invent your own pizza toppings (€7). Daily noon–2.30pm & 7–11pm (until 11.30pm Sat & Sun).

Antico Mola Fondamenta degli Ormesini, Cannaregio 2800 ☎041 717 492; map p.634. Canalside, family-run place that's popular with locals. Serves excellent food at reasonable prices (around €25). There is also a garden at the rear. Mon, Tues & Thurs–Sun 8.15am–4pm & 6.30–10pm.

Birraria La Corte Campo San Polo 2168 ☎041 275 0570, ⓦbirrarialacorte.com; map pp.636–637. Huge restaurant in a quiet part of the square with a lovely courtyard. Pizzas €7. Daily noon–2.30pm & 6–10.30pm.

Dreams Planet Pub Calle Casellerie, Castello 5281 ☎041 522 0808; map p.634. A 5min walk from Piazza San Marco, *Dreams Planet* is an international pub that screens sporting events until 2am. Serves a vast range of pizzas and delicious seafood. A bit pricey but the tourist menus are good value. Daily 11am–2am.

Pizzeria Tortuga Campo dei Gesuiti, Cannaregio 4888 ☎041 241 2654, ⓜpizzeriatortuga.com; map p.634. Excellent pizzeria-bar located near the waterfront. Serves a large choice of bruschetta and speciality salads. Pizzas from €6. Tues–Sun 10am–10.30pm.

DRINKING AND NIGHTLIFE

Venice is short on clubbing action, but there are plenty of bars, particularly around Campo Santa Margherita and Campo San Giacomo, where you can relax and enjoy some evening drinks. Many bars close around 8pm.

Al Timon Fondamenta degli Ormesini, Cannaregio 2754 ☎041 524 6066; map p.634. Great late-night bar by the water's edge that has a wonderful wine selection (glass from €5). Mon–Sat 6pm–1am, Sun 11am–1am.

Al Volto Calle Cavalli, San Marco 4081, near Campo S. Luca ☎041 522 8945; map pp.636–637. Stocks over one hundred wines from Italy and elsewhere and serves up a different risotto every day at lunchtime for €6. No credit cards. Fri–Tues 10am–2pm & 5–10.30pm.

Blues Café Calle dei Preti, Dorsoduro 3778, behind the Scuola di San Rocco; map pp.636–637. One of the few places you can enjoy a burger in Venice. Good coffee and

17

large choice of bottled beers. There is live music on Fri & Sat nights. Burgers, wraps and sandwiches €6.50. Mon–Fri 10am–2am, Sat & Sun 3pm–2am.

Dai Zemei Off the Rughetta del Ravano, San Polo 1045, ☎ 041 520 8596; map pp.636–637. Run by the twins who give this place its name, this traditional *enoteca* on a tiny side street serves a huge range of great *cechetti*. Beer €3. Mon–Sat 8.30am–8.30pm (Sun until 7pm).

★ **Il Caffe** Campo Santa Margherita 2963; map p.634. This tiny bar draws a large crowd. Either stand outside or join the chilled-out throng who sit in the square. Medium beer €4. Mon–Sat 7am–midnight.

Orange Campo Santa Margherita, Dorsoduro 3054 ⓦ orangebar.it; map p.634. As the name implies, this place is bright orange. A laidback, modern bar in a lively, atmospheric square. Buffet served 6–8pm. Medium beer €5. Daily 9am–2am.

Osteria Blues Bar All'Alba Ramo del Fontego dei Tedeschi, San Marco 5370/71; map pp.636–637. Popular wine bar by the Rialto bridge; pick from their large wine menu or scribble a message on the tastefully graffitied walls inside. Glass of wine from €3. Tues–Sun 9am–1am.

ENTERTAINMENT

To find out about concerts and events going on throughout the city head to one of the tourist offices (see p.638). Alternatively, check out websites ⓦ hellovenezia.com, ⓦ musicinvenice.com or ⓦ veniceconcerts.com.

Opera The city's opera house, La Fenice, has been completely rebuilt after a calamitous fire in 1996 (☎ 041 786 511, ⓦ www.teatrolafenice.it) and puts on excellent performances. Tickets range €15–200.

Jazz Live jazz takes place throughout the year at the popular Venice Jazz Club (Fondamenta dello Squero 3102; ☎ 340 150 4985, ⓦ venicejazzclub.com).

Festivals and events The most famous celebrated annual event is Carnival (Carnevale), which occupies the ten days leading up to Lent, finishing on Shrove Tuesday with a masked ball, dancing in the Piazza San Marco, street parties, pageants and performances. The Biennale (ⓦ labiennale.org) organizes international arts events throughout the year, including the Venice Film Festival.

DIRECTORY

Exchange Strada Nuova 4194 (daily 9am–6.30pm).
Hospital Ospedale Civilie Riuniti di Venezia, Campo Santi Giovanni e Paolo, Castello 6777 (☎ 041 523 0000).
Internet Calle dell'Occa, Cannaregio 4426a (daily 10am–10.30pm; €3/hr).
Police Fondamenta di San Lorenzo (☎ 041 270 5511).
Post office Calle de le Acque, San Marco 5016, not far from the Rialto bridge (Mon–Fri 8.30am–2pm, Sat 8.30am–1pm).

BOLOGNA

BOLOGNA is the oldest university town in Europe (the institution dates back to the eleventh century) and teems with students and bookshops. Known for its left-wing politics, "Red Bologna" has long been the Italian Communist Party's spiritual home. The birthplace of Marconi boasts some of the richest food in Italy, a busy cultural life and a convivial café and bar scene.

WHAT TO SEE AND DO

The compact, colonnaded city centre is famous for its 38km of covered arcades, built to cover the horses brought to Bologna by the first university students, and is still startlingly medieval in plan.

Piazza Maggiore and around

Buzzing **Piazza Maggiore** is the heart of the city, dominated by the basilica of **San Petronio**, and was originally intended to have been larger than St Peter's in Rome. On the piazza's western edge, the Palazzo D'Accursio holds the **Museo Morandi** (Tues–Fri 9am–6.30pm, Sat & Sun 10am–6.30pm; free), dedicated to the works of one of Italy's most important twentieth-century painters. Just north of the square, in the centre of Piazza del Nettuno, is the marble and bronze **Fountain of Neptune**, a famous emblem of the city. Created by Giambologna in the late sixteenth century, it shows the sea god lording it over an array of cherubs, mermaids and dolphins. Northwest of the piazza, at Via Don Minzoni 14, is the new **MAMbo** Modern Art Museum of Bologna (Tues, Wed & Fri noon–6pm, Thurs, Sat & Sun noon–8pm; €6; ⓦ mambo-bologna.org). Housed in an ex-bakery, the museum contains works by Italian and international artists and hosts regular temporary exhibitions by contemporary artists.

Archiginnasio

Bologna's university – the **Archiginnasio** – was founded at more or less the same time as the Piazza Maggiore, though it didn't get a special building until 1565. The most interesting portion is the **Teatro Anatomico** (Mon–Fri

9am–6.45pm, Sat 9am–1.45pm; €6), the original medical faculty dissection theatre, whose tiers of seats surround a professor's chair, covered with a canopy supported by figures known as *gli spellati* – the skinned ones.

Piazza San Domenico

Heading south down Via Garibaldi, **Piazza San Domenico** is the site of the church of **San Domenico**, built in 1251 to house the relics of St Dominic. The angel and figures of saints Proculus and Petronius were the work of a very young Michelangelo. It also holds a crucifix by Pizzano.

Due Torri

At Piazza di Porta Ravegnana, the **Torre degli Asinelli** (daily 9am–6pm, closes 5pm Nov–March; €3) and perilously leaning **Torre Garisenda** are together known as the Due Torri, the only significant survivors of 180 towers that were scattered across the city during the Middle Ages, when possession of the towers determined the ranks of power within the city. Superstition holds that any student who enters these towers before graduation won't graduate at all. The climb up the 498 steps to the top of the Torre degli Asinelli is tough and takes about fifteen minutes but you'll be rewarded with spectacular views over Bologna's rooftops.

ARRIVAL AND DEPARTURE

By plane Bologna's airport (ⓦ bologna-airport.it) is northwest of the centre, linked by Aerobus (every 15min; 25min; ⓦ atc.bo.it; €6) to the train station and Via dell'Indipendenza in the centre of town.

By train The train station is on Piazza delle Medaglie d'Oro – about a 15min walk to the centre along Via dell'Indipendenza, or take bus #30 or #25 (€1.20; €1.50 on board).

Destinations Ferrara (every 30min; 30min–1hr); Florence (frequent; 30min–1hr); Genoa (hourly; 3–4hr); Milan (every 30min; 2–3hr); Rimini (every 30min; 1hr 30min); Rome (frequent; 2hr–2hr 30min); Turin (10 direct daily; 2hr 30min–3hr 30min); Venice (frequent; 1hr 30min–2hr); Verona (hourly; 1hr–1hr 30min).

By bus All long-distance buses terminate in Piazza XX Settembre, next to the train station. Bus company Sena (ⓦ sena.it) runs services to Naples, Rome and Siena.

Destinations Naples (2 daily; 8hr); Rome (1 daily; 5hr 45min); Siena (2 daily; 2hr 40min).

INFORMATION

Tourist office Piazza Maggiore 1e (Mon–Sat 9am–7pm, Sun 10am–5pm; ☎ 051 239 660, ⓦ bolognawelcome.it); provides the free quarterly English-language magazine *L'Ospite* di *Bologna*.

Discount passes The 48-hour Bologna Welcome Card costs €20 and includes free admission to many of the major museums, plus either free public transport for 24 hours or a free shuttle bus to and from Bologna's airport.

Internet Internet Point at Via Altabella 12E (Mon–Fri 10am–midnight; €1.50/hr). Bologna offers free wi-fi; to register, go to ⓦ comune.bologna.it or ask at the Public Relations office at Piazza Maggiore 6 (Mon–Sat 8.30am–7pm).

Cinema There's a free open-air cinema in Piazza Maggiore in the summer (June–Sept) showing arty and black-and-white films – ask at the tourist office (see above) for details.

GETTING AROUND

On foot Walking is the best way to see Bologna, as the compact centre can be crossed in under 30min.

City Red Bus This bus (ⓦ www.cityredbus.com) offers a day ticket for just €12 and is a great way to explore Bologna outside the city centre.

Bike rental Autorimessa Pincio, Via dell'Indipendenza 71z (4min walk from the train station; €1.50/hr, €15/day; ☎ 051 249 081).

ACCOMMODATION

Trade fairs take place several times a year (March to early May & Sept–Dec are peak times), during which prices can double – so it's best to book ahead. There's a free accommodation booking service in the tourist office (☎ 051 648 7607).

Albergo Pallone Via del Pallone 4 ☎ 051 421 0533, ⓦ albergopallone.it. Basic but clean place in a somewhat unattractive building. Rooms are a bit clinical, but it has a friendly hostel feel and good staff. No breakfast. Double **€59**

Hostel San Sisto-Due Torri Via Viadagola 5 & 14 ☎ 051 501 810, ⓦ ostellodibologna.com. A 25min bus ride from town (#93 from Via Dei Mille or Via Irenenio from 6am–8pm, every 30min; at night take bus #21/B from across the road from the station or Via Marconi, hourly 8pm–12.40am; the hostel's stop is San Sisto). This large friendly HI hostel is in a quiet location well out of the centre. It has big dorms, a sitting room and lots of outdoor space. Dorm **€18**, double **€46**

Panorama Via Livraghi 1 ☎ 051 221 802, ⓦ hotel panoramabologna.it. Friendly mother-and-daughter-run

17

place. Located near Piazza Maggiore, rooms are spacious and bright and some have lovely views over the hills. They also have a 4-bed room. Double €75, 4-bed room per person €25
★ **Pensione Marconi** Via Marconi 22 ☎ 051 262 832, ⓦ pensionemarconi.it. This one-star doesn't look particularly inviting, but the 44 rooms inside are clean if basic. Ask for a room at the back, as it's on a major road. Double €68

EATING

There's a central Coop supermarket at Via Garibaldi 1, 5min south of Piazza Maggiore, as well as some great food markets: the Mercato delle Erbe at Via Ugo Bassi 25 is a covered produce market, while the lively street markets that cram Via Drapperie and Via Orefici, just off Piazza Maggiore, are perfect for snacks and picnics. Many cheap restaurants are in the popular student streets around Piazza Verdi.
AF Tamburini Via Drapperie 2. This renowned deli, its ceiling thick with hanging sausages and hams, sells no end of picnic food. The deli also has an indoor self-service restaurant that does pastas at €5. Mon–Sat 8.30am–8pm, Sun 10am–6.30pm.
Altero Via dell'Indipendenza 33. This popular chain of pizza takeaways does excellent square-shaped pizza by the slice (€2). Sun–Thurs 9am–12.30am, Fri until 1.30am, Sat until 2.30am.
Il Doge Via Caldarese 5. Backstreet pizzeria close to the Due Torri which doles out pizzas for around €7, as well as regional specialities. Tues–Sun noon–3pm & 7pm–midnight.
ITIT Lago Resighi 2f. Modern coffee and sandwich establishment which has great comfy seating and cheap sandwiches. Daily 8am–8pm.
Osteria al 15 Via Mirasole 13. A lovely old-fashioned trattoria with no menu (the waiter recites the day's specials), enormous portions and very fair prices. Full meal €15. Mon–Sat 7.30pm–midnight.

DRINKING

One of the cheapest and liveliest areas is the pub-and-bar-lined Via Zamboni, where the university students hang out. It is also worth heading to Via Mollini, Via Righi and Via dei Pratello for a more local feel.
Bounty Risto Pub Via Delle Moline 6ab. This place does a good value *aperitivo* buffet and has cheap lunchtime deals with dishes at around €6. Daily noon–3am.
English Empire Via Zamboni 24/a. A lively English-style pub; during happy hour (daily 7–9pm), the *aperitivo* buffet is sufficient to make up dinner. Jamming sessions every Mon night 7–10pm. Beer €4. Mon–Fri 11am–3am, Sat & Sun opens at 3pm.
La Scuderia Piazza Verdi 2. Occupying a former stable block on a rough-and-ready square, this huge bar is aimed squarely at students, with occasional live acts, cheap drinks and plenty of room to dance. Mon–Sat 6.30pm–2am.

★ **Mutenye Bar** Via Del Pratello 44. A bit of a jaunt from the centre, but the reward is an unfussy tourist-free bar that has a great choice of beers. Most people stand on the small pavement outside. Happy hour 5.30–8.30pm. Daily 5pm–3am.

PARMA

PARMA is an extremely pleasant town, with dignified streets, large green spaces, a wide range of good restaurants and an appealing air of provincial affluence. The home of Parmesan and Parma ham also offers plenty to see, not least the works of two key late Renaissance artists – Correggio and Parmigianino.

WHAT TO SEE AND DO

Piazza Garibaldi is the fulcrum of Parma, and its cafés and surrounding alleyways are liveliest at night. The mustard-coloured **Palazzo del Governatore** flanks the square, behind which stands the Renaissance church of **Madonna della Steccata**. Inside there are frescoes by a number of sixteenth-century painters, notably Parmigianino. It's also worth visiting the **Duomo**, on Piazza del Duomo in the northeast of the city centre, to see the octagonal **Baptistery** (daily 9am–12.30pm & 3–6.45pm; €6), considered to be Benedetto Antelami's finest work, built in 1196. Frescoes by Correggio are in the **Camera di San Paolo** (Tues–Sun 8.30am–1.30pm; €2), in the former Benedictine convent off Via Melloni, a few minutes' walk north.

East of the cathedral square, it's hard to miss Parma's biggest monument, the **Palazzo della Pilotta**, begun for Alessandro Farnese in the sixteenth century and rebuilt after World War II bombing. It now houses the city's main art gallery, the **Galleria Nazionale** (Tues–Sun 8.30am–1.30pm; €6), whose extensive collection includes more works by Correggio and Parmigianino. The grassy area around the Palazzo is a popular place for a picnic. If you've had enough of all things cultural and fancy checking out some shopping streets, stroll down the wide and laidback **Strada della Repubblica**, or alternatively people-watch from a café on Via Farini, take a walk along the river or escape the heat of the day at the Parco Ducale.

ARRIVAL AND DEPARTURE

By train Parma's train station is a 15min walk from Piazza Garibaldi and most of the buses in the city pass through it; bus #8 is the most direct.

Destinations Bologna (every 30min; 1hr–1hr 30min); Florence (frequent; 1hr 30min–2hr); La Spezia (frequent; 2hr); Milan (frequent; 1hr 30min); Padua (hourly; 2hr 30min; change at Bologna); Torino (frequent; 3hr–3hr 30min; some change at Milan); Venice (every 30min; 3–4hr; change at Bologna or Brescia).

INFORMATION

Tourist office Via Melloni 1a (Tues–Sat 9am–7pm; Mon 9am–1pm & 3–7pm; Sun 9am–1pm; ☎ 0521 218 889, ⓦ turismo.comune.parma.it).

Internet Moving People, Borgo Santa Brigida 7 (Mon–Fri Sat 10am–1.30pm & 3–8.15pm; €1.50/hr). There's free wi-fi in Parma city centre. Ask the tourist office to connect you.

Festivals and events Events include the annual Verdi festival in October (ⓦ teatroregioparma.org or ask at the tourist office), held at the Teatro Regio on Via Garibaldi (☎ 0521 039 300), while in summer (normally July) the city hosts the wonderful Sotto Il Cielo festival, a month-long music and dance celebration (ⓦ comune.parma.it or ask at the tourist office).

ACCOMMODATION

Albergo Amorini Via Gramsci 37 ☎ 0521 983 239. Near the nightlife of Strada D'Azeglio and a 5min walk from the Parco Ducale, this one-star hotel isn't anything special, but it is cheap, cheerful and opposite a large supermarket. Double €65

Foresteria Delle Colonne Via Malfald Di Savoia 7a ☎ 0521 924 368, ⓦ solaresdellearti.it. An arts foundation that offers simple accommodation. To get here take bus #2 from the Teatro Regio to the *capolinea* (the end of the line) and head right – it's round the back of the building opposite the theatre. Reception open 8pm–midnight. Dorm €18

★ **La Pilotta Room & Breakfast** Strada Garibaldi 31 ☎ 0521 281 415, ⓦ lapilotta.it. Duck through the comically small entrance door to this B&B bang in the centre of Parma. Run by the jolly Clementina, rooms are large and clean. There is a kitchen, washing machine and a great balcony with lovingly tended cacti. March–Aug only. Double €65

Ostello della Gioventù Via San Leonardo 86 ☎ 0521 191 7547, ⓦ ostelloparma.it. Excellent large hostel with big rooms and helpful staff. A 25min walk from the centre, or take bus #2 or #13 from the train station to Centro Torri. Dorm €20, double €44

Parmigianino Nove Borgo del Parmigianino 9 ☎ 0521 570 589, ⓦ discovernaples.net/parma. Two tastefully decorated double rooms with en-suite bathrooms and small kitchen areas in the heart of town. Ideal for sightseeing on foot. Double €70

EATING

The more expensive restaurants and cafés are on Piazza Garibaldi, while the cheaper options are along the busy Via Farini. There's a supermarket (Billa) on Via M. D'Azeglio.

★ **Bottiglia Azzurra** Borgo Felino 63 ☎ 0521 285 842. The "Blue Bottle" offers great lunch deals and cosy upstairs dining. Owner Adriano also arranges piano concerts and displays local artwork throughout the year. Mon–Sat 11am–3pm & 6–11pm.

Il Gallo D'Oro Borgo Salina 3 (just off Via Farini) ☎ 0521 208 846. A bit touristy but serves superb unfussy local fare at inexpensive prices. Mains €8. Mon–Sat 7pm–1am.

La Prosciutteria Via Farini 9. Brilliantly stocked-up deli. The friendly staff here will soon have you loaded up with treats for the perfect picnic. Mon–Sat 8.30am–8pm, Sun 9am–1pm.

Sorelle Picchi Via Farini 28. Part of an establishment that includes an excellent deli, this restaurant specializes in cured meats; try the spectacular ravioli. Mains €10. Mon–Sat noon–3pm.

Tonic Via Nazaro Sauro 5 ☎ 0521 508 426. Run by the friendly Edward, this modern bar serves large pastas for great prices. They have regular indie nights. Pasta €6, mains €7. Wed, Thurs & Sun 6.30pm–1am, Fri & Sat until 2am.

DRINKING

In the evening, the best place to head to is lively Via Farini or Strada D'Azeglio, which has a buzzy, youthful atmosphere.

★ **Le Malve Café** Via Farini 12b. At night customers overflow into the streets from this popular hangout. During the day the purple seats outside are the perfect places to people-watch. Beer €4, cappuccino and snack €1.30. Daily 8am–1am.

Peter Pan Strada Luigi Carlo Farini 92. On weekends people of all ages head to this relaxed bar at the far end of Via Farini. Get there early to get tables outside or join the masses on the wide street. *Aperitivo* €7. Daily 7.30am–midnight, closed Sun afternoon.

Surfer's Den Via M. D'Azeglio 62/b. Although nowhere near the sea, this tiny place does feel like a beachside café. It draws a friendly crowd and serves good cocktails. Mon–Thurs 6pm–1am, Fri & Sat until 2am.

RAVENNA

RAVENNA's colourful sixth-century mosaics are one of the crowning

17

achievements of Byzantine art – and undoubtedly the main reason for visiting the town. The mosaics are the legacy of a quirk of fate 1500 years ago, when Ravenna briefly became capital of the Roman Empire, and can be seen in a day. The **Basilica of San Vitale**, ten minutes northwest of the centre, was completed in 548 AD. Its mosaics, showing scenes from the Old Testament and the life of Christ, are in the apse. Across from the basilica is the tiny **Mausoleo di Galla Placidia** (daily: April–Sept 9am–7pm; Oct–March 9am–5.30pm), whose mosaics glow with a deep-blue lustre. Galla Placidia was the daughter, sister, wife and mother of various Roman emperors, and the interior of her fifth-century mausoleum, whose cupola is covered in tiny stars, is breathtaking. East of here, on the Via di Roma, is the sixth-century basilica of **Sant'Apollinare Nuovo** (daily: April–Sept 9am–7pm; Oct–March 9am–5.30pm). Mosaics run the length of the nave, depicting processions of martyrs bearing gifts. Five minutes' walk up Via di Roma, the **Arian Baptistery** has a fine mosaic ceiling (daily: April–Sept 8.30am–7pm; Oct–March 9am–5.30pm; free). Ravenna does have other strings to its bow, including some lovely sandy beaches (take bus #70 from the station).

ARRIVAL AND INFORMATION

By train Ravenna's train station is a 5min walk from the centre.
Tourist office Via Salara 8 (April–Nov Mon–Sat 8.30am–7pm (6pm in winter), Sun 10am–6pm (4pm in winter).
Discount passes A combined ticket (€9.50) is valid for 7 days and covers most of Ravenna's sights; it's available from any of the participating museums. Opening times for all the sights (excluding those specified here) are daily 9am–5pm.

ACCOMMODATION

Hostel Dante Via Aurelio Nicolodi 12 ☎ 0544 421 164, ⓦ hostelravenna.com. A 15min walk east of the town centre, but you can take Metrobus Rosso from opposite the train station. The rooms are sparse, but there's friendly staff and a good, free breakfast. Open March–Nov. Dorm €20, double €52

EATING AND DRINKING

There are small delis near *Hostel Dante* (see above), which sell good picnic grub. For a drink, try one of the smart bars on Piazza del Popolo, but drinks here are expensive.
Babaleus Pizzeria Vicolo Gabbiani 7 ☎ 0544 216 464, ⓦ ristorantebabaleus.com. This cosy and traditional spot serves cheap meals (pizza €5) and does a good-value lunch buffet (€7). Their goose breast risotto is a speciality. Mon, Tues & Thurs–Sun noon–2.30pm & 7pm–midnight.

Central Italy

The Italian heartland of **Tuscany** is one mass of picture-postcard landscapes made up of lovely, walled hill-top towns and rolling, vineyard-covered hills. **Florence** is the first port of call, home to a majestic Duomo, the extensive Uffizi gallery and the elegant Ponte Vecchio. **Siena**, one of the great medieval cities of Europe, is also the scene of Tuscany's one unmissable festival – the Palio – which sees bareback horseriders careering around the cobbled central square, while **Pisa's** leaning tower, a feat of engineering against gravity, and intricately decorated cathedral justifiably attract hordes of tourists. To the east lies **Umbria**, a beautiful region of thick woodland and undulating hills; the capital, **Perugia**, is an energetic student-dominated town, while **Assisi** is famed for its gorgeous setting and extraordinary frescoes by Giotto.

FLORENCE

FLORENCE (Firenze) is undoubtedly the highlight of Tuscany. Its chapels, galleries and museums are works of art in themselves, and every corner brings you face to face with architectural splendour. Some of the most famous pieces in Western art are on display here, including Michelangelo's *David* in the Accademia and Botticelli's *Birth of Venus* in the Uffizi.

WHAT TO SEE AND DO

Florence's major sights are contained within an area that can be crossed on foot in a little over half an hour. From Santa Maria Novella train station, most visitors gravitate towards **Piazza del Duomo,** beckoned by the pinnacle of the dome. **Via dei Calzaiuoli**, which runs south from the Duomo, is the main catwalk of the Florentine *passeggiata*, a broad pedestrianized avenue lined with shops. It ends at Florence's other main square, the **Piazza della Signoria**, fringed on one side by the graceful late fourteenth-century **Loggia della Signoria** and dotted with statues, most famously a copy of Michelangelo's *David*.

The Duomo

The **Duomo** (Mon–Sat 10am–4.30/5pm, Sun 1.30–4.45pm) was built between the late thirteenth and mid-fifteenth centuries. The fourth-largest church in the world, its ambience is more that of a great assembly hall than of a devotional building. The seven stained-glass roundels, designed by Uccello, Ghiberti, Castagno and Donatello, are best inspected from a gallery that forms part of the route to the top of the dome (€6), from where the views are stupendous. Next door to the Duomo stands the **Campanile** (daily 8.30am–7.30pm; €6) begun by Giotto in 1334. As well as offering an impressive bird's-eye view of Florence, this contains several enormous bells and more than fifty intricately carved marble reliefs. Opposite, the **Baptistery** (Mon–Sat 11.15am–7pm, Sun 8.30am–2pm; €5), generally thought to date from the sixth or seventh century, is the oldest building in the city. Its gilded bronze doors were cast in the early fifteenth century by Lorenzo Ghiberti, and described by Michelangelo as "so beautiful they are worthy to be the gates of Paradise". Inside, it is equally stunning, with a thirteenth-century mosaic floor and ceiling and the tomb of Pope John XXIII, the work of Donatello and his pupil Michelozzo.

The Palazzo Vecchio

The tourist-thronged **Piazza della Signoria** is dominated by the colossal **Palazzo Vecchio**, Florence's fortress-like town hall (April–Sept daily 9am–midnight, Thurs closes 2pm; Oct–March daily 9am–7pm, Thurs closes 2pm; €6), begun in the last year of the thirteenth century as the

home of the Signoria, the highest tier of the city's republican government.

The Uffizi

Immediately south of the Palazzo Vecchio, the **Galleria degli Uffizi** (Tues–Sun 8.15am–6.50pm; booking advisable at ⓦfirenzemusei.it; €6.50 plus €4 booking fee) is the greatest picture gallery in Italy. Highlights include Filippo Lippi's *Madonna and Child with Two Angels* and some of Botticelli's most famous works, notably the *Birth of Venus*. While the Uffizi doesn't own a finished painting that's entirely by Leonardo da Vinci, there's a celebrated *Annunciation* that's mainly by him, and Michelangelo's *Doni Tondo*, found in Room 18, is his only completed easel painting.

Bargello

The **Bargello** museum (Tues–Sun 8.15am–1.50pm, closed first, second and fifth Sun, plus second and fourth Mon of month; €4, €7 during exhibitions) lies just northwest of the Uffizi in Via del Proconsolo. The collection contains numerous works by Michelangelo, Cellini and Giambologna. Upstairs is Donatello's sexually ambiguous bronze *David*, the first freestanding nude figure since classical times, cast in the early 1430s.

North: San Lorenzo

The church of **San Lorenzo** (Mon–Sat 10am–5.30pm, Sun 1.30–5.30pm; €3.50), north of Piazza del Duomo, has a strong claim to be the oldest church in Florence. At the top of the left aisle and through the cloisters, the **Biblioteca Medicea-Laurenziana** (Mon–Sat 9am–1.30pm; €3) was designed by Michelangelo in 1524; its most startling feature is the vestibule, a room almost filled by a flight of steps resembling a solidified lava flow. Just east of here, the **Accademia** (Tues–Sun 8.15am–6.50pm; €11 before 4pm, €10 after 4pm), Europe's first school of drawing, is swamped by people in search of Michelangelo's *David*. Finished in 1504, when the artist was just 29, and carved from a gigantic block of marble, it's an incomparable show of technical bravura.

17

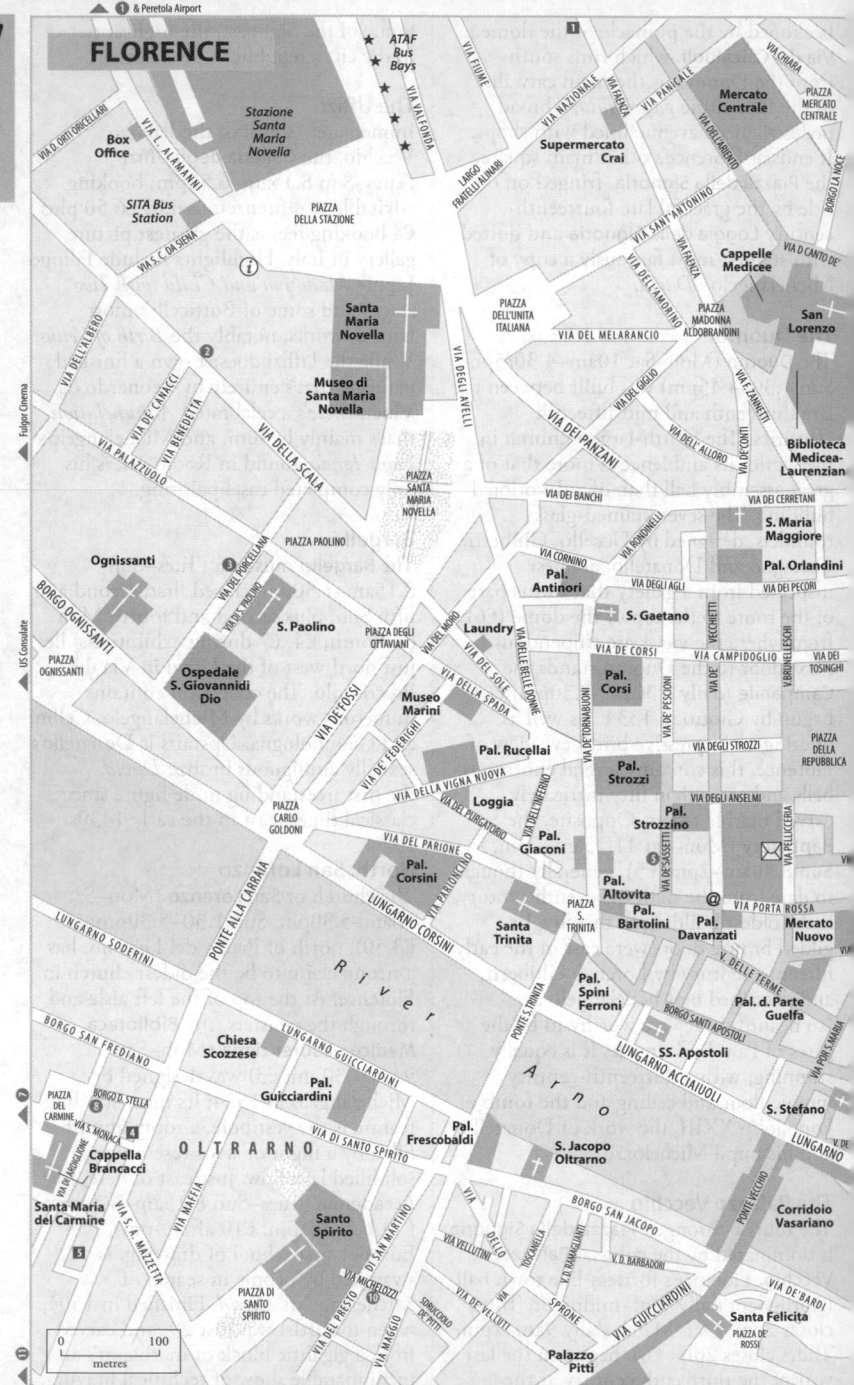

FLORENCE

& Peretola Airport

ATAF Bus Bays

Box Office

Stazione Santa Maria Novella

SITA Bus Station

VIA D. ORTI ORICELLARI
VIA L. ALAMANNI
VIA C. C. DA SIENA
VIA DELLA SCALA
VIA PALAZZUOLO
VIA DEL BENEDETTA
VIA DE' CANACCI
VIA DE' FOSSI
VIA BELLI ALBERO
BORGO OGNISSANTI
VIA DEL PORCELLANA
VIA DE' FEDERIGHI
VIA DELLA VIGNA NUOVA
VIA DEL PARIONE
VIA DE' MORO
VIA DEL MORO
VIA DELLA SPADA
VIA DELLE BELLE DONNE
VIA DEL SOLE
VIA DE' CORSI
VIA DE' PESCIONI
VIA DE' TORNABUONI
VIA DEL PURGATORIO
VIA DELL'INFERNO
VIA DEGLI STROZZI
VIA DEGLI ANSELMI
VIA PARIONCINO

PIAZZA DELLA STAZIONE
PIAZZA DELL'UNITÀ ITALIANA
PIAZZA SANTA MARIA NOVELLA
PIAZZA PAOLINO
PIAZZA DEGLI OTTAVIANI
PIAZZA CARLO GOLDONI
PIAZZA S. TRINITA
PIAZZA OGNISSANTI

VIA FIUME
VIA VALFONDA
VIA NAZIONALE
VIA FARNIA
VIA PANICALE
VIA CHIARA
VIA SANT'ANTONINO
VIA DELL'AMORINO
VIA FAENZA
VIA DEL MELARANCIO
VIA DEGLI AVELLI
VIA DEI PANZANI
VIA DELL'ALLORO
VIA DEI BANCHI
VIA CORNINO
VIA DEL GIGLIO
VIA DE' CONTI
VIA DEI CERRETANI
VIA NONDINELLI
VIA DEGLI AGLI
VIA DEI PECORI
VIA CAMPIDOGLIO
VIA DE' BRUNELLESCHI
VIA DEI TOSINGHI
VIA PORTA ROSSA
V. DELLE TERME
BORGO SANTI APOSTOLI
VIA POR S. MARIA
VIA DE' BARDI

Mercato Centrale
Supermercato Crai
Cappelle Medicee
San Lorenzo
Biblioteca Medicea-Laurenziana
S. Maria Maggiore
Pal. Orlandini
S. Gaetano
Pal. Corsi
Pal. Strozzi
Pal. Strozzino
Pal. Altovita
Pal. Bartolini
Pal. Davanzati
Mercato Nuovo

PIAZZA MERCATO CENTRALE
PIAZZA MADONNA ALDOBRANDINI
PIAZZA DELLA REPUBBLICA

BORGO LA NOCE
VIA D CANTO DE
VIA ZANETTI

Santa Maria Novella
Museo di Santa Maria Novella

Ognissanti
S. Paolino
Ospedale S. Giovanni di Dio
Museo Marini
Pal. Antinori
Pal. Rucellai
Loggia
Pal. Giaconi
Santa Trinita
Pal. Corsini
Pal. Spini Ferroni
SS. Apostoli
Pal. d. Parte Guelfa
S. Stefano

Fulgor Cinema
US Consulate

River Arno

PONTE ALLA CARRAIA
LUNGARNO SODERINI
LUNGARNO CORSINI
LUNGARNO GUICCIARDINI
LUNGARNO ACCIAIUOLI
LUNGARNO
PONTE S. TRINITA
PONTE VECCHIO

BORGO SAN FREDIANO
PIAZZA DEL CARMINE
BORGO D. STELLA
VIA S. MONACA
VIA DI SANT'AGOSTINO
VIA MAFFIA
VIA S. A. MAZZETTA
VIA DEL PRESTO
VIA MAGGIO
VIA MICHELOZZI
VIA DE' VELLUTI
VIA VELLUTINI
VIA DELLO
VIA DI SAN MARTINO
TOSCANELLA
V. D. BARBADORI
SPRONE
SDRUCCIOLO DE' PITTI
BORGO SAN JACOPO
VIA GUICCIARDINI
VIA DE' BARDI

OLTRARNO

Chiesa Scozzese
Pal. Guicciardini
Cappella Brancacci
Santa Maria del Carmine
Santo Spirito
Pal. Frescobaldi
S. Jacopo Oltrarno
Corridoio Vasariano
Santa Felicita
Palazzo Pitti

PIAZZA DI SANTO SPIRITO
PIAZZA DE' ROSSI

0   100
metres

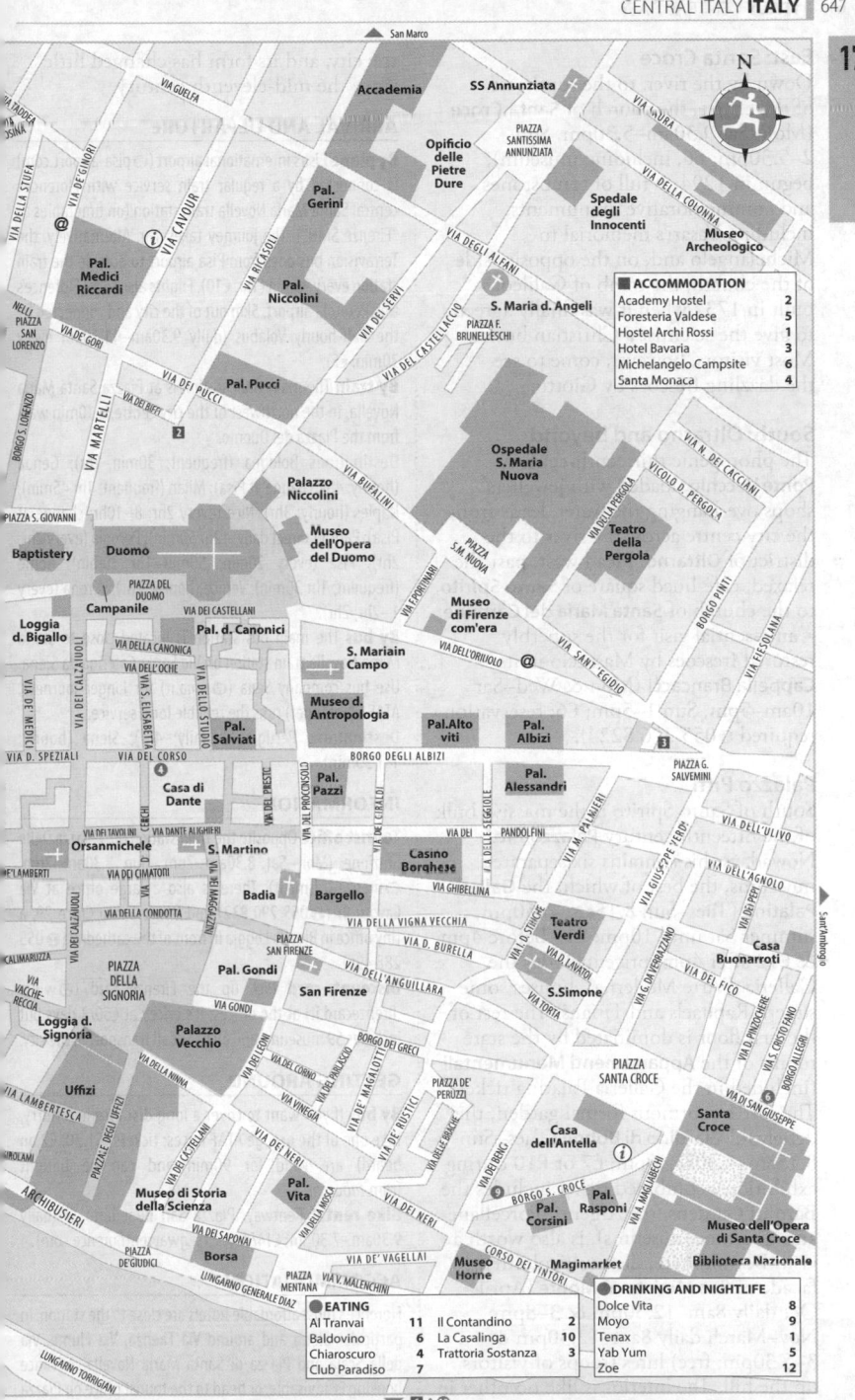

San Marco

N

ACCOMMODATION

Academy Hostel	2
Foresteria Valdese	5
Hostel Archi Rossi	1
Hotel Bavaria	3
Michelangelo Campsite	6
Santa Monica	4

EATING

Al Tranvai	11	Il Contandino	2
Baldovino	6	La Casalinga	10
Chiaroscuro	4	Trattoria Sostanza	3
Club Paradiso	7		

DRINKING AND NIGHTLIFE

Dolce Vita	8
Moyo	9
Tenax	1
Yab Yum	5
Zoe	12

17

East: Santa Croce

Down by the river, to the southeast of the centre, the church of **Santa Croce** (Mon–Sat 9.30am–5.30pm, Sun 2–5.30pm; €6, including museum), begun in 1294, is full of tombstones and commemorative monuments, including Vasari's memorial to Michelangelo and, on the opposite side of the church, the tomb of Galileo, built in 1737 when it was finally agreed to give the scientist a Christian burial. Most visitors, however, come to see the dazzling frescoes by Giotto.

South: Oltrarno and beyond

The photogenic thirteenth-century **Ponte Vecchio**, loaded with jewellers' shops overhanging the water, leads from the city centre across the river to the district of **Oltrarno**. Head west, past the relaxed, café-lined square of **Santo Spirito**, to the church of **Santa Maria del Carmine** – an essential visit for the superbly restored frescoes by Masaccio in its **Cappella Brancacci** (Mon & Wed–Sat 10am–5pm, Sun 1–5pm; €6; reservation required ☎055 276 8224).

Palazzo Pitti

South of Santo Spirito is the massive bulk of the fifteenth-century **Palazzo Pitti**. Nowadays this contains six separate museums, the best of which, the **Galleria Palatina** (Tues–Sun 8.15am–6.50pm, summer Sat until 10pm; €13 before 4pm & €12 after 4pm, price includes the Galleria d'Arte Moderna), houses some superb Raphaels and Titians. The rest of the first floor is dominated by the state rooms of the **Appartamenti Monumentali** (included in the Galleria Palatina ticket). The Pitti's enormous formal garden, the delightful **Giardino di Boboli** (Tues–Sun 8.15am–4.30/7.30pm; €7 or €10 during exhibitions; combined ticket includes the Bardini Gardens, the Argenti, Porcellane and Costume museums), is also worth a visit. Beyond here, the multicoloured facade of **San Miniato al Monte** (April–Oct daily 8am–12.30pm & 3–8pm; Nov–March daily 8am–12.30pm & 3–5.30pm; free) lures troops of visitors up the hill. The interior is like no other in

the city, and its form has changed little since the mid-eleventh century.

ARRIVAL AND DEPARTURE

By plane Pisa's international airport (ⓦ pisa-airport.com) is connected by a regular train service with Florence's central Santa Maria Novella train station (on timetables as "Firenze SMN"). The journey takes 1hr. Alternatively, the Terravision bus goes from Pisa airport to outside the train station every 90min (1hr; €10). Flights also serve Florence's tiny Peretola airport, 5km out of the city and connected by the half-hourly Volabus (daily 9.30am–11.30pm every 30min; €5).

By train The main train station is at Piazza Santa Maria Novella, in the northwest of the city centre, a 10min walk from the Piazza del Duomo.

Destinations Bologna (frequent; 30min–1hr); Genoa (hourly; 4hr; change at Pisa); Milan (frequent; 1hr 45min); Naples (hourly; 3hr); Nice (every 2hr; 8–10hr; change at Pisa); Paris (1 direct daily; 12hr 50min); Perugia (every 2hr; 2hr); Pisa (every 20min; 50min–1hr 30min); Rome (frequent; 1hr 30min); Venice (hourly; 2hr); Verona (every 1–2hr; 2hr).

By bus The main bus station is located close to Santa Maria Novella train station on Via Santa Caterina da Siena. Use bus company Sena (ⓦ sena.it) for longer journeys. ATAF (ⓦ ataf.net) runs the reliable local service.

Destinations Perugia (1 daily; 4hr); Siena (hourly; 1hr 30min).

INFORMATION

Tourist office Opposite the train station on 4 Piazza Della Stazione (Mon–Sat 8.30am–7pm, Sun 8.30am–2pm; ⓦ firenzeturismo.it). There is also a large office at Via Cavour 1r (☎055 290 832) and Borgo Santa Croce 29, a tiny office in Bigallo Loggia in front of the cathedral (☎055 288 496).

Discount card Pick up the Firenze card (ⓦ www .firenzecard.it) at the offices; it's pricey at €50/3 days but includes 59 museums and all use of all transport in the city.

GETTING AROUND

By bus If you want to cover a long distance in a hurry, take one of the orange ATAF buses; tickets (€1.20, €2 on board) are valid for 90min and can be bought from *tabacchi*.

Bike rental Rentway, Piazza San Benedetto 1r (daily 9.30am–7.30pm; €14/day; ⓦ segwayrentflorence.com).

ACCOMMODATION

Florence's most affordable hotels are close to the station, in particular along and around Via Faenza, Via Fiume, Via della Scala and Piazza di Santa Maria Novella. Advance booking is advisable, or head to the tourist office on Piazza

Della Stazione where there is a hotel booking office inside the same building.

Academy Hostel Via Ricasoli 9 ☎ 055 239 8665, ⓦ academyhostel.it. Situated just a short walk from the Duomo, many of the city sights can be reached on foot from this hotel. The rooms and common areas are clean, modern and bright. Dorm €38

Foresteria Valdese Via dei Serragli 49 ☎ 055 212 576, ⓦ istitutogould.it/foresteria. A charming hostel in a religious institute, where many of the generously proportioned rooms have en-suite bathrooms and large terraces – book early. Double €56

★ **Hostel Archi Rossi** Via Faenza 94r ☎ 055 290 804, ⓦ hostelarchirossi.com. Lively, arty and ultra-efficient hostel right by the station with a superb private garden. Cheap evening meals are available. There are also free pizza and pasta nights and free daily walking tours. Dorm €28

★ **Hotel Bavaria** 26 Borgo degli Albizi ☎ 055 234 0313, ⓦ hotelbavariafirenze.it. This wonderful hotel in a sixteenth-century palace has gigantic rooms (room 14 is the largest), stacks of relaxing sitting areas and is a stone's throw from the Duomo. Double €57

★ **Michelangelo Campsite** Piazzale Michelangelo, Viale Michelangelo 80 ☎ 055 681 1977, ⓦ ecvacanze.it. Centrally located campsite with great views. There's also a restaurant and a late-night disco. Walking distance from city centre. Per person plus tent €15.30

Santa Monaca Via Santa Monaca 6, Oltrarno ☎ 055 268 338, ⓦ ostellosantamonaca.com. Very popular hostel in a converted fifteenth-century convent. Located on the southern side of the Arno, it's a 15min walk from the train station. Guests can watch opera at the church next door for only €10 (March–Oct). Dorm €18

EATING

The best place to find picnic food and snacks is the Mercato Centrale, just east of the train station, or Mercato Ambroglio. Both markets close at 2pm. Supermarkets include Il Centro on 57r at Borgo Degli Albizi and the Spar and City supermarkets near the dell'Oriuolo.

Al Tranvai Piazza T. Tasso 14/r ☎ 055 225 197, ⓦ altranvai .it. Named after the tramcar that used to pass nearby, *Al Tranvai* serves good, inexpensive Florentine specialities. Arrive early or book ahead before the locals fill the place. Gnocchi €7. Mon–Sat noon–2.30pm & 7–10.30pm.

Baldovino Via San Giuseppe 22r ☎ 055 241 773, ⓦ baldovino.com. Smart trattoria just off the Piazza Santa Croce that serves an excellent *bistecca Fiorentina*. Pizza €7.50. The tiny *Baldobar* next door serves breakfast. Tues–Sun 7am–1am.

Chiaroscuro Via del Corso 36r ☎ 055 214 247, ⓦ chiaroscurofirenze.it. This small buzzy café serves great coffee. Drinks in-house are very expensive so it might be

best to take them away; takeaway coffee €1.50. Daily 7.30am–9.30pm.

★ **Club Paradiso** Via dell'Orto 24 ☎ 055 223 955. Relax and enjoy the hospitality of the chatty and friendly owner Andrea at this simple restaurant serving great food at low prices. Main meals €6. Mon–Fri noon–2pm & 7–11pm, Sat 7–11pm.

Il Contandino Via Palazzuolo 69–71r ☎ 055 238 2673. This small place is an excellent choice for lunch. For €11 you get a 2-course set lunch, water and wine (€12.50 set dinner). Set meals: lunch noon–5pm; dinner 5–9.40pm. Mon–Fri noon–9.40pm.

La Casalinga Via Michelozzi 9r ☎ 055 218 624, ⓦ trattorialacasalinga.it. People are willing to queue a long time for a table at this great-value trattoria that serves old-style family Italian cooking. Pasta €6. Mon–Sat noon–2.30pm & 7–10pm.

★ **Trattoria Sostanza** 25 Via Porcellana ☎ 055 212 691. Affectionately known as "the trough", this is where the real Florentines have been going for the best *bistecca* (€25) in town since 1869. A simple, no-frills affair, with hearty portions of superlative food. Booking recommended. Mon–Fri 12.30–2pm & 7.30–9.45pm.

DRINKING AND NIGHTLIFE

Mercato Centrale, just east of the train station, has some of Florence's cheapest bars.

Dolce Vita Piazza del Carmine 5 ☎ 055 284 595, ⓦ dolcevitaflorence.com. Trendy cocktail and wine bar that also stages small-scale art exhibitions. Live music every Wed & Thurs. Cocktails €8. Mon–Sat 11am–3am, Sun 5pm–3am.

Moyo Via del Benci 23r ☎ 055 247 9738, ⓦ moyo.it. This chilled-out café and bar on a busy street serves great cocktails; food on offer includes good breakfasts and lunchtime salads, and drinks with buffet until 2am. Large beer/cocktail €6. Food served till 5pm. Daily 8am–2/3am.

Tenax Via Pratese 46 ⓦ tenax.org. Bus #29 or #30. The city's biggest club and one of its leading venues for new and established bands, playing an eclectic mix of indie, trance, modern pop and old classics. Fri & Sat 9.30pm–4am.

Yab Yum Via de' Sassetti 5r ☎ 055 215 160, ⓦ yab.it. City-centre club near the Duomo, playing new dance music. Mon–Sat from 8pm.

Zoe Via Dei Renai 13 ☎ 055 243 111, ⓦ zoebar.it. Atmospheric, chic and modern cocktail bar, with small-scale painting exhibitions, outdoor seating and snack food during the day. Cocktails €7. Daily 8am–3am.

ENTERTAINMENT

For listings information, call in at the box office, Via Delle Vecchie Carceri 50 (☎ 055 210 804), or consult *Firenze Spettacolo* (€2), the *Informa Città* or the *Florentine* (available at the tourist offices).

17

Festivals and events Free concerts and events take place around Florence throughout the summer – see the tourist office (see p.648) for details. In May the Maggio Musicale (ⓦmaggiofiorentino.com) puts on concerts, gigs and other events throughout the city, while the Festa di San Giovanni (June 21–24; ⓦfierasangiovanni.it) sees the city's saint honoured with a massive fireworks display.

DIRECTORY

Consulates UK, Lungarno Corsini 2 ☎055 284 133; US, Lungarno A Vespucci 38 ☎055 266 951, ⓦflorence .usconsulate.gov.

Exchange The city is full of ATMs and exchange bureaus; there is one at 7 Piazza Santa Croce.

Hospitals Santa Maria Nuova, Piazza Santa Maria Nuova 1 ☎055 27 581; ⓦasf.toscana.it. English-speaking doctors are on 24hr call at the Tourist Medical Service, Via Roma 4 ☎055 475 411; ⓦmedicalservice.firenze.it.

Internet Internet Train is at Portarossa, Via Porta Rossa 38r and Via dell'Oriuolo 40r (ⓦinternettrain.it). Also Euro Bangla International on Via Ginori 59r (€1.50/hr).

Police Via Zara 2 ☎055 49 771.

Post office Via Pellicceria 3 (Mon–Sat 8.30am–12.30pm & 3–6pm).

PISA

The Leaning Tower in **PISA** is an iconic image, yet its stunning beauty is often underrated, with its intricate carvings appearing as though they are icing details on a very large wedding cake. It's set alongside the **Duomo** and **Baptistery** on the manicured grass of the lovely **Campo Piazza dei Miracoli**, whose buildings date from the eleventh and twelfth centuries, when Pisa was one of the great Mediterranean powers. Beyond this pretty square, the city synonymous with Galileo, Shelley and Byron may lack the polish of a Siena or a Florence but it is still definitely worth a meander along its charming narrow streets.

WHAT TO SEE AND DO

Leaning Tower

Perhaps the strangest thing about the **Leaning Tower** (daily: April–Sept 8.30am–8.30pm; rest of year times vary; €18; it is advisable to book ahead at ⓦopapisa.it/boxoffice), begun in 1173, is that it has always tilted; subsidence disrupted the foundations when it had reached just three of its eight storeys. For

PISA'S FESTIVALS

Pisa is known for its **Gioco del Ponte**, usually held on the last Sunday in June, when teams from the north and south banks of the river stage a series of "battles", including pushing a seven-tonne carriage over the Ponte di Mezzo. But the town's most magical event is the **Luminara** on June 16, when buildings along the river are festooned with candles to celebrate San Ranieri, the city's patron saint.

the next 180 years a succession of architects was brought in to try to correct the tilt, until 1350 when the angle was accepted and the tower completed. Eight centuries after its construction, it was thought to be nearing its limit, and the tower, supported by steel wires, was closed to the public in the 1990s – though it's open for visits once again now that the tilt (and 3.9m overhang) has been successfully halted.

Duomo

The **Duomo** (daily: April–Sept 10am–8pm; rest of year times vary; free) was begun a century earlier than the Tower, its facade – a delicate balance of black and white marble, and tiers of arcades – setting the model for Pisa's highly distinctive brand of Romanesque. The third building of the Miracoli ensemble, the circular **Baptistery** (daily: April–Sept 8am–8pm, rest of year times vary; €5), is a slightly bizarre mix of Romanesque and Gothic, embellished with statues (now largely copies) by Giovanni Pisano and his father Nicola. The originals are displayed in the Opera del Duomo **museum** (daily: April–Sept 8am–8pm; rest of year times vary; €5) to the east of the Piazza del Duomo.

Camposanto

Along the north side of the Campo Piazza is the **Camposanto** (daily: April–Sept 10am–8pm; rest of year times vary; €5), a cloistered cemetery built towards the end of the thirteenth century. Most of its frescoes were destroyed by Allied bombing in World War II, but two masterpieces survived relatively unscathed in the Cappella Ammanati – a fourteenth-century *Triumph of Death*, and *The Last Judgement*, a ruthless catalogue of horrors painted around the time of the Black Death.

ARRIVAL AND DEPARTURE

By plane Pisa's airport (ⓦpisa-airport.com) is only 1km from the city centre. The best way to the city is by bus. The LAM Rossa (single €1.10; ⓦwww.cpt.pisa.it) leaves every 10–15min to all major points in the city, including the train station.

By train Pisa's picturesque train station is south of the centre on Piazza della Stazione, a 30min walk from Campo dei Miracoli. Take bus LAM Rossa for the 10min journey to the Leaning Tower.

Destinations Florence (every 15min; 1hr–1hr 30min); Lucca (every 30min; 25min); Siena (frequent; 1hr 45min).

By bus A bus shuttles between Florence and Pisa airport (hourly; 1hr 10min).

INFORMATION

Tourist office 14 Piazza Vittorio Emanuele II (Mon–Sat 9am–7pm, Sun 9am–4pm; ☎050 42 291, ⓦpisaunicaterra.it) and at the airport (daily 9.30am–11.30pm; ☎050 502 518).

Discount card A tourist ticket (€9) gives admission to most of Piazza dei Miracoli's sights and museums, but not the Leaning Tower. Available from the main ticket office at Campo Piazza dei Miracoli.

Internet Koine on 5 Via G Carducci (Mon & Fri 10am–8pm, Tues–Thurs 10am–10pm & Sun 2–10pm).

ACCOMMODATION

Campeggio Torre Pendente Viale delle Cascine 86 ☎050 561 704, ⓦcampingtorrependente.it. Large, well-maintained campsite 1km west of Campo Piazza dei Miracoli, with a restaurant, shop and large outdoor swimming pool. Open March–Nov. Per person, plus tent and car **€35**

HI Hostel Via Phillppo Filippo Corridoni 29 ☎0505 201 841, ⓦhihostels.com. An excellent modern hostel a 5min walk from the train station. Great courtyard and facilities. Take advantage of the free walking tours of the city daily (except Mon) at 9am. Dorm **€15**

Hotel Galileo Via S. Maria 12 ☎050 402 21. Excellent budget choice only a short walk from the Tower. Staff speak English. Double **€48**

★ **Michele Guest House** Via Vespucci 103 ☎333 701 483, ⓦguest-house.it. Run by photographer Michele, this excellent B&B has luxurious rooms full of his work. Take advantage of the owner's extensive knowledge of the area. Double **€60**

EATING

Avoid eating around the Tower if you can, as prices here are sky-high for tourists. Most restaurants close on Sundays in Pisa. The best area for restaurants is around the Piazza delle Vettovaglie, and there are fruit markets around Via D. Cavalca.

Caffeteria delle Vettovaglie Piazza delle Vettovaglie 33. Trendy bar-restaurant with a different menu every day. Mains €8. Mon–Sat noon–3pm & 7pm–midnight.

La Bottega del Gelato Piazza Garibaldi. Great *gelato* and a convenient pit stop midway between the station and the Duomo; eat perched on the wall by the river. Daily 10.30am–1am.

Osteria dei Cavalieri Via San Frediano 16. Tucked away behind Piazza dei Cavalieri, this restaurant boasts a great menu and wine list. Pasta dishes €8–9. Mon–Fri 12.30–2pm & 7.45–10pm, Sat 7.45–10pm.

Pizzeria il Montino Via del Monte 1. Super-value pizzeria that serves generous pizzas. It is worth queuing for a table at this popular restaurant. Mon–Sat 10.30am–3pm & 5.30–10.30pm.

Vineria di Piazza Piazza delle Vettovaglie 13. Good soups at decent prices. Soup and fresh bread €6. Mon–Sat 11am–2.30pm & 6.30–10.30pm.

SIENA

SIENA, 60km south of Florence, is the perfect antidote to its better-known neighbour. Self-contained behind excellently preserved medieval walls, its cityscape is a majestic Gothic attraction that you can roam around and enjoy without venturing into a single museum. During the Middle Ages, Siena was one of the major cities of Europe – the size of Paris, it controlled most of southern Tuscany and developed a highly sophisticated civic life, with its own written constitution and a quasi-democratic government.

WHAT TO SEE AND DO

The **Campo** is the centre of Siena in every sense: the main streets lead into it, the Palio (see box, p.653) takes place around its café-lined perimeter, and it's the natural place to gravitate towards. It deserves its reputation as one of Italy's most beautiful squares, and taking a picnic onto the red stones to watch the shadows move around the square is a good way to while away an afternoon.

The Palazzo Pubblico

The **Palazzo Pubblico** (daily 10am–6/7pm) – with its 107m-high bell tower, the **Torre del Mangia** – occupies virtually the entire south side of the square, and although it's

17

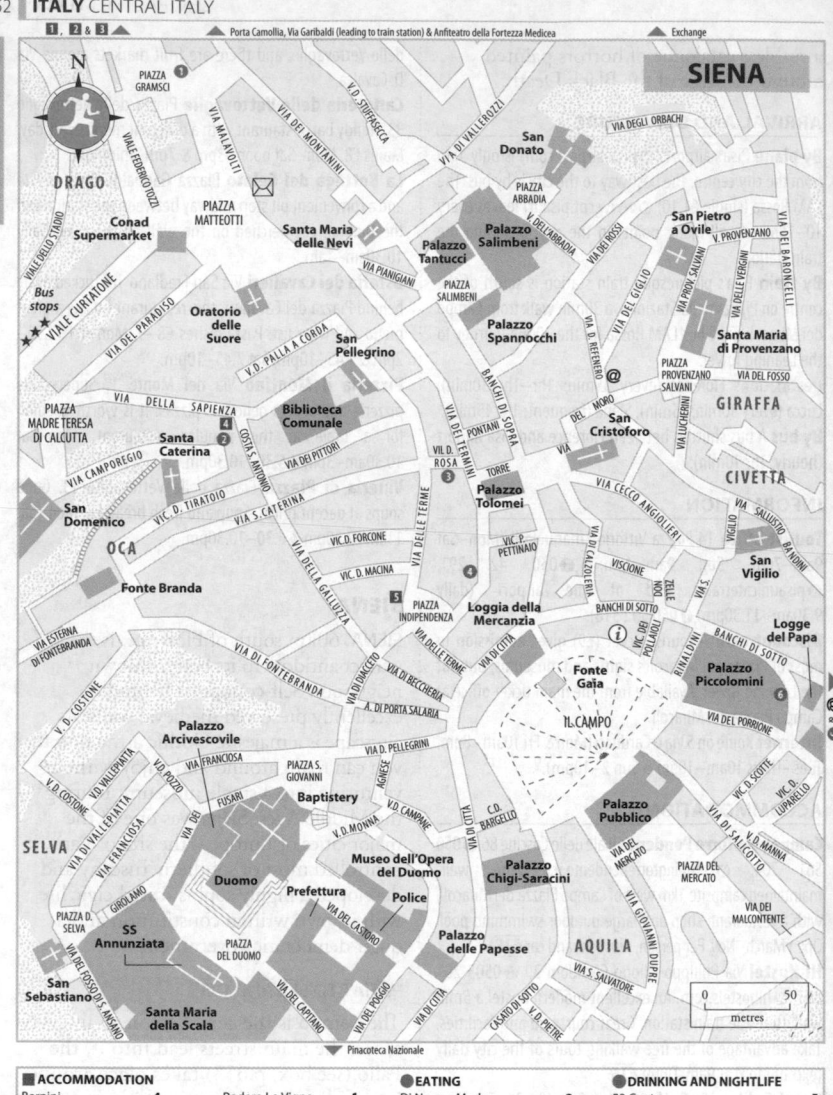

Porta Camollia, Via Garibaldi (leading to train station) & Anfiteatro della Fortezza Medicea | Exchange

SIENA

■ ACCOMMODATION				● EATING		● DRINKING AND NIGHTLIFE	
Bernini	4	Podere Le Vigne	1	Di Nonno Mede	2	53 Cento	5
La Perla	5	Siena HI Hostel	2	Il Ristoro del Papa	6	Barone Rosso	4
Lo Stellino	3			Osteria Da Trombicche	3	The Dublin Post	1

still in use as Siena's town hall, its principal rooms have been converted into a museum (€8, students €4.50), frescoed with themes integral to the secular life of the medieval city.

Around the Campo

Between buildings at the top end of the Campo, the fifteenth-century **Loggia di Mercanzia**, built as a dealing room for merchants, marks the intersection of the city centre's principal streets. From here **Via Banchi di Sotto** leads east to the **Palazzo Piccolomini** and on into the workaday quarter of **San Martino**. From the Campo, Via di Città cuts west across the oldest quarter of the city, fronted by some of Siena's finest private *palazzi*. At

THE SIENA PALIO

The **Siena Palio** is the most spectacular festival in Italy, a minute-and-a-half-long bareback horse race around the Campo contested twice a year (July 2 at 7.45pm and Aug 16 at 7pm) between the seventeen ancient wards – or *contrade* – of the city. Even now, a person's *contrada* frequently determines which churches they attend and where they socialize. There's a big build-up, with trials and processions for days before the big event, and traditionally all Sienese return to their *contrada* the night before the race; emotions run too high for rivals to be together, even if they're husband and wife. The Palio itself is a hectic spectacle whose rules haven't been rewritten since the race began – thus, supposedly, everything is allowed except to gouge your opponents' eyes out. On occasions it can take up to an hour to even start the race due to false starts. For the best view, you need to have found a position on the inner rail by 2pm and to keep it for the next seven hours. Beware that toilets, shade and refreshments are minimal, the swell of the crowd can be overwhelming, and you won't be able to leave the Campo for at least two hours after the race. If you haven't booked a hotel room, reckon on staying up all night (for more info see ⓦ ilpalio.org).

the end of the street, Via San Pietro leads to the **Pinacoteca Nazionale** (Mon 9am–1pm, Tues–Sat 8.15am–7.15pm, Sun 9am–1pm; €4), a fourteenth-century palace housing a roll call of Sienese Gothic painting.

The Duomo

Alleys lead north from here to the **Duomo**, completed to virtually its present size around 1215; plans to enlarge it withered with Siena's medieval prosperity. The building is a delight, its style an amazing mix of Romanesque and Gothic, delineated by bands of black and white marble on its facade. Inside, a startling sequence of 56 panels, completed between 1349 and 1547, features virtually every artist who worked in the city. Midway along the nave, the **Libreria Piccolomini** (daily 10.30am–5.30/7pm; €4), signalled by Pinturicchio's brilliantly coloured fresco of the *Coronation of Pius II*, has superbly vivid frescoes.

Museums

Opposite the Duomo is the complex of **Santa Maria della Scala** (daily 10.30am–5.30pm; €6), the city's hospital for over eight hundred years and now a vast museum that includes the frescoed Sala del Pellegrinaio. The **Museo dell'Opera del Duomo** (daily 10.30am–5.30/7pm; €7), tucked into a corner of the Duomo extension, offers a fine perspective: follow the "Panorama dal Facciatone" signs to steep spiral stairs

that climb up to the top of the building; the views are sensational but the topmost walkway is narrow and scarily exposed.

ARRIVAL AND DEPARTURE

By train The train station is down in the valley 2km northeast of the centre; an escalator from the shopping centre opposite the train station makes reaching the centre easy – it arrives at Antiporto Di Camolia, at the end of Viale Vittoria Emmanuelle 11 and from here it is a pleasant 10min walk to the Campo.

Destinations Florence (hourly; 1hr 30min); Perugia (every 90min; 3hr); Pisa (every 30min; 1hr 50min); Rome (every 2hr; 3–4hr).

By bus Buses stop along Piazza Gramchi, by the Basilica of San Domenico, and are much faster and more frequent from Florence than the trains (for which change at Empoli). See ⓦ sitabus.it for more information.

Destinations Florence (hourly; 90min); San Gimignano (hourly; 1hr; on Sun the journey involves a change at Poggibonsi).

FESTIVALS

Open-air film festival **Cinema in Fortezza** runs from the end of June until the beginning of September. Screenings of the films, varying from slapstick American comedies and world arthouse to old Italian classics, begin at 9.45pm at the Anfiteatro della Fortezza Medicea (€5; ⓦ cinemanuovopendola.it). There are also a number of open-air jazz concerts (ⓣ0577 271 401, ⓦ sienajazz.it) and wonderful operas held in different evocative settings all over Siena and the surrounding areas (ⓦ chigiana.it).

17

INFORMATION

Tourist office Piazza del Campo 56 (April–Oct daily 9.30am–6pm; Nov–March Mon–Sat 9.30am–5.30pm, Sun & public hols 9.30am–12.30pm; ☏ 0577 280 551/283 040, ✆ terresiena.it). You can also book train tickets here.

Discount passes If you plan on doing a lot of sightseeing, there is a whole host of combined ticket options ranging from €10–17. Ask at the tourist office for more details. The free Terre di Siena card offers discounts in many shops, restaurants and hotels.

ACCOMMODATION

In summer, Siena gets ridiculously booked up; it's worth phoning ahead for accommodation, or booking rooms at the Siena Hotels Promotion at Piazza Madre Theresa Di di Calcutta 5 (☏ 0577 288 084, ✆ hotelsiena.com).

★ **Bernini** Via della Sapienza 15 ☏ 0577 289 047, ✆ albergobernini.com. Charming one-star hotel run by a friendly family; the views from the huge windows and wonderful breakfast terrace are breathtaking. Midnight curfew. Double with shared bathroom €65, double with en suite €85

La Perla Piazza Independenza 25 ☏ 0577 747 144, ✆ hotellaperla.com. Small, one-star *pensione* in a great central location. Rooms 26 and 28 are the newest and best, but be warned they are reached by a steep spiral staircase. Double €70

Lo Stellino Via Fiorentina 95 ☏ 0577 51 987, ✆ sienaholidays.com. Pretty hotel with beautifully decorated rooms, next to the HI hostel, with kitchen facilities and a garden. Double €75

★ **Podere Le Vigne** Via Tufi 56 ☏ 0577 286 952, ✆ poderelevigne.it. Picturesque B&B in a typical Tuscan farmhouse a 20min walk from the centre. There is lots of outdoor space to enjoy and the charming Federica also offers cooking lessons. Take bus #54 from the centre. Double €65

Siena HI Hostel Via Fiorentina 89 ☏ 0577 52 212, ✆ ostellosiena.com. A friendly and comfortable hostel. It is 1.5km northwest of the centre; take bus #10 from the train station or Piazza Gramsci, or bus #15 from Piazza Gramsci. If you're coming from Florence, ask the bus driver to let you off at "Lo Stellino". Midnight curfew. Dorm €22

EATING

There is a weekly market at Fortezza Medici every Wednesday. For good picnic supplies try Conad supermarket on Piazza Matteotti, the shopping arcade or one of the many pizza takeaway outlets.

Di Nonno Mede Via Camporegio 2119 ☏ 0577 247 966. Popular pizzeria (pizza €5.50) down a quiet street near San Domenico Basilica. The views from the terrace are unbeatable. Sun–Mon noon–2.30pm & 7–10.30pm.

Il Ristoro del Papa Logge del Papa 1/3 ☏ 0577 284 062. Between Banchi di Sotto and Bia Via del Porrione, this

friendly, unpretentious pizzeria (pizza €6.50) and restaurant has an outdoor seating area and a lively atmosphere. Mon–Sat 12.30–3pm & 7.30pm–midnight.

Osteria Da Trombicche Via delle Terme 66 ☏ 0577 288 089. Small, cosy place with two tables outside; serves delicious home-made pasta (€6) in big brown bowls. Look out for the porcupine on the wall. Mon–Sat 11am–3pm & 5.30–10pm.

DRINKING AND NIGHTLIFE

The lively bars around the Campo, though a bit pricier than elsewhere, are open until late and drinks come with great snacks early in the evening.

53 Cento Viale Pietro Toselli 19 ☏ 0577 280 349. A welcoming bar-cum-restaurant-cum-café: you can enjoy anything from cream-filled cakes in the morning to a glass of champagne in the evening. A fixed-price menu is available at €10. Mon–Wed 8am–1am, Thurs & Fri until 3am, Sat 5pm–3am.

Barone Rosso Via Dei Termini 9 ☏ 0577 286 686. This fun bar is a hit with locals and tourists alike. At weekends local musicians strike up a tune. Daily 9pm–3am.

The Dublin Post Piazza Gramsci 20/21 ☏ 0577 289 089. This Irish pub is right next to the bus station and has three wonderfully cosy rooms and outdoor seating; beer €3. Daily noon until late.

DIRECTORY

Exchange Piazza Tolomei 4 (Mon–Sat 9.30am–7pm).

Internet Netrunner at Via Pantaneto 54 (Mon–Sat 10am–10pm, Sun 3–8pm; €4/hr); Refe Nero, Via Del Refe Nero 18 (Mon–Fri 10am–7.30pm, Sat 9.30am–5pm; €1.70/hr). Discounts with the Terre di Siena card (see above).

Post office Piazza Matteotti 37 (Mon–Fri 8.15am–7pm, Sat 8.15am–1.30pm).

SAN GIMIGNANO

One of the best-known villages in Tuscany, **SAN GIMIGNANO**'s skyline of towers, framed against the classic rolling hills of the Tuscan countryside, has justifiably caught the tourist imagination, and in high season can get uncomfortably busy. The little hill town was a force to be reckoned with in the Middle Ages: it had a large population of fifteen thousand but was hit hard by the Black Death and never quite recovered – today there's half that number.

You can walk across the town in fifteen minutes and around the walls in an hour. The main entrance gate, facing the bus terminal on the south side of town, is **Porta San Giovanni**, from where **Via San**

Giovanni leads to the town's interlocking main squares, **Piazza della Cisterna** and **Piazza del Duomo**. The more austere Piazza Duomo, off to the left, is flanked by the **Collegiata Cathedral** (April–Oct Mon–Fri 10am–7.10pm, Sat 10am–5.10pm, Sun 12.30–7.10pm; Nov–March Mon–Sat 10am–4.40pm, Sun & public hols 12.30–4.40pm; buy tickets at the office on Piazza Luigi Recori €3.50), frescoed with Old and New Testament scenes. The **Palazzo del Popolo** next door (daily: April–Sept 9.30am–7pm; Oct–March 11am–5.30pm; €5, includes Tower, Pinoteca and Palazzo Communale) gives you the chance to climb the 218 steps of the **Torre Grossa**, the town's highest surviving tower. North from Piazza Duomo, **Via San Matteo** is one of the grandest and best preserved of the city streets, with quiet alleyways running down to the walls. The small **Wine Museum** (daily March–Oct 11.30am–6.30pm; Nov–Feb closes 5.30pm; €3 per glass; wine-tasting evenings every Fri 6–8pm; €6 for drink and snacks; call ☎0577 941 267 for details); at the Parco della Rocca, is free to enter and you can enjoy a glass of wine at the adjoining bar while admiring some of the most spectacular views the town has to offer.

ARRIVAL AND DEPARTURE

By train The nearest train station is Poggibonsi, on the Siena–Empoli line; buses run to San Gimignano every hour (€1.60).

By bus Bus is the best way to get here from Poggibonsi, where the train stops. Bus tickets to Florence, Siena and Poggibonsi can be purchased at the tourist office (see below).

Destinations Florence (hourly; 1hr 20min); Poggibonsi (approx every 30min; 30min); Siena (hourly; 1hr).

INFORMATION

Tourist office Piazza del Duomo 1 (daily 9am–1pm & 3–7pm; ☎0577 940 008, ⓦsangimignano.com).

Discount passes Two combined museum tickets are available (€5 or €7.50) at any of the participating sites and at the tourist office.

Internet Café just outside Porta San Matteo (€2/20min).

ACCOMMODATION

Accommodation is expensive, and it's advisable to book in advance. The tourist office can offer assistance in booking

rooms, or try ⓦsienahotelspromotion.com. Finding house numbers in San Gimignano can be difficult as numbers are not clearly marked.

Foresteria del Monastero S Girolamo Via Folgore 30 ☎0577 940 573, ⓦmonasterosangirolamo.it. Run by Benedictine monks, this basic but excellent budget choice in a quiet monastery has comfortable rooms. Booking essential. Dorm €30

Il Boschetto Loc. Santa Lucia 38c ☎0577 940 352, ⓦwww.boschettodipiemma.it. Well-equipped campsite 3km downhill in the village of Santa Lucia. Has a swimming pool and on-site restaurant. €11 per person, plus €9 per tent

Le Vecchie Mura 15 Via Piandornella 15 ☎0577 940 270, ⓦvecchiemura.it. The most fabulous restaurant in San Gimignano (see below) also rents out private rooms with a/c, and dinner on your doorstep. Double €65

Milena Rossi Via Matteoti 3 ☎0577 941 609. A cheap option run by a mother and daughter, who also own Al Taglio pizza joint. Three-person apartment €70, double €55

EATING AND DRINKING

Take a picnic up to the Parco Della Rocca or the Parco di Montestaffoli and enjoy the views of the village and surrounding countryside.

★ **Di Vinorum** Piazza Cisterna 30/Via degli Innocenti 5. Despite the inauspicious entrance on the piazza, this is a lovely spot for an early evening drink. The bar is built into the town wall and has a cool stone interior. The outdoor tables have fantastic views. Wine from €3. Bruschetta from €5. Daily 11am–8pm, reduced opening times in winter.

"Gelateria Dondoli" Piazza Cisterna 1, ⓦgelateria dipiazza.com. Award-winning gelateria right on the piazza. Big queues build up here in high season for the former Gelato World Champion establishment. Easter–Oct daily 9am–midnight; March & Nov until 7pm.

★ **Le Vecchie Mura** Via Piandornella 15 ☎0577 940 270, ⓦvecchiemura.it. Romantic restaurant with wonderful views of the Tuscan hillside from its well-kept terrace. Booking essential. Only open for dinner 6–10pm, closed Tues.

Lucia & Maria Via San Matteo 55 17 ☎ 0577 940 379. The home-made cakes are a delight and the large portions of tasty bruschetta and hearty soups are good value at €6. Thurs–Tues 6.30am–8pm.

Pizza al Taglio Via San Giorgio 110. In a city full of pizza outlets this is ranks as one of the best takeaways; slice and soft drink €3. Daily 7pm–midnight.

PERUGIA

PERUGIA, the Umbrian capital perched on a hill, is an attractive medieval university town dominated by young people of every nationality, many at the Università per

17

Stranieri (Foreigners' University). It's known for its nightlife, people-watching, and chocolate – Italy's most famous chocolate, Perugini, is made here.

WHAT TO SEE AND DO

Perugia hinges on a single street, **Corso Vannucci**, a broad pedestrian thoroughfare. At the far end, the austere **Piazza Quattro Novembre** is backed by the plain-faced **Duomo San Lorenzo** (daily 7.30am–noon & 4–6.30pm) and is interrupted by the thirteenth-century Fontana Maggiore. The lavishly decorated **Collegio di Cambio** (Mon–Sat 9am–1pm & 2–5.30pm, Sun 9am–1pm; €2.60) sits at Corso Vannucci 25. This is the town's medieval money exchange, frescoed by the famous architect Perugino and said to be the most beautiful bank in the world. The Palazzo dei Priori houses the **Galleria Nazionale di Umbria** (daily 8.30am–7.30pm, closed first Mon of each month; €3.25), one of central Italy's best galleries, whose collection includes statues by Cambio, frescoes by Bonfigli and works by Perugino. **Via dei Priori** is a lovely, winding, cobbled street that bends gently through the rambling white buildings. This leads down to Agostino di Duccio's colourful **Oratorio di San Bernardino**, whose richly embellished facade is by far the best piece of sculpture in the city. On the southern side of town, along Corso Cavour, the cloisters of the large church of **San Domenico** hold the **Museo Archeologico Nazionale dell'Umbria** (Mon 2.30–7.30pm, Tues–Sun 8.30am–7.30pm; €2), home of one of the most extensive Etruscan collections around.

ARRIVAL AND DEPARTURE

By train Trains arrive well away from the centre of Perugia on Piazza Vittorio Veneto; buses go from outside the station to Piazza Italia or Piazza Matteotti (20min). Tickets can be bought from the ticket stand for €1.50.
Destinations Assisi (hourly; 20min); Florence (every 2hr; 2hr); Rome (frequent; 2–3hr).
By bus Buses arrive at Pian di Massiano; take the Minimetrò (see above) up to Piazza Italia. Umbria Mobilita (Ⓦapmperugia.it) are the biggest bus operators in Perugia and the surrounding area. Bus #TD, #TS, #R or #G run from the bus terminal to the train station.

THE UMBRIA JAZZ FESTIVAL

One of the most prestigious jazz events in Europe, the **Umbria Jazz Festival** has featured stars such as Dizzy Gillespie and Keith Jarrett. It takes place in July, and while the main events tend to be in Perugia, there are offshoots – performances and workshops that often make use of stunning churches, courts and open-air spaces – in towns across the region (see Ⓦumbriajazz.com).

Destinations Siena (1 daily; 1hr 30min).
By minimetrò The light-rail system takes people up and down the hill of Perugia in 12min (daily; every 2–3min; Mon–Sat 7am–9.20pm, Sun 8.30am–8.30pm, €1.50).

INFORMATION

Tourist office Piazza Matteotti 18 (daily 9am–7pm; ☎ 075 573 6458, Ⓦ perugiaonline.com).
Internet 100diecicaffe at Via Pascoli 23/c (Mon–Fri 7.30am–8pm; €1.50/hr).

ACCOMMODATION

★ **Hotel Rosalba** Via del Circo 7 ☎ 075 572 8285, Ⓦ hotelrosalba.com. Standing alone and impossible to miss with its pink facade and the eccentric and friendly owner runs a great hotel with fresh rooms in a quiet but central location. Double **€70**
Ostello Della Gioventù Via Bontempi 13 ☎ 075 572 2880, Ⓦ www.ostello.perugia.it. Welcoming hostel 2min from the Duomo, with a 1am curfew. Closed between 9.30am and 4pm. Dorm **€18**
San Ercolano Via Del Bovaro 9 ☎ 075 572 4650, Ⓦ santercolano.com. Great budget option, this small hotel in the old town has small clean rooms and friendly staff. Double **€80**
Spagnoli Via Cortonese 4 ☎ 075 501 1366, Ⓦ perugiahostel.com. Located near the train station, this basic hostel is a handy option to save the walk up the hill into town. Dorm **€18**

EATING

Being a student city there are plenty of cheap cafés and takeaways. Co-op supermarket is on Piazza Matteotti 15, while Mercato Coperto (Mon–Sat 8am–2pm) is a covered market off Piazza Matteotti, next to the information centre.
Antica Salumeria Granieri Amato Piazza Matteotti/ Via Fani. This stall has been selling hot roast pork sandwiches since 1916 (€2.50). Mon–Sat 10am–9pm.
★ **Dal Mi'Cocco** Corso Garibaldi 12 ☎ 075 573 2511. They keep it beautifully simple at this local favourite. The

PERUGIA FESTIVALS

As well as its jazz festival, Perugia has a stream of eclectic events throughout the year that are well worth looking up in advance. In mid-October there's a **chocolate festival** (Weurochocolate .com) that lasts for ten days, while the **Christmas market** is splendid in its scale and opulence. See Wregioneumbria.eu for details.

four-course meal costs €13 and the portions are large and hearty. It's best to book. No credit cards. Tues–Sun 1–3pm & 8–10.30pm.

Il Gufo Via della Viola 18 📞075 573 4126, Wosteriailgufo .wordpress.com. Run by Italian and German chefs, the "Owl" tavern specializes in using seasonal ingredients in their unpredictable menu that changes daily. Wed–Sun 6.15pm–1am, Sat & Sun also open noon–3pm.

Mediterranea Piazza Piccinino 11/12 📞075 572 1322. Perugia's best pizzeria and possibly Umbria's finest. It serves a vast selection of tasty, cheap pizzas (€6). Booking recommended. Daily noon–2.30pm & 7.30pm–midnight.

DRINKING AND NIGHTLIFE

Frequented by both local and international students, Perugia's nightlife is varied and lively. If you are not a fan of students, nocturnal Perugia is not for you.

★ **Il Birraio** Via Del Prome 18 📞075 572 5932. This eclectic pub and brewery serves a large selection of beer and food in differently styled rooms that cater for all moods. Tues–Sun 7.30pm–2am.

La Terrazza Via Matteotti, next to tourist office. Outdoor bar with sweeping views over the Umbrian countryside. Cocktails from €5. Open late May–Sept. Daily 11am–2am.

Le Caffe Di Roma Piazza Matteotti 32. A great café for people watching, with outdoor seating; cappuccino only €1. Daily 7am–8pm.

L'Officina Borgo XX Gingro 56 📞075 572 1699. Tucked away so you hardly notice it, this modernist *enoteca's* centrepiece is a glass-walled kitchen. The staff are extremely friendly and the wine is fantastic. Glass of wine €3. Mon–Sat noon–3pm & 7.30–11pm.

Punto di Vista Viale dell'Indipendenza 2. Extremely popular bar with beautiful views of the rolling countryside and snowcapped peaks in the distance. Beer €4. Daily 5.30pm–2.30am; closed in winter.

ASSISI

ASSISI is Umbria's best-known town thanks to St Francis, Italy's premier saint and founder of the Franciscan order. It has a medieval hill-town charm and is easy to navigate around in just a few hours.

The **Basilica di San Francesco**, now restored to its former glory after a devastating earthquake in 1997, is at the end of Via San Francesco (daily April–Oct Upper Basilica 8.30am–6.45pm, Lower Basilica 6am–6.45pm; Nov–March both close 5.45pm). It houses one of the most overwhelming collections of art outside a gallery anywhere in the world. St Francis lies under the floor of the Lower Church, in a crypt only brought to light in 1818. The walls have been lavishly frescoed by artists such as Cimabue and Giotto, and the stained-glass windows cast a dim light that enhances the magical atmosphere. The Upper Church, built to a light and airy Gothic plan, is richly decorated too, with dazzling frescoes about the life of St Francis. A short trek up the steep Via di San Rufino leads to the thirteenth-century **Duomo** (Mon–Fri 7am–12.30pm & 2.30–7pm), which holds the font used to baptize St Francis.

ARRIVAL AND DEPARTURE

By train From the train station, there are half-hourly buses into town.

Tourist office Piazza del Comune 12 (Mon–Sat 8am–2pm & 3–6.30pm, Sun 9am–1pm; 📞075 813 8680)

ACCOMMODATION

Ostello della Pace 177 Via Di Valecchie 📞075 816 767, Wassisihostel.com. Run by a very friendly couple, this hostel is located on a beautiful hillside just below the town. Dorm €18

EATING

Il Duomo Via Porta Perlici 11 📞075 816 326, Wassisiduomo.com. This restaurant in a wonderful medieval building does tasty, stone-oven pizzas (€6) and set menus starting at €12.50. Daily noon–2.30pm & 6.30–11pm (closed Wed in winter).

Lanterna Via S. Rufino 39 📞075 812 385, Wlalanterna ristorantepizzeria.it. If you feel like splashing out, book a table at the romantic and candlelit pizzeria (pizzas €8, tourist menu €16–22). Daily 10am–3.30pm & 6–11pm.

Pizzeria Otello Ristorante Via S. Antonio 📞075 812 415. Great location opposite the church of Sant'Antonio and with outdoor seating. A pizza margherita will set you back just €4.90. Daily noon–2.30pm & 7–11pm.

17

Spoleto

SPOLETO is a tiny hill-top town adorned with small and winding cobbled streets, beautiful Romanesque churches and the remains of an ancient amphitheatre. **Piazza della Libertà** is where you will find the **Museo Archeologico** (daily 8.30am–7.30pm; €4), and where you can also glimpse the ancient arena. From here it's a short walk to the elegant **Duomo** (daily: April–Oct 8.30am–12.30pm & 3.30–7pm; Nov–March 8.30am–12.30pm & 3.30–5.30pm). Inside, the apse frescoes were painted by the fifteenth-century Florentine artist Fra Lippo Lippi – he died shortly after their completion amid rumours that he was poisoned for seducing the daughter of a local noble family. The **Ponte delle Torri**, a photo-favourite, is an astonishing piece of medieval engineering, best seen as part of a circular walk (allow around 5hr 30min) around the base of the **Rocca**. **Piazza del Mercato** and its surrounding streets are a great place to head for a spot of lunch, where there are numerous restaurants offering fixed-price lunch deals.

ACCOMMODATION

Albergo due Porte Piazza della Vittoria 5 ☎ 0743 233 666. If you're looking for somewhere close to the main sights, this hotel run by a cheery owner is a good option. It also offers a mountain bike rental service. Double **€55**
Villa Redenta 1 Via di Villa Redenta ☎ 0743 224 936, ⓦ villaredenta.com. Just a short walk from the station in the lower town, this fabulous villa in verdant surroundings is a haven of tranquillity. Double **€35**

EATING

Pizzeria Zeppelin Piazza della Libertà ☎ 0743 44 900. This fun and friendly pizzeria and snack bar offers cheap and tasty food in the centre of town. Daily 10.30am–9.30pm.
Trattoria del Festivale Via Brignone 6 ☎ 0743 220 993, ⓦ trattoriadelfestival.com. A short walk from Piazza della Libertà, this family-run establishment serves traditional local dishes. A two-course meal costs around €20. Mon–Wed & Fri–Sun noon–2.30pm & 7–10pm.

URBINO

URBINO boasted one of the most prestigious courts in Europe in the fifteenth century, and today the highlight of a visit to this hill-top town is the grand Palazzo Ducale and its impressive collection of Renaissance paintings.

The Palazzo Ducale was built by the extravagant Federico da Montefeltro, the fifteenth-century Duke of Urbino. It is now home to the excellent **Galleria Nazionale delle Marche** (Mon 8.30am–2pm, Tues–Sun 8.30am–7.15pm; €5). Among the paintings in the Appartamento del Duca is Piero della Francesca's strange *Flagellation* and the portrait of *The Mute* by Raphael, who was born in Urbino. The most interesting of the Palazzo's rooms is Federico's Studiolo, a triumph of illusory perspective.

Buzzy **Piazza della Repubblica** is a great place for lunch or a drink.

ARRIVAL AND DEPARTURE

By bus Urbino is hard to reach; the best options are either indirect bus from Perugia (€13; ⓦ umbriamobilita.it) or from Pesaro (€2.75; ⓦ viaggiruocco.eu). All buses stop in Borgo Mercatale; from here follow Via Mazzini to the city's main square the Piazza della Repubblica. From the piazza all the main sights are a steep but short walk away.
Destinations Perugia (daily; 1hr 50min); Pesaro (every 30min, last bus around 9.30pm; 1hr).

INFORMATION

Tourist office Via Puccinotti 35, opposite the Palazzo Ducale (Mon–Sat 9am–1.30pm & 2.30–5.30pm, closed Sun pm; ☎ 0722 2613, ⓦ urbinoculturaturismo.it.

FROM ITALY AND BEYOND

The main arrival and departure port on Italy's eastern coast is the transit town of **Ancona**, with ferries taking you to Croatia, Albania, Greece and Turkey. Ferries leave from Stazione Marittima, a few kilometres north of the train station (take bus #1). All of the ferry companies have ticket offices dotted around the port, plus there are dozens of agencies around town if these happen to be closed. Destinations include: Corfu, Greece (weekly; 15hr); Durrës, Albania (3 weekly in summer; 19hr); Igoumenitsa, Greece (daily; 15hr); Pátra, Greece (daily; 21hr); Split, Croatia (daily; 4hr 30min–10hr); Stari Grad, Croatia (July & Aug only; 2 weekly; 10hr); Vis, Croatia (weekly; 9hr); Zadar, Croatia (daily; 9hr).

17

ACCOMMODATION

Albergo Italia Corso Garibaldi 32 ☎0722 2701, ⓦalbergo-italia-urbino.it. In the heart of the town, this blandly decorated hotel has great views and a pretty courtyard and terrace where breakfast is served. Double **€80**

Hotel San Giovanni Via Barocci 13 ☎0722 2827, ⓦalbergosangiovanniurbino.it. A good, centrally located option. While the decor isn't up to much, the views are stunning. It has a pizzeria downstairs. Double **€46**

EATING AND DRINKING

Dolce Vita Piazza della Repubblica 16 ☎0722 320 711. This fun establishment has tables on the square. You can start your day here with a coffee or enjoy an organic burger later. Mon–Sat 7.30am–2am.

Pizzeria Il Buco Via Cesare Battisti 1. Translated as "the hole", this hole-in-the-wall serves tasty snacks such as *piadine* as well as pizza slices. Mon–Fri 9am–2pm & 5–8pm, Sat 9am–2pm.

Southern Italy

The Italian **south** (*mezzogiorno*) offers a decidedly different experience from that of the north; indeed, few countries are more tangibly divided into two distinct, often antagonistic, regions. **Naples** is the obvious focus of the south, an utterly compelling city just a couple of hours south of Rome. In the **Bay of Naples**, highlights are the resort of Sorrento and the island of **Capri**, crawling with tourists but beautiful enough to be worth your time, while the ancient sites of **Pompeii** and **Herculaneum** are Italy's best-preserved Roman remains. South of Naples, the **Amalfi Coast** is a contender for Europe's most dramatic stretch of coastline. In the far south, **Matera**, jewel of the Basilicata region, harbours ancient cave dwellings dug into a steep ravine. Puglia – the long strip of land that makes up the "heel" of Italy – boasts the Baroque wonders of **Lecce**, and is also useful for ferries to Greece and Croatia.

NAPLES

Wherever else you travel south of Rome, the chances are that you'll wind up in **NAPLES** (Napoli). It's the kind of city people visit with preconceptions, and it rarely disappoints: it is dirty and overbearing; it is crime-ridden; and it is most definitely like nowhere else in Italy – something the inhabitants will be keener than anyone to tell you. One thing, though, is certain: a couple of days here and you're likely to be as staunch a defender of the place as its most devoted inhabitants.

WHAT TO SEE AND DO

The area between the vast and busy Piazza Garibaldi, the city's transport hub, and Via Toledo, the main street a kilometre or so west, makes up the old part of the city – the **Centro Storico**, whose buildings rise high on either side of the narrow, crowded streets. South of here is the busy port, and, to the northwest, Naples' finest museums.

The Duomo

From Piazza Garibaldi, Via dei Tribunali cuts through to Via Duomo, where you'll find the tucked-away **Duomo**, a Gothic building from the early thirteenth century dedicated to San Gennaro, the patron saint of the city, martyred in 305 AD. Two phials of his blood miraculously liquefy three times a year – on the first Saturday in May, on September 19 and on December 16. If the blood refuses to liquefy, disaster is supposed to befall the city. The first chapel on the right as you walk into the cathedral holds the precious phials, as well as Gennaro's skull.

MADRE

A short walk up Via Duomo, Naples' superb modern art museum, **MADRE**, at Via Settembrini 79 (Wed–Mon 10am–7.30pm; €7, student €3.50; Mon free), shows off works by some big-name contemporary artists. The most prominent of these is by Francesco Clemente, a New York-based Neapolitan artist who created the huge, vibrant mural of Naples. The museum also holds works by the likes of Jeff Koons and Anish Kapoor, as well as a massive anchor – symbolizing the city's maritime roots – by Jannis Kounellis.

Spaccanapoli and around

Busy Via dei Tribunali and its parallel, Via San Biagio dei Librai – commonly known as **Spaccanapoli** – make up the heart of the old city and Naples' busiest

17

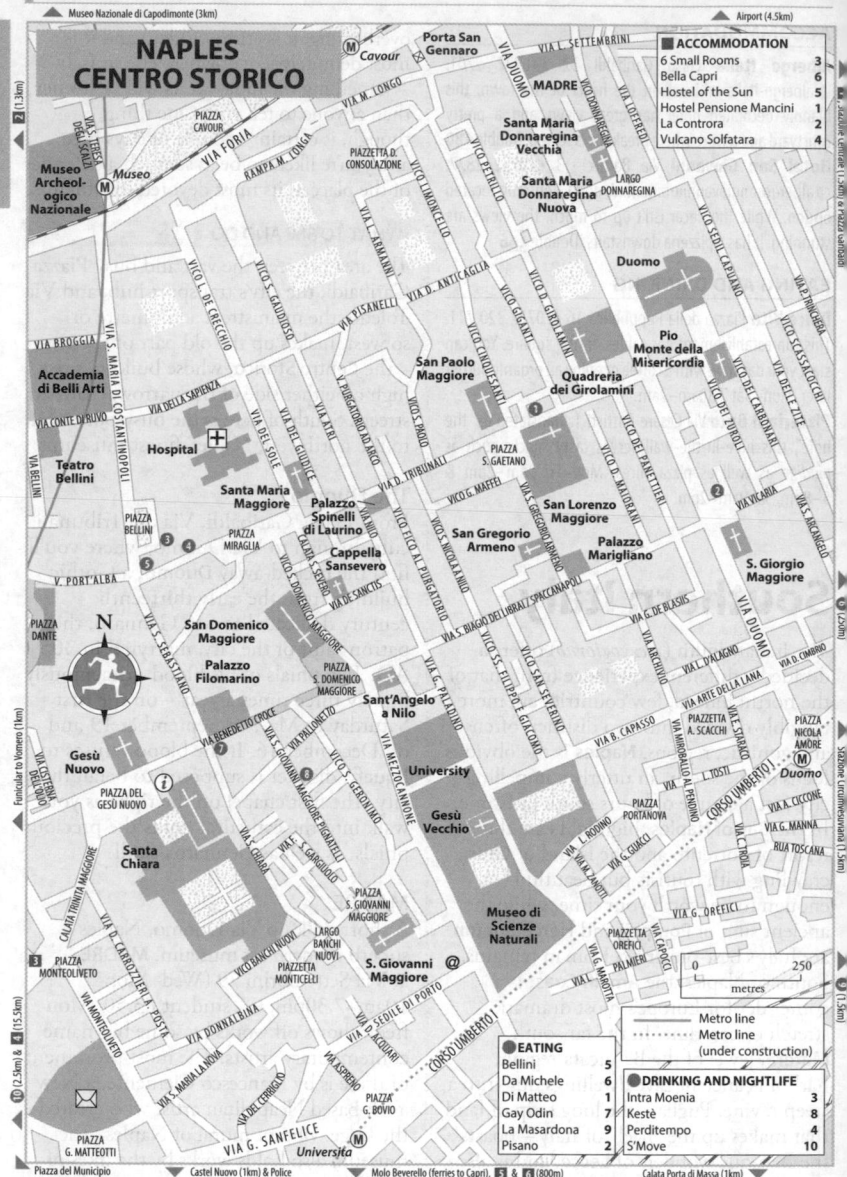

NAPLES CENTRO STORICO

▲ Museo Nazionale di Capodimonte (3km)　　　　　　　　　　▲ Airport (4.5km)

0 _____ 250
metres

——— Metro line
········· Metro line
(under construction)

and architecturally richest quarter. A maelstrom of hurrying pedestrians, revving cars and buzzing scooters, this is the best place to get a sense of the city and its inhabitants. At 253 Via dei Tribunali is the **Pio Monte della Misericordia** (Thurs–Tues 9am–2.30pm; €6, free audioguide), an unassuming jewel of a church thanks to its breathtaking altarpiece: Caravaggio's *Seven Works of Mercy* which elegantly juxtaposes warm acts of charity with ribald picaresque street life, reflecting something of Naples's own appeal. The picture gallery is well worth a visit, containing works by Francesco de Mura, Luca Giordano and others.

Gesù Nuovo and Santa Chiara

West up Spaccanapoli is the **Gesù Nuovo** church, distinctive for its lava-stone faeade, prickled with pyramids that give it an impregnable, prison-like air. Facing the Gesù Nuovo, the church of **Santa Chiara** is quite different, a Provençal-Gothic structure built in 1328 (and rebuilt after World War II). The attached **cloister** (Mon–Sat 9.30am–5.30pm, Sun 10am–2.30pm; €6, student €4.50), covered with colourful majolica tiles depicting bucolic scenes, is one of the gems of the city.

Castel Nuovo

A ten-minute walk south of Santa Chiara, **Piazza del Municipio** is a busy traffic junction that stretches down to the waterfront, dominated by the brooding hulk of the **Castel Nuovo**. Built in 1282 by the Angevins and later the royal residence of the Aragon kings, it now contains the **Museo Civico** (Mon–Sat 9am–7pm; €6), which holds periodic exhibitions – but it's the views from the top terrace that make the entrance fee worthwhile.

Palazzo Reale and around

Some 500m west of the castle, **Piazza del Plebiscito**, with its impressive sweep of columns, was modelled on Bernini's Piazza San Pietro in Rome. On one side of the square, the dignified **Palazzo Reale** (Thurs–Tues 9am–7pm; €4, student €3) was built in 1602 to accommodate a visit by Philip III of Spain. Upstairs, the first-floor rooms are sumptuously decorated with gilded furniture, *trompe-l'oeil* ceilings, and seventeenth- and eighteenth-century paintings.

Just beyond the castle, the opulent **Teatro San Carlo** is the largest opera house in Italy, and one of the most distinguished in the world. The cheapest seats you can book are €50 for opera, €35 for ballet.

Museo Archeologico Nazionale

Arrowing north from the Piazza del Plebiscito, Via Toledo leads to the **Museo Archeologico Nazionale** (Wed–Mon 9am–7pm; €8, student €4), home to the best of the finds from the nearby Roman sites of Pompeii (see p.664) and Herculaneum

(see p.664). The ground floor concentrates on sculpture, the mezzanine houses the museum's collection of mosaics, while upstairs, wall paintings from the villas of Pompeii and Herculaneum are the museum's other major draw. Don't miss the "secret" room of erotic Roman pictures and sculptures, once thought to be a threat to public morality.

Museo Nazionale di Capodimonte

The city's second major museum, the **Museo Nazionale di Capodimonte** (Thurs–Tues 8.30am–7.30pm; €7.50) is a bus ride away from town (#R4 from Via Toledo or #178 from the Museo Archeologico). The former residence of the Bourbon King Charles III, built in 1738, it has a huge and superb collection of Renaissance and Flemish paintings, including a couple of Brueghels, canvases by Perugino and Pinturicchio, an elegant *Madonna and Child with Angels* by Botticelli, and Lippi's soft, sensitive *Annunciation*.

Vomero

Vomero, the district topping the hill immediately above the old city, can be reached by funicular from Corso Vittorio Emanuele, west of the Gesù Nuovo, or Piazza Augusteo near the Teatro San Carlo. A five-minute stroll from the station, the star-shaped fortress of **Castel Sant'Elmo** (Wed–Mon 8.30am–7.30pm; €5) was built in the fourteenth century and hosts occasional exhibitions. Occupying Naples' highest point, its lovely views are only topped by those from the terraced gardens of the **Certosa e Museo di San Martino** (Thurs–Tues 8.30am–7.30pm; €6), a former Carthusian monastery. Now a museum, it contains seventeenth- and eighteenth-century Neapolitan painting and sculpture.

ARRIVAL AND DEPARTURE

By plane Capodichino airport (w gesac.it) is just north of the centre. The red-and-white official airport bus Alibus (every 20min; €3) connects the airport to Piazza Garibaldi and Piazza Municipio.

By bus Most long-distance, inter-regional buses and local buses use Corso Meridionale behind the train station by Piazza Garibaldi.

17

★ **TREAT YOURSELF**

If you're going to splurge on accommodation anywhere in Italy, Naples is the place: your money will go a lot further. Try, for example, **Donna Regina** (Via Settembrini 80; ☎081 446 799, ⓦdiscovernaples.net; double €93), run by a family of artists. A warm and welcoming B&B in a beautifully restored ex-convent, it has spacious, individually furnished rooms with period antiques and wonderfully high ceilings. The walls are jam-packed with books and paintings, giving a cosy touch, while the lively breakfast table adds to the convivial feel. Look at ⓦdiscovernaples.net for more boutique B&Bs in the city.

Destinations Assisi (2 daily; 5hr); Lecce (3 daily; 5hr 30min); Perugia (2 daily; 4hr 30min); Matera (2 daily; 4hr).
By ferry Ferries arrive at Calata Porta di Massa, and are connected with Molo Beverello by free shuttle bus. Hydrofoils dock at Molo Beverello, a short bus ride or a 15min walk from the centre.
Destinations Capri (10 daily; 1hr 20min); Palermo (2 daily; 8hr–10hr 30min).
Destinations Capri (every 30min–1hr; 40min); Sorrento (6 daily; 45min).
By train Trains arrive at Piazza Garibaldi, the main hub of all transport services.
Destinations Lecce (5 daily; 5hr 30min); Palermo (3 daily; 9hr 30min–11hr); Pompeii (from Stazione Circumvesuviana; every 30min; 40min); Rome (hourly; 1hr 10min–2hr 40min); Siracusa (3 daily; 8hr 30min–10hr 30min); Sorrento (from Stazione Circumvesuviana; every 30min; 1hr 5min; reach Amalfi by bus or ferry from Sorrento).

INFORMATION

Tourist office At the train station (daily 9am–8pm) and airport (daily 9am–7pm), but the main tourist office is at Piazza del Gesù Nuovo (Mon–Sat 9am–7pm, Sun 9am–2pm; ☎081 551 2701, ⓦinaples.it).
Discount cards If you are around for more than a day, invest in the Artecard (from €12; sold in the train station, museums and online at ⓦwww.campaniaartecard.it), which is valid on various combinations of city transport, along with free and discounted museum entrance.

GETTING AROUND

Tickets Buy tickets – valid on all city transport – from *tabacchi*. €1.30 tickets are valid for 1hr 30min, €3.70 ones for the day. A 24hr, Unico Costiera ticket also allows you to travel on SITA buses (to Amalfi, for example) and Circumvesuviana trains (for Pompeii). Prices vary

depending on your destination and cost less on weekends. Stamp tickets on board to validate them.
By bus and metro Walking is the best option in the centre, but an extensive bus and metro network is available for the footsore. Useful routes include #R2 between the port and station via Corso Umberto. Underground metros – indicated by a red ⓜ symbol – are fast but only run every 10min or so. Stops include Piazza Garibaldi (for the train station), Piazza Cavour, Piazza Dante and Piazza Vanvitelli in Vomero.
By funicular Funicular railways run up to Vomero and the suburbs of Chiaia, Mergellina and Monte Santo (€1.30).

ACCOMMODATION

6 Small Rooms Via Diodato Lioy 18 ☎081 790 1378, ⓦ6smallrooms.com. Located in a crumbling historical building, this small artsy hostel with quirky murals attracts a laidback boho crowd. Dorm €18, double €45
Bella Capri Via Melisurgo 4 ☎081 552 9494, ⓦbellacapri.it. Right by the port, this hostel offers private rooms with TV and a/c, and a selection of dorms, most with lockers. There's also a little kitchen for guests' use. Ten percent discount with this book. Dorm €21, double with shared bath €55, double with private bath €60
★ **Hostel of the Sun** Via Melisurgo 15 ☎081 420 6393, ⓦhostelnapoli.com. This fun hostel with lively staff has a chilled-out lounge area with board and computer games; dorms have lockers and a/c, while doubles are all equipped with TV and DVD player. There's a buzzing bar and staff organize plenty of tours in the area, including Vesuvius on horseback. Dorm €18, double with shared bath €60, double with private bath €70
Hostel Pensione Mancini Via Mancini 33 ☎081 553 6731, ⓦhostelpensionemancini.com. Family-run hostel right across from the station with one mixed and one female-only dorm; there's a kitchen, a/c in all rooms and free luggage storage. Ten percent discount with this book. Dorm €20, double with shared bath €50, double with private bath €70
★ **La Controra** Piazzetta Trinità alla Cesarea 231 ☎081 549 4014, ⓦlacontrora.com. Clean, funky hostel with a glass lift, modern kitchen and a leafy garden. Dorms all have lockers, individual reading lamps and sockets. Dorm €15, double €64
Vulcano Solfatara Via Solfatara 161, Pozzuoli ☎081 526 2341, ⓦsolfatara.it. Metro to Pozzuoli, then a 10min walk uphill. This well-equipped campsite, on the edge of a volcanic crater, has a swimming pool, minimarket and takeaway. €10 per person, plus €6.50 per tent, 2-person bungalows €54

EATING

Colourful produce markets are found all over the centre; one of the best (daily 8am–1pm) takes up the streets around Via Pignasecca, a few streets west of the Gesù Nuovo.

Bellini Via Costantinopoli 79-80 ⓦ ilbelliniristorante.it. This long-standing favourite serves exceptional *linguine al cartoccchio* – fresh clams, mussels, prawns and squid are cooked with tomato, herbs and pasta in a greaseproof paper bag, served with a little ceremony at your table (€12.50). Lunch only on Sun. Daily 9am–3.30pm & 7pm–1.30am.

Da Michele Via Cesare Sersale 1–3 ⓦ damichele.net. Historic pizzeria serving some of Naples' best pizzas: marinara, margherita or double margherita are the sole choices here, from €4. Arrive early as the queues can get epic (get a ticket from the cash desk), or order to take away if you can't wait. Mon–Sat 10.30am–11pm.

⭐ **Di Matteo** Via Tribunali 94. A must for a truly exceptional pizza (€3–6). Order a *frittatina* (€1) as you wait, a heavenly bundle of pasta, mince, peas, cheese and black pepper, deep-fried. Mon–Fri 8.30am–midnight.

Gay Odin Via Benedetto Croce 61 (plus other branches around the city) ⓦ gay-odin.it. This well-established chocolate shop offers a selection of superb ice creams whose many flavours were inspired by the 300-plus inventive chocolate fillings. €1.70 cup or cone. Mon–Thurs 9am–8.30pm, Fri & Sat 9am–11.30pm, Sun 10am–8.30pm.

La Masardona Via Giulio Cesare Capaccio 27. Truly local street food joint a few minutes from the train station specializing in authentic fried pizzas stuffed with tomatoes, pork scratchings and provola and ricotta cheese (€2); watch owner Enzo at work as he expertly kneads while his wife Anna fries, and enjoy the exquisite result. Tues, Wed, Fri, Sun 7am–3pm, Sat 6.30am–10pm.

⭐ **Pisano** Piazzetta Crocelle ai Mannesi 1. Authentic home-made cooking lovingly prepared by Concetta and Gennaro – just tell them your budget (meals €15–25) and a procession of exquisite dishes will flow to your table. Mon–Sat noon–3.30pm & 6.30–11.30pm.

DRINKING AND NIGHTLIFE

Most clubs close in July and August and move to the beach; the Neapolitans who remain congregate for a beer in the studenty bars around Piazza Bellini and Piazza del Gesù Nuovo.

Intra Moenia Piazza Bellini 70 ⓦ intramoenia.it. This café-cum-bar located in one of the city's most popular nightlife spots is dotted with knick-knacks, books and trinkets for sale, with Thurs jazz, fusion and bossanova sessions at 10pm. Cocktails (€7), beer and wine (both €4). Sun–Thurs 11am–2am, Fri & Sat until 3am.

Kestè Largo San Giovanni Maggiore Pignatelli 26–27 ⓦ keste.it. Fun little bar with tables spilling onto the square attracting a laidback crowd. DJs liven the scene on Wed & Fri plus there are weekly jazz, reggae and rock sessions. Aperitivo at 6.30pm; cocktails €5. Tues–Sun 6.30pm–2.30am.

Perditempo Via San Pietro a Maiella 8 ⓦ perditempodante.blogspot.co.uk. Tiny bar with stacks of new and used CDs and LPs, live music and a cool crowd. Daily 7pm–1.30am, Sat until 2.30am.

S'Move Vico dei Sospiri 10a. This institution in the heart of the lively Chiaia district attracts a hip young crowd who flock here for the cool atmosphere, funky tunes and great cocktails. Daily noon–3am.

DIRECTORY

Consulates UK, Via dei Mille 40 ☎ 081 423 8911; US, Piazza della Repubblica ☎ 081 583 8111.

Exchange At Stazione Centrale (daily 8am–8pm).

Hospital Ambulance ☎ 118; the Guardia Medica Permanente in Palazzo Municipio is open 24hr.

Internet D.M.G., Via Sedile di Porto 63 (Mon–Fri 9am–7pm; €1/hr).

Pharmacy At the train station (24hr).

Police ☎ 113. Main police station is at Via Medina 75 ☎ 081 794 1111.

Post office Piazza Matteotti Giacomo 2 (Mon–Fri 8am–6.30pm, Sat 8am–12.30pm).

THE BAY OF NAPLES

Of the islands that dot the bay, **Capri** is the best place to visit if you're here for a short time. **Sorrento**, the brooding presence of **Vesuvius** and the incomparable Roman sites of **Herculaneum** and **Pompeii** are further draws.

Vesuvius

Its most infamous eruption, in 79 AD, buried the towns and inhabitants of Pompeii and Herculaneum, and **VESUVIUS** has long dominated the lives of those who live on the Bay of Naples. It's still an active volcano – the only one on mainland Europe – and there have been hundreds of (mostly minor) eruptions over the years, the last in 1944 when 28 people died. Considered to be one of the world's most dangerous volcanoes, a future eruption would lead to the evacuation of nearly one million inhabitants who populate the surrounding area.

ARRIVAL AND DEPARTURE

By train and bus Catch the Circumvesuviana train to either Pompeii or Ercolano Scavi. From Pompeii then take the Busvia del Vesuvio bus to 1000m up the volcano (hourly between 9am & 5pm; €22 including entrance ticket). Alternatively, Vesuvio Express minibuses run from Ercolano Scavi (Ercolano; see p.664) train station roughly every half-hour (daily 9am–4pm; 20min; €10 return; ☎ 081 739 3666) to a car park and huddle of souvenir shops and cafés.

17

On foot The walk up to the crater from the bus stop takes about half an hour on marked-out paths. At the top (admission €10; students €8), the crater is a deep, wide, jagged ashtray of red rock emitting the odd plume of smoke. You can walk about halfway round (700m) while soaking in breathtaking sea views. See ⓦvesuviopark.it for information on trails.

Pompeii

Destroyed by Vesuvius, **POMPEII** (daily: 8.30am–7.30pm; ticket office closes 6pm; €11) was, in Roman times, one of Campania's most important commercial centres. Of a total population of twenty thousand, it's thought that two thousand perished in the great eruption of 79 AD, asphyxiated by the toxic fumes of the volcanic debris, their homes buried under several metres of ash and pumice. The full horror of their death is apparent in plaster casts made from the shapes their bodies left in the volcanic ash – gruesome, writhing figures, some with their hands covering their eyes.

Seeing the site will take you half a day at least. Entering from the Pompeii-Villa dei Misteri side, you come across the **Forum**, a slim open space surrounded by the ruins of some of the town's most important official buildings. North of here lies a small baths complex, and beyond, the **House of the Faun**, its "Ave" (Welcome) mosaic outside beckoning you in to view the atrium and the copy of a tiny bronze dancing faun. A few streets southwest, the **Lupanare** was Pompeii's only purpose-built brothel, worth a peek for its racy wall paintings. A short walk from the Porta Ercolano is the **Villa dei Misteri**, the best preserved of all Pompeii's palatial houses, which contains frescoes depicting the initiation rites of a young woman into the Dionysiac Mysteries, an orgiastic cult transplanted to Italy from Greece in the Republican era.

On the other side of the site, the **Grand Theatre** is still used for performances, as is the **Little Theatre** on its far left side. From here, it's a short walk to the **Amphitheatre**, one of Italy's most intact and also its oldest, dating from 80 BC.

Herculaneum

The town of **Ercolano** is the modern offshoot of the ancient site of **HERCULANEUM** (daily: April–Oct 8.30am–7.30pm; ticket office shuts 6pm; €11), situated at the seaward end of Ercolano's main street. A residential town destroyed by the eruption of Vesuvius on August 2, 79 AD, it's much smaller than Pompeii, and as such is a more manageable site – less architecturally impressive, but with better-preserved buildings. Highlights include the **House of the Mosaic Atrium**, with its mosaic-laid courtyard, the large baths complex and the **Casa del Bel Cortile**, which contains a group of skeletons, poignantly lying in the pose they died in.

ARRIVAL AND INFORMATION

By train Ercolano is a 15min hop on the train from Naples on the Circumvesuviana line (€2.10 one-way).
Tourist office Via IV Novembre 82 (Mon–Fri 8.30am–7pm, Sat 8.30am–6pm; ☎081 788 1243, ⓦwww.comune.ercolano.na.it).

SORRENTO

Topping the rocky cliffs close to the end of its peninsula, **SORRENTO**'s inspired location and pleasant climate have drawn travellers from all over Europe for two hundred years. Nowadays it caters mostly to the package-tour industry, but this bright, lively place retains its southern Italian roots. Accommodation and food, though not exactly cheap, are much better value than most of the other resorts along the Amalfi Coast, making it a good base from which to explore the area. Sorrento's centre, **Piazza Tasso**, makes a lively focus for the evening *passeggiata*. The town isn't well provided with beaches: most people make do with the rocks and a tiny, crowded strip of sand at **Marina Grande** – fifteen minutes' walk or a short bus ride from Piazza Tasso.

ARRIVAL AND DEPARTURE

By train Circumvesuviana trains run between Naples and Sorrento (every 30min; 1hr 5min; €4.10, price includes a consecutive metro/bus trip in Naples); the train station is a 5min walk from the centre.
By bus Buses run from outside the train station. Coaches connect the city to Naples Airport (6 daily; 1hr 30min; €10) and buses (every 45min; 1hr 40min; €3.80) to Amalfi (every 45min; 1hr 30min; €2.40) and Rome (1–2 daily; 4hr; €20).
By ferry The port is an uphill walk or short bus ride (buy tickets from *tabacchi*; €1.20) from the centre. Daily departures to Capri (4 daily; 25min; €14.70).

By hydrofoil There are connections to Naples (6 daily; 35min; €12.30) and Capri (every 30min–1hr; 20min; €18.30). Pricey jetfoils connect to Amalfi and Positano (? daily; €39.80 return).

INFORMATION

Tourist office Via de Maio 35, just off Piazza Sant'Antonino (June–Sept Mon–Fri 8.30am–7pm, Sun 9am–1pm; Oct–May Mon–Fri 8.30am–4.15pm; ☎ 081 807 4033, ⊕ sorrentotourism.com).

ACCOMMODATION

Camping Nube d'Argento Via del Capo 21 ☎ 081 878 1344, ⊕ www.nubedargento.com. A 15min walk south from Piazza Tasso up the main road, this campsite has a pool, restaurant, minimart with basic food provisions and wonderful sea views. Closed mid-Jan to mid-March. €12 per person, plus €6 per tent, two-person bungalows €70

⭐ **Seven** Via Iommella Grande 99, Sant'Agnello ☎ 081 878 6758, ⊕ sevenhostel.com. A 20min walk north of town or one stop north on the Circumvesuviana train. Set in a former monastery, this large modern hostel has clean and functional dorms, all with a/c, lockers, individual reading lamps and plugs; the views from the rooftop terrace with deckchairs are, quite simply, breathtaking. Dorm €22, double €80

Ulisse Via del Mare 22 ☎ 081 877 4753, ⊕ ulissedeluxe .com. More of a four-star hotel than hostel, "deluxe" *Ulisse* has sparkling rooms, all with a/c, satellite TV and private bath; there are only two dorms (one male, one female), so book way ahead. Guests have access to the spa next door. Dorm €25, double €80

EATING

⭐ **Da Filippo** Via San Renato 29 ⊕ ristorantedafilippo .com. Exceptional local cuisine with an emphasis on grilled meats, vegetables and fish. The *tagliata di manzo* (€16 for two) is one of the many favourites. *Primi* €6–13, *secondi* €9–20. Free hotel pick-up and drop-off. Fri–Wed 12.30–3pm & 7–11pm.

Mami Camilla Via Cocumella 4 ☎ 081 878 2067, ⊕ mamicamilla.com. Call before 6pm to book a four-course dinner at this cookery school for just €18.

Trattoria Da Emilia Via Marina Grande 62 ☎ 081 807 2720. Right on the seafront with wonderful views of Mount Vesuvius, this trattoria serves great fried local fish (€12) and spaghetti with mussels (€9). Daily noon–3pm & 7–10pm.

DRINKING AND NIGHTLIFE

The main hub of activity is on Piazza Tasso and Piazza Lauro. In summer, the clubbing action takes place at venues out of Sorrento, along the coast. Promoters distribute tickets from midnight onwards; clubs are a 10min taxi ride from here.

Chaplin's Pub Corso Italia 18. True Irish pub serving pints of lager (€5), Guinness and Magners (both €6) with major sporting events shown on screen. Soak up the booze with some fish and chips (€9). Daily 11am–3am.

Fauno Piazza Tasso 13 ⊕ faunonotte.it. Sorrento's only club attracts tourists and locals alike with its themed nights and weekly live music shows. No entry fee, but obligatory €10 spend on drinks. Daily 11.30pm–3am; Oct–March Sat only.

CAPRI

Rising from the sea off the far end of the Sorrentine peninsula, the island of **Capri** is the most sought-after destination in the Bay of Naples. During Roman times the Emperor Tiberius retreated here to indulge in debauchery; more recently the Blue Grotto and the island's remarkable landscape have drawn tourists in their droves. Capri is a busy and expensive place, but it's easy enough to visit as a day-trip (and there's no budget accommodation on the island). In July and August, however, you may prefer to give it a miss rather than fight through the crowds.

WHAT TO SEE AND DO

CAPRI TOWN is a very pretty place, with winding alleyways converging on the tiny main square of Piazza Umberto. The Giardini di Augusto give tremendous views of the coast below and the towering jagged cliffs above. Opposite, take the hairpin path, Via Krupp, down to **MARINA PICCOLA**, a huddle of houses and restaurants around a few patches of pebble beach – pleasantly quiet out of season, though in summer it's heaving. You can also reach the ruins of Tiberius' villa, the **Villa Jovis**, from Capri Town (first to fifteenth of the month Wed–Mon 11am–3pm; sixteenth to last day of the month Mon–Sat 11am–3pm; €2), a steep 45minute trek east. The site is among Capri's most exhilarating, with incredible views.

 ANACAPRI, the island's other main settlement, though less picturesque, is the starting point for some worthwhile excursions: from here a chairlift (daily: March–Oct 9am–5pm; Nov–Feb 9am–3pm; €10 return) carries you up 596m **Monte Solaro**, the island's highest point, where there's a pricey but picturesquely sited café. The island's most famous attraction, the **Blue Grotto**, is an

17

hour's trek down Via Lo Pozzo, but it's best to take a bus from the main square. At €12.50 it's a bit of a rip-off, with boatmen whisking visitors through the grotto in five minutes flat, but the intense, glowing blue of the cave is undeniably beautiful.

ARRIVAL AND DEPARTURE

By ferry Ferries and hydrofoils dock at Marina Grande, from where it's a 20min uphill walk or a short funicular ride (€1.80) to Capri Town, which perches on the hill above. Buses link the main centres – Marina Grande, Capri Town, Marina Piccola and Anacapri – every 10min (€1.80, or €8.60 for a day ticket).

INFORMATION

Tourist office At the port and at Piazza Umberto in Capri Town (June–Sept Mon–Sat 8.30am–8.30pm, Sun 9am–3pm; Oct–May Mon–Sat 9.30am–1.30pm & 3.30–6.45pm, Sun 9am–3pm; ☎081 837 0686, ⓦcapritourism.com).

EATING

Picnics are a good way to avoid paying Capri's inflated restaurant prices.

Capri Pasta Via Canale 12, Capri Town. This local delicatessen offers a great selection of home-made dishes to

go; try the *ravioli caprese* or the *melanzane parmigiana* (both €6). For dessert head to Buonocore nearby for the island's best ice cream. Mon–Sat 8.30am–8pm, Sun 8.30am–2pm.

Le Arcate Via Tommaso de Tommaso 24, Anacapri. Family-run trattoria-pizzeria with a terrace right by the chairlift stop. Wood-fired pizza from €7. Daily noon–3pm & 7pm–midnight.

THE AMALFI COAST

Occupying the southern side of Sorrento's peninsula, the **Amalfi Coast** is one of Europe's most beautiful stretches of coast, its corniche road winding around the towering cliffs. There are no trains; buses from Sorrento and Naples take the coast road – a spectacular ride of hairpin bends with fantastic views of the undulating coastline.

Amalfi

In Byzantine times, **AMALFI** was an independent republic and a naval superpower, with a population of some seventy thousand. Vanquished by the Normans in 1131, it was then devastated

---

BARI AND BRINDISI TRANSPORT

Numerous ferries arrive at the busy ports of **Bari** and **Brindisi** on a daily basis, and the two cities are also served by budget airlines Ryanair and easyJet.

BARI

Ferries serve Albania (Durrës: daily; 9hr); Croatia (Dubrovnik: 6 weekly; 9hr); Montenegro (Bar: 5 weekly; 9hr); and Greece (Igoumenítsa: 2–3 daily; 8–12hr; Corfu: 3 weekly; 8hr; Pátra: daily, 15–21hr). The port is connected with the train station by bus #20/ (every 40min; €1).
Trains to Naples (via Caserta 6 daily; 3hr 40min–5hr) and Lecce (15 daily; 1hr 30min–2hr) leave from the central station in Piazza Aldo Moro; trains to Matera (hourly; 1hr 30min) use the private FAL line, leaving from the small station on the corner of the same piazza.
Buses Marinobus services to Naples depart from Piazza Aldo Moro (6 daily; 3hr–3hr 30min). From the airport, the Pugliarbus runs to Brindisi airport (3–4 daily; 1hr 40min) and to Matera (5 daily; 1hr 15min); bus #16 goes to the central station (every 40min–1hr; €1).
Tourist office Piazza Aldo Moro (daily 8am–8pm; ☎0809 909 341).

BRINDISI

Ferries The central Porto Interno, used by ferries from Albania (Durrës: daily; 5hr; Valona: daily; 8hr 30min; Vlore: 1 daily; 7hr 30min), is a 10min walk from the centre of town; ferries from Greece (Corfu: 3–5 weekly; 7hr 30min; Igoumenítsa: daily; 9hr; Pátra: 6 weekly; 17hr 30min; Kefalloniá: 4–7 weekly; 10–14hr) dock at Costa Morena, 3km southeast of town but linked by free shuttle bus.
Trains The station is a 20min walk west of the port, on Piazza Crispi. Destinations: Lecce (hourly; 30min); Naples (via Taranto or Caserta; 5 daily; 4hr 50min–6hr 30min).
Buses Miccolis buses to Lecce (3 daily; 35min) and Naples (3 daily; 6hr), and Marozzi buses to Rome (5 daily; 4hr 30min–6hr 30min) all depart from Viale Togliatti in the new town. From the airport STP Linea A buses (Linea A; €1) meet arrivals and run into town via the port and train station. COTRAP buses run from the airport to Lecce (50min; €6).
Tourist office Lungomare Margherita 43/44 (daily 10am–1pm & 3–8pm; ☎0831 523 072).

by an earthquake in 1343. A few remnants of Amalfi's past glories survive, and its narrow alleyways and tucked-away piazzas make it fun to wander through. The **Duomo** dominates the main piazza, its toy-town facade topped by a glazed-tiled cupola. St Andrew is buried in its crypt, though the most appealing part of the building is the cloister (daily 9am–7.45pm, earlier in winter; €3) – Arabic in feel, with its whitewashed arches and palms.

Opposite Piazza Gioia, the **Arsenale** (daily 10am–8pm; €2) displays the Tavole Amalfitane – the book of maritime laws that governed the Republic, and the rest of the Mediterranean, until 1570, as well as an exhibition about the evolution of the compass, which was said to have been invented by Amalfitan Flavio Gioia in 1302. Beyond these, the focus is the busy seafront, where there's a crowded **beach**.

ARRIVAL AND DEPARTURE

By bus Buses stop at Piazza Flavio Gioia, on the waterfront.
Destinations Ravello (every 30min; 30min); Rome (Marozzi bus; 3 daily; 5hr 30min); Sorrento (hourly; 1hr 40min); Salerno (hourly; 55min).
By ferry Ferries and hydrofoils use Amalfi's tiny harbour, a stone's throw away from the centre.
Destinations Capri (4 daily; 1hr 30min); Positano (hourly; 30min); Salerno (hourly; 25min); Sorrento (hourly; 50min).
By train The nearest major train station is at Salerno, from where there are SITA buses and ferries to Amalfi.

INFORMATION

Tourist office Corso delle Repubbliche Marinare 27 (Mon–Sat 9am–1pm & 2–6pm; ☎089 871 107, ⓦ amalfitouristoffice.it).

ACCOMMODATION

Almost all the hotels in Amalfi are expensive; it makes sense to base yourself in a hostel in one of the nearby towns, such as Atrani, a 10min bus ride from Amalfi.

A' Scalinatella Piazza Umberto I 5–6, Atrani ☎089 871 492, ⓦhostelscalinatella.com. SITA bus to Atrani or 1km walk from Amalfi. This budget hostel-cum-hotel has small rooms, some with private kitchen, in Atrani, as well as accommodation at a country farmhouse nearby. Note that there are no dorms at the country farmhouse (there are only doubles, twins, 3-and 4-bed privates). Dorm **€25**, double **€70**

Lidomare Largo Piccolomini 9 ☎089 871 332, ⓦ lidomare.it. Located in a building dating back to the 1400s, this pleasant hotel has spacious rooms, some with sea views and all with a/c. Double **€80**

Sant'Andrea Salita Costanza d'Avalos 1 ☎089 871 145, ⓦalbergosantandrea.it. One of the cheaper options in town, this pleasant hotel on the central square has views of the Duomo from most rooms. Double **€80**

EATING

Stock up on food provisions at the grocery Merchiorre Alimentari, just off Piazza dei Dogi; you can order freshly made sandwiches to go for €2.50.

★ **Cuoppo d'Amalfi** Via Supportico dei Ferrari 10, just off Piazza dei Dogi. This little joint offers a selection of dishes sizzled in front of your eyes: take your *cuoppo* – a paper cone filled with shrimps, squid and small local fish (€8) – to the beach with a glass of white wine (€2) and enjoy. Daily noon–midnight.

Da Maria Via Lorenzo d'Amalfi 14 ⓦamalfitrattoriadamaria. com. This welcoming trattoria offers a selection of home-made pastas (€10–18) and wood-fired pizzas (€5–10), all lovingly prepared by the *mamma* and the chefs hard at work in the kitchen. Daily 11.30am–3pm & 6.30–11pm.

Ravello

The best views of the coast are inland from Amalfi, in **RAVELLO**. For a time an independent republic, nowadays it's little more than a large village. What makes it more than worth the thirty-minute bus ride up from Amalfi, however, is its unrivalled location, spread across the top of one of the coast's mountains. The **Duomo** (daily 9am–noon & 5.30–8pm) is a bright eleventh-century church with a richly ornamented interior, but Ravello's real draws are its two villas: by the Duomo are the gardens of the **Villa Rufolo** (daily 9am–8pm, earlier in winter; €5), the spectacular venue for a renowned arts festival in the summer (tickets from €25, some events free; ⓦravellofestival.com); a ten-minute walk south is the stunning **Villa Cimbrone** (daily 9am–sunset; €6), undoubtedly worth a visit for the spectacular views of the coast from the Terrace of Infinity, adorned with eighteenth-century marble busts.

INFORMATION

Tourist office Via Roma 18 (daily: March–Oct 9am–6pm; Nov–Feb 9am–4pm; ☎089 857 096, ⓦravellotime.it).

MATERA

Tucked into the instep of Italy in the Basilicata region, **Matera** is one of the

17

south's most fascinating cities. The main point of interest is its *sassi*, rock dwellings dug out of a ravine. During the 1950s and 1960s the residents were evicted, as the city had degenerated into a slum. New blocks were constructed outside the town to house the population and the *sassi* were left empty, but in 1993 the area was declared a World Heritage Site and has since been slowly repopulated with hotels, restaurants and workshops, as well as starring as the set of many a film, including *The Passion of The Christ*.

The focus of the Sassi district, a warren of rock streets, is the **chiese rupestri** or rock-hewn churches, of which you can visit two, the spectacular **Madonna de Idris** (April–Nov Mon 2.30–7pm & Tues–Sun 10am–7pm; Nov–March Tues–Sun 10.30am–1.30pm; €3), with frescoes dating from the fourteenth century and, adjacent, **Santa Lucia alle Malve** (daily: April–Nov 10am–7pm; Nov–March 10.30am–1.30pm; €3, or €5 for both churches). For an insight into what life was like for the *sassi*-dwellers, stop by the **Casa Grotta**, just below Madonna de Idris (April–Oct 9.30am–7.30pm; Nov–March 9.30am–5.30pm; €2), or the **C'era una Volta** exhibition at Via Fiorentini 251 (daily 8.30am–8pm; €1.50), a *sassi* dwelling with its life-size inhabitants and their furniture sculpted out of the local tufa by generations of the same family. The **Palombaro Lungo Cistern** (daily 9am–1pm & 4–8pm; €3, includes 20min guided tour), entirely dug by hand and with a capacity of over five million litres of water,

served as a vital water supply for inhabitants of the area. Film enthusiasts can visit the **Photographic Cinema Museum** (Via Vetera 34; daily 11am–1pm & 4–6.30pm; €2), with photos and screenings of the city's most iconic film sets.

ARRIVAL AND DEPARTURE

By plane Matera is 60km southwest of Bari airport. Buses operated by Pugliairbus (5 daily; 1hr 15min; €5) run to Piazza Matteotti.

By bus Coaches stop at the Matera Villa Longo station, a 20min walk out of town but connected by bus.

Destinations Naples (2 daily; 4hr); Rome (3 daily; 7hr).

By train The train station, on Piazza Matteotti, is served by the private FAL rail line (ⓦferrovieappulolucane.it) from Bari. If you're travelling from Naples, consider a train running to Ferrandina, 30km outside Matera, from where buses to Matera meet the trains.

INFORMATION

Tourist office There is an infopoint on Via Ridola with sporadic opening hours. Further info on Matera and the region of Basilicata at ⓦdiscoverbasilicata.com and ⓦbasilicataturistica.com.

Tours Bike Basilicata (ⓦbikebasilicata.it) rent mountain bikes (€18/day), while Walk Basilicata (ⓦwalkbasilicata .it) offer hiking tours of the surrounding area.

ACCOMMODATION

★ **La Dolce Vita** Rione Malve 51 ☎0835 310 324, ⓦladolcevitamatera.it. This small, intimate B&B with welcoming management has two beautiful cave-like doubles, as well as two mini apartments equipped with kitchen. Rates include breakfast. Double **€65**

Le Monacelle Via Riscatto 9/10 ☎0835 344 097. This ex-friary is now a smart hotel, with two large dorms sleeping 13 and 16, both nicely decorated with wooden furniture. The latter preserves a wonderful original stone floor. There's a 1am curfew for the dorms. Dorm **€18**, double **€86**

EATING AND DRINKING

L'Arturo Piazza del Sedile 15. This welcoming wine and food shop prepares great sandwiches (€3) and offers excellent cheese and meat boards. Daily 10am–3.30pm & 7pm–midnight.

La Gatta Buia Via Margherita 90/92. Popular restaurant and wine bar with tables on a pretty square offering a selection of creatively prepared local dishes which change monthly. *Primi* €8–10, *secondi* €10–17. Tues–Sun noon–3pm, 7.30pm–midnight.

Oí Marì Via Fiorentini 66 ⓦoimari.it. Authentic Neapolitan pizzas (€4–9) and a selection of regional

---

★ **TREAT YOURSELF**

If you're going to splash out on one of the atmospheric cave hotels, the **Antica Locanda San Martino** (Via Fiorentini 71; ☎0835 256 600, ⓦlocandadisanmartino.it; double €109) is a special choice: a cool, fragrant *sassi* conversion with individual terraces and an underground swimming pool and sauna. The **Hotel Sassi** (Via S. Giovanni Vecchio 89; ☎0835 331 009, ⓦhotelsassi.it; double €90) has gorgeous rooms with film-set-worthy views, some of which can sleep large groups on request to make it more affordable.

dishes made with local ingredients to be enjoyed in a cavernous setting. *Primi* €8.50, *secondi* €7–13. Daily dinner only 8pm–midnight, plus Fri & Sat lunch 1–3pm.

LECCE

LECCE, 40km south of Brindisi port, is often called the "Florence of the south". These alleys may be well trodden, but a real sense of discovery still accompanies a visit to the city's vine-enveloped stonework. Carved from soft sandstone, these buildings were built for wealthy families, churchmen and merchants during the fifteenth to seventeenth centuries, and are among the most beautiful examples of the style. A short walk from the central Piazza Sant'Oronzo is **Santa Croce** (daily 9am–noon & 5–8pm, earlier in winter), the most famous of Lecce's churches, where delicate engravings soften the Baroque outline of the building. Inside, the excess continues with a riot of stars, flowers and foliage covering everything from the top of columns to chapel altarpieces. Lecce's other highlight is the **Piazza del Duomo**, an elegantly proportioned square surrounded by Baroque *palazzi*. The **Duomo** itself (daily 8.30am–12.30pm & 4–7.30pm, earlier in winter) is an explosion of Baroque detail.

ARRIVAL AND DEPARTURE

By plane Lecce is 40km from Brindisi Airport (@ brindisiairport.net); Pugliairbus (9 daily; €7) connects the airport to the City Terminal on Piazza Carmelo Bene in the centre of town.

By train The train station is a 15min walk south of the centre on Viale Oronzo Quarta.

Destinations Bari (9 daily; 1hr 20min–1hr 50min); Bologna (9 daily; 7–9hr); Brindisi (every 30min–1hr; 25min); Naples via Caserta (5 daily; 6hr); Rome (3 daily; 5hr 30min); Turin (2 daily; 13hr); Milan (8 daily; 8–12hr).

By bus Buses arrive at the City Terminal, a 10min walk from the centre; some buses for southern destinations also use the train station.

Destinations Bologna (1 daily; 10hr 50min); Naples (3 daily; 5hr 20min); Palermo (1 daily; 11hr 30min); Rome (4 daily; 8hr).

INFORMATION

Tourist office Via Monte San Michele 20 (Mon–Fri 10am–1pm, Tues & Sun also 3–7pm; @ 0832 314 117, @ viaggiareinpuglia.it).

ACCOMMODATION

B&B Azzurretta Via Vignes 2b @ 0832 242 211 @ bblecce.it. Occupies the top floors of a sixteenth century *palazzo* boasting a glorious terrace. Pleasantly furnished, with large wooden beds and airy rooms. Double **€70**

Centro Storico B&B @ 0832 242 727, @ bedandbreakfast.lecce.it. This attractive B&B occupies the same *palazzo* as B&B Azzurretta (see above). Double without bath **€60**, double with bath **€80**

Le Comari Salentine Via Duca degli Abruzzi 67 @ 348 903 2363, @ lecomarisalentine.it. This itty bitty B&B has three neatly presented rooms decked out in minimalist Ikea furniture; all are spotless, and two have a kitchenette, ideal for self-caterers. Double **€50**

EATING AND DRINKING

In the evenings, the bars that line Piazza Vittorio Emanuele II liven up, with DJs, live music, and tables spilling onto the leafy square.

Caffè Letterario Via G. Paladini 46 @ caffeletterario.org. This arty café-bar with mismatched furniture, board games and knick-knacks dotted about organizes a wealth of arty events, from Wednesday's theatre performances to Thursday's live music shows. Beer €4, cocktails €4.50. Daily 7pm–2.30am.

La Vecchia Osteria Via Dasumno 3. You will see owner and chef Totò hard at work in the kitchen rustling up excellent home-made dishes; the vegetables are mostly home-grown, the olive oil is from Totò's very own olive grove and he even makes the house wine himself. *Primi* €5–12, *secondi* €6–12. Tues–Sun 1–3pm & 8pm–midnight.

★ **Le Zie** Via Costadura 19 @ 0832 245 178, @ lezie trattoria.com. A simple trattoria serving superb home-style cooking – try Puglia's famous *orecchiette* pasta (€8); more adventurous types can go for the local speciality, horsemeat in spicy sauce (€12). The home-made liqueurs at the end are a must-try. Booking is advisable. Sun lunch only. Tues–Sun 12.30–2.30pm & 8–10.30pm.

Sicily

Perhaps the most captivating of Italy's islands, **SICILY** (Sicilia) feels socially and culturally separate from the rest of Italy. Occupying a strategically vital position, the largest island in the Mediterranean has a history and outlook that have less in common with its modern parent than with its erstwhile rulers – from the Greeks who first settled the east coast, in the eighth century BC, through a bewildering array of Romans, Arabs,

17

Normans, French and Spanish, to the Bourbons, seen off by Garibaldi in 1860. Substantial relics remain, and temples, theatres and churches are scattered across the island.

The capital, **Palermo**, is a bustling city with an unrivalled display of Norman art and architecture and Baroque churches. The most obvious other target is the chic eastern resort of **Taormina**. From here you can visit **Mount Etna**, or travel south to the ancient Greek centre of **Siracusa**. To the west, the greatest draw is the grouping of temples at **Agrigento**, the largest concentration of the island's Greek remains.

PALERMO

In its own wide bay beneath the limestone bulk of Monte Pellegrino, **PALERMO** is stupendously sited. Originally a Phoenician, then a Carthaginian, colony, this remarkable city was long considered a prize worth capturing, and under Saracen and Norman rule in the ninth to twelfth centuries it became the greatest city in Europe, famed for the wealth of its court and peerless as a centre of learning. Nowadays it's a brash, exciting city, whose uniquely varied architecture and museums are well worth exploring.

WHAT TO SEE AND DO

Around the Quattro Canti

The heart of the old city is the Baroque **Quattro Canti** crossroads, with **Piazza Pretoria** and its racy fountain just around the corner. In nearby Piazza Bellini, the church of **La Martorana** (Mon–Fri 9.30am–1pm, Wed & Fri also 3.30–5.30pm, Sun 9.30–11am; free) is one of the finest survivors of the medieval city. Its slim twelfth-century campanile and spectacular mosaics make a marked contrast to the adjacent squat chapel of **San Cataldo** (daily 9.30am–12.30pm & 3–6pm; €2.50) with its little Arab red golfball domes representing the Trinity.

Alberghiera

In the district of Alberghiera, a warren of narrow streets, you'll find the deconsecrated church of **San Giovanni degli**

Eremiti (Via dei Benedettini; Mon & Sun 9am–1pm, Tues–Sat 9am–6.30pm; €6), built in 1148. Established on the remains of a mosque, it's topped with five rosy domes and has late thirteenth-century cloisters. From here it's a few paces north to the **Palazzo dei Normanni** (generally Mon–Sat 8.15am–5.40pm, Sun 8.15am–1pm, check ⓦfedericosecondo.org for the latest opening hours; Fri–Mon €8.50, Tues–Thurs €7; entrance on Piazza Indipendenza), the seat of the Sicilian regional parliament. It was originally built by the Saracens and was enlarged by the Normans, under whom it housed the most magnificent of medieval European courts. The beautiful **Cappella Palatina** (closed to visitors Sun from 9.45am–11.15am), the private royal chapel of Roger II, is almost entirely covered in glorious twelfth-century mosaics. The impressive Norman **Cattedrale** (March–Oct Mon–Sat 9am–5.30pm, Sun 8.30am–1pm & 2–7pm; Nov–Feb Mon–Sat 9.30am–1pm, Sun 8.30am–1pm & 2–7pm; free) boasts a fine portal and tombs containing the remains of some of Sicily's most famous monarchs (entry ticket required €1.50).

The Museo Archeologico Regionale, Vucciria and around

The beautiful Neoclassical Teatro Massimo, Italy's largest opera house, built in honour of King Victor Emmanuel II, is on Via Roma. Regular performances take place, and the interior of the theatre can be visited as part of a guided tour (every 20min; 30min; Tues–Sun 9.30am–5pm, last tour at 4.30pm; €8). To the northeast, off Via Roma, the **Museo Archeologico Regionale** (closed for restoration at time of writing; ⓦregione.sicilia.it /beniculturali/salinas) is a magnificent collection of artefacts, mainly from the island's Greek and Roman sites. Two cloisters hold anchors, Bronze Age pottery, coins and jewels retrieved from the sea off the Sicilian coast.

Southeast of the Museo Archeologico is the **Vucciria market** area (daily from 8am), which offers glimpses of the Palermo of old. You can cut through to

CENTRAL PALERMO

■ ACCOMMODATION			● EATING				● DRINKING AND NIGHTLIFE	
A Casa di Amici B&B	2	Casa Orioles	6	Antica Trattoria		Franco "U	Ai Chiavettieri	5
A Casa di Amici		Your Hostel	3	del Monsú	1	Vastiddaru" 4	I Candelai	6
Hostel & Rooms	1	Vespa	4	Bar San Domenico	2	Il Maestro	Qvivi	8
Ai Quattro Canti	5			Cappello	9	del Brodo 7	Taverna Azzurra	3

Sicily's **Galleria Regionale** (Tues–Sat 9am–6.30pm with sporadic Sunday openings; €8), on Via Alloro, in the rough-and-ready La Kalsa district. It's a stunning art collection, with works from the eleventh to the seventeenth centuries.

ARRIVAL AND DEPARTURE

By plane Palermo Airport (☎ 091 702 0273, �ⓦ gesap.it) is 35km west of town. Prestia e Comandè buses meet arrivals and have stops at various city-centre locations before reaching the terminal at the train station – tell the driver where you're going and he can advise where best to get off (55min; €6.10). Trinacria Express run trains to the central station (1hr; €5.80).

Destinations Milan (several daily; 1hr 30min); Naples (2 daily; 55min); Pisa (2 daily; 1hr 25min); Rome (several daily; 1hr).

By train Trains arrive at the Stazione Centrale, at the southern end of Via Roma – buses #101 and #102 run to the centre. Buy tickets (€1.30; valid for 1hr 30min) at *tabacchi* shops or the booth outside the station; they cost more to buy on board.

Destinations Agrigento (10 daily; 2hr 10min); Siracusa (change at Messina; 4 daily; 6hr 30min–7hr 30min); Taormina (change at Messina; 8 daily; 4hr–5hr 20min).

By bus Buses (services run by SAIS and Interbus) are quicker than trains in Sicily, taking scenic cross-country routes rather than lumbering round the coast. The bus terminal is at Piazza Cairoli right by the train station.

17

Destinations Agrigento (every 1hr 30min; 2hr); Naples (1 daily; 12hr); Rome (2 daily; 13hr); Siracusa (3 daily; 3hr 15min); Taormina (change at Catania; hourly; 4hr).

By ferry Services dock just off Via Francesco Crispi, from where it's a 10min walk up Via E. Amari to Piazza Castelnuovo. Destinations Genoa (1 daily; 19hr); Naples (1 daily; 11hr 15min).

INFORMATION

Tourist office The main tourist office is at Via Principe di Belmonte 92 (Mon–Fri 8.30am–2pm & 2.30–6pm; ☎091 585 172, ⓦpalermotourism.com). There's a smaller branch at the airport (Mon–Fri 8.30am–7.30pm, Sat 8.30am–2pm; ☎091 591 698).

GETTING AROUND

By bus Red line and yellow line buses start at the station and do circuits of the centre for €0.52/day.

ACCOMMODATION

A Casa di Amici B&B Via Volturno 6 ☎091 584 884, ⓦwww.acasadiamici.com. Colourful B&B by Teatro Massimo with use of kitchen, helpful staff and exotic percussion instruments dotted around. Dorm €22, double without bath €50, double with bath €70

A Casa di Amici Hostel & Rooms Via Dante 57 ☎091 584 884, ⓦwww.acasadiamici.com. Under construction at the time of writing, this sister hostel to the B&B (see above) has a yoga studio and offers music workshops and bike rental. There's also a café-bar as well as a kitchen for self-caterers. Dorm €22, double without bath €50, double with bath €70

Ai Quattro Canti Piazza del Ponticello 1 ☎339 266 0963 or 091 611 6737, ⓦaiquattrocanti.hostel.com. Intimate little hostel sleeping just twelve – the warm and welcoming owners will take care of you like an old friend; they regularly organize fun nights out to show their guests more of the city's nightlife. Dorm €18

★ **Casa Orioles** Via alla Piazza dei Tedeschi 4 ☎339 874 2001 or 091 652 6890 ⓦcasaorioles.com. This arty B&B in a sixteenth-century building has palatial, beautifully presented rooms with period furniture, all with kitchenette and private bath. There are also larger mini apartments sleeping four. Double €60, apartment €100

Vespa Via Maqueda 331 ☎339 266 0963 or ☎091 611 6737, ⓦvespa.hostel.com. The wonderfully spacious rooms in this old building have high ceilings and are individually decorated with antiques. The couple also give fun little Vespa tours of the city. Double €56

Your Hostel Via Gagini 61 ☎091 320 436, ⓦyourhostel.it. Set on three floors, this functional hostel has a kitchen, laundry facilities and a roof terrace where weekly dinners are held. Most dorms have private bath. Dorm €20, double €50

EATING

The city's markets are a great place to pick up a picnic; try Ballarò, between Piazza Carmine and Piazza Ballarò in the Alberghiera district. There's a GS supermarket in Piazza Marina.

Antica Trattoria del Monsú Via Volturno 41. The cuisine here is in line with traditional Sicilian recipes; tickle your taste buds with a *rustico freddo* (€6), a selection of Palermitan starters, before moving on to *primi* (€6–10), and meat/fish mains (€7–12) or wood-fired oven pizzas (€4–10). Thurs–Tues noon–3pm & 7–11.30pm.

Bar San Domenico Piazza San Domenico. This great little café with plenty of tables on the beautiful square is the perfect pit stop for a refreshing ice cream or a *granita* (both €2). Pasta mains (€5–15) and pizzas (from €4.50). Daily 5am–midnight, Sun & Mon until 8pm.

Cappello Via Colonna Rotta 68 ⓦpasticceriacappello.it. A sweet lover's delight offering all manner of cakes and tarts (from €2.50), as well as artisanal ice cream including lactose-free fruit options, to take away or to enjoy at one of the little tables outside. Thurs–Tues 7am–10pm.

Franco "U Vastiddaru" Corso Vittorio Emanuele 102, corner Piazza Marina. A local hangout with outdoor seating serving traditional *panelle* (fried chickpea flour; €2.50) and *arancini* (€2), as well as the much-loved *focaccia* with *milza* (veal spleen and lung; €2.50). Daily 8am–2am.

Il Maestro del Brodo Via Pannieri 7. Simple Sicilian home cooking with a focus on fish dishes; there's a wonderful buffet selection of antipasti (€8) to choose from. Tues–Sun 12.30–3.30pm, Fri & Sat also 8–11pm; July & Aug lunch only.

DRINKING AND NIGHTLIFE

In summer, nightlife shifts to the beach resort of Mondello, which is full of lively bars, a half-hour bus ride from Palermo (#806 from Teatro Politeama). The Vucciria district, in particular Via dei Chiavettieri, Piazza Rivoluzione and nearby Piazza Maggiore, has scores of bars that are packed most nights of the week. Piazza Marina also attracts a crowd and a half.

★ **Ai Chiavettieri** Via Chiavettieri 16/18. Welcoming bar with handcrafted wooden furniture, attracting a hip artsy crowd who flock here for the great cocktails (€5), selection of over sixty wines (€3.50), cheap *chupitos* (shots €2) and the friendly vibe. Main dishes (€6–13), too. Tues–Sun 7pm–3am.

I Candelai Via dei Candelai 65 ⓦcandelai.it. Laidback place attracting a student crowd here for some of the hottest live music and DJs in Palermo. Soak up the sunset views on the beautiful terrace at aperitivo time 7–9.30pm. Check the website for what's on.

Qvivi Piazza della Rivoluzione 5. A young studenty crowd spills in for the great aperitivo that kicks off as doors open at 6.30pm; drinks are knocked back on the lively square and are sometimes accompanied by live jazz, blues or rock. Tues–Sun 6.30pm–3am.

Taverna Azzurra Discesa Maccheronai 9. A rustic bar attracting a large crowd for the cheap beers (€1.50) and *sangue* (fortified wine €1) enjoyed on the street outside. Mon–Sat 9am–2pm & 5pm–4am.

DIRECTORY

Banks There are plenty of cash machines dotted around town, including Banca Nuova on Via Vittorio Emanuele 194/196.

Consulates UK, Via Cavour 117 ☎091 326 412; US, Via Vaccarini 11 ☎091 305 857

Exchange At the post office.

Hospital Policlino, Via del Vespro 129 ☎091 655 1111.

Internet Teletel Internet Café, Corso Vittorio Emanuele 212 (daily 8.30am–10pm; €2/hr).

Pharmacy 24/7 pharmacy at Via Roma 1.

Police Piazza della Vittoria 8 ☎091 210 111.

Post office Via Roma 320 (Mon–Fri 8.30am–7pm, Sat 8.30am–12.30pm).

TAORMINA

On Sicily's eastern coast, and dominating two grand sweeping bays, **TAORMINA** is the island's best-known resort. The outstanding remains of its classical theatre, with Mount Etna as an unparalleled backdrop, arrested passing travellers when Taormina was no more than a medieval hill village. Nowadays it's rather chichi, full of designer shops and pricey cafés, but still has plenty of charm. Its pedestrianized main street, Corso Umberto I, is lined with fifteenth- to nineteenth-century *palazzi* interspersed with intimate piazzas. The **Teatro Greco** (daily 9am–1hr before sunset; €8) was founded by the Greeks in the third century BC, though most of what's left is a Roman rebuilding from the first century AD, when a deep trench was dug in the orchestra to accommodate animals and gladiators. Don't miss the beautiful **Villa Comunale**, a charming private garden once part of a sumptuous private villa owned by Lady Florence Trevelyan. For breathtaking views of the bay and Mount Etna, climb the steps up the **Via Crucis** footpath to the church of the Madonna della Rocca. From here it's a steep but beautiful uphill walk to the wonderful hamlet of **Castelmola**, one of Italy's most beautiful villages, renowned for its almond wine (for an unusual experience sample a glass at *Bar Turrisi* (see p 674)

The closest beach to Taormina is at **MAZZARÓ**, with its much-photographed islet, **Isola Bella**: it's a scenic thirty-minute descent on foot, or use the cable car (every 15min; €3 each way) from Via Pirandello.

ARRIVAL AND DEPARTURE

By plane The closest airport is Catania (ⓦcatania-airport.com), 45km from town; buses run between the airport and Taormina (11 daily; 1hr25min; €7.90).

By bus The bus terminal is at Via Pirandello, a 5min walk from the centre.

Destinations Catania (every 30min; 1hr 10min); Palermo (via Catania; hourly; 3hr 40min).

By train The train station, Taormina-Giardini Naxos, is way below town – it's a steep 30min walk up or a short bus ride to the centre (€1.70).

Destinations Catania (15 daily; 40–50min); Palermo (via Messina; 12 daily; 4hr 30min–5hr 40min); Siracusa (6 daily; 2hr–2hr 50min).

INFORMATION

Tourist office Palazzo Corvaja, Piazza Santa Caterina (Mon–Fri 8.30am–2.30pm & 3.30–7pm; ☎0942 23 243).

ACCOMMODATION

★ **Hostel Taormina** Via Circonvallazione 13 ☎0942 625 505, ⓦhosteltaormina.com. Welcoming intimate hostel equipped with a kitchen for guests' use, dorms with lockers, and a wonderful terrace with lounge chairs and great views over the bay. The friendly staff are always ready to help and will make you feel at home. Dorm **€22**, double **€66**

Taormina's Odyssey Via Paterno di Biscari 13 ☎349 810 77 33, ⓦtaorminaodyssey.com. Guests at this B&B, with

★ **TREAT YOURSELF**

Smarten up and head to Taormina's luxurious and historic **Grand Hotel Timeo** (Via Teatro Greco 59 ☎0942 627 0200, ⓦgrandhoteltimeo.com), whose guests have included all manner of illustrious figures, from D.H. Lawrence to Somerset Maugham. Sip a cocktail (€12) on the wonderful terrace – the panoramic views over Etna and the bay are, quite simply, breathtaking. Dinner will set you back about €70 per person.

17

pleasantly decorated doubles, and a little dorm sleeping six, mingle over the communal breakfast table. There's also a small terrace and a single room equipped with kitchenette. Dorm €22, single €40, double without bath €60, double with private bath €70

EATING

★ **Bam Bar** Via di Giovanni 45. This pleasant café with outdoor seating serves over twenty natural flavours of icy sweet *granita* (€3.50), including ricotta and pistachio, typically enjoyed with a freshly baked brioche. Heavenly. Tues–Sun 7am–9pm.

★ **Da Cristina** Via Strabone 2. The town's best freshly baked *arancini* (€2.50) come in six exquisite flavours, including pistachio, aubergine and wild fennel; you can also get bargain take-away or eat-in pasta dishes for €5. Daily 7.30am–1am.

Tutti ccá Fratelli Ingegnere 12. The candle-lit tables of this welcoming restaurant line the steps of a quiet cobbled street with views over the Roman Theatre. *Primi* €8–16, *secondi* €10–22. Daily 11am–1am.

DRINKING AND NIGHTLIFE

In town, the action takes place in picturesque but posey Piazza Paladini, off the Corso. Alternatively, the summer beach-bars of nearby Spisone are reachable on foot from Taormina or by bus from Via Pirandello.

★ **Bar Turrisi** Piazza Duomo 19, Castelmola. This unique bar in the beautiful neighbouring village of Castelmola attracts crowds from all over keen to sample traditional almond wine (€3) in an unusual setting – how often have you visited a bar decked out entirely in phallic memorabilia? Daily 9.30am–3am.

Daiquiri Piazza Duomo. This trendy lounge bar knocks up exceptional cocktails – including over ten types of daiquiris and even Pimm's – to be enjoyed on the lantern-lit cushioned seats lining the outdoor steps. Cocktails €8. Daily 5pm–2am.

Déjà vu Piazza Garibaldi 2 ⓦdejavucocktailbar.com. Young, hip lounge bar that attracts a dressed-up crowd. Daily 7.30pm–3.30am.

MOUNT ETNA

Mount Etna's massive bulk looms over much of the coastal route south of Taormina. At 3340m, it is a substantial mountain and the **ascent** is a spectacular trip; the fact that it's also one of the world's biggest volcanoes – and still active – only adds to the draw. Getting up can be costly and is weather-dependent, so get as much advice as possible on the ground beforehand (see box below).

SIRACUSA

SIRACUSA (ancient Syracuse), 115km south of Taormina, was first colonized by the Greeks in 733 BC and grew to become their main power base in Sicily. Today, the city boasts some of the best

---

CLIMBING MOUNT ETNA

The safest and easiest way to ascend Mount Etna is with a **tour** from Taormina (try ⓦetnapeople.com; €68). If you do decide to go it alone, catch the bus (daily, leaves 8am; 1hr) from Catania train station (Catania is approx 50km south of Taormina) up to the huddle of souvenir shops and restaurants at the Rifugio Sapienza (see below), which marks the end of the drivable road up the south side of Etna. To get as high up as possible, you can either take a cable car then a jeep with guide (2hr 30min; €57.50 return), or take the cable car (daily 9am–5pm; €29.50 return) and walk up the remaining 400m. Alternatively, if you're an experienced walker, go on foot: the trip up will take four hours, the return a little less. Take warm clothes, good shoes and glasses to keep the flying grit out of your eyes. The return bus to Catania leaves at 4.30pm, so if you want to walk all the way you'll have to stay the night in the *rifugio*.

If you don't have the time or funds to reach the summit, the **Circumetnea rail service** (€7.25; no service on Sundays; InterRail passes not valid) trundles around the base from **Giarre-Riposto**, thirty minutes by train or bus from Taormina. The whole tour takes three and a half hours and ends in Catania.

ACCOMMODATION

Rifugio Sapienza North Nicolosi, Etna Sud ☏095 915 321, ⓦrifugiosapienza.com. A cosy, chalet-style *rifugio* hotel equipped with central heating for the colder months. Each of the 25 en-suite rooms has a TV, the restaurant's worth a look, and you can reach it on public transport. Breakfast included. €55 per person

Greek archeological remains anywhere, and also has a strong Baroque character in its old town, squeezed onto the island of Ortygia, and connected to the new town by two bridges.

Ortygia

Near the bridge that connects Ortygia to the mainland, the **Temple of Apollo**, built in the sixth century BC, is probably Sicily's most ancient Doric temple. Over the years, it was transformed into a Byzantine church, then an Arab mosque, and into a church again under the Normans. At the centre of the island, the most obvious attraction is the **Duomo** (daily 8am–7pm), set in a piazza studded with Baroque architecture, and itself incorporating twelve fluted columns from the fifth-century BC temple that originally stood here. At the other end of the square, the church of **Santa Lucia** (Tues–Sun 11am–2pm) harbours a Caravaggio painting, the *Burial of Santa Lucia*. Round the corner at Via Capodieci 16 is the severe thirteenth-century facade of the **Galleria Regionale di Palazzo Bellomo** (Tues–Sat 9am–7pm, Sun 9am–1pm; €8), an outstanding collection of medieval art, and paintings by Antonello da Messina.

The Archeological Museum

North of the train station the city is mainly new, though the best of Siracusa's archeological sights are also here. It's a twenty-minute walk to Viale Teocrito (or take bus #12 from Riva Nazario Sauro), from where you walk east for the **Museo Archeologico Regionale** (Tues–Sat 9am–7pm, Sun 9am–2pm; €8 or €13.50 including entrance to Parco Archeologico, valid 3 days), housing a wealth of material from the early Greek colonies, including a wonderful coin and jewellery collection; the museum's highlight is a headless marble *Venus*, sculpted rising from the sea. Round the corner, the ruined **Basilica di San Giovanni** has interesting catacombs (daily 9.30am–12.30pm & 2.30–5.30pm; €8 ticket includes guided tour departing every 30min; 40min).

The Archeological Park

Siracusa's extensive **Parco Archeologico** (daily 9am–2hr before sunset) is a ten-minute walk west of the archeological museum. Here, the **Ara di Ierone II**, an enormous third-century BC altar, is the first thing you see, though the main highlight is the **Teatro Greco**. Cut out of the rock and looking down towards the sea, it hosts a summer season of Greek plays (ⓦindafondazione.org). Nearby, the **Latomia del Paradiso**, a leafy quarry, is best known for the **Orecchio di Dionisio**, an S-shaped cave, 65m long and 20m high, that Dionysius is supposed to have used as a prison.

Buses leaving every two hours make the 55-minute journey to the tumbledown town of **NOTO** – a good day-trip. The town's crumbling suburbs give way to a lovely Baroque centre. Also within easy reach of town are the sandy **beaches** of Fontane Bianche (bus #21 or #22 from Via Rubino; Mon–Sat every 1hr 30min, Sun every 3hr; 25min).

ARRIVAL AND DEPARTURE

By plane Interbus run services from Catania airport (ⓦcatania-airport.com), to Siracusa (hourly; 1hr 15min).

By train Siracusa's train station is on Via Crispi, a 20min walk from Ortygia.

Destinations Agrigento (via Catania and Caltanissetta; 1 daily; 5hr); Catania (8 daily; 1hr 10min); Palermo (via Messina; 4 daily; 7hr 20min); Taormina (10 daily; 2hr).

By bus Buses stop in Corso Umberto, near the train station.

Destinations Agrigento (via Catania; hourly; 4hr 30min); Palermo (3 daily; 3hr 15min); Taormina (hourly; 3hr 10min).

INFORMATION

Tourist office Via Roma 31 (Mon–Sat 8am–8pm, Sun 9.15am–6.45pm; ☎8000 55500, toll-free).

ACCOMMODATION

B&B Artemide Via V. Veneto 9 ☎338 373 9050, ⓦbedandbreakfastsicily.com. Set on two floors, this B&B offers six spacious rooms with a/c and TV; those on the ground floor are fully equipped with kitchenette and share a little courtyard. Double **€60**

Casa Cristina Via Chindemi 8 ☎0931 62 205, ⓦcasacristinasr.it. The airy a/c rooms at this little B&B all have wonderful views over the temple of Apollo; there's a kitchen for guests' use and all-day tea and coffee. Double **€65**

17

Casa Mia Corso Umberto 112 ☎0931 463 349, ⓦbbcasamia.it. More of a small hotel than a B&B, *Casa Mia* has pleasant rooms with a/c and private bath in a nineteenth-century *palazzo*; there's also a pleasant sunny breakfast terrace. Breakfast €10. Double €65

★ **Lol Hostel** Via F. Crispi 94 ☎0931 465 088, ⓦlolhostel.com. Siracusa's only hostel has a spacious funky lounge area, a modern kitchen and immaculate dorms with lockers and reading lamps. Private rooms all have flat-screen TVs and en suite. Dorm €22, double €60

EATING

Fratelli Burgio Piazza Cesare Battisti 4 ⓦsaporiburgio.com. Tickle your taste buds as you explore the food market in the morning, then head to this wonderful deli for a large plate of exceptional cold cuts for €10. Mon–Sat 6.30am–2.30pm.

La Gazza Ladra Via Cavour 8 ☎340 060 2428, ⓦgazzaladrasiracusa.com. The owners of this cosy, itty-bitty restaurant head to the market every morning to stock up on fresh produce, which they lovingly prepare all afternoon. Try the sought-after *pasta alla palermitana* (€9.50). Book ahead. Tues–Sun 7.30–11.30pm.

Spaghetteria Do Scogghiu Via Scinà 11. The interior of this *spaghetteria*, which has been going strong since 1975, is decorated to resemble a typical Sicilian courtyard, replete with hanging washing and dangling marionettes. Spaghetti €6–9.50, meat mains €8, fish mains €12. Tues–Sun 11.30am–3pm & 6–11pm.

DRINKING AND NIGHTLIFE

Nightlife centres on the lively little square of the Corte dei Bottari and Piazzetta San Rocco in Ortygia.

Enoteca Solaria Via Roma 86 ⓦenotecasolaria.com. Laidback wine bar with a few tables dotting the pavement serving Sicilian wines (€3) and tasty nibbles (€5–15). Mon–Sat 10.30am–2pm & 6pm–midnight.

Sale Via Amalfitania 56/2. Happening bar with brick vaulted ceilings and tables spilling onto the lively square; there are live jazz and blues bands on Thurs (Sept–June). Cocktails €5. Daily 6pm–3am.

Tinkitè Via della Giudecca 61/63, corner of Via Minniti A happening little bar-cum-café, serving lovely cakes for breakfast and delicious snacks come *aperitivo* hour (cocktails €5). Sporadic live music bands. Daily 8.30am–1am & 5.30–11pm, Wed 5.30–11pm only.

AGRIGENTO

Halfway along Sicily's southern coast, **AGRIGENTO** is primarily of interest for its substantial Greek remains, strung out along a ridge facing the sea a few kilometres below town. The series of Doric temples here, mostly dating from the fifth century BC, are the most evocative of Sicily's remains. They are also the focus of a constant procession of tour buses, so budget accommodation should be booked in advance (though Agrigento could be a day-trip from Palermo). A road winds down from the modern city to the **Valle dei Templi**; buses from the station drop off at a car park between the two separate zones of **archeological remains** (daily 8.30am–7pm; €10 or €13.50 combined ticket with archeological museum). The eastern zone is home to the scattered remains of the oldest of the temples; the **Tempio di Ercole**, probably begun in the last decades of the sixth century BC; the better-preserved **Tempio della Concordia**, dating to around 430 BC, with fine views of the city and sea; and the doric Tempio di Giunone, probably completed in 440 BC.

The western zone, back along the path and beyond the car park, is less impressive but still worth wandering around. The mammoth construction that was the **Tempio di Giove**, the largest Doric temple ever known, was left in ruins by the Carthaginians and further damaged by earthquakes. Valle dei Templi leads back to the town from the car park via the excellent **Museo Archeologico Regionale** (Tues–Sat 8.30am–7pm, Sun & Mon 8.30am–1.30pm; €8 or €13.50 joint ticket with Valle dei Templi) – an extraordinarily rich collection devoted to local finds. From June/July to mid-September the Valle dei Templi usually opens at **night**: once the sun has set over the ruins, they're spectacularly illuminated by floodlights. Buses #1, #2 and #3 from outside the train station (€1.10 from *tabacchi*, unavailable to buy on board) go to the temples.

ARRIVAL AND DEPARTURE

By plane The closest airports are Catania and Palermo. Regular buses serve Catania airport (hourly; 2hr 40min) and Palermo airport (3 daily; 2hr 30min) from the terminal at Piazza Rosselli.

By bus The bus terminal is at Piazza Rosselli. Destinations Catania (hourly; 2hr 50min); Naples (1 daily; 12hr); Palermo (every 1hr 30min; 2hr); Rome (2 daily; 14hr).

By train Trains arrive at Agrigento Centrale at the edge of the old town (don't get out at Agrigento Bassa). Destinations Palermo (every 2hr; 2hr).

INFORMATION

Tourist office Piazzale Aldo Moro 1 (Mon–Fri 8.30am–2pm & 2.30–7pm, Sat 8.30am–1.30pm; ☎ 0922 593 344, ⓦ www.provincia.agrigento.it).

ACCOMMODATION

★ **Camere a Sud** Via Ficani 6 ☎ 349 638 4424, ⓦ camereasud.it. Welcoming B&B with five cute and cosy rooms, all with private bath, decked out in mellow colours. Staff are exceptionally friendly and there's a pleasant little roof terrace, too. Double **€70**

Hotel del Viale Via del Piave 19 ☎ 0922 20063, ⓦ hoteldelviale.it. Functional hotel with clean and tidy rooms where guests can rent out two-seater electric Renault Twizy cars to zoom around the city's winding streets. Check the website for the latest deals. Double **€79**

Piccolo Gellia Via Atenea 220 ☎ 0922 27157, ⓦ piccologellia.com. An enchanting B&B set in a nineteenth-century building: artsy photos grace the walls, a convivial breakfast table with home-made jam is laid out in the morning and the pets (two cats, one dog and five turtles) make you feel right at home. Double with shared bath **€54**, double with private bath **€64**

EATING AND DRINKING

In town, Piazza San Francesco off Via Atenea livens up substantially in the evenings. Along the beachfront, the area of San Leone has plenty of places offering cheap drinks.

Ambasciata di Sicilia Via Giambertoni 2 ⓦ ristorantelambasciatadisicilia.it. Revel in the wonderful views over the bay as you dig into a hearty plate of *linguine all'ambasciata* (linguine with bacon, calamari and courgette; €9). Tues–Sun noon–3pm & 7–11pm; Mon July & Aug only.

Le Cuspidi Piazza Cavour 19. The best ice creams in town (small cone €1.70), with unusual flavours such as fresh ricotta and almond, as well as the classics. Tues–Sun 7am–midnight.

Mojo Piazza San Francesco 11. Popular bar with thumping music attracting a young crowd who mingle on the square over €5 cocktails. Wed–Sun 7pm–3am.

Sardinia

Just under 200km from the Italian mainland, **SARDINIA** (Sardegna) is often regarded as the epitome of Mediterranean Europe. Its blue seas, white sands and rolling hills are beautiful and its way of life relaxed. Sardinia also holds fascinating vestiges of the various powers – Roman, Carthaginian, Genoese and Pisan – that have passed through, alongside striking remnants of Sardinia's only significant native culture, known as the Nuraghic civilization, in the seven thousand tower-like *nuraghi* that litter the landscape. The capital, **Cagliari**, is worth exploring for its excellent museums and some of the island's best nightlife. From here, it's only a short trip to the renowned ruined city at **Nora**, and the quieter beaches at **Chia**. The other main ferry port and airport is Olbia, in the north, little more than a transit town for the exclusive resorts of the Costa Smeralda. There's a third airport at the relaxed resort of **Alghero** in the northwest.

CAGLIARI

Rising up from its port and crowned by an old citadel squeezed within a protective ring of fortifications, **CAGLIARI** has been Sardinia's capital since at least Roman times and is still the island's biggest town. Nonetheless, its centre is easily explored on foot, with almost all the wandering you will want to do encompassed by the citadel.

WHAT TO SEE AND DO

The citadel

The most evocative entry to the citadel is from the monumental **Bastione San Remy** on Piazza Costituzione. From here, you can potter in any direction to enter its intricate maze. The citadel has been altered little since the Middle Ages, though the tidy Romanesque facade on the mainly thirteenth-century **cathedral** (daily: June–Sept 7.30am–8pm; Oct–May 7.30am–noon & 4–8pm; Mass on Sun 9am, 10.30am, noon & 7pm) in Piazza Palazzo is in fact a fake, added in the twentieth century in the old Pisan style.

Piazza dell'Arsenale

At the opposite end of Piazza Palazzo, a road leads into the smaller **Piazza**

17

dell'Arsenale, site of several museums including the **Museo Archeologico Nazionale** (Tues–Sun 9am–8pm; €3, €5 accumulative ticket with the Pinacoteca). In the same complex, the **Pinacoteca Nazionale** (Tues–Sun 9am–8pm; €5 accumulative ticket) features some glowing fifteenth-century altarpieces, while the **Museo delle Cere** (Tues–Sun 9am–1pm & 4–7pm; €1.55) displays a series of thought-provoking anatomical waxworks executed by Clemente Susini for nineteenth-century medical students.

Towers
Off Piazza Palazzo stands the **Torre San Pancrazio** (Tues–Sun: April–Oct 9am– 1pm & 3.30–7.30pm; Nov–March 9am–5.30pm; €4, €2.50 students under 26), the best preserved of Cagliari's fortified towers, from where it's a 10min walk to the **Torre dell'Elefante** (Tues–Sun: April–Oct 9am–1pm & 3.30–7.30pm; Nov–March 9am–5.30pm; €4, €2.50 students under 26), named after the small carving of an elephant on one side; climb to the top of either for stupendous views over the city and coast.

Beaches
To get to **Poetto Beach**, the long stretch connected to Cagliari, take bus #PF or #PQ from outside the train station – and, in the summer, #PN – for the fifteen-minute ride and get off wherever a patch takes your fancy.

ARRIVAL AND DEPARTURE

By plane The airport (ⓦ cagliari-airport.com) sits beside the Stagno di Cagliari, the city's largest lagoon, a 10min bus ride west of town (€4 one-way, tickets purchased from airport bookshop or coin-only machine in arrivals hall, last bus from airport to Cagliari 11.30pm, last bus from Cagliari to airport 10.30pm).
By boat Cagliari's port lies in the heart of the town, opposite Via Roma. There is a Tirrenia ticket office close to the port (daily 8.30am–12.20pm & 4–6pm; ⓦ tirrenia.it).
Destinations Civitavecchia (1 daily; 15hr); Naples (2 weekly; 16hr); Palermo (1 weekly; 14hr 30min); Trápani (1 weekly; 10hr).
By train The train station is on Piazza Matteotti.
Destinations Alghero (3 daily via Sassari; 4hr 30min); Olbia (1 direct daily; 4hr).

By bus The bus station is on Piazza Matteotti. For more information on buses in Sardinia, see ⓦ arst.sardegna.it.
Destinations Chia (hourly; 1hr 15min); Pula (hourly; 50min).

INFORMATION

Tourist office There are tourist offices at the airport and port (Via Roma 145), and opposite the train and bus stations (daily: April–Sept 8am–8pm; Oct–March 9am–1.30pm & 2–6pm; ☎070 669 255, ⓦcomune.cagliari.it).
Internet *Lamari*, Via Napoli 43 (Mon–Sat 8.30am–9pm; €3/hr). Great breakfast offer at €3 for drink, pastry and 30min internet.

ACCOMMODATION

Albergo Aurora Salita S. Chiar 19 ☎070 658 625, ⓦhotelcagliariaurora.it. Fantastic location near the buzzing Piazza Yenne. The rooms are simply furnished, with some of the original stone walls showing. Ask for room 112; it is large and has the best views. Double €75
★ **Hostel Marina** Piazza Scalette San Sepolcro 2 ☎070 670 818, ⓦhostelmarinacagliari.it. This excellent hostel is located in the heart of the old town, only a short walk from the train station. Enthusiastic staff, an outdoor café and a cinema room. Room 108 is the best. Dorm €22, double €50
★ **La Terraza Sul Porto** Largo Carlo Felice 36 ☎339 876 0155, ⓦlaterrazzasulporto.com. This fabulous B&B close to the centre has a huge kitchen, cheery decor and a stunning roof terrace. Double €50
Rosso e Nero Via Savoia 6 ☎070 656 673, ⓦrossoenerobeb.com. Ideally located for the restaurants of the Stampace area, this small B&B has clean, tastefully decorated rooms. Double €66

EATING

Piazza Yenne is full of outdoor cafés, while the best restaurants are around the streets surrounding Via Sardegna.
La Damigiana Corso Vittorio Emanuele II 115 ☎070 658 277. A simple trattoria a 5min walk from Piazza Yenne run by a mother and son. Seafood menu €25. No credit cards. Tues–Sun noon–3pm & 7–11pm.
Le Patate & Co Scalette San Sepolcro 1. Cheap fried-food restaurant with cosy upstairs seating or tables outside. Calamari and potatoes (potatoes feature heavily on the menu) €7.50. Tues–Sun open until late.
★ **Lillicu** Via Sardegna 78 ☎070 652 970. Locals cram into this excellent trattoria that serves traditional Cagliari food, often at shared long wooden tables. The large portions, excellent seafood and singing waiters make this an unforgettable experience. Pasta and a quart of wine €15. Mon–Sat 1–3pm & 8.30–11pm.

17

L'Isola del Gelato Piazza Yenne 35. This extremely popular *gelateria* serves myriad flavours of ice cream but also offers everything from breakfast cakes to aperitifs. Outdoor seating available. Daily 7am–3am (closes earlier out of season).

Serofino Via Lepanto 6 ☎070 651 795. This large restaurant in the Marina area serves up the cheapest pasta in town. Ragu pasta €5. Mon–Wed & Fri–Sun noon–2.30pm & 7.30–10.30pm.

DRINKING AND NIGHTLIFE

Caffè Librarium Nostrum Via Sante Croce 33/35. One of the best places in Cagliari for a cocktail at sunset. Tues–Sun 7.30am–2am.

Degli Spiriti Via Canelles 34/San Lorenzo 10 ☎070 311 0373. This trendy restaurant, bar and nightclub on Bastion San Remy serves great pizzas (€7) and cocktails, and the views over the city are spectacular. Excellent lunch menu. Tues–Fri 9am–3am.

★ **Mojito** Salita Santa Chiara 25 ☎070 684 439. Tiny, red-draped bar just off Piazza Yenne, with outdoor couches and beanbags in the summer. Beer €4. Tues–Sun 7pm–5am.

PULA AND NORA

The charming little town of **Pula**, an hour south of Cagliari, is a great base to explore **Nora** and the stunning southern beaches at **Chia**.

Nora Archeological Centre

Nora is the site of an **ancient city** (daily: April–Oct 9am–8pm; Nov–March 9am–5.30pm; ☎070 921 470; €5.50), thought to date from the eighth century BC. An administrative, religious and commercial centre for over 1000 years, it was abandoned around the seventh century AD when the Arab invasion forced the inhabitants to retreat inland. The monuments – a theatre, thermal baths (which made use of the natural springs to be found here), a forum, a temple, an aqueduct and noble houses – suggest a sophisticated people, and many of the intricate mosaics decorating the town remain intact.

To get to the ancient city from Pula, take an eight-minute ride on the Follesa bus (☎follesa.com) from Piazza Giovanni XXIII, or follow the signs and walk 25 minutes to get here.

Laguna di Nora

Next to the Nora Archeological Centre is the **lagoon** (daily July & Aug 10am–8pm; June & Sept 10am–7pm; ☎070 920 9544, ☎lagunadinora.it; €8), originally a fish farm and now an environmental park where you can observe nesting birds and local wildlife, paddle around in a **canoe** (€25/3hr, including entry to the lagoon park), or take a **snorkelling** trip to see the Roman remains on the bed of the bay (€25/3hr). Nora beach itself, flanked by the **Torre del Coltellazzo** and the **Torre di Sant Efisio** (which you can climb up for a view over to the mountains of Santa Margherita), is a lovely, family-orientated place for a swim.

Chia

For secluded beaches, take a bus from Pula's Via Lamarmora to **Chia** (hourly; 25min); Chia beach is a five-minute walk from where the bus terminates. From here, white sands lapped by turquoise-blue waters stretch along the west coast for about 4km.

INFORMATION

Tourist office Piazza del Comune (Easter–Sept Mon–Sat 9.30am–12.30pm & 5–7pm; ☎070 920 9033, ☎comune .pula.ca.it).

ACCOMMODATION

If you get stuck for accommodation in Pula, your best bet is to ask at the helpful tourist office. If you fancy some beachside seclusion, try the campsite at Chia beach.

Campeggio Torre Chia ☎070 923 0054, ☎campeggiotorrechia.it. A large campsite just a stone's throw from Chia beach (see above), which has a small on-site shop and restaurant; take a left off the main road from the Chia junction and head towards the sea. €9 per person, plus €13 per tent

Hotel Quattro Mori Via Cagliari 10, Pula ☎070 920 9124. Basic but clean hotel that's also the cheapest accommodation option in town. Double €40

EATING AND DRINKING

Piazza del Popolo in Pula is full of little cafés. Outside the summer months some establishments may be shut.

Mr Jingle's Café Piazza del Popolo 5 ☎070 924 6047. This cheap and cheerful bar/restaurant serves main dishes from €5 and has a lovely upstairs balcony. Daily 7am–2am.

17

ALGHERO

In the northwest of Sardinia, **ALGHERO** is a lively resort with a Catalan flavour. From the **Giardino Pubblico**, the **Porta Terra** is the first of Alghero's seven defensive towers, erected by the prosperous Jewish community before their expulsion in 1492. **Via Roma** runs down from here through the old town's puzzle of lanes to the pedestrianized **Via Carlo Alberto**, home to most of the bars and shops. Turn right to reach **Piazza Civica**, the old town's main square, at one end of which rises Alghero's mainly sixteenth-century **cattedrale** (guided tours organized by the Diocesan Museum ☎079 973 3041; Mon–Sat 10.30am–1pm & 6–9pm; free). The best excursions are northwest along the coast, past the long bay of **Porto Conte** to the point of **Capo Caccia**, where the spectacular sheer cliffs are riddled by deep marine caves. The most impressive of these is the Grotta di Nettuno, or **Neptune's Grotto** (daily: April–Oct 10am–5pm; Nov–March 10am–3pm; €13), a long snaking passage that delves far into the rock and is full of stalagmites and stalactites. To get there, join a boat trip from the port (€15, entrance to the caves not included; 2hr 30min; ⓦnavisarda.it), or take the bus from the Giardino Pubblico G. Manno to Capo Caccia and walk the 654 steps down to the caves (June–Sept 3 daily from 9am; Oct–May 1 daily). If you do have time for another excursion, head down the coast to the picturesque town of **Bosa**. There are four daily buses to this beautiful town and the journey takes an hour.

ARRIVAL AND DEPARTURE

By plane Fertilia airport (ⓦaeroportodialghero.it) is 12km north of the town, and served by the #AIFA bus, for which you can buy tickets on the bus or in most *tabacchi* (90min; €1).
By train Trains arrive 2km north of the centre and are connected to the port by regular local buses.
Destinations Cagliari (5 daily via Sassari; 4hr 30min); Sassari (frequent; 35min).

By bus Long-distance buses arrive in Via Catalogna, on the Giardino Pubblico G. Manno.
Destinations Cagliari (8 daily via Sassari; 6hr approx); Sassari (frequent; 1hr 10min).

INFORMATION

Tourist office Piazza Porta Terra 9 (April–Sept Mon–Sat 8am–8pm, Sun 10am–1pm; Nov–March Mon–Sat 9am–7pm; ☎079 97 054, ⓦalghero-turismo.it).

ACCOMMODATION

Hostal de l'Alguer Via Parenzo 79 ☎079 930 478, ⓦalgherohostel.com. This slightly shabby HI hostel is located in a fairly distant but tranquil spot 5km along the coast at Fertilia, reachable by hourly local bus from Alghero (€1). Dorm **€25**
★ **La Mariposa** ☎079 950 480, ⓦlamariposa.it. Popular, friendly, well-equipped campsite 2km north of town, with direct access to the seaweed-covered beach. April to mid-Oct. **€13** per person, plus tent from **€12**
★ **L'loc D'or B&B** Via Logudoro 26 ☎347 076 3412, ⓦllocdor.com. A 2min walk to the beach and a short distance from the old town. Owner Gemma provides true Sardinian hospitality and a great breakfast. Double **€80**
Mario & Giovanna's B&B Via Canepa 51 ☎339 890 3563, ⓦmarioegiovanna.it. Unmissable with its bright facade, this small, family-run B&B has just three rooms. 15min walk from the old town. Prices fluctuate according to the season. Double **€80**

EATING AND DRINKING

Alghero's restaurants are renowned for seafood, at its best in spring and winter. There's also a supermarket, Conad, at Via Mazzini 1a and Via Don Minzoni, and a great covered food market on Via Sassari.
Casablanca Via Umberto 76 ☎079 983 353. Don't expect top-notch service, but the fresh, large and tasty pizzas (€5) more than make up for this.
Poco Loco Via Gramsci 8 ☎079 983 604. Superb modern pizzeria with live music, internet café and bowling. Try the testing metre-long pizza (€20, serves 4). Large screens showing sport. Daily 7.30pm–1am, closed Mon out of season.
Trattoria Maristella Via Kennedy 9 ☎079 978 172. Tasty, reasonably priced fish restaurant popular with locals. Seafood pasta €10. Mon–Sat 12.30–3pm & 7–11pm, Sun 12.30–3pm

TURAIDA CASTLE, SIGULDA

Latvia

HIGHLIGHTS

❶ **Rīga** Admire the exquisite Art-Nouveau architecture before exploring the expanding bar scene. **See p.686**

❷ **Jūrmala** Join the Latvian summer beach party at this string of seaside resorts. **See p.693**

❸ **Sigulda** Explore the castle ruins and hiking trails of the gorgeous Gauja Valley. **See p.694**

❹ **Ventspils** Vibrant port city with one of Latvia's best beaches. **See p.695**

❺ **Kolka** Explore seaside villages and windswept coast. **See p.696**

HIGHLIGHTS ARE MARKED ON THE MAP ON P.683

ROUGH COSTS

Daily budget Basic €55, occasional treat €60

Drink Aldaris beer €2.50

Food Pork with potatoes and sauerkraut €7

Hostel/budget hotel €18/€30–45

Travel Bus: Rīga–Liepāja €9; train: Rīga–Sigulda €3.50

FACT FILE

Population 2.2 million

Language Latvian; Russian also widely spoken

Currency Euro (€)

Capital Rīga

International phone code ☎ 371

Time zone GMT +2hr

Introduction

Since becoming a member of the European Union in 2004, Latvia has enjoyed a bumpy ride of boom and slump, although the decision to adopt the euro in January 2014 seems to point to a measure of stability in future. The Soviet occupation left the country with a large Russian minority population, and it remains a place divided by language and culture – Rīga in particular is a strikingly bilingual city, although all road signs and public notices are in Latvian. And although it's the boisterous capital to which most visitors are attracted, to experience the true spirit of Latvia you'll need to head into the spectacularly unspoiled countryside, with its lakes, forests and sandy beaches.

The most obvious destination is the capital, **Rīga**. Its architectural treasures, lively nightlife and countless eating options make it a prime destination for budget travellers, and it's also popular with stag parties. Places within easy reach of the capital include the palace of **Rundāle**, while those wishing to hit the beach can head either to the nearby resort area of **Jūrmala** or to the port city of **Ventspils**. In the scenic **Gauja Valley**, the attractive small towns of **Sigulda** and **Cēsis** can both be used as bases for hiking, biking, canoeing and other outdoor pursuits.

CHRONOLOGY

2500 BC The Balts (ancestors of today's Latvians and Lithuanians) occupy present-day Latvia.

1201 German traders found the city of Rīga.

1285 Rīga joins the Hanseatic League, bringing closer economic ties with the rest of Europe.

1330 Rīga Castle is built for the Livonian Knights (it now houses the President of Latvia).

1561 Southern Latvia is conquered by Poland; Catholicism is adopted.

1629 Parts of Latvia are conquered by Sweden.

1721 Sweden loses its Latvian possessions to Peter the Great of Russia.

Late 1800s Cultural and intellectual movements led by the "Young Latvians" increase Latvian national self-consciousness.

1905 Peasant revolt against the rich, land-owning German nobility in Latvia. Brutal repression follows.

1918–1920 Latvia gains independence, despite German and Soviet military attempts to prevent it.

1940 Latvia is taken by the Soviets at the beginning of World War II, then occupied by the Germans a year later.

Both occupations cause horrendous suffering for Latvians.

1945 By the end of the war, Soviet communism is again in control.

1991 Collapse of the Soviet Union brings about the restoration of independence.

1999 Vaira Vike-Freiberga, the first female President of Latvia, takes office.

2004 Latvia joins the EU.

2007 After centuries of disputes, Latvia's borders with Russia are set under a treaty signed by both countries.

2008–11 A period of rapid economic growth is followed by recession.

2014 Latvia adopts the euro.

ARRIVAL AND DEPARTURE

Rīga International Airport (Lidosta Rīga) is served by numerous European airlines, including easyJet, Ryanair, Aer Lingus, Lufthansa and Turkish Airlines as well as Latvia's low-cost airBaltic (ⓦairbaltic .com). You can easily get to the city centre by taking bus #22 (€1) or a taxi, which should cost no more than €20.

Options for cross-border **train** travel are fairly limited, with connections to Moscow and St Petersburg, but not to Lithuania or Estonia. The train lines still exist, however, and services may be reinstated in future. Eurolines (ⓦeurolines-latvia.lv), LuxExpress (ⓦluxexpress.eu) and Ecolines (ⓦecolines.net) offer frequent **bus services** linking Rīga with Tallinn, Vilnius and St Petersburg, among other international destinations.

A daily **ferry** service runs from the Rīga terminal to Stockholm, Sweden

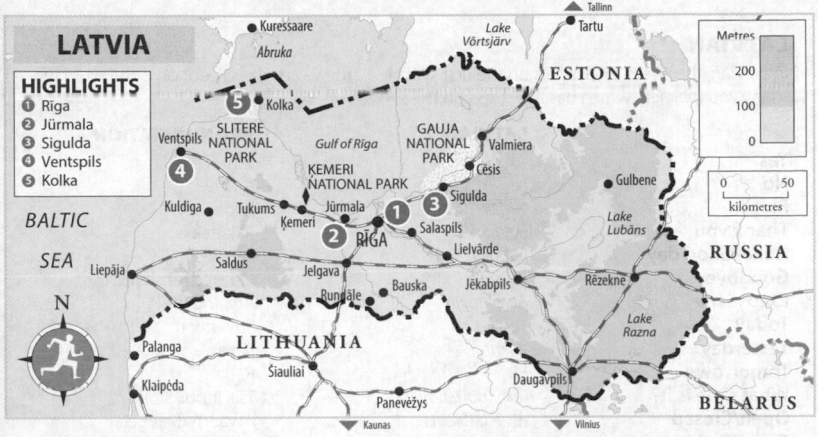

LATVIA

HIGHLIGHTS
1 Rīga
2 Jūrmala
3 Sigulda
4 Ventspils
5 Kolka

18

(⟲tallinksilja.com); as well as daily from Ventspils to Nynäshamn, Sweden (60km from Stockholm).

GETTING AROUND

Rīga has plentiful and cheap public transport. Buy **train** tickets in advance: stations have separate windows for long-distance (*starpilsetu*) and suburban (*pirpilsetu*) trains. Long-distance services are divided into "passenger" (*pasazieru vilciens*) and "fast" (*ātrs*) – both are quite slow but the latter, usually requiring a reservation, stops at fewer places. On timetable boards, look for *atiet* (departure) or *pienāk* (arrival). Check train timetables online at ⟲ldz.lv.

Buses are slightly quicker than trains, though marginally more expensive. Buy long-distance tickets in advance from the ticket counter and opt for an express (*ekspresis*) bus if possible.

A new BalticBike borrowing system (⟲balticbike.lv) allows you to pick up and drop off **bicycles** from various points around Rīga and Jūrmala for €1.50 per hour. Cycling is a particularly good way of getting around the resort areas and small towns.

ACCOMMODATION

Outside Rīga and Jūrmala, you won't find many backpacker hostels, though inexpensive guesthouses and campsites are found in many Latvian towns. **Hostels** are particularly prolific in the centre of Rīga. A number of small-sized, good-value **hotels** and **guesthouses** are also available, but rooms are in short supply during peak season and advance reservations are required in summer. In Rīga and Jūrmala there are agencies offering well-priced **private rooms** (*istabas*) of a reasonable standard. There's a handful of decently equipped **campsites** in Rīga, Jūrmala, Sigulda, Cēsis and Ventspils.

FOOD AND DRINK

While meat or fish and potatoes remain the bedrock of Latvian cuisine, Rīga has something to suit every palate, with a lot of good international cuisine and vegetarian options. **Eating out**, particularly in the capital's classier joints, is fairly expensive, but there are plenty of self-service fast-food places, offering filling meals for around €5–6. Numerous supermarkets and markets make **self-catering** a viable option too.

Restaurants tend to be open from noon to midnight, with bars keeping similar hours (although some are open past 2am). Cafés typically open at 9 or 10am.

Popular national **starters** include cabbage soup (*kāpostu zupa*), sprats with onions (*sprotes ar sīpoliem*) and *pelēkie zirņi* (mushy peas in pork fat). Slabs of pork garnished with potatoes and sauerkraut constitute the typical **main course**, although freshwater fish (*zivs*) is common too. *Rasols* (cubes of potato, ham and gherkin

18

LATVIAN

In Latvian, the stress always falls on the first syllable of the word. The exception is the word for thank you (*paldies*), which has the stress on the second.

	LATVIAN	**PRONUNCIATION**
Yes	*Jā*	Jah
No	*Nē*	Neh
Please	*Lūdzu*	Loodzoo
Thank you	*Paldies*	Paldeeass
Hello/Good day	*Labdien*	Labdeean
Goodbye	*Uz redzēšanos*	Ooz redzehshanwas
Excuse me	*Atvainojiet*	Atvainoyet
Today	*Šodien*	Shwadien
Yesterday	*Vakar*	Vakar
Tomorrow	*Rīt*	Reet
What time is it?	*Cik ir pulkstenis?*	Tsik ir pulkstenis?
Open/Closed	*Atvērts/Slēgts*	Atvaerts/Slaegts
Good/Bad	*Labs/Slikts*	Labs/Slikts
Do you speak English?	*Vai jūs runājat angliski?*	Vai yoos roonahyat angliski?
I don't understand	*Es nesaprotu*	Es nesaprwatoo
How much is…?	*Cik tas maksā…?*	Tsik tas maksah…?
Cheap/Expensive	*Lēts/Dārgs*	Laets/Dahrgs
Student ticket	*Studentu biļeti*	Studentu bilyeti
Boat	*Kuģis*	Kugyis
Bus	*Auto*	Owto
Plane	*Lido*	Lidaw
Train	*Dzelzceļa*	Dzelzcelyuh
Where is the…?	*Kur atrodas…?*	Kur uhtrawduhs…?
Near/Far	*Tuvs/Tāls*	Tuvs/Taals
I'd like…	*Es vēlos…*	Es vaalaws…
I'm a vegetarian	*Es esmu veģetārietis/te (m/f)*	Es asmu vejyetahreatis/te
The bill, please	*Lūdzu rēķinu*	Loodzu rehkyinu
Toilet	*Tualete*	Tuuhlete
One	*Viens*	Viens
Two	*Divi*	Divi
Three	*Trīs*	Trees
Four	*Četri*	Chetri
Five	*Pieci*	Pietsi
Six	*Seši*	Seshi
Seven	*Septiņi*	Septinyi
Eight	*Astoņi*	Astonyi
Nine	*Deviņi*	Devinyi
Ten	*Desmit*	Desmit

drenched in cream) is the staple salad. *Pelmeni* (Russian ravioli) are ubiquitous – you'll find them on most menus.

DRINK

Rīga has excellent **bars**, though some are expensive. Imported **beer** (*alus*) is widely available, but the local brews are fine and also cheaper – the most common brands are Aldaris and Cēsu. Worth trying once is *Rīga Melnais Balzāms* (Rīga Black Balsam), a kind of bitter liqueur (45

percent) made from a secret recipe of roots and herbs, and supposed to cure all ailments.

Coffee (*kafija*) and tea (*tēja*) are usually served black – ask for milk (*piens*) and/or sugar (*cukurs*).

CULTURE AND ETIQUETTE

Latvians are rather reserved and tend to greet each other with solemn handshakes rather than effusive hugs. The distinctive

Russian and Latvian communities do not mix much and some resent being mistaken for the other. In the workplace **women** still tend to fill more traditional roles, and the general attitude to women travelling alone tends to be mildly sexist, although there is little risk of harassment. A ten percent **tip** is appropriate for good service in a restaurant.

SPORTS AND ACTIVITIES

Ice hockey is the national sport, and the revered national team plays at the 12,500-seat Arena Rīga (Skanstes 21, ☎6738 8200, ⊛arenariga.com). You'll need to book in advance for important games.

Outside Rīga there is plenty of scope for **outdoor pursuits**. A number of beautiful **national parks**, best visited in the summer and home to dozens of protected species, offer extensive hiking and biking trails ripe for exploration. Canoeing, rafting and extreme sports such as mountain boarding, quad biking and bungee jumping are on offer around Cēsis and Sigulda in the Gauja Valley. Skiing and snowmobiling take over in winter, while the port of Ventspils attracts kitesurfers.

COMMUNICATIONS

Post offices (*pasts*) are generally open from 8am to 7pm during the week and from 8am to 3pm on Saturdays. Modern **public phones** are operated with either credit cards or magnetic cards (*telekarte*), which are sold at post offices and most newsagents. Using mobile phones from other European countries is fairly inexpensive, but check

roaming charges with your phone company. **Internet cafés** in the capital are becoming obsolete due to the ever-increasing number of **wi-fi hotspots** and free internet and wi-fi offered by guesthouses, hotels and youth hostels.

EMERGENCIES

Theft is the biggest hazard. If you're staying in a cheap hotel, don't leave valuables in your room. Muggings and casual violence are not unknown in Rīga; avoid parks and backstreets after dark. **Police** (*policija*), who are unlikely to speak much English, will penalize you if you're caught drinking in public – expect a stiff fine. Some **strip clubs** and **pubs** are notorious for ripping off drunk foreign males.

Pharmacies (*aptieka*) are well stocked with over-the-counter painkillers, first aid items, sanitary products and the like. In larger cities, they tend to be open from 8am until 8pm. There are 24-hour pharmacies in the capital, where, with some luck, you'll find an English-speaker. **Emergency medical care** is free, but if you fall seriously ill, try and head for home, as many Latvian medical facilities are still lagging behind those in Western Europe.

INFORMATION

Tourist offices run by the Latvian tourist board (⊛latvia.travel) are located at the centre of most major cities and well-touristed towns. Jāņa Sēta (Elizabetes iela 83–85, Rīga) is well stocked with guides,

---

EMERGENCY NUMBERS

Police ☎02; Ambulance ☎03; Fire ☎01; universal emergency number ☎112.

LATVIA ONLINE

⊛**latvia.travel** Detailed website with helpful information on Latvia's attractions, accommodation and transport.
⊛**inyourpocket.com/latvia/riga** Excellent, regularly updated listings and all sorts of practical information about Rīga.
⊛**rigathisweek.lv** Extensive website of *Rīga This Week*, a free listings magazine.

STUDENT AND YOUTH DISCOUNTS

ISIC cards will get you a fifty percent discount off entry to most museums and attractions, and even some restaurants – look for the ISIC sign on doors. HI-affiliated hostels offer discounts for **YHA** card holders.

18

and publishes its own maps. *Rīga in your Pocket* (ⓦinyourpocket.com; €3) is an excellent English-language **listings** guide. *The Baltic Times* (ⓦbaltictimes .com) provides weekly updates on current affairs and events in English while *Rīga This Week* is a detailed listings guide.

MONEY AND BANKS

In January 2014 Latvia adopted the euro (€), which is divided into 100 cents. Notes come as €5, 10, 20, 50, 100, 200 and 500, and **coins** as 1, 2, 5, 10, 20 and 50 cents, and 1 and 2 euros. **Bank** (*banka*) **hours** vary, but in Rīga many are open Monday to Friday from 9am to 5pm, and on Saturdays from 10am to 3pm. Outside the capital, many close at 1pm and most are closed on weekends. **Exchanging cash** is straightforward, even outside banking hours, as Rīga is full of currency exchange offices (*valktas apmaiņa*); shop around to get the best rate. **ATMs** are plentiful nationwide and accept most international cash cards. Credit cards are accepted in an increasing number of establishments.

OPENING HOURS AND HOLIDAYS

Shops are usually open weekdays from either 8 or 10am to 6 or 8pm, and on Saturdays from 10am to 7pm. Some food shops are open until 10pm and are also open on Sundays. In Rīga there are a few 24-hour shops, which sell food and alcohol. Most shops and all banks close on the following **public holidays**: 1 January, Good Friday, Easter Sunday, Easter Monday, May 1, the second Sunday in May, June 23 and 24, November 18, December 25, 26 and 31.

Rīga

RĪGA is the largest, liveliest and most cosmopolitan of the Baltic capitals, with a great selection of accommodation to suit any budget and a wide variety of world cuisine. A heady mixture of the medieval and the contemporary, the city has much to offer architecture and history enthusiasts in the narrow cobbled streets of Old Rīga and the wide boulevards of the New Town, where beautiful examples of Art Nouveau architecture line Strēlnieku iela and Alberta iela.

The city also has all the trappings of a modern capital, with efficient and affordable public transportation, excellent shopping, and a notoriously exuberant nightlife.

WHAT TO SEE AND DO

Old Rīga (Vecrīga), grouped loosely around Town Hall Square (**Rātslaukums**) and Cathedral Square (Doma laukums), forms the city's nucleus and is home to most of its historic buildings. With its cobbled streets, narrow lanes and hidden courtyards, it gives the impression of stepping back in time. To the east, Old Rīga is bordered by Bastejkalns Park, beyond which lies the **New Town** (known locally as "Centrs"). Built during rapid urban expansion between 1857 and 1914, its wide boulevards are lined with four- and five-storey apartment buildings, many decorated with extravagant Art Nouveau motifs.

Town Hall Square

From the doors of St Peter's Church, **Rātslaukums** (Town Hall Square) is straight

---

LOFTY VIEWS

If you want to see the city unfold before you, with its melange of church domes, vast parks, ribbon of river and squat Soviet creations, follow the urban throng to Šķūņu iela to **St Peter's Church** (Pēter baznīca; Tues–Sun; summer 10am–7pm; winter 10am–5pm), a large red-brick structure with a graceful three-tiered spire; climb the tower (€4.50) for excellent panoramic views. Battling the church for the finest vistas of Rīga is "Stalin's Birthday Cake" – the **Academy of Sciences** (April–Sept daily 10am–5pm; €3), a 1950s Empire State Building lookalike at Akadēmijas laukums 1. The 65m skyscraper, adorned with hammers and sickles near the top, has a 360-degree viewing platform on the 17th floor.

Riga Motor Museum (8km) ▲

■ **ACCOMMODATION**
B&B Riga	2
Central Hostel	4
Cinnamon Sally's	5
Dodo Hotel	6
Hotel Multilux	1
Riga Style Hostel	3

Hospital

● **EATING**
Aragats	1
Café Kūkotava	9
Kokanda	4
LIDO Vērmanītis	10
MiiT	7
Muffins & More	3
Raw Garden	6

18

Riga Art Nouveau Museum ❶

Latvian National Art Museum Jews in Latvia Museum

Kronvalda Parks

Esplanāde Cathedral of the Nativity Splendid Palace

National Theatre

Bastejkalns Park

SEE 'OLD RĪGA' MAP

CENTRS

Vērmanes dārzs

Berga Bazārs ❷

OLD RĪGA (VECRĪGA)

Cathedral

St Peter's Church

Daugava

11 NOVEMBRA

Train Station

● **SHOPPING**
Art Nouveau	1
Berga Bazārs	2
Central Market (Centrāltirgus)	3

Bus Station Central Market ❸ Coca-Cola Plaza

Academy of Sciences

● **DRINKING AND NIGHTLIFE**
Bites Blūzs Klubs	2
Chomsky Bar	11
Kaņepes kultūras centrs (KKC)	5
Skyline Bar	8

RĪGA 0 200 metres

N

Riga Ghetto and Latvian Holocaust Museum (20m) ▼ TV Tower & ❻ ▼

ahead and dominated by the **House of the Blackheads** (Melngalvju nams), whose facade is an opulent masterpiece of Gothic architecture and which once served as the headquarters of Riga's bachelor merchants, who adopted the North African, non-white St Maurice as their patron (hence the name "Blackheads"). Largely destroyed in 1941, the House was lovingly reconstructed for the 800th anniversary of Rīga's foundation in 2001.

The ugly oblong structure next door belongs to the **Occupation Museum** (Latvijas okupācijas muzejs), currently closed for long-term renovation – visit the museum's temporary display on Raiņa bulvāris (see p.688).

Museum of the Sun
One of Rīga's most intriguing sights is the quaint and curious **Museum of the Sun** at Vaļņu iela 30 (Saules muzejs; Mon–Sat 10am–7pm; €3), a private collection of artworks, ornaments and cult objects

connected with the fiery life-giving orb in the title. Visually attractive throughout, the display also has interesting things to say about the position of the sun in religion and folk belief, and the development of astronomy.

Cathedral Square
Cathedral Square is dominated by the towering red-brick **Rīga Cathedral** (daily 10am–5pm; €3), established in 1211 and featuring one of the biggest organs in Europe. On the other side of the cathedral, at Palasta 4, is the worthwhile **Museum of Rīga's History and Navigation**, featuring Bronze Age and medieval artefacts, such as a mummified criminal's hand, as well as temporary art exhibitions (Wed–Sun 11am–5pm; €4.50).

Rīga Bourse Art Museum
Opposite the cathedral, the former building of the Latvia stock exchange at Doma laukums 6 contains the **Rīga**

18

Bourse Art Museum (Mākslas muzejs Rīgas birža; Tues–Thurs, Sat & Sun 10am–6pm, Fri 10am–8pm; €3; ⓦ rigasbirza.lv), the nation's collection of old masters and archeological treasures. A small Monet landscape and a Rodin sculpture are the main big-name draws, although the Flemish still lifes and classical antiquities are enough to keep the interest from flagging.

The Castle and the Three Brothers
From Cathedral Square, Pils iela runs down to Castle Square (Pils laukums) and **Rīga Castle** (Rīgas pils), built in 1515 and now home to the Latvian president. Follow Mazā Pils iela from Pils laukums to see the **Three Brothers** (Trīs brāli), three charming medieval houses, one of which, built in the fifteenth century, is thought to be the oldest in Latvia.

Swedish Gate and the Powder Tower
On Torņa iela, you'll find the seventeenth-century **Swedish Gate** (Zviedru vārti), the sole surviving city gate. At the end of Torņa iela is the Powder Tower (Pulvertornis), a vast, fourteenth-century bastion, home to the excellent **War Museum** (Kara muzejs; daily 10am–6pm; free) – three floors of the country's turbulent history, from medieval weaponry to world wars I and II, and Latvia's struggle for independence.

Bastion Hill and the Guild Hall
Bastion Hill (Bastejkalns) – the park that slopes down to the city canal at the end of Torna iela – is a reminder of the city's more recent history: on January 20, 1991, four people were killed by Soviet fire during an attempted crackdown on Latvia's independence drive. Stones bearing the victims' names mark where they fell near the Bastejas bulvāris entrance to the park.

The Freedom Monument
The modernist **Freedom Monument** (Brīvības piemineklis), known affectionately as "Milda", dominates the view along Brīvības bulvāris as it enters the **New Town**, holding aloft three stars symbolizing the three regions of Latvia. Incredibly, the monument survived the Soviet era, and nowadays two soldiers stand guard here in symbolic protection of Latvia's independence.

Occupation Museum
Temporarily housed in the former building of the American Embassy at Raiņa bulvāris 7, the **Occupation Museum** (Latvijas okupācijas muzejs; May–Sept daily 11am–6pm; Oct–April Tues–Sun 11am–5pm; donations; ⓦ okupacijasmuzejs.lv) documents the atrocities committed against Latvia's population by both Nazi and Soviet occupations. Emotion-inducing exhibits include letters to loved ones thrown from trains by Latvians forcibly removed to Siberia, and the simple household items (children's toys,

---

JEWS IN LATVIA

Jews living in Rīga and other parts of Latvia suffered the same fate as Jews in other parts of Eastern Europe when Latvia was overrun by Nazis. The **Rīga Ghetto and Latvian Holocaust Museum** (Maskavas 14a; entry from Krasta; Mon–Fri 10am–6pm; donation; ⓦ rgm.lv), built on the site of the Jewish ghetto behind the Central Market, consists of two outdoor exhibits: a seemingly endless wall of victims' names, and photographs and text illustrating the life of the Jewish community in different parts of Latvia before World War II. On Peitavas iela 6/8, you'll find the last surviving **synagogue** in Rīga; when all the synagogues in the city were burned down by the Nazis in 1941, this building and its treasures – the sacred scrolls – escaped destruction due to its close proximity to other buildings. There's a memorial on Gogoļa iela where the **Great Choral Synagogue** was burnt down in July 1941 with its 300-strong congregation trapped inside. At Skolas 6, you will find a small but gritty and informative **Jews In Latvia Museum** (Mon–Thurs & Sun noon–5pm; donation), telling the history of Jewish life in Latvia from the eighteenth century onwards, including persecution by both Nazis and Soviets, and the survival and "rebirth" of Judaism in independent Latvia.

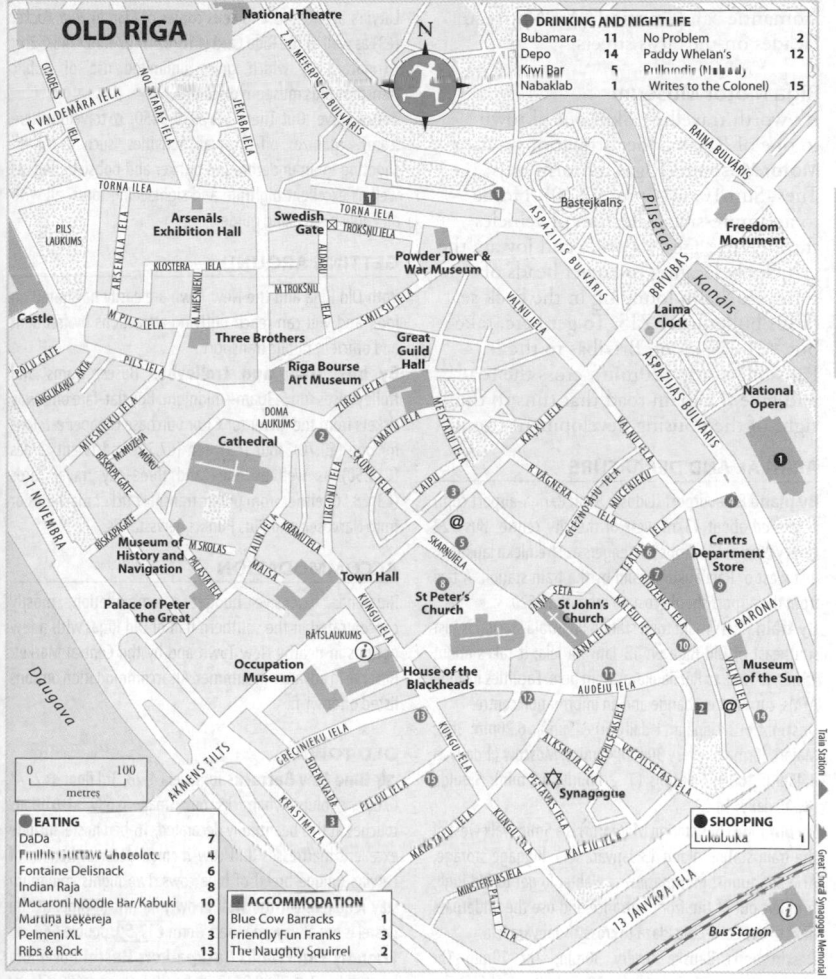

OLD RĪGA

National Theatre

N

● DRINKING AND NIGHTLIFE			
Bubamara	11	No Problem	2
Depo	14	Paddy Whelan's	12
Kiwi Bar	5	Pulkvedis (Nobody	
Nabaklab	1	Writes to the Colonel)	15

Bastejkalns
Freedom Monument

Swedish Gate
Arsenāls Exhibition Hall
Powder Tower & War Museum
Laima Clock

Three Brothers
Great Guild Hall
Rīga Bourse Art Museum
National Opera

Castle
Cathedral

Museum of History and Navigation
Centrs Department Store

Palace of Peter the Great
Town Hall
St Peter's Church
St John's Church

Occupation Museum
House of the Blackheads
Museum of the Sun

Daugava

Synagogue

Train Station
Great Choral Synagogue Memorial

0	100
	metres

●EATING	
DaDa	7
Emīls Gustavs Chocolate	4
Fontaine Delisnack	6
Indian Raja	8
Macaroni Noodle Bar/Kabuki	10
Martiņa Bekereja	9
Pelmeni XL	3
Ribs & Rock	13

■ ACCOMMODATION	
Blue Cow Barracks	1
Friendly Fun Franks	3
The Naughty Squirrel	2

● SHOPPING	
Lukubuka	1

Christian crosses) they fashioned by hand to make life bearable once they got there.

National Art Museum

Esplanade Park runs north from Brīvības bulvāris. At the far end of the park, the **Latvian National Art Museum** (Valsts mākslas muzejs; ⬤lnmm.lv) is closed for restoration until 2015, but its impressive array of nineteenth- and twentieth-century Latvian paintings is worth the wait. In a separate building on Torņa iela 1, the **Arsenāls Exhibition Hall** (Tues, Wed & Fri noon–6pm, Thurs noon–8pm, Sat & Sun noon–5pm; €4) stages cutting-edge temporary exhibitions by contemporary artists.

Rīga Art Nouveau Museum

The **Rīga Art Nouveau Museum** at Alberta iela 12 (Tues–Sun 10am–6pm; €4), housed in the former apartment of renowned artist and engineer Konstantīns Pēkšēns, is a must for anyone with an interest in Art Nouveau. You can view original period furniture and some of Pēkšēns' work, and the visit culminates in the viewing of a short video which will enable you to tell the difference between

18

"romantic" and "vertical" Art Nouveau facades on the city's streets.

Rīga Motor Museum

It's worth travelling 8km out of town to one of Rīga's odder attractions – the **Motor Museum** (Rīgas motormuzejs; Tues–Sun 10am–6pm; €2.30). Home to an impressive collection of vehicles through the ages, its pride and joy are the vehicles belonging to Soviet heads of state: see Stalin lounging in the back seat of his bulletproof ZIS. To get here, take bus #21 east along Brīvibas to the Pansionāts stop (20min), cross the road and take the main road that runs to the right of the housing development (5min).

ARRIVAL AND DEPARTURE

By plane Rīga Airport (Lidosta Rīga; ⍟ riga-airport.com) is located about 13km west of the city centre. Bus #22 (every 20min; €1) drops passengers at Strēlnieku laukums, just west of Rātslaukums, and by the train station. A taxi from the airport should cost no more than €20.

By train Rīga's main train station (Centrālā stacija) is just southeast of Old Rīga on 13 Janvāra iela; it takes about 15min to walk to Rātslaukums from here. Facilities include ATMs, currency exchange and an information centre.
Destinations Liepāja (1 daily Fri & Sun at 6.30pm; 3hr); Majori, Jūrmala (every 30min; 40min); Moscow (1 daily at 4.45pm; 16hr); Salaspils (1–2 hourly; 15 min); Sigulda (8–10 daily; 1hr).

By bus Rīga's bus station (Autoosta) is a 5min walk west of the train station along 13 Janvāra iela; luggage storage, ATM and tourist information available. To get to Old Rīga, turn left out of the front entrance and use the underpass next to the Coca-Cola Plaza to cross 13 Janvāra iela.
Destinations Bauska (every 30min; 1hr 10min–1hr 30min); Kaunas (1–2 daily; 4hr 30min); Klaipēda (3 daily; 5hr); Liepāja (at least 12 daily; 3hr–4hr 30min); Moscow (1 daily; 17hr); Pärnu (9–11 daily; 3hr 30min); Sigulda (at least 8 daily; 1hr 15min); St Petersburg (4 daily; 12–14hr); Tallinn (9–11 daily; 5hr 30min); Tartu (3 daily; 5hr); Vilnius (8 daily; 5hr–5hr 30min).

By ferry The ferry terminal (Jūras pasazieru stacija) is to the north of Old Rīga. Tram #5, #7 or #9 runs from the stop in front of the terminal on Ausekļa iela to Aspazijas bulvāris in the city centre (two stops; €1).
Destinations Stockholm (1 daily; 8hr).

INFORMATION AND TOURS

Tourist information Main tourist office at Rātslaukums 6 in the centre of the Old Town (daily 10am–6pm; ⍟ 6703 7900, ⍟ liveriga.com). It has plentiful information on

Latvia's attractions and sells copies of *Rīga In Your Pocket* (€3) as well as the Rīga Card (€16/€21/€27 for 24/48/72hr; ⍟ rigacard.lv), which gives unlimited use of public transport plus museum discounts.

Tours Travel Out There (⍟ 2938 9450, ⍟ traveloutthere .com) organizes off-the-wall activities, such as AK-47 shooting in an underground bunker and bobsleighing, as well as excellent nightlife and sightseeing tours, all with an English-speaking guide.

GETTING AROUND

Both Old Rīga and the New Town are easily navigated on foot, and you can reach outlying attractions by frequent and efficient public transport.

By bus, tram and trolleybus Buses, trams and trolleybuses run 5.30am–midnight. Buy flat-fare one-way tickets from the driver for €1 or purchase cheaper *e-talons* for one (€0.70), four (€3), ten (€7.20) and twenty rides (€13.50) as well as one- and three-day travel cards (€3/€8.50) either from public transport ticket machines or from Narvesen and Plus Punkts newsstands.

ACCOMMODATION

Rīga has extensive budget accommodation, mostly concentrated in the southern half of Old Rīga, with a few options in nearby New Town and by the Central Market. Reserve in advance in summer. All accommodation options listed offer wi-fi.

OLD TOWN

★ **Blue Cow Barracks** Torna iela 4-2B, 3rd floor ⍟ 2773 6700, ⍟ bluecowbarracks.com; map p.689. Luxurious touches at this beautifully decorated, 16-bed hostel include excellent mattresses and cow-themed decor in honour of Latvia's unique breed of blue cows. Two nights' minimum stay required. Let the staff know your arrival time, as the hostel is not always manned. Dorm €17.50, double €46

Friendly Fun Franks Backpackers Hostel Novembra krastmala 29 ⍟ 2599 0612, ⍟ franks.lv; map p.689. Clean, laddish, Aussie-run hostel for those seeking crush-your-beer-can-against-your-forehead action. Perpetually full and not shying away from hosting stag parties, this firm favourite welcomes you on arrival with a free beer at its 24hr bar. Raucous fun. Dorm €16, double €52

The Naughty Squirrel Backpackers Hostel Kalēju iela 50 ⍟ 6722 0073, ⍟ thenaughtysquirrel.com; map p.689. One of the most sociable places to stay in the Old Town, with daily tours and themed nights – from Movie Night to Latvian Food Night. Lockers are provided, and the location is hard to beat. Dorm €13, double €45

NEW TOWN

B&B Rīga Ģertrūdes iela 43 ⍟ 6727 8505, ⍟ bb-riga.lv; map p.687. A friendly family-run guesthouse in Central

Rīga offering en-suite rooms equipped with cable TV, fridges and microwaves. Breakfast vouchers and airport transfers available. Double €65

Central Hostel E. Birznieka-Upīša iela 20 ☎2232 2663, ⓦ centralhostel.lv; map p.687. The staff are friendly and helpful and the beds (including private rooms) are among the cheapest in the capital, which explains its popularity with local travellers and the odd middle-aged Russian man. Dorm €10, double €30

★ **Cinnamon Sally's** Merkela iela 1, 3rd floor ☎2204 2280, ⓦ cinnamonsally.com; map p.687. More like the luxury apartment of a good friend than a hostel, this place has spacious dorms (with extra touches like the make-up table in the girls' dorm); the combined lounge/kitchen is a great place to socialize and the incomparable Sally herself is always ready for a chat with her guests. Dorm €13, double €30

Dodo Hotel Jersikas iela 1 ☎6724 0220, ⓦ dodohotel .com; map p.687. Budget hotel offering tastefully decorated, spacious en-suite rooms with flat-screen TVs and free wi-fi, as well as a French pancake breakfast (€4), all just a 15min walk or short tram ride from Old Rīga. Double €40

Hotel Multilux Barona iela 37 (entrance from Ģertrūdes) ☎6731 1602, ⓦ hotelmultilux-riga.lv; map p.687. This Art Nouveau building in Central Rīga boasts thoroughly modern en-suite rooms with cable TV, wi-fi and breakfast buffet included in the price. Double €25

Riga Style Hostel Alfrēda Kalniņa 4 ☎6728 0830, ⓦ rigastylehostel.com; map p.687. A good mixture of dorms and private doubles themed after world cities – the London room has a red phone box. It's a clean, design-conscious place with good kitchen facilities, washing machine and wi-fi. Dorm €10, double €40

EATING

Many bars and cafés offer cheap and filling food and there are also plenty of reasonably priced restaurants serving international cuisine.

CAFÉS, CHEAP EATS AND SNACKS

Café Kūkotava Tērbatas iela 10/12; map p.687. Cosy café that not only serves some of the city's best coffee but also tantalizes you with its delectable home-made cakes. Mon–Fri 8am–10pm, Sat & Sun 10am–6pm.

Emihls Gustavs Chocolate inside the Valters un Rapa bookshop, Aspazijas bulvāris 24; map p.689. Try the exquisite chocolate truffles or sip the bliss-in-a-cup white and dark molten chocolate (with a glass of water on the side in case it proves too rich for you). Hot chocolate €2.30. Daily 10am–9pm.

Fontaine Delisnack Teātra iela 2; map p.687. Tucked in an alley behind the Centrs department store, this has quickly become *the* place in the Old Town for freshly flipped gourmet burgers (€4.50), all-day breakfasts and a handful of Asian- and Mexican-inspired snacks – although

the chilli con carne tends to run out by teatime. There's a fully stocked bar if you want to make a night of it. 24hr.

LIDO Vērmanītis Elizabetes iela 65; map p.687. Pretty much everything in the Baltic culinary repertoire is available at this vast order-at-the-counter canteen restaurant, decked out in kitsch-folklore style and patrolled by staff in traditional costume. Mains €3–4. Daily 9am–10pm.

Martiņa Beķereja Vaļņu iela 28; map p.687. Locals queue at the counter of this café-patisserie to stock up on freshly baked *pīrāgi* (from €0.40), doughy parcels filled with bacon bits, shredded cabbage or eggs and leeks. It's also a comfortable city-centre venue for a coffee-and-cake break. Daily 8am–9pm.

★ **MiiT** Lāčplēša iela 10; map p.687. Vegetarian café-bar with sleek modern interior, excellent-value lunch menus (€4.50) and Valmiermuižas beer. *MiiT* also houses a bicycle design workshop and is a popular meeting spot for people of the two-wheeled persuasion. Mon–Thurs 9am–11pm, Fri 9am–2am, Sat 11am–2am.

Muffins and More Ģertrūdes iela 9; map p.687. You'll smell the delicious muffins even before you set foot in this tiny, welcoming café. There are more than a dozen varieties and the blueberry ones just might be the best in Eastern Europe. The "More" of the name consists of soup and baguettes. Muffins €0.90; soup €3.75. Mon–Fri 8am–8pm, Sat 10am–6pm, Sun 11am–6pm.

Pelmeni XL Kaļķu iela 7; map p.689. Popular canteen-style eatery offering six types of *pelmeni* (Russian ravioli) filled with meat or cheese, plus soups and drinks. Gourmet cuisine it ain't, but it *will* fill your belly. €1.50/200g. 24hr.

RESTAURANTS

Aragats Miera iela 15; map p.687. The effusive hostess won't have to tell you off for not finishing your food, because you will: the Armenian-style grilled meats and stews, with the fresh herbs chopped up right at your table, are the best in the city. Mains €9–15. Tues–Sun 1–10pm.

DaDa Audēju iela 16 (Centrs department store); map p.689. Its decor reflects the anarchist art movement but *DaDa* specializes in Mongolian barbecue. Fill up a bowl with fresh meat, seafood, vegetables and noodles, pick a sauce and have it cooked in front of you. Small/large bowl €6.75–10. Mon–Thurs & Sun 10am–10pm, Fri & Sat 10am–midnight.

Indian Raja Skarņu iela 7; map p.689. Authentic, flavourful Indian food in a cosy cellar setting – an expat favourite. The menu is extremely varied and there's plenty for vegetarians. Huge mains €10. Daily noon–11pm.

Kokanda Bruņinieku iela 12; map p.687. This is an excellent choice for inexpensive Central Asian cuisine; try any of the grilled meats or the large, spicy dumplings. Weekday business lunch €6. Daily 11am–11pm.

Macaroni Noodle Bar/Kabuki Audēju iela 14; map p.689. Stylish twin restaurant with minimalist decor offering an extensive menu of excellent home-made pasta

18

18

and noodle dishes, as well as sushi and sashimi platters and bento box weekday lunch specials (€6). Mains €8.30–12. Mon–Thurs & Sun noon–11pm, Fri & Sat 24hr.

Raw Garden Skolas iela 12; map p.687. A stylish, vegan non-dairy restaurant, where no dish is cooked above 45°C, and where you'll either join the crowd of satisfied patrons clamouring for more Thai cucumber soup and papaya-mango cake or leave the premises like Samantha from *Sex and the City*, exclaiming: "I've eaten a f***ing cactus!" Mon–Fri 8.30am–9pm, Sat noon–9pm, Sun 11am–7pm.

Ribs & Rock Grēcinieku iela 8; map p.689. This place is carnivore central and ribs are the star. Whether you order the ones in caraway marinade or the more peculiar "Dark Side of the Moon", featuring Rīga black balsam, you can't go wrong: the tender, flavourful meat just melts off the bone. Mains €12–20. Mon–Fri 2pm–midnight, Sat & Sun noon–midnight.

DRINKING, NIGHTLIFE AND ENTERTAINMENT

The Old Town offers innumerable opportunities for bar-hopping, with a wide range of watering holes (many serve decent food too) filling up with fun-seeking locals seven nights a week. Many double as restaurants during the day but close at 1/2am.

BARS

Chomsky Bar Lačplēša iela 68; map p.687. Looking a bit like a roomy student flat, the gruff but welcoming *Chomsky Bar* is a refreshing alternative to the mass-tourist pubs of the Old Town. A mural of left-wing guru Noam Chomsky sets the tone. Affordable local beers and spirits, and a lively front yard in summer. Mon–Thurs 4pm–midnight, Fri & Sat 4pm–3am.

Kaņepes kultūras centrs (KKC) Skolas iela 15 ⓦ facebook.com/Zoo.KKc; map p.687. Alternative cultural centre offering art exhibitions, occasional theatre and live music, and a supremely mellow bar. Daily 4pm–1am.

Kiwi Bar Skārņu iela 7; map p.689. Appropriately staffed by Kiwis (and Brits), this sports bar's post-hangover Kiwi breakfasts and drink selection are an instant hit with expats and the international backpacker set. Daily 9am–4am.

No Problem Tirgoņu 5/7; map p.689. The best of the capital's beer gardens, *No Problem* boasts a prime spot overlooking Doma laukums (Cathedral Square), over 20 beers on tap, live music nightly and some of the best burgers in town, served by friendly, efficient staff. Daily 11am–3am.

Paddy Whelan's Grēcinieku iela 4; map p.689. Big, lively Irish pub/sports bar bursting at the seams whenever a big match is on, offering 18 kinds of beer and cider on tap, as well as great curry from its Indian menu. Mon–Thurs & Sun 11am–1pm, Fri & Sat 11am–3am.

Skyline Bar Elizabetes iela 55; map p.687. Behold Rīga's splendour from a window seat on the 26th floor of the *Reval Hotel Latvija*. Daily 4pm–2am.

CLUBS AND LIVE MUSIC

Bites Blūzs Klubs Dzirnavu iela 34a ⓦ bluesclub.lv; map p.687. Laidback, unpretentious blues pub festooned with photos of musicians. There are regular live acts, sometimes international. Mon–Fri 11am–3am, Sat 7pm–3am.

Bubamara Audēju iela 8 ⓦ bubamara.lv; map p.689. Underground music bar with acts varying from DJs to rock bands, as well as themed music evenings. Cheap beer and cocktails, and an inexpensive menu of lunchtime food too. Daily noon–3am.

Depo Vaļņu iela 32 ⓦ www.klubsdepo.lv; map p.689. Post-industrial cellar space with alternative DJ nights, live garage bands and an eclectic mix of experimental, reggae, punk, metal and other genres. Daily noon–5am.

Nabaklab Z. A. Mierovica bulvāris 12 ⓦ nabaklab.lv; map p.689. Part art gallery, part bohemian club with live bands, DJs and a summer terrace for enjoying their own *Nabaklab* brew. Mon–Wed & Sun noon–2am, Thurs, Fri & Sat noon–6am.

Pulkvedis (Nobody Writes to the Colonel) Peldu iela 26/28 ⓦ pulkvedis.lv; map. p.689. The sounds at this split-level former bastion of edgy music sometimes degenerate into 80s pop, but when a good DJ is in the house, this easy-going venue filled with a fun-seeking young crowd is the place to be. Entry €4.50. Tues–Thurs 8pm–3am; Fri & Sat 8pm–5am.

CINEMA

Forum Cinemas (Coca-Cola Plaza) 13 Janvāra iela 8 ⓦ forumcinemas.lv; map p.687. Second-largest cinema in northern Europe, with 14 screens. Tickets €6–10.

Splendid Palace Elizabetes iela 61 ⓦ splendidpalace.lv; map p.687. Rīga's oldest cinema, showing art films as well as blockbusters. Tickets €4.50.

SHOPPING

Art Nouveau Rīga Strēlnieku iela 9 ⓦ artnouveauriga .lv; map p.687. Dedicated entirely to Art Nouveau merchandise, such as small plaster faces copied from the decorations on Rīga's facades. Daily 10am–6pm.

Berga Bazārs Elizabetes iela 83/85; map p.687. Soviet kitsch, freshly baked bread, organically grown produce and gourmet food samples. Second and last Sat of each month 9am–3pm.

Central Market (Centrāltirgus) Next to the bus station; map p.687. This row of massive 1930s former Zeppelin hangars is worth visiting just to appreciate the sheer size of it. It sells everything from half a cow to bread, smoked meats and fake designer watches. Daily 8am–5pm.

Lukabuka In the National Opera ticket hall, Aspazijas bulvaris 3 ⓦ lukabuka.lv; map p.689. Art and design bookshop with cards and stationery – they also sell cool comic books (including titles in English) by local independent publisher Kuš!. Mon–Sat 10am–9pm.

DIRECTORY

Embassies Canada, Baznīcas iela 20/22 ☎ 6781 3945; Ireland, Alberta iela 13 ☎ 6703 9370; UK, Alunāna iela 5 ☎ 6777 4700; US, Samnera Velsa 1 ☎ 6710 7000.

Exchange Marika: Brīvības bulvāris 30 and Dzirnavu iela 96 (both 24hr).

Hospital ARS, Skolas iela 5 ☎ 6720 1007. Some English-speaking doctors.

Internet Elik, Kalku 11 (24hr; €1.20/hr).

Left luggage At the bus station (daily 6.30am–11pm; from €0.30/hr, depending on weight). Also lockers at the left-luggage office (Rokas Bagāīas) in the train station basement (4.30am–midnight; €3/day).

Pharmacy Saules aptieka, Brīvības 68 (24hr).

Post office Brīvības bulvāris 32 (Mon–Fri 7.30am–7pm, Sat 9am–3pm).

The rest of Latvia

In summer, the whole of Latvia seems to head to the beach – be it **Jūrmala**, the lively string of seaside resorts near Rīga, or the picturesque port of **Ventspils**, with its unspoiled stretch of sand and its music festival. Nature lovers can head inland to the picturesque little town of **Sigulda**.

JŪRMALA

A 20km string of small seaside resorts lining the Baltic coast west of Rīga, **JŪRMALA** was originally favoured by the tsarist nobility and later drew tens of thousands of holiday-makers from all over the USSR; it continues to be a popular beach resort today. Its wide, clean, sandy **beach** is backed by dunes and pine woods, and dotted with beer tents and climbing frames. It pulses with sun worshippers during the summer, especially during the week-long **music festival** in July.

WHAT TO SEE AND DO

Jomas iela, the pedestrianized main street running east from the station square, teems with people and has a number of excellent restaurants and cafés, as well as craft stalls and art exhibitions. A few paths lead to the beach from Jūras iela, north of Jomas iela. The beach aside, Jūrmala's attractions include the wonderful new interactive **Jūrmala City Museum** (Wed–Sun 11am–5pm; €4.50), which charts the town's history as a popular beach resort. Upstairs is reserved for excellent temporary art and photography exhibitions. Another Jūrmala gem is the **"Inner Light" art gallery** at Omnibusa iela 19 (June–Aug 11am–6pm; Sept–May Sat & Sun noon–6pm; €1.50; ◍jermolajev.lv); local artist Vitaly Yermolayev specializes in the use of eerie glow-in-the-dark paint. Near the beach, at Turaidas iela 1, you'll find the Dzintari (☎ 6776 2117, ◍dzk.lv), an open-air, 2000-capacity concert venue which hosts regular music events in the summer.

ARRIVAL AND INFORMATION

By train Trains leave Rīga's station from platforms 3 and 4. Majori is the main stop for Jūrmala, eleven stops from Rīga.

Destinations Rīga (roughly every 30min until around 11pm; 30min).

By minibus Minibuses depart from Rīga's Central Minibus Station, opposite the train station (every 10min, 6am–midnight; 25min). Take either the Rīga–Sloka or the Rīga–Dubulti minibus and get off in front of the Majori train station.

Tourist information Lienes iela 5 (Mon–Fri 9am–7pm, Sat 10am–5pm, Sun 10am–3pm; ☎ 6714 7900, ◍jurmala.lv). Helpful staff have info on the town's attractions and accommodation. There's a BalticBike stand (see p.683) just outside.

ACCOMMODATION

Elina Lienes iela 43 ☎ 6776 1665, ◍elinahotel.lv. This popular guesthouse has clean en-suite rooms with TV, in a quiet residential street a 10min walk from the beach. Double **€60**

Kempings Nemo Atbalss iela 1, Vaivari ☎ 6773 2350, ◍nemo.lv. Large campsite popular with caravans and families in a pleasant middle-of-the-forest location just behind the beach, with reasonably clean facilities and a water park on site. There are also double rooms in cabins. Camping **€4** per person, plus **€6** per tent, cabin **€15**

EATING AND DRINKING

Picērija Ripo Tirgoņu 21. Step inside this London-double-decker-bus-cum-pizzeria for the best pizza in town – from the classic pepperoni to the more exotic Subaru (horseradish-mayo sauce, minced meat, bacon and pickles). Small pizza €6–10. Daily 10am–11pm.

Sue's Asia Jomas iela 74. Busy restaurant serving large portions of excellent Indian, Thai and Chinese cuisine. The *Tom yum kuung* is spicy and flavoursome (€7). Daily noon–11pm.

Zangezur Jomas iela 80. Popular Armenian restaurant specializing in grilled meats and other tasty dishes, such as

18

18

aubergines with garlic and walnuts. Try the *hinkale* – large meat dumplings (€5). Daily 11am–11pm.

SALASPILS

The concentration camp at **SALASPILS**, 14km southeast of Rīga, is where most of the city's Jewish population perished during World War II. One hundred thousand people died here, including prisoners of war and Jews from other countries, who were herded into the Rīga Ghetto after most of the indigenous Jewish population had been liquidated. The site is marked by monumental sculptures, with the former locations of the barracks outlined by white stones. Look for the offering of toys by the children's barracks and the bunker, inscribed with the words "Behind this gate the earth groans" – here there's a haunting exhibition (open access; free) about the camp.

ARRIVAL AND DEPARTURE

By train To get here take a suburban train from Rīga central station in the Ogre direction and alight at Dārziņi (at least one hourly; 30min), though be aware that the stop is not well signposted; it's the first one to be completely surrounded by pine forest. From here a clearly signposted path leads to the clearing, a 15min walk through the forest.

RUNDĀLE PALACE

One of the architectural wonders of Latvia, Baroque **Rundāle Palace** (Rundāles Pils; daily: May–Oct 10am–6pm; Nov–April 10am–5pm; combined ticket to the palace, exhibitions and gardens €7.50; ⓦrundale .net) is 77km south of Rīga. Its 138 rooms were built in two phases during the 1730s and 1760s, and designed by **Bartolomeo Rastrelli**, the architect responsible for the Winter Palace in St Petersburg. It was privately owned until 1920 when it fell into disrepair, but has largely been returned

to its former glory through meticulous restoration. Each opulent room is decorated in a unique fashion and there are changing art exhibitions both inside the palace and in the vast landscaped gardens.

ARRIVAL AND DEPARTURE

By bus There are frequent buses from Rīga to Bauska (every 30min, 7am–8pm; 1hr 30min); then take a local service to Pilsrundāle (up to 9 daily; 30min). The palace is across the street from the bus stop.

SIGULDA

Dotted with parks and clustered above the southern bank of the River Gauja around 50km northeast of Rīga, **SIGULDA** is Gauja National Park's main centre and a good jumping-off point for exploring the rest of the **Gauja Valley**.

WHAT TO SEE AND DO

From the train station, Raiņa iela runs north into town, passing the bus station. After about 800m a right turn into Baznīcas iela brings you to the impressive seven-hundred-year-old **Sigulda Church** (Siguldas baznīca).

Turaida Castle

Sigulda is home to three castles: Krimulda Castle (Krimuldas pilsdrupas), Sigulda Castle (Siguldas pilsdrupas), a former stronghold of the German Knights of the Sword, and from which you can see **Turaida Castle** (Turaidas pilsdrvpas), the most impressive of the three. Built on the site of an earlier stronghold by the bishop of Rīga in 1214, the castle was destroyed when lightning hit its gunpowder magazine in the eighteenth century. These days, its cellar exhibitions chart the castle's history (daily 10am–5/7pm; €5) and it's possible to climb up the main tower for 360-degree views of the valley below.

LEARN TO FLY

Aerodium, 5km outside Sigulda, (Tues–Fri 4–8pm, Sat & Sun noon–8pm; €25/€30/2min, €9/€13/min thereafter on weekdays/weekends; ☎2838 4400, ⓦaerodium.lv), lets you experience the intense adrenaline rush of skydiving without jumping out of a plane. You hover atop an air current created by a powerful wind tunnel; beginners fly up to 5m above the fan, while professionals reach heights five times that. Book your time slot online. Take any Rīga-bound bus from Sigulda (€1) and ask to be dropped off at the Silciems stop.

You can reach the castle by bus #12 (for Turaida or Krimulda) from Sigulda bus station (several daily; €0.70). Alternatively, take the cable car (every 30min, 10am–6.30pm; €3) across the Gauja River (daredevils can bungee jump from the cable car at 6.30pm Fri–Sun; €30; ⊕bungee.lv) to Krimulda Castle, descend the wooden staircase signposted "Gūtmaņis Cave", then follow the path past the cave – the setting for a legend of "star-crossed lovers". The path turns to the right before rejoining the main road just short of Turaida itself.

The bobsleigh track

West of Sigulda train station along Auseķļa iela is the **bobsleigh track** where you can hurtle down a concrete half-tube at 80km an hour during the summer months (Sat & Sun 11am–6pm; €11/person/ride), or try the exhilarating professional winter bob (Oct–March noon–7pm; €50).

ARRIVAL AND INFORMATION

By train The train station is a 10min walk southwest of the bus station.
Destinations Rīga (up to 9 daily; 1hr 15min).
By bus Frequent buses from Rīga serve Sigulda's bus station, located a 2min walk south of the town centre.
Destinations Rīga (at least hourly; 1hr 15min).
Tourist information Raiņa iela 3, just to the left of the entrance to the bus staion (Mon–Fri 8am–7pm, Sat 9am–2pm; ☎6797 1335, ⊕tourism.sigulda.lv). Helpful multilingual staff can book you into private rooms and provide information on exploring the Gauja Valley. They can also arrange hot-air ballooning (book in advance; ☎2928 8448, ⊕altius.lv) and bungee jumping from the cable car.
Gauja National Park Administration Baznīcas iela 7 (Mon–Fri 8.30am–5pm; ☎6750 9545; ⊕gnp.gov.lv). Located north of the bus and train stations along Raiņa iela, this helpful office provides information on hiking trails in the Gauja National Park, including the popular trail from Sigulda to the village of Ligatne. Hiking map €3.

ACCOMMODATION

Kaķis Pils iela 8 ☎2915 0104, ⊕cathouse.lv. Spotless, compact rooms with a bar and canteen-style restaurant next door. The disco may keep you awake on Fri and Sat. Double €45
Livkalns Pēterala iela 4b ☎6789 5183. This charming hotel's appeal lies in its secluded location, attractive rooms (the more luxurious doubles have own jacuzzis), some

with a/c and satellite TV, and a splendid cellar restaurant serving regional cuisine. Breakfast included. Double €37
Siguldas Pludmale Peldu iela 2 ☎2924 4948, ⊕makars.lv. Large campsite in a shady riverside spot northwest and downhill from the town centre; the only drawback is the queue for the bathroom. Arranges canoeing and rafting trips. Open May–Sept. Camping €6 per person, plus €3 per tent

EATING AND DRINKING

Kaķu Māja Pils iela 8. The *Black Cat* café offers large helpings of inexpensive canteen-style food and a tempting range of cakes in the bakery next door. Main and a drink: €4.75. Daily 11am–midnight.
Zalumnieku Piestātne Kafejnīca Pils iela 9. Another canteen-style place with a roomy, rustic interior serving large portions of Latvian food; pay by weight. Complete meal €4.50 There's also a separate pizza restaurant; medium pizza €5. Daily 11am–10pm.

VENTSPILS

An attractive seaside city, **VENTSPILS**, 200km northwest of Rīga, is Latvia's biggest commercial port. The city's Old Town, with its cobbled streets, its beach – the best in Latvia – and handful of museums, makes Ventspils a great place to while away a couple of days.

WHAT TO SEE AND DO

One of the city's main draws is the long stretch of clean white-sand beach at the town's western end – a worthy recipient of the Blue Flag and popular with sun worshippers, volleyball players and kitesurfers in summer. Still, it's so big that you needn't jostle other beachgoers for elbow space even at the height of peak

---

GAUJA NATIONAL PARK

Encompassing a diverse range of flora and fauna, **Gauja National Park** (⊕gnp.lv) covers over 920 square kilometres of near-pristine forested wilderness, bisected by the 425km Gauja River. The valley is ideal for exploring by bike, as most of the hiking trails are accessible to cyclists. Numerous "wild" campsites are located along the river's banks, and major campsites in Sigulda, Cēsis and Valmiera, at the north end of the park, arrange overnight canoeing and rafting trips.

18

season. In Jūrmalas Park near the beach, you'll find the popular **Beach Aquapark** and also the **open-air museum**, with ethnographic expositions featuring traditional fishermen's dwellings and equipment.

At the northern end of the beach, a long boardwalk, overlooked by a viewing tower, stretches towards the lighthouse. Here you can spot one of several specimens from Ventspils' bizarre **Cow Parade** – the Sailor Cow. Other cow sculptures are found along the Ostas iela promenade that leads east towards the ferry port; don't miss the **Travelling Cow**, shaped like a giant suitcase. South of the promenade lies the Old Town, with its Art Nouveau buildings and attractive **main square**, overlooked by the jolly yellow **Nicholas Evangelical Lutheran Church** and featuring a giant quill sculpture due to the town's popularity with international writers. The Old Town's most interesting feature is the thirteenth-century **Castle of the Livonian Order** at Jāņa iela 17 (Tues–Sun 10am–6pm; €2), home to an excellent interactive museum featuring the history of the city and port and a disturbing exhibit on the Soviet prison in the barracks.

ARRIVAL AND INFORMATION

By bus The bus station is in the centre at Kuldīga iela 5. Destinations Liepāja (6 daily; 2hr 45min–3hr); Rīga (13–16 daily; 2hr 45min–4hr); Talsi (4–5 daily; 1hr 40min).
By ferry Ferries from Travemünde and Lübeck in Germany, Nynashamn in Sweden, St Petersburg in Russia, and Saaremaa in Estonia arrive at the ferry terminal at Dārza iela 6. Check ⓦ stenaline.lt and ⓦ finnlines.com for updated schedules.
Destinations Lübeck, Germany (1 daily Wed & Sat; 7–9hr); Nynashamn, Sweden (1 daily Tues–Thurs, Sat & Sun; 10hr); St Petersburg, Russia (1 daily Fri & Sun; 14hr); Saaremaa, Estonia (check schedule with tourist office); Travemünde, Germany (1 daily Tues & Fri; 27hr 30min).
Tourist information At the ferry terminal building at Dārza iela 6 (May–Sept Mon–Fri 8am–7pm, Sat 10am–5pm, Sun 10am–3pm; Oct–April Mon–Fri 8am–5pm, Sat & Sun 10am–3pm; ☎ 6362 2263, ⓦ visitventspils.com).

ACCOMMODATION

Kupfernams Kārļa iela 5 ☎ 6362 6999, ⓔ hotelkupfernams.lv. Delightful, centrally located guesthouse with funky en-suite attic rooms with sloping roofs. Wi-fi and breakfast included, and there's a good restaurant downstairs. Double €55

Ventspils Piejūras Kempings Vasarnicu iela 56 ☎ 6362 7925, ⓦ camping.ventspils.lv. To the southwest of the city centre, right next to its white sandy beach, this large, popular campsite offers tent spaces and fully equipped 4-person holiday cottages, as well as guest kitchen and sauna. Camping €4.50 per person, plus €4.50 per tent; cottage €36

EATING AND DRINKING

Buginš Lielā iela 1/3. Hearty soups, grilled meats, pastas and more served amid some of the most chaotic decor you're ever likely to see in one place; think taxidermist gone wild in an antique shop. The outdoor terrace makes a good beer garden in summer. Mains €4.50–10. Daily 11am–midnight.
Julius Meinl Kārļa iela at Kuldigas iela. You'll smell it before you see it; this tiny bakery's the best place for fresh bread and for the most amazing cinnamon and poppy seed swirls in Latvia. Daily 9am–10pm.
Kupfernams Kārļa iela 5. Cosy café and restaurant serving tasty local staples such as grilled fish with grated potato pancakes and crêpes with a variety of fillings. Mains €5–8. Mon–Sat 8am–10pm, Sun 8am–6pm.

CAPE KOLKA AND SLĪTERE NATIONAL PARK

To really get away from it all, take a trip to the village of Kolka at the northernmost tip of **Cape Kolka**, where the Gulf of Rīga meets the Baltic Sea, passing through pine forest and numerous coastal villages along the way. Kolka is part of **Slītere National Park**, a former Soviet military base turned protected nature reserve, and there are a number of nature trails to be hiked, not to mention the seemingly endless expanse of virtually deserted beach. In 2005, the coast suffered from an enormous storm and the tangle of fallen trees, strewn across the deserted beach, is testimony to its severity.

ARRIVAL AND DEPARTURE

By bus Direct bus from Rīga (3 daily; 3hr 45min) or from Ventspils (change at Talsi; 3 daily; 1hr 15min–2hr, plus travel time from Ventspils); disembark at "Kolka".

ACCOMMODATION AND EATING

Ūši 10min walk north of the bus stop ☎ 2947 5692, ⓦ kolka.info. You can stay at this friendly guesthouse (go past the church on your left, then a field to your right) or pitch a tent in the adjacent meadow. Meals are provided on request, or you can buy local smoked fish. Double €44, camping €3.60 per person and tent

HILL OF CROSSES (KRYŽIŲ KALNAS), ŠIAULIAI

Lithuania

HIGHLIGHTS

❶ **Genocide Museum, Vilnius** A haunting reminder of man's inhumanity. **See p.705**

❷ **Trakai** A fairytale medieval castle sitting on its own little island. **See p.708**

❸ **Palanga** Lithuania's premier beach resort; the place to hear live music and party all night. See p.712

❹ **Hill of Crosses** A spiritual monument to Lithuanian identity. **See p.712**

❺ **Curonian Spit** A wild, beautiful national park on the Baltic Coast. **See p.713**

HIGHLIGHTS ARE MARKED ON THE MAP ON P.699

ROUGH COSTS

Daily budget Basic €50, occasional treat €70

Drink Utenos beer €1.70

Food *Cepelinai* (potato and meat parcels) €3.50

Hostel/budget hotel €12/€40

Travel Bus: Kaunas–Klaipeda €15; train: Vilnius–Kaunas €5

FACT FILE

Population 3.2 million

Language Lithuanian

Currency Litas (Lt)

Capital Vilnius

International phone code ☎370

Time zone GMT +2hr

Introduction

Lithuania is a vibrant, quirky and largely unspoiled country, which has undergone rapid change since becoming independent from the Soviet Union in 1990. You'll find a lively nightlife, both in Vilnius and on the coast, ample grounds for outdoor pursuits in the national parks and a number of great beaches, as well as a stark contrast between city life and rural simplicity. Fiercely proud of their country, Lithuanians are more exuberant and welcoming than their Baltic neighbours and you are likely to encounter their hospitality everywhere.

19

Lithuania's small size makes getting around inexpensive; even in well-trodden destinations the volume of visitors is low, leaving you with the feeling that there's still much to discover here. **Vilnius**, with its Baroque Old Town and narrow alleys, also boasts a boisterous nightlife, while the second city, **Kaunas**, has an attractive centre and a couple of interesting museums, along with some excellent restaurants and bars. The port city of **Klaipėda** is a convenient overnight point en route to the resorts of **Neringa** (the Curonian Spit), a unique sliver of sand dunes and forest that shields Lithuania from the Baltic Sea, or to **Palanga**, Lithuania's party town, where everyone flocks in the summer for a good time.

CHRONOLOGY

2000 BC The ancestors of the Lithuanians settle in the Baltic region.

1009 AD First recorded mention of the name Lithuania in the Quedlinburg Annals.

1236 Grand Duke Mindaugas unites Lithuania to ward off German crusaders.

1386 After an arranged marriage between the King of Lithuania and the Queen of Poland, Lithuania officially converts to Christianity.

1410 The Polish–Lithuanian alliance defeats the Teutonic Knights, increasing their military influence in the Baltic region.

1547 First Lithuanian book, *The Simple Words of Catechism*, is published.

1795 Russia takes control of Lithuania.

1865 Growth of the liberation movement leads to violent repression by the Russians.

1900 Mass emigration across the world to escape Russian repression.

1918 Lithuania gains independence.

1940 Lithuania is occupied by the Soviet Union.

1941 Lithuania is invaded by Nazi Germany. Thousands of Lithuanian Jews are killed.

1944–5 Soviet occupation returns. Thousands are deported.

1991 (Jan) Soviet crackdown on the independence movement leaves 14 dead.

1991 (Aug) The Soviet Union collapses and Lithuania regains independence.

2004 Lithuania joins the EU; thousands emigrate to work in Western Europe.

2009 Dalia Grybauskaite becomes the country's first female president.

ARRIVAL AND DEPARTURE

Most tourists arrive by **air**; Vilnius airport is served by several European airlines, including budget airlines Wizz Air (w wizzair.com), Norwegian Air Shuttle (w norwegian.com) and Ryanair (w ryanair.com); the latter also flies to Kaunas. Lithuania has poor **rail** connections with its neighbours; international **buses** from neighbouring countries to Vilnius and Kaunas are far more numerous, with plenty of services from Latvia and Estonia. There are also frequent **ferries** from Kiel in Germany, and Karlshamn in Sweden, to Klaipėda on Lithuania's Baltic coast (w krantas.lt).

GETTING AROUND

Buses are slightly quicker, more frequent and more expensive than trains. It's best to buy long-distance bus tickets in advance, and opt for an express (*ekspresas*), to avoid frequent stops. You can also pay

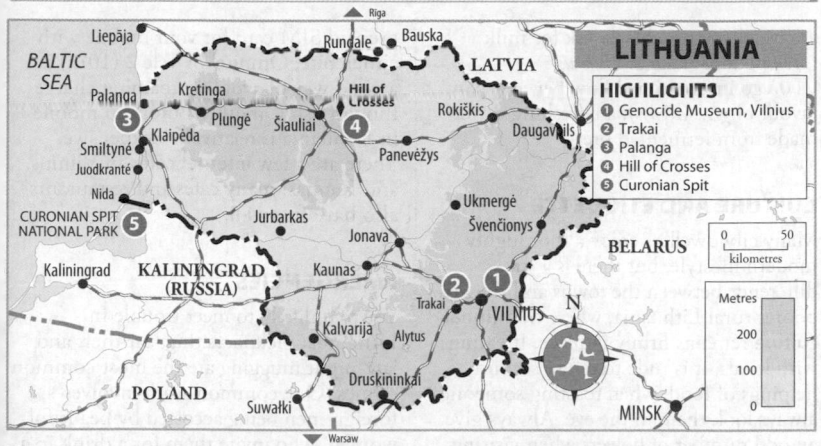

LITHUANIA

HIGHLIGHTS
1. Genocide Museum, Vilnius
2. Trakai
3. Palanga
4. Hill of Crosses
5. Curonian Spit

19

for your ticket on board, although this doesn't guarantee you a seat.

You should also buy long-distance **train** tickets in advance – stations have separate windows for long-distance and suburban (*priemiestinis* or *vietinis*) trains. Long-distance services are divided into "passenger" (*keleivinis traukinys*) and "fast" (*greitas*); the latter usually require a reservation. On timetable boards, look for *isvyksta* (departure) or *atvyksta* (arrival).

In Vilnius and Kaunas public transport is frequent and efficient: buses, trolleybuses and route taxis cover most of the city. The Curonian Spit is best explored by **bicycle**; bike rentals are inexpensive and plentiful.

ACCOMMODATION

A good way to keep accommodation costs down is by staying in **private rooms**, which typically cost 120–140Lt with breakfast. The most reliable agency for these is Litinterp (⊕litinterp.com), which has offices and guesthouses in Vilnius, Kaunas and Klaipėda; the latter can book rooms in Palanga and on the Curonian Spit. Spartan double rooms in **budget hotels** can cost as little as 100Lt; smarter mid-range places charge 140–200Lt.

There are an increasing number of **hostels**, especially in Vilnius and Kaunas, usually charging 30–45Lt per night for a dorm bed; it's best to reserve in advance. There are also plenty of **campsites** in rural areas; expect to pay 10–20Lt per person, and the same per tent.

FOOD AND DRINK

Lithuanian **cuisine** is based on traditional rural fare. Typical starters include marinated mushrooms (*marinuoti grybai*), herring (*silkė*) and smoked sausage (*rukyta desra*) along with cold beetroot soup (*saltibarsčiai*). A popular **national dish** is *cepelinai*, or zeppelins – cylindrical potato parcels stuffed with meat, mushrooms or cheese. Others include potato pancakes (*bulviniai blynai*), and *koldunai* – ravioli-like parcels filed with meat or mushroom. Popular **beer snacks** include deep-fried sticks of black bread with garlic (*kepta duona*) and smoked pigs' ears. Pancakes (*blynai, blyneliai* or *lietiniai*) come in a plethora of sweet and savoury varieties.

Most cafés and bars serve reasonably priced food. Well-stocked supermarkets, such as Iki and Maxima, are found in the main cities and towns. Many restaurants are open between 11am and midnight daily, with cafés open from 8/9am and bars closing at 2am at the earliest.

Beer (*alus*) is popular, local brands being Švyturus, Utenos and Kalnapilis, and so is **mead** (*midus*), Lithuania's former nobleman's drink. The leading local **firewaters** are Starka, Trejos devynerios and Medžiotojų – invigorating spirits flavoured with herbs. Most bars in Vilnius and Kaunas follow contemporary international styles, although there are also plenty of folksy Lithuanian places, while cafés (*kavinė*) come in all shapes and sizes. Coffee (*kava*) and tea (*arbata*)

19

are usually served black; ask for milk (*pienas*) and/or sugar (*cukrus*).

Forego international fizzy beverages in favour of *gira* (kvass), a refreshing drink made from fermented bread.

CULTURE AND ETIQUETTE

Many city dwellers enjoy a thoroughly modern lifestyle, but there is a stark difference between the towns and the far poorer rural Lithuania, where **traditional culture** remains firmly in place. If eating with locals, it is rude to refuse second helpings of food; when toasting someone, always look them in the eye. Always give an odd number of flowers when visiting Lithuanians, as even numbers are for the dead. Shaking hands across the threshold is bad luck. Family ties are strong, and extended family gatherings are common. Women tend to fill traditional roles. Only tip in restaurants to reward good service; ten percent is fair.

SPORTS AND ACTIVITIES

Lithuania's top sport is **basketball**, and locals religiously follow the matches on TV. Try to catch a game at Vilnius's Siemens Arena. Lithuania's **national parks**, as well as the Curonian Spit, offer various opportunities for **outdoor activities** such as hiking, biking and canoeing.

COMMUNICATIONS

In major towns, **post offices** (*pastas*) are open Monday to Friday 8am to 6pm and Saturday 8am to 3pm; in smaller places hours are more restricted. **Stamps** are also available at some kiosks and tourist offices. **Public phones** operate with cards (*telefono kortelė*), which you can purchase at post offices and kiosks. Getting a

prepaid SIM card for your mobile with either Bitė, Omnitel or Tele 2 (10Lt) is a good way of avoiding roaming charges, though using another European mobile in Lithuania is relatively inexpensive. There are a few **internet cafés** in Vilnius and Kaunas; many cafés and restaurants also have free **wi-fi**.

EMERGENCIES

You're unlikely to meet trouble in Lithuania; pickpocketing, car theft and late-night mugging are the most common crimes. One common scam involves foreign men being accosted by beautiful women, who invite them for a drink in a nearby rip-off bar – the victims are then charged extortionate amounts for drinks. The **police** expect to be taken seriously, so be polite if you have dealings with them. **Emergency health care** is free, but if you get seriously ill, head home.

INFORMATION

Most major towns have **tourist offices**, often offering accommodation listings and event calendars in English. The **In Your Pocket** guides to Vilnius, Kaunas and Klaipėda (available from bookshops, newsstands, tourist offices and some hotels; ⓦ inyourpocket.com; 6Lt) are indispensable sources of practical information. Regional **maps** and detailed street plans of Vilnius are available in bookshops and kiosks.

MONEY AND BANKS

Lithuania's currency is the **Litas** (usually abbreviated to Lt), which is divided into 100 centai. Coins come as 1, 2, 5, 10, 20 and 50c, and 1, 2 and 5Lt, with notes of 10, 20, 50, 100, 200 and 500Lt. The litas is pegged to the euro (€1= 3.45Lt). **Bank** (*bankas*) opening hours vary widely from one firm to another (Mon–Fri

---

LITHUANIA ONLINE

ⓦ**vilnius-tourism.lt** Vilnius tourist information.
ⓦ**muziejai.lt** Portal for Lithuanian museums.
ⓦ**lietuva.lt** General information about the country.

EMERGENCY NUMBERS

Fire ❶01; Police ❶02; Ambulance ❶03. For general emergencies call ❶112.

LITHUANIAN

	LITHUANIAN	PRONUNCIATION
Yes	*Taip*	Tape
No	*Ne*	Ne
Please	*Prašau*	Prashau
Thank you	*Ačiu*	Achoo
Hello/Good day	*Labas*	Labass
Goodbye	*Viso gero*	Viso gero
Excuse me	*Atsiprašau*	Atsiprashau
Sorry	*Atleiskite*	Ahtlayskita
Where?	*Kur?*	Kur?
Can you show me?	*Galėtumėt man parodyti?*	Gahlehtumet mahn pahrawdeeteh?
Student ticket	*Studento billetas*	Studantoh bileahtahs
Toilet	*Tualetas*	Tuahlatas
I'd like to try…	*Aš norėčiau išbandyti*	Ahsh nawrehchow ishbahndeeteh
I don't eat meat	*Aš nevalgau mėsos*	Ahsh navahlgow mehrsaus
Bill	*Saskaita*	Sahskaitah
Good/Bad	*Geras/Blogas*	Gerass/Blogass
Near/Far	*Artimas/Tolimas*	Artimass/Tolimass
Cheap/Expensive	*Pigus/Brangus*	Piguss/Branguss
Open/Closed	*Atidarytas/Uždarytas*	Atidaritass/Uzhdaritass
Today	*Šiandien*	Shyandyen
Yesterday	*Vakar*	Vakar
Tomorrow	*Rytoj*	Ritoy
How much is…?	*Kiek kainuoja…?*	Kyek kainwoya…?
What time is it?	*Kiek valandų?*	Kyek valandoo?
I don't understand	*Nesuprantu*	Nessuprantoh
Do you speak English?	*Ar jus kalbate angliškai?*	Ar yoos kalbate anglishkay?
One	*Vienas*	Vyenass
Two	*Du/dvi*	Doh/Dvee
Three	*Trys*	Triss
Four	*Keturi*	Keturee
Five	*Penki*	Penkee
Six	*Šeši*	Sheshee
Seven	*Septyni*	Septinee
Eight	*Aštuoni*	Ashtuonee
Nine	*Devyni*	Devinee
Ten	*Dešimt*	Deshimt

8am–3/4pm is a fairly typical schedule). If you're looking to exchange money or get a cash advance outside banking hours, find an **exchange office** (*valiutos keitykla*). There are plentiful **ATMs** in all major towns as well as at the Curonian Spit; **credit cards** are widely accepted.

OPENING HOURS AND PUBLIC HOLIDAYS

Opening hours for **shops** are 9/10am to 6/7pm. Outside Vilnius, some places take an hour off for lunch; most usually close on Sunday (though some food shops stay open). Most shops and all banks are

STUDENT AND YOUTH DISCOUNTS

An ISIC or an IYTC card will usually get you fifty percent discount on museums and sights, as well as on public transport and some long-distance trains during term time. A YHA card gets discounts at HI-affiliated youth hostels, while ISIC/IYTC cards are accepted at any hostel.

19

closed on the following **public holidays**: January 1, February 16, March 11, Easter Sunday, Easter Monday, May 1, July 6, August 15, November 1, December 25 and 26.

Vilnius

A cosmopolitan city with an ancient, Baroque heart, **VILNIUS** is relatively compact and easy to get to know, with a variety of inexpensive attractions and a lively nightlife. Its numerous churches and palaces jostle for space in the Old Town's windy cobbled alleys, where glitzy restaurants stand incongruously beside dilapidated old buildings. The large student population lends the place a tangible air of energy and optimism. Beguiling, and sometimes downright odd, Vilnius has an addictive quality.

WHAT TO SEE AND DO

At the centre of Vilnius, poised between the medieval and nineteenth-century parts of the city, is **Cathedral Square** (Katedros aikštė). To the south of here along Pilies gatvė and Didžioji gatvė is the **Old Town**, containing perhaps the most impressive concentration of Baroque architecture in northern Europe. West of the square in the **New Town** is Gedimino prospektas, a nineteenth-century boulevard and the focus of the city's commercial and administrative life. The traditionally **Jewish areas** of Vilnius between the Old Town and Gedimino prospektas still retain some sights, and the community that once lived here is remembered in a brace of good museums.

Cathedral Square
Cathedral Square is dominated by the Neoclassical **cathedral** (daily 7.30am–7.30pm), dating from the thirteenth century when a wooden church was built here on the site of a temple dedicated to Perkūnas, the god of thunder. The highlight of the airy, vaulted interior is the opulent **Chapel of St Casimir**, the patron saint of Lithuania. Next to the cathedral on the square is the

white belfry, once part of the fortifications of the vanished Lower Castle. Between the cathedral and the belfry lies a small coloured tile with *stebuklas* (miracle) written on it, marking the spot from where, in 1989, two million people formed a human chain that stretched all the way to Tallinn, Estonia, to protest against Soviet occupation.

The Grand Dukes' Palace
Immediately behind the cathedral stands the **Grand Dukes' Palace** (Valdovu rumai; Tues–Sun 10am–5pm; 10Lt; ⓦ valdovurumai.lt), a twenty-first-century reconstruction of a Renaissance palace that fell into ruin at the end of the eighteenth century. Rebuilt more or less accurately by following old paintings and drawings, the courtyard-edged complex now holds a sumptuous collection of furnishings and artworks displayed in over thirty rooms, reflecting the opulent style in which Lithuania's Grand Dukes might once have lived. Opened in summer 2013, it's one of Lithuania's best-labelled and best-presented collections, and also comes with a gift shop and a café.

Gediminas Castle and Museum
Rising behind Cathedral Square is the tree-clad Castle Hill, its summit crowned by the red-brick **Gediminas Castle** – one of the city's best-known landmarks – founded by Grand Duke Gediminas, the Lithuanian ruler who consolidated the country's independence. The tower houses a little **museum** (May–Sept daily 10am–7pm; Oct–April Tues–Sun 10am–5pm; 5Lt), with displays of armour and models showing the former extent of Vilnius's medieval fortifications. The view of the Old Town from the top is unparalleled. Take the funicular (Tues–Sun 10am–5pm; 3Lt return) from the courtyard of the Applied Art Museum.

The Lithuanian National Museum
About 100m north of the cathedral is the **Lithuanian National Museum**, at Arsenalo 1 (Lietuvos Nacionalinis Muziejus;

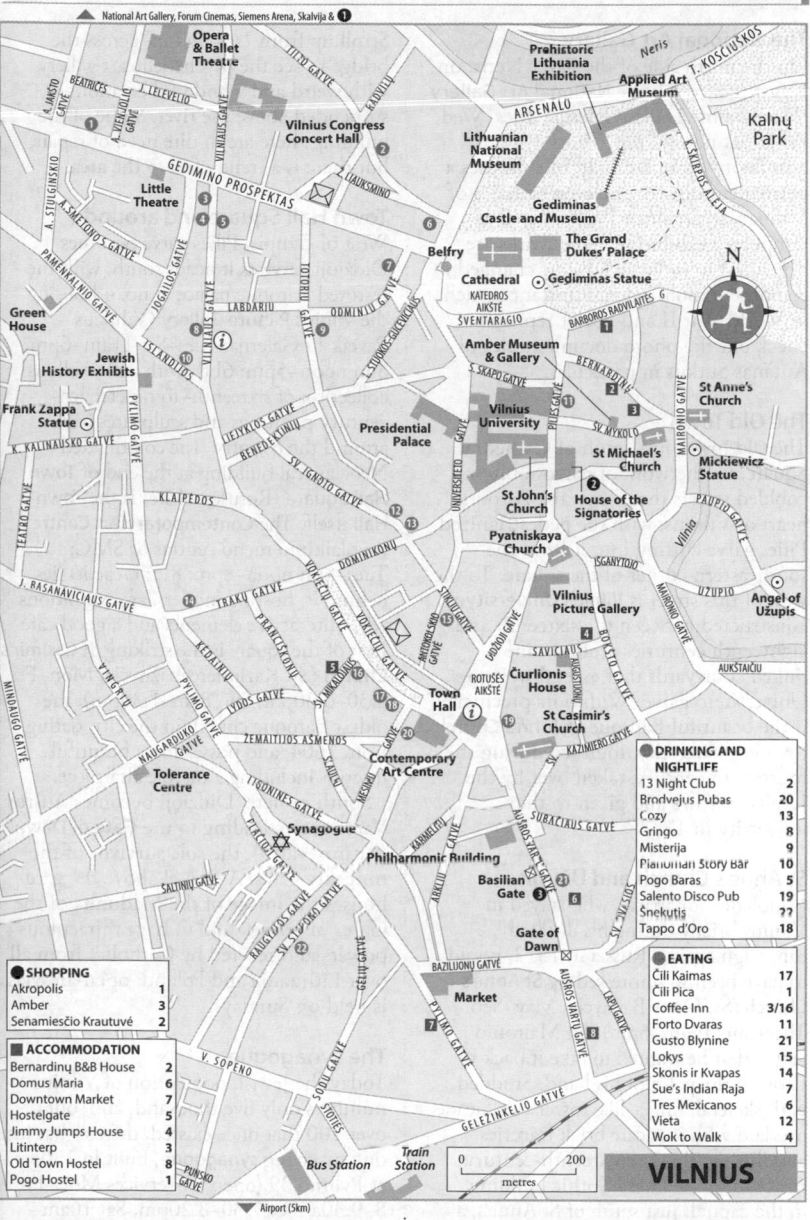

VILNIUS

0 ——— 200
metres

● **DRINKING AND NIGHTLIFE**
13 Night Club	2
Brodvejus Pubas	20
Cozy	13
Gringo	8
Misterija	9
Pianoman Story Bar	10
Pogo Baras	5
Salento Disco Pub	19
Šnekutis	22
Tappo d'Oro	18

● **EATING**
Čili Kaimas	17
Čili Pica	1
Coffee Inn	3/16
Forto Dvaras	11
Gusto Blynine	21
Lokys	15
Skonis ir Kvapas	14
Sue's Indian Raja	7
Tres Mexicanos	6
Vieta	12
Wok to Walk	4

● **SHOPPING**
Akropolis	1
Amber	3
Senamiesčio Krautuvé	2

■ **ACCOMMODATION**
Bernardinų B&B House	2
Domus Maria	6
Downtown Market	7
Hostelgate	5
Jimmy Jumps House	4
Litinterp	3
Old Town Hostel	8
Pogo Hostel	1

▼ Airport (5km)

19

Tues–Sat 10am–5pm, Sun 10am–3pm; 5Lt; ⓦ lnm.lt), which traces the history of Lithuania from prehistoric times to 1940 through an interesting collection of artefacts, paintings and photographs, including a display of wooden crucifixes and ethnographic reconstructions of peasant life. A little further north on Arsenalo, a separate department houses the much snazzier **Prehistoric Lithuania Exhibition** (same hours; 5Lt), displaying flint, iron, bronze and silver objects and covering the history of Lithuanians up to the Middle Ages.

The National Art Gallery

On the north side of the River Neris, on Konstitucijos 22, the **National Art Gallery** (Nacionalinė Dailės Galerija; Tues, Wed, Fri & Sat noon–7pm, Thurs 1–8pm, Sun noon–5pm; ⓦndg.lt; 6Lt) houses a permanent display of eleven galleries of Lithuanian art since 1900, as well as temporary exhibitions. The works are organized to indicate how art changed in response to political circumstances such as World War II and Soviet repression; check out the photo documentaries of Antanas Sutkus in particular.

The Old Town

The **Old Town**, just south of Cathedral Square, is a network of narrow, often cobbled streets that forms the Baroque heart of Vilnius, with the pedestrianized Pilies gatvė cutting into it from the southeastern corner of the square. To the west of this street is **Vilnius University**, constructed between the sixteenth and eighteenth centuries around nine linked courtyards that extend west to Universiteto gatvė. Within its precincts is the beautiful Baroque **St John's Church** (Šv Jono baznyčia), founded during the fourteenth century, taken over by the Jesuits in 1561 and given to the university in 1737.

St Anne's Church and Užupis

Napoleon Bonaparte, who stayed in Vilnius briefly during his ill-fated campaign against Russia in 1812, is said to have been so impressed by **St Anne's Church** (Šv. Onos Bažnyčia; May–Sept Tues–Sun 10am–6pm), on Maironio gatvė, that he wanted to take it back to Paris on the palm of his hand. Studded with skeletal, finger-like towers, its facade overlaid with intricate brick traceries and fluting, this late sixteenth-century structure is the finest Gothic building in the capital. Just south of St Anne's, a bridge over the River Vilnia forms the border of the self-declared independent republic of **Užupis**, home to a flourishing population of artists, bohemians and yuppies (note the locks on the bridge: lovers fasten them here and then throw the key in the river to symbolize their union).

Stroll up from *Užupio Café* across the bridge to see the psychedelic art gallery with weird and wonderful creations suspended above the river. Some of the buildings here are in dire need of repair, but there is a trendy feel to the area.

Town Hall Square and around

West of Užupis, Pilies gatvė becomes Didžioji gatvė as it heads south, with the restored Baroque palace at no. 4 housing the **Vilnius Picture Gallery** (Vilniaus Paveikslų Galerija; Tues–Sat 11am–6pm, Sun noon–5pm; 6Lt), with a marvellous collection of sixteenth- to nineteenth-century paintings and sculptures from around the country. The colonnaded Neoclassical building at the end of **Town Hall Square** (Rotušės aikštė) is the **Town Hall** itself. The **Contemporary Art Centre** (Suolaikinio meno centras or SMC; Tues–Sun noon–8pm; 8Lt; ⓦcac.lt) lies behind it, hosting modern art exhibitions with interactive elements and a good café. East of the square is the striking **St Casimir's Church** (Šv. Kazimiero Bažnyčia; Mon–Fri 4.30–6.30pm, Sun 8am–1.30pm), the oldest Baroque church in the city, dating from 1604, and possessing a beautiful interior including a marble altarpiece.

South of here, Didžioji becomes Aušros Vartų gatvė, leading to the **Gate of Dawn** (Aušros Vartų), the sole survivor of the nine city gates. A chapel above the gate houses the image of the Madonna of the Gates of Dawn, said to have miraculous powers and revered by Catholics from all over Lithuania and Poland; open-air Mass is held on Sundays.

The synagogue

Today the Jewish population of Vilnius numbers only five thousand, and, out of over 100 that once existed, the city has just one surviving **synagogue**, built in 1903, at Pylimo 39 (open for services Mon–Fri 8–9.30am & 7.30–8.20pm, Sat 10am–2pm, Sun 8.45–9.45am & 7.30–8pm).

Jewish Museum

The **Vilna Gaon Jewish State Museum** (Valstybinis Vilniaus Gaono Žydų Muziejus; 5Lt; ⓦwww.jmuseum.lt) is housed in three separate branches. The

JEWISH VILNIUS

Before World War II, Vilnius was one of the most important centres of **Jewish** life in Eastern Europe. The Jews – first invited to settle in 1410 by Grand Duke Vytautas – made up around a third of the city's population, mainly concentrated in the western fringes of the Old Town around present-day Vokiečių gatvė, Žydų gatvė and Antokolskio gatvė. Massacres of the Jewish population began soon after the Germans occupied Vilnius on June 24, 1941, and those who survived the initial killings found themselves herded into two **ghettos**. The smaller of these ghettos centred on the streets of Žydų, Antokolskio, Stiklių and Gaono, and was liquidated in October 1941, while the larger occupied an area between Pylimo, Vokiečių, Lydos, Mikalojaus, Karmelitų and Arklių streets, and was liquidated in September 1943. Most of Vilnius's 80,000 Jewish residents perished in Paneriai forest, 10km southwest of the city.

Jewish History Exhibits at Pylimo 4 (Mon–Thurs & Sun 10am–2pm; free) has displays upstairs on Jewish partisan resistance, life in the Vilnius ghetto, and an exhibit on Lithuanians who risked their lives to save Jews during the Nazi occupation. The **Green House**, slightly uphill at Pamėnkalnio 12 (Mon–Thurs 9am–5pm, Fri 9am–4pm, Sun 10am–4pm; 5Lt), contains a harrowing display on the fate of Vilnius and Kaunas Jews during World War II, including eyewitness accounts, and many extremely disturbing photographs with some captions in English. The most recent addition to the Jewish State Museum is the **Tolerance Centre**, Naugarduko 10/2 (Mon 11am–9pm, Tues–Thurs 10am–6pm, Fri & Sun 10am–4pm; 5Lt), occupying a restored former Jewish theatre. It houses some excellent twentieth-century Jewish artwork, as well as fine religious items and an excellent display in English on the second floor charting the history of Jews in Lithuania from the fourteenth century until the present day.

Frank Zappa statue

On Kalinausko Street, the bronze head of rocker **Frank Zappa** is perched on a column against a backdrop of street art. Civil servant Saulis Paukstys founded the local Zappa fan club and, in 1992, commissioned the socialist-realist sculptor Konstantinas Bogdanas to create this unique memorial.

Gedimino prospektas and the Genocide Museum

Gedimino prospektas, running west from Cathedral Square, is the most important commercial street. On the southern side of **Lukiskių aikštė**, a square around 900m west of Cathedral Square, is Gedimino 40, Lithuania's former KGB headquarters. The building also served as Gestapo headquarters during the German occupation, and, more recently, the Soviets incarcerated political prisoners in the basement. It's now the **Genocide Museum** (Genocido aukų muziejus; entrance at Aukų 2a; Wed–Sat 10am–6pm, Sun 10am–5pm; 6Lt; ⊚genocid.lt /muziejus), its torture cells and execution chamber making a grim impression. Well-labelled, detailed exhibits on Soviet occupation, deportation and Lithuanian partisan resistance are upstairs; the optional English-language audiotape commentary (8Lt) is worthwhile if you want a detailed prison tour.

ARRIVAL AND DEPARTURE

By plane The airport is 5km south of the centre, with regular trains to the central station (every 30min, 6.30am–7.30pm; 7min; 2.50Lt). Buses #1 and #2 (every 30min; 20min; 2.50Lt) will also take you to the centre. A taxi costs around 50Lt.

By train The main train station is at Geležinkelio 16, with 24hr luggage storage in the basement, a 24hr currency exchange, ATMs, detailed timetables, information office and a Maxima supermarket.

Destinations Kaunas (every 30min; 1hr 15min–1hr 45min); Klaipėda (3 daily; 4hr 40min–5hr); Moscow (1–2 daily; 14–16hr); St Petersburg (2 weekly; 18hr 30min); Trakai (8 daily; 40min); Warsaw (1 daily; change at Kaunas and Šestokai; 10hr 30min).

By bus The bus terminal, just across the road from the train station, has luggage storage and an ATM.

Destinations Kaunas (every 20–30min; 1hr 30min–2hr); Klaipėda (hourly; 4hr); Nida (via Klaipėda; 1 daily at 7am; 5hr 50min); Palanga (8 daily, 5hr); Rīga (8 daily; 5hr–5hr

19

30min); Tallinn (5 daily; 9hr); Trakai (every 30min; 30min); Warsaw (2 daily; 9hr).

INFORMATION

Tourist information The multilingual staff of the two main tourist office branches at Vilniaus 22 (Mon–Fri 9am–6pm, Sat & Sun 10am–4pm; ☎5 262 9660, ⓦ vilnius-tourism.lt) and Didžioji 31, in the town hall (☎5 262 6470; same hours), offer advice on accommodation, events listings and festivals (ⓦ vilniusfestivals.lt).

GETTING AROUND

By bus Tickets cost 2Lt from newspaper kiosks or 2.50Lt from the driver. You can buy a one-/three-/ten-day ticket from the kiosk just to the left of the train station near the trolleybus stop for 13/23/46Lt. Validate your ticket by punching it in the machine on board. Alternatively, hail a minibus (normally yellow) at any bus stop in the direction you're going, pay the driver 3–4Lt and you'll be dropped off at the stop you require.
By taxi Prices are usually reasonable and fares should cost no more than 2Lt/km. Phoning ahead guarantees you a better rate; try Ekipažas (☎5 239 5539).

ACCOMMODATION

★ **Bernardinų B&B House** Bernardinu 5 ☎5 261 5134, ⓦ bernardinuhouse.com. Great-value B&B with spacious, tastefully decorated rooms, all with cable TV and some en suite. Offers excursions throughout Lithuania. Breakfast 15Lt extra. Double 170Lt
Downtown Market Pylimo 57 ☎679 85 476, ⓦ downtownmarket.lt. A quirky, friendly boutique hotel close to the Gate of Dawn. The six en-suite rooms are each decorated in market themes (flower market, flea market etc). Organic breakfast included. Double 190Lt
Hostelgate Šv. Mikalojaus 3 ☎638 32 818, ⓦ hostelgate .lt. This bustling central hostel, run by outgoing, helpful staff, offers clean dorms, kitchen, table football and wi-fi. Organized excursions include sauna tours and trips to fire weaponry in the countryside. Dorm 39Lt, double 120Lt
★ **Jimmy Jumps House** Savičiaus 12 ☎607 88 435, ⓦ jimmyjumpshouse.com. Difficult to find but worth it, this backpackers' hostel has a great party feel and offers free walking tours of Vilnius. Kitchen, wi-fi and great waffle breakfast included. Dorm 40Lt, double 120Lt
Litinterp Bernardinų 7 ☎5 212 3850, ⓦ litinterp.com. Stay in the central guesthouse with airy, comfortable rooms and shared bathrooms and kitchenettes, or ask the helpful multilingual staff to book you a private room in the Old Town with a host family (around 180Lt). Book in advance in summer. Breakfast included. Double 140Lt
Old Town Hostel Aušros Vartų 20–10 ☎5 262 5357, ⓦ old townhostel.lt. Cramped, rowdy, but comfortable HI-affiliated hostel near the train and bus stations. Free internet and wi-fi;

★ **TREAT YOURSELF**
Domus Maria Aušros Vartų 12 ☎5 264 4880, ⓦ domusmaria.lt. An oasis of calm in the heart of the city, this hotel has been converted from a seventeenth-century monastery and has a large courtyard to relax in. Some of the bright en-suite rooms look out onto the Gate of Dawn. Double 320Lt

breakfast 5Lt extra. Dorm 35Lt, double 110Lt
Pogo Hostel Barboros Radvilaites 3-1 ☎670 795 91, ⓦ pogo.lt. A bright, neatly renovated town house in the heart of the action, with modern design touches and pop art on the walls. Dorm 45Lt, double 138Lt

EATING

There's a fast-growing range of eating options in Vilnius and a variety of cuisines to match. Bars and cafés serve both snacks and meals, and often represent better value for money than restaurants.

CAFÉS, CHEAP EATS AND SNACKS

Coffee Inn Vilniaus 17; also at Vokiečių 18. It may be a café chain, but it's local and has character, boasting homely mix-and-match furnishings and a young crowd. Excellent coffee, smoothies, muffins, sandwiches, wraps – and cheesecake to die for. Mon–Thurs 7am–10pm, 7am–11pm, Sat 8am–11pm, Sun 8am–10pm.
Forto Dvaras Pilies 16. An excellent place to try fairly authentic *cepelinai* (12Lt) or stuffed potato pancakes (10Lt). Cheap, tasty and filling. Daily 11am–11pm.
Gusto Blynine Aušros Vartų 6. Substantial, tasty crêpes with every imaginable sweet or savoury filling (6Lt). A good place to enjoy Lithuania's legendary potato pancakes. Daily 9am–10pm.
Skonis ir Kvapas Trakų 8. The most beautiful vaulted interior in town. Big pots of tea, Arabian rugs and an affordable range of cakes and hot meals. Drinks 7Lt; mains 8–15Lt. Daily 10am–10pm.

RESTAURANTS

Čili Kaimas Vokiečių 8. Faux-traditional restaurant whose pub-like interior is decorated with agricultural tools, antlers and even a whole tree. The vast menu of Lithuanian dishes includes *cepelinai* (13Lt) and salads (10Lt). Mon–Thurs & Sun 11am–midnight, Fri & Sat 11am–4am.
Čili Pica Gedimino 23. Popular place for inexpensive thin-crust and deep-pan pizzas. Twelve more branches, including one at the Europa shopping mall. Medium pizza 15–18Lt. Mon–Wed & Sun 9am–3am, Thurs–Sat 9am–6am.
Lokys Stiklių 8 ☎5 262 9046. Cosy Lithuanian cellar

restaurant specializing in well-cooked game dishes that are worth the splurge. Beaver stew 30Lt; quail with blackberry sauce 40Lt. Daily noon–midnight.

♠ Sue's Indian Raja Udminių 3 ☎ 5 266 1888. One of the best restaurants in town, this place is popular with expats and locals alike. Gorge yourself on excellent curry (around 30Lt), though be warned that the dishes are authentically spicy. Mon & Sun 11am–10pm, Tues–Sat 11am–11pm.

★ Tres Mexicanos Tilto 2 ☎674 18 600. Run by Mexicans and it shows: try the chocolate chicken (22Lt) or fajitas (24Lt), and wash it down with the house margarita (12Lt). Daily 11am–midnight.

Vieta Šv Ignoto 12. Vegetarian restaurant and wine bar with a regularly changing menu of soups, stews and pies, many with an East-West fusion approach to the spicing. Only problem is they tend to run out of mains come the evening. Mains 12–16Lt. Daily noon–10pm.

Wok To Walk Vilniaus 19. A great little spot where you choose from an array of noodles, rice, vegetables and sauce and it's all wok-fried in front of you. Quick and tasty. Mains 12Lt. Mon–Thurs 11am–10pm, Fri 11am–3am, Sat noon–midnight, Sun noon–8pm.

DRINKING AND NIGHTLIFE

A rapidly developing bar strip along Vilniaus gatve (and adjacent Islandijos) has given Vilnius a new-found every-night-of-the-week buzz. Most bars are open late and many feature DJs at weekends, offering effective competition to the pay-to-enter disco clubs.

BARS

Brodvėjus Pubas Mėsinių 4 ⓦ brodvejus.lt. Popular drinking/dancing venue with live bands (Thurs–Sun) and DJs, and a full menu of snacks and hot meals including lunch specials. Beer 8Lt. Entry 10Lt upwards on music nights. Daily 8pm–2am or later.

Cozy Dominikonų 10. Chilled-out cellar bar with a choice of three rooms, DJ appearances, extensive drinks menu (beers 8Lt) and a bargain two-course business lunch (16Lt). Mon–Thurs 9am–2am, Fri 9am–4am, Sat 10–4am, Sun 10–2am.

Gringo Vilniaus 31. Animated and cheerful café-bar with sofas and tables in the back corner and a constant crush around the bar. One of the key stations on the Vokiečių-Vilnius crawl, it attracts a fair crowd come the weekend. Mon–Wed & Sun 11am–2am, Thurs 11am–3am, Fri & Sat 11am–4am.

Misterija Totorių 18 ⓦ misterija.lt. Lively pub with themed parties, board games and a weekly quiz. A great place to make new friends. Beers 6Lt, cocktails from 10Lt. Mon–Thurs 11am–4am, Fri 11am–6am, Sat 6pm–6am, Sun 6pm–4am.

Pianoman Story Bar Islandijos 1. One of a string of bars along Islandijos, *Pianoman* is in many ways the ideal pub – a good place to sit and talk, watch midweek sport on TV, or enjoy the raw party mood come the weekend. Mon–Thurs 5pm–2am.

Pogo Baras Vilniaus 12 ⓦ pogobaras.lt. This three-room basement bar is something of an indie-rock mecca, with unsigned bands performing on a tiny stage at weekends and a suitably underground soundtrack most other nights. Cheap and tasty Vilniaus beer on tap. Mon–Thurs & Sat 6pm–1am, Fri 6pm–3am, Sun 6–11pm.

Šnekutis Šv. Stepono 8. An excellent place to sample microbrews and ales from all over Lithuania (5Lt) plus traditional dishes (around 12Lt). The rustic decor and tasty beer snacks are a nice touch. Mon–Sat 11am–11pm.

Tappo D'oro Vokiečiu 8. Wine bar with a mildly bohemian edge – It's constantly full of everyone from students to established cultural figures, with the weekend fun usually extending out onto the pavement. Mon–Sat 6pm–3am.

CLUBS

13 Night Club Tilto 13 ⓦ 13nightclub.lt. Cellar club with a relaxed, studenty atmosphere and a relaxed entrance policy. Has regular themed nights. Entry 20Lt. Thurs–Sat 10pm–6am.

Salento Disco Pub Didžioji 28. Various themed nights (most involving foam), cheesy pop tunes, large TV screens and a young and up-for-it crowd. Entry 20Lt. Daily 9pm–6am.

ENTERTAINMENT

Forum Cinemas Akropolis Ozo 25 ⓦ forumcinemas.lt. Modern, multi-screen cinema in Vilnius's largest shopping mall, showing the latest blockbusters in original language, with subtitles. Entry 14–20Lt.

Opera & Ballet Theatre Vienuolio 1 ☎ 5 262 0727, ⓦ opera.lt. Stunning building featuring well-attended performances by local opera and ballet companies.

Siemens Arena Ozo 14 ☎ 5 247 7576, ⓦ siemens-arena .com. Top venue for sports and concerts featuring international stars.

Skalvija Goštauto 2/15 ☎ 5 261 0505, ⓦ skalvija.lt. International art films are shown in this central venue by the river. Entry 6–12Lt.

Vilnius Congress Concert Hall Vilniaus 6/14 ☎ 5 261 8828, ⓦ lvso.lt. Chamber music, orchestra performances and ballet.

SHOPPING

Akropolis Ozo 25. Huge shopping complex around 3km north of town with a variety of clothing and jewellery shops, plus an indoor ice rink and the Vichy Aqua Park with water slides (65Lt). Daily 8am–10pm.

Amber Aušros Vartų 9. An extensive array of amber jewellery and handicrafts. Mon–Fri 10am–7pm, Sat & Sun till 5pm.

19

19

Senamiesčio Krautuvė Literatų 5. Fresh Lithuanian fare including pickles, sausages and cakes, all laid out in baskets for you to sample. Mon–Sat 10am–8pm, Sun 11am–5pm.

DIRECTORY

Banks and exchange ATMs are plentiful. Citadele, outside the station at Geležinkelio 6 (24hr), changes money at decent rates.

Embassies and consulates Australia, Vilniaus 23 ☏ 5 212 3369; Canada, Jogailos 4 ☏ 5 249 0950; Ireland, Gedimino 1 ☏ 5 262 9460; UK, Antakalnio 2 ☏ 5 246 2900; US, Akmenų 6 ☏ 5 266 5500.

Hospital Vilnius University Emergency Hospital, Šiltnamių 29 ☏ 5 216 9069.

Internet Taškas, Jasinskio 1/8 (24hr; 8Lt/hr).

Left luggage Train station has 24hr luggage storage in the basement. Bus station also has baggage room (5.30am–9.45pm).

Pharmacy Eurovaistinė, Ukmergės 282 (Maxima; 24hr); Gedimino Vaistinė, Gedimino 27 (Mon–Fri 7.30am–8pm, Sat & Sun 10am–5pm).

Police Saltoniškiu 19 ☏ 5 271 9731.

Post office Gedimino prospektas 7 (Mon–Fri 7.30am–7pm, Sat 9am–4pm).

TRAKAI

Around 30km west of Vilnius lies the little town of **TRAKAI**, a mix of concrete Soviet-style buildings merging with the wooden cottages of the Karaite community, Lithuania's smallest ethnic minority. Standing on a peninsula jutting out between two lakes, Trakai is the site of two impressive medieval castles and makes for a worthwhile day-trip from the capital.

WHAT TO SEE AND DO

Once you arrive, follow Vytauto gatvė and turn right down Kėstučio gatvė to reach the remains of the **Peninsula Castle**, now partially restored after having been destroyed by the Russians in 1655. Skirting the ruins along the lakeside path, you will see the spectacular **Island Castle** (Salos pilis), one of Lithuania's most famous monuments, accessible by two wooden drawbridges and preceded by souvenir and rowing-boat rental (15Lt) stalls. You can also rent yachts here (80Lt for 40min cruise with skipper). Built around 1400 AD by Grand Duke Vytautas, under whom Lithuania reached the pinnacle of its power, the castle fell into ruin from the seventeenth century until a 1960s restoration returned it to its former glory (May–Sept daily 10am–7pm; March, April & Oct Tues–Sun 10am–6pm; Nov–Feb Tues–Sun 10am–5pm; 14Lt, students 6Lt, permission to take photos 4Lt). The history museum inside displays artefacts discovered while excavating the site.

Trakai is home to three hundred Karaim – a Judaic sect of Turkish origin whose ancestors were brought here from the Crimea by Grand Duke Vytautas to serve as bodyguards. You can learn more about their cultural contribution to Trakai at the **Karaite Ethnographic Exhibition** (22 Karaimų gatvė; Wed–Sun 10am–6pm; 4Lt).

ARRIVAL AND DEPARTURE

By bus and train Take a bus from Vilnius's main bus station (at least one hourly; 35min; last bus from Trakai at 8.45pm) or a train (8 daily; 35min).

EATING

Kybynlar Karaimų 29. Several places in Trakai serve *kibinai*, traditional Karaite pasties stuffed with minced meat, mushrooms or other savoury fillings. This place, just off the main street, has the biggest choice (5–7Lt per pasty), as well as grilled meats and salads. pasty – served up at town cafés. Wash it down with gira, a semi-alcoholic drink made from fermented bread. Mon–Thurs & Sun noon–9pm, Fri & Sat noon–10pm.

The rest of Lithuania

Lithuania is predominantly rural – a gently undulating, densely forested landscape scattered with lakes, and fields dotted with ambling storks in the summer. The major city of **Kaunas**, west of the capital, rivals Vilnius in terms of its historical importance. Further west, the main highlights of the coast are the **Curonian Spit**, whose dramatic dunescapes can be reached by ferry and bus from **Klaipėda**, and **Palanga**, which fills up in summer with thousands of people looking for fun.

KAUNAS

KAUNAS, 98km west of Vilnius and easily reached by bus or rail, is Lithuania's second city, seen by many Lithuanians as the true heart of their country; it served as provisional **capital** during the interwar period of 1920–39. It is undergoing rapid modernization, with the mirror-like exteriors of new buildings reflecting parts of the medieval city wall. While much of Kaunas is a busy urban sprawl, visitors will invariably be drawn to the old heart of the city where the main attractions lie.

WHAT TO SEE AND DO

The most picturesque part of Kaunas is the **Old Town** (Senamiestis), centred on **Town Hall Square** (Rotušės aikštė), on a spur of land between the Neris and Nemunas rivers. The square is lined with fifteenth- and sixteenth-century merchants' houses in pastel stucco shades, but the overpowering feature is the magnificent Town Hall itself, its tiered Baroque facade rising to a graceful 53m tower.

The cathedral and castle

Occupying the northeastern shoulder of the square, the red-brick tower of Kaunas's austere **cathedral** stands at the western end of Vilniaus gatvė. Dating back to the reign of Vytautas the Great, the cathedral was much added to in subsequent centuries. After the plain exterior, the lavish gilt-and-marble interior comes as a surprise: the large statue adorned Baroque high altar (1775) steals the limelight. Predating the cathedral by several centuries is **Kaunas Castle**, whose scant remains survive just northwest of the square. Little more than a restored tower and a couple of sections of wall are left, with temporary art exhibitions inside (6Lt), but in its day the fortification was a major obstacle to the Teutonic Knights.

The New Town

The main thoroughfare of Kaunas's New Town is **Laisvės alėja** (Freedom Avenue), a broad, pedestrianized shopping street running east from the Old Town. At the junction with L. Sapiegos the street is enlivened by a bronze statue of **Vytautas the Great** facing the City Garden. Here, a contemporary memorial composed of horizontal metal shards commemorates the 19-year-old student Romas Kalanta, who immolated himself in protest against Soviet rule on May 14, 1972 and whose death sparked anti-Soviet rioting. Towards the eastern end of Laisvės alėja, the silver-domed **Church of St Michael the Archangel** looms over Independence Square (Nepriklausomybės aikštė). The striking modern building in the northeast corner, with the controversial naked "Man" statue in front, is one of the best art galleries in the country, the **Mykolas Žilinskas Art Museum** (Tues–Sun 11am–5pm; 6Lt), housing a collection of Egyptian artefacts, Japanese porcelain and Lithuania's only Rubens.

The museums

Just north of Unity Square (Vienybės aikštė), a block north of Laisvės, Kaunas has two unique art collections. The **Devil Museum** (Velnių Muziejus), at Putvinskio 64 (Tues–Sun 11am–5pm; 6Lt), houses an entertaining collection of over 2000 devil and witch figures put together by the artist Antanas Žmuidzinavičius and donated from around the world. Diagonally opposite, at Putvinskio 55, the dreamy, symbolist paintings of Mikalojus Čiurlionis, Lithuania's cultural hero credited with the invention of abstract art, are on display in the vast **M. K. Čiurlionis State Art Museum** (same times; 6Lt), along with excellent temporary exhibitions. Nearby, **Tadas Ivanauskas Zoological Museum**, at Laisvės 106 (Tues–Sun 11am–7pm; 5Lt), displays every imaginable animal, bird, insect and sea creature stuffed, pinned or pickled on three spacious floors.

Christ's Resurrection Church

Heading east along V. Putvinskio from the Devil Museum, you'll come to a funicular, leading up to Kaunas's most striking modern church, **Christ's Resurrection Church** (Kristaus Prisikėlimo Bažnyčia). A marvel or an eyesore? You decide. Designed by the man behind the city's Military Museum, Latvian Kārlis Reisons, its 70m tower offers sweeping views of Kaunas (5Lt).

19

19

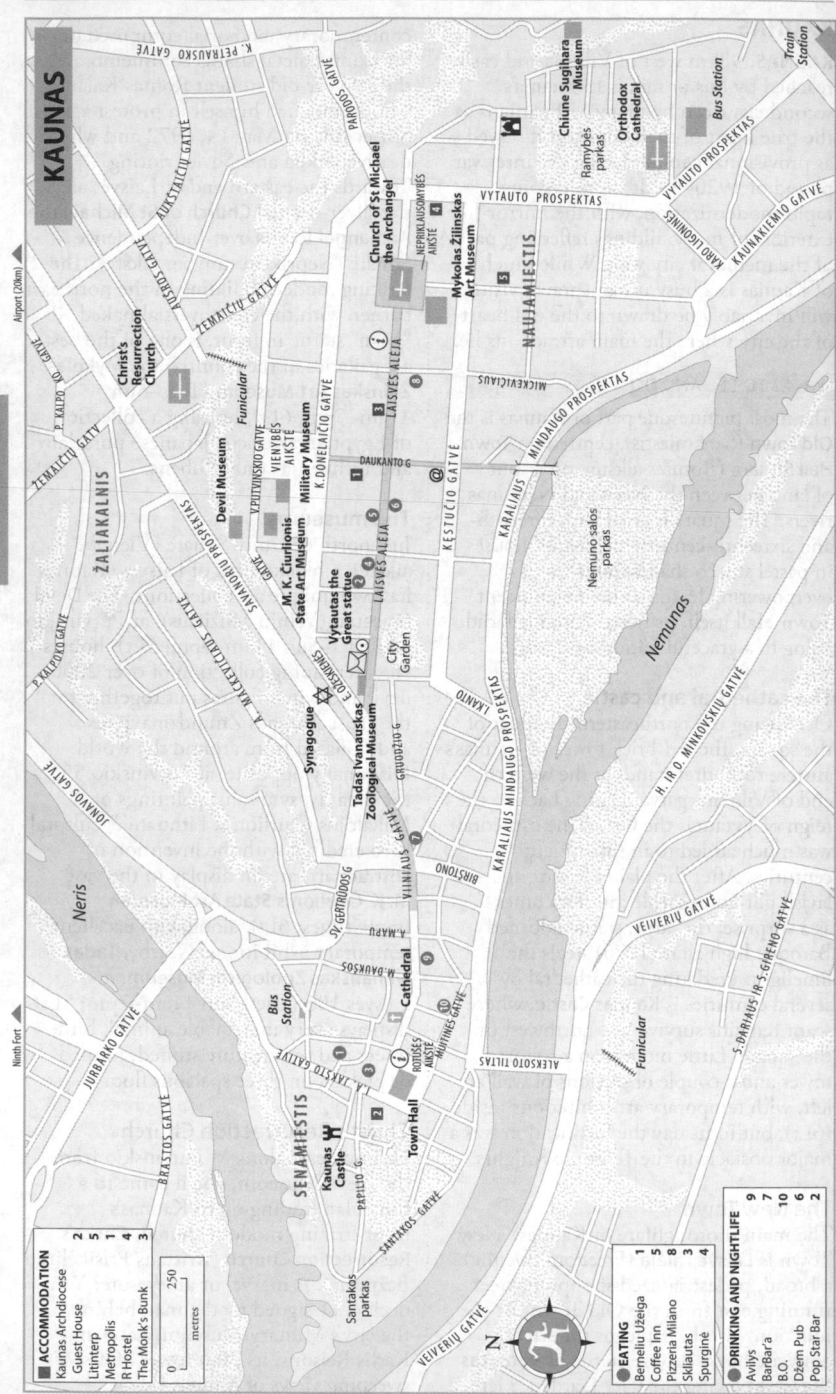

KAUNAS

ACCOMMODATION
Kaunas Archdiocese Guest House	2
Litinterp	5
Metropolis	1
R Hostel	4
The Monk's Bunk	3

● EATING
Bernelių Užeiga	1
Coffee Inn	5
Pizzeria Milano	8
Skliautas	3
Spurginė	4

● DRINKING AND NIGHTLIFE
Avilys	9
BarBar'a	7
B.O.	10
Džem Pub	6
Pop Star Bar	2

Jewish Kaunas

Kaunas has experienced its share of anti-Jewish violence, both during local pogroms and then under the Nazis. During World War II, the city's large Jewish population was all but wiped out; all that remains is the city's sole surviving **synagogue** at Ožeškienės 13 in the New Town, which sports a wonderful sky-blue interior (services Sat 10am–noon) and a **memorial** to the 1700 children who perished at the Ninth Fort (see below). The small and austere former Japanese consulate, at Vaižganto 30 on the other side of the city, is now a **museum to Chiune Sugihara** (May–Oct Mon–Fri 10am–5pm, Sat & Sun 11am–4pm; Nov–April Mon–Fri 11am–3pm; 10Lt), the consul who saved thousands of Jewish lives during the war by issuing Japanese visas against orders.

The **Ninth Fort Museum**, at Žemaičių plentas 73 (Mon & Wed–Sun 10am–6pm; 5Lt), 24km northwest of the centre, is housed in the tsarist-era fortress where the Jews were kept by Nazis while awaiting execution in the killing field beyond; exhibits cover extermination of Jews by the Nazis and the deportation of Lithuanians by the Soviets. A massive, jagged stone memorial crowns the site. Take bus #35 from Kaunas bus station (every 30min) and get off at the IX Fortas stop.

ARRIVAL AND DEPARTURE

By plane Kaunas's international airport is located around 20km north of Kaunas. Bus #29 (2Lt) passes through the Old Town and stops at the main bus and train stations.
By bus and train Kaunas's bus and train stations are both along Vytauto at the southeastern end of the centre, a 10min walk from Laisvės alėja; take any trolleybus passing in front of the stations to the Old Town (2Lt). There is luggage storage at both, and an ATM out on the main street.
Destinations (train) Vilnius (hourly; 1hr 15min–1hr 45min).
Destinations (bus) Klaipėda (hourly; 3hr); Nida (1 daily at 7am; 4hr 10min); Palanga (7 daily; 3hr 30min); Riga (9–14 daily; 4hr–4hr 30min); Tallinn (1 daily via Riga at 9pm; 9hr); Vilnius (every 20–30min; 1hr 30min–2hr); Warsaw (4 weekly; 7hr).

INFORMATION

Tourist information Laisvės 36 (June–Aug Mon–Fri 9am–7pm, Sat 10am–6pm, Sun 10am–3pm; Sept–May Mon–Thurs 9am–6pm, Fri 9am–5pm; ☏37 323 436, ⓦ kaunastic.lt). Provides useful maps and copies of *Kaunas in Your Pocket* (6Lt). There's another office at Rotušės ailūtė 29 (same hours).
Internet Internet Copy 1, at Kęstučio 54/7 (Mon–Fri 7.45am–7pm, Sat 9am–4pm; 5Lt/hr).

ACCOMMODATION

★ **Kaunas Archdiocese Guest House** Rotušės 21 ☏37 322 597, ⓦ kaunas.lcn.lt/sveciunamai. With a hard-to-beat location between two churches, this charming place has clean doubles and free internet. Consumption of alcohol is forbidden. A real bargain. Double **80Lt**
Litinterp Gedimino 28–7 ☏37 228 718, ⓦ litinterp.lt. Ever-reliable guesthouse option offering basic en-suite rooms with kitchenettes. They can also arrange rooms in private residences. Double **140Lt**
Metropolis Daukanto 21 ☏37 205 992, ⓦ metropolishotel.lt. Grand old Soviet hotel in a great location with 75 inexpensive en suites. Free wi-fi and breakfast included. Double **145Lt**
R Hostel Vytauto 83 ☏690 45 329, ⓦ r-hostel.lt. A welcome addition to Kaunas's hostel scene, offering a lounge with table football, beer-tasting evenings and barbecues. Free wi-fi, book exchange and airport pick-up for 17Lt. Dorm **35Lt**, double **110Lt**
The Monk's Bunk Laisves 48–2 ☏620 99 695, ⓔ kaunashostel@gmail.com. Relaxed, traveller-friendly hostel with a great kitchen, poker nights and free wi-fi. Offers free walking tours of the city. Dorm **39Lt**

EATING

Bernelių Užeiga Valančiaus 9 ☏37 200 913. Dine on huge portions of meaty Lithuanian staples in an attractive rustic interior. Mains 10–20Lt. Mon–Wed, Sat & Sun 11am–10pm, Thurs 11am–11pm, Fri 11am–1am.
Coffee Inn Laisvės 72. Great coffee (5Lt), smoothies (7.50Lt) and wraps (8Lt), plus cosy sofas and free wi-fi. Mon–Fri 7am–10pm, Sat 10am–10pm, Sun 10am–9pm.
Pizzeria Milano Mickevičiaus 19. Tucked away in a functional 1930s block, this busy but informal restaurant serves up fairly authentic pizzas (8–11Lt) and pasta dishes (12Lt). Mon–Thurs & Sun 10am–1am, Fri & Sat 10am–2am.
Skliautas Rotušės 26. Set in a courtyard near the town hall, this small bar/restaurant has a brick-vaulted ceiling and evokes the atmosphere of the 1940s with old clocks, photos, candles and interwar music. Pork with cranberry sauce 13Lt. Mon–Thurs 10am–midnight, Fri 10am–2am, Sat 11am–2am, Sun 11am–11pm.
Spurginė Laisvės 84. Traditional café that hasn't changed in decades, dishing out springy Lithuanian doughnuts (*spurgos*), and also tasty small pies stuffed with cabbage, mushroom and other savoury fillings. Mon–Fri 8.30am–8pm, Sat & Sun 9am–7pm.

19

DRINKING AND NIGHTLIFE

Avilys Vilniaus 34. Excellent microbrewery in a cosy cellar offering two types of honey-flavoured beer (8Lt), beer soup and a range of standard meat dishes and beer snacks. Wash down a plate of smoked pigs' ears with a pint of grog (warmed honey beer with extra honey and lemon). Mon–Fri noon–midnight, Fri & Sat noon–2am.

BarBar'a Vilniaus 56. Dress smart, look beautiful and if you make it in, enjoy some cocktails along with Kaunas's pretty young things. Wed–Sat 11pm–5am.

B.O. Muitinės 9. This friendly, popular and unpretentious bar is one of the best places to hook up with a young, arty crowd. Mon–Thurs & Sun 5pm–2am, Fri & Sat 5pm–3am.

Džem Pub Laisvės 59. Take the lift up to this cosy bar with regular live bands, a good range of beers and a superb view of the city. Tues–Thurs 4pm–3am, Fri & Sat 4pm–4am.

Pop Star Bar Vasario 16-osios 2. For the best of the weekend DJ action head to this sixties-themed club offering a floor-filling mix of musical styles. Entry 20Lt. Thurs–Sat 9pm–4am.

KLAIPĖDA

KLAIPĖDA, Lithuania's third-largest city and most important port, lies on the Baltic coast, 275km northwest of Vilnius. Though it has a handful of sights, the city is of more interest as a staging post en route to the Curonian Spit, or to the party town of Palanga.

ARRIVAL AND DEPARTURE

By bus and train Klaipėda's train and bus stations lie on opposite sides of Priestolios gatvė, a 10min walk north of the Old Town.

Destinations (train) Vilnius (3 daily; 4hr 40min–5hr).

Destinations (bus) Kaunas (hourly; 3hr); Liepāja (1 daily at 8.35am; 2hr 35min); Nida (direct: 1–2 Fri–Sun; from Smiltynė: 8 daily; 50min); Palanga (every 30min; 30min); Rīga (4 daily; 4–5hr); Vilnius (hourly; 4–5hr).

By ferry The old ferry terminal at Pilies 4 – which you'll want instead of the new ferry terminal at Nemuno 8 if you don't have a car – has regular departures to Smiltynė, the gateway to the Curonian Spit.

Destinations Smiltynė (June–Aug every 30min, 5am–2am; rest of year at least one hourly, 7am–9pm; 15min).

INFORMATION

Tourist information The tourist office in the Old Town at Turgaus 7 (June–Aug Mon–Fri 9am–7pm, Sat & Sun 10am–4pm; Sept–May Mon–Fri 9am–6pm, Sat 10am–4pm; ☎ 46 412 186, ⊕ klaipedainfo.lt) has internet access (2Lt/30min), rents bikes for 30Lt per day and stocks the excellent *Klaipėda in Your Pocket* (6Lt).

ACCOMMODATION

Klaipėda Hostel Butkų Juzės 7–4 ☎ 46 211 879, ⊕ klaipedahostel.com. Handy if you arrive late, this basic but friendly HI-affiliated hostel is located right next to the bus station. Dorm 44Lt

Litinterp Guest House Puodžių 17 ☎ 46 410 644, ⊕ litinterp.lt. A 15min walk west along S. Daukanto gatvė from the bus and train stations, this is a better bet than *Klaipėda Hostel*, with clean, attractive rooms and a facility for booking private rooms in Klaipėda or Nida (see p.714). Reception open office hours only: Mon–Fri 8.30am–7pm, Sat 10am–3pm. Double 140Lt

EATING

Ararat Liepų 48a. An outstanding Armenian establishment serving tender, delicately spiced grilled meats (from 22Lt), excellent red wine, and Armenian "Ararat" cognac. Mon–Sat noon–midnight, Sun 1–11pm.

Navalis Manto 23. Good places to eat include this modern café-restaurant with tasty sandwiches (10Lt), salads and coffee. The business lunches (Mon–Fri 11am–3pm) are a steal. Daily 8am–8pm.

PALANGA

Around 25km north of Klaipėda, PALANGA is Lithuania's top seaside resort – party central in the summer.

HILL OF CROSSES

Up on a hill, 12km north of the town of Šiauliai, 188km northwest of Vilnius and 170km east of Klaipėda, lies the **Hill of Crosses** (Kryžių Kalnas), an ever-growing, awe-inspiring collection of over 200,000 crosses, statues and effigies. There are many myths surrounding the Hill's origin, some dating back to pagan times, although the most plausible is that it was to commemorate rebels killed in nineteenth-century uprisings against the Russian Empire. In the Soviet era, they were planted by grieving families to commemorate killed and deported loved ones, and kept multiplying despite repeated bulldozing by the authorities. Today, crosses are often planted to give thanks for a happy event in a person's life. To get here, take a train to Šiauliai from Vilnius (5–8 daily; 2hr 30min) or Klaipėda (5 daily; 2hr) and then take a taxi (15min; 25Lt).

WHAT TO SEE AND DO

Palanga's biggest attraction is its white, 18km-long sandy **beach**; throughout the summer months it hosts a number of outdoor all-night music events. The wooden **pier**, jutting into the sea at the end of Basanavičiaus gatvė, is where families and couples gather to watch the sunset (around 10pm in July).

From the beach, head east along pedestrian **Basanavičiaus** with the rest of the human tide, past the street musicians and vendors, countless restaurants, arcade games, amusement park rides and amber stalls. Get fired out of a bungee catapult (50Lt) or dance until morning at one of the clubs on Vytauto gatvė, the main street, or on S. Darius ir S. Girėno gatvė, which leads off Vytauto gatvė to the beach.

The lush Botanical Garden (Botanikos Sodas) houses a fascinating **Amber Museum** (June–Aug Tues–Sat 10am– 8pm, Sun 10am–7pm; Sept–May Tues–Sat 11am–5pm, Sun 11am–4pm; 8Lt; ⓦpgm.lt) with around 25,000 pieces of "Baltic Gold", many with insects and plants trapped inside. The **Anatanas Mončys House Museum** at S. Daukanto 16 (Wed–Sun 11am–5pm; 4Lt) displays unique wooden sculptures, collages and masks made by the twentieth-century Lithuanian sculptor. Visitors are allowed to handle all the exhibits due to the sculptor's will specifying that others can touch his work.

ARRIVAL AND INFORMATION

By bus The bus station on Kretingos gatvė is a couple of blocks away from Basanavičiaus gatvė, the main tourist street.

Destinations Kaunas (9 daily; 3hr 30min); Klaipėda (every 30min; 30min); Rīga via Liepāja (1 daily at 9am; 4hr 30min); Vilnius (7 daily; 6hr).

Tourist information Kretingos 1 (June–Aug Mon–Fri 9am–7pm, Sat & Sun 10am–4pm; rest of the year Mon–Fri 9am–5pm, Sat 10am–2pm; ☎460 48811, ⓦpalangatic.lt). Helpful, multilingual staff can book private rooms, organize excursions and provide information on events in and around town.

ACCOMMODATION

Due to the town's immense summertime popularity, advance bookings are essential. The cheapest option is to haggle with the locals holding up "Nuomojami kambeiriai"

(rooms for rent) signs as the bus enters Palanga, although the quality may vary considerably. Outside of the high season prices can be as much as half of those quoted below.

Ema Jurates gatvė 32 ☎460 48608, ⓦema.lt. This brightly painted guesthouse has seven cute rooms with TV, most featuring cosy attic ceilings, plus a colourfully decorated café on site. Double **100Lt**

Vandenis Birutės 47 ☎460 53530, vandenis.lt. A comfortable hotel away from the bustle, home to a good café-restaurant with outdoor seating and a live music club. All rooms have cable TV and are en suite. Breakfast included. Double **300Lt**

Vila Ramybė Vytauto 54 ☎460 54124, ⓦvilaramybe.lt. A great boutique hotel with colourful themed rooms, all en suite and some with kitchen or balcony. The restaurant-bar downstairs is one of the best in town. Free wi-fi throughout. Breakfast included. Double **350Lt**

EATING, DRINKING AND NIGHTLIFE

1925 Basanavičiaus 4. Bar-restaurant resembling a log cabin, with a rustic wooden interior and an open fire in winter. Also has a pleasant patio garden. Mains around 30Lt. Daily 10am–midnight.

Čagino Basanavičiaus 14. Come to this bright Russian restaurant for good people-watching and ample portions of hearty meat dishes (20Lt), soups and pancakes. Daily noon–midnight.

Exit Nėries 39. Two-tiered entertainment: lively disco with kitschy decor upstairs, and packed nightclub downstairs. Upstairs Mon–Thurs & Sun 7pm–3am, Fri & Sat 9pm–6am; downstairs daily 10pm–6am.

Laukinių Vakarų Salūnas Basanavičiaus 16. Packed with a young crowd and offering nightly karaoke, wet T-shirt competitions and the occasional live band. Cocktails around 14Lt. Mon–Thurs & Sun 9pm–5am, Fri & Sat 9pm–6am.

★ **Žuvinė** Basanavičiaus 37a. Fish restaurant with books on the shelves and a smart interior; the generous portions of well-prepared seafood dishes, such as scorpion fish in orange sauce (25Lt) or spaghetti marinara (36Lt), cannot be faulted. Daily 11am–midnight.

THE CURONIAN SPIT

Shared between Lithuania and Russia's Kaliningrad Province, the **CURONIAN SPIT** is a 98km sliver of land characterized by vast sand dunes and pine forests. Much of the Lithuanian stretch is covered by the Curonian Spit National Park (ⓦnerija.lt). Some of the area can be seen as a day-trip from Klaipėda, though it really warrants a stay of several days to soak up the unique atmosphere.

19

19

CYCLING THE SPIT

The best way to explore the Curonian Spit is by **cycling** along well-marked biking trails that meander through pine forest and along the sand dunes. **Juodkrantė**, 30km away from Nida, is home to **Witches' Hill** (Raganų kalnas), an entertaining wooden sculpture trail in the woods with wonderfully macabre statues of devils, witches and folk heroes. *Vila Flora*, along the waterfront, serves simple but excellent fresh fish (25Lt) and pancakes (12Lt). Heading back towards Nida, stop off at the side of the road to catch a glimpse of the huge **heron and cormorant colony** in the trees. When passing through **Preila**, look for the *rūkyta žuvis* (smoked fish) signs and stop at a smokery for some delicious samples, cheaper here than in Nida. Numerous informal bike rental stalls pop up throughout central Nida in summer (8Lt/hr, 30Lt/day)

ARRIVAL AND DEPARTURE

By ferry and minibus Ferries depart from the quayside towards the end of Žvejų gatvė in Klaipėda (2.90Lt return), sailing to Smiltynė on the northern tip of the spit. From the landing stage, frequent minibuses (11Lt) run south towards more scenic parts of the spit, stopping at the villages of Juodkrantė, Pervalka and Preila, and terminating at Nida, 35km south.

NIDA

NIDA is the most famous village on the spit – a small fishing community boasting several streets of attractive blue- and brown-painted wooden houses. Although there are plenty of visitors in the summertime it never feels crowded. There are several good **restaurants** on Naglių gatvė and Lotmiškio gatvė, as well as along the waterfront. From the end of Naglių, a shore path runs to a flight of wooden steps leading up to the top of the **Parnidis dune** south of the village. From the summit you can gaze out across a Saharan sandscape stretching to Russia's Kaliningrad province. Retrace the trail along the waterfront to see elaborate **weather vanes** with unique designs – each village has its own. Stop by the **Neringa History Museum** (Pamario 53; June–Sept daily 10am–6pm; Oct–May Tues–Sat 10am–5pm; 3Lt), which traces the village's heritage through photos of crow-eating locals and fishing paraphernalia. Also along Pamario is the church cemetery, with **krikštas** – carved wooden grave monuments – placed upright at the foot of the resting body. Nida's long, luxuriant **beach** is on the opposite side of the spit, a thirty-minute walk through the forest from the village.

ARRIVAL AND INFORMATION

By bus Buses from the mainland and from Smiltynė stop on Naglių, Nida's main street. Everything in Nida is within walking distance.

Destinations Kaunas (via Klaipėda; Fri & Sun at 2.45pm; 4hr 30min); Smiltynė (7 daily; 1hr 30min); Vilnius (via Klaipėda; Mon, Fri & Sun at 3.15pm; 5hr 50min).

Tourist information The tourist office at Taikos 4 (June–Aug Mon–Sat 10am–7pm, Sat & Sun 10am–1pm & 2–7pm; Sept–May Mon–Sat 9am–1pm & 2–6pm; ☎ 469 52345, ⓦ visitneringa.com) has info on lodging and events.

ACCOMMODATION

Nida has a few budget guesthouses, but as they tend to fill up in the summer, advance reservations are required. Private rooms (120–150Lt) and local B&Bs (160–200Lt) can be booked via the tourist office.

Inkaro Kaimas Naglių 26 ☎ 469 52123, ⓦ inkarokaimas .lt. A beautifully decorated double, quad and a two-room apartment are on offer at this welcoming seaside guesthouse. All are en suite and have satellite TV and kitchenette. Double **215Lt**, apartment **290Lt**

Misko Namas Pamario 11 ☎ 469 52290, ⓦ miskonamas .com. Colourful house with a range of en-suite rooms and apartments, communal kitchen and a lovely private garden. Breakfast 22Lt; bike rent 17Lt/day. Double **215Lt**, apartment **280Lt**

EATING AND DRINKING

Baras Bangomūša Naglių 5. Homely, informal place, and one of the best spots in Nida to try the local smoked fish. *Koldūnai* (ravioli-like meat parcels; 12Lt) and other Lithuanian dishes also available. Daily 10am–midnight.

In Vino Taikos 32. Enjoy the best views in Nida from the terrace of this popular wine bar on the roof of the *Urbo Kalnas* hotel, uphill from the village centre. Extensive drinks menu, and good tapas. Daily 10am–midnight.

Kuršis Naglių 29. Cosy restaurant offering the gamut of Lithuanian dishes, including roast pike-perch (30Lt) and excellent *šaltibarščiai* (cold beetroot soup; 6Lt). Daily 9am–midnight.

SVETI JOVAN KANEO, OHRID

Macedonia

HIGHLIGHTS

❶ **Skopje** The capital boasts great food, quirky bars and some downright weird architecture. See p.720

❷ **Šutka** Europe's largest Roma community makes for a fascinating day-trip. See p.722

❸ **Sveti Jovan Bigorski** Remote monastery seemingly plucked straight from a fairytale. See p.724

❹ **Bitola** Go off the tourist radar in this charming southern town. See p.724

❺ **Ohrid** Sitting next to a mountain-fringed lake of the same name, this is Macedonia's prettiest and most likeable town. See p.725

HIGHLIGHTS ARE MARKED ON THE MAP ON P.717

ROUGH COSTS

Daily budget Basic €25, occasional treat €35

Drink Wine from €1.60 per bottle

Food *Tavče gravče* (bean casserole) €1.25

Hostel/budget hotel €12/€25

Travel Bus: Skopje–Ohrid €8; train: Skopje–Bitola €4

FACT FILE

Population 2 million

Language Macedonian

Currency Denar (MKD)

Capital Skopje

International phone code ☎389

Time zone GMT +1hr

Introduction

Macedonia is, quite simply, one of Europe's most relaxing travel destinations. Outside the capital it's almost all countryside, with vineyards, mountains, forests and rolling fields lending their hues to a pleasantly green patchwork. Look a little closer at the few urban areas, though, and you'll likely come to understand why the French refer to a mixed salad as a *macédoine*: this hotchpotch of Ottoman rule, Yugoslav domination, Orthodox faith and Albanian influence represents one of Europe's most varied societies.

The capital, **Skopje**, is something of a Yugoslav symphony in grey, though one whose brutal architecture is softened by friendly locals and an appealing Ottoman centre. Most travellers prefer to base themselves around **Lake Ohrid**, a delightful, mountain-fringed expanse straddling the Albanian border. Between Skopje and Ohrid, a glut of immaculately painted **monasteries** competes for your attention; **Sveti Jovan Bigorski** is the most enjoyable, and lies within **Mavrovo**, a national park that provides great hiking opportunities, as well as skiing in the winter.

CHRONOLOGY

168 BC The Macedonian area is absorbed by the Roman Empire.

395 AD The Roman Empire splits, Macedonia falls under Byzantine rule.

447 Attila the Hun rampages through the area.

1394 Five hundred years of Ottoman rule begin.

1878 Russian victory over the Ottoman Empire; Macedonia is ceded to Bulgaria, though soon returned at the instigation of Western powers.

1910 Gonxha Agnesë Bojaxhiu, an ethnic Albanian, now known to the world as Mother Teresa, is born in Skopje.

1912 The Turks are ousted in the Balkan Wars; Macedonia is shared between Serbia and Greece.

1918 The Serb-ruled area that comprises today's Macedonia is given to the Kingdom of Serbs, Croats and Slovenes.

1945 Macedonia becomes part of socialist Yugoslavia.

1963 Over one thousand people killed by an earthquake in Skopje.

1991 Macedonia gains independence from Yugoslavia.

1993 Admitted to the UN as "Former Yugoslav Republic of Macedonia".

2001 Civil war between government and ethnic Albanian insurgents.

2005 Macedonia becomes an official candidate for EU membership.

2014 Projected completion of the "Skopje 2014" project, a gigantic facelift of Macedonia's capital city.

ARRIVAL AND DEPARTURE

Skopje's "Alexander the Great" **airport** (ⓦairports.com.mk) hosts a few Balkan flag carriers and European budget airlines; the one with most connections is Wizz Air (ⓦwizzair.com), whose destinations include London, Brussels and Stockholm. Ohrid also has an international airport but flights are few and far between; Thessaloniki and Sofia are also within striking distance. Most, however, make their way to Macedonia overland. There are a couple of daily **bus** services from

---

"THEN WHAT ARE WE? FYROMANIANS?"

As soon as Macedonia declared independence from Yugoslavia, a different kind of battle broke out along the Greek border, one regarding two matters integral to a new country: **name** and **flag**. Athens objected to the use of the name – the bulk of historical Macedonia now lies under Greek control – and also to a flag featuring the ancient kingdom's sixteen-pointed Vergina Sun. The new nation squeezed into the UN as the "Former Yugoslav Republic of Macedonia", or FYROM for short, and later changed its flag to end a Greek economic blockade. Many nations now recognize the "Republic of Macedonia", but this battle of nomenclature remains locked in stalemate, and is unlikely to end anytime soon.

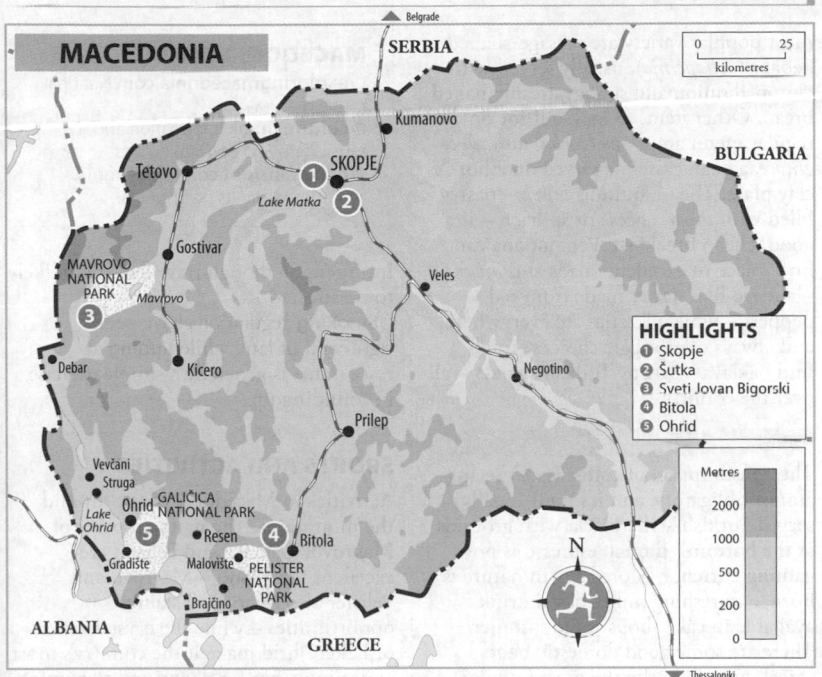

MACEDONIA

SERBIA

Belgrade

BULGARIA

0 — 25
kilometres

Kumanovo

Tetovo
① SKOPJE
② Lake Matka

Gostivar

Veles

MAVROVO
NATIONAL
PARK
③ Mavrovo

Debar
Kicero

Prilep

Negotino

HIGHLIGHTS
① Skopje
② Šutka
③ Sveti Jovan Bigorski
④ Bitola
⑤ Ohrid

Vevčani
Struga
Ohrid GALIČICA
⑤ NATIONAL PARK
Lake
Ohrid ●Resen ④ Bitola
Gradište Malovište
PELISTER
Brajčino NATIONAL
PARK

Metres
2000
1000
500
200
0

N

ALBANIA
GREECE

Thessaloniki

20

Tirana in Albania (via Struga), but poor neighbourly relations mean that there are very few direct services from Greece. In summer you may be able to catch a minibus from Thessaloniki to Skopje; this was once easier by train but the Greek government, in its wisdom, cut off all international services in 2011. Mercifully, the two daily services from Belgrade to Skopje are still running. Citizens of some countries (notably South Africa and India) still need **visas** to enter Macedonia; check ⓦmfa.gov.mk for more information.

GETTING AROUND

Almost all travel in Macedonia is by **bus**. Services are punctual and reasonably frequent, and the vehicles themselves could be worse. Note that buses take one of two routes between Skopje and Ohrid: one through Bitola, and a shorter, more picturesque trip through Kičevo. The limited **train** network suffers from slow and irregular services and is rarely used by visitors. The best domestic line is the thrice-daily service between Skopje and

Bitola, which passes through wonderful mountain scenery.

ACCOMMODATION

Accommodation is not terribly varied but it's generally quite affordable. Skopje's overpriced **hotels** are now supplemented by a few cut-price alternatives (from around €30), while in the hinterlands – including Ohrid – you'll be able to make use of **private rooms**, known as *sobi*; you'll often be met at bus stations by homeowners with rooms to spare. Prices vary wildly depending upon location and facilities, but generally expect to pay from €10 to €30 for a double room. There are now a few **hostels** in Skopje and Ohrid, each costing around €12 for a dorm bed, while **campsites** can be found around the lakes of Ohrid and Prespa; the cost of camping is usually less than €10 per tent.

FOOD AND DRINK

The Macedonian diet is dominated by barbecued **meat** (*skara*), of which the most popular variety are sausage-shaped kebabs (*kebapčinja*), usually served with chopped onion and spongy, freshly baked bread. Other items to look out for on a regular menu are soups (*čorba*) and *tavče gravče*, a bean casserole served on a hot clay plate. The ubiquitous *burek* – pastry filled with meat, cheese or spinach – is a good, cheap **breakfast**. **Vegetarians** can find solace in excellent salads and *ajvar* – a meze-like starter made from red peppers – while pizzerias are everywhere and always offer veggie choices. You'll find baklava – syrupy Turkish **sweets** – all over the country.

DRINK

The consumption of **coffee** (*kafe*) seems almost obligatory, and it's traditionally served Turkish-style (black, with grounds at the bottom), though espresso is now gaining currency. More local in nature is **boza**, a refreshing millet-based drink available in cake shops come summer. There are some good domestic **beers** (*pivo*), with Skopsko the most popular brand, but Macedonia is more famed for uniformly good **wines**. Vranec (red) and Smederevka (white) are two local grape varieties worth trying; you may be lucky enough to find shops selling fresh, home-made concoctions for just 65MKD per litre, but otherwise Tikveš is a reliable, widely sold bottled brand. After 7pm, alcohol can only be bought in bars and licensed restaurants.

CULTURE AND ETIQUETTE

Macedonia is a real mishmash of cultures, and it's very important to take note of a few **political and ethnic issues** – taking Greece's side in the country's naming or flag disputes (see box, p.716) won't win you any friends, nor will promoting Albanian or Macedonian nationalism to the "wrong" side. Only two-thirds of the population are Macedonians of Slav ethnicity – the vast majority of whom belong to the **Orthodox Church** – while most of the remaining third are ethnic Albanian. Tensions still run high between the two groups – 2001 saw a civil war between the government and Albanian

---

> ### MACEDONIA ONLINE
> Ⓦ **exploringmacedonia.com** National tourism portal.
> Ⓦ **culture.in.mk** Information about music, film and performing arts.
> Ⓦ **balkaninsight.com** News from Macedonia and its neighbours.

insurgents – though travellers are unlikely to be affected.

Smoking regulations have been tightened of late, while **tipping** at restaurants is generally a simple exercise in rounding up.

SPORTS AND ACTIVITIES

Activities in Macedonia centre around the mountains. The national parks of Mavrovo, Galičica and Pelister are excellent for **hiking** – Mavrovo and Pelister also offer good **skiing** opportunities – while the crystal waters of Lake Ohrid make it the country's most appealing place for **diving** and **swimming**. The country's empty roads are ideal for **cycling**, but since there are precious few places to rent bikes it makes sense to bring your own.

COMMUNICATIONS

Most **post offices** (*pošta*) are open Monday to Friday 7am to 5pm, and sometimes on Saturday mornings. These are the best places to make **phone calls** or purchase phonecards. International calls are often best made from **internet cafés**, which are easy to find in cities and larger towns; expect to pay around 40MKD per hour. **Wi-fi hotspots** are now fairly widespread, especially in hotels, hostels and cafés.

EMERGENCIES

The crime rate is pretty low by European standards, even in Skopje. However, it's

---

> ### EMERGENCY NUMBERS
> For police, ambulance or the fire department call ☎ 112.

MACEDONIAN

Macedonia uses the **Cyrillic alphabet**, which poses problems with street signs, train and bus timetables. For most of these there's no transliteration into Latin script, but many restaurants have dual-language menus, and a decent level of English is spoken across the country.

	MACEDONIAN	PRONUNCIATION
Yes	Да	Da
No	не	Ne
Please	молам	Molam
Thank you	благодарам	Blago-daram
Hello/Good day	здраво	Zdravoh
Goodbye	до гледање	Dog-led-anyeah
Excuse me	извинете	Eezvee-neteh
Where?	каде?	Ka-deh?
Good	добар	Dobar
Bad	лош	Losh
Near	блиску	Bleeskoo
Far	далеку	Dalekoo
Cheap	евтин	Evteen
Expensive	скап	Skap
Open	отворен	Otvoren
Closed	затворен	Zatvoren
Today	денес	Denes
Yesterday	вчера	Vchera
Tomorrow	утре	Ootre
How much is...?	колку чини тоа...?	Kolkoo chinee toe-ah...?
What time is it?	колку е часот?	Kolkoo eh chasot?
I don't understand	не разбирам	Ne razbee-ram
Do you speak English?	зборувате ли англиски?	Zbo-roo-vateh lee Angliskee?
One	еден	Eh-den
Two	два	Dva
Three	три	Tree
Four	четири	Cheh-tee-ree
Five	пет	Pet
Six	шест	Shest
Seven	седум	Sedum
Eight	осум	Ossum
Nine	девет	Devet
Ten	десет	Deset

prudent to always carry your passport, or a photocopy of the picture page. You'll find **pharmacies** (*apteka*) in all major towns and cities, and a surprising number have English-speaking staff; opening hours vary but some are 24hr. If you need a **hospital**, outside Skopje taxis may be faster than ambulances.

INFORMATION

There are now a few **tourist information offices** dotted around the country. They're slowly starting to learn what travellers require, though many keep irregular hours.

MONEY AND BANKS

The currency is the **denar** (usually abbreviated to MKD), comprising coins of 1, 2, 5, 10 and 50MKD, and notes of 10, 50, 100, 500, 1000 and 5000MKD. Exchange **rates** are currently around 60MKD to the euro, 70MKD to the pound, and 48MKD to the US dollar.

Accommodation prices are usually quoted in euros, though you can also pay in denar. Money can be **exchanged** at an exchange office or bank; the latter are usually open Monday to Friday 8am to 5pm. **ATMs** are easy to find in urban areas, though stock up on cash if you're heading into the sticks.

20

STUDENT AND YOUTH DISCOUNTS

Many museums and galleries offer cut-price student tickets; in practice, a youthful appearance will be acceptable in lieu of an ISIC card. InterRail and Balkan Flexipass tickets are valid.

OPENING HOURS AND HOLIDAYS

Most **shops** stay open until 8pm on weekdays, and mid-afternoon on Saturdays. Sundays are still special in Macedonia – don't expect too much to be open, even in central Skopje. Things also grind to a halt on **public holidays**: January 1, 2 and 7, Orthodox Easter (March or April), May 1 and 24, August 2, September 8 and October 11.

Skopje

Other than the mazy lanes of the delightful, Ottoman-era **Čaršija** district, **SKOPJE** (Скопје) is best described as "appealingly ugly"; the city was ravaged by an earthquake in 1963, its stately buildings replaced by brutal Yugoslav-era designs. These are, in turn, being superseded by the works of **Skopje 2014**, a government-sponsored renovation scheme. Almost universally unpopular with locals, its focal point is a chain of monumental, **Neoclassical buildings** now popping up along the riverfront, joined by literally hundreds of new **statues** (each of a pair of pedestrian bridges sports a full thirty). For the traveller, all of this change is simply rather absorbing, and worth keeping tabs on while you're sampling the city's excellent food and nightlife.

WHAT TO SEE AND DO

The **Čaršija** district north of the river contains the bulk of Skopje's sights, and is the obvious place from which to kick off a trip around the city. The riverfront itself is in flux – new statues are installed on a regular basis, while two pedestrian bridges were under construction at the time of writing.

Čaršija and the Kale

Turkish times linger on in the shape of several mosques – **Mustapha Pasha** is the largest and most intricately decorated

– and two former bathhouses, the copper-domed **Daud Pasha** (daily except Mon 9am–3pm; 100MKD) and the **Čifte Amam** (Mon–Sat: April–Sept 10am–9pm; Oct–March 10am–6pm; 50MKD). These splendid structures are long out of use as hammams, and both now serve as repositories of contemporary art; those seeking history instead can head to the **Museum of Macedonia** (daily except Mon 9am–5pm, 100MKD; Sun free), which is well worth an hour or two. All are outdone, however, by wonderful little **Sveti Spas** (Tues–Fri 9am–5pm, Sat & Sun 9am–3pm; 120MKD), a secluded fourteenth-century monastery. Its church was built mostly underground – under Ottoman rule churches were not allowed to be higher than mosques – and its carved-walnut iconostasis is jaw-dropping. Northwest of Čaršija, and up from the eastern ramparts of the old castle (now closed to visitors), is the excellent **National Museum of Contemporary Art** (Tues–Sat 10am–5pm, Sun 9am–1pm; free), from where you can see the whole of Skopje. The collection, which comprises mainly local art, is not bad, either.

South of the Vardar

Cross the **Stone Bridge** (Kamen Most) and you'll find yourself in Skopje's main square, **Ploštad Makedonija**. You won't be able to miss the gigantic equestrian statue of the original Ali G, Alexander the Great (although, owing to political sensitivities with Greece, its official name is *Warrior on Horse*) – it's by far the largest of the truly bewildering number of statues in the area. Just west of the bridge's southern end are two of the most distinctive Yugoslav buildings in the city. The **Mepso building** is a fusion of Le Corbusier-style design and Communist-era factory, now used as office space; behind it is the **Central Post Office**, a bizarre concrete spaceship whose lavish interior will once more count as a Skopje must-see if repairs following a catastrophic fire in 2013 are successfully made.

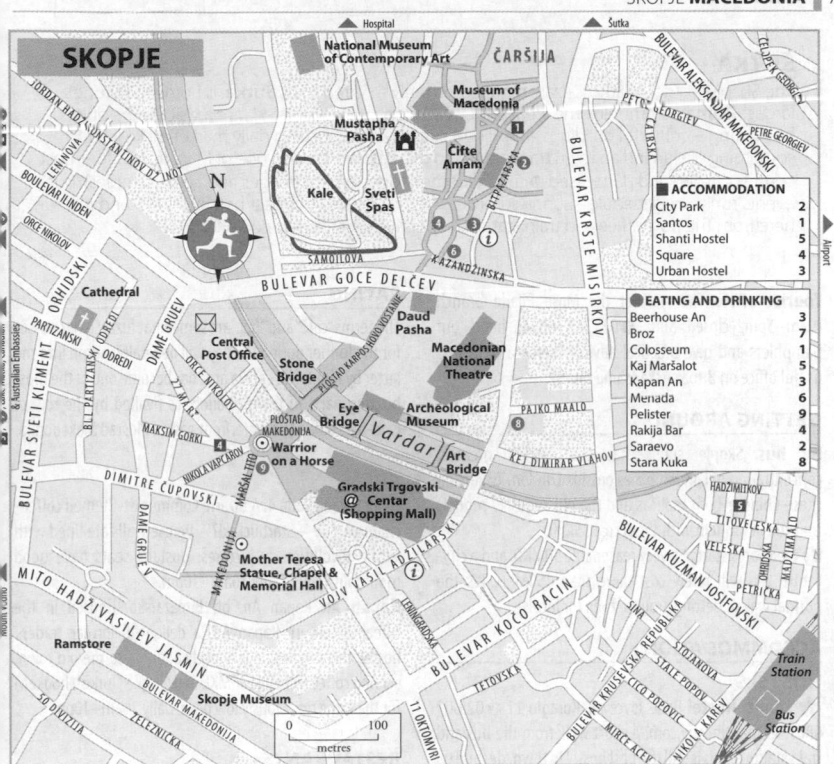

Marking the start of largely pedestrianized **Makedonija**, a crescent of elegant buildings (survivors of the quake) provides some much needed respite from all the new construction. **Mother Teresa** was born further up the road, and a memorial hall, chapel and statue have been placed here in her honour. At the very end of the road, you'll see the imposing **Skopje Museum** (Tues–Sat 9am–5pm, Sun 9am–1pm; free); fronted by a large clock that stopped during the earthquake, it's worth a quick look.

Mount Vodno

Look south from any vantage point in Skopje and you'll see Mount Vodno, within walking distance of the city and topped with a huge cross. The mountain is great for hiking – the 1066m peak is only a couple of hours' walk from central Skopje. In 2011 a cable car entered service from the base of the mountain, whisking visitors to the top in just seven minutes (8am–6pm, closed Mon; 100MKD). To reach the cable car costs 150MKD by taxi and 35MKD on hourly buses from the bus station.

ARRIVAL AND INFORMATION

By plane Skopje's Alexander the Great airport is 21km east of the city. Taxis are expensive at around €20 (1200MKD), though buses are now an option: Vardar Ekspres (w vardarekspres.com.mk) runs shuttles (5–7 daily; 150MKD) to a schedule loosely connected to flight times. You can board at several places; the most useful spots are the bus station, and the central *Holiday Inn*.

By train The train station is located a 20min walk or 100MKD taxi ride southeast of the centre. It's not the kind of place you'll want to hang around for too long.

Destinations Belgrade (2 daily; 9hr); Bitola (3 daily; 3hr–3hr 50min).

By bus The main bus station sits alongside the train station, and is marginally more pleasant.

Destinations Belgrade (12 daily; 7hr); Bitola (12 daily; 2hr 40min); Debar (2 daily; 3hr); İstanbul (5 daily; 12hr); Mavrovi Anovi (7 daily; 1hr 45min); Ohrid (12 daily; 3–4hr); Sofia (5 daily; 8hr); Tirana (2 daily; 10hr).

20

ŠUTKA

The Skopje district of Šuto Orizari, more commonly referred to as **Šutka**, is home to Europe's largest **Roma** community. The area is impoverished and dilapidated, but a visit can be quite fascinating – colourful buildings, litter-lined streets and a bustling daily market make it feel something like an Indian town transported to the Balkans. It's also one of Macedonia's foremost centres of song and dance (see Ⓦculturalcornerstones.org for images and audio samples), but events run to no schedule – sunny summer afternoons are your best bet. Buses #19 and #20 run here from the post office and train station respectively, or it's only 200MKD by taxi.

Tourist office The staff at the Moše Pijade branch (9am–5pm, closed Sun; Ⓣ02 311 6854) hand out pamphlets and give practical advice. There's a new, less useful office on Bitpazarska (same times).

GETTING AROUND

By bus Skopje surely has the world's greatest concentration of London buses outside London. Tickets on these Chinese-built replicas and the old Yugoslav models that run in tandem with them cost 35MKD.
By taxi Fares start at a very reasonable 50MKD, and a city-centre trip will rarely cost more than 150MKD. It's the normal way of getting around, even for locals.

ACCOMMODATION

HOSTELS

★ **Shanti Hostel** Rade Jovcevski Koragin 11 Ⓣ02 609 0807, Ⓦshantihostel.com. A short walk from the bus and train stations, this is still the best hostel in town, despite its slightly cramped common areas. They've also opened up a second hostel around the corner; staff at both are friendly and knowledgeable, and if you fancy a walk into town it's a simple stroll along the river. Dorm €10
Urban Hostel Mother Teresa 22 Ⓣ02 614 2785, Ⓦurbanhostel.com.mk. Good, modern hostel a 20min walk west of the town centre, and accessible on a number of bus routes from the station. The common area is large and inviting, with a piano as its focal point, while the dorm rooms are clean and spacious. Dorm €13

HOTELS

City Park Mihail Cokov 1 Ⓣ02 329 0860, Ⓦhotelcitypark.com.mk. Friendly and modern boutique-style hotel located right next to a park – bring your jogging shoes. You'll almost always be able to knock a little off the rack rate. Double €90
Santos Bitpazarska 125 Ⓣ02 322 6963. One of the very few cheap (and non-seedy) options, its cute little rooms represent great value. You'll see it signed off Bitpazarska. Double €30
Square Nikola Vapcarov 2 Ⓣ02 322 5090, Ⓦhotelsquare.com.mk. Stylish mini-hotel set atop an apartment complex; its thoroughly modern rooms are a pleasant surprise after the Communist-era lifts used to access their floor, and you can gaze down at the Alexander statue as you eat breakfast (included). Double €55

EATING

The terms "café" and "bar" are somewhat fuzzy; what passes for the former during the day will generally morph into the latter by night. The Čaršija area has become one of the most buzzing parts of town, though it's rivalled by the row of café-bars along the waterfront east of Ploštad Makedonija.

CAFÉS

Broz Crvena Voda 4. A bizarre Communist-themed coffee-chain parody – Starbuckski? – whose walls are lined with subtle revolutionary pictures. Upstairs seats have good mountain views. Daily 10am–10pm.
Kapan An Kapan An, off Bitpazarska. Housed in the fifteenth-century Kapan An, a delightful former traders' hostel, this tiny venue is a lovely addition to the old town, serving coffee from just 40MKD and nargile (Turkish hookah) for the same ridiculously low price. Daily 10am–10pm.

RESTAURANTS

Beerhouse An Kapan An, off Bitpazarska. Don't let the name deceive you – this is a classy restaurant in the charming ground level of Kapan An. Extensive and inventive local menu, with grills starting at around 190MKD – the sausages are particularly good. Daily 9am–midnight.
Kaj Maršalot Guro Gakovik 8. Take a trip back to Tito times at this Yugoslav-themed restaurant. The food is little different to what you'll find elsewhere in the city, but where else would you be served by students dressed as Young Pioneers? Daily 8am–midnight.
Pelister Makedonia 1. Hugely popular with locals – you may well struggle to get a seat. Order a pizza (from 260MKD), something more interesting like breaded mozzarella with saffron, or go for the healthy salad bar option. Daily 8am–midnight.
Saraevo Bitpazarska 86. Working men's den with snack-style mains. Ten bite-size *kebapčinja* with bread and onions will set you back just 120MKD, or try a *tavče gravče* for 70MKD. Daily 7am–midnight.
Stara Kuka Pajko Maalo 14. Traditional restaurant serving hearty meals that are worth splurging on; the casseroles are excellent. Walking distance from the centre, and taxi drivers know the name. Mains 250–600MKD. Daily 9am–midnight.

SKOPJE'S FESTIVALS

Buskerfest ⓦ buskerfestmakedonija.com. Over a week of eclectic street performances, usually taking place in May or June

Pivo-Lend ⓦ pivolend.com.mk. Beer festival held each September within the fortress walls.

Skopje Jazz Festival ⓦ skopjejazzfest.com.mk. Acclaimed event featuring musicians from around the world, spread over a week each October.

Skopje Film Festival ⓦ skopjefilmfestival.com.mk. Well worth checking out. Screenings in the Kultura cinema at Luj Paster 2.

Vino-Skop ⓦ vinoskop.com. Wine festival offering the opportunity to taste local produce, usually held in October.

DRINKING AND NIGHTLIFE

BARS & CLUBS

Colosseum Železnička 66. A surprisingly polished house venue that regularly ropes in DJs from overseas. In summer they host outdoor events in Gradski Park. Admission 200MKD. Daily 9pm–late.

Menada Podgraje bb. Overlooking the old Daud Pasha baths, this is a new favourite with Skopje's artier set, largely due to the regular live music sets. Also a great place to head for coffee in the daytime. Daily 10am–late.

Rakija Bar Kaldrma Podgradje 14. The most expensive *rakija* at this buzzing bar costs 120MKD a glass and tastes quite good; the cheapest goes for 50MKD and may well make you heave. Either way, you won't remember in the morning. Daily noon–midnight, weekends to 2am.

ENTERTAINMENT

Macedonian National Theatre Kej Dimitar Vlahov. A new venue, built as part of the Skopje 2014 project, that plays host to ballet and operatic performances. Ticket office 1–8pm; tickets from 200MKD.

Premium Multiplex-style cinema in the Ramstore shopping mall; tickets 150MKD.

DIRECTORY

Embassies and consulates Australia, Londonska 11b ☎ 02 306 1114; Canada, Bulevard Partizanski 17a ☎ 02 322 5630; UK, Salvador Aljende 73 ☎ 02 329 9299; US, Samoilova 21 ☎ 02 311 6180.

Hospital Re-Medika, Makedonska Brigada 18 ☎ 02 260 3100.

Money There are ATMs dotted around the city centre, and in the bus station, which also has exchange booths.

Pharmacy Dimitri Čupovski 13 (24hr).

Post office Orce Nikolov (Mon–Sat 7am–7.30pm, Sun 8am–2pm).

LAKE MATKA

A mere half-hour drive from Skopje, pretty **LAKE MATKA** (Матка езеро) provides an easy break from the grey of the capital. The artificial lake is surrounded by richly forested peaks, and its edges are dotted with restaurants, many of which can only be accessed by **boat**. You'll be approached by boat owners, who typically charge €10 for a short ride around, and a trip to either a restaurant or some nearby **caves**. Ask at the Skopje tourist office about the lake-side guesthouses here. Take bus #60 from the station (9 daily; 35MKD), or hop in a taxi (450MKD).

Western Macedonia

Travellers heading from Skopje to Ohrid have two bus routes to choose from. The first heads south through the major – for Macedonia – city of **Bitola**, a pleasant place with some interesting nineteenth-century architecture. Heading west instead will bring you close to the national park of **Mavrovo**, good for hiking in summer and skiing in winter. This latter route also takes an hour less. **Ohrid** itself is Macedonia's prime attraction, the name referring both to a large, mountain-ringed lake, and the beautiful old town that sits on its northern shore. Just to the east, and sitting next to another pristine lake, is charming **Pelister National Park**.

MAVROVO NATIONAL PARK

Mavrovo National Park (Националниот Парк Маврово; ⓦ npmavrovo.org.mk) spreads its wings over one of Macedonia's most beautiful corners, a rich and rugged

20

20

SKIING IN MAVROVO

The **Zare Lazarevski** resort (ⓦzarelaz
.com) is the place to head for wintertime
fun. The season lasts from Nov 15 to
mid-April, day-passes cost just 1100MKD
(half-day 850MKD), and skis can be rented
for a similar price.

land where rushing streams tumble down
slopes cloaked with pine and birch. There
are a wealth of sights and activities to
choose from – the wonderful monastery
of **Sveti Jovan Bigorski** is a particular
delight to visit. **Camping** and **hiking**
are possible most of the year, while
winter snows make for some of the most
affordable **skiing** and **snowboarding**
in Europe.

Mavrovo

Most travellers base themselves in the little
town of **Mavrovo** (Маврово). Popular with
locals, this resort sits next to a lake of the
same name, but is sadly not accessible on
public transport; to get here, head by bus
to **Mavrovi Anovi**, 8km away on the other
side of the lake, from where it'll be a
150MKD taxi ride. *Hotel Bistra* (ⓣ042
489 002, ⓦbistra.com; double €100) is
right next to the ski slopes; although
rooms here are beyond the budget of most
backpackers, staff can help to organize
(cheaper) private accommodation.

Sveti Jovan Bigorski

Macedonia has no shortage of wonderful
monasteries, but **Sveti Jovan Bigorski**
(Свети Јован Бигорски; free) takes the
biscuit. Tucked away in delightfully bucolic
countryside near the Albanian border, its
whitewashed buildings are edged with dark
wood, and should the fireflies come out to
play in the evening it will feel like you've
stepped into a Hayao Miyazaki anime.
Most of the older buldings were destroyed
in a fire in 2009, though reconstruction
was swift. Travellers can stay for a nominal
fee; this is best arranged through the
hostels or tourist offices of Skopje or
Ohrid. To get here, jump on any bus
heading between Debar and Gostivar (both
accessible from Skopje and Ohrid), and ask
to be let off at the monastery.

BITOLA

Pretty little **BITOLA** (Битола) is one of
Macedonia's few attractive urban centres;
you'll doubtless wonder if it can really be
the second-largest city in the country. Its
laidback air also disguises some historical
pedigree – in the Ottoman era, such was
the importance of this trading hub that a
string of consulates set up on the main
thoroughfare. Amazingly, some remain:
the Turkish one still functions because of
Bitola's sizeable Turkish minority, while
both the UK and France retain a small
diplomatic presence here. All are housed
in splendid nineteenth-century buildings,
more of which line the city's
pedestrianized main road, Maršal Tito.

ARRIVAL AND DEPARTURE

Bitola's train and bus stations sit side by side in contrasting
states of disrepair, a 15min walk south of the centre.

ACCOMMODATION

There's no real reason to stay overnight, but it makes a
convenient break on the Skopje–Ohrid route.
Shanti Hostel ⓣ047 552 034, ⓦshantihostel.com.
Skopje's *Shanti Hostel* team have opened up a new venue
here, in the hope that travellers will pop by on their way to
Greece from the capital. It's a great place, though usually
very quiet. Open April–Oct. Dorm €8

PELISTER NATIONAL PARK

A pristine national park between Bitola
and Ohrid, **Pelister** (Националниот парк
пелистер) overlooks **Lake Prespa**, a
shimmering expanse that, while nowhere
near as deep as Ohrid, boasts surrounding
mountain scenery every bit as beautiful.
On the northern side of the park sits the
small **Pelister ski resort**. From here a spine
trail zigzags south to Malo Ezero, a
picturesque lake at the park's centre. The
lake can also be approached from the
wonderfully unspoilt village of **Brajčino**
(Брајчино), a great hiking base to the
southwest. With its hand-stacked stone
walls it shows almost no signs of the
modern day. Also worth a look is
Malovište (Маловиште), a gorgeous old
village whose population has nose-dived
to almost nothing. Now being thrown
funds to polish up and lure people back,
it's well worth a visit to walk the cobbled

streets, breathe some fresh air and admire this relic of a bygone age.

ARRIVAL AND DEPARTURE

Pelister ski resort is accessible from Bitola: take a bus to Turnovo and then a taxi the rest of the way (€20 all in). Buses to Brajčino leave on the half-hour from Resen, a town on the main Ohrid–Bitola stretch. Malovište is off the Resen–Bitola road; ask to be dropped off the bus in Kažani, from where it's a 4km walk, hitch or taxi ride south.

ACCOMMODATION

It's quite easy to score a *sobi* (private room) in Brajčino; in summer you'll likely be met coming off the bus.

Nikolina's 047 482 222. The only official accommodation in the village is at this homestay-like motel; though unsigned, locals will point you in the right direction. Double **€25**

LAKE OHRID

Vast almost to the point of appearing sea-like, **Lake Ohrid** (Охридско Езеро) is Macedonia's major draw. A backdrop of **mountains** encircles it like a torn sky, looping through Albanian territory on the way back around. This is the only place in the country that can be described as touristy, but even in peak season the combination of Ohrid town's genteel streets and quietly lapping waves produces a relaxed air.

Not only is this one of the **deepest lakes** in Europe – over 300m in places – but it's also one of the oldest. Appropriately, it has played host to lakeside communities since the **Neolithic period**, but it was not until Roman times that **OHRID** (Охрид), on the lake's northeastern fringe, developed as a town. Large basilicas were constructed from the fifth century, and Slavic tribes started moving in shortly after that. Ohrid's importance as a religious centre was maintained under Ottoman rule, the town becoming a tourist destination during the Yugoslav period.

WHAT TO SEE AND DO

Many sights are located among the steep lanes of the walled **Old Town**. There are a couple of monasteries in the area, but most visitors are here for the timeless majesty of **Lake Ohrid** itself – locals swear that the water remains clean enough to

drink, and with visibility of up to 20m they may well be right. Motorized "water-taxis" are available for a 30-minute ride (from 300MKD), though since they dilute both

The Old Town

The best place to start a tour around the Old Town is the **Upper Gate**. In the area immediately to the south you'll find a fascinating **icon gallery** (Tues–Sun 10am–2pm; 100MKD), home to some of the best examples found in the Ohrid area. Staff here should also be able to open up the adjacent **Sveta Bogorodica**, a thirteenth-century church with wonderful interior frescoes.

West of the gate you've a choice of uphill paths; one heads to the **Fortress of Tsar Samoil** (Tues–Sun 9am–4pm; 30MKD), which has a disappointingly messy interior but some superlative views of the town and lake. The other path leads past an old **Roman amphitheatre** to **Sveti Kliment** (daily 8am–8pm; free), a large, modern church inside which you'll see the remains of twelfth-century graves; Saint Clement himself is interred in the far corner. The church is built next to the ruins of another that dates from the fifth century; its foundations (including tremendous mosaics) are on display under a rather ugly shelter.

From Sveti Kliment it's a hop and a skip down the slopes to **Sveti Jovan Kaneo** (daily 8am–5pm; 100MKD), whose lakeside setting makes it Ohrid's most appealing church. The walk east back into town is rather lovely, and passes the tranquil residential enclave of **Kaneo**. Back in the centre you'll find the **National Museum** (Tues–Sun 10am–3pm; 100MKD), full of historical relics and an interesting place to while away an hour or two.

The monasteries

Some 30km south along the eastern shore of the lake is the wonderful monastery of **Sveti Naum**, which lies within walking distance of the Albanian border. Magical grounds surround the seventeenth-century building, whose interior (daily 7am–7pm; 100MKD) is filled with vivid

20

20

> ### THE REPUBLIC OF VEVČANI
> Fancy a quirky half-day trip? Head to **Vevčani**, a village that declared tongue-in-cheek independence after the fall of Communism. The only real evidence of this is its weird banknotes, and even these are rarely available; ask at *Domanska Kuka*, a terrific restaurant. Instead, it's best to come for the pleasant **springs** area, signed uphill from town – the water here may be the best in the Balkans, and the energetic can make use of a 5.2km-long mountain trail. To get here you'll need to take a bus from the town of Struga, located on Lake Ohrid.

frescoes. In the summer you can get here by boat from Ohrid town, and buses (110MKD) run every couple of hours during the day; it'll cost the same in a shared taxi. The road heads between the lake and **Galičica National Park** (ⓦgalicica .org.mk), which is a great place for a hike. On the way to Sveti Naum from Ohrid town you'll pass the village of Gradište, which boasts remains of a Bronze Age village hauled from the bottom of the lake. You can also dive into the surrounding crystal waters from €50 per person (ⓦamfora.com.mk).

Heading north then west instead from Ohrid will eventually bring you to the wonderful lakeside monastery of Kališta, where monks once lived in caves dug into the cliffs – these, and other mural-lined halls, are open to visitors (100MKD), though you'll probably have to ask around for the key.

ARRIVAL AND INFORMATION

By bus The station is inconveniently located 3km north of the Old Town; it'll cost 100MKD by cab, although it's certainly walkable if your bag isn't too big. To get to Debar, it's usually best to catch a bus from nearby Struga (6 daily; 1hr 30min); to get to Struga, you're usually best off grabbing a shared taxi (15min) for 100MKD per person from the main road just north of the tourist area.
Destinations Bitola (6 daily; 1hr 30min); Resen (6 daily; 50min); Skopje (12 daily; 3–4hr).
Tourist office The one inside the bus terminal isn't very helpful (and is often closed); there's a better branch at Partizanska 6 (ⓣ046 260 423).

ACCOMMODATION

There are some great places to stay in Ohrid, but *sobi* (private rooms) are also an option, especially when the hotels are booked up in summer months. You're likely to be met at the bus station by those with rooms to spare. Camping is possible at three sites along the lake between Ohrid and Sveti Naum (around 400MKD/tent).
Di Angollo Just off the main square ⓣ046 260 003,

ⓦapartmanidiangolo.com.mk. So what if the reception is inside a pizza restaurant? The dorms at this simple, central hostel are clean and colourful, and there's a decent little common area. Dorm **€9**
★ **Sunny Lake** Klimentov Univerzitet 38 ⓣ075 629 571, ⓦsunnylakehostel.com. Superb hostel that strikes the tough balance between relaxation and partying. The common areas are great places to meet people, especially in the summer over barbecued meat and a few glasses of *rakija*. Dorm **€12**
Vila Lucija Kosta Abraš 29 ⓣ046 265 608, ⓦvilalucija .com.mk. So close to the lake that you may wake to see your ceiling ashimmer with reflected sunlight. The spick-and-span rooms are excellent value, and come with almost painfully powerful showers. Double **€30**
Vila Sofija Kosta Abraš 64 ⓣ046 254 370, ⓦvilasofija .com.mk. Well-equipped boutique rooms set in a beautiful, traditionally styled building – great value, especially for the €29 single rooms. Double **€49**

EATING AND DRINKING

Ohrid's culinary scene is terribly uninspired for a place with such tourist appeal. In summer, a curl of "beach" bars open up along the lakeside east of the Old Town. More interesting, for some, will be the Skovin Winery (Dimche Malenko 12, just off the main pedestrian square), where a litre of freshly made wine – fired into plastic bottles from petrol-station-like pumps – costs just 65MKD. You can buy regular bottles too, but it's not half as much fun.
Liquid Kosta Abraš 52. This bar is busy most nights with a young and fun-loving clientele, so it's a good place to make new friends, get drunk with existing ones, or combine the two. Daily 6pm–late.
Pandanos Local meals in a superb location overlooking the amphitheatre. Mains aren't the cheapest (from 300MKD), but there are some bargains on the menu; it's quite possible to fill up on their delicious appetizers alone. Daily 9am–9pm.
★ **Potpeš** Kaneo. This new Kaneo restaurant is so close to the lake you can bathe your tootsies in the water as you eat. Prices are generally reasonable, while some items on the menu are just plain cheap, such as the 100MKD hamburger (it puts many a fast-food version to shame). Come for drinks in the evening – the boardwalk stroll alone is quite magical. Daily 11am–11pm.

WHITEWATER RAFTING ON THE TARA RIVER, DURMITOR

Montenegro

HIGHLIGHTS

❶ **Kotor** Head up to St Ivan's Castle for jaw-droppingly beautiful views over Montenegro's prettiest town. **See p.732**

❷ **Budva** The former Yugoslav beach-party place of choice has got its mojo back. **See p.734**

❸ **Cetinje** The one-time Montenegrin capital is a sleepy town dotted with stately old embassy buildings. **See p.737**

❹ **Podgorica** A unique opportunity to go off the tourist radar in a European capital. **See p.738**

❺ **Durmitor National Park** Great for skiing in winter or rafting in the summer. **See p.739**

HIGHLIGHTS ARE MARKED ON THE MAP ON P.729

ROUGH COSTS

Daily budget Basic €30, occasional treat €50

Drink Nikšičko Tamno beer €1 (bottle from shop)

Food *Sarma* €2.50–4

Hostel/budget hotel €20/€50

Travel Bus: Budva–Kotor €3; train: Podgorica–Vlrpazar €1.80

FACT FILE

Population 630,000

Language Montenegrin

Currency Euro (€)

Capital Podgorica

International phone code ☎ 382

Time zone GMT +1hr

21

Introduction

The tiny state of Crna Gora is better known under its Italian name, Montenegro. The English translation – "Black Mountain" – may sound a little bleak, but Montenegro is a land exploding with colour. Carpeted with flowers for much of the year, the country's muscular peaks are dappled with the dark greens of pine, beech and birch from which turquoise streams rush down to a tantalizingly azure blue sea. Fringing it, the coastline is dotted from border to border with beaches of yellow and volcanic grey, and huddles of picturesque, orange-roofed houses – a postcard come to life.

While the **coastline** is most appealing for the traveller, Montenegro's most precious jewel – phenomenally photogenic **Kotor** – sits just a little inland at the end of a fjord-like bay. The beach town of **Budva** is the other real highlight, but you should also try to make time for the ruins of **Stari Bar**. Away from the coast, the country's pleasures are mainly confined to the mountains, particularly the spectacular national park of **Durmitor**, while the old Montenegrin capital of **Cetinje** is also well worth a visit; the present-day capital, **Podgorica**, gets few visitors but certainly has its charms.

CHRONOLOGY

9 AD Roman annexation of the region incorporates most of present-day Montenegro into the province of Dalmatia.
395 The Roman Empire splits into eastern and western halves, with Montenegro lying on the line of division.
990 Slav state of Duklja established.
1190 Successor state of Zeta annexed by Serbia.
1499 Much of Montenegrin interior falls to the Ottoman Empire; the Venetian Empire controls the coast.
1697 Ottomans defeated in the Great Turkish War; Petrović clan assumes control.
1797 Venice falls to Napoleon, who transfers the Gulf of Kotor to Austrian rule.
1878 Montenegro granted independence following the Congress of Berlin.
1918 Kingdom of Serbs, Croats and Slovenes formed, incorporating Montenegro.
1929 Montenegro becomes part of the new Kingdom of Yugoslavia.
1945 Tito becomes prime minister (president from 1953)

and ushers in the era of Communist rule; Podgorica renamed Titograd.
1979 Coast between Bar and Ulcinj damaged by earthquake.
1991 Break-up of Yugoslavia; Montenegro votes to stay with Serbia in a referendum.
2006 Montenegro gains independence following a second referendum.
2012 Montenegro opens negotiations for accession to the EU.

ARRIVAL AND DEPARTURE

Flights to Montenegro are in surprisingly short supply. National flag carrier Montenegro Airlines (⊚montenegro airlines.com) has a monopoly of sorts, and budget carriers have been unable to enter the market. However, Montenegro is easily reached overland from Croatia – there are **buses** along the coast from Dubrovnik (served by budget flights) and Split, though some of these will require a bus change after a short walk across the border. From Serbia, there are several daily buses between Belgrade and the Montenegrin coast, via Podgorica; daily **trains** – including a night service – also run from Belgrade to Bar along the same route. From Bosnia-Herzegovina there are direct buses to Podgorica from Trebinje and Sarajevo. The only decent connections with Albania are twice-daily buses linking Ulcinj and Shkodra, leaving at 7am and 1.15pm; alternatively, *Montenegro Hostel* (see p.733) can

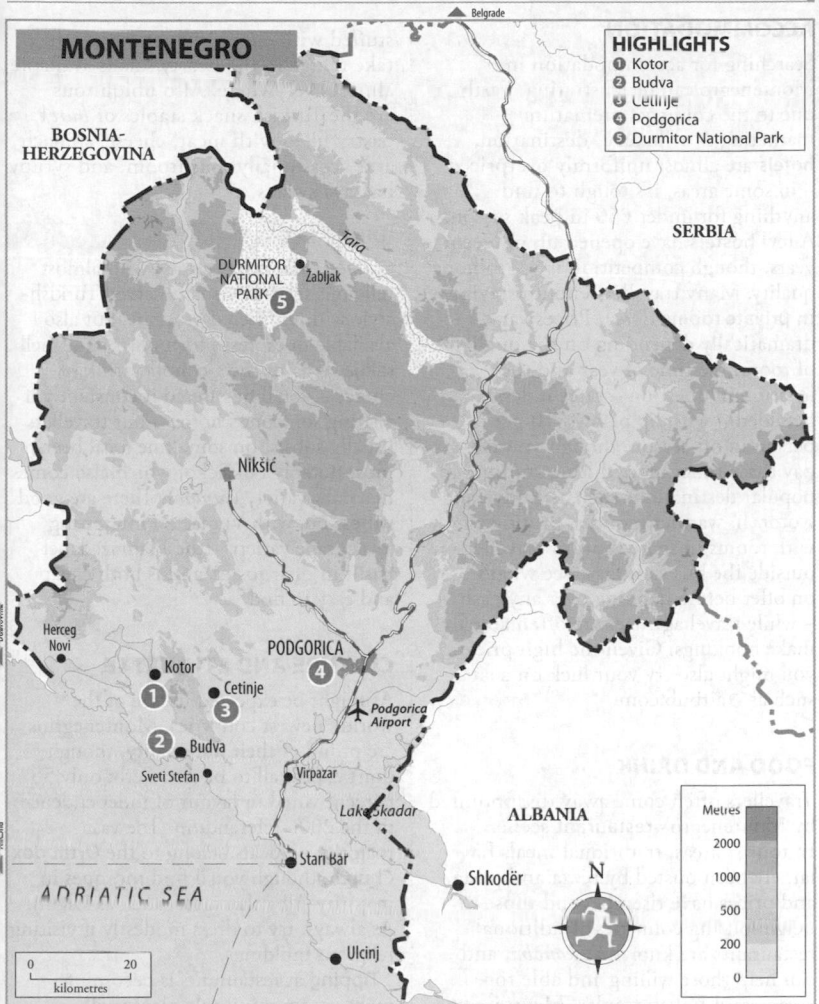

HIGHLIGHTS
❶ Kotor
❷ Budva
❸ Cetinje
❹ Podgorica
❺ Durmitor National Park

organize taxis direct to Tirana from Budva or Kotor for around €35 per person.

Perhaps the most romantic way to arrive in Montenegro is by **ferry** from Italy – Montenegro Lines (ⓦmontenegrolines .net) runs between two and six weekly services to Bar from Bari (from €50).

Note that citizens of some countries, notably South Africa, still need **visas** to enter Montenegro. You may have to apply at a Serbian embassy, since Montenegrin ones remain a little thin on the ground.

GETTING AROUND

For a country with such a small population, the frequency of intercity **buses** is quite remarkable. In addition, Montenegro has poured substantial funds into the upgrading of its main travel arteries, and travel times are accordingly short.

A **train** line heads to Bar from the Serbian border – a beautiful journey. While services are infrequent, prices are dirt-cheap and almost every centimetre of track affords breathtaking views, especially the run into Podgorica from the Serbian border.

21

ACCOMMODATION

Searching for accommodation in Montenegro can be frustrating. Partly due to the country's premature marketing as a "luxury" destination, **hotels** are almost uniformly overpriced – in some areas, it's tough to find anything for under €50 in peak season. A few **hostels** have opened up in recent years, though competition is yet to hone quality. Many travellers end up staying in **private rooms** (*sobe*). Prices vary dramatically depending on the quality of room, the time of year and the location in question – rates in less heralded towns dip below €10 per person in off-season, though you may pay three times more during summer in popular destinations such as Budva and Kotor. In warmer months, proprietors with rooms to spare wait for travellers outside the bus stations – see what's on offer before handing over any cash – while travel agencies are often able to make bookings. Given the high prices, you might also try your luck on a site such as ⓦairbnb.com.

FOOD AND DRINK

Travellers often come away disappointed by Montenegro's **restaurant** scene. In tourist areas, traditional meals have largely been ousted by pizza and pasta, and prices have risen beyond those of neighbouring countries. Traditional restaurants are known as *konoba*, and can help those willing and able to escape said Italian staples. Menu items to look out for include grilled kebabs (*ćevapčići*), cabbage leaves stuffed with mincemeat (*sarma*), bean soup with flecks of meat (*pasulj*), goulash (*gulaš*), and the artery-clogging *karađorđe vasnicla*, a breaded veal cutlet roll stuffed with cheese. **Vegetarians** can take refuge in the hearty salads available almost everywhere. Also ubiquitous are the Turkish snack staples of *burek*, pastry filled with meat, cheese, spinach and occasionally mushroom, and syrupy baklava sweets.

DRINK

Coffee (*kafa*) is consumed with almost religious fervour, usually served Turkish-style with unfiltered grounds, but also available in espresso form. Strong-as-hell **rakija** remains the alcoholic drink of choice – you'll be offered it constantly if visiting someone's home – but travellers usually subsist on some fine local beers, most notably Nikšićko, which also comes in a dark variety (*tamno*). There are good **wines** too, with Vranac an interesting local grape variety – the Plantaže label has it in their roster, and is both cheap and easy to find.

CULTURE AND ETIQUETTE

As might be expected in one of the world's newest countries, Montenegrins are proud of their **nationality**, though don't expect all to be anti-Serb: only 55 percent voted in favour of independence in the 2006 referendum. The vast majority of locals belong to the **Orthodox Church**, though you'll find mosques in majority-Albanian areas, such as Ulcinj. As always, try to dress modestly if visiting religious buildings.

Tipping at restaurants is becoming more common; simple places will expect to keep small change, and posh restaurants to receive up to ten percent of the bill. Despite an official **smoking** ban, Montenegrins still do much of their breathing through slim, tobacco-filled cylinders: non-smokers may have a tough time avoiding the fumes.

SPORTS AND ACTIVITIES

Outdoor activities come in two main flavours: mountain and coastal. **Hiking** is a joy around the peaks of Montenegro's national parks, most notably Durmitor, which is also good for **kayaking**, and

---

MONTENEGRO ONLINE

ⓦ **montenegro.travel** Official tourist board site.

ⓦ **montenegro-investment-news.com** Handy information for expats and visitors.

ⓦ **rivijera.net** Useful listings of coastal accommodation, often including pictures.

MONTENEGRIN

Montenegrin is the official language, though it's essentially the same as Serbian (except that it uses the Roman alphabet rather than Cyrillic). You should be able to get by using Croatian (see box, p.158), with which it has strong similarities, though English is widely spoken in tourist areas.

skiing in winter. On the beach it's a different story, with **watersports** including jets-kiing, parasailing and zorbing available at various points along the coast – Budva is the prime spot, though kayaking around Kotor Bay is a delight.

COMMUNICATIONS

Most **post offices** (*pošta*) are open Monday to Friday 8am to 7pm, Saturday 8am to noon. These are also your best bet for **phone calls** as public phones are in extremely short supply; local landlines are cheap to call, though calls to mobile phones are usually €1 per minute. Getting **online** is becoming easier as many hotels, hostels and cafés have **wi-fi** connections; local **internet cafés** are plentiful, typically charging €1–2 per hour.

EMERGENCIES

Montenegro has a pretty low crime rate as far as muggings and petty theft go, though of course it pays to be vigilant, especially around bus stations. The **police** (*policija*) are generally easy-going, and some speak basic English.

Pharmacies (*apoteka*) tend to follow shop hours, though you'll find emergency 24-hour telephone numbers posted in the windows. If they can't help, you'll be directed to a **hospital** (*bolnica*).

EMERGENCY NUMBERS

Police ☎92; Ambulance ☎94; Fire ☎93.

INFORMATION

Many towns and resorts now have a **tourist information office**, but hours can be infrequent and staff do not always speak English. Although they can advise on local accommodation, it's unlikely that they'll book rooms for you – head to a travel agent instead.

MONEY AND BANKS

Though not yet a member of the EU, Montenegro uses the **euro** (€). **Banks** are generally open Monday to Friday 9am to 6pm and Saturday 9am to noon, while **ATMs** are widespread.

OPENING HOURS AND HOLIDAYS

Most **shops** open Monday to Saturday 9am to 8pm, with many closed on Sundays. Very few museums are open on Mondays, and all shops and banks close on **public holidays**: January 1, 6 and 7, Orthodox Easter (April or May), May 1 and 21, and July 13.

The coast

Blessed with sunshine, pristine beaches lapped by clear Adriatic waters, and appealing, whitewashed old towns, the **Montenegrin coast** has become one of Europe's hottest properties. Heading north–south from Croatia to the Albanian border, you'll first hit charming **Herceg Novi**, before the coast ducks inland to meet magnificent **Kotor** – without doubt the most picturesque town in the land. South of here, the

STUDENT AND YOUTH DISCOUNTS

Quite a few sights and museums now offer discounted fares to students – an ISIC card is useful, but may not be essential if you look to be in the right age bracket. For what it's worth, **InterRail** tickets are valid on Montenegro's one train line (which never costs more than a few euros anyway).

21

littoral swings back out to the beaches of **Budva**, which is something of a party capital during the summer. It's then mountain-edged coast all the way to **Bar**, home to some terrific ruins.

HERCEG NOVI

Developed as a coastal resort during eighteenth-century Austro-Hungarian rule, little **HERCEG NOVI** is a thoroughly likeable town, and yet one that is usually bypassed by tourists. Its steep maze of lanes is lined with stately, crumbling villas, while plants and flowers from around the world abound, bequeathed by countless sailors down the years. Nearby **beaches**, meanwhile, make for excellent swimming.

Most sights are concentrated within Herceg Novi's appealing, walled **Old Town**. At its centre you'll find the **Church of Archangel Michael**, which is barely over a hundred years old, yet looks like it has been around rather longer. From here you can climb the steps to take in views from **Kanli Kula** tower (daily 8am–10pm; €1). Down from the Old Town, the seafront **promenade** makes for a delightful walk. Head east for twenty minutes, then turn inland to find the elegant, seventeenth-century **Savina Monastery** (daily 6am–8pm; free).

ARRIVAL AND INFORMATION

By bus There's a small station on Jadranski put, a 5min walk from the Old Town. Heading south, most buses cross the Bay of Kotor by ferry (no extra charge). Travelling via Kotor increases the following journey times – except to Kotor – by around 45min.
Destinations Bar (6 daily; 2hr 30min); Budva (every 30min–1hr; 1hr 15min); Kotor (hourly; 45min); Podgorica (hourly; 2hr).
Information and tours Tours can be booked through the Black Mountain agency (daily 8am–8pm; ☎ 067 640869, ⊛ montenegroholiday.com), located by the bus station at Pet Danica 21; they also arrange rafting trips to Durmitor (see box, p.739).

ACCOMMODATION AND EATING

There's a dearth of good-value accommodation in town, though the Black Mountain agency (see above) can book private rooms from €10/person. Cafés, bars and restaurants cluster around the harbour.

Autocamp Zelenika Sunčana obala ☎ 067 678631. Campsite 3km east of town; open April–Oct. €12/pitch
Kafana Pod Lozom Trg Nikole Đurkovića. A 2min walk from the church (past the clock tower and turn right), this restaurant cooks up cheap local specialities – you'll be able to fill up for €5. Try the *gulaš*, or the *sarma*. Daily 10am–9pm.

KOTOR

Perched on the edge of a majestic bay, the medieval Old Town of **KOTOR** is the undisputed jewel in Montenegro's crown. Though no longer Europe's best-kept secret, Kotor's sudden elevation to the tour-bus league has failed to dim the timeless delights of its cobbled alleyways and secluded piazzas. Enclosing cafés and churches galore, the town **walls** are themselves glowered down upon by a series of hulking peaks. Down below, a harbour now bustling with sleek yachts marks the end of the **Bay of Kotor**, made fjord-like by the 1000m cliffs that rise almost vertically from the serene waters.

First colonized by the Greeks, Kotor came to prominence in the twelfth century, then passed through Serb, Austro-Hungarian and Bosnian hands before fifteenth-century Ottoman conquests forced it under the protective wing of Venice. Venetian rule ended in 1797, the shape of today's Kotor having been laid out in the intervening years.

WHAT TO SEE AND DO

Kotor's charms are best appreciated by heading to the **Old Town**, *sans* map, and getting lost in the labyrinthine streets. You'll likely enter through the Sea Gate, next to the harbour, and emerge onto the main square, Trg od Oružja. Cafés spill out from glorious buildings, the most notable of which are the old **Rector's Palace** and a leaning **clock tower**. Burrow through the streets and before long you'll end up at **St Tryphon's Cathedral** (daily 8am–7pm; €2), backed by a wall of mountains and perfect for photos; it's well worth the entry fee for a peek inside. Elsewhere there are several churches that merit a look, as well as a fascinating **Maritime Museum**

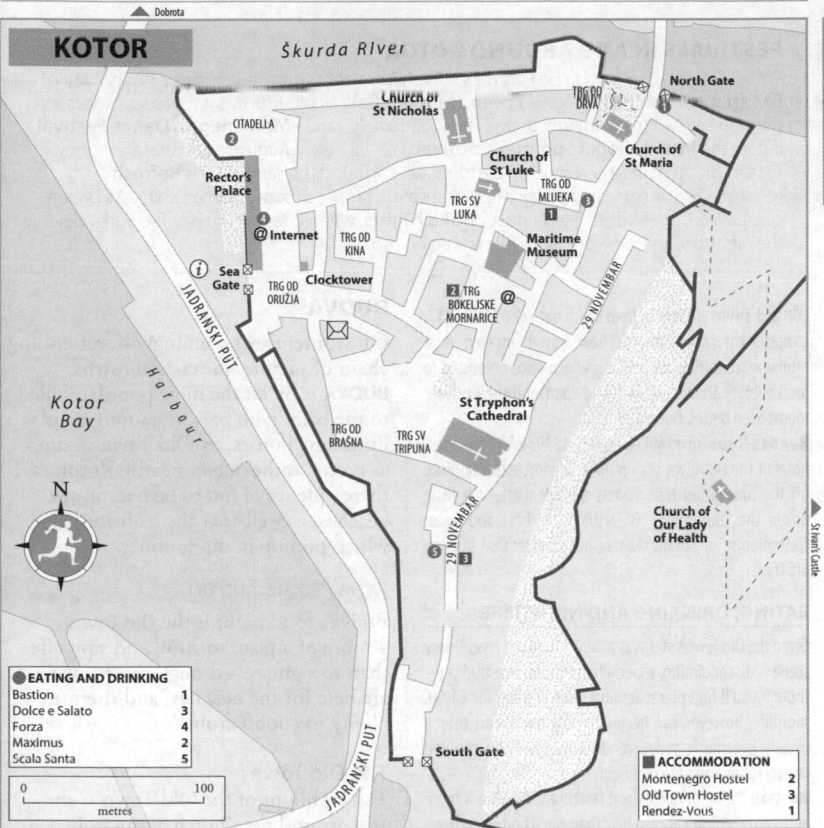

(Sat 8am–3pm, Sun 9am–1pm; €4), a repository of nautical maps and model ships.

The old **fortress walls** (daily 8am–8pm; €3) sit proudly above the town, and make for a rewarding climb. Allow at least ninety minutes for the round-trip to **St Ivan's Castle**, from which you'll have tremendous views of the fjord. On hot summer days it's best to set off early or wait until evening, and note that the first building you come to, the **Church of Our Lady of Health**, is not even halfway up.

ARRIVAL AND INFORMATION

By bus The bus station is a 5min walk south of the Old Town.

Destinations Bar (6 daily; 1hr 45min); Budva (every 30min; 30min); Cetinje (hourly; 1hr); Podgorica (hourly; 1hr 30min).

Tourist office Located just outside the main entrance to the Old Town (daily 8am–5pm; July & Aug to 9pm; ☏ 032 322886, ⓦ tokotor.me), and able to book accommodation.

Tours Both hostels lay on good day-trips; the *Montenegro Hostel*'s famous 12hr "Big Montenegro" tour (€40) covers much of the country.

Bike rental The *Old Town Hostel* rents bikes from €5 per day.

ACCOMMODATION

At all times of year, you're likely to be approached by *sobe* owners as you get off the bus. Rooms are mainly grouped in two areas: Škaljari, uphill from the industrial mess near the bus station, and the more pleasant area of Dobrota, on the bayside just north of the Old Town.

Montenegro Hostel Trg od Muzeja ☏ 069 039751, ⓦ montenegrohostel.com. There's a bit of noise from bars at night and churches in the morning, but the location is excellent – right in the heart of the Old Town – and the rooms in the back are quieter. Dorm __€11__

FESTIVALS IN AND AROUND KOTOR

Kotor's festival year kicks off on February 1, with folk dances and church music on the **day of St Tripun**; this is closely followed by the **Masked Ball**, a colourful event that sees processions through the Old Town. In April there's the wonderfully varied **Montenegrin Dance Festival**, before the **International Summer Carnival** (late July/early August) celebrates the sunny season with theatrical and musical performances. Around the same time is **Refresh** (w refreshfestival.com), a four-day music festival that ropes in some big-name DJs. All pale in comparison, however, to late August's **Boka Nights**, when boats fill the bay, fireworks electrify the night sky, and everyone goes just a little bit mad.

★ **Old Town Hostel** In from south gate ☎ 032 325317, w hostel-kotor.me. Fantastic new hostel, located in a rambling, centuries-old building which once belonged to local nobility. Dorms are spick-and-span, and their private rooms even better. Dorm €10

Rendez-Vous Trg od Mlijeka ☎ 032 323931. The cheapest hotel in the Old Town sits on "Milk Square", a lovely place off the tour-group trail. Rooms are adequate, if a little poky; the "reception" is actually a bar and your "receptionist" one of the waiters, but don't let that put you off. Double €45

EATING, DRINKING AND NIGHTLIFE

Given the Old Town's status as a tourist magnet, its culinary scene is disappointing, especially for those on a budget – though you'll find places serving slices of pizza for €1.50. Nightlife, however, can be surprisingly good, and there's usually live music at weekends, which see the cobbled streets thumping until midnight.

Bastion Trg od Drva. Seafood restaurant offering a more authentic Old Kotor atmosphere than you'll find elsewhere; the interior is far from showy, and the outdoor terrace is located in a charming square. Squid filled with ham and cheese €12, fish salad €5. Daily 9am–10pm.

Dolce e Salato Trg od Mlijeka. Outdoor seats in this quiet square are a perfect place for breakfast – a slice of *burek*, a Turkish coffee and a piece of strudel will come to just €3.10. Daily 7am–3pm.

Forza Trg od Oružja. The best of a whole clutch of cafés on the main square, and a perfect place to watch Kotor strolling by. Don't dare step inside to peek at their cakes – you'll almost certainly emerge €3 lighter and a little heavier elsewhere. Daily 8am–10pm.

Maximus Citadella. Take your pick from several music-themed floors at the biggest nightclub in the country, occasionally host to big-name DJs. Entry can be €10–15 on weekends. Daily 9pm–late.

Scala Santa Just inside the south gate. This attractive restaurant is one of the few places in the Old Town specializing in Montenegrin food, rather than pizza and pasta – try the huge *njeguški* steak (€15), topped with *prosciutto*-like cured ham. Daily 10am–midnight.

BUDVA

Of Montenegro's seemingly never-ending chain of picturesque coastal towns, **BUDVA** is by far the most popular. Filled to the brim with bars, restaurants and limestone houses, its Old Town is almost as pretty as the one in nearby Kotor, and there's plenty of fun to be had on the beaches, as well as at the seafront bars which pop up in the summer.

WHAT TO SEE AND DO

Budva's focal point is the **Old Town** – more of a place to stroll and sip coffee than to sightsee – though most travellers are here for the **beaches**, and there are plenty to choose from.

The Old Town

The highlight of the Old Town is the area around the **Church of the Holy Trinity**, itself home to frescoes that, while far from ancient, are rather beautiful. Looming over this is the fifteenth-century **citadel** (April–Oct 9am–7pm; €2), which offers splendid views of the Adriatic waves pummelling in. Still, you're best advised to save your money and try to hunt down the entrances to the **Old City wall**, which boasts even better views. There are only two of these, meaning that almost no tourists ever get up there – one is just to the left when you enter through the Terra Ferita gate, and the other is down an alley opposite *Hong Kong* restaurant. Also in the Old Town are the **Town Museum** (Tues–Fri 8am–8pm, Sat & Sun 2–8pm; €2), which houses Greek and Roman booty from the ruins being unearthed beneath the citadel, and a **Museum of Modern Art** (Mon–Fri 8am–2pm & 4–7pm, Sat 4–7pm; free).

BUDVA OLD TOWN

Marina

PIZANA

Hong Kong

CARA DUŠANA

BRAĆE BOĆARIĆ

Museum of Modern Art

Pizana Gate

KOTVANOVIĆA

Slovenska Plaza

Terra Ferita Gate

VRZDAK

TRG PALMI

CARA DUŠANA

PETRA I PETROVIĆA

SV MITROV LJUBISE

VUKA KARADŽIĆA

NIKOLE ĐURKOVIĆA

IVO MILIKOVIĆA

NJEGOŠEVA

TRG SLIKARA

Town Museum

ZANOVKI

Ata Agency

TRG PJESNIKA

PETRA I PETROVIĆA

VRANJAK

ADRIATIC SEA

ACCOMMODATION
Astoria	3
Mojo	2
Montenegro Hostel	4
Vila Lux	1

Church of the Holy Trinity

TRG STAROGRADSKI

EATING AND DRINKING
Casper Bar	4
Chest O'Sheas	6
Hotel Mogren	2
Jadran	1
Konoba Stari Grad	5
Mozart	3

Citadel

0   50
metres

N

Beaches and islands

The main beach, **Slovenska Plaža**, curls a few pebbly kilometres east from the Old Town, but far nicer are the sandy **Mogren** beaches, west of the Old Town, which attract a more youthful crowd – just follow the path around the cliffs from the *Mogren Hotel*. Better still is the beach on uninhabited **Sveti Nikola Island**, which you'll see jutting up offshore. In summer, regular water taxis will shuttle you across; prices start at €5 per person, though you'll have to haggle.

WATER ACTIVITIES IN BUDVA

The **Watersports Centre** (⊚ watersport budva.com) on Slovenska Plaža, the main beach, is the place to head for all kinds of watery fun. Jet-skis and parasailing are on offer for the adventurous (€60/hr), while kayaks and pedaloes are a calmer option (€3–5/hr).

ARRIVAL AND INFORMATION

By bus The station is a 15min walk from the Old Town, and a 10min walk from the main beach. A taxi should cost €2 tops; find one whose number starts with ☎ 19. Destinations Bar (hourly; 1hr); Cetinje (every 30min; 1hr); Kotor (every 30min–1hr; 30min); Podgorica (every 30min; 1hr 30min).

Tourist office Njegoševa 28 (daily 9am–6pm; ☎ 033 402550). They won't advise on accommodation, but aren't bad for maps and travel information.

ACCOMMODATION

If you're not met at the bus station – almost a certainty in summer – your best option for private rooms is to head to Ata (☎ 033 452000, ⊚ budvatravelagency.com) in the Old Town who can make bookings for €15–35/room.

21

★ TREAT YOURSELF

Astoria Njegoševa 4 (☎ 033 451110, ⓦ budva.astoriamontenegro.com). Friendly boutique hotel just inside the Old Town, offering artistically designed rooms and wonderful views from a rooftop terrace. Doubles from €129, though off-season you may get a suite for the same price. They also have a hugely popular restaurant that spills out from the town walls.

Mojo Vojvodanska 3 ☎ 069 711986, ⓦ mojobudva.com. Perfectly located between the bus station and the Old Town, this offers a cheap yet relaxing stay in immaculately clean rooms, most of which are private. Double €30

Montenegro Hostel Vuka Karadzića 12 ☎ 069 039751, ⓦ montenegrohostel.com. Colourfully decorated hostel in the Old Town. The three dorms are effectively private rooms with more beds inside (each has its own kitchenette and bathroom), and there's a handy common area up top. Dorm €11

Vila Lux Jadranski put bb ☎ 033 455950, ⓦ vilalux.com. The cheapest hotel in the centre, though you'd never guess it – rooms are just fine, and the free breakfasts will fill you up until lunchtime. Good discounts for single travellers. Double €52

EATING

Restaurant prices are surprisingly reasonable in Budva, though those on a tight budget will be able to fill up on €1.50 slices of pizza around the Old Town.

Hotel Mogren Outside the main Old Town gate. Renovations have transformed this Yugoslav behemoth from 1970s chic to – wait for it – 1980s chic. But its canteen-style dining area is a cheap local favourite, with filling dishes from just €3. They also sell Turkish coffee (€1), boiled up over hot sand. Daily 8am–11pm.

Jadran Slovenska Obala 10. Hugely popular waterfront restaurant whose international menu includes *schnitzels*, mussels or stuffed squid (all €10). In the summer, they even have a bunch of tables on the beach itself. Daily 10am–midnight.

Konoba Stari Grad Njegoševa. One of the better venues in the Old Town, serving excellent seafood dishes – their squid is excellent whether fried, stuffed or grilled, as is the black risotto (all €9). There's a grand beach terrace outside, which also makes this one of the most appealing places for coffee. Daily noon–10pm.

Mozart Just inside the main Old Town gate. Hunt down this café-like place for a filling breakfast, either English-style or something more local; the breaded pancakes (€3.90), filled with sour cream, cheese, mushroom and ham, are as delicious as they are unhealthy. Daily 9am–1am.

DRINKING AND NIGHTLIFE

On summer evenings Budva can be quite wild, especially the open-air bars dotting the harbour road – pole-dancers, *rakija* and Russian tourists are a potent mix.

Casper Bar Cara Dušana 10. The trendiest bar in the Old Town, this is a tiny place with a fun but loungey vibe, and regular DJ sets. Daily 5pm–1am.

Chest O'Sheas Mitrov Ljubiše. Small and appealing Irish pub right in the middle of the Old Town, with sports events on screen and Guinness on tap. Daily noon–1am.

BAR

The pleasant town of **BAR** is literally the first port of call for many visitors to Montenegro, thanks to regular ferry connections with Italy. While the beach is rocky and there are no real attractions in the centre, it's worth at least an afternoon thanks to the magnificent ruins of **Stari Bar** (Jun–Aug 8am–10pm; Sept–May 8am–8pm; €2) – *stari* means old – which sit 5km up the hill. The beauty of its setting is quite staggering – sheer cliffs surround this old town on all sides, and tiny farming communities dot the valleys below. Fragments of pottery found in the area date it as far back as 800 BC, though it wasn't until the **sixth century** that the Byzantine Empire created what you see today; the

SVETI STEFAN

Take a look at any local tourist brochure and you'll soon spot a small, incredibly beautiful island fishscaled with orange roofs. This is **Sveti Stefan**, located a few kilometres south of Budva (most easily accessed by taxi), and visible from the road if you're heading to or from Bar. It's now cordoned off as luxury accommodation, but such is its beauty that people stop all day long to take pictures from the adjacent main road – this, at least, is free. Those with a steady hand may be able to nab a good shot when passing by on a bus.

destruction also in evidence was caused during the Ottoman resistance battles of the 1870s. A trip to Stari Bar should set you back no more than €5 by taxi, or grab one of the marked buses from the main drag or the bus and train stations (every 15min; €1).

ARRIVAL AND INFORMATION

By train The station is located 2km south of town, a €2 taxi ride from the centre.
Destinations Podgorica (4 daily; 1hr); Virpazar (4 daily; 25min).
By bus 300m from the train station; you can often hop on or off buses far nearer the town centre.
Destinations Budva (hourly; 1hr); Kotor (8 daily; 1hr 45min); Podgorica (7 daily; 1hr 45min).
By ferry The terminal is immediately west of the centre, serving daily ferries from Bari year-round (see box, p.666).
Tourist office On the opposite side of the main road from the ferry terminal (Mon–Fri 8am–11.30am & noon–3pm, later in summer; Sat 8am–2pm).

ACCOMMODATION

There are few sobe rooms in central Bar, so it's best to head to Šušanj, a pleasant district hanging over the almost unpronounceable beach of Zukotrlica. It's a 20min walk north along the seafront, or a €2 taxi ride; once there, keep your eyes open for "*sobe*" signs.
Sidro Obala ☎030 312200, ⓦhotelsidro.com. The cheapest hotel in central Bar. Rooms are overpriced, though charming in an old-fashioned kind of way. Double **€44**

EATING AND DRINKING

Kaldrma Stari Bar. Adorable veggie restaurant – think cushions and rugs – near the entrance to the ruins. Opening hours vary; often closed in the winter.
Karađuzović Stari Bar. Small café near the ruins that's great for breakfast; €3 will buy you a slice of *burek*, a Turkish sweetie and an espresso. Daily 9am–7pm.
Pulena Vladimira Rolovića 11. Popular pizza-pub tucked into the fantastic Yugoslav-era Robna Kuka centre on the main drag. They have now added a nice range of local dishes to their Italian roster; you can fill up for under €10. Daily 11am–11pm.

ULCINJ

ULCINJ sits near the Albanian border, and most travellers use the town as a simple conduit between the nations – the twice-daily bus connections to and from Shkodra (see p.728) are the only

scheduled services of any kind linking Albania and Montenegro. You won't need to stay the night, and few foreign travellers choose to, but it's an attractive place for sure – from the bus station, a €3 taxi ride or 30min walk will bring you to the main beach, which sits under a delightful **Old Town**. The latter is a diametric opposite to those in Kotor and Budva – scruffy, unpolished, and quite fascinating as a result.

The interior

The mountains visible from the Montenegrin coast hint at the beauty of its interior, an area sadly bypassed by most travellers. The capital, **Podgorica**, is overlooked by backpackers but certainly merits a visit, while **Cetinje**, the former capital, makes a delightful stopover. Best of all is the mountainous north, particularly **Durmitor**, a spectacular national park where you can hike through unspoilt pastureland, ski past 2000m-plus peaks, or raft through the colossal Tara Canyon.

CETINJE

Sleepy **CETINJE** sits just over the mountainous crest from Budva and Kotor, and is well placed for a visit if you're heading between coast and interior. Cetinje became Montenegro's **capital** on independence in 1878, and of the clutch of embassies that were established, many remain visible today as faded relics of the city's proud past. Though the status of capital has long been passed to Podgorica, many government offices – and, in fact, the presidential seat – remain in Cetinje.

WHAT TO SEE AND DO

Central Cetinje is small enough to walk around in an hour or two, and almost all sights are located on or near **Njegoševa**, a mostly pedestrianized central thoroughfare. The sights listed below are all open daily 9am–5pm, and can be

21

CETINJE'S EMBASSIES

Cetinje's former **embassies** are quite fascinating, and it's fun to track them down – basically, look for any oldish building sporting a crest. Nearest the bus station is the grey **French embassy**, covered with an assortment of lemon and blue tiles. Down on Trg Dvorski, the **Serbian embassy** contains the aforementioned ethnographic museum, and the **Bulgarian** one is now a great café. Further down the road, the crumbling **British embassy** is now a music academy; turn left for the **Turkish embassy**, now home to the University of Cetinje's Faculty of Drama, and the pick of the bunch – the gorgeous, peach-coloured **Russian embassy**.

visited on a €10 combined ticket, or cost from €3 to €5 each.

Trg Dvorski and Trg Revolucije

The **Palace of King Nikola** sits at the southern end of Trg Dvorski. Prior to becoming king in 1910, Nikola was a military leader and poet (as well as a prince, of course), and his old palace is full of regal bric-a-brac. Opposite this is the **Ethnographic Museum**, which mainly features nineteenth-century costumes. Down the road in Trg Revolucie you'll find the **Biliarda**, once the residence of King Petar II, and named after a billiard table – still visible today – that he once had hauled here from Kotor. Near the Biliarda you'll find the **National Museum**, worth visiting for its first-floor art gallery, and nestled into the hillside across the square is **Cetinje Monastery**.

ARRIVAL AND DEPARTURE

By bus Buses pull into a tiny terminal next to the *Sport* hotel. From here it's a 10min walk into town; there's a small map at the station.
Destinations Budva (every 30min; 1hr); Kotor (hourly; 1hr 15min); Podgorica (every 30min; 45min).

ACCOMMODATION AND EATING

Grand Njegoseva st. 1 ☎ 041 231652, ⓦ hotel-grand.me. Yugoslav-era beast at the end of Njegoševa, full of hairdressers, souvenir shops and the like, but the rooms are somewhat bare. Double €60
Restoran Vinoteka Vasa Raičovića. Rich and varied menu of local specialities, including delicious *gulaš* and *sarma*. Dine with a view on the outdoor terrace, or head up to the quiet upper level. Mains €4–10. Daily 10am–8pm.
Sport ☎ 041 231177. Reasonably attractive hotel in the long building next to the bus station; rooms are fresher than you'd expect from the outside. Double €51

PODGORICA

The Montenegrin capital of **PODGORICA** gets precious few backpackers – there's very little cheap accommodation, and not much to see. However, this is the newest capital city in Europe, one of the smallest, and quite possibly the least visited. It also might be the only European capital in which the river water looks positively drinkable – the city centres on the **Morača**, a fast-flowing turquoise river edged by parkland and spanned by a couple of pedestrian bridges, one of which – the Gazela – dives down below street level. There are also some interesting fortress remains in this area, while **Gorica Forest Park** is worth a visit for its pleasant walking trails; it's to the north of town, behind the easy-to-find national stadium.

ARRIVAL AND INFORMATION

By plane The airport lies 11km south of the city. No public transport; taxis €15 (set fare) to the centre.
By train The train station is a 15min walk from the centre. Destinations Bar (10 daily; 1hr); Virpazar (10 daily; 35min).
By bus The terminal is adjacent to the train station. Destinations Bar (7 daily; 1hr 45min); Budva (every 30min; 1hr 30min); Cetinje (every 30min; 30min); Herceg Novi (hourly; 2hr); Kotor (hourly; 1hr 30min); Žabljak for Durmitor National Park (3 daily; 4hr).
Tourist office Slobode 47 (June–Oct Mon–Sat 8am–8pm; Nov–May Mon–Fri 8am–8pm; ☎ 020 667535, ⓦ podgorica.travel). Pretty good for information, and can advise on accommodation.

ACCOMMODATION

Since it can be tough to find a double for under €100, it's important to remember that buses to Budva and Kotor run until fairly late, and trains to the coast even later.
Evropa Orahovačka 16 ☎ 020 623444, ⓦ hotelevropa .co.me. How convenient – Podgorica's cheapest hotel is

located down a side street leading from the train and bus stations. Rooms are good and there's a restaurant downstairs. Double €70

Montenegro Hostel Djecevica 25 ☎069 039751, ⓦ montenegrohostel.com. Yet another addition to the chain. Just a few minutes north from the stations, in a peaceful neighbourhood, it has a pleasant common area and clean, comfy rooms. Dorm €10

EATING AND DRINKING

Restaurants in Podgorica are better value than the hotels, and *burek*-serving snack bars are easy to find. For nightlife, the best streets are Njegoševa and Bokeška – take your pick from the various bars on offer.

Duchovny Centar Njegoševa 27. Scoff down cheap, tasty local fare – mostly veggie – in this church-like restaurant: try the salty pancakes with cream. You can eat for under €5. Daily 8am–10am & 2pm–midnight.

★ **Dvor** Kralja Nikole 36. A little piece of Uzbekistan in Podgorica, located in an eighteenth-century building cheerfully decorated with Central Asian rugs, fabrics, tablecloths and the like. The food is tasty, though portions can be rather small; try the *pilaf* (€6.50). Daily 11am–11pm.

★ **Karver** Obala Ribnice. Charming riverside café set inside an old Turkish bath, whose top was lopped off to make room for a bridge. Squashed it may be, but this is as cool as Podgorica gets – it's a great hangout for evening drinks, and also has a bookshop selling a few English-language cheapies. Latte €1. Daily 9am–11.30pm.

Skalino Inside the Ribnica gorge. What a location – look one way over the crystalline waters of the Morača, or the other at an Ottoman-era bridge. Great for coffee in the day or a beer in the evening; when it's hot you can strip off and have a swim. Daily 9am–11pm; sometimes closed outside summer.

DIRECTORY

Embassies and consulates UK, Bulevar Sveti Petra Cetinjskog 149 ☎020 205460; US, Džona Džeksona 2 ☎020 410500.

Hospital Podgorica Hospital, Ljubljanska 1 ☎020 225125.

Post office Slobode 1 (Mon–Sat 8am–8pm). Has telephones for public use.

LAKE SKADAR

Oozing over the Albanian border, beautiful **Skadar** is the largest lake in the Balkans, and also one of its most untouched. However, since it lies on the train line, it's easily accessible and can make a good stopoff on your way to or from the coast. The main jump-off point is **Virpazar**, a cute little fishing village at the northern end of the lake, a 1km back down the line to Podgorica from the station. From here it's a pleasant walk along the lake's western shore, and though there's nowhere to rent bikes, if you've brought one along you'll be in heaven – an hour's ride will bring into sight a clutch of **offshore monasteries**, though to get any nearer you'll have to search for a boat.

ACCOMMODATION AND EATING

Pelikan Virpazar ☎020 711107, ⓦ pelikan-zec.com. A one-stop shop for lodging, dining and motorboat tours; rooms are homely, though they're outdone by the excellent on-site restaurant, which specializes in lake fish. Double €60

DURMITOR NATIONAL PARK

A land of jagged, pine cloaked mountains and alpine pastureland, **Durmitor** is the most scenic place in inland Montenegro, and a hive of **outdoor activity** throughout the year. Dozens of 2000m-plus peaks drop down to the spectacular **Tara Canyon**,

---

ACTIVITIES IN DURMITOR

There's plenty to do in and around the park, though this area is most famed for its **rafting**, which is among the best in Europe. This can be arranged through agencies on the coast, *Montenegro Hostel* in Kotor or Budva, or in Žabljak itself – try Summit, Njegoševa bb (☎052 360082), or Žabljak Tourist, Svetog Save 37 (☎052 361115) – which charge around €50 per person for a half-day trip. **Hiking** is great from June to September, but do come prepared since this is a wild area, and be warned that the weather can change rapidly, even in summer. The aforementioned agencies can provide maps. Wintertime opens up **skiing** possibilities, and **snowboarding** is on the rise too; the main slopes are accessible from Žabljak, with day-passes costing €15, and ski rental almost the same.

★ **TREAT YOURSELF**

Boskovica Brvnare ☎ 069 541728,
🌐 boskovicabrvnare.com. A little south
of Žabljak (call to be picked up), this
highly appealing, relatively new clutch
of pine-clad chalets makes for great value
– the views are simply stupendous.
Discounts for stays of over five days.
Chalet **€80**

a 1000m-deep rip in the Earth bisected
by a crashing river. Durmitor is a prime
spot for skiing, hiking, camping, rafting
and far more.

The park is centred on the mountain
town of **Žabljak**, accessible by bus
along a bumpy, winding road that can
turn even the stomachs of the locals;
it's a four-hour bus ride from Podgorica
(three daily), though the downhill
return leg only takes three.

ACCOMMODATION

There's plenty of accommodation in the area, though as
elsewhere in the country the hotels are a little dear. Better
for budget travellers are private rooms – from €10 per
person – which you'll be offered on getting off the bus.
Durmitor is also a great place for camping, and there are a
number of sites around the park.

DETAIL IN THE MEDINA, TANGIER

Morocco

HIGHLIGHTS

❶ Tangier The former International Zone retains a delightfully seedy charm. **See p.748**

❷ Chefchaouen Charming little mountain town full of blue houses. **See p.753**

❸ Medina, Fez The world's best-preserved medieval city. **See p.756**

❹ Kasbah des Oudaïas, Rabat Ancient citadel with a splendid gateway. **See p.761**

❺ Jemaa el Fna, Marrakesh A spontaneous open-air circus every evening. **See p.767**

❻ Essaouira Laidback seaside resort that's become famous for its excellent windsurfing. **See p.771**

HIGHLIGHTS ARE MARKED ON THE MAP ON P.743

ROUGH COSTS

Daily budget Basic €25, occasional treat €35

Food *Tagine* €4–5

Drink Pot of mint tea €1

Hostel/budget hotel €8–15

Travel Marrakesh–Casablanca: train €9; bus €5–8

FACT FILE

Population 32.3 million

Languages Arabic, Berber languages, French, Spanish

Currency Dirham (dh)

Capital Rabat

International phone code ☏212

Time zone GMT

Introduction

Just an hour's ferry ride from Spain, Morocco seems worlds away from Europe. It has a deeply traditional Islamic culture and, despite its 44 years of French and Spanish colonial rule, a more distant past constantly makes its presence felt. A visit here is a challenging, intense and rewarding experience.

22

Berbers, the indigenous peoples, make up over half of Morocco's population; only around ten percent of Moroccans claim to be "pure" Arabs. More obvious is the legacy of the colonial period: until independence in 1956, the country was divided into Spanish and French zones, the latter building Villes Nouvelles (new towns) alongside the long-standing Medinas (old towns) in all the country's main cities.

Many people come to Morocco on cheap flights, mainly to Marrakesh, but coming by boat from Europe, your most likely introduction to the country is **Tangier** in the north, still shaped by its heyday of "international" port status in the 1950s. To its south, in the Rif Mountains, the town of **Chefchaouen** is a small-scale and enjoyably laidback place, while inland lies the enthralling city of **Fez**, the greatest of the four imperial capitals (the others are Meknes, Rabat and Marrakesh). The sprawl of **Meknes**, with its ancient walls, makes an easy day-trip from Fez.

The power axis of the nation lies on the coast in **Rabat** and **Casablanca**. "Casa" looks a lot like Marseille, while the elegant, orderly capital, **Rabat**, has some gems of Moroccan architecture. Further south, **Marrakesh** is an enduring fantasy that won't disappoint. The country's loveliest resort, **Essaouira**, a charming walled seaside town, lies within easy reach of both Marrakesh and Casablanca.

CHRONOLOGY

42 AD Romans take control of the coastal regions of Morocco.

600s Arabs conquer Moroccan lands, introducing Islam.

1062 Marrakesh is built by the Berber dynasty of Almoravids.

1195 Almoravids are replaced by the Almohads, who conquer southern Spain.

1269 The capital is moved to Fez.

1415 The Portuguese capture the Moroccan port of Ceuta.

1492 Influx of Jews who have been expelled from Spain.

1860 Spanish wage war with Morocco, ultimately gaining land in Ceuta.

1904 France and Spain divide various areas of influence in Morocco.

1912 Under the terms of the Treaty of Fez, Morocco becomes a French protectorate.

1943 Moroccan Independence Party, Istiqlal, is founded.

1956 Morocco declares independence from France.

1963 First general elections.

1975 Clashes as Morocco forcefully takes back land in the Sahara from the Spanish.

2004 Earthquake along the Mediterranean coast kills over five hundred.

2006 Introduction of cheap flights to Marrakesh leads to a noticeable increase in tourism.

2007 Moroccan Government and Polisario Independence Movement remain unable to come to an agreement regarding the disputed land in the Western Sahara.

2011 Bomb in Marrakesh kills fifteen people – Islamist militants are suspected of involvement.

ARRIVAL AND DEPARTURE

To reach Morocco from Europe you can either fly or take a ferry. The main **airports** are in Casablanca, Fez and Marrakesh, the last of which is served regularly by budget airlines from UK and European airports. Ryanair (Ⓦryanair .com) and easyJet (Ⓦeasyjet.com) both sell cheap online tickets.

Ferries from Algeciras (Spain) take you to the new port of Tangier Med or the Spanish enclave of Ceuta. Ceuta is 3km from the Moroccan town of Fnideq, where you can take buses or shared taxis to Tangier or Tetouan. Tangier Med – also served by ferries from places like Sète, Genoa and Barcelona – is

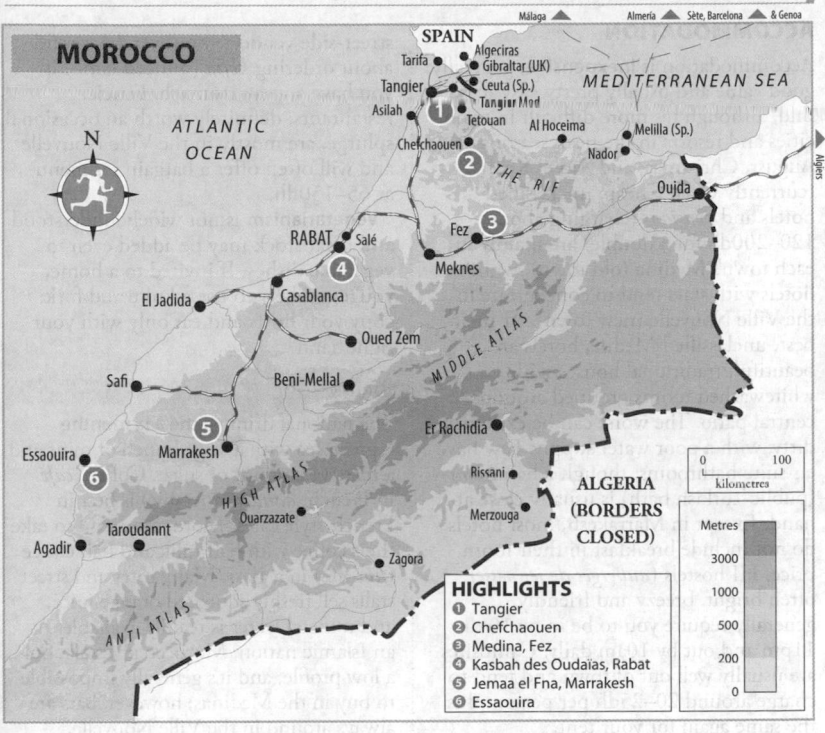

inconveniently situated but has shared *grands taxis* to Tangier. Only ferries from Tarifa (served by a free shuttle bus from Algeciras for ferry ticket holders) actually take you to Tangier, which has all the major transport links, and is itself worth a visit. Boat tickets can be booked online (ⓦtrasmediterranea.es, ⓦbalearia.com and ⓦfrs.es) or at the ports of departure.

GETTING AROUND

BY TRAIN

For travel between the major cities, **trains** are the best option. A table of direct and connecting services to any other station is available at any station ticket office or on the ONCF (national rail company) website (ⓦoncf.ma). Couchettes (145dh extra) are available on trains from Tangier to Marrakesh (10hr 30min), and are worth the money for extra comfort and security. Only direct trains are listed in this chapter.

BY TAXI

Shared *grands taxis* are usually big Peugeots or Mercedes, plying set routes for a set fare, and are much quicker than buses, though the drivers can be reckless. Make clear you only want *une place* (one seat), otherwise drivers may assume you want to charter the whole car. Expect to wait until all six places in the taxi are taken, though you can pay for the extra places if you are in a hurry. Within towns **petits taxis** do short trips, carrying up to three people. They queue in central locations and at stations and can be hailed on streets when they're empty. Payment – usually no more than 15dh – depends on distance travelled.

BY BUS

Buses are marginally cheaper than shared *grands taxis*, and cover longer distances, but are slower. CTM (the national company; ⓦctm.ma) is the most reliable. Supratours (ⓦoncf.ma) run express buses that connect to train services.

22

ACCOMMODATION

Accommodation is **inexpensive**, generally good value and usually pretty easy to find, although it's more difficult in main cities and resorts in the peak seasons: August, Christmas, and Aïd el Kebir (currently Oct). Cheap, unclassified hotels and *pensions* (charging about 120–200dh for a double) are mainly in each town's Medina (old town), while hotels with stars tend to concentrate in the Ville Nouvelle (new town). At their best, unclassified Medina hotels are beautiful, traditional houses with whitewashed rooms grouped around a central patio. The worst can be extremely dirty, with a poor water supply. Few have en-suite bathrooms, though a hammam (public Turkish bath) is usually close at hand. Except in Marrakesh, most hotels do not include breakfast in their room price. HI hostels (*auberges de jeunesse*), often bright, breezy and friendly, generally require you to be in by 10 or 11pm and out by 10am daily. Campsites are usually well out of town and tend to charge around 20–25dh per person plus the same again for your tent.

FOOD AND DRINK

Moroccan cooking is wholesome and filling. The main dish is usually a **tajine** (casserole). Classic *tajines* include chicken with lemon and olives, and lamb with prunes and almonds. The most famous Moroccan dish is **couscous**, a huge bowl of steamed semolina piled with vegetables, mutton, chicken or fish. Restaurant starters include *salade marocaine*, a finely chopped salad of tomato and cucumber, or soup, most often the spicy, bean-based *harira*. Dessert will probably be fruit, yogurt or a pastry. **Breakfast** is cheapest if you buy *msimmen*, *melaoui* (which taste like pancakes), *harsha* (a heavy gritty griddle bread) or pastries from street-side shops and eat them at cafés.

The best **budget meals** are at local diners, where *tajines* or roast chicken with chips and salad are usually under 60dh. Even cheaper are sandwiches and *shwarmas*, which cost 15–20dh from street-side vendors; however, be careful about ordering *kefta* (minced lamb) if you have a weak stomach. Fancier restaurants, definitely worth an occasional splurge, are mostly in the Ville Nouvelle and will often offer a bargain set menu at 65–150dh.

Vegetarianism is not widely understood and meat stock may be added even to vegetable dishes. If invited to a home, you're unlikely to use a knife and fork; copy your hosts and eat only with your right hand.

DRINK

The national drink is **thé à la menthe** – green tea with a large bunch of mint and a massive amount of sugar. Coffee (*café* in French; *qahwa* in Arabic) is best in French-style cafés. Moroccans tend to take their coffee with half milk and half coffee (*nus-nus*) in a glass. Many cafés and street stalls sell freshly squeezed orange juice, and mineral water is readily available. As an Islamic nation, Morocco gives **alcohol** a low profile, and it's generally impossible to buy in the Medinas; however, bars are always around in the Ville Nouvelle. Moroccan wines, usually red, can be very drinkable, while the best-value **beer** is Flag Speciale. Most local bars are male domains; hotel bars, on the other hand, are more mixed and not much more expensive. The big supermarkets sell alcohol; ask a *petit taxi* to take you to the nearest Acima or Marjane.

CULTURE AND ETIQUETTE

Morocco is a Muslim country, and in rural areas particularly, people can be quite **conservative** about dress and displays of affection. It's not the done thing to kiss and cuddle in public, nor even for couples to hold hands. Dress is more conservative in rural areas, though even in the cities you can feel uncomfortable in sleeveless tops, short shorts or skirts above the knee. The heat can also be oppressive, so long, light, loose clothing is best. A shawl allows women to cover up while wearing sleeveless tops.

Be sensitive when taking **photographs**, and always ask permission. In certain

22

SHOPPING

You can pick up bargains throughout Morocco, and you will kick yourself if you go home empty-handed. However, getting a price you can brag about in the hostel requires a willingness to enter into the spirit of **haggling**. The first price you will be given will often be at least three and up to ten times more than you should pay, and, if you're a student, it's always worth pointing that out when you are bargaining. Though quality makes a difference, we've included rough prices for some popular goods you could reasonably fit into a backpack. Fixed-price shops in the Ville Nouvelle also give a good approximation of what you should be paying in the Medina.

• Small kilims (coarse rugs) 500–1500dh
• Leather bags (cheaper in Fez than Marrakesh) 150–500dh
• Leather babouches (slippers) 80–150dh
• Cotton scarves 10–100dh
• Jelaba (traditional Moroccan dress) 100–5000dh

places, particularly the Jemaa el Fna in Marrakesh, people may demand money from you just for happening to be in a shot you have taken. Also note that it is illegal to photograph anything considered strategic, such as an airport or a police station.

When invited into people's homes, remove footwear before entering the reception rooms. If invited for a meal, take a gift: a box of sweets from a posh patisserie usually goes down well.

It is acceptable (and a good idea) to try **bargaining** at every opportunity (see box above). If you do it with a smile, you can often get surprising reductions.

Morocco is inexpensive but poor, and **tips** can make a big difference; it's customary to tip café waiters a dirham or two.

SPORTS AND ACTIVITIES

Casablanca and Essaouira cater to **surfers**: the former has better waves while the latter is excellent for windsurfing. Tangier and Rabat have decent beaches but with less developed services. **Mohammedia**, a thirty-minute ride from both Rabat and Casablanca, is a great destination for surfers.

The Moroccan mountain ranges offer great **hiking** opportunities. Good starting points include: Chefchaouen, in the Rif; Fez and Meknes near the Middle Atlas; and Marrakesh, two hours away from Mount Toubkal – the second-highest mountain in Africa. Consult local tourist information offices or hotels for advice and details of the trails.

Horseriding is an expensive but increasingly popular way of seeing Morocco. *La Roseraie Hotel*, located in the High Atlas, 60km from Marrakesh (☎0524 439128, ☻laroseraiehotel .com), is a great place from which to hire horses and venture into the mountainous countryside. Prices depend on your itinerary but it's not cheap.

Football is Morocco's most popular sport. You will see it being played in every conceivable open space. If you start up a game on a beach it won't be long before you are joined by some Moroccans; equally you'll usually be welcome in pick-up games. All the major cities have teams and money is being poured into new stadiums. For league tables see ☻maroc.net/sports.

COMMUNICATIONS

Post offices (La Poste) are open Monday to Friday 8am to 4.15pm; larger ones stay open until 6pm, and open Saturday 8am to noon. You can also buy stamps at

MOROCCO ONLINE

☻**visitmorocco.com** Moroccan tourist board's website.
☻**babelfan.ma** Arts and culture, including information on festivals throughout Morocco, but in French only.
☻**morocco.com** Huge collection of links to sites about every aspect of Morocco.

22

postcard shops and sometimes at tobacconists. Always post items at a post office. International phone calls are best made with a phonecard (from post offices and some tobacconists). Alternatively, there are privately run *téléboutiques*, open late. You must dial all ten digits of Moroccan phone numbers. Internet access is available pretty much everywhere, and at low rates: 6–10dh per hour is typical.

EMERGENCIES

Street robbery is rare but not unknown, especially in Tangier and Casablanca. Hotels are generally secure for depositing money; campsites less so. There are two main types of **police** – grey-clad *gendarmes*, with authority outside city limits; and the navy-clad *sûreté* in towns. There's sometimes a brigade of "tourist police" too. Moroccan **pharmacists** are well trained and dispense a wide range of drugs. In most cities there is a night pharmacy, often at the town hall, and a rota of *pharmacies de garde* that stay open till late and at weekends. You can get a list of English-speaking doctors in major cities from consulates. Steer clear of marijuana (*kif*) and hashish – it's illegal, and buying it leaves you vulnerable to scams, as well as potentially large fines and prison sentences.

Also be aware that there have been occasional bomb attacks on Western and tourist targets, the most recent occurring in 2011 at a café on Marrakesh's Jemaa el Fna, in which 17 people were killed; you may wish to check the travel advice offered by organizations such as the US State Department (ⓦtravel.state.gov) or UK Foreign Office (ⓦgov.uk/foreign -travel-advice) before visiting.

INFORMATION

There's a **tourist office** (Délégation du Tourisme) run by the Office National Marocain du Tourisme (ONMT) in every

major city, and sometimes also a locally funded Syndicat d'Initiative. They stock a limited selection of leaflets and maps, and can put you in touch with official guides. Travel agencies tend to have a fuller range of brochures regarding local activities. There are scores of "unofficial guides", some of whom are genuine students, while others are out-and-out hustlers (though these have been clamped down on). If they do find you, be polite but firm; note that it's illegal to harass tourists. Tourist offices are usually understocked and often can't give away maps; local bookshops and street-side kiosks are a better bet.

MONEY AND BANKS

The unit of currency is the **dirham** (dh), divided into 100 centimes; in markets, prices may well be in centimes rather than dirhams. There are coins of 10c, 20c, 50c, 1dh, 5dh and 10dh, and notes of 20dh, 50dh, 100dh and 200dh. At the time of writing, £1 = 12.85dh, $1 = 8.50dh, €1 = 11.10dh. You can get dirhams in Algeciras (Spain) and Gibraltar, and can usually change foreign notes on arrival at major sea- and airports. For exchange purposes, the most useful and efficient chain of banks is the **BMCE** (Banque Marocaine du Commerce Extérieur). Post offices will also change cash, and there are **bureaux de change** in major cities and tourist resorts. Many banks give cash advances on credit cards, which can also be used in tourist hotels (but not cheap unclassified ones) and the ATMs of major banks. Banking hours are Monday to Friday 8.15am to 3.45pm (Mon–Fri 9.30am–2pm during the holy month of Ramadan).

OPENING HOURS AND HOLIDAYS

Shops and stalls in the souk (bazaar) areas open roughly 9am to 1pm and 3 to 6pm. Ville Nouvelle shops are also likely to close for lunch, and also once a week, usually Sunday. Islamic religious holidays are calculated on the lunar calendar and change each year. In 2014 they fall (approximately) as follows: January 13 is

---

EMERGENCY NUMBERS
Police – Sûreté ☎19, Gendarmes ☎177; Fire and ambulance ☎15.

MOROCCAN ARABIC

Moroccan Arabic is the country's official language, and there are three Berber languages, but much of the country is bilingual in French. For some useful French words and phrases see p.280.

see p.280.

	MOROCCAN ARABIC
Yes	Eyeh
No	La
Please	Afek/Minfadlik
Thank you	Shukran
Hello	Assalam aleikum
Goodbye	Bissalama
Excuse me	Issmahli
Where?	Fayn?
Good	Mezziyen
Bad	Mish Mezziyen
Near (here)	Krayb (min hina)
Far	Baeed
Cheap	Rkhis
Expensive	Ghalee
Open	Mahlul
Closed	Masdud
Today	El Yoom
Yesterday	Imbarlh
Tomorrow	Ghedda
How much is…?	Shahal…?
What time is it?	Shahal fisa'a?
I (m) don't understand	Ana mish fahim
I (f) don't understand	Ana mish fahma
Do you (m) speak English?	Takellem ingleezi?
Do you (f) speak English?	Takelma ingleezi?
One	Wahad
Two	Jooj
Three	Tlata
Four	Arba'a
Five	Khamsa
Six	Sitta
Seven	Seba'a
Eight	Temeniya
Nine	Tisaoud
Ten	Ashra

22

Mouloud (the birthday of Mohammed); Ramadan (when all Muslims fast from sunrise to sunset) roughly June 28 to July 27; the end of Ramadan is celebrated with Aïd es Seghir (aka Aïd el Fitr), a two-day holiday; October 4 is Aïd el Kebir (when Abraham offered to sacrifice his son for God); October 25 is the Muslim New Year. Non-Muslims are not expected to observe Ramadan, but should be sensitive about not breaking the fast in public. Secular holidays are considered less important, with most public services (except banks and offices) operating normally even during the two biggest ones – the Feast of the Throne (July 30), and Independence Day (Nov 18).

Northern Morocco

The northern tip of Morocco contains enough on its own to justify the short ferry ride over from Spain: in three days or so you could check out the delightfully

22

seedy city of **Tangier** and the picturesque little mountain town of **Chefchaouen** in the Rif Mountains.

TANGIER

For the first half of the twentieth century **TANGIER** (Tanja in Arabic; Tanger in French) was an "International City" with its own laws and administration, attracting notoriety through its flamboyant expat community. With independence in 1956, this special status was removed and the expat colony dwindled. Its mixed colonial history and proximity to Spain means that Spanish is a preferred second language. Today Tangier is a grimy but energetic port, mixing modern nightclubs and seedy Moroccan bars with some fine colonial architecture.

The **Grand Socco**, or Zoco Grande – once the main market square (and, since Independence, officially Place du 9 Avril 1947) – offers the most straightforward approach to the Medina. The arch at the northwest corner opens onto Rue d'Italie, which leads up to the **Kasbah**. To the right, Rue es Siaghin leads to the atmospheric but seedy **Petit Socco**, or Zoco Chico, the Medina's main square.

The Kasbah

To get to the **Kasbah** you can walk from the Petit Socco. Rue des Almohades (aka Rue des Chrétiens) and Rue Ben Raisouli lead to the lower gate. The Kasbah (citadel), walled off from the Medina on the highest rise of the coast, has been the palace and administrative quarter since Roman times. The main point of interest is the former Sultanate Palace, or **Dar el Makhzen** (Mon, Wed, Thurs, Sat & Sun 9am–4pm, Fri 9–11.30am & 1.30–4pm; 10dh), now converted into a museum of crafts and antiquities, which gives you an excuse to look around, though the exhibits are rather sparse.

Beaches

Tangier's best **beaches** are a twenty-minute ride out of town. There are few vendors selling refreshments, so it's best to bring your own food and drink. **Plage Sidi Kacem** has a trendy beach restaurant, *L'Océan* (daily noon–5pm; ☎0539 338137), that rents out deckchairs and serves hamburgers and European food, as well as being licensed. A *petit taxi* from town will cost around 150dh each way.

Caves of Hercules

Perhaps the area's most popular tourist attraction is the **Caves of Hercules** (Grottes d'Hercule), 16km southwest of town, where the sea has eroded the cave entrance to form the shape of Africa. In summer there are very occasional buses (#2 from St Andrew's Church near the Grand Socco), but otherwise you'll have to charter a *grand taxi* to get here (around 250dh for the round trip including waiting time). The caves (9am–sunset; free) have been occupied since prehistoric times, later serving as a quarry for millstones (you can see the erosion on the walls) and in the 1920s becoming a rather exotic brothel.

ARRIVAL AND DEPARTURE

By plane The airport is 15km southwest of the city centre. A *petit taxi* into town is 100dh.

By train All trains terminate at Tanger Ville station 2km east of town. A *petit taxi* into town would be 15dh on the meter, but drivers will usually demand twice that. The overnight train from Tangier to Marrakesh allows you to venture south without losing time.

Destinations Casablanca Voyageurs (8 daily; 4hr 45min); Fez (3 daily; 4hr 30min); Marrakesh (1 nightly; 10hr 30min); Meknes (3 daily; 3hr 50min); Rabat (8 daily; 3hr 40min).

By bus The *gare routière* bus station used by private bus companies and shared *grands taxis* is southeast of the centre on Av Youssef Ben Tachfine, although CTM buses will usually pick up and drop off at the port (and CTM tickets can be bought at the ONCF office in the former Tangier Port railway station).

Destinations Casablanca (31 daily; 6hr); Chefchaouen (7 daily; 3hr); Fez (15 daily; 6hr); Fnideq (for Ceuta) (20 daily; 1hr); Marrakesh (5 daily; 10hr); Meknes (13 daily; 7hr); Rabat (38 daily; 5hr); Tetouan (50 daily; 1hr 30min).

By boat Ferries from Tarifa dock at the terminal immediately below the Medina, while ferries from Algeciras arrive at Tangier Med, 40km east of town.

Destinations from Tangier (city) Tarifa (4 daily; 35min).

Destinations from Tangier Med Algeciras (16–24 daily; 1hr–2hr 30min); Genoa, Italy (2 weekly; 48hr); Gibraltar (2 weekly; 1hr 30min); Sète, France (2 weekly; 35–40hr).

INFORMATION

Tourist information The tourist office is at 29 Bd Pasteur, just down from Place de France (Mon–Fri 8.30am–4.30pm; ☎ 0539 948050).

ACCOMMODATION

There are dozens of hotels and *pensions*, but the city can get crowded in summer, when some places double their prices.

MEDINA HOTELS

Mamora 19 Rue des Postes ☎ 0539 934105. A good-value option with pleasant rooms, some with en-suite showers; make sure you ask for a room facing the mosque, as the views are worth it. Double **250dh**

Olid 12 Rue des Postes ☎ 0539 931310. The rooms here are quite basic, and not the cleanest in town, but the hotel has a certain ramshackle charm, and there's a definite touch of the Jackson Pollocks about the paintwork. Double **150dh**

Pension Palace 2 Rue Mokhtar Ahardane ☎ 0539 936128. Rooms here are simple, all with basins and some with passable showers, giving off a leafy central courtyard. Double **150dh**

VILLE NOUVELLE HOTELS

California 8 Rue Ibn Bennar ☎ 0539 944587. The friendly management and the cosy lived-in feel are the main draw at this hotel with airy rooms. Double **220dh**

⭐ **El Muniria** 1 Rue Magellan ☎ 0539 935337. Pick of Tangier's hotels, decorated in a laidback modern Moroccan style. William Burroughs wrote his most famous book, *The Naked Lunch*, here. Double **250dh**

Magellan 16 Rue Magellan ☎ 0539 372319. Great value for money: sparkling clean with tangerine-coloured public areas and tastefully painted rooms, some en suite (for 50dh extra). Double **200dh**

Pension Madrid 140 Rue de la Plage ☎ 0539 931693. Simple *pension* that'll do the trick for one night; ask for one of the brighter rooms on the sunny courtyard. Double **120dh**

CAMPSITE

Camping Miramonte off Rue Shakespeare, 300m west of Stade Marshan ☎ 0672 207055. Often closed for no apparent reason, so call ahead before trekking out here. Camping **20dh** per person, plus **20dh** per tent, camper van **25dh**

EATING

Tangier is best enjoyed from a café, and the Petit Socco is packed with them, each offering the opportunity to relax and observe the hustle on the street. The two main centres for food in general are the Grand Socco, where you can pick up cheap, filling Moroccan staples, and the more diverse (and licensed) strip on Av d'Espagne.

CAFÉS, CHEAP EATS AND SNACKS

Africa 83 Rue de la Plage. The 55dh (plus 7dh tax) four-course set menu here is one of the best bargains in town, or you can settle for the usual *tajine* and brochette dishes instead (30–40dh). Daily 9am–10pm.

Café Baba 1 Rue Sidi Hosni (take the street into the Dar el Makhzen and turn down the right-hand fork at Place Amrah where it's signposted). Like *Café Hafa*, this place is very popular with Ludo-playing locals. Daily 10am–11.30pm.

Café de Paris Place de France. For a more upmarket choice, head to Tangier's most famous and reputedly oldest café. Daily 5.30am–10pm.

Café Hafa Off Rue Shakespeare by the Punic Tombs. This place is cut into the cliff face and looks across the Mediterranean to Spain. Daily 9am–9pm.

Cinemathèque Cinema Rif, Place 9 Avril, south side of Grand Socco. Young Moroccans and expats hang out at the hip café of this cinema, with tables giving onto the square. Free wi-fi. Tues–Sun 8.30am–9.30pm.

RESTAURANTS

Al Andalus 7 Rue du Commerce. This hole-in-the-wall restaurant with sawdust on the floor doesn't look like much, but they'll fry you up a superb swordfish steak with chips, while you watch, for 65dh. Daily 1pm–midnight.

Anna e Paolo 77 Rue Prince Heritier ☎ 0539 944617. The pastas (55–85dh) are the speciality at this Italian family-run restaurant. Licensed. Mon–Sat noon–3pm & 8–11pm.

Art & Gourmet 4 Place 9 Avril, Grand Socco ☎ 0539 371251. An upmarket French café-cum-restaurant with superb views from the terrace over the Grand Socco, serving dishes such as prawn risotto (160dh), or rabbit in mustard sauce (200dh). Licensed. Daily noon–midnight.

Casa d'Italia Palais Moulay Hafid, Rue Mohamed ben Abdelouahad (off Av Hassan II) ☎ 0539 936348. Located in a beautiful Andalusian-style building with tables set around a little patio, this is a good spot to dig into a pizza (75dh) or a plate of pasta (50–85dh). Popular, so it's wise to book ahead for supper. Licensed. Mon & Wed–Sun noon–3pm & 7–11pm.

Darna Rue Jules Cot. Run by a local nonprofit charity supporting abused women, this restaurant-cum-café serves organically grown food in a pleasant garden setting. Set menus 60dh. Mon–Sat noon–3pm.

El Dorado 23 Rue Allal ben Abdallah. There's a wide variety of marine denizens to be had at this Spanish fish restaurant, as well as couscous on Fri (60dh), paella on Sun (50dh), and pinchitos (little kebabs; 120–160dh per dozen). Daily noon–4pm & 8–11.30pm.

22

22

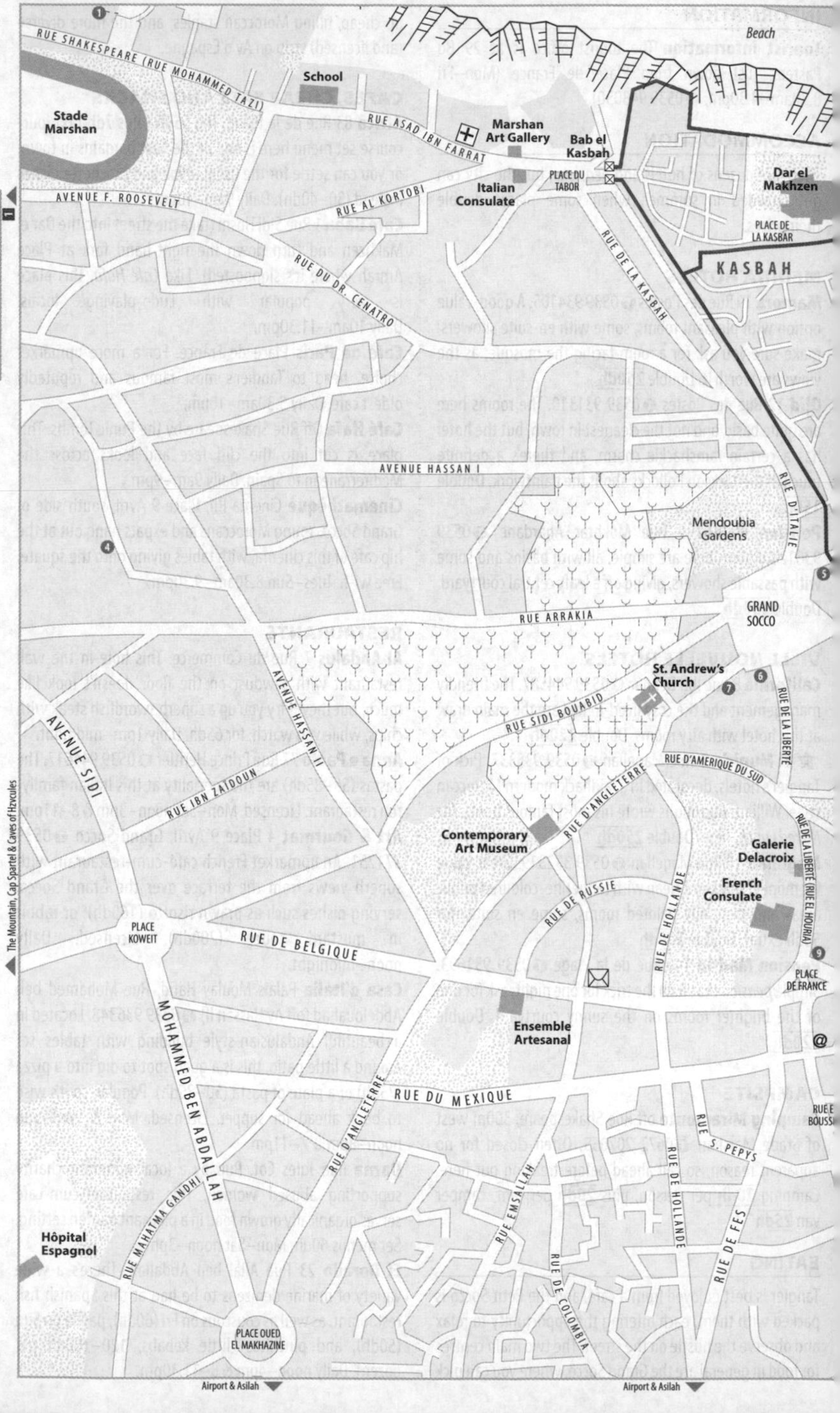

RUE SHAKESPEARE (RUE MOHAMMED TAZI)

Beach

School

Stade Marshan

RUE ASAD IBN FARRAT

Marshan Art Gallery

Bab el Kasbah

Dar el Makhzen

AVENUE F. ROOSEVELT

PLACE DU TABOR

Italian Consulate

PLACE DE LA KASBAR

RUE AL KORTOBI

RUE DU DR. CENATRO

RUE DE LA KASBAH

KASBAH

RUE D'ITALIE

AVENUE HASSAN I

Mendoubia Gardens

RUE ARRAKIA

GRAND SOCCO

St. Andrew's Church

AVENUE SIDI

AVENUE HASSAN II

RUE SIDI BOUABID

RUE DE LA LIBERTÉ

RUE IBN ZAIDOUN

RUE D'AMERIQUE DU SUD

RUE D'ANGLETERRE

Contemporary Art Museum

Galerie Delacroix

French Consulate

RUE LA LIBERTÉ (RUE EL MOURIA)

PLACE KOWEIT

RUE DE BELGIQUE

RUE DE RUSSIE

RUE DE HOLLANDE

PLACE DE FRANCE

@

Ensemble Artesanal

RUE DU MEXIQUE

RUE E BOUSSIT

MOHAMMED BEN ABDALLAH

RUE D'ANGLETERRE

RUE EMSALLAH

RUE S. PEPYS

RUE DE HOLLANDE

RUE DE FES

Hôpital Espagnol

RUE MAHATMA GANDHI

RUE DE COLOMBIA

PLACE OUED EL MAKHAZINE

The Mountain, Cap Spartel & Caves of Hercules

22

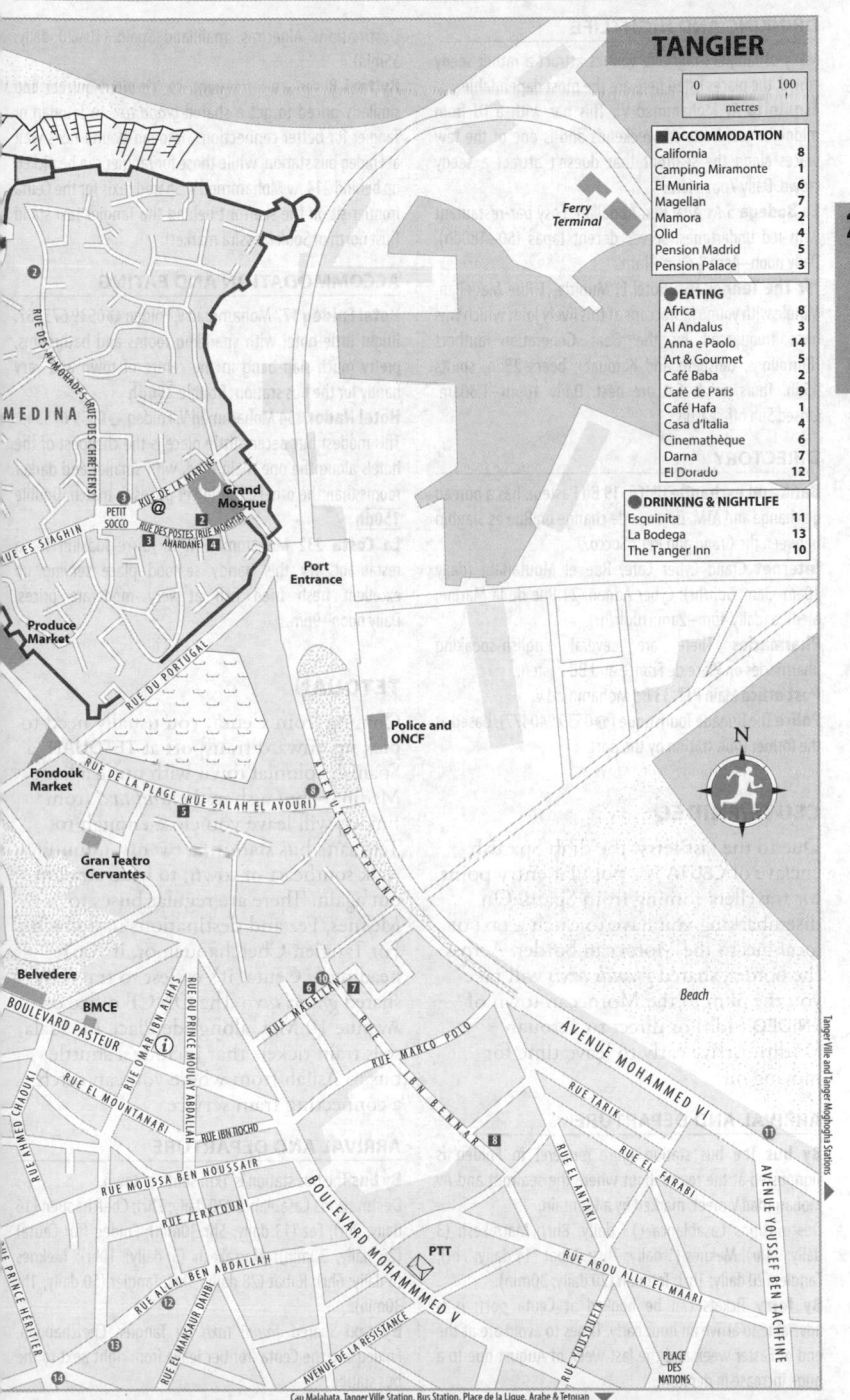

TANGIER

0 ──────── 100
metres

■ **ACCOMMODATION**
California	8
Camping Miramonte	1
El Muniria	6
Magellan	7
Mamora	2
Olid	4
Pension Madrid	5
Pension Palace	3

● **EATING**
Africa	8
Al Andalus	3
Anna e Paolo	14
Art & Gourmet	5
Café Baba	2
Café de Paris	9
Café Hafa	1
Casa d'Italia	4
Cinemathèque	6
Darna	7
El Dorado	12

● **DRINKING & NIGHTLIFE**
Esquinita	11
La Bodega	13
The Tanger Inn	10

Ferry Terminal

MEDINA

RUE DES ALMOHADES (RUE DES CHRÉTIENS)

RUE DE LA MARINE

Grand Mosque

PETIT SOCCO

RUE DES POSTES (RUE MOKHTAR AHARDANE)

RUE ES SIAGHIN

Produce Market

RUE DU PORTUGAL

Port Entrance

Fondouk Market

RUE DE LA PLAGE (RUE SALAH EL AYOURI)

Gran Teatro Cervantes

Police and ONCF

AVENUE D'ESPAGNE

N

Belvedere

BOULEVARD PASTEUR

BMCE

RUE OMAR BEN ATHIS

RUE DU PRINCE MOULAY ABDALLAH

RUE EL MOUNTANARI

RUE AHMED CHAOUKI

RUE MAGELLAN

RUE MARCO POLO

Beach

AVENUE MOHAMMED VI

RUE TARIK

RUE IBN ROCHD

RUE IBN BENNAR

RUE EL FARABI

RUE EL ANTAKI

RUE MOUSSA BEN NOUSSAIR

RUE ZERKTOUNI

BOULEVARD MOHAMMED V

PTT

RUE ALLAL BEN ABDALLAH

RUE EL MANSOUR DAHBI

RUE PRINCE HÉRITIER

AVENUE DE LA RESISTANCE

RUE ABOU ALLA EL MAARI

RUE TOUEDDETTA

PLACE DES NATIONS

AVENUE YOUSSEF BEN TACHFINE

Tanger Ville and Tanger Moghogh Stations

Cap Malabata, Tanger Ville Station, Bus Station, Place de la Ligue, Arabe & Tetouan

22

DRINKING AND NIGHTLIFE

Many of Tangier's nightlife venues attract a rather seedy crowd; the places listed here are the most dependable.

Esquinita Av Mohammed VI. This bar with a DJ from midnight gets lively on weekends and is one of the few places along the seafront that doesn't attract a seedy crowd. Daily 7pm–4am.

La Bodega 5 Av Allal Ben Abdallah. Cosy bar-restaurant with red undertones; serves decent tapas (50–180dh). Daily noon–4pm & 6pm–1am.

★ **The Tanger Inn** Hotel El Muniria, 1 Rue Magellan. Mingle with young Moroccans at this lively joint which was once frequented by the Beat Generation authors (Burroughs, Ginsberg and Kerouac); beers 25dh, spirits 45dh. Thurs, Fri & Sat are best. Daily 10pm–1.30am. Closed Sun off-season.

DIRECTORY

Bank and exchange BMCE, 19 Bd Pasteur, has a bureau de change and ATM. Bureaux de change on Rue es Siaghin between the Grand and Petit Socco.

Internet Grand Cyber Cafe, Rue el Moutanabi (daily 10am–3am; 5dh/hr); Cyber Adnan, 21 Rue de la Marine, Medina (daily 4pm–2am; 10dh/hr).

Pharmacies There are several English-speaking pharmacies on Place de France and Bd Pasteur.

Post office Main PTT, 33 Bd Mohammed V.

Police The Brigade Touristique (☎0539 940477), based at the former train station by the port.

CEUTA/FNIDEQ

Due to the fast ferry, the drab Spanish enclave of **CEUTA** is a popular entry point for travellers coming from Spain. On disembarking you have to catch a taxi or local bus to the Moroccan border. Across the border, shared *grands taxis* will take you the 3km to the Moroccan town of **FNIDEQ** (4dh) or direct to Tetouan (15dh). Arrive early to leave time for moving on.

ARRIVAL AND DEPARTURE

By bus The bus station (*gare routière*) in Fnideq is signposted at the roundabout where the seafront and Av Mohammad V meet, marked by a fountain.

Destinations Casablanca (13 daily; 8hr); Marrakesh (3 daily; 11hr); Meknes (1 daily; 7hr); Rabat (14 daily; 7hr); Tangier (20 daily; 1hr); Tetouan (20 daily; 30min).

By ferry Tickets can be booked at Ceuta port; it is advisable to arrive an hour early. Times to avoid are at the end of Easter week and the last week of August due to a huge increase in demand.

Destinations Algeciras, mainland Spain (10–20 daily; 55min).

By taxi Buses are infrequent, so it's often quicker and similarly priced to get a shared *grand taxi* to Tetouan or Tangier for better connections. Tetouan-bound taxis wait at Fnideq bus station, while those for Tangier can be picked up behind 214 Av Mohammed V. Shared taxis for the Ceuta frontier sit on the seafront behind the Tangier taxi stand (just north of Souk Massira market).

ACCOMMODATION AND EATING

Hotel Fnideq 172 Mohammad V, Fnideq ☎0539 675467. Bright little hotel with sparkling rooms and bathrooms, pretty much slap-bang in the centre of town and very handy for the bus station. Double 250dh

Hotel Nador 134 Mohammad V, Fnideq ☎0539 675345. This modest but decent little place is the cheapest of the hotels along the one main road, with smaller and darker rooms than the others, but lower prices to match. Double 150dh

La Costa 232 Mohammad V. If you're looking for a restaurant, try this handy seafood place serving up excellent fresh fried fish at very moderate prices. Daily noon–9pm.

TETOUAN

Coming from Ceuta, you usually need to pick up onward transport at **TETOUAN**, a Spanish colonial town with quite a large Medina – but a shared *grand taxi* from Fnideq will leave you close enough to Tetouan's bus station, a twenty-minute walk southeast of town, to head straight out again. There are regular buses to Meknes, Fez and destinations nationwide. For Tangier, Chefchaouen or, if you're heading *to* Ceuta, it's easiest to travel by shared *grand taxi*. The ONCF office on Avenue 10 Mai, alongside Place Al Adala, sells train tickets that include a shuttle bus to Asilah from where you can catch a connecting train service.

ARRIVAL AND DEPARTURE

By bus The bus station is 1km south of town.

Destinations Casablanca (20 daily; 7hr); Chefchaouen (16 daily; 2hr); Fez (13 daily; 5hr 30min); Fnideq (for Ceuta) (20 daily; 30min); Marrakesh (3 daily; 10hr); Meknes (6 daily; 6hr); Rabat (28 daily; 5hr); Tangier (50 daily; 1hr 30min).

By taxi Shared *grands taxis* for Tangier, Chefchaouen, Fnideq and the Ceuta frontier leave from right next to the bus station.

ACCOMMODATION

Principe 20 Av Youssef Ibn Tachfine, on the corner of Boulevard de Mouqaouama ☏ 0533 113128. There aren't any hotels by the bus station, but if you're stuck in Tetouan, this is an inexpensive option. Double **140dh**

CHEFCHAOUEN

Shut in by a fold of the Rif Mountains, **CHEFCHAOUEN** (sometimes abbreviated to Chaouen or Xaouen) had, until the arrival of Spanish troops in 1920, been visited by just three Europeans. It's a town of extraordinary light and colour, its whitewash tinted with blue and edged by golden stone walls. *Pensions* are friendly and cheap and Chefchaouen is one of the best places to spend your first few days in Morocco.

The main entrance to the Medina is a tiny arched entrance, Bab el Ain, but the quickest way to negotiate your way to the centre is to get a *petit taxi* to **Place el Makhzen** (ask for the Kasbah), where you will find *Hotel Parador*, an expensive hotel, but a good place to pop into for a beer (23dh) or a swim (100dh). From here it is only a two-minute walk *to* Place Outa el Hammam, where most of the town's evening life takes place. By day the town's focus is the **Kasbah** (Mon, Wed, Thurs, Sat & Sun 9am–1pm & 3–6.30pm, Fri 9am–noon & 3–6.30pm; 10dh), a quiet ruin with shady gardens and a small museum, which occupies one side of the square.

Chefchaouen is best enjoyed pottering around the Medina and relaxing at coffee shops or on your terrace. For the more adventurous there are **hiking** trails that start from the town. Or you can charter a *grand taxi* from Place el Makhzen to go to the **Oued Laou beach** (180dh), about 60km away, or hike along rivers and waterfalls at **Akchour**, a thirty-minute *grand taxi* ride away.

ARRIVAL AND DEPARTURE

By bus Buses arrive at the station southwest of town; it's a 15min uphill walk into the centre, or a 10dh *petit taxi* ride. Buy tickets a day in advance for Fez and Meknes.
Destinations Casablanca (5 daily; 9hr); Fez (11 daily; 5hr); Meknes (3 daily; 5hr 30min); Rabat (7 daily; 8hr); Tangier (7 daily; 3hr); Tetouan (16 daily; 2hr).

By shared taxi Shared *grands taxis* from Tetouan drop you outside the town walls.

ACCOMMODATION

Camping Azilan Rue Sidi Abdelhamid ☏ 0539 986979. Located up on the hill above town, by the modern *Hôtel Asma*. Chefchaouen's campsite is inexpensive but can be crowded in summer. Camping **25dh** per person, plus **20dh** per tent
HI hostel Rue Sidi Abdelhamid ☏ 0666 865355, ✉ sarham03@live.fr. A very inexpensive but basic and somewhat inconveniently located hostel, a 15min walk uphill from town, just by the campsite. Dorm **40dh**
Hotel Andaluz 1 Rue Sidi Salem ☏ 0539 986034. Behind the jolly blue-and-white entrance, the rooms are a bit sombre, but staff are friendly, and there's a very decent English-language book collection. Double **120dh**
Hotel Ouarzazat Rue de Alkharazine ☏ 0539 988990. Rooms are decked out in local furniture and bathrooms are pretty spick and span. Double **120dh**
Pension La Castellena 4 Sidi Ahmed El Bouhali ☏ 0539 986295. The rooms are a little bit small at this perennially popular *pension*, but they're all beautifully decorated, individually furnished and painted by hand with colourful motifs. Double **150dh**

EATING AND DRINKING

Casa Aladin Rue Targi 17, off the north end of Place Outa El Hammam. Two floors and a terrace, beautifully done out in *Arabian Nights* style, as its name suggests, serving great *tajines*, couscous (including vegetarian) and other staple fare (mains 50dh, set menus 85dh). Daily 11am–11pm.
Chez Saild Place Outa El Hammam. A laidback joint perfect to stop by for a mid-afternoon tea (10dh) or a *tajine* (30dh) in the evening; head up to the roof terrace for a view of the square and a welcome breeze on a hot day. Daily 8am–10pm.
Restaurant Al Kasba North end of Place Outa El Hammam. Cushioned partitions and fun decor make this a relaxed place to have a decent spot of food for lunch or dinner (mains 30–50dh, menu 60dh). Daily 8am–10pm.

Central Morocco

Between the mountain ranges of the Rif to the north and the Atlas to the south lie the cities that form Morocco's heart: the great imperial centres of **Meknes** and **Fez**, the modern capital, **Rabat**, and the country's largest city and commercial capital, **Casablanca**.

22

22

MEKNES

More than any other Moroccan town, **MEKNES** is associated with a single figure, the Sultan Moulay Ismail, during whose reign (1672–1727) the city went from provincial centre to spectacular capital showcasing over fifty palaces and 24m of exterior walls. Today Meknes is a more sedate and calm version of Marrakesh, where the Medina's palaces and monuments reward a day's exploration. The town also serves as a perfect base to explore the nearby ancient site of **Volubilis** and holy town of **Moulay Idriss**.

WHAT TO SEE AND DO

The heart of the town, **Place El Hedim**, originally formed the western corner of the Medina, but Moulay Ismail had the houses here demolished to provide a grand approach to his palace quarter. There are a fair few sights to explore leading off the *place*.

The Dar Jamaï and the souks

The **Dar Jamaï** (Mon & Wed–Sun 9am–5pm; 10dh), at the back of Place El Hedim, is a superb example of a nineteenth-century Moroccan palace, and the museum inside is one of the best in Morocco, with a fantastic display of Middle Atlas carpets. The lane immediately to the left of the Dar Jamaï takes you to the Medina's major market street: on your left is **Souk en Nejjarin**, the carpet souk; on your right, leading to the Great Mosque and Bou Inania Medersa, are the fancier goods offered in the **Souk es Sebbat**. The **Bou Inania Medersa** (daily 9am–5pm; 10dh), constructed around 1340–50, has an unusual ribbed dome over the entrance hall, and from the roof you can look out to the tiled pyramids of the Great Mosque.

The Koubba el Khayatine and Moulay Ismail's Mausoleum

Behind the magnificent Bab Mansour (open for occasional exhibitions) is Place Lalla Aouda. Straight ahead and bearing left, you come into another open square, on the right of which is the green-tiled

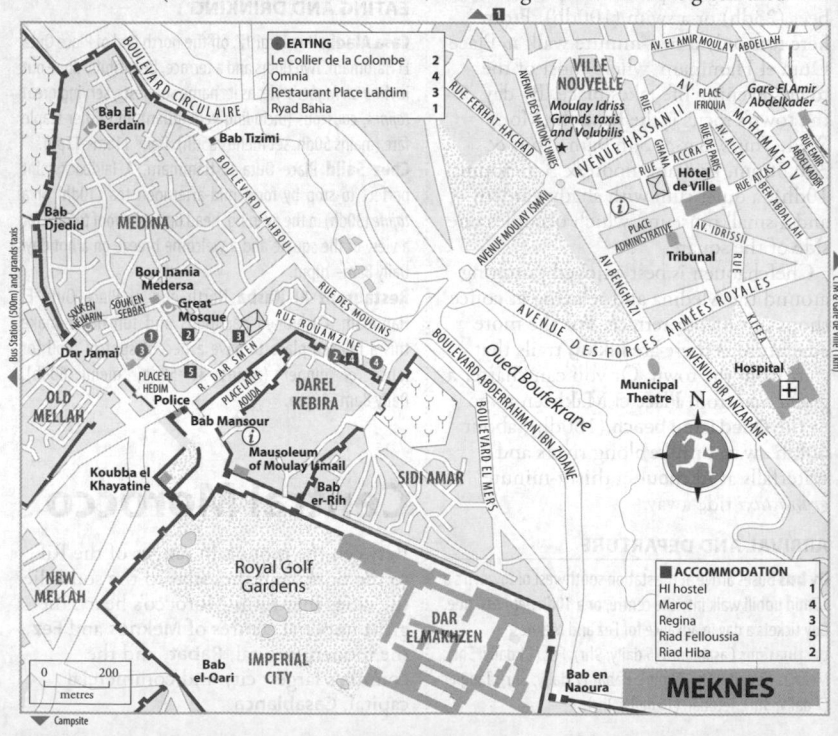

EATING
Le Collier de la Colombe	2
Omnia	4
Restaurant Place Lahdim	3
Ryad Bahia	1

ACCOMMODATION
HI hostel	1
Maroc	4
Regina	3
Riad Felloussia	5
Riad Hiba	2

MEKNES

dome of the **Koubba el Khayatine**, once a reception hall for ambassadors to the imperial court (daily 9am–6pm; 10dh) Below it a stairway descends into a vast series of subterranean vaults, known as the **Prison of Christian Slaves**, though it was probably a storehouse or granary. Nearby is the entrance to **Moulay Ismail's Mausoleum** (daily except Fri 9am–noon & 2.30–6pm; donation of around 10dh expected), where you can approach the sanctuary.

Volubilis and Moulay Idriss

A short *grand taxi* ride from Meknes takes you to two of the most important sites in Morocco's history. **Moulay Idriss**, 25km north of Meknes (10dh by *grand taxi* from Avenue des Nations Unies) was established by the Prophet's great-grandson who is credited with bringing Islam to Morocco. Today, it is a small but bustling town, which Moroccans treat with great respect. It is worth a trip for the views from the top of the town and for an insight into the religious heart of Morocco (particularly true in the festival that takes place in the second week of August). However, non-Muslims are barred from visiting the religious shrines of Moulay Idriss for which the town is famous.

Five kilometres northwest of Moulay Idriss, **Volubilis** (daily 8am–6pm; 10dh; around 40dh by *petit taxi* from Moulay Idriss, or 350dh for return trip plus 2hr waiting time from Meknes) was once the Roman capital of the province; it's still possible to follow the outline of the old city and walk among some well-preserved ruins. A small on-site museum houses Roman artefacts found here.

ARRIVAL AND INFORMATION

By train Meknes has two train stations, both in the Ville Nouvelle. All trains stop at Gare de Ville, but Gare El Amir Abdelkader (some services only) is more central.
Destinations Casablanca Voyageurs (18 daily; 2hr 50min); Fez (22 daily; 40min); Marrakesh (8 daily; 6hr 40min); Rabat (18 daily; 1hr 50min); Tangier (3 daily; 3hr 40min).
By bus and taxi Private buses and most shared *grands taxis* arrive west of the Medina by Bab el Khemis. CTM buses arrive at their terminus on Av de Fès, near the Gare de Ville.
Destinations (private) Casablanca (7 daily; 4hr 30min); Chefchaouen (3 daily; 5hr 30min); Fez (roughly every 30min; 1hr); Marrakesh (2 daily; 9hr); Rabat (12 daily; 3hr); Tangier (8 daily; 7hr); Tetouan (6 daily; 6hr).
Destinations (CTM) Casablanca (7 daily; 4hr); Fez (11 daily; 1hr); Marrakesh (2 daily; 7hr 15min); Rabat (8 daily; 2hr); Tangier (5 daily; 5hr); Tetouan (1 daily; 6hr).
Tourist information Place Hedim, Medina (daily except Fri 10am–12.30pm & 3–5pm, but currently closed afternoons during construction work), and at 27 Place Administrative, Ville Nouvelle (Mon–Fri 8.30am–4.30pm; ☎ 0535 516022).

ACCOMMODATION

The most atmospheric place to stay is in the Medina, where everything is on your doorstep. All places listed here are in the Medina, unless stated otherwise.
HI hostel Ave Okba Ben Nafi, Ville Nouvelle ☎ 0535 524698, ✉ aubergejeune_meknes@hotmail.fr. A 1.5km walk northwest of the city centre, or a 10dh taxi ride. Small rooms, but the place is relatively well maintained and friendly. Breakfast included. Dorm __65dh__, double __160dh__
Maroc 7 Rue Rouamzine ☎ 0535 530075. The spartan rooms on the interior courtyard benefit from a welcome cross-breeze, while the hole-in-the-floor bathrooms could do with similar ventilation. In summer, those on restricted budgets can sleep on the roof terrace for 50dh. Double __200dh__
Regina 19 Rue Dar Smen ☎ 0535 530280. A smile at reception helps compensate for the dingy rooms where the bedsprings may well have supported the weight of one too many *tajine*-fed guests. Shower 5dh. Double __120dh__
Riad Hiba 20 Rue Lalla Aicha Addouya ☎ 0535 460109, ⊕ riadhiba.net. Heavy ornate furnishings and added bonuses like flat-screen cable TV, a/c and wi-fi. Breakfast included. Double __€30__

EATING

There are cheap eats on Rue Rouamzine near *Hôtel Maroc* and you can also pick up inexpensive bites from one of the many restaurants in Place Hedim.
Le Collier de la Colombe 67 Rue Driba ☎ 0535 555041. The speciality here is Atlas mountain trout (90dh), to be savoured on the rooftop terrace with sunset views over the golden Medina. Daily 11.30am–3.30pm & 6.30–11pm.
Omnia 8 Derb Ain El Fouki. Friendly, welcoming restaurant

★ **TREAT YOURSELF**

Riad Felloussia 23 Derb Hammam Jdid ☎ 0535 530840, ⊕ riadfelloussia.com. The quaint labyrinthine corridor leads to a beautiful indoor garden with tiled fountain and cedar beams, and the *Riad's* four suites are beautifully decorated with local fabrics and materials. Breathtaking views from the rooftop terrace, too. Breakfast included. Double __€90__

22

set in a family home courtyard brimming with local knick-knacks. Sit in one of the little cushioned salons as fresh aromas from the menu of the day (70dh) waft out of the kitchen. Daily noon–midnight.

Restaurant Place Lahdim Derb Sidi Amar Bouaouada (just off the northern corner of Place El Hedim). Tuck into some generous portions of tasty Moroccan food (tajines 50–60dh) or unwind on the terrace with some mint tea as you ponder daily life in the square below. Daily noon–9pm.

Ryad Bahia Derb Tiberbarine ☎ 0535 554541. Dig into some home-made food at this pleasant, family-style *riad*; the friendly, well-travelled owners will make you feel at home as the delicious traditional food is prepared (menu 160dh). Daily 11am–10pm.

FEZ (FÈS)

The most ancient of the imperial capitals, **FEZ** (Fès in French) stimulates the senses and seems to exist somewhere between the Middle Ages and the modern world. Some two hundred thousand of the city's half-million inhabitants (though actual figures are probably much higher than official ones) live in the oldest part of the Medina, Fès el Bali.

WHAT TO SEE AND DO

Getting lost is one of the great joys of the Fez Medina. However, if you want a more informed approach, pick up a small green book called "*Fes*" from the paper kiosks; this book corresponds to the tourist trails within the Medina that are marked out by coloured stars. Tour guides also can be employed at the Bab Boujeloud; the official ones wear medallions to identify themselves.

Talâa Kebira

Talâa Kebira, the Medina's main artery, is home to the most brilliant of Fez's monuments, the **Medersa Bou Inania** (daily 9am–5.30pm; closes 4pm during Ramadan, and sometimes closes briefly for prayers; 10dh), which comes close to perfection in every aspect of its construction, with beautiful carved wood, stucco and *zellij* tilework. Continuing down Talâa Kebira you reach the entrance to the **Souk el Attarin** (Souk of the Spice Vendors), the formal heart of the city. To the right, a street leads past the charming **Souk el Henna** – a tree-shaded square where traditional cosmetics are sold – to Place Nejjarin (Carpenters' Square). Here, next to the geometric tilework of the Nejjarin Fountain, is the imposing eighteenth-century **Nejjarin Fondouk**, now a woodwork museum (daily 10am–5pm; 20dh), though the building is rather more interesting than its exhibits. Immediately to the right of the fountain, Talâa Seghira is an alternative route back to Bab Boujeloud, while the alley to the right of that is the aromatic **carpenters' souk**, ripe with the scent of sawn cedar, and top on the list of great Medina smells.

Zaouia Moulay Idriss II

The street opposite the Nejjarin Fountain leads to the **Zaouia Moulay Idriss II**, one of the holiest buildings in the city. Buried here is the son and successor of Fez's founder, who continued his father's work. Only Muslims may enter to check out

---

FEZ ORIENTATION

Fez can be difficult to get to grips with, orientation-wise. The Medina in Fez is uniquely vast and beautiful, with two distinct parts: the newer section, **Fès el Jedid**, established in the thirteenth century, is mostly taken up by the Royal Palace; the older part, **Fès el Bali**, founded in the eighth century on the River Fez, was populated by refugees from Tunisia on one bank – the **Kairaouine** quarter – and from Spain on the other bank – the **Andalusian** quarter. In practice, almost everything you will want to see is in the Kairaouine quarter.

There are several different gates through which you can enter the old city. **Bab Boujeloud** is the most popular and recognizable entry point and is a useful landmark. From here you can turn left at the *Restaurant La Kasbah* to get on to Talâa Kebira, the Medina's main thoroughfare. From the north, **Bab el Guissa** offers another port of entry. For views of the Medina, have a drink at the *Hotel Palais Jamaï* (next to Bab Jamaï) or *Hotel les Merenides*. There's also an impressive view from the Arms Museum in the fort above the bus station (Tues–Sun 8.30–11.30am & 2–5.30pm; 10dh, free on Fri).

22

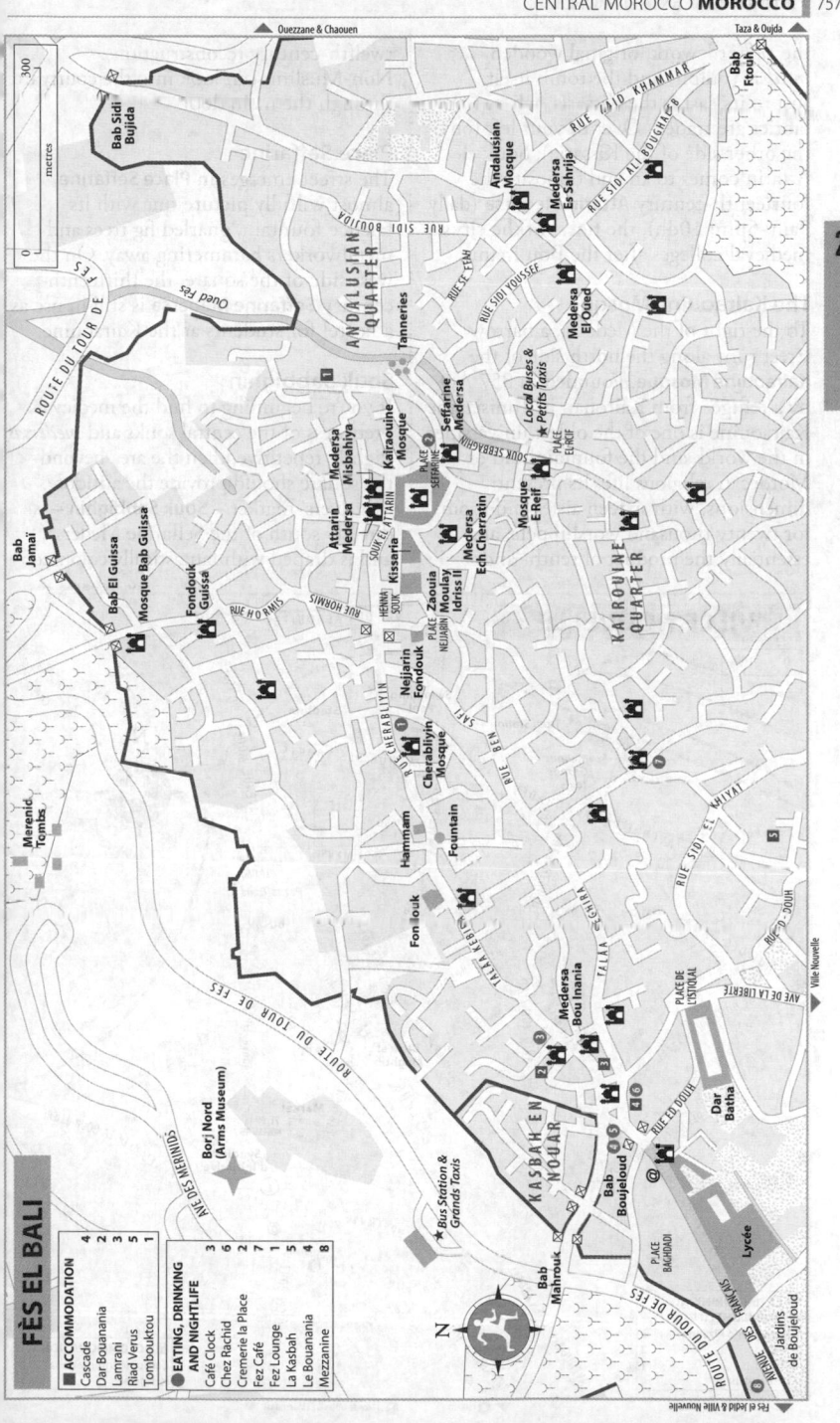

FÈS EL BALI

■ ACCOMMODATION
Cascade	4
Dar Bouanania	2
Lamrani	3
Riad Verus	5
Tombouktou	1

● EATING, DRINKING AND NIGHTLIFE
Café Clock	3
Chez Rachid	6
Cremerie la Place	2
Fez Café	7
Fez Lounge	1
La Kasbah	5
Le Bouanania	4
Mezzanine	8

Ouezzane & Chaouen

Taza & Oujda

Bab Sidi Boujida

Bab Ftouh

FÈS

Oued Fès

ROUTE DU TOUR DE FÈS

ANDALUSIAN QUARTER

Andalusian Mosque

Medersa Es Sahrija

RUE SIDI BOUJIDA

RUE SID KHAMMAR

RUE SE FENI

RUE SIDI YOUSSEF

Medersa El Oued

Tanneries

Seffarine Medersa

Local Buses & Petits Taxis

PLACE SEFFARINE

PLACE EL NIOF

SOUK SEBBAGHIN

Kairaouine Mosque

Medersa Misbahiya

Medersa Attarin

SOUK EL ATTARIN

Kissaria

Medersa Ech Cherratin

Mosque E Reif

KAIROUINE QUARTER

Bab Jamaï

Bab El Guissa

Mosque Bab Guissa

Fondouk Guissa

RUE HORMIS

RUE HORMIS

HENNA SOUK

Zaouia Moulay Idriss II

PLACE NEJJARIN

Nejjarin Fondouk

RUE CHERABLIYIN

Cherabliyin Mosque

RUE BEN

SAFI

RUE SIDI EL MIYAT

Merenid Tombs

Hammam

Fountain

Fonlouk

TALAA KEBIRA

TALAA S'GHIRA

Medersa Bou Inania

PLACE DE L'ISTIQLAL

AVE DE LA LIBERTE

RUE ED DOUH

RUE DU 2 OUH

Ville Nouvelle

★ Bus Station & Grands Taxis

Borj Nord (Arms Museum)

AVE DES MERINIDS

ROUTE DU TOUR DE FÈS

KASBAH EN NOUAR

Bab Boujeloud

Dar Batha

Lycée

Bab Mahrouk

PLACE BAGHDADI

PLACE BAHROUG

RUE FRANÇAIS

Jardins de Boujeloud

MERINIE DES

ROUTE DU TOUR DE FÈS

N

300 metres 0

Fès el Jedid & Ville Nouvelle

22

the *zellij* tilework, original wooden *minbar* (pulpit) and the tomb itself. Just to its east is the Kissaria, where fine fabrics are traded. Over to your left (on the other side of the Kissaria), Souk el Attarin comes to an end opposite the fourteenth-century **Attarin Medersa** (daily 9am–5pm; 10dh), the finest of the city's medieval colleges after the Bou Inania.

The Kairaouine Mosque

To the right of the Medersa, a narrow street runs along the north side of the **Kairaouine Mosque**. Founded in 857 AD by a refugee from Kairouan in Tunisia, the Kairaouine is one of the oldest universities in the world, and the fountainhead of Moroccan religious life. Its present dimensions, with sixteen aisles and room for twenty thousand worshippers, are essentially the product of tenth- and twelfth-century reconstructions. Non-Muslims can look into the courtyard through the main door.

Place Seffarine

The street emerges in **Place Seffarine**, almost wilfully picturesque with its faïence fountain, gnarled fig trees and metalworkers hammering away. On the west side of the square, the thirteenth-century **Seffarine Medersa** is still in use as a hostel for students at the Kairaouine.

Souk Sabbighin

If you're beginning to find the medieval prettiness of the central souks and *medersas* slightly repetitive, then the area beyond the square should provide the antidote. The dyers' market – **Souk Sabbighin** – is directly south of the Seffarine Medersa, and is draped with fantastically coloured

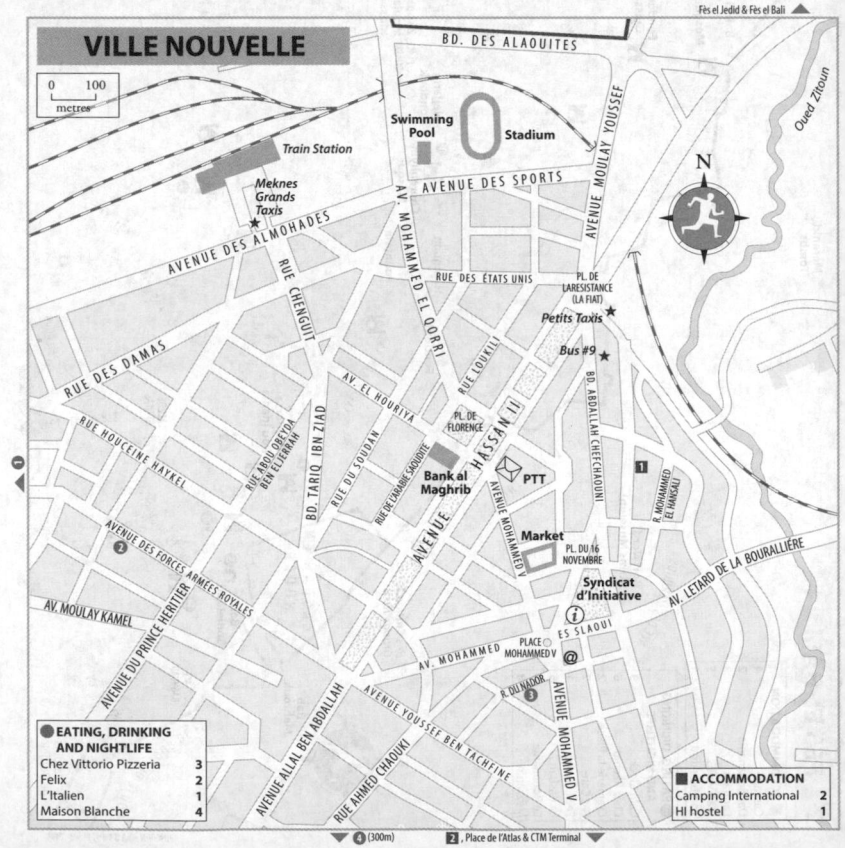

yarn and cloth drying in the heat. Below, workers in grey toil over cauldrons of multicoloured dyes. **Place er Rsif**, nearby, has buses and taxis to the Ville Nouvelle.

The tanneries

The street to the left (north) of the Seffarine Medersa leads to the rather smelly tanneries, constantly visited by tour groups with whom you could discreetly tag along if you get lost. Inside the tanneries water deluges through holes that were once windows of houses. Hundreds of skins lie spread out on the rooftops, above vats of dye and the pigeon dung used to treat the leather. Straight on, the road eventually leads back round to the Attarin Medersa.

ARRIVAL AND DEPARTURE

By train The train station is in the Ville Nouvelle, a 15min walk north of the hotels around Place Mohammed V. If you prefer to stay in the Medina, take a *petit taxi* (10dh), or bus #19 which will drop you off at R'Cif in the Medina; alternatively, walk down to Place de la Résistance (aka La Fiat) and pick up bus #9 to Dar Batha/Place de l'Istiqlal, near the western gate to Fès el Bali, Bab Boujeloud.
Destinations Casablanca Voyageurs (19 daily; 3hr 40min); Marrakesh (8 daily; 7hr 15min); Meknes (22 daily; 30min); Rabat (19 daily; 2hr 50min); Tangier (3 daily; 4hr 20min).
By bus The bus station is just outside the walls near Bab Boujeloud. The terminal for CTM buses is off Rue de l'Atlas, which links the far end of Av Mohammed V with Place de l'Atlas.
Destinations (private) Casablanca (approximately every 30min; 5hr); Chefchaouen (5 daily; 5hr); Marrakesh (6 daily; 7hr); Meknes (approximately every 30min; 1hr); Rabat (approximately every 30min; 4hr); Tangier (9 daily; 6hr); Tetouan (9 daily; 5hr 30min).
Destinations (CTM) Casablanca (5 daily; 5hr); Chefchaouen (2 daily; 5hr); Marrakesh (4 daily; 7hr); Meknes (11 daily; 1hr); Rabat (12 daily; 3hr); Tangier (9 daily; 6hr); Tetouan (4 daily; 5–7hr).
By taxi Shared *grands taxis* mostly operate from the bus station; exceptions include some of those serving Meknes (from the train station).

INFORMATION

Tourist information Place Mohammed V (Mon–Fri 8.30am–4.30pm; ☎0535 623460) can tell you about June's seven-day Festival of World Sacred Music (☎0535 740535, ⊛fesfestival.com) and the five-day cherry festival which usually follows immediately after it in nearby Sefrou.

ACCOMMODATION

There's a shortage of hotel space in all categories, so be prepared for higher-than-usual prices; booking ahead is advisable. For atmosphere and character, the Medina is the place to be.
Camping International Route de Sefrou ☎0535 618061; map opposite; bus #38 from Place de l'Atlas. Located some 4km south of town, this is pricey for a campsite but has good facilities, including a pool in summer. Camping **40dh** per person, plus **30dh** per tent
Cascade Just inside Bab Boujeloud, Fès el Bali ☎0535 638442, ⊛cascadasplaza@gmail.com; map p.757. An old building with a useful public hammam (bath-house) just behind. Rooms are small and basic, but management friendly; the fantastic view from the terrace, where you can drink if you bring your own, is the real draw. Double **140dh**
★ **Dar Bouanania** 21 Derb ben Salem (signposted on Talâa Kebira), Fès el Bali ☎0535 637282, ⊛darbouanania @gmail.com; map p.757. Not quite a *riad*, but the budget equivalent, with spacious rooms and traditional decor for reasonable enough prices. Double **400dh**
HI hostel 18 Rue Abdeslam Seghrini, Ville Nouvelle ☎0535 624085; map opposite. One of Morocco's best hostels – well kept, friendly and spotlessly clean. Breakfast included. Dorm **55dh**
Lamrani Talâa Seghira, Fès el Bali ☎0535 634411; map p.757. Friendly and just opposite a hammam, though a little bit overpriced if there are just one or two of you (the rooms fit four for the same price). Double **200dh**
★ **Riad Verus** 1 Derb Arset Bennis, Batha, Fès el Bali ☎0535 741941, ⊛riadverus.com; map p.757. A snazzy *riad*-cum-hostel with immaculate rooms, most with en suite, as well as a roof terrace and soundproof music lounge. Dorm **€15**, double **€50**
Tombouktou 32 Bis Ouad Zhoune, Fès el Bali ☎0535 638851; map p.757. Slightly gaudy trad Moroccan is the decor of choice at this clean hotel with a/c and cable TV, not to mention two sun patios and excellent food. Double **250dh**

EATING, DRINKING AND NIGHTLIFE

Fès el Bali has two main areas for cheap local food: around Bab Boujeloud and along Rue Hormis (running from Souk el Attarin towards Bab Guissa), while the Ville Nouvelle is mainly home to pricier Western-style restaurants serving European cuisine. There's a lack of drinking places in the Medina itself – those listed here are by far the safest bet.

CAFÉS, CHEAP EATS AND SNACKS

Café Clock 7 Derb El Magana; map p.757. A maze of little comfy salons leads off the three-tiered courtyard; forget *tajines* – you're here for the camel burger (95dh) or the falafel with hummus and tabbouleh (55dh). Daily 8am–10.30pm.

22

22

Chez Rachid Inside Bab Boujeloud; map p.757. One of the friendlier and more welcoming of the numerous street restaurants, with tasty *brochettes* and the usual nosh from 40dh. Daily 9am–10.45pm.

★ **Cremerie La Place** On the northeast corner of Place Seffarine; map p.757. Tiny café perfect for enjoying a tea (10dh) and delectable patisseries (5dh) as you watch the coppersmiths hammering and shaping merchandise under the shade of the picturesque plane tree. Mon–Thurs, Sat & Sun 7am–7pm, Fri 7am–noon.

Fez Café 13 Akbat Sbaa; map p.757. Walk through a beautiful oasis of greenery to reach the shady patio of this quiet café where you can enjoy a detox tea (20dh) or a fresh juice (25dh); the menu changes every day, so there's always something new to try (mains 150–160dh). Daily noon–3pm & 7–10pm.

Fez Lounge 95 Zkak Rouah Talâa Kebira, Fès el Bali ⓦfezlounge.com; map p.757. The tanneries are not far, yet faux leather rules at this Medina hideout where you can sit back and enjoy a *shisha* over a *tartine* (60dh), burger (50dh) or the usual fare (50–80dh). Daily noon–10pm.

La Kasbah Inside Bab Boujeloud; map p.757. The draw here is the roof terrace overlooking the blue gate and the windy Medina alleyways below; the *tajines* (40dh) can be a little insipid, though. Menus 70dh. Daily 9am–10pm.

Le Bouanania Inside Bab Boujeloud; map p.757. Friendly restaurant located in a beautiful building with a cushioned Moroccan salon on the first floor and a roof terrace with commanding views over the ramparts and the blue gate. Mains 45dh, set menu 70dh. Daily 9am–9pm.

BARS AND RESTAURANTS

Chez Vittorio Pizzeria 21 Rue Ibrahim Roudani, nearly opposite *Hôtel Central*; map p.758. Italian restaurant with a wood-fired oven, although the pizzas and pastas are not their strong point; try the steaks and meat dishes instead (110–140dh). Daily noon–3pm & 7–11pm.

★ **L'Italien** Ave Omar Ibnou Khattab, Champs de Course; map p.758. Fun and fashionable restaurant that is by far the best Italian in town, with proper wood-fired pizzas (60–110dh) and exquisite pastas. Daily noon–midnight.

★ **Mezzanine** 17 Ksbat Chams, Av des Français, Fès el Bali; map p.757. Sun yourself on the funky lounge terrace at lunchtime or soak in the trendy atmosphere over a chilled beer (40–55dh) or dinner (mains 50–120dh) as you peer over the city ramparts at the spectacular gardens below. Daily 11am–midnight.

CLUB

Felix *Hotel Tghat*, Av des Forces Armées Royales; map p.758. Moroccan DJs behind the decks do a pretty good job at mixing house, dance and Arabic music. 100dh entry includes one drink. Daily midnight–4am.

★ **TREAT YOURSELF**

Maison Blanche 12 Rue Ahmed Chaouki, Ville Nouvelle, opposite Jnane Palace hotel ⓣ 0535 622727; map. p.758. Fez branch of a trendy Paris restaurant, with sleek couches and illuminated stone walls. Ditch the trainers and head over for some elegant French cuisine with an ever so slight touch of Moroccan. Mains from 230dh. Daily noon–3pm & 5–11pm.

DIRECTORY

Banks and exchange ATMs at Place R'Cif and Bab Boujeloud in the Medina; plenty of banks (all with ATMs) on Mohammed V in the Ville Nouvelle, including BMCE on Place Mohammed V; also on Place de l'Atlas and Place Florence.

Hospital Clinique Agdal, by the French Consulate in the Ville Nouvelle ⓣ 0535 931633.

Internet Cyber Club, corner of Av Mohammed V and Rue el Moujahid el Ayachi, opposite *Hôtel Central* (daily 9am–9pm; 10dh/hr); Cyber Bab Boujeloud, just outside Bab Boujeloud (daily 10am–11pm; 5dh/hr).

Pharmacy Pharmacie Bab Boujeloud, just outside Bab Boujeloud (Mon–Fri 8.30am–12.30pm & 3.30–8pm, Sat 8.30am–1pm). Night pharmacy in the *baladiya* (town hall) on Av Moulay Yousef (daily 9.30pm–8.30am).

Police Bab Boujeloud in the Medina (24/7); the Commissariat Central is on Av Mohammed V in the Ville Nouvelle behind the post office.

Post office Corner of aves Mohammed V and Hassan II, Ville Nouvelle; also in Place Batha and Place des Alaouites, Medina.

RABAT

Often undervalued by tourists, Morocco's capital city, **RABAT**, has a modern political centre (with elegant French architecture), several historical monuments, accessible bars and an ancient Kasbah overlooking a sandy beach. Though it should not take priority over Fez, Marrakesh or Chefchaouen, it is worth a visit if you have the time.

WHAT TO SEE AND DO

Rabat's compact Medina – the whole city until the French arrived in 1912 – is wedged on two sides by the sea and the river, on the others by the twelfth-century Almohad and fifteenth-century Andalusian walls. Laid out in a simple grid, its streets are very easy to navigate.

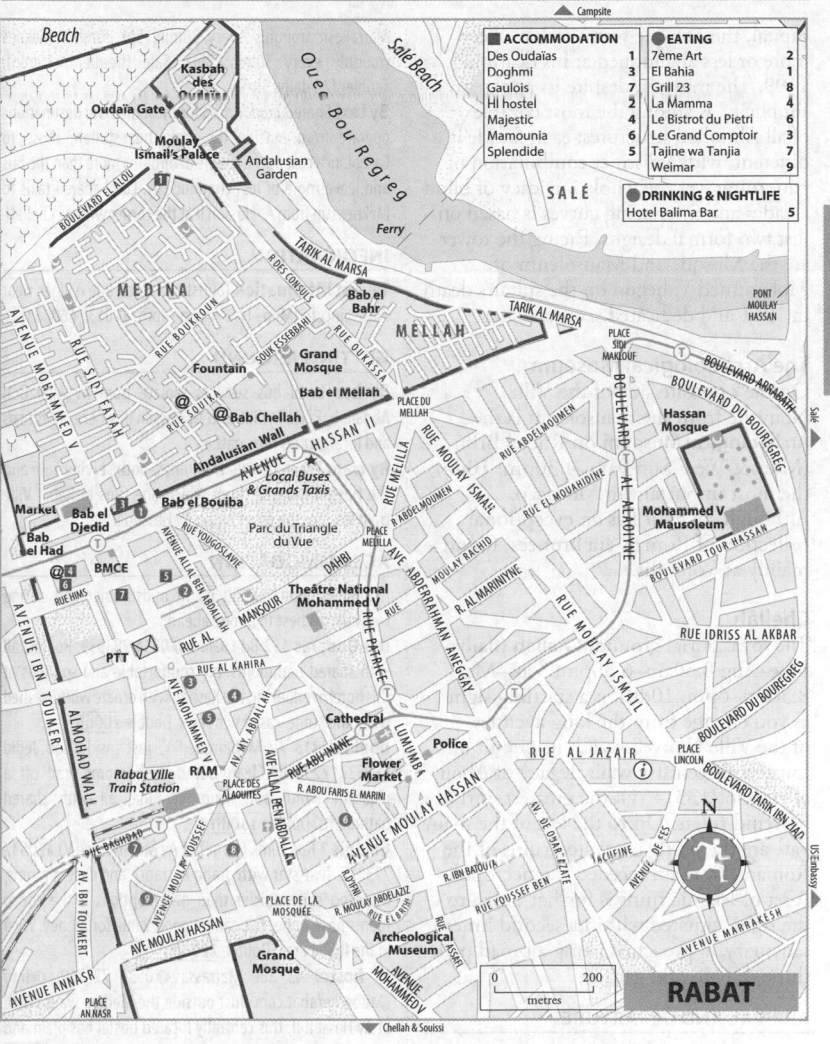

■ ACCOMMODATION		● EATING	
Des Oudaïas	1	7ème Art	2
Doghmi	3	El Bahia	1
Gaulois	7	Grill 23	8
HI hostel	2	La Mamma	4
Majestic	4	Le Bistrot du Pietri	3
Mamounia	6	Le Grand Comptoir	6
Splendide	5	Tajine wa Tanjia	7
		Weimar	9

● DRINKING & NIGHTLIFE	
Hotel Balima Bar	5

22

RABAT

Kasbah des Oudaïas and around

North lies the **Kasbah des Oudaïas**, a charming and evocative quarter whose principal gateway – **Bab el Kasbah** or Oudaïa Gate, built around 1195 – is one of the most ornate in the Moorish world. Its interior is now used for art exhibitions. Down the steps outside the gate, a lower, horseshoe arch leads directly to **Moulay Ismail's Palace** (Mon & Wed–Sun 9.30am–4.30pm; 10dh), which hosts quite an interesting Jewellery Museum. The adjoining **Andalusian Garden** – one

of the most delightful spots in the city – was actually constructed by the French in the last century, though true to Arab Andalusian tradition, with deep, sunken beds of shrubs and flowering annuals.

The Hassan Mosque

The most ambitious of all Almohad buildings, the **Hassan Mosque** (daily 8am–7pm; free), with its vast minaret, dominates almost every view of the city. Designed by the Almohad ruler Yacoub el Mansour as the centrepiece of the new

22

capital, the mosque seems to have been more or less abandoned at his death in 1199. The minaret, despite its apparent simplicity, is among the most complex of all Almohad structures: each facade is different, with a distinct combination of patterning, yet the whole intricacy of blind arcades and interlacing curves is based on just two formal designs. Facing the tower are the Mosque and Mausoleum of Mohammed V, begun on the sultan's death in 1961 and dedicated six years later.

The Archeological Museum

On the opposite side of the Ville Nouvelle from the mausoleum is the **Archeological Museum** on Rue el Brihi (Mon & Wed–Sun 9am–4.30pm; 10dh), the most important in Morocco. Although small, it has an exceptional collection of Roman-era bronzes, found mainly at Volubilis.

Chellah

The royal burial ground, **Chellah** (daily: June–Aug 8.30am–6.30pm; Sept–May 8.30am–6pm; 10dh), is a startling sight as you emerge from the long avenues of the Ville Nouvelle, with its circuit of fourteenth-century walls, legacy of Abou el Hassan (1331–51), the greatest of the Merenid rulers. Off to the left of the main gate are the partly excavated ruins of the Roman city that preceded the necropolis. A set of Islamic ruins is further down to the right, situated within a second inner sanctuary, approached along a broad path through half-wild gardens.

ARRIVAL AND DEPARTURE

By train The best way to arrive is by train, as Rabat Ville train station is at the heart of the Ville Nouvelle; don't get off at Rabat Agdal station, 2km from the centre.
Destinations Casablanca Port (every 30min; 1hr 10min); Casablanca Voyageurs (27 daily; 1hr); Fez (19 daily; 2hr 20min); Marrakesh (9 daily; 4hr 20min); Meknes (18 daily; 1hr 50min); Tangier (8 daily; 3hr 50min).
By bus The main bus terminal is 3km west of the centre, served by local buses #17, #30 and #41, and by petits taxis. It's easier, if you're arriving by bus from the north, to get off in Salé across the river, and take a tram or shared grand taxi from there into Rabat.
Destinations Casablanca (frequent; 1hr 20min); Essaouira (14 daily; 7hr 30min); Fez (roughly every 30min; 4hr);

Marrakesh (roughly every 30min; 5hr 30min); Meknes (roughly every 30min; 3hr); Salé (frequent; 15min); Tangier (28 daily; 5hr).
By taxi Shared grands taxis for most intercity destinations operate from outside the main bus station; those to Casablanca cost only a couple of dirhams more than the bus and leave more or less continuously. Local shared taxis to Meknes run from Av Hassan II at the corner with Av Chellah.

INFORMATION

Tourist information Tourist office at 2 Rue d'Alger, near Place Lincoln (Mon–Fri 8.30am–4pm; ☎0537 660663).

GETTING AROUND

By bus Local bus services radiate from Av Allal Ben Abdallah, Place Melilla and Av Hassan II, where petits taxis and local grands taxis gather.
By tram There are two tram lines, both serving Salé and the Hassan Mosque, from which one runs to Rabat Ville train station, the other along Av Hassan II.

ACCOMMODATION

Accommodation can fill up in midsummer and during festivals; it's best to phone ahead.
Des Oudaïas 132 Bd Laalou ☎0534 283959. Rooms, all with shared bathrooms, are comfortable and spacious at this hotel overlooking the Kasbah with ornate whitewashed walls and stone-cased windows. Double 200dh
Doghmi 313 Av Mohammed V, just inside Bab Jedid ☎0537 723898. Clean but darkish rooms lead off a pleasant white and azure veranda, all with shared bathrooms. Double 130dh
Gaulois 1 Rue Hims (corner of Av Mohammed V) ☎0537 723022. Two-star with grand entrance and decent rooms, some en suite. Pricier than other options if the cheap rooms have gone, but can be good value for money. Wi-fi in the lobby area. Double 220dh
HI hostel 43 Rue Marrassa ☎0537 725769, ✉info @aubergerabat.com. Just outside the Medina walls north of Av Hassan II, this centrally located hostel has plain and simple dorms with shared bathroom facilities. Dorm 60dh
Majestic 121 Av Hassan II ☎0537 722997, ⊛hotelmajestic.ma. Excellent option for female travellers, with a 24hr reception and porter; rooms are bright and spotless. Double 348dh
★ **Mamounia** 10 Rue Mamounia ☎0537 724479, ✉hotel_mamounia@hotmail.fr. Andalusian-style faux flowerpots give a touch of fun to the hallway of this friendly and centrally located hotel. The rooms are clean if a little garish. Double 100dh
Splendide 8 Rue Ghazza ☎0537 723283. A great option with a leafy courtyard to sit back after a day of exploring the city; some of the clean rooms give onto the central patio. Hot water mornings and evenings only. Double 230dh

EATING

Rabat has a wide range of good restaurants serving both Moroccan and international dishes. The cheapest ones are in the Medina.

★ **7ème Art** Av Allal Ben Abdallah. Trendy good-value café with tables set around a garden area with a fountain, serving all sorts of goodies from hamburgers (22–36dh) to ice creams (30dh for three scoops). Daily 7am–10pm.

El Bahia Av Hassan II, built into the Andalusian wall, near the junction with Av Mohammed V. Sit at one of the tables that line the Andalusian wall or retreat to the leafy inner patio for reasonably priced *tajines* (45–60dh), brochettes (50–55dh) and salads (20–25dh), though service can be slow. Daily 8am–10pm.

Grill 23 386 Av Mohammed V. Cheap but delicious *shwarma* (30–42dh), hamburgers (28–38dh) and panini (30–34dh). Convenient for a takeaway to carry with you on a train journey (it's just up the street from the station). Daily 7am–1am.

La Mamma 6 Rue Tanta, behind the *Hôtel Balima*. Good pasta dishes (50–80dh) and wood-oven pizzas (55–90dh) in a rustic trattoria setting. Daily noon–3pm & 7.30pm–12.30am.

★ **Le Bistrot du Pietri** 4 Rue Tobrouk ☎ 0537 707820. Bar serving delicious bistro-style food accompanied on Tues, Fri & Sat nights by outstanding jazz and world music bands. Book ahead on jazz nights if you want a table. Free entry. Daily 11am–midnight, food served Mon–Fri noon–3pm & daily 7.30–11pm.

Tajine wa Tanjia 9 Rue Baghdad. A lovely little place with low cushioned seating and Moroccan paintings serving a wide range of excellent *tajines* (58–88dh) and *tanjia* (jugged beef or lamb; 110–130dh). Mon–Sat 11am–3pm & 6pm–midnight.

★ **Weimar** 7 Rue Sana'a, inside the Goethe Institute. Studenty, expat hangout serving pastas (45–58dh), salads (15–58dh) and meats (69–90dh), washed down with German beer. Mon–Fri noon–2.30pm & 7–11pm, Sat 7–11pm.

DRINKING AND NIGHTLIFE

Aves Mohammed V and Allal Ben Abdallah have some good cafés, but the best bars are situated in Agdal, a bit of a trek from the centre. Those itching for a boogie should head to the Centre Commercial Prestige along the Route des Zaers, a 10min taxi ride out of town, home to a cluster of nightclubs.

Hotel Balima Bar Av Mohammed V. This bar is conveniently located in the centre of town and has a terrace overlooking the Parliament. Daily 9am–11pm.

DIRECTORY

Banks and exchange Along Av Allal Ben Abdallah and Av Mohammed V. BMCE at the northern end of Av Mohammed V has a bureau de change (daily 8am–8pm).

> ★ **TREAT YOURSELF**
> **Le Grand Comptoir** 279 Av Mohammed V ☎ 0537 201514, ⊕ legrandcomptoir.ma. Classy, Parisian-style brasserie with wonderful 1920s-style decor and live music that ranges from jazz to traditional Moroccan. Serves excellent meat and seafood dishes and a decent selection of wines. Main courses 110–225dh, while a meal with wine will set you back 400–500dh. Mon–Sat noon–midnight.

Embassies Australia represented by Canada; Canada, 13bis Rue Jaâfar as Sadiq, Agdal ☎ 0537 687400; New Zealand represented by the UK; UK, 28 Av SAR Sidi Mohammed, Souissi ☎ 0537 633333; US, 2 Av Mohammed el Fassi (Av Marrakech) ☎ 0537 762265. Irish citizens are covered by their embassy in Lisbon (☎ 00 351 21 330 8200), but have an honorary consul in Casablanca (☎ 0522 272721).

Internet Cheapest places are on or off Rue Souika in the Medina (4dh/hr); also at 113 Av Hassan II by *Hôtel Majestic* (Mon–Sat 9am–8pm; 8dh/hr).

Police Av Tripoli, near the Cathedral. Police post at Bab Jedid and north end of Rue des Consuls.

Post office Halfway down Av Mohammed V.

CASABLANCA

Morocco's main city and economic capital, **CASABLANCA** (or "Casa") is also North Africa's largest port. Casa's Westernized image does not fit with most travellers' stereotype of Morocco but the city offers good food, beaches and fun nightlife.

WHAT TO SEE AND DO

Casablanca's Medina, above the port and recently gentrified, is largely the product of the late nineteenth century, when Casa began its modest growth as a commercial centre. Film buffs will be disappointed to learn that Bogart's *Casablanca* wasn't shot here (it was filmed entirely in Hollywood) – *Rick's Bar* (expensive) commemorates it as a gimmick at 248 Bd Sour Jedid.

Mosquée Hassan II

The awe-inspiring **Mosquée Hassan II** (guided tours only Mon–Thurs, Sat & Sun 9am, 10am, 11am & 2pm; 120dh, students 60dh) is a must-see for all visitors to Casablanca. After Mecca and

Medina, it is the world's third-largest mosque, with space for one hundred and five thousand worshippers and a minaret soaring 200m. Commissioned by the last king, who named it after himself, it cost an estimated US$800m. It's a short taxi ride northeast of the centre.

The beaches

The **Ain Diab beach**, to the west of Mosque Hassan II, and at the end of the tram line, is one of Morocco's best and most easily accessible beaches. Surf lessons and equipment are readily available along the corniche, which runs alongside the beach. Mohammedia, 30km from Casa, is a less crowded option, with better surf. Take the train (15dh) from Casa Port station.

Jewish Museum

Five kilometres south of town, in the suburb of Oasis, the **Musée du Judaïsme Marocain** at 81 Rue Chasseur Jules Gros (Mon–Fri 10am–6pm; 20dh; wheelchair accessible; ☎0522 994940, ⒲casajewishmuseum.com) is the only

Jewish museum in any Muslim country. Many Moroccan Muslims are proud of the fact that Jewish communities have, historically, been protected in Morocco. The museum gives an insight into the disproportionate role that Jews have played in Moroccan life.

ARRIVAL AND DEPARTURE

By plane If you're arriving at Mohammed V airport, catch one of the regular trains (hourly, 6am–10pm; 35min) into Casa Voyageurs train station. *Grands taxis* are extortionately expensive (250–300dh) for the 45min drive.

By train Intercity trains stop only at Casa Voyageurs (2km southeast of the centre). From there, take the sleek new tram into town (7dh); otherwise, it's a 20min walk or a *petit taxi* ride. Note that local services from Rabat (every 30min, 6.30am–8.30pm; 1hr 10min) continue to the more convenient Casa Port station (Gare du Port), between the town centre and the port.

Destinations from Casa Voyageurs Fez (hourly; 3hr 55min); Marrakesh (9 daily; 3hr 15min); Meknes (hourly; 3hr 15min); Rabat (27 daily; 1hr); Tangier (8 daily; 4hr 45min).

By bus Arrive by CTM if possible, as it drops you downtown on Rue Léon l'Africain by the *Sheraton Hotel*. Private buses

22

CASABLANCA

● DRINKING & NIGHTLIFE	
Bao	1
La Cigale	10
Rick's Bar	2
Trica Bar	7

■ ACCOMMODATION	
Camping Oasis	
Dar Bouazza	7
Colbert	5
Du Centre	2
Galia	6
HI Hostel	1
Miramar	4
Mon Rêve	4
Touring	3

● EATING	
Casablanca Café	6
La Bodega	5
La Ligue Arabe	8
La Taverne du Dauphin	4
Port de Pêche	3
Snack Yasmina	9

Ain Sebaa & Mohammedia by road (S111)

use the Gare Ouled Ziane bus station southeast of town on Route des Ouled Ziane.

Destinations (CTM) Essaouira (3 daily; 7hr); Fez (5 daily; 5hr); Marrakesh (15 daily; 3hr 30min); Meknes (8 daily; 4hr); Rabat (22 daily; 1hr 20min); Tangier (5 daily; 5hr 30min); Tetouan (5 daily; 7hr).

Destinations (private) Essaouira (27 daily; 7hr); Fez (roughly every 30min; 5hr); Marrakesh (every 30min; 4hr); Meknes (roughly every 30min; 4hr); Rabat (frequent; 1hr 30min); Tangier (26 daily; 6hr); Tetouan (15 daily; 7hr).

By taxi Most shared *grands taxis* arrive at Gare Ouled Ziane; some from Rabat arrive a block east of the CTM terminal; those from Essaouira come into a station south of the centre on Bd Brahim Roudani in Maarif, a longish walk (2km) but only around 10dh by taxi.

INFORMATION

Tourist information The best information office is the Syndicat d'Initiative at 98 Bd Mohammed V (Mon–Fri 8.30am–4.30pm; ☏0522 221524), where you can also arrange a guided tour by car (2hr 30min; 450dh). The Délégation de Tourisme is south of the centre at 55 Rue Omar Slaoui (Mon–Fri 8.30am–4pm; ☏0522 271177). Further info can be found at ⓦcasablanca.ma, a useful site for news and listings (in French).

Internet LG Net, 81 Bd Mohammed V, first floor (daily 9am–10pm; 6dh/hr).

Police Tourist Police on Bd Felix Houphouët Boigny (☏0522 220393).

ACCOMMODATION

There are plenty of hotels, though they are often near capacity; cheaper rooms in the centre can be hard to find by late afternoon.

HOSTEL

HI Hostel (Auberge de Jeunesse) 6 Place Ahmed Bidaoui ☏0522 220551, ⓔlesauberges@menara.ma. A friendly, well-maintained place just inside the Medina and signposted from the nearby Gare du Port. Breakfast included. Double **150dh**

HOTELS

Colbert 38 Rue Chaouia ☏0522 316136, ⓦhotelcolbert .ma. Huge (103 rooms) well-priced hotel with decent rooms (some with shower), 3 gardens and 2 terraces. Double **150dh**

Du Centre Rue Sidi Balyout ☏0522 446180, ⓔhotelducentrecasablanca@hotmail.fr. A warm welcome at reception, along with clean and pleasant, honey-hued, en-suite rooms, makes this an excellent option in the centre. Double **240dh**

★ **Galia** 19 Rue Ibnou Batouta ☏0522 481694, ⓔgalia_19@hotmail.fr. Wooden artefacts liven up the stairwell at this friendly hotel with welcoming rooms. Free wi-fi. Double **220dh**

Miramar 22 Rue León l'Africain ☏0522 310308. One of the cheapest among the little hotels in the city centre, with some en-suite rooms (otherwise a shower is 10dh). Double **150dh**

Mon Rêve 5 Rue Chaouia ☏0522 311439, ⓔhmonreve @gmail.com. Long-standing budget travellers' favourite, popular among locals as well as the odd tourist. Book ahead. Double **220dh**

Touring 87 Rue Allal Ben Abdallah ☏0522 310216. Refurbished old French hotel that's friendly and excellent value; the best option in an area of cheap hotels. Double **150dh**

CAMPSITE

Camping Oasis Dar Bouazza Rte d'Azzour, 18km from town ☏0671 202536. This campsite is run by the Syndicat d'Initiative, but is rather a long way from town. Electricity costs extra (20dh). Camping **40dh** per person and tent

EATING

Casablanca Café 61 Bd Moulay Youssef at corner of Av Hassan Souktani. Bogart's legendary work comes to life at this pleasant French café with photos, posters and memorabilia scattered about. Superb crêpes (25dh) and coffees (12dh). Daily 6am–10.30pm.

La Bodega 127 Rue Allal Ben Abdallah. Jam-packed with Latino and Spanish memorabilia as well as a large TV screen for sporting events, this lively place serves a decent selection of tapas (35–120dh); once the drinks (45–100dh) start flowing the downstairs bar and little dancefloor liven up a fair amount. Daily noon–4pm & 7pm–12.30am, closed Sun lunch.

La Ligue Arabe On the southern end of Bd Moulay Youssef. Students sip tea (10dh) in the open air as they discuss their latest school day, while others take their mind off their studies with a game of pool or mini football. Games room, too. Daily 8am–10.30pm.

La Taverne du Dauphin 115 Bd Felix Houphouët Boigny ☏0522 221200. One of Casa's most famous and popular spots, with great seafood served in the restaurant and bonhomie dished up in the cramped bar. Mains 46–120dh, menu 115dh. Mon–Sat noon–1am.

★ **Port de Pêche** Just outside the main entrance of the port (no name sign). A true local and a real treat for fish lovers with fresh grilled sardines (20dh) or fried fish (40dh), not to be confused with the upmarket restaurant of the same name the other side of the port entrance. Daily 7am–3am.

Snack Yasmina On the southern end of Bd Moulay Youssef. A real student hangout, this place swarms with youngsters swapping school notes as they feast on panini or more substantial mains (22–30dh). Daily 7am–midnight.

DRINKING AND NIGHTLIFE

There are scores of bars and clubs along the Corniche, 10min west of the centre, playing everything from hip-hop to house music.

Bao Bd de la Corniche, Aïn Diab. African beats and a laidback atmosphere make this a popular spot to get down to the sound of West African rhythms. Entry 100dh. Fri & Sat are the best days. Daily 11pm–4am.

La Cigale 10 Bd Brahim Roudani. The room at the back is where it all takes place – once the first tune is on the jukebox, the night has begun. Beers 20dh, spirits 40dh. Free couscous Fri lunchtime. Daily noon–1am.

Trica Bar 5 Rue al Moutanabi. You could nearly be in NYC at this stylish warehouse bar with brick walls and old-school tunes in the background; if you're seriously thirsty try the two-litre giant mojito (400dh). Daily noon–3pm & 6pm–midnight.

Southern Morocco

Few places on earth can better the abiding memory of the Sahara desert meeting the Atlantic, while **Marrakesh**, with its colourful Medina, is undoubtedly Morocco's best-known city; further south loom the scenic **Atlas Mountains** and west lies the coastal city of **Essaouira**, the country's best windsurfing spot.

MARRAKESH

MARRAKESH (Marrakech in French) is a city of immense beauty; low, pink and tent-like before a great range of mountains. It's an immediately exciting place, especially its ancient Medina. Marrakesh's population is growing and it has a thriving industrial area; the city remains the most important market and administrative centre in southern Morocco.

WHAT TO SEE AND DO

The **Jemaa el Fna** is at the heart of the city, with most things of interest emanating from it. There are lots of cheap *pensions* and hotels near here. To the north of the Jemaa are the famous **souks** of Marrakesh, where you can spend hours getting lost and picking up bargains. Just to the west is the great minaret of the **Koutoubia**

mosque. This towers over the start of Avenue Mohammed V, which connects the Medina to Gueliz, where you can find the train station, CTM office and tourist information as well as some modern cafés, supermarkets and bars. It's a fairly long walk between Gueliz and the Medina, but there are plenty of taxis and the regular buses #1 and #16 between the two. Further west of the Koutoubia, just past Bab Jedid, there is a district of opulent hotels with fantastic, if pricey, bars.

Jemaa el Fna

There's nowhere in the world like the **Jemaa el Fna**: by day it's basically a market, with a few snake charmers and an occasional troupe of acrobats; in the late afternoon it becomes a whole carnival of musicians, storytellers and other entertainers; and in the evening dozens of stalls set up to dispense hot food to crowds of locals, while the musicians and performers continue. If you get tired of the spectacle, or if things slow down, you can move over to one of the numerous cafés' rooftop terraces.

The Koutoubia

Nearly 70m high and visible for many kilometres, the **Koutoubia Minaret** was begun shortly after the Almohad conquest of the city, around 1150, and displays many features that were to become widespread in Moroccan architecture – the wide band of ceramic inlay, the pyramid-shaped merlons, and the alternation of patterning on the facades.

The northern Medina

Just before the red ochre arch at its end, **Souk Smarine** (an important Medina thoroughfare) narrows and you get a glimpse through passageways of the **Rahba Kedima**, a small and fairly ramshackle square whose most interesting features are its apothecary stalls. At the end of Rahba Kedima, a passageway to the left gives access to another, smaller, square – a bustling, carpet-draped area known as **La Criée Berbère**, which is where slave auctions used to be held.

Cutting back to Souk el Kebir, which by now has taken over from the Smarine,

22

22

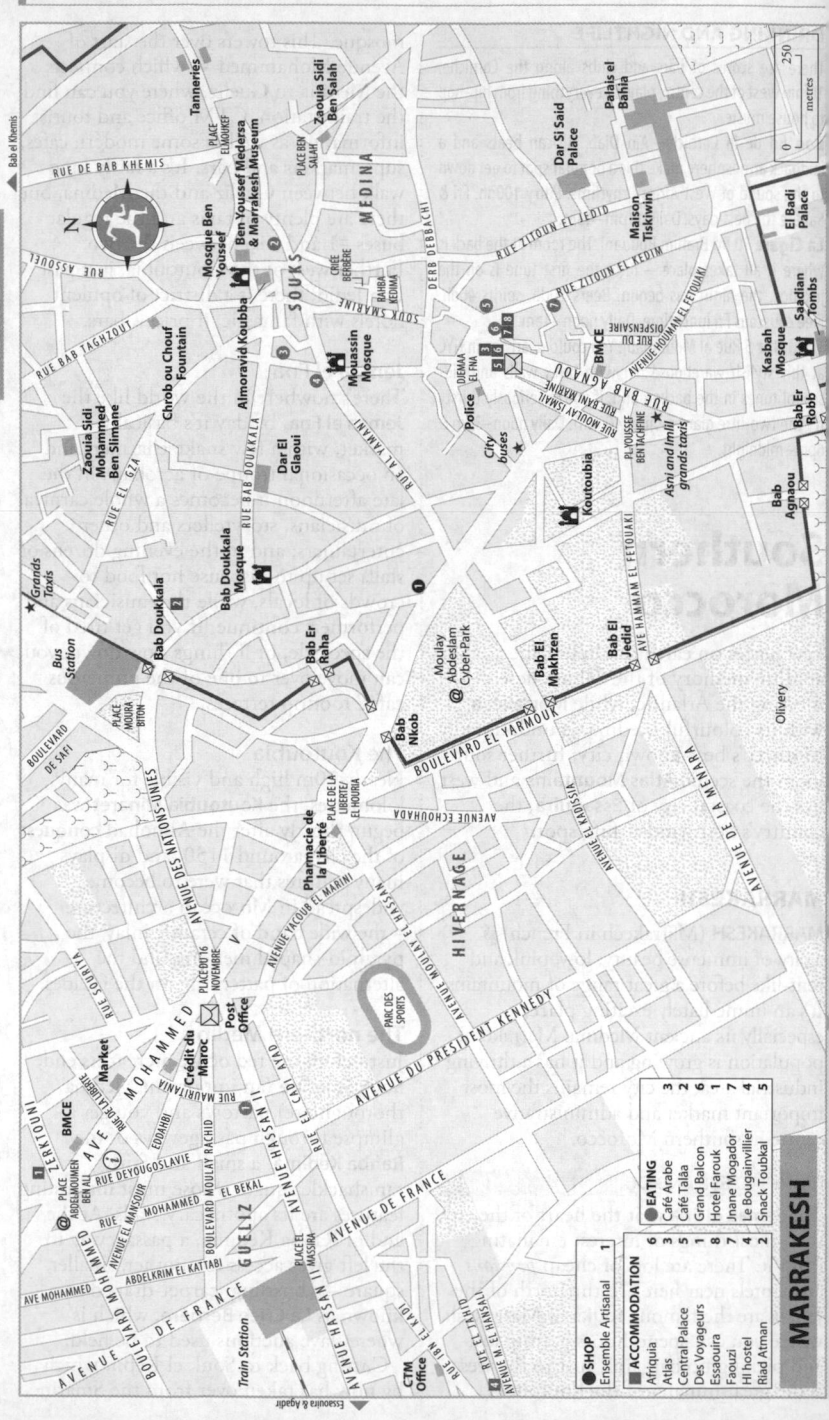

MARRAKESH

● SHOP	
Ensemble Artisanal	1

■ ACCOMMODATION	
Afriquia	6
Atlas	3
Central Palace	2
Des Voyageurs	1
Essaouira	8
Faouzi	7
Hi hostel	4
Riad Atman	5

● EATING	
Café Arabe	3
Café Talâa	2
Grand Balcon	6
Hotel Farouk	1
Jnane Mogador	7
Le Bougainvillier	4
Snack Toubkal	5

you emerge at the **kissarias**, the covered markets at the heart of the souks. Kissarias traditionally sell more expensive products, which today means a predominance of Western designs and imports. Off to their right is **Souk des Bijoutiers**, a modest jewellers' lane, while at the north end is a convoluted web of alleys comprising the **Souk Cherratin**, essentially a leatherworkers' market.

The Ben Youssef Medersa

If you bear left through the leather market and then turn right, you should arrive at the open space in front of the **Ben Youssef Mosque**. The originally fourteenth-century **Ben Youssef Medersa** (daily 9am–6pm; 50dh; combined ticket for this, the Marrakesh Museum and Almoravid Koubba 60dh) – the annexe for students taking courses in the mosque – stands off a side street just to the east. It was almost completely rebuilt in the sixteenth century under the Saadians, with a strong Andalusian influence.

The Marrakesh Museum and Almoravid Koubba

Next door to the Medersa is the **Marrakesh Museum** (daily 9am–6pm; 50dh; combined ticket with Ben Youssef Medersa and Almoravid Koubba 60dh), which exhibits jewellery, art and sculpture, both old and new, in a beautifully restored nineteenth-century palace. Almost facing it, the small **Almoravid Koubba** (daily 9am–6pm; on combined ticket, though closed for restoration at time of writing) is easy to pass by, but it is the only building in the whole of Morocco from the eleventh-century Almoravid dynasty still intact. The motifs you've just seen in the Medersa – the pine cones, palms and acanthus leaves – were all carved here first.

The Saadian Tombs

Sealed up by Moulay Ismail after he had destroyed the adjoining El Badi Palace, the sixteenth-century **Saadian Tombs** (daily 9am–4.45pm; 10dh), accessed by a narrow alley near the Kasbah Mosque south of Jemaa el Fna, are home to two main mausoleums. The finer is on the left as you come in, a beautiful group of three rooms built to house El Mansour's own tomb and completed within his lifetime. The tombs of over a hundred more Saadian princes and royal household members are scattered around the garden and courtyard, their gravestones likewise brilliantly tiled and often elaborately inscribed.

El Badi Palace

Though substantially in ruins, enough remains of Ahmed el Mansour's **El Badi Palace** (daily 9am–4.45pm; 10dh) to suggest that its name – "The Incomparable" – was not entirely immodest. It took a later ruler, Moulay Ismail, over ten years of systematic work to strip the palace of everything moveable or of value, but, even so, there's a lingering sense of luxury. What you see today is essentially the ceremonial part of the palace complex, planned for the reception of ambassadors. To the rear extends the central court, over 130m long and nearly as wide, and built on a substructure of vaults in order to allow the circulation of water through the pools and gardens. In the southwest corner of the complex is the original (and, in its day, much celebrated) *minbar* (pulpit) from the Koutoubia mosque (admission is an extra 10dh, payable at the main gate).

Rue Zitoun el Jedid

Heading north from El Badi Palace, **Rue Zitoun el Jedid** leads back to the Jemaa, flanked by various nineteenth-century mansions. Many of these have been converted into carpet shops or tourist restaurants, but one of them has been kept as a museum, the **Palais el Bahia** (daily 9am–4.30pm; 10dh), former residence of a grand vizier. The name of the building means "The Brilliance"; indeed, it's a beautiful old palace with two lovely patio gardens and some classic painted wooden ceilings. Further north is the **Maison Tiskiwin** (8 Rue de la Bahia; daily 9.30am–12.30pm & 2.30–6pm; 20dh), which houses a superb collection of Moroccan and Saharan artefacts. If you're pressed for time, however, prioritize the lovely **Dar Si Said** palace nearby on Derb Si Said, as it also houses the **Museum of Moroccan Arts** (daily except Tues

22

22

CLIMBING MOUNT TOUBKAL

Imlil, the setting-off point for trekkers wanting to climb **the second-highest peak in Africa**, is within two to three hours' *grand taxi* drive of Marrakesh (30dh for a place, leaving from Place Youssef Tachfine, and usually changing taxis at Asni; 180dh to charter the taxi one-way). Most trekkers set out early to mid-morning from Imlil to stay the night at the Toubkal refuge (5–6hr), which gets crowded in summer. It's best to start from here at first light the next morning in order to get the clearest possible panorama from Toubkal's heights (afternoons can be cloudy). The ascent is not difficult if you are fit, but it can be very cold.

9am–4.45pm; 10dh), with a plethora of interesting historical arts and crafts.

ARRIVAL AND DEPARTURE

By plane The airport, 4km southwest of town, is served by bus #19 to Place Foucauld by the Jemaa and along Avenue Mohammed V (every 30min, 6.30am–9.30pm; 30dh) – *petits taxis* (80dh by day, 120dh by night) are a more convenient option.

By train From the train station, west of Gueliz, cross Ave Hassan II and take bus #8/#10/#14/#66 or a *petit taxi* (10–15dh) for Place Foucauld by the Jemaa.

Destinations Casablanca Voyageurs (9 daily; 3hr 10min); Fez (8 daily; 7hr 10min); Meknes (8 daily; 6hr 30min); Rabat (9 daily; 4hr 15min); Tangier (1 daily; 10hr).

By bus The bus terminal is just outside the northwestern walls of the Medina by Bab Doukkala; from here it's a 20min walk to the Jemaa, or take bus #6/#8/#10/#14/#16 (opposite Bab Doukkala), or a *petit taxi* (8–10dh). CTM buses arrive and depart from their office south of the train station, though you can buy tickets and sometimes pick them up at the main terminal.

Destinations (private) Casablanca (every 30min, 4am–9pm; 3hr 30min); Essaouira (23 daily; 3hr 30min); Fez (6 daily; 8hr); Meknes (5 daily; 7hr); Rabat (roughly every 30min; 5hr 30min); Tangier (4 daily; 10hr).

Destinations (CTM) Casablanca (8 daily; 3hr 30min); Essaouira (2 daily; 3–5hr); Fez (4 daily; 8hr); Meknes (2 daily; 7hr); Rabat (4 daily; 5hr 30min); Tangier (1 daily; 7hr 15min).

INFORMATION

Tourist information Place Abdelmoumen Ben Ali (Mon–Fri 8.30am–4.30pm; ☎ 0524 436131). Keeps limited details of services you might need, though it's best to rely on your hotel; ⊛ ilove-marrakech.com is a good source of information.

ACCOMMODATION

The Medina has the main concentration of cheap accommodation – most of the places quite pleasant – and, unusually, has a fair number of classified hotels too. Given the attractions of the Jemaa el Fna and the souks, this is the first choice. Booking in advance is advisable. All our recommendations are in the Medina unless stated otherwise.

Afriquia 45 Sidi Bouloukate ☎ 0524 442403. Basic but hospitable rooms with a Gaudíesque top-floor terrace. The shady orange trees twitter with swallows, but this means an early-morning wake-up call. En-suites cost 100dh extra). Free wi-fi. Double **150dh**

★ **Atlas** 50 Rue Sidi Bouloukate ☎ 0524 391051, ⊛ hotel-atlas-marrakech.com. Calm and clean hotel set around two courtyards, with decorative iron and woodwork throughout; there's an appealing rooftop chillout lounge for the weary tourist. Excellent rates for single travellers. A/c rooms are twice the price. Double **170dh**

Central Palace 59 Sidi Bouloukate ☎ 0524 440235, ⊛ lecentralpalace.com. A peaceful haven set in a leafy three-tiered courtyard with pleasantly decorated rooms, some en suite. There's also a couscous restaurant on the roof terrace. Double **155dh**

Des Voyageurs 40 Av Zerktouni, Gueliz ☎ 0524 447218. Old-fashioned hotel with welcoming management, spacious rooms and a little patio-cum-garden. Double **220dh**

Essaouira 3 Derb Sidi Bouloukate ☎ 0524 443805. The entrance opens onto a beautiful courtyard with intricately painted woodwork, where vibrant but tastefully tiled rooms might make you dizzy after a heavy night. Double **100dh**

★ **Faouzi** 67 Derb Sidu Bouloukate ☎ 0524 389386, ⊛ faouzihotel.com. Sparkling, excellent-value rooms with luxurious marble plaster walls and modern fittings; the sole drawback is the rather uninspiring roof terrace. Double **180dh**

HI hostel Rue El Jahid, Gueliz ☎ 0524 447713, ✉ marrakech@hotmail.fr. Neat and tidy single-sex dorms, good for those with an early start as it's close to the train station. Hot water costs 10dh extra. Dorm **73.50dh**

★ TREAT YOURSELF

Riad Atman 12 Derb Alaka, Bab Doukkala ⊛ riadatman.com. A peaceful oasis in the heart of the Medina, this welcoming *riad* has four beautifully furnished rooms, all en suite, with a/c, cable TV, cedar wood and intricate ironwork throughout. Breakfast included. Double **€70**

EATING AND DRINKING

The most atmospheric place to eat is the Jemaa el Fna, where food stalls set up around sunset and serve up everything from *harira* soup and couscous to stewed snails and sheep's heads, all eaten at trestle tables. Cheap restaurants gather in the Medina, along with French-style cafés and virtually all the city's bars. You'll find more upmarket places uptown in Gueliz.

Café Arabe 184 Rue Mouassine. Ideal for a beer at sunset, the roof bar teems with foreigners itching for a thirst-quenching snifter (35dh). Daily 10am–midnight.

Café Talâa Souk Chaâria, opposite the Talâa souk entrance. Coffees (10dh), juices (15dh) and teas (10dh) as well as substantial mains (*tajines* from 30dh) at this café with straw stools and parasols. Daily 8am–9pm.

Grand Balcon On top of the *Café Glacier* on Jemaa el Fna. "Obligatory consumption" is what it says and so it is – you won't be allowed in unless you pay for your drinks or passable grub (40–60dh) at the door. The incredible view over the square attracts a large crowd though. Daily 9am–10pm.

Hotel Farouk 66 Av Hassan II, Gueliz. Excellent-value set menu with soup or salad, then couscous, *tajine* or *brochettes*, followed by a choice of desserts, for 50dh. Mains 30–70dh. Daily 11am–9pm.

Jnane Mogador in the *Jnane Mogador* hotel, Derb Sidi Bouloukat by 116 Rue Riad Zitoun el Kedim. The food is decent (mains 40–65dh) and the pretty rooftop terrace will provide a welcome respite from the hustle and hassle of the nearby streets. Daily noon–3pm & 7–9.30pm.

Le Bougainvillier Rue El Mouassine 33. Old French crooners set the mood at this atmospheric café with a leafy sunny patio and little salons, serving panini (50–55dh), sandwiches (50–55dh) and pizzas (50–60dh). Daily 10am–10pm.

⭐ **Snack Toubkal** in the southeast corner of Jemaa el Fna. Despite its touristy appearance, the food here is popular with locals and tourists alike. Try the delicious *tajines* (22–30dh). Daily 5am–1am.

DIRECTORY

Banks and exchange BMCE has branches with adjoining bureaux de change and ATMs in the Medina (Rue Moulay Ismail, facing Place Foucauld) and Gueliz (114 Av Mohammed V).

Internet Moulay Abdeslam Cyber-Park on Av Mohammed V opposite the Ensemble Artisanal (daily 10am–5pm; 5dh/hr); Cyber Siroua, Bd Mohammed Zerkatouni (daily 9am–11pm; 6dh/hr).

Pharmacies and doctor Pharmacie du Progrès, Place Jemaa el Fna at the top of Rue Bab Agnaou; Pharmacie de la Liberté, just off Place de la Liberté (Mon–Fri 9am–12.30pm & 3–7.30pm, Sat 9am–1pm). If you're in need of a doctor, try Dr Abdelmajid Ben Tbib, 171 Av Mohammed V (☎0524 431030).

Police Tourist police on Jemaa el Fna (24/7; ☎0524 384601).

Post office Place du 16 Novembre, midway along Av Mohammed V, and on the Jemaa el Fna (Mon–Fri 8am–6pm, Sat 10am–6pm).

ESSAOUIRA

ESSAOUIRA, the nearest beach resort to Marrakesh, is a lovely eighteenth-century walled seaside town. A favourite with the likes of Frank Zappa and Jimi Hendrix back in the 1960s, its tradition of hippy tourism has created a much more laidback relationship between local residents and foreign visitors than you'll find in the rest of Morocco. Today Essaouira is a centre for arts and crafts in addition to being the country's top windsurfing spot.

WHAT TO SEE AND DO

Essaouira is a simple place to get to grips with orientation wise, and a great place in which to wander; the **ramparts** are an obvious starting point. Heading north along the lane at the end of Place Prince Moulay el Hassan, you can access the **Skala de la Ville** (daily sunrise–sunset), the great sea bastion topped by a row of cannons, which runs along the northern cliffs. At the end is the circular **North Bastion**, with panoramic views. Along the Rue de la Skala, built into the ramparts, are the woodcarving workshops, where artisans use **thuja**, a distinctive local hardwood. You can find another

---

SHOPPING IN THE SOUKS

Marrakesh is famous for its **souks**, where you can buy goods from all over Morocco. Prices are rarely fixed, so before you set out, head to the supposedly fixed-price Ensemble Artisanal (daily 8.30am–7.30pm), on Avenue Mohammed V, midway between the Koutoubia and the ramparts at Bab Nkob, and get an idea of how much things are worth. It pays to bargain hard, as the first price you are told can easily be five or ten times the going rate, with the most obscene prices to be found around the edges of the souks.

22

impressive bastion by the harbour, the **Skala du Port** (daily 9am–5.30pm; 10dh).

The souks

The town's **souks** spread around and to the south of two arcades, on either side of Rue Mohammed Zerktouni, and up towards the **Mellah** (former Jewish ghetto), in the northwest corner of the ramparts. Don't miss the **Marché d'Épices** (spice market) and **Souk des Bijoutiers** (jewellers' market). Art studios and hippie-style clothing shops cluster around Place Chefchaouni by the clock tower. For those wanting to spice up their culinary skills, Atelier Madada (7 bis, rue Youssef El Fassi ☎0524 475512, ⌨lateliermadada.com) offers cookery classes in local specialities.

The beaches

The southern **beach** (the northern one is less attractive) extends for many kilometres, past the Oued Ksob river bed and the ruins of an old fort known as the BorJ el Berod. If you're after **watersports**, Club Mistral (☎0524 783934) on the south beach rents out surfboards, kayaks and wind/kitesurfing gear, and offers lessons too.

ARRIVAL AND INFORMATION

By bus The bus station is about 500m (10min walk) northeast of Bab Doukkala. It's worth taking a *petit taxi* (about 7dh), especially at night,.
Destinations Casablanca (30 daily; 7hr), Marrakesh (25 daily; 3hr 30min); Rabat (14 daily; 8hr 30min).
By taxi Shared *grands taxis* to Marrakesh and Casablanca operate from just next to the bus station, though they may drop arrivals at Bab Doukkala or Place Prince Moulay el Hassan.
Tourist information Tourist office at Av du Caire (Mon–Fri 9am–4pm; ☎0524 783532).

ACCOMMODATION

Accommodation can be tight over Easter and in summer, when advance booking is recommended.
Camping Sidi Magdoul 1km south of town behind the lighthouse (☎0524 472196, ✉campingsidimagdoul @gmail.com. Clean, friendly and well managed, with hot showers, campervan pitches, and an area of soil and trees for pitching tents in. Camping 17dh per person, plus 20–27dh per tent
Cap Sim 11 Rue Ibn Rochd ☎0524 785834, ✉hotelcapsim@menara.ma. The rooms at this refurbished budget hotel with fourth-floor sun terrace are all

beautifully kept and prettily decorated, in colours as warm as the staff welcome. Breakfast included. Double 220dh
Central 5 Rue Dar Eddhab, off Av Mohammed Ben Abdallah ☎0524 783623. The rooms here aren't as attractive as the quaint colonnaded interior patio; ask for the more spacious rooms on the first floor, or one of the single rooms on the roof. Double 100dh
Majestic 40 Rue Laâlouj ☎0524 474909. The lobby and stairs in this budget hotel (formerly the French colonial courthouse) aren't very inspiring, but the rooms are decent enough for the price – nothing fancy, but fresh and clean. Double 130dh
Souiri 37 Rue Attarine ☎0524 475339, ⌨hotelsouiri .com. Very central and deservedly popular, this welcoming little hotel offers a range of rooms, the cheaper ones having shared bathroom facilities. Rooms at the front are considered the best, though those at the back are quieter, and the price includes breakfast. Double 230dh

EATING AND DRINKING

For an informal meal, you can do no better than eat at the line of grills down at the port. Restaurants can be a bit expensive, but there are plenty of places to pick up cheap sandwiches.
Café des Arts 56 Av de l'Istiqlal. Sit at one of the individually painted tables at this little upstairs restaurant decorated with local argan oil flasks and wooden guitars. Live traditional *gnawa* music from 8pm. Mains 40–65dh and set menu 70dh. Daily 10am–4pm & 6pm–midnight.
Dar al Houma 9 Rue el Hajjali. Tuck into some home-style cooking at this vaulted restaurant with heavy drapery. Soups (10–25dh), *tajines* (45–70dh) and salads (12–55dh). Set menus 60(veg)–95dh. Daily 11am–3pm & 6.30–10pm.
Essalam 23 Place Prince Moulay el Hassan. A great-value no-frills restaurant which serves up some of the cheapest set menus in town (30–65dh). The walls are decorated with watercolours by Breton artist Charles Kérival. Daily 8.30am–4pm & 6–10pm.
La Petite Perle 2 Rue el Hajjalli. Sit on cushioned benches in this Berber tent-style restaurant, and dig into a good-value *tajine* (30–50dh) or couscous (35–60dh). Set menus 60dh, 70dh & 75dh. Daily noon–3pm & 7–10.30pm.
Place Marché aux Grains Off Av de l'Istiqlal. This little square is home to some pleasant luncheonettes with outdoor seating serving excellent-value food fresh from the fish market, or three-course *tajine*- or brochette-based set menus from 65dh. Daily 8am–6pm.
Taros Place Moulay Hassan. Along the theme of a boat deck on a Greek island tour, with palm parasols and patio furniture, this jolly rooftop bar is a perfect spot to enjoy an early-evening beer (35dh) or a glass of wine (40dh). Daily 11am–4pm & 6pm–1am.

CANAL, AMSTERDAM

The Netherlands

HIGHLIGHTS

❶ Amsterdam Canals, coffeeshops and world-famous art. **See p.779**

❷ Delft Enjoy wonderful apple cake in Vermeer's home town. **See p.793**

❸ Rotterdam Adventurous architecture and buzzing nightlife. **See p.794**

❹ Utrecht A relaxing antidote to Amsterdam, just 20min from the capital. **See p.797**

❺ Hoge Veluwe National Park Cycle through woods to the world's best collection of Van Goghs. **See p.799**

❻ Maastricht A cosmopolitan university town with a tranquil old quarter. **See p.799**

HIGHLIGHTS ARE MARKED ON THE MAP ON P.775

ROUGH COSTS

Daily budget Basic €55, occasional treat €75

Drink Beer €2.80

Food Pancake €8

Hostel/budget hotel €20–35/€70–95

Travel Train: Amsterdam–Rotterdam €14

FACT FILE

Population 16.7 million

Language Dutch

Currency Euro (€)

Capital Amsterdam

International phone code ☏ 31

Time zone GMT +1hr

Introduction

Despite the popular reputation of its most celebrated city, Amsterdam, the Netherlands is not all sex and drugs (and there's little rock'n'roll). Delve deeper and you will find a diminutive country with a heavyweight cultural heritage: its A-list of art superstars, Rembrandt, Vermeer and Van Gogh, rivals that of any country, and you could easily spend a solid week just scraping the surface of its museums. Dutch cities also provide plenty of architectural eye candy with pretty gabled houses and peaceful canals perfect for aimless wandering, while its flat fertile landscape means cycling can get you almost anywhere, from iconic tulip fields to sandy, dune-backed islands.

23

Though most people travel only to atmospheric **Amsterdam**, nearby is a group of worthwhile towns known collectively as the **Randstad** (literally "rim town"), including **Haarlem** and **Delft** with their old canal-girded centres, and **Den Haag** (The Hague), a stately city with fine museums and easy beach access. The dynamic port city of **Rotterdam** is a showcase for noteworthy architecture and alternative art. Outside the Randstad, life moves more slowly. To the south, the landscape undulates into heathy moorland, best experienced in the **Hoge Veluwe National Park**. Further south lies the compelling city of **Maastricht**, squeezed between the German and Belgian borders.

CHRONOLOGY

58 BC Julius Caesar conquers the area of the present-day Netherlands.

1275 Amsterdam is founded by Count Floris V of Holland.

1477 The Austrian Habsburgs take control.

1500s Protestant Reformation spreads through the Netherlands, leading to wars against the Catholic Habsburg rulers based in Spain.

1579 The Union of Utrecht is signed by seven provinces to form the United Provinces against Spain. The Netherlands are declared independent two years later, heralding a "Golden Age" of trade and colonial expansion.

1603 The Dutch East India Company establishes its first trading post in Indonesia, an area that it would gradually colonize.

1806 Napoleon annexes the Kingdom of Holland for France.

1813 The French are driven out and the Prince of Orange becomes sovereign of the United Netherlands.

1853 Vincent Van Gogh is born.

1914–18 The Netherlands remains neutral during World War I.

1940 Nazi Germany invades the Netherlands, forcing the deportation and murder of Dutch Jews including Anne Frank's family.

1944 Operation Market Garden sees heavy fighting around Arnhem but fails to dislodge German troops.

1947 Anne Frank's diary is published.

1953 More than 1800 killed in severe flooding on Jan 31. The disaster forms the inspiration for the massive Delta land reclamation project.

1975 Cannabis is decriminalized – tourism booms.

1980 Coronation of Queen Beatrix.

1992 The Maastricht Treaty is signed, transforming the European Community into the European Union.

1997 Treaty of Amsterdam clears the way for the introduction of a single European currency.

2001 The Netherlands becomes the first country to legalize same-sex marriage.

2002 Anti-immigration politician Pim Fortuyn is killed shortly before elections.

2004 Film-maker Theo Van Gogh is murdered by a radical Islamist.

2010 Coalition government led by Geert Wilders collapses following dispute over troops in Afghanistan.

2012 Maastricht bans tourists from smoking cannabis in coffeeshops. A nationwide ban fails to be implemented.

2013 Queen Beatrix, aged 75, abdicates in favour of her son Prince Willem-Alexander.

ARRIVAL AND DEPARTURE

High-speed **trains** (ⓦnshispeed.nl/) frequently travel to Amsterdam from Brussels (1hr 49min) and Paris (3hr 16min), with Eurostar trains from London connecting at Brussels Midi

THE NETHERLANDS

23

(total journey time 4hr 37min). German ICE trains also run direct from Amsterdam to Cologne (2hr 38min) and Frankfurt (3hr 46min). Coming from the UK it is cheaper to use the overnight train-ferry-train "Dutch Flyer" service (ⓦstenaline.co.uk/ferry/rail-and-sail) or sail from Harwich to the Hook of Holland or Hull to Rotterdam (ⓦpoferries.com).

Low-cost **airlines** operate flights from across Europe to five Dutch airports: Amsterdam Schiphol, Eindhoven, Groningen, Maastricht and Rotterdam. Of these, Schipol offers by far the widest choice of routes and is a mere 15min by train to Amsterdam Central.

GETTING AROUND

Trains (ⓦns.nl) are fast and efficient, fares relatively low, and the network comprehensive. With any ticket, you're free to stop off en route and continue later that day. Apart from at Schiphol and Amsterdam Central you cannot use **foreign credit or debit cards** at Dutch rail stations (allow time to queue up and pay in cash). **Buses** are rarely used for long-distance journeys except for more

23

remote areas of the country not covered in this guide. The website ⓦ9292ov.nl is a useful journey planner for both trains and buses.

Most Dutch cities have introduced a **public transport chip card system** (ⓦov-chipkaart.nl) for use on metro, trams and buses. You can buy cards valid from one hour (around €2.80) to a couple of days (€12) at station vending machines or on board trams and buses. Remember to tap in and out to log each journey.

There's a nationwide system of **cycle** paths. You can rent bikes cheaply from main train stations and outlets in almost any town and village. Theft is rife: never leave your bike unlocked, and don't leave it on the street overnight – most stations have a storage area. For more on cycling see "sports and outdoor activities".

ACCOMMODATION

Accommodation can be pricey, especially in Amsterdam during peak season. Many of the smaller towns such as Haarlem have few budget options, so it may be cheaper to stay in Den Haag or Rotterdam and make day-trips to the Randstad towns. The cheapest one- or two-star **hotel** double rooms start at around €70; three-star hotel rooms begin around €85. Prices usually include a reasonable breakfast. The national hostel association **Stayokay** (ⓦstayokay.com) runs 27 clean, efficient (and bright orange) hostels nationwide, charging around €20–35 per person including a decent breakfast. If you use them extensively then it may be worth buying a **Stayokay Card**, which costs €17.50 and gives a discount of €2.50 every night. Larger cities have independent hostels with slightly lower prices but a tad more character. There are plenty of well-equipped **campsites**: expect to pay around €6 per person, plus €3–5 for a tent. Some sites also have **cabins** for up to four people, for around €40 a night.

FOOD AND DRINK

Dutch **food** largely revolves around bread, cheese and deep-fat fryers, though there are a few specialities to look out for: *kroketten* (bite-size chunks of meat and cheese sauce deep-fried in breadcrumbs) and *fricandel* (a frankfurter-like sausage). Don't miss *poffertjes*, delicious airy little pancakes dusted in icing sugar. Seafood is often excellent, though the national craze for downing a whole salted herring (*maatjes*) may require some practice. As in Belgium, *frites* and mayo is served on almost any street corner, varying from crispy perfection to sub *McDonald's*.

In **restaurants**, the dish of the day (*dagschotel*) is the cheapest option. Usually the best-value restaurants are **Indonesian** (a legacy of Dutch colonial history), so look forward to lots of lovely *nasi* or *bami goreng* (rice or noodles with meat), *sateh* (peanut sauce marinades) and *rijsttafel* (rice or noodles served with a huge range of tasty side dishes). Another former colony, **Surinam**, has brought South American/Indian fusion cuisine (roti and curried plantain, anyone?) to the streets of major Dutch cities. Turkish-style kebabs (*shoarma*) and falafel are on offer almost everywhere.

DRINK

Sampling the Dutch and Belgian **beers** is a real pleasure, often done in a cosy brown café (*bruine kroeg*, named because of the colour of the tobacco-stained walls); the big brands Heineken, Amstel, Oranjeboom and Grolsch are just the tip of the iceberg. A standard, small glass is *een fluitje*; a bigger glass is *een vaasje*. You may also come across *proeflokalen* or tasting houses, small, old-fashioned bars that close around 8pm, and specialize in **jenever**, Dutch gin, drunk straight; *oud* (old) is smooth, *jong* (young) packs more of a punch.

DRUGS

Purchases of up to 5g of cannabis, and possession of up to 30g (the legal limit) are tolerated; in practice, many "**coffeeshops**" offer discounted bulk purchases of 50g with impunity. Coffeeshops in city centres – neon-lit dives pumping out Bob Marley on a loop – are worth avoiding. Less touristy districts house more congenial,

THE NETHERLANDS ONLINE

w dutchnews.nl English-language news and a useful "Dictionary of Dutchness".
w holland.com National tourist board.
w iamsterdam.com Exhaustive official site of Amsterdam's tourist board.
w invadingholland.com Entertaining blog by an Englishman in Amsterdam.

high-quality outlets. When you walk in, ask to see the **menu**, which lists the different hashes and grasses on offer. Take care with spacecakes (cakes or biscuits baked with hash), mainly because you can never be sure what's in them, and don't ever buy from street dealers. All other narcotics are illegal, and don't even entertain the notion of taking a "souvenir" home with you.

CULTURE AND ETIQUETTE

The Dutch are renowned for their liberal and laidback attitude, so there isn't much in the way of etiquette to observe. Don't be embarrassed about speaking to locals in **English** – unlike many of their fellow Europeans, the Dutch are happy to converse in English and are generally helpful. **Tipping** is generally not expected and service charges are often added to the bill in restaurants. Many bars and cafés continue to allow **smoking** (tobacco, that is), despite a national ban. **Prostitution** is legal, regulated and somewhat in your face in the form of window brothels in Amsterdam and other cities.

SPORTS AND ACTIVITIES

The Netherlands is a nation of **cyclists**, and you won't have any problems finding cycle paths or bikes for rent. With most of the country's major towns located cheek by jowl in the Randstad, cycling from city to city is very easy. If you're looking for a more rural experience, the island of Texel and the Hoge Veluwe National Park near Arnhem are ideal, with the park even providing free bicycles for visitors. **Football** is also extremely popular, with the season running from September to May and matches held on

Sunday at around 2.30pm, with occasional games on Wednesday too. The major teams are PSV Eindhoven, Feyenoord in Rotterdam, and Amsterdam's Ajax.

COMMUNICATIONS

Wi-fi **internet access** is available in most cafés, hostels and hotels; just ask for a password. Libaries and many museums also offer free wi-fi. KPN, T-Mobile and Vodafone are the main mobile operators and offer a range of SIM-only deals. **Public phones** are rapidly disappearing, with only a few of them left near train stations, mainly for tourists. Phonecards are available from TNT stores and VVVs (see p.778). The Dutch postal service is now run by TNT and dedicated post offices can be hard to find (look instead for shops bearing the TNT logo). **Stamps** are sold in most supermarkets, bookshops and hotels. Post international items in the "Overige" slot.

EMERGENCIES

The Netherlands is one of the safest countries in Europe, and most brushes with the law involve tourists who have overindulged in coffeeshops or bars or both (note that urinating in the street carries a €50 fine). **Pharmacies** (*apotheek*) are open Monday to Friday 8.30am to 5.30pm; if they are closed there'll be a note of the nearest open pharmacy on the door. When in need of a doctor, enquire at the reception of your accommodation; otherwise head for any hospital (*ziekenhuis*). If you need the emergency services, police, ambulance and fire are all on ☏112.

DISCOUNT CARDS

The **European Youth Card** (w european youthcard.org) offers discounts at most museums, galleries and tourist attractions throughout the country, as well as theatre, film and other leisure activities. Amsterdam and Rotterdam also offer tourist cards (see p.785 & p.798), with Rotterdam's being by far the best deal.

23

INFORMATION

Official Dutch tourist offices known as VVVs are usually in town centres or by train stations and have information in English, including maps and accommodation lists; they will also book rooms for a small charge.

MONEY AND BANKS

The Dutch currency is the **euro** (€). **Banking hours** are Monday 1 to 5/6pm, Tuesday to Friday 9am to 5/6pm; in larger cities some banks also open Thursday 7 to 9pm and occasionally on Saturday mornings. **GWK exchange offices** at train stations open late daily.

You can also change money at most VVV tourist offices though rates are worse. **ATMs** are widespread.

OPENING HOURS AND HOLIDAYS

Many **shops** stay closed on Monday morning, although markets open early. Otherwise, opening hours tend to be 9am to 5.30/6pm, with many shops closing late on Thursdays or Fridays. Sunday opening is becoming increasingly common, with many shops open between noon and 5pm. In major cities, night shops (*avondwinkels*) open 4pm to 1/2am. **Museum** times are generally Tuesday to Saturday 10am to 5pm,

DUTCH

	DUTCH	PRONUNCIATION
Yes	*Ja*	Yah
No	*Nee*	Nay
Please	*Alstublieft*	Alstooblee-eft
Thank you	*Dank u/Bedankt*	Dank yoo/Bedankt
Hello/Good day	*Hallo*	Halloh
Goodbye	*Dag/Tot ziens*	Dahg/Tot Zeens
Excuse me	*Pardon*	Pardon
Where?	*Waar?*	Waah?
Good	*Goed*	Gud
Bad	*Slecht*	Slecht
Near	*Dichtbij*	Dichtbye
Far	*Ver*	Vare
Cheap	*Goedkoop*	Gudkoop
Expensive	*Duur*	Dooer
Open	*Open*	Open
Closed	*Gesloten*	Gesloten
Push	*Duwen*	Doowen
Pull	*Trekken*	Trekken
Today	*Vandaag*	Vandahg
Yesterday	*Gisteren*	Histehren
Tomorrow	*Morgen*	Morgen
How much is...?	*Wat kost...?*	Wat kost...?
I don't understand	*Ik begrijp het niet*	Ick bechripe het neet
Do you speak English?	*Spreekt u Engels?*	Spraicht oo Engells?
One	*Een*	Ayn
Two	*Twee*	Tway
Three	*Drie*	Dree
Four	*Vier*	Veer
Five	*Vijf*	Vife
Six	*Zes*	Zess
Seven	*Zeven*	Zayven
Eight	*Acht*	Acht
Nine	*Negen*	Nehen
Ten	*Tien*	Teen

Sunday 1 to 5pm, although these vary widely. Shops and banks are closed, and museums adopt Sunday hours, on **public holidays:** January 1, Good Friday, Easter Sunday and Monday, April 30, May 5, Ascension Day, Whitsun and Monday, December 25 and December 26.

Amsterdam

AMSTERDAM is a "bucket-list" city for most travellers. Its relaxed attitude to drugs and vice attract thousands of thrill-seekers, yet beyond the haze of cannabis and the gaudy Red Light District is an inherently liveable, cosmopolitan capital packed with world-class attractions. Of these, the holy trinity of the reborn **Rijksmuseum** and revamped **Van Gogh Museum** plus the heart-rending **Anne Frank House** – is reason enough to visit.

Gradually growing from a fishing village at the mouth of the River Amstel to a major European trading centre, Amsterdam accommodated its expansion with the cobweb of **canals** that gives the city its distinctive and elegant shape today, and around which a *gezellig* café culture has been established.

In the 1960s Amsterdam emerged as a fashionable centre for the alternative movement, famously hosting John Lennon and Yoko Ono's "Bed-In for Peace". This period bestowed a unique character on the city, which still takes a progressive approach to social issues and culture. Despite a more conservative shift in recent years, Amsterdam is showing little sign of slowing down. Its youthful feel was perhaps encapsulated by the 2013 **abdication of Queen Beatrix**. Stepping down in favour of her son Willem-Alexander, she told her subjects "I am convinced that the responsibility for our country should move to the next generation".

WHAT TO SEE AND DO

Amsterdam's compact **Old Centre** contains many of the city's attractions, and it takes only about forty minutes to stroll from one end to the other. Centraal Station lies on the centre's northern edge,

and from here the city fans south in a web of concentric canals (*grachts*), surrounded by expanding suburbs. To the south is the city's main square and energetic party venue, **Leidseplein**, with the leafy **Vondelpark** and Museum quarter just over the Singelgracht to the south. The **Jordaan** to the northwest features mazy cobbled streets and dreamy canals, and offers perfect strolling territory. North and east of Centraal Station are the expanding **docklands**, full of sleek modern architecture, bars and restaurants.

Centraal Station and the Damrak
The cathedral-esque **Centraal Station** is most people's first impression of Amsterdam. Exiting the station you're greeted with chaotic **Stationsplein** which has for years resembled a building site crisscrossed with tram tracks, cyclists, buses and pedestrians, a legacy of the Metro works due to continue until 2020. From here, the busy thoroughfare **Damrak** marches into the heart of the city, lined with overpriced restaurants and bobbing canal boats, and flanked on the left first by the Modernist stock exchange, the **Beurs van Berlage** (now a concert hall), and then by the enormous De Bijenkorf department store.

The Red Light District
East of Damrak, the infamous **Red Light District**, stretching across two canals – Oudezijds Voorburgwal and Oudezijds Achterburgwal – is a curious mixture of unabashed sleaze (live sex shows and vibrator shops) and some quite lovely cafés, restaurants and bars. It's perhaps more fun to visit the place at night, when the seediness is somehow less glaring and the neon-lit window brothels down narrow passageways become strangely scenic (just be prepared for the ladies aggressively tapping their windows as you pass). A few frivolous attractions worth seeking out here include the **Condomerie**, the world's first condom speciality shop (see p.788), and the **Hash Marihuana Hemp Museum** at Oudezijds Achterburgwal 148 (daily 10am–11pm; €9). Similarly frolicsome is the **Erotic**

23

23

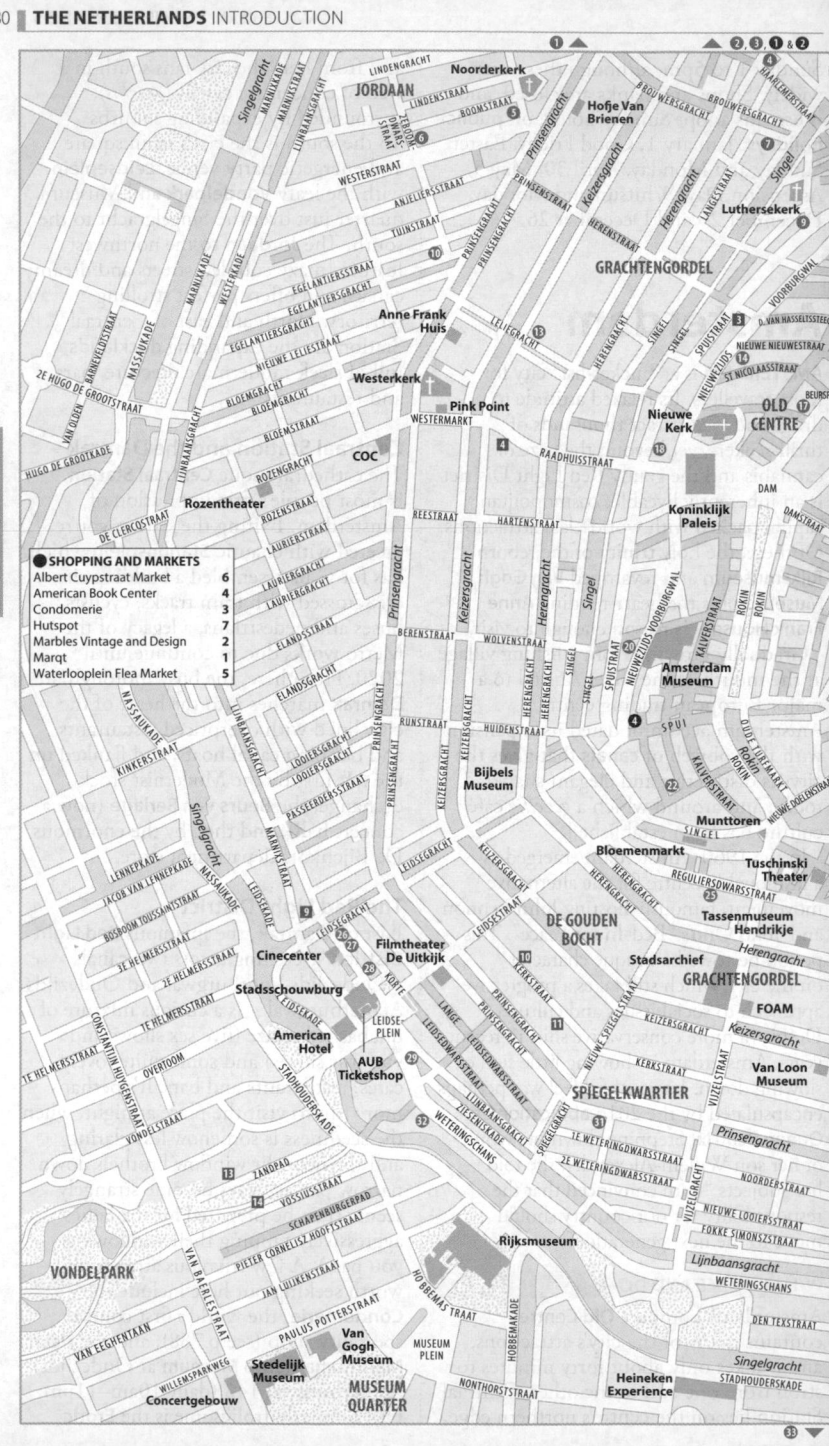

● SHOPPING AND MARKETS
Albert Cuypstraat Market	6
American Book Center	4
Condomerie	3
Hutspot	7
Marbles Vintage and Design	2
Marqt	1
Waterlooplein Flea Market	5

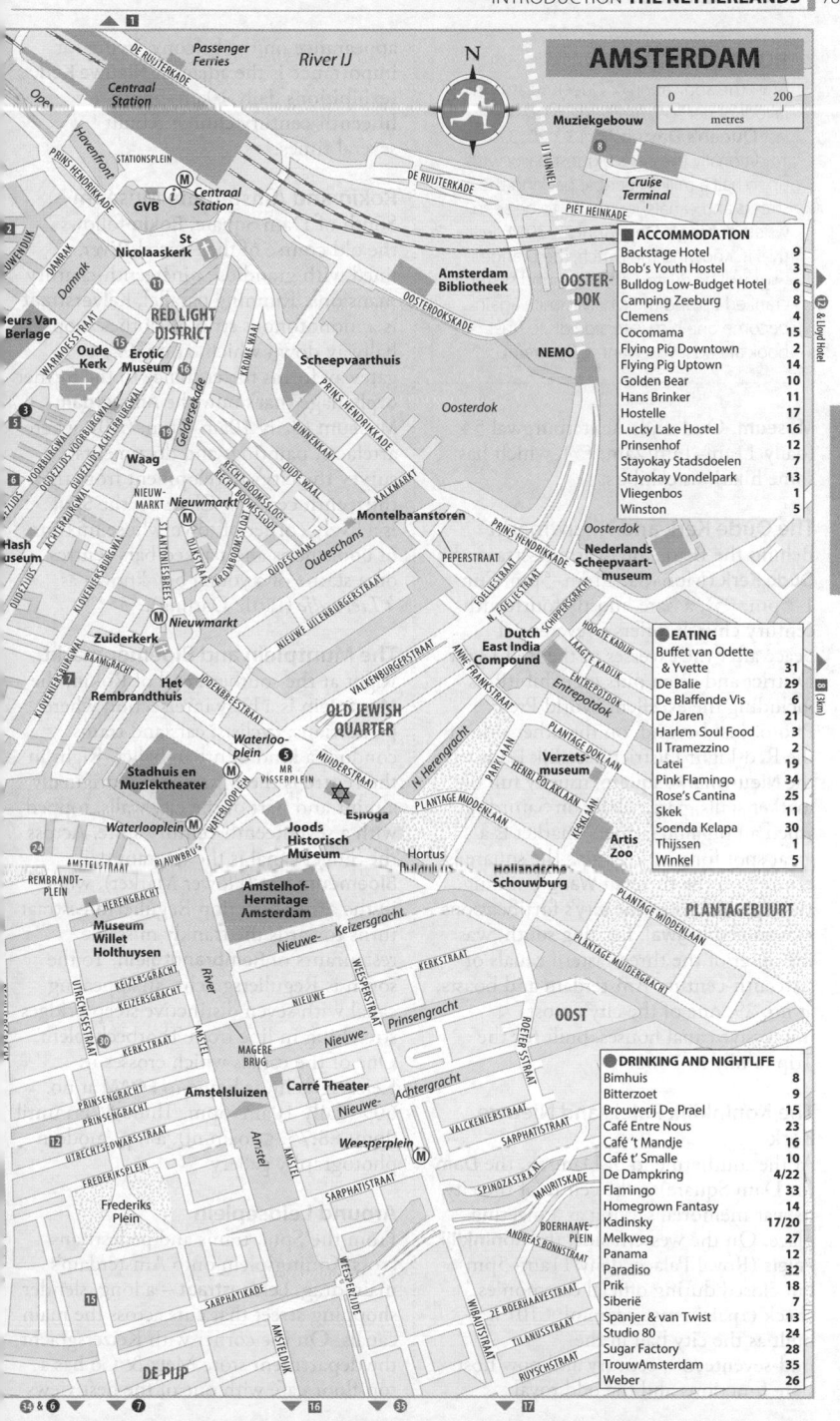

AMSTERDAM

0 — 200 metres

23

■ **ACCOMMODATION**

Backstage Hotel	9
Bob's Youth Hostel	3
Bulldog Low-Budget Hotel	6
Camping Zeeburg	8
Clemens	4
Cocomama	15
Flying Pig Downtown	2
Flying Pig Uptown	14
Golden Bear	10
Hans Brinker	11
Hostelle	17
Lucky Lake Hostel	16
Prinsenhof	12
Stayokay Stadsdoelen	7
Stayokay Vondelpark	13
Vliegenbos	1
Winston	5

● **EATING**

Buffet van Odette & Yvette	31
De Balie	29
De Blaffende Vis	6
De Jaren	21
Harlem Soul Food	3
Il Tramezzino	2
Latei	19
Pink Flamingo	34
Rose's Cantina	25
Skek	11
Soenda Kelapa	30
Thijssen	1
Winkel	5

● **DRINKING AND NIGHTLIFE**

Bimhuis	8
Bitterzoet	9
Brouwerij De Prael	15
Café Entre Nous	23
Café 't Mandje	16
Café t' Smalle	10
De Dampkring	4/22
Flamingo	33
Homegrown Fantasy	14
Kadinsky	17/20
Melkweg	27
Panama	12
Paradiso	32
Prik	18
Siberië	7
Spanjer & van Twist	13
Studio 80	24
Sugar Factory	28
TrouwAmsterdam	35
Weber	26

ROYAL REVELRY

After the abdication of Queen Beatrix in favour of her son, Amsterdam saw its last **Queen's Day** on April 30, 2013. Traditionally the city's biggest party with up to half a million people packing the streets and canals, it remains to be seen whether **King's Day** (April 27, 2014) will rival it. Knowing the Dutch, the orange wigs will be dusted off, the sound systems cranked up and the city will once again become one big waterside disco (just book ahead if you want to be there).

23 Museum, Oudezijds Achterburgwal 54 (daily 11am–1am/2am; €7), which has some hilarious exhibits.

The Oude Kerk and Nieuwmarkt

Behind the Beurs, off Warmoesstraat, the **Oude Kerk** (Mon–Sat 11am–5pm, Sun 1–5pm; €5), a bare, mostly fourteenth-century church, offers a reverential peace after the excesses of the Red Light District and often puts on exhibitions including the excellent World Press Photo. Just beyond, on the other side of the Red Light District, Zeedijk leads to the **Nieuwmarkt square**, usually full of market stalls, particularly on Saturday when an organic farmers' market is a great spot for picnic treats. The square is centred on the turreted **Waag** building, an original part of the city's fortifications. **Kloveniersburgwal**, heading south, was the outer of the three eastern canals of sixteenth-century Amsterdam and boasts, at no. 29, one of the city's most impressive canal houses, built for the Trip family in 1662.

The Koninklijk Paleis and Nieuwe Kerk

At the southern end of Damrak, the **Dam** (or Dam Square) is the centre of the city, its war memorial serving as a meeting place. On the western side, the **Koninklijk Paleis** (Royal Palace; daily 11am–5pm but closed during official ceremonies, check ⓦpaleisamsterdam.nl; €10) was built as the city hall in the mid-seventeenth century and now hosts state functions and the odd royal

appearance on the balcony. Vying for importance is the adjacent **Nieuwe Kerk** (exhibitions daily 10am–5pm), a fifteenth-century church rebuilt several times.

Rokin and Amsterdam Museum

South of Dam Square, **Rokin** follows the old course of the Amstel River, lined with grandiose nineteenth-century mansions. Running parallel, **Kalverstraat** is a monotonous strip of clothes shops, halfway down which, at no. 92, a gateway forms the entrance to the former orphanage that's now the **Amsterdam Museum** (daily 10am–5pm; €10), where artefacts, paintings and documents survey the city's development from the thirteenth century. Close by, the **Spui** is a lively corner of town whose mixture of bookshops and packed bars centres on a statue of a young boy known as *'t Lieverdje* (Little Darling).

The Muntplein and Bloemenmarkt

Right at the southern end of Rokin, the **Muntplein** is a busy intersection where pedestrians, cyclists, cars and trams conduct a kind of urban ballet. Right in the centre is the Munttoren – originally a mint and part of the city walls, topped with a seventeenth-century spire. Across the Singel canal is the fragrant daily **Bloemenmarkt** (Flower Market), while in the other direction Reguliersbreestraat turns towards the frankly missable restaurants of **Rembrandtplein**. To the south is Reguliersgracht, an appealing canal with seven distinctive steep bridges stretching in line from Thorbeckeplein. One of the canals which crosses it, Keizersgracht, is home to **FOAM** at no. 609 (daily 10am–6pm, Thurs & Fri until 9pm; €8.75; ⓦfoam.nl), a hip, modern photography gallery.

Around Leidseplein

From the Spui, trams and pedestrians cross Koningsplein onto Amsterdam's main drag, **Leidsestraat** – a long, slender shopping street that cuts across the main canals. On the corner with Keizersgracht, the department store Metz & Co has a top-floor café with one of the best views

AMSTERDAM CYCLING: A ROUGH GUIDE

Visitors quickly grasp that Amsterdam is a **cyclist's city**, usually by narrowly avoiding being mowed down outside Central Station. Pretty much all Amsterdammers own a bike (*fiets*) and around two-thirds use them every day to get around. If you're thinking of joining them, it's worth bearing in mind some tips:
• start off with a bicycle tour (try Mike's or Yellow Bike, see p.785); you'll get your bearings and learn some useful road etiquette.
• to warn the locals that you're a beginner, rent a bright-red cycle from MacBike (W macbike.nl). If you want to blend in, try a classic Dutch *burco* from Ajaxbike (W ajaxbike.nl).
• beware tram tracks (these can buckle a wheel in seconds). You can't take a bike on a tram, but trains are okay providing you have the right ticket.
• always lock your bike to something solid. Bike thieves simply carry off cycles that only have a wheel lock.
• a lot of traditional Dutch bikes have pedal brakes rather than handlebar brakes – you might want to pay a little more for a regular bike.

23

of the city. Leidsestraat broadens at its southern end into **Leidseplein**, home to a vast Apple store and lined with indentikit bars and clubs that form the hub of the city's mainstream nightlife. On the far corner, the **Stadsschouwburg** is the city's prime performance space after the Muziektheater.

The Jordaan and Anne Frank House

West of Centraal Station and across Prinsengracht, the **Jordaan** is a beguiling area of narrow canals, narrower streets and architecturally varied houses. With some of the city's best bars and restaurants, alternative clothes shops and good outdoor markets, especially those on the square outside the **Noorderkerk** (which hosts an antique and household goods market on Mondays and a popular farmers' market on Saturdays), it's a wonderful area to wander through. It is most famous, however, for the **Anne Frank House** (daily: mid-March to Oct 9am–9pm, Sat and July & Aug until 10pm; Nov to mid-March 9am–7pm, Sat until 9pm; €9; W annefrank.org), where the young diarist lived, at Prinsengracht 267. It's deservedly one of the most popular tourist attractions in town (buy a timed entry ticket online or visit early or late to avoid the queues). Anne, her family and friends went into hiding from the Nazis in 1942, staying in the house for two years until they were betrayed and taken away to labour camps. The plain, small rooms have been well

preserved, and include moving details such as the film-star pin-ups on Anne's bedroom wall and video interviews with her former classmates.

On the Prinsengracht, south of Anne Frank House, stands the **Westerkerk** (Mon–Fri 10am–5pm, Sat 11am–3pm; free), burial place of Rembrandt. You can climb its impressive 85m tower (Mon–Sat 10/11am–6/8pm; guided tours every 30min; €7.50).

The Vondelpark

The lush **Vondelpark** – immediately south of the buzzing Leidseplein – is the city's most enticing open space, packed in summer with young Amsterdammers lazing by the lake and listening to music; in June, July and August there are free concerts every Sunday at 2pm. Southeast of the park is a residential district, with designer shops and delis along chic **P.C. Hooftstraat** and **Van Baerlestraat**, and some of the city's major museums grouped around the grassy wedge of **Museumplein**.

The Rijksmuseum

Reopened in 2013 after a decade-long renovation (it was only supposed to be closed for three years), the **Rijksmuseum** (daily 9am–7pm; €15; W rijksmuseum .nl) has retaken its place as one of the world's premier art museums. From the Museumstraat entrance a vast, light-flooded atrium welcomes you in to the chronologically organized collection

23

which ranges from Dutch masters (pre-eminent among them Rembrandt, Frans Hals and Vermeer) to Van Gogh self-portraits and some wonderful Southeast Asian and Japanese art. Pride of place still goes to Rembrandt's huge *The Night Watch,* but don't miss the wonderful Dutch landscapes by Jan van Goyen, the intricate scale model of an East India Company merchant ship and the comically smug 1642 portrait of one Gerard Andriesz Bicker (son of the mayor of Amsterdam) by Bartholomeus van der Helst (all covered in the excellent multimedia tour; €5). To avoid the worst of the queues, buy an e-ticket online.

The Van Gogh Museum and Stedelijk Museum

An Amsterdam institution for forty years, the **Van Gogh Museum** at Paulus Potterstraat 7 (daily 9am–5pm/6pm, May–Sept Fri until 10pm; €15; Ⓦvangoghmuseum.nl) has recently been given a spring-clean and new decor to better complement the artist's varied palette. The collection includes Van Gogh's early years in Holland including the dark, rather creepy *The Potato Eaters*, continuing to the much celebrated works he produced after moving to Arles in the south of France, where he painted vivid canvases like *The Yellow House* and the *Sunflowers* series (again, book online to avoid the queues). Along the street, the bold new-look **Stedelijk Museum of Modern Art** (Tues–Sun 10am–5pm, Thurs until 10pm; €15; Ⓦstedelijk.nl) was the third Museumplein gallery to reopen in 2013 with a €15 price tag and a series of much-needed improvements, including acres of new exhibition space. Highlights include Picasso's *Seated Woman with Fish-Hat*, as well as major work by Van Gogh, Mondrian, Kandinsky and Matisse.

The Heineken Experience and De Pijp

The vast **Heineken Experience** at Stadhouderskade 78, east from the Rijksmuseum (Mon–Thurs 11am–7.30pm, Fri–Sun 11am–8.30pm; €18; Ⓦheinekenexperience.com), provides a slick overview of one of the

Netherlands' biggest brands, with a couple of free beers thrown in afterwards (for something with a bit more flavour, try **De Prael**; p.787). South of here is the neighbourhood known as **De Pijp** (The Pipe) after its long canyon-like streets of brick tenements. This has always been one of the city's closest-knit communities, and one of its liveliest, with numerous inexpensive Surinamese and Turkish restaurants mixed in with hip bars and organic delis. The main focus is lengthy **Albert Cuypstraat**, whose food and clothes **market** (see p.788) is the largest in the city. Just south is the lovely landscaped **Sarphatipark**.

Waterlooplein and the Rembrandt House

East of Rembrandtplein across the Amstel, the large, squat **Muziektheater** and **Stadhuis** (commonly known as Stopera) flank **Waterlooplein**, home to the city's excellent **flea market** (see p.789). Behind, Jodenbreestraat was once the main street of the Jewish quarter (emptied by the Nazis in the 1940s); no. 6 is **Het Rembrandthuis** (Rembrandt House; daily 10am–6pm; €12.50; Ⓦrembrandthuis.nl), which the painter bought in 1639 at the height of his fame. The main attraction here is the house itself, decorated in seventeenth-century style, rather than its relatively modest collection of Rembrandt etchings.

The Jewish Quarter and Hermitage Amsterdam

The award-winning **Joods Historisch Museum**, at Nieuwe Amstelstraat 1 (Jewish Historical Museum; daily 11am–5pm; closed Yom Kippur; €12; Ⓦjhm.nl), is cleverly housed in a complex of Ashkenazi synagogues dating from the late seventeenth century and gives a vivid impression of Amsterdam's long-gone Jewish ghetto, while interactive pieces explain Jewish customs.

From here it's a short stroll towards the River Amstel and the **Hermitage Amsterdam** at Amstel 51 (daily 10am–5pm; €15; Ⓦhermitage.nl), the first foreign branch of Russia's leading art

HIT THE DOCKS

Amsterdam isn't all cute canals and cobbled streets. For a change of perspective head out to the striking modern architecture and wide-open spaces of the **eastern docklands**. A short tram ride (#26) or cycle ride east of Centraal Station, you'll find the futuristic Muziekgebouw performance venue (Ⓦmuziekgebouw.nl) and the reborn *Lloyd Hotel* (Ⓦlloydhotel.com), a unique one- to five-star hotel and "cultural embassy". Even if you can't stump up €100 for one of the one-star rooms you're welcome to wander around its huge light-filled exhibition spaces.

A 10min (free) ferry ride north of Centraal Station takes you to the former shipyards of the Amsterdam Shipping Company. This area is being rapidly redeveloped and boasts a couple of cool places to eat and drink. Check Ⓦndsm.nl for more information.

museum in St Petersburg, possessing an extensive collection of paintings of Old Masters, as well as Oriental art and Post-Impressionist work.

ARRIVAL AND DEPARTURE

By plane Schiphol airport, 15km southwest of Amsterdam, is connected by high-speed Fyra train to Centraal Station (every 10min, hourly 1–5am; 15min; €3.90).

By train Centraal Station is the hub of all bus and tram routes and just 5min walk from central Dam Square.
Destinations Arnhem (for Hoge Veluwe National Park; every 15min; 1hr 10min); Brussels (every 1–2hr; 1hr 49min); Cologne (every 2hr; 2hr 38min); Den Haag HS (every 10min; 45min); Den Helder (every 30min; 1hr 15min); Frankfurt (every 2–3hr; 3hr 46min). Haarlem (every 10min; 15min); Leiden (every 15min; 35min); Maastricht (every 30min; 2hr 24min); Paris (hourly; 3hr 16min); Rotterdam (every 10min; 40min–1hr 10min); Texel (via Den Helder; every 30min; 1hr 15min); Utrecht (every 10min; 27min).

By bus International buses arrive at Amstel Station, 10min south of Centraal Station by metro.
Destinations Brussels (hourly; 2hr 45min); Cologne (7 daily; 4hr 15min); Frankfurt (7 daily; 6hr 15min); London (7 daily; 10hr); Paris (6 daily; 7hr).

INFORMATION AND TOURS

Tourist office The main VVV is opposite Centraal Station, at Stationsplein 10 (Mon–Wed 9am–5pm, Thurs–Sat 9am–6pm, Sun 10am–5pm; ☎0900 400 4040, Ⓦiamsterdam.com), and there's also an office in the airport arrivals hall (daily 7am–10pm).

Discount card The Iamsterdam City Card (€42/52/62 for 24/48/72hr; Ⓦiamsterdam.com) covers city transport and entry to many attractions. Given the price, though, it's only worth considering if you're planning on hitting a lot of museums (note that it doesn't include the Rijksmuseum or Anne Frank House).

Bike tours Mike's Bike Tours (☎020 622 7970, Ⓦmikesbiketoursamsterdam.com), at Kerkstraat 134,

does a good three-hour city tour for €20. Yellow Bike, at Nieuwezijds Kolk 29 (☎020 620 6940, Ⓦyellowbike.nl), offers similar excursions for €25.

GETTING AROUND

By public transport There's an excellent network of trams, buses and metro (all daily 6/7am–midnight). The GVB public transport office in front of Centraal Station (Mon–Fri 7am–9pm, Sat & Sun 10am–6pm; ☎0900 8011, Ⓦgvb.nl) has free route maps and sells chip cards (see p.776). After midnight, night buses take over, running roughly hourly from Centraal Station to most parts of the city (one-way ticket €4).

By bike Most hostels rent bikes for around €10 per day. Otherwise try MacBike (from €9.75 per day; ☎020 620 0985, Ⓦmacbike.nl), which has convenient branches at Centraal Station, Leidseplein, Marnixstraat and Waterlooplein, or the slightly cheaper Ajax Bike (from €8.50 per day; ☎0615 6 8 4831, Ⓦajaxbike.nl) in De Pijp.

ACCOMMODATION

In high season, and at weekends throughout the year, It's always worth booking ahead, or you'll find almost everywhere full. Many hostels also demand a three night minimum stay.

HOSTELS

Bob's Youth Hostel Nieuwezijds Voorburgwal 92 ☎020 623 0063, Ⓦbobsyouthhostel.nl. Lively and smoky, this is a legendary backpackers' favourite, a 10min walk southwest of Centraal Station. Also has apartments with kitchens. Dorm **€25**

Bulldog Low-Budget Hotel Oudezijds Voorburgwal 220 ☎020 620 3822, Ⓦbulldog.nl. Part of the *Bulldog* coffeeshop chain, this super-smart hostel has a bar, DVD lounge, roof terrace and laundry facilities. Accommodation ranges from dorms with TVs and showers to doubles and apartments. Dorm **€33**, double **€95**

★ **Cocomama** Westeinde 18 ☎020 627 2454, Ⓦcocomama.nl. Located in a former brothel, this "boutique" hostel with themed dorms sleeping up to six people and lovely en-suite private rooms has a pleasant,

23

23

smoke-free communal/kitchen area and cute little garden (plus friendly house cat). Dorm **€36**, double **€120**

Flying Pig Downtown Nieuwendijk 100 ☎020 420 6822, ⊛flyingpig.nl. Popular hostel near Centraal Station run by ex-backpackers. Selling points include its unique queen-sized bunks (good value if you are happy to "spoon" with a friend) free kitchen, internet, an all-night bar and no curfew; not for faint-hearted non-smokers. There's also the slightly quieter *Flying Pig Uptown* branch by the Vondelpark at Vossiusstraat 46 (☎020 400 4187; tram #1/#2/#5 to Leidseplein, then a 5min walk). Both branches dorm **€31**, double **€90**

Hans Brinker Kerkstraat 136 ☎020 622 0687, ⊛hans -brinker.com; tram #1/#2/#5 to Prinsengracht. Well-established and raucously popular no-frills cheapie with a bright café attached (meals €5–7). Tongue-in-cheek approach to customer service (see website). Dorm **€25**, double **€80**

Hostelle Frankemaheerd 2 ☎020 770 3504, ⊛hostelle .com. Tasteful, clean, female-only hostel – the antithesis of the "pack 'em in" party hostels in town. The only catch is the less than central location near the Amsterdam Bijlmer Arena, a 15min metro ride from Centraal Station (though it is convenient for the airport). Dorm **€20**, double **€72**

Stayokay Stadsdoelen Kloveniersburgwal 97 ☎020 624 6832, ⊛stayokay.com. The cleanest and most conventional hostel in the city centre. Like all *Stayokays* you'll find spotless dorms, a decent buffet breakfast but something of a personality bypass. Usually booked solid in summer when you'll be bumped to their Zeeburg branch in the eastern docklands. Dorm **€29**, double **€80**

Stayokay Vondelpark Zandpad 5 ☎020 589 8996, ⊛stayokay.com. Of the three *Stayokay* hostels this has the most appealing location in the leafy Vondelpark. With 536 beds it is a bit of a monster, though, so can feel institutional at busy times. Dorm **€29**, double **€80**

Winston Warmoesstraat 129 ☎020 623 1380, ⊛winston.nl. This self-consciously young and hip hostel has funky rooms individually decorated with alternative art and a busy ground-floor bar that has occasional live music. A 10min walk from Centraal Station. Dorm **€36**, double **€79**

HOTELS

Backstage Hotel Leidsegracht 114 ☎020 624 4044, ⊛backstagehotel.com; tram #1, #2 or #5 to Prinsengracht. Cool, rock-themed hotel with theatre mirrors, PA spotlights and flight cases as furniture. Triple, quad and five-person rooms offer decent value for groups. Facilities include free internet, a 24hr bar and pool table. Double **€115**

Clemens Raadhuisstraat 39 ☎020 624 6089, ⊛clemenshotel.com; tram #13/#17 to Westermarkt. Clean, neat and good value for money, with breakfast included. Ask for a quieter room at the back. Double **€100**

Golden Bear Kerkstraat 37 ☎020 624 4785, ⊛goldenbear.nl; trams #1/#2/#5 to Kerkstraat. The first gay hotel in the city, with clean and spacious rooms. Minimum stay of three nights March–Nov if the weekend is included. Double **€77**

Prinsenhof Prinsengracht 810 ☎020 623 1772, ⊛hotelprinsenhof.com. Housed in an eighteenth-century canal house. Only two rooms are en suite, but a hearty breakfast is included and service couldn't be friendlier. Double **€75**

CAMPSITES

Camping Zeeburg Zuider IJdijk 20 ☎020 694 4430, ⊛campingzeeburg.nl; tram #26 from Centraal Station to Zuiderzeeweg or night bus #359 to Flevoweg. Located on an island amid trees, this site also offers two-person cabins. Free wi-fi. Open all year. Camping **€11.50** per person and tent, cabin **€50**

Vliegenbos Meeuwenlaan 138 ☎020 636 8855, ⊛vliegenbos.com; bus #32, #33 or night bus #361 from Centraal Station. Located a 10min ferry ride away in Amsterdam North, this site is well equipped with a homely restaurant and lots of shade. Open April–Sept. Camping **€8.70** per person, plus **€2.50** per tent

EATING

Amsterdam has many ethnic restaurants, especially Indonesian, Surinamese and Thai, as well as *eetcafés* that serve decent, well-priced food in an unpretentious setting.

CAFÉS

Buffet van Odette & Yvette Prinsengracht 598. Crowded little place selling home-made quiches, salads and soups (from €7.50) as well as mouthwatering cakes to satisfy the sweetest tooth. Mon & Wed–Sun 10am–9pm.

De Balie Kleine-Gartmanplantsoen 10, Leidseplein ☎020 625 1721. Busy, buzzy theatre café in tourist central, Leidseplein. Grab a toastie (€4) or an Italian salad (€9) in the lovely high-ceilinged dining room. Daily 10am–10pm.

De Jaren Nieuwe Doelenstraat 20–22, near Muntplein. Modern, grand café with a waterside terrace – a perfect place for people-watching and newspaper-browsing in the sun. Sandwiches from €5. Mon–Thurs & Sun 9.30am–1am, Fri & Sat 9.30am–2am.

Il Tramezzino Haarlemmerstraat 79. Richly filled sandwiches (€2.95) based on an old Venetian recipe, washed down with superb espresso in an up-to-the-minute setting. Mon & Wed–Sat 9am–6pm, Sun 9.30am–5pm.

★ **Latei** Zeedijk 143. Great soups, sandwiches and unbeatable apple pie plus a great-value dinner menu (Thurs–Sat; from €10), featuring cuisine from around the world. Mon–Wed 8am–6pm, Thurs & Fri 8am–10pm, Sat 9am–10pm, Sun 11am–6pm.

★ **TREAT YOURSELF**

Lucky Lake Hostel ⓦluckylake.nl; metro to Holendrecht station then shuttle bus (€1). If Amsterdam's nightlife has left you a little frazzled, a stay at this rural idyll might be in order. Located in a peaceful location by the manmade Vinkeveen lakes 15km southeast of central Amsterdam, it offers a mixture of brightly decorated caravans (trailers), cabins sleeping two to three, four-bed dorms and a small campsite (bring your own tent). Rent a bike or kayak or chill out in a hammock. You'll soon want to stay longer than you booked. Open April to mid-Sept. Dorm **€26**, cabin/caravan **€29** per person, camping **€15** per tent

Thijssen Brouwersgracht 107. An old-time local favourite, perfect to linger over coffee or fresh mint tea with a magazine. The tiny terrace gives good views of the bustling market. Mon–Thurs & Sun 8am–1am, Fri & Sat 8am–3am.

Winkel Noordermarkt 43, opposite the Noorderkerk. Popular local hangout on Sat mornings during the farmers' market. Famously delicious apple cake. Quiches €5, evening mains from €11.50. Mon 7am–1am, Tues–Thurs 8am–1am, Fri 8am–3am, Sat 7am–3am, Sun 10am–1am.

RESTAURANTS

De Blaffende Vis Westerstraat 118 ☎020 625 1721. Great bar-restaurant in the Jordaan. Popular with students and gets raucous at weekends. *Dagschotel* around €8–9. Mon 7.30am–1am, Tues–Thurs 8.30am–1am, Fri 8.30am–3am, Sat 9am–3am, Sun 10am–3am.

★ **Harlem Soul Food** Haarlemmerstraat 77 ☎020 330 14 98. Stylish New Orleans-style joint knocking out filling nachos (€8), jerk chicken (€5.40), plus more sophisticated evening dishes (crayfish salad €14). Daily 10am–10pm.

Pink Flamingo Gerard Douplein 8 ☎020 670 3274. The best and most inventive pizzas in town (from €9.50) in a lovely little square in De Pijp. Try the gorgonzola, fig and parma ham Basquiat. Daily 6pm–3am.

Rose's Cantina Reguliersdwarsstraat 40 ☎020 625 9797. Long-established Mexican restaurant with attractive garden. Fajitas from €16 and a wicked cocktail selection. Mon–Thurs & Sun 5pm–1am, Fri & Sat 5pm–3am.

★ **Skek** Zeedijk 4-8. Lively student-run bar/kitchen on busy Zeedijk. The signature skekburger (veggie or meat) with home-made salsa and mayo (€13.50) is hard to resist. Mon 4am–1am, Tues–Thurs noon–1am, Fri & Sat noon–3am, Sun noon–1am.

Soenda Kelapa Utrechtsestraat 89 ☎020 627 9416. A small Indonesian restaurant with no frills but generous portions of excellent food. Chicken *sateh rijsttafel* €17.50. Daily 6–11pm.

DRINKING AND NIGHTLIFE

There is a distinction between bars and coffeeshops, where smoking dope is the primary pastime (ask to see the menu). You must be 18 or over to enter these, and don't expect alcohol to be served. Drinks cost around fifty percent more than in a bar, but entry prices are low and there's rarely any kind of door policy. Check ⓦ djguide.nl to see who's hitting the decks.

BARS

★ **Brouwerij De Prael** Oudezijds Voorburgwal 30. Excellent working microbrewery in the heart of the Red Light District. Order a rack of four tasters for €5. Don't miss the 11.5 percent "Willy"– Heineken it ain't. Tues–Sat noon–midnight, Sun noon–11pm.

Café t' Smalle Egelantiersgracht 12. Classic brown café with 250 years of drinking heritage, stained-glass windows and a lovely candlelit vibe and canalside terrace. Mon–Thurs & Sun 10am–1am, Fri & Sat 10am–2am.

Flamingo 1e van der Helststraat 37. This hipster hangout in De Pijp is perfect for an alfresco drink in summer. Cosy inside with a good range of Belgian brews on tap. Mon–Thurs & Sun 10am–1am, Fri & Sat 10am–3am.

Spanjer & van Twist Leliegracht 60. A popular place which is perfect for laidback summer afternoons, with chairs overlooking the quietest canal in Jordaan. Also serves lunch and dinner. Daily 10am–1am.

Weber Marnixstraat 397. Popular bar, just off the Leidseplein, attracting musicians, students and young professionals. Crowded and noisy on weekends. Daily 8pm–3/4am.

COFFEESHOPS

★ **De Dampkring** Handboogstraat 29 & Haarlemmerstraat 44. With colourful decor and a refined menu, this coffeeshop is known for its good-quality hash (the branch on Haarlemmerstraat is the pick of the two). Daily 10am–1am.

Homegrown Fantasy Nieuwezijds Voorburgwal 87a. Part of the Dutch Passion seed company, selling the widest range of (mostly Dutch) marijuana in Amsterdam. Friendly staff. Mon–Thurs noon–11pm, Fri & Sun noon–midnight.

Kadinsky Zoutsteeg 9 & Rosmarijnsteeg 9, both in the old centre. Sensational chocolate-chip cookies, scrupulously accurate deals and a background of jazz dance. Daily 10am–1am.

Siberië Brouwersgracht 11. Slightly off the beaten tourist track, very relaxed and friendly – worth a visit whether you want to smoke or not. Mon–Thurs & Sun 11am–11pm, Fri & Sat 11am–midnight.

23

23

CLUBS

Bitterzoet Spuistraat 2 ⓦ bitterzoet.com. Popular club right by Centraal Station with an eclectic mix of nights, featuring live bands as well as DJs. Daily 8pm–3/4am.

Panama Oostelijke Handelskade 4 ⓦ panama.nl. Club-cum-restaurant overlooking the River IJ with frequent live music, salsa and big-name DJ nights (the likes of Armin van Buuren and Tiesto have performed here). Thurs–Sun 9pm–3am.

Studio 80 Rembrandtplein 17 ⓦ studio-80.nl. This club, basically a big black room below touristy Rembrandtplein, is the best place to discover up-and-coming DJs. Wed–Sat 11pm–3/5am.

Sugar Factory Lijnbaansgracht 238 ⓦ sugarfactory.nl. The choice of the clubs around Leidseplein. Something on pretty much every night – also hosts arts events. Mon & Wed–Sun 11pm–5am.

★ **TrouwAmsterdam** Wibautstraat 127 ⓦ trouwamsterdam.nl; tram #3 to Wibaustraat/Ruyschstraat. Vast industrial club built into a former newpaper printing press, a wee trek south of the centre but worth the trip. Fri–Sun 11pm–5am.

LIVE MUSIC

Bimhuis Piet Heinkade 3 ☎ 020 788 2188, ⓦ bimhuis.nl; tram #25/#26 to stop Muziekgebouw/Bimhuis from Centraal Station. Premier jazz venue. Tues–Sat 3–6.30pm and concert evenings till 11pm.

Melkweg Lijnbaansgracht 234 ☎ 020 531 8181, ⓦ melkweg.nl. Music, theatre, photography, film and media arts all under one roof. There are quality DJs playing at the weekend, a monthly film programme, theatre, gallery, bar and restaurant. Check online schedule for opening times.

Paradiso Weteringschans 6–8 ⓦ paradiso.nl. The city's most atmospheric music venue, located in a converted church near the Leidseplein and hosting local as well as international acts such as Lady Gaga and the odd soul legend. Check online schedule for opening times.

ENTERTAINMENT

Amsterdam buzzes with places offering everything from English-language comedy to arthouse cinema. Grab a copy of *A-mag* from the tourist office or visit the "what's on" section of ⓦ iamsterdam.com for the latest listings. Last-minute tickets are sold by the aptly named ⓦ lastminuteticketshop.nl.

★ **Boom Chicago** Rozentheater, Rozengracht 117 ☎ 020 217 0400, ⓦ boomchicago.nl. Rapid-fire improv energetically performed by Americans who delve deep into the Dutch, and indeed their own, psyche with hilarious results. Tickets from €19.

Cinecenter Lijnbaansgracht 236 ☎ 020 623 6615, ⓦ cinecenter.nl. Arthouse cinema showing lots of Woody Allen and French-language films. The bar is a perfect place to wear a black polo-neck and thoughtfully stroke your beard. Tickets €9.

Concertgebouw Concertgebouwplein 2–6 ☎ 020 671 8345, ⓦ concertgebouw.nl. Catch world-renowned orchestras playing amid wonderful acoustics. Summer concerts and free lunchtime performances on Wed. There are CJP discounts, and "Sprint Seats" for under-30s sold 45min before the start of each concert for €10.

Filmtheater De Uitkijk Prinsengracht 452 ☎ 020 623 7460, ⓦ uitkijk.nl. The oldest film theatre in Amsterdam, and one of the more intimate. Screenings range from Team America to the latest from Almodóvar. Tickets €9.

GAY AMSTERDAM

Amsterdam has one of the biggest and best-established gay scenes in Europe. The nationwide organization COC, at Rozenstraat 14 (☎ 020 626 3087, ⓦ cocamsterdam.nl), can provide information, and has a café and popular club nights. Otherwise check ⓦ gayamsterdam.com.

Café Entre Nous Halvemaansteeg 14. Intimate little café-bar with friendly staff who gradually ramp up the music and fun after about 10pm. Daily 9pm–late.

Café 't Mandje Zeedijk 63. Legendary gay bar dating from 1927, painstakingly renovated in 2008 and now as welcoming and quirky as ever (check out the ties hanging from the ceiling). Tues–Thurs 4pm–1am, Fri & Sat 2pm–3am, Sun 2pm–1am.

Prik Spuistraat 109. Frequently voted as Amsterdam's best gay bar, with tasty cocktails, smoothies and snacks, and DJs on weekends. Daily 4pm–1/3am.

SHOPPING AND MARKETS

Albert Cuypstraat Market Albert Cuypstraat. Amsterdam's biggest market stretches for over 1km along De Pijp's longest street. As well as cheap clothes and homewares you'll find plenty of ethnic food stalls. Mon–Sat 9am–5pm.

American Book Center Spui 12 ⓦ abc.nl. This vast English-language bookshop is packed with travel guides, fiction and US/UK magazines. Mon–Wed noon–8pm, Thurs–Sat 10am–8pm, Sun 11am–6.30pm.

Condomerie Warmoestraat 141 ⓦ condomerie.com. Among the grim sex shops of the Red Light District, the *Condomerie* is worth seeking out for its playful displays and exhaustive range of condoms. Mon–Sat 11am–6pm, Sun 1–5pm.

★ **Hutspot** Van Woustraat 4 ⓦ hutspotamsterdam.com. Cavernous, cool concept store on the edge of Albert Cuypstraat with men's and women's fashion, a lovely upstairs café and even a traditional barber shop. Mon–Sat 10am–7pm, Sun 10am–6pm.

Marbles Vintage and Design Haarlemmerdijk 64. Rack upon rack of well-priced vintage fashion and accessories on one of Amsterdam's coolest streets. Daily 11am–7pm.

Marqt Haarlemmerstraat 165 ⓦ marqt.nl, Amsterdam's answer to *Whole Foods*: a wonderful micro supermarket with specialist cheese and meat deli, perfect for picnics (no cards). Daily 9am–10pm.

Waterlooplein Flea Market Waterlooplein ⓦ waterloopleinmarkt.nl. Perfect for an afternoon browse, this historic flea market bristles with everything from bicycle parts to Afghan rugs. Mon–Sat 9am–6pm.

DIRECTORY

Embassies and consulates In Den Haag (p.793).

Exchange GWK Travelex in Centraal Station and on Damrak 1–5 and 86, Kalverstraat 150, Leidsestraat 103 and Leidseplein 31a.

Hospital De Boelelaan 1117 ☎ 020 444 4444.

Internet Wi-fi is available at all hostels and hotels, and pretty much all cafés and restaurants. If you need a terminal try the Central Library, 500m east of Centraal Station at Oosterdokskade 143 (daily 10am–10pm; €1/30min).

Left luggage Centraal Station (daily 7am–11pm; from €3.30/24hr).

Post office No post office as such, though TNT mail services are available at the Ako newsstand (daily 10am–8pm) close to Rembrandtsplein, and branches of Albert Heijn supermarkets (including Jodenbreestraat 21 near the Rembrandt House Museum).

Police Dial ☎ 0900 8844 and the operator will direct you to the nearest police station.

The Randstad

The string of towns known as the **Randstad**, or "rim town", situated amid a typically Dutch landscape of flat fields cut by canals, forms the country's most populated region and still recalls the landscapes painted in the seventeenth-century heyday of the provinces. Much of the area can be visited as day-trips from Amsterdam. **Haarlem** is worth a look for the outstanding Frans Hals Museum, while to the south, the university centre of **Leiden** makes a pleasant detour before you reach the refined tranquillity of **Den Haag** (The Hague) and the modern urban landscape of **Rotterdam**. Nearby **Delft** and **Gouda** repay visits too, the former with one of the best-preserved centres in the region.

HAARLEM

Just over fifteen minutes from Amsterdam by train, **HAARLEM** is a handsome, mid-sized town that can be easily absorbed in a few hours. It also makes a good alternative base to Amsterdam at busy times, especially thanks to its excellent new B&B/hostel. Those after a decent pint will also love the **Jopenkerk**, a church converted into a brewery.

WHAT TO SEE AND DO

The core of Harlem is **Grote Markt** and the adjoining Riviervischmarkt, flanked by the gabled, originally fourteenth-century **Stadhuis** and the impressive bulk of the **Grote Kerk** (Mon–Sat 10am–4pm; €2.50). Inside, the mighty Christian Müller organ of 1738 is said to have been played by Handel and Mozart. The town's main attraction is the wonderful **Frans Hals Museum**, at Groot Heiligland 62 (Tues–Fri 10am–5pm, Sat & Sun 11am–6pm; €13), a five-minute stroll from Grote Markt in the Oudemanhuis almshouse. It houses a number of his lifelike seventeenth-century portraits, including the *Civic Guard* series, which established his reputation.

23

ARRIVAL AND INFORMATION

By train The train station is north of the centre, about a 10min walk from the Grote Markt.

Destinations Amsterdam CS (every 10min; 15min); Delft (every 30min; 40min); Den Haag HS (every 30min; 30min); Leiden (every 10min; 20min).

Tourist office Verwulft 11 (April–Sept Mon–Fri 9.30am–5.30pm, Sat 9.30am–5pm, Sun noon–4pm; Oct–March Mon 1–5.30pm, Tues–Fri 9.30am–5.30pm, Sat 10am–5pm; ☎ 0900 616 1600, ⓦ haarlemmarketing.nl).

ACCOMMODATION

★ **Hello I'm local** Spiegelstraat 4 ☎ 023 844 6916, ⓦ helloimlocal.nl. Fabulous twelve-room "boutique" B&B/hostel with three dorms sleeping 8–14 and nine doubles/twins and quads, each beautifully decorated and many boasting lovely views. Dorm **€29**, double **€80**

Stayokay Haarlem Jan Gijzenpad 3 ☎ 023 537 3793, ⓦ stayokay.com; bus #2, direction Noord. Inconveniently located out of town on a main road (15min by bus from the train station), but otherwise this HI hostel is of the usual high standard. Dorm **€25**, double **€58**

23

EATING AND DRINKING

De Roemer Botermarkt 17. Wood-panelled brown café serving quality sandwiches and salads (try the Roemer salad with smoked chicken, bacon and apple for €8.30) and a daily changing dinner menu (from €11.90). Mon–Sat 10am–1/2am, Sun noon–1am.

De Vlaminck Warmoesstraat 3. Takeaway serving classic crispy Dutch *frites* served with a dollop of fresh mayo. Mon–Sat 11.30am–5/6pm, Sun noon–5pm.

★ **Jopenkerk** Vestestraat 1 ⓦ jopen.nl. Haarlem has a long history of brewing beer, and the Jopen brand, based in this brilliantly converted church, is an attempt to revive it. Pick three beers from their tasting menu and something to soak it up in the attached café (mains €8.50). Daily 10am–1am.

XO Grote Markt 8, ⓦ xo-haarlem.nl. Up-to-the-minute café-restaurant serving a youthful clientele (lunch menu from €7.50, dinner €15). Great terrace and DJs on weekends. Mon–Sat 9.30am–1/3am, Sun 10.30am–1am.

LEIDEN

The charm of **LEIDEN** lies in the peace and prettiness of its gabled streets and canals, though the town's museums are varied and comprehensive enough to merit a visit. It also has a thriving student population thanks to a university consistently rated one of Europe's finest.

WHAT TO SEE AND DO

The most appealing quarter is **Rapenburg**, a peaceful area of narrow pedestrian streets and canals that is home to the country's best archeological museum, the **Rijksmuseum Van Oudheden** (National Museum of Antiquities; Tues–Sun 10am–5pm; €9.50; ⓦ rmo.nl). Outside sits the first-century AD Temple of Teffeh, while inside are more Egyptian artefacts, along with classical Greek and Roman

sculptures and exhibits from prehistoric, Roman and medieval times. Across Rapenburg, a network of narrow streets converges on the Gothic **Pieterskerk**. East of here, Breestraat marks the start of a vigorous **market** (Wed & Sat), which sprawls right over the sequence of bridges into Haarlemmerstraat, the town's major shopping street. Close by, the **Burcht** (daily 10am–10pm; free) is a shell of a fort, whose battlements you can clamber up for views of the town centre. The **Molenmuseum de Valk**, on Molenwerf at 2e Binnenvestgracht 1 (Tues–Sat 10am–5pm, Sun 1–5pm; €4), is a museum housed in a classic Dutch windmill. Walk west along the 2e Binnenvestgracht and soon you'll hit the **Rijksmuseum voor Volkenkunde** (National Museum of Ethnology; Tues–Sun 10am–5pm; €8.50), with an impressive collection of artefacts from every continent.

ARRIVAL AND INFORMATION

By train Leiden's train station is on the northwest edge of town next to the bus station.

Destinations Amsterdam CS (every 15min; 35min); Amsterdam Schiphol (every 10min; 20min); Delft (every 15min; 20min); Den Haag HS (every 10min; 10min); Haarlem (every 10min; 20min); Rotterdam (every 10min; 30min); Utrecht (every 30min; 40min).

Tourist office Right outside the train station at Stationsweg 41 (Mon–Fri 8am–6pm, Sat 10am–4pm, Sun 11am–3pm; ☏ 071 516 6000, ⓦ www.leiden.nl).

ACCOMMODATION

Flying Pig Beach Hostel Parallel Boulevard 208, Noordwijk ☏ 071 362 2533, ⓦ flyingpig.nl; bus #40 or #44 from Leiden to the lighthouse square in Noordwijk. This relaxed beachside outpost of the *Flying Pig* chain is a

FLOWER POWER: THE KEUKENHOF

Along with Haarlem to the north, Leiden and Delft are the best bases for seeing the famous Dutch **bulbfields** that flourish in spring. The view from the train as you travel from Haarlem to Leiden can be sufficient in itself as the line cuts directly through the main growing areas, the fields divided into stark geometric blocks of pure colour. Should you want to get closer, make a beeline for **Lisse**, home to the **Keukenhof** (mid-March to mid-May daily 8am–7.30pm; €15; ⓦ keukenhof.nl), the largest flower gardens in the world. Some six million blooms are on show for their full flowering period, complemented by five thousand square metres of greenhouses. Bus #54 (every 30min; 25min) runs to the Keukenhof from Leiden bus station. To skip the queues, it's worth getting Connexxion's combined bus and entry ticket (€20; available from Leiden Station as well as Schiphol and Amsterdam VVV).

30min bus ride from Leiden in the resort town of Noordwijk (if you don't fancy the bus, a VW campervan runs here from their other hostels; €4). The bar is a real traveller hangout; you could be forgiven for thinking you were in South America. Dorm €25, double €90

Pension Witte Singel Witte Singel 80 ☎071 512 4592 ⓦ www.pension-ws.demon.nl. Pleasant canalside B&B on the edge of the old town with clean, affordable rooms, some with shared bathroom. Double €50

EATING AND DRINKING

Barrera Rapenburg 56. Buzzy canalside café-bar with big sandwiches and a lip-smacking Rapen'Burger (€11). Mon–Thurs & Sun 10am–1am, Fri & Sat 10am–2am.

De Bonte Koe Hooglandsekerk-choorsteeg 13. The "spotted cow" is a typical Dutch brown café tucked away in a narrow alley with tiled walls and a large beer selection. Mon–Thurs 4pm–1am, Fri 4pm–3am, Sat 12.30pm–3am, Sun 1.30pm–1am.

La Bota Herensteeg 9–11 by the Pieterskerk. Hidden studenty spot which serves great-value food and beers. *Dagschotel* €6.50. Daily 5pm–1am, kitchen 5–10pm.

DEN HAAG

With its urbane atmosphere, **DEN HAAG (THE HAGUE)** is different from any other Dutch city. Since the sixteenth century it has been the Netherlands' political capital and from 1945 the home of the International Court of Justice. For the visitor the main attraction is its wonderful **museums** packed with Dutch masters and its proximity to **Scheveningen**, the Netherlands' biggest beach resort. Staying here can be pricey – many of the city's hotels and restaurants are in the expense-account category – but among all this, Den Haag does have cheaper and livelier bars and restaurants.

WHAT TO SEE AND DO

The modern and historical centres of the city interweave about a 1km north of Den Haag HS station, with the main sights clustered together. More attractions – including the seaside at **Scheveningen** – are further north, all of which are easily accessible on public transport.

The Binnenhof, Mauritshuis and around

Right in the centre, the **Binnenhof** is the home of the Dutch parliament and incorporates elements of the town's thirteenth-century castle set around a pretty, tree-lined lake. Immediately east of here is the **Mauritshuis** at Korte Vijverberg 8, a magnificent seventeenth-century mansion housing an extensive range of Flemish and Dutch paintings including Vermeer's *Girl with a Pearl Earring* and *View of Delft*, and one of Rembrandt's final self-portraits. After a major renovation project (during which many paintings were moved to the Gemeentemuseum; see below) the place is due to reopen in mid 2014 (check ⓦ mauritshuis.nl for the latest opening hours). For an artistic contrast don't miss the nearby **Escher in Het Paleis** (Tues–Sun 11am–5pm; €9; ⓦ escherinhetpaleis.nl) at Lange Voorhout 74, dedicated to the Dutch master of optical illusion, M.C. Escher.

23

Panorama Mesdag and the Gemeentemuseum

Panorama Mesdag, just west of the pedestrianized shopping area of town at Zeestraat 65 (Mon–Sat 10am–5pm, Sun noon–5pm; €10), is an astonishing 360-degree painting of seaside scenes of Scheveningen from the 1880s. North, the **Gemeentemuseum**, Stadhouderslaan 41 (Tues–Sun 11am–5pm; €14.50; ⓦ gemeentemuseum.nl; bus #24/tram #17 from Centraal Station), contains superb collections of musical instruments, Islamic ceramics and modern art, with the world's largest collection of Mondrian paintings. The attached **Museum of Photography** and **GEM** contemporary art museum can be accessed with a combined ticket (€16.50).

Scheveningen

Just 4km from Den Haag city centre and easily accessible by tram #1, **Scheveningen** is a big brash beach resort with all the usual attractions like a pier, casino and Sea Life Centre. In summer Scheveningen becomes a kind of mini Ibiza thanks to its beachside bars and surfers tackling the (bone-chilling) North Sea swells. To soak up the surfy vibe visit **FAST**, a unique "surfer village" fashioned out of shipping

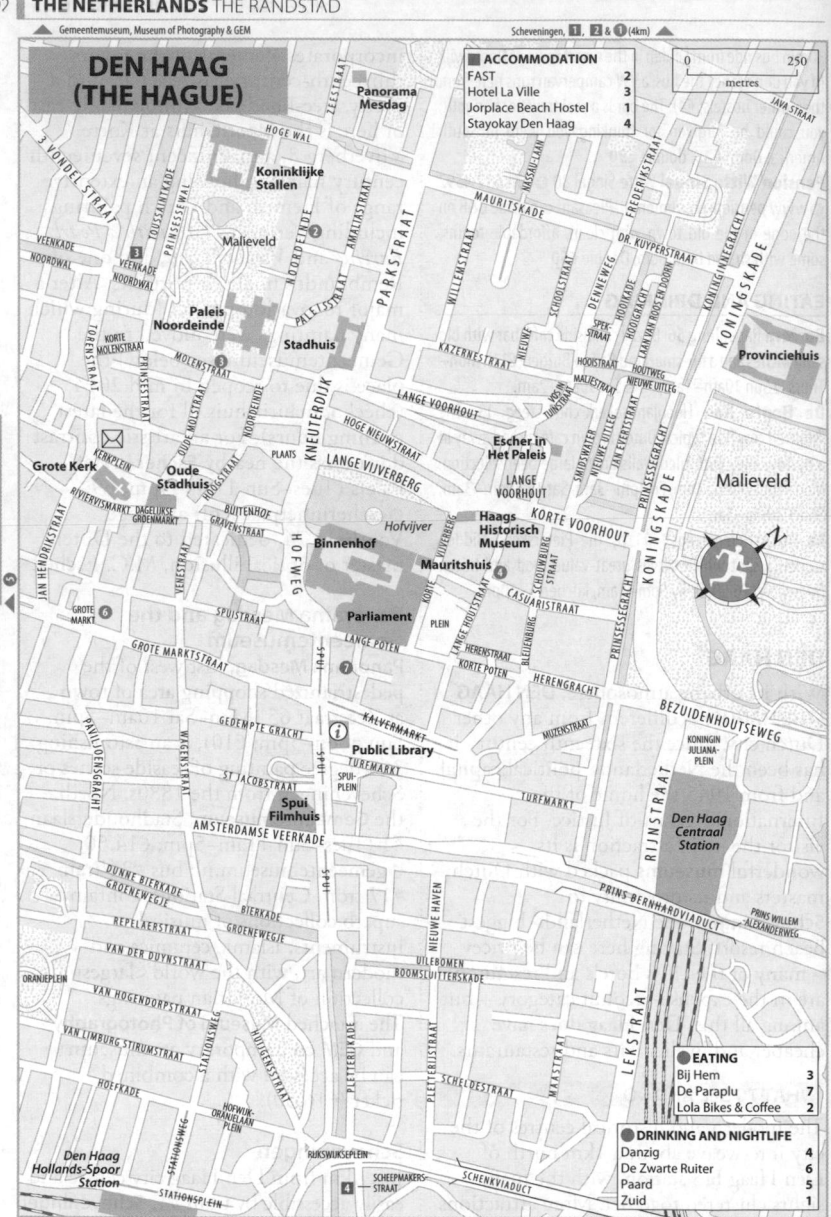

▲ Gemeentemuseum, Museum of Photography & GEM · Scheveningen, **1**, **2** & **1** (4km) ▲

DEN HAAG (THE HAGUE)

■ **ACCOMMODATION**

FAST	2
Hotel La Ville	3
Jorplace Beach Hostel	1
Stayokay Den Haag	4

0 — 250 metres

● **EATING**

Bij Hem	3
De Paraplu	7
Lola Bikes & Coffee	2

● **DRINKING AND NIGHTLIFE**

Danzig	4
De Zwarte Ruiter	6
Paard	5
Zuid	1

containers (see opposite). Another way to experience the sands is to take a "fat bike" tour with Lola Bikes (see opposite).

ARRIVAL AND INFORMATION

By train The city has two train stations – Den Haag Central (CS) and Den Haag Hollands Spoor (HS), the latter

about 1km southeast, close to the *Stayokay* hostel. There are frequent rail services between the two (5min) or you can take tram #1. Trains generally arrive at, and depart from, both stations, so your choice will be down to which is closest to your accommodation. The exceptions are the slow intercity trains to Belgium which only stop at HS (connecting to the Thalys service at Rotterdam is much faster), and services to Schiphol which are slightly more frequent from CS.

Destinations Amsterdam CS (every 10–15min; 50min); Amsterdam Schiphol (every 15–20min; 28min); Antwerp (Den Haag HS only; every 2hr; 1hr 32min); Brussels (Den Haag HS only; every 2hr; 2hr 13min); Delft (every 10–15min; 10min); Gouda (every 15min; 40min); Haarlem (every 30min; 30min); Leiden (every 10–15min; 12min); Rotterdam (every 10min; 20min).

Tourist office Spui 68, inside the public library (Mon noon–8pm, Tues–Fri 10am–8pm, Sat 10am–5pm, Sun noon–5pm; ☎0900 340 3505, ⓦdenhaag.com). Scheveningen has its own VVV info kiosk at the pier (April–Oct Sat & Sun 11am–5pm; ⓦscheveningen.nl).

GETTING AROUND

By tram Trams are the best way to get around Den Haag and out to Scheveningen. A day card costs €7.70. Line #1 runs between the train stations, then continues north to the beach.

ACCOMMODATION

DEN HAAG

Hotel La Ville Veenkade 5 ☎070 346 3657, ⓦhotellaville .nl; tram #17 to Noordwal. Stylishly decorated, good-value hotel that usually undercuts the city's only other budget option, *easyHotel*. Also has apartments with kitchenette, sleeping up to four. Double €75, apartment €85

Stayokay Den Haag Scheepmakersstraat 27 ☎070 315 7878, ⓦstayokay.com. Den Haag's clean, efficient *Stayokay* is a short stroll from HS station. The area is perfectly safe, though you might be surprised to see Amsterdam-style window prostitutes a few streets away. Dorm €29, double €60

SCHEVENINGEN

FAST Strandweg 1A ☎070 358 6749, ⓦfastthehague .com. This beach hostel/campsite/surf shop with attached bar-restaurant is located about 1km south of central Scheveningen. The basic dorms housed in recycled shipping containers are not for everyone, but the camping area is pleasant enough, staff friendly and there's a distinct community feel in summer. Dorm €20, camping €15 per person and tent

★**Jorplace Beach Hostel** Keizerstraat 296, Scheveningen ☎070 338 3270, ⓦjorplace.nl. Not exactly on the beach (for that try FAST; see above), but this hugely popular hostel is near enough to offer surfing and kite-surfing lessons. There's also a disco in the basement and a VW camper (with double bed; priced at standard double rate) in the garden. Dorm €19, double €60

EATING

Bij Hem Molenstraat 21a. Inventive sandwiches (try the

Surinam spicy chicken, €8.50) and some excellent mains (Moroccan lamb with rice, €16.75) await at this bright little café-restaurant on one of the city's most chi-chi streets. Mon–Thurs 11am–11pm, Fri & Sat 11am–1am, Sun 10am–11pm.

De Paraplu Bagijnestraat 9. Tucked away in a tiny alley, this simple *eetcafé* is always jam-packed with people looking for good food at a reasonable price. Known for its Giant Plu-burger and juicy *sateh*. Mon 5–10pm, Tues–Fri noon–3pm & 5–10pm, Sat & Sun 5–10pm.

★**Lola Bikes & Coffee** Noordeinde 91, ⓦlolabikesandcoffee.nl. Bike shop/espresso bar with cool artwork and retro cycles hanging on the wall. Don't miss their Fatbike Experience cycle tour of the beach and dunes (every Sun 8.30am; €26.50). Daily 8am–6pm.

DRINKING AND NIGHTLIFE

Danzig Lange Houtstraat 9 ⓦdanzig.nl. Basement dance bar, hugely popular with students for its free entrance and cheap beer. Thurs–Sat 11pm–4am/5am.

De Zwarte Ruiter Grote Markt 27 ⓦgmdh.nl/zwarte -ruiter. Your best bet on the popular Grote Markt square, "The Black Rider" attracts a more alternative crowd with live bands and a great terrace. Daily 11am–1am.

Paard Prinsegracht 12 ⓦpaard.nl. Den Haag's main music venue, often featuring international acts (Florence and the Machine and Calvin Harris have appeared), and frequent DJ nights (many with free entry). Check online for the full schedule, show times and early bird discounts.

Zuid Wieringse Pad Stroke 11, Duindorp ⓦgmdh.nl /strandpaviljoen-zuid; tram #12 to Duindorp and follow the signs. Popular beach bar-restaurant south of the main Scheveningen strands. Also hosts live music and DJ sets. Summer daily 9am–midnight.

DIRECTORY

Embassies and consulates Australia, Carnegielaan 4, Den Haag ☎070 310 8200; Canada, Sophialaan 7, Den Haag ☎070 311 1600; Ireland, Dr Kuyperstraat 9, Den Haag ☎070 363 0993; New Zealand, Eisenhowerlaan 77N, Den Haag ☎070 346 9324; UK, Lange Voorhout 10, Den Haag ☎070 427 0427; US, Lange Voorhout 102, Den Haag ☎070 310 2209.

DELFT

DELFT, 2km inland from Den Haag, is perhaps best known for **Delftware**, the delicate blue and white ceramics to which the town gave its name in the seventeenth century, and as the home of the painter **Johannes Vermeer**. With its gabled red-roofed houses standing beside tree-lined canals, the town has a faded

23

23

tranquillity – though one that can suffer beneath the tourist onslaught in summer.

WHAT TO SEE AND DO

Delft's main square, the **Markt**, is framed by the impressive **Nieuwe Kerk** (April–Oct Mon–Sat 9am–6pm; Nov–March Mon–Fri 11am–4pm, Sat 10am–5pm; €3.50, tower €3.50) and the Renaissance **Stadhuis** opposite. William the Silent – leader of the struggle for Dutch independence in the sixteenth century – is buried in the Nieuwe Kerk and you can climb the 370 steps of the tower for spectacular views. West of here, **Wynhaven**, an old canal, leads to Hippolytusbuurt and the Gothic **Oude Kerk** (same hours and ticket as Nieuwe Kerk), perhaps the town's finest building, with an unhealthily leaning tower. Vermeer fans should check out the **Vermeer Centrum** (daily 10am–5pm; €8) at Voldersgracht 21. Although there are no actual Vermeer paintings, only reproductions, the studio space explaining Vermeer's technique is worth a visit.

A fifteen-minute walk south of the centre at Rotterdamsweg 196 is the **Royal Delft Experience** (daily 9am–5pm; Nov to mid-March closed Sun; €12) where you can see Delftware being painstakingly painted.

ARRIVAL AND INFORMATION

By train From Delft's train station, aim for the big steeple you see on exit and it's a 10min walk north to the Markt. Destinations Amsterdam (every 15min; 1hr); Den Haag HS (every 10min; 7min); Rotterdam (every 10min; 12min). **Tourist office** Delft's VVV, called TIP, is just north of the Markt at Hippolytusbuurt 4 (April–Sept Mon & Sat 10am–5pm, Tues–Fri 9am–6pm, Sun 10am–4pm; Oct–March Mon 11am–4pm, Tues–Sat 10am–4pm, Sun 10am–3pm; ☎05 215 40 51, ⊕www.delft.nl).

ACCOMMODATION

Jorplace City Hostel Delft Voldersgracht 17–18 ⊕jorplace.nl. Bang in the centre of historic Delft, this friendly little hostel has three airy dorms (6, 12 and 24 beds). There's an attached bar, and both long- and paddle-boards for rent. Dorm €19
Soul Inn B&B Willemstraat 55 ☎015 215 7246, ⊕soulinn.nl. A small hotel, with imaginative, 1970s-themed decor and quirky rooms (mostly with shared facilities). Handy location for the station. Double €60

EATING AND DRINKING

Kobus Kuch Beestenmarkt 1. A gem of a café-restaurant – don't miss the famous *appeltaart met slagroom* (apple pie with cream; €3.40). Open late for drinks, too. Mon–Sat 9.30am–1am, Sun 10am–1am.
Locus Publicus Brabantse Turfmarkt 67. Popular local bar, serving a staggering array of beers as well as a good selection of cheap snacks. Bitterballen €3. Mon–Thurs 11am–1am, Fri & Sat 11am–2am, Sun noon–1am.
★ **Lunchcafé Vrij** Branantse Turfmarkt 61. Buzzing little café specializing in Portuguese tapas (€12.50) and piri-piri sandwiches (€7.50) served with artisan bread. Tues–Sat 9am–5pm, Sun 10.30am–5.30pm.
Zondag Voldersgracht 7. "Every day is Sunday" at this relaxed café on pretty Voldersgracht. Good coffee and snacks (club sandwich €7.95), plus a decent range of beers. Daily 10am–5.30/6pm.

ROTTERDAM

Looming skyscrapers, gritty docklands – **ROTTERDAM** is the Netherlands but not as we know it. The largest seaport in Europe, Rotterdam's unique urban landscape is largely a result of the hammering it received during World War II when bombing completely levelled the city. Today, with its elegant Erasmus bridge, playful Blaak cube houses and the vast Tetris-block "De Rotterdam", the city can boast some of the most aventurous architecture in the world. There's also plenty to keep you entertained, including a great museum park, the bohemian Witte de Wittstraat artistic quarter and, last but not least, the welcoming and independent-spirited Rotterdammers themselves.

WHAT TO SEE AND DO

You can get a feel for the city by walking from Centraal Station (or taking tram #7 from just outside) down to the Museumpark along Mauritsweg. More idiosyncratic attractions lie further east, while Delfshaven is a short, and rewarding, journey southwest.

The Museumpark and around

The impressive **Boijmans Van Beuningen Museum**, at Museumpark 18–20 (Tues–Sun 11am–5pm; €12.50; ⊕boijmans.nl), has a superb collection of works by Monet, Van Gogh, Picasso,

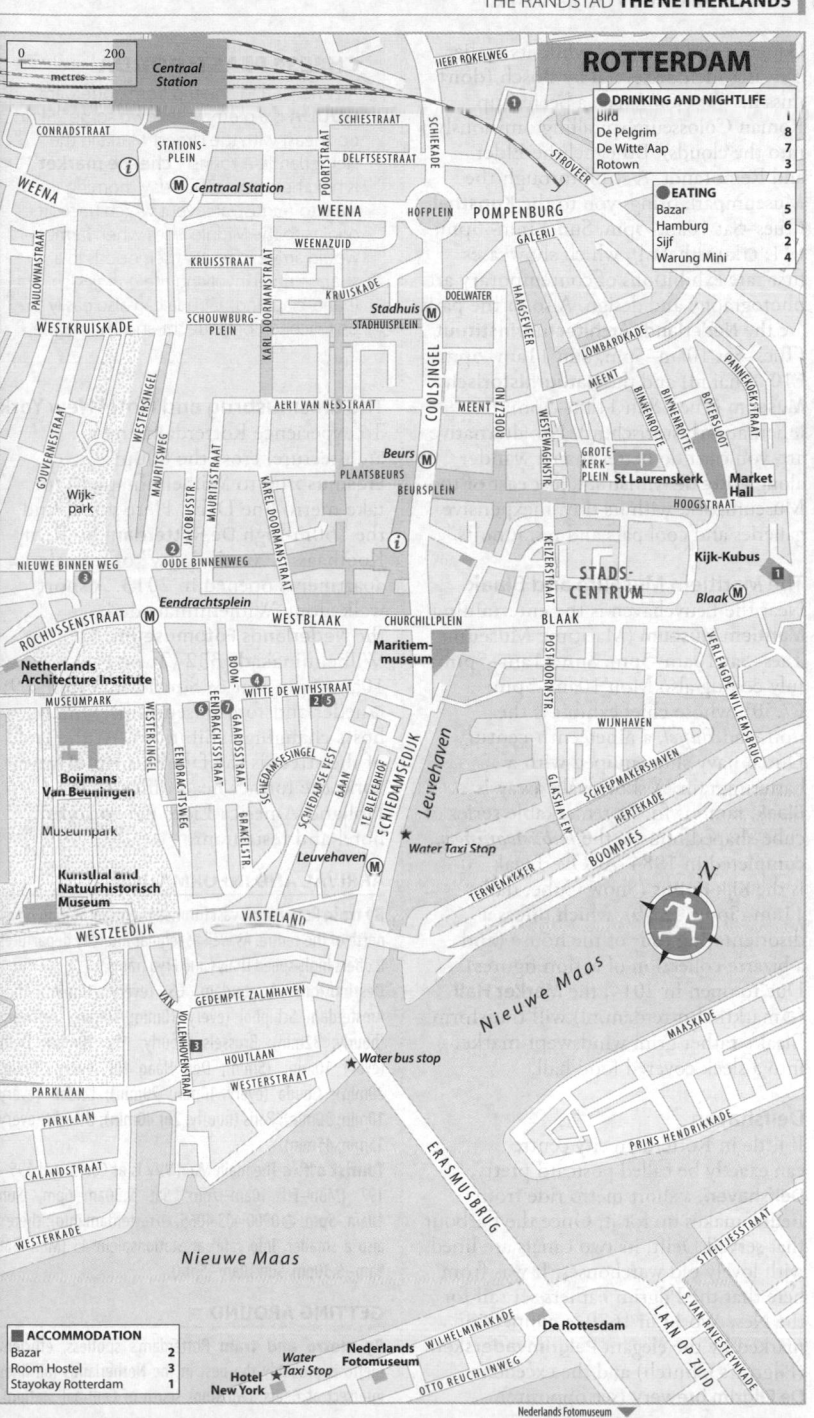

ROTTERDAM

DRINKING AND NIGHTLIFE
Bird	i
De Pelgrim	8
De Witte Aap	7
Rotown	3

EATING
Bazar	5
Hamburg	6
Sijf	2
Warung Mini	4

ACCOMMODATION
Bazar	2
Room Hostel	3
Stayokay Rotterdam	1

23

23

Gauguin and Cézanne, while its earlier canvases include several by Bosch (don't miss his *Tower of Babel*, a beefed-up Roman Colosseum spiralling ominously into the clouds), Brueghel the Elder and Rembrandt. A stroll through the Museumpark brings you to the **Kunsthal** (Tues–Sat 10am–5pm, Sun 11am–5pm; €11; ⍟kunsthal.nl), which showcases first-rate exhibitions of contemporary art, photography and design. Also in the park are the **Nederlands Architectuurinstituut** (Tues–Sat 10am–5pm, Sun 11am–5pm; €10; ⍟nai.nl) and the **Natuurhistorisch Museum** (Tues–Sun 11am–5pm; €6; ⍟hetnatuurhistorisch.nl). For alternative art, you can't do better than a wander along **Witte de Withstraat**, just east of the Museumpark, with its tiny, inexpensive galleries and cool bars and restaurants.

The Maritiem Museum and Blaak

Near the Leuvehaven is the entertaining **Maritiem Museum** (Maritime Museum; Tues–Sat 10am–5pm, Sun 11am–5pm; July & Aug also Mon 10am–5pm; €7.50), whose chief exhibit is the iron-clad *Buffel*, a nineteenth-century Dutch navy ship equiped with a battering ram. A short walk away is **Blaak**, famous for its remarkable series of cube-shaped houses, the *kubuswoningen*, completed in 1984. At Overblaak 70 is the **Kijk-Kubus** (Show Cube; daily 11am–5pm; €2.50), which offers a disorientating tour of the house (and a bizarre collection of action figures). Due to open in 2014, the **Market Hall** (⍟markthalrotterdam.nl) will transform Blaak's rather grim windswept market into a sleek covered food hall.

Delfshaven

If little in Rotterdam city centre can exactly be called postcard pretty, **Delfshaven**, a short metro ride from Beurs, makes up for it. Once the harbour that served Delft, its two canals are lined with lovely old warehouses. It was from here that the Pilgrim Fathers set sail for the New World in 1620, a connection marked by the elegant **Pelgrimvaderskerk** (Pilgrim's Church) and the excellent **De Pilgrim brewery** (see opposite).

CHEESE FEAST: GOUDA

An enchanting day-trip from Rotterdam, **GOUDA** is a pretty little town some 25km northeast with the largest Markt in the Netherlands. A touristy **cheese market** is held here every Thursday morning from June to August, an event which traces its origins to the Middle Ages when farmers would arrive to barter their goods in a strange ritual involving the *handjeklap* (hand-clapping). Gouda can also easily be reached from Utrecht and The Hague.

The Erasmusbrug and Hotel New York

To experience Rotterdam's new architecture, cross the 800m **Erasmusbrug** to Wilhelminaplein (or take metro line D/E). Here you'll find the 150m-high **De Rotterdam** by Rem Koolhaas, a "vertical city" of upscale apartments opened in 2013. A short walk along Wilhelminakade is the **Nederlands Fotomuseum**, Wilhelminakade 332 (Tues–Fri 10am–5pm, Sat & Sun 11am–5pm; €9; ⍟nederlandsfotomuseum.nl), which hosts changing exhibitions. At the end of the street is the fabulous **Hotel New York**, the former head office of the Holland-America Line, now a stylish hotel and restaurant.

ARRIVAL AND INFORMATION

By train Rotterdam's vast futuristic Centraal Station is just north of the centre. As well as regular intercity departures it offers high-speed Thalys and Frya trains.

Destinations Amsterdam CS (every 10min; 1hr); Amsterdam Schiphol (every 10min; 50min); Antwerp (hourly; 32min); Brussels (hourly; 1hr 10min); Delft (every 10min; 15min); Den Haag HS (every 10min; 20min); Gouda (every 10min; 20min); Leiden (every 10min; 30min); Paris (hourly; 2hr 40min); Utrecht (every 15min; 45min).

Tourist office The main Main VVV is at Coolsingel 195–197 (Mon–Fri 10am–7pm, Sat 9.30am–6pm, Sun 10am–5pm; ☎0900 403 4065, ⍟rotterdam.info); there's also a smaller "info café" at Stationsplein 45 (Mon–Sat 9am–5.30pm, Sun 10am–5pm).

GETTING AROUND

By metro and tram Rotterdam's spotless, efficient metro is probably the best in the Netherlands (all lines intersect at Beurs, two stops south of Centraal Station).

Both metro and tram services use the ov-chipkaart system (€3.50 for 2hr).

By water bus This fast ferry runs every 30min from near the Erasmusbrug to Dordrecht, 15km south (Mon–Fri 7am–8pm, Sat 8am–9m, Sun 11am–7.30pm; €2–6; ov-chipkaart accepted; ⓦwaterbus.nl). On the way you can see Rotterdam's vast docklands as well as the famous windmills at Kinderdijk.

By water taxi Departing from Leuvehaven and Veerhaven, these boats (from €2.90; ⓦwatertaxi rotterdam.nl) are a fun way to cross the Maas to and from *Hotel New York* (see opposite).

ACCOMMMODATION

Bazar Witte de Withstraat 16 ☎010 206 5151, ⓦhotelbazar.nl. Popular Middle Eastern-style hotel in trendy Witte de Withstraat (nearest metro Beurs). The rooms are each individually designed, so choose your favourite from the website before you book. Double €80

★ **Room Hostel** Van Vollenhovenstraat 62 ☎010 282 7277, ⓦroomrotterdam.nl; from Centraal Station, take tram #7 to Westerstraat or tram #8 to Vasteland. Funky hostel with a vibrant bar and quieter lounge, and a friendly springer spaniel. The helpful staff organize events for guests. Dorm €18.50, double €53

Stayokay Rotterdam Overblaak 85–87 ☎010 436 5763, ⓦstayokay.com. A short walk from Blaak station, this HI hostel is located inside the famous cube houses, so make sure your stomach can handle the disorientating experience after one beer too many. Dorm €24.50, double €59

EATING

The best places for cheap and tasty food are Oude and Nieuwe Binnenweg, and Witte de Withstraat.

Bazar Witte de Withstraat 16. Popular bar/restaurant serving excellent Turkish/Lebanese food (*lahmacun* €5.90, shish kebab €12.75) with colourful surroundings and a lively atmosphere. Mon–Fri 8am–1am, Sat 9am–2am, Sun 9am–midnight.

★ **Hamburg** Witte de Withstraat 94B. The best burgers in town (free-range Black Angus, chicken or tofu from €6.90) at this new US-style diner. Mon–Wed 4–11pm, Thurs–Sun noon–11pm.

Sijf Oude Binnenweg 115. One of the many agreeable pub-style places along this stretch. Mains are reasonable: €14.50, including unlimited fries and salad, or cheaper daily specials for €10–12. Daily 10am–midnight/1am.

Warung Mini Witte de Withstraat 47. A cheap-and-cheerful canteen dishing up hefty portions of decent Surinamese and Chinese from €7.50. Open until 6am at the weekend to satisfy those late-night cravings. Mon–Thurs noon–midnight, Fri noon–6am, Sat 4pm–6am, Sun 4pm–midnight.

DRINKING AND NIGHTLIFE

Bird Raampoortstraat 26 ⓦbirdrotterdam.nl. You'll find anything from jazz to Latin to hip-hop at this club/restaurant under the arches of the Hofbogen viaduct. Tues–Thurs & Sun 11am–1am Fri & Sat 11am–4am.

★ **De Pelgrim** Aelbrechtskolk 12 ⓦwww.pelgrimbier .nl. Microbrewery housed in a grand building on Delfshaven, producing excellent craft ales including a tasty IPA and the punchy 7.3-percent "Mayflower Triple". The attached restaurant offers well-priced soups, salads and bar snacks (*bitterballen* €5.95). Wed–Sun noon–midnight.

De Witte Aap Witte de Withstraat 78 ⓦdewitteaap.nl. Small but bustling bar – extremely popular with students – hosting DJs on weekends, as well as rotating art exhibitions. Daily 1pm–late.

Rotown Nieuwe Binnenweg 17–19 ⓦrotown.nl. Music café hosting frequent gigs by up-and-coming bands. The kitchen knocks up decent sandwiches (€5.20), toasties and burgers (€9.50). They also run the funky, industrial-looking Bar3 next door. Daily 11am–2am.

UTRECHT

A short hop from Amsterdam, **UTRECHT** makes for a relaxing break from the capital. With its world-class university (home to 30,000 students), stunning medieval architecture and canals full of people lazily boating about in summer, it has an almost Oxbridge feel, though without being quite so clogged with tourists. The city is perhaps best known for the 1713 **Peace of Utrecht**, a series of treaties which ended the War of the Spanish Succession.

WHAT TO SEE AND DO

Though its historic centre is perfect for aimless wandering, there are surprisingly few stellar sights in Utrecht. The focal point is the fourteenth-century **Dom Tower**, which at over 110m is the highest church tower in the country. A guided tour (April–Sept hourly 11am–4pm; Oct–March noon, 2pm & 4pm; €9) takes you unnervingly close to the top, from where you can see Rotterdam and Amsterdam on a clear day. The **Central Museum** (Tues–Sun 11am–5pm; €11; ⓦcentraalmuseum.nl; bus #2), around 1km south of the centre at Nicolaaskerkhof 10, is worth a visit if you still have a hankering for Dutch

23

23

UTRECHT FROM THE WATER
The best way to experience the low-slung canals and architecture of Utrecht is from the water. Kanoverhuur (April–Sept daily 10am–8pm; €5/hour; ⓦ kanoverhuur utrecht.nl) rents kayaks and Canadian-style canoes throughout the summer. The main Oudegracht and Nieuwegracht loop can be done in under an hour.

art (here it's mostly by local Utrecht artists). The **DickBruna Huis** next door (same hours and ticket) is devoted to the creator of children's favourite and global bestselling rabbit Miffy.

ARRIVAL AND INFORMATION

By train Utrecht's train station is located inside the large Hoog Catharijne shopping centre. Follow the signs and you will eventually be spat out at Vrendenburg which leads to the main canal, Oudegracht.
Destinations Amsterdam (every 15min; 30min); Arnhem (every 15min; 35min); Gouda (every 10min; 20min); Maastricht (every 30min; 2hr); Rotterdam (every 15min; 40min).
Tourist office Close to the Dom Tower at Domplein 9 (Mon–Fri 10am–6pm, Sat 10am–5pm, Sun noon–5pm; ☎ 0900 128 8732, ⓦ utrechtyourway.nl).

ACCOMMODATION

Stayokay Utrecht-Bunnik Rhijnauwenselaan 14 ☎ 030 656 1277, ⓦ stayokay.com; bus #40 or #41 from the train station to Rhijnauwen. Peaceful, family-orientated HI hostel located a good 5km out of the centre in an old country manor house. Dorm €25.50, double €59
★ **Strowis** Boothstraat 8 ☎ 030 238 0280, ⓦ www .strowis.nl; bus #3/#4/#8/#11 to the Janskerkhof. Great hostel with a lovely garden, a kitchen and free internet access in the relaxing lounge. It's walkable from the train station, or you can take the bus. Dorm €18, double €60

EATING, DRINKING AND NIGHTLIFE

Broodje Mario Oudegracht 132. This market stall selling pizza slices and the famous Mario sandwich with cheese, salami and red pepper is a local institution. Fill up for only €3. Daily 10am–6pm.
Café Ledig Erf Tolsteegbrug 3. Great canalside pub with a lovely terrace overlooking the Oudegracht and Singel. Excellent range of Belgian and Dutch beers. Daily 10am–midnight/1am.
Ekko Bemuurde Weerd WZ 3 ⓦ ekko.nl. Alternative rock and dance venue with live performances by international artists and DJs. The café serves a well-priced veggie three-course

meal for €12.50 on Thurs and Fri evenings. Concerts generally Thurs–Sun from 7pm, full programme online.
★ **The Village** Voorstraat 46. Probably the hippest café in Utrecht – all exposed brickwork, bearded baristas and boasting a great location for people-watching. Mon–Fri 8am–6pm.

Beyond the Randstad

Outside the Randstad towns, the Netherlands is relatively unknown territory to visitors. To the north, there's superb cycling and hiking to be had through scenic **dune reserves** and delightful villages, with easy access to pristine beaches, while the island of **Texel** offers the country's most complete beach experience, and has plenty of birdlife. The **Hoge Veluwe National Park**, near Arnhem, boasts one of the Netherlands' best modern art museums and has cycle paths through a delightful landscape. Further south the landscape slowly fills out, moving into a rougher countryside of farmland and forests, and eventually into the hills around **Maastricht**, a city with a vibrant, pan-European feel.

TEXEL

The largest of the islands off the north coast – and the easiest to get to (2hr from Amsterdam) – **TEXEL** (pronounced "tessel") offers diverse and pretty landscapes, and is one of Europe's most important bird-breeding grounds.

WHAT TO SEE AND DO

Texel's main settlement, **DEN BURG**, makes a convenient base and has bike rental outlets. On the coast 3km southeast of Den Burg is **OUDESCHILD**, home to the **Maritiem en Juttersmuseum** (Beachcombers' Museum; Tues–Sat 10am–5pm, Sun noon–5pm; July & Aug also Mon 10am–5pm; €8.50), a fascinating collection of marine junk and, just on the way into town, the **Texelse Brewery** (tours Tues–Fri 2pm & 3pm, Sat 2pm, 3pm & 4pm) which offers regular

HOGE VELUWE NATIONAL PARK

Just north of the town of **Arnhem** (80km from Amsterdam/55km from Utrecht) is the huge, privately owned **Hoge Veluwe National Park** (daily: April 8am–8pm; May & Aug 8am–9pm; June & July 8am–10pm; Sept 9am–8pm; Oct 9am–7pm; Nov–March 9am–6pm; €8.40; ⓦhogeveluwe.nl). Apart from being a wonderful place to hike and cycle (there are 1700 free "White Bikes" to use), it's also home to the superb **Kröller-Müller Museum** (Tues–Sun 10am–5pm; €16 including park admission; ⓦkmm.nl), a collection of fine art put together by Helene Kröller-Müller. The museum includes nearly three hundred paintings by Van Gogh, plus works by Picasso, Seurat, Léger and Mondrian, and is surrounded by an imaginative **sculpture garden**.

The quickest route to the park from Amsterdam is to take a train to Apeldoorn (every 30min; 1hr) and then take bus #108 to Hoenderloo from where it's a short walk to the entrance. If you fancy staying over, there's an excellent **campsite** near the Hoenderloo entrance (open April–Oct; €7 per person and tent).

23

tastings. In the opposite direction is DE KOOG, with a good sandy beach and the **EcoMare nature centre**, at Ruijslaan 92 (daily 9am–5pm; €9; ⓦecomare.nl), a bird and seal sanctuary as well as natural history museum: from here you can visit the **Wad**, the banks of sand and mud to the east of the island, where seals and birds gather.

ARRIVAL AND INFORMATION

By boat Ferries from the town of Den Helder on the mainland (bus #33 from the station to the port) depart every hour (20min; €2.50 return ticket). Once on Texel, various buses greet the ferry's arrival and depart for destinations across the island.

Tourist office Den Burg's VVV is at Emmalaan 66 (Mon–Fri 9am–5.30pm, Sat 9am–5pm; ☏0222 314 741, ⓦtexel.net).

Discount card The Rotterdam Welcome Card (€10/13.50/17.50 for 24/48/72hr) covers city transport and provides up to fifty-percent discounts on attractions. It comes with a booklet full of discount vouchers for shops, restaurants and tours.

ACCOMMODATION

Camping is the most popular option here, with good campsites dotted around the island. The VVV website has a full list including some funky yurt options.

Kogerstrand Badweg 33 ☏0222 317 208, ⓦtexelcampings.nl. Campsite set among the beachside dunes in De Koog, the island's busiest resort. Part of a network of four sites across the island. Closed Nov–March. Camping €8.75 per person and tent

Stayokay Texel Haffelderweg 29 ☏0222 315 441, ⓦstayokay.com. HI hostel on the outskirts of Den Burg that's more suited to families and groups, although it has a big bar and terrace. Dorm €22, double €52

EATING AND DRINKING

De Pangkoekehuus Kikkertstraat 9, De Cocksdorp. Cosy pancake house in the small village of Cocksdorp near the northern tip of the island. Delicious filled pancakes for around €8. Daily noon–9pm.

De Twaalf Balcken Weverstraat 20. The *Tavern of the Twelve Beams* is a Texel institution, an *eetcafé* serving well-priced salads, tortilla and ribs (mains from €12.25). Mon–Thurs 10am–1.30am, Fri & Sat 10am–3am, Sun 5pm–1.30am.

Van der Star Heemskerckstraat 15, Oudeschild. Well-priced seafood café located on Oudeschild harbour. It's pretty basic – plastic chairs and tables – but you won't care when you taste the deliciously fresh fish. Daily noon–8pm.

MAASTRICHT

Squashed between the Belgian and German borders, MAASTRICHT is one of the most delightful cities in the Netherlands. A university town popular with foreign students, it made a fitting location for the 1992 treaty that established the modern EU and the euro (you'll find € symbols decorating the pavement). It's worthy of a couple of nights to explore properly. If you can, try to time your visit to coincide with the excellent **pinkpop music festival** (mid-June; ⓦpinkpop.nl) in nearby Landgraaf.

WHAT TO SEE AND DO

A short walk from the train station is the trendy **Wijk quarter**, home to a cluster of bars, restaurants and the city's most interesting shopping street,

23

Rechstraat. From here the pretty Sint Servaasbrug leads west over the Maas River to the old town.

The old town and caves

The heart of the old town is busy **Markt square**, set around the impressive seventeenth-century **Stadhuis**. South of here are several notable churches, the most affecting being the **Onze Lieve Vrouw Basiliek** (daily 7.30am–5pm; free) which houses a beautiful Gothic chapel of Our Lady, full of flickering candles.

Continuing south brings you to the ancient **city walls** and the **university quarter**, with its pretty cobbled streets, shady squares and affordable cafés. You can explore a series of defensive tunnels beneath the city walls at **Casemates** (€5.25), though far more impressive are the labyrinthine **Zonneburg Caves**, a short boat ride away (gaslit tours in English daily 12.30pm & 2pm; €13.25 including boat trip; ⓦmaastrichtunderground.nl).

Bonnefantenmuseum

On the east side of the river is the city's main art gallery, **Bonnefantenmuseum**, at Avenue Céramique 250 (Tues–Sun 10.30am–5pm; €9; ⓦbonnefanten .nl). Designed by Aldo Rossi, it's situated in the newest part of Maastricht, **Céramique**, which offers a complete contrast to the feel of the historic city. The collection ranges from Old Masters to contemporary artists, but the building itself, with its stunning cupola and monumental stairs, is just as impressive.

ARRIVAL, INFORMATION AND TOURS

By train The train station is on the east side of town, a 5min walk from the Sint Servaasbrg Bridge. The nearest high-speed international services depart from Liège in Belgium.

Destinations Amsterdam (every 30min; 2hr 30min); Eindhoven (for Rotterdam or Den Haag; every 30min; 1hr); Liège (hourly; 35min); Utrecht (every 30min; 2hr).

Tourist office The VVV is at Kleine Staat 1, at the end of the main shopping street (May–Oct Mon–Sat 9am–6pm, Sun 11am–3pm; Nov–April Mon–Fri 9am–6pm, Sat 9am–5pm; ☏ 043 325 2121, ⓦ vvvmaastricht.eu).

★ **Maastricht Running Tours** ⓦ maastrichtrunning tours.nl. Grab some exercise and discover hidden historical details on this excellent 6km running tour. Group rates from €12.50.

ACCOMMODATION

Camping Mooi Bemelen Gasthuis 3 ☏ 043 407 1321, ⓦ mooibemelen.nl; bus #53. The most convenient campsite, just 10min east of town by bus. Open all year. Camping **€4** per person, plus **€2.40** per tent

De Hofnar Keizer Karelplein 13 & Capucijnenstraat 35 ☏ 043 351 0396, ⓦ hofnarmaastricht.nl. Good-value B&B with two locations near the old town. The pick of the two is on Capucijnenstraat, a cute little cottage dating from 1730. Double **€50**

Stayokay Maastricht Maasboulevard 101 ☏ 043 750 1790, ⓦ stayokay.com. HI hostel with a big riverside terrace and a lovely light-filled restaurant and bar area. A few minutes' walk from the centre and 15min from the station. Dorm **€29**, double **€71**

EATING AND DRINKING

★ **Coffeelovers** Dominican Square 1. A stylish café within a bookshop in a beautiful converted church. The great coffee is a perfect accompaniment to browsing the books. Mon–Fri 8am–6pm, Sat & Sun 10am–7pm.

Take One Café Rechstraat 28. Over 100 varieties of beer are sold in this Maastricht institution run by a husband-and-wife team. Be prepared to be quizzed in depth on your taste preferences. Mon & Thurs–Sun 4pm–2am.

Tasty Thai Rechstraat 29 ⓦ tastythai.nl. Fast, flawless Thai food (mains €8.90), served up in a canteen-esque restaurant on boutique-lined Rechstraat. Mon 3–9pm, Tues–Sun noon–9pm.

★ **Zondag** Wijckerbrugstraat 42. Cool café-bar with huge windows and a great corner location, serving snacks, soups and salads until 10pm, after which DJs and stiff cocktails are the order of the day. There's also an amazingly good chip shop across the road. Daily 10am–late.

LOFOTEN ISLANDS

Norway

HIGHLIGHTS

❶ **Oslo Opera House** Gorgeous, sprawling arts space. **See p.809**

❷ **Grünerløkka** Buzzy, trendy Oslo neighbourhood with plenty of nightlife. **See p.813**

❸ **Norwegian Canning Museum** Engaging, history-rich exhibitions. **See p.814**

❹ **Bryggen** Atmospheric Bergen quarter with gorgeous wooden structures. **See p.816**

❺ **Balestrand** Quaint, fjordside village with glacier access. **See p.819**

❻ **Lofoten** Stunning Arctic archipelago with evocative architecture. **See p.824**

❼ **Northern Lights** Fiery swathes of celestial illumination. **See p.827**

HIGHLIGHTS ARE MARKED ON THE MAP ON P.803

ROUGH COSTS

Daily budget Basic €80, occasional treat €115

Drink Beer €8

Food Meatballs with potatoes €20

Hostel/budget hotel €35–45/€80

Travel Train: Oslo–Bergen €33–90; bus: Oslo–Trondheim €11–53

FACT FILE

Population 5.1 million

Language Norwegian

Currency Norwegian krone (kr)

Capital Oslo

International phone code ☎47

Time zone GMT +1hr

Introduction

Norway's extraordinary, postcard-perfect landscapes put the country at the top of any bucket list. Though its high prices will stretch your wallet, the payoff comes in the country's mix of likeable, easy-going cities and magnificent wilderness – during summer, you can hike up a glacier in the morning and thaw out in an urban bar in the evening, watching the sun dip below the horizon for all of half an hour, if at all. Deeper into the countryside, you'll find vast stretches of forests surrounded by distinctive glacier-formed landscapes. And because of Norway's small population, it really is possible to travel for hours in this natural grandeur without seeing a soul.

Beyond **Oslo** – a pretty, laconic and increasingly cosmopolitan capital surrounded by mountains and fjords – the major cities of interest are historic **Trondheim**, **Bergen**, on the edge of the fjords, and northern **Tromsø**. Anyone with even a passing fondness for the great outdoors should head to the **western fjords**: dip into the region from Bergen or **Ålesund**, or linger in one of the many quiet waterside towns and villages. Further north, deep in the Arctic Circle, the astounding **Lofoten Islands** have some of the most striking mountain scenery and clearest water in Norway. To the north of here, the tourist trail focuses on the long journey to **Nordkapp**, the northernmost accessible point in Europe; the route leads through **Finnmark**, one of the last strongholds of the Sámi and their herds of reindeer. Tourism reaches its height from June to August when opening hours are long and activities plentiful; the rest of the year, you'll find many establishments closed unless you're in major towns.

CHRONOLOGY

10,000–2000 BC Seal- and reindeer-hunting tribes move into present-day Norway.
800–1050 AD Norwegian Vikings become a dominant force in Europe.
900 King Harald becomes the first ruler of a united Norway.
1030 The Norwegians adopt Christianity.
1262 Norway increases her empire, forming unions with Greenland and Iceland.
1350 Almost two-thirds of the population die during the Black Death.

1396 The Kalmar Union unites Norway with Denmark and Sweden under a single ruler.
1536 Sweden leaves the Kalmar Union, leaving Norway under Danish control.
1814 Norwegian hopes of independence are dashed after Sweden invades and takes control.
1905 Parliament declares independence from Sweden. Haakon VII is crowned the first king of an independent Norway in 525 years.
1911 Explorer Roald Amundsen's expedition is the first to reach the South Pole ahead of the ill-fated Scott expedition.
1913 Norway becomes one of the first countries in the world to give women the vote.
1914 Norway remains neutral during World War I.
1940–45 German forces overrun Norway in 60 days and exterminate half of Norway's Jewish population, before the country is liberated in May 1945.
1960s The discovery of oil and gas in the North Sea leads to greater economic prosperity.
1981 Gro Harlem Brundtland becomes Norway's first female prime minister.
2005 Prime Minister Kjell Bodevik is defeated in the general elections, and is replaced by Labour candidate Jens Stolenberg.
2011 Right-wing extremist Anders Breivik kills 77 people in a shooting spree on litøya island and the bombing of a government building in Oslo.
2013 Oslo surpasses Tokyo as the world's most expensive city to live in.

ARRIVAL AND DEPARTURE

The four busiest **airports** for budget travellers are Oslo, Bergen, Trondheim and Stavanger. The main low-cost carriers are Ryanair, which serves Oslo, and Norwegian (ⓦnorwegian.no), which covers all main Norwegian cities. SAS

NORWAY

```
0          250
   kilometres
```

Metres
2000
1000
400
0

NORWEGIAN SEA

Arctic Circle

HIGHLIGHTS
① Oslo Opera House
② Grünerløkka
③ Norwegian Canning Museum
④ Bryggen
⑤ Balestrand
⑥ Lofoten
⑦ Northern Lights

Nordkapp
Honningsvåg
Hammerfest
Kirkenes
⑦
Alta   Lakselv
Tromsø   RUSSIA
             Karasjok
⑥ Lofoten
Islands   Narvik
Svolvær
Å   Kiruna
Bodø
Fauske
Mo-i-Rana

SWEDEN

Gulf of Bothnia

FINLAND

24

Trondheim
Ålesund   Åndalsnes
Geirangerfjord   Østersund
Nordfjord   Dombås
           Jostedalsbreen
Stryn   Glacier
⑤ Balestrand Mundal
Sognefjord Flåm
Bergen   Finse
⑥   Lillehammer
          ①
② OSLO
Haugesund   JOTUNHEIMEN
            NATIONAL PARK
        Preikestolen
        (Pulpit Rock)   Sandefjord
Stavanger   Larvik
③
        Kristiansand

HELSINKI

STOCKHOLM

TALLINN
ESTONIA

BALTIC SEA

Hirtshals ▽   ▽ Gothenburg & Denmark

(🌐sas.no) also flies to most main destinations in the country, with partner airline Widerøe (🌐wideroe.no) covering the smaller towns.

Norway's long coastline is served by Color Line (🌐colorline.com), DFDS Seaways (🌐dfdsseaways.com) and Fjordline (🌐fjordline.com) **ferry** companies; between them, they ply routes between Oslo, Kiel and Copenhagen, Bergen, Stavanger and Hirtshals.

There are international **trains** to Oslo from Stockholm and Gothenburg in Sweden and to Trondheim from Östersund. International **buses** run from various Swedish cities to Oslo, Narvik and Bodø (🌐swebusexpress.se and 🌐gobybus.se), and from northern Finland to northern Norway (🌐eskelisen -lapinlinjat.com).

GETTING AROUND

Public transport is very reliable, but in the winter (especially in the north), services can be cut back severely. Regional bus, ferry and train timetables are available at all tourist offices.

There are four main **train** routes, linking Oslo to Stockholm in the east, to Kristiansand and Stavanger in the southwest, to Bergen in the west and to Trondheim and on to Bodø in the north. Buying online can save you upwards of 75 percent on train tickets, provided you buy a few days in advance. InterRail and Eurail **rail passes** are valid in Norway, and also give substantial discounts on some major ferry crossings and certain long-distance bus routes. For timetables, check 🌐nsb.no. You'll need to use a combination of ferries and **buses**

PLANNING YOUR TRIP

Travelling the length of Norway involves serious logistical planning, since each part of the country is covered by its own baffling array of buses and boats. Furthermore, some bus routes are only open in summer. Below are some useful websites to assist you with planning.

ⓦ **nsb.no** Norway train timetables and tickets.

ⓦ **rutebok.no** National boat and bus timetables.

ⓦ **nor-way.no** National bus company connecting all major cities up to Trondheim.

ⓦ **177nordland.no** Buses and ferries in Nordland, from Trondheim northwards.

ⓦ **boreal.no** Buses and ferries in regions all over the country.

ⓦ **hurtigruten.no** Timetables and tickets for Norway's main coastal ferry.

ⓦ **fjord1.no** Boats and buses in the western fjords.

ⓦ **torghatten-nord.no** Ferries to the Lofoten Islands from the mainland.

principally in the western fjords and mainly buses in the far north. Long-distance bus tickets can be expensive, though seats are always guaranteed and tickets are usually bought on board; in addition, the country's principal bus company, Nor-Way Bussekspress (ⓦnor-way.no), offers special rates for some online purchases.

Travelling by **ferry** is one of the real pleasures of a trip to Norway. The **Hurtigruten** – "rapid route" (ⓦhurtigruten.no) ferry – still retains its traditional role of connecting remote coastal towns, linking Bergen with Kirkenes, on the Russian border in the far north with passages once a day. If you purchase a relatively inexpensive deck ticket, you can roll out your sleeping bag in the lounge at night and use the showers. The Hurtigbåt (fast coastal ferry) runs along part of this route.

Flying, if you book in advance and particularly if you are travelling long distances, is far quicker and often cheaper than taking a bus; check ⓦwideroe.no or ⓦnorwegian.no for offers.

Norway is a great place for **cycling**, but be prepared for narrow mountain roads, long distances and many tunnels that are closed to non-motorized traffic. Bike Norway (ⓦbike-norway.com) has all the information you need.

ACCOMMODATION

Accommodation is cheapest in summer, the peak season. For budget travellers as well as hikers, climbers and skiers, **hostels** provide the accommodation mainstay;

most are run by Norske Vandrerhjem (ⓦvandrerhjem.no), but there are some excellent and less regimented independent hostels.

Expect to pay 250–300kr for a dorm bed, and 500–600kr for a double room. Sleeping bags are not allowed, but bringing a sleeping bag liner saves paying bed linen costs (50kr). The more expensive hostels nearly always include breakfast in the price of the room. HI members get a fifteen percent discount. Some HI hostels close between 11am and 4pm, there's often an 11pm/midnight curfew and most hostels tend to be inconveniently located. Many hostels close altogether during the winter months.

There are around four hundred official **campsites** around the country (ⓦcamping.no), plenty of them easily reached by public transport. Expect to pay 120–160kr per night for two people using a tent. Sites also often have **cabins** (*hytter*), usually four-bedded affairs with kitchen facilities, with prices ranging between 250 and 750kr. Many campsites come equipped with a guest kitchen, lounge, wi-fi access and sauna. A Camping Card Scandinavia (CCS), available from campsites or online (ⓦcamping.no), gives you numerous discounts. DNT (Norwegian Mountain Touring Club; ⓦturistforeningen.no) maintains 460 **mountain huts** along popular wilderness routes in Norway's national parks, which range from staffed lodges to unmanned huts with kitchen facilities (pick up the key at the nearest DNT office). You can **camp rough** in any

MINIPRIS

If you book train and bus tickets and internal flights online, well enough in advance, the **Minipris**, or budget price, can enable you to travel long distances, such as Oslo to Bergen or Trondheim to Bodø, for as little as 199kr (train) and 99kr (bus).

wild area in Norway as long as you are at least 150m from houses or water sources, and leave no trace.

Hotels are generally pricey, although summer discounts can get you a double room for as little as 650kr. **Guesthouses** (*pensjonat* or *gjestehus*) cost around 650kr for a double, and B&Bs (⊕bbnorway .com) can offer even better deals. Tourist offices in larger towns can often fix you up with a **private room** in someone's house for around 400–500kr for a double. Finally, in the Lofoten Islands, **sjøhus** (literally "sea houses") and **rorbuer** (converted fishermen's cabins) can be rented from 500kr per cabin and sleep between two and eight people.

FOOD AND DRINK

Norwegian **food** can be excellent: fish is plentiful, as is the controversial whale meat, while reindeer steak and elk can be sampled in the north. However, eating well on a tight budget can be difficult. Breakfast (*frokost*) – bread, cheese, eggs, jam, cold meat and fish buffet, washed down with unlimited tea and coffee – is usually decent at hostels, and very good in hotels. If it isn't included in the room rate, reckon on an extra 55–75kr.

Picnic food is the best stand-by, and most supermarkets sell disposable barbecues for spontaneous fry-ups. **Fast-food** alternatives include kebab and burger joints, *pølse* (hot dogs) and pizza slices at any Narvesen or 7-Eleven, and sandwiches and cakes at Deli de Luca branches in Oslo, Bergen and Stavanger. Food markets sell *smørbrød*, huge open sandwiches heaped with a variety of garnishes. In the larger towns, traditional cafés (*kaffistovas*) serve

high-quality Norwegian food at reasonable prices. At lunchtime (*lunsj*), most restaurants offer a separate lunch menu (mains 140–180kr) or cheaper daily specials (*dagens rett*), while dinner (*middag*) can be prohibitively expensive. All large towns have authentic Thai, Chinese and Indian restaurants which offer cheaper meals than their Norwegian equivalents. Restaurant business hours are 11am/noon to 3pm for lunch and 4/6 to 11pm for dinner.

DRINK

Due to heavy regulation and taxing, alcohol prices are among the highest in Europe. Buying from the supermarkets and **Vinmonopolet** (state-run off-licences) is cheapest: in a bar, **beer** costs around 70kr for 500ml. It comes in three strengths: class I is light, class II is what you get in supermarkets, while class III is the strongest and only available at Vinmonopolet. In the cities, bars stay open until at least 1am, if not later; in the smaller towns, they tend to close at 11pm. Look out for the national drink, *aquavit*, served ice-cold in little glasses; at forty percent ABV, it's real headache stuff. Outside bars and restaurants, **wines** and **spirits** can only be purchased from Vinmonopolet; opening hours are usually Monday–Wednesday 10am–4/5pm, Thursday 10am–5/6pm, Friday 9am–4/6pm, Saturday 9am–1/3pm. You have to be 18 to buy wine and beer, 20 to buy spirits. No shop will sell you alcohol on a Sunday.

CULTURE AND ETIQUETTE

Norwegian people are generally scrupulously polite, helpful and self-deprecating. The famous **Nordic reserve** is apparent, but usually evaporates under the influence of direct friendliness or, failing that, alcohol – which Norwegians consume in large quantities.

In most restaurants it's common to round up the bill, whereas in upmarket places a ten percent **tip** is generally expected. Almost everyone speaks excellent English, even in the most isolated towns.

NORWEGIAN

	NORWEGIAN	PRONUNCIATION
Yes	*Ja*	Ya
No	*Nei*	Ney
Please	*Vær så snill*	Veyr saw snil
Thank you	*Takk*	Takk
Hello/Good day	*God morgen/God dag*	God mor-gan/Go-daag
Goodbye	*Adjø*	Ad-yur
Excuse me	*Unnskyld*	Ewn-shewl
Where is?	*Hvor er…?*	Vor ayr…?
Good	*God*	God
Bad	*Dårlig*	Dawr-lig
Near	*Nær*	Neyr
Far	*Langt*	Laangt
Cheap	*Billig*	Billig
Expensive	*Dyrt*	Deert
Open	*Åpen*	Aww-pen
Closed	*Stengt*	Stengt
Today	*I dag*	Ee-daag
Yesterday	*I går*	Ee-gawr
Tomorrow	*I morgen*	Ee maw-ren
How much is it?	*Hvor myer koster det?*	Vor mew-e kaws-ter de?
What time is it?	*Hva er klokka?*	Vaa eyr klaw-ka?
I don't understand	*Jeg forstår ikke*	Yai fawr-stawr ik-ke
Do you speak English?	*Snakker du engelsk?*	Snack-er doo eyng-elsk?
Help!	*Hjelp!*	Yelp!
Cheers!	*Skål!*	Skol!
One	*En*	En
Two	*To*	Taw
Three	*Tre*	Trey
Four	*Fire*	Fee-reh
Five	*Fem*	Fem
Six	*Seks*	Seks
Seven	*Sju*	Shoo
Eight	*Åtte*	Aw-teh
Nine	*Ni*	Nee
Ten	*Ti*	Tee

24

SPORTS AND OUTDOOR ACTIVITIES

Every type of snow-based sport is enjoyed in Norway, but **skiing** (both cross-country and downhill) is the national winter pastime and is taken very seriously indeed. In the north of the country, **dogsledding** and **snowmobile trips** can also help you make the most of the snow, though you pay dearly for the privilege, while **sailing** and **kayaking** are great ways to enjoy the western fjord region. The chill, clear waters around the Lofoten Islands are prime **snorkelling**, **diving** and **whale-watching** territory, while Norway's vast national parks are a hiker's dream. There are plentiful hiking and climbing routes, as well as glacier walk excursions, with transport details and maps available from local tourist offices and DNT offices.

COMMUNICATIONS

Most accommodation options offer (usually) **free wi-fi** access, and most libraries have free internet access for at least 15 minutes at a time. **Post office** opening hours are Monday to Friday 9am to 5pm, Saturday 10am to 2pm. Most public phones only accept **phonecards**, available in a variety of denominations from kiosks.

EMERGENCY NUMBERS
Police ❶ 112; Ambulance ❶ 113; Fire
❶ 110.

EMERGENCIES

Violent crime is extremely rare, hence the national shock at the 2011 massacre of 77 civilians by a right-wing extremist. Hotels, pharmacies and tourist offices have lists of local **doctors** and dentists. Norway is not in the EU, but reciprocal health agreements mean EU citizens get free hospital treatment with an EHIC card.

INFORMATION

Every town has a helpful **tourist office** (⊚visitnorway.com). Many book accommodation, some rent out bikes and change money. During the high season – late June to August – they normally open daily for long hours; outside of these months, they mostly adopt shop hours, and many close down altogether in winter. Some cities, such as Oslo, Bergen and Stavanger, also have local DNT offices (Den Norske Turistforening; ⊚turistofreningen.no) which stock hiking maps and information on Norway's national parks.

MONEY AND BANKS

Norway's currency is the **krone** (kr), divided into 100 øre. Coins come in 50 øre, 1kr, 5kr, 10kr and 20kr denominations; notes are in 50kr, 100kr, 200kr, 500kr and 1000kr denominations. At the time of writing €1 = 7.80kr; £1 = 9kr; and US$1 = 5.90kr.

Banking hours are Monday to Friday 8am to 3pm, Thursday till 5pm. Most airports and some train stations have exchange offices, open evenings and weekends. **ATMs** are commonplace even in the smaller towns, and credit cards are accepted pretty much everywhere.

OPENING HOURS AND HOLIDAYS

Supermarkets are open Monday to Friday 9am to 9pm and on Saturdays 9am to 6pm. Opening hours for **shops** are Monday to Wednesday and Friday 10am to 5pm, Thursday 10am to 7pm, Saturday 10am to 2pm. Almost everything is closed on Sunday, the main exceptions being newspaper and snack-food kiosks (*Narvesen*) and takeaway food stalls. Most businesses are closed on **public holidays**: January 1, Maundy Thursday, Good Friday, Easter Sunday and Monday, May 1 (Labour Day), Ascension Day (mid-May), May 17 (Norway's National Day), Whit Monday, December 25 and 26.

Oslo

Today's **OSLO** is largely the work of the late nineteenth and early twentieth centuries, an era reflected in the wide avenues, dignified parks and gardens, solid buildings and long, classical vistas. Oslo's residents enjoy the trappings of metropolitan life that are a stone's throw from dense forest and sandy beaches.

24

WHAT TO SEE AND DO

Once unfairly dubbed one of the world's most boring capitals, Oslo has been on the up in recent years. The city is blessed with a clutch of first-rate museums and sights, a growing number of (admittedly generally expensive) cafés and restaurants, and a hip bar, clubbing and live music scene, all of which will keep you happily occupied for a few days.

Oslo Cathedral and Stortinget

The **cathedral** (Domkirke; Mon–Thurs & Sun 10am–4pm, Fri 4pm–midnight, Sat midnight–6am, 10am–4pm) is located just off Karl Johans gate. Its elegant interior and striking altarpiece are well

---

STUDENT AND YOUTH DISCOUNTS
Students and under-26s nearly always get a discount on transport on presentation of an **ISIC** card, as well as about thirty percent off most sights and museums and inexpensive meals in some student restaurants.

24

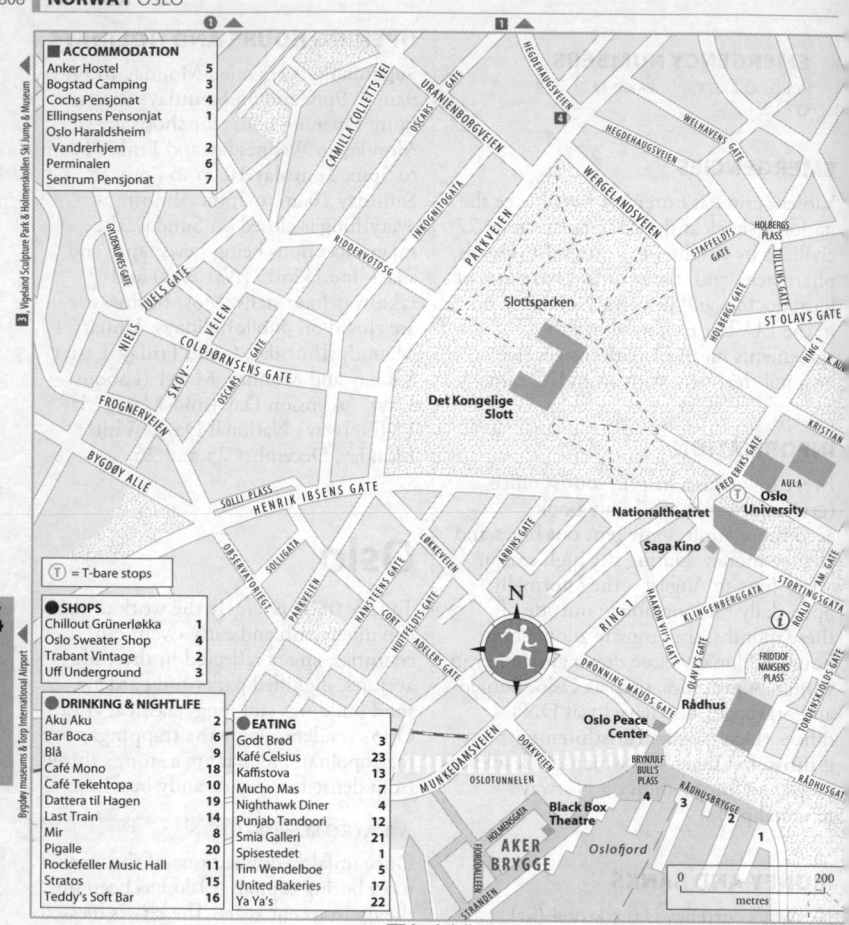

ACCOMMODATION

Anker Hostel	5
Bogstad Camping	3
Cochs Pensjonat	4
Ellingsens Pensjonat	1
Oslo Haraldsheim Vandrerhjem	2
Perminalen	6
Sentrum Pensjonat	7

ⓣ = T-bare stops

SHOPS

Chillout Grünerløkka	1
Oslo Sweater Shop	4
Trabant Vintage	2
Uff Underground	3

DRINKING & NIGHTLIFE

Aku Aku	2
Bar Boca	6
Blå	9
Café Mono	18
Café Tekehtopa	10
Dattera til Hagen	19
Last Train	14
Mir	8
Pigalle	20
Rockefeller Music Hall	11
Stratos	15
Teddy's Soft Bar	16

EATING

Godt Brød	3
Kafé Celsius	23
Kaffistova	13
Mucho Mas	7
Nighthawk Diner	4
Punjab Tandoori	12
Smia Galleri	21
Spisestedet	1
Tim Wendelboe	5
United Bakeries	17
Ya Ya's	22

Bus to Bygdøy Museum   Ferry to Bygdøy Museums

worth a visit. From here, it's a brief stroll up Karl Johans gate to the **Stortinget**, the parliament building, an imposing chunk of neo-Romanesque architecture that was completed in 1866. In front of the parliament, a narrow park-piazza flanks Karl Johans gate; in summer, it teems with promenading city folk, while in winter, people flock to its floodlit open-air skating rinks.

National Gallery

At Universitetsgata 13, you'll find the **National Gallery** (Nasjonalgalleriet; daily 10am–5pm, Thurs until 7pm; 50kr; ⓦnasjonalgalleriet.no), home to Norway's largest and best collection of fine art. A room devoted to Edvard

Munch holds an original version of the famous *Scream*, and there are also wonderfully striking landscapes by Johan Christian Dahl, Caspar David Friedrich and Thomas Fearnley.

City Hall

You can't miss the monolithic brickwork of the massive City Hall near the waterfront. The **Rådhus** (daily 9am–4pm, July till 6pm; free) opened in 1950 to celebrate the city's 900th anniversary. Venture inside to admire some beautiful carved-wood depictions of Norse myths and an enormous hall decorated with a mural by several prominent Norwegian artists – this is where the Nobel Peace Prize is awarded on December 10 each year.

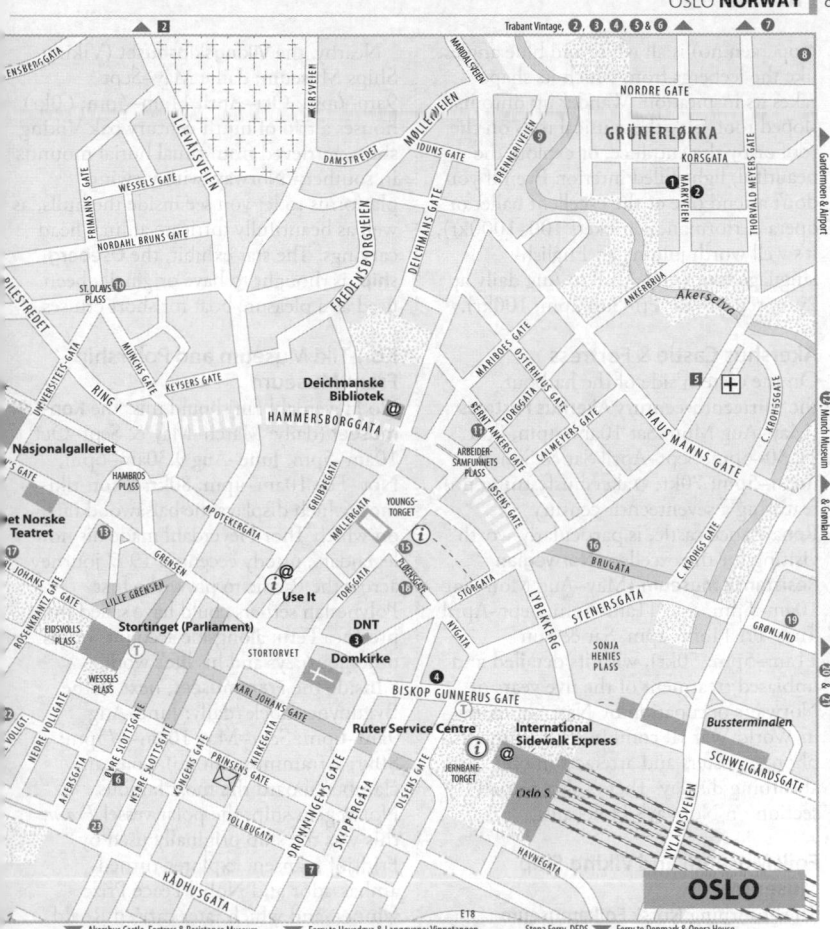

Nobel Peace Center

No visitor to Oslo should miss the **Nobel Peace Center** (mid-May to Sept daily 10am–6pm, closed Mon rest of year; 80kr; ⓦnobelpeacecenter.org), a state-of-the-art interactive museum charting the history of the world's most prestigious prize and the lives and work of its winners. The excellent temporary exhibitions often include cutting-edge shows of modern photography.

Holmenkollen Ski Jump & Museum

At the revamped **Ski Jump & Museum** (daily: May & Sept 10am–5pm; June–Aug daily 9am–8pm; Oct–April 10am–4pm; 110kr; ⓦholmenkollen .com), the ski-jump tower gives you an exhilarating view of the city and of the ski jump itself, which attracts the world's best ski jumpers during the annual ski festival in March. The absorbing museum immerses you in the 4000-year history of skiing, while the entertaining **ski-jump** simulator (separate entry fee: 50kr), complete with movement and sound effects, is not for the weak of stomach. Take T-bane line 1 towards Frognerseteren and alight at Holmenkollen.

Oslo Opera House

One of the most striking pieces of architecture in Oslo, the **Opera House** (foyer Mon–Fri 10am–11pm, Sat 11am–11pm, Sun noon–10pm;

Ⓦoperaen.no) is all white and blue angles, like the icebergs from which its shape takes its inspiration. Wander up onto its sloped roof, play the musical rods on the roof or by the entrance, or explore the beautiful, light-filled interior. Even if you don't attend one of the excellent ballet or opera performances (tickets 100–1000kr), it's well worth joining an English-language **tour** (mid-April to Aug daily at 2pm; rest of year Fri–Sun 2pm; 100kr).

Akershus Castle & Fortress

On the eastern side of the harbour, the thirteenth-century **Akerhus Fortress** (May–Aug Mon–Sat 10am–4pm, Sun 12.30–4pm; Sept–April Sat & Sun noon–5pm; 70kr; Ⓦakershusfestning.no), featuring a seventeenth-century Renaissance castle, is particularly worth visiting for the excellent **Norwegian Resistance Museum** (May–Aug Mon–Sat 10am–5pm, Sun 11am–5pm; Sept–April Tues–Fri 11am–4pm, Sat & Sun 11am–5pm; 50kr), with its detailed and unbiased treatment of the five years of Norway's occupation by Nazi Germany in World War II, combining documents, photos, posters and artefacts in one absorbing display. There's also a small section on Norway's Holocaust.

Folk Museum and Viking Ship Museum

The absorbing **Norsk Folkemuseum** (mid-May to mid-Sept daily 10am–6pm; mid-Sept to mid-May Mon–Fri 11am–3pm, Sat & Sun 11am–4pm; 110kr), at Museumsveien 10, combines an extensive collection of nineteenth-century household objects belonging to the wealthy Siboni family with folk art and an open-air display of around 150 buildings from different periods of Norwegian history.

Nearby, the **Vikingskipshuset** (Viking Ships Museum; daily: May–Sept 9am–6pm; Oct–April 11am–4pm; 60kr) houses a trio of ninth-century oak Viking ships, retrieved from ritual burial mounds in southern Norway, with viewing platforms to let you see inside the hulls, as well as beautifully intricate animal head carvings. The star exhibit, the **Oseberg ship**, is thought to have originally been used as a pleasure boat for short cruises.

Kon-Tiki Museum and Polarship Fram Museum

No Heyerdahl fan should miss the **Kon-Tiki museet** (daily: March–May & Sept–Oct 10am–5pm, June–Aug 9.30am–6pm, Nov–Feb 10am–4pm; 80kr; Ⓦkon-tiki .no), which displays the balsawood raft on which Thor Heyerdahl made his now legendary, utterly eccentric 1947 journey across the Pacific to prove the first Polynesian settlers could have sailed from pre-Inca Peru, alongside accounts of his other journeys and his life's work.

Inside the **Frammuseet**, next to the Bygdøynes dock (daily: June–Aug 9am–6pm; Sept–May 10am–4/5pm; 80kr; Ⓦframmuseum.no), you can clamber aboard the most famous Norwegian ship, the polar vessel *Fram*; this was the ship originally used by Fridtjof Nansen, explorer-turned-ambassador and Nobel Peace Prize winner, and which later carried Roald Amundsen to Antarctica in 1912, allowing him to beat the ill-fated Robert Falcon Scott to the South Pole. Complete with most of its original fittings, the interior gives a superb insight into the life and times of these early polar explorers.

Munch Museum

The **Munch-museet**, Tøyengata 53 (June–Aug daily 10am–5pm; Sept–May

---

GETTING TO THE BYGDØY PENINSULA

The leafy **Bygdøy peninsula** is easily reachable by **ferry**, which leaves from the Rådhusbrygge (pier 3; April–Oct 8am–8.45pm, every 20min; shorter hours outside summer months; 40kr on board or 27kr from kiosk), stopping first at Dronningen pier (15min from Rådhusbrygge) for the Viking Ship and Folk museums, and then the Bygdøynes piers (20min) for the Kon-Tiki and Fram Polarship museums.

Alternatively, take **bus** #30 (every 15min), which runs from Oslo S.

Mon & Wed–Sat 11am–4pm, Sun 11am–5pm; 75kr; ⓦmunch.museum.no), is reachable by T-bane or bus #20: get off at Tøyen. Born in 1863, **Edvard Munch** is Norway's most famous painter. His lithographs and woodcuts are on display here, as well as his early paintings and the great signature works of the 1890s. The museum owns one of two versions of *The Scream*, stolen in 2004 and returned about two years later in mysterious circumstances.

Vigeland Sculpture Park

Reachable by tram #12 from the centre (get off at Vigelandsparken), Frogner Park's star feature is the open-air **Vigeland Sculpture Park** (free access), which commemorates another modern Norwegian artist, Gustav Vigeland. Vigeland started on the sculptures in 1924 and was still working on them when he died in 1943. A long series of life-size bronze and granite figures frowning, fighting and playing leads up to the central fountain, an enormous bowl representing the burden of life, supported by straining, sinewy bronze Goliaths, with an intricately carved obelisk towering behind it.

ARRIVAL AND DEPARTURE

By plane Oslo Gardermoen International Airport is located 50km north of the city centre. It's served by the FlyToget express train (4.18am–midnight, 20min, every 10min; 190kr; ⓦflytoget.no), though the cheaper and slower NSB (Norwegian rail) intercity and local trains also stop at Gardermoen (hourly, fewer on Sat; 30min; 120kr). The Flybussen airport bus (Mon–Fri & Sun every 15–20min, Sat every 30min; 55min; 150kr one-way, 250kr return; ⓦflybussen.no) runs to the bus terminal at Galleri Oslo. Ryanair flights land at Torp airport, located 110km southwest. Torp-Ekspressen buses connect arriving flights (1hr 30min; 200kr one-way, 330kr return; ⓦtorpekspressen.no) and the Galleri Oslo bus terminal.

By train All trains arrive at Oslo Sentralstasjon (Oslo S), at the eastern end of the city centre.

Destinations Åndalsnes (3–4 daily; 5hr 30min); Bergen (4–5 daily including overnight sleeper train; 6hr 30min–8hr); Gothenburg (up to 3 daily; 4hr); Stavanger via Kristiansand (3–5 daily, including overnight sleeper train; 7hr 30min–8hr 40min); Stockholm (up to 3 daily; 6hr–7hr 30min); Trondheim (2–4 daily; 6hr 40min–8hr).

By bus The Galleri Oslo bus terminal is connected to Oslo S by a pedestrian bridge; it handles long-distance and international buses.

OSLO PASS

Given the average cost of a museum in Oslo, if you're planning on much sightseeing, an **Oslo Pass** can save you a considerable amount of money. Available at the tourist offices, the Oslo Pass is valid for 24/48/72hr, and costs 270/395/495kr. Students with valid ID get an additional twenty percent off.

Destinations Ålesund (2 daily; 10hr); Åndalsnes (2 daily; 8hr); Bergen (3–4 daily; 10hr–11hr 30min); Balestrand (3 daily; 8hr 30min); Stavanger (6–7 daily; 9–10hr); Kristiansand (6 daily; 5hr); Trondheim (2–3 daily; 8hr 30min).

By boat DFDS Ferries (ⓦdfdsseaways.com) from Denmark arrive at the Vippetangen quay, a 15min walk south of Oslo S (take bus #60 to the centre), while Color Line Ferries (ⓦcolorline.no) from Germany dock at Hjortneskaia, some 3km west of the city centre; take tram #13 or bus #33 to the centre.

INFORMATION

Tourist office The main branch is at Fridtjof Nansens plass 5 (May–Sept daily 9am–6pm; Oct–April Mon–Fri 9am–5pm; Sat & Sun 9am–4pm; ☎81 53 05 55, ⓦvisitoslo.com), with a second branch just outside Oslo S in the Trafikanten centre (Mon–Fri 7am–8pm, Sat & Sun 8am–6pm), which supplies a comprehensive timetable booklet for Oslo. Both issue free city maps and sell the useful Oslo Pass (see box above).

Youth information The youth information office, Use It, at Møllergata 3 (☎24 14 98 20, ⓦuse-it.no), aimed at backpackers under the age of 26, provides free luggage storage and internet, and books inexpensive accommodation.

Hiking information Den Norske Turistforening (DNT) has an office in the centre at Storgata 3 (☎22 82 28 22, ⓦturistforeningen.no), selling hiking maps, equipment and DNT membership, and giving general advice and information on route planning.

City listings All information offices provide *Streetwise* – a free budget guide to Oslo – as well as the excellent English-language *Oslo Official Guide* and *What's on in Oslo*.

GETTING AROUND

By trams and bus Trams run on six lines and have 99 stops, crossing the centre from east to west. Most bus routes converge at Oslo S and Carl Berners plass.

By metro The *Tunnelbanen* (T-bane) has six lines, all of which also run along the loop of track circling the centre from Majorstuen in the west to Tøyen in the east.

By boat Numerous local ferries cross the Oslofjord to the south of the centre, connecting the city with its outlying districts and archipelagos.

24

Tickets Local transport tickets cost a flat fare of 30kr; a 24hr travel pass, available from Trafikanten, as well as ticket machines at many stops and Narvesen and 7-Eleven kiosks, is 80kr. Night buses cost 55kr.

ACCOMMODATION

Book in advance, particularly in Aug and Sept. Private rooms in family-run B&Bs (from 300kr for a single & 450kr for a double) can be booked by the Trafikanten tourist office outside Oslo S or Use-It (ⓦ use-it.no).

HOSTELS

Anker Hostel Storgata 55 ☎ 22 99 72 00, ⓦ ankerhostel .no. Enormous, clean and friendly hostel on the edge of the hip Grunerløkka district, attracting an international clientele. Amenities include guest kitchens and a bar. Attached hotel has somewhat better-turned-out rooms for 890kr. Dorm 210kr, double 580kr

★ **Oslo Haraldsheim Vandrerhjem** Haraldsheimveien 4, Grefsen ☎ 22 22 29 65, ⓦ haraldsheim.no. Best of the HI hostels, 4km northeast of the centre, consisting mostly of four-bed dorms, many en suite. Take tram #15 or bus #31 from the bottom of Storgata to the Sinsenkrysset stop, from where it's a signposted 5–10min walk. Dorm 255kr, double 610kr; breakfast included

Sentrum Pensjonat Tollbugaten 8 ☎ 22 33 55 80, ⓦ sentrumpensjonat.no. This friendly hostel has a super-central location and the most comfortable beds of all of Oslo's hostels, though the train station area does get a little dodgy at night. Dorm 290kr, double 750kr

HOTELS AND GUESTHOUSES

Cochs Pensjonat Parkveien 25 ☎ 23 33 24 00, ⓦ cochspensjonat.no. Pleasant guesthouse just north of the royal palace, with spartan rooms, some with kitchenettes. The cheapest rooms have shared bathrooms. Triple/quad from 285kr per person, double 700kr

Ellingsens Pensjonat Holtegata ☎ 25 22 60 03 59, ⓦ ellingsenspensjonat.no. Lovely B&B in a nineteenth-century home with bright, high-ceilinged rooms, some with shared bathrooms. Look for the big white house. Double 700kr

Perminalen Øvre slottsgate 2 ☎ 24 00 55 00, ⓦ perminalen.no. A very spartan hostel-like hotel in a central location, with budget prices and all en-suite doubles and singles. Dorm 340kr, double 860kr

CAMPSITE

Bogstad Camping Ankeveien 117 ☎ 22 51 08 00, ⓦ bogstadcamping.no. Large, busy campsite in a good location by a lake, 9km from the city centre, with guest kitchen and nearby restaurant. Take bus #32 from Oslo S. Two-person tent 185kr, four-bed huts 925kr

EATING

For those carefully counting their kroner, United Bakeries (Karl Johans gate 37) and Godt Brød (Thorvald Meyersgate 49) are best for freshly baked bread and doorstop sandwiches. You can also buy a bag of freshly cooked prawns from a fishing boat at the Rådhusbrygge pier, or head to the open-air market on Youngstorget (Mon–Sat 7am–2pm).

Kafé Celsius Rådhusgata 19 ⓦ kafecelsius.no. Great little café-bar in refurbished old premises off a cobbled square, with a fetching courtyard for sunny days and fresh, light dishes such as couscous salad (159kr). Tues–Sat 11.30am–1am, Sun 1–10pm.

Kaffistova Rosenkrantz gate 8 ⓦ kaffistova.com. Set in a hotel, this self-service café feels a bit like a school cafeteria but serves burgers, open sandwiches and traditional Norwegian dishes such as meatballs and reindeer cakes at very fair prices. Sandwiches from 89kr; mains from 129kr. Mon–Fri 11am–9pm, Sat & Sun 11am–7pm.

Mucho Mas Thorvalds Meyersgate 36 ⓦ muchomas.no. Cute, relaxed bar-restaurant that does a roaring trade in less-than-authentic (but still tasty) Mexican food. The portions are enormous. Mains from 100kr. Mon–Thurs & Sun noon–midnight, Fri & Sat noon–3am.

★ **Nighthawk Diner** Seilduksgata 15 ⓦ nighthawk diner.com. Immensely popular replica 1930s diner, complete with original jukebox. The burgers are not cheap (from 135kr) but are truly excellent; most dishes are organic, and the blueberry milkshakes are to die for. Mon 7am–11pm, Tues & Wed 7am–midnight, Thurs 7am–1am, Fri 7am–2.30am, Sat 10am–2.30am, Sun 10am–11pm; kitchen closes 9pm Mon & Sun, 11pm otherwise.

Punjab Tandoori Grønland 24 ⓦ punjabtandoori.no. Superb curries at bargain prices served at this simple, canteen-style restaurant in Grønland; mains from 70kr. Mon–Sat 11am–11pm, Sun noon–10pm.

Spisestedet Hjelmsgate 3 ⓦ spisestedet.vpweb.co.uk. A centrally located vegetarian restaurant with a thirty-year reputation; there's an emphasis on organic produce, and dishes are mostly vegan. Meal 50–100kr. Mon–Thurs 2–8pm, Fri 2–7.30pm.

Tim Wendelboe Grünersgata 1 ⓦ timwendelboe.no. Run by an award-winning barista, this café serves high-quality coffee that's slightly above average in price. Mon–Fri 8.30am–6pm, Sat & Sun 11am–5pm.

★ **Ya Ya's** Øvre Vollgate 13 ⓦ yayas.no. The *som tum* (green papaya salad) at this superb Thai restaurant is spicy enough to satisfy the harshest of critics, the red curry is authentic down to the tiny pea aubergines and the decor (complete with artificial thunderstorm during meal) manages to convince you that you're in a tropical Thai garden. Mains 159kr. Daily 4–10pm.

DRINKING AND NIGHTLIFE

Oslo's hippest cafés and bars can be found in the trendy

★ **TREAT YOURSELF**

Smia Galleri (Oplandsgata 19 ☎ 2219 5920, ⓦ smiagalleri.no), with quirky decor and wrought metal sculptures on the patio, is a local favourite, its imaginative dishes including reindeer heart with lingonberry-aquavit jelly and grilled monkfish with chorizo and gnocchi. Their three-, four- and five-course dinner specials (450/495/545kr) are a real highlight of eating in Oslo. To get here, take bus #37 from Oslo S towards Helsfyr T-bane and disembark at Vålerenga.

Grünerløkka area, as well as the immigrant district of Grønland. The capital also has a lively music scene, with everything from local bluegrass bands to metal to clubs featuring top DJs. For entertainment listings, consult the *Streetwise* guide, published by Use-It (see p.811).

BARS

Aku Aku Thorvald Meyersgate 32 ⓦ akuaku.no. Tiki bar with a South Pacific vibe, great tropical cocktails and a boat strapped to the ceiling that belonged to Thor Heyerdahl, on loan from the Kon-Tiki Museum. Try their signature Chilli Punch. Mon & Tues 6pm–1am, Wed & Thurs 5pm–2am, Fri 4pm–3.30am, Sat 2pm–3.30am, Sun 2pm–1am.

Bar Boca Thorvald Meyers gate 30. Tiny, friendly 1950s retro bar in Grünerløkka, with great cocktails. Live jazz once or twice weekly. Get there early. Mon–Thurs 11am–1am, Fri & Sat 11am–3am, Sun noon–1am.

Café Tekehtopa St Olavs plass 2 ⓦ cafetekehtopa.rhli .org. This busy little bar, set within a former pharmacy, draws in a student crowd on account of its quirky environs and wide range of draught and bottled beers. They also serve inexpensive pizzas, salads and omelettes. Mon–Thurs 10am–1am, Fri 10am–3am, Sat noon–3am, Sun noon–1am; kitchen closes 11pm.

★ **Dattera til Hagen** Grønland 10 ⓦ dattera.no. This multifaceted Grønland gem is a café by day and a lively tapas bar at night, sometimes with a DJ on its small, upstairs dancefloor. There's a massive beer garden and great food. Mon & Tues 11am–1am, Wed & Thurs 11am–2am, Fri & Sat 11am–3am, Sun noon–1am.

Mir Toftesgate 69 ⓦ lufthavna.no. Adorably oddball bar tucked away in a courtyard, complete with old aeroplane seats, candlelight and even a book exchange, popular with local rockers. Live music and other events three or four nights a week. Daily 8pm–1am.

Stratos Youngstorget 2 ⓦ stratos.as. Set atop a large Art Deco tower, this inviting summer rooftop bar has great panoramas and even better cocktails from a brickwork

setting. Accessible by lift. Mid-June to mid-Aug Tues–Sat 3pm–3am, Sun 8pm–3am.

Teddy's Soft Bar Brugata 3. A local stalwart, this genuine 1950s US dive bar is a good place to wind down with a beer or a milkshake. Mon–Sat 11am–3am.

CLUBS

Café Mono Pløensgate 4 ⓦ cafemono.no. Popular rock 'n' roll bar-club just by Youngstorget. Decor and music are rock-themed; you can often catch local and international bands here. Mon–Sat 11am–3am, Sun 6pm–3am.

Pigalle Grønlandleiret 15 ⓦ olympen.no. Hit the dancefloor at this popular nightclub – the city's first ever – or enjoy a sedate drink at the adjoining *Olympen* bar, decked out like an old courtroom with chandeliers. Fri & Sat 9pm–3am.

LIVE MUSIC

★ **Blå** Brenneriveien 9c ⓦ blaaoslo.no. Cultural nightspot that's rated in the top 100 jazz clubs in the world, featuring primarily live jazz, but DJs, salsa and metal nights, public debates and poetry readings feature too. Open daily, hours dependent on acts; till 3.30am at weekends.

Last Train Karl Johans gate 45 ☎ 22 41 52 93, ⓦ lasttrain .no. Premier hard rock club with great live bands and gritty decor. Mon–Fri 3pm–3.30am, Sat 6pm–3.30am.

Rockefeller Music Hall Torggata 16 ⓦ rockefeller.no. One of Oslo's major concert venues, hosting well-known and up-and-coming bands – mostly rock or alternative.

ENTERTAINMENT

Black Box Theatre Stranden 3 ⓦ blackbox.no. Cutting-edge alternative dance and theatre at this arty venue in Aker Brygge.

Saga Kino Stortingsgata 28 ⓦ osloklno.no. Six-screen cinema showing the latest Hollywood blockbusters and other international films. Tickets around 100kr.

SHOPPING

Chillout Grünerløkka Markveien 55 ⓦ chillout.no. Excellent travel shop stocking a wide range of guidebooks, maps and travel gear, with a little café serving perk-me-ups to assist with the browsing. Mon–Fri 10am–7pm, Sat 10am–6pm, Sun noon–6pm.

Oslo Sweater Shop Biskop Gunnerus' gate 3 ⓦ shopatnorway.com. Classic Norwegian sweaters are not known for being affordable, but this shop – the largest selection in the city – frequently has items on sale. Also sells trolls, shoes and *bunads* (national dress). Mon–Fri 10am–6pm, Sat 10am–3pm.

Trabant Vintage Markveien 56 ⓦ trabantclothing.com. Pick up vintage and vintage-inspired fashions at this impeccably cool Grünerløkka boutique. Other location at Youngstorvet 4 specializes in rock-related designs. Mon–Fri noon–6pm, Sat 11am–5pm.

24

JOTUNHEIMEN NATIONAL PARK

North of Oslo, 1151-square-kilometre **Jotunheimen** is the country's largest and most popular national park. Its valleys, lakes and mountains are a veritable playground for hikers and climbers. The park boasts northern Europe's highest peak, Galdhøpiggen (2469m), Sognefjellet – thought to be Norway's most scenic road (and a tough challenge for serious cyclists)– and numerous trails with DNT staffed huts along most of them. Popular hikes include the precarious Besseggen ridge, which scythes its way between two glacial lakes; the Hurrungane massif, with fabulous views from the summit of Fanaråken (2069m); and Galdhøpiggen, a tough day-hike showcasing some dramatic glaciers. You'll need to equip yourself with Staten kartveerk's *Jotunheimen Aust* and *Jotunheimen Vest* maps, and Oslo's DNT office (see p.811) can help you with trip planning. Public transport to the park only runs between late June and mid-August, so check schedules in advance.

UFF UnderGround Storgata 1 ⓦuffnorge.org. Special branch of the popular charity shop, with added cool – the clothing here tends towards youth- and streetwear, with some genuine treasures to be found. Mon–Fri 11am–7pm, Sat 11am–6pm.

DIRECTORY

Embassies and consulates Canada, Wergelandveien 7, 4th Floor ☏ 22 99 53 00; Ireland, Håkon VII's gate 1, 5th Floor ☏ 22 01 72 00; UK, Thomas Heftyes gate 8 ☏ 23 13 27 00; US, Henrik Ibsens gate 48 ☏ 22 44 85 50.

Exchange Forex, Fridtjof Nansens plass 6 & Oslo S.

Hospital Oslo Kommunale Legevakten, Storgata 40 ☏ 22 93 22 93. 24hr emergency clinic.

Internet International Sidewalk Express (Oslo S, next to west exit; 24hr; 30kr/hr).

Left luggage Oslo S (daily 4.30am–1am) has luggage lockers, as does Use-It (see p.811); 24hr from 50kr.

Pharmacy Jernbanetorgets Apotek (24hr), Jernbanetorget 4b ☏ 23 35 81 00, opposite Oslo S.

Post office Prinsens gate and Kikegate (Mon–Fri 9am–6pm, Sat 9am–3pm).

Southern Norway

Regular trains run from Oslo to the lively harbour town of **Stavanger** on the south coast via Kristiansand. Near Stavanger, the spectacular **Lysefjord** accounts for some of the most dramatic landscape in this half of the country and features one of Norway's biggest hiking attractions: **Preikestolen (Pulpit Rock)** – a dramatic clifftop viewpoint overlooking the fjord far below. The region's forests provide ample opportunity for camping and walking, while watersports, sailing in particular, are popular on the many lakes

and beaches; and Stavanger has a vibrant harbourside bar and restaurant scene.

STAVANGER

STAVANGER is a breezily charming seaside city that has grown sleek and prosperous as the hub of Norway's oil industry. The presence of a thriving university gives the town a real buzz, and there's a number of excellent but unpretentious bars that wouldn't be out of place in any of the Scandinavian capitals.

WHAT TO SEE AND DO

The heart-shaped pond, **Breiavatnet**, in the compact town centre is a helpful reference point; the twelfth-century **Norman cathedral** (June–Aug daily 11am–7pm; Sept–May Mon–Sat 11am–4pm; free) is just north of here and the pretty harbour is visible from the cathedral steps.

Stavanger's delightful **old town** is just northwest of the cathedral – stroll around the charming cobbled streets and unique shops or drop into the entertaining **Norwegian Canning Museum** at Øvre Strandgate 88 (daily 10am–4pm; 70kr), part of the multi-site **Stavanger Museum** (ⓦmuseumstavanger.no), which takes you through the twelve-step process of canning fish – a traditional local industry – from the salting to the smoking and packing; freshly smoked sardines are available to taste. Further east along the harbour, the superb **Norwegian Petroleum Museum** (daily June–Aug 10am–7pm; Sept–May Mon–Sat 10am–4pm, Sun 10am–6pm; 100kr; ⓦnorskolje.museum .no) is a slick, well-designed, interactive space lovingly detailing the history of Norway's most important industry. A definite must.

ARRIVAL AND DEPARTURE

By plane The airport, 15km south of the city, is connected to the bus station by regular *flybussen* (daily from 3.30am–12.30am, Sat till 2.20am; every 20–30min; 20min; 100kr one-way, 150kr return).

By train The train station is on Jernbaneveien, facing Breiavatnet, in the city centre by the small lake.

Destinations Oslo via Kristiansand (2–4 daily; 8–9hr).

By bus The bus terminal is right next to the train station.

Destinations Bergen (up to 12 daily; 5hr 15min–6hr); Kristiansand (2–4 daily; 4hr 15min).

By boat International ferries from Denmark arrive at the town's northernmost quay, by Sandvigå. Domestic ferries to Bergen and nearby towns leave from Jorenholmen on the eastern side of the harbour.

Destinations Bergen (3–5 daily; 4hr); Hirsthals, Denmark (1 daily; 10–12hr); Haugesune (2–4 daily; 1hr 20min).

INFORMATION

Tourist office Opposite the cathedral at Domkirkeplassen 3 (June–Aug daily 9am–8pm; Sept–May Mon–Fri 9am–4pm, Sat 9am–2pm; ☎ 51 85 92 00, ⓦ regionstavanger.com).

ACCOMMODATION

Budget accommodation anywhere near the centre is hard to come by; book ahead.

Mosvangen Vandrerhjem Henrik Ibsengate 19 ☎ 51 54 36 36, ⓦ vandrerhjem.no. Basic but comfortable hostel (summer only), right next to *Stavanger Camping Mosvangen*. Free internet; breakfast 50kr. Dorm 200kr, double 545kr

Stavanger Bed and Breakfast Vikedalsgate 1a ☎ 51 56 25 00, ⓦ stavangerbedandbreakfast.no. Extremely popular B&B near the centre with cosy rooms (some with own showers), the best breakfast in town, a book

exchange and nightly waffles and coffee for guests. Double 790kr

Stavanger Camping Mosvangen Thensvoll 1b ☎ 51 53 29 71, ⓦ stavangercamping.no. Campsite by a lake, 25min walk from the centre (take bus #4 and ask for directions). Open April–Sept. 40kr per person, plus 80kr per tent, cabins from 450kr

EATING

Akropolis Greek Restaurant Sølvberggata 14 ⓦ akropolis-stavanger.com. Authentic Greek spot for those hankering for *moussaka*, grilled meats, big salads and more. The Sunday lunch buffet is particularly good value (190kr). Daily 11am–midnight.

★ **Bøker & Børst** Øvre Holmegate 32 ⓦ bokerogborst .webs.com. Relaxed, book-lined café-bar on a street of candy-coloured houses. There's a regular calendar of events with jazz nights, local folk-pop bands and DJs every Sat. Daily 10am–2am.

Food Story Hospitalgata 15 ⓦ foodstory.no. Deli and café specializing in organic food and innovative dishes, such as salad with marinated beef and baked cod in blood orange butter sauce, as well as focaccia and sandwiches. Mains 169–199kr. Mon–Sat 10am–4pm.

Naree Thai Breigata 22 ⓦ nareethairestaurant.no. Cheap and cheerful Thai restaurant, popular with visitors and the capital's Thai population, with some great spicy dishes. Lunch mains 79–89kr; dinner mains from 140kr. Mon–Thurs noon–10pm, Fri & Sat noon–11pm, Sun 1–10pm.

DRINKING AND NIGHTLIFE

Checkpoint Charlie Larshertevigsgate 5 ⓦ checkpoint .no. Student favourite, combining Eastern-bloc chic and loud indie and rock music, as well as DJs and live music several nights a week. The monthly "Forbidden Emotions" night (on Thurs), playing songs you'd otherwise be too embarrassed to request, is a highlight. Daily 7pm–3.30am.

★ **Sting** Valberget 3 ⓦ cafe-sting.no. This charming café-bar serves wine by weight, as well as decently priced food. Live music, poetry readings, art exhibitions and jazz

24

PREIKESTOLEN (PULPIT ROCK)

The region's biggest highlight, **Pulpit Rock** is responsible for one of Norway's most arresting images: people balancing precariously on the edge of the sheer cliff with a 604m drop into Lysefjord below. In the summer months, two separate companies – **Boreal** (ⓦ boreal.no) and **Tide Reiser** (ⓦ tideresier.no) – run combination boat-and-bus return trips to the start of the trail (from 140kr). Ferries leave for Tau from the Stavanger pier (every 30min; 45min; 45kr one-way), followed by buses (85kr one-way) to the *Preikestolhytta Fjellstue & Vandrerhjem* (ⓦ preikestolenfjellstue.no), Preikestolen's lodge/youth hostel at the foot of the trail. The hike up to Pulpit Rock consists of an uneven, sometimes steep, path strewn with large rocks, along with stretches of boggy ground. The highest section of the trail runs right by the cliff edge and the view of Lysefjord from the top of the cliff is vertigo-inducingly incredible. Reasonably fit hikers can make it to the top in an hour and a half; sturdy footwear is essential.

in the tiny downstairs club, plus an outdoor terrace at back with harbour views. Mon–Thurs noon–midnight, Fri & Sat noon–2am, Sun 3pm–midnight.

Bergen and the fjords

The **fjords** are the most familiar and alluring image of Norway – huge forested clefts in the landscape which dwarf the large ferries that pass along them. Bergen is a handy springboard for the fjords, notably the **Flåm valley** and its inspiring mountain railway, which trundles down to the Aurlandsfjord, a tiny arm of the mighty **Sognefjord** – Norway's longest and deepest. North of the Sognefjord, **Nordfjord** is the smaller and less stimulating, though there's superb compensation in the **Jostedalsbreen** glacier (Europe's largest), which nudges the fjord from the east. The tiny S-shaped **Geirangerfjord**, further north again, is magnificent too – narrow, sheer and rugged.

BERGEN

Norway's first capital, **BERGEN** is now the second-biggest city in Norway but somehow doesn't feel like it, perhaps because of its air of calm, and the cobbled streets of its centre are remarkably easy to walk around. It's one of the rainiest places in rainy Norway, but benefits from a lovely setting among seven hills, and is altogether one of the country's most enjoyable cities, with a lively student scene.

WHAT TO SEE AND DO

There's plenty to see in Bergen, from fine old buildings to a series of good museums. The city is also in the heart of **fjord country**, within easy reach of some of Norway's most stunning scenic attractions.

Torget and Bryggen

The obvious place to start a visit is **Torget**, an appealing harbourside plaza that's home to the best fish market in the country.

From here, it's a short stroll round to **Bryggen**, where a string of distinctive, brightly painted wooden buildings (now a UNESCO protected site) lines the waterfront. These once housed the city's merchants and now hold shops, restaurants and bars. Although most of the original structures were destroyed by fire in 1702, they carefully follow the original Hanseatic German design. Among them, the **Hanseatic Museum** (May–Sept daily 9am–5pm; rest of year Tues–Sat 11am–2pm, Sun 11am–4pm; 60kr; ⊚www .museumvest.no), an early eighteenth-century merchant's dwelling kitted out in late Hansa style, is the most diverting.

Nearby, the **Bryggens Museum** (mid-May to Aug daily 10am–4pm; Sept to mid-May Mon–Fri 11am–5pm, Sat noon–3pm, Sun noon–4pm; 70kr) features a series of imaginative exhibitions that attempts to re-create local medieval life. To get the most out of these two museums, it's worth taking the **tour** (June–Aug daily at 11am & noon at Bryggens Museum; 120kr), which takes in both.

Rasmus Meyer Samlinger

The pick of Bergen's four art museums is the **Rasmus Meyer Samlinger**, at Rasmus Meyers Allé 7 (daily 11am–5pm; closed Mon mid-Sept to mid-May; 100kr), which holds an extensive collection of Norwegian paintings spread across four buildings spanning the eighteenth to early twentieth centuries, including several works by Edvard Munch and beautiful landscapes by Thomas Fearnley and J.C. Dahl.

Aquarium and VilVite

Bergen's other attractions include the large **Aquarium** at Nordnessbakken 4 (daily 9am–7pm May–Aug; Sept–April 10am–6pm; 150–200kr; ⊚akvariet.no), featuring a shark tunnel and fish and sea mammals from around the world. For hands-on fun, it's well worth heading to **VilVite** at Thormølensgate 51 (late June to mid-Aug daily 10am–5pm, mid-Aug to late June Tues–Fri 9am–3pm, Sat & Sun 10am–5pm; 180kr; ⊚vilvite.no), a superb interactive science museum where you can defy gravity by riding a bicycle upside down.

24

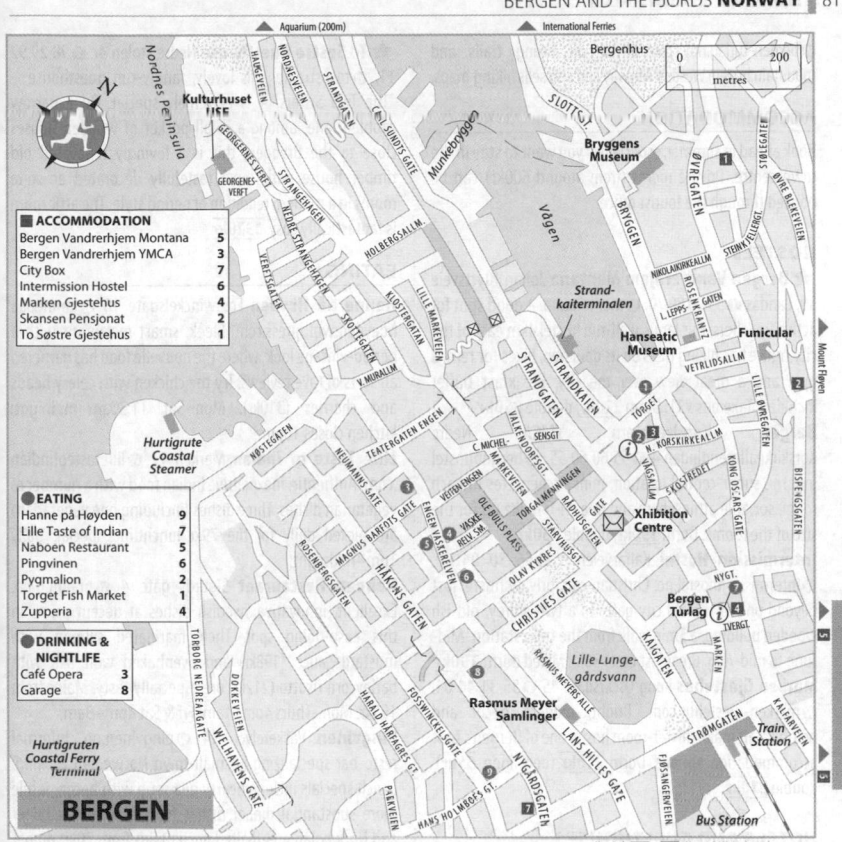

ARRIVAL AND DEPARTURE

By plane The airport, 20km south of the city, is connected to the bus station by regular *flybussen* (every 13–20min. 5am–9pm, Sat till 4pm; 45min; 100kr; w flybussen.no), which stops at Torget, the main bus station and the *Radisson SAS Royal Hotel.*

By train The train station faces Strømgaten, a 5min walk southeast of the head of the harbour.

Destinations Flåm (via Myrdal and Voss; up to 6 daily; 3hr 10min–4hr 30min); Oslo (up to 5 daily; 6hr 30min–7hr 40min).

By bus The bus station is adjacent to the train station.

Destinations Ålesund (1 daily at 8am; 9hr 30min); Flåm (up to 6 daily; 3hr); Oslo (express 3 weekly, 9hr; otherwise 1–3 daily, 11hr); Stavanger (up to 12 daily; 5hr); Trondheim (1 daily at 4.20pm; 14hr 20min).

By boat International ferries and cruise ships arrive at Skoltegrunnskaien quay on the east side of the harbour; domestic Fjord1 (w fjord1.no) and Flaggruten (w flaggruten .no) ferries and catamarans line up on the opposite side of the harbour at the Strandkaiterminalen. A bus (5pm daily; 50kr)

runs to the Hurtigruten ferry terminal near Nøstebryggen, a 25min walk from the *Radisson SAS Royal Hotel.*

Destinations Norled (w norled.no) high speed ferry to Balestrand (1–2 daily at 8am & 4.30pm; 4hr); Flåm (July–Sept only; 1 daily via Balestrand at 8am; 5hr 30min); Hurtigruten coastal ferry to Ålesund (nightly at 8pm; 12hr 45min).

INFORMATION

Tourist office Vågsallmenningen 1 (May & Sept daily 9am–8pm; June–Aug daily 8.30am–10pm; Oct–April Mon–Sat 9am–4pm; ☎ 55 55 20 00, w visitbergen.com). Issues maps and the excellent *Bergen Guide* booklet, books Norway in a Nutshell and other trips, and sells the very worthwhile Bergen Card (200kr/24hr 260kr/48hr), which allows travel on all the city's buses and free entrance to (or discounts for) most of the city's sights, including sightseeing trips.

Hiking information The Bergen Turlag DNT office at Tverrgaten 4–6 (Mon–Wed & Fri 10am–4pm, Thurs 10am–6pm, Sat 10am–2pm; ☎ 55 33 58 10,

Ⓦbergen-turlag.no) can advise on hiking trails and mountain huts in Western Norway and also sells hiking maps.

ACCOMMODATION

Book ahead in summer, especially if you want to stay in the town centre. Private rooms (from around 600kr) can be booked through the tourist office.

HOSTELS

★ **Bergen Vandrerhjem Montana** Johan Blyttsveie 30, Landås ☎55 20 80 70, Ⓦmontana.no. A good spot for active travellers, this large, well-run hostel 4km east of the city centre has hiking trails on its doorstep, bikes for rent, a gym and a great view over the city. Breakfast buffet included. Take bus #31. Dorm 220kr, double 850kr

Bergen Vandrerhjem YMCA Nedre Korskirkeallmenningen 4 ☎55 60 60 55, Ⓦbergenhostel .no. The super-central location, mini kitchenettes in each room, sociable atmosphere and free wi-fi make up for the size of the rooms. Dorm 190kr, double 950kr

Intermission Hostel Kalfarveien 8 ☎55 30 04 00, Ⓦintermissionhostel.no. Christian-run, private hostel just beyond one of the old city gates in a two-storey, old-ish wooden building, a 5min walk from the train station. Mid-June to mid-Aug. Breakfast costs 30kr. Mixed dorm 190kr

Marken Gjestehus Kong Oscarsgate 45 ☎55 31 44 04, Ⓦmarken-gjestehus.com. Bright, modern decor and helpful staff make this 21-room hostel one of Bergen's best accommodation options. Dorm 210kr (bed linen 65kr), double 810kr

HOTELS AND GUESTHOUSES

City Box Nygårdsgaten 31 ☎55 31 25 00, Ⓦcitybox.no. *City Box*'s slick, modern design extends to its booking system; you book online and use your booking number to check yourself in and print your key card at the door. Rooms are chic with minimalist decor (the cheaper ones share bathrooms); there's free wi-fi too. Double from 700kr

Skansen Pensjonat Vestrelidsallmenningen 29 ☎55 31 90 80, Ⓦskansen-pensjonat.no. This attractive seven-room B&B inside a nineteenth-century stone house sits just above the funicular entrance. Excellent views, a Norwegian breakfast and the welcoming couple who run it make it a top place to stay. Double 800kr

★ **To Søstre Guesthouse** Nedre stølen 4c ☎98 29 92 11, Ⓦtosostre.no. This lovely, family-run guesthouse – "The Two Sisters" – is extremely special. On a narrow cobbled lane, among a small pocket of wooden houses close to the Bryggen, this is a lovingly renovated old timber house with three tastefully decorated en-suite rooms in a modern rendition of period style. The attic room is fantastically cosy. 1320kr

EATING

Hanne på Høyden Fosswinckelsgate 18 Ⓦhannepaa hoeyden.wordpress.com. Sleek, smart restaurant with a period-vintage look, where the nouvelle food has garnered all sorts of rave reviews. Try the chicken with celery heads and cherries (310kr). Mon–Sat 11.30am–midnight; kitchen closes 10pm.

Lille Taste of Indian Marken 12 Ⓦlilletasteofindian .com. Authentic, inexpensive Indian food with a number of vegetarian dishes. Three dishes (including one vegetarian) are picked daily for the 79kr lunchtime special. Daily 1pm–midnight.

Naboen Restaurant Sigurds gate 4 Ⓦgrannen.no. Excellent, innovative Swedish dishes at decent prices in this easy-going spot. Their marinated salmon with mustard sauce (198kr) and ovenbaked wolf fish with barleycorn risotto (212kr) are especially tasty. Mains from 195kr. Mon–Thurs 4pm–1am, Fri & Sat 4pm–3am.

Pingvinen Vaskerelven 14 Ⓦpingvinen.no. Informal resto-bar specializing in small-town Norwegian cooking. Lunch specials include hearty pea soup with bacon, while more substantial dinner dishes feature whale, reindeer and Norwegian meatballs. Lunch mains from 70kr; dinner mains from 170kr. Daily 11am–3am.

★ **Pygmalion** Nedre Korskirke allmenning 4 Ⓦpygmalion.no. Cosy organic brick-and-candles café with modern art on the walls and a good choice of vegetarian dishes, including salads, pancakes and ciabattas. Salads 120–150kr, pancakes from 80kr. Daily 9am–11pm.

Torget Fish Market Torget. Feast your eyes on the colourful displays of fish and seafood, shop for local smoked salmon, venison salami and cloudberry jam, or grab one of the delicious open sandwiches (50kr). June–Aug daily 7am–9pm, Sept–May Mon–Sat 7am–4pm.

Zupperia Vaskerelven 12 Ⓦzupperia.no. Choose from an

LOFTY VIEWS

If it's not raining, take a ride on the **Fløibanen**, a funicular railway (every 15min: Mon–Fri 7.30am–11pm/midnight, Sat 8am–11pm/midnight, Sun 9am–11pm/midnight; 80kr return), which runs to the top of **Mount Fløyen** (320m), from where there are incredible panoramic views over the city and the fjord beyond. For even better views, take the shuttle bus from Torget (May–Sept 9am–6pm) to the **Ulriksbanen cable car** (without/with bus 145/245kr), which takes you up Mount Ulriken (620m). From here, you can hike the well-marked trail to the top of Mount Fløyen and come back down on the funicular.

BERGEN'S FESTIVALS

Bergen International Festival
(w festspillene.no) Twelve days of music, ballet, folklore and drama in May/June.
Borealis (w borealisfestival.no) A big music festival in late March, celebrating all genres of music.
Octoberfestival Beer-related festivities at Bergen's version of Oktoberfest.

almost endless menu of soups (from 59kr) including Thai chicken and reindeer with wild mushrooms. More solid dishes include salads, burgers and meat and fish mains. Two other branches at Nordahl Bruns gate 9 and Torget 13. Mon–Fri noon–11pm, Sat 1–11pm, Sun 2–11pm.

DRINKING AND NIGHTLIFE

Café Opera Engen 18 w cafeopera.org. Arty café by day that serves some of the city's best coffee transforms into a hot nightspot, playing soul, blues and funk on Wed & Thurs, hip-hop on Fri and reggae on Sat. Mon 10am–12.30am, Tues 10am–2am, Wed–Fri 10am–3.30am, Sat 11am–3.30am, Sun 11am–11.30pm.
Garage Christies gate 14 w garage.no. Near-darkness and sticky floors in the club downstairs, playing anything from rockabilly to soul, and a friendly bar upstairs. Look out for the unusual door handles – they're trophies handed out in the Norwegian equivalent of the Grammies, donated by musicians.

FLÅM VALLEY

One of the most spectacular attractions in the region is the **Flåmsbana**, a remarkable railway line that plummets 866m from the village of Myrdal into the verdant, mountainous **Flåm valley** and the **Aurlandsfjord**. The track is one of the steepest anywhere in the world, making a wondrously dramatic journey, stopping en route at the impressive Kjosfoss waterfall. You can take one of the daily trains from Bergen to Flåm via Myrdal and sometimes also Voss (up to 7 daily; 3hr 15min–4hr 30min; from 558kr) or alternatively combine the Flåmsbana with a fjord cruise with Norway in a Nutshell (see box, p.820).

Flåm

The village of **FLÅM**, the train's destination, lies alongside meadows and orchards on the Aurlandsfjord, a matchstick-thin branch of the Sognefjord. There are some excellent opportunities for both kayaking and hiking: hikers can get off the train at **Berekvam** station, the halfway point, and stroll down from there, or else walk from Flåm to Berekvam and then hop on the train. Flåm itself is a tiny village that has been developed for tourism to within an inch of its life, but out of season – or on summer evenings, when the day-trippers have gone – it can be a pleasantly restful place. The **tourist office** (daily: May & late Sept 8.30–11.30am & noon–4pm; June to mid-Sept 8.30am–8pm; 57 63 33 13, w visitflam.com) by the train station can book ferry tickets and provide information on local hikes. If you're staying overnight, the excellent *Flåm Camping* (57 63 21 21, w flaam -camping.no; late March to Sept only; camping 105kr per person, dorm 230kr, single 380kr), across the river, has a large campsite and sparkling hostel facilities. You can pick up groceries at the Coop behind the tourist office or grab a large helping of Norwegian staples at the dockside café (mains 149kr).

SOGNEFJORD AND JOSTEDALSBREEN

With the exception of Flåm, the southern shore of the **Sognefjord** remains sparsely populated and relatively inaccessible, whereas the north shore boasts a couple of very appealing villages. Pretty **Balestrand** makes an ideal base for excursions to the breathtaking **Jostedalsbreen glacier**.

Balestrand

A particularly pretty place to base yourself is **BALESTRAND**, a scenic tourist destination since the mid-nineteenth century. The beauty of the fjord aside, there is little to see in town apart from the quaint little stave church of **St Olaf**, though Fjærland and Jostedalsbreen (see box, p.821) are within easy striking distance; daily excursions from Balestrand will take you to the village, glacier museum and glacier itself for around 685kr.

24

NORWAY IN A NUTSHELL

If you're short of time, **Norway In a Nutshell** (⟨w⟩fjordtours.com) specializes in coordinating tours of the fjord country, using either Bergen or Oslo as the starting/finishing point. These range from day-trips to the Flåm valley, Sognefjord and Hardangerfjord to multi-day excursions up and down the coast. Guides are not provided; Norway In a Nutshell simply saves you the trouble of trying to coordinate the complex local boat and bus timetables by booking the relevant transport for you. Pick up the tickets at the train station or the Bergen tourist office using the reference number provided.

ARRIVAL AND INFORMATION

By bus Buses from Bergen (via Vadheim) and Flåm (via Sogndal) arrive at Balestrand's minuscule harbourfront.
Destinations Bergen (3 daily; 4–6hr); Oslo (3 daily; 8hr 10min–8hr 50min).
By boat Boats from Bergen and Flåm arrive at the small dock just north of the *Kviknes* hotel.
Destinations Aurland (May–Sept; 1–2 daily; 1hr 45min); Bergen (2 daily; 4hr); Flåm for passengers (May–Sept; 1–2 daily; 2hr); Flåm via Dragsvik and Vangsnes for vehicles (every 40min–1hr; 30min).
Tourist office At the harbourfront (mid-June to mid-Aug Mon–Sat 7.30am–6pm; rest of year Mon–Fri 10am–5.30pm; ☎57 69 12 55, ⟨w⟩visitbalestrand.no); it provides a map of hikes around the village.

ACCOMMODATION AND EATING

Cider House Sjøtunsvegen 32, ⟨w⟩ciderhuset.no. Summertime-only restaurant specializing in innovative local dishes with a Turkish influence made from organic produce and home-made cider. Give the white scallops with caviar appetizer (100kr) or *manti*, Turkish dumpling main (205kr), a try. Late June to late Aug daily 4–10pm.
Kafé Me Snakkast Holmen 13. A simply furnished café with an outdoor terrace, just behind the tourist office. They serve inexpensive local dishes, such as salads (from 80kr) and soups, plus cakes, ice cream and wine. June–Aug daily 10am–10pm, Sept–May Fri 10.30am–6pm, Sat 10.30am–4pm.
Sjøtun Camping Sjøtunsvegen 1 ☎95 06 72 61, ⟨w⟩sjotun.com. This fully equipped campsite is a 10min walk along the shoreline road. June to mid-Sept only. **30kr** per person, plus **90kr** per tent; four-person cabin **270kr**

ÅLESUND

An overnight ferry ride from Bergen, the fishing and ferry port of **ÅLESUND**, which many Norwegians consider to be the best place to live in the country, is immediately – and quite obviously – different from any other Norwegian town. In 1904, a disastrous fire destroyed the town centre, which was then speedily rebuilt largely in the German Jugendstil (Art Nouveau) style, though with original touches, such as the recurring dragon motif. The finest buildings are concentrated on the main street, **Kongensgate**, and around the slender, central harbour and the **Brosundet**. The excellent **Jugendstil Art Nouveau Centre** (June–Aug 10am–5pm; Sept–May Tues–Sun 11am–4pm; 70kr; ⟨w⟩jugendstilsenteret.no) tells the story of Art Nouveau and the rebuilding of the city through the entertaining visual "From Ashes to Art Nouveau" exhibition.

Not to be missed is the vast **Atlantic Ocean Park** (June–Aug Mon–Fri & Sun 10am–7pm, Sat till 4pm; Sept–May Tues–Sun 11am–4pm; 130kr; ⟨w⟩atlanterhavsparken.no), 3km from the town centre. As one of the best aquariums in Norway, it provides a comprehensive introduction to the North Atlantic undersea world. In summer, a special bus known as Akvariebussen runs from a bus stop just south of St Olaf's plass (Mon–Sat hourly from 9.55am–1.55pm; 40kr).

ARRIVAL AND DEPARTURE

By plane Ålesund's airport is located on Vigra island just outside of town. *Flybussen* (80kr; 25min) are timed to correspond with flight arrivals and departures.
Destinations Bergen (3 daily; 45min); Edinburgh (1 daily via Oslo); London Gatwick (2 daily via Oslo); Oslo (up to 10 daily; 55min); Trondheim (2 daily; 40min).
By bus The town's bus station is by the waterfront on Sjøgata, a few metres south of the Brosundet.
Destinations Åndalsnes (2 daily; 2hr 20min); Bergen (at least 2 daily; 7hr); Trondheim (2–3 daily; 7hr 30min).
By boat The Hurtigruten ferry docks just north of the tourist office by the harbour.
Destinations Hurtigruten ferry to: Bergen (daily at 12.45am; 13hr); Geiranger (mid-April to mid-Sept daily at 9.30am; 3hr 45min); Trondheim (April to mid-Sept daily at 9.30am; 23hr; rest of year daily at 3pm; 15hr).

INFORMATION

Tourist office On the harbourside at Skateflukaia 1 (June–Aug daily 8.30am–6pm; Sept–May Mon–Fri 9am–4pm); ☎ 70 15 76 00, ⓦ visitalesund-geiranger .com), this branch hands out a free walking tour booklet covering Ålesund's architectural highlights.

ACCOMMODATION

Ålesund Vandrerhjem Parkgata 14 ☎ 70 11 58 30, ⓦ vandrerhjem.no. Central HI hostel in a creaky but clean old building, with self-catering facilities. Dorm **300kr**, double **750kr**

EATING AND DRINKING

Anno Apotekergata 9 ⓦ annobar.no. Sleek bar, with atmospheric lighting, hardwood floors and leather banquettes, plus an outside terrace. Mon–Thurs 11am–11pm, Fri & Sat 11am–3am, Sun 1–8pm.

Lille Løvenvold Løvenvold gate 2 ⓦ home.no/lille lovenvold. Grooviest café in town, with red walls, retro furniture, great coffee and cheap sandwiches to soak up the beer. DJs most weekends. Mon–Sat 11am–11pm, Sun 2–11pm.

Lyspunktet Kipervikgata 1 ⓦ lyspunktet.as. Modern café with a massive chandelier and generous coffees. Big slouchy sofas, tacos (135kr), burgers (169kr) and imaginative meaty dishes at low prices. Mon noon–5pm, Tues–Fri 10am–10pm, Sat noon–5pm, Sun noon–6pm.

Maki Brosundet Hotel, Apotekergata 5 ⓦ brosundet .no. Immaculate, intimate restaurant, with harbour views and an always excellent, locally sourced menu. Mains average around 280kr. Mon–Sat 6–11pm.

GEIRANGERFJORD

Inland from Ålesund lies the S-shaped **Geirangerfjord**, one of the region's smallest and most breathtaking fjords. It cuts deeply inland, before terminating at the small village of **Geiranger**, which is invaded daily by cruise-ship passengers in summer. Many impressive waterfalls can be seen throughout the fjord, and the sheer cliffs rising on either side dwarf the cruise ships passing through.

It's best to approach the Geirangerfjord by bus from the north, if you can, as the views are prettiest from this direction. From Åndalsnes (see below), the nerve-racking hairpin bends of the wonderfully scenic **Trollstigen Highway** climb through some of the country's highest mountains before sweeping down to the tiny Norddalsfjord. From here, it's a quick ferry ride and dramatic journey along the Ørnevegen, the Eagle's Highway, for a first view of the Geirangerfjord.

ARRIVAL AND DEPARTURE

By bus The twice-daily bus only runs between Geiranger and Åndalsnes from late June to August (currently at 12.25 and 6.10pm; check timetables in advance at ⓦ rutebok.no; 3hr).

By boat An enjoyable alternative to taking the bus, with fantastic views, is to take the Hurtigruten ferry from Ålesund (mid-Apr to Aug only; daily at 9.25am; 3hr 45min); the same ferry heads back to Ålesund at 1.30pm.

ÅNDALSNES

Whether you're coming from the south via treacherous Trollstigen, or from Oslo by train (via Dombås) on the incredible Rauma line to the Isfjord, arriving in **ÅNDALSNES** is nothing short of spectacular. Its magnificent setting amid lofty peaks and looking-glass water makes for a good day hike up a mountain overlooking the town.

24

VISITING THE JOSTEDALSBREEN GLACIER

The **Jostedalsbreen glacier** is a vast ice plateau that dominates the whole of the inner Nordfjord region. The glacier's 24 arms – or nodules – melt down into the nearby valleys, giving the local rivers and glacial lakes their distinctive blue-green colour. The glacier is protected within the **Jostedalsbreen Nasjonalpark**, and it's possible to organize **glacier walks** on Nigardsbreen, its longest arm, with Jostedalen Breførarlag, based in Jostedalen village (June–Sept; from 250kr; ⓦ bfl.no). Walks range from two-hour excursions to all-day, fully equipped hikes. If you just want to see the glacier, it's possible to do so on a day-trip from Bergen (the ferry from Balestrand to Fjærland – Norway's book capital – from where the bus takes you to the glacier, is timed to meet the boat from Bergen), though an overnight stay in Balestrand is highly recommended. Along the way, the bus makes a stop at the diverting **Glacier Museum** (April, May, Sept & Oct 10am–4pm; June–Aug 9am–7pm; 120kr; ⓦ bre .museum.no), which features an interesting panoramic film on the glacier and climate change.

ARRIVAL AND INFORMATION

By train The train station is located at Jernbanegata 1.
Destinations Dombås (2 daily; 1hr 40min); Oslo (4 daily
via Dombås or Lillehammer; 5hr 30min–6hr).

By bus Buses arrive to the same complex as the train
station.

Destinations Ålesund (2–3 daily; 2hr 10min); Geiranger
(mid-June to Aug only; daily 8.20am, also Mon–Fri & Sun
5.15pm, Sat 3.45pm; 3hr 10min).

Tourist office North of town, next to the train station
(July–Aug Mon–Fri 8am–4pm, Sat & Sun 8am–2pm, rest
of the year Mon–Fri 9am–3pm; ☎71 22 16 22,
ⓦ visitandalsnes.com).

ACCOMMODATION

Åndalsnes Hostel Setnes ☎71 22 13 82,
ⓦ aandalsnesvandrerhjem.no. Located 1.5km outside of
town, the HI-affiliated hostel is a great place to stay
overnight. The bus to and from Geiranger stops right
outside. Dorm 290kr, double 710kr

24 Central and Northern Norway

The long, thin counties of **Trøndelag** and
Nordland mark the transition from
pastoral southern to blustery northern
Norway. Trondheim, Trøndelag's appealing
main town, is easily accessible from Oslo
by train. In **Nordland**, you reach the **Arctic
Circle**, beyond which the land becomes
ever more spectacular, not least on the
exquisite, mountainous **Lofoten Islands**.
Further north still, the provinces of
Tromsø and **Finnmark** appeal to those who
appreciate untamed, severe natural beauty,
with the lively university town of **Tromsø**
the obvious stopping (and jumping-off)
point. As for Finnmark, many visitors
head straight for **Nordkapp**, from where
the midnight sun is visible between early
May and the end of July, while those
interested in Sámi culture go east towards
Finland and the Sámi town of **Karasjok**.

TRONDHEIM

TRONDHEIM, a loveable and atmospheric
city with much of its partly
pedestrianized eighteenth-century centre
still intact, has been an important

Norwegian power base for centuries, its
success guaranteed by the excellence of its
harbour. The early Norse parliament, or
Ting, met here, and the city was once a
major pilgrimage centre.

WHAT TO SEE AND DO

Easy-going Trondheim possesses a
marvellous cathedral and several low-key
sights, as well as a clutch of good
restaurants, cafés and popular student bars.

Nidaros Cathedral and Archbishop's Palace

The colossal **Nidaros Cathedral** –
Scandinavia's largest medieval building,
gloriously restored following the ravages
of the Reformation and several fires
– remains the focal point of the city
centre (early June to mid-Aug Mon–Fri
9am–6pm, Sat 9am–2pm, Sun 1–4pm;
mid-Aug to early June Mon–Sat
9am–2pm, Sun 9–4pm; guided tours:
May to mid-Sept 4 daily; 30min; tower:
mid-June to mid-Aug Mon–Fri 10am–
5pm, Sat 10am–12.30pm, Sun
1–3.30pm; cathedral 70kr, tower 30kr;
ⓦnidarosdomen.no). Taking Trondheim's
former name (Nidaros means "mouth of
the River Nid"), the heavily restored
cathedral is dedicated to King Olav,
Norway's first Christian ruler, who was
buried here. Thereafter, it became the
traditional burial place of Norwegian
royalty and, since 1814, the place of
coronation for Swedish and Norwegian
monarchs. Highlights of the interior
include the Gothic choir and the
gargoyles on the pointed arches.

Behind the cathedral, lies the heavily
restored twelfth-century Archbishop's
Palace (May to early June & early Aug to
mid-Sept Mon–Sat 10am–3pm, Sun
noon–4pm; early June to early Aug
Mon–Fri 10am–5pm, Sat 10am–3pm,
Sun noon–4pm; mid-Sept to April
Tues–Sat 11am–2pm, Sun noon–4pm;
70kr), home to the **Norway Crown Regalia**
(70kr; combined ticket with cathedral
and palace museum 140kr) – the crowns,
sceptres and ermine ceremonial robes are
beautifully presented in the atmospheric
cellar. Another wing of the palace houses
the absorbing **Army and Resistance**

Museum (June–Aug Mon–Fri 10am–4pm, Sat & Sun noon–4pm; free). Its most interesting section is on the top floor and sensitively recalls the German occupation during World War II.

Torvet

Torvet is the main city square, a spacious open area anchored by a statue of Olav Tryggvason, perched on a stone pillar. The broad and pleasant avenues of Trondheim's centre that radiate out from here date from the late seventeenth century.

Sverresborg Trøndelag Folkemuseum

One of the best open-air museums in Norway, the **Folk Museum** (June–Aug daily 11am–6pm; Sept–May Mon–Fri 11am–3pm, Sat & Sun noon–4pm; June to mid-Aug 125kr, rest of year 70kr; ⓦ sverresborg.no) is worth the short bus ride from the centre. You can ramble along the paths that take you through the vast outdoor exhibition, which consists of beautifully preserved old buildings from different parts of Norway, including a twelfth-century stave church and tiny houses with grass growing on roofs. There's also a superb restaurant next door. Take Stavset-bound bus #8 along Dronningens gate.

Munkholmen

If you have an extra day in Trondheim, and the weather's fine, squeeze in a day-trip by ferry (every hour on the hour: late May & late Aug to early Sept 10am–4pm; June to mid-Aug 10am–6pm; 70kr return) to the "Monk's Island" from the harbour. This lovely island with a great beach has a rich history: it was originally the town's execution grounds, but later housed a monastery, which then became a prison and finally a customs house before becoming the recreation spot that it is today.

ARRIVAL AND DEPARTURE

By train The city's train terminal, Sentralstasjon, is on the northern edge of the centre, a 10min walk from the main square, Torvet.
Destinations Bodø (2 daily; 10hr); Oslo (4 daily via Dombås, Lillehammer and Oslo Gardermoen airport; 6hr 30min–7hr 45min); Stockholm (2 daily; 12hr).

By bus The bus terminal, Rutebilstasjon, is next to the train station.
Destinations Ålesund (3–4 daily; 7hr); Bergen (1 daily; 14hr); Oslo (1–3 daily; 8hr 30 min).
By boat The all-year Kystekspressen (ⓦ kystekspressen .no) passenger express boat from Kristiansund (1–3 daily; 3hr 15min) docks at the Pirterminalen, 15min walk north of the train/bus stations. The quay for the Hurtigruten coastal boat is near the Pirterminalen, another 300m or so to the north. Local buses #2 and #46 run from the Pirabadet swimming pool, in between the two quays, to Sentralstasjon.
Destinations Hurtigruten to Ålesund (daily at 10pm; 14hr); Bodø (daily at noon; 24hr 30min).

INFORMATION

Tourist office On Torvet, the main square, at Munkegata 19 (June–Aug Mon–Fri 8.30am–6pm, Sat & Sun 10am–4pm; rest of year Mon–Fri 9am–4pm, Sat 10am–2pm; ⓣ 73 80 76 60, ⓦ visitmytrondheim.no).

ACCOMMODATION

The tourist office can book private rooms from 400kr.

★ **Pensjonat Jarlen** Kongens gate 40 ⓣ 73 51 32 18, ⓦ jarlen.no. Friendly central guesthouse, each of its rooms bar the single have a gleaming bathroom, a kitchenette, a comfortable armchair and free wi-fi. Double **690kr**

Singsaker Sommerhotell Rogertsgata 1 ⓣ 73 89 31 00, ⓦ sommerhotell.singsaker.no. Charming summer-only hotel/hostel with a nice courtyard a short walk or bus ride on bus #63 from the centre. Mid-June to mid-Aug. Dorm **255kr**, double **667kr**

Trondheim InterRail Center Elgeseter gate 1 ⓣ 73 89 95 38, ⓦ tirc.no. Bargain-basement summer lodgings in the unusual, big, red and round building just over the bridge at the south end of Prinsens gate. Offers basic mixed-dorm accommodation with breakfast. No curfew and an extremely lively crowd. Early July to early Aug. Dorm **250kr**

Trondheim Vandrerhjem Weidemannsveien 41 ⓣ 73 87 44 50, ⓦ trondheim-vandrerhjem.no. Completely razed and rebuilt in 2013, this modern building calls to mind something of a designer hospital, but the dorms are spacious and only sleep 4–5. A 20min, 2km hike east from the centre, or to save your legs, take any bus up Innherredsveien and ask the driver to let you off as close as possible. Open all year. Dorm **345kr**, doubl **540kr**.

EATING AND DRINKING

★ **Baklandet Skydsstasion** Øvre Bakklandet 33 ⓦ skydsstation.no. Serves up tasty traditional dishes and is particularly famous for its bacalao (mains from 200kr). Daily: June–Aug 10am–1am, Sept–May 11am–1am.
Bar Passiar Dokkparken 4 ⓦ dokkhuset.no. Managing to straddle that fine line between trendy and pretentious, this

24

high-ceilinged spot is the pick of the bars along the Nedre Elvehavn dockside strip, not least for its roof terrace. Mon–Thurs 3–11.30pm, Fri 3pm–2.30am, Sat noon–2.30am.

Bare Blåbær Innherredsveien 16, Nedre Elvehavn ⓦ barebb.no. Run by the same folks who operate the nearby *Bar Passiar* (see p.823), this fast-moving café-restaurant offers excellent-value stone-baked pizzas (from 90kr) which make it very popular with a youthful clientele. A separate area better known as *Bær & Bar* has house and electro DJs spinning till late. Mon–Thurs 11am–1.30am, Fri & Sat 11am–2.30am, Sun 11am–1.30am.

Café 3B Brattørgata 3B ☎ 73 51 15 50, ⓦ cafe3b.no. Rock 'n' roll and indie club-cum-bar, where you can drink well into the wee hours. One of the grooviest places in town. Daily 6pm–2.30am.

★ **Vertshuset Tavern** Sverresborg Allé 11 ⓦ tavern .no. This creaky wooden tavern with tiny rooms serves up superb traditional Norwegian dishes – from the meatballs with lingonberry sauce to huge plates of smoked salmon with warm potato salad. Mains from 155kr. Mon–Fri 4pm–midnight, Sat & Sun 2pm–midnight.

24   BODØ

North of Trondheim, it's a long, 730km haul beyond the Arctic Circle to **BODØ**, literally the end of the line: this is where all trains and many long-distance buses from the south terminate. The nine-hour train trip is a rattling good journey, with the scenery becoming wilder and bleaker the further north you go. Bodø is also a stop on the Hurtigruten coastal boat route and the main port of departure for the Lofoten Islands.

ARRIVAL AND INFORMATION

By train Trains arrive to Jernbaneveien 99 on the northeast edge of the city centre, immediately next to the ferry terminal. Most days, it's possible to get off a night train from Trondheim (1 daily; 9hr 45min) and catch a ferry to the Lofoten Islands straight away (see opposite), or take a bus north to Narvik via Fauske (2 daily; 6hr 30min).
Destinations Bodø (2 daily; 10hr); Oslo (4 daily; 6hr 30min–7hr 45min); Stockholm (2 daily; 12hr); Verdal (hourly; 1hr 40min).
By bus The station for long-distance Nor-Way Bussekspress buses is located at the Sentrumsterminalen, at the far end of Sjøgata.
Destinations Ålesund (3–4 daily; 7hr); Bergen (1 daily; 14hr); Oslo (1–3 daily; 8hr 30min).
Tourist office At Sjøgata 3 (June–Aug Mon–Fri 9am–8pm, Sat 10am–6pm, Sun noon–8pm; Sept–May Mon–Fri 9am–3.30pm; ☎ 75 54 80 00, ⓦ visitbodo.com).

They give out information on connections to the Lofoten Islands, rent out bikes and also issue a detailed town and district guide.

ACCOMMODATION

Bodøsjøen Camping Båtstøveien 1 ☎ 75 56 36 80, ⓦ bodocamp.no. This year-round lakeside campsite is set roughly 3km to the southeast of the centre, near the Bodin Church. Flanked by a ridge of evergreens are 45 cabins of various shapes and sizes. Cabin 250kr, tent 130kr

City Hotell Storgata 39 ☎ 75 52 04 02, ⓦ cityhotellbodo .no. Nearly two dozen simple, unassuming en-suite rooms are on offer at this bargain-price hotel-cum-guesthouse a few blocks west of the train station. Free wi-fi. 750kr

EATING, DRINKING AND NIGHTLIFE

Løvolds Kafé Tollbugata 9. A quayside spot with a traditional and inexpensive Norwegian menu of canteen-style dishes featuring local ingredients. Mains around 120kr. Mon–Fri 9am–6pm & Sat 9am–3pm.

Rock Café Tollbugata 13B ☎ 75 50 46 33. Bodø's largest nightclub, this place sees local DJs and the occasional live band. Fri & Sat 9pm to 3am.

LOFOTEN ISLANDS

A skeletal curve of mountainous rock stretched out across the Norwegian Sea, the **Lofoten Islands** rise dramatically out of the clear waters as you approach. Snow-covered mountains loom behind tidy little fishing villages with cod drying on traditional wooden racks. Life moves (much) more slowly up here, but there's plenty to keep an active traveller occupied: the islands are perfect for rambling, cycling, sea kayaking, sailing, diving, snorkelling and even whale watching – to say nothing of the cross-country ski opportunities come wintertime. The weather is exceptionally mild, and there's plentiful **accommodation** (ⓦ lofoten.info) in *rorbuer* (originally fishermen's huts), hostels and campsites.

ARRIVAL AND DEPARTURE

Outside the summer months, transport to and from the islands is reduced, so check the timetables.
By plane You can fly to the Lofoten Islands from either Bodø or Tromsø with Widerøe (ⓦ wideroe.no).
By bus Lofotenekspressen (☎ 177 or ☎ 75 77 24 10, ⓦ 177nordland.com) provides the main bus service from the mainland to the Lofoten, departing Narvik twice daily

for Svolvær (2 daily; 4hr), then arriving at Å roughly four hours later. There are also indirect buses from Bodø to Svolvær via Fauske and other towns.

By boat The Hurtigruten calls at two ports in the Lofoten Islands, Stamsund and Svolvær (daily from Bodø: 3pm; 4/6hr; daily from Tromsø: 1.30am; 17/19hr; 300kr), while the southern Lofoten car ferry (ⓦtorghatten-nord.no) leaves Bodø for Moskenes, Værøy and Røst (June–Aug 1–2 daily except Sun; 3hr 30min/5hr 15min/7hr 15min; 163kr per person), or there's one just to Moskenes (June–Aug 6 daily, 1 on Sun at 1.45am; 4hr). Torghatten Nord (ⓣ90 62 07 00, ⓦwww.torghattennord.no) operates the Nordlandexpressen Hurtigbåt passenger express boat service between Bodø and Svolvær (1 daily; 3hr 30min–3hr 45min), as well as normal ferries between Bodø and Moskenes (2–3 daily; 3hr 15min), with stops at Værøy and Røst.

Austvågøy

The main town on **Austvågøy**, the largest and northernmost island of the Lofoten group, is **SVOLVÆR**, a transport hub and home to the excellent **War Memorial Museum** (Fiskergata 12; Mon–Sat 10am–midnight, Sun noon–3pm & 6–10pm; by appointment out of season; 50kr; ⓦlofotenkrigmus.no), a well-presented private collection of rare World War II objects that chronicle the British commando raids on Lofoten (ask the proprietor to tell you about Hitler's last drawings). Nearby **Magic Ice** (daily: mid-June to mid-Aug noon–11pm; rest of year 6–10pm; 95kr) is a quayside gallery (and ice bar) depicting Lofoten life in winter by means of giant ice sculptures, many carved anew annually by international ice artists.

ARRIVAL AND INFORMATION

By boat The Hurtigbåt passenger express boat from Bodø (344kr; see opposite) docks about 1km west of the town centre, whereas the northbound Hurtigruten (see p.804) docks in the centre, at varying times between 8.50am and 11.30pm.

By bus Lofotenekspressen buses depart Narvik twice daily for Svolvær (3hr 30min). The Svolvær bus station is located just in front of the Hurtigruten dock.

Destinations Å (1 daily, 3hr 15min); Harstad (2–4 daily; 3hr 45min); Kabelvåg (15 daily; 10min); Leknes (3–6 daily; 1hr 30min); Narvik (2 daily; 4hr 25min).

Tourist office The busy tourist office (late May to mid-June Mon–Fri 9am–4pm & Sat 10am–2pm; mid- to late June Mon–Fri 9am–8pm, Sat 10am–2pm & Sun 4–8pm;

late June to early Aug Mon–Fri 9am–10pm, Sat 9am–8pm & Sun 10am–8pm; early Aug to late Aug Mon–Fri 9am–8pm, Sat 10am–2pm; Sept to mid-May Mon–Fri 9am–3.30pm; ⓣ76 06 98 07, ⓦlofoten.info) is located just off the main town square near the harbour; they have maps, accommodation lists and public transport details for all the Lofoten Islands.

ACCOMMODATION

Rica Hotel Svolvær Lamholmen Island ⓣ76 07 22 22, ⓦrica.no. Attractive, above-average chain hotel with small but comfortable rooms, half of which offer a balcony. **910kr**

Svinøya Rorbuer Svinøya ⓣ76 06 99 30, ⓦsvinoya.no. These well-appointed red *rorbuer* range from plain to fancy, and there are standard hotel-style rooms as well as apartment-sized suites. *Rorbuer* **1050kr**, double **1550kr**

Svolvær Sjøhus Parkgata ⓣ76 07 03 36, ⓦsvolver-sjohuscamp.no. A few of the thirteen modest rooms here have bunk beds, and some share a kitchen, while others have self-contained kitchenettes. To get here from the square, turn right up the hill along Vestfjordgata, and it's to the right, past the library. Double **540kr**

EATING

Børsen Spiseri Gunnar Bergs vei 2 ⓣ76 06 99 30, ⓦsvinoya.no. Lofoten's best place for an evening meal is set within a gorgeous old 1828-era waterfront building across the bridge to Svinøya island. The speciality here is stockfish, but you could do worse than try the smoked whale roll appetizer (114kr). Reservations recommended. Daily 6–10pm. Closed Mon–Wed in winter.

Du Verden Torget 15 ⓣ76 07 09 75, ⓦcafeduverden.no. Located right at the town's central square, celebrity chef Roy Magne Berglund's creative menu features dishes ranging from sushi (135kr for a king crab roll) to pizza to classic seafood plates. It's not the cheapest but it's very good. Mon–Thurs 11am–midnight, Fri & Sat 11am–3am.

Vestvågøy

The next large island to the southwest, **Vestvågøy**, is the one that really captivates most travellers, due in no small part to the atmospheric village of **STAMSUND**, whose older buildings are strung along a rocky, fretted seashore. The scenery on this island is truly spectacular, and hikers are rewarded with stunning views.

ARRIVAL AND DEPARTURE

By plane The island's airport is located 15km west of Stamsund, in the dull administrative centre of Leknes. Destinations Bodø (8 daily; 25min).

By bus Regular buses run between Stamsund and Leknes,

24

from where you can catch another bus to Å or Svolvær. Buses arrive at the lot alongside the Hurtigruten quay.
Destinations Leknes (3–7 daily; 25min).

By boat The Hurtigruten (see p.804) calls here on its way north from Bodø.
Destinations Honningsvåg (1 daily; 41hr); Svolvær (1 daily; 2hr); Tromsø (1 daily; 19hr).

ACCOMMODATION AND EATING

Skjærbrygga ☎ 76 05 46 00, ⌨ skjaerbrygga.no. This stylishly decorated old *Rorbuer* hosts a café and an excellent restaurant featuring fresh local ingredients (mains around 250kr; the café is more affordable), including smoked whale and great fish soup. Prices drop outside of high season. Rorbuer 1250kr

Stamsund Vandrerhjem ☎ 76 08 93 34, ⌨ hihostels .no. About 1km from the port, this HI hostel with self-catering facilities consists of several *rorbuer* and a *sjøhus* perched over a bonny, pin-sized bay. You can borrow rowing boats and lines to take out on the water and barbecue your catch on the veranda overlooking the bay. March to mid-Oct. Dorm 160kr

Flakstadøya and Moskenesøya

By any standard, the two Lofoten Islands, **Flakstadøya** and **Moskenesøya**, are extraordinarily beautiful, their rearing peaks crimping a sea-shredded coastline studded with a string of fishing villages. Remarkably, the E10 road travels along almost all of this dramatic shoreline, by way of tunnels and bridges, to **MOSKENES**, the **ferry port** midway between Bodø and the remote, southernmost islands of **Værøy** and **Røst**.

The delightful village of **Å**, a huddle of old houses on stilts wedged in tight between the grey-green mountains and the surging sea, is located somewhat at the end of the E10 road, 6km south of Moskenes. Highlights in town include the **Norwegian Fishing Village Museum** (late June to late Aug daily 10am–6pm; rest of the year Mon–Fri 10am–3.30pm; 60kr), a collection of buildings devoted to traditional trades, such as the 1844 bakery which still bakes amazing cinnamon buns (15kr), and the excellent **Tørrfiskmuseum** (Stockfish Museum; early to late June Mon–Fri 11am–4pm; late June to late Aug daily 10am–5.30pm; 40kr). Extending one's knowledge of all things fishy is this great collection on stockfish, the air-dried fish that served as the staple diet of most

Norwegians well into the twentieth century. Presided over by a gregarious curator, you'll learn more than you ever wanted to know about the history of this very typical Norwegian foodstuff.

ARRIVAL AND DEPARTURE

By bus The local Lofoten Ekspressen (⌨ 177nordland .com) buses run the length of the E10, stopping at most destinations between Narvik and Å.
Destinations Reine (2–7 daily; 30min), Leknes (late June to late Aug 2–7 daily; 1hr 45min) and Svolvær via Leknes (2–5 daily; 3hr 15min); less frequently the rest of the year.

By boat Ferries sail between Bodø and Moskenes, Værøy and Røst. Buses don't always coincide with sailings to and from Moskenes though, so if you're heading from the ferry port to Å, time your arrival correctly or you'll either have to walk the fairly easy 5km or take an expensive taxi.
Destinations Bodø (2–3 daily; 4hr 15min); Røst (2–3 daily; 3hr 45min); Værøy (2–3 daily; 6hr 30min).

INFORMATION

Tourist office A helpful office is set right at the Moskenes jetty (March–April & Sept Mon–Fri 10am–2pm; May Mon–Fri 10am–5pm; early June to mid-June and mid-Aug to late Aug daily 10am–5pm; mid-June to early Aug daily 9am–7.30pm; ☎ 98 01 75 64, ⌨ lofoten-info.no).

ACCOMMODATION AND EATING

Å Rorbuer ☎ 76 09 11 21, ⌨ lofoten-rorbu.com. This collection of buldings in town features *rorbuer* of various shapes and sizes. One of the newer buildings contains a cosy bar, with seagull-egg bar snacks, and the town's only restaurant to speak of, *Brygga*, which serves very good seafood (lunch specials 125kr; dinner mains significantly pricier). Rorbuer 1750kr

Gammelgården Bakery Sørvågen, in the Norwegian Fishing Village Museum ☎ 76 09 14 88. Built in the late nineteenth century, with a gabled slate roof, this is where temporary fishery labourers would be housed in season. Now, it is possibly Lofoten's best bakery, cooking excellent cinnamon buns in an original, vintage oven. Mid-June to mid-Aug daily 10am–4pm.

Hostel Å ☎ 76 09 12 11, ⌨ hihostels.no. This quaint, remote, accredited hostel has an assortment of smart one- to eight-bedded *rorbuer* that surround the dock, as well as the facilities of the adjacent *sjøhus*, which offers comfortable and equally smart hotel-standard rooms. Open year-round. Dorm 200kr, double 420kr, rorbuer 850kr

Moskenes Camping Moskenesvågen ☎ 99 48 94 05. A mere 150m from the ferry port is this very basic waterside (and mostly gravel) campsite, with a small patch of grass to pitch a tent. May–Aug. 120kr per tent

TROMSØ

Friendly **TROMSØ**, the "gateway to the arctic", is the de facto capital of northern Norway. Set on an island, connected to the mainland by large bridges, and surrounded by dramatic mountains and craggy shoreline, it offers easy access to the multitude of winter and summer activities on offer.

WHAT TO SEE AND DO

TROMSØ has two cathedrals, a clutch of interesting museums and a lively nightlife, patronized by its significant student population.

Domkirke and the Polar Museum

In the centre of town, you can't miss the striking woodwork of the **Domkirke**. From the church, it's a short walk north along the harbourfront to one of the most diverting museums in the city, the **Polar Museum**, Søndre tollbodgate 11 (daily: mid-June to mid-Aug 10am–7pm; rest of year 11am–5pm; 50kr; ⓦpolarmuseum.no), whose varied displays include skeletons retrieved from the permafrost of Svalbard and accounts of expeditions by polar explorers Fridjof Nansen and Roald Amundsen.

Polaria

Also on the waterfront, **Polaria**, Hjalmar Johansens gate 12 (daily: mid-May to Aug 10am–7pm; rest of year noon–5pm; ⓦpolaria.no; 120kr), the city's star attraction, draws coach-loads of tourists to see the 3pm feeding of the bearded seals. This state-of-the-art aquarium combines its tanks of cold-water fish with a walk-through seal tunnel, displays about the region's fragile ecosystem and a stunning panoramic film on Svalbard.

Arctic Cathedral

Across the long Tromsø Bridge from the centre, the white, pointy, ultramodern **Ishavskatedralen** (June to mid-Aug daily 9am–7pm, Sun 1–7pm; mid-Aug to May 2/3/4–6pm; 40kr; midnight sun concerts in summer 140kr; ⓦishavskatedralen.no; bus #20, #24, #26 or #28 from city centre) is outstanding, its shape inspired by the Hoja mountain in the sea near Tromsø. It's made up of eleven immense triangular concrete sections representing the eleven Apostles left after the betrayal, with a stunning stained-glass window.

Tromsø University Museum

This excellent anthropological and geological **museum** (June–Aug daily 9am–6pm, Sept–May Mon–Fri 10am–4.30pm, Sat noon–3pm, Sun 11am–4pm; 50kr; ⓦuit.no/tmu) should not be missed by anyone with an interest in all things northern. Apart from the excellent displays on both traditional and modern Sámi culture, complete with ceremonial objects, traditional dress and household implements, downstairs you can learn about the Aurora Borealis phenomenon – how it works – as well as create your own. Take bus #37 from the centre.

ARRIVAL AND INFORMATION

By bus Long-distance buses arrive and depart from the Prostneset (car park adjacent to the tourist office).

24

THE NORTHERN LIGHTS AND THE MIDNIGHT SUN

Tromsø's northerly location but relatively mild climate has made it one of the most popular spots in the world from which to view the **Northern Lights**, or Aurora Borealis, which are seen here almost daily between November and April. Caused by solar winds as they hit the Earth's atmosphere, they light up the sky in shimmering waves of blue, yellow and green – a spectacle of celestial proportions.

In the summertime there's an entirely different Arctic phenomenon to behold: the breathtaking **midnight sun**. In Tromsø you're so far north that the sun never actually dips beneath the horizon. Head for Fjellheisen, a cable car that runs to the top of **Mount Storsteinen** (take bus #26 and ask for a cable-car return ticket; late May to mid-Aug 10am–1am; rest of the year 10am–5pm; 130kr) between May 18 and July 25 around midnight, and you'll see the sun, hovering over the horizon in the west, setting the sky spectacularly aglow.

24

ART IN TROMSØ

Tromsø has a couple of excellent art museums which are both free. The **Art Museum of Northern Norway** (Sjørgata 1; Tues–Sun noon–5pm) focuses on beautiful landscape paintings by northern Norwegian artists, as well as modern sculpture and photography exhibitions, while **Perspektivet** (Storgata 95; Tues–Sun 11am–5pm) stages cutting-edge photography exhibitions, the most recent including "Last Days of the Arctic".

Destinations Alta (late June to mid-Aug daily at 4pm; 6hr 30min); Bodø (daily at 10am; 12hr 30min); Svolvær (daily at 10am; 9hr 20min).

By boat The Hurtigruten coastal boat docks in the centre of town at the foot of Kirkegata.

Destinations Honningsvåg (daily at 6.30pm; 17hr); Svolvær (daily at 1.30am; 17hr 30min).

Tourist office Kirkegate 2, near the Domkirke (mid-May to Aug Mon–Fri 9am–7pm, Sat & Sun 10am–6pm; rest of year Mon–Fri 9am–4pm, Sat 10am–4pm; ☎ 77 61 00 00, ⓦ visittromso.no); produces a comprehensive Tromsø guide and has two free internet terminals (15min).

ACCOMMODATION

ABC Hotell Nord Parkgate 4 ☎ 77 66 83 00, ⓦ hotellnord .no. Basic but comfortable budget hotel with an all-day buffet, comfortable guest lounge, fridges in rooms and bike rental (150kr/day), 400m from the centre of town. Free wi-fi and student discounts available. Double <u>725kr</u>

AMI Hotell Skolegate 1 ☎ 77 62 10 00, ⓦ amihotel.no. Good-value family-run hotel up the hill from the centre of town, with free wi-fi, free tea and coffee in the communal lounges, and discounts for longer stays and for students. Double <u>790kr</u>

Tromsø Camping Elvestrandvegen ☎ 77 63 80 37, ⓦ tromsocamping.no. Reasonably handy waterside site, about 2km east of the cathedral, on the mainland side of the main bridge, with 55 modern and "rustic" cabins. Open year-round. Take bus #20 or #24. <u>130kr</u> per tent for two people, cabin <u>1049kr</u>

EATING

You can buy freshly caught cooked prawns straight off the boats at the Stortorget pier, and on weekdays a Thai food stall on Stortorget sells succulent spicy chicken and pork skewers (25kr).

★ **Aunegården** Sjøgata 29 ⓦ aunegarden.no. Ultra-popular restaurant and café in a gorgeous century-old building serving good sandwiches, salads from 109kr, plus coffee and heavenly cakes fresh from the on-site bakery

(try the semolina pudding with cloudberries, 97kr). Mon–Sat 10.30am–11.30pm, Sun noon–5.30pm.

De 4 Roser Grønnegate 38–46 ⓦ de4roser.no. The best coffee (cappuccino 32kr) in Tromsø is served in this refined café-restaurant whose award-winning baristas specialize in latte art. Regular dishes include a pulled-pork sandwich (135kr) and Alfredo ravioli (155kr). Daily 10am–10pm.

Kafé Globus Storgata 30 ⓦ globuskafe.no. Popular Eritrean café with a global menu that includes pitas, salads, Moroccan meat dishes and *injera* – a large, sponge-like pancake topped with mounds of spicy beef curry, lentils and wilted spinach (175kr). Mon–Fri 10am–7pm, Sat 11am–5pm.

Verdensteatret Storgata 93b ⓦ verdensteatret.no. Popular café-bar housed in Norway's oldest movie theatre that attracts an arty young crowd with its cheap lunch food, drinks, independent film screenings and pumping DJ nights. Mon–Thurs 11am–2am, Fri & Sat 11am–3.30am, Sun 1pm–2am.

DRINKING AND NIGHTLIFE

Blå Rock Café Strandgate 14/16 ⓦ blarock.no. Much-loved multistorey bar covered with rock memorabilia; doubles as a chilled café serving sumptuous burgers during the day and a hot DJ venue Thurs–Sat. Mon–Thurs 11.30am–2am, Fri & Sat 11.30am–3.30am, Sun 1pm–2am.

Driv Tollbugata 3 ⓦ driv.no. Cosy student café-bar in a waterfront warehouse near the polar museum where the food and beer is cheap and the company cheerful and welcoming. Mon–Thurs 2pm–1.30am, Fri 4pm–3am, Sat 2pm–3am.

Ølhallen Pub Storgata 4 ⓦ olhallen.no. With its cosy cellar decor and winning location (attached to the Mack Brewery), the city's favourite pub serves a full range of microbrews (67kr/pint). Mon–Fri 10am–6pm, Sat 9am–6pm.

Studenthuset Driv Søndre tollbogate 3b ⓦ driv.no. Built in the early 1900s as a fishermen's warehouse, and now dining out on its exposed beams and planking, this three-tiered student hangout never wants for its share of barflies. Live music on Wed & Thurs, and club nights on Fri & Sat. Mon–Thurs noon–2am, Fri & Sat noon–3.30am.

★ TREAT YOURSELF

Emma's Drømmekjokken Kirkegata 8. "Emma's Dream Kitchen" serves sublime locally sourced fare from Arctic char to reindeer at prices to match. At the downstairs café, *Emma's Under*, prices are slightly lower but the dishes, such as whale steak in peppercorn sauce or grilled fish, are just as delicious. Lunch mains from 139kr. Daily 11am–10pm.

TROMSØ FESTIVALS

Northern Lights Festival ⓦ nordlys festivalen.no. Six days of music, held at the end of January.

Sámi Week ⓦ msm.no. Early February festival which includes reindeer racing, rope tossing and traditional Sámi food and handicrafts held in places all over the region.

Midnight Sun Marathon ⓦ msm.no. Held on a Saturday in June; there's also a half-marathon.

FINNMARK, MAGERØYA AND NORDKAPP

Beyond Tromsø, the northern tip of Norway, **FINNMARK**, enjoys no less than two and a half months of permanent daylight on either side of the summer solstice. Here, the bleak and treeless island of **Magerøya** is connected to the northern edge of the mainland by an ambitious combination of tunnels and bridges.

Alta

A modest Northern Norwegian town, **ALTA**'s primary claim to fame is the most extensive area of **prehistoric rock carvings** in northern Europe, which are impressive enough to have been designated a UNESCO World Heritage Site. The settlement is also the only place to stay overnight if you're heading north from Tromsø towards Nordkapp, since there is only one bus daily (4pm; 6hr 30min; 510kr).

Alta's prehistoric rock carvings form part of the **Alta Museum** (Altaveien 19; May to mid-June daily 8am–5pm; mid-June to Aug daily 8am–8pm; Sept–April Mon–Fri 8am–3pm, Sat & Sun 11am–4pm; 90kr; ⓦ alta.museum .no). The museum itself has displays of rock art and some of the social history behind these carvings, touching upon the role of religion and commerce in the region. A limited local bus service – *bybussen* – runs from the main Alta bus station south to the borough of **Bossekop** and the museum (Mon–Sat every 30min–1hr; 10min).

Count on at least an hour to view the carvings and appreciate the site

(Helleristningene i Hjemmeluft), accessed along the E6. The carvings extend down the hill from the museum to the fjordside along a clear and easy-to-follow footpath and boardwalk that stretches for just under 3km. On the trail, there are a dozen or so vantage points offering close-up views of the carvings, recognizable though highly stylized representations of boats, animals and people picked out in red pigment.

ARRIVAL AND INFORMATION

By bus Long-distance buses arrive at the tourist office in the centre of Alta.

Destinations Hammerfest (1–4 daily; 2hr); Honningsvåg (2–4 daily; 4hr); Kautokeino (1–3 daily except Sat; 2hr 15min); Narvik (1 daily; 9hr 25min); Tromsø (1 daily; 7hr).

Tourist office The main branch is located at Bjørn Wirkolas vei 11, in the same building as the bus terminal (June & Aug daily 9am–6pm; July daily 9am–8pm; Sept–May Mon–Fri 9am–3.30pm, Sat 10am–3pm; ☎ 78 44 50 50, ⓦ visitalta.no). It issues free town maps, will advise on hiking the Finnmarksvidda and help with finding accommodation.

ACCOMMODATION AND EATING

Alfa-Omega Markedsgata 16 ☎ 78 44 54 00, ⓦ alfaomega-alta.no. Omega is the continental eatery; Alfa is the no-holds-barred bar, whose vague Cuban aesthetic manages to attract more than its share of fortysomethings. Mon–Wed 8pm–midnight, Thurs 7pm–1am, Fri 6pm–2.30am, Sat noon–2.30am.

Alta River Camping ☎ 78 43 43 53. This well-equipped site is set on a large green riverside plot, with tent spaces here as well as hotel-style rooms and cabins, some of which have en-suite baths, plus a sauna right on the water. Located about 5km out of town along Highway 93. Open year-round. Tent __170kr__, double __400kr__, cabin __600kr__

Bårstua Gjestehus Kongleveien 2a ☎ 78 43 33 33, ⓦ baarstua.no. Of Alta's several guesthouses, this is the most appealing, located just off the E6 on the north side of town. The eight rooms are large and pleasant enough and all of them have kitchenettes. __830kr__

Honningsvåg

The fishing village of **HONNINGSVÅG**, Magerøya's only significant settlement and a place that claims to be the most northerly "city" in the world, is your last port of call before Nordkapp – the North Cape – just 34km away.

24

ARRIVAL AND DEPARTURE

By plane Widerøe (w wideroe.no) operates flights from Tromsø and Hammerfest to Honningsvåg airport.

Destinations Hammerfest (1–3 daily; 25min); Tromsø (1–3 daily; 1hr 30min).

By bus Buses from the mainland, including the long-distance Nord-Norgeekspressen, pull into the bus station at the southern end of the village.

Destinations Alta and Skaidi, for Hammerfest (1–3 daily); Nordkapp (mid-May to mid-Aug 3 daily; mid-Aug to mid-Sept 2 daily; 45min).

By boat Hurtigruten coastal boats dock at the jetty, adjacent to the bus station, with northbound boats arriving at 11.45am and departing 3.15pm; southbound, the boats don't overlay here, arriving at 6am and departing 15min later; the northbound service is met by special Nordkapp excursion buses – details on board.

Destinations Tromsø (1 daily; 18hr).

ACCOMMODATION AND EATING

Arctico Icebar Sjøgata 1 w articoicebar.com. Opened a decade ago by two transplanted Spaniards, this large storage freezer offers a wintertime arctic experience in the spring- and summertime ice bar. 135kr entrance, which includes two (non-alcoholic) drinks. Daily: April to mid-Oct 9am–9pm.

Corner Fiskeriveien 2 w corner.no. This modern bistro serves fresh seafood (as you would expect) – try the sautéed herb-baked king crab symphony (125kr) – but also does good burgers and stews, and even whale steak (229kr). Daily 10am–11pm (kitchen closes 9pm).

Nordkapp Camping Skipsfjorden ☎78 47 33 77, w nordkappcamping.no. Set outside of Honningsvåg on the road to Nordkapp, this is a good bet for camping out in the middle of nowhere. Free wi-fi. May to mid-Sept. Tent **140kr**, cabin **585kr**

Nordkapp Vandrerhjem Kobbhullveien 10 ☎91 82

4156, w hihostels.no/nordkapp. The town's HI Hostel is a 20min walk north of Honningsvåg – and just 1km from the end of the tunnel from the mainland. Self-catering facilities, but no café or restaurant. May–Dec. Dorm **330kr**, double **760kr**

Nordkapp

While the 307m-high cliff known as **Nordkapp** isn't actually the northernmost point of mainland Europe (that honour belongs to Knivskjellodden, reached along an 18km signposted track from Highway E69), it is as far north as you can get by public transport. It's a hassle to reach, but there is something exhilarating about this bleak, wind-battered promontory, bespeckled with grazing reindeer. It is the only viewpoint in Norway that you have to pay to visit, though officially you're paying to enter the blight on the landscape that is **Nordkapphallen** (North Cape Hall; daily: early to mid-May & Sept to mid-Oct 11am–3pm; mid-May to Aug 11am–1am; mid-Oct to April 12.30–2pm; 235kr), a flashy tourist centre that contains Europe's northernmost (and possibly its most expensive) souvenir shop, café, restaurant, bar, panoramic movie theatre, chapel and post office.

ARRIVAL AND DEPARTURE

By bus Regular buses run between Honningsvåg and Nordkapp.

Destinations Honningsvåg (late May to mid-Aug 6 daily; 45min; 490kr return, including entrance to the Nordkapphallen).

THE SÁMI IN NORWAY

Norway's original inhabitants, the Sámi, have survived as reindeer herders in the north of the country for over 11,000 years. Though their traditions and culture were long under threat, both by modern society and the Norwegian state, today's Sámi are very much alive and kicking; they have their own independence day, their own flag and even their own parliament in the town of **Karasjok**. A detour to Karasjok, linked by twice-daily buses from Alta and Lakselv, is particularly worthwhile, and you can take a guided tour of the **Sámi Parliament** (Kautokeinoveien 50; late June to mid-Aug hourly from 8.30am–2.30pm; rest of the year Mon–Fri 1pm; free), visit the **Sámi National Museum** (Mari Boine geaidnu 17; June–Aug daily 9am–3pm; rest of year Tues–Fri 9am–3pm; 75kr), with its displays of traditional clothing, tools and art by contemporary Sámi artists, or take a more light-hearted look at Sámi culture at the **Sápmi Park** (Porsangerveien; daily: Jan–May 10am–2pm; June to mid-Aug 9am–7pm; mid-Aug to late Aug 9am–4pm; Sept Mon–Fri 9am–4pm; 120kr; w visitsapmi.no), an excellent high-tech theme park. A great place to stay is the *Engholm's Design Lodge* (w engholm.no), a collection of rustic cabins 6km south of Karasjok along the Rv92, which doubles as the town's HI hostel and arranges husky safaris in winter; hearty meals available.

MARKET SQUARE, WROCŁAW

Poland

HIGHLIGHTS

❶ Night out in Warsaw Live it up in the bars of the country's dynamic capital. **See p.842**

❷ Sopot Relax on the vast stretch of white sand near this lively summertime resort. **See p.846**

❸ Kazimierz, Kraków Explore Poland's Jewish heritage in this hip neighbourhood. **See p.850**

❹ Tatra Mountains Hike among jagged alpine peaks and enjoy unique mountain culture. **See p.854**

❺ Wrocław Discover this elegant gem, unspoilt by tourist hordes. **See p.856**

HIGHLIGHTS ARE MARKED ON THE MAP ON P.833

ROUGH COSTS

Daily budget Basic €40, occasional treat €60

Drink Vodka (50ml shot) €1

Food *Żurek* soup €2–3

Hostel/budget hotel €10/€30

Travel Train: Warsaw–Kraków €13; bus: €10

FACT FILE

Population 38.5 million

Language Polish

Currency Złoty (zł/PLN)

Capital Warsaw

International phone code ☏48

Time zone GMT +1hr

25

Introduction

Poland has long been a nation steeped in tradition and history, although the past twenty years have witnessed such dizzying economic development that the country is starting to feel more and more like Western Europe. Still, beneath the gleaming surface lies a culture firmly rooted in Eastern hospitality and community values, and fascinating reminders of the turbulent past are everywhere. Poland is also a land of considerable natural beauty, whose idyllic lakes, beaches and mountains provide a nice contrast to the urban buzz of the cities.

The capital **Warsaw** is a fascinating hybrid, its historic centre rubbing up against neighbourhoods of communist-era grey, glittering modern office blocks and energetic pockets of vibrant nightlife. **Kraków**, the ancient royal capital in the south, is the real crowd-puller, rivalling the elegance of Prague and Vienna, while **Gdańsk** in the north offers an insight into Poland's turbulent history as well as its Baltic-riviera beach life. In the west, **Wrocław** charms visitors with its stately architecture and buzzy student life, while **Poznań** offers a mixture of historical attractions and urban diversions that is quintessentially Polish. The **Tatra Mountains** on the Slovak border offer exhilarating hiking and affordable skiing.

CHRONOLOGY

966 AD Mieszko I unites Slav tribes to create the Polish state.

1025 Bolesław I, Mieszko's son, is crowned the first King of Poland.

1300s Gdańsk and several other northern cities join the Hanseatic League, and trade prospers.

1386 Polish queen Jadwiga marries Lithuanian Grand Duke Jogaila, creating a dynastic union between the two countries.

1410 Polish-Lithuanian forces defeat the Teutonic Knights at the Battle of Grunwald.

1500s The Renaissance sweeps through Poland, giving it significant cultural importance in Europe.

1700s Russia, Prussia and Austria divide Poland–Lithuania between them in the Three Partitions.

1863 The January Uprising against Russian authority is brutally repressed.

1918 An independent Polish state is created following the collapse of German, Russian and Austro-Hungarian empires.

1939 Poland is invaded by Nazi Germany, beginning World War II.

1945 By the end of the war more than six million Poles are dead. Soviets drive out the Nazis and occupy large parts of Poland; the country's borders shift 200km west.

1947 Polish communists win fixed elections.

1978 Karol Wojtyła, Archbishop of Kraków, is elected Pope, taking the name John Paul II.

1980 A strike in Gdańsk, led by Lech Wałęsa, leads to the formation of Solidarity, a free trade union.

1981 Communist leaders attempt to stamp out Solidarity by declaring martial law.

1990 Wałęsa becomes the first popularly elected president of Poland.

2004 Poland accedes to the EU.

2010 A plane carrying conservative President Lech Kaczyński and over 90 dignitaries crashes near Smolensk, Russia, killing everyone on board. Later that year, moderate Bronisław Komorowksi is elected president.

2011 Parliamentary elections return the moderate government of right-of-centre Prime Minister Donald Tusk to power.

ARRIVAL AND DEPARTURE

Several budget **airlines** fly into Warsaw, Kraków, Gdańsk, Wrocław and Poznań.

Poland has **rail** connections with all its neighbouring countries. Several direct trains arrive daily in both Kraków and Warsaw from Prague, Budapest and Vienna, while Poznań, Wrocław and Warsaw all have regular connections to Germany.

Several Polish **bus** companies, including Eurolines (ⓦeurolines.pl), provide services from all major European capitals to Warsaw, Kraków, Gdańsk and other Polish cities. On the southern border,

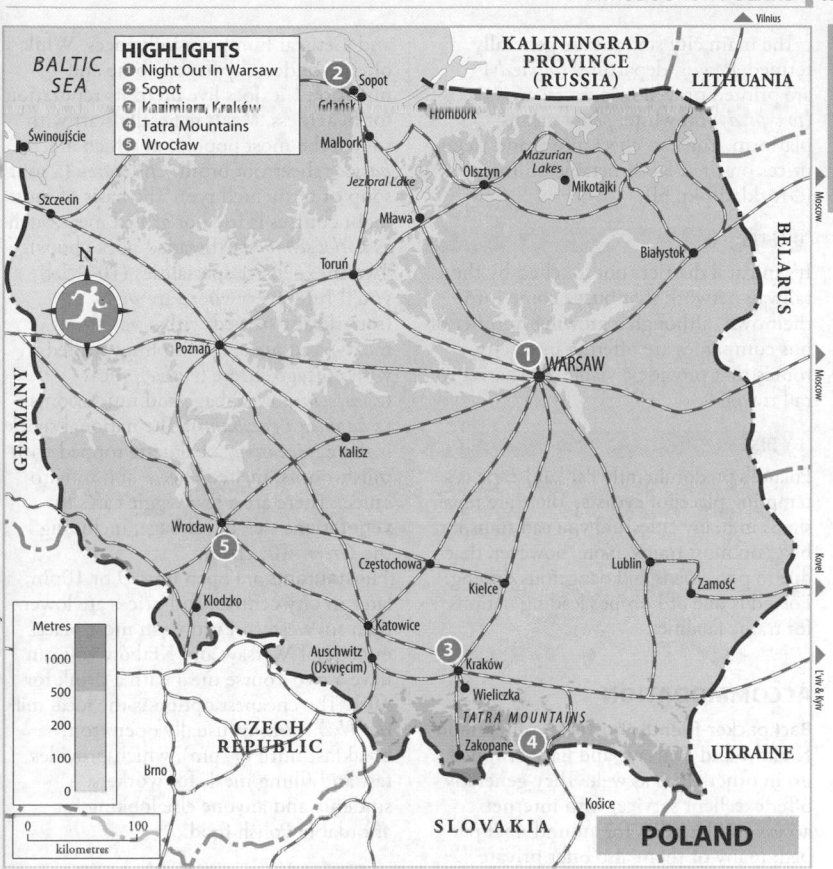

POLAND

there are daily public buses to Zakopane from the Slovakian resort of Poprad.

GETTING AROUND

BY TRAIN

The Polish railway companies operate many different types of **train**. International passes such as Eurail and InterRail are valid for all of them. If you are buying individual-journey tickets, however, beware that tickets valid for one type of service are rarely valid for another. Biggest of the rail companies is PKP Intercity, which runs InterCity (EIC), Express (EX) and TLK trains. EIC and EX trains run on premium routes (such as Warsaw–Kraków or Warsaw–Gdańsk) and only stop at major cities. They're the fastest, most comfortable

but also most expensive means of getting around, and seat reservations (*miejscówka*; 10–12.50zł) are compulsory. TLK are only slightly slower than EIC trains but are significantly cheaper, and often operate long cross-country routes.

The Przewozy Regionalne company is responsible for running Regio, InterRegio, RegioExpress and RegioPlus services; Regio are usually local services that travel at snail-like speeds and stop at every wayside halt; InterRegio, RegioExpress and RegioPlus are faster, longer-distance trains that frequently link important cities. To complicate matters further, Koleje Mazowieckie operates local trains in Warsaw and central Poland, while the Warsaw Municipal Transport company (ZKM) operates commuter trains in and around the capital.

25

The main city stations are generally termed *główny*; departures (*odjazdy*) are printed on yellow posters; arrivals (*przyjazdy*) on white; *peron* means platform. You can check times and ticket prices on the PKP timetable online (ⓦrozklad-pkp.pl).

BY BUS

It's in rural districts not touched by the railway network that **buses** come into their own, although a growing number of bus companies are offering inter-city routes that provide a viable alternative to rail travel.

BY BIKE

Poland's predominantly flat landscape is a tempting place for **cyclists**. There are repair shops in many cities and you can transport bikes on most trains. Note, however, that due to poor roads and dangerous driving, Poland is one of Europe's leading nations for traffic fatalities.

ACCOMMODATION

Backpacker-friendly hostels proliferate in Kraków and Warsaw, and have cropped up in other cities as well. They generally offer excellent service, with internet access and laundry, for around 45zł per bed; many of them also offer private doubles too. There's a small but growing choice of **apartments** and **B&Bs** in the cities, and family-run **pensions** in rural resorts. Prices in these categories hover around 100–150zł for a double room. Many tourist offices can also find you cheap rooms in **private houses** (*kwatera prywatna*; 70–80zł).

Polish **campsites** are often a fair distance from town centres and are not always much cheaper than a hostel dorm bed (20–40zł). Though some of these sites have excellent facilities, in others you'll find a toilet and little else. For a list of campsites in Poland, check ⓦeurocampings.co.uk/en/europe/poland.

FOOD AND DRINK

Poles are passionate about their food, and their cuisine is an intriguing mix of Slavic and Central European influences. While often wonderfully flavoursome and nutritious, it does live up to its reputation for heaviness. **Meals** generally start with soups, the most popular of which are *barszcz* (beetroot broth) and *zurek* (a sour soup of fermented rye). The basis of most main courses is fried or grilled meat, such as *kotlet schabowy* (breaded pork chops). Two inexpensive specialities (10–15zł) you'll find everywhere are *bigos* (sauerkraut stewed with a variety of meats) and *pierogi*, dumplings stuffed with cottage cheese (*ruskie*), meat (*z mięsem*), or cabbage and mushrooms (*z kapustą i grzybami*). The national snack is the *zapiekanka*, a baguette topped with mushrooms, melted cheese and tomato sauce. There are a few veggie cafés for **vegetarians** sick of cabbage, including the *Green Way* chain.

Restaurants are open until 9 or 10pm, later in city centres, and prices are lower than in Western Europe: in most places outside of Warsaw and Kraków you can have a two-course meal with a drink for 40zł. The cheapest option is the local **milk bar** (*bar mleczny*; usually open from breakfast until 6/7pm), which provides fast and filling meals for workers, students and anyone else looking for affordable Polish food.

DRINK

The Poles can't compete with their Czech neighbours when it comes to **beer** (*piwo*), but a growing range of microbreweries is beginning to challenge the bland national brands. Even in Warsaw, you won't pay more than 12zł for a half-litre. Tea (*herbata*) and coffee (*kawa*) are both popular; the former comes with lemon rather than milk. But it's **vodka** (*wódka*), ideally served neat and cold, which is the national drink (see box, p.842).

CULTURE AND ETIQUETTE

As a nation in which around 75 percent of people are practising Roman Catholics, Poland maintains fairly conservative religious and social customs, especially in the countryside where men are often still seen as the breadwinners. Poland's young,

EMERGENCY NUMBERS

Fire, police and ambulance ☎ 112.

urban population tend to be both more relaxed and wilder than their parents. Yet Poles of all ages are also warm, passionate people, fond of handshakes and of lively, informal conversation over a vodka. Table manners follow the Western norm and it is common to reward good service with a ten percent **tip**, though Poles will sometimes leave less.

SPORTS AND OUTDOOR ACTIVITIES

The most popular **sport** is football, and the national and top league teams often attract sell-out crowds. Poles are enthusiastic **cyclists** and the pavements of Warsaw and Kraków are increasingly full of them. For most **hikers**, the highlight of Poland is the Tatra Mountains in the south, though the country's 23 national parks offer plenty of opportunities for beautiful walks and horseriding. **Watersports** are concentrated around Sopot in the north and Mazury in the northeast, while the **skiing** season (Nov–Feb) brings tourists flocking to southern mountain resorts like Zakopane.

COMMUNICATIONS

The ubiquity of wi-fi in city centres and bars has led to a steep decline in the number of **internet cafés**, but they do still exist here and there, charging 4–6zł per hour. Main post offices (*Poczta*) are usually open Monday to Saturday 8am to 8pm; branches close earlier. For public phones you'll need a card (*karta telefoniczna*), available at post offices and RUCH newsagent kiosks.

POLAND ONLINE

🅦 **poland.travel/en** The official tourist website with general details on Poland's major sights and visa information.
🅦 **thenews.pl** Polish radio's English-language service, focusing on national news and current events.
🅦 **culture.pl** News and essays on Polish cultural events and history.

EMERGENCIES

Poland is a very safe country to travel in, though inevitably thefts from dorms and pickpocketing do occur. Safely store your valuables whenever possible and, on night trains, lock your compartment when you sleep. Polish **police** (*policja*) are courteous but unlikely to speak English. **Medical care** can be basic and most foreigners rely on the expensive private medical centres run by Medicover (☎ 500 900 500, 🅦 medicover.pl). For non-prescription medication, local pharmacists are helpful and often speak English.

INFORMATION

Most cities have a **tourist office** (*informacja turystyczna*, or IT), usually run by the local municipality, though some are merely private agencies selling tours.

MONEY AND BANKS

Currency is the **złoty** (zł/PLN), divided into 100 groszy. Coins come in 1, 2, 5, 10, 20 and 50 groszy, and 1, 2 and 5 złoty denominations; notes as 10, 20, 50, 100 and 200 złoty. At the time of writing, €1=4.3zł, US$1 = 3.3zł and £1= 5zł. **Banks** (usually Mon–Fri 7.30am–5pm, Sat 7.30am–2pm) and exchange offices (*kantors*) offer similar exchange rates. Major credit cards are widely accepted,

STUDENT AND YOUTH DISCOUNTS

The major cities offer **tourist cards** (available for one day or longer) that give discounts on transport and at the main sights. Your ISIC card can halve entry prices for museums and city transport, especially in Warsaw, and cut inter-city train fares by a third. A Hostelling International card can earn you up to 25 percent off at public hostels.

POLISH

English	POLISH	PRONUNCIATION
Yes	*Tak*	Tahk
No	*Nie*	Nyeh
Please	*Proszę*	Prosh-eh
Thank you	*Dziękuję*	Djen-ku-yeh
Hello/Good day	*Dzień dobry*	Djen doh-brih
Goodbye	*Do widzenia*	Doh veed-zen-yah
Excuse me/Sorry	*Przepraszam*	Psheh-pra-shahm
Today	*Dzisiaj*	Djyish-eye
Yesterday	*Wczoraj*	Vchor-eye
Tomorrow	*Jutro*	Yoo-troh
What time is it?	*Która godzina?*	Ktoo-rah go-djee-nah?
I don't understand	*Nie rozumiem*	Nyeh roh-zoom-yem
How much is…?	*Ile kosztuje…?*	Ill-eh kosh-too-yeh…?
Do you speak English?	*Pan/i/mówi po angielsku?*	Pahn/ee/movee poh ahn-gyel-skoo?
Where is the…?	*Gdzie jest…?*	G-djeh yest…?
entrance	*wejście*	vey-shche
exit	*wyjście*	viy-shche
toilet	*toaleta*	to-a-le-ta
hotel	*hotel*	ho-tel
hostel	*schronisko/hostel*	sro-nees-ko
church	*kościoł*	kosh-choow
What time does the… leave/arrive?	*O ktorej odchodzi/ przychodzi…?*	O ktoo-rey ot-ho-djee/ pshih-ho-djee…?
boat	*łódź*	woodj
bus	*autobus*	aw-tow-boos
plane	*samolot*	sa-mo-lot
train	*pociąg*	po-chonk
I would like a…	*Proproszę…*	Po-pro-she…
Bed	*Łóżko*	woosh-ko
Single room	*Pokoj jednoosobowy*	Po-koi yed-no-o-so-bo-vi
Double room	*Pokoj lózkiem*	Po-koi woosh-kyem
Cheap	*Tani*	Tah-nee
Expensive	*Drogi*	Droh-gee
Open	*Otwarty*	Ot-var-tih
Closed	*Zamknięty*	Zahmk-nee-yen-tih
One	*Jeden*	Yed-en
Two	*Dwa*	Dvah
Three	*Trzy*	Trshih
Four	*Cztery*	Chter-ih
Five	*Pięć*	Pyench
Six	*Sześć*	Sheshch
Seven	*Siedem*	Shedem
Eight	*Osiem*	Oshem
Nine	*Dziewięć*	Djyev-yench
Ten	*Dziesięć*	Djyesh-ench

and **ATMs** are common in cities. Euros are not widely accepted.

OPENING HOURS AND HOLIDAYS

Most shops open on weekdays from 10am to 6pm, and all but the largest close on Saturday at 2 or 3pm and all day Sunday. RUCH kiosks, selling public transport tickets (*bilety*), open at 6 or 7am. Most museums and historic monuments are closed once a week. Entrance tends to be inexpensive, and is often free one day of the week. **Public**

holidays are: January 1, Easter Monday, May 1, May 3, Corpus Christi (May/June), August 15, November 1, November 11, December 25 and 26.

Warsaw

Packed with a bizarre mix of gleaming office buildings and grey, Communist-era apartment blocks, **WARSAW** (Warszawa) often bewilders backpackers. Yet if any city rewards exploration, it is the Polish capital. North of the lively centre are stunning Baroque palaces and the meticulously reconstructed Old Town; to the south are two of Central Europe's finest urban parks; and in the east lie reminders of the rich Jewish heritage extinguished by the Nazis.

Warsaw became the capital in 1596 and initially flourished as one of Europe's most prosperous cities. Absorbed by the Russian Empire in 1815, it wasn't until 1918 that Warsaw again became the capital of an independent Poland. The Germans invaded in 1939 and herded the city's large Jewish population into a ghetto, prior to their transportation to the death camps. The Warsaw Uprising of 1944 so infuriated Hitler that he ordered the total destruction of the city, leaving 850,000 Varsovians dead and 85 percent of Warsaw in ruins. Rebuilt after the war, the historic core of the city now stands at the centre of a dynamic, fast-developing metropolis.

WHAT TO SEE AND DO

The main sights are on the western bank of the Wisła (Vistula) River where you'll find the central business and shopping district, **Śródmieście**, grouped around Centralna station and the nearby Palace of Culture. The more picturesque **Old Town** (Stare Miasto) is just to the north.

The Old Town

The title **Old Town** (Stare Miasto) is, in some respects, a misnomer for the historic nucleus of Warsaw. After World War II the beautifully arranged Baroque streets were destroyed, only to be painstakingly reconstructed so accurately that the area has been named a UNESCO World Heritage Site. The Old Town comes alive in the summer, as tourists, street performers and festivals take over the cobblestone streets. Plac Zamkowy (Castle Square), on the south side of the Old Town, is the obvious place to start a tour.

Royal Castle

On the east side of Castle Square is the thirteenth-century **Royal Castle**, now home to the Castle Museum (May–Sept Mon–Wed, Fri & Sat 10am–6pm, Thurs 10am–8pm, Sun 11am–6pm; Oct–April Tues–Sat 10am–4pm, Sun 11am–4pm; 22zł, audioguide 17zł; ⓦzamek-krolewski.pl). Though the structure is a replica, many of its furnishings are originals. After passing the lavish Royal Apartments of King Stanisław August, you visit the **Ballroom** with its allegorical ceiling paintings symbolizing the *Apotheosis of the Genius of Poland*.

Old and New Town squares

On ul. Świętojańska, north of the castle, stands St John's Cathedral, the oldest church in Warsaw. A few metres away, the **Old Town Square** (Rynek Starego Miasta) is one of the most remarkable bits of postwar reconstruction anywhere in Europe. Flattened during the Uprising, its three-storey merchants' houses have been rebuilt in near-flawless imitation of the Baroque originals. It's also home to the **Warsaw Historical Museum** (closed at the time of writing, due to reopen by 2014; ⓦmhw.pl), where an English-language film shows poignant footage of the vibrant, multicultural 1930s city and the ruins left in 1945. Crossing the ramparts heading north brings you to the **New Town Square** (Rynek Nowego Miasta) at the heart of the so-called New Town (Nowe Miasto), the town's commercial hub in the fifteenth century but now a quiet spot to escape the bustling Old Town.

The Royal Way

Lined with historic buildings, the road that runs south from pl. Zamkowy along

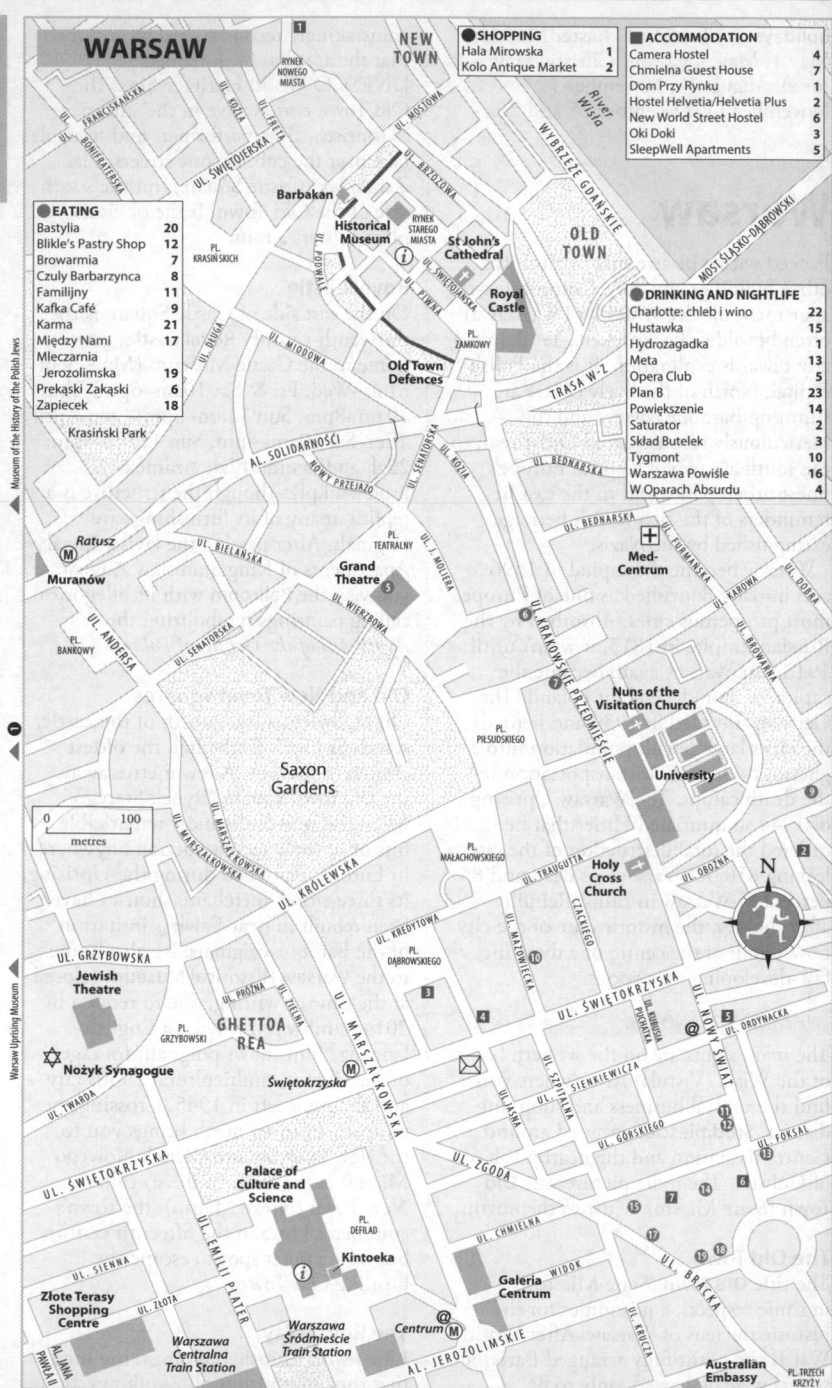

WARSAW

SHOPPING
Hala Mirowska	1
Kolo Antique Market	2

ACCOMMODATION
Camera Hostel	4
Chmielna Guest House	7
Dom Przy Rynku	1
Hostel Helvetia/Helvetia Plus	2
New World Street Hostel	6
Oki Doki	3
SleepWell Apartments	5

EATING
Bastylia	20
Blikle's Pastry Shop	12
Browarmia	7
Czuly Barbarzynca	8
Familijny	11
Kafka Café	9
Karma	21
Między Nami	17
Mleczarnia Jerozolimska	19
Prekąski Zakąski	6
Zapiecek	18

DRINKING AND NIGHTLIFE
Charlotte: chleb i wino	22
Hustawka	15
Hydrozagadka	1
Meta	13
Opera Club	5
Plan B	23
Powiększenie	14
Saturator	2
Skład Butelek	3
Tygmont	10
Warszawa Powiśle	16
W Oparach Absurdu	4

Museum of the History of the Polish Jews

Warsaw Uprising Museum

the streets of **Krakowskie Przedmieście** and Nowy Świat to the palace of Wilanów, on the city's outskirts, is the old **Royal Way**. One highlight is the **Church of the Nuns of the Visitation**, one of the few buildings in central Warsaw to have come through the war unscathed. Much of the rest of Krakowskie Przedmieście is occupied by university buildings, including several fine Baroque palaces and the **Holy Cross Church**. Sealed inside a column to the left of the nave is an urn containing Chopin's heart.

Chopin Museum

Warsaw's most lavish tribute to its favourite son is the achingly modern **Chopin Museum**, east of Krakowskie Przedmieście at ul. Okolnik 1 (Tues–Sun noon–8pm; 22zł; ⓦchopin.museum). With interactive handsets to guide visitors through exhibits on the musician's life, it's a must for Chopin enthusiasts, but only 100 people are allowed into the museum at a time so tickets must be reserved in advance.

The Copernicus Centre

Downhill from the Chopin Museum on the banks of the river, the Copernicus Centre at Wybrzeże Kościuszkowskie 20 (Tues–Fri 9am–6pm, Sat & Sun 10am–7pm; 22zł; ⓦkopernik.org.pl) is a hands-on science museum in a spectacularly contemporary building. The display is mostly intended to entertain children and game-playing adults, and the wealth of touch-screen computers, physical tests and mind-bending challenges can keep you occupied for hours. Visitors expecting an old-school museum may well be disappointed – and there's certainly not much here about Copernicus himself.

National Museum

At the southern end of Nowy Świat and east along al. Jerozolimskie is the **National Museum** (Tues–Fri 10am–4pm, Sat & Sun 10am–6pm; 15zł, free Sat; ⓦmnw .art.pl), housing an extensive collection of archeology and fine art, as well as Christian frescoes from eighth- to thirteenth-century Sudan. The contemporary galleries upstairs contain an all-embracing introduction to Polish modern art.

Palace of Culture and Science

West of the National Museum lies the commercial heart of the city, the Centrum crossroads from which ul. Marszałkowska, the main north–south road, cuts across al. Jerozolimskie running east–west. Towering over everything is the **Palace of Culture and Science**, a post-World War II gift from Stalin whose vast interior now contains theatres, a swimming pool and a nightclub. The platform on the thirtieth floor (Mon–Thurs & Sun 9am–8pm, Fri & Sat 9am–11pm, 20zł; ⓦpkin.pl) offers impressive views of the city.

Jewish Ghetto

West of the New and Old towns is the former **ghetto** area, in which an estimated 380,000 Jews – one-third of Warsaw's total population – were crammed from 1939 onwards. By the war's end, the ghetto had been razed to the ground, with only around three hundred Jews and just one synagogue, the **Nożyk Synagogue** at ul. Twarda 6, left. You can still get an idea of what Jewish Warsaw looked like on the miraculously untouched ul. Próżna.

Museum of the History of the Polish Jews

Located in the midst of the former ghetto area at Anielewicza 6, the **Museum of the History of the Polish Jews** (Mon & Wed–Sun 10am–6pm; 12zł; ⓦjewish museum.org.pl) is worth visiting for the building alone – a futuristic glassy slab filled with organic, curvy surfaces. The display pays tribute to the rich Jewish civilization that flourished on the soil of Poland, until all but snuffed out by the Holocaust. The painted wooden ceiling of the seventeenth-century Gwozdziec synagogue is one obvious highlight. Opposite the museum is the **Ghetto Heroes Monument**, commemorating the doomed Warsaw Ghetto Uprising of April 1943, when lightly armed ghetto inhabitants took on the might of the German SS.

25

Jewish Cemetery

Walk west from the Museum of the History of the Polish Jews or take tram #22 from Centralna Station to ul. Okopowa 49/51 to reach the vast, overgrown **Jewish Cemetery** (Cmentarz Zydowski; Mon–Thurs 10am–5pm, Fri 9am–1pm, Sun 11am–4pm; 8zł), one of the few still in use in Poland.

Warsaw Uprising Museum

About 1.5km west of Centrum is the **Warsaw Uprising Museum** at ul. Grzybowska 79 (Mon, Wed & Fri 8am–6pm, Thurs 8am–8pm, Sat & Sun 10am–6pm; 14zł, free Mon; ⓦ1944.pl; tram #22 from Centralna Station). Set in a century-old brick power station, this ultra-modern audio-visual museum retells the grim story of how the Varsovians fought and were eventually crushed by the Nazis in 1944 – a struggle that led to the deaths of nearly two hundred thousand Poles and the destruction of most of the city. Special attention is given to the equivocal role played by Soviet troops, who watched passively from the other side of the Wisła as the Nazis defeated the Polish insurgents. Only after the city was a charred ruin did they move across to "liberate" its few remaining inhabitants.

Łazienki Park

About 2km south of the commercial district, on the eastern side of al. Ujazdowskie, is the much-loved **Łazienki Park** (bus #116, #180 or #195 from Nowy Świat). Once a hunting ground, the area was bought in the 1760s by King Stanisław August, who turned it into a park and built the Neoclassical **Łazienki Palace** (Tues–Sun 9am–6pm; 17zł) across the lake. But the park itself is the real attraction, with its oak-lined paths alive with peacocks and red squirrels.

Wilanów Palace

The grandest of Warsaw's palaces, **Wilanów** (May–Sept Mon, Wed, Sat & Sun 9.30am–6.30pm, Tues, Thurs & Fri 9.30am–4.30pm; Oct–April Mon & Wed–Sat 9.30am–4.30pm, Sun 10.30am–4.30pm; 20zł, free Sun

Oct–April; ⓦwilanow-palac.pl) makes an easy excursion from the centre: take bus #180 south from Krakowskie Przedmieście or Nowy Świat to its terminus. Converted in the seventeenth century from a small manor house into the "Polish Versailles", the palace displays a vast range of decorative styles, a mixture mirrored in the delightful palace **gardens** (daily 9am–sunset; 5zł, free Thurs).

ARRIVAL AND DEPARTURE

By plane Okęcie airport is 8km southwest of the Old Town. Suburban trains run from the airport to Warszawa Śródmieście (near Centrum) every 30min and Warszawa Centralna every hour (both 6.30am–10.30pm; 25min). Outside these hours night bus #N32 runs into town.

By train The main train station, Warszawa Centralna, is in the modern centre just west of the Centrum crossroads.
Destinations Berlin (2 daily; 5hr 45min); Budapest (2 daily; 11hr 30min); Gdańsk (11 daily; 4hr 30min); Kraków (hourly; 2hr 45min–5hr); Poznań (hourly; 2hr 45min–4hr); Prague (3 daily; 8hr 30min–12hr); Sopot (11 daily; 5hr 20min); Toruń (10 daily; 3hr); Vienna (3 daily; 8hr 30min–9hr 30min); Wrocław (hourly; 5hr–6hr 30min); Zakopane (2 daily; 7–9hr).

By bus The main bus station, Dworzec PKS, is located right next to the Warszawa Zachodnia train station, 3km west of Centralna Station. Catch eastbound buses #127, #130, #158 or #517 into town.
Destinations L'viv (2 daily; 10hr); Rīga (1–2 daily; 13hr); Tallinn (1–2 daily; 17hr); Wrocław (1 daily; 6hr 30min); Vilnius (2 daily; 8–10hr).

INFORMATION

Tourist information In the Old Town Square at 19/21 (daily: May–Aug 9am–9pm; March & April, Sept & Oct 8am–7pm; Nov–Feb 8am–6pm; ☏22 194 31, ⓦwarsawtour.pl). There are also IT offices at the Palace of Culture and the airport.

Travel agents STA Travel, ul. Krucza 41/43 (☎22 529 3800), can reserve international or domestic flights and train tickets, and sells ISIC Cards.

GETTING AROUND

Tickets Tickets for trams, buses and the metro (single trip of up to 20min duration 3.40zł; 40min 4.60zł; 1hr 6.40zł) are available at green RUCH kiosks or automatic ticket machines. Always punch your tickets in the machines on board, as Warsaw's inspectors are extremely thorough. There are also good-value 1-day/3-day passes available (15zł/30zł), which should be punched the first time you use them. Tickets for students (*ulgowy*) are half-price, but you need to show ID.

25

By bus Well-developed if busy system that runs until around 11pm; after that, night buses leave every 30min from behind the main train station.

By tram A crowded but efficient means of transport, running till 11pm.

By metro A small subway system running north–south through the centre of town is the fastest way to get around; at the moment its route is very limited, but a new east–west line should be operational by late 2014.

By taxi Generally with an initial charge of 8zł, then around 3zł/km, 4.50zł/km after 10pm and on Sun. English is spoken at Ele (☎ 22 811 1111) and Glob (☎ 19668).

ACCOMMODATION

Warsaw has many good private hostels, mainly in Śródmieście; all the hostels listed below offer free internet, breakfast and free/cheap laundry services unless otherwise stated. Hotels tend to be pricier than elsewhere in Poland.

HOSTELS

Camera Hostel ul. Jasna 22 ☎ 22 828 8600, �🌐 camerahostel.com. Functional dorms with film-themed decor, good range of social areas and hard-to-beat central location. Dorm 40zł, double 150zł

Dom Przy Rynku Rynek Nowego Miasta 4 ☎ 22 831 5033, �🌐 cityhostel.net. Small and friendly place with the most affordable rooms in the Nowe Miasto. Open daily July & Aug, weekends only the rest of the year. Dorm 55zł, double 120zł

Hostel Helvetia ul. Sewerynów 7 30 ☎ 22 826 7108, �🌐 hostel-helvetia.pl. Dead central yet in a quiet street, this nicely furnished hostel has plenty of showers, a women's dorm and a separate apartment. They also offer swish doubles and apartments in *Helvetia Plus* a 3min walk away (reception at the Helvetia) – breakfast is included at both locations. Dorm 55zł, double 200zł

★ **New World Street Hostel** ul. Nowy Świat 27 ☎ 22 828 1282, �🌐 nws-hostel.pl. Friendly staff and a cosy common room (complete with board games and books) make this the pick of Warsaw's hostels. While the in-hostel atmosphere is calming, neighbouring streets are packed with bars. Dorm 47zł, double 185zł

Oki Doki pl. Dąbrowskiego 3 ☎ 22 828 0122, �🌐 okidoki .pl. With its eccentric, individually designed rooms and bar (0.5lt beer 7zł), this hostel has the liveliest feel of any in town. Breakfast available for 15zł. Dorm 450zł, double 170zł

APARTMENTS

Pragapartments ☎ 792 217 313, �🌐 pragapartments.pl. A superb option if you're aiming to stay on the up-and-coming east bank of the Wisła river, offering a mixture of smartly-furnished, 2-person studio, 1-room and 2-room apartments in different locations in the Praga district. Studio 220zł, 1-room apartment 190zł

★ **SleepWell Apartments** ul. Nowy Świat 62 ☎ 600 300 749, ⌨ sleepwell-warsaw.pl. Located just off Warsaw's main café strip, this restored apartment offers fairly small rooms (they're very cute en-suite doubles rather than "apartments" in the real sense of the word), decked out in bold, kitschy colours. Double 227zł

B&B

Chmielna Guest House ul. Chmielna 13 ☎ 22 828 1282, ⌨ chmielnabb.pl. Surprisingly intimate place for such a central location, with seven rooms arranged around a spacious living room and adjoining kitchen. Some rooms are quite small and share a bathroom in the hallway, but all are stylishly decorated with soothing colours. Double 190zł

EATING

CAFÉS, CHEAP EATS AND SNACKS

Blikle's Pastry Shop ul. Nowy Świat 35. Mouthwatering array of pastries, cakes and chocolates. Blikle's is renowned throughout the nation for its soft springy doughnuts (*paczki*), but there's a lot more besides. Cake slices 3.50zł. Daily 10am–10pm.

Czuly Barbarzynca ul. Dobra 31. Bookshop/café buzzing with students; serves excellent cappuccino, leaf teas and cakes, and has a swing in the middle of the room. Fruit pies 10zł. Daily 10am–10pm, Sun noon–10pm.

Familijny ul. Nowy Świat 29. Conveniently located milk bar serving good soups, pancakes and traditional Polish dishes for just a couple of złoty. A Warsaw student favourite. Mains 5–10zł. Mon–Fri 7am–8pm, Sat & Sun 9am–5pm.

★ **Kafka Café** ul. Obozna 3. Tasty sandwiches (12zł), pasta dishes (20zł) and strong coffee make this stylish café popular with a student crowd, who spill out onto the lawn chairs outside in the summer. Mon–Fri 9am–10pm, Sat & Sun 10am–10pm.

Karma pl. Zbawiciela 3/5. Coffee shop popular with a studenty, young professional and style-conscious crowd, offering a tempting range of pastries and sandwiches, plus good views of the picturesque plac Zbawiciela and its rumbling parade of trams. Sandwiches 15zł. Mon–Fri 9am–10pm, Sun 10am–10pm.

Mleczarnia Jerozolimska al. Jerozolimskie 32. Traditional dishes cheaply priced, served in friendly style in a neat bright environment. Soups for as little as 5zł, mains not much more. Mon–Fri 10am–8pm, Sat noon–6pm, Sun noon–5pm.

Prekąski Zakąski cnr Krakowskie Przedmiescie & ul. Ossolińskich. All dishes are priced 8zł at this legendary stand-up snack bar; simply point at the herring, pie or steak tartare painted on the wall, pay, and wait for your plate to arrive. Drinks are all 4zł, vodka too. 24hr.

25

POLAND'S ELIXIR: VODKA STRIKES BACK

The tipple most associated with Poland, **vodka** is making a major comeback after decades of being overshadowed in the fashion stakes by imported Western drinks. Traditionally made from cereal grains, potatoes or beets, Polish vodka is usually served chilled and neat – although increasingly mixed with fruit juice. Żubrówka, infused with bison grass, is delicious on its own or mixed with apple juice. Other vodkas usually consumed as down-in-one shots include Żołądkowa Gorzka (an amber-coloured herbal vodka), Wiśniówka (from cherries) and the honey-flavoured Krupnik.

RESTAURANTS

Bastylia ul. Mokotowska 17. Legendary pancake bar with a chic interior, serving up a large number of sweet and savoury pancakes. Pancake with prosciutto and gruyère 24zł. Daily 8am–10pm.

Browarmia ul. Królewska 1. Roomy beer hall and grill-restaurant with a hugely popular street-facing terrace, brewing its own pilsner and wheat beers (from 13zł/0.5 litre). Use them to wash down a grilled chicken sandwich (27zł), the pork knuckle (49zł) or a steak (67zł). Daily noon–midnight.

Między Nami ul. Bracka 20. Cultured, gay-friendly café-restaurant that's excellent for a light meal, with some innovative vegetarian choices and a pleasant summer patio. Mains 18–35zł. Mon–Thurs 10am–11pm, Fri & Sat 10am–midnight, Sun 2–11pm.

Zapiecek al. Jerozolimskie 28. A wide variety of *pierogis*, *golabki* (stuffed cabbage leaves), *nalesniki* (pancakes) and other traditional Polish specialities, served by waitresses decked out in folk costumes. *Pierogis* 20zł. Daily 11am–11pm.

DRINKING AND NIGHTLIFE

The bar scene in Warsaw has really taken off over the last decade, and the city now genuinely provides a great night out that rivals Prague and needn't blow your budget. Praga, across the river, boasts a lively, bohemian bar scene – an interesting alternative to the more glitzy hangouts you'll find downtown.

BARS

Charlotte: chleb i wino al. Wyzwolenia 18 (entrance on pl. Zbawiciela). Chic and spacious café-bar dishing out coffee and croissants during the daytime, wine and spirits at night. Outdoor seating beneath plac Zbawiciela's colonnades. Mon–Fri 9am–11pm, Sat 10am–midnight, Sun 10am–10pm.

★ **Meta** ul. Foksal 21. A time capsule stuffed with pop-cultural ephemera from the 70s and 80s, *Meta* serves up vodka shots, excellent small-brewery beers (Kasztelan 6zł) and late-night snacks (including the most popular steak tartare in town). Daily 11am–6am.

Plan B al. Wyzwolenia 18. Leading hipster hangout on the popular pl. Zbawiciel, featuring red sofas, rickety wooden chairs and a standing-room-only terrace in the spring and summer. Mon–Sat 1pm–3am, Sun 4pm–2am.

Skład Butelek ul. 11 Listopada 22, Praga. Wonderfully quirky gathering place for Warsaw's creative types, serving obscure Ukrainian beers in an old factory. 0.5lt beer 9zł. Wed–Sat 7pm–3am.

W Oparach Absurdu ul. Zabkowska 6, Praga. Chaotic, lively and decorated with all the haphazard charm of a flea market. 0.5lt beer 8zł. Daily noon–3am.

Warszawa Powiśle ul. Kruckowskiego 3b. Located in the UFO-shaped former ticket hall of the Warszawa-Powiśle station, this self-styled "kiosk for wódka and culture" serves drinks and snacks (burgers 10zł) until late. Summer evenings bring the best out in the place, when crowds spill across the pavement out front. Daily 10am–3am.

CLUBS AND LIVE MUSIC

Hustawka ul. Bracka 20a. Artistically renovated old palace in a courtyard behind Bracka, transformed into a nightclub that draws in both hipsters and young professionals. Cocktails from 15zł. Mon–Fri noon–4am, Sat & Sun 4pm–4am.

Hydrozagadka ul. 11 Listopada 22 ⓦhydrozagadka .waw.pl. Courtyard bar-cum-nightclub featuring a bare-bones interior: expect to hear leftfield DJs, and the kind of visiting indie bands that attract an informed alternative audience. Cover 25–50zł. Fri, Sat and gig nights (check the website) 7pm–4am.

Opera Club pl. Teatralny 1. Dancefloors and semi-private rooms scattered through the cavernous chambers beneath the Grand Theatre, making for a novel night out. Cocktails 19–25zł. Fri & Sat 10pm–5am.

Powiększenie Nowy wiat 27, ⓦpowiekszenie.pl. Rambling bar with a concert space in the basement, offering a mixture of club nights and live alternative rock. Beer 8zł. Daily 11am–3am.

Saturator ul. 11 Listopada 22, Praga. Pulling in adventurous souls from all over town with its anything-goes attitude, this place grooves well into the wee hours. Cocktails 12zł. Thurs–Sun 7pm–4am.

Tygmont ul. Mazowiecka 6/8 ⓦtygmont.com.pl. The city's top jazz club, with a regular gig roster, retro discos and a stylish, upmarket clientele. Entrance 10zł and upwards depending on event. Tues–Thurs 9pm–2am, Fri & Sat 7pm–3am.

25

MARKETS AND MALLS

For mainstream **fashion brands**, first explore the gleaming Złote Terasy shopping centre, behind Centralna train station, before passing through to the mainly pedestrianized streets of ul. Chimielna and ul. Nowy Świat. The daily Hala Mirowska market on al. Jana Pawła II is the place to go for **fresh fruits and vegetables**, while **antique** hunters should head for the Koło Antique Market on ul. Obozowa (Sun 7am–2pm; trams #13 & #23 from the Old Town), where you'll find everything from war medals to old Christian icons.

ENTERTAINMENT

A wealth of cultural festivals brings the city to life in summer, especially the Warsaw "Summer Jazz Days" in June, and "Jazz in the Old Town" (a series of outdoor concerts) throughout July and Aug. Films are usually shown in their original language with Polish subtitles. Tickets 17–30zł.

Grand Theatre (Teatr Wielki) pl. Teatralny 1 ☎ 22 692 3288, ⓦ teatrwielki.pl. Worth visiting just for its Neoclassical facade, but it also hosts the best of Poland's National Opera. 20–130zł depending on seats.

Kinoteka pl. Defilad 1 ⓦ kinoteka.pl. Multiplex in the Palace of Culture and Science showing the latest blockbusters.

Muranów ul. Gen. Andersa 1 ⓦ muranow.gutekfilm.pl. Art-house cinema that screens a range of films from around the world.

DIRECTORY

Embassies and consulates Australia, ul. Nowogrodzka 11 ☎ 22 521 3444, ⓦ poland.embassy.gov.au; Canada, ul. Matejki 1/5 ☎ 22 584 3100, ⓦ canadainternational.gc.ca /poland-pologne; Ireland, ul. Mysia 5 ☎ 22 849 6633, ⓦ embassyofireland.pl; New Zealand, al. Ujazdowskie 51 ☎ 22 521 0500, ⓦ nzembassy.com/poland; South Africa, ul. Koszykowa 54 ☎ 22 622 1031, ⓦ southafrica.pl; UK, ul. Kawalerii 12 1 ☎ 22 311 0000, ⓦ gov.uk/government /world/poland; USA, ul. Ujazdowskie 29/31 ☎ 22 504 2000, ⓦ poland.usembassy.gov.

Exchange The Old Town has a host of *kantor* stores that exchange foreign cash, though you will have to shop around for the best rates. Interchange Poland at ul. Chmielna 30 (Mon–Fri 8am–10pm, Sat & Sun 9am–10pm) is also a reliable option.

Hospitals The nearest public hospital to the centre is the Praski, al. Solidarności 67 (☎ 22 619 1979). The private Damian clinic at ul. Foksal 3/5 (☎ 22 566 2222, ⓦ damian .pl) has English-speaking staff and 24hr service.

Internet *Arena Cafe*, Centrum metro station (daily 7am– midnight; 6zł/hr).

Left luggage Centralna Station has a 24hr left-luggage room and lockers with storage for up to ten days.

Pharmacies There is a 24hr pharmacy on the top floor of Centralna train station.

Post office ul. Świętokrzyska 31/33 (24hr).

Northern Poland

Even in a country accustomed to shifting borders, **northern Poland** presents an unusually tortuous historical puzzle. Successively the domain of the Teutonic Order, Hansa merchants and the Prussians, it's only in the last seventy years that the region has become definitively Polish. The conurbation of **Gdańsk**, **Sopot** and **Gdynia**, known as the Tri-City, lines the Baltic coast with its dramatic shipyards and sandy beaches, while highlights inland include the medieval centres of **Malbork** and **Toruń**.

GDAŃSK

Both the starting point of World War II and the birthplace of the anti-communist Solidarity movement, **GDAŃSK** has played more than a fleeting role on the world stage. Traces of its past are visible in the steel skeletons of shipyard cranes and the Hanseatic architecture of the old town. After all the social and political upheavals of the last century, the city is now busy reinventing itself as a tourist hub.

WHAT TO SEE AND DO

With its medieval brick churches and narrow eighteenth-century merchants' houses, Gdańsk certainly looks ancient. But its appearance is deceptive: by 1945, the core of the city lay in ruins, and the present buildings are almost complete reconstructions.

The Main Town (Główne Miasto)

Huge stone gateways guard both entrances to ul. Długa, the main thoroughfare. Start from the sixteenth-century gate at the top, **Brama Wyżynna**,

25

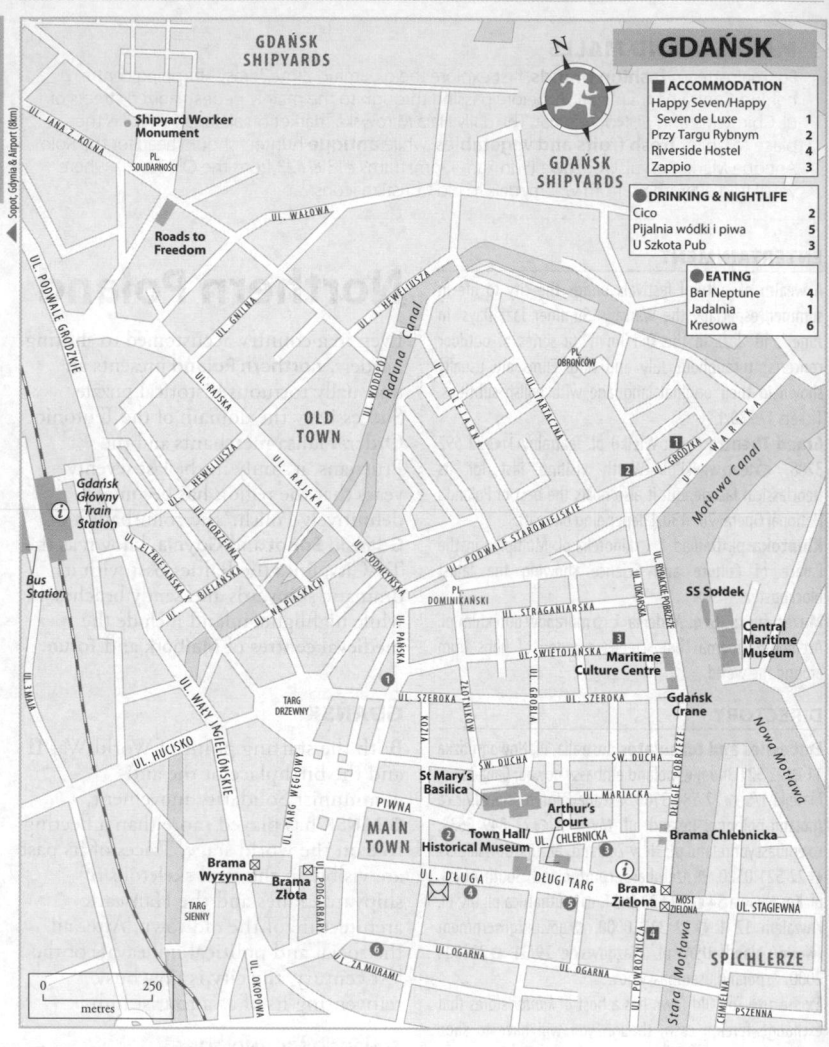

and carry on east through the nearby Brama Zlota. You'll soon come across the imposing Town Hall, which houses a **Historical Museum** (June–Sept Mon 10am–3pm, Tues–Sat 10am–6pm, Sun 11am–6pm; Oct–May Tues 10am–3pm, Wed–Sat 10am–4pm, Sun 11am–4pm; 10zł, free Mon June–Sept & Tues Oct–May) with shocking photos of the city's wartime destruction.

Further down, the street opens onto the wide expanse of ul. Długi Targ, where the ornate facade of **Arthur's Court** (same

hours as Historical Museum; 10zł) stands out among the fine mansions. The surrounding streets are also worth exploring, especially ul. Mariacka, brimming with amber traders, at the end of which stands **St Mary's Basilica** (Mon–Sat 9am–5.30pm, Sun 1–5pm), the largest church in Poland.

The waterfront and the Maritime Museum

At the end of ul. Długi Targ the archways of **Brama Zielona** open directly onto the waterfront. Halfway down is the fifteenth-century **Gdańsk Crane**, the biggest in medieval Europe, part of the **Central Maritime Museum** (July & Aug daily 10am–6pm; Jan–June & Sept–Nov Tues–Sun 10am–4pm; Dec Tues–Sun 10am–3pm; 8zł; ⓦcmm.pl). Highlights include an exhibition of primitive boats; for an extra 8zł you can also tour the cargo ship SS *Soldek* docked outside. The museum's new annexe on the opposite banks of the river, the Maritime Culture Centre (same times; 12zł), has four fascinating floors of interactive displays covering storms and sea life as well as boats from around the world.

The shipyards

Further north loom the cranes of the famous Gdańsk **shipyards**, crucible of the struggle to topple communism in Poland. Poignantly set outside the shipyard gates is the monument to the workers killed during peaceful anti-government demonstrations in 1970. Ten years later, the Solidarity union led by Lech Wałęsa turned a shipyard strike into a snowballing national movement. It's an inspiring story, told in the **Roads to Freedom** exhibition in the Solidarity offices at ul. Piastowskie 24, across from the shipyard gates (May Sept Tues Sun 10am–6pm; Oct–April 10am–5pm; 6zł). A brand-new exhibition and conference hall, the **European Solidarity Centre** (ⓦecs.gda.pl), is due to open its doors in the shipyard area in late 2014.

ARRIVAL AND DEPARTURE

By plane Gdańsk Lech Wałęsa airport lies 8km from the city centre. Bus #210 (every 20min; 3zł) runs to Gdańsk Central Station (see below). Taxis cost 50–80zł.

By train Make sure to get off at the Główny (Central) Station, a 10min walk northwest of ul. Długa, the heart of the Main Town.

Destinations Kraków (5 daily; 9hr 45min–11hr); Malbork (every 30min; 1hr); Poznań (5 daily; 4–5hr); Sopot (every 15min; 20min); Toruń (9 daily; 3hr 40min); Warsaw (11 daily; 4hr 30min); Wrocław (3 daily; 7hr–8hr 30min).

By bus The bus station is just behind the train station, reached via an underpass.

Destinations Riga (1 daily; 16hr); Tallinn (1 daily; 21hr); Vilnius (1 daily; 11hr).

INFORMATION

Tourist information Tourist office at Długi Targ 28/29 (Mon–Sat 9am–5pm, Sun till 4pm; ☏058 301 4355, ⓦgdansk4u.pl). There are also offices at the airport (24hr) and the train station (Mon–Fri 9am–7pm, Sat till 5pm, Sun till 4pm).

ACCOMMODATION

★ **Happy Seven** ul. Grodzka 16 ☏58 320 8601, ⓦhappyseven.com. Bright hostel with all the amenities you could wish for, plus playfully decorated, comfortable rooms and free internet. *Happy Seven de Luxe*, a few doors away (reception is at Happy Seven), offers comfy doubles. Dorm 50zł, double 230zł

Przy Targu Rybnym ul. Grodzka 21 ☏58 301 5627, ⓦgdanskhostel.com.pl. A bit worn around the edges, but centrally located and with a good mixture of dorms and privates. Also rents out bikes (20zł/day). Dorm 35zł, double 100zł

Riverside Hostel ul. Powroznicza 18/24 ☏58 718 3854, ⓦriverside-hostel.pl. Situated among historic dockside warehouses, this hostel combines relaxing social areas and fully equipped kitchen with neat, classy dorms and some cute doubles. Dorm 50zł, double 160zł

Zappio ul. Swietojanska 49 ☏58 322 0174, ⓦzappio.pl. Budget hotel and youth hostel in a beautiful prewar building, with big windows and period woodwork. Dorm 55zł, double 150zł

EATING

Bar Neptune ul. Długa 33/34. Spruced-up milk bar with the usual Polish *barszcz*, *pierogi* and pork-chop fare. Dishes tend to run out well before closing time. Mains from 5zł. Mon–Fri 7.30am–6pm, Sat & Sun 10am–5pm.

Jadalnia ul. Panska 69. This popular cellar comes with cheap beer and hearty Polish meals. 0.5lt beer 5zł; mains 12–22zł. Mon–Fri 10am–10pm, Sat & Sun till midnight.

★ **Kresowa** ul. Ogarna 12. Cuisine from the Polish-Lithuanian-Ukrainian borderlands (*kresy*), served in a refined atmosphere for a reasonable price. Much of the food is based on historic recipe books: don't miss out on the *Zrazy Radziwilowskie* (beef rolls stuffed with mushrooms; 27zl). Other mains 20–40zł. Daily 10am–10pm.

DRINKING AND NIGHTLIFE

Local clubbers prefer the nightlife in Sopot (see p.846), but there are several bars on Piwna and Chlebnicka to keep you entertained.

Cico ul. Piwna 28/30. "Come in and Chill Out" is the appropriate motto for this stylish bar, which also does good coffees and light meals. Cocktails 15–22zł. Daily 8am–midnight.

25

Pjalnia wódki i piwa ul. Długi targ 35/38. One of Poland's new breed of round-the-clock drinks-and-snack bars, serving vodka shots, beer (4zł), herring snacks and *gzik* (sour cream, onion and cottage cheese; 8zł) in a communist-era interior. 24hr.

U Szkota Pub ul. Chlebnicka 9/10. A friendly Scottish pub that comes complete with kilted waiters and Belhaven Scottish Ale on tap, alongside Irish beers such as Kilkenny and Guinness on tap (14zł for 0.4lt). Mon–Thurs & Sun 4pm–1am, Fri & Sat 4pm–2am.

SOPOT

Some 15km northwest of Gdańsk lies Poland's trendiest coastal resort, which boasts Europe's longest wooden pier (512m) and a broad stretch of golden sand. With its vibrant nightlife, **Sopot** is a magnet for young party animals. All roads lead to the beach, where aside from lounging you can meander up the pier (entry 5.50zł May–Sept), on which you'll find boat tours operating in summer.

ARRIVAL AND INFORMATION

By train The train station lies 400m west of the beach and a 5min walk from the main street, ul. Monte Cassino.

Tourist information The tourist office is on the way to the pier at plac Zdrojowy 2 (daily: June to mid-Sept 10am–8pm; mid-Sept to May 10am–6pm; ☎58 550 3783, ✆sts.sopot.pl), and helps with accommodation, which fills up quickly in summer.

Internet Net Cave, ul. Pułaskiego 7a (Mon–Sat noon–8pm; 5zł/hr).

ACCOMMODATION

Cheap accommodation can be hard to find in Sopot. Your best bet is to look for "Wolny Pokoj" (free room) signs in private houses, where you can rent rooms for around 50zł/person.

Central Hostel ul. Monte Casino 15 ☎53 085 8717, ✆hostelcentral.pl. Bang in the centre of town, this hostel is sparsely furnished but has a lively party atmosphere and sunny rooms. Dorm 60zł, double 250zł

★ **Siesta Hostel** ul. Krasickiego 11 ☎79 063 9011, ✆siestahostel.pl. A homely hostel 5min from the train station, with a big garden strung with hammocks, and bicycles for rent (20zł/day). Dorm 60zł, double 170zł

EATING

For best value, avoid ul. Monte Cassino and head for the restaurants around 1km south along the beach.

Bar Przystan al. Wojska Polskiego 11. A touristy but great-value restaurant with a big glass-enclosed dining

OPEN'ER FESTIVAL

Taking place just north of Gdańsk and Sopot at Gdynia's Kosakovo airfield, the **Open'er Festival** (✆opener.pl) in early July is one of Europe's largest outdoor rock events. It's very much Central Europe's answer to Reading or Roskilde: 2013's line-up included Arctic Monkeys, Blur, Nick Cave, Kings of Leon and Tame Impala. Four-day tickets weigh in at around 450zł; add an extra 100–120zł for camping.

room right above the beach. Fresh Baltic fish such as cod, halibut or flounder 9–10.50zł/100g. Daily 11am–11pm.

Dobra Kuchnia ul. Jagiełły 6/1. The best place for reasonably priced Polish classics in the centre. Mains 10–20zł. Mon–Thurs noon–9pm, Fri–Sun noon–10pm.

DRINKING AND NIGHTLIFE

Czekolada ul. Bohaterow Monte Cassino 63 ✆klubczekolada.pl. The most trendy club in town for the well-dressed student crowd, with a dancefloor-friendly mix of house, electro, R'n'B and hip-hop. Wed–Sun 9pm–late.

Soho ul. Monte Cassino 61. Along the main drag not far from the pier, with colourful interiors that draw in the punters all night long. Fri & Sat 10pm–4am.

MALBORK

The spectacular fortress of **MALBORK** (Tues–Sun: mid-April to mid-Sept 9am–7pm; rest of year 10am–3pm; high season 39.50zł, low season 29.50zł; ✆zamek.malbork.pl) was built as the headquarters of the Teutonic Order in the fourteenth century and still casts a threatening shadow over an otherwise sleepy town. As the Teutonic Knights sank into deep financial crisis, they were eventually forced to sell the castle in the mid-fifteenth century. The place was then employed as a royal residence and a stopover for Polish monarchs en route between Warsaw and Gdańsk.

You enter over a moat and through the daunting main gate, before reaching an open courtyard. Brooding above is the **High Castle**, which harbours the centrepiece of the Knights' austere monasticism – the vast **Castle Church** with its faded chivalric paintings. You'll be given an English audioguide for the three-hour self-guided tour, or, in July and

August, you can opt for a live tour instead (both are included in the ticket price).

ARRIVAL AND DEPARTURE

By train The train station is about a 10min walk south of the castle; there are regular trains to and from Gdańsk (every 30min; 1hr).

TORUŃ

Once one of the most beautiful medieval towns in Central Europe, **TORUŃ** was founded by the Teutonic Knights and is still rich with their architectural legacy. It's also famous for being the birthplace of Nicolaus Copernicus, whose house still stands. Now a friendly university city, with bars and cafés sprinkled throughout the compact streets, Toruń combines lively nightlife with its status as a UNESCO World Heritage Site.

WHAT TO SEE AND DO

The highlight of Toruń is the mansion-lined Market Square (Rynek) and its fourteenth-century Town Hall, now the **District Museum** (Tues–Sun: May–Sept 10am–6pm; Oct–April 10am–4pm; 10zł), with a fine collection of nineteenth-century paintings and intricate woodcarvings. South of the Rynek at ul. Kopernika 15/17, the **Copernicus Museum** (same hours as District Museum; 10zł), in the house where the great man was born, contains a fascinating model collection of his original instruments as well as facsimiles of the momentus *De Revolutionibus* and a selection of early portraits. The large, Gothic **St John's Cathedral** (Mon–Sat 8.30am–7.30pm, Sun 4.30–7.30pm; 3zł), at the eastern end of ul. Kopernika, has a tower offering panoramic views over the city (April–Oct only; 3zł extra). Further north stands the **Contemporary Art Centre** at Waly Gen. Sikorskiego 13 (Tues–Sun: July & Aug noon–6pm; Sept–June 10am–6pm; 10zł), a modern building hosting cutting-edge art exhibitions.

ARRIVAL AND DEPARTURE

By train Toruń Główny, the main train station, is 2km south of the river; buses #22, #25 and #27 (every 10min; 2.50zł) run from outside the station to pl. Rapackiego on the western edge of the Old Town, the first stop after crossing the bridge.

Destinations Gdańsk (9 daily; 3hr 40min); Kraków (2 daily; 7hr 30min–8hr 30min); Poznań (9 daily; 2hr 30min); Warsaw (10 daily; 3hr); Wrocław (2 daily; 5hr).

By bus The bus station is on ul. Dąbrowskiego, just north of the centre.

INFORMATION

Tourist information Tourist office at Rynek Staromiejski 25 (Mon & Sat 9am–4pm, Tues–Fri 9am–6pm; May–Sept also Sun 9am–4pm; ☎ 56 621 0931, ⌨ it.torun.pl).
Internet Ksero, ul. Franciszkanska 5; 5zł/hr (Mon–Fri 8am–7pm, Sat 9am–2pm).

ACCOMMODATION

Orange Plus ul. Jeczmienna 11 ☎ 56 651 8457, ⌨ hostelorange.pl. A bright, cosy hostel with friendly staff, comfortable dorms, relaxing social areas but not much of a kitchen. Dorm 30zł, double 90zł
Tor-Host ul. Prosta 2/25 ☎ 78 868 5820, ⌨ tor-host.pl. Hostel in a nicely renovated top-floor apartment with kitchen facilities and attractive double rooms, good value for solo travellers. Dorm 25zł, double 90zł

EATING

Manekin ul. Wysoka 5. The perfect place for pancake lovers, with a lengthy menu of innovative meat, veg and sweet fillings (8–13zł). It's not all batter – soups and salads also feature. Daily 10am–midnight.
Oberza ul. Rabiańska 9. Cosy restaurant near the Market Square offering quick, traditional buffet meals such as stuffed cabbage parcels or pork chop with plums, served up in a farmhouse interior. Mains 13zł. Daily 11am–9pm.
Pierogarnia Most Paulinski 2/10. Specializes both in standard *pierogi* and the giant oven-baked variety (12–20zł) in a creative range of flavours. They also do *czeburki* – deep-fried parcels of pastry stuffed with savoury fillings (20zł). Daily 10am–11pm.
Pod Arkadami ul. Rozana 1. Clean, bright milk bar on the Market Square serving filling soups and potato dishes. Potato pancakes 6zł. Mon–Fri 9am–7pm, Sat & Sun 9am–4pm.

DRINKING AND NIGHTLIFE

Bar Mockba Rynek Staromiejski 22. There's a fun mix of

> ### PIERNIKI
> You can't leave Toruń without trying the local **pierniki**, or gingerbread, which has been made here since the town was founded. *Pierniczek* on Żeglarska 25 offers a mouthwatering range.

25

hip-hop and rock in this communist-themed cellar club on the main square. 0.5lt beer 6zł. Daily 1pm–late.

★ **Café Fajka** ul. Małe Garbary 1. Chilled-out place filled with cushions, offering a huge range of cocktails and shishas that bubble milk or gin instead of water. Cocktails from 10zł. Mon–Wed & Sun 3pm–2am, Thurs–Sat till 3am.

Southern Poland

Southern Poland attracts more visitors than any other region in the country, and its appeal is clear from a glance at the map. The **Tatra Mountains** bordering Slovakia are the most spectacular in the country, snowcapped for much of the year and markedly alpine in feel. The former royal capital of **Kraków** is an architectural gem and the country's intellectual heart. Pope John Paul II was archbishop here until his election in 1978, but equally important are the city's Jewish roots: before the Holocaust, this was one of Europe's most vibrant Jewish centres. This multicultural past echoes in the old district of Kazimierz, and its culmination is starkly enshrined at the death camps of **Auschwitz-Birkenau**, 50km west of the city.

KRAKÓW

KRAKÓW was the only major city in Poland to come through World War II essentially undamaged, and its assembly of monuments has since been hailed as one of Europe's most compelling by UNESCO. The city's Old Town (Stare Miasto) swarms with visitors in summer, but retains an atmosphere of *fin-de-siècle* stateliness, its streets a cavalcade of churches and palaces. A university centre, Kraków has a tangible buzz of arty youthfulness and enjoys a dynamic nightlife.

WHAT TO SEE AND DO

Kraków is bisected by the River Wisła, with virtually everything of interest on the north bank. At the heart of the **Old Town** is the Main Square, with **Wawel Hill**, ancient seat of Poland's kings and Church, and the rejuvenated old Jewish suburb of **Kazimierz** lying to the south.

The Market Square

The largest square in medieval Europe, the Market Square (Rynek Główny) is now a broad expanse with the vast **Cloth Hall** (Sukiennice) at its centre, ringed by magnificent houses and towering spires. Originally a collection of outdoor market stalls, the Cloth Hall was first built in 1300 and reconstructed during the Renaissance, and still houses a bustling covered market.

The Rynek Underground

Central Kraków's newest and most entertaining tourist attraction is the **Rynek Underground** (April–Oct Mon 10am–8pm, Tues 10am–4pm, Wed–Sun 10am–10pm; Nov–March Mon & Wed–Sun 10am–8pm, Tues 10am–4pm; closed first Tues of every Month;17zł), an extensive subterranean museum that stretches beneath the market square – it is entered from the eastern side of the Cloth Hall. Recent archeological excavations have been left *in situ* and covered by glass walkways, allowing you to explore the layout of the medieval marketplace. The display also features touch-screen computers, re-created thatched wooden huts and videos of role-playing actors dressed up as medieval traders.

St Mary's Church

On the east side of the Market Square is the Gothic **St Mary's Church** (Mon–Sat 11.30am–6pm, Sun 2–6pm; 6zł), the taller of its two towers, which you can climb during the summer months (May–Aug Tues, Thurs & Sat 9–11.30am & 1–5.30pm; 5zł), topped by an amazing

---

THE HEJNAŁ

Legend has it that during one of the thirteenth-century **Tatar raids** on Kraków, a guard watching from the tower of St Mary's Church saw the invaders approaching and blew his trumpet, only for his alarm to be cut short by an arrow through the throat. Every hour a local fireman now plays the sombre melody (*hejnał*) from the same tower, halting abruptly at the point when the guard is supposed to have been hit.

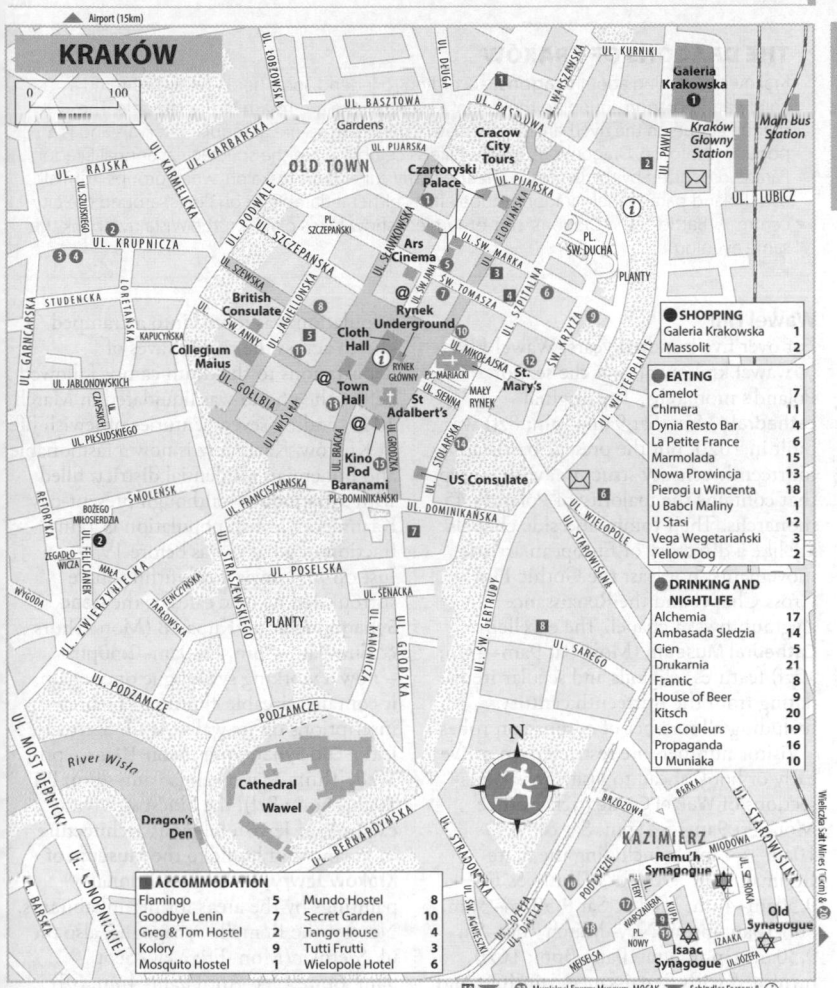

KRAKÓW

▲ Airport (15km)

● SHOPPING
| Galeria Krakowska | 1 |
| Massolit | 2 |

● EATING
Camelot	7
Chimera	11
Dynia Resto Bar	4
La Petite France	6
Marmolada	15
Nowa Prowincja	13
Pierogi u Wincenta	18
U Babci Maliny	1
U Stasi	12
Vega Wegetariański	3
Yellow Dog	2

● DRINKING AND NIGHTLIFE
Alchemia	17
Ambasada Sledzia	14
Cien	5
Drukarnia	21
Frantic	8
House of Beer	9
Kitsch	20
Les Couleurs	19
Propaganda	16
U Muniaka	10

■ ACCOMMODATION
Flamingo	5	Mundo Hostel	8
Goodbye Lenin	7	Secret Garden	10
Greg & Tom Hostel	9	Tango House	4
Kolory	2	Tutti Frutti	3
Mosquito Hostel	1	Wielopole Hotel	6

ensemble of spires. Inside is the stunningly realistic triptych high altar (1477–89), an intricate woodcarving depicting the Virgin Mary's Quietus among the apostles.

Czartoryski Palace

A few blocks north of the Rynek on ul. Pijarska sits the **Czartoryski Palace**, usually home to Kraków's finest art collection, although it is closed until 2014 for renovation. When it reopens, one undoubted highlight will be Poland's most treasured old master, Leonardo da Vinci's extraordinary *Lady with an Ermine*.

The university

West from the Rynek is the university area, whose first element was the fifteenth-century **Collegium Maius** building at ul. Jagiellońska 15. Now it's the **University Museum** (Mon–Fri 11am–2.20pm, Sat 11am–1.20pm; 16zł). Entrance is by guided tour only – the museum office will sign you up for the next English-language tour, departing at regular intervals throughout the day. Inside, the ground-floor rooms retain the mathematical and geographical murals once used for the teaching of figures like Copernicus, one of the university's earliest students.

25

THE DRAGONS OF KRAKÓW

Kraków has a thing about **dragons**: according to legend, local hero Krak slaughtered a child-eating dragon, founding the city of Kraków in the aftermath of the struggle. The dragon statue on the riverbank below Wawel Hill breathes fire at regular intervals and is a popular photo-op. Dragon-lore, meanwhile, is celebrated in the spectacular annual Dragon Parade organized by the Groteska Theatre (early June; ◍groteska.pl), when groups from all over Poland parade their dragons (huge affairs either inflatable or on floats) around the city centre. A "Battle of the Dragons" son-et-lumière show takes place on the Wisła riverbank the same evening.

Wawel Hill

For over five hundred years, Wawel Hill (◍wawel.krakow.pl) was the seat of Poland's monarchy. The original **cathedral** (Mon–Sat 9am–5pm; 8zł) was built in 1020, but the present basilica is a fourteenth-century structure, with a crypt that contains the majority of Poland's 45 monarchs. Their tombs and side chapels are like a directory of European artistic movements, not least the Gothic Holy Cross Chapel and the Renaissance Zygmuntowska chapel. The excellent **Cathedral Museum** (Mon–Sat 9am–4pm; 12zł) features religious and secular items dating from the thirteenth century, including all manner of coronation robes.

Visitor numbers are restricted, so arrive early or book ahead to visit the various sections of **Wawel Castle** (ticket office Mon–Fri 9am–5.45pm, Sat & Sun 10am–4.45pm), including the State Rooms (April–Oct Tues, Thurs & Fri 9.30am–4pm, Wed & Sat 9.30am–3pm, Sun 10am–3pm; Nov–March Tues–Sat 9.30am–3pm, Sun 10am–3pm; 16zł), furnished with Renaissance paintings and tapestries, and the grand Royal Private Apartments (Tues–Sun 9.30am–5pm, Sat & Sun 11am–6pm; 21zł). Much of the original contents of the Royal Treasury and Armoury (same times as the State Rooms; 16zł) were sold to pay off royal debts, but still feature some fine works, including the Szczerbiec, the country's original coronation sword.

Kazimierz

A **Jewish centre** from the fourteenth century onwards, Kraków's Kazimierz district had grown by 1939 to accommodate some 65,000 Jews. After the Nazis took control, however, this population was forced into a cramped ghetto across the river. Waves of deportations to the death camps followed before the ghetto was liquidated in March 1943, ending seven centuries of Jewish life in Kraków. Kazimierz is now a fashionable and bohemian residential district, filled with **synagogues** – although present-day Kazimierz's Jewish population is a tiny fraction of what it was before 1939. Just off pl. Nowy, a colourful square surrounded by chic cafés, is the **Isaac Synagogue** at ul. Kupa 18 (Mon–Thurs & Sun 9am–8pm, Fri 9am–2.30pm) – now a working synagogue once again, it contains sizeable chunks of Hebrew inscriptions on its walls. At ul. Szeroka 24 is the **Old Synagogue** (Mon 10am–2pm, Wed, Thurs & weekends 9am–4pm, Fri 10am–5pm; 9zł), the oldest surviving example of Jewish religious architecture in Poland and home to the **Museum of Kraków Jewry**, with its traditional paintings by the area's former inhabitants. Nearby, the Remu'h Synagogue, also on ul. Szeroka (Mon–Fri: May–Sept 9am–6pm; Oct–April 9am–4pm; 6zł) contains lovely original furnishings; in the cemetery behind the synagogue you'll find restored eighteenth-century gravestones.

At the southern end of Kazimierz, the **Municipal Engineering Museum** at św Wawrzynca 15 (Tues–Sun 10am–4pm; 8zł) contains a fantastic display of vehicles in a former tram depot.

MOCAK Museum of Contemporary Art

The former industrial district of Podgorze/Zabłocie just across the river from Kazimierz is one of contemporary Kraków's fastest-developing districts, thanks in part to the opening of this new art museum at ul. Lipova 4 (Tues–Sun 11am–7pm; 10zł; Tues free; ⊛mocak .com.pl) in 2011. Occupying renovated buildings that once formed part of Oskar Schindler's Emalia Factory (see below), it contains a compelling collection of Polish contemporary art and hosts a regular programme of big-name exhibitions.

The Schindler Factory

Immediately next door to MOCAK, this is the place where German industrialist Oskar Schindler manufactured enamel pots during World War II, purposefully employing over a thousand Kraków Jews in order to save them from the death camps – a tale immortalized in Steven Spielberg's Oscar-winning film, *Schindler's List*. The factory is now home to a superbly arranged display entitled **Kraków Under Nazi Occupation** (Mon 10am–4pm, Tues–Sun 10am–8pm; closed first Mon of month; 19zł), which fills several rooms with photo displays, period newsreels and survivor interviews. Telling the stories of both Jewish and Gentile Kraków with equal weight, it's an engrossing and rewarding experience.

Wieliczka salt mines

Ten kilometres from Kraków is the "underground salt cathedral" of **Wieliczka**, 300km of subterranean tunnels that have been used to mine salt since the thirteenth century (daily: April–Oct 7.30am–7.30pm; Nov–March 8am–5pm). The ticket price includes a tour (68zł English, 49zł Polish), which passes by an underground lake and a number of impressive statues and edifices – including chandeliers – carved out of rock salt. Trains to Wieliczka-Rynek run from Kraków Głowny roughly every hour.

ARRIVAL AND DEPARTURE

By plane Kraków airport is situated 15km west of the city centre. It's easiest to catch the free shuttle bus to the airport's train station, which has regular trains to Kraków Głowny (every 30min, 5.14am–10.44pm; 18min; 19zł). The equivalent taxi ride is 70zł.
By train Kraków Głowny, the central train station, is located a 5min walk northeast from the city's historic centre.
Destinations Berlin (1 daily; 10hr); Bratislava (1 daily; 8hr); Budapest (1 daily; 10hr 30min); Gdańsk (6 daily; 8hr);

Oświęcim/Auschwitz (15 daily; 1hr 45min); Poznań (10 daily; 7hr 30min); Prague (1 daily; 9hr 30min); Toruń (3 daily; 8hr); Warsaw (hourly; 2hr 30min); Wrocław (hourly; 5hr); Zakopane (1 daily; 4hr).
By bus The main bus station is located directly opposite the train station. Nearby Eurolines (see p.33) runs services to all major European capitals.
Destinations Zakopane (every 20min; 2hr).

INFORMATION AND TOURS

Tourist information The municipal tourist office (Mon–Fri 8am–8pm, Sat & Sun 9am–5pm; ☎012 430 2646, ⊛krakow.pl) operates information booths at three central locations: the circular pavilion in the Planty near the train station underpass; the Town Hall Tower on Rynek Głowny; the Wyspiański 2000 Pavilion on plac Wszystkich Świętych; and ul. Jozefa 7 in Kazimierz.
Tourist card The Kraków Tourist Card (2/3 days for 60/80zł; ⊛krakowcard.com) gives you free entrance to all the major museums, as well as discounts at some of the city's pricier restaurants, shops and tour providers.
Tours You'll be bombarded with tour offers for the city and surrounding sights, but these are often rushed and cost four times as much as public transport. If you do want a tour, try Cracow City Tours at ul. Floriańska 44 (daily 9am–9pm; ☎12 421 1327, ⊛cracowcitytours.pl), which offers a wide range of itineraries and discounts for students.

ACCOMMODATION

The number of hostels has mushroomed in the last few years, but it is still worth booking ahead if you want to stay in the most central spots. All hostels have free wi-fi, breakfast and cheap laundry services.

HOSTELS

Flamingo ul. Szewska 4 ☎12 422 0000, ⊛flamingo -hostel.com. A clean, colourful place on a street full of bars, attracting a lively party crowd. Dorm 55zł, double 190zł
Goodbye Lenin ul. Grodzka 34 ☎12 430 3053, ⊛goodbyelenin.pl. Funky, mural-adorned backpacker base with a full kitchen and bright, spacious rooms. There's also another branch at Berka Joselewicza 23. Dorm 40zł, double 150zł
★ **Greg & Tom Hostel** ul. Pawia 12/7 ☎12 422 4100, ⊛gregtomhostel.com. The ideal hostel for those who want home comforts as well as a place to crash, this suave option opposite the train station offers single beds in snazzily designed dorms (no bunks), neat doubles and relaxing social/kitchen space. Dorm 55zł, double 170zł
Mosquito Hostel Rynek Kleparski 4/6 ☎12 430 1461, ⊛mosquitohostel.com. Comfortable and sharply decorated hostel just round the corner from the Stary Kleparz market, offering a mixture of dorms and privates, buffet breakfast and a cosy galley kitchen. Dorm 55zł, double 150zł

★ **TREAT YOURSELF**

Wielopole Hotel ul. Wielopole 3; ☎ 12 422 1475, ⊛ wielopole.pl. If you want a break from hostel parties and busy city streets, try this stylish but intimate hotel ideally poised between the Old Town and Kazimierz. Here you'll find spacious but cosy apartments, satellite TV and free internet access. Breakfast included. Double **479zł**

★ **Mundo Hostel** ul. Sarego 10 ☎ 12 422 6113, ⊛ mundohostel.eu. Probably the most beautiful hostel in Kraków, with each room decorated according to a different national theme. Relaxing kitchen-cum-lounge, and a decent-sized breakfast. Dorm **50zł**, double **160zł**

Secret Garden ul. Skawinska 7 ☎ 12 430 5445, ⊛ thesecretgarden.pl. Spacious, bright and cheerful hostel on a quiet street which provides hotel-like standards at hostel prices – there's a high proportion of privates, a roomy kitchen, and a swish first-floor TV lounge. Dorm **45zł**, double **150zł**

Tutti Frutti ul. Floriańska 29 ☎ 12 428 0028, ⊛ tuttifruttihostel.com. This welcoming hostel, also with 4-bed apartments, does the basics (especially breakfast) very well and also provides guides for guests seeking the best places to go out. Dorm **49zł**, apartment **260zł**

HOTEL

Kolory ul. Estery 10 ☎ 12 421 0465, ⊛ kolory.com.pl. Bright en-suite rooms above *Les Couleurs* café (see opposite), all with TV, folk-style design details and wi-fi coverage. Some rooms overlook the lively plac Nowy; marginally quieter rooms are at the back. Double **230zł**

B&B

Tango House ul. Szpitalna 4 ☎ 12 429 3114, ⊛ tangohouse.pl. Hidden in a secluded courtyard just round the corner from the main square, *Tango* is a B&B of two halves: the old part has a spectacular nineteenth-century staircase and parquet-floored en suites in soothing citrus colours, while the new part houses smart studios with kitchenettes. All rooms come with flat-screen TV, electric kettle and wi-fi. Double **260zł**

EATING

Kraków's centre is renowned for its restaurants and cafés, which offer much beyond the Polish culinary staples.

CAFÉS, CHEAP EATS AND SNACKS

Camelot ul. św. Tomasza 15. A chic, artsy café with wooden furnishings, peasant-art motifs on the walls, and occasional cabaret shows in the basement. Excellent desserts, including the best apple pie in town (12.50zł).

Chimera ul. św. Anny 3. Expansive buffet selection in a soothing courtyard, with attractively priced main courses, a salad bar and plenty of vegetarian choices. Single portions 4zł, plateful 16zł. Daily 11am–10pm.

★ **Nowa Prowincja** ul. Bracka 3–5. Homely, relaxed café owned by local musical legend Grzegorz Turnau, with a wonderful wooden loft, thick hot chocolate and Kraków's best lattes (8zł). Daily 9am–11pm.

La Petite France ul. św. Tomasza 25. An attractive deli-bistro with five small tables and a row of stools pushed against the street-facing window ledge. This is a fantastic place to tuck into what is arguably the best quiche in Kraków (8zł) or a more filling baguette sandwich (12zł). Daily 8am–10pm.

U Babci Maliny ul. Slawkowska 17. Upmarket milk bar with a mountain hut interior, serving suitably wholesome Polish classics. Mains 9–18zł. Mon–Fri 9am–7pm, Sat & Sun 10am–5pm.

U Stasi ul. Mikolajska 16. Lunchtime classic favoured by locals, hidden behind a pizzeria, with unusually friendly service and delicious *knedle* (dumplings) stuffed with plums (7zł). Mon–Fri 12.30pm until the food runs out.

Vega Wegetariański ul. Krupnicza 22. Inexpensive but innovative veggie dishes in an order-at-the-counter place that's also very comfy to sit and eat in. Think tofu, beans, lots of grains and lots of greens. Mains 10–15zł. Daily 9am–9pm.

RESTAURANTS

Dynia Resto-Bar ul. Krupnicza 20. The city's most stylish student hangout has some delicious smoothies (7zł) and amazing breakfasts (10–21zł), healthy salad-or-pasta lunches and seductive desserts. Mon–Fri 8am–10pm, Sat & Sun 9am–10pm.

Pierogi u Wincenta ul. Bozego Ciala 12. Tiny six-table place with a huge selection of own-recipe *pierogi*, including plenty of vegetarian options (such as *pierogi* with broccoli and feta) too. Mon–Wed & Sun noon–10pm, Thurs noon–11pm, Fri & Sat noon–midnight.

Yellow Dog ul. Krupnicza 9/1. Lounge-bar atmosphere and a Singapore-themed menu that delivers a dependable range of Chinese, Malaysian and Indian dishes (mains 20–30zł) with a handful of vegetarian choices. Daily noon–10pm.

★ **TREAT YOURSELF**

Marmolada ul. Grodzka 5. Traditional Polish cuisine with an Italian twist – the Saltimbocca veal (50zł) and roast goose with cherries (52zł) are both memorably rich and satisfying, although there is a lot more to choose from. With candles on the tables and floral decor, it's as relaxing as they come. Daily noon–10pm.

DRINKING AND NIGHTLIFE

For best value head to Kazimierz or the student quarter to the west of the Old Town.

BARS

★ **Alchemia** ul. Estery 5. Murky, quirky and always packed, this candlelit rabbit warren has live jazz on the weekends and a stuffed crocodile over the bar. 0.5lt beer 7.50zł. Daily 9am–4am.

Ambasada Sledzia ul. Stolarska 8/10. The *"Herring Embassy"* doffs an ironic cap to the drinking culture of the communist era (all drinks are priced at 4zł, all food including marinated herring and porky-looking jellied meats at 8zł), while providing a trendily minimalistic matt-black-wall interior in which to consume it. Frequently packed to the gills. 24hr.

Drukarnia Nadwiślańska 1 Ⓦdrukarniaclub.pl. Roomy bar just over the river from Kazimierz, with several rooms decked out in different styles, from arty Parisian café to brash party pub. There's also a basement-level club venue hosting regular DJs and live music. Mon–Thurs & Sun 9am–1am, Fri & Sat 9am–4am.

House of Beer ul. św. Tomasza 35. This roomy and convivial Old-Town pub is the ideal place to plough your way through a selection of the increasingly excellent ales turned out by Poland's small breweries. Guest ales on tap (from 7zł/0.5lt). Daily 2pm–2am.

Les Couleurs ul. Estery 10. A smoky and colourful Parisian-style café-bar serving light meals and alcoholic beverages of every description. Cocktails around 14zł. Mon–Thurs & Sun 8am–midnight, Fri & Sat 8am–2am.

Propaganda ul. Miodowa 12. The People's Republic lives on in this popular hangout, cluttered with propaganda posters, old uniforms and antique radios. 0.5lt beer 7zł. Daily 11am–3am.

CLUBS

Cien ul. św Jana 15. Funk, house and retro DJs entertain a young and glamorous crowd. You'll need to queue at weekends. Cover 25zł. Tues–Sun 9pm–5am.

Frantic ul. Szewska 5. With two dancefloors, there's plenty of space here for grooving to a mix of r'n'b and old-school hits. Cocktails from 15zł. Wed–Sat 9pm–4am.

Kitsch ul. Dajwór 16. A mixture of over-the-top and downright shabby decor sets an appropriately camp tone for this gay/straight/who cares disco on the eastern fringes of Kazimierz. Daily 9pm–5/7am.

U Muniaka ul. Floriańska 3. The city's best live jazz from 9.30pm every night. 0.33lt beer 9zł. Entrance free/25zł depending on who's playing. Daily 7pm–2am.

ENTERTAINMENT

Cinema tickets are 11–19zł throughout the city.

Ars ul. św. Jana 6 Ⓦ ars.pl. Offers a mixture of Hollywood and international art films in an old-style cinema.

Kino Pod Baranami Rynek Główny 27 Ⓦ kinopodbaranami.pl. Screens a range of Western, Polish and Bollywood titles in an old-fashioned cinema setting.

SHOPPING

Touristy Floriańska and the boutiques in the Rynek contain a few bargain art dealers among the overpriced souvenirs. Kazimierz is filled with reasonably priced galleries and secondhand shops and, on Sun, pl. Nowy becomes a colourful flea market of cheap clothes and jewellery.

Galeria Krakowska just next to the train station. An international "mall experience", with all the fashionable global brands that you could wish for, in addition to a large Carrefour supermarket. Mon–Sat 9am–10pm, Sun 10am–9pm.

Massolit Felicjanek 4. You can find a good selection of English used books, including translations of Polish authors, at this café/bookshop, where you can also trade in your old books for new reading material. Mon–Fri 8am–8pm, Sat 10am–8pm, Sun noon–8pm.

DIRECTORY

Consulate US ul. Stolarska 9 ☎ 12 424 5100.

Exchange To avoid the large commission charged at the banks, check the *kantor* exchanges that fill the streets around the Rynek for the best rates.

Hospital Gabriel Narutowicz Hospital (Szpital im. Gabriela Narutowicza) north of the Old Town at ul. Prądniczka 35 (☎ 012 416 2266).

Internet Garinet, ul. Floriańska 18 (daily 9am–10pm; 6zł/hr).

KRAKÓW FESTIVAL CITY

In spring and summer hardly a week goes by in Kraków without at least one cultural **festival** taking place. Many events are held on the Main Market Square, or in outdoor locations elsewhere in the city. Stand-out events include the Jewish Culture Festival (June/July; Ⓦ jewishfestival.pl), with exhibitions, seminars and immensely enjoyable Klezmer concerts in Kazimierz; the Summer Jazz Festival (July/Aug; Ⓦ cracjazz.com), with big names taking to a variety of outdoor stages; and Coke Live Festival (Aug; Ⓦ livefestival.pl) with three days of international pop-rock (2013's line-up included Franz Ferdinand and Florence and the Machine) on Błonie meadow – camping is available.

25

Left luggage The train station has a left-luggage depot (7am–10pm; 5zł/24hr).

Pharmacies Grodzka, ul. Grodzka 26 (Mon–Fri 8am–9pm, Sat 9am–6pm, Sun 10am–5pm), and Pod Złotą Głową, Rynek Główny 13 (Mon–Fri 9am–9pm, Sat 9am–4pm).

Post office ul. Westerplatte 20 (Mon–Fri 7.30am–8.30pm, Sat 8am–2pm, Sun 9–11am).

AUSCHWITZ-BIRKENAU (OŚWIĘCIM)

Lying 70km west of Kraków and within easy day-trip range, the complex of camps known as **AUSCHWITZ-BIRKENAU** (W auschwitz.org.pl) has become synonymous with World War II and the Holocaust. The camps lie on the western fringes of **OŚWIĘCIM**, which is in all other respects a perfectly nondescript middle-sized Polish town.

Auschwitz was established by the Germans in 1940 to house Polish political prisoners but swiftly expanded to accommodate Soviet POWs. The Birkenau annexe, built in 1941 to cope with growing numbers, became the site of one of the Nazi regime's most notorious death camps: about 1.3 million people, ninety percent of them Jews, were murdered here. The Germans failed to destroy the camp before they left and over 60,000 prisoners survived – which is why the horrors perpetrated here are so well documented. The two sites, Auschwitz and Birkenau, are 3km apart, but are linked by shuttle bus. Together they are visited by over 1.3 million visitors a year.

Auschwitz

Most visitors start at Auschwitz (daily 8am–dusk with English-language tours on the hour 9.30am–3.30pm; guided tour 40zł; non-guided visits free), which is 3km west of Oświęcim town centre. From May to October participation in guided tours is compulsory between 10am and 3pm, so if you want to visit the Auschwitz site on your own, arrive outside these times. Once beyond the entrance gate (bearing the notorious cast-iron inscription *Arbeit Macht Frei*), the site consists of a series of red-brick barrack blocks, many of which contain a museum display relating to a particular

aspect of the camp or a particular nation whose citizens were deported here.

Block 13 contains an account of Europe's Roma and Sinti communities (an estimated 20,000 of whom died here); block 5 contains rooms full of spectacles, prosthetic limbs, pots and pans, all confiscated from inmates of the camp and abandoned here when the Germans retreated. The prison blocks finish by a gas chamber and a pair of ovens where the bodies were incinerated.

Birkenau

The enormous **Birkenau** camp (same hours as Auschwitz; allow 1–2hr to fully explore the site) was designed as a death camp in 1942, when the Nazis developed their policy of exterminating European Jewry. Large gas chambers at the back of the camp were damaged but not destroyed by the fleeing Nazis in 1945. Victims arrived in closed trains, and those who were fit to work (around 25 percent) were immediately separated from those who were driven straight to the gas chambers. The railway line is still there, just as the Nazis abandoned it. One of the few buildings still standing here is the so-called Sauna, where the newly arrived were undressed, shaved and assigned camp clothes – a matter-of-fact museum display takes you methodically through the process.

ARRIVAL AND DEPARTURE

By bus You can catch one of the regular buses (2–3 hourly; 1hr 45min) to the main Auschwitz site from Kraków's main bus station. There's an hourly shuttle-bus service (April–Oct) to the Birkenau section from the car park at Auschwitz. Taxis are also available; otherwise it's a 3km walk.

THE TATRAS AND ZAKOPANE

Some 80km long, with peaks of up to 2500m, the **Tatras** are the most spectacular part of the mountain range extending along Poland's border with Slovakia. They are as beautiful as any mountain landscape in northern Europe, the ascents leading along boulder-strewn trails beside woods and streams and culminating in breathtaking, windswept peaks. The peaks

INTO SLOVAKIA
The coach company Strama runs 5 daily
buses (2 daily out of season) to **Poprad**
(2hr; 20zł; ⓦstrama.eu), a Slovakian skiing
and hiking centre.

are topped with snow for most of the year,
making it a great area for skiing (from
mid-Dec to March). The mountains are
a protected national park and as such
harbour lots of wildlife: if you're lucky
you could glimpse rare species such as
lynx, golden eagles and brown bear.

The main base for skiing and hiking on
the Polish side is the extremely popular and
lively resort of **Zakopane**. There are good
road and rail links with Kraków 60km to
the north, as well as several mountain
resorts across the border in Slovakia.

WHAT TO SEE AND DO

Skiing here is cheap, with the premier
slopes of Kasprowy Wierch just a few
minutes out of town, and plenty of places
in the town centre to rent equipment.
Hikers may want to avoid the 9km path
to the lovely but busy Morskie Oko Lake
in high season, but there's no shortage of
other, more secluded trails. Świat, at ul.
Orkana 1/4 (☎693 022 944, ⓦswiat.biz
.pl), organizes **rafting** tours (with
English-speaking guides) on the nearby
Dunajec River. Zakopane's **market** at the
bottom of ul. Krupówki sells a wide
range of traditional local goods, including
oscypek (smoked sheep's cheese) and small
woodcarvings. This latter local tradition
is intriguingly displayed in the whimsical
wooden tombs of the nearby Old
Cemetery (Stary Cementarz).

ARRIVAL AND DEPARTURE

By train The station is on ul. Kosciuszki, a 10min walk east
of the pedestrianized main street, ul. Krupówki.
Destinations Kraków (1 daily; 4hr); Warsaw (2 daily; 7–9hr).
By bus The bus station is located next to the train station.
Destinations Kraków (every 20min; 2hr).

INFORMATION

Tourist information Tourist office just west of the
stations at ul. Kościuszki 17 (March–June & Sept to mid-
Dec Mon–Fri 9am–5pm; July & Aug daily 9am–5pm;
☎018 201 2211, ⓦzakopane.pl).

Tatra National Park Information Centre near the park
entrance at ul. Chałubińskiego 44 (daily: Jan–April & Oct
7am–4pm; May & June 7am–5pm; July & Aug 7am–6pm;
Nov & Dec 7am–3pm; ☎18 202 3300, ⓦtpn.pl); provides
good-quality maps and information on hiking routes.
Internet Ksero, ul. Galicy 8 (Mon–Fri 7.30am–11pm, Sat
& Sun 10am–11pm; 5zł/hr).

ACCOMMODATION

Finding a place to stay is rarely a problem in Zakopane as,
in addition to the hostels, many homeowners in town offer
private rooms.
★ **Goodbye Lenin** ul. Chłabówka 44 ☎18 200 1330,
ⓦgoodbyelenin.pl. Lying 3.5km out of town, this cosy
house in the woods is the perfect place to focus on hiking
and skiing. Call ahead for a ride from the bus station. Dorm
35zł, double 120zł
Hotel Fian ul. Chałubińskiego 38 ☎18 201 5071, ⓦfian
.pl. With a sauna and jacuzzi to ease hiking aches, this place
also prides itself on the "gastronomic experience" offered
by its resident chef. Breakfast included. Double 235zł
Stara Polana ul. Nowotarska 59 ☎18 206 8902,
ⓦstarapolana.pl. A warm wood-panelled interior,
satellite TV and friendly service make this hostel excellent
value. Dorm 60zł, double 160zł
Villa Orla ul. Kościeliska 50 ☎18 201 2697, ⓦorla.com.pl.
Traditional partly-timbered house with cosy rooms, many
with sloping attic ceilings. The buffet breakfast is served up
in a sunny room stuffed with vintage clocks. Double 160zł

EATING, DRINKING AND NIGHTLIFE

Head to the area around ul. Krupówki where you'll find
plenty of lively bars and restaurants.
Bar Mleczny ul. Krupówki 1, entrance from ul. Nowotarska.
Pricey for a milk bar, but still the cheapest eats in town with
hearty Polish mains for 9–15zł. Daily 9am–7pm.
Genesis pl. Niepodległości 1. The town's lager-and-lasers-
type club attracts Poland's top DJs at weekends. 5zł cover
(more on weekends). Summer daily 9pm–5am; winter
Thurs–Sun 9pm–5am.
Owczarnia ul. Galicy 4. Giant grilled steaks, *kielbasa*
(sausage) and local trout are the specialities in this lively
grill-house. Mains 12–35zł. Daily 10am–midnight.
Paparazzi ul. Galicy 8. This chic cocktail bar has some
leafy outdoor seating and fruity drinks (from 17zł). Mon–
Fri 4pm–1am, Sat & Sun noon–1am.

Western Poland

Tossed for centuries back and forth
between the Poles, Germans and Czechs,
Poland's southwestern province of Silesia

25

is a fascinating blend of cultures, languages and architectural styles. Its main city, **Wrocław**, is the focus of Poland's new economic dynamism. Vibrant **Poznań** to the north, the heart of the original Polish nation, is one of the country's oldest cities and a key commercial link to Western Europe.

WROCŁAW

WROCŁAW (pronounced "vrots-waf"), the fourth-largest city in Poland, is used to rebuilding. For centuries – and in common with Breslau – it was largely dominated by Germans, but this changed after the war, as thousands of displaced Poles flocked to the decimated city. The various influences are reflected in Wrocław's architecture, with its mammoth Germanic churches, Flemish-style mansions and Baroque palaces. The latest rebuilding came after a catastrophic flood in the early 1990s, which left most of the centre underwater. Fortunately, the reconstruction that followed has left the pretty Old Town rejuvenated and without the tourist mobs of Kraków. The city has also been actively reaching out to foreign investors in both technology and finance. This, along with a lively university scene, lends Wrocław a vigorous air of economic and cultural well-being.

WHAT TO SEE AND DO

Wrocław's historical centre is delineated by the former city walls, bordered by a moat and a shady park, and by the River Odra to the north, whose pretty islands are home to a handful of churches.

The Market Square

In the heart of the town is the vast **Market Square** (Rynek) and the thirteenth-century town hall, with its magnificently ornate facades. The hall is now the **Town Museum** (Wed–Sat 10am–5pm, Sun 10am–6pm; 20zł). In the northwest corner of the square are two curious Baroque houses known as **Jaś i Małgosia** (Hansel and Gretel), linked by a gateway giving access to **St Elizabeth's**, the finest of Wrocław's churches. Its 90m tower (Mon–Sat 10am–7pm, Sun noon–7pm; 5zł) is the city's most prominent landmark.

Jewish quarter

Southwest of the square lies the former **Jewish quarter**, whose inhabitants were driven from their tenements during the Third Reich. One of the largest synagogues in Poland, the **Synagoga pod Białym Bocianem** (Synagogue Under the White Stork), lies hidden in a courtyard at ul. Włodkowica 9. Visits can be arranged through the Jewish Information Centre (Mon–Thurs 10am–5pm, Fri 10am–4pm, Sun 11am–4pm; 6zł; ☎71 787 3902).

The Racławice Panorama and the National Museum

East of the city centre, a rotunda houses the famous **Panorama of the Battle of Racławice** (mid-April to Sept daily 9am–5pm; Oct Tues–Sun 9am–5pm; Nov to mid-April Tues–Sun 9am–4pm; shows every 30min but expect queues; 25zł, including entrance to the National Museum). This painting – 120m long and 15m high – was commissioned in 1894 for the centenary of the Russian army's defeat by Tadeusz Kościuszko's militia at Racławice, a village near Kraków. You can also visit the nearby **National Museum** (Wed–Fri & Sun 10am–5pm, Sat 10am–6pm; closes 1hr earlier Oct–March; 15zł, Sat free), with its fun and colourful exhibition of twentieth-century Polish installation artists like Jozef Szajna.

University quarter

North of the Market Square is the historic and buzzing **university quarter**, full of bargain eateries and tiny bookshops. At its centre is the huge Collegium Maximum, whose Aula Leopoldina assembly hall, upstairs at pl. Uniwersytecki 1 (daily except Wed 10am–3.30pm; 10zł), is one of the greatest secular interiors of the Baroque age.

Wyspa Piasek and Ostrów Tumski

Northeast from the Market Hall, the Piaskowy Bridge leads to the attractive island of **Wyspa Piasek** and the fourteenth-century church of St Mary of the Sands, with its majestically vaulted ceiling. Two elegant little bridges connect the island with **Ostrów Tumski**, the city's ecclesiastical heart, home to several

Baroque palaces and the vast Cathedral of St John the Baptist.

ARRIVAL AND DEPARTURE

By plane Take bus #406 to the (reasonably central) train station from the airport (30min; 3zł). The equivalent taxi ride costs 40–50zł.

By train The main train station, Wrocław Główny, faces the broad boulevard of ul. Piłsudskiego, a 15min walk south of the Market Square.

Destinations Berlin (1 daily; 4hr 50min); Dresden (3 daily; 3hr 30min); Gdańsk (3 daily; 7hr–8hr 30min); Kraków (hourly; 5hr); Poznań (hourly; 3hr–3hr 30min); Toruń (2 daily; 5hr); Warsaw (hourly; 5hr–6hr 30min).

By bus The main station is just to the south of the train station.

INFORMATION

Tourist information The tourist office at Rynek 14 (daily 9am–7pm; ☎71 344 03111, ⓦwroclaw-info.pl) books accommodation.

Internet Internet Navigator, ul. Igielna 14 (daily 9am–midnight; 4zł/hr).

ACCOMMODATION

Boogie Hostel ul. Ruska 35 ☎71 342 4472, ⓦboogiehostel.com. Spacious and colourful, with clean, modern rooms and a tendency to attract a party crowd. Dorm 40zł, double 130zł

Cinnamon ul. Kazimierza Wielkiego 67 ☎71 344 5858, ⓦcinnamonhostel.com. Pleasant, airy rooms and friendly, attentive-to-detail staff make this spice-themed hostel a winner. Board games in the common room help to keep things sociable. Dorm 35zł, double 135zł

Grampa's Hostel pl. św. Macieja 2/1 ☎71 787 8444, ⓦgrampahostel.com. On the north bank of the Odra, this bright, clean and friendly place has plenty of common-room space. Free wi-fi and breakfast included. Dorm 37zł, double 135zł

Mleczarnia ul. Włodkowica 5 ☎71 787 7570, ⓦmleczarniahostel.pl. Comfortable, bohemian hangout, situated in an old building above a candlelit coffee bar. Retro furnishings and vintage lamps add to the atmosphere. Dorm 45zł, double/apartment 220zł

Stop Wroclaw ul. Sienkiewicza 31 ☎51 911 5075, ⓦstopwroclaw.pl. Just north of the centre across the river, this cute and welcoming guesthouse offers small but comfortable rooms, with access to a kitchen and free tea/coffee. Four-person apartments also available. Double 100zł, apartment 250zł

EATING

Bazylia ul. Kuźnicza 42. Stylishly minimalist canteen, with food priced by weight (2.59zł/100g) and a wonderful view

★ TREAT YOURSELF

JaDka restaurant ul. Rzeznicza 24/25. A meal at this renowned restaurant may not be cheap (though some classics like *pierogi* come in at only 21–36zł), but you can be assured of world-class Polish cuisine and excellent service. Daily 1–10pm.

onto the Collegium. Expect tasty soups, vegetable side dishes, chicken escalopes and lots of salads. Daily 8am–7pm.

Kuchnia Marche ul. Świdnicka 53. Excellent range of Polish and international cuisine in a lively, family-friendly setting. Mains 10–20zł. Mon–Fri 9am–9pm, Sat & Sun noon–9pm.

Mis ul. Kuźnicza 48. Extremely popular and well-known milk bar that provides quick, filling grub for the student crowd. Mains 4zł. Mon–Fri 7am–6pm, Sat 8am–5pm.

Pod II Strusiem ul. Ruska 61. Set in a rejuvenated former lavatory, this place dishes out some tasty pizzas (12.50–20zł). Particularly good for those who like their pizzas hot – the Ognista ("Fiery One") comes in four varying levels of spiciness; Level Four is definitely a challenge. Mon–Sat 11am–midnight, Sun noon–midnight.

DRINKING AND NIGHTLIFE

Bezsennosc ul. Ruska 51. Just 10min away from the Rynek in the bar-packed Pasaz Niepolda courtyard, this graffiti-lined cellar resounds to a fun mix of indie, electronic and reggae tunes. Cocktails 14–17zł. Mon–Wed & Sun 7pm–3am, Thurs–Sat 7pm–5am.

Kalambur ul. Kuznicza 29a. This ornate Art Nouveau pub, with its period bronze-work and retro vibe, is a hangout for theatre types and hosts occasional live music. 0.5lt beer 7.50zł. Mon–Thurs & Sun noon–2am, Fri & Sat noon–4am.

Nagi Kamerdyner ul. św. Mikolaja. Retro-Americana bar that looks like something out of pulp-film noir, serving up cheap drinks and traditional snacks (*pierogi*, white sausage, herring) to an every-night-is-Fri-night crowd. All snacks 8zł, all shots 4zł. Mon–Thurs 5pm–4am, Fri & Sat 5pm–7am, Sun 5pm–3am.

POZNAŃ

Thanks to its position on the Berlin–Warsaw rail line, **POZNAŃ** is many visitors' first taste of Poland. It's a city of great **diversity**, encompassing tranquil medieval quarters, a fine main square, dynamic business districts and an arty-bohemian subculture.

WHAT TO SEE AND DO

The sixteenth-century **town hall** that dominates the **Old Town Square** (Stary

25

Rynek) has a striking eastern facade, which frames a frieze of notable Polish monarchs. Inside is the **Poznań Historical Museum** (mid-June to mid-Sept Tues–Thurs 11am–5pm, Fri noon–9pm, Sat & Sun 11am–6pm; mid-Sept to mid-June Tues–Thurs 9am–3pm, Fri noon–9pm, Sat & Sun 11am–6pm; 7zł; Sat free), worth visiting for the Renaissance Great Hall on the first floor. East of the Old Town Square, a bridge crosses to the quiet holy island of **Ostrów Tumski**, dominated by Poland's oldest cathedral, the **Cathedral of St John the Baptist**. Most of the building was reconstructed after the war, and Poland's first two monarchs are buried in the crypt. Anyone with even a passing interest in architecture should also take a look at the wonderfully renovated **Stary Browar** southwest of the centre at Półwiejska 32 (Mon–Sat 9am–9pm, Sun 10am–8pm; ⓦstarybrowar5050.com), a nineteenth-century brewery impressively transformed into a cultural centre and shopping mall.

ARRIVAL AND DEPARTURE

By plane Poznań's airport is 7km west of the Old Town and is served by bus #59 (30min; 3.80zł), which runs to the Rondo Kaponiera just north of the train station, and by bus #L to the station itself (3.80zł). The 10min taxi ride from the airport is 40–50zł.

By train The main train station, Poznań Główny, is 2km southwest of the historic quarter; tram #5 runs from the western exit on ul. Glogowska to the city centre.

Destinations Berlin (4 daily; 2hr 50min); Gdańsk (5 daily; 4–5hr); Kraków (10 daily; 7hr 30min); Toruń (9 daily; 2hr 30min); Warsaw (hourly; 2hr 45min–4hr); Wrocław (hourly; 3hr–3hr 30min).

By bus The main bus terminal is a 15min walk south from the Old Town Square, at the intersection of ul. Ratajczaka and ul. Królowej Jadwigi.

INFORMATION

Tourist information Tourist office at Stary Rynek 59/60 (May–Oct Mon–Sat 10am–8pm, Sun 10am–6pm; Oct–April Mon–Fri 10am–6pm, Sat & Sun 10am–5pm; ⓣ61 852 6156, ⓦcim.poznan.pl).

GETTING AROUND

By public transport Poznań's public transport works on a timed basis; a 15min (2.80zł) ticket should be adequate for any travel within the centre.

ACCOMMODATION

The city's trade fairs, which take place throughout the year (July & Aug excepted), can cause hotel prices to double, so always book ahead.

Melange ul. Rybaki 6a ⓣ 50 707 0107, ⓦmelangehostel .com. In a slightly tatty old building 10min south of the centre, but the rooms are comfortable and nicely decorated, and staff are friendly. Dorm **35zł**, double **110zł**

Melody Hostel Stary Rynek 67 (entrance on ul. Kozia) ⓣ61 851 6060. Central location, a good choice of either dorms or privates, popular-music-themed decor and a buffet breakfast make this an outstanding choice. Dorm **50zł**, double **130zł**

Mini Hotelik al. Niepodległości 8a ⓣ61 633 1416. This little place not far from the train station may look a bit frumpy, but its rooms are clean, good value and have TVs. Some have shared facilities, others are en suite. Double **139zł**

EATING

Café Ptasie Radio ul. Kościuszki 74. A favourite with the arty elite, this sophisticated and cosy café provides good breakfasts, pasta dishes, salads and dishy desserts. Mains 19zł. Daily 8am–noon.

Republica Roz pl. Kolegracki 2a. Pretty little café, all teapots and florals, serving cakes, tea and an assortment of hot drinks to warm body and soul. Drinks 6zł. Mon–Fri 8am–midnight, Sat 9am–midnight, Sun 11am–midnight.

Spaghetti Bar Piccolo ul. Rynkowa 1. The buffet here comprises simple but tasty spaghetti dishes that are ready as you enter. Mains from 4zł. Mon–Sat 10am–9pm, Sun noon–9pm.

Warung Bali ul. Zydowska 1. Authentic Indonesian food that hasn't been blanded out to suit Central European taste buds, served in a bright interior. Mains from 35zł. Mon–Thurs noon–10pm, Fri & Sat noon–11pm, Sun noon–9pm.

DRINKING AND NIGHTLIFE

Brovaria Stary Rynek 73. This bar in the Old Town Square may be predictably pricey, but the house-brewed *piwo* is some of Poland's finest. 0.5lt mulled honey beer 9zł. Daily 10am–1am.

Cuba Libre ul. Wrocławska 21. A Latin dance club popular with the student crowd, offering the best late-night party in town. 0.5lt beer 8zł. Mon–Wed 9pm–3am, Thurs–Sat 9pm–5am, Sun 9pm–1am.

La Rambla ul. Wodna 5/6. Superb, snug wine bar with an international choice of tipples and a tapas-like selection of nibbles. Mon–Thurs & Sun 1pm–midnight, Fri & Sat 1pm–2am.

Za kulisami ul. Wodna 24. Cosy two-room affair stuffed full of vintage domestic oddments and old books. Attracts a colourful and varied student-to-mad-professor crowd. Draught honey beer 9zł. Mon–Thurs 4pm–1am, Fri & Sat 4pm–3am, Sun 6pm–1am.

STEAM TRAIN, DOURO VALLEY

Portugal

HIGHLIGHTS

❶ **A night out in Lisbon** Check out the Bairro Alto and dance till dawn. **See p.874**

❷ **Queima das Fitas, Coimbra** Join in this university town's end-of-term celebrations in May. **See p.879**

❸ **Port wine lodges, Porto** Numerous lodges offer tours and tastings. **See p.883**

❹ **The Douro Rail Route** Beautifully scenic line along the Douro river valley. **See p.887**

❺ **The Algarve beaches** The Ilha de Tavira has some of the best. **See p.894**

HIGHLIGHTS ARE MARKED ON THE MAP ON P.861

ROUGH COSTS

Daily budget Basic €45, occasional treat €65

Drink Bottle of *vinho verde* €3

Food Grilled sardines €8

Hostel/budget hotel €20/€45

Travel Train: Lisbon–Faro €21.20–22.20; bus: Porto–Lisbon €19

FACT FILE

Population 10.8 million

Language Portuguese

Currency Euro (€)

Capital Lisbon

International phone code ☎351

Time zone GMT +1hr

Introduction

Although Portugal is perhaps best known for the "fun in the sun" resorts of the Algarve, there's much more to the Iberian Peninsula's lesser-visited country than beautiful beaches. Portugal is geographically diverse yet small enough to travel around easily, with lively cities, mountain ranges, rural villages and a stunning coastline all within easy reach of each other. Another draw is the relaxed, laidback pace of life, meaning that, even in the biggest metropolises, stress and bustle are remarkably rare. And most importantly for the budget traveller, Portugal is, by Western European standards at least, a cheap place to visit.

26

Scenically, some of the most interesting parts of the country are in the north: the **Minho**, a verdant area home to Portugal's only national park; and the sensational gorge and valley of the **Douro**, followed along its course by the spectacular Douro Rail Route. For contemporary Portugal, spend some time in **Lisbon** and **Porto**, the two major cities, both treasure-troves of cultural attractions with big party scenes to boot. And if it's monuments you're after, head to the centre of the country – above all, **Coimbra** and **Évora** – which retain a faded grandeur. The coast is virtually continuous beach, and apart from the **Algarve** and a few pockets around Lisbon and Porto, resorts remain relaxed, often sleepy. The loveliest of all are the wild, isolated beaches of the southern **Alentejo**.

CHRONOLOGY

219 BC The Romans capture the Iberian Peninsula from the Carthaginians, taking the settlement of "Portus Cale" in the process.

711 The Islamic Moors take control of large parts of present-day Portugal.

868 Establishment of the First County of Portugal, within the Kingdom of León.

1095 Crusaders help Portuguese to defeat the Moors.

1139 Afonso I, of the Burgundy dynasty, declares himself king of an independent Portugal.

1386 The Treaty of Windsor, the oldest diplomatic alliance in the world, is signed between England and Portugal, securing mutual military support.

1500s Portugal builds a large empire with colonies across the world including Mozambique, Goa and Brazil.

1580 During a succession crisis, Philip II of Spain invades and crowns himself Philip I of Portugal.

1703 Signing of the Methuen trade treaty with England, following which port wine becomes popular internationally.

1755 An enormous earthquake destroys much of Lisbon.

1822 Brazil declares independence from Portugal.

1916 Portugal joins World War I on the side of the Allies.

1926 Military coup sees Portugal fall under a right-wing dictatorship that would last until 1974.

1939 Portugal remains neutral during World War II.

1974 Government overthrown in a near bloodless coup.

1975 Independence is granted to all Portuguese African colonies.

1976 First free elections are held.

1986 Portugal joins the European Community.

2007 Mass demonstrations against the Portuguese government's economic reforms.

2012 Unemployment exceeds fifteen percent as Portugal struggles through the ongoing European sovereign debt crisis.

ARRIVAL AND DEPARTURE

The three most useful **airports** in mainland Portugal are Faro, Lisbon and Porto. Faro and Lisbon in particular are well linked to the rest of Europe by the budget airlines (notably easyJet), with services to and from Faro increasing during the summer rush. **Bus** is the quickest and most convenient method of overland transport from Spain, particularly if you are arriving from the south. Common daily routes include Seville–Faro, Seville–Lisbon and Madrid–Lisbon. **Trains** are a more costly but usually more comfortable option; the Madrid–Lisbon *trenhotel* runs nightly.

PORTUGAL

HIGHLIGHTS
1. A night out in Lisbon
2. Queima das Fitas, Coimbra
3. Port wine lodges, Porto
4. The Douro Rail Route
5. The Algarve beaches

ATLANTIC OCEAN

SPAIN

26

GETTING AROUND

BY TRAIN

CP (ⓦcp.pt) operates Portugal's **trains**, which are very reasonably priced – particularly in the case of suburban services from Porto and Lisbon. Those designated *Regionais* stop at most stations. *Intercidades* are twice as fast and more expensive. The fastest and most luxurious are the *Rápidos* (known as "Alfa"), which speed between Lisbon, Coimbra and Porto. **InterRail passes** are valid, though you must reserve a seat on Alfa services (payable at the train station; €5). You can check timetables online

(select "*Horários y preços*") or call the information line on ☎808 208 208.

BY BUS

The **bus** network, made up of many regional companies, is more comprehensive and services are often faster, while for long journeys buses can sometimes be slightly cheaper than trains. On a number of major routes (particularly Lisbon–Algarve), express coaches can knock hours off standard multiple-stop bus journeys; Rede Expressos (ⓦrede-expressos.pt) is the largest bus operator. Other key operators include Rodonorte in the north

26

(@rodonorte.pt), Rodotejo in the Ribatejo (@rodotejo.pt), Rodoviária do Alentejo in the Alentejo (@rodalentejo .pt) and EVA in the Algarve (@www .eva-bus.com). For 24hr national bus information call ☎707 22 33 44.

Cycling is popular, though there are few facilities to support cyclists. In the north and centre of the country the terrain is hilly, flattening out south of Lisbon. Bikes can be transported on trains for free, as long as there is space. Bus companies' policies vary so enquire before travelling.

ACCOMMODATION

There are more than fifty state-owned **youth hostels** in Portugal (*Pousadas de Juventude*; @pousadasjuventude.pt); most stay open all year and some impose a curfew. All require a valid HI card; for details see @hihostels.com. Alternatively, these hostels in Portugal can provide you with a guest card, which must be stamped every night that you stay (€2 per stamp); once you have five stamps you're a fully paid-up member of HI. A dormitory bed costs €12–17, depending on season and location; double and twin rooms in these hostels cost €23–47. There is also a growing number of **independent hostels**, particularly in Lisbon and Porto; they're a pricier alternative to official youth hostels but tend to be more conveniently located, and the best have hotel-quality facilities, plus free access to wi-fi and a well-stocked kitchen.

In almost any town you should be able to find a single room for around €30 and a double for under €50; cities are slightly more expensive. The main budget stand-bys are *pensions*, or *pensões*. Hotels,

often present only in larger towns and cities, tend to be more expensive. Seaside resorts invariably offer cheaper **rooms** (*quartos*) in private houses; tourist offices have lists. At the higher end of the scale are **pousadas** (@pousadas.pt), often converted from old monasteries or castles, which charge at least four-star hotel prices. No matter what type of accommodation you select, **breakfast** will usually be included (exceptions are noted in this chapter).

Portugal has more than two hundred **campsites**, most small and attractively located, and all remarkably inexpensive – you'll rarely pay more than €5 a person, plus an additional fee for your tent. You can get a map list from any tourist office, or find details online at @roteiro -campista.pt. Camping rough is banned; beach areas are especially strict about this.

FOOD AND DRINK

Portuguese **food** is cheap and served in plentiful portions. Virtually all cafés dish up a basic meal for less than €10, and for a little more you have the run of most of the country's restaurants. **Snacks** include *tosta mistas* (cheese and ham toasties), *pastéis de bacalhau* (cod fishcakes) and *sandes* (sandwiches). In **restaurants** you can usually have a substantial meal by ordering a *meia dose* (half-portion), or *uma dose* (one portion) between two. Most serve an *ementa turística* (set meal), which can be good value, particularly in *pensões* that serve meals, cheaper workers' cafés or *churrasqueiras* (grill restaurants serving meat and fish dishes). It's often worth opting for the *prato do dia* (dish of the day), usually the cheapest dish on the menu, and, if you're on the coast, going for fish and seafood.

SURFING IN PORTUGAL

Portugal is a surfer's paradise, with some of Europe's best beaches for catching waves. Popular spots include **Peniche** in central Portugal, **Guincho beach** near **Cascais** in Lisbon, the **Alentejo coast** and, in the **Algarve**, Lagos and Sagres. First-timers would do well to try a **surf school** such as Peniche Surf Camp (€452 for a week in high season; @penichesurfcamp.com) or The Surf Experience in Lagos (€467 for a week in high season; @surf-experience.com); accommodation is included in courses. For those with a bit more experience, equipment is available for rent in all popular surfing spots (around €60–70 for a week's board rental).

Meals usually begin with uninvited appetizers (from bread, butter and olives to more elaborate entrées), which often carry a hefty price tag; if in doubt ask, and don't be afraid to send these items back or ignore them. Typical **dishes** include *sopa de marisco* (shellfish soup), *caldo verde* (finely shredded kale leaves in broth) and *bacalhau* (dried cod, cooked in myriad ways). *Caldeirada* is a fish stew cooked with onions and tomatoes, *arroz marisco* a similar stew cooked with seafood and rice. *Cabrito assado* (roast kid) is common in the north of the country, while down south you're sure to see chicken piri-piri (chicken with chilli sauce) on the menu. **Puddings** include *arroz doce* (rice pudding) and *pudim molotoff* (a kind of lightly toasted meringue drenched in caramel sauce). **Cakes** – *bolos* or *pastéis* – are often at their best in *pastelarias* (patisseries), though you'll also find them in cafés and *casas de chá* (tearooms). Among the best are custard tarts (*pastéis de nata*).

DRINK

Portuguese **wines** (*tinto* for red, *branco* for white) are very inexpensive and of high quality. The fortified **port** (*vinho do Porto*; see p.882) and madeira (*vinho da Madeira*) wines are the best known. The light, slightly sparkling **vinhos verdes** are produced in the Minho, and are excellent served chilled. **Brandy** is available in two varieties, Macieiera and Constantino, while Lisbon specializes in the cherry brandy *Ginjinha*, which is served at tiny hole-in-the-wall bars throughout the city. The two most common Portuguese **beers** (*cervejas*) are Sagres and Super Bock.

CULTURE AND ETIQUETTE

Portugal is a **Catholic** country, so it's wise to show respect when visiting churches (bare shoulders should be covered up and short skirts may be frowned upon), and avoid visiting during services, which take place on Sundays and sometimes on other days at around 9.30am. It's also a good idea to learn a few basic phrases in **Portuguese** (see box, p.864); it will certainly endear you to locals. Outside the main tourist areas, French is more widely understood than English. In restaurants, it is usual to **tip** five to ten percent if you're satisfied with the service.

Lone women travellers should face no problems, but might attract a bit of curiosity from locals.

SPORTS AND OUTDOOR ACTIVITIES

In Portugal, **football** isn't just a sport: it's a national passion. During all major matches, the streets fall quiet as people flock inside – usually to restaurants and bars – to watch the television. The three biggest and most successful football clubs are FC Porto, Sporting Lisbon and Benfica. **Surfing** is also popular (see box opposite), and has grown to become a key part of Portugal's tourist industry. Portugal's **natural parks** (*parques naturais*) and its one **national park**, the Parque Nacional de Peneda-Gerês in the Minho, provide superb hiking opportunities. More information about the parks can be found at ⓦportal.icn.pt, and tourist offices located near parks can provide maps and other details. In the Algarve, pick up a copy of the excellent *Trails in the Algarve* booklet, a guide to walking routes in the region, available for €7 from tourist offices.

COMMUNICATIONS

Internet cafés are common (€1.50–3/hr), and wi-fi is available at nearly every hostel. There are also wi-fi hotspots in most town centres, but you'll usually need to join and pay a small fee for

---

PORTUGAL ONLINE

ⓦ**visitportugal.com** Tourist board site, with information and advice.

ⓦ**oportocool.wordpress.com** The latest hip hangouts in Porto.

ⓦ**spottedbylocals.com/lisbon** Up-to-the-minute recommendations from Lisbon residents.

ⓦ**algarveuncovered.com** Detailed site dedicated to the Algarve region.

26

PORTUGUESE

	PORTUGUESE	PRONUNCIATION
Yes	*Sim*	Sing
No	*Não*	Now
Please	*Por favor*	Por favor
Thank you	*Obrigado* [said by men]/	Obrigado/obrigada
	Obrigada [said by women]	
Hello/Good day	*Olá*	Orla
Goodbye	*Adeus*	Adayoosh
Excuse me	*Desculpe*	Deskulp
Where?	*Onde?*	Ond?
Good	*Bom*	Bom
Bad	*Mau*	Maw
Near	*Perto*	Pertoo
Far	*Longe*	Lonje
Cheap	*Barato*	Baratoo
Expensive	*Caro*	Karoo
Open	*Aberto*	Abertoo
Closed	*Fechado*	Feshardoo
Today	*Hoje*	Oje
Yesterday	*Ontem*	Ontaygn
Tomorrow	*Amanhã*	Amanya
How much is…?	*Quanto é?*	Kwantoo eh…?
What time is it?	*Que horas são?*	Kay orash sow?
I don't understand	*Não compreendo*	Now comprendoo
Do you speak English?	*Fala Inglés?*	Farla inglayz?
Where is the station?	*Onde é a estação?*	Ond e a estasow?
On the left/right	*A esquerda/direita*	A eeshkerdah/deeraitah
A ticket to…	*Um bilhete para…*	Oom beelyet para…
What time is the train/	*A que horas é o comboio/*	A kay oras e o convoyo/
bus to…?	*autocarro para…?*	autocarro para…?
I would like a room	*Queria um quarto*	Kereea um kwarto
(single/double)	*individual/casal*	individooal/cazal
May I see the room?	*Posso ver o quarto?*	Posso ver o kwarto?
A table for one/two	*Uma mesa para uma*	Uma mehzah para ooma
	pessoa/duas pessoas	pessoa/duash pessoash
I'm a vegetarian	*Sou vegetariano/a*	So vejetarianoh/ah
A bottle of water/wine	*Uma garrafa de água/vinho*	Ooma garrafuh de
		aigua/vinyo
One	*Um/Uma*	Oom/ooma
Two	*Dois/Duas*	Doysh/dooash
Three	*Três*	Treysh
Four	*Quatro*	Kwatroo
Five	*Cinco*	Sinkoo
Six	*Seis*	Saysh
Seven	*Sete*	Set
Eight	*Oito*	Oytoo
Nine	*Nove*	Nove
Ten	*Dez*	Desh

access. **Post offices** (*correios*) are generally open Monday to Friday 9am to 6pm, Saturday 9am to noon. If you want to use a smartphone for web access and Skype calls in Portugal, consider buying a local sim card. Lycamobile (ⓦlycamobile.com) offers unlimited 3G with its €5 pre-pay sim card, available from most newsagents.

26

EMERGENCY NUMBERS
All emergencies ☎ 112.

EMERGENCIES

Lisbon and the larger tourist areas have seen increases in **petty crime**, such as street theft. Pilfering from dorms is relatively rare, but it's always wise to use the lockers provided or buy a padlock for your luggage. Travel on trains and buses is safe, with thefts a rarity. Portuguese **police** are stationed in most towns, and can be recognized by their dark blue uniforms. Lisbon and Porto have separate **tourist police** to deal with issues affecting visitors.

For minor health complaints go to a **pharmacy** (*farmácia*); pharmacists generally speak good English and can dispense many drugs without a prescription. Normal opening hours are Monday to Friday 9am to 1pm and 3 to 7pm, Saturday 9am to 1pm. A sign at each one will show the nearest 24hr pharmacy. You can get the address of an English-speaking doctor from a pharmacy, hotel or consular office.

INFORMATION

You'll find a **tourist office** (*turismo*) in almost every town. Staff can help you find a room (usually with commercial partners), and provide local maps and leaflets.

MONEY AND BANKS

Portugal's currency is the euro (€). **Banks** are open Monday to Friday 8.30am to 3pm; in Lisbon and in the Algarve, **exchange offices** may open in the evening to change money. ATMs are easy to find and credit cards are widely accepted.

OPENING HOURS AND HOLIDAYS

Shop **opening hours** are notoriously fickle. As a general guide, most open Monday to Friday 9am to 12.30/1pm and then again from 2/2.30 to 6/6.30pm, plus Saturday 9am to 12.30/1pm. Larger supermarkets tend to stay open until 8pm, but most shops are closed on Sunday, with some exceptions in the Algarve. Museums, churches and monuments open from around 9/10am to 6pm, with many state institutions free from 10am until 2pm on Sunday; almost all, however, close on Mondays and at Easter; smaller places often close for an hour or more at lunch. Restaurants often close on Sunday evenings. The main **public holidays** are: January 1, February carnival, Good Friday, April 25, May 1, Corpus Christi, June 10, June 13 (Lisbon only), August 15, October 5, November 1, December 1, December 8 and December 25.

Lisbon and around

There are few more immediately likeable European capitals than **LISBON** (*Lisboa*). A lively city, it remains in some ways curiously provincial, and rooted as much in the 1920s as the 2010s. Wooden trams clank up outrageous gradients, past mosaic pavements, Art Nouveau cafés and the medieval quarter of Alfama, which hangs below the São Jorge castle. The city invested heavily for Expo 98 and the 2004 European Football Championships, reclaiming run-down docks and improving communication links, and today it combines an easy-going pace and manageable scale with a vibrant, cosmopolitan identity.

Lisbon has a huge amount of historic interest. Though the Great Earthquake of

STUDENT AND YOUTH DISCOUNTS

If you're under 30 it's worth investing in a **European Youth Card** (ⓦeuropeanyouthcard.org; €10 for Portugal), which often gives the holder sixty percent off admission costs, plus discounts on train and bus travel, and accommodation in official youth hostels. Some sights offer a less significant discount on production of a valid university card.

1755 (followed by a tsunami and fire) destroyed most of the grandest buildings, several monuments from Portugal's sixteenth-century golden age survived and frantic reconstruction led to the building of many impressive new palaces and churches across the city's seven hills.

26 WHAT TO SEE AND DO

Many of Lisbon's historical sights, such as the Sé (cathedral) and the Castelo de São Jorge, are located in the centre's eastern portion, best reached by following Rua de Conceição and its continuations as they wind away from the **Baixa**, the city's eighteenth-century core, towards the ancient district of **Alfama**. The city centre can be explored on foot, but a quick hop on a **tram** or **elevador** is definitely a less strenuous way of scaling Lisbon's hills. Public transport is also necessary to reach outlying sights such as those located in **Belém**, 6km west of the centre, and the **Fundação Calouste Gulbenkian**, north of the city's main artery, the Avenida da Liberdade. The Baixa is the city's principal shopping district, with more elegant and trendy boutiques located in **Chiado** and **Bairro Alto** respectively. Bairro Alto is also the area to head for food, *fado* and fun, as it is home to many of the city's best bars and restaurants.

Baixa

The heart of the capital is the lower town – the **Baixa** – Europe's first great example of Neoclassical design and urban planning. It's an imposing quarter of rod-straight streets, some streaming with traffic, but most pedestrianized with mosaic cobbles. The Baixa's northernmost boundary is **Rossio Square** (officially Praça dom Pedro IV), the area's hub, busy at almost all hours of the day and night and housing some old-style cafés and the grand **Teatro Nacional**. At the waterfront end of the Baixa lies the city's other main square, the beautiful arcaded **Praça do Comércio**. Between the two on Rua Augusta is **MUDE** (Design and Fashion Museum; Tues–Sun 10am–6pm; free), an evolving exhibition space which takes its name from the Portuguese word for movement. MUDE features changing temporary exhibitions as well as a permanent collection giving an excellent overview of modern design and fashion.

The Sé

Lisbon's **Sé** or cathedral (Tues–Sat 9am–7pm, Mon & Sun 9am–5pm; free) stands on Largo da Sé in the city centre's eastern portion. The oldest church in Lisbon, it was founded in 1147 to commemorate the city's reconquest from the Moors, and occupies the site of the principal mosque of Moorish Lishbuna. Like so many of Portugal's cathedrals, it is Romanesque and restrained in both size and decoration. It was damaged in the 1755 earthquake, and was extensively restored in the 1930s.

Castelo de São Jorge

East of the Baixa, Rua Augusto Rosa and its continuations wind up towards the castle, past the **Miradouro de Santa Luzia**, which offers spectacular views over the River Tejo. The **Castelo de São Jorge** (daily: March–Oct 9am–9pm; Nov–Feb 9am–6pm; €7.50) contains the restored remains of the Moorish palace that once stood here, and its ramparts and towers boast some excellent views of the city, particularly from the **camera obscura**, which has half-hourly viewings in summer.

Alfama

The **Alfama quarter**, tumbling from the walls of the Castelo to the banks of the Tejo, is the oldest part of Lisbon, and one of its most beautiful, thanks to its picturesque narrow alleyways and breathtaking hilltop views. Despite a definite tourist presence, the quarter retains a largely traditional feel. The **Feira da Ladra**, Lisbon's rambling flea market, fills the Campo de Santa Clara at the northeastern edge of Alfama, from dawn until dusk every Tuesday and Saturday. Also worth a visit is the nearby church of **São Vicente de Fora** (Tues–Sun 10am–6pm; €4), a former monastery containing some exquisite eighteenth-century *azulejos* (tiles). The church also houses, in almost complete sequence, the bodies of all Portuguese kings from João IV, who restored the monarchy in 1640, to

Manuel II, who lost it and died in exile in England in 1932.

Chiado
Between the Baixa and Bairro Alto, halfway up the hill, lies an area known as **Chiado**, which suffered much damage in a fire in 1988 but has been elegantly rebuilt by Portugal's premier architect, Álvaro Siza Viera. It remains the city's most affluent quarter, centred on **Rua Garrett** and its fashionable shops and chic cafés. The **Elevador de Santa Justa** (€5 return), built by Eiffel disciple Raul Mésnier de Ponsard, is an elaborate wrought-iron lift which transports passengers from Rua de Santa Justa in the Baixa to a platform next to the ruined Gothic arches of the **Convento do Carmo**. Once Lisbon's largest church, it was half-destroyed by the 1755 earthquake, becoming perhaps even more beautiful as a result, its vaulted arches reaching dramatically towards the sky. It now houses an **archeological museum** (Mon–Sat: June–Sept 10am–7pm; Oct–May 10am–6pm; €3.50) which, alongside sculptures from the original church, also contains an eclectic assortment of treasures from prehistoric times to the modern day.

Bairro Alto
High above and to the west of the Baixa is the vibrant quarter of **Bairro Alto**, Lisbon's after-dark playground. Its narrow streets are lined with trendy clothing outlets, *fado* clubs, and a multitude of

> ### ★ TREAT YOURSELF
> **Bairro Alto Hotel** Praça Luís de Camões 2 Ⓜ Baix-Chiado; map p.871. Ride the gold mesh lift to the top floor of this boutique hotel for drinks with a view (most cocktails €9.50). The pint-sized terrace is an ideal spot to watch the sunset; gaze over the Tejo to the Ponte 25 de Abril and the statue of Christ the Redeemer on the opposite bank. The exclusive elegance of the setting justifies the cost of that cosmopolitan, though the price of a double room is, not unsurprisingly, outwith the scope of this guide. Daily 10.30am–1am.

bars and restaurants. The district can be reached by two funicular-like trams – the Elevador da Glória from Praça dos Restauradores or the Elevador da Bica from Rua de São Paulo (€3.60 for up to two trips).

The Fundação Calouste Gulbenkian
The **Fundação Calouste Gulbenkian** is a ten-minute walk north of Lisbon's main park, the Parque Eduardo VII – or take the metro to São Sebastião. The Foundation, established by the oil magnate and prolific collector Calouste Gulbenkian, helps finance various aspects of Portugal's cultural life, including the two art galleries located here. The **Museu Calouste Gulbenkian** (Tues–Sun 10am–6pm; €4, free Sun 10am–2pm) is Portugal's greatest museum, divided into two distinct parts – the first devoted to Egyptian, Greco-Roman, Islamic and Oriental arts, the second to European. There's also a stunning room full of Art Nouveau jewellery by René Lalique. Across the gardens, the **Centro de Arte Moderna** (same hours; €5, joint ticket €8) houses works by all the big names from the twentieth-century Portuguese scene, as well as top British artists such as Antony Gormley and David Hockney.

Museu Nacional de Arte Antiga
The **Museu Nacional de Arte Antiga** (Tues 2–6pm, Wed–Sun 10am–6pm; €5; tram #15 from Praça do Comércio), another of Lisbon's top art museums, is situated near the riverfront to the west of the city at Rua das Janelas Verdes 95. Its core is formed by fifteenth- and sixteenth-century Portuguese works, the masterpiece being Nuno Gonçalves' St Vincent Altarpiece. There are also Portuguese ceramics, textiles and furniture on display, as well as decorative arts from Asia and Africa.

Museu do Oriente
Set in a converted *bacalhau* warehouse down on the docks en route to Belém, the vast **Museu do Oriente** (Av Brasília, Doca de Alcântara Norte; Tues–Sun 10am–6pm, Fri until 10pm, with free entry after 6pm; otherwise €5; tram #15

26

LISBON

Parque das Nações & Oriente Train Station

Parque da Bela Vista

Oceanário de Lisboa & Airport

AV. DOS ESTADOS UNIDOS DA AMÉRICA

AV. ALMIRANTE GAGO COUTINHO

AV. ARREIRO

PR. DR. FRANCISCO DE SÁ CARNEIRO

Areeiro Ⓜ

AV. ALMIRANTE REIS

RUA MORAIS SOARES

PENHA DE FRANÇA

CAMPO PEQUENO

AV. JOÃO XXI

AV. G. JUNQUEIRO

Alameda Ⓜ

Arroios Ⓜ

AV. ALMIRANTE REIS

RUA ANTÓNIO PEDRO

RUA DOS ARROIOS

R. PASCOAL DE MELO

AV. DA ROMA

PR. DE LONDRES

PR. DE

Entrecampos Ⓜ

Entrecampos Station

Praça de Touros

R. DO ARCO DO CEGO

DU BOCAGE

DEFENSORES DE CHAVES

AV. OSCAR MONTEIRO TORRES

AV. DUQUE D'ÁVILA

Saldanha Ⓜ

AV. CASAL RIBEIRO

L. DE DONA ESTEFÂNIA

RUA DONA ESTEFÂNIA

RUA JACINTA MARTO

AVENIDA DA REPÚBLICA

AVENIDA DA REPÚBLICA

BOMBARDA

VALMOR

Campo Pequeno Ⓜ

AV. B. GARCIA

AV. VIS. DE

AV. ELIAS

AV. MIGUEL

AV. JOÃO CRISÓSTOMO

CINCO DE OUTUBRO

PR. DUQUE SALDANHA

ESTEFÂNIA

RUA GOMES FREIRE

R. GONÇALVES CRESPO

R. ANDRADE CORVO

CORONEL FERREIRA DO AMARAL

RUA DE SANTA

DE

R. M. DE SÁ DA BANDEIRA

AV. DUQUE D'ÁVILA

South African Embassy

R. PEDRO NUNES

AV. FONTES PEREIRA DE MELO

Picoas Ⓜ

Parque Ⓜ

Estádio José Alvalade

US Embassy

RUA DA BENEFICÊNCIA

AV. DE BERNA

Fundação Calouste Gulbenkian

Museu Gulbenkian

Centro de Arte Moderna

S. Sebastião Ⓜ

RUA TOMÁS RIBEIRO

AV. ANTÓNIO AUGUSTO DE AGUIAR

AVENIDA SIDÓNIO PAIS

PR. DO MARQUÊS DE POMBAL (ROTUNDA)

Marquês Ⓜ

Parque Eduardo VII

AV. DOS COMBATENTES

PR. DE ESPANHA

Praça de Espanha Ⓜ

RUA R. ORTIGÃO

AVENIDA CARDEAL

RUA MARQUÊS DE FRONTEIRA

RUA CASTILHO

RUA RODRIGO DA FONSECA

AV. J. A. DE AGUIAR

RUA DAS AMOREIRAS

Estádio da Luz

AV. COLUMBANO BORDALO

Sete Rios Station

Bus Station

GULBENKIAN

AVENIDA CALOUSTE

CAMPOLIDE

Aqueduto das Águas Livres

RUA PROF. O. DA CAMARA

RUA DO ARCO DO CARVALHO

CALÇADA DA QUINTINHA

AV. E. D. PACHECO

British Hospital

Estrada da Luz

ESTRADA DAS LARANJEIRAS

AV. DAS FORÇAS ARMADAS

Jardim Zoológico Ⓜ

Zoo

Palácio Marquês de Fronteira

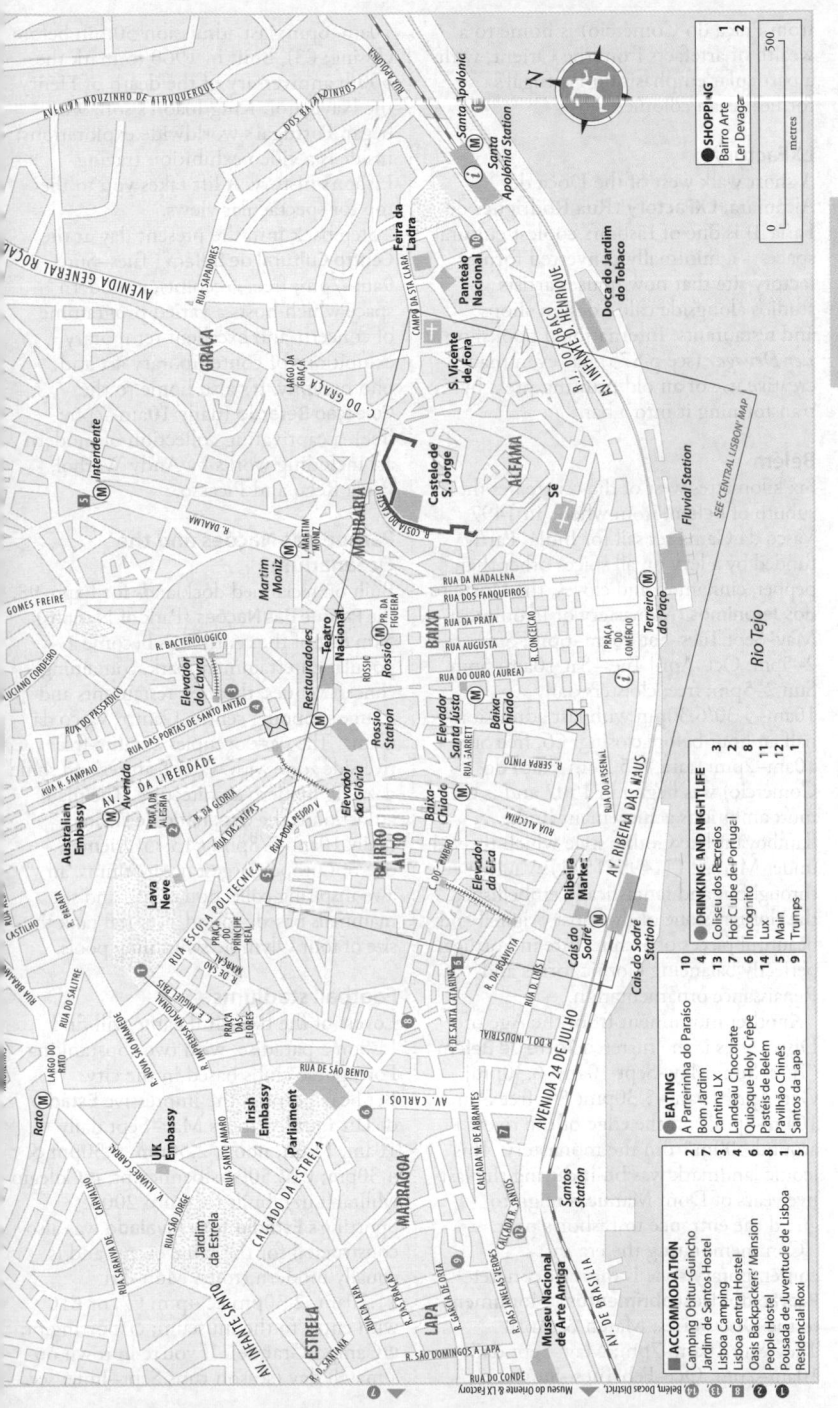

● SHOPPING
Bairro Arte 1
Ler Devagar 2

● EATING
A Parreirinha do Paraíso 2
Bom Jardim 7
Cantina LX 3
Landeau Chocolate 4
Quiosque Holy Crêpe 6
Pastéis de Belém 8
Pavilhão Chinês 1
Santos da Lapa 5

● DRINKING AND NIGHTLIFE
Coliseu dos Recreios 10
Hot Cube de Portugal 4
Incógnito 13
Lux 7
Main 2
Trumps 6

■ ACCOMMODATION
Camping Obitur-Guincho 2
Jardim de Santos Hostel 7
Lisboa Camping 3
Lisboa Central Hostel 4
Oasis Backpackers' Mansion 6
People Hostel 8
Pousada de Juventude de Lisboa 1
Residencial Roxi 5

26

from Praça do Comércio) is home to a wealth of artefacts from the Orient, with a particular emphasis on Portugal's former Asian colonies.

LXFactory

A short walk west of the Doca de Alcântara, **LXFactory** (Rua Rodrigues de Faria 3) is one of Lisbon's coolest cultural spaces – a minimally converted former factory site that now houses artists' studios alongside cafés, design shops and restaurants. International bookshop *Ler Devagar* (see p.875) has even made creative use of an old printing press by transforming it into a bar.

Belém

Six kilometres west of the centre lies the suburb of **Belém**, from where, in 1497, Vasco da Gama set sail for India. Partly funded by a levy on all spices other than pepper, cinnamon and cloves, the **Mosteiro dos Jerónimos** (Monastery of Jerónimos; May–Sept Tues–Sat 10am–6pm; Sun 2–5pm; Oct–April Tues–Sat 10am–5pm, Sun 2–5pm; free; cloisters daily 10am–5.30/6.30pm with last admission half an hour before closing; €6, free Sun 10am–2pm; tram #15 from Praça do Comércio) was begun in 1502 and is the most ambitious achievement in the flamboyant late Gothic style which thrived under Manuel I (1495–1521). Vaulted throughout and fantastically embellished, the cloister is one of the most original and beautiful pieces of architecture in Portugal, perfectly balancing Gothic forms and Renaissance ornamentation.

Another monument from the Age of Discoveries is the turreted **Torre de Belém** (Tues–Sun: May–Sept 10am–6.30pm; Oct–April 10am–5.30pm; €5, free Sun 10am–2pm), on the edge of the river around 500m from the monastery. This iconic landmark was built during the last five years of Dom Manuel's reign to guard the entrance to Lisbon's port.

Commemorating the era in contemporary style is the vast concrete **Padrão dos Descobrimentos** (Monument to the Discoveries; March & April Tues–Sun 10am–7pm; May–Sept daily 10am–7pm; Oct–Feb Tues–Sun

10am–6pm; last admission 30min before closing; €3), built in 1960 to mark the 500th anniversary of the death of Henry the Navigator, King João I's son, who began Portugal's worldwide explorations; inside is a video exhibition tracing Lisbon's history. A lift takes you to the top for spectacular views.

Step back into the present day at the **Centro Cultural de Belém** (Tues–Sun 9am–7pm; free; ⒲ccb.pt), a modern space which hosts a varied programme of concerts and excellent temporary exhibitions of contemporary art and photography. It's also home to the **Colecçao Berardo** (daily 10am–7pm; free), a captivating collection of modern art including works by Andy Warhol, Paula Rego and Picasso.

Parque das Nações and the Oceanarium

Built on reclaimed docklands for Expo '98, the **Parque das Nações** (Park of Nations), 5km east of the centre, has become a popular entertainment park, containing concert venues, theatres, restaurants and a large shopping centre, Centro Vasco da Gama. The park occupies a traffic-free riverside zone with water features and some dazzling modern architecture. The main attraction is the **Oceanário de Lisboa** (daily 10am–7/8pm; €13; ⒲Oriente), one of Europe's largest oceanariums, an awe-inspiring collection of fish and sea mammals based around a central tank the size of four Olympic swimming pools.

Football stadiums

Lovers of the beautiful game will find Lisbon a paradise, with two top-ranking Portuguese clubs based in the city. Benfica's home is the impressive **Estádio da Luz** (guided tours May–Sept daily 10am, 11am, noon, 2.30pm, 3.30pm & 4.30pm; €12.50; ⒲slbenfica.pt; ⒲Colegio Militar/Luz), built for Euro 2004. Sporting's **Estádio Jose Alvalade** was also constructed for the same event, and is equally modern (tours Mon–Fri 11.30am, 2.30pm & 4pm; €7, or €10 with entry to the museum; ⒲sporting.pt; ⒲Campo Grande). If you're in town on a match day (season runs Sept–June; see

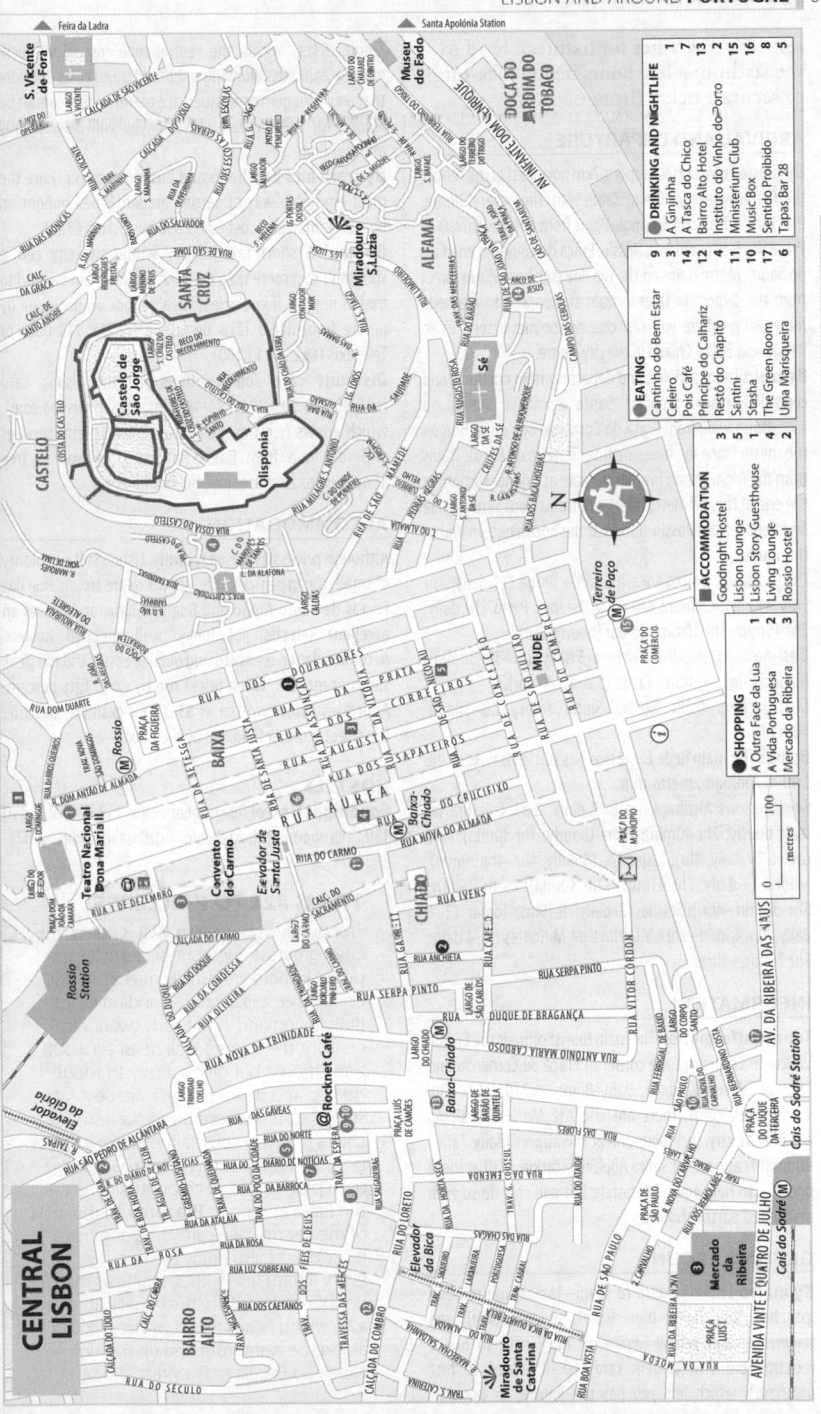

CENTRAL LISBON

26

● DRINKING AND NIGHTLIFE
A Ginjinha	7
A Tasca do Chico	1
Bairro Alto Hotel	13
Instituto do Vinho do Porto	2
Ministerium Club	15
Music Box	16
Sentido Proibido	8
Tapas Bar 28	5

● EATING
Cantinho do Bem Estar	9
Celeiro	3
Pois Café	14
Príncipe do Calhariz	12
Restô do Chapitô	4
Sentini	5
Stasha	11
The Green Room	10
Uma Marisqueira	17
	6

● ACCOMMODATION
Goodnight Hostel	3
Lisbon Lounge	1
Lisbon Story Guesthouse	2
Living Lounge	2
Rossio Hostel	3

● SHOPPING
A Outra Face da Lua	1
A Vida Portuguesa	2
Mercado da Ribeira	3

26

respective websites for fixtures), head to the stadium a few hours before kick-off to secure a ticket (from €20).

ARRIVAL AND DEPARTURE

By plane From Portela airport, 7km northeast of the centre, the Aerobus (every 20min, 7am–9pm, then every 30min, 9–11pm; 20min; €3.50 single) runs from outside arrivals to Praça dos Restauradores, Rossio, Praça do Comércio and Cais do Sodré. Metro trains on the red line (see below) run direct from the airport to Oriente train station and to Alameda metro stop where you can change for metro services to Rossio and Baixa-Chiado in the city centre.

By train Trains arriving and departing from northern and central Portugal stop at Santa Apolónia Station, a 15–20min walk from Praça do Comércio or a quick hop on the metro (take the blue line from Terreiro do Paço). Trains from the Algarve and Évora terminate at Oriente station, at the end of the red metro line. Local trains from Sintra arrive and depart from Rossio station at the northwestern end of the square.

Destinations from Santa Apolónia Braga (13 daily; 3hr 30min–5hr); Coimbra (20 daily; 2–3hr); Porto (18 daily; 2hr 45min–3hr 10min); Tomar (hourly; 2hr).

Destinations from Oriente Faro (5 daily; 3hr–3hr 30min); Madrid (nightly; 10hr); Tavira (5 daily; 4–5hr).

Destinations from Rossio Sintra (every 20–30min; 40min).

By bus The main Rede Expressos bus station is next to the Jardim Zoológico metro stop.

Destinations Alcobaça (up to 7 daily; 2hr); Coimbra (at least hourly; 2hr 20min); Évora (hourly; 1hr 30min); Faro (up to 19 daily; 4hr); Lagos (7–10 daily; 4hr–4hr 30min); Madrid (3 daily; 7hr 45min–11hr 30min); Porto (hourly; 3hr 30min–4hr); Seville (2 daily; 8–9hr); Tomar (2–6 daily; 1hr 45min–2hr); Vila Nova de Milfontes (3–4 daily; 3hr 30min–4hr).

INFORMATION

Tourist information The main tourist office is the Lisboa Welcome Centre, on the corner of Praça do Comércio and Rua do Arsenal (daily 9am–8pm; ☎210 312 700, ⓦ visitlisboa.com). There are also Ask Me Lisboa kiosks around the city, including one at the airport (daily 7am–midnight) and one at Santa Apolónia station. Staff at these booths can help you book hotels, but will only do so with associated partner hotels.

GETTING AROUND

By metro Lisbon's metro (6.30am–1am; ⓦ metrolisboa .pt) has four lines: blue (*azul*), green (*verde*), red (*vermelha*) and yellow (*amarela*). You'll have to buy a rechargeable Viva Viagem card (€0.50, added to first purchase), which lets you pay per journey or per day.

Single tickets within the central zone cost €1.40 each, while a 24hr pass allowing unlimited travel costs €6. Note that a Viva Viagem card issued at a metro station cannot be loaded for use on train services (you will need to buy another one).

By tram and bus Trams and buses (ⓦ carris.pt) are the most enjoyable way of getting around. When bought on board, tram tickets cost €2.85 and bus tickets €1.80.

By taxi A short taxi journey within the city centre shouldn't cost more than €10–12, but taxis can be hard to find at night – if you're leaving a bar or club book one by phone from Rádio Táxis de Lisboa (☎218 119 000) or Teletáxis (☎218 111 100).

Discount card Tourist offices sell the Lisboa Card (€18.50/€31.50/€39 for 24/48/72hr; ⓦ askmelisboa.com), which allows free travel on buses, trams, metro services and the train from Rossio to Sintra, as well as free admission to 25 museums and monuments.

ACCOMMODATION

Although prices have risen recently, Lisbon still has plenty of small, cheap *pensões*, many of which are around Rua das Portas de Santo Antão and Rua da Glória, and boasts an excellent selection of funky, well-equipped hostels. Accommodation is easy to find outside Easter and the peak summer months, when prices rise by up to fifty percent. Addresses below written as 53-3°, for example, describe the street number followed by the floor.

HOSTELS

Goodnight Hostel Rua dos Correeiros 113-2° ☎213 430 139, ⓦ goodnighthostel.com; ⓜ Rossio; map p.871.

TRAM #28 TO PRAZERES

The picture-book **tram #28** is one of the city's greatest rides, but because it's so popular there are usually queues to get on and most likely only standing room. Built in England in the early twentieth century, the trams are all polished wood and chrome and give a distinctly rough ride up and down Lisbon's steepest streets, at times coming so close to shops that you could almost take a can of sardines off the shelves. From Graça, the tram plunges down through Alfama to the Baixa and up to **Prazeres**, to the west of the centre. Take care of belongings as pickpockets also enjoy the ride. If you fancy a tram ride without quite as many people on board, try the equally attractive #25, which heads from Casa dos Bicos along the waterfront and up through Lapa and Estrela to Prazeres.

Friendly and well-designed hostel in the heart of the Baixa. There's a TV lounge, and a guitar for evening sing-alongs. Dorm €18, double €50

★ **Jardim de Santos Hostel** Largo Vitorino Damásio 4-2° ☎ 213 974 666, ⊛ jardimdesantoshostel.com; ⓜ Cais do Sodré (trams #25 and #28 also stop nearby); map pp.868–869. Wooden floors and colourful "string art" displays thread their way through this second-floor hostel, which has roomy dorms, a relaxed lounge and knowledgeable staff. Not the most central location but still within easy reach of the main sights. Dorm €16, double €50

Lisboa Central Hostel Rua Rodrigues Sampaio 160 ☎ 309 881 038, ⊛ lisboacentralhostel.com; ⓜ Marquês de Pombal; map pp.868–869. Sturdy bunks, a TV room and a small outdoor terrace make this friendly and well-maintained hostel a good, sociable option. Some private rooms are en suite. Dorm €21, double €64

Lisbon Lounge Rua de São Nicolau 41, Baixa ☎ 213 462 061, ⊛ lisbonloungehostel.com; ⓜ Rossio; map p.871. Upmarket hostel near Rossio with spacious, airy dorms and an impressive kitchen where nightly 3-course meals are served for €10. Dorm €25, double €64

Living Lounge Rua do Crucifixo 116-2°, Baixa ☎ 213 461 078, ⊛ lisbonloungehostel.com; ⓜ Baixa-Chiado; map p.871. *Lisbon Lounge*'s conveniently located sister hostel has huge individually designed rooms; bike rental is offered and there's free tea and coffee. Dorm €25, double €64

Oasis Backpackers' Mansion Rua de Santa Catarina 24, Chiado ☎ 213 478 044, ⊛ oasislisboa.com; ⓜ Baixa-Chiado; map pp.868–869. Lively, well-equipped hostel with its own bar, located below the Miradouro de Santa Catarina. Dorm €23, double €75

People Hostel Rua dos Jerónimos 16, in Belém ☎ 218 289 567, ⊛ peoplehostel.com; tram #15E from Cais do Sodré; map pp.868–869. Clean but slightly cramped, this cheap and brightly painted hostel has a vague pop-art theme running throughout. Laundry service and bike rental (€7.50/day) available. Great location near the Mosteiro do Jerónimos. Dorm €12, double €44

Pousada de Juventude de Lisboa Rua Andrade Corvo 46 ☎ 213 532 696, ⊛ pousadasjuventude.pt; ⓜ Picoas; map pp.868–869. Well-run hostel with good facilities and en-suite doubles, located near Parque Eduardo VII. Dorm €18, double €46

Rossio Hostel Calçada do Carmo 6-2° ☎ 213 426 004, ⊛ rossiohostel.com; ⓜ Rossio; map p.871. Immaculately clean, efficiently run and well-designed hostel with large dorms and excellent doubles. Dorm €21, double €60

PENSIONS AND HOTELS

★ **Lisbon Story Guesthouse** Largo de São Domingos 18, Baixa ☎ 218 879 392, ⊛ lisbonstoryguesthouse.com; ⓜ Rossio; map p.871. Combining the best of hostel and

hotel, *Lisbon Story* offers eight simple yet stylish private rooms with a Lisbon theme, a kitchen and a lounge stocked with travel books. Great breakfast. Double €50

Residencial Roxi Avenida Almirante Reis 31 2°-3° ☎ 218 126 341, ⊛ residencialroxi.com; ⓜ Intendente; map pp.868–869. Clean, simple rooms in a worn-out, wedge-shaped building north of the centre. It's cheap, but lacks a little soul. Double €30

CAMPSITES

Camping Obitur-Guincho Lugar da Areia, Guincho ☎ 214 870 450, ⊛ orbitur.pt; train from Cais do Sodré to Cascais, then bus to Guincho; map pp.868–869. A well-located site 12km out of the city in surfer's paradise Guincho, with a restaurant, supermarket and sports facilities. Camping €6.50 per person, plus €8.60 per tent

Lisboa Camping Parque Florestal Monsanto ☎ 217 628 100, ⊛ lisboacamping.com; bus #714 from Praça Figueira; map pp.868–869. Well-equipped campsite in a large park 6km west of the centre, with pool and shops. The entrance is on Estrada da Circunvalação on the park's west side. Camping €7.50 per person, plus €7 per tent

EATING

Lisbon has some great cafés and restaurants serving large portions of food at reasonable prices. Lunch is particularly good value, with plenty of bargain dishes of the day and set menus on offer. Alongside the usual Portuguese restaurants serving grilled meat and fish, there are lots of seafood places, and inexpensive options offering food from former colonies (including Angola, Goa and Macau). Many restaurants are closed Sun.

CAFÉS, CHEAP EATS AND SNACKS

A Parreirinha do Paraíso Rua do Paraíso 40; ⓜ Santa Apolónia; map p.868–869. Hectic canteen with paper tablecloths and service without a smile. However, the pork and pepper skewers (€5.50) are good value, and competently done. Daily 7am–midnight.

Celeiro Rua 1 de Dezembro 65; ⓜ Rossio; map p.871. Just off Rossio, this inexpensive self-service place sits in the basement of a health-food supermarket and offers tasty vegetarian spring rolls, quiches, pizza and the like from around €6. There's also a streetside café offering drinks and snacks. Café Mon–Fri 9am–6pm & Sat 9am–5pm.

Landeau Chocolate LXFactory, at Rua Rodrigues Faria 103; tram #15E from Cais do Sodré or Praça do Comércio; map pp.868–869. You might smell this café before you see it. The dreamy scent of the devilishly good chocolate cake (€3.50) wafts into the street, drawing in a steady stream of locals and tourists. Tues–Sun noon–7pm.

Pastéis de Belém Rua de Belém 84–92; tram #15E from Cais do Sodré or Praça do Comércio; map pp.868–869. This huge, well-known *pastelaria* could easily have made the

26

26

move into tourist-trap territory, but its deliciously flaky *pastéis de nata* still go for just €1.05. Daily 8am–11pm/midnight.

Pois Café Rua São João da Praça 93–95, Baixa; ⓜ Terreiro do Paço; map p.871. Eclectically furnished café with a relaxed atmosphere and plenty of international books and papers to peruse. Serves brunch, quiche, sandwiches (from €6.40) and daily specials, including vegetarian options. Tues–Sun 11am–10pm.

Quiosque Holy Crêpe Rua das Francesinhas, in the park just south of the parliament building; bus #706 from Cais do Sodré to Assembleia República; map pp.868–869. This little green kiosk serves up sweet and savoury crêpes (from €3.50) in quiet, leafy surroundings. Mon & Sun noon–7/8pm, Tues–Sat noon–10pm/midnight.

Santini Rua do Carmo 9, Chiado; ⓜ Baixa-Chiado map p.871. Italian-American-style ice-cream parlour serving more than a dozen divine home-made flavours. Pay before choosing which ones you'll go for. Daily 11am–midnight.

The Green Room Rua do Cais do Sodré 16; ⓜ Cais do Sodré; map p.871. Cool, veggie-friendly café with a blackboard full of salads, soups and breakfasts (from €3.50) to choose from. Daily 9am–midnight.

RESTAURANTS

Bom Jardim Trav. De Santo Antão 11–18; ⓜ Restauradores; map pp.868–869. A fairly touristy restaurant, so popular that it's spread into three buildings on either side of a pedestrianized alley, with some outdoor seats as well. The grilled sea bream costs €12.10. Daily noon–11.30pm.

Cantina LX Rua Rodrigues de Faria 103; tram #15E from Cais do Sodré or Praça do Comércio; map pp.868–869. Former factory canteen serving mains like flaked *bacalhau* for €13. There's a well-shaded seating area around the side. Daily noon–3pm & 7.30–11pm.

Cantinho do Bem Estar Rua do Norte 46, Bairro Alto; ⓜ Baixa-Chiado; map p.871. The staff might be stroppy, but this tiny place is great value for money – its portions of Portuguese classics (around €12.50) feed two with ease. Go early. Tues–Sun noon–2.30pm & 7–11.30pm.

Príncipe do Calhariz Calçada da Combro 28–30; ⓜ Baixa-Chiado; map p.871. Busy barbecue joint doing grilled chicken and fillets of fish. Not so hungry? Go for one of the half portions (€5.50). Mon–Fri & Sun noon–3pm & 7–10.30pm.

Restô do Chapitô Rua Costa do Castelo 7, Castelo; ⓜ Terreiro do Paço; map p.871. Two-in-one venue with tapas and barbecued meat served in a buzzing courtyard, and more expensive international dishes on offer in the upstairs restaurant. Both have excellent river views. Mon–Fri noon–midnight, Sat & Sun 7.30pm–midnight/2am.

★ **Santos da Lapa** Rua Sao Joao da Mata 30, Santos; ⓜ Cais do Sodré or train to Santos; map pp.868–869. Simple, wood-panelled place serving punchy plates of Portuguese regional specialities, from sausage cooked in

red wine to goat and gizzards. The tapas-style dishes start at just €1.50, and a draught beer is only 50c. Wed 6pm–midnight, Thurs–Sat 6pm–2am, Sun 4pm–midnight.

Stasha Rua das Gaveas 33, Bairro Alto; ⓜ Baixa-Chiado; map p.871. Lively place offering a creative international menu full of well-priced meat, fish and vegetarian options. The risotto with prawns is a bargain at €8.50. Tues–Sun noon–3.30pm and 7.30pm–midnight.

Uma Marisqueira Rua dos Sapateiros 177; ⓜ Baixa-Chiado; map p.871. Locals love this small, tiled restaurant in the Baixa, where authentic Portuguese meals start at €5.50. Daily noon–10pm.

DRINKING, NIGHTLIFE AND ENTERTAINMENT

The densest concentration of bars and clubs is in Bairro Alto. In summer, crowds spill out of bars and into the streets, creating a festive atmosphere. More expensive late-night action can be found in the Docas (Docklands) district, just east of the 25 de Abril bridge (take tram #15), where the Doca de Alcântara and the Doca de Santo Amaro (further from the city) house waterfront bars and clubs in converted warehouses. Lisbon's gay scene centres around Praça do Príncipe Real in the north of Bairro Alto. Clubs don't really get going until at least 2am and tend to stay open till 6am. Admission fees range from €10 to €20 (usually including a drink). What's-on listings can be found in the monthly *Agenda Cultural*, available free at tourist offices, or at ⓦ lisbon.angloinfo.com.

BARS

A Ginjinha Largo de São Domingos 8, Baixa; ⓜ Rossio; map p.871. The original *ginjinha* (cherry brandy) bar, this small stand-up place located in lively Largo de São Domingos is a great place to start a night out in Lisbon. Small shot of Ginjinha €1.10. Daily 9am–10pm.

Instituto do Vinho do Porto Rua de São Pedro de Alcântara 45, Bairro Alto; ⓜ Restauradores; map p.871. Over 200 types of port, with ten-year-old tawnies for €2.90 a glass. Mon–Fri 11am–midnight, Sat 2pm–midnight.

Pavilhão Chinês Rua Dom Pedro V 89, Bairro Alto; ⓜ Rato; map pp.868–869. Ideal for a cocktail (€7.50), this famous (and pricey) drinking den is decorated with kitsch toys and models. Daily 6pm–2am.

Sentido Proibido Rua da Atalaia 34, Bairro Alto; ⓜ Baixa-Chiado; map p.871. Smoky late-night bar that plays a mixture of cheese, indie and rock, and has a happy hour 8–9pm. Otherwise, a large beer is €3. Daily 2pm–midnight/2am.

Tapas Bar 28 Travessa Fieis de Deus 28, Bairro Alto; ⓜ Baixa-Chiado; map p.871. Skip the overpriced food and pull up a cushion for a drink (beer €3) on the steps outside. The location attracts buskers, whose music adds to the street-party vibe. Daily 4.30pm–1.30am.

CLUBS

Incógnito Rua Poiais de São Bento 37, Bairro Alto ⓦincognitobar.com; ⓜBaixa-Chiado/Cais do Sodré; map pp.868–869. Student-friendly mainstay spinning synth, new wave and indie until the early hours. Wed–Sat 11pm–4am.

Lux Av Infante Dom Henrique Armázem A, opposite Santa Apolónia station ⓦluxfragil.com; ⓜSanta Apolónia; map pp.868–869. The city's best-known club, often hosting top DJs and electronic acts, like Fatboy Slim and Hot Chip. See website for specific events and times.

Main Av 24 de Julho 68, opposite Santos station; ⓜCais do Sodré; map pp.868–869. Swanky place with a minimalist vibe and house tunes, attracting diners and dancers. Wed–Sat 8pm–6am.

Ministerium Club Praça do Comércio ⓦministerium.pt; ⓜTerreiro do Paço; map p.871. Fresh from the US, Ibiza and beyond, big-name DJs come to rock Lisbon's former finance ministry. Sat only; see website for specific event details.

Trumps Rua da Imprensa Nacional 104b, Rato ⓦtrumps .pt; ⓜRato; map pp.868–869. The biggest gay venue in Lisbon, with themed parties in the summertime and a year-round "hetero-friendly" policy. Fri & Sat 11.45pm–6am.

FADO AND LIVE MUSIC

A Tasca do Chico Rua do Diário de Notícias 39; ⓜBaixa-Chiado; map p.871. Make like the locals and catch some amateur *fado* in this bar during the week. Free entry. Daily 6pm–2/3am, with performances on Mon & Wed

Coliseu dos Recreios Rua Portas de Santo Antão 96 ⓦcoliseulisboa.com; ⓜRestauradores; map pp.868–869. Portuguese stars fill much of the programme, but this concert hall also attracts international bands. See website for specific event times.

Hot Clube de Portugal Praça da Alegria 48 ⓦhotclubedeportugal.org; ⓜAvenida; map pp.868–869. The longest-running jazz club in Portugal, with live performances five nights a week. Tues–Sat 10pm–2am.

Music Box Rua Nova do Carvalho 24 ⓦmusicboxlisboa .com; map p.871. Live music venue near Cais do Sodré, with a schedule packed full of DJs and bands playing almost every musical style imaginable. Mon–Sat with gigs from 10.30pm/midnight; club nights 1am/4am–6am.

SHOPPING

A Outra Face da Lua Rua da Assunção 22; ⓜBaixa-Chiado; map p.871. Vintage emporium stocking a mishmash of goodies, from clothing to toys. There's also an in-store café, with home-made meals for around €7. Daily 10am–8pm.

A Vida Portuguesa Rua Anchieta 11; ⓜBaixa-Chiado; map p.871. From tiles to sardines, if it's Portuguese, you'll find it here. Many of the old-fashioned brands on sale would have disappeared had this chain store not made them cool again. Daily 10/11am–8pm.

Bairro Arte LXFactory, on Rua Rodrigues Faria; tram #15E from Cais do Sodré or Praça do Comércio; map pp. 868–869. One of three *Bairro Arte* shops in Lisbon (the others are in Bairro Alto and Chiado), selling all manner of quirky retro junk. Worth a browse. Daily 9/10am–midnight.

Ler Devagar LXFactory, on Rua Rodrigues Faria; tram #15E from Cais do Sodré or Praça do Comércio; map pp. 868–869. Well-stocked bookshop that has vertiginous shelves stacked with Portuguese reads, plus foreign-language titles. Tues–Sat noon–midnight/2am, Sun 11am–10pm.

Mercado da Ribeira Av 24 de Julho; ⓜCais do Sodré; map p.871. The city's main food market, which is also home to a variety of craft stores and flower stalls; afternoons are flowers only. Mon–Fri 6am–2pm & 3–7pm, Sat 6am–2pm.

DIRECTORY

Banks and Exchange Main bank branches in the Baixa. Exchange office at the airport (24hr) and at Santa Apolónia station (daily 8.30am–3pm).

Embassies Australia, Av da Liberdade 198-2° ☎213 101 500; Canada, Av da Liberdade 196–200 ☎213 164 600; Ireland, Av da Liberdade 200-4° ☎213 308 200; South Africa, Av Luis Bívar 10 ☎213 192 200; UK, Rua de São Bernardo 33 ☎213 924 000; US, Av das Forças Armadas ☎217 273 300.

Hospital British Hospital, Rua Tomás da Fonseca ☎217 213 400.

26

FADO

Difficult to classify but often described as falling somewhere between the blues and flamenco, the emotional and melodramatic musical genre of **fado** (literally "fate") is as typically Portuguese as custard tarts and Cristiano Ronaldo. *Fado* has its roots in early nineteenth-century Alfama, where it thrived until the early twentieth century, when it was subject to censorship. Despite the authorities' efforts, the genre continued to develop, and still features in the charts today thanks to a new generation of performers. Lisbon is the best place to hear *fado*, specifically in Bairro Alto, where many restaurants put on performances (from €15 upwards, including dinner), although Coimbra also has its own style (see p.8/9). To get the most out of a show, first visit the modern **Museu do Fado** at Largo do Chafariz de Dentro 1 (Tues–Sun 10am–6pm; €5), which gives an excellent audioguide introduction to the history of the genre and its brightest stars, including *grande dame* Amália Rodrigues and younger talent Joana Amendoeira.

26

Internet Rocknet Café at Rua do Norte 58, Bairro Alto (Mon–Sat 5pm–2am; 80c/15min).

Left luggage Available at Oriente (daily 6.40am–10pm) and Santa Apolónia (daily 6.40am–9.45pm) stations from €1/hr.

Pharmacy Throughout the city, including Farmácia Estácio, Rossio Square (Mon–Fri 9am–1pm & 2.30–7pm).

Post office Praça do Município 6 (Mon–Sat 8.30am–6.30pm).

Tourist police Praça dos Restauradores (☎ 213 421 634).

BEACHES AROUND LISBON

The coast around Lisbon offers ample opportunities to escape from the summer heat of the capital. Half an hour south of the capital, dunes stretch along the **COSTA DA CAPARICA**, a thoroughly Portuguese resort popular with surfers and crammed with restaurants and beach cafés. Solitude is easy enough to find, though, thanks to the **transpraia** (mini-railway) that runs along the 8km of dunes in summer.

Another popular seaside escape is the former fishing village of **CASCAIS**, forty minutes to the west of the city, which boasts three beaches and a campsite. Cascais has a particular appeal to surfers due to its proximity to Guincho beach (see box, p.862), reached by local bus, which has hosted the World Surfing Championships.

ARRIVAL AND DEPARTURE

Costa da Caparica Ferry from Cais do Sodré in Lisbon to Cacilhas (every 15–20min), then the 135 TST bus (every 20min). Buses stop along Avenida Doutor Aresta Branco, close to the main square Praça da Liberdade, and a 5min walk east of the beach.

Cascais Train from Cais do Sodré (every 15–30min; 40min).

SINTRA

The cool, hilltop woodland setting of **SINTRA** once attracted Moorish lords and the Portuguese kings from Lisbon during the summer months; the palaces they constructed remain among Portugal's most spectacular attractions. Sintra is best seen on a day-trip from Lisbon, as its hotels and restaurants are pretty pricey. That said, there are certainly enough sights to keep you occupied for several days. Combined tickets bring the price

of admission to the sights down; enquire at the tourist office for the latest offers.

WHAT TO SEE AND DO

An amalgamation of three villages, Sintra can be confusing, but there are plenty of local buses connecting the sights.

Palácio Nacional

The **Palácio Nacional** (daily 9.30am–6pm; €8.50), about fifteen minutes' walk from the train station, is an obvious landmark, with its distinctive conical chimneys. The palace probably existed under the Moors, but takes its present form from the rebuilding commissioned by Dom João I and his successor, Dom Manuel, in the fourteenth and fifteenth centuries. Its style is a fusion of Gothic and the latter king's Manueline additions. The **chapel** and its adjoining chamber are well worth seeing, as is the curious Magpies Room, decorated with hundreds of paintings of the birds with the motto "*Por Bem*" ("For the good") in their beaks.

Quinta da Regaleira

Also within walking distance of the centre is another must-see site, the beautiful **Quinta da Regaleira** (daily: Feb, March & Oct 10am–6.30pm; April–Sept 10am–8pm; Nov–Jan 10am–5.30pm; €6, or €10 for guided visits booked in advance on ☎ 219 106 650). One of Sintra's most elaborate private estates, it lies ten minutes' walk west of the Palácio Nacional on the Seteais–Monserrate road. The house and its fantastic gardens were built at the beginning of the twentieth century by an Italian theatrical set designer for one of the richest industrialists in Portugal. One highlight is the **Initiation Well**, inspired by the initiation practices of the Knights Templar and Freemasons. The vast gardens are full of surprising delights, with chapels, follies and fountains at every turn.

Monserrate

Beyond Quinta da Regaleira, the road leads past a series of beautiful private estates to recently renovated **Monserrate** (park 9.30am–8pm, last ticket 7pm; palace 9.30am–7pm, last ticket 6.15pm;

€7) – about an hour's walk – a Moorish-style folly of a palace whose 75-acre **garden**, filled with exotic trees and subtropical shrubs and plants, extends as far as the eye can see.

Moorish castle and Palácio da Pena

Two of Sintra's main sights can be reached on bus #434 (the €5 ticket allows you to hop on and off at each one), starting at the train station. The bus stops outside the Praça da República tourist office before proceeding to the ruined ramparts of the **Castelo dos Mouros** (Moorish castle; daily 9.30am–8pm, last ticket 7pm; €7), from where the views over the town and surrounding countryside are extraordinary. Further on, the bus stops at both entrances to the immense **Pena Park**, at the top end of which rears the fabulous **Palácio da Pena** (Tues–Sun: April–Sept 9.45am–7pm; Oct–March 9.45am–5.30pm; €13.50, including access to the park, or €12.50 if ticket bought 9.30–10.30am), a wild, nineteenth-century fantasy of domes, towers and a drawbridge that doesn't draw. The cluttered, kitschy interior has been preserved as left by the royal family on their flight from Portugal in 1910.

ARRIVAL AND INFORMATION

By train Trains run from Lisbon's Rossio station to the centre of Sintra. From here it's a 10min stroll southeast to the main tourist office.

Destinations Lisbon (Rossio) (every 15–30min; 40min).

Tourist information There's one small tourist office at the train station (daily 10am–6pm) and a larger one (daily 9.30am–6pm, until 7pm Aug; ☎ 219 231 157) just off the central Praça da República.

ACCOMMODATION AND EATING

★ **Café Saudade** Av Doutor Miguel Bombarda 6. On the site of an old cheesecake factory, with beautifully ornate ceilings, this café/gallery near the train station does excellent salads for €6. Daily 8.30am–8pm/midnight.

Estrada Velha Rua Consiglieri Pedroso 16. On the road to the Quinta da Regaleira, this good-value café serves sandwiches, crêpes (from €3) and other quick bites. Daily 11am–2am.

Piela's Av Desiderio Cambournac 1 ☎ 219 241 691, ⓦ cafepielas.com Pleasant *pension* in Estefania, above central Sintra. All rooms are en suite, with clean tiled bathrooms, and there's a small café at street level. Double **€60**

Central Portugal

The Beiras, Estremadura and Ribatejo regions that comprise central Portugal have played crucial roles in each phase of the nation's history – and the monuments are here to prove it. The vast plains of the Beiras are dominated by **Coimbra**, an ancient university town and Portugal's former capital, perched high above the Beira Litoral. Below the Beiras lie Estremadura and Ribatejo, both comparatively small areas of fertile rolling hills, which boast an extraordinary concentration of vivid architecture and engaging towns. **Alcobaça** in Estremadura and **Tomar** in the wine-producing Ribatejo are two of the most striking, both housing famously grand religious monuments.

ALCOBAÇA

The pretty town of **Alcobaça** is dominated by the vast, beautiful **Mosteiro de Santa Maria de Alcobaça** (daily: April–Sept 9am–7pm; Oct–March 9am–5pm; €6, free Sun until 2pm). From its foundation in 1147 until its dissolution in 1834, this Cistercian monastery was one of the greatest in the world. Its **church** (free) is one of the largest in Portugal, with a Baroque facade that conceals an interior stripped of most of its later adornments and restored to its original simplicity.

The monastery's most precious treasures are the fourteenth-century **tombs** of Dom Pedro and Dona Inês de Castro, sculpted with incredible detail to illustrate the story of Pedro's love for Inês, the daughter of a Galician nobleman (see box, p.878).

The monastery's most impressive room is the **kitchen**, featuring a gigantic conical chimney, and a stream tapped from the river to provide Alcobaça's famously gluttonous monks with a constant supply of fresh fish.

ARRIVAL AND INFORMATION

By bus Alcobaça's bus station is a 5min walk from the monastery in the centre of town, across the bridge.

Destinations Coimbra (1 daily; 1hr 25min); Lisbon (7 daily; 1hr 50min); Porto (1–2 daily; 4hr 30min); Tomar (3 daily; 2hr).

26

TILL DEATH DO US PART: DOM PEDRO AND DONA INÊS DE CASTRO

Dom Pedro's father, Afonso V, forbade his marriage to **Dona Inês de Castro**, which nevertheless took place in secret. Afonso ordered Inês's murder, and Pedro waited for his succession to the throne before exhuming her corpse and forcing the royal circle to acknowledge her as queen by kissing her decomposing hand. Their tombs have been placed foot to foot so that on Judgement Day the lovers may rise and immediately see one another.

26

Tourist information Tourist office at Rua 16 de Outubro 7, a short walk north of the monastery (daily 10am–1pm & 2–6pm; ☎ 262 582 377).

ACCOMMODATION AND EATING

Pensão Corações Unidos Rua Frei António Brandão 39 ☎ 262 582 142. Neat, clean *pensão* with modern bathrooms facing the monastery. The restaurant below serves good-value regional cooking (mains €8). Double €40

Real Baça Directly opposite the monastery on Praça 25 de Abril. Relaxed *pastelaria* with a good selection of local pastries and cakes (around €1), plus ice-cold drinks. Daily 8am–8pm.

Ti Fininho Rua Frei António Brandão 34. Cheap grilled fish and meats, omelettes, and wine by the jug at this weary-looking restaurant a short walk from the monastery. *Bacalhau á casa* €8. Daily 10am–3.30pm & 6–10pm.

TOMAR

Riverside **TOMAR** is famous for its spectacular headquarters of the Portuguese branch of the Knights Templar, which overlooks the town from a wooded hill. It's also an attractive town in its own right – especially during the lively **Festa dos Tabuleiros**, a festival of music and dancing, held once every four years at the beginning of July.

WHAT TO SEE AND DO

Built on a simple grid plan, Tomar's centre preserves its traditional charm, with whitewashed houses lining narrow cobbled streets. West of the central Praça da República is the former Jewish quarter, where at Rua Joaquim Jacinto 73 you'll find an excellently preserved fourteenth-century synagogue, now the **Museu Luso-Hebraicoa Abraham Zacuto** (daily 10am–1pm & 2–7pm; free), one of the few surviving synagogues in Portugal. There's a bit of contemporary interest at **NAM** on Rua Gil de Avô (Tues–Sun: April–Sept 10am–6pm; Nov–March

10am–5pm; free), a three-floor modern art gallery exhibiting works mostly by Portuguese artists.

A fifteen-minute walk uphill from the town centre, the **Convento de Cristo** (daily 9am–5.30/6.30pm; €6) is set among pleasant gardens (free) with excellent views of the surrounding woodland. Founded in 1162 by Gualdim Pais, first Master of the Knights Templar, it was the Order's headquarters. At the heart of the complex, surrounded by serene cloisters, is the **Charola**, the high-ceilinged, sixteen-sided temple from which the knights drew their moral conviction. The beautiful adjoining two-tiered **Principal Cloister** is one of the purest examples of the Renaissance style in Portugal.

ARRIVAL AND INFORMATION

By train The train station is on Av dos Combatentes de Grande Guerra, 10min south of the town centre. Destinations Coimbra (up to 11 daily; 2hr 30min); Lisbon (15 daily; 2hr).

By bus Buses pull in at a lot beside the train station. Destinations Coimbra (1 daily; 2hr 10min); Porto (1 daily; 4hr).

Tourist information Tourist office at the top of Av Dr Cândido Madureira (daily: May–Sept 10am–1pm & 3–7pm; Oct–April 9.30am–1pm & 2.30–6pm).

ACCOMMODATION

Parque de Campismo ☎ 249 329 824. Tomar's campsite is a short walk east of Rua Marquês de Pombal. It's a good-sized site with plenty of trees providing shade and a helpful front desk. Camping €4 per person, plus €5 per tent

Residencial União Rua Serpa Pinto 94 ☎ 249 323 161. Faded but passable *pensão* in a nineteenth-century building on the main street. Cheap walk-up rates and a friendly, English-speaking owner. Double €50

EATING AND DRINKING

Café Paraíso Rua Serpa Pinto 127. A Tomar institution with mirrored walls and a quirky vibe, ideal for a drink (espresso 65c) at any time of day. Mon evening only, Tues–Sat 8am–2am, Sun 8am–8pm.

La Bella Rua Serpa Pinto 149. The once-modern decor is looking a little tatty, but the well-made pizzas (from €6.50) make this Italian restaurant/late-night lounge worth a visit. Daily noon–2am.

COIMBRA

COIMBRA was Portugal's capital from 1143 to 1255 and ranks behind only Lisbon and Porto in historic importance. Its university, founded in 1290, was the only one in Portugal until the beginning of the twentieth century.

WHAT TO SEE AND DO

For a provincial town Coimbra has significant architectural riches. Its many students create a rather vivacious atmosphere during term time – especially in May, when they celebrate the end of the academic year with the **Queima das Fitas**, a symbolic tearing or burning of their gowns and faculty ribbons followed by some serious partying. This is when you're most likely to hear the Coimbra *fado*, distinguished from the Lisbon version by its mournful pace and complex lyrics. During the summer months, the atmosphere is rather more subdued.

The old town

Old Coimbra sits on a hill on the right bank of the River Mondego, with the university crowning its summit. The main buildings of the **Old University** (March–Oct daily 9am–7pm; Nov–Feb Mon–Fri 9am–5pm, Sat & Sun 10am–4pm; €7), dating from the sixteenth century, are set around a courtyard (entrance free) dominated by a Baroque clock tower and a statue of João III. The **chapel** is covered with *azulejos* and intricate decoration, but takes second place to the **library**, a Baroque fantasy with *trompe-l'oeil* ceilings. It also has some unusual inhabitants: a colony of bats. Other areas included in the visit are the graduation hall and the academic prison. Halfway down the hill towards the centre stands the solid and simple **Sé Velha** (Old Cathedral; Mon–Sat 10am–6pm; €2), one of Portugal's most important Romanesque buildings.

Central Coimbra

Restraint and simplicity certainly aren't the chief qualities of the flamboyant **Igreja de Santa Cruz** (Mon–Fri 9am–5pm, Sat 9am–noon & 2–5.30pm, Sun 4–5.30pm; €2.50), at the bottom of the hill on Praça 8 de Maio. It houses the tombs of Portugal's first kings, Afonso Henriques and Sancho I, and an elaborately carved pulpit.

Across the river, the beautifully restored convent of **Santa Clara a Velha** (Tues–Sun: May–Sept 10am–7pm; Oct–April 10am–5pm; €5) is worth seeing now you have the chance: a century ago, it had all but disappeared under the rising tide of the Mondego. The nuns moved to higher and higher floors before abandoning the convent for **Santa Clara a Nova** up the hill in 1677. There's now a visitor centre detailing life in medieval Portugal as well as a film of the restoration process with English subtitles (Mon–Sat 8.45/9am–6.45/7pm, Sun 9am–6.45/7pm).

Other areas of interest include the epicentre of the students' social scene, **Praça da República**, a ten-minute walk from Praça 8 de Maio up Rua Olímpio Nicolau Rui Fernandes, and the rambling **Botanic Garden** (Mon–Sat: April–Sept 9am–8pm; Oct–March 9am–5.30pm; free), which sits in the shadow of the sixteenth-century **aqueduct** to the east of Praça da República.

ARRIVAL AND DEPARTURE

By train Intercity trains stop at Coimbra B, 3km north of the city, from where there are frequent connecting services to Coimbra A in the town centre.
Destinations Lisbon (hourly; 2–3hr); Porto (hourly; 1hr 20min–2hr); Tomar (up to 11 daily; 2hr 30min).
By bus The bus station is on Av Fernão de Magalhães, a 15min walk from the centre – turn right out of the bus station and head down the main road. Some buses from the north stop on Av Emídio Navarro.
Destinations Alcobaça (1–2 daily; 1hr 30min); Lisbon (at least hourly; 2hr 20min); Porto (at least 11 daily; 1hr 30min).

INFORMATION

Tourist information The main tourist office is near the bridge, on Largo da Portagem (summer Mon–Fri

26

9am–8pm, Sat & Sun 9am–5.30pm; winter Mon–Fri 9am–6pm, Sat & Sun 9.30am–12.30pm & 1.30–5.30pm; ☎ 239 488 120, ⊕ turismodecoimbra.pt).

GETTING AROUND

By bus The main hub for Coimbra's local buses is Av Emídio Navarro near Coimbra A train station. Buses #7, #10 and #11 run from here to Praça da República. A one-way journey bought on board costs €1.60; 3 tickets bought in advance at a newsstand cost €2.20.

ACCOMMODATION

Grande Hostel de Coimbra Rua Antero de Quental 196 ☎ 239 108 212, ⊕ grandehostelcoimbra.com. Long-running hostel near Praça da República, set in a big old house with a garden, lounge and kitchen providing free fruit. A good place to meet fellow travellers. Dorm €18, double €40

Pousada de Juventude Rua Dr. Henrique Seco 14 ☎ 239 822 955, ⊕ pousadasjuventude.pt; bus #7 from Av Emídio Navarro. Basic but cheap hostel 10min north of Praça da República. Dorm €13, double €28

Serenata Next to Sé Velha at Largo Sé Velha 21–23 ☎ 239 853 130, ⊕ serenatahostel.com. Palatial hostel with a hotel-like living room, games room and sun terrace, plus names of famous Portuguese figures running along its walls. Dorm €14, double €31

EATING, DRINKING AND NIGHTLIFE

Most of the town's restaurants can be found tucked away in the alleys between Largo da Portagem – the place to head for cafés – and Praça 8 de Maio.

Adega Paço do Conde Rua Paço do Conde 1. Atmospheric, locally renowned *churrasqueira* serving tasty barbecued meat and fish (around €9). Mon–Sat 11am–3.30pm & 7–11pm.

Café Tropical Praça da República. A favourite haunt of students, with outdoor tables and cheap drinks (small beer €1). Mon–Sat 10am–2am, Sun 2pm–2am.

Fado ao Centro Rua do Quebra Costas 7. A good place to hear Coimbra *fado*, with nightly performances (€10 for 50min) at 6pm. The price includes a glass of port wine. Although it doesn't open till evening, tickets are sold throughout the day. Note that it isn't a bar, however, and is only open for the duration of the performance. Daily at 6pm.

Jardim da Manga Rua Olímpio Nicolau Rui Fernandes. Self-service café serving up good-value meals in a pretty spot by an elaborate domed fountain. Mains around €8.50. Daily 8am–midnight.

The Rock Planet Rua Almeida Garrett 1. Three floors of fun, combining a restaurant with a bar and club. Live rock bands, DJs and themed party nights make this place a student favourite. Tues–Sat 10pm–6am.

Northern Portugal

Porto, the country's second-largest city, is an attractive and convenient centre from which to explore this region. Magnificently set on a rocky cliff astride the River Douro, it is perhaps most famous for the port-producing suburb of **Vila Nova de Gaia**, supplied by vineyards further inland along the river. The **Douro Valley** is traced by a spectacular rail route, though sadly the branch line along the Corgo to the pretty town of **Vila Real** is now defunct – the town is nevertheless a good base for exploration of the Parque Natural do Alvão, and the main centre for transport connections into the isolated rural region of **Trás-os-Montes** – literally "behind the mountains".

In the northwest, the **Minho**, considered by many to be the most beautiful part of the country, is a lush wilderness of rolling mountain forests and rugged coastlines (the Costa Verde), with some of the most unspoilt beaches in Europe. A quietly conservative region, its towns have a special charm and beauty, among them the religious centre of **Braga**, and the self-proclaimed birthplace of the nation, **Guimarães**, both of which can be visited by day-trip from Porto, but which also make good bases from which to explore the rest of the Minho.

PORTO

Capital of the north, **PORTO** (sometimes called "Oporto" in English) is very different from Lisbon – unpretentious and unashamedly commercial, yet extremely welcoming. As the local saying goes: "Coimbra sings; Braga prays; Lisbon shows off; and Porto works." Already possessing considerable appeal, the city received something of a makeover thanks to funding received for Euro 2004, and now boasts an efficient metro system, state-of-the-art football stadium and a top concert venue, the Casa da Música.

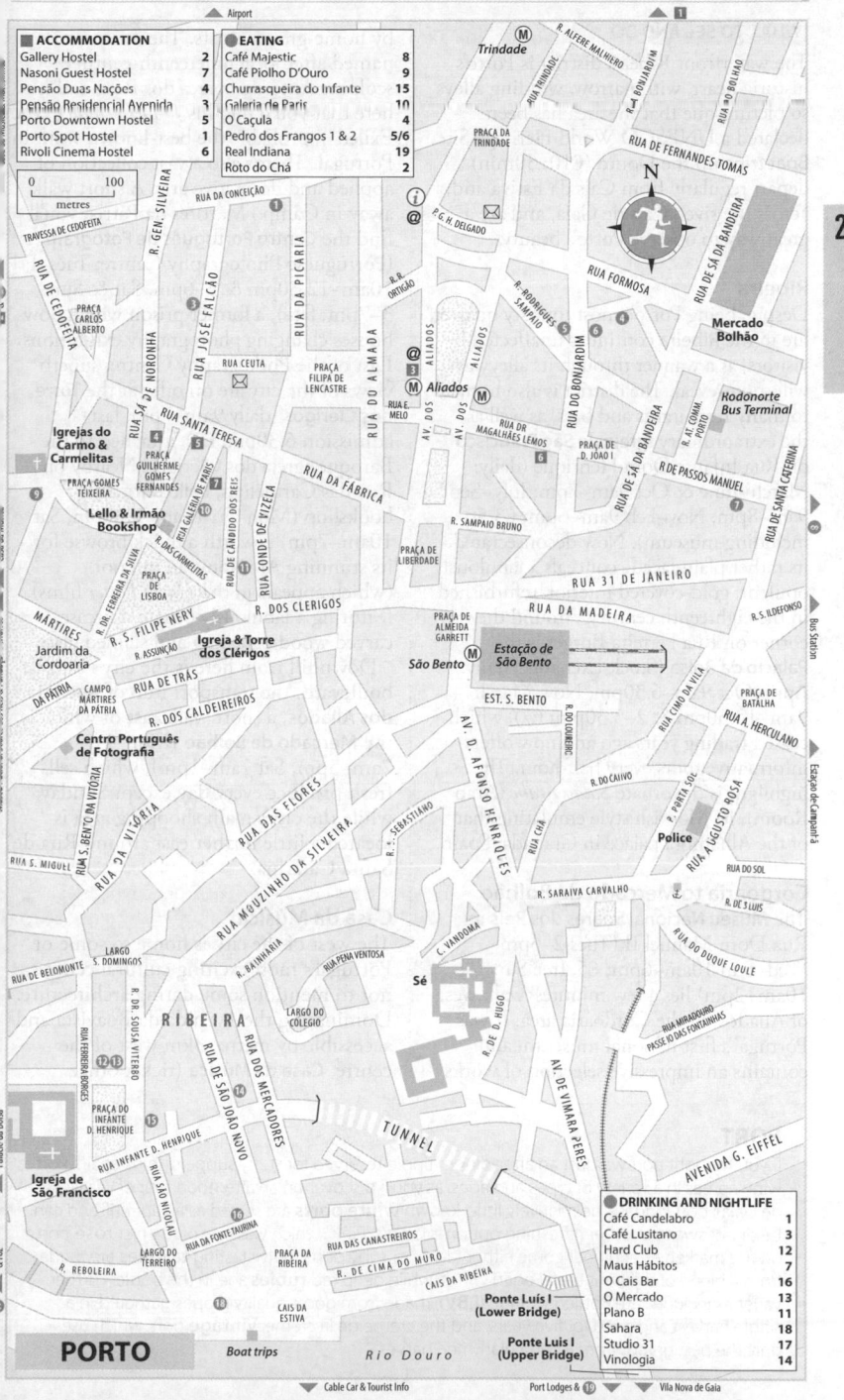

■ ACCOMMODATION
Gallery Hostel — 2
Nasoni Guest Hostel — 7
Pensão Duas Nações — 4
Pensão Residencial Avenida — 3
Porto Downtown Hostel — 8
Porto Spot Hostel — 1
Rivoli Cinema Hostel — 6

● EATING
Café Majestic — 8
Café Piolho D'Ouro — 9
Churrasqueira do Infante — 15
Galeria de Paris — 10
O Cáçula — 4
Pedro dos Frangos 1 & 2 — 5/6
Real Indiana — 19
Roto do Chá — 2

● DRINKING AND NIGHTLIFE
Café Candelabro — 1
Café Lusitano — 3
Hard Club — 12
Maus Hábitos — 7
O Cais Bar — 16
O Mercado — 13
Plano B — 11
Sahara — 18
Studio 31 — 17
Vinologia — 14

PORTO

Airport

Trindade

Mercado Bolhão

Kodonorte Bus Terminal

Igrejas do Carmo & Carmelitas

Lello & Irmão Bookshop

Igreja & Torre dos Clérigos

São Bento

Estação de São Bento

Centro Português de Fotografia

Jardim da Cordoaria

Police

RIBEIRA

Sé

Igreja de São Francisco

TUNNEL

Rio Douro

Boat trips

Ponte Luís I (Lower Bridge)

Ponte Luís I (Upper Bridge)

Cable Car & Tourist Info

Port Lodges &

Vila Nova de Gaia

26

The waterfront Ribeira district is Porto's historic heart, with narrow, winding alleys so picturesque that the area has been declared a UNESCO World Heritage Site. **Boat trips** up the Douro (€10; 50min) depart regularly from Cais da Estiva and, across the river, Cais de Gaia, and are a great way to observe Porto's beauty.

Ribeira

Despite being Porto's most touristy quarter, life in the **Ribeira** continues unaffected by visitors, as a wander through its alleyways will soon reveal. The district is also home to many restaurants and bars, as well as the extraordinary **Igreja de São Francisco** on Rua Infante Dom Henrique (daily: March–June & Oct 9am–7pm; July–Sept 9am–8pm; Nov–Feb 9am–6pm; €3.50 including museum). Now deconsecrated, its rather plain facade conceals a fabulously opulent, gold-covered interior, refurbished in the eighteenth century. Around the corner on Rua Ferreira Borges is the **Palácio da Bolsa** (Stock Exchange; daily: April–Oct 9am–6.30pm; Nov–March 9am–12.30pm & 2–5.30pm; €7), which ceased trading years ago and now offers informative tours every half-hour. The highlight is the ornate *Salão Árabe* (Arab Room), its Moorish style emulating that of the Alhambra palace in Granada, Spain.

Cordoaria to Mercado de Bolhão

The **Museu Nacional Soares dos Reis** at Rua Dom Manuel II (Tues 2–6pm, Wed–Sun 10am–6pm; €5, free Sun 10am–2pm) lies a few minutes' walk west of Aliados, in the Cordoaria area. It was Portugal's first national museum, and contains an impressive selection of works by home-grown artists. The museum is named after local nineteenth-century sculptor António Soares dos Reis, and it's here that you'll find his *O Desterrado* ("The Exiled"), probably the best-known work in Portugal. There's also a vast collection of applied and decorative arts. A short walk away in Campo Mártires da Pátria, you'll find the **Centro Português de Fotografia** (Portuguese Photography Centre; Tues–Fri 10am–12.30pm & 3–6pm, Sat & Sun 3–7pm; free), a former prison which now houses changing photography exhibitions. East of the Photography Centre, superb views of the city are on offer at the **Torre dos Clérigos** (daily 9am–7pm, last admission 6.30pm; €2), attached to the Baroque Igreja dos Clérigos. Nearby on Rua das Carmelitas, **Lello & Irmão** bookshop (Mon–Fri 10am–7.30pm, Sat 10am–7pm) is worth a quick browse for its stunning Art Nouveau interior (which appears in the *Harry Potter* films), featuring a fabulously ornate staircase, carved wood panelling and stained glass.

Downhill from here is the city's biggest boulevard, the transport hub of **Avenida dos Aliados**, a short walk east of which is the **Mercado de Bolhão** (Mon–Fri 7am–5pm, Sat 7am–1pm), which sells fresh produce every day except Sunday, while the city's main shopping area is located a little further east around Rua de Santa Catarina.

Casa da Música

The west of the city is home to some of Portugal's most exciting cultural centres, not to mention some daring architecture. Dominating the Avenida da Boavista and accessible by metro, 3km west of the centre, **Casa da Música** (ticket office

---

PORT

If you thought port was just an after-dinner tipple reserved for stuffy suppers, think again. Port wine comes in a variety of types and ages, as you'll discover on an afternoon tour of Vila Nova de Gaia's port lodges. The relatively little-known **white ports** are served as an aperitif, and can be dry or sweet; another refreshing option is Croft's "Pink", which was one of the first **rosé** ports on the market. After dinner come either tawny or ruby ports: nutty-tasting **tawnies** are made from a blend of different barrel-aged wines, while deep red **rubies** age in the bottle. Further varieties include Late Bottled Vintage (**LBV**), made from good-quality grapes gathered in a single harvest and aged for five years, and the crème de la crème, **Vintage** port, which uses only the best grapes from a particularly fine harvest.

Mon–Sat 10am–7pm, Sun 10am–6pm; English tours daily 10am–4pm; €4; ⓦcasadamusica.com) is a vast, irregularly shaped and strangely beautiful white concrete confection designed by Rem Koolhaas. Concerts are held here almost every night of the year (see website for details), though you can have a peek at its impressive interior for free. For a more in-depth exploration, there are daily guided tours in English.

Fundação Serralves

Three kilometres west of Casa da Música is another architectural gem and one of Porto's key attractions, the **Fundação Serralves** (Tues–Sun 10am–5pm, until 7/8pm Sat & Sun April–Oct; €7, park only €3; free Sun 10am–1.30pm; bus #201 from Aliados to Avenida Gomes da Costa), which comprises the modernist **Museum of Contemporary Art**, hosting an exciting array of temporary exhibitions by Portuguese and international artists, and the Art Deco **Serralves Villa** (which also hosts occasional exhibitions), set in a vast, beautiful park. If the exhibition isn't to your taste, skip it and head straight for the **park**, encompassing everything from formal gardens to wild woods, and even a farm featuring species from northern Portugal.

Foz do Douro

The coastline at **Foz** makes an easy escape from the city, reached via tram #1 (€2.50 one-way) from Rua Nova da Alfândega. The old wooden tram clanks along the coastline to Passeio Alegre, from where you can take a one-hour stroll along the beachside promenade to the curiously named **Castelo do Queijo** (Cheese Castle) before taking bus #502 back to the centre. For much of the year the Atlantic Ocean is too chilly for all but the hardiest of swimmers, but the beaches fill up with sun-worshippers once summer rolls round. Foz is also home to a buzzing nightlife scene.

Vila Nova de Gaia

South of the river and essentially a city in its own right, **Vila Nova de Gaia** (usually referred to as Gaia) is dominated by the

port trade. From the Ribeira, the names of the various companies, spelled out in neon letters above the terracotta roofs of the wine lodges, leave you in no doubt as to what awaits you. You can walk to Gaia across the **Ponte Dom Luís I**: the most direct route to the lodges is across the Lower Bridge from the Cais da Ribeira, but taking the metro across the top level to the Jardim do Morro stop has the bonus of breathtaking views. Another scenic option is the **Teleférico de Gaia** cable car (daily: early April to early Oct 10am–8pm; mid-Oct to March 10am–6pm; €2.50 each way), which connects Vila Nova de Gaia's waterfront with the top level of the bridge (though doesn't actually cross the river). The port lodges offer **tours**, which generally explain the histories of both the company and of port production, and end with a tasting session. Most lodges charge €3–4 for the most basic tours, which conclude with tastings of one or two ports, with more expensive options such as vintage ports available for an extra fee.

It's worth trekking up the hill to Taylor's, as at the end of the €3 guided tour, you'll be able to try a Late Bottled Vintage. The tourist information kiosk on Avenida Diogo Leite (Mon–Fri 10am–6pm, Sat 10am–1pm & 2–6pm) has the helpful *Caves do Vinho do Porto* leaflet, which outlines timetables and prices of tours. If all this sampling whets your appetite, head to *Vinologia* (see p.885) to learn and taste more.

ARRIVAL AND DEPARTURE

By plane From the Francisco Sá Carneiro airport, 10km north of the city, take metro line E (roughly 6am–1am; €2.30, including purchase of rechargeable Andante card) to the centre.

By train Most trains from the south stop at the distant Estação de Campanhã; you may need to change here for a connection to the central Estação de São Bento (frequent; 5min). Metro line B will also take you into the centre from Campanhã.

Destinations Braga (every 30min–1hr; 40min–1hr 5min); Coimbra (hourly; 1hr 30min–2hr); Guimarães (every 1–2hr; 1hr–1hr 15min); Lisbon (hourly; 2hr 45min–3hr 30min).

By bus The main bus terminal (Rede-Expressos) is on Rua Alexandre Herculano, a short walk east of São Bento, while the Rodonorte terminal is at Rua Ateneu Comercial do Porto 19, off Rua de Passos Manuel.

26

26

Destinations Amarante (15 daily; 50min); Braga (every 30min; 1hr–1hr 30min); Coimbra (8–10 daily; 1hr 30min); Guimarães (up to 4 daily; 1hr 40min); Lisbon (at least hourly; 3hr 30min).

INFORMATION

Tourist information The tourist office is just north of Av dos Aliados at Rua Clube dos Fenianos 25 (daily: June–Oct 9am–8pm; Nov–May 9am–7pm; ☎ 222 393 472, ⓦ www.portoturismo.pt). There is also an *iPoint* information desk at the Fundação Serralves museum (Mon–Fri 10am–7pm, Sat & Sun 10am–7/8pm).

Tourist passes All tourist offices sell the Porto Card, which offers free public transport and free or discounted entry to most of the city's sights (1/2/3-day for €10.50/€17.50/€21.50). A cheaper alternative is the one-day "walker" card (€5), which excludes public transport but still provides the same discounts.

GETTING AROUND

Tickets The blue Andante card covers the metro, tram, the funicular from opposite the Ponte Luís I to Praça da Batalha, and most bus lines. It costs €0.50, added to the price of your first ticket, and is available at the airport, in all metro stations and in the main tourist office. Once purchased, it can be loaded with one-way journeys or 24hr passes. Whichever you choose, remember that your card must be validated at the start of each trip (or part thereof). When using a "Z2" (zone 2) pass, for example, you can change freely between vehicles within that zone, revalidating the card each time. When you first validate the card, you are given an hour. As long as your final validation of the card falls within that hour, you will be able to continue to your final destination without paying for a new single-trip pass – so long as it is within the same zone. If you revalidate the card after the first hour is up, you will be charged for a new pass.

By metro Porto's sleek, six-line metro system (daily, roughly 6am–1am) is cheap and efficient. The lines meet at Trindade station, which also houses an Andante shop (Mon–Fri 8am–7.30pm, Sat 9am–4.30pm, Sun 10am–4.30pm). A single trip in the centre costs €1.20, and a 24hr pass, valid on all forms of transport, costs €3.95.

By bus One-way bus tickets can be purchased on board for €1.80, but the Andante scheme offers better value.

By taxi Taxis are cheap and plentiful; two useful ranks are located at Praça da Ribeira and the Rotonda da Boa Vista, near Casa da Música.

ACCOMMODATION

Well-located, good-value rooms are on offer in the streets to the east and west of Av dos Aliados. There are also some bargain rooms in the slightly run-down area around Praça da Batalha, east of Estação de São Bento. In addition to *residenciais* and *pensões*, Porto now has some central, well-equipped hostels.

HOSTELS

★ **Gallery Hostel** Rua Miguel Bombarda 222 ☎ 224 964 313, ⓦ gallery-hostel.com; ⓜ Aliados/Trindade. Superb, spacious, hostel-cum-gallery in Porto's emerging artists' quarter. The house, built in 1906 and carefully restored, has its own library, bar and TV room. The helpful family running it offer free tours and trips to local galleries. Dorm €20

Nasoni Guest Hostel Rua Galerias de Paris 82 ☎ 222 083 807, ⓦ facebook.com/nasoni82; ⓜ Aliados/São Bento. Individually themed doubles and dorms that share a bright, top-floor living room, plus a kitchen and small terrace. Dorm €18, double €42

Porto Downtown Hostel Praça Guilherme Gomes Fernandes 66–1° ☎ 220 018 094, ⓦ portodowntownhostel .com; ⓜ Aliados. Friendly, spotlessly clean and central place with different-sized dorms and three double rooms. There's also an inviting lounge and a decent kitchen. Dorm €15, double €42

Porto Spot Hostel Rua Gonçalo Cristovao 12 ☎ 224 085 205; ⓜ Trindade. A little further out, this smart and sociable hostel has key-card access, clean minimalist rooms and a garden. Dorm €18, double €50

Rivoli Cinema Hostel Rua Dr Magalhães Lemos 83 ☎ 220 174 634, ⓦ rivolicinemahostel.com; ⓜ Aliados/São Bento. Efficiently run, cinema-themed hostel which offers dorms and spacious twin rooms. There's also a roof terrace. Dorm €21, double €44

PENSIONS AND HOTELS

Pensão Duas Nações Praça Guilherme Gomes Fernandes 59 ☎ 222 081 616, ⓦ duasnacoes.com.pt; ⓜ Aliados/São Bento. A deservedly popular option, with bright, decently sized rooms, most of which are en suite. No breakfast. Dorm €13.50, double €28

Pensão Residencial Avenida Av dos Aliados 141 ☎ 222 009 551, ⓦ pensaoavenida.planetaclix.pt; ⓜ Aliados. Sparklingly clean rooms with smart, modern bathrooms; the location's good but you have to climb a lot of stairs to reach the rooms. Double €45

EATING

Porto's culinary speciality is the mighty *francesinha* – a gut-busting sandwich of steak, ham and *Linguiça* sausage, covered in a layer of melted cheese and a spicy beer and tomato sauce; an acquired taste. Restaurants are good value, particularly the workers' cafés, which usually offer a set menu at lunchtime (but close around 7.30pm and at weekends). Prime areas are Rua do Almada and Rua de São Bento da Vitória. For international options, head to the riverside Cais de Gaia complex, which offers Italian, Indian and other international flavours.

CAFÉS, CHEAP EATS AND SNACKS

Café Majestic Rua de Santa Catarina 112; ⓜ Bolhão /Aliados. Voted one of the world's most beautiful cafés, with *belle époque* mirrors and cherubs adorning its walls. Perfect for an elegant (if expensive) snack (sandwiches from €8). Mon–Sat 9.30am–midnight.

Café Piolho D'Ouro Praça de Parada Leitão; ⓜ São Bento. Near the university, this diner is popular with students and serves incredibly cheap food throughout the day, before morphing into a packed bar at night. *Francesinha* €7.50. Daily 7am–4am.

Churrasqueira do Infante Praça do Infante Dom Henrique; ⓜ São Bento. A wide selection of good-value grilled meat and fish makes this *churrasqueira* a great budget option in the Ribeira. Grilled chicken €3.50. Mon–Sat noon–3.30pm & 6.30–10.30pm.

★ **Galeria de Paris** Rua Galeria de Paris 56; ⓜ Aliados. A curio-cluttered hangout doing excellent buffet lunches, usually with grilled fish, chicken and plenty of healthy salad (€4.50). Daily 11am–4am.

Pedro dos Frangos 1 & 2 Rua do Bonjardim; ⓜ Aliados. Cheap-and-cheerful café/restaurants on opposite sides of the road, serving great-value spit-roasted chicken (just €8.50 for a whole one with chips). Daily 11.30am–10.30pm.

Roto do Chá Rua Miguel Bombarda 457; ⓜ Aliados. Choose from around 300 different brews (from €1.50) at this chilled-out tea shop, a 15min walk from the metro station. There's a tranquil garden at the back. Mon–Fri noon–8pm, Sat noon–midnight, Sun 1–8pm.

RESTAURANTS

O Caçula Travessa do Bonjardim 20; ⓜ Aliados. Smart spot near Aliados serving a select menu of inventive international fish, meat and vegetarian dishes in generous portions. The three-course menu of the day, which often includes dishes like rump steak, costs €7.95. Mon–Thurs & Sun noon–midnight, Fri & Sat noon–2am.

Real Indiana Cais de Gaia 360; ⓜ Jardim do Morro. Tasty Indian dishes served in a modern first-floor space with beautiful river views. Good for vegetarians. *Saag aloo* €9.50, with meaty mains for around €13.50. Daily noon–3pm & 7–11pm.

DRINKING AND NIGHTLIFE

The Ribeira area offers a fairly laidback drinking scene, while Cais de Gaia is a good option for sophisticated sipping. Livelier late-night bars (open until around 4am at weekends) can be found around Rua de Cândido dos Reis, near Aliados. Most of the city's big clubs are in the outlying Matosinhos district or near Foz.

BARS

★ **Café Candelabro** Rua da Conceição 3; ⓜ Aliados. Low-key and cool with bookcase-lined walls and huge glasses of

quality wine for €1.60. Also a popular spot for breakfast, with croissants warmed up behind the bar. Mon–Sat 10am–2am.

Café Lusitano Rua de José Falcão 137; ⓜ Aliados. Fun and lively bar with chandeliers dangling from the ceiling, art on the walls and a mixed gay/straight crowd. Tues–Thurs 9.30pm–2am, Fri & Sat 10pm–4am.

O Cais Bar Rua da Fonte Taurina 2; ⓜ São Bento. Relaxed bar with a clientele as varied as the soundtrack. Serves lots of foreign beers and jugs of sangria for €9. Daily 9.30pm–3am.

O Mercado Praça do Infante Dom Henrique, outside *Hard Club*; ⓜ São Bento. Skip the indoor restaurant in favour of the terrace bar, which overlooks Jardim do Infante Dom Henrique, and grab yourself a cool glass of port and tonic (€6). Tues–Sun noon–3am.

Plano B Rua de Cândido dos Reis 30; ⓜ Jardim do Morro. A popular late-night bar with weekend DJs and a programme of live music and performance art. Tues & Wed 10pm–2am, Thurs 10pm–4am, Fri & Sat 10am–6pm.

Sahara Caís da Estiva 4; ⓜ São Bento/Jardim do Morro. Glittery, Arabian-style bar tucked away in a cavern-like space by the waterfront. Apple tobacco fills the air while young locals and tourists sip beer (€2). Daily 3pm–2am.

★ **Vinologia** Rua de São João Novo 46; ⓜ São Bento. Innovative bar offering a huge selection of port (from €3/glass), with knowledgeable, friendly staff. Even an expert could learn a lot here. Mon–Thurs 4–10pm, Fri–Sun 4pm–midnight.

CLUBS

Porto's clubs are mostly outside the city centre; catch the #500 to Foz or one of the night buses from Aliados or Casa da Música if you can't afford a taxi.

Hard Club Mercado Ferreira Borges, Praça do Infante Dom Henrique ⓦ hard-club.com; ⓜ São Bento. Porto's main venue for international DJs, housed in a huge former market building. Gets going around 10pm–2am; see website for specific event times.

Maus Hábitos Rua Passos Manuel 178-4° ⓦ maushabitos .com; ⓜ Bolhão. Cultural space and bar opposite the Coliseu do Porto theatre, hosting live bands, singer-songwriters and pumping DJ sets. Check the website for listings. Also does veggie lunches until 3pm on weekdays. Mon & Tues 12.30–3pm, Wed, Thurs & Sun 12.30–3pm & 10pm–2am, Fri & Sat 12.30–3pm & 10pm–4am.

Studio 31 Rua Passeio Alegre, 564, Foz. DJs from across Portugal come here to play funky house, old hits, and plenty in between. Wed–Sun 10pm–4am.

DIRECTORY

Internet OnWeb at Praça General Humberto Delgado 291, just downhill from the tourist office (Mon–Fri 10am–2am, Sat & Sun 2pm–2am; €2/2hr).

Left luggage At Trindade metro station (from €1/hr).

Tourist police Rua Clube dos Fenianos 11.

26

BRAGA

Capital of the Minho, **BRAGA** is also Portugal's religious capital – the scene of spectacular **Easter celebrations** with torchlight processions. But it's not all pomp and ceremony; it's also a lively university town, with a compact and pretty historical centre.

Rua Andrade Corvo leads from the train station to the centre, entered via the sixteenth-century **Arco da Porta Nova**.

The City

Just beyond the city gate lies the oldest cathedral in the country, the extraordinary **Sé** (Tues–Sun 9am–12.30pm & 2–5.30/6.30pm), which dates back to 1070 and encompasses Gothic, Renaissance and Baroque styles. The most impressive areas of the Sé, the Gothic chapels – especially the *Capela dos Reis* (Kings' Chapel), built to house the tombs of Henry of Burgundy and his wife Theresa, the cathedral's founders – and the upper choir may only be visited by guided tour (same hours as cathedral; €5 for tour of museum, chapels and sacristy). Nearby is the **Museu dos Biscaínhos** (Rua dos Biscaínhos; Tues–Sun 10am–12.15pm & 2–5.30pm; €2), a beautiful seventeenth-century mansion housing a collection of decorative arts, painting and sculpture. Just behind the palace lies the lovely **Jardim de Santa Bárbara**, an oasis of topiary and rose gardens. Braga's main square, the buzzing, café-lined **Praça da República**, is a short walk northwest of the garden.

Bom Jesus do Monte

Braga's real gem is **Bom Jesus do Monte**, set on a wooded hillside 3km above the city – its glorious ornamental stairway is one of Portugal's best-known images. A monumental place of pilgrimage, Bom Jesus was created by Braga's archbishop in the early eighteenth century. The #2 bus runs from Avenida da Liberdade in Braga to Bom Jesus twice every hour (€1.65). Save the ancient wooden funicular (€1.20) for the return journey and ascend the wide, tree-lined staircases to watch Bom Jesus's

simple allegory unfold. Each landing holds a small fountain and a chapel containing rather crumbling tableau depictions of the life of Christ, leading up to the Crucifixion scene on the altar of the Neoclassical church which sits atop the staircase. Beyond the church are wooded gardens and a number of hotels and restaurants.

ARRIVAL AND INFORMATION

By train Braga's train station is almost 1km west of the centre, down Rua Andrade Corvo.
Destinations Lisbon (roughly hourly; 3hr 30min–5hr); Porto (at least hourly; 1hr 15min–1hr 40min).
By bus The bus station, a regional hub, is north of the centre on Av General Norton de Matos.
Destinations Coimbra (7 daily; 2hr 40min); Guimarães (2–7 daily; 25min); Lisbon (up to 15 daily; 4hr 30min); Porto (roughly hourly; 1hr); Vila do Gerês (for Parque Nacional da Peneda-Gerês; every 1–2hr Mon–Fri, 7 on Sat and 3 on Sun; 1hr 20min).
Tourist information At the corner of Praça da República and Av da Liberdade (Mon–Fri 9am–1pm & 2–6.30pm, Sat 10am–1pm & 2–6pm; ☎ 253 262 550, ⓦ cm-braga.pt).

ACCOMMODATION

Campismo Parque da Ponte ☎ 253 273 355; bus #9 or #18 from Av da Liberdade. Cheap, basic campsite 2km south of central Braga, complete with its own pool. Camping **€2.35** per person, plus **€2.90** per tent
Pop Hostel Rua do Carmo 61–3° ☎ 253 058 806, ⓦ bragapophostel.blogspot.com. A small hostel near the bus station, brightened by cheery art and a terrace with views across Braga. Has a female-only dorm. Dorm **€17**, double **€42**
Pousada de Juventude Rua de Santa Margarida 6 ☎ 253 263 279, ⓦ pousadasjuventude.pt. Fairly basic but good value, with eight-bed dorms and en-suite doubles. Dorm **€12**, double **€27**

EATING AND DRINKING

A Brasileira Largo Barão de São Marinho. Bustling café in the pedestrianized centre with drinks and light meals served at pavement tables. Sandwiches from €2.15. Daily 8am–midnight/2am.
Churrasqueira da Sé Rua dom Paio Mendes 25. Popular little grill restaurant serving barbecued veal chops for €11.90. Mon, Tues & Thurs–Sun 9.30am–9.30pm.
Mercearia Café Rua dom Paio Mendes 59. Funky minimarket with a small restaurant, where the menu runs from canned fish to plates of meat and cheese (from €12). For a good-value snack try the house speciality: a Portuguese burger made from Barrosã beef (€5.50). Mon–Thurs 10am–9pm, Fri & Sat 10am–midnight.

GUIMARÃES

The first capital of Portugal, **GUIMARÃES** remains an atmospheric and beautiful university town. In recent years its prosperity has been helped by the fact that it was named (along with Maribor in Slovenia) as the 2012 European Capital of Culture. The town's chief attraction is the hilltop **castle** (daily 10am–6pm, tower closed at lunchtime; free), whose square keep and seven towers are an enduring symbol of the emergent Portuguese nation. Built by the Countess of Mumadona and extended by Henry of Burgundy, it became the stronghold of his son, Afonso Henriques, Portugal's first independent king. Afonso launched the Reconquest from Guimarães, which was replaced by Coimbra as the capital city in 1143.

Other key sights include the **Archbishop's Palace** (daily 10am–6pm; €5, free Sun 10am–2pm) near the castle, a fifteenth-century building which was perfectly restored and used as a presidential residence for Salazar, Portugal's former dictator; and the **Igreja de Nossa Senhora da Oliveira** on Largo da Oliveira (Mon–Sat 8.30am–noon & 3.30–7.30pm, Sun 9am–1pm & 5–8pm; free), a beautiful convent church founded by Countess Mumadona, in the picturesque medieval centre. The pretty **Praça de Santiago** is a popular spot for an alfresco coffee during the day, and comes alive again at night.

ARRIVAL AND INFORMATION

By train The train station is south of town, connected to the centre by Av D. Afonso Henriques.
Destinations Braga (up to 14 daily; 2hr 10min); Porto (hourly; 1hr 15min).
By bus Guimarães's bus station is a 15min walk west of town in a vast shopping centre. Follow Av Conde de Margaride to reach the town centre.
Destinations Braga (2–8 daily; 25min); Coimbra (3 daily; 2hr–2hr 30min); Lisbon (2 daily; 5hr); Porto (1–4 daily; 1hr–1hr 15min); Vila Real (2–7 daily; 1hr).
Tourist information Tourist office on the corner of Av D. Afonso Henriques and Alameda de São Damaso (Mon–Fri 9.30am–6.30pm, Sat 10am–1pm & 1.30–6.30pm, Sun 10am–1pm; ☎ 965 025 234, ⓦ guimaraesturismo.com).

ACCOMMODATION AND EATING

Pousada de Juventude Largo da Cidade 8 ☎ 253 421 380, ⓦ pousadasjuventude.pt. Stylish, modern hostel with excellent facilities: the best-value accommodation in town. Dorm €14, double €38
Residencial das Trinas Rua das Trinas 29 ☎ 253 517 358, ⓦ residencialtrinas.com. Well run *residencial* in the historic centre, with clean, comfortable en-suite rooms, free wi-fi and in-room TVs. Double €35

EATING AND DRINKING

Cozinha Regional Santiago Praça de Santiago. One of four restaurants battling for the tourist buck on this pretty square, with good regional specialities at fair prices. Fish of the day €7.50. Mon–Sat noon–3pm & 6.30–10pm.
Pátria Wine House Travessa da Pereira 151. Soft rock is played to the wine aficionados who frequent this smart little bar with bottle-lined walls. If wine's not your tipple, don't fret: the beer (€1.30) comes in frozen glasses. Mon–Thurs 11am–midnight, Fri 11am–2am, Sat 10am–2am.

THE DOURO RAIL ROUTE

The Douro Valley, a narrow, winding gorge for the majority of its route, offers some of the most spectacular scenery in Portugal. The **Douro Rail Route**, which joins the river about 60km inland (shortly after Livração) and then sticks to it across the country, is one of those journeys that needs no justification other than the trip itself.

Porto is a good place to begin a trip, though there are also regular connections along the line as far as **Peso da Régua**, the depot through which all port wine must pass on its way to Porto. Beyond Régua, there are less frequent connections to **Tua**

26

PARQUE NACIONAL DA PENEDA-GERÊS

Encompassing mountains, valleys and moors, Portugal's only designated national park is heaven for nature lovers, with ample opportunities for hiking, as well as more extreme sports. The main bases for exploration are the spa town of **Vila do Gerês** and **Ponte da Barca**, where the park's Regional Development Association, Adere-PG, is located. It's worth visiting them at Largo da Miséricordia 10 in Ponte da Barca (Mon–Fri 9am–12.30pm & 2.30–6pm; ⓦ adere-pg.pt) for information on walking routes and accommodation, including a booking service. Vila do Gerês is easily reached by bus from Braga, though to get to Ponte da Barca you'll need your own transport.

26

and **Pocinho**, which marks the end of the line. The trip from Porto to Pocinho takes just over three hours (€13).

VILA REAL

From Peso da Régua, a narrow-gauge line used to branch off through the mountains destined for **VILA REAL**. Now the only way to reach this gateway to Trás-os-Montes – and the closest this rural province gets to a city – is by bus or car.

Vila Real is a lively little spot with an invitingly laidback atmosphere and some surprisingly sophisticated shopping. It also makes a great base for exploration of the nearby **Parque Natural do Alvão**, a mountainous park containing an impressive variety of flora and fauna given its petite size (only 72 sq km). Also close to Vila Real is the **Palacio de Mateus** (May–Oct 9am–7.30pm; Nov–April 9am–6pm; house and gardens €9.50, gardens only €6; bus #1 from Rua Gonçalo Cristóvão with direction UTAD – ask driver where to get off), instantly recognizable as the house depicted on labels of Mateus Rosé wine. This palatial Baroque residence is still inhabited by the Mateus family, but certain rooms (including the well-stocked library) can be visited by guided tour. The mansion is set in well-tended formal gardens.

ARRIVAL AND INFORMATION

By bus Rede Expressos services from Porto, Braga and Peso da Régua stop at the junction of Rua Dom António Valente da Fonseca and Avenida Cidade de Orense, northwest of the centre.
Destinations Braga (up to 10 daily; 1hr 30min); Lisbon (up to 12 daily; 5–6hr); Porto (7–10 daily; 1hr 30min).
Tourist information Vila Real's small tourist office is at Av Carvalho Araújo 94 (April–Oct daily 9am–noon & 2–5.30pm; Nov–March Mon–Fri 9am–noon & 2–5.30pm).

ACCOMMODATION AND EATING

Churrasqueira Real Rua Teixeira de Sousa 14. Popular grill place a 2min walk from the tourist office, serving half chickens for €5 each. Mon–Sat noon–midnight.
Parque de Campismo Av I de Maio. A 15min walk northeast of the centre, this good campsite is located in a quiet spot on the edge of town, with low per-night prices. Camping €3.75 per person, plus €2.30 per tent

Residencial Montanhês 1km east of town on Rua das Botelhas ☎ 259 323 787. Basic roadside B&B, a 15min walk downhill from the centre. Rooms come with a TV and an en-suite bathroom, while those closest to reception manage to pick up a wi-fi signal. Double €25
Residencial Real Rua Combatentes da Grande Guerra 5 ☎ 259 325 879, ⊛ residencialreal.com. The best-value accommodation in the centre of Vila Real is this charming, well-kept guesthouse, with the bonus of breakfast in the downstairs *pastelaria* (Mon–Sat 7am–midnight). Double €40

Southern Portugal

The huge, sparsely populated plains of the **Alentejo**, southeast of Lisbon, are overwhelmingly agricultural, dominated by vast cork plantations. This impoverished province provides nearly half of the world's cork but only a meagre living for its rural inhabitants. Visitors to the Alentejo often head for **Évora**, the province's dominant and most historic town. But the **Alentejo coast**, the Costa Azul, is a breath of fresh air after the stifling plains of the inland landscape, and offers a low-key alternative to the busy Algarve.

With its long, sandy beaches and picturesque rocky coves, the southern coast of the **Algarve** is the most visited region in the country. West of **Faro**, the region's capital, you'll find the classic postcard images of the Algarve – a series of tiny bays and coves, broken up by rocky outcrops and fantastic grottoes, which reach their most spectacular around the resort of **Lagos**. To the east of Faro lie the less developed sandy offshore islets, **the Ilhas** – which front the coastline for some 40km – and the lower-key towns of **Olhão** and **Tavira**. In summer it's wise to book accommodation in advance, as the Algarve is a popular package-holiday destination.

ÉVORA

ÉVORA, a UNESCO World Heritage Site, is one of southern Portugal's most attractive towns and worth a day's exploration. The Romans and the Moors were in occupation for four centuries apiece, leaving their stamp in the tangle of narrow alleys that rise steeply among the whitewashed houses. Most of the monuments, however, date from the fourteenth to the sixteenth centuries, when, with royal encouragement, the city was one of the leading centres of Portuguese art and architecture.

WHAT TO SEE AND DO

The **Templo Romano** in the central square is the best-preserved Roman temple in Portugal, its remains consisting of a small platform supporting more than a dozen granite columns with a marble entablature. Next to the temple lies the church of the **Convento dos Lóios**. The convent is now a luxury *pousada*, but the church (Tues–Sun 10am–12.30pm & 2–6pm; €3), dedicated to São João Evangelista, contains beautiful *azulejos* and an ossuary under the floor. Nearby, the Romanesque **cathedral** (daily 9am–12.20pm & 2–4.50pm, museum closed Mon; cloisters and cathedral €2.50, museum €3.50) was begun in 1186, about twenty years after the reconquest of Évora from the Moors. The most memorable sight in town is the **Capela dos Ossos** (daily 9/10am–12.45pm & 2.30–5.15pm; €2) in the church of **São Francisco**, just south of Praça do Giraldo. A gruesome reminder of mortality, the walls and pillars of this chilling chamber are covered with the bones of more than five thousand monks; an inscription over the door reads, *Nós ossos que aqui estamos, Pelos vossos esperamos* – "We bones here are waiting for your bones". Just below the church lies a beautiful, shady park with resident peacocks, a duck pond and a small café.

ARRIVAL AND INFORMATION

By bus Évora's bus station is 1km west of the old town.
Destinations Albufeira (for the Algarve, 3–4 daily; 3hr 15min–3hr 30min); Lagos (1 or 2 daily in high season; 4hr–4hr 30min); Lisbon (up to 20 daily; 1hr 30min–2hr).
By train Trains pull in south of the old town, a 15min walk from the central Praça do Giraldo.

Destinations Lisbon (4 daily; 1hr 25min).
Tourist information Tourist office on Praça do Giraldo (April–Oct Mon–Fri 9am–7pm; Nov–March daily 9am–6pm; ☎ 266 730 030).

ACCOMMODATION

Évora's tourist appeal pushes accommodation prices over the norm. In addition to the places listed below, there are also some attractive *turismo rural* properties in the nearby countryside; the tourist office has details.

★ **Hostel Namaste** Largo Doutor Manuel Alves Branco, 12 ☎ 266 743 014, ⓦ hostelnamasteevora.pt. Cool, breezy house in a quiet part of town with a shady courtyard, a sun terrace and big, bright dorms and en-suite doubles. There's a ten percent discount for artists, teachers and students. Dorm €17, double €45

Parque de Campismo Estrada de Alcáçovas ☎ 266 705 190; bus #41 from Praça do Giraldo. This well-equipped campsite is 2km out of town on the Alcáçovas road. Camping €5.80 per person, plus €8 per tent

Pensão Giraldo Rua dos Mercadores 27 ☎ 266 705 833. Clean, basic rooms in an atmospheric old building; the doubles with en suite (€5 extra) are more spacious. Double €30

Residencial Policarpo Rua Freiria de Baixo 16 ☎ 266 702 424, ⓦ pensaopolicarpo.com. Beautiful, rambling old place full of rustic charm. Alongside doubles, there are also rooms sleeping three or four. Double €38

EATING AND DRINKING

A Choupana Rua dos Mercadores 20. Pick a stool along the wooden bar or a seat in the attached restaurant, looked after by bow-tied waiters, and tuck into some tasty tapas. The calamari and coriander salad (€5) is a real zinger. Daily noon–3pm & 7–10pm.

Dom Joaquim Rua dos Penedoa 6. Smart restaurant near the city walls offering more creative cuisine than most in Évora. Mains from €11.50. Anyone fancy "rancid lard of the saint" for dessert? Daily noon–3pm & 7–10.30pm.

★ **TREAT YOURSELF**

The Évora Inn 11 Rua da República ☎ 266 744 500, ⓦ evorainn.com. Tucked away just off Praça do Giraldo is this daringly different kind of guesthouse, with smart, individually styled rooms that focus on concepts like pop, travel and revolution. All of the double rooms and (slightly pricier) suites come equipped with high-end designer furnishings by the likes of Philippe Starck, and in the communal areas there are pieces by Portuguese artists. Double €50

26

26

O Antão Rua João de Deus 5. The place to come for regional specialities such as Alentejo rabbit (€13). Tues 7–10.50pm, Wed–Sun noon–3pm & 7–10.50pm.

THE ALENTEJO COAST

Starting south of Lisbon, the **Alentejo coast** features towns and beaches as inviting as those of the Algarve. Some of the most attractive are the pint-sized resort of **Vila Nova de Milfontes**, and the surfers' haven of **Zambujeira do Mar**, at the southern point of the coastline stretch. Though exposed to the winds and waves of the Atlantic, with colder waters, the Alentejo coast is fine for summer swimming and far quieter than the Algarve. Outside the summer season, the area is blissfully peaceful. **Surfing** is popular along the Alentejo coast; first-timers can have lessons at Surf Milfontes in Vila Nova de Milfontes (from €35; ☎969 483 334, ⓦsurf milfontes.com).

Vila Nova de Milfontes

The attractively low-key resort of **VILA NOVA DE MILFONTES** sits on the estuary of the River Mira, whose sandy banks merge into the coastline. This is the most popular as well as one of the most beautiful resorts in the region, its streets lined with houses and hotels painted in the typical Alentejan white and blue. Adding to the charm is a handsome little castle and an ancient port, reputed to have harboured Hannibal and his Carthaginians during a storm.

Zambujeira do Mar

Southwest of Odemira, southern Alentejo's main inland town, is the tiny village of **ZAMBUJEIRA DO MAR**. Here a large cliff provides a dramatic backdrop to the beach, which is prime **surfing** territory. The place livens up in summer, with a music festival featuring mostly Portuguese bands held every August, but it's still quieter than Vila Nova de Milfontes.

ARRIVAL AND DEPARTURE

By bus Local bus services and express buses from Lisbon (Rede Expressos; ⓦrede-expressos.pt) take you within easy reach of the whole coastline, stopping at Vila Nova de Milfontes (3hr 30min–3hr 55min) and Zambujeira do Mar (4hr 5min). Rede Expressos bus #81 runs between Vila Nova de Milfontes and Zambujeira do Mar. Note that there are no direct transport connections between Zambujeira and the Algarve.

Destinations from Vila Nova de Milfontes Lagos (1 daily; 2hr); Portimão (1 daily; 2hr 20min); Sagres (1 daily July–Sept only; 2hr); Zambujeira do Mar (4–5 daily; 35min).

ACCOMMODATION

Accommodation is plentiful in both Vila Nova de Milfontes and Zambujeira do Mar, but it's wise to book ahead during the summer months.

VILA NOVA DE MILFONTES

Campiférias To the southwest of *Camping Milfontes* ☎283 996 409, ⓦcampingcampiferias.com. Cheaper and more modest than nearby *Camping Milfontes*, with a restaurant and games room. Camping **€4.10** per person, plus **€3.35** per tent

Camping Milfontes Pousadas Novas, just north of town ☎283 996 140, ⓦcampingmilfontes.com. Well-equipped campsite with its own saltwater pool. There are also bungalows and two-person tepees for rent. Camping **€4.40** per person, plus **€4.40** per tent

Casa Amarela Rua Dom Luis Castro e Almeida Dorms ☎283 996 632, ⓦcasaamaramilfontes.com. Dorm beds, attractive en-suite rooms and a guest kitchen can be found at this backpackers' favourite. Reductions for longer stays. Dorm **€20**, double **€65**

ZAMBUJEIRA DO MAR

Camping Zambujeira About 1km east of the cliffs ☎283 961 172, ⓦcampingzambujeira.com. Campsite with 2-person apartments, plus its own minimarket and pools. Camping **€6** per person, plus **€7** per tent, apartment **€70**

FARO

FARO is the capital of the Algarve, with excellent beaches within easy reach, but as regional capitals go, it's surprisingly laidback. While its suburbs may be modern, Faro retains an attractive historic centre south of the marina.

WHAT TO SEE AND DO

The **Cidade Velha**, or Old Town, is a semi-walled quarter entered through the eighteenth-century town gate, the **Arco da Vila**. Here you'll find the majestic **Sé** (Mon–Fri 10am–6.30pm, last admission 6pm, Sat 10am–1pm, last admission 12.30pm; €3 including cathedral museum and outdoor bones chapel, which offers superb views from its bell tower. The nearby **Museu Municipal** (summer: Tues–Fri 10am–7pm, Sat & Sun 11.30am–6pm; winter: Tues–Fri 10am–6pm, Sat & Sun 10.30am–5pm; €2) is housed in a sixteenth-century convent on Largo Dom Alfonso III; the most striking exhibit is a third-century Roman mosaic of Neptune and the four winds, unearthed near Faro train station.

Faro's most curious sight is the Baroque **Igreja do Carmo** (Mon–Fri 10am–1pm & 3–5pm, Sat 10am–1pm), near the central post office on Largo do Carmo. A door to the right of the altar leads to a macabre **Capela dos Ossos** (€1), its walls decorated with bones disinterred from the adjacent cemetery. The nearby **beach** (Praia de Faro) can be reached by bus from the Avenida da República stop opposite the bus station, or by boat from the harbour. Up to five boats a day also go to the more tranquil **Ilha do Farol**; the tourist information office has timetables or you can check the website of local operator Silnido (ⓦsilnido.com).

ARRIVAL AND DEPARTURE

By plane Taxis from the airport, 6km west of town, to the centre cost €10–12, or take bus #14 or #16 (up to 24 daily, 5am–11.15pm; 20min; €1.95). To get to the airport, catch the bus from the stop opposite the bus station.

By train The train station is a couple of minutes' walk north beyond the central bus station, up Av da República.

Destinations Lagos (8–9 daily; 1hr 40min); Lisbon (5 daily; 3hr); Olhão (up to 15 daily; 10min); Tavira (11–15 daily; 35–45min).

By bus Buses use the station behind the *Hotel Eva*, just north of the marina.

Destinations Évora (3–4 daily; 4hr–4hr 30min); Lagos (6 daily; 2hr 10min); Lisbon (up to 15 daily; 4hr–4hr 30min); Olhão (several per hour; 20min); Seville, Spain (2–6 daily; 4hr 40min); Tavira (up to 11 daily; 1hr).

INFORMATION

Tourist information The main tourist office is near the harbour at Rua da Misericórdia 8 (Mon & Sat 9.30am–1pm & 2–5.30pm, Tues–Fri 9.30am–5.30pm; ☎ 289 803 604, ⓦturismodoalgarve.pt); there's also a branch at the airport (daily 8am–11.30pm).

★ **TREAT YOURSELF**

Vila Termal das Caldas de Monchique ☎ 282 910 910, ⓦmonchiquetermas .com. In Serra de Monchique above Portimão (60km north of Faro) nestles this tiny spa resort centred around natural thermal springs. Weary travellers can lounge in the spa for €15 per day, but staying overnight can also be a bargain: out of season, luxurious hotel rooms are available for comparatively little. Regular buses (see ⓦfrotazul -algarve.pt for exact schedule) run between Monchique and Portimão (8 daily; 30 min). Double **€45**

26

ACCOMMODATION

Blablabla' Hostel Rua Miguel Bombarda 12 ☎ 915 591 888, ✉ blablabla.rooms@gmail.com. Slightly cramped, but a good back-up option when *Casa D'Alagoa* is full. The private rooms and dorms share a sunny terrace and a small kitchen. Dorm **€22**, double **€56**

★ **Casa D'Alagoa** Praça Alexandre Herculano 27 ☎ 289 813 252, ⓦfarohostel.com. Beautifully restored, 300-year-old house converted into a sociable hostel with its own courtyard, kitchen and roof terrace. Clean dorms, solid wooden bunks with proper mattresses and lots of late-night sangria sessions. Dorm **€25**, double **€80**

Pousada de Juventude Rua da Polícia de Segurança Pública 1 ☎ 289 826 521, ⓦpousadasjuventude.pt. Basic but friendly hostel a 10min walk east of the centre; some rooms are en suite. Dorm **€15**, double **€42**

Residencial Adelaide Rua Cruz dos Mestres 7 ☎ 289 802 383, ⓦadelaideresidencial.net. Bright, simply styled en-suite rooms with a/c, cable TV and free wi-fi. Welcoming staff. Double **€70**

EATING AND DRINKING

Adega Nova Rua Francisco Barreto 24. A good-value restaurant always crammed with locals, who come for dishes like grilled squid and salad (€12.90). Daily noon–11pm.

Columbus Rua Dr Francisco Gomes. Late-night disco bar close to the harbour with a relaxed, friendly atmosphere and tangy mojitos (€4.80). Daily noon–4am.

Faz Gostos Rua do Castelo 13. Upmarket but good-value restaurant mixing locally sourced ingredients with flavours from further afield. Prawn curry €14.50. Mon–Fri noon–3pm & 7–11pm/midnight.

Jam Bar Rua do Rasquinho 26. Huge cocktails, €1 beers, plus guitars and an electric drum kit for anyone who fancies a jam. Popular with the hostel crowd. Mon–Sat 9pm–4am.

26

Vasco da Gama Rua Vasco da Gama 47. Tourist-oriented restaurant on a quiet side street, churning out reasonably priced Portuguese food, including *bacalhau* and sardines. Most main courses around €10. Daily 10.30am–11.30pm.

LAGOS

The seaside town of **LAGOS** is one of the Algarve's most popular destinations and attracts large numbers of visitors each summer, drawn by its beautiful beaches and lively nightlife. Lagos was also favoured by Henry the Navigator, who used it as a base for African trade. Europe's first slave market was built here in 1441 in the arches of the Customs House, which still stands in the Praça da República near the waterfront.

WHAT TO SEE AND DO

On the waterfront and to the rear of the town are the remains of Lagos's once impregnable fortifications, devastated by the Great Earthquake. One rare and beautiful church which did survive was the **Igreja de Santo António**; decorated around 1715, its gilt and carved interior is wildly obsessive, every centimetre filled with cherubic youths struggling with animals and fish. The church is part of – and can be visited in tandem with – the adjacent **Museu Municipal** (Tues–Sat 10am–6pm; €3), housing an eclectic collection of artefacts including Roman busts and deformed animal foetuses.

Lagos's main attraction, however, is its splendid array of beaches, the most secluded of which lie below extravagantly eroded cliff faces south of town. **Praia de Dona Ana** is considered the most picturesque, though its crowds make the smaller coves of **Praia do Pinhão**, down a track just opposite the fire station, and **Praia Camilo**, a little further along, more appealing. Over the river east of Lagos is a splendid sweep of sand – **Meia Praia** – where there's space even at the height of summer. Meia Praia is an ideal destination for **watersports** enthusiasts, as various companies based here offer sailing, sea kayaking and waterskiing lessons, and it's also popular with surfers. Those who like to keep their feet dry might prefer an excursion to the extraordinary rock formations around **Ponta da Piedade**, a headland that can be viewed by boat (from €10 for an hour, or €15 for longer trips) from the marina. Smaller boats have the advantage of gaining access to some of the smaller grottoes.

ARRIVAL AND INFORMATION

By train The train station is across the river, a 15min walk from the centre across the swing bridge to the marina.
Destinations Faro (8–9 daily; 1hr 40min); Lisbon (5 daily; 4hr).
By bus The bus station is slightly closer to the town centre, just off the main Av dos Descobrimentos.
Destinations Faro (6 daily; 2hr 10min); Lisbon (11–13 daily; 3hr 45min); Seville, Spain (2–6 daily; 5hr 30min).
Tourist information The tourist office is inside the old town hall on Praça Gil Eanes, in the central pedestrianized zone (Mon–Fri 9am–6/7pm, Sat & Sun 9.30am–1pm & 2–5.30pm; ☎ 282 763 031). The *Good Times Guide to Lagos* includes a map of the local area. Find it in hostels, bars and restaurants around town.

ACCOMMODATION

Algarve Surf Hostel Urb Cerro das Mos Lote 55 ⓦ algarvesurfschool.com. Villa-style hostel a 15min walk from the centre and set around a swimming pool, with sociable areas for playing pool, drinking and barbecuing. Arranges surf trips to nearby beaches. Dorm __€26__, double __€80__

Campismo da Trindade Rossio da Trindade ☎ 282 763 893. Small, busy campsite close to the sea and just south of the town centre. To reach it, follow the main road 200m beyond the fort. Open all year. Camping __€8__ per person and tent.

Gold Coast Hostel Rua Gil Vicente 48 ☎ 916 594 225, ⓔ goldcoast_hostel@yahoo.com. Friendly, relaxed hostel with a shared kitchen and a cool outdoor terrace. Not as party-focused as other Lagos hostels. Dorm __€23__

Jah Shaka Surf Villa Estrada da Luz-Burgau, on the outskirts of Luz, about 8km west of Lagos ☎ 282 764 848, ⓦ jahshakasurf.com. Well-equipped villa, plus a pool, TV room and volleyball court. The best dorm has sea views and a big en-suite bathroom. The owners can arrange land- and sea-based activities in the area. Call to arrange free pick-up from town or take a taxi (€15). Dorm __€30__, double __€80__, camping __€20__ per person and tent

Pensão Caravela Rua 25 de Abril 16 ☎ 282 763 361. Rooms at this old-fashioned hostel right in the centre of town are basic but well kept, providing a reasonable alternative to sleeping in a dorm. Double __€35__

Pousada de Juventude Rua Lançarote de Freitas 50 ☎ 282 761 970, ⓦ pousadasjuventude.pt. Busy, well-equipped hostel in a central location, with both the beach and the main after-dark watering holes within easy reach. Dorm €17, double €45

Rising Cock Hostel Travessa do Forno 14 ☎ 968 758 785, ⓦ risingcock.com. Popular party hostel with a female-only dorm and free crêpes for breakfast. Facilities are a little worn out, but this is still the best place for meeting other travellers. Dorm €25

EATING, DRINKING AND NIGHTLIFE

Key areas for restaurants and nightlife are the streets around central Praça Gil Eanes, with the cheaper options further back from the water. Avoid the restaurants around the marina, which tend to charge over the odds for very average food.

★ **Bora Café** Rua Conselheiro Joaquim Machado 17. Close to the main drag but better value than its neighbours, offering decent tapas (around €4 a plate) among wind chimes and cushioned benches. Mon–Sat 8.30am–10pm, Sun 10am–8.30pm.

Croissanteria 29 Rua da Estrema 29. Humble Portuguese café selling freshly baked croissants (from €1.60). More than 30 different fillings to choose from. Mon–Sat 8am–7pm.

Eddie's Bar Rua 25 de Abril 99. Friendly, smoky bar on the main drag, with loud music, TV football and 2 for 1 cocktails 9–11pm. A beer will cost you €3. Daily 2pm–2am.

Fresco Rua Senhora do Loreto. Glass-fronted corner café selling fresh, international dishes with good veggie options and a three-course menu that changes daily (€8.50). Daily 9am–4/10pm.

Moinho Rua do Hospital São João de Deus. Whitewashed windmill from the 1980s converted into a cheap bar/café, with rosemary bushes and fragrant pink flowers running around its perimeter. A small local beer is just 65c. Daily 9.30am–2am.

Nahnahbar Travessa do Forno. A good spot for dinner or drinks, with home-made burgers served up by a young, international team. Shots cost €1 11pm–midnight. Tues–Sun 6pm–late.

No Patio Rua Lançarote de Freitas 46 ☎ 282 763 777. Run by a British expat chef, *No Patio* ("on the patio") offers beautifully prepared fusion cuisine at a reasonable price. Main courses €8–15. Reservations recommended. Tues–Sat 7pm–late.

OLHÃO AND THE ISLANDS

OLHÃO, 8km east of Faro, is the largest fishing port in the Algarve and an excellent base for visiting the local sandbank islands. The pedestrianized centre, close to the seafront, is pretty yet free of tourist hordes, ensuring the town retains much of its charm.

WHAT TO SEE AND DO

Although Olhão has no sights to speak of, its café-strewn centre is worth a wander, and there's a busy market on Avenida 5 de Outubro. The town's main attraction, however, is its close proximity to, and good connections with, two of the sandbank islands that comprise the **Ria Formosa Natural Park**. The islands of Armona and Culatra boast some superb, spacious beaches, so expansive that they still feel uncrowded even in the height of summer. Ferries to the islands operate year-round, and depart regularly (up to 13 daily) from the jetty to the left of the municipal gardens. The service to **Armona** (30min; €3.60 return) drops you off at a long strip of holiday chalets and huts that stretches right across the island on either side of the main path. On the ocean side, the beach disappears into the distance and a short walk will take you to totally deserted stretches of sand. Boats to **Culatra** (30min; €3.60 return) call first at Praia da Culatra, a vast expanse of sand stretching away from Culatra town. The same service then makes its way to **Praia do Farol** (1hr; €4.20 return), considered to be one of the most beautiful beaches on the sandbank islands. Heading east, away from the holiday homes, the beach becomes quieter, and eventually leads to the peaceful Praia dos Hangares.

ARRIVAL AND INFORMATION

By train The train station is just east of Av da República, towards the north of town.
Destinations Faro (at least 9 daily; 10min); Lisbon (5 daily; 3hr 20min–4hr 45min); Tavira (up to 15 daily; 25min).
By bus The bus station is nearby, to the west of the Avenida.
Destinations Lisbon (8–9 daily; 3hr 30min–4hr 45min).
Tourist information Tourist office at Largo Sebastião Martins Mestre (Tues–Sat 9.30am–1pm & 2–5.30pm; ☎ 289 713 936).

ACCOMMODATION AND EATING

Camping Olhão ☎ 289 700 300. Large, well-equipped campsite 2km east of town. In summer a bus runs from near the municipal garden. Camping €4.20 per person, plus €3.10 per tent

Pensão Bela Vista Rua Teófilo Braga 65 ☎ 289 702 538. Offers neat and tidy en-suite rooms with a/c; the restaurant beneath offers excellent local dishes from €6. Double €30

26

26

★ **Pensão Bicuar** Rua Vasco da Gama 5 ☎ 289 714 816, ⓦ pensionbicuar.com. Spotless Australian-run guesthouse with a kitchen, roof terrace, and pleasant rooms (sleeping up to four) with shower and sink. Bikes available at €8/day. Minimum two nights' stay in July & Aug. Double €49

Ria Formosa Av 5 de Outubro 14. This is the locals' favourite restaurant along the main waterfront road, serving decent seafood and rice dishes. Daily noon–3pm & 7–11pm/midnight.

TAVIRA

TAVIRA is a handsome little town made up of cobbled streets, and split into two pretty halves by the River Gilão. The Romans and Moors who once ruled Tavira left behind monuments that contribute to the town's appeal, but the main tourist attractions, the superb island beaches of the **Ilha de Tavira**, actually lie offshore. Boats to the island depart from the quayside on Rua do Cais from June to mid-September (12 daily; 20min; €2 return), with year-round boats from Quatro Águas (every 30min; 5min; €1.50 return), 2km east of town. The beach is backed by dunes and stretches west almost as far as Fuzeta, 14km away. Despite some development – a small chalet settlement, a **campsite**, and a handful of bars and restaurants facing the sea – it's still easy to find your own peaceful patch of sand.

Back in central Tavira, it's worth wandering up to the remains of the **Moorish castle** (Mon–Fri 8am–5pm, Sat & Sun 10am–7pm; free), perched high above the town, with its walls enclosing a pretty garden that affords splendid views. Close to the castle, at Calçada da Galeria 12, a former water tower has been converted into a **camera obscura**, offering views of the town (Mon–Sat 10am–5pm; €3.50).

ARRIVAL AND INFORMATION

By train The train station is 1km southeast of the town centre, at the end of Av Doutor Mateus Teixeira de Azevedo. Destinations Faro (around 14 daily; 35–45min); Olhão (up to 14 daily; 25min).

By bus Buses pull up at the terminal by the river, a 2min walk from the central square, Praça da República. Destinations Lisbon (up to 9 daily; 4hr–5hr 30min).

★ **TREAT YOURSELF**

Aquasul Rua Dr Augusto Silva Carvalho 13 ☎ 281 325 166. Perfectly cooked international dishes, stonebaked pizzas and changing daily specials are the order of the day at friendly *Aquasul*. Seasonal starters include beetroot carpaccio with goat's cheese and rocket (€6.50), followed by mains like confit of duck with red cabbage (€14). The setting is pretty and peaceful, with pastel-coloured tables spilling out of the restaurant into a pedestrianized cobbled street. Tues–Sat 6–10pm.

Tourist information Praça da República 5 (Mon & Sat 9.30am–1pm & 2–5.30pm, Tues–Fri 9.30am–5.30pm, with extended hours July & Aug; ☎ 281 322 511, ⓦ turismodoalgarve.pt).

ACCOMMODATION

Camping Tavira Ilha de Tavira ☎ 281 321 709, ⓦ campingtavira.com. Busy campsite with a great location on the Ilha de Tavira; follow the path opposite the ferry dock to reach it. Open April–Sept. Camping €12 per person and tent.

Pousada de Juventude Rua Miguel Bombarda 36 ☎ 217 232 101, ⓦ pousadasjuventude.pt. New-ish hostel with excellent facilities, including a relaxed communal lounge area, simple dorms and attractive private rooms (some of which have en-suite facilities). Dorm €15, twin €40

Residencial Lagoas Rua Almirante Cândido dos Reis 24 ☎ 281 328 243, ✉ al.lagoas@hotmail.com. Long-established pension in an old house with small rooms, some of which have en-suite facilities. There are two sun terraces, the highest of which has views across Tavira. Double €30

EATING AND DRINKING

Bica Rua Almirante Cândido dos Reis 22–24. Basic setting, but the food speaks for itself: fresh, tasty portions of Portuguese classics such as fried squid (€7.50). Daily noon–3pm & 7–10pm.

Brisa do Rio Rua Dr Augusto Silva Carvalho 6–8. Often packed, this restaurant a short stroll up from the waterfront serves some seriously good fish dishes (the grilled salmon is a steal at just €9). Daily 6–11pm.

Tavira Lounge Rua Gonçalo Velho. A smart riverside place that acts as a café/ice-cream parlour by day (try the *gelato*; €1.70) and a restaurant/tapas bar by night. Big salads from €7. Mon–Thurs noon–10.30pm/1am, Fri & Sat noon–1/3am.

PEŞTERA VILLAGE, CARPATHIAN MOUNTAINS

Romania

HIGHLIGHTS

❶ Bucharest Stalinist architecture, pretty residential streets, plus good dining and nightlife. **See p.901**

❷ Sighişoara Beautiful medieval citadel in the heart of Transylvania, with authentic Dracula connections. **See p.910**

❸ The Carpathians Stunning mountain scenery under two hours from the capital. **See p.910**

❹ Museum of Traditional Folk Civilization, Sibiu A fascinating open-air museum of Romanian village architecture, set in a scenic landscape. **See p.912**

HIGHLIGHTS ARE MARKED ON THE MAP ON P.897

ROUGH COSTS

Daily budget Basic €25, occasional treat €40

Drink Beer €1.80; bottle of Romanian wine €5

Food *Tochitura moldoveneasca* (Moldavian stew) €2

Hostel/budget hotel €10/€30

Travel Bus: Bucharest–Braşov €10; train: €10

FACT FILE

Population 19 million

Language Romanian

Currency Leu (RON); plural: lei

Capital Bucharest

International phone code ☏40

Time zone GMT +2hr

Introduction

Nowhere in Eastern Europe defies preconceptions quite like Romania. It still suffers from a poor image abroad, but don't be put off – this intriguing country, dotted with picturesque towns and rural communities following traditions little changed since the Middle Ages, is easily accessible and a pleasure to explore.

27

Romanians trace their ancestry back to the Romans and tend to stress their Latin roots, although they have Balkan traits too. Viewing their future as firmly within the Euro-Atlantic family, they were delighted to join NATO and then, in 2007, the European Union.

The capital, **Bucharest**, is perhaps daunting for the first-time visitor – its savage recent history is only too evident, not least in the form of the Communist-era Centru Civic – but parts of this once-beautiful city have retained their appeal. More attractive by far, and easily accessible on public transport, is **Transylvania**, an ancient region offering some of the most beautiful mountain scenery in Europe as well as a uniquely multi-ethnic character. Its chief cities, such as Braşov, Sibiu and Sighişoara, were built by Saxon (German) colonists, and there are also strong Hungarian and Roma (Gypsy) presences here. In the border region of the **Banat**, also highly multi-ethnic, Timişoara is Romania's most Western-looking city and famed as the birthplace of the 1989 revolution.

CHRONOLOGY

513 BC The Dacian tribe inhabit the area of present-day Romania.

106 AD The Roman Emperor Trajan conquers the Dacian tribe.

271 Following attacks from the Goths, the Romans withdraw from the area.

1000s Hungary conquers and occupies parts of present-day Romania.

1200s Division of Romanian population into different principalities including Wallachia, Moldavia and Transylvania.

1400s Principalities of Moldavia, Transylvania and Wallachia come under attack from the Turkish Ottomans but remain independent.

1448 Vlad "the Impaler" becomes Prince of Wallachia; he is later credited as the inspiration for the character of Dracula.

1700s The Austrian Habsburgs take control of large parts of the Romanian principalities after military successes over the Ottomans.

1862 After battling for independence, Wallachia and Moldavia unite to form Romania. Bucharest is declared the capital.

1878 Romania's claim to independence is formalized by the Treaty of Berlin.

1881 Carol I is named the first King of Romania.

1918 After invasion by the central powers during World War I, Romania is freed and her borders increased.

1939–45 Romania sides with Germany at start of World War II, but changes allegiance to the Allies towards the end. Soviets take large parts of Romanian territory.

1947 Soviet influence remains and the Communist Party comes into power in Romania.

1965 Nicolae Ceauşescu becomes Communist Party leader and adopts a foreign-policy stance independent of the Soviets.

1989 Revolution leads to the overthrow of the Communist regime.

2004 Romania joins NATO.

2007 Romania joins the European Union.

2012 Following almost a decade of strong economic growth, severe recession and austerity measures trigger widespread unrest and the resignation of Prime Minister Emil Boc.

2014 Romanians are permitted to work without restriction throughout the EU.

ARRIVAL AND DEPARTURE

All flights in and out of Bucharest use Otopeni (Henri Coandă) airport, but there are half a dozen regional airports (of which Timişoara and Cluj-Napoca are the most important), served by a growing number of budget airlines such as Wizz Air (ⓦwizzair.com), Blue Air (ⓦblueairweb.com) and Carpatair (ⓦcarpatair.com).

Map showing Romania, its neighbouring countries (Hungary, Ukraine, Moldova, Bulgaria, Serbia), cities, the Carpathian and Făgăraş Mountains, and the Black Sea.

ROMANIA

HIGHLIGHTS
1. Bucharest
2. Sighişoara
3. The Carpathians
4. Museum of Traditional Folk Civilization, Sibiu

27

Travelling to Romania by **train** is fairly simple via Paris, Vienna and Budapest, and there are also through trains from Prague, Belgrade, Sofia and Kiev. This will usually cost more than flying into the country, but works well as part of a larger Europe-wide trip using a pass or the point-to-point ticket options offered by the rail contacts listed on p.33, including **InterRail** (for European residents) and **Eurail** (for non-European residents).

GETTING AROUND

InterCity **trains** are the fastest and most comfortable; they're followed by InterRegio trains which stop more often. Regio trains stop everywhere and are generally grubby and crowded. Some overnight trains have **sleeping carriages** (*vagon de dormit*) and **couchettes** (*cuşet*) for a modest surcharge. Seat reservations are required for all fast trains, and are automatically included with locally purchased tickets. You'll also need a seat reservation for **international trains** even if you do not require one before entering Romania, so be sure to book a seat before departure or face a fine. The best place to **buy tickets** and book seats is at the local Agenţia SNCFR (generally open Mon–Fri 7.30am–7.30pm, Sat 8am–noon; @cfr.ro); at the station tickets are slightly cheaper but available only one hour in advance. Wasteels, a Europe-wide youth rail travel agency, has offices in Bucharest's Gara de Nord station and in Braşov's station (@triptkts.ro; both Mon–Fri 8am–7pm, Sat 8am–2pm) and offers discounts for under-26s. Both **InterRail** and **Eurail** are valid.

The **bus** (*autobuz*) network can be confusing so it's best to check bus times in advance at @autogari.ro. There are also **minibus** (*maxitaxi*) services on the busy routes; although fast and frequent, they are often crowded and the driving can be manic. They do also make some surprisingly long inter-city journeys;

expect to pay the same as the Regio train fare or a bit more. Buses are more comfortable for longer journeys.

Taxis are cheap and an attractive alternative to crowded public transport, but be sure to choose a taxi with a clearly marked company name, and check that the meter is working.

ACCOMMODATION

Decent **hostels** have become widespread in recent years and you can expect to pay around 40–50 lei for a dorm bed. Cheaper **hotels** cost 80–130 lei for a basic en-suite double; breakfast is normally an extra 15–20 lei. In season (June–September) you may come across locals at train or bus stations offering **private rooms** (*cazare la persoane particulare*), particularly in the more touristy areas of Transylvania and the coastal resorts; expect to pay around 50 lei per person. Most **campsites** are fairly basic; you'll pay around 30 lei per night for tent space. Outside national parks, officials will generally turn a blind eye if you are discreet about camping wild.

FOOD AND DRINK

Breakfast (*micul dejun*) is typically a fairly light meal of bread rolls, butter and jam and an omelette washed down with a coffee (*cafea*). The most common **snacks** are bread rings (*covrigi*), flaky pastries (*pateuri*) filled with cheese (*cu brânză*) or meat (*cu carne*), and spicy grilled sausages (*mici*) and meatballs (*chiftele*). Menus in most **restaurants** concentrate on grilled meats, or *friptura*. *Cotlet de porc* is the common pork chop, while *mușchi de vacă* is fillet of beef.

Traditional **Romanian dishes** can be delicious. The best known of these is *sarmale* – pickled cabbage stuffed with rice, meat and herbs, usually served with sour cream – and *tochitură moldovenească*, a pork stew, with cheese, polenta (*mămăligă*) and a fried egg on top. **Vegetarians** could try asking for *cașcaval pane* (hard cheese fried in breadcrumbs), *ghiveci* (mixed fried veg), *ardei umpluții* (stuffed peppers), or vegetables and salads.

DRINK

Most **cafés** (*cafénea* or *cofetărie*) serve a range of coffee and cakes, as well as ice cream and alcoholic drinks. Coffee, whether *cafea naturală* (finely ground and brewed Turkish-style), *filtru* (filtered) or *nes* (instant), is usually drunk black and sweet; ask for it *cu lapte* or *fără zahăr* if you prefer it with milk or without sugar. **Cakes** and **desserts** are sweet and sticky, as throughout the Balkans. Romanians also enjoy pancakes (*clătite*) and pies (*plăcintă*) with various fillings.

Evening **drinking** takes place in outdoor beer gardens, *cramas* (beer cellars), restaurants, and in a growing number of Western-style cafés and bars. Try *ţuică*, a powerful plum brandy taken neat; in rural areas, it is home-made and often twice distilled to yield fearsomely strong *palincă*. Most **beer** (*bere*) is German-style lager. Romania's best **wines** are Grasa (white) and Feteasca Neagră (red), and the sweet dessert wines of Murfatlar.

CULTURE AND ETIQUETTE

Generally speaking, Romanians tend to be very open and friendly people. They will think nothing of striking up a conversation on buses and trains, even if they don't speak much English, and will try their best to communicate through any language barrier.

When speaking to older people, it is respectful to address them using either

ROMANIA ONLINE

ⓦ **romaniatourism.com** Official tourism site.
ⓦ **mountainguide.ro** Hiking information and links.
ⓦ **eco-romania.ro** Association of ecotourism operators.
ⓦ **inyourpocket.com** Bucharest guide.
ⓦ **bucharestlife.net** Regularly updated blog by long-term resident and editor-in-chief of the In Your Pocket guides.
ⓦ **sapteseri.ro** Listings guide for most large cities.
ⓦ **nineoclock.ro** An excellent online and daily print English-language newspaper.

Domnul (Mr) or *Doamnă* (Mrs), while shaking someone's hand is the most common and familiar way of **greeting** – although bear in mind that a Romanian man may well kiss a woman's hand on introduction. The welcoming attitude of the Romanians may mean you are invited to someone's home; it is considered polite to bring a small **gift** with you, which you should also wrap. A bottle of wine, chocolates or flowers are all appropriate – although if you do bring flowers you should ensure an odd number of blooms, as even-numbered bouquets are strictly for funerals.

Tipping in restaurants is not necessary, although it will be appreciated.

Over the past decade, Romania has been remarkably progressive in its attitude towards gay and lesbian culture; Accept (❶021 2525620, ⓦaccept -romania.ro) is the best source of up-to-date information on the scene.

SPORTS AND ACTIVITIES

Romania's landscape is dominated by the spectacular Carpathian Mountains. A continuation of the Alps, they encircle Transylvania and provide the country with a rocky backbone perfect for activities ranging from hiking and skiing to caving and mountain biking.

The main mountain ranges, the Bucegi, the Făgăraş, the Apuseni and the Retezat, provide the best-known destinations for **hiking**. There are numerous well-marked trails allowing day-trips or longer expeditions, sleeping in a mountain refuge (*cabana*); these are usually very friendly and sociable places, and make good bases for hiking, caving or climbing. All of the trails are marked on the excellent Hartă Turistica (ⓦharta -turistica.ro) maps, which can be found in hiking shops and bookshops in most major towns. Some *cabanas* also sell maps. Spring and summer are the best seasons to explore the mountains, and a large number of trails should only be attempted in warmer weather.

Romania also offers some of Europe's cheapest **skiing** and **snowboarding** between November and April

(ⓦski-in-romania.com). There are several major ski and snowboarding resorts in Romania, the most popular of which is Poiana Braşov, near Braşov. Other resorts include Sinaia, Buşteni and Predeal – all on the main road north from Bucharest – Păltiniş near Sibiu, Borşa to the north in Maramureş, and Ceahlău and Durău on the border of Moldavia. Although Borşa is arguably the best resort for beginners, the larger resorts all have a number of easy and medium pistes and at least one black run.

COMMUNICATIONS

Post offices (*poşta*) in major cities are open Monday to Friday 7am to 8pm, Saturday 8am to noon; in smaller places they may close an hour or two earlier. You can **phone** from the orange cardphones or post offices. Phonecards (10 or 15 lei – get the latter for international calls) are available from post offices and news kiosks. Cheap **SIM cards** are available from Romania's three main mobile network providers (Cosmote, Orange and Vodafone). **Wi-fi** is available in hostels and hotels, and in many cafés, bars and restaurants. **Internet cafés** are now rare.

EMERGENCIES

Watch out for pickpockets in crowded buses and trams and don't leave bags unattended. There has been a proliferation of ATMs throughout the country in recent years, but it's best to stick to those located within or outside banks whenever possible.

EU residents carrying a European Health Insurance Card are entitled to free medical treatment in Romania, but are advised to have travel insurance nonetheless as state hospitals outside Bucharest and other large towns may not be up to Western standards. Bucharest's central emergency **hospital** is up to

> ### EMERGENCY NUMBER
> In all emergencies call ❶112.

27

ROMANIAN

	ROMANIAN	PRONUNCIATION
Yes	*Da*	Da
No	*Nu*	Noo
Please	*Vă rog*	Ve rog
Thank you	*Mulţumesc*	Mult-sumesk
Hello/Good day	*Salut/bună ziua*	Saloot/boona zhewa
Goodbye	*La revedere*	La re-ve-dairy
Excuse me	*Permiteţi-mi*	Per-mi-tets-may
Where?	*Unde?*	Oun-day?
Good	*Bun/bine*	Boon/Bee-ne
Bad	*Rău*	Rau
Near	*Apropriat*	A-prope-reeat
Far	*Departe*	D'par-tay
Cheap	*Ieftin*	Yeftin
Expensive	*Scump*	Scoomp
Open	*Închis*	Un-keez
Closed	*Deschis*	Des-keez
Today	*Azi*	Az
Yesterday	*Ieri*	Ee-airy
Tomorrow	*Mâine*	Mwee-ne
How much is...?	*Cât costa...?*	Cuut costa...?
What time is it?	*Ce ora este?*	Che ora est?
I don't understand	*Nu înţeleg*	Noo unts-eledge
Do you speak English?	*Vorbiţi Englezeste?*	Vor-beetz eng-lay-zeste?
One	*Un, una*	Oon, oona
Two	*Doi, doua*	Doy, doo-a
Three	*Trei*	Tray
Four	*Patru*	Pat-ru
Five	*Cinci*	Chinch
Six	*Şase*	Shass-er
Seven	*Şapte*	Shap-tay
Eight	*Opt*	Opt
Nine	*Nouă*	No-ar
Ten	*Zece*	Zay-chay

Western standards, while Medicover Unirii, at 64–66 Marasesti Blvd (**☎**021 3353940, **⊛**medicover.ro), also offers Western-standard care, with English-speaking doctors. **Pharmacies** (*farmacie*) are open Monday to Saturday from 9am until 6pm, though most towns and cities should have one that's open 24 hours.

INFORMATION

Tourist offices (marked "Tourist Information Centre") can be found in the country's most visited towns and cities.

MONEY AND BANKS

Romania's currency is the new **leu** (plural lei, international code RON), comprising

coins of 1, 5, 10 and 50, and notes of 1, 5, 10, 50, 100, 200 and 500 lei. At the time of writing, exchange rates were around €1=4.35 lei, £1=5.10 lei and US$=3.35 lei. Some hotels, rental agencies and other services quote prices in euros. There are plenty of **ATMs** throughout the country. **Changing money** is best done at banks, which are generally open Monday to Friday between 9am and 4pm; you will need your passport. Never change money on the streets. **Credit cards** are accepted in most hotels, restaurants and shops.

OPENING HOURS AND HOLIDAYS

Shop **opening hours** are Monday to Friday 9am to 6pm, Saturday 9am to

1pm, with many food shops open until 10pm (or even 24hr), including weekends. Museums and castles also open roughly 9am to 6pm, though most are closed on Mondays. **National holidays** are: January 1 and 2, Easter Monday, May 1, December 1, December 25 and 26.

Bucharest

Arriving in **BUCHAREST** (Bucureşti), most tourists want to leave as quickly as possible; yet to do so would mean missing out on Romania's most vibrant city. The capital does have its fair share of charm and elegance – it just takes a little seeking out. Among the ruptured roads and disintegrating buildings you'll find leafy squares, beautiful, eclectic architecture (albeit often crumbling), and dressed-up young Romanians bringing a touch of glamour to the surroundings. What's more, it's a dynamic city, changing faster than any other in Romania as new office towers sprout up and shops and bars multiply.

Head south of the centre into the Centru Civic and you'll come across myriad unfinished projects from Ceauşescu's reign – seeing the true scale of what a dictatorship can set in motion is something you won't forget, and reason enough to spend a day or two in the capital.

WHAT TO SEE AND DO

The heart of the city lies to the north of the **Dâmboviţa River**, between two north–south avenues; it's a jumble of modern hotels, ancient Orthodox churches and decaying apartment blocks, relieved by the buzzing **historic quarter** and some attractive parks. Beyond lies Ceauşescu's monstrously compelling **Centru Civic**, centred on the extraordinary **Palace of Parliament**. The northern outskirts, dotted with woodlands and lakes, are freezing in winter and hot and dusty in the summer.

Piaţa Revoluţiei

Most inner-city sights are within walking distance of Calea Victoriei, an avenue of vivid contrasts, with vestiges of *ancien régime* elegance in among the apartment blocks, glass and steel facades, and cake shops. Fulcrum of the avenue is **Piaţa Revoluţiei**, created during the 1930s on Carol II's orders to ensure a field of fire around the Royal Palace.

On the north side of the square is the **Athénée Palace Hotel** (now a Hilton), famous for its role as an "intelligence factory" from the 1930s until the 1980s, with its bugged rooms, tapped phones and informer prostitutes. To its east are the grand **Romanian Atheneum**, the city's main concert hall, and the **University Library**, torched, allegedly by the Securitate, in the confusion of the 1989 revolution, but since rebuilt and reopened.

To the southeast of the square is the former Communist Party HQ, now the **Senate**, where Nicolae Ceauşescu made his last speech from a low balcony on December 21. His speech drowned out by booing, the dictator's disbelief was broadcast to the nation just before the TV screens went blank. He and his wife Elena fled by helicopter from the roof, but were captured and executed on Christmas Day.

The Royal Palace

The **Royal Palace**, on the western side of Piaţa Revoluţiei, now contains the excellent **National Art Museum** (Wed–Sun: May–Sept 11am–7pm; Oct–April 10am–6pm; 15 lei; ⓦmnar.arts.ro), the highlight of which is a marvellous collection of medieval and modern Romanian art, featuring the country's most revered painter, Grigorescu, and the great modern Romanian sculptor Brâncuşi; there are also impressive works by El Greco, Rembrandt and Brueghel.

The Creţulescu Church and Cişmigiu Park

Standing opposite the Senate, the eighteenth-century **Creţulescu Church** is the city's most celebrated historic building. Badly damaged during the 1989

27

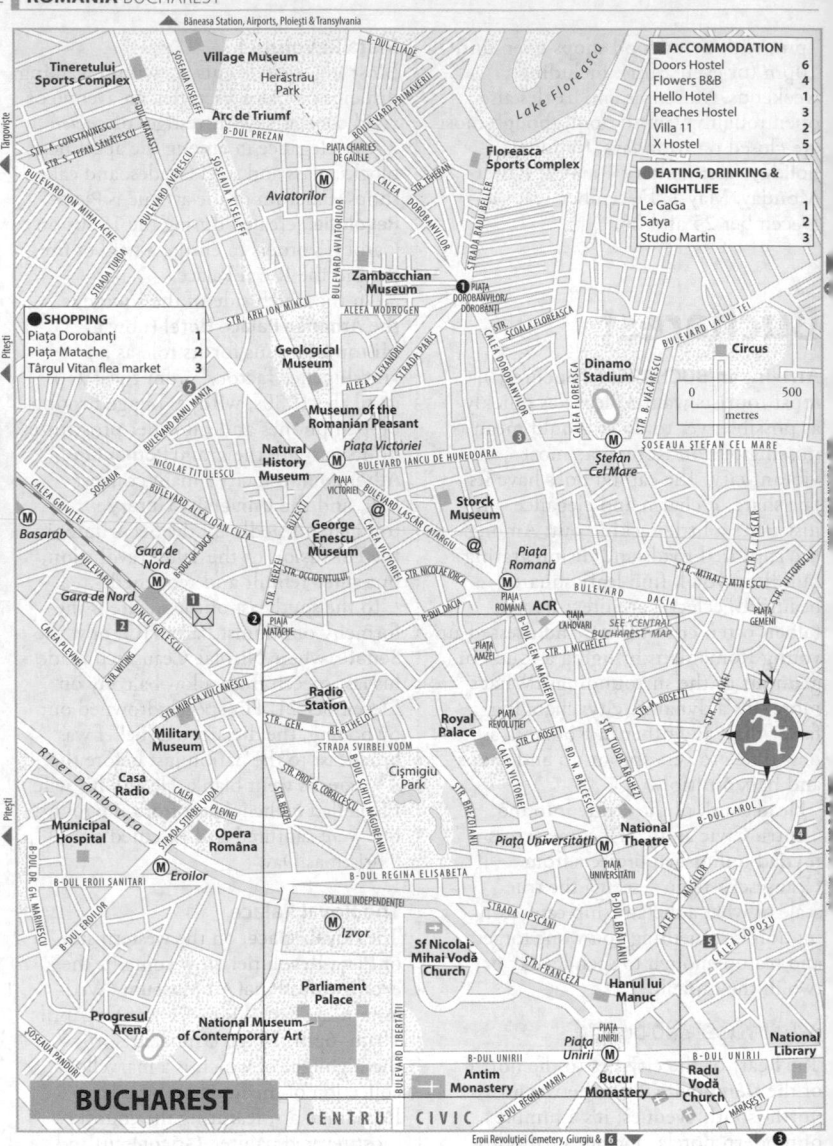

Băneasa Station, Airports, Ploieşti & Transylvania

BUCHAREST

CENTRU   CIVIC

Eroii Revoluţiei Cemetery, Giurgiu &

ACCOMMODATION

Doors Hostel	6
Flowers B&B	4
Hello Hotel	1
Peaches Hostel	3
Villa 11	2
X Hostel	5

EATING, DRINKING & NIGHTLIFE

Le GaGa	1
Satya	2
Studio Martin	3

SHOPPING

Piaţa Dorobanţi	1
Piaţa Matache	2
Târgul Vitan flea market	3

fighting, but now handsomely restored, it fronts a tangle of streets wending west towards **Cişmigiu Park**, Bucharest's oldest, containing a boating lake, playgrounds, summer terrace cafés and chess players.

The Military Museum

West of Cişmigiu Park, near the Gara de Nord station, the **Military Museum**

(Tues–Sun 9am–5pm; 6 lei) has a fine display on the army's role during the 1989 revolution. Among the most moving exhibits are the personal belongings of both civilians and soldiers, including the blood-splattered uniform worn by the then Minister of Defence, General Vasile Milea, who was executed after refusing to carry out orders to shoot civilians.

The historic centre

The regeneration of Bucharest's **historic centre**, known locally as Lipscani after the street of the same name, at the southern end of B-dul Brătianu, is ongoing, and it's now the focal point for the city's best nightlife, with a massive recent influx of bars, cafés and restaurants. Just southwest of Strada Lipscani stands the diminutive **Stavropoleos Church**; built in the 1720s, it has gorgeous, almost arabesque, patterns decorating its facade, and an elegant columned portico.

The Centru Civic

The infamous **Centru Civic** was Ceauşescu's pet urban project. After an earthquake in 1977 damaged much of the city, Ceauşescu took the opportunity to remodel the entire southern portion of central Bucharest as a monument to Communism. By the early 1980s bulldozers had moved in to clear the way for the Victory of Socialism Boulevard (now Bulevardul Unirii), taking with them thousands of architecturally significant houses, churches and monuments. Now colossal apartment blocks line Bulevardul Unirii, at 4km long and 120m wide slightly larger – intentionally so – than the Champs-Élysées on which it was modelled. The eastern end of the boulevard is now a banking district, while the other end is dominated by the Parliament Palace.

Parliament Palace

The **Parliament Palace** (Palatul Parlamentului) – also known as Casa Nebunului ("Madman's House") – is supposedly the second-largest administration building in the world. Started in 1984 – but still not complete despite the toil of 100,000 workers – the building contains 1100 rooms and a nuclear shelter, and now houses the Romanian Parliament and a conference centre. Guided tours in English (daily 10am–4pm; 25 lei, plus 30 lei for the use of cameras; ✪www.cdep.ro) start to the right of the entrance as you face the building and should be booked a day in advance. You must bring your passport to gain entry.

National Museum of Contemporary Art

Occupying a vast space within the Parliament Palace is the glass-fronted **National Museum of Contemporary Art** (Wed–Sun 10am–6pm; 5 lei; ✪www.mnac.ro). On display are works by top contemporary artists, both Romanian and foreign, while the gallery also hosts regular temporary exhibitions.

Piaţa Universităţii

You're bound to pass through busy **Piaţa Universităţii**, overshadowed by the *Hotel Intercontinental* on B-dul Carol I. This is where students pitched their post-revolution City of Peace encampment, which was violently overrun, together with the illusion of true democracy, by the miners called in by President Iliescu to "restore order" in June 1990. The miners returned to Bucharest in 1991, this time in protest against the government rather than to protect it.

Museum of the Romanian Peasant

Stretching north from Piaţa Victoriei, Şoseaua Kiseleff leads into the more pleasant, leafy suburbs. At no. 3, the **Museum of the Romanian Peasant** (Muzeul Ţăranului Român; Tues–Sun 10am–6pm; 6 lei; ✪muzeultaranului roman.ro) is a must-see, giving an insight into the country's varied rural traditions, with exhibits on everything from costume and textiles to painted glass icons; to the rear there's a beautiful wooden church, as well as an excellent souvenir shop. In the basement there's a fascinatingly curious exhibition of Communist iconography, featuring one of the very few paintings still remaining of Ceauşescu.

Herăstrău Park and the Village Museum

Just to the north of the museums, traffic heading for the airports and Transylvania swings around a familiar-looking Arc de Triumf, commemorating Romania's participation on the side of the Allied victors in World War I. To the right, in **Herăstrău Park** (the city's largest), is the **Village Museum** (Muzeul Satului; daily

27

9am–5pm; 10 lei; ⓦmuzeul-satului.ro), a fabulous ensemble of wooden houses, churches, windmills and other structures from various regions of the country.

ARRIVAL AND DEPARTURE

By plane Otopeni (Henri Coandâ) airport is 17km north of the centre; ignore all offers of a taxi within the terminal and book one at an official desk within the airport. Alternatively, take the #783 bus from under the international arrivals hall – before boarding you'll need to buy an Activ Card (3.70 lei) from a booth within the airport. The journey from the airport to the centre is 7 lei (charge before boarding) and the Activ Card can be recharged for use on buses, trams and the metro.

By train Virtually all trains terminate at the Gara de Nord, from where it's a 30min walk into the centre, or a short ride on the metro (change lines at Piaţa Victoriei to reach Piaţa Universităţii). Taxi drivers are ready to pounce at the main entrance, but check that the tariff displayed in the taxi window is not more than 2 lei per km. Bus #780 connects Gara de Nord with the airport.

Destinations Braşov (hourly; 2hr 45min); Sibiu (3 daily; 5hr 30min); Sighişoara (7 daily; 5hr); Timişoara (7 daily; 8hr 30min).

By bus Bucharest still doesn't have a central bus station, but at least there's now a decent website (ⓦautogari.ro) listing daily schedules along with the relevant departure and arrival points. Buses for Braşov and Sighişoara depart from Autogara Ritmului (walking distance from Piaţa Iancului metro station) and buses for Sibiu and Timişoara depart from Autogara Militari (next to Păcii metro station).

Destinations Braşov (hourly; 3hr 30min); Sibiu (8 daily; 5hr); Sighişoara (8 daily; 5hr 30min); Timişoara (3 daily; 11hr 30min).

INFORMATION

Tourist information The main tourist information office is in the Piaţa Universităţii underpass at Universitate metro station (Mon–Fri 9am–6pm, Sat 10am–1pm; ☎0746 252922). There are two other, much smaller, booths – one on the main concourse in the Gara de Nord (daily 9am–9pm; ☎0371 155063) and the other within Piaţa Unirii metro station (daily 10am–6pm; ☎0725 217318). All the offices stock free city maps as well as the excellent English-language listings magazine *Bucharest in Your Pocket* (also in hotels).

GETTING AROUND

Public transport Although crowded, public transport is efficient and very cheap. Trams, buses and trolleybuses run from the early hours until 11pm, after which night buses take over, running hourly from Piaţa Unirii. The most useful lines of the metro system are the M2 (north–south) and M3 (a near-circle).

Tickets Activ Cards costing 3.70 lei can be bought from kiosks at major stops and are valid for all forms of public transport in Bucharest. The cards can be charged with credit that is debited every time you swipe them over the orange terminals within buses, trams and trolleybuses (1.30 lei for a single journey), or at the entrance to metro stations (2 lei per journey). It's also possible to buy a ticket that's valid for use on any mode for one hour (5 lei) or for 24 hours (16 lei).

By taxi Fares are cheap, at about 2 lei/km; the most reputable companies are Cristaxi (☎021 9461), Cobalcescu (☎021 9451) or Meridian (☎021 9444) – make sure the meter is running.

ACCOMMODATION

Bucharest is jammed with great hostels, most of which offer private rooms as well as dorm beds, and there's also a reasonable choice of affordable hotels.

HOSTELS

Doors Hostel Str. Olimpului 13 ☎021 3362127, ⓦdoorshostel.com; map p.902. Clean, spacious hostel with a lovely garden, just a short walk from Piaţa Unirii metro station. Dorm 38 lei, double 110 lei

Funky Chicken Hostel Str. Gen. Berthelot 63 ☎021 3121425, ⓦfunkychickenhostel.com; map opposite. Located a 10min walk from Gara de Nord, this is a well-established hostel with clean, simply furnished rooms, helpful staff and a friendly vibe. Dorm 35 lei

Midland Hostel Str. Biserica Amzei 22 ☎021 3145323, ⓦthemidlandhostel.com; map opposite. This modern hostel has a great central location, with large dorms sleeping between six and fourteen; breakfast, internet and lockers included. Laundry is extra. Dorm 40 lei

Peaches Hostel Str. Ozari 52 ☎0761 971967, ⓦpeaches .ro; map p.902. Within walking distance of Piaţa Muncil metro station on a quiet street, this smart hostel features hammocks and a vast shared bathroom. Dorm 35 lei, double 110 lei

Puzzle Hostel Str. Luigi Cazzavillan 44 ☎0733 128887, ⓦpuzzlehostel.ro; map opposite. A 10min walk from Gara de Nord, this place is a mixture of very smart dorms and private rooms within an attractive old house. Dorm 40 lei, double 130 lei

Villa 11 Str. Institutul Medico-Militar 11 ☎0722 495 900, ⓦvila11.hostel.com; map p.902. Friendly, family-run hostel just a 5min walk from Gara de Nord, with two-, three- and six-bed rooms, some with bathroom. Price includes a pancake breakfast. Laundry and bike rental available. Dorm 50 lei, double 150 lei

X Hostel Str. Balcesti 9 ☎021 3127613, ⓦxhostel; map p.902. Its party hostel reputation is well deserved, so

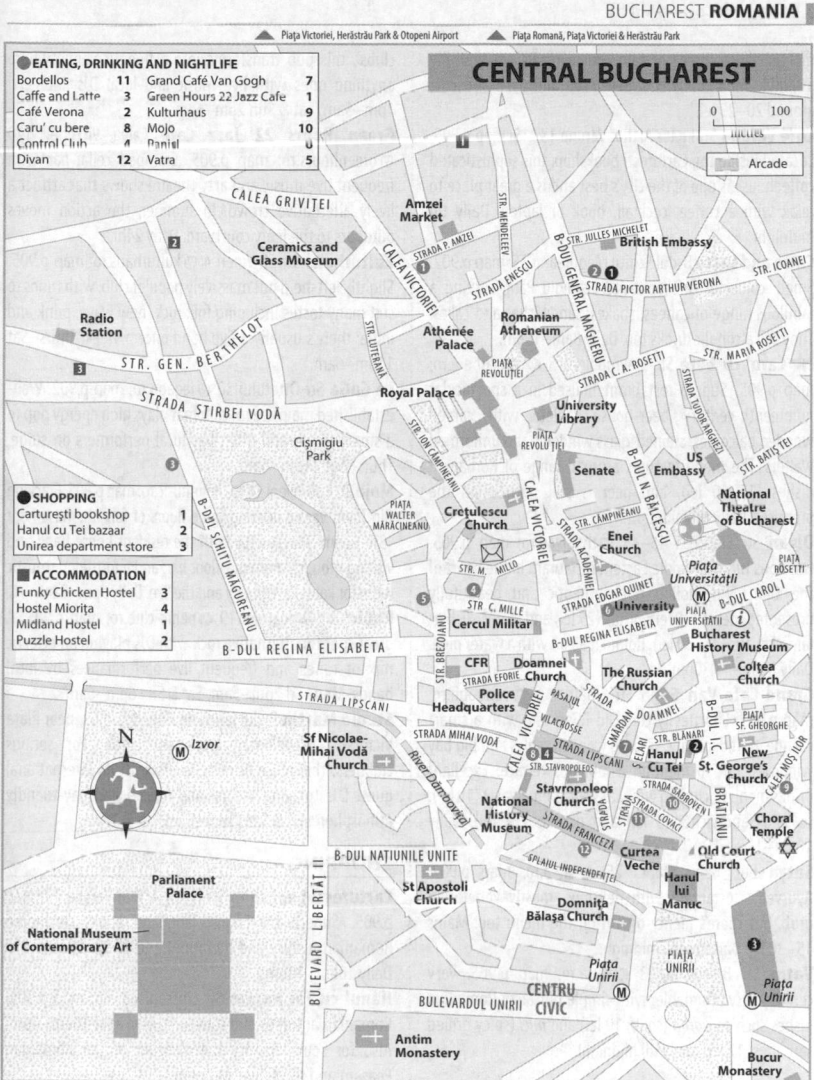

▲ Piața Victoriei, Herăstrău Park & Otopeni Airport   ▲ Piața Romană, Piața Victoriei & Herăstrău Park

CENTRAL BUCHAREST

● EATING, DRINKING AND NIGHTLIFE

Bordellos	11	Grand Café Van Gogh	7	
Caffe and Latte	3	Green Hours 22 Jazz Cafe	1	
Café Verona	2	Kulturhaus	9	
Caru' cu bere	8	Mojo	10	
Control Club	4	Daniel	6	
Divan	12	Vatra	5	

0 ─────── 100
metres

▢ Arcade

● SHOPPING

Cartureşti bookshop	1
Hanul cu Tei bazaar	2
Unirea department store	3

■ ACCOMMODATION

Funky Chicken Hostel	3
Hostel Miorița	4
Midland Hostel	1
Puzzle Hostel	2

27

don't come here in search of a good night's sleep. In its favour are modern facilities and a central location close to Piața Unirii metro station. Dorm 50 lei, double 200 lei

HOTELS

★ **Flowers B&B** Str Plantelor 2 ☎ 021 3119848, ⓦ www .flowersbb.ro; map p.902. First-rate and very hospitable bed and breakfast, with elegant en-suite rooms and a lovely summer terrace. Take bus #65 or #85 to B-dul Carol I, from where it's a 5min walk. Breakfast included. Double 200 lei
Hello Hotel Calea Grivitei 43 ☎ 0372 121 800, ⓦ hellohotels .ro; map p.902. A 2min walk from the train station, this large,

modern hotel has colourful, good-sized rooms with wall-mounted TVs. Breakfast is extra. Double 200 lei
Hostel Miorița Str Lipscani 12 ☎ 021 3120361, ⓦ hostel -miorita.ro; map above. A hotel rather than a hostel, the homely *Miorița* has a great central location, with six spacious en-suite rooms and cable TV. Breakfast included. Double 150 lei

EATING

Bucharest's thriving restaurant scene has a wide selection of ethnic cuisines to choose from, as well as traditional Romanian food. Look out for restaurants offering daily set

27

menus; these three- or four-course meals are typically available Mon to Fri between noon and 5pm and cost around 20–25 lei.

Café Verona Str Pictor Arthur Verona 13–15; map p.905. Located inside the Cărtureşti bookshop, this sophisticated coffeehouse is one of the city's best and is a great place to relax with a coffee, cocktail, book or laptop. Daily till midnight.

Caffe and Latte B-dul Schitu Măgureanu 35; map p.902. Small, colourful café opposite Cişmigiu Park, serving a fabulous range of coffees, shakes, sandwiches and cakes. They sell alcoholic drinks too. Daily 8am–10pm.

★ **Caru' cu bere** Str Stavropoleos 5 ⓦ carucubere.ro; map p.905. Superb restaurant housed in a spectacular nineteenth-century beer-house replete with carved wooden balconies, stained-glass windows and uniformed waiters. The menu features a broad range of Romanian dishes (15–50 lei), and beer is still brewed on the premises. Daily till midnight.

Divan Str Franceză 46–48 ⓦ thedivan.ro; map p.905. Fabulous Turkish/Middle Eastern restaurant in the heart of the Old Town, doling out authentic and beautifully presented mezes (15 lei), pittas (25 lei) and mains such as lamb kebabs (25–30 lei). Round it all off with a water pipe. Daily noon–11.30pm.

Grand Café Van Gogh Str Smârdan 9 ⓦ vangogh.ro; map p.905. Effortlessly cool Old Town café with a smart orange-tinted interior, smooth wooden tables and big bay windows, not to mention a fabulous terrace. Excellent drinks menu (including wine) as well as breakfasts (10 lei), toasted sandwiches (9 lei) and platters (28 lei). Daily 10am–1am.

Satya Bul. Banu Manta 25 ⓦ satya.ro; map p.902. Ayurvedic restaurant with delicious, mostly vegetarian grub, but there's plenty of fish on the menu too. Mains 15–30 lei. Daily noon–midnight.

Vatra Str Brezoianu 23 ⓦ vatra.ro; map p.905. Very central, very affordable, with simple but tasty Romanian dishes such as *ciorba* (soup; 10 lei) and *mici* (spicy grilled sausages; 12 lei). Daily till midnight.

DRINKING AND NIGHTLIFE

Bucharest's historic quarter is awash with bars, pubs and clubs; in summer, the clubs and restaurants around the lake in Herăstrău Park are popular. For more detailed information on the city's nightlife check out the free local listings guide *Sapte Seri* (ⓦ sapteseri.ro) or *Bucharest in Your Pocket* (ⓦ inyourpocket.com/romania/bucharest).

Bordellos Str Selari 9–11; map p.905. One of the burgeoning number of Old Town hangouts, this vibrant pub has good draught beers, great tapas and big screens for all your sporting kicks. Daily 10am–5am.

Control Club Str Constantin Mille 4 ⓦ control-club-ro; map p.905. Marketed as "the club for people who don't like

clubs", this pub transforms into a frenetic venue where anything goes with live music and local DJs. Mon–Fri 1pm–5am, Sat & Sun 2pm–6am.

Green Hours 22 Jazz Cafe Calea Victoriei 120 ⓦ greenhours.ro; map p.905. Cramped cellar-bar with frequent live music and arty theatre shows that attract a lively alternative crowd. In summer, the action moves outdoors to the leafy courtyard. Daily 24hr.

Kulturhaus Str Sf. Vineri 4 ⓦ kulturhaus.ro; map p.905. Slightly left-field but massively popular club, with tunes to suit many tastes including folk rock, new wave, punk and indie; there's usually a live band once a week. Thurs–Sat 11pm–6am.

Le GaGa Str Ottetului 30 ⓦ legaga.ro; map p.902. Well-established mainstream club that plays high energy pop to a smart crowd and often has local performers on stage. Thurs–Sat 11pm–6am.

Mojo Str Gabroveni 14 ⓦ mojomusic.ro; map p.905. Cracking Old Town venue offering three floors of fun: the basement "Brit Room" for gigs (by both the resident house band and visiting groups); a ground-floor bar; and a top-floor acoustic room for karaoke, comedy and the like. Daily 9pm–5am.

Panic! Str Academiei 19 ⓦ panic-club.ro; map p.905. A great spot for alternative rock with DJs playing an eclectic mix of tunes and frequent live performances by local bands. Mon–Fri 2pm–5am, Sat & Sun 6pm–6am.

Studio Martin B-dul Iancu de Hunedoara 61, near Piaţa Victoriei ⓦ studiomartin.ro; map p.902. For serious clubbers, this place attracts ravers with its international guest DJs (playing techno and house) and gay-friendly atmosphere. Fri & Sat 11pm–5am.

SHOPPING

Cartureşti bookshop Str Pictor Arthur Verona 13; map p.905. Superb for English-language books (including Romanian history and literature) and all kinds of music. Daily 10am–10pm.

Hanul cu Tei bazaar Str Lipscani 63–65; map p.905. Romanian antiques and souvenirs. Mon–Sat 10am–6pm. Also for souvenirs, try the Museum of the Romanian Peasant and the Village Museum.

Piaţa Dorobanţi and Piaţa Matache The best of the city's daily food markets. Both 6am–2pm. See map p.902

Târgul Vitan flea market Calea Vitan (Dristor I metro); map p.902. The city's largest flea market is chaotic yet fascinating. Sun only 8am–4pm.

Unirea department store Piaţa Unirii 1; map p.905. Built during the Communist era, this enormous central shopping centre is a good place to find familiar labels. Daily 10am–10pm.

DIRECTORY

Embassies and consulates Australia, Str Praga 3 ⓣ 021 2062200; Canada, Str Tuberozelor 1–3 ⓣ 021 307 5000;

Ireland, Str Buzesti 50–52 ☎021 310 2161; UK, Str J. Michelet 24 ☎021 201 7200; US, bul Liviu Librescu 4–5 ☎021 200 3300.

Hospitals Spitalul Clinic de Urgenţa, Calea Floreasca 8 ☎021 599 2300; Medicover Unirii, 64–66 bul. Marasesti ☎021 310 1599, ⓦmedicover.com.

Internet Most hotels, hostels, bars, cafés and restaurants offer free wi-fi, but dedicated cafés are increasingly rare.

Left luggage *Bagaj de mână* (4 lei; open 24hr) at the Gara de Nord, opposite platforms 4 and 5.

Pharmacies Sensiblu has branches throughout the city. Its 24hr pharmacy is at Str Radu Beller 6. Helpnet has a 24hr one at bul. Ion Mihalache 92.

Police bul. Lascăr Catargiu 22 ☎021 2125684.

Post office Str M. Millo 12 (Mon–Fri 7.30am–8pm).

Transylvania

From Bucharest, trains carve their way north through the spectacular **Carpathian mountain range** into the heart of **Transylvania**. Thanks to centuries of migration and colonization, the region's population is a mix of Romanians, Magyars, Germans, Roma and others. The 1920 Trianon Treaty placed the region within the Romanian state, but the character of many towns still reflects those past patterns of settlement, even if only through architecture. With their defensive towers and fortified churches, the most striking of them are the former seats of Saxon power. Indeed, **Sighişoara** (the most picturesque of the lot) could be the Saxons' cenotaph: their houses and churches remain, yet the living culture has evaporated, as it threatens to do in **Braşov** and **Sibiu**.

The Carpathians, meanwhile, offer Europe's cheapest skiing in winter and

wonderful hiking during the summer, along with caves, alpine meadows, dense forests sheltering bears, and lowland valleys with quaint villages.

BRAŞOV

With an eye for trade and invasion routes, the medieval Saxons sited their largest settlements near Transylvania's mountain passes. **BRAŞOV**, which they called Kronstadt, grew prosperous as a result, and Saxon dominance lasted until the Communist government brought thousands of Moldavian villagers to work in the new factories. As a result, there are two parts to Braşov: the Gothic and Baroque centre beneath Mount Tâmpa, which looks great, and the surrounding sprawl of flats, which doesn't. The central square, surrounded by restored merchants' houses, is now the heart of a buzzing city with a raft of exciting bars and restaurants.

WHAT TO SEE AND DO

Buses from the station will leave you near the central square, **Piaţa Sfatului**. Leading northeast from the square, the pedestrianized **Strada Republicii** is the hub of Braşov's social and commercial life.

Piaţa Sfatului

Piaţa Sfatului is overshadowed by the Gothic pinnacles of the city's most famous landmark, the **Black Church** (Tues–Sat 10am–7pm, Sun noon–7pm; 6 lei), which stab upwards like a series of daggers. An endearingly monstrous hall-church that took almost a century to complete (1383–1477), it is so-called for its soot-blackened walls, the result of

---

THE FORTIFIED CHURCHES OF TRANSYLVANIA

Transylvania's Saxon legacy is clearly apparent in the fortified churches erected throughout the region's villages following the migration of the Saxons to Romania under King Géza II in 1150. The Mioritics Association, in conjunction with UNESCO, is dedicated to preserving the fortified churches and developing tourism around them (ⓦfortified-churches.com). Despite this, the majority are not well known and there is little information available. However, most are accessible with their original gate-key, which is usually kept by one of the elder villagers for safekeeping. Simply ask in the village for the key-holder, who should be able to open up the church and show you around. It is normal to pay them a small amount (about 5 lei) for their trouble.

being torched by the Austrian army in 1689. Inside, by contrast, the church is startlingly white, with oriental carpets creating splashes of colour along the walls of the nave. In summer (June–Sept Tues at 6pm), the church's 4000-pipe organ is used for concerts.

The fifteenth-century council house (Casa Sfatului) in the centre of Piaţa Sfatului now houses the **History Museum** (Tues–Sun 9am–5pm; 7 lei), which has a small exhibition dedicated to the Saxon guilds that dominated Braşov in medieval times.

Mount Tâmpa

A length of fortress wall runs along the foot of **Mount Tâmpa**, behind which a **cable car** (daily 9.30am–5.45pm, Mon from noon; 8 lei) whisks tourists to the summit. However, the trails up offer a challenging walk (1hr) and some fantastic views.

Museum of the Bârsa Land Fortifications

Of the original seven bastions (towers maintained by the city's trade guilds), the best preserved is that of the weavers, on Strada Coşbuc. This complex of wooden galleries and bolt holes now contains the **Museum of the Bârsa Land Fortifications** (Tues–Sun 10am–5.30pm; 6 lei). Inside are models and weaponry recalling the bad old days when the region was repeatedly attacked by Tatars, Turks, and by Vlad the Impaler, who left hundreds of captives on sharp stakes to terrorize the townsfolk. The Saxons' widely publicized stories of Vlad's cruelty unwittingly contributed to Transylvania's dark image and

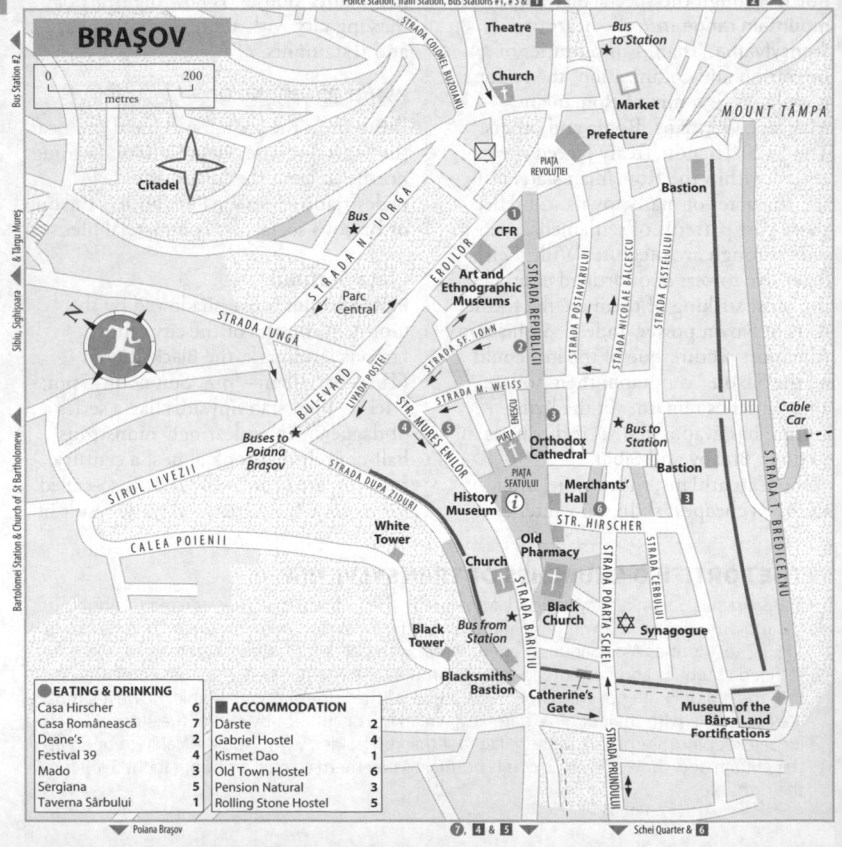

● EATING & DRINKING		■ ACCOMMODATION	
Casa Hirscher	6	Dârste	2
Casa Românească	7	Gabriel Hostel	4
Deane's	2	Kismet Dao	1
Festival 39	4	Old Town Hostel	6
Mado	3	Pension Natural	3
Sergiana	5	Rolling Stone Hostel	5
Taverna Sârbului	1		

eventually caught Bram Stoker's attention as he conceived *Dracula*.

ARRIVAL AND DEPARTURE

By train Braşov's train station is northeast of the old town, 2km from the centre – take bus #4 into town or spend around 8 lei on a taxi.

Destinations Bucharest (hourly; 2hr 45min); Sibiu (6 daily; 2hr 30min); Sighişoara (12 daily; 2hr 15min); Timişoara (1 daily; 10hr).

By bus Buses arrive and depart from either Autogari 1 next to the train station, or Autogari 2, a 5min walk east of the train station opposite the football stadium.

Destinations From Autogari 1: Bucharest (hourly; 3hr 30min); Sibiu (6 daily; 2–3hr); Sighişoara (10 daily; 2hr). From Autogari 2: Bran (every 30min Mon–Fri, hourly Sat & Sun; 45min); Timişoara (2 daily; 9hr 30min); Zărneşti (hourly Mon–Fri, Sat 8 daily, Sun 3 daily; 1hr).

INFORMATION AND TOURS

Tourist office In the History Museum, Piaţa Sfatului 30 (daily 9am–7pm; ☎0268 419 078, ⓦbrasovtravelguide.ro).

Tours Active Travel at Str Toamnei 2 (☎0268 321515, ⓦactivetravel.ro) is a well-established agency that runs hiking, biking, rafting and skiing trips throughout the region as well as tours of Braşov and day-trips to Bran castle.

Internet Most hotels, hostels, bars, cafés and restaurants offer free wi-fi.

ACCOMMODATION

Dârste 6km southeast of Braşov at Calea Bucureşti 285 ☎0268 339 967, ⓦcampingdirste.ro. Modern campsite with cabins; bus #17 from the centre or #35 from the station. Camping 13 lei, double cabin from 55 lei

Gabriel Hostel Str Vasile Saftu 41a ☎0744 844 223. Located in the historic Schei district (bus #51), this quiet, pleasant place has small dorms with segregated male and female bathrooms and a kitchen. Dorm 40 lei, double 95 lei

Kismet Dao Str Neagoe Basarab 8 ☎0268 514 296, ⓦkismetdao.com. Busy, popular hostel just 5min from the centre, with decent dorms and private rooms, and a large kitchen. Dorm 40 lei, double 135 lei

Old Town Hostel Str Prundului 39 ☎0368 428204, ⓦoldtownbrasov.com. Excellent central hostel with spacious, clean dorms and laundry, towels, and a free drink thrown in too. Dorm 35 lei

★ **Pension Natural** Str Castelului 58 ☎0744 321 273, ⓦpensiuneanatural.ro. Immaculate little family-run hotel with a tranquil garden beside the city walls. Double 220 lei

Rolling Stone Hostel Str Piatra Mare 2a ☎0268 513 965, ⓦrollingstone.ro. Friendly, sociable hostel with clean, attractive dorms, private rooms and immaculate bathrooms. Pleasant garden terrace with pool and basement bar. Dorm 32 lei, double 115 lei

EATING AND DRINKING

Casa Hirscher Piaţa Sfatului 12–14 ⓦcasahirscher.ro. This lovely restaurant, housed in an atmospheric seventeenth century building, serves quality Romanian and international specialities. Mains 20–50 lei. Daily 9am–midnight.

Casa Românească Piaţa Unirii 15. Friendly and cheap restaurant convenient for the hostels, with a courtyard offering views of the *piaţa*. Traditional Romanian cuisine, and good-sized portions. Mains 15–30 lei. Daily 11am–midnight.

Deane's Str Republicii 19 ⓦdeanes.ro. Perennially popular Irish boozer which puts on some form of entertainment most evenings (music, comedy, karaoke, quizzes). Live sport on TV and a darts room too. Daily 10am–1am.

Festival 39 Str Republicii 62. A great place to drink, Braşov's best-known bar is full of the strangest things – from badly stuffed animals to plastic trophies. Daily 7am–midnight.

Mado Str Republicii 10 ⓦmado.ro. Popular restaurant with outdoor seating and a spacious interior. The dishes include traditional Romanian and Turkish specialities; you can also try some Romanian wines, such as *vin fiert*, the hearty and spicy hot tipple favoured in rural Transylvania during winter. Home-made cakes too. Mains 15–35 lei. Daily 10am–midnight.

Sergiana Str Mureşenilor 28. Serves wholesome and tasty Transylvanian food in its warren of atmospheric cellars. Mains 15–30 lei. Daily 11am–1am.

Taverna Sârbului Str Republicii 55 ⓦtavernasarbului .ro. Capacious brick-cellar restaurant dishing up gut-busting portions of meat-heavy Romanian and Serbian food. Mains 15–23 lei. Daily noon–midnight.

BRAN

Cosy little **BRAN**, 28km southwest of Braşov, is situated at the foot of the stunning Bucegi Mountains. Despite what you may hear, its **castle** (daily 9am–6pm, Mon from noon; 25 lei; ⓦbran-castle.com) has only tenuous associations with Dracula, aka Vlad the Impaler, who may have attacked it in 1460. Hyperbole is forgivable, though, as Bran really does look like a vampire count's residence. The castle was built in 1377 by the Saxons of Braşov to safeguard what used to be the main route into Wallachia, and it rises in tiers of towers and ramparts from among the woods, against a glorious mountain background. A warren of stairs, nooks and chambers around a small courtyard,

27

the interior is filled with elaborately carved four-poster beds, throne-like chairs and portraits of grim-faced boyars.

ARRIVAL AND DEPARTURE

Hotels and hostels throughout the country arrange trips to Bran Castle, while Brașov-based Active Travel runs day-trips on Tues, Thurs and Sat.
By bus Buses from Brașov arrive in the centre of town, in view of the castle.

ACCOMMODATION

Pension Carina Str Principala 484 ☎0268 238303, ⓦpensiunea-carina.ro. Sporting some bright colour schemes, this pleasant guesthouse is smart and modern, with a lovely garden. Double 125 lei
The Guesthouse Str General Traian Mosoiu 365B ☎0745 179475, ⓦguesthouse.ro. A comfortable place run by an affable British expat, set in a large garden, with kitchen facilities and immaculate en-suite doubles. Double 130 lei

RÂȘNOV AND ZĂRNEȘTI

For a more low-key, but no less satisfying, experience than Bran, try nearby RÂȘNOV, where the hilltop fortress (daily 8am–8pm; 6 lei) and the views are stunning. North of Bran is ZĂRNEȘTI, a charming small town that is the perfect jumping-off point for trips into the Făgăraș Mountains.

ARRIVAL AND DEPARTURE

Buses between Bran and Brașov stop at Râșnov. There's a regular bus service between Zărnești and Moeciu de Jos (southwest of Bran) which you can pick up in Bran.

ACCOMMODATION

Pensiunea Mosorel 1 Str Dr Senchea 162, Zărnești ☎0744 368432, ⓦpensiuneamosorel.ro. Charming family-run guesthouse with large en-suite rooms,

delicious home-cooked food, and a pleasant garden with space for tents. Double 120 lei, camping 12 lei per person
Pensiunea Mosorel 2 Just south of Zărnești ☎0745 024471, same website. For a near-medieval mountain escape, spend a night here in the picturesque hamlet of Magură, on the flanks of the Piatra Craiului Mountains. Phone ahead and the owners will pick you up from Zărnești's bus station. Double 120 lei

SIGHIȘOARA

The citadel of **SIGHIȘOARA**, perched on a hill overlooking the Târnave Mare valley, presents a forbidding silhouette of looming battlements and needle spires; it seems fitting that this was the birthplace of Vlad Țepeș, the man known to posterity as **Dracula**. Look out for the Medieval Arts and the Inter-ethnic Cultural **festivals** held annually in July and August, when Sighișoara may be overrun by thousands of beer-swillers.

WHAT TO SEE AND DO

The route from the train station to the centre passes the **Romanian Orthodox Cathedral**, its gleaming white, multifaceted facade a striking contrast to the dark interior. Across the **Târnave Mare** river, the **citadel** dominates the town from a hill whose slopes support a jumble of ancient houses. Steps lead up from the lower town's main square, **Piața Hermann Oberth**, to the main gateway, above which rises the mighty **clock tower**. This was built in the fourteenth century when Sighișoara became a free town controlled by craft guilds – each of which had to finance the construction of a bastion and defend it in wartime.

WOLF AND BEAR TRACKING IN THE CARPATHIANS

Romania has the largest **wolf** and **brown bear** populations in Europe. Transylvanian Wolf (☎0744 319 708, ⓦtransylvanianwolf.ro) is an organization offering guided walks (around 300 lei for up to 5 people, 65 lei for each extra person) tracking wolves, bears, red deer and lynx under the eagle eye of Dan Marin, an award-winning tracker who works closely with conservation organizations and the new Piatra Craiului National Park.

In winter there's the chance to see some spectacular snow-covered landscapes, and take part in sleigh rides and cross-country skiing. Treat yourself and stay in the Marins' spectacular family guesthouse (Str I. Metianu 108, Zărnești; 215 lei per person), where all meals (breakfast, dinner and packed lunch) are home-cooked and included in the price. Birdwatching and botany tours are also available.

Sighişoara grew rich on the proceeds of trade with Moldavia and Wallachia, as attested by the regalia and strongboxes in the clock tower's **museum** (Tues–Sun 10am–3.30pm; 6 lei). The ticket also gives access to the seventeenth-century **torture chamber** and the **Museum of Armaments** next door, with its small and poorly presented "Dracula Exhibition".

In 1431 or thereabouts, the child later known as Dracula was born at Strada Muzeului 6 near the clock tower. At the time his father – Vlad Dracul – was commander of the mountain passes into Wallachia, but the younger Vlad's privileged childhood ended eight years later, when he and his brother Radu were sent to Anatolia as hostages to the Turks. There Vlad observed the Turks' use of terror, which he would later turn against them, earning the nickname of "The Impaler". Nowadays, Vlad's birthplace is a mediocre tourist restaurant.

ARRIVAL AND INFORMATION

By train Sighişoara's train station is on the northern edge of town, on Str Libertăţii.
Destinations Braşov (12 daily; 2hr 15min); Bucharest (6 daily; 5hr); Sibiu (3 daily; 2hr 30min).
By bus The bus station is close to the train station on the same road. For Sibiu change buses at Braşov.
Destinations Braşov (9 daily; 2hr); Bucharest (9 daily; 5hr 30min).
Tourist office Opposite the clock tower at Piaţa Muzeului 6 (Tues–Sun 10am–6pm; ☎0788 115511, ⓦinfosighisoara.ro).

ACCOMMODATION

Backpackers are met at the train and bus stations by runners for the town's many excellent private rooms.
Burg Hostel Str Bastionului 4–6 ☎0265 778489, ⓦburghostel.ro. Central, atmospheric hostel in a seventeenth-century building with clean dorms and doubles. There's a bar in the cellar, internet access and free wi-fi. Breakfast isn't included, but there is a good-value restaurant in the courtyard. Dorm 45 lei, double 100 lei
Gia Hostel Str Libertăţii 41 ☎0265 772486, ⓦhotelgia .ro. A simple hotel that doubles as a hostel and offers dorms, doubles and triples. No breakfast, but shared kitchen available. Conveniently close to the train station. Dorm 45 lei, double 110 lei
Private room Str Cojocarilor 1 ☎0744 119211, ⓔcristinafaur2003@yahoo.de. The private rooms offered by the Faur family in the citadel are some of the town's

★ **TREAT YOURSELF**
Casa cu Cerb Str Şcolii 1 ☎0265 774 625, ⓦcasacucerb.ro. This extremely classy hotel occupies a seventeenth-century mansion with an abundance of atmospheric period features. It's a good choice for romantics, with bathtubs big enough for two, while the most expensive rooms have four-poster beds. The restaurant is among the town's best. 260 lei

best. Guests have use of a kitchen, and bicycle rental is available. Dorm 45 lei, double 120 lei
Villa Franka Camping Str Dealu Garii ☎0265 771046. Boasting wonderful views from its hilltop position high above the train station, this idyllic tree-shaded campsite (open April–Nov) also has clean wooden bungalows and a good restaurant. Camping 13 lei per person, double bungalow 95 lei

EATING AND DRINKING

Casa cu Cerb Str Şcolii 1. In the hotel of the same name, this is one of the best restaurants in the citadel, with good breakfasts, light meals and more expensive dinners. There's also a lovely, sunny outdoor seating area. Mains 20–45 lei. Daily 10am–11pm.
Culture Pub In the basement of the *Burg Hostel* (see above), with some live rock/pop music, mainly weekend evenings. Daily till 3am.
International Café Piaţa Cetăţii 8. A cosy café serving delicious and filling sandwiches and cakes (10 lei), and just about the only quiche (12 lei) in Transylvania. Mon–Sat: summer 8am–9pm; winter 10am–6pm.
Quattro Amici Str Octavian Goga 12. In the lower town, this enjoyable pizzeria offers fabulous oven-baked pizzas and fresh salads, and there's outdoor seating facing a field. Mains 10–25 lei. Daily 10am–11pm.
Rustica Str 1 Decembrie 1918 58. Hearty, wholesome Romanian food, such as *mititei* (spicy grilled sausages) and *sarmalute* (cabbage leaves stuffed with minced meat and rice), served up in nice surroundings. The bar is popular at night, and there's a good breakfast menu too. Mains 15–25 lei. Daily 10am–11pm.

SIBIU

The narrow streets and gabled houses of SIBIU's older quarters are the stuff of fairytales. Like Braşov, Sibiu was founded by Germans invited by Hungary's King Géza II to colonize strategic regions of

27

27

Transylvania in 1143. Its inhabitants dominated trade in Transylvania and Wallachia, but their citadels were no protection against the tide of history which eroded their influence after the eighteenth century. The Saxon community is now mostly gone from Romania, but Sibiu still has stronger and more lucrative links with Germany than any other Transylvanian town, and its stint as European Capital of Culture in 2007 meant its buildings were handsomely refurbished. The city also stages some cracking festivals, not least the International Theatre Festival in late May, with open-air stages across all the main squares.

To reach the old town cross the square from the train station and follow Str Gen. Magheru to **Piața Mare**, one of three conjoined squares that form the centre.

Piața Mare

On the western side of Piața Mare stands the handsome eighteenth-century **Brukenthal Palace**, housing the eponymous **museum** (daily 10am–6pm; 20 lei; ⓦbrukenthalmuseum.ro), one of the finest in Romania with an evocative collection of works by Transylvanian and Western painters – look out for Jan van Eyck's *Man in Blue Turban*. The city's **History Museum** (Tues–Sun 10am–6pm; 12 lei) is nearby in the impressive Old City Hall. On the northern side of Piața Mare, the huge Catholic church stands next to the **Council Tower** (daily 10am–6pm), which offers fine views to the Carpathians.

The cathedral

Just beyond the Council Tower, on Piața Huet, the **Evangelical Cathedral** (closed for long-running renovations at the time of writing) is a massive Gothic hall-church raised during the fourteenth and fifteenth centuries.

Museum of Traditional Folk Civilization

Set aside most of a day to explore Sibiu's wonderful open-air **Museum of**

Traditional Folk Civilization (Muzeul Astra; daily 9am–5pm; 15 lei; ⓦmuzeulastra.ro) at Piața Mica 11, south of the centre; take trolleybus #1 to the end of the line. Set against a mountain backdrop, the museum offers a fantastic insight into rural life, with authentically furnished wooden houses, churches and mills; there's also a traditional inn serving local food and drink.

ARRIVAL AND INFORMATION

By train Sibiu's train station is on Piața 1 Decembrie 1918, 400m northeast of the main square.

Destinations Brașov (6 daily; 3hr); Bucharest (3 daily; 6hr); Sighișoara (3 daily; 2hr 30min); Timișoara (3 daily; 7hr).

By bus The bus station is adjacent to the train station. For Sighișoara change buses at Brașov.

Destinations Brașov (6 daily; 2hr 45min); Bucharest (5 daily; 5hr 15min); Timișoara (4 daily; 6hr 15min).

Tourist office Sibiu's central tourist office is inside the City Hall at Str Samuel von Brukenthal 2 (Mon–Fri 9am–8pm, Sat & Sun 10am–6pm; ☎0269 208 913, ⓦturism.sibiu.ro).

ACCOMMODATION

Ela Str Nouă 43 ☎0269 215197, ⓦela-hotels.ro. A friendly, family-run hotel, with a pleasant garden, eight spotless en-suite rooms and a guest kitchen. From the train station take Str 9 Mai, turn right onto Str Rebreanu, then first left onto Str Nouă. Breakfast is 15 lei. Double **100 lei**

★ **Felinarul Hostel** Str Felinarului 8 ☎0269 250282, ⓦfelinarulhostelsibiu.ro. Delightful hostel with a courtyard café in the old town that's rustically styled and simply furnished with quaint antique furniture. The well-travelled owners keep the place spotlessly clean and are a great source of local information; they can also organize trips around Sibiu and beyond. Dorm **50 lei**, double **100 lei**

Old Town Hostel Piața Mică 26 ☎0269 216445, ⓦhostelsibiu.ro. Located above a historic pharmacy in a 450-year-old building, the hostel has three large, airy dorms and also offers en-suite doubles at a different location. Breakfast is not included but there's a kitchen, plus free tea and coffee and internet access. The hostel can also arrange bike rental. Dorm **50 lei**, double **150 lei**

Podul Minciunilor Str Azilului 1 ☎0269 217259, ⓦela -hotels.ro. A small, central, family-run guesthouse near the Liar's Bridge, with five en-suite doubles and one triple. No breakfast. Double **100 lei**

Sibiu Travelers Hostel Str Teilor 4 ☎0269 238161,

ⓦ sibiutravelershostel.com. Spotless dorms a short walk from the train station and 10min northwest of the centre. Laundry and breakfast included. Dorm __50 lei__

EATING AND DRINKING

Crama Sibiu Vechi Str Ilarian 3 ⓦ sibiulvechi.ro. Traditional Transylvanian restaurant in the cellar of a fifteenth-century building. This is the best place for something typically Romanian such as *tochitură* (meat stew), *ghiveci* (vegetable stew) or *fasole batută* (mashed beans), served by staff in national costume. There's also live folk music and cheap wine on tap. Mains 15–40 lei. Daily noon–midnight.

Go In Piaţa Mica 9 ⓦ goin-sibiu.ro. Popular central restaurant serving great pizzas (12–22 lei) and pasta. Cocktails are good too. Daily 9.30am–midnight.

Imperium Club Str Bălcescu 24 ⓦ imperiumsibiu.ro. Cool, classy brick-cellar bar with regular jazz sessions, piano concerts on Sun, and evenings of stand-up comedy (rarely in English, but fun to watch nonetheless). Good beer too. Daily 6pm–2am.

La Turn Piaţa Mare 1 ⓦ laturn.com. Atmospheric spot next to the Council Tower with an impressive range of seafood and Italian dishes. Mains 15–35 lei. Daily 10am–midnight.

Mara's Steakhouse Str Bălcescu 21 ⓦ marasibiu.ro. Excellent local food is served up here, including some superb game. They also have a large selection of wines, including Romanian varieties. Mains 15–45 lei. Daily 9am–midnight.

The Banat

Once a much larger territory that now lies between Romania and neighbouring Hungary and Serbia, the featureless plains of **Banat** were ruled from **Timişoara** until the Turks conquered it in 1552; they governed until 1716 when they were ousted by the Habsburgs. The region's current frontiers were drawn up during the Versailles conference of 1918–20. Today, Romanian Banat is still home to a diverse population that for centuries has included Slovaks, Bulgarians, Ukrainians and Germans living alongside Serbians, Romanians and Hungarians. Besides the picturesque villages scattered throughout the region, the Banat's main attraction (and unofficial capital) is Timişoara with its thriving cultural scene and old town centre packed with historic buildings.

TIMIŞOARA

The engaging city of **TIMIŞOARA**, 250km west of Sibiu near the Serbian border and the rail junction at Arad, is Romania's most West-leaning city, its good location and multilingual inhabitants attracting much foreign investment. The city's fame abroad rests on its crucial role in the overthrow of the Ceauşescu regime. A Calvinist minister, Lászlo Tökes, stood up for the rights of the Hungarian community and, when the police came to evict him on December 16, 1989, his parishioners barred their way. The bloody riots that ensued inspired the people of Bucharest to follow, so that Timişoara sees itself as the guardian of the revolution.

27

Approaching from the train station, you'll enter the centre at the attractive pedestrianized Piaţa Victoriei, with fountains and flowerbeds strewn along its length. North of here, antique trams trundle past the Baroque **Town Hall** on the central Piaţa Libertăţii, while two blocks further north is the vast Piaţa Unirii.

Piaţa Victoriei

The focal point of Piaţa Victoriei is the huge **Romanian Orthodox Cathedral**, completed in 1946 with a blend of neo-Byzantine and Moldavian architectural elements – this is where most of the protesters were gunned down in 1989. At the opposite end, the unattractive Opera House stands near the **castle**, which now houses the **Museum of the Banat** (closed for long-term renovation at the time of writing), with a broad collection of archeological and historical artefacts.

Piaţa Unirii

Piaţa Unirii is dominated by the monumental **Roman Catholic** and **Serbian Orthodox cathedrals**. Built between 1736 and 1773, the former (to the east) is a

27

fine example of Viennese Baroque; the latter is roughly contemporaneous and almost as impressive.

The Museum of the Revolution

Located at Strada Popa Şapcă 3–5 (but accessed via Strada Oituz northeast of Piaţa Unirii) is the superb **Museum of the Revolution** (Mon–Fri 10am–6pm, Sat 9am–2pm; free), which soberly documents the remarkable events of December 1989, courtesy of photos, newspaper cuttings and film footage, including the extraordinary moment when the Ceauşescus were informed of their impending execution.

Banat Village Museum

Situated 5km northeast of the centre and accessible by tram (#1 and #2) or bus (#46), the wonderful **Banat Village Museum** (Tues–Sat 10am–6pm, Sun noon–8pm; 4.50 lei; ⓦmsbtm.ro) is an outdoor affair featuring a fascinating ensemble of nineteenth-century cottages collected from local villages and reconstructed within the museum's wooded grounds. Architectural styles include German, Slovak, Hungarian, Ukranian and Romanian. With the same ticket, visitors can also view the city's **Ethnographic Museum** collection that further illustrates the region's ethnic diversity.

ARRIVAL AND INFORMATION

By train Timișoara Nord train station is a 15min walk west of the centre along B-dul Republicii.
Destinations Brașov (1 daily; 10hr); Bucharest (4 daily; 9hr); Sibiu (2 daily; 7hr).
By bus The central bus station (Autogara Autotim) lies opposite the train station.
Destinations Brașov (3 daily; 9hr); Bucharest (2 daily; 11hr 30min); Sibiu (4 daily; 6hr 15min).
Tourist information The tourist office (Mon–Fri 9am–8pm, Sat 9am–5pm; ☎0256 437 973, ⓦtimisoara-info.ro), on the ground floor of the opera building at Str Alba Iulia 2, has maps and copies of the free quarterly English-language guide *Timișoara What Where When* as well as the Romanian-language weekly listings guide *Șapte Seri* (ⓦsaptseri.ro).

ACCOMMODATION

Camping International 4km west of town on Aleea Pădurea Verde ☎0256 217086, ⓦcampinginternational .ro. Open all year, this well-kept campsite also has huts sleeping one to four people. Take trolleybus #11 from the train station or centre. Camping 30 lei per person, double huts 110 lei
Freeborn Hostel Str Patriarch Miron Cristea 3 (street also known as Asanesti), Apartment 1 ☎0743 438534, ⓦfreebornhostel.com. Very central hostel with two spacious dorm rooms and a double, each with their own bathroom. There's also a shaded courtyard with barbecue and table tennis. Dorm 40 lei, double 130 lei
Hostel Costel Str Petru Sfetca 1 (street also known as Vidra) ☎0356 262487, ⓦhostel-costel.ro. Lovely hostel with huge dorm rooms in a stylishly refurbished old house, just a short walk northeast from the centre. Dorm 40 lei, double 130 lei

EATING, DRINKING AND NIGHTLIFE

There's a useful 24hr supermarket, Stil, on Str Mărășești (at Str Lazăr), a short walk northwest of Piaţa Libertăţii. During the summer, party animals should head for the plethora of canalside bars behind the cathedral.
Baroque Piaţa Unirii 14. This place lives up to its name, with wrought-iron tables and chairs outside and a decadent array of teas, coffees, milkshakes and hot chocolate (both alcoholic and non-alcoholic). Breakfasts for around 15 lei, hot drinks from 5 lei. Daily 8am–1am.
Club 30 Piaţa Victoriei 7. In the Cinema Timiș, this small basement club has good jazz and blues, often live. Daily 6pm–3am.
Cora Pizzaria Str Eugeniu de Savoya 13 ⓦpizzeriacora .ro. First-rate pizzeria located in the heart of the city (15–30 lei). Daily 10am–1am.
Harold's Aleea Studenţilor 17 ⓦharolds.ro. Understated and classy restaurant in a studeny area, with a wide selection of international and vegetarian options, including the large "Harold's Vegetarian Plate" – good for sharing at 40 lei. Most mains about 16 lei. Daily 11.30am–midnight.
Java Coffee House Str Rodnei 6. This dark bar on the southeastern corner of Piaţa Unirii is a fine place for a coffee or something stronger. Drinks range from the classic to the more inventive, including their "ice cream chocolate coffee". Drinks 6–20 lei. Daily 24hr.
Piranha Club Str Alecsandri 5. A popular drinking den with a range of cocktails and truly eye-catching surroundings, complete with fish tanks, live lizards and snakes. Open around the clock, it's also a pleasant place for morning coffee.

THE PETER AND PAUL FORTRESS, ST. PETERSBURG

Russia

HIGHLIGHTS

❶ **The Kremlin** See the Orlov diamond, stunning churches and the world's biggest cannons at the historical and political heart of Russia. **See p.924**

❷ **Banya** Purge your pores in style at Moscow's Sandunovsky baths. **See p.925**

❸ **Moscow nightlife** Party in style until the wee hours in the Russian capital, home to some of the world's best nightlife. **See p.929**

❹ **The Hermitage** View thousands of priceless treasures at Russia's premier museum. **See p.930**

❺ **Peter and Paul Fortress** Caper along the battlements and take a dip in the Neva River. See p.932

HIGHLIGHTS ARE MARKED ON THE MAP ON P.917

ROUGH COSTS

Daily budget Basic €60, occasional treat €75

Drink Beer (*pivo*) €3

Food Pancake (*blini*) €1.50

Hostel/budget hotel €15–25/€45

Travel Train: Moscow–St Petersburg from €25

FACT FILE

Population 142 million

Language Russian

Currency Ruble (R)

Capital Moscow

International phone code ❼ 7

Time zone GMT +4hr

Introduction

European Russia stretches from the borders of Belarus and Ukraine to the Ural mountains, over 1000km east of Moscow; even without the rest of the vast Russian Federation, it constitutes by far the largest country in Europe. Formerly a powerful tsarist empire and a Communist superpower, Russia continues to be a source of fascination for travellers. While access is still made relatively difficult by lingering Soviet-style bureaucracy – visas are obligatory and accommodation usually has to be booked in advance – independent travel is increasing every year, and visitors are doubly rewarded by the cultural riches of the country and the warmth of the Russian people.

Moscow, Russia's bustling capital, combines the frenetic energy of an Eastern city with the cosmopolitan feel of a Western one. With its dense human traffic and show-stopping architecture – from the Kremlin's tsarist palaces and onion domes of St Basil's Cathedral, through the monumental relics of the Communist years to today's massive building projects – the metropolis can feel rather overwhelming. By contrast, with its beautiful canals and graceful buildings, **St Petersburg**, Russia's second city, is nicknamed "the Venice of the north". Founded as a seaport by the eighteenth-century tsar Peter the Great, who wanted the Russian fleet to be the strongest in the world, the city was intended to emulate the best of Western European elegance. Today, its people are more relaxed and friendly than the capital's, and its position in the delta of the River Neva is unparalleled, giving it endless watery vistas. Uneven – and often ostentatious – wealth creation in both cities has made them twin figureheads for Russia's recent high-speed renaissance.

CHRONOLOGY

862 AD A Scandinavian warrior, Rurik, founds the state of Rus' (Русь).

989 Grand Duke Vladimir I adopts Orthodox Christianity.

1552 Ivan the Terrible conquers the Tatars and builds the famous domed St Basil's Cathedral in Red Square, Moscow.

1613 Michael Romanov is elected as Tsar of Russia, ushering in 300 years of Romanov rule.

1725 Peter the Great builds the new capital of St Petersburg after defeating Sweden in the Great Northern War.

1751 First recorded reference to "vodka" is made in a decree made by Empress Elizabeth.

1812 Napoleon invades Russia but is defeated.

1869 Tolstoy writes *War and Peace*.

1892 Tchaikovsky composes the famous ballet, *The Nutcracker*.

1905 Revolution leads to the masses gaining both a constitution and a parliament.

1914 Russia enters World War I on behalf of the Allies.

1917 The October Revolution witnesses the Communist Bolsheviks, led by Lenin, overthrowing the monarchy and government.

1924 Joseph Stalin takes control of the Soviet Union.

1941 The Nazis invade Russian territory; after intense fighting and victory at Stalingrad, the Red Army repel the Germans from Russia.

1961 Yuri Gagarin becomes the first human to travel into space aboard the *Vostok*.

1962 The Cuban Missile Crisis heightens tensions with the US during the Cold War.

1991 The Soviet Union collapses; many former Soviet countries declare independence. Boris Yeltsin is elected President.

1999 Yeltsin resigns and is replaced by Vladimir Putin.

2007 Russian relations with the US deteriorate over their plans to install anti-missile launchers around Russia's borders.

2008 Russia goes to war with Georgia over Georgia's offensive against Southern Ossetia.

2009 President Medvedev announces Russia's rearmament plan, which includes nuclear force.

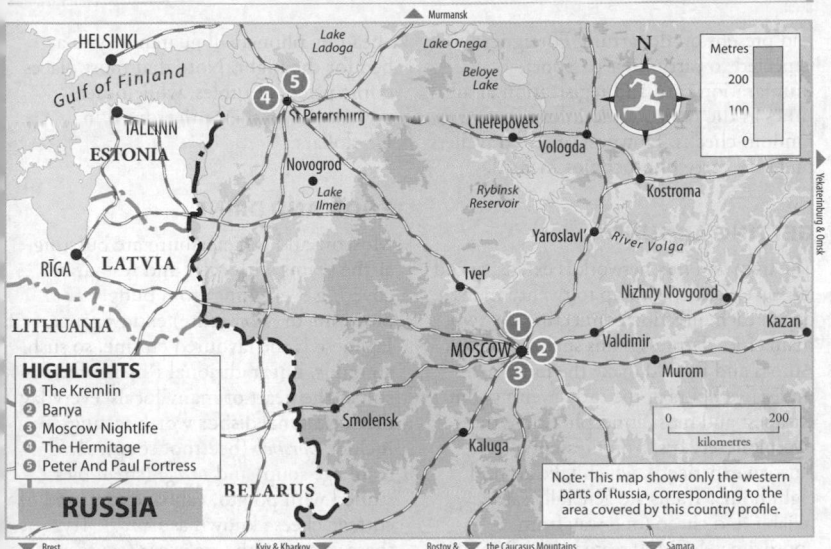

HIGHLIGHTS
❶ The Kremlin
❷ Banya
❸ Moscow Nightlife
❹ The Hermitage
❺ Peter And Paul Fortress

RUSSIA

Note: This map shows only the western parts of Russia, corresponding to the area covered by this country profile.

2011 Russia wins bid to host the football World Cup in 2018.
2012 Putin is sworn in for his second stint as President in May; protests ensue. In August Russia joins the WTO.

ARRIVAL AND VISAS

International flights serve Moscow's Sheremetyevo and Domodedovo airports and St Petersburg's Pulkovo Airport. All **airports** are connected with their respective cities by regular and efficient public transport. Besides being the main hub for all domestic **trains**, including the trans-Siberian ones, Moscow is served by trains from Rīga, Tallinn, Warsaw, Berlin and Budapest, while European train routes into St Petersburg include arrivals from Helsinki, Rīga and Vilnius. Train stations in both Moscow and

VISA CONTACTS

Ⓦ **russianembassy.net** Russian embassies and consulates.
Ⓦ **www.scottstours.co.uk** Visa service as well as tailor-made tours, handy for travellers combining Russia with Ukraine, Belarus, the Baltics or Central Asia.
Ⓦ **visatorussia.com** Provides an efficient visa service.

St Petersburg are well connected to the metro; all Moscow's *vokzal* (train stations) link to a stop on the (brown) circle line. The most convenient way to come to St Petersburg for travellers arriving from the Baltic States may be by **bus**, as they are more frequent than trains. **Ferries** into St Petersburg from Helsinki arrive at the Vasilyevskiy Island ferry terminal.

All tourists travelling to Russia require a **tourist visa**, which entitles visitors to a 30-day stay in the country. To obtain a visa, travellers need to have been "invited" by a hotel or hostel (note that hostels charge a fee for invitation letters). If booking **accommodation** in advance, your hotel or hostel can provide this document for you. Should you wish to find accommodation upon arrival, you can obtain a letter of invitation through a **visa agency** (see box above) for a fee, which states that you will be staying at a randomly selected hotel – there is no obligation to actually do so once in Russia. Once you arrive in the country, your hotel/hostel will **register your visa** (hostels charge for this). Note that it's important to register within seven working days of your arrival. At the airport you will also be given an **immigration card** which you must keep

28

and present on departure. Foreigners are expected to carry their passport, immigration card and registration at all times as the police sometimes carry out random checks. However, many travellers prefer to carry **photocopies** instead.

GETTING AROUND

The **train** and **bus** network is extensive and largely efficient, with up to twenty trains a day in each direction connecting the two main cities. Express trains such as Sapsan, Aurora and Er-200 make the journey in under five hours in the early evening, but cheapest and most atmospheric are the **overnight** services, a quintessentially Russian experience, which take around eight hours. Trains are generally safe, reliable and cheap (one-way from approximately R400 seated only, R2500 in a couchette). Buy tickets in advance from Leningradskiy station in Moscow or Moskovskiy station in St Petersburg. Regular buses connect the two cities, but the long ten- to twelve-hour journey (R1000) rarely makes it worth the while. **City transport** in Moscow and St Petersburg centres on the punctual metro; overground transport includes buses, trams, trolleybuses and minibuses (*marshrútki*). Official taxis can be very expensive, whereas unofficial ones are not necessarily safe – people do use them, but unpleasant incidents are not unknown. **Bike** rental in St Petersburg offers a pleasant way to see the city's quieter outer corners, but cycle in Moscow at your peril. As you make your way around the cities, know that the word "ulitsa" (street) is often abbreviated as "ul.", "pereulok" (lane) becomes "per.", "ploshchad" (square) becomes "pl.", and "naberezhnaya" (embankment) becomes "nab.".

ACCOMMODATION

Hostels tend to be safer, cleaner and more pleasant than cheap **hotels**, many of which have "economy" rooms unaltered since Soviet times. The standard rate is around R700–800 for a dorm bed for a night; aim to reserve three to four weeks in advance in the summer. Booking ahead by phone will guarantee you a bed for the night. Note that most places quote prices in rubles, while others prefer to keep their prices fixed in US dollars.

FOOD AND DRINK

Moscow and St Petersburg are bursting at the seams with cafés and restaurants covering everything from budget blowouts to *elitni* (elite) extravagance. Japanese is the favoured cuisine, so sushi abounds, but traditional Russian food is still at the heart of many locals' everyday diets. **National dishes** worth tasting include *borshch* (beetroot soup), *shchi* (cabbage soup) and *pirogi* (small pies stuffed with potato, cabbage or a kind of cottage cheese known as *tvorog*). Try these at one of the *stolovaya* (canteen-style) restaurants, such as *Dachniki* in St Petersburg (see p.936). Cheap *blini*, available from the ubiquitous and much-loved *Teremok* fast-food chain, subdivide into *blinchiki*, pancake wraps stuffed with meat or berries, and flat pancakes, served with honey, condensed milk, *smetana* (sour cream) or *krasnaya ikra* (red caviar). In summer, Russians go mad for *morozhenoe* (ice cream), sold at a fraction of the Western price.

DRINK

Vodka (*vódka*) is, of course, the national drink, knocked back in one gulp and chased with a bite on black bread or salted cucumber. **Beer** (*pivo*) is essential in summer; try Baltika (rated in strength from 3 to 9), Stariy Melnik or Nevskoe. Be sure to sample the excellent semi-sweet Georgian **wines** too (Khvanchkara was Stalin's favourite). For cheap eating and drinking, stock up at a *produkti* (small grocery shop), or at *rynki* (markets), scattered across both cities, though concentrated in the suburbs. These sell the full range of Russian dairy delights such as *kefir* (sour milk), plus salami, sausages and cheap fresh fruit and vegetables. Traditionally, breakfast is eaten between 7am and 9am and lunch between 1pm and 2pm; evening meals tend to be taken around 8pm.

28

CULTURE AND ETIQUETTE

Although the Western practice of eating out is now widespread, Russians love to entertain at home; if you're invited over, always bring a small present: men traditionally offer flowers while women bring chocolates. **Tipping** is the norm only at high-end eating and drinking establishments, with five to ten percent given as standard. In **churches**, women should cover their head and shoulders, and men in shorts may be refused entry; you'll also notice that locals avoid turning their back to the iconostasis that screens the altar. Russians are rather superstitious: you'll see people rubbing the noses of the dog statues at the Metro Ploshchad Revolyutsii in Moscow for good luck. Old-fashioned chivalry is alive and well, with men opening doors for women and offering to help with heavy lifting. You'll notice, too, that young people give up their seats to the elderly on public transport: follow their example before being told to.

Russia has a negative attitude towards homosexuality and, in 2013, passed a law banning any so-called "propaganda" supportive of "non-traditional" sexual orientations.

SPORTS AND ACTIVITIES

Spectator sports centre on **football**, with Moscow's biggest teams being Dinamo (Leningradskiy prospekt 36 ☏495 612 7172, ⓦfcdynamo.ru; ⓜDinamo) and Spartak (Luzhniki Stadium, Luzhnetskaya nab. 24 ☏495 637 0259, ⓦspartak.com; ⓜSportivnaya), while Petersburgers support Zenit (Petrovskiy stadium, 2nd Petrovskiy Island ☏812 535 4613, ⓦfc-zenit.ru; ⓜSportivnaya).

Skating is as much part of Russian culture as drinking vodka or eating *blinis*. Moscow has plenty of likely spots in winter, including the frozen-over paths at the vast Gorky Park (Krymskiy Val ul. 9; ⓜPark Kultury) or the smaller, more intimate Hermitage Garden at ul. Karetniy Ryad 3 (ⓦPushkinskaya). You can also skate year-round at the covered rink in Gorky Park. A great place for winter **sledging** in Moscow is on the Sparrow Hills (Vorobyovy Gory; ⓜUniversitet), where you can overlook Moscow State University, the largest of the city's collection of 1950s Stalinist-Gothic skyscrapers, collectively known as the "seven sisters". Summer or winter, **swim** in the open air at the Chayka (Turchaninov per. 3/1; ⓜPark Kultury), or Luzhniki (Luzhnetskaya nab. 24; ⓜsportivnaya) lidos. Cycling enthusiasts can see St Petersburg with a **bike tour** (Skatprokat Rent a Bike, Goncharnaya ul. 7 ⓦskatprokat.ru; ⓜPl. Vosstaniya). Alternatively, take a **guided walk** (Peter's Walking Tours, ⓦpeterswalk.com; R650 for 4–5hr).

COMMUNICATIONS

Most **post offices** are open Monday to Saturday 8am to 7pm, and blue postboxes are affixed to walls across both cities. However, local mail is slow and not particularly reliable, so for urgent letters use DHL. **Internet cafés** are abundant and cheap, and most hostels offer internet access and wi-fi for free, while virtually all cafés and restaurants also have **wi-fi**. For **international calls** get a pre-paid international phonecard such as the Zebra Telecom card or Evroset card, usable from any phone. Ask at a bank or telecoms kiosk for a *telefonnaya karta*. Non-Russian **mobiles** work on roaming via local providers, but you'll pay a fortune. You could also consider getting a local SIM card for R200–400 (bring your passport with you to buy one). Note that when calling a local number from a Russian mobile or landline you need to dial 8 before the number. However, if dialling from an international mobile the 8 is not necessary. Dial the country code +7 followed directly by the number.

28

EMERGENCY NUMBERS

Police ☏02; Ambulance ☏03; Fire ☏01. Moscow rescue service (for help with any incidents while holidaying in Moscow) ☏495 937 9911. You'll be connected to an English-speaking operator.

RUSSIAN

	RUSSIAN	PRONUNCIATION
Yes	да	Da
No	нет	Nyet
Please	пожалуйста	Pazháaloosta
Thank you	спасибо	Spaséeba
Hello/Good day	здравствуйте	Zdrávstweetye
Goodbye	до свидания	Da svidáaneya
Excuse me	извините	Izvinéetye
Sorry	простите	Prostitye
Where?	где?	Gdye?
Good/Bad	хороший/плохой	Khoróshee/Plokhóy
Near/Far	близко/далеко	Bléezki/Dalyekó
Cheap/Expensive	дешевый/дорогой	Deshóvy/Daragóy
Open/Closed	открыто/закрыто	Otkryto/Zakryto
Today	сегодня	Sevódnya
Yesterday	вчера	Vcherá
Tomorrow	завтра	Závtra
How much is...?	сколько стоит...?	Skólka stóyit...?
What time is it?	Который час?	Katóree chass?
I don't understand	я не понимаю	Ya ne ponimáyou
Do you speak English?	вы говорите по-английски?	Vwee gavoréetye po angliyski?
Where are the toilets?	где туалет?	Gdye tualyét?
My name is...	меня зовут...	Menyá zavóot...
What is your name?	как вас зовут?	Kak vas zavóot?
I don't speak Russian	я не говорю по-русски	Ya nye gavaryóo pa-róosski
Can I have....	можно...	Mózhna...
Tea	чай	Chay
Beer	пиво	Péeva
Juice	сок	Sok
I am a vegetarian	я вегетарианец	Ya vegetariyánets
The bill, please	счет пожалуйста	Shchyot, pazhálooista
Men's toilet (often seen as M)	мужчины	Moózhshini
Women's toilet (often seen as Ж)	женщины	Zhénshini
Breakfast	завтрак	Závtrak
One	один	Adéen
Two	два	Dva
Three	три	Tree
Four	четыре	Chetéeri
Five	пять	Pyat
Six	шесть	Shest
Seven	семь	Syeem
Eight	восемь	Vósyem
Nine	девять	Déyvyat
Ten	десять	Déysyat

EMERGENCIES

Beware of **petty crime**, particularly pickpockets in the metro and in bus and train stations during rush hour. Don't leave valuables in your hotel room. If you are dark-skinned exercise extra caution, especially at night, as racist attacks are not unknown. Your embassy will be able to advise you on what to do if you get robbed. The **police** (полиция) wear blue-grey uniforms; always make sure you have photocopies of your passport, visa,

STUDENT AND YOUTH DISCOUNTS

"Foreigner prices" at museums and galleries are often steeper than for Russian citizens, though most museums offer tickets for foreign **students** which cost half or two-thirds of the full price. An ISIC card is your best bet, though other student cards often work too. Ask for *adeen studyencheskiy bilyet* (one student ticket) in your most authentic accent.

immigration card and registration on you, as they do stop people at random and often look for an excuse to fine you. When traversing busy roads, look for an underground crossing (*perekhod*/переход) as many drivers do not honour zebra crossings. High-street **pharmacies** (*aptéka*) offer many familiar medicines over the counter. Foreigners tend to rely on expensive **private clinics** for treatment, so travel insurance is essential. St Petersburg **water** may still contain the giardia parasite, which can cause severe diarrhoea – metranidazol is the cure and can be bought over the counter. The tap water of both cities contains high levels of heavy metals, so it's best to drink the bottled stuff.

INFORMATION

St Petersburg is well prepared for visitors, with numerous tourist offices dotted around town. The main Tourist Information Office (Sadovaya ul. 14; Nevsky prospekt) has plenty of maps and information in English. **Moscow** didn't get an official Tourist Information Office (Pl. Revolyutsii 2/3; Okotniy Ryad) until 2012. For up-to-the-minute restaurant and bar listings see the excellent *In Your Pocket* guide (inyourpocket .com/russia) which you can pick up at some hotels, as well as at restaurants catering to expats. Hostel and hotel receptions carry leaflets and maps, and you can get the latest bar, restaurant and entertainment listings and reviews from **English-language papers**. The *Moscow Times* and the more ponderously pro-Kremlin *Moscow News* are well established, while *Element* is directed at young city-dwellers (elementmoscow .ru). Find **maps** in English at bookshops like Dom Knigi (larger branches in Moscow at Tverskaya ul. 8/7; Tverskaya and ul. Novy Arbat 8; Arbatskaya).

A useful website with detailed practical advice is waytorussia.net.

MONEY AND BANKS

Russia's currency is the **ruble**, divided into 100 kopeks. There are coins of 1, 5, 10, 20 and 50 kopeks and 1, 2, 5 and 10 rubles, and notes of 10, 50, 100, 500, 1000 and 5000 rubles. Everything is paid for in rubles, although some hostels make a habit of citing prices in either euros or dollars. At the time of writing £1=R48, €1=R41 and US$1=R31. Only **change money** in an official bank or currency exchange. Most **exchange offices** are open Monday to Saturday 10am to 8pm or later, and **ATMs** are plentiful. In general, prices in both cities range from "New Russian" levels down to what the average local salary will cover, making many shops, bars and cafés affordable for the budget-conscious traveller.

OPENING HOURS AND HOLIDAYS

Most **shops** are open Monday to Saturday 10am to 8pm or later; Sunday hours are slightly shorter. **Museums** tend to open 9am to 5pm, with last ticket sales an hour before closing time, and they are invariably shut one day a week, with a day each month put aside for cleaning. **Churches** are accessible from 8am until the end of evening service. **Clubs** open late – many until 6am – or don't close at all, morphing into early-morning cafés.

Russian **public holidays** fall on the following dates: January 1 (New Year's Day) and 7 (Christmas), February 23 (Defender of the Motherland Day), March 8 (Women's Day), May 1 (Labour Day), May 9 (Victory Day), June 12 (Russia Day) and November 4 (Day of Popular Unity).

28

Moscow

Russia's capital, **MOSCOW** (Москва), is a modern, energetic city, but its chaotic spirit is never far beneath the surface: people bribe their way into nightclubs or out of scrapes with the law, supercars tussle for space with barely roadworthy wrecks and, come nightfall, the party mindset is truly no-holds-barred.

■ ACCOMMODATION	
Backpacker Ecohostel	5
Chillax	2
Da!	6
Godzillas	1
HM	7
iVan	3
Napoleon	4

A humble wooden town in the twelfth century, contemporary Moscow is Russia's Manhattan, with brash and opinionated locals, a "whatever, whenever" approach to retail and a startling contrast between its glitzy, cosmopolitan heart, catering to a well-heeled elite, and pockets of extreme poverty. For visitors, the city is, above all, an assault on the senses – spend 24 hours navigating its golden-domed churches, people-crushed subway, designer shops

DRINKING & NIGHTLIFE

Gogol	3
Gypsy	18
Kitayskiy Letchik Dzhao Dao	13
Krizis Zhanra	9
Liga Pap	4
Masterskaya	7
Propaganda	8
Solyanka	16

EATING

Art Lebedev	11
Jagganath	6
Khachapuri	2
Kvartira 44	10
Lyudi kak Lyudi	14
Mari Vanna	5
Mayak	12
Projektor	15
Sisters Grimm	1
Varenichnaya Pobeda	17

28

▼ Kolomenskoe & Domodedovo Airport

and cliquey nightspots, and you'll need another 24 to recover.

WHAT TO SEE AND DO

Moscow's centre is compact enough to explore on foot, with the general **layout** a series of concentric circles and radial lines emanating from Red Square and the Kremlin. You can map the city's principal sights as strata of its history: the old Muscovy that Russians are eager to show; the now retro-chic Soviet-era sites such as VDNKh and Lenin's Mausoleum; and the exclusive restaurants and shopping malls that mark out the "New Russia".

Every visitor to Moscow is irresistibly drawn to **Red Square**, the historic and spiritual heart of the city. The name (*Krasnaya ploshchad*) derives from *krasniy*, the old Russian word for beautiful. The Lenin Mausoleum squats beneath the ramparts of the **Kremlin** and, facing it, sprawls **GUM**: the State Department Store in Soviet times, it is now devoted to costly fashion outlets. At the southwest end stands the incomparable St Basil's Cathedral. Opposite it you'll find the Historical Museum, directly behind which a golden circle on the ground marks Moscow's Kilometre Zero. In front of St Basil's Cathedral is the fenced-off Lobnoe Mesto (Place of Executions) where Ivan the Terrible and Peter the Great presided over public beheadings and hangings during their respective reigns.

The Lenin Mausoleum and Kremlin wall

In post-Communist Russia, the **Lenin Mausoleum**, which houses Vladimir Ilyich Ulianov's embalmed corpse (Tues–Thurs & Sat 10am–1pm; free; ⓦlenin.ru; queue at the Alexander Gardens entrance to Red Square), can be seen as either an awkward reminder of the old days or a cherished relic. Descend past stony-faced guards into the dimly lit chasm where the leader's body lies. Stopping or giggling will earn you stern rebukes. Behind the Mausoleum, the **Kremlin wall** – 19m high and 6.5m thick – contains a **mass grave** of Bolsheviks who perished during the battle for Moscow in 1917. The ashes of an array of luminaries, including writer Maxim Gorky and the first man in space, Yuri Gagarin, are here too. Beyond lie the graves of a select group of Soviet leaders, each with his own bust; Stalin still gets the most flowers.

St Basil's Cathedral

With its multicoloured onion domes silhouetted against the skyline where Red Square slopes down towards the Moskva River, **St Basil's Cathedral** (daily 11am–5pm; R250, student R150; ⓦsaintbasil.ru) is perhaps the most instantly recognisable symbol of Russia. The exterior is far more impressive than the interior, however, which consists of a stone warren of small chapels and souvenir stalls. Built in 1561 to celebrate Ivan the Terrible's capture of the Tatar stronghold of Kazan in 1552, its name commemorates St Basil the Blessed, who foretold the fire that swept through Moscow in 1547.

The Kremlin

Brooding and glittering in the heart of the capital, the **Kremlin** (Aleksandrovsky Sad; Fri–Wed 10am–5pm; R350, student R100; ⓦkreml.ru; ⓜBorovitskaya) is both the heart of historical Moscow and home to its present-day parliament, the Duma. Its founding is attributed to Prince Yuriy Dolgorukiy, who built a wooden fort here in about 1147. Look out for the **Tsar Cannon**, cast in 1586: one of the largest

KREMLIN ETIQUETTE

You may only purchase **tickets** for the set entry times to the Armoury and the Diamond Fund an hour before the session; Soviet-style bureaucracy prevents you from purchasing a ticket in advance. Even if you are in possession of a ticket, you will still have to queue for both attractions separately and watch tour groups and people with connections being ushered in before you. It's all part of the experience..

★ TREAT YOURSELF

Get the city grit out of your skin at the exquisitely elaborate **Sandunovsky baths** (Neglinnaya ul. 14 bldg 83–7 Ⓦsanduny.ru; ⓂKuznetskiy Most), patronized by Muscovites since 1896. Join Russian businessmen and socialites in the *banya*, a wooden hut heated with a furnace, where you are invited to sweat out impurities, get beaten energetically with birch twigs, and finally plunge into ice-cold water. Men's and women's baths are separate, with the women's section more like a modern spa. A three-hour session costs R1300. Daily 8am–10pm.

---

cannons ever made, and intended to defend the Saviour Gate, it has never been fired. Close by looms the earthbound, broken **Tsar Bell**, the largest bell in the world, cast in 1655. **Cathedral Square** is the historic heart of the Kremlin, dominated by the magnificent, white **Ivan the Great Bell Tower**. Of the square's four key churches, the most important is the **Cathedral of the Assumption**, with a spacious, light and echoing interior, walls and pillars smothered with icons and frescoes, and temporary exhibitions housed in its belfry. The **Cathedral of the Archangel** houses the tombs of Russia's rulers from Grand Duke Ivan I to Tsar Ivan V, while the golden-domed **Cathedral of the Annunciation** hides some of Russia's finest icons, including works by Theophanes the Greek and Andrey Rublev.

The Armoury Chamber

The unmissable **Armoury Chamber** (ticketed entry at 10am, noon, 2.30pm and 4.30pm; R700, student R200), inside the Kremlin, boasts a staggering array of treasures, among them the tsars' coronation robes, jewellery and armour. A separate part of the Armoury Chamber houses the **Diamond Fund** (ticketed entry Fri–Wed at twenty-minute intervals 10am–1pm and 2–5pm; R500) – a priceless collection of jewels, it includes the 190-karat Orlov Diamond which belonged to Catherine the Great, and the world's largest sapphire.

The Museum of Modern History

The **Museum of Modern History** at Tverskaya ul. 21 (Tues, Wed & Fri 10am–6pm, Thurs, Sat & Sun 11am–7pm, closed last Fri of the month; R250; Ⓦsovr.ru; ⓂTverskaya) brings the Communist past alive with striking displays of Soviet propaganda posters, photographs and state gifts, although there's a frustrating lack of English translation.

The Pushkin Museum of Fine Arts

Founded in 1898 in honour of the famous Russian poet, the **Pushkin Museum of Fine Arts** at Volkhonka ul. 12 (Tues–Sun 10am–7pm, Thurs until 9pm; R400, student R200, separate fee for Impressionist wing; Ⓦarts-museum.ru; ⓂKropotkinskaya) holds a hefty collection of **European paintings**, from Italian High Renaissance works to Rembrandt, and an outstanding display of Impressionist works.

Cathedral of Christ the Saviour

Built as a symbol of gratitude to divinity for having aided the Russians' defeat of Napoleon in 1812, the **Cathedral of Christ the Saviour** (daily 10am–6pm; Ⓦxxc.ru; ⓂKropotkinskaya), opposite the Pushkin Museum of Fine Arts at Volkhonka ul. 15, was demolished in 1931 in favour of a monument to socialism. The project was soon abandoned; years later, under Khrushchev's rule, the site was turned into the world's largest public swimming pool. In 1994 the Cathedral was rebuilt and is now a symbol of Moscow's (and Russia's) post-Communist religious revival.

House-Museums

Admirers of Bulgakov, Chekhov, Gorky, Tolstoy and Stanislavsky will find their former homes preserved as museums. Anton Chekhov lived at Sadovaya-Kudrinskaya ul. 6, in what is now the **Chekhov House-Museum** (Tues & Sat 11am–6pm, Wed & Fri 2–8pm, Thurs 2–9pm; R100, student R60; ⓂBarrikadnaya), containing humble personal effects, while the **Gorky House-Museum** (Wed–Sun

28

11am–5.30pm, closed last Thurs of the month; free; ⓂArbatskaya) on the corner of Povarskaya ulitsa and ulitsa Spiridonovka is worth seeing purely for its raspberry-pink Art Nouveau decor. Leo Tolstoy admirers should head to the wonderfully preserved **Tolstoy Memorial Estate** on ul. Lva Tolstogo 21 (Tues, Wed, Fri & Sun 11am–6pm, Thurs noon–8pm, closed last Fri of the month; R200, student R100; ⓂPark Kultury) where the Tolstoy family lived after moving to Moscow from their country estate in 1881, and where the novelist wrote *War and Peace*. The **Bulgakov Museum**, at Bolshaya Sadovaya ul. 10 (daily 1–11pm, Fri & Sat until 1am; free; ⓂMayakovskaya), is the house where the novelist lived from 1921 to 1924. There are nightly tours (1–6am; R1000; Russian only). Thespians should not miss the **Stanislavsky House-Museum** (Wed & Fri noon–7pm, Thurs, Sat & Sun 11am–6pm; R120, student R40; ⓂTverskaya) at Leontyevskiy per. 6, where the renowned theatre director and founder of the Moscow Arts Theatre Constantin Stanislavsky once lived with his wife and children. Stanislavsky transformed his house into a makeshift theatre, with regular performances taking place in the main hall, while the adjoining dining area served as a make-up studio and held furniture for rehearsals.

Patriarch's Ponds
One of Moscow's most exclusive neighbourhoods, **Patriarch's Ponds** (ⓂTverskaya) is a pleasant spot for a summer stroll or an ice-skate on its frozen waters in the depths of winter – note that there's just one pond, despite the name. The area is also known for being the location of the opening scene of Mikhail Bulgakov's magical realist novel *T he Master and Margarita*.

Novodevichiy Convent
A cluster of domes shining above a fortified rampart belongs to the lovely **Novodevichiy Convent** (Wed–Mon 10am–5.30pm, closed first Mon of month; R150, student R60; Ⓦshm.ru; ⓂSportivnaya), founded by Ivan the

Terrible in 1524. At its heart stands the white Cathedral of the Virgin of Smolensk. In its **cemetery** lie numerous famous writers, musicians and artists, including Gogol, Chekhov, Stanislavsky, Bulgakov and Shostakovich.

The Tretyakov Gallery
Founded in 1892 by the financier Pavel Tretyakov, the **Tretyakov Gallery** at Lavrushinskiy per. 10 (Tues–Sun 10am–6pm, Thurs & Fri until 9pm; R360, student R220; Ⓦtretyakovgallery .ru; ⓂTretyakovskaya) displays an outstanding collection of pre-Revolutionary Russian art. Icons are magnificently displayed, and the exhibition continues through to the late nineteenth century, with the politically charged canvases of the iconic realist Ilya Repin and the Impressionist portraits of Valentin Serov, including *The Girl with Peaches*, one of the gallery's masterpieces.

The Tretyakov Gallery at Krymskiy Val
Opposite the entrance to Gorky Park at Krymskiy Val 10, the **Tretyakov Gallery at Krymskiy Val** (Tues–Sun 10am–7.30pm, Thurs until 10pm; R360, student R220; Ⓦtretyakovgallery.ru; ⓂPark Kultury) takes a breakneck gallop through twentieth-century Russian art, from the avant-garde of the 1910s and 20s to contemporary artists. Full and illuminating commentary in English is a bonus.

Gorky Park
Gorky Park on ul. Krymskiy Val (ⓂPark Kultury) is a large park occupying an area of 300 acres along the river. In the winter the frozen-over paths become one of the city's largest ice rinks, while in the summer Muscovites stroll the area savouring an ice cream. The park underwent major renovations in 2011 and now hosts contemporary art projects, design fairs and even has free wi-fi access. You can rent bikes, rollerblades and paddle boats in the warmer months.

VDNKh
To see Soviet triumphalism at its most prolific, visit the Exhibition of

Economic Achievements, or **VDNKh** (Ⓦvvcentre.ru; ⓂVDNKh), with its statue upon statue of ordinary workers in heroic poses. Adding to the scene is the permanent exhibition centre – host to everything from fairs and festivals to concerts and congresses – housed in the grandiose Stalinist architecture of the All-Union Agricultural Exhibition of 1939, and the People's Friendship Fountain, flanked by Soviet maidens, each symbolizing a Soviet republic. One of the most hubristic Soviet monuments ever built is the **Space Obelisk**, which bears witness to Soviet designs on the stratosphere. Unveiled in 1964 – three years after Gagarin orbited the earth – it's a sculpture of a rocket blasting nearly 100m into the sky on a plume of energy clad in shining titanium. The giant Ferris wheel, small amusement park and numerous food vendors help to create a fairground-like atmosphere. For a fantastic view over the VDNKh, take the lift to the 25th floor of *Hotel Cosmos* across Prospekt Mira.

ARRIVAL AND DEPARTURE

By plane Flights from Western Europe arrive either at Sheremetyevo, 30km north of the centre, or Domodedovo, 45km to the south. Aeroexpress trains run between Shremetyevo and Belorusskiy station, connected to ⓂBelorusskaya, on the green and brown lines (every 30min 5am–12.30am; 35min; R320). Trains to and from Domodedovo serve Paveletsky station (every 30min 6am–midnight; 50min; R320) which is connected to ⓂPaveletskaya; shuttle buses run between Domodedovo and ⓂDomodedovskaya (every 15min 6am–midnight, hourly midnight–6am; 30min; R120), 20km south of the centre.
By train All mainline stations are conveniently located by a metro station. Trains from Vilnius and Warsaw arrive at Belorusskiy station (Belorusskiy vokzal, Tverskaya Zastava pl. 7; ⓂBelorusskaya) while Rizhsky station (Rizhsky vokzal, Rizhskaya pl. 79/3; ⓂRizhskaya) serves Latvian destinations such as Rīga. Leningradskaya station (Leningradsky vokzal, Komsomolskaya pl. 3; ⓂKomsomolskaya) is the departure point for frequent trains to St Petersburg; Kievsky station (Kievsky vokzal, Kievskogo vokzala pl. 2; ⓂKievskaya) is the final destination for trains from Kiev and Odessa, while Yaroslavsky station (Yaroslavsky vokzal, Komsomolskaya pl. 5; ⓂKomsomolskaya) is the starting point for trans-Siberian adventures.

28

> **MOSCOW ONLINE**
> Ⓦ**a-a-ah.com** Plenty of information on Moscow's best sights, as well as events calendars with concerts, performances and films.
> Ⓦ**kultura.mos.ru** Moscow's tourist information portal.
> Ⓦ**moscowfreetour.com** Sign up here for free guided tours of the city.

Destinations Helsinki (1 daily; 14hr); Rīga (1 daily; 16hr); St Petersburg (standard service: 13 daily; 7–9hr; Sapsan express: up to 5 daily; 4hr); Tallinn (1 daily; 15hr 30min); Vilnius (1 daily; 14hr); Warsaw (1 daily; 17hr 30min).
By bus Ecolines buses from Germany and the Baltic States terminate at Leningradskiy pr. 37/6 (near ⓂDinamo), 6km north of the city centre, or Rizhsky Station (ⓂRizhskaya), 8km to the north. Moscow's main bus station with intercity departures is at Uralskaya ul. 2 (ⓂShcholkovskaya), 16km northeast of the city centre. Most long-distance foreign destinations require a change at Rīga.
Destinations Vilnius (1 daily; 15hr); Rīga (1 daily; 14hr 30min); St Petersburg (21 daily; 10–12hr).

INFORMATION

Tourist office The tourist office is located just north of Red Square at Pl. Revolyutsii 2/3 (Mon, Wed & Fri–Sun 10am–6pm, Thurs 11am–9pm; ⓂPloshchad Revolyutsii). There is a 24/7 hotline (☎800 220 0001 free within Russia or ☎495 663 1393, Ⓦtravel2moscow.com) that provides visitors with information on major sights and attractions in English.

GETTING AROUND

By bus Buses cost R30 per journey; stops are marked with yellow signs.
By metro With its Soviet mosaics, murals and statuary, Moscow's metro (5.30am–1am) is world-famous and is by far the best way to get around, given the city's congested roads. Stations are marked with a large "M" and you can plan your journey on Ⓦmetroway.ru. A one-way fare costs R30; you can also buy a card of five (R150) or eleven (R300) journeys (ask at the *kassa* for *pyat/odinnatsat póezdok*).
By minibus *Marshrutki* are cheap (around R30 a journey). They wait to fill up with passengers, then take the route advertised on the side. You can ask to get out at any point. Pay the driver on board.
By tram and trolleybus Moscow's terrible traffic means trolleybuses and trams are often at a standstill, although they can at times be useful to tackle a major road such as the Garden Ring. Stops have blue-and-white signs. Most routes operate from 5am to 1am; fares cost R30 on board; the same tickets are used for buses.

ACCOMMODATION

HOSTELS

Backpacker Ecohostel Starosadsky per. 5/8 bldg.3 ☎ 916 535 5727, ⓦ backpacker-hostel.ru; ⓜ Kitay-gorod/ Chistye Prudy. Moscow's first sustainable hostel is spotlessly clean and all dorms have lockers and shared bathrooms. There's Soviet paraphernalia for sale, too. Dorm R550, double R2400

Chillax 2-y Kolobovskiy per. 9/2 ☎ 495 620 5959, ⓦ chillax-hostels.com; ⓜ Trubnaya. The dorms at this small friendly hostel can get a bit cramped, and the intimate bathrooms may be a bit much for some, but staff are helpful. Events are organized for guests, from parties to games nights. No privates. Dorm R550

Da! Arbat 11, 4th floor ☎ 495 691 5577, ⓦ da-hostel.ru; ⓜ Arbatskaya. This large hostel set over two floors offers two spacious living areas with beanbags and PlayStation, kitchen amenities and wi-fi throughout. Rooms are on the small side, but the great location on a bustling pedestrianized street makes up for it. Dorm R650, double R2900

★**Godzillas** Bolshoi Karetniy 6 ☎ 495 699 4223, ⓦ godzillashostel.com; ⓜ Tsvetnoy bulvar/Tverskaya. Relaxed, popular hostel a short walk from the centre. Rooms are pleasantly decorated with quirky wallpaper, minimalist furniture and parquet floors. Helpful staff provide lots of Moscow information. Dorm US$28, double US$75

HM Maly Afanasyevskiy per. 1/33 ☎ 495 778 8501, ⓦ hostel-moscow.com; ⓜ Arbatskaya. Quiet little hostel smack in the centre of town, with just three dorms (two single-sex, one mixed). There's also a kitchen, living area, free laundry and wi-fi. Dorm R800

iVan Petrovsky per. 1/30-1, apt.23 ☎ 916 407 1178, ⓦ ivanhostel.com; ⓜ Chekhovskaya. Clean hostel located just off swanky ul. Petrovka with free morning coffee, all-day tea and single-sex dorms with lockers. There is an annexe with similar amenities in the building next door. Dorm R750, double R2500

Napoleon Maly Zlatoustinskiy per. 2, 4th floor ☎ 495 628 6695, ⓦ napoleonhostel.com; ⓜ Kitay-gorod. Standards have dropped at what was once Moscow's best hostel, but staff remain as friendly as ever and it's in an excellent location to sample the city's nightlife. There's a small lounge area with TV, as well as a kitchen for guests' use; staff take care of laundry at an extra cost. Dorm R650, double R2500

EATING

Take advantage of the great-value business lunches offered by cafés and restaurants during the week between noon and 4pm.

CANTEENS AND CAFÉS

Art Lebedev Bol. Nikitskaya 35; ⓜ Arbatskaya. This itty-bitty café attracts a literary crowd. Come for light breakfasts (R170) and salads (R230), or more substantia dishes such as *vareniki* (Ukrainian dumplings with cheese, potatoes or cherries; R270) and home-made *pelmeni* (meat dumplings; R310). Daily 8.30am–11pm.

Jagganath Kuznetskiy most 11; ⓜ Kuznetskiy Most. Make your way through a little health-food shop to get to this veggie canteen. Fresh salads and soups (both from R80), curries and light cakes make a nice change from the carb-heavy and dairy dishes found elsewhere in the city. Mon–Fri 8am–11pm, Sat & Sun 10am–11pm.

★**Khachapuri** B. Gnezdnikovskiy 10 ⓦ hacha.ru; ⓜ Tverskaya. Some of the city's tastiest Georgian grub is served at this cosy and inexpensive café, with live piano recitals laid on in the evenings. The exquisite meat *khinkali* (large dumplings; R80) and the *khachapuri* (bread oozing with melted cheese; R120) are unmissable. Superb-value business lunches (R210–500). Mon–Fri 10am–11pm, Sat & Sun from 11am.

Lyudi kak Lyudi Solyanskiy Tupik 1/4 ⓦ ludikakludi .com; ⓜ Kitay-gorod. Small café with a cosy wine cellar feel. Feast on tasty sandwiches (R150) and pies (R130) as well as more substantial dishes like lasagne (R120), washed down with a freshly prepared juice (R130). Daily 8am–11pm, Fri & Sat until 6am.

Varenichnaya Pobeda Arbat 29; ⓜ Arbatskaya. This café-cum-restaurant, decorated with all manner of Soviet knick-knacks, rustles up over 90kg of exquisite handmade *vareniki* (Ukrainian dumplings; R150) every day. Daily 10am–midnight.

RESTAURANTS

Kvartira 44 Bol. Nikitskaya 22/2; ⓜ Arbatskaya. Wooden furniture and crimson decor give this place an intimate, Parisian feel. Live piano music on Fri nights. Mains from R320. Daily noon–2am, Fri & Sat until 4am.

★ TREAT YOURSELF

Mari Vanna Spiridonevskiy per. 10a ☎ 495 650 65 00, ⓦ marivanna.ru; ⓜ Tverskaya. Set out like a 1960s Soviet flat, with mock black-and-white TV, floral decor and old-world memorabilia, this expat favourite is a great little place to savour traditional Russian dishes. The exquisite *borshch* soup (R450) is presented at the table with a little fanfare, and the home-made meat *pelmeni* (R650) are just superb. Make sure to try the cherry *vareniki* for dessert (dumplings; R270). Roaming pets add to the welcoming homely atmosphere, as does the doorbell you need to ring upon arrival. Daily 9am–midnight.

★ **Mayak** Bol. Nikitskaya 19; ⓜ Arbatskaya. With its heavy furnishings, parquet floors and an old-school piano this popular restaurant located above a theatre is set out like an oversized Soviet drawing room. The crowd, a mix of foreigners and bohemian Muscovites, ensures a convivial vibe, and the beef stroganoff (R490) is reliably good. Daily noon–6am.

★ **Projektor** Slavyanskaya pl. 2/5; ⓜ Kitay-gorod. This hip addition to Moscow's dining and nightlife scene serves an array of beautifully presented international dishes at knockdown prices. It does a fantastic cocktail too – sit back in one of the partitioned sofa areas and choose from a 40-strong list, with the Apple Jack (R380) and Crusoe-inspired Robinson (R450) particularly good. Resident DJs liven things up with funky jazz music on Fri and Sat from 10pm. Daily 24hr.

Sisters Grimm Stoleshnikov per. 11; ⓜ Teatralnaya. Tucked away in a courtyard, this quiet little place is a perfect spot for a bite before heading to its next-door neighbour *Gogol* (see below) until the early hours. The international menu includes big juicy burgers (R325) as well as lighter meals such as salads (R190) and soups (R240). Mon–Fri noon–midnight, Sat & Sun until 2am.

DRINKING AND NIGHTLIFE

Moscow's famous nightlife is marred by the practice of "face control", excluding the not-so-beautiful people from *elitni* clubs. The venues listed here are largely accessible. There are scores of trendy bars and clubs on Krasny Oktyabr (Red October), previously the site of a chocolate factory, located across the river from ⓜ Kropotkinskaya and now home to some of Moscow's hippest nightlife.

BARS

Gogol Stoleshnikov per. 11 ⓦ gogolclubs.ru; ⓜ Teatralnaya. Fun, friendly and good-value place hosting edgy bands (gigs R200–1000). It's best in summer when you can savour grilled *shashlik* in the courtyard at the back, and sip a cocktail or two (R210–330). Daily noon–5am.

Kitayskiy Letchik Dzhao Dao Lubyanskiy proezd 25/12 ⓦ jao-da.ru; ⓜ Kitay-gorod. Descend to this artfully scuffed-up basement labyrinth, which hosts some outstanding alternative bands at weekends (R200–500). Mon–Thurs 11am–6am, Fri & Sat noon–8am, Sun noon–6am.

Liga Pap Bolshaya Lubyanka 24 ⓦ ligapap.ru; ⓜ Turgenevskaya. It's a sports bar at heart, but this place attracts a decidedly hip crowd. The large projector and array of plasma TVs dotted around the faux-vaulted brick and wooden interior means you won't miss any of the action. Beer by the pint costs from R150. Daily 24hr.

CLUBS

Note that all the venues listed below act as a café by day, restaurant in the early evening, and both bar and club at night. All have free entry unless otherwise stated.

Gypsy Bolotnaya nab. 3/4, Krasny Oktyabr ⓦ bargipsy.ru; ⓜ Kropotkinskaya. This trendy club with an eclectic mix of decor and music attracts crowds of Muscovites who revel nightly on the rooftop terrace. There's pretty strict face control so make sure you look the part. Daily noon–6pm.

Krizis Zhanra Pokrovka 16/16, bldg. 1 ⓦ kriziszhanra.ru; ⓜ Kitay-gorod. Peer over the split-level balcony of this popular indie haunt at expats and Russians alike stomping around to 90s classics. Live bands, too. Mon–Fri 11.30am–5am, Sat & Sun 11am–6am.

Masterskaya Treatralny Proezd 3, bldg.3 ⓦ mstrsk.ru; ⓜ Lubyanka. Alternative club that attracts a young bohemian crowd. Live concerts at weekends (R100–800). Daily noon–6am.

Propaganda Bolshoy Zlatoustinsky per. 7 ⓦ propagandamoscow.com; ⓜ Kitay-gorod. With this popular club's bare brick walls and bright lights, you might be backstage at a Hollywood film set. Mild face control so best to book a table for dinner to ensure entry. Gay nights on Sun. Daily noon–6am.

★ **Solyanka** Solyanka 11/6 ⓦ s-11.ru; ⓜ Kitay-gorod. Stylish club that attracts renowned house and electro DJs. Alcoholic drinks start at around R250. Free entry before 11pm, R500 after. Mon–Fri 10am–6am, Sat & Sun 11am–6am.

ENTERTAINMENT

Theatre, classical music and ballet all have superb vintages in Russia and won't necessarily break the bank, provided you ask for the cheapest ticket available (*samiy deshoviy bilyet*).

LIVE MUSIC

B2 Bolshaya Sadovaya 8 ⓦ b2club.ru; ⓜ Mayakovskaya. With a capacity of 2000 people, B2 is a staple venue on the live music scene, with a variety of bands playing anything from jazz to ska music. Thurs & Sun R400 after 8pm, Fri & Sat R600 after 8pm, free beforehand. Concert admission from R300. Daily noon–6am.

Tchaikovsky Concert Hall Triumfalnaya pl. 4/31 ⓦ meloman.ru; ⓜ Mayakovskaya. Soak in some classical music at Moscow's premier musical venue. The hall has excellent acoustics and hosts all manner of performances, from soloist acts to symphony orchestras. Tickets start at R100.

THEATRE

Bolshoi Theatre Teatralnaya pl. 1 ⓦ bolshoi.ru; ⓜ Teatralnaya. The sumptuous, recently renovated theatre is home to the world's most famous ballet and regularly stages operas and operettas. Tickets from R2500.

CINEMA

The cinemas listed below screen films in their original language.

28

28

35MM Pokrovka 47/24 ⓦ kino35mm.ru; ⓜ Chistye Prudy. Specializes in independent foreign films.

Dome Cinema Olimpiyskiy pr. 18/1 ⓦ domecinema.ru; ⓜ Prospekt Mira. Latest blockbuster films as well as occasional independent screenings.

Rolan Cinema Chistoprudny Boulevard 12a ⓦ 5zvezd.ru; ⓜ Chistye Prudy. Art-house films – mainly new classics – and festival screenings.

SHOPPING

Dorogomilovsky Market Mozhaisky Val 10; ⓜ Kievskaya. Plenty of fresh produce on offer, including cheeses, meats, fish and seafood as well as an excellent selection of fruit and veg. Daily 8am–8pm.

Vernissage at Izmaylovo Izmailovskoye shosse 73; ⓜ Partizanskaya. Open-air market with Moscow's best (and cheapest) Soviet paraphernalia and memorabilia including coins, fur hats, *matrioshka* dolls, Soviet posters and postcards. In winter make sure you get there before 3pm. It is open daily but you're best going at weekends 9am–6pm when there are more stalls.

DIRECTORY

Embassies Australia, Podkolokolny per. 10a/2 ☎ 495 956 6070, ⓜ Kitay-gorod; Canada, Starokonyushenny per. 23 ☎ 495 925 6000, ⓜ Kropotkinskaya; Ireland, Grokholski per. 5 ☎ 495 937 5911, ⓜ Prospekt Mira; New Zealand, Povarskaya 44 ☎ 495 956 3579, ⓜ Barrikadnaya; UK, Smolenskaya nab.10 ☎ 495 956 7200, ⓜ Smolenskaya; US, Novinskiy bulvar 19 ☎ 495 728 5577, ⓜ Smolenskaya.

Health European Medical Center, Spiridonovskiy per. 1 ☎ 495 933 6655, ⓦ emcmos.ru, ⓜ Tverskaya; ZAO International Medical Clinic, 31 Grokholskiy per. 31, 10th floor ☎ 495 937 5760, ⓦ sosclinic.ru, ⓜ Prospekt Mira. Both recognized by international insurance companies.

Internet Centre Internet Club, Kuznetskiy Most 12, ⓜ Kuznetskiy most (Mon–Fri 9am–midnight, Sat & Sun from 10am; R90/hr).

Pharmacies 24hr pharmacies at Stariy Arbat 15, ⓜ Arbatskaya and at Tverskaya ul. 11, ⓜ Okotniy Ryad.

Post offices Main Post Office, Tverskaya 7, ⓜ Tverskaya (Mon–Fri 8am–1pm & 2–8pm, Sat 9am–1pm & 2–6pm). Express postal service: DHL, Tverskaya ul. 3, ⓦ dhl.ru; ⓜ Okotniy Ryad.

St Petersburg

ST PETERSBURG (Санкт-Петербург), Petrograd, Leningrad and St Petersburg again – the city's succession of names mirrors Russia's turbulent history. Founded in 1703 by **Peter the Great** as

a "window in the West", self-assured, future-focused St Petersburg still retains more of a Western European feel than Moscow more than three hundred years on. A sophisticated capital of the tsarist Empire, the cradle of the Communist Revolution of 1917, and a symbol of Russian stoicism due to the city's heroic endurance of a three-year Nazi siege during World War II, present-day St Petersburg has eased into modernity without sacrificing any of its old-world magnificence and charm, with shopping malls and nightclubs sitting alongside opulent palaces. The pace of life here is relaxed, and the people are more open and laidback than their Muscovite counterparts. The best **time to visit** is during the midsummer White Nights (mid-June to mid-July), when darkness never falls, and the partying can reach fever pitch. From May to October all bridges across the River Neva are raised from 1am to 5am – a beautiful sight, best experienced from a boat.

WHAT TO SEE AND DO

St Petersburg's centre lies on the south bank of the Neva, with the curving River Fontanka marking its southern boundary. The area within the Fontanka is riven by a series of avenues fanning out from the golden spire of the Admiralty on the Neva's south bank. Many of the city's top sights are located on and around **Nevsky prospekt**, the backbone and heart of the city for the last three centuries, stretching from the Alexander Nevsky Monastery to Palace Square. Across the Neva is **Vasilevskiy Island**, home to the Kuntskamera, while over the Birzhevoy Bridge lies the Peter and Paul Fortress. To the east of the centre, beyond the River Fontanka, lies the **Smolniy Institute**, where the Bolsheviks fomented revolution in 1917.

The Winter Palace and Hermitage

Sited on the banks of the River Neva, the 200m-long Baroque **Winter Palace** is the city's largest and most opulent, and was the official residence of the tsars, their court and 1500 servants until the revolution of 1917. Today the building houses one of the world's greatest museums, the **Hermitage** (Tues–Sun 10.30am–6pm, Wed until 9pm; R400, free to students, free admission first Thurs of every month; ⓦhermitagemuseum.org; ⓜAdmiralteyskaya), launched as Russia's first public art museum in 1852. The Hermitage collection embraces over three million treasures and works of art, from ancient Scythian gold and giant malachite urns to Cubist pieces. After the elaborately decorated staterooms and the Gold Collection, the most popular section covers modern European art from the nineteenth and twentieth centuries, with an array of works by Picasso, Gauguin, Van Gogh, Rodin, Monet and Renoir.

Kazan Cathedral

Curving **Kazan Cathedral** (daily 9am–6pm; ⓜNevsky prospekt), built between 1801 and 1811, was modelled on St Peter's in Vatican City and is unique in die-straight St Petersburg. The cathedral was built to house a venerated icon, Our Lady of Kazan, reputed to have appeared miraculously overnight in Kazan in 1579 and later transferred to St Petersburg, where it resided until its disappearance in 1904. In Soviet times the cathedral housed the Museum of Atheism, dedicated to proving that "religion is the opium of the people". Today it teems once more with worshippers.

The Church of the Saviour on the Spilled Blood

The multicoloured, onion-domed **Church on Spilled Blood** at 26 Kanala Groboedova embankment (Thurs–Tues 11am–7pm, last entry 6pm; R250, student R150; ⓦcathedral.ru; ⓜNevsky prospekt) was built in 1882 on the very spot where Tsar Alexander II was assassinated by student radicals a year earlier. With a stunning mosaic-covered interior, the church is one of St Petersburg's most striking landmarks, quite unlike the dominant Neoclassical architecture.

The Russian Museum

The Mikhailovsky Palace, worth a visit for its beautifully decorated rooms alone, houses the main part of the **Russian Museum** (4 Inzhenernaya ul.; Mon 10am–5pm, Wed & Fri–Sun until 6pm, Thurs 1–9pm; R220, student R50; ⓦrusmuseum.ru; ⓜGostiny dvor). Its collection of Russian art is the world's finest, ranging from fourteenth-century icons to the particularly impressive avant-garde collection from the early twentieth century in the Benois Wing.

The Summer Garden

Most popular of all St Petersburg's public gardens is the **Summer Garden** (Wed–Sun 10am–8pm; ⓦrusmuseum.ru; ⓜGostiny dvor) on Kutuzov Embankment, commissioned by Peter the Great in 1704 and rebuilt by Catherine the Great in the informal English style that survives today. Also charming are the Mikhailovsky Gardens behind the Russian Museum (May–Sept daily 10am–10pm, rest of the year until 8pm, closed in April; same website), and Marsovo Pole (the Field of Mars) on the other side of the River Moyka where a flame burns for the fallen of the Revolution and civil war (1917–21).

The Admiralty and Decembrists' Square

The **Admiralty**, perched at the northwestern end of Nevsky prospect (ⓜAdmiralteyskaya), was founded in 1704 as a fortified shipyard. It extends 407m along the waterfront from Palace Square to **Decembrists' Square**, named after a group of reformist officers who, in December 1825, marched three thousand soldiers into the square in a doomed attempt to proclaim a constitutional monarchy. Today, Decembrists' Square is dominated by the *Bronze Horseman*, Falconet's 1778 statue of Peter the Great and the city's unofficial symbol.

St Isaac's Cathedral

Looming above Decembrists' Square, **St Isaac's Cathedral** (Thurs–Tues

28

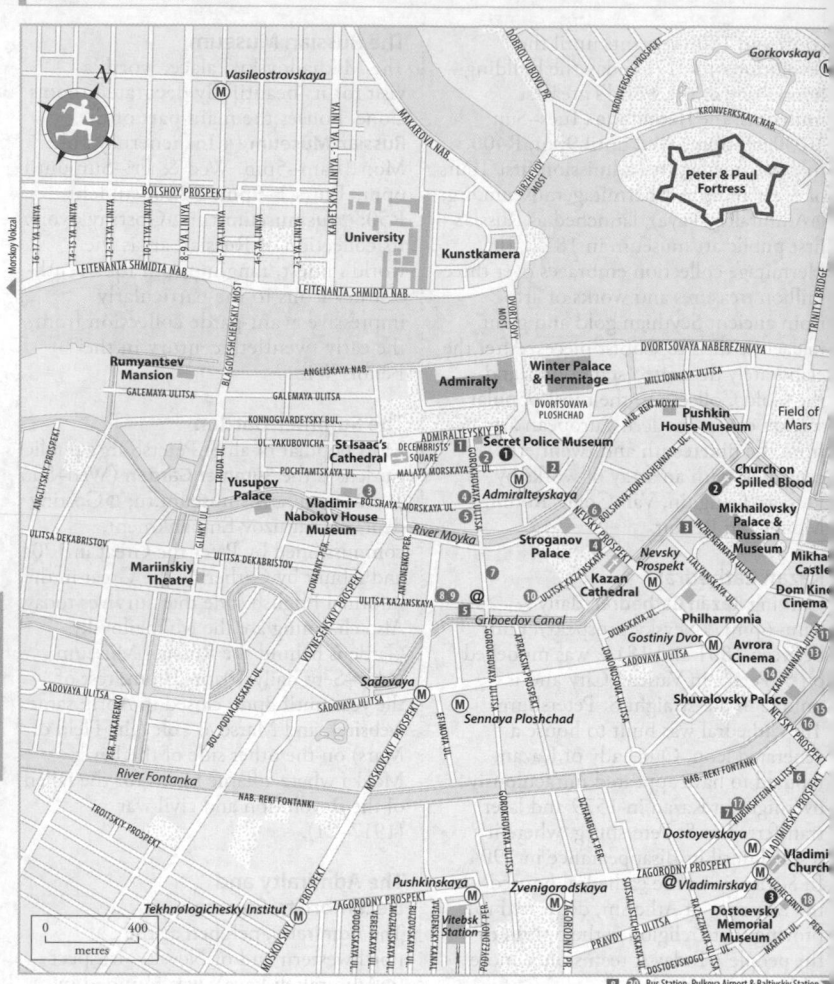

8 , 20 , Bus Station, Pulkova Airport & Baltiyskiy Station

11am–7pm; colonnade until 5pm or
11pm in summer; R250, student
R150, colonnade R150; ⓦcathedral.ru;
ⓜAdmiralteyskaya) is one of the glories
of St Petersburg's skyline, its gilded
dome the third largest in Europe.
The opulent interior is equally
impressive, decorated with fourteen
kinds of marble. Climb the 262 steps
to the outside colonnade to appreciate
the cathedral's height (101.5m) and
for an expansive view of the city.
During White Nights from June 1 to
August 20 the colonnade is open
until 4.30am.

The Peter and Paul Fortress

Across the Neva from the Winter Palace
stands the **Peter and Paul Fortress**, built
to secure Russia's hold on the Neva
delta. The Fortress (daily 8.30am–8pm;
free; ⓦspbmuseum.ru; ⓜGorkovskaya)
shelters a cathedral as well as rotating
exhibitions in the Engineers' and
Commandant's House. Completed in
1733, the Dutch-style Peter and Paul
Cathedral (Mon, Thurs & Fri 10am–
6pm, Tues 10am–5pm, Sat
10am–5.45pm, Sun 11am–6pm; R220,
student R100) remained the tallest
structure in the city until the 1960s.

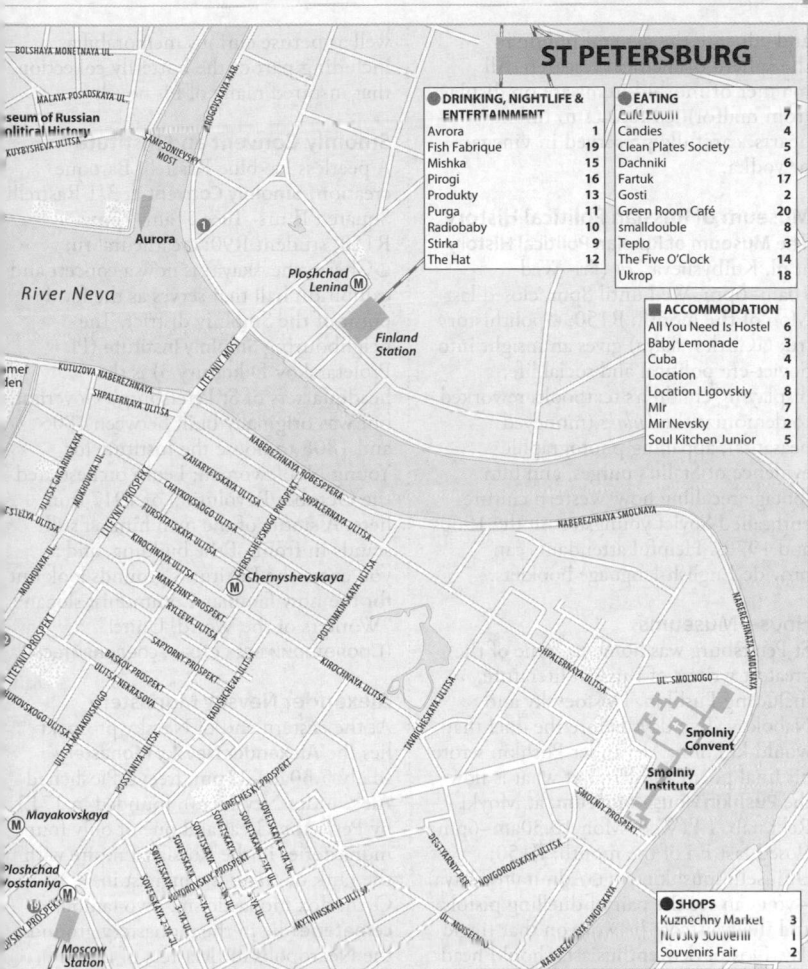

ST PETERSBURG

● DRINKING, NIGHTLIFE & ENTERTAINMENT

Avrora	1
Fish Fabrique	19
Mishka	15
Pirogi	16
Produkty	13
Purga	11
Radiobaby	10
Stirka	9
The Hat	12

● EATING

Café Zoom	7
Candies	4
Clean Plates Society	5
Dachniki	6
Fartuk	17
Gosti	2
Green Room Café	20
smalldouble	8
Teplo	3
The Five O'Clock	14
Ukrop	18

■ ACCOMMODATION

All You Need Is Hostel	6
Baby Lemonade	3
Cuba	4
Location	1
Location Ligovskiy	8
Mir	7
Mir Nevsky	2
Soul Kitchen Junior	5

● SHOPS

Kuznechny Market	3
Nevsky Souvenir	1
Souvenirs Fair	2

28

Sited around the nave are the tombs of **Romanov monarchs** from Peter the Great onwards, excluding Peter II, Ivan VI and Nicholas II. The Nevskaya panorama walk (daily 10am–9pm; separate ticket required R150, student R120), along the rooftops of the fortifications, gives an excellent view of the Winter Palace.

Cruiser Aurora

Anchored a short walk along the Neva from the Peter and Paul Fortress is the **Cruiser Aurora** (Tues–Thurs, Sat & Sun 10.30am–4pm; entry by advance ticket booking only 📞 812 230 8440; R300, student R100; 🌐 aurora.org.ru; Ⓜ Gorkovskaya), the famous battle ship that fired the opening shot of the revolution of 1917.

Kunstkamera

Don't miss the **Kunstkamera** at Universitetskaya nab. 3, Vasilevsky Island (Tues–Sun 11am–6pm, closed last Tues of the month; R200; 🌐 kunstkamera.ru; Ⓜ Vasileostrovskaya), Russia's oldest public museum, founded by Peter the Great in 1714 in order to promote scientific research and educate the general public in the sphere of medical research. All manner of morbid items are on display, from malformed fetuses to infants' hearts, carefully preserved in vinegar or vodka.

Museum of Russian Political History

The **Museum of Russian Political History** at ul. Kuibysheva 2/4 (Fri–Wed 10am–6pm, Wed until 8pm, closed last Mon of the month; R150; ⓦpolithistory .ru; ⓜGorkovskaya) gives an insight into Soviet-era political and social life, displaying children's textbooks reworked to demonize the *kulaks* (moneyed peasants), appalling photographic evidence of Stalin's purges, and film footage recalling how Western culture enthralled Soviet youngsters in the 1960s and 1970s. Helpful attendants can provide English-language booklets.

House-Museums

St Petersburg was home to some of the greatest writers of Russian literature, including Pushkin, Dostoevsky and Nabokov. Two days before the duel that would kill him, Alexander Pushkin wrote his final poem and letter at what is now the **Pushkin House-Museum**, at Moyki Reki nab. 12 (Wed–Mon 10.30am–6pm, closed last Fri of the month; R150; ⓦmuseumpushkin.ru; ⓜAdmiralteyskaya) – you can see the pair of duelling pistols and the waistcoat he wore on that tragic day. Dostoevksy enthusiasts should head to the **Dostoevsky Memorial Museum** at Kuznechny per. 5/2 (Tues–Sun 11am– 6pm; R160, student R80; ⓦmd.spb.ru; ⓜVladimirskaya), where the novelist resided briefly in 1846 and then again from 1878 until his death three years later. Here he initially worked on his first story *The Double*, and later on his last novel *The Brothers Karamazov*. The former home of the prose master behind *Lolita* is the **Vladimir Nabokov House-Museum** at Bolshaya Morskaya 47 (Tues–Fri 11am–6pm, Sat & Sun noon–5pm; free entry; ⓦnabokov museum.org; ⓜAdmiralteyskaya), where the novelist lived until 1917. You can watch a video interview with Nabokov as well as peruse curious memorabilia, including part of the butterfly collection that inspired many of his novels.

Smolniy Convent and Institute

A peerless ice-blue Rastrelli Baroque creation, **Smolniy Convent** at 3/1 Rastrelli Square (Thurs–Tues 11am–7pm; R150, student R90; ⓦcathedral.ru; ⓜChernyshevskaya) is now a concert and exhibition hall that serves as the focal point of the Smolniy district. The neighbouring **Smolniy Institute** (Pl. Proletarskoy Diktatury 3) is the headquarters of St Petersburg's Governor, but was originally built between 1806 and 1808 to house the Institute for Young Noblewomen; Lenin orchestrated the October Revolution of 1917 from here. A statue of the man himself still stands in front of the building, and as you enter the Institute's grounds look out for the now familiar Communist slogan: "Workers of the World, Unite!" (Пролетарии всех стран, соединяйтесь!).

Alexander Nevsky Monastery

At the eastern end of Nevsky prospekt lies the **Alexander Nevsky Monastery** (daily 5.30am–11pm; free; ⓜPloshchad Aleksandra Nevskogo), founded in 1713 by Peter the Great and one of only four monasteries in the Russian Empire with the rank of *lavra*, the highest in Orthodox monasticism. Two famous **cemeteries** lie in the monastery grounds: the Necropolis for Masters of the Arts, where Dostoevsky, Rimsky-Korsakov, Tchaikovsky and Glinka lie, and, directly opposite, the Lazarus Cemetery, the oldest in the city with elaborately decorated tombs. Tickets are required for entry to both (Fri–Wed: April–Oct 9.30am–6pm; Fri–Wed: Nov–March 9.30am–5.30pm; R200).

Rumyantsev Mansion

Along the Neva embankment to the west of the Admiralty, the focal point of the **Rumyantsev Mansion** at Angliyskaya nab. 44 (Thurs–Tues 11am–6pm, Tues until 5pm; R120, student R70; ⓦspbmuseum .ru; ⓜSadovaya) is the exhibition on Leningrad during the Great Patriotic

War, which details the horrors of life in a desperate city, besieged by the Nazis between 1941 and 1944. The most harrowing exhibit is the diary of 11-year-old Tanya Savicheva, who continued going to school as, one by one, her entire family died of starvation.

Yusupov Palace

Purchased by the aristocratic Yusupov family in 1830, the elaborately decorated **Yusupov Palace** at Nab. reki Moyki 94 (daily 11am–5pm; R500, student R380, including audioguide; ⊙Nevsky prospekt) was the scene of the murder of the sinister monk, Rasputin, deemed to have had undue influence over the royal family. You can see a wax likeness of him down in the cellar where he was poisoned by Felix Yusupov and his associates in 1916 (additional ticket required: R300, student R180). When the poison failed to take effect, they shot him, rolled him up in a carpet and threw him in the river; he finally died from drowning, having clawed his way through much of the ice.

ARRIVAL AND DEPARTURE

By plane International flights arrive at Pulkovo Airport (☎812 704 3444), Terminal 2. Take a shuttle bus (#K3 or #113; R30) or city bus #13 (both modes approximately every 15min) three stops from the end of the metro line (⊙Moskovskaya). Shuttle bus #K3 continues on to ⊙Sennaya in the centre of town.

By train Services from Helsinki use Finland station (Findlyanskiy vokzal) at Pl. Lenina 6 (⊙Ploshchad Lenina). Trains from Rīga and Vilnius terminate at Vitebsk station (Vitebskiy vokzal) on Zagorodny Prospekt (⊙Pushkinskaya). Trains from Moscow draw into Moscow station (Moskovskiy vokzal) on Pl. Vosstaniya (⊙Ploshchad Vosstaniya).

Destinations Helsinki (standard service: 1 daily; 6hr 30min; Sapsan express: 2 daily; 3hr 30min); Moscow (standard service: 13 daily; 7–9hr; Sapsan express: up to 5 daily; 4hr); Rīga (1 daily; 13hr); Vilnius (1 daily; 13hr).

By bus Most buses arrive at the central bus station, Nab. Obvodnogo kanala 36, ⊙Obvodny kanal. Buses from the Baltic States use Baltiyskiy station at Nab. Obvodnogo kanala 120, ⊙Baltiyskaya. You can purchase bus tickets online via Lux Express (⊙luxexpress.eu) or at the ticket office by the bus station to the Baltic States. Scandinavia (call ☎901 314 56 74 to book, ⊙scandinavia.spb.ru) run minibuses to

Helsinki, departing from the corner of Ligovsky Prospekt and Nevsky prospekt by *Hotel Oktyabrskaya* (⊙Ploshchad Vosstaniya).

Destinations Helsinki (3 daily, 8hr); Moscow (21 daily; 10–12hr); Rīga (9 daily; 10hr); Tallinn (10 daily; 6hr); Tartu (3 daily; 6hr); Warsaw (5 daily; 26hr).

By ferry St. Peter Line (⊙stpeterline.com) operates ferries year-round (except in Jan) to Helsinki and then on to Stockholm and Tallinn. They dock at the Morskoy vokzal, Morskoy Slavy 1 (⊙Vasileostrovskaya), at the western end of Vasilevskiy Island (metro or minibus from the centre).

INFORMATION

The main tourist office centre at Sadovaya ul. 14 (Mon–Fri 10am–7pm, Sat noon–6pm; ☎812 982 8253, ⊙visit -petersburg.com; ⊙Nevsky prospekt) has plenty of material in English.

GETTING AROUND

By metro The St Petersburg metro, the deepest in the world, runs from 5.30am to midnight. Small numbers of journeys (R28 a journey) are sold using tokens (*zhetoni*), which you feed into ticket machines. For ten or more rides to be used over a fixed number of days, buy a plastic card.

By bus and trolleybus Often the best way to navigate a major road like Nevsky prospekt, overground transport is more useful in the compact city centre than the metro, with its lengthy escalators. Buy tickets from the driver (R25).

By minibus *Marshrutkas* (yellow in St Petersburg) are cheap (R35 a journey) and cheerful. The #K-147 goes from Moskovskiy vokzal train station right to the upper end of Nevsky prospekt.

By boat One of the best ways to see the city is by boat (May–Oct) – either a private motorboat from any bridge on Nevsky prospekt (from R2000/hr/boat), or a large tour boat from behind the Hermitage (R300/person). AngloTourismo (☎921 989 4722, ⊙anglotourismo.com) offer guided tours in English (R600) from the pier on Fontanka next to Shuvalovsky Palace at Nab. reki Fontanki 21 (⊙Gostiny dvor). Try the excellent "St Petersburg by Night" boat tour (R750), which takes in the more spectacular of the city's bridges, illuminated as they are being raised for the night.

ACCOMMODATION

HOSTELS

★ **All You Need Is Hostel** Rubinshteina 6 ☎921 950 0574, ⊙youneedhostel.com; ⊙Mayakovskaya. An immaculate new addition, with spacious dorms and a communal area full of comfy beanbags, a TV and PlayStation, and all manner of musical instruments to try

28

28

your hand at. Rates include breakfast, and bike rental is offered. Dorm R650, double R2500

Baby Lemonade Inzhenernaya 7 ☎812 570 7943, ✉babylemonadehostel@gmail.com; Ⓜ Gostiny dvor. This cute, intimate hostel has two pleasant dorms and a double; the bunks are decked out with privacy curtains and the colourful kitchen is a great spot to mingle. Dorm R835, double R3200

Cuba Kazanskaya 5, 4th floor ☎812 921 7115, Ⓦcubahostel.ru; Ⓜ Nevsky prospekt. Pick the dorm name that corresponds to your favourite colour and you'll sleep surrounded by your favourite hues. Dial 41 at the buzzer downstairs. Mixed dorm R490, double R2700

Location Admiralteysky prospekt 8 ☎812 490 6429, Ⓦlocation-hostel.ru; Ⓜ Admiralteyskaya. A stone's throw away from the Hermitage, this little place with bare brick walls has small mixed dorms and a bright modern kitchen (microwave only) where guests congregate over the free tea and coffee. Staff are helpful and friendly. No doubles. Dorm R750, twin R1400

Location Ligovskiy Ligovskiy prospekt 74 ☎812 329 1274, Ⓦlocation-hostel.ru; Ⓜ Ligovskiy prospekt. The much larger sister hostel to the other *Location* shares this former bread factory building with an arts centre. With over 150 beds, rooms are a bit poky but the laidback communal area and marvellously cheap neighbouring *Green Room Café* (see below) make up for it. Dorm R650, double R1400

Mir Rubinshteina 15/17 ☎911 755 7844, Ⓦmirhostel.com; Ⓜ Dostoyevskaya. With a bright, open-plan kitchen and homely touches such as rugs on the floors and a piano in the hallway, this hostel has a welcoming feel. Dorms are spacious, staff are friendly and the premises are kept in good nick. Rates include breakfast. Dorm R650, double R2600

Mir Nevsky Nevsky prospekt 16 ☎911 755 6001, Ⓦmirhostel.com; Ⓜ Admiralteyskaya. Contented travellers here regularly scribble their comments in colourful chalk on the walls of the attractive, parquet-floored communal area. Dorms are clean and spacious and staff even take care of your laundry at no extra cost. Rates include breakfast. Dorm R650, double R2600

★**Soul Kitchen Junior** Nab. reki Moyki 62/2, apt.9 ☎965 816 3470, Ⓦsoulkitchenhostel.com; Ⓜ Admiralteyskaya. Cool and funky hostel that boasts a large modern kitchen and bright spacious dorms with individual reading lamps, lockers and privacy curtains. Premises are kept spick-and-span, and staff organize activities ranging from pub crawls to Hermitage trips. Dorm R800, double R3000

EATING

CAFÉS

Café Zoom Gorokhovaya 22 Ⓦcafezoom.ru; Ⓜ Nevsky prospekt. Pick a book off one of the shelves or sit back with

a board game at this pleasant little café that specializes in healthy, tasty and affordable grub. Hearty breakfast omelettes (from R90), as well as great soups and salads (R120). Mon–Fri 9am–midnight, Sat 11am–midnight, Sun 1pm–midnight.

Candies Gorokhovaya 11 Ⓦcoffeeroom-spb.ru; Ⓜ Admitaleyskaya. A quirky place with mismatched chairs and an eclectic mix of other furniture offering exceptional home-made teas (R230), lemonades (R230), milk-based drinks (R180) and desserts (R100), as well as light mains and breakfast until 4pm. Daily 9am–11pm; 24hr in summer.

Green Room Café Ligovskiy prospekt 74; Ⓜ Ligovskiy prospekt. Join the young, artsy crowd at this buzzing café which boasts a leafy interior and great cheap grub. Mains run R110–160 and there's plenty on offer for vegetarians (R80–130). Art exhibitions take place within the same building. Daily 9am–11pm, Fri & Sat until 6am.

smalldouble Kazanskaya 26; Ⓜ Sennaya ploshchad. This tiny café serves a wide range of coffees (R60) that go perfectly with their homemade cookies (R30), croissants (R50) and cakes (R140). Mon–Fri 8.30am–10pm, Sat & Sun 11am–10pm.

The Five O'Clock Karavannaya 11/64; Ⓜ Gostiny dvor. *Alice in Wonderland*-inspired café, perfect for a quick refuelling stop. Teas from R90, cakes R160. Daily 10am–11pm.

Ukrop Marata 23 Ⓦcafe-ukrop.ru; Ⓜ Vladimirskaya. Bright and airy veggie café with leafy flowerpots and knick-knacks dotted around its two floors; downstairs is the cheaper self-service (R80 per serving) while upstairs the café serves more refined vegetarian dishes, including their renowned vegetable tartar (R260). Daily noon–10pm.

RESTAURANTS

Clean Plates Society Gorokhovaya ul. 13 Ⓦcleanplates .ru; Ⓜ Admiralteyskaya. This newcomer serves good-value food in a laidback, modern setting with a hint of faded glamour. Try the tasty club burger (R280). Daily noon–2am, Fri & Sat until 6am.

Dachniki Nevsky prospekt 20; Ⓜ Admiralteyskaya. Laid out in true Russian *dacha* style with log cabin-style walls, chintzy curtains and Soviet films running back-to-back on the TV screen. The traditional food is excellent, from meat *pelmeni* (meat dumplings; R190) to *vareniki* (Ukrainian dumplings with potatoes, cheese or cherries; R140), as well as a range of soups (R120). Daily noon–1.30/2am.

Fartuk Rubinshteina 15/17; Ⓜ Dostoyevskaya. This family-run place has a welcoming feel, with its communal wooden table, large open windows and exposed brick walls. The cuisine is mostly Mediterranean, with mains starting at R210. Thurs–Sat 10am–1am, Sun–Wed 11am–midnight.

Gosti Malaya Morskaya 13 ⓦgdegosti.ru; ⓜAdmiralteyskaya. Frilly and floral as a grandmother's parlour, this ground-floor café-bakery is a great little spot for some traditional Serbian pançakes (R140) while the upstairs restaurant serves international dishes in four rooms, including a library and kitchen, set out like a Russian flat. Daily 8am–2am.

★ **Teplo** Bol. Morskaya 45; ⓜAdmiralteyskaya. This gem of a place serves up international cuisine in a warren of cosy partitioned rooms, some with sofas, that will have you lingering longer than you intended. Mains R500. Fri & Sat 1pm–1am, Sun–Thurs 9am–midnight.

DRINKING AND NIGHTLIFE

BARS

Mishka Nab. reki Fontanki 40 ⓦmishkabar.ru; ⓜNevsky prospekt. Hipsters flock to this basement joint for the house, fusion and electro beats that kick in at 10pm. Daily noon–3am, Fri & Sat until 6am.

Pirogi Nab. reki Fontanki 40 ⓦpiterogi.ru; ⓜNevsky prospekt. Café, restaurant, bar, club, concert and exhibition hall, this 24/7 place attracts a laidback, studenty crowd with great-value food (mains R179) and drinks (cocktails R130). Music varies from rock to dance.

★ **Produkty** Nab. reki Fontanki 17; ⓜNevsky prospekt. The retro decor of this little old-school bar includes a juke box and countless odds and ends brought over from Berlin. It's a great spot to sip a cocktail (R250) as you enjoy some new-wave favourites spun by the DJ. Daily 2pm–2am, Fri & Sat until 6am.

Stirka Kazanskaya 26 ⓦ40gradusov.ru; ⓜSennaya. This small grungy haunt attracts an alternative crowd. When live bands aren't playing you can lounge about on the worn sofas and enjoy the decent sound system. Beers R140. Mon–Fri 11am–1am, Fri & Sat until 4am.

CLUBS

Fish Fabrique Ligovskiy Prospekt 53 ⓦfishfabrique .ru; ⓜPloshchad Vosstaniya. With regular gigs (admission R100–300), this is a grungy venue in the heart of a complex which also houses exhibition spaces and artists' studios; live music usually on Thurs, Sat & Sun 5pm–6am.

Purga Nab. reki Fontanki 11 ⓦpurga-club.ru; ⓜMayakovskaya. You'll either love or hate the two *Purga* clubs; *Purga I* hosts New Year celebrations nightly, complete with an address by a Soviet leader, while neighbouring *Purga II* is the place to go with your other half for a mock wedding. Rowdy fun. *Purga I*: daily 4pm–6am, *Purga II*: Fri & Sat 8pm–6am. Both R400 Fri & Sat.

Radiobaby Kazanskaya 7 ⓦradiobaby.com; ⓜNevsky prospekt. A cool place full of young hipsters who come back again and again for their favourite local DJs. Daily 6pm–6am.

ENTERTAINMENT

Theatres tend to close for the summer until mid-Sept. For listings and events pick up the quarterly freebie *Where St Petersburg*, *In Your Pocket* or the Friday *St Petersburg Times*.

LIVE MUSIC

Avrora Pirogovskaya nab. 5/2 ☎812 907 1917, ⓦavrora -zal.ru; ⓜPloshchad Lenina. A wide range of bands, from pop to folk and punk, perform in the 1000-capacity concert hall, while the more intimate B.B. King Hall hosts smaller gigs. Daily noon–10pm.

The Hat Belinskogo 9; ⓜMayakovskaya. Set out like an old New York City bar, this smoky drinking hole attracts barflies looking for some live jazz and a few whiskies (there are thirty types). Jam sessions daily at 10.30pm. Daily 7pm–late.

CLASSICAL, OPERA AND BALLET

Marlinskiy Theatre Teatralnaya pl. 1 ☎812 326 4141, ⓦmariinsky.ru; ⓜSadovaya. Tickets €8–120. Opera and ballet performances at 7pm, matinees at noon.

Philharmonia Mikhaylovskaya ul. 2 ☎812 312 9871, ⓦwww.philharmonia.spb.ru; ⓜNevsky prospekt. Draws international classical musicians as well as Russia's finest. Performances at 7pm. Tickets from R250.

CINEMA

Avrora Nevsky prospekt 60 ⓦavrora.spb.ru; ⓜNevsky prospekt. Screens original-language mainstream films.

Dom Kino Karavannaya 12 ⓦdomkino.spb.ru; ⓜGostiny dvor. Specializes in art-house movies, as well as international cinema weeks.

SHOPPING

Kuznechny market Kuznechniy per. 3; ⓜVladimirskaya. With its mouthwatering displays of sweets and cakes, salted cucumbers, sausages, plaited cheese rinds and caviar, this is the place to come for Russian speciality foods. Daily 8am–8pm, Sun until 7pm.

Nevsky Souvenir Nevsky prospekt 3; ⓜNevsky prospekt. Pick up high-quality (though not cheap) Russian souvenirs here, as well as the obligatory *matrioshka* dolls. There's also stunning amber jewellery by local artists, plus Fabergé-style ornaments made from real eggs. Daily 10am–9pm.

Souvenirs Fair Nab. kanala Griboedova 1, opposite the Church of the Saviour on the Spilled Blood; ⓜNevsky prospekt. Nearly 200 stalls open all year round with plenty of souvenirs from paintings to handicrafts. Daily 9am–6pm.

DIRECTORY

Consulates Australia, Nab. reki Moyki 11 ☎812 315 1100, ⓜNevsky prospekt; UK, pl. Proletarskoy Diktatury 5

28

⊕ 812 320 3200, Ⓜ Chernyshevskaya; US, Furshtadtskaya ul. 15 ⊕ 812 331 2600, Ⓜ Chernyshevskaya.

Internet 59°57', ul. Kazanskaya 26, Ⓜ Sennaya (daily 24hr; R100/hr); there's another branch at Razezzhaya 1 Ⓜ Dostoyevskaya (daily 24hr; R80/hr).

Health MEDEM International Clinic & Hospital, ul. Marata 6 ⊕ 812 336 3333, Ⓜ Mayakovskaya; American Medical Clinic, Nab. reki Moyki 78 ⊕ 812 740 2090, Ⓜ Sadovaya.

Pharmacy Petropharm, Nevsky prospekt 22–24 (24hr).

Post offices Main office at Pochtamskaya ul. 9 (Mon–Sat 9am–8pm, Sun 10am–6pm; Ⓜ Nevsky prospekt). Express letter post: DHL (Nevsky prospekt 10; Mon–Fri 9am–9pm, Sat & Sun 10am–4pm; Ⓦ dhl.ru; Ⓜ Admiralteyskaya).

DAY-TRIPS FROM ST PETERSBURG

The Imperial palaces of **Peterhof** and **Tsarskoe Selo**, half an hour to an hour outside the city, are both splendid day-trips. Although entering the palaces is increasingly expensive, you can slip away from the crowds into the surrounding parks. As you leave St Petersburg on the bus, look out for the awe-inspiring war monument to Leningrad's World War II sacrifice, and Lenin "hailing a taxi" near Finland station.

The Peterhof

Most visitors with time for just one day-trip opt for **Peterhof** (Grand Palace Tues–Sun 10.30am–7pm, closed last Tues of month; R550, student R300; park daily 9am–8pm; R450, student R250), 29km west of St Petersburg, known as the "Russian Versailles" and famed for its marvellous fountains and impressive cascades. Though originally built between 1709 and 1724 for Peter the Great, each of the subsequent rulers made their mark here. Travel by hydrofoil in summer (every 30min 10am–7pm; R650 each way or R1100 return; 30–40min) from outside the Winter Palace or take minibus #224, #300 or #424 from Ⓜ Avtovo, or #103 or #420 from Ⓜ Leninsky prospekt.

Tsarskoe Selo and Pavlovsk

The small town of **Tsarskoe Selo** (also known as Pushkin, after the "Russian Shakespeare" who was educated at the neighbouring Lyceum school), 30km south of St Petersburg, centres on the **Catherine Palace** (palace: Wed–Mon 10am–6pm, open until 9pm the first three Mon of the month, closed last Mon of the month; R320; grounds: daily 7am–9pm; R100, student R50). The ostentatious blue-and-white Baroque structure built by Catherine the Great is surrounded by a richly landscaped park. Scottish architect Charles Cameron's elegant Neoclassical gallery stretches high above it. To get to Pushkin, take minibus #342 or #545 from Ⓜ Moskovskaya or #186 from Ⓜ Kupchino; alternatively, take a train to Detskoe Selo from Vitebsky station, then bus #371 or #382.

The same minibuses take you 5km further south to the more intimate **Pavlovsk Palace** (Sat–Thurs 10am–5pm; closed first Mon of the month; palace R450, student R250; grounds R150, student R80), its magnificent Neoclassical interior set amid luxurious 1500-acre grounds.

CITY HALL, SUBOTICA

Serbia

HIGHLIGHTS

❶ **Belgrade** Explore the nightlife and café culture of Serbia's hectic, hedonistic capital city. **See p.944**

❷ **Novi Sad** Admire the view from Petrovaradin, the hilltop fortress that hosts the EXIT Festival every summer. **See p.950**

❸ **Subotica** Enjoy the city's unspoilt feel and fantastical Secessionist architecture. **See p.953**

❹ **Studenica Monastery** The finest of Serbia's fresco-laden, medieval monastic churches. **See p.954**

HIGHLIGHTS ARE MARKED ON THE MAP ON P.941

ROUGH COSTS

Daily budget Basic €25, occasional treat €40

Drink Beer (0.5l) €1

Food *Pljeskavica* (hamburger) €1–2

Hostel/budget hotel €12/€35

Travel Bus: Belgrade–Novi Sad €6; train: Belgrade–Niš €7

FACT FILE

Population 7.5 million (excluding Kosovo)

Language Serbian

Currency Dinar (din)

Capital Belgrade

International phone code ☎ 381

Time zone GMT +1hr

29

Introduction

Serbia is a buzzy and boisterous country, compact enough for visitors to sample both Belgrade's urban hedonism and the gentler pace of the smaller towns or national parks within a few days – and it's one of Europe's most affordable destinations to boot. Grittier than its blue-eyed neighbour Croatia, it is nevertheless an integral part of any backpacker's Balkan tour: at the heart of the region, it gives easy access to the cluster of cultures and histories crammed into this small corner of Europe.

Serbia's young, European-minded population brings a bubbling energy to its bars, cafés and clubs, producing an adrenaline-charged nightlife unmatched anywhere else in the Balkans. The general determination to have a good time confounds the expectations of many a traveller, arriving with memories of the 1990s, when Serbia's name was not often off war reporters' lips. Today, it's just as likely to attract headlines for its crop of world-class tennis players or the annual EXIT festival in Novi Sad.

Serbia's capital, **Belgrade**, is a sociable, hectic city that energizes and exhausts by turns. Northwest of the city on the iron-flat Vojvodina Plain sits lovely **Novi Sad**, window to the **Fruška Gora** hills, while further north – a stone's throw from the border with Hungary – enchanting **Subotica** is sprinkled with early twentieth-century Secessionist architecture. Deep in the mountainous tract of land to the south of Belgrade are three key struts of Serbia's religio-cultural heritage – Žiča, Studenica and Sopoćani **monasteries**. East of here, **Niš** is a pleasant small city to pause in en route to or from Bulgaria or Macedonia.

CHRONOLOGY

168 BC The Romans defeat the Illyrian tribe and establish their rule of the area of present-day Serbia.

630 AD Serbs settle in the region.

1166 Stefan Nemanja, leader of the Serbs, declares independence from Byzantine rule.

1219 The Serbian Orthodox Church is established.

1389 The Ottomans defeat the Serbs in the Battle of Kosovo, ushering in four centuries of direct rule.

1804 National hero Karađorđe ("Black George") begins the First Serbian Uprising against the Ottomans.

1913 The Ottomans lose their remaining authority in Serbia during the Balkan wars.

1918 Following World War I the Kingdom of Serbs, Croats and Slovenes is formed.

1929 The Kingdom is renamed Yugoslavia.

1945 Following World War II, Serbia is absorbed into Socialist Yugoslavia.

1989 Slobodan Milošević, a Serbian communist, becomes President of Serbia.

1992 The wars of the disintegration of Yugoslavia begin. Fighting ends three years later.

1993 The International Criminal Tribunal for the former Yugoslavia is set up in The Hague to try those accused of war crimes.

1998 Serbia launches a violent campaign against the ethnic Albanian community in Kosovo, costing thousands of lives.

1999 NATO's "Operation Merciful Angel" – a ten-week war from the air to end Milošević's ethnic cleansing campaign – drives Yugoslav National Army forces out of Kosovo.

2000 Mass protests lead to the resignation of Milošević.

2003 Serbian prime minister, Zoran Đinđić, is assassinated in Belgrade.

2006 Milošević dies in prison, awaiting trial at the International Criminal Tribunal for the former Yugoslavia on charges of genocide.

2006 Montenegro peacefully gains independence from Serbia.

2008 Kosovo declares independence from Serbia after nine years under UN administration. Serbia does not recognize Kosovo as an independent state.

2011 Ratko Mladić arrested and transferred to the War Crimes Tribunal in The Hague.

2013 EU announces that accession talks will begin in 2014.

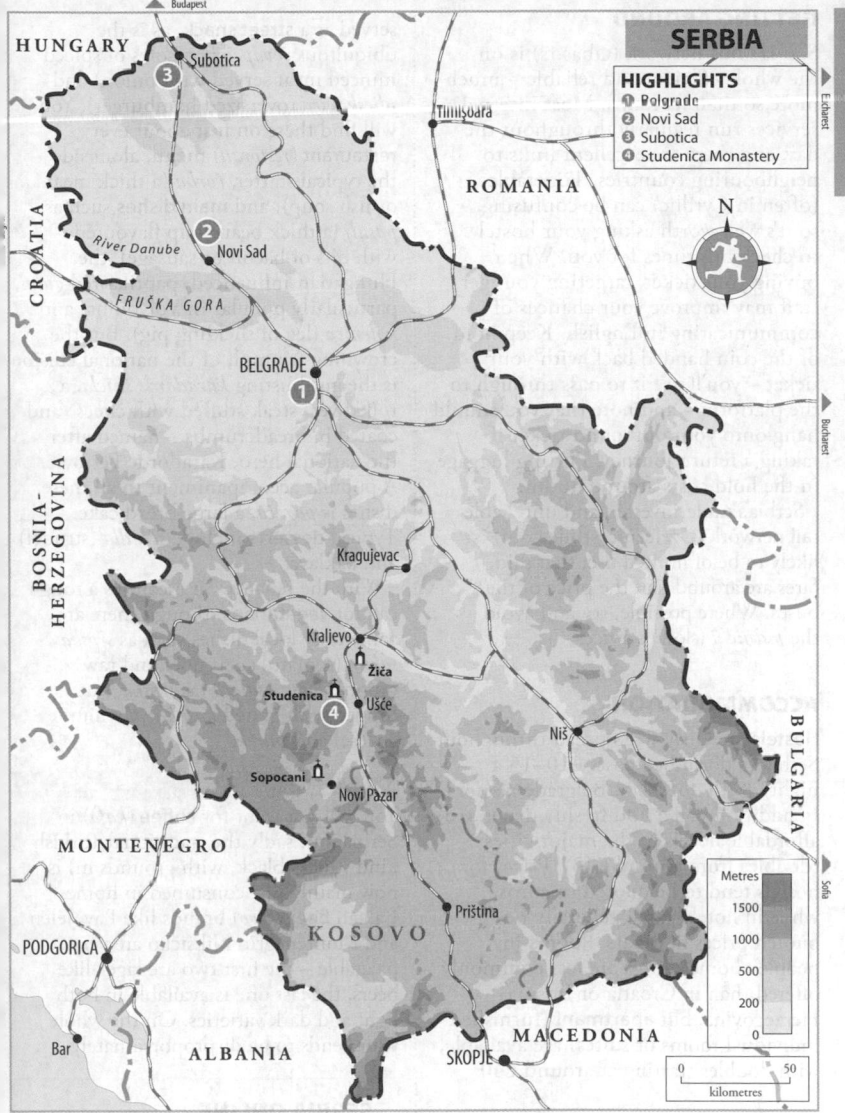

SERBIA

HIGHLIGHTS
1. Belgrade
2. Novi Sad
3. Subotica
4. Studenica Monastery

ARRIVAL AND DEPARTURE

Flight operators from the UK include Wizz Air (wwizzair.com) and the Yugoslav national airline JAT (wjat.com), inherited by Serbia. Cuts to services mean that Serbia's **rail** connections with neighbouring countries are now fairly limited: from Belgrade there are currently two daily services to Budapest in Hungary, two to

Podgorica (and Bar on the coast) in Montenegro, two to Skopje in Macedonia, one to Sofia in Bulgaria (via Niš), and one to Zagreb in Croatia. For the time being there are no services to Romania or Bosnia. No visas are needed for nationals of the US, Canada, Australia, New Zealand, UK, Republic of Ireland, or any EU country staying in Serbia for up to ninety days.

29

GETTING AROUND

Serbia's **bus** network (ⓦbas.rs) is on the whole efficient and reliable – much more so than its trains. Most internal services run regularly throughout the day, and there are excellent links to neighbouring countries. Timetables (often in Cyrillic) can be confusing, so it's well worth asking your hostel to check bus times for you. When buying your ticket, targeting younger staff may improve your chances of communicating in English. Keep hold of the coin handed back with your ticket – you'll use it to pass through to the platform – and note that you should hang onto your outbound ticket if taking a return journey. Putting luggage in the hold costs around 40din.

Serbia's underinvested and unreliable **rail** network (ⓦzeleznicesrbije.com) is likely to be of limited use; that said, fares are around half the price of the buses. Where possible, try and avoid the *putnički* (slow) services.

ACCOMMODATION

Hostels are fairly widespread throughout Serbia (a dorm bed costs €10–15 a night), with dozens in Belgrade alone. In addition you'll find freshly decorated, affordable **hotels** in the major cities (doubles from around €40). Prices for hostels tend to be quoted in euros, while in hotels you'll generally be quoted prices in dinars. **Rooms** in people's homes (*sobe*) are less commonly offered than in Croatia or Bosnia-Herzegovina, but **apartmani** (furnished individual rooms or suites) are available, with doubles starting at around €40.

FOOD AND DRINK

In common with other Balkan countries, Serbian **cuisine** is overwhelmingly dominated by meat, and many dishes manifest Turkish or Austro-Hungarian influences. **Breakfast** (*doručak*) typically comprises a coffee, roll and cheese or salami, while also popular is *burek*, a greasy, flaky pastry filled with cheese (*sa sirom*) or meat (*sa mesom*). *Burek* is also served as a **street snack**, as is the ubiquitous *čevapčići* (rissoles of spiced minced meat served with onion) and *pljeskavica* (oversized hamburger). You will find these on just about every **restaurant** (*restoran*) menu, alongside the typical starter, *čorba* (a thick meat or fish soup), and **main dishes** such as *pasulj* (a thick bean soup flavoured with bits of bacon or sausage), the Hungarian-influenced, paprika-red *gulaš*, particularly popular in Vojvodina, and *kolenica* (leg of suckling pig). But the crowning triumph of the national cuisine is the gut-busting *karađorđe šnicla*, a rolled veal steak stuffed with cheese and coated in breadcrumbs – named after the national hero, Karađorđe Petrović. A popular accompaniment to all these dishes is *pogača*, a large bread cake. Typical **desserts** include *strudla* (strudel) and baklava.

With the reliance on meat, it's a tough call for **vegetarians**, though there are some tasty local dishes such as *srpska salata* (tomato, cucumber and raw onion), *šopska salata* (as *srpska*, but topped with grated *kashkaval* white cheese) and *burek*.

You will not want for **coffee** (*kafa*) in Serbia, but sadly the traditional Turkish kind (thick, black, with grounds in) is now mainly just consumed in homes. Balkan **beer** (*pivo*) brands like Lav, Jelen and Montenegrin Nikšićko are very palatable – the first two are lager-like beers, the last one is available in both light and dark varieties. On the whole **wine** tends to be disproportionately

---

SERBIA ONLINE

ⓦ**belgradian.com** Comprehensive English-language site covering everything from local transport information to the fast-changing nightlife scene.
ⓦ**b92.net** Venerable broadcasting station and the driving force behind anti-Milošević demonstrations during the 1990s; it remains the country's most newsworthy site.
ⓦ**serbia.travel** Official tourist board site.

pricey on restaurant menus, but Montenegrin Vranac and Macedonian Tikveš are more affordable. Everyone should sample *slijvovica* – plum *rakija* – but pace yourself to avoid waking up with a shocked head and raw throat.

CULTURE AND ETIQUETTE

Even though tourists are quite a rarity in some parts, part of the charm of travel in Serbia is a sense of "live and let live" – you are unlikely to be quizzed intrusively or pestered to buy wares. Serbian culture as a whole is far from conservative – a fact you'll quickly grasp from the fashion choices youngsters make. You should cover arms and legs in Orthodox churches, however. **Tipping** in restaurants is not essential, but in the nicer places you should leave ten percent.

SPORTS AND ACTIVITIES

Serbia's countryside is beautiful, varied and never more than a short bus ride away. In the summer, **hike** or walk in the Fruška Gora National Park (®npfruskagora.co.rs); in winter hit the **ski** slopes with Balkan daredevils at Kopaonik National Park (®eng.infokop .net). The locals love their **football**, and a derby between Belgrade's Red Star (®crvenazvezdafk.com) and FK Partizan (®partizan.rs) is invariably fiery, and frequently violent (outside the ground). For something more sedate, head to Novi Sad's FK Vojvodina (®fkvojvodina.com). Basketball, too, is a major spectator sport, with both Red Star (®kkcrvenazvezda.rs) and Partizan (®kkpartizan.rs) the dominant forces.

SERBIAN

Serbia uses the **Cyrillic alphabet** as well as the Latin one. Many street signs (see box, p.946) and bus and train timetables are in Cyrillic only, so it's worth being able to decode at least the first few letters of a word. Serbian, like Bosnian, is very closely related to Croatian (see p.158) and all three languages will be understood in all three countries.

EMERGENCY NUMBERS

Police ☎92; Ambulance ☎94; Fire ☎93; Road assistance ☎987.

COMMUNICATIONS

Wi-fi is available in a good number of cafés, and is increasingly widespread in Belgrade and Novi Sad public spaces. Most hostels and hotels offer it as standard. **Internet cafés** are now rare, but where you do find one, expect to pay around 100din per hour. **Public phones** use Halo cards, sold with 300din and 600din credit at post offices, kiosks and tobacconists. Most **post offices** (*pošta*) are open Monday to Friday 8am to 7pm. **Stamps** (*markice*) can also be bought at newsstands.

EMERGENCIES

The **crime** rate, even in Belgrade, is low by European standards, though the usual precautions apply; be particularly wary of pickpockets on the city buses.

Pharmacies (*apoteka*) tend to follow shop hours of around Monday to Friday 8am to 8pm and Saturday 8am to 3pm.

INFORMATION

All the towns covered in this chapter have a **tourist information office** (*turističke informacije*), stocking good-quality materials in English. Another good source of information is *In Your Pocket* (®inyourpocket .com), which currently publishes both print and online guides to Belgrade, Novi Sad and Niš.

MONEY AND BANKS

The currency is the **dinar** (usually abbreviated to din), comprising coins of 1, 2, 5, 10 and 20din (and also 50 para coins – 100 para equals 1din), and notes of 10, 20, 50, 100, 200, 1000 and 5000din. At the time of writing exchange rates were €1 = 110din, £1 = 130din, and US\$1 = 85din. **Exchange offices** (*menjačnica*) are everywhere, while **ATMs** are widely available in towns. Credit/

29

debit cards are accepted in most hotels, restaurants and shops.

OPENING HOURS AND HOLIDAYS

Most **shops** open Monday to Friday 8am to 7/8pm (sometimes with a break for lunch), plus Saturday 8am to 2pm, and sometimes later in Belgrade. Most **museums** are open Tuesday to Sunday 9/10am to 5/6pm. Shops and banks close on **public holidays**: January 1, 2 and 7, February 15, and May 1 and 2. The Orthodox Church celebrates Easter between one and five weeks later than the other churches.

Belgrade

BELGRADE (Београд; Beograd) is a vigorous, high-energy city, especially in spring and summer, when all ages throng the streets at all hours. With a seemingly endless supply of bars and clubs, the city's pulsing nightlife is one of the unexpected high points on any European itinerary.

The city sits at a strategic point on the junction of the Danube and Sava rivers, something that has proved a source of weakness as well as strength over the ages: Belgrade has been captured as many as sixty times by Celts, Romans, Huns, Avars and more. The onslaught continued right through the twentieth century, when the city suffered heavy shelling during World War II and in 1999 withstood 78 days of NATO airstrikes.

Visually, the mingling and merging of architectural styles can be off-putting, particularly when a row of beautiful older frontages is interrupted by a postwar interloper. Yet this mishmash also makes the city what it is: alongside all the Yugoslav experimentation, the grand nineteenth-century buildings and Art Nouveau facades bear eloquent witness to the days of Ottoman and Austro-Hungarian rule.

WHAT TO SEE AND DO

The city's most attention-grabbing attraction is the **Kalemegdan Fortress**,

while just outside the park's boundary is the **Old City**, whose dense lattice of streets conceals Belgrade's most interesting sights. South of here is Belgrade's central square, **Trg Republike**, and the old bohemian quarter of **Skadarlija**, centred on charming, cobbled Skadarska, beyond which lie several more sights worth seeing, including the Church of St Sava, one of the world's largest Orthodox churches. For a spot of rest and recuperation, head west across the Sava to the verdant suburb of **Zemun**, in New Belgrade, or further south towards the island of **Ada Ciganlija**, Belgrade's own miniature beach resort.

Kalemegdan Fortress

Splendidly sited on an exposed nub of land overlooking the confluence of the Sava and Danube rivers, **Kalemegdan Park** is dominated by the **fortress** (ⓦbeogradskatvrjava.co.rs) of the same name. The whole complex is a paean to Serbian heroism, topped with the proud Victory Monument of 1912. Originally built by the Celts in the third century BC, before expansion by the Romans, the fortress has survived successive invasions; most of what remains is the result of a short-lived Austrian occupation in the early eighteenth century. The best of the attractions is the **Military Museum** (Tues–Sun 10am–5pm; 150din), where a history thick with conflict is divertingly presented; one of its most prized acquisitions is part of a US stealth bomber downed during the 1999 conflict.

The Orthodox Cathedral and museum

Leaving the park and crossing Pariska, you'll find yourself in the oldest part of the city. On Kneza Sime Markovića is the city's main **Cathedral Church**, a modest, rather stark Neoclassical edifice built in 1840 and featuring a fine Baroque tower; it's also the resting place for several members of the mighty Obrenović dynasty, as well as Serbia's greatest literary hero, Vuk Karadžić. Opposite, at Kralja Petra 5, stands the

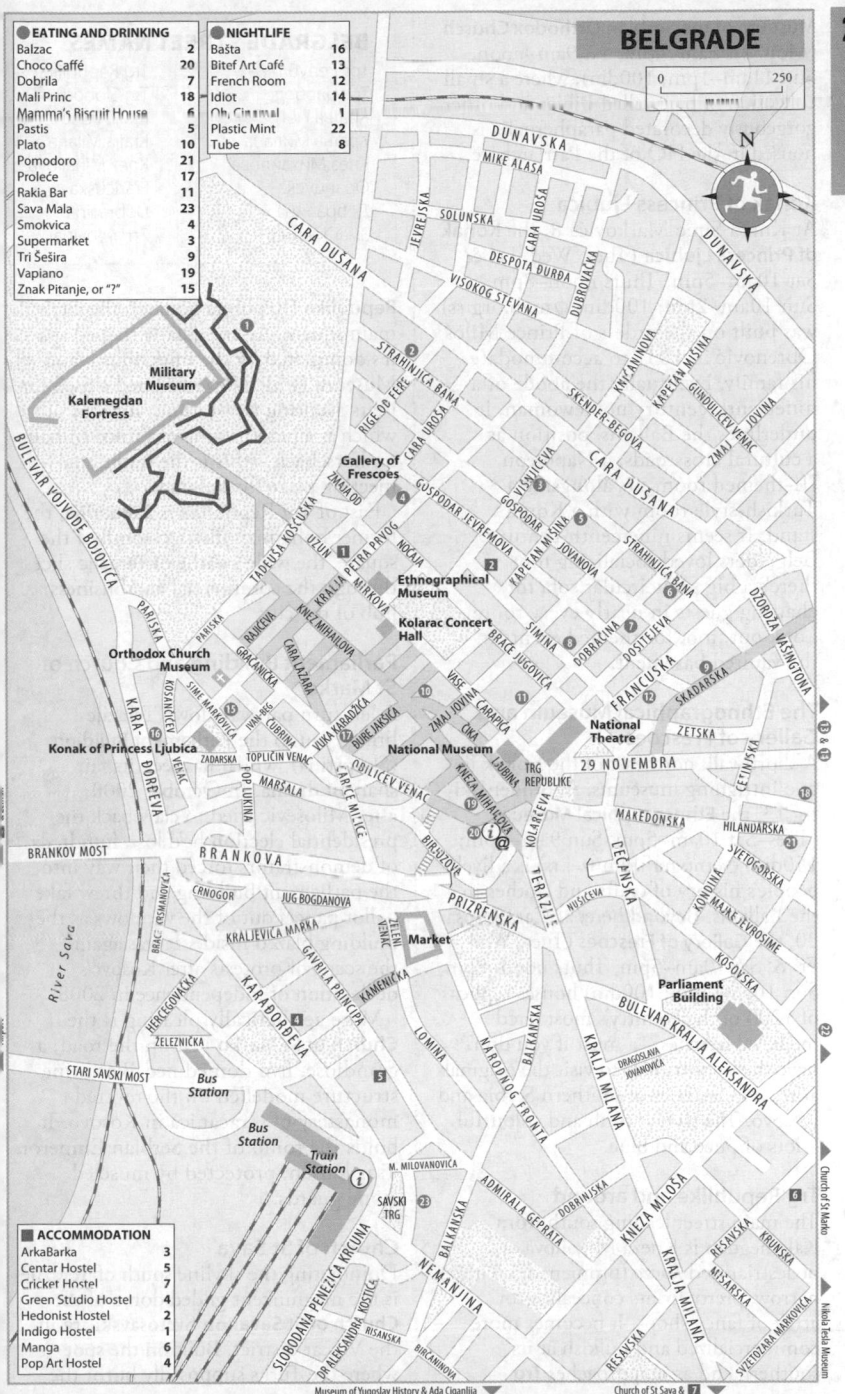

EATING AND DRINKING

Balzac	2
Choco Caffé	20
Dobrila	7
Mali Princ	18
Mamma's Biscuit House	6
Pastis	5
Plato	10
Pomodoro	21
Proleće	17
Rakia Bar	11
Sava Mala	23
Smokvica	4
Supermarket	3
Tri Šešira	9
Vapiano	19
Znak Pitanje, or "?"	15

NIGHTLIFE

Bašta	16
Bitef Art Café	13
French Room	12
Idiot	14
Oh, Cinema!	1
Plastic Mint	22
Tube	8

BELGRADE

0   250

ACCOMMODATION

ArkaBarka	3
Centar Hostel	5
Cricket Hostel	7
Green Studio Hostel	4
Hedonist Hostel	2
Indigo Hostel	1
Manga	6
Pop Art Hostel	4

29

Museum of the Serbian Orthodox Church
(Mon–Fri 8am–4pm, Sat 9am–noon,
Sun 11am–1pm; 100din), where a small
collection of bejewelled Bibles and other
gorgeously decorated paraphernalia is
housed in the HQ of the Patriarchate.

Konak of Princess Ljubica

At Kneza Sime Markovića 8, the **Konak
of Princess Ljubica** (Tues, Wed, Fri &
Sat 10am–5pm, Thurs noon–8pm,
Sun 10am–2pm; 100din; ⓦmgb.org.rs)
was built on the orders of Prince Miloš
Obrenović in 1831 to accommodate
his family. Eventually the abode of a
nineteenth-century noblewoman, it
underlines the Balkans' position as
a cultural crossroads: a Napoleon
III-themed room sits alongside a
Turkish-style room with a Koran
stand. It seems nineteenth-century
Belgraders loved socializing too:
there's a big semicircular sofa for
chatting guests in nearly every room.
Look out, too, for themed events in
the vaulted basement.

The Ethnographical Museum and Gallery of Frescoes

A short walk northeast of the Konak lie
two intriguing museums. At Studentski
trg 13, the **Ethnographical Museum**
(Tues–Sat 10am–5pm, Sun 9am–2pm;
150din; ⓦetnografskimuzej.rs) is a lively
people's history of crafts and clothes in
the Balkans. Beyond here, at Cara Uroša
20, the **Gallery of Frescoes** (Tues, Wed,
Fri & Sat 10am–5pm, Thurs noon–8pm,
Sun 10am–2pm; 100din) houses replicas
of 1200 of the country's most fêted
medieval frescoes – a must if you don't
have the opportunity to visit the originals
at the monasteries of southern Serbia and
Kosovo. The style is fresh and colourful
– lots of puce and blue.

Trg Republike and around

The main street leading south from
Kalemegdan is Kneza Mihailova, a
pedestrianized *korzo* (promenade) with
narrow, pretty fronts concealing an
array of fancy shops. It becomes more
commercialized and hulkish at its
southern end as it approaches **Trg**

BELGRADE STREET NAMES

Трг Републике	Trg Republike
Трг Слободе	Trg Slobode
Краља Петра	Kralja Petra
Краља Милана	Kralja Milana
Кнез Михаилова	Knez Mihailova
Француска	Francuska
Добрачина	Dobračina
Змај Јовина	Zmaj Jovina

Republike (Republic Square), the city's
main square. An irregularly shaped space,
it's dominated by the imperious National
Museum (which has remained closed for
years awaiting renovation), in front of
which is a grand statue of Prince Mihailo
on horseback – this is the traditional
meeting place for Belgraders.

East of Trg Republike is **Skadarlija**, the
former bohemian district; south of the
square, the wide swathe of **Terazije** slices
through the commercial and business
hub of the city.

Parliament Building and Church of St Marko

A left turn partway down Terazije
brings you to the **Parliament Building**
(Skupština), which has seen its fair
share of drama. In October 2000,
after Milošević tried to claw back the
presidential election he'd lost, hundreds
of demonstrators forced their way into
the parliament building and threw fake
ballot papers out of the windows as the
building blazed inside. It was again
the scene of protests after Kosovo's
declaration of independence in 2008.

More aesthetically pleasing is the
Church of St Marko just up the road, a
grandiose, five-domed neo-Byzantine
structure modelled on the revered
monastery of Gračanica in Kosovo. It
holds the tomb of the Serbian Emperor,
Tsar Dušan, protected by muscled
stone guards.

Church of St Sava

Dominating the skyline south of Terazije
is the magnificent gilded dome of the
Church of St Sava, on Svetosavski trg in
the Vračar district. Built on the spot
where the Turks supposedly burnt the

bones of the founder of the Serbian Orthodox Church in 1594, it is a perfect example of the way religious and national identities fuse here. Standing some 70m high, it also stakes a fair claim to be one of the largest Orthodox churches in the world, with a cavernous interior that has been under stop-start construction for over a hundred years. The church is a twenty-minute walk south of Trg Republike.

Nikola Tesla Museum
A short walk north of the Church of St Sava, at Krunska 51, is the engaging **Nikola Tesla Museum** (Tues–Fri 10am–6pm, Sat & Sun 10am–3pm; 150din; ⍟tesla-museum.org), which celebrates the pioneering work of the eponymous nineteenth-century inventor and engineer. Tesla (1856–1943) is credited with inventing the AC current, while other notable achievements include the development of wireless communications and remote control technologies. Alongside papers, tools and personal effects, the museum contains the urn with his ashes. Demonstrations of his experiments are usually held hourly.

The Museum of Yugoslav History
Well worth the trip is the **Museum of Yugoslav History** (Tues–Sun 10am–4pm; 200din; bus #40 or #41 from Kneza Miloša), located around 1.5km south of the centre on Botićeva 6. The centrepiece of the complex is the House of Flowers, designed in 1975 as Tito's winter garden and now housing the former president's tomb. The adjoining **museum** holds a wealth of exhibits pertaining to the former Yugoslavia's convoluted history, but inevitably the focus is on Tito himself, notably a bewildering array of gifts presented to him by foreign dignitaries, and thousands of batons used in the annual "relay of youth" which took place on 25 May each year to celebrate Tito's birthday.

Ada Ciganlija and Ada Bridge
In the summer months Belgraders flock to **Ada Ciganlija** (literally, "gypsy island"), a stretch of wooded park along the bank of the Sava just south of the centre. The island's sandy beaches have earned it the local nickname "Belgrade's seaside", and city dwellers enjoy its giant water slides, waterskiing and naturist area; there's even bungee-jumping. A gleaming new addition to the Belgrade skyline is the **Ada Bridge**, which skirts the easternmost tip of the island; a seven-span superstructure over 950m long, and rising to a height of some 200m, it is the largest single pylon suspension bridge in the world – the views of it from the island are stunning. To get to Ada Ciganlija, take bus #53 or #56 from Zeleni Venac.

Zemun
If you're after peace and quiet, head across the Sava River to New Belgrade and the west bank suburb of **Zemun**, a jumble of low-slung houses and narrow winding streets centred around the hilly waterside district of Gardoš, which holds the Baroque **Nikolajevska Church**, the city's oldest Orthodox church. To get here, take bus #15 from Zeleni Venac, or bus #83 from outside the train station, and alight on Glavna, the main street.

ARRIVAL AND DEPARTURE

By plane Belgrade's Nikola Tesla airport (☎11 209 4000, ⍟beg.aero) is 18km northwest of the city in Surčin, and connected to the centre by bus #72 (5.15am–midnight, Mon–Fri every 30min, Sat & Sun hourly; 140din), which departs from in front of the departures hall (one level above arrivals) and terminates at the Zeleni Venac market. If you wish to travel to the centre by taxi, avoid the sharks in the arrivals hall and instead head to the Taxi Info sign, where you can order a taxi for 1800din (€18).

By train The main train station (*železnička stanica*) is on Savski trg, a 15min walk southwest of the centre. Note that bus arrivals stop by the park across the road from the bus station itself.

Destinations Budapest (2 daily; 8hr); Ljubljana (1 daily; 10hr); Niš (6 daily; 4hr 30min–6hr); Novi Sad (11 daily; 1hr 30min); Skopje (2 daily; 9hr 30min); Subotica (7 daily; 3hr 30min–5hr); Zagreb (1 daily; 7hr 30min).

By bus The main bus station (*autobuska stanica*) is adjacent to the train station on Železnička. Note that bus arrivals stop by the park across the road from the station itself.

Destinations Kraljevo (every 1hr–1hr 30min; 2hr); Niš

29

(every 1hr–1hr 30min; 3hr); Novi Pazar (every 1hr–1hr 30min; 3hr); Novi Sad (every 30–45min; 1hr 20min); Sarajevo (7 daily; 7–8hr); Subotica (every 45min–1hr; 3hr 30min); Zagreb (5 daily; 5–6hr).

INFORMATION

Tourist information The main information centre is at Knez Mihailova 5 (Mon–Sat 9am–9pm, Sun 10am–3pm; ☎ 11 263 5622, ⊛ tob.rs/en), with other branches at the railway station (Mon–Sat 7am–1.30pm) and at the airport arrivals hall (daily 9am–9.30pm). You can pick up good maps and, occasionally, *Belgrade in Your Pocket*, at all of them.

GETTING AROUND

By bus, trolleybus and tram There's an extensive network of buses, trolleybuses and trams throughout the city; the cheapest way to travel is to buy a BusPlus pass (40din), which you load with credit (72din per journey); these can be bought from a kiosk or newsstand; alternatively, pay once you get on (145din) – either way, make sure you validate the ticket in the machine on board. Night buses depart from Trg Republike, operating between midnight and 4am (145din payable on the bus).

By taxi Give short shrift to the baying mob at the bus station and under no circumstances take a taxi from outside the train station; instead, grab one from the street or at any small rank; better still, call one of the following reliable firms: Beogradski Taxi (☎ 11 9801), Pink Taxi (☎ 11 9803) and Beotaxi (☎ 11 970). It is 170din from the outset, after which it's around 65din per km.

ACCOMMODATION

Belgrade can now count on a stack of terrific hostels, many within striking range of the stations, alongside an affordable, if not particularly exciting, crop of centrally located budget hotels.

ArkaBarka Bulevar Nikole Tesle bb ☎ 64 925 3507, ⊛ arkabarka.net. This floating hostel is a cool concept exactingly executed, with snug cabin-like rooms, on-board entertainment (playlists on the laptop), and drinks on deck (the small balcony edging the raft). To reach it, head towards the river through Ušće Park. Breakfast included. Dorm €15, double €40

Centar Hostel Gavrila Principa 46a ☎ 11 761 9686, ⊛ hostelcentar.com. Compact, quiet hostel near the bus and train stations, with four- to seven-bed dorms, triples, doubles and singles; every room has a TV and computer, while each floor has its own bathroom and kitchen. Breakfast not included. Dorm €13, double €42

Cricket Hostel Makenzijeva 46 ☎ 11 244 1966, ⊛ crickethostel.com. Small, warm and friendly hostel with doubles, triple and quads, each with TV and some with

balcony. There are laptops for use and wi-fi throughout. A 20min walk south of the stations, bus #83 or trams #9 or #12 to Slavija Square. Breakfast not included. Dorm €12, double €26

Green Studio Hostel Karađorđeva 69 ☎ 11 263 3626, ⊛ greenstudiohostel.com. Directly opposite the bus station drop-off point, this cheap, welcoming hostel – an airy loft conversion – has neat rooms and a cool, convivial communal space. Laundry is free. Breakfast not included. Dorm €10, double €32

★ **Hedonist Hostel** Simina 7 ☎ 11 328 4798, ⊛ hedonisthostelbelgrade.com. Occupying an old town house, this fantastic hostel is a superb antidote to the ubiquitous apartment-style places that proliferate – bare brick walls and low, wooden-beam ceilings lend it considerable charm. There's also a chill room with PlayStation, and the chirpy owners lay on regular barbecues in the pretty garden. A massage room and bike rental are available too. Breakfast not included. Dorm €11, double €50

Indigo Hostel Uzun Mirkova 10 ☎ 11 262 6333, ⊛ indigohostel.com. In a super location, the classy *Indigo* offers four smart, wood-furnished rooms (single, double, four- and six-bed), each with a balcony, and there's also a fully equipped studio apartment. Breakfast not included. Dorm €13, double €34

Manga Resavska 7 ☎ 11 324 3877, ⊛ mangahostel.com. Opened by enthusiastic couchsurfers, *Manga* occupies a small chalet, with a range of colourfully decorated dorms and a cosy exposed-brick cellar where guests share dinner with the staff. Breakfast not included. Dorm €10, double €36

Pop Art Hostel Karađorđeva 69 ☎ 11 218 5908, ⊛ poparthostel.com. In the same building as *Green Studio*, this place is as funky as its name suggests, with four superbly conceived rooms (sleeping two, four, six and eight), themed on artists Warhol and Basquiat, The Doors frontman Jim Morrison, and cartoonist Stan Drake. Breakfast not included. Dorm €14, double €44

EATING

Belgrade's restaurant scene has improved markedly in recent years and you'll now find an increasing number of ethnic restaurants alongside those serving traditional Serbian food, all at easy-on-the-pocket prices. If you fancy a spot of open-air (though entirely unexceptional) dining, complete with live music and a bit of tourist tack, then head to one of the traditional tavernas lining Skadarska.

Balzac Strahinjića Bana 13. A good spot for alfresco dining, this sparky little place hits a wide range of price points, from chicken risotto (650din) to salmon fillet (1150din). It also offers a cracking-value two-course menu of the day (noon–5pm) for 600din. Mon–Sat 9am–midnight.

Pomodoro Hilandarska 32. This fairly simple-looking place knocks up some of the city's best pizzas (650din) from its wood-burning stove, in addition to some terrific pasta dishes and cooked breakfasts. Mon–Sat 9am–midnight, Sun noon–midnight.

Proleće Vuka Karadžića 11. There's no fuss or fanfare at this very ordinary-looking restaurant, just a steady flow of locals tucking into honest Serbian grub such as *sarma* (cabbage leaves stuffed with ground pork and rice) with *sauerkraut* (510din), white beans with roast pork (530din) and *šopska salata* (350din; cheese, tomato and cucumber salad). Daily 9am–11pm.

Sava Mala Savski trg 7. This restaurant's location, opposite the stations, couldn't be any less distinguished, but don't let that put you off. Perfect for a pre- or post-journey fill-up, the menu offers the standard Serbian grills (680din) plus dishes like *prebanac* (Serbian beans) and the mighty *karađorđe šnicla* (stuffed veal steak). Daily 8am–11pm.

★ **Smokvica** Kralja Petra 73. Named after the fig tree that shades its slightly wonky stone-and-brick terrace, the "little fig" is a terrific place to tuck into a scrumptious *smokvica* burger (500din) or grilled veggie roll (320din); also available are country-themed breakfasts, with a different one each day of the week (400din). Daily 9am–midnight.

Tri Šešira Skadarska 29. Skadarlija's oldest restaurant, *The Three Hats* is a great place to be introduced to the robust charms of Serbian dining – the mixed grill (600din) includes no less than six types of meat. It's all rather hammed up for the tourists, but great fun if you can bear that. Daily 11am–midnight.

Vapiano Obilićev venac 29. The premise is simple but cool: pizzas, pastas and salads made with fresh ingredients before your eyes. Collect a card as you enter, place your order and they'll rustle up the meal in minutes. The lunch deal (11am–3pm) is a snip at 580din. Daily 9am–11.30pm.

Znak Pitanje, or **"?"** Kralja Petra 6. Run through with atmosphere and history, and furnished with low wooden tables and stools, the city's oldest inn is the best place to get your chops round a gut-busting *pljeskavica* with *kajmak* (500din). Daily 8am–midnight.

DRINKING AND NIGHTLIFE

Not for nothing is Belgrade now regarded as one of Europe's foremost party towns. There are a staggering number of places to drink and dance, with heavy concentrations along Strahinjića bana (known as "Silicon Valley", and not for its technological innovations), Obilićev venac and Njegoševa, to name but three streets. In summer, it's all aboard the *splavovi* – floating bars and clubs – to dance the night away. Most are concentrated on the bank of the Danube behind the *Hotel Jugoslavija* – a

conspicuous block on the main road towards Zemun – and along the Sava around the Brankov Bridge; two of the most popular are *Freestyler* and *Blaywatch*. Most clubs don't get going until at least 11pm and usually stay open until around 4am.

BARS AND CAFÉS

Choco Caffé Obilićev venac 30. Chocoholics will love this place; coffee, shakes, sundaes and the like – and if that isn't enough of a sugar rush, pop into the adjoining chocolate shop. Daily 9am–midnight.

Dobrila Dobračina 30. Neat venue with bare-brick walls, funky square bar, cushioned wooden benches and a small stage for regular evenings of live music. Daily 10am–2pm.

Mali Princ Palmotićeva 27. In the shadow of a giant linden tree, this refined little coffeehouse makes for a relaxing stop, with a range of coffees and some delectable cakes and chocolates. Mon–Sat 8am–midnight, Sun 10am–midnight.

Mamma's Biscuit House Strahinjića Bana 72a. By day this cool, curiously named café satisfies those seeking great coffee and cake; by night it services a more boisterous drinking crowd. Daily 9am–1am.

Pastis Strahinjića Bana 52b. This French-style bistro bar is one of the street's more down-to-earth venues, with drinkers huddling round wooden barrels. Decorative baguettes and a mini *bicyclette* complete the look. Daily 10am–2am.

Plato Akademski Plato 1. Serbs are a literary lot, and this bookshop-cum-café by the philosophy faculty is a Belgrade institution. The loungey outdoor terrace is a fun place to kick back, and there's live jazz at weekends. Mon–Sat 10am–2am, Sun noon–2am.

Rakia Bar Dobračina 5. How could you come to Belgrade and not sample a glass or two of the country's finest? This place has in excess of one hundred varieties – your only problem will be deciding which ones to try, and how many. Daily 9am–midnight.

★ **Supermarket** Corner of Strahinjića Bana and Višnjića. If Belgrade hasn't already sharpened your sense of the surreal, check out this vast "concept store", a warehouse with a futuristic aesthetic. Snack on sushi (750din), sip a freshly squeezed juice (320din) or nurse a cocktail (500din). Daily 9am–midnight, Fri & Sat until 1am.

CLUBS AND LIVE MUSIC

★ **Bašta** Mala Stepenice 1A. Just one of the many new venues down by the currently very cool Beton Hala Complex near Brankov Bridge, *Bašta* (meaning "The Garden") is a stupendously ace jazz café-cum-club, with live music (jazz, blues, soul, bossa nova) most nights of the week. One not to miss.

29

Bitef Art Café Skver Mire Trailović 1. Ever-popular café offering a regular and energetic programme of live funk, soul and jazz – as well as an eclectic mix of cultural events – in a converted Evangelical church.

French Room Francuska 12. Superb underground venue, blasting out dub and techno at weekends, and more straightforward rock and pop during the week. There are no signs – it's through a courtyard next to a residential building.

Idiot Dalmatinska 13, 1km southeast of Džordža Vašingtona, off Ruzveltova. Students and artists swarm into this small basement club by the Botanic Gardens. The terrace, too, is a great spot in warmer weather.

Oh, Cinema! Gračanička 18. Views of the Danube and live music draw crowds on summer weekends, when the club stays open till dawn.

Plastic Mint Takovska 34. Although not quite the mega-popular venue of yore, this split-level two-in-one club (consisting of *Plastic* and *Mint*) still pumps out some of the best house music in Belgrade; often visited by international DJs and pop stars. Thurs–Sat.

Tube Simina 21. This super-cool underground warren is the city's top dog for all strands of electronica, attracting some of Europe's leading DJs; the defining feature of its superbly conceived interior is a narrow, 25m-long dancefloor. Thurs–Sat.

ENTERTAINMENT

Tickets for concerts and events are on sale at the Bilet Servis ticket agency, inside the Kulturni Centar at Trg Republike 5 (Mon–Fri 9am–8pm, Sat 10am–8pm).

Kolarac Concert Hall Studentski trg 5 ⓦkolarac.rs. Hosts many of the concerts of the Beogradska Filharmonija. Box office Mon–Fri 10am–8pm; tickets 200–500din.

National Theatre Francuska 3 ⓦnarodnopozoriste .co.rs. Tickets to opera, ballet and plays are a bargain, ranging from 100–800din. Box office 11am–3pm & 5pm till performance.

SHOPPING

Kalenić Pijaca Maksima Gorkog bb. Belgrade's biggest open-air food market, a 20min walk southeast of Trg Republike in the Vračar district (just east of St Sava's). You can stock up on edible souvenirs or essentials for hostel cooking: smallholders sell fresh fruit and veg, breads, honey and national delicacies like *kajmak* (clotted cream) and *ajvar* (pepper and aubergine puree). Daily 6am–7pm.

Ušće Shopping Centre Bulevar Mihajla Pupina 4. Across the river in New Belgrade, the city's premier shopping complex harbours some 150 shops, as well as a host of entertainment facilities. Daily 10am–10pm.

DIRECTORY

Embassies and consulates Australia, Vladimira Popovića 38–40 ☎11 330 3400; Canada, Kneza Miloša 75 ☎11 306 3000; Ireland, Kosančićev venac 2/1 ☎11 218 3581; UK, Resavska 46 ☎11 306 0900; US, Kneza Miloša 50 ☎11 361 9344.

Exchange There are "Menjačnica" signs everywhere.

Hospital Emergency Centre, Pasterova 2 ☎11 361 8444 (24hr).

Internet Top floor of the Vulcan Bookshop, near tourist information at Sremska 4 (130din/hr). Free wi-fi in Studentski trg.

Left luggage (пртљаг – *prtlag*). At bus and train stations (120din/24hr).

Pharmacies Prvi Maj, Kralja Milana 9 ☎11 324 1349; Sveti Sava, Nemanjina 2 ☎11 264 3170. Both 24hr.

Police Savski trg 2 ☎11 264 5764.

Post office Zmaj Jovina 17 (Mon–Sat 8am–7pm).

Northern Serbia

North of Belgrade, stretching up towards the Hungarian border and spanning the southern part of the fertile Pannonian Plain, is **Vojvodina**, one of Serbia's most ethnically eclectic regions, with a large Hungarian minority. The region's capital, **Novi Sad**, is a charming spot that's a feasible day-trip from the capital or a handy springboard north to **Subotica** and Hungary. It's also an ideal base for forays into **Fruška Gora**, the gently undulating hills to the south peppered with medieval Orthodox monasteries.

NOVI SAD AND AROUND

Situated on the main road and rail routes towards Budapest some 75km northwest of Belgrade, **NOVI SAD** (Нови Сад) has long charmed visitors with its comely buildings – remnants of Austro-Hungarian rule. Today it's an emphatically young town – especially in the summer, when thousands of international revellers swarm to Petrovaradin Fortress for the four-day EXIT festival.

WHAT TO SEE AND DO

The hub of the city is **Trg Slobode** (Freedom Square), a spacious plaza bounded on either side by the neo-Gothic **Catholic Church of the Virgin Mary** and the neo-Renaissance town hall. Running east from here is bustling Zmaj Jovina, which, together with the adjoining bar-filled alleyway Laze Telečkog and wide, pedestrianized Dunavska, forms the town's central nexus of streets for eating, drinking and socializing. At the bottom end of Dunavska, occupying no. 35, the enlightening **Museum of Vojvodina** (Tues–Fri 9am–5pm, Sat & Sun 10am–6pm; 100din; ⓦmuzejvojvodine .org.rs) explores the region's many nationalities, including its significant Hungarian, Romanian and Slovak minorities; the prize exhibit, however, is a gold-plated Roman parade helmet.

Sun-lovers should head for the **Štrand** (May–Sept; 50din), a sandy beach on the Danube's north bank, opposite the fortress, which has bars, cafés and a "school's out" vibe.

The south bank and Petrovaradin Fortress

Novi Sad developed in tandem with the huge **Petrovaradin Fortress** (open access) on the Danube's south bank. The fortress rises picturesquely from rolls of green hillside, its delicate lemon-yellow buildings set inside sturdy fortifications. It took its present shape in the eighteenth century when the Austrians tried to create an invincible barrier against the Turks. Unfortunately its defences quickly became outdated, and

the authorities decided to imprison independent-minded troublemakers here instead – including Karađorđe and, a century later, a young Tito. The fortress **museum** (Tues–Sun 10am–6pm; 100din) relays the history of both the fortress and the town, though is more interesting for its wealth of eighteenth- and nineteenth-century applied art. As you approach from town, look out for the **plaque** on the right of the bridge commemorating Oleg Nasov, who was killed during the NATO bombing – Novi Sad was one of the cities hardest hit in the spring of 1999, losing all its bridges.

Beyond the fortress, climb the steps to the right of the church; you'll arrive just under the **clock tower**. From this vantage point, the functional twentieth-century architecture of Novi Sad itself looks less alluring than the fortress does from the opposite bank, but the views of the surrounding countryside are magnificent.

Sremski Karlovci

On the eastern fringes of the Fruška Gora National Park, the enchanting small town of **Sremski Karlovci** (Сремски Карловци) makes for a great little trip out of Novi Sad. Its main square, Branka Radičevića, with the Orthodox and Catholic churches side by side and the Four Lions fountain, is highly picturesque, but Sremski Karlovci's status as a national treasure comes courtesy of its speciality wine, **Bermet**,

---

MONASTERIES AROUND NOVI SAD

Shadowing the city to the south are the low rolling hills of the **Fruška Gora**, once an island in the now evaporated Pannonian Sea. These days, its orchards and vineyards comprise a national park carved up by a web of simple hiking trails. The hills – known among devotees as the Holy Mountain – also house sixteen monasteries (there were once 35). About 15km south of Novi Sad, just off the main road before the village of Irig, is **Novo Hopovo**, where a Byzantine church is housed within a picturesque monastery. Not far off are two more sixteenth-century monastic churches: elegant white **Krušedol** and **Vrdnik-Ravanica**, which has Tsar Lazar's collarbone on display.

Accessing the monasteries is nigh on impossible without a car; a good local **car rental** firm in Novi Sad is Autotehna (Balzakova 29; ☎21 474 516, ⓦautotehna.com); expect to pay around €35–40 for a day's rental. Alternatively, contact the tourist office in Sremski Karlovci (see p.952), who can, with some warning, organize group sightseeing tours of the main monasteries (around 1200din) or arrange for a driver (around 2000din for 3hr).

29

made exclusively here since 1770. Drunk with desserts or as an aperitif, Bermet was popular in the Austro-Hungarian court and served on board the *Titanic*'s maiden voyage. The tourist information office on the main square can point you to the delightful **wine cellar** owned by the Živanović family (Mitropolita Stratimirovića 86b; daily 10am–7pm), where you can buy your own supplies – swing open the side-gate to enter their orchard; there's also a quaint beekeeping museum. Alternatively, relax with a glass or two on the outdoor decking of the hotel of the same name on the main square.

Sremski Karlovci is a ten-minute taxi ride from Novi Sad (around 500din); catch a cab from the rank on Ilije Ognjanovića.

ARRIVAL AND DEPARTURE

By train Novi Sad's train station is just under 1km north of the centre on Bulevar Jaše Tomića. Heading for the centre, bus #4 (50din) departs from in front of it, while walking takes about 30min; head straight down Bulevar Oslobođenja and turn left into Jevrejska at the market. A taxi into the centre should cost no more than 200din.
Destinations Belgrade (every 2hr; 2hr); Budapest (2 daily; 6hr); Subotica (10 daily; 2hr).
By bus The bus station is adjacent to the train station.
Destinations Belgrade (every 30–45min; 1hr 20min); Sarajevo (2 daily; 8hr); Subotica (every 30min–1hr; 1hr 30min).

INFORMATION

Tourist information Mihaila Pupina 9 and Modena 1 (Mon–Fri 7.30am–6pm, Sat 10am–3pm; ☎ 21 421 811,

---

★ **TREAT YOURSELF**

Zak Šafarikova 6 ☎ 021 447 545. Novi Sad's finest restaurant, with exquisitely thought-out dishes such as deer fillet with red cabbage and juniper sauce (1200din), and chocolate leaves with white mousse and morello cherries. Fine wines and impeccable service round things off beautifully. Mon–Fri 8am–11pm, Sat 10am–1am, Sun 11am–11pm.

ⓦ turizamns.rs). There's free wi-fi in many public spaces, including Trg Slobode – ask the tourist office to give you the password.

ACCOMMODATION

All of Novi Sad's accommodation gets booked up well in advance of the EXIT Festival, and just about all of them double their prices for this period.
Hostel 021 Pavla Papa 6 ☎ 63 573 073. Located on a small side street across from the National Theatre, the clean and welcoming *021* has four- to six-bed dorms, a triple and a double with TV, plus a spacious communal area and a small kitchen. Breakfast not included. Dorm €10, double €30
Hostel Downtown Njegoševa 2 ☎ 21 524 818, ⓦ hostelnovisad.com. A quiet, unassuming hostel just a few paces along from the main square, with large dorms, kitchen and laundry facility. Breakfast not included. Dorm €12, double €40
Hotel Mediteraneo Ilije Ognjanovića 10 ☎ 21 427 135, ⓦ hotelmediteraneo.rs. A step up in comfort from the town's hostels, this hotel has bright, fresh, nautical-themed rooms decorated in a fetching lime green and chocolate brown colour scheme. Breakfast included. Double €62, three-person apartment €78
Sova Hostel Ilije Ognjanovića 26 ☎ 21 527 556, ⓦ hostelsova.com. Located just off the main square, the "owl" is an appealing apartment hostel offering funky four- to ten-bed rooms, a cosy communal space, and kitchen. Breakfast not included. Dorm €10, double €32

EATING AND DRINKING

Astal Saren Mite Ružića 4. The aroma of grilled meat will have you sniffing out this homely little Serbian diner, located up a tiny side street off Laze Telečkog; big, calorific plates of grilled sausages, *ćevapi* (a type of kebab) and *pljeskavica*, served with roast or fried potatoes and pickled salad (450din). Daily 9am–11pm.
Café Nublu Žarka Zrenjanina 12. Welcoming, gay-friendly café/bar located at the back of the city's best bookshop; the bare-bricked interior is replete with dimly lit lanterns, quirky clocks and lots of mismatched furniture,

---

THE EXIT FESTIVAL

For four days at the beginning of July the grounds of Petrovaradin Fortress are overrun by **EXIT Festival** revellers (ⓦ exitfest.org). Now established as one of the premier music events in Europe, EXIT attracts some of the very biggest names in pop, techno and hip-hop (the 2013 line-up included Snoop Doggy Dog, The Prodigy and Bloc Party). Buy tickets and camping passes via the website. You can rent rooms in Novi Sad for the duration: check ⓦ exittrip.org, which helps with booking accommodation and transport.

while the colourfully graffitied garden terrace completes the look. Daily 9am–11pm.

Divan Dućan Laze Telečkog 6. This tiny café-bar is crammed with eye-catching art and antiques: it's rather like drinking cocktails in a toy-box. Soya caramel macchiato 155din, martinis and cocktails 250din. Mon–Sat 9am–midnight, Sun 11am–11pm.

Foody Modena 1–3. Committed cost-cutters will warm to this bright, functional canteen, with soups, sandwiches, *pljeskavica* (150din) and much more. Sit down or takeaway. Mon–Sat 7.30am–11pm, Sun 9.30am–11pm.

Gusan Zmaj Jovina 4. Narrow brick-vaulted cellar restaurant doling out juicy mixed grills and kebabs (600din); alternatively, just stop by for a beer at the long wooden bar or outside on the buzzy terrace. It's through a passageway by the Diesel shop sign. Daily 8am–midnight.

Kuća Mala Laze Telečkog 4. A refreshing antidote to the string of brasher venues along this street, the "little house", with its homely decor and checked tablecloths, is great for a hot sandwich (200din), pizza (680din) or bowl of pasta. Daily 8am–11pm.

SUBOTICA

Some 175km north of Belgrade, Vojvodina's second city, **SUBOTICA** (Суботица; Hungarian: Szabadka), is a wonderful counterpoint to the capital, its Secessionist buildings, green spaces, wide pavements and burghers riding around on old-fashioned bicycles all contributing to its unspoilt, wholesome air. Just a stone's throw from Hungary, Subotica feels tangibly more like its northern neighbour. Historically, the ties are close: Subotica reached its apotheosis in the years of the Austro-Hungarian Empire, when it was granted the status of a Royal Free Town.

WHAT TO SEE AND DO

The heart of the town is grassy **Trg Republike**, fronted by a hulking city hall built in 1912; its gingerbread-like windows and colourfully patterned roof are almost too gaudy to look at in full sunlight. In front stands a brilliant blue fountain. Adjoining Trg Republike is Trg Slobode, behind which runs the Korzo, a busy pedestrianized street featuring the fairytale **Piraeus Bank** building, with its door and windows

straight out of a medieval castle, created by architects Dezsó Jakab and Marcell Komor at the start of the twentieth century.

Further out, northwest of the city centre is another Jakab/Komor collaboration: the dignified but now deserted 1902 **synagogue**, where a moving plaque remembers the "4000 Jewish citizens with whom we lived and built Subotica".

Likovni Susret Contemporary Art Gallery

Occupying the wildly colourful 1904 mansion of architect Ferenc Raichle, Raichle on Rajhlov Park Square is the **Likovni Susret Contemporary Art Gallery** (Mon & Sat 8am–noon, Tues–Fri 8am–6pm; 100din), exhibiting work by local artists. The real draw, however, is the attention-seeking interior decor, from the cutesy hearts at the entranceway to the bulbous alcoves upstairs.

Cathedral of St Theresa

A five-minute walk west of the centre, on Harambašićeva, the **Catholic Cathedral of St Theresa** is a curiously moving place; in the surrounding square, the scattered statues are a poignant mix of classical piety (the two hands clasped in prayer) and postwar brutalism (the enormous monument to the "victims of fascism" who died during World War II).

ARRIVAL AND DEPARTURE

By train The train station dominates one side of Rajhlov Park, a 5min walk from the centre.
Destinations Belgrade (6 daily; 3hr 30min–5hr); Budapest (2 daily; 2hr 30min); Novi Sad (10 daily; 2hr).
By bus The bus station is on Senćanski Put, a 15min walk from the centre on the road to Novi Sad.
Destinations Belgrade (hourly; 3hr 30min); Novi Sad (hourly; 1hr 30min); Szeged, Hungary (every 2hr; 1hr 30min).

INFORMATION

Tourist information Trg Slobode 1, to the rear of the City Hall (Mon–Fri 8am–6pm, Sat 9am–1pm; ☎ 24 670 350, ⓦ visitsubotica.rs). There are plenty of brochures and maps on both the town and Lake Palić.

29

ACCOMMODATION

Hotel Patria Đure Đakovića bb ☎ 24 554 500, ⓦ hotelpatria.rs. Between the bus station and the centre, this budget four-star hotel proves you get more bang for your buck outside Belgrade. Breakfast included. Double **€60**

Incognito Huga Badalića 3, left off Maksima Gorkog ☎ 62 666 674, ⓦ hostel-subotica.com. This large hostel is a 5min walk from the central square, with basic but clean rooms, all with TV and wi-fi. Breakfast not included. Dorm **€10**, double **€24**

EATING AND DRINKING

Boss Matije Korvina 7–8. Just behind the Likovni Susret mansion, this atrium pizzeria and bar is where people come to be seen; the adjoining statue-strewn courtyard is a fabulous place to sup a beer. Pizza 450din. Daily 7.30am–midnight.

Népkör Žarka Zrenjanina 11. Outstanding Hungarian food in a lovely townhouse 5min north of the cathedral. Someone's had fun with the menu (fancy "a pageant of local cheeses" or "concealed brains"?). *Gulaš* to share 150din; set menu 300din. Mon–Sat 10am–10pm, Sun 10am–4pm.

Stara Picerija Matije Korvina 5. Opposite *Boss*, on a cute cobbled alleyway, this place excels at pizza (450din), hot sandwiches and much more besides; attractive interior and cheerful feel-good classics on the stereo. Mon–Sat 7am–midnight, Sun 9am–midnight.

Southern Serbia

South of Belgrade, the softly rolling hillsides studded with low red-roofed houses are the setting for three of the country's most precious medieval monasteries: **Žiča**, **Studenica** and **Sopoćani**. Elsewhere, the south's main city, **Niš**, conveniently straddles major road and rail routes to Bulgaria and Macedonia, and is an attractive small town with some fascinating sights.

ŽIČA, STUDENICA AND SOPOĆANI

In the hilly stretch south from the town of Kraljevo – itself some 170km south of Belgrade – to Novi Pazar lie some of Serbia's most impressive **monasteries**. Just 4km southeast of Kraljevo, **Žiča** was a thirteenth-century creation of St Sava – Serbia's patron saint and the first archbishop of the independent Serbian Church – with a vivid red exterior that evokes the red Serbs use to paint eggs at Easter.

The first and greatest of the Serbian monasteries, however, is **Studenica**, set against the wild, roaming slopes some 12km (and accessible by bus) from the village of Ušče. It was established in 1190 by Stefan Nemanja, founder of the Nemanjić dynasty, whose marble tomb lies in the Church of the Virgin Mary. Studenica's **superb frescoes** were the work of an innovative but still anonymous Greek painter who created *trompe-l'oeil* frescoes to resemble mosaics.

Around 16km from Novi Pazar is the **Sopoćani** monastery, a thirteenth-century construction that once stretched across a whole complex but of which only the Holy Trinity Church remains. *The Assumption of Virgin Mary* is the most famous of its unusually large Byzantine frescoes; the bright colours and expressive faces are said to prefigure the Italian Renaissance.

NIŠ

The pleasant university town of **NIŠ** (Ниш), 235km southeast of Belgrade, is a useful stopover point between Belgrade and Sofia or Skopje. Its inhabitants have a definite small-town pride, as well they might: this is the birthplace of Constantine, the Roman emperor responsible for the conversion of the

---

VISITING THE MONASTERIES

While Žiča is easily accessible by **bus** from Kraljevo (every 30–45min; 50din), you'll need a **car** if you want to see more than one monastery in a day. In Niš try Inter Rent-A-Car (P.C. Ambasador Lok 23; ☎ 18 528 852, ⓦ rentacarnis.rs) or Autotehna (Svetozara Markovića 1; ☎ 18 246 222, ⓦ autotehna.com); prices start at around €40 per day. If you have more time, you could try public buses: on the Kraljevo–Novi Pazar route, you can get off at Ušče, from where there are 2–3 daily buses to Studenica.

whole empire to Christianity. Its collection of intriguing – if macabre – sights is a gritty reminder of the darker sides to Serbia's history, but the focus in the cafés and bars crammed with students is all on having a good time.

WHAT TO SEE AND DO

The city's centrepiece is its main square, **Trg Kralja Milana**, which sits across the Nišava River from **Niš Fortress**.

The fortress

A Roman fortress once stood here – a circle of Roman tombstones remains inside – but the current fortifications date from the beginning of the eighteenth century. Enter from the main İstanbul Gate facing the bridge; inside, the town authorities have put real effort into making this a place residents can enjoy, with the beautiful **mosque of Bali Bey** converted into an exhibition space, and the row of cafés in the shadow of the fortress's inner wall a cool spot to unwind. Each August the whole fortress is given over to the Nišville jazz festival (ⓦnisville.com).

The first of the city's rather grim sights is to your right as you leave the fortress: look out for the miniature blue-domed **memorial chapel** perched on the lawn, which commemorates the local people killed in the NATO bombings.

Ćele Kula

East of the centre on Brače Taskoviča, **Ćele Kula** (The Skull Tower; Tues–Sun 9am–6pm; 150din; take any bus towards Niška Banja) makes for gruesome sightseeing. It dates from 1809, when Stevan Sinđelić, commander of a nationalist uprising, found his men surrounded by the Turkish army on nearby Čegar Hill and took drastic action against his adversaries, firing into his gunpowder supplies and blowing up most of the Turks and all the Serbs around him. Following the battle, to deter future rebellion the ruling Pasha ordered that the heads of the Serbian soldiers killed in the battle be stuffed and mounted on the tower; 952 went into creating this macabre totem pole, though today only 58 remain.

Crveni Krst

The derelict **Crveni Krst** (Red Cross; Tues–Sun 9am–6pm; 150din) concentration camp, a ten-minute walk down busy Bulevar 12 Februar from the bus station, is powerfully evocative: the hand-painted German signs for the washroom, messroom and kitchen make it all seem very recent. The barbed-wire fences and watchtowers, so familiar from camps in Poland and Germany, are a reminder that the displacement and genocide of millions was a truly pan-European operation. The camp was closed at the time of writing, so check with the tourist office first.

ARRIVAL AND DEPARTURE

By train The train station is 2km west of town on Dimitrija Tucovića. Buses #1, #5 and #6 all run to the centre.
Destinations Belgrade (6 daily; 4hr 30min–6hr); Skopje (2 daily; 4hr 45min); Sofia (1 daily; 5hr).
By bus The bus station is a 5min walk from town, west of the fortress on Bulevar Februar 12.
Destinations Belgrade (every 30–45min; 3hr); Kraljevo (6 daily; 3hr); Skopje (6 daily; 4–5hr); Sofia (2 daily; 2hr 30min).

INFORMATION

Tourist information Voždova Karađorđa 7 (Mon–Fri 8am–7pm, Sat 9am–2pm; ☏ 18 523 118, ⓦ visitnis.com) and inside the fortress (Mon–Fri 9am–8pm, Sat 9am–4.30pm, Sun 10am–3pm; ☏ 18 250 222).

ACCOMMODATION

Downtown Hostel Kej Kola Srpskih Sestara 3/2 ☏ 18 526 756, ✉ office@downtownhostel.rs. Occupying a renovated apartment just metres from the riverfront, this enthusiastically run place conceals an eight-bed dorm and several doubles (all with a/c), plus a well-equipped kitchen and lounge. Dorm €12, double €30
Hostel Niš Dobrička 3a ☏ 18 513 703, ⓦ hostelnis.rs. A spotless hostel with engaging owners – this should be your first port of call. There are two-, four- and eight-bed rooms, and it's just a few minutes' walk west from the fortress entrance. Breakfast not included. Dorm €11, double €32

EATING AND DRINKING

Cobbled Kazandžijsko Sokače (Tinker's Alley), just south of Trg Kralja Milana, is the town's social hub, thronging with café-bars.
★ **Hamam** Tvrđava bb. Named after the Turkish baths it's housed in (just inside the fortress entrance), this is the

29

place to try some grilled lamb or oven-baked fish (400–500din); frequent evenings of live music enliven proceedings. Daily 10am–midnight.

Mamma Nade Tomić 10. Quirkily designed pizzeria with a terrific wood-fired oven; serious carnivores should have a stab at the house pizza, which comes topped with five types of meat (500din). Mon–Sat 10am–midnight, Sun noon–11pm.

Sinđelić Nikole Pašića 36. Named after the kamikaze general behind the Tower of Skulls episode,

Sinđelić excels at simple, hearty Serbian food; try the gourmet *pljeskavica*, stuffed with pork and spices (500din). Located near the Kalča shopping mall. Daily 8am–1am.

Spark Strahinjića bana 2a. The city's most vibrant club, there's loads of great stuff going on here, such as live turbo-folk (a bizarre hybrid of folk and dance music), gypsy bands, electronica parties and occasional foreign acts. A good time guaranteed. Thurs–Sun 11pm–5am.

SPIŠ CASTLE

Slovakia

HIGHLIGHTS

❶ **Bratislava** Try out the chic coffeehouses
and cool underground bars. **See p.963**

❷ **Banská Štiavnica** Climb a volcano or swim
in a mine. **See p.968**

❸ **High Tatras** Admire the majesty of Slovakia's
highest peaks. **See p.970**

❹ **Levoča** Explore the crumbling backstreets
of this beautiful walled town. **See p.973**

❺ **Spiš Castle** Step into the Middle Ages at
this atmospheric pile. **See p.974**

❻ **Košice** Enjoy this laidback and youthful
southern city. **See p.974**

HIGHLIGHTS ARE MARKED ON THE MAP ON P.959

ROUGH COSTS

Daily budget Basic €30, occasional treat €40

Drink Beer €1.70

Food Gnocchi with bacon €4

Hostel/budget hotel €15/€30

Travel Bratislava–Košice (train): 5hr–6hr 35min, €14

FACT FILE

Population 5.4 million

Language Slovak

Currency Euro (€)

Capital Bratislava

International phone code ☎421

Time zone GMT +1hr

Introduction

Hungarians and Turks came to Slovakia for its natural resources, and so does the modern tourist. Broad, sprawling mountains mean good skiing and snowboarding, Karst is for caving, and the rambling hilly midlands are a hiker's paradise.

30

Bratislava is a badger sett of cobbled streets, low arches and tiny squares. It's small enough to explore in a day, but big enough to hold your interest for a long weekend. In Central Slovakia is lovely **Banská Štiavnica**, a UNESCO-protected medieval mining town in a lunar landscape of dead volcanoes. East and north are the **High Tatras**, as decent a mountain range as any in Central Europe. They've long been the site of enthusiastic skiing, hiking and sonnet-writing. Heading east towards Ukraine is the wild, rocky **Spiš** region, home to medieval mammoth **Spiš Castle** and the twelfth-century walled town of **Levoča**. Continuing south, almost to the Hungarian border, you'll find Slovakia's second city, the lively town of **Košice**.

Sharing borders with Poland, the Czech Republic, Austria, Hungary and Ukraine, Slovakia is landlocked, with high mountains in the north, low mountains in the centre, hills to the west, and the Danube basin to the south. The population is fairly diverse, with over half a million ethnic **Hungarians**, hundreds of thousands of **Roma** (Gypsies), and several thousand **Rusyns** in the east.

CHRONOLOGY

450 BC Celts inhabit present-day Slovakia.

623 AD Samo becomes King of the Slavs after defeating the Avarians near Bratislava.

828 First Christian church consecrated in Slovakia.

863 First Slavic alphabet written in Greater Moravia by saints Cyril and Methodius.

895 The Magyars (Hungarians) gradually begin to conquer and occupy the territory.

1241 Mongol invasion of Slovakia results in heavy losses.

1526 Hungary loses Buda to the Turks; the Habsburgs move their capital to Bratislava.

1800s Growth in Slovak nationalism.

1895 Czechs and Slovaks form a strategy of mutual cooperation against dual monarchy Austria-Hungary.

1918 The independent republic of Czechoslovakia is established on the defeat of Austria-Hungary in World War I.

1939 Germany takes Sudetenland in Czechoslovakia, before occupying the rest of the country.

1945 Slovak National Uprising against German occupation is successful, but thousands of Slovakian Jews have already been sent to the camps.

1948 The Communist Party comes into power in Czechoslovakia.

1989 The Velvet Revolution heralds the end of Communism in Czechoslovakia.

1993 Czechoslovakia splits peacefully into two states.

2004 Slovakia joins NATO and the EU.

2009 The euro replaces the Slovak crown as the national currency.

ARRIVAL AND DEPARTURE

Slovakia's main international airport is M.R. Štefánika, often referred to as **Bratislava Airport** (☏ 2 3303 3353, ⦿ bts .aero), 9km northeast of central Bratislava. There are also international airports in **Košice**, operating flights to and from Prague, Vienna, London and Dublin, and in Poprad, operating mainly business flights to and from various European cities. Another option is to fly into Vienna; the two capitals are only 60km apart, flights to Vienna are often cheaper, and Eurolines (10 daily; 1hr 10min) and Postbus (18 daily; 1hr 30min–1hr 40min) both run shuttle-bus connections for €10–15 one-way. For a more romantic arrival, there's the Vienna–Bratislava hydrofoil (see p.965).

Slovakia has good **rail connections** with Austria, Hungary, Poland and the Czech Republic. Most international trains terminate at Bratislava, but trains from Budapest, Kraków and Prague also run to Košice, and there's a direct service between Prague and Poprad.

Eurolines buses connect European cities to Bratislava (ⓦeurolines.sk), and **Student Agency's** (ⓦstudentagencybus .com) domestic and international coaches are cheap and comfortable.

GETTING AROUND

BY TRAIN

Train journeys are slow but scenic. Slovak Railways (Železnice Slovenskej Republiky or ŽSR; ☎18188, ⓦslovakrail.sk) runs fast *rýchlik* trains that stop at major towns; *osobný* (local) trains stop everywhere. You can buy **tickets** (*lístok*) for domestic journeys at the station (*stanica*) before or on the day of departure. Supplements are payable on all EuroCity (EC) trains, and occasionally for InterCity (IC) and Express (Ex) trains of Slovak Railway trains. ŽSR runs reasonably priced sleepers and couchettes. Book in advance no later than six hours before departure. **InterRail** is valid; **Eurail** requires supplements. Find train timetables online at ⓦcp.atlas.sk.

BY BUS

Buses (*autobus*) cover a more extensive network. The state bus company is Slovenská Autobusová Doprava or SAD.

Buy your **ticket** from the driver or book in advance from the station if you're travelling at the weekend or early in the morning on one of the main routes. Bus timetables are available online at ⓦcp.atlas.sk.

BY BICYCLE

Although much of Slovakia is mountainous and not ideal for **cyclists**, the countryside around Bratislava has well-maintained bike paths that stretch into Austria and Hungary. More demanding rides can take you into the Little Carpathians. Most trains allow bikes.

ACCOMMODATION

New B&Bs are opening all the time, and hostels are on the rise. There's no network of **hostels** in Slovakia, though a few are affiliated to HI (ⓦhihostels .com). Bratislava has plenty of good private hostels, and in the High Tatras you can find chalet-style **boarding houses** (*chata*) scattered over the mountains, with basic dorm beds from €8 per bed. There are plenty of **campsites** in Slovakia, which usually rent out basic wooden huts (*chata*), fun if you share with friends.

In summer the cheapest accommodation is **university halls**; ask at the local tourist office for details. **Private rooms** are also cheap, and can be organized through the local tourist office as well. If you're a student, get hold of an ISIC (International Student Identity Card), as you'll need it to get student rates. Check websites for online booking discounts. Smaller places are often understaffed so pre-book and give an estimated arrival time, or you might find yourself locked out.

FOOD AND DRINK

Slovak **cuisine** is an edifice resting on three mighty columns: the potato, the pig and the cabbage. Because of their many neighbours, you'll find hints of Polish, Hungarian and Ukrainian delights as well. Main courses are usually a combination of meat with potatoes (*zemiaky*), or dumplings. Slovak dumplings (*halušky*) are small and smooth, like gnocchi. Meat is usually breaded and fried, or cooked in a sauce. The main meal of the day is lunch, which starts with **soup** (*polievka*) – perhaps garlic (*cesnaková*) or sauerkraut (*kapustnica*). You can often find game meats, like boar, rabbit and venison, on menus, as well as pork, beef, chicken, duck and goose.

A classic mid-morning **snack** is *párok*, a hot frankfurter. A Slovak delicacy is *jaternica*, made from pig's blood and rice. *Bryndza*, sheep's cheese made in the region since the Middle Ages, is light, salty and delicious. *Bryndzové halušky*, the national dish, is dumplings served with *bryndza* and bacon. Another favourite is *pirohy*; unleavened boiled dumplings stuffed with cheese, a little like ravioli. Hungarian goulash is popular, and so is *langoše* – deep-fried dough topped with crushed garlic, cheese, ketchup or sour cream.

Some popular **desserts** are strudel (apple or curd cheese), *palacinky* (crêpes filled with chocolate, fruit or jam, and usually cream) and *lievance*, which look like Scotch or American pancakes, and are served with hot fruit. An unusual Slovak speciality is sweet noodles (*rezance*), with poppy seeds and butter or curd cheese and sugar.

Outside the major cities, **closing time** is usually 9 or 10pm. Pubs often have cheap lunchtime deals from 11.30am to 1.30pm.

DRINK

The Romans brought **wine** to Slovakia. Vineyards in the southeast produce good whites, the most distinctive being Tokaj, a sweet dessert wine. For a few weeks in September you can get fresh *burčák*, a fruity, bubbly semi-fermented white with which Slovaks and Czechs toast the harvest. *Slivovica*, made with plums, and *borovička,* made with juniper berries, are popular spirits, but Slovaks will gladly make alcohol from any fruit. The national soft drinks are Kofola, an aniseedy Coca-Cola substitute, and Vinea, made with red or white grapes. The best-known bottled **beer** is Zlatý Bažant (Golden Pheasant). You'll find a pub (*krčma – pivnica* is different) in every town, as well as a wine bar (*vináreň*), which will usually have later closing hours and often doubles as a nightclub. The legal drinking age is 18 and you may be asked for ID in shops, pubs or clubs. **Coffee** is traditionally served strong and black, but American-style coffeehouses are popularizing cappuccino, latte and the like. Teahouses (*čajovňa*) are popular, especially with young people, and stock dozens of types of **tea**.

CULTURE AND ETIQUETTE

Learning a few Slovak words helps break down Slovak reserve, even just "hello", "goodbye" and "thank you" (see box, p.962). If you've been travelling eastwards, your Czech will do fine, as all Slovaks understand Czech (an equation which doesn't work in reverse).

When **tipping**, Slovaks round up to the nearest euro or two, but as a foreigner it's courteous to tip ten percent. When you are introduced to strangers, shake hands, and don't use first names when addressing older people. Casual greetings like *ahoj* are only for close friends. Wish fellow diners a good meal (*dobrú chuť*) before starting, and make a toast (*na zdravie*) before drinking. If you are invited to a Slovak home you must take off your shoes at the door, even when told not to (they're just being polite), and if you're invited to eat, bring wine or chocolates.

SPORTS AND ACTIVITIES

Slovaks love football and **ice hockey**, which you can see live on screens in bars across the Republic. You can go to ice hockey games in stadiums from September to April (ⓦhcslovan.sk, in Bratislava); tickets cost between €13 and €50 and can be bought from the arena on match days. There's plenty of **hiking**, **skiing**, **snowboarding** and **rafting** in the High Tatras (ⓦtatry.sk) and caving in the Slovak Karst in east Slovakia (ⓦssj.sk). Walking is a popular national pastime, and if there wasn't so much woodland, the woods would be full on Saturday afternoons.

COMMUNICATIONS

Most **post offices** (*pošta*) open Monday to Friday 8am to 5pm. You can buy stamps (*známky*) from tobacconists (*trafika*) and street kiosks, and it's also worth asking in anywhere that sells postcards. Cheap local calls can be made from any phone, but for international calls it's best to buy a **phonecard** (*telefónna karta*) from a tobacconist or post office. You'll find an **internet café** in most towns; the average charge is €3 per hour.

SLOVAKIA ONLINE

ⓦ **slovakia.org** Political, historical, cultural and economic information.
ⓦ **slovakia.travel** Tourist information in a variety of languages with travel tips and event information.
ⓦ **spectator.sme.sk** English-language weekly with news and listings.
ⓦ **slovak-republic.org** Upcoming events and attractions as well as other travel information.

EMERGENCY NUMBERS

Police ❶ 158; Ambulance ❶ 155; Fire ❶ 150; General emergency ❶ 112.

EMERGENCIES

Violent crime is fairly rare and pickpocketing or petty theft is the biggest danger. You should carry a photocopy of your passport with you, as ID is required by law. Small ailments can be dealt with by the **pharmacist** (*lekáreň*); for bigger problems go to the nearest **hospital** (*nemocnica*).

INFORMATION

Most towns have some kind of **tourist office** (*informačné centrum*), usually with English-speaking staff. In summer they're generally open Monday to Friday 9am to 6pm, Saturday and Sunday 9am to 2pm; in winter they tend to close an hour earlier and all day Sunday. **Maps** are available from tourist offices, bookshops and some hotels. The Slovak for town plan is *plán mesta*.

MONEY AND BANKS

The euro was introduced in Slovakia in 2009. **Credit** and **debit cards** are accepted in upmarket hotels and restaurants and some shops, and there are plenty of **ATMs** in larger towns. **Exchange offices** (*zmenáreň*) can be found in big hotels, travel agencies and department stores, but it's usually better value to change your money in a bank.

OPENING HOURS AND HOLIDAYS

Opening hours for local shops are in the region of 9am to 6pm on weekdays and 9am to noon Saturdays, with supermarkets staying open later and

STUDENT DISCOUNTS

To get a student discount (which is often as much as fifty percent) you'll need an ISIC, as most places won't accept your university ID card.

30

30

SLOVAK

	SLOVAK	PRONUNCIATION
Yes	*Áno*	Uh-no
No	*Nie*	Nyeh
Please	*Prosím*	Pro-seem
Thank you	*Ďakujem*	Dya-koo-yem vam
Hello/Good day	*Dobrý deň/Ahoj*	Dob-rie den[y]/a-hoy
Goodbye	*Dovidenia*	Do-vid-en-ya
Excuse me	*Prepáčte*	Pre-patch-teh
Where	*Kde*	Gde
Good	*Dobrý*	Dob-rie
Bad	*Zlý*	Zlee
Near	*Blízko*	Bli-sko
Far	*Ďaleko*	D[y]a-lek-o
Cheap	*Lacný*	Lats-nie
Expensive	*Drahý*	Dra-hie
Open	*Otvorený*	Ot-vor-eh-nie
Closed	*Zatvorený*	Zat-vor-eh-nie
Today	*Dnes*	Dnes
Yesterday	*Včera*	Ftch-er-a
Tomorrow	*Zajtra*	Zuyt-ra
How much is…?	*Koľko stojí…?*	Kol-ko stat[y]…?
What time is it?	*Koľko je hodín?*	Kol-ko ye hod-in?
I don't understand	*Nerozumiem*	Ne-ro-zoom-yem
Do you speak English?	*Hovoríte po anglicky?*	Hov-or-i-te po ang-lits-ky?
Entrance	*Vchod*	FHod
Exit	*Výstup*	VeeStoop
Ticket	*Lístok*	Leestok
Hotel	*Hotel*	Hotel
Toilet	*Záchod*	ZaHod
Square	*Námestie*	Nahmestee
Station	*Stanica*	Stani-tza
Do you have a…?	*Máte…?*	Ma-te…?
Single room	*Jednoposteľovú izbu*	yed-no-pos-tye-lyo-voo iz-bu
One	*Jeden*	Yed-en
Two	*Dva*	Dva
Three	*Tri*	Tri
Four	*Štyri*	Shtir-i
Five	*Päť*	Pyat[y]
Six	*Šesť*	Shest[y]
Seven	*Sedem*	Sed-em
Eight	*Osem*	Oss-em
Nine	*Deväť*	Dev-yat[y]
Ten	*Desať*	Dess-at[y]

sometimes on Sundays. Smaller rural shops close for an hour at lunchtime. Opening hours for **sights** and **attractions** are usually Tuesday to Sunday 9am to 5pm. Out of the season hours are often restricted to weekends and holidays. Most **castles** are closed in winter. When visiting a sight,

ask for English (*anglický*) text. Admission rarely costs more than €4. **Public holidays** include January 1, January 6, Good Friday, Easter Monday, May 1, May 8, July 5, August 29, September 1, September 15, November 1, November 17, December 24, 25 and 26.

Bratislava

Sitting on both sides of the Danube in the southwest corner of Slovakia, **BRATISLAVA** is a festive city, with meandering streets and tiny but grand buildings. With its rural atmosphere, on a hot afternoon a flock of sheep wouldn't look out of place grazing on Františkánske Square. The Old Town showcases the skill of Slovak town planners, who crammed a city's worth of palaces, shops, cafés, pubs, restaurants, museums and churches into a few blocks.

The area has been settled since the Neolithic era (about 500 BC), making it centuries older than Prague or Budapest. It has always been an international city – Romans, Hungarians, Germans, Austrians, Turks, Czechs, Jews and Roma have all left their mark. The locals are less weary and cynical than the natives of most capitals, characterized by a friendly reserve.

WHAT TO SEE AND DO

Old Town (Staré Mesto) lies on the north bank of the Danube, 1km south of the train station, east of the stout **castle** and southwest of the shops and housing blocks of **New Town** (Nové Mesto). A pedestrian zone stretches between Hodžovo námestie in the north down to the river in the south. South of the city is Hungary and west is Austria. Bratislava is the only capital city that borders two independent countries.

Old Town

You can enter the Old Town via the only surviving medieval gateway, **Michalská brána a veža** (St Michael's Gate and Tower; Tues–Fri 10am–5pm, Sat & Sun 11am–6pm; €4.50), which contains a military museum and a tower with a view. Michalská and Ventúrska, two halves of one street, are lined with stately **Baroque palaces**, the university library and dozens of places to eat. At number 10 is **Mozart House**, where the six-year-old Mozart performed for the Palffy clan, and at Michalská 1 is the former Hungarian parliament.

A little northeast are the adjoining squares of the **Old Town** – Hlavné námestie and Františkánske námestie. Hlavné, dotted with street cafés, hosts the Christmas and Easter markets, and a few stalls most weeks. On Františkánske, you'll find the Rococo **Mirbach Palace** (Františkánske nám. 11; Tues–Sun 11am–6pm; €3.50, students €2), home of the City Gallery's Baroque collection.

Primate's Palace

Neoclassical **Primate's Palace** (Primaciálne nám 1; Tues–Sun 10am–5pm; €3.50) contains the Hall of Mirrors, where Napoleon and Austrian Emperor Franz I signed the Peace of Pressburg (as Bratislava was then called) in 1805. In 1903 city authorities restored the palace, and discovered six seventeenth-century English tapestries concealed behind the plaster, which are now the palace's other main attraction.

Cathedral of St Martin

On the edge of Old Town is the fine Gothic Cathedral of St Martin. This was the **coronation church** for the kings and queens of Hungary between 1563 and 1830, and houses the remains of the seventh-century saint Joan the Merciful.

30

ACTIVE BRATISLAVA

Cycling and **rollerblading** along the Danube, towards Austria (upstream) or Hungary (downstream), are popular activities. For information on bike rental see p.966. The Small Carpathian mountains surrounding Bratislava are beautiful and make for a good day's **cycling** or **walking**; see ⓦ bratislavasightseeing.com or call ☎ 09 0768 3112 for suggested routes and guided tours.

Action Park offers a number of activities including zorbing, kiting, bungee trampoline and a shooting gallery (zorbing/€6, shooting €35–45 /1hr, ⓦ actionpark.sk).

30

EATING AND DRINKING

Bratislava Flag	3
Ship Restaurant	3
Bratislavský	13
mestiansky pivovar	1
Caffe L'Aura	5
Góvinda	9
Greentree Caffe	14
Nu Spirit Bar	4
Pizza Mizza	8
Prašná Bašta	7
Shtoor	
Sladovňa:	
House of Beer	

● NIGHTLIFE

Al Faro	15
Dopler	10
Dubliner	6
Harley Saloon	16
Norton Club	11
Nu Spirit Club	12

● SHOPPING

AuPark	3
Eurovea Shopping Mall	2
Oxford Books	1

■ ACCOMMODATION

A1 Hostel	5
Art Hostel Taurus	6
Downtown	1
Backpacker's Hostel	4
Hostel Blues	2
Hostel Possonium	7
Portus	3
Zlaté piesky Intercamp	

Lumière Cinema

Tesco

Canadian Consulate

Blue Church

Komenský University

Natural History Museum

Hydrofoil Terminal

River Danube

Primate's Palace

Old Town Hall & City Museum

Slovak National Theatre

Reduta Palace

Jesuit Church

Slovak National Gallery

Michalská veža (St Michael's Gate)

Mirbach Palace

Trinitarian Church

Mozart House

British Embassy

Pálffy Palace

US Embassy

Museum of Clocks

Cathedral of St Martin

NOVÝ MOST SNP

Castle

National Council of the Slovak Republic

BRATISLAVA

Nový most

Road bridge **Nový most** ((formerly Most SNP; New Bridge), nicknamed UFO because at one end there's a building that looks like a flying saucer speared by a twig, represents a whimsical moment in Slovak communist functionalism. You can ascend the tower by elevator and dine at the restaurant, which looks like the *Starship Enterprise* (daily 10am–11pm), or gaze at Bratislava from the viewing deck – locals say it's the best view of the city, because it doesn't contain Nový most.

The castle and museums

Bratislava's **castle** (*hrad*; daily 9am–6/8pm) sits on a strategic hill between the Alps and Carpathians, first fortified in 3500 BC. On a clear day you can see Slovakia, Austria and Hungary. The current building, a boxy four-towered rectangle, is a 1950s reconstruction of Emperor Sigismund's fifteenth-century castle, which burnt down in 1811. The castle houses two museums: the **Slovak Historical Museum** (Historické Múzeum), which displays historical artefacts and antiques, and the Music Museum (Hudobné múzeum), with local folk instruments, scores and recordings (Tues–Sun 9am–5pm; €4 for Historical Museum, €2 for the Music Museum; ⓦsnm.sk). Winding down the castle hill is what's left of the former Jewish quarter (Židovská), which contains the **Museum of Clocks** on Židovská 1 (Tues–Fri 10am–5pm, Sat & Sun 11am–6pm; €2.30, students €1.50; ⓦmuzeum.bratislava.sk).

Slovak National Gallery

There are two entrances to the **Slovak National Gallery** (Tues–Sun 10am–6pm; €3.50, students €1.30; ⓦsng.sk): the entrance on the embankment leads to the main building, a converted barracks housing the main collection, while the entrance on Štúrovo námestie leads to the **Esterházy Palace** wing, used for temporary exhibitions, mostly modern.

The Blue Church

A short walk east from the Old Town is the Church of St Elizabeth (Kostol svätej Alžbety) or **Blue Church** (Modrý kostolík), which rises out of the suburbs like an Art Nouveau wedding cake. Built in the early twentieth century, the church is in the Hungarian Secessionist style, playfully combined with oriental, Romanesque and classical features. It's consecrated to a medieval princess and saint, a native of Bratislava, who risked her rank by giving alms to the poor; she stars in some mosaics inside.

Bratislava-on-Sea

Every year hundreds of tonnes of sand are dropped on the banks of the Danube to give locals a taste of the beach. **Tyršovo nábrežie**, on the south bank facing the Old Town, is friendly, hot and crowded. Entry, hammocks, deckchairs, parasols and sports equipment are free, and there are cocktail bars, live music, table football, volleyball and snack bars.

ARRIVAL AND DEPARTURE

By plane From Bratislava Airport (ⓣ 2 3303 3353, ⓦbts .aero), take bus #61 to the main train station, and from there walk or catch the tram into the centre. You can also take a taxi (see p.966).

By train Main station, Bratislava-Hlavná stanica, is within walking distance – 1km north – of the centre, or you can take bus #93. Some trains, particularly those heading for west Slovakia, pass through Bratislava Nové Mesto station, 4km northeast of the centre, which is linked to town by tram #6.

Destinations Brno (5 daily; 1hr 25min); Košice (approx hourly; 5hr–6hr 35min); Poprad (approx 10 daily; 3hr

---

DAY-TRIP TO AUSTRIA

From Bratislava it takes 1hr 30min to get to Vienna by **hydrofoil**. Add that to higher prices in Austria and there's an argument for making Vienna a day-trip rather than an overnight affair. You can catch the hydrofoil from Rázusovo Nábrežie Embankment (up to 3 daily; €20–35 one-way, depending on the day and time; reservations required; ⓦtwincityliner.com). For a less scenic, cheaper trip you can get a bus (Slovaklines; 1hr 30 min; €12.60, student €6.90; ⓦslovaklines.sk; from the main bus station).

30

50min–4hr 35min); Prague (to Praha-Hlavní nádraží; 5 daily; 4hr 10min).

By bus The main bus station is Bratislava autobusová stanica, on Mlynské nivy, just over 1km east of the centre. Trolleybus #210 connects it to the main train station, while #206 goes to the centre.

Destinations Bánska Štiavnica (2 direct buses daily; 3hr 20min); Brno (approx hourly; 1hr 35min–1hr 45min); Poprad (4 direct daily; 5hr 55min–7hr 45min); Prague (Florenc station; hourly; 4hr 15 min).

INFORMATION

Tourist office Klobučnícka 2 (April–Oct daily 9am–7pm; Nov–March daily 9am–6pm; ☎02 216 186, ⓦbratislava .sk). There's also a branch at the airport with varying hours, usually opening 8.30–9.30am and closing 1.30–7.30pm.

Discount card The Bratislava City Card is available from both the centre and airport tourist offices: it lasts for up to three days, costs up to €15, and gets you discounts to city attractions, a one-hour walking tour, and free transport (excluding night buses).

GETTING AROUND

Walking is the only way to see the pedestrianized Old Town, but it's less than five minutes end to end so you're unlikely to get tired.

By tram, bus and trolleybus Buses are slower than trams and trolleybuses. Public transport runs from 4.30am until approximately 11pm. Night buses run roughly every hour; you'll need a night ticket (€1.60), and to let the driver know where you're going, as the stops are by request only.

Tickets Buy your ticket before you board and validate it in one of the orange machines inside. Inspectors target routes going to the airport and bus and train terminals; fines are €50. Buy one-way tickets from machines at the tram terminus and newsagents: €0.70/15min; €0.90/up to 60min. A day-pass costs €4.50 and a three-day pass €10; you can buy these from shops at both the main bus and train stations (ⓦimhd.sk). You also need a half-fare ticket for bulky luggage.

By bike See ⓦbratislava.info/trips/bike for information on cycling in Bratislava. Bikes can be rented from Bratislava Sightseeing, also known as Luca Tours (☎0907 683 112, ⓦbratislavasightseeing.com; €6/hr; €18/day), and they also run bike tours. The "Bike Point" is in the *UFO* restaurant car park, Viedenská cesta. There are no designated bike paths in Bratislava.

By taxi Taxis are equipped with a meter, but even so it's normal to bargain the price before your journey. It's best to order in advance rather than hailing one on the street; try Radio Taxi (☎16303) or Personal Express (☎0903 588 070, ⓦpersonalexpress.sk), which takes bookings by email.

ACCOMMODATION

You can book centrally located private rooms through the tourist office (see above).

A1 Hostel Heydukova 1 ☎09 4428 0288, ⓦa1hostel bratislava.com. Neat and slightly characterless, but the location is fantastic, prices are low, there's a kitchen and they have bikes for rent. Dorm €15, double €42

Art Hostel Taurus Zámocká 24–26 ☎01 2207 22401, ⓦhostel-taurus.com. Gleaming white, central hostel with only eight rooms. There's a dining area, sofas dotted around and a stage and musical instruments in case you want to jam. All rooms contain a private bathroom and locker. Breakfast included. Dorm €14.99, double €50

Downtown Backpacker's Hostel Panenská 31 ☎02 5464 1191, ⓦbackpackers.sk. Arty, colourful HI-affiliated hostel on the edge of the Old Town with 24hr reception, a restaurant-bar, common room with a tuneless old piano, books and games. Smoking is allowed in the foyer, and there's a kitchen and laundry room. Dorm €15, twin without bathroom €50

★ **Hostel Blues** Špitálska 2 ☎09 0520 4020, ⓦhostelblues.sk. Great concrete slab of a building which unexpectedly contains a warm, inviting hostel. The space given over to socializing (bar/reception with live weekly concerts, living room and a big kitchen) makes for a friendly atmosphere, and the staff are friendly and well informed. Rooms and dorms (single-sex or mixed) are clean and towels are provided. Dorm €16, double €64

Hostel Possonium Šancová 20 ☎02 2072 0007, ⓦpossonium.sk. Great little hostel a 3min walk from the station, which means a 5min tram ride to the Old Town. There's a popular horror-themed bar (inspired by the film *Hostel*) and a garden where guests chat and barbecue in the summer. Some of the dorms are pretty small, but all have intriguing wall decor. Dorm €17, double €54

Portus Paulínyho 10 ☎09 1197 8026, ⓦportus.sk. Well-located *pension* close to the river. Large dull rooms, but gleaming bathrooms and friendly staff. Double €70

Zlaté piesky Intercamp ☎02 4425 7373, ⓦintercamp .sk. Lakeside campsite 8km northeast of the city centre. Lifeguard services and a beach, as well as two restaurants on site. Take tram #4 from town to the end stop, Zlaté Piesky. Camping (May to mid-Oct) €3.50 per person, chalet (sleeps three) €30

EATING

CAFÉS

Caffe L'Aura Rudnayovo nám 4. Packed with creaking chairs, antique pitchers and cracked oil paintings, this unruly café-bar is a good place to wait out a rainstorm. In better weather sit on the terrace overlooking the cathedral. Billiards €5/hr. Sun–Thurs 10am–midnight, Fri 9am–1am, Sat noon–1am.

Greentree Caffe Ventúrska 20 ⓦgreentreecaffe.com.

Part of a likeable Italian-owned local chain. There are five dotted around town, and this is the newest and best, in an atmospheric vaulted cellar Mon–Thurs 8am–8.30pm, Fri 8am–9pm, Sat & Sun 9am–8.30pm.

Shtoor Štúrova 8 w shtoor.sk. Elegant but laidback café modelled on the glamorous coffeehouses of interwar Austria-Hungary. Freshly baked cakes, hearty sandwiches, and famous spiced home-made lemonade. There's a second branch on Panská. Mon–Fri 8am–10pm, Sat & Sun 10am–10pm.

RESTAURANTS

★ **Bratislava Flag Ship Restaurant** Nám SNP 8 w bratislavskarestauracia.sk. Cavernous, echoing restaurant with decor that's half Charles Dickens half Las Vegas. The food is very decent and inexpensive, the atmosphere is warm and there's a terrace on the square. Mains €4–13. Mon–Sat 10am–midnight, Sun noon–midnight.

Bratislavský meštiansky pivovar Drevená 8 w mestianskypivovar.sk. Old-style pub that brews its own beer and serves meaty Slovak staples. It can be hard to get a table on a Fri night. Mains €7–18, daily special €4.50. Mon–Thurs & Sat 11am–midnight, Fri 11am–1am, Sun 11am–11pm.

Góvinda Obchodná 30 w govinda.sk. Good, inexpensive Indian vegetarian buffet on a busy shopping street. A plate of food is roughly €3.50. Mon–Fri 11am–7pm, Sat 11.30am–5pm.

Pizza Mizza Tobrucká 5 w pizzamizza.sk. Reckoned to be the smartest pizza joint in Bratislava (though that's not saying much), *Pizza Mizza* is a decent place for a cheap, filling meal (pizza €4–14). They're dotted all over town, and if you don't feel like leaving your hotel you can get home delivery via the website. Mon–Fri 10am–11pm, Sat & Sun 11am–11pm.

Prašná Bašta Zámočnícka 11 w prasnabasta.sk. Tucked in a quiet courtyard off Michalská gate is *Prašná Bašta*, an elegant, low-key restaurant loved by locals. The delicious food combines Slovak and international flavours, there's a handsome vaulted interior, summer terrace and live jazz and classical music. Mains €7–19. Daily 11am–11pm.

Sladovňa: House of Beer Ventúrska 5. Decent local cuisine and good beer, outdoor seating (street or courtyard) in summer, and an atmospheric beer cellar in winter. Mains €7–15. Mon–Wed 11am–1am, Thurs–Sat 11am–2am, Sun 11am–11pm.

DRINKING AND NIGHTLIFE

Al Faro Eurovea Shopping Mall, Pribinova 8/A w alfaro .sk. Strange to say, one of the nicest places for a cold drink on a hot evening is the mall: Eurovea, a 15min walk from Old Town, has a row of bars, cafés and restaurants along the riverbank, and *Al Faro* has a summer terrace on a pier over the river furnished with sofas and parasols. Mon–

Thurs 9am–10pm, Fri & Sat 9am–11pm, Sun 9am–9pm.

Dopler Prievozská 18. Bratislava's biggest and most raucous nightclub is a taxi ride from the centre, popular with students and high schoolers. Mon–Sat 9pm–5am.

Dubliner Sedlárska 6 w irish-pub.sk. Busy Irish pub providing sports games and live music at the weekends. Located on a street of bars, so if this one doesn't work you have plenty of nearby options. Daily 9am–3am.

Harley Saloon Rebarborová 1/a w harley.sk. Big place, heaving at weekends, with kitsch music (Bryan Adams often reminisces about the summer of '69). It's on the edge of town so you'll need to take a trolley bus or taxi. Mon–Thurs 10am–midnight, Fri 10am–6am, Sat 11am–6am, Sun 11am–midnight.

Norton Club Panská 29. British motorcycle-theme bar, though you are unlikely to meet any bikers as it's on a pedestrian street. Sun–Wed 2pm–midnight, Fri–Sat 2pm–2am.

Nu Spirit Club Šafárikovo nám 7 w nuspirit.sk. Nudisco, drum'n'bass, funk, hip-hop, house and disco, DJ nights, stand-up comedy, live concerts and jam sessions. The owners also run a good bar on Medená St (same name). Mon–Fri 10am–3am, Sat 5pm–3am, Sun 5pm–1am.

ENTERTAINMENT

The tourist office stocks *Kam do mesta* (free). The weekly *Slovak Spectator*, available from kiosks and hotels, has news and listings. There are open-air classical music concerts in summer in courtyards and squares across the city, such as outside the Jesuit church by Michalská. Ask at the tourist office for details, or check w bkis.sk.

Slovak National Theatre w snd.sk. Encompassing two sites is the impressive modern New Slovak National Theatre (Pribinova 17), and the Historic Slovak National Theatre (Hviezdoslavovo nám). Tickets can be bought at either building one hour before the performance (€8–30). Some of the less well-known performances in the studio cost as little as €3.

Reduta Palace On the corner of nám Štúra and Medená. This is home to the Slovak Philharmonic Orchestra (w filharm.sk).

Lumière Cinema Špitálska 4 w aic.sk/kinolumiere. Arthouse joint in the centre showing old and new Slovak, European and world films.

Cinema City In the Eurovea Shopping Mall, Pribinova 8 w cinemacity.sk. Cinema showing new releases.

SHOPPING

Michalská and Ventúrska streets in the Old Town are good for souvenir shopping – good bets are ceramics and wooden items.

AuPark Einsteinova 18 w aupark.sk. Large town mall with a Cinema City and foodcourt. Mon–Fri 10am–9pm, Sat & Sun 9am–9pm.

FESTIVALS

Bratislava hosts a raft of excellent festivals, especially for music-lovers. Here are a few of the best:

Cultural Summer Ⓦbkis.sk. Performance festival from June to September which floods Bratislava with theatre, opera, visual arts and dance.

Coronation Celebration Ⓦbratislava-info .sk. Once a year (check website for current date and king) history-lovers don their codpieces and stockings to celebrate the coronation of a certain ruler.

Jazz Days Ⓦbjd.sk. Brief but exuberant jazz festival which has been held every year since 1975. Typically held in October.

Bratislava Music Festival Ⓦbhsfestival .sk. Classical music heavyweight organized by the Slovak Philharmonic every September and October, holding about 25 chamber and symphonic concerts each year.

Eurovea Shopping Mall Pribinova 8 Ⓦeurovea.com. A 15min walk from the Old Town, Eurovea contains riverside bars and restaurants (see p.967) and a multiplex cinema (see p.967). Daily 10am–9pm.

Oxford Books Laurinská 9 Ⓣ02 5262 2029, Ⓦoxfordbookshop.sk. Good browsing and a wide selection of English-language books. Mon–Fri 10am–7pm, Sat 10am–5pm.

DIRECTORY

Embassies and consulates Canada, Mostová 2 Ⓣ02 5920 4031; UK, Panská 16 Ⓣ02 5998 2020; US, Hviedoslavovo nám 5 Ⓣ02 5443 3338.

Hospital Poliklinika Ružinov, Ružinovská 10 (trams #8, #9, #14 and #50; Ⓣ02 4827 9111, Ⓦruzinovskapoliklinika .sk).

Internet There's free wi-fi access in certain parts of town, including Primaciálne nám, Hlavné nám and Františkánske nám. If you're after a café, try Wi-fi Café (Mon–Fri 9am–9pm, Sat & Sun 11am–8pm), Tatracentrum, Hodžovo nám. 4. It has free use of computers when you buy a drink, plus wi-fi.

Left luggage Main train station (daily 6.30am–11pm).

Pharmacies Lekáreň Pod Manderlom, nám SNP 20 (Ⓣ02 5443 2952). Lekáreň Pokrok, Račianske Mýto 1 (24hr; Ⓣ02 4445 5291, Ⓦlekarenpokrok.sk).

Police Foreign police and passport services, Hrobáková 44 (Ⓣ09 6103 6866).

Post office Slovenská pošta, nám SNP 35 (Mon–Fri 7am–8pm, Sat 7am–6pm, Sun 9am–2pm).

Central Slovakia

If you're partial to an undulating hill or a winding mossy way, **Central Slovakia** is your kind of place. Quiet and agrarian, it's the heart of Slovakia; the cradle of Romantic Nationalism in the nineteenth century and the seat of the Slovak National Uprising in 1944. The way of life is slow, as are the trains, but what it lacks in zip it repays in beauty.

BANSKÁ ŠTIAVNICA

Lying in a great caldera created by the collapse of a volcano, **BANSKÁ ŠTIAVNICA** is Slovakia's oldest mining town. In the third century the Huns discovered precious metal here, and by the Middle Ages it was the largest source of gold and silver in the Hungarian Empire. During the Ottoman Wars the town sprouted fortifications, watchtowers and a castle to repel marauding Turks. As the metal reserves dwindled the inhabitants migrated, leaving the town unmodernized. Nowadays the population of about 10,000 is divided between the blue-collar descendants of mining families, and hotel-owning entrepreneurs from out of town, who tolerate each other grudgingly.

WHAT TO SEE AND DO

Main square **Námestie sv Trojice** is dominated by the Holy Trinity column, a red marble monolith marking the end of the plague in 1711. Southeast is Radničné Námestie, the Gothic Church of St Catherine and the Town Hall (Radnica), the latter with a clock that marks hours with its big hand and minutes with its little hand – according to an unusually credible local legend it was the work of a drunk clockmaker. Continuing southeast you'll come to the minimalist **New Castle** (Nový Zámok) and **Church of Our Lady of the Snows**.

The Old Castle
To the west of the main square is the **Old Castle** (Starý zámok; May–Sept daily 9am–5pm; Oct–April Wed–Sat 8am–4pm; €4), not a castle at all but a fortified Romanesque church used as a storage facility for municipal wealth. It's part of the Slovak Mining Museum, and exhibits Baroque sculptures, archeological remains and medieval blacksmithery. You can also discover life was like in a medieval jail.

Klopačka
Up Λ. Sládkoviča street is the **Clapping Tower** (Klopačka), home to a giant clapping contraption built for waking up miners. Today it claps for the amusement or irritation of tourists, and contains a teahouse (see p.970).

Museums
Štiavnica is museum-rich. First up is the **Jozef Kollár Gallery** on Námestie sv Trojice, which exhibits everything from medieval madonnas to twentieth-century watercolours. A few doors down is the **Mineral Museum**, which houses exhibits on the technical development of mining. **New Castle** contains a little museum about the Ottoman Wars in Slovakia. All of these museums are run by the **Slovak Mining Museum** (w muzeum.sk) and have the same opening hours and prices (May–Sept Tues–Sat 9am–5pm; Oct–April Mon–Fri 8am–4pm; €2).

At the **Open Air Mining Museum** (J.K. Hella 12; April–June & Sept–Oct Tues–Sun 9am–5pm; July & Aug Mon noon–5pm, Tues–Sun 9am–6pm; tours hourly; €5), 1.5km from town, you can take a trip down the old mines, while 3km from town the **Museum of St Anton** (72 Svätý Anton; always open Tues–Sat 9am–3pm, with some seasonal early opening and late closing – see w msa.sk; €5–7, depending on how much of the museum you wish to see) is the kind of tapestry-heavy, trophy-stuffed manse that helps to while away a rainy morning.

Around Banská Štiavnica
The hills around Štiavnica are perfect for strolling, berry-picking and idling. Centuries of mining with gunpowder left the hills scarred with pits, which in time became lakes. On a hot day you can hike, swim, picnic, and be back by teatime. The most interesting walk is up to **Calvary** (Kalvária, 1km northeast of Old Town), a cluster of red and white Baroque chapels and churches perched on an inactive volcano, each one representing a stage in Christ's journey to the cross. Hiking maps are available at the tourist office and hotels.

ARRIVAL AND DEPARTURE
By train The train station is a 2km walk through the suburbs from the old town. There's no direct train-only service to Bratislava.

By bus The bus stop is 100m closer to town than the train station, and is next to the big Billa supermarket at Križovatka, a steep climb up to the centre.

Destinations Bratislava (8 indirect services daily, change in Žarnovica or Žiar nad Hronom; 3hr 20min–3hr 50min); Nitra (indirect with a change in Žiar nad Hronom, 3 daily; 2hr 5min–2hr 40min); Poprad (indirect with a change in Zvolen, 3 daily; 3hr 40min–4hr 5min).

INFORMATION
Tourist office Nám sv Trojice 3 (daily: May–June & Sept 9am–5pm; Oct–April 9am–6pm; July & Aug 8am–4pm; ☎ 04 694 9653, w banskastiavnica.sk, w banskastiavnica .org). Go in through the gate and turn right.

GETTING AROUND
Public transport You can walk from one side of the Old Town to the other in 10min. Cheap shuttle buses run through town; you can stop them anywhere by waving, and the fare is €0.50. Taxis are useful if you want to get out into the country but operators rarely speak English, so ask your hotel or hostel to order and agree the fee for you. Firms include Jo-Ma taxi (☎ 09 1018 0380) and F-Taxi (☎ 09 10 525 999).

ACCOMMODATION
Archanjel Radničné nám 10b ☎ 915 365 371, w archanjel.com. Smart rooms in an old townhouse above a local bar, with a shared kitchenette. The rooms aren't perfect (leaky showers, skimpy curtains), but good value for an en-suite room. Double **€35**

Hostel 6 Andreja Sladkovica 6 ☎ 905 106 706 w hostel6 .sk. Neat hostel with friendly staff and good views. 3-, 5- or 6-bed dorms. Dorm **€13**

30

30

SPA TREATMENT

If the weather's bad, hop on a bus at Križovatka and whizz over to **Sklené Teplice Spa** (Ul. A. Pechá 2; €7.50/hr; ⓦ kupele-skleneteplice.sk). You'll be instructed to jump into hot springs and take cold showers alternately, an ordeal that leaves you exhausted to the point of relaxation. The spring is at 42°C, with high levels of magnesium and calcium, and the spa claims it heals visitors with muscle and locomotive conditions. There's also a pool, saunas and massage.

Hostel Juraj A. Pechá 2 ☎ 0905 382 885, ⓦ stiavnica.sk /hosteljuraj. Štiavnica's cheapest; a rambling, echoey hostel and campsite below the castle. Camping €6 per person plus pitch, dorm €8, double €24

Penzion Kachelman Kammerhofská 18 ☎ 045 692 23 19, ⓦ kachelman.sk. Large and pristine hotel located halfway between the bus station and the centre. There's a restaurant, pizzeria, sauna and jacuzzi on site. Double €40

★ **Penzion Nostalgia** Višňovského 3 ☎ 0904 434 043, ⓦ penzion-nostalgia.sk. Possibly the nicest B&B in Slovakia, *Nostalgia* is a seventeenth-century townhouse with a wood-burning stove, oak beams and linen sheets. It's right in the centre of town, with views of the Old Town synagogue. Breakfast €4.50. Double €35, apartment €45

EATING AND DRINKING

Art Café Akademická 2. Bustling café, bar, exhibition space and sometime-cinema. It stocks a good range of local wines. Follow the staircase behind their terrace for views of the town. Sun–Thurs 11am–11pm, Fri & Sat 11am–2am.

Čajovňa Klopačka A.Sládkoviča 7 ⓦ klopacka.com. Teahouse of the red cushion, smoky incense variety popular with Slovak students. There are 150 types of tea and water pipes. Mon–Thurs 11am–11pm, Fri & Sat 10am–midnight, Sun 10am–11pm.

★ **Kaviareň Divná pani** Andreja Kmeťa 8 ⓦ divnapani .sk. Decorated like a flamboyant Roman library, this café-bar is called "madwoman", but "charmingly eccentric lady" would be kinder. There's beer on tap, liquors, coffee and cakes, columns, statues and old books. The advertised closing times are often pushed back on busy nights. Mon–Thurs 7.30am–10pm, Fri 7.30am–midnight, Sat 8.30am–midnight, Sun 9am–10pm.

Pivovar ERB Novozámocká 2 ⓦ erb-breweries.sk. Shiny tourist-orientated microbrewery and restaurant with specialities including smoked pork knuckles and sausages in vinegar brine. Mains €8–22. Sun–Thurs 11am–10pm, Fri & Sat 11am–midnight.

★ **Terasa u Blažkov** Jazero Počúvadlo. If you're in town on a balmy Friday or Saturday evening, take a long hike to *Terasa u Blažkov* (7km from Štiavnica). It's a traditional rustic night out with a whole pig roasted on a spit, fresh bread, salad and a folk band. Dinner is €5–7 and the taxi home around €7 more. It starts at 5pm, and if you arrive early you can swim in the adjoining lake. June–Sept daily 10am–11pm.

Tulsi Radničné nám 13 ⓦ tulsi.sk. Banska's "sushi and chocolate bar" provides a break from *pirohy* and a sporting chance for vegetarians. Mains €3.50–9. Daily menu €3.50. Mon–Thurs 11am–10pm, Fri 11am–11pm, Sat noon–11pm, Sun noon–9pm.

U Mateja Akademická 4. This small inn opposite *Grand Hotel Matej* is the place for a meat and dumpling binge. The food is popular with locals and there's terrace seating in the summer. Mains €4–8. Sun–Thurs noon–10pm, Fri & Sat noon–11pm.

THE TATRAS

Lying on the border with Poland, the **HIGH TATRAS** (Vysoké Tatry) are visible from space. The highest peak, pyramid-shaped Gerlach, is the tallest mountain in northern and eastern Central Europe at 2,655m high. The beauty and splendour of the mountains made them a magnet for Romantic and Nationalistic types in the eighteenth century, and in 1844 a student in Bratislava wrote a song beginning with the words "There is lightning over the Tatras" – today the national anthem. The mountains are awash with rare flora and fauna, and if you're lucky you might glimpse a lynx, wild boar, brown bear or Tatra chamois (goat-antelope).

Poprad is an excellent transport hub, directly linked with Bratislava, Prague, Budapest and Kraków; however, there's not much happening to keep you there. From Poprad you can catch a train or bus to the **Smokovec** resorts (divided into two adjoining halves, Nový (new) and Starý (old), bustling ski resort **Tatranská Lomnica**, or spindly **Ždiar**, one endless street of painted wooden cabins. Wherever you stay you'll want to move between the villages; if you're using public transport you'll have to plan ahead a little because the trains and buses are erratically timed.

ARRIVAL AND DEPARTURE

By train The main-line train station for the Tatras is Poprad-Tatry in Poprad. From there tiny red electrical trains (TEZ; hourly; 25min to Starý Smokovec; €1.50) trundle across the mountains, linking Poprad with Smokovec and Tatranská Lomnica.

Destinations (from Poprad) Bratislava (10 daily; 3hr 50min–4hr 35min); Košice (hourly; 1hr 15min–1hr 50min).

By bus Buses also move between the cities listed above, but the train is usually quicker and more convenient. Ždiar isn't on the train line so you'll have to get the bus, which leaves Poprad roughly hourly and takes an hour.

Destinations (from Poprad) Levoča (hourly; 15–45min); Prešov (6 daily; 1hr 5min–2hr).

By plane There is a small airport on the western outskirts of Poprad, Poprad-Tatry (☎52 776 3875, ⊛airport -poprad.sk), which runs infrequent flights to and from a number of European countries including the UK.

INFORMATION

Tourist office In Poprad: at the western end of námestie sv Egidia in the Dom Kultúry building (Mon–Fri 9am–5pm, Sat 9am–noon; July & Aug Mon–Fri 9am–6pm, Sat 9am–1pm; ☎052 16 186, ⊛poprad.sk). In Starý Smokovec: down the road to your right as you face the *Grand Hotel* (daily 10am–4pm; ☎052 442 34 40, ⊛tatry .sk). In Tatranská Lomnica: on the main street opposite *Penzión Encián* (Mon–Fri 8am–3.30pm; ☎052 446 81 19, ⊛tatry.sk).

ACTIVITIES

AquaCity Športová 1, Poprad ⊛aquacity.sk. AquaCity has outdoor thermal pools (30–38°C) and a 50m pool, toboganing, a beauty centre, massage, slides, restaurants, bars and a club. Perfect for a break after a few days' skiing. €15–24 for a 3hr package. Daily 8am–10pm.

Belianska Cave The north slope of Kobylí Hill, near to Tatranská Kotlina (☎05 2446 7375, ⊛ssj.sk). A 70min tour of Belianska Cave, which was discovered by gold prospectors in the 1700s, leads you past subterranean waterfalls, stalagmites and the Music Hall – so-called because of the melodious sound of water drops on the still pool. It's below freezing even in summer, so dress warmly. The nearest bus stop is Tatranská Kotlina. Tour times 9.30am, 11am, 12.30pm & 2pm; times fluctuate, so check beforehand. €7, students €6.

Climbing To go climbing you'll need a valid membership card for a recognized climbing club, or a guide. Certified guides are available at the Association of Mountain Guides (Spolok horských vodcov), but they're expensive, starting at €168/hike (Vila Alica, Starý Smokovec; ☎05 428 170, ⊛tatraguide.sk).

Bikes, scooters and tubing Tatry Motion rental, Starý Smokovec (☎09 114 10945, ⊛vt.sk) and Tatranská Lomnica (☎09 031 12200, ⊠info@vt.sk). Scooter €7.50/ ride, bike €12/day, tubing (at Hrebienok) €4/5 rides. There's also a bike park (⊛vt.sk) at Hrebienok (accessible by funicular from Starý Smokovec) with easy and difficult routes; bikes €35/day (9am–6pm dependent on weather).

Rafting at Červený Kláštor Pieniny sport centrum, Červený Kláštor 45, Pieniny National Park (☎09 0747 7412, ⊛rafting-pieniny.sk). It's a little over two hours by bus to the Dunajec River in Pieniny National Park, on the Slovak–Polish border, but worth the trip. You can rent a kayak, canoe or mountain bike or take a rafting trip with a guide. May–Sept only; equipment rental 9am–6pm. Bus Poprad–Červený Kláštor, with a change in Spišská St.Ves (5 daily; 2hr 20min).

Skiing and snowboarding The season is Dec–March. Tatranská Lomnica is an ideal place to ski and snowboard, with heated chairlifts and cable cars, long runs, routes for all abilities, good black runs plus off piste. Bachledova Dolina is a great, affordable option – a day-pass is €20, ski rental is €10, and the restaurants on the slopes are cheap too. There's a 2km run, beginners' slopes in the villages (Strednica and Strachan), and blue, red and black routes at Bachledova. Štrbské Pleso hosts national and international skiing events and it's a beautiful place, but it's pricey and the skiing is pretty similar to Lomnica. See ⊛skibachledova.sk and ⊛tatry.sk for more.

Tatrabob Tatranská Lomnica 29 ☎09 4450 3069, ⊛tatrabob.com. Pint-sized mountainside roller coaster plus archery. €3/ride.

MOUNTAIN SAFETY

On average, twenty people a year die in the High Tatras. Keep safe by hiking with two or more people and making sure someone knows where you are going. Wear layers, a waterproof and windproof coat, and hiking boots. Always take plenty of water and some food. Buy a whistle – the emergency signal is 6 blasts. Weather conditions change fast, so check the prognosis before you leave; the Mountain Rescue Service in Starý Smokovec will give you a forecast. If you get in trouble, call Mountain Rescue (☎18300) right away. Don't think of them as an easy fall-back, though; they charge a large fee for call-outs.

30

30

ACCOMMODATION

In high season (ski season and high summer) prices often double. All prices listed are for high season. The tourist offices in any of the resorts can help you arrange accommodation.

★ **Ginger Monkey Hostel** Ždiar 294 ☎ 05 2449 8084, ⓦ gingermonkey.eu. Many the eye of a hardened backpacker mists at the mention of *Ginger Monkey*, a wooden-cabin hostel on the edge of Ždiar. There are chickens in the garden, books in the kitchen, mountains out the window and a yellow dog for company. From Poprad, the bus stop is the fourth in Ždiar – keep an eye out for the sign that says "Petrol Station 500m" and alight at the next stop. Breakfast included. Dorm €13, double €32

Hotel Café Razy Námestie sv. Egídia 58, Poprad ☎ 05 2776 41 01, ⓦ hotelcaferazy.sk. New hotel on Poprad's main square offering large and comfortable two-floor rooms. Friendly staff and a decent breakfast (€5). Located above a restaurant so may be noisy until they close. Double €42

Penzion Aqualand Štefánikova 893, Poprad ☎ 421 903 412 482, ⓦ aqualand.sk/en/pension. This *pension*, a 10min walk from the bus and train stations, is neat and friendly. Plus, guests get a discount at the waterpark in case bad weather is keeping you from hiking or biking outdoors. Dorm €15, double €45

Penzion Mon Ami Nový Smokovec 31 ☎ 05 2442 3024, ⓦ monami.sk. Clean, comfortable B&B in a traditional wood-framed guesthouse on the high street in Smokovec, with views over the mountains. All rooms are doubles with en suite. €20 per person

Penzion Slalom Tatranská Lomnica 94 ☎ 05 2446 7216, ⓦ slalom.sk. Friendly little B&B close to both bus and train stations. Nearly all rooms have a balcony. Double €41

Penzión Ždiar Ždiar 460 ☎ 05 2449 8138, ⓦ penzionzdiar.sk. Large, friendly wooden guesthouse with equine equipment and painted plates on the walls.

Rooms for 1–5 people. €8 per person, en-suite room €12 per person

MOUNTAIN CABINS

For an authentic mountain experience hike to one of the wooden huts (*chata*) in the hills. Sleeping is often in dorms, and most huts offer dinner and breakfast.

Bilíkova Chata ☎ 52 442 2439, ⓦ bilikovachata.sk. Hotel-like hut, with wood-panelled dorms, single and double rooms for a cosy lie down after a long hike. Breakfast €4.50. €25 per person

Zbojníčka ☎ 09 0363 8000, ⓦ zbojnickachata.sk. All oak beams and open fires, with one dorm sleeping 16. Breakfast is included. Dorm €21

EATING AND DRINKING

Cukráreň Tatra Starý Smokovec 66. Follow the warm scent of vanilla to this delightful *cukráreň* (the nearest translation is "sugary"), which serves great cakes, ice cream, chocolate and real coffee. Daily 9am–7pm.

Hotel Atrium Bowling Bar Nový Smokovec 42. An amusing evening out in a village low on nightlife. Daily 9am–1am.

Humno Tatranská Lomnica 14640 ⓦ humnotatry.sk. Swish alpine chalet that's a bar, café, pub, and on Fridays and Saturdays a nightclub (the best in the mountains). There's an open fire, leather sofas, a snow plough coming out the wall (the DJ booth) and a cadillac once belonging to Madonna. Mains €5.50–18.50. Sun–Thurs 11am–midnight, Fri & Sat 11am–4am.

Rustika Ždiar 334. Road-sign-strewn wood shack serving toothsome, inexpensive pizzas. Pizza €4.50, monster pizza (50cm) €12. Daily 2–10pm.

Sabato Sobotské nám 6, Poprad ⓦ sabato.sk. Medieval-style restaurants combine large slabs of meat and ludicrously dressed waiters, and this is a nice example of the genre. Mains €8–21. Mon–Sat 11am–11pm.

Tatratom Ždiar 288. Traditional pub serving excellent, old-timey meals. The garlic soup is hot and piquant, and

---

ON YER HIKE

If you're not a hiker, there are plenty of shorter routes to leave the heel unblistered. Ask for maps or recommendations at any of the tourist offices.

Štrbské pleso–Popradské pleso A scenic stroll between two lakes that takes less than two hours. On the way you'll pass the Symbolic Cemetery, a memorial garden to those who died in the Tatras.

Biela voda–Chata pri Zelenom plese Takes a little under 3 hours, and it ends on a high, with beautiful mountain panoramas around the chalet.

Kriváň peak When you've got your mountain legs, hike up this high, hook-nosed peak (2495m – a hike for summer only), beloved of Slovak Romantic poets. It's one of the highest mountains in the Tatras and the walk takes a full day. You can start from Štrbské pleso and follow the red trail towards Podbanské. Peruse our safety tips (see box, p.971) before starting out.

the fruit dumplings are dreamy. Mains €4–9. Daily 9am–7pm.

U Friga Nový Smokovec 44. Pizza and *halušky* in comfy environs. Mains €3.90–6.50. Mon–Sat 5–10pm.

Vila Park Tatranská Lomnica. Decent modern Slovak food with a sunny summer terrace overlooking the village green, 3min from the train station. Mains from €5. Daily noon–10pm.

East Slovakia

Slovakia's **east** (východoslovenský kraj) has one foot in the past. Protected from the west by the Tatras, traditional dialects and folk customs thrive, and the land is bleaker and grander than the west. Stretching northeast up the Poprad Valley to the Polish border, and east along the River Hornád towards Prešov, is the **Spiš** region, for centuries a semi-autonomous province in the Hungarian kingdom.

LEVOČA

What inspired the great Hungarian writer Kálmán Mikszáth to make **LEVOČA** the star of his 1910 revenge saga *The Black Town* is a mystery. The medieval town is as neat and respectable as a privet hedge, and if there are any passions seething they're well buried. The town's main attraction is the wonderful religious art at the Church of St James, but it's also a good base for visiting **Spiš castle** (see box, p.974), and a gateway to beautiful Slovak Paradise National Park.

WHAT TO SEE AND DO

Levoča is a grid-plan town. The main streets run from **Námestie Majstra Pavla** (the main square) to the city walls, becoming darker and shabbier as they go. Churches, hotels and museums congregate in the main square, with the cheaper *pensions*, hostels and pubs scattered near the town walls. From the north side of **Námestie Majstra Pavla** you can see the graceful white church at Mariánska hora (Mary's Mountain), a Catholic pilgrimage.

Church of St James

The splendid **Church of St James** (Chrám sv Jakuba; Tues–Sat 8.30am–4pm) soars above the north side of the main square. It houses a magnificent 5.5m-high wooden altarpiece containing the *Last Supper*, and a baby-faced Madonna, both the work of sixteenth-century master-carver Pavol of Levoča. The church can only be entered with a guide, and tours (€2) are conducted on the hour. The ticket office is opposite the main entrance. A small and uninspiring **museum** (daily 9am–5pm; €1.50), dedicated to Master Pavol, stands opposite the church and exhibits replicas of the art in the church.

Town Hall and Lutheran Church

Between St James and the squat, Neoclassical **Lutheran church** (Evanjelický kostol) is a wrought-iron contraption called the **Cage of Shame** (*klietka hanby*), built in a flourish of sixteenth-century misogyny: women caught on the streets after dark were imprisoned here overnight in their petticoats, heads shorn, as an example to other females. The third building on the square is the old **Town Hall** (daily 9am–5pm, €3.50, ticket is also valid for the Spiš Museum). The **Spiš Museum** (daily 9am–5pm; ⓦsnm.sk) exhibits paintings and icons.

ARRIVAL AND INFORMATION

By bus The bus station is 1km southeast of the old town. If you're coming from the east, alight one stop earlier at the Košice gate.

Destinations Poprad (15 daily; 35–50min); Košice (3 daily; 2hr 25min).

By train Levoča is not on the train line, but you can get a taxi or catch a bus to Spišská Nová Ves (#11 twice hourly; 20min) and from there catch the direct train to Bratislava (6 daily; 4hr 55min), which also stops at Poprad.

Tourist office Nám Majstra Pavla 58 (daily 9am–noon & 12.30–5pm; ☎ 053 451 37 63, ⓦ levoca.sk).

ACCOMMODATION

Barbakan Košická 15 ☎ 53 451 43 10, ⓦ barbakan.sk. The kind of solid, old-fashioned hotel that smells of floor wax and pink soap. Breakfast €5. Single **€28**, double **€44**

30

30

SPIŠ CASTLE

An endless mass of ramshackle bone-white walls, roads and broken towers, **Spiš Castle** (Spišský hrad; daily: April & Oct 9am–4pm; Nov 10am–4pm; May–Sept 9am–6pm, last entry 5pm; €5, students €3; ⓦ spisskyhrad.com) is a monumental twelfth-century fortress built over a much older castle. It's a bleak, dreamlike place, so isolated that the only sounds are birds and crickets. Inside are exhibits giving a clear picture of medieval life (short and dirty), audioguides and a tower to climb. You can catch a bus from Levoča to Spišské Podhradie for €1 (2 hourly; 30min) and then it's about an hour's walk to the castle.

Oaža Nová 65 ☎ 053 451 4511, ⓦ oaza.weblib.sk. Well-scrubbed, no-frills accommodation in a family-run boarding house a few minutes' walk from the main square. You can get a room or share (either with friends or strangers). A good option on a tight budget. Dorm **€10**

Rekreačné zariadenie Levočská Dolina ☎ 421 53 451 2705, ⓦ rzlevoca.sk. Campsite with wooden bungalows and a *pension* 5km northwest of town with bike rental, a café, sauna and whirlpool. Camping **€3** per person plus **€1.50** per pitch, bungalow rental **€6.50** per person, *pension* (double) **€37**

EATING

Arkáda Nám Majstra Pavla 26 ⓦ arkada.sk. Vaulted cellar tavern stashed under one of the bigger hotels. Draught beer, local wine and Slovak staples. You'll also find similar food, decor and prices at *U Troch Apoštolov* (nám Majstra Pavla 11), further up the main square. Mains €5–14. Daily 9am–10pm.

Planéta Nám Majstra Pavla 38a ⓦ planetalevoca.sk. Every sleepy provincial town needs a *Planéta*; a café at 4pm, a restaurant at 7pm and a bar at 10pm. The menu is simple (pizza, salads, pasta) but fresh. Lunch menu €4, dinner menu €4.50. May–Sept Mon–Fri 8am–11pm, Sat & Sun 11am–10.30pm; Oct–April Mon–Fri 8am–10pm, Sat & Sun 9.30am–10pm.

Peko Spiš Košicka ulica. The town's best bakery. Mon–Fri 6am–6pm, Sat 6am–noon.

Restaurácia Slovenka Nám Majstra Pavla 62. Cheap filling Slovak food with good service. Mains €4–10. Daily 10am–10pm.

Restaurácia U Leva Nám Majstra Pavla 24 ⓦ uleva.sk. The nicest mid-range restaurant in Levoča, combining Mediterranean (carpaccio, *insalata caprese*) and Slavic dishes (duck breast with cherry sauce, chicken liver with wild mushrooms), and doing both well. Mains €6–12. Daily 10am–10pm.

Tatra Food Nám Majstra Pavla 54a ⓦ tatrafood.sk. Pleasant snack bar with cheap baguettes, kebabs, milkshakes and desserts in the municipal theatre building. Sandwiches €1–2.50. Mon–Thurs 8am–7pm, Fri 8am–10pm, Sat noon–10pm.

KOŠICE

KOŠICE was once a vital commercial crossroad for the Hungarian Empire, and today the pleasing centre forms a kilometre-long promenade, lined with historical buildings, churches, cafés and restaurants. Warm days see residents emerging in packs to enjoy the sun and listen to the musical fountain located in the park next to the State Theatre. A lively university town, Košice was named the European Capital of Culture for 2013, leading to a number of new and improved attractions. If Kraków (see p.848) or Budapest (see p.551) are in your travel plans, the city makes a great mid-way stopping point for a couple of days.

WHAT TO SEE AND DO

Košice's action is pretty much centred on its main street, **Hlavná**, which is lined with parks interspersed with some historical sites. Wandering the side streets provides some interesting sightseeing; this is also where you'll find various places to stay.

St Elizabeth's Cathedral

The symbol of the city's patron, **St Elizabeth's Cathedral** (Dóm svätej Alžbety; Mon 1–5pm, Tues–Fri 9am–5pm, Sat 9am–1pm; €1.50) is the country's largest place of worship. It houses an intriguing rare Gothic double spiral staircase and a sundial dating from 1477. The cast-iron altar, reportedly the only one in Europe, is said to have been crafted from weapons used in World War I. For a view of the town and out to the hills, climb the 60m-high northern tower.

WARHOL'S ROOTS

Pop artist **Andy Warhol** has Slovak roots; his parents immigrated to the US in the early 1900s. Born Andrej Varhola Jr, the artist has been commemorated in the town of Medzilaborce (120km north of Košice) with the Andy Warhol Museum of Modern Art, which displays his works of art and artefacts from his childhood and life. There's one direct bus and one direct train to Medzilaborce daily, each taking about 2hr 30min. Or you can arrange a tour at the tourist office in Košice, which includes a visit to Warhol's parents' village.

30

St Michael's Chapel

Smaller, and more charming, **St Michael's Chapel** (Kaplnka Sv. Michala; Mon–Fri 9.15am–6pm, Sat 9.15am–noon; €1.50) sits next to St Elizabeth's and was originally surrounded by the city's cemetery, which has now been turned into an attractive park.

Lower Gate

Reconstruction of Hlavná street in the mid-1990s uncovered the original gateway to the city and parts of the original fortifications. **Lower Gate** (Dolná brána; May–Sept Tues–Sun 10am–6pm; €0.90) has been turned into an underground museum of sorts in which you can see these ancient constructions.

Vojtech Löffler Museum

Famed local sculptor Vojtech Löffler donated a significant body of work to the city, leading Košice to open this **museum** (Alžbetina 20; Tues–Sat 10am–6pm, Sun 1–5pm; €1, admission free Fri mornings), dedicated to him and his work. In addition to his sculptures and painted portraits of local personalities, the museum also gives space to contemporary artists.

ARRIVAL AND INFORMATION

By plane Košice's airport (w airportkosice.sk) is 6km south of the city and offers regular flights to Bratislava, as well as internationally to Prague and Vienna.

By train The train station is a 10min walk from the city centre; head through the park and down Mlynská. There's a left luggage desk in the train station.

Destinations Bratislava (10 daily; 5hr–6hr 30min); Budapest (1 daily; 3hr 30min); Kraków (1 nightly train, 9hr 30min; 1 daily, 8hr 45min); Poprad (hourly; 1hr–1hr 50min); Prague (1 nightly train, 9hr; 2 daily, 8hr 15 min–9hr 30min).

By bus The bus station is next to the train station. Check w eurobus.sk for international connections.

Destinations Budapest (1 daily; 3hr); Levoča (3 daily; 2hr); Prešov (hourly; 30–55min).

Tourist office Hlavná 59, in the Old Town Hall (Mon–Fri 10am–6pm, Sat 10am–3pm; ☏055 625 8888, w visitkosice.eu).

ACCOMMODATION

Krmanova Krmanova 14 ☏ 55 623 05 65, w krmanova .sk. Clean and friendly, *Krmanova* could probably do with an upgrade; however, the price and convenient location to the bus and train stations make it a good choice. Breakfast is included. Double €46 (weekend), €58 (weekday)

Rokoko Gorkého 9 ☏ 55 796 68 00, w rokoko.sk. *Rokoko* has clean, good-sized doubles and is about a 5min walk from the main square. Breakfast is included. Double €68

Villa Regia Dominikánske námestie 3 ☏ 625 65 10, w villaregia.sk. Located in the shadow of the Dominican Church, this hotel offers contemporary rooms in warm colours. Their restaurant is one of the best in town, serving up delicious marinated ribs and traditional Slovak mushroom soup. Breakfast is included. Double €65

EATING AND DRINKING

Aida Hlavná 44 w aida-cukraren.sk. Confectionery overload in this most famous of Košice's sweet shops. Summer sees a massive queue for ice cream; you can snag a slice of fresh cake for under a euro. Daily 8am–8pm.

Bageteria Hlavná 102 w bageteria.com. Chain sandwich shop selling fresh and affordable flavours, ranging from ham and cheese to Indian and Balkan. Sandwiches from around €2. Mon–Thurs 8am–9pm, Fri 8am–11pm, Sat & Sun 9am–9pm.

Diesel Pub Hlavná 92 w irishpubkosice.com. The ubiquitous Irish pub; Košice's is large, with a great back garden, and offers regular disco nights. Decent food with Guinness, Kilkenny and Cashel's Cider on draught. Mon–Wed 11am–midnight, Thurs & Fri 11am–2.30am, Sat 4pm–2.30am, Sun 4–11pm.

30

FESTIVALS AND EVENTS

Some of the city's festival highlights include Košice City Day (the first week in May), followed by the City Festival at the end of the month, both offering a variety of middle-aged entertainment including crafts, historic parades, knight fighting and more such merriment. There's a birthday party for Andy Warhol at the beginning of August (see box, p.975) and the Košice Wine Festival in mid-September. The oldest marathon in Europe, the Košice Peace Marathon, is run on the first Sunday in October.

Med Malina Hlavná 8 ⓦ www.medmalina.sk. For a taste of Central European slow food, eaten in a room reminiscent of Granny's, head to *Med Malina* on the main square. Try the traditional Polish soup, *žurek*, or splurge on roast duck with potato pancakes. Mains €4.20–11.20. Mon–Sat 10am–11pm, Sun 10am–10pm.

Pivovar Golem Dominikánske námestie 15 ⓦ pivovar -golem.sk. The only place in Košice still brewing beer, theirs is light to say the least. However, they make up for it with generous portions of heavy Slovak pub food served up in two large rooms, one with more of a dining feel, the other all pub with views to the brewing vats. Mains €4.40–5.30. Daily 10am–10pm.

PIRAN

Slovenia

HIGHLIGHTS

❶ **Old Town, Ljubljana** Wonderful architecture, a hilltop castle and atmospheric riverside bars. **See p.984**

❷ **Škocjan Caves** Magnificent underground canyon. **See p.988**

❸ **Piran** Historic coastal town with gorgeous Venetian Gothic architecture and. **See p.989**

❹ **Lake Bohinj** The pearl of Slovenia's alpine lakes. **See p.991**

❺ **Soča Valley** Stunningly scenic location for hiking, rafting and skiing. **See p.992**

❻ **Ptuj** Slovenia's oldest, most endearing settlement. **See p.995**

HIGHLIGHTS ARE MARKED ON THE MAP ON P.979

ROUGH COSTS

Daily budget Basic €45, occasional treat €65

Drink *Pivo* (beer) €2.50 for half a litre

Food Pizza €5–7

Hostel/budget hotel €18/€60

Travel Train: Ljubljana–Maribor €9; bus: Ljubljana–Bled €7

FACT FILE

Population 2 million

Language Slovene

Currency Euro (€)

Capital Ljubljana

International phone code ☎ 386

Time zone GMT +1hr

Introduction

Stable, prosperous and welcoming, Slovenia is a charming and comfortable place to travel, with architecturally grand, cultured cities, and lush pine-forested countryside, perfect for hiking and biking in summer and skiing in winter. The country managed to avoid much of the strife that plagued other nations during the messy disintegration of the Yugoslav Republic, and has integrated quickly with Western Europe, joining the eurozone at the start of 2007. Administered by German-speaking Habsburg overlords until 1918, Slovenes absorbed the culture of their rulers while managing to retain a strong sense of ethnic identity through their Slavic language.

31

Slovenia's sophisticated capital, **Ljubljana**, is a delight, pleasantly compact and cluttered with fabulous Baroque and Habsburg buildings. A short ride away, the Julian Alps provide stunning mountain scenery, most accessible at the majestic twin lakes of **Bled** and **Bohinj**, while the **Soča Valley**, skirting the country's western border, is even more memorable. Further south are spectacular caves, notably at **Postojna** and **Škocjan**, while the short stretch of Slovenian coast is punctuated by two starkly different towns: historic **Piran** and party-oriented **Portorož**. In the eastern wine-making regions, **Ptuj** is Slovenia's oldest and best-preserved town, while the country's second city, **Maribor**, is a worthwhile stopover point on the way to Austria.

CHRONOLOGY

181 BC The Romans conquer the area of present-day Slovenia.

550 AD Slavs begin to inhabit the area.

600s The first Slovenian state, the Duchy of Carantania, is established.

745 The Frankish Empire takes over Carantania, and converts the Slavs to Christianity.

1267 Coastal Istria officially becomes the territory of the Venetian Republic. It remains under Venetian rule until 1797.

1335 The Habsburgs take control of Slovenian regions through marriage.

1550 The first book is published in the Slovenian language.

1867 Slovenia is brought under the direct control of Austria.

Late 1800s Growth of Slovenian nationalism.

1918 Following the collapse of the Austro-Hungarian Empire after World War I, Slovenia is incorporated into the Kingdom of the Serbs, Croats and Slovenes.

1929 The Kingdom is renamed Yugoslavia.

1945 After being occupied by the Germans during World War II, a liberation force led by Slovenian General Tito incorporates Slovenia into the Republic of Socialist Yugoslavia.

1950s The industrialization of Slovenia leads to rapid economic development.

1980 General Tito dies; disintegration of Yugoslavia begins.

1990 Slovenians vote for independence in a referendum.

1991 Slovenia declares its independence from Socialist Yugoslavia, leading to a ten-day war with the Yugoslav army. The Slovenians win.

2003 The oldest wooden wheel in the world, thought to be 5000 years old, is discovered in Slovenia.

2004 Slovenia joins NATO as well as the EU.

2007 Slovenia is the first former Communist state to adopt the European single currency.

2012 Maribor is the European Capital of Culture.

ARRIVAL AND DEPARTURE

Flight operators from the UK include easyJet (⊚easyjet.com), flying from London Stansted; Wizz Air (⊚wizzair .com), flying from Luton; and the Slovenian national carrier, Adria (⊚adria .si), flying from London Gatwick. Slovenia is well connected to its four neighbouring countries – Austria, Croatia, Hungary and Italy – by both **bus** and **train**. Currently, there are international train services from Ljubljana to Zagreb, Vienna and Belgrade. There are more options by bus from Ljubljana, including services to Zagreb,

SLOVENIA

Salzburg

Graz & Vienna

AUSTRIA

HUNGARY

Budapest

Villach

Jesenice

Maribor

❻ Ptuj

ITALY

POHORJE MASSIF

Mt Triglav
(2864m)

Bled

Lesce

Savinja River

Bovec

JULIAN ALPS

Lake
Bled

Kobarid

Tolmin

*Lake
Bohinj*

❹

Most na Soči

Soča River

Nova Gorica

❶

LJUBLJANA

N

ZAGREB

Lipica

Divača

Postojna

Trieste

❷

Piran

❸

Koper

CROATIA

Portorož

Rijeka

Belgrade

Metres
1500
1000
500
200
0

ADRIATIC
SEA

Pula

HIGHLIGHTS
❶ Old Town, Ljubljana
❷ Škocjan Caves
❸ Piran
❹ Lake Bohinj
❺ Soča Valley
❻ Ptuj

0   40
kilometres

31

Belgrade, Budapest and Sarajevo. Access to the Slovene coast is also straightforward: buses arrive daily from Trieste (Italy) and Pula (Croatia), and between April and October you can travel by **catamaran** between Venice and Piran/Izola.

GETTING AROUND

Slovene Railways (Slovenske železnice; ⓦslo-zeleznice.si) is smooth and efficient. **Trains** (*vlaki*) are divided into slow (LP), and Intercity (IC) express trains, as well as the fast Inter City Slovenia trains (ICS) between Ljubljana and Maribor. Seat reservations (*rezervacije*; €3.50) are obligatory for all services marked on a timetable with a boxed R (effectively, all ICS trains and some international services). Most timetables have English notes; "departures" is *odhodi*, "arrivals" is *prihodi*. Eurail and InterRail passes are valid.

The **bus** network consists of an array of local companies offering a comprehensive and reliable service, with buses reaching a far wider range of destinations than trains, though services are significantly reduced on Sundays. Towns such as Ljubljana, Maribor and Koper have big bus stations, where you can buy your tickets in advance – elsewhere, simply pay the driver or conductor. You'll be charged extra for cumbersome items of baggage.

Slovenia is a superb destination for **cycling**, with quiet roads, fabulous scenery and a well-established network of adventurous Alpine trails for mountain bikers. The lakes, the Soča Valley and the eastern wine roads are all pleasant places to explore on two wheels, and many hotels and hostels rent bikes for free or a small charge. The website ⓦmtb.si is a useful resource for mountain bikers.

ACCOMMODATION

Accommodation is universally clean and good quality. Slovenia has a decent spread of **hostels**, many of which are highly original in their conception. In addition,

31

★ TREAT YOURSELF

Slovenia's quiet roads and inspiring scenery make the country a driver's dream. If you can stretch your budget to a few days of **car rental**, you will afford yourself unlimited access to rural and mountainous regions such as the Soča Valley, which can prove challenging to reach using public transport. There are branches of most major car rental companies at Ljubljana airport; typical costs are €35 per day, €120 per week.

you'll find basic student dorms (*dijaški dom*) that significantly boost capacity during the summer. Hostels are not especially cheap; expect to pay about €18–22 per person per night in high season; student dorms are around €10. **Campsites** are numerous and generally have very good facilities, often including sporting equipment, restaurants and shops; two people travelling with a tent can expect to pay €20–30, and the majority of campsites are open from April or May to September. Camping rough without permission is punishable by a fine.

In the capital, double rooms at a two-star hotel start around €60. Family-run *pensions* and tourist farms in rural areas, especially the mountains, offer many of the same facilities as hotels but usually at a lower price. **Private rooms** (*zasebne sobe*) are available throughout Slovenia, with bookings often made by the local tourist office or travel agents like Kompas. Rooms are pretty good value at about €35–50 for a double, although stays of three nights or less can be subject to a surcharge in peak season. Self-catering **apartments** (*apartmaji*) are also plentiful in the mountains and on the coast.

FOOD AND DRINK

Slovene **cuisine** draws on Austrian, Italian and Balkan influences. There's a native tradition, too, based on age-old peasant recipes, which you may encounter at tourist farms across the country; but traditional Slovene dishes are becoming harder to find on restaurant menus increasingly dominated by Italian pizzas and pastas. For breakfast and snacks, *okrepčevalnice* (snack bars) and street kiosks dole out *burek*, a flaky pastry filled with cheese (*sirov burek*) or meat (*burek z mesom*). Sausages come in various forms, most commonly *kranjska klobasa* (big spicy sausages). Menus in a restaurant (*restavracija*) or inn (*gostilna*) will usually include roast meats (*pečenka*) and schnitzels (*zrezek*). Goulash (*golaž*) is also common. Two traditional dishes are *žlikrofi*, ravioli filled with potato, onion and bacon; and *žganci*, once the staple diet of rural Slovenes, a buckwheat or maize porridge often served with sauerkraut. Few local dishes are suitable for **vegetarians**, though international restaurants usually offer a choice of dishes without meat. On the coast you'll find plenty of fresh fish (*riba*), mussels (*žkoljke*) and squid (*kalamari*). Typical **desserts** include strudel filled with apple or rhubarb; *žtruklji*, dumplings with fruit filling; and *prekmurska gibanica*, a delicious local cheesecake.

DRINK

Daytime **drinking** takes place in small café-bars, or in a *kavarna*, where a range of cakes, pastries and ice cream is usually on offer. **Coffee** (*kava*) is generally served with milk (*kava z mlekom*), or strong and black, as is tea (*čaj*), unless specified otherwise. Slovene beer (*pivo*) is refreshingly crisp and is dominated by two brands: Laško, from the town of the same name, and Union, from Ljubljana. Most breweries also produce *temno pivo* ("dark beer"), a Guinness-like stout. Although still somewhat under the radar, Slovenian **wine** (*vino*) is superb; *črno* is red, *belo* is white. If you can't make it to any of the country's beautiful wine-growing regions, Ljubljana has several excellent wine bars, while most restaurants should have a decent selection. Favourite aperitifs include *slivovka* (plum brandy), the fiery *sadjevec*, a brandy made from various fruits, and the gin-like *brinovec*.

SLOVENIA ONLINE

Ⓦburger.si Superb interactive maps and panoramic photos.

Ⓦinyourpocket.com/slovenia
Up-to-date and irreverant online listings from the ever reliable In *Your Pocket* series.

Ⓦslovenia.info Official tourist board site.

Ⓦvisitljubljana.com Detailed information on sights and events in the capital.

CULTURE AND ETIQUETTE

Slovenes are welcoming people, who are only too willing to help tourists. The predominant religion is Catholicism, and respectful attire (no sleeveless tops or above-the-knee skirts) should be worn inside churches and around religious sites. Although **tipping** is not obligatory, it is polite to round the bill up to a convenient figure in restaurants and when taking a taxi.

SPORTS AND OUTDOOR ACTIVITIES

There are few more active nations in Europe than Slovenia – the most popular **spectator sports** are basketball, handball and football, in addition to several prestigious skiing competitions and rowing regattas each year.

The country's dramatic and varied landscape – particularly in the Soča Valley (see p.992) – provides superb opportunities for a host of outdoor pursuits, most obviously **hiking**, **climbing** and **cycling** in summer, and **skiing** in winter. Moreover, the country's mountains, forests, lakes and rivers provide ample opportunity for adventure-seekers, with **rafting**, **canyoning** and **paragliding** among the most popular activities. Local tourist offices have comprehensive relevant information.

EMERGENCY NUMBERS

Police ☎113; Ambulance & Fire ☎112.

COMMUNICATIONS

Wi-fi is widely available, offered free in most hostels and hotels and in many public spaces. Most tourist information offices will have a PC for use. Most **post offices** (*pošta*) are open Monday to Friday 8am to 6/7pm and Saturday 8am to noon. Stamps (*znamke*) can also be bought at newsstands.

Public **phones** use cards (*telekartice*; €7.90 or €14.60), available from post offices, kiosks and tobacconists. Make long-distance and international calls at a post office, where you're assigned to a cabin. Better still, buy a **SIM card** from a kiosk or newsstand; these typically cost around €7, which includes €5 starting credit. The main Slovenian mobile operators are Mobitel, Simobil and Tušmobil.

EMERGENCIES

The **police** (*policija*) are generally easy-going and likely to speak some English. **Pharmacies** (*lekarna*) are typically open Monday to Friday from 7am to 7/8pm, Saturday 7am to 1pm, and a rota system covers night-time opening; details are in the window of each pharmacy.

INFORMATION

Just about every town and resort has a well-stocked and helpful **tourist information office**, which can usually arrange accommodation too. Many of these offices stock an excellent range of hiking and cycling maps, as well as copies of the superb *In Your Pocket* Guides (usually free). A very high standard of English is spoken almost everywhere.

STUDENT AND YOUTH DISCOUNTS

Even if you already have the EURO< 26 card (see p.44), consider purchasing the affiliated SŽ-EURO<26 (€18; from most train stations) to get an additional 30 percent off train fares within Slovenia, and 25 percent off international rail travel.

SLOVENE

	SLOVENE	PRONUNCIATION
Yes	*Ja*	Ya
No	*Ne*	Ne
Please	*Prosim*	Proseem
Thank you	*Hvala*	Huala
Hello/Good day	*Živijo/dober dan*	Zheeveeyoh/dohburr dhan
Goodbye	*Nasvidenje*	Nasveedehnye
Excuse me	*Dovolite mi, prosim*	Dovoleeteh mee, proseem
Where?	*Kje?*	Kye?
Good	*Dobro*	Dobro
Bad	*Slabo*	Slabo
Near	*Blizu*	Bleezoo
Far	*Daleč*	Daalech
Cheap	*Poceni*	Potzenee
Expensive	*Drago*	Drago
Open	*Odprto*	Odpurto
Closed	*Zaprto*	Zapurto
Today	*Danes*	Danes
Yesterday	*Včeraj*	Ucheray
Tomorrow	*Jutri*	Yutree
How much is…?	*Koliko stane…?*	Koleeko stahne…?
What time is it?	*Koliko je ura?*	Koleeko ye oora?
I don't understand	*Ne razumem*	Ne razoomem
Do you speak English?	*Ali govorite angleško?*	Alee govoreete angleshko?
One	*Ena*	Ena
Two	*Dve*	Dve
Three	*Tri*	Tree
Four	*Štiri*	Shteeree
Five	*Pet*	Pet
Six	*Šest*	Shest
Seven	*Sedem*	Sedem
Eight	*Osem*	Osem
Nine	*Devet*	Devet
Ten	*Deset*	Deset

MONEY AND BANKS

Slovenia's currency is the **euro** (€). **Banks** (*banka*) generally open Monday to Friday 9am to noon and 1 to 5pm, Saturday 8.30am to 11am/noon. You can also change money in tourist offices, post offices, travel agencies and exchange bureaux (*menjalnica*). **Credit cards** are accepted in most hotels, restaurants and shops, while **ATMs** are widespread.

OPENING HOURS AND HOLIDAYS

Most **shops** open Monday to Friday 8am to 7pm and Saturday 8am to 1pm, with a few also open on Sunday mornings. Museum times vary, but many close on Mondays. All shops and banks are closed on the following **public holidays**: January 1 and 2, February 8, Easter Monday, April 27, May 1 and 2, June 25, August 15, October 31, November 1, December 25 and 26.

Ljubljana

Prosperous and elegant, the Slovene capital **LJUBLJANA** gracefully fans out from its castle-topped hill, the old centre marooned in the shapeless modernity that stretches out across the plain. The city's museums, galleries and architecture are only part of the picture; above all, Ljubljana is a place to meet people and enjoy the nightlife.

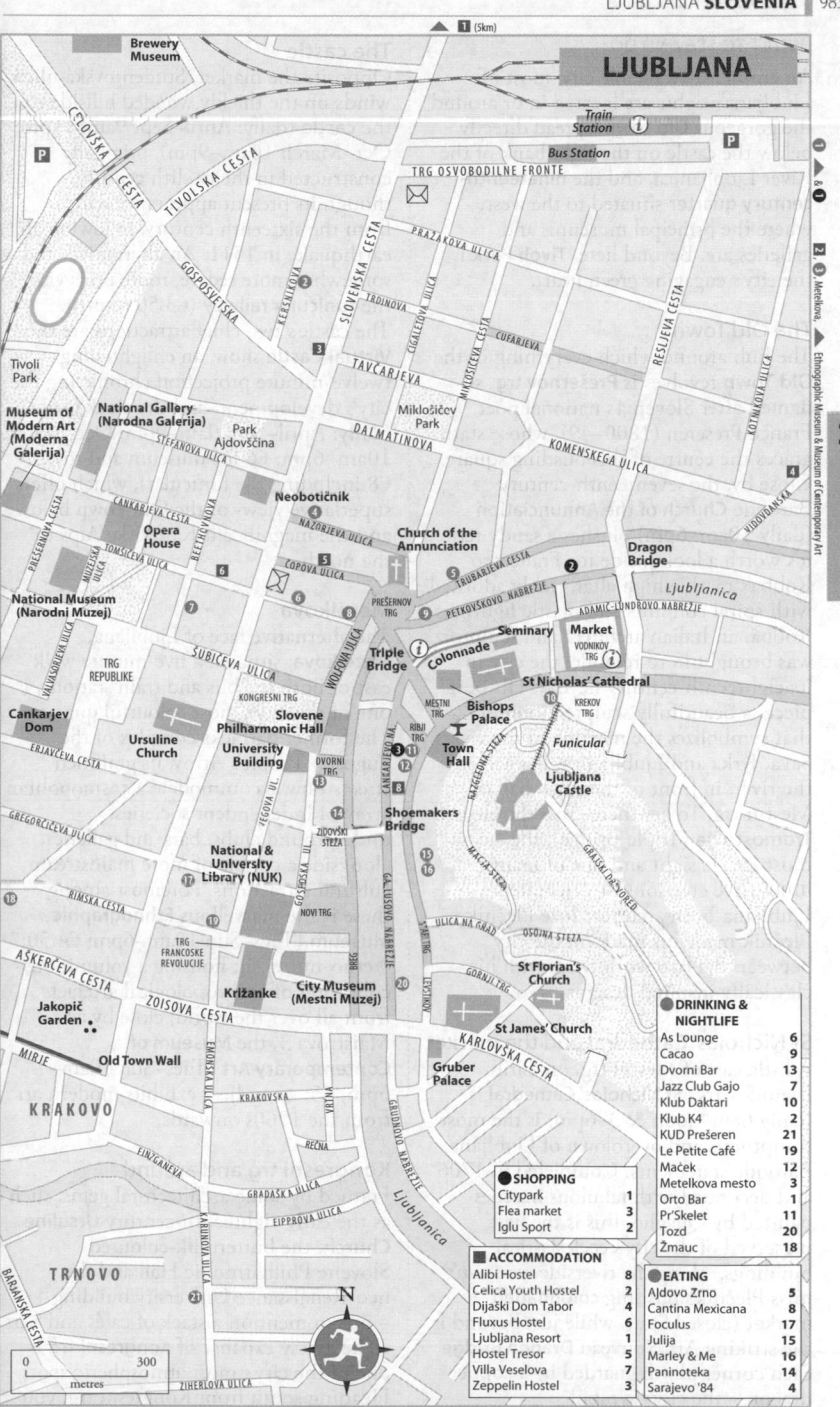

LJUBLJANA

31

Brewery Museum

Train Station

Bus Station

TRG OSVOBODILNE FRONTE

CELOVŠKA CESTA

TIVOLSKA CESTA

GOSPOSVETSKA

PRAŽAKOVA ULICA

SLOVENSKA CESTA

KERSNIKOVA

TRDINOVA

CIGALETOVA ULICA

MIKLOŠIČEVA CESTA

ČUFARJEVA

RESLJEVA CESTA

KOTNIKOVA ULICA

TAVČARJEVA

Tivoli Park

Museum of Modern Art (Moderna Galerija)

National Gallery (Narodna Galerija)

Park Ajdovščina

Miklošičev Park

DALMATINOVA

KOMENSKEGA ULICA

KRIŽEVNIŠKA

ŠTEFANOVA ULICA

CANKARJEVA CESTA

National Museum (Narodni Muzej)

PREŠERNOVA CESTA

WOLFOVA ULICA

MUZEJSKA

TOMŠIČEVA ULICA

BLEIWEISOVA

Neobotičnik

Opera House

NAZORJEVA ULICA

ČOPOVA ULICA

Church of the Annunciation

TRUBARJEVA CESTA

Dragon Bridge

Ljubljanica

PETKOVŠKOVO NABREŽJE

ADAMIČ-LUNDROVO NABREŽJE

PREŠERNOV TRG

Triple Bridge

Colonnade

Seminary

Market

VODNIKOV TRG

ZIDOVSKA STEZA

SUBIČEVA ULICA

TRG REPUBLIKE

KONGRESNI TRG

Slovene Philharmonic Hall

MESTNI TRG

Bishops Palace

St Nicholas' Cathedral

KREKOV TRG

Cankarjev Dom

Ursuline Church

University Building

RIBJI TRG

Town Hall

Funicular

Ljubljana Castle

ERJAVČEVA CESTA

JENGOVA UL.

DVORNI TRG

GALLUSOVO NABREŽJE

KARLOVŠKA CESTA

GREGORČIČEVA ULICA

Shoemakers Bridge

ZIDOVSKA STEZA

MAČKA STEZA

GRAJSKI DREVORED

RIMSKA CESTA

National & University Library (NUK)

NOVI TRG

KRIŽEVNIŠKA

ULICA NA GRAD

OSOJNA STEZA

AŠKERČEVA CESTA

TRG FRANCOSKE REVOLUCIJE

Jakopič Garden

Old Town Wall

MIRJE

ZOISOVA CESTA

Križanke

City Museum (Mestni Muzej)

GORNJI TRG

St Florian's Church

KRAKOVO

EMONSKA ULICA

KRAKOVSKA

VRTNA

REČNA

GRADAŠKA ULICA

EIPPROVA ULICA

FINŽGARJEVA

St James' Church

Gruber Palace

GRUDNOVO NABREŽJE

Ljubljanica

TRNOVO

BARANSKA CESTA

KARUNOVA ULICA

ZIHERLOVA ULICA

0   300   metres

N

SHOPPING

Cityparks	1
Flea market	3
Iglu Sport	2

ACCOMMODATION

Alibi Hostel	8
Celica Youth Hostel	2
Dijaški Dom Tabor	4
Fluxus Hostel	6
Ljubljana Resort	1
Hostel Tresor	5
Villa Veselova	7
Zeppelin Hostel	3

DRINKING & NIGHTLIFE

As Lounge	6
Cacao	9
Dvorni Bar	13
Jazz Club Gajo	7
Klub Daktari	10
Klub K4	2
KUD Prešeren	21
Le Petite Café	19
Maček	12
Metelkova mesto	3
Orto Bar	1
Pr'Skelet	11
Tozd	20
Žmauc	18

EATING

Ajdovo Zrno	5
Cantina Mexicana	8
Foculus	17
Julija	15
Marley & Me	16
Paninoteka	14
Sarajevo '84	4

31

WHAT TO SEE AND DO

An eminently walkable city, most of Ljubljana's sights are located in or around the gorgeous **Old Town**, spread directly below the castle on the right bank of the River Ljubljanica, and the **nineteenth-century quarter** situated to the west, where the principal museums and galleries are. Beyond here, **Tivoli Park** is the city's engaging green heart.

The Old Town

The hub around which everything in the **Old Town** revolves is **Prešernov trg**, so named after Slovenia's national poet, France Preseren (1800–49), whose statue graces the centre of this bustling square. Close by, the seventeenth-century Baroque **Church of the Annunciation** (daily 10am–6pm) blushes a sandy red; it's worth a look inside for Francesco Robba's marble high altar, richly adorned with spiral columns and plastic figurines. Robba, an Italian architect and sculptor, was brought in to remodel the city in its eighteenth-century heyday. His best piece, a beautifully sculpted **fountain** that symbolizes the meeting of the rivers Sava, Krka and Ljubljanica, lies across the river, in front of the town hall on Mestni trg. To get there cross the elegant **Tromostovje** (Triple Bridge), the city's most iconic sight and one of many innovative creations by celebrated Ljubljana-born architect Jože Plečnik. Plečnik made his mark on the city between the two world wars with his classically inspired designs.

St Nicholas' Cathedral and the market

A little east of Mestni trg, on Ciril-Metodov trg, **St Nicholas' Cathedral** (daily 6am–noon & 3–6pm) is the most sumptuous and overblown of Ljubljana's Baroque statements. Completed in 1706 and decorated with fabulous frescoes painted by Quaglio, this is the best preserved of the city's ecclesiastical buildings. Along the riverside, you can't miss Plečnik's bustling **colonnaded market** (closed Sun), while just beyond is the striking Art Nouveau **Dragon Bridge**, each corner plinth guarded by a copper dragon – the city's symbol.

The castle

Opposite the market, Študentovska ulica winds up the thickly wooded hillside to the **castle** (daily: April–Sept 9am–11pm; Oct–March 10am–9pm), originally constructed in the twelfth century, though its present appearance dates from the sixteenth century, following an earthquake in 1511. An alternative, and somewhat more sedate, route up is via the **funicular railway** (€3.50 return). The castle's two chief attractions are the **Virtual Castle** show, an enlightening twelve-minute projection chronicling the city's development, and the **clock tower** (daily: April–Sept 9am–9pm; Oct–March 10am–6pm; €6 for museum and tower, €8 including the funicular), which offers superlative views of the Old Town below and the magnificent Kamniške Alps to the north.

Metelkova

The alternative face of Ljubljana, **Metelkova**, situated a five-minute walk east of both the bus and train stations, is one of the city's most colourful quarters. The former barracks complex of the Yugoslav People's Army, its graffitied streets now accommodate a cosmopolitan array of independent societies, underground clubs, bars and galleries, alongside a couple of more mainstream cultural attractions. Foremost among these is the marvellous **Ethnographic Museum** (Tues–Sun 10am–6pm; €4.50; ⓦetno-muzej.si), housing a voluminous collection of anthropological artefacts from all over the world; close by at Maistrova 3, the **Museum of Contemporary Art** (Tues–Sun 10am–6pm; €5; ⓦmg-lj.si) exhibits modern art from the 1960s onwards.

Kongresni trg and around

Framed by some architectural gems, such as the early eighteenth-century **Ursuline Church**, the buttermilk-coloured Slovene Philharmonic Hall and the neo-Renaissance University building – not to mention a stack of cafés and bars – the grassy expanse of **Kongresni trg** is one of the city's most atmospheric spots. Heading south from Kongresni trg, you can't miss the chequered pink, green and grey brickwork of the **National and University Library**, arguably Plečnik's greatest work. Just behind here, the fine **City Museum** (Tues–Sun 10am–6pm; €4) is devoted to the lives and times of the city's inhabitants (*ljubljancani*), though do keep an eye out for the usually excellent temporary exhibitions held here. Virtually next door is the seventeenth-century monastery complex of **Križanke**, originally the seat of a thirteenth-century order of Teutonic Knights, now an atmospheric concert venue. In the centre of Trg Francoske revolucije, opposite, the **Illyrian Monument** was erected in 1929 in belated recognition of Napoleon's short-lived attempt to create a fiefdom of the same name centred on Ljubljana.

Museums west of Slovenska

The town's leafy cultural quarter boasts several impressive museums and galleries. The best of these is the **National Gallery** at Prešernova 24 (Tues–Sun 10am–6pm; €5; ⊛ng-slo.si), which is rich in local medieval Gothic work, although most visitors gravitate towards the halls devoted to the Slovene Impressionists, and in particular the outstanding paintings by Ivan Grohar and Rihard Jakopič. Diagonally across from here the **Museum of Modern Art** at Tomšičeva 14 (Tues–Sun 10am–6pm; €5; ⊛mg-lj.si) effectively takes over from where the National Gallery stops, showcasing more experimental work from the mid-twentieth century onwards. Lastly, the grand **National Museum** (daily 10am–6pm, Thurs till 8pm; €4; ⊛nms.si), at Prešernova 20, has intermittently interesting displays of archeological finds and artefacts relevant to Slovene history; the building also houses the **Natural History Museum** (same hours and ticket), whose star exhibit is the only complete mammoth skeleton found in Europe.

Tivoli Park

Beyond the galleries lies elegant **Tivoli Park**, an expanse of lawns and tree-lined walkways leading to dense woodland. It's a lovely retreat from the busy city centre.

A Baroque villa at the edge of the park contains the **National Museum of Contemporary History** (Tues–Sun 10am–6pm; €3.50; ⊛www.muzej-nz.si), with interactive displays and carefully presented artefacts creating an evocative journey through Slovenia's conflict-riddled twentieth-century history, including some fascinating footage of the Ten-Day War in 1991.

ARRIVAL AND DEPARTURE

By plane Ljubljana's Jože Pučnik airport (☎04 206 1981, ⊛lju-airport.si) is in Brnik, 25km north of the city, and connected by bus (weekdays hourly, every 2hr at weekends; 50min; €4.10), or the quicker shuttle bus (€9). Taxis should cost around €35–40.

By train The train station (*železniška postaja*) is on Trg Osvobodilne fronte, a 10min walk north of the centre.

Destinations Divača (hourly; 1hr 30min); Koper (3 daily; 2hr 30min); Maribor (hourly; 1hr 45min–2hr 30min); Postojna (hourly; 1hr); Ptuj (2 daily; 2hr 30min).

By bus The station (*Avtobusna postaja*) is beside the train station.

Destinations Bled (hourly; 1hr 20min); Bohinj (hourly; 2hr); Bovec (4 daily; 3hr 30min–4hr 15min); Divača (7 daily; 1hr 30min); Kobarid (3 daily; 3–5hr); Koper (10 daily; 2hr); Maribor (4 daily; 2hr 30min–3hr); Piran (6 daily; 2hr 45min); Portorož (5 daily; 2hr 30min); Postojna (hourly; 1hr).

INFORMATION AND TOURS

Tourist information The Slovenian Tourist Information Centre (STIC) is at Krekov trg 10 (June–Sept daily 8am–9pm; Oct–May Mon–Fri 8am–7pm, Sat & Sun 9am–5pm; ☎01 306 4576), with the main Ljubljana Tourist Information Office (TIC) next to the Triple Bridge on Stritarjeva ulica (daily: June–Sept 8am–9pm; Oct–May 8am–7pm; ☎01 306 1215, ⊛visitljubljana.com); there's another branch in the arrivals hall at the airport (daily 10am–10pm). You can pick up *Ljubljana in Your Pocket* at all of these.

Tourist card The Ljubljana Tourist Card, Urbana (€35 for three days, €30 for two days), is available from all the tourist offices and entitles you to free travel on Ljubljana's buses, free bike rental, one free guided tour and entrance to most museums and galleries; there's a ten percent discount if you buy online.

Walking and boat tours The Ljubljana Tourist Information Office organizes a range of pleasant 2hr walking tours (April–Sept; €10) of the Old Town, as well as special interest tours. On the water, Barka Ljubljanica offer 30min river cruises, which depart from Novi trg on the hour between 11am and 9pm (€5).

31

31

GETTING AROUND

City transport Ljubljana's buses are cheap and frequent; there are no cash fares on buses, so you must buy an Urbana public transport card (€2), available at tourist information offices, news kiosks and post offices, and top it up with credit for your journeys, which cost €1.20.

Bikes Bikes can be rented from various central docking stations including the Central Market and Tivoli Park through Ljubljana's "Bicike" scheme (register at ⓦ bicikelj .si; free up to 1hr, €1/2hr, €2/3hr). There are also bikes available from the Slovenian Tourist Information Centre (€2/2hr, €8/day).

ACCOMMODATION

Ljubljana now has a terrific stock of hostels, in addition to student dorms (*dijaški dom*), which generally become available in late June/early July. Decently priced budget hotels are few and far between.

HOSTELS

Alibi Hostel Cankarjevo Nabrežje 27 ☎01 251 1244, ⓦ alibi.si. Super location in the heart of the Old Town for this sprawling hostel, with graffitied walls and large communal spaces. No kitchen. Dorm €19, double €50

★ **Celica Youth Hostel** Metelkova 8 ☎01 230 9700, ⓦ hostelcelica.com. Brilliantly original hostel in a former military prison at the centre of artistic Metelkova, with bright dorms and two/three-bed "cells", each designed by a different architect or artist. Breakfast included. Expect concerts, exhibitions and parties here too. Dorm €23, double €60

Dijaški Dom Tabor Vidovdanska 7 ☎01 234 8840, ⓦ hostel.ddt.si. Busy, central student hostel, with decent, very cheap beds on offer in July and Aug only. Breakfast included. Dorm €11, double €38

Fluxus Hostel Tomšičeva 4 ☎01 251 5760, ⓦ fluxus -hostel.com. Quiet and understated, but deservedly popular hostel in a beautiful old building; friendly host and a stylish yet homely feel. Dorm €18, double €60

★ **Hostel Tresor** Čopova ulica 38 ☎01 200 9060, ⓦ hostel-tresor.si. This former bank building has been utilized to great effect: the spacious dorms are wonderfully bright and the old vaults now function as the breakfast room and games/chill-out area. Superb atrium too. Breakfast included. Dorm €26, double €66

Villa Veselova Veselova 14 ☎059 926 721, ⓦ v-v.si. Charming hostel in a historic villa bordering peaceful Tivoli Park, with large, airy dorms and one en-suite private. Breakfast included. Dorm €22, double €60

Zeppelin Hostel Slovenska 47 ☎059 191 427, ⓦ zeppelinhostel.com. Sociable, centrally located option with four-, six-, and ten-bed dorms as well as doubles with or without bathroom. Breakfast included. Dorm €23, double €54

CAMPING

Ljubljana Resort Dunajska 270 ☎01 568 3913, ⓦ ljubljanaresort.si. Superbly equipped site 4km north of the centre in Ježica; also has chalets sleeping four, a water park, restaurant, bar and shop. Bus #6 or #8 from Slovenska cesta. €12.90 per person, plus €5.50 per tent

EATING

The streets of Ljubljana's Old Town are packed with restaurants to suit all budgets, and during the warmer months it's lovely to dine alfresco on the banks of the Ljubljanica. For snacks, head to the many kiosks and stands near the stations selling *burek*, *pljeskavica* and the local *gorenjska* sausages. There's a lively food market on Vodnikov trg (closed Sun) where you can pick up tasty seasonal produce, while the nearby Market Colonnade is packed with little food shops selling breads, cheeses, sandwiches and the like. Every Friday on neighbouring Pogačarjev trg, the open-air kitchen is great for street food at bargain prices.

RESTAURANTS

Ajdovo Zrno Trubarjeva 7. Excellent veggie canteen in a pleasant courtyard, with a self-service salad bar, soups, sandwiches and tortillas (€3–4), plus daily specials like cannelloni and risotto. Mon–Fri 11am–7pm.

Cantina Mexicana Knafljev prehod. On a lively alleyway between Slovenska cesta and Wolfova ulica, this colourfully painted restaurant serves decent Mexican fajitas and tortillas (€8–12), as well as cocktails. Mon, Tues & Sun 9am–1am, Wed–Sat 10am–3am.

Foculus Gregorčičeva 3. Wonderfully decorated pizzeria with an enormous menu of cheap pizza and salad options from €6. Daily 11am–midnight.

Julija Stari trg 9. Refined, atmospheric Old Town restaurant with a menu of delicious salads, pasta and risotto (€9–12). Daily 11am–midnight.

Marley & Me Stari trg 9. Next to *Julija*, here's another enticing possibility on this busy little Old Town street, with well-prepared Mediterranean classics such as tagliatelle with shrimp (€11). Daily 11am–11pm.

Paninoteka Jurčičev trg 3. Cracking riverside setting by the Shoemaker's Bridge for this cool sandwich bar serving a range of piping-hot panini, ciabattas and wraps. Takeaway too. Daily 8am–11pm.

★ **Sarajevo '84** Nazorjeva ulica 12. Decked out with sporting paraphernalia in homage to Sarajevo's staging of the winter Olympics, this fun Bosnian restaurant serves, among other things, the classic Balkan grilled meats, *čevapčiči* and *pljeskavica* (€7). Mon–Fri 10am–midnight, Sat noon–midnight, Sun noon–10pm.

DRINKING AND NIGHTLIFE

Despite its diminutive size, Ljubljana has an impressively varied and energetic choice of bars and clubs, and a leisurely stroll along the banks of the Ljubljanica will yield a locale every 20m or so. Similarly, you'll find plenty of places along Mestni trg and Stari trg, and around Kongresni trg. The city has always maintained a strong independent spirit, manifest in numerous progressive venues offering a wide programme of alternative events. *Ljubljana In Your Pocket* is your best bet for the most up-to-date listings.

CAFÉS AND BARS

Cacao Petkovškovo Nabrežje 3. This stylish riverside café-bar serves the city's best ice cream; take your pick from delicious flavours like pistachio, melon and forest strawberry (€1.50 per scoop), or just kick back with a refreshing fruit juice or coffee. Daily 8am–midnight.

★ **Dvorni Bar** Dvorni trg 2. If you don't get to Slovenia's beautiful wine-growing regions, fear not; this classy bar has offerings from all over the country, be it the straw-coloured Rebula from Goriška Brda or the ruby-red Teran from the Karst (€3/glass). Mon–Sat 8am–1am, Sun 9am–midnight.

Klub Daktari Krekov trg 7. The decor really makes this convivial place special, with restored antique furniture, corner piano and shelves packed with books. Live music, cabaret and jam sessions. Daily 9am–midnight.

Le Petite Café Trg Francoske revolucije 4. This cosy, long-standing Parisian-style café, in a lovely spot by Križanke, is perfect for a big mug of *bela kava* (white coffee) during the day or a glass of wine later on. Daily 7.30am–1am.

Maček Krojaška 5 ⓦ sobe-macek.si. This lively, bohemian café bar is arguably the most popular of the riverside watering holes, its large terrace perfect for a glass of wine. Mon–Sat 9am–1am, Sun 9am–11pm.

Pr'Skelet Ključavničarska ulica 5. The name's a bit of a giveaway: this cavernous bar has swinging skeletons and doors hidden in bookcases. Two-for-one cocktails make the outdoor terrace the best value on the riverfront. Daily 9am–11pm.

Tozd Galusovo Nabrežje 27. Located down by the quieter, southern stretch of the river, this is a great spot to cool off with a beer at sundown; the funky brick and enamel interior is plastered with all manner of random objects. Daily 8.30am–midnight.

Žmauc Rimska 21. The graffiti-daubed exterior of this happy, hippy dive gives some indication of what to expect; the small buzzy terrace is packed throughout the day. Mon–Sat 7.30am–1am, Sun 6pm–1am.

CLUBS AND LIVE MUSIC

As Lounge Čopova 5 (entrance on Knafljev prehod). The cellar beneath this upmarket restaurant transforms into a classy club with DJs and a cocktail-sipping crowd.

Jazz Club Gajo Beethovnova 8 ⓦ jazzclubgajo.com. Suitably atmospheric venue for the genre, with quality live offerings and jam sessions every Mon.

Klub K4 Kersnikova ⓦ klubk4.org. Legendary stalwart of Ljubljana's alternative scene with a terrific rota of music: mainly electronic, but also rock, jazz and folk, plus a gay and lesbian night every Sun.

KUD Prešeren Karunova 14 ⓦ www.kud.si. Superb gig venue and cultural centre in Trnovo that also hosts regular literary events, workshops and art exhibitions. Also stages the excellent *Trnfest* festival in Aug.

★ **Metelkova mesto** Metelkova cesta ⓦ metelkovamesto.org. The city's counter-cultural hub, with a left-field cluster of clubs, bars and galleries; one of the most banging venues here is *Gala Hala*, with several live performances a week during the summer.

Orto Bar Grablovičeva 1 ⓦ orto-bar.com. Energetic club east of the train station; also one of the city's principal rock venues, with typically one or two gigs a week.

ENTERTAINMENT AND EVENTS

Ljubljana has a busy calendar of dance, music and theatre at its purpose-built venues.

Cankarjev Dom Prešernova 10 ☎ 01 241 7100, ⓦ cd-cc .si. The city's cultural headquarters, hosting major orchestral and theatrical events, art exhibitions, and folk and jazz concerts.

National Opera and Ballet Theatre Župančičeva 1 ☎ 01 241 1740, ⓦ opera.si. An impressive nineteenth-century Neoclassical theatre staging ballet and opera.

LJUBLJANA FESTIVALS

There's a wonderful roster of exciting annual festivals in the capital.

Druga Godba ☎ 01 430 8260, ⓦ drugagodba.si. Brilliant two-day annual world music festival in May featuring concerts at atmospheric venues throughout the city.

International Summer Festival ☎ 01 241 6026, ⓦ ljubljanafestival.si. Long-running programme of internationally renowned orchestral artists, with concerts at various venues between July and mid-Sept.

Ljubljana Jazz Festival ⓦ ljubljanajazz.si. Ljubljana's five-day jazz festival is up there with the best in Europe; better still, most concerts take place at the wonderful Križanke open-air theatre.

SHOPPING

Citypark Šmartinska 152 @ citypark.si. Slovenia's largest shopping centre, out on the northeastern fringes of the capital, with more than a hundred stores. Buses #2, #7, #12 and #27. Mon–Sat 9am–9pm, Sun 9am–3pm.

Flea market Wonderful antiques market along the right bank of the Ljubljanica where, among other things, you can pick up Tito-era memorabilia. Sun 8am–2pm.

Iglu Sport Petkovškovo 31 @ iglusport.si. Stocks camping and outdoor gear; useful for trips to the lakes or mountains. Mon–Fri 9am–2pm & 3–7.30pm, Sat 9am–1pm.

DIRECTORY

Embassies and consulates Australia, Železna cesta 14 ☎ 01 234 8675; Canada, Trg Republike 3 ☎ 01 252 4444; Ireland, Palaca Kapitelj, Poljanski nasip 6 ☎ 01 300 8970; UK, Trg Republike 3 ☎ 01 200 3910; US, Prešernova 31 ☎ 01 200 5500.

Exchange At the train station and at post offices.

Hospital Zaloška Cesta 2 ☎ 01 522 5050, @ kclj.si.

Internet Most of the city centre has wi-fi coverage (free for 1hr). There are PCs at the Slovenian Tourist Information Centre on Krekov trg (€1/30min).

Left luggage Lockers at the train station (€2–3/24hr depending on locker size).

Pharmacy Centralna Lekarna on Prešernov trg (Mon–Fri 7.30am–8pm, Sat 8am–3pm, Sun 9am–2pm; ☎ 01 230 6100); 24hr pharmacy at Prisojne 7 ☎ 01 230 6230.

Post office Slovenska cesta 32 (Mon–Fri 8am–7pm, Sat 8am–noon) and Pražakova ulica 3.

Southwest Slovenia

Not to be missed while you're in Ljubljana is a visit to either the **Postojna** or **Škocjan caves** – both spectacular, and both easily manageable either as a day-trip from the capital or en route south to the coast. A trip easily combined with Postojna is to **Predjama Castle**, a sombre fortress craftily embedded into the karst landscape. On the small stretch of Adriatic coastline are a number of charismatic towns, heavily influenced by a legacy of Venetian rule. Of these, **Piran** is by far the most rewarding, its fishing-village charm and gorgeous architecture contrasting starkly with the brash modernity of neighbouring **Portorož**.

POSTOJNA

Hourly trains run the 65km route from Ljubljana to **POSTOJNA**, but as the walk to the caves is shorter from the bus stop, most people opt for this mode of transport. Once in the town, signs direct you to the **caves** (daily: May, June & Sept 9am–5pm; July & Aug 9am–6pm; April & Oct 10am–4pm; Jan–March, Nov & Dec 10am–3pm; tours every 1–2hr; 90min; €23; @ postojnska-jama.eu). Inside, a train whizzes you through spectacular preliminary systems before the guided 1.5km walking tour starts. The vast and fantastic jungles of rock formations are breathtaking and there's also an opportunity to catch a rare glimpse of the cave-dwelling "human fish", a blind amphibian that can live for up to 100 years, before the climactic finale of the 40m-high "concert hall". Bring a jacket and appropriate footwear; the air inside the caves is decidedly chilly. To avoid the considerable crowds, visit first thing in the morning or late afternoon.

PREDJAMA CASTLE

Nine kilometres northwest of the caves, but not served by public transport, is the precariously sited **Predjama Castle** (daily: Jan–March, Nov & Dec 10am–4pm; April & Oct 10am–5pm; May, June & Sept 9am–6pm; July & Aug 9am–7pm; €9). Built into and around an elevated cave entrance in the midst of the dramatic karst landscape, this sixteenth-century fortress is a striking sight and affords excellent views of the surrounding countryside. Its damp, sparsely filled interior is less rewarding, though it is fun exploring the many passageways, galleries and alcoves, and you can see weaponry and artefacts dating back to its heyday as the castle of the legendary knight Erazem Lueger. The easiest way to get here is to rent bikes from the *Hotel Sport* at Kolodvorska 1 in Postojna (€15/day).

ŠKOCJAN CAVES

Much less visited, but even more dramatic than Postojna, the **Škocjan**

Caves are a stunning system of echoing chambers, secret passages and collapsed valleys carved out by the Reka River, which begins its journey some 50km south near the Croatian border. Daily **tours** (June–Sept hourly, 10am–5pm; Oct–May 2–3 daily, 10am–3pm; €15; ⓦpark-skocjanske-jame.si) take you through several stalactite-infested chambers and halls, before you reach the breathtaking **Murmuring Cave**, reputedly the world's largest subterranean canyon; here you get to cross the remarkable, vertiginous 45m-high **Cerkvenik Bridge**, under which the Reka flows. To get here follow the 3km footpath from Divača train station (see map at the station).

PORTOROŽ

Easily reached by bus from the train terminus in Koper, **PORTOROŽ** ("Port of Roses") sprawls at the beginning of a long, tapering peninsula that projects like a lizard's tail north into the Adriatic. Popular since the end of the nineteenth century for its mild climate and the health-inducing properties of its salty mud baths, today the resort's big draw is high-rise hotels, glitzy casinos and buzzing nightlife. The main "beach" is just a continuation of the concrete promenade, and though there's not a great deal of culture here, the town's vibrant bars and clubs are unrivalled on this stretch of the coast.

ARRIVAL AND INFORMATION

By bus The small, principal bus terminal is on the main coastal strip, Obala, though buses stop all along here.
Tourist office Just down from the bus terminal at Obala 16 (July & Aug daily 9am–7pm; Sept–June Mon–Sat 9am–5pm, Sun 10am–2pm; ☎05 674 2220, ⓦportoroz.si).

ACCOMMODATION

Private rooms (double €30–50) can be booked through Maona, at Obala 14b (☎05 674 0363, ⓦmaona.si), or Turist Biro at Obala 57 (☎05 674 1055, ⓦturistbiro-ag.si).
Hostel Panorama Šentjane 25 ☎04 674 7289, ⓦhostel-portoroz.eu. Pleasant small hostel located halfway between Portorož and Piran, with fine views of the Istrian coast. There's no public transport up to here, so expect a stiff 30min walk. Breakfast included. Dorm **€25**, double **€56**

EATING AND DRINKING

Take your pick from any number of beachside bars and clubs, many of which stay open until dawn.
Alaya Sprawling, tropically themed open air beach bar just south of the main beach and watersports centre, which also stages live music and regular party nights.
Cacao Obala 14. Near the tourist office, this laidback bar sports a cool, loungey interior and deck terrace facing the beach.

PIRAN

PIRAN, at the tip of the peninsula, 4km from Portorož, couldn't be more different. Its web of arched alleys, tightly packed ranks of houses and little Italianate squares is delightful. The centre, 200m around the harbour from the bus station, is **Tartinijev trg**, a striking, marble-surfaced square fringed by Venetian palaces and an imposing Austrian town hall. The square is named after Giuseppe Tartini, an eighteenth-century Italian violinist and composer who was born in a cream villa up a small flight of stairs on the square's east side; now a **commemorative house** (daily: July & Aug 9am–noon & 6–9pm; Sept–May 11am–noon & 5–6pm; €2), it features scores, diaries and letters as well as his death mask. From the square's eastern edge, follow Rozmanova ulica all the way up to the commanding Baroque **Church of St George**, crowning a spectacular spot on the far side of Piran's peninsula. Climb the monumental belfry (€1) for superlative views of the Adriatic.

ARRIVAL AND INFORMATION

By bus Buses pull up on Cankarjevo nabrežje, a 5min seafront walk from the main square, Tartinijev trg.
Destinations Ljubljana (7 daily; 2hr 45min); Portorož/Koper (every 15–20min; 10/45min); Trieste (Mon–Sat 1 daily; 1hr 30min).
Tourist information Tartinijev trg 2 (July & Aug daily 9am–7pm; Sept–June Mon–Fri 9am–5pm & Sat 10am–2pm; ☎05 673 4440, ⓦportoroz.si).

ACCOMMODATION

Private rooms (double €30–50) can be booked through Maona, at Cankarjevo nabrežje 7 (☎05 674 0363, ⓦmaona.si), between the bus station and the square.
Alibi Hostels Bonifacijeva 11 & 14 and Trubarjeva 60 ☎03 136 3666, ⓦalibi.si. Three historic houses, with

31

two- and four-bedded rooms imaginatively decorated with a theme from a different region, town or attraction in Slovenia. No kitchens. Dorm **€25**, double **€50**

Fiesa Camping Fiesa 57b ☎05 674 6230. Decent site 1km east of Piran (follow the path from the Church of St George). Open May–Sept. **€11.50** per person

Val Hostel Gregorčičeva 38a ☎05 673 2555, ⓦhostel-val.com. Friendly and well run, with a homely guesthouse feel; two-, three- and four-bedded rooms, laundry facilities and a good restaurant. Breakfast included. Dorm **€25**, double **€60**

EATING AND DRINKING

Da Noi Prešernovo nabrežje. Popular, cellar-like bar, with a cool, breezy seafront terrace too. Daily until 3am in the summer.

Fontana Trg 1 Maja. A local favourite on account of its excellent service and good choice of reasonably priced fresh fish: a filling plate of sardines is €6. Balkan grilled meats too. Daily 3pm–midnight.

Pirat Zupančičeva 24. A pleasant antidote to the town's touristy restaurants, with no-frills seafood served in copper bowls and a good-value daily tourist menu for €10. Daily 10am–11pm.

Pri Mari Dantejeva ulica 17. Just beyond the bus station, this warm, *gostilna*-style place offers some terrific dishes like spicy squid pasta, and fillet of tuna on a bed of rocket salad (€10). Tues–Sat noon–10pm, Sun 2–6pm.

Northwest Slovenia

Within easy reach of Ljubljana are the stunning mountain lakes of **Bled** and **Bohinj**. The magnificent **Soča Valley**, on the western side of the Julian Alps, is much less touristed, and small towns such as **Kobarid** and **Bovec** are excellent bases for hiking and adventure sports.

BLED

The lake resort of **BLED** has all the right ingredients for a memorable visit – a placid mirror lake with a romantic island, a medieval cliff-top castle and a backdrop of snowcapped mountains. In summer, the lake is the setting for a whole host of watersports – including major rowing contests – and in winter the surface becomes a giant fairytale skating rink.

Perhaps the most visited place outside of the capital, Bled manages to retain a magical calm despite the hordes of tourists.

WHAT TO SEE AND DO

The best way to appreciate the lake is to walk around it: a leisurely stroll should take no more than two hours. Otherwise, a constant relay of stretched gondolas leaves from below the *Park Hotel*, by the *Pension Mlino*, and by *Vila Prešeren*, ferrying tourists back and forth to Bled's picturesque **island** (€12 return). With an early start (and by renting your own rowing boat (€10–15/hr) from the Castle Boat House or *Pension Pletna*), you can beat them to it. Crowning the island, the Baroque **Church of Sv Marika Božja** (€3) is the last in a line of churches on a spot that's long held religious significance: under the present building lie remains of a pre-Roman temple.

From the north shore a couple of paths wind steeply uphill to **Bled Castle** (daily: April–May 8am–8pm; June–Oct 8am–9pm; Nov–March 8am–6pm; €8), originally an eleventh-century fortification whose present appearance dates from the seventeenth; the museum contains a well-presented collection of local artefacts relating to the settlement of Bled, and the lovely courtyard has magnificent views across the lake and towards the Alps. In the shade of the castle rock lies a clean, well-equipped **bathing area** with changing rooms (June to late Sept). **Bikes** can be rented (€5/3hr, €10/day) from any number of places, providing an excellent way to see the surrounding area; the circumference of the lake can be cycled in thirty minutes.

★ TREAT YOURSELF

On selected dates between mid-May and early October, an old-fashioned steam train plies the line between Jesenice and Nova Gorica, passing through Bled Jezero and Bohinjska Bistrica, providing a wonderful scenic option as it chugs steadily through the mountains. Tickets cost €41 return and must be booked in advance (ⓦabc-tourism.si).

Vintgar Gorge

The main attraction in the outlying hills is the **Vintgar Gorge** (April 20 to Oct daily 8am–7pm; €4), 4km north of town, an impressive defile accessed via a series of wooden walkways and bridges suspended from the rock face. To get here, take the daily tourist bus (10am June–Sept, additional bus at 9am July & Aug; return at 12.30pm; €2.30) to the village of Zasip, climb to the hilltop chapel of **Sv Katarina** and pick up a path through the forest to the gorge entrance.

ARRIVAL AND DEPARTURE

By train Trains from Ljubljana stop at Bled-Lesce, 4km southeast of Bled, from where there are regular buses (€1.80) to the lake. Trains on the Jesenice–Nova Gorica branch call at Bled Jezero, a 5min walk from the northwest corner of Bled.

Destinations Ljubljana (every 1–2hr; 40min–1hr); Bohinjska Bistrica (4–6 daily; 20min); Most na Soči for the Soča Valley (4–6 daily; 55min).

By bus The station is a 5min walk northeast of the lake on Grajska cesta.

Destinations Ljubljana (hourly; 1hr 15min); Ribčev Laz for Lake Bohinj (hourly; 40min).

INFORMATION

Tourist office Cesta svobode 10, opposite the *Park Hotel* (April–June, Sept & Oct Mon–Sat 8am–7pm, Sun 11am–5pm; July & Aug Mon–Sat 8am–9pm, Sun 10am–6pm; Nov–March Mon–Fri 8am–6pm, Sun 8am–1pm; ☎ 04 574 1122, ⓦ bled.si).

ACCOMMODATION

Private rooms are available through Kompas in the shopping centre at Ljubljanska 4 (☎ 04 572 7501, ⓦ kompas-bled.si).

★ **Camping Bled** Kidričeva 10 ☎ 04 575 2000, ⓦ sava -hotels-resorts.com. Beautifully located amid the pines at the western end of the lake, this family-friendly campsite has first-rate facilities. For glampers there are some superb wooden huts with double beds and hot tubs; the breakfast basket (€9) is fab. €13 per person camping; €65 per hut

Pension Bledec Grajska 17 ☎ 04 574 5250, ⓦ youth -hostel-bledec.si. This low-key hostel's comfortable dorms and doubles feature traditional furniture; each has its own bathroom. No kitchen but a good restaurant. Breakfast included. Dorm €22, double €56

Travellers Haven Riklijeva cesta 1 ☎ 05 904 4226, ⓦ travellers-haven.si. Close to *Pension Bledec*, with tastefully furnished dorms, a homely kitchen and common area, and free bike rental and laundry facilities. Breakfast

not included but there's a supermarket opposite. Dorm €21, double €48

EATING AND DRINKING

The best places for eating are in the hillside area between Bled's bus station and castle, though several *pensions* on the lake's perimeter offer decent food too. The ugly concrete shopping centre on Ljubljanska is home to some strangely popular bars.

Chilli Cesta svobode 9. Popular bar and restaurant with a pleasant terrace and an appropriately spicy menu of Mexican and Mediterranean dishes from around €8. Daily 11am–1am.

Gostilna Pri Planincu Grajska 8. Opposite the bus station, this historic pub and restaurant has been serving up hearty Slovene home cooking since 1903; the mixed grill (€12.50) is worth chomping into after a hard day's hike. Daily 9am–11pm.

Smon Grajska 3. No less of a local Institution, "The Bear" café is the best place to try the ubiquitous Bled *Kremna Rezina* (cream cake; €2.50) alongside a steaming mug of *bela kava* (white coffee). Daily 7.30am–9pm.

LAKE BOHINJ

From Bled hourly buses make the 25km trip through the verdant, mist-laden Sava Bohinjka Valley to **Lake Bohinj**. In appearance and character Lake Bohinj is utterly different from Bled: the lake crooks a narrow finger under the wild mountains, evergreen woods slope gently down to the water, and in the relative absence of visitors, a lazy stillness hangs over all.

Ribčev Laz

RIBČEV LAZ (referred to as Jezero on bus timetables), at the eastern end of the lake, is where most facilities are based. **Walking trails** lead round both sides of the lake (the 12km circumference can be walked in around four hours), or north onto the eastern shoulders of the Triglav range. One route leads north from the enchanting village of Stara Fužina into the Voje valley, passing through the dramatic **Mostnica Gorge** (€2.50), a local beauty spot.

Ukanc, Mount Vogel and the Valley of the Seven Lakes

About 5km from Ribčev Laz at the western end of the lake is the hamlet of

31

31

UKANC (sometimes referred to as Zlatorog), where a **cable car** (daily 7am–7pm, every 30min; closed Nov; €13.50 return) whizzes you vertiginously up to the summit of **Mount Vogel** (1540m) in no time – if the Alps look dramatic from the lakeside, from Vogel's summit they're breathtaking. Ukanc is also the starting point for a one-hour walk north to the photogenic **Savica Waterfalls** (daily weather permitting 8am–8pm; €2.50). From here, the serious hiking can commence, either as a day-trip to the **Valley of the Seven Lakes** – an area strewn with eerie boulders and hardy firs – or as an expedition to scale Mount Triglav itself.

ARRIVAL AND DEPARTURE

By train Trains on the Jesenice–Nova Gorica line call at Bohinjska Bistrica, from where two morning shuttle buses run the 4km back towards Bled.
Destinations From Bohinjska Bistrica: Bled Jezero (4–6 daily; 20min); Most na Soči for the Soča Valley (4–6 daily; 35min).
By bus Buses stop outside the *Hotel Jezero* in Ribčev Laz, terminating in Ukanc on the lake's southwestern corner.
Destinations Bled (hourly; 40min); Bohinjska Bistrica (hourly; 15min); Ljubljana (hourly; 1hr 45min).

INFORMATION

Tourist office Ribčev Laz 48, just up from the main bus stop next to the Mercator supermarket (July & Aug Mon–Sat 8am–8pm, Sun 8am–6pm; Sept–June Mon–Sat 8am–6pm, Sun 9am–3pm; ☎ 04 574 6010, ⓦ bohinj -info.com). There's free public wi-fi in the immediate vicinity of Ribčev Laz.

ACCOMMODATION

The tourist office offers a plentiful choice of private rooms and apartments around Ribčev Laz and in the idyllic villages of Stara Fužina and Studor, 1km and 3km north respectively.
Hostel Pod Voglom Ribčev Laz ☎ 04 572 3461, ⓦ hostel-podvoglom.com. Rather old-fashioned hostel occupying a prime lake-shore spot some 2km along the road to Ukanc; all rooms have four beds with shared facilities, and there's a major programme of activities available. Breakfast included. Dorm €19, double €44
★ **Studor 13 Hostel** Studor 13, Srednja Vas ☎ 03 146 6707, ⓦ studor13.si. Exceptional hostel in a tastefully renovated historic house 3km from the lake, with two-, four- and eight-bed rooms and a self-catering kitchen.

Free pick-up from Bohinj. Breakfast included. Dorm €25, double €50
Zlatorog Ukanc 2 ☎ 04 572 3482. Simple, pleasant campsite on the lake's western tip; conveniently located for trips up the mountains. May–Sept; €9 per person

EATING AND DRINKING

Gostišče Erlah Ukanc 67. Good-value fish dishes such as fresh trout kebab (€7) and grilled salmon feature on the menu at this friendly inn at the western end of the lake. Mon–Thurs noon–9pm, Fri–Sun 11am–10pm.
Pizzerija Ema Srednja Vas 73. The fabulous mountain views from the terrace and *Ema's* extensive menu of affordable, tasty pizzas and pasta dishes more than justify the 4km hike from the lake to the pretty village of Srednja Vas. Daily 9.30am–11pm.

THE SOČA VALLEY

On the other, less touristy side of the mountains from Bohinj, the brilliantly turquoise **River Soča** streaks through the western spur of the Julian Alps, running parallel with the Italian border. During World War I, the Soča marked the front line between the Italian and Austro-Hungarian armies; now memorial chapels and abandoned fortifications nestle incongruously amid awesome Alpine scenery. The valley is a major centre for activity-based tourism, with the river providing first-class **rafting** and **kayaking** conditions throughout the spring and summer, and the mountain slopes perfect for **skiing** and **snowboarding** in winter. The main tourist centres are **Kobarid** and **Bovec**, both small towns boasting a range of walking possibilities. The GZS 1:50,000 Zgornje Posočje **map** covers trails in the region.

Kobarid

It was at the little Alpine town of **KOBARID** that German and Austrian troops finally broke through Italian lines in 1917, almost knocking Italy out of World War I in the process. The 29 months of fighting in the region are relayed in the superb **Kobarid Museum**, Gregorčičeva 10 (April–Sept Mon–Fri 9am–6pm, Sat & Sun 9am–7pm; Oct–March daily 10am–5pm; €5), via a twenty-minute multimedia presentation and a series of sobering photographs, maps and mementoes. It's also the starting point for the superb **Kobarid Historical Trail** (3–5hr), a steep 5km loop where remote woodland paths are punctuated by forgotten wartime landmarks. From the town's main square you climb up to a striking three-tiered **Italian War Memorial**, opened by Benito Mussolini in 1938, before hiking further into the hills to see surviving military fortifications. At the trail's farthest point from town bubbles the **Kozjak waterfall** (40min walk), less impressive for its height than for the cavern-like space that it has carved out of the surrounding rock. Maps of the trail are available from the museum and tourist office.

ARRIVAL AND INFORMATION

By bus Buses stop on the small main square, Trg Svobode.
Destinations Bovec (3–5 daily; 20min); Ljubljana (2 daily; 3hr 30min).

Tourist office Trg Svobode 16 (July & Aug daily 9am–8pm; Sept–June Mon–Fri 9am–1pm & 2–4pm, Sat 10am–2pm; ☎05 380 0490, ⓦlto-sotocje.si). Adjoining the museum, the excellent Walk of Peace information centre provides a wealth of info on the valley's World War I sights and organizes guided walks.

ACCOMMODATION

Camp Koren Drežniške Ravne 33 ☎05 389 1311, ⓦkamp-koren.si. 500m out of town near the end of the historical walk trail, this superbly well-equipped site also has six log cabins sleeping up to six. €12 per person, chalet €65

Hostel X-Point Trg Svobode 6 ☎05 388 5308, ⓦxpoint .si. Clean, modern hostel run by the adventure sports company; two- and four-bed rooms, shared bathrooms and self-catering kitchen. Dorm €16, double €40

EATING AND DRINKING

Pri Vitku Pri Malnih 41. Small, welcoming place in a residential street a 10min walk south of town (follow signs), offering pizza, pasta and grilled meat dishes (€6). Daily noon–midnight.

Topli Val Trg Svobode 1. Inside the *Hotel Hvala*, this classy restaurant has a marvellous fish and seafood menu featuring the likes of trout, crayfish and mussels (€15). Daily noon–10pm.

Bovec

Twenty five kilometres up the valley from Kobarid, the village of **BOVEC** straggles

---

ADVENTURE SPORTS

In Kobarid the main **adventure sports** company is X-Point, at Trg Svobode 6 (☎05 388 5308, ⓦxpoint.si); they organize rafting (€37), kayaking (€40) and canyoning (€45), among other activities guaranteed to raise your heart rate. Popular outfits in Bovec include Soča Rafting (☎05 389 6200, ⓦsocarafting.si), opposite the tourist office at Trg Golobarskih žrtev 14, and Avantura (☎41 718 317, ⓦavantura.org), further down the same street, who specialize in tandem paragliding (€125). They all offer similar prices for activities.

31

between imperious mountain ridges. Thanks to its status as a winter ski resort, it has a greater range of accommodation options and sporting agencies than Kobarid; as a result, it enjoys a more vibrant atmosphere. The quickest route into the mountains from here is provided by the **gondola** that departs on the hour 1km south of the village (June–Sept 8am–4pm; €13 return), which ascends to the pasture-cloaked Mount Kanin over to the west.

ARRIVAL AND INFORMATION

By bus Buses terminate outside the *Letni Vrt* restaurant on the main square, Trg Golobarskih žrtev.
Destinations Kobarid (3–5 daily; 20min).

Tourist office Trg Golobarskih žrtev 8 (July & Aug daily 9am–8pm; Sept–June Mon–Fri 9am–5pm, Sat & Sun 9am–1pm; ☎05 384 1919, ⓦbovec.si).

ACCOMMODATION

Eco Camp Canyon Soča 38 ☎041 383 662, ⓦadrenalinecheck.com. Some 12km from Bovec, Europe's first sustainable outdoor hostel offers camping, dorms and hammocks right on the river. Free pick-ups. Camping €11 per person, hammock €13, dorm €15

Eastern Slovenia

The lush landscapes to the east of Ljubljana – where many of the country's most reputable vineyards are concentrated – are generally less explored by travellers. But as host to Slovenia's

31

second city, **Maribor**, and oldest settlement, **Ptuj**, which lie on the main routes to Austria and Hungary respectively, the region can reward the passing visitor with its rich historical heritage, traditional culture and fine wine.

MARIBOR

Located 122km northeast of Ljubljana, **MARIBOR** is perched snugly on the Drava River between hillside vineyards and the Pohorje mountain range. Though beset by war and occupation, the old town's beautiful architecture preserves myriad historical and cultural influences, and the nightlife is second only to Ljubljana.

WHAT TO SEE AND DO

Maribor's main attractions are condensed in a pedestrianized centre, beginning on Trg Svobode. Here Maribor Castle houses the **regional museum** (Tues–Sat 9am–1pm & 3–7pm, Sun 9am–1pm; €3), which presents particularly fine ethnological and cultural history sections. Across the square is the labyrinth of underground catacombs that make up the **Vinag Wine Cellar** (Mon–Fri 9am–6pm, Sat 8am–1pm), where you can stop by to sample some of the region's acclaimed vintages (€5 for five wines). On the western fringe of the pedestrianized zone sits the photogenic **Slomškov trg**, a serene, leafy opening surrounded by a few landmarks, including the university building and the elegant **Slovene National Theatre**. Opposite the university, and mimicking its distinct yellow colour, is the sixteenth-century Gothic **Cathedral Church** (daily 10am–6pm), with a bell tower that offers fantastic views to the edges of the city and beyond. South of Slomškov is Maribor's most charming square, **Glavni trg**, which epitomizes the hotchpotch architectural styles of the city. Its centrepiece is the Baroque **Plague Memorial**, erected after the deadly disease wiped out a third of the town's population in the seventeenth century.

Lent

Between Glavni and the Drava River, the streets become narrow and uneven, as you enter the oldest part of town, **Lent**, which hosts a myriad of open-air events during the Lent festival in late June each year, comprising two entertaining weeks of street theatre, dance performances and jazz, rock and classical concerts. It is here that the world's oldest productive vine, a protected national monument, grows majestically outside the **Old Vine House** (daily: May–Oct 10am–8pm; Nov–April 10am–6pm; free). Inside, a small exhibition complements the range of top-quality, reasonably priced local vintages, some of which you can taste (€4).

Pohorje

Just a short bus ride (#6 to vzpenjača; €1.10) or cycle southwest from the centre is the sprawling **Pohorje** mountain range. Take the hourly cable car (daily 8am–8pm; €10 return) up the slope, where – depending on the season – you can hike, mountain bike, horseride and ski, or simply sit and admire the glorious views of Maribor and the countryside surrounding it. The website ⓦpohorje.org has detailed information on activities in the area.

ARRIVAL AND DEPARTURE

By train Partizanska cesta 50. Turn left out of the exit and the road curves directly into the town centre. Left luggage lockers €2–3/24hr.
Destinations Ljubljana (every 45min–2hr; 2hr); Graz (2 daily; 1hr); Ptuj (8 daily; 1hr); Vienna (2 daily; 3hr 40min).
By bus Mlinska ulica 1 (just off Partizanska cesta).
Destinations Ljubljana (4 daily; 3hr); Ptuj (every 30–45min; 40min).

INFORMATION

Tourist office Partizanska cesta 6a, next to the Franciscan church (Mon–Fri 9am–7pm, Sat & Sun 9am–6pm; ☎02 234 6611, ⓦmaribor-pohorje.si). They rent out bikes (€10/day) and provide helpful cycling maps to explore the vineyards. There is free wi-fi in public spaces throughout the city.

ACCOMMODATION

The tourist office can book private accommodation (from €20/person).

Hostel Pekarna Ob železnici 16 ☏059 180 880, ⓦmkc -hostelpekarna.si. Part of Maribor's foremost alternative cultural centre, this sparky hostel in Tabor (on the south side of the Drava) offers four-bed dorms as well as doubles and small apartments. Dorm €17, double €42

Lollipop Hostel Maistrova ulica 17 ☏04 024 3160, ⓔlollipophostel@yahoo.com. Small, clean hostel 5min from the park with kitchen facilities and a homely common room. Free city tours given by the English owner. Dorm €20

EATING AND DRINKING

Gril Ranca Dravska 10. Down in the riverside Lent district, this is fast food Serbian style, with the likes of *čevapčiči* and *pljeskavica* grilled meats (€6) comprising the bulk of the menu. Mon–Sat 11am–11pm.

KGB Vojašniški trg 5 ⓦklub-kgb.si. The most popular joint in Maribor, this lively underground cellar bar attracts all ages, with an eclectic programme of regular live music. Mon–Sat 7pm–2am.

Satchmo Jazz Klub Strossmayerjeva ulica 6 ⓦsatchmo .si. Hosts high-calibre jazz and rock sessions, but also ideal for a mellow drinking session. Daily 7pm–2am.

Takos Mesarski prehod 3. Tucked away on a cobbled alley, this cheap-and-cheerful Mexican also serves cocktails, becoming a club at weekends. Mon–Thurs 11am– midnight, Fri & Sat till 3am, Sun 11am–4pm.

Toto Café Slomškov Trg 13. Popular, brightly painted courtyard café-bar with a studenty feel near the university. Mon–Sat 7am–midnight, Sun 3–10pm.

PTUJ

PTUJ is arguably Slovenia's most attractive town, rising up from the Drava valley in a flutter of red roofs, and topped by a charming castle. The streets themselves are the main attraction, with scaled-down mansions standing shoulder to shoulder on scaled-down boulevards and medieval fantasies crumbling next to Baroque extravagances.

WHAT TO SEE AND DO

Ptuj's main street is **Prešernova ulica**, an atmospheric thoroughfare which snakes along the base of the castle-topped hill. At its eastern end is **Slovenski Trg**, home to a fine-looking sixteenth-century bell tower (though now just a souvenir shop) and the **Church of St George**, dating from the twelfth century, with an interior distinguished by some spectacular frescoes. From here

Prešernova leads to the **Archeological Museum** (mid-April to Nov daily 10am–5pm; €4), housed in what was a Dominican monastery until the eighteenth century. Although it may still be closed owing to extensive renovation work, its likeably dishevelled cloisters usually display medieval and modern stone carvings. At either end of Prešernova, cobbled paths wind up to the **castle** – featuring an agglomeration of architectural styles from the fourteenth to the eighteenth centuries – which now houses the carefully presented collections of the **Ptuj Regional Museum** (daily: mid-Oct to April 9am–5pm; May to mid-Oct 9am–6pm; €4). In particular, look out for the colourful displays of *kurenti* masks, which appear each February as part of the Kurent carnival, one of the country's most celebrated events.

ARRIVAL AND DEPARTURE

By train The station is on Osojnikova cesta, a 5min walk northeast of town.

Destinations Ljubljana (2 daily; 2hr 25min); Maribor (8 daily; 1hr).

By bus The station is 200m from the train station.

Destinations Maribor (every 45min–1hr; 45min).

INFORMATION

Tourist information Slovenski trg 5 (daily: May–Sept 9am–8pm; Oct–April 9am–6pm; ☏02 779 6011, ⓦptuj.info). More helpful is The Centre for Free Time Activities, just across from the bus station in the modern buildings at Osojnikova 9 (Mon–Fri 9am–6pm; ☏02 780 5540, ⓦcid.si).

ACCOMMODATION

Kurent Osojnikova cesta 9 ☏02 771 0814, ⓔyhptuj @csod.si. Large, rather anonymous, hostel with functional dorms sleeping between two and six, some with bathrooms. Breakfast included. Dorm €19

★ **Musikafe** Vrazov trg 1 ☏02 787 8860, ⓦmuzikafe.si. Seven beautifully conceived rooms brimming with colour and creativity in this warm and welcoming B&B. Breakfast included. Double €52

Terme Ptuj Pot v Toplice ☏02 749 4100, ⓦsava-hotels -resorts.com. Across the river, 2km west of town, guests at this pleasant resort-style campsite can also use the on-site Thermal Park pools and saunas. Camping €17 per person; four-person bungalow €90

31

31

EATING AND DRINKING

Gostilna PP Novi trg 2. Cheap and very cheerful canteen-style joint knocking up fast and filling daily specials (€4–5), though it's best known for its local chicken dishes (€4–5). Mon–Sat 9am–8pm, Sun noon–4pm.

★ **Musikafe** Vrazov trg 1. Wonderful hangout which combines an inviting stone terrace with a richly painted, retro furnished interior where you can chill out to an eclectic playlist. Superb live music in both the garden (summer) and cellar (winter). Daily 8am–11pm, Fri & Sat till midnight.

Ribič Dravska ulica 9. The exceptional seafood at this riverside restaurant with a lovely terrace overlooking the Drava justifies the slightly higher price tag. Daily 10am–11pm.

MUSEO GUGGENHEIM, BILBAO

Spain

HIGHLIGHTS

❶ Madrid World-class museums and legendary nightlife. **See p.1004**

❷ Alhambra, Granada Evocative Moorish palace atop this charming Andalucian city. **See p.1038**

❸ Barcelona Perhaps Europe's most alluring city. **See p.1054**

❹ San Sebastián Stunning beaches and mouth-watering cuisine. **See p.1073**

❺ Museo Guggenheim, Bilbao The building is as big an attraction as the art it houses. See p.1075

❻ Santiago de Compostela The end point of Europe's most famous pilgrim trail. **See p.1080**

HIGHLIGHTS ARE MARKED ON THE MAP ON P.999

ROUGH COSTS

Daily budget Basic €55, occasional treat €75

Drink €1.70–2.50 per *caña* (small beer)

Food *Menú del día* €10–12

Hostel/budget hotel €16–28/€27–50

Travel Madrid–Barcelona: bus €32–39; train €43–84

FACT FILE

Population 47.3 million

Languages Spanish, Catalan, Basque, Galician, Aranese

Currency Euro (€)

Capital Madrid

International phone code ☎ 34

Time zone GMT +1hr

Introduction

Spain has so much more to offer than the clichés of bullfights, crowded beaches, paella and flamenco. You don't have to travel for very long to discover ancient castles, world-class museums, idyllic whitewashed villages, isolated coves and beaches, and a wealth of art and architecture. The separate kingdoms that made up the original Spanish nation are still very evident today, encompassing a medley of languages, cultures and traditions.

Of the regions, vibrant **Catalunya** in the northeast is fiercely independent of spirit; the fishing region of **Galicia** in the northwest a seafood lover's dream; the **Basque country** a remarkable contrast between post-industrial depression and world-class architecture and food; and **Castilla y León** and the **south** still, somehow, quintessentially "Spanish". There are definite highlights: the three great cities of **Barcelona**, **Madrid** and **Seville**; the Moorish monuments of **Andalucía** in the south and the Christian ones of **Castilla y León** in the west; beach life on the islands of **Ibiza**, **Costa del Sol** or on the more deserted Costa de la Luz near **Cádiz**; some of the best trekking in Europe in the **Pyrenees**, and winter sports in **Andorra**.

Spain can be visited all year round, though Madrid, Extremadura and parts of Andalucía get unbearably hot in the summer. Depending on what you're after, you can party at numerous quirky local festivals, engage in all manner of outdoor pursuits, sample the seasonal and regional specialities, take in the varied architecture that traces Spain's multicultural heritage and enjoy some of Europe's best nightlife. The country has suffered crippling economic woes of late, with unemployment among the under-30s as high as 55 percent. Still, there are reasons to be cheerful, not least the national team's recent footballing triumphs.

CHRONOLOGY

1000 BC Phoenicians colonize the Iberian Peninsula, establishing the cities of Cádiz and Málaga.
400s BC Carthaginians exert power over large parts of present-day Spain.

200s BC The Romans capture "Hispania" during the Punic Wars and rule it for over 500 years.
711 AD The Islamic Moors conquer Spain, and Moorish culture flourishes.
1085 With the capture of Toledo, Spanish Christians begin to diminish the influence of the Moors in Spain.
1480 The Spanish Inquisition persecutes non-Christians, leading to mass conversions and expulsion of Jews.
1492 Christopher Columbus discovers lands in the Americas for the Spanish Crown.
1605 The world's first "novel", *Don Quixote* by Cervantes, is published.
1714 The British capture Gibraltar.
1800s Spanish colonies in the Americas gain their independence.
1931 Surrealist artist Salvador Dalí completes his most famous painting, *The Persistence of Memory*.
1936 The Spanish Civil War breaks out as Nationalist forces led by General Franco defeat Republican forces.
1939 Spain remains neutral at the outbreak of World War II.
1975 Franco dies and is replaced by King Juan Carlos.
1977 First free elections are held in almost four decades.
2004 Bombs detonated on busy Madrid trains leave 191 people dead. An Islamic group takes responsibility.
2007 The government's struggle with Basque separatists, ETA, continues as the group end their ceasefire.
2008 Spain's construction boom brought to an end by international financial meltdown and unemployment soars from 6 percent to 20 percent. Spain wins the UEFA European Football Championship.
2010 Spain wins the FIFA World Cup.
2013 Spain's unemployment rate climbs to record high, with 55 percent of under-30s out of work.

ARRIVAL AND DEPARTURE

The quickest — and cheapest — way to get to Spain is on one of the budget-airline **flights** (Vueling, easyJet, Ryanair and Norwegian Air). All major airlines serve Barcelona and Madrid. Other

HIGHLIGHTS
- ❶ Madrid
- ❷ Alhambra, Granada
- ❸ Barcelona
- ❹ San Sebastián
- ❺ Museo Guggenheim, Bilbao
- ❻ Santiago de Compostela

SPAIN

major airports include Alicante, Málaga, Valencia, Seville and Mallorca. **Trains** from France serve San Sebastián (from Biarritz), Barcelona (from Toulouse and Perpignan) and Girona (from Perpignan), while trains from Portugal run from Lisbon to Madrid via Cáceres and from Porto to Santiago de Compostela. Regular **ferries** from Morocco serve the ports of Algeciras, Gibraltar and Tarifa.

GETTING AROUND

Spain's public transport is budget traveller-friendly. While the high-speed trains are often more comfortable than buses for longer journeys, they are rather more expensive.

BY TRAIN

RENFE (ⓦrenfe.es) operates three types of train: *cercanías* (local commuter trains); *media distancia* (intercity trains), and *larga distancia* (long-distance) express trains which include

the high-speed *AVE* (Madrid–Barcelona and Madrid–Seville) and *Euromed* (Valencia–Barcelona) trains and the somewhat slower *Alaris* (Madrid–Valencia) and *Altaria* (Madrid–Alicante). To avoid queuing, buy tickets online from the RENFE website and print the ticket out at the station. Return fares (*ida y vuelta*) often get a ten to twenty percent discount, as do advance online bookings. **InterRail** and **Eurail** passes are valid on all RENFE trains and also on *Euromed*; additional supplements are charged on the fastest trains. Book well in advance, especially at weekends and holidays. The InterRail Spain Pass is only worth it if you're planning on a lot of train travel within a short space of time.

BY BUS

Alsa (ⓦalsa.es) is the biggest **bus** company, covering most of the country. There are regular services between major cities, and many smaller villages are accessible only by bus. In some cases it is

32

ON YOUR BIKE

Though few large Spanish cities have cycle lanes, Spain is becoming more bicycle friendly, with **public bicycle** systems introduced in cities such as Barcelona, Seville, Valencia, Mérida and Zaragoza; dozens of pick-up/drop-off points are scattered around the streets.

faster to take the bus than a regional train. Frequency is reduced on Sundays and holidays. For long-distance buses, you can buy your ticket in advance.

BY BOAT

Regular ferries and hydrofoils connect mainland Spain to the Balearic Islands and Tangier, Ceuta and Melilla. Acciona Trasmediterránea (𝕨 trasmediterranea.es) is the main national ferry company; you can book seats or sleeping berths for its fast, modern passenger ferries on its website. The Balearic Islands are served by Iscomar (𝕨 www.iscomar.com) and Baleària (𝕨 balearia.com) ferries.

ACCOMMODATION

Book accommodation well in advance if planning on staying during a festival. Prices in popular areas drop in low season.

HOTELS AND HOSTELS

There are several types of budget accommodation available. **Pensiones** (P) are simple guesthouses without breakfast, most rooms sharing a bathroom. Slightly more expensive are **hostales** (H) – budget hotels – offering single and double rooms, mostly en-suite, with TV, heating and air conditioning. Madrid, Barcelona and other popular destinations have a large network of centrally located independent **hostels** with a full range of facilities, such as guest kitchen, lockers and tour booking. Beds are generally €22–28. HI-affiliated **youth hostels** (*albergues juveniles*; 𝕨 reaj.com) can be inconveniently located and are sometimes block-reserved by school

groups. At €17–27 per person (more without an HI card), they offer basic accommodation in dorms, usually including breakfast. Most of these options now offer free wi-fi.

CASAS RURALES, CAMPING AND REFUGIOS

Nationwide, **agroturismo** (𝕨 agroturismorural.com) and **casa rural** programmes offer cheap accommodation in rural areas. "*Camas y comidas*" ("beds and meals") in private houses cost around €40 for a double, and €20 for a single. Tourist offices have full lists. There are hundreds of **campsites** throughout Spain, charging around €5 per person plus the same for a tent; see 𝕨 vayacamping.net. In popular mountain areas you'll find *refugios* (mountain shelters) offering dorm-style accommodation on a first-come, first-served basis (€10–15 per night). Some have a cooking area and/or serve hot meals; bring your own bedding and cooking equipment.

FOOD AND DRINK

Bars and cafés are best for **breakfast**, which can consist of *churros con chocolate* (tubular deep-fried doughnuts dipped in thick drinking chocolate), *tostadas* (toast), or *tortilla* (omelette). **Coffee** and **pastries** are available at the many excellent *pastelerías* and *confiterías*, while *bocadillos* (sandwiches) are available everywhere. *Tabernas*, *tascas*, *bodegas*, *cervecerías* and bars all serve **tapas** or *pintxos*: tiny sandwiches, mini portions of meat, *tortilla* or fried potatoes with *alioli* for €1.50–4.50 a plate; the most elaborate tapas are found in the Basque country. Their big brothers, **raciones** (€8–15), make a sufficient meal in themselves. Most restaurants offer a weekday lunchtime two- or three-course meal, *menú del día* (€10–12), or *platos combinados* (€7–10), a single dish such as meat with fries and a side of salad, drink included. **Fish** and **seafood** are excellent, particularly regional specialities such as Galician fish stew (*zarzuela*), grilled octopus and *gambas a la plancha* (grilled prawns).

Spain's national dish is the rice-based paella, which can be made with seafood, meat and vegetables. There's also *fideuá* (similar to paella but made with vermicelli instead of rice), especially popular in Valencia and Alicante. Andalucía's staples include *gazpacho* and *salmorejo* – cold summer soups, with Granada and Almería adding North African food to the mix, such as Moroccan tagines. Inland Spain is famous for its *carnes asados* (roasted meats), hearty stews and delicious **cured meats** – particularly *jamón iberico bellota* – a highly prized dry-cured ham. Big cities, notably Madrid, Barcelona and Seville, cater best to **vegetarians**, while gourmets should make a beeline for the Basque country and Catalunya – the two regions responsible for some of the most adventurous cuisine in the world. San Sebastián in particular is known for its proliferation of bars serving imaginative tapas and for its Michelin-starred places.

DRINK

Wine (*vino*) – either *tinto* (red), *blanco* (white) or *rosado/clarete* (rosé) – is usually very good. The best red is Rioja, and Catalunya produces the best whites, especially Penedès or Peralada; Catalunya is also home to *cava* – a sparkling white wine that's champagne in everything but name. Vino de Jerez, Andalucían **sherry**, is served chilled and either *fino/jerez seco* (dry), *amontillado* (medium) or *oloroso/jerez dulce* (sweet). *Cerveza*, lager-type **beer**, includes San Miguel, Cruz Campo, Alhambra, Keler and Estrella del Galicia. In bars, you usually order a *caña* (small glass) of beer with your tapas. *Tinto de verano* (red wine spritzer) is a popular summer drink. **Sangría**, a red wine-and-fruit punch, and **sidra**, a dry cider most typical in Asturia and the Basque Country, are well worth sampling. **Coffee** is invariably espresso, unless you specify *cortado* (with a drop of milk), *con leche* (a more generous amount) or *americano* (weaker black coffee). **Tea** is drunk black, though you can order it *con leche*, and most eating establishments offer *infusiones* (herbal teas).

CULTURE AND ETIQUETTE

Lunch is usually eaten 2–4pm and dinner from 8pm. In the largest Spanish cities, a lot of shops, tourist offices and restaurants stay open all day, whereas smaller towns and especially villages are dead between 1–4pm. **Tipping** ten percent in restaurants is considered generous. When paying by credit/debit card in shops, you will need photo ID.

SPORTS AND ACTIVITIES

The beaches on the south coast are the best for **swimming**, while the north coast (and Spain's southernmost tip) are ideal for watersports such as **windsurfing** and **surfing**: Playa de Zurriola in San Sebastián is a popular choice, as is Santander's Sardinero beach. Tarifa, at the southernmost tip of Spain, is a year-round paradise for kitesurfers and windsurfers. The Mediterranean waters of Costa Brava and Costa del Sol, as well as the Balearic Islands, offer numerous good scuba-diving and snorkelling spots. Whitewater junkies can head to Catalunya's Noguera Pallaresa River, or Cantabria's Carasa River for kayaking, hydrospeed and rafting. There are great paragliding destinations along the Mediterranean coast and in Aragón. The Aragonese Pyrenees, Picos de Europa and the Sierra Nevada, in Andalucía, are excellent in winter for **skiing** and equally good for **hiking** in summer. The **Camino de Santiago** (see box, p.1079) makes a superb long-distance hike or bike ride. Outside the main cities, Spain has numerous scenic and challenging cycling options throughout the country, including *bici todo terreno* (off-road tracks for mountain bikes).

SPECTATOR SPORTS

A match at Real Madrid's Estadio Santiago Bernabéu is a must for any **football** fan (☎913 984 300, ⌨realmadrid.es), as is a game at the Camp Nou, FC Barcelona's 100,000-seater stadium (☎902 189 900, ⌨fcbarcelona.com). For something quite different, try the electrifying spectacle of **bull runnings** (or *encierros*), the most

32

famous of which take place every July in Pamplona during the week-long Fiesta de San Fermín (see box, p.1071). While **bullfighting** remains a subject of great passion in Madrid and Andalucía (particularly in Seville, Málaga and Ronda), its popularity is waning with the younger generation, and it has been outlawed in Catalunya since 2012.

COMMUNICATIONS

Post offices (*correos*) are open Monday to Friday 8.30am to 2pm, Saturday 9am to noon. The cheapest way to make international phone calls is online via Skype, ever easier thanks to the growing number of wi-fi hotspots. Blue public **payphones** take prepaid phonecards (*tarjetas telefónicas*), available from tobacconists and newspaper kiosks; in larger cities, there are lots of discount call centres (*locutorios*). The international access code is ☏00, the Spain country code is ☏34 and local area codes are incorporated into the phone numbers. If you have an unlocked mobile phone, buying a prepaid SIM card is inexpensive. **Internet** cafés are becoming rarer due to the proliferation of free wi-fi.

EMERGENCIES

Violent crime is rare, but watch out for pickpockets and scam artists. Be particularly vigilant around market areas and during fiestas. Report robberies to the **Policía Nacionál**; you can report your loss by phone (☏902 102112) or online under *Denuncias* at ⓦpolicia.es. For minor **health** complaints, go to a pharmacy (*farmacía*). In more serious cases, head to *Urgencias* at the nearest **hospital**, or get the address of an English-speaking doctor from the nearest consulate, *farmacía* or tourist office.

EMERGENCY NUMBERS
For the police, ambulance services or fire brigade, call ☏112.

INFORMATION

The **Spanish National Tourist Office** (*Información* or *Oficina de Turismo*) has a branch in virtually every major town, giving away detailed city maps and brochures on attractions. There are also provincial or regional *Turismos*, stocking information on the entire province.

MONEY AND BANKS

Currency is the euro (€). **Banks** have branches in all but the smallest towns, open Monday to Friday 8.30am to 2pm; some also open Saturday 9am to 1pm. The best exchange rates for foreign currencies are available from most banks. In tourist areas, you'll also find **casas de cambio**, with more convenient hours, but worse exchange rates. **ATMs** (*cajeros automáticos*) are widespread and all major credit cards (particularly Visa and MasterCard) are widely accepted in many shops, restaurants and hotels, especially in larger cities.

OPENING HOURS AND HOLIDAYS

Shops **open** Monday to Saturday 9am to 8pm; some open for a shorter time on Sunday. Smaller towns take a **siesta** between 1 and 4pm. Tapas bars are typically open from lunchtime until late, while restaurants are typically open 1–4pm and 8–11pm or 1–11pm, with many closed on Sunday evenings and on Mondays. In nightclubs, things only really get going after midnight. Shops and banks are closed on the following public holidays: January 1 and 6, March 19, the week before Easter Monday, May 1, June 24, July 25,

---

SPAIN ONLINE
ⓦ **spain.info** Comprehensive website of the Spanish tourist board.
ⓦ **guiadelocio.com** Nationwide restaurant and entertainment listings, updated weekly (in Spanish only).
ⓦ **gospain.org** Useful links directory.

SPANISH

	SPANISH	PRONUNCIATION
Yes	Sí	See
No	No	Noh
Please	Por favor	Por fahvor
Thank you	Gracias	Grath-yass
Hello/Good day	Hola	Ola
Goodbye	Adiós	Ad-yoss
Excuse me	Con permiso	Con pairmeeso
Sorry (strong)	Lo siento	Loh see-en-toh
Sorry (mild)	Perdón	Pear-don
Where?	¿Donde?	¿Donday?
Good	Bueno	Bwaynoh
Bad	Malo	Maloh
Near	Próximo	Prox-eemo
Far	Lejos	Layhoss
Cheap	Barato	Bar-ahto
Expensive	Caro	Cahro
Open	Abierto	Ahb-yairto
Closed	Cerrado	Thairrado
Today	Hoy	Oy
Yesterday	Ayer	A-yair
Tomorrow	Mañana	Man-yana
Toilet	Aseo/baño	Ahseyoh/ bahnio
I don't eat meat	No como carne	Noh cohmoh carnay
The bill	La cuenta	Lah kwentah
How much is…?	¿Cuánto cuesta…?	¿Kwanto kwesta…?
What time is it?	¿Tiene la hora?	¿Tee-eynay-la ora?
Do you speak English?	¿Habla inglas?	¿Ahblah eenglays?
Where is…?	¿Dónde está…?	¿Don-des-ta…?
I don't understand	No entiendo	Noh ent-yendo
I would like…	Quisiera…	Ki-si-yeah-ra
One	Un/Uno	Oon/Oon-oh
Two	Dos	Doss
Three	Tres	Tress
Four	Cuatro	Kwatro
Five	Cinco	Theenko
Six	Seis	Say-eess
Seven	Siete	See-ettay
Eight	Ocho	Oh-cho
Nine	Nueve	Nwa-vay
Ten	Diez	Dee-yeth

32

August 15, October 12, November 1, December 6, 8 and 24.

FESTIVALS

Each town and city celebrates its own annual **fiesta** in honour of its patron saint. Don't miss: Pamplona's **San Fermín** festival (second week of July) – the famous running of the bulls; **La Tomatina** in Buñol, near Valencia (second to last or last Wed in Aug) – messy fun with tomatoes; **Semana Santa** (week leading up to Easter Sunday) in Seville, Málaga and Córdoba – spectacular processions, feasting and fireworks, followed by Seville's **Feria de Abril** (late April); the decadent **Carnaval** in Cádiz (Feb/March); and Valencia's **Las Fallas** (March 15–19) – processions, fireworks and carousing around the clock.

Madrid

When Philip II moved the seat of government to **MADRID** in 1561 his aim was to create a symbol of Spanish unification and centralization. Given its lack of natural advantages, such as a sea port, and extreme temperatures in winter and summer, it was only the determination of successive rulers to promote a strong central capital that ensured its success.

WHAT TO SEE AND DO

Today, Madrid's streets are a beguiling mix of old and new, with narrow, atmospheric alleys and wide, open boulevards. It is also home to some of Spain's best art, from the Museo del Prado's world-renowned classical collection, to the impressive modern works at the Reina Sofía. Galleries and numerous sights aside, much of Madrid's charm comes from immersing yourself in the daily life of the city and tapping into its frenetic energy: hanging out in the traditional cafés and *chocolaterías* or the summer *terrazas*, packing the lanes of the Sunday Rastro flea market, or playing very hard and very late in a thousand bars, clubs and discos.

Puerta del Sol and the Plaza de Cíbeles

Central **Puerta del Sol** is officially the centre of the nation: a stone slab in the pavement outside the main building on the south side marks **Kilómetro Zero**, from where six of Spain's *Rutas Nacionales* (National Routes) begin. The city's emblem, a statue of a bear pawing a *madroño* bush, lies on the north side. To the west, c/Arenal heads directly towards the Teatro Real and Palacio Real, but there's more of interest along **c/Mayor**, one of Madrid's oldest thoroughfares, which runs southwest through the heart of the medieval city. Down c/Alcalá to the east, the Cibeles fountain is the unofficial bathing spot for Real Madrid fans who congregate here to celebrate their team's victories.

Plaza Mayor

Plaza Mayor is one of the most important architectural and historical landmarks in Madrid and the centrepiece of Madrileño life for centuries. In this beautiful seventeenth-century square, *autos-da-fé* (trials of faith) and executions were held by the Inquisition, kings were crowned, demonstrations, festivals and bullfights staged. These events were watched by up to 50,000 spectators and by royalty from the frescoed **Real Casa de la Panadería** (Royal Bakery). Today, the plaza is a pleasant place to have a drink or sprawl on the cobbles with young Madrileños and tourists. In summer, it's an outdoor theatre and music stage, in autumn, a book fair, and a Christmas market in mid-December.

Palacio Real

Palacio Real, or Royal Palace, on C de Bailén (daily 10am–6pm; €10, students €5; ⓦpatrimonionacional.es; ⓜÓpera), built after the earlier Muslim Alcázar burned down in 1734, was the principal royal residence until Alfonso XIII went into exile in 1931, but is now used only on state occasions. The building, which claims more rooms than any other European palace, features a **library** with one of the biggest collections of books, manuscripts, maps and musical scores in the world; an **armoury** with an unrivalled and often bizarre collection of weapons dating back to the fifteenth century, including armour for war horses and children; and an original **pharmacy** – a curious mixture of alchemist's den and early laboratory. Take your time to contemplate the extraordinary opulence of the place: acres of Flemish and Spanish tapestries, endless Rococo decoration, bejewelled clocks and pompous portraits of the monarchs.

The Gran Vía

Central Plaza de España, home to the statues of Cervantes, Don Quixote and Sancho Panza, joins **Gran Vía**, once the capital's major thoroughfare, which effectively divides the old city to the south from the newer parts. Permanently crowded with shoppers and sightseers, the street is appropriately named, with quirky Art Nouveau and Art Deco facades fronting its banks, offices and apartments, and huge posters on the theatres. At its far end, by the magnificent cylindrical **Edificio Metropolis**, it joins with c/Alcalá on the approach to Plaza de Cibeles. Just across the junction is the majestic old **Real Academia de Bellas Artes** (museum Tues–Sun 10am–3pm; €5, free Wed; ⓦrabasf.insde.es; ⓜSevilla), a cultural centre for up-and-coming artists and a great spot for a coffee.

Museo del Prado

Madrid's **Museo del Prado**, on Paseo del Prado (Tues–Sat 10am–8pm, Sun 10am–7pm; €14/21.60 combined ticket with Museo Thyssen-Bornemisza and Centro de Arte Reina Sofía; ⓦwww .museodelprado.es; ⓜAtocha), has been one of Europe's key art galleries ever since it opened in 1819. It holds a collection of over 8600 paintings, including the world's finest collections of Goya, Velázquez, Rubens and Bosch. The central downstairs gallery houses the **early Spanish collection**, and a dazzling array of portraits and religious paintings by El Greco, among them his mystic and hallucinatory *Crucifixion* and *Adoration of the Shepherds*. Beyond this are the Prado's **Italian** treasures: superb Titian portraits of Charles V and Philip II, as well as works by Tintoretto, Bassano, Caravaggio and

---

MADRID FOR FREE

You can see most of Madrid's top sights for free, as long as you time your visits carefully. Get there as close to the set times as possible, or you'll have to contend with crowds of like-minded penny-pinchers. Free entry is as follows: **Centro de Arte Reina Sofía** (Mon, Wed–Fri & Sat 7–9pm, Sun 3–7pm; always free to university students); **Museo del Prado** (Tues–Sat 6–8pm, Sun & hols 5–8pm; always free to under-25 EU students); **Palacio Real** (Wed & Thurs 3–6pm for EU citizens). Many other sights also offer reduced rates for students or people under 26.

Veronese. Upstairs are Goya's unmissable *Pinturas negras* (*Black Paintings*), so called due to their dark hues and the distorted appearance of their subjects, hinting at the artist's unsettled state of mind. The outstanding presence among Spanish painters is Velázquez – among the collection are intimate portraits of the family of Felipe IV, most famously his masterpiece *Las Meninas*.

Museo Thyssen-Bornemisza

The **Museo Thyssen-Bornemisza** (Tues–Sun 10am–7pm; €9; ⓦmuseothyssen.org; ⓜBanco de España) occupies the grand Palacio de Villahermosa, diagonally opposite the Prado. In 1993, this prestigious site played a large part in Spain's acquisition of what was perhaps the world's greatest private art collection, belonging to the late Baron Thyssen-Bornemisza. There are important works from every major period and movement – from Duccio and Holbein, through El Greco and Caravaggio, to Schiele and Rothko; from a strong showing of nineteenth-century Americans to some very early and very late Van Goghs; and side-by-side hangings of parallel Cubist studies by Picasso, Braque and Mondrian.

Centro de Arte Reina Sofía

As well as the collection of twentieth-century art, the **Centro de Arte Reina Sofía**, at c/Santa Isabel 52 (Mon & Wed–Sat 10am–9pm, Sun 10am–2.30pm; €8; ⓦmuseoreinasofia.cs; ⓜAtocha), features a cinema, excellent art and design bookshops, a print, music and photographic library and edgy temporary exhibitions. However, it is **Picasso's Guernica** – his signature Cubism piece – that most visitors come to see, and rightly so. Superbly displayed along with its preliminary studies, this icon of twentieth-century Spanish art and politics – a response to the Fascist bombing of the Basque town of Guernica in the Spanish Civil War – carries a shock that defies all familiarity. Other halls are devoted to **Dalí** and Surrealism, early twentieth-century Spanish artists including **Miró** and post-World War II

32

32

ACCOMMODATION

Albergue Juvenil	1
Cat's Hostel	6
Chic & Basic Colors	4
Hostal Acapulco	2
Hostel La Posada de Huertas	5
Las Musas Residence	7
Los Amigos Hostel	3

DRINKING, NIGHTLIFE AND ENTERTAINMENT

Amor de Madre	9	Kikekeller	12
Café Central	24	La Boca del Lobo	18
Café Manuela	8	La Escalera	
Cardamomo	20	de Jacob	30
Casa Patas	25	La Venencia	21
Corral de la Morería	26	Mi madre era	
El Barco	10	una groupie	28
El Clandestino	11	Moby Dick	3
El Imperfecto	17	Samsara	19
El Viajero	29	Serrano 41	4
Kapital	32	Tupperware	6

(200m) & 2

CALLE DIVINO PASTOR

El Centro
Cultural
Conde
Duque

Las
Comendadoras

Montserrat

PLAZA DE LAS
COMENDADORAS

C. DAOIZ

PLAZA
DOS
DE MAYO

C. VELAR

CALLE PALMA

CALLE SAN VICENTE FERRER

Centro Princesa
(Cinema)

CALLE ESPIRITU SANTO

S. Marcos

Noviciado

MALASAÑA

Parque
del
Oeste

Torre de
Madrid

Edificio
España

Pza. de España

Museo
Cerralbo

Plaza
de
España

GRAN VÍA

Templo de
Debod

S. Antonio de
los Alemanes

Parque de
la Montaña

San
Plácido

Jardines
de Ferraz

S. Martín

Príncipe
Pío

Sto. Domingo

Palacio de
la Prensa

S. JACOMETREZO

Jardines de
Sabatini

Convento de
la Encarnación

Cine Callao

Callao

GRAN VÍA

Jardines
del Cabo
Noval

Descalzas
Reales

PLAZA DEL
CARMEN

Palacio
Real

Ópera

PLAZA DE
SAN MARTÍN

Armería
Real

PLAZA DE
ISABEL II

Teatro
Real

PUERTA
DEL SOL

Campo
del
Moro

Iglesia de
Santiago

San Ginés

Sol

Catedral
Ntra. Sra. de
la Almudena

San
Nicolás

PLAZA MAYOR

CUESTA DE LA VEGA

Casa de
la Villa

Los
Lujanes

Parque Emir
Mohamed

Muralla
Árabe

Capitanía
General

Casa de Cisneros

La Basílica
de San
Miguel

Palacio de
Santa Cruz

CALLE DE SEGOVIA

Capilla
del Obispo

San
Pedro

Jardines
de las
Vistillas

San
Andrés

Museo
de San Isidro

San
Isidro

Tirso De
Molina

Hemeroteca
National

San Francisco
el Grande

LA LATINA

La Latina

LAVAPIÉS

San
Cayetano

La
Paloma

Puerta
De Toledo

La Corrala

Estadio Vicente Calderón

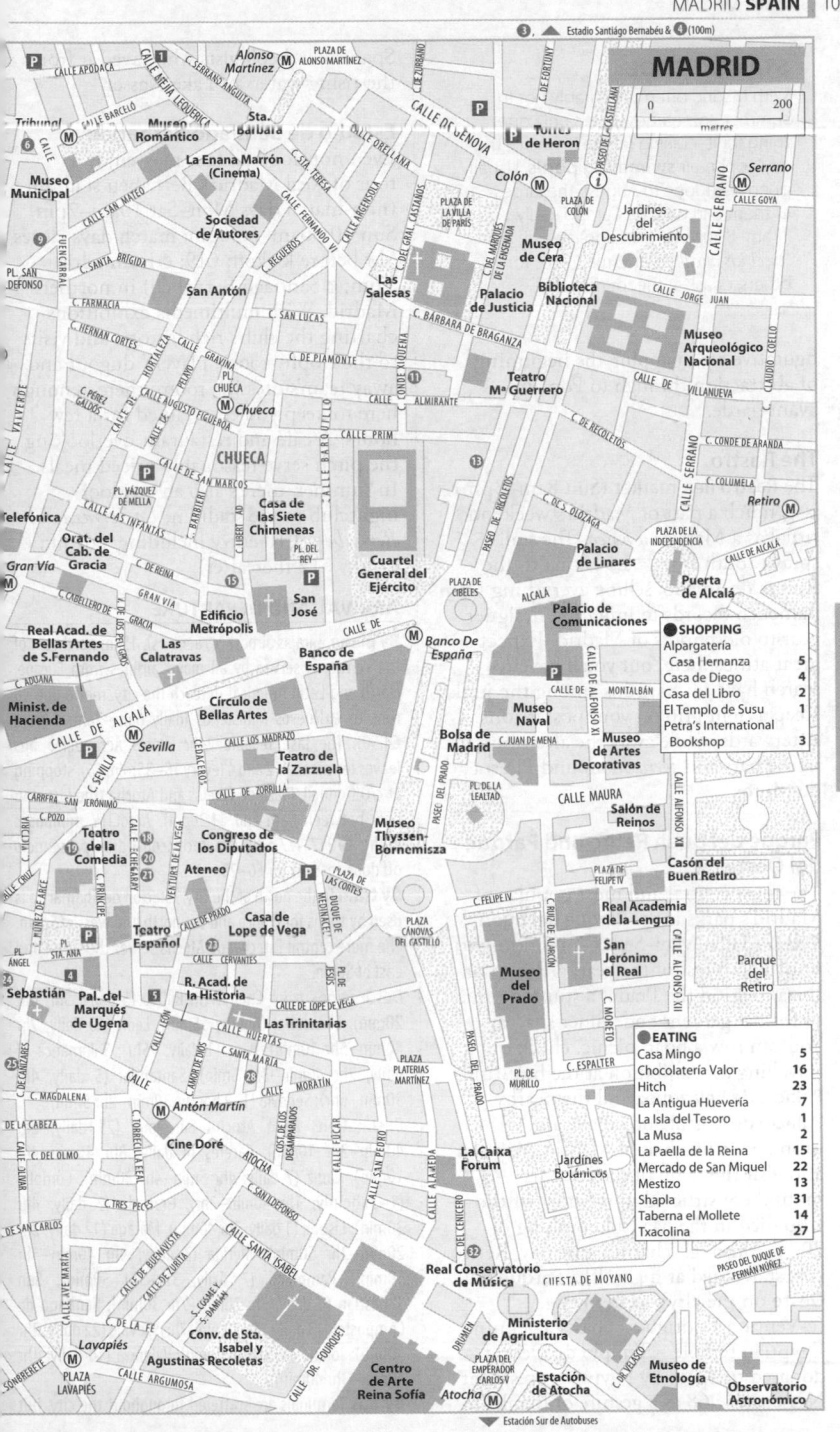

3 ▲ Estadio Santiago Bernabéu & **4** (100m)

MADRID

0 —————————— 200
metres

SHOPPING
Alpargatería	
Casa I lernanza	5
Casa de Diego	4
Casa del Libro	2
El Templo de Susu	1
Petra's International Bookshop	3

32

EATING
Casa Mingo	5
Chocolatería Valor	16
Hitch	23
La Antigua Huevería	7
La Isla del Tesoro	1
La Musa	2
La Paella de la Reina	15
Mercado de San Miguel	22
Mestizo	13
Shapla	31
Taberna el Mollete	14
Txacolina	27

32

STAYING COOL

With Madrid often unbearably hot In summer, sometimes there's only one thing for it – taking refuge in one of the city's open-air **swimming pools**. Usually open from June to August, the largest of them is in Casa de Campo (daily 11am–8.30pm; €5; ⓜLago). Search for "*piscinas aire libre*" at ⓦmadrid.es for others, or ask at the tourist office.

figurative art, mapping the beginning of abstraction through to Pop and avant-garde.

The Rastro

The **Rastro flea market** (Sun 8am–3pm) is as much a part of Madrid's weekend ritual as a Mass or a *paseo*. The stalls sprawl south from ⓜLa Latina to the Ronda de Toledo, selling everything from flamenco records to imitation designer gear to old photos of Madrid. Expect a great atmosphere, but you'll have to search hard for bargains among the junk. Keep a tight grip on your possessions. Afterwards, while away the afternoon in the bars and *terrazas* around Puerta de Moros.

Parque del Buen Retiro and Parque del Oeste

The most central and most popular of Madrid's parks is the **Parque del Buen Retiro** (daily: May–Sept 6am–midnight; until 11pm rest of the year; ⓜRetiro or Ibiza) behind the Prado, a stunning mix of formal gardens and wilder spaces. You can row a boat, picnic, check out a travelling art exhibition at the beautiful **Palacio de Velázquez** and the nearby **Palacio de Cristal** and, above all, promenade like half of Madrid. You can also visit the "Hill of the Absents" – a mound constructed in memory of those who died in the Madrid bombing of 2004. Although charming by day, Retiro is best avoided at night. The **Parque del Oeste** on the city's western edge (ⓜVentura Rodríguez) boasts a genuine Egyptian temple – Templo de Debod, donated to Spain by Egyptian president Nasser in 1968 as a gesture of thanks to

Spanish archeologists who saved it from the rising waters of Lake Nasser.

Estadio de Santiago Bernabéu

Even non-football fans may enjoy a tour of Real Madrid's Bernabéu stadium (non-match days Mon–Sat 10am–7pm, Sun 10.30am–6.30pm; match days closes 5hr before kickoff; €19; ⓦrealmadrid .com; ⓜSantiago Bernabéu) in northern Madrid. With multimedia exhibitions charting the club's rich history, and visits to the trophy room, players' dugout and away team's dressing room, there's enough here to keep you entertained for a few hours. A café and restaurant overlooking the pitch serve reasonably priced meals. In summer, there's also an outdoor nightclub in the stadium, *La Terraza del Bernabéu* (€10 entry including a drink; drinks €12 thereafter).

ARRIVAL AND DEPARTURE

By plane Barajas airport (ⓦaena.es), 15km northeast of the centre, is served by all major airlines from Europe, North and Latin America. To reach the city, metro line #8 runs to ⓜNuevos Ministerios (daily 6am–2am; 12min; €4.50). The fast, reliable 24hr Exprés Aeropuerto bus leaves terminals 1, 2 and 4 (every 15–35min; €5), stopping at c/O'Donnell, Plaza de Cibeles and Atocha (the last stop only between 6am and 11.30pm). AeroCITY minibuses (24hr; ☎917 477 570, ⓦaerocity.com) drop passengers off door-to-door for €6–20.

By train In the north of the city, Estación de Chamartín is used by trains for France and the north and west of Spain. The more central Estación de Atocha serves the south and east of Spain.

Destinations from Chamartín Bilbao (5 daily; 5hr–6hr 20min); El Escorial (hourly; 55min); León (10 daily; 2hr 40min–5hr 10min); Paris (1 daily; 15hr); Salamanca (7 daily; 2hr 40min–3hr 5min); Santander (5 daily; 4hr 30min–6hr); Segovia (1–2 hourly; 30min–2hr 5min).

Destinations from Atocha Barcelona (25 daily; 2hr 40min–3hr 10min); Cáceres (4 daily; 3hr 45min–4hr 10min); Cádiz (7 daily; 4hr 5min–4hr 30min); Córdoba (1–2 hourly; 1hr 40min–2hr); Granada (2 daily; 4hr 30min); Lisbon (1 daily; 7hr 40min); Málaga (12 daily; 2hr 20min–2hr 50min); Mérida (3 daily; 4hr 40min–5hr 50min); Pamplona (7 daily; 3hr–3hr 50min); San Sebastián (6 daily; 5hr 20min–7hr 30min); Santiago de Compostela (3 daily; 5hr 30min–7hr); Seville (22 daily; 2hr 30min); Toledo (13 daily; 30min); Valencia (16 daily; 1hr 40min–3hr 40min).

By bus Terminals are scattered throughout the city, but

the two main stations are the Estación del Sur (Ⓜ Méndez Alvaro) on c/Méndez Alvaro, south of Estación de Atocha, for destinations south, east and west of Madrid, and the Intercambiador de Avenida de América (Ⓜ Avenida de América) for destinations in the north.

Destinations Alicante (5–8 daily; 5hr–6hr 30min); Almería (2 daily; 10hr 30min); Barcelona (20 daily; 7hr 30min–8hr); Bilbao (13 daily; 4hr 10min–4hr 45min); Cáceres (7 daily; 4hr–4hr 30min); Cádiz (13 daily; 12hr 45min–16hr 30min); El Escorial (hourly; 1hr); Granada (14 daily; 4hr 30min–5hr); León (10 daily; 3hr 30min–4hr 15min); Málaga (4–8 daily; 6hr); Mérida (10 daily; 4hr 15min–5hr); Pamplona (8 daily; 5hr–6hr 30min); Salamanca (22 daily; 2hr 30min–3hr); San Sebastián (9 daily; 6hr); Santander (8 daily; 5hr 45min); Santiago de Compostela (5 daily; 8–9hr); Segovia (10 daily; 1hr 30min); Seville (8 daily; 6hr); Toledo (every 30min 6.30am–10pm; 1hr 15min); Trujillo (12 daily; 2hr 40min–4hr); Valencia (13 daily; 3hr 15 min–4hr 15min).

INFORMATION

Tourist information Centro de Turismo de Madrid is at Plaza Mayor 27 (daily 9.30am–8.30pm; ☏ 91 588 163 651, ⓦ www.esmadrid.com; Ⓜ Sol). Branches at Plaza de Colón (Ⓜ Colón) and Terminal 4 at the airport (same hours). Events listings are detailed in free English-language monthly *In Madrid* (ⓦ in-madrid.com) and Spanish *Guía del Ocio* (ⓦ guiadelocio.com).

GETTING AROUND

By bus Buses (ⓦ emtmadrid.es) run from 6.30am to midnight; there are also 26 night-bus *búhos* (owls) in the centre from Plaza de Cibeles (midnight–6am; every 15min). Single fare €1.50.

By metro The metro (ⓦ metromadrid.es) runs 6.05am–2am. Fares are €1.50–2 within central zone A, or €12.20 for a 10-journey ticket that is also valid on buses.

By taxi Taxi ranks are located throughout the city centre. Fares start from €2.15 6am–9pm during the week; higher fares in the evening and at weekends. Charges per km are €1–1.20, and supplementary charges apply for journeys to and from the airport, train and bus stations.

ACCOMMODATION

The best budget accommodation is in the area surrounding buzzing, pedestrianized Plaza Santa Ana. Other good areas include Gran Vía and along c/Fuencarral towards Chueca and Malsaña.

HOSTELS

Albergue Juvenil c/Mejia Lequerica 21 ☏ 915 939 688, ⓦ ajmadrid.es; Ⓜ Alonso Martínez or Tribunal. The stylish decor mixes modern furnishings and graffiti murals and no dorm has more than 6 beds. Facilities include a gym, TV/

DVD/games room and laundry. Breakfast included. Dorm: under-26s **€20**, over-26s **€22.50**

Cat's Hostel c/Cañizares 6 ☏ 913 692 807, ⓦ catshostel .com; Ⓜ Antón Martín. Party hostel located in a converted eighteenth-century palace with beautiful central patio. Rooms are a bit cramped but there's a lively cellar bar, nightly tapas bar crawls, and free wi-fi. Dorm **€19**, double **€70**

★ **Hostel La Posada de Huertas** c/de las Huertas 21 ☏ 914 295 526, ⓦ posadadehuertas.com; Ⓜ Antón Martín. Spacious, secure and colourful dorms with lockers in the heart of Madrid's nightlife. Helpful staff, nightly tapas bar tours, free breakfast, wi-fi and kitchen facilities are just some of the perks. Dorm **€20**

Las Musas Residence c/Jesus y María 12, 3rd floor ☏ 915 394 984, ⓦ lasmusasresidence.com; Ⓜ Tirso de Molina. This spick-and-span hostel is a favourite with international backpackers who congregate in its large kitchen/lounge before hitting the many nearby bars and clubs. Dorm **€14**, double **€45**

Los Amigos Hostel c/Arenal 26 ☏ 915 592 472, ⓦ losamigoshostel.com; Ⓜ Ópera. Popular, friendly hostel with bright dorms, lockers, kitchen and internet. Dorm **€21**, double **€60**

HOTELS

Chic & Basic Colors c/de las Huertas 14, 2nd floor ☏ 914 296 935, ⓦ chicandbasic.com; Ⓜ Antón Martín. The name says it all: it's chic, sleek, and brightly coloured. Each minimalist, comfortable room comes with both flat-screen TV and free wi-fi, and the location is hard to beat. Double **€80**

Hostal Acapulco c/de la Salud 13, 4th floor ☏ 915 311 945, ⓦ hostalacapulco.com; Ⓜ Gran Vía. You're guaranteed not to go loco here: the spotless, sunny rooms with marble floors and balconies overlook cute little Plaza del Carmen. Double **€65**

EATING

Madrid has an incredible variety of restaurants, and it's easy to dine out on a tight budget. Most tapas bars are known for a particular speciality – Madrileños will have a drink and a tapa in one bar before moving on to another. They only really get going around 10.30pm. Most places serve food 1–4pm and 8–11.30pm; opening hours come at the end of reviews where this is not the case.

CAFÉS AND TAPAS BARS

Some of the best areas to enjoy tapas are La Latina, Chueca and Sol, with myriad bars clustered along the little streets.

Chocolatería Valor Postigo de San Martín; Ⓜ Callao. One of the best spots in town for *chocolate con churros*, with an incredible array of dipping chocolate for the doughnuts.

32

Hitch c/Cervantes 8; Ⓜ Antón Martín. Café by day, arty bar by night, this versatile spot screens classic films and football games, holds photography contests and makes to-die-for goat's cheese and caramelized onion tapas (€3.50).

Mercado de San Miguel Plaza de San Miguel; Ⓜ Sol. Transformed into a gleaming modern venue with numerous food counters and perpetually busy tables, one of Madrid's oldest markets is now a top spot for tapas (from €1), drinks and people-watching.

★ **Taberna El Mollete** c/de la Bola 4; Ⓜ Opera. Nab a table in the tiny loft dining space, sip your wine and savour the *morcilla* croquettes and the *huevos rotos* (fried potatoes with egg), or push your way to the popular bar for a beer.

Txacolina c/de la Cava Baja 26; Ⓜ Latina. Busy bar renowned for its imaginative, elaborate Basque *pintxos*. Wash them down with *txacoli*, a dry Basque white wine.

RESTAURANTS

Casa Mingo Paseo de la Florida 34; Ⓜ Príncipe Pío. Asturian cider house with a cheap, no-nonsense menu. If the roast chicken doesn't grab you, go for the *chorizo a la sidra* (€8).

★ **La Antigua Huevería** c/San Vicente Ferrer 28; Ⓜ Tribunal. "The old egg shop" is a cosy little restaurant/ bar serving great eggs (from €9) and, appropriately, *huevos rotos* – eggs lightly scrambled over potato, onion and sometimes ham or sausage.

La Isla de Tesoro c/de Manuela Malasaña 3; Ⓜ Bilbao. Veggie restaurant worth seeking out for its eclectic decor and a menu that changes daily but often features vegetable goulash, Thai vegetable curry and other internationally inspired dishes. *Menú del día* €11.

La Musa c/Manuela Malasaña 18 ⓦ grupolamusa.com; Ⓜ Bilbao. Always heaving with a young clientele, the food here is deliciously different – try the fried green tomatoes with goat's cheese (€6.20). There's another branch on Plaza de la Paja.

La Paella de la Reina c/de la Reina 39; Ⓜ Gran Vía. This is where Madrileños head to sate their rice cravings. Like any good *arrocería*, this place only cooks paella for two people or more, so take a friend. The *arroz negro* (€16.50/ person) is delicious.

★ **Mestizo** c/Recoletos 13 ⓦ madrid.mestizomx.com; Ⓜ Retiro. This authentic Mexican restaurant packs some real heat, with an extensive menu of quesadillas, tamales, filled tacos and enchiladas, plus something rarely found outside of Mexico – tortillas stuffed with *cuitlacoche*, a black corn fungus (€8.80).

Shapla c/Lavapiés 42; Ⓜ Lavapiés. No-frills Indian restaurant serving bargain curries, including plenty of vegetarian options. Try the *dhal* (€4) washed down with a mango *lassi*.

DRINKING AND NIGHTLIFE

Clubs open from midnight until well beyond dawn; the best areas are the hipster haunt of Malasaña, gay-friendly Chueca and multicultural Lavapiés/Antón Martín.

BARS

Amor de Madre c/San Joaquín 14; Ⓜ Tribunal. A skateboarder's paradise in terms of decor, "mother's love" is a laidback, friendly bar right in the heart of Malasaña.

Café Manuela c/San Vicente Ferrer 29; Ⓜ Tribunal. Splashes of marble and gilt trims give this place a certain old-fashioned grandeur, but the vibe's relaxed. Enjoy a milkshake or cocktail over a board game.

El Clandestino c/de Barquillo 34; Ⓜ Chueca. Immensely popular bar serving great mojitos to an accompaniment of indie/rock music, sometimes live.

El Imperfecto c/Coloreros 5; Ⓜ Sol. Far from being imperfect, this is an excellent cocktail bar with an intriguingly decorated interior. There's live jazz on Tues.

El Viajero Plaza de la Cebada 11; Ⓜ La Latina. Ideal spot for a beer on a warm night, when you can gaze out at the city's comings and goings from the open-air rooftop *terraza*.

Kikekeller c/Corredera Baja de San Pablo 17; Ⓜ Callao No, it's not a design shop, but a trendy bar where the furniture's for sale and the waiters wear leather skirts. Perfect people-watching territory.

La Venencia c/Echegaray 7; Ⓜ Sevilla or Sol. Old-school sherry bar where nothing seems to have changed for years (except perhaps the quantity of dust on the bottles behind the bar). Sherry from €1.70 a glass.

CLUBS

Kapital c/Atocha 125; Ⓜ Atocha. Popular megaclub with seven levels and a roof terrace featuring different dancefloors – everything from hip-hop to salsa to r'n'b. All this fun doesn't come cheap – and you need to dress up – but the €20 admission includes one drink. Fri & Sat midnight–6am.

Mi madre era una groupie c/Santa Polonia 5; Ⓜ Antón Martín. One for the less-than-hardcore clubbers, this little place has a friendly atmosphere and a playlist that features Britpop and classic hits. Free entry. Thurs–Sat until 3.30am.

Samsara c/Cruz 7; Ⓜ Sol. Fun, unpretentious place popular with a young crowd, playing mostly chart music. Entry €10. Wed–Sat 10pm–6am.

Serrano 41 c/Serrano 41 ⓦ serrano41.com; Ⓜ Serrano. Chic venue playing a mix of pop and house and funk, frequented by well-heeled Madrileños. Sunday's hip-hop night is particularly popular. Strict door policy, so look smart. Entry from €10. Wed–Sun 11pm–5.30am.

Tupperware Corredera Alta de San Pablo 26; Ⓜ Tribunal. This little club is fun through-and-through, from its über-kitsch decor to its eclectic playlist – soul, indie and Sixties and Seventies classics, enjoyed by a 30-something crowd. Free entry. Daily 9pm–3am.

ENTERTAINMENT

Big rock concerts are usually held at Palacio Vistalegre, Utebo 1 (ⓜOporto), and La Peineta stadium, Avda Arcentales (ⓜLas Musas). Flamenco is at its best in the summer, especially during the Suma Flamenca, a fortnight of special concerts in June (ⓦmadrid.org/sumaflamenca).

CINEMA

Cine Doré c/Santa Isabel 3; ⓜAntón Martín. Offers a bargain (€2.50) programme of classic films, a pleasant bar and, in summer, an outdoor *cine-terraza*; home to the Filmoteca Nacional (national film library).

Cines Princesa c/de la Princesa 3; ⓜPlaza de España. Films shown in their original language – from English-language Hollywood blockbusters to international art films.

La Enana Marrón Travesía de San Mateo 8 ⓦwww .laenanamarron.org; ⓜAlonzo Martínez. Artsy and independent Spanish-language films and alternative theatre.

LIVE MUSIC

Café Central Plaza del Ángel 10 ⓦcafecentralmadrid .com; ⓜSol. Attracting big international musicians, this is one of the best places in the world to hear live jazz. Open from noon for drinks, with music nightly from 10pm; get here before 9pm to secure weekend tickets (€10–15).

El Barco c/del Barco 34 ⓦbarcobar.com; ⓜTribunal. Popular bar/club in Malasaña with a varied programme of gigs, from flamenco to rock. Nightly from 10pm.

La Boca del Lobo c/Echegaray 11 ⓦlabocadellobo.com; ⓜSevilla. Dark, atmospheric venue with a reputation for showcasing new rock and alternative acts, as well as funk, roots, ska and fusion. Entry free–€10. Live music from around 9.30pm, followed by DJs. Open Wed–Sat.

La Escalera de Jacob c/de Lavapiés 11 ⓦlaescaleradejacob.es; ⓜAntón Martín. Intimate, multifaceted venue with fusion, soul, jazz, funk and indie nights, a loyal local following and some great live performances. Nightly from 10pm.

Moby Dick Avda de Brasil 5 ⓦmobydickclub.com; ⓜSantiago Bernabéu. Popular nautical-themed venue attracting live rock bands, both local and international.

BULLFIGHTING

Plaza de Toros Monumental de las Ventas c/de Alcalá 237; ⓜVentas. Hosts some of the year's most prestigious events, especially during the May/June San Isidro festivities; ticket prices start from around €3 for standing *sol* (sun) tickets, with *sombra* (shade) tickets from €5. Tickets for all but the biggest events are available at the box office (☎913 562 200, ⓦlas-ventas.com).

FLAMENCO

Cardamomo c/Echegaray 15 ⓦcardamomo.es; ⓜSevilla. Atmospheric bar with nightly *tablaos* (performances). Pricey (from €39 including drink), but the shows are some of the city's most authentic. Daily 9pm–3.30am.

Casa Patas c/Cañizares 10 ⓦcasapatas.com; ⓜAntón Martín. Classic flamenco club with bar and restaurant, and incredible shows. Best nights Thurs & Fri from 8.30pm; can get rather crowded. Entrance €35–40 with dinner. Check website for performance times.

Corral de la Morería c/de la Morería 17 ⓦcorraldelamoreria.com; ⓜÓpera. Venerable flamenco venue that's been going strong for over 50 years, thanks to the quality of its nightly performers. Entrance €30–45. Daily 8.30pm–2.30am; check website for show schedules.

SHOPPING

The main shopping streets are Gran Vía (where you'll find international and Spanish chain stores) and c/Fuencarral (for Spanish and international brands and designers, plus some independent shops). If you're looking for quirky clothing or jewellery, try the boutiques and vintage stores of Chueca and Malasaña. The area from Plaza Mayor to Puerta de Toledo is filled with shops selling everything from religious icons to embroidered shawls – great for browsing and picking up the odd authentic souvenir, but often quite expensive.

Alpargatería Casa Hernanza c/de Toledo 18; ⓜOpera. This purveyor of traditional rope-soled sandals and shoes has been in business since 1840.

Casa de Diego Puerta del Sol 12; ⓜSol. The place to go for handcrafted *abanicos* (fans). Prices for more basic models start at under €10.

Casa del Libro Gran Vía 29; ⓜGran Vía. A huge bookshop with a large selection in English.

El Templo de Susu c/del Espíritu Santo 1; ⓜTribunal. One of Malasaña's best-stocked vintage emporiums.

Petra's International Bookshop c/de Compomanes 13; ⓜÓpera. Lets you swap your old books for other secondhand ones.

DIRECTORY

Embassies Australia, Torre Espacio, Paseo de la Castellana 259d, 24th floor ☎913 536 600; Canada, Torre Espacio, Paseo de la Castellana 259d ☎913 828 400; Ireland, Paseo de la Castellana 46, 4th floor ☎914 364 093; New Zealand, c/de Pinar 7 ☎915 230 226; UK, Torre Espacio, Paseo de la Castellana 259d ☎917 146 300; US, c/Serrano 75 ☎915 872 200.

32

Exchange Large branches of most major banks on c/ Alcalá and Gran Vía and ATMs throughout the city centre. Round-the-clock currency exchange at the airport; Banco Central is best for AmEx travellers' cheques.

Hospitals Anglo-American Medical Unit (Unidad Médica) at c/del Conde de Aranda 1 (☎914 351 823, ⓦunidadmedica.com; ⓜRetiro) has Spanish- and English-speaking staff. Hospital General Gregorio Marañón at c/del Doctor Esquerdo 46 (☎915 868 000; ⓜSáinz de Baranda) is the main public hospital.

Left luggage Estación de Atocha has lockers (daily 5.30am–10.20pm); Estación de Chamartín also has lockers (daily 7am–11pm). There is a *consigna* (left luggage) at the Estación Sur de Autobuses (6.30am–midnight). There are also 24hr *consignas* at the airport terminals 1, 3 and 4.

Pharmacies Farmacia Mayor at c/Mayor 13 (☎913 664 616) and Farmacia Velázquez at c/Velázquez 70 (☎915 756 028) are both open 24hr.

Post office Main post office at Paseo del Prado 1, Plaza de Cibeles (ⓜBanco de España).

32

Day-trips from Madrid

Surrounding the capital are some of Spain's most fascinating cities, all an easy day-trip from Madrid or a convenient stopoff on the main routes out.

EL ESCORIAL

Fifty kilometres northwest of Madrid, nestled in the foothills of the Sierra de Guadarrama, are **SAN LORENZO DEL ESCORIAL** and the monastery of **El Escorial** (Tues–Sun 10am–6pm; €10, free Wed for EU citizens). The city grew around this enormous, severe-looking building, which resembles a fortress rather than a palace. Start at the monastery's west gateway, which leads into the **Patio de los Reyes** and the impressive Basilica. Move on to the **Salas Capitulares**, outside and around to the left, to see works by El Greco, Velázquez and Ribera. Nearby, the staircase next to the Sacristía leads down to the **Panteón de los Reyes**, the final resting place of virtually all Spanish monarchs since Charles V, where they lie in gilded tombs (guided/audioguide visits only). You'll pass the **Pudrería**, where corpses are left to rot for twenty years, and the eerie **Panteón de los Infantes**, with tiny marble coffins. The spartan Habsburg apartments inside the **Palace** itself, inhabited by Philip II, house the chair that supported his gouty leg and the deathbed from which he looked down into the church.

ARRIVAL AND INFORMATION

By train From both of Madrid's train stations, C8 *cercanías* run to El Escorial (hourly; 1hr; €1.25). Take a connecting local bus up to the town centre (€1.20); otherwise it's a 20min walk uphill.

By bus Bus #661 runs between Moncloa and the bus station in El Escorial (every 15min weekdays, hourly on weekends; 50min). From here, it's a 10min walk to the monastery.

Tourist office c/Grimaldi 2 (Tues–Sat 10am–2pm & 3–6pm, Sun 10am–2pm; ☎918 905 313, ⓦsanlorenzoturismo.org).

SEGOVIA

Located 87km northwest of Madrid, **SEGOVIA** has a remarkable number of architectural achievements for a small city. Known to locals as the "stone ship", from a bird's-eye view the city resembles a boat, with its three most celebrated attractions at the stern, bow and mast: the Alcázar, Aqueduct and cathedral, respectively.

The Aqueduct

The **Aqueduct**, a magnificent structure that looms over the Plaza del Azoguejo, stretches over 800m and towers 30m high. As if these dimensions weren't impressive enough, the entire structure stands up without a drop of mortar. No one knows exactly when it was built, but it was probably around the end of the first century AD under the Emperor Trajan.

The cathedral

Dominating the Plaza Mayor in the heart of the old city, the **cathedral** (daily 9.30am–6.30pm; €3, free Sun mornings) takes the Gothic style to its extreme, with pinnacles and flying buttresses tacked on at every conceivable point.

The Alcázar

Beside the cathedral, c/Daoiz leads on to a small park in front of the **Alcázar** (daily: April–Sept 10am–7pm; Oct–March 10am–6pm; €4.50, free for EU citizens third Tues of every month; tower access €2). This extraordinary castle with narrow towers and turrets, rebuilt in 1862 after the original was destroyed by fire, is said to have inspired Walt Disney's design for Sleeping Beauty's castle. Inside, you can admire the splendid Sala de Reyes, the three-dimensional frieze depicting all the monarchs of Asturias, Castilla and León, the peculiar "pine cones" decorating the ceiling in the Sala de Las Piñas, and, of course, the unsurpassed view of the city and the snow-tipped mountains behind it from the summit of the Torre de Juan II. It's worth investing in an audioguide (€2), as information inside the Alcázar is scarce.

Vera Cruz

The most impressive of Segovia's churches is **Vera Cruz** (Tues–Sun 10.30am –1.30pm & 4–7pm; closed Nov; €1.75), a remarkable twelve-sided building in the valley facing the Alcázar, erected by the Knights Templar in the early thirteenth century.

ARRIVAL AND INFORMATION

By train The fast AVE train (up to 17 daily; 28min; €10) from Madrid Chamartín stops at Segovia-Guiomar station, 7km from town: take bus #11 to the Aqueduct (every 15min; €1).

By bus Frequent buses (every 45min; 1hr 30min; €8.10) run from Madrid's Paseo de Florida bus station (Ⓜ Príncipe Pío). The entrance to the old city is a 10min walk up Avda de Fernández Ladreda.

Tourist office Plaza del Azoguejo 1 (daily 10am–7pm, Sat until 8pm; ☎ 921 466 720, ⓦturismodesegovia.com); guided city tours available (€13.50/person, minimum 4 people).

ACCOMMODATION AND EATING

Hostal Juan Bravo c/de Juan Bravo 12 ☎ 921 463 413, ⓦ hostaljuanbravo.blogspot.com.es. Superbly located, friendly *hostal*, its spotless rooms brightened up with cheerful art prints. Request one of the back rooms for the awesome views of the Sierra de Guadarrama. Double €45
La Judería c/Judería Vieja 5. Great for vegetarians, this restaurant offers fresh Indian cuisine, with a few Spanish

dishes thrown in for good measure. The three-course *menú degustación* (€15) will fill you up for an afternoon's sightseeing. Daily 1–3.30pm & 8–11pm.
Maribel c/Padre Claret 16. A local favourite which specializes in Segovia's delicacy of *cochinillo asado* (suckling pig), although the roast lamb is also excellent. Prices are moderate too – around the €12 mark for generous portions. Mon lunch only, closed Tues, otherwise 1–4pm & 8–11pm.

TOLEDO

Capital of medieval Spain until 1560, UNESCO World Heritage Site **TOLEDO** is the spiritual heart of Catholic Spain and a city redolent of past glories. Set in a bleak landscape, the haphazard maze of cobbled streets rests on a rocky mound isolated on three sides by a looping gorge of the Río Tajo. To see the city at its finest, lose yourself in the backstreets or stay the night; by 6pm, the tour buses have all gone home.

The Catedral

The **Catedral** is at the heart of the city (Mon–Sat 10am–6.30pm, Sun 2–6.30pm; €8 including audioguide). This Gothic construction took almost three centuries to complete (1227–1493) and is bursting with treasures from numerous great artists. The sacristy and museums are home to the most opulent paintings, most notably by Zurbarán, Velázquez and El Greco. Behind the Capilla Mayor's huge altarpiece is the Baroque *Transparente*, with marble cherubs and clouds, especially magnificent when the sun reaches through the strategically placed opening in the roof above.

The Alcázar and around

Inside the Alcázar fortress, the splendid cavernous interior of the Museo de Ejército (Army Museum; Tues & Thurs–Sun 11am–5pm; €5, free Sun) houses an impressive collection of medieval weaponry and armour, model soldiers, scale models of fortifications, dioramas and much more. In 1936, during the Civil War, some 600 barricaded Nationalists held out against relentless Republican attack for over two months until finally relieved by one of Franco's armies. North of here, the **Museo**

32

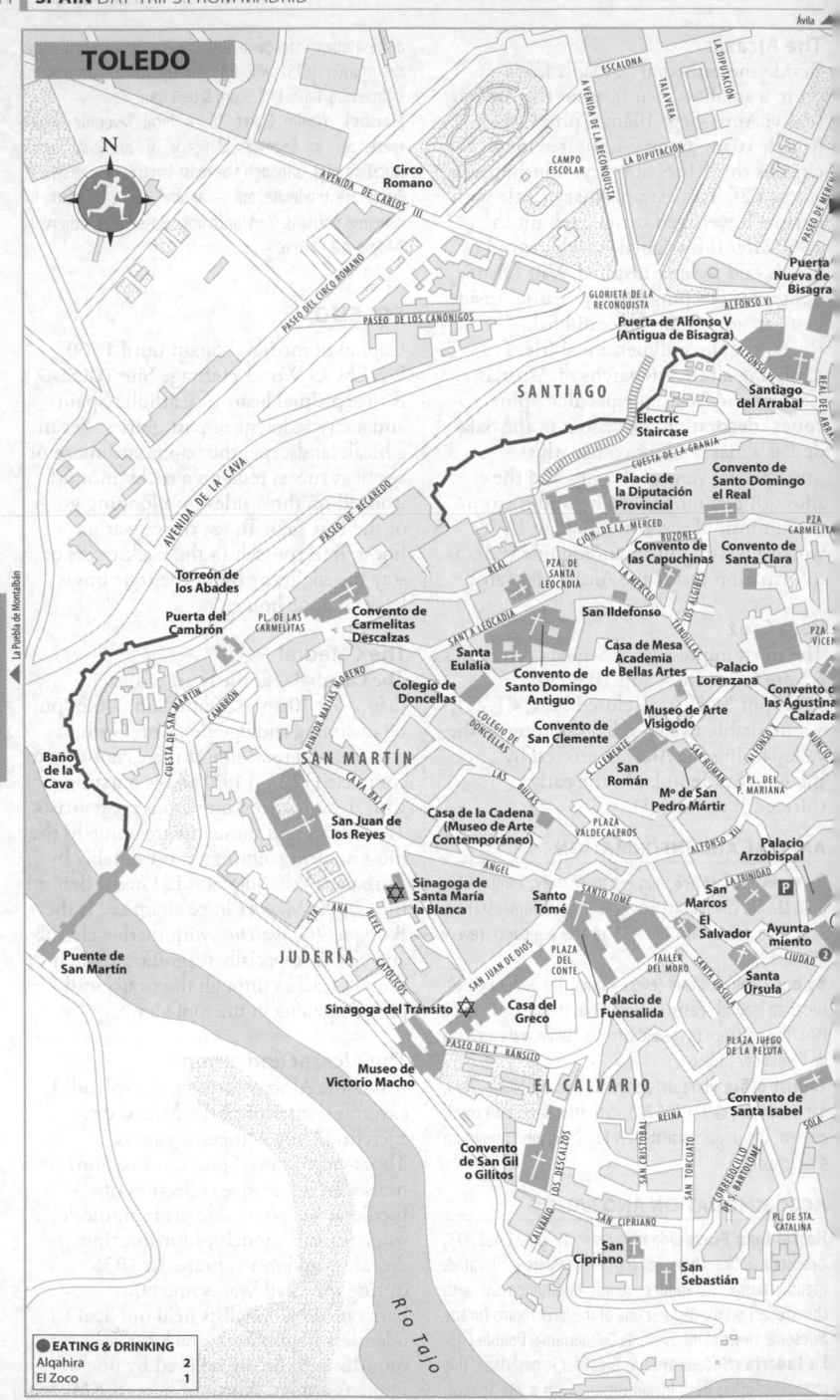

Ávila ▲

TOLEDO

◀ La Puebla de Montalbán

N

Circo Romano

CAMPO ESCOLAR

AVENIDA DE CARLOS III

ESCALONA

TALAVERA

AVENIDA DE LA RECONQUISTA

LA DIPUTACIÓN

LA DIPUTACIÓN

Puerta Nueva de Bisagra

PASEO DEL CIRCO ROMANO

GLORIETA DE LA RECONQUISTA

PASEO DE LOS CANÓNIGOS

ALFONSO VI

Puerta de Alfonso V (Antigua de Bisagra)

ALFONSO VI

REAL DEL ARRA...

SANTIAGO

Santiago del Arrabal

Electric Staircase

CUESTA DE LA GRANJA

AVENIDA DE LA CAVA

PASEO DE RECAREDO

Palacio de la Diputación Provincial

CJON. DE LA MERCED

BUZONES

Convento de Santo Domingo el Real

PZA. CARMELIT...

Convento de las Capuchinas

LA MERCED

Convento de Santa Clara

Torreón de los Abades

REAL

PZA. DE SANTA LEOCADIA

ALJIBES

FENDILLAS

PZA. VICEN...

Puerta del Cambrón

PL. DE LAS CARMELITAS

Convento de Carmelitas Descalzas

SANTA LEOCADIA

San Ildefonso

Casa de Mesa Academia de Bellas Artes

Palacio Lorenzana

Convento de las Agustinas Calzadas

PINTOR MATÍAS MORENO

Santa Eulalia

Convento de Santo Domingo Antiguo

Museo de Arte Visigodo

NÚNCIO

ALFONSO

CUESTA DE SAN MARTÍN

CAMBRÓN

Colegio de Doncellas

COLEGIO DE DONCELLAS

SAN ROMÁN

Baño de la Cava

SAN MARTÍN

CAVA BAJA

LAS BULAS

Convento de San Clemente

S. CLEMENTE

Convento de San Clemente

San Román

PL. DEL P. MARIANA

ALFONSO

Casa de la Cadena (Museo de Arte Contemporáneo)

PLAZA VALDECALEROS

Mº de San Pedro Mártir

San Juan de los Reyes

STA. ANA

REYES

ÁNGEL

ALFONSO XII

Palacio Arzobispal

Sinagoga de Santa María la Blanca

Santo Tomé

SANTO TOMÉ

LA TRINIDAD

San Marcos

P

CATÓLICOS

SAN JUAN DE DIOS

PLAZA DEL CONTE

El Salvador

Ayuntamiento

CIUDAD...

JUDERÍA

TALLER DEL MORO

Santa Úrsula

SANTA ÚRSULA

Sinagoga del Tránsito

Casa del Greco

Palacio de Fuensalida

PASEO DEL T. RÁNSITO

PLAZA JUEGO DE LA PELOTA

Museo de Victorio Macho

EL CALVARIO

REINA

Convento de Santa Isabel

SOLA...

Río Tajo

CANALÓN

LOS DESCALZOS

Convento de San Gil o Gilitos

SAN CRISTÓBAL

SAN TORCHAJO

CORRELILLO DE S. BARTOLOMÉ

PL. DE STA. CATALINA

San Cipriano

SAN CIPRIANO

San Sebastián

Puente de San Martín

Puente de San Martín

● EATING & DRINKING

| Alqahira | 2 |
| El Zoco | 1 |

32

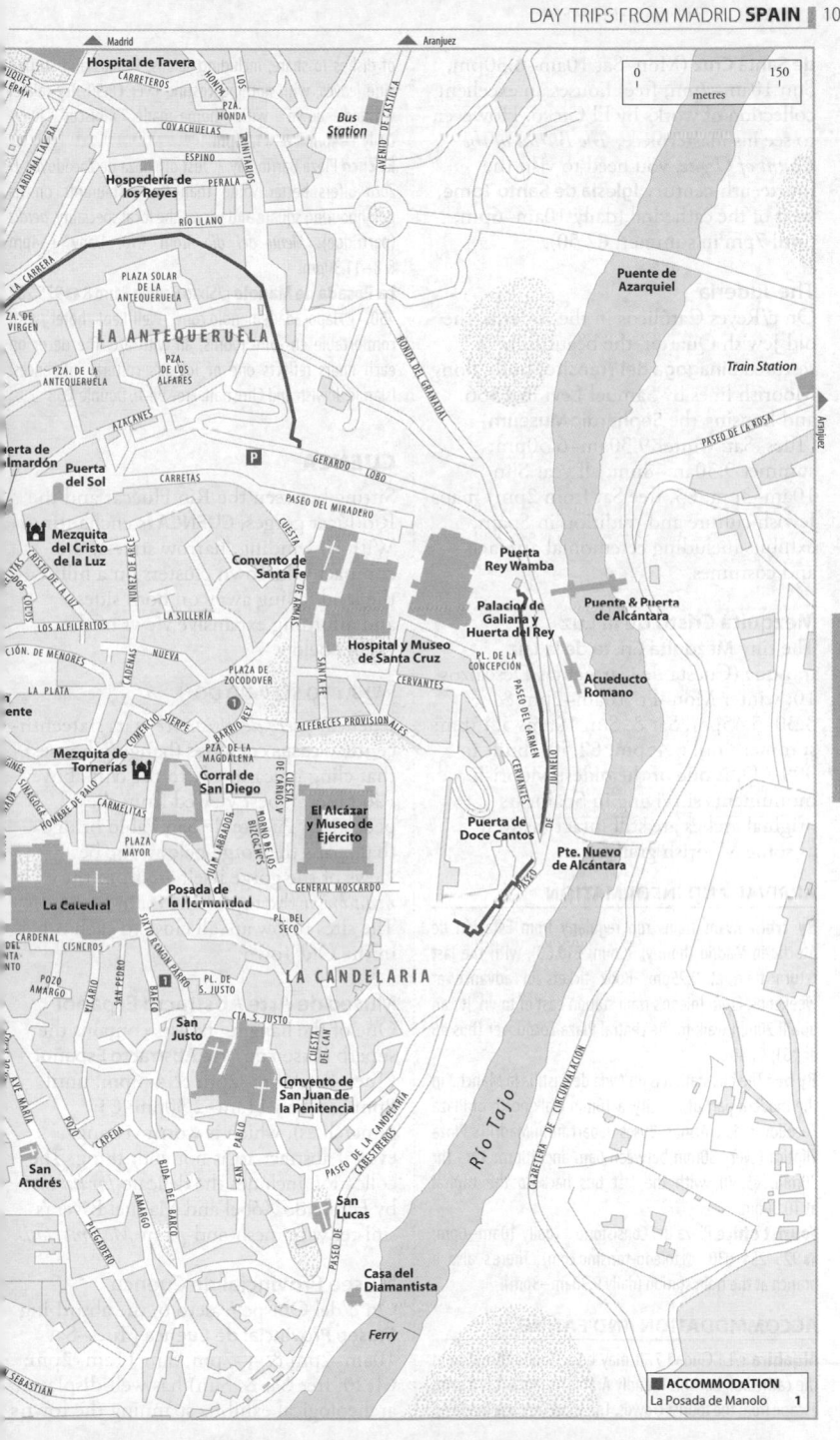

Madrid   Aranjuez

Hospital de Tavera
CARRETEROS
HONDA
LOS
PZA.
HONDA
COVACHUELAS
TRINITARIOS
ESPINO
Hospedería de
los Reyes   PERALA
RÍO LLANO

Bus
Station

AVENIDO DE CASTILLA

LA CARRERA
CARDENAL TAVERA
UQUES
ERMA
PLAZA SOLAR
DE LA
ANTEQUERUELA
ZA DE
VIRGEN

Puente de
Azarquiel

LA ANTEQUERUELA
PZA. DE LA
ANTEQUERUELA
PZA.
DE LOS
ALFARES

RONDA DEL GRANADAL

Train Station

AZACANES

Aranjuez

uerta de
lmardón
Puerta
del Sol
CARRETAS
GERARDO LOBO

PASEO DE LA ROSA

P

PASEO DEL MIRADERO

Mezquita
del Cristo
de la Luz
CRISTO DE LA LUZ
SANTAS
JUSTA Y RUFINA
LA SILLERÍA
NUEVA
Convento de
Santa Fe

Puerta
Rey Wamba

Palacio de
Galiana y
Huerta del Rey
PL. DE LA
CONCEPCIÓN

Puente & Puerta
de Alcántara

LOS ALFILERITOS
CIÓN. DE MENORES
LA PLATA
ente

CADENAS
PLAZA DE
ZOCODOVER

Hospital y Museo
de Santa Cruz

CERVANTES

Acueducto
Romano

32

Mezquita de
Tornerías
GINES
SINAGOGA
HOMBRE DE PALO
COMERCIO SIERPE
BARRIO REY
PZA. DE LA
MAGDALENA
Corral de
San Diego
CARMELITAS
PLAZA
MAYOR

ALFÉRECES PROVISIONALES

CUESTA DE CARLOS V

CUESTA
DE ARMAS

SANTA FE

HORNO DE LOS
BIZCOCHOS
JUAN LABRADOR
El Alcázar
y Museo de
Ejército

CERVANTES

PASEO DEL CARMEN

Puerta de
Doce Cantos

CERVANTES

DE JUANELO

Pte. Nuevo
de Alcántara

La Catedral
CARDENAL
DEL
NTA
NTO
CISNEROS
SAN PEDRO
SIXTO RAMÓN PARRO
BACA
POZO
AMARGO
VICARIO
Posada de
la Hermandad
GENERAL MOSCARDÓ
PL. DEL
SECO

PASEO DE

CARRETERA DE CIRCUNVALACIÓN

PL. DE
S. JUSTO
LA CANDELARIA

AVE MARÍA
POZO
CAPEDA
San
Justo
CTA. S. JUSTO
CUESTA
DEL CAN
Convento de
San Juan de
la Penitencia

Río Tajo

San
Andrés
PABLO
REYES
RDA. DEL BARCO
AMARGO
PLEGADERO
PASEO DE LA CANDELARIA
CABESTREROS
San
Lucas
PASEO DE

Casa del
Diamantista

N SEBASTIÁN

Ferry

0   150
metres

ACCOMMODATION
La Posada de Manolo   1

de Santa Cruz (Mon–Sat 10am–6.30pm, Sun 10am–2pm; free) houses an excellent collection of works by El Greco. However, to see his masterpiece, *The Burial of the Count of Orgaz,* you need to visit the fourteenth-century **Iglesia de Santo Tomé**, west of the cathedral (daily 10am–6pm, until 7pm in summer; €2.50).

The Judería

On c/Reyes Católicos in the **Judería**, the old Jewish Quarter, the beautifully restored **Sinagoga del Tránsito**, built along Moorish lines by Samuel Levi in 1366 and housing the **Sephardic Museum** (Tues–Sat: winter 9.30am–6.30pm; summer 9.30am–8pm; all year Sun 10am–3pm; €3, free Sat from 2pm) maps Jewish culture and tradition in Spain, exhibits including ceremonial artefacts and costumes.

Mezquita Cristo de la Luz

The tiny **Mezquita Cristo de la Luz** mosque (Cuesta de Carmelitas Descalzos 10; winter Mon–Fri 10am–2pm & 3.30–5.45pm, Sat & Sun 10am–5.45pm; summer until 6.45pm; €2.50), built in 999 AD, is one of the oldest Moorish monuments surviving in Spain. Its original arches are still intact (as well as some Moorish graffiti).

ARRIVAL AND INFORMATION

By train Avant trains run regularly from Estación de Atocha in Madrid (hourly; 30min; €10.60), with the last return train at 9.25pm. Book tickets in advance at weekends. From Toledo's train station east of town, it's an uphill 20min walk to the central Plaza Zocódover (bus #5 or #61; €1.40).

By bus The bus station is on Avda de Castilla la Mancha in the modern part of the city, a 10min walk north of Plaza Zocódover via c/Armas. Buses depart from Madrid's Plaza Elíptica (every 30min between 6am and 10pm; 1hr–1hr 30min; €5.40), with the last bus back to the capital at 10.30pm.

Tourist office Plaza del Consistorio 1 (daily 10am–6pm; ☎925 254 030, ⓦtoledo-turismo.com). There's also a branch at the train station (daily 9.30am–3pm).

ACCOMMODATION AND EATING

Alqahira c/La Ciudad 7. It may be a stone's throw from the cathedral, but this friendly Arabic restaurant is a calm escape from the tourist crowds. The short menu is made up of dishes to share, including salads, kebabs and stuffed vine leaves, with nothing costing over €8.50. Try falafel washed down with home-made hibiscus juice. Daily 1–4pm & 8–11.30pm.

El Zoco Plaza Barrio Rey 7. Just off Plaza de Zocódover, *El Zoco* offers better value than the restaurants on its neighbouring square and serves the local speciality, *perdiz* (partridge). *Menú del día* from €10. Daily 1–4pm & 8–11.30pm.

La Posada de Manolo c/Sixto Ramón Parro 8 ☎ 925 282 250, ⓦlaposadademanolo.com. Well-kept hotel with comfortable en-suite rooms, all with a/c. The decor on each floors reflects one of Toledo's cultural influences: Islamic, Jewish and Christian. Free wi-fi. Double €68

CUENCA

Sitting between the Río Huécar and the Río Júcar gorges, **CUENCA** is enchanting. With its winding, narrow streets, the compact Old Town clusters on a hill, the land falling away on both sides and affording expansive views of the valleys below.

WHAT TO SEE AND DO

Cuenca's *pièce de résistance* is its sixteenth-century **casas colgadas** (hanging houses) that cling precariously to the cliff above Río Huécar, best viewed from the pedestrian Puente de San Pablo bridge that spans the gorge below. The best views of the gorge itself are from the *mirador* at the top of the main street. The sites below are all close to each other in the Old Town.

Museo de Arte Abstracto Español

One of the hanging houses contains the superb **Museo de Arte Abstracto Español** (Tues–Sat 11am–2pm & 4–6pm, until 8pm Sat, Sun 11am–2.30pm; €3; ⓦmarch.es), which is worth visiting even if abstract art is not your thing. The collection includes the delicate *Jardín Seco* by Fernando Zóbel and Manuel Rivera's sinister wire-mesh-and-paint *Metamorfosis*.

Museo Provincial de Cuenca

On c/del Obispo Valero 6, the absorbing **Museo Provincial de Cuenca** (Tues–Sat 10am–2pm & 4–7pm, Sun 11am–2pm; €1.20, free Sat & Sun) has well-displayed archeological exhibits spanning the town's history from the Bronze Age to the eighteenth century. Highlights include an extensive Roman collection and a large hoard of gold coins, uncovered in 2010.

The Catedral
The mostly Gothic **Catedral** (daily 9am–2pm & 4–7pm; €3), built on the base of a former mosque, dominates the main square and features some splendid stained-glass windows.

ARRIVAL AND INFORMATION

By train Slow trains for Madrid use the station on central c/Mariano Catalina, a block from the bus station. High-speed trains arrive at the AVE station 3km outside of Cuenca; the #12 bus connects it to the town's bus station (every 15min; €1.20).
Destinations Madrid (6 daily; 1hr 10min–3hr 30min); Valencia (6 daily; 1hr 15min–4hr).
By bus The bus station is on c/Fermín Caballero, a 10min walk from Cuenca's Old Town.
Destinations Madrid (8 daily; 2hr 10min–2hr 30min); Toledo (1 daily; 2hr–3hr 20min).
Tourist office Plaza Mayor (Mon–Sat 10am–2pm & 5–7pm, Sun 9am–2.30pm; shorter hours in winter; ☎ 969 176 100, ⌨ turismocuenca.com). Pick up a free booklet here, *Paseos por Cuenca*, which details picturesque walks starting from the Old Town.

ACCOMMODATION, EATING AND DRINKING

Bar Clásicos c/Severo Catalina 5. Little bar serving good-value lunch menus (€10). Arrive early to grab a table on the terrace overlooking the Río Júcar. Daily 1–4pm & 8–11.30pm.
La Bodeguita de Basilio c/Fray Luís de León 3. One of the town's best watering holes, this place is ideal for those on a budget – each drink (around €3) comes with a sizeable free tapa. Daily 1–4pm & 8–11.30pm.
Posada de San Julián c/de las Torres 1 ☎ 969 211 704. At the foot of the hill leading up into the Old Town, this comfortable place has simple rooms with their own toilets (but shared showers), wi-fi access and a popular restaurant on the ground floor. Double €38

Extremadura

The harsh environment of **Extremadura**, west of Madrid, is known as the "cradle of the conquistadors". Remote before and forgotten since, the area enjoyed a

brief golden age when the conquerors of the Americas returned with their gold to live in a flourish of splendour. **Cáceres** preserves an entire town built with conquistador wealth, the streets crowded with the ornate mansions of returning empire-builders, as does **Trujillo**, the birthplace of Francisco Pizarro. An even more ancient past is tangible in the wonders of **Mérida**, the most completely preserved Roman city in Spain. The province attracts fewer tourists in June and July, as temperatures get unbearably hot.

TRUJILLO
Little **TRUJILLO** is the birthplace of key figures who shaped the fate of the New World; much of the town's wealth is a direct result of the conquerors' plunders.

WHAT TO SEE AND DO

The town, a charming maze of russet-coloured houses and mansions topped with storks' nests, has at its heart the large, pedestrianized Plaza Mayor, just beneath the fortress walls of the Old Town and overlooked by a statue of Francisco Pizarro. In the southwestern corner of the plaza stands the elaborate **Palacio de la Conquista**, built for Hernando Pizarro, the brother of Francisco Pizarro – the swineherd turned conqueror of Peru – and his wife, the daughter of Francisco's union with Inés, his Incan consort; their carved images are on the corner. Across the plaza is the **Iglesia de San Martín** (Mon–Sat 10am–2pm & 4–7pm, Sun 10am–12.30pm; €1.40), which contains the family tombs of Francisco de Orellana, the first European to sail down the Amazon. West of the plaza is the **Palacio Juan Pizarro Orellana**, decorated with the coats of arms of the town's two most powerful families. In the Old Town uphill, encased within the crumbling medieval walls, head for the **Casa Museo Pizarro** (Mon–Sat 10am–2pm & 4–7pm; summer 5–8pm; €1.40), a sixteenth-century house with exhibits covering the history of the Pizarro family and the conquest of the Americas. Nearby is the

32

Gothic **Iglesia Santa María Mayor** (Mon–Sat 10am–2pm & 4–7pm; €1.40); from its Romanesque tower, you get all-encompassing views of the town, surrounded by arid plains. There's an even better view from the restored tenth-century Moorish **castle** (daily 10am–2pm & 4–7pm; summer 5–8pm; €1.40).

ARRIVAL AND INFORMATION

By bus The station is in the Lower Town, 5min walk from the Plaza Mayor.

Destinations Cáceres (8 daily; 40min); Madrid (up to 12 daily; 3–4hr); Mérida (3–4 daily; 1hr 15min).

Tourist office Plaza Mayor (daily 10am–2pm & 4.30–7.30pm; ☎927 322 677, ⓦturismotrujillo.com). Sells discounted combined tickets (€4.70–5.30) for Trujillo's top attractions.

ACCOMMODATION AND EATING

El Burladero Plaza Mayor 7. A large selection of tapas on offer, including excellent cured meats. Wash it down with some local wine. Daily 1–11.30pm.

Emilia Plaza del Campillo. Good-value restaurant serving *extremeño* specialities, such as *migas* (breadcrumbs fried with chorizo), served as part of the lunchtime menú del *día* (€9.60); an evening three-course set menu costs €18. Daily 1–4pm & 9–11.30pm.

Pensión Plaza Mayor Plaza Mayor ☎927 322 313, ⓦtrujilloplazamayor.com. Light, bright rooms with wi-fi access, superbly located on the Plaza Mayor. Double €45

CÁCERES

Old **CÁCERES** was built largely on the plunders of the New World and is home to the University of Extremadura. The Ciudad Monumental – a maze of tiny, winding streets, lined with immaculate historical buildings – is enclosed by medieval stone walls, with storks nesting on every rooftop.

WHAT TO SEE AND DO

Almost every building in the **Plaza Mayor** is magnificent, featuring ancient walls pierced by the low **Arco de la Estrella**, the **Torre del Horno**, one of the best-preserved Moorish mud-brick structures in Spain, and the **Torre del Bujaco** – whose foundations date back to Roman times and which you can climb for a great view of the city (Mon–Sat 10am–2pm &

5.30–8.30pm, Sun 10am–2pm; €2.50). Another must-see is the **Museo de Cáceres** (Tues–Sat 9am–2.30pm & 5–8pm, Sun 10.15am–2.30pm; EU citizens free, non-EU €1.20), on the Plaza de las Veletas, which has jewellery, statuary, national costume and fine arts sections and whose highlight is the *aljibe* (cistern) of the original Moorish Alcázar, with rooms of wonderful horseshoe arches. The **Casa de Toledo-Montezuma** lies through the Estrella gate, and was where a follower of Cortés brought back a daughter of the Aztec emperor as his bride. Near the Plaza de San Jorge is the *judería* (former Jewish quarter) – narrow lanes of whitewashed houses with window boxes of bright flowers. On c/Cuesta del Marqués 4, you'll find the **Museo Yusuf Al Burch**, a traditionally decorated Moorish house (Tues–Sun 10am–2pm & 6–8pm; €1.50) complete with a harem and an original water cistern.

ARRIVAL AND DEPARTURE

By train The station is 3km out of town. Bus #L1 runs every 15min to central Plaza de San Juan, near the Plaza Mayor.

Destinations Madrid (5 daily; 4hr); Mérida (5 daily; 1hr).

By bus The station faces the railway station across the Carretera Sevilla.

Destinations Madrid (7 daily; 3hr 40min–5hr); Salamanca (4 daily; 3hr 30min); Seville (8 daily; 4hr); Trujillo (6 daily; 40min).

INFORMATION

Tourist office Plaza Mayor 1 (Mon–Fri 9am–2pm & 4–6pm, summer 8am–3pm, Sat & Sun 10am–2pm year-round; ☎927 010 834, ⓦturismo.ayto-caceres.es).

ACCOMMODATION

Albergue Las Veletas c/Margallo 36 ☎927 211 210. Bright, spacious dorms and rooms with modern furnishings and a/c. Friendly staff make it popular with groups of young Spaniards. Breakfast available for €3.50. Dorm €19, double €45

Hostal Goya Plaza Mayor 11 ☎927 247 482. Simple, old-fashioned en-suite rooms with a/c. In a prime location: you pay €10 extra for a view of Plaza Mayor. Double €48

EATING AND DRINKING

Babel c/de Luís Sergios Sánchez 7. Arty café-bar where you can sip a coffee by day or a cocktail by night, with occasional art exhibitions. Daily 1–4pm & 8–11.30pm.

El Asador c/Moret 34. Moderately priced restaurant and tapas bar serving dishes from Extremadura. Try the €10 roast chicken. Daily 1–4pm & 8–11.30pm.

Mesón Ibérico Plaza San Juan 10. Traditional restaurant serving local specialities. Try the excellent hams and cheeses, or the *conejo al ajillo* (rabbit in garlic sauce). *Menú del día* €12.50. Daily 1–4pm & 8–11.30pm.

MÉRIDA

MÉRIDA, 70km south of Cáceres, contains one of Europe's most remarkable concentrations of Roman monuments, including two impressive aqueducts.

WHAT TO SEE AND DO

The beautiful **Teatro Romano** and **Anfiteatro** were gifts to the city from Marcus Agrippa in around 15 BC. The stage is in a particularly good state of repair, and in July and August it's the scene for a season of classical plays (ⓦfestivaldemerida.es; tickets from €12). In its day, up to fifteen thousand people would gather in the adjacent amphitheatre to watch gladiatorial combats and wild animal fights. By the theatre's entrance is the superb **Museo Nacional de Arte Romano** (April–Sept Tues–Sat 9.30am–8.30pm & Sun 10am–3pm; Oct–March Tues–Sat 9.30am–6.30pm & Sun 10am–3pm; €3, free Sat pm, Sun am and for EU students), with an impressive collection including portrait statues of Augustus, Tiberius and Drusus, plus some glorious mosaics, coins and other Roman artefacts. Further south, behind the Plaza de Toros, is the **Casa de Mitreo** – the remains of a Roman villa with an impressive mosaic. To the east of town you'll find the outline of the **Circo Romano**, which accommodated up to 30,000 people during chariot races. Also worth seeing is the magnificent **Puente Romano**, the pedestrian Roman bridge across the Río Guadiana on the city's west side – 60 arches long, and defended by an enormous Moorish **Alcazaba fortress**, built in 835 AD.

An **Entrada Conjunta** (combined ticket; €12) gives access to all six archeological sites (check at tourist office for latest timetables).

ARRIVAL AND DEPARTURE

By train The station is a 10min walk along c/Mártir Santa Eulalia from the town centre.

Destinations Cáceres (4 daily; 1hr); Madrid (4 daily; 4hr 30min–5hr 30min).

By bus Mérida's bus station is on Avda de la Libertad, a 15min walk across the Lusitania bridge or a short bus ride (bus #4 or #6) to the city centre.

Destinations Madrid (8 daily; 4hr 15min); Salamanca (5 daily; 4hr 10min–5hr); Seville (5 daily; 2hr 15min –2hr 45min).

INFORMATION

Tourist office Paseo Sáenz de Buruaga (daily 9.30am–2pm & 4.30–7.30pm; ☏924 330 722, ⓦturismomerida.org).

ACCOMMODATION

El Flor de Al-Andalus Avda Extremadura 6 ☏924 313 356, ⓦlaflordeal-andalus.es. Guesthouse with rooms decorated in Moorish style and scrupulously clean private bathrooms. Close to the train station and main attractions. Double €52

Hostal El Alfarero c/Sagasta 40 ☏924 303 183, ⓦhostalalfarero.com. The pick of the budget options in the centre – its tastefully decorated en suites come with TV and a/c. Enjoy good-quality local cuisine at the *Mesón El Alfarero* next door. Double €50

EATING AND DRINKING

All the below are open daily 1–4pm & 8–11.30pm.

Casa Nano c/Castelar 3. Friendly restaurant offering well-priced set menus (from €12) of local specialities, including lamb with plums.

Convivium c/de Sagasta 21. Thriving tapas bar specializing in *tortillinas* (mini potato omelettes) with fillings as varied as aubergine, prawns and chorizo. The *tortillina*, gazpacho and drink combo is a steal at only €3.

Mesón El Yantar Avda José Álvarez Saez de Buruaga 12. Snack on the best hams of the region, sample local *extremeño* dishes, or raid the shop for gourmet meats and cheeses to take home.

Castilla y León

The foundations of modern Spain were laid in the kingdom of **Castilla y León**, west and north of Madrid. A land of frontier fortresses – the *castillos* from which it takes its name – it became the most powerful and centralizing force of the Reconquest. The monarchs of this

32

triumphant and expansionist age were enthusiastic patrons of the arts, endowing their cities with superlative monuments above which, quite literally, tower the great Gothic cathedrals of **Salamanca** and **León**.

SALAMANCA

SALAMANCA is home to arguably the oldest and what was once the most prestigious university in Europe. It's a small place, but with many golden sandstone monuments and an attractive Plaza Mayor. As if that weren't enough, Salamanca's student population ensures their town is lively at night during term time.

WHAT TO SEE AND DO

For a postcard-worthy view of Salamanca, cross the city's oldest surviving monument, the much-restored, 400m-long **Puente Romano** (Roman Bridge) at the southern end of the Old Town. Then start your exploration proper at the grand **Plaza Mayor**, its centre enclosed by a four-storey refined Baroque building decorated with iron balconies and medallion portraits, the restrained elegance of the designs heightened by the changing position of the sun. Be sure to wander Salamanca's streets by night, when the glorious architecture is subtly lit by street lights; the pedestrian Calle de la Compañía has the best views.

Casa de las Conchas and the Universidad

The celebrated fifteenth-century **Casa de las Conchas** at c/Compañía 2 (Mon–Fri 9am–9pm, Sat 9am–2pm & 4–7pm, Sun 10am–2pm & 4–7pm; free), or House of Shells, is so called because its facades are decorated with rows of carved scallop shells, symbol of the pilgrimage to Santiago de Compostela. It now houses a library. From here, c/Libreros leads to the **Patio de las Escuelas Menores** and the Renaissance entrance to the **Universidad** (Mon–Sat 10am–7pm, Sun 10am–1pm; €10). The ultimate achievement of Plateresque art, a Spanish style characterized by ornate decoration, this reflects the tremendous reputation of

Salamanca in the early sixteenth century, when it was Europe's greatest university with the most important astronomy department in the world, consulted by Columbus before he set off on his sea voyage. Spotting the legendary "*rana de suerte*" (lucky frog) on its intricately sculpted facade allegedly brings you a year of good luck (spoiler: look closely at the skulls on the right column). The university's highlight is its incredible **library**, with its carved wooden ceiling and a collection of around 2800 manuscripts, a contrast to the rather plain lecture theatres also open to visitors.

The cathedrals

Sumptuous and intricate, the late Gothic **Catedral Nueva** (daily 9am–8pm) was begun in 1512, and acted as a buttress for the Catedral Vieja, which was in danger of collapsing. Entry to the **Catedral Vieja** (daily 10am–7.30pm; €4.75) is inside the Catedral Nueva. Tiny by comparison and a stylistic hotch-potch of Romanesque and Gothic, its most striking feature is the fifteenth-century Renaissance altarpiece, its 54 tablets depicting the life of Christ. As you look at the Catedral Nueva from the Plaza de Anaya, try to spot the ice-cream cone and the astronaut, carved into the Puerta de Ramos during the last restoration. Inside the cathedral, you will find yourself dwarfed by its monolithic proportions. If time and money are short, skip the Catedral Vieja and head straight for the **Ieronimus exhibition** (entrance from the Plaza de Juan XXIII, at the southwestern corner of the Catedral Nueva; daily 10am–7.15pm; €3.75). A visit affords views of both the old and new cathedrals and excellent views over Old Salamanca, plus history and art exhibitions hidden in a maze of little rooms.

The convents

The **Convento de San Esteban** (daily 10am–2pm & 4–8pm, closed Sun pm and Mon & Tues am; €3) is a short walk down c/Tostado from the Plaza de Anaya. Although the Gothic-Renaissance cloisters here are magnificent, those at the **Convento de las Dueñas** are even more beautiful (Mon–Sat 10.30am–12.45pm

32

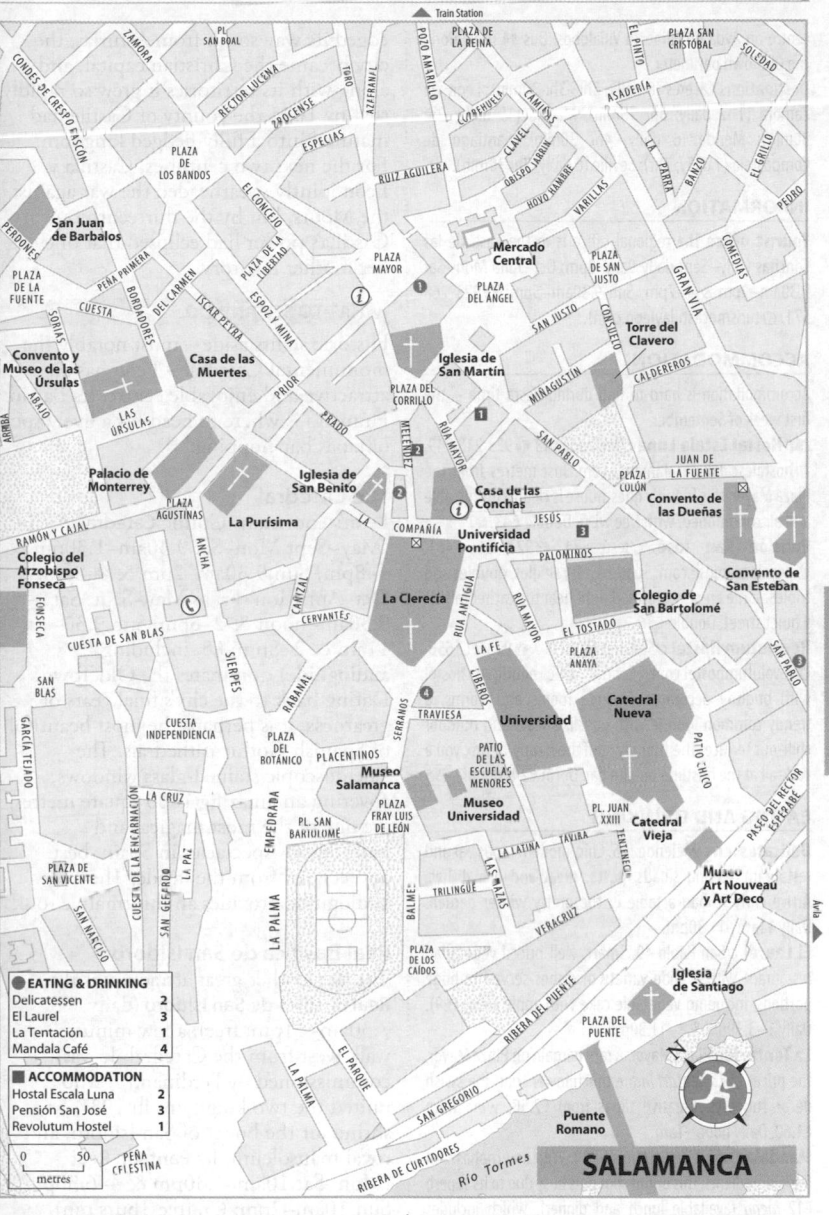

SALAMANCA

● **EATING & DRINKING**
Delicatessen	2
El Laurel	3
La Tentación	1
Mandala Café	4

■ **ACCOMMODATION**
Hostal Escala Luna	2
Pensión San José	3
Revolutum Hostel	1

0 ———— 50
metres

32

& 4.30–7.30pm; €2). Built on an irregular pentagonal plan, its upper-storey capitals are wildly carved with writhing demons and human skulls.

ARRIVAL AND DEPARTURE

By train On foot, the main Salamanca station is 15min northeast of the centre. Bus #11 runs to the historical centre. The Salamanca–Alamedilla stop is more central; a 10min walk to Plaza Mayor down Gran Vía.

Destinations Barcelona (1 daily; 8hr 30min); Bilbao (3 daily; 4hr 55min–6hr 18min); Madrid (8 daily via Ávila; 2hr 40min); San Sebastián (3 daily; 5hr 20min–6hr 20min).

By bus The station is a 10min walk northwest from the

centre on Avda de Filiberto Villalobos. Bus #4 runs along the Old Town perimeter.

Destinations Cáceres (8 daily; 3hr–3hr 30min); León via Zamora (1–2 daily; 3hr 15min); Madrid (15 daily; 2hr 30min); Mérida (6 daily; 4hr 30min); Santiago de Compostela (1 daily; 7hr); Seville (6 daily; 7hr 30min).

INFORMATION

Tourist office The regional office is in the Casa de las Conchas (July–Sept daily 9am–8pm; Oct–June Mon–Sat 9.30am–2pm & 4–7pm, Sun 9.30am–5pm; ☎923 268 571, ⊛turismocastillayleon.com).

ACCOMMODATION

Accommodation is hard to find during fiesta time – the first week of September.

★ **Hostal Escala Luna** c/Mélendez 13 ☎923 218 749, ⊛hostalescalalunasalamanca.com. Just metres from the Plaza Mayor, this friendly guesthouse is clean, comfortable and air conditioned, with free wi-fi. Double €43.50

Pensión San José c/Jesús 24 ☎923 265 461, ⊛pensionsanjose.com. Spotless, airy singles, doubles and triples, some en-suite, located right near the cathedrals on a quiet street. Double €36

Revolutum Hostel c/Sánchez Barbero 7 ☎923 217 656, ⊛revolutumhostel.com. Central, chic boutique hostel with brightly decorated en-suite rooms and dorms, a trendy common lounge with egg-like seats and outdoor chill-out terrace. The friendly staff are happy to mix you a cocktail at the bustling on-site bar. Dorm €24, double €55

EATING AND DRINKING

Delicatessen c/Mélendez 25. Chic, modern tapas bar and restaurant serving salads, pasta, meat and fish dishes. Arrive early to bag a table in the pretty winter garden. Daily 11am–11.30pm.

El Laurel c/San Pablo 49. Smart, well-priced vegetarian restaurant with a wide variety of dishes served in huge portions, including vegetable cake with apple sauce (€9). Daily 1–3.30pm & 8–11.30pm.

La Tentación Plaza Mayor. A rare bargain on Plaza Mayor, the prices at *La Tentación* are much lower than the swish decor suggests. Creative tapas from €2.50, wine from €1.60. Daily noon–1am.

Mandala Café c/de Serranos 9–11. With an emphasis on fresh ingredients, this bright spot gets busy due to its superb €12 *menú* (available lunch and dinner), which includes dishes like *arroz negro*, and a number of vegetarian choices – try the stuffed aubergine. Daily 1–4pm & 8–11pm.

LEÓN

The old *barrio* of **LEÓN** is steeped in history: in 914 AD, as the Reconquest

edged its way south from Asturias, the city became the Christian capital, and along with its territories it grew so rapidly that by 1035 the county of Castile had matured into a fully fledged kingdom. For the next two centuries, Castilla y León jointly spearheaded the war against the Moors, but by the thirteenth century Castilla's power had eclipsed that of even her mother territory.

WHAT TO SEE AND DO

Historic sights aside – most notably the monumental Catedral – León has an attractive and enjoyable centre. Its Barrio Húmedo is where to head for a lively spot of tapas bar-hopping.

The Catedral

León's enormous Gothic **Catedral** (May–Sept Mon–Sat 9.30am–1.30pm & 4–8pm, Sun 9.30am–2pm & 4–8pm; Oct–Apr Mon–Fri as May–Sept, Sat 9.30am–noon & 2–6pm, Sun 9.30–11am & 2–8pm; €5, including audioguide) dominates the Old Town. Dating back to the city's final years of greatness, it is perhaps the most beautiful of Spanish Gothic cathedrals. The kaleidoscopic stained-glass windows, covering an amazing 1800 square metres, are one of the most magical and harmonious spectacles in Spain, best appreciated from the inside. The audioguide provides an informative tour.

Real Basílica de San Isidoro

The city's other great attraction is the **Real Basílica de San Isidoro** (daily 7.30am–11pm; free), a few minutes' walk west from the Catedral. It was commissioned by Ferdinand I, who united the two kingdoms in 1037, as a shrine for the bones of San Isidoro, and royal mausoleum. Its **Panteón Real** (Mon–Sat 10am–1.30pm & 4–6.30pm, Sun 10am–2pm; €5, free Thurs pm), a pair of twelfth-century, crypt-like chambers, features some of the most imaginative and impressive paintings of Romanesque art, as well as a mummified finger of San Isidoro. It once contained the bones of eleven kings and twelve queens, but now lies empty, the French troops having destroyed the graves during the Napoleonic wars.

Convento de San Marcos

The opulent **Convento de San Marcos**, on the Plaza de San Marcos west of the city's old pedestrianized quarter, was built in 1168 for the Knights of Santiago, one of several chivalric orders founded in the twelfth century to lead the Reconquest. It served as a resting point for weary pilgrims on their way to Santiago de Compostela, and is now part of a sumptuous *Parador* hotel, though non-guests can peek inside at the beautiful cloisters. The church's sacristy houses the small **Museo de León** (Tues–Sat 10am–2pm & 4–7pm, Sun 10am–2pm; €0.60), containing some beautiful statuary and portraits of the Knights of Santiago.

Museo de Arte Contemporaneo (MUSAC)

A short walk north of the Monasterio San Marcos is the award-winning **Museo de Arte Contemporaneo** (Tues–Fri 11am–2pm & 5–8pm, Sat & Sun 11am–3pm & 5–9pm; €5, free Sun pm; ⓦmusac.es), its exterior covered with 37 shades of glass, known for its excellent, thought-provoking temporary exhibitions by contemporary artists, which include Spanish and international photography, sculpture and video installations.

ARRIVAL AND DEPARTURE

By train The train station is at the end of Avda de Palencia across the bridge from the city centre. The *casco antiguo* (old city) is a 10min walk along Avda de Ordoño II.
Destinations Barcelona (3 daily; 8hr–8hr 40min); Bilbao (1 daily; 4hr 50min); Madrid (10 daily; 2hr 50min–4hr 45min); San Sebastián (1 daily; 5hr); Santiago de Compostela (1 daily; 5hr 40min).
By bus The bus station is near the train station on Paseo Ingeniero Saenz de Miera.
Destinations Cáceres (3 daily; 6hr 15min); Madrid (10 daily; 3hr 30min–4hr); Santander (7 daily; 5hr–5hr 40min); Seville (3 daily; 10hr 30min); Zaragoza (3 daily; 6hr 15min–9hr 15min).

INFORMATION

Tourist office Pl. de la Regla 2 (Mon–Sat 9.30am–2pm & 4–7pm, Sun 9.30am–5pm; ☎987 237 082,

★ TREAT YOURSELF

Real Colegiata de San Isidoro Plaza de Santo Martino 5 ☎987 075 088, ⓦhotelrealcolegiata.es. Rest your weary bones in the super-comfortable beds at this hotel, stunningly located in the Colegiata section of the Real Basílica de San Isidoro church complex (see opposite). Set around a beautiful cloister, it's a surprisingly affordable oasis of luxury if you book out-of-season deals. Doubles from **€70**.

ⓦ turismocastillayleon.com). There's another branch at Pl. San Marco (same hours) which offers cheap bike rental (from €3 per half day).

ACCOMMODATION

Hostal San Martín Plaza Torres de Omaña 1, 2º ☎987 815 187, ⓦsanmartinhostales.com. Plain, bright rooms (some en-suite) and a warm welcome near Barrio Húmedo. Double **€31**
Pensión La Torre de San Isidoro c/La Torre 3, 1º ☎987 225 594, ⓦlahiguera.net/torresanisidoro. Spacious, good-quality rooms with private bathrooms. The friendly owner offers laundry service and free wi-fi. Double **€41**

EATING AND DRINKING

Free tapas is the name of the game in the Barrio Húmedo around Plaza San Martín.
Bar Altar c/Platerías 2. Lively, friendly tapas bar a few metres from the Plaza Mayor with a range of free tapas plus cheap *montaditos* (small sandwiches). Daily 1–11.30pm.
El Llar Plaza San Martín 9. Stalwart Leónese bar with dark wood interior and terracotta walls. The *patatas allioli* (potatoes with garlic mayonnaise) – free with every drink – are brilliant. Daily 1–4pm & 7.30pm–1am.
Molly Malone c/Cardiles 2. Popular in equal measure with locals and visitors, this lively Irish pub has Guinness on tap and nightly live music. Daily 1–11.30pm.
Parilla Louzao c/Juan Madrazo 4. Smart but moderately priced restaurant serving local meat dishes in large portions. Try the pork chops (€25 to share). Daily 1–4pm & 8–11.30pm.

Andalucía

The southern region of **Andalucía**, the parched, passionate home of **flamenco** and the **bullfight**, is all tradition and fierce

32

pride. Evidence of the **Moors'** sophistication remains visible to this day in **Córdoba**, in **Seville**, and, particularly, in **Granada's Alhambra**. Extending to either side of **Málaga** is the **Costa del Sol**, Europe's most developed resort area, but you can find unspoiled beaches even there, and along the **Costa de la Luz**, on the way to **Cádiz**, one of Spain's oldest cities. Andalucía is also where Europe stops and Africa begins: from **Tarifa**, a kite-surfer and windsurfer hub on Europe's most southerly tip, that great continent appears almost close enough to touch.

SEVILLE (SEVILLA)

SEVILLE (Sevilla) is the great city of the Spanish south, one of the earliest Moorish conquests (in 712 AD) and, as part of the Caliphate of Córdoba, the second city of al-Andalus. Under the Almohad dynasty, Seville became the capital of the last real Moorish empire in Spain from 1170 until 1212 before being conquered by Fernando III in 1248. Its monopoly on trade with the New World meant the city grew in wealth and influence; centuries on, it remains one of the most prosperous and beautiful of Spain's cities. Illustrious history aside, it is Seville's vitality that remains the great attraction, expressed on a grand scale at the city's two great festivals: **Semana Santa**, the week before Easter, and the **Feria de Abril**, a week at the end of April. While thoroughly modern, the soul of the city lies in its historic latticework of narrow streets, patios and plazas, where minarets jostle for space among cupolas and palms, and in its atmospheric flamenco bars.

WHAT TO SEE AND DO

Seville's three architectural gems – the Alcázar, Catedral and La Giralda – occupy the southern corner of the popular *barrio* of Santa Cruz.

La Giralda and the Catedral

Topped with four copper spheres, the 90m-tall **La Giralda** (Mon–Sat 11am–5pm, Sun 2.30–6.30pm; €8), erected by the Almohads between 1184 and 1198, still dominates the skyline today, and you can ascend the former minaret for a remarkable view of the city. The Giralda was so venerated by the Moors that they wanted to destroy it before the Christian conquest of the city. Instead, in 1402 it became the bell tower of the **Catedral**, the world's largest Gothic church, and third-largest cathedral after St Peter's and St Paul's. Its centre is dominated by a vast Gothic *retablo* composed of 45 carved scenes from the life of Christ, making up the largest altarpiece in the world. The cathedral is also the final resting place of Christopher Columbus. On your way out, linger inside the Patio de los Naranjas – the courtyard studded with 66 orange trees where ritual ablutions would have been performed before entering the mosque.

The Alcázar

Across Plaza del Triunfo from the cathedral lies the **Alcázar** (April–Sept daily 9.30am–7pm; Oct–March Tues–Sat

---

SEMANA SANTA SURVIVAL

Semana Santa (Holy Week) is the most exciting time to be in Seville, with its eerie processions of robed and hooded faithful from different *hermanidades* (brotherhoods). To navigate your way around the city during this frenetic time, here are some tips:
• Do all your sightseeing in the mornings, since most processions take place in the afternoons and evenings.
• Find out the day's procession routes and make sure you know how to get back to where you're staying.
• Stock up on water and snacks, as many central shops will be closed.
• To get past a procession, shuffle along the side, NOT down the middle.
• Don't sit on the wooden chairs along the procession routes; the city's wealthiest residents will have paid up to €800 for each one.
• Splurge on a balcony space (€60) for an unobstructed view.

9.30am–5pm, Sun 9.30am–1.30pm; €8.75; ⊕alcazarsevilla.org), a site that rulers of Seville have occupied from the time of the Romans. Rebuilt and added to numerous times, under the Almohad dynasty, the complex was turned into an enormous citadel, forming the heart of the town's fortifications. Parts of the walls survive, but the palace was rebuilt in the Christian period by Pedro the Cruel (1350–69). His works, some of the best surviving examples of Mudéjar architecture, form the nucleus of the Alcázar today. The perfectly proportioned patios, beautiful tile work, gilded ceilings, tranquil gardens and calligraphy carved into the palace walls – reminiscent of Granada's Palacios Nazaríes – encourage wandering the complex for hours.

Torre del Oro
By the river, west of the Catedral, stands the twelve-sided **Torre del Oro** (Mon–Fri 9.30am–6.45pm, Sat & Sun 10.30am–6.45pm; €3), built in 1220 as part of the Alcázar fortifications and named after the gold brought back to Seville from the Americas and stored here. There are excellent views of the city from the top and the nautical museum inside features models of ships from the Spanish Armada, early diving equipment and seafarers' maps.

Plaza de Toros de la Maestranza
Even if you're not planning on attending a *corrida* (see box, p.1029), it's worth taking a tour of Seville's venerable **bullring** (Paseo de Cristóbal Colón 12; half-hourly tours 9am–7pm, until 3pm on bullfight days; €6.50; ⊕real maestranza.com) – one of the oldest, and certainly one of the most beautiful, in Spain. The tour explains the role of the bullfighting team, while the museum features costumes of famous bullfighters and *corrida*-related paintings and sketches by Goya, a bullfighting aficionado.

The Museo de Bellas Artes
There's superb art at the **Museo de Bellas Artes** on Plaza del Museo (Tues–Sat 10am–8.30pm, Sun 10am–5pm; €1.50, free for EU citizens), housed in a beautiful former convent. Highlights include paintings by Murillo, as well as Zurbarán's *Carthusian Monks at Supper* and El Greco's portrait of his son.

Metropol Parasol
Designed by German architect Jürgen Mayer H., the 2011 **Metropol Parasol** dominates Plaza de la Encarnación. Allegedly the largest wooden building in the world, it resembles a cluster of giant mushrooms. The Roman ruins discovered during its construction are beautifully presented under glass (daily 11am–2pm & 3–8pm; €2) and you can take the lift (€1.30) up to Level 2 where a panoramic walkway winds its way about the structure, affording unique views of the city.

Triana
Across the river lies the **Triana** *barrio* that was once home to the city's gypsy community. At Triana's northern edge is **La Cartuja** (Tues–Sat 11am–9pm, Sun 11am–3pm; €3), a fourteenth-century former Carthusian monastery, where Columbus allegedly planned his early voyages – home to the **Centro Alnaluz de Arte Contemporáneo** (⊕caac.es), which hosts edgy painting, sculpture and photography exhibitions by international and local artists.

Isla Mágica
Just north of the Triana lies an amusement park with a New World theme (June–Aug daily 11am–11pm, fewer days in low season: Nov–March closed; €32; ⊕islamagica.es) and a selection of adrenaline-charged rides. Highlights include the "Anaconda", the "Wet'n'Wild" ride with almost vertical drops and the "Jaguar" – a stomach-churning roller coaster with 360-degree turns.

ARRIVAL AND DEPARTURE
By plane Los Amarillos (⊕losamarillos.es) shuttle bus runs every 30min from Seville's domestic and international Aeropuerto San Pablo to Avda del Cid and the train station (5.45am–12.45am; 30min; €2.50).
By train Estación Santa Justa is north of the centre, on Avda Kansas City; bus #C1 (€1) connects it to the centre and to the San Sebastián bus station.

32

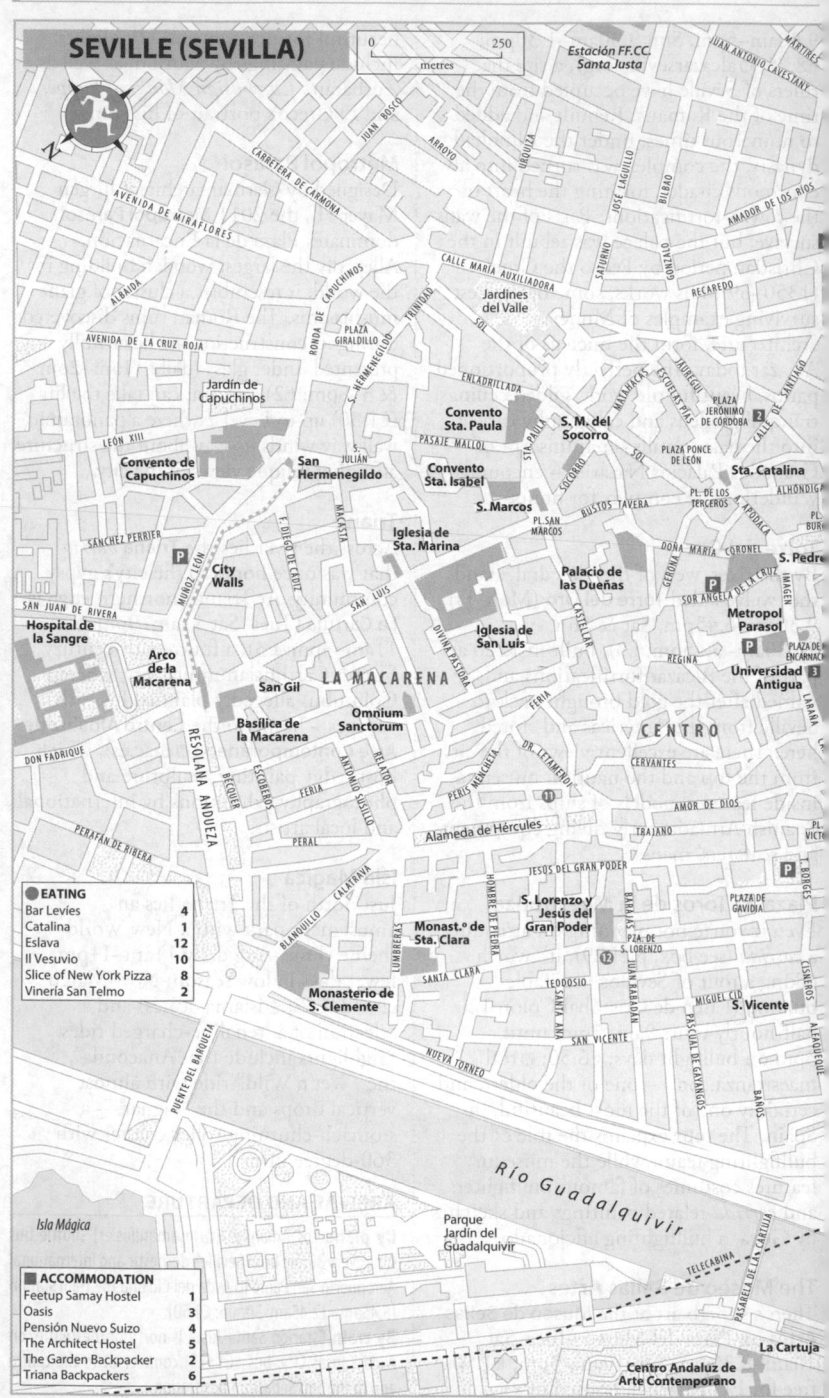

SEVILLE (SEVILLA)

0 — 250
metres

Estación FF.CC. Santa Justa

Jardines del Valle

Convento Sta. Paula

S. M. del Socorro

Convento Sta. Isabel

S. Marcos

San Hermenegildo

Jardín de Capuchinos

Convento de Capuchinos

Sta. Catalina

Iglesia de Sta. Marina

Palacio de las Dueñas

S. Pedro

Metropol Parasol

Universidad Antigua

Iglesia de San Luis

Hospital de la Sangre

City Walls

Arco de la Macarena

San Gil

Basílica de la Macarena

Omnium Sanctorum

LA MACARENA

CENTRO

Alameda de Hércules

Monast.º de Sta. Clara

S. Lorenzo y Jesús del Gran Poder

Monasterio de S. Clemente

S. Vicente

Isla Mágica

Parque Jardín del Guadalquivir

Río Guadalquivir

La Cartuja

Centro Andaluz de Arte Contemporáno

EATING

Bar Levíes	4
Catalina	1
Eslava	12
Il Vesuvio	10
Slice of New York Pizza	8
Vinería San Telmo	2

ACCOMMODATION

Feetup Samay Hostel	1
Oasis	3
Pensión Nuevo Suizo	4
The Architect Hostel	5
The Garden Backpacker	2
Triana Backpackers	6

32

SAN BERNARDO

32

Jerez & Cádiz

Remedios

Extremadura

DRINKING, NIGHTLIFE & ENTERTAINMENT

Bar Garlochí	7
Bodega Santa Cruz	6
Casa Anselma	13
Casa de la Memoria de Al Andalus	5
Fun Club	11
La Carbonería	3
P Flaherty Irish Pub	9

Destinations Almería (4 daily; 5hr 30min–5hr 45min); Barcelona (7 daily; 5hr–11hr 30min); Cádiz (15 daily; 1hr 30min–2hr); Córdoba (every 30min 6.50am–9.35pm; 40min–1hr 20min); Granada (4 daily; 3hr); Madrid (17 daily; 2hr 30min–6hr 40min); Málaga (12 daily; 2hr–2hr 30min); Valencia (4 daily; 4hr–7hr 30min).

By bus The main bus station is at Plaza de Armas, but buses for destinations within Andalucía (plus Barcelona, Alicante and Valencia) leave from the more central terminal at Plaza de San Sebastián. Bus #C3 connects the two.

Destinations Almería (3 daily; 5hr 45min); Cáceres (5 daily; 4hr); Cádiz (11 daily; 1hr 45min); Córdoba (11 daily; 2hr); Granada (10 daily; 3hr 30min); Madrid (14 daily; 6hr); Málaga (12 daily; 2hr 45min); Mérida (10 daily; 3hr); Ronda (5 daily; 2hr 30min); Tarifa (3 daily; 3hr 30min).

INFORMATION

Tourist office Plaza del Triunfo (Mon–Fri 9am–7pm, Sat 10am–2pm & 3–7pm, Sun 10am–2pm; ☎ 954 210 005, ⓦ visitsevilla.es and ⓦ andalucia.org). Another useful website is ⓦ discoversevilla.com.

ACCOMMODATION

The most attractive area to stay is the maze-like Barrio Santa Cruz, near the Catedral. During Easter Week and the Feria de Abril, prices double; book several months in advance.

Feetup Samay Hostel Avda. Menéndez Pelayo 13 ☎ 955 100 160, ⓦ samayhostels.com. Top budget choice in a modern, marble-floored building with light, spacious and secure en-suite dorms, breakfast, and a large roof terrace. Dorm €12, double €47

Oasis c/Compañia 1 ☎ 954 293 777, ⓦ hostelsoasis.com. Fantastic backpacker favourite, with helpful staff and clean dorms on several floors festooned with greenery. Rooftop pool and excellent breakfast included. Great for nightly tapas bar crawls. Dorm €10.50, double €70

Pensión Nuevo Suizo c/Azofaifo 7 ☎ 954 229 147, ⓦ nuevosuizo.com. This friendly, creaky wooden house that's right in the heart of the action (particularly during Semana Santa) offers free breakfast and teas and coffees. Some rooms share bathrooms. Double €46

★ **The Architect Hostel** c/Joaquín Guichot 8, 1st floor ☎ 955 324 640, ⓦ thearchitectbackpacker.com. This relatively new hostel stands out thanks to its staff, who offer plenty of help and advice when you're in town. On top of that, the place is spotless, the beds comfortable and the location super-central. Dorm €12

The Garden Backpacker c/Santiago 19 ☎ 954 223 866, ⓦ thegardenbackpacker.com. With a tranquil back garden, sun-lounge area and bustling bar serving up free sangría, this ever-popular central hostel has tours (walking and tapas) organized daily. Dorm €13

Triana Backpackers c/Rodrigo de Triana 69 ☎ 954 459 960, ⓦ trianabackpackers.com. Friendly and sociable place

in the Triana, whose staff organize lots of guest events, such as a tapas night. Clean dorms inside the attractively tiled building have a/c – a godsend in summer. Dorm €15

EATING

There are numerous choices in the Barrio Santa Cruz, the streets around Plaza Nueva and Triana. Seville is also one of the great bastions of the tapa. Opening hours are daily 1–4pm & 8–11pm unless otherwise stated.

Bar Levíes c/San José 15. Packed at night with a young crowd, this informal bar serves large portions of regional tapas, plus pizza and beer. Try the *salmorejo* (thick, savoury gazpacho) or the *solomillo al whisky* (steak cooked in whisky). Tapas €2.50–5. Daily 7.30pm–midnight.

Catalina Paseo Catalina de Ribera 4. Vegetarians are welcome at this restaurant with an appealing outdoor terrace; the sumptuous aubergines with grilled goat's cheese is one of the house specials. Mains €9–14.

★ **Eslava** c/Eslava 3 ⓦ espacioeslava.com. The tatty furniture and paper tablecloths at this award-winning tapas bar do not detract from the tenderest beef in cheese sauce, the perfectly seared scallops, the *almejas* (clams) and more. Be prepared to wait for a table. Tapas from €3.75. Tues–Sat 12.30pm–midnight, Sun 12.30–4.30pm.

Il Vesuvio c/Sierpes 54. At this authentic Italian restaurant, choose from a short menu of home-made pasta and fish or steak mains, then finish off with a better-than-average tiramisu. Mains from €9.

Slice of New York Pizza c/Alemanes 13. This place's made-to-order pizza has met with the approval of visiting New Yorkers, particularly the veggie options. Order a whole pizza or a single gooey slice (from €3).

Vinería San Telmo Paseo Catalina de Ribera 4. This tapas bar with alfresco terrace has a wonderful signature dish – the *rascocielo* or "skyscraper" of smoked salmon, grilled aubergine, goat's cheese and tomatoes. Tapas €3.50.

DRINKING AND NIGHTLIFE

The Plaza Alfalfa area, north of the Catedral, is particularly lively at night. The other main area for nightlife, popular with tourists and Seville's gay population, is just across the river in Triana, on c/Betis. Opening hours are daily 1–4pm & 8–11pm unless otherwise stated.

Bar Garlochí c/Boteros 4. Weird and wonderful bar popular with *Sevillanos*, with a mock-Semana Santa theme and a sacrilegious house special – the Sangre de Cristo cocktail.

Bodega Santa Cruz c/Rodrigo Caro 1. Perpetually popular bar covered in bullfighting posters and serving inexpensive tapas (€2.30–3.20) – try the *pringá*, a meaty sandwich and local speciality.

Fun Club Alameda de Hércules 86 ⓦ funclubsevilla.com. A live music club that's most definitely fun; live bands play a mix of funk, jazz and Latino. Entry €5–7 on live music nights. Thurs–Sun 11.30pm–late.

BULLFIGHTING

The season starts with the Feria de Abril and continues until October, with most *corridas* held on Sunday evenings. Love it or hate it, Seville's bullring is probably the best in Spain, with only bullfighters who have "made it", such as El Cid and El Juli, fighting on its sands. Tickets from the Plaza de Toros de la Maestranza, Paseo de Colón 12 (☎ 902 5223 506), go from as little as €15 for a *sol* (sun-exposed) seat; more for *sombra* (shade).

P Flaherty Irish Pub c/Alemanes 7. Lively expat haunt next to the Catedral, with Guinness on tap, a wide selection of beers, good pub grub and sports on TV.

FLAMENCO

Flamenco music and dance goes on at dozens of places in the city. Head to one of the following bars, or go to c/ Rodrigo de Triana, the home of a handful of flamenco academies.

Casa Anselma c/Pagés de Corro 49. Thick with cigarette smoke and packed with local flamenco aficionados, all waiting for a spontaneous performance to break out. There's no sign; it's on the corner of c/Alfarería in the Triana neighbourhood. Mon–Sat from midnight.

Casa de la Memoria de Al Andalus c/Ximénez de Enciso 28 ☎ 954 560 670, ⓦ casadelamemoria.es. Fantastic daily performances at this intimate cultural centre (100 spaces daily) at 7.30/9/10.30pm, depending on the season. Book tickets in advance (€15).

La Carbonería c/Levíes 18. Tapas bar in an old coal merchant's building, with free flamenco performances at 11pm and midnight most nights.

DIRECTORY

Exchange There are numerous banks, ATMs and *cambios* along Avda de la Constitución in the centre, as well as at the train and bus stations.

Hospital Hospital Universitario Virgen Macarena, Avda Dr Fedriani 3 (☎ 950 080 000), has English-speaking doctors. For an ambulance, call ☎ 061.

Left luggage Coin-operated lockers at the train station. *Consignas* at both bus stations.

Post office Avda de la Constitución 32.

CÁDIZ

CÁDIZ is among the oldest settlements in Spain, founded about 1100 BC by the Phoenicians, and has long been one of the country's principal ports. In the eighteenth century it enjoyed a virtual monopoly on the Spanish–American trade in gold and silver. Central Cádiz, built on a peninsula island, entices with its grand open squares, narrow alleyways and high, turreted houses. It's also the spiritual home of flamenco, and has a tremendous atmosphere – slightly seedy, somewhat in decline, but still full of mystique. Cádiz's big party time is its annual **Carnaval**, complete with frenzied costumed revelry, normally held in February and early March.

WHAT TO SEE AND DO

With its winding alleys, backstreets and cafés, Cádiz is fascinating to wander around.

Torre Tavira

For 360-degree views of the city, climb the **Torre Tavira** at Marqués del Real Tesoro 10 (daily: May–Sept 10am–8pm; Oct–April 10am–6pm; €5; ⓦ torretavira .com), tallest of the city's 126 lookout towers – a legacy of the pirate age. The ticket price includes tours showcasing the *camera obscura* – a device that uses mirrors to zoom in on any part of the city and project a live image onto a flat surface inside the tower.

Catedral Nueva and Torre de Poniente

The huge, white, sea-facing **Catedral Nueva** (Mon–Sat 10am–6.30pm, Sun 1.30–6.30pm; €5, free Tues–Fri 7–8pm & Sun 11am–1pm) is a blend of High Baroque and Neoclassical styles as a result of it taking 116 years to build, decorated entirely in stone. Climb the adjacent **Torre de Poniente** (daily: mid-June to mid-Sept 10am–8pm; rest of year 10am–6pm; €5) for splendid views of the city.

Museo de Cádiz

The spacious, well-lit interior at the **Museo de Cádiz** on Plaza de Mina (Tues 2.30–8.30pm, Wed–Sat 9am–8.30pm, Sun 9.30am–2.30pm; €1.50, free for EU citizens) perfectly showcases the Phoenician marble sarcophagi, Roman statuary and other archeological treasures. Upstairs are masterpieces by Zurbarán

32

and Murillo – including the last altarpiece he painted before a fatal fall from the scaffolding.

Coastal walk and beaches

You can also enjoy a 4.5km **coastal walk** that runs along the outside of the Old Town, taking in two beautiful parks – the Alameda Apodaca, running along the Bay of Cádiz, and the large, sculpted Parque Genovés, home to numerous exotic plants. Cádiz also has two main **beaches**: the often-crowded little crescent Playa de la Caleta at its western end, complete with Castillo San Sebastian (Tues–Sun 11am–7.30pm; €2), and Playa de la Victoria's wide stretch of white sand (take bus #1 south along Avda del Puerto).

ARRIVAL AND DEPARTURE

By train The station is at the southeastern end of the Old Town, a 5min walk from the Plaza de San Juan de Dios.
Destinations Córdoba (3 daily; 3hr–3hr 30min); Madrid (10 daily; 4hr 20min–4hr 50min); Seville (15 daily; 1hr 30min–2hr).

By bus The bus station is opposite the train station.
Destinations Almería (1 daily at 3pm; 7hr); Granada (3 daily; 5hr); Málaga (3 daily; 4hr); Ronda (1–2 daily; 3hr); Seville (8 daily; 2hr); Tarifa (6 daily; 1hr 45min).

INFORMATION

Tourist office *Turismo municipal* office, Paseo de Canalejas (Mon–Fri 8.30am–6pm, Sat & Sun 9am–5pm; ☎ 956 241 001), and regional tourist office, Avda Ramón de Carranza 1 (Mon–Fri 9am–7.30pm, Sat & Sun 10am–2pm; ☎ 956 203 191).

ACCOMMODATION

Cadiz Inn Backpackers c/Botica 2 14 ☎ 956 262 309, ⊛ cadizbackpackers.es. A super-central location, helpful staff and sunny roof terrace for chilling out are some of the perks here. On the downside, the single bathroom generates queues, and the tiny double is overpriced. Dorm €18, double €50

Casa Caracol c/Suárez de Salazar 4 ☎ 956 261 166, ⊛ hostel-casacaracol.com. This chilled-out backpacker favourite has laidback staff, open-plan dorms, home cinema and a plethora of activities on offer, from yoga to salsa classes. You'll never lack for company during their rooftop parties. Dorm €17

Pensión España c/Marqués de Cádiz 9 ☎ 956 285 500, ⊛ pensionespana.com. This friendly, central guesthouse offers clean singles, doubles and triples, most with shared bathrooms. Double €40

EATING AND DRINKING

For drinks and seafood, head to c/Virgen de la Palma in the Barrio de la Viña, just east of Playa de la Caleta, or to Plaza de Las Flores. Opening hours are daily 1–4pm & 8–11pm unless otherwise stated.

El Aljibe c/Plocia 25. Trendy, stone-walled, wooden-beamed bar with some of Cadiz's most inventive tapas on the menu. Try the likes of squash and prawn lasagne, goat's cheese on nutty bread with blueberry sauce and baby squid in ink. Tapas €2.40–4.

Freiduría Las Flores Plaza de Las Flores. A Cádiz institution, this *freiduría* (fry shop) serves up large, cheap portions of all kinds of fish. Try the excellent *cazón adobo* (marinated shark in batter) or the *tortilla de camarónes* (shrimp patty). Tapas €1.60–3.40.

La Sidrería de El Populo c/Mesón 16. This tiny spot – all exposed stone and low lighting – specializes in Asturian cuisine, such as chicken cooked in cider, plus the flavourful tipple itself. The €7.50 "two tapas and a cider" deal is good value. Mon–Sat noon–11pm.

Taberna El Tío de la Tiza Plaza Tío de la Tiza s/n. *Bodega* with outdoor seating serving up excellent gazpacho, *salmorejo* and large helpings of cooked *gambas* (prawns). Mains from €7.

TARIFA

If there is one thing that defines tiny **TARIFA**, it is the prevailing, massively powerful wind, which has made the southernmost point in mainland Europe one of the world's most popular kitesurfing and windsurfing destinations. There's a good feel to the place, with its laid-back atmosphere and compact maze of narrow streets. Africa seems very close, too, and is easily accessible, via the daily ferry that runs to Tangier in Morocco (see box opposite).

WHAT TO SEE AND DO

There are two principal things to keep you occupied: making the most of the waves and the wind and going in search of whales.

Kitesurfing and windsurfing

The 10km white, sandy **beaches**, **Playa de los Lances** and **Ensenada de Valdevaqueros**, are the places for water-sports. You can book a course or rent equipment from a number of outfitters on c/Batalla del Salado, including Art of Kiting at no. 47 (☎ 605 031 880, ⊛ artofsurfing.com) and the Wave Bandits Kite School at c/Braille 22 (☎619 471 735, ⓦwavebandits.com). Competition keeps prices down, with a four-hour kitesurfing "baptism" costing €75.

Whale-watching

The Strait of Gibraltar is an excellent place for spotting killer whales, pilot whales, sperm whales and dolphins. Several different operators run daily two-hour **whale-watching** boat **trips**, including Firmm at c/Pedro Cortéz 4 (April–Oct; €30; ☎956 627 008, ⓦfirmm.org), dedicated to research and conservation of the local population of marine mammals, and Whalewatch Tarifa at Avda de la Constitución 6 (☎956 627 013, ⓦwhalewatchtarifa.net), a non-profit conservation association.

ARRIVAL AND DEPARTURE

By bus Comes (☎956 684 038, ⓦtgcomes.es) buses arrive at the bus station at Batalla del Salado 13. The town centre is a 10min walk south.

Destinations Algeciras (6 daily; 30min); Cádiz (5 daily; 1hr 45min); La Línea de la Concepción (6 daily; 1hr 30min–2hr); Málaga (2 daily; 2hr); Seville (3 daily; 3hr).

By boat FRS at Avenida Andalucía 16 (☎956 681 830, ⓦfrs.es) runs fast ferries to Tangier, Morocco (see box below).

INFORMATION

Tourist office Paseo de la Alameda (daily 10am–2pm; also 6–8pm Mon–Fri June–Sept; ☎956 680 993, ⓦaytotarifa.com).

ACCOMMODATION

From July to mid-Sept, book accommodation well in advance. Campsites near the main windsurfing beaches include *Tarifa* (☎956 604 778) and *Paloma* (☎956 684 203), both fully equipped and with their own pools.

Hostal Africa c/María Antonia Toledo 12 ☎956 680 220 ⓦhostalafrica.com. Popular with kitesurfers, this central guesthouse has attractive marble-floored rooms, some en-suite, and a covered roof terrace for lounging around. Cheaper rooms share bathrooms. Double **€50**

Melting Pot Hostel c/Turriano Gracil 5 ☎956 682 906, ⓦmeltingpothostels.com. Backpacker and kitesurfer haven with fully equipped kitchen, cosy lounge/bar and helpful staff. En-suite dorms are somewhat cramped, but the ambience is great. Dorm **€20**, double **€56**

EATING AND DRINKING

Bamboo c/Paseo Alameda 2. Bob Marley and trance on the stereo, fantastic breakfasts, smoothies and fresh juices. Turns into a spacey surfer bar after dark. Daily 10am–2am.

Chilimosa c/Peso 6. Compact vegetarian restaurant/takeaway serving up healthy food with an eastern twist. The changing menu includes the *plato degustación* (€7), featuring falafel, hummus, salad and more. Don't miss the cheesecake. Daily 1–4pm & 8–11pm.

★ **Lola** c/Guzmán el Bueno 5, ⓦlollatarifa.com. In the evenings, tables spill out of this friendly flamenco bar onto the street. The shining stars on the tapas menu include the seared tuna, fresh, garlicky prawns and *el revuelto de abuela* (fancy scrambled eggs) – the perfect hangover cure. Tapas from €4.50. Daily 7.30pm until late.

GIBRALTAR

Backed by the enormous Rock, visible from many kilometres away, and long

32

MOROCCO-BOUND

The main reason to visit the gritty, busy post of **Algeciras** is to take a ferry to **Tangier** in Morocco, or the Spanish enclave of **Ceuta**. FRS ferries (ⓦfrs.es) are the fastest and most frequent: buy tickets directly from their office at the port. More salubrious departure points for Tangier are Tarifa (see opposite), with FRS offering guided one- and two-day trips (bring your passport) as well as straightforward ferry tickets (1-/2-day-trip €60/89; ☎956 681 830, ⓦfrs.es; see above), and Gibraltar.

From Algeciras Ceuta (2–5 daily; 1hr; €31 one-way), Tangier (4 daily; 30min; €31 one-way).

From Gibraltar Tangier (Fri & Sun 1 daily; 30 min; €46).

From Tarifa Tangier (5–8 daily; 35min; €37 one-way).

If arriving in Algeciras, transport to other Spanish cities from the bus station on c/San Bernardo and the adjacent train station is as follows:

By train Córdoba (2 daily; 3hr 15min); Granada (2 daily; 4hr 15min); Madrid (2 daily; 5hr 20min); Ronda (4 daily; 1hr 30min–1hr 45min).

By bus Granada (5 daily; 3hr 45min–5hr 30min); La Línea (every 30min; 45min); Málaga (every 30min; 1hr 45min–3hr); Tarifa (6 daily; 30min).

32

coveted for its strategic position at the entrance to the Mediterranean, the British territory of **GIBRALTAR**, at the southern tip of Spain, has been the source of tension between the two countries for nearly three hundred years since it was ceded to **Britain** under the Treaty of Utrecht. Relations were particularly strained at the time of writing, with Spain enforcing tough, time-consuming border checks.

Now a somewhat clichéd slice of Britain perched next to the Spanish mainland, Gibraltar comes complete with red postboxes, Marks & Spencer, chippies and, of course, the pound.

WHAT TO SEE AND DO

The town is dominated by the huge **Rock of Gibraltar**, the area's main attraction and thought, in antiquity, to be a pillar of Hercules.

The Rock and nature reserve

Take the **cable car** running from Red Sands Road (daily: May–Oct 9.30am–7.15pm; Nov–April 9.30am–5.15pm; £6.50/8 one-way/return; £16 combined entry to nature reserve) to the top of the rock for spectacular views of the coastline. Signs from the cable-car exit lead you to the **nature reserve** (daily 9.30am–7.15pm; £10). A fifteen-minute signposted walk takes you south to the immense **St Michael's Cave** – once home to the Rock's Neolithic inhabitants, and currently home to colourfully lit stalactites and stalagmites. From here, a road leads down and north past the cable car's middle station and the **Apes' Den** – the home of the peninsula's famous simian residents (see box below) – to the

Great Siege Tunnels, carved out of the rock by the British during the siege of 1779–83, full of antique cannons and descriptions of battles. A ten-minute walk down and west arrives at the **Gibraltar, A City Under Siege** wax figure exhibition (best viewed at twilight for the ultimate spooky effect), and on your way down to the town along Willis's Road, you'll pass the fourteenth-century **Tower of Homage** – one of the few remains of the Moorish era.

Gibraltar Museum

For a thorough overview of Gibraltar's history, pop into the **Gibraltar Museum** on Bomb House Lane (Mon–Fri 10am–6pm, Sat 10am–2pm; free). In the warren of rooms you'll encounter everything from Neanderthal finds to fourteenth-century Arabic baths, before moving on to the British capture of Gibraltar, its role in World War II and present-day self-determination. Standout exhibits include an Egyptian mummy washed up nearby in the nineteenth century, and a Neanderthal skull.

ARRIVAL AND DEPARTURE

By bus Buses run from several Spanish destinations to La Línea. To get to Gibraltar, simply walk across the border and follow Winston Churchill Ave into town (10min).
Destinations La Línea to: Algeciras (every 30min; 45min); Cádiz (4 daily; 2hr 30min); Málaga (3–5 daily; 2hr 30min); Seville (4 daily; 5hr).

INFORMATION

Tourist office Grand Casemates Square (Mon–Fri 9am–5.30pm, Sat 10am–3pm, Sun 10am–1pm; ☎ 350 507 62, ⓦ visitgibraltar.gi).

ACCOMMODATION

Cannon Hotel 9 Cannon Lane ☎ 350 200 517 11, ⓦ cannonhotel.gi. Central no-frills cheapie with dated decor. Rooms border on tiny, and the place could be cleaner, but English breakfast is included. Cheaper rooms share facilities. Double **£42**
Con Dios Marina Bay, off Bayside Road ☎ 350 200 517 55, ⓦ gibraltarbedandbreakfast.com/condiosco. Those with sea legs can bed down in one of the four cabins aboard this comfortable yacht, moored in Marina Bay. The hosts are helpful, a light breakfast is thrown in, and the deck is wonderful come sunset. Cabins from **£50**; prices almost halved for single occupancy.

> ### APES OF THE ROCK
>
> The so-called "apes" are, in fact, tailless Barbary macaques, thought to have been brought over to the Spanish mainland by the Moors. Visitors must not feed them, as that can result in both a hefty fine and a savage bite. Don't walk around the nature reserve with food visible, but if they do jump on you, keep still and remain calm.

EATING

Bianca's 7 Admiral's Walk, Marina Bay, ⓦbiancas.gi. Ample English breakfasts, large portions of fish and chips, salads, and meaty mains served at this seafront restaurant. Mains from £0. Daily 8.30am–10pm.

★ **Verdi Verdi** International Commercial Centre, Casemates Square, ⓦverdiverdi.com. The freshly prepared dishes at this cute café range from "Not Quite Welsh Rarebit" to home-made quiches, falafel wraps and poached hake. Mon–Fri 7.30am–5pm.

RONDA

Built on an isolated ridge of the sierra, and ringed by dark, angular mountains, the spectacular *pueblo blanco* of **RONDA**, a large cluster of attractive whitewashed houses, was made famous in Hemingway's *For Whom The Bell Tolls*. The town is split in two by a gaping river **gorge** with a sheer drop, spanned by an incredible eighteenth-century arched bridge from which hundreds of people were thrown to their deaths during the Spanish Civil War.

WHAT TO SEE AND DO

Most sights of interest lie in the tiny, atmospheric old quarter on the eastern side of the gorge.

Plaza de Toros y Museo Taurino

In the modern Mercadillo quarter, the Plaza de Toros (**bullring**), Spain's oldest, is where three generations of the Romero family shaped the rules of bullfighting into what they are today during the eighteenth and nineteenth centuries (daily 10am–8pm; €6.50). The on-site **Museo Taurino** showcases a wealth of *corrida* memorabilia, including numerous *trajes de luz* – the colourful individual costumes of the *matadores*.

Old Quarter sights

The principal gate of the town, through which the Christian conquerors passed, stands beside the **Alcázar**, destroyed by the French in 1809. Sights in the Old Quarter include the well-preserved thirteenth- and fourteenth-century **Baños Árabes** (daily 10am–7pm, Sat & Sun 10am–3pm; €3, free Mon), with their distinctive horseshoe arches,

reachable via a long flight of cobbled steps and a path along a section of the old city wall. The **Palacio de Mondragón** (Mon–Fri 10am–7pm, Sat & Sun 10am–3pm; €3), located on its namesake plaza, was probably once the palace of the Moorish kings and is now home to exhibitions on the history of the area. On the nearby Plaza Duquesa de Parcent stands the **Iglesia de Santa María de Mayor** (Mon–Sat 10am–8pm, Sun 10am–12.30pm & 2–8pm; €4), built on the site of Ronda's main mosque. The whimsical **Museo Lara** at c/de Armiñán 29 (daily 11am–7pm; €4; ⓦmuseolara.org) is home to an ever-expanding private collection of antique objects, ranging from watches and eighteenth- and nineteenth-century weaponry (look out for a tiny pocket pistol with five barrels) to early cameras and antique horse carriages. A macabre exhibit on witchcraft and the Inquisition is (fittingly) located in the cellar.

Local walks

The Old Quarter's **Jardínes de Forestier** ascend the gorge in a series of stepped terraces, offering superb views of the river, the bridge and the remarkable stairway of the **Casa del Rey Moro**, an early eighteenth-century mansion on the north side of the gorge. For that classic shot of the Puente Nuevo that spans the gorge, take the path down from the Plaza María Auxiliadora to one of the **viewpoints**. This is a section from one of the eight day hikes, ranging from 2.5km to 9.1km, outlined in a booklet available at the tourist office (€5).

ARRIVAL AND DEPARTURE

By train The train station is several blocks north of Pl. Redondo, along Avda Andalucía, a 15min walk from the Old Quarter.

Destinations Algeciras (5 daily; 1hr 30min–1hr 50min); Córdoba (2 daily; 1hr 45min); Granada (3 daily; 2hr 30min); Madrid (2 daily; 4hr); Málaga (daily at 4.55pm; 1hr 50min).

By bus The bus station is near Plaza Redondo.

Destinations Cádiz (3 daily; 2hr); Granada (2 daily; 3hr 30min); Málaga (7 daily; 3hr 30min); Seville (3–5 daily; 2hr 30min).

32

32

INFORMATION

Tourist office Opposite the entrance to the bullring at Plaza de Toros (Mon–Fri 10am–7pm, Sat 10am–2pm & 3–5pm, Sun 10am–2.30pm; ☎952 187 119, ⓦturismoderonda.es).

ACCOMMODATION

Hotel Morales c/Sevilla 51 ☎952 871538. This friendly, central cheapie lives up to its "friendly hotel" moniker, thanks to the warmth of its staff. The tiled en-suite rooms are spotless. Double €40

Hotel San Francisco c/María Cabrera 18 ☎952 873 299, ⓦsanfranciscoronda.com. Elegant budget option, with Moorish archways in the dining room and cosy rooms equipped with a/c. Double €52

EATING AND DRINKING

All opening hours are daily 1–4pm & 8–11pm.

Bodega San Francisco c/Ruedo Alameda, just outside the Carlos V gate. Old-school tapas bar crowded with locals, serving fantastic *gambas al ajillo* (garlic prawns), mini-pinchos (grilled meat on sticks), *patatas bravas* and other favourites. Tapas from €2.50.

La Vita E Bella c/Nueva 5. Cheerful, homely Italian joint serving up delicious home-made pasta dishes. Try the seafood pasta or the *penne* with cheese and truffles. Mains from €8.

Tragatapas c/Nueva 4. Ronda's most imaginative tapas, such as pork cheeks with white truffle and fusion mains such as curried duck and spicy mussels. Tapas from €2.40; mains €8–20.

MÁLAGA

MÁLAGA is the second city of the south after Seville, one of the oldest in Spain, and also the gateway to the rest of the Costa del Sol, the richest resort area in the Mediterranean.

WHAT TO SEE AND DO

While the clusters of high-rises are not attractive, the historic centre (Old Town) has plenty of charm, and boasts the second most popular art museum in Spain.

The Picasso museums

Málaga's most famous native son, born here in 1881, is honoured in the immensely popular **Museo Picasso Málaga**, c/San Agustín 8 (Tues–Thurs & Sun 10am–8pm, Fri & Sat 10am–9pm; permanent collection €6, temporary exhibition €4.50, combined ticket €9; ⓦmuseopicassomalaga.org), which displays an intimate collection spanning Picasso's entire career; temporary exhibitions feature his contemporaries. Serious fans shouldn't miss the **Casa Natal de Picasso**, Plaza de la Merced 15 (daily 9.30am–8pm; closed holidays; €2, free with the Museo Picasso Málaga combined ticket; ⓦfundacionpicasso.es), where the artist was born, with choice works of his displayed upstairs.

Catedral

Founded in 1528, Málaga's **cathedral** (Mon–Thurs 10am–5.30pm, Fri 10am–5pm; €5) towers above the Old Town from its location on Calle Molina Lario. It features a melange of architectural styles, having taken 260 years to complete: its interior is Renaissance and Baroque while the northern entrance is Gothic. Since it features one tower when the original plans included two, it is affectionately known as La Manquita (One-armed Woman).

Alcazaba and Castillo de Gibralfaro

Just east of the Old Town rises Mount Gibralfaro where the Moorish citadels of the 1057 **Alcazaba** (all year: Mon 9am–6pm; Tues–Sun: April–Oct 9.30am–8pm; Nov–March 8.30am–7.30pm; €2.20) and **Castillo de Gibralfaro** (Tues–Sun: April–Oct 9.30am–8pm; Nov–March 9am–6pm; €2.10, joint ticket with Alcazaba €3.50), built in the eighth century by Abd ar-Rahman I and rebuilt in the fourteenth and fifteenth, tower above the ruins of a Roman theatre. The viewpoint on the way to the castle offers spectacular views of the town.

Centro de Arte Contemporáneo (CAC)

Housed inside a converted 1930s wholesale market on Calle Alemana, this cutting-edge **contemporary art museum** (Tues–Sun: April–Oct 10am–2pm & 5–9pm; Nov–March 10am–8pm; free; ⓦcacmalaga.org) features exhibits of twentieth- and twenty-first-century installations, painting and sculpture by international artists.

Beaches

Sunbathers favour the white-sand Playa de la Malagueta, ten minutes' walk from the Old Town. The old fishing villages of El Palo and Pedregalejo, 4km east of the centre, boast grey-sand **beaches** and a promenade lined with some of the best **fish and seafood restaurants** in the province; catch bus #11 along Paseo del Parque.

ARRIVAL AND DEPARTURE

There are ATMs and luggage storage at both the bus and train stations.

By plane Málaga's Pablo Picasso Airport (952 048 484, aena.es) is linked to the train station by electric train (every 20min 5.30am–10.30pm; €2.20); continue another stop to Málaga Centro: Alameda for the city centre. The airport bus (#75) leaves every 20–30min between 7am and midnight for the city centre, via the main bus station (€1.30).

By train The train station is across the road from the bus station. Take buses #3 and #4 to the city centre.

Destinations Barcelona (7 daily; 5hr–12hr 40min); Córdoba (18 daily; 50min–2hr 25min); Madrid (10 daily; 2hr 30min); Seville (11 daily; 2hr 45min); Valencia (3 daily; 4hr 15min–8hr 30min).

By bus The bus station (952 350 061) on the Paseo de los Tilos is a 15min walk southwest of the Old Town. Take buses #4 and #12 to and from the Alameda Principal.

Destinations Almería (2 daily; 3hr–4hr 30min); Córdoba (4 daily; 2hr 30min); Granada (18 daily; 1hr 30min–2hr); Madrid (8 daily; 6hr); Ronda (8 daily; 2hr 30min); Seville (8 daily; 2hr 30min).

INFORMATION

Tourist office Plaza de la Marina (March–Sept Mon–Fri 9am–8pm, until 6pm rest of the year; 952 122 020, malagaturismo.com).

ACCOMMODATION

Casa Babylon c/Pedro de Quejana 3 952 267 228, casababylonhostel.com. Colourful, sociable and full of character, this is the place to meet fellow travellers, though don't count on getting much sleep if your room is near the common room. The location – in the middle of Málaga's historical centre – is hard to beat. Dorm €15, double €40

La Casa Mata c/Molinillo del Aceite 8 951 252 776. On the edge of the Old Town, this quiet secure hostel features a single dorm and bright private rooms, a well-stocked kitchen and friendly, helpful management. The singles are tiny. Call ahead if arriving after 8pm. Dorm €18, double €48

Melting Pot Hostel Avda del Pintor Joaquin Sorolla 30 952 600 571, meltingpothostels.com. A stone's throw from the beach (a bus ride from the centre), this friendly hostel has spotless dorms (without a/c), there's an on-site café-bar serving affordable meals, and daily walking tours and nightly pub crawls encourage socializing between the guests. Dorm €13

EATING AND DRINKING

Málaga specialities – *fritura malagueña* (battered and fried fish and squid) and *espeto* – sardines grilled on bamboo spears – are found at seaside restaurants along the El Palo and Pedregalejo beaches.

Al-Yamal c/Blasco de Garay 7 restaurantearabeal -yamal.net. Málaga's proximity to Africa is reflected in the flavoursome tagines, grilled meats and couscous dishes of this intimate Moroccan restaurant. The fresh mint tea with orange blossom stands out and the meal deal for two (Mon–Thurs) – several dishes with wine at €15 apiece – is a bargain. Mon–Sat 1–4pm & 8–11pm.

El Piano c/San Juan de Letran 13. This tiny, award-winning vegan spot is more of a takeaway than a restaurant, with locals and visitors alike popping in for delicious quiche, dahl, falafel, veggie burgers and more. Mains from €4. Tues–Sat 1–4pm & 8–11pm.

★ **Tapas de Cervantes** c/Cárcer 8. In this cramped, atmospheric bar you'll be sitting cheek by jowl with other diners, hungrily awaiting tapas such as pork shoulder with pumpkin and pineapple and lamb stew with couscous. Get there early, as the place gets packed. Tapas from €3.75. Tues–Sat 1–4pm & 8–11pm.

CÓRDOBA

CÓRDOBA was once the largest city of Roman Spain, and for three centuries the heart of the great medieval caliphate of the Moors, as well as the second-largest headquarters of the dreaded Inquisition. It's an engaging, atmospheric city, easily explored on foot.

WHAT TO SEE AND DO

For visitors, Córdoba's main attraction is a single building: **La Mezquita** – the grandest and most beautiful mosque ever constructed by the Moors in Spain. This stands right in the centre of the city, surrounded by the labyrinth of old Jewish and Moorish quarters.

32

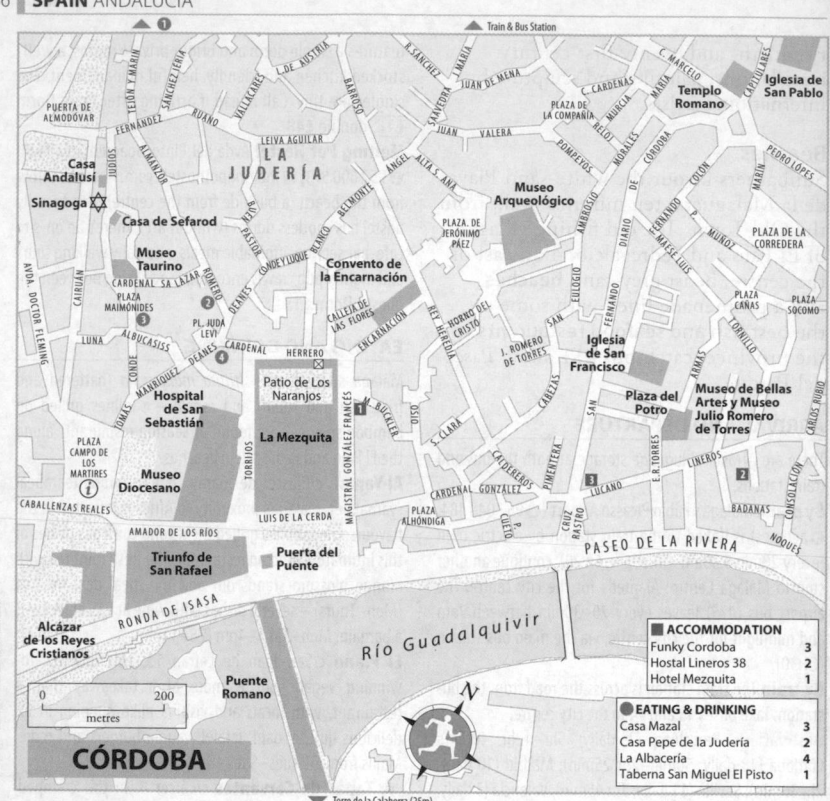

32

Map of **CÓRDOBA**

Train & Bus Station

LA JUDERÍA

Río Guadalquivir

0 200
metres

ACCOMMODATION
Funky Cordoba	3
Hostal Lineros 38	2
Hotel Mezquita	1

EATING & DRINKING
Casa Mazal	3
Casa Pepe de la Judería	2
La Albacería	4
Taberna San Miguel El Pisto	1

Torre de la Calahorra (25m)

La Mezquita

Córdoba's domination of Moorish Spain began thirty years after the conquest, in 756 AD, when the city was placed under **Abd ar-Rahman I**, who established control over all but the north of Spain. He began the building of the Great Mosque – in Spanish, **La Mezquita** (Mon–Sat 8.30am–6pm, Sun 8.30–10.30am & 2–6pm; €8, free Mon–Sat 8.30–10am) – which is approached through the **Patio de los Naranjos**, a classic Islamic court preserving both its orange trees and fountains for ritual purification before prayer. Inside, nearly a thousand twin-layered red and white archways combine to mesmerizing effect, the harmony culminating only at the foot of the beautiful **mihrab** (prayer niche), decorated with gold mosaic cubes – a gift from Nicephoras II Phocas, the Christian emperor of Byzantium. In the centre of one of the most beautiful mosques in the world, you'll find the incongruous presence of a Renaissance cathedral, built in 1523, though it's the mihrab that commands most of the attention.

La Judería and around

North of La Mezquita lies **La Judería**, Córdoba's old Jewish quarter, a fascinating network of narrow, atmospheric lanes and small plazas. Near the heart of the quarter, at c/Maimonides 18, is a tiny fourteenth-century **synagogue** with fine stuccowork (Tues–Sat 9.30am–2pm & 3.30–5.30pm, Sun 9.30am–1.30pm; €0.30, free for EU citizens), one of only three in Spain that survived the Jewish expulsion of 1492. Nearby, on the corner of c/Judíos and c/Averroes, the beautiful fourteenth-century **Casa de Sefarad** (Mon–Sat 11am–6pm, Sun 11am–2pm; €4; ⓦcasadesefarad.es) explores the Sephardic-Judaic tradition. Its collections include weavings with gold thread and ceremonial objects; upstairs, exhibits are devoted to the contribution of Sephardic Jews to Islamic Córdoba and their persecution by the Inquisition. Some evenings there are excellent live flamenco shows.

Alcázar de los Reyes Cristianos

Near the Mezquita is the thirteenth-century **Castle of the Christian Monarchs** (Tues–Fri 8.30am–7pm, Sat & Sun 8.30am–2.30pm; €4, free on Fri), originally home to Alfonso X and then the headquarters of the Inquisition between 1490 and 1821. Highlights include the beautiful sculpted gardens, a third-century Roman sarcophagus and the view from one of the Alcázar's towers.

Museo Julio Romero de Torres

Located on the tiny Plaza del Potro, the ever-popular **Museo Julio Romero de Torres** (Tues 2.30–8.30pm, Wed–Sat 9am–8.30pm, Sun 9am–2.30pm; €4, free on Fri) features the work of the namesake local painter, whose signature works depicted curvy Córdoban women.

Puente Romano and Torre de la Calahorra

Across the pedestrianized **Puente Romano** (Roman Bridge) stands the fourteenth-century **Torre de la Calahorra** (daily: Oct–April 10am–6pm; May–Sept 10am–2pm & 4.30–8.30pm; €4.50), housing an entertaining museum; the talking dioramas bring the history of Islamic Córdoba to life. There's a great view of the Mezquita from the top of the tower, and also across the bridge at night.

ARRIVAL AND DEPARTURE

By train The train station is along the Glorieta de las Tres Culturas, 1km northwest of the old town.

Destinations Barcelona (13 daily; 4–10hr); Cádiz (20 daily; 2hr 30min–3hr 30min); Granada (2 daily; 2hr 20min); Madrid (every 30min 7am–10pm; 1hr 45min–5hr); Málaga (13 daily; 1hr–2hr 30min); Seville (every 30min 6.50am–11.20pm; 45min–1hr 30min).

By bus The bus station is behind the train station. Bus #3 (€1.50) runs down c/San Fernández, just east of the Judería.

Destinations Granada (7 daily; 2hr 30min); Madrid (6 daily; 4hr 45min); Málaga (5 daily; 2hr 45min); Seville (6 daily; 1hr 45min).

INFORMATION

Tourist office Opposite the Alcázar (daily 9am–2pm & 5–7pm; ⓣ 902 201 774, ⓦ turismodecordoba.org).

ACCOMMODATION

Funky Cordoba c/Lucano 12 7 ⓣ 957 473 234, ⓦ funkycordoba.com. The pros: great central location, helpful staff, en-suite a/c rooms and dorms, Pop Art-style decor, roof terrace for chilling out, guest kitchen. Cons: the place could be cleaner and breakfast is not included. Dorm **€14**, double **€40**

Hostal Lineros 38 c/Lineros 38 ⓣ 957 482 517, ⓦ hostallineros38.com. Live out your Arabian Nights fantasy at this Moorish-style guesthouse that's more hotel than hostel, with luxurious four-poster beds and hammam-style bathrooms. Double **€52**

Hotel Mezquita Plaza Santa Catalina 1 ⓣ 957 475 585, ⓦ hotelmezquita.com. Friendly hotel practically on top of Córdoba's biggest attraction, with mid-sized en suites and a dining area/lobby that looks like a cross between an antique shop and a museum. Wi-fi downstairs only. Double **€55**

EATING AND DRINKING

Córdoba's cuisine is some of the best in Andalucía. Don't miss dishes such as *salmorejo* (a thicker, more savoury gazpacho), *ajoblanco* (cold garlic and almond soup) or the *rabo de toro* (oxtail). Opening hours are daily 1–4pm & 8–11pm unless otherwise stated.

★ **Casa Mazal** c/Tomas Conde 3 ⓦ casamazal.com. A tiny passageway leads into a beautiful cobbled courtyard adorned with flowers of the city's only Sephardic restaurant. Not only are their vegetarian dishes (rice with grilled vegetables, aubergine pâté with home-made bread) the best in town, but their couscous is perfection. Mains €8–18.

Casa Pepe de la Judería c/Romero 1 ⓦ casapepejuderia.com. Prop up the bar at this Cordoban institution; their *salmorejo* and *berenjenas con miel* (aubergines with honey) are some of the best in town. Tapas from €5; mains from €13.

La Albacería c/Deanes 1. Try the melt-in-your-mouth lamb with couscous, *croquetas* made with Cabrales cheese and served with apple sauce, an oxtail dish with chocolate, or the "potato volcano". Tapas from €3.

Taberna San Miguel El Pisto Pl. San Miguel 1. Over a hundred years old, this Córdoba institution serves excellent Montilla wine, accompanied by regional tapas, such as *rabo de toro* or *callos en salsa picante* (tripe in spicy sauce). Tapas from €3.50. Closed Sun & Aug.

32

32

GRANADA

If you see only one town in Spain, it should be **GRANADA**, with its wonderful backdrop of the **Sierra Nevada** mountains, and Spain's most visited monument, the **Alhambra**. Granada was established as an independent kingdom in 1238 by **Ibn Ahmar**, a prince of the Arab Nasrid tribe. The Moors of Granada maintained their autonomy for two and a half centuries, but by 1490 only the city itself remained in Muslim hands. On January 2, 1492, Granada fell to the army of Ferdinand and Isabella following a seven-month siege, and the Christian Reconquest of Spain was complete, followed by the expulsion of Jews from Spain and the persecution of its Muslim population. Today Granada is a vibrant city, combining modern infrastructure with astounding Moorish architecture and an exuberant nightlife.

WHAT TO SEE AND DO

The main attraction of the town is the **Alhambra**, the stunning Moorish palace complex set up on a hill overlooking the city. However, Granada's centre has some fine architecture of its own, including the **cathedral** and the **Capilla Real**. On an adjacent hill to the Alhambra lies the **Albaicín** – a maze of tiny, cobbled medieval streets, whitewashed houses with Moorish touches still in evidence. In fact, Granada retains much of its North African legacy, from the *teterías* offering shisha and sweet pastries to the Arabic doorways of its houses, and traditional Arabic baths.

The Alhambra: the Alcazaba and the Palacios Nazaríes

The standard approach to the **Alhambra** is along the Cuesta de Gomérez that climbs uphill from Plaza Nueva, either on foot or by taking the Alhambra bus (#30) from the Gran Vía (every 8min between 7am and 11pm; €1.20). The earliest, most ruined part of the fortress is the **Alcazaba**, furthest from the main entrance. It was this building's distinctive hue that gave the complex its name, as "al-Hambra" means "red" in Arabic. At the summit is the **Torre de la Vela**; from both the tower and the ramparts there's a fine view of the whitewashed houses clustered on the hillside opposite.

The buildings in the **Palacios Nazaríes** – undoubtedly the Alhambra's gem – show a brilliant use of light and space with ornamental stucco decoration, in rhythmic repetitions of supreme beauty. Elegant Arabic inscriptions from the Koran cover the palace walls. Look closely, and you'll see the remains of ancient paint behind the calligraphy; try to imagine what the palace once looked like in all its splendour. The sultans used the **Palacio del Mexuar**, the first series of rooms, for business and judicial purposes. In the **Serallo**, beyond, they received distinguished guests: here is the royal throne room, known as the **Hall of the Ambassadors**, the largest room of the palace. The last section, the **Harem**, formed their private living quarters. These are the most beautiful rooms of the palace, and include the **Patio de los Leones** with its elegant, fluted columns and the restored lions around the fountain, which have become the archetypal images of Granada. It's worthwhile coming back

ALHAMBRA PRACTICALITIES

Tickets for the Alhambra (daily: mid-March to mid-Oct 8am–7pm; mid-Oct to mid-March until 5pm; €13; ⓦalhambradegranada.org) are limited, so buy well in advance online (€1 booking fee; ⓦalhambra-tickets.es), and collect them from the Alhambra ticket office; bring ID and the credit card used to purchase the ticket. If online tickets are sold out, get to the ticket office no later than 5.30am on the day. You can also buy advance tickets from the Servicaixa machines in the Alhambra grounds (daily: March–Oct 8am–7pm; Nov–Feb 8am–5pm). When you purchase your ticket, you also book a 30-minute assigned slot for the star attraction of **Palacios Nazaríes**. Nocturnal visits to the Palacios Nazaríes (March–Oct Tues–Sat 10–11.30pm; Nov–Feb Fri & Sat 8–9.30pm; €8) also need to be booked in advance; if you plan to visit the Alhambra on two consecutive days, a joint night/day ticket costs €15.

The **Bono Turístico Granada** (3-day/5-day €33.50/37.50; ⓦgranadatur .com) lets you jump the lengthy queues at top sights and gets you into a range of museums throughout the city, with a handful of free bus trips thrown in. Purchase it in advance and collect it from the tourist information office.

to the Palacios Nazaríes at night, to see the serene reflection in the perfectly proportioned pool of the Patio de los Arrayanes and the buildings subtly lit up.

The Alhambra: the Palacio de Carlos V and the Generalife

Next to the Palacios Nazaríes is the **Palacio de Carlos V**, an ostentatious piece of Renaissance architecture, with a circular courtyard where bullfights once took place, which was built by its namesake Charles V, the grandson of Ferdinand and Isabella. A wing of the Palacios Nazaríes was demolished to make way for it. The palace's lower floor is home to the Museo de la Alhambra (Tues–Sat 9am–2.30pm; free), which showcases a collection of Islamic artefacts, such as a fourteenth-century chessboard, handwritten Korans and fine tile work, while upstairs, the Museo de Bellas Artes (Tues 2.30–8pm, Wed–Sat 9am–2.30pm, Sun 9am–2.30pm; €1.50, free for EU citizens) features a small collection of Hispano-Moorish paintings and sculpture. From here, a short walk takes you to the **Generalife**, the cypress-shaded gardens and summer palace of the sultans.

The Albaicín

Opposite the Alhambra, framed by the Gran Vía on the west and the Carrera del Darro to the south, is the old Arab quarter of the **Albaicín**, a higgledy-piggledy collection of whitewashed houses and mansions with courtyard gardens seemingly piled on top of one another along steep, cobbled streets. Getting lost in this picturesque labyrinth is a pleasure, but mind your valuables particularly during the siesta hours when the odd opportunistic mugging can occur. From here, you can wind your way

up to the **Mirador de San Nicolás** for the quintessential Alhambra view, with the Sierra Nevada backdrop – it's particularly stunning (and crowded) at sunset. Bus #31 runs to the mirador from Plaza Nueva (every 10min 7am–11pm; €1.20).

The Capilla Real and the Cathedral

The **Capilla Real** (April–Oct Mon–Sat 10.30am–1.30pm & 4–7.30pm, Sun 11am–1.30pm & 4–7pm; Oct–March closed Sun; €3.50) along Calle Oficios was built in the first decades of Christian rule as a mausoleum for Ferdinand and Isabella. Although their tombs are simple, in the sacristy you'll find Isabella's sceptre and crown, as well as Ferdinand's sword. Adjoining the Capilla Real, the stark Gothic-Baroque bulk of Granada's **Cathedral** (Mon–Sat 10.45am–1.30pm & 4–8pm, Sun 4–8pm; Nov–March Sun until 7pm; €3.50), built on the site of the former mosque, has an attractive Renaissance interior.

32

ARRIVAL AND DEPARTURE

By plane The airport lies 17km west of the centre; Autocares J González (ⓦautocaresjosegonzalez.com) buses run to Gran Vía de Colón (6 daily; 30min; €3). Taxis cost €20–24.

By train The station is 1.5km west of the centre on Avda de Andaluces, off Avda de Constitución, connected to the centre by buses #4, #6, #7 and #11. Destinations Almería (4 daily; 2hr 30min); Barcelona (1–2 daily; 11hr 30min); Córdoba (2 daily; 2hr 30min); Madrid (3 daily; 4hr 30min–6hr); Ronda (3 daily; 2hr 30min); Seville (4 daily; 3hr–3hr 15min); Valencia (1–2 daily; 6hr 30min–7hr 40min).

By bus The station is in the northwest of the city on Carretera de Jaén; buses #3 and #33 run to Gran Vía de Colón (every 10min; 15min).

★ **TREAT YOURSELF**

Immerse yourself (literally) in the city's Moorish culture at the oldest Arabic baths in Spain – the **Hammams de Al-Andalus** (c/Santa Ana 16; daily sessions every 2hr 10am–midnight; bath only €24, with massage €36; ☎958 229 978, ⓦhammam.es). Book your session in advance, then alternate in semi-darkness between the hot pools, the cold pool and sips of hot, sweet tea.

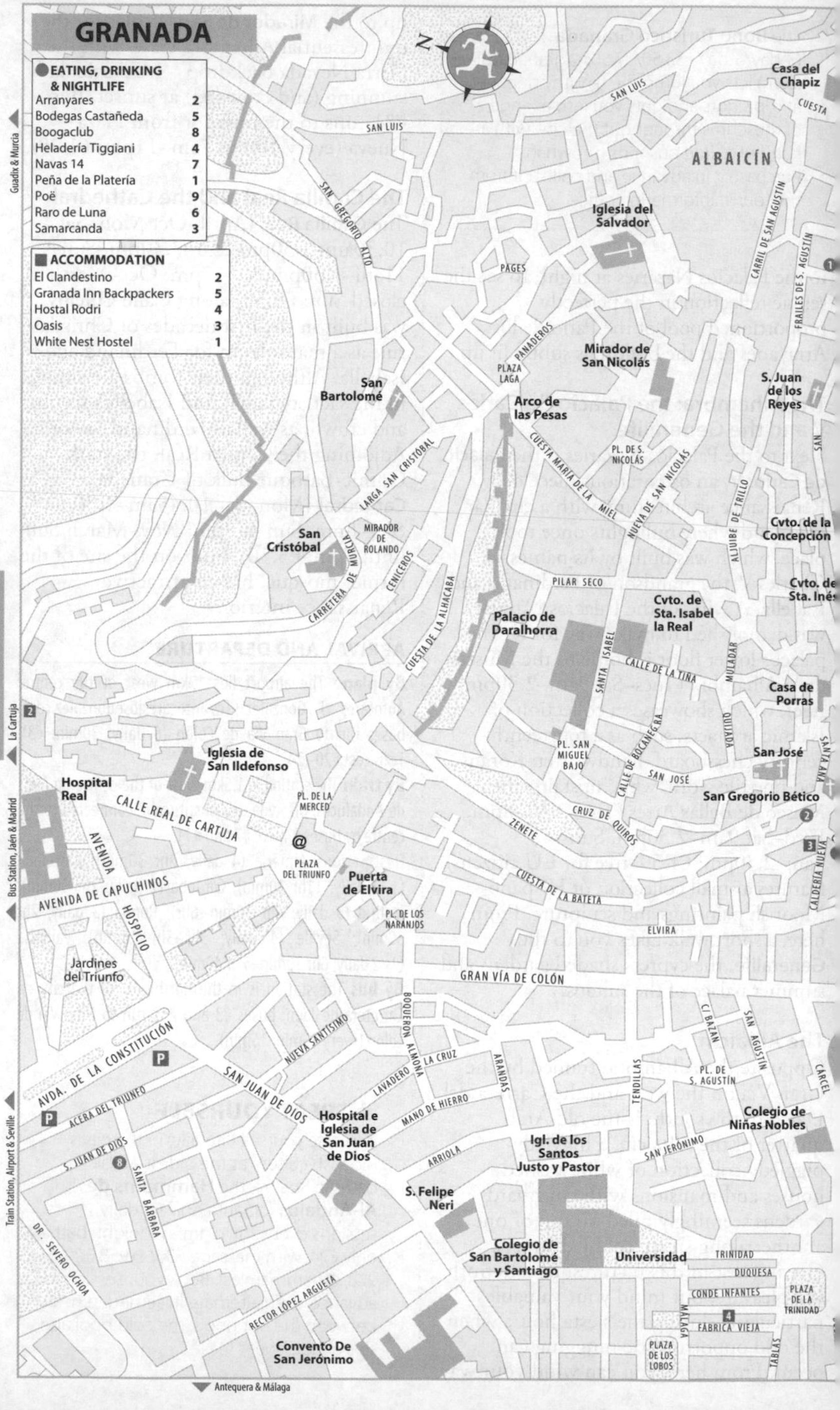

GRANADA

● EATING, DRINKING & NIGHTLIFE

Arranyares	2
Bodegas Castañeda	5
Boogaclub	8
Heladería Tiggiani	4
Navas 14	7
Peña de la Platería	1
Poë	9
Raro de Luna	6
Samarcanda	3

■ ACCOMMODATION

El Clandestino	2
Granada Inn Backpackers	5
Hostal Rodri	4
Oasis	3
White Nest Hostel	1

Guadix & Murcia

La Cartuja

Bus Station, Jaén & Madrid

Train Station, Airport & Seville

32

ALBAICÍN

SAN LUIS

CUESTA

Casa del
Chapiz

SAN LUIS

SAN GREGORIO ALTO

CABRIL DE SAN AGUSTÍN

FRAILES DE S. AGUSTÍN

PAGES

Iglesia del
Salvador

S. Juan
de los
Reyes

PADEROS

PLAZA
LAGA

Mirador de
San Nicolás

PL. DE S.
NICOLÁS

CUESTA MARÍA DE LA MIEL

NUEVA DE SAN NICOLÁS

ALJIBE DE TRILLO

San
Bartolomé

Arco de
las Pesas

PL. DE S.
NICOLÁS

Cvto. de la
Concepción

LARGA SAN CRISTÓBAL

Cvto. de
Sta. Inés

San
Cristóbal

MIRADOR
DE
ROLANDO

MURCIA

CENTECEROS

PILAR SECO

Cvto. de
Sta. Isabel
la Real

MIRADOR

Casa de
Porras

CARRETERA DE MURCIA

CUESTA DE LA ALHACABA

Palacio de
Daralhorra

SANTA ISABEL

CALLE DE LA TIÑA

San José

San Gregorio Bético

CALDERERÍA NUEVA

PL. SAN
MIGUEL
BAJO

CALLE DE BACANEGRA

VELETINO

MULIADER

SAN ANA

Hospital
Real

Iglesia de
San Ildefonso

CALLE REAL DE CARTUJA

PL. DE LA
MERCED

SAN JOSÉ

CRUZ DE QUIROS

@

AVENIDA

ZENETE

PLAZA
DEL TRIUNFO

Puerta
de Elvira

CUESTA DE LA BATETA

AVENIDA DE CAPUCHINOS

HOSPICIO

PL. DE LOS
NARANJOS

ELVIRA

Jardines
del Triunfo

GRAN VÍA DE COLÓN

BOQUERÓN

ALMONA

C. BAZAN

SAN AGUSTÍN

AVDA. DE LA CONSTITUCIÓN

NUEVA SANTÍSIMO

LAVADERO

LA CRUZ

ARANDAS

PL. DE
S. AGUSTÍN

CARCEL

P

SAN JUAN DE DIOS

TENDILLAS

Colegio de
Niñas Nobles

ACERA DEL TRIUNFO

MANO DE HIERRO

P

Hospital e
Iglesia de
San Juan
de Dios

S. JUAN DE DIOS

ARRIOLA

Igl. de los
Santos
Justo y Pastor

SAN JERÓNIMO

SANTA BÁRBARA

S. Felipe
Neri

DR. SEVERO OCHOA

Colegio de
San Bartolomé
y Santiago

Universidad

TRINIDAD

DUQUESA

CONDE INFANTES

PLAZA
DE LA
TRINIDAD

MÁLAGA

FÁBRICA VIEJA

RECTOR LÓPEZ ARGUETA

Convento De
San Jerónimo

PLAZA
DE LOS
LOBOS

TABLAS

Antequera & Málaga

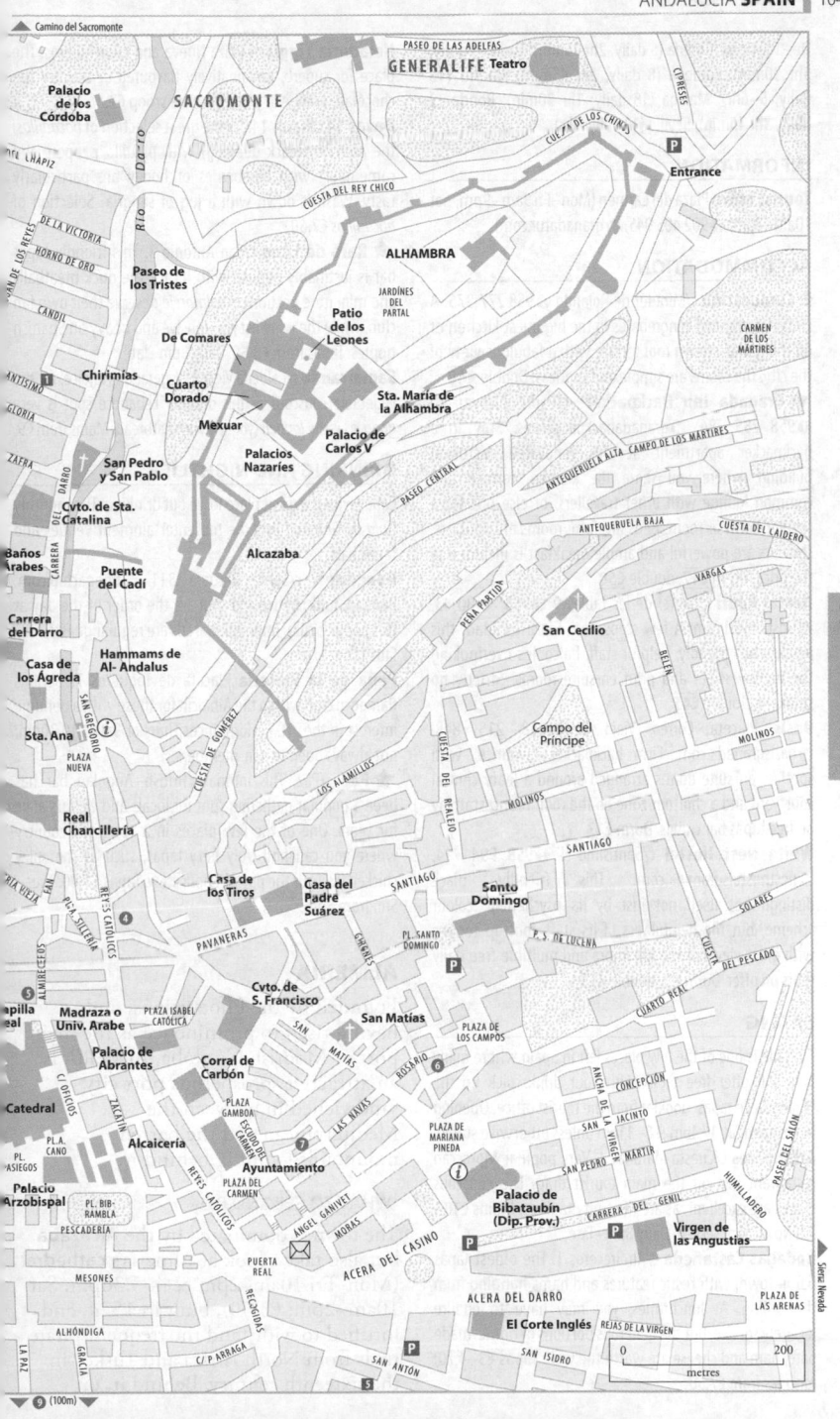

Destinations Almería (5 daily; 2hr 15min); Cádiz (4 daily; 5hr 30min); Córdoba (8 daily; 2hr 45min); Madrid (10 daily; 5–6hr); Málaga (18 daily; 1hr 30min); Ronda (2 daily; 3hr 45min); Seville (10 daily; 3hr).

INFORMATION

Tourist office Plaza del Carmen (Mon–Fri 9am–9pm, Sat 10am–8pm; ☎ 902 405 045, ⊛ granadatur.com).

ACCOMMODATION

El Clandestino c/Miradór de Rolando ☎ 958 277 875. A chilled-out crowd congregates in the big guest kitchen or on the guitar-strewn roof terrace with a fabulous view of the city. The rooms are simple and spotless. Double €40

★ **Granada Inn Backpackers** c/Padre Alcover 10 ☎ 958 285 284, ⊛ granadabackpackers.es. Stay in a backpacker apartment at this renovated historical building, where you share the kitchen, terrace and common lounge with other travellers, or else opt for a regular dorm or room. Beds are firm, rooms are spotless, showers are powerful and ample breakfast is included in the price. Dorm €17, double €50

Hostal Rodri c/Laurel de las Tablas 9 ☎ 958 28 80 43, ⊛ hostalrodri.com. A few steps from Plaza Trinidad, this *pension* has friendly, helpful staff, balconies overlooking the narrow street and prim en-suite rooms. Strictly no smoking. Double €45

Oasis Placeta Correo Viejo 3 ☎ 958 215 848, ⊛ oasisgranada.com. Firm backpacker favourite, with spotless en-suite dorms arranged around a leafy central courtyard and a chill-out zone on the roof. Young staff lay on free tapas bar crawls. Dorm €13

White Nest Hostel c/Santísimo 4 ☎ 958 994 714, ⊛ nesthostelsgranada.com. This friendly place distinguishes itself not just by its psychedelic colour scheme, but the helpfulness of its staff, rooftop terrace with great views of the Alhambra and multiple free daily tours on offer. Dorm €9, double €38

EATING

Granada is one of the few places left in Spain where many bars still offer free tapas with your drink: pick up the "Granada de tapas" booklet from the tourist office. Opening hours are daily 1–4pm & 8–11pm unless otherwise stated.

Arranyares c/Cuesta Marañas 4. Very popular Moroccan restaurant just off the main tourist drag. The couscous dishes are excellent, as are the fruity tagines. Mains €10–22. No alcohol served. Daily 8pm–late.

Bodegas Castañeda c/Almireceros 1. The oldest tapas bar in town, with rustic features and hams hanging from the ceiling. At lunchtimes, you may have to endure leisurely service, but the generous portions of home-made pâté, ham and cheese are worth the wait. Tapas €3–4.70; *raciones* from €7.50.

Heladería Tiggiani Plaza Nueva and c/Cuchilleros. The place for superb, imaginatively flavoured *gelato*; try the chocolate orange or pistachio. One scoop €2.

Navas 14 c/Navas 14. Try the great selection of *bocadillos*; the *morcilla* (black pudding) with piquillo peppers and camembert with blueberries or honey are particularly tasty. Wash it down with a jug of sangría. Selection of *bocadillos* €7.50.

★ **Raro de Luna** c/San Antonio 3. This friendly tapas bar is justifiably popular with locals: the duck meatballs and miniature portions of *salmorejo* deserve their own fan club, while the wine list is extensive and heavy on Spanish tipples. Tapas from €3.50. Daily 8pm–late.

Samarcanda c/Caldería Vieja 3. Vegetarians rejoice, for the vegetable couscous at this outdoor Lebanese spot is very good, as is the *labneh* (yogurt) with flatbread. Mains from €9.

DRINKING AND NIGHTLIFE

Calle Elvira is a great place to go out drinking. The monthly *Guía de Granada* lists the top entertainment venues and tapas bars.

Boogaclub c/Santa Barbara 311 ⊛ boogaclub.com. Reggae, funk, house and soul are the order of the day at this popular club; international DJs are regular guests. Fri–Sun 11pm–7am.

Peña de la Platería Placeta de Toqueros 7. Serious flamenco club within the Albaicín for those with a genuine interest in the art. Performances Thurs or Sat at 10.30pm; not always open to non-members.

★ **Poë** c/Paz. This intimate British–Angolan bar has been a popular gathering spot for locals and visitors alike for years. One of the few places in a spice-shy country where you can find truly fiery tapas, such as the spicy chicken livers or the piri-piri pork stew. Tapas €1.40. Tues–Sun from 8pm.

ALMERÍA

Founded by the Phoenicians, and having risen to prominence as the main port of Moorish Córdoba, **ALMERÍA** is an attractive, prosperous port city sandwiched in between the Mediterranean and the barren mountains looming behind it.

WHAT TO SEE AND DO

The town is dominated by the **Alcazaba**, but also take a look at Almería's **cathedral** (Mon–Fri 10am–2pm & 4–5.30pm, Sat 10am–2pm; €3.50), built in 1524, and fortified to withstand the frequent pirate raids from North Africa and Turkey in the sixteenth century. Behind it, on

THE GOOD, THE BAD AND THE CORNY

In the 1960s and the 1970s, the rocky desert landscape north of Almería was used as the setting for such Hollywood classics as *Lawrence of Arabia* and later for the likes of *Indiana Jones and the Last Crusade*, as well as around 150 "spaghetti Westerns"; Clint Eastwood's career was launched here in *A Fistful of Dollars*. You can visit the Wild West sets to watch a bank hold-up and shoot-out (two shows daily at noon and 5pm) at **Mini Hollywood** (April–Oct daily 10am–9pm; €22; ⓦ oasysparquetematico.com), where the ticket also includes entry to the adjoining Reserva Zoológica. Nearby **Fort Bravo** (daily 10am–9pm; €17.90; ⓦ fortbravo.es) offers similar attractions. The two are located around 25km north of Almería, off the Tabernas turn-off from the A92. You'll need your own car to get out there, which you can rent from any major car rental at Almería airport.

c/Pintor Díaz Molina 9, the **Centro Andaluz de la Fotografía** (11am–2pm & 5.30–9.30pm; free) houses excellent temporary photography exhibitions by top international names.

Alcazaba

The grand, crumbling, tenth-century **Alcazaba** (April–Sept Tues–Sat 9am–8.30pm, Sun 9am–3pm; Oct–March Tues–Sat 9am–6.30pm, Sun 9am–3pm; €2.50, free with EU passport) was built into the hillside by the Córdoba Caliph Abd-ar Rahman III and subsequently altered by the Christian monarchs. During its heyday, the fortress complex held up to 20,000 people and was said to rival Granada's Alhambra with the beauty of its palaces and sculpted gardens. Little remains, but it's worth visiting if only for the fabulous coastal views.

ARRIVAL AND DEPARTURE

By plane To reach Almería airport, 10km east of the city, catch the #L22 bus from outside the bus/train station.
By train Both buses and trains pull in at the combined Estación Intermodal on Carretera La Ronda, a 10min walk from the city centre. No luggage storage available.
Destinations Barcelona (1–2 daily; 13hr 30min–14hr 30min); Granada (4 daily; 2hr 30min); Madrid (3 daily; 6hr 30min–7hr 15min); Seville (4 daily; 5hr 30min–5hr 45min); Valencia (1–2 daily; 8hr 30min– 9hr 30min).
By bus Buses use the same Estación Intermodal as trains.
Destinations Granada (8 daily; 2hr 15min); Madrid (5 daily; 7hr); Málaga (8 daily; 3hr 15min); Seville (2 daily; 5hr 45min); Valencia (5 daily; 8hr 30min).

INFORMATION

Tourist office c/Parque Nicolás Salmerón at Martínez Campos (Mon–Fri 9am–7pm, Sat & Sun 10am–2pm; ☎ 950 175 220, ⓦ turismoalmeria.com).

ACCOMMODATION

Hotel La Perla Plaza del Carmen 7 ☎ 950 238 877, ⓦ www.hotellaperla.es. Multistorey budget hotel with compact, spotless en-suite rooms and pleasant staff. Little character, but it's hard to beat the central location. Wi-fi is temperamental. Double **€38**
Hotel Nuevo Torreluz Plaza de las Flores 10 ☎ 950 234 399, ⓦ torreluz.es. Well-located, four-star hotel turned friendly cheapie. Think warm colours, firm beds and compact, comfy en suites. Double **€45**
Hotel Sevilla c/de Granada 23 ☎ 950 230 009, ⓦ hotelsevillaalmeria.net. Spick-and-span a/c rooms with thimble-sized but modern bathrooms at this centrally located hotel. Double **€40**

EATING AND DRINKING

La Receta c/Tenor Iribarne 2. Perch on the comfiest bar stools you'll ever experience at this trendy bar, and order from the long list of tapas, such as the *albóndigas*

32

EL CABO DE GATA

Only 15km east of Almería lies Cabo de Gata, a **national park** comprising dramatic cliffs, desolate scrubland, low-key fishing villages and some of the most beautiful unspoiled beaches in the south. You can explore the park on a bike, enjoy incredible views of the coast from Torre Vigia Vela Blanca (an eighteenth-century watchtower), camp at the seaside villages and enjoy the pristine beauty of Playa de los Genoveses – the cape's prettiest beach. The only village you can reach by bus from Almería is San José, where you'll also find the greatest variety of accommodation and the National Park information office (Avda de San José 27; daily 10am–2pm & 5–8pm; ⓦ degata .com). There are two or three daily buses from Almería with Autocares Bernardo (ⓦ autocaresbernardo.com).

(meatballs) or the signature smoked salmon with guacamole. Tapas from €1.50. Daily 8pm until late.

★ **Taberna Vasca Añorga** c/Padro AlfonsoTorres 4. Basque mini-masterpieces are the order of the day at this cosy little bar – choose from the likes of cod with smoked potato foam or grilled foie gras with apple sauce, and wash them down with a glass of Txacolí. Tapas from €3. Daily 8.30pm until late.

★ **Tetería Almedina** c/Aurora Paz 2 ⓦ teteriaalmedina .com. A local legend, this cosy Moorish-themed restaurant really delivers when it comes to tagines, couscous and anything with aubergine. Try the superb *rghifa* pancakes, washed down with one of the many teas. Mains €8–10. Daily 11am–11pm.

Valencia and Alicante

Much of the coast around **Valencia** and further south on the **Costa Blanca** has been insensitively overdeveloped, suffering from mass package tourism and its associated ills. The main cities, however – vibrant **Valencia** and relaxed **Alicante** – are appealing and worth a stop for anyone travelling along the east coast.

VALENCIA

VALENCIA has been working hard to shed its provincial reputation and is emerging as an exciting, cosmopolitan city to rival Madrid and Barcelona. The City of Arts and Sciences complex is the best example of this, but Valencia's exuberance is also evident in its diverse nightlife. The city can also take pride in its museums, easily accessible beach, and, of course, its main festival: the world-famous **Las Fallas**. Also in the region are international music festival **Benicassim** and the riotous **Tomatina**, held in Buñol.

WHAT TO SEE AND DO

A few blocks north of the train station, the adjoining squares of **Plaza de la Reina** and **Plaza de la Virgen** are Valencia's heartbeat, with many of its principal sights nearby. Pedestrianized Plaza de la Virgen is a perfect spot to while away an hour with a drink and a cathedral view.

The most interesting area for wandering is the maze-like **Barrio del Carmen**, with its arty, bohemian atmosphere. Stretching north of the Mercado Central up to the river bed of the Río Turia, it's full of historic buildings being renovated and stylish cafés opening up next to crumbling townhouses. Valencia's beach, **Playa de la Malvarrosa**, is easily accessible (bus #1 from Torres Serranos and metro line #5 to Maritim-Serrería).

The town centre

Plaza de la Reina is home to the impressive thirteenth-century **Catedral** (Oct–April Mon–Sat 10am–5.30pm, Sun 2–7.30pm; May–Sept Mon–Sat 10am–5.30pm, Sun 2–6.30pm; €4.50), whose bell tower, the **Miguelete** (daily 10am–7.30pm; €2), gives stunning city views. Southwest of the cathedral lies the enormous **Mercado Central**, a modernist iron and glass structure housing over one thousand stalls selling local fruit, vegetables and seafood until 2pm (closed Sun). Opposite is the city's former silk exchange, La Lonja (entrance at c/de la Lonja 2; mid-March to mid-Oct Tues–Sat 10am–7pm, Mon & Sun 10am–5pm; mid-Oct to mid-March Tues–Sat 10am–6pm, Mon & Sun 10am–5pm; €2, free Sun), a stunning Gothic building whose main hall features intricately crafted spiral columns and a vaulted ceiling.

The museums

Art lovers will find **IVAM**, the modern art museum at c/Guillém de Castro 118 (Tues–Sun 10am–7pm; €2, free Sun; ⓦivam.es), a treat, with its permanent sculpture collection plus two floors of changing exhibitions of work by Spanish and international artists. The highlight of the city's museums, however, is the **Ciudad de las Artes y las Ciencias** (City of Arts and Sciences; see website for times; €36.25 for 3-day ticket to all sights; ☎902 100 031, ⓦcac.es). Sitting at the end of the Jardines del Turia, a 7km-long landscaped park that was built in the old river bed of the Río Turia, this breathtaking collection of futuristic concrete, steel and glass architecture

32

comprises five buildings, four of which were designed by locally born superstar architect Santiago Calatrava. The complex includes the **Hemisfèric**, an eyeball-shaped IMAX **cinema** (€8.80), a vast **science museum** (€8), a huge **aquarium** with beluga whales, sharks and turtles (€27.90), and a dramatic pistachio nut-shaped **arts centre**. The complex itself is free to enter, and well worth a visit to check out the architecture if you can't afford museum entry. Take bus #19 from Plaza del Ayuntamiento, or #35 from Avenida Marqués de Sotelo.

ARRIVAL AND DEPARTURE

By plane Valencia airport is 8km west of the centre, and is accessible by metro (lines #3 and #5; 25min; 5.30am–10.30pm; €3.90).

By train Trains to and from Alicante and Murcia use the central Estació del Nord on c/Xàtiva (⓶Xàtiva). Trains between Madrid and Barcelona use the Estació Joaquim Sorolla, 500m further south.

Destinations Alicante (10 daily; 1hr 35min–2hr 15min); Barcelona (15 daily; 3hr–5hr 20min); Granada (1 daily; 7hr 40min); Madrid (16 daily; 1hr 40min–3hr 40min).

By bus The station is northwest of the centre, on the far bank of the Río Turia river bed (⓶Turia); bus #8 (or a 30min walk) to Pl. del Ayuntamiento.

Destinations Alicante (20 daily; 2hr 30min–5hr); Barcelona (10 daily; 4hr–5hr 45min); Madrid (13 daily; 4hr); Seville (3 daily; 9hr 45min–11hr 40min).

By ferry Bus #19 connects the Balearic Ferry Terminal with Pl. del Ayuntamiento.

Destinations Ibiza (6 weekly; 6hr 30min); Mahon (1 weekly; 15hr); Palma (6 weekly; 8hr).

INFORMATION

Tourist office Municipal: Pl. de la Reina 19 (Mon–Sat 9am–7pm, Sun 10am–2pm; ⓣ963 153 931, ⓦturisvalencia.es). Regional: c/Paz (c/Pau) 48 (Mon–Fri

9am–8pm, Sat 10am–8pm, Sun 10am–2pm; ☎963 986 422, ⓦcomunitatvalenciana.com). Both hand out the free English-language listings guides such as *Hello Valencia* and *24-7 Valencia* (ⓦ247valencia.com).

Discount cards The Valencia Tourist Card (€15/20/25 for 1/2/3 days, or €10 for 3 days without transport) gives you unlimited travel on buses and metro and discounts in some museums, shops and restaurants. Available at tourist offices or at ⓦvalenciatouristcard.com.

GETTING AROUND

By bus and metro Most of Valencia's key sights are walkable from the town centre, but the public transport system is efficient and easy to use. Bus journeys cost €1.50, the metro €2 for journeys within the central zone A and €4 to the airport (plus €0.50 for reloadable card).The metro runs from 5.30am–midnight.

ACCOMMODATION

Although prices given here are for high season, many hostels put prices up further for Las Fallas.

Center Valencia c/Samaniego 18 ☎963 914 915, ⓦcenter-valencia.com; ⓜXàtiva. Clean, basic dorms with good facilities, including free internet, roof terrace, laundry service and breakfast. Dorm €13

★ **Hôme Youth Hostel** c/La Lonja 4 ☎963 916 229, ⓦhomehostelsvalencia.com; ⓜXàtiva. One of two *Hôme* hostels in the city. Well-designed, comfortable accommodation with kitchen, free internet and TV room, in a great central location. Dorm €23, double €56

Pensión París c/Salvá 12 ☎963 526 766, ⓦpensionparis .com; ⓜColón. Bright, clean, spacious rooms at budget prices, in a central location. Double €32

Red Nest Hostel c/Paz (c/Pau) 36 ☎963 427 168, ⓦrednesthostel.com; ⓜColón. Bright, fun decor and lots of communal space, with pool table and table football. Dorm €17, double €45

EATING

There are plenty of decent options near the Mercado Central and in the Barrio del Carmen, but avoid touristy places too near the plazas de la Reina and de la Virgen.

Most restaurants serve food daily 1–4pm and 8–11.30pm; exceptions cited below.

La Lluna c/San Ramón 23. Filling vegetarian grub plus organic beers and wines in a homely atmosphere. The bargain €8 weekday lunch menu features treats such as a spinach and squash "cake". Closed Mon.

★ **La Marcelina** Avda Neptuno 8. A smart choice for tasty beachside paella, with a lunchtime tasting menu (€20) that includes garlic bread, a selection of fried fish and a choice of five rice dishes, including a delicious *arroz negro* (black rice with squid). Closed Mon, Sun 1–4pm only.

Pepita Pulgarcita c/Caballeros (c/Cavallers) 19. Tapas (from €5.50 for one or €6.50 to share) and light meals are available in this stylish yet unpretentious restaurant. Closed Mon.

Taberna Botijo c/San Dionisio 1. A relaxed spot for home-made tapas, including daily specials such as oven-baked potatoes topped with roquefort (€3). Daily 9am–1pm.

DRINKING AND NIGHTLIFE

The action in Valencia is quite widely dispersed, but the city centre's best nightlife is in the Barrio del Carmen (c/Caballeros, c/Quart and c/Alta). The best gay bars and clubs are in and around c/Quart. Clubs open around 11pm.

Dub Club c/Jesús 91; ⓜJesús. The emphasis is on reggae at this little club. Entry is usually free, but there's a charge for live gigs (usually at weekends).

Music Box c/Pintor Zariñena 6. One of Valencia's most popular clubs, playing a variety of pop and dance music and open until late (Wed–Sat only).

Radio City c/Santa Teresa 19 ⓦradiocityvalencia.com. Barrio del Carmen bar with a varied programme of exhibitions, films, dance and music performances. Free entry most nights; see website for programme. Tues is flamenco night and costs €7 including a drink.

DIRECTORY

Banks Main branches of most banks are around Pl. del Ayuntamiento or along c/Xàtiva near the train station.

Hospital Hospital General, Avda Tres Cruces 2, at Avda del Cid; ☎961 972 000; ⓜNou d'Octubre.

FESTIVALS

The famous **Las Fallas** (ⓦfallasfromvalencia.com) are held annually from March 15 to 19, when hundreds of papier-mâché caricatures are paraded and then burnt in the streets of Valencia amid a riot of fireworks in a tribute to St Joseph, the patron saint of carpenters. Summer heralds a host of festivals in and around Valencia: the **Festival Internacional de Benicassim** (ⓦfiberfib.com) is a four-day music festival in the beach town of Benicassim, between Barcelona and Valencia, featuring well-known indie, pop and electronica acts; or indulge in some childhood fantasies at **La Tomatina** (ⓦlatomatina.info), essentially an enormous public tomato fight that takes place on the last Wednesday in August, in the tiny town of Buñol, one hour to the west of the city.

Internet Work Center, c/Paz 25 (open 24 hours; internet €2/hr).

Left luggage Lockers at the train station (by platform 6; daily 8am–9pm; €2.40–4/24hr) and the bus station (24/7: €3–4/24hr). You'll need the exact change.

Pharmacies Farmacia Valero, Plaza de la Reina 1 (☎ 963 384 555). Pharmacies run a rota for night-time and Sunday opening, posted in all pharmacy windows.

Police Gran Vía de Ramón y Cajal 40 (☎ 963 539 539).

Post office Pl. del Ayuntamiento 24.

ALICANTE

ALICANTE is a thoroughly Spanish city, despite its proximity to a strip of package holiday resorts. With good beaches nearby, lively nightlife and plenty of cheap hotels, it's worth a short stopover.

WHAT TO SEE AND DO

Wide esplanades give the town an elegant air, and around the Plaza de Luceros and along the seafront *paseo* you can relax beneath palm trees at terrace cafés. Try to time your visit to coincide with the **Hogueras fiesta** of processions, fire and fireworks, which culminates in an orgy of burning on the night of June 23/24. The cliff-top fortress of **Castillo de Santa Bárbara** (daily April–Sept 10am–10pm; Oct–March 10am–8pm; €2.40 for the lift, free Sun; last ascent is at 7.20pm, last descent 7.40pm) is Alicante's main sight, with pleasant park areas and a tremendous view from the top. Access to the lift is from beach-side Avenida de Jovellanos via a tunnel. Also worth a visit is the **Museum of Contemporary Art** (Tues–Sat 10am–8pm, Sun 10am–2pm; free) on Plaza de Santa María, a light, airy space with a permanent collection of twentieth-century (mostly Spanish) art, including works by Miró and Picasso, plus temporary exhibitions. **Playa Postiguet** is the city beach, but it gets crowded in summer: try the beaches at **Playa San Juan**, ten minutes from the town, on the half-hourly #L3 tram.

ARRIVAL AND DEPARTURE

By plane The airport is 12km south of town. The #L6 airport bus (every 20min 6.10am–11.10pm; €2.75) stops near the train station and at Pl. Luceros.

By train The main train station is on Avda Salamanca, a 20min walk from the town centre.

> ### ★ TREAT YOURSELF
>
> **El Portal** c/Bilbao 2 ☎ 965 143 269, ⓦelportaltaberna.com. Gourmet *tapas* and *raciones* served at the bar or in the chic restaurant. The menu features lots of local produce, including a salad made with Raf tomatoes and tuna belly (€6), and creative options such as baked scallops with cauliflower, almonds and truffles (€8). Daily 1.30–4.30pm & 8–11.30pm.

Destinations Barcelona (8 daily; 4hr 45min–5hr 35min); Madrid (7 daily; 3hr 15min); Valencia (12 daily; 1hr 30min–3hr).

By bus Local and long-distance services arrive at the bus station on c/Portugal, a 15min walk from the town centre. Destinations Barcelona (8 daily; 7hr 45min–9hr 15min); Granada (6 daily; 5hr–6hr 40min); Madrid (9 daily; 4hr 15min–6hr 15min); Málaga (7 daily; 5hr–6hr 50min); Valencia (22 daily; 2hr 30min–5hr 20min).

INFORMATION

Tourist office Avda Rambla Méndez Nuñez 23 (Mon–Fri 9am–6pm, Sat & Sun 10am–2pm ☎ 965 200 000, ⓦalicanteturismo.com). There are others inside the train and bus stations, and at the airport.

ACCOMMODATION

Outside July and August, finding accommodation should be easy, with most budget options concentrated at the lower end of the Old Town, especially on c/San Fernando, c/Jorge Juan and c/Castaño.

Albergue Juvenil La Florida Avda de Orihuela 59 ☎ 965 918 250, ⓦivaj.es. Fairly institutional HI hostel (card obligatory), with café and laundry facilities. From October to June many spaces are reserved for students, so booking ahead is essential. Under-25s **€11.50**, over-25s **€15.50**, full-board **€21.50/25.50**

Camping Costa Blanca c/Convento 143, El Campello ☎ 965 630 670, ⓦcampingcostablanca.com. In a small town, Campello, 10km to the north of Alicante, and close to the beach. Accessible by L1 or L3 tram, or bus #21. Also has bungalows sleeping 4–6 people. **€6** per person plus **€6** per tent, bungalow **€72**

★ **Hostal Les Monges Palace** c/San Agustín 4 ☎ 965 215 046, ⓦlesmonges.es. Elegant, stylishly decorated rooms, with excellent facilities for the price. Great central location. Double **€53**

Pensión San Nicolás c/San Nicolás 14 ☎ 965 217 039, ⓦalicantesannicolas.com Comfortable rooms (some en-suite) with little extras such as kettles and bathrobes, plus a fridge for visitor use. Close to the nightlife, so can be noisy at weekends. Double **€40**

32

EATING AND DRINKING

Known locally as El Barrio, the concentration of streets stretching north from the main Rambla to the castle contains over a hundred bars and is without a doubt the best place for eating and drinking. Another key area for nightlife is c/Castaños, which fills with revellers on summer nights. For eating, it can be hard to find budget options now that Alicante's gastronomic scene is booming; avoid touristy places on the Esplanade.

Ali Oli c/Miguel Soler 12. Relaxed wine and tapas bar serving local and national wines by the glass, plus a selection of meats and cheeses. Mon–Fri noon–4pm & 8pm–midnight, Sat & Sun 8pm–midnight.

Desdén c/Labradores 22, El Barrio. Lively, late-opening bar playing dance, jazz and funk music. Several similar options on the same street. Open daily until late.

★ **El Cisne de Oro** c/César Elguezábal 23. Popular tapas bar full of locals sampling delicious Alicante specialities, such as *pulpo* and *pastel de tortilla*. Daily 1–4pm & 8–11pm.

DIRECTORY

Consulate UK, Pl. Calvo Sotelo 1–2 ☎ 965 216 022.
Internet Some *locutorios* (phone offices) have internet access, including c/San Fernando 7 (Mon–Fri 10am–9pm, Sat 11am–9pm, Sun closed).
Post office Plaza Gabriel Miró 7.

The Balearic islands

The largest **Balearic islands** – Ibiza, Mallorca and Menorca – each maintain a character that is distinct from the mainland and from each other. **Ibiza** is synonymous with all-night summer clubbing, though it also boasts some lovely beaches and traditional villages. While **Mallorca**, the largest of the Balearics, attracts mass tourism with brash resorts crammed along the Bay of Palma, away from these there are soaring pine-forested mountains, traditional villages, lively fishing ports, incredible cycling terrain, beautiful coves and the Balearics' one real city, **Palma**. The furthest island from the mainland, **Menorca**, is more tranquil than its sisters, its topography less dramatic. Along with an abundance of unspoilt coves lapped by waters turquoise enough to rival the Caribbean, Menorca is also famous for

the prehistoric monuments that dot the island. Prices on all the Balearic islands are considerably above the mainland, and from mid-June to mid-September budget **rooms** are in short supply, so book in advance.

GETTING TO THE ISLANDS

Ferries from mainland Spain and inter-island connections are relatively expensive considering the distances involved, and special **flight** deals from the Spanish mainland with Vueling mean it can be cheaper, as well as quicker, to fly; in the summer months, there are plenty of international flights to all three islands. The three main ferry companies are Acciona **Trasmediterranea** (@trasmediterranea.es), **Balearia** (@www.balearia.com) and **Iscomar** (@www.iscomar.com); they operate from Barcelona, Valencia and Denia (just south of Valencia) on the mainland and have connections to and between Ibiza, Palma, Port d'Alcúdia, Maó and Ciutadella on the islands. Ferry timetables and prices vary hugely, and some services, particularly the fast boats, only run in summer. For the latest fares and schedules, see @directferries.co.uk, a useful one-stop shop (in English) for all routes and services.

IBIZA

IBIZA (Eivissa in Catalan) is an island of excess. Internationally heralded as one of the world's top clubbing destinations, each summer Europe's best DJs play at its clubs, attracting large numbers of people looking to party 24/7. Yet it also has a quieter side, particularly in the north, with beautiful beaches and a bohemian vibe, a legacy from the 1960s when the island was a hippy hang-out.

WHAT TO SEE AND DO

IBIZA CITY is the most attractive place on the island. Set around a dazzling natural harbour, it's one of the Mediterranean's most cosmopolitan small capitals. The mighty city walls enclose the ancient quarter of **D'alt Vila**, with its labyrinthine alleyways, attractive Gothic cathedral, and the excellent **Museu d'Art Contemporani** (Ronda de Narcís Puget; Tues–Fri 10am–1.30pm & 4–6pm, Sat & Sun 10am–1.30pm; free). Next to D'alt Vila, the port area is a maze of streets lined with bustling bars and expensive boutiques, with a small, lively produce market just opposite the fortress entrance. The island's second town, **SANT ANTONI** (accessible by bus #3 from Ibiza City; every 30min 7.30am–midnight), is handy for club access but rather charmless. To make the most of this compact island and to explore its isolated coves and traditional villages, it's well worth renting a car.

ARRIVAL AND DEPARTURE

By plane The airport is 7km southwest of Ibiza City. Regular bus #10 (daily 6.50am–11.50pm; €3.50) connects it to the port area via the city centre.

By boat The terminal on Passeig des Moll serves ferries to and from the mainland and Mallorca; boats from Formentera arrive at the terminal on Avda Santa Eularia.

By bus Ibiza is covered by a good network of buses. For timetables see ⓦ ibizabus.com.

INFORMATION

Tourist office On Plaça de la Catedral (Mon–Sat 10am–2pm & 5–9pm, Sun 10am–2pm; ☎ 971 399 232, ⓦ eivissa.es). There's another handy branch by the port at c/Antoni Riquer 2; both stock an excellent booklet on the 23 cycle routes around the island.

ACCOMMODATION

Camping Cala Nova Platja Cala Nova ☎ 971 331 774, ⓦ campingcalanova.com. Located 20km north of Ibiza Town – but only 50m from the Cala Nova beach. Good watersports base; bungalows available. Buses run from nearby Santa Eulària 11 times daily (except Wed & Sun). **€7.80** per tent, plus **€8.50** per person

Hostal Cala Boix Cala de Boix ☎ 971 335 224 ⓦ hostalcalaboix.com. Located by one of Ibiza's most

★ **TREAT YOURSELF**

Sa Nansa Av 8 de Agosto 27 ☎ 971 318 750. A meal here does not come cheap, but you will get to taste some of the best paella and *fideuá* in the Balearics, served by the friendly chef. Bring a friend, since portions are for two. Mains around €17 per person. Booking advisable on weekend evenings. Daily 1–4pm & 8–11pm.

beautiful beaches in the northeast, this whitewashed guesthouse offers spacious, bright rooms with terraces. Good restaurant attached. Double **€60**

Hostal Giramundo c/Ramón Muntaner ☎ 971 307 640, ⓦ hostalgiramundoibiza.com. Brightly coloured backpacker joint with themed rooms, thimble-sized toilets and an in-house bar-café, just a block from Figueretes beach and a 10min walk from the centre of Ibiza City. Dorm **€27**, double **€66**

Hostal Las Nieves c/Juan de Austria 18 ☎ 971 190 319 ⓦ hostalibiza.com. Clean and friendly *hostal* several blocks away from the Old Town. Double **€70**

Hostal Rosalía c/Rosalía 5, Sant Antoni ☎ 971 340 709, ⓦ hostalrosalia.com. Refurbished budget hotel with a small pool, popular with clubbers who like to stay a short walk away from *Es Paradis*. Prices drop steeply outside Aug. Double **€89**

EATING AND DRINKING

Opening hours are daily 1–4pm & 8–11pm unless otherwise stated.

Bar La Bodega c/Manel Sorà, Ibiza City. Eclectic decor and great tapas distinguish this popular bar, right near the entrance to D'alt Vila. It's hard to go wrong with the beef cheek, meatballs or grilled squid. Tapas from €4.

Bistrot el Jardín Mercado Viejo, Ibiza City. Right next to the produce market, this lively café specializes in incredible salads – a rarity in Spain. Try the goat's cheese, pear and honey, or the Oriental, washed down with a fresh fruit juice. Mains €7.50. Mon–Sat 10am–2pm & 5–8pm, Sun 10am–2pm.

32

DETOUR TO FORMENTERA

Just 20km south of Ibiza Town, the fourth-largest Balearic island, **Formentera**, lures day-trippers from Ibiza with its appealing beaches backed by sand dunes (Ses Illetes, Llevant and Migjorn are particularly good), and alternating landscapes of rugged cliffs and fields. Formentera is small enough to be explored end-to-end by bike in a day: numerous kiosks rent bicycles at the harbour. Plentiful mid-range restaurants focus on seafood and rice dishes; most tend to be open May–Oct. Baleària–Trasmapi ferries (ⓦ www.balearia.com) run at least ten times daily during peak season (one-way from €16.50), while Mediterranea-Pitiusa (ⓦ medpitiusa.net) lay on eleven fast ferries daily.

Can Costa c/Sa Creu 19. Family-run restaurant serving no-nonsense Spanish dishes. The soup is filling enough to be a meal in itself, or keep going with grilled meat and fish and home-made desserts. Mains from €7. Closed Sun.

Comidas Bar San Juan c/Vicent Soler s/n. Long-standing family-run restaurant-bar, with outstanding fish dishes. Arrive early to avoid queuing and expect to share tables. Closed Sun. Mains from €7.

Tapas Restaurant & Lounge Bar Cami des Reguero 4, Sant Antoni. Yes, it attracts a large tourist contingent, but their *patatas bravas* and spicy calamari stand out, and the roast dinners tempt homesick Brits. Tapas from €4.50, mains from €11.

CLUBS

Ibiza's world-famous temples to hedonism draw hundreds of thousands of revellers during the party season (June–Sept), the entertainment provided by world-class DJs. The action tends to take place 1–6am, with each megaclub specializing in a different theme, be it foam parties, fancy dress or even striptease. Entry fees can be anything between €25 and €65, not including drinks (from €10 each); look out for touts selling discounted tickets around the port bars each night, and club promoters handing out free invites on the beaches. Ibiza also has one of the best gay scenes in Europe, with a lot of the action centred in the port and another cluster of bars on c/de la Virgen; many mainstream clubs hold a weekly gay night. The Discobus (check ⓦ discobus.es for timetables; €3 one-way/€12 for 5 trips) links most of these clubs with the centre of town. Alternatively, head to Platja d'en Bossa to party day and night at the famous beach bar *Bora Bora* (ⓦ boraboraibiza .net; free entry).

Amnesia Ibiza Town–Sant Antoni road, km6 ⓦ amnesia .es. Dance area surrounded by a massive tropical glasshouse filled with palm trees, a superb sound system that DJs Mar T, Les Schmitz and Caal Smith make good use of, and the island's most popular gay night, La Troya, which is held here on Wed. May–early Oct.

Anfora c/San Carlos 7, Dalt Vila ⓦ disco-anfora.com. Ibiza's only dedicated gay club.

Es Paradis c/Salvador Espriu 2, Sant Antoni ⓦ esparadis .com. Glass pyramid, roofless dancefloor, and pounding sound system. Extremely popular for its water parties (Tues & Fri), when the dancefloor is flooded, and Sun night Neon Paint Party. June–late Sept.

Pacha Avda 8 d'Agost ⓦ pacha.com. Think: mirror balls, large dancefloor with a capacity of over three thousand; a variety of music, including Spanish pop, soul and funk, but predominantly techno and house; DJs such as David Guetta; and a chillout terrace. May–Oct.

Privilege Ibiza Town–Sant Antoni road, km7 ⓦ privilegeibiza.com. One of the biggest clubs in the world, with a capacity for 10,000 and the DJs doing

BEST OF THE BEACHES
Of Ibiza's many beaches, particular gems include the following: **Cala Llenya**, 2km northeast of Santa Eulària, with calm azure waters against a backdrop of pine trees; tiny, sheltered **Cala Mastella**, covered in bark-like Poseidonia seagrass; **Cala Boix** with its deep, turquoise water and a steep descent; golden-sand Platges de Comte on the western tip of the island; and the long white crescent behind a pine grove that is **Platja de Ses Salines**, south of the airport, past the salt marsh, accessible by bus #11 (hourly 9.30am–7.30pm).

their thing from a cabin suspended above the pool. June–early Oct.

Space Platja d'en Bossa ⓦ space-ibiza.es. Vast dance space accommodating up to 12,000 revellers, with a plethora of chill-out zones and a roster of A-list DJs such as Carl Cox. Since things kick off mid-afternoon, you can take a boat to Platja d'en Bossa from Ibiza City (€6 return). June–mid-Oct.

MALLORCA

MALLORCA has a split identity. There are sections of its coast where the concrete curtain of high-rise hotels and shopping centres is continuous, but these parts are easy to avoid. Elsewhere the island is as appealing as it gets in the Mediterranean, particularly in the northwest where several stunning coves and pretty villages are framed by the dramatic backdrop of the rugged Tramuntana mountains. The northwest and northeast coasts also hold great appeal for serious cyclists, with steep switchback bends extending down to the Sa Calobra cove and running all the way to Cap de Formentor, Mallorca's northernmost tip.

Palma

Much to the surprise of many visitors, **PALMA** is an attractive, historic and cosmopolitan city filled with atmospheric narrow streets, stylish boutiques and lively bars and restaurants. The main focal point is the vast Gothic **cathedral** (Mon–Fri 10am–5.15pm, Sat 10am–2.15pm; €4) at c/del Palau Reial 9, which was built in recognition of the Christian Reconquest of

★ **TREAT YOURSELF**

Hidden in the labyrinthine La Lonja, behind a large wooden door, **Abaco** (c/Sant Joan 1, just off C/Apuntadores) looks like a cross between a market and an antiques store, with fruit draped over the elegant staircase, copious flowers and even caged birds. The cocktails are some of the best in town – at €16 a pop, they'd better be.

Mallorca, and later worked on by Gaudí. Next door is the imposing **Palau de l'Almudaina** (Mon–Fri 10am–5.45pm, Sat 10am–1.15pm; €2.50), an Islamic fort turned royal residence; you can visit the spartan chambers and royal apartments. A short walk away, at Porta de Santa Catalina 10, the contemporary glass-and-concrete **Es Baluard** (Tues–Sun 10am–8pm; €6, €4 temporary exhibitions, free Tues) houses an equally contemporary collection of twentieth-century art and excellent temporary exhibitions.

ARRIVAL AND INFORMATION

By plane Palma airport, 8km east of the city, is served by bus #1 (every 15min; €2.50) to the Passeig Mallorca.
By boat The large ferry port is 3.5km west of the city centre, connected to Palma by bus #1.
Tourist office Plaça de la Reina 2 (Mon–Fri 9am–8pm, Sat 9am–2pm; ☎ 971 712 216, ☜ infomallorca.net).
Car rental Palma airport has plenty of options, or try Europcar along the seafront in Palma proper (Avda Ingeniero Gabriel Roca 19 ☎ 902 105 055).

ACCOMMODATION

Hostal Apuntadores c/Apuntadores 8 ☎ 971 713 491, ☜ palma-hostales.com. Centrally located multistorey cheapie with tiled rooms, friendly English-speaking management and a roof terrace offering great views of the city. Double **€50**
Hostal Brondo c/Ca'n Brondo 1 ☎ 971 720 507, ☜ hostalbrondo.com. Stylish hotel, tastefully decorated in traditional Mallorcan style. Rooms are quieter than the options on c/Apuntadores but only come with wash basin. Double **€75**
Hostal Terramar c/Berlin 9, El Arenal ☎ 971 739 931, ☜ hostalterramar.com. A stone's throw from the beach in El Arenal, 4km south of Palma, this friendly hostel is great value for money; breakfast is included and some rooms are en suite with sea views. Bus #25 connects you to Palma. Dorm **€15**, double **€38**

EATING AND DRINKING

The best place to go strolling in search of food is the largely pedestrianized La Lonja. Opening hours are daily 1–4pm & 8–11pm unless otherwise stated.
★ **Bar El Día** c/Apuntadores 18. Simple tapas bar, overflowing with locals, that specializes in large portions of *patatas alioli*, garlicky *gambas al ajillo*, *pimentos padrón* and more. Tapas from €4. Closed Mon.
Celler Pagès Off c/Apuntadores at c/Felip Bauza 2. Small, unpretentious restaurant serving traditional Mallorcan food – try the stuffed marrows with home-made mayonnaise. Good-value lunch menu at €14. Closed Sun.
★ **Tasca Gastrobar** c/Blaquerna 6 ☜ tasca deblanquerna.com. The most affordable of the three Marc Fosh institutions in Palma, this contemporary bar tempts with the likes of goat's cheese, beetroot and hazelnut dressing salad, braised beef cheek with smoked bacon and incredible white chocolate cheesecake, all beautifully presented. Dishes €7–12.50. Closed Sun & Mon.
★ **Ummo** c/Sant Magi 66. Modern tapas bar serving 13 award-winning, delicious mouthfuls such as peppers stuffed with mushrooms and veal cheek, as well as daily specials and lunchtime set menu. Tapas from €3. Closed Mon

Sóller and around

Set beneath the dramatic Tramuntana mountains, where the air is scented by orange and lemon groves, the beautiful town of **SÓLLER** is dominated by the Baroque Església de San Bartolomé. Don't miss the superb local ice cream at the Sa Fabrica de Gelats (☜ gelatsoller.com) on

32

PALMA–SÓLLER TRAIN RIDE

The **train ride from Palma to Sóller** (5–7 daily; €12.50 one-way, €19.50 return; ☜ trendesoller .com) is definitely worth the trip. Built in 1912 to carry fruit to Palma, the wooden carriages rattle along the narrow-gauge railway through the dusty outskirts of the capital before a cross-country climb up mountain passes and through tunnels, passing almond groves, unruffled lakes and craggy peaks topping a thousand metres. In Sóller, you can then hop on the antique 1913 trolley that rumbles down to Port de Sóller (1–2 hourly; €5 one-way, combined ticket with train €28), where you find a small sandy cove suitable for bathing and good fish restaurants.

CYCLING MALLORCA

The rugged terrain, pine forests and winding roads along Mallorca's northwestern coast make for some challenging cycling, and lycra-clad enthusiasts tackle it in droves. Don't miss the scenic ride to Cap de Formentor – the **lighthouse** at the island's northernmost tip. When you climb to the first viewpoint, past the Port de Pollença, a minor road winds its way uphill to your right. If you reach the top, there are fantastic views of the island from the perilous watchtower. Heading south along the Ma-10, it's well worth stopping in Pollença for the Calvari – a 365-stone-step climb to the hilltop chapel. Further southwest, the most picturesque of Mallorca's turquoise-water coves, Sa Calobra, is reached by a series of steep hairpin bends. Bikes are available at rental outlets in Palma and in Alcúdia on the north coast; they can be transported in the luggage section of buses.

the Plaça de Mercat. The best way to get here is by train (see box, p.1059). From Sóller it's only 2km to the picturesque village of **Biniaraix**, and another 2km to **Fornalutx**. The winding Ma-10 hugs the coast, heading southwest, passing through the mountain village of **Deià**, the former home of Robert Graves, before arriving in **Valdemossa**, famous for its monastery where Chopin and George Sand stayed in 1838–9.

Eastern Mallorca

While many beaches along Mallorca's east coast have been ruined by mass tourism, the beaches north of Cala Ratjada are still relatively unspoiled, with white sand and clear waters. Inland there is the quiet town of Artà, dominated by a fourteenth-century hilltop fortress, from which you get a fantastic view of the surrounding countryside, while south along the coast, near the town of Porto Cristo, are the island's most spectacular caves – Coves del Drac (⊕cuevasdeldrach.com for tour times; €14), known for their vast size, strange rock formations and subterranean lake.

ARRIVAL AND DEPARTURE

By bus Frequent buses from Palma run to Artà and Cala Ratjada, but to get to the caves and some of the more isolated beaches you need your own wheels.

MENORCA

In 1993 **MENORCA** was declared a biosphere reserve, and as such the island has largely avoided the rampant development seen elsewhere in the Balearics. Instead, idyllic coves, tranquil

bays and rolling countryside, dotted with prehistoric sights, take their place. It's possible to get to some of the beaches with local transport from the main towns of **Maó** or **Ciutadella**, but you'll need your own wheels if you want to discover the more isolated beauty spots. Cycling is a great option as the roads are flat and quiet.

Maó

As most visitors stay in resorts along the coast, the Menorcan capital of **MAÓ** is relatively free from tourists and so retains an authentic feel, its lovely old streets lined with Georgian houses and picturesque squares. Across the bay from Maó, 12km away, is the vast nineteenth-century **Fortalesa de la Mola** (June–Sept daily 10am–8pm, shorter hours rest of year; €8; ⊕fortalesalamola.com), reachable only by car, while local buses provide access to nearby attractions, such as the lunar landscape of the **Cap de Favaritx**, the whitewashed seaside town of **Fornells** – home of Menorca's signature dish, *caldereta de langosta*, slow-cooked lobster stew – or the beach resorts in the southeast, such as **Cala en Porter**.

ARRIVAL AND DEPARTURE

By plane Menorca's international airport is 5km southwest of Maó. Buses (€1.60) run every 30min from 6am to midnight to Maó's central bus station.

By bus There are hourly TMSA buses to Ciutadella (45min), while five daily Autos Fornells buses run to Fornells (30min). There are also less frequent buses from Ciutadella that pass near some of the southern beaches.

By boat Ferries from Palma and Barcelona arrive at Maó harbour, a short walk from the town centre.

32

MENORCA'S PREHISTORIC SITES

Unlike its neighbours, Menorca is dotted with stone constructions dating as far back as 2000 BC. There are three types of edifices: *taulas*, unique to Menorca, are horseshoe-shaped constructions with T-shaped pillars at the centre; *talayots* are stone mounds that served as ancient watchtowers; *navetas* are constructions that resemble upturned boats and possibly served as tombs or places of gathering. The most impressive include **Naveta des Tudons** (Tues–Sun 9.15am–8.30pm, Sun until 3pm; €2), a large, intact stone burial chamber near the 40km mark along the Ciutadella–Maó road, and **Torre d'en Galmés** (same hours; €3), where you can check out the three hilltop *talayots* and underground chambers. Outside set hours and peak season the sites can be visited free of charge.

INFORMATION

Tourist office Plaça S'Esplanada (Mon–Fri 9am–1.30pm & 5–7.30pm, Sat 9am–2pm; ☎971 355 952, ⓦmenorca.es).

Bicycle rental Autos Mahon Rent, Moll de Levant 35–36 ⓦautosmahonrent.com. Rents bicycles (€15/24hr), scooters and cars.

ACCOMMODATION

Hostal La Isla c/Santa Caterina 4 ☎971 366 492, ⓦhostal-laisla.com. The rooms at this friendly guesthouse are on the compact side, but all come with TV and private bath; decent bar downstairs. Double €56

Posada Orsi c/Infanta 19 ☎971 364 751. Brightly coloured though ageing rooms and roof terrace make this a reasonable choice. Cash only. Double €47

EATING AND DRINKING

The best places for eating and drinking are down by the port, where the plentiful bars and restaurants are open mainly in July and Aug, and around Plaça Bastió, an appealing square with lots of tapas options.

Cristinal y Gradinata C/Isabel II. A collection of old radios, hats and beer bottles adorns the shelves of this delightful bistro bar. Serves an excellent range of artisan beers and liquor at night; tapas and coffee during the day. Mon 8.30am–3pm, Tues–Fri 8.30am–3pm & 7–11.30pm, Sat noon–3pm & 7–11.30pm.

Mirador Café Plaça Espanya 2. A friendly bohemian spot with great views for tapas (€1.50–6), loose-leaf teas and live music or film screenings. Closed Sun.

★ **Ses Forquilles** Rovellada de Dalt 20. The informal decor belies the quality of the gourmet food on offer. Feast on suckling pig, black pudding and honey sandwiches, tuna tataki, steak, imaginative tapas and desserts. Tapas from €3, mains from €10. Closed Sun.

Ciutadella and around

Well-preserved **CIUTADELLA** has a lovely old quarter and harbour and is Menorca's prettiest town. Wandering around the narrow, cobbled streets and quiet plazas, lined with colourful houses and seventeenth-century churches, is a real pleasure. Nearby are some of the most beautiful and secluded virgin beaches in the Mediterranean, such as **Cala Turqueta** (10km) and **Macarella** (13km) – both have soft white sand and turquoise waters and are about a twenty-minute drive from Ciutadella (also easily reachable by bike) through countryside and pine forest. There are no facilities at Turqueta, so bring a picnic. A short walk from Macarella over the white stone gorge takes you to the even prettier bay of **Macarelleta**.

ARRIVAL AND DEPARTURE

By bus TMSA (ⓦtmsa.es) buses arrive and depart from Plaça dels Pins, a few minutes' walk from the centre of town.

Destinations Maó (hourly; 45min).

By boat Ferries from Alcúdia in Mallorca arrive at the ferry port about 4km south of the centre. Buses sometimes meet the boats to ferry passengers to town.

Bicycle and motorbike rental Velos Joan, c/Sant Isidre 30 (☎971 381 576, ⓦvelosjoan.com).

INFORMATION

Tourist office Plaça Catedral 5 (Mon–Sat 8.30am–3pm & 5–9pm; ☎971 382 693, ⓦmenorca.es).

ACCOMMODATION

Hostal Residencia Oasis c/Sant Isidre 33 ☎971 382 197. Comfortable, spacious rooms set back from a pretty courtyard in the Old Town and run by a friendly elderly couple. No internet; closed June–Sept. Double €50

Hotel Geminis c/Josepa Rossinyol 4 ☎971 384 644, ⓦhotelgeminismenorca.com. Light, bright a/c rooms (some with balcony) in an attractive salmon-coloured hotel with small pool, a couple of minutes' walk from the Old Town. Weak wi-fi. Double €62

32

EATING AND DRINKING

The produce market (Plaça Francesc Netto and Plaça Llibertat, Mon–Sat mornings) is a good place to pick up provisions for a picnic. For nightlife, hit the port, where bars and clubs (in high season) stay open until 6am.

Ca'n Nito c/Plaça d'es Born 11. A lively bar on the main square, popular for drinks and a fantastic range of tapas. *Platos combinados*, such as roast chicken with side (€9), also available. Daily 9am–late.

★ **La Guitarra** c/Nostra Senyora dels Dolors 1. Family-run restaurant serving traditional Menorcan specialities, such as *caldereta de llagosta* (lobster stew) – Menorca's most famous and expensive dish – and *fideuá* (paella-like noodle dish), in an atmospheric cellar. Mains from €15. Mon–Sat 1–4pm & 8–11pm.

La Rosa de Habana c/Sa Rosa dels Vents. Inexpensive Cuban specials (mains from €7), such as Cuban-style chicken and *ropa vieja* (beef stew), are served at this friendly spot. Fast food such as pizza and burgers also available, but Cuban food is the star. Daily 1–4pm & 8–11pm.

32

Catalunya

With its own language, culture and, to a degree, government, **Catalunya** (Catalonia in English) has a unique identity. **Barcelona**, the capital, is very much the main event – one of the most vibrant and exciting cities in Europe. Inland, the monastery of **Montserrat**, Catalunya's premier sight, is perched on one of the most unusual rock formations in Spain and makes for a great day-trip. To the north, the rugged **Costa Brava** is slowly shedding its erstwhile unfortunate touristy image and boasts the best beaches in the region, along with some appropriately wacky and wonderful homages to Surrealist artist Salvador Dalí. Just south of Barcelona, the beach town of **Sitges** draws visitors with its beaches and a raucous Gay Pride event in June.

BARCELONA

Cool and hip as they come, **BARCELONA** is Catalunya's elegant and self-confident modern capital. A thriving port, and the most prosperous commercial centre in the Iberian peninsula, its sophistication and cultural dynamism are way ahead of the rest of Spain – the city seems far more in tune with Milan and Paris than with Madrid or Lisbon. Barcelona also evolved a quirky and very individual identity of its own, most perfectly expressed in the eccentric Art Nouveau architecture of **Antoni Gaudí** and his contemporaries, but also evident in the huge diversity of the city's cultural events.

WHAT TO SEE AND DO

Though it boasts outstanding **Gothic** and **Art Nouveau** buildings, and some great museums – most notably those dedicated to Picasso, Miró and Catalan art – Barcelona's main appeal lies in getting lost in the narrow side streets of the **Barri Gòtic** (Gothic Quarter), rising, eating and drinking late, hitting the beach or lazing in the parks, and generally soaking up the atmosphere. As in any large city, beware of pickpockets.

La Rambla

One of the most popular avenues in Europe, **La Rambla** teems with sightseers, tourist bars, postcard stalls and human statues. As it bisects the city, La Rambla remains a useful point of reference, so it's worth strolling down to orient yourself before getting lost in the more interesting maze of side streets in the Barri Gòtic to the east or El Raval to the west. If you are walking down La Rambla towards the sea, just off to your right is the highly photogenic **La Boqueria**, the city's main food market (Mon–Sat 8am–8.30pm; ⓦboqueria .info), a splendid gallery of sights and smells that's frequented by locals and tourists alike. By the namesake metro station stands the **Liceu**, Barcelona's celebrated opera house (daily guided tours of the interior at 10am, €10; visit without guide daily at 11.30am, noon, 12.30pm and 1pm; €5; ⓣ934 859 914, ⓦliceubarcelona.cat). Further south, just off La Rambla and into the Barri Gòtic, is the elegant nineteenth-century **Plaça Reial**, crowded with hundreds of alfresco diners and drinkers. Across La Rambla and just into El Raval, **Palau Güell** (daily: April–Oct 10am– 8pm, Nov–March 10am–5pm; €12;

CATALAN (CATALÀ)

	CATALAN	PRONUNCIATION
Yes	*Sí*	See
No	*No*	Noh
Please	*Si us plau*	See-uus-plow
Thank you	*Graciés*	Gra-see-ess
Hello/Good day	*Hola*	Oh-la
Goodbye	*Adéu*	A-day-uu
Excuse me	*Perdoni*	Perdoni
Where?	*On?*	On?
Good	*Bon/Bona*	Bon/Bonna
Bad	*Mal*	Mal
Near	*Aprop*	Aprop
Far	*Lluny*	Yoon
Cheap	*Barat*	Barat
Expensive	*Car*	Carr
Open	*Obert*	Oo-berrt
Closed	*Tancat*	Tun-cat
Today	*Avui*	A-boo-ee
Yesterday	*Ahir*	A-hear
Tomorrow	*Demà*	Du-maa
How much?	*Quant val?*	Kwant val?
What time is it?	*Quina hora és?*	Kina ora es?
I don't understand	*No ho entenc*	No oo antenk
Do you speak English?	*Parles anglès?*	Par-les ang-lays?
One	*Un/Una*	Oon/Oona
Two	*Dos/Dues*	Doss/Doo-guz
Three	*Tres*	Trays
Four	*Quatre*	Kwa-tra
Five	*Cinc*	Sing
Six	*Sis*	Seess
Seven	*Set*	Set
Eight	*Vuit*	Bweet
Nine	*Nou*	No
Ten	*Deu*	Dayoo

32

ⓦpalauguell.cat) at c/Nou de la Rambla 3–5 is a must for any Gaudí fan: the interiors showcase some of his best work and are simply breathtaking. Right at the harbour end of La Rambla, Columbus stands perilously perched atop a tall, grandiose column, the **Mirador de Colom** (daily 8.30am–8.30pm; €4). Take the lift to his head for a bird's-eye view of the city.

El Raval

The once-notorious red-light district of **El Raval** lies on the west side of La Rambla. With its two universities and numerous bars, clubs and arts centres, Raval is now one of the most authentic areas of the city. For a taste of the area's regeneration, walk up the **Rambla de Raval** – a boulevard with pavement cafés and bars – on your way to the **Museu d'Art Contemporani de Barcelona** or **MACBA** (Mon & Wed–Fri 11am–7pm, Sat 10am–8pm, Sun 10am–3pm, open in summer till 8pm Mon & Wed, midnight Thurs & Fri; €7.50 to visit the whole museum, individual exhibitions less; ⓦmacba.cat), an arresting white-walled and glass edifice, which houses a permanent collection of Spanish and Catalan art from the 1950s onwards, as well as thought-provoking temporary exhibitions by international and national artists. Next door is the **Centre de Cultura Contemporània de Barcelona** or **CCCB** (Tues, Wed & Fri–Sun 11am–8pm,

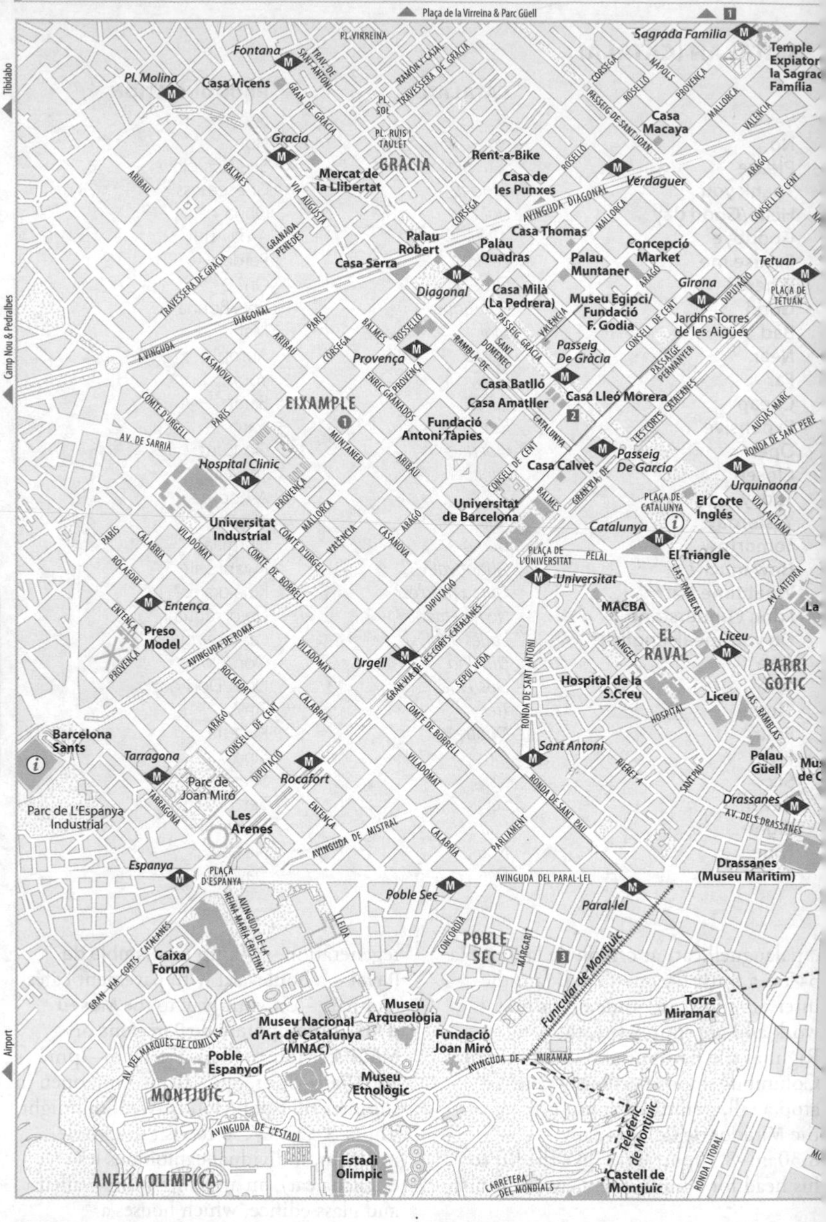
Plaça de la Virreina & Parc Güell
1
Tibidabo
Camp Nou & Pedralbes
Airport
PL. VIRREINA
Fontana
Pl. Molina
Casa Vicens
Sagrada Familia
Temple Expiator la Sagrad Família
Casa Macaya
Gracia
Mercat de la Llibertat
GRÀCIA
Rent-a-Bike
Casa de les Punxes
Verdaguer
Palau Robert
Casa Thomas
Palau Quadras
Casa Serra
Palau Muntaner
Concepció Market
Tetuan
PLAÇA DE TETUAN
Diagonal
Casa Milà (La Pedrera)
Museu Egipci/ Fundació F. Godia
Girona
Jardins Torres de les Aigües
Provença
Passeig De Gràcia
Casa Batlló
Casa Amatller
Casa Lleó Morera
EIXAMPLE
Fundació Antoni Tàpies
2
Hospital Clinic
Passeig De Gracia
Casa Calvet
Urquinaona
Universitat de Barcelona
PLAÇA DE CATALUNYA
El Corte Inglés
Universitat Industrial
Catalunya
El Triangle
PLAÇA DE L'UNIVERSITAT
Universitat
MACBA
Entença
Preso Model
EL RAVAL
Liceu
Urgell
BARRI GÒTIC
Hospital de la S.Creu
Barcelona Sants
Tarragona
Sant Antoni
Palau Güell
Rocafort
Parc de Joan Miró
Parc de L'Espanya Industrial
Les Arenes
Drassanes
Espanya
PLAÇA D'ESPANYA
Drassanes (Museu Maritim)
Poble Sec
Paral·lel
POBLE SEC
3
Caixa Forum
Funicular de Montjuïc
Torre Miramar
Museu Arqueològia
Museu Nacional d'Art de Catalunya (MNAC)
Fundació Joan Miró
Poble Espanyol
Museu Etnològic
MONTJUÏC
Teleferic de Montjuïc
Estadi Olimpic
ANELLA OLÍMPICA
Castell de Montjuïc
AVINGUDA DIAGONAL
GRAN VIA DE LES CORTS CATALANES
AVINGUDA DEL PARAL·LEL
AVINGUDA DE MISTRAL
AVINGUDA DE ROMA
AVINGUDA DE L'ESTADI
AV. DEL MARQUÈS DE COMILLAS
AVINGUDA DE MIRAMAR
CARRETERA DEL MONDIALS
RONDA LITORAL
RONDA DE SANT ANTONI
RONDA DE SANT PAU
LAS RAMBLAS

32

Thurs 11am–10pm; €4.50 one exhibition, €6 two or more; ⓦcccb.org). Firmly at the cutting edge of contemporary culture, this creative space hosts film cycles, exhibitions, installations and more, including Sónar (see box, p.1063).

Barri Gòtic

The **Barri Gòtic** dates principally from the fourteenth and fifteenth centuries, when Catalunya reached the height of its commercial prosperity. The quarter is centred on **Plaça de Sant Jaume**, just behind which lies Barcelona's **cathedral**

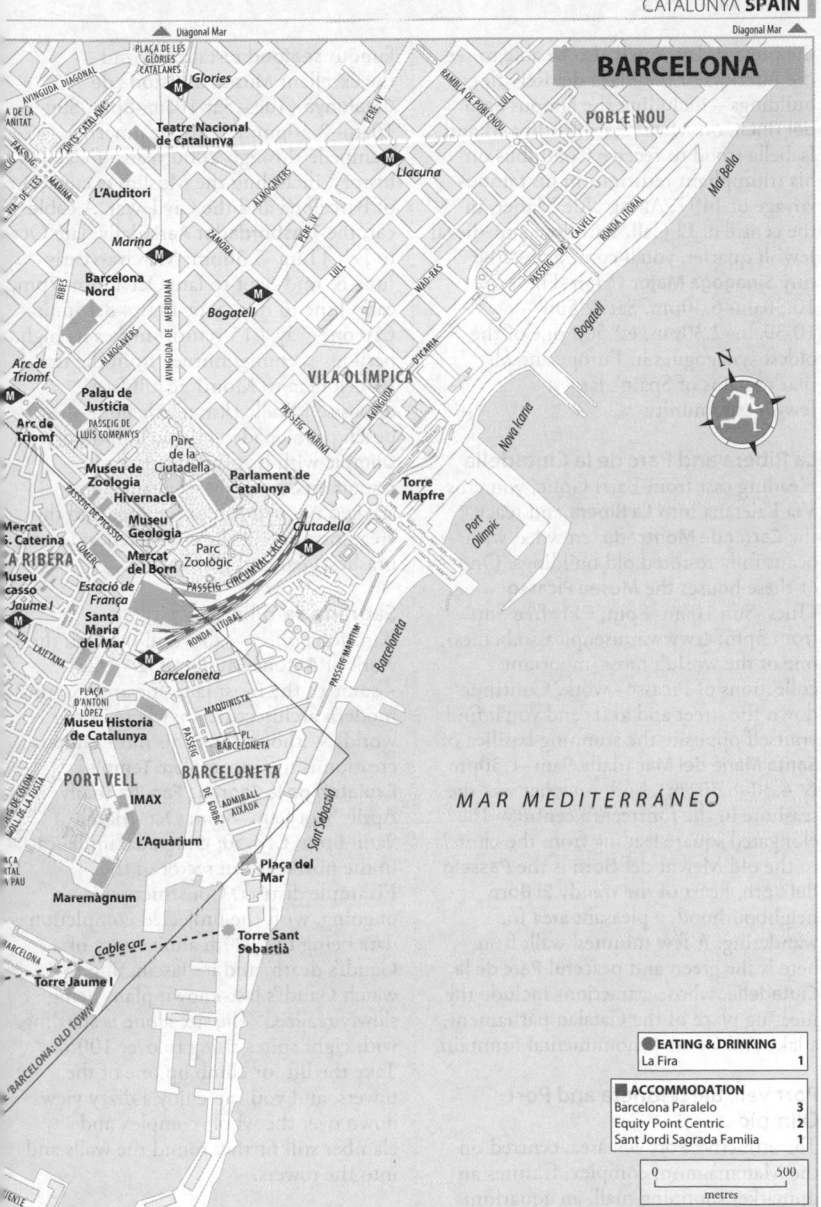

BARCELONA

Diagonal Mar

PLAÇA DE LES GLORIES CATALANES — Glories

POBLE NOU

Teatre Nacional de Catalunya

L'Auditori

Llacuna

Marina

Barcelona Nord

Bogatell

Mar Bella

VILA OLÍMPICA

Arc de Triomf

Arc de Triomf

Palau de Justicia

Parc de la Ciutadella

Museu de Zoologia

Parlament de Catalunya

Torre Mapfre

Hivernacle

Museu Geologia

Ciutadella

Mercat S. Caterina

LA RIBERA

Museu Picasso

Mercat del Born

Parc Zoològic

Estació de França

Jaume I

Santa Maria del Mar

Port Olímpic

Barceloneta

PLAÇA D'ANTONI LÓPEZ

Museu Historia de Catalunya

PL. BARCELONETA

MAQUINISTA

PORT VELL

BARCELONETA

IMAX

MAR MEDITERRÁNEO

L'Aquàrium

Plaça del Mar

Maremàgnum

Cable car

Torre Sant Sebastià

Torre Jaume I

BARCELONA: OLD TOWN

● EATING & DRINKING
La Fira | 1

■ ACCOMMODATION
Barcelona Paralelo | 3
Equity Point Centric | 2
Sant Jordi Sagrada Familia | 1

0 ————— 500
metres

32

(La Seu; daily 8am–12.45pm & 5.15–8pm; free, but €5 1–5pm; ⓦcatedralbcn.org), one of Spain's great Gothic buildings. Barcelona's finest Roman remains were uncovered nearby, beneath the beautiful **Plaça del Rei**, and now form part of the wonderful **Museu** **d'Història de la Ciutat** (Tues–Sat 10am–7pm, Sun 10am–8pm; €7, free first Sat of the month from 4pm & Sun from 3pm; ⓦwww.museuhistoria.bcn.es), which takes you into the nitty-gritty of the city's development, all the way from its Roman fish sauce-making factory to the present day. You'll also be able to see the interiors of the Plaça del Rei's finest buildings – including the famous **Saló del Tinell**, on whose steps Ferdinand and Isabella stood to receive Columbus on his triumphant return from his famous voyage of 1492. Along c/de Marlet, in the centre of El Call, Barcelona's medieval Jewish quarter, you'll come across the tiny **Sinagoga Major** (Mon–Fri 10.30am–6.30pm, Sat & Sun 10.30am–2.30pm; €2.50), one of the oldest synagogues in Europe and all that remains of Spain's largest Jewish community.

La Ribera and Parc de la Ciutadella

Heading east from Barri Gòtic, you cross Vía Laietana into **La Ribera** and reach the **Carrer de Montcada**, crowded with beautifully restored old buildings. One of these houses the **Museu Picasso** (Tues–Sun 10am–8pm; €11, free Sun from 3pm; ⓦwww.museupicasso.bcn.es), one of the world's most important collections of Picasso's work. Continue down the street and at its end you'll find yourself opposite the stunning basilica of **Santa Maria del Mar** (daily 9am–1.30pm & 4.30–8.30pm), built on what was the seashore in the fourteenth century. The elongated square leading from the church to the old Mercat del Born is the **Passeig del Born**, heart of the trendy **El Born** neighbourhood, a pleasant area for wandering. A few minutes' walk from here is the green and peaceful **Parc de la Ciutadella**, whose attractions include the meeting place of the Catalan parliament, a lake and Gaudí's monumental fountain.

Port Vell, Barceloneta and Port Olímpic

The attractive **Port Vell** area, centred on the Maremàgnum complex, features an upmarket shopping mall, an aquarium with an 80m-long shark tunnel, IMAX cinema and a multitude of expensive restaurants. The other side of the port, past the marina, the **Barceloneta** district, in contrast, is one of the few remaining *barris* harbouring genuine local Catalan life. Here, you'll find popular and not terribly clean **beaches**, the city's most

famous **seafood** restaurants and the excellent **Museu d'Història de Catalunya** (Tues–Sat 10am–8pm, Sun 10am–2.30pm; €5; ⓦmhcat.net), a stampede through 2000 years of Catalan history, including the Muslim occupation of Barcelona and the Civil War. A **cable car**, the **Trasbordador Aeri** (daily: late Oct to Feb 11am–5.30pm; March to early June & mid-Sept to late Oct 11am–7pm; early June to mid-Sept 11am–8.15pm; €10 one-way, €15 return) makes its high, perilous-seeming journey from the tip of Barceloneta to Montjuïc hill (see opposite). Walk 1km north along the beach promenade and you'll find **Port Olímpic** with its myriad bars and restaurants. At night, the tables are stacked up, dancefloors emerge and the area hosts one of the city's liveliest (and brashest) bar and club scenes.

Sagrada Família

Barcelona offers – above all through the work of **Antoni Gaudí** (1852–1926) – some of the most fantastic and exciting modern architecture anywhere in the world. Without doubt his most famous creation is the incomplete **Temple Expiatori de la Sagrada Família** (daily: April–Sept 9am–8pm; Oct–March 9am–6pm; €13.50; ⓦsagradafamilia.cat), in the northeastern sector of the Eixample district. Construction is ongoing, with the projected completion date being the 100th anniversary of Gaudí's death, and it's fascinating to watch Gaudí's last-known plans being slowly realized. The size alone is startling, with eight spires rising to over 100m. Take the lift, or climb up one of the towers, and you can enjoy a dizzy view down over the whole complex and clamber still further round the walls and into the towers.

L'Eixample

Barcelona's Eixample (the street-grid zone) abounds with wonderful modernista (Art Nouveau) buildings. The top two are Gaudí's **Pedrera** at Passeig de Gràcia 92 (daily: March–Oct 9am–8pm; Nov–Feb 9am–6.30pm; €16.50; ⓦlapedrera.com) and, nearby, his

Casa Batlló at Passeig de Gràcia 43 (daily 9am–8pm; €20.35/16.30; ⓦcasabatllo .cat), a wonderfully surreal residential building; check out the front window in the form of a dragon's mouth. Inside, you'll find no straight lines – just curves, twists and undulations. Casa Batlló shares a block with two other great Art Nouveau buildings, the Casa Amatller at no. 41 and the Casa Lléo Morera at no. 35.

Barcelona's other Art Nouveau masterpiece is the 1908 **Palau de la Música Catalana** concert hall in c/Sant Pere Més Alt (daily 10am–6pm; tours every 30min; €15, with limited places so buy in advance; ⓦpalaumusica.org), where the multicoloured columns of the facade are just a taster the wonders within, in particular the amazing stained-glass roof.

Gràcia and Parc Güell

The residential neighbourhood of **Gràcia**, north of the centre, has a bohemian, village-like feel, and is a good place for an authentic night out. Popular with arty student types, the bars are best stumbled upon by chance – try your luck around the Plaça de la Virreina.

In the eastern part of Gràcia, **Parc Güell** (daily: winter 10am–6pm; summer 10am–8pm; free) is Gaudí's most ambitious project after the Sagrada Família. This almost hallucinatory experience consists of a hillside park featuring, among other creations, giant decorative lizards and a vast Hall of Columns, containing a small **museum** (daily 10am–6pm; €6) with some of the furniture Gaudí designed. To get here, take the metro to Vallcarca or Lesseps (15min walk from either) or bus #24 from Plaça de Catalunya to the eastern side gate.

Montjuïc

The green hill of **Montjuïc**, with its winding paths and botanical gardens, provides a refuge from the bustle of the city, while at the same time featuring a couple of great museums and a superbly sited castle. You can approach it from **Plaça d'Espanya** and walk from there up the imposing Avenida de la Reina María Cristina, past the **Font Mágica**, a large fountain that comes alive with lights to the tune of "Barcelona" by Freddie Mercury and Montserrat Caballé in the evenings. To start with the castle, take the **Funicular de Montjuïc** (daily, from 7.30am weekdays or 9am weekends until 10pm in summer, or 8pm in winter; every 10min; fare included in metro tickets), from Paral.lel metro station to the start of the **Telefèric de Montjuïc** (daily: March–May & Oct 10am–7pm; June–Sept 10am–9pm; Nov–Feb 10am–6pm; €7.30 one-way, €10.50 return), which in turn leads to the **Castell de Montjuïc** (daily: April–Sept 9am–9pm, Oct–March 9am–7pm; free), an eighteenth-century fortress that offers magnificent city views.

MNAC, the Poble Espanyol and the Fundació Joan Miró

The Palau Nacional, set at the back of Montjuïc, is the grand peach-coloured home to one of Spain's great art museums, the **Museu Nacional d'Art de Catalunya** or **MNAC** (Tues–Sat 10am–7pm, Sun 10am–2.30pm; €11, free first Sun of month; ⓦmnac.es). Its enormous bounty includes a Romanesque collection that is the best of its kind in the world and a substantial number of Gothic, Baroque and Renaissance works, as well as a large modern art section and changing temporary exhibits. Nearby is

32

DAY-TRIP: MONTSERRAT

The bulbous mountains of **Montserrat**, 60km northwest of Barcelona, make for an interesting day-trip out of the city. As well as some short hikes (1–3hr) through the national park's unusual rock formations, the main attraction is the Benedictine monastery, with its well-preserved sixteenth-century basilica housing a twelfth-century image of La Moroneta, patron saint of Catalunya. To get here, take the R5 train from Plaça Espanya (every hour at 36min past; 1hr 5min) to Montserrat Aeri (for the cable car), or to Monistrol de Montserrat (for the rack railway to the town).

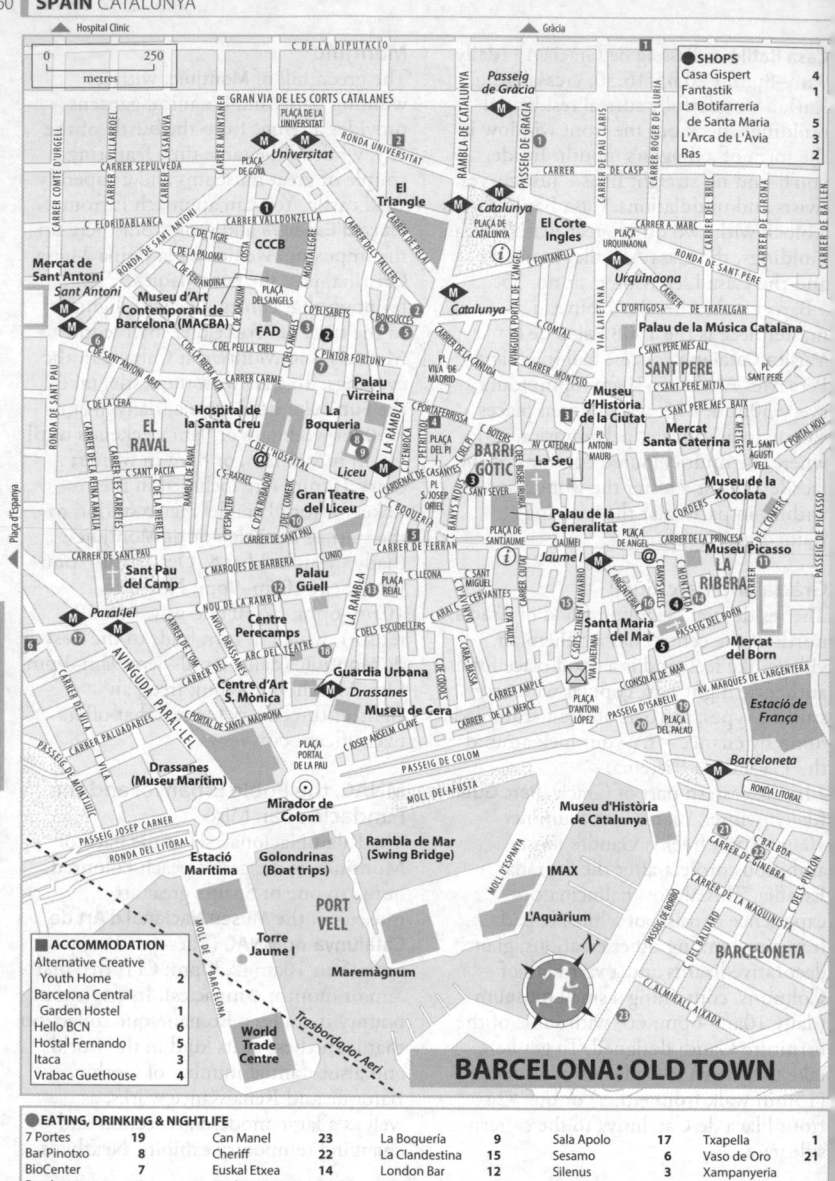

BARCELONA: OLD TOWN

● SHOPS
Casa Gispert	4
Fantastik	1
La Botifarrería de Santa Maria	5
L'Arca de L'Avia	2
Ras	3

■ ACCOMMODATION
Alternative Creative Youth Home	2
Barcelona Central Garden Hostel	1
Hello BCN	6
Hostal Fernando	5
Itaca	3
Vrabac Guethouse	4

● EATING, DRINKING & NIGHTLIFE
7 Portes	19	Can Manel	23	La Boquería	9	Sala Apolo	17	Txapella	1
Bar Pinotxo	8	Cheriff	22	La Clandestina	15	Sesamo	6	Vaso de Oro	21
BioCenter	7	Euskal Etxea	14	London Bar	12	Silenus	3	Xampanyeria	
Boadas	2	Jamboree	13	Moog	18	Taller de Tapas	16	Can Paixano	20
Buenas Migas	4	Julivert Meu	5	Organic	10	Tlaxcal	11		

the **Fundació Joan Miró** (Tues, Wed, Fri & Sat: Oct–June 10am–7pm; July–Sept 10am–8pm, Thurs 10am–9.30pm, Sun 10am–2.30pm; €10; ⓦbcn.fjmiro.es), devoted to the largest collection of works by one of the greatest Catalan artists, with Miró's drawings, bold abstract paintings, sculpture and textile creations on display in an appealing, light-filled building. Downhill and to the west of MNAC is the **Poble Espanyol** or "Spanish Village" (Mon 9am–8pm, Tues–Thurs 9am–2am, Fri 9am–4am, Sat 9am–5am, Sun 9am–midnight; €9.50;

ⓦpoble-espanyol.com), consisting of replicas of famous or characteristic buildings from all over Spain, and with a lively club scene at night.

ARRIVAL AND INFORMATION

By plane The main Aeroport del Prat is 12km southwest of the city centre and is linked by train (daily 5.42am–11.38pm, every 30min; €3.50) to Barcelona Sants, and Pg. de Gràcia in the city centre, both served by ⓜL3 to Liceu or Pl. de Catalunya. The Aerobús (6am–1am, every 5–10min from Terminal 1, every 10–20min from Terminal 2; €5.90; ⓦaerobusbcn.es) runs to Pl. d'Espanya and Pl. de Catalunya. Some Ryanair flights land at Girona Barcelona airport near Girona (see p.1065).

By train Barcelona Sants (ⓜSants) is the city's main train station, for national and some international arrivals – many national buses also stop here. Estació de França (ⓜBarceloneta) is the terminal for long-distance Spanish and European express and intercity trains.

Destinations Girona (1–2 hourly; 1hr 10min–1hr 45min); Madrid (1–2 hourly; 2hr 40min–9hr); Tarragona (2–4 hourly; 35min–1hr 45min); Valencia (15 daily; 3–4hr); Zaragoza (1–2 hourly; 1hr 30min–5hr 30min).

By bus The main bus terminal for international and long-distance services is the Estació del Nord (ⓦbarcelonanord.com; ⓜArc de Triomf).

Destinations Alicante (9 daily; 7hr–9hr 45min); Madrid (17 daily; 7hr 20min–8hr 5min); Valencia (9 daily; 4hr–4hr 30min); Zaragoza (20 daily; 3hr 30min–4hr).

By ferry Balearics ferries dock at the Estació Marítima (ⓜDrassanes). Acclona Transmediterranea (ⓦtrasmediterranea.es) and Balearia (ⓦbalearia.com) are the main ferry companies with regular services from Barcelona to Palma de Mallorca, Maó on Menorca and Ibiza Town. Grandi Navi Veloci ferries (ⓦwww.gnv.it) run three or more luxury ferries to Genoa, Italy (19hr), while Grimaldi Ferries (ⓦwww.grimaldi-lines.com) run to Civitavecchia not far from Rome, Livorno in Tuscany and Porto Torres in Sardinia.

INFORMATION

Tourist office Plaça de Catalunya (daily 8.30am–8.30pm; ☏932 853 834, ⓦbarcelonaturisme .com; ⓜCatalunya).

GETTING AROUND

By metro and bus The easiest way of getting around is by metro (Mon–Thurs & Sun 5am–midnight, Fri till 2am, all night Sat). Numerous bus routes (ⓦtmb.cat; roughly 6am–10.30pm) pass through Plaça de Catalunya; every bus stop displays route maps. Yellow night buses run between 11pm and 3/5am every 30–45min; all pass through Plaça de Catalunya. Pick up a free transport map at TMB customer service centres at Barcelona Sants, and at Universitat, Diagonal, La Sagrera and Sagrada Familia metro stations.

Tickets Ticket prices for bus and metro are as follows: zone 1 single (covers all major sights) €2; a ten-ride *targeta* "T-10" €9.75 which is valid for the train to El Prat airport; 1/2/3-day pass €6.95/12.80/18.50.

Discount cards The Barcelona Card, available from any tourist office (2/3/4/5 days €37/47/56/62), covers all city transport including to/from airport, plus between 15 and 50 percent discounts at many museums and some tours, shops and restaurants. Worthwhile only if you're planning on huge amounts of sightseeing in a short period. The Articket (€30, available at the tourist office and participating museums; ⓦarticketbcn.org) covers entry to six of the city's main art galleries: it's worth getting if you plan on visiting at least four of them. Student ticket prices in museums and galleries are often only available to those who are both a student and under 25.

Bicycles Many hostels rent out bikes, or try Rent-a-Bike, c/Perill 28 (€7/day; ☏931 845 936, ⓦrentabikebarcelona .com). We (c/Montjuic del Bisbe 3–5; ☏934 122 853, ⓦwebarcelona.com) offer themed, self-guided cycling and walking tours that use their iPhones and app (half-day/full day €35/50).

Taxis The black-and-yellow taxis charge a minimum of €2.10, plus €0.95/km 8am–8pm weekdays, €1.20 at other times: a cross-town journey costs around €8–12.

ACCOMMODATION

Accommodation in Barcelona is among the most expensive in Spain, and you're strongly advised to book ahead, particularly at busy times such as Sónar (see box, p.1063) and September's Festes de la Mercè, when the city celebrates its patron saint with a riot of *castellers* (human castles) and other revelry. Most of the cheapest accommodation is in the side streets off and around La Rambla and in El Raval. Try ⓦhostelbarcelona.com to help you find hostels.

★ **Alternative Creative Youth Home** Ronda de la Universitat 17 ☏635 669 021, ⓦalternative-barcelona .com; ⓜCatalunya; map p.1060. Great location, friendly atmosphere that encourages communal dinners (without this being a party hostel), wonderfully helpful staff and fast broadband. Dorm €33

Barcelona Central Garden Hostel c/Roger de Llúria 41 ☏935 006 999, ⓦbarcelonacentralgarden.com; ⓜCatalunya; map p.1060. Near the main attractions, with lovely patio, common area with book exchange, and sparsely decorated but comfortable rooms. Quiet time after midnight guarantees a good night's sleep. Dorm €24, double €52

Barcelona Paralelo c/Salva 62 ☏934 439 885, ⓦwww .districthostel1.com; ⓜParal.lel; map pp.1056–1057.

32

While the dorms are on the small side, the staff are helpful and group dinners encourage camaraderie among guests. Great atmosphere. Dorm **€26**, double **€70**

Equity Point Centric Passeig de Gràcia 33, Eixample ☎ 932 156 538, ⓦ equity-point.com; Ⓜ Passeig de Gràcia; map pp.1056–1057. A beautiful old mansion conversion right near La Rambla and Plaça Catalunya with comfy beds, great terrace bar and decent guest kitchen. The staff aren't particularly helpful, though. Breakfast included. Dorm **€22**

Hello BCN c/Lafont 8–10, Poble Sec ☎ 934 428 392, ⓦ hellobcnhostel.com; Ⓜ Paral.lel; map p.1060. Secure, well-located hostel popular with a young crowd. Crowded dorms but an excellent common room with great atmosphere; also has gym, kitchen, bike rental and a bar. Dorm **€28**, double **€100**

Hostal Fernando c/Ferran 31, Barri Gòtic ☎ 933 017 993, ⓦ hfernando.com; Ⓜ Liceu; map p.1060. Refurbished stone-walled *hostal* offering spacious, sparkling rooms, plus top-floor dorm accommodation and tapas bar downstairs. Breakfast included. Dorm **€24**, double **€77**

Itaca c/Ripoll 21 ☎ 933 019 751, ⓦ itacahostel.com; Ⓜ Jaume I; map p.1060. Jolly little hostel in the heart of Barri Gòtic, with spacious mixed dorms (and one women-only dorm), plus plenty of communal spaces, helpful staff and a small kitchen. Dorm **€28**, double **€70**

★ **Sant Jordi Sagrada Familia** c/Freser 5 ☎ 934 460 517, ⓦ santjordihostels.com; Ⓜ Sant Pau/Dos de Maig; map pp.1056–1057. Not far from its namesake attraction, this super-clean, skater-trendy hostel scores high points for the sociable vibe, huge guest kitchen and group nights out. Great place to meet people. Dorm **€21**

★ **Vrabac Guethouse** c/Portaferrissa 14 ☎ 663 494 029, ⓦ vrabacguesthouse.wordpress.com; Ⓜ Liceu; map p.1060. Lovely small guesthouse in Barrio Gòtic, its individually decorated rooms arranged around a peaceful central courtyard. Good breakfast is included and the owner is very helpful. Double **€80**

EATING

Barcelona is a reasonably expensive place to eat out. The best bet for a cheap meal is to take advantage of the lunchtime *menú del día* many places offer Mon–Fri – you can get three courses with wine and bread for as little as €10. For picnics, head for La Boquería market off La Rambla. There are many excellent tapas bars in the Old Town; avoid the overpriced ones on La Rambla. Opening hours are daily 1–4pm & 8–11pm unless otherwise stated.

★ **7 Portes** Passeig d'Isabel II 14; Ⓜ Barceloneta; map p.1060. Expect white linen, smart-looking career waiters and expertly cooked large portions of paella, *arroz negro* (rice in sepia ink) and *fideuá*. One of the few *arrocerías* where you can order a paella for one. Mains €15.

Bar Pinotxo La Boquería; Ⓜ Liceu; map p.1060. Perpetually busy with locals, this tapas bar at the back of La Boquería dishes up such delights as caramel pork belly or seared squid. Tapas from €4. Sept–July Mon–Sat 6am–5pm.

BioCenter c/Pintor Fortuny 25 ⓦ restaurantebiocenter .es; Ⓜ Catalunya; map p.1060. One of the best-value vegetarian lunchtime menus in town – €10 weekdays, €12.50 weekends. Or order curried tofu, gnocchi and veggie chips with dips à la carte.

Buenas Migas Pl. Bonsuccés 6; Ⓜ Catalunya or Liceu; map p.1060. Small café in the heart of arty Raval, serving delicious pizza, quiche slices, cake and good coffee. Set menus from €8.50.

Can Manel Pg. Joan de Borbó 60 ⓦ canmanel.es; Ⓜ Barceloneta; map p.1060. *Bodega* with large wooden barrels, specializing in grilled meats and Catalan favourites such as *calçotes* (grilled spring onions). Good-value €12 *menú del día*, and the sangría made with cava is very refreshing. Closed Mon & Sun eve.

Cheriff c/Ginebra 15; Ⓜ Barceloneta; map p.1060. Traditional restaurant famous for its paella and fish dishes. Mains from €15; bring a friend if you want to order a rice dish.

Euskal Etxea Placeta de Montcada 1 ⓦ euskaletxea taberna.com; Ⓜ Jaume I; map p.1060. Basque *taberna* specializing in a great range of mouthwatering *pintxos* (tapas) from €2 each.

Julivert Meu c/ Bonsuccés 7, El Raval; Ⓜ Catalunya; map p.1060. Stone-walled, wooden-beamed bar serving an excellent selection of traditional Catalan dishes. Eat well for €15–20.

★ **La Boquería** La Rambla; Ⓜ Liceu; map p.1060. Barcelona's most famous produce market, heaving with locals and tourists. Shop here for fruit, veg, chorizo, jamón, cheese, bread, cake and fresh fruit juices, and head for the tapas stalls at the back for lunch or snacks. Mon–Sat 8am–8.30pm.

Organic c/Junta de Comerc 11; Ⓜ Liceu; map p.1060. Bright little organic vegetarian restaurant with a hippy vibe. Three courses (including all-you-can-eat salad buffet) for €11, though desserts are not a strong point. Another branch at the back end of La Boquería market does takeaway.

★ **Sesamo** c/Sant Antoni Abat 52; Ⓜ Sant Antoni; map p.1060. Vegetarians rejoice, for this cheerful spot serves "food with no beasts". Three-course lunches are a steal at €8 and there are fresh juices and pastries if you're not too hungry. Closed Wed & Sun eve.

Silenus c/Angels 8; Ⓜ Liceu; map p.1060. The full set lunch isn't cheap (€16) but there's a cheaper, no-dessert menu (€12) at this modern European restaurant serving the likes of gnocchi, duck with caramel and incredible lavender ice cream.

Taller de Tapas c/de l'Argentería 51; Ⓜ Jaume I; map p.1060. One of several city-centre branches of this popular

SÓNAR

If electronica is your thing, make sure you're in town for **Sónar** (w sonar.es), an internationally respected multimedia art and progressive music festival, held every June in Barcelona. Day tickets bought online cost €45, night tickets €70, while a three-day, two-night pass will set you back **€170**.

chain of tapas bars offering slabs of tortilla, grilled prawns and other simple, filling dishes in relaxed surroundings. Another branch at La Rambla 49. Tapas from €4.50.

Tlaxcal c/Comerç 27 w tlaxcal.com; m Jaume I; map p.1060. Trendy Mexican joint with thirteen types of tacos and fantastic home-made salsas. Weekday lunchtimes are a bargain, with fresh guacamole, a portion of tacos and dessert for €10.50. Closed Mon.

Txapella Passeig de Gràcia 8–10; m Passeig de Gràcia; map p.1060. Basque *pintxo* bar with over fifty tiny elaborate sandwiches on the menu. Choose anything from grilled calamari to prawn with bacon, steak tartare and plain ol' *jamón serrano*. Pintxos from €1.75.

DRINKING AND NIGHTLIFE

Barcelona's nightlife is some of Europe's best, though it's not cheap. The high-tech theme palaces are concentrated mainly in the Eixample, especially around c/Ganduxer, Avda Diagonal and Vía Augusta. Laidback and/or alternative places can be found in the streets of El Raval, while the waterfront Port Olímpic area is a more mainstream summer-night playground, where the big, brash identikit clubs are. Music bars close at 3am, the clubs at 4 or 5am, though later at weekends. For listings, pick up a copy of *Butxaca*, a free weekly guide available in most bars and clubs (w butxaca.com), or buy the weekly *Guía del Ocio* from any newsstand (w guiadelociobcn.com). The thriving gay scene in Barcelona (w gaybarcelona.net) is prevalent in the so-called Gaixample, a few square blocks northwest of the main university.

BARS

Boadas c/Tallers 1, El Raval; m Catalunya; map p.1060. Old-fashioned cocktail bar just off La Rambla once frequented by Hemingway, with three mixologists creating the signature daiquiris and over thirty types of gin. Mon–Thurs noon–2am, Fri & Sat noon–3am.

La Clandestina Baixada de Viladecols 2; m Jaume I; map p.1060. Relax with a water pipe, glass of wine, beer or strong, sweet Turkish coffee at this bohemian joint. Fri & Sat 10am–midnight, Sun–Thurs 10am–10pm.

⭐ **La Fira** c/Provença 171; m Provença; map pp.1056–1057. Only in Barcelona – fairground rides and circus

paraphernalia adorn this long-standing theme bar. Tues–Sat from 11pm till late.

London Bar c/Nou de la Rambla 34–36; m Liceu; map p.1060. Here you can prop up the bar that Picasso and Miró once graced, or check out the live acts on the small stage at the back.

Vaso de Oro c/Balboa 6; m Barceloneta; map p.1060. A tiny but lively bar, packed with locals and serving a good selection of artisan beer. Closed Sept.

Xampanyeria Can Paixano c/Reina Cristina 7; m Barceloneta; map p.1060. The place to sip champagne while snacking on tiny sandwiches. Very popular (read: very, very crowded). Mon–Sat 9am–10.30pm, Sun to 1pm.

CLUBS

Jamboree Pl. Reial 17 w masimas.com/jamboree; m Liceu; map p.1060. Cavernous basement club with an international crowd dancing to hip-hop, funk and r'n'b (cover charge around €10), with live acts earlier in the evening at 8 and 10pm. Daily until 5.30am.

Moog c/Arc del Teatre 3 w masimas.com/moog; m Drassanes; map p.1060. From disco to drum'n'bass with regular appearances from top UK and Euro DJs. Despite the large, industrial setting the atmosphere is relaxed and both gay- and straight-friendly. Cover charge €10. Daily midnight–5am.

Sala Apolo c/Nou de la Rambla 113 w sala-apolo.com; m Paral.lel; map p.1060. Live gigs from international acts and burgeoning stars from the worlds of alternative electronica, rock and techno. "Nasty Mondays" are very popular. Daily 11.30pm–5am.

SHOPPING

The big names of the fashion industry occupy the Passeig de Gràcia and the shopping centre Maremagnum. The crooked passages of La Ribera and El Born are home to dozens of little boutiques, while in El Raval, numerous trendy vintage shops lie along the Carrer de la Riera Baixa. There are also a number of excellent speciality food retailers in the city, and chocolate shops are scattered throughout the Ciutat Vella.

Casa Gispert c/Sombrerers 23 w casagispert.com; m Barceloneta or Jaume I; map p.1060. Freshly roasted nuts, dried fruits, speciality chocolates and *turrons* (marzipan and nougat bars), with sweet teeth catered to since 1851.

Fantastik c/Joaquín Costa 62; m Universitat; map p.1060. A potpourri of crafts and knick-knacks from all over the world – perfect for quirky last-minute gifts.

La Botifarrería de Santa María c/Santa María 4; m Barceloneta or Jaume I; map p.1060. Sells fabulous speciality hams, cheeses and their famous *botifarras* (Catalan sausages).

L'Arca de L'Àvia c/Banys Nous 20; m Liceu; map p.1060. An

32

incredible collection of vintage clothing – so much so that these guys have supplied the set of *Titanic* and other films.

Ras c/Doctor del Dou 10; ⓜ Universitat; map p.1060. Beautiful bookshop and gallery selling books on art and architecture, as well as photography.

DIRECTORY

Consulates Canada, Pl. de Catalunya 9 ☎ 934 127 236, 1st floor, 2a; Ireland, Gran Vía Carles III 94 ☎ 934 915 021; UK, Avda Diagonal 477, 13th floor, Eixample ☎ 933 342 194; US, Pg. Reina Elisenda de Montcada 23, Sàrria ☎ 932 802 227.

Exchange Most banks are located in Pl. de Catalunya and Pg. de Gràcia. ATMs and money exchange available at the airport, Barcelona Sants, the Pl. Catalunya tourist office, and at *casas de cambio* throughout the centre.

Hospitals 24hr accident and emergency centres at the following: Hospital Clínic, c/Villaroel 170 ☎ 932 275 400, ⓜ Hospital Clínic; Hospital dos de Maig, c/Dos de Maig 301, ⓜ Sant Pau–Dos de Maig.

Left luggage Lockers at Sants station (daily 5.30am–11pm) and at Locker (Estruc 36, Barri Gòtic, ⓜ Catalunya; daily 9am–9pm).

Pharmacies At least one *farmacía* in each neighbourhood is open nights and weekends. Try Farmàcia Clapés (La Rambla 98, ⓜ Liceu).

Police Guàrdia Urbana (City Police), La Rambla 43 ☎ 092, ⓜ Liceu; open 24hr.

Post office Pl. Antoni López, Barri Gòtic, ⓜ Jaume I (Mon–Fri 8.30am–9.30pm, Sat 8.30am–2pm).

THE COSTA BRAVA

Stretching for 145km from the French border to the town of Blanes, the **Costa Brava** (Rugged Coast) boasts wooded coves, high cliffs, popular beaches and deep blue water. The more rugged northern part, dominated by the spectacular **Cap de Creus** headland and park, and the whitewashed fishing town of **Cadaqués**, is the most attractive yet least crowded, with a natural appeal all its own. Inland is **Girona**, the beautiful medieval capital of the region, and **Figueres**, Dalí's birthplace and home to his outrageous **museum**. Buses in the region are almost all operated by SARFA (☎ 902 302 025, ⓦ sarfa.es), with an office in every town. To visit the smaller and more picturesque coves, a car or bike is useful, or walk the fabulous Camí de Ronda necklace of footpaths running along the coastline.

Figueres

The northernmost parts of the Costa Brava are reached via **FIGUERES**, a provincial Catalan town with a lively *rambla*. The town's major highlight is the most visited museum in Spain after El Prado, the surrealist creation that is the **Teatre-Museu Dalí** (March–June & Oct 9.30am–6pm; July–Sept 9am–8pm; Nov–Feb 10.30am–6pm; Oct–May closed Mon; €12; ⓦ salvador-dali.org). Born in Figueres, Dalí died here in the tower and the museum showcases some of his most eccentric work. The extraordinary pink facade, topped with enormous eggs and suits of armour balancing baguettes on their heads, sets the tone for the exhibitions inside, which include collages, sculptures and mechanical contraptions requiring audience participation, and ticket price includes entry to the Dalí Jewels exhibition – 39 precious creations based on the artist's designs. Between late July and late August, the whole experience gets even more surreal during cava-fuelled night visits (daily 10pm–1am; €13).

ARRIVAL AND DEPARTURE

By train To make your way into the centre of town (about 600m), simply follow the "Museu Dalí" signs from the train station.

Destinations Barcelona (hourly; 1hr 50min–2hr 20min); Girona (hourly; 30–40min); Madrid (daily at 3.49pm; 5hr 20min).

By bus The bus station is around 200m away from the train station, towards the city centre. SARFA buses run to Cadaqués (4–8 daily; 1hr).

INFORMATION

Tourist office Pl. del Sol (July–Sept Mon–Sat 9am–8pm, Sun 10am–2pm; Jan–Feb Mon–Fri 10am–2pm; spring and autumn hours vary; ☎ 972 503 155, ⓦ figueresciutat.com).

ACCOMMODATION AND EATING

It's easy to go to Figueres as a day-trip from either Barcelona or coastal destinations, but it might be worth staying overnight to beat the bussed-in crowds. The restaurants around Museu Dalí tend to be sub-par and overpriced.

Creperie Bretonne c/Cap de Creus 6. The decor draws on the absurdist theme, and the wide range of sweet and savoury stuffed crêpes and salads (set lunch menu from €7) is equally enticing. Daily 1–4pm & 8–11pm.

Hostal Sanmar c/Rec Arnau 31 ☎972 509 813, ⓦhostalsanmar.com. Motel-style accommodation 200m north of the Old Town. Worn furnishings, but clean and perfectly acceptable for an overnight stay. Double **€60**

Cadaqués

The picture-postcard fishing village of **CADAQUÉS**, an hour by SARFA bus (4–8 daily; 1hr) from Figueres, with whitewashed houses, tiny beaches and narrow cobbled streets straddling a hill topped by an imposing church, was Salvador Dalí's home from 1930 to 1982, and attracted an arty crowd during its heyday. The tiny fishing village of Portlligat, 1.25km walk from Cadaqués, features the **Casa-Museu Dalí** (by advance booking only; closed early Jan to mid-Feb; €11; ☎972 251 015, ⓦsalvador-dali.org), a labyrinthine ramble of a house decorated according to the whims of Dalí and his beloved wife. Bizarre ornaments catch your eye in every room and a visit to the artist's intimate quarters offers an enthralling glimpse into his private life.

INFORMATION

Tourist office Carrer del Cotxe 2 (☎972 258 315; late June–mid-Sept Mon–Sat 9am–9pm, Sun 10am–1pm & 5 8pm; shorter hours rest of year).

ACCOMMODATION

Camping Cadaqués Ctra Port-Lligat 17 ☎972 258 126. Campsite in an attractive location with a large pool that's only open in summer; very basic facilities. Open April–Sept. **€9.60** per person, plus **€10.40** per tent
Hostal Vehí Carrer de l'Església 5 ☎972 258 470, ⓦhostalvehi.com. Friendly budget hotel near the church, with wonderfully clean rooms and an irritating wi-fi policy (switched off between 10pm and 8am); cheaper rooms shared facilities. Double **€55**

EATING AND DRINKING

For a drink or a meal, the seafront is the liveliest. Look out for suquet – the town's signature fish and potato stew.
Pilar c/de la Miranda. Some of Cadaqués's best paella and other rice dishes, as well as grilled fish and seafood. Mains €16–20. Daily 1–4pm & 8–11pm, closed Sun eve.

Girona

GIRONA, 37km south of Figueres and 100km from Barcelona, is one of Spain's loveliest unsung cities, with alleyways winding around its compact old town, the **Barri Vell**, through the atmospheric streets of **El Call**, the beautifully preserved medieval Jewish quarter. The star attraction here is the **Museu d'Història dels Jueus de Girona** (Mon–Sat 10am–8pm, Sun 10am–2pm; €2) at Carrer de la Força 8, an excellent museum that tells the story of Catalonia's second most important Jewish community, from daily rituals to contributions to medieval medicine and relentless persecution by the Inquisition. Girona was fought over every century since the Romans first set foot here, and is dominated by its towering **cathedral** (daily: April–Oct 10am–8pm; Nov–March 10am–7pm; €5, free Sun) nearby. The town's eclectic past is tangible in its **medieval walls**, which you can walk on for a great view of the city from above.

Girona is also popular with hikers and cyclists who use the city as a base for the many great routes in the area, details of which are available at the tourist office.

ARRIVAL AND DEPARTURE

By plane The airport (ⓦbarcelona-girona-airport.com), served by Ryanair flights from the UK, 11km out of town, is connected to Girona's bus/train station by Sagalés (ⓦsagales.com) buses.
By train The station is off the Barcelona Crta, a 10min walk southwest from the centre.
Destinations Barcelona (2–4 hourly; 40min–1hr 20min); Figueres (hourly; 30–40min); Madrid (10 daily; 4hr–10hr 20min).
By bus The station is next to the train station.
Destinations Barcelona (3–5 daily; 1hr 20min); Cadaqués (2–3 daily; 1hr 45min).

INFORMATION

Tourist office c/Joan Maragall 2 (Mon–Fri 8am–8pm, Sat 8am–2pm & 4–8pm, Sun 9am–2pm; ☎872 975 975, ⓦgirona.cat).

ACCOMMODATION

Girona can easily be visited as a day-trip from Barcelona but staying overnight allows you to soak in the atmosphere after crowds of day-trippers leave.
Equity Point Hostel Pl. de Catalunya 23 ☎972 312 045, ⓦequitypoint.com. Great location in the historical centre, helpful staff, large chill-out lounge, rooftop terrace and spacious, secure rooms and dorms make this the best backpacker choice in town. Dorm **€16**, double **€56**

32

Pensió Margarit c/Ultònia 1 ☎972 201 066, ⓦhotelmargarit.com. Between the train station and the Old Town, this budget hotel offers comfortable rooms, though light sleepers beware: walls are thin and the sound really carries. Double €57

EATING AND DRINKING

For evening drinking it's best to head into the Barri Vell or the area around Pl. Independència, where you'll find most of the bars and clubs.

Creperie Bretonne c/Cort eial 14. Quirky spot where the bus serves as the kitchen, turning out large helpings of sweet and savoury crêpes. Crêpes €6–8. Daily 1–4pm & 8–11pm.

Txalaka c/Bonastruc de Porta 4. Lively Basque *pintxo* (€2.50–4) bar where you help yourself to the tiny elaborate sandwiches on the counter, wash them down with *txacoli* (young white Basque wine) and pay according to the number of toothpicks/dishes. Mon–Sat 1–4pm & 8–11pm.

Andorra

32

A tiny country nestled in the Pyrenees, Andorra is one of the oldest nations in Europe. Set up by Charlemagne in the eighth century as a buffer between France and the Islamic Moors, it became an independent, democratic principality in 1993. It's the only country in the world with Catalan as its official language, although Spanish and French are also widely spoken, as is basic English.

Duty-free shopping, winter sports and summer hiking are the main attractions of this picturesque alpine nation: the capital, **Andorra la Vella**, offers the widest range of accommodation and cuisine, while next-door **Escaldes-Engordany** lays claim to the biggest thermal spa in Europe. To the northwest is the popular ski resort of **Pal-Arinsal**, while the hills around **Ordino** boast challenging trails and splendid valley views. East of Ordino, a road weaves through appealing mountainscapes to **Canillo**, home to a captivating Romanesque chapel, and near the French border are sleepy **Soldeu** and the busy ski slopes of **Grandvalira**.

ARRIVAL AND INFORMATION

Andorra doesn't have an airport, but regular buses link the tiny nation to the nearest international ones three to four hours' drive away, in Barcelona (225km) and Toulouse (180km). Alsina Graells (☎902 335 533, ⓦmovelia.es) has eight daily services from Barcelona (€28), as does Nadal Autocars (Andorra ☎805 151, ⓦautocarsnadal.com; from €28), while Novatel (☎803 789, ⓦandorrabybus.com) does airport transfers from both Barcelona (€32; 5 daily) and Toulouse (from €35; 2 daily). Alternatively, you can travel by rail from Zaragoza or Barcelona Sants to Lleida and then take one of several daily Montmantell minibuses (☎973 982 949 or Andorra ☎807 444, ⓦmontmantell.com; €20) from the street in front of the train station directly to Andorra la Vella.

The international phone code for Andorra is ☎376 and the currency is the euro.

ENTRY REQUIREMENTS

Passports are required to cross the Andorran border. You'll be asked to show your passport when buying a bus ticket.

GETTING AROUND

Its small size makes Andorra easy to get around – most places can be visited as day-trips from Andorra la Vella, with efficient public bus links to most towns and villages.

ACCOMMODATION

Good **budget hotels** are scarce, and most of the cheapest, located in the capital, have zero charm. Prices peak in high season – July to August (when reservations are a must) and December to March – expect to pay at least €50 for a double room in most places. As a lower-priced alternative, there are many well-equipped **campsites** throughout

EMERGENCY NUMBERS

Police ☎110; Ambulance and Fire ☎118; Medical ☎116; Mountain Rescue ☎112.

Andorra, and in summer you can stay for free in one of the 26 state-run **refugis** – simple mountain cabins; information is available at tourist offices. Camping in the wild is illegal except around *refugis*.

ANDORRA LA VELLA

The name of the national capital **ANDORRA LA VELLA** is a bit of a misnomer: "Old Andorra" is for the most part a spread-out collection of ski lodges, touristy restaurants, bars and ageing storefronts that cater to duty-free shoppers and skiers. Yet its setting has undeniable appeal: sited at the confluence of three rivers, the city boasts a stunning backdrop of towering mountains.

WHAT TO SEE AND DO

The capital is bisected by the Avinguda del Príncep Benlloch, which further east becomes the shop-filled Avinguda de Meritxell and then, on towards neighbouring Escaldes-Engordany, Avinguda de Carlemany. Towards the western end of town, **Barri Antic** is the capital's old quarter, with pleasant cobbled streets and quiet *plaças*; at its centre is the **Casa de la Vall**, one of the

oldest – and smallest – parliaments in Europe.

ARRIVAL AND DEPARTURE

By bus Most international buses use the Central d'Autobusos, located just southeast of the small Parc Central, 5min south of the city centre. Buses to Lleida run by Montmantell (ⓦ montmantell.com) leave from Caldea Spa but can also make several stops in the centre on request. Domestic buses run along Avda Meritxell and connect the capital to all the main towns and villages. Check ⓦ transportpublic.ad for schedules.

★ **TREAT YOURSELF**

The **Caldea Spa** (opening hours vary, check website for details; €34.80 for 3hr, €28 for 2hr evening session; ☎ 800 999, ⓦ caldea.com; bus #L1 from Avda Príncep Benlloch), 1km east of Casa de la Vall, in Escaldes-Engordany, is the largest health centre on the continent, pumping in water from the nearby thermal springs to offer everything from Turkish baths to exfoliating hydro-massages. The mountain views from the outdoor lagoon are particularly spectacular. The thermal water is rich in sodium, silica and sulphur and is reputed to have considerable therapeutic effects for skin and respiratory ailments.

32

ANDORRA LA VELLA (BARRI ANTIC)

● EATING & DRINKING	
1940	1
Borda Pairal 1630	6
Cerveseria L'Abadia	3
La Cava	2
L'Escenari de Pizzes	4
Papanico	5

■ ACCOMMODATION	
AWA Festa Brava	2
Camping Valira	3
Pensió Garcia	1

Map labels: Punt Fresc Supermarket; CI L'ALZINARET; C/LLACUNA; C/LES CANALS; AV. PRÍNCEP BENLLOCH; C/DR NEQUI; PLAÇA GUILLEMÓ; C/MOSSEN C. VERDAGUER; ANTIC CARRER MAJOR; C/M JANER; Buses to Caldea, La Massana and Arisal; C/MOSSEN TREMOSA; Casa de la Vall; C/VALL; PLAÇA PRÍNCEP BENLLOCH; Sindicatura; Església de St Esteve; Casa Rectoral; RAMBLA MOLINES; PLAÇA REBÉS; C/DR VILANOVA; PLAÇA; AVINGUDA MERITXELL; Grans Magatzems Pyrénées; CAMÍ DE LA GRAU; Parc Infantil; C/D VILANOVA; Centre de Congresos; PLAÇA DEL POBLE; Cinema MDRN; National Tourist Office; C/DR. VILANOVA; C/PRADA CASADET; Llieda Buses; C/PRAT DE LA CREU; N; 0 50 metres; ⑥ & Bus Station

Margin labels: Municipal Tourist Office, French and; Spanish Post Offices & Hospital; (600m)

Destinations Barcelona (15 daily; 3–4hr); Lleida for Zaragoza and Madrid (4–6 daily; 2hr 30min); Toulouse (2 daily; 3hr 15min).

INFORMATION

Tourist office Municipal: Plaça de la Rotonda (Mon–Sat 9am–7pm, Sun 10am–1pm; ☎873 103). National: c/Dr Vilanova 13 (Mon–Sat 9am–7pm, July and Aug also Sun 10am–1pm; ☎820 214, ⓦvisitandorra.com).

ACCOMMODATION

★ **AWA Festa Brava** c/La Llacuna 7 ☎820 741. Just off Avda Meritxell, this shiny hotel offers en-suite rooms decked out in creams and browns, with TVs, strong wi-fi and a tanning salon if you're that way inclined. Double **€44**

Camping Valira Avda. de Salou ☎722 384, ⓦcampvalira.com. Just 10min from the city centre; the not-quite-in-the-wild camping facilities are good and there's a pool and restaurant. Open all year round. **€6.10** per person plus **€6** tent, bungalow **€70**

Pensió Garcia Avda. Príncep Benlloch 51 ☎820 868. Drab but clean rooms smelling of stale smoke in a "hotel" that time forgot, with wi-fi that doesn't function and friendly elderly management. Bring own towel if you're bigger than a Hobbit. Double **€36**

EATING AND DRINKING

Avda Princep Benlloch and Avda Meritxell are lined with small supermarkets.

1940 Avda Princep Benlloch 20 ⓦrestaurant1940.com. Decor reflects the name and the food is a good mix of grilled meats, fondue, gnocchi and sublime French onion soup. One of the few places open on a Sunday. Mains from €12. Daily 1–4pm & 8–11pm.

Borda Pairal 1630 c/Dr Vilanova 7. Traditional Andorran restaurant serving local specialities (from €10). Check out *trinxat* (bacon with cabbage and slabs of potato) and *escudella* (vegetable stew with a huge meatball and sausages). Tues–Sat 1–4pm & 8–11pm, Sun 1–4pm.

Cerveseria L'Abadia Cap del Carrer 2. Up the stairs from the Pl. Guillemó, this popular local pub has Leffe, Hoegaarden and Becks on draught. Daily till 1–2am, or 3am at weekends and in summer.

La Cava c/Mossen Cinto Verdaguer 7. Contemporary restaurant with attentive staff and superlative rice dishes. You can order a paella for one, as well as exemplary *fideuá*. Mains from €13. Mon–Sat 1–4pm & 8–11pm, Sun 1–4pm.

L'Escenari de Pizzes Avda Dr Mitjavila 19. Small, cosy restaurant with some of the best pizza in Andorra. Mains from €9. Mon–Sat 1–4pm & 8–11pm, Sun 1–4pm.

Papanico Avda. Príncep Benlloch 4. Busy, bustling bar-restaurant serving tapas from around €3.70 and *platos combinados* from €11. Daily 1–4pm & 8–11pm.

DIRECTORY

Hospital Hospital Nostra Senyora de Meritxell, just next to Caldea Spa (☎871 000).

Internet Selenites, c/l'Alziranet 5, at c/Mossè Enric Marfany, off Pl. Guillemó (€3/hr).

Pharmacy Les Tres Creus, c/Canals 5 (☎820 212, ⓦfarmacialestrescreus.com).

Post offices Spanish PO at c/Joan Maragall 10 (Mon–Fri 8.30am–2.30pm, Sat 9.30am–1pm); French PO at c/Pere d'Urg 1 (Mon–Fri 8.30am–2.30pm, Sat 9.30am–noon).

LA MASSANA

A twenty-minute bus ride away through a verdant valley, **LA MASSANA** makes for an easy day-trip from Andorra la Vella (bus #L5 or #L6 from Avda. Princep Benlioch, every 15min 7am–9pm, €1.50). The town, presided over by a modern church clock tower, is also a good base for hiking or skiing – get information at the helpful tourist office (Avda. Sant Antoni 1, Pl. les Fontetes; Mon–Sat 9am–1pm & 3–7pm, Sun same hours when the ski station is open; ☎835 693, ⓦlamassana.ad) and pick up the booklet *36 Interesting Itineraries of Ordino and La Massana*, which covers all the walks in great detail (€2.50).

PAL AND ARINSAL

At the western end of La Massana commune lies **PAL** (bus #M2 from La Massana, 4 daily), one of the best-preserved villages in Andorra, hugging the slopes that veer up to Pal-Arinsal, part of the popular Vallnord ski complex (ⓦvallnord.com). Pal is also a great base for summertime activities – ask at the tourist office in La Massana for details. Head back down to La Massana to take the road up to **ARINSAL**, 2km northwest (bus #L5 from Avda. Princep Benlloch in Andorra la Vella via La Massana, every 30min 7.15am–8.45pm, €3.40), which is much bigger than Pal – it is also a great base for summer treks and known for its lively **nightlife**.

32

ACCOMMODATION AND EATING

El Cau c/Arinsal 5, Arinsal. Popular restaurant, bar and club with themed nights such as "beach party" and "Seventies disco". Open till 3am.

Hotel Xalet Verdu Prat de Verdu s/n, Arinsal ☎ 900 100 710, ⊚ hotelhusaxaletverdu.com. All rooms come with satellite TV, and there's a swimming pool for après-ski use. Double €51

Surf Next to the cable car station, Arinsal. The most popular place in town, this is an Argentinian steakhouse until 11.30pm before becoming a raucous bar-club until 4am during the ski season.

The Pyrenees

The area around the Spanish Pyrenees is little visited – most tourists who come here travel straight through, but in so doing they miss out on some of the most wonderful scenery in Spain, and some of the country's most attractive trekking, with several beautiful **national parks** as a focus for exploration. To the south lies Aragón, and most especially its capital, **Zaragoza**, with its fine architecture and stately pace of life. One place that attracts tourists is **Pamplona**, the capital of **Navarra** and famous for its bull-running fiesta, but a great place to visit at any time of the year.

ZARAGOZA

ZARAGOZA is the capital of Aragón, and easily its largest and liveliest city, with over half the province's one million inhabitants and the majority of its industry. There are some excellent bars and restaurants tucked in among its remarkable monuments, and it's also a handy transport centre, with good connections into the Pyrenees and east towards Barcelona.

WHAT TO SEE AND DO

Many places of interest are clustered around the Plaza del Pilar, near the Río Ebro. Other beautiful medieval monuments are a short walk away. Try and be in town for the October **Fiestas del Pilar**, a lively festival in honour of the town's patron saint.

Aljafería

The city's only surviving legacy from Moorish times, the **Aljafería** (April–Oct daily 10am–2pm & 4.30–8pm; Nov–March Mon–Sat 10am–2pm & 4.30–6.30pm, Sun 10am–2pm, sometimes closed Thurs & Fri am for parliamentary meetings, check with tourist office; €3, free on Sun; ⊚ cortesaragon.es), was built in the eleventh century by the independent dynasty of Beni Kasim. After Zaragoza was reconquered in 1118, the palace was Christianized and used by the *reconquista* kings of Aragón. From the original design, the foremost relic is a tiny and beautiful mosque adjacent to the second courtyard, the intricately decorated **Patio de Santa Isabel**. From here, the **Grand Staircase** (added in 1492) leads to a succession of rooms remarkable chiefly for their carved ceilings.

Basílica de Nuestra Señora del Pilar

The most imposing of the city's churches, majestically fronting the Río Ebro, is the **Basílica de Nuestra Señora del Pilar** (daily: summer 6.45am–9.30pm; winter 6.45am–8.30pm). It takes its name from the column that the Virgin is said to have brought from Jerusalem during her lifetime to found the first Marian chapel in Christendom. Topped by a diminutive image of the Virgin, the pillar forms the centrepiece of the Holy Chapel and is the focal point for pilgrims, who line up to kiss an exposed section encased in a silver sheath. Visitors can climb the **tower** (daily 10am–1.30pm & 4–7.30pm, €3) for excellent city views.

San Salvador

In terms of beauty, the interior of the Basilica de Nuestra Señora del Pilar can't compare with the nearby Gothic-Mudéjar cathedral, **San Salvador**, or **La Seo** (summer Mon–Fri 10am–6.30pm, Sat 10am–11.30am, 1–6pm & 7.30–8.30pm, Sun 10–11.30am, 1–6pm & 7.30–8.30pm; winter Mon–Fri 10am–1.30pm & 4–6pm, Sat 10am–noon & 4–6pm, Sun 10–11.30am & 4–6.30pm; €4), at the far end of the pigeon-thronged Plaza del Pilar.

32

Roman remains

The city has brought to light its Roman past through several underground excavations: there's the **Forum** and **River Port** (close to La Seo), as well as the **Roman Baths** and the **amphitheatre** on c/San Jorge (all Tues–Sat 10am–1.30pm & 5–8.30pm, Sun 10am–2pm; €4, free first Sun of the month, combined ticket €7). Following the semicircle of c/Coso and c/Cesar Augusto, the **Roman walls** are steadily being excavated; the best place to view them is at c/Echegaray at the junction with c/Coso, where remains of towers and ramparts can be seen.

ARRIVAL AND DEPARTURE

Zaragoza's modern Delicias station serves all train and bus destinations. It's on Avda. Navarra, about a 30min walk from the centre and connected by bus #51 to Paseo de Pamplona, at the southern end of Avda. de la Independencia (every 10min). Some regional trains also call at the more central Goya station.

By train Barcelona (1–2 hourly; 1hr 30min–4hr 45min); Bilbao (2 daily; 4hr 20min); Madrid (20 daily; 1hr 20min–4hr 10min); Pamplona (5 daily; 1hr 45min–2hr 15min).
By bus Barcelona (20 daily; 3hr 30min–4hr); Madrid (22 daily; 4hr); Pamplona (8–10 daily; 2hr–2hr 45min).

INFORMATION

Tourist office Pl. del Pilar (daily 10am–8pm; ☎976 201 200, ⓦzaragozaturismo.es); also at Torreón de la Zuda, and in Delicias train station and airport (all same hours and phone). There's an English information line on ☎902 142 008.
Discount card The Zaragoza Card, available at the tourist office (24hr €18/48hr €21/72hr €24, with discount if bought on line; ⓦzaragozacard.com), includes entrance to all the city's museums and monuments, a day on the tourist bus, public transport use and various discounts in hotels, bars and restaurants.
Internet Conecta-T (Mon–Fri 10am–11pm, Sat & Sun 11am–11pm; €2/hr), c/Murallas Romanas 4, opposite the Mercado Central.

ACCOMMODATION

Hostal Descanso c/San Lorenzo 2 ☎976 291 741. Light, bright rooms, each with basin and some overlooking the attractive Pl. de San Pedro. Shared bathroom. Double €35
★ **Hotel Sauce** c/Espoz y Mina 33 ☎976 205 050, ⓦhotelsauce.com. Worth a stay for the name alone, *Hotel Sauce* has a prime location around the corner from Pl. del Pilar, comfortable, en-suite rooms and friendly staff. The

on-site café serves great home-made cakes. Free wi-fi. Double €49
Pensión Iglesias c/Verónica 14-2º ☎976 293 161, ⓦbedandbreakfast-pensioniglesias.com. In a great location with some rooms overlooking the Roman amphitheatre. Doubles have basins and a shower but separate toilets. Double €25

EATING AND DRINKING

El Tubo, the name given to the streets around c/Estébanes and c/Libertad, is the best place for bar-hopping and tapas, while the bars around the church of Santa María de Magdalena have a more bohemian, alternative vibe. The districts of El Casco, La Paz and Bohemia are best for late-night bars and dancing. Those self-catering can try Zaragoza's main fresh-food market, Mercado Central, on c/Caesar Agosto (Mon–Sat until 2pm). Most places open 1–4pm and 8–11.30pm.

★ **Baobab** c/Arzobispo Apalolaza. Smart veggie restaurant which manages to make meat-free dining appeal to committed carnivores. The €12.50 weekday lunch menu includes treats such as aubergine *tarte tatin*. Near the university (tram to Plaza San Francisco).
Café Tertulia Actual c/Don Jaime I 28. Great lunchtime menu for €9 (€12 on weekends), and art exhibitions inside. Also open until late for drinks.
El Angel del Pincho c/Jordán de Urries 5. Tiny tapas bar specializing in Argentinian *empanadillas* (pies) and Japanese tempura dishes – an unusual combination that has made this place a local favourite.
Gran Café Zaragozano c/Coso 35. A lively place for breakfast or drinks throughout the afternoon and evening. Quirky decor, from barbers' chairs to transparent flooring.
Taberna Doña Casta c/Estebanes 6. This popular bar elevates the humble *croqueta* to an art form, with delicious specialities including *arroz negro*. Even ever-popular jamón is paired with walnut for a tasty twist.
Wok Japonés c/Don Jaime I 34. Stylish Japanese restaurant done out in black with an impressive all-you-can-eat buffet featuring sushi, tempura, salad and seafood. €10.75 at lunchtime (noon–4pm), €16.15 at dinner (8pm–midnight).

PARQUE NACIONAL DE ORDESA

For summertime walking, there's no better destination than the **Parque Nacional de Ordesa** (ⓦordesa.net), focused on a vast, trough-like valley flanked by imposingly striated limestone palisades. From Zaragoza's Intercambiador de Actur you'll need to take a bus to **Sabiñánigo** (up to 9 daily;

1hr 45min) and from there catch a bus to **Torla**, the best base for the park. Note that bus services between Torla and Sabiñánigo are very limited, so plan your journey well – see ⓦalosa.es for more details. At Torla, a regular shuttle bus takes you to and from the park (the park is not accessible by car), but trekkers should opt instead for the lovely trail (1hr 30min) on the far side of the river, well marked as the GR15.2. Further **treks** can be as gentle or as strenuous as you like, the most popular outing being an all-day trip to the **Circo de Soaso** waterfalls. For detailed information on the park, contact either Torla's tourist office (July–Sept Thurs–Tues 9.30am–1.30pm & 5–9pm; ⓣ974 486 378) or the park's **Centro de Visitantes**, which is also in Torla (daily 9am–2pm & 4–6pm; ⓣ974 486 472).

ACCOMMODATION

Reserve well in advance for accommodation in July and August; even the three campsites, *San Antón* (ⓣ974 486 063), *Río Ara* (ⓣ974 486 248) and *Valle de Bujaruelo* (ⓣ974 486 348), strung out between 1km and 3km north, often fill up.

Refugio Lucien Briet c/A'rruata ⓣ974 486 221, ⓦordesa.net/refugio-lucienbriet. Simple *refugio* in the middle of Torla offering good-value meals. Dorm €10, double €40

PAMPLONA

PAMPLONA (Iruña in Basque) has been the capital of the old kingdom of Navarra since the ninth century, and long before that was a powerful fortress town defending the northern approaches to Spain. Even now it has something of the appearance of a garrison city, with its hefty walls and elaborate pentagonal citadel.

WHAT TO SEE AND DO

Though most visitors flood the city during the Fiestas de San Fermín (see below), the compact and lively streets of the Old Town have plenty to look at. Highlights include the elaborately restored Gothic **cathedral** with its magnificent cloister and the **Museo Diocesano** (Mon–Sat 10am–6pm; €5; ⓦcatedraldepamplona.com) with its collection of religious art, and the colossal **city walls** and **citadel**. Don't miss the excellent **Museo de Navarra** (Tues–Sat 9.30am–2pm & 5–7pm, Sun 11am–2pm; €2, free Sat pm & Sun; ⓦcfnavarra.es/cultura/museo); besides the wealth of archeological treasures, from Paleolithic tools to vast Roman mosaics, funereal offerings and an intricately carved eleventh-century chest from Islamic

32

SAN FERMÍN: THE RUNNING OF THE BULLS

From midday on July 6 until midnight on July 14, Pamplona embraces the riotous nonstop celebration of the **Fiestas de San Fermín**. The focus is the **encierro**, or the running of the bulls – which has evolved from a way of herding cattle to the market to a nail-bitingly exciting spectacle. The *mozos* (runners) are a mix of daring locals and outsiders, mostly male (women were originally forbidden from participating, but some still do) and fuelled by alcohol and bravado. The course – from the Plaza Santo Domingo to the bullring – is 825m long. At 8am two rockets are fired to signify the release of the six bulls from their corral and the participants start running. Once you're in, you're in till the end; if you lose your nerve halfway through the run and try to scramble up the wall alongside the course, you'll be pushed back in. Particularly dangerous parts are where c/Mercaderes meets c/Estafeta and the slope down from c/Estafeta to the bullring. Every year there are gorings, particularly when a bull becomes separated from the rest of the herd. The spectacle is over in minutes; to watch the *encierro* it's essential to arrive early and to stake out a spot along the route. If you can't afford a spot on a balcony, buy a ticket for the bullring to watch the end of the proceedings, when bullocks with padded horns are let loose on the crowd inside the bullring. The bulls that participate in the *encierro* are then killed in the afternoon bullfights. If you watch the actual running, you won't be able to get into the bullring, so go on two separate mornings to see both. At midnight on July 14, there's a mournful candlelit procession, the **Pobre De Mí**, to wind up the festivities. See ⓦsanfermin.com for more details. There's also a PETA-organized anti-bullfighting event, the **Running of the Nudes** (ⓦrunningofthenudes.com), held two days before the first bull run; participants mostly wear a red scarf and plastic horns, but little else.

Spain, there's a superb art collection – from medieval and Renaissance ecclesiastical works to Navarrese art from the nineteenth and twentieth centuries.

ARRIVAL AND DEPARTURE

By train 800m from the old part of town; bus #9 runs every 15min to the end of Paseo de Sarasate, a short walk from the central Pl. del Castillo – there is a RENFE ticket office at c/Estella 8.

Destinations Barcelona (5 daily; 3hr 15min–4hr 15min); Madrid (4 daily; 3hr 15min); San Sebastián (2 daily; 1hr 45min); Zaragoza (9 daily; 1hr 45min– 2hr 30min).

By bus c/Yanguas Miranda in front of the citadel.

Destinations San Sebastián (11–15 daily; 1hr); Zaragoza (7–12 daily; 2hr–2hr 55min).

INFORMATION

Tourist office Avda. Roncesvalles 4 (Mon–Fri 9am–7pm, Sat 10am–2pm & 4–7pm, Sun 10am–2pm; ☏848 420 420, ⊚turismo.navarra.es), opposite the monument to the running of the bulls.

ACCOMMODATION

Rooms are in short supply during summer, and at fiesta time you've virtually no chance of a place without booking months in advance. Most accommodation options quadruple their prices during San Fermín, so you're better off staying nearby (San Sebastián is a viable option) and travelling to Pamplona to enjoy the night-long festivities and early morning running of the bulls. Many end up sleeping rough; remember that there is safety in numbers – head for one of the many parks such as Vuelta del Castillo or Media Luna and bring a sleeping bag. Prices below are high season, outside of fiesta time.

Ezcaba Camping ☏948 330 315, ⊚campingezcaba .com. Some 7km out of town, on the road to France, reached by bus #4 and with a large swimming pool. Fills up several days before the fiesta. **€6** per person plus **€6.50** per tent

★ **Hostel Hemingway** c/Amaya 26-1º ☏948 983 884, ⊚hostelhemingway.com. The only proper hostel in town, with funky decor, large guest kitchen, awesome bathrooms and staff who go out of their way to help. Downside? Creaky wooden floors. Dorm **€20**

Pensión Arriazu c/Comedías 14 ☏948 210 202, ⊚hostalarriazu.com. Fourteen prim, pastel-shaded rooms at this former theatre in a you-can't-get-more-central-than-that location. Double **€51**

Pensión El Camino c/San Gregorio 12 ☏638 206 664, ⊚pamplonainn.com. A luxurious budget option (albeit with temperamental wi-fi), with spacious en-suite studios equipped with bathtubs. The owner is not on site, so call him with your arrival time. Double **€50**

EATING AND DRINKING

Self-caterers can hit the Caprabo supermarket (daily 9.30am–9.30pm), upstairs in the Mercado de Santo Domingo, the town's main produce market (Tues–Sat 9.30am–2pm & 5–7pm). The highest concentration of eateries and bars is along c/San Nicolás and c/Estafeta in the Casco Antiguo.

★ **Baserri** c/San Nicolás 32. Popular bar serving award-winning, creative tapas. Try the venison with mushrooms and fruit dressing or smoked cod in black olive emulsion (€2.50), or go for a range of sandwiches (jamón and Roquefort, tortilla, squid; €5) or the good-value set menu (€14). Daily 1–11pm.

El Churrero de Lerin c/Estafeta 5. Three different kinds of churros served with thick hot chocolate to sate your sweet tooth. Try the cream-filled ones (€1.50 each). Daily 9am–8pm.

Sarasate c/San Nicolás 19. A great vegetarian restaurant that serves the likes of couscous salad and baked aubergines stuffed with spinach. Daily set menu €15. Daily 1–4pm, Fri & Sat also 8.30–11pm.

The north coast

Spain's **north coast** veers wildly from the typical conception of the country, with a rocky, indented coastline full of cove beaches and fjord-like *rías*. It's an immensely beautiful region – mountainous, green and thickly forested, with frequent rains often shrouding the countryside in a fine mist. In the east, butting against France, is the **País Vasco** (**Euskadi**, or **Basque Country**), with a strongly independent character. Note that the Basque language, Euskera, bears no relation to Spanish, or any other known language (we've given the alternative Basque names where popularly used) – it's perhaps the most obvious sign of Spain's strongest separatist movement.

San Sebastián is the big seaside attraction, with superb beaches and some of the most imaginative food in Spain. There are any number of lesser-known, equally attractive coastal villages all the way to **Bilbao** – home to the iconic Guggenheim – and beyond. To the west lies pastoral **Cantabria**, centred on the port of **Santander**, with more good beaches and superb trekking in the mountains of the **Picos de Europa**. In the far west, green and lush **Galicia** is Spain's main fishing region; unsurprisingly, its population goes crazy for all manner of seafood. This province also treasures its independence, and Gallego, which has much in common with Portuguese, is still spoken by around 85 percent of the population. For travellers, the obvious highlights are the world-class city of **Santiago de Compostela**, the greatest goal for pilgrims in medieval Europe, and the strenuous, 800km **Camino de Santiago**, one of Europe's finest hikes.

SAN SEBASTIÁN

The undisputed queen of Basque resorts, **SAN SEBASTIÁN** (Donostia) has excellent beaches and is acknowledged worldwide as an exceptional gastronomic centre, with more Michelin stars than any other European city bar Paris. San Sebastián has always been a fashionable place to escape the heat of the southern summers, and in July and August it's packed with well-to-do families. Its summer **festivals** include annual rowing races between the villages along the coast, and an International Jazz Festival (late July; ⓦheinekenjazzaldia.com) that attracts top performers to play in different locations around town.

WHAT TO SEE AND DO

San Sebastián is beautifully situated around the deep, still bay of **La Concha**. The **Parte Vieja** (old quarter) sits on the eastern promontory, while newer development has spread inland along the banks of the River Urumea and around the edge of the bay to the foot of **Monte Igeldo**.

Parte Vieja

The **Parte Vieja**'s cramped and noisy streets are where crowds congregate in the evenings to wander among the small bars and shops or sample the shellfish from the traders down by the fishing harbour. Here, too, are the town's chief sights: the gaudy Baroque facade of the church of **Santa María** and the more elegant and restrained, sixteenth-century **San Vicente**. The centre of the Old Town is the Plaza

de la Constitución, known locally as "La Consti"; the numbers on the balconies of the buildings around the square date back to the days when it was used as a bullring. Behind La Consti, winding footpaths crisscross up to the top of **Monte Urgull**. From the mammoth figure of Christ on its summit, there are great views out to sea and back across the bay to town.

Aquarium

By the waterfront at the foot of Monte Urgull, the superb **Aquarium** (Semana Santa–October daily 10am–9pm, rest of the year Mon–Fri 10am–7pm, till 8pm Sat & Sun; €13; ⓦaquariumss.com) consists of two sections: a naval history museum explores the Basque country's relationship with the sea, with numerous models of boats and nets through the ages, plus a section on whaling and the local regatta; the aquarium itself features a shark tunnel as well as rays, eels, jellyfish and some of more curious denizens of the deep, such as razorfish, lionfish and the hovercraft-like cuttlefish.

Monte Igeldo

For wonderful views of the curving bay, the city and the mountains beyond, head to the top of **Monte Igeldo**: take bus #16 or walk around the coastline to its base, from where a **funicular** (spring & June daily 11am–9pm; July & Aug 10am–10pm; rest of the year Thurs–Tues 11am–6pm; ⓦwww.monteigeldo.es; €3 return) will carry you to the summit.

City beaches

La Concha beach is the most central and most celebrated, a wide crescent of yellow sand stretching round the inlet from the town. Out in La Concha bay is a small island, **Isla de Santa Clara**, which makes a good spot for picnics; glass-bottom boats leaves from the Paseo Mollaberria (June–Sept 10am–8pm; every 60–90min; €3.80; tours of the bay €6; ⓦmotorasdelaisla.com).

Ondarreta, considered the best beach in San Sebastián for swimming, lies beyond the rocky outcrop that supports the **Palacio Miramar**, west of La Concha. Far less crowded, and popular with surfers,

32

Playa de Zurriola and the adjacent Playa de Gros have breakwaters to shield them from dangerous currents, with the latter particularly good for beginners; Pukas (Avda Zurriola 24; Mon–Sat 10am–1.30pm & 4–8pm; ☎943 320 068, ⓦpukasurf.com) offers surf lessons, wetsuit and board rental. Weekend surf courses cost €53; board rental is €10 for an hour or €25 for a day.

ARRIVAL AND DEPARTURE

By train The RENFE train station is across the Río Urumea on Paseo de Francia, a 10–15min walk to the historical centre.

Destinations Barcelona (2 daily; 6hr); Madrid (5 daily; 5hr 20min–7hr 30min); Pamplona (2 daily; 1hr 40min); Salamanca (2 daily; 6hr); Zaragoza (2 daily; 3hr 40min).

By bus National buses arrive at Pl. Pío XII, a 20min walk or a bus journey (#26, #28; €1.60) from the Parte Vieja. Buy tickets from the appropriate *taquilla* along Paseo de Bizkaia or Avda de Sancho El Sabio at least 30min before boarding (and note that some close for lunch).

Destinations Bilbao (13–25 daily; 1hr 10min); Madrid (7–9 daily; 5–6hr); Pamplona (11–15 daily; 1hr–1hr 30min).

INFORMATION

Tourist office Alameda del Boulevard 8 (Mon–Thurs 9.30am–1.30pm & 3.30–7pm, Fri & Sat 10am–7pm, Sun 10am–2pm; ☎943 481 166, ⓦsansebastianturismo .com). Runs good local walking tours (tickets from €10; book at ⓦsansebastianreservas.com).

ACCOMMODATION

During busy July and August prices are inflated. High season extends to September when the popular cinema festival takes place.

Pensión Amaiur c/31º de Agosto 44 ☎943 429 654, ⓦpensionamaiur.com. Incredible attention to detail marks out the *Amaiur*: the charming owners have thought of everything, from lending beach towels to organizing book exchanges. All rooms are well equipped and stylish. Double €57

Pensión Aussie c/San Geronimo 23-2º ☎943 422 874, ⓦpensionaussie.com. Rooms decked out in soothing pastels in a great central location. No wi-fi, though, and the owners charge €1 for 15min of internet. Double €55

★ **Pensión Larrea** c/Narrica Kalea 21-1º ☎943 422 694, ⓦpensionlarrea.com. Run by a super-helpful *señora*, this *hospedaje* offers sparkling mid-sized rooms with polished wooden floors, tiny balconies and soundproof windows, and powerful, spacious showers in the shared bathrooms. Double €48

Roger's House c/Juan de Bilbao 13-3º ☎943 433 856, ⓦhostel-rogers-house.com. One of the very few actual hostels (as opposed to *pensiones*), *Roger's* caters to surfers and backpackers, with helpful staff, surf boards for rent and surfing lessons arranged as part of the deal. Dorm €18

EATING AND DRINKING

Food in the Basque country is considered some of the best in Spain and it's easy to see why in San Sebastián. The Parte Vieja is crammed with bars serving gourmet *pintxos* (tapas), washed down with Basque country cider or Txacolí (young white wine). Opening hours are daily 1–4pm & 8–11pm unless otherwise stated.

A Fuego Negro c/31º Agosto 31. Spoof posters decorate this ultra-modern bar, and experimental *pintxos* include the amazing pig's ear with Mexican *mole* ice cream, seared cod with spelt, and chicken livers with beetroot hearts. *Pintxos* from €3.50.

★ **Atari Gastroteka** c/Mayor l8. An array of *pintxos*, both cold (try the jamón, goat's cheese and onion marmalade) and hot (the beef cheeks and seared foie gras are superb). More substantial meals also offered – finish off with a divine brownie served alongside passion-fruit ice cream. During busy times be prepared to wait. Tapas from €5 each.

Borda Berri c/Fermín Cabetón 12. The daily *pintxos* at this superb bar are chalked up on the blackboard; the best include melt-in-your-mouth calf's cheek cooked in red wine. *Pintxos* from €3.50.

Kata 4 c/Santa Catalina 4. The speciality at this friendly bar is oysters: seven different types are offered (€2.50). Otherwise, try a *tosta* with jamón or duck and goat's cheese (€6.50), or small helpings of risotto with foie gras (€3.50), or squid croquettes (€2.50). Mon–Thurs 8am–11pm, Fri & Sat 9am–midnight, Sun noon–4pm.

La Muralla c/Embeltrán 3 ☎943 433 508 ⓦrestaurantelamuralla.com. Sleek restaurant serving Basque specialities such as flavourful fish soup, tender beef cheeks and grilled cod with garlic sauce. The three-course weekday menu (€24) is good value; at weekends choose between two taster menus (€28/31; wine included). Evening reservations recommended.

★ **TREAT YOURSELF**

Bodegón Alejandro c/Fermín Calbetón 4 ☎943 427 158, ⓦbodegonalejandro .com. This is the most affordable of the three great restaurants established in San Sebastián by Michelin-starred chef Martín Berasategui, with a menu that is seasonal, whimsical and draws strongly on local ingredients. The tasting menu costs €38.50. Closed Sun & Tues night & Mon.

NIGHTLIFE

Bar Ondarra Av de Zurriola 16. This beachfront bar gets packed with locals at weekends. Open daily.

Etxe Kalte c/Mari 11, Jazz, urban soul and hip-hop in a relaxed, low-key bar with DJs. Free entry. Tues–Thurs & Sun 6pm–4am, Fri & Sat 6pm–5am.

BILBAO

Although traditionally a gritty industrial city, **BILBAO** (Bilbo), has been given a makeover in the last couple of decades and is now a must for any lover of art or architecture. A state-of-the-art metro, designed by Norman Foster, links the city's widely spread attractions: the monumental titanium-and-glass Museo Guggenheim by Frank Gehry – along with Jeff Koons' puppy sculpture in flowers – is the city's highlight, while the airport and one of the many dramatic river bridges are Calatrava-designed, and the compact Casco Viejo (Old Town) is a beguiling maze of medieval streets. The city's vibrant, friendly atmosphere, elegant green spaces and some of the best *pintxo* bars in Euskadi combine to make Bilbao an appealing destination. From the first Saturday after August 15, the whole city goes totally wild during the annual bullfighting extravaganza, **La Semana Grande**, with scores of open-air bars, live music and impromptu dancing.

WHAT TO SEE AND DO

The **Casco Viejo**, the old quarter on the east bank of the river, is focused on the beautiful **Teatro Arriaga**, the elegantly arcaded **Plaza Nueva** and the fourteenth-century Gothic **Catedral de Santiago**

FEVE RAIL LINE

If you're not in a great hurry, you may want to make use of the independent **FEVE rail line** (ⓦ feve.es; rail passes not valid). The 650km track begins at Bilbao and follows the coast west, with inland branches to Oviedo and León, all the way to El Ferrol in Galicia. It may be both slower and pricier than taking buses, but this atmospheric coastal chug skirts beaches, crosses rivers and snakes through a succession of limestone gorges.

ARTEAN PASS

If you're planning to visit both the Guggenheim and the Museo de Bellas Artes, the joint ticket Artean Pass (€13.50) saves you a few euros.

(Tues–Sat 10am–1pm & 4–7pm, Sun 10.30am–1.30pm).

Museo Guggenheim

A good route leads from the Casco Viejo down the river past the Campo Volantín footbridge and the more imposing Puente Zubizuri to the sensual, gleaming titanium curves of the **Museo Guggenheim** (daily 10am–8pm; Sept–June closed Mon; €13; ⓦ guggenheim-bilbao.es), described as "the greatest building of our time" by architect Philip Johnson. Replacing an industrial wasteland, the Guggenheim, with its promontories, soaring columns, and wonderful use of light inside its vast atrium, is at least as interesting as the treasures it houses. The permanent collection, which includes works by Kandinsky, Klee, Mondrian, Picasso, Chagall and Warhol, to name a few, is housed in traditional galleries, while the superb temporary exhibitions and individual artists' collections are displayed in the huge sculpted spaces nearer the river.

Museo de Bellas Artes

A five-minute walk from the Guggenheim, on the edge of the Parque de Doña Casilda de Hurriza, is the **Museo de Bellas Artes** (Tues–Sun 10am–8pm; €6, free on Wed; ⓦ museobilbao.com), which focuses on three main themes: classical art, such as works by Goya, Murillo, Zurbarán and El Greco; more recent art by the likes of Gauguin; and Basque art, such as sculpture by Quintín de Torre. There are also some fine temporary exhibitions.

ARRIVAL AND DEPARTURE

By plane From the airport (ⓣ 902 404 704, ⓦ aena.es), 12km north of town, the Bizkaibus #A3247 runs to Pl. Moyúa in the centre (daily 6.15am–midnight; every 30min; 30min; €1.30).

32

32

By train The FEVE and RENFE train stations are located at Abando, just over the river from the Casco Viejo.

Destinations Barcelona (2 daily; 6hr 40min); Madrid (3 daily; 5hr–6hr 30min); Santander (FEVE; 3 daily; 2hr 45min–3hr).

By bus Buses arrive at Termibús in San Mamés, connected to the train station by *cercanías* trains to the Casco Viejo by metro.

Destinations Barcelona (6 daily; 8hr); Madrid (15 daily; 4–5hr); San Sebastián (13–26 daily; 1hr 10min); Santander (21–25 daily; 1hr 15min).

INFORMATION

Tourist office Pl. Ensanche 11 (Mon–Fri 9am–2pm & 4–7pm; ☎ 944 795 760, ⓦ bilbao.net), with another useful branch in the Guggenheim (Mon–Sat 10am–7pm, Sun 10am–6pm), and at the airport.

GETTING AROUND

Standard metro rates are €1.45 for a single journey in the central zone, €4.50 for a day-pass; single tickets on the *cercanías* trains cost €1.60, while EuskoTran tram line tickets are €1.30 for a single, €3.65 for a day-pass (validate your ticket in the platform's machine before boarding). The 1-/2-/3-day Bilbaocard (€6/10/12), available from tourist offices, offers reduced rates on city transport and entry to sights, while Creditrans (denominations of €5/10/15) passes offer significantly reduced transport costs; purchase at any metro or tram station.

ACCOMMODATION

In summer and at weekends, booking ahead is advisable.

Ganbara Hostel c/Prim 13 ☎ 944 053 930, ⓦ ganbarahostel.com. A couple of minutes' walk from the Casco Viejo, this hostel houses backpackers in en-suite dorms that are rather cramped compared to the spacious chillout areas. Could be cleaner. Dorm €18.50

Pensión Arias c/Pablo Azola 13-2° ☎ 944 270 651, ⓦ hostalarias.es. Clean, rather nondescript rooms with shared facilities, presided over by an overly helpful *señora* who insists on holding on to the front door key. Double €45

Pensión Mendez c/Santa María 13-4° ☎ 944 160 364, ⓦ pensionmendez.com. Attractive rooms right in the middle of the Casco Viejo, all with balcony. Popular so book ahead. Double €30

Pil Pil Hostel Av Sabino Arana 14 ☎ 944 345 544, ⓦ pilpilhostel.com. Bright decor, spacious twelve-person dorms with lockers and a backyard patio for socialising are just some of this central hostel's perks. The breakfast is rather basic. Dorm €20

EATING AND DRINKING

The highest concentration of *pintxo* bars is around Plaza

Nueva in Casco Viejo. Opening hours are daily 1–4pm & 8–11pm unless otherwise stated.

Bar Negresco Pl. Nueva 10. A younger crowd flocks to this compact bar for €1 *pintxos*, slabs of tortilla (€5), and *bocatas* (sandwiches). The eight *pintxos* and glass of *txacoli* deal (€19.50) tempts the hungry.

Gure Toki Pl. Nueva 12. Great selection of cold *pintxos* (such as goat's cheese with mango) but, for a real treat, hot delights are chalked up on the board. You can't go wrong with the tiny Wagyu beefburgers or the mushroom risotto with foie gras. *Pintxos* from €1.80.

Porrue Alameda Rekalde 4 ⓦ porrue.com. Elegant contemporary restaurant specializing in dishes with a creative twist. Expect the likes of spinach risotto with crispy Vietnamese rice, delectable *fideuá* with cuttlefish and perfectly grilled cuts of meat. Mains from €16. Closed Sun evenings.

★ **Sorginzulo** Pl Nueva 12. Tiny, friendly tapas bar that specializes in grilled calamari, though the other *pintxos* – foie gras with figs, lamb skewers and much more – are also delectable, and there are salads (€9) and *raciones* (from €7.50) for those wanting more substantial nourishment.

DIRECTORY

Hospital Santa Marina, Ctra. Santa Marina 41 ☎ 944 006 900.

Post office Alameda Urquijo 19, Ensanche.

SANTANDER

Long a favourite summer resort of Madrileños, the port of **SANTANDER** has an elegant feel to it. Though it was severely damaged by fire in 1941, leaving the town with few historical buildings of interest, the setting along the Bahía de Santander is nothing short of spectacular and the beaches are excellent.

WHAT TO SEE AND DO

While the city's main draw is its wealth of white-sand beaches, there are also a couple of entertaining museums. All attractions are easily reachable either on foot or by catching city buses along the coastal road.

Museo de Arte Moderno y Contemporáneo

The three floors at the excellent **Museo de Arte Moderno y Contemporáneo** (c/de Rubio 6; Tues–Sat 10am–1pm & 6–9pm, Sun 11am–1.30pm; free) feature twentieth-century paintings, sculpture, photography and installations, with an emphasis on artists from Santander and wider Cantabria.

Museo Marítime del Cantábrico
Located along the waterfront c/de San Martín de Bajamar, the well-presented **Museo Marítimo del Cantábrico** (daily 10am–7.30pm; closed Mon Oct–April; €8) is a thorough immersion into Cantabria's long relationship with the sea. On the ground floor, enormous whale skeletons overlook the entrance to a shark-infested **aquarium**. The other two floors focus on Cantabria's nautical history from prehistoric times to the present, with models of boats and nets, displays on life at sea, and the Cantabrian sailors' contribution to world exploration.

The beaches
Heading east of the town centre along the **Bahía de Santander** you reach the **beaches** in the following order: Playa de Los Peligros, Playa de Magdalena, Playa de Bikinis, Playa del Camello, Playa de la Concha and Playa El Sardinero. The first three beaches are sheltered by cliffs, with calm waters, while the 1.25km stretch of white sand that is Playa El Sardinero faces the ocean, its waves attracting surfers in autumn and winter. Playa de Bikinis nestles along the south side of the Península de Magdalena, a wooded headland featuring the **Palacio Real de Magdalena**, the summer residence of the royal family until 1930. Playa El Sardinero is divided in two by the **Jardínes de Piquío**, an attractive palm-studded park with benches overlooking the beach from above. From the north end of the beach, a beautiful cliff-side trail skirts the headland, leading to the **El faro de Cabo Mayor** lighthouse. Buses #1, #4, #7 and #15 run to the beaches along the waterfront from the centre; #4 also leaves from the bus station (€1.30). If you find these too crowded, make for **Playa del Somo** (which has a surf school, boards to rent and a summer campsite) or **Playa del Puntal**, just before Somo; jump on a *lancha*, a cheap

taxi-ferry (every 30–60min 9.30am–7.30pm; €4.50 return; ⓦlosreginas.com) from Los Reginas, on the waterfront by the Palacete del Embarcadero.

ARRIVAL AND DEPARTURE

By plane The airport is 5km from town, served by Vueling and Iberia flights to main Spanish cities and Ryanair flights from major European destinations. Buses run to Santander bus station (every 30min between 6.30am and 10.30pm).

By train The RENFE and FEVE train stations are centrally located near the waterfront at Plaza de las Estaciones.
Destinations Madrid (3 daily; 4hr 30min); Bilbao (FEVE; see box, p.1075; 3 daily; 2hr 45min); Oviedo (FEVE; see box, p.1075; 1 daily; 4hr 30min).

By bus The station is over the road from the train stations.
Destinations Bilbao (22–26 daily; 1hr 30min); Oviedo (8–10 daily; 2hr 15min–3hr 15min); Santiago de Compostela (2 daily; 7hr 15min–9hr 45min).

INFORMATION

Tourist office Municipal: Jardines de Pereda (mid-June to mid-Sept daily 9am–9pm; mid-Sept to mid-June Mon–Fri 9am–7pm, Sat 10am–7pm, Sun 10am–2pm; ☎942 203 000, ⓦsantander.es). Regional: inside the Mercado del Este, c/ de Hernán Cortés 4 (same hours; ☎901 111 112, ⓦturismodecantabria.com).

ACCOMMODATION

Some places shut down outside the peak summer season of mid-June to mid-September.

Hospedaje Magallanes c/Magallanes 22 ☎942 236 939, ⓦhospedajemagallanes.com. Located in the city centre, this multistorey guesthouse is simple but bright, clean and good value. Double **€59**

Hostal Cabo Mayor c/Cádiz 1 ☎942 211 181, ⓦhcabomayor.com. Conveniently located near the bus station, these plush en-suite rooms have lighthouse prints on walls and ultra-comfortable beds. Double **€65**

Hostel B&B&B c/Méndez Núñez 6 25 ☎942 227 817. Great central location, five dorms for four to eight people, equipped with comfy beds and lockers and a good bathroom-to-guest ratio. Dorm **€23**

Pensión Madrid 21 c/Madrid 21-1° ☎942 214 494, ⓦpensionensantander.com. A friendly landlady presides over several clean rooms with tired decor and shared bathrooms, located close to the train and bus stations. Very little English spoken. Double **€40**

EATING AND DRINKING

The richest pickings are found along c/Daoíz y Velarde and c/Hernán Cortés. Opening hours are daily 1–4pm & 8–11pm unless otherwise stated.

32

Bodegas la Conveniente c/Gómez Oreña 9. Catering to lovers of all things battered and fried, this mix of traditional *bodega* and chic piano bar serves heaped platters of cured meats, cheeses, *croquetas* and *rollos* (deep-fried cheese wrapped in ham). *Raciones* from €7.

Cañadio c/Gómez Oreña 15. Well-lit, contemporary restaurant with red decor and leather seats, generous tapas and imaginative mains such as partridge pie with *salmorejo* (a thicker, more savoury gazpacho) or tuna burger. Mains from €10. Closed Sun.

★ **días desur** c/Hernán Cortés 47. Cutting-edge bar with white industrial decor and plenty of mirrors, serving imaginative global tapas. Try the spiced veal brochettes with couscous, the "Sofia Loren" (grilled veggies with goat's cheese in a martini glass) or the divine mini-burgers with purple mustard. Tapas from €1.50. Daily 8am–1.30am.

La Casa del Indiano c/Hernán Cortés 4, inside the Mercado del Este. Locals gather at the counters of this tapas bar inside the market for €1 tapas on Thurs afternoons; try the generous helpings of *patatas indianas* (€3.20), grilled foie gras, goat's cheese, caramelized onion and walnut *bocadillos* (€2). Closed Sun evening.

PARQUE NACIONAL PICOS DE EUROPA

The **Picos de Europa** (ⓦpicosdeeuropa .com) offers some of the finest hiking, canoeing and other mountain activities in Spain, with August the peak season. The densely forested national park boasts two glacial lakes, a series of peaks over 2400m high, and wildlife including otters and bears. The weather in the mountains is notoriously capricious, so bring warm and waterproof gear regardless of the time of year.

ARRIVAL AND INFORMATION

By bus From Oviedo, at least seven daily ALSA buses run to Cangas de Onís, a major gateway to the park; there are at least three buses daily from Cangas de Onís to Covadonga, a village on the park's northwestern edge.

By car From Santander, about 80km to the east, the park is reached by passing through San Vicente de la Barquera, Unquera and Cares; alternative access is from Oviedo in the south.

Tourist office Cangas de Onís has a tourist office (Mon–Fri 8.30am–2.30pm, Sat 9am–2pm & 4–7pm; closed Sat Sept–June; ⓣ985 848 614, ⓦcangasdeonis .com/turismo)

ACCOMMODATION

Hospedería del Peregrino ⓣ985 846 047, ⓦpicosdeuropa.net/peregrino. Basic rooms at an atmospheric old building in Covadonga in the park. Double **€40**

La Posada del Monasterio ⓣ985 848 553, ⓦposadamonasterio.com. Private hotel in a former monastery in La Vega-Villanueva, 2km northwest of Cangas de Onís; the management organizes canoeing, hiking and other park activities. Dorm **€12**, double **€50**

Pensión Torreón Cangas de Onís ⓣ985 848 211, ⓦpensiontorreon.es. Eight simple, comfortable en-suite rooms, some with views of an ancient bridge. Double **€40**

OVIEDO

The capital of the ancient principality of Asturias under King Alfonso II, thriving **OVIEDO** is best known for its *sidrerías* (cider bars), whose waiters artfully sling the smoky-tasting local brew (more like scrumpy than commercial cider) from above head height into glasses held at waist level to give it some fizz. The *sidrerías* are concentrated in the attractive Old Town in the heart of the city, a warren of beautiful squares and narrow streets.

WHAT TO SEE AND DO

Though a sizeable place, Oviedo is easy to navigate on foot as most attractions are found in and around the compact old quarter. Look out for the profusion of street sculptures strewn across the city, which include a statue of Woody Allen (who expressed a fondness for Oviedo) on c/Milicias Nacionales and an enormous bottom on c/Pelayo.

Catedral de San Salvador and the Cámara Santa

Oviedo has a couple of unusual ninth-century churches, dating from a time when Asturias was an independent kingdom, and the only part of Spain under Christian rule. One of these churches, the **Cámara Santa**, now forms part of the city's otherwise Gothic **Cathedral** (Mon–Fri 10am–2.30pm & 4–8pm, Sat 10am–2.30pm & 4–6pm; entry to Cámara Santa €3, €5 including Diocesan Museum and cloister). The treasures here include a jewel-studded gold cross donated by Alfonso II, and the Santo Sudario, a bloodstained cloth said to have been wrapped round Christ's head (displayed just three times a year).

Iglesia de San Julián de los Prados

The ninth-century **Iglesia de San Julián de los Prados** (Mon 10am–12.30pm, Tues–Fri 10am–12.30pm & 4–5.30pm, Sat 9.30am–noon & 3.30–5pm; €1.20, Mon free) is on c/Selgas, ten minutes northeast of the old quarter, next to the Oviedo–Gijón highway, with colourful frescoes, and a "secret chamber" in the walls.

Museo de Bellas Artes

The **Museo de Bellas Artes** at c/Santa Ana 1 (Tues–Sat 10.30am–2pm & 4.30–8.30pm, Sun 10.30am–2.30pm; free; ⓦmuseobbaa.com) has a fine collection of Old Masters and a few modern masterpieces, among them the portraits of the twelve Apostles by El Greco, a couple of Goyas, a Rubens or two, a Picasso and a Dalí. You may also spot the dark and ominous *Muerte de Abel* by Diego Polo and a striking self-portrait by José Agustín Meléndez.

ARRIVAL AND DEPARTURE

By train RENFE and FEVE trains both leave from the train station on Avda de Santander, a 10min walk northwest of the old quarter.

Destinations León (7 daily; 2–3hr); Madrid (6 daily; 5–7hr); Santander (FEVE; see box, p.1075; 2 daily; 4hr 45min); Zaragoza (daily at 8.36am; 8hr).

By bus On Avda de Pepe Cosmen, 200m north of the train stations.

Destinations Bilbao (9–10 daily; 3hr 35min–5hr 30min); Madrid (18–21 daily; 5hr 15min–6hr); Santander (8–12 daily; 2hr 15min–3hr 15min); Santiago de Compostela (8–10 daily; 4hr 45min–7hr).

INFORMATION

Tourist office Municipal: Pl. de la Constitución 4 (Mon–Sat 10am–6pm; ☏ 985 086 060, ⓦturismo.ayto-oviedo .es), with booths at c/Marquéz de Santa Cruz 1 (daily 10am–2pm & 4.30–7.30pm) and in the bus station (daily 10am–2pm & 4.30–7.30pm). Regional: c/Cimadevilla 4 (Mon–Sat 10am–7pm; ☏ 985 300 202, ⓦasturias.es).

ACCOMMODATION

Hostal Álvarez c/Independencia 14 2º ☏ 985 252 673, ⓦ hostalalvarez.com. Clean, unremarkable en-suite rooms within easy reach of both the bus and train stations and Old Town. Smokers welcome. Double **€30**

Hostal Arcos c/Magdalena 3-2º ☏ 985 214 773, ⓦ hostal-arcos.com. Ten spick-and-span rooms in an unbeatable location in the heart of the old quarter. Double **€50**

Hostal Oviedo c/Uría 43-2º ☏ 985 241 000, ⓦ hostaloviedo.com. Directly opposite the train station on a busy street, this guesthouse has spacious en-suite rooms decorated in warm colours. Double **€35**

EATING AND DRINKING

If you fall in love with Asturian food, there are several shops dotted around the Old Town where you can buy cider, cheese and meats to take away.

THE CAMINO DE SANTIAGO

The most famous Christian pilgrimage in the world, the **Camino de Santiago** – or Way of St James – traces a route through France and Spain to Santiago de Compostela (Saint James of the Field of Stars), the supposed burial place of St James the Apostle and the third-holiest site in Christendom after Jerusalem and Rome. There are several routes, but the majority of pilgrims take the so-called Camino Francés into Galicia, which includes the toughest climb over the mountains. Pilgrims identify themselves by attaching a large scallop shell to their backpack and many carry a *credencial*, or "pilgrim passport", available from tourist offices and *refugios*, that permits overnight stay in some mountain refuges. Accommodation along the way consists mostly of pilgrim *albergues*, where you can sleep in a basic dorm for €5–10. Along the way, pilgrims collect stamps in order to receive a Compostela (certificate of completion) from the Church authorities. To be eligible, you must walk at least 100km or cycle 200km of the 800km-long route. Aside from those motivated by faith, people are drawn by the physical challenge of the long hike, the stunning countryside, and the spiritual benefits of a temporary retreat from hectic urban life; while half the pilgrims come from Spain, the rest make up a very international crowd. For more details, see ⓦxacobeo.es.

30 y Tantos c/Servantes 7 ⓦ 30ytantos.es. Stylish bar-restaurant, a 15min walk northwest of the Old Town, with imaginative takes on traditional dishes, such as *huevos rotos* (scrambled eggs) with exotic additions, as well as goat's cheese salad and standout tapas (try the mini-hamburgers and "potatoes from hell"). Tapas from €3.50, mains from €9. Daily 1.30–4pm & 8–11pm.

Bar El Bar-Baro Pl. de la Constitución. Attractive setting, inexpensive cocktails (€4) and unusual teas, as well as Asturian favourites on the menu – think platters of Cabrales cheese and smoked meats, as well as a very reasonable *menú* (€10). Daily 1–11.30pm.

★ **Tierra Astur** c/de Gascona 1. This atmospheric *sidrería* fills up with local diners on a daily basis, thanks to its extensive menu of Asturian favourites (the hearty *fabada* stew, wild mushrooms scrambled with eggs and prawns, platters of local meats and cheese). Wash it down with their award-winning cider or get some produce to take away from the attached deli. Mains €8–12. Daily 1.30–4.30pm & 8–11.30pm.

SANTIAGO DE COMPOSTELA

SANTIAGO DE COMPOSTELA, built in warm golden granite, is one of the most beautiful of all Spanish cities and deservedly declared a national monument. The **pilgrimage to Santiago** (see box, p.1079) captured the imagination of medieval Christian Europe on an unprecedented scale, peaking at half a million pilgrims each year during the eleventh and twelfth centuries. The route continues to be well trodden by the faithful, as well as hikers and cyclists who enjoy the challenge, ensuring that the medieval streets of Galicia's regional capital are filled with a lively buzz.

WHAT TO SEE AND DO

With many pedestrianized areas, picturesque plazas and a wealth of beautiful architecture, Santiago is ideal to discover on foot. Most sights are clustered near each other in the compact historic **Old Town**. The large **Parque de Alameda** separates the old centre from the modern new town, which boasts many bars and cafés.

Catedral de Santiago

All roads lead to the **cathedral** (daily 7am–9pm, visits allowed outside Mass), on Praza do Obradoiro. The fantastic granite pyramid adorned with statues of the saint was built in the mid-eighteenth century by an obscure Santiago-born architect, Fernando Casas y Novoa. Just inside this facade is the building's original west front: the stupendous **Pórtico de Gloria**. So many millions have pressed their fingers into the roots of its sacred Tree of Jesse that five deep holes have been worn into the solid marble. Behind, the **High Altar** symbolizes the spiritual climax of the pilgrimage. Visitors climb steps behind the altar to the *Most Sacred Image of Santiago*, kiss his bejewelled cape, place their hands on the silver scallop shell on the back of his throne and receive a Latin certificate called a Compostela – a procedure that's seven centuries old. The elaborate pulley system in front of the altar is for moving the immense incense burner – **El Botafumeiro** – which, operated by eight priests, is swung in a vast ceiling-to-ceiling arc across the transept. This takes place only during certain festival services (check with the tourist office). Visiting the **cathedral museum** (June–Sept Mon–Sat 10am–2pm & 4–8pm, Sun 10am–2pm; Oct–May Mon–Sat 10am–1.30pm & 4–6.30pm, Sun 10am–1.30pm; €5) is worthwhile, as is a tour of the cathedral roof (€10), which offers stupendous views of the Old Town.

The convents and monasteries

The enormous Benedictine **San Martín Pinario monastery** stands close to the cathedral, the vast altarpiece in its church depicting its patron riding alongside St James. Nearby is the **Convento de San Francisco**, reputedly founded by the saint himself during his pilgrimage to Santiago. In the north of the city are Baroque **Convento de Santa Clara**, with a unique curving facade, and, a little southwards, **Convento de Santo Domingo de Bonaval**. This last is perhaps the most interesting of the buildings, featuring a magnificent seventeenth-century triple stairway, each spiral leading to a different storey of a single tower.

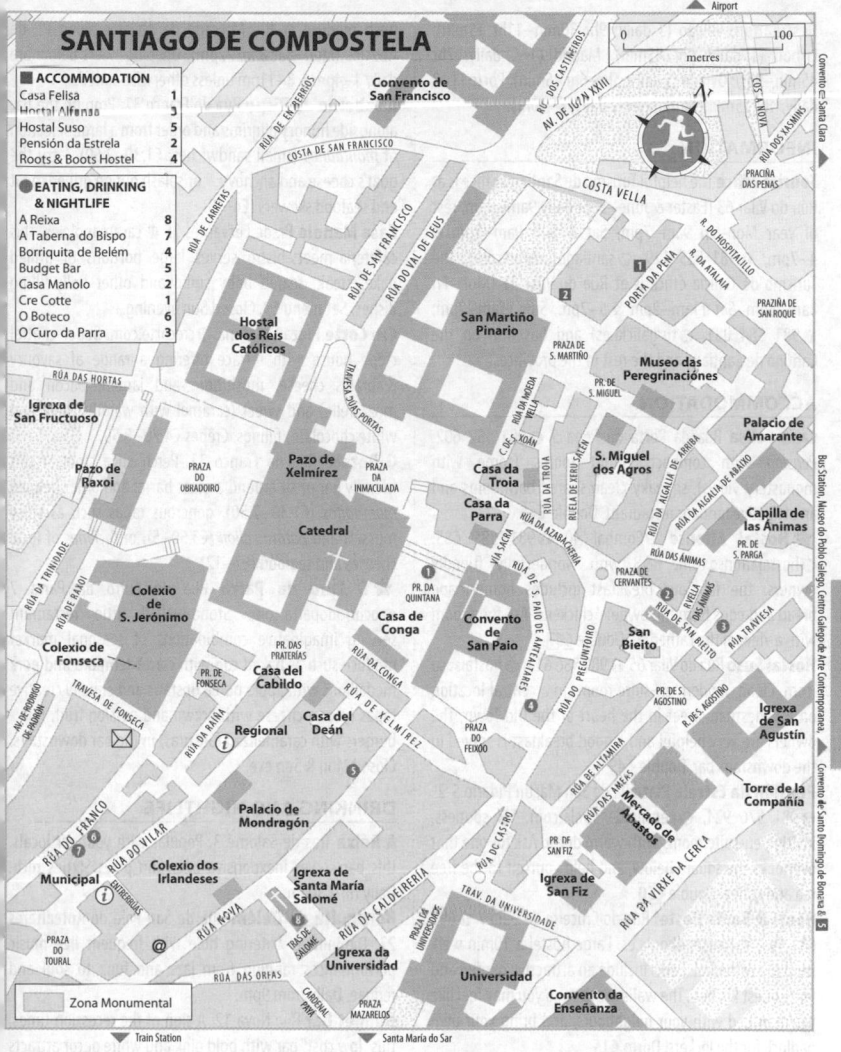

SANTIAGO DE COMPOSTELA

■ ACCOMMODATION

Casa Felisa	1
Hostal Alfonso	3
Hostal Suso	5
Pensión da Estrela	2
Roots & Boots Hostel	4

● EATING, DRINKING & NIGHTLIFE

A Reixa	8
A Taberna do Bispo	7
Borriquita de Belém	4
Budget Bar	5
Casa Manolo	2
Cre Cotte	1
O Boteco	6
O Curo da Parra	3

Zona Monumental

The museums

Museo do Pobo Galego at Rúa San Domingos de Bonaval is a fascinating glimpse into Galician culture (Tues–Sat 10am–2pm & 4–8pm, Sun 11am–2pm; €3, Sun free; ⓦmuseodopobo.es), from the region's fishing history to traditional crafts. Just next door is the **Centro Galego de Arte Contemporánea** (Tues–Sun 11am–8pm; free; ⓦcgac.org), a striking wave-like gallery designed by Portuguese architect Álvaro Siza that hosts temporary exhibitions by international artists.

ARRIVAL AND DEPARTURE

By plane Lavacolla airport, 11km northeast of town (ⓣ981 547 500, ⓦaena.es), is linked to the bus and train stations by Freire buses (every 30min; €3).

By train The train station is a 15min walk south of the Old Town along Rúa do Horreo.

Destinations Bilbao (daily; 10hr 35min); León (daily; 5hr 40min); Madrid (2 daily; 7hr 15min–9hr 30min); Porto (2 daily, changing at Vigo; 5hr 10min–6hr 20min).

By bus The bus station is on Praza de Camillo Díaz Baliño, a 20min walk northeast of the town centre; bus #5 (€1) runs every 16–30min to Pr. Galicia at the old city's southern edge.

Destinations Bilbao (3 daily; 9hr 30min–11hr 15min); Lisbon (1 daily; 9hr 45min); Madrid (4–5 daily; 7hr 45min–9hr); Oviedo (5 daily; 5hr–6hr 45min); Porto (1–2 daily; 4hr 15min); Santander (2 daily; 8–10hr).

INFORMATION

Tourist office The helpful Turismo de Santiago office is at Rúa do Vilar 63 (Easter & June–Sept daily 9am–9pm; rest of year Mon–Fri 9am–7pm, Sat & Sun 9am–2pm & 4–7pm; ☎981 555 129, ⓦsantiagoturismo.com). The Turismo de Galicia office is at Rúa do Vilar 32 (Mon–Fri 8am–8pm, Sat 11am–2pm & 5–7pm, Sun 11am–2pm; ☎981 584 081, ⓦturgalicia.es) and has info on the Camino de Santiago and the rest of the province.

ACCOMMODATION

Casa Felisa Rúa da Porta da Pena 5 ☎981 582 602. *Pension* with compact, bright rooms (some with monastery views), squeaky-clean shared bathrooms and an attractive outdoor restaurant. Double €40

★**Hostal Alfonso** c/Pombal 40 ☎981 585 685, ⓦhostalalfonso.com. B&B with wonderfully friendly owners; the fabulous breakfast includes home-made bread and eggs from the owners' chickens. Ask for a room with a view of the cathedral. Double €67

Hostal Suso Rúa do Vilar 65 ☎981 586 611, ⓦhostalsuso.com. Clean, modern en-suite rooms in a central location on a pedestrian street in the heart of the Old Town. The owners are very helpful and a good breakfast is served in the downstairs bar. Double €49

Pensión da Estrela Plazuela de San Martín Pinario 5-2º ☎981 576 924, ⓦpensiondaestrela.com. Six spotless, inviting en-suite rooms with warm decor. Ask for one that overlooks the square below, and help yourself to the free tea and coffee. Double €50

Roots & Boots Hostel Rúa do Cruceiro do Gaio 7 ☎699 631 594, ⓦrootsandboots.es. Large hostel a 10min walk from the cathedral. Perks include an attractive garden and large guest kitchen. The walls are thin, so you may feel like you're in bed with your neighbours, and bring your own padlock for the lockers. Dorm €15

EATING

There are plenty of inexpensive restaurants and tapas bars in the historic centre, particularly Rúa do Franco and Rúa da Raíña. Galicia is famous for its seafood, so expect all sorts of gifts from the sea, as well as the province's signature dish, *polvo á feira* (boiled, spicy octopus), and the famous *tarta de Santiago* (almond cake). Self-caterers can purchase fresh produce at the Mercado de Abastos along Pl. de Abastos (Mon–Sat 8am–2pm). Opening hours below are daily 1–4pm & 8–11pm unless otherwise stated.

A Taberna do Bispo Rúa do Franco 37. Prop up the bar alongside hungry pilgrims and order from a large selection of *montaditos* (small sandwiches; €1.30–2.50) – try the goat's cheese and anchovy – or splash out on grilled meat and seafood skewers (€6–9).

Casa Manolo Pr. de Cervantes 25 ⓦcasamanolo.es. This cafeteria-meets-bistro serves large portions of grilled hake, steak, seared baby squid and other belly-filling dishes. Set menu €9. Closed Sun evening.

Cre Cotte Praza Quintana ⓦcrecotte.com. Super-central crêpe house with terrace offering a range of savoury (Cabrales cheese, mushroom and jamón, bacon and mozzarella) and sweet (caramel with walnuts, dark and white chocolate) fillings. Crêpes €4.70–8.50.

O Boteco Rúa do Franco 31. Perch on a stool at this friendly bar or sit around a giant barrel and order heaped *montaditos* (€1.30–2.50), generous tapas such as spicy mussels and *patatas alioli* (€3.50–5), or *raciones* of local cheeses and seafood (€7–12).

★**O Curro da Parra** Rúa do Curro da Parra 7 ⓦocurrodoparra.com. Stone-walled little restaurant serving imaginative combinations of seasonal market produce such as baked cod with carrot tempura and pork medallions with apple purée upstairs and equally creative tapas (young cheese with prawn and passion fruit, mini-burgers with caramelized foie gras) in the bar downstairs. Closed Mon & Sun eve.

DRINKING AND NIGHTLIFE

A Reixa Tras de Salomé 3. Popular with younger locals, this bar serves inexpensive beer and plays Sixties rock. Daily till 2.30am.

Borriquita de Belém Rúa de San Paio de Antealtares 22. Diminutive watering hole with frequent live music performances ranging from jazz and funk to soul and reggae. Daily from 9pm.

Budget Bar Rúa Nova 12. A sign of the recession times, this "low cost" bar with bold pink and white decor attracts a young local clientele with its €1 *cañas* of beer and €4 cocktails. Daily till 2.30am.

DIRECTORY

Pharmacies Pr. do Toural 11 (24hr); Cantón do Toural 1 (daily 8am–midnight).

Post office Rúa do Franco 4. Mon–Fri 8.30am–8.30pm, Sat 9.30am–2pm.

Sweden

HIGHLIGHTS

❶ **Stockholm** Perhaps the most beautiful setting of any European capital. **See p.1089**

❷ **Gothenburg** Hop on a tram and explore Sweden's second city. **See p.1098**

❸ **Malmö** Fun-sized city with its own sandy beaches. **See p.1103**

❹ **Gotland** Join the summer exodus to Sweden's party island. **See p.1107**

❺ **Inlandsbanan** Whistle past endless forests en route to Lapland. **See p.1109**

❻ **Icehotel** A chilly treat worth breaking the budget for. **See p.1111**

HIGHLIGHTS ARE MARKED ON THE MAP ON P.1085

ROUGH COSTS

Daily budget Basic €65, occasional treat €85

Drink *Spendrups* draught beer (40cl) €5

Food *Korv med bröd* (Swedish hotdog) €2.40

Hostel/budget hotel Dorm bed €27/hotel room €75

Travel Train: Stockholm–Gothenburg €90; bus: Stockholm–Gothenburg €38

FACT FILE

Population 9.5 million

Language Swedish

Currency Swedish krona (kr)

Capital Stockholm

International phone code ☏46

Time zone GMT +1hr

33

Introduction

Sweden combines stylish, sophisticated cities with a vast wilderness of dense forests and crystal-clear mountain lakes. Quality of life is high, almost everyone speaks fluent English, and even a short visit here leaves you with the impression that the Swedes have somehow got things "right". While the country is not entirely populated by blonde, blue-eyed sauna-loving eco-warriors, you'll find plenty to reinforce the stereotype.

As with the rest of Scandinavia, Sweden can prove a challenge for the budget traveller. However, it's still considerably cheaper than Norway. If you stick to hostels, eat out only at lunch and resist the temptation to buy a round of drinks, you can still manage to explore beyond a flying visit.

First on the list for almost any traveller is **Stockholm**. One of Europe's most beautiful capital cities, it's a bundle of islands hosting a picture-postcard old town, fine museums and the country's most active nightlife. Although Stockholm laps up most of the international attention, Sweden's other main cities – **Gothenburg** and **Malmö** – are both eminently likeable, and well worth exploring for a couple of days each. The university towns of **Lund** and **Uppsala** make excellent day-trips from Malmö and Stockholm respectively.

During summer, Sweden's interior beckons with the opening of the 1300km **Inlandsbanan** rail line running along the spine of the country past pine forests and shimmering lakes as far as the **Arctic Circle**. Summer is also the time to join the rush to **Gotland**, Sweden's Baltic island escape. If you're in Sweden between December and mid-April, you shouldn't miss the chance to splurge on a night at the *Icehotel* near **Kiruna**, in the country's far north.

CHRONOLOGY

98 AD Tacitus refers to a Scandinavian tribe known as the "Suiones".
800s The Swedish Vikings become a powerful force in Europe over the following few centuries.
1255 City of Stockholm founded.
1397 The Kalmar Union unites Sweden with Denmark and Norway through a marriage arrangement.

1520 Hundreds of nobles are killed by Danish forces during the "Stockholm Bloodbath". A counter-attack is led by Swede Gustav Vasa.
1523 Gustav is crowned King Gustav I and leads the Protestant Reformation of Sweden.
1536 Sweden leaves the Kalmar Union, asserting independence.
1628 The *Vasa* battleship sinks outside Stockholm – a national embarrassment now turned into a money-spinning tourist attraction.
1721 Sweden is defeated by a coalition led by Russia in the Great Northern War, ending the success of the Swedish Empire.
1814 Sweden invades and conquers Norway.
1901 First Nobel Prize ceremony held, as part of the will of Swedish inventor Alfred Nobel.
1905 Sweden peacefully concedes Norwegian independence.
1914 Sweden remains neutral during World War I.
1939 Sweden declares neutrality during World War II.
1943 The first IKEA store is opened by founder Ingvar Kamprad.
1974 ABBA top the charts after winning the Eurovision Song Contest with "Waterloo".
1986 Prime Minister Olof Palme is assassinated in Stockholm; the crime is still unresolved.
1995 Sweden joins the EU after a closely fought referendum.
2003 Swedish voters reject the adoption of the euro.
2006 After twelve years of rule, the Social Democrats lose an election to the centre-right Alliance for Sweden.
2010 A four-day celebration ends with Crown Princess Victoria marrying a "commoner" at Stockholm Cathedral.
2012 Opinion polls show increased support for the far-right Sweden Democrats party (Sverigedemokraterna), which gained its first parliamentary seats two years earlier.

ARRIVAL AND DEPARTURE

Most travellers arrive and depart from one of Stockholm's three international **airports**. The largest and most

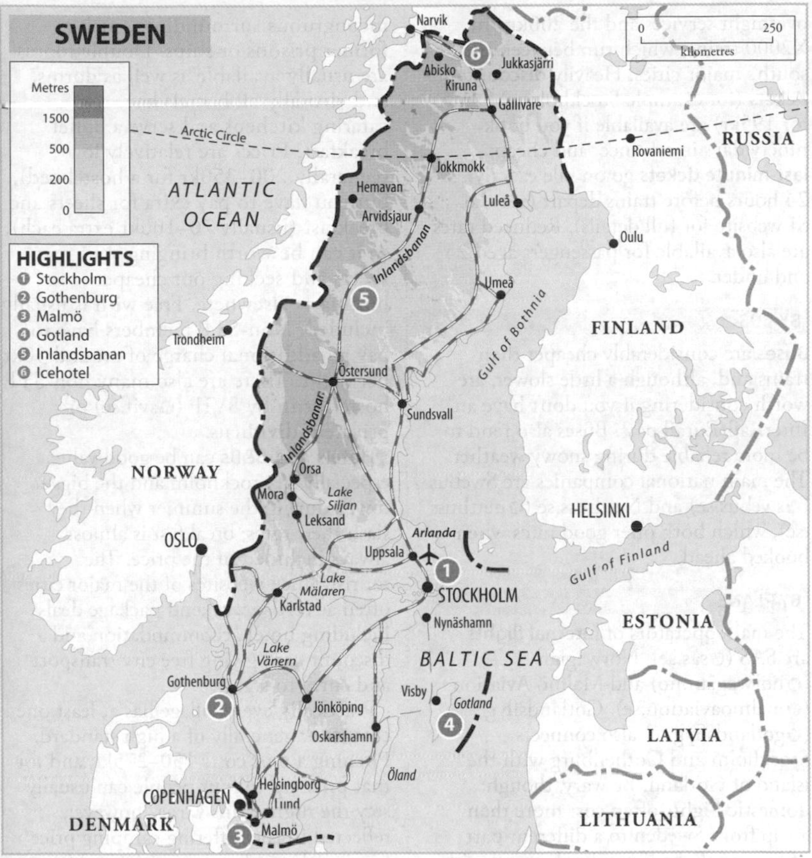

SWEDEN

Metres
1500
500
200
0

HIGHLIGHTS
1 Stockholm
2 Gothenburg
3 Malmö
4 Gotland
5 Inlandsbanan
6 Icehotel

Narvik

Abisko
Kiruna
Jukkasjärvi
Gällivare

Arctic Circle

RUSSIA

ATLANTIC
OCEAN

Hemavan
Arvidsjaur

Jokkmokk
Luleå

Rovaniemi

Oulu

Trondheim

Inlandsbanan

Umeå

FINLAND

Östersund

Gulf of Bothnia

Sundsvall

NORWAY

Inlandsbanan

Orsa
Mora
Leksand

Lake
Siljan

HELSINKI

Arlanda

OSLO

Lake
Mälaren
Karlstad

Uppsala

Gulf of Finland

STOCKHOLM

Nynäshamn

ESTONIA

Lake
Vänern

BALTIC SEA

Gothenburg

Jönköping

Visby
Gotland

LATVIA

Oskarshamn

Öland

COPENHAGEN

Helsingborg
Lund

Malmö

DENMARK

LITHUANIA

0   250
kilometres

convenient, Arlanda, is served by the big international carriers like Finnair and SAS, plus a few of the budget airlines like easyJet and Norwegian. Ryanair uses Skavsta and Västerås airports, both around 100km from Stockholm; the budget airline also flies in and out of Gothenburg, a three- to four-hour train ride from Stockholm.

International **trains** and **buses** from Norway and Denmark stop at Stockholm, Malmö and Gothenburg. In the north, Kiruna is the first stop in Sweden for visitors arriving from northern Norway.

International **ferry routes** include: Stockholm–Tallinn (Estonia), Helsinki and Turku (Finland); Helsingborg–Helsingør (Denmark); Gothenburg–Kiel (Germany) and Frederikshavn (Denmark).

GETTING AROUND

BY TRAIN

The most comfortable way to explore Sweden is by train. The extensive **state-run rail network**, SJ (⊕sj.se), runs as far north as Abisko, 250km inside the Arctic Circle. There are also other companies in charge of regional routes (all of them are visible on the SJ website). The scenic **Inlandsbanan** line (⊕inlandsbanan.se), which travels through central and northern Sweden, is privately run and only operates from June to August (see box, p.1109). **InterRail** and **Eurail** passes are valid on all trains, but you must book a seat in advance (65kr for X2000 services; 230kr for a bed in a six-berth sleeper compartment) for

33

overnight services and the 200km/hr X2000 trains, which run between the south's major cities. Heavily **discounted tickets** (for example Stockholm–Malmö for 195kr) are available if you book ninety days in advance, and cheap **last-minute tickets** go on sale exactly 24 hours before trains depart (see the SJ website for full details). Reduced rates are also available for passengers aged 25 and under.

BY BUS

Buses are considerably cheaper than trains and, although a little slower, are worth considering if you don't have an InterRail/Eurail pass. Buses also tend to be more reliable during snowy weather. The main national companies are Swebus (Ⓦswebus.se) and Nettbuss.se (Ⓦnettbuss .se), which both offer good rates when booked ahead.

BY PLANE

The main operators of **internal flights** are SAS (Ⓦsas.se), Norwegian (Ⓦnorwegian.no) and Malmö Aviation (Ⓦmalmoaviation.se). Gotlandsflyg (Ⓦgotlandsflyg.se) also connects Stockholm and Gothenburg with the island of Gotland. Be wary, though: domestic flights often cost more than a trip from Sweden to a different part of Europe. Even if you book ahead with SAS, for example, a one-way flight from Stockholm to Kiruna will set you back around 1000kr.

BY BOAT

Ferries can help you make the most of Sweden's long coastline and the mass of disparate islands that speckle the cold blue water. Information on accessing the islands of Stockholm's archipelago and Gotland is given later in the chapter (see p.1097 & p.1108).

ACCOMMODATION

Sweden has an excellent network of well-maintained **hostels** (*vandrarhem*) mostly operated by STF (Ⓦsvenskaturistforeningen.se). They are found all over the country, often in

incongruous surroundings, such as former prisons or ships. Double rooms are usually available as well as dorms, and virtually all hostels have self-catering kitchens and serve a buffet breakfast. Prices are relatively low (generally 200–350kr for a hostel bed), but you have to pay extra for sheets and breakfast (usually 70–100kr extra each), so it can be worth bringing your own sheets and seeking out cheaper breakfasts elsewhere. Free wi-fi is usually included. Non-STF members have to pay an additional charge of around 50kr per night. There are also many non-STF hostels, run by SVIF (Ⓦsvif.se) or private individuals.

Hotels and **B&Bs** can be good value, especially in Stockholm and the bigger towns during the summer when they slash their rates; breakfast is almost always included in the price. The tourist-office websites of the major cities often advertise weekend package deals including hotel accommodation and a discount card giving free city transport and entry to sights.

Practically every village has at least one **campsite**, generally of a high standard. Pitching a tent costs 150–275kr, and for that price up to four people can usually stay the night. This varies, however, reflected in the differing camping price formats throughout the chapter. Most sites are open from June to September, some year-round. Many sites also have cabins, usually with kitchen equipment but not sheets, for around 600–700kr for a two-bedded affair. For a list of campsites, and how to get the Camping Key Europe (150kr), which you need to pitch a tent in many campsites, see Ⓦcamping.se. Swedish law permits free, wild camping for one night at a time, but there are strict rules about what you can and cannot do. For helpful pointers in English, visit the Naturvårdsverket website (Ⓦswedishepa.se).

FOOD AND DRINK

Thanks in part to IKEA, Swedish meatballs (*köttbullar*) are familiar across the world. However, there is rather more to the national cuisine than this. **Seafood** is particularly good, with marinated salmon (*gravlax*) and herring (*strömming*), the latter pickled, smoked and even fermented, being served everywhere; you'll often find them offered as part of a classic **smörgåsbord** buffet with potato salad, rye bread, cheeses and fruit. Other specialities include reindeer and elk (both surprisingly tasty), crayfish (especially on the west coast) and sweet cloudberries (delicious with ice cream).

Breakfast (*frukost*) is invariably a help-yourself buffet of juice, cereals, bread, boiled eggs, jams, salami and coffee or tea. For **snacks**, a *gatukök* (simple takeaway) or *korvkiosk* (hot-dog stand) will serve hot dogs, burgers, chips and the like for around 50kr. Coffee shops are predominantly where Swedes come to *fika* (chat over coffee and cake), but usually they also serve a good range of *smörgåsar* – open sandwiches piled high with toppings (40–70kr) – and freshly made salads.

Lunchtime (*lunch*; usually served around noon) is, from a budget traveller's perspective, the best time to eat out, with most places offering a **set meal** (*dagens rätt*) of a main dish with bread, salad and coffee at 70–120kr. Otherwise meals in restaurants, especially at **dinner** (*middag*), can be expensive: 250–350kr for two courses, plus drinks. Much cheaper are kebab shops, pizzerias and simple Thai restaurants.

DRINK

Sweden remains one of the most expensive places in Europe to **drink alcohol**. In a bar or pub you'll pay around 40kr for a 40cl glass of one of the main national brands, *Spendrups* or *Falcon*. Order a Guinness or an imported lager, and the price will rise to around 70kr. In clubs, it's normal for a cocktail (or even just a shot with a mixer) to cost upwards of 100kr.

No surprise, then, that many Swedes load up on shop-bought alcohol before hitting the town. The only places licensed to sell drinks with an alcohol content above 3.5 percent are the government-run **Systembolaget** shops, where alcohol costs around a third of what you'll pay in a bar (you need to be at least 20 years old to buy alcohol at Systembolaget, as opposed to 18 in bars). There are at least one or two branches in even the smallest towns, but opening hours are deliberately restrictive, with most shops closing in the early evening. All outlets are closed on Sundays.

CULTURE AND ETIQUETTE

Swedes are a mix of apparent contradictions: fiercely patriotic yet globally minded, confident yet self-deprecating, orderly yet creative. Throughout the country you'll find the small ritual of *fika* – a verb that means something like "to have a coffee and a bun and a chat with a friend or two" – is a common pastime, along with singalongs and complaining about winter. **Traditional festivities** like Midsummer's Day and Easter inspire enormous enthusiasm, and on holidays young and old alike head for the countryside to celebrate. The vast majority of Swedes speak some **English** and most speak it with disarming fluency, so Anglophone travellers will have no problem striking up conversations.

SPORTS AND OUTDOOR ACTIVITIES

Football is Sweden's national sport, with a club or two in most of the main cities. Naturally enough, **winter sports** are where the Swedes excel on the world stage, and skiing, snowboarding and ice hockey are all very popular. The best ski resorts are in Åre, Kittelfjäll, Riksgränsen

---

SWEDEN ONLINE

ⓦ **cityguide.se** Up-to-date events listings in the main Swedish cities.
ⓦ **thelocal.se** English-language news, views, listings and blogs on life in Sweden.
ⓦ **kokblog.johannak.com** Quirky, illustrated food blog featuring Swedish recipes.

33

SWEDISH

	SWEDISH	PRONUNCIATION
Yes	Ja	Ya
No	Nej	Nay
Please	Varsågod	Vaa-show-go
Thank you	Tack	Tak
Hello/Good day	Hej	Hay
Goodbye	Hejdå	Hay-dor
Excuse me	Ursäkta	Urh-shekta
Where?	Var?	Vaar?
Good	Bra	Braa
Bad	Dålig	Doo-ah-lig
Near	Nära	Nehra
Far	Avlägsen	Arv-lessen
Cheap	Billig	Billi
Expensive	Dyr	Deyur
Open	Öppen	Upp-en
Closed	Stängd	Stengd
Today	I dag	Ee dag
Yesterday	I går	Ee gor
Tomorrow	I morgon	Ee morron
How much is…?	Vad kostar det…?	Vaa kostar day…?
What time is it?	Hur mycket är klockan?	Hoor mucker er clockan?
I don't understand	Jag förstår inte	Yaa fur-stor int-eh
Do you speak English?	Talar du engelska?	Taalar doo eng-ul-ska?
One	Ett	Ett
Two	Två	Tvo
Three	Tre	Tree-a
Four	Fyra	Feera
Five	Fem	Fem
Six	Sex	Sex
Seven	Sju	Shoo
Eight	Åtta	Otta
Nine	Nio	Nee-o
Ten	Tio	Tee-o

and Ramundberget. In summer, everyone flocks to Sweden's exquisite, unpolluted lakes and to Stockholm's archipelago for **swimming**, **kayaking** and **sailing**. Sweden is a fantastic place for **hiking**, with some of Europe's most unspoilt wildernesses to explore. The most trekked path is the 500km Kungsleden (King's Trail; see p.1112).

COMMUNICATIONS

The Swedish **postal service** scrapped normal post offices in 2001. Instead, you can send and receive mail and buy stamps at supermarkets, newsagents and tobacconists (look for the blue postal sign). **Free wi-fi** is widely available in cafés, bars and restaurants across the country, and you can usually get a decent mobile internet connection, even in the remotest parts of the north.

EMERGENCIES

The **police** are generally courteous and fluent in English. Medical treatment is free for anyone with a European Health Insurance Card (EHIC), although a small administration fee may be charged (around 300kr for a consultation with a doctor). **Pharmacies** operate normal shop opening hours with a rota system for late

EMERGENCY NUMBERS
All emergencies ☎ 112.

STUDENT AND YOUTH DISCOUNTS

The main cities all have **tourist cards** or passes, which offer either free or discounted entry to museums, free or discounted use of local transport (often including ferries), and sometimes other goodies, such as discounts in cafés and restaurants. An **ISIC card** can halve the price of museums, and attract variable discounts on accommodation, shops, restaurants and transport (for example, up to 20 percent off at Swebus and up to 30 percent off train journeys with SJ). Most state-run museums are free for under 25s.

opening. Stockholm has a 24-hour pharmacy (see p.1097).

INFORMATION

Almost all towns have a **tourist office**, giving out good-quality maps and timetables; they are also usually able to book accommodation and rent out bikes. Information on regional tourist offices can be found at ⓦvisitsweden.com. If you want a detailed map to use when you go hiking, try ⓦkartbutiken.se (Swedish only), which stocks a wide range.

MONEY AND BANKS

Sweden's currency is the **krona** (abbreviated to kr; plural: kronor). There are coins of 1kr, 5kr and 10kr, and notes of 20kr, 50kr, 100kr, 500kr and 1000kr. At the time of writing €1 was worth 8.3kr, US$1 was 6.4kr, and £1 was 9.7kr. **Banks** are generally open Monday to Friday 9.30am to 3pm, but most have later opening hours (until around 6pm) at least one day per week. Outside these hours you can **change money** at airports and ferry terminals, as well as at Forex offices, which usually offer good rates

CASHLESS SWEDEN

Sweden is well on its way to becoming one of the world's first **cashless societies**. In 2012, just three per cent of all of the country's transactions involved notes and coins. Despite the locals' preference for paying with plastic, almost all bars, shops, restaurants and supermarkets do (for the time being at least) still accept cash. On many buses and trams, however, that option no longer exists – so make sure you buy your ticket from the station in advance.

(minimum 50kr commission). **ATMs** are plentiful.

OPENING HOURS AND HOLIDAYS

Generally, **shops** open Monday to Friday 9am to 6pm, and on Saturday from 9am to 1/4pm. Most larger stores stay open until 8/10pm, and the majority are also open until 8/10pm on Sundays. Banks, offices and shops close on **public holidays** (Jan 1, Jan 6, Good Fri, Easter Sun & Mon, May 1, Ascension, Whit Sun & Mon, June 20 & 21, Nov 1, Dec 24–26 & 31). They may also close early the preceding day.

Stockholm

With the air of a grand European capital yet on a small, Scandinavian scale, **STOCKHOLM** is a vibrant and instantly likeable city. Built across fourteen islands, water and green space dominate the landscape, but there are still plenty of distinctly urban attractions to fill your days, from elegant museums and royal palaces to achingly cool bars and clubs.

WHAT TO SEE AND DO

Taking a **boat tour** is the classic way to see Stockholm. Once you've checked into your accommodation, head straight to Strömkajen, the harbour fronting the *Grand Hotel*, where operators sell tickets for sightseeing trips (see p.1094). Once you have a fix on the city's layout you can cover most ground on foot or take the T-bana **metro** for cross-city trips.

The key **sights** are Gamla Stan (the Old Town), Vasa Museum, Moderna Museet (modern art museum), the Fotografiska photography museum and Sodermalm's

33

SoFo neighbourhood. Aside from these it's best, in summer at least, to stroll around the parks and gardens (especially Djurgården) or take a trip to the Stockholm Archipelago. In winter, the city's ice rinks and cosy coffee houses come into their own.

Central Station and the Stadshuset

The first impression of Stockholm for most people is the vast and sometimes confusing **Central Station**, the city's main transport hub. Cityterminalen, the bus station, is just across the road and the Ⓜ Centralen metro station is underneath. A short walk west across the Stadshusbron bridge to Kungsholmen is one of the city's most recognizable buildings: the **Stadshuset** (City Hall) at Hantverkargatan 1 (daily guided tours only, in English hourly 10am–3pm; April–Oct 100kr; Jan–March & Nov–Dec 70kr; Ⓜ Centralen), which hosts the annual Nobel Prize banquet. Climbing the hall's 106m-high **tower** (May–Sept daily 10am–4/5.15pm; 40kr), which is topped by three golden crowns, is worth the effort for unrivalled views of the city.

Gamla Stan

One of the best-preserved medieval towns in Europe, **Gamla Stan** is packed with sights to explore. However, the real joy is in simply strolling around, particularly in the evening after the tourists depart and the lamp-lit streets become more intimate.

Stortorget, the main square, is surrounded by beautiful terracotta and saffron-coloured eighteenth-century buildings – look out for no. 7 where you'll see a cannonball lodged into the wall, supposedly fired during the Stockholm Bloodbath of 1520. Art shops, restaurants and bars line the surrounding narrow streets. The informative **Nobelmuseet** at Stortorget 2 (June–Aug daily 10am–8pm; Sept–May Tues 11am–8pm, Wed–Sun 11am–5pm; 100kr; Ⓦ nobelmuseum.se) showcases the work of Nobel Prize winners since 1901.

Gamla Stan: Kungliga Slottet

The monumental **Kungliga Slottet** (Royal Palace; Ⓜ Gamla Stan) is a beautiful Renaissance successor to Stockholm's original castle. The Swedish Royals don't actually live here, having relocated to the Drottningholm Palace 10km west of the city, but no one seems to have told the royal guards who put on a display of pomp, pageantry and shouting at the daily changing of the guard (Mon–Sat 12.15pm, Sun 1.15pm). Inside are the royal **apartments** (mid-May to mid-Sept daily 10am–5pm; mid-Sept to early May Tues–Sun noon–4pm; 150kr), a dazzling collection of regal furniture, tapestries and Rococo decoration, while the **Treasury** (same times as apartments; 150kr) displays ranks of regalia, including jewel-studded crowns and a sword belonging to the 16th-century Swedish king Gustav Vasa.

Gamla Stan: Storkyrkan

Close to the royal palace, Stockholm's cathedral, **Storkyrkan** (daily 9am–4pm, with tours in English Wed 10.15am and Thurs 9.15am; 40kr), was consecrated in 1306 and is where the monarchs of Sweden are married and crowned. Inside, look for the animated fifteenth-century sculpture of St George and the Dragon, which incorporated elk horns into the design, and the royal pews, which look more like golden thrones.

Gamla Stan: Riddarholmen

Just west of Gamla Stan, Riddarholmen or "Knights' Island" is home to Stockholm's only preserved medieval monastery, the thirteenth-century **Riddarholmskyrkan** (mid-May to mid-Sept daily 10am–5pm; 40kr). Until 1950 it was used as the burial

---

STOCKHOLM BY KAYAK

Seeing Stockholm by boat is one thing, but getting right down to water level on a **kayak** gives you a terrific sense of freedom – you can stop off just about anywhere – and a unique view of the city. The best place to rent kayaks is **Kafé Kajak** at Smedsuddsvägen 23 on Kungsholmen (daily 11am/noon–5pm, closed for winter once water freezes; 200kr/2hr; Ⓦ kafekajak.se).

place for Swedish monarchs but today its role is purely aesthetic, with its pointy latticework spire visible from much of the city.

The Royal Swedish Academy of Fine Arts

Between now and 2017, when the Nationalmuseum finally reopens after years of renovations, **The Royal Swedish Academy of Fine Arts**, at Fredsgatan 12 (wkonstakademien.se; wCentralen), will house some of Sweden's most valuable artistic treasures. Taking up three of the academy's galleries, temporary exhibitions (daily 10am–6/8pm; 100kr) will show selected parts of the Nationalmuseum's collection, which includes Rembrandts, Renoirs and pieces by Swedish artists such as Carl Larsson.

Moderna Museet

Stockholm's answer to London's Tate Modern or New York's Guggenheim, **Moderna Museet** (Tues–Sun 10am–6/8pm; 120kr; free 6–8pm Fri) on Skeppsholmen certainly keeps up with its rivals in terms of grand modernist architecture, though the art collection plays second fiddle in some respects. Connoisseurs will appreciate the large selection of Cubist painting as well as lesser-known works by Picasso and Dalí, plus a peppering of American pop art. There's also a restaurant with great views over the city.

Norrmalm and Östermalm

Modern Stockholm lies immediately north of Gamla Stan. It's split into two distinct sections: the central **Norrmalm** and the classier, residential streets of **Östermalm** to the east. Norrmalm was redeveloped in the 1970s and is dominated by high-rises and the huge public-square-cum-roundabout, Sergels Torg. Taking up most of the east side of the square is the **Kulturhuset** (Tues–Fri 9am–7pm, Sat & Sun 11am–5pm; free), an interesting mix of exhibition space, art gallery, cinema, theatre and meeting place. Norrmalm is also home to Stockholm's biggest department stores, Åhléns City and NK, as well as H&M's

flagship store on Hamngatan. Kungsträdgården, the huge tree-lined plaza known for its summer concerts and winter ice-skating, marks Norrmalm's eastern boundary.

Östermalm, east of Norrmalm, is the address of choice for upmarket Stockholmers. It also hosts the city's most exclusive nightlife – particularly on Stureplan, where you'll find legions of designer-clad revellers queuing round the block for ultra-expensive nightclubs. The main attractions during the day are the **Östermalms Saluhall** food market (see p.1097) and **Historiska Muséet** (May–Aug daily 10am–5pm; Sept–April Tues & Thurs–Sun 11am–5pm, Wed 11am–8pm; 80kr, free on Fri; whistoriska.se; wKarlaplan). Highlights here include a Stone Age household and a mass of Viking weapons, boats and, most interestingly, gold – over 52kg of the stuff.

Södermalm and Långholmen

Stockholm's hippest island is **Södermalm**, just south of Gamla Stan. Head south from the traffic hub of Slussen along Götgatan, past Medborgarplatsen, to arrive at the central district of **SoFo** (South of Folkungagatan), which bristles with cool bars, clubs and boutiques. To the west of central Södermalm, **Hornstull** is SoFo's quieter cousin, with a cluster of bars and restaurants along Hornsgatan and around Bergsundstrand. It's a short walk north from here to the peaceful island of **Långholmen**, whose leafy woodlands and small sandy beach are perfect for summertime picnics.

Fotografiska

Behind the brick facade of a former customs building that hugs Södermalm's north coast is **Fotografiska** (Mon–Wed & Sun 9am–9pm; Thurs–Sat 9am–11pm; 110kr; wfotografiska.eu), Stockholm's contemporary photography centre. Here, 2,500 square metres of exhibition space is given over to inspirational pictures by local and international snappers. On Thursdays, Fridays and Saturdays, when the museum is open late, there's usually live music in the upstairs bistro.

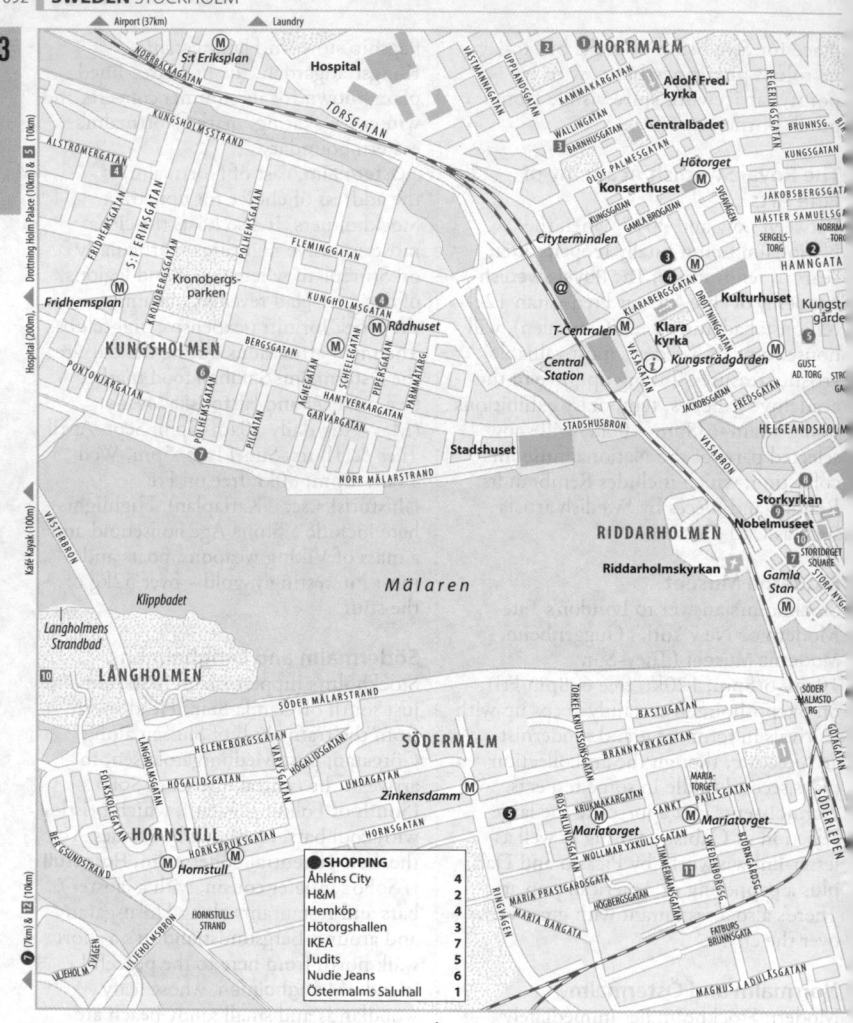

● SHOPPING	
Åhléns City	4
H&M	2
Hemköp	4
Hötorgshallen	3
IKEA	7
Judits	5
Nudie Jeans	6
Östermalms Saluhall	1

Djurgården and its museums

A former royal hunting ground,
Djurgården is the nearest large expanse of
park to the city centre and home to
several interesting museums. You could
walk to the park from Central Station,
but it's quite a hike: it's quicker to take a
bus, tram or ferry instead. Bus #44 makes
the journey from Karlaplan, while tram
#7 runs from Sergels Torg, via
Nybroplan. Ferries leave year-round from
Slussen, dropping off at the Allmänna
Gränd jetty.

On the west shore of Djurgården,
Vasa Museet (daily: June–Aug

8.30am–6pm; Sept–May 10am–5pm
with late opening Wed; 130kr;
ⓦvasamuseet.se;) is one of the country's
top tourist attractions, displaying a
famous Swedish design disaster: the
top-heavy *Vasa* warship, which sank in
Stockholm harbour just twenty minutes
into its maiden voyage in 1628.
Preserved in mud, the ship was raised in
1961 and painstakingly restored. It
really is an incredible sight close up and
the museum does an excellent job of
evoking the atmosphere of the time.
The palatial **Nordiska Muséet** (daily
10am–5pm with late opening and free

Tallink Silja Line Ferry Terminal

STOCKHOLM

0   200
metres

ÖSTERMALM

Karlaplan
KARLAPLAN

Östermalmstorg
Östermalms Saluhall

LADUGÅRDSGÄRDET

Östermalmstorg

Historiska
Muséet

DJURGÅRDSBRUNNSVÄGEN

N

STRANDVÄGEN

Nybrosviken

Kungsträdgården

Djurgårdsbrunnsviken

ROSENDALSVÄGEN

Grand Hotel

Nationalmuseum
(closed until 2017)

Nordiska
Muséet

Summer only

Vasa Muséet

Skansen

DJURGÅRDEN

Vaxholm-
bolaget
Boats

ngliga
lottet

Moderna
Muséet

ABBA:
The Museum

Strömmen

GAMLA
STAN

ska kyrkan

SKEPPSHOLMEN

Allmänna
Grand Jetty

KASTELLHOLMEN

All year

KARL
JOHANS
TORG

BECKHOLMEN

Slussen

Saltsjön

KATARINAVÄGEN
STADSGÅRDSLEDEN

Fotografiska

Viking Line
Terminal

Medborgarplatsen

SOFO

NYTORGET

● EATING	
Café Schweizerkonditoriet	8
Creperie Fyra Knop	13
Grill	1
Hermitage	10
Koh Phangan	17
La Neta	14
Noodle Mama	4
Nystekt Strömming	12
Vurma	6

■ ACCOMMODATION	
Af Chapman	6
Ångby Camping	5
Bredäng	12
Castanea	8
City Backpackers	3
Gärdet	1
Hotel Micro	2
Långholmen	10
Old Town Hostel	7
Old Town Lodge	9
Stockholm Hostel	4
Tre Små Rum	11

● DRINKING & NIGHTLIFE	
Debaser	11
East	3
Garlic & Shots	16
Kelly's	15
Mälarpaviljongen	7
Naglo Vodkabar	5
Snotty	19
Stampen	9
Sturecompagniet	2
Vampire Lounge	18

entry Wed Sept–May; 100kr; ⓦnordiska
museet.se), nearby, showcases Swedish
cultural history in an accessible fashion,
with a particularly interesting section
on the Sami – the indigenous people of
Sweden's northern reaches.

Further south on the western shore
of Djurgården, at Djurgårdsvägen 68,
is Stockholm's latest blockbuster
attraction, **ABBA: The Museum** (daily:
May–Aug 10am–8pm; Sept–April
noon–8pm; 195kr; ⓦabbathemuseum.
com), which uses interactive exhibits
to tell the story of Sweden's most
successful band.

ARRIVAL AND DEPARTURE

By plane The main airport is Arlanda, 37km north.
A high-speed rail line connects it with Central
Station (every 5–10min; 20min; 260kr one-way,
490kr return; half-price with ISIC card or free with
InterRail/Eurail; under 25s also get a discount;
ⓦarlandaexpress.com). Alternatively, buses (45min;
99kr one-way, 198kr return; ⓦflygbussarna.se) run
frequently into the city, arriving at Cityterminalen.
Skavsta and Västerås airports, each around 100km from
the capital, are also well connected by bus (1hr 20min;
129kr one-way, 248kr return; discount for under 25s;
ⓦflygbussarna.se).

By train Trains arrive and depart from Central Station, a
busy terminal on Vasagatan in Norrmalm. All branches of

33

> ★ **TREAT YOURSELF**
>
> **Jumbo Stay** Jumbovägen 4, Arlanda
> Airport ☎08 593 60 400, ⓦjumbostay
> .com. Flying visit? Consider treating
> yourself to a night at a working hotel and
> hostel built into the shell of an old Boeing
> 747. Up front in the flight deck, with two
> adjustable beds and a flat-screen TV, the
> Cockpit Suite (1625kr) is the reserve of
> first-class travellers. Thankfully there's
> cheaper accommodation further back in
> the fuselage, where cattle class used to
> be. Dorm <u>450kr</u>, double <u>650kr</u>

the Tunnelbana, Stockholm's metro, meet at ⓜCentralen, the station directly below Central Station.

Destinations Copenhagen (up to 5 daily; 5hr); Gothenburg (at least hourly; 3hr by X2000, 5hr by Intercity); Jönköping (1 daily; 3hr 15min); Kiruna (1 nightly; 18hr); Lund (at least hourly; 4hr 15min); Malmö (at least hourly; 4hr 30min); Nynäshamn (every 30min; 1hr); Oslo (1 daily; 6hr); Östersund (3–4 daily; 6hr); Umeå (up to 4 daily; 6hr); Uppsala (several per hour; 40min).

By bus Cityterminalen, adjacent to Central Station, handles almost all bus services, both domestic and international.

Destinations Gothenburg (up to 15 daily; 6–7hr); Jönköping (up to 16 daily; 4–5hr); Lund (4 weekly; 8hr); Malmö (5 weekly; 8hr 30min); Nynäshamn (1 daily; 1hr); Oslo (3 daily; 8hr); Östersund (2 weekly; 7hr 30min); Umeå (2–3 daily; 9hr); Uppsala (up to 13 daily; 1hr 10min).

By ferry Viking Line ferries serving Baltic destinations arrive and depart from Stadsgårdskajen in Södermalm, towards the south of the city. The terminal is a 30min walk from Central Station, or 15min from ⓜSlussen. The main terminals for Tallink Silja Line ferries – Frihamnen and Värtahamnen – are in the northeastern reaches of the city, both around a 15min walk from ⓜGärdet station. Polferries from Gdansk and Gotland ferries from Visby dock at Nynäshamn, 58km south of the city centre.

Destinations from Stadsgårdskajen Mariehamn (3 daily; 6hr 25min).

Destinations from Värtahamnen Helsinki (Helsingfors; 1 daily; 17hr); Tallinn (1 daily; 15hr); Turku (4 daily; 10hr 30min–12hr).

Destinations from Frihamnen Riga (1 daily; 17hr).

Destinations from Nynäshamn Gdansk (at least 6 monthly; 19hr); Visby (up to 5 daily; 3hr 15min).

GETTING AROUND

Tickets Buses, trams and trains (both T-bana/underground and local) are operated by Storstockholms Lokaltrafik (SL; ⓦsl.se). In zone A, it costs 36kr (20kr for

under-20s) for up to 75min of travel on trams, T-bana services and buses – buy tickets from the automatic machines. If you're going to travel around the city a lot, it's worth buying the SL Access card (20kr from SL ticket offices) and loading it with a 24/72hr pass (115kr/230kr). Alternatively, use the Stockholm Card (see below).

By metro The clean, efficient Tunnelbana (T-bana; Mon–Thurs & Sun 5am–roughly 1am, Fri & Sat 24hr) is worth considering once you've tired of walking. There are three lines (red, green and blue).

By bus There are four main "blue bus" lines that run across the city centre, numbered #1 to #4; numerous other lines serve suburban destinations. Buy tickets before you board.

By tram Trams run between Sergels Torg in Norrmalm and Waldermarsudde, on the southern tip of Djurgården.

By ferry Frequent ferries link Slussen with Djurgården, travelling via Skeppsholmen. Individual tickets cost 45kr. In future it may also be possible to take a ferry from Slussen to the Fotografiska museum (see p.1091), but at the time of writing the route was still being tested.

By taxi Taxis are expensive (the meter starts at 45kr) and only really a good option if you are in a group. Due to the risk of overcharging, it's best to stick with one of the main companies; try Taxi Stockholm (☎08 15 0000, ⓦtaxistockholm.se).

By bike The Stockholm City Bikes scheme (April–Oct only; ⓦcitybikes.se) offers a quick, affordable way to rent cycles from around 100 locations across the city. Buy the city bike card at the tourist office or an inner-city hostel/hotel (165kr/3 days) and then swipe it at the bike stand to unlock a cycle (max hire time 3hr).

INFORMATION AND TOURS

Tourist information The helpful main tourist office is at Vasagatan 14 in Norrmalm, just across from Central Station (May to mid-Sept Mon–Fri 9am–7pm, Sat 9am–4pm, Sun 10am–4pm; late Sept to April same times but closes 6pm Mon–Fri; ☎08 508 28 508, ⓦvisitsweden.com). There's also an office inside Terminal 5 at Arlanda Airport. Both offices sell the Stockholm Card (495/650/795/1,050kr for 1/2/3/5/ days), which gives unlimited use of city transport (except Flygbussarna airport buses and Arlanda Express trains), free boat tours and free entry to more than 80 museums and attractions.

Boat tours Strömma (ⓦstromma.se) runs a hop-on, hop-off boat tour (late April to early Sept; 100kr/24hr) stopping at the Vasa Museum, Skeppsholmen (Moderna Muséet) and Gamla Stan. Buy tickets online or at the main office at Nybroplan. Winter sightseeing tours also available.

ACCOMMODATION

HOSTELS

★ **Af Chapman** Flaggmansvägen 8, Skeppsholmen ☎08 463 22 66, ⓦstfchapman.com. A Stockholm landmark, *Af*

Chapman is a tall sailing ship converted into probably the world's most elegant hostel. If you can't get a bed on board (from 375kr) there are cheaper rooms on dry land in the hostel building, which houses the reception and a breakfast room plus a decent café. Dorm 265kr, double 850kr

Castanea Kindstugatan 1, Gamla Stan ☎ 08 22 35 51, ⊛ castaneahostel.com. The Old Town location of this quiet, second-floor hostel (just a few min from the Royal Palace) takes some beating. Inside are clean, bright dorms. Dorm 265kr, double 760kr

★ **City Backpackers** Upplandsgatan 2a, Norrmalm ☎ 08 20 69 20, ⊛ citybackpackers.org. Fun, sociable hostel with everything from private en-suite rooms to 12-bed dorms. Free pasta, wi-fi and, this being Sweden, sauna. Dorm 230kr, double 640kr

Gärdet Sandhamnsgatan 59, Östermalm ☎ 08 463 22 99, ⊛ stfturist.se/gardet; ⓜ Gärdet and 10min walk, or blue bus #1 from Cityterminalen to Östhammarsgatan and 50m walk. There are 53 modern rooms at this hotel/hostel on the edge of a quiet park, northeast of the centre. It's a pleasant 2km walk from here to Djurgården and the Vasa Museum. Double 855kr

Långholmen Långholmsmuren 20, Långholmen ☎ 08 720 85 00, ⊛ langholmen.com; ⓜ Hornstull, turn left and follow the signs. Located within an old prison on leafy Långholmen island. Spend the night in a converted cell: there are single-sex dorms with shared facilities, plus en-suite doubles and pricier hotel rooms. Dorm 255kr, double 740kr

Old Town Hostel Stora Nygatan 22, Gamla Stan ☎ 08 20 77 17, ⊛ oldtownhostel-stockholm.com. Good-value, subterranean hostel with dorms, a kitchen and a chill-out room arranged in a warren of arched corridors. Some rooms are larger than others, so ask to see several before choosing. Dorm 180kr

Stockholm Hostel Alströmergatan 15, Kungsholmen ☎ 07 156 55 25, ⊛ stockholmhostel.se; ⓜ Fridhemsplan, and a few mins walk. It's not in the best location and you have to book an entire room, but this bright, clean hostel is still a sociable option, with a huge, spotless kitchen and bathrooms in every room. Double 790kr

HOTELS AND PENSIONS

Hotel Micro Tegnérlunden 8, Norrmalm ☎ 08 545 455 69, ⊛ hotelmicro.se. Bargain prices for central Stockholm. The rooms are windowless but pleasant enough and there are clean men's and women's bathrooms along each corridor. Online discounts. Double 645kr

Old Town Lodge Baggensgatan 25, Gamla Stan ☎ 08 20 44 55, ⊛ oldtownlodge.se. This cosy little place in the heart of the Old Town dates back to the 1600s. As a result its 19 rooms are a little small, but they feel modern inside and are most certainly comfortable. Note, though, that the cheapest rooms are windowless. Double 715kr

Tre Små Rum Högbergsgatan 81, Södermalm ☎ 08 641 23 71, ⊛ tresmarum.se; ⓜ Mariatorget. The name means "three small rooms" but there are now seven at this good-value hotel in the heart of Södermalm. A delicious buffet breakfast is served in the lovely kitchen area and there are cycles for rent for 150kr/day. Double 795kr

CAMPSITES

Ängby Camping Blackebergsvägen 25 ☎ 08 37 04 20, ⊛ angbycamping.se; ⓜ Ängbyplan, then a 5–10min walk. Basic campsite 10km west of the city on Lake Mälaren, close to the beach. Open all year. Camping 140kr per person and tent

Bredäng Stora Sällskapets Väg ☎ 08 97 70 71, ⊛ bredangcamping.se; ⓜ Bredäng, and 10min walk. Decent spot with hostel and restaurant on site, 10km southwest of the centre by Lake Mälaren. Open late March to early Oct only. Camping 135kr per person and tent, dorm 220kr, double 420kr

EATING

CAFÉS, CHEAP EATS AND SNACKS

Café Schweizerkonditoriet Västerlånggatan 9, Gamla Stan ⓜ Gamla Stan. The most homely and welcoming café in a very touristy (and expensive) part of the old town. Coffee is served in great big cereal bowls, and you can get a tasty salmon pie with salad for 95kr. Daily 7am–7pm, occasionally longer on weekends.

Hermitage Stora Nygatan 11, Gamla Stan ⓜ Gamla Stan. Cheery, old-town canteen serving vegetarian food from around the world. On weekdays the lunch buffet (11am–3pm) costs 110kr. Mon–Fri 11am–8pm, Sat & Sun noon–8pm.

La Neta Östgötagatan 12B ⓜ Medborgarplatsen. Minimalist Mexican place selling great tacos and quesadillas, fast-food style. Both this place and its sister restaurant on Barnhusgatan, sell five small tacos for 90kr. Mon–Fri 11am–9pm, Sat noon–9pm.

Noodle Mama Kungsholmsgatan 22 ⓜ Rådhuset. Steaming bowls of soba noodles with fragrant meat and vegetables (from 79kr) are served at this *kawaii* Japanese kitchen in Kungsholmen. Mon–Fri 10.30am–9pm, Sat & Sun 11.30am–8pm.

Nystekt Strömming Södermalmstorg, just outside the T-bana stop ⓜ Slussen. This tiny but well-known takeaway cart serves fried herring on Swedish crisp bread (*knäckebröd*) for 35kr. It's always busy, and rumour has it that the food works wonders on a hangover. Daily 10am–9pm.

Vurma Polhemsgatan 15 ⓜ Rådhuset. Kitsch and cosy café that has its own bakery. The *Vurma* brand has become something of a Stockholm institution, with five branches now open across the city. Good option for breakfast (from 50kr). Mon–Fri 7am–6pm, Sat & Sun 8am–6pm.

33

RESTAURANTS

Creperie Fyra Knop Svartensgatan 4, Södermalm ⓜ Medborgarplatsen/Slussen. Good-value crêpes (from 50kr) are served in this dark, evocative restaurant, which is fashionably tatty and often packed. Mon–Fri 5–11pm, Sat & Sun noon–11pm.

★ **Grill** Drottninggatan 89, Norrmalm ⓜ Rådmansgatan. It's the lavish boudoir-style decor (with velvety sofas and mannequins standing in the windows) that first lures passing shoppers into *Grill*. But the daily lunch buffet (110kr), with tasty dishes like seafood paella on offer, also happens to be great value. Mon–Fri 11.15am–2pm & 5pm–1am, Sat 4pm–1am, Sun 3–11pm.

Koh Phangan Skånegatan 57, Södermalm ☎ 08 642 50 40; ⓜ Medborgarplatsen. Very popular Thai restaurant-bar with an interior resembling a tropical forest. The food – vegetable curries (from 151kr), *pad thai* (165kr) and the like – struggles to match the decor, but it's competently put together. Listen out for the hourly thunderstorm noises that rattle through the restaurant. Booking recommended. Mon–Fri 4pm–1am, Sat & Sun 1pm–1am.

DRINKING AND NIGHTLIFE

BARS AND PUBS

East Stureplan 13, Östermalmstorg ⓜ Östermalmstorg. Lively Japanese bar-restaurant with a heated outdoor area. Always packed at weekends, when DJs play late into the night. Mon–Fri 11.30am–3am, Sat & Sun 5pm–3am.

Garlic & Shots Folkungagatan 84 ⓜ Medborgarplatsen. Garlic is offered with just about everything at this American-style bar – including the draught beer. For something a little sweeter, check out the excellent list of long and short drinks. Daily 5pm–1am.

★ **Kelly's** Folkungagatan 49, Södermalm ⓜ Medborgarplatsen. Big, brash and student-friendly rock bar right near Medborgarplatsen, serving what must be some of the city's cheapest beer (24kr 4–10pm). If you don't have a coat to hang up (20kr) it's free to get in, too. Min age 23. Daily 4pm–3am.

Snotty Skånegatan 90, Södermalm ⓜ Medborgarplatsen. One for the hipsters, *Snotty* is a cramped bar-restaurant with old LPs on the walls and indie playing through the speakers. Mains around 185kr. Daily 5pm–midnight.

Vampire Lounge Östgötagatan 41, Södermalm ⓜ Medborgarplatsen. Subterranean cocktail bar – comfy red sofas, bare stone walls and hip clientele. Kick-start your evening with a Vampire Martini cocktail, or go for a cheap beer (36kr 5–7pm). Min age 20/21. Mon–Fri 5pm–1am, Sat and summer months 7pm–1am.

CLUBS AND LIVE MUSIC

Debaser Karl Johans Torg 1 ⓦ debaser.se; ⓜ Slussen or Gamla Stan. Legendary live music venue and club, attracting great local and international bands, and packing in hundreds of energetic partygoers. Entry and min age varies; see website. Mon–Thurs & Sun 7pm–1am when events are scheduled, otherwise Fri & Sat 7pm–3am.

Stampen Stora Nygatan 5, Gamla Stan ⓦ stampen.se; ⓜ Gamla Stan. Two floors of jazz, swing and blues, right in the heart of the old town. Live music almost every night. Mon–Thurs 5pm–1am, Fri & Sat 8pm–2am.

Sturecompagniet Sturegatan 4 ⓦ sturecompagniet.se; ⓜ Östermalmstorg. This Stockholm staple boasts a terrific light-show with house and techno sounds blaring long into the night. Dress to impress and start queuing early. Over-23s only. Thurs–Sat 10pm–3am.

GAY STOCKHOLM

Mälarpaviljongen Norr Mälarstrand 64, ⓦ malarpaviljongen.se; ⓜ Rådhuset. Open-air bar-restaurant down by the water with great views of Gamla Stan. It attracts a mixed gay/straight crowd and puts on events during the annual Stockholm Pride. April–Sept daily 11am–1am.

Naglo Vodkabar Regeringsgatan 4 ⓦ naglo.com; ⓜ Kungsträdgården. Small, gay-friendly bar/club with around seventy different types of vodka on offer. Plays pop until the early hours. Min age 23. Mon–Sat 9pm–3am.

SHOPPING

FASHION AND LIFESTYLE

Åhléns City Klarabergsgatan 50, near the T-bana stop ⓜ Centralen. Sweden's biggest department store is the place to stock up on Björn Borg undies and skinny Acne jeans. Mon–Fri 1am–9pm, Sat 10am–7pm, Sun 11am–7pm.

H&M Hamngatan 37 ⓜ Hötorget. The main Stockholm branch of one of Sweden's biggest retail success stories; wall-to-wall with cut-price fashion. Mon–Fri 10am–8pm, Sat 10am–6pm, Sun 11am–6pm.

IKEA Modulvägen 1, Skärholmen (7km southwest of Stockholm). If you're dying to see the world's largest IKEA then hop on one of the free shuttle buses leaving from Vasagatan 18 (Mon–Fri on the hour 10am–7pm). Daily 10am–8pm.

Judits Hornsgatan 75 ⓦ judits.se; ⓜ Zinkensdamm. Fantastic secondhand clothes emporium with shoes and accessories at affordable prices. Mon–Fri 11am–6pm, Sat 11am–4.30pm.

Nudie Jeans Skånegatan 75 ⓦ nudiejeans.com; ⓜ Medborgarplatsen. Organic khakis and jeans draw style-conscious Stockholmers to this concept store on Skånegatan. Mon–Fri 11am–6.30pm, Sat 11am–5pm, Sun noon–4pm.

FOOD AND MARKETS

Hemköp Directly below Åhléns City, Mäster Samuelsgatan 57. Super-central supermarket with an excellent deli counter and an in-house bakery. Mon–Fri 7am–10pm, Sat & Sun 10am–9pm.

Hötorgshallen Hötorget ⓦ hotorgshallen.se; ⓜ Hötorget. A truly international market, selling everything from oolong tea and Gruyère cheese to fresh Finnish bread. There's a branch of Systembolaget here, too (closes at 3pm on Sat). Mon–Thurs 10am–6pm, Fri 10am–6.30pm, Sat 10am–4pm.
Östermalms Saluhall Östermalmstorg ⓜ Östermalmstorg. Pig out in style at this neo-Gothic food hall, built in 1888. Wine bars and restaurants surround the stalls. Mon–Thurs 9.30am–6pm, Fri 9.30am–7pm, Sat 9.30am–4pm.

DIRECTORY

Embassies Australia, Klarabergsviadukten 63, 8th floor ☏ 08 613 29 00; Canada, Klarabergsgatan 23, 6th floor ☏ 08 453 30 00; Ireland, Hovslagargatan 5 ☏ 08 54 50 40 40; UK, Skarpögatan 6–8 ☏ 08 671 30 00; US, Dag Hammarskjöldsväg 31 ☏ 08 783 53 00.
Hospital St Görans Sjukhus, St Göransplan 1 ☏ 08 587 010 00, ⓦ www.stgoran.se/in-english (24hr).
Internet Sidewalk Express, Cityterminalen (29kr/2hr).
Left luggage Lockers in Central Station and Cityterminalen (60/70kr per 24hr, depending on size).
Pharmacy Apoteket C.W. Scheele, Klarabergsgatan 64 ☏ 07 714 504 50 (24hr).
Post office You can send packages from the information desks in branches of Hemköp and Ica, with a branch of the latter on Kungsholmstorg, just north of Strömkajen (daily 8am–11pm).

Around Stockholm

One of the key excursions from Stockholm is to the royal palace of Drottningholm, on the shores of Lake Mälaren, west of the capital. In summer the pine-clad islands of Stockholm's **archipelago** make an enticing escape from the city while history buffs should head to the elegant town of **Uppsala**, a short train ride away.

DROTTNINGHOLM PALACE

Just 10km west of Stockholm, the **Drottningholm Palace** (April & Oct Fri–Sun 11am–3.30pm; May–Aug daily 10am–4.30pm; Sept daily 11am–3.30pm; Nov–March Sat & Sun noon–3.30pm; 100kr; ⓦ kungahuset.se) is a Versailles-like monument to excess dating from the mid-seventeenth century.

The Swedish royal family made it their permanent residence in 1981, and, while you're unlikely to spot any of them, you are free to wander through sections of the palace on guided tours and visit the manicured gardens.

ARRIVAL AND DEPARTURE

By boat The best way to get here is on one of the majestic old steam ships which leave from the quay near Stadshusbron five times a day (mid-April to Oct; 180kr return; ⓦ stromma.se).
By metro and bus You can also reach it on the less regal combination of T-bana to Brommaplan followed by the #177 bus.

THE STOCKHOLM ARCHIPELAGO

For 80km east of the capital stretches the **Stockholm archipelago** (Stockholms Skärgård), made up of 30,000 islands, most of which are little more than lumps of rock rising up from the sea. In summer, the area bristles with tourists, day-trippers, sailing boats and locals making use of their summer homes.

ARRIVAL AND DEPARTURE

By boat Boats to some of the islands leave from Strömkajen in Stockholm and are run by Waxholmsbolaget (☏ 08 614 64 50, ⓦ waxholmsbolaget.se; from 45kr one-way). If you're sticking around for a while, invest in a Båtluffakortet (island-hopping card, 420kr), a pass that entitles you to five days of unlimited transport on Waxholmsbolaget routes; it's available online at ⓦ visitskargarden.se and at the tourist office, where you can also pick up a boat timetable.

Vaxholm and Kyrkogårdsön

Just an hour's scenic boat ride from Stockholm and also connected by road, **Vaxholm** is the most easily accessible of the archipelago islands, which means it can be swamped with visitors in summer. However, it's still a charming spot, only 3.2km long and with an elegant harbour on its eastern edge, where you'll find restaurants, cafés and shops.

An hour's ferry ride north of Vaxholm is the cute little island of **Kyrkogårdsön**, which locals rave about. Siaröfortet is the name of the island's small naval fort, built during World War I. The fort has been turned into a museum but the real

33

attraction is the island's indented coastline – perfect for kayaking and swimming.

ARRIVAL AND INFORMATION

By ferry Blidösundsbolaget ferries do day-trips from Strömkajen to Kyrkogårdsön (May to mid-Aug; 200kr return; ⓦ blidosundsbolaget.se; get off at Siaröfortet).

Tourist information Vaxholm's tourist office is at Torget 1, a short walk north from the harbour (May & Sept Mon–Fri 11am–4pm, Sat & Sun 11am–3pm; June–Aug Mon–Fri 10am–6pm, Sat & Sun 10am–3pm; Oct–April Mon–Fri 10am–3pm, Sat & Sun 10am–2pm; ☏ 08 541 314 80).

ACCOMMODATION

STF hostel South across the bridge at Per Brahesväg 1, Vaxholm ☏ 08 541 750 60, ⓦ bogesundsslottsvandrarhem .se; bus #681 from Söderhamnsplan (near the harbour) until you reach Bogesunds Gård. Though accommodation is expensive on the island itself, this peaceful hostel is a good choice. Dorm 245kr, double 490kr

STF youth hostel By the beach, Kyrkogårdsön ☏ 08 243 090, ⓦ svenskaturistforeningen.se. If you want to stay on Kyrkogårdsön, this is a lovely hostel with a wood-fired sauna. Open mid-May to mid-Oct only. Dorm 250kr, double 580kr

UPPSALA

Forty minutes' train ride north of Stockholm, the pretty university town of **UPPSALA** makes an excellent day-trip. Just north of the restaurant- and bar-lined River Fyris, which bisects the town, you'll find the vast Gothic **Domkyrkan** (daily 8am–6pm), Scandinavia's largest cathedral. Poke around and you'll find the tombs of Reformation rebel monarch Gustav Vasa and his son Johan III, as well as local hero Carl Linnaeus, the famous botanist.

Also worth seeking out are the remarkable royal burial mounds at **Gamla (Old) Uppsala**. Thought to have been created by the Svea tribe some 1500 years ago, they were once the site of gruesome human sacrifices – with unfortunate victims strung up from a tree. The place where this took place is marked by the **Gamla Uppsala Kyrka** (daily 9am–4/6pm), a church built when the Swedish kings first took baptism in the new faith. The worthwhile **Gamla Uppsala Museum** (March & April Mon, Wed, Sat & Sun noon–4pm; May–Aug daily 10am–4pm; 60kr) fills you in on all the background.

ARRIVAL AND INFORMATION

By train Trains pull in at Uppsala Resecentrum, a couple of blocks northeast of the river.
Destinations Stockholm (at least 3 per hour; 40min); Leksand/Mora (twice daily; 2hr 30min–3hr 10min); Östersund (around 4 daily; 4hr 20min–6hr 30min).

By bus Swebus and Nettbuss services to Stockholm are frequent, departing from Stationsgatan.
Destinations Stockholm (at least hourly; 1hr).

Tourist information Signs show the way to the cathedral and tourist office at Kungsgatan 59 (Mon–Fri 10am–6pm, Sat 10am–3pm; ☏ 018 727 48 00, ⓦ destinationuppsala.se).

ACCOMMODATION AND EATING

Max Stora Torget 6–8 (the main square). This fast-food joint is part of a nationwide chain giving customers free coffee and details of each burger's carbon footprint. Most meals 60–70kr. Mon & Tues 10am–10pm, Wed & Thurs 10am–3am, Fri & Sat 10am–5am, Sun 10am–midnight.

Uppsala City Hostel St Persgatan 16, northwest of the station off Kungsgatan ☏ 018 10 00 08, ⓦ uppsalacity hostel.se. Conveniently located hostel with good-value dorms and rooms in satisfyingly simple Swedish style. Dorm 220kr, double 500kr

Southern Sweden

Southern Sweden is dominated by endless expanses of farmland, and its coastline is famous for its superb beaches. Local dialects are strong and cause much mirth among metropolitan Stockholmers. Yet to portray the area as a rural backwater would do it a disservice. Here you'll find the gritty port city of **Gothenburg**, which buzzes with student life. South of here, **Malmö** is Sweden's culturally diverse gateway to the rest of Europe, while **Lund**, a medieval cathedral and university town, is an essential day-trip. Lying 90km off the southern coast in the Baltic Sea is the attractive and historically important island of **Gotland**, whose beaches and bars are awash with visitors over the summer.

GOTHENBURG

Sweden's second city, **GOTHENBURG** (Göteborg, pronounced *Yuh-teh-borr*) is

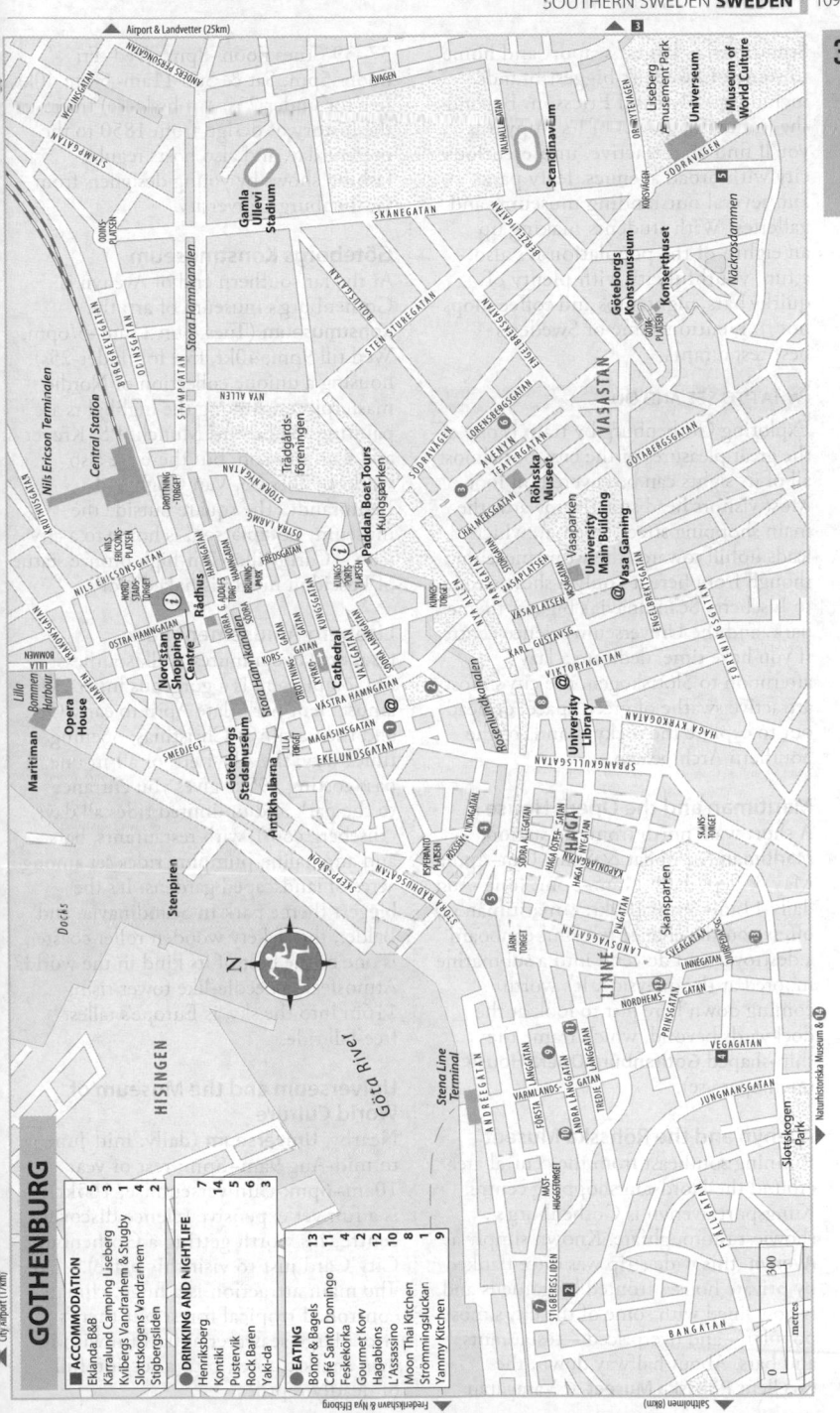

GOTHENBURG

■ ACCOMMODATION
Eklanda B&B	5
Kärralund Camping Liseberg	3
Kvibergs Vandrarhem & Stugby	1
Slottsskogens Vandrarhem	4
Stigbergsliden	2

● DRINKING AND NIGHTLIFE
Henriksberg	7
Kontiki	14
Pustervik	5
Rock Baren	6
Yaki-da	3

● EATING
Bönor & Bagels	13
Café Santo Domingo	11
Feskekörka	4
Gourmet Korv	2
Hagabions	12
L'Assassino	10
Moon Thai Kitchen	8
Strömmingsluckan	1
Yammy Kitchen	9

City Airport (17km)

Airport & Landvetter (25km)

Lilla
Bommen
Hatbour

Maritiman

Opera
House

HISINGEN

Göta River

Docks

Stenpiren

Frederikshavn & Nya Elfsborg

Stena Line
Terminal

N

Central Station

Nils Ericson Terminalen

Nordstan
Shopping
Centre

Rådhus

Göteborgs
Stadsmuseum

Antikhallarna

Gamla
Ullevi
Stadium

Trädgårds-
föreningen

Paddan Boat Tours
Kungsparken

Cathedral

University
Library

HAGA

LINNÉ

Skansparken

Slottsskogen
Park

Scandinavium

Liseberg
Amusement Park

Universeum

Museum of
World Culture

Göteborgs
Konstmuseum

Konserthuset

VASASTAN

Röhsska
Museet

University
Main Building

Vasaparken

@ Vasa Gaming

Näckrosdammen

Naturhistoriska Museum & ▲

Saltholmen (8km)

0   300   metres

33

Scandinavia's largest seaport and home to some of Sweden's biggest brands, including Volvo and Ericsson. Beyond the industrial gloom of its shipyards you'll find an attractive, unpretentious city with broad avenues, leafy parks and several outstanding museums and galleries. With students making up an eighth of the population it's also a fun, youthful city with plenty of quirky bars, nightclubs and coffee shops – not to mention some of Sweden's best restaurants.

WHAT TO SEE AND DO

Exploring Gothenburg by tram is one of the great pleasures of the city, but almost all of its sights can be covered on foot. Most visitors head straight towards the main shopping street, Avenyn, which leads uphill towards the Konstmuseum, though from here it's only a short stroll to Liseberg, Scandinavia's biggest theme park, and the Universeum science centre. If you have time, dedicate a lazy afternoon to Slottsskogen, the city's most attractive swathe of green space, or head out to explore the rocky islands of the Southern Archipelago.

Maritiman and the Opera House

A short walk north from the station, **Maritiman** (April Sat & Sun 11am–4pm; May & Sept daily 11am–5pm; June–Aug daily 11am–6pm; 100kr; ⓦmaritiman.se) offers you the chance to clamber aboard a destroyer and descend into a submarine moored at the quayside. It's worth coming down here just to look at the dockyards beyond, which frame the ship-shaped **Gothenburg Opera House** (ⓦen.opera.se).

Avenyn and the Röhsska Museet

Running southeast from the central area around the Nordstan shopping centre, Kungsportsavenyn is Gothenburg's showiest thoroughfare. Known simply as **Avenyn**, this wide strip was once flanked by private houses fronted by gardens and is now lined with some of the city's most popular – and overpriced – restaurants and bars. About halfway down, the excellent **Röhsska Museet** at Vasagatan

37–39 (Tues noon–8pm, Wed–Fri noon–5pm, Sat & Sun 11am–5pm; 40kr, free for under 25s; ⓦrohsska.se) traces the history of design from 1850 to the present day, and also hosts regular fashion shows by young designers from Gothenburg University.

Göteborgs Konstmuseum

At the far southern end of Avenyn is Gothenburg's museum of art, the **Konstmuseum** (Tues–Sun 11am–5/6pm, Wed till 9pm; 40kr, free for under-25s), housing a unique collection of Nordic masterpieces. Among the highlights are paintings by Edvard Munch, P.S. Krøyer and Carl Larsson, but there are also works by Picasso, Van Gogh and Rembrandt. The square outside the museum, **Götaplatsen**, is home to a city icon – Carl Milles' 7m-high bronze statue of Poseidon in all his naked glory.

Liseberg Amusement Park

Liseberg, five minutes' walk southeast of Götaplatsen, is a gorgeous inner-city amusement park (late April to early Oct, and then again at Christmas; opening times vary; the Allt-i-ett, or all-in-one, pass costing 395kr gives you entrance to the park and unlimited rides all day; ⓦliseberg.com), with restaurants, bars and adrenaline-pumping rides set among acres of landscaped gardens. It's the biggest theme park in Scandinavia, and Balder, the rickety wooden roller coaster, is one of the best of its kind in the world. Atmosfear, a needle-like tower rising 116m into the sky, is Europe's tallest free-fall ride.

Universeum and the Museum of World Culture

Nearby, **Universeum** (daily: mid-June to mid-Aug 9am–8pm; rest of year 10am–6pm; ⓦuniverseum.se; 165kr) is a fun yet expensive science discovery centre (it's worth getting a Gothenburg City Card just to visit this place). The main attraction is a huge, climate-controlled tropical forest but there's also a large seawater aquarium with its own shark tunnel, plus a section full of deadly reptiles.

Adjacent to Universeum, the **Museum of World Culture** (Tues–Sun 11am/noon 5pm, Wed till 8pm; 40kr, more to access certain galleries; ⓦvarldskulturmuseet.se) runs exhibitions on global issues such as HIV/Aids, human trafficking and fair trade as well as more upbeat topics such as Bollywood and hip-hop. There are also regular screenings of English and foreign-language films.

Haga and Linnégatan

The old working-class district of **Haga**, a few minutes' walk west of Avenyn, is now a picturesque area of cobbled streets lined with cafés, clothing boutiques and antique shops. Tree-lined **Linnégatan**, further west still, is a prettier and more refined version of Avenyn, with relaxed bars and restaurants leading almost all the way to Slottsskogen.

Slottsskogen Park and the Naturhistoriska Museum

Slottsskogen (tram #1, #2 or #6 to Linnéplatsen) is the city's largest park, a lovely expanse of woodland, lakes and wide paths perfect for joggers and cyclists. Several vantage points offer sweeping views over the city and there's also a small zoo area with penguins and a seal pond. The nearby **Naturhistoriska Museum** (Tues–Sun 11am–5pm; 40kr, under-25s free; ⓦgnm.se) houses the world's only stuffed blue whale. It was once possible to go inside the huge marine mammal, but since a couple of visitors were caught in a compromising embrace in its mouth, the whale has been kept as a purely visual exhibit.

Southern Archipelago

Saltholmen (the southernmost stop on tram #11) is the jumping-off point for trips to Gothenburg's craggy **Southern Archipelago**. Ferries run from here to inhabited islands like Vargö, Bränö and Styrsö, which make great spots for swimming and sunbathing in the summertime. Tram tickets are valid for ferry journeys, too.

ARRIVAL AND DEPARTURE

By plane The main airport, Gothenburg Landvetter, is 25km east of the city; buses (every 20min; 30min; 99kr/89kr if booked online; ⓦflygbussarna.se) connect to the Nils Ericson terminal next to Central Station. Gothenburg City airport, used by budget airlines Ryanair and Wizz Air, is a corrugated steel building 17km north of the city; bus departures and arrivals are roughly synchronized with flights (25min; 79kr/69kr if booked online; ⓦflygbussarna.se).

By train Trains arrive and depart from Central Station on Drottningtorget, just north of the centre; an underground walkway leads into Nordstan, the city's biggest shopping mall.

Destinations Copenhagen (hourly; 3hr 50min); Helsingborg (hourly; 2hr); Lund (hourly; 3hr); Malmö (hourly; 3hr 10min); Oslo (3 daily; 4hr); Stockholm (at least hourly; 3hr by X2000, 5hr by Intercity).

By bus Buses from all destinations use the Nils Ericson bus terminal, which adjoins Central Station. For onward travel to regional destinations like Copenhagen and Oslo, served by Swebus (ⓦswebus.se) and Nettbuss (ⓦnettbuss.se), the best advice is to book ahead online.

Destinations Copenhagen (up to 7 daily; 4hr 30min–5hr); Helsingborg (up to 18 daily; 2hr 40min); Lund (up to 15 daily; 3hr–3hr 30min); Malmö (up to 20 daily; 3hr 30min–4hr); Oslo (up to 21 daily; 3hr 30min–4hr); Stockholm (up to 15 daily; 6–7hr).

By boat Stena Line ferries from Frederikshavn in Denmark and Kiel in Germany dock within a 20min walk of the centre. Trams #3, #9 and #11 run from nearby Masthuggstorget to the centre.

Destinations Frederikshavn (4 daily; 2hr–3hr 30min); Kiel (1 daily; 14hr 30min).

INFORMATION AND TOURS

Tourist information Gothenburg has two helpful and well-informed tourist offices: a main office on the canal front at Kungsportsplatsen 2 (June–Aug daily

---

FIVE MUSEUMS FOR THE PRICE OF ONE

Pay the 90kr admission fee at the Naturhistoriska Museum and you'll automatically receive a **pass** that lets you visit the Konstmuseum, Röhsska Museet and two other city museums (Sjöfartsmuseet Akvariet and Göteborgs Stadsmuseum) as many times as you like over a twelve-month period.

33

9.30am–6/8pm; Sept–May Mon–Sat 9.30am–2/5pm; ☎031 368 4200, ⓦgoteborg.com) and a glass kiosk in the middle of the Nordstan shopping mall (Mon–Fri 10am–8pm, Sat 10am–6pm, Sun noon–5pm). Both tourist offices sell the Gothenburg City Card (315/425/565kr for 24/48/72hr), giving unlimited bus and tram travel, free or half-price museum and attraction entry, free Paddan boat tours and a fifty percent discount on a day-trip to Frederikshavn in Denmark.

Internet Vasa Gaming at Aschebergsgatan 11 (daily 10am–midnight; 20kr/hr).

Boat tours Open-topped Paddan boats (ⓦstromma.se) take tourists on 50min tours (April–Oct; 155kr or free at certain times with Gothenburg City Card) along the city's canals. Boats depart from Kungsportsplatsen.

GETTING AROUND

By tram There are 13 colour-coded tram routes operated by Västtrafik – pick up a map from any hotel or tourist office, or use the English-language journey planner at ⓦvasttrafik.se. Tickets (24kr or free with Gothenburg City Card) can usually be bought from the on-board vending machines. A more reliable option is the Västtrafikkort, which can be purchased at any branch of Pressbyrån. You pay a 50kr deposit for the card, and can then top it up with 100, 200 or 500kr at a time. Touch the card against the on-board scanner when you start each journey and, for inner-city trips, you'll pay 18.60kr.

By bike Cycle paths criss-cross the city. You can rent bikes (200kr/day) from Cykelkungen at Chalmersgatan 19 (ⓦcykelkungen.se) or buy a three-day pass for the city's bike rental scheme, Styr & Ställ (10kr; ⓦwww .goteborgbikes.se). The first 30min of every journey is free.

ACCOMMODATION

Gothenburg can be an affordable place to treat yourself to a proper a hotel room, thanks to the Gothenburg Package (from 645kr/person), run by the city tourist board. This deal gets you a double room in a central hotel, with breakfast and a free Gothenburg City Card worth 315kr – book ahead at ⓦgoteborg.com.

★ **Eklanda B&B** Eklandagatan 3 ☎031 18 79 94, ⓦeklandabohb.com. High up in an attractive townhouse near Universeum and Liseberg (no sign outside), this privately run B&B has two immaculate doubles that share a bathroom and a relaxed lounge area. Rates include a buffet breakfast. Booking essential. Double **495kr**

Kärralund Camping Liseberg Olbergsgatan ⓦliseberg.se; from Brunnsparken in the city centre, take tram #5 to Welandergatan (direction Torp). Busy campsite 4km from the centre aimed mostly at families visiting the Liseberg amusement park. There is also a youth hostel on site (dorms only, holding up to four people, and you must book the whole room). Prices

stated per person and tent sleeping up to four people. Camping **295kr** per tent, dorm **995kr**

Kvibergs Vandrarhem & Stugby Lilla Regementsvägen 35 ☎031 43 50 55, ⓦvandrarhem.com; tram #7 or #11 towards Kviberg. A 10min ride from the centre, this peaceful place offers a range of decent accommodation, from dorms (though you have to rent the entire room) to private rooms. There are also self-contained, five-person wooden cabins with kitchens. Double **556kr**, cabin **1350kr**

★ **Slottskogens Vandrarhem** Vegagatan 21 ☎031 42 65 20, ⓦsov.nu; tram #1, #2 or #6 to Olivedalsgatan. This huge hostel is in a great location near Slottskogen park, 2min walk from Linnégatan. There's a sauna, free wi-fi and a chill-out area for meeting other travellers, and dorms come with lockers built into the bunks. Dorm **195kr**, double **540kr**

Stigbergsliden Stigbergsliden 10 ☎031 24 16 20, ⓦhostel-gothenburg.com; tram #3, #9 or #11 from the city centre to Stigbergstorget. Comfortable hostel in a charming, nineteenth-century sailor's mission, close to the Stena Line ferry terminal and the bars of Andra Långgatan. Check-in closed noon–4pm. Dorm **235kr**, double **675kr**

EATING

CAFÉS, CHEAP EATS AND SNACKS

Bönor & Bagels Linnégatan 48. Cracking little café on one of the city's most attractive streets. Grab a latte (32kr), some soup and a bagel (from 65kr), then sit outside and watch the trams roll by. Mon–Sat 9.30am–6/7pm, Sun 10am–6.30pm.

Café Santo Domingo Andra Långgatan 4a. With stacks of old LPs for sale and Dominican coffee steaming away on the counter, this roomy record store attracts a mixed crowd of music lovers. The vegetarian soup (served Mon–Fri) costs 50kr. Live bands every Fri. Mon–Fri 9.30am–6.30/8.30pm, Sat 10am–4pm.

Feskekörka Rosenlundsvägen by the waterfront. Built in 1874, this lively church-like building (its name literally means fish church) is where locals come to stock up on locally caught crayfish or natter over a takeaway shellfish salad from Kerstins Delikatesser (79kr). Tues–Fri 10am–6pm and Sat 10am–3pm.

Gourmet Korv Södra Larmgatan 6. Choose from 50 different kinds of hotdog sausage – including one flavoured with cognac and juniper berries – at this tiny yet central kiosk. The sausage of the day, served with potato salad and a drink, costs 72kr. A second branch in Nordstan has longer hours. Mon–Fri 10am–6pm, Sat 11am–4pm.

Hagabions Linnégatan 21. Eat vegetarian food or drink a creamy glass of Stigbergets IPA (brewed in Gothenburg; 65kr) at this film-themed café inside an arthouse cinema showing pictures from around the globe. Mon–Fri 5pm–1am, Sat & Sun 1pm–1am.

Strömmingsluckan On the car park near Magasinsgatan 17. Insanely popular takeaway van serving a truly Swedish take on fast food: fried herring with mashed potatoes and lingonberries (55kr). Mon–Fri 11am–3pm and Sat noon–4pm.

RESTAURANTS

L'Assassino Andra Långgatan 35. A crispy pizza and a glass of red wine at this student-friendly Italian place will cost you just 79kr (Wed–Sat 5–7pm). Local artists show off their work on the walls, and there's a quiz every Tues. Mon–Sat 5pm–1/2am.

★ **Moon Thai Kitchen** Storgatan 1. Still the best Thai restaurant in town, with twinkling fairy lights strewn across its interior, and surprisingly authentic curries (from 119kr) grouped according to spiciness and cost. Tues–Thurs 11am–11pm, Fri 11am–1am, Sat noon–1am, Sun noon–11pm.

Yammy Kitchen Andra Långgatan 5. For sizzling soups and beef stews, look no further than this Korean-run place, whose huge menu also includes sushi boxes (from 72kr). Veggie and vegan options are available, too. Mon–Thurs 11am–10pm, Fri 11am–11pm, Sat 2–11pm, Sun 2–9pm.

DRINKING AND NIGHTLIFE

For cheap beer and good times, Andra Långgattan ("second long street") is a safe bet – it's one of the few places you can buy a beer for under 45kr and there are plenty of cheap Indian and Thai restaurants.

Henriksberg Stigbergsliden 7. A fun place to meet Swedish students, with cheap beer (from 39kr) and pub games like pool and indoor shuffleboard helping to keep things consistently lively. Upstairs is a terrace with views over the harbour, and at weekends bands play in the venue downstairs. Tues–Thurs 5pm–midnight, Fri & Sat 3/4pm–2am.

Kontiki Storängsgatan 2; nearest tram stop Botaniska Trädgården. This cosy Polynesian-style hangout near Slottskogen, complete with little bamboo "huts" for diners, is a welcome escape on those long winter nights. Expect live music and long, fruity cocktails (96kr). Summer Wed–Sat 5pm–1/2am; winter Fri & Sat 5pm–1/2am.

Pustervik Järntorgsgatan 14. Live bands and/or DJs play almost nightly at this former theatre, which draws in a good mix of local talent and international acts. Try to visit on Mon (free entry) when you can take part in the venue's surreal ping-pong competition. Mon–Sat 11am/noon–2/3am, Sun 5–10pm.

Rock Baren Kristinelundsgatan 14. Two floors of noisy rock 'n' roll action, just steps from the swanky clubs of Avenyn. Head in between 5–9pm for the daily happy hour, when a draught beer costs just 29kr. Minimum age 20. Daily 5pm–2/3am.

Yaki-da Storgatan 47. Homely sofas, framed portraits and old-fashioned lampshades decorate the themed rooms of this sprawling club, just off Avenyn. The well-mixed Manhattans (114kr) are easier on the tongue than they are on the wallet. Minimum age 23, entry around 150kr. Wed, Fri & Sat 10pm–3/4am.

MALMÖ

Linked to Denmark by the impressive Öresund Bridge, **MALMÖ** is Sweden's most cosmopolitan city. More than a hundred languages are spoken on its streets and you'll find Turkish and Thai food as popular as meatballs and herring. In fact, Malmö didn't even become Swedish until 1658, having been Denmark's second city for generations. Today it's Sweden's third-largest town, an attractive mix of chocolate-box medieval squares and striking modern architecture, most notably the Turning Torso skyscraper, Scandinavia's tallest building.

WHAT TO SEE AND DO

Mostly flat and home to an extensive cycle network, Malmö is the perfect place to rent a bike and explore at leisure. Most of the sights are squeezed into the compact medieval centre, although the **beaches** and modern **docklands** to the north make a tempting excursion. South of the old centre is the bohemian district of **Möllevångstorget**, where you'll find many of the best places to eat and drink.

Stortorget

The city's main square, **Stortorget** is as impressive today as it must have been when it was first laid out in the sixteenth century. It's flanked on one side by the imposing **Rådhus** (town hall), built in 1546 and covered with statuary and spiky accoutrements. To its rear stands the fine Gothic **St Petri Kyrka** (daily 10am–6pm), while to the south runs **Södergatan**, Malmö's main pedestrianized shopping street.

Lilla Torg

A late sixteenth-century spin-off from Stortorget, **Lilla Torg** is everyone's favourite part of the city. Edged by cafés and restaurants, it's usually pretty crowded at night, with drinkers kept

33

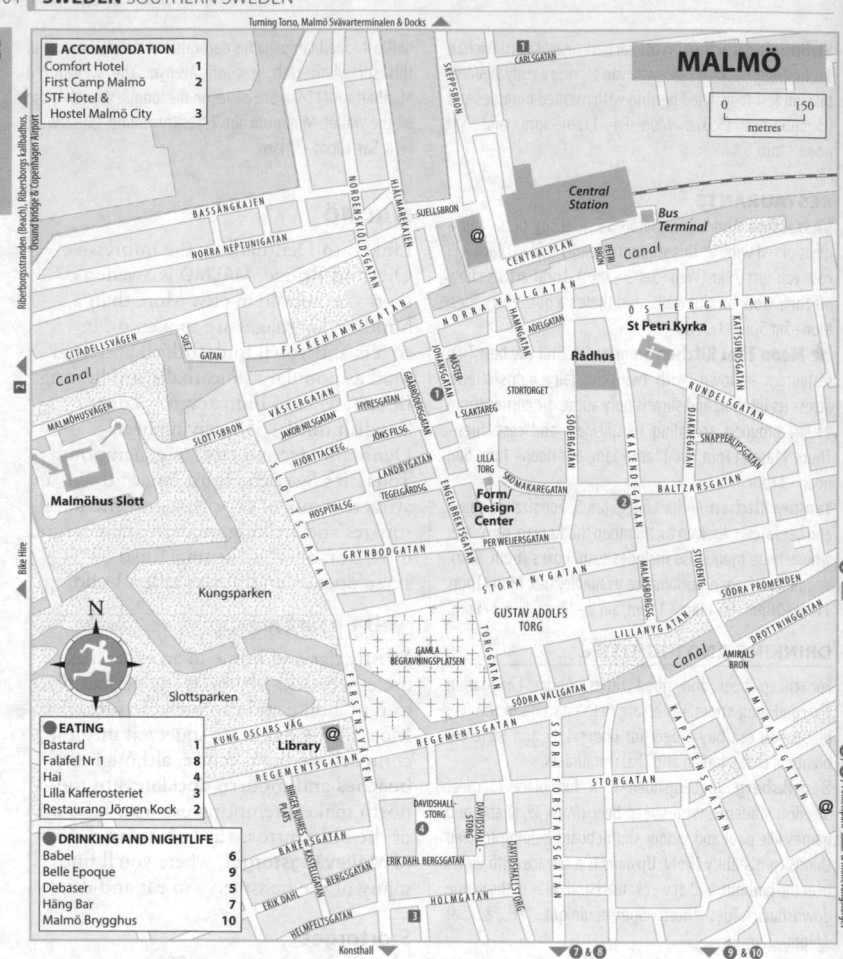

■ **ACCOMMODATION**
Comfort Hotel — 1
First Camp Malmö — 2
STF Hotel &
Hostel Malmö City — 3

MALMÖ

0 — 150
metres

● **EATING**
Bastard — 1
Falafel Nr 1 — 8
Hai — 4
Lilla Kafferosteriet — 3
Restaurang Jörgen Kock — 2

● **DRINKING AND NIGHTLIFE**
Babel — 6
Belle Epoque — 9
Debaser — 5
Häng Bar — 7
Malmö Brygghus — 10

warm under patio heaters and bars handing out free blankets. On the south side of the square, through an archway, is the **Form/Design Center** (Tues–Sat 11am–5pm, Sun noon–4pm; free; ⓦformdesigncenter.com), which showcases cutting-edge Swedish furniture, textiles and lighting. Upstairs is a café stocked with magazines and journals on design trends.

Malmöhus Slott
Handsome **Malmöhus Slott** is a low, heavily fortified castle defended by a deep moat and two circular keeps. Taking its current form in the mid-sixteenth century, when Danish king Christian III

wanted to assert his power over the region, the castle was later used as a prison. Now it houses **Malmö Museer** (daily 10am–5pm; 40kr; ⓦmalmo.se /museer), a disparate but fascinating collection of exhibitions on everything from geology to photography – and an aquarium, too. Small lakes and an old windmill dot the three leafy parks that surround the castle grounds.

The Turning Torso and Öresund Bridge
A good twenty-minute walk or five-minute cycle ride north of the station is Malmö's most iconic sight, the 190m-high **Turning Torso** skyscraper. A towering

helix of glass and steel, the structure was completed in 2005 and remains Scandinavia's tallest building. You can't go up in the tower, but the area immediately around it is still worth a wander. On a wall just to the west is an electronic eye (made from LEDs by Swedish artist Annika Svenbro), which seems to change its appearance throughout the day. Heading coastward takes you to a viewpoint of the **Öresund Bridge**, the 17km engineering marvel that links the city with Copenhagen, a journey of just 35min by train.

The beach

Ribersborgsstranden, or "Ribban", as city residents call it, is Malmö's artificial sandy beach, created in the 1920s. A long access path, busy in summer with rollerbladers and cyclists, leads down to the sections of beach, each indicated by a jetty. Just offshore is Ribersborgs Kallbadhus (May–Aug Mon, Tues, Thurs & Fri 9am–8pm, Wed 9am–9pm, Sat & Sun 9am–6pm; Sept–April Mon, Tues, Thurs & Fri 10am–7pm, Wed 10am–8pm, Sat & Sun 9am–6pm; 55kr; w ribersborgskallbadhus.se), where nude locals come to take a dip in the icy sea and warm up in one of the five oven-like saunas.

Möllevångstorget

Known as **Möllan**, this giant cobbled square towards the south of the city was once the heart of working-class Malmö. By day it hosts a busy market selling everything from cassava to Arabic sweets, while by night it becomes the alternative hangout of choice for the city's student population.

ARRIVAL AND DEPARTURE

By plane Copenhagen/Kastrup Airport is just 20min by train from Malmö's Central Station; trains leave round the clock and cost 107kr. Malmö's own airport, Sturup, is used mostly by Swedish airlines flying to domestic destinations and the odd Ryanair or Wizz Air service to Spain, the UK or Poland. It's 30km southeast of the city; buses run once or twice per hour (40min; one-way journey costs 109kr, or 99kr if booked online; w flygbussarna.se).

By train All trains terminate at Central Station, including the local Pågatåg services that run from Helsingborg and Lund (rail passes are valid). Trains bound for Copenhagen, on the other side of the Öresund Bridge, also depart from here.

Destinations Copenhagen (every 20min; airport 20min, city 35min); Gothenburg (hourly; 3hr 10min); Helsingborg (roughly every 20min; 40–50min); Lund (every 10min; 10–15min); Stockholm (hourly; 4hr 30min).

By bus The main bus terminal, served by local buses and long-distance Swebus and Nettbuss services, is just east of Central Station on Centralplan. Occasionally, long-distance buses drop off and pick up at Malmö Svävarterminalen, 600m north of the train station.

Destinations Copenhagen (up to 9 daily; airport 45min, city 1hr); Gothenburg (up to 20 daily; 3hr 30min–4hr); Lund (up to 16 daily; 25min); Helsingborg (up to 18 daily; 50min–1hr 15min); Stockholm (4 weekly; 8hr 25min); Oslo (up to 13 daily; 7hr 30min–8hr).

INFORMATION

Tourist information The main tourist office is across from the train station at Skeppsbron 2 (Mon–Fri 9am–5pm, Sat & Sun 10am–2.30pm; t 040 34 12 00, w malmotown.com). They sell the Malmö Card (100kr), which gives free museum entry, plus discounts at shops and cafés across the city.

Internet The city library at Kung Oscars Väg 11 offers free internet access (Mon–Fri 10am–6/8pm, Sat & Sun 11am–5pm).

GETTING AROUND

By bus City buses are run by Skånetrafiken (w skanetrafiken.se), whose desk inside the glass part of the train station (Mon–Fri 6am–8pm, Sat 9am–6pm, Sun 10am–6pm) sells a 24hr pass that allows unlimited travel on inner-city bus routes (65kr).

By bike Bike rental available from Fridhems Cykelaffär, Tessins Väg 13, about two blocks along Tessins Väg west from the castle (150kr for the first day, then 100kr/day thereafter).

ACCOMMODATION

Comfort Hotel Carlsgatan 10c t 040 33 04 40, w choice .se. Bright, comfortable rooms just a 2min walk from Central Station. Room rates include free organic breakfast, wi-fi and access to the on-site gym. Book ahead for the best deal. Double **690kr**

First Camp Malmö Strandgatan 101 t 040 15 51 65, w firstcamp.se; bus #4 from Central Station. Huge beachside campsite with views of the Öresund Bridge. Camping **20kr** per person, plus **200kr** per tent

STF Hotel & Hostel Malmö City Rönngatan 1 t 040 611 62 20; bus #2 or #8 from the train station to Davidshall.

33

Comfortable, clean and very popular STF hostel 1km south of the centre in a great location for nightlife and shops. Dorm 240kr, double 550kr

EATING

Bastard Mäster Johansgatan 11. There aren't many animal parts the tattooed chefs at *Bastard* won't cook. Its adventurous menu includes dishes like blood sausage with apple and pine nuts, and raw ox with mustard (both 135kr). Tues–Thurs 5pm–midnight, Fri & Sat 5pm–2am.

Falafel Nr 1 Bergsgatan 37. Malmö is known for its falafel, and this simple Lebanese place (where a spicy falafel wrap costs 35kr) is by far the locals' favourite. Daily 11am/noon–10pm.

Hai Davidshallstorg 5. Malmö's best sushi and sashimi is served in this buzzing restaurant on elegant Davidshallstorg. There's a new lunch menu (85kr) every weekday. Mon–Fri 11.30am–10/11pm, Sat noon–11pm, Sun 3–10pm.

Lilla Kafferosteriet Baltzarsgatan 24. Caffeine-hungry Swedes flock to this mustard-coloured café, which specializes in coffee made from newly roasted beans. The breakfast buffet (8–11am on weekdays; 85kr) is a great way to kick-start the day. Mon–Fri 8am–7pm, Sat 10am–5pm, Sun 11am–5pm.

Restaurang Jörgen Kock Inside the Frans Suell och Jörgen Kocks Gymnasium (high school) at Kungsgatan 44. Lunch at this restaurant, run by students in training, includes a hot main, salad, and a dessert. At 68kr, it's unbeatable value. Mon–Fri 11.30am–12.45pm during term time.

DRINKING AND NIGHTLIFE

★ **Babel** Spångatan 38 ⓦ babelmalmo.se. This old red-brick church spends most of its time shaking to the sounds of local bands, but it also hosts club nights, comedy shows and documentary screenings. Entry usually 60–140kr. Hours vary with each event; see website.

Belle Epoque Södra Skolgatan 43 ⓦ belle-epoque.se. Eating here is expensive (mains around 200kr) so come later on in the evening, when DJs play to a young crowd of cocktail-sipping party people. Tues–Sat 5.30pm–1am.

Debaser Norra Parkgatan 2 ⓦ debaser.se. The Malmö branch of the popular Stockholm club/venue. Live music, DJ nights, dancing and drinking. Entry often free before 10pm. May–Sept Mon–Fri 3pm–midnight/3am, Sat & Sun noon–midnight/3am; Oct–April Wed–Sat 7pm–3am. See website for specific event times.

Häng Bar Kristianstadsgatan 7b. With a covered seating area out front and a menu that features cheap nibbles like crayfish tails with bread (69kr), this is a decent spot for slurping a beer (from 45kr) and people-watching. Mon–Fri 5pm–1am, Sat & Sun 11am–1am.

Malmö Brygghus Bergsgatan 33. Sup pale ales, pilsners and porters at the city's only microbrewery. The pub is open late, and on Fri and Sat you can take a tour of the brewery itself (250kr). Mon–Sat 4/5pm–1am.

LUND

Just a short hop inland from Malmö, the pretty university town of **LUND** makes for a pleasant afternoon wander. It's often voted one of the best places to live in Sweden, and with its quaint cobbled streets, relaxed pace of life and mix of well-heeled residents and students from across the world, it's easy to see why. The high student population may account for the huge number of bikes you'll see across the city.

The main sight in town is the impressive, twin-towered **cathedral** (Mon–Fri 8am–6pm, Sat & Sun 9.30am–5/6pm), one of Scandinavia's finest medieval buildings. Inside is a quirky attraction: a fifteenth-century astronomical clock from which two mechanical knights pop out and clash swords as the clock strikes (Mon–Sat noon & 3pm, Sun 1pm & 3pm). Surrounding the cathedral are several grand nineteenth-century buildings belonging to the university. Also nearby is the entrance to the vast **Kulturen** open-air museum (May–Aug daily 10am–5pm; 120kr; Sept–April Tues–Sun noon–4pm; 90kr; ⓦ kulturen.com), a village in itself – full of perfectly preserved cottages and permanent exhibitions covering everything from Viking weapons to modernist design. Student discounts offered.

ARRIVAL AND INFORMATION

By train The train station is towards the west of town, an easy walk from the centre.

Destinations Gothenburg (hourly; 3hr); Helsingborg (every 10min; 30–40min); Malmö (every 5–10min; 10min); Stockholm (hourly; 4hr 20min).

By bus Frequent buses arrive and depart from the train station.

Destinations Gothenburg (5–6 daily; 3hr 25min); Copenhagen (1–2 daily; 1hr 35min).

Tourist information The tourist office is just off Stortorget at Botulfsgatan 1a (Mon–Fri 10am–6pm, Sat 10am–2/3pm, plus June–Aug Sun 11am–3pm; ☏ 046 35 50 40, ⓦ visitlund.se).

GETTING AROUND

By bike To rent a bike head to Fridhems Cyckelaffär at Brodgatan 32, a 10min walk from the train station (150kr for first day, 100kr/day thereafter).

ACCOMMODATION AND EATING

Since Lund's famous train hostel closed down, there's been a shortage of affordable rooms (nearby Malmö is a much better bet for budget travellers).

CheckInn Hantverksgatan 6 ☎072 329 08 00, ⓦ checkinn.se. If you get stuck in Lund, this hotel-style B&B in a pretty green house (with single and double rooms) is one of the cheaper spots. Doubles discounted by 100kr Fri & Sat. Double **995kr**

Saluhallen Mårtenstorget 1. This indoor market has all the ingredients you need to put together a cheap picnic. Inside, Widerbergs Gröna Deli sells a tasty smoked salmon salad (65kr). Most shops Mon–Fri 10am–6pm, Sat 9.30am–3pm.

GOTLAND

Sweden's largest island, **GOTLAND** is packed with historical intrigue, lined with great beaches, and, in summer at least, full of partying students. The star attraction is the beautifully preserved medieval town of **Visby** though the rest of the island is also well worth exploring, especially by bike or car.

WHAT TO SEE AND DO

Once the Baltic's main trading centre, **VISBY** is a heavily fortified and beautifully preserved medieval town, full of crumbling churches and cute half-timbered houses. The best approach is to simply get lost in its warren of cobbled alleyways, using the thirteenth-century walls circling the town as a reference point. After a while you'll find your way to the main open space, **Stora Torget**, where bars and restaurants cater to a happy crowd of holidaying Swedes.

Visby's museums

Established in the late nineteenth century, **Gotlands Fornsal** (Tues–Sun 11am–4pm; 100kr, free for visitors under 20; ⓦ gotlandsmuseum.se) has exhibitions about everything from Viking rune stones and gold to the macabre discovery of shallow graves that held the bones of townsfolk executed in the Middle Ages.

Behind the museum is Visby's art gallery or **Konstmuseum** (Tues–Sun noon–4pm; 50kr, or free on same day with entry to Gotlands Fornsal), mostly focused on paintings by islanders and Swedes from further afield.

Visby cathedral and church ruins

Visby's graceful **cathedral**, St Maria (daily 9am–5pm), is a short walk west of Stora Torget. Its three towers, two octagonal and one square, can be seen for kilometres around. Of the town's ruined churches, the most impressive and photogenic are **St Hans** on St Hansgatan and **St Katarina** on the eastern side of Stora Torget.

The rest of the island

Tofta Strand, 20km south of Visby (take bus #10 or rent a car; see p.1108), is one of the island's most picturesque sandy beaches. It's packed out in summertime, especially during week 29 (otherwise known as Stockholm Week; most Swedes can tell you off the top of the head which week of the year we are in) when rich kids from the capital invade the island, sending prices sky-high. To avoid the crowds it's often worth checking out the beaches on the eastern side of the island instead. Buses run across the island but services are infrequent, so renting a car makes things easier. With your own wheels you can also take a trip up to **Fårö**, Gotland's tiny sister island (the ferry is free, with frequent crossings during summer), where you'll find the beach resort of Sudersand, and the mysterious-looking sea stacks known as Langhammars, on the wind-battered north coast. Halfway to the ferry port on Gotland, the caves at **Lummelunda**, a 14km drive north of Visby (May–Sept only; 130kr), make for an interesting stop. Take bus #61 from Visby if using public transport.

ARRIVAL AND INFORMATION

By plane Several airlines, including Gotlandsflyg (ⓦ gotlandsflyg.se), SAS (ⓦ sas.se) and Norwegian (ⓦ norwegian.com), fly to Gotland, with year-round services running from Stockholm, Gothenburg and Helsingborg, plus summer-only flights from as far afield as

33

Oslo and Helsinki. Book ahead and it's possible to fly Stockholm–Visby one-way for around 400kr, even in high season. The airport is 4km north of Visby. An infrequent bus service runs into the centre of town in summer (June–Aug; see ⓦflygbussarna.se for times). Otherwise, a taxi costs 120–150kr.

By ferry Visby is accessible by ferry from the mainland ports of Nynäshamn, a 1hr train ride south of Stockholm, and Oskarshamn, in Sweden's southwest. Both crossings are run by Destination Gotland (☎0771 22 33 00, ⓦdestinationgotland.se), arriving at the harbour, a 10–15min walk west of Visby. One-way tickets start at 258kr for adults and 206kr for under-25s. If you have an InterRail pass you're eligible for a discount, but you'll need to call ahead to get it.

Destinations Nynäshamn (for Stockholm; up to 5 daily; 3hr 15min); Oskarshamn (for southern Sweden; up to 3 daily, 3hr).

Tourist Information Donners Plats 1, near the ferry terminal (May–Sept daily 9am–5/6pm; Oct–April Mon–Fri 8am–4pm; ☎0498 20 17 00, ⓦgotland.info).

GETTING AROUND

By bus Visby's main bus terminal is beyond the town wall to the east, on Kung Magnus Väg. Tickets for single trips start at 15kr.

By car Car rental at Mickes Biluthyrning, down by the ferry terminal (☎0498 26 62 62, ⓦmickesbiluthyrning.se; 300kr/day summer, otherwise 250kr/day). Good selection of old VWs and the like at bargain prices.

By bike Bike rental from Gotlands Cykeluthyrning, Skeppsbron 2, near to the tourist office (June–Aug daily 9am–6pm, with limited hours in May & Sept; from 85kr/day; ☎0498 21 41 33, ⓦgotlands cykeluthyrning.se).

ACCOMMODATION

Accommodation prices skyrocket in summer, putting all but the cheapest hostels out of the reach of budget travellers. However, some of Gotland's mid-range hotels cut their rates by as much as fifty per cent at colder times of the year, making a winter break more affordable.

STF Hostel Lärbro/Grannen Around 1km north of Lärbro, in the north of the island ☎0498 22 50 33, ⓦsvenskaturistforeningen.se. In a peaceful wooded area 35km from Visby, this no-frills hostel has small rooms, a sauna and a sociable TV area. Double 430kr

Visby Fängelse Skeppsbron 1 ☎0498 20 50 60, ⓦvisbyfangelse.se. Striking youth hostel in a converted prison near the waterfront, with beds in "cells" that sleep between 2 and 6 guests. Book ahead in summer. Dorm 290kr, double 730kr

Visby Logi St Hansgatan 31/Hästgatan 14 ☎070 752 20 55, ⓦvisbylogi.se. Two beautiful historic homes in the heart of Visby converted into double and single rooms (shared bathroom). No breakfast but kitchen facilities available. Double 650kr

Visby Strandby 4km northeast of Visby. Holiday houses and a pleasant campsite just beside Snäckviken beach, about 4km from the town centre. Discount on camping prices for under-25s. Camping 270kr per 2 people and tent, cabin 999kr

EATING, DRINKING AND NIGHTLIFE

Black Sheep Arms St Hansgatan 51. English-style bar serving up pub grub (fish and chips 159kr) and a wide selection of beers; a favourite with locals and tourists alike. Mon–Fri 5–11pm, Fri & Sat 5pm–1am.

Gutekällaren Stora Torget ⓦgutekallaren.com. With bars inside and out, this club complex is heaving with bronzed, dressed-up twenty-somethings all summer, when it attracts Sweden's top DJ talent. Entry sometimes free before 11pm. June–Aug daily 9/10pm–2am.

Hamnplan 5 Hamnplan 5. This club-restaurant by the water is best visited on a Fri night, when dishes on the special after-work menu (including a chorizo and pineapple burger) cost 99kr. Music varies from live reggae to funky house. Fri 4pm–2am, Sat 10pm–2am.

★ **Munkkällaren** St Hansgatan 40 ⓦmunkkallaren.se. Visby nightlife stalwart with live bands and a big party vibe later in the evening, particularly on Thurs and Fri. The restaurant serves up decent grub, and a Spendrups beer costs just 37kr during happy hour (6–7pm Wed, Thurs and Sat, plus 5–9pm Fri). Daily 5/6pm–2am.

Surfers Södra Kyrkogatan 1 ⓦsurfersvisby.se. An unusual concept for medieval Visby: sweet and peppery Szechuan food served tapas style, with each dish costing 80kr (70kr for takeaway orders). Good cocktail list too. Wed–Sun 6pm–late.

Central Sweden

The rural Sweden of most visitors' imaginations begins in the central areas of the interior: vast tracts of forest, peaceful lakes and log cabins. Deep-blue **Lake Siljan**, at the heart of the province of Dalarna, is a major draw, particularly in midsummer when it's a focus of festivities celebrating the long days and warm weather. From here one of Europe's classic rail journeys, the **Inlandsbanan**, begins its slow route north to the Arctic Circle via the towns of Orsa and Östersund.

THE INLANDSBANAN

The **Inlandsbanan** (Inland Railway), which cuts a route through 1300km of Sweden's best-looking scenery, ranks among the most enthralling of European train journeys. The quaint, toy-like line links central Sweden with Gällivare in the north, a two-day trip if attempted without a break. The full railway (☎0771 53 53 53, ☻inlandsbanan.com) is open from June to the end of August only.

Tickets Fares are calculated per kilometre – for example, Mora to Östersund costs 482kr, Östersund to Gällivare is 962kr; reserving a seat costs 30kr per journey.

Discounts and rail cards InterRail and Eurail pass holders travel for free apart from the optional seat reservation fee. Students receive a 25 percent discount. The Inlandsbanan Card (1795kr) offers unlimited travel on the line for fourteen days.

LAKE SILJAN

Lake Siljan (☻siljan.se) holds a special, misty-eyed place in the Swedish heart. Thousands head here in summer to stay at its iconic red lakeside cabins, paddle lazily in canoes and kayaks and hike deep into the surrounding countryside. If you happen to be here around Midsummer's Eve (*midsommarafton*), head to the town of **Leksand** at the south end of the lake, which holds a huge festival with maypole dances and longboat races.

Mora, at the north end of Siljan, has more facilities and is the starting point for the Inlandsbanan rail route (see box above). Right near the *STF Mora hostel* is the finish line for Vasaloppet – the gruelling 90km-long cross-country ski race held annually on the first Sunday in March. The small museum here (summer daily 10am–5pm, rest of year Mon, Tues, Wed & Fri 8am–4.30pm; free; ☻vasaloppet.se) tells the story of the event's ninety-year history.

ARRIVAL AND INFORMATION

By train From Stockholm, direct trains (at least 3 daily; roughly 4hr) make the scenic journey to Mora. There's also a direct service from Gothenburg (1 daily; 6hr 30min).

Tourist information The tourist office (Mon–Fri 10am–5pm, Sat 10am–2pm; ☎0250 59 20 20) across from Morastrand station gives out information on activities around the lake.

ACCOMMODATION

STF Mora 600m northeast of the tourist office at Fredsgatan 6 ☎0250 381 96. Rustic but welcoming hostel in a pleasant location by the Vasaloppet finish line. Sauna on site. Dorm 250kr, double 600kr

ORSA

The Inlandsbanan, having begun in Mora, makes its first stop at **ORSA**, fifteen minutes up the line, where the nearby **Orsa Björnpark** (daily 10am–3/6pm; 190kr; ☻orsabjornpark.se; bus #118 to Grönklitt) provides the best chance to see the brown bears that roam over swathes of central Sweden. In winter, there's some great skiing, snowshoeing and walking to be done here.

ACCOMMODATION

Grönklitts Vandrarhem ☎0250 462 00, ☻orsa gronklitt.se. The Orsa Björnpark's on-site hostel has nice clean rooms in a building at the foot of one of the slopes. Dorm 350kr

ÖSTERSUND

ÖSTERSUND, halfway point on the Inlandsbanan, is a very provincial but welcoming town on the shores of **Lake Storsjön**. It's most famous for the Loch Ness-style monster, the Storsjöodjur, said to inhabit the lake. More prosaically the town is also a major inland rail junction: as well as the Inlandsbanan, routes head east to Stockholm and west to Trondheim in Norway.

WHAT TO SEE AND DO

Apart from monster-spotting (there are eight official "observation points" along the lakeshore), the main thing to do is visit **Jamtli** (daily 11am–5pm; closed Mon Sept–May; 60kr), a family-friendly, partly open-air **museum**, fifteen minutes' walk north from the centre along Rådhusgatan. The key exhibits are the ninth-century **Överhogdal tapestries**,

33

whose simple hand-woven patterns of horses, dogs and other beasts date from the Viking Age.

From near Östersund's **harbour** you can take the bridge over the lake to **Frösön** island, site of the original Viking settlement here. In the colder months, when the lake freezes and is turned into an enormous winter park, it's possible to skate or walk from one side to the other.

ARRIVAL AND DEPARTURE

By plane Daily SAS flights from Stockholm land at Åre Östersund Airport on Frösön, a 15min bus ride from the city centre. Bus journeys are scheduled to match flight times. See ⓦ stadsbussarna.se for exact times.

By train It's a 5min walk north into the centre from Östersund Centralstation.

Destinations Gällivare, for trains to Kiruna (1 daily; 14hr); Mora (1 daily, summer only; 6hr); Orsa (1 daily, summer only; 5hr 45min); Stockholm (3 daily; 5–8hr); Trondheim (2 daily; 3hr 40min); Uppsala (3 daily; 4hr 15min–6hr 45 min).

By bus The main bus station is on Gustavs III Torg, off Rådhusgatan.

Destinations Kiruna, via Gällivare (1 daily; 12hr 45min); Mora (1–2 daily; 5hr 15min); Orsa (1–2 daily; 4hr 45min); Stockholm, via Örnsköldsvik (1 daily; 14hr).

INFORMATION

Tourist information The tourist office is at Rådhusgatan 44 (Mon–Fri 9am–5pm; June–Aug until 5/7pm and also Sat & Sun 10am–3/5pm; ☏ 063 14 40 01, ⓦ visitostersund.se).

ACCOMMODATION

Frösö Camping ☏ 063 432 54, ⓦ froso.nordiccamping .se; bus #3 from the centre. The most picturesque of Östersund's campsites. Open mid-May to mid-Sept. Camping **230kr** per person and tent

Jamtli Hostel ☏ 063 12 20 60, ⓦ jamtli.com. Quaint, appealing hostel in the grounds of Jamtli museum, with bright, clean dorms. Booking ahead is essential. Dorm **250kr**

Östersund Ledkrysset Biblioteksgatan 25 ☏ 063 10 33 10, ⓦ ostersundledkrysset.se. The most modern and sociable of the city's hostels, with immaculate dorms and private rooms housed in an attractive former fire station near the centre. Dorm **220kr**, double **700kr**

EATING AND DRINKING

Captain Cook Hamngatan 9. Australian-themed drinking haunt with decent food to boot. Try the *Jämtländska korvar* – local reindeer, elk and lamb sausages

DINE WITH LOCALS

Östersund is no culinary capital, but there's plenty of good **local food** to wrap your taste buds around – from elk and wild mushrooms to tangy Jämtland cheese. One of the best ways to find out what the locals eat, and to get tips on what to see and do in the area, is to visit a family for dinner. The local tourist board's website (ⓦ visitostersund.se) lists more than half a dozen families waiting to welcome guests over for dinner (250kr/person).

served with chanterelles (135kr). Tues–Thurs 5–10pm/ midnight, Fri & Sat 4/5pm–2am.

Wedemarks Konditori Prästgatan 27. Popular bakery with a cosy downstairs lunch bar and some delicious prawn-topped open sandwiches (67kr). Mon–Fri 8am–6pm, Sat 10am–4pm, Sun noon–4pm.

Northern Sweden

Northern Sweden – Swedish Lapland – is the wildest, strangest part of the country. The region is famous for the northern lights and midnight sun as well as the Sámi people – reindeer herders who were once the sole inhabitants here. The Sámi are still visible, especially in the small town of **Jokkmokk**, which almost straddles the Arctic Circle. A couple of hundred kilometres further north, **Kiruna** is the access point for the celebrated **Icehotel**, a once-in-a-lifetime stay if you're feeling flush.

ARRIVAL AND DEPARTURE

By plane and train The most atmospheric way to reach the far north of the country is the Inlandsbanan rail line (see box, p.1109), although you can also get here via regular rail services from Stockholm and by air to Kiruna. Flights also run to the east-coast city of Luleå, which has a direct train to Kiruna and Abisko.

THE ARCTIC CIRCLE AND JOKKMOKK

After brief stops at Arvidsjaur and Moskosel, the Inlandsbanan finally crosses the **Artic Circle** at a point 7km south of Jokkmokk. Painted white rocks indicate this latitudinal milestone, making it an essential photo stop; killjoys will point out that the real Arctic Circle (66°33') has shifted a further kilometre north owing to changes in the earth's orbit but no one seems to care.

JOKKMOKK itself is a welcome oasis after hours on a tiny train. The town is a renowned handicraft centre, with a Sámi educational college keeping the language and culture alive, and a lively winter market. The **Ájtte Museum** (mid-June to mid-Aug daily 9am–6pm; rest of year Tues–Fri 10am–4pm, Sat 10am–2pm; 70kr) on Kyrkogatan takes a respectful look at Sámiculture. The permanent exhibitions house vivid Sámi costumes and a fascinating section on how the industrial age has affected the region and its people. Jokkmokk's **Great Winter Market** (first Thurs, Fri & Sat of Feb; ⊚jokkmokksmarknad.se) is the best and busiest time to visit; you'll need to book accommodation a good six months in advance.

INFORMATION

Tourist information The tourist office is at Stortorget 4 (Mon–Fri 8.30am–noon & 1–4pm, with extended hours in summer; ☏0971 222 50, ⊚www.turism.jokkmokk.se).

ACCOMMODATION

Jokkmokk Camping Center ☏0971 12370, ⊚jokkmokkcampingcenter.com. If you're washed out from the long journey to get here, try this campsite which also has family-friendly, 2-bed cabins and heated swimming pools in a lakeside location 3.5km east of Jokkmokk. Camping 155kr per tent, cabin 695kr
Villa Åsgård Åsgatan 20 ☏070 366 46 45, ⊚facebook .com/VillaAsgard. A good alternative to camping, where you'll find modern rooms in a grand 1920s house. Dorm 250kr, double 700kr

KIRUNA

With its nearby airport, rail connections to Norway and proximity to the *Icehotel* (see box below), **Kiruna**, 145km north of the Arctic Circle, has become the unlikely tourist hub for Swedish Lapland. The city is dominated by its iron ore mine, the world's largest, and became a focus during World War II, when the supply of iron was fought over by the Germans and Allies. Be sure to take plenty of photos of Kiruna as you walk around: the vast mine is continuing to expand, threatening the city's vital infrastructure, and many of today's landmarks have already been scheduled for demolition. Between now and 2035, 2,500 homes plus shops, schools and many of Kiruna's best-known buildings – including the huge town hall – will be knocked down and rebuilt 3km to the east.

To see why the city has to move, you can take a tour of the **mine** (in English at 3pm daily; book ahead at the tourist office; 295kr), run by mining company LKAB. Descending more than 500m below the surface, you'll learn about the mine's history and the techniques used for extracting iron ore.

ARRIVAL AND DEPARTURE

By plane Kiruna's airport is 10km southwest of the city. An airport bus (50kr, cash only) runs during the summer and winter seasons; otherwise take a shared taxi (350kr/car).
By train At the end of Aug 2013, the old brick-built train station at Bangårdsvägen, a 10min walk west of the centre, will close. A new temporary station, 1.5km north, will replace it as part of the huge city-moving project.
Destinations Abisko Turiststation (3 daily; 1hr 30min); Luleå (up to 5 daily; 3hr 30min–4hr 30min); Narvik (3 daily; 3hr); Stockholm (1 daily; 18hr).

★ TREAT YOURSELF

Icehotel 17km west of Kiruna in the small village of Jukkasjärvi ⊚icehotel.com; bus #501 from Kiruna, get off at Jukkasjärvi. If you've made it this far north, a visit to Sweden's world-famous *Icehotel* is a tempting prospect. Although the hotel operates year-round, the obvious time to come is Dec–April when the fairytale-like ice structure is in place; a visitor pass (325kr) allows you a look inside the rooms. If you can stump up the cash, you could consider spending a night in its igloo-like conditions; temperatures hover around –5°C to –8°C although you'll be toasty warm, wrapped up tight in an army sleeping bag and lying on reindeer skins. A cheaper alternative is a night in the hotel's regular, heated chalets. Double 4000kr, chalet 1330kr

33

By bus The bus station is at the top of Skolgatan, just across the road from the city hall (look for the clock tower). Destinations Luleå (1–2 daily; 5hr 10min); Gällivare (2–3 daily; 1hr 30min–1hr 50min); Jukkasjärvi (for the *Icehotel*; at least 2 daily; 30min–1hr).

INFORMATION AND TOURS

Tourist information Inside Folkets Hus, on the main square at Lars Janssonsgatan 17 (Mon–Sat 8.30am–4.30/6pm; ☎ 0980 188 80, ☜ kirunalapland.se).

Tours If you want to get out into the countryside but don't fancy doing it alone, contact Kiruna Guidetur (☎ 098 08 11 10, ☜ kgt.se), which arranges elk safaris, snowmobile excursions (including a trip from Kiruna to the *Icehotel*) and dogsled rides.

ACCOMMODATION

Camp Ripan Campingvägen 5 ☎ 0980 630 00, ☜ ripan .se/en. Family-oriented campsite with an on-site restaurant, sauna and swimming pool. You can even rent an igloo for the night (Dec–April only, weather dependent). Camping 160kr per tent, double 1275kr, igloo 600kr

Kiruna Vandrarhem Bergmästaregatan 7 ☎ 0980 171 95, ☜ kirunahostel.com. Sociable hostel a 5min walk from the bus station, with TV, sauna and kitchen facilities. Breakfast costs 70kr. Dorm 250kr, double 500kr

Yellow House Hantverkaregatan 25 ☎ 0980 137 50, ☜ yellowhouse.nu. Cosy independent hostel across not one but two yellow houses. Advance booking recommended in summer. Dorm 170kr, twin 440kr

EATING AND DRINKING

Bishops Arms Föreningsgatan 6. English-style pub selling burgers (145kr) and overpriced beer. Options are limited in Kiruna, though, and this place acts as one of the few social hubs. Mon–Thurs 4–11pm/midnight, Fri 3pm–1am, Sat noon–1am, Sun 4–10pm.

Landströms Kök & Bar Föreningsgatan 11. More expensive than the *Bishops Arms* pub, with most mains 200–270kr, but the menu covers specialities like reindeer and Arctic char. Mon–Sat 6pm–11pm/1am.

Thai Kitchen Vänortsgatan 8. A friendly little Thai place near the tourist office, where you can enjoy a yellow curry with king prawns for 80kr. Mon–Fri 11am–9pm, Sat noon–8pm.

ABISKO AND THE KUNGSLEDEN TRAIL

Sweden's premier trek, the **Kungsleden** (King's Trail) winds through 500km of wilderness from Abisko, 98km west of Kiruna, south to Hemavan. Mountain huts are spaced every 10–20km along the route to allow for a day's walk between them. The northern section of the trail between Abisko and Kebnekaise (86km) is the most popular and well worth tackling if you have around a week to spare. **Abisko**, just an hour and twenty minutes by train from Kiruna on the Narvik line, is considered one of the world's best places for watching the Northern Lights. For more information on each section of the trail visit ☜ stfturist.se.

ACCOMMODATION

Abisko Turiststation ☜ abisko.nu. This incredibly popular hostel/hotel is the starting point for the King's Trail, and the slopes around the outpost are popular with skiers and snowboarders alike. Dorm 390kr, double 1395kr

Switzerland

HIGHLIGHTS

❶ Lausanne Lively and extremely hilly town in a beautiful setting on Lake Geneva. **See p.1121**

❷ Luzern Covered wooden bridges, lake cruises and mountain views. **See p.1125**

❸ Zürich Trendy bars, cutting-edge clubs and a beautiful medieval old town. **See p.1128**

❹ Jungfrau region Breathtaking scenery plus unlimited hiking and adventure sports. See p.1132

❺ The Matterhorn Towering, world-famous mountain peak, with guaranteed skiing and snowboarding year-round. **See p.1135**

HIGHLIGHTS ARE MARKED ON THE MAP ON P.1115

ROUGH COSTS

Daily budget Basic €50, occasional treat €80

Drink Beer €5

Food Fondue €20

Hostel/budget hotel €30/€100

Travel Train: Geneva–Zürich €84; bus: St Moritz–Lugano €73

FACT FILE

Population 7.9 million

Languages German, French, Italian, Romansch

Currency Swiss Franc (Fr.)

Capital Bern

International phone code ☏41

Time zone GMT +1hr

Introduction

All the quaint stereotypes are true – cheese, chocolate, clocks, obsessive punctuality – but there's much more to Switzerland than this. The major cities are cosmopolitan and vibrant, transport links are excellent, and the scenery takes your breath away. Switzerland is diverse and multilingual – almost everyone speaks some English along with at least one of the four official languages.

34

The most visited Alpine area is the picturesque **Bernese Oberland**, but the loftiest Alps are further south, where the Toblerone-peaked **Matterhorn** looms above **Zermatt**. Of the northern German-speaking cities, **Zürich** has tons of sightseeing and nightlife and provides easy access to the tiny principality of **Liechtenstein**. **Basel** and the capital, **Bern**, are quieter, each with an attractive historic core, while **Luzern** lies in an appealing setting of lakes and mountains. In the French-speaking west, **Geneva** and **Lausanne** are at the heart of Suisse-Romande. South of the Alps, Italian-speaking **Ticino** seems a world apart, particularly the palm-fringed lakeside resorts of **Lugano** and **Locarno**.

CHRONOLOGY

800–58 BC A Celtic tribe, the Helvetians, inhabit what is now Switzerland.
58 BC Julius Caesar conquers the Helvetians.
1291 AD Three valleys unite against Habsburg rule, forming the basis of the Swiss Confederation.
1388 The Swiss Confederation defeats the Habsburgs.
1536 Protestant Reformation in Switzerland led by Calvin.
1719 Liechtenstein becomes an independent principality of the Holy Roman Empire.
1803 The Swiss start to produce chocolate.
1803–15 Nine cantons join the confederation, including most of the non-German-speaking ones, giving the country's present frontiers.
1864 Red Cross founded in Geneva.
1914 Switzerland remains neutral during World War I.
1920 The League of Nations headquarters are based in Geneva.
1921 Liechtenstein adopts Swiss currency.
1939–45 Swiss neutrality during World War II tainted by the acceptance of Nazi plunder by Swiss banks.
1959 An agreement known as the "magic formula" is established between four parties in order to share power.

1971 Swiss women are among the last in Europe to gain the vote.
1993 Liechtenstein elects Europe's youngest leader, Mario Frick, at the tender age of 28.
1998 Swiss banks agree to pay US$1.25 billion in compensation to Holocaust survivors and families.
2013 Swiss tennis number one, Roger Federer, is the most successful male player in the history of the game, having won seventeen Grand Slam titles.

ARRIVAL AND DEPARTURE

Switzerland's main **airports** are at Geneva (wgva.ch), Zürich (wzurich-airport.com) and Basel (weuroairport.com), and to a lesser extent Bern (wflughafenbern.ch). Travelling to Switzerland from the continent, it's most likely you'll arrive by **train**. Services run from Paris to Geneva, Lausanne, Basel, Bern and Zürich. Geneva is also reached by trains from Lyon, southern France and Barcelona. Travelling via Strasbourg, or southwestern Germany, you'll probably arrive at Basel. Zürich is the main hub for trains from Bavaria, Austria, Italy and Eastern Europe. The most scenic way to arrive is by **ferry**, crossing Lake Maggiore from Italy, Lake Geneva from France or Lake Constance from Germany.

GETTING AROUND

Public transport is comprehensive. **Train** travel is comfortable, hassle-free and extremely scenic, with many mountain routes attractions in their own right. The national network, run by SBB-CFF-FFS, is seamlessly integrated with the many routes, especially Alpine lines, operated by local companies. **Buses** take over where the rails run out – generally yellow

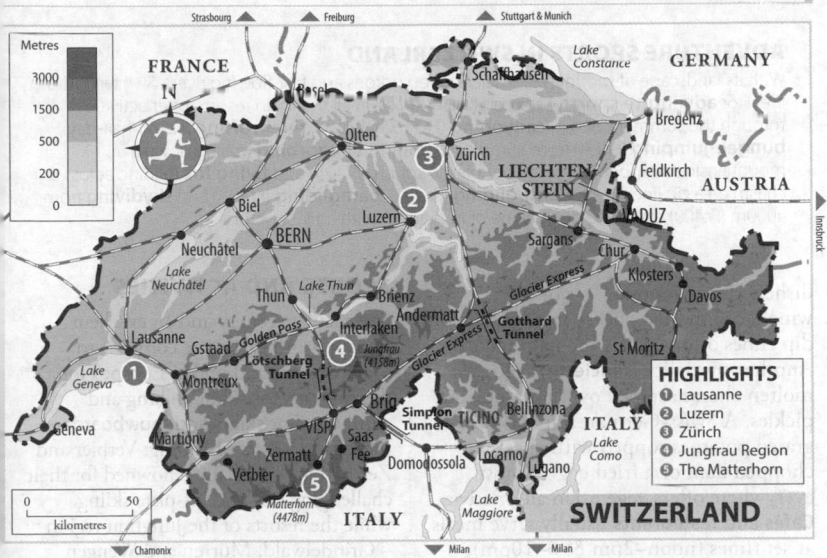

postbuses, departing from train station forecourts. InterRail, Eurail and various Swiss Passes (specified in the text as "IR", "ER" and "SP" respectively) give free travel on SBB and most minor lines, plus discounts on boats, cable cars and mountain railways. Bargain Supersaver tickets are available up to two weeks in advance at ⓦrail.ch. Postbuses (along with city transport and many museums) are free with Swiss Passes – although some routes over Alpine passes require a supplement – but not with Eurail or InterRail. There are also regional passes such as the Tell Pass in central Switzerland (ⓦtell-pass.ch), the Berner Oberland Regional Pass (ⓦregionalpass -berneroberland.ch) or the Léman-Alpes Regional Pass (ⓦgoldenpass.ch), giving some days of free travel and others at half-price. Most lake **ferries** run only from April to October, and may duplicate routes covered more cheaply and quickly by rail.

ACCOMMODATION

Accommodation, though admittedly expensive, is nearly always excellent. Tourist offices can often book rooms for free; some have boards (with a courtesy phone) on the street or at the train station, giving hotel details. When you check in, ask for a **guest card**, giving free local transport and other discounts. **Hostels** (*Jugendherberge*; *Auberge de Jeunesse*; *Albergo/Ostello per la Gioventù*) offer great value for money (book ahead June–Sept). **HI hostels** (ⓦyouthhostel.ch) are universally excellent, with doubles as well as small dorms. Non-HI members pay Fr.6 extra. A rival group known as Swiss Hostels (ⓦswisshostels.com) has lively hostels that are less institutional and more likely to have kitchens, often centrally located and priced to compete; they're specified "SH" in the text. Typically a dorm bed costs around Fr.35. **Campsites** are clean and well equipped, charging Fr.8–13 per person plus Fr.9–12 per tent. Many require an international camping carnet. Camping outside official sites is illegal. **Hotels** are first-rate, but will stretch your budget; shared-bath doubles start around Fr.100 (average Fr.120), en suites around Fr.140.

FOOD AND DRINK

Eating out in Switzerland can punch a hole in your wallet. Burgers, pizza slices, kebabs and falafel are universal **snack** standbys, as are pork *Bratwürst* sausages. Dairy products find their way into most

34

ADVENTURE SPORTS IN SWITZERLAND

With its landscape of mountains, glaciers, deep gorges and fast-flowing rivers, Switzerland is ideal for **adventure sports**. Dozens of companies, in all the main resorts, offer activities through the summer, such as **canyoning** (Fr.110/half-day), **river-rafting** (Fr.100/half-day), **bungee-jumping** (Fr.130 from 85m; Fr.170 from 134m), **zorbing** (rolling down a mountainside strapped inside a giant plastic sphere; Fr.125) and **flying fox** (gliding across a chasm on a zip line; Fr.40). **Hang-gliding** (Fr.220), **paragliding** (Fr.170) and **skydiving** from 4000m (Fr.400) can all be done alone or in tandem with an instructor.

dishes: cheese **fondue** – a pot of wine-laced molten cheese into which you dip cubes of bread – is the national dish. Another speciality is **raclette** – piquant molten cheese scraped over potatoes and pickles. A Swiss-German staple is **rösti**, grated potatoes topped with cheese, chopped ham or a fried egg. Almost everywhere offers vegetarian alternatives. **Cafés** and **restaurants** usually serve meals at set times (noon–2pm & 6–10pm), with only snacks available in between. To get the best value, make lunch your main meal, and opt for the dish of the day (*Tagesmenu, Tagesteller, Tageshit*; *plat/assiette du jour, piatto del giorno*) – substantial nosh for around Fr.18 or less. The same meal in the evening, or choosing à la carte anytime, can cost double. Major department stores, and some Coop or Migros supermarkets, have excellent-value self-service restaurants: a small/large plate costs about Fr.9/15, with as much fresh salad or hot food as you can pile onto it. There are supermarkets in most large stations, which open late seven days a week. Cafés are open from breakfast till midnight or 1am and often sell alcohol; **bars** and **pubs** tend to open from late afternoon into the evening only. **Beers** are invariably excellent, at Fr.5–8 for a glass (*e'Schtange, une pression, una birra*). Even the simplest places have **wine**, most affordably as *Offene Wein, vin ouvert, vino aperto* – a handful of house reds and whites chalked up on a board (small glass Fr.4–5).

CULTURE AND ETIQUETTE

It's not customary to **tip**; if you're impressed by the service, just round up your bill to the nearest franc.

SPORTS AND ACTIVITIES

Spectacular scenery and an excellent transport infrastructure combine to make Switzerland one of Europe's top destinations for skiing, hiking and climbing. For **skiers and snowboarders**, the choice is overwhelming: Verbier and Zermatt are especially renowned for their challenging on- and off-piste skiing, while the resorts of the Jungfrau region – Grindelwald, Mürren and Wengen – cater better for intermediates. A lift pass should cost Fr.55–65 for a day or Fr.280 upwards for six days. Glaciers at Saas Fee and Zermatt allow summer skiing. The Swiss love hiking, and with over 65,000km of marked trails, most of them revealing stunning Alpine vistas, it's not hard to see why – the Jungfrau and Zermatt regions are particularly popular. Hiking trails are clearly signed in yellow; red signs mark the nationwide **cycling** network. Bikes (and trailers, e-bikes etc) can be rented from main stations (from Fr.27 half-day, Fr.35 day), and in summer the largest cities also have free bike schemes (such as Zuri-rollt and Genève'roule). Ask at tourist offices or consult ⓦmyswitzerland.com for routes and tips.

COMMUNICATIONS

Main **post offices** open Monday to Friday 7.30am to 6pm, Saturday 8 to 11am. Most **public phones** take phonecards (*taxcards*), available from post offices and news kiosks, as well as credit cards; some take Swiss and euro coins. Kiosks sell discount cards for

EMERGENCY NUMBERS

Police ☎117; Fire ☎118; Ambulance ☎144.

SWITZERLAND AND LIECHTENSTEIN ONLINE

ⓦ **myswitzerland.com** Tourist office site – vast, detailed and authoritative.

ⓦ **postbus.ch** and ⓦ **sbb.ch** Details of the postbus and rail networks, including Alpine routes.

ⓦ **swissinfo.org** News database in English, with good links.

ⓦ **tourismus.li** The Liechtenstein tourist board.

---

cheap international calls. **Wi-fi** internet access (known as WLAN) is widespread, available at cafés (Fr.4–12/hr) or free at many hotels and hostels.

EMERGENCIES

You'll have to pay **hospital** (*Spital, hôpital, ospedale*) bills up-front and claim expenses back later. Every district has one local **pharmacy** (*Apotheke, pharmacie, farmacia*) open outside normal hours; each pharmacy has a sign telling you where the nearest open one is.

INFORMATION

Tourist offices (*Verkehrsverein* or *Tourismus*; *Office du Tourisme*; *Ente Turistico*) are invariably located near the train station and always extremely useful. Most staff speak English. Opening hours in smaller towns involve a long lunch and can be limited at weekends and out of season. All have accommodation and transport lists, and maps.

MONEY AND BANKS

Both Switzerland and Liechtenstein use the **Swiss franc** (CHF or Fr.), divided into 100 Rappen (Rp), centimes or centisimi (c). There are coins of 5c, 10c, 20c, 50c, Fr.1, Fr.2 and Fr.5, and notes of Fr.10, Fr.20, Fr.50, Fr.100, Fr.200 and Fr.1000. It's easiest to **change money** in train stations. **Banks** usually open Monday to Friday 8.30am to 4.30pm; some in cities and resorts also open Saturday 9am to

4pm. **Post offices** give a similar exchange rate to banks, and **ATMs** are everywhere. Many shops and services, especially in tourist hubs, accept euros. At the time of writing, €1 was roughly equal to Fr.1.23, US\$1 to Fr.0.93 and £1 to Fr.1.45.

OPENING HOURS AND HOLIDAYS

Shop hours are Monday to Friday 9am to 7pm, Saturday 8.30am to 4pm, sometimes with a lunch break and earlier closing in smaller towns. Many **museums** and attractions close on Monday. Almost everything is closed on **public holidays**: January 1, Good Friday and Easter Monday, Ascension Day, Whit Monday, December 25 and 26. In Switzerland, shops and banks close for all or part of the national holiday (Aug 1) and on a range of local holidays. Liechtenstein keeps May 1 as a public holiday, and August 15 as the national holiday.

Lake Geneva

French-speaking Switzerland, or Suisse Romande, occupies the western third of the country, comprising the shores of **Lake Geneva** (Lac Léman) and the hills and lakes to the north. **Geneva**, at the southwestern tip of the lake, was once a haven for freethinkers from across Europe; now it's a city of diplomats and big business, but you'll see its more relaxed side by the lake on a warm day. Visible from the city is **Mont Blanc**, Western

---

STUDENT AND YOUTH DISCOUNTS

With an ISIC card, you can take advantage of student discounts (up to fifty percent) at almost all **museums** and galleries. Although there is no student discount on cable-car tickets, during the winter season many resorts offer a youth discount on **lift passes**.

34

Europe's highest mountain (4807m). Halfway around the lake, **Lausanne** is full of young people; it's a cultured, energetic town acclaimed as the skateboarding capital of Europe. It also has breathtaking views across the water to the French Alps. Further east is the stunning medieval **Château de Chillon**, which drew Byron and the Romantic poets. On a sunny day, the train ride around the beautiful northern shore is memorably scenic, but the excellent boat service (ER & SP free, IR 50 percent; ⓦcgn.ch) brings home the full grandeur of the setting.

GENEVA

The struggle of **GENEVA** (Genève) for independence is inextricably linked with Puritanism. By 1602, when it won independence from Savoy, the city's religious zeal had painted it as the "Protestant Rome". Geneva joined the Swiss Confederation only in 1815, with a reputation for joylessness which it still struggles to shake off. Today, there is plenty for budget travellers, with its beautiful Old Town and many galleries.

WHAT TO SEE AND DO

The **Rive Gauche**, on the south bank, is a grid of waterfront streets comprising the main shopping and business districts, and above them the Old Town. Further south is **Carouge**, characterized by artisans' shops and picturesque Italianate architecture. Behind the grand hotels lining the northern **Rive Droite** waterfront is the main station and the cosmopolitan (and in places sleazy) **Les Pâquis** district, full of cheap ethnic eateries. Further north are the dozens of international bodies headquartered in Geneva, including the UN.

Rive Gauche and the Old Town

On the Rive Gauche, beyond the ornamental flowerbeds of the Jardin Anglais, erupts the roaring 140m-high plume of Geneva's trademark **Jet d'Eau**. South of Rive Gauche is the main thoroughfare of the **Old Town**, the steep, cobbled Grande Rue. Here, among jewellery shops and galleries, you'll find the atmospheric seventeenth-century **Hôtel de Ville** and the arcaded armoury. A block away is the late Romanesque **Cathédrale St-Pierre** (June–Sept Mon–Fri 9.30am–6.30pm, Sat 9.30am–5pm, Sun noon–6.30pm; Oct–May Mon–Sat 10am–5.30pm, Sun noon–5.30pm), with an incongruous Neoclassical portal and a plain, soaring interior. Tucked behind the cathedral in the eighteenth-century Maison Mallet, the **Musée Internationale de la Réforme** (Tues–Sun 10am–5pm; Fr.13; ⓦmusee-reforme.ch) documents Geneva's contribution to the Reformation. Just beyond is the hub of the Old Town, **Place du Bourg-de-Four**, a picturesque split-level square ringed by cafés. Alleys wind down from here to a lovely terrace, the Promenade de la Treille, with the world's longest wooden bench (126m). Beneath this is the austere **Wall of the Reformation** (1909–17), with statues of the leading reformist preachers, in the university park.

The Musée d'Art et d'Histoire

Just east of the Old Town is the **Musée d'Art et d'Histoire**, 2 rue Charles Galland (Tues–Sun 11am–6pm; free; ⓦville-ge.ch /mah). The first floor houses a superb collection of armour and weaponry, fine panelled interiors and silverware, while the basement holds a huge archeological collection. Upstairs, the art collection includes three rooms of Hodlers and Konrad Witz's famous altarpiece, made for the cathedral in 1444, with Christ and the fishermen transposed to Lake Geneva.

Bâtiment d'Art Contemporain

A former factory west of the Old Town at 28 rue des Bains, the **Bâtiment d'Art Contemporain** now houses top-quality contemporary art galleries, notably MAMCO (Tues–Fri noon–6pm, Sat & Sun 11am–6pm; Fr.8, students Fr.6; free first Wed of month 6–9pm and first Sun; ⓦmamco.ch), the Centre d'Art Contemporain de Genève (Tues–Sun 11am–6pm; Fr.5, free first Sun of month; ⓦcentre.ch) and the Centre Photographique de Genève (Tues–Sun 11am–6pm; free; ⓦcentrephotogeneve .ch), as well as a cinema, restaurant and nightclub.

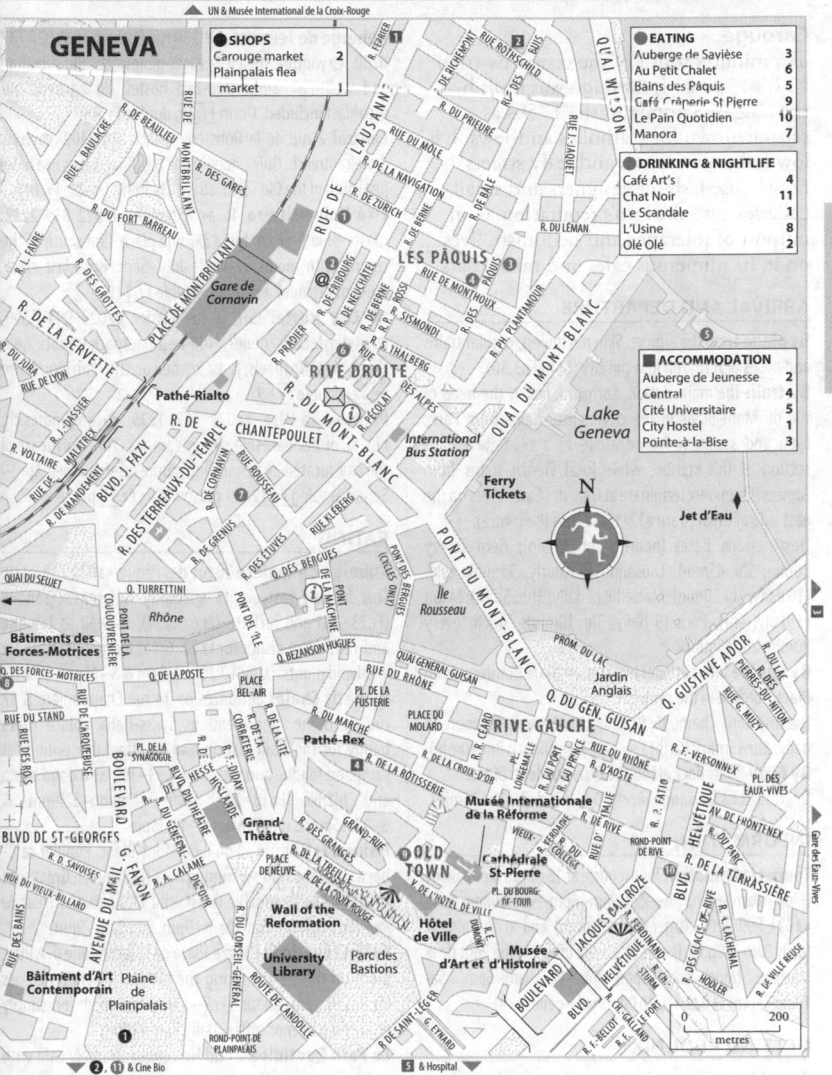

GENEVA

▲ UN & Musée International de la Croix-Rouge

● SHOPS
Carouge market	2
Plainpalais flea market	1

● EATING
Auberge de Savièse	3
Au Petit Chalet	6
Bains des Pâquis	5
Café Crêperie St Pierre	9
Le Pain Quotidien	10
Manora	7

● DRINKING & NIGHTLIFE
Café Art's	4
Chat Noir	11
Le Scandale	1
L'Usine	8
Olé Olé	2

■ ACCOMMODATION
Auberge de Jeunesse	2
Central	4
Cité Universitaire	5
City Hostel	1
Pointe-à-la-Bise	3

34

▼ ❷, ⓫ & Cine Bio   ❺ & Hospital ▼

Palais des Nations and Museé International de la Croix-Rouge

About 1km north of the station stands the imposing UN complex (tram #13 or #15 to Nations). One-hour tours of the **Palais des Nations** (April–June Mon–Sat 10.30am, noon, 2.30pm & 4pm; July & Aug Mon–Sat 10.30am–4pm; Sept–March Mon–Fri 10.30am, noon, 2.30pm & 4pm; Fr.12, student Fr.10; passport required; ⓦunog.ch) start in the new wing (entry 14 av. de la Paix) and continue to

the original Palais des Nations, built from 1929–38 to house the League of Nations. The highlight is the Council Chamber, with allegorical ceiling murals by José-Maria Sert. Just beyond the UN is the thought-provoking **Museé International de la Croix-Rouge** (Tues–Sun 10am–5pm, April–Oct until 6pm; Fr.10/7, pay what you want first Sat of the month; ⓦmicr.ch; bus #8 or #F to Appia), newly refurbished to illustrate the Red Cross's response to humanitarian crises.

34

Carouge

Ten minutes south of the centre by tram #12, #13 or #14, **Carouge** was built by the king of Sardinia in the 1750s as a separate town for Catholics and Jews. Its low Italianate houses and leafy streets now house fashion designers and small galleries, and the area's reputation as an outpost of tolerance and hedonism lives on in its numerous cafés and music bars.

ARRIVAL AND DEPARTURE

By plane From the airport, 5km northwest, regular trains and buses (#5/10) run into the city (both Fr.3.50).

By train The main station, Cornavin, lies at the head of rue du Mont-Blanc in the city centre. Trains from Paris, Lyon and southern France arrive in a separate French section of this station, while local French trains from Annecy/Chamonix terminate at Gare des Eaux-Vives on the east side of town (tram #12/16/17 into the centre).

Destinations Basel (hourly; 2hr 35min); Bern (every 30min; 1hr 45min); Lausanne (6 hourly; 35min); Lyon (10 daily; 1hr 50min); Marseille (2 daily; 3hr 35min); Milan (3 daily; 4hr); Paris (9 daily; 3hr 10min); Zürich (every 30min; 2hr 45min).

By bus The international bus station (Gare Routière) is on Place Dorcière in the centre.

Destinations Chamonix (2 daily; 2hr 45min); Grenoble (5 daily; 2hr 15min); Paris (3 weekly; (overnight); 8hr 30min).

By ferry Boats dock along the Quai du Mont-Blanc.

Destinations Lausanne (April–Oct 1–2 daily; 3hr 35min).

INFORMATION

Tourist information Tourist office at 18 rue du Mont-Blanc (Mon 10am–6pm, Tues–Sat 9am–6pm, Sun 10am–4pm; ☎022 909 7000, ⓦgenevatourism.ch) and at the airport (daily 8am–10pm). There's also a city office on the Pont de la Machine (Mon noon–6pm, Tues–Fri 9am–6pm, Sat 10am–5pm; ☎022 418 20 00, ⓦville-geneve.ch).

GETTING AROUND

By public transport The Geneva Transport Card allows free public transport for the duration of your stay including the train to the airport and the *mouette* ferries across the mouth of the lake.

By bike Bikes can be rented at Place de Montbrillant 17 behind the station (8am–6/9pm daily; Fr.12/half-day, Fr.20/day). The Genève'roule scheme (May–Oct daily 9am–7pm) provides free bikes form the same address, and at temporary locations across the city.

ACCOMMODATION

Be sure to pick up a Geneva Transport Card (see above) when checking in.

Auberge de Jeunesse (HI) 30 rue Rothschild ☎022 732 6260, ⓦyouthhostel.ch & ⓦyh-geneva.ch. Big, bustling and well-maintained 360-bed hostel. No kitchens but breakfast included. Dorm **Fr.29**, double **Fr.85**

Central 2 rue de la Rôtisserie ☎022 818 8100, ⓦwww .hotelcentral.ch. Quiet, good-value top-floor rooms in a hotel just south of the Old Town, all with balcony. Double **Fr.105**

Cité Universitaire 46 av Miremont ☎022 839 2222, ⓦcite-uni.unige.ch; bus #3. Huge place 3km south of the centre, with rooms available July–Sept. Breakfast extra. Student discount available. Double **Fr.110**

★ **City Hostel** (SH) 2 rue Ferrier ☎022 901 1500, ⓦcityhostel.ch. Friendly 100-bed backpacker place near the station. No meals, but a kitchen on each corridor. Dorm **Fr.32**, double **Fr.89**

Pointe-à-la-Bise ☎022 752 1296, ⓦcampingtcs.ch; bus #E or #G. Lakeside site in Vésanaz, 7km northeast of the city, located by a charming nature reserve. Open April–Sept. Camping **Fr.12** per person, plus **Fr.10** per tent

EATING

Auberge de Savièse 20 rue des Pâquis ☎022 732 8330. This friendly restaurant's speciality is fantastic fondue (Fr.23–28) and raclette (Fr.6.50/34), as well as lasagne and vegetarian dishes for Fr.22. Great for groups; book for weekend nights. Daily 10.30am–3pm & 5–11pm.

Au Petit Chalet Entrances on 14 rue Chapponière & 17 rue de Berne. Unpretentious Swiss-Italian place that's handy for the train station and an affordable option for sampling fondue and raclette (Fr.23–30); also good pasta and pizzas (Fr.18–23). Mon–Fri noon–2.30pm & 6–11.15pm, Sat & Sun noon–11.15pm.

Bains des Pâquis 30 quai du Mont-Blanc. Popular café-bar at the lakefront swimming area (Fr.2 entry). Great spot to soak up some sun. Breakfast until 11.30am, then *plat du jour* (Fr.14). Mon–Sat 10am–9pm, Sun 9am–9pm.

Café-Crêperie St Pierre Place de la Taconnerie 6. A little place on the terrace facing the cathedral, serving crêpes (Fr.8–20) and salads (Fr.7–19). Also good for simply enjoying a beer or coffee. Daily 8am–10pm.

Le Pain Quotidien 21 bd Helvétique. Homely café with delicious pastries (Fr.4.50), quiche (Fr.17), salads or pasta, plus a range of newspapers. Daily 7/8am–6pm.

Manora 6 rue Cornavin. Deli counters on the ground floor of this department store sell good takeaway *foccacine* (Fr.3), pizza slices (Fr.4.30) and curries (Fr.4.50). There's also a self-service restaurant and roof terrace, serving salads, pizza and dishes of the day from Fr.11. Deli Mon–Sat 8.30am–6/9pm, restaurant Mon–Sat 9am–6/9pm.

DRINKING AND NIGHTLIFE

Café Art's 17 rue des Pâquis. Café-bar with a relaxed bohemian feel. Good simple food, beer Fr.8 for half a litre, cocktails Fr.15. Daily 8/11am–2am.

Chat Noir 13 rue Vautier, Carouge ⓦchatnoir.ch. Bar and cellar venue with DJs and live music (anything from world to techno) Tues–Sat 6pm–4am.

Le Scandale 24 rue de Lausanne ⓦlescandale.ch. Funky bar with comfy armchairs and DJs several nights a week. It also serves food; dish of the day Fr.17 and drinks from Fr.5. Mon & Sat 5pm–2am, Tues–Fri 11am–2am.

L'Usine 4 place des Volontaires ⓦusine.ch. Converted factory hosting a plethora of arts and music events. Zoo (ⓦlezoo.ch) runs club nights (hip-hop, breakbeat, electronica) and leREZ puts on gigs. See website for times.

★ **Olé Olé** 11 rue de Fribourg. Tapas bar with personality, offering cocktails at Fr.15, glasses of wine at Fr.5 and bottles of beer at Fr.8. Chalk boards list a host of tapas dishes for Fr.10 plus salads and burgers. Mon–Fri 11am–2am, Sat 5pm–2am.

ENTERTAINMENT

In July and Aug films are screened on the lakeside Quai Gustave-Ador (ⓦorangecinema.ch), and from mid-July to mid-Aug mainstream Hollywood films are screened in the open air by the lakeside at Port-Noir.

Cinéma Bio 47 rue St-Joseph, on the Place du Marché, Carouge ⓦcinema-bio.ch. A charming arthouse cinema with two screens, dating from 1912. Films cost Fr.11/16.50.

Pathé-Rex Rue Confédération 8. Located on the Rive Gauche, this smaller cousin to the Rialto cinema shows recent blockbusters for Fr.18 (2-D only).

Pathé-Rialto Bd James-Fazy 2. This multiplex, close to Cornavin station, shows recent blockbusters for Fr.19, as well as 3-D films (Fr.3 extra).

SHOPPING AND MARKETS

Carouge market Carouge in general is a good choice for affordable and whimsical shopping; it's crammed with cute boutiques and hosts a colourful market. Wed & Sat 8am–1.30pm.

Plainpalais flea market Head for this flea market near the Old Town, where you can pick up anything from old records and retro kitchenware to gemstones. Wed & Sat 6am–6pm.

DIRECTORY

Consulates Australia, 2 chemin des Fins ☎022 799 9100; Canada, 5 av. de l'Ariana ☎022 919 9200; New Zealand, 2 chemin des Fins ☎022 929 0350; US, 7 rue Versonnex ☎022 840 5160. Embassies are in Bern.

Exchange At the train station by the ticket office (Mon–Fri 7am–8pm, Sat 7am–7pm, Sun 9am–1.30pm & 2.30–5.50pm).

Hospital Hôpitaux Universitaires, 2 rue Gabrielle-Perret-Gentil ☎022 372 8120.

Internet Charly's Checkpoint, 7 rue de Fribourg (Mon–Sat 9am–midnight, Sun 1–11pm; Fr.1/15min or Fr.3/hr).

Left luggage At the train station (4.30am–12.45am; Fr.4/7); also lockers (24hr, Fr.6/9).

Post office 18 rue du Mont-Blanc (Mon–Fri 7.30am–6pm, Sat 9am–4pm).

Pharmacy Amavita, in the train station (Mon–Sat 7am–11pm, Sun 10am–11pm).

LAUSANNE 34

LAUSANNE is attractive and vibrant, set on a succession of south-facing terraces above Lake Geneva, with the Old Town at the top, the train station and commercial districts in the middle, and the former fishing village of **Ouchy**, now prime territory for waterfront café-lounging and strolling, at the bottom. Switzerland's biggest university makes this a lively, fun city. For chilled-out bars, head for the trendy Flon district.

WHAT TO SEE AND DO

To reach the central **Place St-François** from the train station, walk up the steep **rue du Petit-Chêne**, or take the metro to **Flon**; from the metro platforms, lifts raise you to the level of the giant Grand Pont, between **Place Bel-Air** on the left and Place St-François on the right. From here, rue St-François drops down into a valley and up again to the cobbled **Place de la Palud**, an ancient, fountained square flanked by the Renaissance town hall.

The Cathedral and around

From Place de la Palud the medieval Escaliers du Marché lead up to the **Cathedral** (Mon–Sat 7am–7pm, Sun 8am–7pm, winter closes 5.30pm; ⓜBessières), a fine Romanesque-Gothic jumble. Opposite, in the former bishop's palace, is the **Musée Historique** (Tues–Thurs 11am–6pm, Fri–Sun 11am–5pm; also Mon July & Aug; Fr.8/students Fr.5, first Sat of month free, combined with MUDAC Fr.15/8; ⓦlausanne.ch/mhl), covering the history of the canton of Vaud. Next door is the **MUDAC Musée de Design et d'Arts Appliqués Contemporains** (Tues–Sun 11am–6pm; also Mon July & Aug; Fr.10, students Fr.5; ⓦmudac.ch), displaying contemporary glass and temporary exhibitions upstairs.

34

Lausanne suffered many medieval fires, and is the last city in Europe to keep alive the tradition of the **nightwatch**: every night, on the hour (10pm–2am), a sonorous-voiced civil servant calls from the cathedral tower "C'est le guet; il a sonné l'heure" ("This is the nightwatch; the hour has struck").

Collection de l'Art Brut

Ten minutes' walk west of Palud on Avenue Vinet (or bus #2, #3 or #21 to Beaulieu), the fascinating **Collection de l'Art Brut**, 11 av des Bergières (Tues–Sun 11am–6pm; July & Aug also Mon; Fr.10, students Fr.5, free first Sat of month; ⓦartbrut.ch), is devoted to utterly absorbing "outsider art".

Ouchy, the Olympic Museum and Museé de l'Elysée

Ouchy's waterfront hosts regular free music events all summer, and people come down here for a spot of café sunbathing or rollerblading. In a fine lakefront park just to the east sits the **Olympic Museum** (daily 9am–6pm; Nov–March closed Mon; Fr.15, students Fr.10; ⓦolympic.org), newly reopened with high-tech displays on the history of the Games. Above it in the same park is the **Musée de l'Elysée**, an excellent photography museum (Tues–Sun 11am–6pm; Fr.8, students Fr.4, free first Sat of month).

ARRIVAL AND DEPARTURE

By train From the train station the metro's Line 2 runs down to Ouchy by the lake and up to Flon, Riponne and Bessières, for the cathedral area.

Destinations Basel (every 30min; 2hr 10min); Bern (every 30min; 1hr 10min); Geneva (6 hourly; 35min); Milan (3 daily; 3hr 20min); Paris (5 daily; 3hr 40min); Zermatt (hourly, change at Visp; 3hr); Zürich (every 30min; 2hr 10min).

By ferry The ferry port is located on Allée des Bacounis – out of Ouchy metro station to the lake and just to the left/east. Note that ferries run mid-April to mid-Dec only.

Destinations Chillon (1 daily; 1hr 45min); Geneva (1–2 daily; 3hr 35min); Montreux (2–4 daily; 1hr 30min).

INFORMATION

Tourist information Lausanne has two tourist offices (ⓣ021 613 7392, ⓦwww.lausanne-tourisme.ch): one in the train station (daily 9am–7pm), the other facing Ouchy metro station (daily 9am–7pm; Oct–April closes 6pm).

ACCOMMODATION

Camping Vidy ⓣ021 622 5000, ⓦcampinglausannevidy .ch; bus #1/2/6 west to Maladière and 5min walk (past the ruins of Roman Lousana). Large lakeside campsite with basic, two-person bungalows (no WC or shower), supermarket and restaurant (April–Sept). Open all year. Camping **Fr.8.50** per person, plus **Fr.16** per tent; bungalow **Fr.56**

Jeunotel (HI) 36 chemin du Bois-de-Vaux ⓣ021 626 0222, ⓦyouthhostel.ch/lausanne. Huge HI place beside *Vidy* campsite with four-bed dorms and rooms, plus cheap meals on request (Fr.13.40). Dorm **Fr.36**, double **Fr.93**

★ **Lausanne Guest House** (SH) 4 chemin des Epinettes ⓣ021 601 8000, ⓦlausanne-guesthouse.ch. Fabulous, friendly hostel with lake views, kitchen, garden, four-bed dorms and rooms. Dorm **Fr.37**, double **Fr.98**

Pension Bienvenue 2 rue du Simplon ⓣ021 616 2986, ⓦpension-bienvenue.ch. Respectable women-only guesthouse behind the station. Long stays available. Very clean and friendly, with shared WCs and showers, wi-fi, kitchen and a good breakfast. Double **Fr.120**

EATING

Café Romand Place St-François 2. Bustling, heartwarming place with cosy alcoves for beer, coffee or heavy Swiss fare. Dish of the day Fr.18.50. Mon–Sat 11.30am–11pm.

Café Saint François Place St-François 5. Soak up the sun at this French-style café by the church; choose from its ever-changing lunch menu. Dish of the day Fr.14.50–19, Sun brunch Fr.17.50, takeaway pastries Fr.4.50. Mon–Fri 7am–7pm, Sat 8am–6.30pm, Sun 9am–6pm.

Laxmi Escaliers du Marché 5. Reasonably authentic North Indian food, with plenty of vegetarian choices (Fr.25); the all-you-can-eat lunch buffet is popular, and takeaways are also available. Mon–Sat 11.30am–2pm & 6.30–11pm, Sun 6.30–11pm.

Le Barbare Escaliers du Marché 27. Perfect little café among the Old Town's rooftops. There's a sun-trap terrace for summer and it's cosy inside in winter. Mon–Sat 8.30am–midnight.

Manora Rue Pichard 3. Excellent self-service cafeteria, with a wide range of wholesome hot and cold food for Fr.12 or under. Mon–Fri 8.30/9am–7pm, Sat 8am–6pm.

DRINKING AND NIGHTLIFE

Bleu Lézard 10 rue Jenni Enning ⓦbleu-lezard.ch. Fashionable, lively café-bar with regular live music sets downstairs and excellent, seasonal, veggie-friendly food (including Sun brunch). Mon–Thurs 7am–1am, Fri 7am–2am, Sat 8am–2am, Sun 8am–1am.

LAUSANNE FESTIVALS

Lausanne's big party is the free **Festival de la Cité** in early July (ⓦ festivaldelacite .ch), featuring music, dance and drama on open-air stages in the Old Town. June is also a great time to visit, with the **Fête à Lausanne**, a weekend of fairground attractions, the **Chocolate Festival** (ⓦ chocolate-festival.ch) of electronic music, and the **Fête de la Musique** (ⓦ fetemusiquelausanne.ch).

Brasserie Au Château 1 place du Tunnel ⓦ bierreduchateau.ch. Bar with tasty home-brewed beers, pub grub and funky music (DJs Thurs–Sat). Mon–Sat 11am–1/2am, Sun 4pm–1am.

D! Club Place Centrale, Flon ⓦ dclub.ch. Popular club in a former theatre with live acts, and DJs spinning electro and house. Thurs is student night. Wed–Sat, 11pm/ midnight–5am.

Le V.O. 11 place du Tunnel ⓦ voclub.ch. Unpretentious jazz café-bar and live venue with regular live acts and DJs Thurs–Sat. No entry fee. Daily 5pm–5am.

MAD (Moulin à Danse) 23 rue de Genève, Flon ⓦ mad .ch. At the hub of trendy Flon, housing four dancefloors with cutting-edge DJs, plus a theatre, art galleries and alternative-style café. Daily 11pm–5am.

DIRECTORY

Exchange At the train station (Mon–Wed & Fri 8am–6.30pm, Thurs 8am–8.30pm, Sat 8am–6pm, Sun 9am–1.20pm & 2.40–6pm).

Left luggage At the train station (Mon–Fri 8.30am–6.45am, Sat & Sun 9am–1pm & 2–6.30pm).

CHÂTEAU DE CHILLON

The highlight of a journey around Lake Geneva, or en route to Zermatt, is the spectacular thirteenth-century **Château de Chillon** (daily: April–Sept 9am–7pm; March & Oct 9.30am–6pm; Nov–Feb 10am–5pm; Fr.12, students Fr.10; ⓦ chillon.ch), one of the best-preserved medieval castles in Europe. Take the hourly train to Veytaux-Chillon, the ferry (dating from 1904) from Lausanne or Montreux (Fr.48/17; 4/day), or it's a 45-minute walk or a short ride on bus #1 east from Montreux station (every 10min). Your first glimpse of the castle, jutting into the lake and framed by craggy mountains, is simply unforgettable.

MONTREUX JAZZ FESTIVAL

The sleepy lakeside town of Montreux livens up during its star-studded **Montreux Jazz Festival** (ⓦ montreux jazz.com), held in the first half of July. Over 45 years it's pulled in the likes of Miles Davis and Ray Charles, but "jazz" is now something of a misnomer; these days the festival features big-name acts from all genres of popular music. Check online for tickets (Fr.65–240), or just join the street parties and free entertainment around the lake.

François Bonivard, a Genevan priest, was imprisoned in the gloomy dungeons from 1530 to 1536; the story captured the imagination of Lord Byron, who wrote his poem *The Prisoner of Chillon* after sailing here with Shelley in 1816. Upstairs you'll find grand halls, lavish bedchambers and dreamy lake views.

The Swiss heartland

The Mittelland – between Lake Geneva and Zürich, flanked by the Jura range to the north and the high Alps to the south – is a region of lakes, gentle hills and some higher peaks. There's a wealth of cultural and historical interest in the cities of **Basel**, **Luzern** and the federal capital, **Bern**. Wherever you are, the mountains are never more than a couple of hours away by train.

BASEL

Astride the Rhine where Switzerland, France and Germany touch, **BASEL** (Bâle in French) is a logical staging post en route north. Despite a reputation for insularity, it has become a pan-European hub. Certainly, it feels like a working city – neither as picturesque as Bern or Luzern, nor as vibrant as Zürich. Yet it's a wealthy place and boasts first-rate museums and galleries, in addition to some superb contemporary architecture. It also holds a

34

massive three-day **carnival** in February or March (⊛fasnacht.ch), beginning at 4am on the Monday after Mardi Gras.

The River Rhine curves through the city, flowing from east to north. On the south/west bank (1km north of the main station) is the historic Old Town, centred on **Barfüsserplatz**. Across the river, on the north bank, lies **Kleinbasel**, historically scorned by the city's merchants as a working-class quarter. Nowadays, the steps down to the Rhine are a popular place to catch the sun.

Historisches Museum and the Münster

The city's pre-eminence in the fifteenth and sixteenth centuries is amply demonstrated in the **Barfüsserkirche**, home since 1894 to the **Historisches Museum** (Tues–Sun 10am–5pm; Fr.12; free first Sun of month); don't miss the sumptuous medieval tapestries hidden behind protective blinds. On a terrace between the river and the Historisches Museum is the **Münster** (summer Mon–Fri 10am–5pm, Sat 10am–4pm, Sun 11.30am–5pm; winter Mon–Sat 11am–4pm, Sun 11.30am–4pm), which contains, in the north aisle, the tomb of Renaissance humanist Erasmus. Behind the church is the Pfalz terrace, perfect for a picnic.

Kunstmuseum and Museum für Gegenwartskunst

Just east of the Old Town at St Alban-Graben 16, Basel's **Kunstmuseum** (Tues–Sun 10am–6pm; Fr.15; free first Sun of month) has a dazzling array of twentieth-century art, plus an outstanding medieval collection, including many works by the Holbein family. Tucked away by the river, the **Museum für Gegenwartskunst** (Museum of Contemporary Art; Tues–Sun 11am–5pm; Fr.12) contains installations by Frank Stella and Joseph Beuys.

Museum Jean Tinguely

On the north bank of the Rhine at Paul Sacher-Anlage 2, the beautiful **Museum Jean Tinguely** (Tues–Sun 11am–6pm; Fr.15, students Fr.10; ⊛tinguely.ch) is dedicated to one of Switzerland's best-loved artists. Tinguely used scrap metal, plastic and everyday junk to create room-sized Monty Pythonesque machines, veering between grotesque and comical, that – with the touch of a button – judder into life, clanking and squeaking.

ARRIVAL AND DEPARTURE

By train Basel has two train stations serving three countries. The main Basel SBB is in Switzerland, but has a notionally French section entitled Bâle SNCF at its west end which handles trains from Paris and Strasbourg. Trams #8 and #11 shuttle to Barfüsserplatz. Some trains from Germany terminate at the notionally German Badischer Bahnhof (Basel Bad. for short), on the north side of the river, from where tram #6 runs to Barfüsserplatz.
Destinations Frankfurt (hourly; 2hr 50min); Geneva (hourly; 2hr 35min); Interlaken (hourly; 2hr); Lausanne (every 30min; 2hr 10min); Lugano (hourly; 3hr 45min); Luzern (2 hourly; 1hr 10min); Paris (6 daily; 3hr); Strasbourg (hourly; 1hr 30min); Zürich (every 15min; 1hr).

INFORMATION

Tourist information Tourist offices at Steinenberg 14 (Mon–Fri 9am–6.30pm, Sat 9am–5pm, Sun 10am–3pm; ☎061 268 6868, ⊛basel.com) and in the main train station (Mon–Fri 8.30am–6pm, Sat 9am–5pm, Sun 9am–3pm). Either office can provide a full list of Basel's museums and galleries. If you stay overnight you're entitled to a Mobility Ticket, giving free city transport; ask for it when you check in.
Basel Card This card (Fr.20/27/35 for 24/48/72hr) grants free museum entry, free city tours and discounts at restaurants, bars and clubs.

ACCOMMODATION

Basel Backpack (SH) Dornacherstr. 192 ☎061 333 0037, ⊛baselbackpack.com; tram #15 or #16 to Tell Platz. Good hostel in a funky renovated factory/arts complex behind the station. Colour-coded dorms or numbered guesthouse rooms, bar, kitchen and industrial-style bathrooms. Dorm Fr.32, double Fr.99
Jugendherberge St Alban (HI) St Alban-Kirchrain 10 ☎061 272 0572, ⊛youthhostel.ch. Superbly refurbished silk factory in the central yet semi-secret St-Alban-Tal. Dorm Fr.42, double Fr.122

EATING

Mr Wong Gerbergasse 74. Popular cafeteria-style joint just off Barfüsserplatz serving large and affordable, if not particularly authentic, portions of Chinese-style fast food. Noodle dishes from Fr.12. Daily 11am–11pm/midnight.
Parterre Klybeckstr. 1. Lively Kleinbasel hangout, with busy outside terrace and a creative, vegetarian-friendly

★ **TREAT YOURSELF**

Au Violon Im Lohnhof 4 ☎061 269 8711, ⓦau-violon.com. Comfortable, stylish Old Town hotel (once a prison), next to St Leonhard's Church. There are fourteen converted "cell rooms" (all en suite), or you can opt for a grander "police office" with great views over the Old Town. Double __Fr.160__

menu; mains Fr.26–39. No hot food on Sun. Mon–Wed 9am–11pm, Thurs–Sat 9am–midnight, Sun 11am–11pm.
Zum Roten Engel Andreasplatz. Busy little café serving coffees, cakes and muffins to a studenty clientele, in a pedestrianized cobbled square. Mon–Sat 9am–midnight, Sun 10am–10pm.

DRINKING AND NIGHTLIFE

Atlantis Klosterberg 13 ⓦatlan-tis.ch. A Basel institution for many years, this classy restaurant and lounge-bar hosts jam-packed club nights at weekends. Entry Fr.15. Club Fri & Sat 11pm–4am, restaurant Tues–Thurs 11.30am–2pm & 5pm–midnight, Fri 11.30am–2pm & 5–11pm, Sat 6–11pm.
Bird's Eye Kohlenberg 20 ⓦbirdseye.ch. Basel's main jazz venue, with weekly residencies. Entry Fr.12. June–Aug Wed–Sat 8–11.30pm; Sept–May Tues–Sat 8–11.30pm.
★ **eoipso** Dornachstr. 192. Trendy, spacious industrial bar in a buzzing factory complex behind the train station. Mon evening bar only. Mon 11am–midnight, Tues–Thurs 11am–1am, Fri 11am–2am, Sat 5pm–2am.
Fischerstube Rheingasse 45. Atmospheric Kleinbasel beer hall with an older clientele and a range of bar snacks. Dish of the day Fr.16–19. Mon–Fri 10am–2pm & 4pm–midnight, Sat 2pm–1am, Sun 2pm–late.
Kaserne Klybeckstr. 1b ⓦkaserne-basel.ch. Alternative hangout with a varied live music, theatre and dance programme. Becomes Basel's premier gay/lesbian meeting point on Tues. Events mainly Thurs–Sat around 8pm; closed July.

LUZERN (LUCERNE)

An hour south of Basel is beautiful **LUZERN**, offering captivating mountain views, lake cruises and a picturesque medieval quarter.

WHAT TO SEE AND DO

To the right of the train station, you're greeted by the striking KKL concert hall; busy Pilatusstrasse is to the left, where, 100m further along, you'll find the

Sammlung Rosengart gallery (daily: April–Oct 10am–6pm; Nov–March 11am–5pm; Fr.18, students Fr.10), with a superb collection of twentieth-century art, notably by Picasso and Klee. The alleyways of the Old Town span both riverbanks, linked by two covered wooden bridges. The fourteenth-century **Kapellbrücke** was rebuilt after a fire in 1993; some of the seventeenth-century paintings fixed to its roof beams have been replaced by facsimiles. Northeast of the Old Town is **Löwenplatz**, dominated by the absorbing **Bourbaki Panorama** (daily: April–Oct 9am–6pm; Nov–March 10am–5pm; Fr.12; SP free), a 110m by 10m circular mural, depicting the flight of General Bourbaki's 87,000-strong army into Switzerland during the Franco-Prussian War. Just off the square is the **Löwendenkmal**, a dying lion hewn out of a cliff-face to commemorate seven hundred Swiss mercenaries killed by French revolutionaries in 1792.

A pleasant 2km stroll east along the lakeside (or train, boat, or bus #6/8/24) lies the **Verkehrshaus** (daily 10am–5pm, summer to 6pm; Fr.30, or Fr.40 including IMAX cinema; ER 25 percent off, SP 50 percent; ⓦverkehrshaus.ch), a vast transport museum complex containing space capsules, railway locomotives, cable cars and a planetarium.

Lake Luzern

You shouldn't leave Luzern without taking a trip on the lake (every 30min; Fr.11–45, day ticket Fr.69, ER & SP free, IR 50 percent reduction; ⓦlakelucerne .ch), Switzerland's most beautiful and dramatic by far, the thickly wooded slopes rising sheer from the water.

ARRIVAL AND INFORMATION

By train The station sits at the south end of the Seebrücke, facing the docks for boats on Lake Luzern.
Destinations Basel (2 hourly; 1hr); Bern (hourly; 1hr); Interlaken (hourly; 2hr); Lausanne (hourly; 2hr 10min); Zürich (every 30min; 45min).
Tourist information Tourist office at Zentralstr. 5 (May–Oct Mon–Sat 8.30am–7pm, Sun 9am–5pm; Nov–March Mon–Fri 8.30am–5.30pm, Sat 9am–5pm, Sun 9am–1pm; ☎041 227 1717, ⓦluzern.org), on the west side of the railway station.

34

GETTING AROUND

By public transport Everything in the centre is easily reached on foot, but the Luzern Card (Fr.19/27/33 for 1/2/3 days) gives free bus and train travel within the city plus half-price admission to eleven museums.

By bike Bikes can be rented at the Velostation on the east side of the station (daily 7/8am–7pm), the HI hostel or *Backpackers Lücerne*.

ACCOMMODATION

Backpackers Lucerne (SH) Alpenquai 42 ☎041 360 0420, ⓦbackpackerslucerne.ch. A friendly place, with kitchen and bike rental but no breakfast, a 10min walk east from the station along the lake. Dorm Fr.32, double Fr.74

HI Jugendherberge Am Rotsee, Sedelstrasse 12 ☎041 420 8800, ⓦyouthhostel.ch/luzern; bus #18. A friendly modern hostel not far from the centre (the bus takes a roundabout route from the Bahnhof to Jugendherberge); a bit of a maze but lots of pleasant common areas. Dorm Fr.32, double 47.40

Lido Lidostr. 19 ☎041 370 2146, ⓦcamping -international.ch. A shady lakeside site near the transport museum, open all year. Also with bunk-bed dorms (holding up to 8). Camping Fr.10 per person, plus Fr.10 per tent, dorm Fr.25

EATING AND DRINKING

There's a good range of cafés and restaurants on both sides of the river; picnic supplies are available at the station.

Bourbaki Löwenplatz 11. As well as an arthouse cinema, this place encompasses a café-bar (serving panini and salads from Fr.7.50) and the *Angolo* pasta & pizza restaurant, with a Fr.14 lunch menu. Café-bar daily 9am–11.30pm, restaurant Mon–Sat 11am–10pm, Sun noon–9pm.

Café Suisse Gerbergasse 11. A splendidly traditional café, serving authentic Swiss dishes and a dish of the day (Fr.15.50–17.50). Mon–Sat 9am–12.30am, Sun 10am–7pm.

LUZ Bahnhofplatz. On the lake by the station is this lovely café with cheap food, such as würst, baked potatoes and salads (all from Fr.7.50), or ciabattas from Fr.10. Daily from 7.30am with variable closing time.

Manora Weggisgasse 5. Excellent self-service cafeteria with a wide range of salads and daily specials (Fr.10–14) plus free wi-fi. Mon–Wed 9am–6.30pm, Thurs & Fri 9am–9pm, Sat 8am–4pm.

Roadhouse Pilatusstr. 1. A lively pub facing the west side of the station, with jam sessions, live gigs and themed parties most weekends. Daily 7/9am–4am.

World Café In the KKL building, Europaplatz 1. This place has changing specials with a global twist from Fr.18, as well as real coffee and a wine bar. Daily 9am–8pm.

ENGELBERG

Under fifty minutes from Luzern by train is the picturesque Alpine resort of **ENGELBERG**, from where a revolving cable car (Fr.86 return; ER, IR & SP fifty percent reduction) serves the snowbound summit of Mount Titlis (3239m), the highest point in Central Switzerland (ⓦtitlis.ch). Here you can hit the snow year-round, with countless rental deals for snowboards, as well as for mountain bikes, scooters and DevilBikes.

BERN

Of all Swiss cities, **BERN** is the most immediately charming. Crammed onto a steep-sided peninsula in a crook of the River Aare, the city's quiet, cobbled lanes, lined with arcaded sandstone buildings, have changed little in five hundred years. It's sometimes hard to remember that this petite town of just 130,000 people is the nation's capital.

WHAT TO SEE AND DO

The heart of Bern's compact old town is **Spitalgasse**. Heading east from the Bahnhofplatz, this becomes **Marktgasse**, Kramgasse and then Gerechtigkeitsgasse, before crossing the river to the **Bärengraben** (bear pits). The main museums are on Helvetiaplatz, on the south bank of the river, across the Kirchenfeldbrücke.

The Old Town and the Münster

Marktgasse, lined with attractive seventeenth- and eighteenth-century buildings and arcaded boutiques, leads you past various landmarks, such as the distinctively top-heavy Zytglogge, a medieval city gate converted to a clock tower in the sixteenth century. To the left in Kornhausplatz, the most notorious of Bern's fountains, the horrific **Kindlifresserbrunnen**, depicts an ogre devouring a baby. Münstergasse, one block south, takes you to the fifteenth-century Gothic **Münster** (Mon–Sat 10am–5pm, Sun 11.30am–5pm), with a magnificently gilded high-relief *Last Judgement* above the main entrance. Its 444-stepped tower (closes 30min earlier;

Fr.5), the tallest in Switzerland, offers terrific views. Munsterplattform, nearby, hosts a craft market on the first Saturday of the month from March to November.

The Bärengraben

At the eastern end of the centre, the Nydeggbrücke crosses the river to the **Bärengraben**, Bern's famed bear pits, which held generations of morose shaggies from the early sixteenth century to 2009. The new Bear Park (open access), sloping down to the river, houses four bears in far better conditions than before. Legend has it that the town's founder, Berchtold V of Zähringen, named Bern after killing one of the beasts during a hunt.

The Kunstmuseum

Bern's **Kunstmuseum**, near the station at Hodlerstrasse 8 (Tues 10am–9pm, Wed–Sun 10am–5pm; Fr.7; ⓦkunstmuseumbern.ch), is one of the country's best art galleries, especially strong on twentieth-century art, notably Matisse, Kandinsky, Braque, Picasso and Hodler.

The Historisches Museum

The vast Historisches Museum (Tues–Sun 10am–5pm; Fr.13, students Fr.8; ⓦbhm .ch), on Helvetiaplatz, south of the river, details the country's history and also houses the superb Einstein Museum (same hours, Fr.18, students Fr.13), documenting the physicist's eventful family life and his chequered early career. Exhibits include examples of young Albert's schoolwork, complete with scathing marginalia.

Zentrum Paul Klee

East of the centre at Ostring, the **Zentrum Paul Klee** (Tues–Sun 10am–5pm; Fr.20; ⓦzpk.org; bus #12) has the world's largest collection of works by the artist, who spent much of his life in Bern. The building is a stunning, triple-arched design by the star Italian architect Renzo Piano.

ARRIVAL AND INFORMATION

By train The train station is on Bahnhofplatz, to the west of the Old Town.

Destinations Basel (every 30min; 55min); Geneva (every 30min; 1hr 40min); Interlaken (every 30min; 55min); Lausanne (every 30min; 1hr 5min); Luzern (hourly; 1hr);

Milan (3 daily; 3hr); Paris (2 daily; 4hr); Zermatt (hourly, change at Visp; 2hr 10min); Zürich (every 30min; 1hr).

Tourist information Tourist office in the train station (Mon–Sat 9am–7pm, Sun 10am–6pm; ☎031 328 1212, ⓦbern.com). Staff sell the Bern Card (Fr.20/31/38 for 24/48/72hr), which allows free public transport and discounts.

GETTING AROUND

34

Bern's Old Town is compact and can easily be covered on foot.
By bus Bus #12 runs from the train station through the Old Town to the Bärengraben and then to the Zentrum Paul Klee.
By bike Bike rental available all year at the Velostation in the Bahnhof (daily 8/10am 7pm; first 4hr free, but you need photo ID and Fr.20 deposit and must return bikes the same day; ⓦbernrollt.ch). Also May–Oct at Hirschengraben and Zeughausgasse.

ACCOMMODATION

Bern Backpackers/Hotel Glocke (SH) Rathausgasse 75 ☎031 311 3771, ⓦbernbackpackers.com. Very central hostel (if a little noisy) with large common area and good kitchen; no breakfast. Dorm **Fr.37**, double **Fr.98**
Camping Eichholz Strandweg 49 ☎031 961 2602, ⓦcampingeichholz.ch; tram #9 from south of Bahnhofplatz to Wabern. Good-value riverside campsite with kitchen and restaurant. Open April–Sept. Camping **Fr.7.50** per person, plus **Fr.7/9** per tent
HI Hostel Weihergasse 4 ☎031 311 6316, ⓦyouthhostel .ch/bern. Good hostel in a quiet riverside site just below the Bundeshaus. Breakfast included. Dorm **Fr.35**, double **Fr.93**
Landhaus (SH) Altenbergstr. 4 ☎031 331 4166, ⓦlandhausbern.ch. Excellent hostel in an old house near the Bärengraben. Full of character, with wonky wooden stairs leading to a modern extension, and a lively downstairs bar (live jazz on Thurs). Dorms have neat 2-bed cubicles. Breakfast included with doubles only. Dorm **Fr.33**, double **Fr.120**

EATING AND DRINKING

For picnic supplies and takeaways, try the supermarket at the train station, or visit the produce market in Bärenplatz.
Altes Tramdepot Grosser Muristalden 6. Microbrewery with fantastic views across the river to the Old Town, serving Swiss cuisine such as rösti from Fr.17 or *flammkuchen* from Fr.18. Daily: summer 10am–12.30am; winter 11am–12.30am.
Anker Kornhausplatz 16. Cheery place for local beer and dishes such as rösti (Fr.21) or fondue (Fr.24.50). Mon–Fri 8am–11.30pm, Sat 9am–midnight, Sun 9.30am–6pm.
★ **Le Lötschberg** Zeughausgasse 16. Relaxed, trendy wine bar and deli serving a range of cheese platters, veggie dishes (Fr.17–35) and salads (Fr.11–18). Mon–Thurs 9am–midnight, Fri & Sat 9am–12.30am, Sun 11am–11pm.

34

Tibits Bahnhofplatz. Excellent vegetarian self-service place, with a great selection of salads and hot dishes. Pay by weight. Mon–Wed 6.30am–11.30pm, Thurs–Sat 6.30am–midnight, Sun 8am–11pm.

NIGHTLIFE

Bern hosts a huge open-air rock event (ⓦ gurtenfestival .ch) in July.

Dampfzentrale Marzilistr. 47 ⓦ dampfzentrale.ch. Lively arts centre offering live music, dance and clubs (Sat), plus food and drink. Mon–Thurs 11am–11.30pm, Fri 11am–12.30am, Sat 2pm–12.30am, Sun 10am–11pm, closed Mon & Sun Oct–March.

Reitschule Neubrückstr. 8 ⓦ reitschule.ch. Cultural and political arts squat at the heart of the alternative clubbing scene, also hosting theatre, films and flea markets. See website for events and times.

DIRECTORY

Embassies Canada, Kirchenfeldstr. 88 ☎ 031 357 3200; Ireland, Kirchenfeldstr. 68 ☎ 031 352 1442; UK, Thunstr. 50 ☎ 031 359 7700; US, Sulgeneckstr. 19 ☎ 031 357 7011.

Hospital Inselspital, Freiburgstr. (☎ 031 632 2464).

Internet Weblane, Kramgrasse 47 (basement; daily 9am–11pm; Fr.4/30min).

Left Luggage In the station (Mon–Sat 8am–7pm, Sun 10am–7pm; lockers 6am–1am; left luggage Fr.7/10, lockers Fr.6/9).

Pharmacy Bahnhof Apotheke, in the station (daily 6.30am–10pm).

Post office Schanzenstr. 4, behind the station; also at Kramgasse 1.

ZÜRICH

A beautiful city, set astride a river and turned towards a crystal-clear lake and distant snowy peaks, **ZÜRICH** has plenty to recommend it. Niederdorf's steep cobbled alleys are great to wander around, with an engaging café culture and a wealth of nightlife, whereas to the northwest of the centre a former industrial quarter, popularly known as "Züri-West", has become home to many of the city's trendiest clubs. Whether wandering the streets of the Old Town, window-shopping in Bahnhofstrasse or day-tripping to the Rhine Falls, you may end up spending longer here than originally planned.

WHAT TO SEE AND DO

Across the River Limmat from the station, the narrow lanes of the medieval **Niederdorf** district stretch south, quiet during the day and bustling after dark. The waterfront is lined with fine Baroque *Zunfthäuser* (guildhalls), arcaded lower storeys fronting the quayside and now mostly upmarket restaurants. One block in is **Niederdorfstrasse**, initially tacky, but offering plenty of opportunities to explore atmospheric cobbled side alleys and secluded courtyards: Lenin lived at Spiegelgasse 14 in 1917 (pre-Revolution).

The Grossmünster

Just south of Niederdorfstrasse is Zürich's trademark **Grossmünster** (Great Minster; daily: mid-March to Oct 9am–6pm; Nov to mid-March 10am–5pm), where Huldrych Zwingli, father of Swiss Protestantism, began to preach the Reformation in 1519. Its exterior is largely fifteenth-century, while its twin towers were topped with distinctive octagonal domes in the seventeenth century. The interior is austere apart from the intensely coloured choir windows (1933) by Augusto Giacometti and the Romanesque crypt which contains an oversized fifteenth-century statue of Charlemagne.

The Kunsthaus

Switzerland's best gallery, the **Kunsthaus** (Tues, Sat & Sun 10am–6pm, Wed–Fri 10am–8pm; Fr.16, students Fr.11, more for temporary shows, free Wed; ⓦ kunsthaus.ch), is up the hill from the Grossmünster via several alleys. Some fascinating Gothic paintings are followed by Venetian masters, fine Flemish pieces and the greatest Swiss artists, Fuseli, Böcklin, Hodler, Segantini, Vallotton and Klee. The collection of international twentieth-century art is also stunning.

West of the centre

The **west bank** is the main commercial district, while further west are the coolest hangouts and the best street life. Tram #8 towards Hardplatz will deliver you to relaxed **Helvetiaplatz**, from where funky **Langstrasse** heads north – lowlife bars rubbing shoulders with avant-garde

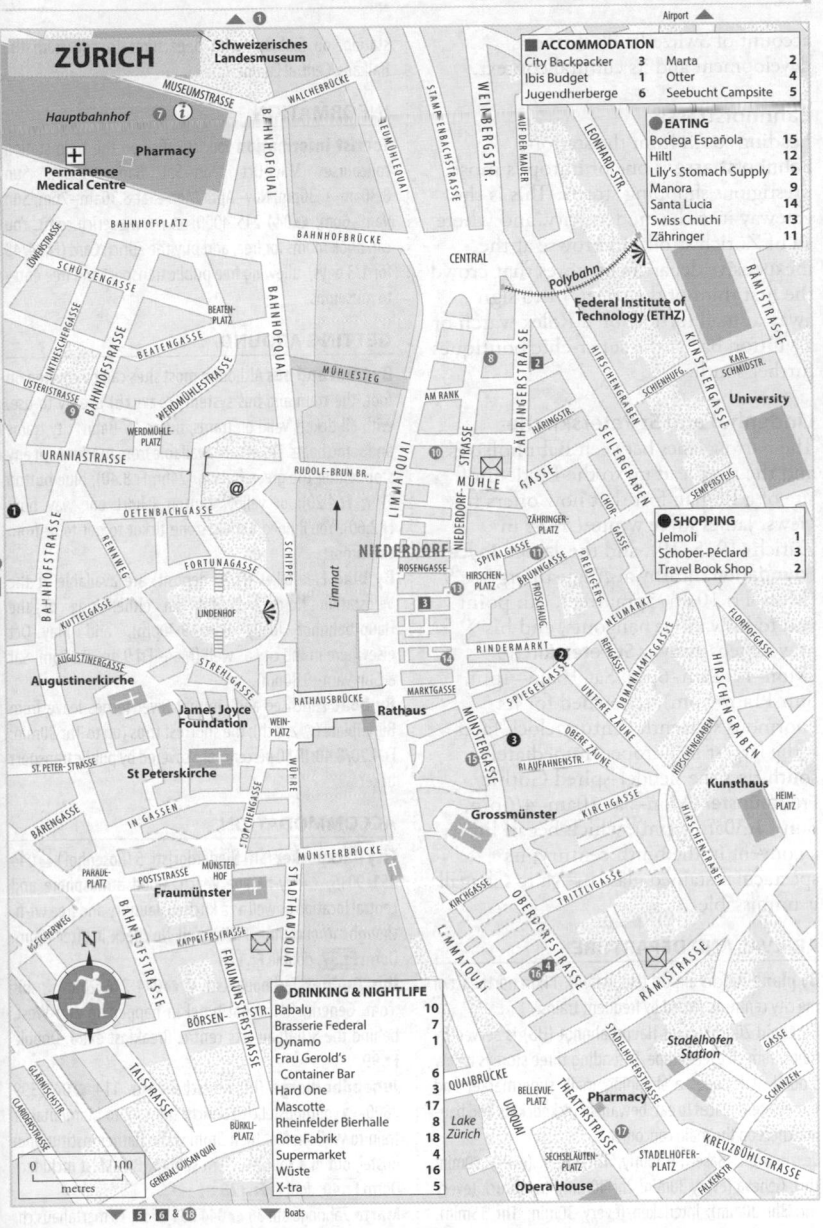

ZÜRICH

■ ACCOMMODATION			
City Backpacker	3	Marta	2
Ibis Budget	1	Otter	4
Jugendherberge	6	Seebucht Campsite	5

● EATING	
Bodega Española	15
Hiltl	12
Lily's Stomach Supply	2
Manora	9
Santa Lucia	14
Swiss Chuchi	13
Zähringer	11

● SHOPPING	
Jelmoli	1
Schober-Péclard	3
Travel Book Shop	2

● DRINKING & NIGHTLIFE	
Babalu	10
Brasserie Federal	7
Dynamo	1
Frau Gerold's Container Bar	6
Hard One	3
Mascotte	17
Rheinfelder Bierhalle	8
Rote Fabrik	18
Supermarket	4
Wüste	16
X-tra	5

galleries, the smells of kebabs and pizza mixing with the aroma of marijuana. This fascinating street is a mixture of styles and cultures – Swiss-German blending with French-African, Turkish, Balkan, East Asian and Latin American.

Schweizerisches Landesmuseum

Immediately north of the main station, the **Landesmuseum** or Federal History Museum, at Museumstr. 2 (Tues–Sun 10am–5pm, Thurs till 7pm; Fr.10; ⓦnationalmuseum.ch), gives the definitive

34

account of Switzerland's tortuous development and its cultural context.

Bahnhofstrasse

Leading south from the station, **Bahnhofstrasse** is one of Europe's most prestigious shopping streets. This is the gateway into the modern city, and where all of Zürich strolls, to browse at the inexpensive department stores that crowd the first third of the street, or to sign away a small fortune on a Rolex watch or a Vuitton bag at the super-chic boutiques further south.

Lindenhof and St Peterskirche

The narrow lanes between Bahnhofstrasse and the river lead up to the Lindenhof, site of a Roman fort that now offers fine views. James Joyce wrote *Ulysses* in Zürich (1915–19), and the **James Joyce Foundation**, nearby at Augustinergasse 9 (Mon–Fri 10am–5pm; free), can point you to his various hangouts, and his grave. Steps away is **St Peterskirche** (Mon–Fri 8am–6pm, Sat 10am–4pm, Sun 11am–5pm), renowned for its enormous sixteenth-century clock faces – the largest in Europe. Immediately south rises the slender-spired Gothic **Fraumünster** (Mon–Sat 10am–4/6pm, Sun 11.30am–6pm), which began life as a convent in the ninth century; its spectacular stained glass by Marc Chagall is unmissable.

ARRIVAL AND DEPARTURE

By plane Zürich's airport (Flughafen), 11km northeast of the city centre, is served by frequent trains.

By train Zürich's giant Hauptbahnhof (HB) is served by trains from all over Europe. Extending three storeys below ground, it includes a shopping mall, supermarket and some decent places to eat; beware of pickpockets and bag-snatchers on the main concourse.

Destinations Basel (4 hourly; 1hr); Bern (every 30min; 1hr); Geneva (every 30min; 2hr 40min); Innsbruck (every 2hr; 3hr 30min); Interlaken (every 30min; 1hr 55min); Lausanne (every 30min; 2hr 10min); Lugano (hourly; 2hr 40min); Luzern (every 30min; 45min); Milan (6 daily; 3hr 40min); Munich (4 daily; 4hr 15min); Paris (6 daily; 4hr); Sargans (2 hourly; 55min); Schaffhausen (2 hourly; 40min); St Moritz (change at Chur; hourly; 3hr 20min); Stuttgart (every 2hr; 3hr); Vienna (6 daily; 7hr 45min).

By bus The bus station is located 50m north of the train station, on Sihlquai, with departures to and from the Balkans/Central Europe.

INFORMATION

Tourist information Tourist office on the train station concourse (May–Oct Mon–Sat 8am–8.30pm, Sun 8.30am–6.30pm; Nov–April Mon–Sat 8.30am–7pm, Sun 9am–6pm; ☎044 215 4000, ⬥www.zuerich.com). You can book rooms for free, and buy the Zürich Card (Fr.24/48 for 1/3 days), allowing free public transport and free entry to museums.

GETTING AROUND

By tram and bus Although most sites can be covered on foot, the tram and bus system (⬥zvv.ch) is easy to use, with all tickets valid on trams, buses, "S-Bahn" city trains and some boats. Tickets are available from machines at any stop: either the green button (24hr; Fr.8.40); blue button (1hr; Fr.4.20); or yellow button (short one-way hop; Fr.2.60). You'll need a multi-zone ticket to get to or from the airport.

By bike Free bikes (Fr.20 deposit) are available at the Velostation Nord and Sud, on either side of the Hauptbahnhof (daily 8am–9.30pm), and May–Oct elsewhere in the city as well (Mon–Fri 9am–9.30pm, Sat & Sun 9am–9.30pm).

By boat Zürichsee and Limmat River ferries leave from Bürkliplatz (⬥zsg.ch); the shortest trips (up to 1hr 30min; Fr.4.20/8.40; IR 50 percent) are covered by public transport tickets.

ACCOMMODATION

City Backpacker (SH) Niederdorfstr. 5 (Rosenhof) ☎044 251 9015, ⬥city-backpacker.ch. Good atmosphere and central location as well as a kitchen, laundry and free wi-fi, though rather cramped when full. No check-in after 10pm. Dorm **Fr.37**, double **Fr.118**

Ibis Budget Technoparkstr. 2 ☎044 276 2000, ⬥ibis .com. Generic, functional hotel in happening Züri-West, behind the Schiffbau arts centre. Breakfast extra. Double **Fr.99**

Jugendherberge (HI) Mutschellenstr. 114 ☎043 399 7800, ⬥youthhostel.ch/zuerich; tram #7 to Morgental or train to Wollishofen, then 5min walk. Rather institutional hostel, out in a southwestern suburb. Breakfast included. Dorm **Fr.40**, double **Fr.128**

Marta Zähringerstr. 36 ☎044 251 4550, ⬥martahaus.ch. Clean Old Town budget hotel with cabin dorms and doubles, plus café, internet and laundry. Dorm **Fr.40**, double **Fr.150**

Otter Oberdorfstr. 7 ☎044 251 2207, ⬥wueste.ch. Quirky and friendly hotel with themed rooms, plus a dreamy top-floor apartment and balcony rooms with stunning Old Town views, and a lively bar. Breakfast included; bathrooms are shared. Double **Fr.150**

Seebucht Campsite Seestr. 559 ☎ 044 482 1612; bus #161 or #165 from Bürkliplatz to Stadtgrenze. Well-serviced site on the lakeside, 2km south of the centre. Open May–Sept. Camping **Fr.8** per person, plus **Fr.13** per tent

EATING

A wander through the Niederdorf district will turn up dozens of eating options, among them sausage, noodle and French-fry stands, plus beer halls serving daily specials for about Fr.13.

Bodega Española Münstergasse 15. Atmospheric Spanish restaurant (with recommended paella) upstairs and shady tapas bar below. Tapas from Fr.10. Daily 10am–midnight.

Hiltl Sihlstr. 28 Top-quality vegetarian buffet, with budget takeaway prices. Daily specials Fr.16.50. Mutates into a trendy cocktail bar with DJs at weekends. Restaurant Mon–Sat 6am–midnight, Sun 8am–midnight, bar Thurs–Sun 11pm–4am.

Lily's Stomach Supply Langstr. 197. Bustling pan-Asian noodle-bar, serving huge stir-fries from Fr.15 (Fr.10 takeaway, until 10pm). Mon–Thurs 11am–midnight, Fri & Sat 11am–1am, Sun 3–11pm.

Manora 5th floor of Manor store, Bahnhofstr. 75. Excellent self-service cafeteria, with a wide range of wholesome hot and cold food for Fr.13 or less. Mon–Sat 9am–8pm.

Santa Lucia Marktgasse 21. Popular local chain, serving a wide selection of good-value pasta and pizza dishes from Fr.16. Daily 11.30am–2am.

Swiss Chuchi Rosengasse 10. Fantastic people-watching opportunities in summer when tables spill out onto the Hirschenplatz. Huge portions of fondue or raclette for Fr.25. Daily 11.30am–11.15pm.

Zähringer Zähringerplatz 11. Cooperative-run café-bar with an alternative-minded clientele and simple, substantial vegetarian, vegan and carnivore's menus (Fr.24–28). Mon 6pm–midnight, Tues–Sun 9am–midnight.

DRINKING AND NIGHTLIFE

Zürich boasts lively music venues and a booming club scene. The hip quarter around Langstrasse, west of the centre, is full of DJ bars, while the best clubs hide themselves in the former industrial quarter of Züri-West. Mid-Aug sees the Street Parade (🕸 street-parade.ch), a hedonistic Saturday of techno street dancing. The ZüriTipp (🕸 zueritipp.ch) listings magazine is available at the tourist office.

BARS

Babalu Schmidgasse 6. Trendy little DJ-bar with Brazilian cocktails and thumping house music on an Old Town side-street. Mon–Fri 5pm–late, Sat 6pm–late.

Brasserie Federal In the Hauptbahnhof. A great range of beers, as well as soups, salads and full meals. Soups Fr.5, salads Fr.9, mains from Fr.18. Daily 11am–midnight.

Frau Gerold's Container Bar Geroldstr. 23 🕸 fraugerold.ch. Literally in, and on, shipping containers next to the railway in Züri-West, doubling as a garden centre. Mon–Sat 11am–midnight, Sun noon–8pm.

Hard One Hardstr. 260 🕸 hardone.ch. Stylish, dimly lit lounge bar with roof terrace (until 11.30pm), serving cocktails, champagne and bar snacks. Tues–Thurs 6pm–2am, Fri 6pm–4am, Sat 9pm–4am.

Rheinfelder Bierhalle Niederdorfstr. 76. Founded in 1870 and still the best of the beerhalls, filled with locals and serving cheap and filling daily specials. Daily 9am–midnight.

Wüste In *Hotel Otter*, Oberdorfstr. 7. Mellow, relaxed cellar bar located near the Grossmünster and attracting a bohemian crowd. Mon–Thurs 4pm–midnight, Fri & Sat 4pm–2am.

X-tra Limmatstr. 118 🕸 x-tra.ch. Spacious and stylish bar-restaurant, with popular upstairs lounges and club hosting DJs and a surprising range of gigs, from folk to electro. Wed–Sat 9/10pm–late.

CLUBS

Dynamo Wasserwerkstr. 21 🕸 dynamo.ch. City-run youth centre hosting courses, theatre groups and alternative, punkish bands. There's also a restaurant. Gig nights start around 7/8pm, though don't fill up till later.

Mascotte Theaterstr. 10 🕸 mascotte.ch. Most popular of the Old Town clubs. Renowned for its Tues rock/metal "Karaoke from Hell" night. Mon–Sat 11pm–late.

Rote Fabrik Seestr. 395 🕸 rotefabrik.ch. Alternative bands, big-name DJs, art studios, a cheap and funky restaurant (closed Mon) and a great riverside bar, all in a former factory complex. Tues–Sun 11am–midnight.

Supermarket Geroldstr. 17 🕸 supermarket.li. Popular gay friendly Züri-West club, attracting international DJs playing techno, electronica and house till the early hours. Thurs–Sat 8pm–late.

SHOPPING

Kirchgasse has a high concentration of secondhand bookshops, antiques shops and galleries, while Niederdorfstrasse and Viaduktstrasse are crammed with boutiques from grungy indie fashions to fabulous jewellery.

Flea market Bürkliplatz 🕸 flohmarktbuerkliplatz.ch. Since 1971, this has been the place to look for jewellery, antiques and other secondhand treasures. May–Oct Sat 8am–4pm.

Jelmoli Bahnhofstrasse/Seidengasse. Founded in 1833, this continues to be the country's leading department store, offering all kinds of services as well as anything you might want to buy. Mon–Sat 9am–8pm.

Schober-Péclard Napfgasse 4. Good option for over-the-top chocolates and cakes, from either the jewel-like shop or the upstairs café. Mon–Wed 8am–7pm, Thurs–Sat 8am–11pm, Sun 9am–7pm.

34

Travel Book Shop Rindermarkt 20. Good selection of maps and travel guides, roughly half of which are in English, and many of which are on hiking and climbing. Mon noon–6.30pm, Tues, Wed & Fri 9am–6.30pm, Thurs 9am–8pm, Sat 9am–5pm.

DIRECTORY

Banks and exchange At the station (daily 6.30am–9.30pm) or UBS, Bahnhofstr. 45 & 72 (Mon–Fri 8.15am–4.30pm).

Consulates Ireland, Claridenstr. 25 ☎044 289 2515; UK, Hegibachstr. 47 ☎044 383 6560; US, Dufourstr. 101 ☎043 499 2960. Embassies are in Bern.

Hospital Permanence Medical Centre, Bahnhofplatz 15 ☎044 215 4444 (reception daily 7am–10pm).

Internet *Cafe.ch*, Uraniastr. 3 (Mon–Sat 7/8am–11pm & Sun 10am–10pm).

Left luggage North side of the station (daily 7.30am–7.45pm).

Pharmacy Bellevue, Theaterstr. 14 ☎044 266 6222; and Bahnhof Apotheke, Bahnhofplatz 15 ☎044 225 4242 (both 24hr).

Post office Sihlpost, Kasernenstr. 95, beside the station (Mon–Fri 6.30am–10.30pm, Sat 6.30am–8pm, Sun 10am–10.30pm).

THE RHINE FALLS

A great excursion from Zürich is the half-day trip north to the **Rhine Falls** (🌐rhinefalls.com), Europe's largest waterfalls, 3km west of **SCHAFFHAUSEN**. They are magnificent, not so much for their height (just 23m) as for their impressive breadth (150m) and sheer drama, with spray rising in a cloud of rainbows above the forested banks and the turreted castle, **Schloss Laufen** (now an HI hostel), on the south bank. Come on the national holiday, August 1, for the famous fireworks display. In summer, the best views are from daredevil boats (Fr.6–17; 🌐maendli.ch), which scurry about in the spray from Schloss Laufen or Schlössli Wörth, across the river, from where a restaurant gives a great view of the falls.

Take a train to Schaffhausen then bus #1 to Neuhausen Zentrum, or a local train to either Laufen am Rheinfall (below the castle; April–Oct) or Neuhausen; you can also walk (30min) from Schaffhausen to the bridge above the falls.

The Swiss Alps

South of Bern and Luzern, and east of Lake Geneva, lies the grand Alpine heart of Switzerland, a massively impressive region of classic Swiss scenery – high peaks, sheer valleys and cool lakes – that makes for great summer hiking and world-class winter sports. The Bernese Oberland, centred on the **Jungfrau Region**, is the most accessible and tourised area, but beyond this first great wall of peaks is another even more daunting range on the Italian border in which the **Matterhorn** is the star attraction.

THE JUNGFRAU REGION

The spectacular **Jungfrau Region** is named after a grand triple-peaked ridge – the Eiger, Mönch and Jungfrau – which crests 4000m. Switzerland's most popular **mountain railway**, which celebrated its centenary in 2012, trundles south from **Interlaken** before coiling up across mountain pastures, and tunnelling clean through the Eiger to emerge at the **Jungfraujoch** (3454m), an icy, windswept col just beneath the Jungfrau summit. Touted relentlessly as the "Top of Europe", it's a scenic but very slow journey (2hr 20min from Interlaken, with two changes to progressively smaller trains) and also extremely pricey; it's only worthwhile on a clear day, for the spectacular panoramic views from the Sphinx Terrace (3571m) to Germany's Black Forest in one direction, and across a gleaming wasteland to the Italian Alps in the other. Bring your sunglasses.

The cable-car ride up the **Schilthorn** (2970m) gets second billing, but is in fact quicker, cheaper, offers a more scenic ride up and has better views from the top. A return trip from Interlaken takes six hours to the Jungfraujoch, or four hours to the Schilthorn (both allowing an hour at the summit). Taking the first train of the day (6.30am) brings discounts on both routes.

The most beautiful countryside is the **Lauterbrunnen valley**, overlooked by the village of **Mürren**, an excellent base for

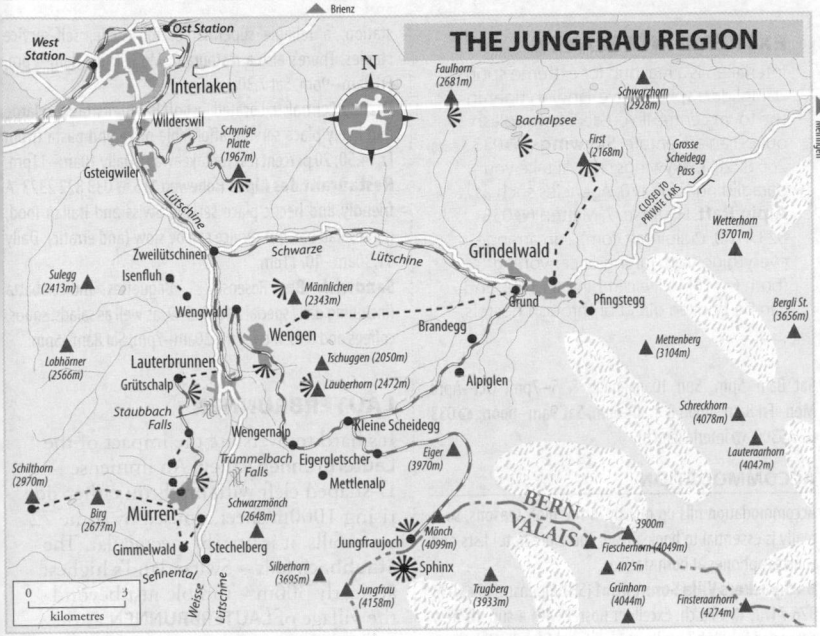

THE JUNGFRAU REGION

winter skiing and summer hiking, as is **Grindelwald**, in the next valley east. Interlaken is the region's transport hub, but the sheer volume of tourists passing through can make it a less than restful place to stay.

ARRIVAL AND DEPARTURE

By train There are two routes up the Jungfrau from Interlaken, changing trains at either Lauterbrunnen or Grindelwald (it's normal to go up one way and down the other). The routes meet at the spectacularly sited station of Kleine Scheidegg, where you change for the final pull to the Jungfraujoch. The adult return-trip fare from Interlaken to the Jungfraujoch is a budget-crunching Fr.197.60 (IR no discount; ER 25 percent discount; SP free to Grindelwald and Lauterbrunnen, then half-price to Kleine Scheidegg and 25 percent off to the top) – but the discounted "Good Morning" and "Good Afternoon tickets", valid if you travel up on the first or second trains of the day (at 6.30am & 7.20am from Interlaken Ost), or leave Kleine Scheidegg after 3.30pm, cost Fr.145 from Interlaken, and Fr.135 from Lauterbrunnen or Grindelwald.

By cable car The Schilthorn cable-car prices, compared to the Jungfraujoch ride, are a bargain. From Stechelberg to the top is Fr.98.60 return, from Mürren Fr.77 (IR no discount; ER 25 percent discount; SP free to Mürren, then 50 percent). Going up before 8.55am or after 3.25pm knocks the fare down to Fr.74 (Fr.57.80 from Mürren).

INTERLAKEN

INTERLAKEN is centred on its long main street, Höheweg, which is lined with cafés and hotels, and has a train station at each end, though the best way to arrive is by boat. The town lies on a neck of land between two of Switzerland's loveliest lakes, and it exists chiefly to amuse the trippers on their way to the mountains. Coming from Luzern, you could get out at Brienz and do the last stretch to Interlaken Ost by boat (ER & SP free, IR 50 percent). Likewise, from the Bern/Zürich direction, you could take a boat from Thun to Interlaken West.

ARRIVAL AND INFORMATION

By train Interlaken West station serves the town centre; from here Bahnhofstr. leads east, becoming the main street, Höheweg, with Interlaken Ost station, the main interchange, at its far end.
Destinations Bern (every 30min; 55min); Grindelwald (every 30min; 35min); Jungfraujoch (change at Grindelwald or Lauterbrunnen, then Kleine Scheidegg; every 30min; 2hr 20min); Lauterbrunnen (every 30min; 20min); Luzern (hourly; 2hr); Zürich (change at Bern; every 30min; 2hr).
Tourist information Tourist office beneath the town's tallest building at Höheweg 37 (May–Sept Mon–Fri 8am–6pm, Sat 8am–4pm; July & Aug Mon–Fri 8am–7pm,

34

EXTREME INTERLAKEN

Interlaken is a real hub for extreme sports; paragliders spiral above, landing right in the town centre. If you decide to splash out on an adventure, **Skywings** (☎033 266 8228, ⓦskywings.ch) will take you paragliding for Fr.170. Agencies such as **Alpin Raft**, Hauptstr. 7, Matten (☎033 823 4100, ⓦalpinraft.com), can arrange everything from rafting or canyoning (both Fr.110) to ice climbing (Fr.180), and can be booked direct or through hostels.

Sat 8am–5pm, Sun 10am–noon & 5–7pm; Oct–April Mon–Fri 8am–noon & 1.30–6pm, Sat 9am–noon; ☎033 826 5300, ⓦinterlaken.ch).

ACCOMMODATION

Accommodation fills up quickly in the high seasons, so it really is essential to book ahead. There are hotel lists and courtesy phones at both stations.

Backpackers Villa Sonnenhof (SH) Alpenstr. 16 ☎033 826 7171, ⓦvilla.ch. Excellent hostel with a superb new extension; peaceful, well equipped and friendly. Excellent deals with local restaurants. Dorm **Fr.37**, double **Fr.106**

Balmer's Herberge (SH) Hauptstr. 23–33, Matten ☎033 822 1961, ⓦbalmers.com. With a DJ bar and summer beer garden, this sociable hostel 10min south of town is the hub of Interlaken's lively backpacker scene. Dorm **Fr.30.50**, double **Fr.93**, tented dorm **Fr.25**

Camping Jungfraublick Gsteigstr. 80, Matten ☎033 822 4414, ⓦjungfraublick.ch. At the southern exit from town, a clean, modern site with a solar-heated outdoor pool and a view to die for. Camping **Fr.9** per person, plus **Fr.9** per tent

Jugendherberge Bahnhofplatz Ost ☎033 826 1090, ⓦyouthhostel.ch/interlaken. A big, brand-new HI hostel right by Interlaken Ost station, with rooms for up to six, many en suite and some with balcony, plus internet access, billiards and good food. Dorm **Fr.36**, double **Fr.126.60**

EATING, DRINKING AND NIGHTLIFE

In the evenings most backpackers congregate at one of the busier hostel bars: *Balmer's Herberge* (see above) is the most popular and has cheap beer.

Club Caverne Hauptstr. 36, Matten ⓦcaverne.ch. Located in the *Funny Farm* hostel, this place attracts party-goers till the small hours with its pumping house music and maverick staff. Daily 10.30pm–1.30am.

Coop Opposite Interlaken Ost station, with a smaller branch at Höheweg 26. Huge supermarket with a restaurant. Main branch daily 8am–5/6.30pm, smaller branch Mon–Sat 6am–10.30pm.

Migros Rugenparkstrasse 1. Opposite Interlaken West

station, a reliable supermarket for cheap, self-service staples. There's also a restaurant. Mon–Thurs 8am–7pm, Fri 8am–9pm, Sat 7.30am–5pm.

PizPaz Centralstr. Located just off Bahnhofstrasse, a large and lively place serving affordable pizza and pasta (from Fr.14.50; 20 percent less for takeaway). Daily 10am–11pm.

Restaurant des Alpes Höheweg 115 ☎033 822 2323. A friendly and hectic place serving Swiss and Italian food; good salad bar, but service can be slow (and erratic). Daily 11.30am–10/11pm.

Sandwich Bar Rosenstr. 5. Baguettes and ciabatta (including daily specials) for Fr.5–9, as well as salads, soups, coffees and teas. Mon–Fri 7.30am–7pm, Sat 8am–5pm.

LAUTERBRUNNEN

It's hard to overstate the impact of the **Lauterbrunnen valley**. An immense U-shaped cleft with bluffs on either side rising 1000m sheer, doused by some 72 waterfalls, it is utterly spectacular. The **Staubbach falls** – Switzerland's highest at nearly 300m – tumble just beyond the village of **LAUTERBRUNNEN** at the valley entrance.

From Lauterbrunnen, it's a scenic half-hour walk, or an hourly postbus, 3km up the valley to the spectacular **Trümmelbach falls** (April–June & Sept–Nov 9am–5pm; July & Aug 8.30am–6pm; Fr.11), a series of thunderous waterfalls – fed by the glaciers above – which have carved corkscrew channels inside the valley walls. The bus continues 1.5km to the end of the road at **STECHELBERG**; the **cable-car** station for Gimmelwald, Mürren and the Schilthorn is 1km before the hamlet.

ARRIVAL AND INFORMATION

By train Lauterbrunnen station (served by trains from Interlaken Ost) is opposite the cable-car station for Mürren.

Tourist information The tourist office is just south of the station (June–Sept daily 8.30am–noon & 2–6.30pm; Oct–May Tues–Sat 9am–noon & 1.30–5pm; ☎033 856 8568, ⓦlauterbrunnen.ch).

ACCOMMODATION

Camping Jungfrau ☎033 856 2010, ⓦcamping -jungfrau.ch. Great views and facilities, including a decent restaurant for Swiss dishes, pizza and pasta, plus a minimarket. Also has family chalets (minimum week-long rental). Camping **Fr.13** per person, plus **Fr.13** per tent, chalet **Fr.1090**

HIKING IN THE JUNGFRAU REGION

Hiking some sections of the Jungfrau Region, up or down, is perfectly feasible in summer, and can save a great deal on train tickets. Excellent transport networks and vista-rich footpaths linking all stations mean that with a hiking map – such as the *Wanderkarte Wengen-Mürren-Lauterbrunnental* (1:40,000) – you can see and do a great deal in a day.

SH Valley Hostel ☎ 033 855 2008, ⊛ valleyhostel.ch. A cosy place with 7 dorms (4–8 bunk beds in each, most with balcony) and just one double, plus kitchen, laundry and drying facilities. Dorm **Fr.28**, double **Fr.66**

MÜRREN AND UP TO THE SCHILTHORN

The cable car sets out north of Stechelberg and leaps the valley's west wall to reach the little-visited hamlet of **GIMMELWALD**, continuing to the car-free village of **MÜRREN**. It's worth the journey for the views: from here, the valley floor is 800m straight down, and a dazzling panorama of snowy peaks fills the sky. Mürren is also accessible from Lauterbrunnen by taking a cable car to **Grütschalp** and a spectacular little cliff-edge train from there (one-way Fr.10.80/return Fr.21.60; IR no discount; ER 25 percent discount; SP free). It's easy to do a loop by cable car and train. A cable car continues from Mürren on a breathtaking ride (20min) to the 2970m peak of the **Schilthorn** (⊛ schilthorn.ch), where you can enjoy exceptional panoramas and sip cocktails in the revolving *Piz Gloria* restaurant, famed as Blofeld's hideout in the Bond film *On Her Majesty's Secret Service.*

ACCOMMODATION

Mountain Hostel ☎ 033 855 1704, ⊛ mountain hostel.com. A superb self-catering chalet hostel with beer (and pizza) terrace. Open mid-April to Oct. Dorm **Fr.33**

GRINDELWALD

Valley-floor trains from Interlaken Ost also run to the more popular resort of **GRINDELWALD**, nestling under the craggy trio of the Wetterhorn, Mettenberg and Eiger. Numerous trails around **Pfingstegg** and especially **First** – both reached by gondolas from Grindelwald – offer excellent hiking.

INFORMATION

Tourist information 200m east of the station (daily 8/9am–6pm; ☎ 033 854 1212, ⊛ grindelwald.com).

ACCOMMODATION

Camping Gletscherdorf ☎ 033 853 1429, ⊛ gletscherdorf.ch. A quiet site by a stream to the east of the village, with electric hook-ups and a basic food kiosk. Open May to late Oct. Camping **Fr.8** per person, plus **Fr.9** per tent
HI Jugendherberge Geissstutzstr. 12 ☎ 033 853 1009, ⊛ youthhostel.ch/grindelwald. Located in a quiet lane above the village, this is an excellent hostel in a huge chalet with restaurant and massive mountain-view terrace. Closed mid-April to mid-May & mid-Oct to early Dec. Dorm **Fr.36.70**, double **Fr.121.40**
Mountain Hostel (SH) ☎ 033 854 3838, ⊛ mountain hostel.ch. A well-run place on the valley floor by Grindelwald-Grund station (served by trains from Grindelwald to Kleine Scheidegg). Dorm **Fr.37**, double **Fr.94**

ZERMATT AND THE MATTERHORN

The shark's-tooth **Matterhorn** (4478m) is the most famous of Switzerland's mountains; for most people, the Matterhorn stands for Switzerland like the Eiffel Tower stands for France. One reason it's so famous is that it stands alone, its impossibly pointy shape sticking up from an otherwise uncrowded horizon above **ZERMATT**; another is that the quintessential Swiss chocolate, Toblerone, was modelled on it.

WHAT TO SEE AND DO

Zermatt's main street is thronged year-round with an odd mix of professional climbers, glacier skiers, tour groups, backpackers and fur-clad socialites. No cars are allowed in the town; electric buses ferry people between the train station at the town's northern end and the cable-car terminus 1km south. All Zermatt's cable cars and trains bring you to trailheads and spectacular views: opposite the station, Gornergrat-Bahn trains (ER 25 percent discount, SP 50

34

percent; cheaper after 1.40pm) give spectacular Matterhorn views (sit on the right) as they climb all the way to the **Gornergrat**, where there's a magnificent panorama including Switzerland's highest peak, the **Dufourspitze** (4634m). On summer Thursdays, GGB trains leave Zermatt at dawn for a breathtaking Alpine sunrise and a wildlife hike (Fr.81, SP Fr.60). At the south end of Zermatt a cable car climbs to the **Schwarzsee** (2583m), in summer the start of a zigzag hike (2hr) to the *Hörnli Hut* (3260m), on the flank of the Matterhorn itself. Lifts to **Trockener Steg** give access to 21km of ski runs and a snowboard half-pipe that are open all summer long (day pass Fr.75; SP 50 percent). If the weather is less kind, the **Matterhorn Museum** on Kirchplatz (daily: July–Sept 11am–6pm; Oct–June 2–6pm; Fr.10; SP free) has striking modern displays on all aspects of local life.

ARRIVAL AND INFORMATION

By train The only access to Zermatt is on the spectacular narrow-gauge MGB train line (ER no discount, IR 50 percent, SP free; ⓦ mgbahn.ch); change at Visp from main-line trains. The most celebrated way to arrive is on the *Glacier Express*, a day-long journey from St Moritz by panoramic train (reserve at any train station; ER 25 percent discount, IR Youth Pass 50 percent, SP free; ⓦ glacierexpress.ch).
Destinations Brig (hourly; 1hr 24min); St Moritz (1–4 daily; 7hr 50min); Visp (hourly; 1hr 10min).
Tourist information Tourist office outside the station (mid-June to Sept daily 8.30am–6pm; rest of year Mon–Sat 8.30am–noon & 1.30–6pm, Sun 9.30am–noon & 4–6pm; ⓦ zermatt.ch). There's a hotel list and courtesy phone here.
Snow and Alpine Centre This centre at Bahnhofstr. 58 (daily 8am–noon & 4–7pm; ☎027 966 2460, ⓦ alpincenter-zermatt.ch) runs fixed-rope courses for Fr.135 and ice climbing for Fr.190. It's the place to book climbing guides and also ski/snowboard lessons (Mon–Fri 8am–noon & 3–7pm, Sat & Sun 5am–9pm).

ACCOMMODATION

Hotel Tannenhof Englischer Viertel 3 ☎027 967 3188, ⓦ rhone.ch/tannenhof. Good-value hotel that's popular with climbers. Cosy doubles, with or without private bathroom. Double __Fr.110__
Matterhorn Campsite Bahnhofstr. ☎027 967 3921, ⓦ campingzermatt.ipeak.ch. Though there's no car access to this campsite (located just north of the train station), there's a bus stop for access to the cable cars. Open June–Sept. Camping __Fr.11__ per person and tent

Matterhorn Hostel (SH) Schluhmattstr. 32 ☎027 968 1919, ⓦ matterhornhostel.com. Friendly staff and a lively bar with food, but rather cramped and in need of a revamp. Dorm __Fr.36__, double __Fr.92__
Zermatt Youth Hostel Staldenweg. 5, Winkelmatten ☎027 967 2320, ⓦ youthhostel.ch/zermatt. Excellent HI hostel above the town centre in a sustainably constructed modern building. Good meals. Dorm __Fr.36__, double __Fr.106__

EATING AND DRINKING

Brown Cow Bahnhofstr. 41. Popular pub, serving reasonably priced snacks: soups and hot dogs (from Fr.9) and burgers (Fr.12). Also the *Broken Bar* disco. Bar daily 9am–2am; food till 10.30pm, disco daily 10pm–3.30am.
Grampi's Bahnhofstr. 70. Lively pub with an astonishing human jukebox who can sing virtually any song you'd care to name, and plays keyboard and trumpet to boot. There's a disco downstairs and a pizzeria upstairs. Daily 9am–2am.
Papperla Pub Steinmattstr. 34 at Kirchstr. Zermatt's most popular après-ski (or after-hike) spot, this wood-panelled pub serves up draught beers and live music. Daily 11am–4am.

Ticino

Italian-speaking **Ticino** (Tessin in German and French) occupies the balmy, lake-laced southern foothills of the Alps. It's a little pocket of Italy in Switzerland and radically different in almost every way: culture, food, architecture, attitude and driving style owe more to Milan than Zürich, although Switzerland has controlled the area since the early 1500s. The main attractions are the lakeside resorts of **Locarno** and **Lugano**, where mountain scenery meets subtropical flora. The best way to enjoy these chic towns is to join the locals promenading with ice creams.

Unless you approach from Italy, there's only one train line in – through the 15km **Gotthard Tunnel**. The climb to the tunnel is famous for its spiralling contortions: trains pass Wassen's onion-domed church three times, first far above, then on a level (but going the wrong way), and finally far below.

LOCARNO

A branch line heads west from Bellinzona (whose three superb castles are on UNESCO's World Heritage list) to

LOCARNO, a charming town on **Lake Maggiore** with piazzas overhung by subtropical shrubbery. Overrun with the rich and wannabe-famous on summer weekends and during its world-class film festival (early August), it manages to retain a sun-drenched cool.

WHAT TO SEE AND DO

The **Piazza Grande**, where exquisitely groomed locals parade on warm summer nights, is near the lake, with the Renaissance Old Town rising gently behind. The fifteenth-century church of **Madonna del Sasso** (daily 6.30am–6.45pm) is an impressive ochre vision high on a crag. It's a glorious walk up (or down); or take the funicular (Fr.7.20 return) from just west of the station to Orselina, Ticino's greatest photo-op, looking down on the church and lake.

From here a cable car climbs steeply to **Cardada** amid fragrant pine woods with walking routes; a spectacular chairlift whisks you further up to **Cimetta**, where the restaurant terrace offers a view you won't forget in a hurry.

A short bus ride east of Locarno is Valle Verzasca, where you can re-enact the opening of the James Bond film *Goldeneye* by bungee-jumping a world-record 220m off the Verzasca Dam (April–Oct daily; Fr.255; book on ☎091 780 7800, ⓦtrekking.ch) – in July and August, you can jump by moonlight.

ARRIVAL AND INFORMATION

By train Station 150m northeast of Piazza Grande.
Destinations Basel (every 2hr; 4hr 10min); Bellinzona/Giubiasco (for Lugano; 3 hourly; 20min); Domodossola (for Brig and southwestern Switzerland; 7–11 daily; 1hr 45min); Luzern (every 2hr; 3hr); Zürich (every 2hr; 3hr 10min).
By boat The landing stage is between the train station and Piazza Grande; boats (late March to mid-Sept; ⓦnavigazionelaghi.it) sail to nearby Swiss and Italian resorts.
Destinations Ascona (hourly; 20–30min); Stresa (for Milan; 2 daily; 2hr 20min–3hr 30min).
Tourist information Tourist office in the Casino opposite the landing stage (Mon–Fri 9am–6pm; March–Oct also Sat 10am–6pm, Sun 10am–1.30pm & 2.30–5pm; ☎091 791 0091, ⓦascona-locarno.com).

ACCOMMODATION

Delta campsite Via Respini 7 ☎091 751 6081, ⓦcampingdelta.com. Expensive but well-equipped campsite 20min walk south by the lake (just past the lido). Open March–Oct. Camping Fr.13 per person, plus Fr.21 per tent, caravan rental Fr.56
HI hostel "Palagiovani" Via Varenna 18 ☎091 756 1500, ⓦyouthhostel.ch/locarno; bus #1/#2/#7 from opposite the station to Cinque Vie. Friendly hostel 10min walk from the centre. Dorm Fr.31, double Fr.102

EATING AND DRINKING

Cantina Canetti Piazza Grande 13. Little place at the west end of the Piazza Grande with simple local cooking (from Fr.14) and live accordion on weekend nights. Mon–Sat 8.30am–11pm, Sun 9am–12.30pm.
Manora Via Stazione 1. Self-service chain facing the train station, with good, cheap meals for Fr.14 or under. Daily: April–Oct 7.30/8am–10pm; Nov–March 7.30/8am–9pm.

LUGANO

With its tree-lined promenades and piazzas, **LUGANO** is Ticino's most alluring resort, less touristy than Locarno but twice as chic. The centre of town is **Piazza della Riforma**, a café-lined square by the lovely **Lago di Lugano**. Through the maze of steep lanes northwest of Riforma, Via Cattedrale dog-legs up to the **Cattedrale San Lorenzo**, with its fine Renaissance facade, fragments of interior frescoes and spectacular views from its terrace. Also from Riforma, narrow Via Nassa – home to big-name boutiques – heads southwest to the medieval church of **Santa Maria degli Angioli**, home to a stunning wall-sized fresco of the Crucifixion. A little further south is the **Museo d'Arte**, Riva Caccia 5 (Tues–Sun 10am–6pm; Fr.12, students Fr.8; ⓦmdam.ch), with world-class exhibitions; a little further still is the modestly named district of Paradiso, from where a funicular rises 600m to San Salvatore, a rugged sugarloaf pinnacle offering fine views of the lake and surrounding countryside. Boats and buses open up the lakeside scenery, as well as cable cars that reach many other peaks, some with fine ridge hikes between them.

ARRIVAL, INFORMATION AND TOURS

By train Lugano's train station overlooks the town from the west, linked to the centre by a short funicular (SP free) or by steps down to Via Cattedrale.

34

34

Destinations Luzern (hourly; 2hr 30min); Milan (every 2hr; 1hr); Zürich (hourly; 2hr 40min).
By bus Postbuses bookable at the train station.
Destinations St Moritz (mid-June to mid-Oct daily, otherwise 3 weekly; 4hr).
Tourist information Tourist office on Palazzo Civico, off Riforma (Mon–Fri 9am–7pm, Sat 9am–6pm, Sun 10am–6pm; ☎ 091 913 3232, ⊛ lugano-tourism.ch).
Tours Boat tours around the lake (April–Oct; Fr.4.20–26.60, SP free; ⊛ lakelugano.ch) depart from directly opposite the tourist office.

ACCOMMODATION

HI hostel Via Cantonale 13, Savosa ☎ 091 966 2728, ⊛ youthhostel.ch/lugano; bus #5 to Crocifisso from 200m north of the train station. Excellent, quiet hostel with a large garden and swimming pool. Dorm **Fr.37**, double **Fr.96**
Hotel Pestalozzi Piazza Indipendenza ☎ 091 921 4646, ⊛ pestalozzi-lugano.ch. Centrally located (150m from the lake), with clean, white, recently refurbished rooms, a great (alcohol-free) restaurant and friendly staff. Double **Fr.116**
TCS Camping Lugano La Piodella Via alle Foce 4 ☎ 091 994 7788, ⊛ campingtcs.ch. One of several lakeside campsites in Muzzano, 3km west by FLP train from the platform opposite the main station. Camping **Fr.13** per person, plus **Fr.25** per tent
La Tinèra Via dei Gorini, behind Riforma. Classic locals' restaurant hidden in a basement, with great pasta and tasty Ticinese chicken stews (Fr.19) and *zabaglione* to finish. Mon–Sat 11.30am–3pm & 5.30–10.30pm.
Manora Salta Chiattone. Inexpensive self-service (dishes of the day Fr.10–14), plus pizza (Fr.11–14) in the evening. There's also an outside terrace. Hot food served until 9pm. Mon–Sat 7.30am–10pm, Sun 10am–10pm.

Liechtenstein

Barely larger than Manhattan, **Liechtenstein** is the world's sixth-smallest country. It's an unassuming place squashed between Switzerland and Austria, ruled over by His Serene Highness Prince Hans Adam II. The country has made a mint from nursing some Fr.90 billion in numbered bank accounts. The main reason to visit is the novelty value – you can see the whole country in an easy day-trip from Zürich, less than two hours away by train. Swiss francs are legal tender, but the phone system is separate (country code ☎ 423).

VADUZ

From Sargans train station on the Zürich–Chur line, bus #1 shuttles over the Rhine (no border controls) in half an hour to the capital **VADUZ**, a tiny town bulging with glass-plated **banks** and squadrons of aimless visitors. The central hub is the post office, where all buses stop, set between the main highway, Äulestrasse, and pedestrianized Städtle. On either side are the sleek **Kunstmuseum** (Tues–Sun 10am–5pm, Thurs till 8pm; Fr.12, students Fr.8, combined ticket with Landesmuseum Fr.15/10), displaying temporary art exhibitions drawing on the prince's private collection and other donations, and the **Landesmuseum** (Tues–Sun 10am–5pm, Wed till 8pm; Fr.8, students Fr.5), with excellent coverage of local history. Perched on the forested hillside above is the prince's sixteenth-century **castle** (no public access).

ARRIVAL AND INFORMATION

By bus Buses stop on Vaduz's main street, by the post office. They serve all of Liechtenstein, as well as connecting to Sargans in Switzerland, and to Feldkirch in Austria, from where trains serve Bregenz, Innsbruck and Vienna.
Destinations Feldkirch (Austria; hourly; 30min); Sargans (Switzerland; every 30min; 25min).
Tourist information Städtle 39 (daily 9am–5pm; Nov–April closed Sat & Sun; ☎ 239 6300, ⊛ tourismus.li).

ACCOMMODATION

HI hostel Schaan-Vaduz Untere Rüttigasse 6 ☎ 232 5022. Quiet rural location, looking out over fields and mountains, 5min from Mühleholz bus stop and 2km north of Vaduz. Open March–Oct. Dorm **Fr.34.50**, double **Fr.87**
Mittagsspitze campsite ☎ 392 3677, ⊛ campingtriesen.li. Tranquil rural campsite with swimming pool, 5km south near the Säga bus stop. Camping **Fr.9** per person, plus **Fr.6** per tent

EATING AND DRINKING

Burg Brasserie Städtle 15. Sandwiches, burgers and salad buffet from Fr.12, also pizza, pasta and free wi-fi; upstairs is the slightly grander *Cesare* Italian restaurant. Brasserie Mon–Fri 8.30am–midnight, Sat & Sun 9.30am–midnight, restaurant Mon–Fri 11.30am–2pm & 6–10.50pm.
Café im Kunstmuseum Städtle 32. Stylish café/sushi bar in the art museum serving salads, soups and sweets. Mon, Tues, Sat & Sun 9am–6pm, Wed–Fri 9am–11pm.

FAIRY CHIMNEYS, CAPPADOCIA

Turkey

HIGHLIGHTS

❶ **İstanbul** A sensory overload with historical sights, fantastic nightlife and delicious cuisine. **See p.1145**

❷ **Ephesus** One of the world's best-preserved ancient cities. **See p.1162**

❸ **Kaş** A great base for beaches, ancient sites and adventure sports. **See p.1166**

❹ **Olympos** Explore well-preserved ruins in a tranquil valley and spend the night in a rustic treehouse. **See p.1167**

❺ **Cappadocia** A lunar landscape, complete with eerie caves and underground cities. **See p.1173**

HIGHLIGHTS ARE MARKED ON THE MAP ON P.1141

ROUGH COSTS

Daily budget Basic €25, occasional treat €40

Drink *Rakı* €3.50, beer (*Efes*) €3

Food Kebab with side order €5-6

Hostel/budget hotel €11 (dorm)/€25–50

Travel Bus: İstanbul–Ankara €14

FACT FILE

Population 75.6 million

Area 783,562 sq km

Language Turkish

Currency Turkish lira (TL)

Capital Ankara

International phone code ☏90

Time zone GMT +2hr

Introduction

Turkey has multiple identities. Poised between East and West, it's a place where mosques coexist with churches, and Roman remnants crumble alongside ancient Hittite sites. The country is politically secular, though the majority of the population is Muslim, and it's an immensely rewarding place to travel, not least because of the people, whose reputation for friendliness and hospitality is richly deserved.

35

Much of the country's delights are inexpensive pleasures. Whether it's indulging in tasty *gözleme* pancakes or dancing in backstreet bars, there are plenty of activities to consume your time but not your budget.

Most visitors begin their trip in **İstanbul**, a heady mixture of European shopping districts, Ottoman architecture and Anatolian cultural influences. South from here are small country towns swathed in olive groves and several ancient sites, most notable of all **Ephesus**. Beyond the functional city of **İzmir**, the **Aegean coast** is Turkey at its most developed, with large numbers drawn to hedonistic party resorts such as **Bodrum** and **Marmaris**. Beyond here, the aptly named Turquoise Coast is home to resorts such as **Fethiye** and **Kaş**, famous for their fabulous water- and adventure-sports facilities. Further inland is spectacular **Cappadocia**, with its well-known rock churches, subterranean cities and landscape studded with cave dwellings. Further north, **Ankara**, Turkey's capital, is a planned city whose contrived Western feel gives some indication of the priorities of the modern Turkish Republic. Further south, **Konya** is best known as the birthplace of the Sufi sect.

CHRONOLOGY

1250 BC According to Homer's *Iliad* Troy is cleverly taken by the Greeks who sneak into the city in a wooden horse.
334 BC Alexander the Great marches through Anatolia, present-day Turkey.
129 BC Romans conquer Anatolia.
54 AD St Paul brings Christianity to Anatolia.
330 Emperor Constantine founds Constantinople, calling it the new Rome and establishing the Byzantine Empire.
1288 The Islamic Ottoman Empire starts to expand across present-day Turkey.
1526 The Ottomans defeat the Habsburgs, taking large areas of Europe.
1832 Following more than ten years of heavy fighting, the Greeks gain independence from Ottoman Turkey.
1918 The Ottomans enter World War I on the side of Germany and are defeated by the Allies.
1923 After its War of Independence, Turkey is declared a republic led by President Mustafa Kemal Atatürk.
1928 The Turkish constitution declares Turkey to be a secular state.
1938 Atatürk dies on November 10.
1945 Turkey remains neutral during World War II, lending nominal assistance to the Nazis while outwardly supporting the Allies.
1960 Army takes power in a coup that encounters minimal resistance, dismissing the ruling Democrat Party and hanging its leaders.
1980 Once more the army overthrows government and takes control. Governance is given back to civilians a couple of years later.
1993 Tansu Çiller becomes Turkey's first female Prime Minister.
2005 Talks about Turkish accession to the EU are held.
2007 Tens of thousands of secularists protest in Ankara against Islamist Prime Minister Erdogan's proposed run for president.
2010 İstanbul becomes a European Capital of Culture. Nine Turkish citizens aboard a Gaza-bound relief ship are killed by Israeli commandoes.
2011 Ten thousand Syrian refugees flood over the border into Turkey. Erdogan criticizes his former ally Assad.
2013 Protests against plans to develop İstanbul's Taksim Gezi Park turn into a summer of demonstrations and discontent across the country. The heavy-handed response by the government and police is condemned at home and abroad.

ARRIVAL AND DEPARTURE

Tourist **visas** (€15–45 depending on nationality) are required for individuals from most countries and can be got upon arrival. You'll need to pay cash and queue

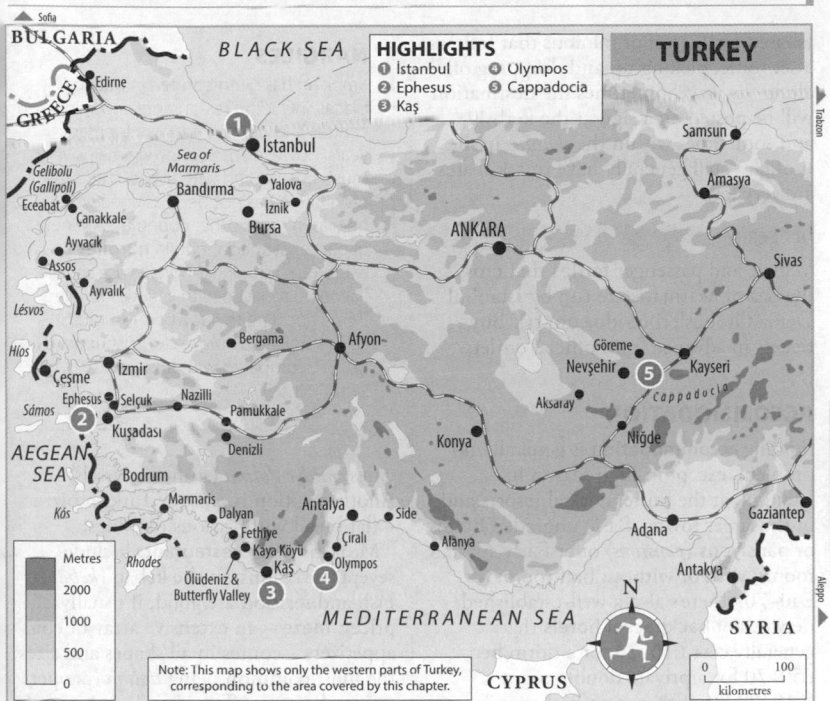

up before joining the queue for passport control. Visas usually last for three months and enable visitors to travel between Turkey and neighbouring countries.

The most common point of **arrival** is İstanbul, with **overland travellers** arriving at the bus station some distance from the centre. **International flights** to İstanbul arrive at either Atatürk Airport (wataturk airport.com) on the European side or Sabiha Gökçen (wsgairport.com), used by many budget carriers, on the Anatolian side. For those heading to Turkey's Turquoise Coast, Antalya's international airport is the most convenient for the region's many resorts. If you're travelling to Turkey **by sea** you're likely to arrive at either Kuşadası or Marmaris where ferries connect Turkey with the Greek islands.

GETTING AROUND

BY TRAIN

The **train** system, run by TCDD (wtcdd .gov.tr) is limited, and many kilometres of track are currently closed for major engineering works. Long-distance train travel is possible, but you'll need to check their website for the latest news on routes. Cheap sleeper cabins are available on overnight services. Reservations are only necessary at weekends or on national holidays. An ISIC card gets a twenty percent discount. InterRail passes are valid, Eurail aren't.

BY BUS

The **long-distance bus** network is extensive, reliable and affordable. Most destinations are served by several competing firms, which all have ticket booths at the bus station (*otogar* or terminal) from which they operate, as well as an office in the town centre. Book ahead if you're travelling in high season or on a public holiday. **Fares** vary only slightly between companies: expect to pay about 10TL per 100km. Bus companies usually provide a free shuttle bus between the *otogar* and town centre. For short hops you're most likely to use a **dolmuş** (shared taxi), a **car** or **minibus** that follows a set route, picking up and dropping off along the way. Sometimes the destination will be posted on a sign at the kerbside, and sometimes within the *dolmuş* itself, though you'll generally have to ask. Fares are very low.

BY FERRY

Vehicle and passenger **ferries** that cross the Sea of Marmaris are run by İstanbul Deniz Otobüsleri (@ido.com.tr). Buy tickets in advance from official outlets.

35 ACCOMMODATION

Finding **accommodation** is generally no problem, except in high season in İstanbul, at the busier coastal resorts and in the larger towns. Basic ungraded **hotels** or **pansiyons** (*pensions*) offer fairly spartan rooms, with or without bathroom, for €40–70. There's also a well-established network of **backpacker hotels** that generally cost €10–20 for a dorm bed, €50–70 for a private double room (€10–20 less if there's no bathroom). You'll also find triple and quad rooms offered at attractive rates at most hotels. Many resort-based places close in winter, so it's wise to call ahead. Almost everywhere offers wi-fi and a/c in each room, and, unless otherwise indicated, includes a Turkish buffet breakfast in the price. **Campsites** are common only on the coast and in national parks and cost around €8–13 per person.

FOOD AND DRINK

At its finest, Turkish food is one of the world's great cuisines, yet prices are on the whole affordable. **Breakfast** (*kahvaltı*) served at hotels and *pansiyons* is usually a buffet, offering bread with butter, cheese, cucumber, tomatoes, olives, jam, honey, and tea or coffee. Many workers start the morning with a *börek* (1.50TL) or a *poça*, pastries filled with meat, cheese or potato that are sold at a tiny *büfe* (stall/café) or at street carts. Others make do with a simple *simit* (sesame-seed bread ring). Snack vendors hawk *lahmacun*, small "pizzas" with meat-based toppings, and, in coastal

NARGILES

Smoking has been banned in public places, including restaurants, shopping centres and public transport, for many years. However, the country remains very much enamoured with tobacco and the prohibition has not been as effective here as in some other countries. A variety of bars exist specializing in **nargile** (waterpipe) smoking. *Nargiles* use special flavoured tobacco with varieties ranging from chocolate to strawberry. In touristy cafés smoking a *nargile* can cost upwards of 15TL compared with less than 10TL in a locals' joint.

cities, *midye dolma* (stuffed mussels). Another option is *pide*, or Turkish pizza – flat bread with various toppings.

Meat dishes in **restaurants** include several variations on the kebab (*kebap*). Fish and seafood are good, if usually pricey. **Meze** – an extensive array of cold appetizers – comes in all shapes and sizes, the most common being *dolma* (peppers or vine leaves stuffed with rice), *patlican salata* (aubergine in tomato sauce) and *acılı* (a mixture of tomato paste, onion, chilli and parsley). Many budget restaurants are alcohol-free, especially in smaller, more conservative cities.

For **dessert**, there's every imaginable concoction at a *pastane* (sweet shop): best are the honey-soaked baklava, and a variety of milk puddings, most commonly *sütlaç*. Other sweets include *aşure* (Noah's pudding), a sort of rosewater jelly laced with pulses, raisins and nuts; and *lokum* or Turkish delight.

Restaurant **opening hours** vary widely but in general are open all day; some open as early as 7am, others open for lunch at around 11am and close between 11pm and 1am. In smaller cities, such as Bursa and Edirne, many tend to shut by around 9pm. Bars are generally open 11am or noon–2am. Clubs are usually open after 11pm until 5/6am.

DRINK

Tea (*çay*) is the national drink, with sugar on the side but no milk. **Turkish coffee** (*kahve*) is strong, bitter and served in tiny cups. Nescafé pretty much holds a monopoly on instant coffee, but fresh filter coffee and even international favourites like flat whites and lattes are cropping up in trendier cafés. **Fruit juices** (*meyva suyu*) can be excellent but are usually sweetened. You'll also come across **ayran**, watered-down yogurt, which makes a refreshing drink. The main locally brewed brands of **beer** (*bira*) are Efes Pilsen and Tuborg. The national aperitif is anis-flavoured *rakı* – a strong spirit consisting of 45 percent alcohol. It's usually topped up with water and enjoyed with *meze* or a *nargile* (see box opposite).

CULTURE AND ETIQUETTE

Turkey's unspoken codes of conduct can catch the first-time visitor off guard. Away from the main cities you should **dress modestly** and avoid shorts and revealing attire – this is particularly important the further east you travel. If you are a female traveller, it is essential to take a headscarf or shawl if you plan on **visiting a mosque**. These are generally open during daylight hours, except for prayer time (around half an hour following the call to prayer). Both sexes should remember to remove their shoes.

In almost every sphere of social interaction, **tea drinking** plays an important role. You'll notice shop salesmen commonly invite you to peruse their goods over tea.

Although interaction between Turkish men and women is quite formal, single **female travellers** may experience harassment and should take care,

---

HAGGLING

Shopping in Turkey requires more than just money. In bazaars, market stalls and independent shops, you should try **haggling** – the original price quoted can be three times the price of the item's actual value. Avoid displaying too much enthusiasm over your desired item, and if the price quoted sounds expensive, inform the shopkeeper that you would like to shop around for a better deal – this might result in a better offer.

---

particularly in the evenings. Note also that, while many young Turkish women visit bars and clubs, few of them go out unaccompanied at night, and you should observe this rule away from tourist areas.

SPORTS AND ACTIVITIES

Undoubtedly Turkey's most popular sport is **football**, with Galatasaray, Beşiktaş and Fenerbahçe (all from İstanbul) being three of the nation's favourite teams. All of these clubs boast huge stadiums, but 19 Mayıs stadium, located in Ankara, is also home to three clubs and big games. To find out about games and buy tickets, visit ⓦbiletix.com. Most tour operators in the established resorts have information about both summer and winter **adventure sports**. **Scuba diving** is popular, and Kaş in particular offers some of the best in the Med. Other picturesque spots along the coast have skies full of **paragliders**, while **cyclists** and **hikers** will find all manner of great trails, not least the Lycian Way from Fethiye to Antalya.

COMMUNICATIONS

Most **post offices** (PTT) open Monday to Saturday 9am to 5pm, with main branches open till 7/8pm and also on Sun. Use the *yurtdışı* (overseas) slot on postboxes. **Phone calls** can be made from Turk Telecom booths and the PTT. Post offices and kiosks sell phonecards (30, 60 and 100 units) and also have metered phones. Some payphones accept credit cards. Numerous private phone shops (*Köntürlü telefon*) offer metered calls at dubious, unofficial rates. For longer stays it might be worthwhile purchasing a cheap phone, or at least a SIM card, locally. There are **internet** cafés in most towns, but almost every hotel and hostel has free wi-fi and often a computer for use by residents. Many bars, cafés, restaurants – and even the long-distance buses – also have free **wi-fi**.

EMERGENCIES

Street **crime** is uncommon and theft is rare; however, lone women should pay

35

TURKISH

	TURKISH	PRONUNCIATION
Yes	Evet	Evet
No	Hayır/yok	Hi-uhr/yok
Please	Lötfen	Lewtfen
Thank you	Teşekkürler/mersi/sağol	Teshekkewrler/sa-ol
Hello/Good day	Merhaba	Merhabuh
Goodbye	Hoşçakalın	Hosh-cha kaluhn
Excuse me	Pardon	Pardon
Where?	Nerede?	Neredeh?
Good	İyi	Eeyee
Bad	Kötü	Kurtew
Near	Yakın	Yakuhn
Far	Uzak	Oozak
Cheap	Ucuz	Oojooz
Expensive	Pahalı	Pahaluh
Open	Açık	Achuhk
Closed	Kapalı	Kapaluh
Today	Bugün	Boogewn
Yesterday	Dün	Dewn
Tomorrow	Yarın	Yaruhn
How much is?	Ne kadar...?	Ne kadar...?
What time is it?	Saatiniz var mı?	Saatiniz var muh?
I don't understand	Anlamıyorum	Anlamuh-yoroom
Do you speak English?	İngilizce biliyor musunuz?	Eengeeleezjeh beeleeyor moosoonooz?
Sorry	Özür dilerim	Erzer delereem
Do you have?	...var mı?	Öva mur?
I would like	...istiyorum	Öe-stee-yo-rum
What is your name?	Adınız ne?	A-denurz nay?
I'd like the bill	Hesabı Istiyorum	Hes-ab ee-stee-yo-rum
One	Bir	Bir
Two	İki	Iki
Three	Üç	Ewch
Four	Dört	Durt
Five	Beş	Besh
Six	Altı	Altuh
Seven	Yedi	Yedi
Eight	Sekiz	Sekiz
Nine	Dokuz	Dokuz
Ten	On	On

attention and be very wary of going out alone after dark. **Police** wear dark blue uniforms with baseball caps, with their division – *trafik*, *narkotik*, etc – clearly marked. There's a tourist police centre at Yerebatan Cad 6 (☎0212 527 4503) in Sultanahmet with some English-speaking officers. In rural areas, you'll find the camouflage-clad Jandarma, a division of the regular army. For minor **health** complaints, head for the nearest pharmacy (*eczane*). Night-duty pharmacists are known as *nöbetçi*; the current rota is posted in every pharmacy's front window. For more serious ailments, go to a hospital (*klinik*) – either public or the much higher-quality and cleaner private (Özel Hastane).

EMERGENCY NUMBERS
Police ☎155; Ambulance ☎112; Fire ☎110.

TURKEY ONLINE

ⓦ **goturkey.com** Turkey's official tourism portal.

ⓦ **timeoutistanbul.com/en** A reliable listings site for the latest exhibitions, gigs and films.

ⓦ **turkeytravelplanner.com** Turkey expert's personal guide to the country.

INFORMATION

Most towns of any size have a **tourist office** (Turizm Danışma Bürosu), generally open Monday to Friday 8.30am to 12.30pm and 1.30 to 5.30pm. Staff usually speak English, and should be able to help you with accommodation, and you'll generally find a good range of brochures and maps.

MONEY AND BANKS

Currency is the **Turkish lira** (TL), divided into 100 kuruş. (In March 2012, Prime Minister Erdogan unveiled a new symbol for the lira (₺), but prices are still generally indicated using TL.) There are coins of 1, 5, 10, 25, 50 kuruş and 1TL, and notes of 1, 5, 10, 20, 50 and 100TL. £1 = 3TL, €1 = 2.5TL, US$1 = 1.9TL. Exchange rates for foreign currency are always better inside Turkey. Many *pensions* and hotels, particularly in the popular destinations, also quote prices in **euros**, particularly for more expensive options, and you can usually pay in either euros or Turkish lira.

Banks open Monday to Friday 8.30am to noon and 1.30pm to 5pm; some, notably Garanti Bankasi, are open at lunchtimes and on Saturday. Some of the **exchange booths** run by banks in coastal resorts, airports and ferry docks charge a small commission. Private exchange offices have competitive rates and no commission. Almost all banks have ATMs. **Post offices** in sizeable towns also sometimes change cash and cheques.

OPENING HOURS AND HOLIDAYS

Shops are generally open Monday to Saturday 9am to 7/8pm, and possibly Sunday, depending on the owner. There are two **religious holidays. Kurban Bayramı** (the Feast of the Sacrifice) falls on October 3 to 7 in 2014 and September 22 to 26 in 2015. **Şeker Bayramı** (Sugar Holiday), meanwhile, marks the end of the Muslim fasting month of Ramadan. If either falls midweek, the government may choose to extend the holiday period to as much as nine days. Many shops and restaurants close as their owners return to their home towns for the holiday. Banks and public offices are also closed on the **secular holidays**: January 1, April 23, May 19, August 30, October 28 and 29.

İstanbul

Arriving in **İSTANBUL** can result in sensory overload: backstreets teem with traders pushing handcarts, the smell of grilled food from roadside vendors lingers in the air and the call to prayer rings out from tall minarets. Yet this is merely one aspect of modern İstanbul. With the bustling bars, cafés, boutiques and art galleries in Beyoğlu, a distinctly continental influence also pervades.

İstanbul is the only city in the world to have played capital to consecutive Christian and Islamic empires, and retains features of both. Named

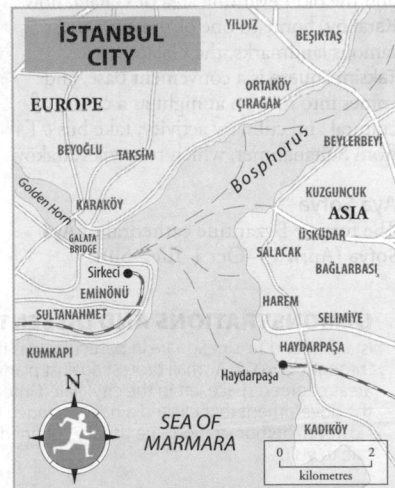

35

Byzantium after the Greek colonist Byzas, the city was an important trading centre. In the fourth century it was renamed **Constantinople** when Constantine chose it as the new capital of the Roman Empire. The city later became an independent empire, adopting the Greek language and Christianity as its religion. In 1453 the city was captured by the Ottoman **Mehmet the Conqueror**. By the nineteenth century, the glory days of the Ottoman empire were over. After the War of Independence (1919–23), the territorial boundaries of modern-day Turkey were set and İstanbul lost its status as the **capital** to Ankara under the country's leader, **Mustafa Kemal Atatürk**. The city remains the country's economic and cultural heart, though, with a population of 13.5 million.

WHAT TO SEE AND DO

The city is divided in two by the **Bosphorus**, a stretch of water that runs between the Black Sea and the Sea of Marmara, dividing Europe from Asia. At right angles to it, the inlet of the **Golden Horn** cuts the European side in two. It is this European section (also known as Old İstanbul) where most visitors spend their time, wandering around the cobbled streets and tourist sites in **Sultanahmet** or exploring the arty district of **Beyoğlu**. Sandwiched between the two is **Eminönü** and the old Levantine area of Galata, now **Karaköy**, home to one of the city's most famous landmarks, the Galata Tower. **Taksim Square** is a convenient base, and comes into its own at night as a centre of cultural and culinary activity; take bus #T4 from Sultanahmet, which runs via Karaköy.

Aya Sofya

The former Byzantine cathedral of **Aya Sofya** (April 15–Oct 1 Tues–Sun 9am–6pm; Oct 2–May 14 Tues–Sun 9am–5pm; 25TL), readily visible thanks to its massive domed structure, is perhaps the single most compelling sight in the city. Commissioned in the sixth century by the Emperor Justinian, it was converted to a mosque in 1453, after which the minarets were added; it's been a museum since 1934. For centuries this was the largest enclosed space in the world, and the interior – filled with shafts of light from the high windows around the dome – is still profoundly impressive. There are a few features left over from its time as a mosque – a mihrab (niche indicating the direction of Mecca), a mimber (pulpit) and the enormous wooden plaques which bear sacred names of God, the Prophet Mohammed and the first four Caliphs. There are also remains of abstract and figurative mosaics.

Topkapı Palace

Immediately north of Aya Sofya, **Topkapı Palace** (daily except Tues 9am–6pm; 25TL) is İstanbul's second unmissable sight. Built between 1459 and 1465, the palace was the centre of the Ottoman Empire for nearly four centuries. The ticket office is in the first courtyard, followed by the beautifully restored Divan, containing the Imperial Council Hall in the second courtyard. Around the corner is the Harem, well worth the additional 15TL (tickets sold outside Harem entrance). The only men once allowed in here were eunuchs and the imperial guardsmen, who were only employed at certain hours and even then blinkered. Back in the main body of the palace, in the third courtyard, the throne room was where the sultan awaited the outcome of sessions of the Divan. Be sure to take in some of the spectacular views of the Bosphorus as you explore.

DEMONSTRATIONS AND DISSENT

İstanbul, and Taksim Square in particular, was the scene of several demonstrations and clashes throughout 2013. A small protest against plans to redevelop Taksim Gezi Park (one of the few areas of green space left in the city) flared into a much larger expression of dissatisfaction with the government that elicited a heavy-handed response and unrest across the country. However, demonstrations are usually confined to central open-air spaces and İstanbul remains safe to visit.

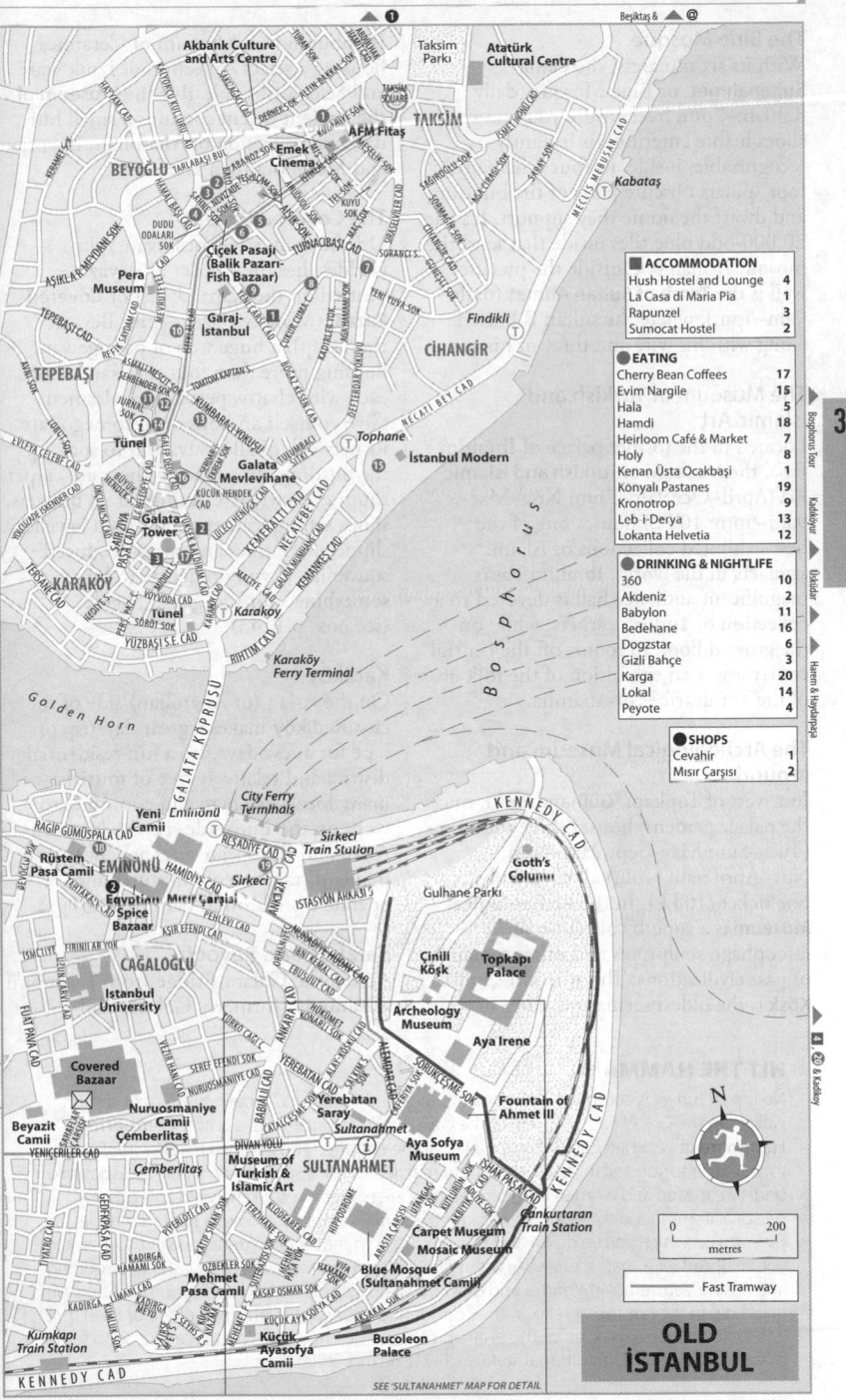

Beşiktaş & @

ACCOMMODATION
Hush Hostel and Lounge	4
La Casa di Maria Pia	1
Rapunzel	3
Sumocat Hostel	2

EATING
Cherry Bean Coffees	17
Evim Nargile	15
Hala	5
Hamdi	18
Heirloom Café & Market	7
Holy	8
Kenan Üsta Ocakbaşı	1
Konyalı Pastanes	19
Kronotrop	9
Leb-i-Derya	13
Lokanta Helvetia	12

DRINKING & NIGHTLIFE
360	10
Akdeniz	2
Babylon	11
Bedehane	16
Dogzstar	6
Gizli Bahçe	3
Karga	20
Lokal	14
Peyote	4

SHOPS
Cevahir	1
Mısır Çarşısı	2

35

Bosphorus tour ▶
Kadıköy ▶
Üsküdar ▶
Harem & Haydarpaşa ▶
& Kadıköy ▶

0 ———— 200
metres

———— Fast Tramway

OLD İSTANBUL

SEE 'SULTANAHMET' MAP FOR DETAIL

35

The Blue Mosque

With its six minarets, the **Camii Sultanahmet**, or Blue Mosque (daily 8.30am–7pm; free; ensure you remove shoes before entering), is instantly recognizable; inside, its four "elephant foot" pillars obscure parts of the building and dwarf the dome they support. It's the 20,000-odd blue tiles inside that lend the mosque its name. Outside the precinct wall is the **Tomb of Sultan Ahmet** (daily 9am–4pm), where the sultan is buried along with his wife and three of his sons.

The Museum of Turkish and Islamic Art

Located in the former palace of Ibrahim Paşa, the **Museum of Turkish and Islamic Art** (April–Oct 9am–7pm; Nov–Mar 9am–5pm; 10TL) houses one of the best-exhibited collections of Islamic artefacts in the world. Ibrahim Paşa's magnificent audience hall is devoted to a collection of Turkish carpets, while on the ground floor, in rooms off the central courtyard, is an exhibition of the folk art of the Yörük tribes of Anatolia.

The Archeological Museum and around

Just west of Topkapı, **Gülhane Parkı**, once the palace gardens, houses three museums (Tues–Sun: May–Sept 9am–6pm; Nov–April 9am–4pm) all covered by one ticket (10TL). In the **Archeological Museum** is a superb collection of sarcophagi, sculptures and other remains of past civilizations. The adjacent **Çinili Köşk** is the oldest secular building in

İstanbul, now a Museum of Ceramics housing a select collection of İznık ware and Selçuk tiles. Nearby, the **Museum of the Ancient Orient** contains a small but dazzling collection of Anatolian, Egyptian and Mesopotamian artefacts.

The Covered Bazaar

Off the main street of Divan Yolu Caddesi lies the district of Beyazıt, centred on the Kapalı Çarşı or **Covered Bazaar** (Mon–Sat 9am–7pm; Beyazıt tram stop), a huge web of passageways housing more than four thousand shops, each with chatty, persuasive salesmen. Give yourself an hour or so to negotiate its network of alleyways and to soak up the bustling atmosphere. There are carpet shops everywhere catering for all budgets, shops selling leather goods, gold jewellery, slippers, ceramics and mass-produced souvenirs. If you do decide to buy something, don't forget to haggle (see box, p.1143).

Kadiköy

On the Asian (or Anatolian) side of the city, **Kadiköy** makes a great day-trip or base for a few days. It's a fun residential district and relatively free of tourists; many locals live here and commute to work on the Euro side. Ferries between Asian and European sides are cheap and frequent, take twenty minutes and operate from around 6am to 11.30pm.

Karaköy and Beyoğlu

Across the Galata Bridge from Eminönü is **Karaköy** (formerly Galata) and

---

HIT THE HAMMAM

No trip to Turkey is complete without a trip to a traditional Turkish bath. In İstanbul, a short walk from the Grand Bazaar, is one of the city's finest historical public baths, **Çemberlitaş Hammam** at VezirHan Cad 8, Çemberlitaş. At the entrance you'll be given a *peştamal* (cotton towel) to wrap yourself in, and a scrubbing mitt; ladies will also be given a pair of disposable underwear. Men and women bathe in separate areas. Once you've changed and put any personal items in a locker you'll be led into the *sıcaklık*, a hot room with a heated marble platform on which you lie down and relax for fifteen minutes or so until you start to sweat. If you've opted for a soap scrub, your attendant will spend fifteen minutes washing, scrubbing and rinsing you, removing grime and dead skin cells. Otherwise you wash yourself. Afterwards, take a dip in the hot tub or relax in the cool lounge afterwards with a cup of tea or fresh fruit juice. Allow at least an hour for the entire process. Basic entry 45TL; entrance plus soap scrub by an attendant 69TL (traditional style) or 117TL (luxury style).

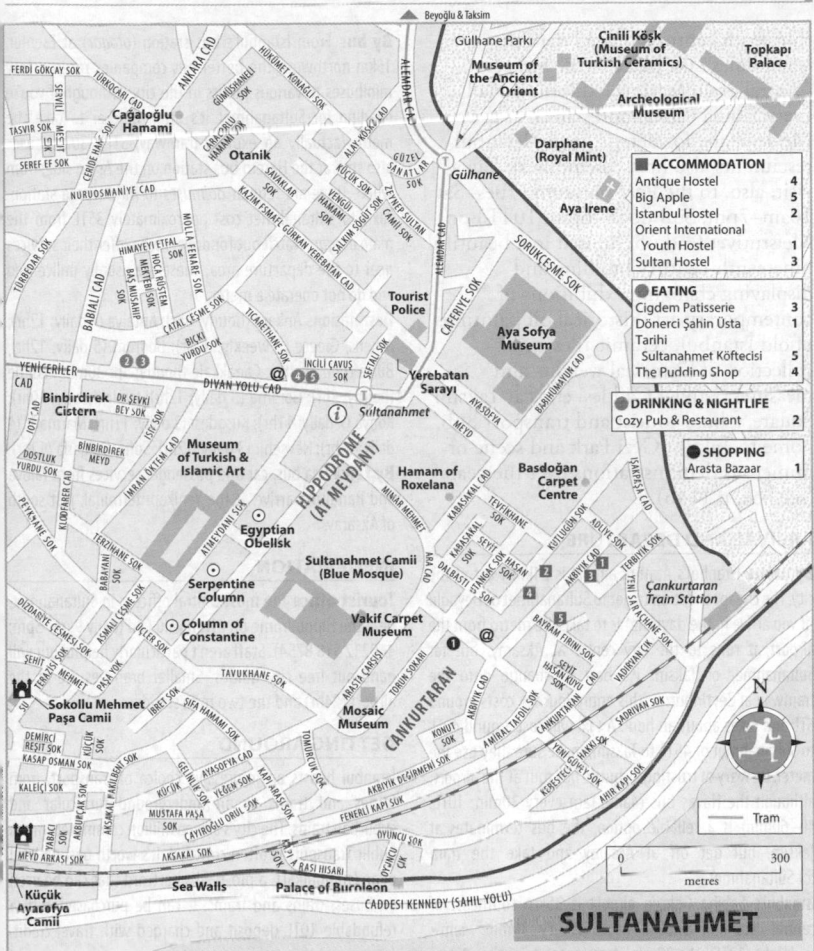

Beyoğlu & Taksim

Gülhane Parkı

Çinili Köşk (Museum of Turkish Ceramics)

Topkapı Palace

Museum of the Ancient Orient

Archeological Museum

FERDİ GÖKÇAY SOK

ANKARA CAD

HÜKÜMET KONAĞI SOK

ALEMDAR CAD

Darphane (Royal Mint)

Çağaloğlu Hamamı

TÜRKOCAĞI CAD

GÜMÜŞHANELİ SOK

CEBECİ HAMAM SOK

ALAY KÖŞKÜ SOK

Gülhane

TASVİR SOK

İBNÜ SİNA

ZEYNEP SULTAN CAMİİ SOK

Aya İrene

SEREF EF SOK

Otanik

CERİDE HAC SOK

SANTRAL SOK

KÜÇÜK SOK

YENGÜL HAMAMI SOK

SALİM SOK SULTAN SOK

SALİM SÖĞÜT SOK CAMİİ SOK

SORUKÇEŞME SOK

■ **ACCOMMODATION**

NURUOSMANİYE CAD

KAZIM İSMAİL GÜRKAN CAD YEREBATAN CAD

Antique Hostel 4
Big Apple 5
İstanbul Hostel 2
Orient International Youth Hostel 1
Sultan Hostel 3

TÜRBEDAR CAD

BABIALİ CAD

HİMAYEYİ ETFAL

HOCA RÜSTEM MEKTEBİ SOK

MOLLA FENARİ SOK

BAŞ MUSAHİP

CAFERİYE SOK

Aya Sofya Museum

●**EATING**

Çiğdem Patisserie 3
Dönerci Şahin Usta 1
Tarihi Sultanahmet Köftecisi 5
The Pudding Shop 4

ÇATAL ÇEŞME SOK

BİCKİ YURDU SOK

TİCARETHANE SOK

İNCİLİ ÇAVUŞ SOK

SETHAL SOK

YENİÇERİLER CAD

DİVAN YOLU CAD

Yerebatan Sarayı

BARBİHATÜR CAD

AYASOFYA MEYD

●**DRINKING & NIGHTLIFE**

Cozy Pub & Restaurant 2

Binbirdirek Cistern

DR ŞEVKİ BEY SOK

Sultanahmet

35

İDİL SOK

İSEÇ SOK

Museum of Turkish & Islamic Art

AYASOFYA

Basdoğan Carpet Centre

İŞARESİ CAD

●**SHOPPING**

Arasta Bazaar 1

DOSTLUK YURDU SOK

BİNBİRDİREK MEYD

İMRAN ÖKTEM CAD

Hamam of Roxelana

TEVFİKHANE SOK

KUTLUGÜN SOK

ADLİYE SOK

TERBİTTİK SOK

PEYKHANE SOK

KLODFARER CAD

ATMEYDANI SOK

HİPPODROME (AT MEYDANI)

MİMAR MEHMET

KABASAKAL CAD

ŞEVKİ HASAN

DALBASTI

SEYİT HASAN

KUTLUGÜN SOK

ARBUK SOK

YENİ AKÇEME SOK

Çankurtaran Train Station

TERZİHANE SOK

Egyptian Obelisk

Sultanahmet Camii (Blue Mosque)

ÜÇLER SOK

BAYRAM FİRİNİ SOK

BATRAM FİRİNİ SOK

SADRIVAN SOK

DEDDİYE ÇEŞMESİ SOK

BARABANİ SOK

AŞMALI ÇEŞME SOK

Serpentine Column

Column of Constantine

Vakif Carpet Museum

TORUN SOKAKTI

VADİ KAPI SOK

ŞEHİT MEHMET PAŞA SOK

ARASTA ÇARŞISI

CANKURTARAN

ŞEYİT HASAN KUYU CAD

TAVUKHANE SOK

Mosaic Museum

KONUT SOK

AMİRAL TAFDİL SOK

CANKURTARAN CAD

N

Sokollu Mehmet Paşa Camii

İBRET SOK

ŞİFA HAMAMI SOK

YENİ SARAÇHANE SOK

AHIR KAPI SOK

DEMİRCİ REŞİT SOK

KASAP OSMAN SOK

KÜÇÜK SOK

GELİN SOK

KÜÇÜK AYASOFYA CAD

YEŞİL DÖVEY SOK

KÜRESTECİ

KALEİÇİ SOK

AKBIYIK DEĞİRMENİ SOK

■

BARABACI SOK

AKSARAY PARİLLBEVI SOK

MUSTAFA PAŞA SOK

KÜÇÜK ÇAYIROĞLU ORUL SOK

KAPI AĞASI SOK

FENERLİ KAPI SOK

Tram

■

MEYD ARKASI SOK

AKSAKAL SOK

OYUNCU SOK

BAŞİ HİSARI SOK

OYUNCU SOK

0 300 metres

Küçük Ayasofya Camii

Sea Walls

Palace of Buçeleon

CADDESİ KENNEDY (SAHİL YOLU)

SULTANAHMET

Beyoğlu. Karaköy was previously the capital's "European" quarter, and has been home to Jewish, Greek and Armenian minorities. Today you'll find boutiques, crafts shops and small art galleries, and it's where locals and clued-up overseas visitors meet in international coffee shops, world-class restaurants and lively clubs; this is the place to come for a night out without the tourist hordes you get in Sultanahmet. The **Galata Tower** (daily 9am–7.30pm; 10TL), built in 1348, is the area's most obvious landmark; its viewing galleries, café (Turkish coffee 5TL, beer 8TL) and ridiculously

expensive restaurant offer the best panoramas of the city, with queues to match. **İstanbul Modern** by the Bosphorus (Tues–Sun 10am–6pm; 15TL) is worth a visit too. With a focus on modern art from contemporary Turkish artists as well as international talent, this is Turkey's answer to the Tate Modern in London.

Up towards İstiklâl Caddesi, Beyoğlu's main shopping boulevard, an unassuming doorway leads to the courtyard of the **Galata Mevlevihane** (9am–4pm, closed Wed; 5TL), a former monastery and ceremonial hall of the Whirling Dervishes, a sect founded in the

35

thirteenth century. Staged dervish ceremonies take place at the Sirkeci Central Train Station Exhibition Hall every Sunday afternoon (check at the Mevlevihane for details; many İstanbul restaurants also host ceremonies). Pay a visit, also, to the **Pera Museum** (Tues–Sat 10am–7pm; Sun noon–6pm; 10TL) on Meişrutiyet Cad 65, housed in a beautiful nineteenth-century building and displaying changing exhibitions of contemporary art, historical oil paintings of old İstanbul, ceramic tiles and a collection of historical weights and measures. Istiklâl Caddesi ends at Taksim Square, a busy tourist and transport hub, home to Taksim Gezi Park and scene of numerous demonstrations over the years (see box, p.1146).

ARRIVAL AND DEPARTURE

By plane İstanbul's Atatürk airport is 24km west of the city. The cheapest option to get to Sultanahmet or Beyoğlu (if you arrive in the daytime) is to take the metro from the airport; it runs to the city centre at Aksaray, but for Sultanahmet or Taksim it's best to change onto the tramway at Zeytinburnu; this entire journey costs around 6TL and takes about an hour. A taxi will cost around 40TL to Sultanahmet or 45TL to Taksim; make sure they use the meter. Be wary of trusting a shuttle bus tout at the airport, although the Havaş bus (4am–1am every 30min; 10TL; 40–60min) is a reliable option; the bus terminates at Taksim, but get off at Aksaray and take the tram for Sultanahmet.

İstanbul's Sabiha Gökçen airport is 35km southeast of central İstanbul. Shuttle buses (every 30min; 4am–midnight, 12TL; 1hr 30min) terminate at Taksim. A taxi from Sabiha Gökçen airport to Sultanahmet will cost around 90TL.

By train Trains from Europe terminate at Sirkeci station (although at the time of writing works on the line necessitate a change onto a bus at Çerkezköy for the last leg, which is linked to Sultanahmet by a short tram ride (3TL). Haydarpaşa station, the terminal for trains from Asia on the east bank of the Bosphorus, was also closed at the time of writing for the construction of high-speed rail lines and the Marmary Rail Transport Project, due for completion in 2015. Until then you'll need to take a bus to Eskişehir, 314km east of İstanbul, for trains to Turkish cities to the east. Check their site (@tcdd.gov.tr) for the latest developments.

Destinations Ankara (10 daily via Eskişehir; 5hr 30min); Konya (3 daily; 8hr); Edirne (1 daily; 5hr); London (5 days); Sofia, Bulgaria (1 daily; 13hr).

By bus From İstanbul's bus station (*otogar*) at Esenler, 15km northwest, the better bus companies run courtesy minibuses to various points in the city, although if you're heading for Sultanahmet it's often quicker to take the metro (actually an express tramway; 3TL). Some buses also stop at the Harem bus station on the Asian side, from where there are regular *dolmuşes* to Haydarpaşa station. Taxis to Sultanahmet cost approximately 35TL from the main *otogar*. Watch out for drivers who offer their services near to the departure area. These are usually unlicensed and do not operate a meter.

Destinations Ankara (hourly; 6hr); Antalya (4 daily; 12hr); Athens, Greece (2 weekly; 22hr); Bodrum (5 daily; 12hr); Bursa (hourly; 4hr); Çanakkale (hourly; 5hr 30min); Edirne (hourly; 3hr); Göreme (5 daily; 12hr); İzmir (hourly; 10hr); Konya (7 daily; 11hr); Kuşadası (3 daily; 11hr); Marmaris (4 daily; 13hr); Nevşehir (3 daily; 12hr); Sofía, Bulgaria (12hr).

By ferry Sea bus, car and passenger services from Yalova and Bandirma arrive at the Yenikapı terminal, just south of Aksaray.

INFORMATION

Tourist office The most central office is in Sultanahmet, near the Hippodrome on Divan yolu Cad (daily 9am–5pm; ☎0212 518 8754). Staff aren't particularly helpful but will hand out free city guides. Smaller branches are at the airport (24hr) and the two train stations.

GETTING AROUND

İstanbul boasts an impressive choice of transport, from ferries and trams to an underground furnicular and suburban trains. The city's eleven million commuters mean public transport is often crowded. It's worth getting hold of an İstanbulkart, a pre-paid smartcard that can be used on buses, trains and trams. It can be purchased with a refundable 10TL deposit and charged with travel credit. Journeys work out cheaper per trip.

By train There's a municipal train network running along the Marmara shore – west from Sirkeci station on the European side, and east from Haydarpaşa on the Asian (allow at least 1hr to get to the Asian station from the centre). Either use a *jeton* (plastic token; 3TL), purchased in advance at bus stations, newspaper kiosks or fast-food booths, or present the İstanbulkart.

By bus İstanbul's buses are either run by the municipality, and are marked by an "IETT" logo, or one of several private companies. The main bus stops boast large route maps and lists of services. Most services run from early in the morning (around 6.30am) to late at night (11.30pm). Use *jetons* (3TL) or the İstanbulkart.

By tram The European side has two tram lines, one running from Kabataş through Sultanahmet to outlying suburbs; buy *jetons* (3TL) from a booth before you enter the platform. The other "toy" tram runs along Istiklâl Cad from Beyoğlu to Taksim using an antique tram; pay with a *jeton* or the İstanbulkart (3TL).

Dolmuş *Dolmuşes* have their point of departure and destination displayed somewhere about the windscreen or painted on the bonnet. Several depart the streets around Taksim Square to various points in the city, useful for avoiding the trek downhill to the river and back up again if you're heading to Sultanahmet.

By boat Regular ferries run between Eminönü and Karaköy on the European side, and Üsküdar, Kadıköy and Haydarpaşa in Asia; buy your ticket (3TL one-way) from the dockside kiosks. Ferries depart every 15–20min from around 6am to 11.30pm; crossings take 20min. There are also sightseeing hop-on-and-off boats that cruise the Bosphorus. These leave from the Boğaz Iskelesi terminal near the Eminönü tram stop and stop at either Rumeli Kavağı or Anadolu Kavağı, distant villages up the Bosphorus on the European and Asian sides respectively. The cruise takes approximately 1hr 45min each way and the last return boat from Anadolu Kavağı in summer is late afternoon, after which you'll need to take a bus or *dolmuş*.

ACCOMMODATION

There are numerous small hotels and *pansiyons* in Sultanahmet, particularly around Yerebatan Cad and the backstreets between the Blue Mosque and the sea. Taksim is a great base, and is handy for nightlife and boutique shopping and bustling cafés. From Eminönü and Aksaray, many buses pass through either Karaköy or Taksim, or both. Kadıköy on the Asian side offers a less touristy option.

SULTANAHMET

Antique Hostel Kutlugün Sok 51 ☎0212 638 1637, ⓦantiquehostel.com; map p.1149. The rooms are a little stuffy but good-looking nonetheless. The sea-view terrace is perched atop the city like an eyrie, with an island bar and decent food available (mains 12–15TL). Wi-fi and breakfast included. All rooms have a/c. Dorm €18, double €50

Big Apple Akbıyık Cad Bayram Fırını Sok No 12 ☎0212 517 7931, ⓦhostelbigapple.com; map p.1149. The place as a whole has a slightly sombre feel but the dorm decor gets nicer as you ascend floors, and there's a great view from the roof terrace where there's a bar and music in the evenings. Dorm €15, double €85

İstanbul Hostel Kutlugün Sok 35 ☎0212 516 9380, ⓦistanbulhostel.net; map p.1149. Friendly long-running hostel, with 68 beds plus a terrace and bar. The basement dorm is justifiably popular and they offer log fires during the winter. Hostel guests get ten-percent discount in the restaurant. Dorm €14, double €70

Orient International Youth Hostel Akbıyık Cad 9 ☎0212 517 9493, ⓦorienthostel.com; map p.1149. A large hostel with 150 beds and probably the best views of

> **LIVE LIKE A LOCAL**
>
> **La Casa di Maria Pia** Yeni Carsi Cad 37, Beyoğlu (☎0541 624 5462, ⓦlacasadi mariapia.com); map p.1147. If you're planning on staying for a week or so in İstanbul then renting an apartment is a good, affordable option. This quirky spot offers five apartments, all of which are named after animals, as well as a studio flat. Each space is imaginatively quirkily decorated with *objets* collected by the owner. Fully equipped kitchenettes in the apartments. Prices start at €65 per night.

any of the area's rooftop bars. Locals play backgammon in the shade downstairs and keep an eye on the international backpacker clientele. Free wi-fi and laptops. Dorm €11, double €40

Sultan Hostel Akbıyık Cad 17 ☎0212 516 9260, ⓦsultanhostel.com; map p.1149. The bar-restaurant is a social focal point on this, the main hostel street, with music blaring and dorm beds empty until the early hours. Abrupt staff and not somewhere for a good night's sleep, but a lively spot. Fine views from the terrace and top-floor 20-bed dorm. Dorm €11, double €60

BEYOĞLU

★ **Rapunzel** Bereketzade Camii Sok 3 ☎0212 292 5034, ⓦrapunzelistanbul.com; map p.1147. Hard to find, but worth the effort. Housed in a more original building than many others, it features nineteenth-century stone walls and all manner of decorative curiosities. Staff are young and full of tips and ideas for making the most of your time in the city. Dorm €18, single €55

Sumocat Hostel Alı Hoca Aralık Sok 9 ☎0212 292 7866, ⓦsumocathostel.com; map p.1147. A small and basic hostel in Galata housed in a renovated nineteenth-century building offering funkily decorated rooms and a warm welcome. Close to the bars and nightlife of Beyoğlu. Breakfast and wi-fi included. All rooms have a/c. Kitchen. Dorm €14, double €56

KADIKÖY

Hush Hostel and Lounge Rasimpaşa Mah, Rıhtım Cad, İskele Sok 46, Kadıköy ☎0216 450 4363, ⓦhushhostel istanbul.com; map p.1147. This spacious and clean hostel has a well-equipped kitchen, roof terrace and a large back garden. Buffet breakfast, wi-fi and use of computer included. Dorm €13, single €30.

EATING

İstanbul offers all the range of food and drink you'd expect from a major world city, and provides a number of top

35

35

spots to sample Turkish delights. From high-end restaurants with prices to match to super-cheap street carts, there are plenty of ways to fill up. Fresh orange and pomegranate juice are worth picking up from street stalls; corn on the cob, less so. Sultanahmet has some decent restaurants, although the principal concentrations are in Beyoğlu and Taksim. The Balık Pazarı, particularly, behind the Çiçek Pasajı (off Istiklâl Cad), is a great area for meze, kebabs and fish. The Beşiktaş neighbourhood is also worth a visit. In Kadiköy you'll find plenty of bars (many with live music) and restaurants but relatively few tourists.

CAFÉS
İstanbul has undergone a coffee renaissance in recent years, and while strong, thick, traditional Turkish coffee is still available everywhere, international brews are increasingly sold at new coffee shops.

Cherry Bean Coffees Camekan Sok 10, Galata-Beyoğlu; map p.1147. Small and friendly independent café on a cute boutique-lined street that serves up deliciously creamy lattes, frothy cappuccinos plus teas. Daily 9am–9pm.

Cigdem Patisserie Divan Yolu Cad 62; map p.1149. One of many patisseries in the area but one of the best, with 40 years of experience serving delectable baklava (6TL per portion). Daily 8am–11pm.

★ **Evim Nargile** Meclis-i Mebusan Cad, Tophane; map p.1147. In front of İstanbul Modern (the city's principal modern art gallery) you will find a kind of *nargile* bazaar – a string of eye-poppingly colourful cafés merging into one other. This is just one of them, sporting PVC beanbags. Daily 9am–late.

★ **Heirloom Café & Market** Adile Naşit Sok 6; map p.1147. Hard to find (their only sign looks like a homeless person's piece of cardboard) but worth seeking out. A quiet spot set in the garden of a 115-year-old building offering "pour over" coffee (6TL) made from Italian espresso machines, as well as pastries, panini and salads (8–15TL). Daily 8.30am–8.30pm

GET YOUR FRESH FISH HERE
Fresh fish and seafood are delicious in İstanbul. Avoid the pricey Bosphorus restaurants and dine alongside the locals in the open air on the river banks. At both ends of **Galata Bridge** you can buy freshly grilled fish sandwiches (5TL) from fishermen with mobile carts or fresh off a bobbing boat. At the Karaköy end walk past the fish market, settle down at the plastic chairs and tables and order crisp fried calamari, a whole grilled fish, chips and salad for around 12–15TL. Times vary but food served generally until 10pm daily.

Holy Hacıoğlu Sok 1/B; map p.1147. Vintage armchairs, an indie soundtrack and haughty staff combine to make this an unashamedly hipster spot, but the lattes (7TL) are justifiably popular. Mon–Sat 10am–8pm.

Konyalı Pastanesi Ankara Cad, by the tram stop near Sirkeci train station, Eminönü; map p.1147. This place goes back to 1897 and they have their Turkish coffee down to a T. Couple it with the rich sesame *çörek*. Mon–Sat 7am–8pm.

Kronotrop Yeniçarşi Cad 5; map p.1147. There's no room to sit down in this popular spot, but their take-out flat white (6TL) and Americano (5TL) coffees are from freshly roasted single origin beans and sublime. Mon–Sat 8.30am–8pm, Sun 11am–7pm.

RESTAURANTS
SULTANAHMET
Dönerci Şahin Üsta Nuruosmaniye Kılıçlar Sok 7; map p.1149. Proper authentic kebabs (10TL) served from an establishment the size of an en-suite bathroom. Justifiably popular with locals working in the bazaar and sold out and closed up by mid-afternoon. Mon–Sat 10am–3pm.

The Pudding Shop (Lale Restaurant) Divan Yolu Cad 6; map p.1149. Dating back to 1957, this Sultanahmet hotspot became the essential meeting place for hippies making the trek to India in the 1960s. It's still popular, offering canteen-style dining (vegetarian bean dishes for 10TL; kofte at 15TL) and its famous desserts. Daily 7am–11pm.

Tarihi Sultanahmet Koftecisi Divan Yolu Cad; map p.1149. An İstanbul institution popular with celebrities (many of whose mugs beam down from the wall). You'll probably have to queue, especially as lunchtime, but the kofte (12TL) – six meaty fingers of lamb with a flash of pink inside, accompanied by chillies, chilli sauce and bread rolls – are sufficient recompense. Takeaway available too. Daily 11am–11pm.

BEYOĞLU AND EMINÖNÜ
Hala Istiklâl Cad 137; map p.1147. If you don't want to wander too far from the main Beyoğlu thoroughfare then this is the most authentic purveyor of *mantı* and *gözleme* (7–10TL) nearby. You'll see the women making the pancakes in the window. Daily until late.

Hamdi Tahmis Cad Kalçin Sok 17 ☎ 0212 528 0390; map p.1147. Third-floor restaurant next to the spice bazaar. Fresh meze and köfte are all served to a high standard. Highly recommended and touristy but the views of the Golden Horn are irresistible. Reservations advised. Mains 12–18TL. Daily 11am–midnight.

★ **Kenan Üsta Ocakbaşi** Kurabiye Sok 18; map p.1147. Master grillsman Kenan has been perfecting his art for four decades, and a visit to his basement charcoal grill to watch him in action is a must. Locals gather around the huge fire pit as he cooks meat to perfection before sending it out with a red onion and coriander garnish, lightly toasted *lavaş* (tortilla-style bread) and a variety of fresh meze. You'll leave full and contented for around 20TL. Daily 10am–2pm.

Leb i Derya Kumbaracı Yokuşu 57 6, Tünel; map p.1147. This is one of the best bar-restaurants from which to see the city from up high. The food and the cocktails are as good as the view, though prices are not budget. Expect to part with at least 50TL per head. The street is steep and narrow, leading off from the main drag, İstiklâl Cad. Mon–Thurs & Sun 11am–2am, Fri & Sat 11am–3am.

Lokanta Helvetia General Yazgan Sok 8/a; map p.1147. It may be small but the buffet-style lunches and dinners make this one of Beyoğlu's best bargains (it's 12TL/plate). Mon–Sat 8am–10pm.

DRINKING AND NIGHTLIFE

Backpackers tend to gather in the bars on Akbıyık Cad in Sultanahmet, but Beyoğlu is a much better choice, especially around Nevizade Sok where you'll find a hip arty international crowd hanging out. In Kadıköy go to Kadife Sok, aka "bar street", for the liveliest places.

BARS

★ **360** Misir Apartmani 32 309, İstiklâl Cad, Tünel ⓦ 360istanbul.com; map p.1147. Actually a restaurant, bar and club, as its name suggests this place has panoramic views best appreciated at night. At weekends the place rocks till the small hours, but it's really all about the view. Mon–Thurs noon–2am, Fri noon–4pm & 6pm–4am, Sat 6pm–4am, Sun 6pm–2.30am.

Akdeniz Nevizade Sok 25, Beyoğlu; map p.1147. Rambling, multistorey student bar, with rock music and cheap drinks. Some of the artwork is a bit dodgy but it's a great spot to chill out with friends – or on your own – with an Efes or two. Daily until late.

Badehane General Yazgan Sok 5; map p.1147. A popular, bohemian student spot specializing in cheap beer and live bands in the winter. One of the top spots in Beyoğlu for easy-on-the-wallet boozing. Daily 9am–2am.

Cozy Pub & Restaurant Divan Yolu Cad 66; map p.1149. A dark wood-panelled bar on a corner perfect for people-watching that's been serving the locals and tourists alike since 1846. Order some Turkish or international food (20–30TL) or just a beer (7TL) and observe the human traffic flowing by. Daily 10am–2am.

Gizli Bahçe Nevizade Sok 27, Beyoğlu; map p.1147. Cutting-edge dance music in a dilapidated Ottoman town-house bar. Probably looks like a squat in daylight. This is hipster İstanbul, with languidly cool staff. Daily noon–2am.

Karga Kadife Sok 16, Kadıköy; map p.1147. A hip yet friendly bar spread across several floors and furnished with lots of dark chunky wood tables. DJs and live music. Daily 11am–2am.

Lokal 4 Tünel Meydanı, Tünel; map p.1147. A chic spot on a quieter street offering drinks in semi-darkness and a variety of main meals for around 20TL. Mon–Thurs 7.30am–1am, Fri & Sat 7.30am–5am, Sun 10am–1am.

CLUBS

Babylon Şehbender Sok 3, Asmalı Mescit Tünel, Beyoğlu ⓦ babylon.com.tr; map p.1147. More of a gig and performance venue than a club, it attracts the most exciting, alternative Turkish and international acts. Tues–Thurs 9.30pm–2am, Fri & Sat 10pm–3am.

Dogzstar Kartal Sok 3, Kat 3 ⓦ dogzstar.com; map p.1147. A pioneering club on the city's music scene, spread over three floors, which seeks out innovative, genre-bending musicians and bands. Entrance fee varies depending on acts. Daily 6pm–5am.

Peyote Sahne Sok 24, Beyoğlu ⓦ peyote.com.tr; map p.1147. Run by people in bands (generally a good sign), this live music club boasts several floors and a much-needed roof terrace for cooling after. Beers are around 7TL and entry charges start from 10TL. Daily 10pm–4am.

ENTERTAINMENT

For listings pick up monthly *Time Out İstanbul* from newsstands, bookshops, hotels and hostels.

AFM Fitaş İstiklal Cad 24–26. A popular ten-screen cinema near Taksim Square, with a pub upstairs. Open daily; Wed is discount day.

Akbank Culture and Arts Centre (Akbanksanat) İstiklal Cad 8, Beyoğlu. A multipurpose centre boasting café, dance studio, music room, library and theatre. The centre hosts film festivals and the annual Akbank Jazz Festival Tues–Sun 10.30am–7.30pm.

Garajistanbul Kaymakan Reşit Bey Sok 11, Beyoğlu. A hip performing arts venue in a converted car park, offering cutting-edge films, art projects and workshops. Opening hours vary depending on the programme.

SHOPPING

İstanbul is famous for its bazaars, where you can pick up pretty much anything, from mass-produced trinkets and souvenirs to hand-woven carpets. Shops lining İstiklâl Cad are the place to head for clothes (you'll find European and American brands here) and the network of narrow streets in Beyoğlu is home to numerous boutiques, secondhand and vintage shops, as well as owner-maker artist studios where you can buy one-off craft items for affordable prices.

BAZAARS

Arasta Bazaar Mimar Mehmet Ağa Cad 14, Sultanahmet; map p.1149. Good for handmade crafts and carpets. Daily from 10am.

35

35

Mısır Çarşısı (Egyptian Spice Bazaar) Çiçek Pazarı Sok, 5min southwest of Eminönü tram stop; map p.1147. Everything from spices to jewellery, natural apple tea and aphrodisiacs including chewy sweet-like blocks of Viagra. Daily 8am–7.30pm.

SHOPS

Cevahir Büyükdere Cad 22, Şişli; map p.1147. One of the biggest shopping malls in the city, spread over six floors and offering a number of food outlets and a multiplex cinema. Another open-air shopping centre, Kanyon, is located nearby at Büyükdere Cad 185. Daily 10am–10pm.

DIRECTORY

Consulates Australia, Askerocagi Cad 15, Elmadag, Şişli 34367 ☎ 0212 243 1333; New Zealand, İnönü Cad No 48 3, Taksim 80090 ☎ 0212 244 0272; UK, Meşrutiyet Caddesi No.34, Beyoğlu ☎ 0212 334 6400; US, Kaplıcalar Mevkii Sok 2, Istinye 34460 ☎ 0212 335 9000.

Hospitals American Hospital, Güzelbahçe Sok 20, Nişantaşı ☎ 0212 444 3777; International Hospital, İstanbul Cad 82, Yeşilköy ☎ 0212 468 4444.

Internet Wi-fi is available at almost every café or hostel, but numerous internet cafés dot the city. Try Adeks at Barbaros Bulvari 49.

Left luggage Facilities are available at both of the city's airports, Atatürk (18TL for a suitcase) and Sabiha Gökçen (comparable prices). Open 24 hours daily.

Police Tourist Police, Yerebatan Cad, Sultanahmet ☎ 0212 527 4503.

Post office The central office is on Büyük Postane Caddesi (☎ 0212 526 1200).

The Sea of Marmara

Despite their proximity to İstanbul, the shores and hinterland of the Sea of Marmara are relatively neglected by foreign travellers – but there are good reasons to explore the region: not least **Bursa**, the first Ottoman capital, which has some of the finest monuments in the Balkans. Many visitors also stop off at the extensive World War I battlefields and cemeteries of the **Gelibolu** peninsula (Gallipoli), using either the port of **Eceabat** as a base, or, more commonly, **Çanakkale**. The border town of **Edirne**, meanwhile, is a charming spot to break a journey into Europe.

BURSA

Draped along the leafy lower slopes of Uludağ, a mountain which towers more than 2000m above, **BURSA** – first capital of the Ottoman Empire and the burial place of several sultans – is a charming city in which to spend a few days. Gathered here are some of the finest early Ottoman monuments in Turkey, in a tidy and appealing city centre.

WHAT TO SEE AND DO

Flanked by the busy Atatürk Caddesi and the compact **Koza Parkı**, with its fountains, benches and cafés, is the heart of Bursa. On the far side looms the fourteenth-century **Ulu Camii**, whose interior is dominated by a huge *şadırvan* pool for ritual ablutions. A little way north is Bursa's covered market, the **Bedesten**, given over to the sale of jewellery and precious metals, and the **Koza Hanı**, flanking the park, still entirely occupied by silk and brocade merchants.

Yeşil Camii, Yeşil Türbe and the Art Museum

Across the river to the east, the **Yeşil Camii** (daily 8am–8.30pm) is easily the most spectacular of Bursa's imperial mosques. The nearby hexagonal **Yeşil Türbe** (daily 8am–noon & 1–7pm) contains the sarcophagus of Çelebi Mehmet I and assorted offspring. Just north of Yeşil Türbe is the small **Museum of Turkish and Islamic Art** (Tues–Sun 9am–noon & 1–7pm; 10TL), with Çanakkale ceramics, glass items and clothing. The peaceful courtyard is a nice place to chill out.

The Hisar and around

West of the centre, the **Hisar** ("citadel") district was Bursa's original nucleus. Narrow lanes wind up past dilapidated Ottoman houses, while walkways clinging to the rock face offer fabulous views. The best-preserved dwellings are a little way west in medieval **Muradiye**, where the Muradiye Külliyesi mosque and *medrese* complex was begun in 1424. This is the last imperial foundation in Bursa, although it's most famous for its tombs, set in lovingly tended gardens.

THE EVIL EYE

Take a short stroll around any Turkish town and it won't be long until you spot one of the ubiquitous **evil eye** symbols. This circular blue and white emblem with a dot in the middle is a good luck charm designed to ward off evil spirits. As well as being proudly displayed in homes and businesses, the symbol is also printed on pendants, bracelets and brooches.

ARRIVAL AND INFORMATION

By bus The bus station is 5km north on the main road to İstanbul, from where bus #38 (every 15min) runs to Koza Parkı.

Destinations Çanakkale (hourly; 5hr); İstanbul (hourly; 3hr); İznik (hourly; 2hr).

Tourist office Corner of Koza Parkı (Mon–Fri 8am–noon & 1–5pm, Sat 9am–12.30pm & 1.30–6pm; ☎0224 220 1848).

ACCOMMODATION

Hotel Çeşmeli Gümüşçeken Cad 6 ☎0224 224 1511. A Female-run place with a handy location that makes up for its somewhat quaint aesthetic. Centrally located with an excellent self-service breakfast. Double 140TL

Hotel Güneş İnebey Cad 75 ☎0224 222 1404. Cheap, clean and friendly. Extremely basic but full of character. Prices are cheaper if you can forgo a bath for the night. Breakfast is 8TL extra. Double 70TL

Kitap Evi Kavaklıdere Cad, Burçüstü Sok 21 ☎0224 225 4160, ⓦkitapevi.com.tr. This one-time bookshop has been turned into a swish boutique hotel. The place to come if you need pampering – one room boasts a private hammam. Double €85, suite with private hammam €145

EATING AND DRINKING

Everything closes pretty early in Bursa with the exception of popular baklava cafés. Sakarya Cad is a pretty cobbled street of fish and seafood restaurants that fill with post-work locals after dark. Mains around 15TL.

Çiçek Izgara Belediye Cad 15. An elegant restaurant with a slightly inflated price to match. However, the food is reliable and the main Ottoman-inspired dishes, including *köfte* and *sütlü tel kadayıfı*, are worth a try. Mains 10–15TL. Mon–Sat 10am–midnight.

Kebapçı İskender Ünlü Cad 7 ⓦiskender.com.tr. A local institution. Queues form early at lunch and the restaurant closes early, but it's a great choice for trying Bursa's speciality, the *İskender kebap* – lamb with tomato sauce, yoghurt and hot butter poured from a saucepan at the table (19.50TL). Daily 11am–6.30pm.

Safran Ortapazar Cad, Arka Sok 4, Hisar. A comfortable little restaurant in a hotel of the same name offering grilled meats, meze and vegetables in olive oil for around 30TL for a three-course meal. Daily from 6.30am to around 10pm.

ÇANAKKALE

ÇANAKKALE is a progressive, modern city celebrated for its setting on the Dardanelles and is a popular base for visiting Gelibolu (Gallipoli) and Troy. There's a big university here, and the 15,000-odd students, together with Aussie and Kiwi backpackers visiting Gallipoli, make for a busy nightlife scene. You'll find no shortage of bars, clubs and budget places to eat, and English-speaking voices drift across the seafront nightly. Almost everything of interest – park, **Naval Museum** (Tues, Wed & Fri–Sun 9am–noon & 1.30–5pm; 4TL) and **Archeological Museum** (daily 8am–noon & 1–5.30pm; 5TL) – is within walking distance of the ferry docks, close to the start of the main Demircioğlu Caddesi. Stroll past the Trojan horse on the seafront promenade near the ferry terminal; you might recognize the wooden structure from the 2004 film *Troy*.

ARRIVAL AND INFORMATION

By bus The bus station is on the coastal highway, Atatürk Cad, a 15min walk from the waterfront; if you're arriving from İstanbul, get off at the ferry terminal in the centre of the city rather than at the bus station.

Destinations İstanbul (6 daily; 5hr); İzmir (4 daily; 6hr); Selçuk (4 daily; 7hr).

By ferry Ferries run hourly between Çanakkale and Eceabat and take 25min. Tickets can be bought at the ferry terminal for 2.50TL.

CROSSING TO BULGARIA

Edirne (see p.1157) is a popular base for travellers crossing the border into **Bulgaria**. Regular buses leave from Edirne to Plovdiv and tickets cost 35–40TL. If visiting Edirne for the day, bring your passport along even if you don't intend to cross the border. Officials at the bus station may ask to see it to make sure you haven't entered Turkey illegally.

35

35

Tourist office Beside the ferry docks (daily 8.30am–5.30/7pm depending on season; ☎0286 217 1187).

ACCOMMODATION

Except for a crowded couple of weeks during the Çanakkale/Troy Festival (mid-Aug), or on ANZAC Day (April 25), when the town is inundated with Antipodeans, you'll have little trouble finding budget accommodation.

Anzac House Hostel Cumhuriyet Meydanı 61 ☎0286 213 2550, ⍟anzachouse.com. A pretty basic hostel offering well-kept rooms over several floors. Bathrooms are shared and there's no lift. Breakfast is 5TL extra. Dorm 25TL, single 45TL, double/twin 75TL.

★ **Grand Anzac Hotel** ⍟anzachotel.com. One of several Anzac hotels run by the same owners (try the Comfort Anzac, Anzac or Kervansarary – below – if this one is full). A big and buzzy popular spot in the centre of the city, with a large indoor/outdoor breakfast area and supper for €5–10. Single €40, double €55.

Kervansaray Hotel Fetvane Sok No 13 ☎0286 217 7777, ⍟otelkervansaray.com. The former home of an Ottoman judge: you'll find big plush rooms, a pretty garden and a quality buffet breakfast waiting in the morning. Be sure to get a room in the main, old building, as the annexe at the back of the garden has far less character. Single €45, double €60.

Yellow Rose Kemal Paşa Mah ☎0286 217 3343, ⍟yellowrose.4mg.com. A good-value hostel with a homely feel that lets you economize further by using the kitchen. Breakfast can be taken near the table-tennis tables in the attractive garden. Dorm 25TL, single 30TL, double 60TL.

EATING AND DRINKING

The seafront is jammed with restaurants and some of the best bars are tucked away in the streets just behind. Be sure also to seek out the *peynir helvası* – the city's famous cheese dessert – it's much tastier than it sounds.

★ **Cevahir** Fetvane Sok 15/a. Small, family-run corner café serving tasty home-style Turkish food. Buffet-style food served on small, medium and large plates (6–8TL); salad and bread included. Dishes might include aubergine

and chicken, sweet grated carrot with yogurt, or bean salad. Daily until early evening.

Gülen Pide Cumhuriyet Meydanı 27/a. Popular kebab and pizza joint on the main road leading from the ferry dock. Try the *Gülen* kebab (22TL) or a *pide* pizza (5.50–8.50TL). Their sister restaurant across the road, *Gülen Pizza*, serves conventional (and far less interesting) pizza as well as French fries and cheeseburgers. Daily 9am–10.30pm.

Sardunya Fetvane Sok 11. One of several *ev yemekleri* (home-style cooking) places, but a local's favourite offering filling stews and salads. Daily noon–10pm.

Seaside Eski Balikhane Sok 3. One of the better seafront restaurants, offering fresh fish for around 30TL per head, live entertainment and a relaxed atmosphere. Daily until around 11pm.

THE GELIBOLU (GALLIPOLI) PENINSULA

Though endowed with splendid scenery and beaches, the slender **Gelibolu** (Gallipoli) peninsula, which forms the northwest side of the Dardanelles, is known chiefly for its grim military history. In April 1915 it was the site of a plan, devised by Winston Churchill, to land Allied troops, many of them **Australian** and **New Zealand** units, with a view to putting Turkey out of the war. Huge strategic mistakes, as well as a fierce opposition headed by the gifted officer Mustafa Kemal (later known as Atatürk), led to the dismal failure of the operation, incurring massive casualties. This was the first time Australians and New Zealanders had seen action under their own commanders, and the date of the first landings, April 25, is celebrated as **ANZAC Day**.

WHAT TO SEE AND DO

The World War I battlefields and Allied cemeteries are by turns moving and

---

BATTLEFIELD TOURS

Various companies offer **battlefield tours** from Çanakkale or further afield from İstanbul or Kusadasi. Fez Travel (⍟feztravel.com) run all manner of one- to eight-day tours. Their one-day Trooper Tour to Gallipoli starts and finishes in İstanbul and includes visits to Lone Pine, ANZAC Cove and the Gallipoli Museum, and lunch in a local restaurant. It will set you back €93 (£79) but is worth shelling out for. There are special tours to coincide with the ANZAC Day service, although much is booked up for the centenary in 2015 already. Argeus Travel (⍟argeus.com) is another popular operator. If you have time, it's more relaxing to stay overnight in Çanakkale and investigate some of the local operators. The Anzac hotel chain offers tours, as does the *Anzac House Hostel* (see above).

numbing in the sheer multiplicity of graves, memorials and obelisks. The first stop on most tours is the **Kabatepe Information Centre and Museum** (daily 9am–1pm & 2–6pm; 10TL), beyond which are the **Beach**, **Shrapnel Valley** and **Shell Green** cemeteries, followed by **Anzac Cove** and **Arıburnu**, site of the ill-fated ANZAC landing. Most tourists then bear right for **Büyük Anafartalar** village and **Çonkbayırı hill**, where there's a massive New Zealand memorial and a Turkish memorial detailing Atatürk's words and deeds. Working your way back down towards the orientation centre, you pass **The Nek**, **Walker's Ridge** and **Quinn's Post**, where the trenches of the opposing forces lay within a few metres of each other: the modern road corresponds to no-man's-land.

ARRIVAL AND DEPARTURE

By bus Buses from İstanbul to Çannakale stop at Eceabat. Destinations İstanbul (6 daily; 5hr).
By ferry Ferries run hourly between Çanakkale and Eceabat and take 25min.

ACCOMMODATION

Crowded House Hostel İsmetpaşa Mah Hüseyin Avni Sok 4, Eceabat ✆ 0286 814 1565, ⓦ crowdedhousegallipoli .com. A 30min ferry ride from Çanakkale in Eceabat, this hostel offers 26 rooms all with private bathroom, and an outdoor restaurant and bar serving barbecued meat and fish. Double **€30**

EDIRNE

Bordering both Greece and Bulgaria, the small sleepy town of **EDIRNE** boasts an impressive number of elegant monuments. It springs to life for the week-long oil-wrestling festival of Kırkpınar (end of June) but is a relaxing alternative to İstanbul (some 230km southeast) at any time of year.

WHAT TO SEE AND DO

You can see the sights on foot in a day. The best starting point is the **Eski Camii** (open to visitors during daylight hours aside from prayer times, free) bang in the centre, the oldest mosque in town, begun in 1403. Just across the way, the **Bedesten** was Edirne's first covered market and was

restored in the 1980s. The beautiful **Üç Şerefeli Camii** (also open to visitors outside prayer times and free) dates from 1447 and has four idiosyncratic minarets, the tallest of which has three galleries for the muezzin. A little way east of here is the masterly **Selimiye Camii** (open daily, free), designed by Minar Sinan. Its four slender minarets, among the tallest in the world, also have three balconies; the interior is most impressive, its dome planned to surpass that of Aya Sofya in İstanbul. The main **Archeological Museum** (Tues–Sun 9am–5pm; 5TL), just northeast of the mosque, contains an assortment of Greco-Roman fragments and some Neolithic finds. A stroll south in the direction of Karaağaç, crossing the iconic Mecidiye bridge over the river Meriç, is also a pleasant way to spend a morning.

ARRIVAL AND INFORMATION

By train The train station is 5km southeast of the centre. Dolmuşes run into town from here (2TL). Destinations İstanbul twice daily (5hr).
By bus The bus station is 8km southeast of the centre. When you arrive, walk through the terminal to the car park on the other side – here you'll find dolmuşes that go to the centre of town (2TL). Get off either near the main shopping area or at the Eski Camii mosque. Destinations Ankara (10pm & 11am; 10hr); Çanakkale (4 daily; 4hr 30min); İstanbul (every 30min; 2hr 30min); İzmir (4 daily; 10hr); Plovdiv, Bulgaria (3hr).
Tourist office Hürriyet Meydani 17 (daily 8.30am–5.30pm; ✆ 0284 213 9208).

ACCOMMODATION

Efe Hotel Maarif Cad 13 Kaleiçi ✆ 0284 213 6166, ⓦ efehotel.com. Smart boutique hotel with impressive rooms, all manner of quirky knick-knacks strewn about, and an outdoor bar. Breakfast included. Double **140TL**
Hotel Aksaray Alipaşa Ortakapı Cad ✆ 0284 212 6035. A small pension with a friendly welcome, but the rooms are slightly scruffy and it feels a bit like an eldery relative's home. No breakfast. Double **85TL**
Tashan Hotel Cavusbey Mahallesi Agacpazari Cad 4 ✆ 0284 225 1413. A characterful new addition in Edirne, housed in a 500-year-old building in the centre of town. Thoughtfully renovated with cool brick walls and wooden floors. Breakfast served in a quiet courtyard. Double **90TL**

EATING AND DRINKING

Hanedan Karaağaç Mah. İki Köprü Arasi Cad 2. A

35

well-situated riverside spot offering meze from 5TL and a variety of kebabs (13–19TL). Daily until late evening.

Meşhur Edirne Ciğercisi Balıkpazarı Osmaniye Cad 43. You can have anything you want as long as it's liver, freshly floured and quickly deep-fried. Proper fast food, served with lots of onion and salad. An Edirne delicacy. Closes early evening.

Niyazi Usta Alipaşa Ortakapı Cad 9. Another renowned *ciğercis* (liver purveyor), where the fried slices (10TL) are piled high and served with *cacık* (cucumber and yoghurt, 4TL). The walls are adorned with photos of smiling celebrities. Closes at 9.30pm.

Pena Cafe Pub Alipaşa Ortakapı Cad 6. Sash windows usher cool breezes into this café-bar made up of small rooms with wooden floorboards and panelling. A youthful atmosphere in a middle-aged-feeling town. Daily 9am–1pm.

The Aegean coast

The **Aegean coast** is, in many ways, one of Turkey's most enticing destinations, home to some of the best of its antiquities and the most appealing resorts. The city of İzmir serves as a base for day-trips to nearby sights and beaches. Visitors continuing south will be spoilt for sightseeing choices as the territory is rich in Classical, Hellenistic and Roman ruins, notably **Ephesus** and the remains inland at **Hierapolis** – sitting atop the famous pools and mineral formations of **Pamukkale**. The coast itself is better down south, too, and although the larger resorts, including **Kuşadası**, have been marred by the developers, **Bodrum** still has a certain charm despite the growing number of hedonistic holidaymakers.

İZMIR

İZMIR – ancient Smyrna – was mostly burned down in the Greco-Turkish war of 1919–22, and was built pretty much from scratch afterwards. Nowadays it's Turkey's third-largest city, a booming, cosmopolitan and relentlessly modern place that's home to around four million people. Orientation can be confusing in places, but most points of interest lie near each other and walking is the most enjoyable way of exploring, especially along the waterfront.

WHAT TO SEE AND DO

İzmir doesn't have a single centre, although the district of **Konak**, where you'll find a busy park, the city bus terminal and **Konak Pier** on the waterfront, is where visitors spend most time. Head north and you'll reach the **Kültür Parkı**, a large park with regular outdoor entertainment, particularly in the summer. Continue in the same direction and you'll soon reach the district of **Alsançak** – the hub of evening entertainment with alfresco bars and restaurants and, on the seafront, the **Atatürk Museum** (Tues–Sun 8.30am–5.30pm) on Atatürk Caddesi. This beautiful nineteenth-century seafront house is where Atatürk stayed when he visited the city in the 1930s. If you fancy a walk, head south along the waterfront for about twenty minutes to the city's free elevator, **Asansör**, which has wonderful views over the city and Gulf of İzmir.

Archeological Museum and Ethnography Museum

Southwest of the Konak Camii is İzmir's **Archeological Museum** (Tues–Sun 8.30am–noon & 1–5.30pm; 8TL). The collection consists of finds from all over İzmir province, including some stunning marble statues and sarcophagi. Next door in an old Turkish house is the charming **Ethnography Museum** (Tues–Sun 8.30am–noon & 1–5.30pm; free) where you can learn about the local tradition of camel wrestling and see examples of Anatolian crafts such as clog-making, lacemaking and the ubiquitous "evil eye" beads.

Kemeraltı Bazaar

Immediately east of Konak is **Kemeraltı**, İzmir's bazaar. The main drag, Anafartalar Caddesi, is lined with clothing, jewellery and shoe shops; Fevzipaşa Bulvarı and the alleys just south are strong on leather garments.

35

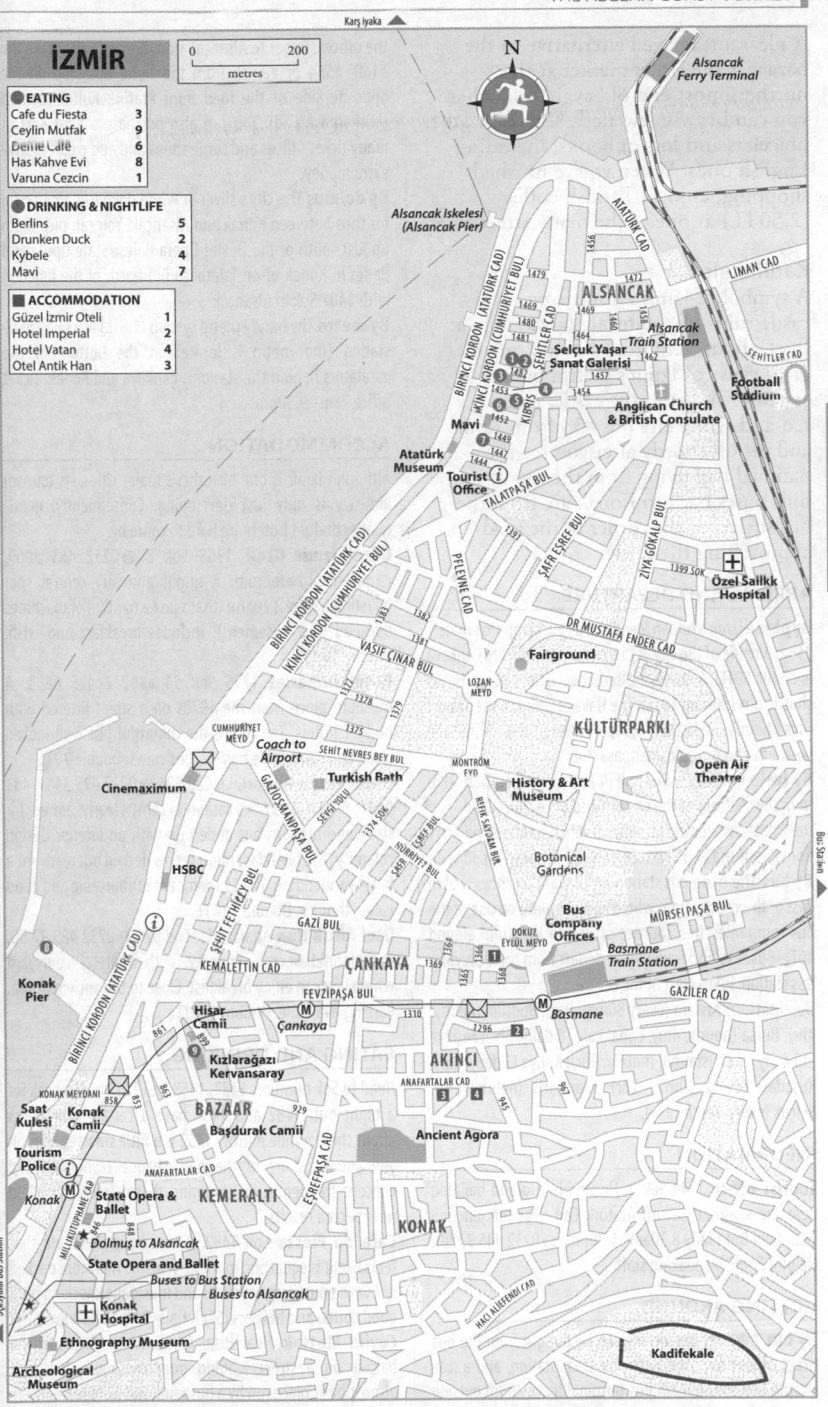

İZMİR

0 — 200 metres

● EATING
Cafe du Fiesta	3
Ceylin Mutfak	9
Deniz Café	6
Has Kahve Evi	8
Varuna Cezcin	1

● DRINKING & NIGHTLIFE
Berlins	5
Drunken Duck	2
Kybele	4
Mavi	7

■ ACCOMMODATION
Güzel İzmir Oteli	1
Hotel Imperial	2
Hotel Vatan	4
Otel Antik Han	3

Karşıyaka

N

Alsancak Ferry Terminal

Alsancak İskelesi (Alsancak Pier)

ALSANCAK

Selçuk Yaşar Sanat Galerisi

Alsancak Train Station

Football Stadium

Anglican Church & British Consulate

Mavi

Atatürk Museum

Tourist Office

Özel Sağlık Hospital

Fairground

KÜLTÜRPARKI

Coach to Airport

Cinemaximum

Turkish Bath

History & Art Museum

Open Air Theatre

HSBC

Botanical Gardens

Bus Company Offices

Basmane Train Station

Konak Pier

ÇANKAYA

Hisar Camii

Çankaya

Basmane

AKINCI

Kızlarağazı Kervansaray

Konak Pier

Saat Kulesi

Konak Camii

Başdurak Camii

BAZAAR

Ancient Agora

Tourism Police

Konak

State Opera & Ballet

KEMERALTI

Dolmuş to Alsancak

State Opera and Ballet

KONAK

Buses to Bus Station

Buses to Alsancak

Konak Hospital

Ethnography Museum

Archeological Museum

Kadifekale

35

A pleasant, relaxed alternative to the bazaar is the street market at the northernmost end of Sevgi Yolu, where you can browse jewellery, scarves, leather bracelets and lots of books, including English ones. When you've finished shopping, enjoy a Turkish coffee (2.50TL) at one of the many street cafés.

Kadifekale

A symbol of İzmir's historic past, the castle ruins of **Kadifekale** (always open; free), about 3km from Konak, provide great views of İzmir's metropolitan expanse. To get to the castle, take a red-and-white city bus #33 from Konak and get off shortly after you see the national flag flying from the top of the hill. Buses back to Konak are from the bus shelter at the corner of the road approaching the castle.

ARRIVAL AND DEPARTURE

By plane İzmir's Adnan Menderes airport is approximately 15km outside of the city. A taxi from the airport to Çankaya is about 50TL. A cheaper alternative is to catch a Havaş shuttle bus (30min; 10TL). The Havaş service to the airport runs hourly 3.30am–11.30pm every day from the northern end of Gaziosmanpaşa Bul.

By train Intercity trains pull in at Basmane station, 1km from the seafront at the eastern end of Fevzipaşa Bul.
Destinations Denizli (3 daily; 5–6hr); İstanbul via ferry from Bandirma (1 daily; 10hr); Selçuk (8 daily; 1hr 30min).

By bus The main bus station for onward journeys is 8km east of the centre, from where you can jump on one of the bus companies' free shuttles or grab a taxi from around 40TL. Buses to and from Çeşme depart from the Uçkuyular bus station 10km west of the centre.
Destinations Ankara (every 30min; 8hr); Bodrum (hourly; 4hr); Bursa (hourly; 6hr); Çanakkale (8 daily; 5hr); Fethiye (15 daily; 7hr); İstanbul (hourly; 9hr); Konya (1 daily; 8hr); Kuşadası (every 30min; 2hr); Marmaris (hourly; 4hr); Selçuk (every 40min; 1hr).

INFORMATION

Tourist office 1344 Sok 2. Housed in a grand building near the seafront just off Atatürk Cad near the junction with Gazi Bul (daily 8.30am–5.30pm; ☎0232 445 7390). Helpful English-speaking staff.

GETTING AROUND

By bus Intercity bus tickets can be bought from the bus ticket offices near the Basmane train station, and a free shuttle bus to the main bus terminal leaves from outside the offices. To get to Alsancak from Konak (1.8TL) take the #169, #554 or #8, all from the same bus stop on the opposite side of the road from Atatürk Kültur Merkezi (Mithatpaşa Cad). You can also purchase a Kent Kart at many ticket offices and some shops and add credit to save extra money.

By dolmuş The city's silver or white *dolmuşes* are usesful for trips between Konak and Alsancak. You can pick them up just south of the Devlet Opera Balesi/State Opera and Ballet in Konak or on Talatpaşa Bul north of the junction with 1407 Sok in Alsancak.

By metro The handy metro system (1.8TL) links Basmane station (the metro is located at the bottom of the escalators behind the station), Çankaya and Konak. Ticket office 7am–9.30pm.

ACCOMMODATION

Although İzmir is one of Turkey's major cities, its tourism industry is only just developing. Consequently, good-quality budget hotels are hard to come by.

Güzel İzmir Oteli 1368 Sok 8 ☎0232 483 5069, ⓦguzelizmirhotel.com. A bright and airy central spot boasting a fitness centre (that's just a handful of machines dumped in a basement). Includes breakfast and wi-fi. Double 100TL

Hotel Imperial 1296 Sok 54 ☎0232 425 6883. A museum piece from the 1970s on a street littered with budget hotels. The rooms are mournful but well looked after, and some have half-decent views. Double 70TL

Hotel Vatan Anafartalar Cad 626 ☎0232 425 3461, 483 0637 & 484 5681, ⓦvatanotel.com. Clearly aimed for sleek and modern but ended up with an interior design calamity; the breakfast room seems decked out ready for a fairytale wedding. The 25 rooms are comfortable and good value, though. Double 120TL

Otel Antik Han Anafartalar Cad 626 ☎0232 489 27 50, ⓦotelantikhan.com. Friendly, with a pretty courtyard where you can enjoy breakfast. Close to the ancient agora. Parking available. Double 110TL

EATING AND DRINKING

Head to Sok numbers 1482, 1453 and 1452 in Alsancak for a night out. 1482 and 1453 have a certain grunginess about them, while narrow 1452 is a little smarter, though still young. Many of the bars change ownership and concept frequently, so exploring these streets can yield unexpected results.

Cafe du Fiesta Sok 1482. A wood-panelled café that feels like it is squatting in a 150-year-old mansion, packed out with teenagers, students and musicians knocking back good coffee and burgers (5TL). Daily 9am–11.30pm.

Ceylin Mutfak Near Hisar Camii. At the heart of the bazaar on a street leading from the mosque is this atmospheric place run by a husband-and-wife team. There are only three tables outside. The *köfte* (5TL) is grilled to perfection. Daytime only.

★ **Defne Café** 1452 Sok. Cosy little place on a cute side street where Efes is 6TL and a steak sandwich is just 9TL. Open for lunch and dinner.

Has Kahve Evi Konak Pier. A lovely setting on a breezy terrace at the far end of the pier. Take a look and weigh up whether the view merits the inflated price of the coffee. Open until early evening.

Varuna Cezcin 1482 Sok. A busy bar and restaurant full of students taking advantage of happy hour (until 9pm) and chowing down on international cuisine including Pad Thai (12TL). Licence plates all over the walls and booming rock music add to the atmosphere. Meal and a drink around 20TL. Open until late.

NIGHTLIFE

Opening hours vary, but most clubs and bars stay open until midnight and beyond.

Berlins Sok 1453. Jugs of mojitos and a thumping reggae and r'n'b soundtrack are the order of the day here.

Drunken Duck 1482 Sok 15. A small but friendly bar with live music and mildly inebriated locals.

Kybele 1453 Sok 28. Live music club specializing in alt-rock and jazz with a tiny stage and super-speedy bar staff. Entrance price varies depending on who's playing (generally 15–30TL).

ENTERTAINMENT

Bostanlı Karşıyaka Açıkhava Tiyatrosu Cemal Gürsel Cad. Hasan Ali Yücel Blv. Large concert hall hosting regular pop concerts in Konak Pier.

Cinemaximum Atatürk Cad 19. Cinema with recent Hollywood releases. Student discount available.

Mavi Cumhuriyet Bul 206, Alsançak. Music venue in an atmospheric old building. Things kick off around 10pm.

State Opera and Ballet Milli Kütüphane Cad, Konak ☎0232 484 3692. A diverse programme of concerts ranging from classical to jazz and pop.

KUŞADASI

KUŞADASI is Turkey's most bloated resort, yet the old town has its charms even when the place is heaving with the football shirts of numerous boozy Brits and Australians. Ferry services link it with the Greek island of Sámos, while the resort is a port of call for Aegean cruise ships, which disgorge vast numbers in summer.

WHAT TO SEE AND DO

Liman Caddesi runs from the ferry port up to Atatürk Bulvarı, the main harbour esplanade, from which pedestrianized Barbaros Hayrettin Bulvarı ascends the hill. To the left of here, the **Kale** district, huddled inside the town walls, is the oldest and most appealing part of town, with a mosque and some fine traditional houses. Kuşadası's most famous beach, **Kadınlar Denizi**, 3km southwest of town, is a popular strand, usually too crowded for its own good in season. The best beach in the area is **Pamucak**, at the mouth of the Küçük Menderes River, 15km north, an exposed 4km stretch of sand that is comparatively less developed; in season it's served by regular *dolmuşes* from both Kuşadası and Selçuk.

ARRIVAL AND INFORMATION

By bus The combined *dolmuş* and long-distance bus station is about 2km out, past the end of Kahramanlar Caddesi on the ring road to Söke, while the *dolmuş* stop is closer to the centre on Adnan Menderes Bulvarı.

Tourist office The tourist office (Mon–Fri 8am–5pm; summer also Sat & Sun; ☎0256 614 1103) is right by the ferry port.

ACCOMMODATION AND EATING

Avlu Cephane Sok 15/a. Serves a wide range of kebabs, stews, steamed vegetables and meze in an outdoor courtyard (mains 7–10TL). Daily 8am–midnight.

Sezgin Hotel and Guesthouse Arsanlar Cad 68 ☎0256 614 4225, ☞sezginhotel.com. A great, value spot boasting a lovely garden and swimming pool. Double **€35**

35

FERRIES TO GREECE

Every day in high season (April to October), a morning (8.30am) and afternoon (5pm) ferry leaves from Kuşadası to the Greek island of **Sámos** (€35 one-way, €40 day return, €55 open return; 1hr 15min). Returning ferries depart from Greece at the same times. Meander on Kıbrıs Cad (right by the ferry port ☎0256 614 3859, ☞meandertravel.com) runs up to two boats daily in summer. From Sámos, a popular follow-on destination is the party island **Íos** (see p.558). Tickets from Sámos to Íos can be bought from ITSA or By Ship travel agents located near the pier.

35

SELÇUK

Once a small farming village, **SELÇUK** was catapulted into the tourism limelight by its proximity to the ruins of **Ephesus**, once the wealthy capital of Roman Asia and now a UNESCO World Heritage Site. Pleasant Pamucak beach (see p.1161) is easily accessible by a *dolmuş* ride or by bike (9km).

WHAT TO SEE AND DO

The sights and attractions in Selçuk itself can easily be seen in a day. **Ayasoluk** hill (daily 8.30am–5.30pm; 5TL) to the northwest of the centre is the traditional burial place of St John the Evangelist, who died here around 100 AD; it boasts the remains of a basilica built by Justinian that was one of the largest Byzantine churches in existence. Just behind the tourist office, the **Efes Archeological Museum** (due to reopen in summer 2014) has galleries of finds from Ephesus, while beyond the museum, 600m along the road towards Ephesus, are the scanty remains of the **Artemision** or sanctuary of Artemis.

Ephesus

With the exception of Pompeii, **Ephesus** (Efes in Turkish; daily 8am–5.30pm; 25TL), 3km southwest of Selçuk, is the largest and best-preserved ancient city around the Mediterranean. Originally situated close to a temple devoted to the goddess Artemis, its location by a fine

---

SURVIVING EPHESUS

Ephesus is Turkey's most popular tourist site and often swarming with visitors, mostly from the cruise ships which drop off in Kuşadasi. Be sure to visit early in the morning to avoid the worst of the crowds and blistering heat (you can easily walk to the site, but most accommodation offers free drop-offs from Selçuk). If you're tempted to hire a guide, do so at the tourist office in Selçuk rather than the sharks touting their services at the site itself (audioguides are available but there are few information boards). Remember to bring a hat and water (there's next to no shade).

---

harbour was the source of its wealth and resulted in an array of fine buildings.

In the centre of the site is the **Arcadian Way**, which was once lined with hundreds of shops and illuminated at night. The nearby theatre has been partly restored to allow its use for open-air concerts; climb to the top for views of the surrounding countryside. About halfway along Marble Street is a footprint, a female head and a heart etched into the rock – an alleged signpost for a brothel. Across the intersection looms the elegant **Library of Celsus**, erected by the consul Gaius Julius Aquila between 110 and 135 AD. Just uphill, a Byzantine fountain looks across the Street of the Curetes to the **public latrines**, a favourite photo opportunity with visitors.

ARRIVAL AND DEPARTURE

By train The train station lies a little east of the aqueduct. Destinations İstanbul (5 daily; 10hr); İzmir (6 daily; 1hr 30min).

By bus and dolmuş The bus and *dolmuş* terminal is a few mins' walk south from the centre of town. Ephesus is a quick taxi ride or 40min walk away.
Destinations by bus: Bodrum (3–4 direct daily; 3hr); Marmaris (one direct daily; 4hr). By dolmuş: Kuşadasi (frequent til 8–9pm; 30min); Pamucak beach (hourly; 30min); Şirince (every 30min until 7pm).

INFORMATION

Tourist office Opposite the bus terminal. Efficient rather than helpful, and no use for hotel or restaurant recommendations (daily 8.30am–noon & 1–5.30pm; winter Sat & Sun only; ☎0232 892 6945.

ACCOMMODATION

ANZ Guesthouse 1064 Sok 12 ☎0232 892 6050, ⊚anzguesthouse.com. Popular backpacker choice with bicycles for rent. Free breakfast buffet on roof terrace. Check a few rooms as some are better than others. Dorm €10, double €30

Atilla's Getaway Acarlar Köyü ☎0232 892 3847, ⊚atillasgetaway.com. A long-term favourite offering a variety of accommodation options, swimming pool, bar and numerous hammocks. A little out of town but the management shuttle to and from Selçuk centre several times daily. Campsite €8, dorm €16, single €26

Boomerang Guest House 1047 Sok 10 ☎0232 892 4879, ⊚ephesusboomerangguesthouse.com. A centrally located and spotlessly clean establishment comprising a number of private rooms and a decent twelve-bed dorm. There's a roof terrace and residents get ten-percent discount in the restaurant. Dorm **€10**, double **€40**

★ **Homeros Pansiyon** Atatürk Mah Asmalı/1048 Sok 17 ☎0232 892 3995, ☜homerospension.com. This super-friendly family-run *pension* is one of the best places to stay in the area. The bedrooms (some with a balcony, all with a/c) are cosy and are richly decorated with colourful carpets, blankets and knick-knacks. Roof terrace has fabulous views of the town. Home-cooked dinner 18TL. Free pick-up from the bus or train station and bikes available. Double **80TL**

Nişanyan House Şirince village ☎0232 898 3208, ☜nisanyan.com. A peaceful boutique hotel high on the hillside with a private hammam and spectacular views. Rooms are individually decorated and the traditional Turkish breakfast is made on site by the talented kitchen staff. Double **120TL**

Wallabies Hostel Cengiz Topel Cad 2 ☎0232 892 3204, ☜wallabieshostel.com. A family affair, headed up by Mehmet (aka Geoff). Some rooms have views of the Roman aqueduct and nesting storks (the best is room 305). Includes breakfast. Single **30TL**, double **50TL**

EATING AND DRINKING

Café Carpouza Argenta Cad 6. This popular café is run by the municipality so prices for the coffees and beer are reasonable. A meatball sandwich will fill you up for around 5TL. Daily 9am–midnight.

★ **Mehmet and Alibaba Kebab House** 1047 Sok 4/a ☎0232 892 3872. By far the most popular restaurant in town. While the food is decent enough (ranging from kebabs at 13TL to generous plates of mixed veg meze 10TL), the owners are the reason to visit. Mehmet is particularly chatty and affable, and will run you to Ephesus on his motorbike, picking you up when you're finished. Apple tea, orange tea and regular tea are free to diners. Daily 9am–11.30pm.

Old House 1005 Sok 1/a. Carefully prepared mains including grills and Turkish standards 10–14TL served up in a shady little garden courtyard. Daily 8am–midnight.

Selçuk Köftesi Şahabettin Dede Cad. Easily overlooked because of its basic, rather bland appearance but, with forty years' experience behind it, this place is all about the food. Smoky bread cooked in a wood oven, known as Şirince bread, accompanies mains. Soups 4–5TL, meaty mains around 10TL and a mixed grill for 15TL. Daily 6am–10pm.

BODRUM

In the eyes of its devotees, **BODRUM** – ancient Halicarnassos – with its whitewashed houses and subtropical gardens, is an attractive Turkish resort, a quality outfit in comparison to its upstart Aegean rivals. However, it's increasingly overrun by boozy tourists at one end and chic sailor types at the other.

WHAT TO SEE AND DO

The town's centrepiece is the **Castle of St Peter** (Tues–Sun 9am–6.30pm; 20TL), built by the Knights of St John over a Selçuk fortress between 1437 and 1522. Inside, the various towers house a **Museum of Underwater Archeology**, which includes coin and jewellery rooms, Classical and Hellenistic statuary, and Byzantine relics retrieved from two wrecks. The **Carian Princess Hall** (Tues–Fri 9am–noon & 2–4.30pm; 5TL extra) displays the skeleton and sarcophagus of a fourth-century BC noblewoman unearthed in 1989. There is also the **Glass Wreck Hall** (Tues–Fri 9am–noon & 2–4.30pm; 5TL extra) containing the wreck and cargo of an ancient Byzantine ship, which sank near Marmaris. Note that some of these displays may be closed without warning, though you can always bank on enjoying the fantastic views of the water from various vantage points in the castle. Immediately north of the castle lies the bazaar, from where you can stroll up to Türkkuyusu Caddesi to see what's left of the **Mausoleum** (Tues–Sun 8.30am–4.30pm; 8TL), the burial place of Mausolus, ruler of Halicarnassos from 376–353 BC and the origin of the word mausoleum.

ARRIVAL AND DEPARTURE

By bus The bus station is 500m up Cevat Şakir Cad, which divides the town roughly in two.
Destinations Fethiye (6 daily; 5min); İstanbul (hourly; 12hr); İzmir (hourly; 4hr); Kuşadası (3 daily; 3hr); Marmaris (14 daily; 3hr 15min); Selçuk (hourly; 3hr).
By ferry Ferries dock at the jetty west of the castle. Bodrum Ferryboat Association (☎0252 316 0882, ☜bodrumferryboat.com) runs ferries to Kos and Datça, while Bodrum Express Lines (☎0252 316 1087, ☜bodrumexpresslines.com) handles hydrofoils to Kos, Rhodes and domestic services to Marmaris.
Destinations Datça (two daily; 90min); Kos (2 daily; 1hr); Rhodes (daily; 2hr).

35

PAMUKKALE AND THE "GATEWAY TO HELL"

The rock formations of **PAMUKKALE** (literally "Cotton Castle"), 190km east of Selçuk, are well worth a detour, a series of white terraces saturated with dissolved calcium bicarbonate, bubbling up from the feet of the Çal Dağı mountains beyond. The spring emerges in what was once the ancient city of **Hierapolis**, the ruins of which would merit a stop even if they weren't coupled with the natural phenomenon. Access to the travertine terraces is 20TL, while up on the plateau is Pamukkale Thermal Baths, home to the sacred pool of the ancients (daily 8am–6.30pm; 30TL), open for bathing in the 35°C mineral water.

The archeological zone of Hierapolis lies behind the Pamukkale terraces and admission is by the same entrance fee. Its main features include a **Temple of Apollo** and the infamous, albeit inconspicuous, **plutonium cavern**, where a toxic mixture of sulphur dioxide and carbon dioxide brews. Archeologists have recently noted that the spot matches several historical descriptions of the "gateway to Hell".

35

INFORMATION

Tourist office Baris Square 48, close to the jetty (Mon–Fri 8am–noon, 1–5.30pm; summer daily 8.30am–5.30pm ☎0252 316 1091). Friendly staff will help you book accommodation and boat trips.

ACCOMMODATION

Bodrum Backpackers Atatürk Cad 37/b ☎0252 313 2762, ⊕bodrumbackpackers.net. Lively backpackers' hostel– not the place to go if you want some beauty sleep. During the summer, when all the beds are full, you can sleep on the terrace for 15TL. Breakfast and wi-fi included. Dorm/singles 35TL, double 40TL

Hotel Güleç Üçkuyular Cad 22 ☎0252 316 5222, ⊕hotelgulec.com. Pretty standard accommodation considering the price, but nice and secluded from the chaos. It's on a quiet street a short walk from the beach and bars. Breakfast included. Double 140TL, triple 160TL

Hotel Kalender Cevat Şakir Mah İnönü Cad Bitez Sok 15 ☎0252 319 5229, ⊕hotelkalender.com. In the Gumbet neighbourhood, a little way out, but free pick-up from the bus station is offered. Bright, simple rooms with chairs and tables set outside around a central swimming pool. Breakfast included. Single €40, double €60

Mars Otel Turgut Reis Cad, İmbat Çıkmazı 29. ☎0252 316 6559, ⊕marsotel.com. Clean, friendly and great value – and quiet, despite its central location. Free rides to the *otogar* and free Turkish bath if you stay for at least three nights. Small swimming pool and bikes for rent. Breakfast included. Single 90TL, double 118TL

EATING AND DRINKING

Bodrum is packed with places hugging the shoreline, and offers numerous opportunities to dine in the dark on the sand. Many places are complacent and pricey but there are a few gems to be found if you dig a little.

Berk Balık Cumhuriyet Cad 167. A fish and meze restaurant at the far end of the bar strip. Quality varies but it's always busy and buzzy. Mains 15–20TL. Open late.

Otantik Ocabaşı Atatürk Cad Çarşı Mah 46. Decent prices considering the location (opposite *Bodrum Backpackers*), probably thanks to the very high turnover. Offers all the grilled meats and *pide* options you'd expect from a traditional Turkish spot. Daily until around midnight.

Ox Wine and Burger Bar Cumhuriyet Cad 175. A decent burger joint with a spectacular wine list, if you're starting to tire of Efes and kebabs. Not too pricey considering the location. Gourmet burger, chips saltier than the Dead Sea and beer around 30TL. Daily noon–midnight.

NIGHTLIFE

Hadigari 1025 Sok 2. A Bodrum stalwart that still pulls in 2000-odd punters on summer nights. Find it at the marina near Bodrum Castle and dance till daybreak under the stars. Open til 5am on weekends.

Halikarnas Far end of bar strip, near *Mavi* and *Berk Balık*. A renowned and recently renovated nightclub with an entry price to match (expect to pay at least 30TL to get in and bring a stuffed wallet if you want to drink). However, the place is enormous, the atmosphere electric, and varied themed shows will keep you on your feet until dawn. Daily 10pm–late.

The Mediterranean coast

The first stretch of Turkey's Mediterranean coast, dominated by the Akdağ and Bey mountain ranges and known as the "**Turquoise Coast**", is its most popular, famed for its pine-studded shore, minor ruins and beautiful scenery. In the west, **Fethiye** is a perfect base for visits to **Ölüdeniz**, **Kaya Köyü** and **Butterfly Valley**. The scenery becomes increasingly spectacular as you head towards the site of **Olympos**, and **Kaş**, which offers great scuba diving, before reaching the port and major city of **Antalya**.

FETHIYE

FETHIYE is well sited for access to some of the region's ancient sites, many of which date from the time when this area was the independent kingdom of Lycia. The best **beaches**, around **Ölüdeniz lagoon**, are now much too crowded for comfort, but Fethiye is still a charming market town and has been able to spread to accommodate increased tourist traffic.

WHAT TO SEE AND DO

Fethiye itself occupies the site of the Lycian city of Telmessos, little of which remains other than the impressive ancient theatre, and a number of Lycian rock tombs on the hillside. You can also visit the remains of the medieval fortress behind the harbour area of town. In the centre of town the tiny **museum** (Tues–Sun 8am–5pm; 3TL) has some fascinating exhibits from local sites, a good ethnographic section and will keep you occupied for about an hour. There are numerous boats on the harbour offering **island-hopping trips** (see below).

Kaya Köyü

One of the most dramatic sights in the area is the ghost village of **Kaya Köyü** (Levissi), 7km out of town, served by *dolmuşes* from the old bus station. The village was abandoned in 1923, when its Anatolian-Greek population was relocated, and all you see now is a hillside covered with more than two thousand ruined cottages and an attractive basilica.

Ölüdeniz lagoon

The warm waters of **Ölüdeniz lagoon** make for pleasant swimming although the crowds can reach saturation level in high season – in which case the nearby beaches of Belceğiz and Kidrak are better bets. Ölüdeniz is about two hours on foot from Kaya Köyü or a thirty-minute *dolmuş* ride from Fethiye.

ARRIVAL AND DEPARTURE

By bus Fethiye's bus station is 2km east of the centre.
Destinations İstanbul (3 daily; 14hr); Kaş (hourly; 4hr); Marmaris (hourly; 3hr).
By dolmuş *Dolmuşes* leave from near the mosque (Yeni Camii), which is beyond the town hall and the PTT on Atatürk Cad.
Destinations Kaya Köyü (30min; hourly); Ölüdeniz (hourly; 30min).

INFORMATION, TOURS AND ACTIVITIES

Tourist office Close to the theatre, near the harbour at Fevzi Kakmak Cad 9/d (summer: Mon–Fri 8am–8pm & Sat 10am–5pm; winter: Mon–Fri 8am–noon, 1–5pm; ☎0252 612 1527).
Tours Daily boat tours generally cost 40–60TL, lasting from 10.30am–6.30pm. Tickets can be bought through your accommodation.
Scuba diving Divers Delight (ⓦdiversdelight.com) runs several diving courses as well as try-a-dive day-trips (€50) and snorkelling for non-divers (€15).

ACCOMMODATION

Duygu Pension Karagözler Ordu Cad 54 ☎0252 614 3563, ⓦduygupension.com. Eleven rooms, some with amazing views of the bay, kept in great condition. Swimming pool and free bus station pick-up. Family-run and friendly. Double 80TL
★ **Ferah Pension (Monica's Place)** Karagözler Orta Yol 23 ☎0252 614 2816, ⓦferahpension.com. This *pansiyon* has lovely sea views from the upstairs rooms. There's also a beautiful garden in which to while away many an hour chatting with the affable owner Monica and her husband. Free transfers from the bus station. Excellent food. Double 80TL
Irem Pansiyon Fevzi Çakmak Cad 61 ☎0252 614 3985, ⓦirempansiyon.com. A rather hotel-like *pansiyon*, the rooms are bland and basic but fine, with a/c and en suite. Double 50TL
V-Go Guest House Fevzi Çakmak Cad 109 ☎0252 612 5409, ⓦv-gohotel.com. Large and convivial hotel offering 34 rooms, two bars, pool and nightly barbecues (grilled meat and meze 15–20TL). A good place to meet fellow travellers. Dorm €10, double €36

EATING AND DRINKING

Capkin B Hamam Sok 16. This place is heaving after 11pm with locals, expats and in-the-know tourists. It's an upstairs bar accessed by a stairs leading off a side street and rocks with live music from Turkish bands most nights (you'll probably hear it before you see it). Daily noon–late.
Car Cemetery Bar Hamam Sok 33. Look out for the car bonnet protruding incongruously from the wall along

35

Fethiye's liveliest street. This is a hip spot where shots and tasty cocktails are the order of the day (or night). Tues–Sat 6pm–4am.

Meğri Lokantasi Carşı Cad. This *lokanta*, a humbler version of *Meğri Restaurant* round the corner, has a nice setting by the duck pond and delivers good traditional Turkish grub. Mains 15–20TL. Daily 9.30am–1am.

Mercan Balık Restaurant Hal ve Balık Pazarı, Zabıta Bürosu Yanı. One of numerous restaurants surrounding the little fish market which will cook the fish you buy and give you salad and bread into the bargain. The fish market can get popular with tourists so arrive early. Open daily.

★ **The Duck Pond** Eski Cami Sok 41. Bag a table next to the pond in welcome shade, sip on a beer (5TL) and nibble on a plate of the best mixed meze in town (20TL for 2–3 people) or treat yourself to a Turkish casserole. Daily till late.

KAŞ

KAŞ sprang to prominence after about 1850, when it established itself as a Greek fishing and timber port. It is beautifully located, nestled in a small curving bay below rocky cliffs. But what was once a sleepy fishing village is fast becoming an **adventure-sports centre** for backpackers, with nightlife to match (see below).

WHAT TO SEE AND DO

Scattered around the streets and to the west are the remains of ancient **Antiphellos**, one of the few Lycian cities to bear a Greek name, small in number but nevertheless impressive. Five hundred metres west of town lies an almost complete **Hellenistic theatre**, behind which is a unique Doric tomb named Kesme Mezar, again almost completely intact. Kaş is also well situated for the nearby ruins of Kekova and Patara. On Fridays there is a big market behind the bus station.

ARRIVAL AND INFORMATION

By bus and dolmuş All buses and *dolmuşes* arrive at the small bus station just north of the town at the top of Elmalı Cad.

Destinations Antalya (2 daily; 7hr); Bodrum (3 daily; 6hr); Fethiye (15 daily; 2hr).

Tourist office In the town square at Cumhuriyet Maydanı 5 (May–Oct Mon–Fri 8.30am–7pm, Sat & Sun 10am–7pm; Nov–Apr Mon–Fri 9am–5pm; ☎0242 836 1238).

ACTIVITIES

Kaş is a handy base for paragliding and mountain biking, and offers some of the best scuba diving in Turkey. Many of the *pansiyons* listed can organize these activities, or try one of the numerous operators in town, such as Bougainville (☎0242 836 3737, ⍾bougainville-turkey.com).

ACCOMMODATION

Most *pansiyons* are located in the streets close to the bus station, particularly around Recep Bilgin Cad and immediately beyond.

Ateş Pension Yeni Cami Sok 3 ☎0242 836 1393, ⍾atespension.com. Meals can be eaten up on the pleasant rooftop terrace, where a BBQ with up to fifteen meze will set you back 20TL. Check the rooms – prices are negotiable on the less pleasant ones. You can use the pool at the *Hideaway Hotel* across the road. Double 90TL

★ **Hideaway** Eski Kilise Arkasi 7 ☎0242 836 1887, ⍾hotelhideaway.com. Situated at the fringes of the village, so views are spectacular. A rooftop bar serves margaritas (16TL) and proper coffee. Renovated bathrooms and swimming pool. A cut above the rest in town. Double 130TL

Hilal Pension Süleyman Yıldırım Cad ☎0242 836 1207, ⍾korsan-kas.com. The really helpful owner here can help with all manner of excursions and activities. The rooms are decent and you can often feast on reasonably priced fish from the barbecue in the evening. A convivial spot. Double 70TL

Meltem Atatürk Buluari Meltem Sok ☎0242 836 18 55, ⍾kasmeltempansion.com. Lovely, airy bedrooms (most have balconies), with cooling tiled floors, plus a great

---

BUTTERFLY VALLEY

Popularized in the 1980s by hippies, **Butterfly Valley** (Kelebek Vadisi) is a peaceful spot worth a detour. Boasting a deserted beach, a handful of shady restaurants, a waterfall and not much else, it's reached by boat from Ölüdeniz (3 return trips daily), and usually open from March to October. As the name would suggest, it's home to a colony of butterflies, including the Jersey Tiger, although they can be pretty elusive. You can get a feel for the place in a day, but if you want to linger longer basic accommodation is on offer – in tents (50TL), bungalows (60TL) or wood huts with a roof terrace (670TL); prices include a buffet breakfast and dinner. Book via ⍾thebutterflyvalley.blogspot.co.uk.

ACTIVE OLYMPOS

Olympos, with its beautiful scenery, calm warm sea and plenty of sunshine, is perfect for anyone who likes outdoor life. *Kadir's* (p.1168) offer a whole host of activities. You could try scuba diving (from €30 for a dive from the beach), trekking part of the Lycian Way to Mount Musa (€35 per person), a half-day sea kayak tour (55TL) or an introduction to rock climbing on natural rock (55TL). If you're heading to Fethiye, opt for the three-night *gület* boat trip with V-Go (☎0252 612 2113, ⊛boatcruiseturkey.com; from €129 per person), which stops en route at archeological sites, small villages and Butterfly Valley (see box opposite).

terrace with hammocks. Extremely friendly owners serve up fresh orange juice and other fruit and veg from the family farm just out of town. Call for pick-up from the bus station. Double **90TL**

EATING AND DRINKING

Bar Celona Uzunçarşı Gürsoy Sok 2/a. The soundtrack's a little dated (think Chris Rea and Status Quo) but it's well placed on the corner of a pedestrian street and perfect for people-watching over a beer (8TL). Daily until late.

Kas'ım Öztürk Sok 15. Chicken stew, *pide* pizzas and good old kebabs are all cooked to delicious perfection. Perpetually popular. Daily 9am–11pm.

Smiley's Yat Limanı Girişi. Taking advantage of their prime position, they hike prices up for fresh fish, but it's possible to fill up more frugally on soup or meze (both 12TL). A local's favourite and the banter with owner Smiley is entertaining. Daily 8am–2am.

Sultan Garden Hükümet Cad. Set in an atmospheric spot up the hill across the harbour and offering excellent meze, this family business has played host to several weddings. Daily until late.

OLYMPOS

The Lycian site of **OLYMPOS**, 50km before Antalya, is located on a beautiful sandy bay and the banks of a largely dry river. It's an idyllic location with a small village that is now firmly on the backpacker circuit. You can while away several hours rambling among the overgrown **ruins** (5TL, including access to the beach) before chilling out on the sand. The ruins include some recently excavated tombs, the walls of a Byzantine church and a theatre, though most seats are long gone. On the north side of the river are more striking ruins, including a well-preserved marble temple entrance. Beyond is a Byzantine bathhouse, with mosaic floors, and a Byzantine canal that would have carried water to the heart of the city.

Çirali and the Chimaera

A 1.5km walk along the pebbly beach from Olympos is the quieter holiday village of **ÇIRALI**. About an hour's well-marked stroll above the village's citrus groves flickers the dramatic **Chimaera** (open 24hr; 4TL), a series of eternal flames issuing from cracks in the bare rock, and particularly beautiful at night (take a torch for the walk there and back); many hostels in Olympos organize trips here for a small fee. The Chimaera fires have been burning since antiquity, and inspired the Lycians to worship the god Hephaestos (or Vulcan to the Romans).

ARRIVAL AND INFORMATION

By bus Catch any Kaş–Antalya bus to the minibus stop on the main highway, 11km up from the shore; in season a minibus departs every 15min from the main road to Olympos. In winter minibuses run but there are fewer of them so be prepared to take a taxi from the main road to Olympos village. There are also one or two minibuses a day from Antalya to Çıralı in season.

Money Note that there are no banks or ATMs in Olympos or Çıralı, so make sure you have enough cash before arriving. Many of the *pansiyons* can accept card payment for accommodation. There's no tourist office but hotels can help with tours and travel plans.

ACCOMMODATION

Most places in the area offer a choice of dorm bed or private bungalow.

Bayram's ☎0242 892 1243, ⊛bayrams.com. Accommodation ranges from bungalow shacks to treehouses. Excellent facilities include laundry service and internet access. Prices include breakfast and dinner. Treehouse double **50TL**, bungalow **140TL**

Deep Green Bungalows ☎0242 892 1090, ⊛olympos deepgreen.com. Fire pits and hammocks are dotted among peaceful gardens while live music in the summer kicks things up a notch. Friendly and relaxed atmosphere. Open May–Oct. Breakfast and dinner included. Dorm **45TL**, bungalow **130TL**

35

35

★ **Kadir's** ☎0242 892 1250, ⊛kadirstreehouses.com
With 338 dorm and bungalow beds mostly set in
treehouses plus space for campers, a volleyball court, the
eclectic *Hangar Bar* for cocktails and the lively *Bull Bar*
alfresco nightclub (from midnight till very late), it's no
surprise this is the backpacker hangout of choice. No TVs in
the rooms. Dorm 25TL, bungalow 140TL
Orange ☎0242 892 1317, ⊛olymposorangepension
.com. Professionally run and offering better-quality cabins
than others. Good wholesome grub too, including a decent
vegetarian buffet. Prices can be bargained down a little.
Dorm 30TL, bungalow 140TL
Şaban ☎0242 892 1265, ⊛sabanpansion.com. Tranquil,
treehouse-style *pansiyon* set among pomegranate and
lemon trees and low-slung hammocks with excellent
home-made Turkish food offered as part of the room rate
and a friendly, relaxed atmosphere. English and German
spoken. Hammocks slung in shady spots. Dorm 30TL,
bungalow 120TL
Sheriff Pension ☎0242 892 1301, ⊛olympos.biz. A
friendly *pension* with a bit more of a party vibe. 40 clean
bungalows on stilts, accommodating 100 people. Orange
and pomegranate trees provide shade from the summer
sun; in the evenings you can chat and dance around the
campfire outside the bar. Includes breakfast and dinner.
Double 140TL

EATING AND DRINKING

Most hotels provide evening meals, but there's plenty of
shady restaurants with locals preparing stuffed *gözleme*
pancakes.
Cactus Café Chilled-out place playing reggae in Olympos
village set amid a pretty orange grove. Basic fare such as
omelettes, salads, sandwiches and pasta dishes (5–10TL).
Beer 7TL. Open daily.
Çirali Gözleme Çıralı village between the Orange Market
and Olympos Rent A Car, close to the *Orange Motel*. The
most succulent specimens of *gözleme* hereabouts.
Open daily.
Zakkum Olympos village. Another great spot to fill up on
cheap *gözleme*. Choose from meat, cheese, potato or
spinach–or all of the above–for less than 10TL. Open daily.

ANTALYA

ANTALYA is blessed with an ideal climate
and a stunning setting, and, despite the
grim appearance of its concrete sprawl,
it's an agreeable place – although the
main area of interest for visitors is
confined to the relatively small old
quarter. A short bus ride away are the
charming **Düden** falls, perfect on a hot
summer day. Antalya's principal

attraction, however, is situated on
the outskirts of the city – **Aspendos**,
a Roman theatre that still holds
live performances.

WHAT TO SEE AND DO

Antalya is dominated by the **Yivli Minare**
or "Fluted Minaret", erected in the
thirteenth century. Downhill from here is
the old **harbour**, recently restored and site
of the evening promenade. North is the
bazaar, while south, beyond the Saat
Kalesi (clock tower), lies Kaleiçi or the
old town, with every house now a carpet
shop, café or *pansiyon*. On the far side, on
Atatürk Caddesi, the triple-arched
Hadrian's Gate recalls a visit by the
emperor in 130 AD; Hesapçı Sokak leads
south past the Kesik Minare to a number
of tea gardens.

The Antalya Museum

The one thing you shouldn't miss is the
Antalya Museum (Tues–Sun 9am–7pm;
15TL), one of the top five archeological
collections in the country; it's on the
western edge of town at the far end of
Kenan Evren Bulvarı, easily reachable by
a tram that departs from the clock tower
in Kaleiçi.

Düden falls

A small but nonetheless enchanting
waterfall, **Düden falls** attracts a large
number of visitors. The upper falls
provide the best visual spectacle and
are situated in the middle of a park.
There is even a precarious walkway
carved out to enable visitors to walk
behind the falls. To get to the falls from
Kaleiçi, either take a *dolmuş* or book
onto one of the boat tours offered at
the harbour (around €20 per person
but prices are negotiable).

ARRIVAL AND INFORMATION

By plane The airport is 12km northeast; Havaş buses into
town depart from the domestic terminal, 5min walk from
the international terminal, while city-centre-bound
dolmuşes pass nearby.
By bus Antalya's main bus station is 7km north of town.
From the bus station take bus #93 to Hadrian's Gate
(*Üçkapılar*) then walk into the old town.
Destinations Fethiye, by inland route (6 daily; 4hr); İzmir

(6 daily; 9hr 30min); Kaş (6 daily; 5hr); Konya (6 daily; 5hr 30min); Olympos (every 30min; 2hr).

Tourist office A 15min walk west from the clock tower on Cumhuriyet Cad (daily 8am–6/7pm; ☎0242 241 1747).

GETTING AROUND

By tram The tram runs along Atatürk Cad, ending its route at the museum. Tickets (1.75-2.30TL) can be bought on board.

ACCOMMODATION

Most budget accommodation is in the area sandwiched between Hadrian's Gate and the back of the bazaar.

Blue Sea Garden Hotel Kılçarslan Mah Hesapçı Sok 65 ☎0242 248 8213, ⓦhotelblueseagarden.com. The rooms are not exactly a knockout but most guests spend their time in the hotel's garden anyway, which has a pool, small restaurant area, music playing and a laidback party atmosphere. Double 100TL

Lazer Pension Hesapçı Sok 61 ☎0242 242 7194, ⓦlazerpansiyon.com. Friendly and good location, but room quality varies. Try and get one of the wood-panelled spots upstairs. Includes breakfast in the pleasant garden. Dorm €10, double €35

Sabah Pansiyon Hesapçı Sok 60/a ☎0242 247 5345, ⓦsabahpansiyon.com. Backpacker-friendly place with decent rooms and a sleepy courtyard. Price includes breakfast. Double 75TL

White Garden Kaleiçi Kılıçaslan Hesapçı Geçidi 9 ☎0242 241 9115, ⓦwhitegardenpansion.com. Charming Ottoman restoration; fifteen immaculate rooms with large en suites. The owners also run the nearby *Secret Palace Hotel* and *Hadrians*, two equally pretty establishments with shady gardens, charging comparable prices. Double 65TL

EATING AND DRINKING

Antalya's restaurants and bars are generally open from the morning until late evening, unless otherwise specified.

★ **Art Café and Meyhane** Hesapçı Sok 51. Laidback café (wood floors, exposed brickwork, quirky chairs/ tables) popular with students from Antalya's uni. There's live music every night, an open-mic music night on Fridays and film screenings on Sundays. Mains might include fresh grilled fish or chicken stew for 10–15TL.

Parlak Restaurant Kazım Özalp Cad Zincirlihan 7. It might not look too appealing from the outside but this popular spot is worth a visit. Try the slow-roasted chicken or lovely fresh meze. Meze 4–8TL, mains 12–25TL.

Salman Patisserie Fevzi Çakmak Cad. Uluç Apt 7 ☎0242 316 7738, ⓦsalmanpatisserie.com. Treat yourself to a sumptuous breakfast buffet or baklava and a top-notch cappuccino. Open during the daytime.

Seraser Karanlık Sok 18 ☎0242 247 6015. A cut above the budget joints in town, serving well-presented fresh fish and other Turkish delights. Good for a special night out.

★ **Sim Restaurant** Kaledibi Sok 7. Tucked away from the crowds, but well worth seeking out. A charming husband-and-wife-run place; tables are either upstairs in a small dining room decorated with antiques or outdoors on the quiet street beneath shady vines. Salads (10TL), calamari (18TL) and kebabs (20TL) are all well prepared.

Topçu Kebap 1885 Kazım Özalp Cad 21. They have been honing their kebabs since 1885, and hordes descend every lunchtime to enjoy them. Near the square by the tram stop. Kebabs 12–15TL. Closed evenings. Mon–Sat 9am–9.30pm.

Central Turkey

35

Sandwiched between the Black Sea and the Mediterranean, Central Turkey, or **Anatolia**, comprises several interesting spots. **Ankara** grew as a result of immigration from the Anatolian villages to become the metropolis it is now. Southeast of here is the bizarre landscape of **Cappadocia**, where water and wind have created fantastic forms from the soft tufa rock, including forests of cones, table mountains and canyon-like valleys. Further south still, **Konya** is best known as the birthplace of the mystical Sufi sect and makes a convenient place to stop over between Cappadocia and the coast.

ANKARA

Modern **ANKARA** is really two cities, a double identity that is due to the breakneck pace at which it has developed since being declared capital of the Turkish Republic in 1923. Until then Ankara – known as Angora – had been a small provincial city, famous chiefly for the production of soft goat's wool. This city still exists, in and around the old citadel that was the site of the original settlement. The other Ankara is the modern metropolis that has grown up around a carefully planned attempt to create a seat of government worthy of a modern, Western-looking state. Often overlooked, it merits a detour of a couple of days, especially if you're travelling from İstanbul to Cappadocia.

35

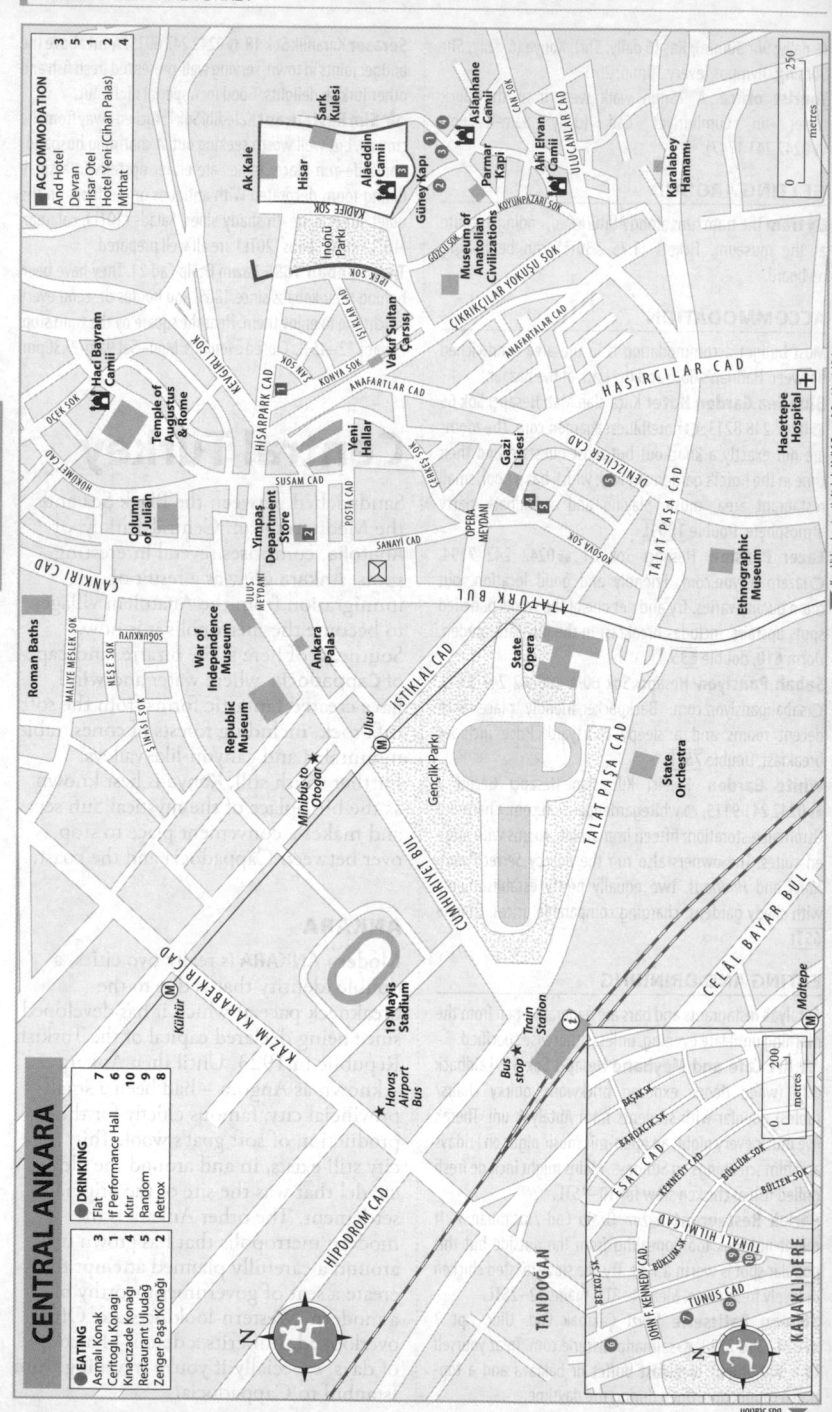

CENTRAL ANKARA

● EATING
Asmali Konak	3
Ceritoglu Konagi	1
Kinaczade Konağı	4
Restaurant Uludağ	5
Zenger Paşa Konağı	2

● DRINKING
Flat	7
If Performance Hall	6
Kitir	10
Random	9
Retrox	8

■ ACCOMMODATION
And Hotel	3
Devran	5
Hisar Otel	1
Hotel Yeni (Cihan Palas)	2
Mithat	4

WHAT TO SEE AND DO

The city is bisected north–south by **Atatürk Bulvarı**, and everything you need is within easy reach of this broad and busy street. At the northern end, **Ulus Meydanı**, a large square and an important traffic intersection marked by a huge equestrian Atatürk statue, is the best jumping-off point for the old part of the city – a village of narrow cobbled streets and ramshackle wooden houses centring on the **Hisar**, Ankara's old fortress and citadel. To the south, the modern shopping district of **Kızılay** sees Turkish students congregate on its streets. At night, the area is awash with entertainment, bars and restaurants, as are the neighbouring districts of **Kavaklıdere** and **Çankaya**.

The Museum of Anatolian Civilizations

Located in Ulus, at the end of Kadife Sokak, is the **Museum of Anatolian Civilizations** (daily 8.30am–6.15pm; 15TL), which boasts an incomparable collection of archeological objects housed in a restored Ottoman *bedesten*, or covered market. Hittite carving and relief work form the most compelling section of the museum, mostly taken from Carchemish, near the present Syrian border. There are also Neolithic finds from Çatal Höyük, the site of one of Anatolia's oldest settlements and widely regarded as the world's first "city".

Hisar

A steep walk up Hisarpark Cad brings you to the **Hisar**, a small citadel amid the old city walls. Most of what can be seen today dates from Byzantine times, with substantial Selçuk and Ottoman additions. Inside the confines, follow the steps leading up the hill and look out for the flag flying in the distance as you wend your way through the narrow lanes, and you'll soon reach **Ak Kale**, a castle ruin which provides a perfect perch for viewing Ankara from above. A walk around the rest of the Hisar will let you amble in and out of the alleys that intersect the ramshackle houses as local kids shout greetings. Continue to head south and you'll find the twelfth-century mosque, **Alâeddin Camii**, along with a series of touristy souvenir stalls selling handmade carpet bags, jewellery and crockery.

Roman Ankara

What's left of Roman Ankara lies north of Ulus Meydanı. First stop is the **Column of Julian** on Hükümet Meydanı. Close by are the ruins of the **Temple of Augustus and Rome**, built in honour of Augustus around 20 BC. Northeast of here are the remains of Ankara's **Roman baths** (daily 8.30am–noon & 1–5.30pm; 5TL). Only the foundation stones that supported the heating and service areas remain.

ARRIVAL AND DEPARTURE

By plane Esenboğa airport is 28km north of town. Havaş buses (10TL) meet incoming Turkish Airlines flights; a taxi will set you back around 70TL.

By train Ankara's pleasant and airy train station (with English announcements) is at the corner of Talat Paşa Cad and Cumhuriyet Bul, from where frequent buses run to Kızılay and Ulus. A high-speed line linking Ankara with İstanbul is due to be completed in 2014; until then you'll have to travel part of the way to Eskişehir on the high-speed route and the rest on a bus.

Destinations İstanbul (10 daily via Eskişehir; 5hr 30min total journey time); İzmir (2 daily overnight; 13hr); Konya (8 daily; 2hr).

By bus The bus station is 5km to the southwest. Some companies run minibuses to the centre, otherwise take a *dolmuş* or the easy and convenient Ankaray rapid transit system (3.50TL return) to Kızılay (10min) and change onto the metro (same ticket) for Ulus (red line towards Batıkent), where most of the budget hotels are located.

Destinations Antalya (12 daily; 7hr); Bodrum (10 daily; 12hr); Bursa (hourly; 5hr 30min); İstanbul (every 30min; 6hr); İzmir (hourly; 8hr); Konya (hourly; 3hr); Nevşehir (12 daily; 4hr 30min).

INFORMATION

Tourist office There's a small but helpful tourist office in the train station offering maps and ideas for day-trips nearby (Mon–Fri 8.30am–5.30pm, closed on weekends; ☏ 0312 231 5572).

GETTING AROUND

By bus As well as displaying numbers, buses in Ankara also display the names of their destinations, so it's easy to work out which one to catch. Buy bus tickets

35

(1.6TL) in advance from kiosks next to the main bus stops (it's a good idea to stock up, as some areas have no kiosks). They should be inserted into the machine next to the driver. Most buses stop running between midnight and 1am.

By metro/Ankaray The metro runs from Batıkent in the northwest and splits at Kızılay where it becomes the Ankaray (light railway). The Ankaray heads to either Aşti (where the bus station is based) or Dikimevi in the east. Tickets (3.50TL for two journeys, 8.75TL for five) can be bought from the ticket offices inside the station. In the summer, the metro stops running at midnight and in the winter it terminates at 11pm.

ACCOMMODATION

Most of the cheaper hotels are in the streets east of Atatürk Bul in the Ulus district. Standards are pretty basic across the board.

And Hotel Istek Sok 2, Ulus ☎0312 310 2304, ⓦandbutikhotel.com. Smart hotel with clean and pleasant rooms. Double `120TL`

Devran Opera Meydanı, Ulus ☎0312 311 0485. Friendly welcome and professional feel. Great views of the city and stadium but could do with a lick of paint and plaster in parts. Bathrooms are clean and rooms have TVs. Breakfast costs an additional 5TL. Double `70TL`

Hisar Otel Hisarpark Cad 6, Ulus ☎0312/ 311 9889. Rooms in a much more presentable state than similarly priced options, some with better views than others. Shower cubicles, TV and firm beds. Single `25TL`

Hotel Yeni (Cihan Palas) Sanayi Cad 5/b, Ulus ☎0312 310 4720, ⓦhotelyeni.com. A good couple of notches up from the rest of the town's more affordable hotels. Quiet and respectable and open to a quick haggle on room prices. Double `€50`

Mithat Opera Meydanı, Tavus Sok 2, Ulus ☎0312 311 5410, ⓦotelmithat.com.tr. The welcome might not be that warm, and some of the showers are practically above the toilet, but the place is clean and tidy and conveniently located. On a bustling street full of alfresco electronics shops. Double `€40`

EATING

Ulus is home to a number of decent lunchtime spots while you'll need to head south to Kızılay and Kavaklıdere for evening sustenance. The latter in particular is home to a revitalized restaurant scene. *Pide* and kebab places are dotted about the city and stuffed mussels are another popular street-corner option.

Asmalı Konak Kalekapısı Sok 14, Hisar. Great range of fresh meze (7TL) in an atmospheric old building looking out onto a peaceful courtyard. Open daily until early evening.

Ceritoglu Konagi Kalekapisi Sokak, Hisar ☎0312 324

3622. A quirky café offering *kahvalti* (breakfast) (10TL) and filling *gözleme* for a mere 5TL. Daily till late.

Kınacızade Konağı Kalekapısı Sok 28, Hisar. Guns, waistcoasts, records, tankards and hookahs are just some of the random objects hanging from the walls in this intriguing spot. Mains range from 12–15TL, and while the quality isn't impeccable, the setting makes up for it. Daily 8am–1am.

Restaurant Uludağ Denizciler Cad 54, Ulus. It doesn't look like much from the outside but it offers perhaps the best *Iskender kebab* in Ankara. Closes around 9pm.

Zenger Paşa Konağı Doyran Sok 13, Hisar. Just climbing up to the restaurant is a treat. On the way up you will see women sitting by a fire making flatbreads. Reasonable prices considering the wonderful views, and delicious *pide* and grilled meats. Mon–Sat 10am–midnight.

DRINKING AND NIGHTLIFE

Eski Yeti İnkılap Sok 6, Kızılay. A lively spot on a busy bar street entertaining enthusiastic drinkers with live muisc inside and a large courtyard outside. Daily until late.

Flat Tunus Cad 54, Kavaklıdere ☎0312 466 6311. Marking its territory by flames and Balearic tunes, this spot serves top cocktails to a hip, young crowd while a shot bar on the pavement aims to entice more in. A sign reads "Music, drinks, people", which has it about right. Daily 3pm–3am.

★ **Kıtır** Tunalı Hilmi Cad 114 24, Kavaklıdere. A sprawling treat, full of locals packed into wooden booths and perusing beer-stein-shaped menus to a thumping rock and pop soundtrack. Hot dogs and *kokorec* (lamb's intestines, 20TL) are popular, but their salads (12TL) are large and offer an alternative if you've overdosed on meat. Wash it down with a large Efes beer (8.50TL) or two. Daily until late.

Random Tunalı Hilmi Cad 114, Kavaklıdere. Tucked away in the bowels of *Kıtır*, this busy, intimate bar is reliably popular with a young crowd. Daily 9am–1am.

Retrox Tunus Cad 53, Kavaklıdere ☎0312 465 0053. A dark and convivial spot, where the lights are low and the conversation kept to a murmur. Brick walls and black-and-white photography add to the ambience. Opening hours vary but closes at 1am on Fri and Sat.

ENTERTAINMENT

Anadolu Gösteri Kongre Merkezi Türkocağl Cad Balgat. Large performance hall for theatre or music concerts. See ⓦbiletix.com for tickets.

If Performance Hall Tunus Cad 14/a, Kavaklıdere ☎0312 418 9506, ⓦifperformance.com. Bands perform nightly – a stalwart of the Ankara music scene.

DIRECTORY

Embassies Australia, Nehenhatun Cad 83, Gaziosmanpaşa ☎0312 459 9500; Canada, Cinnah Cad 58, Çankaya

📞 0312 409 2700; New Zealand, Iran Cad 13 4, Kavaklıdere
📞 0312 467 9054; UK, Şehit Ersan Cad 46/a, Çankaya
📞 0312 455 3344; US, Atatürk Bul 110, Kavaklıdere
📞 0312 455 5555.
Hammam Karacabey Hamami, Talat Paşa Bul 101 (daily 10am–1pm; from 20TL).
Hospital Hacettepe University Medical Faculty, west of Hasırcılar Sok, Sıhhıye 📞 0312 305 1080.
Internet Chatlak Net Café Fevzi Çakmak Sok 22-B Kızlay.
Left luggage The train station has lockers you can use 24 hours.
Post office Merkez Postahane, on Atatürk Bul, Ulus.

CAPPADOCIA

A land created by the complex interaction of natural and human forces over vast spans of time, **CAPPADOCIA**, around 150km southeast of Ankara, is a superlative visual experience. Its weird (and it must be said, somewhat phallic) formations of soft, dusty rock have been adapted into caves and even underground cities over centuries by many cultures. A short flight from İstanbul, Cappadocia is an essential destination thanks to the wide selection of competitively priced accommodation, restaurants and activities on offer. Many backpackers choose to stay in the touristy hotspot of **Göreme**, but alternatives include sleepier **Uçhisar** or **Ürgüp**, a small town where many of the old abandoned cave dwellings have been renovated into smart guesthouses and private homes. Less appealing is the working city of **Nevşehir**, which acts as a transport hub for the region.

WHAT TO SEE AND DO

A relatively easy 1km walk from Göreme village, the **Göreme Open-Air Museum** (daily 8am–6.15pm; 15TL) is the site of more than thirty cave churches, mainly dating from the ninth century to the end of the eleventh century and a treasure-trove of detailed frescoes in dark recesses – many of which have been defaced in distant centuries. Outdoor pursuits include walking in the valleys, in particular **Ihlara Valley**; allow two to four hours per walk and don't miss a stop at one of the rustic farmer-run teashops en route.

Note that there are no detailed maps of the area and waymark signs tend to be arrows painted on rocks. The best routes are Pigeon Valley between Göreme and Uçhisar, and the Red Valley from Ortahisar to the village of Çavuşin. The open-air museum at **Zelve** (daily 8am–5pm, 8TL), meanwhile, was occupied for some 4000 years until as recently as the 1920s, and was the site of a monastery from the ninth to the thirteenth centuries.

Derinkuyu and Kayamaklı

Among the most extraordinary phenomena of the Cappadocia region are the remains of a number of underground settlements, some of them large enough to have accommodated up to 30,000 people. The cities are thought to date back to Hittite times, though the complexes were later enlarged by Christian communities. Most thoroughly excavated is **Derinkuyu** (daily 8am–5.30/7pm; 15TL), 29km from Nevşehir and accessible by *dolmuş*. The city is well lit, and the original ventilation system still functions remarkably well, though some of the passages are small and cramped. The excavated area (less than half of the total) consists of eight floors and includes stables, wine presses and a dining hall or schoolroom with two long, rock-cut tables, plus a cruciform church and dungeon. Some 10km north of Derinkuyu is **Kaymakli** (daily 8am–5.30/7pm; 15TL), where only five of its underground levels have been excavated to date.

ARRIVAL AND DEPARTURE

By plane The region is served by two main airports, Kayseri Erkilet Airport about an hour away from Göreme, and Nevşehir, which is much closer and more convenient. Taxis and shuttles run from the latter but your hotel may arrange transport.
Destinations from Nevşehir İstanbul (2 daily; 90min).
By bus Direct services arrive at the Göreme bus station, located in front of Müze Cad, in the centre of town. However, some firms will drop you off in Nevşehir, from where you'll have to continue by local bus or *dolmuş*. The *dolmuş* runs between Nevşehir and Ürgüp, calling at Göreme, several times an hour from 7am to 11pm. You

35

shouldn't have to wait long for a ride. When buying your bus ticket, be sure to check the end destination. Destinations from Nevşehir Ankara (daily; 5hr); Konya (4 daily; 3hr).

INFORMATION, TOURS AND ACTIVITIES

Numerous travel agencies masquerading as tourist information centres offer tours of the region, which take in the best of Cappadocia's panoramic points, underground cities, monasteries and other attractions.

Tourist office By Göreme bus station (daily 5am–8pm), it offers accommodation lists and maps but not much in the way of help.

Tour operators: Nomad Travel (ⓦ nomadtravel.com.tr) offer various one-day tours (prices for tours vary, but expect to pay around 100–120TL). Their Green Tour includes Derinkuyu Underground City, a 4km hike in Ihlara Valley, lunch in Belisirma Village, Silime Monastery, Pigeon Valley and the obligatory stop at an onyx factory/gift shop. Argeus Travel (ⓦ argeus.com.tr) specialize in cycling and hiking trips (between $435 and $755 for a three-night hiking tour including accommodation, depending on group size), while bicycles, mopeds and jeeps can be rented from a number of spots in Göreme. Ürgüp Balloons (ⓣ0384 341 5636, ⓦ urgupballoons.com; standard flight €150, deluxe flight €230) are one of the numerous companies offering a spectacular hot-air balloon ride at dawn.

GETTING AROUND

By dolmuş *Dolmuşes* operate regularly between Cappadocia's villages, departing Göreme for example every 15min from 7am to around 10.30pm.

ACCOMMODATION

Cave hotels are the most popular form of accommodation in Cappadocia but there are alternatives – often with great views – for those not keen on a night underground. Some hostels/hotels can be tricky to find, though most are walkable from bus stations. If you're staying in another village, ask your accommodation, as many will arrange a free transfer from the bus station.

GÖREME

Köse Pansion Ragıp Üner Cad, Göreme ⓣ0384 271 2294, ⓦ kosepension.com. Large, homely *pansiyon* near the bus station with swimming pool, shady outdoor and rooftop areas to relax in. The mattress-strewn dorm (sleeping bag rental 2.50TL) is in a large wooden hall on the roof. Free wi-fi. Breakfast (6TL) and evening meal (20TL) served daily. Dorm 15TL, doubles 80TL

Rock Valley Pension Isali Mah., Iceri Dere Sok, Göreme ⓣ0384 271 2153, ⓦ rockvalleycappadocia.com. Attractive wooden dorm with heating chimney for snugness. Big pool

with the valley looming up all around. A pleasant, low-key option. Breakfast included. Dorm 30TL, double 50TL

Shoestring Kazım Erin Sok 23, Göreme ⓣ0384 271 2450, ⓦ shoestringcave.com. A warm, sociable atmosphere. Quality beds and bedding make these cave rooms very cosy indeed. Dorm €8, doubles €25

UÇHISAR

★ **Kale Konak** Kale Sok 9, Uçhisar ⓣ0384 219 2828, ⓦ kalekonak.com. A wonderfully cosy and labyrinthine hotel at the foot of Uçhisar Castle. All fifteen rooms are spectacular and the affable owner keeps large tour groups away. A private session in the marble hammam (free) is the ultimate indulgence. A top place to blow the budget for a night or two. Doubles €120

ÜRGÜP

★ **Esbelli Evi** Esbelli Sok 8, Ürgüp ⓣ0384 341 3395, ⓦ esbelli.com. Magnificent views and sumptuous boutique rooms in caves with private terraces and secret gardens at one of Cappadocia's finest – and oldest – hotels. Laptops with Skype in each room. Well worth stretching your budget for. Includes breakfast. Doubles €120

EATING AND DRINKING

In Göreme, several restaurants and bars are on Müze Cad, behind the bus station. Most places in the region are open every day until quite late in the evening during high season.

GÖREME

Anatolia Kitchen Müze Cad 1, Göreme. Offers local wine as well as beer. A peaceful, shady spot serving cheap lunch options (*pide* and pizza, around 12TL, kebabs 15TL) and more substantial choices (slow-cooked stews in clay pots 20TL), a couple of minutes from the bus station.

Dibek Hakkı Paşa Meydanı, Göreme. It won't take long for someone to tell you about this place's *testi kebap* (28TL) but it takes the restaurant a long time to cook it – you need to order it when you make your reservation. The building is nearly 500 years old.

Göreme Restaurant Muze Caddesi 18, Göreme. With kilim and cushions on the floor this place has a warm feel (welcome in sometimes chilly Göreme). Meze starters at 7.50TL and a variety of vegetarian dishes make a nice change from the meat & bread staples elsewhere.

Kale Terasse Müze Cad, Göreme. Offering kebabs, salads and a range of set three-course meals with soups 16–20TL, this shady spot in the centre of town offers reasonably priced sustenance after a long day exploring.

ÜRGÜP

★ **Ziggy's** Yunak Mah, Tevfik Fikret Cad 24, Ürgüp. Delicious meze, superlative mains (including a spectacular liver dish), an outdoor terrace and charming owners make this an essential, if pricier, stop. Booking essential. Around 50–60TL per head including local wine.

KONYA

Roughly midway between Antalya and Nevşehir, **KONYA** is a relatively unremarkable city but an essential place of pilgrimage for the Muslim world – the home of Celaleddin Rumi or the Mevlâna ("Our Master"), the mystic who founded the Mevlevî or **Whirling Dervish** sect, and the centre of Sufic mystical practice and teaching.

The Mevlâna Museum

The **Mevlâna Museum** (Mon 10am–6.30pm, Tues–Sun 9am–6.30pm; 3TL) is housed in the first lodge (*tekke*) of the Mevlevî dervish sect, at the eastern end of Mevlâna Bulvarı, recognizable by its distinctive fluted turquoise dome. Inside are the tombs of the Mevlâna, his father and other notables. The original *semahane* (ceremonial hall) exhibits some of the musical instruments of the first dervishes, the original illuminated poetical work of the Mevlâna, and a 500-year-old silk carpet from Selçuk Persia (supposedly the finest ever woven). In the adjoining room, a casket containing hairs from the beard of the Prophet Mohammed is displayed alongside illuminated medieval Korans and other sacred texts.

Karatay Tile Museum

Built by Emir Celaleddin Karatay in the thirteenth century, the interior of the **Karatay Tile Museum** (Alâeddin Bulvarı; daily 8am–noon & 1–5pm; 3TL) is equally as fascinating as the ceramics on show, with a beautifully decorated domed central ceiling and ornamental green tiles.

ARRIVAL AND DEPARTURE

By plane Konya's airport is 18km from the city. Havaş has started an 8TL transfer to and from the airport (40TL by taxi). Catch one from the taxi rank at the airport, and head to the Turkish Airlines office at Feritpaşa Cad 10/b in the city for the return journey.

By train The train station is 2km out of the centre at the far end of Istasyon Cad, connected to the centre by regular *dolmuş*.

Destinations Ankara (8 daily 1hr 50min); Eskişehir (for İstanbul 2 daily; 2hr); İzmir (1 daily; 11hr).

By bus The bus station is 10km out of town, from where the *otogar dolmuş* and tramway connects with the town centre. Follow the tramway signs and purchase a pass at the small ticket booth.

Destinations Ankara (hourly; 3hr 20min); Antalya (25 daily; 5hr 30min); İstanbul (every 40min; 9hr); Nevşehir (10 daily; 3hr 30min).

35

INFORMATION

Tourist office Azize Mahallesi, Aslanli Kişla Caddesi 5. By the Mevlâna Museum and very helpful. Daily 8am–5pm; ☎ 0032 353 4021, ext 147.

Internet Internet cafés are around Alâeddin Hill, next to the *McDonald's* or Ince Minare Medresesi.

GETTING AROUND

By tram The city has one main tram line running from Alâeddin in the centre to the outskirts via the Otogar. Buy tickets from booths by the stops.

ACCOMMODATION

Deluxe Otel Ayanbey Sok 22 ☎ 0332 351 1546. All 25 rooms are en suite with a/c, minibar and flat-screen TV at this hotel, with a business-style feel but impressive for the money. Little English but welcoming nonetheless. Double 90TL

Hotel Bella Aziziye Caddesi 15 ☎ 0332 353 8793, ⓦ hotelbella.comtr. Rooms are a little snug but beds are comfy. En-suite bathrooms come with basic showers; rooms equipped with flatscreen TVs and wi-fi throughout. Double 70TL

Rumi Hotel Durakfakih Sok 5 ☎ 0332 353 1121, ⓦ rumihotel.com. A comfortable and very centrally located hotel opposite the Mevlâna Museum with spectacular views from the rooftop breakfast terrace. Large rooms and decent bathrooms. Double 175TL

★ **Ulusan** Off Alâeddin Cad on side road behind the PTT ☎ 0332 351 5004, ✉ ulusanhotel@hotmail.com. A

WHIRLING DERVISH CEREMONY

This meditational ceremony, where worshippers spin around to draw closer to God, is held at the Mevlâna Cultural Centre near the museum. The ceremony is free and takes place every Saturday night. No need for a ticket; just turn up (8pm winter; 9pm summer). You'll find plenty of background reading on ⓦ mevlana.net.

family-run place helmed by an eccentric and amiable host with great English. Stuffed toys and knick-knacks throughout. Shared bathrooms but decent rooms and a home-away-from-home feel. Double 80TL

EATING AND DRINKING

Konya has a handful of half-decent restaurants but no reputable bars or pubs to speak of. Locals prefer to hang out around a *nargile*, and few women venture out at night alone. The area around Alâeddin Parkı is where younger people congregate, although there's not a lot to do there either.

Konark Konya Mutfağı Mengüç Cad 66. Slap-bang in the middle of pretty much nowhere, this slightly ramshackle place is a 10min trek from town but worth the wander for budget eats. Barely anything exceeds 10TL and a two-course meal will set you back around 16TL. The

yoğurt çorbasi, with yoghurt, butter, chickpea and mint, is a great starter. Waiters will entertain with napkin tricks and provide free drinks at the end. Daily 11am–10pm.

Mevlevi Sofrası Nazimbey Cad 1/a. Smart, spacious terrace with sweeping views of the museum garden. If you're hungry after a museum visit, try the *adana kebap* 8TL. Daily 8am–11pm.

Osmanlı Çarsisi Ince Minare Sokak. A classic *nargile* and coffee place with Ottoman-style rooms spread over several floors. It is behind the Ince Minare Medresesi on an atmospheric street flooded with green lights. Daily until late.

Somatci Akcesme Mahallesi Menguc Cad 36. A converted Ottoman house on a quiet and atmospheric cobbled street serving traditional food to a mostly local clientele. Photos on the wall are testament to the many happy punters since it opened. Don't let the confusing blackboard outside put you off. Daily until late.

PECHERSKA LAVRA ORTHODOX MONASTERY, KYIV

Ukraine

HIGHLIGHTS

❶ **Chornobyl Museum, Kyiv** Learn about the world's worst nuclear accident and the heroism of those who cleared it up. **See p.1183**

❷ **Pecherska Lavra, Kyiv** Experience Orthodox-Christian spirituality first-hand in this centuries-old religious site. **See p.1184**

❸ **Odesa** Soak up the sun then party all night at Arkadia beach. **See p.1187**

❹ **L'viv Old Town** Lose yourself in the café-filled alleys and courtyards of this Central European jewel. **See p.1189**

HIGHLIGHTS ARE MARKED ON THE MAP ON P.1179

ROUGH COSTS

Daily budget Basic €40, occasional treat €60

Drink *horilka* (vodka; 50ml shot) €1

Food Ukrainian *borshch* €0.80

Hostel/budget hotel €8/€30

Travel Train: Kyiv–Odesa €10; bus €18

FACT FILE

Population 45.7 million

Languages Ukrainian, Russian

Currency Hryvnia (Hr/UAH)

Capital Kyiv

International phone code ☏ 380

Time zone GMT +3hr

Introduction

The second-largest country in Europe, Ukraine has not always had clearly defined frontiers and has spent large tracts of its history under foreign rule. Even today the issue of "Ukrainianness" is viewed differently by people living in different regions of the country: Ukrainians living in Kyiv and the east may well speak the Russian language at home and on the streets, while those living in L'viv and the west speak Ukrainian in all social situations and are enormously proud of the fact.

Despite being a country of large distances and time-consuming travel, Ukraine is not as far away as you might think, and its three key cities are well worth fitting in to a wider European trip. Ukraine's fast-paced capital **Kyiv** offers a fascinating insight on a country in the throes of transformation, with chic boutiques and slick bars sprouting up along broad, cobbled boulevards. Glittering church domes and steeples show off the city's medieval glories. One of Europe's great maritime cities, **Odesa** exudes a sense of Tsarist-Empire grandeur, while its bars and beaches provide a vibrant hedonistic edge. In total contrast is the western city of **L'viv**, a Central European city that looks like an estranged cousin of Vienna or Prague, and has the cultural attractions and café life to match. Situated within easy travelling distance of Central European cities, L'viv is the one Ukrainian city that you should squeeze into your itinerary.

CHRONOLOGY

Tenth century AD A strong Slav state known as "Rus" emerges, centred on Kyiv.

988 Prince Vladimir of Kyiv accepts Christianity.

1240 Kyiv is sacked by the Tatars.

1362 After the Battle of the Blue Waters, much of Ukraine is absorbed into the Grand Duchy of Lithuania.

1569 The Union of Lublin creates the Polish–Lithuanian Commonwealth, with most of Ukraine falling under direct Polish rule.

1648 Cossack leader Bohdan Khmelnitskyi leads an uprising against the Commonwealth.

1654 Khmelnitskyi swears allegiance to Tsarist Russia, bringing Ukraine into the orbit of Moscow.

1709 An anti-Russian revolt under Ivan Mazepa is defeated.

1780s Russia drives the Ottoman Turks from southern Ukraine and the Crimea.

1794 Russian Empress Catherine the Great founds the Black Sea port of Odesa.

1917–21 The Russian Revolution sparks failed attempts to re-create an independent Ukrainian state. Central and Eastern Ukraine are absorbed into the Soviet Union, while Western Ukraine becomes part of Poland.

1932–33 Stalinist collectivization policies lead to the Holodomor or Great Famine, resulting in anything between 2.5 and 7.5 million deaths.

1941 Nazi Germany invades Ukraine, meeting fierce resistance in Kyiv and Odesa.

1945 International borders are redrawn: Western Ukraine is absorbed into the Ukrainian Soviet Republic.

1986 A fire at the Chornobyl power plant leads to the world's worst nuclear accident.

1991 The USSR is dissolved and Ukraine becomes an independent state.

2004 Viktor Yanukovych wins a presidential election regarded by many as fraudulent. Popular protests spark the so-called Orange Revolution. A re-vote ordered by the Supreme Court is won by pro-Western Viktor Yushchenko.

2005 The Orange Revolution runs out of steam: President Yushchenko falls out with Prime Minister Yulia Tymoshenko.

2009 Old-style conservative Viktor Yanukovych is elected president.

2012 Ukraine hosts the European Football Championships together with Poland.

ARRIVAL AND DEPARTURE

The main hub for arrivals **by air** is Kyiv Borispil, which is served by major European and transatlantic airlines. The smaller Kyiv Zhulyany is used by the budget carrier Wizz Air, while the airports at Odesa and L'viv receive a limited number of flights from other European cities. Kyiv Central Railway

Station (sometimes marked on timetables as Kyiv Pasazhirs'kyi) is the main international **train station**, served by overnight trains from Budapest, Kraków and Warsaw. The western Ukrainian city of L'viv is by far the easiest to reach from Central Europe, served by trains from Bucharest, Budapest and Kraków, and **buses** from Kraków, Warsaw and Prague.

GETTING AROUND

Ukraine's principal cities are a long distance apart and travelling between them usually takes a whole day or night. Trains and buses are frequently booked solid days in advance so it is wise to plan ahead. **Public transport** in Ukraine's cities is cheap, with flat fares rarely exceeding 2Hr. Many urban transport routes are operated by privately owned **minibuses** known as *marshrutki*. They are speedier than regular buses and trams, but can be overcrowded.

BY TRAIN

Train is the cheapest way to travel. However, there is only one daytime train each way on the Kyiv–L'viv and Kyiv–Odesa routes; all other services are overnight. The cheapest tickets are for so-called *platskart* or third class, a cramped open carriage in which the (relatively hard) seats are turned into bunks at night. The next step up is *kupe*, a second-class

compartment with four bunks, while *luks* are private one- or two-person sleeping compartments that are three times more expensive. Whichever class you travel in, your carriage will be controlled by an attendant (*provodnitsa*) who serves you tea but who also prevents you from wandering around from carriage to carriage. Dining cars are rare, so bring your own food and drink. **Train stations** (*vokzal*) are confusing places with little in the way of Latin-script labelling and a proliferation of counters selling different types of ticket. Counters selling tickets for today are marked "Dobovoho prodazhu"; those for advance bookings are marked "Poperednyoho prodazhu". International tickets are bought from counters marked "Mizhnarodnoho spolucheniya".

BY BUS

Intercity bus services are slightly quicker than trains and usually run during daylight hours, although tickets are more expensive. Companies such as Avtolyuks (ⓦautolux .ua) and Gunsel (ⓦgunsel.com.ua) operate services between Kyiv and Odesa, and Kyiv and L'viv. They have booking offices at the main bus stations (*avtovoksal*) in each city. Avtolyuks operate "VIP" services between Kyiv and Odesa that are quicker and slightly more expensive than the regular buses; tickets sell out fast and should be booked well in advance.

36

ACCOMMODATION

Backpacker **hostels** are common in the main cities. They're often rough-and-ready affairs in converted apartments, although most will offer a mixture of multi-bed dorms and private doubles, with a kitchen and/or common room to lounge around in and socialize.

Hotels are the most unpredictable category of accommodation, with informal B&Bs, Soviet-era concrete blocks and modern business-oriented establishments all charging similar prices for hugely varying levels of comfort. In Kyiv it is difficult to find an acceptably habitable double room for less than $100/€80/800Hr; prices are cheaper in Odesa and L'viv.

Local agencies rent out **private rooms** and apartments to tourists in Odesa, where a small self-catering apartment can work out cheaper than a double room in a hotel.

FOOD AND DRINK

Ukrainian cities are well supplied with restaurants (*restoran*), and cafés and pubs frequently have a full menu of food. Cheap and convenient are the self-service **canteens** (*stolova*), which serve local food and help-yourself salads at hard-to-resist prices.

Ukraine is one of the original homelands of **borshch**, the pinky-hued beetroot soup. Ukrainian *borshch* often includes cabbage, along with bits of pork or other meat. A summer alternative to *borshch* is *okroshka*, a cold soup consisting of sour milk, cucumber, bits of ham and boiled egg. Other staples include *varenyky*, ravioli-like parcels of dough with potato, cottage cheese or minced-meat fillings; *sirniki*, cylindrical little cheese cakes with a sweet-and-savoury taste; and a whole range of pancakes (*mlintsi*) stuffed with a variety of ingredients. Pork, beef and chicken figure prominently among the main courses; fish (particularly anchovy and mackerel) is common on the Black Sea coast. Buckwheat (*hrechka*) is a staple side order, while bread with *salo* (pork fat) is a traditional snack. Central Asian dishes once popular across the Soviet Union and still ubiquitous in Ukraine include *shashlik* (shish-kebab) and *cheburek* (a deep-fried meat pasty).

DRINK

Horilka (vodka) is very much the national drink. It usually comes in classic, clear form, although flavoured varieties are also available – *medova s pertsem* (honey vodka with hot red pepper) is the one you must try at least once. The standard measure for spirits is 0.50cl (almost a double by Western standards), so consume in moderation. Ukrainian **beer** (*pivo*) is on the whole excellent, with Obolon, Slavutich, L'vivske and Chernihivske among the main mass-market brewers. Most produce a regular lager-type brew (*svitle*) alongside a dark porter (*tamne*) and a "white" unfiltered beer (*bile*). In addition, an increasing number of brewpubs serve up their own-brand ales, and a good number of small-scale breweries (notably Stare Misto in Western Ukraine) are producing a cracking range of tasty beers.

There is a handful of domestic red and white **wines** from the Crimea, although most bars and restaurants in Kyiv and L'viv tend to serve European, Australian and American imports.

Hookah pipes (*kalyan*) with flavoured tobaccos are very popular among young adults and are a regular feature of Ukrainian bars.

CULTURE AND ETIQUETTE

The majority of Ukrainians are Orthodox Christians. In churches and monasteries, women should cover their heads and shoulders (there may well be stalls outside selling cheap scarves and shawls for precisely this purpose), while men should don long trousers. **Tipping** is not required if you are just having a drink in a café, but ten percent is common in restaurants.

SPORTS AND OUTDOOR ACTIVITIES

Football is the most popular spectator sport, with Shakhtar Donetsk (UEFA Cup winners in 2009) and Dinamo Kyiv enjoying mass support. Karpaty L'viv have had their moments, playing in the group stages of the Europa League in 2010.

36

Ukraine's main **hiking** area is in the smooth green hills of the Carpathian range, with the 2061m Mount Hoverla (Ukraine's highest) the main target. The trailheads are a good three to four hours' drive southeast of L'viv so you will need to plan a two- to three-day trip to make the most of it.

COMMUNICATIONS

Post offices (*Poshta*) in major cities are open Monday to Saturday 9am to 9pm, Sunday 10am to 5pm. Public phones on the street are increasingly rare and can only be used for local calls. They take phonecards (purchased at the post office). Long-distance and international calls are best made from a **telephone office** (usually attached to the main post office), where you pay a deposit before being assigned a

cabin to make your call. Cheap international calls are also available at many of the internet cafés spread throughout city centres. If you are travelling with a laptop, wi-fi internet access is free of charge in many hostels, hotels and city-centre cafés.

EMERGENCIES

Ukraine is a relatively safe country to travel in, although tourists are frequently the target of pickpockets and petty thieves. Ukrainian **police** occasionally carry out spot checks on foreigners so always carry your passport with you. They rarely speak English.

High-street **pharmacies** (*apteka*) sell familiar medicines over the counter. Each city has a 24hr pharmacy in the centre. Staff in Ukrainian public **hospitals** are

36

UKRAINIAN

	UKRAINIAN	PRONUNCIATION
Yes	*Так*	Tak
No	*Ні*	Nyi
Please	*Будь ласка*	bood-la-ska
Thank you	*Дякую*	dya-koo-yoo
Hello/Good day	*Доброго дня*	do-bro-ho dnya
Goodbye	*До побачення*	do po-ba-che-nya
Excuse me/sorry	*Вибачте*	vee-bach-teh
Today	*Сьогодні*	syo-hod-nyi
Yesterday	*Вчора*	Fcho-ra
Tomorrow	*Завтри*	Zaf-tra
I don't understand	*Я не розумію*	Ya ne roz-um-i-yoo
How much?	*Скільки?*	Skil-ki?
Do you speak English?	*Ви розмовляєте*	Vi roz-mov-lya-ee-tee
	англійською мовою?	an-hlee-sko-yoo mo-vo-yoo?
Where is the..?	*Де?*	Deh?
Hotel	*Готель*	Hotel
Bus	*Автобус*	Af-to-boos
Plane	*Літак*	Li-tak
Train	*Поїзд*	Po-yizd
I would like a...	*Я хочу*	Ya ho-chu
Open	*Відчинено*	Vid-chi-ne-no
Closed	*Зачинено*	Za-chi-ne-no
One	*Один*	O-din
Two	*Два*	Dva
Three	*Три*	Tri
Four	*Чотири*	Cho-ti-ri
Five	*П'ять*	Pyat
Six	*Шість*	Shist
Seven	*Сім*	Sim
Eight	*Вісім*	Vi-sim
Nine	*Дев'ять*	Dev-yat
Ten	*Десять*	Des-yat

EMERGENCY NUMBERS
Fire ☎ 101; Police ☎ 102; Ambulance ☎ 103.

unlikely to speak English and you are advised to seek private treatment in the event of illness or injury – so make sure you are insured before you travel.

INFORMATION

L'viv is the only Ukrainian city that has a **tourist information office** and Latin-alphabet signage in the streets. In Kyiv and Odesa, hostel staff and private tourist agencies are the most likely sources of information.

MONEY AND BANKS

Currency is the **hryvnia** (Hr/UAH), divided into 100 kopinky. Coins come in 1, 2, 5, 10, 25 and 50 kopinky denominations; and notes in 1, 2, 5, 10, 20, 50, 100 and 200 hryvnias. At the time of writing, £1 = 12.5Hr, €1 = 10.50Hr, US$1 = 8Hr. Banks (Mon–Fri 9am–6pm, Sat 9am–noon) and exchange offices (*obmin valyut*) offer similar exchange rates. Credit cards are accepted in larger hotels and city-centre shops, but will be refused elsewhere. ATMs are fairly widespread.

OPENING HOURS AND HOLIDAYS

An increasing number of shops in Ukrainian cities are open 10am to 6pm daily, although some have restricted hours on Saturdays and are closed on Sundays. Most museums and historic sights are closed one day a week, and one day at the end of the month for cleaning. **Public holidays** are January 1, January 7, March 8, Easter Sunday & Monday, May 1, May 9, June 28 and August 24.

Kyiv

Sprawling, energetic but never overwhelming, **KYIV** (Київ) combines the stately aura of a great historical city with the raw vigour of a rapidly changing society. Golden-domed churches recall the city's role as the birthplace of Christian Rus – the medieval Slav civilization that subsequently gave rise to both the Ukrainian and Russian nations. Designer-label boutiques, flashy bars and top-of-the-range jeeps offer a jarringly contemporary contrast. With attractions aplenty and a fast-developing nightlife scene, it's a city that is easy to enjoy. It also remains an easy-to-explore capital despite its scale: walking distances between the main sights are not too taxing, and the city's metro system provides quick and cheap transport from one neighbourhood to the next.

WHAT TO SEE AND DO

At the heart of the city is **Khreschatyk**, a broad, tree-lined boulevard bordered by fashion stores, glitzy cafés and imposing government buildings. A brace of historic churches occupies the high ground above, while downhill to the northeast is Podil, an area of serene Neoclassical buildings bordered by residential streets. Linking the two is **Andriivs'kyi uzviz** ("St Andrew's Descent"), the winding cobbled street that best captures the atmosphere of nineteenth-century Kyiv. A short southbound hop on the metro is **Kyivo-Pecherska Lavra**, a rambling monastery complex famous for its icon-rich churches and candlelit catacombs. Bordering the monastery complex to the south, a swathe of riverside park is dominated by **Rodina Mat'**, the imperious statue that symbolizes Soviet Ukraine's struggles against Nazi Germany during the "Great Patriotic War" of 1941–45.

Khreschatyk and around

Lined by shops and cafés, Khreschatyk is the place where many Kyivans come to sip coffee during the day and stroll on summer evenings. At its southwestern end, the boutiques of the Metrograd underground shopping centre provide a contemporary contrast to the pre-World War I Besarabs'kyi Rynok, the indoor market hall that fills daily with fresh produce.

Opposite the Rynok on the corner of Velyka Vasylkivs'ka and Baseina, the **Pinchuk Art Centre** (Tues–Sun noon–9pm;

free) displays contemporary art on four storeys, with major international names featuring heavily in the programme. The top-floor café is decked out in minimallst all-white style and comes with roofline views of downtown Kyiv.

Maidan nezalezhnosti

A horseshoe-shaped square at the eastern end of Khreschatyk, Maidan nezalezhnosti or "Independence Square" has long served as the symbolic heart of the city. During the Soviet period it hosted a statue of Lenin, removed by pro-independence protesters in 1991 and replaced in 2001 with a gilded **statue of Berehynia**, the pre-Christian spirit adopted by romantically inclined Ukrainians as some kind of all-protecting mother-goddess. In December 2004 the square was the scene of mass demonstrations that presaged the so-called Orange Revolution.

St Sofia's Cathedral

Beckoning visitors with its vivacious cluster of green and golden domes, **St Sofia's Cathedral** at Volodymyrs'ka 24 (Mon, Tues & Wed–Sun 10am–5pm; complex 3Hr; cathedral and museums 50Hr) was founded by Prince of Rus Yaroslav the Wise in 1037. Inside the church is Kyiv's most stunning collection of medieval frescoes and mosaics, with scenes in the central dome including Christ Pantocrator surrounded by angels, and a resplendent Virgin with outstretched arms lower down.

St Michael's Golden-Domed Cathedral

Standing opposite St Sofia's at the far end of a long square, **St Michael's** (daily 8am–7pm) was demolished by the Soviets in the 1930s and faithfully reconstructed six decades later. A medieval church given a thorough Baroque makeover in the eighteenth century, it was the first church in Kyiv to sport gilded domes, a practice later picked up by most of the other churches in the city. The church interior contains fragments of original twelfth-century mosaics and frescoes, taken to

St Petersburg in 1937 and returned to Kyiv in 2008.

Andriivs'kyi uzviz

Still paved with its original cobblestones and lined with nineteenth-century houses, the steep and winding **Andriivs'kyi uzviz** is one of the few streets to have preserved its pre-Revolutionary appearance. It is also Kyiv at its most tourist-laden, lined with stalls selling Ukrainian embroidered shirts, Soviet-era collectables and souvenir tat. At the top of the street is St Andrew's Church (daily except Wed 10am–6pm), designed by Baroque master Bartolomeo Rastrelli, its slender dome-topped towers spearing skywards like a gargantuan clump of divine asparagus. Halfway down, the **Mikhail Bulgakov Museum** at no. 13 (Mon, Tues & Thurs–Sun 10am–5pm; 30Hr) fills the novelist's former home with a theatrically arranged collection of exhibits, drawing attention to the more fantastical elements of the author of *The Master and Margarita*'s work. At the bottom of the street, the **One Street Museum** at no. 2 (Tues–Sun noon–6pm; 20Hr) recalls the area's Tsarist-era heyday through a collection of period costumes and sepia photographs.

The Chornobyl Museum

Main sight of the Podil area is the **Chornobyl Museum** at proulok Khoreviy 1 (Natsіonal'nіy muzei Chornobyliu; Mon–Fri 10am–6pm, Sat 10am–5pm; 10Hr; English-language audioguide

---

CHORNOBYL TOURS

Tours of the 30km exclusion zone around the **Chornobyl reactor** are offered by a growing number of local tour agencies. A **day-long trip** will pass near the reactor before visiting the ghost town of Pripyat alongside other eerily deserted sites within the exclusion zone. Despite the high levels of radiation within the zone, one day's exposure is thought to be too insignificant to have an adverse effect on a visitor's health. Per-person prices range from $150–450 depending on how many individuals have signed up for the tour. Tours are likely to be advertised by hostels in Kyiv; otherwise contact one of the agencies in town (see p.1185).

36

36

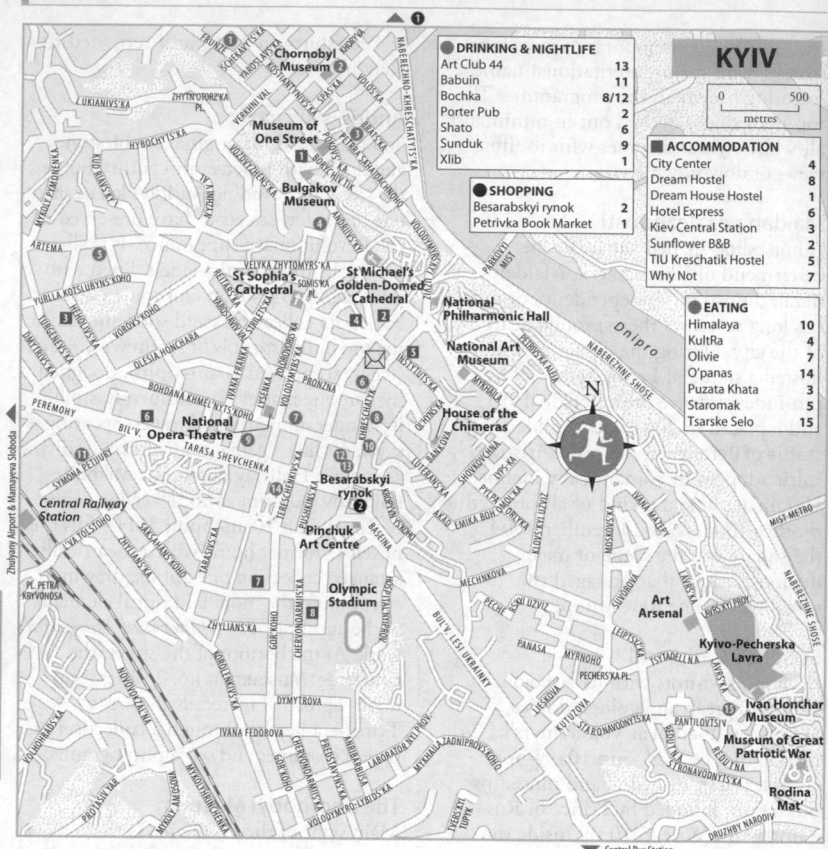

KYIV

0   500
metres

● **DRINKING & NIGHTLIFE**

Art Club 44	13
Babuin	11
Bochka	8/12
Porter Pub	2
Shato	6
Sunduk	9
Xlib	1

■ **ACCOMMODATION**

City Center	4
Dream Hostel	8
Dream House Hostel	1
Hotel Express	6
Kiev Central Station	3
Sunflower B&B	2
TIU Kreschatik Hostel	5
Why Not	7

● **SHOPPING**

Besarabskyi rynok	2
Petrivka Book Market	1

☐ **EATING**

Himalaya	10
KultRa	4
Olivie	7
O'panas	14
Puzata Khata	3
Staromak	5
Tsarske Selo	15

50Hr), an informative and frequently moving account of the events of April 1986 – when an explosion at Chornobyl nuclear power station, 100km north of Kyiv, released a radioactive plume of smoke that travelled over much of Central Europe. The 50,000-strong city of Pripyat was evacuated, and a 30km exclusion zone established – it still exists today. The museum is mostly labelled in Ukrainian, although the photographs and newsreels on display tell the story eloquently enough. It's certainly an affecting tribute to the emergency crews who risked their lives in the aftermath of the disaster.

Kyivo-Pecherska Lavra

Few sights in Kyiv pack the historical and spiritual punch of **Pecherska Lavra**, the "Cave Hermitage" founded on a bluff overlooking the River Dnipro in the eleventh century. Located 1.5km southeast of Khreschatyk, just beyond the Arsenal'na metro station, this sprawling complex of churches, monastery buildings and museums is regarded as the birthplace of Ukrainian and Russian Orthodoxy, and is swarming with pilgrims all year round.

The Lavra is divided into two parts, the **Upper Lavra** to the northwest and the Lower Lavra to the southeast. The Upper Lavra centres on the **Cathedral of the Dormition** and its accompanying bell tower, a five-storey Baroque beauty topped by a gilded dome. Also inside the Upper Lavra compound is the worthwhile **Museum of Ukrainian Folk Art** (Mon & Wed–Sun 10am–6pm; 20Hr), containing the phantasmagorical paintings of self-taught village artist Mariya Pryimachenko.

Highlight of the **Lower Lavra** is the system of caves used by medieval monks as burial vaults, the dry subterranean air helping to mummify many of the bodies laid to rest there. Entrance to the largest group of catacombs, the **Near Caves**, is inside the **Church of the Raising of the Cross** (daily 9am–6pm). Among the coffins stored in niches are the Lavra's founder, Anthony of Athos, eleventh-century folk hero Ilya Muromets, and twelfth-century chronicler Nestor.

The Ivan Honchar Museum

Right outside the Lower Lavra's boundary wall, the **Ivan Honchar Museum**, Ivana Mazepy 29 (Tues–Sun 10am–5.30pm; 15Hr), is an attractively arranged ethnographical collection rich in ceramics, costumes and musical instruments. Look out for trademarks of Ukrainian culture such as the brightly embroidered *rushniki*, long narrow drapes embroidered with geometric fertility symbols.

Rodina Mat'

Rising imperiously from the riverbank to the south of Pecherska Lavra, the 68m-high sword-wielding statue of **Rodina Mat'** ("Homeland Mother") was raised in 1981 in memory of Kyiv's suffering in World War II. Constructed from plates of steel bolted together, she looks like a cross between a classical goddess and a gargantuan robot. The statue's cone-shaped pedestal holds a Museum of the Great Patriotic War (as World War II was known in the Soviet Union; Tues–Sun 10am–5pm; 10Hr), recalling Kyiv's two-year occupation by the Germans. An open-air section of the museum (daily 9am–7pm; 2Hr) is packed with post-World War II Soviet hardware, MIG jets and rocket launchers included.

Mamayeva sloboda

If there is one historical community associated with the Ukraine then it's the Cossacks – and it's only fitting that they have their own theme park in the shape of **Mamayeva sloboda** (daily 10am–6pm; 100Hr; ⓦmamayeva-sloboda.ua). Situated 7km west of the centre on vul. Dontsya (trolleybus #27 from

ⓂShulyavs'ka), it's basically a re-creation of a typical seventeenth-century Cossack settlement, complete with thatched dwellings and a timber-built church. Displays of folk crafts, horseriding and swordsmanship are held at weekends, and traditional dishes washed down with vodka are available in the *Shynok* restaurant (open till 11pm).

ARRIVAL AND DEPARTURE

By plane Most international flights arrive at Boryspil 29km southeast of the city, which has three main terminals (B, D and F). The terminals are within a 5–10min walk of each other, and there is also a shuttle bus connecting them all. Sky Bus buses from the stops in front of terminals B and F run to the Central Railway Station (every 15min, 6am–8pm, then every 30–45min till 6am the following morning; 50min; 28Hr). Some budget flights arrive at Zhulyani airport, which is 8km west of the centre (bus #9 runs to the central train station).

By train International trains terminate at the Central Railway Station (Tsentralnyi vokzal) on the western fringes of the centre. Leave the main exit and turn left to find the Voksal'na metro station: downtown Khreschatyk is only two stops from here.

Destinations Budapest (1 daily; 25hr); Kraków (change at L'viv and Przemysl; 1 daily; 14hr); L'viv (7 daily; 5hr–9hr 20min); Moscow (3 daily; 10–13hrs); Odesa (4 daily; 8hr 30min–11hr); Warsaw (1 daily; 18hr).

By bus Kyiv's Central Bus Station (Tsentralnyi avtovoksal) is at pl. Moskovska 4km southwest of the centre. Demiivs'ka metro station is a 5min walk west of the bus station; otherwise taxis will take you into town for 50–60Hr.

Destinations L'viv (4 daily; 8hr); Odesa (8 daily; 5hr 30min–7hr 30min); Warsaw (4 weekly; 16hr).

INFORMATION AND TOURS

Tours Free Tours (ⓣ066 851 855, ⓦfreetours.kiev.ua) offer a daily choice of two 3hr walking tours of city sights; Solo East, Prorezna 10 (ⓣ044 279 3505, ⓦ.tourkiev.com), offer Chornobyl tours; Tour2Kiev (ⓣ044 451 6171, ⓦtour2kiev.com) also do day-trips to Chernobyl.

GETTING AROUND

By bus and trolleybus One-way tickets cost 1.50Hr and should be bought from newspaper kiosks before boarding.

By metro Kyiv has three metro lines (red, blue and green). All of them intersect at central Khreschatyk. One-way fares cost 2Hr; buy a plastic token from the *kassa* and push it into the slot at the entrance barriers. You can travel with a compact rucksack on the metro but not large items of luggage.

36

36

By minibus Yellow-coloured *marshrutki* operate on many routes. Pay the driver (2–3Hr; the price will be displayed on the side of the bus).

ACCOMMODATION

HOSTELS

City Center Sofiivs'ka 2 apt 10 ☎ 098 263 6506 & 044 278 5246, ✉ hostel.happy@mail.ru; ⓜ Maidan Nezalezhnosti. Bright and airy apartment with a mixture of social space, dorms and private rooms. Not the quietest of locations but it does come with a balcony overlooking the main square. Dorm <u>100Hr</u>, double <u>360Hr</u>

Dream Hostel Chervonoarmiys'ka 47 ☎ 066 244 1447, ⓦ dream-hostel.com; ⓜ L. Tolstoho. Bright and pleasant hostel with two dorms, a quad and a double, within striking distance of both Khreschatyk and the national football stadium. There's a slump-in-a-beanbag common room, and breakfast for a few extra hryvnia. Dorm <u>100Hr</u>, double <u>280Hr</u>

Dream House Hostel Andriivskyi uzviz 2-D ☎ 044 580 2169, ⓦ dream-family.com; ⓜ Kontraktova. New offshoot for the Dream team (see above), in a courtyard just off Kyiv's most characterful pedestrianized street. Common areas are chic and spacious, dorms and privates neat and modern. Dorm <u>100Hr</u>, double <u>380Hr</u>

Kiev Central Station Hoholivs'ka 25, apt 11 ☎ 093 758 7468, ⓦ kievcentralstation.hostel.com; ⓜ Universytet. In a nicely kept apartment with parquet floors and cheerful colours, this is the most convenient hostel for early-morning getaways, with the central train station a 15–20min walk away. The usual mix of doubles and dorms, plus kitchen-diner chill-out zone. Dorm <u>90Hr</u>, double <u>350Hr</u>

TIU Kreschatik Hostel Khreshchatyk 8b, apt 11 ☎ 066 932 3676, ⓦ tiu-kreschatik.com.ua; ⓜ Maidan Nezalezhnosti. Small, intimate and friendly place with only one dorm and one private. The decent-sized lounge helps generate a family atmosphere. Dorm <u>130Hr</u>, double <u>250Hr</u>

Why Not Saksahans'koho 30/3a ☎ 063 688 3880, ⓦ whynothostels.com; ⓜ L. Tolstoho. A colourful collection of rooms ranging in size from a 10-bed dorm to quads and doubles, located a short 1km walk southwest of Khreschatyk. Kitchen and chill-out room. Dorm <u>70Hr</u>, double <u>270Hr</u>

HOTELS

Hotel Express Shevchenka 38/40 ☎ 044 234 2113, ⓦ expresskiev.com; ⓜ Universytet. This ungainly tower block is a perfectly situated 10min walk from the train station and has frumpy but acceptably clean en-suite rooms with TV and tiny balcony. The top-floor breakfast room (complete with tropical fish) is a major plus. Double <u>820Hr</u>

Sunflower B&B Kostel'na 9–41 ☎ 044 279 3846, ⓦ sunflowerhotel.kiev.ua; ⓜ Maydan Nezalezhnosti. Superbly central but secretively tucked away in a courtyard, this intimate B&B offers bright rooms, warm colours and friendly customer service. Double <u>1000Hr</u>

EATING

Himalaya Khreschatyk 23 ⓜ Khreschatyk. Occupying a glassy pavilion set back from the main boulevard, this well-established Indian restaurant serves authentic food with plenty of spice – and a good range of vegetarian options. Mains from 80Hr. Daily 11.30am–11.30pm.

KultRa Volodymyrs'ka 4 ⓜ Zoloti vorota. Café-restaurant themed on the culture of medieval Kievan Rus – with nothing (potatoes for example) that was subsequently imported to Europe. Organic bread, soup served in a half-pumpkin, fried fish and a gorgeous range of sweet and savoury pancakes. Occasional concerts and literary evenings pull in the cultured crowd. Mains 100Hr. Daily 10am–11pm.

Olivie Khmel'nyts'koho 16 ⓜ Teatral'na. A self-service canteen with a long line of dishes laid out on hotplates, this is a good place to sample local favourites such as *kievski kotlet* (chicken kiev), *vareniki* (ravioli-like dumplings stuffed with savoury fillings), and more. Main courses 15–25Hr. Daily 8am–10pm.

O'panas Tereschenkivs'ka 10 ⓜ Teatral'na. This restaurant in Taras Shevchenko park has plenty of garden seating and an interior that looks like a giant-sized peasant's hut. The menu is Ukrainian-international, ranging from *vareniki* with cabbage (55Hr) to rib-eye steak (220Hr). Daily 10am–11pm.

Puzata Khata Sahaidachnoho 24 ⓜ Kontraktova. Cafeteria with roomy second-floor dining room overlooking Kontraktova pl, and staff dressed in folksy costumes serving a broad range of Ukrainian dishes. A convenient place to grab a bite in Podil, with *borshch* from 6Hr. Daily 8am–11pm.

Staromak Artema 37/41 ⓜ Zoloti vorota. Czech-themed restaurant a 10min walk west of the cathedrals, serving thirst-quenching Ferdinand and Krušovice beers, accompanied by a long menu of meat-heavy mains (roast duck with dumplings 147Hr). Daily 10am–2am.

Tsarske Selo Ivana Mazepy 42/1 ⓜ Arsenal'na. Ukrainian food, wait-staff dressed in traditionally embroidered blouses, and an interior strong on wooden benches and wall-mounted textiles. Hearty pork and chicken dishes from 60Hr. Daily 8am–1am.

DRINKING AND NIGHTLIFE

Art Club 44 Khreschatyk 44b ⓦ club44.com.ua; ⓜ Khreschatyk. Live rock, jazz, blues and world music with acts ranging from local cover bands to cutting-edge alternative. Face control, but not as strict as in some of the other clubs. Admission 40–50Hr. Daily 10am–2/3am.

★ **Babuin** Simona Petlyura 10 ⓜ Universytet. A bookshop, café and drinks bar rolled into one, the "baboon" is a mellow and rather chic place decked out in orangey colours and oriental-looking lanterns. Long popular with an arty crowd, there's a menu that takes in everything from salads to steaks, and a functions room that hosts literary events and live jazz. Daily 10am–1am.

Bochka Khmelnyts'koho 3 ⓜTeatral'na. Popular microbrewery pub serving their own brew on tap alongside plenty of other Ukrainian beers. There's also an extensive menu of main meals and snacks. Set in a courtyard with a colonnaded terrace decorated with hanging baskets, it's a relaxing spot for a beer. The other branch of *Bochka*, in the courtyard behind Khreshchatyk 21, has a more raucous beer-hall feel. Both 24hr.

Porter Pub Spas'ka 13 ⓜKontraktova. Best of the drinking venues in the Podil district, with Ukrainian and Czech beers on tap, and outdoor seating on the street-facing wooden decking. Live cover bands at weekends. Daily 11am–1am.

Shato Khreschatyk 24 ⓜKhreschatyk. Pricier than most and occasionally slightly snobbish, this roomy brewpub is still one of the few spots along Khreschatyk that has a street-side terrace. Excellent own-brand beer, and traditional snacks such as cheese platters, sausages and pigs' ears. 24hr.

Sunduk Mykhailivs'ka 16 ⓜUniversytet. A laidback and cosy pub on a quiet but central street, serving up its own-brew lager beer as well as more mainstream names. The food menu ranges from pizza to ribs, and there's a pleasant outdoor terrace under the trees. Daily 11am–11pm.

Xlib Frunze 12 ⓜKontraktova. Pronounced "hlib", this minimally decorated warehouse-style space concentrates on quality of music (house, trance, techno, dub reggae) rather than kitsch decor and bad-attitude bouncers. Occasional live gigs too. Admission 40–50Hr. Thurs–Sat 11pm–6am.

SHOPPING

Besarabskyi rynok ⓜL. Tolstoho. A pungent collection of fresh fruit, vegetables, fish and flowers in a nineteenth-century covered market hall. Tins of caviar 200Hr. Daily 8am–6pm.

Petrivka Book Market ⓜPetrivka oskovsky. A warren of stalls selling new and secondhand books, maps, stationery and computer software. Daily 9am–5pm.

DIRECTORY

Embassies Canada, Kostelna 13a ☎590 3100, ⓦkyiv .gc.ca; Ireland, Shchorsa 44 ☎285 5902, ⓦirishconsulate .kiev.ua; UK, Desyatynna 9 ☎490 3660, ⓦgov.uk /government/world/ukraine; US, Sikorsky 4 ☎521 5000, ⓦukraine.usembassy.gov.

Hospital American Medical Center Berdychivs'ka 1 (☎044 490 7600; ⓜLuk'yanivs'ka).

Internet At the Post Office, Khreshchatyk 22 (24hr; 10Hr/hr).

Left Luggage At the central train station: luggage lockers in the basement – buy a token from the cashier (24hr; 14Hr/item). Also at the bus station (6am–10.30pm; 7–10Hr/item).

Pharmacy 03 Apteka Shevchenka 58 (24hr).

Post office Khreshchatyk 22 (Mon–Sat 8am–9pm, Sun 9am–7pm).

Odesa

Founded by Russian Empress Catherine the Great in 1794, **ODESA** (Одеса) is both busy port and beach resort, exuding a seductive blend of commercial swagger and riviera-town style. Well-preserved nineteenth-century buildings provide a sense of historical grandeur, while the bars of Deribasivs'ka and nightclubs at the nearby beaches ensure that you're never too far away from a party. It's a town popular with tourists all over the Russian-speaking world, and a holiday atmosphere reigns for much of the spring and summer.

WHAT TO SEE AND DO

With a grid of predominantly nineteenth-century streets, Odesa is a welcoming and easily stroll-able city. The pedestrianized, café-lined strip of Deribasivs'ka is the centre's main focal point, with a deliciously pink-and-cream Art Nouveau shopping arcade at its western end providing an irresistible architectural flourish. From Deribasivs'ka, Yekaterynyns'ka curves down towards the Potemkin Stairs and the port area, passing stately rows of Neoclassical buildings on the way. Odesa's sandy beaches spread for several kilometres along the southeastern side of the city; the most famous of them is Arkadia, a twenty-minute tram ride from the centre.

The Potemkin Stairs

Completed in 1841, the 192-step sweep of the Potemkin Stairs was immortalized in Sergei Eisenstein's 1925 film *Battleship Potemkin* – in which Tsarist troops march remorselessly down the steps firing on demonstrators, famously upsetting a baby's pram on the way. It remains one of the most iconic locations in the whole Ukraine, and it's here that every visitor to Odesa comes to be photographed.

The tree-lined Prymors'ka promenade runs either side of the top of the steps. At the eastern end of the promenade a statue of Alexander Pushkin (resident here 1823–24) stands in front of **Odesa City Hall**, a Neoclassical building boasting a Corinthian columned portico.

36

Beaches

Stretching east of town is a string of sandy beaches, each backed by a clutch of cafés and restaurants. They are linked by Trasazdoroviya ("The Path of Health"), a tree-shaded path that runs along the coast from central Odesa – pick it up from the Monument to the Unknown Sailor in Shevchenko Park. Nearest to the centre is **Lanzheron**, packed with city folk on summer weekends. One kilometre further on is **Otrada**, famous for the rudimentary cable car (each car resembling a metal bucket) that links the beach to bul. Frantsuzsky, the main street that runs along the high ground above.

Best known of the beaches is **Arkadia**, 5km from the centre (near the terminus of tram #5 if you don't fancy the walk), and main focus of the city's party life. It's a small but undoubtedly beautiful crescent of sand, much of which is administered by beach-side cafés renting out sun loungers and parasols (70–80Hr for the day). On the edges are "free" stretches of beach where you can lay your towel – although they are crowded at weekends.

Odesa catacombs

Stay at one of Odesa's backpacker hostels and you'll inevitably be offered the chance to go on a tour of Odesa's so-called **catacombs**, the honeycomb of tunnels carved by nineteenth-century limestone miners and used by anti-Nazi partisans during World War II. Led by local speleologists, the tours are unofficial, at-your-own-risk affairs that pay scant regard to health-and-safety regulations – you may get a pair of overalls but you're unlikely to be issued a hard hat. The tours usually focus on the catacombs near Nerubays'ke, 10km north of Odesa, and frequently include a visit to the **Partizanska Slava** memorial complex, where a few short stretches of tunnel have been opened as an official museum. Expect to pay 180–220Hr per person for the guided tour and taxi transfer.

ARRIVAL AND INFORMATION

By plane Odesa airport is 12km south of the centre. Marshrutka #117 runs from here to the central Yekaterins'ka.
By train Odesa train station is 2km south of the main

downtown area. Bus #220 runs from here to Hrets'ka, a stone's throw from the main Deribasivs'ka.
Destinations Kyiv (4 daily; 8hr 30min–11hr); L'viv (1 daily; 12hr).
By bus Odesa's central bus station is 4km west of the centre at Kolontayivs'koi 58. Tram #5 runs from here to the train station.
Destinations Kyiv (8 daily; 5hr 30min–7hr 30min).
Maps Empik, Deribasivs'ka 14, is a bookshop that sells maps of Odesa and surrounding region. Daily 10am–8pm.

GETTING AROUND

By bus, trolleybus and tram Tickets (1.50Hr) are bought from conductors on board.

ACCOMMODATION

The Kvartirne byuro at Odesa train station (opposite platform 4; daily 8am–noon & 1–5pm; ☎ 048 727 4133) has a choice of private rooms (60–100Hr) and apartments (from 300Hr) in locations across the city. Outside the train station, unofficial landladies hawk rooms (*kvartiri*) at cheaper prices – have a map handy to check locations before accepting any offers.
Babushka Grand Mala Arnauts'ka 60 ☎ 630 705 535. Conveniently close to the train station, *Babushka* offers a taste of Odesa's faded glories, with nineteenth-century chandeliers and ceiling mouldings presiding over a snug collection of dorm beds and privates. It's a good place for mellow socializing and staff have good local knowledge. Dorm 125Hr, double 375Hr
Deribas Deribasivs'ka 27 ☎ 048 700 0521, ☜ hotel -deribas.com. Hidden in an alleyway linking Deribasivs'ka with pl. Hrets'ka, and initially difficult to find, this apartment-hotel offers pristine modern doubles and 3- to 4-person studios in a superbly central spot. Free wi-fi, but no breakfast. Double 550Hr
Magic Bus Backpackers Pushkins'ka 8, apt 14 ☎ 978 333 358, ☜ magicbushostel.com. Central, converted apartment comprising two private doubles and two dorms, homely kitchen and common room. Dorm 115Hr, double 350Hr
★ **TIU Front Page** Koblevs'ka 42 ☎ 968 344 074. A fine old apartment with creaky floors, high ceilings, and a welcoming living room and kitchen-diner, *Front Page* has a good mix of dorms and private doubles. Friendly staff and a family atmosphere as well. Dorm 115Hr, double 380Hr

EATING

Bazilik Deribasivs'ka 1. Cute café with arty-rustic interior and a terrace shaded by tassled awnings, serving good teas and coffees and an extensive menu of Mediterranean-influenced food. Salads (60Hr), pastas (55Hr). Daily 9am–midnight.
Fat Mozes Yekateryns'ka 8/10. Cosy restaurant with booth seating inside and a 4-table terrace overlooking the

street. The short but varied menu of regional cuisine takes in Moldavian mincemeat kebabs, local fish and meaty stews. Mains in the 70Hr range. Daily 11am–11pm.

Pizza Olio Gavanna 7 and Bunina 35. Justifiably popular Mediterranean-themed place serving up speedy and reliable thin-crust pizzas and a range of pasta dishes, with mains in the 45–60Hr bracket. Daily 9am–11pm.

Robin Bobin Saborna 2. Occupying a comfy timber porch facing a leafy park, *Robin Bobin* offers traditional Ukrainian dishes and also plenty of salt- and freshwater fish. Try the pan-fried fillets of pike-perch (*sudak*) for 70Hr. Daily 10am–11pm.

Tavriya Galereya Afina, pl. Hrets'ka 3–4. Smart self-service restaurant with passable main courses and good pastries and cakes, in the basement of the Afina shopping mall. There's also an express pizzeria, sushi bar and supermarket on the same floor. Pile your tray high for under 40Hr. Daily 8am–10pm.

DRINKING AND NIGHTLIFE

Fanconi Katerynyns'ka 15. Swish café-bar whose street-facing terrace is hugely popular with the mid-evening cocktail-sipping crowd. The menu takes in sushi, cakes, ice cream and other fancy food. 24hr.

Ibiza Arkadia ⓦ ibiza.ua. Popular beach club with a dancefloor right by the sea and bizarre white pods that serve as "VIP" boxes, with a busy programme of DJs and Ukrainian pop stars throughout the summer. May–Sept 10pm–5am.

Itaka Arkadia ⓦ itaka-club.com.ua. With palm trees, swimming pools and fluted columns reminiscent of a classical Greek temple, this is an enjoyably kitsch beach club pulling in international DJs and party-hungry locals. May–Sept 9pm–5am.

Pivnoy sad Havanna 6. Brew pub with a big subterranean dining hall and a terrace facing the lush lawns of the city garden. With a couple of own-brand lagers and porters there's plenty of ale to sample, plus a food menu taking in soups, grilled sausages and other pub grub. Daily 11am–midnight.

Rock and Roll Dvoryans'ka 7. One of several local bars squeezed into the streets west of pl. Soborna, with inexpensive draught beer, quirky-but-cool pop rock sounds, and an odd mixture of comfy chairs and sofas. Live bands at weekends. Daily 10am–midnight.

ENTERTAINMENT

National Opera Chaikovs'koho 1 ☏ 048 722 2230, ⓦ opera.odessa.ua. Nothing sums up Odesa's *belle époque* more than the grandeur of its opera house, erected in 1883. It hosts top-quality performances from the classic opera and ballet repertoire, and tickets are comparatively cheap.

SHOPPING

Novy rynok Torhova. Not the biggest of Odesa's markets but certainly the handiest central place to stock up on picnic provisions, with smoked Black Sea mackerel, fresh cheese and other scrumptious local produce. Daily 7am–6pm.

Pl. Soborna This centrally located square fills up daily with stalls selling crafts and souvenirs in spring and summer. Daily 9am–9pm.

Starokonny rynok Starokonny pereulok; tram #5 to Kosvenna. A neighbourhood market near the bus station that hosts a huge flea market on Sun, with vendors laying out their wares on the pavements of several surrounding streets. Old clothes, crockery, kids' toys, Soviet-period junk and more. Sun 7am–3pm.

L'viv

Home to a burgeoning café scene and an ever-growing stock of backpacker hostels, forward-looking **L'VIV** (Львів) represents Ukraine at its most tourist-friendly. For centuries subject to Polish then Habsburg overlords, L'viv still looks and feels like a slice of Central Europe, its welter of Catholic, Orthodox and Armenian churches attesting to a multi-cultural past. Historically the centre of the Ukrainian national movement, L'viv remains an avowedly Ukrainian-speaking city. With uneven cobbled streets, creaky-floored art galleries and trams screeching their way around tracks that were laid generations ago, the city has the look of a well-preserved nineteenth-century survivor. A night spent exploring the city's addictively eccentric bars will soon dispel any ideas that this is just a museum piece.

36

WHAT TO SEE AND DO

A fistful of churches and palaces lies within a pedestrian-friendly **Old Town**, its neat grid of streets arranged around the spacious Rynok (Market Square). An irregular circle of broad boulevards and park-like greenery separates the Old Town from the nineteenth-century suburbs beyond. A short hike up **Visokyi Zamok** hill, just north of the Old Town, provides an expansive panorama of central L'viv and is a good way to get your bearings.

36

The Rynok

Surrounded by stately mansions and a warren of courtyards, the Rynok is the centre of L'viv's social life, abuzz with outdoor cafés in the summer. At its centre is the Neoclassical **Town Hall** or Ratusha, its castellated **tower** (Tues–Sun 10am–6pm; 10Hr) a nineteenth-century copy of an earlier medieval version. Most eye-catching of the buildings on the Rynok's eastern side is the **Black House** at no. 4, with statues of saints protruding from its grime-encrusted sixteenth-century facade. Next door at no. 6 is the **Kornyakt Palace**, famous for its arcaded Renaissance courtyard (nowadays a daytime café).

Around the Old Town

Just off the southwestern corner of the Rynok, the fourteenth-century **Latin Cathedral** (the city's main Catholic church) contains a show-stopping sequence of Baroque altarpieces. Have your camera at the ready for the adjacent **Boim Chapel**, at Katedral'na 1 (Tues–Sun 10am–5pm; 10Hr), encrusted both inside and out with an animated collection of seventeenth-century statuettes. Although built on the model of medieval Armenian churches, the **Armenian Cathedral**, a block north of the square on Virmens'ka, contains a delicious collection of Art Nouveau frescoes by Józef Mehoffer and Jan Henryk Rosen.

Arguably the finest of L'viv's churches, the **Bernardine Cathedral** on pl. Soborna boasts a Dutch-Renaissance facade and bulbous belfry, its profile recognizable from countless tourist brochures.

Fragments of L'viv's fortifications still survive along Pidval'na, where the sixteenth-century **Arsenal** at no. 5 (Mon, Tues & Thurs–Sun 10am–5pm; 20Hr) contains a display of helmets, breastplates, pikes and early firearms.

Prospekt Svobody

Running along L'viv's Old Town to the west is **Prospekt Svobody** ("Freedom Avenue"), a broad two-lane street with a strip of fountain-splashed park running up the middle. Presiding haughtily over the scene is L'viv Opera House, dating from 1900 and topped with a trio of winged statues symbolizing the arts.

Diagonally opposite at Svobody 20, the **National Museum** (Tues–Sun 10am–6pm; 20Hr) holds an impressive collection of Ukrainian Orthodox icons.

The Brewery Museum

Two kilometres northwest of the centre at bul. Kleparivs'ka 18, L'viv's brewery was a highly respected brand throughout the Habsburg and Soviet eras, and (although now owned by a well-known multinational) continues to churn out well-regarded local-recipe brews. Right beside the brewery gate is the **Brewery Museum** (admissions Mon & Wed–Sun at 10.30am, noon, 1.30pm, 3pm, 4.30pm & 5.30pm; museum 10Hr, museum and beer tasting 20Hr), a small but entertaining display that tells the history of beer brewing from its origins in the ancient Middle East to the present day. There's a diorama of ale-making friars (beer brewing in L'viv was actually founded by the Jesuits in 1715), and a model of L'viv brewery as it looked in 1860.

Occupying the huge barrel-vaulted cellars underneath the museum, the **Robert Doms House of Beer** (daily noon–midnight) is named after the Swiss entrepreneur who owned the brewery in the mid-nineteenth century, and serves up draught L'vivs'ke by the litre.

Lychakivs'ke Cemetery

Entered from Mechnikova 3km southeast of the centre, **Lychakivs'ke Cemetery** (daily 10am–6pm; 10Hr; tram #7 or #8 to Pekars'ka) is one of Central Europe's classical burial grounds, park-like in its landscaped beauty and brimming with over two centuries' worth of fine funerary monuments. Originally laid out in 1786, it is now a museum reserve: indeed the sheer profusion of ornate family chapels, sculpted angels and statues of the deceased gives the place the appearance of an outdoor art gallery. The southeastern corner of the cemetery is dominated by the so-called **Cemetery of the Eagles**, a memorial complex built by the interwar Polish state to commemorate the (mostly very young) volunteers who beat off pro-independence Ukrainian forces in the winter of 1918/1919. Right next to it is a towering, pillar-top statue of the **Archangel Michael**, honouring the Ukrainians who fell in the very same conflict.

Folk Architecture Museum

Spread over a forested hillside to the north of Lichakivs'ke Cemetery at Chernecha Hora 1 (daily 9am–6pm; 10Hr; tram #2, #7 or #8 to Mechnikova then walk uphill), this collection of timber-built houses and barns from all over Western Ukraine provides the ideal introduction to the region's much-cherished rural traditions. The most spectacular buildings are the fairytale Carpathian churches, their belfries raised in pagoda-like tiers.

ARRIVAL AND DEPARTURE

By plane L'viv airport is 6km southwest of the city centre. Trolleybus #9 (40min; 1Hr) and *marshrutka* #95 (35min; 2Hr) run into town; otherwise a taxi costs 80–120Hr.

By train The train station is 2km west of the centre at the top of Chernivets'ka. ATMs are in the arrivals hall, and the "lux" waiting room (3Hr/hr) offers free wi-fi. Trams #1 & #9 run to the centre. Taxis vary between 30–60Hr depending on how gullible you look. International tickets are sold from a counter upstairs in the "Hall of Enhanced Comfort". Reservations for international trains frequently sell out a few days in advance, so don't bank on leaving town this way.
Destinations Budapest (1 daily; 13hr); Kraków (1 daily; 8hr); Odesa (1 daily; 12hr).

By bus The main bus station is at bul. Striys'ka 109, 6km southeast of the centre. Trolleybus #4 runs to Shota Rustaveli, a 10min walk south of the main square. A taxi will set you back 50–60Hr. *Marshrutki* minibuses from Medyka-Shehyni (the Polish–Ukraine border) arrive at the train station.
Destinations Prague (5 weekly; 17hr); Rīga (4 weekly; 16hr).

INFORMATION

Tourist information The tourist office in the town hall, Rynok 1 (Mon–Fri 10am–8pm, Sat 10am–7pm, Sun 10am–6pm; ☎032 254 6079, ⓦtouristinfo.lviv.ua), has free town maps and can advise on accommodation.
Maps Knigarnya E, pr. Svobody 7 (Mon–Fri 10am–8pm, Sat 10am–3pm), is the place to stock up on maps.

GETTING AROUND

By tram, bus and trolleybus Almost everything in central L'viv is walkable but you will need to use the city's mixture of trams, buses and trolleybuses to get to train and bus stations as well as outlying attractions such as Lychakivs'ke Cemetery and the Folk Architecture Museum. Buy single-journey tickets (1Hr) from kiosks or from the driver.

ACCOMMODATION

Art Hostel Rynok 3 apt. 4 ☎032 297 5195, ⓦarthostel .lviv.ua. Located up several flights of magnificently creaky stairs, this hostel looks directly out onto the main square, with a multi-bed dorm, a private double and a small kitchen. Breakfast available for an extra few hryvnia. Dorm 85Hr, double 220Hr
Central Square Hostel Rynok 5 ☎095 225 6654, ⓦcshostel.com. Historical building in a square-side location, with two bunk-bed dorms, a very spacious private double, a social room and a kitchen. Dorm 95Hr, double 350Hr
George Mitskievycha 1 ☎032 232 6236, ⓦgeorgehotel .com.ua. A charming Habsburg-era hotel that has retained many of its interior features, the *George* offers high ceilings, sturdy furnishings and parquet floors at decidedly old-school prices. En suites cost 160Hr extra. Double 420Hr
Kosmonaut Sichovych striltsiv 6 ☎032 260 1602, ⓦthekosmonaut.com. A bit tatty round the edges but superbly welcoming, *Kosmonaut* continues to lead the way when it comes to cultivating a friendly, sociable and informative hostel environment. A range of 12- to 4-bed dorms in an off-street courtyard, and breakfast is included in the price. Dorm 100Hr
Old City Hostel Beryndy 3 ☎032 294 9644, ⓦoldcityhostel.lviv.ua. This new hostel in a nineteenth-century apartment block with plush furnishings and parquet floor will suit those who prefer their accommodation to be squeaky clean. There's a fully equipped kitchen. Dorm 100Hr, double 320Hr

EATING

Amadeus Katedral'na pl. 7. For quality pan-European cuisine in a picturesque city-centre square, you can't do much better than *Amadeus*. The food ranges from humble *varenyky* (stuffed pastry parcels) to fancy Adriatic seafood with plenty of pork-chop fare in between; expect to fork out 100–150Hr for mains. Daily 11am–11pm.
Kumpel Vynnychenka 7. Microbrewery and restaurant whose huge copper vats form an attractive centrepiece to the dining room. Steaks, stews, sausages and schnitzels are the main items on the menu. Wash it down with *Kumpel*'s own-brand *svitle* (a pale refreshing lager) or *burshtinove* (a more rounded brown-coloured ale). Mains 80–100Hr. Daily 11am–midnight.
L'vivs'ka maysternya shokoladu Serbs'ka 3. Strong coffee, velvety drinking chocolate and in-house ice creams. The delectable range of own-brand, handmade chocolates makes repeat visits a near-certainty. Daily 10am–8pm.
Myasa ta spravedlivost Bernardine Monastery courtyard (access from Halyts'ka pl). An open-sided barn with medieval torture masks hanging from the beams, "Meat and Justice" serves up sausage, chicken, steak and other grilled fare, with staff dressed in serving-wench garb and food

36

36

arriving on wooden platters. Theatrical it may be, but young locals love it. Mains 35–70Hr. Daily 11am–midnight.

Pid zolotoyu rozoyu Staroevreys'ka 48. Ukrainian-Jewish restaurant named after the Golden Rose synagogue (which stood nearby until World War II), offering a good range of traditional dishes like *cholent* (meat and barley stew) and stuffed carp. The interior is dark, woody and atmospheric, and the outdoor terrace comes with views of the town walls. There are no prices on the menu, and you are invited to bargain your bill at the end of your meal. Daily noon–midnight.

Puzata Khata Sichovykh Striltsiv 12. City-centre branch of the trusty self-service canteen chain, especially strong on *varenyky*, *mlintsi* and other Ukrainian staples. Frequently packed with Polish tour groups, who know a good culinary bargain when they see one. Fill up your plate for under 40Hr. Daily 8am–10pm.

Stargorod pl. Mytna. A huge pub-restaurant with a vaguely Czech theme, serving excellent own-brewed beer (half litre/20Hr) accompanied by meat-heavy dishes such as sausage (60Hr) and roast duck (115Hr). The roomy interior incorporates a re-creation of L'viv main square, and the beer garden is truly vast. 24hr.

DRINKING AND NIGHTLIFE

BARS

Bilya Diani Rynok. With chairs and tables scattered around the statue of Diana in the Rynok's southwestern corner, this outdoor café is the ideal place for a thirst-quenching beer, serving up own-brand light and dark ales as well as a range of nibbles – the *sudzhuk* (spicy beef sausage) platter goes down a treat. May–Sept daily 10am–11pm.

Buket vina Staroevreys'ka 5 & 15. Wine bar with two branches on the same street, serving Crimean reds on tap and a few more fancy international choices by the bottle. Both get busy in summer: join the overspill clinking glasses outside on the pavement. Daily 11am–10pm.

Dim lehend Staroevreys'ka 48. The five-storey "House of Legends" begins with a souvenir shop on the ground floor and a sequence of wackily decorated drinking rooms above, culminating with a dizzying roof terrace. Fills nightly with young L'vivians enjoying draught beers and a menu of snacks. Daily 11am–2am.

★ **Dzyha** Virmens'ka 35. Cult art centre comprising a gallery, a café-pub (*Pid Klepsydroyu*) with a varied food menu, and an upstairs performance space (*Kvartyra 35*) that hosts folk and jazz concerts as well as being a cool place to drink. Daily 11am–midnight.

Gasova Lyampa Virmens'ka 20. Head down the steps and then up a spiral staircase to reach this characterful bar occupying four cramped storeys of a tall and narrow house. Draught beers and meaty snacks are served up in rooms decorated with pictures of gas lamps and oil derricks: a

statue of Ignacy Lukasiewicz, oil pioneer and inventor of the kerosene lamp, sits outside. Daily 11am–2am.

Kabinet Vynnychenka 12. Literary café with book-filled shelves and a programme of cultural events, *Kabinet*'s collection of armchairs and sofas makes it an ideal venue for a relaxing evening drink. Also menu of inexpensive eats. Daily 10am–11pm.

Masoch Serbs'ka 7. Author of *Venus in Furs* Leopold von Sacher-Masoch was born in L'viv in 1836, and this café-bar serves as some kind of kinky tribute. The decor (lacy fabrics, whips) is charming rather than over-the-top, and cocktails (from 45Hr) have corny names like *Burning Desire*. Your bill is delivered in a high-heeled shoe. Daily 11am–1am.

Zenik Mytnyk Kostyushka 1. A modern bar with bold red colours, table football, and occasional live music or karaoke, *Zenik* offers a contemporary riposte to the historically-themed places around the main square. It's next door to the Ukrainian customs administration, which helps to explain the pictures of border guards ("Mytnyk") on the walls. Mon–Fri 8am–2am, Sat & Sun 10am–2am.

CLUBS

Metro Zelena 14 ⓦ metroclub.com.ua. Big city-centre club with a dancefloor policy ranging from commercial Euro-pop to cutting-edge trance and techno. Good social mix of local youngsters and international students. Cover 25–50Hr. Daily 9pm–6am.

Picasso bul. Zelena 88 ⓦ picasso.lviv.ua. Seventeen years old and still going strong, *Picasso* is the place to catch incoming DJs and live jazz and rock acts. Open as a café during the daytime. Cover 30–100Hr depending on event. Café noon–8pm; gigs and club nights 8/10pm–4am.

SHOPPING

Krakivsky rynok ul. Bazarna. Covered market with fruit, veg and dairy products, bordered by a lively strip of outdoor clothes stalls. Daily 8am–3pm.

Souvenir market cnr Teatral'na and Lesi Ukrainky. Open-air stalls selling embroidered tablecloths and blouses, near-antique collectables and kitschy souvenir trash by the bag-load. Daily 9am–6pm.

DIRECTORY

Banks and exchange ATMs and exchange offices are scattered throughout the centre.

Hospital Emergency dept, Mykolaychuka 9 (ⓣ 032 252 7590).

Internet Medea, Kryva Lypa 9. Computers (10Hr/hr; 24hr).

Left luggage At the train station (24hr with breaks at 11am–noon & 2–3am; 10Hr/item).

Pharmacy Apteka, cnr Brativ Rohatyntsiv & Halyts'ka (24hr).

Post office Slovats'koho 1 (Mon–Fri 9am–7pm, Sat 10am–4pm, Sun 10am–3pm).

Small print and index

A ROUGH GUIDE TO ROUGH GUIDES

Published in 1982, the first Rough Guide – to Greece – was a student scheme that became a publishing phenomenon. Mark Ellingham, a recent graduate in English from Bristol University, had been travelling in Greece the previous summer and couldn't find the right guidebook. With a small group of friends he wrote his own guide, combining a highly contemporary, journalistic style with a thoroughly practical approach to travellers' needs.

The immediate success of the book spawned a series that rapidly covered dozens of destinations. And, in addition to impecunious backpackers, Rough Guides soon acquired a much broader readership that relished the guides' wit and inquisitiveness as much as their enthusiastic, critical approach and value-for-money ethos.

These days, Rough Guides include recommendations from budget to luxury and cover more than 120 destinations around the globe, as well as producing an ever-growing range of eBooks.

Visit **roughguides.com** to find all our latest books, read articles, get inspired and share travel tips with the Rough Guides community.

Rough Guide credits

Editors: Neil McQuillian, Brendon Griffin, Lucy Kane, Helen Abramson and Andy Turner
Layout: Anita Singh
Cartography: Rajesh Chhibber
Picture editor: Raffaella Morini
Proofreader: Jan McCann
Managing editor: Monica Woods
Assistant editor: Dipika Dasgupta
Production: Charlotte Cade

Cover design: Nicole Newman, Rhiannon Furbear-Williams, Anita Singh
Editorial assistant: Olivia Rawes
Senior pre-press designer: Dan May
Operations coordinator: Helen Blount
Creative operations manager: Jason Mitchell
Publisher: Joanna Kirby
Publishing director (Travel): Clare Currie

Publishing information

This fourth edition published March 2014 by
Rough Guides Ltd,
80 Strand, London WC2R 0RL
11, Community Centre, Panchsheel Park,
New Delhi 110017, India
Distributed by Penguin Random House
Penguin Books Ltd,
80 Strand, London WC2R 0RL
Penguin Group (USA)
345 Hudson Street, NY 10014, USA
Penguin Group (Australia)
250 Camberwell Road, Camberwell,
Victoria 3124, Australia
Penguin Group (NZ)
67 Apollo Drive, Mairangi Bay, Auckland 1310,
New Zealand
Penguin Group (South Africa)
Block D, Rosebank Office Park, 181 Jan Smuts Avenue,
Parktown North, Gauteng, South Africa 2193
Rough Guides is represented in Canada by Tourmaline
Editions Inc. 662 King Street West, Suite 304, Toronto,
Ontario M5V 1M7
Printed in Singapore by Toppan Security Printing Pte. Ltd.
© Rough Guides 2014

Maps © Rough Guides
Contains Ordnance Survey data © Crown copyright and
database rights 2014
No part of this book may be reproduced in any form
without permission from the publisher except for the
quotation of brief passages in reviews.
1208pp includes index
A catalogue record for this book is available from the
British Library
ISBN: 978-1-40933-736-2
The publishers and authors have done their best to
ensure the accuracy and currency of all the information
in **The Rough Guide to Europe on a Budget**, however,
they can accept no responsibility for any loss, injury, or
inconvenience sustained by any traveller as a result of
information or advice contained in the guide.
1 3 5 7 9 8 6 4 2

MIX
Paper from
responsible sources
FSC™ C018179
www.fsc.org

Help us update

We've gone to a lot of effort to ensure that the fourth edition of **The Rough Guide to Europe on a Budget** is accurate and up-to-date. However, things change – places get "discovered", opening hours are notoriously fickle, restaurants and rooms raise prices or lower standards. If you feel we've got it wrong or left something out, we'd like to know, and if you can remember the address, the price, the hours, the phone number, so much the better.

Please send your comments with the subject line "Rough Guide Europe on a Budget Update" to ✉ mail @uk.roughguides.com. We'll credit all contributions and send a copy of the next edition (or any other Rough Guide if you prefer) for the very best emails.

Find more travel information, connect with fellow travellers and plan your trip on ⓦ roughguides.com

Acknowledgements

Eleanor Aldridge Big thanks to everyone at Rough Guides, particularly Monica for sending me off to France in the first place, Brendon for the excellent editing and Alice, Emma, Keith and Neil for the updating tips. Thanks, too, to Rosemary and Alan for the support and proofreading, Charlie for the insider scoop in Paris and Izzy for the helpful contacts and pre-trip cocktails. Last but not least, thanks to all those who provided advice and assistance along the way.
Lauren Atherton Provence-Alpes-Côte d'Azur Tourism Board, Bouches-du-Rhône Tourism Board and the Vaucluse Tourism Board. Thank you to Mum, Dad, Michael and Martin, Quil and all my dear friends. And thank you to Michael.
Tim Burford Julie Melet of Switzerland Tourism and Alexia Hungerbühler of Schweizer Jugendherbergen/Swiss Youth Hostels.

Tim Chester Ceyda Pekenc and Ulku Dirioglu at Redmint Communications.
Kiki Deere Adriana Vacca at ENIT for her help and support coordinating my trip, Roberta Evangelisti in Rome, Manuela Barzan in Campania, Marcella di Feo and Dora in Basilicata, Nadia Fortunato and Debora in Puglia, and Roberta Ianni in Sicily. Thanks also to all of those who helped me along the way, in particular Lubna Khan, Alessia and Ory in Rome, Tillo and Luca in Naples and Francesco in Taormina.
Natasha Foges The White Hart Inn in Bath and Whitesands Lodge at Sennen for their kind hospitality, Anna-Louise Clegg for providing the perfect Cornish bolt hole, Keith Drew for some great Bristol tips, Harriet Foges for a memorable day in Oxford, Joey Valentine for fun and games on buses and trains, and

Will Widén for keeping me company all the way to Land's End.

John Malathronas Agnes Zsebo-Ferenczi, Karin Jones (Hungary), Christina Köpf, Gisela Moser, Tomma Profke, Sabrina Lillich, Karoline Graf, Christina Möller, Cathrin Tronser, Monika Schmid, Brigitte Ohel, Susanne Fick and Jürgen Schmidt (Germany).

Jo-Ann Titmarsh Erika Carpaneto at Torino Turismo, Roberta Romoli at the Florence Tourist Office and all the friends who offered me lifts around the country.

Andy Turner would like to say *dank je* to Lotje and all

the staff at Cocomama (including Joop the cat), Rachel and Pepijn at misc eatdrinksleep, Kim Heinen at Rotterdam Marketing and Raoul Spronken of Maastricht Running Tours.

Kate Turner Charlynne and Nathalie for the company, Suriñe for her Zaragoza tips, and Adela and Jane for their expertise on the Madrid clubbing scene.

Steve Vickers Jenna Osborne, Brendon Griffin, Monica Woods, Visit Portugal and Jan Svensson at SJ. Special thanks also to Karin Ingesten for her help along the way.

Photo credits

All photos © Rough Guides except the following:
(Key: b-below/bottom; c-centre; l-left; r-right; t-top)

p.1 4Corners: Colin Dutton/SIME
p.2 Getty Images: DESEO
p.4 Corbis: Antonino Bartuccio/SOPA
p.5 Corbis: Atlantide Phototravel
p.9 4Corners: Johanna Huber/SIME (t). Corbis: Frans Lemmens (b)
p.10 Alamy: Alex Paillon (b). Robert Harding Picture Library: Image Broker (t); Stuart Black (c)
p.12 Robert Harding Picture Library: Adam Burton
p.13 Corbis: Henrik Trygg/Johnér Images (b); Michele Falzone/JAI (c). Photoshot: Angel Manzano (t)
p.14 Dreamstime.com: Jackq (b); Nikolai Sorokin (c). Robert Harding Picture Library: Hans-Peter Merten (t)
p.15 Alamy: David Saunders (b). Getty Images: Massimo Pizzoti (t). Photoshot: TTL (cl). Robert Harding Picture Library: Roy Rainford (cr)
p.16 Corbis: Gonzales Photo/Demotix (b); Stefano Rellandini/Reuters (c). Getty Images: Peter Muhly/AFP (t)
p.17 Corbis: Cathal McNaughton/Reuters (bl); Juan Ferreras/epa (tr); Marko Djurica/Reuters (br). Robert Harding Picture Library: age fotostock (tl)
p.18 Alamy: Hilke Maunder (b). Getty Images: Sean Gallup (cl); UIG via Getty Images (t). Photoshot: Karl F. Schöfmann (cr)
p.19 Alamy: Art Directors & TRIP (b); CuboImages srl (t). Getty Images: Julian Love (c)
p.20 Corbis: Franck Guiziou/Hemis (cr); Hans Huber/Westend61 (t). Getty Images: Arctic-Images (cl); Maya Karkalicheva (b)
p.21 Getty Images: Henn Photography (c); IIC/Axiom (t); Slow Images (b)
p.22 Corbis: Wolfgang Weinhäupl/Westend61
p.28 Corbis: Atlantide Phototravel
p.47 Getty Images: Christian Kober
p.61 Robert Harding Picture Library: Roy Rainford
p.87 Dreamstime.com: Erik De Graaf
p.113 Dreamstime.com: Lianem
p.127 Dreamstime.com: Hristo Shanov
p.153 Dreamstime.com: Marcelkudla

p.183 Dreamstime.com: Frantisek Chmura
p.207 Photoshot: I TL
p.237 Dreamstime.com: Oleksiy Mark
p.255 Corbis: Doug Pearson/JAI
p.275 Corbis: Sylvain Sonnet/Hemis
p.351 Dreamstime.com: Pavel Losevsky
p.415 Dreamstime.com: Rob Van Esch
p.495 Dreamstime.com: Radist
p.603 Corbis: Radius Images
p.681 Corbis: Walter Bibikow/JAI
p.697 Robert Harding Picture Library: Eitan Simanor
p.715 Dreamstime.com: Ollirg
p.741 Dreamstime.com: Kompasstudio
p.773 Photoshot: Hoferichter
p.801 Dreamstime.com: Bettina Schwarz
p.831 Dreamstime.com: Neirfy
p.859 Dreamstime.com: Richard Semik
p.895 Dreamstime.com: Emi Cristea
p.915 Dreamstime.com: Sborisov
p.939 Photoshot: Tibor Bognar
p.957 Dreamstime.com: Richard Semik
p.977 Dreamstime.com: Europhotos
p.997 Dreamstime.com: Pedro Antonio Salaverría Calahorra
p.1083 Dreamstime.com: Oleksiy Mark
p.1113 Dreamstime.com: Mihai-bogdan Lazar
p.1139 Dreamstime.com: Adisa
p.1177 Dreamstime.com: Jojjik

Front cover Berner Oberland, Switzerland © Alamy Images: Jon Arnold Images Ltd/Alamy
Back cover Food stalls, people and Koutoubia Mosque at sunset, Jemaa el Fna square, Marrakesh, Morocco (t) © Corbis: Matthew Williams-Ellis/Robert Harding World Imagery; Tourists along the waterfront of the Nyhavn canal, Copenhagen, Denmark (br) © Corbis: Paul Mounce; Metro station with Art Nouveau style by Hector Guimard, Paris, France (bl) © Corbis: Perousse Bruno/Hemis

3 1502 00783 5265

Index

Maps are marked in grey

Map symbols

The symbols below are used on maps throughout the book

✈	Airport	☼	Viewpoint	◠	Cave		
★	Transport stop	🛆	Waterfall	⚠	Campsite		
⛴	Boat	✡	Synagogue	—	Wall		
🚂	Train	≋	Swimming pool	- - - -	Path		
🚌	Bus	⊙	Statue	— —	Ferry Route		
@	Internet café/access	♟	Museum	●- -●- -●	Cable Car		
✉	Post office	⊤	Fountain/gardens	⌁⌁⌁⌁⌁	Funicular		
(i)	Tourist office	⊠	Gate		Church		
🛆	Windmill	⊖	London Underground		Building		
+	Hospital	(S)	S-bahn		Pedestrianized area		
◆	Place of interest	(M)	Metro		Market		
∴	Ruins	(U)	U-bahn		Stadium		
🛆	Monastery	(T)	Tram stop		Park/national park		
🕌	Mosque	P	Parking		Beach		
🏰	Castle	▲	Mountain peak		Marsh		
🏛	Stately home	⌃⌃	Mountain range		Glacier		
🏛	Monument	⌢⌢	Rocks		Christian cemetery		
❋	Ferris wheel	///	Hill		Jewish cemetery		
⚘	Lighthouse	⌣	Bridge		Muslim cemetery		

Listings key

■	Accommodation
●	Eating/drinking/nightlife
●	Shop

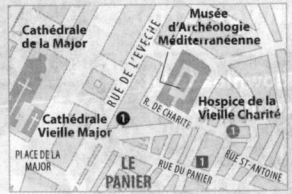

Download the free Rail Planner App

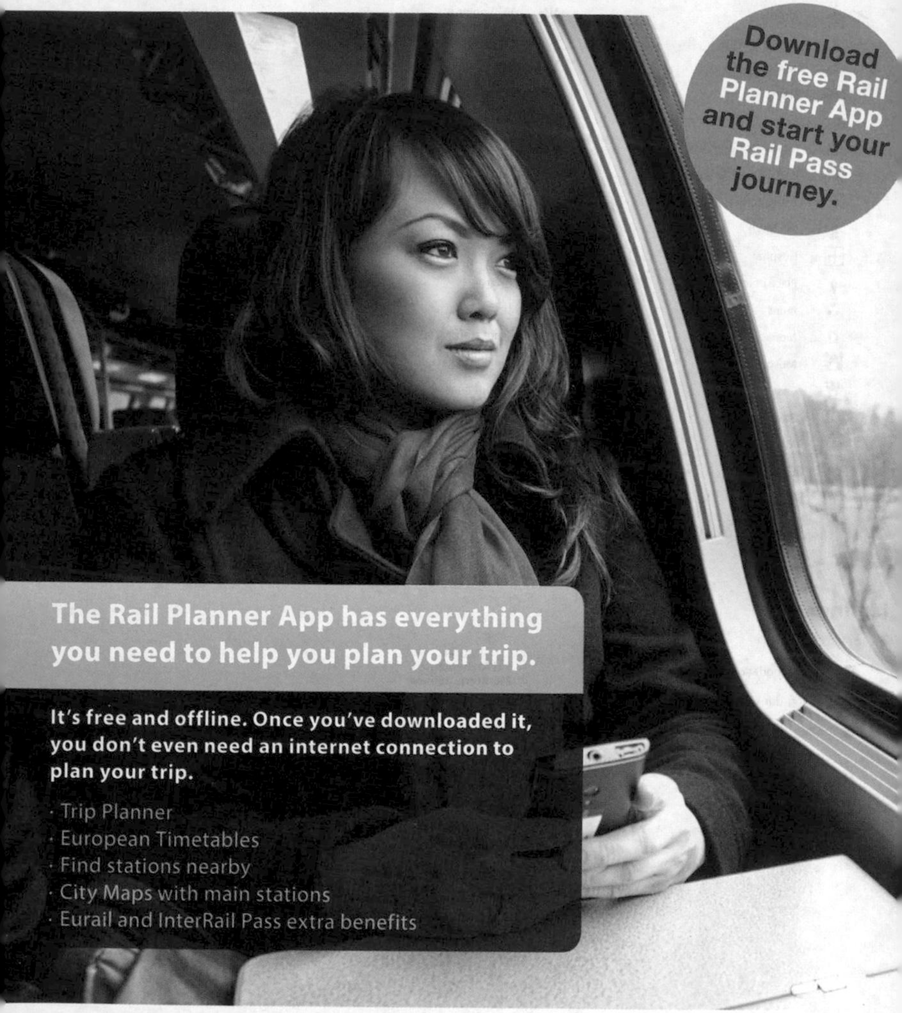

Download the free Rail Planner App and start your Rail Pass journey.

The Rail Planner App has everything you need to help you plan your trip.

It's free and offline. Once you've downloaded it, you don't even need an internet connection to plan your trip.

· Trip Planner
· European Timetables
· Find stations nearby
· City Maps with main stations
· Eurail and InterRail Pass extra benefits

Still unique.
Still luxurious.
Still lots of beds.
Still run by girls.
Only difference,
no more hourly rates.

18

COCO MAMA

COCOMAMA, Amsterdam's only boutique hostel in a former luxurious brothel

www.cocomama.nl

SO NOW WE'VE TOLD YOU HOW TO MAKE
THE MOST OF YOUR TIME, WE WANT YOU
TO STAY SAFE AND COVERED WITH OUR
FAVOURITE TRAVEL INSURER

 WorldNomads.com
keep travelling safely

RECOMMENDED BY
ROUGH
GUIDES

GET AN ONLINE QUOTE
roughguides.com/travel-insurance

MAKE THE MOST OF YOUR TIME ON EARTH™

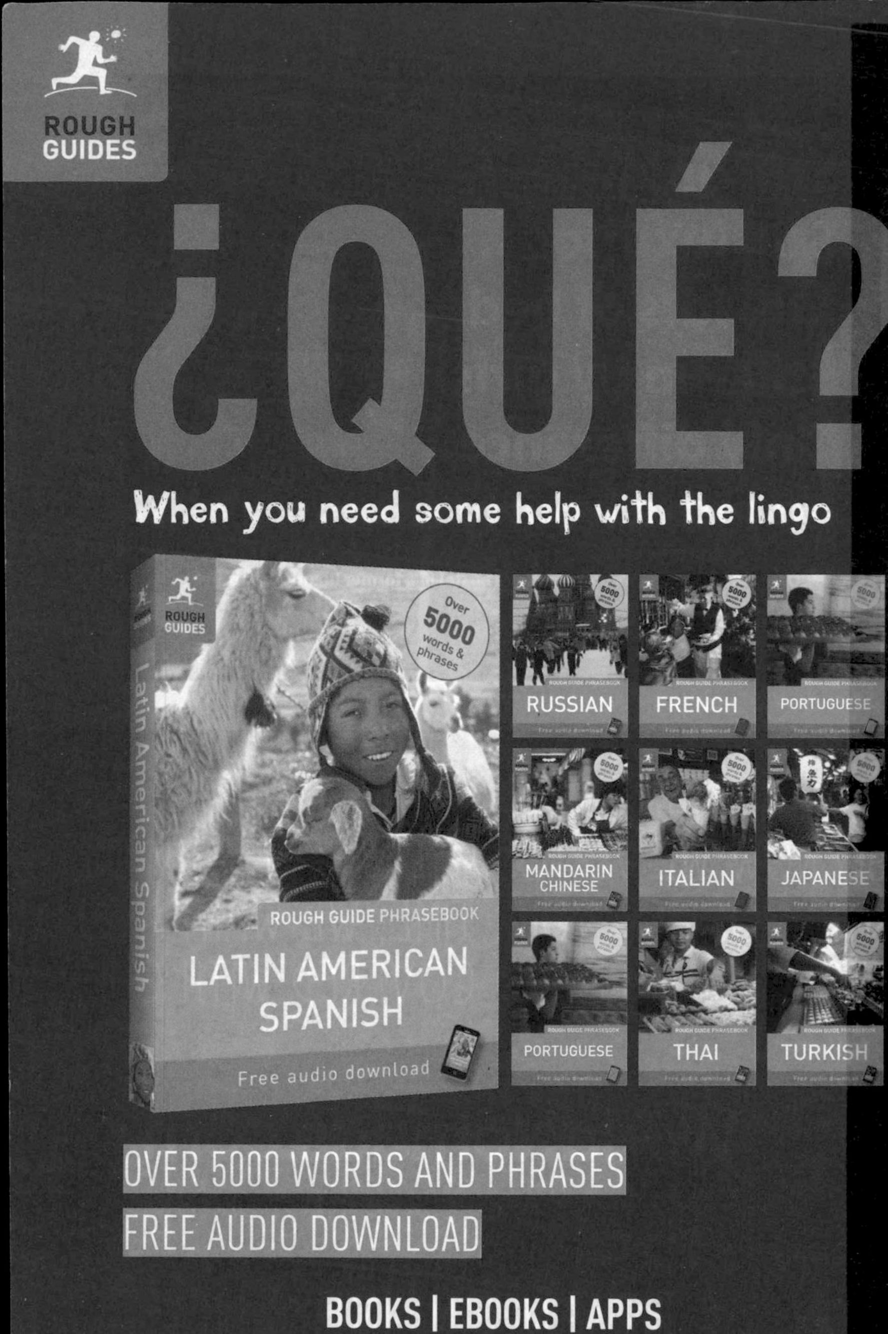

ROUGH
GUIDES

¿QUÉ?

When you need some help with the lingo

Over
5000
words &
phrases

RUSSIAN

FRENCH

PORTUGUESE

MANDARIN
CHINESE

ITALIAN

JAPANESE

ROUGH GUIDES

ROUGH GUIDE PHRASEBOOK

LATIN AMERICAN
SPANISH

Free audio download

PORTUGUESE

THAI

TURKISH

OVER 5000 WORDS AND PHRASES

FREE AUDIO DOWNLOAD

BOOKS | EBOOKS | APPS